CHASE'S
CALENDAR OF EVENTS
2001

CB
CONTEMPORARY BOOKS

☆ Chase's 2001 Calendar of Events ☆

NTC/CONTEMPORARY PUBLISHING GROUP, INC.
4255 WEST TOUHY AVENUE
LINCOLNWOOD, ILLINOIS 60712-1975
FAX: (847) 679-2595
PHONE: (847) 679-5500

Printed in USA

— NOTICE —

Events listed herein are not necessarily endorsed by the editors or publisher. Every effort has been made to assure the correctness of all entries, but neither the authors nor the publisher can warrant their accuracy. IT IS IMPERATIVE, IF FINANCIAL PLANS ARE TO BE MADE IN CONNECTION WITH DATES OR EVENTS LISTED HEREIN, THAT PRINCIPALS BE CONSULTED FOR FINAL INFORMATION.

ILLUSTRATIONS

Woodcuts at the beginning of each month are from *The Shepheards Calendar,* by Edmund Spenser, London, 1579. The woodcuts of people at various types of work are from a collection of drawings by Swiss painter and print maker Jost Amman, that was published in Leipzig in the 16th century. Many are from *The Book of Days,* by R. Chambers, London, 1864. Other engravings used in this book have been selected to represent almanac, advertising and book illustrations of the 15th–19th and early 20th centuries. Some interior art courtesy of Dover Publications Inc.

Chase's 2001 calendar of events,
Chicago, Contemporary Books   (c. 2001)

752 p., ill.
Includes index and tables.
Published annually since 1958.
Previous title: (1992–1994): Chase's Annual Events: The Day-by-Day Directory
                (1984–1991): Chase's Annual Events
                (1958–1983): Chases' Calendar of Annual Events
1. Calendars, 2. Almanacs, 3. Holidays, 4. Festivals, 5. Chronology,
6. Anniversaries, 7. Manners and customs, 8. Year-books. I. Title.

D11.5C48   ISBN: 0-8092-9554-7
LC 57-14540   529.3 (calendars)
ISSN: 0740-5286   394.26 (holidays)

☆ *Chase's 2001 Calendar of Events* ☆

TABLE OF CONTENTS

★ in text indicates Presidential Proclamations

WELCOME TO *CHASE'S 2001*—THE 44th EDITION

2001: A Space Odyssey

In 1966 movie director Stanley Kubrick asked Arthur C. Clarke to write a book from which Kubrick could make a film. The resulting 1968 movie *2001: A Space Odyssey* introduced HAL (Heuristically programmed ALgorithmic computer, although some sources say the letters HAL were chosen because they precede IBM). Written before the first men had landed on the moon, the book was prescient in many ways. Clarke gave the world's population as six billion (achieved in 1999). He described an international space station; the US started building one with the Russians in 1999. A character in the book reads the news on his electronic newspad, just as millions do today. *2001: A Space Odyssey* will undoubtedly be a popular video rental in the year 2001.

What's New At Chase's This Year?

The new millennium is finally here. However, most of the celebrating took place at the end of 1999. See page 61 for an explanation of why 2001 is the first year of the third millennium.

Visit our Web site at www.chases.com where you'll find free updates to this 2001 edition. This is where we post events for which 2001 dates were set too late to be included in this book and also note people listed in Birthdays Today who have died since *Chase's* went to press.

Process for Declaring Special Observances

How do special days, weeks and months get created? The President has the authority to declare any commemorative event by proclamation, but this is done infrequently. In 1999, for example, the President issued 100 proclamations. A good number of those were proclamations, such as Mother's Day and Bill of Rights Week, for which there was legislation giving continuing authority for a proclamation to be issued each year. The White House Clerk's Office initiates the issuing of these proclamations each year, since they are mandated by authorizing legislation.

Until January 1995, Congress had been active in seeing that special observances were commemorated. Members of the Senate and House could introduce legislation for a special observance to commemorate people, events and other activities they thought worthy of national recognition. Because these bills took up a disproportionate amount of time on the part of senators and representatives and their staffs, when Congress met in January 1995 to review and reform its rules and procedures, it was decided to discontinue this process. However, the Senate still does issue commemorative resolutions which do not have the force of law. Some state legislatures and governors proclaim special days, as do mayors of cities.

How do organizations promote awareness about an event or concern that they feel deserves recognition by the public? They can send their information to us for free listing in THE standard reference book for event and observance information—*Chase's Calendar of Events*.

Types of Events in Chase's

PRESIDENTIAL PROCLAMATIONS: In addition to the complete list of proclamations issued Jan 1, 1999–June 15, 2000, we have included in the day-by-day directory proclamations that have continuing authority and those that have been issued consistently since 1995. The most recent proclamations can be found on the World Wide Web at the Federal Register Online: www.access.gpo.gov.

NATIONAL DAYS AND STATE DAYS: Public holidays of other nations are gleaned from United Nations documents and from information we obtain from tourism agencies. Technically, the United States has no national holidays. Those holidays proclaimed by the president only apply to federal employees and to the District of Columbia. Governors of the states proclaim holidays for their states. In practice, federal holidays are usually pro-claimed as state holidays by the governors as well. Some governors also proclaim commemorative days that are unique to their states.

SPONSORED EVENTS: Events for which there is individual or organizational sponsorship are listed with the name of the event, inclusive dates and place of observance, brief description, approximate attendance and the sponsor's name and contact information. We obtain information for these events directly from the sponsors.

ASTRONOMICAL PHENOMENA: Information about eclipses, equinoxes and solstices, moon phases and other astronomical information is calculated largely from data prepared by the US Naval Observatory's Nautical Almanac Office and Her Majesty's Nautical Almanac Office.

HISTORIC ANNIVERSARIES, FOLKLORIC EVENTS AND BIRTHDAYS: Dates for these entries have been gathered from a wide range of reference books. Most birthdays here are for people who are deceased. Usually, living persons are listed under "Birthdays Today." Dates for historic events can be assumed to be Gregorian calendar (New Style) dates unless (OS) appears after the date. This means it is an Old Style or Julian date. Most of America's founding fathers were born before 1752, when Great Britain and its colonies adopted the Gregorian calendar. As an example of this, we list George Washington's birthday as Feb 22, 1732, the Gregorian or New Style date. However, when he was born Great Britain and its colonies began the year on March 25th, not January 1, so his Julian birthdate was Feb 11, 1731.

RELIGIOUS OBSERVANCES: Principal observances of the Christian, Jewish, Muslim and Baha'i faiths are presented with background information from their respective calendars. We include anticipated dates for Muslim holidays. When known, religious and secular events of China, India and Japan are also listed. There is no single Hindu calendar and different sects define the Hindu lunar month differently. There is no single lunar calendar that serves as a model for all Buddhists, either. Therefore, we are not able to provide the dates of many religious holidays for these faiths.

Omissions/Errors

The omission of an event usually means that information was not available in time for inclusion. Errors in dates are most often the result of tentative information that was later changed by the sponsoring organization.

We welcome the submission of new entries. Instructions for this are on page 752. Final selection and format of information included in Chase's is, of course, the decision of the editors.

Acknowledgments

Thanks to the many people who helped in the process of compiling this 2001 edition: the reference staffs at the Evanston, Lincolnwood and Skokie public libraries, Steve Gietschier of The Sporting News and Buck Trewicky.

Special thanks to our colleagues at NTC/Contemporary Publishing: Richard Spears, Phil Elliott, Martha Best, Michelle Davidson, Gigi Grajdura, Terry Stone, Pam Juarez, Jeanette Wojtyla and Denise Duffy-Fieldman.

In Memoriam

The year 2000 saw the death of Harrison V. Chase, professor emeritus at Florida State University. He compiled *Chases' Calendar of Annual Events* with his brother William D. Chase from the first edition in 1958 to 1970. This 2001 edition of *Chase's* is dedicated to his memory.

July 2000

Sandy Whiteley, MLS, Editor
Kim Summers, Assistant Editor

Spotlight *Banner 2001 Events*

The following section focuses on milestone anniversaries in 2001. In Spotlight on the Past we highlight 10 different years, from 250 years ago to 25 years ago, and provide a sample of important events. In Spotlight on the World and Spotlight on America, we give more detailed information on some landmark events that are being commemorated in 2001. If observances are planned, addresses are provided for further information. In Spotlight on Education, we provide brief histories of some colleges and universities that are celebrating tercentennials, bicentennials, sesquicentennials, etc. Spotlight on People concentrates on milestone birth or death anniversaries in 2001. Spotlight on 2001 highlights the International Year of Volunteers and the IAAF World Championships. And we hope Spotlight on the Millennium clears up the debate—did the third millennium begin in 2000 or does it begin in 2001?

Spotlight *Contents*

1751 *250 years ago*

Landmark World Events

Feb 20 Philip Stanhope, the Earl of Chesterfield, introduced legislation in the House of Lords to substitute the Gregorian calendar for the Julian calendar still in use in Great Britain and its colonies. The Gregorian calendar had first been introduced in Catholic countries in 1582 and in most other Protestant countries in the early 1700s. Stanhope's British Calendar Act passed and the "New Style" calendar became effective the following year. At the same time, the beginning of the year was changed from Mar 25 to Jan 1. As a result, 1751 in Great Britain and its North American colonies only had 282 days.

May 5 The power of the Inquisition was curbed in Portugal.

August–September Robert Clive, English soldier and colonial administrator, captured several towns in India, defeating the territorial ambitions of the French.

- Royal Worcester Porcelain Co founded.
- British Parliament forbade the issuance of paper money by any of its colonies.

Landmark US Events

May 11 At the urging of Benjamin Franklin, the governor of Pennsylvania approved a law for more humane treatment of the insane.

Aug 13 The Academy and College of Philadelphia opened, with Benjamin Franklin as its president. Later this institution would become the University of Pennsylvania.

- Sugar cane was introduced into Louisiana from Hispaniola by Jesuit priests. It was used to make rum.
- Coaches ran regularly between New York and Philadelphia.
- Easton, PA, was founded by Thomas Penn.
- George Washington made a trip to Barbados. His journal of the trip was later published.

Culture

PUBLICATIONS

Fiction

- *Amelia*, by Henry Fielding
- *The Adventures of Peregrine Pickle*, by Tobias Smollett
- *The Life of Harriot Stuart*, by Charlotte Ramsay Lennox, the first novel written by an author born in America (though she was living in Britain when she wrote it).

Nonfiction

- *Experiments and Observations in Electricity, Made at Philadelphia in America*, by Benjamin Franklin, was published in London.
- *Observations . . . Made by Mr John Bartram in His Travels from Pennsylvania to Lake Ontario*, by America's first botanist
- *Importance of Settling and Fortifying Nova Scotia*
- *Proposal for Uniting the Kingdoms of Great Britain and Ireland*
- *An Enquiry Concerning the Principles of Morals*, by David Hume
- *Philosophica Botanica*, by Carl von Linne (Linnaeus)

THE *ENCYCLOPÉDIE*

The first volume of Denis Diderot and Jean d'Alembert's *Encyclopédie* was published this year. It was to have been a translation of an English work, Ephraim Chamber's *Cyclopaedia*, but it was expanded until it was an entirely new work. Diderot issued a prospectus for the encyclopedia in 1750. The first seven volumes were published between 1751 and 1757. The work was then suppressed by the censors because of its bold statements about religious liberty, freedom of thought and political freedom. Diderot published the last ten volumes without authorization, 1765–66. Eleven volumes of illustrations were also prepared by Diderot. The *Encyclopédie* championed the rationalism of the Enlightenment and was a major factor in the intellectual preparation for the French Revolution of 1789.

Notes

- In this year's edition of *Poor Richard's Almanack* Benjamin Franklin wrote "Time is money."

Poetry

- "An Elegy Written in a Country Churchyard," by Thomas Gray

Notes

June Children's publisher John Newbery introduced *Lilliputian Magazine*, the first magazine for children.

THEATER

- *Gil Blas*, by Edward Moore

MUSIC

- *Platée*, opera by Rameau

ART

- *Gin Lane*, by William Hogarth
- *Artist, Wife and Child*, by Thomas Gainsborough
- *Reclining Girl*, by François Boucher

Science

- Benjamin Huntsman invented crucile process for casting steel.
- Swedish mineralogist Axel Cronstedt isolated the element nickel.
- British anatomist Robert Whytt experimented with the spinal cord, distinguishing between voluntary and reflex actions.

Obits

- Colonial statesman and scholar James Logan

1776 *225 years ago*

Landmark World Events

DECEMBER Captain James Cook began his third world voyage. He reached the coast of Oregon and mapped as far north as the Bering Strait. He discovered the Hawaiian Islands, where he was killed in 1779.
- The Bolshoi Ballet was established at Moscow.
- Potemkin, a favorite of Czarina Catherine II, organized the Russian Black Sea fleet. Russia's Black Sea ports were the only ones that did not freeze over in the winter.

Landmark US Events

JAN 1 Norfolk, VA, burned by the British.
FEB 7 The first prison reform society founded: the Philadelphia Society for Relieving Distressed Prisoners Owing to the War of Independence.
MAR 4 American marines captured Fort Nassau in the Bahamas. They captured large military stores which they brought back to Connecticut.
MAR 17 British troops evacuated Boston after Revolutionary troops seized Dorchester Heights. Evacuation Day is a holiday in Boston and Suffolk County, MA. George Washington's troops occupied Boston by Mar 20. More than 1,000 Bostonians loyal to the crown fled by ship to Halifax, NS.
MARCH The Privateering Resolution was passed by the Continental Congress, allowing colonists to fit out armed vessels.
APR 3 George Washington received an honorary doctor of laws degree from Harvard College.
APR 6 American ports were opened to trade with nations other than Britain.
MAY 2 An American mission to France obtained a loan to support the war effort against Britain.
MAY 4 Rhode Island declared its independence from Great Britain.
MAY The Continental Congress learned that Great Britain was hiring German mercenaries to fight in America.
MAY–JULY American troops withdrew from Canada after a succession of defeats.
JUNE 7 Richard Henry Lee of Virginia introduced a resolution into the Second Continental Congress: ". . . that these united colonies are, and of right ought to be, free and independent states." (*See also* Spotlight on America.)
JUNE 11 Committee appointed to draft a declaration of independence from Britain.

1776 *continued*

June 12 Committee appointed to draw up Articles of Confederation which would create a union of the states.

June 28 Charleston, SC, successfully defended against the British.

July 3 The Continental Congress authorized the hiring of shipbuilders to construct warships on Lake Champlain.

July 4 Declaration of Independence adopted by the Continental Congress (but not signed).

July 4 The Continental Congress approved a resolution calling for the design of a Great Seal for the new country. The seal was not designed and used until 1782.

July 8 The ringing of the Liberty Bell in Philadelphia summoned citizens to the first public reading of the Declaration of Independence by Colonel John Nixon.

July 9 Statue of King George III pulled off its pedestal by patriots in New York.

July 12 John Dickinson's "Articles of Confederation and Perpetual Union" were delivered to Continental Congress. After revision, the Articles of Confederation were adopted by the Congress on Nov 5, 1777. The Articles were not ratified by all the states until 1781.

Aug 1 Francis Salvador of South Carolina was the first Jewish soldier to be killed in the American Revolution. He was called the "Southern Paul Revere" because of his warning of the approach of the British fleet to Charleston.

Aug 14 The Continental Congress passed a law granting land to British and Hessian soldiers if they deserted from the British army.

Aug 27 Revolutionary forces defeated in the Battle of Brooklyn and retreated to Manhattan by boat.

Sept 6 The first submarine attack in history took place when the one-man *Turtle* moved beside a British warship in New York harbor and attached a bomb. The bomb drifted loose before it exploded so no damage was inflicted.

Sept 9 The Continental Congress resolved that the words United States were to replace United Colonies.

Sept 15 The Continental Army evacuated New York City, which was occupied by the British.

Sept 21 The state of Delaware was formed when its constitution was approved at New Castle.

Sept 22 Captain Nathan Hale was executed by the British for spying. He said "I only regret that I have but one life to lose for my country."

September Benjamin Franklin was chosen by the Continental Congress to represent the US in negotiations with the French.

Oct 9 San Francisco de Asis Mission founded in what would become San Francisco, CA, the sixth of the 21 missions founded by Franciscan monks in California to Christianize and educate the Indians. It survived the earthquake of 1909 and is today the oldest building in San Francisco and is known as Mission Delores. On Nov 1, San Juan Capistrano Mission was founded by Father Junipero Serra, the seventh in the chain of missions.

Oct 11 In the first battle of Lake Champlain, Continental forces led by General Benedict Arnold suffered heavy losses but managed to stall the British.

Nov 16 Battle of Fort Washington, NY, in which 2,800 Revolutionary soldiers surrendered to more than 3,000 Hessian soldiers. Fort Lee, NJ, surrendered Nov 18 and Washington began his retreat across New Jersey.

Nov 30 British peace commissioners offered a pardon to all those who would declare their allegiance to King George III within 60 days.

Dec 5 Phi Beta Kappa founded at the College of William and Mary. Though founded as a social fraternity, in 1831 it became an honorary society. It admits men and women graduates of American universities who have distinguished themselves in scholarship in the liberal arts and sciences.

Dec 8 Washington and his troops crossed the Delaware River from New Jersey into Pennsylvania.

Dec 12 The Continental Congress fled from Philadelphia to Baltimore.

Dec 21 Benjamin Franklin arrived in Paris to help negotiate treaties and seek loans.

Dec 26 The Battle of Trenton won by the Americans. George Washington and his troops had re-crossed the Delaware the day before to attack Hessian troops at Trenton.

- Eight states drafted new constitutions; two already had republican government due to former colonial charters.
- Philadelphia with a population of 26,000 was the largest city in the colonies; New York City had 22,000 residents.
- Paul Revere started a gunpowder factory at Canton, MA.
- The Continental Congress instituted a national lottery to support governmental activities.
- Ann Lee founded the first community of Shakers at Watervliet, NY.

Culture

PUBLICATIONS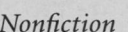

Nonfiction

- *The Wealth of Nations*, by Adam Smith
- *The Decline and Fall of the Roman Empire*, volume 1, by Edward Gibbon
- *A Dialogue Concerning the Slavery of the Africans*, by Samuel Hopkins
- *The Battle of Bunkers-Hill*, by Hugh H. Brackenridge

Jan 10 Thomas Paine's *Common Sense* was published. It sold 500,000 copies within a few months, a huge number relative to the size of the population.

Dec 19 Paine released *The American Crisis*, the first issue of a series of pamphlets, which began with the words "These are the times that try men's souls."

Poetry

- A poem by black poet Phillis Wheatley appeared in the *Pennsylvania* magazine. It was addressed to General George Washington, with whom she had corresponded.

THEATER

- A play by the German writer Friedrich Maximilian von Klinger performed in Leipzig, Germany, gave its name to the *Sturm und Drang* ("Storm and Stress") romantic school.
- The anonymous play *The Blockheads*, a satire on the British, was performed in Boston.

MUSIC

- *Concertos No. 6–8*, by Mozart
- *Symphonies No. 66, 67*, by Haydn
- The first Viennese waltz music appeared in Vincente Martin's opera, *Una Cosa Rara*.

ART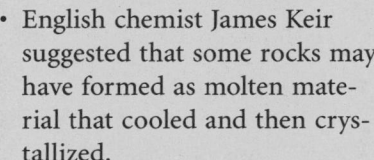

- *John the Baptist*, by Joshua Reynolds
- *Mrs James Smith and Grandson*, by Charles Willson Peale
- *Helen Brought to Paris*, by Benjamin West
- *Portrait of Roger Sherman*, by Ralph Earl

Science and Technology

- English chemist James Keir suggested that some rocks may have formed as molten material that cooled and then crystallized.
- Swedish chemist Karl Wilhelm Scheele discovered uric acid in kidney stones.
- US engineer David Bushnell built a hand-powered submarine, the *Turtle*, which was used during the Revolution.
- Marsh gas (methane) was discovered in Italy by physicist Alessandro Volta.
- Invisible ink was developed by Sir James Jay. It was used in diplomatic correspondence by American patriots.

Obits

- Patriot Nathan Hale, executed by the British
- David Hume, Scottish philosopher

Spotlight on the Past *milestone anniversary years*

1801 *200 years ago*

Landmark World Events

Jan 1 As the Act of Union of 1800 took effect, Britain and Ireland were combined under the same government with the name United Kingdom. Catholics were excluded from voting. The Union Jack became the official flag of the UK.

Feb 9 The Treaty of Lunéville, following France's defeat of Austria, marked the virtual destruction of the Holy Roman Empire. France gained all territory west of the Rhine.

Mar 8 During the Napoleonic Wars, combined British and Ottoman troops established a foothold in French-occupied Egypt. By June Napoleon had captured Egypt as a launching point for an attack on India. Egypt was restored to the Ottoman Empire in 1802. Britain attempted to blockade Napoleonic France. In turn, British ships were excluded from many European ports.

July 15 The Concordat of 1801 between Napoleon Bonaparte and Pope Pius VII reestablished the Catholic Church in France.

Oct 1 Preliminaries of peace were signed between Britain and France.

- The first British census showed a population of about 10.5 million in England, Scotland and Wales. The 1991 census counted a population of 55.7 million, including Northern Ireland. A census will be taken in 2001.
- Alexander I became Czar of Russia. His father, Paul I, was strangled by army officers who had failed to force his abdication.
- Pierre Toussaint L'Ouverture achieved control of Santo Domingo (today's Haiti). A French force later regained control of the island and L'Ouverture was captured and died in a French prison in 1803.

Landmark US Events

Jan 20 John Marshall appointed fourth chief justice of the Supreme Court. During his 34-year tenure, he molded the Constitution by the wisdom of his interpretations and raised the stature of the Court.

Feb 17 After a tie vote in the electoral college and 35 tie votes in the House of Representatives, Thomas Jefferson was elected president and Aaron Burr vice president. Both men had garnered more votes than incumbent John Adams.

Feb 27 The District of Columbia was placed under the jurisdiction of Congress.

February Congress passed the Judiciary Act, creating 16 circuit courts.

Mar 3 During the final days of his presidency, John Adams made "midnight" appointments of federal judges, appointing as many Federalists as possible. Incoming president Thomas Jefferson protested.

Mar 4 Thomas Jefferson was the first American president to be inaugurated in Washington, DC.

Mar 7 Massachusetts enacted the first voter registration law.

June 7 The first booksellers' organization was founded at New York City, the American Company of Booksellers.

June President Thomas Jefferson ordered US Navy ships to the Mediterranean in protest against raids on US ships by North African pirates. This led to the First Barbary War or Tripolitan War.

Nov 10 Tennessee was the first state to outlaw dueling.

- Congregationalists and Presbyterians agreed through the Plan of Union to carry religion to frontier settlements. One of the most successful cooperative endeavors in US history, it allowed ministers to serve in either church.
- Meriwether Lewis was named secretary to his friend President Jefferson. Later he was appointed by Jefferson to lead

an expedition with William Clark to the Pacific Coast.
- Johnny Appleseed arrived in the Ohio Valley with his seeds.
- A bakery in Milton, MA, introduced the first biscuits to be called "crackers" because of the noise made when eaten.
- Philadelphia established the first major municipal waterworks in the US.
- About 200 newspapers were being published in the US, 20 of them dailies.
- Crane & Co started a cotton pulp business in Dalton, MA, to make stationery and currency pulp for the US mint.
- The University of South Carolina was founded. (*See also* Spotlight on Education.)

Culture

PUBLICATIONS

Fiction
- *Jane Talbot, a Novel*, by Charles Brockden Brown
- *Belinda*, by Maria Edgeworth

Nonfiction
- *How Gertrude Teaches Her Children*, by Swiss educator Johann Pestalozzi, set forth his theories of education.
- *Manual of Parliamentary Practice, for the Use of the Senate of the United States*, by Thomas Jefferson
- *Trial of Republicanism*, by Peter Porcupine (William Cobbett)
- "An Inquiry into the Causes and Effects of . . . Cow Pox," by Edward Jenner

Poetry
- *Thalaba*, epic poem by Robert Southey

Notes
- *The New York Evening Post* began publication.

THEATER
- *The Maid of Orleans*, by Schiller, first performed in Leipzig, Germany.

MUSIC
- *Piano Sonatas No 12–15*, by Beethoven
- *The Creation Mass*, by Haydn
- Songbooks such as the *Vermont Harmony, New England Harmony* and the *American Harmony* were published.
- *The Fourth of July (A Grand Military Sonata)*, by James Hewitt

ART
- *The Envoys of Agamemnon*, by Jean Auguste Dominique Ingres
- *The Infant Christ and Saint John*, by John Trumbull
- *Rubens Peale with a Geranium*, by Rembrandt Peale
- *Calais Pier*, by J.M.W. Turner

Science and Technology
- The element columbium (niobium) isolated by Charles Hatchett and vanadium by Andres del Rio.
- Giuseppe Piazzi discovered the first asteroid, Ceres, at his observatory in Palermo, Sicily.

- Jacquard loom (with pattern controlled by punch cards) designed by Joseph-Marie Jacquard. This was the precursor of punched cards used with early computers. It was exhibited at the Paris Industrial Exposition of 1801.
- The first factory to extract sugar from beets opened in Silesia in Central Europe.
- The cause of astigmatism was discovered by English physician Thomas Young.
- For the first time, an entire building in Paris was illuminated by gas.
- Robert Hare of Philadelphia invented the hydrogen-oxygen blowpipe, the ancestor of modern-day welding torches.
- E.I. DuPont built a gunpowder plant near Wilmington, DE.

Obits
- Benedict Arnold, Revolutionary War traitor
- German novelist and poet Novalis

1826 *175 years ago*

Landmark World Events

MAR 14 General Congress of South American States convened by Simón Bolívar at Panama. The congress ended without agreement on uniting the South American republics.

JUNE The Janissaries, the politically powerful army of the Ottoman Empire, were slaughtered on the orders of Sultan Mahmud II.

- The colony of Western Australia founded.
- The First Anglo-Burmese War ended. Burma was forced to cede some territory to Britain. By 1885, all of Burma was under British rule.

Landmark US Events

APR 26 John James Audubon left Louisiana for England in hopes of finding a publisher for his drawings of birds and mammals.

AUG 22 Jedediah Strong Smith led the first overland expedition from the Great Salt Lake to California. He helped chart the American West.

SEPT 13 A rhinoceros was exhibited for the first time in the US, in New York City at Peale's Museum and Gallery of Fine Arts.

OCT 7 The first US railroad was built at Quincy, MA. Horse-drawn wagons carrying granite were pulled along rails.

- Pennsylvania passed a law making kidnapping a felony, nullifying the federal Fugitive Slave Law of 1793.
- Kansas City founded as a trading post on the Missouri River.
- Memphis, TN, incorporated.
- American Society for the Promotion of Temperance organized in Boston.
- Mr Lord and Mr Taylor opened a dry goods store in New York City.
- Work began on the Pennsylvania Main Line Canal between Philadelphia and Pittsburgh.
- New York state granted a charter to the Mohawk and Hudson Railroad, later to be the New York Central.
- Charles Babbage compiled the first reliable actuarial tables used to calculate risk for insurance premiums.
- Maryland removed religious qualifications for voting.
- John Randolph and Henry Clay fought a duel; neither man was hurt.
- Former president James Madison was named rector of the University of Virginia.
- Western Reserve University was chartered and opened. Later it merged with the Case Institute of Technology to form Case Western Reserve University.
- Lafayette College founded at Easton, PA.

Culture

PUBLICATIONS *Fiction*

- *Vivian Grey*, by Benjamin Disraeli
- *The Last of the Mohicans*, by James Fenimore Cooper
- *Woodstock*, by Sir Walter Scott

Nonfiction

- *Memoirs*, by Casanova
- First edition of *Burke's Peerage*

Poetry

- *Poems I*, by Henry Wadsworth Longfellow

Notes

- The newspaper *Le Figaro* was founded at Paris.
- *The Juvenile Miscellany*, a bimonthly magazine for children edited by Lydia Maria Frances Child.

THEATER

- Edwin Forrest made his New York debut in *Othello*.

MUSIC

- *String Quartet No 16*, by Beethoven
- *Midsummer Night's Dream Overture*, by Mendelssohn
- *The Siege of Corinth*, by Rossini
- *Symphonie Fantastique*, by Berlioz
- "The Erie Canal" (anonymous) was a popular song.

ART

- *Illustrations on Job*, by William Blake
- *Greece on the Ruins of Missolonghi*, by Delacroix

- *The Butcher's Table*, by Francisco Goya
- *John Adams*, by Gilbert Stuart

Science and Technology

MAY 5 The first railroad tunnel was built on the Liverpool & Manchester railway in England.
- The element bromine discovered by Antoine-Jérôme Balard.
- John Walker devised sulphur friction matches, called "Lucifers."
- Otto Unverdorben obtained aniline from indigo, used for dye, to make explosives and drugs.
- Nicephore Niepce, a French doctor, produced the first photograph from nature using pewter plates and a camera obscura. It required an eight-hour exposure.
- Samuel Morey received a patent on an internal combustion engine.

Obits

- John Adams, second president of the US, and Thomas Jefferson, third president, died on the same day: July 4.

- Stamford Raffles, founder of Singapore
- René Laënnec, inventor of the stethoscope
- German composer Carl Maria von Weber
- Philippe Pinel, advocate for humane treatment of the insane
- French gastronome Brillat-Savarin
- Gulf Coast smuggler Jean Laffite

"ALL THE NEWS THAT'S FIT TO PRINT"

On Sept 18, 1851, *The New York Times* debuted as the *New-York Daily Times*. At the time, the city had a population of 500,000, most of whom lived south of 14th Street. New York City already had many newspapers, including *The Herald*, *The Tribune* and *The Sun* but they sold for 2 cents while *The Times* was a penny. The paper was founded by two Albany bankers and a journalist, Henry Raymond, who had worked for Horace Greeley's *Tribune*. Presenting the news free from scandal and appealing to intelligent conservatives, *The Times* was an immediate success. Active in politics, Raymond was given the title "Godfather of the Republican Party." In 1867 the word Daily was dropped from the newspaper's title.

The Times weathered the Civil War draft riots and exposed the Boss Tweed ring. However, by the 1890s the paper was almost bankrupt. On Aug 13, 1896 *The Times* was purchased by Adolph Ochs, a newspaper publisher from Tennessee. Ochs extended coverage of the business and financial world and took as his credo "To give the news impartially, without fear or favor." Under his direction, the newspaper thrived and became firmly established as a newspaper of record. In 1905 *The Times* moved uptown to Broadway and 42nd Street to what became known as Times Square.

While publicly held, the controlling interest in the newspaper is held by the Sulzberger family, descendents of Adolph Ochs. Today *The Times* has the third largest circulation among American newspapers, with its national edition distributed all across the country, and is the most influential newpaper in the US.

For more information:

Diane McNulty
The New York Times
229 W 43 St
New York, NY 10036
E-mail: mcnuldc@nytimes.com
Web: www.nytimes.com

1851 *150 years ago*

Landmark World Events

MAY 1 The Great Exhibition of the Industry of All Nations opened in the Crystal Palace in Hyde Park, London. It was the first international exposition of manufactured products. It included the first public showing of photography. American Cyrus McCormick exhibited his reaper.

DEC 2 Napoleon III, nephew of Napoleon I, carried out a coup d'etat in France. He dissolved the Assembly and the following year was made emperor of France.

- The 1851 British census showed that the population of Ireland had declined to 6 million from 8 million before the famine. The population continued to drop through emigration well into the 20th century.
- Australian gold rush began when gold was discovered in New South Wales. Immigrants pouring in from abroad more than doubled Australia's population in ten years.
- Victoria was made a separate colony in Australia.
- China's population was 450 million, having grown rapidly since the introduction of American crops such as corn, potatoes and peanuts. Today the population is 1.3 billion.
- David Livingstone discovered the Zambezi River in Africa.

Landmark US Events

APR 29 The deed of trust founding the Cooper Union for the Advancement of Science and Art, a college at New York City, forbade discrimination because of race, religion or color.

JUNE 2 Maine passed a prohibition law, the first US state to do so.

JULY 23 The Sioux gave up all land in Iowa and most land in Minnesota by signing the Treaty of Traverse des Sioux.

DEC 24 Fire devastated the Library of Congress, housed in the Capitol, destroying 35,000 volumes, some of which had been sold to Congress by Thomas Jefferson.

- The Normal School for Colored Girls was founded at Washington, later to become the District of Columbia Teachers College.
- The Illinois Central Railroad was chartered.
- Western Union was founded to provide telegraph services.
- Travelers Aid founded with a grant of $1 million from Bryan Mullanphy of St. Louis to assist those who were going west. St. Louis was the usual starting place for westbound travelers.
- Des Moines, IA, and Portland, OR, founded.
- Coe College founded at Cedar Rapids, IA; Northwestern University founded at Evanston, IL; University of Minnesota founded at Minneapolis; Santa Clara University founded at Santa Clara, CA, University of the Pacific founded at Santa Clara, CA, and Westminster College founded at Fulton, MO. (See also Spotlight on Education.)

THE YMCA

On Dec 29 the first YMCA in the US was opened in Boston. It was modeled on an organization started in London in 1844. Today there are 2,284 YMCA's in 10,000 communities in all 50 states. YMCA programs serve 16.9 million people each year, including more than 8 million children. YMCAs in the US are part of a 120-country worldwide movement, the World Alliance of YMCAs.

For more information:

YMCA of the USA
National Media Relations Office
101 N Wacker Dr
Chicago, IL 60606
Phone: (312)977-4809
Web: www.ymca.net
or call your local YMCA

Culture

PUBLICATIONS

Fiction

- *House of the Seven Gables*, by Nathaniel Hawthorne
- *Moby-Dick*, by Herman Melville

Nonfiction

- *History of the Conspiracy of the Pontiac*, by Francis Parkman
- *Social Statistics, or the Conditions Essential to Human Happiness Specified*, by Herbert Spencer
- *The Stones of Venice*, vol 1, by John Ruskin

Poetry

- *The Golden Legend*, by Henry Wadsworth Longfellow

Music

- *Twelve Transcendental Études*, by Franz Liszt
- *Rigoletto*, opera by Verdi, first performed in Venice.
- *Fantasy on "God Save the Queen"*, by Louis Moreau Gottschalk
- "Old Folks At Home," by Stephen Foster
- "The Arkansas Traveler," anonymous

Art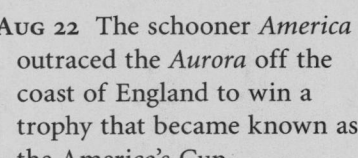

- *Arab Attacked by a Lion*, by Delacroix
- *The Annunciation*, by Dante Gabriel Rossetti
- *Christ in His Parents' Home*, by John Millais

- *The Stone Breakers*, by Gustav Courbet
- *Washington Crossing the Delaware*, by Emanuel Leutze

Science and Technology

Jan 8 Using a pendulum, French physicist Jean Foucault proved that the Earth rotates on its axis.

May 6 Linus Yale patented the Yale lock.

May 6 First patent for a refrigerator was granted to Dr. John Gorrie of Apalachicola, FL. He wanted to cool hospital rooms for yellow fever patients.

Aug 12 Isaac Singer was granted a patent on his continuous-stitch sewing machine. It was an improvement on the 1846 design by Elias Howe.

Nov 11 First US patent for a telescope issued to Alvan Clark of Cambridge, MA.

- German botanist Hugo von Mohl proposed that new cells are created by cell division.
- First telegraph cable laid beneath the English Channel.

- First high-speed flash photograph taken by William Fox Talbot.
- Improved method of converting iron into steel developed by William Kelly of the US. Generally known as the Bessemer process after the English inventor.
- Lord Kelvin completed development of his principles for the heat pump.
- James Russell of Baltimore introduced mass-produced ice cream.
- Bigelow carpet loom developed.
- Hermann von Helmholtz developed the ophthalmoscope.

Sports

Aug 22 The schooner *America* outraced the *Aurora* off the coast of England to win a trophy that became known as the America's Cup.

Obits

- British painter J.M.W. Turner
- American author James Fenimore Cooper

Fugitive Slaves

The Fugitive Slave Act of 1850 had provided for paid federal marshalls to ensure the return of runaway slaves. Many Northern states refused to tolerate the presence of slave-catchers in their midst. Free blacks battled bounty hunters intent on capturing fugitive slaves in Christiana, PA. Group of free blacks rescued escaped slave Shadrack from federal authorities in Boston. In Syracuse, NY, another runaway slave was rescued. In Boston an attempt by abolitionists to rescue Thomas Sims failed. There were serious confrontations between state courts, arguing that the Fugitive Slave Act was unconstitutional, and federal courts upholding the law. As the abolitionist movement grew, no further attempts to uphold this law were made in northern states after 1854.

1851 *continued*

- British author Mary Shelley (*Frankenstein*)
- American nature artist John James Audubon
- Photography pioneer Louis Daguerre
- Deaf educator Thomas Gallaudet
- American diplomat Joel Poinsett, after whom the poinsettia is named.
- Reformer Sylvester Graham, after whom the graham cracker is named.
- Danish physicist Hans Oersted, after whom the unit of magnetic field strength is named.

1876 *125 years ago*

Landmark World Events

MAY 24 The expedition that began modern oceanography ended as the HMS *Challenger* returned to England after circumnavigating the Earth over four years.

JUNE 2 Bulgarian hero Hristro Botev fell while fighting the Turks. Bulgaria attained its independence in 1878. Serbia and Montenegro also rebelled against Ottoman rule.

- Queen Victoria was declared Empress of India by Parliament.
- Heinrich Schliemann discovered the tombs of the Mycenaean kings in Greece.
- A famine in India from 1876 to 1878 killed five million people. Famine in northern China killed nine million between 1876 and 1879.
- The Plimsoll Mark, a marking on cargo vessels devised by Samuel Plimsoll, came into use to prevent the overloading of ships.
- Porfirio Diaz began his 34-year dictatorship as president of Mexico. He was overthrown by a revolution in 1911.
- The University of Montreal was founded as a branch of Laval University. It became independent in 1919.

Landmark US Events

JAN 1 The first citywide Mummer's Parade was held in Philadelphia in honor of the centennial celebration of the Declaration of Independence. Mummer's celebrations in America date back to colonial times but what had been uncoordinated neighborhood celebrations now turned into a citywide parade. This parade is still held every New Year's Day.

INVENTION OF THE TELEPHONE

Alexander Graham Bell, a professor of vocal physiology at Boston University, took the telegraph which transmitted code by turning an electric signal off and on and turned it into a mechanism for transmitting the human voice. Some of his backers called it the "talking telegraph."

In 1873 Bell and his assistant Thomas J. Watson began investigating telegraph technology, looking for a way to take sound waves and turn them into electric signals. On Mar 10, 1876, in Boston, Bell sent the first complete intelligible sentence to his assistant in the next room ("Mr Watson, come here, I want you"). He had received a patent on this instrument three days before. In June he exhibited the telephone for the first time at the Centennial Exposition in Philadelphia. In October he received the first one-way long distance call in Canada over a distance of 8 miles. The same month he conducted the first two-way conversation between Boston and Cambridge, MA. Other people improved on Bell's invention and by 1880 most of the components of the telephone had been developed. In 1895 there were 339,000 telephones in the US; today there are 162 million.

Spotlight on the Past *milestone anniversary years*

May 16–18 The Greenback Party, founded in 1875, nominated Peter Cooper of New York for president. The party advocated the withdrawal of all US currency and the issuance of "greenbacks," federal promissory notes, in its place. The party had a candidate in one more federal election but disappeared by the 1890s.

Aug 1 Colorado was admitted to the Union as the 38th state.

Aug 2 Wild Bill Hickok was killed playing poker in a Deadwood, SD, saloon.

Nov 7 Though Samuel J. Tilden won the popular vote for the US presidency, Rutherford B. Hayes won the electoral vote and became the 19th president.

November Tammany Hall leader William Marcy "Boss" Tweed was captured in Spain where he had fled after his conviction for the embezzlement of public funds.

- Congress repealed the Southern Homestead Act of 1866 which had set aside nearly 50 million acres of southern land for settlement by former slaves.
- Congress appropriated $200,000 for the completion of the Washington Monument in Washington, DC, the cornerstone of which had been laid in 1848. The completed monument was dedicated in 1885.
- The American Medical Association admitted its first woman member.
- The first PhD awarded to an African-American was granted to Edward Alexander Bouchet by Yale University in physics.
- Johns Hopkins University was founded at Baltimore, MD. (*See also* Spotlight on Education.)

100 Years of Independence

The Centennial Exposition in Philadelphia which opened on May 10 commemorated a century of independence with exhibits in more than 150 buildings on 236 acres in Fairmount Park. One of the buildings, Memorial Hall, still stands today. Nearly nine million people attended the Exposition and 35 foreign countries were represented. Bell's telephone, Edison's duplex telegraph, the Westinghouse air brake and a refrigerator car were among the displays. They were powered by the huge Corliss Steam Engine, the largest engine ever built up to that time. The Kudzu vine was introduced from Asia, intended for erosion control and as forage for livestock. Bananas were a sensation, selling for 10 cents each. Philadelphia was the second largest city in the US at the time. Although not a financial success, the exposition promoted unification of the nation after the Civil War.

The Battle of Little Bighorn

On June 25 Lt Colonel George Custer and his Seventh Cavalry were wiped out by Sioux and Cheyenne Indians in the Battle of Little Bighorn in Montana, also known as Custer's Last Stand.

The most dramatic of the Indian wars were those on the northern Great Plains. Indians had been moved west of the Mississippi as pioneers took their lands. By the 1850s settlers were moving west of the Mississippi as well. After the Civil War, army troops were available to force Indian tribes onto reservations. The Sioux, led by Crazy Horse, joined with the northern Cheyenne to resist. In June a three-pronged army invasion moved into Sioux country. On June 17, Crazy Horse stopped the southern prong at the Battle of the Rosebud. Crazy Horse then went to a camp at the Little Bighorn River with a large contingent of Sioux and Cheyenne, including Sitting Bull. On June 25, Custer attacked the camp with 600 troopers of the Seventh Cavalry. Custer and about 225 men were killed and the rest barely escaped. This so-called massacre stunned the nation. The army intensified its efforts to move Native Americans onto reservations. Today the site where this battle took place is Little Bighorn Battlefield National Monument.

1876 *continued*

- Order of Eastern Star, women's auxiliary of Masons, was founded.
- Appalachian Mountain Club founded.
- Meharry Medical College was established to train black doctors.
- The US Coast Guard Academy was established.
- The Society for Ethical Culture was founded at New York City by Felix Adler.

Culture

Publications

Fiction

- *Daniel Deronda*, by George Eliot
- *The Adventures of Tom Sawyer*, by Mark Twain
- *Roderick Hudson*, by Henry James

Nonfiction

- *Effect of Cross and Self-fertilization in the Vegetable Kingdom*, by Charles Darwin

- "Declaration of Rights of the Women of the United States," by Elizabeth Cady Stanton and Matilda Joselyn Gage of the National Woman Suffrage Association was presented to the vice president of the US at the Centennial Exposition in Philadelphia.

Poetry

- *The Hunting of the Snark*, by Lewis Carroll
- *The Flood of Years*, by William Cullen Bryant
- *The Afternoon of a Faun*, by Stephane Mallarmé

Notes

- *McCall's* magazine began publication under the title *The Queen*. The periodical was created to promote McCall's sewing patterns but grew to become a general magazine for women.

Classical Music

- *Symphony No 1*, by Brahms
- *Vakula the Smith*, by Tchaikovsky
- *Symphony No 5*, by Anton Bruckner
- *Götterdämmerung*, by Wagner
- The theater in Bayreuth, Germany, opened with the first complete performance of Wagner's *Ring* cycle.

Popular Music

- "I'll Take You Home Again, Kathleen," by Thomas Westendorf
- "The Rose of Killarney," by John R. Thomas and G. Cooper
- "The Honored Dead March," by John Philip Sousa
- "What a Friend We Have in Jesus," by Ira David Sankey and Horatius Bonar

Art

- *The Absinthe Drinkers*, by Degas
- *The Swing*, by Renoir

The Beginning of Professional Librarianship

On Oct 6 the American Library Association was founded at a meeting of 103 librarians in Philadelphia. It is the world's oldest and largest professional association for librarians. Prominent in the founding of the association was Melvil Dewey who this year copyrighted the Dewey Decimal Classification system that he had developed while a student and librarian at Amherst College. Also this year, the federal government published *Public Libraries in the United States of America*, the first federal survey of libraries. Charles Cutter published his *Rules for a Printed Dictionary Catalog*. *Library Journal*, the oldest independent library publication in the US, was first published Sept 30, 1876, as *American Library Journal*. The managing editor was Melvil Dewey and the general editor was Richard Rogers Bowker. Samuel Swett Green of the Worcester (MA) Public Library called on librarians to establish reference services in their libraries.

- *The Chess Players*, by Thomas Eakins
- *Breezing Up*, by Winslow Homer

Notes
- The Boston Museum of Fine Arts was completed. It was the first museum in the US built specifically for that purpose.

Science and Technology

Apr 20 American Chemical Society founded at New York City.

Aug 8 Edison patented the mimeograph machine which was used through the 1960s at which time it was superseded by the photocopier.

Nov 7 First cigarette-making machine patented.

- Scientist Robert Koch discovered how anthrax works. Not long after, Pasteur developed a vaccine to protect against the disease.
- Swedish chemist Alfred Nobel patented gelatinous dynamite.
- The element scandium discovered by Lars Nilson.

New Products

- "Mrs Lydia E. Pinkham's Vegetable Compound," a medicine for "women's weakness" which was 18 percent alcohol, was sold by mail order.
- The Bissell carpet sweeper was patented.
- Heinz's Tomato Ketchup was patented.
- Swede Gustav de Laval patented the cream separator.

- The first Fred Harvey restaurant with its "Harvey Girls" opened at the Santa Fe Railroad depot at Topeka, KS. By 1901 there were 47 Fred Harvey restaurants at major rail depots.
- First I. Magnin store opened in San Francisco.
- Pharmaceutical firm Eli Lilly opened in Indianapolis, IN.
- Seth Thomas Clock Co introduced the wind-up alarm clock.
- Thomas Edison began building an industrial research laboratory at Menlo Park, NJ, which he called the "invention factory."
- American Bankers Association formed.
- W. Atlee Burpee Co founded at Philadelphia to sell livestock by mail. Burpee entered the mail-order seed business in 1882.

Sports

Feb 2 National League of Professional Baseball Clubs organized at New York City.

Apr 26 First baseball game that was a shutout, when the Chicago White Stockings beat Louisville, 4–0.

May 2 First baseball players to hit home runs were Ross Barnes of the Chicago White Stockings and Charles "Baby" Jones of the Cincinnati Reds. Chicago won the game, 15–9.

July 20–21 First intercollegiate track meet was held at Saratoga, NY.

Nov 23 The Intercollegiate Football Association was founded at Springfield, MA. Columbia, Harvard and Princeton were the three charter members. The number of men on a team was standardized at 15 and the size of the field at 140 by 70 yards.

Dec 6 Yale was first collegiate football champion.

- Baseball player and manager Albert Spalding started a sporting goods business.

Obits

- French author George Sand
- Frontiersman Wild Bill Hickok
- Mexican General Santa Anna, who defeated the defenders of the Alamo.
- Union General Daniel Butterfield, composer of bugle call "Taps."

1901 *100 years ago*

Landmark World Events

JAN 1 Commonwealth of Australia founded. (*See also* Spotlight on the World.)

JAN 22 Death of Britain's Queen Victoria at age 82. She had reigned for 64 years, longer than any other monarch, and ruled over the one-quarter of the world that made up the British Empire. Succeeded by her son Edward VII who was 59 years old.

JANUARY Robert Falcon Scott began his first expedition to Anarctica. During the three-year expedition, he surveyed the coast and discovered the Edward VII Peninsula. On a second journey in 1912 Scott and his party died after reaching the South Pole.

JUNE Cuba was forced to incorporate into its constitution the Platt Amendment which allowed US military intervention in Cuban affairs. As part of this agreement, the US acquired indefinite rights to the Guantanamo Bay naval base.

SEPT 7 The Peking Protocol ended the Boxer Rebellion of 1900. As a result, China was essentially a subject nation to the West.

DEC 10 First Nobel Prizes awarded in literature, chemistry, physics, peace and medicine. In 1969 a Nobel Prize in economics was established.

- Beriberi killed thousands in the Philippines after the introduction of polished white rice by US occupation forces after the Spanish-American War.
- The first section of the Trans-Siberian railroad opened.

Landmark US Events

JAN 10 Oil was discovered in Texas at Spindletop Hill. Though oil had been pumped from Pennsylvania wells since 1859, it was mainly used to make kerosene for lighting. The huge supply of Texas oil made gasoline a practical power source and fueled a new industrial revolution.

MAR 12 Industrialist Andrew Carnegie offered the city of New York $5.2 million for the construction of 65 branch libraries. Eventually Carnegie would fund 2,509 libraries in the English-speaking world. He had sold his Carnegie Steel Corporation to US Steel this year for $250 million.

APR 25 New York began requiring registration of automobiles, the first state to do so. License plates bore the owner's initials.

MAY 21 Connecticut passed the first legislation regulating the speed of cars. They were limited to 12 MPH in the country and 8 MPH within city limits.

MAY 30 The Hall of Fame for Great Americans was dedicated on the Bronx campus of New York University, the first "hall of fame" in the US. Twenty-nine Americans were honored. Today there are 98 bronze busts commemorating distinguished Americans. The last to be added was Franklin Delano Roosevelt in 1993. In 1973 NYU sold the campus to Bronx Community College.

JULY 4 William Howard Taft was installed as the first governor-general of the Philippines.

SEPT 2 Vice president Theodore Roosevelt, speaking at the Minnesota State Fair, said "Speak softly and carry a big stick."

SEPT 6 President McKinley was assassinated by an anarchist at the Pan-American Exposition at Buffalo, NY. Vice president Theodore Roosevelt became president on Sept 14. At 42, he was the youngest president the US had ever had.

OCT 16 Booker T. Washington was the first African American to be invited to dine at the White House.

OCT 24 Anna Edson Taylor became the first person to go

over Niagara Falls in a barrel and survive.

Nov 27 The Army War College established at Washington, DC.

Nov 28 Alabama adopted a new constitution which disenfranchised blacks through the use of literacy and property tests. It also had a grandfather clause that said a man couldn't vote if his grandfather had not voted before him. Louisiana had passed such a law in 1898.

November Robert M. LaFollette elected reform governor of Wisconsin.

- The average life expectancy for white females in the US was 51 years; for white males it was 48 years.
- US citizenship was granted to the Five Civilized Tribes (Cherokees, Creeks, Choctaws, Chickasaws and Seminoles). Citizenship wasn't granted to all Native Americans until 1924.
- The Library of Congress began printing catalog cards for itself and depository libraries, forming a union catalog of 600 libraries. The next year it began selling these cards to American libraries. This service was discontinued in 1997, after hundreds of millions of cards had been sold.
- Rockefeller Institute for Medical Research founded at New York City; today known as Rockefeller University.
- Texas Woman's University founded.

Culture

PUBLICATIONS

Fiction

- *Buddenbrooks*, by Thomas Mann was published in Germany. It did not become available in English until 1924.
- *Kim*, by Rudyard Kipling
- *The Octopus*, by Frank Norris
- *The Marrow of Tradition*, by Charles Chesnutt
- *Alice of Old Vincennes*, by Maurice Thompson
- *Mrs Wiggs of the Cabbage Patch*, children's book by Alice Hegan

Nonfiction

- *The Making of an American*, autobiography of Jacob Riis
- *The Life of the Bee*, by Maurice Maeterlinck

Poetry

- *Lincoln and Other Poems*, by Edwin C. Markham

Notes

- *Parents* magazine began as *Children: The Magazine for Parents*.

THEATER

- *The Three Sisters*, by Chekhov, premiered in Moscow.
- *The Way of the World*, by Clyde Fitch
- *The Dance of Death*, by August Strindberg
- *The Governor's Son*, a musical by George M. Cohan, starring The Five Cohans

CLASSICAL MUSIC

- *Piano Concerto No 2*, by Rachmaninoff

- *Three Harvest Home Chorales*, by Charles Ives

Popular Music

- "The Pride of Pittsburgh March," by John Philip Sousa
- "I Love You Truly," by Carrie Bond
- "High Society," by Porter Steele

ART

- *The Gold in Their Bodies*, by Gauguin
- *Seated Woman*, sculpture by Aristide Maillol
- *Opera Messalina*, by Toulouse-Lautrec
- *Central Park*, by Maurice Prendergast
- *East Entrance, City Hall, Philadelphia*, by John Sloan
- *After the Bath*, by Mary Cassatt
- *The Man Cub*, sculpture by A. Stirling Calder
- Frank Lloyd Wright constructed what some consider to be his first Prairie Style house, in Highland Park, IL.

Science and Technology

Feb 25 US Steel was incorporated with a capitalization of $1 billion, the largest company to that date. It was formed by a merger of the Carnegie Company and nine other steel companies.

July German doctor Robert Koch proposed that the bubonic plague was transmitted by rats.

Aug 27 Walter Reed and his research team published their

1901 *continued*

findings from Cuba that yellow fever is transmitted by mosquitos.

OCTOBER The Hartford (CT) Electric Company began generating electricity using a steam turbine.

Nov 16 The automobile exceeded the speed of 60 m.p.h. for the first time in the US at a race in Brooklyn sponsored by the Long Island Automobile Club.

DEC 2 The first safety razor, designed by King Camp Gillette, was patented. Until this time, men shaved with a straight edge razor they sharpened on a leather strap.

DEC 12 Marconi demonstrated the potential of wireless communication when he received signals from Cornwall, England, at St. John's, Newfoundland, Canada. He broadcast the single letter "S" across the Atlantic. This led to the development of radio and television.

- The element europium discovered by Eugene Demarcay.
- The first accurate determination of the sun's distance from the Earth was made by Scottish astronomer David Gill.
- The hormone epinephrine was isolated. Known by its trade name Adrenalin.
- The hydrogenation of fats extended the shelf life of foods.
- Victor Talking Machine Co formed by Emile Berliner and Eldridge Johnson. Their gramophone was called "Victrola." A dog and "His Master's Voice" became their registered trademark.
- Monsanto Chemical and US Gypsum founded.
- Bergdorf Goodman opened in New York City, Nordstrom's in Seattle. Macy's opened its first department store on 34th Street in New York City.

New Products

- Pierce Motorette car launched, forerunner of the Pierce-Arrow.
- The Oldsmobile was the first American car to be made in quantity, with 600 cars sold this year. This was the real beginning of the American automobile industry.
- The first automobile speedometer was made, calibrated from 0 to 35.
- The first US-made motorcycle, the Indian, was released.
- First Christmas tree lights sold by Edison General Electric Co.
- The first powdered instant coffee was sold at the Pan-American Exposition in Buffalo.
- Campbell's introduced powdered milk.
- Quaker Oats was established to market rolled oats cereal.
- Clicquot Club, the first nationally marketed ginger ale, was launched at Boston.
- First electric vacuum cleaner developed by Hubert Booth of England.

Sports

JAN 8–11 The American Bowling Congress held its first national tournament in Chicago.

JUNE 14–17 The first professional open golf championship was held at Hamilton, MA.

- Field hockey was introduced into the US.
- Charlotte Cooper Sterry won women's singles at Wimbledon.
- Bill Larnard won the US Open (tennis).
- *Columbia* (USA) won the America's Cup.
- The Chicago White Sox were the first champions of the American League.
- Michigan was college football champion.
- Ping-Pong was a craze.

Obits

- Benjamin Harrison, 23rd president
- William McKinley, 25th president
- British Queen Victoria
- French painter Henri de Toulouse-Lautrec
- Italian opera composer Giuseppe Verdi

- English children's book illustrator Kate Greenaway
- Swiss author Johanna Spyri (*Heidi*)
- English opera impresario Richard D'Oyly Carte
- Historian Herbert Baxter Adams

1926 *75 years ago*

Landmark World Events

JANUARY Abdul Aziz ibn Saud became king of Hejaz and changed the country's name to Saudi Arabia.

FEB 17 A new legal code in Turkey outlawed polygamy. This was part of the new civil, commercial and penal codes based on European models adopted by Turkey this year.

APR 21 Princess Elizabeth Windsor born, later to become Queen Elizabeth II.

APR 29 Sixty percent of France's debt from World War I was cancelled by the US.

MAR 11 Eamon de Valera resigned as head of Sinn Fein, a political party dedicated to achieving a unified independent Ireland. He entered Irish Free State politics and in 1932 was elected president of Ireland (which did not include Northern Ireland).

MAY 4 A general strike in Britain had begun as a strike of 1,200,000 coal miners but spread to other industries. Nearly half of Britain's workforce stayed home.

MAY 9 Piloting a Fokker monoplane Lt Commander Richard Byrd and Floyd Bennett were hailed as the first men to fly over the North Pole. However, this was later disputed.

JULY 3–4 Nazi party rally at Weimar attended by 7,000–8,000 people.

SEPT 6 The Chinese Civil War began. It was to last until 1949, with an interruption from 1936 to 1945 for World War II. On this day Komintang forces led by General Chiang Kai-shek seized Hankou, which became their capital.

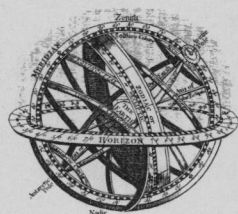

DEC 11 Hitler published the second volume of *Mein Kampf*.

DEC 25 Yoshihito, emperor of Japan, died and was succeeded by his son Hirohito, who was in power for 62 years, becoming Japan's longest-reigning emperor. He ruled through World War II and died in 1989.

- Joseph Goebbels was made Gauleiter of Berlin.
- At the Imperial Conference it was declared that all members of the British Commonwealth of Nations were equal in status, and independent of the others, although associated together under a common crown.
- A new constitution in Lebanon tried to provide for representation of all religious communities, with a Maronite Christian president, a Sunni Muslim prime minister and a Shiite Muslim speaker of the chamber.

Landmark US Events

MAY 10 US Marines landed in Nicaragua following an uprising by General Augusto Sandino.

MAY 22 A bill was signed by President Calvin Coolidge establishing Great Smoky Mountains (NC, TN) and Shenandoah (VA) National Parks. Mammoth Cave (KY) was authorized later that month.

MAY 31–NOV 30 America's sesquicentennial was celebrated in Philadelphia with an exposition. It was not adequately funded and many pavilions remained unfinished on opening day. Innovations on display included talking motion pictures, radio advertising and a public address system.

JULY 2 The US Army Air Service was renamed the Army Air Corps. The Air Force did not became independent of the Army until 1947.

SEPTEMBER The Ford Motor Co introduced the 8-hour workday and 5-day week.

OCT 25 The Supreme Court ruled that the president has the authority to remove executive officers from their positions. Previously consent of the Senate was required.

Spotlight on the Past *milestone anniversary years*

1926 *continued*

- Howard University named Mordecai W. Johnson its first black president. Howard had been founded in 1867.
- US Route 66 opened, linking Chicago and Los Angeles. The highway was decommissioned in 1985.
- Restoration of colonial Williamsburg, VA, founded in 1699, was begun by John D. Rockefeller.
- Evangelist Aimee Semple McPherson disappeared and was presumed dead; later it was discovered that she was having a tryst with her lover.
- Sarah Lawrence College founded at Bronxville, NY, and Long Island University at Brooklyn, NY.
- Illegal traffic in liquor spawned a huge criminal industry since 1919—a $3.6 billion business.
- Airmail service inaugurated between Chicago and St. Louis, with Charles Lindbergh as pilot.
- New York City celebrated its tercentennial with a parade up Broadway. Peter Minuit, director of the Dutch West India Company, had landed on Manhattan Island in 1626.

Culture

PUBLICATIONS 📖

Fiction

- *Exiles*, by James Joyce
- *The Castle*, by Franz Kafka, published posthumously.
- *Show Boat*, by Edna Ferber
- *The Sun Also Rises*, by Ernest Hemingway
- *Soldier's Pay*, William Faulkner's first novel
- *Topper*, by Thorne Smith
- *The Murder of Roger Ackroyd*, by Agatha Christie
- *Clouds of Witness*, by Dorothy Sayers
- *Winnie the Pooh*, by A.A. Milne
- *The Little Engine that Could*, children's book by Watty Piper

Nonfiction

- *Song Index: An Index to More Than 12,000 Songs . . .*, by Minnie Sears
- *Seven Pillars of Wisdom*, by T.E. Lawrence ("Lawrence of Arabia")
- *Abraham Lincoln, The Prairie Years*, by Carl Sandburg
- *The Microbe Hunters*, by Paul de Kruif
- *The Stream of Life*, by Julian Huxley

Poetry

- *Dark of the Moon*, by Sara Teasdale
- *The Weary Blues*, Langston Hughes's first book of poetry
- *Enough Rope*, by Dorothy Parker
- *The Bridge*, by Hart Crane

Notes

MAR 10 Book-of-the-Month Club founded. It sells books by mail, on subscription. *Lolly Willowes* by Sylvia Townsend Warner was the first offering. By the end of the year there were 40,000 subscribers.

APRIL *Amazing Stories*, the first science fiction magazine, debuted. It continued publication until 1994.

- Sinclair Lewis turned down the Pulitzer Prize for *Arrowsmith*.

THEATER

- *The Great God Brown*, by Eugene O'Neill
- *Oh, Kay!*, with music by George and Ira Gershwin and starring Gertrude Lawrence
- *The Girl Friend*, with music by Richard Rodgers and Lorenz Hart
- *The Desert Song*, operetta by Sigmund Romberg, Otto Harbach and Oscar Hammerstein
- *Sex*, written by and starring Mae West, was closed down by the police.
- *The Plough and the Stars*, by Sean O'Casey, opened in Dublin.

Dance

APRIL First Martha Graham modern dance recital

FILM

All silent films except Don Juan

- *Metropolis*, directed by Fritz Lang, released in Germany.

- *What Price Glory?*, directed by Raoul Walsh
- *La Bohème*, starring Lillian Gish and Erich von Stroheim
- *The Black Pirate*, with Douglas Fairbanks
- *Battling Butler*, with Buster Keaton
- *Don Juan*, first film with synchronized musical score and sound effects on phonograph records (but no dialogue). It starred John Barrymore and Mary Astor.
- *Flesh and the Devil*, starring Greta Garbo and John Gilbert
- *Mantrap*, starring Clara Bow
- *Putting Pants on Philip*, Laurel and Hardy's first film as a duo

RADIO

- "Auction Bridge Game"
- "Betty Crocker Magazine of the Air," recipes and homemaking tips
- "Cook's Travelogue"
- "The Eveready Hour," variety show, one of NBC's first programs
- "The Happiness Boys," with two of radio's first stars who sang and told jokes
- "Housekeeper's Chat," sponsored by the US Agriculture Department
- "Men's Conference," a Sunday afternoon religious talk program
- "Synagogue Service"
- "Sam 'n' Henry" debuted on local radio in Chicago. In 1929 it premiered on the NBC network as "Amos 'n' Andy."

OCTOBER Demagogue Father Charles Coughlin began his long series of radio broadcasts from Detroit. Eventually he attacked Roosevelt, Commu-nism, Jews and promoted fascism.

Nov 15 The National Broadcasting Company (NBC) radio network was founded by David Sarnoff with 24 stations. The first broadcast was on this day from the Waldorf-Astoria Hotel in New York City. This was the beginning of network radio.

CLASSICAL MUSIC

- *Sanctus*, by Virgil Thomson
- *Piano Concerto*, by Aaron Copland
- *Piano Concerto No 4*, by Rachmaninoff
- *Turandot* , opera by Puccini, first performed at Milan.

Notes

- Arturo Toscanini became the head of the New York Philharmonic.

POPULAR MUSIC

- "Baby Face," by Harry Akst and B. Davis
- "Tip-Toe Through the Tulips," by Joseph Burke and A. Dubin
- "Birth of the Blues," by R. Henderson and B. DeSylva
- "Bye, Bye Blackbird," by R. Henderson and M. Dixon
- "Are You Lonesome Tonight," by R. Turk and L. Handman
- "If You See My Savior, Tell Him That You Saw Me," by Thomas Andrew Dorsey, considered to be the first gospel song.

ART

- *Lover's Bouquet*, by Marc Chagall
- *Odalisque with Tambourine*, by Henri Matisse
- *Dog Barking at the Moon*, by Joan Miró
- *Lobster Telephone*, sculpture by Salvador Dalí
- *Eleven AM*, by Edward Hopper
- *Black Iris*, by Georgia O'Keeffe

Science and Technology

JANUARY The Pasteur Institute in Paris announced an anti-tetanus serum.

MAR 7 First transatlantic radiotelephone conversation between New York City and London. Commercial service became available the following year.

MAR 16 The first liquid-fuel powered rocket was launched by Robert Hutchings Goddard at Auburn, MA.

APR 28 The term wave mechanics introduced by nuclear physicist Erwin Schrodinger to describe the motion of electrons in terms of wave motion.

OCT 19 The semiautomatic rifle was patented by John Garand of Maryland.

- Insulin was obtained in pure crystalline form. Insulin had been discovered in 1921.
- Riboflavin or vitamin B-1 isolated by D.T. Smith and E.G. Hendrick of the US. It prevents beriberi.
- The cause (a dietary deficiency) and cure for pellagra were discovered by American pathologist Joseph Goldberger.
- German physiologist Rudolf Magnus discovered how the inner ear regulates balance.

1926 *continued*

- John Logie Baird demonstrated a workable TV system. The BBC began broadcasting experimental TV programs in 1929, using Baird's system.

New Products

- The first long-playing (LP) record was developed by Thomas Edison. It was 12 inches in diameter, one-half-inch thick and weighed two pounds. It was played with a diamond stylus.
- The first pop-up toaster was marketed.
- The slide fastener was named the zipper and replaced buttons on blue jeans.
- The first steam irons went on sale.
- Mass production of safety glass begun by Libby Owens.
- Mies van der Rohe tubular steel chair manufacturered by Thonet.
- Q-Tips first sold (under the name Baby Gays).
- Hershey's Chocolate Syrup introduced.
- IGA (Independent Grocers of America) launched at Pough-keepsie, NY. Independent grocers organized to compete with corporate giants such as A&P.
- Canned ham first marketed by the Hormel Company of Austin, MN.
- First factory ships for freezing and processing fish were used by British and French.

- First company devoted to commercial production of hybrid corn seed, Pioneer Hi-Bred International, founded.
- The first White Tower restaurant opened in Milwaukee.
- Erik Rotheim of Norway invented the aerosol can.
- The first waterproof watch was sold by Rolex.
- Cellophane was developed by DuPont.
- Burma-Shave unveiled its rhyming roadside signs.

Sports 🏀

Aug 6 Nineteen-year-old Gertrude Ederle of New York became the first woman to swim the English Channel; she beat the world record by two hours.

Sept 23 Gene Tunney defeated Jack Dempsey to win the world heavyweight boxing title.

- Montreal Maroons won the Stanley Cup.
- Bobby Jones won the US Open (golf).
- René Lacoste won the US Open (tennis).
- St. Louis Cardinals won the World Series, beating New York Yankees.
- Cubs Park was renamed Wrigley Field.
- Alabama and Stanford were college football champions.
- Miniature golf was invented in Tennessee.

Obits

- Horticulturalist Luther Burbank
- American West artist Charles Russell

- Actor Rudolph Valentino
- American painter Mary Cassatt
- French artist Claude Monet
- Magician and escape artist Harry Houdini
- Markswoman Annie Oakley
- Socialist presidential candidate Eugene Debs
- Pilot Bessie Coleman
- Spanish architect Antonio Gaudí
- German poet Rainer Maria Rilke
- British author Ronald Firbank
- American book publisher Henry Holt
- Newspaper publisher Edward Scripps
- Builder of the Brooklyn Bridge Washington Roebling
- Harvard University president Charles W. Eliot
- British author Israel Zangwill (*Children of the Ghetto*)
- The last Ottoman sultan, Mehmet VI, in Italy

1951 *50 years ago*

Landmark World Events 📺

Jan 4 The city of Seoul in South Korea was captured for the second time by North Korean and Chinese troops.

Mar 14 Seoul was retaken by UN forces.

Apr 11 General Douglas MacArthur was relieved of command of the Korean War by President Truman because MacArthur wanted to extend the war by bombing Chinese bases in Manchuria.

MacArthur received a hero's welcome on his return to the US on Apr 20.

MAY 3 Festival of Britain opened by King George VI at London. Commemorating the centenary of the Crystal Palace Exhibition of 1851, this festival was the official celebration of Britain's recovery from World War II. There were fairgrounds on the South Bank in London and events at 37 other sites in Britain.

MAY 23 A Tibetan-Chinese agreement was signed under which Tibet became an autonomous region of China. Supposedly under the rule of the Dalai Lama, Tibet was actually under Chinese control. In 1959 the Dalai Lama fled to India.

JUNE UN forces pushed as far north as the 38th parallel in Korea.

JULY 20 Jordan's King Abdullah was assassinated in Jerusalem. His son Talal succeeded him briefly; his younger son Hussein ascended the throne in 1953 and served until his death in 1999.

JULY Korean War peace talks started in Panmunjon but a peace treaty wasn't signed until 1953.

DEC 24 Libya gained its independence from Italy. Parts of Libya had been occupied by Italy as early as 1911; the whole country had come under Italian control by 1932.

- Winston Churchill became British prime minister again, having last served 1940–45.
- Eamon de Valera became prime minister of Ireland again, having served 1931–48. He would serve one more term, 1957–59.
- Iran's prime minister nationalized the oil industry, precipitating a crisis with Britain.
- Volcanic eruptions in the Philippines and Papua New Guinea killed several thousand people.
- South Africa suspended participation in the UN General Assembly because of controversy over its control of South-West Africa. In 1990 South-West Africa finally gained independence as Namibia.

Landmark US Events

JAN 15 Supreme Court ruled that a speaker who presents "a real and present danger" can be arrested.

APR 6 Julius and Ethel Rosenberg sentenced to death for treason for passing atomic secrets to the Soviet Union. They were executed in 1953.

MAY 18 The United Nations moved from its temporary headquarters at Lake Success, NY, to its permanent home in Manhattan.

JUNE Robert Maynard Hutchins resigned as president of the University of Chicago, ending a 21-year term.

JULY 9 President Truman asked Congress to formally end the state of war between the US and Germany.

SEPT 20 The first shopping mall opened in Seattle. Fourteen days later another opened in Framingham, MA.

SEPT 24 New Yorker George Jorgensen went to Denmark for a sex change operation, the first American to do so. The 25-year-old adopted the name Christine Jorgensen.

NOV 1 US exploded history's first hydrogen bomb in the skies over the Marshall Islands.

NOV 10 First direct-dial, coast-to-coast telephone call was made when the mayor of Englewood, NJ, called his counterpart in Alameda, CA. This introduced the use of area codes to the public. Prior to this, long-distance calls required the assistance of an operator.

NOV 27 A rocket intercepted an airplane for the first time, over White Sands Proving Grounds, NM.

DEC 27 The US Postal Service introduced the first right-hand-drive car specifically designed for mail delivery. It was a Crosley.

- United Auto Workers president Walter Reuther was elected president of the CIO. He helped the CIO merge with the AFL in 1955.
- The Senate, led by Senator Estes Kefauver, investigated organized crime.
- The Nature Conservancy founded.
- Recording for the Blind began in New York City.

1951 *continued*

Culture

PUBLICATIONS

Fiction

- *Catcher in the Rye*, by J.D. Salinger
- *Requiem for a Nun*, by William Faulkner
- *From Here to Eternity*, by James Jones
- *The Caine Mutiny*, by Herman Wouk
- *The End of the Affair*, by Graham Greene
- *The Ballad of the Sad Café*, short stories by Carson McCullers
- *A Question of Upbringing*, by Anthony Powell, the first of 12 volumes in his A Dance to the Music of Time series
- *Spartacus*, by Howard Fast

Nonfiction

- *A Man Called Peter*, by Katherine Marshall
- *The Sea Around Us*, by Rachel Carson
- *White Collar*, by C. Wright Mills
- *The Origins of Totalitarianism*, by Hannah Arendt
- *God and Man at Yale*, by William F. Buckley, Jr
- *Speak, Memory*, autobiography of Vladimir Nabokov

Poetry

- *Complete Poems*, by Carl Sandburg
- *Collected Poems*, by Marianne Moore

Notes

- "Dennis the Menace," comic strip by cartoonist Hank Ketcham debuted.

THEATER

- *The King and I*, with music by Richard Rodgers and Oscar Hammerstein, starring Gertrude Lawrence and Yul Brynner
- *Paint Your Wagon*, with music by Lerner and Loewe
- *The Rose Tattoo*, by Tennessee Williams
- *I Am a Camera*, based on Christopher Isherwood's *Goodbye to Berlin*, starring Julie Harris. It later formed the basis for the musical *Cabaret*.
- *Top Banana*, musical starring Phil Silvers

FILM

- *The African Queen*, starring Katherine Hepburn and Humphrey Bogart (who won the Oscar for Best Actor).
- *A Streetcar Named Desire*, starring Marlon Brando and Vivian Leigh (who won the Oscar for Best Actress).
- *Death of a Salesman*, starring Fredric March and Mildred Dunnock
- *An American in Paris*, with Gene Kelly and Leslie Caron, won the Oscar for Best Picture.
- *A Place in the Sun*, directed by George Stevens, who won the Oscar for Best Director, starring Elizabeth Taylor, Montgomery Clift and Shelley Winters.
- *Show Boat*, with Ava Gardner and Howard Keel

- *Quo Vadis?*, with Deborah Kerr and Robert Taylor
- *The Red Badge of Courage*, with Audie Murphy
- *Detective Story*, with Kirk Douglas and Eleanor Parker
- *The Great Caruso*, with Mario Lanza
- *Alice in Wonderland*, Disney's animated version
- *Kon-Tiki*, Oscar-winning documentary based on previous year's bestseller.
- *Bedtime for Bonzo*, starring Ronald Reagan
- *I Was a Communist for the FBI*, with Frank Lovejoy
- *The Thing*, horror/sci-fi classic

RADIO

- "Barrie Craig: Confidential Investigator"
- "City Hospital"
- "The Hardy Family," a comedy based on the successful series of movies, starring Mickey Rooney.
- "Hollywood Sound Stage," a drama anthology
- "Meet Millie," situation comedy that moved to TV in 1952.
- "Howdy Doody," an audio version of the TV program for children
- "Pete Kelly's Blues," crime drama starring Jack Webb
- "Rocky Jordan," adventure series starring George Raft

- "Silver Eagle," a children's adventure series
- "Wild Bill Hickok," juvenile western adventure program that went on TV in 1952.

Television

- "Mr Wizard," science program for children with Don Herbert that ran for 14 years and was revived in 1983.
- "Strike It Rich," game show
- "Ernie Kovacs," comedy show
- "Amos'n'Andy," based on the popular radio show, with an all-black cast. (The radio version had used a white cast.) The next network program with an all-black cast was 1972's "Sanford and Son."
- "The Sammy Kaye Show," with bandleader Sammy Kaye
- "Love of Life," soap opera that ran for 28 years, introducing such stars as Christopher Reeve, Warren Beatty and Peter Falk.
- "Search for Tomorrow," soap that ran for 35 years, introducing stars Don Knotts, Susan Sarandon, Kevin Kline and Olympia Dukakis.
- "The Red Skelton Show," variety show hosted by the famous comedian.
- "I Love Lucy," starring Lucille Ball and Desi Arnaz
- "See It Now," public affairs show hosted by Edward R. Murrow which had premiered as "Hear It Now" on radio the year before.
- "The Dinah Shore Show," variety show hosted by the popular singer.
- "Dragnet," crime show starring Jack Webb

- "The Roy Rogers Show," starring Roy Rogers and Dale Evans as themselves
- "Sky King," adventure show about a rancher who uses his plane to help victims and chase bad guys.
- "Kukla, Fran & Ollie" went national, after having appeared on Chicago television.

Notes

June 25 The first commercial color TV telecast was a one-hour special broadcast on CBS from New York to four other cities. Among the program's stars were Ed Sullivan, Garry Moore, Robert Alda and Arthur Godfrey.

Sept 4 On the first coast-to-coast television broadcast President Harry Truman discussed the newly signed peace treaty with Japan. The program was broadcast to 97 of the 104 television stations then in existence.
- There were 10.6 million TV sets in use in the US.

Classical Music

- *Billy Budd*, opera by Benjamin Britten
- *The Pilgrim's Progress*, by Ralph Vaughan Williams
- *Trouble in Tahiti*, by Leonard Bernstein
- *Amahl and the Night Visitors*, by Gian Carlo Menotti. This was the first opera specifically written for television.
- *The Rake's Progress*, opera by Igor Stravinsky

Popular Music

- "In the Cool, Cool, Cool of the Evening," by Hoagy Carmichael and Johnny Mercer
- "Cold Cold Heart," by Hank Williams
- "Unforgettable," by Irving Gordon, recorded by Nat King Cole
- "Kisses Sweeter Than Wine," by J. Newman and P. Campbell, recorded by the Weavers
- "Be My Love," by N. Brodszky and Sammy Cahn
- "Syncopated Clock," by Leroy Anderson
- "How High the Moon," recorded by Les Paul and Mary Ford
- "Cry," recorded by Johnnie Ray
- "Come On-a My House," recorded by Rosemary Clooney
- "Frosty the Snowman," recorded by Mitch Miller and the Gang
- "Harbor Lights," recorded by Sammy Kaye
- "My Heart Cries for You," by Guy Mitchell
- "Hello, Young Lovers," by Rodgers and Hammerstein, from *The King and I*
- "They Call the Wind Maria" and "I Talk to the Trees," from *Paint Your Wagon*

Notes

- Cleveland disk jockey Alan Freed applied the term rock-and-roll to popular music.
- The Modern Jazz Quartet was founded by Dave Brubeck.

1951 *continued*

ART

- *Baboon and Young*, sculpture by Picasso
- *Christ on the Cross*, by Salvador Dalí
- *Silent Music*, by Ben Shahn
- *Rooms by the Sea*, by Edward Hopper
- *Echo No 2*, by Jackson Pollock

Science and Technology

FEB 1 An atomic explosion was seen on television for the first time as an NBC camera on Mt Wilson in California captured a blast at Frenchman Flat, NV.

FEB 15 The first nuclear reactor to be used in medical therapy was opened at Brookhaven National Laboratory in New York.

MARCH Ohio Bell Telephone Company marketed a telephone answering machine which could be rented for $12.50 a month.

JUNE 14 UNIVAC computer, designed for the Census Bureau, was unveiled at Philadelphia. This was the first commercial electronic computer. By 1958, there were 1,000 of these massive computers in use in the US.

JUNE 14 A live human birth was televised for the first time on closed-circuit TV at a meeting of the American Medical Association in Atlantic City.

JULY 24 African "killer" bees escaped from a lab in Saō Paolo, Brazil. The hyperaggressive bees have since spread throughout the Western Hemisphere.

AUGUST Deutsche Grammophon released the first 33-rpm long-playing record.

NOV 29 First underground nuclear test at Frenchman Flat, NV.

DEC 20 The Experimental Breeder Reactor in Idaho produced the first electricity to be generated by nuclear energy.

- Helicopters were first used by the US military to move wounded to field hospitals during the Korean War.
- Grace Hopper of Remington Rand developed the first compiler computer program. It translated programming code into machine language.
- The junction transistor was developed by William Shockley.
- US surgeon John Gibbon Jr created the first heart-lung machine.
- The first birth control pill was developed by Gregory Pincus and John Rock. It underwent clinical trials beginning in 1954 and was put on the market in 1960.
- French obstetricians Fernand Lamaze and Pierre Vellay introduced the Lamaze method of natural childbirth, which they had studied in the Soviet Union and which became widely used in the US in the 1960s.

New Products

- Chrysler introduced power steering in its cars.
- The Weber grill was invented in Palatine, IL, by George Stephens, an employee of the Weber Brothers Metal Works.
- Liquid correction fluid was created by Bette Nesmith to correct typing mistakes.
- Tropicana Products founded.
- Cyclamates approved for consumer use as a sweetener by the Food and Drug Administration.

Sports

FEB 25 The first Pan-American games held at Buenos Aires, Argentina.

MAR 2 The first National Basketball Association All-Star Game was played at Boston, MA.

SEPT 11 Swimming from England to France, American Florence Chadwick became the first woman to swim the English Channel both ways. She had swum from France to England in 1950.

OCT 3 "The Shot Heard Round the World" as Bobby Thomson hit a three-run home run at the bottom of the ninth inning to give the New York Giants a 5–4 victory over the Brooklyn Dodgers in the deciding game of the National League play-off.

- Ben Hogan won the Masters and the US Open.
- Sam Snead won the PGA Championship.
- Maureen Connelly won the US Open (tennis), at 16 the youngest woman ever to do so.
- In the World Series New York Yankees beat New York Giants. Rookie Willie Mays, 20, played for the Giants and Mickey Mantle, 19, for the Yankees.
- Michigan won the Rose Bowl.
- Tennessee was college football champion.
- NCAA Basketball championship won by Kentucky.
- Rochester Royals became NBA champions.
- Toronto Maple Leafs won Stanley Cup.

Obits

- Newspaper magnate William Randolph Hearst
- Novelist Sinclair Lewis
- Documentary filmmaker Robert Flaherty
- French author André Gide
- Austrian philosopher Ludwig Wittgenstein
- Comedienne Fanny Brice
- Cereal manufacturer W.K. Kellogg
- Austrian car designer Ferdinand Porsche
- Austrian composer Arnold Schoenberg
- French General Henri Pétain, hero of World War I
- Painter John Sloan
- Baseball player Shoeless Joe Jackson
- American statesman Charles Dawes

- Hungarian-American composer Sigmund Romberg (*The Student Prince*)
- *New Yorker* editor Harold Ross

1976 *25 years ago*

Landmark World Events

Feb 26 Spain completed its withdrawal from the Sahara. The previous year King Hassan II of Morocco launched the "Green March," in which 300,000 Moroccans marched into the territory and claimed it.

Mar 24 Isabel Perón was deposed as the leader of Argentina by the military, which then began a bloody reign. An estimated 30,000 people "disappeared" between 1976 and 1983.

Apr 16 India announced that it would begin paying citizens to be sterilized as a population control measure.

May Syria intervened in the Lebanese civil war.

June 16 Soweto, South Africa, uprising of students against the forced use of the Afrikaans language in school and poor education for blacks left 575 dead.

June 26 The CN Tower, one of the world's tallest buildings, opened in Toronto.

July 2 North and South Vietnam reunified as Socialist Republic of Vietnam with Hanoi as capital.

July 4 Israeli commandos rescued 103 hostages held at Entebbe, Uganda airport by Palestinian hijackers.

July 29 The worst earthquake in modern times, a magnitude 8.2, left 250,000 dead in Tangshan, China.

August A women's peace movement was launched in Northern Ireland. Its leaders, Mairead Corrigan and Betty Williams, would win the Nobel Peace Prize.

September The unrest of the cultural revolution in China which had begun in 1966 came to an end with the deaths of Chou En-Lai in January and Mao Tse-tung this month. Red Guards, and later the People's Liberation Army, had destroyed the bourgeoisie and any opposition within the Communist Party. On Oct 11 in a purge of radicals by the new government, the Gang of Four, which included Mao's widow, were arrested, expelled from the Communist Party and imprisoned. This was followed by massive political and economic reorganization.

Oct 16 A peace conference was held in Riyadh, Saudi Arabia, to end the Lebanese civil war. While full-scale fighting ceased, the war continued until 1991.

1976 *continued*

Nov 18 The Spanish Parliament passed a bill to establish a democracy after 37 years of dictatorship. Dictator General Francisco Franco had died the previous year.

• The world's population was four billion.

Landmark US Events

Feb 10 Soviet use of radiation against the US embassy in Moscow was revealed. It is believed that at least two US ambassadors were killed as a result of the more than 25 years of microwave radiation.

Mar 20 Heiress Patty Hearst was convicted of armed robbery and sentenced to seven years in prison.

Mar 29 Washington, DC, subway opened.

Mar 31 The New Jersey Supreme Court ruled that the comatose Karen Anne Quinlan could be removed from her artificial respirator, as her family wished. Although she lived until 1985 after being detached from the machine, this right-to-die case set an important precedent.

Apr 1 Conrail, a federally funded corporation, took over the operation of six bankrupt railroads in the northeast.

June After the US ambassador to Lebanon and an associate were murdered by Muslim guerrillas in Beirut, Americans were urged to leave Lebanon. The bloody Lebanese civil war had begun the year before.

July 2 The Supreme Court ruled that the death penalty was not inherently cruel and unusual punishment, reversing a 1972 decision. Two-thirds of Americans surveyed supported the death penalty.

July 4 During America's bicentennial celebration six million people watched tall ships sail into New York harbor and there were fireworks coast-to-coast.

July 6 Queen Elizabeth II arrived in Philadelphia and presented a copy of the Liberty Bell as a bicentennial gift. On July 17 she opened the Summer Olympics in Montreal.

July 27 A form of pneumonia that became known as Legionnaires' disease killed 29 people attending an American Legion convention in Philadelphia.

July Congresswoman Barbara Jordan was the first African American speaker to deliver the keynote speech at the Democratic National Convention.

Sept 20 Presidential candidate Jimmy Carter admitted in a *Playboy* interview to having "committed adultery in my heart many times."

Sept 20 The House of Bishops of the Episcopal Church approved a revised Book of Common Prayer, the first major revision in 427 years.

Sept 30 California passed the first right-to-die law, allowing physicians to withhold life-sustaining treatment from terminally ill patients under some conditions.

Sept 30 Congress approved a new copyright law extending protection for 50 years after the death of an author, artist or composer. The legislation took effect in 1978.

Oct 15 Walter Mondale and Robert Dole participated in the first-ever debate of vice presidential candidates.

Oct 21 President Gerald Ford signed the Resource Conservation and Recovery Act, which established federal standards for the disposal of toxic waste.

Nov 2 Barbara Mikulski of Maryland became the first person of Polish descent to be elected to Congress.

• Women were enrolled for the first time at the US military academies.

• Australian Rupert Murdoch bought the New York *Post*.

• Legislation was passed making casino gambling legal at Atlantic City, NJ. The first casinos opened in 1978.

• Bill Clinton was elected Arkansas attorney general.

• Al Gore, Jr was elected to the US House of Representatives for the first time.

• As a result of the death of Elijah Muhammad the previous year, the Black Muslims split into the Nation of Islam (led by Louis Farrakhan) and the American Muslim Mission (led by Muhammad's son Wallace Muhammad).

• Imported cars accounted for 18 percent of total US car sales.

Culture

PUBLICATIONS 📖

Fiction

- *Roots*, by Alex Haley. Was a TV miniseries the following year.
- *The Thorn Birds*, by Colleen McCullough
- *Trinity*, by Leon Uris
- *1876*, by Gore Vidal
- *The Spectator Bird*, by Wallace Stegner
- *The Woman Warrior*, by Maxine Hong Kingston
- *The Great Santini*, by Pat Conroy
- *Salem's Lot*, by Stephen King
- *Interview with the Vampire*, by Anne Rice

Notes

- Saul Bellow won the Nobel Prize for Literature.

Nonfiction

- *The Uses of Enchantment: The Meaning and Importance of Fairy Tales*, by Bruno Bettleheim
- *The Hite Report*, a survey of the sex life of Americans by Shere Hite
- *Scoundrel Time*, memoir by Lillian Hellman
- *Lyndon Johnson and the American Dream*, by Doris Kearns
- *Racial Equality in America*, by John Hope Franklin

Poetry

- *Collected Poems, 1930–1976*, by Richard Eberhart
- *Another Republic*, by Mark Strand
- *The Zodiac*, by James Dickey

THEATER

- *Joseph and the Amazing Technicolor Dream Coat*, by Andrew Lloyd Webber and Tim Rice
- *California Suite*, by Neil Simon, starring Tammy Grimes and Jack Weston
- *Evita*, based on the life of Eva Perón, by Andrew Lloyd Webber
- *Bubblin' Brown Sugar*, African American review
- *The Belle of Amherst*, based on the life of Emily Dickinson, starring Julie Harris
- *Annie*, musical based on *Little Orphan Annie*
- *Pacific Overtures*, by Stephen Sondheim
- *Your Arms Too Short to Box with God*, gospel musical

Dance

- *Push Comes to Shove*, by choreographer Twyla Tharp, blended ballet and jazz.

FILM

- *A Star Is Born*, starring Barbra Streisand and Kris Kristofferson
- *Rocky*, starring Sylvester Stallone, won Best Picture Oscar and director John Avildsen

won the Oscar for Best Director.
- *Network*, starring Peter Finch (Oscar for Best Actor) and Faye Dunaway (Oscar for Best Actress).
- *All the President's Men*, starring Jason Robards, Robert Redford and Dustin Hoffman, told the Watergate story.
- *Taxi Driver*, directed by Martin Scorsese, starred Robert De Niro and Jodie Foster.
- *King Kong*, remake with Jessica Lange and Jeff Bridges
- *Silver Streak*, with Gene Wilder, Richard Pryor
- *Carrie*, horror flick starring Sissy Spacek
- *Little Big Man*, starring Dustin Hoffman
- *Cousin, Cousine*, French film

TELEVISION

- First miniseries, "Rich Man, Poor Man," starring Peter Strauss and Nick Nolte
- "Laverne and Shirley," sitcom starring Penny Marshall and Cindy Williams
- "The Gong Show," talent show for people with no talent, hosted by Chuck Barris.
- "The Muppet Show," comedy-variety show spin-off of "Sesame Street"
- "Charlie's Angels," crime show starring Farrah Fawcett-Majors, Kate Jackson and Jaclyn Smith
- "Alice," comedy based on the film *Alice Doesn't Live Here Anymore*, starring Linda Lavin and Polly Holliday

- "Quincy, M.E.," medically-oriented crime show starring Jack Klugman
- "Family Feud," game show hosted by Richard Dawson.
- "Family," drama starring Sada Thompson and James Broderick
- "Wonder Woman," starring Lynda Carter
- "Mary Hartman, Mary Hartman," parody of soap operas starring Louise Lasser
- "The MacNeil-Lehrer Report," PBS's contribution to the evening news, began as a half-hour show and in 1983 expanded to an hour.

Notes

- Barbara Walters became the first woman to anchor a network evening news program. She cohosted the "ABC Evening News" with Harry Reasoner.

CLASSICAL MUSIC

- *Sirius*, by Stockhausen
- *Symphony No 1*, by Gian Carlo Menotti
- *Montezuma*, opera by Roger Sessions

Notes

MAY 18 The "Concert of the Century" was held at Carnegie Hall to raise money to refurbish the building. Musical greats Leonard Bernstein, Yehudi Menuhin and Vladimir Horowitz participated.

OCT 19 Avery Fisher Hall at Lincoln Center in New York reopened after a construction project to improve acoustics.

POPULAR MUSIC

- "Evergreen," by Barbra Streisand
- "Handy Man," by James Taylor
- "Bohemian Rhapsody," by Queen
- "Disco Duck," by Rick Dees
- "Don't Go Breaking My Heart," by Elton John and Kiki Dee
- "50 Ways to Leave Your Lover," by Paul Simon
- "I Write the Songs," by Barry Manilow
- "Play That Funky Music," by Wild Cherry
- "Love to Love You Baby," by Donna Summer
- "Saturday Night," by the Bay City Rollers
- "Tonight's the Night," by Rod Stewart
- "You Should Be Dancing," by the Bee Gees
- "She's Gone," by Hall and Oates
- "Kiss and Say Goodbye," by the Manhattans
- "Dancing Queen," by Abba
- *Songs in the Key of Life*, by Stevie Wonder
- *Rumours*, by Fleetwood Mac
- *The Sun Sessions*, by Elvis Presley
- *Hotel California*, by The Eagles
- *Live!*, by Bob Marley and the Wailers
- *Presence*, by Led Zeppelin

ART

- *Sea Boots*, by Andrew Wyeth
- *Atlantis*, by Will Barnet
- *So Many Different Colors*, by Jim Dine
- *Linda*, by Chuck Close

- Christo completed "Running Fence," a 24.5-mile sculpture in California.

Science and Technology

JAN 13 Raymond Kurzweil introduced the Kurzweil machine which reads printed material aloud to the blind.

JAN 21 The first supersonic passenger plane, the Concorde, was put into service by Air France and British Airways. Air France flew from Paris to Rio de Janeiro in three hours.

APR 16 A US–German rocket made the closest-ever approach to the sun, getting within 27 million miles.

JULY 6 *Soyuz 21* launched by the Soviet Union. Astronauts spent 48 days on the space station *Salyut*.

JULY 20 America's *Viking 1* robot, carrying life-detection labs, made a successful first-ever landing on Mars, where it took photos. Designed to work for only 90 days, it operated for 6½ years before falling silent. *Viking 2* landed on Mars Sept 3, and the Soviet spacecraft *Luna 24* soft-landed on the Moon Aug 18.

SEPT 17 US space shuttle *Enterprise*, the first reusable manned spacecraft, was unveiled. It was launched the following year.

- The American Panel of Atmospheric Chemistry warned that the Earth's ozone layer might be being destroyed by chlorofluorocarbons from spray cans and refrigeration systems.
- Red food dye No 2 was banned in the US.
- The Ebola virus was discovered in the Congo.
- Roger Guillemin discovered endorphins.
- Har Gobind Khorana and colleagues constructed the first artificial gene, a major step in genetic engineering.
- The charm (a subatomic particle) was discovered at the Stanford Linear Accelerator.

New Products

- College dropouts Steve Wozniak and Steven Jobs founded Apple Corporation in a garage. The Apple I computer kit released this year sold largely to electronic hobbyists. Not until the Apple II was released in 1977 did sales really take off.
- VHS video format released.
- Perrier water was introduced into the US.
- Microsoft was registered as a trade name.
- Citizens band radio was popular, with $3 billion in sales.
- Fax machines gained widespread use.

Sports

- At the Winter Olympics in Innsbruck, Austria, skater Dorothy Hamill emerged as a star.
- Pittsburgh Steelers beat Dallas in the Super Bowl.
- Pittsburgh was the college football champion.
- UCLA won the Rose Bowl.
- Indiana won NCAA basketball championship.
- Boston Celtics won the NBA championship for the 13th time.
- The 18 teams of the National Basketball Association merged with four of the six teams in the American Basketball Association.
- Montreal Canadiens won their 19th Stanley Cup.
- Janet Guthrie was the first women to compete in the Indianapolis 500.
- Jerry Pate won the US Open (golf).
- Jimmy Connors and Chris Evert won the US Open (tennis).
- Bjorn Borg won the first of his five singles titles at Wimbledon; Chris Evert won the women's singles title.
- At the Summer Olympics in Montreal, Romanian gymnast Nadia Comaneci scored the first perfect "10" in gymnastic history.
- Cincinnati Reds beat New York Yankees in the World Series.

Obits

- Chinese leaders Mao Tse-tung and Chou En-lai
- Actor/singer Paul Robeson
- Mystery author Agatha Christie
- Author Dalton Trumbo
- Songwriter Johnny Mercer
- British composer Benjamin Britten
- Film director/choreographer Busby Berkeley
- Actor Lee J. Cobb
- Actress Rosalind Russell
- Movie pioneer Adolph Zukor
- Industrialist and aviator (and finally recluse) Howard Hughes
- WWII commander Field Marshal Bernard Montgomery
- Sculptor and creator of the mobile Alexander Calder
- Chicago mayor Richard J. Daley
- Painter Josef Albers
- Painter Max Ernst
- Artist Man Ray
- Architect and designer Alvar Aalto
- German philosopher Martin Heidegger
- Oil billionaire J. Paul Getty
- Film director Fritz Lang
- English actress Dame Edith Evans
- German-American singer Lotte Lehmann
- Chinese-American writer Lin-Yü-t'ang

University of Glasgow

1451 • 550 years ago

Glasgow University was founded by Pope Nicholas V in a letter from Rome dated Jan 7, 1451. This is still the authority by which the university confers degrees. (St. Andrews University, the first Scottish university, had also been founded by papal bull in 1413.) Scotland had and still has a distinct and more popular tradition in education than England. The majority of early students were the sons of ministers, burgesses and farmers. Increasingly, students sought education and not preparation for the ministry. In the 18th century fewer noblemen's sons came to Glasgow—they went to Oxford or Cambridge. While most students were the sons of ministers or professional men, increasing numbers of students were the sons of weavers, workmen and tenant farmers. Large numbers came from Presbyterian northern Ireland and smaller numbers from England, mostly dissenters excluded by religious tests from Oxford, Cambridge and Dublin.

Among the famous people associated with the university was economist Adam Smith, who was both a student and a professor there. James Watt was instrument maker to the university, repairing its first observatory instruments. It was at the university that he first experimented on the properties of steam engines. Glasgow's most eminent scientist was physicist William Thomson, Lord Kelvin, who studied thermodynamics.

In 1870 the university sold its downtown campus and moved to a new campus at Gilmorehill. Women were admitted to all Scottish universities in 1892.

Glasgow University now has more than 14,000 undergraduates and 3,200 graduate students in eight faculties.

For information:

University of Glasgow 2001 Celebration
Glasgow, Scotland, UK
Phone: (44) (141) 330 2001
Fax: (44) (141) 330 6243
E-mail: 2001@gla.ac.uk
Web: glasgow2001.gla.ac.uk

Australia Becomes a Nation

1901 • 100 years ago

The Australian continent was the last to be colonized by Europeans, having been first discovered in 1606. In 1768 the British government supported an expedition to the Pacific for geographical research. Led by Captain James Cook, the group arrived at the east coast of Australia in 1770. Naming the land New South Wales, Cook claimed it for Great Britain.

Because the American Revolution had ended the British practice of transporting convicts to North America, the British government adopted a plan to send them to New South Wales. In 1788 the first fleet of 11 ships filled with 736 convicts arrived. Free settlers trickled in starting in 1793, lured by free land and cheap convict labor. Transportation of convicts continued on a large scale to New South Wales until 1840 and to Western Australia until 1868. About 160,000 people were sentenced to this penal colony and when their terms expired they rarely returned to Britain. In 1851 the discovery of gold in New South Wales changed the course of Australian history. Immigrants pouring in to seek gold more than doubled the population in ten years.

In 1850 the Australian continent was made up of several separate colonies and territories. That year the British Parliament passed the Australian Colonies Government Act and the colonial legislatures were permitted to frame constitutions for themselves. By 1859 all the colonies except Western Australia became self-governing. During the last two decades of the 19th century, the growth of railroads made the formation of a central federal government feasible. The first federal convention took place in Sydney in 1891 but because of a severe economic depression little was accomplished. In 1895 the colonial premiers called another convention, agreeing to submit any constitution it might draw up to the voters and, if it was accepted, to ask the British Parliament to enact it as law. In 1897 the convention adopted a draft constitution and referendums passed in Victoria, South Australia and Tasmania but failed in New South Wales.

A second referendum in 1899 resulted in all five eastern colonies accepting an amended constitution for a federal government. The Commonwealth Constitution Bill was passed by the British Parliament in the spring of 1900 and Queen Victoria gave her Royal Assent. The Commonwealth of Australia was instituted on Jan 1, 1901.

On Jan 1, 2001, a Centenary of Federation parade will be held in Sydney to celebrate this event.

New Australian State

The Northern Territory will become the nation's seventh state in 2001 subject to a popular vote. The territory accounts for 17 percent of the Australian land mass but only has a population of 190,000. Its capital is Darwin and it is the site of the popular tourist destination, Ayer's Rock.

An Australian Republic?

For the last decade Australians have debated changing their form of government, abandoning the constitutional monarchy with the British queen as head of state and becoming a republic within the British Commonwealth. In February 1998 a Constitutional Convention met to discuss this issue. At a referendum held Nov 6, 1999, Australians voted to maintain the constitutional monarchy. Reportedly many people voted against the referendum because it would have had the president of Australia elected by the Australian Parliament rather than by popular vote. This issue undoubtedly will be brought up again.

For more information

Embassy of Australia
1601 Massachusetts Ave NW
Washington, DC 20036
Phone: (202) 797-3000
Web: www.austemb.org

Detroit Founded

1701 • 300 years ago

On July 24, 1701, Antoine de la Mothe Cadillac landed on the shores of the Detroit River and founded a fort and trading post, Fort Pontchartrain, which later would become the city of Detroit. Claimed for the king of France and considered part of Canadian west, in 1760 the region passed from French to English control. In 1763 the fort survived a five-month seige by the chief of the Ottawa, Pontiac, against British rule. During the American Revolution Detroit was the western headquarters of the British administration, although most of the population was French-speaking until 1800.

When the Michigan Territory was organized in 1805, Detroit was made the capital. Detroit was the administrative center for the direction of US relations with Indians of the northwest. After the completion of the Erie Canal in 1824, Detroit's population began to grow rapidly. In 1837 Michigan gained statehood with Detroit as its capital. Ten years later the capital moved to Lansing but Detroit remained the principal manufacturing and commercial city. Prior to the Civil War Detroit was one of the main outlets of the Underground Railroad by which slaves escaped to Canada.

The opening of the first auto manufacturing plant in 1899 marked the beginning of a new era in Detroit. Between 1900 and 1930 the population swelled to more than one and a half million people. There was a great migration to the city, especially from the South. While the population of Detroit has decreased to about a million, it is still one of the world's major automobile manufacturing centers.

The city will celebrate its 300th anniversary July 20–22 with a parade of historic ships, ranging from canoes to classic "tall ships" and schooners. A Celebrity Homecoming Concert will feature Detroit's greatest headliners. Celebrations will also take place in the city and around the region throughout 2001.

For information:

Detroit 300
Albert Kahn Bldg, Ste 310
7430 Second Ave
Detroit, MI 48202
Phone: (877) 338-2001
Web: www.Detroit300.org

Declaration of Independence

1776 • 225 years ago

In the Halifax Resolves passed in April 1776, North Carolina was the first colony to instruct its delegates to the Second Continental Congress meeting in Philadelphia to vote for independence. On May 15 the Virginia Convention passed a resolution instructing its delegates to vote for independence. On June 7, Richard Henry Lee of Virginia introduced a resolution into the Second Continental Congress: ". . . that these United Colonies are, and of right ought to be, free and independent states, that they are absolved from all allegiance to the British Crown, and that all political connection between them and the State of Great Britain is, and ought to be, totally dissolved." However, there were still some members of Congress who wanted to pursue reconciliation so consideration of the Lee Resolution was postponed as Congress recessed for three weeks.

Before recessing, the Second Continental Congress had appointed a committee consisting of Thomas Jefferson, John Adams, Benjamin Franklin, Roger Sherman and Robert Livingston to draft a declaration of independence. Jefferson chaired the committee and prepared the first draft, which he submitted to Adams and Franklin. After they made changes, the revised document was submitted to the Congress when it reconvened on July 1. The next day 12 colonies voted in favor of Lee's legislation which dissolved the bond with Great Britain (New York abstained). Then Jefferson's declaration was debated. After several days of discussion, on July 4 Congress approved the text as amended. That day it was signed by John Hancock, the president of the Congress, and Charles Thomson, secretary.

The Declaration ranks as one of the greatest documents in human history, reflecting philosophical ideas from the Enlightenment on social and political justice. It described the colonies' reasons for proclaiming their freedom from British rule and stated that all people have certain rights, including the right to change a government that denies them their liberties. The eloquent language of the Declaration stirred the hearts of Revolutionary patriots, and it also encouraged Europeans in their aspirations for a democratic form of government.

The committee that drafted the Declaration was also charged with seeing that it was printed. On July 5, copies were dispatched around the colonies and to the commanders of Continental troops. (There are 24 copies of this first printed version in existence today.) The next day the Declaration of Independence was published in the *Pennsylvania Evening Post* and on July 8, there was the first public reading of the Declaration in Philadelphia by John Nixon, commander of the Philadelphia City Guard. The following day it was read to George Washington's troops in New York City.

On July 9, New York officially approved the actions of Congress, so that all 13 colonies were now in agreement. On July 19, Congress ordered that the Declaration be copied onto parchment so that it could be signed by every member. The Declaration was signed by the delegates on Aug 2, although George Washington, Patrick Henry and others were busy elsewhere that day. Eventually 56 delegates placed their signatures on the parchment version of the Declaration. A few delegates who had voted for adoption of the Declaration never signed, because they clung to the idea of reconciliation or thought the action was premature.

The parchment copy of the Declaration followed Congress through its many moves during the Revolutionary War. On Dec 12, 1776, Congress fled to Baltimore and the Declaration went with them. Later the document returned to Philadelphia, then went to York, PA, to Princeton, NJ, Annapolis, MD, and Trenton, NJ. On Jan 18, 1777, Congress ordered a second printing of the Declaration, this time to include the names of all the signers. (The first printing had carried only the names of Hancock and Thomson.)

The parchment copy of the Declaration moved to New York City in 1785, where Congress was meeting, and then accompanied Congress back to Philadelphia where it stayed from 1790 to 1800. When the US government moved to the new capital in Washington, DC, in 1800 the Declaration accompanied it. It was housed in three different locations in the city. In 1814, with Washington ready to fall to the British during the War of 1812, the Declaration was taken to Leesburg, VA. When the Declaration was returned to Washington, it was housed at the Patent Office and at the State Department. In 1876 it was returned to Philadelphia for a few months where it was exhibited at the Centennial Exposition which commemorated 100 years of American independence.

Over the years, the Declaration had been exposed to bright light as it was exhibited in government buildings and the signatures had faded so much as to be invisible. By 1903, the Declaration was put away in a case so that light would not fade it further. However, it was not being stored in a fireproof container so in 1921 the Declaration and the Constitution were transferred to the Library of Congress, where there was a staff skilled in archival preservation and where the documents could be safely displayed. In 1941, concerned that the war raging in Europe might reach the United States, the Librarian of Congress had the Declaration and the Constitution stored in a vault at Fort Knox in Kentucky. In 1944 the documents were returned to the Library.

In 1952, the Declaration made its last move, to the National Archives, which had opened in 1933. An exhibition hall with murals depicting the signers of the Declaration and Constitution was part of the National Archives building but only after 20 years of political wrangling were the documents actually placed there. Today they are exhibited alongside the Bill of Rights and other important records in American history.

For information:

National Archives
Seventh and Pennsylvania Ave NW
Washington, DC 20408
Web:www.nara.gov/exhall/charters

Spotlight on Education *milestone anniversary years*

College and University Founding Anniversaries

The more than 3,000 colleges and universities across the US range from private to state-supported, small to large, liberal-arts based to technically oriented. The following is a selection of colleges and universities celebrating a founding anniversary in 2001.

Yale University

1701 • 300 years

The third oldest institution of higher learning in the US, Yale was chartered as the Collegiate School of Connecticut on Oct 9, 1701. Its religious roots were in Congregationalism. The first bachelor's degree was awarded in 1703. Originally located at Saybrook, CT, the school moved to New Haven in 1716. In 1718, Elihu Yale, a retired London merchant who had been born in New England, made a donation to the school which resulted in its being renamed Yale College. In 1752, Connecticut Hall, the college's first permanent building, was completed.

New Haven was invaded by the British during the American Revolution but the college continued its steady growth. The medical school was chartered in 1810, the divinity school had its beginnings in 1822 and the law school in 1824. The opening of the Trumbull Gallery gave Yale the first college-connected art museum in the country. The forerunner of the graduate school was founded in 1847 and the first PhD was granted in 1861, the first to be awarded in the US, but the institution's name wasn't changed to Yale University until 1887. In 1933 Yale established its residential college plan which attempts to provide for undergraduates in a large university the educational and social advantages of a a small college.

Women had been admitted to the graduate school beginning in the late 19th century but Yale first admitted women undergraduates in 1969. Today Yale College with 5,200 undergraduates is the largest unit of the university, which has a total enrollment of 11,000. Yale's tercentennial commemoration will last from October 2000 to October 2001.

For information:

Janet Lindner
Tercentennial Office
Yale University
New Haven, CT 06520
Phone: (203) 432-0300
Web:
www.yale.edu/about/tercenten
nial.html

University of South Carolina

1801 • 200 years

One of the oldest state universities in the country, the University of South Carolina is the first to be continuously supported by annual appropriations from the state government. The South Carolina legislature granted a charter for South Carolina College on Dec 19, 1801. The college was opened Jan 10, 1805, with nine students and a faculty of two. The first degree was conferred in 1806. The college was closed in 1862 when the entire student body volunteered for service in the Civil War. The college buildings were used as a Confederate military hospital. The college was reopened as the University of South Carolina in 1865. Conflict led to the school being closed in 1877. It reopened in 1880 as the South Carolina College of Agriculture and Mechanic Arts, the state's land-grant institution. In 1893 the land-grant status was transferred to the new Clemson University and the name University of South Carolina was used again starting in 1906.

In 1964 the university was reorganized as the University of South Carolina System, with seven branches around the state. Today the university has 26,000 students on the main Columbia campus, 16,000 of whom are undergraduates.

For information:

Sally Tibshrany McKay
Executive Director, Bicentennial
University of South Carolina
Columbia, SC 29208
Phone: (803) 777-7700
Web: www.sc.edu

Coe College

1851 • 150 years

Coe College had its beginnings in the parlor of the home of Rev. Williston Jones, minister of the Presbyterian Church in Cedar Rapids, IA. It was his dream to educate young men for the ministry to serve churches in the Midwest. When he opened his preparatory school in 1851, he called it the "School for Prophets." Two years later, when he was canvassing churches in the east for funds to send three of his students to eastern seminaries, an uneducated Durham, NY, farmer named Daniel Coe pledged $1,500, urging Jones instead to start his own college in the frontier town of Cedar Rapids, with the stipulation that it be open to both men and women. With Rev. Jones' blessing, the Cedar Rapids Collegiate Institute was incorporated in August of 1853 by a group of Cedar Rapids leaders who organized as the college's first board of directors. They used Daniel Coe's money to purchase 80 acres of farmland on what was then the edge of Cedar Rapids and which remains today the site of the Coe campus.

The small college suffered through several difficult financial years and changes in identity until the Iowa Presbyterian Synod agreed to establish Coe as a denominational college, on the condition that the Coe Collegiate Institute be presented to the synod completely free of debt. This challenge was met by the school's vice president, a young industrialist named T.M. Sinclair, who personally liquidated the school's debts and paved the way for its incorporation on February 2, 1881, as Coe College. Three years later, in June of 1884, two students were graduated from Coe College, fledgling teachers and direct heirs of Daniel Coe's legacy to "the educational wants of a great and growing west."

Today Coe is a nationally known independent liberal arts college that retains its historical affiliation with the Presbyterian Church. Coe's 1,250 students hail from most states and 20 foreign countries. The college will commemorate this milestone with a sesquicentennial celebration from September 2000 to Founders Day in December 2001.

For information:

Sher Jasperse
Director of Public Relations
Coe College
Cedar Rapids, IA 52402
Phone: (319) 399-8686
Web: www.coe.edu

Northwestern University

1851 • 150 years

On May 31, 1850, nine men active in civic and charitable affairs in Chicago met to discuss founding a college under the patronage of the Methodist Church to serve the people of the Northwest Territory. On Jan 28, 1851, the act of incorporation for The North Western University was signed by the Illinois governor. The founders searched as far south as Indiana and as far north as Winnetka, IL, for a tract of land for the campus, finally settling in 1853 for lakefront property in what would later be called Evanston, after one of the university's founders, John Evans. North Western University opened its doors on Nov 5, 1855, with two professors and ten students. The first four undergraduate degrees were given in 1859. In 1863, "North" and "Western" were joined and the university has been known as Northwestern ever since. On June 23, 1869, the trustees considered coeducation and women were admitted the following year. In 1873 the Evanston College for Ladies was incorporated into Northwestern as the Woman's College and its president, Emma Willard, became a Northwestern dean. In 1870 the trustees approached the Chicago Medical College about a merger which resulted in the university's medical school; the university became affiliated with a law school in 1873.

In 1896 the first PhDs were awarded. Also that year representatives from Northwestern, and the universities of Chicago,

Wisconsin, Minnesota, Michigan, Illinois and Purdue established a permanent faculty organization to supervise inter-collegiate sports. It became known as the Western Conference and, eventually, the Big Ten. By 1900, Northwestern's enrollment had grown to 2,700 students, making it then the third largest American university, after Harvard and Michigan.

Today Northwestern is one of the nation's leading private research and teaching institutions, with more than 14,000 students, 8,000 of them undergraduates.

For information:

Monica Metzler
Sesquicentennial Director
Northwestern University
555 Clark St
Evanston, IL 60208-2376
Phone: (847) 467-7241
E-mail: m-metzler@nu.edu
Web: www.NU150.north
western.edu

University of Minnesota

1851 • 150 years

In February 1851, seven years before Minnesota became a state, the Minnesota territorial legislature created the University of Minnesota as a preparatory school. It was located on a site in St. Anthony, later to be called Minneapolis. The school opened on Nov 26, 1851, with 20 pupils and one teacher. Financial problems caused the school to close in 1861 but it reopened in 1867.

On Sept 15, 1869, it was reorganized as an institution of higher education with 18 students and a faculty of nine. The university now included a land-grant college established under the Morrill Act of 1862. The first two students graduated in 1873; the first master's degree was awarded in 1880 and the first doctorate in 1888. In 1881 land was purchased for the St. Paul campus and in 1888 the School of Agriculture was opened there. The colleges of law and medicine were also established in 1888.

Today the university has three branch campuses, with a student body of 37,000 on the Twin Cities campus, of whom 23,000 are undergraduates.

For information:

Office of University Relations
University of Minnesota
Minneapolis, MN 55455
Phone: (612) 625-5000
Web: www.umn.edu

Santa Clara University

1851 • 150 years

Founded by the Society of Jesus, Santa Clara was established on the site of the Mission Santa Clara de Assis, the eighth of the original California missions, instituted in 1777. The Mission remains at the heart of the university. Founded as Santa Clara College, it was a preparatory school and did not offer college courses until 1853. In 1912, the institution became the University of Santa Clara when

the schools of engineering and law were added. In 1928 the preparatory school was separated from the university.

For 110 years, Santa Clara was an all-male establishment. In the fall of 1961, women were admitted as undergraduates and Santa Clara became the first coeducational Catholic university in California. In 1985, the university adopted Santa Clara University as its official name.

Located in the heart of California's Silicon Valley, today the university has a total enrollment of 7,700, including 4,400 undergraduate students.

For information:

Media Relations
Santa Clara University
500 El Camino Real
Santa Clara, CA 95053-1500
Phone: (409) 554-5126
Web: www.scu.edu

Spotlight on Education *milestone anniversary years*

University of the Pacific

1851 • 150 years

In 1851 California Wesleyan University became California's first chartered college. The first degrees were awarded in 1858. In 1871 the campus was moved from Santa Clara to San Jose and it became the state's first coeducational college. In 1911 the name was changed to College of the Pacific and it moved to Stockton in 1924. In 1956 the graduate school was founded and in 1961 the college was renamed University of the Pacific. In 1962 the College of Physicians and Surgeons in San Francisco became Pacific's School of Dentistry and in 1966 the McGeorge School of Law merged with Pacific. Today 4,000 undergraduate and graduate students are enrolled on the Stockton campus, with an additional 1,200 at the Law School in Sacramento and 450 at the Dental School in San Francisco.

For information:

University Relations
University of the Pacific
3601 Pacific Ave
Stockton, CA 95211
Phone: (209) 946-2311
Web: www.uop.edu

Westminster College

1851 • 150 years

The Reverend William W. Robertson has been called the "Father of Westminster College." During a meeting of the Presbytery of Missouri in 1849, Robertson introduced a resolution to inquire into "an institution of learning to be under the care of the Synod." Two years later Robertson and other Presbyterians from Fulton, MO, secured a charter from the state legislature for the establishment of Fulton College. In 1852 the Presbyterian Synod voted to assume control of the new institution and renamed it Westminster College. By 1854 Westminster had 114 students, all of them men.

Winston Churchill made his famous "Iron Curtain" speech at Westminster College in 1946. Each year 20,000 visitors come to Westminster to see the Winston Churchill Memorial and Museum which is housed in a 17th-century church designed by Sir Christopher Wren. It pays homage to Churchill's life and career in British politics. In addition, a monument designed by Churchill's granddaughter, constructed from eight sections of the Berlin Wall, stands next to the Memorial.

Westminster College admitted women for the first time in 1979. Today this independent liberal arts college has 650 students.

For information:

College Relations
Westminster College
501 Westminster Avenue
Fulton, MO 65251
Phone: (573) 592-5311
Web: www.wcmo.edu

Johns Hopkins University

1876 • 125 years

Johns Hopkins University was the first in North America to be founded on the model of the European research institution, in which research and the advancement of knowledge were linked to teaching. The university is named for its first benefactor, Baltimore merchant Johns Hopkins, who gave $7 million for the establishment of the university and a hospital, the largest philanthropic bequest in US history at that time. The University opened Feb 22, 1876, with the inauguration of its first president, Daniel Coit Gilman. The first PhDs were granted in 1878, while the first undergraduate degrees were awarded in 1879. Women were admitted to graduate study in 1907 and as undergraduates in 1970.

The Peabody Institute, a leading professional school of music founded in 1857, has been affiliated with Johns Hopkins since 1977 and became a division of the university in 1985. The Applied Physics Laboratory, located between Baltimore and Washington, is devoted entirely to research and development and is known for its contributions to space exploration and national security.

Today this private university enrolls 16,000 students, of whom 3,400 are undergraduates.

For information:

Office of News and Information

Johns Hopkins University
100 Homewood
3003 N Charles St
Baltimore, MD 21218
Phone: (410) 516-7160
Web: www.jhu.edu

Texas A&M University

1876 • 125 years

Texas A&M, the state's first public institution of higher education, opened on Oct 4, 1876, as the Agricultural and Mechanical College of Texas. The school owes its origin to the Morrill Act of 1862, which established the nation's land-grant college system. Today it is a land-grant, sea-grant and space-grant institution. The graduate school was opened in 1924 and doctoral programs were added in 1936. In 1963 women were first enrolled on a conditional basis; the university became coeducational in 1971.

In 1963 the name of the institution was changed to Texas A&M University to more accurately reflect its expanding role. The initials "A" and "M" are a link to the university's past; they no longer represent any specific words as the school's curriculum has grown to include not only agriculture and engineering, but architecture, business, education, geosciences, liberal arts, medicine, science and veterinary medicine. The university's enrollment is 43,000, with undergraduates numbering 17,000. The Texas A&M University System includes five additional campuses.

For information:

University Relations
Texas A&M University
College Station, TX 77843
Phone: (409) 845-4641
Web: www.tamu.edu

California Polytechnic University

1901 • 100 years

Cal Poly was founded by the California legislature as a vocational high school, California Polytechnic School, on Mar 8, 1901. Classes were first held on Oct 1, 1903, at this three-year high school; a fourth year was added in 1916. In 1937 the name was changed to California Polytechnic State School and the first bachelor's degree was awarded May 28, 1942. In 1947 the school became California Polytechnic State College and in 1949 the first master's degrees were granted. In 1972 university status was attained. Today Cal Poly is part of the 23-campus California State University system. It has more than 16,000 students and offers bachelor's and master's degrees. The largest programs are in agriculture and engineering.

For information:

Public Affairs
California Polytechnic University
San Luis Obispo, CA 93407
Phone: (805) 756-1111
Web: www.calpoly.edu

Idaho State University

1901 • 100 years

Idaho State University was founded as the Academy of Idaho in 1901. The two-year preparatory school opened Sept 22, 1902, with 40 students and four faculty members. It was coeducational and tuition was free to in-state students. In 1915 the academy became the Idaho Technical Institute. In 1927 the school was placed under the University of Idaho and became UI-Southern Branch which offered junior-college type classes. For many years, the school struggled to become a four-year college.

On Mar 3, 1947, UISB became Idaho State College, a four-year, degree-granting college. In the 1950s, master's degrees were first offered and in 1963 university status was achieved.

Today Idaho State University has more than 12,500 students. Several thousand more attend classes on the Idaho Falls campus and through distance learning classes given off campus and on the Internet. The university will celebrate its centennial during 2001–02.

For information:

Denise Bowen
Centennial Celebration
Red Hill Bldg, Rm 110
Campus Box 8042
Pocatello, ID 83209-8042
Phone: (208) 236-3091
Web: www.isu.edu

Entertainment

SIGMUND LUBIN

Birth • Apr 20, 1851 • 150 years

Pioneer film executive, born at Breslau, Germany. With interests in optics and photography, Lubin produced short subject movies as early as 1897, including a pillow fight between his daughters. Directly competing with Thomas Edison, Lubin dominated the film industry by recreating the 1897 boxing match between Gentleman Jim Corbett and Robert Fitzsimmons. Lubin's production company was based in Philadelphia and had the Liberty Bell as its trademark. Other Lubin films include *The Battle of Gettysburg, An Interrupted Nap* and *Relentless Dalton.* Died at Atlantic City, NJ, Sept 10, 1923.

DANIEL FROHMAN

Birth • Aug 22, 1851 • 150 years

Theater producer and manager, born at Sandusky, OH. Frohman began his career in 1879 in New York City where he managed several theaters. He established the Daniel Frohman Stock Company at the Lyceum Theater in New York. He served on the "theatrical trust," an organization set up by his brother, Charles, that controlled many US theaters. His plays included *A Lady of Quality* and *The Day of Days.* He and his brother were the most famous theatrical producers of their time. Died at New York, NY, Dec 26, 1940.

MATA HARI

Birth • Aug 7, 1876 • 125 years

Born Margaretha Geertruide Zelle at Leeuwarden, Netherlands. Known as a seductive spy, Mata Hari began her dancing career in Paris in 1905 as Lady MacLeod. During World War I, she was a member of the German secret service and acquired military secrets from Allied officers. Accused of spying by the French, she was arrested in Paris in 1917, tried and sentenced to death. She was shot by a firing squad at Vincennes, France, Oct 15, 1917.

MURAT BERNARD "CHIC" YOUNG

Birth • Jan 9, 1901 • 100 years

Born at Chicago, IL. Cartoonist best known for his popular comic strip "Blondie." Young began the strip in 1930 with Blondie and her husband Dagwood Bumstead. Later Young added such characters as Mr. Dithers, Dagwood's boss, Baby Dumpling, Cookie and Daisy, the dog. By the 1960s "Blondie" was appearing in more than 1,500 newspapers across the world. The strip also was the source of the "Dagwood" sandwich, a multilayered concoction he would make to satisfy his late-night hunger. A motion picture as well as a television and radio series were created from the comic strip. Young died at St. Petersburg, FL, Mar 14, 1973.

CLARK GABLE

Birth • Feb 1, 1901 • 100 years

One of Hollywood's leading male stars, Clark Gable was born William Clark Gable at Cadiz, OH. His portrayal of the romantic hero, in roles such as Rhett Butler in *Gone With the Wind,* made him famous. He starred with such actors and actresses as Spencer Tracy and Jean Harlow. In 1934 he won an Academy Award for *It Happened One Night* and was nominated for awards for his roles in *Mutiny on the Bounty* and *Gone With the Wind.* Other films included *The Finger Points, Red Dust, Boom Town* and *The Misfits.* He died at Hollywood, CA, Nov 16, 1960.

ZEPPO MARX

Birth • Feb 25, 1901 • 100 years

Born Herbert Marx at New York, NY, Zeppo Marx, the youngest of the five brothers, began acting with his brothers, Groucho, Chico and Harpo in 1918 when he replaced Gummo. Known for their comedy on stage, screen and radio, The Marx Brothers had several vaudeville acts including *The Four Nightingales* and *The Six Musical Mascots.* In the 1920s, the brothers had several successful films including *The Cocoanuts, Animal Crackers, Duck Soup* and *Monkey Business.* Zeppo went on to become a theatrical agent in the 1930s, worked on machines for the war effort during World War II and was a commercial fisherman. He died at Palm Springs, CA, Nov 30, 1979.

GARY COOPER

Birth • May 7, 1901 • 100 years

Born Frank James Cooper at Helena, MT, Gary Cooper was one of Hollywood's most popular and charismatic motion-picture stars of the 1920s and 30s. Cooper began his career in 1924 as a cowboy extra and a stunt man. He became a leading man in *The Virginian* in 1929. Cooper's other works included *Mr Deeds Goes to Town, A Farewell to Arms* and *Pride of the Yankees.* Cooper won Academy Awards for his performances in *High Noon* and *Sergeant York.* In 1961 the Academy honored him with a Special Award for his contributions to the film industry. He died at Hollywood, CA, May 13, 1961.

FUZZY KNIGHT

Birth • May 9, 1901 • 100 years

Born John Forest Knight at Fairmont, WV. Featured in more than 200 westerns, Knight was also a musician, singer and bandleader. He starred with such greats as Tex Ritter and Johnny Mack Brown. Films include *Wanderer of the Wasteland, Mountain Justice, She Done Him Wrong* and *The Plainsman.* Died at Hollywood, CA, Feb 23, 1976.

NELSON EDDY

Birth • June 29, 1901 • 100 years

Actor, baritone, born at Providence, RI. Eddy performed his first concert recital in Philadelphia in 1928 after winning a contest. He signed a seven-year contract with Metro-Goldwyn-Mayer in 1933 and starred in many successful musicals, among them *Naughty Marietta* and *Rose Marie* with Jeanette MacDonald. He and MacDonald were the most popular screen duo of their day. After his last film, *I Married an Angel,* he toured and sang internationally. He collapsed while performing in Australia and died at Miami Beach, FL, Mar 6, 1967.

ED SULLIVAN

Birth • Sept 28, 1901 • 100 years

Known as "the Great Stone Face," Ed Sullivan was born at New York, NY. He began his media career as a Broadway columnist for the *New York Daily News.* From 1948–55 he hosted the popular variety show "Toast of the Town," later renamed "The Ed Sullivan Show." Sullivan was known for introducing new talent and having such celebrities as the Beatles, Rodgers and Hammerstein, and Dean Martin and Jerry Lewis perform on his show. He entertained audiences for more than two decades. Died at New York, NY, Oct 13, 1974.

WALT DISNEY

Birth • Dec 5, 1901 • 100 years

Producer and animator, Walt Disney was born at Chicago, IL. Disney's career began when he and Ub Iwerks developed the character Oswald the Rabbit. After producing several short films, the two created Mickey Mouse. Disney produced his own short with music and voices, *Steamboat Willie,* with himself providing the voice for Mickey Mouse. Disney went on to create Donald Duck, Minnie Mouse and Pluto, and to produce full-length films such as *Snow White and the Seven Dwarfs* and *Fantasia.* He also produced live-action feature films such as *Treasure Island* and *Mary Poppins.* Theme parks, based on Disney's characters, opened in 1955 in California and in 1971 in Florida. He died at Los Angeles, CA, Dec 15, 1966.

MARLENE DIETRICH

Birth • Dec 27, 1901 • 100 years

Known for her sensuality and sophistication, Marlene Dietrich was one of the most glamorous film stars of Hollywood. Born at Berlin, Germany, Dietrich first studied the violin and then took up acting in the late 1920s. She studied acting under Austrian film director Max Reinhardt. Her first performance was as Lola-Lola in the 1930 film *The Blue Angel*. Other films include *Shanghai Express, The Devil Is a Woman, Witness for the Prosecution* and *Judgment at Nuremberg*. She died at Paris, France, May 6, 1992.

Literature

RICHARD SHERIDAN

Birth • Oct 30, 1751 • 250 years
Dramatist and politician, born at Dublin, Ireland. Sheridan's works brought together wit and 18th-century sensibility. His first play, *The Rivals*, has proven to be one of the most enduring of all English comedies. The 1777 play *School for Scandal* is another example of Sheridan's satires on society. Other works include *The Critic*, a play, and the comic opera *The Duenna*. In 1780, Sheridan entered Parliament as a member of the Whig party. He died at London, England, July 7, 1816.

E.T.A. HOFFMANN

Birth • Jan 14, 1776 • 225 years
Born Ernst Theodor Wilhelm at Konigsberg, Germany. Composer, writer and painter, Hoffmann was known for his sinister and supernatural characters. His vivid fantasies and fairy tales were inspirations for opera composers such as Richard Wagner, Jacques Offenbach and Paul Hindemith. *The Nutcracker*, by Peter Tchaikovsky, was also based on a Hoffmann novel. Hoffmann composed several ballets and operas including *Arlequin* and *Undine*. Other works include *The Tales of Hoffmann* and various collections of short stories. He died at Berlin, June 25, 1822.

CARLO COLLODI

Birth • Nov 24, 1826 • 175 years
Born Carlo Lorenzini at Florence, Italy, Collodi is best remembered for the creation of Pinocchio, the puppet brought to life who has childhood adventures. Collodi began his journalism career in 1848 with the newspaper *Il Lampione*. Pinocchio first appeared in 1881 in the *Children's Magazine*. Collodi's success resulted from his ability to show children in a realistic light, making it easy for young people to follow and identify with his stories. Died at Florence, Oct 26, 1890.

MARY SHELLEY

Death • Feb 1, 1851 • 150 years
Novelist, whose best known work is *Frankenstein, or The Modern Prometheus*. Born at London, England, Aug 30, 1797, Shelley's first work was published in 1818. After her husband Percy Shelley's death in 1822, she spent time publishing his works including *Posthumous Poems* and *Poetical Works*. Her other novels include *Valperga, Falkner* and *The Fortunes of Perkin Warbeck*. Her 1826 novel about the end of the human race by plague, *The Last Man*, is considered her best novel. She died at London.

JAMES FENIMORE COOPER

Death • Sept 14, 1851 • 150 years
Considered the first major American novelist, Cooper's frontier adventures brought him international fame. His frontier character Natty Bumppo was featured in *The Pioneers, The Last of the Mohicans, The Prairie, The Pathfinder* and *The Deerslayer*. Born at Burlington, NJ, Sept 15, 1789. Cooper began a new trend in literature in his work *The Spy*, that combined 17th- and 18th-century Scotland with an American Revolutionary War setting. His father, William Cooper, was the founder of a frontier settlement now called Cooperstown, NY. Cooper died at Cooperstown.

JACK LONDON

Birth • Jan 12, 1876 • 125 years
Novelist and short story writer whose works deal with elements of survival. Born at San Francisco, CA, London often told of his own adventures in his stories. *The Cruise of the Snark* was an account of his experiences in the South Pacific. Other works include *Call of the Wild, White Fang, The Son of the Wolf* and *Burning Daylight*. In 17 years, London finished 50 works of fiction and nonfiction. Although some of his works seem crude and overly realistic, London is one of the most translated and read American authors. He died near Santa Rosa, CA, Nov 22, 1916.

IRVIN COBB

Birth • June 23, 1876 • 125 years

Born at Paducah, KY, Cobb began his writing career at the *Paducah Daily News*. In 1904 he became a staff writer for the *Evening World* and *Sunday World* in New York City. He is best remembered for his novels of Judge Priest, a Kentucky judge. His works include *Back Home* and *Old Judge Priest*. When his Judge Priest novels went to the big screen, he moved to California and began an acting career. His films include *The Young in Heart* and *The Arkansas Traveler*. He died at New York, NY, Mar 10, 1944.

SHERWOOD ANDERSON

Birth • Sept 13, 1876 • 125 years

A great influence on American literature during World Wars I and II. Novelists such as William Faulkner and Ernest Hemingway are said to have been affected by his writings. His 1919 collection of short stories, *Winesburg, Ohio*, gained him fame as a mature author. Other works include *Many Marriages, The Triumph of the Egg* and *Beyond Desire*. Born at Camden, OH, he died at Colon, Panama, Mar 8, 1941.

GEORGE SAND

Death • June 8, 1876 • 125 years

Born Amandine Aurore Lucile Dupin at Paris, France, July 1, 1804. Known for her romantic novels, Sand's works conveyed her beliefs as a liberated woman. Her 1832 novel, *Indiana,* protests the social issues that bind a wife to her husband and her quest to find true love. It was this novel that earned Sand immediate recognition and fame. Other works include *Horace, Leone Leoni* and *Marianne*. She is best remembered today for her liaisons with such famous men as Chopin. She died at Nohant, France.

BARBARA CARTLAND

Birth • July 9, 1901 • 100 years

A popular romantic novelist, born at Hatfield, England. Since her first novel, *Jigsaw*, in 1923, Cartland produced more than 600 books. Her novels center around romance, but she also wrote books on health, food and beauty. Cartland is included in the *Guinness Book of Records* for writing 26 books in one year (1983). She died at Hertfordshire, England, May 21, 2000.

Music

VINCENZO BELLINI

Birth • Nov 3, 1801 • 200 years

Born at Catania, Sicily, Bellini earned his international reputation with the opera *Il Pirata*, written in 1827 for La Scala. His compositions greatly influenced the works of Richard Wagner, Frederic Chopin and Franz Liszt. Known for his vocal melodies, Bellini's other works include *I Capuleti ed i Montecchi*, *La sonnambula* and *Norma*. Bellini died at Puteaux, France, Sept 23, 1835.

STEPHEN FOSTER

Birth • July 4, 1826 • 175 years

Known for his popular songs and ballads, Stephen Foster was born at Lawrenceville, PA. Influenced by his sisters, black church services, minstrel shows and black laborers in Philadelphia, Foster wrote and composed more than 200 songs. In 1849 Foster began to write songs for Edwin P. Christy's show. He wrote "Old Folks at Home" or "Suwannee River" for the show. Originally the song had Christy's name on it until 1879 when it was finally credited to Foster. Other compositions include "Camptown Races," "My Old Kentucky Home" and "Oh! Susanna." He died at New York, NY, Jan 13, 1864.

PABLO CASALS

Birth • Dec 29, 1876 • 125 years

Cellist and conductor, born at Venrell, Spain. Casals was known for his technique and interpretations. In 1896 he became the chief cellist in Barcelona at the Gran Teatro del Liceo. He was instrumental in founding the École Normale de Musique in Paris and establishing an orchestra in Barcelona. An antifascist, Casals left Spain and retired from performing in 1946 to protest the recognition of the Franco regime in Spain but in 1950 resumed playing and conducting. He died at Rio Pedros, Puerto Rico, Oct 22, 1973.

WAYNE KING

Birth • Feb 16, 1901 • 100 years
The "Waltz King," born at Savannah, IL. King was a prominent bandleader in the 1930s and has often been compared to Lawrence Welk and Fred Waring. His works include "Lazy River," a song with Hoagy Carmichael, "Josephine," "Dream a Little Dream of Me" and the Wayne King Orchestra theme song "The Waltz You Saved for Me." He died at Paradise Valley, AZ, July 16, 1985.

RUDY VALLEE

Birth • July 28, 1901 • 100 years
A popular singer of the 1920s and 1930s, Vallee was born at Island Pond, VT. He was a professional musician who could play the drums, clarinet and saxophone. In 1928 he formed his own dance band called the Connecticut Yankees in which he became the lead singer. He went on to Hollywood to star as a singer in *Vagabond Lover*. In 1967 he performed his last role in *How To Succeed in Business Without Really Trying*. His trademark songs include "My Time Is Your Time" and "The Whiffenpoof Song." He died at North Hollywood, CA, July 3, 1986.

GIUSEPPE VERDI

Death • Jan 27, 1901 • 100 years
A leading 19th-century opera composer, Verdi was born at Le Roncole, Italy, Oct 10, 1813. He began his operatic career by composing works for the philharmonic society and the church. His first opera, *Oberto*, was performed at La Scala in 1839. Other works include *Rigoletto*, *Don Carlo*, *Otello*, *La Traviata*, *Aida* and *Falstaff*. He died at Milan, Italy.

Art

JOHN CONSTABLE

Birth • June 11, 1776 • 225 years
Born at Suffolk, England, John Constable was a 19th century landscape artist. His paintings accurately depicted the English countryside. Although his father brought him up for the church and then the family business, he was encouraged to pursue painting by Sir George Beaumont, a landscape painter and patron of the arts. In 1829 Constable was elected to the Royal Academy. His works include *The Hay-Wain* and *Hadleigh Castle*. He died at London, England, Mar 31, 1837.

THOMAS COLE

Birth • Feb 1, 1801 • 200 years
Landscape artist, born at Lancashire, England. Cole was a founder of the Hudson River school and sketched and painted a series of landscape pictures of the Hudson River Valley. His style included capturing the minute details of a landscape but he was also capable of grand, imaginary scenes as well. His works include *The Ox-Bow*, a series of paintings titled *The Course of Empire* and a religious series titled *The Cross of the World*. *The Voyage of Life* was a series of four paintings depicting life from infancy to old age. He died at Catskill, NY, Feb 11, 1848.

JOSEPH PAXTON

Birth • Aug 3, 1801 • 200 years
Landscape gardener and designer, born near Woburn, England. Known for his glass and iron structures, Paxton was the architect of the Crystal Palace built for the 1851 Great Exhibition in London. While working at Chatsworth, a Derbyshire estate, he built a conservatory and a lily house. He also designed eclectic houses and planned a number of public parks. For 20 years, Paxton was a member of Parliament for Coventry. He died at Sydenham, England, June 8, 1865.

JOHN JAMES AUDUBON

Death • Jan 27, 1851 • 150 years
Ornithologist, naturalist and artist, born at Haiti, Apr 26, 1785. Audubon is best remembered for his drawings and paintings of North American birds. After

several failed business ventures, Audubon considered publishing his artistic works. He went to London and had the *Birds of America* published in four volumes. This was followed by *Ornithological Biography* and *A Synopsis of the Birds of North America*. After establishing a reputation, he returned to America and published several more books. He died at New York, NY.

WILLIAM JOHNSON

Birth • Mar 18, 1901 • 100 years

African American artist, born at Florence, SC. Influenced by works of Vincent Van Gogh, Paul Gauguin and Henry O. Tanner, Johnson painted in Europe for several years during the 1930s. He left Europe because Hitler was destroying African American art. His works include *Minnie, Going to Church* and *Mom and Dad*. He died at Islip, NY, Apr 13, 1970.

History

WILLIAM PRESCOTT

Birth • Feb 20, 1726 • 275 years

Historian, born at Groton, MA. Prescott was seen by many as America's first scientific historian. His works included the *History of the Conquest of Mexico* and the *History of the Conquest of Peru*. Archaeological and anthropological findings have proven Prescott's visions of these cultures to be romanticized and distorted but his sympathy for them won him the designation of greatest Anglo-American histo-

rian of the Latin-American world. He died at Pepperell, MA, Oct 13, 1795.

MARY BEARD

Birth • Aug 5, 1876 • 125 years

Social reformer and historian, born at Indianapolis, IN. The wife of Charles Beard, Mary collaborated on several books with her husband including *The Rise of American Civilization* and *The Basic History of the United States*. She worked for women's suffrage and labor reforms both in England and in the US. She also wrote and lectured about women's contributions to society. Her works include *Women's Work in Municipalities* and *Women as a Force in History*. She died at Phoenix, AZ, Aug 14, 1958.

Exploration

CHRISTOPHER COLUMBUS

Birth • 1451 • 550 years

Explorer, known as "Admiral of the Ocean Sea," born at Genoa, Italy. With the backing of Ferdinand V and Isabella I of Spain, Columbus set off to reach India by sailing west. During his voyage he discovered a majority of the Caribbean Islands including Cuba and Hispaniola. On his voyage of 1498 he reached Venezuela and found a continent.

He died at Valladolid, Spain, May 21, 1506.

American Politics

ABRAHAM CLARK

Birth • Feb 15, 1726 • 275 years

Patriot and signer of the Declaration of Independence, born at Elizabethtown, NJ. He served in the Continental Congress and was a delegate to the Annapolis Convention in 1786. Clark opposed a US constitution unless there was a Bill of Rights added to it. He served in the House of Representatives from 1791–94. He died at Elizabethtown, Sept 15, 1794.

LEWIS MORRIS

Birth • Apr 8, 1726 • 275 years

Born at Morrisania Manor at Westchester County, NY. Signer of the Declaration of Independence, Morris held many state positions in New York and New Jersey including chief justice of the province of New York and governor of New Jersey. Morris believed that drafting a Declaration of Independence to separate from Great Britain was a legislative duty to promote patriotism. He died at his childhood home, Morrisania Manor, Jan 22, 1798.

OLIVER WOLCOTT

Birth • Nov 20, 1726 • 275 years

Statesman, born at Windsor, CT. Signer of the Declaration of Independence, Wolcott also had an integral part in the settlement of the conflict with the Iroquois in 1784, which was resolved by the Second Treaty of Fort Stanwix. He served as Connecticut's lieutenant governor from 1787–96 and its governor from 1796–97. Wolcott died at Litchfield, CT, Dec 1, 1797.

HENRY DEARBORN

Birth • Feb 23, 1751 • 250 years

Born at Hampton, NH, Dearborn was an army officer and congressman. From 1793–97 he served in Congress for the state of Massachusetts, in 1801 was appointed secretary of war by Thomas Jefferson and was the US minister to Portugal from 1822–24. During the War of 1812, he was dismissed from his post as senior major general by President James Madison for failing to invade Canada. Fort Dearborn, which was once located where downtown Chicago is now, was named for him. Dearborn died at Boston, MA, June 6, 1829.

JAMES MADISON

Birth • Mar 16, 1751 • 250 years

Born at Port Conway, VA, James Madison was the fourth president of the US serving from 1809–17. Known as a founding father, Madison was instrumental in the planning of the Constitution and helped draft The Federalist Papers. He was a member of the House of Representatives and was secretary of state during the Louisiana Purchase. He died at Montpelier, VT, June 28, 1836.

WILLIAM SEWARD

Birth • May 16, 1801 • 200 years

Born at Florida, NY, William Seward is best remembered for his role in the purchase of Alaska in 1867 which was referred to as "Seward's Folly." He served as governor of New York where he established himself as the head of the anti-slavery faction of the Whig party. After the collapse of the Whig party, Seward became the recognized head of the Republican party. He served as secretary of state under Abraham Lincoln and Andrew Johnson, 1861–69. His last public act was the purchase of Alaska. He died at Auburn, NY, Oct 10, 1872.

JULIA DENT GRANT

Birth • Jan 26, 1826 • 175 years

Wife of the 18th president of the US, born at St. Louis, MO. Julia Dent met Ulysses S. Grant through her brother, a classmate of Grant's at West Point. Dent and Grant were married in 1848 and had four children. During the Civil War when her husband was called to serve as general, Julia frequently joined him near the scene of battle. She died at Washington, DC, Dec 14, 1902.

JOHN ADAMS

Death • July 4, 1826 • 175 years

Born at Braintree, MA, Oct 30, 1735, John Adams served as both the first vice president and the second president of the US (1797–1801). A lawyer, Adams supported state constitutions and defended the soldiers involved in the Boston Massacre. A delegate to the Second Continental Congress, he also served on the committee that drafted the Declaration of Independence. He was elected to the House of Representatives in 1772. He was the father of the sixth president of the US. He died at Quincy, MA, on the same day as Thomas Jefferson.

Thomas Jefferson

Death • July 4, 1826 • 175 years

The third president of the US (1801–09), born at Albermarle County, VA, Apr 13, 1743. Known as the author of the Declaration of Independence, Jefferson's most noted achievement during his presidency was the Louisiana Purchase in 1803. One of his last major accomplishments during his lifetime was the planning and construction of the University of Virginia. He died at Charlottesville, VA.

Nellie Tayloe Ross

Birth • Nov 29, 1876 • 125 years

Ross was the first woman in the US to be elected governor and the first woman to be director of the US mint. Born at St. Joseph, MO, Ross became the governor of Wyoming in 1924 and in 1926 was vice chairman of the Democratic National Committee. In 1933, Franklin D. Roosevelt appointed Ross director of the US Mint. While Ross was director, the Roosevelt dime, the Jefferson nickel and the steel penny were introduced. She died at Washington, DC, Dec 20, 1977.

Roy Wilkins

Birth • Aug 30, 1901 • 100 years

Born at St. Louis, MO, Wilkins served as the executive director of the National Association for the Advancement of Colored People (NAACP) from 1955–77. He first joined the NAACP staff as an editor for their publication *The Crisis*. In 1963 he helped organize the March on Washington. Because of his belief in nonviolence and rejection of all forms of racism, Wilkins was appointed chairman of the US delegation to the International Conference on Human Rights. In 1977 he was awarded the position of director emeritus of the NAACP. He died at New York, NY, Sept 9, 1981.

William McKinley

Death • Sept 14, 1901 • 100 years

The 25th president of the US (1897–1901), William McKinley was born at Niles, OH, Jan 29, 1843. McKinley favored high tariffs to protect US industries from foreign competition. President during the Spanish-American War, McKinley declared Puerto Rico, the Philippines and other islands US dependencies. He was reelected in 1900 but was shot Sept 6, 1901, while attending the Pan-American Exposition at Buffalo. He died at Buffalo, NY.

Benjamin Harrison

Death • Mar 13, 1901 • 100 years

Born at North Bend, OH, Aug 20, 1833, Benjamin Harrison was the 23rd president of the US (1889–93) and grandson of the ninth president William Henry Harrison. Harrison advocated expanding US influence and aggressive foreign policies. During his presidency the Sherman Antitrust Act was passed, banning business combinations in foreign trade, and the Sherman Silver Purchase Act was passed, putting more money into circulation. He died at Indianapolis, IN.

World Politics

Robert Walpole

Birth • Aug 26, 1676 • 325 years

Statesman and the first British prime minister, born at Norfolk, England. As a member of the House of Commons, Walpole established his reputation as a firm, eloquent speaker. Because of his forcefulness, he was appointed secretary of war in 1708 and treasurer of the Navy in 1710. He lost the seat of treasurer when the Tory Party took over power in the House of Commons. Walpole was impeached in 1712 for corruption when he served as secretary of war, was found guilty and sent to the Tower of London. He returned to the House of Commons several years later as the first lord of the Treasury and chancellor of the Exchequer, positions he held until 1742. He died at London, England, Mar 18, 1745.

MOHAMMED ALI JINNAH

Birth • Dec 25, 1876 • 125 years

Born at Karachi, Mohammed Ali Jinnah was the founder and first governor-general of Pakistan, 1947–48. Known as the "ambassador of Hindu-Muslim unity," he headed the Muslim League in 1935 and proposed the creation of a new Muslim state carved out of India. In 1947 Pakistan was created. Jinnah was regarded as the father of the nation of Pakistan. He died at Karachi, Sept 11, 1948.

EMPEROR HIROHITO

Birth • Apr 29, 1901 • 100 years

The longest-reigning monarch of Japan, Emperor Hirohito ruled from 1926 until his death in 1989. He was the first emperor to break the imperial silence when he made a radio broadcast announcing Japan's surrender to the Allies in 1945. Japan became a constitutional monarchy in 1946. Hirohito was also the first emperor to travel abroad when he went to Europe in 1971. Born at Tokyo, he died there, Jan 7, 1989, whereupon his son, Akihito, became the next emperor of Japan.

Military
PRINCE LEOPOLD I

Birth • July 3, 1676 • 325 years

Founder of the Prussian military system, Prince Leopold I was born at Dessau, Prussia. He was a commander during the War of Spanish Succession and fought in Germany, France, Italy and the Netherlands. Leopold was credited with introducing the ramrod, the modern bayonet and the marching step. With these innovations, he produced a disciplined infantry that was victorious for Frederick II. He died at Dessau, Apr 7, 1747.

DAVID FARRAGUT

Birth • July 5, 1801 • 200 years

US admiral during the Civil War, David Farragut led his navy to capture the port of New Orleans, where the South was receiving most of its war supplies. He went on to capture several Mobile Bay, AL, forts. By forcing these strongholds to surrender, this battle became one of Farragut's greatest victories. He was made a full admiral in 1866. Born near Knoxville, TN, he died at Portsmouth, NH, Aug 14, 1870.

BENEDICT ARNOLD

Death • June 14, 1801 • 200 years

Revolutionary War officer, whose name has become synonymous with traitor. Born at Norwich, CT, Jan 14, 1741, Benedict Arnold served as a general during the Revolutionary War but changed his allegiance and warned the British of an American invasion of Canada. After his British contact was captured and hanged, Arnold escaped. He further blemished his reputation when he led an invasion of New London, CT in 1781. He died at London, England.

Religion and Philosophy
DAVID HUME

Death • Aug 25, 1776 • 225 years

David Hume, philosopher, historian and economist, born at Edinburgh, Scotland, May 7, 1711. An empiricist, Hume believed only in what can be experienced by the human senses. His book, *A Treatise of Human Nature*, is categorized into understanding, the passions of man and morals and feelings. He died at Edinburgh.

BRIGHAM YOUNG

Birth • June 1, 1801 • 200 years

Religious leader who was the second president of the Mormon church. Born at Whittingham, VT, Young led Mormons to Nauvoo, IL after they were driven out of Missouri. After the death of Joseph Smith, Young replaced him as head of the Mormon church. In 1846, Young moved the Mormons to Salt Lake City. He is said to have had more than 20 wives and 47 children. He died at Salt Lake City, UT, Aug 29, 1877.

Eugenio Pacelli (Pope Pius XII)

Birth • Mar 2, 1876 • 125 years

Eugenio Pacelli was born at Rome, Italy. As Pope Pius XII, he was head of the Roman Catholic Church during World War II and postwar reconstruction. His encyclicals addressed the contemporary moral and theological issues of the Church, the most popular being *Divino Afflante Spiritu*, meaning *With the Help of the Divine Spirit*. He died at Castel Gandolfo, Oct 9, 1958.

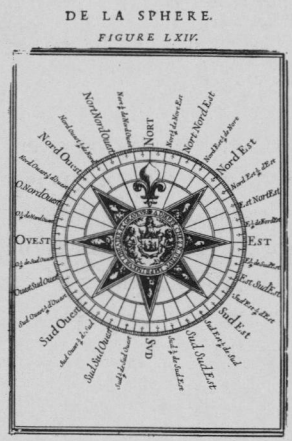

DE LA SPHERE.
FIGURE LXIV.

Science

James Hutton

Birth • June 3, 1726 • 275 years

Geologist, born at Edinburgh, Scotland. Hutton is best remembered for his theory of uniformitarianism which states that the Earth's crust has been formed by natural processes over thousands of years. Hutton also stated that pressure and heat caused particles to solidify into rocks. His geological theories were published in his two-volume work, *Theory of the Earth*. Died at Edinburgh, Mar 26, 1797.

Amedeo Avogadro

Birth • Aug 9, 1776 • 225 years

Scientist, born at Turin, Italy, who formulated Avogadro's law, which stated that when at the same temperature and pressure, equal volumes of gases have the same number of molecules. Although he formulated his hypothesis in 1811, it was not accepted until the 1850s. For more than 20 years, Avogadro was professor of physics at Turin. He died at Turin, July 9, 1856.

Peter Barlow

Birth • Oct 13, 1776 • 225 years

An optician and mathematician, Barlow is best remembered for the noncolor distorting telescope lenses named for him. He performed experiments and helped develop the electric telegraph. In 1814, Barlow published *New Mathematical Tables*, which listed the factors and functions of all numbers up to 10,000. He died at Kent, England, Mar 1, 1862.

Henri Dutrochet

Birth • Nov 14, 1776 • 225 years

Born at Neon, France, Henri Dutrochet is best known for his discovery of osmosis, the process in which a solvent diffuses through a semipermeable membrane. His scientific contributions include the osmometer, to detect osmotic pressure and a way to find heat production in both muscle tissue and in plants. He believed all basic processes in organisms were similar and these processes could be explained both physically and chemically. He died at Paris, France, Feb 4, 1847.

George Biddell Airy

Birth • July 27, 1801 • 200 years

Scientist and astronomer, born at Northumberland, England. Airy served as the director of the Royal Greenwich Observatory for more than 45 years. In 1827 he created a lens that corrected astigmatism. He measured gravity and by swinging a pendulum calculated the average density of the Earth. He died at London, Jan 2, 1892.

Walter Reed

Birth • Sept 13, 1851 • 150 years

Born at Gloucester County, VA, Walter Reed is best remembered for his study of yellow fever. A pathologist and bacteriologist, Reed led the experiment that determined that yellow fever is passed through the bite of a mosquito. He began his experiments during the Spanish-American War in 1898. The Walter Reed Hospital in Washington, DC, is named for him. He died at Washington, DC, Nov 22, 1902.

J.J.R. MacLeod

Birth • Sept 6, 1876 • 125 years

Born at Cluny, Scotland, MacLeod is known for his work and theories of metabolism. Together with Sir Frederick Banting and Charles H. Best, he discovered insulin in 1821. He received the Nobel Prize for Physiology or Medicine in 1923. MacLeod's theories have been published in *Practical Physiology* and *Physiology and Biochemistry in Modern Medicine*. He died at Aberdeen, Scotland, Mar 16, 1935.

Linus Pauling

Birth • Feb 28, 1901 • 100 years

Chemist, born at Portland, OR. Pauling is best known for his study of molecular structures in connection with quantum mechanics. He formed the theory of electronegativity that explained the behavior of electrons in a covalent bond. He was awarded the Nobel Prize for Chemistry in 1954 and the Nobel Peace Prize in 1962. Died at Big Sur, CA, Aug 19, 1994.

Charles B. Huggins

Birth • Sept 22, 1901 • 100 years

Born at Halifax, Nova Scotia, Canada, Huggins discovered the relationship between hormones and certain cancers. His experiments proved that both prostate cancer and breast cancer need certain hormones to grow. He received the Nobel Prize for Physiology or Medicine with Peyton Rous in 1966. He died at Chicago, IL, Jan 12, 1997.

Enrico Fermi

Birth • Sept 29, 1901 • 100 years

Physicist, born at Rome, Italy. Known for directing the first chain reaction with nuclear fission, Fermi designed the atomic pile in 1942. He received the Nobel Prize for Physics in 1938. The US Department of Energy's Enrico Fermi Award is named for him as well as Element 100, fermium. Died at Chicago, IL, Nov 28, 1954.

Margaret Mead

Birth • Dec 16, 1901 • 100 years

Born at Philadelphia, PA, Margaret Mead studied aspects of culture and psychology in regard to behavior. She authored 23 books including *Coming of Age in Samoa, Continuities in Cultural Evolution* and *Growing Up in New Guinea*. An anthropologist, Mead served as a curator at the American Museum of Natural History. She was posthumously given the Presidential Medal of Freedom in 1979. She died at New York, NY, Nov 15, 1978.

Inventors

Gail Borden

Birth • Nov 9, 1801 • 200 years

Born at Norwich, NY, Borden developed a process for condensing milk. In 1829 he moved to Texas and was an integral part in developing the city of Galveston, founding the first Texas newspaper and writing the Texas state constitution. He died at Borden, TX, Jan 11, 1874.

Melvil Dewey

Birth • Dec 10, 1851 • 150 years

Born at Adams Center, NY. American librarian best known as the creator of the Dewey Decimal Classification for libraries and for the creation of library science as a curriculum. He established the *Library Journal* in 1876 with R.R. Bowker and Frederick Leypoldt and was also one of the founders of the American Library Association. Credited with reorganizing the New York state library to be more efficient, Dewey was involved with reform movements for simplified spelling and the metric system. He died at Lake Placid, FL, Dec 26, 1931.

Asa Candler

Birth • Dec 30, 1851 • 150 years

Born near Villa Rica, GA, Candler bought the formula for the popular Coca-Cola soft drink in 1887 and developed it into the money-making industry it is today. Also a philanthropist, Candler donated money to Emory College for its expansion into a university. His generosity also provided for the teaching hospital next to the university's medical school. He died at Atlanta, GA, Mar 12, 1929.

Sports

Bill Dinneen

Birth • Apr 5, 1876 • 125 years

Born at Syracuse, NY. Baseball player and umpire, Dinneen pitched for 12 years and played in the 1903 World Series. Two weeks after retiring as a player, he joined the American League as an umpire and became known as a balls-and-strikes umpire with a heated temper. He died at Syracuse, Jan 13, 1955.

Frank Cavanaugh

Birth • Apr 28, 1876 • 125 years

Football coach, born at Worcester, MA. During World War I Cavanaugh became known as the "Iron Major." After the war he began coaching and established Boston College and Fordham as major national foot-

ball powers. He died at Marshfield, MA, Aug 29, 1933.

Percy Haughton

Birth • July 11, 1876 • 125 years

American college football coach, born at Staten Island, NY. Haughton coached the Harvard University football team from 1908–16 and won 71 games, lost 7 and tied 5. A Harvard football and baseball player himself, Haughton taught his players the hidden ball play, forward pass and lateral pass. He died at New York, NY, Oct 27, 1924.

Three Finger Brown

Birth • Oct 19, 1876 • 125 years

Born Mordecai Peter Centennial Brown at Nyesville, IN. Three Finger Brown lost his forefinger and use of his little finger on his right hand after a farming accident. With his nasty curveball and pitching control, Three Finger Brown was one of the key components in the Cubs winning two World Series and four national pennants from 1906–10. He died at Terre Haute, IN, Feb 14, 1948. He was elected posthumously into the Baseball Hall of Fame in 1949.

Arthur Wirtz

Birth • Jan 22, 1901 • 100 years

Hockey Hall of Fame executive and sports administrator, born at Chicago, IL. Wirtz was responsible for bringing Sonja Henie to the United States after the 1936 Olympics and established the

first ice show. Owner of the Chicago Blackhawks and part owner of the Chicago Bulls, Wirtz was inducted into the Hockey Hall of Fame in 1971. He died at Chicago, July 21, 1983.

FAT FREDDIE FITZSIMMONS

Birth • July 28, 1901 • 100 years

Born at Mishawaka, IN, Fitzsimmons was a National League right-handed pitcher. Although his best pitch was a knuckleball, he was best known for his windup in which he completely twisted his body to face second base before delivering the pitch. He began his career with the minor leagues and then joined the New York Giants in 1925. After retiring, he became a coach and a manager. Died at Yucca Valley, CA, Nov 18, 1979.

HENRI COCHET

Birth • Dec 14, 1901 • 100 years

Born at Lyon, France. Tennis player, known as one of the Four Musketeers, along with Jean Borotra, René Lacoste and Jacques Brugnon. Cochet won the French championship five times and Wimbledon twice, in 1927 and in 1929. With the other Musketeers, he helped secure the Davis Cup for France for six consecutive years from 1927 to 1932. Cochet turned professional in 1933 but was reinstated to amateur status in 1945. He was elected to the International Tennis Hall of Fame in 1976. Died at Saint-Germain-en-Laye, France, Apr 1, 1987.

Miscellaneous

CHARLES H. DOW

Birth • Nov 6, 1851 • 150 years

Journalist who cofounded Dow Jones & Company and *The Wall Street Journal*. Born at Sterling, CT, Dow was the first to compile the average of US stock prices in 1884. This eventually led to the Dow-Jones Industrial averages that are calculated today. His reputation as a financial analyst was made as the first editor of *The Wall Street Journal*, first published July 8, 1889. Died at Brooklyn, NY, Dec 4, 1902.

JOEL POINSETT

Death • Dec 12, 1851 • 150 years

Born at Charleston, SC, Mar 2, 1799, Poinsett was a US statesman and an amateur botanist. After serving in the South Carolina legislature, he became a member of the House of Representatives. On a special mission to Mexico in the mid-1820s, he brought back to the US a flowering plant that was later named for him, the poinsettia. He served as the first minister to Mexico, 1825–29 and secretary of war, 1837–41. Poinsett also helped found the National Institute for the Promotion of Science and the Useful Arts. He died near Statesburg, SC.

CLARA MAASS

Birth • June 28, 1876 • 125 years

Born at East Orange, NJ. American nurse, known for the selfless act of volunteering to go to Cuba in 1900 and treat patients with yellow fever. She was the only woman and the only American to participate in the program. On Aug 18, 1901, Maass became and ill and died less than a week later. She died at Havana, Cuba, Aug 24, 1901.

FRANK GANNETT

Birth • Sept 15, 1876 • 125 years

American publisher, born at Bristol, NY. Known for his business ventures, Gannett bought many daily newspapers in several US cities and often merged them. His first merger was in 1907 when he joined the New York-based *Elmira Star* and the *Gazette*. His angle was to pursue the advertising and circulation possibilities of a one-newspaper town, while eliminating competition. By 1954 Gannett's corporation included 22 newspapers, four radio stations and three television stations. Today Gannett Co, Inc publishes 74 newspapers and operates 22 television stations. Gannett died at Rochester, NY, Dec 3, 1957.

Goodwill Games

Aug 29–Sept 9

The fifth Goodwill Games will be held in Brisbane, Queensland, Australia. The Games will feature 14 sports and more than 1,300 of the finest athletes in the world. Athletes are invited based on rankings and performances in major international competitions, including Olympic Games, world championships and past Goodwill Games. Millions in prize money will be awarded. The sports include:

- Artistic gymnastics
- Athletics
- Basketball
- Beach volleyball
- Boxing
- Cycling
- Diving
- Figure skating
- Rhythmic gymnastics
- Surf lifesaving
- Swimming
- Trampoline
- Triathlon
- Weight lifting

For information:

2001 Goodwill Games Brisbane Ltd
GPO Box 2110
Brisbane, Queensland 4121, Australia
Phone: (61) 7 3233 2001
Fax: (61) 7 3233 2000
E-mail: info@2001gwgbrisbane.com.au
Web: www.goodwillgames.com

IAAF World Championships

Aug 3–12

The International Amateur Athletic Federation will have its Eighth World Championships in Athletics at Edmonton, Alberta, Canada. This is the first time they will have been held in North America. The Championships take place every two years and attract more than 3,000 athletes, coaches and team officials from over 200 countries. The Championships are the third largest sporting event in the world, after the Summer Olympics and World Cup Soccer, and will have a TV viewing audience of four billion people.

The Championships will feature 24 men's and 22 women's events, including:

- 100 m, 200 m, 400 m, 800 m, 1500 m, 5000 m, 10,000 m, and marathon
- 100 m (women's), 110 m (men's), 400 m hurdles and 3000 m steeplechase (men's)
- 4 x 100 m and 4 x 400 m relays
- 20 km and 50 km (men's) walks
- High jump
- Long jump
- Triple jump
- Pole vault
- Shot put
- Discus
- Hammer
- Javelin
- Heptathlon (women's)
- Decathlon (men's)

For information:

Edmonton 2001
PO Box 2001
Edmonton, AB, Canada T5J 5A5
Phone: (780) 821-2001
Web: www.2001.edmonton.com

Spotlight on 2001 Events

International Year of Volunteers

In November 1997, the United Nations General Assembly proclaimed 2001 as the International Year of Volunteers. Aimed at increased recognition, facilitation, networking and promotion of volunteering, the year provides a unique opportunity to highlight the achievements of the millions of volunteers worldwide who devote some of their time to serving others, and to encourage more people to engage in volunteer activity. In addition to the 123 governments that supported the proclamation of 2001 as the International Year of Volunteers, hundreds of organizations worldwide have expressed their support of the endeavor.

The US Committee for the International Year of Volunteers consists of more than 20 organizations representing the voluntary sector. It is chaired by the Points of Light Foundation and the Association of Junior Leagues.

For information:

Team IYV
External Relations Group
United Nations Volunteers
Postfach 260111
D-53153 Bonn, Germany
Phone: (49) (228) 815 2000
E-mail: team@iyv2001.org
Web: www.iyv2001.org

Jeux de la Francophonie/ Francophone Games

July 14–24

The fourth Francophone Games will be held in Canada at Hull, Quebec and Ottawa, Ontario. More than 2,600 athletes and artists from 50 French-speaking countries will participate. Artists will be awarded medals just like the athletes. The first Francophone Games were held in Morocco in 1989; the 2005 Games will be in Niger.

The sports competitions for 2001 are:
- Athletics (men and women)
- Basketball (women)
- Boxing (men)
- Soccer (men)
- Judo (men and women)
- Table tennis (men and women)
- Beach volleyball (men and women)
- Handisport

The arts competitions for 2001 are:
- Song
- Storytelling
- Dance
- Literature
- Painting
- Photography
- Sculpture
- Busking (street performance)

For information:

Rheal Leroux
Executive Dir, 2001 Jeux de la Francophonie
Phone: (613) 749-5389
Fax: (613) 741-9906
E-mail: rheal@leroux.ca
Web: www.jeux2001.ca

The Calendar

Welcome to the third millennium! With the excitement of the digits rolling from 19 to 20, it didn't matter much to global partygoers in December 1999 that the beginning of the next millennium was still a year away. There has been a lot of confusion about just when one millennium ends and the new one begins. Here's the straight scoop as explained by the Royal Observatory Greenwich.

Why Wasn't It 2000?

A millennium is a period of 1,000 years. The Gregorian calendar is divided into two periods, BC (before Christ) and AD (anno Domini, which means "in the year of our Lord"), based on the date medieval Christians thought Jesus Christ was born. However, in the eighth century when this system started to be widely used, there was no Year 0 designated because there was no Roman numeral for zero. So, the first year of the first millennium was AD 1 and the year 1000 was the 1,000th year, which means that Jan 1, 1001, was the first day of the second millennium and Jan 1, 2001 (or 01/01/01), is the first day of the third millennium. Of course, no one knows exactly when Christ was born. Researchers think he was born some time between 12 BC and 4 BC which means that technically the new millennium began several years ago. It is significant to note that this event has meaning only for societies that use the Gregorian calendar. Countries that use the Japanese, Jewish or Islamic calendars did not celebrate a new millennium.

For more info:

Web: www.rog.nmm.ac.uk/leaflets/new_mill.html

Although most millennial celebrations are long over, the website Everything 2000: Your One-Stop Resource for the New Millennium at www.everything 2000.com monitors continuing millennial activities.

Millennium Gardens

The US Department of Agriculture is urging Americans to grow Millennium Gardens to strengthen their communities. For a school, home or community garden to qualify as a Millennium Garden it must be planted or improved by the end of 2001 and the gardener must:

- Share vegetables with an organization that feeds the hungry or with needy families in the area
- Give flowers or ornamental plants to hospitals, nursing homes and shut-ins
- Practice sound conservation methods
- Bring people together to learn about how plants enhance communities

Register as a Millennium Garden project and receive a certificate of participation.

To register:

Millennium Gardens
National Arboretum,
USDA/ARS
3501 New York Ave NE
Washington, DC 20002-1958
Phone: (202) 720-2593
Web: www.gardening.usda.gov

Glossary

DOMINICAL LETTER

The basis of a perpetual calendar used in the Christian church to determine the date on which Sundays fall in a particular year. Knowing the Dominical Letter (A to G) of a year gives the entire order of days in that year.

EPACT

The number of days in the age of the Moon on Jan 1 of any year. Each year has an epact number that allows the dates of all full moons for the year to be calculated. It is used to determine the date of Easter. The epact is supposed to be an improvement over the Golden number (below) for this purpose.

ERAS

Counting years from a particular date as year one. The era of Nabonassar, named after King Nabonassar of Babylon, dated time from the eighth century BC. The ancient Greeks counted years from the Olympics. A period of four years was called an Olympiad, so an event would be described as having occurred in the second year of the 92nd Olympiad. The Seleucid era used in the Asian part of the Roman Empire was named after a Roman general, Seleucus. Year one was 312 BC, the year he captured Babylon. The Romans counted years from the reign of an emperor or the founding of Rome. The Diocletian era, for example, was counted from AD 284. The Roman Era (AUC) had year one as 753 BC, the traditional founding date of Rome. The Byzantines dated their era back to what they thought was the creation in 5508 BC. The Roman Indiction, an era introduced by the Emperor Constantine, dated time in 15-year intervals (indictions) from AD 313. The Jewish calendar counts from the year established as the date of the creation (3760 BC) and the Muslim calendar from the flight into exile of Muhammad (AD 622). The Japanese count years from the beginning of an emperor's reign, the Chinese calendar dates time from 2637 BC and the Indian Saka era dates time from AD 78.

The Gregorian calendar counts years from the birth of Christ. In the sixth century a monk named Dionysius Exiguus realized that it was the 525th year since the birth of Christ. (We now know that he was slightly off in this calculation; Christ is thought to have been born in 4 BC.) He saw an opportunity to replace the system of calculating years from pagan emperors, who often had been great persecuters of Christians, and instituted a system whereby time is calculated from the birth of Christ. Years are designated as AD (from Latin for "in the year of our Lord"). This system was not widely adopted, however, until the eighth century when it was popularized by the Venerable Bede. Since the system of Roman numerals available to Dionysius and Bede lacked a zero, time was divided at 1 BC and 1 AD; there was no year zero.

GOLDEN NUMBER

The position of any year in the 19-year Metonic cycle, a lunisolar cycle discovered by the Greek astronomer Meton. In modern times it has been used to determine the date of Easter.

GREGORIAN CALENDAR

This solar calendar, used in most countries of the world today, was designed on the order of Pope Gregory to improve on the Julian calendar, which over time had grown to exceed the seasons by ten days. In 1582, ten days were deleted from the year as a correction and the Gregorian calendar was adopted in Catholic Europe. To reflect the fact that the solar year has 365.24219 days, not 365.25 days as used in the Julian calendar, the cycle of leap years was changed so that century years must be evenly divisible by 400 to be leap years. Hence, 1600 and 2000 were leap years, 1900 was not. The Gregorian calendar is still 25 seconds longer than the true solar year but will not gain a full day for some 3,400 years.

This calendar, often called New Style as opposed to Old Style (Julian), was adopted in Roman Catholic countries in 1582, but Great Britain and its colonies (including North America) did not switch until 1752. (Great Britain also changed the beginning of the year to January at this time; it had been Annunciation Day, Mar 25.) The Gregorian calendar was not adopted in Russia and Greece until the twentieth century.

ISLAMIC CALENDAR

This lunar calendar has 354 days and thus is shorter than the solar year. As a result, the fixed holidays in the Islamic calendar move "backward" about 11 days each year in relation to the seasons. In roughly 32 years, Ramadan, the Islamic month of fasting, moves back through the entire solar year. If Ramadan occurs in January one year, about 16 years later it will occur in June. Many Islamic countries use the Gregorian calendar for civil purposes and the Islamic calendar determines the days of religious holidays. The Islamic era began with year one on July 16, 622, the date of the flight into exile of the Prophet Muhammad.

Jewish Calendar

This lunisolar calendar is regulated by both the moon and the sun. The average year is a lunar year with 354 days; adjustments are made by adding a leap month about every three years so that major Jewish holidays fall into their proper season. From year to year, Jewish dates vary from their Gregorian equivalents. For example, the state of Israel was founded on Iyar 5, 5708. In 1948, when this event occurred, the Gregorian date was May 14th. However, in 2001 the Gregorian equivalent is Apr 28th. But the addition of the extra month periodically means that this holiday will always occur in the spring. The Jewish calendar dates year one from 3761 BC, the assumed date of creation.

Julian Calendar

This solar calendar was commissioned by Julius Caesar in 46 BC. Up until that time, the Romans had used a lunar calendar. It had increasingly grown out of sync with the seasons, so the year 46 BC was lengthened to 445 days to make the adjustment. From then on, the year was 365 days long, with a leap year every fourth year. Julian dates are now usually identified as Old Style.

The numbering of years varied, usually dating time from the reign of a Roman emperor. The Julian calendar was used for more than 1,600 years and is still used by Orthodox Christian churches to determine some religious holidays. *See* Gregorian Calendar for the successor to the Julian calendar.

Julian Period and Julian Day

This system of calculating time, which is used by astronomers, is not related to the Julian Calendar. A Frenchman, Joseph Justus Scaliger, conceived these measures in 1582 and named them after his father, Julius Scaliger. The Julian Period is composed of 7,980 years. Scaliger selected Jan 1, 4713 BC as day one of the period, which will be complete in 3267. Individual Julian days are counted from the beginning of the Julian Period and each day has its own number. Currently, more than 2,451,000 Julian days have elapsed. Astronomical reference books have tables to facilitate converting any date into its Julian-day number for calculations involving large time intervals.

Roman Calendars

Prior to the adoption of the Julian calendar in 46 BC, the Romans used various lunar

calendars. The Romans, like many other civilizations, started the year in March; hence the names of the months September, October, November and December have their roots in seven (sept), eight (oct), nine (nov) and ten (dec), when they are our ninth, tenth, eleventh and twelfth months. About 451 BC the calendar was rearranged to have the year begin in January

Solar Cycle

A cycle designed to show the relation between the day of the week and the day of the month. Because the 365 days in the year are not evenly divisible by the seven days in a week (there is one day left over), if one year begins on a Sunday, the next year must begin on a Monday. During a leap year, with its added day, the calendar leaps ahead from, for example, Sunday to Tuesday. Thus, a perpetual calendar has 14 possible arrangements for days of the year, seven for leap years and seven for nonleap years.

It took 28 years (a solar cycle) for these 14 calendars to occur in the same order in the Julian calendar. In the Gregorian calendar it takes 400 years.

NATIONAL DAYS OF THE WORLD FOR 2001

(Compiled from publications of the U.S. Department of State, the United Nations and from information received from the countries listed.)

Most nations set aside one or more days each year as national public holidays, often recognizing the anniversary of the attainment of independence, or the birthday of the country's ruler. Below, the national days are listed alphabetically. It should be noted that in some countries the Gregorian Calendar date of observance varies from year to year. See the Index and the main chronology for further details of observance, and for numerous holidays in addition to the national days listed here.

Afghanistan	Aug 19
Albania	Nov 28
Algeria	Nov 1
Andorra	Sept 8
Angola	Nov 11
Antigua and Barbuda	Nov 1
Argentina	May 25
Armenia	Sept 21
Australia	Jan 26
Austria	Oct 26
Azerbaijan	May 28
Bahamas	July 10
Bahrain	Dec 16
Bangladesh	Mar 26
Barbados	Nov 30
Belarus	July 3
Belgium	July 21
Belize	Sept 21
Benin	Aug 1
Bhutan	Dec 17
Bolivia	Aug 6
Bosnia and Herzegovina	Mar 1
Botswana	Sept 30
Brazil	Sept 7
Brunei Darussalam	Feb 23
Bulgaria	Mar 3
Burkina Faso	Dec 11
Burundi	July 1
Cambodia	Nov 9
Cameroon	May 20
Canada	July 1
Cape Verde	July 5
Central African Republic	Dec 1
Chad	Aug 11
Chile	Sept 18
China	Oct 1
Colombia	July 20
Comoros	July 6
Congo	Aug 15
Congo, Democratic Republic of	June 30
Costa Rica	Sept 15
Cote D'Ivoire	Aug 7
Croatia	May 30
Cuba	Jan 1
Cyprus	Oct 1
Czech Republic	Oct 28
Denmark	Apr 16
Djibouti	June 27
Dominica	Nov 3
Dominican Republic	Feb 27
Ecuador	Aug 10
Egypt	July 23
El Salvador	Sept 15
Equatorial Guinea	Oct 12
Eritrea	May 24
Estonia	Feb 24
Ethiopia	May 28
Fiji	Oct 10
Finland	Dec 6
Former Yugoslav Republic of Macedonia	Aug 2
France	July 14
Gabon	Aug 17
Gambia	Feb 18
Georgia	May 26
Germany	Oct 3
Ghana	Mar 6
Great Britain*	(Tentative) June 9
Greece	Mar 25
Grenada	Feb 7
Guatemala	Sept 15
Guinea	Oct 2
Guinea-Bissau	Sept 24
Guyana	Feb 23
Haiti	Jan 1
Holy See	Oct 22
Honduras	Sept 15
Hungary	Aug 20
Iceland	June 17
India	Jan 26
Indonesia	Aug 17
Iran	Feb 11
Iraq	July 17
Ireland	Mar 17
Israel	Apr 28
Italy	June 2
Jamaica	Aug 6
Japan	Dec 23
Jordan	May 25
Kazakhstan	Oct 25
Kenya	Dec 12
Kiribati	July 12
Korea, Democratic People's Republic of	Sept 9
Korea, Republic of	Aug 15
Kuwait	Feb 25
Kyrgyzstan	Aug 31
Lao People's Democratic Republic	Dec 2
Latvia	Nov 18
Lebanon	Nov 22
Lesotho	Oct 4
Liberia	July 26
Libyan Arab Jamahiriya	Sept 1
Liechtenstein	Aug 15
Lithuania	Feb 16
Luxembourg	June 23
Madagascar	June 26
Malawi	July 6
Malaysia	Aug 31
Maldives	July 26
Mali	Sept 22
Malta	Sept 21
Marshall Islands	May 1
Mauritania	Nov 28
Mauritius	Mar 12
Mexico	Sept 16
Micronesia (Federated States of)	Nov 3
Moldova, Republic of	Aug 27
Monaco	Nov 19
Mongolia	July 11
Morocco	Mar 3
Mozambique	June 25
Myanmar	Jan 4
Namibia, Republic of	Mar 21
Nauru	Jan 31
Nepal	Dec 28
Netherlands	Apr 30
New Zealand	Feb 6
Nicaragua	Sept 15
Niger	Dec 18
Nigeria	Oct 1
Norway	May 17
Oman	Nov 18
Pakistan	Mar 23
Panama	Nov 3
Papua New Guinea	Sept 16
Paraguay	May 15
Peru	July 28
Philippines	June 12
Poland	May 3
Portugal	June 10
Qatar	Sept 3
Romania	Dec 1
Russian Federation	June 12
Rwanda	July 1
Saint Christopher (St Kitts) and Nevis	Sept 19
Saint Lucia	Feb 22
Saint Vincent and the Grenadines	Oct 27
Samoa	June 1
San Marino	Sept 3
Sao Tome and Principe	July 12
Saudi Arabia	Sept 23
Senegal	Apr 4
Seychelles	June 18
Sierra Leone	Apr 27
Singapore	Aug 9
Slovakia	Sept 1
Slovenia	June 25
Solomon Islands	July 7
Somalia	Oct 21
South Africa	Apr 27
Spain	Oct 12
Sri Lanka	Feb 4
Sudan	Jan 1
Suriname	Nov 25
Swaziland	Sept 6
Sweden	June 6
Switzerland	Aug 1
Syrian Arab Republic	Apr 17
Tajikistan	Sept 9
Tanzania, United Republic of	Apr 26
Thailand	Dec 5
Togo	Apr 27
Tonga	June 4
Trinidad and Tobago	Aug 31
Tunisia	Mar 20
Turkey	Oct 29
Turkmenistan	Oct 27
Tuvalu	Oct 1
Uganda	Oct 9
Ukraine	Aug 24
United Arab Emirates	Dec 2
United Republic of Tanzania	Apr 26
United States of America	July 4
Uruguay	Aug 25
Uzbekistan	Sept 1
Vanuatu	July 30
Venezuela	July 5
Vietnam	Sept 2
Yemen	May 22
Yugoslavia	Apr 27
Zambia	Oct 24
Zimbabwe	Apr 18

*Trooping of the Colour—Queen's official birthday.

Januarye.

JANUARY 1 — MONDAY
Day 1 — 364 Remaining

MONDAY, JANUARY ONE, 2001. Jan 1. First day of the first month of the Gregorian calendar year, Anno Domini 2001, being the first Common Year after Leap Year, the first year of the third millennium, and (until July 4th) 225th year of American independence. 2001 will be year 6714 of the Julian Period, a time frame consisting of 7,980 years, which began at noon, universal [Greenwich] time, Jan 1, 4713 BC. Astronomers will note that Julian Day number 2,451,910 begins at noon, universal time (representing the number of days since the beginning of the Julian Period). New Year's Day is a public holiday in the US and in many other countries. Traditionally, it is a time for personal stocktaking, for making resolutions for the coming year and sometimes for recovering from the festivities of New Year's Eve. Financial accounting begins anew for businesses and individuals whose fiscal year is the calendar year. Jan 1 has been observed as the beginning of the year in most English-speaking countries since the British Calendar Act of 1751, prior to which the New Year began Mar 25 (approximating the vernal equinox). Earth begins another orbit of the sun, during which it, and we, will travel some 583,416,000 miles in 365.2422 days. New Year's Day has been called "Everyman's Birthday," and in some countries a year is added to everyone's age Jan 1 rather than on the anniversary of each person's birth. Today's date has the unusual abbreviation of 01/01/01.

ACADIA NATIONAL PARK ESTABLISHED: ANNIVERSARY. Jan 1, 1919. Maine's Sieur de Monts National Monument, authorized in 1916, was established as Lafayette National Park in 1919. The name was changed to Acadia National Park by an act of Congress in 1929.

THE ARC OF THE US: ANNIVERSARY. Jan 1. To celebrate the founding of the nation's largest volunteer-based organization addressing all aspects of mental retardation. Established in 1950 as the "National Association of Parents and Friends of Mentally Retarded Children." For info: Liz Moore, The Arc, 500 E Border St, Ste 300, Arlington, TX 76010. Phone: (817) 261-6003. Fax: (817) 277-3491. E-mail: lizmoore@metronet.com. Web: www.TheArc.org.

ATTENTION TO DREAMS AND DESIRES DAY. Jan 1. A day to honor the millions of people who have been told they are afflicted with Attention Deficit Disorder. It is no coincidence that this day is celebrated on the first day of the year. It is a new beginning for positive possibilities and the perfect opportunity to give ADD a whole new meaning. From now on, let's turn our Attention to Dreams and Desires! There is a simple way to feel confident, balanced and happy regardless of what others may have told you. You have the power to attract and create desired results in your life with amazing ease, if you choose to do so. Today is the perfect day to enjoy a second chance and a clean slate! For info: Jacquelyn Aldana, Box 1341, Los Gatos, CA 95031-1341. Phone: (408) 353-2050. Fax: (408) 353-HOME.

AUSTRALIA: CENTENARY OF FEDERATION PARADE. Jan 1. Sydney, New South Wales. A parade to celebrate 100 years of Australian nationhood.

AUSTRALIA: COMMONWEALTH FORMED: 100th ANNIVERSARY. Jan 1, 1901. On this day, the six colonies of Victoria, New South Wales, Queensland, South Australia, Western Australia and Northern Territory were united into one nation. The British Parliament had passed the Commonwealth Constitution Bill in the spring of 1900, and Queen Victoria signed the document Sept 17, 1900.

BALD EAGLE WATCH MONTH. Jan 1–31. Indoor programs and educational exhibits from 10 AM–3 PM on Jan 6, 13, 20 and 27 at Cassville, Wisconsin, Municipal Building. Outdoor viewing of eagles from wildlife observation dock at Riverside Park (Mississippi River) and at Nelson Dewey State Park. Est attendance: 1,000. For info: Tourism Coord, Cassville Tourism, PO Box 576, Cassville, WI 53806. Phone: (608) 725-5855. Fax: (608) 725-2192. E-mail: casstour@pcii.net. Web: www.cassville.org.

BILLIONAIRE BACHELOR BITES THE BULLET: WEDDING ANNIVERSARY. Jan 1, 1994. America's most eligible billionaire, Bill "Mr Microsoft" Gates, married Melinda French, a marketing manager at Microsoft. Under tight security to protect privacy, the wedding took place at Lanai Island, HI.

BONZA BOTTLER DAY™. Jan 1. (also Feb 2, Mar 3, Apr 4, May 5, June 6, July 7, Aug 8, Sept 9, Oct 10, Nov 11 and Dec 12). To celebrate when the number of the day is the same as the number of the month. Bonza Bottler Day™ is an excuse to have a party at least once a month. Created by the late Elaine Fremont and continued by her family, Bonza Bottler Day is now celebrated in many countries. Logo buttons are available for $2 (includes postage and handling). For info: Gail M. Berger, Bonza Bottler Day, 109 Matthew Ave, Poca, WV 25159. Phone: (304) 776-7746. E-mail: gberger5@aol.com.

BOOK BLITZ MONTH. Jan 1–31. Focuses attention on improving authors' relationships with the media in order to create a best-selling book. Free book PR evaluation available. Annually, the month of January. For info: Barbara Gaughen, Media 21, 7456 Evergreen Dr, Santa Barbara, CA 93117. Phone: (805) 968-8567. Fax: (805) 968-5747. E-mail: barbara@rain.org.

BREAD MACHINE BAKING MONTH. Jan 1–31. Encourage the use of bread machines and accessories for use in the home to enjoy home-baked breads. For info: Cindy Reishus, Bread Machine Industry Assn, PO Box 1832, Milwaukee, WI 53201. Phone: (800) 471-0828. E-mail: BMIAORG@yahoo.com. Web: www.breadmachine.org.

BRYCE CANYON NATIONAL PARK ESTABLISHED: ANNIVERSARY. Jan 1, 1928. Utah's Bryce Canyon National Monument, created in 1923, was established as a national park and preserve.

CELEBRATION OF LIFE MONTH. Jan 1–31. The month of January, being the first month of the year, signifies the new year, a new beginning, a new life, a new happiness in many lives each year. Each community has a new hope to begin a new page in their lives. Remember always to value the gift of life for all Americans pursuing life, liberty, happiness and justice for all citizens. For info: Judith Natale, CEO & Founder, Natl Children & Family Awareness of America, 3060 Rt 405 Hwy, Muncy, PA 17756-8808. Phone: (888) MAA-DESK. E-mail: MaaJudith@aol.com. Web: hometown.aol.com/MaaJudith/Pa.

CELEBRATION OF LIFE WEEK. Jan 1–7. The purpose of this week is to impress upon people all over the world the preciousness of life and the importance of all living things. For complete information and many famous quotations about life, send $4 to cover printing, handling and postage. For info: Dr. Stanley Drake, Pres, Intl Soc of Friendship and Good Will, 8592 Roswell Rd, Ste 434, Atlanta, GA 30350-1870.

CIRCUMCISION OF CHRIST. Jan 1. Holy day in many Christian churches. Celebrates Jesus's submission to Jewish law; on the octave day of Christmas. See also: "Solemnity of Mary,

Mother of God" (Jan 1) for Roman Catholic observance since 1969 calendar reorganization.

COPYRIGHT REVISION LAW SIGNED: 25th ANNIVERSARY.
Jan 1, 1976. The first major revision since 1909 of laws governing intellectual property in the US was signed by President Ford. It took effect two years later on Jan 1, 1978. The act (Public Law 94–553) contains substantial revisions of the principles governing acquisition and duration of copyright and deals with issues that have been raised in recent years concerning photocopying and the use of copyrighted works by public broadcasting and cable television systems.

CUBA: ANNIVERSARY OF THE REVOLUTION.
Jan 1. National holiday celebrating the overthrow of the government of Fulgencio Batista in 1959 by the revolutionary forces of Fidel Castro, which had begun a civil war in 1956.

CUBA: LIBERATION DAY.
Jan 1. A national holiday that celebrates the end of Spanish rule in 1899. Cuba, the largest island of the West Indies, was a Spanish possession from its discovery by Columbus (Oct 27, 1492) until 1899. Under US military control 1899–1902 and 1906–09, a republican government took over Jan 28, 1909, and controlled the island until overthrown Jan 1, 1959, by Fidel Castro's revolutionary movement.

CZECH-SLOVAK DIVORCE: ANNIVERSARY.
Jan 1, 1993. As Dec 31, 1992, gave way to Jan 1, 1993, the 74-year-old state of Czechoslovakia separated into two nations—the Czech and Slovak Republics. The Slovaks held a celebration through the night in the streets of Bratislava amid fireworks, bell ringing, singing of the new country's national anthem and the raising of the Slovak flag. In the new Czech Republic no official festivities took place, but later in the day the Czechs celebrated with a solemn oath by their parliament. The nation of Czechoslovakia ended peacefully though polls showed that most Slovaks and Czechs would have preferred that it survive. Before the split Czech Prime Minister Vaclav Klaus and Slovak Prime Minister Vladimir Meciar reached an agreement on dividing everything from army troops and gold reserves to the art on government building walls.

DIET RESOLUTION WEEK.
Jan 1–7. This week emphasizes the importance of watching your weight by focusing on the type—not the amount—of food you put on your plate. Resolve to take it off by consuming minimally processed, less-refined carbohydrate foods. Slim down permanently with whole grains, legumes, fresh fruits and vegetables. Eat more but weigh less for life. Delete meat and other animal foods to make miniscule meals and calorie counting obsolete. Start the year off right by eating light with every bite! For info: Vegetarian Awareness Network, Communications Center, PO Box 321, Knoxville, TN 37901-0321. Phone: (877) VEG-DIET.

ELLIS ISLAND OPENED: ANNIVERSARY.
Jan 1, 1892. Ellis Island was opened on New Year's Day in 1892. Over the years more than 20 million individuals were processed through the stations. The island was used as a point of deportation as well: in 1932 alone, 20,000 people were deported from Ellis Island. When the US entered WWII in 1941, Ellis Island became a Coast Guard Station. It closed Nov 12, 1954, and was declared a national park in 1956. After years of disuse it was restored and in 1990 it was reopened as a museum.

EMANCIPATION PROCLAMATION TAKES EFFECT: ANNIVERSARY.
Jan 1, 1863. Abraham Lincoln, by executive proclamation of Sept 22, 1862, declared that on this date " . . . all persons held as slaves within any state or designated part of a state, the people whereof shall then be in rebellion against

the United States, shall be then, thenceforward, and forever, free. . ." Slaves in the four slave states that had not seceded from the Union (Delaware, Maryland, Kentucky and Missouri) were not freed until the passage of the 13th Amendment in 1865. See also: "Thirteenth Amendment to the Constitution Ratified" (Dec 6).

ENGLAND: LONDON PARADE.
Jan 1. London. The biggest parade of its kind in the world attracts a million people on the streets of the capital. The route starts at noon in Parliament Square, and goes along Whitehall, round Trafalgar Square and up Piccadilly. Dozens of the world's top marching bands, thousands of cheerleaders and the amazing eight-story-high cartoon character balloons all add to the fun. Est attendance: 1,000,000. For info: Mark Phillips, The London Parade, Research House, Fraser Road, Perivale, Greenford, Middlesex, England UB6 7AQ. Phone: (44) (20) 8566 8586. Fax: (44) (20) 8566 8494. E-mail: markp@londonparade.co.uk. Web: www.londonparade.co.uk.

EURO INTRODUCED: ANNIVERSARY.
Jan 1, 1999. The Euro, the common currency of 11 members of the European Union, was introduced for use by banks. The value of the currencies of the 11 nations (Austria, Belgium, Finland, France, Germany, Ireland, Italy, Luxembourg, the Netherlands, Portugal and Spain) is locked in at a permanent conversion rate to the Euro. On Jan 1, 2002, Euro bills and coins will begin circulating and other currencies will be phased out.

FAT FREE LIVING MONTH.
Jan 1–31. Healthy living is achievable. Try for at least one month to reduce the fat in your diet. Fat Free Living, Inc is devoted to helping others "take the fat out" in the hope of preventing many of the diseases associated with high fat/high cholesterol diets. The first month of the New Year is the perfect time to change your life. For info: Fat Free Living Inc, 15202 N 50th Place, Scottsdale, AZ 85254. Phone: (888) 328-3731. E-mail: fatfree@dancris.com. Web: www.fatfreeliving.com.

FEDEX ORANGE BOWL FOOTBALL GAME.
Jan 1. Miami, FL. Est attendance: 75,000. For info: Lisa Franson, Orange Bowl Committee, 601 Brickell Key Dr, Ste 206, Miami, FL 33131. Phone: (305) 371-4600. Web: www.orangebowl.org.

FIRST MONDAY TRADE DAYS.
Jan 1. (Also the 1st Monday of every month and the preceding Sunday.) Jackson County Courthouse Square, Scottsboro, AL. One of the Deep South's oldest and largest trade days where bartering, haggling and swapping of goods has not passed on with time; blend of antique shows, craft fairs, rummage sales. Believed to have begun in the mid-1850s when Jackson County Circuit Court used to meet on the first Monday of each month, thus attracting tradesmen. Est attendance: 7,500 per month. Est attendance: 7,500. For info: Rick Roden, Exec Dir, Scottsboro-Jackson County Chamber of Commerce, 407 E Willow St, Scottsboro, AL 35768. Phone: (256) 259-5500 or (800) 259-5508. Fax: (256) 259-4447. Web: www.sjcchamber.org.

FORSTER, E.M.: BIRTH ANNIVERSARY.
Jan 1, 1879. Edward Morgan Forster, English author born at London, England, is remembered for his six novels: *Where Angels Fear to Tread* (1905), *The Longest Journey* (1907), *A Room with a View* (1908), *Howard's End* (1910), *A Passage to India* (1924) and the posthu-

	S	**M**	**T**	**W**	**T**	**F**	**S**
		1	2	3	4	5	6
January	7	8	9	10	11	12	13
2001	14	15	16	17	18	19	20
	21	22	23	24	25	26	27
	28	29	30	31			

mously published *Maurice* (1971). He also achieved eminence for his short stories and essays, and he collaborated on the libretto for an opera, Benjamin Britten's *Billy Budd* (1951). Forster died at Coventry, England, June 7, 1970.

FRANCE: THE PARIS PARADE. Jan 1. Paris. The parade begins at 2 and its route takes in much of Montmartre and passes Sacre Coeur. International participation of marching bands, floats, vehicles, animals, etc. Est attendance: 100,000. For info: Robert Bone, The Paris Parade Festival, Research House, Fraser Road, Perivale, Middlesex, England UB6 7AQ. Phone: (44) (181) 566-8586. Fax: (44) (181) 566-8494.

"GET A LIFE" DAY. Jan 1. Start the New Year off right with a coaching special to benefit the Friends of AIDS CARE of Hampshire County. You will receive 10 minutes of personal coaching for $10. If you want to be ready for the year 2001, start now by keeping your 2000 resolutions. Get focused and motivated with the help of a professional coach and benefit a good cause too. Annually, New Year's Day. For info: Sandy Maynard, Catalytic Coaching, 1722 19th St NW, #508, Washington DC, 20009. Phone: (202) 884-0063. Fax: (202) 884-0063. Web: www.sandy-maynard.com.

GREENBERG, HANK: BIRTH ANNIVERSARY. Jan 1, 1911. Henry Benjamin (Hank) Greenberg, Baseball Hall of Fame first baseman and outfielder, born at New York, NY. One of the game's most prodigious sluggers, Greenberg hit 331 home runs and drove in 1,276 runs in only nine full seasons. Baseball's first Jewish superstar, Greenberg entered the army after playing just 19 games in 1941 and did not return to the Detroit Tigers until midway through the 1945 season. His grand slam on that season's last day won the pennant for the Tigers and propelled them toward a World Series triumph. Inducted into the Hall of Fame in 1956. Died at Beverly Hills, CA, Sept 4, 1986.

HAITI: INDEPENDENCE DAY. Jan 1. A national holiday commemorating the proclamation of independence in 1804. Haiti, occupying the western third of the island Hispaniola (second largest of the West Indies), was a Spanish colony from the time of its discovery by Columbus in 1492 until 1697, then a French colony until the proclamation of independence in 1804.

HANGOVER HANDICAP RUN. Jan 1. Veteran's Park, Klamath Falls, OR. Two-mile fun run at 9 AM New Year's Day morning. The first-place male and female finishers each take home a beercan trophy. Est attendance: 100. For info: Hangover Handicap, 1800 Fairmont, Klamath Falls, OR 97601. Phone: (541) 882-6922. Fax: (541) 883-6481.

HOOVER, JOHN EDGAR: BIRTH ANNIVERSARY. Jan 1, 1895. Known as J. Edgar Hoover, born at Washington, DC. He led the Palmer Raids and was director of the FBI from 1924–1972. During his time as director, Hoover practiced modern investigative techniques, improved FBI agent training and increased FBI funding from Congress. He died May 2, 1972, at Washington, DC.

INTERNATIONAL BIODIVERSITY OBSERVATION YEAR 2001–2002. Dec 29, 2000–Dec 31, 2002. IBOY will focus global attention on the Earth's biodiversity. It is a grassroots effort of the international scientific community to assemble a wide array of projects exploring various aspects of biodiversity. The educational, arts and media communities are also encouraged to put forth proposals for programs. The offical launch date for IBOY is Dec 29, 2000, the United Nations Day of Biological Diversity. For info: Dr Gina Adams, Natural Resource Ecology Laboratory, Natural & Environmental Sciences Bldg, Colorado State Univ, Fort Collins, CO 80523-1499. Phone: (970) 491-1984. Fax: (970) 491-3945. E-mail: iboy@nrel.colostate.edu. Web: www.nrel.colostate.edu/IBOY.

INTERNATIONAL "GET OVER IT" MONTH. Jan 1–31. A month devoted to letting go of the past and getting over whatever is bugging you about anyone or anything. The ritual chant for the month is a hearty "GET OVER IT" that is spoken with earnest gusto upon awakening in the morning as one looks in the bathroom mirror. This chant releases endorphins and leads to greater vitality and a renewed optimism about life and its inherent possibilities. For info: Doug Stevenson, Doug Stevenson Unlimited, 2104 Sussex Ln, Colorado Springs, CO 80909. Phone: (800) 773-0265. Fax: (719) 574-2605.

INTERNATIONAL LIFE BALANCE MONTH. Jan 1–31. Ever feel like a tumbleweed being blown about with no control because of all the demands put on your time? Overwhelmed by all your choices? Those choices can cause stress and isolation. This month is focused not on New Year's resolutions, but on making better strategic decisions yearlong to get your life in balance. Includes the importance of balancing time for self, family and friends. For info: Sheryl Nicholson, Strategic Survival!, 1404 Corner Oaks Dr, Brandon, FL 33510. Phone: (813) 684-3076. Fax: (813) 662-0780. E-mail: sspeaker@aol.com. Web: www.Sheryl.com.

IT'S OKAY TO BE DIFFERENT!. Jan 1–31. A month dedicated to teaching children to be tolerant and accepting of different races, cultures and religions. Author Ramona Winner published a children's picture book with English/Spanish text exquisitely celebrating the uniqueness of each individual. Endorsed by educators and loved by children. For info: BrainStorm 3000, PO Box 42246, Santa Barbara, CA 93140. Phone: (805) 961-9810. E-mail: brainstorm3000@earthlink.net.

JAPANESE ERA NEW YEAR. Jan 1–3. Celebration of the beginning of the year Heisei Thirteen, the 13th year of Emperor Akihito's reign.

JOHN E. TEAMER BLACK-EYED PEA DINNER AND AWARDS CEREMONY. Jan 1. San Francisco, CA. Annual dinner celebrating the Southern tradition of eating one's way into good luck and prosperity throughout the coming year. Named in honor of the man who introduced this tradition to MACT-SFBA. Est attendance: 100. For info: Men of All Colors Together-San Francisco Bay Area, 2261 Market St, PMB No 629, Ste 600, San Francisco, CA 94114. Phone: (415) 675-0201. E-mail: mactsfba@go.to. Web: go.to/MACTSFBA.

KLIBAN, B(ERNARD): BIRTH ANNIVERSARY. Jan 1, 1935. Cartoonist B. Kliban was born at Norwalk, CT. He was known for his satirical drawings of cats engaged in human pursuits, which appeared in the books *Cat* (1975), *Never Eat Anything Bigger than Your Head & Other Drawings* (1976) and *Whack Your Porcupine* (1977), and on T-shirts, greeting cards, calendars, bedsheets and other merchandise, creating a $50 million industry before his death at San Francisco, CA, Aug 12, 1990.

LOVE YOURSELF MONTH. Jan 1–31. Make loving yourself the most important of all New Year's resolutions. Love yourself, pamper yourself, cherish yourself, reward yourself every day this month and benefit for the rest of the year with your positive attitude. For info: Dr. Ava Cadell, Ph.D., 9000 Sunset Blvd, #1115, Los Angeles, CA 90069. Phone: (310) 276-8623. E-mail: acadell@earthlink.net.

MARCH OF DIMES BIRTH DEFECTS PREVENTION MONTH. Jan 1–31. To heighten awareness of birth defects and how they may be prevented, to inform the public about the work of the March of Dimes and to offer opportunities to new volunteers for service in the prevention of birth defects. For info: March of Dimes Birth Defects Foundation, 1275 Mamaroneck Ave, White Plains, NY 10605. Phone: (914) 997-4600.

MEXICO: ZAPATISTA REBELLION: ANNIVERSARY. Jan 1, 1994. Declaring war against the government of President Carlos Salinas de Gortari, the Zapatista National Liberation Army seized four towns in the state of Chiapas in southern Mexico in 1994. The rebel group, which took its name from the early 20th-century Mexican revolutionary Emiliano Zapata, issued a declaration stating that they were protesting discrimination against the Indian population of the region and against their severe poverty.

MUMMERS PARADE. Jan 1. Philadelphia, PA. World famous New Year's Day parade of 20,000 spectacularly costumed Mummers in a colorful parade that goes on all day. Est attendance: 100,000. For info: Mummers Parade, 1100 S 2nd St, Philadelphia, PA 19147. Phone: (215) 636-1666. E-mail: mummersmus@aol.com. Web: www.mummers.com.

NATIONAL BE ON-PURPOSE MONTH. Jan 1–31. An observance to encourage us to start the new year by putting our good intentions into action, personally and professionally, and to trade confusion for clarity as we balance our lives with more meaning and purpose. For info: Kevin W. McCarthy, The On-Purpose School for Leaders, PO Box 1568, Winter Park, FL 32790-1568. Phone: (407) 657-6000. Fax: (407) 645-1345.

NATIONAL BOOK MONTH. Jan 1–31. When the world demands more and more of our time, National Book Month invites everyone in America to take time out to treat themselves to a unique pleasure: reading a good book. Readers participate

in National Book Month annually through literary events held at schools, bookstores, libraries, community centers and arts organizations. The organization also sponsors the annual National Book Awards. For info: Natl Book Foundation, 260 Fifth Ave, Rm 904, New York, NY 10001. Phone: (212) 685-0261. Fax: (212) 235-6570. E-mail: NatBkFdn@mindspring.com. Web: www.nationalbook.org.

NATIONAL CLEAN UP YOUR COMPUTER MONTH. Jan 1–31. Dedicated to the education of computers users with simple tips and methods to increase the efficiency of their systems. For info: Denise Hall, 24797 State St, Elberta, AL 36530. Phone: (334) 986-6652. E-mail: denise@specterweb.com. Web: specterweb.com.

NATIONAL ENVIRONMENTAL POLICY ACT: ANNIVERSARY. Jan 1, 1970. The National Environmental Policy Act of 1969, established the Council on Environmental Quality and made it federal government policy to protect the environment.

NATIONAL EYE CARE MONTH. Jan 1–31. Sponsored by the American Academy of Ophthalmology, National Eye Care Month promotes awareness of eye health and the importance of medical eye care and prevention to avoid eye injuries and disease. Free information is available to media and organizations to increase awareness at a local and community level. Fax a copy of your mailing label with your request. For info: American Academy of Ophthalmology, PO Box 7424, San Francisco, CA 94140-7424. Phone: (415) 561-8500. Fax: (415) 561-8533. E-mail: PIMR@aao.org. Web: www.eyenet.org.

NATIONAL GEOGRAPHY BEE, SCHOOL LEVEL. Jan 1–12. (Begins Nov 27, 2000.) Principals must register their

schools by Oct 15, 2000. Nationwide contest involving millions of students at the school level. The Bee is designed to encourage the teaching and study of geography. There are three levels of competition. A student must win school-level Bee in order to win the right to take a written exam. The written test determines the top 100 students in each state who are eligible to go on to the state level. National Geographic brings the state winner and his/her teacher to Washington for the national level in May. Alex Trebek moderates the national level. For info: Natl Geographic Bee, Natl Geographic Soc, 1145 17th St NW, Washington, DC 20036. Phone: (202) 857-7001.

NATIONAL GLAUCOMA AWARENESS MONTH. Jan 1–31. Between two and three million people suffer from glaucoma. Nearly half do not know they have the disease—it causes no early symptoms. Prevent Blindness America will provide valuable information about this "sneak thief of sight." Organizations are encouraged to educate the community through screenings, forums and programs. For info: Prevent Blindness America®, 500 E Remington Rd, Schaumburg, IL 60173. Phone: (800) 331-2020. Fax: (847) 843-8458. Web: www.preventblindness.org.

NATIONAL HIGH-TECH MONTH. Jan 1–31. Recognizing the dramatic effect high-tech products and services have had on the way we live now and how they will change the way we live in the 21st century. Promoting high-tech education and solutions in the home and in business. Annually, the month of January. For info: Kathleen Quinn, Pres, ProQuest/2020, 826 Carriage Hill Dr, Glenview, IL 60025-5401. Phone: (847) 998-9950. Fax: (847) 998-9945. E-mail: NHTM2000@aol.com. Web: www.cluelessnomore.com.

NATIONAL HOT TEA MONTH. Jan 1–31. To celebrate one of nature's most popular, soothing and relaxing beverages; the only beverage in America commonly served hot or iced, anytime, anywhere, for any occasion. For info: Joseph P. Simrany, Pres, The Tea Council of the USA, 420 Lexington Ave, Ste 825, New York, NY 10170. Phone: (212) 986-6998. Fax: (212) 697-8658.

NATIONAL LOSE WEIGHT/FEEL GREAT WEEK. Jan 1–6. To inspire individuals to incorporate fitness into their daily routine and make exercise a priority, whether it be to promote weight loss or maintain overall good health and physical condition. For info: Jana Angelakis, PEX Personalized Exercise, 924 Broadway, 3rd Floor, New York, NY 10010. Phone: (212) 254-1915. Fax: (212) 254-7912. E-mail: pexinc@pexinc.com. Web: www.pexinc.com.

NATIONAL MAILORDER GARDENING MONTH. Jan 1–31. There's no better way to beat the winter "blahs" than by curling up with a few colorful garden catalogs and spending some time dreaming and scheming about next spring's garden. Many catalogs offer tips and information on how to create a beautiful garden. For a MGA Garden Catalog Guide, which contains information on more than 135 garden catalogs and magazines, send $2 to the Mailorder Gardening Association. For info: Camille Chioini, Exec Dir, Mailorder Gardening Assn, PO Box 2129, Columbia, MD 21045. Phone: (410) 730-9713. Fax: (410) 730-9619. E-mail: consumer@mailordergardening.com. Web: www.mailordergardening.com. Media contact: Randall Schultz, Schultz Communications. Phone: (505) 822-8222.

NATIONAL PERSONAL SELF-DEFENSE AWARENESS MONTH. Jan 1–31. To educate women and teens about realistic self-defense options that could very well save their lives. NSDI/S.A.F.E. Program (TM) seminars and related events nationally emphasize being totally prepared . . . realizing that awareness + risk reduction = 90% of self-defense while the other 10% is physical . . . and waking up to the fact that the key to their own safety lies in themselves. For info: Natl Self-Defense Inst Inc, PO Box 398355, Miami, FL 33239-8355. Phone: (305) 868-NSDI. Fax: (305) 867-6634. E-mail: nsdi@worldnet.att.net.

NATIONAL POVERTY IN AMERICA AWARENESS MONTH. Jan 1–31. To promote public awareness of the continuing existence of poverty and social injustice in America. Individuals are encouraged to support efforts to eradicate poverty by

		S	M	T	W	T	F	S
January			1	2	3	4	5	6
2001		7	8	9	10	11	12	13
		14	15	16	17	18	19	20
		21	22	23	24	25	26	27
		28	29	30	31			

increasing their understanding of the causes and practical solutions and by active participation and support for anti-poverty programs. Sponsored by the Catholic Campaign for Human Development, the largest private funder of self-help programs for the poor and disenfranchised in the US, regardless of religion, race or ethnic origin. For info: Barbara Stephenson, CCHD, US Conference of Catholic Bishops, 3211 Fourth St NE, Washington, DC 20017-1194. Phone: (202) 541-3364.

NATIONAL REACHING YOUR POTENTIAL MONTH.
Jan 1–31. A time dedicated to encouraging and motivating people of all ages toward a happier and fuller life by realizing and reaching their full potential. For info: Dr. Clifford Lee, The Eagle Company, PO Box 150263, Longview, TX 75615. Phone: (903) 295-2149. E-mail: TheEagleCo@aol.com. Web: www.TheEagleCo.com.

NATIONAL YOURS, MINE AND OURS MONTH.
Jan 1–31. Blending families and creating positive step-relationships can be one of the most challenging aspects of a couple's remarriage. Each member of the family is affected in different ways. This observance focuses on what parents and children can expect as a step or blended family and offers tips for a smooth transition and enhanced long-term relationships. Annually, the month of January. For info send SASE to: Teresa Langston, Dir, Parenting Without Pressure, 1330 Boyer St, Longwood, FL 32750-6311. Phone: (407) 767-2524.

NEW YEAR'S DAY.
Jan 1. Legal holiday in all states and territories of the US and in most other countries. The world's most widely celebrated holiday.

NEW YEAR'S DISHONOR LIST.
Jan 1. Since 1976, America's dishonor list of words banished from the Queen's English. Overworked words and phrases (e.g., *uniquely unique, first time ever, safe sex*). Send nominations to following address. For info: PR Office, Lake Superior State University, Sault Ste. Marie, MI 49783. Phone: (906) 635-2315. Fax: (906) 635-2623. Web: www.lssu.edu.

NEW YEAR'S RESOLUTIONS WEEK.
Jan 1–7. To show people how, why and what resolutions/goals should be set and the necessary action steps to make this new year the best ever! For info: Gary Ryan Blair, The GoalsGuy, 911 East Klosterman Rd, Tarpon Springs, FL 34689. Phone: (877) GOALSGUY. Fax: (800) 731-GOAL. E-mail: nyrw@goalsguy.com. Web: www.goalsguy.com.

OATMEAL MONTH.
Jan 1–31. "Celebrate oatmeal, a low-fat, sodium-free, whole grain that when eaten daily as a part of a diet that's low in saturated fat and cholesterol may help reduce the risk of heart disease. Delicious recipes, helpful hints and tips from Quaker® Oats, The Oat Expert, will make enjoying the heart health benefits oatmeal has to offer easy, convenient and, above all, delicious." For info: The Oat Expert, 225 W Washington, Ste 1625, Chicago, IL 60606. Phone: (312) 629-1234.

OURHOUSE.COM FLORIDA CITRUS BOWL.
Jan 1. Orlando, FL. Postseason college football game matching two teams selected from the Big Ten and Southeastern Conferences. Sponsors: OurHouse.com and The Florida Department of Citrus. Est attendance: 70,000. For info: Florida Citrus Sports, One Citrus Bowl Place, Orlando, FL 32805. Phone: (407) 423-2476. Fax: (407) 425-8451. E-mail: fcsmedia@psinet.com. Web: www.fcsports.com.

OUTBACK BOWL GAME.
Jan 1. Raymond James Stadium, Tampa, FL. The New Year's Day Outback Bowl Game brings together top college football teams for postseason play. In addition, the bowl is highlighted by a variety of special events, sports activities, concerts and private functions. Est attendance: 65,000. For info: Mike Schulze, Tampa Bay Bowl Assn, 4511 N Himes Ave, Ste 260, Tampa, FL 33614. Phone: (813) 874-2695.

OWN YOUR SHARE OF AMERICA.
Jan 1–Dec 31. A year-long program sponsored by the National Association of Investors Corporation (NAIC) designed to promote, encourage and teach individuals to invest in common stock. Addresses individual's concerns about investing and focuses on the individual investor's value to the securities market. For a free pamphlet on investing and the Own Your Share of America campaign, contact NAIC. For info: Natl Assn of Investors Corp, 711 W Thirteen Mile Rd, Madison Heights, MI 48071. Phone: (888) OWN-A-STOCK. Fax: (248) 583-4880. Web: www.oysa.org.

PENGUIN PLUNGE.
Jan 1. Mackerel Cove, Jamestown, RI. Annual plunge into the icy waters of Narragansett Bay to benefit Rhode Island Special Olympics. Annually, Jan 1. Est attendance: 2,000. For info: Rhode Island Special Olympics, 33 College Hill Rd, Bldg 31, Warwick, RI 02886. Phone: (401) 823-7411. Fax: (401) 823-7415.

PHILIPPINES: BLACK NAZARENE FIESTA.
Jan 1–9. Manila. A traditional nine-day fiesta honors Quiapo district's patron saint. Cultural events, fireworks and parades culminate in a procession with the life-size statue of the Black Nazarene. Procession begins at the historic Quiapo Church.

POLAR BEAR SWIM.
Jan 1. Sheboygan Armory, Sheboygan, WI. Each New Year's Day at 1 PM, more than 450 daring swimmers brave Lake Michigan's ice floes. Most are costumed, all are crazy. Refreshments and free live entertainment from 10 AM–6 PM. Sponsor: Sheboygan Polar Bear Club. Est attendance: 2,000. For info: Sheboygan CVB, 712 Riverfront Dr, Ste 101, Sheboygan, WI 53081. Phone: (920) 452-6443.

PORTLAND CENTER STAGE.
Jan 1–Apr 22. (Season began Sept 26, 2000. Also Oct 3–Dec 31, 2001.) Portland, OR. A seven-month season of six plays by classical and contemporary playwrights in the Newmark Theatre of the Portland Center for the Performing Arts. Est attendance: 90,000. For info: Portland Center Stage, PO Box 9008, Portland, OR 97207. Phone: (503) 274-6588. Fax: (503) 796-6509. Web: www.pcs.org.

REVERE, PAUL: BIRTH ANNIVERSARY.
Jan 1, 1735 (OS). American patriot, silversmith and engraver, maker of false teeth, eyeglasses, picture frames and surgical instruments. Best remembered for his famous ride Apr 18, 1775, celebrated in Longfellow's poem, "The Midnight Ride of Paul Revere." Born at Boston, MA, died there May 10, 1818. See also: "Paul Revere's Ride: Anniversary" (Apr 18).

ROSE BOWL GAME.
Jan 1. Pasadena, CA. Football conference champions from Big Ten and Pacific-10 meet in the Rose Bowl game. Tournament of Roses has been an annual New Year's Day event since 1890; Rose Bowl football game since 1902. Michigan defeated Stanford 49–0 in what was the first postseason football game. Called the Rose Bowl since 1923, it is preceded each year by the Tournament of Roses Parade. Sponsored by AT&T. Est attendance: 100,000. For info: Bridget Schinnerer, Program Coordinator, Rose Bowl Stadium, 1001 Rose Bowl Drive, Pasadena, CA 91103. Phone: (626) 449-4100. Fax: (626) 449-9066. Web: www.tournamentofroses.com.

ROSS, BETSY: BIRTH ANNIVERSARY. Jan 1, 1752 (OS). According to legend based largely on her grandson's revelations in 1870, needleworker Betsy Ross created the first stars-and-stripes flag in 1775, under instructions from George Washington. Her sewing and her making of flags were well known, but there is little corroborative evidence of her role in making the first stars-and-stripes. The account is generally accepted, however, in the absence of any documented claims to the contrary. She was born Elizabeth Griscom at Philadelphia, PA, and died there Jan 30, 1836.

RUSSIA: NEW YEAR'S DAY OBSERVANCE. Jan 1–2. National holiday. Modern tradition calls for setting up New Year's trees in homes, halls, clubs, palaces of culture and the hall of the Kremlin Palace. Children's parties with Granddad Frost and his granddaughter, Snow Girl. Games, songs, dancing, special foods, family gatherings and exchanges of gifts and New Year's cards.

SAINT BASIL'S DAY. Jan 1. St. Basil's or St. Vasily's feast day observed by Eastern Orthodox churches. Special traditions for the day include serving St. Basil cakes, each of which contains a coin. Feast day observed Jan 14 by those churches using Julian calendar.

SENIOR-SPIRIT MONTH. Jan 1–31. Senior-Spirit.com spotlights "the new" 50+ senior woman. She's vital, she's energetic and committed to making these years the best of her life. Special events celebrating what the National Council on Aging calls "Vital Aging." Topics include "The Web, E-mail and More," "Financial Strategies for Seniors," "Grandmother/Grandchild: Loving and Learning," "Senior Women's Travel: Your Travel Days Are Not Over." Senior-Spirit will announce Senior-spirit Women of the Year award to three women. Send nominations by Nov 30, 2000. For info: Senior-Spirit.com. Phone: (212) 838-1740. Fax: (212) 826-8710. E-mail: maryann@poshnosh.com. Web: www.senior-spirit.com.

SEW FOR THE CURE(tm). Jan 1–Dec 31. Aiming to raise $1 million for breast cancer research and education through sewing, SFTC joins sewing consumers, retailers and suppliers with special events, sales, programs and products. Check with your local American Sewing Guild Chapter (www.asg.org) for more details. For info: Home Sewing Foundation. Phone: (212) 714-1633. Web: www.sewforthecure.com.

SILENT RECORD WEEK. Jan 1–7. To commemorate the anniversary of the invention of the silent record in 1960, which was played on Detroit jukeboxes. The following year a Silent Record Concert and Recording Session featured emcee Henry Morgan, Soupy Sales and the 120-piece Hush Symphonic Band. [Originated by the late W.T. Rabe of Sault Ste. Marie, MI.]

SOLEMNITY OF MARY, MOTHER OF GOD. Jan 1. Holy Day of Obligation in Roman Catholic Church since calendar reorganization of 1969, replacing the Feast of the Circumcision, which had been recognized for more than 14 centuries. See also: "Circumcision of Christ" (Jan 1).

SOUTHWESTERN BELL COTTON BOWL CLASSIC. Jan 1. Dallas, TX. 65th annual. Postseason football game matching the #2 team from the Big 12 with the Southeastern Conference (SEC) division champion, division runner-up or a team with a comparable record. Est attendance: 68,000. For info: Cotton Bowl Athletic Assn, Box 569420, Dallas, TX 75356-9420. Phone: (214) 634-7525. Ticket Office: (888) 792-BOWL. E-mail: mail@swbellcottonbowl.com.

STOCK EXCHANGE HOLIDAY (NEW YEAR'S DAY). Jan 1. The holiday schedules for the various exchanges are subject to change if relevant rules, regulations or exchange policies

are revised. If you have questions, phone: American Stock Exchange (212) 306-1000; Chicago Board of Trade (312) 435-3500; Chicago Board of Options Exchange (312) 786-5600; New York Stock Exchange (212) 656-2065; Pacific Stock Exchange (415) 393-4000; Philadelphia Stock Exchange (215) 496-5000.

SUDAN: INDEPENDENCE DAY: 45th ANNIVERSARY. Jan 1. National holiday. Sudan was proclaimed a sovereign independent republic in 1956, ending its status as an Anglo-Egyptian condominium (since 1899).

TOURNAMENT OF ROSES PARADE. Jan 1. Pasadena, CA. 112th annual parade. Rose Parade starting at 8:00 AM, EST, includes floats, bands and equestrians. Theme: "Fabric of America." Est attendance: 1,000,000. For info: Pasadena Tournament of Roses Assn, 391 S Orange Grove Blvd, Pasadena, CA 91184. Phone: (626) 449-4100. Fax: (626) 449-9066. Web: www.tournamentofroses.com.

UNITED KINGDOM: NEW YEAR'S HOLIDAY. Jan 1.

UNITED NATIONS: ASIAN AND PACIFIC DECADE OF DISABLED PERSONS: YEAR NINE. Jan 1–Dec 31. The decade 1993–2002 was proclaimed on Apr 23, 1992, by the Economic and Social Commission for Asia and the Pacific (ESCAP) and was endorsed by the General Assembly on Dec 16, 1992 (Res 47/88), to give further impetus to the implementation of the World Programme of Action concerning Disabled Persons in the ESCAP region and to strengthen regional cooperation in achieving the goals. Info from: United Nations, Dept of Public Info, New York, NY 10017.

UNITED NATIONS: DECADE FOR HUMAN RIGHTS EDUCATION: YEAR SEVEN. Jan 1–Dec 31. On Dec 23, 1994, the General Assembly proclaimed this decade for 1995–2004, and welcomed the Plan of Action for the Decade submitted by the Secretary-General (Res 49/184). The Assembly expressed its conviction that human rights education should constitute a lifelong process, by which people learn respect for the dignity of others. Info from: United Nations, Dept of Public Info, New York, NY 10017.

UNITED NATIONS: DECADE FOR THE ERADICATION OF POVERTY: YEAR FIVE. Jan 1–Dec 31. General Assembly, Dec 20, 1995, (Res 50/107 II), proclaimed 1997–2006 (the decade following the International Year for the Eradication of Poverty—1996) to be a time for governments and organizations to pursue implementation of the recommendations of the major UN conferences on this issue, particularly the World Summit for Social Development held in Copenhagen in March 1995. Info from: United Nations, Dept of Public Info, New York, NY 10017.

UNITED NATIONS: INTERNATIONAL DECADE FOR A CULTURE OF PEACE AND NON-VIOLENCE FOR THE CHILDREN OF THE WORLD: YEAR ONE. Jan 1–Dec 31. The General Assembly (Res 53/25) invites religious bodies, educational institutions, artists and the media to support this decade for the benefit of every child of the world. Member states are invited to ensure that the practice of peace and non-violence is taught at all levels in their societies, including in educational institutions.

UNITED NATIONS: INTERNATIONAL DECADE OF THE WORLD'S INDIGENOUS PEOPLE: YEAR EIGHT. Jan 1–Dec 9. Proclaimed by the General Assembly, Dec 21, 1993 (Res 48/163), this decade (1994–2003) focuses international attention and cooperation on the problems of indigenous people in a range of areas, such as human rights, health, education, development and environment. Governments are encouraged to include representatives of these people in planning and executing goals and activities for the decade. Info from: United Nations, Dept of Public Info, New York, NY 10017.

UNITED NATIONS: INTERNATIONAL YEAR OF MOBILIZATION AGAINST RACISM, RACIAL DISCRIMINATION, XENOPHOBIA AND RELATED INTOLERANCE. Jan 1–Dec 31. This observance (General

January 2001	S	M	T	W	T	F	S
		1	2	3	4	5	6
	7	8	9	10	11	12	13
	14	15	16	17	18	19	20
	21	22	23	24	25	26	27
	28	29	30	31			

Assembly Re 53/132 III) aims at drawing the world's attention to the objectives of the 2001 World Conference on Racism, Racial Discrimination, Xenophobia and Related Intolerance and giving momentum to the political commitment to eliminate those phenomena. For more info: United Nations, Dept of Public Info, New York, NY 10017.

UNITED NATIONS: INTERNATIONAL YEAR OF VOLUNTEERS. Jan 1–Dec 31. A year to enhance the recognition, facilitation, networking and promotion of volunteer service in order to encourage service from an expanded number of individuals. The United Nations Volunteer Program is the focal point for the year. Info from: United Nations, Dept of Public Info, New York, NY 10017. Web: www.iyv2001.org.

UNITED NATIONS: SECOND INDUSTRIAL DEVELOPMENT DECADE FOR AFRICA: YEAR NINE. Jan 1–Dec 31. On Dec 22, 1989, the General Assembly proclaimed the decade for the years 1991–2000 for the purpose of mobilizing increased political commitment to and financial and technical support for the industrialization of Africa. On Dec 22, 1992 (Res 47/177), the Assembly changed the time period for the decade to 1993–2002. Info from: United Nations, Dept of Public Info, New York, NY 10017.

UNITED NATIONS: YEAR OF DIALOGUE AMONG CIVILIZATIONS. Jan 1–Dec 31. The General Assembly (Res 53/22) invites governments, international organizations and non-governmental organizations to implement cultural, educational and social programs to promote the concept of dialogue among civilizations, including organizing conferences and seminars and disseminating information on the subject. For more info: United Nations, Dept of Public Info, New York, NY 10017.

UNIVERSAL HOUR OF PEACE. Jan 1. A synchronized hour starting at noon (Greenwich Mean Time) dedicated to creating peace throughout our planet. Every man, woman and child is asked to spend the hour in meditation, prayer, conversation, listening to beautiful music or whatever helps them concentrate on peace. The simple truth is "living peaceably begins by thinking peacefully." To add your name to the "Millions for Peace" list, e-mail your name, city, state/country to som@som.org. An hour cassette tape of the Universal Peace Covenant voiced in seven languages is available at no charge by Contacting SOM. One hour of peace, a world of difference. For info: Dr. Barbara Condron, Intl Coord, School of Metaphysics, World HQ, HCR 1, Box 15, Windyville, MO 65783. Phone: (417) 345-8411. Fax: (417) 345-6668. E-mail: som@som.org. Web: www.som.org.

VIEWING THE DELLS EAGLES. Jan 1–31. River's Edge Resort, Wisconsin Dells, WI. Mid-winter bald eagle watching. Watch the eagles soar overhead and comb the open waters of the beautiful Wisconsin River. For info: Angie Rizner, Wisconsin Dells Visitors Bureau, PO Box 390, Wisconsin Dells, WI 53965. Phone: (800) 223-3557. E-mail: info@wisdells.com. Web: www.wisdells.com.

WALKER, DOAK: BIRTH ANNIVERSARY. Jan 1, 1927. Ewell Doak Walker, Jr, Pro Football Hall of Fame and Heisman Trophy running back, born at Dallas, TX. Walker won the Heisman Trophy in 1948, playing for SMU, and went on to an outstanding pro career with the Detroit Lions. He was a handsome, humble player during a time when football players could become national heroes. Inducted into the Hall of Fame in 1986. Died at Steamboat Springs, CO, Sept 27, 1998.

WAYNE, "MAD ANTHONY": BIRTH ANNIVERSARY. Jan 1, 1745 (OS). American Revolutionary War general whose daring, sometimes reckless, conduct earned him the nickname "Mad Anthony" Wayne. His courage and shrewdness as a soldier made him a key figure in the capture of Stony Point, NY (1779), preventing Benedict Arnold's "delivery" of West Point to the British, and in subduing hostile Indians of the Northwest Territory (1794). He was born at Waynesboro, PA and died at Presque Isle, PA, Dec 15, 1796.

WESTERN PACIFIC HURRICANE SEASON. Jan 1–Dec 31. Most hurricanes occur from June 1 through Oct 1, though the season lasts all year. (Western Pacific: West of International Dateline.) Info from: US Dept of Commerce, Natl Oceanic and Atmospheric Admin, Rockville, MD 20852.

Z DAY. Jan 1. To give recognition on the first day of the year to all persons and places whose names begin with the letter "Z" and who are always listed or thought of last in any alphabetized list. For info: Tom Zager, 4545 Kirkwood Dr, Sterling Heights, MI 48310.

ZWINGLI, ULRICH: BIRTH ANNIVERSARY. Jan 1, 1484. Swiss clergyman, theologian, and reformer, born at Wildhaus, St. Gall, Switzerland. Ordained a Catholic priest, he converted to Protestantism. While serving as a military chaplain in the Second War of Kappel, Zwingli was killed on Oct 11, 1531. A monument marks the place where he fell during the battle.

BIRTHDAYS TODAY

Valentina Cortese, 76, actress (*The Barefoot Contessa, Juliet of the Spirits*), born Milan, Italy, Jan 1, 1925.

Ernest F. Hollings, 79, US Senator (D, South Carolina), born Charleston, SC, Jan 1, 1922.

Helmut Jahn, 61, architect, born Nuremberg, Germany, Jan 1, 1940.

Gary Johnson, 48, Governor of New Mexico (R), born Minot, ND, Jan 1, 1953.

Tony Knowles, 58, Governor of Alaska (D), born Tulsa, OK, Jan 1, 1943.

Frank Langella, 61, actor (*The Twelve Chairs, Lolita*), born Bayonne, NJ, Jan 1, 1940.

Don Novello (Father Guido Sarducci), 58, actor, comedian ("The Smothers Brothers Show," "Saturday Night Live"), born Ashtabula, OH, Jan 1, 1943.

J.D. Salinger, 82, author (*Catcher in the Rye, Franny & Zooey, Seymour: An Introduction*), born New York, NY, Jan 1, 1919.

JANUARY 2 — TUESDAY
Day 2 — 363 Remaining

ASIMOV, ISAAC: BIRTH ANNIVERSARY. Jan 2, 1920. Although Isaac Asimov was one of the world's best-known writers of science fiction, his almost 500 books dealt with subjects as diverse as the Bible, works for preschoolers, college textbooks, mysteries, chemistry, biology, limericks, Shakespeare, Gilbert and Sullivan and modern history. During his prolific career he helped to elevate science fiction from pulp magazines to a more intellectual level. Some of his works include the *Foundation Trilogy, The Robots of Dawn, Robots and Empire, Nemesis, Murder at the A.B.A.* (in which he himself was a character), *The Gods Themselves* and *I, Robot*, in which he posited the famous Three Laws of Robotics. His *The Clock We Live On* is an accessible explanation of the origins of calendars. Asimov was born near Smolensk, Russia, and died at New York, NY, Apr 6, 1992.

55-MPH SPEED LIMIT: ANNIVERSARY. Jan 2, 1974. President Richard Nixon signed a bill requiring states to limit highway speeds to a maximum of 55 mph. This measure was meant to conserve energy during the crisis precipitated by the embargo imposed by the Arab oil-producing countries. A plan, used by some states, limited sale of gasoline on odd-numbered days for cars whose plates ended in odd numbers and even-numbered days for even-numbered plates. Some states limited purchases to $2–$3 per auto and lines as long as six miles resulted in some locations. See also: "Arab Oil Embargo Lifted: Anniversary" (Mar 13).

GEORGIA: RATIFICATION DAY. Jan 2, 1788. By unanimous vote, Georgia became the fourth state to ratify the Constitution.

HAITI: ANCESTORS' DAY. Jan 2. Commemoration of the ancestors. Also known as Hero's Day. Public holiday.

HAPPY MEW YEAR FOR CATS DAY. Jan 2. Felines, ever above mere humans in the great chain of being, have a day unto themselves to celebrate the "mewness" of a new time. Annually, Jan 2. © 2000 WH. For info: Thomas and Ruth Roy, Wellcat Holidays, 2418 Long Ln, Lebanon, PA 17046. Phone: (717) 279-0184. E-mail: wellcat@supernet.com. Web: www.wellcat.com.

JAPAN: KAKIZOME. Jan 2. Traditional Japanese festival gets under way when the first strokes of the year are made on paper with the traditional brushes.

MILLER, ROGER: 65th BIRTH ANNIVERSARY. Jan 2, 1936. Country and western singer, songwriter and musician "King of the Road" Roger Miller was born at Ft Worth, TX. Miller won 11 Grammy Awards and a Tony (1986 for the score to the Broadway play *Big River*). He died Oct 25, 1992, at Los Angeles, CA.

MOON PHASE: FIRST QUARTER. Jan 2. Moon enters First Quarter phase at 5:31 PM, EST.

NATIONAL THRIFT WITH FLAIR DAY. Jan 2. After Christmas shopping, consumers need to take stock of how to save money and keep the money they already have in the New Year. Events in conjunction with this day will help busy consumers find inexpensive alternatives for budget-busting sinkholes while keeping what's important in life. Info on how to get rid of debt and start anew in the new year. Annually, Jan 2. For info: The Penny Orchid—"Thrift With Flair," PO Box 642335, San Francisco, CA 94164-2335. Phone: (415) 563-7458. Fax: (415) 563-3246. E-mail: thepennyorchid@hotmail.com. Web: www.thepenny-orchid.com.

NOKIA SUGAR BOWL CLASSIC. Jan 2. Louisiana Superdome, New Orleans, LA. Bowl alliance national championship football classic. The Sugar Bowl originated in 1935. Est attendance: 75,000. For info: Nokia Sugar Bowl, Louisiana Superdome, Mezzanine Level, 1500 Sugar Bowl Dr, New Orleans, LA 70112. Phone: (504) 525-8573 or (504) 525-4867.

RUSSIA: PASSPORT PRESENTATION. Jan 2. A ceremony for 16-year-olds, who are recognized as citizens of the country. Always on the first working day of the New Year.

SPACE MILESTONE: *LUNA 1* (USSR). Jan 2, 1959. Launch of robotic moon probe that missed the moon and became the first spacecraft from Earth to orbit sun.

SPAIN CAPTURES GRANADA: ANNIVERSARY. Jan 2, 1492. Spaniards took the city of Granada from the Moors, ending seven centuries of Muslim rule in Spain.

SWITZERLAND: BERCHTOLDSTAG. Jan 2. National holiday. Commemorates the founding of the city of Berne by Duke Berchtold V in the 12th century.

January 2001	S	M	T	W	T	F	S
		1	2	3	4	5	6
	7	8	9	10	11	12	13
	14	15	16	17	18	19	20
	21	22	23	24	25	26	27
	28	29	30	31			

TAFT, HELEN HERRON: BIRTH ANNIVERSARY. Jan 2, 1861. Wife of William Howard Taft, 27th President of the US, born at Cincinnati, OH. Died at Washington, DC, May 22, 1943.

THOMAS, MARTHA CAREY: BIRTH ANNIVERSARY. Jan 2, 1857. The second president of Bryn Mawr College, Martha Carey Thomas gained a reputation for her insistence that the education of women should be as rigorous as that of men. A zealous suffragist, she served as the first president of the National College Women's Equal Suffrage League. Thomas promoted Bryn Mawr's Summer School for Women in Industry (opened in 1921) to provide a liberal education for working women. Born at Baltimore, MD, she died at Philadelphia, PA, Dec 2, 1935.

WOLFE, JAMES: BIRTH ANNIVERSARY. Jan 2, 1727. English general who commanded the British army's victory over Montcalm's French forces on the Plains of Abraham at Quebec City in 1759. As a result, France surrendered Canada to England. Wolfe was born at Westerham, Kent, England. He died at the Plains of Abraham of battle wounds Sept 13, 1759.

BIRTHDAYS TODAY

Jim Bakker (James Orsen), 62, former TV evangelist, born Muskegon, MI, Jan 2, 1939.

Tia Carrere, 34, actress (*Wayne's World, True Lies*), born Honolulu, HI, Jan 2, 1967.

David Cone, 38, baseball player, born Kansas City, MO, Jan 2, 1963.

Christopher Durang, 52, playwright, actor (*The Secret of My Success, Heaven Help Us*), born Montclair, NJ, Jan 2, 1949.

Cuba Gooding, Jr, 33, actor (*Jerry Maguire, As Good As It Gets*), born The Bronx, NY, Jan 2, 1968.

Dennis Hastert, 59, Speaker of the House, born Aurora, IL, Jan 2, 1942.

Wendy Philips, 49, actress ("Promised Land," "Homefront"), born Brooklyn, NY, Jan 2, 1952.

Richard Riley, 68, US Secretary of Education (Clinton administration), born Greenville, SC, Jan 2, 1933.

Renata Tebaldi, 79, opera singer, born Pesaro, Italy, Jan 2, 1922.

Christy Turlington, 32, model, born San Francisco, CA, Jan 2, 1969.

JANUARY 3 — WEDNESDAY
Day 3 — 362 Remaining

ALASKA: ADMISSION DAY: ANNIVERSARY. Jan 3. Alaska, which had been purchased from Russia in 1867, became the 49th state in 1959. The area of Alaska is nearly one-fifth the size of the rest of the US.

"THE ARSENIO HALL SHOW" TV PREMIERE: ANNIVERSARY. Jan 3, 1989. Arsenio Hall became the first African-American to host a successful syndicated late-night talk show. The show attracted a younger audience than that of Johnny Carson's "The Tonight Show" and effectively limited the impact of CBS's 1989 late-night entry, "The Pat Sajak Show." Hall was successful in booking soul and rap music acts that had rarely been seen on other shows. His was also the show on which presidential candidate Bill Clinton appeared, playing the saxophone in dark glasses. Hall was named by *TV Guide* (June 1990) as its first "TV Person of the Year."

ATTLEE, CLEMENT RICHARD: BIRTH ANNIVERSARY. Jan 3, 1883. English leader of the Labour Party and prime minister (July 1945–October 1951). Born at London, England; died there Oct 8, 1967.

CONGRESS ASSEMBLES. Jan 3. The Constitution provides that "the Congress shall assemble at least once in every year. . . ." and the 20th Amendment specifies "and such meeting shall begin at noon on the 3rd day of January, unless they shall by law appoint a different day."

COOLIDGE, GRACE ANNA GOODHUE: BIRTH ANNIVERSARY. Jan 3, 1879. Wife of Calvin Coolidge, 30th president of the US, born at Burlington, VT. Died at Northampton, MA, July 8, 1957.

DAVIES, MARION: BIRTH ANNIVERSARY. Jan 3, 1897. Born at Brooklyn, NY, Marion Cecilia Douras became Marion Davies and made her first appearance on film in 1917. Her romantic and professional involvement with newspaper magnate William Randolph Hearst ensured the type of publicity that would launch her to stardom. Her films included *When Knighthood Was in Flower*, *The Patsy* and *Show People*. Davies died at Hollywood, Sept 23, 1961.

DRINKING STRAW PATENTED: ANNIVERSARY. Jan 3, 1888. A drinking straw made out of paraffin-covered paper was patented by Marvin Stone of Washington, DC. It replaced natural rye straws.

FIRST FEMALE CONGRESSIONAL PAGE: ANNIVERSARY. Jan 3, 1939. Gene Cox, 13, served on the House floor as aide to her father, Representative Eugene Cox (D-GA), on opening day of the 76th Congress. She was paid $4 for three hours of work and there were no objections to her one-day service. More than 30 years later, however, there was much debate when Senator Jacob Javits (R-NY) nominated a female to be a real Senate page.

LENNON-ONO ALBUM CONFISCATION: ANNIVERSARY. Jan 3, 1969. John Lennon and Yoko Ono posed nude for the cover of their album *Two Virgins*. On this day, a shipment of 30,000 of the albums was confiscated by police at Newark, NJ, as a violation of pornography statutes.

"LOOK UP AND LIVE" TV PREMIERE: ANNIVERSARY. Jan 3, 1954. CBS broadcast this inspirational show on Sunday mornings for 24 years. The Reverend Lawrence McMasters appeared in the early years and Merv Griffin hosted the show in 1955. Pamela Ilott, executive producer, was also director of religious programming for CBS News.

MEMENTO MORI. Jan 3. "Memento, mori," Italian for "Remember, you die," is also the title of a novel by Muriel Spark. We suggest posting the words at home and at work, not to be morbid, but to remind us to cherish all that we have today. . .for tomorrow may never arrive. ©2000 WH. For info: Thomas and Ruth Roy, 2418 Long Ln, Lebanon, PA 17046. Phone: (717) 279-0184. E-mail: Wellcat@supernet.com. Web: www.Wellcat.com.

MOTT, LUCRETIA (COFFIN): BIRTH ANNIVERSARY. Jan 3, 1793. American teacher, minister, antislavery leader and (with Elizabeth Cady Stanton) one of the founders of the women's rights movement in the US. Born at Nantucket, MA, she died near Philadelphia, PA, Nov 11, 1880.

"QUEEN FOR A DAY" TV PREMIERE: 45th ANNIVERSARY. Jan 3, 1956. NBC/ABC game show on which prizes were awarded to the contestant who evoked the most sympathy from the studio audience. The show began some 11 years earlier on the radio with Jack Bailey hosting. Five women were chosen from the audience to appear on stage. Each related her story of misfortune and explained what she needed to remedy the situation and the audience would vote by applause. The lucky winner was then given the royal treatment—crown, scepter and red robe—plus a prize to help with her problem. This soon became the top-rated daytime show. In 1969 the show went into syndication with Dick Curtis as host, but it didn't last long.

RAUH, JOSEPH L. JR: 90th BIRTH ANNIVERSARY. Jan 3, 1911. Political activist Joseph L. Rauh, Jr, was born at Cincinnati, OH. In 1947 he cofounded Americans for Democratic Action (ADA), which supports liberal causes. Rauh helped create the minority civil rights plank at the 1948 Democratic National Convention—a foundation for the federal civil rights legislation in the 1960s. He served on the executive board of the NAACP and was general counsel to the Leadership Conference on Civil Rights. He died Sept 3, 1992, at Washington, DC.

STURGES, JOHN: 90th BIRTH ANNIVERSARY. Jan 3, 1911. Motion picture director John Sturges, born at Oak Park, IL, was known for his action movies. He received an Academy Award nomination in 1955 for *Bad Day at Black Rock*. He also directed *Gunfight at the OK Corral* (1956), *The Magnificent Seven* (1960), *The Great Escape* (1963) and his last film *The Eagle Has Landed* (1977). He died Aug 18, 1992, at San Luis Obispo, CA.

TOLKIEN, J[OHN] R[ONALD] R[EUEL]: BIRTH ANNIVERSARY. Jan 3, 1892. Author of *The Hobbit* (1937) and the trilogy *The Lord of the Rings*. Though best known for his fantasies, Tolkien was also a serious philologist. Born at Bloemfontein, South Africa, he died at Bournemouth, England, Sept 2, 1973.

WIND CAVE NATIONAL PARK ESTABLISHED: ANNIVERSARY. Jan 3, 1903. President Theodore Roosevelt signed a bill on this date establishing South Dakota's Wind Cave a national park and preserve. It was the first national park established for the preservation of a cave.

BIRTHDAYS TODAY

Joan Walsh Anglund, 75, author, illustrator of children's books (*Crocus in the Snow*, *Bedtime Book*), born Hinsdale, IL, Jan 3, 1926.

Victor Borge (Borge Rosenbaum), 92, comedian, pianist, born Copenhagen, Denmark, Jan 3, 1909.

Dabney Coleman, 69, actor ("Buffalo Bill," *Nine to Five, Tootsie*), born Austin, TX, Jan 3, 1932.

Mel Gibson, 45, actor (*Braveheart, Lethal Weapon*), born New York, NY, Jan 3, 1956.

Robert Marvin (Bobby) Hull, 62, Hockey Hall of Fame left wing, born Point Anne, Ontario, Canada, Jan 3, 1939.

Robert Loggia, 71, actor (*An Officer and a Gentleman, Scarface*), born Staten Island, NY, Jan 3, 1930.

Danica McKellar, 26, actress ("The Wonder Years," *Sidekicks*), born La Jolla, CA, Jan 3, 1975.

Victoria Principal, 51, actress ("Dallas"), born Fukuoka, Japan, Jan 3, 1950.

Stephen Stills, 56, musician, songwriter, born Dallas, TX, Jan 3, 1945.

JANUARY 4 — THURSDAY
Day 4 — 361 Remaining

AMERICAN HISTORICAL ASSOCIATION: ANNUAL MEETING. Jan 4–7. Boston, MA. Approximately 180 sessions will be held covering a wide range of scholarly, professional and pedagogical topics dealing with world history. Est attendance: 4,200. For info: Sharon K. Tune, Asst Dir, American Historical Assn, 400 A St SE, Washington, DC 20003. Phone: (202) 544-2422. Fax: (202) 544-8307. E-mail: aha@theaha.org. Web: www.theaha.org.

AMNESTY FOR POLYGAMISTS: ANNIVERSARY. Jan 4, 1893. President Benjamin Harrison issued a proclamation granting full amnesty and pardon to all persons who had since Nov 1, 1890, abstained from unlawful cohabitation of a polygamous marriage. This was intended in the main for a specific group of elderly Mormons who had continued in the practice of contracting serial marriages. Amnesty was based on the condition that those pardoned must obey the law in the future or be "vigorously prosecuted." The practice of polygamy was a factor interfering with attainment of statehood for Utah.

BRAILLE, LOUIS: BIRTH ANNIVERSARY. Jan 4, 1809. The inventor of a widely used touch system of reading and writing for the blind was born at Coupvray, France. Permanently blinded at the age of three by a leatherworking awl in his father's saddlemaking shop, Braille developed a system of writing that used, ironically, an awl-like stylus to punch marks in paper that could be felt and interpreted by the blind. The system was largely ignored until after Braille died in poverty, suffering from tuberculosis, at Paris, Jan 6, 1852.

"THE CATHOLIC HOUR" TV PREMIERE: ANNIVERSARY. Jan 4, 1953. Produced in cooperation with the National Council of Catholic Men, this show ran for 17 years, alternating from week to week with "The Eternal Light" and "Frontiers of Faith."

"COLLEGE BOWL" TV PREMIERE: ANNIVERSARY. Jan 4, 1959. Originally, a quiz show on CBS. Two colleges sent a team of their best and brightest to the academic competition. "College Bowl" was sponsored by General Electric and hosted by Allen Ludden (1959–62) and Robert Earle (1962–70). More recent incarnations of "College Bowl" have appeared on NBC and Disney with Pat Sajak and Dick Cavett as hosts.

EARTH AT PERIHELION. Jan 4. At approximately 4 AM, EST, planet Earth will reach Perihelion, that point in its orbit when it is closest to the sun (about 91,400,000 miles). The Earth's mean distance from the sun (mean radius of its orbit) is reached early in the months of April and October. Note that Earth is closest to the sun during Northern Hemisphere winter. See also: "Earth at Aphelion" (July 4).

GENERAL TOM THUMB: BIRTH ANNIVERSARY. Jan 4, 1838. Charles Sherwood Stratton, perhaps the most famous midget in history, was born at Bridgeport, CT. He eventually reached a height of three feet, four inches and a weight of 70 pounds. Discovered by P.T. Barnum in 1842, Stratton, as "General Tom Thumb," became an internationally known entertainer and performed before Queen Victoria and other heads of state. On Feb 10, 1863, he married another midget, Lavinia Warren. Stratton died at Middleborough, MA, July 15, 1883.

GRIMM, JACOB: BIRTH ANNIVERSARY. Jan 4, 1785. Librarian, mythologist and philologist, born at Hanau, Germany. Best remembered for *Grimm's Fairy Tales* (in collaboration with his brother Wilhelm). Died at Berlin, Germany, Sept 20, 1863.

HOLLOWAY, STERLING: BIRTH ANNIVERSARY. Jan 4, 1905. Actor Sterling Holloway prospered in films and television, but he is probably best remembered as the voice of Winnie the Pooh. He provided the voices for characters in several full-length animated features, including *Alice in Wonderland* (the Cheshire Cat), *The Aristocats* and *The Jungle Book*. Born at Cedartown, GA, he died Nov 22, 1992, at Los Angeles, CA.

MYANMAR: INDEPENDENCE DAY. Jan 4. National Day. The British controlled the country from 1826 until 1948 when it was granted independence. The country's name was changed to the Union of Myanmar in 1989 to reflect that the population is made up not just of the Burmese but of many other ethnic groups as well.

NASHVILLE FISHING EXPO. Jan 4–7. Tennessee State Fairgrounds, Nashville, TN. Annual event featuring the latest in fishing tackle, rods, reels, boats, boating equipment, guide services and other accessories. Daily seminars by BASS pros. Est attendance: 10,000. For info: Cindy Crabtree, Esau, Inc, PO Box 50096, Knoxville, TN 37950. Phone: (865) 588-1233 or (800) 588-ESAU. Fax: (865) 588-6938. Web: www.esaushows.com.

January 2001	S	M	T	W	T	F	S
		1	2	3	4	5	6
	7	8	9	10	11	12	13
	14	15	16	17	18	19	20
	21	22	23	24	25	26	27
	28	29	30	31			

NEWTON, ISAAC: BIRTH ANNIVERSARY. Jan 4, 1643. Sir Isaac Newton was the chief figure of the scientific revolution of the 17th century, a physicist and mathematician who laid the foundations of calculus, studied the mechanics of planetary motion and discovered the law of gravitation. Born at Woolsthorpe, England, he died at London, England, Mar 31, 1727. Newton was born before Great Britain adopted the Gregorian calendar. His Julian (Old Style) birth date is Dec 25, 1642.

"NIGHT COURT" TV PREMIERE: ANNIVERSARY. Jan 4, 1984. NBC sitcom set in an urban courtroom. The original cast included Harry Anderson as Judge Harry T. Stone, John Larroquette as prosecutor Dan Fielding, Richard Moll as court officer Bull Shannon and Selma Diamond as court officer Selma Hacker. Karen Austin as clerk Lana Wagner, and Paula Kelly as public defender Liz Williams, were gone after one season; Ellen Foley then became PD Billie Young but was replaced by Markie Post in 1985 as PD Christine Sullivan. Charles Robinson joined the cast as clerk Mac Robinson in 1985. Diamond died in 1985 and Florence Halop, who then appeared as court officer Florence Kleiner, died in 1986. Marsha Warfield was then brought aboard as Court Officer Roz Russell. Mel Tormé made a few appearances as himself, Harry's idol. The last telecast was July 1, 1992.

NIXON'S REJECTION OF SENATE ORDER: ANNIVERSARY. Jan 4, 1974. President Richard Nixon rejected the Senate Watergate Committee's subpoenas seeking White House tapes and documents.

POLISH-AMERICAN IN THE HOUSE: ANNIVERSARY. Jan 4, 1977. Maryland Democrat Barbara Mikulski took her seat in the US House of Representatives, the first Polish-American ever to do so. An able voice for female as well as working class Baltimore constituents of the 3rd District, Ms Mikulski went on to be elected to the US Senate.

POP MUSIC CHART INTRODUCED: 65th ANNIVERSARY. Jan 4, 1936. *Billboard* magazine published the first list of best-selling pop records, covering the week that ended Dec 30, 1935. On the list were recordings by the Tommy Dorsey and the Ozzie Nelson orchestras.

RUSH, BENJAMIN: BIRTH ANNIVERSARY. Jan 4, 1746. Physician, patriot and humanitarian of the American Revolution, born on a plantation at Byberry, PA. Rush was a signer of the Declaration of Independence, and his writings on mental illness earned him the title "Father of Psychiatry." His tract *Inquiry* attacked the common wisdom of the time that alcohol was a positive good. He was the first American to call alcoholism a chronic disease. Benjamin Rush died at Philadelphia, PA, Apr 19, 1813.

SAN DIEGO BOAT SHOW. Jan 4–7. San Diego Convention Center, San Diego, CA. Annual show is largest one-stop nautical sports event on the West Coast and features a wide selection of boats and accessories, plus informative boating and fishing seminars. For info: NMMA, 200 East Randolph Dr, Ste 5100, Chicago, IL 60601. Phone: (312) 946-6200. Fax: (312) 946-0388. Web: www.boatshows.com.

SETON, ELIZABETH ANN BAYLEY: FEAST DAY. Jan 4. First American-born saint (beatified Mar 17, 1963; canonized Sept 14, 1975). Born at New York, NY, Aug 28, 1774, Seton was the founder of the American Sisters of Charity, the first American order of Roman Catholic nuns. She died at Baltimore, MD, Jan 4, 1821.

TRIVIA DAY. Jan 4. In celebration of those who know all sorts of facts and/or have doctorates in uselessology. For info: Robert L. Birch, Puns Corps, Box 2364, Falls Church, VA 22042-0364. Phone: (703) 533-3668.

UTAH: ADMISSION DAY: ANNIVERSARY. Jan 4. Utah became the 45th state in 1896.

BIRTHDAYS TODAY

Dyan Cannon, 64, actress (Oscar nominations for *Heaven Can Wait, Bob and Carol and Ted and Alice*), born Tacoma, WA, Jan 4, 1937.

Patrick Cassidy, 39, actor ("Bay City Blues," *Longtime Companion*), born Los Angeles, CA, Jan 4, 1962.

Dave Foley, 38, actor ("NewsRadio"), born Toronto, Ontario, Canada, Jan 4, 1963.

Ann Magnuson, 45, actress, performance artist ("Anything but Love," *Clear and Present Danger*), born Charleston, WV, Jan 4, 1956.

Julia Ormond, 36, actress (*Legends of the Fall, Sabrina*), born Surrey, England, Jan 4, 1965.

Floyd Patterson, 66, former boxer, born Waco, NC, Jan 4, 1935.

Barbara Rush, 74, actress ("Peyton Place," *Magnificent Obsession, Hombre*), born Denver, CO, Jan 4, 1927.

Donald Francis (Don) Shula, 71, Pro Football Hall of Fame coach and player, born Paineville, OH, Jan 4, 1930.

Michael Stipe, 41, singer (REM), born Decatur, GA, Jan 4, 1960.

Jane Wyman (Sarah Jane Faulks), 87, actress ("Falcon Crest," *Magnificent Obsession*; Oscar for *Johnny Belinda*), born St. Joseph, MO, Jan 4, 1914.

JANUARY 5 — FRIDAY

Day 5 — 360 Remaining

AILEY, ALVIN: 70th BIRTH ANNIVERSARY. Jan 5, 1931. Born at Rogers, TX, Alvin Ailey began his noted career as a choreographer in the late 1950s after a successful career as a dancer. He founded the Alvin Ailey American Dance Theater, drawing from classical ballet, jazz, Afro-Caribbean and modern dance idioms to create the 79 ballets of the company's repertoire. He and his work played a central part in establishing a role for blacks in the world of modern dance. Ailey died Dec 1, 1989, at New York, NY.

"ALL MY CHILDREN" TV PREMIERE: ANNIVERSARY. Jan 5, 1970. This ABC show became TV's top-rated soap opera by the 1978–79 season, and even today the show keeps viewers glued to the screen. "All My Children" was created by Agnes Nixon, who had written for "Search for Tomorrow," "Another World" and "One Life to Live." Set in a place called Pine Valley, NY, the show focused on the Tyler and Martin families. The story includes the illegitimate child of Dr. Tyler, Erica Kane (played by Susan Lucci), who became one of daytime TV's most popular characters. Lucci had been nominated more than a dozen times for an Emmy, and finally won one in 1999. This serial has included in its cast Hugh Franklin as Dr. Charles Tyler and Ruth Warrick as his wife, Phoebe; son Lincoln has been played by James Karen, Paul Dumont, Nicholas Pryor and Peter White, daughter Ann by Diana De Vegh, Joanna Miles, Judith Barcroft and Gwyn Gilliss.

ASARAH B'TEVET. Jan 5. Hebrew calendar date: Tevet 10, 5761. The Fast of the 10th of Tevet begins at first morning light and commemorates the beginning of the Babylonian siege of Jerusalem in the 6th century BC.

CARVER, GEORGE WASHINGTON: DEATH ANNIVERSARY. Jan 5, 1943. Black American agricultural scientist, author, inventor and teacher. Born into slavery at Diamond Grove, MO, probably in 1864. His research led to the creation of synthetic products made from peanuts, potatoes and wood. Carver died at Tuskegee, AL. His birthplace became a national monument in 1953.

DECATUR, STEPHEN: BIRTH ANNIVERSARY. Jan 5, 1779. American naval officer (whose father and grandfather, both also named Stephen Decatur, were also seafaring men) born at Sinepuxent, MD. In a toast at a dinner in Norfolk in 1815, Decatur spoke his most famous words: "Our country! In her intercourse with foreign nations may she always be in the right; but our country, right or wrong." Mortally wounded in a duel with Commodore James Barron, at Bladensburg, MD, on the morning of Mar 22, 1820, Decatur was carried to his home in Washington where he died a few hours later.

ELVIS PRESLEY'S BIRTHDAY CELEBRATION. Jan 5–8. Graceland, Memphis, TN. Special birthday proclamation on Jan 8 as well as other Elvis birthday events at Graceland. For info: Graceland, 3734 Elvis Presley Blvd, Memphis, TN 38116. Phone: (800) 238-2000 or (901) 332-3322. Web: www.elvis-presley.com.

ENGLAND: LONDON INTERNATIONAL BOAT SHOW. Jan 5–14. Earls Court Exhibition Centre, London. One of the largest international boat shows in the world, displaying more than 600 craft, plus accessories for the marine enthusiast. Est attendance: 175,000. For info: British Marine Industries Federation/Natl Boat Shows Ltd, Meadlake Place, Thorpe Lea Rd, Egham, Surrey, England TW20 8BF. Phone: (44) (178) 223 600. Fax: (44) (178) 443-9678. Web: www.bigblue.org.uk.

FIVE-DOLLAR-A-DAY MINIMUM WAGE: ANNIVERSARY. Jan 5, 1914. Henry Ford announced that all worthy Ford Motor Company employees would receive a minimum wage of $5 a day. Ford explained the policy as "profit sharing and efficiency engineering." The more cynical attributed it to an attempt to prevent unionization and to obtain a docile workforce that would accept job speedups. To obtain this minimum wage an employee had to be of "good personal habits." Whether an individual fit these criteria was determined by a new office created by Ford Motor Company—the Sociological Department.

ITALY: EPIPHANY FAIR. Jan 5. Piazza Navona, Rome, Italy. On the eve of Epiphany a fair of toys, sweets and presents takes place among the beautiful Bernini Fountains.

LONGHORN WORLD CHAMPIONSHIP RODEO. Jan 5–7. Tulsa Convention Center, Tulsa, OK. More than 500 cowboys and cowgirls compete in seven professional contests ranging from bronco riding to bull riding for $100,000+ and world championship points. Featuring colorful opening pageantry and Big, Bad BONUS Bulls. Season opener for Longhorn rodeos nationally. 11th annual. Est attendance: 16,000. For info: W. Bruce Lehrke, Pres, Longhorn World Chmpshp Rodeo Inc, PO Box 70159, Nashville, TN 37207. Phone: (615) 876-1016. Fax: (615) 876-4685. E-mail: lhrodeo@idt.net. Web: www.longhornrodeo.com.

PICCARD, JEANNETTE RIDLON: BIRTH ANNIVERSARY. Jan 5, 1895. First American woman to qualify as free balloon pilot (1934). One of first women to be ordained as Episcopal priest (1976). Pilot for record-setting balloon ascent into stratosphere (from Dearborn, MI, Oct 23, 1934) (57,579 ft) with her husband, Jean Felix Piccard. See also: "Piccard, Jean Felix: Birth Anniversary" (Jan 28). Identical twin married to identical twin. Born at Chicago, IL. Died at Minneapolis, MN, May 17, 1981.

ROMAN CATHOLIC/EASTERN ORTHODOX MEETING: ANNIVERSARY. Jan 5, 1964. Pope Paul VI and Patriarch Athenagoras of Jerusalem met in the Holy Land for the first meeting in five centuries between a Roman Catholic pontiff and an Eastern Orthodox patriarch.

RUFFIN, EDMUND: BIRTH ANNIVERSARY. Jan 5, 1794. Born at Prince George County, VA, Edmund Ruffin was an American agriculturist whose discoveries about crop rotation and fertilizer were influential in the early agrarian culture of the US. He published the *Farmer's Register* from 1833 to 1842, a journal that promoted scientific agriculture. A noted politician as well as a farmer, he was an early advocate of Southern secession whose views were widely circulated in pamphlets. As a member of the Palmetto Guards of Charleston, he was given the honor of firing the first shot on Fort Sumter Apr 12, 1861. According to legend, after the South's defeat he became despondent and, wrapping himself in the Confederate flag, took his own life on June 18, 1865, at Amelia County, VA.

SOUTHWEST ANTIQUE SHOW AND SALE. Jan 5–7. Yuma Civic and Convention Center, Yuma, AZ. A fine collection of antiques and collectibles. Sponsor: Jack Black Enterprises. Est attendance: 3,500. For info: Mktg Dept, Yuma Civic and Conv Ctr, 1440 Desert Hills Dr, Yuma, AZ 85365. Phone: (520) 344-3800. Fax: (520) 344-9121.

STAMP EXPO. Jan 5–7. Travelodge Hotel, Long Beach, CA. Annual expo. Est attendance: 7,500. For info: Intl Stamp Collectors Soc, PO Box 854, Van Nuys, CA 91408. Phone: (818) 997-6496. Fax: (818) 988-4337. E-mail: iibick@aol.com. Web: www.bick.net.

TWELFTH NIGHT. Jan 5. Evening before Epiphany. Twelfth Night marks the end of medieval Christmas festivities and the end of Twelfthtide (the 12-day season after Christmas ending with Epiphany). Also called Twelfth Day Eve.

WYOMING INAUGURATES FIRST WOMAN GOVERNOR IN US: ANNIVERSARY. Jan 5, 1925. Nellie Tayloe (Mrs William B.) Ross became the first woman to serve as governor upon her inauguration in Wyoming. She had previously finished out the term of her husband, who had died in office. In 1974 Ella Grasso of Connecticut became the first woman to be elected governor in her own right.

BIRTHDAYS TODAY

Suzy Amis, 39, actress (*Titanic, Judgement Day*), born Oklahoma City, OK, Jan 5, 1962.

Mike DeWine, 54, US Senator (R, Ohio), born Springfield, OH, Jan 5, 1947.

Warrick Dunn, 26, football player, born Baton Rouge, LA, Jan 5, 1975.

Robert Duvall, 70, actor (*A Civil Action, The Godfather*), born San Diego, CA, Jan 5, 1931.

Umberto Eco, 69, author (*In the Name of the Rose*), born Alessandria, Italy, Jan 5, 1932.

Diane Keaton (Diane Hall), 55, actress (Oscar for *Annie Hall; The First Wives Club, The Other Sister*), born Los Angeles, CA, Jan 5, 1946.

Pamela Sue Martin, 47, actress (*The Poseidon Adventure*, "The Nancy Drew Mysteries," "Dynasty"), born Westport, CT, Jan 5, 1954.

Walter Frederick "Fritz" Mondale, 73, former US vice president and senator, born Ceylon, MN, Jan 5, 1928.

Charlie Rose, 59, newscaster, TV host, born Henderson, NC, Jan 5, 1942.

W.D. Snodgrass, 75, poet, born Wilkinsburg, PA, Jan 5, 1926.

JANUARY 6 — SATURDAY

Day 6 — 359 Remaining

ARMENIAN CHRISTMAS. Jan 6. Christmas is observed in the Armenian Church, the oldest Christian national church.

CARNIVAL SEASON. Jan 6–Feb 27. A secular festival preceding Lent. A time of merrymaking and feasting before the austere days of Lenten fasting and penitence (40 weekdays between Ash Wednesday and Easter Sunday). The word *carnival* probably is derived from the Latin *carnem levare*, meaning "to remove meat." Depending on local custom, the carnival season may start any time between Nov 11 and Shrove Tuesday. Conclusion of the sea-

January *2001*	S	M	T	W	T	F	S
		1	2	3	4	5	6
	7	8	9	10	11	12	13
	14	15	16	17	18	19	20
	21	22	23	24	25	26	27
	28	29	30	31			

son is much less variable, being the close of Shrove Tuesday in most places. Celebrations vary considerably, but the festival often includes many theatrical aspects (masks, costumes and songs) and has given its name (in the US) to traveling amusement shows that may be seen throughout the year. Observed traditionally in Roman Catholic countries from Epiphany through Shrove Tuesday.

CONCLUSION OF HOLY YEAR 2000. Jan 6. An estimated 13 million people traveled to Rome to celebrate the Great Jubilee of the Incarnation of Christ. For info: Great Jubilee 2000, Vatican City, 00120. Web: www.vatican.va/

EPIPHANY or TWELFTH DAY. Jan 6. Known also as Old Christmas Day and Twelfthtide. On the twelfth day after Christmas, Christians celebrate the visit of the Magi, the first Gentile recognition of Christ. Epiphany of Our Lord, one of the oldest Christian feasts, is observed in Roman Catholic churches in the US on a Sunday between Jan 2 and 8. Theophany of the Eastern Orthodox Church is observed in churches using the Gregorian calendar (Jan 19 in those churches using the Julian calendar). This feast day celebrates the manifestation of the divinity of Jesus at the time of his baptism in the Jordan River by John the Baptist.

GIBRAN, KAHLIL: BIRTH ANNIVERSARY. Jan 6, 1883. Lebanese-American poet (*The Prophet*) and artist. Born at Bsherri, Lebanon, he died Oct 10, 1931, at New York, NY.

GREAT FRUITCAKE TOSS. Jan 6. Manitou Springs, CO. What do you do with leftover fruitcake? Toss, hurl, launch competitions. Annually, the first Saturday in January. For info: Manitou Springs Chamber of Commerce, 354 Manitou Ave, Manitou Springs, CO 80829. Phone: (800) 642-2567. Web: www.manitousprings.org.

"HALLMARK HALL OF FAME" TV PREMIERE: ANNIVERSARY. Jan 6, 1952. Carried at different times by ABC, CBS, NBC and PBS, this was a top quality dramatic anthology series. Originally titled "Hallmark Television Playhouse," the program was sponsored by Hallmark Cards and hosted by Sarah Churchill until 1955. A few of the presentations were *Hamlet*, with Maurice Evans and Ruth Chatterton (Apr 26, 1953); *Moby Dick*, with Victor Jory (May 16, 1954); *Macbeth*, with Maurice Evans, Dame Judith Anderson and House Jameson (Nov 28, 1954); *Alice in Wonderland*, with Eva LeGallienne, Elsa Lanchester and Reginald Gardiner (Oct 23, 1955). The list goes on with splendid performances by many highly acclaimed actors and actresses.

INTERNATIONAL RESPECT-FULL LIVING DAY. Jan 6. Living every day of your life with respect for yourself and others is crucial to living with joy and meaning, the keys to happiness and success. Contact us for keynote presentations, training, seminars, media interviews, ideas you can implement immediately to improve your life, along with a list of activities being held around the world. Special programs for youth organizations and schools. Annually, Jan 6. For info: Rhonda Patras, The Respect Lady, Empowering U™, 724 Irving Ave NW, Elk River, MN 55330. Phone: (763) 441-0197. Fax: (413) 208-4145. E-mail: info@empoweringu.net. Web: www.empoweringu.net.

ITALY: LA BEFANA. Jan 6. Epiphany festival in which the "Befana," a kindly witch, bestows gifts on children—toys and candy for those who have been good, but a lump of coal or a pebble for those who have been naughty. The festival begins on the night of Jan 5 with much noise and merrymaking (when the Befana is supposed to come down the chimneys on her broom, leaving gifts in children's stockings) and continues with joyous fairs, parades and other activities throughout Jan 6.

JAMAICA: MAROON FESTIVAL. Jan 6. Commemorates the 18th-century Treaty of Cudjoe. While Jamaica was a Spanish colony, its native inhabitants (Arawaks) were exterminated. The Spanish then imported African slaves to work their plantations. When the Spanish were driven out (1655), the black slaves fled to the mountains. The "Maroons" (fugitive slaves) were permitted to settle in the north of the island in 1738.

JOAN OF ARC: BIRTH ANNIVERSARY. Jan 6, 1412. Born at the village of Domrémy, in the Meuse River valley of France (probably in 1412). Turned over to an ecclesiastical court by the British, she was tried for heresy and burned to death at the stake May 30, 1431, at age 19; in reality, she was executed for the military action she'd taken against the British on behalf of Charles VII of France.

JOHNSON, BAN: BIRTH ANNIVERSARY. Jan 6, 1863. Byron Bancroft (Ban) Johnson, Baseball Hall of Fame executive, born at Cincinnati, OH. Johnson transformed the minor league Western League into the major league American League in 1901. He ruled as president with an iron hand and was eased out of power by the league's owners in 1927. Inducted into the Hall of Fame in 1937. Died at St. Louis, MO, Mar 28, 1931.

KANE COUNTY FLEA MARKET. Jan 6–7. (also Feb 3–4, Mar 3–4, Mar 31–Apr 1, May 5–6, June 2–3, June 30–July 1, Aug 4–5, Sept 1–2, Oct 6–7, Nov 3–4 and Dec 1–2). Kane County Fairgrounds, Randall Road between Rtes 64 and 38. Saturday, Sunday 7–4. Free parking. Admission $5, children under 12 free. One of the largest antique and collectible flea markets in the Midwest or anywhere. For more than 30 years it has just kept getting bigger and better. If it was ever made, you will probably be able to find it here! Est attendance: 15,000. For info: St. Charles CVB, 311 N Second St, Ste 100, St. Charles, IL 60174. Phone: (800) 777-4373 or (630) 377-6161. Web: www.visit-stcharles.com.

"THE LAST WORD" TV PREMIERE: ANNIVERSARY. Jan 6, 1957. CBS talk show moderated by Dr. Bergen Evans that aired Sunday afternoons and was dedicated to discussing the English language. Three guest celebrities or authorities along with John Mason Brown, permanent panelist, would discuss questions submitted by viewers about language.

MALESKA, EUGENE T.: 85th BIRTH ANNIVERSARY. Jan 6, 1916. *New York Times* crossword puzzle editor, Maleska was born at Jersey City, NJ. He invented new puzzle formats and clue styles for crossword puzzles in 1977 after a career in education. Maleska died Aug 3, 1993, at Daytona Beach, FL.

MIRROR LAKE CANDLELIGHT CROSS-COUNTRY SKIING. Jan 6 (also Jan 20 & Feb 10). Mirror Lake State Park, Baraboo, WI. Nordic skiing by candlelight on state park trails. Park provides lit cooking grills and a warming fire. For info: Wisconsin Dells Visitors Bureau, Angie Rizner, PO Box 390, Wisconsin Dells, WI 53965. Phone: (800) 223-3557. E-mail: info@wisdells.com. Web: www.wisdells.com.

MIX, TOM: BIRTH ANNIVERSARY. Jan 6, 1880. American motion picture actor, especially remembered for western cowboy films. Born at Driftwood, PA. Died near Florence, AZ, Oct 12, 1940.

NATIONAL SMITH DAY. Jan 6. The commonest surname in the English-speaking world is Smith. There are an estimated 2,382,500 Smiths in the US. This special day honors the birthday in 1580 of Captain John Smith, the leader of the English colonists who settled at Jamestown, VA, in 1607, thus making him one of the first American Smiths. On this special day, all derivatives, such as Goldsmith, are invited to participate. For info: Adrienne Sioux Koopersmith, 1437 W Rosemont, 1W, Chicago, IL 60660-1319. Phone: (773) 743-5341. Fax: (773) 743-5395. E-mail: adrienne@21stcentury.net.

NATIONAL WESTERN STOCK SHOW AND RODEO. Jan 6–21. Denver, CO. One of the nation's largest livestock shows with more than 30 breeds of animals, rodeo performances, horse shows, Mexican rodeos, PBR bull riders and cutting horse and sheep shearing contests. 95th annual. Est attendance: 630,000. For info: Natl Western Stock Show and Rodeo, 4655 Humboldt St, Denver, CO 80216. Phone: (303) 297-1166 or 800 336 6977. Fax: (303) 292-1708. Web: www.nationalwestern.com.

NEW MEXICO: ADMISSION DAY: ANNIVERSARY. Jan 6. Became 47th state in 1912.

PAN AM CIRCLES EARTH: ANNIVERSARY. Jan 6, 1942. A Pan American Airways plane arrived in New York to complete the first around-the-world trip by a commercial aircraft.

"PRO BOWLER'S TOUR" TV PREMIERE: ANNIVERSARY. Jan 6, 1962. ABC's weekly coverage of bowling tournaments with anchorman Chris Schenkel and Nelson Burton, Jr. Schenkel was previously assisted by Jack Buck (1962–64) and Billy Welu (1964–74).

SALOMON, HAYM: DEATH ANNIVERSARY. Jan 6, 1785. American Revolutionary War patriot and financier was born at Lissa, Poland, in 1740 (exact date unknown). Salomon died at Philadelphia, PA.

SANDBURG, CARL: BIRTH ANNIVERSARY. Jan 6, 1878. American poet, biographer of Lincoln, historian and folklorist, born at Galesburg, IL. Died at Flat Rock, NC, July 22, 1967.

SMITH, JEDEDIAH STRONG: BIRTH ANNIVERSARY. Jan 6, 1799. Mountain man, fur trader and one of the first explorers of the American West, Smith helped develop the Oregon Trail. He was the first American to reach California by land and first to travel by land from San Diego, up the West Coast to the Canadian border. Smith was born at Jericho (now Bainbridge), NY, and was killed by Comanche Indians along the Santa Fe Trail in what is now Kansas May 27, 1831.

SPACE MILESTONE: *LUNAR EXPLORER* (US). Jan 6, 1998. NASA headed back to the moon for the first time since the Apollo 17 flight 25 years before. This unmanned probe searches for evidence of frozen water on the moon and found evidence of ice in late 1998.

THOMAS, DANNY: BIRTH ANNIVERSARY. Jan 6, 1912. Comedian Danny Thomas was born Muzyad Yakhoob, later Amos Jacobs, at Deerfield, MI. Thomas began his entertainment career as a radio actor and nightclub comedian and then went on to movies in the late 1940s and early 1950s. His greatest fame came from his television show "Make Room for Daddy" (1953–64), and later as a television producer. Thomas was also a tireless philanthropist and fundraiser who founded St. Jude's Children's Research Hospital at Memphis, TN. Thomas died Feb 6, 1991, at Los Angeles, CA.

THREE KINGS DAY. Jan 6. Major festival of Christian Church observed in many parts of the world with gifts, feasting, last lighting of Christmas lights and burning of Christmas greens. Twelfth and last day of the Feast of the Nativity. Commemorates visit of the Three Wise Men (Kings or Magi) to Bethlehem.

"WHEEL OF FORTUNE" TV PREMIERE: ANNIVERSARY. Jan 6, 1975. This daytime quiz show was originally hosted by Chuck Woolery. In 1981 Pat Sajak became host, assisted by Vanna White. A nighttime version was added in 1983. Not to be confused with the human interest show rewarding people who had done good deeds, hosted by Todd Russell, that premiered in 1952.

WILDERNESS WILDLIFE WEEK OF NATURE. Jan 6–14. Heartlander Country Resort, Pigeon Forge, TN. A no-cost week of walks, talks and workshops led by experts in their various fields. Est attendance: 10,000. For info: Pigeon Forge Dept of Tourism, 2450 Parkway, PO Box 1390, Pigeon Forge, TN 37868. Phone: (800) 251-9100 or (423) 429-7350. Fax: (423) 429-7362. Web: pigeon-forge.tn.us.

BIRTHDAYS TODAY

Joey Lauren Adams, 30, actress (*Chasing Amy, Big Daddy*), born Little Rock, AR, Jan 6, 1971.
Rowan Atkinson, 46, British actor ("Mr Bean"), born Newcastle-on-Tyne, England, Jan 6, 1955.
E.L. Doctorow, 70, writer (*Ragtime, Welcome to Hard Times*), born New York, NY, Jan 6, 1931.
Bonnie Franklin, 57, actress ("One Day at a Time," *The Kettles in the Ozarks*), born Santa Monica, CA, Jan 6, 1944.
Lou Harris, 80, public opinion analyst, author, born New Haven, CT, Jan 6, 1921.
Louis Leo (Lou) Holtz, 64, former Notre Dame football coach, born Follansbee, WV, Jan 6, 1937.
Howard M. (Howie) Long, 41, sportscaster, former football player, born Somerville, MA, Jan 6, 1960.
Nancy Lopez, 44, LPGA Hall of Fame golfer, born Torrance, CA, Jan 6, 1957.
Anthony Minghella, 47, writer, director (*The English Patient*), born Isle of Wight, England, Jan 6, 1954.
Gabrielle Reece, 31, pro volleyball player, born La Jolla, CA, Jan 6, 1970.
Earl Scruggs, 77, musician, born Cleveland County, NC, Jan 6, 1924.
John Singleton, 33, director, screenwriter (*Boyz N the Hood*), born Los Angeles, CA, Jan 6, 1968.
Loretta Young, 88, actress (Oscar for *The Farmer's Daughter*; "The New Loretta Young Show"), born Salt Lake City, UT, Jan 6, 1913.

JANUARY 7 — SUNDAY

Day 7 — 358 Remaining

CHRISTMAS EPIPHANY CELEBRATION. Jan 7. St. John's Lutheran Church, Isanti, MN. Celebrate the holiday season through lessons and carols all done in German. A traditional German Christmas tree graces the historic church on the National Register of Historic Sites. We'll heat up the wood stove, but dress warmly. Annually, the Sunday closest to the Epiphany. For info: Valorie Arrowsmith, Isanti County Historical Society, PO Box 525, Cambridge, MN 55008. Phone: (763) 689-4229. Fax: (763) 689-4229. E-mail: varrow2@ecenet.com.

January 2001	S	M	T	W	T	F	S
		1	2	3	4	5	6
	7	8	9	10	11	12	13
	14	15	16	17	18	19	20
	21	22	23	24	25	26	27
	28	29	30	31			

EMPEROR HIROHITO: DEATH ANNIVERSARY. Jan 7, 1989. After ruling Japan for 62 years as its longest-reigning ruler, Emperor Hirohito died at Tokyo of cancer at 6:33 AM on Jan 7, 1989. His only son, Crown Prince Akihito, succeeded him to the throne later that day.

"FAME" TV PREMIERE: ANNIVERSARY. Jan 7, 1982. NBC series centered on life at New York's High School of the Performing Arts. Based on the movie, it featured four of the film's actors in the same parts: Debbie Allen as dance teacher Lydia Grant, Albert Hague as music instructor Benjamin Shorofsky, Lee Curreri as student Bruno Martelli and Gene Anthony Ray as dancing student Leroy Johnson. Also in the cast were Erica Gimpel as Coco Hernandez, Carol Mayo Jenkins as English teacher Elizabeth Sherwood, P.R. Paul as student Montgomery, Lori Singer as cellist Julie Miller, Valerie Landsburg as student Doris Schwartz, Carlo Imperato as Danny Amatullo, Michael Thoma as drama teacher Crandall, Morgan Stevens as drama teacher Reardon and Carmine Caridi as Angelo Martelli. The last telecast aired on Aug 4, 1987.

FILLMORE, MILLARD: BIRTH ANNIVERSARY. Jan 7, 1800. 13th president of the US (July 10, 1850–Mar 3, 1853). Fillmore succeeded to the presidency upon the death of Zachary Taylor, but he did not get the hoped-for nomination from his party in 1852. He ran for president in 1856 as candidate of the "Know-Nothing Party," whose platform demanded, among other things, that every government employee (federal, state and local) should be a native-born citizen. Fillmore was born at Summerhill, NY, and died at Buffalo, NY, Mar 8, 1874. Now his birthday is often used as an occasion for parties for which there is no other reason.

FIRST BALLOON FLIGHT ACROSS ENGLISH CHANNEL: ANNIVERSARY. Jan 7, 1785. Dr. John Jeffries, a Boston physician, and Jean-Pierre Francois Blanchard, French aeronaut, crossed the English Channel from Dover, England, to Calais, France, landing in a forest after being forced to throw overboard all ballast, equipment and even most of their clothing to avoid a forced landing in the icy waters of the English Channel. Blanchard's trousers are said to have been the last article thrown overboard.

FIRST US COMMERCIAL BANK: ANNIVERSARY. Jan 7, 1782. The first commercial bank in the US, the Bank of North America, was opened at Philadelphia.

GARDENIA, VINCENT (VINCENT SCOGNAMIGLIO): BIRTH ANNIVERSARY. Jan 7, 1922. Stage, screen and television performer Vincent Gardenia was born at Naples, Italy. Gardenia once estimated he had played 500 parts in his lifetime. He received two Oscar nominations, one for playing a baseball manager in *Bang the Drum Slowly* and again for the role of patriarch of a goofy Brooklyn family in *Moonstruck*. He won a Tony for his part in *The Prisoner of Second Avenue* and an Emmy for his portrayal in *Age Old Friends*. Vincent Gardenia died Dec 9, 1992, at Philadelphia, PA.

GERMANY: MUNICH FASCHING CARNIVAL. Jan 7–Feb 27. Munich. From Jan 7 through Shrove Tuesday is Munich's famous carnival season. Costume balls are popular throughout carnival. "High points on Fasching Sunday (Feb 25) and Shrove Tuesday (Feb 27) with great carnival doings outside at the Viktualienmarkt and on Pedestrian Mall."

INTIMATE APPAREL MARKET WEEK. Jan 7–11. Also Mar 5–7, May 7–10, Aug 6–8 and Nov 5–7. Market week dates for the intimate apparel industry. For info: Mary Howell, Dir of Product Divisions, American Apparel Mfgs Assn, 2500 Wilson Blvd, Ste 301, Arlington, VA 22201. Phone: (703) 524-1864. Fax: (703) 522-6741. Web: www.americanapparel.org.

JAPAN: NANAKUSA. Jan 7. Festival dates back to the 7th century and recalls the seven plants served to the emperor that are believed to have great medicinal value—shepherd's purse, chickweed, parsley, cottonweed, radish, hotoke-no-za and aona.

JAPAN: USOKAE (BULLFINCH EXCHANGE FESTIVAL). Jan 7. Dazaifu, Fukuoka Prefecture. "Good Luck" gilded wood bullfinches, mixed among many plain ones, are sought after by the throngs as priests of the Dazaifu Shrine pass them out in the dim light of a small bonfire.

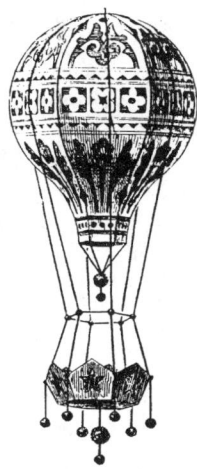

MONTGOLFIER, JACQUES ETIENNE: BIRTH ANNIVERSARY. Jan 7, 1745. Merchant and inventor born at Vidalon-lez Annonay, Ardèche, France. With his older brother, Joseph Michel, in November 1782, conducted experiments with paper and fabric bags filled with smoke and hot air, which led to the invention of the hot-air balloon and human's first flight. Died at Serrieres, France, Aug 2, 1799. See also: "First Balloon Flight: Anniversary" (June 5); "Aviation History Month" (Nov 1).

OLD CALENDAR ORTHODOX CHRISTMAS. Jan 7. Some Orthodox Churches celebrate Christmas on the "Old" (Julian) calendar date.

POL POT OVERTHROWN: ANNIVERSARY. Jan 7, 1979. Pol Pot's Cambodian government fell to combined forces of Cambodian rebels and Vietnamese soldiers.

RUSSIA: CHRISTMAS OBSERVANCE. Jan 7. National holiday.

"SOMEDAY WE'LL LAUGH ABOUT THIS" WEEK. Jan 7–13. We've all used the expression, "Someday we'll laugh about this!" Why wait? It usually takes less than seven days for people to violate 90 percent of their New Year's resolutions. This week helps us to remember the art of laughing at ourselves. This week tickles the yoke and joke of perfectionism while encouraging people to strive for excellence at the same time. This week is a great way to start the new year—laughing at the humorous human condition. For a free information packet on the positive power of humor send a stamped (99 cents) self-addressed envelope. For info: Dr. Joel Goodman, The Humor Project, Inc, 480 Broadway, Ste 210-C, Saratoga Springs, NY 12866-2288. Phone: (518) 587-8770. Fax: (518) 587-8771. E-mail: chase@HumorProject.com. Web: www.HumorProject.com.

TRANSATLANTIC PHONING: ANNIVERSARY. Jan 7, 1927. Commercial transatlantic telephone service between New York and London was inaugurated. There were 31 calls made the first day.

UNITED KINGDOM: SOLID GOLD HAT DAY. Jan 7. Royal Square, St. Helier, Jersey, United Kingdom. The Island hosts its annual party to elect the king for the year. At 12 minutes past 12, a cannon is fired, and the Hatmeister announces the name of the new Monarch, and crowns him with the Solid Gold Hat. Islanders must avoid eye contact with the king for the whole year, and each Islander grants the king one rabbit and a liter of homemade sherry. Annually, the first Sunday of the New Year. Est attendance: 1,000. For info: Peter Mac, 6 Tunnell St, Jersey, United Kingdom, JE2 4LU. Phone: (153) 488-7799.

William Blatty, 73, novelist (*The Exorcist*), screenwriter, born New York, NY, Jan 7, 1928.

Nicolas Cage, 37, actor (*Leaving Las Vegas, Con Air*), born Long Beach, CA, Jan 7, 1964.

Katie Couric, 44, cohost ("Today Show"), born Arlington, VA, Jan 7, 1957.

Dustin Diamond, 24, actor ("Saved by the Bell"), born San Jose, CA, Jan 7, 1977.

Erin Gray, 49, actress ("Buck Rogers in the 25th Century," "Silver Spoons"), born Honolulu, HI, Jan 7, 1952.

Kenny Loggins, 53, singer (Loggins and Messina, "Your Mama Don't Dance"), songwriter ("What a Fool Believes" with Michael McDonald, won three Grammys), born Everett, WA, Jan 7, 1948.

Terry Moore, 72, actress ("Empire," *Gaslight, Come Back Little Sheba*), born Los Angeles, CA, Jan 7, 1929.

Paul Revere, 63, singer, pianist (Paul Revere & the Raiders), born Boise, ID, Jan 7, 1938.

Jann Wenner, 54, journalist, publisher, *Rolling Stone* magazine, born New York, NY, Jan 7, 1947.

JANUARY 8 — MONDAY
Day 8 — 357 Remaining

AT&T DIVESTITURE: ANNIVERSARY. Jan 8, 1982. In the most significant antitrust suit since the breakup of Standard Oil in 1911, American Telephone and Telegraph agreed to give up its 22 local Bell System companies ("Baby Bells"). These companies represented 80 percent of AT&T's assets. This ended the corporation's virtual monopoly on US telephone service.

BATTLE OF NEW ORLEANS: ANNIVERSARY. Jan 8, 1815. British forces suffered crushing losses (more than 2,000 casualties) in an attack on New Orleans, LA. Defending US troops were led by General Andrew Jackson, who became a popular hero as a result of the victory. Neither side knew that the War of 1812 had ended two weeks previously with the signing of the Treaty of Ghent, Dec 24, 1814. Battle of New Orleans Day is observed in Louisiana.

BIDDLE, NICHOLAS: BIRTH ANNIVERSARY. Jan 8, 1786. American lawyer, diplomat, statesman and financier who served as president of the Second Bank of the United States. Born at Philadelphia, PA, he died there Feb 27, 1844.

CHOU EN-LAI: 25th DEATH ANNIVERSARY. Jan 8, 1976. Anniversary of the death of Chou En-Lai, premier of the State Council of the People's Republic of China. He was born in 1898 (exact date unknown).

COLLINS, WILLIAM WILKIE: BIRTH ANNIVERSARY. Jan 8, 1824. English novelist, author of *The Moonstone* (one of the first examples of detective fiction), *The Woman in White* and *The Dead Secret*. Born at London, England, he died there Sept 23, 1889.

DOW-JONES TOPS 2,000: ANNIVERSARY. Jan 8, 1987. The Dow-Jones Index of 30 major industrial stocks topped the 2,000 mark for the first time.

EARTH'S ROTATION PROVED: 150th ANNIVERSARY. Jan 8, 1851. Using a device now known as Foucault's pendulum in his Paris home, physicist Jean Foucault demonstrated that the Earth rotates on its axis.

ENGLAND: PLOUGH MONDAY. Jan 8. Always the Monday after Twelfth Day. Work on the farm is resumed after the festivities of the 12 days of Christmas. On preceding Sunday ploughs may be blessed in churches. Celebrated with dances and plays.

FERRER, JOSE: BIRTH ANNIVERSARY. Jan 8, 1912. Award-winning actor, producer, writer and director was born at Santurce, Puerto Rico. Nominated three times for an Academy Award, he won best actor for his role in *Cyrano de Bergerac*. In addition, Ferrer was awarded Tonys and Critics' Circle prizes during half a century in the entertainment world. He died Jan 26, 1992, at Coral Gables, FL.

FOURTEEN POINTS PROPOSED: ANNIVERSARY.

Jan 8, 1918. In a speech before a hastily convened joint session of Congress, President Woodrow Wilson presented Fourteen Points for a just peace. The proposal called for reduction of armaments to the lowest point consistent with domestic safety, "open covenants openly arrived at," self-determination of governments and the creation of a League of Nations to preserve peace. Wilson was unable to obtain Allied agreement to his proposals.

GREECE: MIDWIFE'S DAY or WOMEN'S DAY. Jan 8.

Midwife's Day or Women's Day is celebrated Jan 8 each year to honor midwives and all women. "On this day women stop their housework and spend their time in cafés, while the men do all the housework chores and look after the children." In some villages, men caught outside "will be stripped . . . and drenched with cold water."

JAPAN: COMING-OF-AGE DAY. Jan 8. National holiday for

youth of the country who have reached adulthood during the preceding year. Annually, the second Monday in January.

NATIONAL BUBBLE BATH DAY. Jan 8. A day of rest, relax-

ation and taking a little time to pamper ourselves. A day to be good to ourselves, without being seen as selfish, is a great comfort and a great luxury. For info: Bree Dorrance, Davenport College, 8200 Georgia St, Merrillville, IN 46410. Phone: (219) 840-0749.

NATIONAL CLEAN-OFF-YOUR-DESK DAY. Jan 8. To pro-

vide one day early each year for every desk worker to see the top of the desk and prepare for the following year's paperwork. Annually, the second Monday in January. For info: A.C. Moeller, Box 71, Clio, MI 48420-1042.

NATIONAL GRAVES' DISEASE AWARENESS WEEK.

Jan 8–12. Graves' disease is an abnormality in the autoimmune system, causing production of antibodies which attach to the thyroid, enlargement of the gland and overproduction of thyroid hormone. Similar antibodies may also cause swelling of the eye muscles and swelling in the skin on the front of the lower leg. Graves' disease occurs in less than ¼ of one percent of the general population. Most people with Graves' disease are treated and then managed on hormone replacement. Because some people with Graves' disease are misdiagnosed and because it is an illness that occurs in all age groups, education and support continue to be vital. Annually, the second week in January. For info: Natl Graves' Disease Foundation, PO Box 1969, Brevard, NC 28712. Phone: (828) 877-5251. Fax: (828) 877-5250. E-mail: ngdf@citcom.net. Web: www.ngdf.org.

NATIONAL JOYGERM DAY. Jan 8. Myriads of merry mirth-

makers harvesting hugs, happiness and humor; validating vision, vigor and vitality; wallowing in the willingness and wish to change their lives from obvious boredom to beneficent beatitudes. Goal: Rise from muck and mire of misery and lace life with love and laughter. For info: Joygerm Junkie Joan E. White, Founder, Joygerms Unlimited, PO Box 219, Eastwood Station, Syracuse, NY 13206-0219. Phone: (315) 472-2779.

January 2001

S	M	T	W	T	F	S
	1	2	3	4	5	6
7	8	9	10	11	12	13
14	15	16	17	18	19	20
21	22	23	24	25	26	27
28	29	30	31			

PRESLEY, ELVIS AARON: BIRTH ANNIVERSARY. Jan

8, 1935. Popular American rock singer, born at Tupelo, MS. Although his middle name was spelled incorrectly as "Aron" on his birth certificate, Elvis had it legally changed to "Aaron," which is how it is spelled on his gravestone. Died at Memphis, TN, Aug 16, 1977.

SAINT GUDULA'S FEAST DAY. Jan 8. Virgin, patron saint

of the city of Brussels. Died Jan 8, probably in the year 712. Her relics were transferred to the church of St. Michael in Brussels.

SHOW AND TELL DAY AT WORK. Jan 8. Since students

have show and tell at school, adults should get to do the same. Sponsored by Wellcat Holidays (© 2000 WH). For info: Thomas or Ruth Roy, 2418 Long Ln, Lebanon, PA 17046. Phone: (717) 279-0184. E-mail: wellcat@supernet.com. Web: www.wellcat.com.

SIRANI, ELISABETTA: BIRTH ANNIVERSARY. Jan 8,

1638. Born at Bologna, Italy, Elisabetta Sirani was one of the few women Renaissance artists. Among the 190 pieces done by her during her short life was the 1663 *Virgin and Child*, which was chosen by the US Postal Service as the 1994 traditional holiday stamp. While in her 20s Sarani established a painting school for women. When she died at her native Bologna Aug 28, 1665, the entire city went into mourning for her.

UNIVERSAL LETTER-WRITING WEEK. Jan 8–14. The

purpose of this week is for people all over the world to get the new year off to a good start by sending letters and cards to friends and acquaintances, not only in their own country, but to people throughout the world. For complete information and suggestions about writing good letters, send $4 to cover expense of printing, handling and postage. For info: Dr. Stanley Drake, Pres, Intl Soc of Friendship and Goodwill, 8592 Roswell Rd, Ste 434, Atlanta, GA 30350-1870.

WAR ON POVERTY: ANNIVERSARY. Jan 8, 1964. Pres-

ident Lyndon Johnson declared a War on Poverty in his State of the Union address. He stressed improved education as one of the cornerstones of the program. The following Aug 20, he signed a $947.5 million anti-poverty bill designed to assist more than 30 million citizens.

BIRTHDAYS TODAY

Shirley Bassey, 64, singer ("Goldfinger"), born Cardiff, Wales, Jan 8, 1937.

David Bowie (David Robert Jones), 54, musician, actor (*The Labyrinth*), born London, England, Jan 8, 1947.

Bob Eubanks, 63, game-show host ("The Newlywed Game"), born Flint, MI, Jan 8, 1938.

Vladimir Feltsman, 49, Russian pianist, born Moscow, USSR, Jan 8, 1952.

Slade Gorton, 73, US Senator (R, Washington), born Chicago, IL, Jan 8, 1928.

Stephen Hawking, 59, British physicist, author (*A Brief History of Time*), born Oxford, England, Jan 8, 1942.

Yvette Mimieux, 60, actress (*The Light in the Piazza, The Time Machine*, "The Most Deadly Game"), born Los Angeles, CA, Jan 8, 1941.

Kathleen Noone, 55, actress ("Party of Five," "Sunset Beach"), born Hillsdale, NJ, Jan 8, 1946.

Charles Osgood, 68, CBS newsman, born New York, NY, Jan 8, 1933.

Soupy Sales (Morton Supman), 71, comedian ("The Soupy Sales Show" may hold record for pies in the face), born Wake Forest, NC, Jan 8, 1930.

Bob Taft, 59, Governor of Ohio (R), born Boston, MA, Jan 8, 1942.

JANUARY 9 — TUESDAY
Day 9 — 356 Remaining

ALL STATES PICNIC (FOR SENIOR CITIZENS). Jan 9. Yuma, AZ. Seniors from all over the US and Canada gather for picnic lunch, entertainment and fun. Sponsor: City of Yuma Parks and Recreation Department. Est attendance: 1,200. For info: Mktg Dept, Yuma Civic and Conv Center, 1440 Desert Hills Dr, Yuma, AZ 85365. Phone: (520) 344-3800. Fax: (520) 344-9121.

AVIATION IN AMERICA: ANNIVERSARY. Jan 9, 1793. A Frenchman, Jean-Pierre Francois Blanchard, made the first manned free-balloon flight in America's history at Philadelphia, PA. The event was watched by President George Washington and many other high government officials. The hydrogen-filled balloon rose to a height of about 5,800 feet, traveled some 15 miles and landed 46 minutes later in New Jersey. Reportedly Blanchard had one passenger on the flight—a little black dog.

CATT, CARRIE LANE CHAPMAN: BIRTH ANNIVERSARY. Jan 9, 1859. American women's rights leader, founder (in 1919) of National League of Women Voters. Born at Ripon, WI, she died at New Rochelle, NY, Mar 9, 1947.

CONNECTICUT RATIFIES CONSTITUTION: ANNIVERSARY. Jan 9, 1788. By a vote of 128 to 40, Connecticut became the fifth state to ratify the Constitution.

FAKE HOWARD HUGHES BIOGRAPHY: ANNIVERSARY. Jan 9, 1972. Reclusive billionaire Howard Hughes held a telephone news conference to state that the biography about him written by Clifford Irving was a fake.

HAWAIIAN ISLANDS HUMPBACK WHALE NATIONAL MARINE SANCTUARY LECTURE SERIES. Jan 9. (also Feb 12, Mar 12, Apr 10, May 8, June 12, July 10, Aug 14, Sept 11, Oct 9, Nov 13 and Dec 11.) Kihei, Maui, HI. The Sanctuary is host to a free evening lecture series on a variety of ocean-related topics such as humpback whales, Native Hawaiian fishing practices, boating safety, marine debris, life on an atoll, etc. The goal of these lectures is to bring together various sectors of the marine community to increase public knowledge and encourage positive discussion about our environment. Tentatively, the second Tuesday of every month. Est attendance: 600. For info: Claire Cappelle, Hawaiian Islands Humpback Whale Natl Marine Sanctuary, 726 South Kihei Rd, Kihei, HI 96753. Phone: (800) 831-4888. Fax: (808) 874-3815. E-mail: claire.cappelle@noaa.gov.

"IT TAKES A THIEF" TV PREMIERE: ANNIVERSARY. Jan 9, 1968. ABC's adventure series starred Robert Wagner as Alexander Mundy, an unlikely thief who agrees to conduct secret government missions instead of serving out his prison term. Malachi Throne costarred as Noah Bain, chief of the SIA and Mundy's employer. Fred Astaire sometimes made recurring cameo appearances as Mundy's father.

LUNAR ECLIPSE. Jan 9. Total eclipse of the moon. Moon enters penumbra at approximately 12:43 PM, EST, reaches middle of eclipse at 3:20 PM and leaves penumbra at 5:57 PM. Visible in western half of Australia, Asia, Africa, Europe (including British Isles), Greenland, Northern Canada and Northern Alaska.

MOON PHASE: FULL MOON. Jan 9. Moon enters Full Moon phase at 3:24 PM, EST.

NIXON, RICHARD MILHOUS: BIRTH ANNIVERSARY. Jan 9, 1913. Richard Nixon served as 36th vice president of the US (under President Dwight D. Eisenhower) Jan 20, 1953, to Jan 20, 1961. He was the 37th president of the US, serving Jan 20, 1969, to Aug 9, 1974, when he resigned the presidency while under the threat of impeachment. First US president to resign that office. He was born at Yorba Linda, CA, and died at New York, NY, Apr 22, 1994.

PANAMA: MARTYRS' DAY. Jan 9. Public holiday.

PERIGEAN SPRING TIDES. Jan 9. Spring tides, the highest possible tides, occur when New Moon or Full Moon falls within 24 hours of the moment the Moon is nearest Earth (perigee) in its monthly orbit at 3 PM, EST. These tides are not named for the season of spring but for the German *springen*, "to leap up."

PHILIPPINES: FEAST OF THE BLACK NAZARENE. Jan 9. Culmination of a nine-day fiesta. Manila's largest procession takes place in the afternoon of Jan 9, in honor of the Black Nazarene, whose shrine is at the Quiapo Church.

RAPE SURVIVOR DAY. Jan 9. When something extraordinarily calamitous like rape happens, most survivors feel a compelling need to tell their stories and be heard and supported by family and friends. Unfortunately, tales of rape can make listeners uncomfortable—so much that we listeners back off, telling survivors to just "put it all behind them." This day is our opportunity to listen well to friends and family members who have survived rape. Annually, Jan 9. For info: Veritas Programming, PO Box 446, Putney, VT 05346-0446. Phone: (802) 387-4356. Fax: (802) 387-4828. E-mail: veritas@sover.net. Web: www.sover.net/~schw-cof.

"RAWHIDE" TV PREMIERE: ANNIVERSARY. Jan 9, 1959. CBS western that kept them dogies [cattle] rollin' home from northern Texas to Sedalia, KS. The series featured Eric Fleming (1959–65) as trail boss Gil Favor, Clint Eastwood as Rowdy Yates, ramrod and trail boss after Fleming's departure from the show, Jim Murdock as Mushy, Paul Brinegar as the cook, Wishbone, Steve Raines as Quince, Rocky Shahan as Joe Scarlet, Sheb Wooley as scout Pete Nolan, Robert Cabal as Hey Soos, John Ireland as Jed Colby, David Watson as Ian Cabot and Raymond St. Jacques as Simon Blake. (St. Jacques was the first African American regular on the series.) Also remembered for its rollicking theme song.

US LANDING ON LUZON: ANNIVERSARY. Jan 9, 1945. US forces began the final push to retake the Philippines by attacking at the same location where the Japanese had begun their invasion nearly four years earlier. General Douglas MacArthur landed 67,000 troops in the Gulf of Lingayen on the western coast of the big island of Luzon. The Japanese offered little opposition to the landing itself but fought fiercely against Allied advancement, particularly around Clarke Field, the major air base in the islands.

YORBA LINDA, CALIFORNIA: NIXON BIRTHDAY HOLIDAY. Jan 9. Yorba Linda, the birthplace in 1913 of former president Richard M. Nixon, became the first community officially to declare his birth anniversary a public holiday. In announcing the declaration Sept 20, 1989, Mayor Henry Wedaa said, "We're not here to judge history—we're here to recognize it." The first observance by Yorba Linda's municipal employees took place in 1990.

YOUNG, MURAT BERNARD "CHIC": 100th BIRTH ANNIVERSARY. Jan 9, 1901. The comic strip "Blondie" was created by Murat Bernard "Chic" Young in 1930. Originally about a jazz-age flapper who marries a playboy from a socially prominent family, "Blondie" soon changed its direction: two children and a dog were added to the cast, Dagwood became a working stiff and the strip focused on middle-class family situations and problems. "Blondie" introduced America to the "dagwood," an enormous sandwich made during Dagwood's late-night forays in the refrigerator. Chic Young was born at Chicago, IL, and died at St. Petersburg, FL, Mar 14, 1973.

BIRTHDAYS TODAY

Joan Baez, 60, folksinger, born Staten Island, NY, Jan 9, 1941.

Tyrone Curtis ("Muggsy") Bogues, 36, basketball player, born Baltimore, MD, Jan 9, 1965.

Bob Denver, 66, actor ("The Many Loves of Dobie Gillis," "Gilligan's Island"), born New Rochelle, NY, Jan 9, 1935.

Richard Allen (Dick) Enberg, 66, sportscaster, born Mount Clemens, MI, Jan 9, 1935.

Sergio Garcia, 21, golfer, born Borriol, Spain, Jan 9, 1980.

Crystal Gayle (Brenda Gayle Webb), 50, singer ("Don't It Make My Brown Eyes Blue"), born Paintsville, KY, Jan 9, 1951.

Bill Graves, 48, Governor of Kansas (R), born Salina, KS, Jan 9, 1953.

Judith Krantz (Judith Tarcher), 73, author (*Dazzle, Scruples*), born New York, NY, Jan 9, 1928.

Dave Matthews, 34, singer, musician (The Dave Matthews Band), born South Africa, Jan 9, 1967.

Joely Richardson, 36, actress (*101 Dalmatians*), born London, England, Jan 9, 1965.

Byron Bartlett (Bart) Starr, 67, former football coach, Pro Football Hall of Fame quarterback, born Montgomery, AL, Jan 9, 1934.

Susannah York, 60, actress (*Tom Jones; They Shoot Horses, Don't They?; Superman*), born London, England, Jan 9, 1941.

JANUARY 10 — WEDNESDAY

Day 10 — 355 Remaining

COMMON SENSE PUBLISHED: 225th ANNIVERSARY. Jan 10, 1776. More than any other publication, *Common Sense* influenced the authors of the Declaration of Independence. Thomas Paine's 50-page pamphlet sold more than 500,000 copies within a few months of its first printing.

HENRIED, PAUL: BIRTH ANNIVERSARY. Jan 10, 1908. Actor Paul Henried once estimated that he had played in or directed more than 300 feature or made-for-TV films. Though a staunch anti-Nazi, his early film parts included a number of German roles, including *Goodbye Mr Chips* and *Night Train*. He eventually moved away from the German stereotype in such films as *Of Human Bondage, The Four Horsemen of the Apocalypse* and as Victor Laslo in *Casablanca*. His film career cut short by the anti-Communist blacklist in Hollywood during the 1940s, Henried found a second calling as a director, with more than 80 episodes of TV's "Alfred Hitchcock Presents" to his credit. Born at Trieste, Austria, he died Mar 29, 1992, at Pacific Palisades, CA.

JEFFERS, ROBINSON: BIRTH ANNIVERSARY. Jan 10, 1887. American poet and playwright. Born at Pittsburgh, PA, he died at Carmel, CA, Jan 20, 1962.

LEAGUE OF NATIONS FOUNDING: ANNIVERSARY. Jan 10, 1920. Through the Treaty of Versailles, the League of Nations came into existence. Fifty nations entered into a covenant designed to avoid war. The US never joined the League of Nations, which was dissolved Apr 18, 1946.

"MASTERPIECE THEATRE" TV PREMIERE: 30th ANNIVERSARY. Jan 10, 1971. Television at its best, PBS's long-running anthology series consists of many highly acclaimed original and adapted dramatizations. Many are produced by the BBC. Alistair Cooke and Russell Baker have hosted the program. The first presentation was "The First Churchills." Other notable programs include: "Jude the Obscure," "The Six Wives of Henry VIII" and "Elizabeth R" (1972); "Upstairs Downstairs" (1974–77); "I, Claudius" (1978); "The Jewel in the Crown" (1984); "Bleak

House" (1985); and "A Tale of Two Cities" (1989). "The Muppet Show" had a take-off of the show with Kermit the Frog playing the host.

SAN ANTONIO SPORT, BOAT AND RV SHOW. Jan 10–14. San Antonio Convention Center, San Antonio, TX. 45th boating, travel, hunting, fishing, camping, RVs and recreation show. For info: Mike Coffen, Double C Productions, Inc, PO Box 1678, Huntsville, TX 77342. Phone: (409) 295-9677 or (800) 574-9650. Fax: (409) 295-8859. E-mail: doublec@lcc.net. Web: www.lcc.net/~doublec.

SPACE MILESTONE: *SOYUZ 17* (USSR). Jan 10, 1975. Launched on this date, cosmonauts A. Gubarev and G. Grechko completed a 30-day space flight, landing Feb 9. Cosmonauts spent 28 days aboard *Salyut 4*, orbiting space station. With the exception of *Soyuz 19*, the *Soyuz* craft were now used as ferries to the *Salyut* space stations. More than 20 more flights were made.

SPACE MILESTONE: *SOYUZ 27* (USSR). Jan 10, 1978. Launched on this date, cosmonauts Vladimir Dzhanibekov and Oleg Makarov linked with *Salyut 6* space station, which was already occupied by crew of *Soyuz 26*. Returned to Earth Jan 16 in *Soyuz 26*.

UNITED NATIONS GENERAL ASSEMBLY: 55th ANNIVERSARY. Jan 10, 1946. On the 26th anniversary of the establishment of the unsuccessful League of Nations, delegates from 51 nations met at London, England, for the first meeting of the UN General Assembly.

US AND VATICAN ESTABLISH DIPLOMATIC RELATIONS: ANNIVERSARY. Jan 10, 1984. The US and Vatican established full diplomatic relations after a break of 117 years.

WOMEN'S SUFFRAGE AMENDMENT INTRODUCED IN CONGRESS: ANNIVERSARY. Jan 10, 1878. Senator A.A. Sargent of California, a close friend of Susan B. Anthony, introduced into the US Senate a women's suffrage amendment known as the Susan B. Anthony Amendment. It wasn't until Aug 26, 1920, 42 years later, that the amendment was signed into law.

BIRTHDAYS TODAY

Pat Benatar (Patricia Andrejewski), 48, singer, born Brooklyn, NY, Jan 10, 1953.

George Edward Foreman, 52, boxer, born Marshall, TX, Jan 10, 1949.

Gisele Mackenzie, 74, singer ("Hard to Get," regular on "Your Hit Parade"), born Winnipeg, Manitoba, Canada, Jan 10, 1927.

Glenn Robinson, 28, basketball player, born Gary, IN, Jan 10, 1973.

Rod Stewart, 56, singer, musician ("Maggie May," "Do Ya Think I'm Sexy?"), born Glasgow, Scotland, Jan 10, 1945.

JANUARY 11 — THURSDAY

Day 11 — 354 Remaining

CUCKOO DANCING WEEK. Jan 11–17. To honor the memory of Laurel and Hardy, whose theme, "The Dancing Cuckoos," shall be heard throughout the land as their movies are seen and their antics greeted by laughter by old and new fans of these unique masters of comedy. [Originated by the late William T. Rabe of Sault Ste. Marie, MI.]

"DESIGNATED HITTER" RULE ADOPTED: ANNIVERSARY. Jan 11, 1973. American League adopted the "designated hitter" rule, whereby an additional player is used to bat for the pitcher.

FIRST BLACK SOUTHERN LIEUTENANT GOVERNOR: 15th ANNIVERSARY. Jan 11, 1986. L. Douglas Wilder was sworn in as lieutenant governor of Virginia. He was the first black elected to statewide office in the South since Reconstruction. He later served as governor of Virginia.

FLORIDA CITRUS FESTIVAL. Jan 11–21. Polk County Fairgrounds, Winter Haven, FL. Celebrating Diamond Jubilee featuring an industry-wide fresh fruit competition, citrus fruit

January 2001	S	M	T	W	T	F	S
		1	2	3	4	5	6
	7	8	9	10	11	12	13
	14	15	16	17	18	19	20
	21	22	23	24	25	26	27
	28	29	30	31			

displays, an automated fresh fruit packing line and appearances by Miss Florida Citrus. FFA and 4-H exhibits, crafts and horticultural competitions, livestock exhibits, giant-sized midway and big-name country and western entertainers. Parade Saturday, Jan 20. Est attendance: 160,000. For info: Exec Dir, Florida Citrus Showcase, 211 Avenue G SW, Winter Haven, FL 33882. Phone: (863) 292-9810. Web: www.citrusfestival.com.

HAMILTON, ALEXANDER: BIRTH ANNIVERSARY.
Jan 11, 1755. American statesman, an author of *The Federalist* papers, first secretary of the treasury, born at British West Indies. Engaged in a duel with Aaron Burr the morning of July 11, 1804, at Weehawken, NJ. Mortally wounded there and died July 12, 1804.

HOSTOS, EUGENIO MARIA: BIRTH ANNIVERSARY.
Jan 11, 1839. Puerto Rican patriot, scholar and author of more than 50 books. Born at Rio Canas, Puerto Rico, he died at Santo Domingo, Dominican Republic, Aug 11, 1903. The anniversary of his birth is observed as a public holiday in Puerto Rico.

INTERNATIONAL THANK YOU DAYS.
Jan 11–18. A week of time to thank someone from your past or present who did something nice for you. Write, call, fax or e-mail him or her and say thank you. [©1994] For info: Adrienne Sioux Koopersmith, Thanks Alot, 1437 W Rosemont, #1W, Chicago, IL 60660-1319. Phone: (773) 743-5341. Fax: (773) 743-5395. E-mail: adrienne@21stcentury.net.

JAMES, WILLIAM: BIRTH ANNIVERSARY.
Jan 11, 1842. American psychologist and philosopher of distinguished family that included his brother, novelist Henry James. "There is no worse lie," he wrote in *Varieties of Religious Experience* (1902), "than a truth misunderstood by those who hear it." Born at New York City, he died at Chocorua, NH, Aug 26, 1910.

MacDONALD, JOHN A.: BIRTH ANNIVERSARY.
Jan 11, 1815. Canadian statesman, first prime minister of Canada. Born at Glasgow, Scotland, he died June 6, 1891, at Ottawa. His birth anniversary is observed in Canada.

MOROCCO: INDEPENDENCE DAY.
Jan 11. National holiday. Commemorates the date in 1944 when the Independence Party submitted a memo to the Allied authorities asking for independence under a constitutional regime. Morocco gained independence from France in 1956.

NEPAL: NATIONAL UNITY DAY.
Jan 11. Celebration paying homage to King Prithvinarayan Shah (1723–75), founder of the present house of rulers of Nepal and creator of the unified Nepal of today.

PAUL, ALICE: BIRTH ANNIVERSARY.
Jan 11, 1885. Women's rights leader and founder of the National Woman's Party in 1913, advocate of an equal rights amendment to the US Constitution. Born at Moorestown, NJ, she died there July 10, 1977.

THEODOSIUS I: BIRTH ANNIVERSARY.
Jan 11, 347. Roman emperor known as Theodosius the Great was born at Cauca, Gallaecia, in Spain. In 379 Theodosius was summoned by the emperor Gratian to become emperor of the east. On Feb 28, 380, without consulting religious authorities, he issued the edict that made the Nicene Creed (in which God the Father, the Son and the Holy Spirit are all of the same substance) binding on all subjects. Only those who accepted it would be considered Christians; this was the first recorded use of that designation. Theodosius engaged in a continuing struggle with the west for power. He prohibited pagan worship, but the various emperors of the west had strong connections with pagan aristocracy. The two sides came to blows in 394. His final victory in September of that year was seen as a divine victory in which the Christian God had triumphed over the Roman gods. Theodosius died in January, 395.

US SURGEON GENERAL DECLARES CIGARETTES HAZARDOUS: ANNIVERSARY.
Jan 11, 1964. US Surgeon General Luther Terry issued the first government report saying that smoking may be hazardous to one's health.

WARMEST YEAR ON RECORD DECLARED: ANNIVERSARY.
Jan 11, 1999. NASA declared 1998 the warmest year on record. Global surface temperatures increased by 0.34 of a degree Fahrenheit. The average temperature of 58.496 degrees Fahrenheit eclipsed the previous record set in 1995. The 1998 warmth was associated partly with a strong El Niño, a periodic warming of the Pacific Ocean.

BIRTHDAYS TODAY

Mary J. Blige, 30, pop singer, born The Bronx, NY, Jan 11, 1971.

Jean Chretien, 67, 20th prime minister of Canada, born Shawinigan, Quebec, Canada, Jan 11, 1934.

Clarence Clemons, 59, musician, singer, born Norfolk, VA, Jan 11, 1942.

Ben Daniel Crenshaw, 49, golfer, born Austin, TX, Jan 11, 1952.

Jim Hightower, 58, radio host, author (*Hard Tomatoes, Hard Times; Eat Your Heart Out*), born Denison, TX, Jan 11, 1943.

Naomi Judd, 55, country singer ("Have Mercy," "Why Not Me"), born Ashland, KY, Jan 11, 1946.

Christine Kaufmann, 56, actress (*Taras Bulba, Bagdad Cafe*), born Lansdorf Graz, Austria, Jan 11, 1945.

Rod Taylor, 71, actor (*The Birds*, "Masquerade"), born Sydney, Australia, Jan 11, 1930.

Grant Tinker, 75, TV executive, born Stamford, CT, Jan 11, 1926.

Stanley Tucci, 41, actor (*Pelican Brief*, "Murder One"), born Katonah, NY, Jan 11, 1960.

JANUARY 12 — FRIDAY
Day 12 — 353 Remaining

AFRICAN AMERICAN ARTS FESTIVAL.
Jan 12–Mar 16. Greensboro, NC. A series of arts events held in celebration of the cultural achievements of local, regional and national black artists in all disciplines of the arts (music, dance, visual arts, literature and theater). Annually, during the months of January, February and March. Sponsors: Miller Brewing Company. Est attendance: 20,000. For info: Karen Drake, Community Events Dir, United Arts Council of Greensboro, PO Box 877, Greensboro, NC 27402. Phone: (336) 373-7523. Fax: (336) 373-7553.

"ALL IN THE FAMILY" TV PREMIERE: 30th ANNIVERSARY.
Jan 12, 1971. Based on the success of the British comedy "Till Death Us Do Part," Norman Lear created CBS's controversial sitcom "All in the Family." The series was the first of its kind to realistically portray the prevailing issues and taboos of its time with a wickedly humorous bent. From bigotry to birth control, few topics were considered too sacred to discuss on air. Ultra-conservative Archie Bunker (played by Carroll O'Connor) held court from his recliner, spewing invective at any who disagreed with him. Jean Stapleton portrayed Archie's dutiful wife, Edith. Sally Struthers and Rob Reiner rounded out the cast as Archie's ultra-liberal daughter and son-in-law, Gloria and Mike "Meathead" Stivic.

"BATMAN" TV PREMIERE: 35th ANNIVERSARY.
Jan 12, 1966. ABC's crime-fighting show gained a place in Nielsen's top 10 ratings in its first season. The series was based on the DC Comics characters created by Bob Kane in 1939. Adam West starred as millionaire Bruce Wayne and superhero alter ego, Batman. Burt Ward co-starred as Dick Grayson/Robin, the Boy Wonder. An assortment of villains guest-starring each week included: Cesar Romero as the Joker, Eartha Kitt and Julie Newmar as Catwoman, Burgess Meredith as the Penguin and Frank Gorshin as the Riddler. Some other stars making memorable appearances included Liberace, Vincent Price, Milton Berle, Tallulah Bankhead and Ethel Merman. The series played up its comic-strip roots with innovative and sharply skewed camera angles, bright bold colors and wild graphics. Although the last telecast was Mar 14, 1968, "Batman's" memorable theme song, composed by Neal Hefti, can be heard today with some 120 episodes in syndication. Many Batman movies have been made, the first in 1943. The most recent was *Batman & Robin*, released in 1997 and starring George Clooney and Chris O'Donnell.

"THE BELL TELEPHONE HOUR" TV PREMIERE: ANNIVERSARY. Jan 12, 1959. NBC's musical series ran semi-regularly for nearly 10 seasons. The Bell Telephone Orchestra was conducted by Donald Voorhees.

BURKE, EDMUND: BIRTH ANNIVERSARY. Jan 12, 1729. British orator, politician and philosopher, born at Dublin, Ireland. "Superstition is the religion of feeble minds," he wrote in 1790, but best remembered is "The only thing necessary for the triumph of evil is for good men to do nothing," not found in his writings but almost universally attributed to Burke. Died at Beaconsfield, England, July 9, 1797.

CONGRESS AUTHORIZED USE OF FORCE AGAINST IRAQ: 10th ANNIVERSARY. Jan 12, 1991. The US Congress passed a resolution authorizing the president of the US to use force to expel Iraq from Kuwait. This was the sixth congressional vote in US history declaring war or authorizing force on another nation.

"DYNASTY" TV PREMIERE: 20th ANNIVERSARY. Jan 12, 1981. The popular ABC prime-time serial focused on the high-flying exploits of the Denver-based Carrington family. The series had a weekly wardrobe budget of $10,000 with many elegant costumes designed by Nolan Miller. In addition to the juicy storylines, many tuned in worldwide to view the palatial mansions and lavish sets. John Forsythe played patriarch Blake Carrington with Linda Evans as his wife, Krystle. Joan Collins played Alexis, Blake's scheming ex-wife and arch business rival. Other cast members included Kathleen Beller, Pamela Bellwood, Diahann Carroll, Jack Coleman, John James, Heather Locklear, Pamela Sue Martin, Ted McGinley, Michael Nader, Catherine Oxenberg, Emma Samms and Gordon Thomson. Notable guest stars included William Campbell, James Farentino, George Hamilton, Charlton Heston, Rock Hudson, Billy Dee Williams and others.

FARMER, JAMES: BIRTH ANNIVERSARY. Jan 12, 1920. Civil Rights leader, born at Marshall, TX. Farmer was one of the founders of CORE, the Congress of Racial Equality, a volunteer organization established in 1942 to improve race relations and eliminate discriminatory practices. Farmer led the nonviolent fight to desegregate buses and terminals in 1961, known as the Freedom Rides. He received the Presidential Medal of Freedom in 1998. Died at Fredericksburg, VA, July 9, 1999.

HANCOCK, JOHN: BIRTH ANNIVERSARY. Jan 12, 1737 (OS). American patriot and statesman, first signer of the Declaration of Independence. Born at Braintree, MA, he died at Quincy, MA, Oct 8, 1793. Because of his conspicuous signature on the Declaration, Hancock's name has become part of the American language, referring to any handwritten signature, as in "Put your John Hancock on that!"

HAYES, IRA HAMILTON: BIRTH ANNIVERSARY. Jan 12, 1922. Ira Hayes was one of six US Marines who raised the American flag on Iwo Jima's Mount Suribachi, Feb 23, 1945, following a US assault on the Japanese stronghold. The event was immortalized by AP photographer Joe Rosenthal's famous photo and later by a Marine War Memorial monument at Arlington, VA. Hayes was born on a Pima Indian Reservation at Arizona. He returned home after WWII a much celebrated hero. A hero to everyone except himself, Hayes was unable to cope with fame. He was found dead of "exposure to freezing weather and overconsumption of alcohol" on the Sacaton Indian Reservation at Arizona, Jan 24, 1955.

	S	**M**	**T**	**W**	**T**	**F**	**S**
January		1	2	3	4	5	6
2001	7	8	9	10	11	12	13
	14	15	16	17	18	19	20
	21	22	23	24	25	26	27
	28	29	30	31			

LONDON, JACK: 125th BIRTH ANNIVERSARY. Jan 12, 1876. American author of more than 50 books: short stories, novels and travel, stories of the sea and of the far north, many marked by brutal realism. His most widely known work is *The Call of the Wild*, the great dog story published in 1903. London was born at San Francisco, CA. He died by suicide Nov 22, 1916, near Santa Rosa, CA.

MISSION SANTA CLARA DE ASIS: FOUNDING ANNIVERSARY. Jan 12, 1777. California mission to the Indians founded.

MOTOR SPORTS SPECTACULAR. Jan 12–14. MultiPurpose Events Center, Wichita Falls, TX. Monster truck racing, AMA-sanctioned motor cross racing. Est attendance: 6,000. For info: Wichita Falls CVB, 1000 5th St, Wichita Falls, TX 76301. Phone: (940) 716-5500. Fax: (940) 716-5509. E-mail: MPEC@wf.net. Web: www.wichitafalls.org.

NATIONAL HANDWRITING DAY. Jan 12. Popularly observed on birthday of John Hancock to encourage more legible handwriting.

NC RV AND CAMPING SHOW. Jan 12–14. Special Events Center, Greensboro Coliseum Complex, Greensboro, NC. A display of the latest in recreation vehicles and accessories by various dealers. Est attendance: 11,000. For info: Apple Rock Advertising & Promotion, 1200 Eastchester Dr, High Point, NC 27265. Phone: (336) 881-7100. Fax: (336) 883-7198.

SEATTLE BOAT SHOW. Jan 12–21. Stadium Exhibition Center, Seattle, WA. Huge display of new boats, accessories and services. A second show, Seattle Boat Show at Shilshole Bay Marina, scheduled for Aug 25–29. Large boats (25 ft or longer) on display in Puget Sound with more than 70 accessories and 150 trailer boats dealers on land. Est attendance: 80,000. For info: NW Marine Trade Assn, 1900 N Northlake Way, #233, Seattle, WA 98103. Phone: (206) 634-0911. Fax: (206) 632-0078. Web: www.seattleboatshow.com.

TANZANIA: ZANZIBAR REVOLUTION DAY. Jan 12. National day. Zanzibar became independent in December 1963, under a sultan.

WINTHROP, JOHN: BIRTH ANNIVERSARY. Jan 12, 1588 (OS). American colonial governor of Massachusetts Bay Colony, born at Edwardston, England. Governor Winthrop kept a diary of events in the Massachusetts Bay Colony, published nearly two centuries later (in 1825–26), titled *The History of New England from 1630 to 1649*. Died at Boston, MA, Mar 26, 1649 (OS).

WOMEN DENIED VOTE: ANNIVERSARY. Jan 12, 1915. The US House of Representatives rejected a proposal to give women the right to vote. Women gained the right to vote in 1920.

YUMA HOME SHOW. Jan 12–14. Yuma Civic and Convention Center, Yuma, AZ. Public exhibit—home improvement, construction, renovation, remodeling and decorating. Annually, the second weekend in January. Est attendance: 17,000. For info: Yuma Civic & Convention Center, 1440 Desert Hills Dr, Yuma, AZ 85365. Phone: (520) 344-3800. Fax: (520) 344-9121.

BIRTHDAYS TODAY

Kirstie Alley, 46, actress (Emmy for "Cheers"; *Look Who's Talking*, "Veronica's Closet"), born Wichita, KS, Jan 12, 1955.

Jeff Bezos, 37, founder (Amazon.com), born New Mexico, Jan 12, 1964.

Joe Frazier, 57, former boxer, born Beaufort, SC, Jan 12, 1944.

HAL, 4, computer in *2001: A Space Odyssey*, by Arthur C. Clarke, "born" Urbana, IL, Jan 12, 1997.

Rush Limbaugh, 50, talk-show host ("The Rush Limbaugh Show"), born Cape Girardeau, MO, Jan 12, 1951.

Ray Price, 75, country singer, born Perryville, TX, Jan 12, 1926.

Luise Rainer, 89, actress (Oscars for *The Great Ziegfield* and *The Good Earth*), born Vienna, Austria, Jan 12, 1912.

Howard Stern, 47, radio and TV personality ("The Howard Stern Show"), born Queens, NY, Jan 12, 1954.

JANUARY 13 — SATURDAY

Day 13 — 352 Remaining

ALGER, HORATIO, JR: BIRTH ANNIVERSARY. Jan 13, 1834. American clergyman and author of more than 100 popular books for boys (some 20 million copies sold). Honesty, frugality and hard work assured that the heroes of his books would find success, wealth and fame. Born at Revere, MA, he died at Natick, MA, July 18, 1899.

ANCIENT CHINESE TANGRAM PUZZLE CHALLENGE. Jan 13. Burlington, WI. Try to solve some of the hundreds of puzzles derived from the same seven pieces of this Chinese puzzle challenge. Create your own set to go, too. For info: Hall of Puzzles, 533 Milwaukee Ave, Burlington, WI 53105. Phone: (262) 763-3946.

CHASE, SALMON PORTLAND: BIRTH ANNIVERSARY. Jan 13, 1808. American statesman, born at Cornish, NH. US senator, secretary of the treasury and chief justice of the Supreme Court. Salmon P. Chase spent much of his life fighting slavery (he was popularly known as "attorney general for runaway Negroes"). He was one of the founders of the Republican Party and his hopes for becoming candidate for president of the US in 1856 and 1860 were dashed because his unconcealed anti-slavery views made him unacceptable. Died at New York, NY, May 7, 1873. His portrait may be seen on US currency (the $10,000 bill).

CORRIDOR OF DEATH: ANNIVERSARY. Jan 13, 1943. The suffering of the people of Leningrad during the German siege of that city was one of the greatest tragedies of World War II. More than half the population of Russia's second largest city died during the winter of 1942. On Jan 13, 1943, Soviet troops broke through German lines and opened a 10-mile-wide corridor south of Lake Ladoga. Within a week supplies were arriving in the city by way of this narrow opening. Because fierce German bombardment of the passage continued for another year, the pass came to be called the "Corridor of Death." The siege finally ended Jan 27, 1944, after 880 days.

DeSOTO'S WINTER ENCAMPMENT. Jan 13. Tallahassee, FL. Hernando DeSoto's Winter Camp at Apalachee Village Anhyca (present-day Tallahassee) interpreted with living history, craft demonstrations, exhibits, etc. Est attendance: 1,000. For info: DeSoto's Winter Encampment, 1022 DeSoto Park Dr, Tallahassee, FL 32301. Phone: (850) 922-6007. Fax: (850) 488-0366.

EAGLE DAYS. Jan 13–14. Milford Nature Center/Fish Hatchery, Junction City, KS. Learn more about the magnificent bird that is our national emblem. Meet both a live bald eagle and a golden eagle! Guides with spotting scopes and binoculars will be waiting to show you eagles as they roost and soar around Milford Lake. Sponsor: Kansas Wildlife and Parks; US Army Corps of Engineers. Est attendance: 700. For info: Milford Nature Center, 3115 Hatchery Dr, Junction City, KS 66441. Phone: (785) 238-5323. Fax: (785) 238-5775.

FULLER, ALFRED CARL: BIRTH ANNIVERSARY. Jan 13, 1885. Founder of the Fuller Brush Company, born at Kings County, NS, Canada. In 1906 the young brush salesman went into business on his own, making brushes at a bench between the furnace and the coal bin in his sister's basement. Died at Hartford, CT, Dec 4, 1973.

MINORITY SCIENTISTS SHOWCASE. Jan 13–15. St. Louis, MO. Open new doors to future science careers and interests during Martin Luther King, Jr, weekend with hands-on activities and information available as part of a free program. Meet and talk with African-Americans working in science-related fields throughout the St. Louis area. Annually, Martin Luther King, Jr, weekend. Est attendance: 2,000. For info: Bev Pfeifer-Harms, St. Louis Science Center, 5050 Oakland Ave, St. Louis, MO 63110. Phone: (314) 289-4419. Fax: (314) 533-8687. E-mail: bpharms@slsc.org. Web: www.slsc.org.

MODEL RAILROAD SHOW. Jan 13–14. Wilson Lodge, Oglebay, Wheeling, WV. Train enthusiasts will find nearly 80 train exhibitors displaying and selling their wide variety of items. Est attendance: 1,700. For info: Steve Mitch, Theater Director, Good Zoo, Oglebay, Rt 88 N, Wheeling, WV 26003. Phone: (304) 243-4034. Fax: (304) 243-4110. Web: www.oglebay-resort.com.

NEW WORK OF THE NEW YEAR. Jan 13–31. St. Simons Island, GA. It is designed to present new artists, new work, new techniques to the public. For info: Mittie B. Hendrix, Dir, Coastal Center for the Arts, 2012 Demere Rd, St. Simons Island, GA 31522. Phone: (912) 634-0404. E-mail: coastalart@thebest.net.

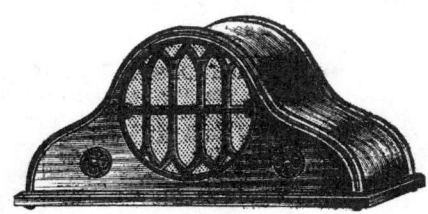

RADIO BROADCASTING: ANNIVERSARY. Jan 13, 1910. Radio pioneer and electron tube inventor Lee De Forest arranged the world's first radio broadcast to the public at New York, NY. He succeeded in broadcasting the voice of Enrico Caruso along with other stars of the Metropolitan Opera to several receiving locations in the city where listeners with earphones marveled at wireless music from the air. Though only a few were equipped to listen, it was the first broadcast to reach the public and the beginning of a new era in which wireless radio communication became almost universal. See also: "First Scheduled Radio Broadcast: Anniv" (Nov 2).

SIGHT-SAVING SABBATH. Jan 13–14. Religious congregations throughout the US are invited to participate in this nondenominational observance. The emphasis will be on periodic eye examinations as a way to prevent vision loss to diseases like glaucoma. For info: Prevent Blindness America®, 500 E Remington Rd, Schaumburg, IL 60173. Phone: (800) 331-2020. Fax: (847) 843-8458. Web: www.preventblindness.org.

★**STEPHEN FOSTER MEMORIAL DAY.** Jan 13. Presidential Proclamation 2957 of Dec 13, 1951 (designating Jan 13, 1952), covers all succeeding years. (PL82–225 of Oct 27, 1951.) Observed on the anniversary of Foster's death, Jan 13, 1864, at New York, NY. See also: "Foster, Stephen: Birth Anniversary" (July 4).

TOGO: LIBERATION DAY. Jan 13. National holiday. Commemorates 1967 uprising.

WELCOME BACK SNOWBIRDS PANCAKE BREAKFAST. Jan 13 (tentative). El Centro, CA. Annually, the second Saturday in January. Est attendance: 2,500. For info: El Centro Chamber of Commerce, Box 3006, El Centro, CA 92244. Phone: (760) 352-3681. Fax: (760) 352-3246. Web: www.elcentrochamber.com.

BIRTHDAYS TODAY

Kevin Anderson, 41, actor (*Hoffa, Rising Sun*), born Gurnee, IL, Jan 13, 1960.

Keith Coogan, 31, actor (*Adventures in Babysitting, Cousins*), born Palm Springs, CA, Jan 13, 1970.

Patrick Dempsey, 35, actor (*Heaven Help Us, In the Mood*), born Lewiston, ME, Jan 13, 1966.

Nicole Eggert, 29, actress ("Baywatch," "Charles in Charge"), born Glendale, CA, Jan 13, 1972.

Frank Gallo, 68, artist, sculptor, born Toledo, OH, Jan 13, 1933.

Julia Louis-Dreyfus, 40, actress ("Seinfeld"), born New York, NY, Jan 13, 1961.

Jay McInerney, 46, writer (*Bright Lights, Big City*), born Hartford, CT, Jan 13, 1955.

Penelope Ann Miller, 37, actress (*Adventures in Babysitting, The Freshman, Carlito's Way*), born Los Angeles, CA, Jan 13, 1964.

Richard Moll, 58, actor ("Night Court," *Wicked Stepmother, The Flintstones*), born Pasadena, CA, Jan 13, 1943.

Charles Nelson Reilly, 70, actor ("The Ghost and Mrs Muir," "Match Game PM"), born New York, NY, Jan 13, 1931.

Robert Stack, 82, actor (Emmy for "The Untouchables"), host ("Unsolved Mysteries"), born Los Angeles, CA, Jan 13, 1919.

Frances Sternhagen, 71, actress (*The Tiger Makes Out, Misery*; stage: *The Good Doctor*), born Washington, DC, Jan 13, 1930.

Gwen Verdon, 75, actress (*Cocoon*; stage: *Damn Yankees, High Button Shoes*), born Los Angeles, CA, Jan 13, 1926.

JANUARY 14 — SUNDAY

Day 14 — 351 Remaining

ARNOLD, BENEDICT: BIRTH ANNIVERSARY. Jan 14, 1741 (OS). American officer who deserted to the British during the Revolutionary War and whose name has since become synonymous with treachery. Born at Norwich, CT. Died June 14, 1801, at London, England.

FIRE THE BOSS WEEK. Jan 14–20. Who doesn't dream of firing the boss? Well in North America todays, tens of thousands of people have already punched their last time clock and headed home to work. They've said goodbye to corporate politics, commuter traffic and they don't ask permission from anyone for anything! Celebrates the courage, vision and stick-to-it-iveness of those home-based pioneers who have already kissed the boss goodbye. . .and offers hope to those who long to be free. For an instant report on "How To Fire the Boss: 5 Steps to Freedom" e-mail: how-to-fire-the-boss@sendfree.com. For info: Shelia Martin, 250 H St, Blaine, WA 98230. Phone: (604) 535-3636. E-mail: sheila@we-build-dreams.com. Web: www.we-build-dreams.com.

FIRST CAESAREAN SECTION: ANNIVERSARY. Jan 14, 1794. Dr. Jesse Bennett, of Edom, VA, performed the first successful Caesarean section. The patient was his wife.

HOUSTON MARATHON. Jan 14. Houston, TX. 29th annual citywide race in conjunction with the Health & Fitness Expo (Jan 12–13). Est attendance: 7,000. For info: Greg D. Goss, Houston Marathon, 720 North Post Oak Rd, #335, Houston, TX 77024. Phone: (713) 957-3453. Fax: (713) 957-3406. E-mail: marathon@ghg.net. Web: www.houstonmarathon.com.

INTERNATIONAL PRINTING WEEK. Jan 14–20. To develop public awareness of the printing/graphic arts industry. Annually, the week including Ben Franklin's birthday, Jan 17. For info: Kevin P. Keane, Exec Dir, Intl Assn of Printing House Craftsmen, 7042 Brooklyn Blvd, Minneapolis, MN 55429-1370. Phone: (612) 560-1620. Web: www.iaphc.org.

January 2001	S	M	T	W	T	F	S
		1	2	3	4	5	6
	7	8	9	10	11	12	13
	14	15	16	17	18	19	20
	21	22	23	24	25	26	27
	28	29	30	31			

LET MEN BE OUR HEROES WEEK. Jan 14–20. Men don't get to be heroes very often, so why not create opportunities for them to shine? Let this week be a time to celebrate and enjoy their masculine qualities that make us feel more like women. Let's bridge the ever-widening gap that keeps men and women apart. For info: Kara Oh, author of Men Made Easy. Phone: (877) 636-6233. E-mail: KaraOh@MenMadeEasy.com.

MAURY, MATTHEW FONTAINE: BIRTH ANNIVERSARY. Jan 14, 1806. Naval officer, born at Fredericksburg, VA. Maury established oceanography as a branch of science and revolutionized the recording of oceanographic data as a superintendent of the Naval Observatory. Died at Lexington, VA, Feb 1, 1873.

MUSICAL TRIBUTE TO DR. MARTIN LUTHER KING. Jan 14. Abraham Lincoln's Birthplace National Historical Site, Hodgenville, KY. Local Baptist and Methodist choirs present a selection of hymns and spirituals in commemoration of Dr. King's birthday. Est attendance: 125. For info: Patsy Cobb, 2995 Lincoln Farm Rd, Hodgenville, KY 42748. Phone: (502) 358-3137.

OUTCAULT, RICHARD FELTON: BIRTH ANNIVERSARY. Jan 14, 1863. When Richard Felton Outcault was asked by the *New York World*'s Sunday editor to submit drawings for use with their new process for printing color pictures, colored comics or "funny papers" were born. Outcault's first color drawing, titled "Origin of a New Species," was published Nov 18, 1894. The first regular colored strip, "Hogan's Alley," drawn by Outcault, began appearing with its main character's blustery comments written across his nightshirt. It was Outcault's strip "Buster Brown" that brought him celebrity and fortune. Outcault was born at Lancaster, OH, and died Sept 25, 1928, at Flushing, NY.

RATIFICATION DAY. Jan 14, 1784. Anniversary of the act that officially ended the American Revolution and established the US as a sovereign power. On Jan 14, 1784, the Continental Congress, meeting at Annapolis, MD, ratified the Treaty of Paris, thus fulfilling the Declaration of Independence of July 4, 1776.

ROACH, HAL: BIRTH ANNIVERSARY. Jan 14, 1892. American film writer, director and producer Harold Eugene (Hal) Roach was born at Elmira, NY. He pioneered film comedy as chief of his own studio for nearly 40 years. During that time he produced, and sometimes directed and wrote, nearly 1,000 movies. Roach is noted for originating the *Our Gang* comedies in 1922 and for introducing Laurel and Hardy to film audiences. He won Academy Awards for the short films *The Music Box* (1931) and *Bored of Education* (1936). Roach produced the film version of Steinbeck's novel *Of Mice and Men* in 1939. In 1984 he won an honorary Academy Award for career achievement. Roach died Nov 2, 1992, at Los Angeles, CA.

"SANFORD AND SON" TV PREMIERE: ANNIVERSARY. Jan 14, 1972. NBC sitcom which gained immediate popularity depicting an African American father and son engaged in the junkyard business. Norman Lear and Bud Yorkin developed the comedy series based on the British "Steptoe and Son." The name Sanford came from John Sanford, the real name of comedian Redd Foxx, who played Fred Sanford. His son, Lamont, was played by Demond Wilson. Others appearing on the show were Whitman Mayo as Grady, Slappy White as Melvin, LaWanda Page as Aunt Esther, Gregory Sierra as Julio, Nathaniel Taylor as Rollo, Raymond Allen as Uncle Woody, Don Bexley as Bubba Bexley, Lynn Hamilton as Donna Harris, Howard Platt and Hal Williams as Hoppy and Smitty, Pat Morita as Ah Chew, Marlene Clark as Janet and Edward Crawford as Roger. The last telecast was Sept 2, 1977.

SCHWEITZER, ALBERT: BIRTH ANNIVERSARY. Jan 14, 1875. Alsatian philosopher, musician, physician and winner of the 1952 Nobel Peace Prize was born at Kayserberg, Upper Alsace, and died at Lambarene, Gabon, Sept 4, 1965.

SPACE MILESTONE: *SOYUZ 4* (USSR). Jan 14, 1969. First docking of two manned spacecraft (with *Soyuz 5*) and first interchange of spaceship personnel in orbit by means of space walks.

SPECIAL EDUCATION WEEK. Jan 14–21. A week-long series of events, workshops, seminars and informational activities designed to support the families of school-age children with disabilities. Explore laws, regulations, entitlements and strategies parents need in order to insure their children get the best education available. For info: Seth Krauss, 6753 El Cajon Blvd, San Diego, CA 92115. Phone: (619) 433-3322. Fax: (619) 460-0423. Web: www.hizhonor.com.

SWITZERLAND: MEITLISUNNTIG. Jan 14. On Meitlisunntig, the second Sunday in January, the girls of Meisterschwanden and Fahrwangen, in the Seetal district of Aargau, Switzerland, stage a procession in historical uniforms and a military parade before a female General Staff. According to tradition, the custom dates from the Villmergen War of 1712, when the women of both communes gave vital help that led to victory. Popular festival follows the procession.

"TODAY" TV PREMIERE: ANNIVERSARY. Jan 14, 1952. NBC program that started the morning news format we know today. Captained by Dave Garroway, the show was segmented with bits and pieces of news, sports, weather, interviews and other features that were repeated so that viewers did not have to stop their morning routine to watch. The segments were brief and to the point. Sylvester Weaver devised this concept to capitalize on television's unusual qualities. What used to take three hours to broadcast live across the country was done in two with videotape on a delayed basis. The addition of chimpanzee J. Fred Muggs in 1953 helped push ratings up. There have been a number of hosts over the years, from John Chancellor and Hugh Downs to Tom Brokaw, Bryant Gumbel and Matt Lauer. Female hosts (originally called "Today Girls") include Betsy Palmer, Florence Henderson, Barbara Walters, Jane Pauley and Katie Couric.

WHIPPLE, WILLIAM: BIRTH ANNIVERSARY. Jan 14, 1730. American patriot and signer of the Declaration of Independence. Born at Kittery, ME, he died at Portsmouth, NH, Nov 10, 1785.

BIRTHDAYS TODAY

Jason Bateman, 32, actor ("Chicago Sons," "The Hogan Family"), born Rye, NY, Jan 14, 1969.
Julian Bond, 61, legislator, civil rights leader, born Nashville, TN, Jan 14, 1940.
Faye Dunaway, 60, actress (Oscar for *Network*; *Bonnie and Clyde*, *Chinatown*), born Bascom, FL, Jan 14, 1941.
Marjoe Gortner, 56, ex-evangelist, actor, singer, born Long Beach, CA, Jan 14, 1945.

Lawrence Kasdan, 52, filmmaker (*The Bodyguard*, *The Big Chill*, *Mumford*), born Miami Beach, FL, Jan 14, 1949.
Shannon Lucid, 58, astronaut, born Shanghai, China, Jan 14, 1943.
Andy Rooney, 82, writer, columnist ("60 Minutes," *Pieces of My Mind*), born Albany, NY, Jan 14, 1919.
Nina Totenberg, 57, broadcast journalist, correspondent ("Nightline"), born New York, NY, Jan 14, 1944.
Emily Watson, 34, actress (*Angela's Ashes*, *The Boxer*), born London, England, Jan 14, 1967.
Carl Weathers, 53, actor (*Rocky, Happy Gilmore*), born New Orleans, LA, Jan 14, 1948.

JANUARY 15 — MONDAY
Day 15 — 350 Remaining

ACE, GOODMAN: BIRTH ANNIVERSARY. Jan 15, 1899. Radio and TV writer, actor, columnist and humorist. With his wife, Jane, created and acted in the popular series of radio programs (1928–45) "Easy Aces." Called "America's greatest wit" by Fred Allen. Born at Kansas City, MO; died at New York, NY, Mar 25, 1982, soon after asking that his tombstone be inscribed "No flowers, please, I'm allergic."

ALPHA KAPPA ALPHA SORORITY FOUNDED: ANNIVERSARY. Jan 15, 1908. Founded at Howard University at Washington, DC, by Ethel Hedgeman Lyle, Alpha Kappa Alpha was the first organization of its type for black women. It was incorporated Jan 29, 1913.

BRITISH MUSEUM: ANNIVERSARY. Jan 15, 1759. On this date, the British Museum opened its doors at Montague House in London. Incorporated by an act of Parliament in 1753, following the death of British medical doctor and naturalist Sir Hans Sloane, who had bequeathed his personal collection of books, manuscripts, coins, medals and antiquities to Britain. As the national museum of the United Kingdom, the British Museum houses many of the world's most prized treasures. The national library moved to separate facilities in 1997.

FIRST SUPER BOWL: ANNIVERSARY. Jan 15, 1967. The Green Bay Packers won the first NFL–AFL World Championship Game, defeating the Kansas City Chiefs, 35–10, at the Los Angeles Memorial Coliseum. Packers quarterback Brett Starr was named the game's Most Valuable Player. Pro football's title game later became known as the Super Bowl and is now played on the last Sunday in January.

"HAPPY DAYS" TV PREMIERE: ANNIVERSARY. Jan 15, 1974. This nostalgic comedy set in Milwaukee in the 1950s starred Ron Howard as teenager Richie Cunningham with Anson Williams as his best friend "Potsie" Weber and Don Most as his best friend Ralph Malph. Tom Bosley and Marion Ross played Richie's parents and his sister, Joanie, was played by Erin Moran. The most memorable character was The Fonz—Arthur "Fonzie" Fonzarelli—played by Henry Winkler. "Happy Days" remained on the air until July 12, 1984, and has been in syndication ever since. "Laverne and Shirley" was a spin-off.

"HILL STREET BLUES" TV PREMIERE: 20th ANNIVERSARY. Jan 15, 1981. Immensely popular NBC police series created by Stephen Bochco and Michael Kozoll that focused more on police officers than on crime. The show was very realistic and highly praised by real policemen. It won a slew of Emmys and ran for seven seasons. Cast: Daniel J. Travanti as Captain Frank Furillo, Veronica Hamel as public defender Joyce Davenport, Michael Conrad as Sergeant Phil "Let's be careful out there" Esterhaus, Barbara Bosson as Fay Furillo, and as the wonderfully drawn cops, Bruce Weitz (Mick Belker), Taurean Blacque (Neal Washington), Kiel Martin (Johnny LaRue), Joe Spano (Henry Goldblume), James B. Sikking (Howard Hunter), René Enríquez (Ray Calletano), Michael Warren (Bobby Hill), Betty Thomas (Lucy Bates), Ed Marinaro (Joe Coffey) and Charles Haid (Andy Renko). The last telecast was on May 19, 1987.

HUMANITARIAN DAY. Jan 15. One of the three Emancipation Days of Respect that highlights the three key principles of the American Civil Rights renaissance of the 1960s. Wearing white shows visible respect for all the unsung humanitarians, regardless of their race, that challenged and changed the USA system of white supremacy practices. The Emancipation D.o.R. promotes practice of unity, respect and remembrance and focuses awareness on the global economical impact of slavery and unjust laws of segregation. The days of Respect are held on the anniversary of Dr. Martin Luther King, Jr's birth to show unity, respect and remembrance for all who changed America's unjust laws of racial segregation. It kicks off Humanitarian Week. See also: "Victims of Violence Holy Day" (Apr 4) and "Emancipation Dream Day" (Aug 28). For info: Dee D. Smith Simmons, Global Committee Commemorating Emancipation Days of Respect, PO Box 21050, Chicago, IL 60621. Phone: (773) RESPECT (737-7328).

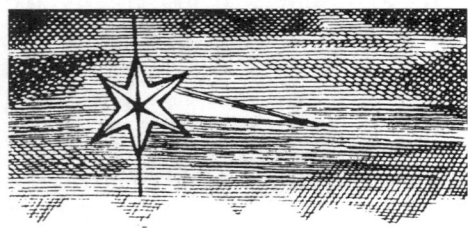

KING, MARTIN LUTHER, JR: BIRTH ANNIVERSARY. Jan 15, 1929. Black civil rights leader, minister, advocate of nonviolence and recipient of the Nobel Peace Prize (1964). Born at Atlanta, GA, he was assassinated at Memphis, TN, Apr 4, 1968. After his death many states and territories observed his birthday as a holiday. In 1983 the Congress approved HR 3706, "A bill to amend Title 5, United States Code, to make the birthday of Martin Luther King, Jr, a legal public holiday." Signed by the president on Nov 2, 1983, it became Public Law 98–144. The law sets the third Monday in January for observance of King's birthday. First observance was Jan 20, 1986. See also: "King, Martin Luther, Jr: Birthday Observed" (Jan 15).

KING, MARTIN LUTHER, JR: BIRTHDAY OBSERVED. Jan 15. Public Law 98–144 designates the third Monday in January as an annual legal public holiday observing the birth of Martin Luther King, Jr. First observed in 1986. In New Hampshire, this day is designated Civil Rights Day. See also: "King, Martin Luther, Jr: Birth Anniversary" (Jan 15).

LEE-JACKSON-KING DAY IN VIRGINIA. Jan 15. Annually, the third Monday in January.

LIVINGSTON, PHILIP: BIRTH ANNIVERSARY. Jan 15, 1716. Merchant and signer of the Declaration of Independence, born at Albany, NY. Died at York, PA, June 12, 1778.

MAN WATCHERS WEEK. Jan 15–20. A week of appreciation for men who are well worth watching. List of activities available. For info: Suzy Mallery, Suzy Mallery's Man Watchers Inc, 2923 Woodwardia Dr, Los Angeles, CA 90077. Phone: (310) 474-9906. Fax: (310) 474-8607. E-mail: manwatchrs@aol.com. Web: manwatchers.com.

★**MARTIN LUTHER KING, JR, FEDERAL HOLIDAY.** Jan 15. Presidential Proclamation has been issued without request each year for the third Monday in January since 1986.

MOLIERE DAY: BAPTISM ANNIVERSARY. Jan 15, 1622. Most celebrated of French authors and dramatists, Jean Baptiste Poquelin, baptized at Paris, France, Jan 15, 1622, took the stage name Molière when he was about 22 years old. While playing in a performance of his last play, *Le Malade Imaginaire* (about a hypochondriac afraid of death), Molière became ill and died within a few hours at Paris, Feb 17, 1673.

NATIONAL FRESH SQUEEZED JUICE WEEK. Jan 15–19. Drinking fresh squeezed juice is a great healthy way of living. For info: Bob O'Brien, PO Box 2356, Secaucus, NJ 07096. Phone: (201) 860-1595. Fax: (201) 865-4775. E-mail: bobconsumeradvocate@excite.com.

NATIONAL THANK GOD IT'S MONDAY! DAY. Jan 15. Besides holidays, such as President's Day, being celebrated on Mondays, people everywhere start new jobs, have birthdays, celebrate promotions and begin vacations on Mondays. A day in recognition of this first day of the week. For info: Dorothy Zjawin, 61 W Colfax Ave, Roselle Park, NJ 07204. Phone: (908) 241-6241. Fax: (908) 241-6241.

PENTAGON COMPLETED: ANNIVERSARY. Jan 15, 1943. The world's largest office building with 6.5 million square feet of usable space, the Pentagon is located in Virginia across the Potomac River from Washington, DC, and serves as headquarters for the Department of Defense.

QUARTERLY ESTIMATED FEDERAL INCOME TAX PAYERS' DUE DATE. Jan 15. For those individuals whose fiscal year is the calendar year and who make quarterly estimated federal income tax payments, today would be one of the due dates (Jan 15, Apr 16, June 15 and Sept 17, 2001).

SIEGMEISTER, ELIE: BIRTH ANNIVERSARY. Jan 15, 1909. American composer Elie Siegmeister was born at New York, NY. He composed eight symphonies and eight operas and a number of other concertos, chamber pieces and orchestral works using folk, jazz and street songs to create a contemporary American classical music. He died Mar 10, 1991, at Manhasset, NY.

STOCK EXCHANGE HOLIDAY (MARTIN LUTHER KING DAY). Jan 15. The holiday schedules for the various exchanges are subject to change if relevant rules, regulations or exchange policies are revised. If you have questions, phone: American Stock Exchange (212) 306-1000; Chicago Board of Options Exchange (312) 786-5600; Chicago Board of Trade (312) 435-3500; New York Stock Exchange (212) 656-2065; Pacific Stock Exchange (415) 393-4000; Philadelphia Stock Exchange (215) 496-5000.

TRAIN FOR PARIS: ANNIVERSARY. Jan 15, 1945. The civilian populations of England and France had their first direct contact since May 1940 when a boat train left London's Victoria Station headed for Paris.

BIRTHDAYS TODAY

Charo (Maria Martinez), 50, singer, actress ("Chico and the Man"), born Murcia, Spain, Jan 15, 1951.

Chad Lowe, 33, actor ("Now and Again," "Life Goes On," *Nobody's Perfect*), born Dayton, OH, Jan 15, 1968.

Rod MacLeish, 75, broadcast journalist, born Bryn Mawr, PA, Jan 15, 1926.

Andrea Martin, 54, actress (*Wag the Dog, Anastasia*, "SCTV"), born Portland, ME, Jan 15, 1947.

Margaret O'Brien, 64, actress (*Little Women, Meet Me in St. Louis*), born San Diego, CA, Jan 15, 1937.

Edward Teller, 93, physicist, born Budapest, Hungary, Jan 15, 1908.

Mario Van Peebles, 44, actor (*Love Kills, Judgment Day*), born Mexico City, Mexico, Jan 15, 1957.

January *2001*	S	M	T	W	T	F	S
		1	2	3	4	5	6
	7	8	9	10	11	12	13
	14	15	16	17	18	19	20
	21	22	23	24	25	26	27
	28	29	30	31			

JANUARY 16 — TUESDAY
Day 16 — 349 Remaining

BRITISH AIR RAID ON BERLIN: ANNIVERSARY. Jan 16, 1943. In the first bombing of Germany since the Casablanca Conference, the British Royal Air Force began heavy bombing of Germany by day and night to bring about "the progressive destruction and dislocation of the German military, industrial and economic system, and for the undermining of the morale of the German people." The RAF used their new "target indicator" bombs to mark targets for their bombers.

CIVIL SERVICE CREATED: ANNIVERSARY. Jan 16, 1883. The US Congress passed a bill creating the civil service.

COAL CONSERVATION ORDERED: ANNIVERSARY. Jan 16, 1918. In a precursor of things to come, 75 New York schools closed down for lack of coal on Jan 2, 1918. On Jan 16, by order of US Fuel Administrator Harry A. Garfield, all industry east of the Mississippi not crucial to the war effort was shut down. Factories remained closed for five days. In addition, the following nine Mondays became days of leisure for a large segment of the American workforce as further attempts were made to reserve coal for troop transport, ships and merchant vessels.

DEAN, DIZZY: 90th BIRTH ANNIVERSARY. Jan 16, 1911. Jay Hanna "Dizzy" Dean, major league pitcher (St. Louis Cardinals) and Baseball Hall of Fame member was born at Lucas, AR. Following his baseball career, Dean established himself as a radio and TV sports announcer and commentator, becoming famous for his innovative delivery. "He slud into third," reported Dizzy, who on another occasion explained that "Me and Paul [baseball player brother Paul "Daffy" Dean] . . . didn't get much education." Died at Reno, NV, July 17, 1974.

"DONNY AND MARIE" TV PREMIERE: 25th ANNIVERSARY. Jan 16, 1976. ABC show hosted by brother-and-sister act Donny and Marie Osmond. There were seven other talented siblings in the Osmond family who appeared on the show at times along with regulars Jim Connell and Hank Garcia. The sister-and-brother team could sing, dance and perform on ice skates.

EISENHOWER ASSUMES COMMAND: ANNIVERSARY. Jan 16, 1944. General Dwight D. Eisenhower arrived in London to assume command of the Supreme Headquarters Allied Expeditionary Forces in Europe (SHAEF). Having demonstrated his organizational abilities in North Africa as well as his strength as an arbitrator of inter-Allied rivalries, Eisenhower was charged with the most far-reaching push of the war—the invasion of France.

EL SALVADOR: CIVIL WAR ENDED: ANNIVERSARY. Jan 16, 1992. A peace treaty was signed in Mexico City ending the 12-year civil war that had claimed 75,000 lives. On Feb 1, a cease-fire went into effect.

JAPAN: HARU-NO-YABUIRI. Jan 16. Employees and servants who have been working over the holidays are given a day off.

MERMAN, ETHEL: BIRTH ANNIVERSARY. Jan 16, 1909. Musical comedy star famous for her belting voice and brassy style. Born Ethel Agnes Zimmerman on Jan 16, 1909 (or 1912—the date changed the older she got, but most sources say 1909) at Queens, NY. Died Feb 15, 1984, at New York, NY.

MICHELIN, ANDRE: BIRTH ANNIVERSARY. Jan 16, 1853. French industrialist who, along with his brother Edouard, started the Michelin Tire Company in 1888, manufacturing bicycle tires. They were the first to use demountable pneumatic tires on cars. Born at Paris, France; died there Apr 4, 1931.

MOON PHASE: LAST QUARTER. Jan 16. Moon enters Last Quarter phase at 7:35 AM, EST.

NATIONAL NOTHING DAY: ANNIVERSARY. Jan 16. Anniversary of National Nothing Day, an event created by newspaperman Harold Pullman Coffin and first observed in 1973 "to provide Americans with one national day when they can just sit without celebrating, observing or honoring anything." Since 1975, though many other events have been listed on this day, light-hearted traditional observance of Coffin's idea has continued. Coffin, a native of Reno, NV, died at Capitola, CA, Sept 12, 1981, at the age of 76.

PERSIAN GULF WAR BEGINS: 10th ANNIVERSARY. Jan 16, 1991. Allied forces launched a major air offensive against Iraq to begin the Gulf War. The strike was designed to destroy Iraqi air defenses, command, control and communication centers. As Desert Shield became Desert Storm, the world was able to see and hear for the first time an initial engagement of war as CNN broadcasters, stationed at Baghdad, covered the attack live.

PROHIBITION (EIGHTEENTH) AMENDMENT: ANNIVERSARY. Jan 16, 1919. Nebraska became the 36th state to ratify the prohibition amendment and the 18th Amendment became part of the US Constitution. One year later, Jan 16, 1920, the 18th Amendment took effect and the sale of alcoholic beverages became illegal in the US with the Volstead Act providing for enforcement. This was the first time that an amendment to the Constitution dealt with a social issue. The 21st Amendment, repealing the 18th, went into effect Dec 6, 1933.

RELIGIOUS FREEDOM DAY. Jan 16, 1786. The legislature of Virginia adopted a religious freedom statute that protected Virginians against any requirement to attend or support any church and against discrimination. This statute, which had been drafted by Thomas Jefferson and introduced by James Madison, later was the model for the First Amendment to the US Constitution.

★ **RELIGIOUS FREEDOM DAY.** Jan 16. Commemorates the adoption of a religious freedom statute by the Virginia legislature in 1786.

SERVICE, ROBERT WILLIAM: BIRTH ANNIVERSARY. Jan 16, 1874. Canadian poet, born at Preston, England. Lived in the Canadian northwest for many years and perhaps is best remembered for such ballads as "The Shooting of Dan McGrew" and "The Cremation of Sam McGee" and for such books as *Songs of a Sourdough*, *Rhymes of a Rolling Stone* and *The Spell of the Yukon*. Died at France, Sept 11, 1958.

SOUTHWEST SENIOR INVITATIONAL GOLF CHAMPIONSHIP. Jan 16–19. Yuma Golf and Country Club, Yuma, AZ. A 36-hole medal play tournament, limited to 120 players 50 and older. For info: Caballeros de Yuma, Inc, Box 5987, Yuma, AZ 85366-5987. Phone: (520) 343-1715. Fax: (520) 783-1609. Web: www.caballeros.org.

BIRTHDAYS TODAY

Debbie Allen, 51, dancer, choreographer, singer, actress ("Fame"), born Houston, TX, Jan 16, 1950.

John Carpenter, 53, movie director (*Halloween, The Thing*), born Carthage, NY, Jan 16, 1948.

David Chokachi, 33, actor ("Baywatch"), born Plymouth, MA, Jan 16, 1968.

Anthony Joseph (A.J.) Foyt, Jr, 66, former auto racer, born Houston, TX, Jan 16, 1935.

Marilyn Horne, 67, opera singer, born Bradford, PA, Jan 16, 1934.

Katy Jurado, 74, actress (*High Noon, One-Eyed Jacks*), born Guadalajara, Mexico, Jan 16, 1927.

Eartha Kitt, 73, singer, born North, SC, Jan 16, 1928.

Jack Burns McDowell, 35, baseball player, born Van Nuys, CA, Jan 16, 1966.

Ronnie Milsap, 57, singer ("[There's] No Gettin' Over Me"), born Robinsville, NC, Jan 16, 1944.

Francesco Scavullo, 72, fashion photographer, born Staten Island, NY, Jan 16, 1929.

JANUARY 17 — WEDNESDAY
Day 17 — 348 Remaining

"BARETTA" TV PREMIERE: ANNIVERSARY. Jan 17, 1975. CBS series starring Robert Blake as Baretta, a police detective who defied his superiors and solved his cases in a most unorthodox manner—usually by figuring it out while talking to his pet cockatoo, Fred, or his informant, Rooster (played by Michael D. Roberts). Commanding officer Lieutenant Hal Brubaker was played by Edward Grover. The last telecast aired on June 1, 1978.

CABLE CAR PATENT: ANNIVERSARY. Jan 17, 1871. Andrew Hallikie received a patent for a cable car system that began service in San Francisco in 1873.

FIRST NUCLEAR-POWERED SUBMARINE VOYAGE: ANNIVERSARY. Jan 17, 1955. At 11 AM, EST, the commanding officer of the world's first nuclear-powered submarine, the *Nautilus*, ordered all lines cast off and sent the historic message: "Under way on nuclear power." Highlights of the *Nautilus*: keel laid by President Harry S Truman June 14, 1952; christened and launched by Mrs Dwight D. Eisenhower Jan 21, 1954; commissioned to the US Navy Sept 30, 1954. It now forms part of the *Nautilus* Memorial Submarine Force Library and Museum at the Naval Submarine Base New London at Groton, CT.

FRANKLIN, BENJAMIN: BIRTH ANNIVERSARY. Jan 17, 1706. "Elder statesman of the American Revolution," oldest signer of both the Declaration of Independence and the Constitution, scientist, diplomat, author, printer, publisher, philosopher, philanthropist and self-made, self-educated man. Author, printer and publisher of *Poor Richard's Almanack* (1733–58). Born at Boston, MA, Franklin died at Philadelphia, PA, Apr 17, 1790. His birthday is commemorated each year by the Poor Richard Club of Philadelphia with graveside observance. In 1728 Franklin wrote a premature epitaph for himself. It first appeared in print in Ames's 1771 almanac: "The Body of BENJAMIN FRANKLIN/Printer/Like a Covering of an old Book/Its contents torn out/And stript of its Lettering and Gilding,/Lies here, Food for Worms;/But the work shall not be lost,/It will (as he believ'd) appear once more/In a New and more beautiful Edition/Corrected and amended/By the Author."

"FRONTLINE" TV PREMIERE: ANNIVERSARY. Jan 17, 1983. PBS hour-long independently produced documentaries hosted by Jessica Savitch. The programs often created controversy, focusing on a variety of political, military and social issues. Judy Woodruff replaced Savitch, who was killed in an auto accident in the fall of 1983.

"THE GOLDBERGS" TV PREMIERE: ANNIVERSARY. Jan 17, 1949. Originally broadcast by CBS, this show was one of the earliest TV sitcoms. The show centered around a Jewish mother and her family living in The Bronx and later in the suburbs. Gertrude Berg created the hit radio show before she wrote, produced and starred as Molly Goldberg in the television version. Contributing actors and actresses included Philip Loeb, Arlene McQuade, Tom Taylor, Eli Mintz, Menasha Skulnik and Arnold Stang.

HUTCHINS, ROBERT MAYNARD: BIRTH ANNIVERSARY. Jan 17, 1899. American educator, foundation executive and civil liberties activist, born at Brooklyn, NY. He was president and later chancellor of the University of Chicago, where he introduced many educational concepts, including the Great Books program. Died at Santa Barbara, CA, on May 14, 1977.

IKE'S FAREWELL: 40th ANNIVERSARY. Jan 17, 1961. President Dwight D. Eisenhower, in his farewell address to the nation on national radio and television, spoke the sentences that would be the most quoted and remembered of his presidency. In a direct warning, he said, "In the councils of government, we must guard against the acquisition of unwarranted influence, whether sought or unsought, by the military-industrial complex. The potential for the disastrous rise of misplaced power exists and persists."

ILLINOIS SNOW SCULPTING COMPETITION. Jan 17–20. Rockford, IL. Teams from around the state create enormous works of frozen art, as they compete to represent Illinois in national snow sculpting competition. In case of inclement weather, event may be postponed. Sponsor: Rockford Park District. Est attendance: 100,000. For info: Patricia Hayes, Rockford Park District, 1401 N Second St, Rockford, IL 61107-3086. Phone: (800) 521-0849 or (815) 987-8800. Fax: (815) 987-1631. E-mail: rpdmail@inwave.com. Web: www.rockfordparks.org.

JAPAN SUFFERS MAJOR EARTHQUAKE: ANNIVERSARY. Jan 17, 1995. Japan suffered its second most deadly earthquake in the 20th century when a 20-second temblor left 5,500 dead and more than 21,600 people injured. The epicenter was six miles beneath Awaji Island at Osaka Bay. This was just 20 miles west of Kobe, Japan's sixth-largest city and a major port that accounted for 12 percent of the country's exports. Measuring 7.2 on the Richter scale, the quake collapsed or badly damaged more than 30,400 buildings and left 275,000 people homeless.

JUDGMENT DAY. Jan 17. No need to wait 'til it's too late. All you need to do to see how you measure up to the standards of your God is simple: look in the mirror. There's your judgment. ©2000 Wellcat Holidays & Herbs. For info: Thomas Roy, 2418 Long Ln, Lebanon, PA 17046. Phone: (240) 332-4886. E-mail: wellcat@supernet.com. Web: www.wellcat.com.

LUMUMBA, PATRICE: 40th DEATH ANNIVERSARY. Jan 17, 1961. The first prime minister of the Democratic Republic of the Congo (Zaire), nationalist and Pan-Africanist Lumumba was assassinated. Born at Stanleyville in the Belgian Congo (today's Katako Kobme, Kasai Province, Congo), July 2, 1925. For info: Gebregeorgis Yohannes, Intl Patrice Lumumba Soc, PO Box 21365, Oakland, CA 94620. Phone: (510) 658-0462. Fax: (510) 658-6685. E-mail: lumumba@africansun.org. Web: www.africansun.org/lumumba.

MEXICO: BLESSING OF THE ANIMALS AT THE CATHEDRAL. Jan 17. Church of San Antonio at Mexico City or Xochimilco provide best sights of chickens, cows and household pets gaily decorated with flowers. (Saint's day for San Antonio Abad, patron saint of domestic animals.)

NATIONAL SOCCER COACHES ASSOCIATION OF AMERICA NATIONAL CONVENTION. Jan 17–21. Indianapolis Convention Center, Indianapolis, IN. The NSCAA is the largest single-sport coaching organization in the US. The NSCAA annual convention is the largest gathering of soccer coaches in the world. The convention features clinics, lectures, exhibits and national awards. Est attendance: 6,200. For info: NSCAA, 6700 Squibb Rd, Ste 215, Mission, KS 66202. Phone: (800) 458-0678 or (913) 362-1747. Fax: (913) 362-3439. Web: www.nscaa.com/.

PALOMARES HYDROGEN BOMB ACCIDENT: 35th ANNIVERSARY. Jan 17, 1966. At 10:16 AM, according to villagers, fire fell from the sky over Palomares, Spain. An American B-52 bomber carrying four hydrogen bombs collided with its refueling plane, spilling the bombs (two of which had "chemical explosions," scattering radioactive plutonium over the area). In a cleanup, American soldiers burned crops, slaughtered animals and removed tons of topsoil (which was sent to South Carolina for burial). More than 19 years later, in November 1985, the Nuclear Energy Board permitted villagers to see their medical reports for the first time.

January 2001	S	M	T	W	T	F	S
		1	2	3	4	5	6
	7	8	9	10	11	12	13
	14	15	16	17	18	19	20
	21	22	23	24	25	26	27
	28	29	30	31			

PGA OF AMERICA FOUNDED: 85th ANNIVERSARY.
Jan 17, 1916. Golf great Walter Hagen and some 30 other pro golfers met and formed the Professional Golfers' Association of America and also developed the idea for a national championship. Rodman Wanamaker provided the trophy and the $2,580 purse for the first PGA Championship, which was played Apr 10, 1916, at the Siwanoy course at Bronxville, NY. The winner was British golfer Jim Barnes, who also won the second competition—not held until 1919 because of World War I. In 1921 Walter Hagen became the first American to win, a feat he accomplished four more times—in 1924, '25, '26 and '27.

POLAND: LIBERATION DAY.
Jan 17, 1945. Celebration of liberation from Nazi oppression on this day, of the city of Warsaw by Soviet troops. Special ceremonies at the Monument to the Unknown Soldier in Warsaw's Victory Square (which had been called Adolf Hitler Platz during the German occupation).

QUEEN LILIUOKALANI DEPOSED: ANNIVERSARY.
Jan 17, 1893. Hawaiian Queen Liliuokalani, the last monarch of Hawaii, lost her throne when the monarchy was abolished by the "Committee of Safety," with the foreknowledge of US minister John L. Stevens, who encouraged the revolutionaries. The Queen's supporters were intimidated by the 300 US Marines sent to protect American lives and property. Judge Sanford B. Dole became president of the republic and later was Hawaii's first governor after the US annexed it by joint resolution of Congress on July 7, 1898. Hawaii held incorporated territory status for 60 years. President Dwight D. Eisenhower signed the proclamation making Hawaii the 50th state on Aug 21, 1959.

RUSH, WILLIAM: DEATH ANNIVERSARY.
Jan 17, 1833. First American-born sculptor. William Rush's work in wood and clay included busts of many notables, American and European alike; carved wooden female figureheads for ships; the masks of Tragedy and Comedy seen at the Actor's House outside Philadelphia, PA; and the *Spirit of Schuylkill* in Fairmount Park in Philadelphia. In 1805 Rush and others founded the Pennsylvania Academy of the Fine Arts. Rush was born at Philadelphia in 1756.

SAINT ANTHONY'S DAY.
Jan 17. Feast day honoring Egyptian hermit who became the first Christian monk and who established communities of hermits; patron saint of domestic animals and patriarch of all monks. Lived about AD 251–354.

SOUTHERN CALIFORNIA EARTHQUAKE: ANNIVERSARY.
Jan 17, 1994. An earthquake measuring 6.6 on the Richter scale struck the Los Angeles area about 4:20 AM. The epicenter was at Northridge in the San Fernando Valley, about 20 miles northwest of downtown Los Angeles. A death toll of 51 was announced Jan 20. Sixteen of the dead were killed in the collapse of one apartment building. More than 25,000 people were made homeless by the quake and 680,000 lost electric power. Many buildings were destroyed and others made uninhabitable due to structural damage. A section of the Santa Monica Freeway, part of the Simi Valley Freeway and three major overpasses collapsed. Hundreds of aftershocks occurred in the following several weeks. Costs to repair the damages were estimated at 15–30 billion dollars.

BIRTHDAYS TODAY
Muhammad Ali (born Cassius Marcellus Clay, Jr), 59, former heavyweight champion boxer, who changed his name after converting to Islam, born Louisville, KY, Jan 17, 1942.
Jim Carrey, 39, actor (*Dumb and Dumber, The Truman Show, Ace Ventura*), comedian ("In Living Color"), born Newmarket, Ontario, Canada, Jan 17, 1962.
David Caruso, 45, actor ("NYPD Blue," *An Officer and a Gentleman*), born Forest Hills, NY, Jan 17, 1956.
James Earl Jones, 70, actor (*The Great White Hope; Roots: The Next Generations*), born Arktabula, MS, Jan 17, 1931.
Newton Minow, 75, former head of the Federal Communications Commission (1961–63), called television a "vast wasteland," born Milwaukee, WI, Jan 17, 1926.
Sheree North, 68, actress (*Marilyn, How to Be Very Very Popular*), born Dawn Bethel, Los Angeles, CA, Jan 17, 1933.
Maury Povich, 62, talk-show host, born Washington, DC, Jan 17, 1939.
Vidal Sassoon, 73, hair stylist, born London, England, Jan 17, 1928.
Betty White, 77, actress ("Mary Tyler Moore," "The Golden Girls"), animal rights activist, born Oak Park, IL, Jan 17, 1924.
Paul Young, 45, singer ("Every Time You Go Away"), born Luton, England, Jan 17, 1956.
Donald William (Don) Zimmer, 70, former baseball manager and player, born Cincinnati, OH, Jan 17, 1931.

JANUARY 18 — THURSDAY
Day 18 — 347 Remaining

CANADA: ICEWINE FESTIVAL.
Jan 18–21. Sun Peaks Resort, Kelowana, BC, Canada. For info: Okanagan Wine Fest Soc, 1527 Ellis St, Kelowana, BC, Canada V1Y 2A7. Phone: (250) 861-6654. Fax: (250) 861-3942. E-mail: info@owfs.com. Web: www.owfs.com.

FIRST BLACK US CABINET MEMBER: 35th ANNIVERSARY.
Jan 18, 1966. Robert Clifton Weaver was sworn in as Secretary of Housing and Urban Development, becoming the first black cabinet member in US history. He was nominated by President Lyndon Johnson. Weaver died at New York, NY, July 17, 1997.

FLOOD, CURT: BIRTH ANNIVERSARY.
Jan 18, 1938. Curtis Charles (Curt) Flood, baseball player, born at Houston, TX. Flood was one of baseball's best center fielders in the 1960s, batting .293 over 15 seasons and playing spectacular defense. After the 1969 season, he refused to accept a trade from the St. Louis Cardinals to the Philadelphia Phillies. "I am not a piece of property to be bought and sold irrespective of my wishes," he said in a letter to Commissioner Bowie Kuhn. The resulting lawsuit went to the Supreme Court where Flood lost. But his stand, taken because he did not want to switch teams, paved the way for the end of baseball's reserve clause and the advent of free agency. Died at Los Angeles, CA, Jan 20, 1997.

GET TO KNOW YOUR CUSTOMER DAY.
Jan 18 (also Apr 19, July 20 and Oct 19). Set aside the third Thursday of each quarter to get to know your customers even better. For example, salespeople might plan to take a customer out to lunch, not to sell, but to learn more about their needs and why they like doing business with them. Executives could get out from behind the desk and go into the field. For info: Shep Hyken, Shepard Presentations, 711 Old Ballas Rd, Ste 215, St. Louis, MO 63141. Phone: (314) 692-2200. E-mail: Shep@hyken.com. Web: www.hyken.com.

GRANT, CARY: BIRTH ANNIVERSARY.
Jan 18, 1904. Known as a romantic leading actor, Grant was born at Bristol, England. For more than three decades Grant entertained with his wit, charm, sophistication and personality. His films include *Topper, The Awful Truth, Bringing Up Baby* and *Holiday*. Died at Davenport, IA, Nov 29, 1986.

HARDY, OLIVER: BIRTH ANNIVERSARY. Jan 18, 1892. Born at Atlanta, GA, Hardy teamed up with Stan Laurel in 1926 to form the comedy team of Laurel and Hardy. Among their most popular films: *From Soup to Nuts, Babes in Toyland, Swiss Miss.* Hardy died at Hollywood, Aug 7, 1957.

ICEBOX DAYS XXI. Jan 18–21. International Falls, MN. Smoosh racing, "Freeze Yer Gizzard Blizzard Run," turkey bowling, ski races, mutt races and beach party. Est attendance: 5,000. For info: Kallie L. Briggs, Chamber of Commerce, 301 2nd Ave, International Falls, MN 56649. Phone: (800) 325-5766 or (218) 283-9400. Fax: (218) 283-3572. E-mail: intlfall@intlfalls.org. Web: www.intlfalls.org.

INDIANA MOTORCYCLE & WATERCRAFT EXPOSITION. Jan 18–21. Indiana State Fairgrounds, Indianapolis, IN. For info: Kevin Renfro, VP, 2511 E 46th St, Ste E-2, Indianapolis, IN 46205. Phone: (800) 892-1723 or (317) 546-4344. Fax: (317) 546-3002. E-mail: insportshow@iquest.net.

INTERNATIONAL FINALS RODEO. Jan 18–20. State Fair Arena, Oklahoma City, OK. The top 15 money winning IPRA cowboys and cowgirls compete for world championship titles in seven events. Prize money more than $275,000. Trade show, dances, Bucking Stock Sales. Est attendance: 50,000. For info: Jane Kirton, Event Coordinator, Intl Finals Rodeo, PO Box 83377, Oklahoma City, OK 73148. Phone: (405) 235-6540. Fax: (405) 235-6577. E-mail: info@iprarodeo.com.

"THE JEFFERSONS" TV PREMIERE: ANNIVERSARY. Jan 18, 1975. CBS sitcom about an African American family (formerly neighbors of the Bunkers on "All in the Family") who moved to Manhattan's East Side, thanks to the success of George Jefferson's chain of dry cleaning stores. Having a format similar to "All in the Family," the show featured a black bigot, George Jefferson. Particularly memorable were the racial slurs Jefferson used against the mixed-marriage neighbors, Tom and Helen Willis. The show was able to humorously introduce subjects such as mixed marriage on a prime-time series. Cast included Sherman Hemsley as George Jefferson, Isabel Sanford as Louise Jefferson, Mike Evans and Damon Evans as Lionel, Franklin Cover and Roxie Roker as the mixed couple and Berlinda Tolbert as their daughter, Jenny and Paul Benedict as the British bachelor neighbor Bentley. The last episode aired July 23, 1985.

KAYE, DANNY: BIRTH ANNIVERSARY. Jan 18, 1913. American entertainer Danny Kaye was born David Daniel Kaminski at Brooklyn, NY. Kaye became a star in films, international stage performances and television. His most notable films are *The Secret Life of Walter Mitty* (1947) and *Hans Christian Andersen* (1952), as well as the classic *White Christmas.* He hosted the television show *The Danny Kaye Show* in the 1960s. In addition, Kaye helped raise millions of dollars for the United Nations International Children's Emergency Fund (UNICEF) and musicians' pension plans. He died Mar 3, 1987, at Los Angeles, CA.

LAUGHLIN DESERT CHALLENGE. Jan 18–21. Laughlin, NV. Off-road race with spectator appeal during the Laughlin Leap, a hugh-jump contest for trucks, crew competitions and event entertainment. For info: Phone: (800) 452-8445.

MACKINAW CITY WINTERFEST. Jan 18–21. Mackinaw City, MI. Professional snow sculptors create beautiful works of art from blocks of snow. Professional judging as well as People's Choice Awards are given. Gumbo cook-off, live cajun style music and Saturday night fireworks. Est attendance: 5,000. For info: Mackinaw Area Tourist Bureau, PO Box 160, Mackinaw City, MI 49701. Phone: (800) 666-0160. Web: www.mackinawcity.com.

POOH DAY: A.A. MILNE: BIRTH ANNIVERSARY. Jan 18, 1882. Anniversary of the birth of A(lan) A(lexander) Milne, English author, especially remembered for his children's stories: *Winnie the Pooh* and *The House at Pooh Corner.* Also the author of *Mr Pim Passes By, When We Were Very Young* and *Now We Are Six.* Born at London, England, died at Hartfield, England, Jan 31, 1956.

ROGET, PETER MARK: BIRTH ANNIVERSARY. Jan 18, 1779. English physician, best known as author of Roget's *Thesaurus of English Words and Phrases,* first published in 1852. Roget was also the inventor of the "log-log" slide rule. He was born at London, England, and died at West Malvern, Worcestershire, England, Sept 12, 1869.

RUFFIN, DAVIS ELI (DAVID): 60th BIRTH ANNIVERSARY. Jan 18, 1941. American popular singer David Ruffin was born at Meridian, MS. He was one of the original members of the Motown singing group the Temptations, which began in Detroit in the 1960s. Ruffin left the group in 1968 to pursue a solo career. He and the other original members of the Temptations were inducted into the Rock and Roll Hall of Fame in 1989. Ruffin died June 1, 1991, at Philadelphia, PA.

SUNDANCE FILM FESTIVAL. Jan 18–28. Park City, UT. "The premier US festival for American independent filmmakers." Est attendance: 15,000. For info: Sundance Institute, PO Box 3630, Salt Lake City, UT 84101. Phone: (801) 328-FILM. E-mail: institute@sundance.org. Web: www.sundance.org.

"TED MACK'S ORIGINAL AMATEUR HOUR" TV PREMIERE: ANNIVERSARY. Jan 18, 1948. This immensely popular show, featuring host Ted Mack, introduced amateurs performing their talents on live television. It debuted as a regularly scheduled broadcast on the Dumont network. The show had been a long-running success on radio as "Major Bowes' Original Amateur Hour" until the death of Edward Bowes. Mack became host of the radio show a year later. While a few episodes were televised in 1947, the show did not air weekly until this date. The program ran until 1970 and also continued on radio until 1952.

VERSAILLES PEACE CONFERENCE: ANNIVERSARY. Jan 18, 1919. French President Raymond Poincare formally opened the (World War I) Peace Conference at Versailles, France. It proceeded under the chairmanship of Georges Clemenceau. In May the conference disposed of Germany's colonies and delivered a treaty to the German delegates on May 7, 1919, fourth anniversary of the sinking of the *Lusitania.* Final treaty-signing ceremonies were completed at the palace at Versailles, June 28, 1919.

WEBSTER, DANIEL: BIRTH ANNIVERSARY. Jan 18, 1782. American statesman and orator who said, on Apr 6, 1830, "The people's government, made for the people, made by the people, and answerable to the people." Born at Salisbury, NH; died at Marshfield, MA, Oct 24, 1852.

WEEK OF CHRISTIAN UNITY. Jan 18–25. From the Conversion of St. Peter (Jan 18) to the Conversion of St. Paul (Jan 25).

BIRTHDAYS TODAY

John Boorman, 68, filmmaker (*Deliverance, Excalibur*), born Shepperton, England, Jan 18, 1933.

Kevin Costner, 46, actor (*Field of Dreams, Dances with Wolves* [Oscar for directing], *Bull Durham*), born Compton, CA, Jan 18, 1955.

Ray Dolby, 68, inventor of the Dolby Sound System for sound recording, born Portland, OR, Jan 18, 1933.

Jane Horrocks, 37, actress (*Little Voice*), born Lancashire, England, Jan 18, 1964.

Evelyn Lear, 70, opera singer, born New York, NY, Jan 18, 1931.

Jesse L. Martin, 32, actor ("Law & Order," "Ally McBeal"), born Rocky Mountain, VA, Jan 18, 1969.

Mark Messier, 40, hockey player, born Edmonton, Alberta, Canada, Jan 18, 1961.

January 2001

S	M	T	W	T	F	S
	1	2	3	4	5	6
7	8	9	10	11	12	13
14	15	16	17	18	19	20
21	22	23	24	25	26	27
28	29	30	31			

JANUARY 19 — FRIDAY
Day 19 — 346 Remaining

ARBOR DAY IN FLORIDA. Jan 19. The third Friday in January is Arbor Day in Florida, a ceremonial day.

CÉZANNE, PAUL: BIRTH ANNIVERSARY. Jan 19, 1839. Post-impressionist painter born at Aix-en-Provence, France. Still-lifes and landscapes were his preferred subjects. Cézanne died Oct 23, 1906, at Aix.

CONFEDERATE HEROES DAY. Jan 19. Observed on anniversary of Robert E. Lee's birthday. Official holiday in Texas.

"48 HOURS" TV PREMIERE: ANNIVERSARY. Jan 19, 1988. CBS prime-time newsmagazine-type program airing each week with Dan Rather as anchorman and Bernard Goldberg as main correspondent.

HELMS, EDGAR J.: BIRTH ANNIVERSARY. Jan 19, 1863. Born near Malone, NY, Reverend Dr. Helms became a minister to a parish of poor immigrants in Boston's South End. In that capacity he developed the philosophy and organization that eventually became Goodwill Industries. Helms died Dec 23, 1942, at Boston.

HISTORIC BIRTHDAY PARTIES IN LEXINGTON. Jan 19–21. Lexington, VA. Celebrates the birthdays of Robert E. Lee and Stonewall Jackson. Annually, Jan 19–21. For info: Lexington Visitors Bureau, 106 E Washington St, Lexington, VA 24450. Phone: (540) 463-3777. Fax: (540) 463-1105. E-mail: lexington@rockbridge.net.

INTERNATIONAL SING-OUT DAY™. Jan 19 (also Feb 1). Break out in song today like they do in the musicals. Sing out your words in conversations instead of speaking them. You can even add a few dance steps if you like. In 2001, Sing Out Day™ happens on Donald and Phillip Everly (The Everly Brothers') birthdays. For info: Adrienne Sioux Koopersmith, 1437 W Rosemont, #1W, Chicago, IL 60660. Phone: (773) 743-5341. Fax: (773) 743-5395. E-mail: adrienne@21stcentury.net.

JOPLIN, JANIS: BIRTH ANNIVERSARY. Jan 19, 1943. Possibly the most highly regarded white female blues singer of all time, Janis Joplin was born at Port Arthur, TX. Joplin's appearance with Big Brother and the Holding Company at the Monterey International Pop Festival in August 1967 launched her to superstar status. Among her recording hits were "Get It While You Can," "Piece of My Heart" and "Ball and Chain." She died of a heroin overdose Oct 4, 1970, at Hollywood, CA, at the age of 27.

LEE, ROBERT E.: BIRTH ANNIVERSARY. Jan 19, 1807. Greatest military leader of the Confederacy, son of Revolutionary War General Henry (Light Horse Harry) Lee. His surrender Apr 9, 1865, to Union General Ulysses S. Grant brought an end to the Civil War. Born at Westmoreland County, VA, he died at Lexington, VA, Oct 12, 1870. His birthday is observed in Florida, Kentucky, Louisiana, South Carolina and Tennessee. Observed on third Monday in January in Alabama, Arkansas and Mississippi.

"THE MILLIONAIRE" TV PREMIERE: ANNIVERSARY. Jan 19, 1955. The CBS drama that had all of America hoping to find Michael Anthony on their doorstep. Mr John Beresford Tipton was a millionaire who made a hobby of giving away million dollar checks anonymously to unknown people to see how they handled the sudden wealth. Michael Anthony, played by Marvin Miller, was Mr Tipton's personal secretary and the star of "The Millionaire." No one ever saw Mr Tipton but his voice would greet Anthony at the opening of each show and issue instructions for delivery of the next check. Anthony would then find the recipient and give him or her the check, explaining that the recipient had to agree never to divulge the amount or how it was acquired.

POE, EDGAR ALLAN: BIRTH ANNIVERSARY. Jan 19, 1809. American poet and story writer, called "America's most famous man of letters." Born at Boston, MA, he was orphaned in dire poverty in 1811 and was raised by Virginia merchant John Allan. In 1836 he married his 13-year-old cousin, Virginia Clemm. A magazine editor of note, he is best remembered for his poetry (especially "The Raven") and for his tales of suspense. Died at Baltimore, MD, Oct 7, 1849.

SCOTLAND: CELTIC CONNECTIONS. Jan 19–Feb 4. Royal Concert Hall, Glasgow. Much acclaimed festival with music from around the world. For info: Glasgow Royal Concert Hall, Glasgow, Strathclyde, Scotland. Phone: (44) (141) 353-8050. Fax: (44) (141) 353-8001.

SEWARD POLAR BEAR JUMP FESTIVAL. Jan 19–21. Resurrection Bay, Seward, AK. Volunteers collect pledges to jump into bay in costumes. Festivities include golf tournament, parade, dog weight pull, dogsled race, Polar Bear Expo/Trade Show, ski-joring, Bachelor/Bachelorette Auction, ice bowling, talent show, Seafood Feed and much more. Benefits local nonprofit organizations and the American Cancer Society. The actual "Plunge" takes place on Saturday, Jan 20. Est attendance: 2,500. For info: Seward Polar Bear Jump Fest, PO Box 386, Seward, AK 99664. Phone: (907) 224-5230. Fax: (907) 224-4085. E-mail: northern-nights@seward.net.

SOUTHWESTERN EXPOSITION LIVESTOCK SHOW AND RODEO. Jan 19–Feb 4. Fort Worth, TX. Western-flavored extravaganza. World's first indoor rodeo added in 1918 (45 acres under roof). Prize livestock (over 22,000 head) displays, horse shows, midway, commercial exhibits and quality family-oriented entertainment. Est attendance: 817,500. For info: Delbert Bailey, PO Box 150, Fort Worth, TX 76101-0150. Phone: (817) 877-2400. Fax: (817) 877-2499. Web: www.fwssr.com.

TIN CAN PATENT: ANNIVERSARY. Jan 19, 1825. Ezra Daggett and Thomas Kensett obtained a patent for a process for storing food in tin cans.

WATT, JAMES: BIRTH ANNIVERSARY. Jan 19, 1736 (OS). Scottish engineer and inventor, born at Greenock, Scotland. The modern steam engine grew out of his efficiency-improving inventions. Died at Heathfield, England, Aug 25, 1819.

WINGS OVER WILLCOX/SANDHILL CRANE CELEBRATION. Jan 19–21. Willcox, AZ. Tours to the Willcox Playa and Wetlands to see Sandhill Cranes, a Hawk Stalk tour, Plovers, Longspurs and much more. Visit Cochise Lake and see the waders. Workshops on wildlife. Seminars on birdwatching by various experts, a banquet, silent auction and a whole lot more. Est attendance: 1,000. For info: Willcox Chamber of Commerce. Phone: (800) 200-2272 or (520) 384-2272. Web: www.wingsoverwillcox.com.

BIRTHDAYS TODAY

Desi Arnaz, Jr, 48, singer, actor, born Los Angeles, CA, Jan 19, 1953.

Michael Crawford, 59, actor, singer (*Phantom of the Opera*), born Salisbury, Wiltshire, England, Jan 19, 1942.

Phil Everly, 62, singer, with brother Don (The Everly Brothers), born Brownie, KY, Jan 19, 1939.

Shelley Fabares, 59, actress ("The Donna Reed Show," "Coach," sang "Johnny Angel"), born Santa Monica, CA, Jan 19, 1942.

Richard Lester, 69, director (*The Four Musketeers, Superman II & III*), born Philadelphia, PA, Jan 19, 1932.

Robert MacNeil, 70, broadcast journalist, born Montreal, Quebec, Canada, Jan 19, 1931.

Dolly Parton, 55, singer ("Jolene"), actress (*Nine to Five*), born Sevier County, TN, Jan 19, 1946.

Javier Perez de Cuellar, 81, Peruvian diplomat, former UN Secretary General, born Lima, Peru, Jan 19, 1920.

William Ragsdale, 40, actor ("Brother's Keeper," "Herman's Head"), born El Dorado, AR, Jan 19, 1961.

Simon Rattle, 46, British orchestra conductor, born Liverpool, England, Jan 19, 1955.

Jean Stapleton (Jeanne Murray), 78, actress (*Klute*; Emmy for "All in the Family"), born New York, NY, Jan 19, 1923.

Fritz Weaver, 75, actor (*Holocaust, Marathon Man*), born Philadelphia, PA, Jan 19, 1926.

JANUARY 20 — SATURDAY
Day 20 — 345 Remaining

AFRMA FANCY RAT AND MOUSE ANNUAL SHOW.
Jan 20 or 27 (to be determined). Hacienda Heights, CA. Annual show where trophies are awarded to the winners. As urban sprawl continues to limit the space needed to keep dogs and cats, rats and mice as pets are emerging as an ideal substitute. They provide all the pleasure and satisfaction of a warm, cuddly, intelligent and friendly pet companion. The American Fancy Rat and Mouse Association (AFRMA) was founded in 1983 to promote and encourage the breeding and exhibition of fancy rats and mice, to educate the public on their positive qualities as companion animals and to provide information on their proper care. Est attendance: 100. For info: AFRMA (CAE), PO Box 2589, Winnetka, CA 91396-2589. Phone: (909) 685-2350. Fax: (818) 592-6590. E-mail: craigr@afrma.org. Web: www.afrma.org.

AQUARIUS, THE WATER CARRIER. Jan 20–Feb 19. In the astronomical/astrological zodiac, which divides the sun's apparent orbit into 12 segments, the period Jan 20–Feb 19 is identified, traditionally, as the sun-sign of Aquarius, the Water Carrier. The ruling planet is Uranus or Saturn.

BALD EAGLE APPRECIATION DAYS. Jan 20–21. Riverfront, Keokuk, IA. Features trained personnel stationed at observation points for viewing the American bald eagle. Indoor exhibits at Keosippi Mall and live eagle demonstrations. Est attendance: 10,000. For info: Kirk Brandenberger, Dir of Tourism, Keokuk Area Conv and Tourism Bureau, 329 Main, Keokuk, IA 52632. Phone: (800) 383-1219 or (319) 524-5599. Fax: (319) 524-5016. E-mail: keokukia@interl.net. Web: www.keokuktourism.com.

BRAZIL: NOSSO SENHOR DO BONFIM FESTIVAL.
Jan 20–30. Salvador, Bahia, Brazil. Our Lord of the Happy Ending Festival is one of Salvador's most colorful religious feasts. Climax comes with people carrying water to pour over church stairs and sidewalks to cleanse them of impurities.

BRAZIL: SAN SEBASTIAN'S DAY. Jan 20. Patron Saint of Rio de Janeiro.

BURNS, GEORGE: BIRTH ANNIVERSARY. Jan 20, 1896. Comedian George Burns was born at New York City. He began in vaudeville without much success until he teamed up with Gracie Allen, who became his wife. As Burns and Allen, the two had a long career on radio, in film and with their hit TV show, "The George Burns and Gracie Allen Show." More recently he played the role of God and the Devil in the *Oh, God!* movies. He lived to be 100, and died Mar 9, 1996 at Los Angeles, CA.

CAMCORDER DEVELOPED: ANNIVERSARY. Jan 20, 1982. Five companies (Hitachi, JVC, Philips, Matsushita and Sony) agreed to cooperate on the construction of a camera with a built-in videocassette recorder.

January *2001*	S	M	T	W	T	F	S
		1	2	3	4	5	6
	7	8	9	10	11	12	13
	14	15	16	17	18	19	20
	21	22	23	24	25	26	27
	28	29	30	31			

CHINESE NEW YEAR FESTIVAL. Jan 20–Feb 4. San Francisco, CA. North America's largest Chinese community salutes the Year of the Snake. Activities include Chinatown Flower Market Fair; Miss Chinatown USA Pageant with Coronation Ball; Chinese New Year Parade (Feb 3); Chinatown Community Street Fair, which showcases the diversity of Chinese culture from Chinese opera and ballet, traditional dance and ancient dynastic costumes to martial arts. Booths feature cooking demonstrations, calligraphy and arts and crafts. Est attendance: 700,000. For info: Chinese Chamber of Commerce, New Year Festival, 730 Sacramento, San Francisco, CA 94108. Phone: (415) 391-9680. Fax: (415) 982-4720.

DELCHAMP'S SENIOR BOWL FOOTBALL GAME. Jan 20. Ladd-Peebles Stadium, Mobile, AL. All-star football game featuring the nation's top collegiate seniors on teams coached by National Football League coaching staffs. Proceeds go to charities. 52nd annual. Est attendance: 40,700. For info: Vic Knight, PR Dir, Senior Bowl, 63 S Royal St, Ste 100, Mobile, AL 36602. Phone: (334) 438-2276. Fax: (334) 432-0409. E-mail: srbowl@seniorbowl.com. Web: www.seniorbowl.com.

EINSTEIN ON WINE. Jan 20. Tampa, FL. Fundraiser for MOSI Science Center held by BEAM (Be Enthusiastic About MOSI). Events include wine tastings, food and a silent auction. Est attendance: 1,500. For info: Mktg Dept, MOSI, 4801 E Fowler Ave, Tampa, FL 33617-2017. Phone: (813) 987-6000. Fax: (813) 987-6310.

FELLINI, FEDERICO: BIRTH ANNIVERSARY. Jan 20, 1920. Director and screenwriter Federico Fellini was born at Rimini, Italy. Four of Fellini's movies won Oscars for best foreign-language film: *La Strada* (1956), *The Nights of Cabiria* (1957), *8½* (1963) and *Amarcord* (1974). He received an honorary Oscar in 1993 in recognition of his cinematic accomplishments. Fellini died Oct 31, 1993, at Rome.

FUN-IN-THE-SUN POSTCARD SALE. Jan 20–21. Las Palmas Hotel, Orlando, FL. Sale of antique and modern postcards by 20 dealers. Est attendance: 300. For info: John H. McClintock, Dir, Postcard Soc, Inc, Box 1765, Manassas, VA 20108. Phone: (703) 368-2757.

GRAY, HAROLD LINCOLN: BIRTH ANNIVERSARY. Jan 20, 1894. The creator of *Little Orphan Annie* was born at Kankakee, IL. The comic strip featuring the 12-year-old Annie, her dog Sandy and her mentor and guardian Oliver "Daddy" Warbucks began appearing in the *Chicago Tribune* in 1924. While controversial for its strong conservative views, the strip was highly popular for its stories demonstrating the values of perseverance, independence and courage. Gray created the strip for 44 years until his death May 9, 1968, at La Jolla, CA, at age 74.

GUINEA-BISSAU: NATIONAL HEROES DAY. Jan 20. National holiday.

HULA BOWL MAUI ALL STAR CLASSIC. Jan 20. War Memorial Stadium, Kahului, Maui, HI. College all-star football classic. 55th annual. Est attendance: 23,000. For info: Hula Bowl Office, 1110 University Ave, Ste 403, Varsity Building, Honolulu, HI 96826-1508. Phone: (808) 947-4141. Fax: (808) 947-6648. E-mail: higames@aloha.net. Web: calendar.gohawaii.com/.

INAUGURATION DAY. Jan 20. The 20th Amendment provides that "The terms of the President and Vice President shall end at noon on the 20th day of January . . . and the terms of their successors shall then begin . . ." A quadrennial event and holiday in the District of Columbia. Today the 43rd president of the United States will be inaugurated. See also: "Old Inauguration Day" (Mar 4).

INAUGURATION DAY PUBLIC HOLIDAY OBSERVANCE. Jan 20. The US Code, Title 5, Section 6103(c) declares "January 20 of each fourth year after 1965, Inauguration Day, is a legal public holiday for the purpose of statutes relating to pay and leave of employees." Note: Title 5 concerns Government Organization and Employees.

JOHN MARSHALL APPOINTED CHIEF JUSTICE: 200th ANNIVERSARY. Jan 20, 1801. John Marshall was appointed chief justice of the US Supreme Court.

LEE, RICHARD HENRY: BIRTH ANNIVERSARY. Jan 20, 1732. Signer of the Declaration of Independence. Born at Westmoreland County, VA, he died June 19, 1794 at his birthplace.

LESOTHO: ARMY DAY. Jan 20. Lesotho.

MUSEUM OF AMERICAN GLASS: MID-WINTER EXHIBIT. Jan 20–Mar 4. Wheaton Village, Millville, NJ. "Curator's Choice" exhibit of fine glass items. Est attendance: 6,000. For info: Wheaton Village, 1501 Glasstown Rd, Millville, NJ 08332-1566. Phone: (856) 825-6800 or (800) 998-4552. Fax: (856) 825-2410. E-mail: mail@wheatonvillage.org. Web: www.wheatonvillage.org.

PAUL BUNYAN SLED DOG RACES, WEIGHT PULL, SKIJORING AND MUTT RACES. Jan 20–21. Lake Bemidji, Bemidji, MN. 29th annual competition. For info: Bemidji Area Chamber of Commerce, Box 850, Bemidji, MN 56619-0850. Phone: (800) 458-2223. Web: www.paulbunyan.net/paulbunyansleddograces.

PENGUIN AWARENESS DAY. Jan 20. Jenkinson's Aquarium, Point Pleasant Beach, NJ. Learn all about the African penguin families at Jenkinson's Aquarium and the status of penguins in the wild. Children will enjoy penguin storytelling as well as appearances by our mascot Perky the Penguin. Penguins are fed at 11 AM and 3:30 PM. Crafts and face painting 1–4 PM. Free buttons will be given away to the first 300 visitors. Est attendance: 600. For info: Liz Carletta, Education Coord, Jenkinson's Aquarium, 300 Ocean Ave, Point Pleasant Beach, NJ 08742. Phone: (732) 899-1212. Fax: (732) 899-1717. E-mail: aquarium@jenkinsons.com. Web: www.jenkinsons.com.

PHILIPPINES: ATI-ATIHAN FESTIVAL. Jan 20–21. Kalibo, Aklan. One of the most colorful celebrations in the Philippines, the Ati-Atihan Festival commemorates the peace pact between the Ati of Panay (pygmies) and the Malays, who were early migrants in the islands. The townspeople blacken their bodies with soot, don colorful and bizarre costumes and sing and dance in the streets. The festival also celebrates the Feast Day of Santo Niño (the infant Jesus). Annually, the third weekend in January.

TIP-UP TOWN USA™ 2001. Jan 20–21 (also Jan 27–28). Houghton Lake, MI. 51st annual. Michigan's largest winter festival featuring ice-fishing contests, softball on the ice, three polar bear dips, two parades, carnival, vendors, monster-truck rides, arts and crafts, fireworks, World's Longest Poker Run & Scavenger Hunt, Mid-week Snowmobile Drag Races and much more. Est attendance: 150,000. For info: Chamber of Commerce, 1625 W Houghton Lake Dr, Houghton Lake, MI 48629. Phone: (800) 248-5253. E-mail: hlcofc@freeway.net. Web: www.houghtonlakechamber.net.

US REVOLUTIONARY WAR: CESSATION OF HOSTILITIES: ANNIVERSARY. Jan 20, 1783. The British and US Commissioners signed a preliminary "Cessation of Hostilities," which was ratified by England's King George III Feb 14 and led to the Treaties of Paris and Versailles, Sept 3, 1783, ending the war.

WICHITA WEST BULLFEST. Jan 20. Multi-Purpose Events Center, J.S. Bridgewell Agricultural Center, Wichita Falls, TX. Bullriding at its best—local and area riders compete. Est attendance: 2,500. For info: Wichita Falls Conv & Visitors Bureau, 1000 5th St, Wichita Falls, TX 76301. Phone: (940) 716-5500 or (940) 691-2738. Fax: (940) 716-5509. E-mail: MPEC@wf.net. Web: www.viewscape.com or www.wf.net.

WISCONSIN DELLS FLAKE OUT FESTIVAL. Jan 20–21. Noah's Ark Waterpark, Wisconsin Dells, WI. Wisconsin-sanctioned snow sculpting competition. Winners will compete in the National Snow Sculpting Competition. Other activities include ice carving demonstrations, snowman making, turkey bowling, sleigh rides,

ice skating, glowing hot-air balloons on Saturday evening and much more. Est attendance: 20,000. For info: Angie Rizner, Wisconsin Dells Visitors Bureau, PO Box 390, Wisconsin Dells, WI 53965. Phone: (800) 223-3557. E-mail: info@wisdells.com. Web: www.wisdells.com.

BIRTHDAYS TODAY

Edwin "Buzz" Aldrin, 71, former astronaut, one of first three men on moon, born Montclair, NJ, Jan 20, 1930.

Arte Johnson, 67, comedian, actor (Emmy for "Rowan & Martin's Laugh-In"), born Chicago, IL, Jan 20, 1934.

Lorenzo Lamas, 43, actor ("Falcon Crest," "Renegade"), born Los Angeles, CA, Jan 20, 1958.

David Lynch, 55, director ("Twin Peaks," *Blue Velvet*), writer, producer, born Missoula, MT, Jan 20, 1946.

Bill Maher, 45, comedian, TV host ("Politically Incorrect with Bill Maher"), born New York, NY, Jan 20, 1956.

Patricia Neal, 75, actress (*Breakfast at Tiffany's, Hud, The Subject Was Roses*), born Packard, NY, Jan 20, 1926.

Natan (Anatoly) Scharansky, 53, expatriate Soviet dissident, born Donetsk, USSR, Jan 20, 1948.

Skeet Ulrich, 32, actor (*Scream*), born New York, NY, Jan 20, 1969.

Otis Dewey "Slim" Whitman, 77, singer (first country performer to play at the London Palladium), born Tampa, FL, Jan 20, 1924.

JANUARY 21 — SUNDAY
Day 21 — 344 Remaining

ALLEN, ETHAN: BIRTH ANNIVERSARY. Jan 21, 1738. Revolutionary War hero and leader of the Vermont "Green Mountain Boys." Born at Litchfield, CT, he died at Burlington, VT, Feb 12, 1789.

BALDWIN, ROGER NASH: BIRTH ANNIVERSARY. Jan 21, 1884. Founder of the American Civil Liberties Union, called the "country's unofficial agitator for, and defender of, its civil liberties." Born at Wellesley, MA, he died Aug 26, 1981, at Ridgewood, NJ.

BRECKINRIDGE, JOHN CABELL: BIRTH ANNIVERSARY. Jan 21, 1821. 14th vice president of the US (1857–61), serving under President James Buchanan. Born at Lexington, KY; died there May 17, 1875.

BROWNING, JOHN MOSES: BIRTH ANNIVERSARY. Jan 21, 1855. World famous gunmaker and inventor who was taught gunsmithing by his Mormon pioneer father, Jonathan Browning, was born at Ogden, UT. Starting the J.M. & M.S. Browning Arms Company with his brother, he designed guns for Winchester, Remington, Stevens and Colt arms companies, as well as American and European armies. Browning had more gun patents than any other gunsmith in the world. He is best known worldwide for inventing the machine gun in 1890 and the automatic pistol in 1896. He died suddenly Nov 26, 1926, at age 71, while at Belgium on business. The company he founded, known now as Browning Arms Company, is located at Morgan, UT.

FIRST CONCORDE FLIGHT: 25th ANNIVERSARY.
Jan 21, 1976. The supersonic Concorde airplane was put into service by Britain and France.

HEALTHY WEIGHT WEEK. Jan 21–27. People who diet the first week in January and blow it the second are ready for eating and living in healthier ways by the third week—Healthy Weight Week. This is a week to learn healthy lifestyle habits that last a lifetime and prevent weight problems, rather than cause them, as dieting does. For info: Francie M. Berg Editor/Publisher, Healthy Weight Journal, 402 S 14th St, Hettinger, ND 58639. Phone: (701) 567-2646. Fax: (701) 567-2602. E-mail: hwj@healthy-weight.net. Web: www.healthyweight.net.

JACKSON, THOMAS JONATHAN "STONEWALL": BIRTH ANNIVERSARY. Jan 21, 1824. Confederate general and one of the most famous soldiers of the American Civil War, best known as "Stonewall" Jackson. Born at Clarksburg, VA (now WV). He died of wounds received in battle near Chancellorsville, VA, May 10, 1863.

KIWANIS INTERNATIONAL: ANNIVERSARY. Jan 21, 1915. First Kiwanis Club chartered at Detroit, MI.

LEE BIRTHDAY CELEBRATIONS. Jan 21. Alexandria, VA. The birthdays of Revolutionary War Colonel "Light Horse Harry" Lee and his son Civil War General Robert E. Lee are celebrated at the Lee-Fendall House. Refreshments, period music, house tours. Admission. Est attendance: 125. For info: Marketing Coordinator, Alexandria Conv and Visitors Assn, 221 King St, Alexandria, VA 22314. Phone: (703) 838-4200. Fax: (703) 838-4683. E-mail: acva@FunSide.com. Web: www.FunSide.com.

MARGARET BRENT DEMANDS A POLITICAL VOICE: ANNIVERSARY. Jan 21, 1648. Margaret Brent made her claim as America's first feminist by demanding a voice and vote for herself in the Maryland colonial assembly. Brent came to America in 1638 and was the first woman to own property in Maryland. At the time of her demands she was serving as secretary to Governor Leonard Calvert. She was ejected from the meetings, but when Calvert died she became his executor and acting governor, presiding over the General Assembly.

NATIONAL CREATIVE FRUGALITY WEEK. Jan 21–27. Christmas has come and gone and for many Americans the credit card bills are now rolling in. Give your budget a break by participating in National Creative Frugality Week. Participants are encouraged to have fun as they experiment with frugality and resourcefulness. Whether you're new to frugal living or have been doing it for years, use this holiday to challenge yourself to learn a new skill or try a new money-saving technique. For info: Nancy Twigg, Editor, Counting the Cost Newsletter, 8715 Brucewood Ln, Knoxville, TN 37923. Phone: (865) 531-3947. E-mail: counting.the.cost@excite.com. Web: www.countingthecost.com.

NATIONAL HUGGING DAY™. Jan 21. Since hugging is something everyone can do and since it is a healthful form of touching, this day should be spent hugging anyone who will accept a hug, especially family and friends. The most "Huggable People" of the year will be announced. Nominations accepted through Jan 10. For more info, please send SASE to: Kevin C. Zaborney, PO Box 64, Fairgrove, MI 48733-0064. Phone: (517) 693-6666. E-mail: holidaymaker@loveslife.com. Web: holidaymaker.loveslife.com.

NATIONAL NURSE ANESTHETISTS WEEK. Jan 21–27. To provide recognition for the nation's 27,000 certified registered nurse anesthetists (CRNAs), who have been providing safe anesthesia care for more than 100 years. CRNAs administer more than 65 percent of the anesthesia in the US each year. For info:

Christopher Bettin, PR Dir, Amer Assn of Nurse Anesthetists, 222 S Prospect, Park Ridge, IL 60068. Phone: (847) 692-7050. Fax: (847) 692-6968. Web: www.aana.com.

SAN DIEGO MARATHON & HALF MARATHON. Jan 21. Plaza Camino Real, Carlsbad, CA. Race open to runners, walkers, race walkers and disabled. Post-race festival with refreshments, entertainment, massages and more. Friday and Saturday (Jan 19–20) is the All About Fitness Expo under the Big Top at the Plaza Camino Real. For info: San Diego Marathon, 511 S Cedros Ave, Solana Beach, CA 92075. Phone: (858) 792-2900. E-mail: imisdm@aol.com.

SOLO–PRENEURING WEEK. Jan 21–27. Control your own destiny by taking charge of your work and your life. This week is set aside to plan and prepare for the work you were meant to do, and to celebrate those who are following a path of their own choosing. Whether you are an employee, a business owner, or just contemplating your place in the workforce, resolve to learn how you can do work that is satisfying and fulfilling, create your own job security, prepare for an uncertain future, and have fun doing work you love. Free articles available for publishers and webmasters at IdeaLady.com/content.htm. For info: Cathy Stucker, Special Interests Publishing, 4646 Hwy 6, PMB 123, Sugar Land, TX 77478. Phone: (281) 265-7342. Fax: (281) 265-9727. E-mail: cathy@idealady.com. Web: www.idealady.com.

TOPS CLUB, INC: ANNIVERSARY. Jan 21. Milwaukee, WI. TOPS (Take Off Pounds Sensibly) is the leading, international, non-profit weight-loss support group. Founded in 1948 in Milwaukee, WI, by Esther Manz, a homemaker, TOPS has grown to almost 300,000 members in 11,700 chapters worldwide. It is dedicated to providing its members with information, motivation and fellowship in attaining and maintaining physician-prescribed weight-loss goals. For info: Susan Trones, TOPS Club Inc, 4575 S Fifth St, Milwaukee, WI 53207. Phone: (414) 482-4620 or (800) 932-8677. Web: www.tops.org.

WOLFMAN JACK: BIRTH ANNIVERSARY. Jan 21, 1938. Wolfman Jack was born Robert Smith at Brooklyn, NY. He became famous as a disc jockey for radio stations at Mexico in the 1960s. Wolfman Jack was influential as a border radio voice because the Mexican station broadcast at 250,000 watts, five times the legal limit for American stations at the time, and therefore he was heard over a vast part of the US. During his night shift he played blues, hillbilly, and other black and white music that wasn't getting a lot of exposure. He later appeared on American radio, movies and television as an icon of 1960s radio. Wolfman Jack died July 1, 1995, at Belvidere, NC.

WORLD RELIGION DAY. Jan 21. To proclaim the oneness of religion and the belief that world religion will unify the peoples of the earth. Baha'i-sponsored observance established in 1950 by the Baha'is of the US. Annually, the third Sunday in January. For info: Dir, Bahai's of the US, Office of Public Information, 866 UN Plaza, Ste 120, New York, NY 10017-1822. Phone: (212) 803-2500. Fax: (212) 803-2573. E-mail: usopi-ny@bic.org. Web: www.us.bahai.org.

BIRTHDAYS TODAY

Robbie Benson (Robert Segal), 45, actor ("Search for Tomorrow," *Ode to Billie Joe*), born Dallas, TX, Jan 21, 1956.

Geena Davis, 44, actress (Oscar for *The Accidental Tourist*; *Thelma and Louise*, "Buffalo Bill"), born Ware, MA, Jan 21, 1957.

Mac Davis, 59, actor, songwriter ("The Mac Davis Show," *North Dallas Forty*), born Lubbock, TX, Jan 21, 1942.

Placido Domingo, 60, opera singer, one of the "Three Tenors," born Madrid, Spain, Jan 21, 1941.

Jill Eikenberry, 54, actress ("LA Law"), born New Haven, CT, Jan 21, 1947.

Gary Locke, 51, Governor of Washington (D), born Seattle, WA, Jan 21, 1950.

Jack William Nicklaus, 61, golfer, born Columbus, OH, Jan 21, 1940.

	S	M	T	W	T	F	S
January		1	2	3	4	5	6
2001	7	8	9	10	11	12	13
	14	15	16	17	18	19	20
	21	22	23	24	25	26	27
	28	29	30	31			

Billy Ocean, 51, musician, songwriter, born London, England, Jan 21, 1950.

Hakeem Abdul Olajuwon, 38, basketball player, born Lagos, Nigeria, Jan 21, 1963.

Detlef Schrempf, 38, basketball player, born Leverkusen, West Germany, Jan 21, 1963.

Paul Scofield, 79, actor (*A Man for All Seasons, Quiz Show*; stage: *A Man for All Seasons*), born Hurstpierpoint, England, Jan 21, 1922.

JANUARY 22 — MONDAY
Day 22 — 343 Remaining

ALLIED LANDING AT ANZIO: ANNIVERSARY. Jan 22, 1944. A predominately American Allied force of 36,000 men was landed at Anzio on Italy's western coast. Commanding officer John P. Lucas failed to take the initiative but instead fortified his original position and thus possibly missed an early opportunity to retake Rome. The Allies entered Rome more than four months later, June 4, 1944.

ALLIES TAKE NEW GUINEA: ANNIVERSARY. Jan 22, 1943. In the first land victory over the Japanese in World War II, American and Australian soldiers overcame the last pockets of resistance west and south of Sanananda on New Guinea. Three thousand Allies were killed in the battle. The Japanese lost 7,000. Of the 350 prisoners taken, most were Chinese and Korean laborers attached to the Japanese forces. Almost no Japanese allowed themselves to be taken prisoner, preferring to commit hara-kiri than to surrender.

AMPÈRE, ANDRE: BIRTH ANNIVERSARY. Jan 22, 1775. Physicist, student of electrical and magnetic phenomena, founder of the science of electrodynamics. Born at Lyons, France, from his early childhood, tragedy and depression pursued him. His father was executed during the French Revolution. Ampère died at Marseilles, France, June 10, 1836. The epitaph he selected for his tombstone was *tandem felix* ("happy at last"). The ampere, a unit of electrical current, is named for him.

ANSWER YOUR CAT'S QUESTION DAY. Jan 22. If you will stop what you are doing and take a look at your cat, you will observe that the cat is looking at you with a serious question. Meditate upon it, then answer the question! Annually, Jan 22. [© 2000 by WH] For info: Tom or Ruth Roy, Wellcat Holidays, 2418 Long Ln, Lebanon, PA 17046. Phone: (717) 279-0184. E-mail: wellcat@supernet.com. Web: www.wellcat.com.

BACON, FRANCIS: BIRTH ANNIVERSARY. Jan 22, 1561. Statesman and essayist, born at London, England. One may guess that Bacon was of short stature as he wrote (*Apothegms*), "Wise nature did never put her precious jewels into a garret four stories high: and therefore . . . exceeding tall men had ever very empty heads." Died at London, Apr 9, 1626.

BALANCHINE, GEORGE: BIRTH ANNIVERSARY. Jan 22, 1904. Born Georgi Militonovitch Balanchivadze at St. Petersburg, Russia, George Balanchine became one of the leading influences in 20th-century ballet. He choreographed more than 200 ballets including *Concerto Barocco, Apollo, Orpheus, Firebird, Swan Lake, Waltz Academy* and *The Nutcracker*. In 1933 he was invited to the US by Boston philanthropist Lincoln Kirstein to establish a school for American dancers. Together they founded the School of American Ballet in 1934 and then formed several ballet companies, including the New York City Ballet, which was led by Balanchine. Died at New York, NY, Apr 30, 1983.

CELEBRATION OF LIFE DAY. Jan 22. Celebrated each year as a day to recognize the value, the gift and the life of ourselves and our children and grandchildren in America. Each child and each life is held as a precious gift and should be treated with the highest respect and dignity of human life. A day to celebrate the gift of life. For info: Judith Natale, CEO & Founder, Natl Children & Family Awareness of America, Administrative Headquarters, 3060 Rt 405 Hwy, Muncy, PA 17756-8808. Phone: (888) MAA-DESK. E-mail: MaaJudith@aol.com.

CHAMPAGNES FRANCE DAY. Jan 22. New York, NY. A date which coincides with Saint Vincent's Day in France, honoring the patron saint of vine growers. Champagnes France Day, held by the Champagne Wines Information Bureau, celebrates the uniqueness of Champagne wines and reminds us that Champagne only comes from La Champagne, France. The day also marks the annual culmination of the Champagnes France Challenge, a national contest aimed at creating greater awareness of, and interest in, Champagne wines. Annually, every Jan 22. For info: Jean-Louis Carbonnier, Champagne Wines Information Bureau, 800 Second Ave, New York, NY 10017. Phone: (212) 682-6300, ext 203 or (800) 64-CHAMPagne. Fax: (212) 697-0910. E-mail: info@champagnes.com. Web: www.champagnes.com.

DIRECT DEPOSIT WEEK. Jan 22–26. Encouraging people to use the faster, safer, smarter way of getting paid by using payroll direct deposit. For info: Rossana Czelusniak, Communications & Mktg, Electronic Payments Network, 1500 Harbor Blvd, Weehawken, NJ 07087. Phone: (201) 319-5477. Fax: (201) 319-5455. E-mail: webmaster@nych.org. Web: www.ezpay.org.

"EMERGENCY!" TV PREMIERE: ANNIVERSARY. Jan 22, 1972. This NBC program was introduced in midseason up against "All in the Family." It surprised everyone by becoming quite popular. The fast-paced action of the fire department paramedics saving lives by giving victims emergency treatment and then taking them to the hospital demonstrated the steps taken during actual emergency situations. The last episode aired Sept 3, 1977.

GRIFFITH, DAVID (LEWELYN) WARK: BIRTH ANNIVERSARY. Jan 22, 1875. D.W. Griffith, pioneer producer-director in the American motion picture industry, best remembered for his film *Birth of a Nation* (1915). Born at LaGrange, KY. Died at Hollywood, CA, July 23, 1948.

"LAUGH-IN" TV PREMIERE: ANNIVERSARY. Jan 22, 1968. Actually the name of this NBC comedy was "Rowan and Martin's Laugh-In." Funny men Dan Rowan and Dick Martin hosted the show, but they seemed staid next to the show's other regulars, most of whom were young unknowns, including Dennis Allen, Chelsea Brown, Judy Carne, Ruth Buzzi, Ann Elder, Richard Dawson, Teresa Graves, Arte Johnson, Goldie Hawn, Alan Sues, Jo Anne Worley and Lily Tomlin. The show moved fast from gag to gag with heads popping out of bushes or doors in the big wall. The show brought a new energy to comedy as well as new phrases to our vocabulary ("You bet your sweet bippy," "Sock it to me"). The last telecast was May 14, 1973.

"OZARK JUBILEE" TV PREMIERE: ANNIVERSARY. Jan 22, 1955. ABC country and western music show hosted by Red Foley from Springfield, MO. Brenda "(Open Up Your Heart and) Let the Sunshine In" Lee appeared on the show at age 10 as one of the regulars. Other regulars included Smiley Burnette, Bobby Lord, Wanda Jackson, Suzi Arden and Webb Pierce.

PONSELLE, ROSA: BIRTH ANNIVERSARY. Jan 22, 1897. Formerly Rosa Melba Ponzilla, soprano Ponselle was born at Meriden, CT. Her career changed direction from vaudeville to opera when she was discovered by Enrico Caruso at the age of 21. Ponselle made her operatic debut at the Met in Verdi's *La forza del destino.* Her career spanned 19 seasons at the Met, and included performances at London and Florence. Ponselle died May 25, 1981, at Baltimore.

QUEEN VICTORIA: 100th DEATH ANNIVERSARY. Jan 22, 1901. Queen Victoria died at age 82 after a reign of 64 years, the longest in British history. She had ruled over the one-quarter of the world that was the British Empire. Born May 24, 1819, at London, she died at Osborne, England.

ROE v WADE DECISION: ANNIVERSARY. Jan 22, 1973. In the case of *Roe v Wade*, the US Supreme Court struck down state laws restricting abortions during the first six months of pregnancy. In the following two decades debate has continued to rage between those who believe a woman has a right to choose whether to continue a pregnancy and those who believe that aborting such a pregnancy is murder of an unborn child.

SAINT VINCENT'S FEAST DAY. Jan 22. Spanish deacon and martyr who died AD 304. Patron saint of wine growers. Old weather lore says if there is sun on this day, good wine crops may be expected in the ensuing season.

SOCIETY FOR THE PRESERVATION & ENCOURAGEMENT OF BARBER SHOP QUARTET SINGING IN AMERICA (SPEBSQSA) MID-WINTER CONVENTION. Jan 22–28. Jacksonville, FL. Members meet for administrative conferences, shows and contest to select national Seniors Quartet Champion. Est attendance: 1,200. For info: Crystal Miller, Mktg & Public Relations Coord, SPEBSQSA, Inc, 6315 Third Ave, Kenosha, WI 53143. Phone: (800) 876-SING. E-mail: cmiller@spebsqsa.org. Web: www.spebsqsa.org.

STRINDBERG, AUGUST: BIRTH ANNIVERSARY. Jan 22, 1849. Swedish novelist and dramatist often called Sweden's greatest playwright. Born at Stockholm and died there of cancer on May 14, 1912, at age 63.

UPJOHN, RICHARD: BIRTH ANNIVERSARY. Jan 22, 1802. American architect and founder of the American Institute of Architects in 1857. A Gothic revivalist, he designed many churches. Among his works were Trinity Chapel, New York, NY; Corn Exchange Bank Building, New York, NY; Central Congregational Church, Boston, MA. Born at Shaftesbury, England, he died Aug 17, 1878, at Garrison, NY.

VINSON, FRED M.: BIRTH ANNIVERSARY. Jan 22, 1890. The 13th Chief Justice of the US, born at Louisa, KY. Served in the House of Representatives, appointed Director of War Mobilization during WWII and Secretary of the Treasury under Harry Truman. Nominated by Truman to succeed Harlan F. Stone as Chief Justice of the US Supreme Court. Died at Washington, DC, Sept 8, 1953.

	S	M	T	W	T	F	S
January		1	2	3	4	5	6
	7	8	9	10	11	12	13
2001	14	15	16	17	18	19	20
	21	22	23	24	25	26	27
	28	29	30	31			

BIRTHDAYS TODAY

Linda Blair, 42, actress (*The Exorcist, Airport*), born Westport, CT, Jan 22, 1959.

Seymour Cassell, 64, actor (*Faces, Dick Tracy, Honeymoon in Vegas*), born Detroit, MI, Jan 22, 1937.

Olivia D'Abo, 34, actress ("The Wonder Years," "The Single Guy"), born London, England, Jan 22, 1967.

Balthazar Getty, 26, actor (*Lost Highway*), born Los Angeles, CA, Jan 22, 1975.

John Hurt, 61, actor ("And the Band Played On," *The Elephant Man*), born Lincolnshire, England, Jan 22, 1940.

Diane Lane, 36, actress (*A Little Romance, Rumble Fish*), born New York, NY, Jan 22, 1965.

Piper Laurie (Rosetta Jacobs), 69, actress (*Fighting for My Daughter*, "Twin Peaks"), born Detroit, MI, Jan 22, 1932.

Steve Perry, 52, lead singer (Journey), born Hanford, CA, Jan 22, 1949.

Joseph Wambaugh, 64, author, ex-police officer (*The Blooding, Fugitive Nights*), born East Pittsburgh, PA, Jan 22, 1937.

JANUARY 23 — TUESDAY
Day 23 — 342 Remaining

"BARNEY MILLER" TV PREMIERE: ANNIVERSARY. Jan 23, 1975. ABC sitcom about a New York precinct captain starred Hal Linden as Captain Barney Miller. The 12th Precinct gang included Barbara Barrie as Miller's wife, Abe Vigoda as Detective Phil Fish, Max Gail as Sergeant Stan Wojciehowicz, Gregory Sierra as Sergeant Chano Amenguale, Jack Soo as Sergeant Nick Yemana, Ron Glass as Detective Ron Harris and a host of others.

BLACKWELL, ELIZABETH, AWARDED MD: ANNIVERSARY. Jan 23, 1849. Dr. Elizabeth Blackwell became the first woman to receive an MD degree. The native of Bristol, England, was awarded her degree by the Medical Institution of Geneva, NY.

BULGARIA: BABIN DEN. Jan 23. Celebrated throughout Bulgaria as Day of the Midwives or Grandmother's Day. Traditional festivities.

CARTER REINSTATES SELECTIVE SERVICE REGISTRATION: ANNIVERSARY. Jan 23, 1980. President Jimmy Carter, saying he planned to "revitalize" the Selective Service System, reinstated registration and pledged to use military force, if necessary, to protect the Persian Gulf from Soviet aggression.

HEWES, JOSEPH: BIRTH ANNIVERSARY. Jan 23, 1730. Signer of the Declaration of Independence. Born at Princeton, NJ, he died Nov 10, 1779 at Philadelphia, PA.

"THE KING FAMILY SHOW" TV PREMIERE: ANNIVERSARY. Jan 23, 1965. ABC musical variety show featuring the singing and playing of the King sisters and other descendents of William King Driggs, who organized the family musical group in the 1930s. Including spouses, children, grandchildren and great-grandchildren, some three dozen members of the King family have appeared on camera at one time.

KOVACS, ERNIE: BIRTH ANNIVERSARY. Jan 23, 1919. Comedian and television pioneer, born at Trenton, NJ. Throughout the '40s and '50s Ernie Kovacs made a name for himself hosting his own shows including "The Ernie Kovacs Show" and "Ernie In Kovacsland" and a variety of quiz shows. He died in an automobile accident at Los Angeles, Jan 13, 1962.

MANET, ÉDOUARD: BIRTH ANNIVERSARY. Jan 23, 1832. Painter born at Paris, France. Among his best-known paintings are *Olympia* and *Déjeuner sur l'herbe.* Manet died Apr 30, 1883, at Paris.

RID THE WORLD OF FAD DIETS AND GIMMICKS DAY. Jan 23. The "worst" weight loss products and programs of the year are announced—the 10th annual Slim Chance Awards—by Healthy Weight Network and the National Council

Against Health Fraud. Diet quackery defrauds, disables and kills. List of 2001 awards plus diet quackery information available. For info: Francie M. Berg, Editor/Publisher, Healthy Weight Network, 402 S 14th St, Hettinger, ND 58639. Phone: (701) 567-2646. Fax: (701) 567-2602. E-mail: hwj@healthyweight.net. Web: www.healthyweight.net.

SONORA SHOWCASE. Jan 23–24. Yuma, AZ. A fiesta to promote the state of Sonora, Mexico, features dancers, food and beverage samples, vacation information and curios. Est attendance: 4,500. For info: Mktg Dept, Yuma Civic and Conv Ctr, 1440 Desert Hills Dr, Yuma, AZ 85365. Phone: (520) 344-3800. Fax: (520) 344-9121.

STENDHAL: BIRTH ANNIVERSARY. Jan 23, 1783. French author Marie Henri Beyle, whose best-known pseudonym was Stendhal. Best remembered are his novels *The Red and the Black* (1831) and *The Charterhouse of Parma* (1839). Born at Grenoble, France, he died at Paris, Mar 23, 1842.

STEWART, POTTER: BIRTH ANNIVERSARY. Jan 23, 1915. Associate Justice of the Supreme Court of the US, nominated by President Eisenhower Jan 17, 1959. (Oath of office, May 15, 1959.) Born at Jackson, MI, he retired in July 1981 and died Dec 7, 1985, at Putney, VT, five days after suffering a stroke. Buried at Arlington National Cemetery.

TWENTIETH AMENDMENT TO US CONSTITUTION RATIFIED: ANNIVERSARY. Jan 23, 1933. The 20th Amendment was ratified, fixing the date of the presidential inauguration at the current Jan 20 instead of the previous Mar 4. It also specified that were the president-elect to die before taking office, the vice president-elect would succeed to the presidency. In addition, it set Jan 3 as the official opening date of Congress each year.

TWENTY-FOURTH AMENDMENT TO US CONSTITUTION RATIFIED: ANNIVERSARY. Jan 23, 1964. Poll taxes and other taxes were eliminated as a prerequisite for voting in all federal elections by the 24th Amendment.

USS *PUEBLO* SEIZED BY NORTH KOREA: ANNIVERSARY. Jan 23, 1968. North Korea seized the USS *Pueblo* in the Sea of Japan, claiming the ship was on a spy mission. The crew was held for 11 months. The vessel was confiscated. Accompanying the crew when they were released—on Dec 22, 1968— was the body of Seaman Duane D. Hodges, the only crewman killed.

BIRTHDAYS TODAY

Richard Dean Anderson, 51, actor ("General Hospital," "MacGyver"), born Minneapolis, MN, Jan 23, 1950.

Princess Caroline, 44, born Monte Carlo, Monaco, Jan 23, 1957.

Tom Carper, 54, Governor of Delaware (D), born Beckley, WV, Jan 23, 1947.

Gil Gerard, 58, actor ("Buck Rogers," "Sidekicks"), born Little Rock, AR, Jan 23, 1943.

Patrick Capper (Pat) Haden, 48, sportscaster, former football player, born Westbury, NY, Jan 23, 1953.

Rutger Hauer, 57, actor (*Blade Runner*), born Breukelen, Netherlands, Jan 23, 1944.

Frank R. Lautenberg, 77, US Senator (D, New Jersey), born Paterson, NJ, Jan 23, 1924.

Jeanne Moreau, 73, actress (*Jules and Jim, Viva Maria*), born Paris, France, Jan 23, 1928.

Gail O'Grady, 38, actress ("NYPD Blue"), born Detroit, MI, Jan 23, 1963.

Chita Rivera (Conchita del Rivero), 68, singer, actress (*The Kiss of the Spider Woman*, "The New Dick Van Dyke Show"), born Washington, DC, Jan 23, 1933.

Tiffani-Amber Thiessen, 27, actress ("Beverly Hills 90210," "Saved by the Bell," *Son-in-Law*), born Long Beach, CA, Jan 23, 1974.

JANUARY 24 — WEDNESDAY
Day 24 — 341 Remaining

ACHELIS, ELISABETH: BIRTH ANNIVERSARY. Jan 24, 1880. Calendar reform advocate, author of *The World Calendar*, born at Brooklyn, NY. Her proposed calendar made every year the same, with equal quarters, each year beginning on Sunday, Jan 1, and each date falling on same day of week every year. Died at New York, NY, Feb 11, 1973.

BOLIVIA: ALACITIS FAIR. Jan 24–26. La Paz. Traditional annual celebration by Aymara Indians with prayers and offerings to god of prosperity.

BRICKHOUSE, JACK: BIRTH ANNIVERSARY. Jan 24, 1916. Born John Beasley Brickhouse at Peoria, IL. A legend in Chicago broadcasting, Brickhouse was the play-by-play voice for the first baseball game televised by WGN, an exhibition game between the Cubs and the White Sox on Apr 16, 1948. He broadcasted Cubs games for 40 years, Chicago Bears games for 24 years and some Chicago Bulls and White Sox games. In 1983, he received the Ford C. Frick Award. Died at Chicago, IL, Aug 6, 1998.

CALIFORNIA GOLD DISCOVERY: ANNIVERSARY. Jan 24, 1848. James W. Marshal, an employee of John Sutter, accidentally discovered gold while building a sawmill near Coloma, CA. Efforts to keep the discovery secret failed, and the gold rush of 1849 was under way.

CHINESE NEW YEAR. Jan 24. Traditional Chinese lunar year falls on the first day of the first lunar month; it follows the winter solstice. The New Year can begin any time from Jan 10 through Feb 19. Begins year 4699 of the ancient Chinese calendar, designated as the Year of the Snake. Generally celebrated until the Lantern Festival 15 days later, but merchants usually reopen their stores and places of business on the fifth day of the first lunar month (Jan 28, 2001). This holiday is celebrated as Tet in Vietnam. See also: "China: Lantern Festival" (Feb 7).

FDR's "UNCONDITIONAL SURRENDER" STATEMENT: ANNIVERSARY. Jan 24, 1943. At the end of the Casablanca Conference, 1943, Franklin D. Roosevelt and Winston Churchill held a press conference. Roosevelt stated, "Peace can come to the world only by the total elimination of German and Japanese war power. That means the unconditional surrender of Germany, Italy and Japan." This position calling for "unconditional surrender" has subsequently been criticized by some as having prolonged the war.

"THE FIGHT OF THE WEEK" TV PREMIERE: ANNIVERSARY. Jan 24, 1953. For 11 years, you could catch a boxing match every week on TV. Jack Drees announced the matches the first few seasons; Don Dunphy succeeded him.

FIRST CANNED BEER: ANNIVERSARY. Jan 24, 1935. Canned beer went on sale for the first time, at Richmond, VA.

GOODSON, MARK: BIRTH ANNIVERSARY. Jan 24, 1915. Producer and creator of TV game shows, Mark Goodson was born at Sacramento, CA. His career in entertainment began in radio where he created his first game show, "Pop the Question." He later teamed with Bill Todman and that partnership led to "What's My Line?," "I've Got a Secret," "Password," "The Price Is Right" and "Family Feud." He died Dec 18, 1992, at New York, NY.

JUST DO IT DAY—MAKE THE CONNECTION. Jan 24. This is the day to honor "you" and to connect people and places. This is the day to plan a vacation or arrange to journey with a new travel companion rather than travel solo! This is the day to connect the "link," you select the "from" and "to." Annually, the third Wednesday in January. For info: Joy Babock, JoyLinks— Wedding Links, Travel links, Single Travelers Links, 666 Main St, Ste 210, Watertown, MA 02472. Phone: (617) 924-6840. E-mail: joy@joylinks.com. Web: joylinks.com.

MOON PHASE: NEW MOON. Jan 24. Moon enters New Moon phase at 8:07 AM, EST.

NATIONAL COMPLIMENT DAY. Jan 24. This day is set aside to compliment at least five people. Not only are compliments appreciated by the receiver, they lift the spirit of the giver. Compliments provide a quick and easy way to connect positively with those you come in contact with. Giving compliments forges bonds, dispels loneliness and just plain feels good. Annually, the fourth Wednesday in January. For info: Debby Hoffman, Positive Results Seminars, 12 Campion Circle, Concord, NH 03303-3410. Phone: (603) 225-0991. E-mail: prseminars@compuserve.com. or Katherine Chamberlin, Heart to Heart Seminars, 724 Park Ave, Contoocook, NH 03229-3089. Phone: (603) 746-6227. E-mail: Kathiecham@aol.com

NATIONAL SCHOOL NURSE DAY. Jan 24. A day to honor and recognize the school nurse, School Nurse Day has been established to foster a better understanding of the role of school nurses in the educational setting. Annually, the fourth Wednesday in January. Brochures available for purchase. For info: Judy Barker, Adm Asst, Natl Assn of School Nurses, Inc, PO Box 1300, Scarborough, ME 04070-1300. Phone: (207) 883-2117. Fax: (207) 883-2683. E-mail: nasnweb@aol.com.

PONTIAC SILVERDOME CAMPER, TRAVEL AND RV SHOW. Jan 24–28. Pontiac Silverdome, Pontiac, MI. This event brings together buyers and sellers of RVs, motor homes, campers and camping accessories, as well as buyers and sellers of camping vacations and travel destinations. Est attendance: 30,000. For info: Mike Wilbraham, ShowSpan, Inc, 1400 28th St SW, Grand Rapids, MI 49509. Phone: (616) 530-1919. Fax: (616) 530-2122.

SIOUX EMPIRE FARM SHOW. Jan 24–27. Sioux Falls, SD. Winter farm and livestock show featuring all classes of livestock, commercial exhibits, horse pull, consumer programs and a women's show. Est attendance: 30,000. For info: Sioux Empire Farm Show, Chamber of Commerce, 200 N Phillips Ave, #102, Sioux Falls, SD 57104. Phone: (605) 373-2016. Fax: (605) 336-6499. E-mail: agbus@siouxfalls.org.

SPACE MILESTONE: *COSMOS 954* (USSR) FALLS. Jan 24, 1978. Nuclear-equipped reconnaissance satellite launched Sept 18, 1977. Fell into Earth's atmosphere and burned over northern Canada. Some radioactive debris reached ground on Jan 24, 1978.

SPACE MILESTONE: *DISCOVERY* (US). Jan 24, 1985. Space shuttle *Discovery* launched from and returned to Kennedy Space Center, FL, deploying eavesdropping satellite in secret, all-military mission, Jan 24–27, 1985.

WHARTON, EDITH: BIRTH ANNIVERSARY. Jan 24, 1862. American author (*The Age of Innocence, Ethan Frome*) and Pulitzer Prize winner. Born at New York, NY. Died at Pavillon Colombe, France, Aug 11, 1937, of a stroke.

BIRTHDAYS TODAY

Ernest Borgnine, 84, actor ("McHale's Navy," "The Single Guy"), born Hamden, CT, Jan 24, 1917.
Neil Diamond, 60, singer, composer ("Cracklin' Rosie," "Song Sung Blue"), born Coney Island, NY, Jan 24, 1941.
Nastassja Kinski, 41, actress (*Tess, The Hotel New Hampshire*), born Berlin, Germany, Jan 24, 1960.
Matthew Lillard, 31, actor (*Scream*), born Lansing, MI, Jan 24, 1970.
Aaron Neville, 60, singer, songwriter, born New Orleans, LA, Jan 24, 1941.
Michael Ontkean, 51, actor ("Twin Peaks," *Slap Shot*), born Vancouver, British Columbia, Canada, Jan 24, 1950.

January 2001	S	M	T	W	T	F	S
		1	2	3	4	5	6
	7	8	9	10	11	12	13
	14	15	16	17	18	19	20
	21	22	23	24	25	26	27
	28	29	30	31			

Mary Lou Retton, 33, Olympic gold medal gymnast, born Fairmont, WV, Jan 24, 1968.
Oral Roberts, 83, evangelist, born Tulsa, OK, Jan 24, 1918.
Yakov Smirnoff, 50, comedian ("What a Country," "Night Court"), born Odessa, USSR, Jan 24, 1951.
Maria Tallchief, 76, former ballet dancer, born Fairfax, OK, Jan 24, 1925.

JANUARY 25 — THURSDAY

Day 25 — 340 Remaining

AMERICAN CLUB'S WOMEN'S WELLNESS RETREAT. Jan 25–28. The American Club, Kohler, WI. An empowering four-day retreat focusing on the issues of wellness, spirituality and self-renewal. Experts in the fields of women's health and wellness, mid-life issues and natural healing offer ways to balance one's personal and professional life. Advance reservations required. Est attendance: 150. For info: The American Club, Highland Dr, Kohler, WI 53044. Phone: (920) 208-4676. Fax: (920) 457-0299. Web: www.americanclub.com.

BOYLE, ROBERT: BIRTH ANNIVERSARY. Jan 25, 1627 (OS). Irish physicist, chemist and author who formulated Boyle's Law in 1662. Born at Lismore, Ireland, he died at London, England, Dec 30, 1691 (OS).

BURNS, ROBERT: BIRTH ANNIVERSARY. Jan 25, 1759. Beloved Scottish poet ("Oh wad some power the giftie gie us To see oursels as others see us!"). Born at Ayrshire, Scotland, he died at Dumfries, Scotland, July 21, 1796. His birthday is widely celebrated as Burn's Nights, especially in Scotland, England and Newfoundland.

CAPONE, AL: DEATH ANNIVERSARY. Jan 25, 1947. Gangster Alphonse ("Scarface") Capone, who dominated organized crime in Chicago throughout Prohibition, died at age 48 at Miami after suffering from syphilis. Capone was born Jan 17, 1899, at Naples, Italy, and moved with his family to Brooklyn, NY.

CURTIS, CHARLES: BIRTH ANNIVERSARY. Jan 25, 1860. The 31st vice president of the US (1929–33). Born at Topeka, KS, he died at Washington, DC, Feb 8, 1936.

FIRST SCHEDULED TRANSCONTINENTAL FLIGHT: ANNIVERSARY. Jan 25, 1959. American Airlines opened the jet age in the US with the first scheduled transcontinental flight on a Boeing 707 nonstop from California to New York.

FIRST TELEVISED PRESIDENTIAL NEWS CONFERENCE: 40th ANNIVERSARY. Jan 25, 1961. Beginning a tradition that survives to this day, John F. Kennedy held the first televised presidential news conference five days after being inaugurated the 35th president.

FIRST WINTER OLYMPICS: ANNIVERSARY. Jan 25, 1924. The first Winter Olympic Games opened in Chamonix, France, with athletes representing 16 nations. The ski jump, previously unknown, thrilled spectators. The Olympics offered a boost to skiing, which would make enormous strides in the next decade.

KNOXVILLE FISHING EXPO. Jan 25–28. Jacob Building, Chilhowee Park, Knoxville, TN. Annual event featuring the latest in fishing tackle, rods, reels, boats, boating equipment, guide services and other accessories. Est attendance: 13,000. For info: Cindy Crabtree, Esau, Inc, PO Box 50096, Knoxville, TN 37950. Phone: (865) 588-1233 or (800) 588-ESAU. Fax: (865) 588-6938. Web: www.esaushows.com.

MACINTOSH DEBUTS: ANNIVERSARY. Jan 25, 1984. Apple's Macintosh computer went on sale this day for $2,495. It wasn't until mid-1985, however, that sales began to take off and this computer began to replace the Apple II model.

MAUGHAM, W. SOMERSET: BIRTH ANNIVERSARY. Jan 25, 1874. English short story writer, novelist and playwright born at Paris, France. Among his best-remembered books: *Of Human Bondage, Cakes and Ale* and *The Razor's Edge*. Died at Cap Ferrat, France, Dec 16, 1965.

MILLS, FLORENCE: BIRTH ANNIVERSARY. Jan 25, 1896. The leading black American singer and dancer of the Jazz Age and the Harlem Renaissance was born Florence Winfree at Washington, DC. She appeared in Langston Hughes's *Shuffle Along* in 1921 and *Plantation Review* on Broadway in 1922, then at the London Pavilion in *Dover Street to Dixie* in 1923. Offered a spot in the *Ziegfeld Follies,* she turned it down and joined in creating a rival show with an all-black cast. Mills was the first black woman to appear as a headliner at the Palace Theatre. She was so revered for her efforts to create opportunities for black entertainers and to bring the unique culture of blacks to Broadway that more than 150,000 people filled the streets of Harlem to mourn her when she died at New York City, Nov 1, 1927, at age 31.

A ROOM OF ONE'S OWN DAY. Jan 25. For anyone who knows or longs for the sheer bliss and rightness of having a private place, no matter how humble, to call one's own. [© 2000 by WH] For info: Tom or Ruth Roy, Wellcat Holidays, 2418 Long Ln, Lebanon, PA 17046. Phone: (717) 279-0184. E-mail: wellcat@supernet.com. Web: www.wellcat.com.

WOMEN'S HEALTHY WEIGHT DAY. Jan 25. A day to honor American women of all sizes and confirm that beauty, talent and love cannot be weighed. Corporate winners of the Women's Healthy Weight Media Contest will be announced—businesses that portray a healthy, realistic look for women. This is a day to appreciate women in all their diversity and reject the national obsession with thinness that is shattering the lives of women, young girls and their families. For info: Francie M. Berg, Editor/Publisher, Healthy Weight Journal, 402 S 14th St, Hettinger, ND 58639. Phone: (701) 567-2646. Fax: (701) 567-2602. E-mail: hwj@healthyweight.net. Web: www.healthyweight.net.

WOOLF, VIRGINIA: BIRTH ANNIVERSARY. Jan 25, 1882. English writer, critic and novelist, author of *Jacob's Room* and *To the Lighthouse.* Born at London, England. After completing her last novel, *Between the Acts,* she collapsed under the strain and drowned herself in the River Ouse near Rodmell, England, on Mar 28, 1941.

BIRTHDAYS TODAY

Corazon "Cory" Aquino, 78, former president of the Philippines, born Tarlac Province, Philippine Islands, Jan 25, 1923.
Conrad Burns, 66, US Senator (R, Montana), born Gallatin, MO, Jan 25, 1935.
Chris Chelios, 39, hockey player, born Chicago, IL, Jan 25, 1962.
Ernie Harwell, 83, sportscaster, born Washington, GA, Jan 25, 1918.
Dean Jones, 70, actor (*Tea and Sympathy, The Love Bug, Beethoven*), born Decatur, AL, Jan 25, 1931.
Dinah Manoff, 43, actress (stage: *I Ought to Be in Pictures* [Tony Award]; "Soap," "Empty Nest"), born New York, NY, Jan 25, 1958.
Edwin Newman, 82, journalist, author ("Comet," *A Civil Tongue*), born New York, NY, Jan 25, 1919.
Leigh Taylor-Young, 56, actress ("Peyton Place," "Dallas," *I Love You, Alice B. Toklas*), born Washington, DC, Jan 25, 1945.

JANUARY 26 — FRIDAY

Day 26 — 339 Remaining

AMERICANA INDIAN AND WESTERN ART SHOW AND SALE. Jan 26–28. Yuma, AZ. Indian and Western paintings, rugs and jewelry. Est attendance: 8,000. For info: Mktg Dept, Yuma Civic and Conv Ctr, 1440 Desert Hills Dr, Yuma, AZ 85365. Phone: (520) 344-3800. Fax: (520) 344-9121.

AUGUSTA FUTURITY. Jan 26–Feb 3. Augusta, GA. Brings together the top cutting horses and riders in the world to compete for purse and awards of more than $800,000. Sponsors: Wrangler, John Deere, Manna Pro Feed Company, Ariat Boots, CellularOne, *Augusta Chronicle,* E-Z-Go Textron, KMC Telecom, Gist Silversmiths, American Hat Company, COMCAST Cable,

ConAgra Feed Co, Caldwell's Horse & Saddle Co and Manna Pro Feed Co. Est attendance: 42,000. For info: Skip Peterson, Dir of Mktg, Augusta Futurity, PO Box 936, Augusta, GA 30903. Phone: (706) 823-3370 or (706) 823-3417. Web: www.augusta-futurity.com.

AUSTRALIA: AUSTRALIA DAY—FIRST BRITISH SETTLEMENT: ANNIVERSARY. Jan 26, 1788. A shipload of convicts arrived briefly at Botany Bay (which proved to be unsuitable) and then at Port Jackson (later the site of the city of Sydney). Establishment of an Australian prison colony was to relieve crowding of British prisons. Australia Day, formerly known as Foundation Day or Anniversary Day, has been observed since about 1817 and has been a public holiday since 1838. Observed Jan 26 if a Monday, otherwise on the first Monday thereafter (Jan 29 in 2001).

BIG BAND WEEKEND. Jan 26–28. Asheville, NC. 10th annual. Two orchestras, two gala balls and dance instructions are featured at this annual event. Est attendance: 1,400. For info: Grove Park Inn Resort, 290 Macon Ave, Asheville, NC 28804. Phone: (800) 374-0050 or (828) 252-2711. Fax: (828) 253-7053. Web: www.groveparkinn.com.

COLEMAN, BESSIE: BIRTH ANNIVERSARY. Jan 26, 1893. Born at Atlanta, TX, Bessie Coleman would not take no for an answer, especially where it concerned her dreams of flying. Because of her race and gender, she was denied admission to aviation school programs in the US. She therefore worked as a manicurist earning her way to Paris. There she received an international pilot's license from the Fédération Aéronautique Internationale in 1921. Upon return, "Queen Bess" took part in numerous acrobatic air exhibitions where her stunt-flying and "figure eights" won her many admirers. She avidly encouraged others to follow in her footsteps. Coleman, however, perished in a plane crash during a practice session, at Jacksonville, FL, Apr 30, 1926.

DENTAL DRILL PATENT: ANNIVERSARY. Jan 26, 1875. George F. Green, of Kalamazoo, MI, patented the electric dental drill.

DOMINICAN REPUBLIC: NATIONAL HOLIDAY. Jan 26. An official public holiday celebrates the birth anniversary of Juan Pablo Duarte, one of the fathers of the republic.

"THE DUKES OF HAZZARD" TV PREMIERE: ANNIVERSARY. Jan 26, 1979. This comedy/action show ran for seven seasons and featured car chases. Brothers Bo Duke (John Schneider) and Luke Duke (Tom Wopat) were the good guys, fighting crooked law enforcement in their rural southern community. Other characters included Daisy Duke (Catherine Bach), Uncle Jesse Duke (Denver Pyle), Sheriff Roscoe P. Coltrane (James Best), Deputy Enos Strate (Sonny Shroyer) and Boss Hogg (Sorrell Booke).

EAGLES, ETC. Jan 26–28. Bismarck, AR. To see bald eagles in the wild and to learn about and observe birds of prey. Est attendance: 600. For info: Park Naturalist, DeGray State Park, 2027 State Park Entrance Rd, Bismarck, AR 71929-8194. Phone: (800) 737-8355. Fax: (501) 865-2880. E-mail: interpreter@cei.net. Web: www.degray.com.

FRANKLIN PREFERS TURKEY: ANNIVERSARY. Jan 26, 1784. In a letter to his daughter, Benjamin Franklin expressed his unhappiness over the choice of the eagle as the symbol of America. He preferred the turkey.

FUN AT WORK DAY. Jan 26. Plan an activity that will result in fun and laughter in your work environment. Laughter releases tension and builds rapport. When we enjoy our work we are more productive. Annually, the last Friday of January. For info: Diane C. Decker, Quality Transitions. Phone: (847) 394-0994. E-mail: dcdecker@msn.com.

GRANT, JULIA DENT: 175th BIRTH ANNIVERSARY. Jan 26, 1826. Wife of Ulysses Simpson Grant, 18th president of the US. Born at St. Louis, MO, died at Washington, DC, Dec 14, 1902.

HITLER YOUTH DEPLOYED: ANNIVERSARY. Jan 26, 1943. Due to the need for more men at the front, the Nazis began manning anti-aircraft batteries within Germany with members of the Hitler Youth who were aged 15 and up. This was 10 days after the British had begun the heavy bombing of Berlin and other German cities. See also: "British Air Raid on Berlin: Anniversary" (Jan 16).

INDIA: REPUBLIC DAY. Jan 26. National holiday. Anniversary of Proclamation of the Republic, Basant Panchmi. In 1929, Indian National Congress resolved to work for establishment of a sovereign republic, a goal that was realized Jan 26, 1950, when India became a democratic republic and its constitution went into effect.

LOTUS 1-2-3 RELEASED: ANNIVERSARY. Jan 26, 1983. This spreadsheet software drove demand for the IBM PC, just as the introduction of VisiCalc had for the Apple II in 1979.

MacARTHUR, DOUGLAS: BIRTH ANNIVERSARY. Jan 26, 1880. US general and supreme commander of Allied forces in Southwest Pacific during World War II. Born at Little Rock, AR, he served as commander of the Rainbow Division's 84th Infantry Brigade in World War I, leading it in the St. Mihiel, Meuse-Argonne and Sedan offensives. Remembered for his "I shall return" prediction when forced out of the Philippines by the Japanese during WW II, a promise he fulfilled. Relieved of Far Eastern command by President Harry Truman on Apr 11, 1951, during the Korean War. MacArthur died at Washington, DC, Apr 5, 1964.

MICHIGAN: ADMISSION DAY: ANNIVERSARY. Jan 26. Became 26th state In 1837.

"MIKE HAMMER" TV PREMIERE: ANNIVERSARY. Jan 26, 1984. Mike Hammer was a gritty, urban detective created by writer Mickey Spillane. Originally a TV series in the '50s, CBS revived the series with Stacy Keach as the hard-boiled detective. Production was stopped while Keach was briefly imprisoned for a drug charge in 1984 but the series returned in 1986. The series also featured Don Stroud as NYPD Captain Pat Chambers, Kent Williams as Assistant DA Barrington, Lindsay Bloom as Hammer's secretary Velda, Danny Goldman as "Ozzie the Answer," Donna Denton as "The Face" and Lee Benton as Jenny the bartender.

ROCKY MOUNTAIN NATIONAL PARK ESTABLISHED: ANNIVERSARY. Jan 26, 1915. Under President Woodrow Wilson, the area covering more than 1,000 square miles in Colorado became a national park.

SAINT PAUL WINTER CARNIVAL. Jan 26–Feb 4. St. Paul, MN. Minnesota's largest tourist attraction and the nation's oldest and largest winter festival. The 115-year-old St. Paul Winter carnival provides 10 fun-filled days with more than 100 indoor and outdoor events celebrating the thrills and chills of wintertime fun. Est attendance: 250,000. For info: Saint Paul Festival and Heritage Foundation, 429 Landmark Ctr, 75 W 5th St, St. Paul, MN 55102. Phone: (651) 223-4700. Fax: (651) 223-4707. Web: www.winter-carnival.com.

SUGARLOAF'S SPRING CHANTILLY CRAFT FESTIVAL. Jan 26–28. Capital Expo Center, Chantilly, VA. This show, now in its 3rd year, features 350 nationally recognized craft designers and fine artists displaying and selling their original creations. Craft demonstrations, live music, food, hourly gift certificate drawings and more. Est attendance: 30,000. For info: Sugarloaf Mountain Works, 200 Orchard Ridge Dr, #215, Gaitherburg, MD 20878. Phone: (800) 210-9900. E-mail: smworks@sugarloafcrafts.com. Web: www.sugarloafcrafts.com.

TOAD HOLLOW DAY OF ENCOURAGEMENT. Jan 26. A day to give and receive a word of encouragement. For info: Ralph Morrison, Dir, Toad Hollow, PO Box 151, Fulton, MI 49052. Phone: (800) 574-8623.

VAN HEUSEN, JIMMY: BIRTH ANNIVERSARY. Jan 26, 1913. Jimmy Van Heusen was born Edward Chester Babcock at Syracuse, NY. He was a composer of many popular songs with his lyricist partners Johnny Burke and Sammy Cahn. One of his 76 songs that Frank Sinatra recorded was "My Kind of Town." Van Heusen won four Academy Awards for songs in movies such as *Going My Way* (1944). He was inducted into the Songwriters Hall of Fame when it was founded in 1971. Van Heusen died Feb 7, 1990, at Rancho Mirage, CA.

WINTER IN THE LUDINGTON AREA. Jan 26–28 (also Feb 2–4). Ludington, MI. Ice and snow sculpture competition, indoor sidewalk sale, antique show and sale, marathon race and cross country ski race. Est attendance: 5,000. For info: Ludington Area Chamber of Commerce, 5827 W US 10, Ludington, MI 49431. Phone: (800) 542-4600. Fax: (231) 845-6857. E-mail: visitlud@carrinter.net. Web: www.ludingtoncvb.com.

BIRTHDAYS TODAY

Anita Baker, 43, singer ("Sweet Love," "Rhythm of Love"), born Toledo, OH, Jan 26, 1958.

Vince Carter, 24, basketball player, born Daytona Beach, FL, Jan 26, 1977.

Father George Harold Clements, 69, Roman Catholic priest, civil rights leader, born Chicago, IL, Jan 26, 1932.

Angela Davis, 57, political activist, born Birmingham, AL, Jan 26, 1944.

Ellen DeGeneres, 43, comedienne, actress ("Ellen"), born New Orleans, LA, Jan 26, 1958.

Philip Jose Farmer, 83, science fiction writer, born Peoria, IL, Jan 26, 1918.

Jules Feiffer, 72, cartoonist, writer, born New York, NY, Jan 26, 1929.

Scott Glenn, 59, actor (*The Right Stuff, Silverado*), born Pittsburgh, PA, Jan 26, 1942.

January 2001	S	M	T	W	T	F	S
		1	2	3	4	5	6
	7	8	9	10	11	12	13
	14	15	16	17	18	19	20
	21	22	23	24	25	26	27
	28	29	30	31			

Wayne Gretzky, 40, Hockey Hall of Famer, born Brantford, Ontario, Canada, Jan 26, 1961.

Paul Newman, 76, actor (Oscar for *The Color of Money; Cat on a Hot Tin Roof, Butch Cassidy and the Sundance Kid*), director (*Rachel, Rachel; The Glass Menagerie*), born Cleveland, OH, Jan 26, 1925.

Andrew Ridgeley, 38, musician, born Bushey, England, Jan 26, 1963.

David Strathairn, 51, actor (*LA Confidential*), born San Francisco, CA, Jan 26, 1950.

Robert George (Bob) Uecker, 66, sportscaster, former baseball player, actor, born Milwaukee, WI, Jan 26, 1935.

Eddie Van Halen, 44, guitarist ("Jump," "Right Now"), born Nijmegen, Netherlands, Jan 26, 1957.

JANUARY 27 — SATURDAY

Day 27 — 338 Remaining

APOLLO I: SPACECRAFT FIRE: ANNIVERSARY. Jan 27, 1967. Three American astronauts, Virgil I. Grissom, Edward H. White and Roger B. Chaffee, died when fire suddenly broke out at 6:31 PM in *Apollo I* during a launching simulation test, as it stood on the ground at Cape Kennedy, FL, Jan 27, 1967. First launching in the Apollo program had been scheduled for Feb 27, 1967.

BLACK HILLS STOCK SHOW AND RODEO. Jan 27–Feb 4. Rapid City, SD. Events include PRCA rodeos, ranch rodeo, timed sheepdog trials, draft horse events, livestock shows and sales, buffalo show and sale, bucking horse and bull sale, stockman banquet and ball and commercial exhibits. Est attendance: 250,000. For info: Black Hills Stock Show & Rodeo, 800 San Francisco, Rapid City, SD 57701. Phone: (605) 355-3861.

BROOKFIELD ICE HARVEST. Jan 27. Brookfield, VT. Demonstrations of ice harvesting using the original equipment near the Brookfield Floating Bridge, one of only two such bridges remaining in the US today. Annually, the last Saturday in January. Est attendance: 1,000. For info: Al Wilder, PO Box 405, Brookfield, VT 05036. Phone: (802) 276-3959. Fax: (802) 276-3023.

COWBOY POETRY GATHERING. Jan 27–Feb 3. Elko, NV. Soulful poetry and music performed by working cowboys. The event, which includes workshops, jam sessions, Western art and buckaroo trappings exhibits, attracts an international audience. For info: Phone: (775) 738-7508.

DODGSON, CHARLES LUTWIDGE (LEWIS CARROLL): BIRTH ANNIVERSARY. Jan 27, 1832. English mathematician and author, better known by his pseudonym, Lewis Carroll, creator of *Alice's Adventures in Wonderland*, was born at Cheshire, England. *Alice* was written for Alice Liddell, daughter of a friend, and first published in 1886. *Through the Looking-Glass*, a sequel, and *The Hunting of the Snark* followed. Dodgson's books for children proved equally enjoyable to adults, and they overshadowed his serious works on mathematics. Dodgson died at Guildford, Surrey, England, Jan 14, 1898.

FARMERS MARKET. Jan 27 (tentative). El Centro, CA. Annually, the last Saturday in January. Est attendance: 25,000. For info: El Centro Chamber of Commerce, Box 3006, El Centro, CA 92244. Phone: (760) 352-3681. Fax: (760) 352-3246. Web: www.elcentrochamber.com.

GERMANY: DAY OF REMEMBRANCE FOR VICTIMS OF NAZISM. Jan 27. Since 1996 commemorated on this day, the date in 1945 that Soviet soldiers liberated the Auschwitz concentration camp in Poland.

GOMPERS, SAMUEL: BIRTH ANNIVERSARY. Jan 27, 1850. Labor leader, first president of the American Federation of Labor, born at London, England. Died Dec 13, 1924, at San Antonio, TX.

GUNPOWDER PLOT TRIAL: ANNIVERSARY. Jan 27, 1606. The surviving conspirators in the "Gunpowder Treason," a plot to blow up Parliament and the king of England on Nov 5, 1605, were brought to trial and convicted at London, Jan 27, 1606. Four days later they were executed. An inscription on a contemporary engraving states: "The heads of Percy and Catesby after they were dead, were cut off and set upon the ends of Parliament House. Friday the last of Jan, 1606, were executed in Parliament Yard: T. Winter, Rokenvood, Keys and Guido Fawkes, their quarters were placed over London gates and their heads upon London Bridge." See also: "Guy Fawkes Day" (Nov 5).

ICE FEST. Jan 27–28. Ligonier, PA. A weekend of ice-carving demonstrations as blocks of ice are turned into works of art. Est attendance: 10,000. For info: Rachel Roehrig, Ligonier Chamber of Commerce, 120 East Main St, Ligonier, PA 15658. Phone: (724) 238-4200. Fax: (724) 238-4610. E-mail: ligonier@ligonier.com.

KERN, JEROME: BIRTH ANNIVERSARY. Jan 27, 1885. American composer born at New York City; died there Nov 11, 1945. In addition to scores for stage and screen, Kern wrote many memorable songs, including "Who," "Make Believe," "Ol' Man River," "Bill," "Smoke Gets in Your Eyes," "Lovely to Look At," "I Won't Dance," "The Way You Look Tonight," "All the Things You Are" and "The Last Time I Saw Paris."

"LAVERNE AND SHIRLEY" TV PREMIERE: 25th ANNIVERSARY. Jan 27, 1976. This ABC sitcom was a spin-off of the popular TV show "Happy Days" that was also set during the late '50s in Milwaukee, WI. Penny Marshall (sister of series co-creator, Garry Marshall) starred as Laverne DeFazio with Cindy Williams as Shirley Feeney. The two friends worked at a brewery and shared a basement apartment. Also featured in the cast were: Phil Foster as Laverne's father, Frank DeFazio; David L. Lander as co-worker Andrew "Squiggy" Squiggman; Michael McKean as co-worker Lenny Kosnowski; Betty Garrett as landlady Edna Babish and Eddie Mekka as Carmine Ragusa, Shirley's sometime boyfriend.

LONGWOOD GARDENS WELCOME SPRING. Jan 27–Apr 6. Kennett Square, PA. Indoor conservatory display features thousands of colorful, fragrant spring bulbs, green lawns, orchids and roses. Est attendance: 90,000. For info: Longwood Gardens, PO Box 501, Kennett Sq, PA 19348-0501. Phone: (610) 388-1000. Web: www.longwoodgardens.org.

McKINLEY DAY. Jan 27. McKinley Museum, Canton, OH. A celebration of the birth anniversary of President William McKinley with special activities all day. For info: McKinley Museum, 800 McKinley Monument Dr NW, Canton, OH 44711. Phone: (330) 455-7043. Web: www.mckinleymuseum.org.

MOZART, WOLFGANG AMADEUS: BIRTH ANNIVERSARY. Jan 27, 1756. One of the world's greatest music makers. Born at Salzburg, Austria, into a gifted musical family, Mozart began performing at age three and composing at age five. Some of the best known of his more than 600 compositions include the operas *Marriage of Figaro, Don Giovanni, Cosi fan tutte* and *The Magic Flute*, his unfinished Requiem Mass, his C major symphony known as the "Jupiter" and many of his quartets and piano concertos. He died at Vienna, Dec 5, 1791.

ORANGE CITY BLUE SPRING MANATEE FESTIVAL. Jan 27–28. Valentine Park, Orange City, FL. Now in its 16th year, this festival was created to raise awareness of the endangered West Indian manatee. It features more than 90 arts and crafts exhibitors, most of whom honor the manatee in a variety of mediums. Children's games, family entertainment, animal and environmental exhibits and food vendors round out the event. For info: Orange City Blue Spring Manatee Festival Office, Phone: (904) 775-9224.

ORCHID SHOW. Jan 27–Mar 1. Missouri Botanical Garden, St. Louis, MO. Spectacular display of the Garden's vast orchid collection. For info: Missouri Botanical Garden, PO Box 299, St. Louis, MO 63166-0299. Phone: (314) 577-5142 or (800) 642-8842. Fax: (314) 577-9598. E-mail: anne.shepherd@mobot.org. Web: www.mobot.org.

RICKOVER, HYMAN GEORGE: BIRTH ANNIVERSARY. Jan 27, 1900. American naval officer, known as the "Father of the Nuclear Navy." Admiral Rickover directed development of nuclear reactor-powered submarines, the first of which was the *Nautilus*, launched in 1954. Rickover was noted for his blunt remarks: "To increase the efficiency of the Department of Defense," he said, "you must first abolish it." The four-star admiral retired (unwillingly) at the age of 81, after 63 years in the navy. Born in Russia, Rickover died at Arlington, VA, July 9, 1986, and was buried at Arlington National Cemetery.

SCIENCE EXPO 2001. Jan 27. St. Ann School, Milford, CT. 10th annual Expo and open house with hands-on activities for all ages, special guests and exhibits covering a broad range of fields; a journey through the many faces of scientific discovery. Annually, the last Saturday in January to coincide with the beginning of Catholic Schools Week. 11–3. Admission $3; under 2 free. Est attendance: 1,200. For info: St. Ann School, 64 Ridge St, Milford, CT 06460. Phone: (203) 878-2738.

TEXAS COLLECTORS' GUN & KNIFE SHOW. Jan 27–28. (also Mar 17–18, Aug 18–19, Oct 13–14 and Dec 1–2.) Multi-Purpose Events Center Exhibit Hall, Wichita Falls, TX. The largest gun, knife and shooting sports show and sale in the area. Buy, sell, swap. Est attendance: 5,000. For info: Wichita Falls CVB, 1000 5th St, Wichita Falls, TX 76301. Phone: (940) 716-5500. Fax: (940) 716-5509. E-mail: MPEC@wf.net. Web: www.viewscape.com or www.wf.net.

THOMAS CRAPPER DAY. Jan 27, 1910. Born at Thorne, Yorkshire, England, in 1836 (exact date unknown), Crapper is often described as the prime developer of flush toilet mechanism as it is known today. The flush toilet had been in use for more than 100 years; Crapper perfected it. Founder, London, 1861, of Thomas Crapper & Co, later patentees and manufacturers of sanitary appliances. Died Jan 27, 1910. [Editor's Note: The date of Crapper's death has been revised based on info sent by Dr. Andy Gibbons of the International Thomas Crapper Society, who has viewed Crapper's gravestone and obtained a copy of his death certificate. Ken Grabowski sent further info.]

UNIVERSITY KIWANIS PANCAKE FESTIVAL. Jan 27. Multi-Purpose Events Center, J.S. Bridwell Center, Wichita Falls, TX. 45th annual. A day of food and fun, featuring the world's "best pancakes." Est attendance: 9,500. For info: Wichita Falls CVB, 1000 5th St, Wichita Falls, TX 76301. Phone: (940) 716-5500. Fax: (940) 716-5509. E-mail: MPEC@WF.net. Web: www.viewscape.com or www.wf.net.

VIETNAM PEACE AGREEMENT SIGNED: ANNIVERSARY. Jan 27, 1973. US and North Vietnam, along with South Vietnam and the Viet Cong, signed an "Agreement on ending the war and restoring peace in Vietnam." Signed at Paris, France, to take effect Jan 28 at 8 AM Saigon time, thus ending US combat role in a war that had involved American personnel stationed in Vietnam since defeated French forces had departed under terms of the Geneva Accords in 1954. This was the longest war in US history with more than one million combat deaths (US: 47,366). However, within weeks of the departure of American troops the war between North and South Vietnam resumed. For the Vietnamese, the war didn't end until Apr 30, 1975, when Saigon fell to Communist forces.

WHIPTOP CONTEST. Jan 27. Spinning Top Museum, Burlington, WI. The traditional whiptop played with often in winter to play and keep warm. Whiptop is used by most North American Indian tribes, the British and many island cultures. For info: Spin-

ning Top Museum, 533 Milwaukee Ave (Hwy 36), Burlington, WI 53105. Phone: (262) 763-3946.

WINTERFEST. Jan 27. American Legion Hall, Grand Blanc, MI. All kinds of cans and brewery memorabilia such as steins, coasters, signs, mirrors, neon signs, etc. $10 general admission includes display table if desired, available on first-come, first-served basis. Includes food and beverages and door prize raffle tickets. Kids under eight free. Est attendance: 200. For info: Gene Goulet, Pres, Mid-Michigan Chapter, Beer Can Collectors of America, 5306 Lippincott, Burton, MI 48519. Phone: (810) 742-5353. E-mail: davevanh@aol.com.

BIRTHDAYS TODAY

Mikhail Baryshnikov, 53, ballet dancer, actor (*White Nights, The Turning Point*), born Riga, Latvia, USSR, Jan 27, 1948.
(Anthony) Cris Collinsworth, 42, sportscaster, former football player, born Dayton, OH, Jan 27, 1959.
Mairead Corrigan, 57, pacifist, Nobel Peace Prize winner, born Belfast, Northern Ireland, Jan 27, 1944.
James Cromwell, 59, actor (*The People vs Larry Flynt; Star Trek: First Contact*), born Los Angeles, CA, Jan 27, 1942.
Troy Donahue, 64, actor ("Surfside 6," "Hawaiian Eye," *Parrish*), born New York, NY, Jan 27, 1937.
Bridget Fonda, 37, actress (*Single White Female, Lake Placid*), daughter of Peter Fonda, born Los Angeles, CA, Jan 27, 1964.
Julie Foudy, 30, soccer player, born San Diego, CA, Jan 27, 1971.
Skitch Henderson, 83, bandleader ("The Tonight Show"), born Halstad, MN, Jan 27, 1918.
Mordecai Richler, 70, author (*The Apprenticeship of Duddy Kravitz*), born Montreal, Quebec, Canada, Jan 27, 1931.
Mimi Rogers, 45, actress (*The Doors, The Rapture*), born Coral Gables, FL, Jan 27, 1956.

JANUARY 28 — SUNDAY
Day 28 — 337 Remaining

"BARNABY JONES" TV PREMIERE: ANNIVERSARY. Jan 28, 1973. CBS drama about a mild-mannered, milk-drinking (but don't say milquetoast) private eye who comes out of retirement following his son's murder. Cast included Buddy Ebsen as Barnaby Jones, Lee Meriwether as Barnaby's widowed daughter-in-law, Betty Jones, John Carter as Lieutenant Biddle and Mark Shera as Jedediah Jones.

CATHOLIC SCHOOLS WEEK. Jan 28–Feb 3. A national celebration focusing on the uniqueness of Catholic schools. Many schools plan special activities celebrating their Catholic heritage. Jointly sponsored by the National Catholic Educational Association and the US Catholic Conference. Annually, beginning on the last Sunday in January. For info: Natl Catholic Educational Assn, 1077 30th St NW, Ste 100, Washington, DC 20007-3852. Phone: (202) 337-6232. Web: catholicschoolsweek.org.

CHALLENGER SPACE SHUTTLE EXPLOSION: 15th ANNIVERSARY. Jan 28, 1986. At 11:39 AM, EST, the Space Shuttle *Challenger* STS-51L exploded, 74 seconds into its flight and about 10 miles above the earth. Hundreds of millions around the world watched television replays of the horrifying event that killed seven people, destroyed the billion-dollar craft, suspended all shuttle flights and halted, at least temporarily, much of the US manned space flight program. Killed were teacher Christa McAuliffe (who was to have been the first ordinary citizen in space) and six crew members: Francis R. Scobee, Michael J. Smith, Judith A. Resnik, Ellison S. Onizuka, Ronald E. McNair and Gregory B. Jarvis. [See also individual names.]

CHINESE LUNAR NEW YEAR FESTIVAL: YEAR OF THE SERPENT (SEA-EH NIEN). Jan 28. Baltimore, MD. Dragon/Lion (Mo Tze) performance, Chinese culture, indoor program, evensong and traditions. Light brunch by advance subscription reservation ($10) no later than Dec 15. Est attendance: 500. For info: Lillian Lee Kim, Grace and St. Peter's Parish, 524

	S	M	T	W	T	F	S
January		1	2	3	4	5	6
	7	8	9	10	11	12	13
2001	14	15	16	17	18	19	20
	21	22	23	24	25	26	27
	28	29	30	31			

Anneslie Rd, Baltimore, MD 21212-2009. Phone: (410) 539-1395 or (410) 377-8143.

"FANTASY ISLAND" TV PREMIERE: ANNIVERSARY.
Jan 28, 1978. You knew you were a bona fide "star" in the '70s when you received a casting call from "Fantasy Island." Young and old stayed home on Saturday night to watch Mr Roarke introduce yet another hapless lot of guest stars anxious to live out their fantasies in camp splendor. Ricardo Montalban starred as our prescient guide, Mr Roarke, with Hervé Villechaize as Tattoo, Wendy Schaal as Mr Roarke's goddaughter, Julie, and Christopher Hewett as Mr Roarke's assistant, Lawrence. The show's run of 130 episodes, ending on Aug 18, 1984, was produced by Aaron Spelling and Leonard Goldberg. Who can forget Tattoo's opening lines each week, "De plane, de plane!"

GREAT SEAL OF THE US: AUTHORIZATION ANNIVERSARY.
Jan 28, 1782. Congress resolved that the secretary of the Congress should "keep the public seal, and cause the same to be affixed to every act, ordinance or paper, which Congress shall direct. . . ." Although the Great Seal did not exist yet, the Congress recognized the need for it. See also: "Great Seal of the United States: Anniversary" (July 4 and Sept 16).

GREENWICH ARTS CENTER OPEN HOUSE.
Jan 28. Arts Center, Greenwich, CT. An alternative to football on Super Bowl Sunday, the 12th annual Open House features theater, dance and music performances, plus art demonstrations and gallery exhibits. Artists' studios will be open. Refreshments. Noon–4; free. Annually, on Super Bowl Sunday. Est attendance: 700. For info: Greenwich Arts Council, 299 Greenwich Ave, Greenwich, CT 06830. Phone: (203) 622-3998.

HOBBY INDUSTRY ASSOCIATION ANNUAL CONVENTION AND TRADE SHOW.
Jan 28–31 (classes begin Jan 27). Anaheim Convention Center, Anaheim, CA. 60th annual showcase for wholesale and retail buyers to view and order craft and hobby products. Est attendance: 20,000. For info: Hobby Industry Assn, 319 E 54th St, Elmwood Park, NJ 07407. Phone: (201) 794-1133. Fax: (201) 797-0657. E-mail: hia@ix.netcom.com. Web: www.hobby.org.

ISRAELI SIEGE OF SUEZ CITY ENDS: ANNIVERSARY.
Jan 28, 1974. The Israeli army lifted its siege of Suez City, freed encircled Egyptian troops and turned over 300,000 square miles of Egyptian territory to the UN, thereby ending the occupation that started during the October 1973 war.

MacKENZIE, ALEXANDER: BIRTH ANNIVERSARY.
Jan 28, 1822. The man who became the first Liberal prime minister of Canada (1873–78) was born at Logierait, Perth, Scotland. He died at Toronto, Apr 17, 1892.

MARTÍ, JOSÉ JULIAN: BIRTH ANNIVERSARY.
Jan 28, 1853. Cuban author and political activist born at Havana, Cuba, Martí was exiled to Spain, where he studied law before coming to the US in 1890. He was killed in battle at Dos Rios, Cuba, May 19, 1895.

PICCARD, AUGUSTE: BIRTH ANNIVERSARY.
Jan 28, 1884. Scientist and explorer, born at Basel, Switzerland. Made record-setting balloon ascent into the stratosphere on May 27, 1931 and also ocean depth descents and explorations. Twin brother of Jean Felix Piccard. Died at Lausanne, Switzerland, Mar 24, 1962. See also: "Piccard, Jean Felix: Birth Anniversary" (Jan 28).

PICCARD, JEAN FELIX: BIRTH ANNIVERSARY.
Jan 28, 1884. Scientist, engineer, explorer, born at Basel, Switzerland. Noted for cosmic-ray research and record-setting balloon ascensions into stratosphere. Reached 57,579 ft in sealed gondola piloted by his wife, Jeannette, in 1934. Twin brother of Auguste Piccard. Died at Minneapolis, MN, Jan 28, 1963. See also: "Piccard, Jeannette Ridlon: Birth Anniversary" (Jan 5) and "Piccard, Auguste: Birth Anniversary" (Jan 28).

STANLEY, HENRY MORTON: BIRTH ANNIVERSARY.
Jan 28, 1841. Explorer born at Wales and leader of the expedition to find the missing missionary-explorer David Livingstone,

who had not been heard from for more than two years. Stanley began the search in Africa on Mar 21, 1871, finally finding the explorer at Ujiji, near Lake Tanganyika, on Nov 10, 1871, whereupon he asked the now-famous question: "Dr. Livingstone, I presume?" Stanley died at London, England, May 10, 1904.

SUPER BOWL XXXV.
Jan 28. Atlanta, GA. The battle between the NFC and AFC champions. Annually, the last Sunday in January. For info: PR Dept, The Natl Football League, 280 Park Ave, New York, NY 10017. Phone: (212) 758-1500. Web: www.nfl.com.

BIRTHDAYS TODAY

Alan Alda (born Alphonso D'Abruzzo), 65, actor (*Paper Lion, The Four Seasons*, "M*A*S*H"), director, born New York, NY, Jan 28, 1936.

John Beck, 58, actor ("Dallas," *Sleeper, The Big Bus*), born Chicago, IL, Jan 28, 1943.

Susan Howard (Jeri Lynn Mooney), 58, actress ("Dallas"), born Marshall, TX, Jan 28, 1943.

Harley Jane Kozak, 44, actress (*When Harry Met Sally . . ., Parenthood*), born Wilkes-Barre, PA, Jan 28, 1957.

Sarah McLachlan, 33, folksinger, born Halifax, Nova Scotia, Canada, Jan 28, 1968.

Claes Oldenburg, 72, artist, sculptor (*Standing Trowel*), born Stockholm, Sweden, Jan 28, 1929.

Jeanne Shaheen, 54, Governor of New Hampshire (D), born St. Charles, MO, Jan 28, 1947.

Susan Sontag, 68, author (*Against Interpretation, The Volcano Lover: A Romance*), born New York, NY, Jan 28, 1933.

Elijah Wood, 20, actor (*Back to the Future Part II, The Good Son*), born Cedar Rapids, IA, Jan 28, 1981.

JANUARY 29 — MONDAY
Day 29 — 336 Remaining

AUSTRALIA: AUSTRALIA DAY OBSERVANCE.
Jan 29. Public holiday. Commemorates beginning of settlement when Governor Phillip landed at Sydney Cove on Jan 26, 1788. When the date falls other than on a Monday, the holiday is held on the Monday following Jan 26, in order to give a long weekend. First proclaimed a public holiday in 1838. See also: "Australia: Australia Day" (Jan 26).

CHEKHOV, ANTON PAVLOVICH: BIRTH ANNIVERSARY.
Jan 29, 1860. Russian playwright and short story writer, especially remembered for *The Sea Gull, The Three Sisters* and *The Cherry Orchard*. Born at Taganrog, Russia; died July 15, 1904, at the Black Forest spa at Badenweiler, Germany.

FREETHINKER'S DAY.
Jan 29. Annual celebration of the birth of Thomas Paine. For info: Truth Seeker Foundation, 16935 W Bernardo Dr, Ste 103, San Diego, CA 92127. Phone: (800) 321-9054 or (760) 676-0430. Fax: (760) 676-0433. E-mail: tseditor@aol.com. Web: truthseeker.com.

KANSAS: ADMISSION DAY: ANNIVERSARY.
Jan 29. Became the 34th state in 1861.

McKINLEY, WILLIAM: BIRTH ANNIVERSARY.
Jan 29, 1843. 25th president of the US (1897–1901), born at Niles, OH. Died in office, at Buffalo, NY, Sept 14, 1901, as the result of a gunshot wound by an anarchist assassin Sept 6, 1901, while he was attending the Pan-American Exposition.

MILITARY BAN ON HOMOSEXUALS EASED: ANNIVERSARY. Jan 29, 1993. An interim policy on ending the ban on homosexuals in the US military was announced by President William Clinton. The policy ended the questioning of military recruits regarding their sexual orientation but allowed removal of openly homosexual members from active service. President Clinton's announced policy of "don't ask, don't tell, don't pursue" allowed homosexuals to serve in the armed forces as long as they were discreet.

MORMON BATTALION ARRIVAL IN CALIFORNIA: ANNIVERSARY. Jan 29, 1847. The 500 men of the US Mormon Battalion, along with 50 women and children, arrived at San Diego, CA, on this date, having marched 2,000 miles—the longest march in modern military history—since leaving Council Bluffs, IA, on July 16, 1846, to fight in the war against Mexico. In the course of their trek they established the first wagon route from Santa Fe to southern California. Their historic arrival is commemorated each year with a military parade in San Diego's Old Town.

NATIONAL PUZZLE DAY. Jan 29. To recognize different puzzles and games and their creators. Call or write for free information on the origins and creators of puzzles and games. For info: Carol Handz, Coord, Jodi Jill Features, 1705 14th St, Ste 321, Boulder, CO 80302. Phone: (303) 786-9849. Fax: (303) 786-9401. E-mail: Jjillone@aol.com.

PAINE, THOMAS: BIRTH ANNIVERSARY. Jan 29, 1737. American Revolutionary leader, a corset-maker by trade, author of *Common Sense*, *The Age of Reason* and many other influential works, was born at Thetford, England. "These are the times that try men's souls" are the well-known opening words of his inspirational tract *The Crisis*. Paine died at New York, NY, June 8, 1809, but 10 years later his remains were moved to England by William Cobbett for reburial there. Reburial was refused, however, and the location of Paine's bones, said to have been distributed, is unknown.

PEDDLER'S VILLAGE ANNUAL QUILT COMPETITION AND DISPLAY. Jan 29–Apr 1. Peddler's Village, Lahaska, PA. Handmade quilt entries compete for $1,500 in cash prizes in such categories as traditional, Amish, creative, clothing, children's and amateur. A distinguished panel of judges chooses the winners, and quilts are displayed in the Village Gazebo. Open daily to public. Free admission. Est attendance: 150,000. For info: Peddler's Village, Routes 202 & 263, Lahaska, PA 18931. Phone: (215) 794-4000. Fax: (215) 794-4001. Web: www.peddlersvillage.com.

SWEDENBORG, EMANUEL: BIRTH ANNIVERSARY. Jan 29, 1688 (OS). Born at Stockholm, Sweden, Swedenborg is remembered as a scientist, inventor, writer and religious leader. Swedenborg made plans for machine guns, submarines and airplanes and published Sweden's first scientific journal. His study of human anatomy and his search for the soul led him to begin thinking about religion. His writings interpreting the scriptures formed the basis of the Church of the New Jerusalem, which was established by his devotees soon after his death. He died at London, England, Mar 29, 1772.

BIRTHDAYS TODAY

John Forsythe (John Freund), 83, actor ("Bachelor Father," Charlie's voice on "Charlie's Angels," "Dynasty"), born Penn's Grove, NJ, Jan 29, 1918.
Sara Gilbert, 26, actress ("Roseanne"), born Santa Monica, CA, Jan 29, 1975.

January 2001	S	M	T	W	T	F	S
		1	2	3	4	5	6
	7	8	9	10	11	12	13
	14	15	16	17	18	19	20
	21	22	23	24	25	26	27
	28	29	30	31			

Heather Graham, 31, actress (*Lost in Space, Boogie Nights*), born Milwaukee, WI, Jan 29, 1970.
Germaine Greer, 62, author (*Daddy We Hardly Knew You, The Female Eunuch*), born Melbourne, Victoria, Australia, Jan 29, 1939.
Dominik Hasek, 36, hockey player, born Pardubice, Czech Republic, Jan 29, 1965.
Ann Jillian, 50, actress ("It's a Living," *The Ann Jillian Story*), born Cambridge, MA, Jan 29, 1951.
Andrew Keegan, 22, actor (*Independence Day*), born Los Angeles, CA, Jan 29, 1979.
Gregory Efthimios (Greg) Louganis, 41, actor, Olympic gold medal diver, born San Diego, CA, Jan 29, 1960.
Bobbie Phillips, 33, actress ("Murder One," *Red Shoe Diaries*) born Charleston, SC, Jan 29, 1968.
Katharine Ross, 58, actress (*The Graduate*), born Los Angeles, CA, Jan 29, 1943.
Tom Selleck, 56, actor ("Magnum, PI," *Three Men and a Baby, Mr. Baseball*), born Detroit, MI, Jan 29, 1945.
Nick Turturro, 39, actor ("NYPD Blue"), born Queens, NY, Jan 29, 1962.
Oprah Winfrey, 47, TV talk-show host (Emmys for "The Oprah Winfrey Show"), actress (*The Color Purple*), producer (owner of Harpo Studios), born Kosciusko, MS, Jan 29, 1954.

JANUARY 30 — TUESDAY
Day 30 — 335 Remaining

BEATLES LAST PUBLIC APPEARANCE: ANNIVERSARY. Jan 30, 1969. On this day the Beatles performed together in public for the last time. The show took place on the roof of their Apple Studios in London, England, but it was interrupted by police after they received complaints from the neighbors about the noise.

BIRMINGHAM SPORT AND BOAT SHOW. Jan 30–Feb 4. Birmingham/Jefferson Civic Center, Birmingham, AL. For info: Mike Coffen, Double C Productions, Inc, Box 1678, Huntsville, TX 77342. Phone: (409) 295-9677 or (800) 574-9650. Fax: (409) 295-8859. E-mail: doublec@lcc.net. Web: www.lcc.net/~doublec.

BLOODY SUNDAY: ANNIVERSARY. Jan 30, 1972. In Londonderry, Northern Ireland, 13 Roman Catholics were shot dead by British troops during a banned civil rights march. During 1972, the first year of British direct rule, 467 people were killed in the fighting.

CHARLES I EXECUTION: ANNIVERSARY. Jan 30, 1649. English king beheaded by order of Parliament under Oliver Cromwell on this date; considered a martyr by some.

FIRST BRAWL IN THE US HOUSE OF REPRESENTATIVES: ANNIVERSARY. Jan 30, 1798. The first brawl to break out on the floor of the US House of Representatives occurred at Philadelphia, PA. The fight was precipitated by an argument between Matthew Lyon of Vermont and Roger Griswold of Connecticut. Lyon spat in Griswold's face. Although a resolution to expel Lyon was introduced, the measure failed and Lyon maintained his seat.

GANDHI ASSASSINATED: ANNIVERSARY. Jan 30, 1948. Indian religious and political leader, assassinated at New

Delhi, India. The assassin was a Hindu extremist, Ram Naturam. See also: "Gandhi, Mohandas Karamchand (Mahatma): Birth Anniversary" (Oct 2).

MARYLAND ADOPTS ARTICLES OF CONFEDERA-TION: ANNIVERSARY. Jan 30, 1781. Maryland became the last of the 13 original states to adopt the Articles of Confederation.

★**NATIONAL CONSUMER PROTECTION WEEK.** Jan 30–Feb 5.

NATIONAL INANE ANSWERING MESSAGE DAY. Jan 30. Annually, the day set aside to change, shorten, replace or delete those ridiculous and/or annoying answering machine messages that waste the time of anyone who must listen to them. [© 2000 by WH]. For info: Thomas and Ruth Roy, Wellcat Holidays, 2418 Long Ln, Lebanon, PA 17046. Phone: (717) 279-0184. E-mail: wellcat@supernet.com. Web: www.wellcat.com.

OSCEOLA: DEATH ANNIVERSARY. Jan 30, 1838. Osceola was a war leader during the Second Seminole War (1835–1842). During the first two years of the war, he led the fight against removal of the Florida Seminoles to Indian territory. He was captured under a flag of truce in 1837 and imprisoned at Fort Marion in St. Augustine. He was moved to Fort Moultrie at Charleston Harbor, SC, where he died. He was born near present-day Tuskegee, AL, ca.1804.

RAF BOMBS HITLER CELEBRATION: ANNIVER-SARY. Jan 30, 1943. British Royal Air Force Mosquito bombers ran a daylight raid on Berlin timed to coincide with a speech being given by Joseph Goebbels in honor of Hitler's 10th year in power.

ROOSEVELT, FRANKLIN DELANO: BIRTH ANNI-VERSARY. Jan 30, 1882. 32nd president of the US (Mar 4, 1933–Apr 12, 1945). The only president to serve more than two terms, FDR was elected four times. He supported the Allies in WWII before the US entered the struggle by supplying them with war materials through the Lend-Lease Act; he became deeply involved in broad decision making after the Japanese attack on Pearl Harbor Dec 7, 1941. Born at Hyde Park, NY, he died a few months into his fourth term at Warm Springs, GA, Apr 12, 1945.

SCOTLAND: UP HELLY AA. Jan 30. Lerwick, Shetland Islands. Norse galley burned in impressive ceremony symbolizing sacrifice to sun. Old Viking custom. A festival marking the end of Yule. Annually, the last Tuesday in January. For info: Tourist Information Centre, Market Cross, Lerwick, Shetland, Scotland ZE1 0LU. Phone: (44) (595) 693-434. Fax: (44) (595) 695-807.

SCRAPERS CAN COLLECTION FOR KIDS. Jan 30 (also Apr 30, Aug 30 and Nov 30). Porter, TX. Every three months we collect cans nationwide and donate the tabs to charity. This helps kids with serious diseases that range from cancer to tumors. Our donations helps buy medical supplies and also helps the families. Please help make our collection a success. Est attendance: 500. For info: Scrapers, 23766 E Webb St, Porter, TX 77365. Phone: (281) 354-5272. E-mail: scrapcu@hotmail.com. Web: www.hotyellow98.com/scrap.

TET OFFENSIVE BEGINS: ANNIVERSARY. Jan 30, 1968. After calling for a cease-fire during the Tet holiday celebrations, North Vietnam and the National Liberation Front launched a major offensive throughout South Vietnam on that holiday. Attacks erupted in 36 of the 44 provincial capitals and five of the six major cities. In addition, the Viet Cong attacked the US embassy in Saigon, Tan Son Nhut Air Base, the presidential palace and South Vietnamese general staff headquarters. Costing as many as 40,000 battlefield deaths, the offensive was a tactical defeat for the Viet Cong and North Vietnam. The South Vietnamese held their ground and the US was able to airlift troops into the critical areas and quickly regain control. However, the offensive is credited as a strategic success in that it continued the demoralization of American public opinion. After Tet, American policy toward Vietnam shifted from winning the war to seeking an honorable way out.

THOMAS, ISAIAH: BIRTH ANNIVERSARY. Jan 30, 1749. American printer, editor, almanac publisher, historian and founder of the American Antiquarian Society. Born at Boston, MA; died Apr 4, 1831, at Worcester, MA.

TUCHMAN, BARBARA W.: BIRTH ANNIVERSARY. Jan 30, 1912. Historian and journalist Barbara Tuchman's most famous works were her Pulitzer Prize–winning books *The Guns of August* (1962) and *Stilwell and the American Experience in China, 1911–45* (1971). Tuchman was known for making history live, never dry. Other well-known books included *The Proud Tower* (1966) and *The First Salute* (1988). Barbara Wertheim Tuchman was born at New York, NY, and died at Greenwich, CT, Feb 6, 1988.

BIRTHDAYS TODAY

Christian Bale, 27, actor (*Little Women, Empire of the Sun*), born Pembrokeshire, West Wales, Jan 30, 1974.

Brett Butler, 43, comedienne, actress ("Grace Under Fire"), born Montgomery, AL, Jan 30, 1958.

Richard B. Cheney, 60, US Secretary of Defense (Bush administration), born Lincoln, NE, Jan 30, 1941.

Phil Collins, 50, musician, singer, songwriter, born Chiswick, England, Jan 30, 1951.

Charles S. Dutton, 50, actor ("Roc," *Mississippi Masala, Menace II Society*), born Baltimore, MD, Jan 30, 1951.

Gene Hackman, 71, actor (*The French Connection, Bonnie and Clyde, Unforgiven*), born San Bernardino, CA, Jan 30, 1930.

Davey Johnson, 58, baseball manager and former player, born Orlando, FL, Jan 30, 1943.

Dorothy Malone, 76, actress ("Peyton Place"; Oscar for *Written on the Wind*), born Chicago, IL, Jan 30, 1925.

Dick Martin, 79, comedian, actor (Emmy for "Rowan & Martin's Laugh-In"), born Detroit, MI, Jan 30, 1922.

Frank O'Bannon, 71, Governor of Indiana (D), born Louisville, KY, Jan 30, 1930.

Vanessa Redgrave, 64, actress (*Mary, Queen of Scots; Julia*), born London, England, Jan 30, 1937.

Louis Rukeyser, 67, financial commentator, host ("Wall Street Week"), born New York, NY, Jan 30, 1934.

Boris Spassky, 64, former chess player, journalist, born Leningrad, USSR, Jan 30, 1937.

Curtis Strange, 46, golfer, broadcaster, born Norfolk, VA, Jan 30, 1955.

Jody Watley, 40, singer, born Chicago, IL, Jan 30, 1961.

JANUARY 31 — WEDNESDAY

Day 31 — 334 Remaining

FIRST SOCIAL SECURITY CHECK ISSUED: ANNI-VERSARY. Jan 31, 1940. Ida May Fuller of Ludlow, VT, received the first monthly retirement check in the amount of $22.54. Ms Fuller had worked for three years under the Social Security program (which had been established by legislation in 1935). The accumulated taxes on her salary over those three years were $24.75. She lived to be 100 years old, collecting $22,888 in Social Security benefits. See also: "Social Security Act: Anniv" (Aug 14).

GREY, ZANE: BIRTH ANNIVERSARY. Jan 31, 1872. Zane Grey (original name Pearl Grey), American dentist and prolific author of tales of the Old West, was born at Zanesville, OH. Grey eventually wrote more than 80 books that were translated into many languages and sold more than 10 million copies. The novel *Riders of the Purple Sage* (1912) was the most popular. Grey died Oct 23, 1939, at Altadena, CA.

McDONALD'S INVADES THE SOVIET UNION: ANNI-VERSARY. Jan 31, 1990. McDonald's Corporation opened its first fast-food restaurant in the Soviet Union.

MOORE, GARRY: BIRTH ANNIVERSARY. Jan 31, 1915. American television host Garry Moore was born Thomas Garrison Morfit at Baltimore, MD. His best-known shows were "I've

Got a Secret" (1952–67) and "To Tell the Truth" (1969–76). He gave Carol Burnett her break on TV when he made her a regular on "The Garry Moore Show." He died Nov 28, 1993, at Hilton Head Island, SC.

MORRIS, ROBERT: BIRTH ANNIVERSARY. Jan 31, 1734. Signer of the Declaration of Independence, the Articles of Confederation and the Constitution. He was only one of two men who signed all three documents. He was born at Liverpool, England, and died May 7, 1806, at Philadelphia, PA.

NAURU: NATIONAL HOLIDAY. Jan 31. Republic of Nauru. Commemorates independence in 1968 from a UN trusteeship administered by Australia, New Zealand and the UK.

"NIGHT HEAT" TV PREMIERE: ANNIVERSARY. Jan 31, 1985. A joint production of the Canadian network CTV and CBS, "Night Heat" was filmed in a Toronto disguised to represent any big city. The series, which took place mainly after hours, was about two urban cops assigned to the Mid-South precinct and the columnist assigned to cover their cases. Sonny Grosso, a former cop himself, and Larry Jacobson served as producers. Cast principals included: Scott Hylands as veteran detective Kevin O'Brien, Jeff Wincott as his partner, Frank Giambone, and Allan Royal as reporter Tom Kirkwood.

PONTIAC SILVERDOME BOAT, SPORT AND FISHING SHOW. Jan 31–Feb 4. Pontiac Silverdome, Pontiac, MI. This event brings together buyers and sellers of boating, fishing and outdoor sporting products. US and Canadian hunting and fishing trips, as well as other vacation travel destinations, are featured. Est attendance: 35,000. For info: Adam Starr, Show Span, Inc, 1400 28th St SW, Grand Rapids, MI 49509. Phone: (616) 530-1919. Fax: (616) 530-2122. Web: www.showspan.com.

ROBINSON, JACKIE: BIRTH ANNIVERSARY. Jan 31, 1919. Jack Roosevelt Robinson, athlete and business executive, first black to enter professional major league baseball (Brooklyn Dodgers, 1947–56). Voted National League's Most Valuable Player in 1949 and elected to the Baseball Hall of Fame in 1962. Born at Cairo, GA, Jackson died at Stamford, CT, Oct 24, 1972.

SCHUBERT, FRANZ: BIRTH ANNIVERSARY. Jan 31, 1797. Composer, born at Vienna, Austria, and died there of typhus Nov 19, 1828, at age 31. Buried, at his request, near the grave of Beethoven. Schubert last worked on his "Unfinished Symphony" (No 8) in 1822. On the 100th anniversary of his death in 1928 a $10,000 prize was offered to "finish" the work. The protests were so great that the offer was withdrawn.

SCOTCH TAPE DEVELOPED: ANNIVERSARY. Jan 31, 1928. Scotch tape developed by Richard Drew, of the 3M Company.

SLOVIK, EDDIE D.: EXECUTION ANNIVERSARY. Jan 31, 1945. Anniversary of execution by firing squad of 24-year-old Private Eddie D. Slovik. Born at Detroit, MI, Feb 18, 1920, Slovik was assigned to Company G, 109th Infantry, 28th Division, US Army. His death sentence, the first for desertion since the Civil War, has been a subject of controversy. First buried in France, Slovik's remains were exhumed in 1987 for reburial beside his wife, Antoinette, who died in 1979, after years of effort to clear Slovik's name and have his body returned to the US.

SPACE MILESTONE: _APOLLO 14_ (US): 30th ANNIVERSARY. Jan 31, 1971. Launch date of _Apollo 14_. Five days later on Feb 5 astronauts Alan B. Shepard, Jr, and Edgar D. Mitchell landed on the moon (Lunar Module _Antares_). Command Module _Kitty Hawk_ was piloted by Stuart A. Roosa. Pacific splashdown on Feb 9.

SPACE MILESTONE: _EXPLORER 1_ (US). Jan 31, 1958. The first successful US satellite. Although launched four months later than the Soviet Union's _Sputnik_, _Explorer_ reached a higher altitude and detected a zone of intense radiation inside Earth's magnetic field. This was later named the Van Allen radiation belts. More than 65 subsequent _Explorer_ satellites were launched through 1984.

SPACE MILESTONE: _LUNA 9_ (USSR): 35th ANNIVERSARY. Jan 31, 1966. Launch of unmanned mission that accomplished the first soft landing on the moon three days later on Feb 3. Relayed TV photos of the lunar surface.

SPACE MILESTONE: PROJECT MERCURY TEST (US): 40th ANNIVERSARY. Jan 31, 1961. A test of Project Mercury spacecraft accomplished the first US recovery of a large animal from space. Ham, the chimpanzee, successfully performed simple tasks in space.

ZEHNDER'S SNOWFEST (WITH ICE CARVING AND STATE OF MICHIGAN SNOW SCULPTING COMPETITIONS). Jan 31–Feb 5. Frankenmuth, MI. Annual festival also includes ice demonstrations, snow exhibitions by international teams from 10 countries and many children's activities such as a petting zoo, rides and music. Est attendance: 200,000. For info: Linda Kelly, Zehnder's of Frankenmuth, 730 S Main St, Frankenmuth, MI 48734. Phone: (800) 863-7999. Fax: (517) 652-3544. Web: www.zehnders.com.

BIRTHDAYS TODAY

Ernest (Ernie) Banks, 70, Baseball Hall of Fame shortstop, born Dallas, TX, Jan 31, 1931.

Queen Beatrix, 63, Queen of the Netherlands, born Sostdijk, Netherlands, Jan 31, 1938.

Carol Channing (Carol Channing Lowe), 78, actress (stage: _Hello, Dolly!; Thoroughly Modern Millie_), born Seattle, WA, Jan 31, 1923.

Minnie Driver, 30, actress (_Gross Pointe Blank, Good Will Hunting_), born London, England, Jan 31, 1971.

Philip Glass, 64, composer, born Baltimore, MD, Jan 31, 1937.

Johnny (Rotten) Lydon, 45, lead singer (Sex Pistols 1975–77), born near London, England, Jan 31, 1956.

Kelly Lynch, 42, actress (_Mr. Magoo, Drugstore Cowboy_), born Minneapolis, MN, Jan 31, 1959.

Norman Mailer, 78, author (_The Executioner's Song, The Naked and the Dead_), born Long Branch, NJ, Jan 31, 1923.

Stuart Margolin, 61, actor, director, writer ("The Rockford Files" [Emmy Awards, 1979, 1980], _The Big Blue, S.O.B._), born Davenport, IA, Jan 31, 1940.

Suzanne Pleshette, 64, actress ("The Bob Newhart Show"), born New York, NY, Jan 31, 1937.

(Lynn) Nolan Ryan, 54, Baseball Hall of Famer, born Refugio, TX, Jan 31, 1947.

Jean Simmons, 72, actress (_Black Narcissus, The Robe, Elmer Gantry_), born London, England, Jan 31, 1929.

Jessica Walter, 57, actress ("Amy Prentiss," _Play Misty for Me, The Flamingo Kid_), born Brooklyn, NY, Jan 31, 1944.

Februarie.

FEBRUARY 1 — THURSDAY
Day 32 — 333 Remaining

AMD/LOW VISION AWARENESS MONTH. Feb 1–28. Macular degeneration is a leading cause of vision loss. Low vision aids can make the most of remaining vision. Information on eye disease warning signs and on low vision aids will be available. For info: Marketing Dept, Prevent Blindness America, 500 E Remington Rd, Schaumburg, IL 60173. Phone: (800) 331-2020.

AMERICAN HEART MONTH. Feb 1–28. Volunteers across the country spend one to four weeks canvassing neighborhoods and providing educational information about heart disease and stroke. The 2001 theme is "Be An American Heart Saver!" Know the warning signs of a heart attack. Call 911. Give CPR. For info: Call your local chapter of the American Heart Association or News Media Relations, American Heart Association, 7272 Greenville Ave, Dallas, TX 75231. Phone: (800) AHA-USA1. Fax: (214) 369-3685. Web: www.americanheart.org.

★**AMERICAN HEART MONTH.** Feb 1–28. Presidential Proclamation issued each year for February since 1964. (PL88–254 of Dec 30, 1963.)

ANTIQUE VALENTINE EXHIBIT. Feb 1–25. Surratt House and Tavern, Clinton, MD. Display of 19th-century valentines and memorabilia. Est attendance: 500. For info: Surratt House and Tavern, PO Box 427, Clinton, MD 20735. Phone: (301) 868-1121. Fax: (301) 868-8177. Web: www.surratt.org.

BLACK HISTORY MONTH. Feb 1–28. Traditionally the month containing Abraham Lincoln's birthday (Feb 12) and Frederick Douglass's presumed birthday (Feb 14). Observance of a special period to recognize achievements and contributions by African Americans dates from February 1926, when it was launched by Dr. Carter G. Woodson and others. Variously designated Negro History, Black History, Afro-American History, African-American History, Black Heritage and Black Expressions, the observance period was initially one week, but since 1976 the entire month of February. Each year the month has a theme. For info: Assn for Afro-American Life and History, 7961 Eastern Ave, #301, Silver Spring, MD 20910. Phone: (301) 587-5900. Fax: (301) 587-5915. E-mail: ASALH@earthlink.net. Web: www.artnoir.com/asalh/.

BLACK MARIA STUDIO: ANNIVERSARY. Feb 1, 1893. The first moving picture studio was built at Thomas Edison's laboratory compound at West Orange, NJ, at a cost of less than $700. The wooden structure of irregular oblong shape was covered with black tar paper. It had a sharply sloping roof hinged at one edge so that half of it could be raised to admit sunlight. Fifty feet in length, it was mounted on a pivot enabling it to be swung around to follow the changing position of the sun. There was a stage draped in black at one end of the room. Though the structure was officially called a Kinetographic Theater, it was nick-named the "Black Maria" because it resembled an old-fashioned police wagon.

CAMELLIA DAYS. Feb 1–28. Massee Lane Gardens, Fort Valley, GA. 10th annual celebration of the beautiful flower, the camellia. Events include: garden tours and workshops, plant sale, Senior Citizen Day, fashion show and luncheon, Family Fun Day, golf tournament and more. Call for more details and ticket prices. Sponsor: The American Camellia Society. Est attendance: 4,000. For info: Massee Lane Gardens, 100 Massee Lane, Fort Valley, GA 31030. Phone: (912) 967-2722. Fax: (912) 967-2083. E-mail: acs@alltel.net. Web: www.camellias-acs.com.

CAR INSURANCE FIRST ISSUED: ANNIVERSARY. Feb 1, 1898. Travelers Insurance Company issued the first car insurance against accidents with horses.

CARAWAY, HATTIE WYATT: BIRTH ANNIVERSARY. Feb 1, 1878. Born at Bakersville, TN, Hattie Caraway became a US senator from Arkansas when her husband died in 1931 and she was appointed to fill out his term. The following year she ran for the seat herself and became the first woman elected to the US Senate. She served 14 years there, becoming an adept and tireless legislator (once introducing 43 bills on the same day) who worked for women's rights (once cosponsoring an equal rights amendment), supported New Deal policies as well as Prohibition and opposed the increasing influence of lobbyists. Caraway died at Falls Church, VA, Dec 21, 1950.

CELEBRATION OF CHOCOLATE. Feb 1–28. Decatur, IL. Afternoon and evening reservations for private Chocolate Tea Parties. Selection of hot cocoas, imported and domestic boxed chocolates, specialty handcrafted candy and fresh-baked goods from the 1800s, gourmet fudge collection. Est attendance: 1,000. For info: Chocolate Research Library, 202 E North St, Decatur, IL 62523. Phone: (217) 422-7933.

CHATTANOOGA BOAT SHOW. Feb 1–4. Chattanooga, TN. 16th annual show featuring more than 50,000 square feet of boats and 40 booths displaying fishing tackle, marine equipment, water skis and much more. Est attendance: 12,000. For info: Cindy Crabtree, Esau, Inc, PO Box 50096, Knoxville, TN 37950. Phone: (865) 588-1233 or (800) 588-ESAU. Fax: (865) 588-6938. Web: www.esaushows.com.

A DAY FOR HEARTS: CHD AWARENESS DAYS. Feb 1–28. Activities occur throughout February in various cities across the United States. A grass roots effort to promote greater public awareness of congenital heart disorders (CHD). Currently, approximately one in every 100 babies born in the United States will have something wrong with its heart, making congenital heart disorders the number one birth defect. For info: Gabrielle Harlow, 58 Summerhill Park, Crownsville, MD 21032. Phone: (410) 841-2491. Fax: (410) 841-6684. E-mail: CHDQUILT@yahoo.com.

DEARBORN SNOW FRIEZE. Feb 1–4. Dearborn, MI. Snow sculpting competition and community festival to raise funds for charity. A "frieze" is a three-dimensional work of art carved into a vertical surface. The event includes food booths, live musical and family entertainment and a Friday evening "Snow Ball" dance. Est attendance: 3,000. For info: Gail Fisher, City of Dearborn, 13615 Michigan Ave, Dearborn, MI 48126. Phone: (313) 943-3156. Fax: (313) 943-2776.

FEBRUARY IS BERRY FRESH IN THE SUNSHINE STATE. Feb 1–28. Strawberries in February? You bet your snow boots! Though it's cold and dreary in many parts of the country, February is fantastic in Florida where strawberry growers are harvesting their winter crop and shipping handpicked fruit to key markets. Strawberries dipped in chocolate or champagne make an interesting Valentine's Day menu, or consider using the ripe, luscious berry in a variety of treats. For info: Florida Strawberry Growers Assn, PO Drawer 2550, Plant City, FL 33564. Phone: (813) 752-6822. Web: www.straw-berry.org.

FESTIVAL OF THE NORTH. Feb 1–28. Ketchikan, AK. A cultural event encompassing an annual Wearable Art Show, performing, visual and literary arts, including a myriad of workshops.

Annually, the month of February. Est attendance: 1,000. For info: Ketchikan Area Arts and Humanities Council, 338 Main St, Ketchikan, AK 99901. Phone: (907) 225-2211. Fax: (907) 225-4330.

FIRST SESSION OF SUPREME COURT: ANNIVERSARY. Feb 1, 1790. The Supreme Court of the United States met for the first time in New York City with Chief Justice John Jay presiding.

FLAGSTAFF WINTERFEST. Feb 1–28. Flagstaff, AZ. This winter festival, now in its 15th year, showcases Flagstaff's mountain wonderland with more than 100 events including sled dog races, alpine and nordic ski activities, snow games, sleigh rides, snowmobile drag races, concerts, historic walking tours, Native American storytelling and winter workshops. Est attendance: 20,000. For info: Ann Dunlop, Winterfest Coordinator, Flagstaff Chamber of Commerce, 101 W Rte 66, Flagstaff, AZ 86001. Phone: (520) 774-4505. Fax: (520) 779-1209. Web: www.flagstaff.az.us.

FORD, JOHN: BIRTH ANNIVERSARY. Feb 1, 1895. Film director John Ford was born at Cape Elizabeth, ME, as Sean Aloysius O'Feeney; he changed his name after moving to Hollywood. Ford won his first Academy Award in 1935 for *The Informer*. Among his many other films: *The Plough and the Stars, Stagecoach, Young Mr Lincoln, The Grapes of Wrath, How Green Was My Valley, Rio Grande, What Price Glory?, Mister Roberts* and *The Man Who Shot Liberty Valance*. During World War II he served as chief of the Field Photographic Branch of the OSS. Two documentaries made during the war earned him Academy Awards. He died Aug 31, 1973, at Palm Desert, CA.

FREEDOM DAY: ANNIVERSARY. Feb 1, 1865. Anniversary of President Abraham Lincoln's approval of the 13th Amendment to the US Constitution (abolishing slavery): "1. Neither slavery nor involuntary servitude, except as a punishment for crime whereof the party shall have been duly convicted, shall exist within the United States or any place subject to their jurisdiction. 2. Congress shall have power to enforce this article by appropriate legislation." The amendment had been proposed by the Congress Jan 31, 1865; ratification was completed Dec 18, 1865.

GABLE, CLARK: 100th BIRTH ANNIVERSARY. Feb 1, 1901. Actor William Clark Gable's first film was *The Painted Desert* in 1931 during the era when talking films were replacing silent films. He won an Academy Award for his role in the comedy *It Happened One Night*, which established him as a romantic screen idol. Other films included *China Seas, Mutiny on the Bounty, Saratoga, Command Decision, Run Silent Run Deep* and *Gone with the Wind*, for which his casting as Rhett Butler seemed a foregone conclusion due to his popularity as the acknowledged "King of Movies." Gable was born at Cadiz, OH, and died Nov 16, 1960, at Hollywood, CA, shortly after completing his last film, Arthur Miller's *The Misfits*, in which he starred with Marilyn Monroe.

"GENERAL ELECTRIC THEATER" TV PREMIERE: ANNIVERSARY. Feb 1, 1953. CBS's half-hour dramatic anthology series was hosted by Ronald Reagan (in between his movie and political careers). Making their television debuts were Joseph Cotten (1954); Fred MacMurray, James Stewart and Myrna Loy (1955); Bette Davis, Anne Baxter, Tony Curtis and Fred Astaire (1957); Sammy Davis, Jr (1958); and Gene Tierney (1960). Other memorable stars who appeared on the series include: Joan Crawford, Harry Belafonte, Rosalind Russell, Ernie Kovacs, the Marx Brothers and Nancy Davis Reagan.

February 2001

S	M	T	W	T	F	S
				1	2	3
4	5	6	7	8	9	10
11	12	13	14	15	16	17
18	19	20	21	22	23	24
25	26	27	28			

"GOOD TIMES" TV PREMIERE: ANNIVERSARY. Feb 1, 1974. A CBS spin-off from "Maude," which was a spin-off of "All in the Family." "Good Times" featured an African American family living in the housing projects of Chicago. The series portrayed the Evans family's struggles to improve their lot. The cast featured Esther Rolle and John Amos as Florida and James Evans, Jimmie Walker as son J.J., BernNadette Stanis as daughter Thelma, Ralph Carter as son Michael, Johnny Brown as janitor Mr Bookman, Ja'Net DuBois as neighbor Willona Woods, Janet Jackson as Willona's adopted daughter Penny and Ben Powers as Thelma's husband, Keith Anderson.

GREENSBORO SIT-IN: ANNIVERSARY. Feb 1, 1960. Commercial discrimination against blacks and other minorities provoked a nonviolent protest. At Greensboro, NC, four students from the Agricultural and Technical College at Greensboro (Ezell Blair, Jr, Franklin McCain, Joseph McNeill and David Richmond) sat down at a Woolworths store lunch counter and ordered coffee. Refused service, they remained all day. The following days similar sit-ins took place at the Woolworths' lunch counter. Before the week was over they were joined by a few white students. The protest spread rapidly, especially in southern states. More than 1,600 persons were arrested before the year was over for participating in sit-ins. Civil rights for all became a cause for thousands of students and activists. In response, equal accommodation regardless of race became the rule at lunch counters, hotels and business establishments in thousands of places.

HUGHES, LANGSTON: BIRTH ANNIVERSARY. Feb 1, 1902. African American poet and author, born at Joplin, MO. Among his works are the poetry collection *Montage of a Dream Deferred*, plays, a novel and short stories. Hughes died May 22, 1967 at New York, NY.

INTERNATIONAL BOOST SELF-ESTEEM MONTH. Feb 1–28. A month to focus on the importance of nurturing and cultivating self-esteem to beat the winter blahs, to boost morale and to inspire yourself and others to seize new challenges. For info: Valla Dana Fotiades, M.Ed., PO Box 812, West Side Stn, Worcester, MA 01602-0812. Phone: (508) 799-9860. E-mail: Eb1valla@aol.com.

INTERNATIONAL EXPECT SUCCESS MONTH. Feb 1–28. If you want good things to happen to you in the new year, you must "Expect Success. . .then work like there is no other option." For details and information on how to make this your most successful year yet by letting the power of positive expectation work for you, contact Life Power Dynamics. For info: Karla Brandau, Life Power Dynamics, 4985 Chartley Circle, Lilburn, GA 30047. Phone: (770) 923-0883. Fax: (770) 931-2530. E-mail: karla@karlaspeaks.com. Web: www.karlaspeaks.com.

"LATE NIGHT WITH DAVID LETTERMAN" TV PRE-MIERE: ANNIVERSARY. Feb 1, 1982. This is when it all began: the stupid pet tricks, stupid human tricks and the legendary top ten lists. "Late Night" premiered on NBC as a talk/variety show appearing after "The Tonight Show with Johnny Carson." Host David Letterman was known for his irreverent sense of humor and daffy antics. The offbeat show attained cult status among college crowds and insomniacs, as many tuned in to see a Velcro-suited Letterman throw himself against a wall. The show also featured bandleader-sidekick Paul Shaffer, writer Chris Elliott and Calvert DeForest as geezer Larry "Bud" Melman. In 1993, Letterman made a highly publicized exit from NBC and began hosting "The Late Show" on CBS.

LIBRARY LOVERS' MONTH. Feb 1–28. A month-long celebration of school, public and private libraries of all types. This is a time for everyone, especially library support groups, to recognize the value of libraries and to work to assure that the nation's libraries will continue to serve. For info: Stephanie Stokes, 1980 Washington, No 107, San Francisco, CA 94109-2930. Phone: (415) 749-0130. Fax: (415) 749-0735. E-mail: librarylovers @calibraries.org. For great ideas, check our website: www .calibraries.org.

MARFAN SYNDROME AWARENESS MONTH. Feb 1–28. Volunteers across the country distribute items with a heart theme and educational information about Marfan syndrome and related connective tissue disorders that can result in life-threatening cardiovascular problems as well as orthopedic and ophthalmologic handicaps; it affects about 200,000 Americans. Annually, the month of February. For info: Cathie Tsuchiya, National Marfan Foundation, 382 Main St, Port Washington, NY 11050. Phone: (800) 862-7326 or (516) 883-8712. Fax: (516) 883-8040. E-mail: staff@marfan.org. Web: www.marfan.org.

MOON PHASE: FIRST QUARTER. Feb 1. Moon enters First Quarter phase at 9:02 AM, EST.

★**NATIONAL AFRICAN AMERICAN HISTORY MONTH.** Feb 1–28.

NATIONAL CHERRY MONTH. Feb 1–28. To publicize the colorful red tart cherry. Recipes, posters and table tents available. For info: Jane Baker, Mktg Dir, Cherry Marketing Institute, PO Box 30285, Lansing, MI 48909-7785. Phone: (517) 669-4264. Fax: (517) 669-3354. E-mail: jbaker@cherrymkt.org. Web: www .cherrymkt.org.

NATIONAL CHILDREN'S DENTAL HEALTH MONTH. Feb 1–28. To increase dental awareness and stress the importance of regular dental care. For info: American Dental Assn, 211 E Chicago Ave, Chicago, IL 60611. Catalog sales: (800) 947-4746. Web: www.ada.org.

★**NATIONAL FREEDOM DAY.** Feb 1. Presidential Proclamation 2824, Jan 25, 1949, covers all succeeding years (PL80–842 of June 30, 1948).

NATIONAL SIGN UP FOR SUMMER CAMP MONTH. Feb 1–28. Every year more than nine million children continue a national tradition by attending day or resident camps. Building self-confidence, learning new skills and making memories that last a lifetime are just a few examples of what makes camp special and why camp does children a world of good. To find the right program, parents begin looking at summer camps during this month—and sign their children up while there are still vacancies. For info: Public Relations, American Camping Assn, 5000 State Rd 67N, Martinsville, IN 46151. Phone: (765) 342-8456. E-mail: pr@aca-camps.org. Web: www.ACAcamps.org. For a guide to accredited camps, call (800) 428-CAMPS.

NATIONAL SNACK FOOD MONTH. Feb 1–28. Potato chips and other crunchy munchies are promoted as "fun foods" in radio ads, radio contests, publicity and in-store promotions. Sponsors: Snack Food Association and The National Potato Board. For info: Communications Dept, Snack Food Assn, 1711 King St, Alexandria, VA 22314. Phone: (703) 836-4500. Fax: (703) 836-8262. E-mail: sfa@sfa.org.

NATIONAL WEDDINGS MONTH. Feb 1–28. As the "wedding season" gets into high gear, this observance is to call attention to the fact that more than 2.5 million weddings are celebrated in the US each year. For info: Gerard J. Monaghan, Pres, Assn of Bridal Consultants, 200 Chestnutland Rd, New Milford, CT 06776-2521. Phone: (860) 355-0464. Fax: (860) 354-1404. E-mail: office@bridalassn.com. Web: www.BridalAssn.com.

NATIONAL WILD BIRD FEEDING MONTH. Feb 1–28. To recognize that February is one of the most difficult winter months in much of the US for birds to survive in the wild and to encourage people to provide food, water and shelter to supplement the wild birds' natural diet of weed seeds and harmful insects. For info: Sue Wells, Exec Dir, National Bird-Feeding Society, PO Box 23, Northbrook, IL 60065-0023. Phone: (847) 272-0135. E-mail: feedbirds@aol.com.

NORTH CAROLINA SWEETPOTATO MONTH. Feb 1–28. To educate the public about the nutritional benefits and versatility of sweet potatoes. North Carolina farmers want America to know that sweetpotatoes aren't just for turkeys anymore. Available year-round, sweetpotatoes are loaded with beta carotene and vitamin C. They can be boiled, baked, microwaved, grilled, broiled, fried, mashed, sauteed, candied or served raw. North Carolina produces more sweetpotatoes than any other state. For info: Sue Johnson-Langdon, North Carolina SweetPotato Commission, 1327 N Brightleaf Blvd, Ste H, Smithfield, NC 27577. Phone: (919) 989-7323. Fax: (919) 989-3015. E-mail: ncsweetsue@aol .com. Web: www.ncsweetpotatoes.com.

PLANT THE SEEDS OF GREATNESS MONTH. Feb 1–28. Think globally—build for the future—Plant the Seeds of Greatness. If you're unhappy with your present situation, discover how you can remove the barriers and make a change in your life for the better. Use the next 28 days to put to use your own unique prosperity consciousness and plant the seeds for your new career, life objectives or goals. Make a difference for yourself, your family, your business or your community. Take a chance, help yourself or help another unlock the potential for success and plant the seeds of greatness. Get outside of your comfort zone and take action on your ideas and dreams. For info send a LSASE: Lorrie Walters Marsiglio, Lorimar Communications, PO Box 284 CC, Wasco, IL 60183-0284. Phone: (630) 584-9368. E-mail: marsiglio@megsinet.net.

RETURN SHOPPING CARTS TO THE SUPERMARKET MONTH. Feb 1–28. A monthlong opportunity to return stolen shopping carts, milk crates, bread trays and ice cream baskets to supermarkets and to avoid the increased food prices that these thefts cause. Annually, the month of February. Sponsor: Illinois Food Retailers Association. For info: Anthony A. Dinolfo, Grocer-"Retired," 163 Fairfield Dr, New Lenox, IL 60451-3523. Phone: (815) 463-9136.

ROBINSON CRUSOE DAY. Feb 1, 1709 (OS). Anniversary of the rescue of Alexander Selkirk, Scottish sailor who had been put ashore (in September 1704) on the uninhabited island, Juan Fernandez, at his own request after a quarrel with his captain. His adventures formed the basis for Daniel Defoe's book *Robinson Crusoe.* A day to be adventurous and self-reliant.

SAINT LAURENT, LOUIS STEPHEN: BIRTH ANNIVERSARY. Feb 1, 1882. Canadian lawyer and prime minister, born at Compton, Quebec. Died at Quebec City, July 25, 1973.

"THE SECRET STORM" TV PREMIERE: ANNIVERSARY. Feb 1, 1954. "The Secret Storm" lathered up homes for 20 years. The first soap on television, it revolved around the Ames family in fictional Woodbridge and featured a variety of actors and actresses who have moved on to bigger things. Among them are: Bibi Besch, Roy Scheider, Diana Muldaur, Nicolas Coster, Robert Loggia, Laurence Luckinbill, Christina Crawford, Diane Ladd, Troy Donahue and Frances Sternhagen.

WISE HEALTH CONSUMER MONTH. Feb 1–28. Self-care is a proven way to reduce health care costs. For this reason, companies, hospitals and HMOs are offering more self-care programs.

Wise Health Consumer Marketing packet available. For info: American Institute for Preventive Medicine, 30445 Northwestern Hwy, Ste 350, Farmington Hills, MI 48334. Phone: (248) 539-1800 ext 247. Fax: (248) 539-1808.

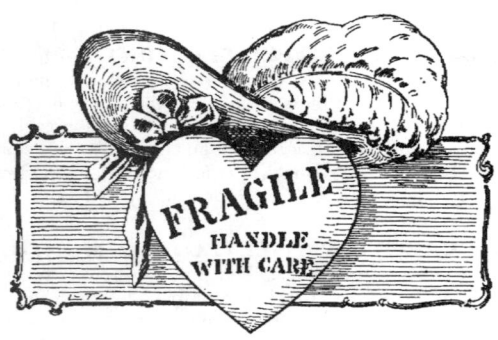

WOMEN'S HEART HEALTH DAY. Feb 1. As American Heart Month begins, here is a day to promote awareness that heart disease is the number one killer of American women. For info: Charlotte Libov, Editor, Women's Health Hot Line, 71 Judson Lane, Bethlehem, CT 06751. Phone and Fax: (203) 266-5904. E-mail: char@libov.com. Web: www.libov.com.

"YOU ARE THERE" TV PREMIERE: ANNIVERSARY. Feb 1, 1953. The program began as an inventive radio show in 1947. News correspondents would comb the annals of history and "interview" the movers and shakers of times past. Walter Cronkite hosted the series on CBS for four seasons. The show's concept was revived for a season in 1971 with Cronkite gearing the program toward children.

BIRTHDAYS TODAY

Michelle Akers, 35, soccer player, born Santa Clara, CA, Feb 1, 1966.

Michael B. Enzi, 57, US Senator (R, Wyoming), born Bremerton, WA, Feb 1, 1944.

Don Everly, 64, singer, musician ("Bye Bye Love," "Wake Up Little Susie"), with brother Phil (The Everly Brothers), born Brownie, KY, Feb 1, 1937.

Sherilynn Fenn, 36, actress ("Twin Peaks," *Wild at Heart*), born Detroit, MI, Feb 1, 1965.

Sherman Hemsley, 63, actor ("The Jeffersons," "Amen"), born Philadelphia, PA, Feb 1, 1938.

Rick James (James Johnson), 49, singer (King of Funk in the '80s, *Street Songs*), born Buffalo, NY, Feb 1, 1952.

Bob Jamieson, 58, broadcast journalist, born Streator, IL, Feb 1, 1943.

Terry Jones, 59, actor, director ("Monty Python's Flying Circus"), born Colwyn Bay, Wales, Feb 1, 1942.

Garrett Morris, 64, comedian ("Saturday Night Live"), born New Orleans, LA, Feb 1, 1937.

Bill Mumy, 47, actor (*Palm Springs Weekend, Twilight Zone—The Movie*, "The Rockford Files"), born El Centro, CA, Feb 1, 1954.

Lisa Marie Presley, 33, daughter of Priscilla and Elvis, born Memphis, TN, Feb 1, 1968.

Pauly Shore, 31, actor ("Pauly," *What He's Got*), born Los Angeles, CA, Feb 1, 1970.

Stuart Whitman, 72, actor ("Cimarron Strip," *The Seekers*), born San Francisco, CA, Feb 1, 1929.

February 2001	S	M	T	W	T	F	S
					1	2	3
	4	5	6	7	8	9	10
	11	12	13	14	15	16	17
	18	19	20	21	22	23	24
	25	26	27	28			

FEBRUARY 2 — FRIDAY
Day 33 — 332 Remaining

AUDEN, WYSTAN HUGH: BIRTH ANNIVERSARY. Feb 2, 1907. Pulitzer Prize–winning Anglo-American poet was born at York, England. "Some books," he wrote in *The Dyer's Hand* (1962), "are undeservedly forgotten; none are undeservedly remembered." Died at Vienna, Austria, Sept 28, 1973.

BABE VOTED INTO BASEBALL HALL OF FAME: 65th ANNIVERSARY. Feb 2, 1936. The five charter members of the brand-new Baseball Hall of Fame at Cooperstown, NY, were announced. Of 226 ballots cast, Ty Cobb was named on 222, Babe Ruth on 215, Honus Wagner on 215, Christy Mathewson on 205 and Walter Johnson on 189. A total of 170 votes were necessary to be elected to the Hall of Fame.

BADGER STATE WINTER GAMES. Feb 2–4. Wausau, WI, and 15 other central Wisconsin communities. 13th annual Olympic-style competition for Wisconsin residents of all ages and abilities featuring 10 sports and opening ceremonies. More than 6,000 athletes in cross-country skiing, downhill skiing, figure skating, ice hockey, ski jumping, snowshoe racing, snowboarding, speed skating and quadrathon. Major sponsors are: AT&T, Ameritech, American Family Insurance, Wisconsin Milk Marketing Board and Ministry Health Care. Member of the National Congress of State Games. Est attendance: 21,000. For info: Badger State Games, PO Box 7788, Madison, WI 53707-7788. Phone: (608) 226-4780. Fax: (608) 226-9550. E-mail: badger@badgerstategames.org. Web: www.badgerstategames.org.

BAN ON AFRICAN NATIONAL CONGRESS LIFTED: ANNIVERSARY. Feb 2, 1990. The 30-year ban on the African National Congress was lifted by South African President F.W. de Klerk. De Klerk also vowed to free Nelson Mandela and lift restrictions on 33 other opposition groups.

BENET, WILLIAM ROSE: BIRTH ANNIVERSARY. Feb 2, 1886. American poet and critic. Born at Fort Hamilton, NY; died at New York, NY, May 4, 1950.

BONZA BOTTLER DAY™. Feb 2. To celebrate when the number of the day is the same as the number of the month. Bonza Bottler Day™ is an excuse to have a party at least once a month. For further information, see Jan 1. For info: Gail M. Berger, 109 Matthew Ave, Poca, WV 25159. Phone: (304) 776-7746. E-mail: gberger5@aol.com.

BULLNANZA. Feb 2–3. Lazy E Arena, Guthrie, OK. Present and past champions in exciting competition in bull riding. Annually, the first Friday and Saturday in February. Est attendance: 14,000. For info: Lazy E Arena, Rte 5, Box 393, Guthrie, OK 73044. Phone: (800) 595-RIDE. Fax: (405) 282-3785. E-mail: arena@lazye.com. Web: www.lazye.com.

CALIFORNIA KIWIFRUIT DAY. Feb 2. National campaign to educate Americans about the nutritional benefits of kiwifruit, the most nutrient-dense fruit (they provide twice the vitamin C of oranges); ways to enjoy kiwifruit and kiwifruit's colorful history. Annually, Feb 2. For info: Katie Mauro, Porter Novelli, 444 Market St, Ste 3000, San Francisco, CA 94111. Fax: (415) 733-1770.

CANADA: ONTARIO WINTER CARNIVAL BON SOO. Feb 2–11. Sault Ste. Marie, ON. One of Canada's largest winter carnivals features more than 125 festive indoor and hearty outdoor events for all ages during an annual 10-day winter extravaganza featuring winter sports, festive dress, entertainment, fireworks and the Fantasy Kingdom winter playground. Est attendance: 100,000. For info: Donna Gregg, Bon Soo Winter Carnival Inc, PO Box 781, Sault Ste. Marie, ON, Canada P6A 5N3. Phone: (705) 759-3000. Fax: (705) 759-6950. E-mail: mrbonsoo@bonsoo.on.ca. Web: www.bonsoo.on.ca.

CANDLEMAS DAY or PRESENTATION OF THE LORD. Feb 2. Observed in Roman Catholic and Eastern Orthodox Churches. Commemorates presentation of Jesus in the Temple and the purification of Mary 40 days after his birth. Candles have been blessed since the 11th century. This marks the end of the Christmas liturgical season. Formerly called the Feast of Purification of the Blessed Virgin Mary. Old Scottish couplet proclaims: "If Candlemas is fair and clear/There'll be two winters in the year."

CORDOVA ICEWORM FESTIVAL. Feb 2–4. Cordova, AK. A multitude of activities for all the family to enjoy: variety show, arts and crafts, basketball tournament, blessing of the fleet, survival suit race, pet show, auction and much more. The legendary 140-ft-long Iceworm, which is propelled by 40 pairs of legs, makes his annual appearance as the finale of the Grand Parade! Cordova is surrounded by the Chugach Mountains and the Prince William Sound on the Gulf of Alaska. Est attendance: 1,500. For info: Darrel Olsen, Dir, Box 768, Cordova, AK 99574. Phone: (907) 424-5756. Fax: (907) 424-3523. E-mail: beedle2@ptialaska .net.

EVERGLADES CITY SEAFOOD FESTIVAL. Feb 2–4. City Park, Everglades City, FL. Fundraiser to improve community center and city park. School children raise funds to pay for prom and other events. Est attendance: 60,000. For info: Betterment Assn of Everglades Area, Inc, PO Box 5029, Everglades City, FL 34139. Phone: (941) 695-4100. Fax: (941) 695-2526. E-mail: evrg1@aol.com.

FLORIDA WILDLIFE AND WESTERN ART EXPO. Feb 2–4. The Lakeland Center, Historic Downtown Lakeland, FL. Featuring more than 200 of the nation's finest wildlife artists, wood sculptors, conservation groups and live wildlife exhibits. Est attendance: 8,000. For info: Michael E. Kessler, Pres, Florida Wildlife Exposition Inc, PO Box 15693, Sarasota, FL 34277. Phone: (941) 364-9453. Fax: (941) 364-9453. E-mail: fwexpo @home.com. Web: www.wildlifeartexpo.com.

GERMAN SURRENDER AT STALINGRAD: ANNIVERSARY. Feb 2, 1943. Two pockets of starving German soldiers remained in Stalingrad on this date. They had received few supplies since Soviet soldiers had encircled the city the previous November. Friedrich von Paulus, whom Hitler had promoted to field marshal only the day before, was forced to seek surrender terms, thereby becoming the first German marshal to surrender. Hitler was furious with von Paulus, believing he should have preferred suicide to surrender. Approximately 160,000 Germans died in the Stalingrad Battle; 34,000 were evacuated by air. Of the 90,000 captured and sent to Siberia on foot, tens of thousands died on the way. This Allied victory is generally considered the psychological turning point of the war.

GETZ, STAN: BIRTH ANNIVERSARY. Feb 2, 1927. American jazz saxophonist Stan Getz was born at Philadelphia, PA. He introduced the cool-jazz style, which became a major movement in the 1950s, and the bossa nova (new wave) style of the 1960s. Getz received 11 Grammy Awards, and was the first jazz musician to win the Grammy Award for Record of the Year (1965) for "The Girl from Ipanema." Died at Mailbu, CA, June 6, 1991.

GREAT NORTHEAST HOME SHOW. Feb 2–4. Pepsi Arena and Empire State Plaza, Albany, NY. The 21st anniversary of the largest consumer home show in the northeast. In addition to exhibits, informative seminars are held throughout the show on topics about the home. Annually, the first full weekend in February. Sponsor: The Times Union Newspaper. Est attendance: 30,000. For info: Tara Sullivan, Dir, Consumer Shows and Special Events, Ed Lewi Assoc, 6 Chelsea Pl, Clifton Park, NY 12065. Phone: (518) 383-6183. Fax: (518) 383-6755.

GROUNDHOG DAY. Feb 2. Old belief that if the sun shines on Candlemas Day, or if the groundhog sees his shadow when he emerges on this day, six weeks of winter will ensue.

GROUNDHOG DAY IN PUNXSUTAWNEY, PENNSYLVANIA. Feb 2. Widely observed traditional annual Candlemas Day event at which "Punxsutawney Phil, king of the weather prophets," is the object of a search. Tradition is said to have been established by early German settlers. The official trek (which began in 1887) is followed by a weather prediction for the next six weeks. [Phil made his dramatic film debut with Bill Murray in *Groundhog Day*.]

GROUNDHOG DAY IN SUN PRAIRIE, WISCONSIN. Feb 2. Sun Prairie, WI. To predict the weather for the balance of winter. Prognostication at 7:15 AM, EST, to see if Jimmy the Groundhog has seen his shadow. Persons born on this date are eligible for "official" groundhog birth certificate and/or groundhog club membership (for a small fee). Est attendance: 700. For info: Chamber of Commerce, 109 E Main St, Sun Prairie, WI 53590. Phone: (608) 837-4547. Fax: (608) 837-8765.

GROUNDHOG DAYS. Feb 2–4. Historic Woodstock Square, Woodstock, IL. Thanks to Bill Murray and the *Groundhog Day* movie, Woodstock celebrates with ice sculpting demonstrations, walking tour of filming sites, breakfast and Woodstock Willie's prognostication. Est attendance: 500. For info: Woodstock Chamber of Commerce, 136 Cass St, Woodstock, IL 60098. Phone: (815) 338-2436. Fax: (815) 338-2927. E-mail: chamber@stans .com.

GROUNDHOG JOB SHADOW DAY. Feb 2. Students spend part of the day in the workplace "shadowing" an employee as he or she goes through a normal day on the job. Job Shadow Day demonstrates the connection between academics and careers and introduces students to the requirements of professions and industries. Local contacts can be found on the website. Planning kit available. For info: Groundhog Job Shadow Day. Phone: (410) 810-7910. E-mail: jobshadow@dc.ogilvypr.com. Web: www .jobshadow.org.

HALAS, GEORGE: BIRTH ANNIVERSARY. Feb 2, 1895. George ("Papa Bear") Halas, Pro Football Hall of Fame coach and owner, born at Chicago, IL. After playing football at the University of Illinois and baseball with the New York Yankees, Halas helped to found the National Football League and the Chicago Bears in 1920. As coach of the Bears for 40 years, he compiled a record of 324 wins, 151 losses and 31 ties. Charter member of the Hall of Fame, 1963. Died at Chicago, IL, Oct 31, 1983.

HOMESTEAD CHAMPIONSHIP RODEO. Feb 2–4. Homestead, FL. Rodeo features cowboy- and cowgirl-athletes competing in seven championship events including calf roping, steer wrestling, bareback riding, saddle bronc riding, barrel racing and bull riding event. For info: Homestead Rodeo Assn, PO Box 1432, Homestead, FL 33090-1432. Phone: (305) 247-3515. Web: www.homesteadrodeo.com.

IMBOLC. Feb 2. (Also called Imbolg, Candlemas, Lupercalia, Feast of Pan, Feast of Torches, Feast of Waxing Light, Brigit's Day and Oimelc.) One of the "Greater Sabbats" during the Wiccan year, Imbolc marks the recovery of the Goddess (after giving birth to the Sun, or the God, at Yule) and celebrates the anticipation of spring. Annually, Feb 2.

JOYCE, JAMES: BIRTH ANNIVERSARY. Feb 2, 1882. Irish novelist and poet, author of *Dubliners, A Portrait of the Artist as a Young Man, Ulysses* and *Finnegans Wake*, was born at Dublin, Ireland. "A man of genius," he wrote in *Ulysses*, "makes no mistakes. His errors are volitional and are portals of discovery." Of *Finnegans Wake* Joyce is reported to have replied to an academic whose letter had asked for clues to its meaning, "If I can throw any obscurity on the subject, let me know." (From AP story, "1000 years of Irish Memories. . . ." by Hugh A. Mulligan.) Joyce died at the age of 58 of peritonitis at Zurich, Switzerland, Jan 13, 1941, and was buried there.

LONGHORN WORLD CHAMPIONSHIP RODEO. Feb 2–4. State Fair Coliseum, Columbus, OH. Held in conjunction with Ohio Beef Expo and Ohio Deer & Turkey Expo. More than 300 cowboys and cowgirls compete in six professional contests ranging from bronc riding to bull riding for top prize money and world championship points. Featuring colorful opening pageantry and Big, Bad BONUS Bulls. 27th annual. Est attendance: 18,000. For info: W. Bruce Lehrke, Pres, Longhorn World Championship Rodeo, Inc, PO Box 70159, Nashville, TN 37207. Phone: (615) 876-1016. Fax: (615) 876-4685. Web: www.longhornrodeo.com.

LUXEMBOURG: CANDLEMAS. Feb 2. Traditional observance of Candlemas. At night children sing a customary song wishing health and prosperity to their neighbors and receive sweets in return. They carry special candles called *Lichtebengel* symbolizing the coming of spring.

MEXICO: DIA DE LA CANDELARIA. Feb 2. All Mexico celebrates. Dances, processions, bullfights.

MOOSE STOMPERS WEEKEND. Feb 2–4. Houlton, ME. Human curling, human dogsled racing, potato peeling contest, wiffle snow ball, giant sliding hill for children, snowmobiling activities, cross-country skiing, skating, bonfire, snowmobile light parade, snowshoe races, Moose Stompers ball, fireworks and much more. For info: Greater Houlton Chamber of Commerce, 109 Main St, Houlton, ME 04730. Phone: (207) 532-4216. E-mail: chamber@rcn.com. Web: www.greaterhoulton.com.

NC RV AND CAMPING SHOW. Feb 2–4. Charlotte Merchandise Mart, Charlotte, NC. A display of the latest in recreation vehicles and accessories by various dealers. Est attendance: 15,000. For info: Apple Rock Advertising & Promotion, 1200 Eastchester Dr, High Point, NC 27265. Phone: (336) 881-7100. Fax: (336) 883-7198.

NRA/NWRA RODEO FINALS. Feb 2–4. MetraPark Arena, Billings, MT. Rodeo action at its best—24th annual finals. A fun-filled rodeo weekend in cowboy country! Est attendance: 16,000. For info: Northern Rodeo Assn, PO Box 1122, Billings, MT 59103. Phone: (406) 252-1122. Fax: (406) 252-0300.

PERCHVILLE USA. Feb 2–4. Tawas Bay, East Tawas, MI. A winter festival with ice-fishing contests, polar bear swims, IWPA dog weight pulls, softball tournaments and many children's activities. Annually, the first weekend in February. Est attendance: 10,000. For info: Amy Dittenber, Tawas Area Chamber of Commerce, Box 608, Tawas City, MI 48764-0608. Phone: (517) 362-8643 or (800) 55-TAWAS.

THE RECORD OF A SNEEZE : ANNIVERSARY. Feb 2, 1893. One day after Thomas Edison's "Black Maria" studio was completed at West Orange, NJ, a studio cameraman took the first "close-up" in film history. *The Record of a Sneeze*, starring Edison's assistant Fred P. Ott, was also the first motion picture to receive a copyright (1894). See also: "Black Maria Studio: Anniversary" (Feb 1).

SARANAC LAKE WINTER CARNIVAL. Feb 2–11. Saranac Lake, NY. Come and join the family fun with fireworks and entertainment, food booths and much more. Annually, the first two full weekends in February. For info: Saranac Lake Winter Carnival, Saranac Lake Chamber of Commerce, 30 Main St, Saranac Lake, NY 12983. Phone: (518) 891-1990 or (800) 347-1992.

TREATY OF GUADALUPE HIDALGO: ANNIVERSARY. Feb 2, 1848. The war between Mexico and the US formally ended with the signing of the Treaty of Guadalupe Hidalgo, signed in the village for which it was named. The treaty provided for Mexico's cession to the US of the territory that became the states of California, Nevada, Utah, most of Arizona, and parts of New Mexico, Colorado and Wyoming, in exchange for $15 million from the US. In addition, Mexico relinquished all rights to Texas north of the Rio Grande. The Senate ratified the treaty Mar 10, 1848.

WALTON, GEORGE: DEATH ANNIVERSARY. Feb 2, 1804. Signer of the Declaration of Independence. Born at Prince Edward County, VA, 1749 (exact date unknown). Died at Augusta, GA.

WHALE OF A WINE & ART FESTIVAL. Feb 2–4. Curry County Fairgrounds, Gold Beach, OR. Toasting the yearly trek of the gray whales, this annual celebration showcases Oregon's vintages. Food tasting, art auction, seminars, live music, art displays and whale watching. Est attendance: 1,000. For info: Gold Beach Chamber of Commerce, 29279 Ellensburg Ave, #3, Gold Beach, OR 97444. Phone: (800) 525-2334. Fax: (541) 247-0188. E-mail: goldbeach@harborside.com. Web: www.goldbeach.org.

"WHAT'S MY LINE?" TV PREMIERE: ANNIVERSARY. Feb 2, 1950. This popular game show premiered on CBS and ran for 17 years in prime time. A panel of four celebrities figured out the professions of the contestants and the identities of the mystery guests by asking yes-or-no questions. The first panel consisted of poet Louis Untermeyer, columnist Dorothy Kilgallen, New Jersey Governor Harold Hoffman and psychiatrist Dr. Richard Hoffman. Yankee Phil Rizzuto was the first mystery guest. John Daly hosted.

WORLD OF WHEELS. Feb 2–4. Multi-Purpose Events Center Exhibit Hall, Wichita Falls, TX. Features spectacular customized, modified and restored vehicles of all sizes, shapes and colors. Famous television stars, exciting entertainment and fun for all ages. Est attendance: 14,000. For info: Wichita Falls Conv & Visitors Bureau, 1000 5th St, Wichita Falls, TX 76301. Phone: (940) 716-5500 or (940) 855-0499. Fax: (940) 716-5509. E-mail: MPEC @WF.net. Web: www.viewscape.com or www.wf.net.

BIRTHDAYS TODAY

Christie Brinkley, 48, model, born Monroe, MI, Feb 2, 1953.

Sean Michael Elliott, 33, basketball player, born Tucson, AZ, Feb 2, 1968.

Farrah Fawcett, 54, actress, model ("Charlie's Angels," *The Burning Bed*), born Corpus Christi, TX, Feb 2, 1947.

Bo Hopkins, 59, actor ("The Rockford Files," "Dynasty," *American Graffiti*), born Greenwood, SC, Feb 2, 1942.

Simon MacCorkindale, 49, actor, producer, screenwriter ("Falcon Crest," *Death on the Nile, Jaws 3-D*), born Isle-of-Ely, England, Feb 2, 1952.

Robert Mandan, 69, actor ("Soap," "Days of Our Lives"), born Clever, MO, Feb 2, 1932.

Graham Nash, 59, musician, singer, born Blackpool, England, Feb 2, 1942.

Liz Smith, 78, journalist, author, born Fort Worth, TX, Feb 2, 1923.

Tom Smothers, 64, comedian, folksinger (brother of Dick Smothers, "The Smothers Brothers Comedy Hour"), born New York, NY, Feb 2, 1937.

Elaine Stritch, 76, actress (*Company*, sang "The Ladies Who Lunch"), born Birmingham, MI, Feb 2, 1925.

Michael T. Weiss, 39, actor ("The Pretender"), born Chicago, IL, Feb 2, 1962.

	S	M	T	W	T	F	S
February					1	2	3
2001	4	5	6	7	8	9	10
	11	12	13	14	15	16	17
	18	19	20	21	22	23	24
	25	26	27	28			

FEBRUARY 3 — SATURDAY
Day 34 — 331 Remaining

ARIZONA RENAISSANCE FESTIVAL. Feb 3–Mar 25. (Saturdays, Sundays and Presidents' Day [Feb 19] only.) Apache Junction, AZ. Enjoy your best day out in history. Find yourself surrounded by medieval merriment with knights, kings, maidens and minstrels. Stroll through acres of amusements, shoppes and non-stop revelry as you join our village celebration. The official sister event to the Robin Hood Festival in Sherwood Forest, England. Est attendance: 265,000. For info: Arizona Renaissance Festival, 12601 E Highway 60, Apache Junction, AZ 85219. Phone: (520) 463-2600.

AZALEA/CAMELLIA FLOWER SHOW. Feb 3–Mar 11. Garfield Park Conservatory and Lincoln Park Conservatory, Chicago, IL. More than 1,000 blooming azaleas representing more than 40 varieties, some of which are decades old, the progeny of plants shown at the 1893 Columbian Exposition. A naturalized woodland setting and brilliant floral contrast include flowering trees and shrubs, spring bulbs and annuals. More than 100 blooming camellias are displayed in the recently renovated Horticulture Hall and beautiful showroom. For info: Garfield Park Conservatory, 300 N Central Park Ave, Chicago, IL 60624. Phone: (312) 746-5100. Fax: (773) 638-1777. Web: www.garfield-conservatory.org or Lincoln Park Conservatory, 2400 N Stockton Dr, Chicago, IL 60614. Phone: (312) 742-7736.

BEARGREASE SLED DOG MARATHON. Feb 3–9. Duluth, MN. To commemorate John Beargrease, a Chippewa sled dog mail carrier along the north shore of Lake Superior from 1887–1900. A 400-mile endurance race with mushers and dogs from the US and Canada. Est attendance: 10,000. For info: Beargrease, Box 500, Duluth, MN 55802. Phone: (218) 722-7631. Fax: (218) 722-3675. E-mail: info@beargrease.com. Web: www.beargrease.com.

BIFOCALS AT THE MONITOR LIBERATION DAY. Feb 3. Wearers of bifocals who work at computer monitors suffer greatly year round. It's time to stop the head bob-and-wave. Throw the spectacles away and glue your face to the screen! ©2000 Wellcat Herbs & Holidays. For info: Thomas & Ruth Roy, 2418 Long Ln, Lebanon, PA 17046-1708. Phone: (230) 332-4886. E-mail: wellcat@supernet.com. Web: www.wellcat.com.

BLACKWELL, ELIZABETH: BIRTH ANNIVERSARY. Feb 3, 1821. First woman physician. Born near Bristol, England, she and several other members of her family were active abolitionists, women's suffrage advocates and pioneers in women's medicine. Her family moved to New York State in 1832, and she received a medical doctor's degree at Geneva, NY, in 1849. She established a hospital in New York City with an all-woman staff, where she recruited and trained nurses for service in the Civil War. Returning to England in 1869, she continued to teach and practice medicine until her death at Hastings, England, May 31, 1910.

CANADAFEST. Feb 3–4. Hollywood, FL. Annual event held on the beach and boardwalk featuring Canadian and American entertainment, arts and crafts, community exhibits and international food. Est attendance: 90,000. For info: Roguey Doyle, City of Hollywood, Dept of Parks, Recreation & Cultural Arts, 1940 Harrison St, Ste 101, Hollywood, FL 33020. Phone: (954) 921-3404.

CIVIL WAR PEACE TALKS: ANNIVERSARY. Feb 3, 1865. Abraham Lincoln and his Secretary of State, William Seward, met to discuss peace with Confederate Vice President Alexander Stephens and others at Hampton Roads, VA. The meeting, which took place on board the ship *River Queen*, lasted four hours and produced no positive results. The Confederates sought an armistice first and discussion of reunion later, while Lincoln was insistent that recognition of Federal authority must be the first step toward peace.

"THE DAY THE MUSIC DIED:" ANNIVERSARY. Feb 3, 1959. The anniversary of the death of rock-and-roll legend Charles Hardin "Buddy" Holly. "The Day the Music Died," so-called in singer Don McLean's song "American Pie," is the date on which Holly was killed in a plane crash in a cornfield near Mason City, IA, along with J.P. Richardson (otherwise known as "The Big Bopper") and Richie Valens. Holly was born Sept 7, 1936, at Lubbock, TX.

DOLL SHOW. Feb 3. Yuma Civic and Convention Center, Yuma, AZ. Assorted antique, handmade and collector's item dolls on display and for sale. Also, miniature furniture and doll-making supplies on sale. Sponsor: Yuma Doll Club. Annually, the first Saturday in February. Est attendance: 750. For info: Marketing Dept, Yuma Civic and Conv Ctr, 1440 Desert Hills Dr, Yuma, AZ 85365. Phone: (520) 782-5797 or (520) 344-3800. Fax: (520) 344-9121.

ENDANGERED SPECIES ACT: ANNIVERSARY. Feb 3, 1973. President Richard Nixon signed the Endangered Species Act into law.

FIFTEENTH AMENDMENT TO US CONSTITUTION RATIFIED: ANNIVERSARY. Feb 3, 1870. The 15th Amendment granted that the right of citizens to vote shall not be denied on account of race, color or previous condition of servitude.

FIRST SECURITY BOULDER MOUNTAIN TOUR. Feb 3. Galena Lodge, Sun Valley, ID. A 30K cross-country race from Galena Lodge to the Sawtooth National Recreation Area (SNRA) headquarters. For info: Sun Valley/Ketchum Chamber of Commerce, Box 2420, Sun Valley, ID 83353. Out-of-state phone: (800) 634-3347; Idaho phone: (208) 726-3423. Fax: (208) 726-4533. E-mail: sunval@micron.net. Web: www.visitsunvalley.com.

FIRST SECURITY WINTER GAMES OF IDAHO. Feb 3–25. Idaho Falls, Sun Valley, Boise, McCall and Kellogg, ID. Idaho's official winter sports competition—four weekends of competition in ice hockey, figure skating, alpine skiing, freestyle skiing, telemark skiing, snowboarding and cross-country skiing with 3,000 participants. For info: Winter Games of Idaho, PO Box 15214, Boise, ID 83715. Phone: (800) 442-3794. Fax: (208) 393-2187.

FOUR CHAPLAINS MEMORIAL DAY. Feb 3, 1943. Commemorates four chaplains (George Fox, Alexander Goode, Clark Poling, John Washington) who sacrificed their life belts and lives when the SS *Dorchester* was torpedoed off Greenland during WWII.

GREELEY, HORACE: BIRTH ANNIVERSARY. Feb 3, 1811. Newspaper editor born at Amherst, NH. Founder of the *New York Tribune* and one of the organizers of the Republican Party, Greeley was an outspoken opponent of slavery. Best remembered for his saying, "Go West, young man." Died Nov 29, 1872, at New York City.

HALFWAY POINT OF WINTER. Feb 3. On this day, 45 days of winter will have elapsed and the equivalent remain before Mar 20, 2001, which is the spring equinox and the beginning of spring.

HOGGETOWNE MEDIEVAL FAIRE. Feb 3–4 and 10–11. Alachua County Fairgrounds, Gainesville, FL. 15th annual faire features jousting, birds of prey, medieval arts and crafts, food and continuous entertainment on eight stages. Est attendance: 60,000. For info: Linda Piper, City of Gainesville, Dept of Cultural Affairs, PO Box 490 Sta. 30, Gainesville, FL 32602. Phone: (352) 334-5064. Fax: (352) 334-2146.

I HATE FINANCIAL PLANNING AWARENESS WEEK. Feb 3–10. Does the thought of financial planning make you want to pull out your hair and scream? Do you count yourself among the 77 percent of Americans who hate financial planning or among the 72 percent of Americans who don't have a financial plan? A week dedicated to helping people who hate financial planning learn how to deal with money matters and how to manage and invest money. For info: Arlene Wheaton, PR Mgr, IHateFinancialPlanning.com. Phone: (612) 372-5784 or Stephen Dupont, Carmichael Lynch Spong. Phone: (612) 375-8525. Web: IHateFinancialPlanning.com.

INCOME TAX BIRTHDAY: SIXTEENTH AMENDMENT TO US CONSTITUTION: RATIFICATION ANNIVERSARY. Feb 3, 1913. The 16th Amendment was ratified, granting Congress the authority to levy taxes on income. (Church bells did not ring throughout the land and no dancing in the streets was reported.)

JAPAN: BEAN-THROWING FESTIVAL (SETSUBUN). Feb 3. Setsubun marks the last day of winter according to the lunar calendar. Throngs at temple grounds throw beans to drive away imaginary devils.

JOHNSTON, JOSEPH: BIRTH ANNIVERSARY. Feb 3, 1807. Born near Farmville, VA, and died Mar 21, 1891, at Washington, DC. Confederate general in the Civil War whose troops were never directly defeated. Longstanding differences with Jefferson Davis, president of the Confederacy, prevented him, however, from reaching his full potential.

KISSIMMEE SLOUGH SHOOTOUT AND RENDEZVOUS. Feb 3–4. Ah-Tah-Thi-Ki Museum, Big Cypress Reservation, FL. Seminole War reenactment. Living history camps, Seminole dancing, Indian arts and crafts, pioneer traders and archery contest. Annually, the first weekend in February. Est attendance: 1,000. For info: Tom Gallaher, Ah-Tah-Thi-Ki Museum, HC-61, Box 21A, Clewiston, FL 33440. Phone: (954) 792-0745. Fax: (954) 583-9893. E-mail: Museum@semtribe.com. Web: www.seminoletribe.com.

KITES ON ICE. Feb 3–4. Frank Lloyd Wright Convention Center, Lake Monona, Madison, WI. Kite flyers from around the world will hold demonstrations and shows on the ice and inside the Convention Center. Est attendance: 75,000. For info: Madison Festivals, Inc, 7818 Big Sky Dr, Ste 205, Madison, WI 53719. Web: www.madfest.org.

LAURA INGALLS WILDER GINGERBREAD SOCIABLE. Feb 3. Pomona, CA. The 34th annual event commemorates the birthday (Feb 7, 1867) of the renowned author of the Little House books. The library has on permanent display the handwritten manuscript of *Little Town on the Prairie* and other Wilder memorabilia. Entertainment by fiddlers, craft displays, apple cider and gingerbread. Annually, the first Saturday in February. Est attendance: 200. For info: Marguerite F. Raybould, Friends of the Pomona Public Library, 625 S Garey Ave, Pomona, CA 91766. Phone: (909) 620-2017. Fax: (909) 620-3713.

LIBERACE MEMORIAL MASS. Feb 3. St. Viator's Church, Las Vegas, NV. Liberace, "Mr Showmanship," was known throughout the world for his beautiful music, his costumes and candelabra. He was honored with an astounding array of awards, including two Emmys, six gold albums and two stars on the Hollywood Walk of Fame. Annually, the first Saturday in February. For info: Jamie G. James, James Agency, PR, 3630 Coldwater Canyon Ave, Studio City, CA 91604. Phone: (818) 508-4902. Fax: (818) 508-0562. E-mail: Jjames@liberace.org.

MACKINAW MUSH SLED DOG RACE. Feb 3–4. Mackinaw City, MI. Largest sled dog race in the continental US. Various sled dog teams race short and speed races to compete for cash prizes. Musher banquet is held on Friday and Saturday nights with live entertainment. Est attendance: 4,000. For info: Brad Jones, Mackinaw Area Tourist Bureau, 708 S Huron, PO Box 160, Mackinaw City, MI 49701. Phone: (800) 666-0160. Web: www.mackinawcity.com.

MARRIAGE OF THE PORT CEREMONY. Feb 3–17. Bryan, TX. Old Portuguese tradition in which a superb hearty red wine is fortified by adding brandy to the barrel. After considerable aging the result is gold medal-winning Papa Paulo Port. The ceremony takes place during each $5 tour of the winery and guests are treated to tastings of port and wedding cake. For info: Cindy Seaton, Messina Hof Wine Cellars, 4545 Old Reliance Rd, Bryan, TX 77808. Phone: (979) 778-9463. Fax: (979) 778-1729.

MICHENER, JAMES: BIRTH ANNIVERSARY. Feb 3, 1907. American author, born at New York, NY. His *Tales of the South Pacific* was the basis for the popular musical, *South Pacific*. A prolific author, his other works include *Sayonara, Iberia, Hawaii, Centennial* and *Texas*. Died at Austin, TX, Oct 17, 1997.

MID-WINTER ANTIQUES AND COLLECTIBLE SHOW AND SALE. Feb 3–4. Millville, NJ. Snow, rain or shine, the sale will go on. Est attendance: 2,000. For info: Wheaton Village, 1501 Glasstown Rd, Millville, NJ 08332. Phone: (800) 998-4552 or (856) 825-6800. Fax: (856) 825-2410. E-mail: mail @wheatonvillage.org. Web: www.wheatonvillage.org.

NATIONAL MEN'S GROOMING DAY. Feb 3. Established by David Raccuglia, founder and president of American Crew, the leading manufacturer of quality grooming products for men, this annual event celebrates the importance of the men's market in the hair care industry. American Crew has an in-depth understanding of men's individual grooming needs and is able to bring this important client into professional salons. Annually, the first Saturday in February. For info: Rob Wilcox, American Crew, 1732 Champa St, Denver, CO 80202. Phone: (800) 598-CREW.

NAUVOO LEGION CHARTERED: ANNIVERSARY. Feb 3, 1841. Created by Illinois Charter and comprised of 5,000 Mormon men under the command of Lieutenant General Joseph Smith, the Nauvoo Legion was considered the "largest trained soldiery in the US" except for the US Army.

NORTH AMERICA'S COLDEST RECORDED TEMPERATURE: ANNIVERSARY. Feb 3, 1947. At Snag, in Canada's Yukon Territory, a temperature of 81 degrees below zero (Fahrenheit) was recorded on this date, a record low for all of North America.

OCEAN COUNTY WILDFOWL ART AND DECOY SHOW. Feb 3–4. Brick High School, Brick, NJ. 140 artists and carvers, decoy-carving competitions, decorative and gunning decoys, junior competition; free seminars on decoy carving, decoy painting and flat art painting. Annually, the first weekend in February. Est attendance: 4,000. For info: Janet Sellitto, Show Coord, Ocean County YMCA, 1088 Whitty Rd, Toms River, NJ 08755. Phone: (732) 341-9622. Fax: (732) 341-1629. Web: www.ocymca.org.

PERRY'S "BRR" (BIKE RIDE TO RIPPEY). Feb 3. Perry, IA. Winter bike riding. Twenty-two miles of frigid fun. Annually, the first Saturday in February. Est attendance: 2,000. For info: John Doyle, Chamber of Commerce, 1226 Second St, Perry, IA 50220. Phone: (515) 465-4601. Fax: (515) 465-2256. E-mail: perrychmbr@aol.com. Web: www.perryia.org.

RAILROAD AND HOBBY SHOW. Feb 3–4. West Springfield, MA. Now expanded to three buildings, nearly 5½ acres with more than 30 operating layouts; displays; art; railroads; Shortline, Tourist and Class 1 railroads; flea market, dealers and more. Est attendance: 25,000. For info: Robert Buck, PO Box 718, Warren, MA 01083-0718. Phone: (413) 436-0242. Fax: (413) 436-7013.

ROCKWELL, NORMAN: BIRTH ANNIVERSARY. Feb 3, 1894. American artist and illustrator especially noted for his realistic and homey magazine cover art for the *Saturday Evening Post*. Born at New York, NY, he died at Stockbridge, MA, Nov 8, 1978.

ROLEX 24 AT DAYTONA. Feb 3–4. Daytona International Speedway, Daytona Beach, FL. 39th annual running of the most prestigious endurance race in North America (exotic purpose-built race cars). Sponsor: Rolex Watch. For info: Daytona Intl Speedway, PO Box 2801, Daytona Beach, FL 32120-2801. Phone: (904) 947-6782. Fax: (904) 947-6791. Web: www.daytonausa.com.

February 2001	S	M	T	W	T	F	S
					1	2	3
	4	5	6	7	8	9	10
	11	12	13	14	15	16	17
	18	19	20	21	22	23	24
	25	26	27	28			

SHOW OF WHEELS. Feb 3–4. Lea County Fairgrounds, Lovington, NM. Car show presented by the Lovington Chamber of Commerce. Featuring antiques, classics, streetrods, motorcycles and minitrucks. A swapmeet, commercial exhibits and games will be an exciting part of the show. RV parking available. For info: Lovington Chamber of Commerce, 201 S Main St, Lovington, NM 88260. Phone: (505) 396-5311 or (505) 396-3661. Fax: (505) 396-2823. E-mail: visitus@leaconet.com. Web: www.leaco.net.

SPACE MILESTONE: *CHALLENGER STS-10* (US). Feb 3, 1984. Shuttle *Challenger* launched from Kennedy Space Center, FL, with a crew of five (Vance Brand, Robert Gibson, Ronald McNair, Bruce McCandless and Robert Stewart). On Feb 7 two astronauts became the first to fly freely in space (propelled by their backpack jets), untethered to any craft. Landed at Cape Canaveral, FL, Feb 11.

STEIN, GERTRUDE: BIRTH ANNIVERSARY. Feb 3, 1874. Avant-garde expatriate American writer, perhaps best remembered for her poetic declaration (in 1913): "Rose is a rose is a rose." Born at Allegheny, PA; died at Paris, France, July 27, 1946.

WASHINGTON'S BIRTHDAY CELEBRATION. Feb 3–18. Laredo, TX. Founded in 1898, the event celebrates the cultures of both the US and Mexico with festivities ranging from the Jalapeño Festival to parades, fireworks and a carnival. The largest celebration of George Washington's birthday in the nation. Est attendance: 500,000. For info: Washington's Birthday Celebration Assn, 1819 E Hillside Rd, Laredo, TX 78041. Phone: (956) 722-0589. Fax: (956) 722-5528. E-mail: wbca@icsi.net.

WORLD SHOVEL RACE CHAMPIONSHIPS. Feb 3–4. Angel Fire, NM. This famous event highlights thrilling competition in production and modified divisions for several age groups. "Modified" competition reaches speeds of 75 mph. Spectator competition on stock grain scoop shovels. Est attendance: 3,000. For info: Angel Fire Resort, PO Drawer B, Angel Fire, NM 87710. Phone: (800) 633-7463 or (505) 377-4237. Fax: (505) 377-4395. E-mail: events@angelfireresort.com. Web: www.angelfireresort.com.

BIRTHDAYS TODAY

Shelley Berman, 75, comedian ("Mary Hartman, Mary Hartman"), born Chicago, IL, Feb 3, 1926.

Joey Bishop (Joseph Abraham Gottlieb), 83, actor ("The Joey Bishop Show," "Liar's Club"), born New York, NY, Feb 3, 1918.

Thomas Calabro, 42, actor ("Melrose Place"), born Brooklyn, NY, Feb 3, 1959.

Blythe Danner, 58, actress (*Butterflies Are Free, Brighton Beach Memoirs, Mr and Mrs Bridge*), born Philadelphia, PA, Feb 3, 1943.

Vlade Divac, 33, basketball player, born Prijepolje, Yugoslavia, Feb 3, 1968.

Morgan Fairchild (Patsy McClenny), 51, actress ("Dallas," "Falcon Crest," "Flamingo Road," "North and South"), born Dallas, TX, Feb 3, 1950.

Keith Gordon, 40, actor, director (*All That Jazz, Dressed to Kill, A Midnight Clear*), born New York, NY, Feb 3, 1961.

Robert Allen (Bob) Griese, 56, sportscaster, Pro Football Hall of Fame quarterback, born Evansville, IN, Feb 3, 1945.

Nathan Lane, 45, actor (Tony for *A Funny Thing Happened on the Way to the Forum*; *The Birdcage*, "Encore! Encore!"), born Jersey City, NJ, Feb 3, 1956.

Bibi Osterwald, 81, actress ("Bridget Loves Bernie"), born New Brunswick, NJ, Feb 3, 1920.

Paul S. Sarbanes, 68, US Senator (D, Maryland), born Salisbury, MD, Feb 3, 1933.

Francis Asbury (Fran) Tarkenton, 61, Pro Football Hall of Fame quarterback, born Richmond, VA, Feb 3, 1940.

Maura Tierney, 36, actress ("NewsRadio," "ER"), born Boston, MA, Feb 3, 1965.

FEBRUARY 4 — SUNDAY
Day 35 — 330 Remaining

APACHE WARS BEGAN: ANNIVERSARY. Feb 4, 1861. The period of conflict known as the Apache Wars began at Apache Pass, AZ, when Army Lieutenant George Bascom arrested Apache Chief Cochise for raiding a ranch. Cochise escaped and declared war. The wars lasted 25 years under the leadership of Cochise and, later, Geronimo.

CARDIAC REHABILITATION WEEK. Feb 4–10. For info: American Assn of Cardiovascular and Pulmonary Rehabilitation, 7611 Elmwood Ave, Ste 201, Middleton, WI 53562. Phone: (608) 831-6989. Fax: (608) 831-5122. E-mail: aacvpr@tmahq.com.

CLEAR LAKE AREA EPICUREAN EVENING. Feb 4. Friendswood, TX, at Baybrook Mall. Come and enjoy tasting food from area restaurants while being entertained by local performers. For info: Clear Lake Area Chamber of Commerce, 1201 Nasa Rd One, Houston, TX 77058. Phone: (281) 488-7676. Fax: (281) 488-8981.

COCONUT GROVE BRIDAL EXPO. Feb 4. Coconut Grove, Santa Cruz, CA. Features more than 60 booths with every aspect needed for that perfect wedding, reception and honeymoon. Est attendance: 2,000. For info: Jan Bollwinkel-Smith, Communications Mgr, Santa Cruz Beach Boardwalk, 400 Beach St, Santa Cruz, CA 95060-5491. Phone: (831) 423-5590. Fax: (831) 460-3336. E-mail: publicity@scseaside.com. Web: www.beachboardwalk.com.

GET PAID TO SHOP WEEK. Feb 4–10. Love to shop? Got those post-holiday, maxed-out credit cards, can't go to the mall blues? Start getting paid to go shopping as a mystery shopper. Businesses use thousands of mystery shoppers to tell them what their customers won't—the truth about service, cleanliness and more. And if you work up an appetite shopping, mystery shoppers also get paid to eat out in restaurants. Free information and articles available for publishers and webmasters at IdeaLady.com/content.htm. Annually, the first full week in February. For info: Cathy Stucker, 4646 Hwy 6, PMB #123, Sugar Land, TX 77478. Phone: (281) 265-9727. E-mail: cathy@idealady.com. Web: idealady.com.

GROUNDHOG RUN. Feb 4. Kansas City, MO. 19th annual. The only 10K, 5K underground run in the world takes place on the Sunday closest to Groundhog Day at the Hunt Midwest Enterprises SubTropolis. More than 2,200 runners from all over the country participate in this event to benefit Children's TLC. Est attendance: 2,200. For info: Children's TLC, 3101 Main St, Kansas City, MO 64111-1921. Phone: (816) 756-0780. Fax: (816) 756-1677. Web: www.childrenstlc.org.

KOSCIUSKO, THADDEUS: BIRTH ANNIVERSARY. Feb 12, 1746. Polish patriot and American Revolutionary War figure. Born at Lithuania, he died at Solothurn, Switzerland, Oct 15, 1817.

LINDBERGH, CHARLES AUGUSTUS: BIRTH ANNIVERSARY. Feb 4, 1902. American aviator Charles "Lucky Lindy" Lindbergh was the first to fly solo and nonstop over the Atlantic Ocean, New York to Paris, May 20–21, 1927. Born at Detroit, MI; died at Kipahula, Maui, HI, Aug 27, 1974. See also: "Lindbergh Flight: Anniversary" (May 20).

SRI LANKA: INDEPENDENCE DAY. Feb 4. Democratic Socialist Republic of Sri Lanka observes National Day. Public holiday. On Feb 4, 1948, Ceylon (as it was then known) obtained independence from Great Britain. The country's name was changed to Sri Lanka in 1972.

SWITZERLAND: HOMSTROM. Feb 4. Scuol. Burning of straw men on poles as a symbol of winter's imminent departure. Annually, the first Sunday in February.

TORTURE ABOLITION DAY: ANNIVERSARY. Feb 4, 1985. Twenty countries signed a UN document titled "Convention Against Torture and Other Cruel, Inhuman or Degrading Treatment or Punishment." Adopted Dec 10, 1984, by the UN General Assembly, it defined torture as any act "by which severe pain or suffering, whether physical or mental, is intentionally inflicted" to obtain information or a confession. While the US did sign the document, signing is only a preliminary stage that must be followed by ratification—which the US has never done.

USO: 60th BIRTHDAY. Feb 4. To honor the civilian agency founded in 1941 that provides support worldwide for US service people and their families. The United Service Organizations (USO) centers have served as a home away from home for hundreds of thousands of Americans.

BIRTHDAYS TODAY

Gabrielle Anwar, 30, actress (*Scent of a Woman*), born Laleham, England, Feb 4, 1971.

Clint Black, 39, country singer, songwriter, born Katy, LA, Feb 4, 1962.

David Brenner, 56, comedian, born Philadelphia, PA, Feb 4, 1945.

Gary Conway, 65, actor ("Burke's Law," *I Was a Teenage Frankenstein*), born Boston, MA, Feb 4, 1936.

Alice Cooper (Vincent Damon Furnier), 53, singer, songwriter, born Detroit, MI, Feb 4, 1948.

Oscar de la Hoya, 28, boxer, born Los Angeles, CA, Feb 4, 1973.

Lisa Eichhorn, 49, actress (*The Vanishing, King of the Hill*), born Reading, PA, Feb 4, 1952.

Pamela Franklin, 51, actress (*The Prime of Miss Jean Brodie, The Legend of Hell House*), born Tokyo, Japan, Feb 4, 1950.

Betty Friedan, 80, author (*The Feminine Mystique*), founder, the National Organization for Women (NOW), born Peoria, IL, Feb 4, 1921.

Michael Goorjian, 30, actor ("Party of Five"), born San Francisco, CA, Feb 4, 1971.

Rod Grams, 53, US Senator (R, Minnesota), born Princeton, MN, Feb 4, 1948.

Rosa Lee Parks, 88, civil rights leader who refused to give up her seat on the bus, born Tuskegee, AL, Feb 4, 1913.

J. Danforth (Dan) Quayle, 54, 44th US Vice President, born Indianapolis, IN, Feb 4, 1947.

John Schuck, 61, actor ("McMillan and Wife," *McCabe and Mrs Miller, Dick Tracy*), born Boston, MA, Feb 4, 1940.

Lawrence Taylor, 42, Pro Football Hall of Fame linebacker, born Williamsburg, VA, Feb 4, 1959.

February 2001	S	M	T	W	T	F	S
					1	2	3
	4	5	6	7	8	9	10
	11	12	13	14	15	16	17
	18	19	20	21	22	23	24
	25	26	27	28			

FEBRUARY 5 — MONDAY
Day 36 — 329 Remaining

CARRADINE, JOHN: 95th BIRTH ANNIVERSARY. Feb 5, 1906. American film actor John Carradine was born Richmond Reed Carradine at Greenwich Village, NY. He appeared in more than 200 films. Frequently observed wandering the streets in a velvet suit and satin cape while reciting Shakespeare, he became known as "the Bard of the Boulevard." Died Nov 27, 1988, at Milan, Italy.

FAMILY-LEAVE BILL: ANNIVERSARY. Feb 5, 1993. President William Clinton signed legislation requiring companies with 50 or more employees (and all government agencies) to allow employees to take up to 12 weeks unpaid leave in a 12-month period to deal with the birth or adoption of a child or to care for a relative with a serious health problem. The bill became effective Aug 5, 1993.

INTERNATIONAL PERSONAL AND BUSINESS COACHING WEEK. Feb 5–11. To provide a week each year to educate the public about the value of working with a personal or business coach and to provide an opportunity for coaches and their clients to acknowledge the results and progress made through the coaching process. Annually, the first week in February. For info: Jerri N. Udelson, MCC, Entrepreneurial Consulting Services, 72 Fresh Pond Parkway, Cambridge, MA 02138. Phone: (617) 491-5748. E-mail: JerriU@aol.com.

LINCOLN, ABRAHAM: OREGON BIRTHDAY OBSERVANCE. Feb 5. Observed annually in Oregon on the first Monday in February. See also: "Lincoln, Abraham: Birth Anniversary" (Feb 12).

LONGEST WAR IN HISTORY: ENDING ANNIVERSARY. Feb 5, 1985. The Third Punic War, between Rome and Carthage, started in the year 149 BC. It culminated in the year 146 BC, when Roman soldiers led by Scipio razed Carthage to the ground. The desolated site was cursed and rebuilding forbidden. On this date, 2,131 years after the war began, Ugo Vetere, mayor of Rome, and Chedli Klibi, mayor of Carthage, met at Tunis to sign a treaty of friendship officially ending the Third Punic War.

MEXICO: ANNIVERSARY OF THE CONSTITUTION. Feb 5. Present constitution, embracing major social reforms, adopted in 1917.

NATIONAL SCHOOL COUNSELING WEEK. Feb 5–9. Promotes school counseling in the school and community. For info: American School Counselor Assn, 801 N Fairfax St, Ste 310, Alexandria, VA 22314 Phone: (800) 306-4722. Fax: (703) 683-1619. E-mail: asca@schoolcounselor.org. Web: www.schoolcounselor.org.

PEEL, ROBERT: BIRTH ANNIVERSARY. Feb 5, 1788. English statesman, established the Irish constabulary (known as the "Peelers"). Later, as England's Home Secretary, he reorganized the London police, thereafter known as "Bobbies." Born at Lancashire, England, he died July 2, 1850, at London from injuries received in a fall from his horse.

STEVENSON, ADLAI EWING: BIRTH ANNIVERSARY. Feb 5, 1900. American statesman, governor of Illinois, Democratic candidate for president in 1952 and 1956, US representative to the UN, 1961–65. Born at Los Angeles, CA. Died at London, England, July 14, 1965. Not to be confused with his grandfather, Vice President Adlai Ewing Stevenson. See also: "Stevenson, Adlai Ewing: Birth Anniversary" (Oct 23).

WEATHERMAN'S [WEATHERPERSON'S] DAY. Feb 5. Commemorates the birth of one of America's first weathermen, John Jeffries, a Boston physician who kept detailed records of weather conditions, 1774–1816. Born at Boston, Feb 5, 1744, and died there Sept 16, 1819. See also: "First Balloon Flight Across English Channel: Anniversary" (Jan 7).

WITHERSPOON, JOHN: BIRTH ANNIVERSARY. Feb 5, 1723. Clergyman, signer of the Declaration of Independence and reputed coiner of the word *Americanism* (in 1781). Born near Edinburgh, Scotland. Died at Princeton, NJ, Nov 15, 1794.

BIRTHDAYS TODAY

Henry Louis (Hank) Aaron, 67, baseball executive, Baseball Hall of Fame outfielder, all-time home run leader, born Mobile, AL, Feb 5, 1934.

Roberto Alomar, 33, baseball player, born Ponce, Puerto Rico, Feb 5, 1968.

Bobby Brown, 32, singer, dancer ("My Prerogative," "Every Little Step"), born Roxbury, MA, Feb 5, 1969.

Red Buttons (Aaron Chwatt), 82, actor ("The Red Buttons Show," "The Double Life of Henry Phyfe"), born The Bronx, NY, Feb 5, 1919.

Father Andrew Greeley, 73, Roman Catholic priest and author (*Happy Are the Merciful, An Occasion of Sin*), born Oak Park, IL, Feb 5, 1928.

Christopher Guest, 53, writer, comedian (Emmy for writing *Lily Tomlin*; "Saturday Night Live"), born New York, NY, Feb 5, 1948.

Barbara Hershey (Barbara Hertzstein), 53, actress (*Hannah and Her Sisters, With Six You Get Eggroll*, "The Monroes"), born Los Angeles, CA, Feb 5, 1948.

David Alan Ladd, 54, actor, producer (*A Dog of Flanders, The Day of the Locust*), born Los Angeles, CA, Feb 5, 1947.

Jennifer Jason Leigh (Morrow), 39, actress (*Miami Blues, Rush, Backdraft*), born Los Angeles, CA, Feb 5, 1962.

Laura Linney, 37, actress (*Primal Fear, The Truman Show*), born New York, NY, Feb 5, 1964.

Jane Bryant Quinn, 60, financial writer (*Everyone's Money Book*), born Niagara Falls, NY, Feb 5, 1941.

Charlotte Rampling, 55, actress (*Georgy Girl, Farewell My Lovely*), born Sturmer, England, Feb 5, 1946.

David Selby, 60, actor ("Falcon Crest," *Rich and Famous*), born Morgantown, WV, Feb 5, 1941.

Roger Thomas Staubach, 59, Pro Football Hall of Fame quarterback, born Cincinnati, OH, Feb 5, 1942.

Darrell Waltrip, 54, auto racer, born Owensboro, KY, Feb 5, 1947.

FEBRUARY 6 — TUESDAY
Day 37 — 328 Remaining

ACCESSION OF QUEEN ELIZABETH II: ANNIVERSARY. Feb 6, 1952. Princess Elizabeth Alexandra Mary succeeded to the British throne (becoming Elizabeth II, Queen of the United Kingdom of Great Britain and Northern Ireland and Head of the Commonwealth) upon the death of her father, King George VI, Feb 6, 1952. Her coronation took place June 2, 1953, at Westminster Abbey at London.

BURR, AARON: BIRTH ANNIVERSARY. Feb 6, 1756. 3rd vice president of the US (Mar 4, 1801–Mar 3, 1805). While vice president, Burr challenged political enemy Alexander Hamilton to a duel and mortally wounded him July 11, 1804, at Weehawken, NJ. Indicted for the challenge and for murder, he returned to Washington to complete his term of office (during which he presided over the impeachment trial of Supreme Court Justice Samuel Chase). In 1807 Burr was arrested, tried for treason (in an alleged scheme to invade Mexico and set up a new nation in the West) and acquitted. Born at Newark, NJ, he died at Staten Island, NY, Sept 14, 1836.

DUMP YOUR "SIGNIFICANT JERK" DAY. Feb 6. It's time to take out the garbage and get rid of that "Jerk" boyfriend or girlfriend. Annually, the Tuesday of the week before Valentine's Day. For info: Marcus P. Meleton Jr, Sharkbait Press, PO Box 11300, Costa Mesa, CA 92627. Phone: (949) 645-0139. E-mail: SharkbaitP@aol.com. Web: www.sharkbaitpress.com.

GREAT AMERICAN PIZZA BAKE. Feb 6–13. Pizza parlors, restaurants and volunteer agencies nationwide create healthy pizza recipes to increase the public's awareness of the benefits of controlling high cholesterol levels through diet. For info: Frederick S. Mayer, Pres, Cholesterol Council of America, c/o PPSI, 101 Lucas Valley Rd, #210, San Rafael, CA 94903. Phone: (415) 479-8628. Fax: (415) 479-8608. E-mail: ppsi@aol.com. Web: www.ppsinc.org.

MARLEY, BOB: BIRTH ANNIVERSARY. Feb 6, 1945. With his group, The Wailers, Bob Marley was one of the most popular and influential performers of reggae music, an "off-beat-accented Jamaican" music closely associated with the political/religious Rastafarian movement (admirers of the late Ethiopian emperor Haile Selassie, who was formerly called Ras Tafari). Marley was born at Rhoden Hall in northern Jamaica. Died of cancer at Miami, FL, May 11, 1981.

MASSACHUSETTS RATIFIES CONSTITUTION: ANNIVERSARY. Feb 6, 1788. By a vote of 187 to 168, Massachusetts became the sixth state to ratify the Constitution.

MID-WINTER'S DAY CELEBRATION. Feb 6. Ann Arbor, MI. To create euphoria by fiat in celebration that winter is half over. For info: Richard Ankli, The Fifth Wheel Tavern, 639 Fifth St, Ann Arbor, MI 48103.

NEW ZEALAND: WAITANGI DAY. Feb 6. National Day. Commemorates signing of the Treaty of Waitangi in 1840 (at Waitangi, Chatham Islands, New Zealand). The treaty, between the native Maori and the European peoples, provided for development of New Zealand under the British Crown.

NORMAN ROCKWELL'S COLONIAL SIGN PAINTER COVER FOR *THE SATURDAY EVENING POST*: ANNIVERSARY. Feb 6, 1926. This Norman Rockwell cover for the *Post* was the first to appear in full color. It depicted a Rockwell kindred spirit—a Colonial sign painter.

PAY-A-COMPLIMENT DAY. Feb 6. Practice this simple act of kindness and pay a compliment to co-workers, family members or a stranger on the street or in the elevator in your office building. Go ahead, make someone feel a little happier today. [©1995] For info: Adrienne Sioux Koopersmith, 1437 W Rosemont, #1W, Chicago, IL 60660-1319. Phone: (773) 743-5341. Fax: (773) 743-5395. E-mail: adrienne@21stcentury.net.

REAGAN, RONALD WILSON: 90th BIRTHDAY. Feb 6, 1911. 40th president of the US (1981–89). Former sportscaster, motion picture actor, governor of California (1967–74); he was the oldest and the first divorced person to become president. Born at Tampico, IL. Married actress Jane Wyman in 1940 (divorced in 1948); married actress Nancy Davis, Mar 4, 1952.

RUTH, "BABE": BIRTH ANNIVERSARY. Feb 6, 1895. One of baseball's greatest heroes, George Herman "Babe" Ruth was born at Baltimore, MD. The left-handed pitcher—"the Sultan of Swat"—hit 714 home runs in 22 major league seasons of play and played in 10 World Series. Died at New York, NY, Aug 16, 1948.

TRUFFAUT, FRANÇOIS: BIRTH ANNIVERSARY. Feb 6, 1932. Born at Paris, France, Truffaut was the most popular and successful French film director of his time. His films include *The 400 Blows, Jules and Jim, The Last Metro* and *The Story of Adele H.* He died at Paris, Oct 21, 1984.

BIRTHDAYS TODAY

Sarah Brady, 59, handgun control activist, born Alexandria, VA, Feb 6, 1942.

Tom Brokaw, 61, journalist, born Yankton, SD, Feb 6, 1940.

Natalie Cole, 51, singer ("This Will Be," "Unforgettable"), born Los Angeles, CA, Feb 6, 1950.

Fabian (Fabian Forte), 58, singer, actor, born Philadelphia, PA, Feb 6, 1943.

Mike Farrell, 62, actor ("M*A*S*H," "Providence"), born St. Paul, MN, Feb 6, 1939.

Zsa Zsa (Sari) Gabor, 82, actress (*Ninotchka, Special Tonight*), born Budapest, Hungary, Feb 6, 1919.

Gayle Hunnicutt, 58, actress ("Dallas," *The Wild Angels, Marlowe*), born Fort Worth, TX, Feb 6, 1943.

Barry Miller, 43, actor (stage: *Biloxi Blues* [Tony Award]; *Saturday Night Fever, The Last Temptation of Christ*), born Los Angeles, CA, Feb 6, 1958.

Kathy Najimy, 44, actress ("Veronica's Closet," *Sister Act*), born San Diego, CA, Feb 6, 1957.

Gigi Perreau, 60, actress (*Bonzo Goes to College, Tammy Tell Me True*), born Los Angeles, CA, Feb 6, 1941.

Ronald Wilson Reagan, 90, 40th US president, former sportscaster and actor (*The Winning Team*), born Tampico, IL, Feb 6, 1911.

Rip Torn (Elmore Torn, Jr), 70, actor ("The Larry Sanders Show," *The Blue and the Gray*), born Temple, TX, Feb 6, 1931.

Robert Townsend, 44, actor, director (*The Five Heartbeats, The Mighty Quinn*), born Chicago, IL, Feb 6, 1957.

Michael Tucker, 57, actor ("LA Law"), born Baltimore, MD, Feb 6, 1944.

Mamie Van Doren, 68, actress (*High School Confidential, Three Nuts in Search of a Bolt*), born Rowena, SD, Feb 6, 1933.

FEBRUARY 7 — WEDNESDAY

Day 38 — 327 Remaining

ART OF COMMUNICATIONS WEEK. Feb 7–14. Make your Valentine's Day a memorable one. Compliment your partner every day, emotionally and physically. Communicate your needs, wants and desires using positive reinforcement and tokens of your appreciation, love and happiness. For info: Dr. Ava Cadell, Ph.D., 9000 Sunset Blvd, #1115, Los Angeles, CA 90069. Phone: (310) 276-8623. E-mail: acadell@earthlink.net.

BALLET INTRODUCED TO THE US: ANNIVERSARY. Feb 7, 1827. Renowned French danseuse Mme Francisquy Hutin introduced ballet to the US with a performance of *The Deserter*, staged at the Bowery Theater, New York, NY. A minor scandal erupted when the ladies in the lower boxes left the theater upon viewing the light and scanty attire of Mme Hutin and her troupe.

BLAKE, EUBIE: BIRTH ANNIVERSARY. Feb 7, 1883. James Hubert "Eubie" Blake, American composer and pianist, writer of nearly 1,000 songs (including "I'm Just Wild About Harry" and "Memories of You"). Born at Baltimore, MD. Recipient of the Presidential Medal of Freedom in 1981. Last professional performance was in Jan 1982. Died at Brooklyn, NY, five days after his 100th birthday, Feb 12, 1983.

February 2001	S	M	T	W	T	F	S
					1	2	3
	4	5	6	7	8	9	10
	11	12	13	14	15	16	17
	18	19	20	21	22	23	24
	25	26	27	28			

CHINA: LANTERN FESTIVAL. Feb 7. Traditional Chinese festival falls on 15th day of first month of Chinese lunar calendar year. Lantern processions mark end of the Chinese New Year holiday season. See also: "Chinese New Year" (Jan 24).

DESERT FOOTHILLS MUSICFEST. Feb 7–25. Carefree/Cave Creek, AZ, in four venues. Arizona's premier winter classical music festival celebrates the music of the millennium with 12 events over a 19-day period. Nine concerts, four daytime "Festival Insights" (lecture, mini-concerts). Features the Festival Chamber Ensemble, pianist Leon Bates with an all-Gershwin program, classical-flamenco guitarist Dennis Koster, Phoenix Symphony Orchestra and jazz piano great Paul Smith. Est attendance: 4,800. For info: Desert Foothills, Musicfest Publicity, PO Box 5254, Carefree, AZ 85377. Phone: (480) 488-0806. Fax: (480) 488-2310. E-mail: info@azmusicfest.org. Web: www.azmusicfest.org.

DICKENS, CHARLES: BIRTH ANNIVERSARY. Feb 7, 1812. English social critic and novelist, born at Portsmouth, England. Among his most successful books: *Oliver Twist, The Posthumous Papers of the Pickwick Club, David Copperfield* and *A Christmas Carol*. Died at Gad's Hill, England, June 9, 1870, and was buried at Westminster Abbey.

ELEVENTH AMENDMENT TO US CONSTITUTION (SOVEREIGNTY OF THE STATES): RATIFICATION ANNIVERSARY. Feb 7, 1795. The 11th Amendment to the Constitution was ratified, curbing the powers of the federal judiciary in relation to the states. The amendment reaffirmed the sovereignty of the states by prohibiting suits against them.

GRENADA: INDEPENDENCE DAY: ANNIVERSARY. Feb 7. National Day. Commemorates independence from Great Britain in 1974.

LEARNING DISABILITIES ASSOCIATION OF AMERICA INTERNATIONAL CONFERENCE. Feb 7–10. New York Hilton, New York, NY. Est attendance: 5,200. For info: Learning Disabilities Assn of America, 4156 Library Rd, Pittsburgh, PA 15234. Phone: (412) 341-1515. Fax: (412) 344-0224. Web: www.ldanatl.org.

LEWIS, SINCLAIR: BIRTH ANNIVERSARY. Feb 7, 1885. American novelist and social critic. Recipient of Nobel Prize for Literature (1930). Among his novels: *Main Street, Babbitt* and *It Can't Happen Here*. Born Harry Sinclair Lewis at Sauk Center, MN. Died at Rome, Italy, Jan 10, 1951.

LOVE MAY MAKE THE WORLD GO 'ROUND, BUT LAUGHTER KEEPS US FROM GETTING DIZZY WEEK. Feb 7–14. This week is dedicated to Victor Borge's notion that "Laughter is the shortest distance between two people" and Joel Goodman's notion that "Seven days without laughter makes one weak." This is a chance to lighten your relationships and to reinforce the connection between "heart" and "hearty laughter." Annually, the week leading up to and including Valentine's Day. To receive a free live-love-laugh info packet on the positive power of humor, send a stamped (99 cents) SASE. For info: Dr. Joel Goodman, The HUMOR Project, Inc, 480 Broadway, Ste 210-C, Saratoga Springs, NY 12866-2288. Phone: (518) 587-8770. Fax: (518) 587-8771 E-mail: chase@HumorProject.com. Web: www.HumorProject.com.

MORE, SIR THOMAS: BIRTH ANNIVERSARY. Feb 7,
1478. Anniversary of birth of lawyer, scholar, author, Lord Chancellor of England, martyr and saint at London, England. Refusing to recognize Henry VIII's divorce from Queen Catherine, the "Man for All Seasons" was found guilty of treason and imprisoned in the Tower of London, Apr 17, 1534. He was beheaded at Tower Hill on July 6, 1535, and his head displayed from Tower Bridge. Canonized in 1935. Memorial observed on June 22.

NATIONAL GIRLS AND WOMEN IN SPORTS DAY. Feb
7. Celebrates and honors all girls and women participating in sports. Recognizes the passage of Title IX in 1972, the law that guarantees gender equity in federally-funded school programs, including athletics. Sponsored by Girls Inc, the Girl Scouts, the National Association for Girls and Women in Sports, the Women's Sports Foundation and the YWCA. For info: Women's Sports Foundation, Eisenhower Park, East Meadow, NY 11554. Phone: (516) 542-4700.

NORTHWEST FLOWER AND GARDEN SHOW. Feb
7–11. Washington State Convention Center, Seattle, WA. Est attendance: 80,000. For info: Northwest Flower and Garden Show, 1515 NW 51st St, Seattle, WA 98107. Phone: (206) 789-5333. Fax: (206) 784-5545. Web: www.gardenshow.com.

SPACE MILESTONE: *STARDUST* (US). Feb 7, 1999. *Stardust* began its 3 billion-mile journey to collect comet dust on this date. The unmanned mission is to meet up with Comet Wild–2 in January 2004 and the comet samples will reach Earth in January 2006. This is the first US mission devoted solely to a comet. NASA plans three more over a four-year period.

TAIWAN: LANTERN FESTIVAL AND TOURISM DAY.
Feb 7. Fifteenth day of the First Moon of the lunar calendar marks end of New Year holiday season. Lantern processions and contests.

WAVE ALL YOUR FINGERS AT YOUR NEIGHBORS
DAY. Feb 7. After all the challenges our neighbors and we have faced, it's time to put it all aside for at least one day. Wave "hello" to everybody and mean it. Annually, Feb 7. © 2000 WH. For info: Thomas and Ruth Roy, Wellcat Holidays, 2418 Long Ln, Lebanon, PA 17046. Phone: (717) 279-0184. E-mail: wellcat @supernet.com. Web: www.wellcat.com.

BIRTHDAYS TODAY

Hector Babenco, 55, director (*Ironweed, Kiss of the Spider Woman*), born Buenos Aires, Argentina, Feb 7, 1946.

Eddie Bracken, 81, actor (*Miracle of Morgan's Creek, Hail the Conquering Hero*), born New York, NY, Feb 7, 1920.

Oscar Brand, 81, folksinger, born Winnipeg, Manitoba, Canada, Feb 7, 1920.

Garth Brooks, 39, country singer ("Friends in Low Places"), born Tulsa, OK, Feb 7, 1962.

Miguel Ferrer, 47, actor ("Twin Peaks;" *Star Trek III; Hot Shots! Part Deux*), born Santa Monica, CA, Feb 7, 1954.

Juwan Howard, 28, basketball player, born Chicago, IL, Feb 7, 1973.

Herb Kohl, 66, US Senator (D, Wisconsin), born Milwaukee, WI, Feb 7, 1935.

Pete Postlethwaite, 56, actor (*Amistad; The Lost World: Jurassic Park; Brassed Off*), born London, England, Feb 7, 1945.

Chris Rock, 35, actor, comedian ("Saturday Night Live," *Beverly Hills Ninja*), born Brooklyn, NY, Feb 7, 1966.

James Spader, 41, actor (*sex, lies, and videotape; Wolf*), born Boston, MA, Feb 7, 1960.

Gay Talese, 69, author (*The Kingdom and the Power, Unto the Sons*), born Ocean City, NJ, Feb 7, 1932.

FEBRUARY 8 — THURSDAY
Day 39 — 326 Remaining

BOY SCOUTS OF AMERICA FOUNDED: ANNIVER-
SARY. Feb 8, 1910. The Boy Scouts of America was founded at Washington, DC, by William Boyce, based on the work of Sir Robert Baden-Powell with the British Boy Scout Association.

DEAN, JAMES: 70th BIRTH ANNIVERSARY. Feb 8,
1931. American stage, film and television actor who achieved immense popularity during a brief career. Born at Fairmont, IN. Best remembered for his role in *Rebel Without a Cause*. Died in an automobile accident near Cholame, CA, Sept 30, 1955, at age 24. Stamp collectors made the US postal stamp bearing Dean's likeness the most popular stamp of 1996.

FLORIDA STATE FAIR. Feb 8–19. Florida State fairgrounds,
Tampa, FL. The fair features the best arts, crafts, competitive exhibits, equestrian shows, livestock, entertainment and food found in Florida. Also not to be missed is "Cracker Country," where cultural and architectural history has been preserved. Est attendance: 545,000. For info: Sherry Powell, Mktg & Advertising Mgr, Florida State Fair, PO Box 11766, Tampa, FL 33680. Phone: (813) 621-7821 or (813) 622-PARK. Web: www .floridastatefair.com.

HOUSTON LIVESTOCK SHOW AND RODEO. Feb
8–Mar 4. Astrodome Complex, Houston, TX. Livestock show with more than 35,000 entries. Rodeo action and top-name musical entertainment. Est attendance: 1,900,000. For info: Mktg Dept, Houston Livestock Show and Rodeo, Box 20070, Houston, TX 77225-0070. Phone: (713) 791-9000. Fax: (713) 794-9528. Web: www.hlsr.com or www.rodeohouston.com.

JAPAN: HA-RI-KU-YO (NEEDLE MASS). Feb 8. Ha-Ri-
Ku-Yo, a Needle Mass, may be observed on either Feb 8 or Dec 8. Girls do no needlework; instead they gather old and broken needles, which they dedicate to the Awashima Shrine at Wakayama. Girls pray to Awashima Myozin (their protecting deity) that their needlework, symbolic of love and marriage, will be good. Participation in the Needle Mass hopefully leads to a happy marriage.

JAPAN: SNOW FESTIVAL. Feb 8–12. Sapporo, Hokkaido.
Huge, elaborate snow and ice sculptures are erected on the Odori-Koen Promenade.

KURSK RETAKEN: ANNIVERSARY. Feb 8, 1943. One year
and three months after being taken by the Nazis, the important railroad junction of Kursk was retaken by the Red Army. This city had served as a principal center of north/south communication and was an essential post for the German army in their chain to the Ukraine.

LAUGH AND GROW RICH DAY. Feb 8. Recognition of laugh-
ter's power to add to the bottom line. People are more effective, tend to remember things better and laughter helps to lower the turnover rate. For info: Rick Segel, 1 Wheatland St, Burlington, MA 01803. Phone: (781) 272-9995. Fax: (781) 272-9996.

MARTHA GRIFFITHS SPEAKS OUT AGAINST SEX
DISCRIMINATION: ANNIVERSARY. Feb 8, 1964. During the congressional debate over the 1964 Civil Rights Act, Representative Martha Griffiths delivered a memorable speech advocating the prohibition of discrimination based on sex. Her efforts resulted in adding civil rights protection for women to the 1964 Act. She later successfully led the campaign for the Equal Rights Amendment in the House of Representatives.

MARY, QUEEN OF SCOTS: EXECUTION ANNIVER-
SARY. Feb 8, 1587. Mary Stuart, the queen regent of Scotland, was beheaded at Fotheringhay, England, her death warrant having been sealed by Queen Elizabeth I on Feb 1. Mary, the daughter of James V of Scotland by his second wife, Mary of Guise, was born Dec 7 or 8, 1542, at Linlithgow, Scotland, and became queen a week later upon the death of her father, although she did not begin governing until after the death of her mother in 1561. She was forced to abdicate in favor of her son (James VI)

when the people turned against her after she married the Earl of Bothwell, who was believed to be the murderer with Mary's knowledge of her second husband (her cousin Henry Stewart, Lord Darnley). She fled to England for protection, only to find herself a prisoner for the rest of her life. She was tried and sentenced to death in 1586 because of her involvement in a plot to assassinate Elizabeth. She was buried at Peterborough, but in 1612 her body was moved to Henry VII's Chapel at Westminster, where a tomb was erected by her son. Essentially, Mary Stuart was a victim of the political intrigue and Protestant–Roman Catholic conflicts that surrounded the Reformation and Henry VIII's ecclesiastical revolution.

MILWAUKEE/NARI HOME IMPROVEMENT SHOW.
Feb 8–11. Wisconsin State Fair Park, West Allis, WI. Cosponsored by Milwaukee/NARI Home Improvement Council and the *Milwaukee Journal Sentinel*, this show is of particular interest to homeowners planning a remodeling project for their home. More than 300 exhibitors in a no-pressure setting. Educational seminars by home improvement experts, a remodeler's showcase with the latest innovations plus guided tours and colorful garden areas. Annually, the second Thursday through Sunday in February. Est attendance: 35,000. For info: Mary Fox-Hagner, Exec Dir, Milwaukee/NARI Home Improvement Council, 13390 Watertown Plank Rd, PO Box 668, Elm Grove, WI 53122-0668. Phone: (414) 789-4800. Fax: (414) 789-4805. E-mail: nari@execpc.com. Web: www.milwaukeenari.com.

MOBIUS ADVERTISING AWARDS.
Feb 8. Chicago, IL. Selection and recognition of the world's most outstanding television and radio commercials, print advertising and package designs. Founded in 1971. Est attendance: 500. For info: J.W. Anderson, Chairman, The Mobius Advertising Awards, 841 N Addison Ave, Elmhurst, IL 60126-1291. Phone: (630) 834-7773. Fax: (630) 834-5565. E-mail: mobiusinfo@mobiusawards.com. Web: www.mobiusawards.com.

MOON PHASE: FULL MOON.
Feb 8. Moon enters Full Moon phase at 2:12 AM, EST.

NEW ORLEANS BOAT SHOW.
Feb 8–11. Louisiana Superdome, New Orleans, LA. Annual show of boat and marine products, fishing equipment and resort info. Informative boating and fishing seminars. For info: NMMA, Sherron F. Smith, Show Mgr, 3500 N Causeway Blvd, Ste 1060, Metairie, LA 70002. Phone: (504) 846-4446. Fax: (504) 846-4443. Web: www.boatshows.com.

OMAHA LAWN FLOWER AND PATIO SHOW.
Feb 8–11. Omaha Civic Auditorium, Omaha, NE. For info: Robert P Mancuso, Pres, Mid-America Expositions, Inc, PO Box 24851, Omaha, NE 68124-0851. Phone: (800) 475-SHOW or (402) 346-8003. Fax: (402) 346-5412. Web: www.showofficeonline.com.

OPERA DEBUT IN THE COLONIES: ANNIVERSARY.
Feb 8, 1735. The first opera produced in the colonies was performed at the Courtroom, at Charleston, SC. The opera was *Flora; or the Hob in the Well*, written by Colley Cibber.

February 2001	S	M	T	W	T	F	S
					1	2	3
	4	5	6	7	8	9	10
	11	12	13	14	15	16	17
	18	19	20	21	22	23	24
	25	26	27	28			

PERIGEAN SPRING TIDES.
Feb 8. Spring tides, the highest possible tides, occur when New Moon or Full Moon falls within 24 hours of the moment the Moon is nearest Earth (perigee) in its monthly orbit at 2 PM, EST. These tides are not named for the season of spring but for the German *springen*, "to leap up."

REENACTMENT OF COWTOWN'S LAST OLD WEST GUNFIGHT.
Feb 8. White Elephant Saloon, Fort Worth, TX. Annual reenactment of Fort Worth's last Old West gunfight, which took place on Feb 8, 1887, between White Elephant Saloon owner Luke Short and former Marshal T.I. "Longhaired Jim" Courtright. Annually, Feb 8. Est attendance: 400 For info: Joe Dulle, Owner, 108 E Exchange Ave, Fort Worth, TX 76106-8210. Phone: (817) 624-9712. Fax: (817) 625-9663.

SEMINOLE TRIBE FESTIVAL, POWOW AND PRCA RODEO.
Feb 8–11. Hollywood Reservation, Hollywood, FL. The Seminole Tribe of Florida hosts dancers representative of more than 100 tribes from across North America. Featured events include Seminole art show, all-Indian rodeo and seldom seen deep-water alligator wrestling. Annually, the second weekend in February. Est attendance: 30,000. For info: Buster Baxley, Seminole Tribe of Florida, 6300 Stirling Rd, Hollywood, FL 33024. Phone: (954) 967-3434. Fax: (954) 967-3483. E-mail: bbaxley@semtribe.com. Web: www.seminoletribe.com.

SHERMAN, WILLIAM TECUMSEH: BIRTH ANNIVERSARY.
Feb 8, 1820. Born at Lancaster, OH, General Sherman is especially remembered for his devastating march through Georgia during the Civil War and his statement "War is hell." Died at New York, NY, Feb 14, 1891.

SPACE MILESTONE: *ARABSAT-1*.
Feb 8, 1985. League of Arab States communications satellite launched into geosynchronous orbit from Kourou, French Guiana, by the European Space Agency.

SPACE MILESTONE: *BRASILSAT-1 (BRAZIL)*.
Feb 8, 1985. Brazilian communications satellite launched into geosynchronous orbit from Kourou, French Guiana, by the European Space Agency.

TU B'SHVAT.
Feb 8. Hebrew calendar date: Shebat 15, 5761. The 15th day of the month of Shebat in the Hebrew calendar year is set aside as Hamishah Asar (New Year of the Trees or Jewish Arbor Day), a time to show respect and appreciation for trees and plants.

VERNE, JULES: BIRTH ANNIVERSARY.
Feb 8, 1828. French writer, sometimes called "the father of science fiction," born at Nantes, France. Author of *Around the World in Eighty Days, Twenty Thousand Leagues Under the Sea* and many other novels. Died at Amiens, France, Mar 24, 1905.

BIRTHDAYS TODAY

Brooke Adams, 52, actress (*Days of Heaven, Gas Food Lodging*), born New York, NY, Feb 8, 1949.

Gary Coleman, 33, actor ("Diff'rent Strokes," *The Kid from Left Field*), born Zion, IL, Feb 8, 1968.

John Grisham, 46, author (*The Firm, The Client*), born Jonesboro, AR, Feb 8, 1955.

Robert Klein, 59, comedian, actor ("Comedy Tonight," *They're Playing Our Song*), born New York, NY, Feb 8, 1942.

Ted Koppel, 61, journalist (anchor of "Nightline"), born Lancashire, England, Feb 8, 1940.

Jack Lemmon (John Uhler III), 76, actor (*Mr Roberts, Grumpy Old Men*), born Boston, MA, Feb 8, 1925.

Alonzo Mourning, 31, basketball player, born Chesapeake, VA, Feb 8, 1970.

Nick Nolte, 60, actor (*48 HRS, Grace Quigley, Prince of Tides*, "Rich Man, Poor Man"), born Omaha, NE, Feb 8, 1941.

Mary Steenburgen, 48, actress (*Melvin and Howard, Parenthood, Back to the Future Part III*), born Newport, AR, Feb 8, 1953.

John Williams, 69, pianist, conductor (formerly with Boston Pops), composer (scores for *Jaws, Star Wars, Jurassic Park, Schindler's List*), born New York, NY, Feb 8, 1932.

FEBRUARY 9 — FRIDAY
Day 40 — 325 Remaining

ALLIES RETAKE GUADALCANAL: ANNIVERSARY.
Feb 9, 1943. In a major strategic victory, the American 161st and 132nd Regiments retook Guadalcanal in the Solomon Islands on this date after a six-month-long battle. More than 9,000 Japanese and 2,000 Americans were killed. The fierce resistance by the Japanese was an indication to the Allies of things to come. Guadalcanal put the Allies within striking distance of Rabaul.

BEHAN, BRENDAN: BIRTH ANNIVERSARY. Feb 9, 1923. Irish playwright and poet born at Dublin, Ireland. Died there Mar 20, 1964.

CANADA: FESTIVAL DU VOYAGEUR. Feb 9–18. Winnipeg, MB. More than 400 shows, food and "joie de vivre" of the fur-trade era. Sled dog races, snow sculptures, costumed interpreters in historic Fort Gibraltar, arts and crafts display and sale, French-Canadian cuisine and much more at Western Canada's largest winter festival. Est attendance: 200,000. For info: Festival du Voyageur, 768 Tache Ave, Winnipeg, MB, Canada R2H 2C4. Phone: (204) 237-7692. Fax: (204) 233-7576. E-mail: voyageur@festivalvoyageur.mb.ca. Web: www.festivalvoyageur.mb.ca.

GOLD RUSH DAYS. Feb 9–11. Wickenburg, AZ. Annual community-wide celebration of the Old West: rodeo, parade, carnival, gold panning. Named one of the top 100 events in North America by the American Bus Association. Annually, the second full weekend in February. Est attendance: 60,000. For info: Chamber of Commerce, 216 N Frontier St, Wickenburg, AZ 85390. Phone: (520) 684-5479 or (520) 684-0977. Fax: (520) 684-5470. E-mail: info@wickenburgchamber.com. Web: www.wickenburgchamber.com.

GYPSY ROSE LEE: BIRTH ANNIVERSARY. Feb 9, 1914. American ecdysiast and author whose real name was Rose Louise Hovick, born at Seattle, WA. Her autobiography, *Gypsy*, was made into a Broadway musical and a motion picture. Died at Los Angeles, CA, Apr 26, 1970.

HARRISON, WILLIAM HENRY: BIRTH ANNIVERSARY. Feb 9, 1773. 9th president of the US (Mar 4–Apr 4, 1841). His term of office was the shortest in our nation's history—32 days. He was the first president to die in office (of pneumonia contracted during inaugural ceremonies). Born at Berkeley, VA, he died at Washington, DC, Apr 4, 1841.

LEBANON: ST. MARON'S DAY. Feb 9. Holiday of Lebanon's Maronite Christian community. St. Maron was a Syrian hermit of the 4th–5th centuries.

LONGHORN WORLD CHAMPIONSHIP RODEO. Feb 9–11. Cincinnati Gardens, Cincinnati, OH. More than 200 cowboys and cowgirls compete in six professional contests ranging from bronc riding to bull riding for top prize money and world championship points. Featuring colorful opening pageantry and Big, Bad BONUS Bulls. 27th annual. Est attendance: 24,000. For info: W. Bruce Lehrke, Pres, Longhorn World Chmpshp Rodeo, Inc, PO Box 70159, Nashville, TN 37207. Phone: (615) 876-1016. Fax: (615) 876-4685. E-mail: lhrodeo@idt.net. Web: www.longhornrodeo.com.

LOWELL, AMY: BIRTH ANNIVERSARY. Feb 9, 1874. American poet born at Brookline, MA. Died there May 12, 1925.

NATIONAL BASKETBALL ASSOCIATION ALL-STAR WEEKEND. Feb 9–11. MCI Center in Washington, DC. For info: Brian McIntyre, Sr VP, Communications, Natl Basketball Assn, Olympic Tower, 645 Fifth Ave, New York, NY 10022. Phone: (212) 407-8000.

NATIONAL "DAV" DAY. Feb 9. "DAV" stands for Develop Alternative Vices. A day to change your habits, improve yourself and become your own person so that things you do today will affect you positively tomorrow. Annually, Feb 9. For info send a SASE to: Kevin Davenport, 5304 Regency Way, Rockford, IL 61114.

NC RV AND CAMPING SHOW. Feb 9–11. Charlie Rose Agri Expo Center, Fayetteville, NC. A display of the latest in recreation vehicles and accessories by various dealers. Est attendance: 5,000. For info: Apple Rock Advertising & Promotion, 1200 Eastchester Dr, High Point, NC 27265. Phone: (336) 881-7100. Fax: (336) 883-7198.

RUSK, (DAVID) DEAN: BIRTH ANNIVERSARY. Feb 9, 1909. US diplomat Dean Rusk was born at Cherokee County, GA. He served as US secretary of state from 1961 to 1969, during which time he supported US involvement in the Vietnam War. He died Dec 20, 1994, at Athens, GA.

TUBB, ERNEST: BIRTH ANNIVERSARY. Feb 9, 1914. Country and western singer, born at Crisp, TX. Ernest Tubb was the sixth member to be elected to the Country Music Hall of Fame and the headliner on the first country music show ever to be presented at Carnegie Hall. His first major hit, "Walking the Floor Over You," gained him his first appearance at the Grand Ole Opry in 1942, and he attained regular membership in 1943. He died Sept 6, 1984, at Nashville, TN.

VEECK, BILL: BIRTH ANNIVERSARY. Feb 9, 1914. William Louis (Bill) Veeck, Jr, Baseball Hall of Fame executive born at Chicago, IL. Veeck was baseball's premier promoter and showman as an owner of several teams. He integrated the American League, sent a midget to the plate to start a game and, in general, sought to provide fans with entertainment in addition to baseball. Inducted into the Hall of Fame in 1991. Died at Chicago, IL, Jan 2, 1986.

WAR TIME: ANNIVERSARY. Feb 9, 1942. US clocks were advanced one hour at 2 AM as the nation went on War Time to conserve electricity. President Roosevelt had signed this daylight savings bill on Jan 20.

WELLS FARGO BANK CUP. Feb 9–11. Winter Park Resort, Winter Park, CO. 26th annual. Elite disabled skiers compete head to head on a dual giant slalom course in the World Disabled Invitational. A purse of more than $13,000 is up for grabs. Amateur races, silent auction and charity dinners benefit the National Sports Center for the Disabled. Est attendance: 10,000. For info: Winter Park Resort, PO Box 36, Winter Park, CO 80482. Phone: (970) 726-1580. Fax: (970) 726-1572. E-mail: wpinfo@mail.skiwinterpark.com. Web: www.winterparkresort.com.

YUMA SQUARE AND ROUND DANCE FESTIVAL. Feb 9–11. Yuma Civic and Convention Center, Yuma, AZ. Square and round dance enthusiasts from Southern California and Arizona participate. Est attendance: 2,000. For info: Marketing Dept, Yuma Civic and Conv Ctr, 1440 Desert Hills Dr, Yuma, AZ 85365. Phone: (520) 344-3800. Fax: (520) 344-9121.

BIRTHDAYS TODAY

Mia Farrow (Maria de Lourdes Villers), 56, actress ("Peyton Place," *Rosemary's Baby, Hannah and Her Sisters*), born Los Angeles, CA, Feb 9, 1945.

Kathryn Grayson (Zelma Hedrick), 78, actress (*Kiss Me Kate, The Kissing Bandit*), born Winston-Salem, NC, Feb 9, 1923.

Carole King, 59, singer, songwriter, born Brooklyn, NY, Feb 9, 1942.

Judith Light, 52, actress ("One Life to Live," "Who's the Boss?"), born Trenton, NJ, Feb 9, 1949.

Roger Mudd, 73, journalist (former anchorman "ABC Evening News"), born Washington, DC, Feb 9, 1928.

Joe Pesci, 58, actor (*Raging Bull, Goodfellas, My Cousin Vinny*), born Newark, NJ, Feb 9, 1943.

Charles Shaughnessy, 46, actor ("Days of Our Lives," "The Nanny"), born London, England, Feb 9, 1955.

Janet Suzman, 62, actress (*Nicholas and Alexandra, A Dry White Season*), born Johannesburg, South Africa, Feb 9, 1939.

Travis Tritt, 38, country and western singer (*Country Club*), born Marietta, GA, Feb 9, 1963.

Alice Walker, 57, author (*The Color Purple, Possessing the Secret of Joy, Meridian*), born Eatonton, GA, Feb 9, 1944.

FEBRUARY 10 — SATURDAY

Day 41 — 324 Remaining

ALBRECHT–KEMPER VALENTINE DINNER. Feb 10. Albrecht–Kemper Museum of Art, St. Joseph, MO. An elegant way for "sweet'arts" to celebrate and also support the museum's major winter fund-raiser. Est attendance: 150. For info: Information Desk, AKMA, 2818 Frederick Ave, St. Joseph, MO 64506. Phone: (816) 233-7003. Fax: (816) 233-3413. E-mail: AKMA @albrechtkemper.org. Web: www.albrecht-kemper.org.

"ALL THE NEWS THAT'S FIT TO PRINT": ANNIVERSARY. Feb 10, 1897. The familiar slogan "All the News That's Fit to Print" has appeared on page one of *The New York Times* since Feb 10, 1897. It had first appeared on the editorial page on Oct 25, 1896. Although in 1896 a $100 prize was offered for a slogan, owner Adolph S. Ochs concluded that his own slogan was better.

AMERICAN BOWLING CONGRESS CHAMPIONSHIPS TOURNAMENT. Feb 10–June 30. Albuquerque, NM. 98th annual. The largest participatory sporting event in the world features more than 50,000 bowlers from around the US and the world. Bowlers compete for titles in singles, doubles, five-player team and all events categories in arena setting. Lanes are especially built for the tournament in convention centers around the US each year. Opening ceremonies are on Feb 12 and include celebrities, traditional "Joe Bowler" selection and recognition of dignitaries. Est attendance: 100,000. For info: Michael Deering, American Bowling Congress, 5301 S 76th St, Greendale, WI 53129-0500. Phone: (414) 423-3309. Fax: (414) 421-3013.

ANDERSON, DAME JUDITH: BIRTH ANNIVERSARY. Feb 10, 1898. Film and stage actress Dame Judith Anderson was born Frances Margaret Anderson at Adelaide, Australia. She was nominated for an Academy Award in 1941 for her role in Alfred Hitchcock's film *Rebecca*. In 1960 she was made Dame Commander of the British Empire by Queen Elizabeth II. She died Jan 3, 1992, at Santa Barbara, CA.

BLACKPOWDER HISTORICAL FAIR. Feb 10–11. Northbridge Mall, Albert Lea, MN. Reenactors and craftsmen from seven states dress in full costume and sell their colonial period items. Entertainment, food and drink, workshops and demonstrations. Est attendance: 5,000. For info: Big Island Rendezvous Inc, 202 North Broadway, Albert Lea, MN 56007. Phone: (800) 658-2526. Fax: (507) 373-0344.

BRECHT, BERTOLT: BIRTH ANNIVERSARY. Feb 10, 1898. German playwright born at Augsburg, Germany. His plays, such as *Mother Courage*, reflect his Marxist and antimilitary world view. Also wrote *The Threepenny Opera* in collaboration with composer Kurt Weill. Died at East Berlin, Aug 14, 1956.

CASA LARGA FIRE & ICE WEEKEND. Feb 10–11. Casa Larga, Fairport, NY. Celebrate the harvest of our Fiore Delle Stella Ice wine. Tours and tasting available both days. For info: Casa Larga Vineyards, 27 Emerald Hill Circle, Fairport, NY 14450. Phone: (716) 223-4210. Web: www.casalarga.com.

CHOCOLATE FEST. Feb 10–11. Garfield Park Conservatory, Chicago, IL. A free weekend celebration of chocolate. Children's activities include chocolate leaf dipping and Valentine card decorations under the only chocolate producing trees in Chicago. Experts will lecture on history and production of chocolate and demonstrate cooking with chocolate. A free sample tasting of the different types of chocolate plus Candy College Library cards and bookmarks. Est attendance: 3,000. For info: Garfield Park Conservatory Alliance, 300 N Central Park Ave, Chicago, IL 60624. Phone: (773) 638-1766, ext 14. Fax: (773) 638-1777. Web: www .garfield-conservatory.org.

CHOCOLATE FESTIVAL. Feb 10–11. Browning Mansion, Galesburg, IL. A chocolate lover's dream! Homemade and commercially made chocolates, tortes, cakes, pies and creams—all you can eat for a small admission fee. Annually, the weekend closest to Valentine's Day. Est attendance: 700. For info: Galesburg Area CVB, PO Box 60, Galesburg, IL 61402-0060. Phone: (309) 343-2485. Fax: (309) 343-2521. E-mail: visitors@galesburg.org. Web: www.galesburg.org/visitors.

CORVETTE AND HIGH PERFORMANCE WINTER MEET. Feb 10–11. Puyallup, WA. Buy, sell and show cars and parts—new, used and reproductions. Est attendance: 10,000. For info: Larry Johnson, Show Organizer, PO Box 7753, Olympia, WA 98507. Phone: (360) 786-8844. Fax: (360) 754-1498.

DURANTE, JIMMY: BIRTH ANNIVERSARY. Feb 10, 1893. "The Schnozz," Jimmy Durante, was born at New York City. His first break into show biz came when he was 17 and got a regular job playing ragtime at a saloon at Coney Island. Later his friend Eddie Cantor urged him to try comedy. Durante developed a unique comedic style as a short-tempered but lovable personage. His shtick included slamming down his hat and flapping his arms. His clothing, enormous nose, craggy face, gravelly singing voice and mispronunciations were all part of the persona. Durante, whose career spanned six decades, appeared on TV, stage and screen. His television signoff, "Good night, Mrs Calabash, wherever you are!" became a trademark. Jimmy Durante died at Santa Monica, CA, Jan 29, 1980.

FARM TOY SHOW AND AUCTION. Feb 10. Sauk Centre, MN. More than 25 vendors display farm toy equipment from 9 AM to 4:30 PM, with a consignment auction starting at 5:30 PM. Est attendance: 800. For info: Barb Borgerding, Sauk Centre Chamber of Commerce, PO Box 222, Sauk Centre, MN 56378. Phone: (320) 352-5201. Web: www.saukcentre.com.

FIRST ACTOR TO PERFORM IN TWO CITIES ON THE SAME DAY: ANNIVERSARY. Feb 10, 1887. Nathaniel Carr Goodwin performed at an 11:30 AM matinee of *Turned Up* at Boston, MA, then, following the closing curtain, he returned to New York City on the 1 PM train and that evening performed in *The Mascot* at the Bijou Theatre at 8 PM.

FIRST WORLD WAR II MEDAL OF HONOR: ANNIVERSARY. Feb 10, 1942. Second Lieutenant Alexander Ramsey ("Sandy") Nininger, Jr, was posthumously awarded World War II's first Medal of Honor for heroism at the Battle of Bataan. He had graduated from West Point in 1941 and was on his first assignment after being commissioned.

GOODY'S DASH SERIES RACE. Feb 10. Daytona Beach, FL. 23rd annual race is season kickoff for the NASCAR Goody's Dash Series. Sponsor: Discount Auto Parts. For info: Daytona Intl Speedway, PO Box 2801, Daytona Beach, FL 32120-2801. Phone: (904) 947-6782. Fax: (904) 947-6791. Web: www.daytonausa.com.

LAMB, CHARLES: BIRTH ANNIVERSARY. Feb 10, 1775. Literary critic, poet and essayist, born at London, England. "The greatest pleasure I know," he wrote in 1834, "is to do a good action by stealth, and to have it found out by accident." Died at Edmonton, England, Dec 27, 1834.

MACKINAW WILDERNESS RUN SLED DOG RACE. Feb 10. Mackinaw City, MI. A one-day event in which dog teams run a mid-distance race and compete for cash prizes. Est attendance: 3,000. For info: Mackinaw Area Tourist Bureau, PO Box 160, Mackinaw City, MI 49701. Phone: (800) 666-0160. Web: www.mackinawcity.com.

MALTA: FEAST OF ST. PAUL'S SHIPWRECK. Feb 10. Valletta. Holy day of obligation. Commemorates shipwreck of St. Paul on the north coast of Malta in AD 60.

February 2001	S	M	T	W	T	F	S
					1	2	3
	4	5	6	7	8	9	10
	11	12	13	14	15	16	17
	18	19	20	21	22	23	24
	25	26	27	28			

"MY FRIEND FLICKA" TV PREMIERE: 45th ANNIVERSARY. Feb 10, 1956. CBS series about a boy and his horse based on the children's book by Mary O'Hara. The series was set in the early 1900s on the Goose Bar Ranch in Montana. Johnny Washbrook starred as Ken McLaughlin; Gene Evans as Ken's father, Rob; Anita Louise as Ken's mother, Nell; Frank Ferguson as Gus, the ranch hand; and Wahama, the beautiful Arabian horse, as Flicka.

NATIONAL HOME AND GARDEN SHOW. Feb 10–18. I-X Center, Cleveland, OH. The largest show of its kind in the country with more than 35 feature gardens, 900 exhibitors and three fully decorated and landscaped walk-through model homes. Est attendance: 300,000. For info: Natl Home and Garden Show, PO Box 550–Edgewater Branch, Cleveland, OH 44107. Phone: (216) 529-1300. Fax: (216) 529-0311. E-mail: expoinc@expoinc.com. Web: www.expoinc.com.

PASTERNAK, BORIS LEONIDOVICH: BIRTH ANNIVERSARY. Feb 10, 1890. Russian poet and novelist, born at Moscow, Russia. Best-known work: *Doctor Zhivago*. Died at Moscow, May 30, 1960.

PLIMSOLL DAY. Feb 10, 1824. A day to remember Samuel Plimsoll, "The Sailor's Friend," a coal merchant turned reformer and politician, who was elected to the British Parliament in 1868. He attacked the practice of overloading heavily insured ships, calling them "coffin ships." His persistence brought about amendment of Britain's Merchant Shipping Act. The Plimsoll Line, named for him, is a line on the side of ships marking maximum load allowed by law. Born at Bristol, England, Feb 10, 1824. Died at Folkestone, England, June 3, 1898.

ROMANCE & REMEMBRANCE. Feb 10 (also Feb 14). Indianapolis, IN. Share a romantic evening with your Valentine by immersing yourselves in the beauty of Harrison's historical home. You will be treated to readings from Victorian and contemporary literature written by Indiana authors and interpreted by readers dressed in period costumes. Guests will then enjoy a candlelight dinner in the Museum's Centennial Room. Est attendance: 80. For info: PR Dept, President Benjamin Harrison Home, 1230 N Delaware St, Indianapolis, IN 46202. Phone: (317) 631-1888. Fax: (317) 632-5488.

TILDEN, BILL: BIRTH ANNIVERSARY. Feb 10, 1893. William Tatem (Bill) Tilden, Jr, tennis player, born at Philadelphia, PA. Generally considered one of the greatest players of all time, Tilden won more tournaments than the record books can count. A nearly flawless player, he was also an egotistical showman on the court with an interest in show business. He turned pro in 1930 and continued to win regularly. Died at Hollywood, CA, June 5, 1953.

TREATY OF PARIS ENDS FRENCH AND INDIAN WAR: ANNIVERSARY. Feb 10, 1763. Known in Europe as the Seven Years' War, this conflict ranged from North America to India, with many European nations involved. In North America French expansion in the Ohio River Valley in the 1750s led to conflict with Great Britain. Some Indians fought alongside the French; a young George Washington fought for the British. As a result of the signing of the Treaty of Paris, France lost all claims to Canada and had to cede Louisiana to Spain. Fifteen years later French bitterness over the loss of its North American colonies to Britain contributed to its supporting the colonists in the American Revolution.

TWENTY-FIFTH AMENDMENT TO US CONSTITUTION RATIFIED (PRESIDENTIAL SUCCESSION, DISABILITY): ANNIVERSARY. Feb 10, 1967. Procedures for presidential succession were further clarified by the 25th Amendment, along with provisions for continuity of power in the event of a disability or illness of the president. The 25th Amendment was ratified Feb 10, 1967.

WHITE, WILLIAM ALLEN: BIRTH ANNIVERSARY. Feb 10, 1868. American newspaperman, owner and editor of the *Emporia Gazette*. Coined the phrase "tinhorn politician" and, in one obituary, wrote of the deceased that he had "the talent of a meat-packer, the morals of a money changer and the manners of an undertaker." Born at Emporia, KS, he died there Jan 29, 1944.

WMAS 94.7 FM VALENTINE'S BALL. Feb 10. Northampton, MA. A formal affair for both couples and singles. An evening of music, dancing and prizes. Est attendance: 700. For info: Dina McMahon, PO Box 9500, Springfield, MA 01120. Phone: (413) 737-1414. Fax: (413) 737-1488.

YUMA JAYCEE'S SILVER SPUR RODEO. Feb 10–12. Yuma County Fairgrounds, Yuma, AZ. Three-day rodeo features professional rodeo cowboy action, preceded by a week of activities beginning with parade on Feb 3. Annually, the second weekend in February. Sponsors: KTTI 95.1, Dodge, Pepsi, Best Western Inn Suites and Wrangler. Est attendance: 18,000. For info: Mary Wurther, Rodeo Chair, Silver Spur Rodeo, 4318 W 17th Lane, Yuma, AZ 85366. Phone: (520) 344-5451.

BIRTHDAYS TODAY

Laura Dern, 34, actress (*Blue Velvet, Rambling Rose*), born Los Angeles, CA, Feb 10, 1967.
Donovan (Donovan P. Leitch), 55, singer, songwriter, born Glasgow, Scotland, Feb 10, 1946.
Leonard Kyle (Lenny) Dykstra, 38, former baseball player, born Santa Ana, CA, Feb 10, 1963.
Roberta Flack, 62, singer, born Black Mountain, NC, Feb 10, 1939.
Frank Keating, 57, Governor of Oklahoma (R), born St. Louis, MO, Feb 10, 1944.
Frances Moore Lappe, 57, author (*Diet for a Small Planet, Rediscovering America's Values*), born Pendleton, OR, Feb 10, 1944.
Gregory John (Greg) Norman, 46, golfer, born Melbourne, Australia, Feb 10, 1955.
Leontyne Price, 74, opera singer, born Laurel, MS, Feb 10, 1927.
Mark Andrew Spitz, 51, Olympic gold medal swimmer, born Modesto, CA, Feb 10, 1950.
Robert Wagner, 71, actor ("It Takes a Thief," "Hart to Hart"), born Detroit, MI, Feb 10, 1930.

FEBRUARY 11 — SUNDAY
Day 42 — 323 Remaining

AFRICAN AMERICAN ARTISTS ANNUAL. Feb 11–28. St. Simons Island, GA. Exhibit and promotion of African-American artists, their art and artistic achievements. For info: Mittie B. Hendrix, Dir, Coastal Center for the Arts, 2012 Demere Rd, St. Simons Island, GA 31522. Phone: (912) 634-0404. E-mail: coastalart@thebest.net.

ARCA 200 BONDO/MAR-HYDE. Feb 11. Daytona International Speedway, Daytona Beach, FL. 38th annual running. Season kickoff for the Bondo/Mar-Hyde Series. Sponsor: First Plus Financial. For info: Daytona Intl Speedway, PO Box 2801, Daytona Beach, FL 32120-2801. Phone: (904) 947-6782. Fax: (904) 947-6791. Web: www.daytonausa.com.

BE ELECTRIFIC DAY. Feb 11. A day to honor the birth of Thomas Alva Edison and discover the "electricity" of the body through applied kinesiology and other body energy demonstrations. For info: Carolyn Finch, author of Be Electrific: Understanding Body Language, Electrific Solutions, 51 Cedar Dr, Danbury, CT 06811. Phone: (203) 792-4833. Fax: (203) 743-5675. E-mail: Carolyn@electrific.nai.net. Web: www.electrific.com.

CAMEROON: YOUTH DAY. Feb 11. Public holiday.

CELEBRATION OF LOVE WEEK. Feb 11–17. To stress the importance and value of love in making the world a much better place in which to live. For complete info, send $4 to cover expense of printing, handling and postage. Annually, the second full week of February. For info: Dr. Stanley Drake, Pres, Intl Soc of Friendship and Good Will, 8592 Roswell Rd, Ste 434, Atlanta, GA 30350-1870.

CHILD, LYDIA MARIA: BIRTH ANNIVERSARY. Feb 11, 1802. Born at Medford, MA. As a writer her works included *Hobomok*, about early Salem and Plymouth life, and *The Rebels*, which described pre-Revolutionary Boston. In addition, she produced several practical works including *The Frugal Housewife*, which enjoyed 21 editions, and *The Mother's Book*. In 1833 she and her husband, David Lee Child, published the controversial abolitionist document "An Appeal in Favor of That Class of Americans Called Africans," which called for educating the slaves. Their work for abolition continued with the weekly newspaper *The National Anti-Slavery Standard*, which they published at New York City from 1840–44. Lydia died Oct 20, 1880, at Wayland, MA.

DUNNE, PHILIP: BIRTH ANNIVERSARY. Feb 11, 1908. American screenwriter and director Philip Dunne was born at New York, NY. In 1947 he joined directors John Huston and William Wyler to found the Committee for the First Amendment, which campaigned against the "blacklisting" in Hollywood of anyone suspected of being a communist by the House Un-American Activities Committee. He was also a founder of the Screen Writers Guild. Dunne died June 2, 1992, at Malibu, CA.

EDISON, THOMAS ALVA: BIRTH ANNIVERSARY. Feb 11, 1847. American inventive genius and holder of more than 1,200 patents (including the incandescent electric lamp, phonograph, electric dynamo and key parts of many now-familiar devices such as the movie camera, telephone transmitter, etc). Edison said, "Genius is 1 percent inspiration and 99 percent perspiration." His birthday is now widely observed as Inventor's Day. Born at Milan, OH, and died at Menlo Park, NJ, Oct 18, 1931.

ENABLED ENTREPRENEURS WEEK. Feb 11–17. In recognition of entrepreneurs with disabilities, those who chart their own courses with determination and perseverance, creating businesses for themselves and jobs for people in the community. Show your support this week by identifying these entrepreneurs, getting to know them and their businesses. Encourage networking opportunities with other business owners in your area. Annually, the third week in February. For info: Carol MacKenzie, Communicate with Care, 12 Kayla Circle, Plymouth, MA 02360. Phone: (508) 224-3640.

FIRST WOMAN EPISCOPAL BISHOP: ANNIVERSARY. Feb 11, 1989. The presiding bishop of the Episcopal Church, Bishop Edmond L. Browning, consecrated the Reverend Barbara Clementine Harris as a bishop of the Episcopal Church.

FREELANCE WRITERS APPRECIATION WEEK. Feb 11–17. Freelance writers do more than query editors and write and submit articles and books (nonfiction and fiction). They provide overworked editors with material, as well as inform and entertain readers. Annually, the second week of February. For info:

	S	M	T	W	T	F	S
February					1	2	3
2001	4	5	6	7	8	9	10
	11	12	13	14	15	16	17
	18	19	20	21	22	23	24
	25	26	27	28			

Dorothy Zjawin, Dir, 61 W Colfax Ave, Roselle Park, NJ 07204. Phone: (908) 241-6241. Fax: (908) 241-6241.

FULLER, MELVILLE WESTON: BIRTH ANNIVERSARY. Feb 11, 1833. 8th chief justice of the US Supreme Court. Born at Augusta, ME, he died at Sorrento, ME, July 4, 1910.

GIBBS, JOSIAH WILLARD: BIRTH ANNIVERSARY. Feb 11, 1839. Chemist and professor of physics at Yale, born at New Haven, CT; died there, Apr 28, 1903.

HEART FAILURE AWARENESS WEEK. Feb 11–17. Organized and maintained by the Heart Failure Society of America. The organization promotes the treatment and awareness of heart failure, one of America's silent epidemics. There are current treatments for the disease and HFSA is trying to garner an awareness for this treatable disease. Annually, the week of Valentine's Day. For info: Melinda Lowers, HFSA, Crane Bldg, Pittsburgh, PA 15222. Phone: (412) 402-0161. E-mail: mlowers@bk-pa.com. Web: www.abouthf.org.

HOMES FOR BIRDS WEEK. Feb 11–17. A week to encourage people to clean out, fix up and put up homes for wild birds. For info: John F. Gardner, Pres, Wild Bird Marketplace, 4317 Elm Tree Rd, Bloomfield, NY 14469. Phone: (716) 229-5897. Fax: (716) 229-5448. E-mail: jfg@wildbird.com. Web: www.wildbird.com.

INTERNATIONAL JACKS & PICK-UP STICKS TOURNAMENT. Feb 11. Burlington, WI. Enjoy old fashioned games and enjoy friendly competition, pass on your memories. Exhibit of antique jacks and pick-up sticks. For info: Teacher Place & Parent Resources, 533 Milwaukee Ave, Burlington, WI 53105. Phone: (262) 763-3946.

IRAN, ISLAMIC REPUBLIC OF: NATIONAL DAY. Feb 11. National holiday. Commemorates the revolution that overthrew the Shah in 1979.

JAPAN: NATIONAL FOUNDATION DAY: ANNIVERSARY. Feb 11. Marks the founding of the Japanese nation. In 1872 the government officially set Feb 11, 660 BC, as the date of accession to the throne of the Emperor Jimmu (said to be Japan's first emperor) and designated the day a national holiday by the name of Empire Day. The holiday was abolished after WWII, but was revived as National Foundation Day in 1966. Ceremonies are held with Their Imperial Majesties the Emperor and Empress, the Prime Minister and other dignitaries attending. National holiday.

MANDELA, NELSON: PRISON RELEASE: ANNIVERSARY. Feb 11, 1990. After serving more than 27½ years of a life sentence (convicted, with eight others, of sabotage and conspiracy to overthrow the government), South Africa's Nelson Mandela, 71 years old, walked away from the Victor Verster prison farm at Paarl, South Africa, a free man. He had survived the governmental system of apartheid. Mandela greeted a cheering throng of well-wishers, along with hundreds of millions of television viewers worldwide, with demands for an intensification of the struggle for equality for blacks, who make up nearly 75 percent of South Africa's population.

MANKIEWICZ, JOSEPH L.: BIRTH ANNIVERSARY. Feb 11, 1909. Oscar-winning American film writer, director and producer was born at Wilkes-Barre, PA. He became a Hollywood screenwriter, winning an Oscar nomination for *Skippy* in 1931. He coined the famous W.C. Fields phrase "my little chickadee" for the 1932 film *If I Had a Million*. In 1935 he turned to producing and subsequently made *The Philadelphia Story* and *Woman of the Year*. He began directing in 1946 and his stature grew with such films as *The Late George Apley*, *The Ghost and Mrs Muir*, *A Letter to Three Wives*, *All About Eve*, *Guys and Dolls*, *Cleopatra* and *Sleuth*. Mankiewicz won four Academy Awards for directing and screenwriting. He died Feb 5, 1993, at Mount Kisco, NY.

MATERIALS TESTING WEEK. Feb 11–17. Recognition of the positive role material testing and inspection services provide in quality control and quality assurance for the construction industry. Focusing on the numerous tests, inspections and highly qualified technicians available to the construction industry for help in building a better quality of life for everyone—from bridges and smooth airport runways to sturdy steel high-rises and attractive multi-housing developments. For info: Charlene Moken, Materials Testing Inc, 180 Mill Rd, Edison, NJ 08817. Phone: (732) 248-3777. Fax: (732) 248-7979. Web: material-testing.com.

MOTIVACTION DAY. Feb 11. Both motives and actions are required to produce results. Six weeks after New Year's resolutions, most of us need a reminder to focus on our goals. MotivACTion Day is a day to put aside "busyness" and focus on the business of your life, expand your vision, accelerate your growth and create the plans to achieve your goals. For info: Dr. Rita H. Losee, PO Box 163, Boxford, MA 01921. Phone: (978) 887-0952. Fax: (978) 887-9551. E-mail: ritalosee@excelonline.com. Web: www.motivactionenterprises.com.

★**NATIONAL CHILD PASSENGER SAFETY AWARENESS WEEK.** Feb 11–17. Always the week in February containing Valentine's Day.

NATIONAL FAMILY, CAREER AND COMMUNITY LEADERS OF AMERICA WEEK. Feb 11–17. To call the nation's attention to the activities and goals of the organization and family and consumer sciences education. Theme: "Building Strong Leaders in Families, Careers and Communities." For info: Beth Carpenter, Communications Coord, Family, Career and Community Leaders of America, 1910 Association Dr, Reston, VA 21091. Phone: (703) 476-4900. Fax: (703) 860-2713. E-mail: bcarpenter@fcclainc.org.

NATIONAL RESURRECT ROMANCE WEEK. Feb 11–17. Event focuses on celebrating creative, noncommercialized romance. Encourages men and women to find ways to be romantic every day this week by using their hearts and not their wallets. For info: Michael Webb, Romance Expert and Author, PO Box 1567, Cary, NC 27512. Phone: (888) 476-6268 or (919) 462-0900. E-mail: chase@theromantic.com. Web: www.TheRomantic.com.

SATISFIED STAYING SINGLE DAY. Feb 11. As Valentine's Day approaches, some single folks would like to point out that they're quite content buying candy and flowers for no one but themselves. Live it up. Shadow dance! ©2000 Wellcat Herbs & Holidays. For info: Thomas & Ruth Roy, 2418 Long Ln, Lebanon, PA 17046. Phone: (230) 332-4886. E-mail: wellcat@supernet.com. Web: www.wellcat.com.

SPACE MILESTONE: *ENDEAVOUR* **MAPPING MISSION (US).** Feb 11, 2000. This manned flight spent 11 days in space creating a 3-D map of more than 70 percent of the Earth's surface. It will be the most accurate and complete topographic map of the Earth ever produced.

SPACE MILESTONE: FIRST SOVIET COMMERCIAL SATELLITE MISSION. Feb 11, 1990. Anatoly Solovyov and Aleksandr Balandin departed the Baikonur launching site on the Soviet Union's first satellite mission designed for profit—by producing industrial crystals in the weightlessness of space. The craft arrived at the *Mir* orbital space station on Feb 13. Launching of the *Soyuz* TM-9 capsule was witnessed by four American astronauts and televised live. The mission was hailed as initiating a new level of openness of information about Soviet space projects.

SPACE MILESTONE: *OSUMI* **(JAPAN).** Feb 11, 1970. First Japanese satellite launched. Japan became fourth nation to send a satellite into space.

TOPHER MOUNTAIN CHALLENGE. Feb 11. Winter Park Resort, Winter Park, CO. Held in memory of Christopher "Topher" Sendroy, the Topher Mountain Challenge is a fun ski/snowboard/telemark race consisting of a giant slalom on the top half of the trail, turning into a slalom and finishing with a bump run. Proceeds benefit programs for Grand County at-risk

youth. Est attendance: 100. For info: Winter Park Resort, PO Box 36, Winter Park, CO 80482. Phone: (970) 726-1580. Fax: (970) 726-1572. E-mail: wpinfo@mail.skiwinterpark.com. Web: winterparkresort.com.

VATICAN CITY: INDEPENDENCE ANNIVERSARY. Feb 11, 1929. The Lateran Treaty, signed by Pietro Cardinal Gasparri and Benito Mussolini, guaranteed the independence of the State of Vatican City and recognized the sovereignty of the Holy See over it. Area is about 109 acres.

WATER CLOSET INCIDENT: ANNIVERSARY. Feb 11, 1960. Jack Paar, then host of "The Tonight Show," walked out of his late-night TV show on this date. The incident was prompted by NBC's censoring of a slightly off-color "water closet" joke the previous night. After a meeting with network officials, Paar agreed to return to the show on Mar 7.

WHITE SHIRT DAY. Feb 11. Anniversary of UAW-GM agreement following 44-day sit-down strike at General Motors' Flint, MI, factories in 1937. "Blue-collar" workers traditionally wear white shirts to work on this day, symbolic of workingman's dignity won. Has been observed by proclamation at Flint, MI.

WSBA/WARM 103 EASTER CRAFT SHOW. Feb 11. York, PA. More than 225 quality craft displays will be presented with everything from miniatures and ornaments to quilts, country furniture and wedding crafts for that special occasion. Admission fee. Est attendance: 5,000. For info: Joe Alfano, Asst Promo Dir, PO Box 910, York, PA 17402-0910. Phone: (717) 764-1155. Fax: (717) 252-4708. E-mail: jalfano@suscom.com.

YALTA AGREEMENT SIGNED: ANNIVERSARY. Feb 11, 1945. President Franklin D. Roosevelt, British Prime Minister Winston Churchill and Soviet leader Joseph Stalin signed an agreement at Yalta, a Soviet city on the Black Sea in the Crimea. The agreement contained plans for new blows at the heart of Germany and for occupying Germany at the end of the war. It also called for a meeting in San Francisco to draft a charter for the United Nations.

BIRTHDAYS TODAY

Jennifer Aniston, 32, actress ("Friends," *Picture Perfect*), born Sherman Oaks, CA, Feb 11, 1969.

Paul Bocuse, 75, chef, born Collonges-au-Mont-d'Or, France, Feb 11, 1926.

Brandy (Norwood), 22, singer, actress ("Cinderella," "Moesha"), born Macomb, MS, Feb 11, 1979.

Jeb Bush, 48, Governor of Florida (R), born Midland, TX, Feb 11, 1953.

Mel Carnahan, 67, Governor of Missouri (D), born Birch Tree, MO, Feb 11, 1934.

Sheryl Crow, 39, singer, musician, born Kennett, MO, Feb 11, 1962.

Virginia Johnson, 76, psychologist, born Springfield, MO, Feb 11, 1925.

Mike Leavitt, 50, Governor of Utah (R), born Cedar City, UT, Feb 11, 1951.

Tina Louise, 67, actress ("Gilligan's Island," *The Stepford Wives*), born New York, NY, Feb 11, 1934.

Carey Lowell, 40, actress ("Law & Order"), born New York, NY, Feb 11, 1961.

Sergio Mendes, 60, musician, bandleader, born Niteroi, Brazil, Feb 11, 1941.

Leslie Nielsen, 79, actor (*Naked Gun* films, *Airplane!*, "Peyton Place"), born Regina, Saskatchewan, Canada, Feb 11, 1922.

Burt Reynolds, 65, actor (*Hooper, Deliverance, Cannonball Run*, "Evening Shade"), born Waycross, GA, Feb 11, 1936.

Sidney Sheldon, 84, author (*Bloodline, The Doomsday Conspiracy*), born Chicago, IL, Feb 11, 1917.

FEBRUARY 12 — MONDAY
Day 43 — 322 Remaining

ADAMS, LOUISA CATHERINE JOHNSON: BIRTH ANNIVERSARY. Feb 12, 1775. Wife of John Quincy Adams, 6th president of the US. Born at London, England. Died at Washington, DC, May 14, 1852.

BOB HOPE CHRYSLER CLASSIC. Feb 12–18. La Quinta, CA. The nation's largest sports event for charity. It features PGA pros, celebrities and amateurs. Est attendance: 110,000. For info: Pat Bennett, PR and Production, Bob Hope Chrysler Classic, 39000 Bob Hope Dr, Rancho Mirage, CA 92270. Phone: (760) 346-8184. Fax: (760) 346-6329. E-mail: info@bhcc.com. Web: www.bhcc.com.

DARWIN, CHARLES ROBERT: BIRTH ANNIVERSARY. Feb 12, 1809. Author and naturalist born at Shrewsbury, England. Best remembered for his books *On the Origin of Species by Means of Natural Selection, or the Preservation of Favoured Races in the Struggle for Life* and *The Descent of Man and Selection in Relation to Sex.* Died at Down, Kent, England, Apr 19, 1882.

HARRIS, ROY: BIRTH ANNIVERSARY. Feb 12, 1898. Born at Chandler, OK, Harris was one of the most important composers of this century. He was known for his use of Anglo-American folk tunes. He composed more than 200 works, including 13 symphonies, several ballet scores and much chamber and choral music. His best-known work is his *Third Symphony* (1939). He died at Santa Monica, CA, Oct 1, 1979.

INTERNATIONAL FLIRTING WEEK. Feb 12–18. Celebrating the ancient art of flirting and recognizing the role it plays in the lives of singles seeking a mate, couples looking to sustain their love and those simply exchanging a playful glance with a stranger, acquaintance, colleague, etc. For info: Robin Gorman Newman, 44 Somerset Dr N, Great Neck, NY 11020. Phone: (516) 773-0911. E-mail: rgnewman@aol.com.

LEWIS, JOHN LLEWELLYN: BIRTH ANNIVERSARY. Feb 12, 1889. American labor leader born near Lucas, IA. His parents came to the US from Welsh mining towns, and Lewis left school in the seventh grade to become a miner himself. Became leader of United Mine Workers of America and champion of all miners' causes. Died at Washington, DC, June 11, 1969.

LINCOLN, ABRAHAM: BIRTH ANNIVERSARY. Feb 12, 1809. 16th president of the US (Mar 4, 1861–Apr 15, 1865) and the first to be assassinated (on Good Friday, Apr 14, 1865, at Ford's Theatre at Washington, DC). His presidency encompassed the tragic Civil War. Especially remembered are his Emancipation Proclamation (Jan 1, 1863), his Gettysburg Address (Nov 19, 1863) and his proclamation establishing the last Thursday of November as Thanksgiving Day. Born at Hardin County, KY, he died at Washington, DC, Apr 15, 1865. Lincoln's birthday is observed as part of Presidents' Day in most states, but is a legal holiday in Illinois and an optional bank holiday in Iowa, Maryland, Michigan, Pennsylvania, Washington and West Virginia. See also: "Presidents' Day," (Feb 21).

	S	**M**	**T**	**W**	**T**	**F**	**S**
February					1	2	3
2001	4	5	6	7	8	9	10
	11	12	13	14	15	16	17
	18	19	20	21	22	23	24
	25	26	27	28			

LINCOLN'S BIRTHPLACE CABIN WREATH LAYING. Feb 12. Abraham Lincoln's Birthplace National Historic Site, Hodgenville, KY. A wreath is placed at the door of the symbolic "Birthplace Cabin" in commemoration of the birth of Abraham Lincoln. Refreshments are also served to park visitors. Est attendance: 75. For info: Patsy Cobb, 2995 Lincoln Farm Rd, Hodgenville, KY 42748. Phone: (502) 358-3137.

LOST PENNY DAY. Feb 12. Today is set aside to put all of those pennies stashed in candy dishes, bowls and jars back in circulation. Take those pennies and give them to a shelter or agency that assists the homeless or your local Humane Society. Annually, on President Abraham Lincoln's birthday, the man depicted on the copper penny. [©1995] For info: Adrienne Sioux Koopersmith, 1437 W Rosemont, #1W, Chicago, IL 60660-1319. Phone: (773) 743-5341. Fax: (773) 743-5395. E-mail: adrienne @21stcentury.net.

LUXEMBOURG: BURGSONNDEG. Feb 12. Young people build a huge bonfire on a hill to celebrate the victorious sun, marking the end of winter. A tradition dating to pre-Christian times.

NAACP FOUNDED: ANNIVERSARY. Feb 12, 1909. The National Association for the Advancement of Colored People was founded by W.E.B. Dubois and Ida Wells-Barnett, among others, to wage a militant campaign against lynching and other forms of racial oppression. Its legal wing brought many lawsuits that successfully challenged segregation in the 1950s and '60s.

NATIONAL FIELD TRIAL CHAMPIONSHIP. Feb 12–23. (Monday–Friday only.) Ames Plantation, Grand Junction, TN. To select the national champion all-age bird dog. Est attendance: 7,800. For info: Jim Anderson, Secy/Treas, Natl Field Trial Champion Assn, Box 389, Grand Junction, TN 38039. Phone: (901) 878-1067. Fax: (901) 878-1068. E-mail: amesplantation@ lunaweb.net. Web: www.amesplantation.org.

OGLETHORPE DAY. Feb 12. General James Edward Oglethorpe (born at London, England, Dec 22, 1696), with some 100 other Englishmen, landed at what is now Savannah, GA, on Feb 12, 1733. Naming the new colony Georgia for England's King George II, Oglethorpe was organizer and first governor of the colony and founder of the city of Savannah. Oglethorpe Day and Georgia Day observed on this date.

PAVLOVA, ANNA: BIRTH ANNIVERSARY. Feb 12, 1881. Russian ballerina Anna Pavlova, thought by some to have been the greatest dancer of all time, was born at St. Petersburg, Russia. After performing with great success with the Ballet Russe and other companies, she formed her own company in 1910 and performed on tour for enthusiastic audiences in nearly every country in the world. Pavlova died at The Hague, Netherlands, Jan 23, 1931.

SAFETYPUP'S® BIRTHDAY. Feb 12. This year Safetypup®, created by the National Child Safety Council, joyously celebrates his birthday by bringing safety awareness/education messages to children in a positive, nonthreatening manner. Safetypup® has achieved a wonderful balance of safety sense, caution and childlike enthusiasm about life and helping kids "Stay Safe and Sound." For info: Barbara Handley Huggett, Dir, NCSC, R & D, Box 1368, Jackson, MI 49204-1368. Phone: (517) 764-6070.

UTAH WOMEN GIVEN THE VOTE: ANNIVERSARY. Feb 12, 1870. The women in the Utah Territory were granted the right to vote in political elections—50 years before the 19th Amendment was ratified.

WESTMINSTER DOG SHOW. Feb 12–13. Madison Square Garden, New York, NY. 125th annual. For info: Westminster Kennel Club, 230 Park Ave, Ste 644, New York, NY 10169. Web: westminsterkennelclub.org.

BIRTHDAYS TODAY

Maud Adams, 56, actress (*Killer Force, Octopussy*), born Lulea, Sweden, Feb 12, 1945.

Joe Don Baker, 65, actor (*Charlie Varrick, Cool Hand Luke*), born Groesbeck, TX, Feb 12, 1936.

Ehud Barak, 59, Israeli prime minister, born Mishmar, Hasharon, Israel, Feb 12, 1942.

Judy Blume, 63, author (*Blubber, Superfudge*), born Elizabeth, NJ, Feb 12, 1938.

Josh Brolin, 33, actor (*The Mod Squad, Best Laid Plans*), born Los Angeles, CA, Feb 12, 1968.

Cliff De Young, 54, actor (*Blue Collar, F/X*), born Inglewood, CA, Feb 12, 1947.

Joseph Henry (Joe) Garagiola, 75, sportscaster, former baseball player, born St. Louis, MO, Feb 12, 1926.

Arsenio Hall, 46, comedian, actor (*Coming to America*), former TV talk-show host, born Cleveland, OH, Feb 12, 1955.

Joanna Kerns, 48, actress ("Growing Pains"), former national-caliber gymnast, born San Francisco, CA, Feb 12, 1953.

Chynna Phillips, 33, singer (Wilson Phillips), born Los Angeles, CA, Feb 12, 1968.

Christina Ricci, 21, actress (*Ice Storm, Addams Family Values*), born Santa Monica, CA, Feb 12, 1980.

William Felton (Bill) Russell, 67, Basketball Hall of Fame center and former coach, born Monroe, LA, Feb 12, 1934.

Arlen Specter, 71, US Senator (R, Pennsylvania), born Wichita, KS, Feb 12, 1930.

Franco Zeffirelli, 78, film director (*Otello, Young Toscanini*), born Florence, Italy, Feb 12, 1923.

FEBRUARY 13 — TUESDAY

Day 44 — 321 Remaining

BESS TRUMAN DAY LECTURE. Feb 13. Independence, MO. Each year the Truman Library celebrates the anniversary of Bess Truman's birth with a program featuring a distinguished author speaking on a subject relevant to the role of First Ladies. Previous lecturers include historians Michael Beschloss and Carl Anthony. Est attendance: 200. For info: Larry J. Hackman, Dir, Harry S. Truman Library, US Highway 24 and Delaware St, Independence, MO 64050-1798. Phone: (816) 833-1400. Fax: (816) 833-4368. E-mail: library@truman.nara.gov. Web: www.trumanlibrary.org.

BLACK LOVE DAY. Feb 13. A national, commemorative holiday of observance, celebration, reconciliation and demonstration of love within black community and for the black community, conceived by Ayo-Handy Kendi in 1993. On this day blacks should perform 5 specific acts of love, toward the Creator, toward oneself, within the family, in the community and for the race, and whites are encouraged to demonstrate love through acts of service and self-inventory of their attitudes and behavior toward blacks. Annually, Feb 13. For info: African American Holiday Assn, 1305 Emerson St NW, Washington, DC 20011. Phone: (202) 310-1430. E-mail: aaha@aaha-info.org. Web: aaha-info.org.

CHURCHILL, RANDOLPH HENRY SPENCER: BIRTH ANNIVERSARY. Feb 13, 1849. English politician and the father of Winston Churchill. Born at Blenheim, Woodstock, Oxfordshire, England, he died at London, Jan 24, 1895.

DOW-JONES TOPS 7,000: ANNIVERSARY. Feb 13, 1997. The Dow-Jones Index of 30 major industrial stocks topped the 7,000 mark for the first time.

DRESDEN FIRE BOMBING: ANNIVERSARY. Feb 13, 1945. Dresden, Germany. Allied fire bombing caused a firestorm that destroyed the city and killed 135,000 people.

FIRST MAGAZINE PUBLISHED IN AMERICA: ANNIVERSARY. Feb 13, 1741 (OS). Andrew Bradford published *The American Magazine* just three days ahead of Benjamin Franklin's *General Magazine*.

GET A DIFFERENT NAME DAY. Feb 13. For the pity of the millions of us who hate our birth names. On this day we may change our names to whatever we wish and have the right to expect colleagues, family and friends to so address us. Sponsored by Wellcat Holidays. [© 2000 WH] For info: Thomas or Ruth Roy, 2418 Long Ln, Lebanon, PA 17046. Phone: (717) 279-0184. E-mail: wellcat@desupernet.net. Web: www.wellcat.com.

GRAND CENTER BOAT SHOW. Feb 13–18. Grand Center, Grand Rapids, MI. This event brings together buyers and sellers of power and sail boats, boating accessories, docks, dockominiums and vacation properties. Est attendance: 32,000. For info: Mike Wilbraham, ShowSpan, Inc, 1400 28th St SW, Grand Rapids, MI 49509. Phone: (616) 530-1919. Web: www.showspan.com.

IRWIN WINS FIRST MEDAL OF HONOR: ANNIVERSARY. Feb 13, 1861. Colonel Bernard Irwin distinguished himself while leading troops in a battle with Chiricahua Apache Indians at Apache Pass, AZ (at the time part of the territory of New Mexico). For those actions Irwin later became the first person awarded the new US Medal of Honor, although he didn't actually receive it until three years later (Jan 24, 1864).

NATIONAL CONDOM WEEK. Feb 13–20. To educate consumers, patients, students and professionals on the prevention of sexually transmitted diseases, AIDS and teenage pregnancies. For info: Frederick S. Mayer, Pres, Pharmacists Planning Service, Inc, 101 Lucas Valley Rd, #210, San Rafael, CA 94903. Phone: (415) 479-8628. Fax: (415) 479-8608. E-mail: ppsi@aol.com. Web: www.ppsinc.org.

PIAZZETTA, GIOVANNI BATTISTA: BIRTH ANNIVERSARY. Feb 13, 1682. Prominent 18th-century Venetian painter. Notable among his works are the *Ecstasy of St. Francis* and *Fortune Teller*. Born at Venice, Italy, and died there Apr 28, 1754.

TRUMAN, BESS (ELIZABETH) VIRGINIA WALLACE: BIRTH ANNIVERSARY. Feb 13, 1885. Wife of Harry S Truman, 33rd president of the US. Born at Independence, MO, and died there Oct 18, 1982.

WOOD, GRANT: BIRTH ANNIVERSARY. Feb 13, 1892. American artist, especially noted for his powerful realism and satirical paintings of the American scene, was born near Anamosa, IA. He was a printer, sculptor, woodworker and high school and college teacher. Among his best-remembered works are *American Gothic, Fall Plowing* and *Stone City.* Died at Iowa City, IA, Feb 12, 1942.

WORLD AG EXPO. Feb 13–15. Tulare, CA. The largest farm equipment show in North America. For info: Intl Agri-Center, PO Box 1475, 4450 S Laspina, Tulare, CA 93275. Phone: (800) 999-9186 or (209) 688-1751. Fax: (209) 686-5065. E-mail: info@farmshow.org. Web: www.farmshow.org.

BIRTHDAYS TODAY

Stockard Channing (Susan Stockard), 57, actress (*Six Degrees of Separation, The House of Blue Leaves*), born New York, NY, Feb 13, 1944.

Peter Gabriel, 51, singer, songwriter, born London, England, Feb 13, 1950.

Kelly Hu, 34, actress ("Martial Law," "Nash Bridges"), born Honolulu, HI, Feb 13, 1967.

Carol Lynley, 59, actress (*Harlow, Bunny Lake Is Missing*), born New York, NY, Feb 13, 1942.

Randy Moss, 24, football player, born Rand, WV, Feb 13, 1977.

David Naughton, 50, singer, actor (*An American Werewolf in London, Overexposed*), born Hartford, CT, Feb 13, 1951.

Kim Novak (Marilyn Novak), 68, actress (*Bell, Book and Candle, Vertigo*), born Chicago, IL, Feb 13, 1933.

Eddie Robinson, 82, former college football coach, Jackson, LA, Feb 13, 1919.

George Segal, 67, actor (*A Touch of Class*, "Just Shoot Me"), born Great Neck, NY, Feb 13, 1934.

Jerry Springer, 57, TV host ("The Jerry Springer Show"), born London, England, Feb 13, 1944.

Bo Svenson, 60, actor (*North Dallas Forty, Heartbreak Ridge*), born Goteborg, Sweden, Feb 13, 1941.

Peter Tork (Peter Thorkelson), 57, actor, singer (The Monkees), born Washington, DC, Feb 13, 1944.

Chuck Yeager, 78, pilot who broke sound barrier, born Myra, WV, Feb 13, 1923.

FEBRUARY 14 — WEDNESDAY
Day 45 — 320 Remaining

ARIZONA: ADMISSION DAY: ANNIVERSARY. Feb 14. Became 48th state in 1912.

BENNY, JACK: BIRTH ANNIVERSARY. Feb 14, 1894. American comedian. Born Benjamin Kubelsky, Jack Benny entered vaudeville at Waukegan, IL, at age 17, using the violin as a comic stage prop. His radio show first aired in 1932 and continued for 20 years with little change in format. He also had a long-running television show. One of his most well-known comic gimmicks was his purported stinginess. In 1927 Benny married Mary Livingstone (Sadie Marks). He was born at Chicago, IL, and died Dec 26, 1974, at Beverly Hills, CA.

BIG 12 WOMEN'S SWIMMING CHAMPIONSHIP. Feb 14–17. Austin, TX. Est attendance: 5,000. For info: Big 12 Conference, 2201 Stemmons Freeway, 28th Floor, Dallas, TX 75207. Phone: (214) 742-1212. Fax: (214) 742-2046. Web: www .big12sports.com.

BULGARIA: VITICULTURISTS' DAY (TRIFON ZAREZAN). Feb 14. Celebrated since Thracian times. Festivities are based on cult of Dionysus, god of merriment and wine.

CONGENITAL HEART DEFECT AWARENESS DAY. Feb 14. Public relations/media campaign, special events in cities throughout the United States. For info: Mona Barmash, Children's Health Info Network. Phone: (215) 493-3068. E-mail: mb@tchin .org. Web: www.tchin.org.

ENIAC COMPUTER INTRODUCED: ANNIVERSARY. Feb 14, 1946. J. Presper Eckert and John W. Mauchly demonstrated the Electronic Numerical Integrator and Computer (ENIAC) for the first time at the University of Pennsylvania. This was the first electronic digital computer. It occupied a room the size of a gymnasium and contained nearly 18,000 vacuum tubes. The Army commissioned the computer to speed the calculation of firing tables for artillery. By the time the computer was ready, World War II was over. However, ENIAC prepared the way for future generations of computers.

FERRIS WHEEL DAY. Feb 14, 1859. Anniversary of the birth of George Washington Gale Ferris, American engineer and inventor, at Galesburg, IL. Among his many accomplishments as a civil engineer, Ferris is best remembered as the inventor of the Ferris wheel, which he developed for the World's Columbian Exposition at Chicago, IL, in 1893. Built on the Midway Plaisance, the 250-feet-in-diameter Ferris wheel (with 36 coaches, each capable of carrying 40 passengers), proved one of the greatest attractions of the fair. It was America's answer to the Eiffel Tower of the Paris International Exposition of 1889. Ferris died at Pittsburgh, PA, Nov 22, 1896.

FIRST PRESIDENTIAL PHOTOGRAPH: ANNIVERSARY. Feb 14, 1849. President James Polk became the first US president to be photographed while in office. The photographer was Mathew B. Brady, who would become famous for his photography during the American Civil War.

HANCOCK, WINFIELD SCOTT: BIRTH ANNIVERSARY. Feb 14, 1824. Born at Montgomery, PA, died Feb 9, 1886, at Governor's Island, NY. After serving as Union general in the Civil War, his command of the military division of Texas and Louisiana won him much favor from the Democratic Party because he allowed local civil authorities to retain their power. The Democrats made him their presidential candidate in 1880. He lost to James A. Garfield by a narrow margin.

February *2001*	S	M	T	W	T	F	S
					1	2	3
	4	5	6	7	8	9	10
	11	12	13	14	15	16	17
	18	19	20	21	22	23	24
	25	26	27	28			

LEAGUE OF WOMEN VOTERS FORMED: ANNIVERSARY. Feb 14, 1920. While meeting in Chicago to celebrate the imminent ratification of the 19th Amendment to the Constitution, leaders of the National American Woman Suffrage Association (NAWSA) approved the formation of a new organization—the League of Women Voters. With the vote for women just a few months away, the new organization was created to help American women exercise their new political rights and responsibilities. For info: League of Women Voters of Illinois, 332 S Michigan Ave, Ste 1142, Chicago, IL 60604. Phone: (312) 939-5935. Web: www.lwv.org.

MILWAUKEE BOAT SHOW. Feb 14–18. Midwest Express Center, Milwaukee, WI. This event brings together buyers and sellers of sail and power boats, including fishing boats, pontoons and boating accessories, as well as vacation property and travel destinations. Est attendance: 25,000. For info: Adam Starr, ShowSpan, Inc, 1400 28th St SW, Grand Rapids, MI 49509. Phone: (616) 530-1919. Fax: (616) 530-2122. Web: www.show span.com.

MOON PHASE: LAST QUARTER. Feb 14. Moon enters Last Quarter phase at 10:23 PM, EST.

NATIONAL HAVE-A-HEART DAY. Feb 14. The goal of this celebration of life is to create a new consciousness concerning the impact of our food choices on the environment, world hunger, animal welfare and human health—especially heart health. A vegetarian lifestyle increases longevity and helps prevent—and even reverse—heart disease. Vegetarians live about 15 years longer than nonvegetarians and they suffer less than one-tenth the heart disease death rate of nonvegetarians. For info: Vegetarian Awareness Network, Communications Center, PO Box 321, Knoxville, TN 37901-0321. Phone: (800) USA-VEGE.

OREGON: ADMISSION DAY: ANNIVERSARY. Feb 14. Became 33rd state in 1859.

PROUT, MARY ANN ("AUNT MARY PROUT"): 200th BIRTH ANNIVERSARY. Feb 14, 1801. It is believed most likely that Mary Prout—social activist, humanitarian, educator—was born free on this date at Baltimore, MD. Prout became a teacher and in 1830 founded a day school. Actively involved in her church, she founded a secret society that became the Independent Order of St. Luke to help with the cost of medical care and burial services for needy blacks, an organization that grew to have 1,500 chapters across the nation by 1900. Prout died at Baltimore in 1884.

RACE RELATIONS DAY. Feb 14. A day designated by some churches to recognize the importance of interracial relations. Formerly was observed on Abraham Lincoln's birthday or on the Sunday preceding it. Since 1970 observance has generally been Feb 14.

READ TO YOUR CHILD DAY. Feb 14. "Show your kids you love them: Read to them." To encourage parents and other caregivers to engage in the wonderfully beneficial and delightfully fun practice of reading to children. A packet includes ideas for literacy campaigns plus reproducible flyers on family reading at home and sharing books with babies. Flyers describe the benefits of reading aloud, give tips for oral reading and list books people can read for more information. Annually, on Valentine's Day. RTYCD is a volunteer, nonprofit effort. For packet send business-size SASE plus two first-class stamps tucked inside (to cover photocopy expenses) to Dee Anderson, 1023 25 St, #1, Moline, IL 61265.

SALMAN RUSHDIE'S DEATH SENTENCE: ANNIVERSARY. Feb 14, 1989. Iranian leader Ayatollah Ruholla Khomeini, offended by *The Satanic Verses*, called on Muslims to kill the book's British author, Salman Rushdie. On the following day the Ayatollah offered a $1 million reward for execution of his sentence. Rushdie, fearful for his life, went into hiding. Worldwide protests against the efforts to abridge academic and literary freedoms, countered by protests of Muslim and other religious fundamentalists, stimulated the sales of *The Satanic Verses*, but Rushdie remained virtually a prisoner unable to resume a public life. In 1998 the Iranian government rescinded the death sentence.

SPACE MILESTONE: *NEAR* ORBITS ASTEROID. Feb 14, 2000. The robot spacecraft Near Earth Asteroid Rendezvous (now called *NEAR* Shoemaker) finished circling the asteroid Eros on this day. Eros is called a near-Earth asteroid because its orbit crosses that of Earth and poses a potential collision danger. *NEAR* continued orbiting the asteroid for a year, moving closer to the surface to make more precise measurements. By May 2000, it was in orbit 31 miles from Eros. *NEAR* was launched from Cape Canaveral, FL, Feb 17, 1996.

SPACE MILESTONE: SMM (US). Feb 14, 1980. Unmanned Delta rocket, a "Solar Maximum Mission Observatory," launched on this date. Intended to study solar flares.

TEXOMA FARM AND RANCH SHOW. Feb 14–15. Multi-Purpose Events Center Exhibit Hall, Wichita Falls, TX. Farmers and ranchers from North Texas and Oklahoma come to see the latest in equipment. Seminars and information in new farming and ranching techniques. Est attendance: 8,000. For info: Wichita Falls CVB, 1000 5th St, Wichita Falls, TX 76301. Phone: (940) 716-5500. Fax: (940) 716-5509. E-mail: MPEC@WF.net. Web: www.viewscape.com.

VALENTINE'S DAY. Feb 14. St. Valentine's Day celebrates the feasts of two Christian martyrs of this name. One, a priest and physician, was beaten and beheaded on the Flaminian Way at Rome, Italy, Feb 14, AD 269, during the reign of Emperor Claudius II (who died of the plague less than a year later). Another Valentine, the Bishop of Terni, is said to have been beheaded, also on the Flaminian Way at Rome, Feb 14 (possibly in a later year). Both history and legend are vague and contradictory about details of the Valentines and some say that Feb 14 was selected for the celebration of Christian martyrs as a diversion from the ancient pagan observance of Lupercalia. An old legend has it that birds choose their mates on Valentine's Day. Now it is one of the most widely observed unofficial holidays. It is an occasion for the exchange of gifts (usually books, flowers or sweets) and greeting cards with affectionate or humorous messages. See also: "Lupercalia" (Feb 15).

VALENTINE'S DAY MASSACRE: ANNIVERSARY. Feb 14, 1929. Anniversary of Chicago gangland executions, when gunmen posing as police shot seven members of the George "Bugs" Moran gang.

WALLET, SKEEZIX: "BIRTHDAY." Feb 14. Comic strip character in "Gasoline Alley" by Frank King. First cartoon character to grow and age with the years of publication. Foundling child of Walt and Phyllis Wallet, discovered on doorstep Feb 14, 1921. Skeezix grew through childhood, marriage, military service in WWII, returning home to parenthood and business after the war. Comic strip began in the *Chicago Tribune*, Aug 23, 1919.

FEBRUARY 15 — THURSDAY
Day 46 — 319 Remaining

AFGHANISTAN: SOVIET TROOP WITHDRAWAL: ANNIVERSARY. Feb 15, 1989. The USSR's target of withdrawal of all Soviet troops from Afghanistan by this date was essentially met, ending more than nine years of intervention in a civil war.

AMERICAN ASSOCIATION FOR THE ADVANCEMENT OF SCIENCE ANNUAL MEETING. Feb 15–20. San Francisco, CA. Annual meeting and science innovation exposition. For info: AAAS, 1200 New York Ave NW, Washington, DC 20005. Phone: (202) 326-6450. Fax: (202) 289-4021. Web: www.aaas.org/meetings.

ARLEN, HAROLD: BIRTH ANNIVERSARY. Feb 15, 1905. American composer and songwriter, born at Buffalo, NY. Arlen wrote many popular songs, including "Over the Rainbow" (for which he won 1939 Oscar for best song), "That Old Black Magic," "Blues in the Night" and "Stormy Weather." Died at New York, NY, Apr 23, 1986.

BARRYMORE, JOHN: BIRTH ANNIVERSARY. Feb 15, 1882. American actor of famous acting family. Born John Blythe at Philadelphia, PA, and died at Los Angeles, CA, May 29, 1942. US Postal Service stamp was issued in 1982 featuring Ethel, John and Lionel Barrymore.

BIG TEN WOMEN'S SWIMMING AND DIVING CHAMPIONSHIP. Feb 15–17. Univ of MI, Ann Arbor, MI. Est attendance: 1,500. For info: Sue Ryan, Big Ten Conference, 1500 W Higgins Rd, Park Ridge, IL 60068-6300. Phone: (847) 696-1010. Fax: (847) 696-1110. Web: www.bigten.org or www.bigtenchampionships.com.

CANADA: MAPLE LEAF FLAG ADOPTED: ANNIVERSARY. Feb 15, 1965. The new Canadian national flag was raised in Ottawa, Canada's capital, on this day. The red-and-white flag with a red maple leaf in the center replaced the Red Ensign flag which had the British Union Jack in the upper left-hand corner.

CERMAK, ANTON J.: ASSASSINATION ANNIVERSARY. Feb 15, 1933. At Bay Front Park, Miami, FL, an assassin aiming at President-elect Franklin D. Roosevelt had his aim deflected by a spectator. Cermak, mayor of Chicago, IL, born May 9, 1873, at Kladno, Bohemia, Czechoslovakia, was struck and killed instead. Giuseppe (Joe) Zangara, the 32-year-old assassin, who had emigrated from Italy in 1923, was electrocuted at the Raiford, FL, state prison Mar 20, 1933.

CLARK, ABRAHAM: 275th BIRTH ANNIVERSARY.
Feb 15, 1726. Signer of the Declaration of Independence, farmer and lawyer. Born at Elizabethtown, NJ, and died there Sept 15, 1794.

ENGLAND: CHESTER ANTIQUES AND FINE ART SHOW.
Feb 15–18 (Also Oct 25–28). Chester Racecourse, Cheshire. 50 stands on three floors where all items have been vetted for authenticity and age. Est attendance: 6,000. For info: Penman Fairs, PO Box 114, Haywards Heath, Sussex, England RH16 2YU. Phone: (44) (144) 448-2514. Fax: (44) (144) 448-3412. E-mail: info@penman-fairs.co.uk.

FARLEY, CHRIS: BIRTH ANNIVERSARY.
Feb 15, 1964. Born at Madison, WI. Farley started acting in Chicago's *Second City* and was a regular on "Saturday Night Live." His movie credits include *Black Sheep, Tommy Boy* and *Beverly Hills Ninja*. Farley died Dec 18, 1997, at Chicago.

GALILEI, GALILEO: BIRTH ANNIVERSARY.
Feb 15, 1564. Physicist and astronomer who helped overthrow medieval concepts of the world, born at Pisa, Italy. He proved the theory that all bodies, large and small, descend at equal speed and gathered evidence to support Copernicus's theory that the Earth and other planets revolve around the sun. Galileo died at Florence, Italy, Jan 8, 1642.

LUPERCALIA.
Feb 15. Anniversary of ancient Roman fertility festival. Thought by some to have been established by Romulus and Remus who, legend says, were suckled by a she-wolf at Lupercal (a cave in Palestine). Goats and dogs were sacrificed. Lupercalia celebration persisted until the fifth century of the Christian era. Possibly a forerunner of Valentine's Day customs.

McCORMICK, CYRUS H.: BIRTH ANNIVERSARY.
Feb 15, 1809. Inventor of the reaper, born at Rockbridge County, VA. It is said that Cyrus McCormick's invention of the reaper rates second only to the railroad in the development of the US. Continuing the dream of his father, McCormick constructed a horse-operated reaper which was demonstrated for the first time in a Virginia wheat field in July 1831. He moved his operation to Chicago, IL, in 1847 in order to be closer to the Midwest's expanding wheat fields. His business prospered despite two decades of constant litigation over patent rights. He died May 13, 1884, at Chicago, IL. In 1902–03, his McCormick Harvesting Machine Company was consolidated with other firms to become the International Harvester Company.

MENENDEZ DE AVILES, PEDRO: BIRTH ANNIVERSARY.
Feb 15, 1519. Spanish explorer and naval adventurer. Explored Florida coastal regions for king of Spain and established a fort at St. Augustine in September 1565. Died Sept 17, 1574, at Santander, Spain.

MIAMI INTERNATIONAL BOAT SHOW AND SAILBOAT SHOW.
Feb 15–20. Miami Beach Convention Center, Miami Beach, FL. 60th annual boat show, the biggest in the US and considered the main event for product introductions. With more than 3,000 boats, this show offers an unparalleled opportunity to view the sport's latest products. For info: NMMA, 400 Arthur Godfrey Rd, Ste 310, Miami Beach, FL 33140. Phone: (305) 531-8410. Fax: (305) 534-3139. Web: www.boatshows.com.

February 2001	S	M	T	W	T	F	S
					1	2	3
	4	5	6	7	8	9	10
	11	12	13	14	15	16	17
	18	19	20	21	22	23	24
	25	26	27	28			

REMEMBER THE *MAINE* DAY: ANNIVERSARY.
Feb 15, 1898. American battleship *Maine* was blown up while at anchor in Havana harbor, at 9:40 PM, on this day in 1898. The ship, under the command of Captain Charles G. Sigsbee, sank quickly, and 260 members of its crew were lost. Inflamed public opinion in the US ignored the lack of evidence to establish responsibility for the explosion. "Remember the *Maine*" became the war cry, and a formal declaration of war against Spain followed on Apr 25, 1898.

SIMPLOT GAMES.
Feb 15–17. Holt Arena, Idaho State University, Pocatello, ID. One of the nation's largest indoor high school track and field events, featuring 2,200 top high school athletes from the US and Canada. Est attendance: 20,000. For info: Carol Lish, Exec Dir, Simplot Games, PO Box 912, Pocatello, ID 83204. Phone: (800) 635-9444. Fax: (208) 235-5604. E-mail: clish@simplot.com. Web: www.simplotgames.com.

SPANISH WAR MEMORIAL DAY AND *MAINE* MEMORIAL DAY.
Feb 15. Massachusetts.

SUSAN B. ANTHONY DAY.
Feb 15. Honors one of the first women's right advocates, working especially for the right to vote. Anthony was born on this day in 1820 at Adams, MA. She died Mar 13, 1906, at Rochester, NY.

SUTTER, JOHN AUGUSTUS: BIRTH ANNIVERSARY.
Feb 15, 1803. Born at Kandern, Germany, Sutter established the first white settlement on the site of Sacramento, CA, in 1839, and owned a large tract of land there, which he named New Helvetia. The first great gold strike in the US was on his property, at Sutter's Mill, Jan 24, 1848. His land was soon overrun by gold seekers who, he claimed, slaughtered his cattle and stole or destroyed his property. Sutter was bankrupt by 1852. Died at Washington, DC, June 18, 1880.

TIFFANY, CHARLES LEWIS: BIRTH ANNIVERSARY.
Feb 15, 1812. American jeweler whose name became synonymous with high standards of quality. Born at Killingly, CT, and died at New York, NY, Feb 18, 1902. Father of artist Louis Comfort Tiffany. See also: "Tiffany, Louis Comfort: Birth Anniversary" (Feb 18).

WASHINGTON BOAT SHOW.
Feb 15–18. Washington Convention Center, Washington, DC. Biggest indoor boat show in the mid-Atlantic region. 400+ boats—power and sail—from express cruisers to daysailers to motoryachts to dinghies. Also hundreds of booths with every possible accessory, from electronics and foul weather gear to marinas and destinations. For info: Gail Stafford, Washington Boat Show, 6017 Tower Court, Alexandria, VA 22304. Phone: (703) 823-7960.

BIRTHDAYS TODAY

Adolfo (Adolfo F. Sardina), 68, fashion designer, born Havana, Cuba, Feb 15, 1933.
Marisa Berenson, 53, actress (*Cabaret, Barry Lyndon*), model, born New York, NY, Feb 15, 1948.
Claire Bloom, 70, actress (*A Doll's House, The Spy Who Came In from the Cold*), born London, England, Feb 15, 1931.
Susan Brownmiller, 66, author, feminist (*Against Our Will, Femininity*), born Brooklyn, NY, Feb 15, 1935.
Matt Groening, 47, cartoonist ("The Simpsons"), born Portland, OR, Feb 15, 1954.
Jaromir Jagr, 29, hockey player, born Kladno, Czechoslovakia, Feb 15, 1972.
Harvey Korman, 74, actor, comedian (two Emmys for "The Carol Burnett Show"; *High Anxiety*), born Chicago, IL, Feb 15, 1927.
Melissa Manchester, 50, singer ("Don't Cry Out Loud"), born The Bronx, NY, Feb 15, 1951.
Kevin McCarthy, 87, actor (*Invasion of the Body Snatchers, Buffalo Bill and the Indians*), born Seattle, WA, Feb 15, 1914.
William Mark Price, 37, basketball player, born Bartlesville, OK, Feb 15, 1964.
Jane Seymour, 50, actress (Emmy for "East of Eden"; "Dr. Quinn: Medicine Woman"), born Hillingdon, England, Feb 15, 1951.

FEBRUARY 16 — FRIDAY
Day 47 — 318 Remaining

BERGEN, EDGAR: BIRTH ANNIVERSARY. Feb 16, 1903. Actor, radio entertainer and ventriloquist, voice of Charlie McCarthy, Mortimer Snerd and Effie Klinker. Father of Emmy Award-winning actress Candice Bergen, star of TV's "Murphy Brown." Born at Chicago, IL; died at Las Vegas, NV, Sept 30, 1978.

COWBOY STATE GAMES WINTER SPORTS FESTIVAL. Feb 16–19. Casper, WY. The festival features a variety of winter sporting events for athletes of all ages. Est attendance: 1,600. For info: Eileen Ford, Cowboy State Games, PO Box 3485, Casper, WY 82602. Phone: (307) 577-1125. Fax: (307) 577-8111. E-mail: csg@trib.com.

FLAHERTY, ROBERT JOSEPH: BIRTH ANNIVERSARY. Feb 16, 1884. American filmmaker, explorer and author, called "father of the documentary film." Born at Iron Mountain, MI; died at Dunnerston, VT, July 23, 1951. Films included *Nanook of the North, Moana* and *Man of Aran.*

FRANCE: NICE CARNIVAL. Feb 16–27. Dates from the 14th century and is celebrated each year during the 12 days ending with Shrove Tuesday. Derived from ancient rites of spring, the carnival offers parades, floats, battles of flowers and confetti, a fireworks display lighting up the entire Baie des Anges. King Carnival is burned on his pyre at the end of the event.

GREATER PHILADELPHIA MID-WINTER SCOTTISH AND IRISH MUSIC FESTIVAL AND FAIR. Feb 16–18. Valley Forge Convention Center, King of Prussia, PA. Music, dance, spectacle and song celebrate Ireland and Scotland. All-star lineup of entertainment and a host of ethnic activities, foods and products. Est attendance: 9,000. For info: Wm M. Reid, Jr, Scottish & Irish Festival, PO Box 102, Plymouth Meeting, PA 19462. Phone: (610) 825-7268. Fax: (610) 825-8745. E-mail: eohebrides@aol.com.

HEART 2 HEART DAY. Feb 16. Confide something to your diary—start young and you'll write a whole book before you know it! Annually, two days after Valentine's Day. For info: Fine Print Publishing Co, PO Box 916401, Longwood, FL 32791-6401. Phone: (407) 814-7777. Fax: (407) 814-7677.

INDIANAPOLIS BOAT, SPORT AND TRAVEL SHOW. Feb 16–25. Indiana State Fairgrounds, Indianapolis, IN. Est attendance: 200,000. For info: Kevin Renfro, VP, Ste E-2, Corporate Sq East, 2511 E 46th St, Indianapolis, IN 46205. Phone: (317) 546-4344. Fax: (317) 546-3002. E-mail: insportshow@iguest.net. Web: www.renfrosportshows.com.

JALAPEÑO FESTIVAL. Feb 16–17. Laredo, TX. Celebration of the jalapeño pepper. Events include the world famous Jalapeño Eating Contest, the "Some Like It Hot" Recipe Contest, the crowning of Ms Jalapeño, Jalapeño Olympic games, spicy food, cold drinks, big name entertainment, music and dancing. Held during Laredo's annual Washington's Birthday Celebration. Proceeds benefit youth-oriented charities. Est attendance: 25,000. For info: c/o Anselmo Castro, Jr, Jalapeño Festival, Inc, PO Drawer 1359, Laredo, TX 78042-1359. Phone: (956) 726-6697. Fax: (956) 726-6691. E-mail: anselmo_castro@iboc.com.

KING, WAYNE: 100th BIRTH ANNIVERSARY. Feb 16, 1901. American saxophonist and bandleader, widely known as "the Waltz King," born at Savannah, IL. His own composition, "The Waltz You Save for Me," was his theme song. Died at Paradise Valley, AZ, July 16, 1985.

LITHUANIA: INDEPENDENCE DAY. Feb 16. National Day. The anniversary of Lithuania's declaration of independence in 1918 is observed as the Baltic state's Independence Day. In 1940, Lithuania became a part of the Soviet Union under an agreement between Joseph Stalin and Adolf Hitler. On Mar 11, 1990, Lithuania declared its independence from the Soviet Union, the first of the Soviet republics to do so. After demanding independence, Lithuania set up a border police force and aided young men in efforts to avoid the Soviet military draft, prompting then Soviet leader Mikhail Gorbachev to send tanks into the capital of Vilnius and impose oil and gas embargoes. In the wake of the failed coup attempt in Moscow Aug 19, 1991, Lithuanian independence finally was recognized.

LONGHORN WORLD CHAMPIONSHIP RODEO. Feb 16–18. The Palace of Auburn Hills, Auburn Hills, MI. More than 200 cowboys and cowgirls compete in six professional contests ranging from bronc riding to bull riding for top prize money and world championship points. Featuring colorful opening pageantry and Big, Bad BONUS Bulls. 37th annual. Est attendance: 35,000. For info: W. Bruce Lehrke, Pres, Longhorn World Chmpshp Rodeo, Inc, PO Box 70159, Nashville, TN 37207. Phone: (615) 876-1016. Fax: (615) 876-4685. E-mail: lhrodeo@idt.net. Web: www.longhornrodeo.com.

MID-CONTINENT RAILWAY'S STEAM SNOW TRAIN. Feb 16–18. Mid-Continent Railway Museum, North Freedom, WI. Snow tours aboard authentic steam train. Coach, first class and dinner service available. Est attendance: 3,000. For info: Angie Rizner, Wisc Dells Visitors Bureau, PO Box 390, Wisconsin Dells, WI 53965. Phone: (800) 223-3557. E-mail: info@wisdells.com. Web: www.wisdells.com.

MIDWINTER BLUEGRASS FESTIVAL. Feb 16–18. Hannibal Inn, Hannibal, MO. Annually, the third weekend in February. Est attendance: 3,000. For info: Delbert Spray, Program Dir, Tri-State Bluegrass Assn, RR1, Kahoka, MO 63445. Phone: (573) 853-4344.

NATIONAL DATE FESTIVAL. Feb 16–25. Indio, CA. America's most exotic county fair features Arabian Nights theme, camel and ostrich races, satellite horse wagering, Arabian Nights play, date exhibits and sampling, thousands of competitive exhibits and carnival. Est attendance: 300,000. For info: Riverside County Fair/Natl Date Fest, 46-350 Arabia St, Indio, CA 92201-9990. Phone: (760) 863-8247 or (800) 811-FAIR. Web: www.datefest.org.

NEWPORT WINTER FESTIVAL. Feb 16–25. Newport, RI. More than 60 individual events from food, music and entertainment to skating, hayrides, snow sculptures, ice carving, scavenger hunt and even winter polo demonstrations—fun for all ages. Est attendance: 25,000. For info: Mktg & Events, Inc, 28 Pelham St, Newport, RI 02840. Phone: (401) 847-7666. Web: www.newportevents.com.

OREGON SHAKESPEARE FESTIVAL. Feb 16–Oct 28. An eight-month season of 11 plays by Shakespeare, classical and contemporary playwrights on three stages: the outdoor Elizabethan Stage, the versatile Angus Bowmer Theatre and the intimate Black Swan. Est attendance: 370,000. For info: Oregon Shakespeare Festival, Box 158, Ashland, OR 97520. Phone: (541) 482-4331. Web: www.orshakes.org.

RECREATIONAL VEHICLE SHOW. Feb 16–18 (also Feb 23–25). Timonium State Fairgrounds, Timonium, MD. Mid-Atlantic's oldest, largest and best-attended RV show with exhibitors to display all the latest in motor homes, camping and RV accessories. Est attendance: 20,000. For info: Maryland Recreational Vehicle Assn, 8332 Pulaski Hwy, Baltimore, MD 21237. Phone: (410) 687-6191. Fax: (410) 686-1486.

SMOKY MOUNTAINS STORYTELLING FESTIVAL. Feb 16–17. Patriot Park, Pigeon Forge, TN. Food, bonfire and hayrides with the region's finest yarn-spinners and folklore specialists. Est attendance: 2,500. For info: Pigeon Forge Dept of Tourism, 2450 Parkway, PO Box 1390, Pigeon Forge, TN 37868. Phone: (800) 251-9100 or (423) 453-8574. Fax: (423) 429-7362. Web: www .pigeon-forge.tn.us.

SOUTH COAST WRITER'S CONFERENCE AND FIRE-MAN'S FISH FRY. Feb 16–17. Gold Beach Resort, OR, and Gold Beach Union High School. Keynote speaker followed by a series of workshops and roundtable discussions concerning writing techniques, publishing guidelines and editorial commentary. Est attendance: 350. For info: Gold Beach Chamber of Commerce, 29279 Ellensburg Ave, #3, Gold Beach, OR 97444. Phone: (800) 525-2334. Fax: (541) 247-0188. E-mail: goldbeach @harborside.com. Web: www.harborside.com/gb.

SOUTH TEXAS RANCHING HERITAGE FESTIVAL. Feb 16–18. Kingsville, TX. Cowboy storytelling, craftsmen, ranching rodeo, chuckwagon cook-off and camp cooking. Est attendance: 10,000. For info: Kingsville CVB, 1501 N Hwy 77, Kingsville, TX 78363. Phone: (800) 333-5032. Fax: (361) 592-3227. E-mail: cvb@kingsvilletexas.com. Web: www.kingsvilletexas.com.

SOUTHEASTERN WILDLIFE EXPOSITION. Feb 16–18. Charleston, SC. Spectacular wildlife and nature art exposition showcasing original paintings, prints, sculpture, photography, carvings, collectibles and crafts. Twelve exhibition sites throughout historic Charleston. Est attendance: 43,000. For info: Southeastern Wildlife Exposition, 211 Meeting Street, Charleston, SC 29401. Phone: (843) 723-1748. Web: www.sewe.com.

STAMP EXPO/USA. Feb 16–18. Radisson Hotel, Anaheim, CA. Annual expo. Est attendance: 5,000. For info: Intl Stamp Collectors Soc, PO Box 854, Van Nuys, CA 91408. Phone: (818) 997-6496. Fax: (818) 988-4337. E-mail: iibick@aol.com. Web: www.bick.net.

WHISKEY FLAT DAYS. Feb 16–19. Kernville, CA. Whiskey Flat Days commemorates the old Kernville that was called Whiskey Flat until 1860. We turn back the clock as the parade, stores and residents go back to the 1860s. Frog races, craft booths, rodeo, parade, games for small children, carnival, street dances, puppet shows, costume and whiskerino contests, melodrama and much more. Annually, the third weekend in February. Est attendance: 25,000. For info: Kernville Chamber of Commerce, PO Box 397, Kernville, CA 93238. Phone: (760) 376-2629 or 8003507393. Fax: (760) 376-4371. E-mail: kernvillechamber@ lightspeed.net. Web: www.kernvillechamber.org.

WILSON, HENRY: BIRTH ANNIVERSARY. Feb 16, 1812. 18th vice president of the US (1873–75). Born at Farmington, NH; died at Washington, DC, Nov 22, 1875.

BIRTHDAYS TODAY

Jerome Bettis, 29, football player, born Detroit, MI, Feb 16, 1972.
LeVar Burton, 44, actor ("Roots," "Star Trek: The Next Generation"), born Landsthul, Germany, Feb 16, 1957.
Ice T (born Tracy Morrow), 42, rap singer, born Newark, NJ, Feb 16, 1959.
James Ingram, 45, singer ("Baby, Come to Me" [with Patti Austin]), songwriter, born Akron, OH, Feb 16, 1956.
William Katt, 46, actor ("The Greatest American Hero," *Perry Mason Returns, Carrie*), born Los Angeles, CA, Feb 16, 1955.
George Frost Kennan, 97, historian, diplomat, born Milwaukee, WI, Feb 16, 1904.

	S	M	T	W	T	F	S
February					1	2	3
2001	4	5	6	7	8	9	10
	11	12	13	14	15	16	17
	18	19	20	21	22	23	24
	25	26	27	28			

John Patrick McEnroe, Jr, 42, former tennis player, born Wiesbaden, West Germany, Feb 16, 1959
Barry Primus, 63, actor ("Cagney and Lacey," *Absence of Malice, Down and Out in Beverly Hills*), born New York, NY, Feb 16, 1938.
Leonard F. Woodcock, 90, former labor union official, former ambassador to China, born Providence, RI, Feb 16, 1911.

FEBRUARY 17 — SATURDAY
Day 48 — 317 Remaining

AMERICAN COUNCIL ON EDUCATION ANNUAL MEETING. Feb 17–20. Washington, DC. Est attendance: 1,300. For info: Stephanie Marshall, Amer Council on Educ, One Dupont Circle, Washington, DC 20036. Phone: (202) 939-9410. Fax: (202) 833-4760. E-mail: stephanie_marshall@ace.nche.edu. Web: www.acenet.edu.

BARBER, WALTER LANIER "RED": BIRTH ANNIVERSARY. Feb 17, 1908. One of the first broadcasters inducted into the Baseball Hall of Fame, "Red" Barber was born at Columbus, MS. Barber's first professional play-by-play experience was announcing the Cincinnati Reds opening day on radio in 1934. That game was also the first major league game he had ever seen. He broadcast baseball's first night game (in Brooklyn) on Aug 26, 1939, the 1947 game in which Jackie Robinson broke the color barrier, and Roger Maris's 61st home run in 1961. "Red" Barber died Oct 22, 1992, at Tallahassee, FL.

BRIGHTON FIELD DAY AND RODEO. Feb 17–18. Brighton Indian Reservation, Okeechobee, FL. Arts and crafts, alligator wrestling, PRCA rodeo, animal show, parade and beautiful Native American clothing. Sponsor: Seminole Tribe of Florida. Annually, the third weekend in February. Est attendance: 6,000. For info: Ellen Click, Field Day Contact Person, Rte 6, Box 666, Okeechobee, FL 34974. Phone: (941) 763-4128. Fax: (941) 763-5077.

CANADA: FROSTY FROLICS WINTER CARNIVAL. Feb 17–24. Bancroft, ON. Sled dog races, craft show, Mineral Capital Luge Track competitions and special attractions. Est attendance: 5,000. For info: Bancroft and District Chamber of Commerce, PO Box 539, Bancroft, ON, Canada K0L 1C0. Phone: (613) 332-1513. Fax: (613) 332-2119. E-mail: chamber @commerce.bancroft.on.ca. Web: www.commerce.bancroft.on .ca.

CHICAGO FLAG EXHIBIT CONTROVERSY: ANNIVERSARY. Feb 17, 1989. An exhibit at the School of the Art Institute of Chicago, titled *What is the Proper Way to Display a US Flag?*, consisted of a ledger for viewers to write their impressions but required the viewers to stand on a US flag mounted on the floor to reach the ledger. The exhibit by art student Scott Tyler prompted protests from veterans' groups, a failed lawsuit and an introduction of legislation by Senator Bob Dole to make displaying a US flag on the floor or ground a crime. Although that legislation didn't pass, Congress continues to introduce legislation against flag desecration, most recently in 1999.

CHOCOLATE FESTIVAL. Feb 17. Firehouse Art Center, Norman, OK. Tasting sessions, cooking competitions and tantalizing displays of chocolate as an art form are a treat for the eyes as well as the palate. Annually, the Saturday after Valentine's Day. Est attendance: 2,000. For info: Linda Sexton, Asst Dir, The Firehouse Art Center, 444 S Flood, Norman, OK 73069. Phone: (405) 329-4523.

COCONUT GROVE ARTS FESTIVAL. Feb 17–19. Coconut Grove, FL. More than 300 artists exhibit and sell their work. Various ethnic foods will be offered and nationally known jazz musicians will perform as well. Est attendance: 750,000. For info: Carol Romine, Coconut Grove Assn Inc, 3427 Main Highway, PO Box 330757, Coconut Grove, FL 33133. Phone: (305) 447-0401. Fax: (305) 447-1499. Web: www.coconutgroveartsfest.com.

CORELLI, ARCANGELO: BIRTH ANNIVERSARY. Feb 17, 1633. Italian composer and virtuoso violinist, born at Fusignano, Italy. From his home in Rome, Corelli made extensive and popular concert tours throughout much of Europe. Died at Rome, Italy, Jan 8, 1713.

ESA MID-WINTER SURFING CHAMPIONSHIP. Feb 17. Narragansett Town Beach, Narragansett, RI. Competition in all age categories and specialty events with prizes and trophies. Est attendance: 125. For info: Peter Pan, ESA Dir, 396 Main St, Wakefield, RI 02879. Phone: (401) 789-3399. Fax: (401) 782-0458.

FORT SUMTER RETURNED TO UNION CONTROL: ANNIVERSARY. Feb 17, 1865. After a siege that lasted almost a year and a half, Fort Sumter in South Carolina returned to Union hands on this date. The site of the first shots fired in the American Civil War on Apr 12, 1861, the fort had become a symbol for both sides. As Union attempts to retake it by shelling diminished the fort's capacity with large bombardments, Southern forces managed to hold out with few casualties.

GEORGE WASHINGTON BIRTHNIGHT BANQUET AND BALL. Feb 17. Alexandria, VA. Recreation of dinner, dancing and toasts offered to George Washington in Alexandria. Staged in original setting—Gadsby's Tavern. Eighteenth-century dancing, clothing. Alexandrians portray historic characters including George and Martha Washington. Annually, the Saturday of the federal holiday weekend. Sponsor: George Washington Birthday Celebration Committee. Est attendance: 200. For info: Alexandria Conv and Visitors Assn, 221 King St, Alexandria, VA 22314. Phone: (703) 838-4200. Fax: (703) 838-4683. E-mail: acva@FunSide.com. Web: www.FunSide.com.

GERONIMO: DEATH ANNIVERSARY. Feb 17, 1909. American Indian of the Chiricahua (Apache) tribe was born about 1829 in Arizona. He was the leader of a small band of warriors whose devastating raids in Arizona, New Mexico and Mexico caused the US Army to send 5,000 men to recapture him after his first escape. He was confined at Fort Sill, OK, where he died Feb 17, 1909, after dictating the story of his life for publication.

IROC INTERNATIONAL RACE OF CHAMPIONS. Feb 17. Daytona International Speedway, Daytona Beach, FL. All-star race for the greatest drivers from different forms of racing in the US. For info: Daytona Intl Speedway, PO Box 2801, Daytona Beach, FL 32120-2801. Phone: (904) 947-6782. Fax: (904) 947-6791. Web: www.daytonausa.com.

KROGER ST. JUDE TENNIS INTERNATIONAL. Feb 17–25. Racquet Club of Memphis, Memphis, TN. The world's finest tennis players compete in one of the most prestigious tour events of the year. Est attendance: 63,000. For info: Tom Buford, Kroger St. Jude, Racquet Club of Memphis, 5111 Sanderlin, Memphis, TN 38117. Phone: (901) 765-4400.

LAENNEC, RENE THEOPHILE HYACINTHE: BIRTH ANNIVERSARY. Feb 17, 1781. Famed French physician, author and inventor of the stethoscope, called "father of chest medicine." He wrote extensively about respiratory and heart ailments. Born at Quimper, France, he died there Aug 13, 1826.

MALTHUS, THOMAS: BIRTH ANNIVERSARY. Feb 17, 1766. English economist, author and demographer, born near Dorking, England. Malthusian population theories (especially that population growth exceeds growth of production) provoked great controversy when published in 1798. Died near Bath, England, Dec 23, 1834.

MARDI GRAS PENSACOLA & PENSACOLA BEACH. Feb 17–27. Pensacola & Pensacola Beach, FL. Annual event of street dances, parades, costume and tourist balls, food festivals, 5K run. Est attendance: 100,000. For info: Donna or David McDonald, Boogie Inc, PO Box 8219, Pensacola Beach, FL 32505. Phone: (850) 473-8858. E-mail: mrboogie5@worldnet.att .net. Web: www.boogieinc.com/margra.htm.

McCLURE, SAMUEL SIDNEY: BIRTH ANNIVERSARY. Feb 17, 1857. Irish-American newspaper editor and publisher, founder of newspaper syndicate. Born at County Antrim, Ireland. Died at New York, NY, Mar 21, 1949.

NAPA AUTO PARTS 300 NASCAR BUSCH SERIES RACE. Feb 17. Daytona International Speedway, Daytona Beach, FL. 43rd annual race is season kickoff for the NASCAR Busch series. For info: Daytona Intl Speedway, PO Box 2801, Daytona Beach, FL 32120-2801. Phone: (904) 947-6782. Fax: (904) 947-6791. Web: www.daytonausa.com.

NATIONAL FFA WEEK. Feb 17–24. More than 450,000 FFA members in more than 7,200 chapters across the US, Guam, Puerto Rico and the Virgin Islands organize events and activities fostering and supporting agricultural education and the FFA. FFA is the organization for high school students studying the business, science and technology of agriculture. For info: Natl FFA Organization, 1410 King St, Ste 400, Alexandria, VA 22314. Phone: (800) 772-0939 or (703) 838-5889. E-mail: aboutffa@ffa.org. Web: www.ffa.org.

NATIONAL PTA FOUNDERS' DAY: ANNIVERSARY. Feb 17, 1897. Celebrates the PTA's founding by Phoebe Apperson Hearst and Alice McLellan Birney. For info: Natl PTA, 330 N Wabash, Ste 2100, Chicago, IL 60611. Phone: (312) 670-6782. Fax: (312) 670-6783. E-mail: info@pta.org. Web: www.pta.org.

PEALE, RAPHAEL: BIRTH ANNIVERSARY. Feb 17, 1774. American painter, member of famous family of early American painters, born at Annapolis, MD. Died Mar 4, 1825.

"A PRAIRIE HOME COMPANION" PREMIERE: ANNIVERSARY. Feb 17, 1979. This popular live variety show debuted locally on Minnesota Public Radio in 1974 and was first broadcast nationally on Feb 17, 1979 as part of National Public Radio's Folk Festival USA. It became a regular Saturday night program in early 1980. Host Garrison Keillor's monologues about the mythical Lake Wobegon and his humorous ads for local businesses such as Bertha's Kitty Boutique, Powdermilk Biscuits and the Chatterbox Cafe were accompanied by various musical groups. Broadcast from the World Theater in St. Paul, MN, the show went off the air in 1986. A series of programs were done for cable TV, and Keillor continues to write works of fiction (*Lake Wobegon Days*). In 1994, "A Prairie Home Companion" went back on the air on Public Radio International.

TRIG'S KLONDIKE DAYS. Feb 17–18. Eagle River Derby Track, Eagle River, WI. A re-creation of primitive camps used by early buck-skinners, pioneers, trappers and traders, complete with tomahawk throwing and black powder musket shoot. Additional attractions include a 2-day horse weight-pull reminiscent of Wisconsin's logging days, a chain saw carving competition, a Native American cultural presentation including a ceremonial dance exhibition, lumberjack competition, craft show, dog weight-pull, snow sculpting competition, Northwoods Wildlife Art & Amish Craft Show & Sale and much more. Wisconsin's premiere multi-faceted winter festival. Est attendance: 12,000. For info: Eagle River Chamber of Commerce, PO Box 1917, Eagle River, WI 54521. Phone: (800) 359-6315.

TWIN CITIES' KREWE OF JANUS MARDI GRAS PARADE. Feb 17. Monroe, LA. Festive parade to celebrate Mardi Gras. For info: Tourism Sales Mgr, 1333 State Farm Dr, Monroe, LA 71202. Phone: (800) 843-1872. Fax: (318) 324-1752. E-mail: mwmcvb@centurytel.net. Web: www.bayou.com/visitors.

WHO SHALL I BE DAY?. Feb 17. Hundreds of people have their opinions as to who we are. Today is the day we decide who's right. Today we determine our identities all by ourselves. ©2000 Wellcat Holidays & Herbs. For info: Thomas Roy, 2418 Long Ln, Lebanon, PA 17046. Phone: (240) 332-4886. E-mail: wellcat @supernet.com. Web: www.wellcat.com.

BIRTHDAYS TODAY

Vanessa Atler, 19, gymnast, born Valencia, CA, Feb 17, 1982.

Alan Bates (Arthur Bates), 67, actor (*An Unmarried Woman, Women in Love*), born Derbyshire, England, Feb 17, 1934.

James Nathaniel (Jim) Brown, 65, activist, actor, Pro Football Hall of Famer, born St. Simons Island, GA, Feb 17, 1936.

Ronald DeVoe, 34, singer (Bell Biv DeVoe), born Boston, MA, Feb 17, 1967.

Michelle Forbes, 34, actress ("Homicide: Life On the Street"), born Austin, TX, Feb 17, 1967.

Brenda Fricker, 56, actress (Oscar for *My Left Foot*; *The Field*), born Dublin, Ireland, Feb 17, 1945.

Joseph Gordon-Levitt, 20, actor ("3rd Rock from the Sun," *Halloween H20*), born Los Angeles, CA, Feb 17, 1981.

Lee Hoiby, 75, composer, concert pianist, born Madison, WI, Feb 17, 1926.

Hal Holbrook (Harold Rowe, Jr), 76, actor (*Magnum Force, All the President's Men*), born Cleveland, OH, Feb 17, 1925.

Barry Humphries, 67, actor, comedian, aka Dame Edna Everidge (*Spiceworld*), born Melbourne, Australia, Feb 17, 1934.

Michael Jeffrey Jordan, 38, former basketball player, former minor league baseball player, born Brooklyn, NY, Feb 17, 1963.

Richard Karn, 42, actor ("Home Improvement"), born Seattle, WA, Feb 17, 1959.

Lou Diamond Phillips, 39, actor (*La Bamba, Stand and Deliver*), born Corpus Christi, TX, Feb 17, 1962.

Rene Russo, 47, actress (*Lethal Weapon 3, Ransom*), born Burbank, CA, Feb 17, 1954.

Craig Thomas, 68, US Senator (R, Wyoming), born Cody, WY, Feb 17, 1933.

FEBRUARY 18 — SUNDAY
Day 49 — 316 Remaining

ALEICHEM, SHOLEM: BIRTH ANNIVERSARY. Feb 18, 1859 (OS). Pen name of Russian-born author and humorist Solomon Rabinowitz. Affectionately known in the US as the "Jewish Mark Twain." Died at New York, NY, May 13, 1916.

BUILD A BETTER TRADE SHOW IMAGE WEEK. Feb 18–24. For companies that exhibit at trade shows, this week is set aside to evaluate and improve your exhibit strategies for the upcoming trade show season. For "10 Steps to a Better Trade Show Image" tip sheet, send #10 SASE. Annually, the third full

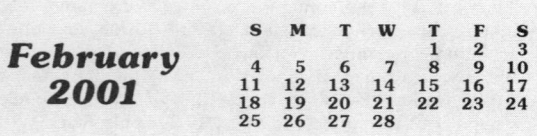

February 2001	S	M	T	W	T	F	S
					1	2	3
	4	5	6	7	8	9	10
	11	12	13	14	15	16	17
	18	19	20	21	22	23	24
	25	26	27	28			

week of February. For info: Marlys K. Arnold, Total Image Specialist, 7885 NW Roanridge Rd, Ste A, Kansas City, MO 64151. Phone: (816) 746-7888. E-mail: marnold@imagespecialist.com. Web: www.imagespecialist.com.

COW MILKED WHILE FLYING IN AN AIRPLANE: ANNIVERSARY. Feb 18, 1930. Elm Farm Ollie became the first cow to fly in an airplane. During the flight, which was attended by reporters, she was milked and the milk was sealed in paper containers and parachuted over St. Louis, MO.

DAVIS, JEFFERSON: INAUGURATION ANNIVERSARY. Feb 18, 1861. In the years before the Civil War, Jefferson Davis was the acknowledged leader of the Southern bloc and a champion of states' rights, but he had little to do with the secessionist movement until after his home state of Mississippi joined the Confederacy Jan 9, 1861. Davis withdrew from the Senate that same day. He was unanimously chosen as president of the Confederacy's provisional government and was inaugurated at Montgomery, AL, Feb 18. Within the next year he was elected to a six-year term by popular vote and inaugurated a second time Feb 22, 1862, at Richmond, VA.

DAYTONA 500. Feb 18. Daytona International Speedway, Daytona Beach, FL. 43rd annual running of the "world's greatest races" is season kickoff for the NASCAR Winston Cup season. For info: Daytona Intl Speedway, PO Box 2801, Daytona Beach, FL 32120-2801. Phone: (904) 947-6782. Fax: (904) 947-6791. Web: www.daytonausa.com.

GAMBIA: INDEPENDENCE DAY: ANNIVERSARY. Feb 18, 1965. National holiday. Independence from Britain granted. Referendum in April 1970 established Gambia as a republic within the Commonwealth.

INTERNATIONAL FRIENDSHIP WEEK. Feb 18–24. Promotion of international friendship and the international language Esperanto. For complete information, send $4 to cover expense of printing, handling and postage. Annually, the last full week in February. For info: Dr. Stanley Drake, Pres, Intl Society of Friendship & Good Will, 8592 Roswell Rd, Ste 434, Atlanta, GA 30350-1870.

NEPAL: NATIONAL DEMOCRACY DAY. Feb 18. Holiday. Anniversary of the 1952 Constitution.

PEABODY, GEORGE: BIRTH ANNIVERSARY. Feb 18, 1795. American merchant and philanthropist, born at South Danvers, MA. He endowed the Peabody Institute in Baltimore, museums at Harvard and Yale and the George Peabody College for Teachers at Nashville, TN. Died at London, England, Nov 4, 1869.

PLANET PLUTO DISCOVERY: ANNIVERSARY. Feb 18, 1930. Pluto, the ninth planet, was discovered by astronomer Clyde Tombaugh at the Lowell Observatory at Flagstaff, AZ. It was given the name of the Roman god of the underworld.

REVOLUTIONARY WAR ENCAMPMENT. Feb 18. Alexandria, VA. Sunday afternoon of Washington's Birthday Weekend. Camp life demonstrated at Fort Ward Museum and Historic Site. British and Colonial uniformed troops engage in a skirmish. Free. Est attendance: 2,000. For info: Marketing Coordinator, Alexandria Conv and Visitors Assn, 221 King St, Alexandria, VA 22314. Phone: (703) 838-4200. Fax: (703) 838-4683. E-mail: acva@Fun Side.com. Web: www.FunSide.com.

TIFFANY, LOUIS COMFORT: BIRTH ANNIVERSARY. Feb 18, 1848. American artist, son of famed jeweler Charles L. Tiffany. Best remembered for his remarkable work with decorative iridescent "favrile" glass. Born at New York, NY; died there Jan 17, 1933. See also: "Tiffany, Charles Lewis: Birth Anniversary" (Feb 15).

WILLKIE, WENDELL LEWIS: BIRTH ANNIVERSARY. Feb 18, 1892. American lawyer, author, public utility executive and politician, born at Elwood, IN. Presidential nominee of the Republican Party in 1940. Remembered for his book, *One World*, published in 1943. Died at New York, NY, Oct 8, 1944.

BIRTHDAYS TODAY

Helen Gurley Brown, 79, author (*Sex and the Office*), publisher (*Cosmopolitan*), born Green Forest, AR, Feb 18, 1922.

Aldo Ceccato, 67, conductor, born Milan, Italy, Feb 18, 1934.

Matt Dillon, 37, actor (*My Bodyguard, Drugstore Cowboy*), born Westchester, NY, Feb 18, 1964.

Milos Forman, 69, film director (Oscars for *Amadeus* and *One Flew Over the Cuckoo's Nest*), born Caslaz, Czechoslavakia, Feb 18, 1932.

Barbara Hale, 80, actress ("Perry Mason"), born DeKalb, IL, Feb 18, 1921.

John Hughes, 51, producer, director (*Home Alone 1 & 2, National Lampoon's Christmas Vacation*), born Lansing, MI, Feb 18, 1950.

George Kennedy, 74, actor (Oscar for *Cool Hand Luke*; "The Blue Knight"), born New York, NY, Feb 18, 1927.

Allan Melvin, 78, actor ("The Brady Bunch," "All in the Family"), born Kansas City, MO, Feb 18, 1923.

Toni Morrison (Chloe Anthony), 70, Nobel Prize-winning novelist (*Beloved, Jazz, Tar Baby, Sula*), born Lorain, OH, Feb 18, 1931.

Juice Newton (Judy Cohen), 49, singer (platinum album *Juice*, gold album *Quiet Lives*), born Virginia Beach, VA, Feb 18, 1952.

Yoko Ono, 68, artist, musician, widow of John Lennon, born Tokyo, Japan, Feb 18, 1933.

Jack Palance, 81, actor (Oscar for *City Slickers*; "Bronk," "Ripley's Believe It or Not"), born Lattimer, PA, Feb 18, 1920.

John Pankow, 47, actor ("Mad About You"), born St. Louis, MO, Feb 18, 1954.

Molly Ringwald, 33, actress (*Sixteen Candles, The Breakfast Club, Pretty in Pink*), born Roseville, CA, Feb 18, 1968.

Greta Scacchi, 41, actress (*White Mischief, Presumed Innocent*), born Milan, Italy, Feb 18, 1960.

Cybill Shepherd, 51, actress (*The Last Picture Show*, "Moonlighting," "Cybill"), born Memphis, TN, Feb 18, 1950.

John Travolta, 46, actor (*Pulp Fiction, Look Who's Talking, Urban Cowboy, Saturday Night Fever*, "Welcome Back Kotter"), born Englewood, NJ, Feb 18, 1955.

John William Warner, 74, US Senator (R, Virginia), born Washington, DC, Feb 18, 1927.

Vanna White, 44, TV personality ("Wheel of Fortune"), born Conway, SC, Feb 18, 1957.

FEBRUARY 19 — MONDAY

Day 50 — 315 Remaining

BOLLINGEN PRIZE: ANNIVERSARY. Feb 19, 1949. On this date, the first Bollingen Prize for poetry was awarded to Ezra Pound for his collection *The Pisan Cantos*. This first award was steeped in controversy because Pound had been charged with treason after making pro-Fascist broadcasts in Italy during World War II.

BROTHERHOOD/SISTERHOOD WEEK. Feb 19–23. A kickoff period for programs emphasizing a commitment to brotherhood/sisterhood. The National Program Office develops educational materials for use during this period that can be used year round. Annually, the third full week in February. Sponsor: The National Conference for Community and Justice (founded as the National Conference of Christians and Jews). For info: The Natl Conference for Community and Justice, 475 Park Ave South, Ste 1900, New York, NY 10016. Phone: (212) 545-1300.

CANADA: FAMILY DAY IN ALBERTA. Feb 19. Annually, the third Monday in February.

COPERNICUS, NICOLAUS: BIRTH ANNIVERSARY. Feb 19, 1473. Polish astronomer and priest who revolutionized scientific thought with what came to be called the Copernican theory, that placed the sun instead of the Earth at the center of our planetary system. Born at Torun, Poland, he died at East Prussia, May 24, 1543.

THE FEMININE MYSTIQUE PUBLISHED: ANNIVERSARY. Feb 19, 1963. Betty Friedan published *The Feminine Mystique* this month, a call for women to achieve their full potential. Her book generated enormous response and revitalized the women's movement in the US.

GARRICK, DAVID: BIRTH ANNIVERSARY. Feb 19, 1717. English actor, theater manager and playwright. Born at Hereford, England; died Jan 20, 1779, at London.

GEORGE WASHINGTON BIRTHDAY CELEBRATION PARADE. Feb 19. Alexandria, VA. Nation's largest parade honoring George Washington. Staged by his hometown. More than 200 units. Floats, bands, antique cars, and equestrian units, bagpipers. Route through historic district. Sponsor: George Washington Birthday Celebration Committee. Free admission. Est attendance: 50,000. For info: Alexandria Conv and Vistiors Association, 221 King St, Alexandria, VA 22314. Phone: (703) 838-4200. Fax: (703) 838-4683. E-mail: acva@FunSide.com. Web: www.FunSide.com.

HEDIN, SVEN: BIRTH ANNIVERSARY. Feb 19, 1865. Explorer and scientist, Sven Anders Hedin was born at Stockholm, Sweden, and died there Nov 26, 1952. His Tibetan explorations provided the first substantial knowledge of that region to the rest of the world.

JAPANESE INTERNMENT: ANNIVERSARY. Feb 19, 1942. As a result of President Franklin Roosevelt's Executive Order 9066, some 110,000 Japanese-Americans living in coastal Pacific areas were placed in concentration camps in remote areas of Arizona, Arkansas, inland California, Colorado, Idaho, Utah and Wyoming. The interned Japanese-Americans (two-thirds were US citizens) lost an estimated $400 million in property. They were allowed to return to their homes Jan 2, 1945.

KNIGHTS OF PYTHIAS: FOUNDING ANNIVERSARY. Feb 19, 1864. The social and fraternal order of the Knights of Pythias was founded at Washington, DC.

PRESIDENTS' DAY. Feb 19. Presidents' Day observes the birthdays of George Washington (Feb 22) and Abraham Lincoln (Feb 12). With the adoption of the Monday Holiday Law (which moved the observance of George Washington's birthday from Feb 22 to the third Monday in February), some of the specific significance of the event was lost and added impetus was given to the popular description of that holiday as Presidents' Day. Present usage often regards Presidents' Day as a day to honor all former presidents of the US, though the federal holiday is still Washington's Birthday. Annually, the third Monday in February.

STOCK EXCHANGE HOLIDAY (WASHINGTON'S BIRTHDAY). Feb 19. The holiday schedules for the various exchanges are subject to change if relevant rules, regulations or exchange policies are revised. If you have questions, phone: American Stock Exchange (212) 306-1000; Chicago Board of Trade (312) 435-3500; Chicago Board of Options Exchange (312) 786-5600; New York Stock Exchange (212) 656-2065; Pacific Stock Exchange (415) 393-4000; Philadelphia Stock Exchange (215) 496-5000.

US LANDING ON IWO JIMA: ANNIVERSARY. Feb 19, 1945. Beginning at dawn, the landing of 30,000 American troops took place on the barren 12-square-mile island of Iwo Jima. Initially there was little resistance, but 21,500 Japanese stood ready underground to fight to the last man to protect massive strategic fortifications linked by tunnels.

WASHINGTON, GEORGE: BIRTHDAY OBSERVANCE (LEGAL HOLIDAY). Feb 19. Legal public holiday (Public Law 90–363) sets Washington's birthday observance on the third Monday in February each year—applicable to federal employees and to the District of Columbia). Observed in all states. See also: "Washington, George: Birth Anniversary" (Feb 22).

BIRTHDAYS TODAY

Prince Andrew, 41, Duke of York, born London, England, Feb 19, 1960.

Justine Bateman, 35, actress ("Family Ties," "Men Behaving Badly"), born Rye, NY, Feb 19, 1966.

Lou Christie, 58, singer ("Lightnin' Strikes Again"), born Glen Willard, PA, Feb 19, 1943.

Jeff Daniels, 46, actor (*The Purple Rose of Cairo, Something Wild, Dumb and Dumber*), born Chelsea, MI, Feb 19, 1955.

Stephen Nichols, 50, actor ("Days of Our Lives," "Santa Barbara"), born Cincinnati, OH, Feb 19, 1951.

Smokey Robinson (William Robinson, Jr), 61, singer, songwriter ("Cruisin'," "Being With You"), born Detroit, MI, Feb 19, 1940.

Seal, 38, British singer-songwriter ("Prayer for the Dying"), born Sealhenry Samuel, London, England, Feb 19, 1963.

Andrew Shue, 34, actor ("Melrose Place"), born South Orange, NJ, Feb 19, 1967.

Amy Tan, 49, author (*The Joy Luck Club*), born Oakland, CA, Feb 19, 1952.

FEBRUARY 20 — TUESDAY

Day 51 — 314 Remaining

ADAMS, ANSEL: BIRTH ANNIVERSARY. Feb 20, 1902. American photographer, known for his photographs of Yosemite National Park, born at San Francisco, CA. Adams died at Monterey, CA, Apr 22, 1984.

DOUGLASS, FREDERICK: DEATH ANNIVERSARY. Feb 20, 1895. American journalist, orator and antislavery leader. Born at Tuckahoe, MD, probably in February 1817. Died at Anacostia Heights, DC. His original name before his escape from slavery was Frederick Augustus Washington Bailey.

EATING DISORDERS AWARENESS WEEK. Feb 20–27. Provides opportunities for eating disorders organizations, mental health professionals, families and concerned individuals around the world to join together to distribute information and plan events relating to eating disorders. Eating Disorders Awareness & Prevention, Inc, 603 Stewart St, Ste 803, Seattle, WA 98101. Phone: (206) 382-3587. Web: members.aol.com/edapinc/edaw.html.

JEFFERSON, JOSEPH: BIRTH ANNIVERSARY. Feb 20, 1829. Distinguished American actor, born at Philadelphia, PA, in a family of actors. Jefferson made his stage debut at the age of three in Kotzebue's *Pizarro*. After many successes, his search for a character both humorous and pathetic centered on Rip Van Winkle, about whom he wrote a short play. Later revised by Dion Boucicault, the play opened with Jefferson in the leading role at London, England, in 1865 and was an immediate suc-

cess. Rip Van Winkle became the signature role for which he was known. Jefferson died at Palm Beach, FL, Apr 23, 1905. He is remembered each year in Chicago when the Joseph Jefferson (Jeff) Awards are presented to recognize excellence in theatrical productions.

NORTHERN HEMISPHERE HOODIE-HOO DAY. Feb 20. At high noon (local time) citizens are asked to go outdoors and yell "Hoodie-Hoo" to chase away winter and make ready for spring, one month away. [© 2000 by WH] For info: Tom or Ruth Roy, Wellcat Holidays, 2418 Long Ln, Lebanon, PA 17046. Phone: (717) 279-0184. E-mail: wellcat@supernet.com. Web: www.wellcat.com.

PISCES, THE FISH. Feb 20–Mar 20. In the astronomical/astrological zodiac, which divides the sun's apparent orbit into 12 segments, the period Feb 20–Mar 20 is identified, traditionally, as the sun sign of Pisces, the Fish. The ruling planet is Neptune.

PRESCOTT, WILLIAM: 275th BIRTH ANNIVERSARY. Feb 20, 1726. American Revolutionary soldier, born at Groton, MA. Died at Pepperell, MA, Oct 13, 1795. Credited with the order, "Don't fire until you see the whites of their eyes," at the Battle of Bunker Hill, June 17, 1775.

ROMMEL STRIKES FROM MARETH LINE: ANNIVERSARY. Feb 20, 1943. After his defeat in Libya in January of 1943, Field Marshal Erwin Rommel retreated to the Mareth Line, an old French frontier position in Tunisia. From there Rommel took the offensive to defeat US forces at Kasserine Pass on this date. He then attacked the 8th Army at Medenine but had to pull back after losing 52 tanks. British General Sir Bernard Montgomery then took the offensive Mar 20, attacking and turning the Mareth Line. The German forces withdrew and shortly thereafter Rommel was recalled to Germany, and his command passed to Italian General Messe, who retreated to Enfidaville.

SPACE MILESTONE: *FRIENDSHIP 7* (US): FIRST AMERICAN TO ORBIT EARTH: ANNIVERSARY. Feb 20, 1962. John Herschel Glenn, Jr, became the first American, and the third person, to orbit Earth. Aboard the capsule *Friendship 7*, he made three orbits of Earth. Spacecraft was *Mercury-Atlas 6*. In 1998 the 77-year-old Glenn went into space again on the space shuttle *Discovery* to test the effects of aging.

SPACE MILESTONE: *MIR* SPACE STATION (USSR): 15th ANNIVERSARY. Feb 20, 1986. A "third-generation" orbiting space station, *Mir* (Peace), was launched without crew from the Baikonur space center at Leninsk, Kazakhstan. Believed to be 40 feet long, weigh 47 tons and have six docking ports. Both Russian and American crews have used the station. After many equipment failures and financial problems, the Russians contemplated taking *Mir* out of service in 1999 but private funding has made it possible for it to stay aloft.

STOTZ, CARL E.: BIRTH ANNIVERSARY. Feb 20, 1920. Carl E. Stotz shaped the summers of millions of kids as the founder of Little League baseball. Born at Williamsport, PA, he organized the first three-team league there in 1939. Died at Williamsport, June 4, 1992.

STUDENT VOLUNTEER DAY. Feb 20. To honor students who give of themselves and of their personal time to improve the lives of others and their communities. Annually, Feb 20. Est atten-

February 2001	S	M	T	W	T	F	S
					1	2	3
	4	5	6	7	8	9	10
	11	12	13	14	15	16	17
	18	19	20	21	22	23	24
	25	26	27	28			

dance: 250. For info: Susquehanna Univ, Center for Service Learning and Volunteer Programs, 514 University Avenue, Selins-grove, PA 17870-1001. Phone: (570) 372-4139. Fax: (570) 372-2745. E-mail: woodsd@susqu.edu.

BIRTHDAYS TODAY

Edward Albert, 50, actor (*Butterflies Are Free, Terminal Entry, Guarding Tess*), born Los Angeles, CA, Feb 20, 1951.

Robert Altman, 76, film director (*M*A*S*H, Nashville*), born Kansas City, MO, Feb 20, 1925.

Charles Barkley, 38, former basketball player, born Leeds, AL, Feb 20, 1963.

Brenda Blethyn, 55, actress (*Secrets and Lies, A River Runs Through It*), born Ramsgate, England, Feb 20, 1946.

Cindy Crawford, 35, model, actress, born DeKalb, IL, Feb 20, 1966.

Sandy Duncan, 55, actress (*Funny Face*, "The Hogan Family," *Peter Pan*), born Henderson, TX, Feb 20, 1946.

Ron Eldard, 38, actor ("Men Behaving Badly," "ER"), born Long Island, NY, Feb 20, 1963.

Philip Anthony (Phil) Esposito, 59, hockey executive, former coach and Hockey Hall of Fame center, born Sault Ste. Marie, Ontario, Canada, Feb 20, 1942.

Stephon Marbury, 24, basketball player, born New York, NY, Feb 20, 1977.

Mitch McConnell, 59, US Senator (R, Kentucky), born Colbert County, AL, Feb 20, 1942.

Jennifer O'Neill, 53, actress (*The Summer of '42*, "Cover-Up"), born Rio de Janeiro, Brazil, Feb 20, 1948.

Sidney Poitier, 74, actor (*In the Heat of the Night*; Oscar for *Lilies of the Field*), born Miami, FL, Feb 20, 1927.

Buffy Sainte-Marie (Beverly Sainte-Marie), 60, Native-American folksinger ("Mister Can't You See," "He's an Indian Cowboy in the Rodeo"), born Craven, Saskatchewan, Canada, Feb 20, 1941.

Patty Hearst Shaw, 47, newspaper heiress who was kidnapped by radical group Symbionese Liberation Army; actress (*Cry-Baby*), born San Francisco, CA, Feb 20, 1954.

French Stewart, 37, actor ("3rd Rock From the Sun"), born Albuquerque, NM, Feb 20, 1964.

Peter Strauss, 54, actor ("Rich Man, Poor Man;" *Soldier Blue*), born Croton-on-Hudson, NY, Feb 20, 1947.

Lili Taylor, 34, actress (*I Shot Andy Warhol, Mrs Parker and the Vicious Circle, Mystic Pizza*), born Glencoe, IL, Feb 20, 1967.

Robert William (Bobby) Unser, 67, auto racer, born Albuquerque, NM, Feb 20, 1934.

Gloria Vanderbilt, 77, fashion designer, artist, born New York, NY, Feb 20, 1924.

James Wilby, 43, actor (*DreamChild, Howard's End*), born Rangoon, Burma, Feb 20, 1958.

Nancy Wilson, 64, singer ("Yesterday's Love Songs/Today's Blues"), born Chillicothe, OH, Feb 20, 1937.

FEBRUARY 21 — WEDNESDAY

Day 52 — 313 Remaining

BANGLADESH: MARTYRS DAY. Feb 21. National mourning day in memory of martyrs of the Bengali Language Movement in 1952. Mourners gather at the Azimpur graveyard.

BATTLE OF VERDUN: 85th ANNIVERSARY. Feb 21. The German High Command launched an offensive on the Western Front at Verdun, France, which became WWI's single longest battle. An estimated one million men were killed, decimating both the German and French armies, before the battle ended on Dec 15, 1916.

BOMBECK, ERMA: BIRTH ANNIVERSARY. Feb 21, 1927. Humorist and writer born at Dayton, OH. Authored many books, including *The Grass Is Always Greener Over the Septic Tank*. Bombeck died at San Francisco, CA, Apr 22, 1996.

CIA AGENT ARRESTED AS SPY: ANNIVERSARY. Feb 21, 1994. Aldrich Hazen Ames and his wife Maria del Rosario Casas Ames were arrested on charges they had spied for the Soviet Union beginning in 1985 and had continued to spy for Russia after the Soviet collapse in 1991. Ames had worked as a counterintelligence officer for the CIA at its headquarters at Langley, VA. Prosecutors said that the pair had been paid about $2.5 million for their activities and were probably responsible for the deaths of at least 10 CIA agents whom Ames had identified for the Soviets. The government considered this to be one of the most serious spy cases ever uncovered in the US. On Apr 28 Aldrich Ames was sentenced to life in prison. Rosario Ames was sentenced to a 63-month prison term in return for her husband's promise to cooperate with authorities.

FIRST WOMAN TO GRADUATE FROM DENTAL SCHOOL: ANNIVERSARY. Feb 21, 1866. Lucy Hobbs became the first woman to graduate from a dental school at Cincinnati, OH.

INTERNATIONAL RESIDENCE HALL STUDENT STAFF RECOGNITION DAY. Feb 21. This is a national day of recognition for students working in university residence halls. Resident Assistants (and RCs, CAs, SAs) serve more than 3.5 million residents in university housing. This day serves to spotlight the efforts and energy put into serving residents! Annually, the third Wednesday in February. For info: Dan P. Oltersdorf. E-mail: dan@residentassistant.com. Web: www.residentassistant.com.

LA FIESTA DE LOS VAQUEROS. Feb 21–25. Tucson, AZ. Tucson celebrates its Old West heritage with parade, PRCA rodeo and other related rodeo events. Est attendance: 55,000. For info: Tucson Rodeo Committee, Inc, PO Box 11006, Tucson, AZ 85734. Phone: (520) 741-2233. Fax: (520) 741-7273.

LIONEL HAMPTON JAZZ FESTIVAL. Feb 21–24. University of Idaho, Moscow, Idaho. College, high school, junior high and elementary school vocal and instrumental jazz ensembles come from all over the US to compete in the festival and attend concerts and clinics given by the world's greatest jazz artists. Annually, Wednesday–Saturday the last full week of February. Est attendance: 40,000. For info: Dr. Lynn J. Skinner, Exec Dir, UI Lionel Hampton Jazz Fest, Lionel Hampton School of Music, Univ of Idaho, Moscow, ID 83844-4014. Phone: (208) 885-6765. Fax: (208) 885-6513. E-mail: jazzdoc@uidaho.edu.

MALCOLM X: ASSASSINATION ANNIVERSARY. Feb 21, 1965. Malcolm X, a black leader who renounced the Black Muslim sect to form the Organization of Afro-American Unity and to practice a more orthodox form of Islam, was shot and killed as he spoke to a rally at the Audubon Ballroom at New York, NY. Three men were convicted of the murder in 1966 and sentenced to life in prison. Born Malcolm Little, the son of a Baptist preacher, at Omaha, NE, May 19, 1925.

***NEW YORKER* PUBLISHED: ANNIVERSARY.** Feb 21, 1925. First issue of the magazine published on this date.

PALMER, ALICE FREEMAN: BIRTH ANNIVERSARY. Feb 21, 1855. Born at Colesville, NY, Alice Freeman Palmer became president of Wellesley College at the age of 27. Under her leadership the school grew into one of the leading women's colleges. She was also instrumental in bringing the women's school Radcliffe College into its association with Harvard University. One of the organizers of the American Association of University Women, she served as its president for two terms. She was appointed the first dean of women at the University of Chicago when it opened in 1892. Palmer died Dec 6, 1902, at Paris.

RICHARD NIXON'S TRIP TO CHINA: ANNIVERSARY. Feb 21, 1972. Richard Nixon became the first US president to visit any country not diplomatically recognized by the US when he went to the People's Republic of China for meetings with Chairman Mao Tse-tung and Premier Chou En-lai. Nixon arrived at Peking on this date, and departed China on Feb 28. The "Shanghai Communique" was issued Feb 27. See also: "Shanghai Communique Anniversary" (Feb 27).

SANDINO, CESAR AUGUSTO: ASSASSINATION ANNIVERSARY. Feb 21, 1934. Nicaraguan guerrilla leader after whom the Sandinistas of the present day are named. Sandino, born in 1893 (exact date unknown), was murdered along with his brother and several aides at Managua on Feb 21, 1934. He and his followers had eluded the occupying force of US Marines as well as the Nicaraguan National Guard from 1927 until 1933. Regarded by the US as an outlaw and a bandit, he is revered as a martyred patriot hero by many Nicaraguans. His successful resistance and the resulting widespread anti-US feeling were largely responsible for inauguration of a US counteraction—the "Good Neighbor Policy" toward Latin American nations during the administration of President Franklin D. Roosevelt.

UNITED NATIONS: INTERNATIONAL MOTHER LANGUAGE DAY. Feb 21. To help raise awareness among all peoples of the distinct and enduring value of their languages. Info from: United Nations, Dept of Public Info, New York, NY 10017. Web: www.un.org.

WASHINGTON MONUMENT DEDICATED: ANNIVERSARY. Feb 21, 1885. Monument to the first president was dedicated at Washington, DC.

BIRTHDAYS TODAY

Christopher Atkins, 40, actor ("Dallas," *The Blue Lagoon*), born Rye, NY, Feb 21, 1961.

William Baldwin, 38, actor (*Born on the Fourth of July*, *Backdraft*), born Massapequa, NY, Feb 21, 1963.

Mary Chapin Carpenter, 43, musician ("Stones in the Road," "Hometown Girl"), born Princeton, NJ, Feb 21, 1958.

Charlotte Church, 15, singer (*Voice of an Angel*), born Wales, Feb 21, 1986.

Tyne Daly, 54, actress (Emmy for "Cagney and Lacey"; *Gypsy*), born Madison, WI, Feb 21, 1947.

Christine Ebersole, 48, actress (*Richie Rich*, *Amadeus*, "Saturday Night Live"), born Chicago, IL, Feb 21, 1953.

David Geffen, 57, record company executive (Geffen Records), born New York, NY, Feb 21, 1944.

Hubert de Givenchy, 74, fashion designer, born Beauvais, France, Feb 21, 1927.

Kelsey Grammer, 46, actor ("Cheers," "Frasier"), born St. Thomas, US Virgin Islands, Feb 21, 1955.

Jennifer Love Hewitt, 22, actress ("Party of Five," "Time of My Life"), born Waco, TX, Feb 21, 1979.

Gary Lockwood, 64, actor (*Splendor in the Grass*, *2001: A Space Odyssey*), born Van Nuys, CA, Feb 21, 1937.

Rue McClanahan, 67, actress ("Maude," "The Golden Girls"), born Healdton, OK, Feb 21, 1934.

William Petersen, 48, actor (*Return to Lonesome Dove*), born Evanston, IL, Feb 21, 1953.

Nina Simone (Eunice Waymon), 68, singer ("I Loves You Porgy," "Trouble in Mind"), born Tryon, NC, Feb 21, 1933.

Olympia J. Snowe, 54, US Senator (R, Maine), born Augusta, ME, Feb 21, 1947.

FEBRUARY 22 — THURSDAY

Day 53 — 312 Remaining

AMERICAN BIRKEBEINER XXIX RACE. Feb 22–24. Cable to Hayward, WI. The largest and most prestigious cross-country ski marathon in North America attracts more than 8,000 participants for the 51K trek. Starting off with the Birkie, skiers of the 23K Kortelopet finish at the halfway point. A nordic festival of related ski events and activities begins Feb 22. Est attendance: 25,000. For info: American Birkebeiner Ski Foundation, Inc, Box 911, Hayward, WI 54843. Phone: (715) 634-5025. Fax: (715) 634-5663. E-mail: birkie@win.bright.net. Web: www.birkie.com.

BADEN-POWELL, ROBERT: BIRTH ANNIVERSARY. Feb 22, 1857. British army officer who founded the Boy Scouts and Girl Guides. Born at London, England, he died at Kenya, Africa, Jan 8, 1941.

BIG TEN MEN'S SWIMMING AND DIVING CHAMPIONSHIP. Feb 22–24. Univ of Minnesota. Est attendance: 2,000. For info: Sue Ryan, Big Ten Conference, 1500 W Higgins Rd, Park Ridge, IL 60068-6300. Phone: (847) 696-1010. Fax: (847) 696-1110. Web: www.bigten.org or www.bigtenchampionships.com.

CANADA: YUKON SOURDOUGH RENDEZVOUS. Feb 22–25. Whitehorse, YT. Mad trapper competitions, flour packing, beard-growing contests, old time fiddle show, sourdough pancake breakfasts, can-can girls, talent shows, etc. Also, many family-oriented activities. Visitors welcome to participate. Est attendance: 20,000. For info: Yukon Sourdough Rendezvous, Box 5108, Whitehorse, YT, Canada Y1A 4S3. Phone: (867) 667-2148 or (888) FUN-N-SNO. Fax: (867) 668-6755. E-mail: ysr@yukon.net. Web: rendezvous.yukon.net/

CARNIVAL DE PONCE. Feb 22–27. Ponce, PR. Carnival, artisans fair, parade with floats and papier-mâché masks. Annually, the six days before Ash Wednesday. Est attendance: 100,000. For info: David Talavera, Tourism Dir, Municipality of Ponce, Ponce, PR 00731. Phone: (809) 841-8044.

CHARRO DAYS. Feb 22–25. Brownsville, TX. Two Nations–Twin Cultures, a true example of international harmony and cooperation between Brownsville, Texas, and Matamoros, Mexico. Starts the last Thursday in February. Colorful celebration of the charro horsemen of Mexico, men of great riding skills. Dances, parades and carnival. Est attendance: 150,000. For info: Charro Days, Inc, PO Box 3247, Brownsville, TX 78523-3247. Phone: (956) 542-4245. Fax: (956) 542-6771. Web: www.charrodays.org.

FLORIDA ACQUIRED BY US: ANNIVERSARY. Feb 22, 1819. Secretary of State John Quincy Adams signed the Florida Purchase Treaty under which Spain ceded Florida to the US. As payment, the US assumed $5 million of claims by US citizens against Spain. Florida became a state in 1845.

INDIANA DEER & TURKEY EXPOSITION. Feb 22–25. Indiana State Fairgrounds, Indianapolis, IN. For info: Kevin Renfro, VP, 2511 E 46th St, Ste E-2, Indianapolis, IN 46205. Phone: (317) 546-4344 or (800) 892-1723. Fax: (317) 546-3002. E-mail: insportshow@iquest.net.

ITALY: FEAST OF THE INCAPPUCCIATI. Feb 22. Gradoli (near Viterbo). On the Thursday before Ash Wednesday the members of the Confraternity of Purgatory make the rounds of the town dressed in traditional hooded robes, bearing a banner and walking to the beat of a drum. They stop at every house to collect foodstuffs in the name of the souls in purgatory; the food is then served at the banquet on Ash Wednesday.

LOWELL, JAMES RUSSELL: BIRTH ANNIVERSARY. Feb 22, 1819. American essayist, poet and diplomat. Born at Cambridge, MA, he died there Aug 12, 1891.

MAYMONT FLOWER & GARDEN SHOW. Feb 22–25. Richmond Centre, Richmond, VA. The 12th annual Maymont Flower & Garden Show is Virginia's largest. Landscape exhibits, lectures and more. Benefits Maymont, a 100-acre Victorian estate two miles from downtown Richmond. Est attendance: 31,000. For info: Maymont Foundation, 1700 Hampton St, Richmond, VA 23220. Phone: (804) 358-7166. Web: www.maymont.org.

February 2001	S	M	T	W	T	F	S
					1	2	3
	4	5	6	7	8	9	10
	11	12	13	14	15	16	17
	18	19	20	21	22	23	24
	25	26	27	28			

MICHIGAN HOME AND GARDEN SHOW. Feb 22–25. Pontiac Silverdome, Pontiac, MI. Products and services for home building/remodeling, home furnishings and interior design, lawn and garden and related areas. On-site constructions, theme gardens, seminars and demonstrations, plus The Standard Flower Show sponsored by The Federated Garden Clubs of Michigan, District 1. Est attendance: 45,000. For info: Mike Wilbraham, ShowSpan, Inc, 1400 28th St SW, Grand Rapids, MI 49509. Phone: (616) 530-1919. Fax: (616) 530-2122. Web: www .showspan.com.

MILLAY, EDNA ST. VINCENT: BIRTH ANNIVERSARY. Feb 22, 1892. American poet ("My candle burns at both ends . . ."), born at Rockland, ME. She died Oct 19, 1950, at Auster-litz, NY.

MONTGOMERY BOYCOTT ARRESTS: ANNIVER-SARY. Feb 22, 1956. On Feb 20 white city leaders of Montgomery, AL, issued an ultimatum to black organizers of the three-month-old Montgomery bus boycott. They said if the boycott ended immediately there would be "no retaliation whatso-ever." If it did not end, it was made clear they would begin arresting black leaders. Two days later, 80 well-known boycotters, including Rosa Parks, Martin Luther King, Jr and E.D. Nixon marched to the sheriff's office in the county courthouse, where they gave themselves up for arrest. They were booked, finger-printed and photographed. The next day the story was carried by newspapers all over the world.

NAIA MEN'S AND WOMEN'S INDOOR TRACK AND FIELD NATIONAL CHAMPIONSHIPS. Feb 22–24. Devaney Sports Center, Lincoln, NE. Individuals compete for All-America honors while teams compete for the national champi-onship. 36th (men) and 21st (women) annual competition. Est attendance: 2,500. For info: Natl Assn Intercollegiate Athletics, 6120 S Yale Ave, Ste 1450, Tulsa, OK 74136. Phone: (918) 494-8828. Fax: (918) 494-8841. E-mail: thasseltine@naia.org. Web: www.naia.org.

PEALE, REMBRANDT: BIRTH ANNIVERSARY. Feb 22, 1778. American portrait and historical painter, son of artist Charles Willson Peale, born at Bucks County, PA. Died at Philadel-phia, PA, Oct 3, 1860.

SAINT LUCIA: INDEPENDENCE DAY: ANNIVER-SARY. Feb 22. National holiday. Commemorates independence of the island in the West Indies from Britain in 1979.

SCHOPENHAUER, ARTHUR: BIRTH ANNIVERSARY. Feb 22, 1788. Philosopher and author, born at Danzig, Germany, and died at Frankfurt am Main, Germany, Sept 21, 1860. Gen-erally regarded as a misanthrope, the never-married Schopen-hauer wrote, in 1819, "To marry is to halve your rights and double your duties."

WADLOW, ROBERT PERSHING: BIRTH ANNIVER-SARY. Feb 22, 1918. Tallest man in recorded history, born at Alton, IL. Though only 9 lbs at birth, by age 10 Wadlow already stood over 6 feet tall and weighed 210 lbs. When Wadlow died at age 22, he was a remarkable 8 feet 11.1 inches tall, 490 lbs. His gentle, friendly manner in the face of constant public attention earned him the name "Gentle Giant." Wadlow died July 15, 1940, at Manistee, MI, of complications resulting from a foot infection.

WASHINGTON, GEORGE: BIRTH ANNIVERSARY. Feb 22, 1732. First president of the US ("First in war, first in peace and first in the hearts of his countrymen" in the words of Henry "Light-Horse Harry" Lee). Born at Westmoreland County, VA, Feb 22, 1732 (New Style). However, the Julian (Old Style) cal-endar was still in use in the colonies when he was born and the year began in March, so the date on the calendar when he was born was Feb 11, 1731. He died at Mount Vernon, VA, Dec 14, 1799. See also: "Washington, George: Birthday Observance (Legal Holiday)" (Feb 19 in 2001).

WOOLWORTHS FIRST OPENED: ANNIVERSARY. Feb 22, 1879. First chain store, Woolworths, opened at Utica, NY. In 1997, the closing of the chain was announced.

Amy Strum Alcott, 45, golfer, born Kansas City, MO, Feb 22, 1956.

George Lee ("Sparky") Anderson, 67, Baseball Hall of Fame manager and player, born Bridgewater, SD, Feb 22, 1934.

Drew Barrymore, 26, actress (*E.T. The Extra-Terrestrial, Irrecon-cilable Differences*), born Los Angeles, CA, Feb 22, 1975.

Michael Te Pei Chang, 29, tennis player, born Hoboken, NJ, Feb 22, 1972.

Jonathan Demme, 57, director (*Silence of the Lambs*), born Cen-tre, MD, Feb 22, 1944.

Paul Dooley, 73, actor (*Slap Shot, Breaking Away, The Player*), born Parkersburg, WV, Feb 22, 1928.

Julius Winfield ("Dr. J") Erving, 51, former basketball player, Basketball Hall of Famer, born Roosevelt, NY, Feb 22, 1950.

William Frist, 49, US Senator (R, Tennessee), born Nashville, TN, Feb 22, 1952.

Nelson Bunker Hunt, 75, business executive, born El Dorado, TX, Feb 22, 1926.

Edward Moore (Ted) Kennedy, 69, US Senator (D, Massachu-setts), born Boston, MA, Feb 22, 1932.

Kyle MacLachlan, 42, actor ("Twin Peaks," *Blue Velvet, The Flint-stones*), born Yakima, WA, Feb 22, 1959.

Miou-Miou, 51, actress (*Entre Nous, La Lectrice*), born Paris, France, Feb 22, 1950.

Jeri Ryan, 33, actress ("Star Trek: Voyager"), born Munich, Ger-many, Feb 22, 1968.

Vijay Singh, 38, golfer, born Lautoka, Fiji, Feb 22, 1963.

Julie Walters, 51, actress (*Educating Rita, Prick Up Your Ears*), born Birmingham, England, Feb 22, 1950.

Jayson Williams, 33, basketball player, born Ritter, SC, Feb 22, 1968.

FEBRUARY 23 — FRIDAY

Day 54 — 311 Remaining

AMERICAN CLUB'S TEDDY BEAR CLASSIC. Feb 23–25. The American Club, Kohler, WI. The creations of more than 60 teddy bear artists from across the country on display—bears, accessories, clothes, supplies, gifts. Many demonstrations. Est attendance: 3,500. For info: The American Club, Highland Dr, Kohler, WI 53044. Phone: (800) 344-2838. Fax: (920) 457-0299. Web: www.americanclub.com.

BIG 12 MEN'S AND WOMEN'S INDOOR TRACK CHAMPIONSHIP. Feb 23–24. Lincoln, NE. Est attendance: 5,000. For info: Big 12 Conference, 2201 Stemmons Freeway, 28th Floor, Dallas, TX 75207. Phone: (214) 774-2121. Fax: (214) 742-2046. Web: www.big12sports.com.

BRUNEI DARUSSALAM: NATIONAL DAY. Feb 23. National holiday observed in Brunei Darussalam, located on the island of Borneo.

DOW-JONES TOPS 4,000: ANNIVERSARY. Feb 23, 1995. The Dow-Jones Index of 30 major industrial stocks topped the 4,000 mark for the first time.

Du BOIS, W.E.B.: BIRTH ANNIVERSARY. Feb 23, 1868. William Edward Burghardt Du Bois, American educator and leader of the movement for black equality. Born at Great Bar-rington, MA, he died at Accra, Ghana, Aug 27, 1963. "The cost of liberty," he wrote in 1909, "is less than the price of repres-sion."

FIRST CLONING OF AN ADULT ANIMAL: ANNIVERSARY. Feb 23, 1997. Researchers in Scotland announced the first cloning of an adult animal, a lamb they named Dolly with a genetic makeup identical to that of her mother. This led to worldwide speculation about the possibility of human cloning. On Mar 4, President Clinton imposed a ban on the federal funding of human cloning research.

GROUND WAR AGAINST IRAQ BEGINS: 10th ANNIVERSARY. Feb 23, 1991. After an air campaign lasting slightly more than a month, Allied forces launched the ground offensive against Iraqi forces. The relentless air attacks had devastated troops and targets in both Iraq and Kuwait. A world that had watched and anticipated "The Mother of All Battles" was surprised at the swiftness and ease with which Allied forces were able to subdue Iraqi forces in 100 hours.

GUYANA: ANNIVERSARY OF REPUBLIC. Feb 23, 1970. National holiday. Guyana in South America became a republic.

HANDEL, GEORGE FREDERICK: BIRTH ANNIVERSARY. Feb 23, 1685 (OS). Born at Halle, Saxony. Germany, Handel and Bach, born the same year, were perhaps the greatest masters of Baroque music. Handel's most frequently performed work is the oratorio *Messiah*, which was first heard in 1742. He died at London, England, Apr 14, 1759. See also: "Bach, Johann Sebastian: Birth Anniversary" [Mar 21].

JAPANESE ATTACK US MAINLAND: ANNIVERSARY. Feb 23, 1942. In the first attack on the US mainland, a Japanese submarine fired 25 shells at an oil refinery at the edge of Ellwood Oil Field 12 miles west of Santa Barbara, CA. One shell made a direct hit on the rigging causing minor damage.

LONGHORN WORLD CHAMPIONSHIP RODEO. Feb 23–25. Von Braun Civic Center, Huntsville, AL. More than 200 cowboys and cowgirls compete in six professional contests ranging from bronco riding to bull riding for top prize money and world championship points. Featuring colorful opening pageantry and Big, Bad BONUS Bulls. 22nd annual. Est attendance: 16,000. For info: W. Bruce Lehrke, Pres, Longhorn World Chmpshp Rodeo, Inc, PO Box 70159, Nashville, TN 37207. Phone: (615) 876-1016. Fax: (615) 876-4685. E-mail: lhrodeo@idt.net. Web: www.longhornrodeo.com.

LOST DUTCHMAN DAYS. Feb 23–25. Apache Junction, AZ. Three-day rodeo competiton (senior pro rodeo), dance, carnival, parade, business vendors in celebration of the legend of the Superstition Mountains and the Lost Dutchman Mine. Est attendance: 30,000. For info: Apache Junction Chamber of Commerce, PO Box 1747, Apache Junction, AZ 85217-1747. Phone: (800) 252-3141. Fax: (480) 982-3234.

MOON PHASE: NEW MOON. Feb 23. Moon enters New Moon phase at 3:21 AM, EST.

NC RV AND CAMPING SHOW. Feb 23–25. NC State Fairgrounds, Raleigh, NC. A display of the latest in recreational vehicles and accessories by various dealers. Est attendance: 12,000. For info: Apple Rock Advertising & Promotions, 1200 Eastchester Dr, High Point, NC 27265. Phone: (336) 881-7100. Fax: (336) 883-7198.

NEWPORT SEAFOOD AND WINE FESTIVAL. Feb 23–25. Newport, OR. Central coastal festival featuring seafood and wines from Oregon, Washington, California and Idaho. Est attendance: 17,500. For info: Rebecah Morris, Special Events Coordinator, Greater Newport Chamber of Commerce, 555 SW Coast Hwy, Newport, OR 97365. Phone: (541) 265-5883. Fax: (541) 265-5589. E-mail: rm@actionnet.net.

February 2001	S	M	T	W	T	F	S
					1	2	3
	4	5	6	7	8	9	10
	11	12	13	14	15	16	17
	18	19	20	21	22	23	24
	25	26	27	28			

PEPYS, SAMUEL: BIRTH ANNIVERSARY. Feb 23, 1633 (OS). Diarist, born at London, England. Wrote Pepys in his diary (Mar 10, 1666): "The truth is, I do indulge myself a little the more in pleasure, knowing that this is the proper age of my life to do it; and, out of my observation that most men that do thrive in the world do forget to take pleasure during the time that they are getting their estate, but reserve that till they have got one, and then it is too late for them to enjoy it." Died at London, England, May 26, 1703 (OS).

RUSSIA: ARMY AND NAVY DAY. Feb 23. Also known as Defender of the Fatherland Day. Wreaths are laid at the Tomb of the Unknown Soldier. Commemorates a 1918 clash with German troops that went down in history as the birthday of the Red Army.

SECOND HONEYMOON WEEKEND. Feb 23–25. This weekend is set aside for all couples to spend some quality time together away from the routine of their everyday lives. Take your significant other aside and experience fun, joy and closeness together. Annually, the weekend immediately after Valentine's Day. [©1996] For info: Adrienne Sioux Koopersmith, 1437 W Rosemont, #1W, Chicago, IL 60660-1319. Phone: (773) 743-5341. Fax: (773) 743-5395. E-mail: adrienne@21stcentury.net.

SHIRER, WILLIAM L.: BIRTH ANNIVERSARY. Feb 23, 1904. American journalist and author William L. Shirer was born at Chicago, IL. As the European correspondent from 1927 to 1934 for the *Chicago Tribune* he became a friend of Mohandas K. Gandhi, the leader of India's independence movement. As a result of this he published *Gandhi: A Memoir* in 1980. His best-known book is *The Rise and Fall of the Third Reich* (1960), in which he used his experiences in Europe with the *New York Herald Tribune*, the Universal News Service and CBS Radio. He died Dec 28, 1993, at Boston, MA.

STAMP EXPO. Feb 23–25. Pasadena Convention Center, Pasadena, CA. Annual expo. Est attendance: 5,000. For info: Intl Stamp Collectors Soc, PO Box 854. Van Nuys, CA 91408. Phone: (818) 997-6496. Fax: (818) 988-4337. E-mail: iibick@aol.com. Web: www.bick.net.

TAYLOR, GEORGE: DEATH ANNIVERSARY. Feb 23, 1781. Signer of the Declaration of Independence. Born 1716 at British Isles (exact date unknown). Died at Easton, PA.

WILLARD, EMMA HART: BIRTH ANNIVERSARY. Feb 23, 1787. Pioneer in higher education for women, born at Berlin, CT. Intent on improving educational opportunities for women, she sent her *Plan for Improving Female Education* to the governor of New York. In it she described her ideal for a girls' school, including the instruction usually offered the girls of her day (music, drawing, painting, penmanship, dancing), as well as adding religious and moral instruction, natural philosophy and domestic science. The New York legislature granted her a charter for the Waterford Academy for Young Ladies. The school later moved to Troy, NY, where it was first named the Troy Female Seminary and later the Emma Willard School. She assisted in the founding of a teachers' training school for girls at Athens, Greece, in 1832. She began the Willard Association for the Mutual Improvement of Female Teachers in 1837, and she authored several textbooks on geography, history and astronomy. Willard died at Troy, NY, Apr 15, 1870.

BIRTHDAYS TODAY

Roberto Martin Antonio (Bobby) Bonilla, 38, baseball player, born New York, NY, Feb 23, 1963.

Sylvia Chase, 63, newscaster, born Northfield, MN, Feb 23, 1938.

Peter Fonda, 62, actor (*Easy Rider, Ulee's Gold*), born New York, NY, Feb 23, 1939.

Edward Lee ("Too Tall") Jones, 50, former football player and boxer, born Jackson, TN, Feb 23, 1951.

Howard Jones, 46, singer (gold album *Dream into Action*), born Southampton, England, Feb 23, 1955.

Patricia Richardson, 50, actress ("Double Trouble," "Home Improvement"), born Bethesda, MD, Feb 23, 1951.

Rodney Slater, 46, US Secretary of Transportation (Clinton administration), born Tutwyler, MS, Feb 23, 1955.

Johnny Winter (John Dawson III), 57, singer, musician (*Still Alive and Well, Second Winter*), born Beaumont, TX, Feb 23, 1944.

FEBRUARY 24 — SATURDAY
Day 55 — 310 Remaining

BIG TEN MEN'S INDOOR TRACK AND FIELD CHAMPIONSHIP. Feb 24–25. Penn State, State College, PA. Est attendance: 1,500. For info: Sue Ryan, Big Ten Conference, 1500 W Higgins Rd, Park Ridge, IL 60068-6300. Phone: (847) 696-1010. Fax: (847) 696-1110. Web: www.bigten.org or www.bigtenchampionships.com.

BIG TEN WOMEN'S INDOOR TRACK AND FIELD CHAMPIONSHIP. Feb 24–25. Purdue University, West Lafayette, IN. Est attendance: 1,500. For info: Sue Ryan, Big Ten Conference, 1500 W Higgins Rd, Park Ridge, IL 60068-6300. Phone: (847) 696-1010. Fax: (847) 696-1110. Web: www.bigten .org or www.bigtenchampionships.com.

BLACK HERITAGE PARADE. Feb 24. Monroe, LA. Informative parade to celebrate Black History Month. Annually, the last Saturday in February. Est attendance: 30,000. For info: Millard Lee, 1206 Walton Ln, Monroe, LA 71202. Phone: (318) 322-2848. Fax: (318) 324-1752. E-mail: mwmcvb@iamerica.net. Web: www.bayou.com/visitors.

BRAIN CHALLENGE AT THE HALL OF PUZZLES. Feb 24. Hall of Puzzles, Burlington, WI. Hands-on brain and logic puzzles to play, solve, outdo yourself! Ring bells upon success plus make a puzzle to take home. Antique logic puzzle exhibit, too. For info: Hall of Puzzles, Teacher Place & Parent Resources, 533 Milwaukee Ave, Burlington, WI 53105. Phone: (262) 763-3946.

BRAZIL: CARNIVAL. Feb 24–27. Especially in Rio de Janeiro, this carnival is said to be one of the last great folk festivals, and the big annual event in the life of Brazilians. Begins on Saturday night before Ash Wednesday and continues through Shrove Tuesday.

CLAM CHOWDER COOKOFF. Feb 24. Santa Cruz Beach Boardwalk, Santa Cruz, CA. Who makes the world's greatest clam chowder? Up to 60 teams compete to find out. Prizes for best booth encourage wacky costumes, elaborate props! Separate categories for restaurants, media and individuals, Boston and Manhattan style chowder. Free admission. Est attendance: 15,000. For info: Jan Bollwinkel-Smith, Communications Mgr, Santa Cruz Beach Boardwalk, 400 Beach St, Santa Cruz, CA 95060-5491. Phone: (831) 423-5590. Fax: (831) 460-3336. E-mail: publicity @scseaside.com. Web: www.beachboardwalk.com.

DEEP CREEK DUNK. Feb 24. Columbia, MD. More than 250 adventurous souls will brave the winter elements to jump into the frigid Deep Creek Lake. Participants gather pledges to benefit Special Olympics Maryland. Est attendance: 400. For info: Tina Bell, 8300 Guilford Rd, Ste A, Columbia, MD 21046. Phone: (800) 541-7544 or (410) 290-7611. Fax: (410) 381-4483. E-mail: tbell@somd.org. Web: www.somd.org.

DORAL-RYDER OPEN. Feb 24–Mar 4. Doral Golf Resort and Spa, Miami, FL. A PGA Tour golf tournament with a full week of events, including a free outdoor pops concert, a skins game, three celebrity pro-ams and the four-day tournament, which features 144 of the top golfers in the world. The Doral-Ryder Open is the nation's largest sports fundraiser for the American Cancer Society. Est attendance: 175,000. For info: Mktg Dir, Doral-Ryder Open, 3600 NW 38th St, Ste 200, Miami, FL 33178. Phone: (305) 477-4653. Fax: (305) 477-4914.

ESTONIA: INDEPENDENCE DAY. Feb 24. National holiday. Commemorates declaration of independence from Soviet Union in 1918. Independence was brief, however; Estonia was again under Soviet control until 1991.

FRENCH WEST INDIES: CARNIVAL. Feb 24–28. Martinique. For five days, business comes to a halt. Streets spill over with parties and parades. Carnival Queen is elected. For info: Martinique Promo Bureau, 444 Madison Ave, 16th Floor, New York, NY 10022. Phone: (800) 391-4909. Fax: (212) 838-7855. E-mail: info@martinique.com. Web: www.martinique.org.

GREGORIAN CALENDAR DAY: ANNIVERSARY. Feb 24, 1582. Pope Gregory XIII, enlisting the expertise of distinguished astronomers and mathematicians, issued a bull correcting the Julian calendar that was then 10 days in error. The correction was a minor one, changing the rule about leap years. The new calendar named for him, the Gregorian calendar, became effective Oct 4, 1582, in most Catholic countries, in 1752 in Britain and the American colonies, in 1918 in Russia and in 1923 in Greece. It is the most widely used calendar in the world today. See also: "Calendar Adjustment Day: Anniversary" (Sept 2) and "Gregorian Calendar Adjustment: Anniversary" (Oct 4).

GRIMM, WILHELM CARL: BIRTH ANNIVERSARY. Feb 24, 1786. Mythologist and author, born at Hanau, Germany. Best remembered for *Grimm's Fairy Tales,* in collaboration with his brother, Jacob. Died at Berlin, Germany, Dec 16, 1859. See also: "Grimm, Jacob: Birth Anniversary" (Jan 4).

HADASSAH: ANNIVERSARY. Feb 24, 1912. Twelve members of the Daughters of Zion Study Circle met at New York City under the leadership of Henrietta Szold. A constitution was drafted to expand the study group into a national organization called Hadassah (Hebrew for "myrtle" and the biblical name of Queen Esther) to foster Jewish education in America and to create public health nursing and nurses training in Palestine. Hadassah is now the largest women's volunteer organization in the US with 1,500 chapters rooted in health care delivery, education and vocational training, children's villages and services and land reclamation in Israel. See also: "Szold, Henrietta: Birth Anniversary" (Dec 21).

HATSUME FAIR. Feb 24–25. Morikami Museum, Delray Beach, FL. Celebrates the coming of spring with demonstrations and performances of Japanese taiko drums, folk dancing, martial arts, plants, orchids and bonsai exhibits. Annually, the last weekend in February. Est attendance: 16,000. For info: Public Relations, The Morikami Museum, 4000 Morikami Park Rd, Delray Beach, FL 33446. Phone: (561) 495-0233. Fax: (561) 499-2557. Web: www.icsi.com/ics/morikami/

HOME AND GARDEN FESTIVAL. Feb 24–25. Multi-Purpose Events Center, Wichita Falls, TX. More than 100 exhibitors providing seminars and demonstrations, home and garden needs and antiques. Est attendance: 30,000. For info: Wichita Falls CVB, 1000 5th St, Wichita Falls, TX 76301. Phone: (940) 716-5500. Fax: (940) 716-5509. E-mail: MPEC@wf.net. Web: www.viewscape.com or www.wf.net.

HOMER, WINSLOW: BIRTH ANNIVERSARY. Feb 24, 1836. American artist, born at Boston, MA. Noted for the realism of his work, from the Civil War reportage to the highly regarded rugged outdoor scenes of hunting and fishing. Died at his home at Prout's Neck, ME, Sept 29, 1910.

JOHNSON IMPEACHMENT PROCEEDINGS: ANNIVERSARY. Feb 24, 1867. In a showdown over reconstruction policy following the Civil War, the House of Representatives voted to impeach President Andrew Johnson. During the two years following the end of the war, the Republican-controlled Congress had sought to severely punish the South. Congress passed the Reconstruction Act that divided the South into five military districts headed by officers who were to take their orders from General Grant, the head of the army, instead of from President Johnson. In addition, Congress passed the Tenure of Office Act, which required Senate approval before Johnson could remove any official whose appointment was originally approved by the Senate. Johnson vetoed this act but the veto was overridden by Congress. To test the constitutionality of the act, Johnson dismissed Secretary of War Edwin Stanton, triggering the impeachment vote. On Mar 5, 1868, the Senate convened as a court to hear the charges against the president. The Senate vote of 35–19 fell one vote short of the two-thirds majority needed for impeachment.

NIMITZ, CHESTER: BIRTH ANNIVERSARY. Feb 24, 1885. Commander of all Allied naval, land and air forces in the southwest Pacific during a portion of WWII, Admiral Chester William Nimitz was born at Fredericksburg, TX. During the final assault on Japan in April 1945, Nimitz resumed command of the entire naval operation in the Pacific which he had shared with MacArthur for some time. Nimitz was one of the signers of the Japanese document of surrender Sept 2, 1945, aboard the USS *Missouri* in Tokyo Bay. Nimitz died Feb 20, 1966, at Treasure Island, San Francisco Bay, CA. The USS *Nimitz* was named in his honor.

ORANGE HISTORICAL SOCIETY ANNUAL ANTIQUE SHOW. Feb 24–25. Amity Jr High School, Orange, CT. More than 30 antique dealers displaying quality collections. Catered luncheon served until 3 PM both days. Saturday 10–5; Sunday 10–4. Admission $4. Annually, the last weekend in February. Est attendance: 1,000. For info: Show Coord, Orange Historical Society, PO Box 784, Orange, CT 06477. Phone: (203) 795-3106.

PARKE COUNTY MAPLE FAIR. Feb 24–25 (also Mar 3–4). Rockville, IN. Headquarters at the 4-H Fairgrounds, one mile north of Rockville on US 41. Pancakes, sausage and maple syrup meals. Largest indoor craft and art show. Farmers' Market, Butcher Shop, tours to the Sugar Camps featuring the unique process of making maple syrup. Annually, the last weekend in February and the first weekend in March. Est attendance: 50,000. For info: Anne Lynk, Covered Bridge Capital, PO Box 165, Rockville, IN 47872. Phone: (765) 569-5226. Fax: (765) 569-3900. E-mail: pci@ticz.com. Web: www.coverbridges.com.

RECORD LOSS FOR GENERAL MOTORS: ANNIVERSARY. Feb 24, 1992. The greatest loss by a US company was suffered by the world's largest industrial company, General Motors Corporation. The $4.45 billion loss for 1991 was announced on Feb 24, 1992.

WAGNER, HONUS: BIRTH ANNIVERSARY. Feb 24, 1874. American baseball great, born John Peter Wagner at Carnegie, PA. Nicknamed the "Flying Dutchman," Wagner was among the first five players elected to the Baseball Hall of Fame in 1936. Died at Carnegie, Dec 6, 1955.

	S	M	T	W	T	F	S
February					1	2	3
2001	4	5	6	7	8	9	10
	11	12	13	14	15	16	17
	18	19	20	21	22	23	24
	25	26	27	28			

FEBRUARY 25 — SUNDAY

Day 56 — 309 Remaining

BACKUS, JIM: BIRTH ANNIVERSARY. Feb 25, 1913. Born James Gilmore Backus at Cleveland, OH. An actor whose career encompassed radio, television and film, Jim Backus is most remembered as the voice behind the near-sighted bumbler, Mr Magoo, and for his portrayal of Thurston Howell III on the popular TV show, "Gilligan's Island." Backus died July 3, 1989, at Santa Monica, CA.

BASCOM, "TEXAS ROSE": BIRTH ANNIVERSARY. Feb 25, 1922. A Cherokee-Choctaw Indian born at Covington County, MS, Rose Flynt married rodeo cowboy Earl Bascom and learned trick roping, becoming known as the greatest female trick roper in the world. She appeared on stage, in movies and on early TV. She toured with the USO during WWII, performing at every military base and military hospital in the US. After the war she entertained servicemen stationed overseas. In 1981 she was inducted into the National Cowgirl Hall of Fame (located at Hereford, TX). She died Sept 23, 1993, at St. George, UT.

BURGESS, ANTHONY: BIRTH ANNIVERSARY. Feb 25, 1917. Author (*A Clockwork Orange*). Born at Manchester, England. Died Nov 25, 1993, at London.

CARUSO, ENRICO: BIRTH ANNIVERSARY. Feb 25, 1873. Operatic tenor of legendary voice and fame, born at Naples, Italy. Died there Aug 2, 1921.

CLAY BECOMES HEAVYWEIGHT CHAMP: ANNIVERSARY. Feb 25, 1964. Twenty-two-year-old Cassius Clay (later Muhammad Ali) became world heavyweight boxing champion by defeating Sonny Liston. At the height of his athletic career Ali was well known for both his fighting ability and personal style. His most famous saying was, "I am the greatest!" In 1967 he was convicted of violating the Selective Service Act and was stripped of his title for refusing to be inducted into the armed services during the Vietnam War. Ali cited religious convictions as his reason for refusal. In 1971 the Supreme Court reversed the conviction. Ali is the only fighter to win the heavyweight fighting title three separate times. He defended that title nine times.

DAVIS, ADELLE: BIRTH ANNIVERSARY. Feb 25, 1905. American nutritionist and author, born at Lizton, IN. Her message "You are what you eat" found an eager readership for her books, including *Let's Cook It Right* (1947) and *Let's Eat Right to Keep Fit* (1954). Davis died of bone cancer at Palo Verdes Estates, CA, May 31, 1974.

FASCHING SUNDAY. Feb 25. Germany and Austria. The last Sunday before Lent.

FENWICK, MILLICENT HAMMOND: BIRTH ANNIVERSARY. Feb 25, 1910. Former fashion model, author, member NJ General Assembly and US congresswoman, Millicent Fenwick was born at New York, NY. A champion of liberal causes, Fenwick pointed to her sponsorship of the resolution creating the commission to monitor the 1975 Helsinki accords on human rights as her proudest achievement. She fought for civil rights, peace in Vietnam, aid for the poor, reduction of military programs, gun control and restrictions on capital punishment. Fenwick, the inspiration for Garry Trudeau's "Doonesbury" character Lacey Davenport, died at Bernardsville, NJ, Sept 16, 1992.

FIRST NATIONAL BANK CHARTERED BY CONGRESS: ANNIVERSARY. Feb 25, 1791. The First Bank of the US at Philadelphia, PA, was chartered. Proposed as a national bank by Alexander Hamilton, it lost its charter in 1811. The Second Bank of the US received a charter in 1816 which expired in 1836. Since that time, the US has had no central bank. Central banking functions are carried out by the Federal Reserve System, established in 1913. See also: "Federal Reserve System: Anniversary" (Dec 23).

FREER, CHARLES LANG: BIRTH ANNIVERSARY. Feb 25, 1856. American art collector who built and endowed the Freer Gallery, which was presented to the Smithsonian Institution in 1906. Born at Kingston, NY, he died at New York, NY, Sept 25, 1919.

HEBRON MASSACRE: ANNIVERSARY. Feb 25, 1994. An American-born Jewish settler in Hebron, Israel, Baruch Goldstein, opened fire with an assault rifle in a crowded mosque, part of a complex sacred to both Jews and Muslims because it is believed to contain the tomb of Abraham and his wife Sarah. Of the more than 400 Muslims gathered for early morning prayers during the holy month of Ramadan, 29 were killed immediately and 150 were wounded. Others, including Goldstein, were crushed in the panic to flee or during subsequent rioting.

ITALY: CARNIVAL WEEK. Feb 25–Mar 3. Milan. Carnival week is held according to local tradition, with shows and festive events for children on Tuesday and Thursday. Parades of floats, figures in the costume of local folk characters Meneghin and Cecca, parties and more traditional events are held on Saturday. Annually, the Sunday–Saturday of Ash Wednesday week.

JOE CAIN PROCESSION. Feb 25. Mobile, AL. Led by Slacabamorinico IV, it honors the man who revived the Mardi Gras in Mobile in 1866 following the War Between the States. Annually, the Sunday before Shrove Tuesday. Est attendance: 100,000. For info: The Rev Wayne Dean, Sr, VP, Joe Cain Society, 1064 Palmetto St, Mobile, AL 36604-3041. Phone: (334) 432-3960. E-mail: revchief@fcbl.net.

KUWAIT: NATIONAL DAY. Feb 25. National holiday.

NATIONAL PANCAKE WEEK. Feb 25–Mar 3. Traditional celebration surrounding Shrove or Pancake Tuesday to recognize the history and continuing popularity of pancakes. For info: Pam Becker, Bisquick Baking Mix, General Mills, Inc, #1 General Mills Blvd, Minneapolis, MN 55426. Phone: (763) 764-2470. Fax: (763) 764-3232.

RENOIR, PIERRE AUGUSTE: BIRTH ANNIVERSARY. Feb 25, 1841. Impressionist painter, born at Limoges, France. Renoir's paintings are known for their joy and sensuousness as well as the light techniques he employed in them. In his later

years he was crippled by arthritis and would paint with the brush strapped to his hand. He died at Cagnes-sur-Mer, Provence, France, Dec 17, 1919.

SHROVETIDE. Feb 25–27. The three days before Ash Wednesday: Shrove Sunday, Monday and Tuesday—a time for confession and for festivity before the beginning of Lent.

SPACE MILESTONE: *SOYUZ 32* (USSR). Feb 25, 1979. Launched from Baikonur space center in Soviet Central Asia. Cosmonauts Vladimir Lyakhov and Valery Ryumin aboard, docked at *Salyut 6* space station Feb 26. Returned to Earth in *Soyuz 34* after what was then a record 175 days in space Aug 19, 1979.

SPECIAL OLYMPICS MARYLAND WINTER GAMES. Feb 25–27. Wisp Ski Resort, McHenry, MD. More than 150 Special Olympics athletes throughout Maryland compete in alpine, cross-country and modified alpine skiing. The 3-day festivities include an elaborate opening and closing ceremony featuring the traditional lighting of the Special Olympics cauldron. For info: Pam Logan, 8300 Guilford Rd, Ste A, Columbia, MD 21046. Phone: (800) 541-7544 or (410) 290-7611. Fax: (410) 381-4483. E-mail: plogan@somd.org. Web: www.somd.org.

"YOUR SHOW OF SHOWS" TV PREMIERE: ANNIVERSARY. Feb 25, 1950. Sid Caesar and Imogene Coca starred in the NBC 90-minute variety program along with Carl Reiner and Howard Morris. The show included monologues, improvisations, parodies, pantomimes and sketches of varying length. Some of its writers were: Mel Tolkin, Lucille Kallen, Mel Brooks, Larry Gelbart, Neil Simon and Woody Allen.

BIRTHDAYS TODAY

Sean Astin, 30, actor (*Rudy, Courage Under Fire*), son of John Astin and Patty Duke, born Santa Monica, CA, Feb 25, 1971.

Diane Baker, 63, actress (*Silence of the Lambs*), born Hollywood, CA, Feb 25, 1938.

Tom Courtenay, 64, actor (*The Dresser, The Loneliness of the Long Distance Runner, Otley*), born Hull, England, Feb 25, 1937.

Larry Gelbart, 73, writer, producer ("M*A*S*H"), born Chicago, IL, Feb 25, 1928.

Karen Grassle, 57, actress ("Little House on the Prairie"), born Berkeley, CA, Feb 25, 1944.

George Harrison, 58, musician and singer (The Beatles), born Liverpool, England, Feb 25, 1943.

Neil Jordan, 51, director, writer (*The Crying Game, Interview with a Vampire*), born County Sligo, Ireland, Feb 25, 1950.

Tea Leoni, 35, actress ("The Naked Truth," *Deep Impact*), born New York, NY, Feb 25, 1966.

Sally Jessy Raphael, 58, talk-show host, born Easton, PA, Feb 25, 1943.

Bob Schieffer, 64, TV newscaster, born Austin, TX, Feb 25, 1937.

FEBRUARY 26 — MONDAY
Day 57 — 308 Remaining

AMERICA'S CUP. Feb 26–Mar 26. Auckland, New Zealand. The world's most prestigious yacht race.

CARNIVAL. Feb 26–27. Period of festivities, feasts, foolishness and gaiety immediately before Lent begins on Ash Wednesday. Ordinarily Carnival includes only Fasching (the Feast of Fools), being the Monday and Tuesday immediately preceding Ash Wednesday. The period of Carnival may also be extended to include longer periods in some areas.

CODY, WILLIAM FREDERIC "BUFFALO BILL": BIRTH ANNIVERSARY. Feb 26, 1846. American frontiersman born at Scott County, IA, who claimed to have killed more than 4,000 buffaloes. Subject of many heroic Wild West yarns, Cody became successful as a showman, taking his acts across the US and to Europe. Died Jan 10, 1917, at Denver, CO.

COMMUNIST MANIFESTO PUBLISHED: ANNIVERSARY. Feb 26, 1848. Written by Karl Marx and Friedrich Engels on the eve of the revolutions of 1848, the *Manifesto* provided ideas for socialist and communist movements.

CYPRUS: GREEN MONDAY. Feb 26. Green, or Clean, Monday is the first Monday of Lent on the Orthodox Christian calendar. Lunch in the fields, with bread, olives and uncooked vegetables and no meat or dairy products.

DAUMIER, HONORE: BIRTH ANNIVERSARY. Feb 26, 1808. French painter and caricaturist famous for his satirical and comic lithographs. Once spent six months in prison for a caricature of Louis Philippe shown as Gargantua consuming the heavy taxes of the citizens. Born at Marseilles, France, he died Feb 11, 1879, at Volmondois, France.

DENMARK: STREET URCHINS' CARNIVAL. Feb 26. Observed on Shrove Monday.

FASCHING. Feb 26–27. In Germany and Austria, Fasching, also called Fasnacht, Fasnet or Feast of Fools, is a Shrovetide festival with processions of masked figures, both beautiful and grotesque. Always the two days (Rose Monday and Shrove Tuesday) between Fasching Sunday and Ash Wednesday.

FEDERAL COMMUNICATIONS COMMISSION CREATED: ANNIVERSARY. Feb 26, 1934. President Franklin D. Roosevelt ordered the creation of a Communications Commission, which became the FCC. It was created by Congress June 19, 1934 to oversee communication by radio, wire or cable.

FOR PETE'S SAKE DAY. Feb 26. A world wonders: after all these years, who is Pete and why do we do or not do things for his sake? ©2000 Wellcat Herbs & Holidays. For info: Thomas & Ruth Roy, 2418 Long Ln, Lebanon, PA 17046. Phone: (240) 332-4886. E-mail: wellcat@supernet.com. Web: www.wellcat.com.

	S	M	T	W	T	F	S
February					1	2	3
2001	4	5	6	7	8	9	10
	11	12	13	14	15	16	17
	18	19	20	21	22	23	24
	25	26	27	28			

GLEASON, JACKIE: 85th BIRTH ANNIVERSARY. Feb 26, 1916. American musician, comedian and actor, Herbert John "Jackie" Gleason was born at Brooklyn, NY. Best known for his role as Ralph Kramden in the long-running television series "The Honeymooners." Died at Fort Lauderdale, FL, June 24, 1987.

GRAND CANYON NATIONAL PARK ESTABLISHED: ANNIVERSARY. Feb 26, 1919. By an act of Congress, Grand Canyon National Park was established. An immense gorge cut through the high plateaus of northwest Arizona by the raging Colorado River and covering 1,218,375 acres, Grand Canyon National Park is considered one of the most spectacular natural phenomena in the world.

HUGO, VICTOR: BIRTH ANNIVERSARY. Feb 26, 1802. French author, born at Besançon, France. "An invasion of armies can be resisted," he wrote in 1852, "but not an idea whose time has come." His most well-known work was the novel *Les Misérables*. Died at Paris, May 22, 1885.

ICELAND: BUN DAY. Feb 26. Children invade homes in the morning with colorful sticks and receive gifts of whipped cream buns (on the Monday before Shrove Tuesday).

ORTHODOX LENT. Feb 26–Apr 7. Great Lent or Easter Lent, observed by Eastern Orthodox Churches, lasts until Holy Week begins on Orthodox Palm Sunday (Apr 8).

READ ME WEEK. Feb 26–Mar 2. National and local celebrities and other volunteers read in classrooms wearing readable clothing with school appropriate messages. For info: Phyllis Frank, Program Coord, Book 'Em!, 2012 21st Ave South, Nashville, TN 37212. Phone: (615) 834-7323. Fax: (615) 297-7323.

SHROVE MONDAY. Feb 26. The Monday before Ash Wednesday. In Germany and Austria, this is called Rose Monday.

STRAUSS, LEVI: BIRTH ANNIVERSARY. Feb 26, 1829. Bavarian immigrant Levi Strauss created the world's first pair of jeans—Levi's 501 jeans—for California's gold miners in 1850. Born at Buttenheim, Bavaria, Germany, he died in 1902.

TELECOMMUTER APPRECIATION WEEK. Feb 26–Mar 4. Sponsored by the American Telecommuting Association, this week is designed to call attention to the benefits to people who telecommute. The individual and family as well as the employer and society benefit when people telecommute. For info: American Telecommuting Assn, 1220 L St, NW, Ste 100, Washington DC, 20005. Phone: (800) ATA-4-YOU. Fax: (800) 465-8638. E-mail: YourATA@aol.com.

TRINIDAD: CARNIVAL. Feb 26–27. Port of Spain. Called by islanders "the mother of all carnivals," a special tradition that brings together people from all over the world in an incredible colorful setting that includes the world's most celebrated calypsonians, steel band players, costume designers and masqueraders. Annually, the two days before Ash Wednesday. For info: Natl Carnival Commission, Tourism and Industrial Development Co, Administration Bldg, Queen Park Savannah, Port of Spain, Trinidad and Tobago, West Indies. Phone: (809) 623-1932. Fax: (809) 623-3848.

VERCORS, JEAN: BIRTH ANNIVERSARY. Feb 26, 1902. Jean Vercors was the author of the first clandestine novel published during the Nazi occupation of France. Vercors, whose real name was Jean-Marcel de Bruller, was best known for his novel *Silence of the Sea*, which he published with Pierre de Lescure for their publishing house, Les Editions de Minuit, after the Nazis occupied France in 1941. Vercors was born at Paris, France, and died there June 10, 1991.

WORLD TRADE CENTER BOMBING: ANNIVERSARY. Feb 26, 1993. A 1,210-lb bomb packed in a van exploded in the underground parking garage of the World Trade Center in New York City, killing six people and injuring more than 1,000 (mostly from smoke inhalation). The powerful blast left a crater 200 feet wide and several stories deep. The cost for damage to the building and disruption of business for the 350 companies with offices in the Center exceeded more than $591 million. Fifteen people—the fundamentalist Moslem cleric Sheik Omar Abdul

Rahman and fourteen of his followers—were indicted for the bombing. Rahman was given a life sentence and the others received prison terms of up to 240 years each.

BIRTHDAYS TODAY

Mason Adams, 82, actor ("Lou Grant," "Morningstar /Eveningstar"), born New York, NY, Feb 26, 1919.

Erykah Badu, 29, pop singer, born Dallas, TX, Feb 26, 1972.

Johnny Cash, 69, singer ("Guess Things Happen That Way," "Ring of Fire"), born Kingsland, AR, Feb 26, 1932.

Fats Domino (Antoine Domino), 73, singer, songwriter ("Ain't That a Shame," "I'm in Love Again," "Blueberry Hill"), born New Orleans, LA, Feb 26, 1928.

Marshall Faulk, 28, football player, born New Orleans, LA, Feb 26, 1973.

Jennifer Grant, 35, actress (*The Evening Star*), born Burbank, CA, Feb 26, 1966.

Betty Hutton (Elizabeth June Thornberg), 80, singer, actress (*Annie Get Your Gun*, "The Betty Hutton Show"), born Battle Creek, MI, Feb 26, 1921.

Tony Randall (Leonard Rosenberg), 81, actor (*Pillow Talk*, "The Odd Couple"), born Tulsa, OK, Feb 26, 1920.

FEBRUARY 27 — TUESDAY

Day 58 — 307 Remaining

ANDERSON, MARIAN: BIRTH ANNIVERSARY. Feb 27, 1897. Born at Philadelphia (some sources say in 1899 or 1902), Anderson's talent was evident at an early age. Her career stonewalled by the prejudice she encountered in the US, she moved to Europe where the magnificence of her voice and her versatility as a performer began to establish her as one of the world's finest contraltos. Preventing Anderson's performance at Washington's Constitution Hall in 1939 on the basis of her color, the Daughters of the American Revolution secured for her the publicity that would lay the foundation for her success in the States. Her performance was rescheduled, and on Apr 9 (Easter Sunday) 75,000 people showed up to hear her sing from the steps of the Lincoln Memorial and the performance was simultaneously broadcast by radio. In 1957 Anderson became the first African-American to perform with the New York Metropolitan Opera. The following year President Eisenhower named her a delegate to the United Nations. She performed at President Kennedy's inauguration and in 1963 received the Presidential Medal of Freedom. Anderson died Apr 8, 1993, at Portland, OR.

ASSOCIATION OF AMERICAN GEOGRAPHERS ANNUAL MEETING. Feb 27–Mar 3. New York, NY. National meeting of members with workshops, paper and poster sessions and field trips. Est attendance: 3,000. For info: Assn of American Geographers, 1710 16th St NW, Washington, DC 20009-3198. Phone: (202) 234-1450. Web: www.aag.org.

BENNETT, JOAN: BIRTH ANNIVERSARY. Feb 27, 1910. American film and television actress was born at Palisades, NJ. Her film career was mostly during the 1930s and 1940s in such films as *Father of the Bride* (1950), after which she became a star of the television cult hit "Dark Shadows" (originally broadcast 1966–71). Died Dec 7, 1990, at Scarsdale, NY.

DOMINICAN REPUBLIC: INDEPENDENCE DAY. Feb 27. National Day. Independence gained in 1844 with the withdrawal of Haitians, who had controlled the area for 22 years.

FARRELL, JAMES THOMAS: BIRTH ANNIVERSARY. Feb 27, 1904. American author, novelist and short story writer, best known for his Studs Lonigan trilogy. Born at Chicago, IL, he died at New York, NY, Aug 22, 1979.

HAMILTON, ALICE: BIRTH ANNIVERSARY. Feb 27, 1869. American pathologist Alice Hamilton was born at New York, NY. She contributed to the workmen's compensation laws by reporting on the dangers to workers of industrial toxic substances. She taught at Harvard Medical School from 1919 until 1935. Hamilton died Sept 22, 1970, at Hadlyme, CT.

ICELAND: BURSTING DAY. Feb 27. Feasts with salted mutton and thick pea soup. (Shrove Tuesday.)

INTERNATIONAL PANCAKE DAY. Feb 27. Liberal, KS. The 2001 International Pancake Race will be the 52nd annual competition between the women of Liberal, KS, and Olney, Bucks, England. The women, wearing the traditional dress, apron and scarf, run a 415-yard "S"-shaped course, carrying a pancake in a skillet. Other events include a breakfast, parade, talent show, eating and flipping contests and the Miss Liberal scholarship pageant. Annually on Shrove Tuesday, the day before Ash Wednesday. Est attendance: 5,000. For info: JoAnn Combs, Exec Secy, PO Box 665, Liberal, KS 67905. Phone: (316) 626-0170. Web: www.pancakeday.com.

KUWAIT LIBERATED AND 100-HOUR WAR ENDS: 10th ANNIVERSARY. Feb 27, 1991. Allied troops entered Kuwait City, Kuwait, four days after launching a ground offensive. President George Bush declared Kuwait to be liberated and ceased all offensive military operations in the Gulf War. The end of military operations at midnight EST came 100 hours after the beginning of the land attack.

LONGFELLOW, HENRY WADSWORTH: BIRTH ANNIVERSARY. Feb 27, 1807. American poet and writer born at Portland, ME. He is best remembered for his classic narrative poems, such as *The Song of Hiawatha, Paul Revere's Ride* and *The Wreck of the Hesperus*. Died at Cambridge, MA, Mar 24, 1882.

MARDI GRAS. Feb 27. Celebrated especially at New Orleans, LA, Mobile, AL, and certain Mississippi and Florida cities. Last feast before Lent. Although Mardi Gras (Fat Tuesday, literally) is properly limited to Shrove Tuesday, it has come to be popularly applied to the preceding two weeks of celebration.

PACZKI DAY. Feb 27. Food lovers pick this day to enjoy these round, sugar-coated, fruit-filled Polish pre-Lenten pastries, pronounced "poonch-kee," available in bakeries nationwide. Paczki Day coincides with Shrove Tuesday or Fat Tuesday, the day before Ash Wednesday. Sponsors: RBA (The Retailer's Bakery Association) and RBA National Paczki Promotion Board. For info: RBA-The Retailer's Bakery Assn, 14239 Park Center Dr, Laurel, MD 20707. Phone: (301) 725-2149 or (800) 884-1500 for a free promotions Paczki kit. E-mail: rba@rbanet.com.

SARAZEN, GEORGE: BIRTH ANNIVERSARY. Feb 27, 1902. Gene Sarazen, golfer, born Eugenio Saraceni at Harrison, NY. Sarazen was one of the game's greatest players and in his later years one of its greatest goodwill ambassadors. The inventor of the sand wedge, Sarazen was also the first to win the modern grand slam (the Masters, US Open, British Open and PGA), although not in the same year. During the 1935 Masters, he hit one of golf's most famous shots, a four-wood for a double eagle on the par-5 fifteenth hole of the final round. The shot enabled him to tie Craig Wood for the lead and defeat him in a playoff. Sarazen's last shot was the traditional ceremonial tee shot to open the 1999 Masters. Died at Marco Island, FL, May 13, 1999.

SHANGHAI COMMUNIQUE: ANNIVERSARY. Feb 27, 1972. On this day, President Richard Nixon and Premier Chou En-Lai released a joint communique (the Shanghai Communique) after Nixon's weeklong visit to the People's Republic of China. The two nations agreed to work toward normalizing relations. Stopping short of establishing diplomatic relations, this was the first step in that direction. The two nations entered full diplomatic relations on Jan 1, 1979, during the Carter administration.

SHROVE TUESDAY. Feb 27. Always the day before Ash Wednesday. Sometimes called Pancake Tuesday. This day is a legal holiday in some counties in Florida.

SHROVETIDE PANCAKE RACE. Feb 27. Olney, Buckinghamshire, England. The pancake race at Olney has been run since 1445. Competitors must be women over 16 years of age, wearing traditional housewife's costume, including apron and head-covering. With a toss and flip of the pancake on the griddle that each must carry, the women dash from marketplace to the parish church, where the winner receives a kiss from the ringer of the Pancake Bell. Shriving service follows. Annually, on Shrove Tuesday.

SPAY DAY USA. Feb 27. An annual, nationwide event designed to end the tragedy of pet overpopulation by encouraging every humane American to take responsibility for having at least one cat or dog spayed or neutered, be it theirs, a neighbor's or a shelter animal. Veterinary clinics, humane societies/shelters, animal protection organizations, individuals and others are encouraged to participate. For info: Doris Day Animal Foundation, Spay Day USA, 227 Massachusetts Ave NE, Ste 100, Washington, DC 20002. Phone: (202) 546-1761. Fax: (202) 546-2193. E-mail: ddaf@ddal.org. Web: www.ddal.org.

TERRY, ELLEN: BIRTH ANNIVERSARY. Feb 27, 1847. Popular English actress (Alice) Ellen Terry was born at Coventry, Warwickshire, Feb 27, 1847. Terry is best known for her portrayal of Shakespeare's heroines, especially Portia, and as theatrical partner of English actor Henry Irving. Together she and Irving dominated both the British and American theater of their day. She died at Small Hythe, Kent, July 21, 1928.

February *2001*	S	M	T	W	T	F	S
					1	2	3
	4	5	6	7	8	9	10
	11	12	13	14	15	16	17
	18	19	20	21	22	23	24
	25	26	27	28			

TWENTY-SECOND AMENDMENT TO US CONSTITUTION (TWO-TERM LIMIT): RATIFICATION ANNIVERSARY. Feb 27, 1950. After the four successive presidential terms of Franklin Roosevelt, the 22nd Amendment limited the tenure of presidential office to two terms.

BIRTHDAYS TODAY

Adam Baldwin, 39, actor (*My Bodyguard, Full Metal Jacket*), born Chicago, IL, Feb 27, 1962.

Michael Bolton, 48, singer ("How Am I Supposed to Live Without You"), born New Haven, CT, Feb 27, 1953.

Alan Guth, 54, physicist, born New Brunswick, NJ, Feb 27, 1947.

Howard Hesseman, 61, actor ("WKRP in Cincinnati," "Head of the Class"), born Salem, OR, Feb 27, 1940.

Charlayne Hunter-Gault, 59, broadcast journalist, born Due West, SC, Feb 27, 1942.

Ralph Nader, 67, consumer advocate, lawyer, born Winsted, CT, Feb 27, 1934.

Grant Show, 38, actor ("Melrose Place," "Ryan's Hope"), born Detroit, MI, Feb 27, 1963.

Elizabeth Taylor, 69, actress (Oscar for *Who's Afraid of Virginia Woolf?; National Velvet, Cleopatra, Cat on a Hot Tin Roof*), AIDS activist, born London, England, Feb 27, 1932.

Joanne Woodward, 71, actress (Oscar for *The Three Faces of Eve; Mr and Mrs Bridge*), born Thomasville, GA, Feb 27, 1930.

James Ager Worthy, 40, former basketball player, born Gastonia, NC, Feb 27, 1961.

FEBRUARY 28 — WEDNESDAY

Day 59 — 306 Remaining

ASH WEDNESDAY. Feb 28. Marks the beginning of Lent. Forty weekdays and six Sundays (Saturday considered a weekday) remain until Easter Sunday. Named for use of ashes in ceremonial penance.

BLONDIN, CHARLES: BIRTH ANNIVERSARY. Feb 28, 1824. Daring French acrobat and aerialist (whose real name was Jean Francois Gravelet), born at St. Omer, France. Especially remembered for his conquest of Niagara Falls. Died Feb 19, 1897, at London. See also: "Charles Blondin's Conquest of Niagara Falls: Anniversary" (June 30).

CANIFF, MILTON: BIRTH ANNIVERSARY. Feb 28, 1907. Creator of the comic strips "Terry and the Pirates®" and "Steve Canyon," Milton Caniff was born at Hillsboro, OH. His strips were noted for their fine draftsmanship and action/adventure story lines. Caniff died Apr 3, 1988, at New York City.

FLORAL DESIGN DAY. Feb 28. A day to commemorate floral designing as an art form. Annually, on Feb 28. For info: Dr. Stephen Rittner, Rittners School of Floral Design, 345 Marlborough St, Boston, MA 02115. Phone: (617) 267-3824. E-mail: stevrt@tiac.net. Web: www.tiac.net/users/stevrt/index.html or www.floralschool.com.

HECHT, BEN: BIRTH ANNIVERSARY. Feb 28, 1894. In the course of his career Ben Hecht wrote in many genres. His newspaper column, "1001 Afternoons in Chicago," popularized human interest sketches. His play *The Front Page*, written with Charles MacArthur, was a hit on Broadway (1928) and in film (1931). He was a successful reporter and his first novel *Eric Dorn*, resulted partly from his time reporting from Berlin after World War I. Hecht wrote or co-wrote a number of successful movie scripts, including *Notorious* and *Wuthering Heights*. Born at New York City, he died there Apr 18, 1964.

LENT BEGINS. Feb 28–Apr 14. Most Christian churches observe period of fasting and penitence (40 weekdays and six Sundays—Saturday considered a weekday) beginning on Ash Wednesday and ending on the Saturday before Easter.

LYON, MARY: BIRTH ANNIVERSARY. Feb 28, 1797. Mary Lyon, born near Buckland, MA, became a pioneer in the field of higher education for women. She founded Mount Holyoke Seminary (forerunner of Mount Holyoke College) in South Hadley, MA, in 1837 at a time when American women were educated primarily by ministers in classes held in their homes. Mount Holyoke was one of the first permanent women's colleges. She died Mar 5, 1849, at South Hadley.

"M*A*S*H": THE FINAL EPISODE: ANNIVERSARY. Feb 28, 1983. Concluding a run of 255 episodes, this 2 ½-hour finale was the most-watched television show at that time—77 percent of the viewing public was tuned in. The show premiered in 1972. See also: "M*A*S*H TV Premiere: Anniversary" (Sept 17).

MONTAIGNE, MICHEL DE: BIRTH ANNIVERSARY. Feb 28, 1533. French essayist and philosopher, born at Perigord, France. "And if you have lived a day," he wrote in Book I of his *Essays*, "you have seen everything. One day is equal to all days. There is no other light, no other night. This sun, this moon, these stars, the way they are arranged, all is the very same your ancestors enjoyed and that will entertain your grandchildren. . . ." Died at Montaigne, France, Sept 13, 1592.

NAIA MEN'S AND WOMEN'S SWIMMING AND DIVING NATIONAL CHAMPIONSHIPS. Feb 28–Mar 3. Burnaby, BC, Canada. Individuals compete for the national championship. 21st annual competitions for women and 45th annual for men. Est attendance: 3,000. For info: Natl Assn of Intercollegiate Athletics, 6120 S Yale Ave, Ste 1450, Tulsa, OK 74136. Phone: (918) 494-8828. Fax: (918) 494-8841. E-mail: jstruckle@naia.org. Web: www.naia.org.

NATO PLANES DOWN SERB JETS: ANNIVERSARY. Feb 28, 1994. In the first military action by the North Atlantic Treaty Organization (NATO) in the two-year-old Bosnian civil war and the first combat action by NATO in its 45-year history, UN-designated American fighter planes shot down four of six Bosnian Serb jets operating in a no-fly zone.

PALME, OLOF: 15th ASSASSINATION ANNIVERSARY. Feb 28, 1986. The popular prime minister of Sweden was shot to death as he left a movie theatre in Stockholm with his wife. A courageous and dominant figure in Swedish politics, Palme, an aristocrat turned socialist, had earned international respect. On the day of his death he had signed (with five other world leaders) an appeal to the leaders of the United States and the Soviet Union to forgo nuclear testing until the next summit meeting. Born on Jan 30, 1927, Palme was the third European head of government to be assassinated since the beginning of World War II (the others: Prime Minister Armand Calinescu of Romania in 1939 and Prime Minister Luis Carrero Blanco of Spain in 1973).

SAINT OSWALD OF WORCESTER FEAST DAY. Feb 28. Bishop of Worcester, England, from 961, and Archbishop of York from 972. Oswald died Feb 29, 992, but Feb 28 is generally celebrated as his Feast Day.

"SMOKELESS" CIGARETTE WITHDRAWN: ANNIVERSARY. Feb 28, 1989. The R.J. Reynolds Tobacco Company stopped marketing Premier, the "smokeless" cigarette, due to poor sales.

TENNIEL, JOHN: BIRTH ANNIVERSARY. Feb 28, 1820. Illustrator and cartoonist, born at London, England. Best remembered for his illustrations for Lewis Carroll's *Alice's Adventures in Wonderland*. Died at London, Feb 25, 1914.

USS *PRINCETON* EXPLOSION: ANNIVERSARY. Feb 28, 1844. The newly built "war steamer," USS *Princeton*, cruising on the Potomac River with top government officials as its passengers, fired one of its guns (known, ironically, as the "Peacemaker") to demonstrate the latest in naval armament. The gun exploded, killing Abel P. Upshur, Secretary of State; Thomas W. Gilmer, Secretary of the Navy; David Gardiner, of Gardiners Island, NY; and several others. Many were injured. The president of the US, John Tyler, was on board and narrowly escaped death.

BIRTHDAYS TODAY

Svetlana Allilueva, 75, daughter of Joseph Stalin, author (*The Faraway Music*), born Moscow, USSR, Feb 28, 1926.

Mario Gabrielle Andretti, 61, former auto racer, born Montona, Trieste, Italy, Feb 28, 1940.

Charles Durning, 78, actor (*Dog Day Afternoon*, "Evening Shade"), born Highland Falls, NY, Feb 28, 1923.

Frank Gehry, 72, architect, born Toronto, Ontario, Canada, Feb 28, 1929.

Robert Sean Leonard, 32, actor (*The Manhattan Project, Dead Poets Society*), born Westwood, NJ, Feb 28, 1969.

Eric Lindros, 28, hockey player, born London, Ontario, Canada, Feb 28, 1973.

Bernadette Peters, 57, singer, actress (*Dames at Sea, Annie Get Your Gun*), born New York, NY, Feb 28, 1944.

Charles Aaron ("Bubba") Smith, 56, actor, former football player, born Beaumont, TX, Feb 28, 1945.

Tommy Tune, 62, actor, singer, dancer (Tony for *My One and Only*; *Will Rogers Follies*, "Dean Martin Presents . . ."), musical theater director, born Wichita Falls, TX, Feb 28, 1939.

John Turturro, 44, actor (*Desperately Seeking Susan, Quiz Show*), born Brooklyn, NY, Feb 28, 1957.

FEBRUARY 29 BIRTHDAYS

Joss Ackland, 72, actor (*The Hunt for Red October, The Sicilian*), born London, England, Feb 29, 1928.

Dennis Farina, 56, actor ("Buddy Faro," *Get Shorty*), born Chicago, IL, Feb 29, 1944.

Arthur Franz, 80, actor (*Sands of Iwo Jima, Caine Mutiny, That Championship Season*), born Perth Amboy, NJ, Feb 29, 1920.

Phyllis Frelich, 56, actress (Tony for *Children of a Lesser God*; *Love Is Never Silent*), born Devil's Lake, ND, Feb 29, 1944.

Jack Lousma, 64, astronaut, born Grand Rapids, MI, Feb 29, 1936.

James Mitchell, 80, actor ("All My Children"), born Sacramento, CA, Feb 29, 1920.

Michèle Morgan (Simone Roussel), 80, actress (*The Fallen Idol*), born Neuilly, France, Feb 29, 1920.

Alex Rocco, 64, actor ("The Famous Teddy Z," *The Godfather, The Stunt Man*), born Cambridge, MA, Feb 29, 1936.

Antonio Sabato, Jr, 28, actor ("Earth 2"), born Rome, Italy, Feb 29, 1972.

March.

MARCH 1 — THURSDAY

Day 60 — 305 Remaining

★**AMERICAN RED CROSS MONTH.** Mar 1–31. Presidential Proclamation for Red Cross Month issued each year for March since 1943. Issued as American Red Cross Month since 1987.

THE ARRIVAL OF MARTIN PINZON: ANNIVERSARY. Mar 1, 1493. Martin Alonzo Pinzon (1440–1493), Spanish shipbuilder and navigator (and co-owner of the *Niña* and the *Pinta*), accompanied Christopher Columbus on his first voyage, as commander of the *Pinta*. Storms separated the ships on their return voyage, and the *Pinta* first touched land at Bayona, Spain, where Pinzon gave Europe its first news of the discovery of the New World (before Columbus's landing at Palos). Pinzon's brother, Vicente Yanez Pinzon, was commander of the third caravel of the expedition, the *Niña*.

ARTICLES OF CONFEDERATION RATIFIED: ANNIVERSARY. Mar 1, 1781. This compact made among the original 13 states had been adopted by the Congress Nov 15, 1777, and submitted to the states for ratification Nov 17, 1777. Maryland was the last state to approve, Feb 27, 1781, but Congress named Mar 1, 1781, as the day of formal ratification. The Articles of Confederation remained the supreme law of the nation until Mar 4, 1789, when the US Constitution went into effect.

BELGIUM: CAT FESTIVAL. Mar 1. Traditional cultural observance. Annually, on the second day of Lent.

"BELIEVE IT OR NOT" TV PREMIERE: ANNIVERSARY. Mar 1, 1949. The series was originally a radio show based on Robert L. Ripley's comic strips describing curiosities. Both the radio program and the NBC TV show were hosted by Robert Ripley until his death in 1949. Robert St. John became Ripley's successor. ABC recreated the show in 1982 with Jack Palance as host.

BIG TEN WOMEN'S BASKETBALL TOURNAMENT. Mar 1–4. Grand Rapids, MI. Est attendance: 2,500. For info: Dennis LaBissoniere, Big Ten Conference, 1500 W Higgins Rd, Park Ridge, IL 60068-6300. Phone: (847) 696-1010. Fax: (847) 696-1110. Web: www.bigten.org.

BIG 12 MEN'S SWIMMING CHAMPIONSHIPS. Mar 1–3. Austin, TX. For info: Big 12 Conference, 2201 Stemmons Frwy, 28th flr, Dallas, TX 75207. Phone: (214) 742-1212. Fax: (214) 753-0145. Web: www.big12sports.com.

	S	M	T	W	T	F	S
March					1	2	3
2001	4	5	6	7	8	9	10
	11	12	13	14	15	16	17
	18	19	20	21	22	23	24
	25	26	27	28	29	30	31

BLACK HILLS PASSION PLAY—FLORIDA. Mar 1–Apr 12. (Note: Not performed every day—call in advance.) Lake Wales Amphitheater, Lake Wales, FL. Spectacular outdoor drama depicting the last seven days in the life of Christ. Cast of more than 200, plus live animals. Est attendance: 40,000. For info: Lake Wales Amphitheater, PO Box 71, Lake Wales, FL 33859. Phone: (800) 622-8383 or (941) 676-1495. Fax: (941) 638-2037.

BOSNIA AND HERZEGOVINA: INDEPENDENCE DAY: 10th ANNIVERSARY. Mar 1. Commemorates independence in 1991.

CRANE WATCH '01. Mar 1–Apr 15. Kearney, NE. "World's Largest Concentration of Cranes." Each spring some 500,000 sandhill cranes (80 percent of the world's population of this species) gather on the Platte River "staging area" during their northward migration. For info: Kearney Visitors Bureau, PO Box 607, Kearney, NE 68847. Phone: (800) 652-9435.

ELLISON, RALPH WALDO: BIRTH ANNIVERSARY. Mar 1, 1914. American writer and educator born at Oklahoma City, OK. Author of the acclaimed novel *Invisible Man* (1952), the story of a young black man's struggle for his own identity in the face of rejection from both whites and blacks. It won the National Book Award in 1953. While only one of his novels was published, Ellison published collections of his essays, reviews and stories in *Shadow and Act* (1964) and *Going to the Territory* (1986). He died Apr 16, 1994, at New York City.

ETHICS AWARENESS MONTH. Mar 1–31. An insurance industry educational event to increase practitioners' awareness of ethical issues within the sector. Sponsors: The American College, American Institute for CPCU, Society of Financial Service Professionals and the CPCU Society. For info: Jennifer Ioannidi, Soc of Financial Service Professionals, 270 S Bryn Mawr Ave, Bryn Mawr, PA 19010-2195. Phone: (888) 243-2258 or (610) 526-2500. Fax: (610) 527-1499. E-mail: jioannidi@financialpro.org. Web: www.financialpro.org.

FESTIVAL OF NATIVE ARTS. Mar 1–3. University of Alaska, Fairbanks. Native cultural event features craft exhibits and sales, demonstrations and dances presented by Native people from all over Alaska. Est attendance: 4,000. For info: Festival of Native Arts, PO Box 756300, Univ of Alaska, Fairbanks, AK 99775-6300. Phone: (907) 474-7181 or (907) 474-6889. Fax: (907) 474-5624. E-mail: fnch@aurora.alaska.edu.

FLORIDA STRAWBERRY FESTIVAL. Mar 1–11. Plant City, FL. Celebration of winter strawberry harvest. Est attendance: 850,000. For info: Patsy Brooks, Gen Mgr, Florida Strawberry Fest, PO Drawer 1869, Plant City, FL 33564-1869. Phone: (813) 752-9194 or (813) 754-1996. Fax: (813) 754-4297. Web: www.flstrawberryfestival.com.

FULTON OYSTERFEST. Mar 1–4. Fulton Navigation Park, Fulton, TX. This salute to the oyster industry features oyster-shucking, raw oyster-eating contests, more than 100 arts and crafts booths, food and fun, live bands and other entertainment. Annually, the first full weekend in March. Est attendance: 30,000. For info: Fulton Oysterfest, PO Box 393, Fulton, TX 78358. Phone: (361) 729-2388. Fax: (361) 729-3248.

GAINES, WILLIAM M.: BIRTH ANNIVERSARY. Mar 1, 1922. The magazine *Mad*, especially popular in the 1960s and 1970s, was founded and published by William Gaines. Alfred E. Neuman, the loony, freckle-faced mascot of the publication, became a pop-culture hero. The magazine, known for its parodies of movies, comic strips and celebrities as well as its satire of politics and social mores, greatly influenced dozens of humorists. Gaines was born at The Bronx, NY. He died June 3, 1992, at New York City.

HUMORISTS ARE ARTISTS MONTH (HAAM). Mar 1–31. To recognize the important contributions made by various types of humorists to the high art of living. For info: Lone Star Publications of Humor, 8452 Fredericksburg Rd, Ste 103, San Antonio, TX 78229. E-mail: lspubs@aol.com. Web: members.aol.com/lspubs/lsindex.html.

ICELAND: BEER DAY. Mar 1. Reykjavik. This event began on Mar 1, 1989, when a 75-year-long prohibition of beer was lifted. Features celebrations in pubs and restaurants all over Reykjavik.

INTERNATIONAL LISTENING AWARENESS MONTH. Mar 1–31. Dedicated to learning more about the impact that listening has on all human activity. To promote the study, development and teaching of effective listening in all settings. For info: James Pratt, PO Box 744, River Falls, WI 54022. Phone: (800) 452-4505 or (715) 425-3377. Fax: (715) 425-0704. E-mail: ilistening@aol.com. Web: www.listen.org.

INTERNATIONAL MIRTH MONTH. Mar 1–31. The merry month of March is set aside to encourage more mirthful moments. Its focus is to show people how to use humor to deal with not-so-funny stuff. Mirth month was founded by Allen Klein, professional speaker and author of *The Healing Power of Humor*. For info: Allen Klein, 1034 Page St, San Francisco, CA 94117. Phone: (415) 431-1913. Fax: (415) 431-8600. E-mail: mirth@allenklein.com. Web: www.allenklein.com.

★**IRISH-AMERICAN HERITAGE MONTH.** Mar 1–31. Presidential Proclamation called for by House Joint Resolution 401 (PL 103–379).

JAPAN: OMIZUTORI (WATER-DRAWING FESTIVAL). Mar 1–14. Todaiji, Nara. At midnight, a solemn rite is performed in the flickering light of pine torches. People rush for sparks from the torches, which are believed to have magic power against evil. Most spectacular on the night of Mar 12. The ceremony of drawing water is observed at 2 AM on Mar 13, to the accompaniment of ancient Japanese music.

JOHN AND MABLE RINGLING MUSEUM OF ART MEDIEVAL FAIR. Mar 1–4. Sarasota, FL. A benefit for the Ringling Museum of Art featuring a 12th-century European village filled with food, arts and crafts, entertainment, armored jousting and a human chess match. Est attendance: 56,000. For info: (April to November) Medieval Fair, 1244 S Canterbury Rd, Ste 306, Shakopee, MN 55379. Phone: (800) 966-8215 or (952) 445-7361. Fax: (952) 445-7380. (Dec to Mar) Medieval Fair, Ringling Museum of Art, 5401 Bay Shore Rd, Sarasota, FL 34243. Phone: (941) 351-8497. E-mail: med.fair@gte.net. Web: www.renaissancefest.com.

KOKOSCHKA, OSKAR: BIRTH ANNIVERSARY. Mar 1, 1886. Born at Pochlarn, Austria. Avant-garde artist, playwright, teacher and humanitarian, his work evoked violent reaction. After viewing a 1911 exhibition of Kokoschka's work, the Archduke Franz Ferdinand is reported to have declared, "This man deserves to have every bone in his body broken." Kokoschka's work was featured in a 1937 Nazi exhibit of "Degenerate Art." Died at Montreux, Switzerland, Feb 22, 1980.

KOREA: SAMILJOL or INDEPENDENCE MOVEMENT DAY. Mar 1. Koreans observe the anniversary of the independence movement against Japanese colonial rule in 1919.

LAND MINE BAN: ANNIVERSARY. Mar 1, 1999. A UN treaty banning land mines took effect on this date. More than 130 nations signed the treaty; the US, Russia and China did not.

LINDBERGH KIDNAPPING: ANNIVERSARY. Mar 1, 1932. 20-month-old Charles A. Lindbergh, Jr, the son of Charles A. and Anne Morrow Lindbergh, was kidnapped from their home at Hopewell, NJ. Even though the Lindberghs paid a $50,000 ransom, their child's body was found in a wooded area less than five miles from the family home on May 12. Bruno Richard Hauptmann was charged with the murder and kidnapping. He was executed in the electric chair Apr 3, 1936. As a result of the kidnapping and murder of the Lindbergh baby, the Crime Control Act was passed on May 18, 1934. It authorized the death penalty for kidnappers who take their victims across state lines.

MENTAL RETARDATION AWARENESS MONTH. Mar 1–31. To educate the public about the needs of this nation's more than seven million citizens with mental retardation and about ways to prevent retardation. The Arc is a national organization on mental retardation, formerly the Association for Retarded Citizens. For info: Chris Privett, The Arc, 1010 Wayne Ave, Ste 650, Silver Spring, MD 20910. Phone: (301) 565-3842. Fax: (301) 565-3542. Web: www.thearc.org/welcome.html.

MILLER, GLENN: BIRTH ANNIVERSARY. Mar 1, 1904. American bandleader and composer (Alton) Glenn Miller was born at Clarinda, IA. He enjoyed great popularity preceding and during World War II. His hit recordings included "Moonlight Serenade," "String of Pearls," "Jersey Bounce" and "Sleepy Lagoon." Major Miller, leader of the US Army Air Force band, disappeared Dec 15, 1944, over the English Channel, on a flight to Paris where he was scheduled to give a show. There were many explanations of his disappearance, but 41 years later, in December 1985, crew members of an aborted RAF bombing said they believed they had seen Miller's plane go down, the victim of bombs being jettisoned by the RAF over the English Channel.

MUSIC IN OUR SCHOOLS MONTH. Mar 1–31. To increase public awareness of the importance of music education as part of a balanced curriculum. The theme for 2001 is "Music. . .Pass It On!" Additional information and awareness items are also available. For info: Deidre Healy, Mgr Special Programs, Music Educators Natl Conference, 1806 Robert Fulton Dr, Reston, VA 20191. Phone: (800) 336-3768. Web: www.menc.org.

NATIONAL CHRONIC FATIGUE SYNDROME AWARENESS MONTH. Mar 1–31. To educate patients, their families, the public and the medical profession about the nature and impact of CFS, "the Thief of Vitality," and related disorders, as well as to encourage and provide research funding. Annually, the month of March. For info: Natl Chronic Fatigue Syndrome and Fibromyalgia Assn, PO Box 18426, Kansas City, MO 64133. Phone: (816) 313-2000 (24-hour info line). Fax: (816) 524-6782. E-mail: NCFSFA@aol.com.

NATIONAL COLLISION AWARENESS MONTH. Mar 1–31. A month of vehicle safety awareness to promote the use of seatbelts, child safety seats, safe driving in inclement weather, obeying speed limits and other safety tips for drivers. For info: Nathan Hostetler, Accurate Autobody, 5550 S Garnett, Tulsa, OK 74146. Phone: (918) 270-0100. Fax: (918) 270-0102. E-mail: LorieHicks@aol.com.

NATIONAL COLORECTAL CANCER AWARENESS MONTH. Mar 1–31. To generate widespread awareness about colorectal cancer and to encourage people to learn more about how to prevent the disease through a healthy lifestyle and regular screening. Founding partners include the Cancer Research Foundation of America, the National Colorectal Cancer Roundtable and the American Digestive Health Foundation. For info: Stephanie Guiffre, Dir of Mktg and Communications, Cancer Research Foundation of America, 1600 Duke St, Ste 110, Alexandria, VA 22314. Phone: (703) 836-4412. Fax: (703) 836-4413. E-mail: sguiffre@crfa.org. Web: www.preventcancer.org.

NATIONAL CRAFT MONTH. Mar 1–31. Promoting the fun and creativity of hobbies and crafts. For info: Hobby Industry Assn, Natl Craft Month, Richartz and Fliss, 400 Morris Ave, Denville, NJ 07834. Phone: (973) 627-8180. Fax: (973) 672-8410. Web: www.i-craft.com. Info also available from: Assn of Crafts and Creative Industries, 1100-H Brandywine Blvd, PO Box 2188, Zanesville, OH 43702-2188. Phone: (614) 452-4541.

NATIONAL FROZEN FOOD MONTH. Mar 1–31. Promotes national awareness of the economical and nutritional benefits of frozen foods. Annually, the month of March. For info: Julie Henderson, VP Communications, Natl Frozen Food Assn, 4755 Linglestown Rd, Ste 300, Harrisburg, PA 17112. Phone: (717) 657-8601. Fax: (717) 657-9862. E-mail: nffm@nffa.org. Web: www.nffa.org.

NATIONAL HUMANE EDUCATION AWARENESS MONTH. Mar 1–31. A monthlong celebration promoting respect, responsibility and reverence toward all living things through education. Highlights of this event include a national search for adult and youth "humaneitarians" who exemplify compassion and concern for others–animals, people and the environment. For info: Sheryl Glidden, PALS Foundation, PO Box 1271, San Luis Obispo, CA 93406. Phone: (805) 544-0984. Web: www.expage.com/page/PALShome.

NATIONAL KIDNEY MONTH. Mar 1–31. Kidney disease may often be silent for many years, until it has reached an advanced stage. The National Kidney Foundation urges everyone to get regular checkups that include tests for blood pressure, blood sugar, urine protein and kidney function. For info: Ellie Schlam, National Kidney Foundation, 30 E 33rd St, New York, NY 10016. Phone: (800) 622-9010 or (212) 889-2210. Web: www.kidney.org.

NATIONAL MARCH TO COLLEGE DAY. Mar 1–31. A day when 7th grade students are invited to spend a day on a college campus as the guests of campus chapters of The National Society of Collegiate Scholars. During the day students will tour campus, hear a lecture, meet other college students and tour residence halls. The day is designed to expose 7th graders to college as a viable option for their future. Annually, any day in March (various on different campuses). For info: Vicki Dehlbom, The Natl Soc of Collegiate Scholars, 11 Dupont Circle NW, Ste 610, Washington, DC, 20036. Phone: (202) 234-5295. Fax: (202) 234-5298. E-mail: dehlbom@nscs.org. Web: www.nscs.org.

NATIONAL NUTRITION MONTH®. Mar 1–31. To educate consumers about the importance of good nutrition by providing the latest practical information on how simple it can be to eat healthfully. For info: The American Dietetic Assn, Natl Center for Nutrition and Dietetics, 216 W Jackson Blvd, Chicago, IL 60606-6995. Phone: (312) 899-0040. Fax: (312) 899-4739. E-mail: nnm@eatright.org. Web: www.eatright.org.

NATIONAL ON-HOLD MONTH. Mar 1–31. A month to recognize everyone who has been placed "on hold" after calling a place of business, and to honor those businesses who make this hold time more enjoyable by supplying informative messages and music for their callers waiting on hold. For info: Audiomax, 470 Sentry Pkwy East, Blue Bell, PA 19422. Phone: (800) 284-4653 or (610) 825-9100. Fax: (610) 825-0703. E-mail: thagerty@audiomax.com. Web: www.audiomax.com.

NATIONAL PIG DAY. Mar 1. To accord to the pig its rightful, though generally unrecognized, place as one of man's most intelligent and useful domesticated animals. Annually, Mar 1. For further information send SASE to: Ellen Stanley, 7006 Miami, Lubbock, TX 79413.

NATIONAL PROFESSIONAL SOCIAL WORK MONTH. Mar 1–31. To honor the social work profession and to recognize the contributions social workers and concerned citizens make within their communities. "Social Worker of the Year" and "Public Citizen of the Year" awards are announced and each winner receives a plaque. For info: Natl Assn of Social Workers, Inc, 750 First St NE, Ste 700, Washington, DC 20002-4241. Phone: (202) 408-8600. Web: www.socialworkers.org.

March 2001

S	M	T	W	T	F	S
				1	2	3
4	5	6	7	8	9	10
11	12	13	14	15	16	17
18	19	20	21	22	23	24
25	26	27	28	29	30	31

NATIONAL TALK WITH YOUR TEEN ABOUT SEX MONTH. Mar 1–31. The importance of frank talk with teenagers about sex is emphasized. Parents are encouraged to provide their teenage children with current, accurate information and open lines for communication, as well as to support their self-esteem, reduce misinformation and guide teenagers toward making responsible decisions regarding sex. Annually, the month of March. For info send SASE to: Teresa Langston, Dir, Parenting Without Pressure (PWOP), 1330 Boyer St, Longwood, FL 32750-6311. Phone: (407) 767-2524.

NATIONAL UMBRELLA MONTH. Mar 1–31. In honor of one of the most versatile and underrated inventions of the human race, this month is dedicated to the purchase of, use of and conversation about umbrellas. Annually, the month of March. For info: Thomas Edward Knibb, 8819 Adventure Ave, Walkersville, MD 21793-7828. Phone: (301) 898-3009. E-mail: tomknibb@juno.com. Media: Please call in advance for interviews.

NATIONAL WOMEN'S HISTORY MONTH. Mar 1–31. A time for reexamining and celebrating the wide range of women's contributions and achievements that are too often overlooked in the telling of US history. Information catalog available. For info: Natl Women's History Project, 7738 Bell Rd, Dept P, Windsor, CA 95492. Phone: (707) 838-6000. Fax: (707) 838-0478. E-mail: nwhp@aol.com. Web: www.nwhp.org.

NATIONAL WRITE A LETTER OF APPRECIATION WEEK. Mar 1–7. Send a letter expressing your gratitude to others, acknowledging the goodness that we find all around us. For info: Larry McManus, 1504 N Richmond Rd, McHenry, IL 60050-1410. Phone: (815) 344-4934. Fax: (815) 344-4934. E-mail: faithhealer@ameritech.net. Web: www.appreciationweek.org.

NEBRASKA: ADMISSION DAY: ANNIVERSARY. Mar 1. Became 37th state in 1867.

NORTH DAKOTA WINTER SHOW. Mar 1–11. Valley City, ND. 11-day agricultural expo featuring world's largest crop show, 8-breed cattle show, culinary arts show and competition, style and needlework show and competition, children's area, four-performance PRCA Rodeo, state team roping and penning championships, draft horse pulls, old-time tractor pull (tractors built prior to 1955), 80-vendor farm toy show and single performance headliner country concert. Annually, beginning the first Thursday in March. Est attendance: 72,000. For info: Dale Hildebrant, Mgr, ND Winter Show, PO Box 846, Valley City, ND 58072. Phone: (701) 845-1401 or (800) 437-0218 Fax: (701) 845-3914. E-mail: ndws@rrnet.com. Web: www.ndws.org.

OHIO: ADMISSION DAY: ANNIVERSARY. Mar 1. Became 17th state in 1803.

OPTIMISM MONTH. Mar 1–31. To encourage people to boost their optimism. Research proves optimists achieve more health, prosperity and happiness than pessimists. Use this monthlong celebration to practice optimism and turn optimism into a delightful, permanent habit. Free "Tip Sheets" available. For info: Dr. Michael Mercer & Dr. Maryann Troiani, The Mercer Group, Inc,

25597 Drake Rd, Barrington, IL 60010. Phone: (847) 382-0690. For media interviews, Victoria Sterling. Phone: (847) 382-6420. E-mail: DrTroiani@aol.com

PEACE CORPS FOUNDED: 40th ANNIVERSARY. Mar 1, 1961. Official establishment of the Peace Corps by President John F. Kennedy's signing of executive order. The Peace Corps has sent more than 153,000 volunteers to 134 countries to help people help themselves. The volunteers assist in projects such as health, education, water sanitation, agriculture, nutrition and forestry. For info: Peace Corps, 1111 20th St NW, Washington, DC 20526. Web: www.peacecorps.gov.

PLAY-THE-RECORDER MONTH. Mar 1–31. American Recorder Society members all over the continent will celebrate the organization's annual Play-the-Recorder Month by performing in public places such as libraries, bookstores, museums and shopping malls. Some will offer workshops on playing the recorder or demonstrations in schools. Founded in 1939, the ARS is the membership organization for all recorder players, including amateurs to leading professionals. Annually, the month of March. For info: American Recorder Soc, PO Box 631, Littleton, CO 80160-0631. Phone: (303) 347-1120. E-mail: recorder@compuserve.com. Web: ourworld.compuserve.com/homepages/recorder.

POISON PREVENTION AWARENESS MONTH. Mar 1–31. To educate parents, grandparents, schoolchildren and PTAs about accidental poisoning and how to prevent it. PPSI is a nonprofit organization. There is a $15 charge for kit materials. Annually, the month of March. For info: Frederick Mayer, Pres, Pharmacists Planning Service, Inc, 101 Lucas Valley Rd, #210, San Rafael, CA 94903. Phone: (415) 479-8628. Fax: (415) 479-8608. E-mail: ppsi@aol.com. Web: www.ppsinc.org.

RAID ON RICHMOND: ANNIVERSARY. Mar 1, 1864. Believing the Confederate capital of Richmond, VA, to be lightly fortified, President Abraham Lincoln ordered a surprise raid to capture the city and free Union prisoners. Federal troops under General Judson Kilpatrick and Colonel Ulric Dahlgren led the attack on this date, but failed when the plan was discovered by Southern forces. In the wake of their retreat, Dahlgren was killed, and two documents were discovered on his body. The incriminating documents contained plans to burn the city and kill Confederate President Jefferson Davis and his cabinet. Confederate General Robert E. Lee complained to the Union commander, George Meade, but a federal investigation was inconclusive.

RETURN THE BORROWED BOOKS WEEK. Mar 1–7. To remind you to make room for those precious old volumes that will be returned to you, by cleaning out all that worthless trash that your friends are waiting for. Annually, the first seven days of March. For info: Inter-Global Society for Prevention of Cruelty to Cartoonists, Al Kaelin, Secy, 3119 Chadwick Dr, Los Angeles, CA 90032. Phone: (323) 221-7909.

ROSACEA AWARENESS MONTH. Mar 1–31. Rosacea Awareness Month has been designated by the National Rosacea Society to raise understanding of this increasingly common disease. Rosacea is a facial skin condition that can cause permanent physical and psychological damage if it is not diagnosed and treated. For info: Natl Rosacea Soc, 800 S Northwest Hwy, Ste 200, Barrington, IL 60010. Phone: (847) 382-8971 or (800) NO-BLUSH. Fax: (847) 382-5567. E-mail: rosaceas@aol.com. Web: www.rosacea.org.

ROZELLE, PETE: 75th BIRTH ANNIVERSARY. Mar 1, 1926. Alvin Ray ("Pete") Rozelle, Commissioner of the National Football League, born at South Gate, CA. Rozelle began his career in the public relations department of the Los Angeles Rams, became general manager and was elected commissioner in 1960. He built the NFL into a sporting power, uniting its development to television. He helped engineer the NFL's merger with the American Football League, created the Super Bowl as America's greatest sports extravaganza, conceived the idea for Monday Night Football and persuaded NFL owners to accept revenue sharing. Died at Rancho Santa Fe, CA, Dec 6, 1996.

SAINT-GAUDENS, AUGUSTUS: BIRTH ANNIVERSARY. Mar 1, 1848. Sculptor, born at Dublin, Ireland. His works include the statue of Lincoln in Lincoln Park, Chicago, and of Admiral Farragut in Madison Square, New York. Saint-Gaudens died at Cornish, NH, Aug 3, 1907.

SHORE, DINAH: BIRTH ANNIVERSARY. Mar 1, 1917. American radio and television personality Dinah Shore was born Frances Rose Shore at Winchester, TN. In addition to recording many hit songs in the 1930s and 1940s, she was one of the first women to be successful as a television host, beginning in the 1950s with the "Dinah Shore Chevy Show." She received 10 Emmys before she died Feb 24, 1994, at Beverly Hills, CA.

SLAYTON, DONALD "DEKE" K.: BIRTH ANNIVERSARY. Mar 1, 1924. "Deke" Slayton, longtime chief of flight operations at the Johnson Space Center, was born at Sparta, WI. Slayton was a member of Mercury Seven, the original group of young military aviators chosen to inaugurate America's sojourn into space. Unfortunately, a heart problem prevented him from participating in any of the Mercury flights. When in 1971 the heart condition mysteriously went away, Slayton flew on the last Apollo Mission. The July 1975 flight, involving a docking with a Soviet Soyuz spacecraft, symbolized a momentary thaw in relations between the two nations. During his years as chief of flight operations, Slayton directed astronaut training and selected the crews for nearly all missions. He died June 13, 1993, at League City, TX.

SWITZERLAND: CHALANDRA MARZ. Mar 1. Engadine. Springtime traditional event when costumed young people, ringing bells and cracking whips, drive away the demons of winter.

UNIVERSAL HUMAN BEINGS WEEK. Mar 1–7. The purpose of this observance is to inspire men and women to become Universal Human Beings in a world that is rapidly becoming a "global village." Annually, Mar 1–7. For complete info send $4 to cover printing, handling and postage. For info: Dr. Stanley Drake, Pres, Intl Soc of Friendship and Good Will, 8592 Roswell Rd, Ste 434, Atlanta, GA 30350-1870.

WALES: SAINT DAVID'S DAY. Mar 1. Celebrates patron saint of Wales (Dewi Sant). Welsh tradition calls for the wearing of a leek on this day.

★**WOMEN'S HISTORY MONTH.** Mar 1–31.

WORKPLACE EYE HEALTH AND SAFETY MONTH. Mar 1–31. Can you see the dangers at your workplace? Accidents at work are a major cause of preventable blindness. Find out more about Prevent Blindness America®'s workplace safety program, The Wise Owl Club, and find out how to make your work environment easier on your eyes. For info: Prevent Blindness America®, 500 Remington Rd, Schaumburg, IL 60173. Phone: (800) 331-2020. Fax: (847) 843-8458. Web: www.preventblindness.org.

YELLOWSTONE NATIONAL PARK ESTABLISHED: ANNIVERSARY. Mar 1, 1872. The first area in the world to be designated a national park, most of Yellowstone is in Wyoming, with small sections in Montana and Idaho. It was established by an act of Congress.

YOUTH ART MONTH. Mar 1–31. To emphasize the value and importance of participation in art in the development of all children and youth. For info: Council for Art Education, Inc, 1280 Main St, PO Box 479, Hanson, MA 02341. Phone: (781) 293-4100. Fax: (781) 294-0808.

BIRTHDAYS TODAY

Catherine Bach, 47, actress ("The Dukes of Hazzard"), born Warren, OH, Mar 1, 1954.

Harry Belafonte, 74, singer ("Mary's Boy Child," "Island in the Sun," "Banana Boat Song"), born New York, NY, Mar 1, 1927.

John B. Breaux, 57, US Senator (D, Louisiana), born Crowley, LA, Mar 1, 1944.

Robert Conrad, 66, actor ("The Wild Wild West"), born Chicago, IL, Mar 1, 1935.

Roger Daltrey, 57, lead singer (The Who), born London, England, Mar 1, 1944.

Timothy Daly, 45, actor (*Diner*, "Wings"), born New York, NY, Mar 1, 1956.

Ron Francis, 38, hockey player, born Sault Ste. Marie, Ontario, Canada, Mar 1, 1963.

Mark-Paul Gosselaar, 27, actor ("Saved by the Bell," "She Cried No"), born Panorama City, CA, Mar 1, 1974.

Yolanda Griffith, 31, basketball player, born Chicago, IL, Mar 1, 1970.

Ron Howard, 47, actor ("The Andy Griffith Show," "Happy Days"); director (*Cocoon, Backdraft*), born Duncan, OK, Mar 1, 1954.

Judith Rossner, 66, novelist (*Looking for Mr Goodbar*), born New York, NY, Mar 1, 1935.

Alan Thicke, 54, actor ("Thicke of the Night," "Growing Pains"), born Kirkland Lake, Ontario, Canada, Mar 1, 1947.

Chris Webber, 28, basketball player, born Detroit, MI, Mar 1, 1973.

Richard (Purdy) Wilbur, 80, former poet laureate of the US, born New York, NY, Mar 1, 1921.

MARCH 2 — FRIDAY

Day 61 — 304 Remaining

BATTLE OF BISMARCK SEA: ANNIVERSARY. Mar 2–4, 1943. Protected by American and Australian fighters, 137 American Flying Fortress and Liberator bombers attacked a Japanese convoy en route from its base at Rabaul to New Guinea on Mar 2, 1943. In the convoy were eight transports carrying 7,000 reinforcements, which were escorted by eight destroyers. All the transports and four of the destroyers were sunk and 3,500 Japanese troops were drowned. Of the 150 Japanese aircraft involved in the fighting, 102 were shot down. The Battle of Bismarck Sea was a major victory for the Allies, ending any efforts by the Japanese to send reinforcements to New Guinea.

BIKE WEEK. Mar 2–11. Daytona Beach, FL. The "World's Largest Motorcycle Event" attracts motorcycle enthusiasts from around the world. Annually, the first two weekends in March. Est attendance: 500,000. For info: Bike Week, c/o The Chamber, 126 E Orange Ave, Daytona Beach, FL 32114. Phone: (904) 255-0981. E-mail: info@daytonachamber.com. Web: www .officialbikeweek.com.

CARNAVAL MIAMI. Mar 2–11. Little Havana, Miami, FL. Ten-day celebration includes 8K run (Mar 2), Carnaval Night (Mar 3), Sun Day on the Mile (Mar 4), Calle Ocho Cooking Contest (Mar 6), Carnaval Miami Golf Classic (Mar 8), Carnaval Miami Sports Festival and Carnaval Miami Internacional (Mar 10) and culminates with Calle Ocho: Open House (Mar 11). Endless entertainment in this 23-block party with musical stages, ethnic foods, dancing and plenty of events for the entire family. Billed as the largest block party in the world with more than a million people in attendance. For info: Kiwanis Club of Little Havana, 701 SW 27th Ave, #900, Miami, FL 33155. Phone: (305) 644-8888. Fax: (305) 644-8693. Web: www.carnavalmiami.org.

March 2001	S	M	T	W	T	F	S
					1	2	3
	4	5	6	7	8	9	10
	11	12	13	14	15	16	17
	18	19	20	21	22	23	24
	25	26	27	28	29	30	31

CHALO NITKA. Mar 2–4. Moore Haven, FL. To promote Lake Okeechobee bass fishing and bring the Seminoles and the rest of the community together for a celebration. *Chalo Nitka* means Bass (Chalo) Day (Nitka) in the Seminole language. Annually, the first three-day weekend in March. Est attendance: 10,000. For info: Exec Dir, Glades County Chamber of Commerce, Box 490, Moore Haven, FL 33471. Phone: (863) 946-0440. Fax: (863) 946-2282.

CORAY, MELISSA BURTON: BIRTH ANNIVERSARY. Mar 2, 1828. Coray was born at Mersey, Ontario, Canada. At the age of 18 she accompanied her Mormon Battalion soldier husband, William Coray, on a 2,000-mile military march on foot from Council Bluffs, IA, to San Diego, CA, then 1,500 more miles across the Sierra Nevada Mountains and the Nevada desert to Salt Lake City, UT, the only woman to make the entire trip. On July 30, 1994, a mountain peak near Carson Pass was named for her, the 2nd peak in California to be named for a woman.

CRAFTSMEN'S CLASSIC ARTS & CRAFTS FESTIVAL. Mar 2–4. State Fairgrounds, Columbia, SC. Arts and crafts. Est attendance: 20,000. For info: Gilmore Enterprises, 1240 Oakland Ave, Greensboro, NC 27403. Phone: (336) 274-5550. Fax: (336) 274-1084.

ETHIOPIA: ADWA DAY. Mar 2, 1896. Ethiopian forces under Menelik II inflicted a crushing defeat on the invading Italians at Adwa.

GEISEL, THEODOR "DR. SEUSS": BIRTH ANNIVERSARY. Mar 2, 1904. Theodor Seuss Geisel, the creator of *The Cat in the Hat* and *How the Grinch Stole Christmas*, was born at Springfield, MA. Known to children and parents as Dr. Seuss, his books have sold more than 200 million copies and have been translated into 20 languages. His career began with *And to Think That I Saw It on Mulberry Street*, which was turned down by 27 publishing houses before being published by Vanguard Press. His books included many messages, from environmental consciousness in *The Lorax* to the dangers of pacifism in *Horton Hatches the Egg* and *Yertel the Turtle*'s thinly veiled references to Hitler as the title character. He was awarded a Pulitzer Prize in 1984 "for his contribution over nearly half a century to the education and enjoyment of America's children and their parents." He died Sept 24, 1991, at La Jolla, CA.

HIGHWAY NUMBERS INTRODUCED: ANNIVERSARY. Mar 2, 1925. A joint board of state and federal highway officials created the first system of interstate highway numbering in the US. Standardized road signs identifying the routes were also introduced. Later the system would be improved with the use of odd and even numbers that distinguish between north-south and east-west routes respectively.

HOME AND GARDEN SHOW. Mar 2–4 (tentative). Florence Events Center, Florence, OR. Features a variety of home improvement, gardening, landscaping and appliance ideas. For info: Florence Event Center, 715 Quince St, Florence, OR 97439. Phone: (888) 968-4086. E-mail: mary@eventcenter.org. Web: www.eventcenter.org.

HOUSTON, SAM: BIRTH ANNIVERSARY. Mar 2, 1793. American soldier and politician, born at Rockbridge County, VA, is remembered for his role in Texas history. Houston was a congressman (1823–27) and governor (1827–29) of Tennessee. He resigned his office as governor in 1829 and rejoined the Cherokee Indians (with whom he had lived for several years as a teenage runaway), who accepted him as a member of their tribe. Houston went to Texas in 1832 and became commander of the Texan army in the War for Texan Independence, which was secured when Houston routed the much larger Mexican forces led by Santa Ana, Apr 21, 1836, at the Battle of San Jacinto. After Texas's admission to the Union, Houston served as US senator and later as governor of the state. He was deposed in 1861 when he refused to swear allegiance to the Confederacy. Houston, the only person to have been elected governor of two different states, failed to serve his full term of office in either. Houston, TX, was named for him. He died July 26, 1863, at Huntsville, TX.

LOG DRIVER'S WEEKEND. Mar 2–4. Houlton, ME. Featuring the "World's Largest Coffee Pot." Radar races and snowmobiling fun. For info: Greater Houlton Chamber of Commerce, 109 Main St, Houlton, ME 04730. Phone: (207) 532-4216. E-mail: chamber@rcn.com. Web: www.greaterhoulton.com.

LONGHORN WORLD CHAMPIONSHIP RODEO. Mar 2–4. ALLTEL Arena, Little Rock, AR. More than 200 cowboys and cowgirls compete in six professional contests ranging from bronc riding to bull riding for top prize money and world championship points. Featuring colorful opening pageantry and Big, Bad BONUS Bulls. 2nd annual in a new facility. Est attendance: 15,000. For info: W.Bruce Lehrke, Pres, Longhorn World Championship Rodeo, PO Box 70159, Nashville, TN 37207. Phone: (615) 876-1016. Fax: (615) 876-4685. E-mail: lhrodeo@idt.net. Web: www.longhornrodeo.com.

MARYLAND HOME AND FLOWER SHOW. Mar 2–4 (also 9–11). Timonium Fairgrounds, Baltimore, MD. The largest display of home building, remodeling and home decorating exhibits in the Baltimore area. Includes educational exhibits, crafts, plant marketplace and displays of landscaped gardens. Est attendance: 72,000. For info: S & L Productions Inc, Crain Overlook, 1916 Crain Hwy, Ste 16, Glen Burnie, MD 21061. Phone: (410) 863-1180. Fax: (410) 863-1187. E-mail: showinfo@slprod.com.

MISSOURI VALLEY CONFERENCE BASKETBALL TOURNAMENT. Mar 2–5. St. Louis, MO. Ten college teams compete with the winner earning an automatic berth in the NCAA tournament. For info: Missouri Valley Conference, 1000 St. Louis Union Station, Ste 105, St. Louis, MO 63103. Phone: (314) 421-0339.

MOON PHASE: FIRST QUARTER. Mar 2. Moon enters First Quarter phase at 9:03 PM, EST.

MOUNT RAINIER NATIONAL PARK ESTABLISHED: ANNIVERSARY. Mar 2, 1899. Located in the Cascade Mountains of Washington state, this is the fourth oldest national park.

NAIA WRESTLING NATIONAL CHAMPIONSHIPS. Mar 2–3. Individuals compete for All-America honors in 12 weight divisions, while teams compete for the national championship. 44th annual competition. Est attendance: 4,000. For info: Natl Assn of Intercollegiate Athletics, 6120 S Yale Ave, Ste 1450, Tulsa, OK 74136. Phone: (918) 494-8828. Fax: (918) 494-8841. E-mail: jkehl@naia.org. Web: www.naia.org.

NATIONAL SALESPERSON'S DAY. Mar 2. Salespeople are essential resources for customers today. The talented salesperson filters the vast amount of information that is available to customers. As salespeople present what is necessary, they help business people make the best purchasing decisions. Salespeople also help consumers make better, quicker decisions with the counsel they offer. The role of the salesperson is continually evolving with the impact of technology. Instead of replacing salespeople, techology makes the role of the salesperson much more sophisticated and essential. For info: Maura Schreier-Fleming, Strategic Selling, 7028 Judi, Dallas, TX 75252. Phone: (972) 380-0200. Fax: (972) 733-0126. E-mail: MauraSF@worldnet.att.net. Web: www.strategicselling.cc.

OTT, MELVIN (MEL): BIRTH ANNIVERSARY. Mar 2, 1909. Baseball Hall of Fame outfielder born at Gretna, LA. Playing for the New York Giants, Ott hit 511 home runs, a National League record until Willie Mays surpassed it in 1966. Inducted into the Hall of Fame in 1951. Died at New Orleans, LA, Nov 21, 1958.

POPE PIUS XII: 125th BIRTH ANNIVERSARY. Mar 2, 1876. Eugenio Maria Giovanni Pacelli, 260th pope of the Roman Catholic Church, born at Rome, Italy. Elected pope Mar 2, 1939. Died at Castel Gandolfo, near Rome, Oct 9, 1958.

READ ACROSS AMERICA DAY. Mar 2. A national reading campaign that advocates that all children read a book the evening of Mar 2. Celebrated on Dr. Seuss's birthday. For info: Natl Education Assn, 1201 16th St NW, Washington, DC 20036. Phone: (202) 822-7830. Fax: (888) 747-READ. Web: www.nea.org/readacross.

RITT, MARTIN: BIRTH ANNIVERSARY. Mar 2, 1914. American film and television director Martin Ritt was born at New York, NY. His best-known films are *Hud* (1963), *Sounder* (1972) and *Norma Rae* (1979). During the 1950s he was blacklisted by McCarthy's anti-Communist crusade. Died Dec 8, 1990, at Santa Monica, CA.

SCHURZ, CARL: BIRTH ANNIVERSARY. Mar 2, 1829. American journalist, political reformer and army officer in Civil War. Born near Cologne, Germany, he died at New York, NY, May 14, 1906.

SNOWFEST. Mar 2–11. North Lake Tahoe and Truckee, CA. Snowfest is a fantastic vacation opportunity, showcasing America's largest concentration of skiing and outdoor recreation combined with the fun, sparkle and excitement of 10 full days of more than 50 special and unique events. Annually, beginning the Friday before the first Sunday in March. Est attendance: 100,000. For info: Festivals at Tahoe, PO Box 5, Crystal Bay, NV 89402. Phone: (775) 832-7625. Fax: (775) 832-2232.

SNOWFEST WINTER CARNIVAL. Mar 2–11. North Lake Tahoe, NV. In its 21st year as the premiere winter carnival in the West, Snowfest offers activities for all ages and abilities. Downhill skiing, dance, torchlight parade, concerts, parties. For info: North Lake Tahoe/Truckee Winter Carnival, PO Box 5, Crystal Bay, NV 89402. Phone: (775) 832-7625. Web: snowfest.com.

SPACE MILESTONE: *PIONEER 10* (US). Mar 2, 1972. This unmanned probe began a journey on which it passed and photographed Jupiter and its moons, 620 million miles from Earth, in December 1973. It crossed the orbit of Pluto, and then in 1983 become the first known Earth object to leave our solar system. On Sept 22, 1987 *Pioneer 10* reached another space milestone at 4:19 PM, when it reached a distance 50 times farther from the sun than the sun is from Earth.

SPACE MILESTONE: *SOYUZ 28* (USSR). Mar 2, 1978. Cosmonauts Alexi Gubarev and Vladimir Remek linked with *Salyut 6* space station Mar 3, visiting crew of *Soyuz 26*. Returned to Earth Mar 10. Remek, from Czechoslovakia, was the first person in space from a country other than the US or USSR. Launched Mar 2, 1978.

TEXAS COWBOY POETRY GATHERING. Mar 2–4. Sul Ross State University, Alpine, TX. Cowboys from Texas and neighboring states gather for poetry readings and music. Includes Trappings of Texas Art and gear show. Est attendance: 5,000. For info: J.J. Tucker, Texas Cowboy Poetry Gathering Committee, PO Box 395, Alpine, TX 79831. Phone: (915) 837-1071 or (915) 837-3237. Fax: (915) 837-8195. Web: www.cowboypoetry.org.

TEXAS INDEPENDENCE DAY. Mar 2, 1836. Texas adopted Declaration of Independence from Mexico.

USA INDOOR TRACK & FIELD CHAMPIONSHIPS. Mar 2–3. Georgia Dome, Atlanta, GA. Annually, the first weekend in March. Est attendance: 12,000. For info: James Thornton, Dir of Special Events, USA Track & Field, 1 RCA Dome, Ste 140, Indianapolis, IN 46225. Phone: (317) 261-0500. Fax: (317) 261-0481. Web: www.usatf.org.

WINTER CARNIVAL. Mar 2–3. Red Lodge, MT. Winter Carnival features parades, snow sculptures, King and Queen contest, Snow Ball, costume contest, Cardboard Classic Race (for which teams design crafts of cardboard for downhill race), live music and prizes. Torchlight parade and spaghetti dinner. Annually, the first weekend in March. Est attendance: 2,000. For info: Red Lodge Area Chamber of Commerce, PO Box 988, Red Lodge, MT 59068. Phone: (888) 281-0625. Fax: (406) 446-1718. E-mail: information@redlodge.com. Web: www.redlodge.com.

WORLD DAY OF PRAYER. Mar 2. An ecumenical event that reinforces bonds between peoples of the world as they join in a global circle of prayer. Annually, the first Friday in March. Sponsor: International Committee for World Day of Prayer. Church Women United is the National World Day of Prayer Committee for the US. For info: Jeanette Zaragoza DeLeon, Dir for Ecumenical Celebrations, Church Women United, 475 Riverside Dr, 5th Fl, New York, NY 10115. Phone: (212) 870-3339 or (800) 298-5551. Fax: (212) 870-2338. E-mail: jzaragoza @churchwomen.org.

BIRTHDAYS TODAY

Jon Bon Jovi (John Bongiovi), 39, singer, songwriter ("You Give Love a Bad Name"), born Sayreville, NJ, Mar 2, 1962.

John Cullum, 71, actor (stage: *Shenandoah, On the Twentieth Century*; "Northern Exposure"), born Knoxville, TN, Mar 2, 1930.

Russell D. Feingold, 48, US Senator (D, Wisconsin), born Janesville, WI, Mar 2, 1953.

Mikhail Sergeyvich Gorbachev, 70, former Soviet political leader, born Privolnoye, Stavropol, Russia, Mar 2, 1931.

John Irving, 59, author (*Cider House Rules, The World According to Garp*), born Exeter, NH, Mar 2, 1942.

Jennifer Jones (Phyllis Isley), 82, actress (Oscar for *The Song of Bernadette*), born Tulsa, OK, Mar 2, 1919.

Eddie Money, 52, musician, born Brooklyn, NY, Mar 2, 1949.

Laraine Newman, 49, comedienne ("Saturday Night Live"), born Los Angeles, CA, Mar 2, 1952.

Doc Watson, 78, singer, musician (*Riding the Midnight Train, Then and Now*), born Deep Gap, NC, Mar 2, 1923.

Tom Wolfe, 70, author, journalist (*The Bonfire of the Vanities, The Right Stuff*), born Richmond, VA, Mar 2, 1931.

	S	**M**	**T**	**W**	**T**	**F**	**S**
March					1	2	3
2001	4	5	6	7	8	9	10
	11	12	13	14	15	16	17
	18	19	20	21	22	23	24
	25	26	27	28	29	30	31

MARCH 3 — SATURDAY
Day 62 — 303 Remaining

ANTIQUE SHOW AND SALE. Mar 3–4. West Platte High School Auditorium, 935 Washington St, Weston, MO. 30–40 selected dealers from several states display a variety of antiques (including furniture) and collectibles for sale to the general public. For info: Weston Development Co, 502 Main, Weston, MO 64098. Phone: (816) 640-2909. Web: ci.weston.mo.us.

ANTIQUES IN SCHOHARIE. Mar 3–4 (also Sept 15–16). Schoharie, NY. Est attendance: 2,000. For info: Donna Reston, Mgr, Schoharie Colonial Heritage Assn, PO Box 554, Schoharie, NY 12157. Phone: (518) 295-7505. E-mail: scha@midtel.net.

BELL, ALEXANDER GRAHAM: BIRTH ANNIVERSARY. Mar 3, 1847. Inventor of the telephone, born at Edinburgh, Scotland, Bell acquired his interest in the transmission of sound from his father, Melville Bell, a teacher of the deaf. Bell's use of visual devices to teach articulation to the deaf contributed to the theory from which he derived the principle of the vibrating membrane used in the telephone. On Mar 10, 1876, Bell spoke the first electrically transmitted sentence to his assistant in the next room: "Mr Watson, come here, I want you." Bell's other accomplishments include a refinement of Edison's phonograph, the first successful phonograph record and the audiometer, and he continued exploring the nature and causes of deafness. He died near Baddeck, Nova Scotia, Canada, Aug 2, 1922.

BETHUNE, NORMAN: BIRTH ANNIVERSARY. Mar 3, 1890. Canadian physician who worked in the front lines during World War I, the Spanish Civil War and the Chinese Revolution. Bethune was born at Gravenhurst, Ontario; he died at age 49 at China while treating a soldier of Mao's Eighth Route Army, Nov 11, 1939. He is said to be the only Western man recognized as a hero of the Chinese Revolution.

BIG TEN WRESTLING CHAMPIONSHIP. Mar 3–4. Northwestern University, Evanston, IL. Est attendance: 10,000. For info: Sue Ryan, Big Ten Conference, 1500 W Higgins Rd, Park Ridge, IL 60068-6300. Phone: (847) 696-1010. Fax: (847) 696-1110. Web: www.bigten.org or www.bigtenchampionships .com.

BIG 12 WRESTLING CHAMPIONSHIP. Mar 3. Stillwater, OK. Est attendance: 2,000. For info: Big 12 Conference, 2201 Stemmons Freeway, 28th Floor, Dallas, TX 75207. Phone: (214) 742-1212. Fax: (214) 742-2046. Web: www.big12sports.com.

BONZA BOTTLER DAY™. Mar 3. To celebrate when the number of the day is the same as the number of the month. Bonza Bottler Day™ is an excuse to have a party at least once a month. For more information, see Jan 1. For info: Gail M. Berger, 109 Matthew Ave, Poca, WV 25159. Phone: (304) 776-7746. E-mail: gberger5@aol.com.

BULGARIA: LIBERATION DAY. Mar 3. Grateful tribute to the Russian, Romanian and Finnish soldiers and Bulgarian volunteers who, in the Russo-Turkish War, 1877–78, liberated Bulgaria from five centuries of Ottoman rule.

FAITH CITY KENNEL CLUB DOG SHOW. Mar 3–4. Multi-Purpose Events Center, Wichita Falls, TX. More than 1,000 dogs in competition in the two-day event. Est attendance: 2,500. For info: Wichita Falls CVB, 1000 5th St, Wichita Falls, TX 76301. Phone: (940) 716-5500. Fax: (940) 716-5509. E-mail: MPEC @WF.net. Web: www.viewscape.com or www.wf.net.

FLORIDA: ADMISSION DAY: ANNIVERSARY. Mar 3. Became 27th state in 1845.

I WANT YOU TO BE HAPPY DAY. Mar 3. A day dedicated to reminding people to be thoughtful of others by showing love and concern, even if things are not going well for them. For info: Harriette W. Grimes, Grandmother, PO Box 545, Winter Garden, FL 34777-0545. Phone: (407) 656-3830. Fax: (407) 656-2790.

IDITAROD TRAIL SLED DOG RACE. Mar 3. 1,150 miles through Alaskan wilderness from Anchorage to Nome, Alaska, along the historic Iditarod Trail. Est attendance: 50,000. For info: Iditarod Trail Committee, PO Box 870800, Wasilla, AK 99687. Phone: (907) 376-5155. Fax: (907) 373-6998. Web: www.iditarod.com.

JAPAN: HINAMATSURI (DOLL FESTIVAL). Mar 3. This special festival for girls is observed throughout Japan. Annually, Mar 3.

MALAWI: MARTYR'S DAY. Mar 3. Public holiday in Malawi.

MISSOURI COMPROMISE: ANNIVERSARY. Mar 3, 1820. In Feb, 1819, a bill was introduced into Congress that would admit Missouri to the Union as a state that prohibited slavery. At the time there were 11 free states and 10 slave states. Southern congressmen feared this would upset the balance of power between North and South. As a compromise, on this date Missouri was admitted as a slave state but slavery was forever prohibited in the northern part of the Louisiana Purchase. In 1854, this act was repealed when Kansas and Nebraska were allowed to decide on slave or free status by popular vote.

"MOONLIGHTING" TV PREMIERE: ANNIVERSARY. Mar 3, 1985. Cybill Shepherd and Bruce Willis starred in ABC's comedy-adventure hour with Allyce Beasley as rhyming receptionist Agnes DiPesto. The premise: former model Maddie Hayes (Shepherd) discovers that the Blue Moon Detective Agency is her only remaining asset after her business manager embezzled her wealth. After deciding to keep the agency, she and her sparring partner, wisecracking detective David Addison (Willis), go off on a series of madcap adventures. The show frequently broke with formula by using the show-within-a-show technique, having characters directly address the camera, shooting sequences in black and white or by going completely off-concept (as in an episode based on Shakespeare's "The Taming of the Shrew"). Last telecast on May 14, 1989, the show foundered due to personality conflicts and production delays.

"MR WIZARD" TV PREMIERE: 50th ANNIVERSARY. Mar 3, 1951. Don Herbert as Mr Wizard explained the mysteries of science while performing experiments in front of wide-eyed children. The series ran on NBC for 14 continuous years. In 1983, Herbert returned to host "Mr Wizard's World" on Nickelodeon.

NATIONAL ANTHEM DAY: 70th ANNIVERSARY. Mar 3, 1931. The bill designating "The Star-Spangled Banner" as our national anthem was adopted by the US Senate and went to President Herbert Hoover for signature. The president signed it the same day.

NENANA TRIPOD RAISING FESTIVAL. Mar 3–4. Nenana, AK. Festival centers around the guessing of the exact time of the ice breakup on the Tanana River. Highlights include the raising of the tripod (Mar 5), Nenana Banana Eating, Weight-Pull Contest (humans and dogs), sled dog races, Kitty Cat Snowmachine races, snowshoe races, craft bazaar and much more. Est attendance: 2,500. For info: Nenana Ice Classic, Box 272, Nenana, AK 99760. Phone: (907) 832-5446. Fax: (907) 832-5888. E-mail: tripod@ptialaska.net. Web: www.ptialaska.net/~tripod.

PHILADELPHIA FLOWER SHOW. Mar 3–10. PA Convention Center, Philadelphia, PA. The largest flower show in the US. The premier event of its kind in the world. Est attendance: 300,000. For info: Pennsylvania Horticultural Soc, 100 N 20th St, 5th Floor, Philadelphia, PA 19103-1495. Phone: (215) 988-8800 or (215) 988-8899. Fax: (215) 988-8810. Web: www.philaflowershow.com.

PULLMAN, GEORGE: BIRTH ANNIVERSARY. Mar 3, 1831. Born at Brocton, NY, George Mortimer Pullman was an inventor and industrialist who became famous for his design and production of the "Pullman" railroad sleeping car. His first attempt at improving railroad sleeping accommodations began in 1858, while working as a contractor for the Chicago & Alton Railroad at Chicago, IL. His initial model was not adopted, but he left Chicago only to return five years later in 1863 with a new design that was enthusiastically received. He secured a patent for the folding upper berth design in 1864 and a second patent for the lower berth design in 1865. By 1867 Pullman and his partner organized the Pullman Palace Car Company, which became the greatest railroad car building organization in the world. In 1881 the town of Pullman, IL, south of Chicago, was formed by Pullman to house his employees. Because rents were not lowered when wages were cut, a strike was initiated and Pullman was eventually forced to give up control of all property in the town not directly required for manufacturing. He died Oct 19, 1897, at Chicago, IL.

RIDGWAY, MATTHEW BUNKER: BIRTH ANNIVERSARY. Mar 3, 1895. American Army officer, Matthew Bunker Ridgway was born at Fort Monroe, VA. As major general commanding the newly formed 82nd Airborne Division, he led it in the invasion of Sicily in July 1943 and the invasion of the Italian mainland in 1944. Ridgway replaced MacArthur as commander of the US Eighth Army in Korea in 1951 and succeeded Eisenhower as Supreme Allied Commander of the North Atlantic Treaty Organization in 1952. He became US Army Chief of Staff in 1953. Ridgway died at Fox Chapel, PA, July 26, 1993.

SAINT PIRAN'S DAY CELEBRATION. Mar 3. Location available after Jan 1. Celebration in honor of St. Piran, patron saint of Cornwall and Cornish peoples. Held to help preserve history and culture of the Cornish (Celtic). Annually, the Saturday nearest Mar 5. Est attendance: 50. For info: Polly Whitman, Pres, Greater Kansas City Cornish Soc, 24 E 68th St, Kansas City, MO 64113-2414. Phone: (816) 444-1963. E-mail: dandpwhit@aol.com.

SOUTHEAST FLORIDA SCOTTISH FESTIVAL AND GAMES. Mar 3. Heritage Park, Plantation, FL. Est attendance: 8,000. For info: Scottish-American Soc of Southeast Florida, 5901 NE 21 Rd, Fort Lauderdale, FL 33308. Phone: (954) 776-5675. E-mail: mfcampbell@juno.com.

TIME MAGAZINE FIRST PUBLISHED: ANNIVERSARY. Mar 3, 1923. The first issue of *Time* bore this date. The magazine was founded by Henry Luce and Briton Hadden.

TOY INVENTING. Mar 3. Burlington, WI. Celebrate inventing and thinking, a family day, invent a toy to take home, meet a US patent holder. See an exhibit of invented toys. For info: Teacher Place & Parent Resources, 533 Milwaukee Ave, Burlington, WI 53105. Phone: (262) 763-3946.

WHAT IF CATS AND DOGS HAD OPPOSABLE THUMBS DAY. Mar 3. We are grateful today that the infinite wisdom of the universe has not allowed cats and dogs to have thumbs. Imagine the cat, able to operate the can opener! Imagine the dog, able to open the refrigerator door! ©1999 Wellcat Herbs & Holidays. For info: Thomas & Ruth Roy, 2418 Long Ln, Lebanon, PA 17046. Phone: (230) 332-4886. E-mail: wellcat@supernet.com. Web: www.wellcat.com.

WILLIAM MCKINLEY'S SECOND INAUGURAL BALL: 100th ANNIVERSARY. Mar 3. Canton, OH. Dancing, gourmet dinner, historical reenactments. Fundraiser to benefit the McKinley Museum. For info: McKinley Museum, 800 McKinley Monument Dr NW, Canton, OH 44708. Phone: (330) 455-7043. Web: www.mckinleymuseum.org.

WOMAN SUFFRAGE PARADE ATTACKED: ANNIVERSARY. Mar 3, 1913. A parade held by the National American Woman Suffrage Association at Washington, DC, on the day before Woodrow Wilson's inauguration turned into a near riot when people in the crowd began jeering and shoving the marchers. The 5,000 women and their supporters were spit upon, struck in the face and pelted with burning cigar stubs while police looked on and made no effort to intervene. Secretary of War Henry Stimson was forced to send soldiers from Fort Myer to restore order.

BIRTHDAYS TODAY

Jessica Biel, 19, actress ("7th Heaven"), born Ely, MN, Mar 3, 1982.

David Faustino, 27, actor ("Married . . . With Children"), born Los Angeles, CA, Mar 3, 1974.

Jacqueline (Jackie) Joyner-Kersee, 39, Olympic gold medal heptathlete, born East St. Louis, IL, Mar 3, 1962.

Tim Kazurinsky, 51, actor, comedian, writer ("Saturday Night Live"), born Johnstown, PA, Mar 3, 1950.

Brian Leetch, 33, hockey player, born Corpus Christi, TX, Mar 3, 1968.

Princess Radziwill (Caroline Lee Bouvier), 68, sister of the late Jackie Kennedy Onassis, born New York, NY, Mar 3, 1933.

Miranda Richardson, 43, actress (*The Crying Game, Enchanted April*), born Lancashire, England, Mar 3, 1958.

Herschel Walker, 39, football player, born Wrightsville, GA, Mar 3, 1962.

MARCH 4 — SUNDAY
Day 63 — 302 Remaining

ADAMS, JOHN QUINCY: RETURN TO CONGRESS ANNIVERSARY. Mar 4, 1830. On this day, John Quincy Adams returned to the House of Representatives to represent the district of Plymouth, MA. He was the first former president to do so and served for eight consecutive terms.

AUTOGRAPH COLLECTING WEEK. Mar 4–10. Celebrating the fun of collecting autographs for love and money! Thousands of adults and children all over the world enjoy obtaining the signatures of the famous, infamous and nearly-famous, and almost everyone has at least one special autograph tucked away somewhere. This week honors a hobby which can be started with little or no money, and allows the hobbyist of any age to build an exciting and valuable collection. Free articles for publishers and webmasters at IdeaLady.com/content.htm. For info: Cathy Stucker, On-Line Autograph Collectors Club, 4646 Hwy 6, PMB 123, Sugar Land, TX 77478. Phone: (281) 265-7342. Fax: (281) 265-9727. E-mail: cathy@idealady.com. Web: www.idealady.com.

	S	M	T	W	T	F	S
March					1	2	3
2001	4	5	6	7	8	9	10
	11	12	13	14	15	16	17
	18	19	20	21	22	23	24
	25	26	27	28	29	30	31

CONGRESS: ANNIVERSARY OF FIRST MEETING UNDER CONSTITUTION. Mar 4, 1789. The first Congress met at New York, NY. A quorum was obtained in the House Apr 1 and in the Senate Apr 5, and the first Congress was formally organized Apr 6. Electoral votes were counted, and George Washington was declared president (69 votes) and John Adams vice president (34 votes).

CONSERVE WATER/DETECT-A-LEAK WEEK. Mar 4–10. To help everyone learn why it is important to conserve our water and how to help accomplish this goal. For info: American Leak Detection, 888 Research Dr, Ste 100, Palm Springs, CA 92262. Phone: (800) 755-6697. Fax: (760) 320-1288. E-mail: sbangs@leakbusters.com. Web: www.leakbusters.com.

COURAGEOUS FOLLOWER DAY. Mar 4. We are a country built on the myth of "rugged individualism," in love with the concept of leadership. But all leaders require followers and, in fact, virtually all of us are followers at some times and leaders at others. This day honors the too often disparaged role of follower. The purpose of this day is to dispell the myth that followers are passive and to raise awareness that good followership is energetic and at times courageous. In fact, only through active and courageous followership can leaders be counted on to use their power wisely and well. For info: Ira Chaleff, Author, Exec Coaching & Consulting Assoc. Phone: (301) 933-3752. Web: www.exe-coach.com.

"THE DICK CAVETT SHOW" TV PREMIERE: ANNIVERSARY. Mar 4, 1968. Dick Cavett began his television career on ABC with a daytime talk show that subsequently became a late-night program competing with Johnny Carson. Cavett, with his Yale background, had a reputation as an "intellectual" host and was particularly adept at the one-man interview. He has since appeared on the CBS, PBS and USA networks hosting a variety of shows.

DING LING: 15th DEATH ANNIVERSARY. Mar 4, 1986. Writer and champion of women's rights, born at Hunan Province, China, in 1904. Ding was a prolific author, having written nearly 300 novels as well as plays, short stories and essays. She received the 1951 Stalin Prize for Literature for her novel *The Sun Shines Over the Sanggan River* (1949). She fell from favor in the 1950s, was exiled and, in 1970, was imprisoned. After the death of Chairman Mao she was freed and during her last years she enjoyed renewed attention and favor. Died at age 82 at Beijing, China.

DRED SCOTT DECISION ANNIVERSARY. Mar 4. Old Courthouse, St. Louis, MO. Annual commemoration of the Mar 6, 1857 Supreme Court decision that ruled that Dred Scott, a slave, was not a citizen and could not sue in the federal courts. Chief Justice Roger Taney wrote that blacks could not be citizens and that Congress had no power to restrict slavery in the territories. The most famous court case in the long slavery controversy. Guest speakers and a reenactment of the Dred Scott trial. For info: Jefferson Natl Expansion Memorial, 10 S Broadway, Ste 1540, St. Louis, MO 63102. Phone: (314) 655-1701.

GREENWOOD, JOAN: 80th BIRTH ANNIVERSARY. Mar 4, 1921. British stage and screen actress Joan Greenwood was born at Chelsea, London. With her husky voice she became best known for playing the roles of coquettes. She died Feb 27, 1987, at London.

GROVER CLEVELAND'S SECOND PRESIDENTIAL INAUGURATION: ANNIVERSARY. Mar 4, 1893. Grover Cleveland was inaugurated for a second but nonconsecutive term as president. In 1885 he had become 22nd President of the US and in 1893 the 24th. Originally a source of some controversy, the Congressional Directory for some time listed him only as the 22nd president. The Directory now lists him as both the 22nd and 24th presidents though some historians continue to argue that one person cannot be both. Benjamin Harrison served during the intervening term, defeating Cleveland in electoral votes, though not in the popular vote.

HELP SOMEONE SEE WEEK OBSERVANCE. Mar 4–10. Rockford, OH. Collect used eyeglasses, offer new glass cases for nursing home residents, arrange visits from guide dogs, have programs or videos about sight. For info: Brooke Reyman, Activities Dir, Shane Hill Nursing Home, 10731 State Rte 118, Rockford, OH 45882-8947. Phone: (419) 363-2620.

HOT SPRINGS NATIONAL PARK ESTABLISHED: ANNIVERSARY. Mar 4, 1921. To protect the Hot Springs of Arkansas the government set aside Hot Springs Reservation on Apr 20, 1832. In 1921 the area became a national park.

HUG A GI DAY. Mar 4. Today is the only calendrical date which is a command—March Fourth. Therefore, today we honor all of the gallant men and women who serve in all branches of the military. We acknowledge and salute the sacrifices they make to keep this the land of the free. [©1996] For info: Adrienne Sioux Koopersmith, 1437 W Rosemont, 1W, Chicago, IL 60660-1319. Phone: (773) 743-5341. Fax: (773) 743-5395. E-mail: adrienne@21stcentury.net.

MARCH 4 YOURSELF. Mar 4. The March 4 Yourself Movement celebrates this day by marching off to work, marching off to school or staying home and taking care of the children. The motto is "March 4th Everyday," symbolizing the commitment to rugged individualism and personal responsibility which are what the US was founded on. Members believe that the solutions to their problems and the keys to their happiness cannot be found anyplace except within themselves. The movement celebrates the individual and recognizes that we get the most out of life when we are getting the most out of ourselves. For info: Pete Martino, PO Box 86, Epsom, NH 03234. Phone: (603) 736-9419. E-mail: martinos@nh.ultranet.com.

NATIONAL PROFESSIONAL PET SITTERS WEEK. Mar 4–10. A week to show appreciation for the pet sitters who work 365 days a year for customers. Annually, the first full week in March. For info: Pet Sitters Intl (PSI), 418 E King St, King, NC 27021. Phone: (336) 983-9222. Fax: (336) 983-3755. E-mail: info @petsit.com. Web: www.petsit.com.

NATURAL BRIDGE BATTLE REENACTMENT. Mar 4. Tallahassee, FL. Reenactment of the Confederate army's victory at the Natural Bridge site, which kept Tallahassee (the state capital) from falling into Union hands. Est attendance: 2,500. For info: Natural Bridge Battlefield State Historic Site, 1022 DeSoto Park Dr, Tallahassee, FL 32301. Phone: (850) 922-6007. Fax: (850) 488-0366.

OLD INAUGURATION DAY. Mar 4. Anniversary of the date set for beginning the US presidential term of office, 1789–1933. Although the Continental Congress had set the first Wednesday of March 1789 as the date for the new government to convene, a quorum was not present to count the electoral votes until Apr 6. Though George Washington's term of office began on Mar 4, he did not take the oath of office until Apr 30, 1789. All subsequent presidential terms (except successions following the death of an incumbent), until Franklin D. Roosevelt's second term, began Mar 4. The 20th Amendment (ratified Jan 23, 1933) provided that "the terms of the President and Vice President shall end at noon on the 20th day of January . . . and the terms of their successors shall then begin."

PENNSYLVANIA DEEDED TO WILLIAM PENN: ANNIVERSARY. Mar 4, 1681. To satisfy a debt of £16,000, King Charles II of England granted a royal charter, deed and governorship of Pennsylvania to William Penn.

PEOPLE MAGAZINE: ANNIVERSARY. Mar 4, 1974. The popular magazine highlighting celebrities was officially launched with the Mar 4, 1974, issue featuring a cover photo of Mia Farrow.

PERKINS, FRANCES: CABINET APPOINTMENT ANNIVERSARY. Mar 4, 1933. Frances Perkins became the first woman appointed to the president's cabinet when she was appointed Secretary of Labor by President Franklin D. Roosevelt.

PULASKI, CASIMIR: BIRTH ANNIVERSARY. Mar 4, 1747. American Revolutionary hero, General Kazimierz (Casimir) Pulaski, born at Winiary, Mazovia, Poland, the son of a count. He was a patriot and military leader in Poland's fight against Russia of 1770–71 and went into exile at the partition of Poland in 1772. He went to America in 1777 to join the Revolution, fighting with General Washington at Brandywine and also serving at Germantown and Valley Forge. He organized the Pulaski Legion to wage guerrilla warfare against the British. Mortally wounded in a heroic charge at the siege of Savannah, GA, he died aboard the warship *Wasp* Oct 11, 1779. Pulaski Day is celebrated on the first Monday of March in Illinois.

ROCKNE, KNUTE: BIRTH ANNIVERSARY. Mar 4, 1888. Legendary Notre Dame football coach born at Voss, Norway. Known for such sayings as "Win one for the Gipper," he died at Cottonwood Falls, KS, Mar 31, 1931.

RONALD AND NANCY REAGAN: WEDDING ANNIVERSARY. Mar 4, 1952. Little Brown Church in the San Fernando Valley, CA. Ronald Reagan was 41 and Nancy Davis (born Anne Frances Robbins) was 30. They were both actors; William Holden served as best man. This was Reagan's second marriage. His first marriage to actress Jane Wyman in 1940 produced daughter Maureen Elizabeth Reagan in 1941, adopted son Michael Edward Reagan (born 1942) in 1945 and daughter Christina Reagan in 1947, who was born prematurely and died within a few days. Nancy and Ronald have two children: Patricia Ann Reagan (Patti Davis), born in 1952, and Ronald Prescott Reagan, in 1958. Reagan was the first US president who had been divorced.

SAVE YOUR VISION WEEK. Mar 4–10. To remind Americans that vision is one of the most vital of all human needs and its protection is of great significance to the health and welfare of every individual. Annually, the first full week in March. For info: American Optometric Assn, 243 N Lindbergh Blvd, St. Louis, MO 63141. Phone: (314) 991-4100. Fax: (314) 991-4101. E-mail: hozinn@theaoa.org. Web: www.aoanet.org/.

★**SAVE YOUR VISION WEEK.** Mar 4–10. Presidential Proclamation issued for the first week of March since 1964, except 1971 and 1982 when issued for the second week of March. (PL88–1942, of Dec 30, 1963.)

"SEZ WHO?" FOURPLAY! MARCH(INETTI'S) MADNESS. Mar 4–26. Marchinetti's Restaurant, Winfield, IL. Two-player man-and-woman teams compete against one another, trying to complete humorous, provocative and otherwise memorable quotes made by basketball personalities. Annually, from the Sunday in March when NCAA Tournament field is announced through Monday, 22 days later, when the championship game is played. Est attendance: 100. For info: Rich Bysina, 853 Lorlyn Dr, #3D, West Chicago, IL 60185. Phone: (630) 876-9615.

SPACE MILESTONE: *OGO 5* (US). Mar 4, 1968. Orbiting Geophysical Observatory (OGO) collected data on sun's influence on Earth. Launched Mar 4, 1968. Six OGOs were launched in all.

SPECIAL OLYMPICS WORLD WINTER GAMES. Mar 4–11. Anchorage, AK. Nearly 7,000 people—athletes, coaches, officials, family and friends— will arrive for the largest international sporting event ever held in Alaska. More than 2,000 athletes from 80 countries will compete in games with the theme "Challenging New Frontiers." For info: Special Olympics Intl, 1325 G St NW, Washington, DC 20005-3104. Phone: (202) 628-3630. Web: www .2001worldgames.org.

TELEVISION ACADEMY HALL OF FAME: FIRST INDUCTEES ANNOUNCED: ANNIVERSARY. Mar 4, 1984. The Television Academy of Arts and Sciences announced the formation of the Television Academy Hall of Fame at Burbank, CA. The first inductees were Lucille Ball, Milton Berle, Paddy Chayefsky, Norman Lear, Edward R. Murrow, William S. Paley and David Sarnoff.

VERMONT: ADMISSION DAY: ANNIVERSARY. Mar 4. Became 14th state in 1791.

YAWM ARAFAT: THE STANDING AT ARAFAT. Mar 4. Islamic calendar date: Dhu-Hijjah 9, 1421. The day when people on the Hajj (pilgrimage to Mecca) assemble for "the Standing" at the plain of Arafat at Mina, Saudi Arabia, near Mecca. This gathering is a foreshadowing of the Day of Judgment. Different methods for "anticipating" the visibility of the new moon crescent at Mecca are used by different Muslim groups. US date may vary.

BIRTHDAYS TODAY

Emilio Estefan, 48, percussionist for the Miami Sound Machine ("Anything for You"), born Havana, Cuba, Mar 4, 1953.
Patricia Heaton, 42, actress ("Everybody Loves Raymond"), born Bay Village, OH, Mar 4, 1959.
Kevin Johnson, 35, former basketball player, born Sacramento, CA, Mar 4, 1966.
Patsy Kensit, 33, actress (*The Great Gatsby, Blame It on the Bellboy*), born London, England, Mar 4, 1968.
Kay Lenz, 48, actress (*Rich Man, Poor Man*), born Los Angeles, CA, Mar 4, 1953.
Miriam Makeba, 69, actress, singer, anti-apartheid activist, born Johannesburg, South Africa, Mar 4, 1932.
Barbara McNair, 67, singer, actress ("The Barbara McNair Show"), born Racine, WI, Mar 4, 1934.
Catherine O'Hara, 47, comedienne, writer ("SCTV Network 90"), actress (*Home Alone*), born Toronto, Ontario, Canada, Mar 4, 1954.
Paula Prentiss (Paula Ragusa), 62, actress ("He & She," *What's New Pussycat?*), born San Antonio, TX, Mar 4, 1939.
Steven Weber, 40, actor ("Wings," *Deception: A Mother's Secret*), born Queens, NY, Mar 4, 1961.
Mary Wilson, 57, singer (original member of the Supremes with Diana Ross and Florence Ballard), born Detroit, MI, Mar 4, 1944.

MARCH 5 — MONDAY

Day 64 — 301 Remaining

AUSTRALIA: EIGHT HOUR DAY or LABOR DAY. Mar 5. Western Australia and Tasmania. Parades and celebrations commemorate trade union efforts during the 19th century to limit working hours. Their slogan: "Eight hours labor, eight hours recreation, eight hours rest!" Annually, the first Monday in March.

BLACKSTONE, WILLIAM: BIRTH ANNIVERSARY. Mar 5, 1595. William Blackstone, born at Durham County, England, was the first settler in what is now Boston, MA, and also the first in what is now Rhode Island. Blackstone came to New England with the Captain Robert Gorges expedition in 1623. When the expedition failed and most returned to England, he stayed and settled on what later became Beacon Hill. In 1634, he sold most of his Boston property and moved to the shores of the river that now bears his name. He died there at what is now Cumberland, RI, May 26, 1675.

BOSTON MASSACRE: ANNIVERSARY. Mar 5, 1770. A skirmish between British troops and a crowd at Boston, MA, became widely publicized and contributed to the unpopularity of the British regime in America before the American Revolution. Five men were killed and six more were injured by British troops commanded by Captain Thomas Preston.

	S	M	T	W	T	F	S
March					1	2	3
2001	4	5	6	7	8	9	10
	11	12	13	14	15	16	17
	18	19	20	21	22	23	24
	25	26	27	28	29	30	31

CHANNEL ISLANDS NATIONAL PARK ESTABLISHED: ANNIVERSARY. Mar 5, 1980. California's Channel Islands Monument, authorized in 1938 by President Franklin D. Roosevelt, consisted of the islands of Anacapa and Santa Barbara. In 1980 President Jimmy Carter signed a bill establishing the Channel Islands National Park consisting of the islands Anacapa, San Miguel, Santa Barbara, Santa Cruz and Santa Rosa Island.

CRISPUS ATTUCKS DAY: DEATH ANNIVERSARY. Mar 5, 1770. Honors Crispus Attucks, possibly a runaway slave, who was the first to die in the Boston Massacre.

CULLIGAN, EMMETT J.: BIRTH ANNIVERSARY. Mar 5, 1893. Emmett J. Culligan, founder of world's largest water treatment organization, was born at Yankton, SD. Culligan first experimented with a water-softening device in the early 1920s—to soften water used to wash his baby's diapers. In 1936 he launched the company from a Northbrook, IL, blacksmith shop. Recipient of Horatio Alger Award in 1969, Culligan died at San Bernardino, CA, June 3, 1970.

EGYPT: GRAND BAIRAM. Mar 5. Muslims celebrate the sacrifice by the Prophet Abraham of killing a ram in place of his son, Ismail. Preceded by pilgrimage to Mecca. Dates vary according to the Muslim lunar calendar.

EID-AL-ADHA: FEAST OF THE SACRIFICE. Mar 5. Islamic calendar date: Dhu-Hijja 10, 1421. Commemorates Abraham's willingness to sacrifice his son Ishmael in obedience to God. It is part of the Hajj (pilgrimage to Mecca). The day begins with the sacrifice of an animal in remembrance of the Angel Gabriel's substitution of a lamb as Abraham's offering. One-third of the meat is given to the poor and the rest is shared with friends and family. Celebrated with gifts and general merrymaking, the festival usually continues for several days. It is celebrated as Tabaski in Benin, Burkina Faso, Guinea, Guinea-Bissau, Ivory Coast, Mali, Niger and Senegal, as Hari Raya Hajj in South East Asia and as Kurban Bayram in Turkey and Bosnia. Different methods for "anticipating" the visibility of the moon crescent at Mecca are used by different Muslim groups. US date may vary.

GERMAN 16-YEAR-OLDS DRAFTED: ANNIVERSARY. Mar 5, 1945. The Nazis began inducting German boys of the Hitler Youth born in or before 1929 into the regular German army, thereby lowering the draft age to 16.

GUAM: DISCOVERY DAY or MAGELLAN DAY. Mar 5. Commemorates discovery of Guam in 1521 by Magellan. Annually, the first Monday in March.

HARRISON, REX: BIRTH ANNIVERSARY. Mar 5, 1908. Born Reginald Carey at Huyton, England. Rex Harrison's career as an actor encompassed more than 40 films and scores of plays. He won both a Tony and an Oscar for the role of Henry Higgins in *My Fair Lady*, perhaps his most famous role. Among other films, he appeared in *Dr. Dolittle, Cleopatra, Blithe Spirit* and *Major Barbara*. He claimed he would never retire from acting, and he was appearing in a Broadway revival of Somerset Maugham's *The Circle* three weeks before his death June 2, 1990, at his home at New York, NY.

HEMLOCK DAY. Mar 5. To honor the legendary Taffy Hemlock, supposed inventrix of a procedure for attaching padlocks around the hem of her skirt so that it would not be blown upward by inquisitive winds that might let her ankles get freckled. Celebrated by the True-Blue Law Society with patent searches to determine when/if the idea was ever patented. For info: Robert L. Birch, Puns Corps, Box 2364, Falls Church, VA 22042-0364. Phone: (703) 533-3668.

HUMAN RESOURCE WEEK. Mar 5–9. This week is set aside to recognize those who work hard to help all employees everywhere every day of the year. Annually, the first full week in March, Monday–Friday. For info: Lavonne Juhl, Human Resources, Summit Manor Health Care Center, 80 Western Ave North, St. Paul, MN 55102.

"IRON CURTAIN" SPEECH: 55th ANNIVERSARY.
Mar 5, 1946. Winston Churchill, speaking at Westminster College, Fulton, MO, established the cold war boundary with these words: "From Stettin in the Baltic to Trieste in the Adriatic an iron curtain has descended across the continent." Though Churchill was not the first to use the phrase *iron curtain*, his speech gave it a new currency and its usage persisted.

MERCATOR, GERHARDUS: BIRTH ANNIVERSARY.
Mar 5, 1512. Cartographer-geographer Mercator was born at Rupelmonde, Belgium. His Mercator projection for maps provided an accurate ratio of latitude to longitude and is still used today. He also introduced the term "atlas" for a collection of maps. He died at Duisberg, Germany, Dec 2, 1594.

MOST BORING FILM AWARDS. Mar 5. 16th annual awards for the most boring films of the previous year. Categories include drama, comedy and others. The announcement of the awards will be posted prior to the event on www.boringinstitute.com. For info: Alan Caruba, Founder, The Boring Inst, PO Box 40, Maplewood, NJ 07040. Phone: (973) 763-6392. E-mail: acaruba@aol.com. Web: www.boringinstitute.com.

NATIONAL PROCRASTINATION WEEK. Mar 5–11. To promote the benefits of relaxing through putting off until tomorrow everything that needn't be done today. For info: Les Waas, Pres, Procrastinators' Club of America Inc, PO Box 712, Bryn Athyn, PA 19009. Phone: (215) 947-9020. Fax: (215) 947-7007. E-mail: lw518@msn.com.

NATIONAL SCHOOL BREAKFAST WEEK. Mar 5–9. To focus on the importance of a nutritious breakfast served in the schools, giving children a good start to their day. Annually, the first full week in March (weekdays). For info: American School Food Service Assn, 1600 Duke St, 7th Fl, Alexandria, VA 22314-3436. Phone: (703) 739-3900. E-mail: asfsa@asfsa.org. Web: www.asfsa.org.

NEWSPAPER IN EDUCATION WEEK. Mar 5–9. A week-long celebration of using newspapers in the classroom as living textbooks. Annually, the first full week in March (weekdays). For info: Mgr Education Programs, Newspaper Assn of America Foundation, 1921 Gallows Rd, Ste 600, Vienna, VA 22182-3900. Phone: (703) 902-1730. E-mail: abboj@naa.org. Web: www.naa.org.

SAINT PIRAN'S DAY. Mar 5. Celebrates the birthday of St. Piran, the patron saint of Cornish tinners. Cornish worldwide celebrate this day. For info: The Cornish American Heritage Soc, 2405 N Brookfield Rd, Brookfield, WI 53045. Phone: (262) 786-9358. E-mail: jjolliff@post.its.mcw.edu.

US BANK HOLIDAY: ANNIVERSARY. Mar 5, 1933. On his first full day in office (Sunday, Mar 5, 1933), President Roosevelt proclaimed a national "Bank Holiday" to help save the nation's faltering banking system. Most banks were able to reopen after the 10-day "holiday" (Mar 4–14), but in the meantime, "scrip" had temporarily replaced money in many American households.

Samantha Eggar, 62, actress ("Samantha and the King," *The Collector*), born London, England, Mar 5, 1939.
Penn Jillette, 46, magician, born Greenfield, MA, Mar 5, 1955.
John Kitzhaber, 54, Governor of Oregon (D), born Colfax, WA, Mar 5, 1947.
Paul Sand (Paul Sanchez), 57, actor ("St. Elsewhere"; Tony Award for *Story Theatre*), born Los Angeles, CA, Mar 5, 1944.
Dean Stockwell, 65, actor (*The Boy with Green Hair*, "Quantum Leap"), born Los Angeles, CA, Mar 5, 1936.
Laurence Tisch, 78, broadcasting executive, born New York, NY, Mar 5, 1923.
Marcia Warfield, 47, actress ("Night Court," "Empty Nest"), born Chicago, IL, Mar 5, 1954.
Michael Warren, 55, actor ("Paris," "Hill Street Blues") born South Bend, IN, Mar 5, 1946.
Fred Williamson, 63, actor ("Julia," "Half Nelson"), former professional football player, born Gary, IN, Mar 5, 1938.

MARCH 6 — TUESDAY
Day 65 — 300 Remaining

BIG 12 WOMEN'S BASKETBALL TOURNAMENT. Mar 6–8. Municipal Auditorium, Kansas City, MO. Est attendance: 25,000. For info: Big 12 Conference, 2201 Stemmons Freeway, 28th Floor, Dallas, TX 75207. Phone: (214) 742-1212. Fax: (214) 742-2046. Web: www.big12sports.com.

BROWNING, ELIZABETH BARRETT: BIRTH ANNIVERSARY. Mar 6, 1806. English poet, author of *Sonnets from the Portuguese*, wife of poet Robert Browning and subject of the play *The Barretts of Wimpole Street*, was born near Durham, England. She died at Florence, Italy, June 29, 1861.

FALL OF THE ALAMO: ANNIVERSARY. Mar 6, 1836. Anniversary of the fall of the Texan fort, the Alamo. The siege, led by Mexican general Santa Anna, began Feb 23 and reached its climax Mar 6, when the last of the defenders was slain. Texans, under General Sam Houston, rallied with the war cry "Remember the Alamo" and, at the Battle of San Jacinto, Apr 21, defeated and captured Santa Anna, who signed a treaty recognizing Texas's independence.

"GENERATIONS" TV PREMIERE: ANNIVERSARY.
Mar 6, 1989. "Generations" was the first daytime serial in which one of the main families was black. Set in Chicago, the series focused on the relationships between the Marshalls and the Whitmores. The cast included Lynn Hamilton, Joan Pringle, Taurean Blacque, James Reynolds, Sharon Brown, Debbi Morgan, Jonelle Allen, Kristoff St. John, Patricia Crowley, Gail Ramsey, Gerard Prendergast and Kelly Rutherford.

GHANA: INDEPENDENCE DAY. Mar 6. National holiday. Commemorates independence from Great Britain in 1957.

"IN THE HEAT OF THE NIGHT" TV PREMIERE: ANNIVERSARY. Mar 6, 1988. NBC's police drama was based on the 1967 movie with the same name. Carroll O'Connor played Mississippi police chief Bill Gillespie who, along with Howard Rollins as Detective Virgil Tibbs, investigated crimes in the rural South. The cast featured Alan Autry as Sergeant Bubba Skinner, Anne-Marie Johnson as Virgil's wife, Althea, David Hart as Deputy Parker William, Hugh O'Connor as Deputy Lonnie Jamison, Christian LeBlanc as Deputy Junior Abernathy, Geoffrey Thorne as Deputy Sweet and Crystal Fox as dispatcher Luanne Corbin. The last telecast aired July 28, 1994, but the program remains popular in reruns.

LARDNER, RING: BIRTH ANNIVERSARY. Mar 6, 1885. Ringgold Wilmer (Ring) Lardner, sportswriter, born at Niles, MI. Lardner wrote about sports for a variety of newspapers, mostly in Chicago. In both his columns and his short stories, he reproduced ballplayers' vernacular speech patterns with great success, thereby laying the groundwork for generations of baseball fiction to come. Lardner abandoned baseball after the Black Sox scandal was exposed. He wrote songs, plays and magazine articles but never the novel that some of his friends thought he should. Taciturn and solemn with a biting sense of humor, Lardner drank and smoked to excess, even after contracting tuberculosis in 1926. Given the J.G. Taylor Spink Award in 1963. Died at East Hampton, NY, Sept 25, 1933.

MICHELANGELO: BIRTH ANNIVERSARY. Mar 6, 1475. Anniversary of the birth, at Caprese, Italy, of Michelangelo di Lodovico Buonarroti Simoni, a prolific Renaissance painter, sculptor, architect and poet who had a profound impact on Western art. Michelangelo's fresco painting on the ceiling of the Sistine Chapel at the Vatican at Rome, Italy, is often considered the pinnacle of his achievement in painting, as well as the highest achievement of the Renaissance. Also among his works were the sculptures *David* and *The Pieta*. Appointed architect of St. Peter's in 1542, a post he held until his death Feb 18, 1564, at Rome.

PEALE, ANNA CLAYPOOLE: BIRTH ANNIVERSARY. Mar 6, 1791. American painter of miniatures and a member of the famous Peale family of artists. Born at Philadelphia, PA; died Dec 25, 1878.

TASTE OF THE TOWN. Mar 6. Multi-Purpose Events Center Exhibit Hall, Wichita Falls, TX. More than 50 restaurants and vendors gather together to show off the best food in town benefiting the Wichita County Chapter of the Red Cross. Est attendance: 2,200. For info: Wichita Falls CVB, 1000 Fifth St, Wichita Falls, TX 76301. Phone: (940) 716-5500. Fax: (940) 716-5509.

TOWN MEETING DAY. Mar 6. Vermont. The first Tuesday in March is an official state holiday in Vermont. Nearly every town elects officers, approves budget items and deals with a multitude of other items in a daylong public meeting of the voters.

TRIUMPH OF AGRICULTURE EXPO. Mar 6–7. Civic Auditorium, Omaha, NE. Est attendance: 30,000. For info: Robert P. Mancuso, Mid-America Expositions, Inc, PO Box 24851, Omaha, NE 68124-0851. Phone: (402) 346-8003. Fax: (402) 346-5412. Web: www.showofficeonline.com.

BIRTHDAYS TODAY

Tom Arnold, 42, actor ("Roseanne," *McHale's Navy, True Lies*), born Ottumwa, IA, Mar 6, 1959.
Christopher Samuel Bond, 62, US Senator (R, Missouri), born St. Louis, MO, Mar 6, 1939.
Sarah Caldwell, 77, conductor, born Maryville, MO, Mar 6, 1924.
L. Gordon Cooper, 74, astronaut, born Shawnee, OK, Mar 6, 1927.

	S	M	T	W	T	F	S
March					1	2	3
2001	4	5	6	7	8	9	10
	11	12	13	14	15	16	17
	18	19	20	21	22	23	24
	25	26	27	28	29	30	31

Gabriel Garcia-Marquez, 73, Nobel Prize-winning author (*A Hundred Years of Solitude, Love in the Time of Cholera*), born Aracaracca, Colombia, Mar 6, 1928.
Dave Gilmour, 57, singer, musician (member Pink Floyd, *The Dark Side of the Moon*), born Cambridge, England, Mar 6, 1944.
Alan Greenspan, 75, economist, Chairman of the Federal Reserve Board, born New York, NY, Mar 6, 1926.
Kiri Te Kanawa, 57, opera singer, born Gisborne, New Zealand, Mar 6, 1944.
Ed McMahon, 78, actor, TV host ("The Tonight Show," "Star Search"), born Detroit, MI, Mar 6, 1923.
Ben Murphy, 59, actor ("Alias Smith and Jones," *Yours, Mine and Ours*), born Jonesboro, AR, Mar 6, 1942.
Shaquille Rashan O'Neal, 29, basketball player, born Newark, NJ, Mar 6, 1972.
Amy Pietz, 32, actress ("Caroline in the City"), born Oakcreek, WI, Mar 6, 1969.
Rob Reiner, 56, actor ("All in the Family"), director (*When Harry Met Sally. . ., This Is Spinal Tap*), born New York, NY, Mar 6, 1945.
Wilver Dornel (Willie) Stargell, 61, Baseball Hall of Fame outfielder and first baseman, born Earlsboro, OK, Mar 6, 1940.
Valentina Tereshkova-Nikolaeva, 64, cosmonaut, born Maslennikovo, USSR, Mar 6, 1937.

MARCH 7 — WEDNESDAY
Day 66 — 299 Remaining

BURBANK, LUTHER: BIRTH ANNIVERSARY. Mar 7, 1849. Anniversary of birth of American naturalist and author, creator and developer of many new varieties of flowers, fruits, vegetables and trees. Luther Burbank's birthday is observed by some as Bird and Arbor Day. Born at Lancaster, MA, he died at Santa Rosa, CA, Apr 11, 1926.

DISTINGUISHED SERVICE MEDAL: ANNIVERSARY. Mar 7, 1918. With US troops fighting in the trenches in France during the First World War, President Woodrow Wilson authorized the creation of a new bronze, beribboned medal to be given to US Army personnel who performed "exceptionally meritorious service."

HOPKINS, STEPHEN: BIRTH ANNIVERSARY. Mar 7, 1707. Colonial governor (Rhode Island) and signer of the Declaration of Independence. Born at Providence, RI, and died there July 13, 1785.

LOUISIANA SPORTSMEN'S SHOW. Mar 7–11. New Orleans, LA. 22nd annual. Louisiana's original sportfishing, hunting and boat show also covering Baton Rouge and the Gulf Coast. Est attendance: 100,000. For info: Bob Del Giorno. Phone: (504) 464-7363. Fax: (504) 835-8692. Web: www.sportsmensshow.com.

MONOPOLY INVENTED: ANNIVERSARY. Mar 7, 1933. Monopoly was mass marketed by Parker Brothers beginning in 1935.

NAIA MEN'S DIVISION II BASKETBALL NATIONAL CHAMPIONSHIP TOURNAMENT. Mar 7–13. Branson, MO. 32-team field competes for the national championship. 9th annual. Est attendance: 30,000. For info: Natl Assn of Intercollegiate Athletics, 6120 S Yale Ave, Ste 1450, Tulsa, OK 74136. Phone: (918) 494-8828. Fax: (918) 494-8841. E-mail: mchiarucci @naia.org. Web: www.naia.org.

NAIA WOMEN'S DIVISION II BASKETBALL NATIONAL CHAMPIONSHIP TOURNAMENT. Mar 7–13. Sioux City, IA. 32-team field competes for the national championship. 9th annual. Est attendance: 12,500. For info: Natl Assn of Intercollegiate Athletics, 6120 S Yale Ave, Ste 1450, Tulsa, OK 74136. Phone: (918) 494-8828. Fax: (918) 494-8841. E-mail: lheeter@naia.org. Web: www.naia.org.

NCAA MEN'S AND WOMEN'S SKIING CHAMPIONSHIPS. Mar 7–10. Middlebury College, Middlebury, VT. Est attendance: 800. For info: Natl Collegiate Athletic Assn, 700 W

Washington Ave, PO Box 6222, Indianapolis, IN 46206-6222. Phone: (317) 917-6222. Fax: (317) 917-6888. Web: www.ncaa.org.

REMAGEN BRIDGE CAPTURE: ANNIVERSARY. Mar 7, 1945. On this date in 1945, a small advance force of the US first Army captured the Ludendorff railway bridge across the Rhine River at Remagen (between Bonn and Coblenz)—the only bridge across the Rhine that had not been blown up by the German defenders—thus acquiring the first bridgehead onto the east bank and the beginning of the Allied advance into Germany, a turning point in World War II.

STOP BAD SERVICE DAY. Mar 7. Celebrating those companies that foster loyalty from customers by giving thorough, professional service. Consumers are encouraged to thank their favorite companies for offering a superior level of services. For info: Margo Chevers, PO Box 1584, Plainville, MA 02762. Phone: (508) 695-8687. Fax: (508) 643-2978. E-mail: margo@MargoChevers.com.

SUEZ CANAL OPENS: ANNIVERSARY. Mar 7, 1869. This waterway across Egypt connecting the Mediterranean and Red seas was built by the French. In 1956, Egyptian president Nasser nationalized the canal, prompting an invasion by the British, French and Israelis. The Six-Day War in 1967 shut down the canal for eight years.

BIRTHDAYS TODAY

Anthony Armstrong-Jones (Lord Snowdon), 71, photographer, born London, England, Mar 7, 1930.
Taylor Dayne, 39, singer ("Love Will Send You Back"), born Long Island, NY, Mar 7, 1962.
Michael Eisner, 59, Disney executive, born Mount Kisco, NY, Mar 7, 1942.
Janet Guthrie, 63, former auto racer, born Iowa City, IA, Mar 7, 1938.
Franco Harris, 51, Pro Football Hall of Fame running back, born Fort Dix, NJ, Mar 7, 1950.
John Heard, 55, actor (*The Milagro Beanfield War, Rambling Rose, The Pelican Brief*), born Washington, DC, Mar 7, 1946.
Ivan Lendl, 41, former tennis player, born Ostrava, Czechoslovakia, Mar 7, 1960.
Willard Herman Scott, 67, weatherman ("Today Show"), friend of centenarians, born Alexandria, VA, Mar 7, 1934.
Daniel J. Travanti, 61, actor ("Hill Street Blues"), born Kenosha, WI, Mar 7, 1940.
Peter Wolf, 55, lead singer (J. Geils Band, "Centerfold"), born Boston, MA, Mar 7, 1946.

MARCH 8 — THURSDAY
Day 67 — 298 Remaining

BEAVERS, LOUISE: BIRTH ANNIVERSARY. Mar 8, 1902. The Hollywood career of Louise Beavers spanned 30 years and more than 125 films. Though she was forced to play stereotypical roles, such as those of maids, her authentic talent was always apparent. Her starring role in the film *Imitation of Life* earned her high praise. Beavers was a member of the Black Filmmakers Hall of Fame. She also played the title role in the TV series "Beulah" (1951–53). Born at Cincinnati, OH; died at Los Angeles, Oct 26, 1962.

BIG TEN MEN'S BASKETBALL TOURNAMENT. Mar 8–11. Chicago, IL. For info: Sue Ryan, Big Ten Conference, 1500 W Higgins Rd, Park Ridge, IL 60068-6300. Phone: (847) 696-1010. Fax: (847) 696-1110. Web: www.bigten.org or www.bigtenchampionships.com.

BIG 12 MEN'S BASKETBALL CHAMPIONSHIP. Mar 8–11. Kemper Arena, Kansas City, MO. Est attendance: 75,000. For info: Big 12 Conference, 2201 Stemmons Freeway, 28th Floor, Dallas, TX 75207. Phone: (214) 742-1212. Fax: (214) 742-2046. Web: www.big12sports.com.

CAXTON'S *MIRROR OF THE WORLD* TRANSLATION: ANNIVERSARY. Mar 8, 1481. William Caxton, England's first printer, completed the translation from French into English of *The Mirror of the World*, a popular account of astronomy and other sciences. In print soon afterward, *Mirror of the World* became the first illustrated book printed in England.

ENGLAND: CRUFTS DOG SHOW. Mar 8–11. National Exhibition Centre, Birmingham, West Midlands. The world's greatest dog show where more than 21,000 top pedigree dogs compete to achieve the title of "Best in Show," the most prestigious award in the world of dogs. Held since 1859. Est attendance: 110,000. For info: Events Department, The Kennel Club, 1 Clarges St, London, England W1Y 8AB. Phone: (44) (171) 493-7838. Fax: (44) (171) 518-1028. Ticket info: (44) (171) 518-1012. Web: www.crufts.org.uk.

GRAHAME, KENNETH: BIRTH ANNIVERSARY. Mar 8, 1859. Scottish author, born at Edinburgh. His children's book, *The Wind in the Willows*, has as its main characters a mole, a rat, a badger and a toad. He died July 6, 1932, at Pangbourne, Berkshire.

INTERNATIONAL (WORKING) WOMEN'S DAY. Mar 8. A day to honor women, especially working women. Said to commemorate an 1857 march and demonstration at New York, NY, by female garment and textile workers. Believed to have been first proclaimed for this date at an international conference of women held at Helsinki, Finland, in 1910, "that henceforth Mar 8 should be declared International Women's Day." The 50th anniversary observance, at Peking, China, in 1960, cited Clara Zetkin (1857–1933) as "initiator of Women's Day on Mar 8." This is perhaps the most widely observed holiday of recent origin and is unusual among holidays originating in the US in having been widely adopted and observed in other nations, including socialist countries. In Russia it is a national holiday, and flowers or gifts are presented to women workers.

KNOXVILLE BOAT SHOW. Mar 8–11. Knoxville Convention Center, Knoxville, TN. 18th annual show featuring more than 50,000 sq ft of boats and 70 booths displaying scuba and marine equipment, water skis and more. Est attendance: 14,000. For info: Cindy Crabtree, Event Coord, ESAU, Inc, PO Box 50096, Knoxville, TN 37950. Phone: (865) 588-1233 or (800) 588-ESAU. Fax: (865) 588-6938. Web: www.esaushows.com.

MOSBY CAPTURES STOUGHTON: ANNIVERSARY. Mar 8, 1863. In a daring raid with his commando-style raiders, Colonel John Mosby captured Union General E.H. Stoughton from his headquarters in Fairfax County Courthouse in Virginia on this date. Mosby's irregular forces patrolled a northern area of Virginia that became known as Mosby's Confederacy. Supported by the local populace and reviled by his Northern enemies, Mosby's Rangers were one of the most successful of the Southern irregular forces.

RUSSIA: INTERNATIONAL WOMEN'S DAY. Mar 8. National holiday.

SYRIAN ARAB REPUBLIC REVOLUTION DAY: ANNIVERSARY. Mar 8, 1963. Official public holiday commemorating assumption of power by Revolutionary National Council.

TA'ANIT ESTHER (FAST OF ESTHER). Mar 8. Hebrew calendar date: Adar 13, 5761. Commemorates Queen Esther's fast, in the 6th century BC, to save the Jews of ancient Persia. Ordinarily observed Adar 13, the Fast of Esther is observed on the previous Thursday (Adar 11) when Adar 13 is a Sabbath.

UNITED NATIONS: INTERNATIONAL WOMEN'S DAY. Mar 8. An international day observed by the organizations of the United Nations system. Info from: United Nations, Dept of Public Info, New York, NY 10017.

UNIVERSAL WOMEN'S WEEK. Mar 8–14. To remind ourselves and others of the value of women of all ages and classes and of their rights and dignity, and to honor outstanding women in the fields of government, business, industry, science, health, education, social work and the cultural arts by election to Universal Hall of Fame. Please send $4 to cover expense of printing, handling and postage. Annually, Mar 8-14. For info: Dr. Stanley Drake, Pres, Intl Soc of Friendship and Good Will, 8592 Roswell Rd, Ste 434, Atlanta, GA 30350-1870.

UPPITY WOMEN DAY. Mar 8. Uppity women from around the world unite in their ability to be themselves, no matter the place and time. For info: Teresa Coronado, 2550 Ninth St, Ste 101, Berkeley, CA 94710. Phone: (510) 649-7190. Fax: (510) 649-7190. E-mail: tcoronado@conari.com. Web: www.conari.com.

US INCOME TAX: ANNIVERSARY. Mar 8, 1913. The Internal Revenue Service began to levy and collect income taxes. The 16th Amendment to the Constitution, ratified Feb 3, 1913, gave Congress the authority to tax income. The US had also levied an income tax during the Civil War. See also: "Lincoln Signs Income Tax" (July 1).

VAN BUREN, HANNAH HOES: BIRTH ANNIVERSARY. Mar 8, 1783. Wife of Martin Van Buren, 8th president of the US. Born at Kinderhook, NY, she died at Albany, NY, Feb 5, 1819.

VIRGINIA SPRING SHOW. Mar 8-11. Showplace Exhibition Center, Richmond, VA. Features hundreds of artisans and craftspeople, food shops, spring entertainment. Holiday Cooking Theatre. 14th annual show. Est attendance: 25,000. For info: Virginia Show Productions, PO Box 305, Chase City, VA 23924. Phone: (804) 372-3996. Fax: (804) 372-3410.

WORLD'S LARGEST CONCERT. Mar 8 (tentative). To celebrate Music in Our Schools Month, the World's Largest Concert is broadcast on PBS stations nationwide and the Armed Forces Television Network overseas. Theme for the 2001 concert is "Music . . . Pass It On!" Send $5 to cover shipping for "Teacher's Guide." Awareness items also available. For info: Deidre Healy, Mgr Special Programs, Music Educators Natl Conference, 1806 Robert Fulton Dr, Reston, VA 20191. Phone: (800) 336-3768. Web: www.menc.org.

BIRTHDAYS TODAY

Cyd Charisse (Tula Finklea), 78, actress (*Silk Stockings*), dancer (*Grand Hotel, Singin' in the Rain*), born Amarillo, TX, Mar 8, 1923.

Susan Clark, 61, actress ("Webster," *Babe*), born Sarnia, Ontario, Canada, Mar 8, 1940.

Micky Dolenz, 56, singer ("I'm a Believer"), actor ("The Monkees," "Circus Boy"), born Los Angeles, CA, Mar 8, 1945.

Kathy Ireland, 38, model, born Santa Barbara, CA, Mar 8, 1963.

Camryn Manheim, 40, actress ("The Practice"), born Caldwell, NJ, Mar 8, 1961.

Freddie Prinze, Jr, 25, actor (*She's All That, I Know What You Did Last Summer*), born Albuquerque, NM, Mar 8, 1976.

Aidan Quinn, 42, actor (*Desperately Seeking Susan*; stage: *A Streetcar Named Desire*), born Chicago, IL, Mar 8, 1959.

Lynn Redgrave, 58, actress (*Georgy Girl*, "House Calls"), born London, England, Mar 8, 1943.

James Edward (Jim) Rice, 48, former baseball player, born Anderson, SC, Mar 8, 1953.

Carole Bayer Sager, 54, singer, songwriter ("That's What Friends Are For," with Burt Bacharach), born New York, NY, Mar 8, 1947.

Raynoma (Mayberry Liles) Gordy Singleton, 64, cofounder of Motown, born Detroit, MI, Mar 8, 1937.

James Van Der Beek, 24, actor ("Dawson's Creek"), born Cheshire, CT, Mar 8, 1977.

	March **2001**	S	M	T	W	T	F	S
						1	2	3
		4	5	6	7	8	9	10
		11	12	13	14	15	16	17
		18	19	20	21	22	23	24
		25	26	27	28	29	30	31

MARCH 9 — FRIDAY
Day 68 — 297 Remaining

ADAMS, RICHARD C.: DEATH ANNIVERSARY. Mar 9, 1988. Richard C. Adams, challenged by the shortage of paintbrushes during World War II, invented the paint roller in 1940, while working in his basement. Adams died at La Mesa, CA.

ALL-NORTHWEST BARBERSHOP BALLAD CONTEST. Mar 9-10. Pacific University, Forest Grove, OR. Barbershop quartets from throughout the Pacific Northwest compete in an 1890s setting. Est attendance: 3,000. For info: Forest Grove Chamber of Commerce, 2417 Pacific Ave, Forest Grove, OR 97116. Phone: (503) 357-3006 or (503) 292-5673. Fax: (503) 357-2367. E-mail: fgchamber@grovenet.net.

AMA NATIONAL HOT-SHOE DIRT TRACK. Mar 9. Daytona Beach Municipal Stadium, Daytona Beach, FL. 11th annual. For info: Daytona Intl Speedway, Box 2801, Daytona Beach, FL 32120-2801. Phone: (904) 947-6782. Fax: (904) 947-6791. Web: www.daytonausa.com.

BARBIE DEBUTS: ANNIVERSARY. Mar 9, 1959. The popular girls' doll debuted in stores. More than 800 million dolls have been sold.

BATTLE OF THE *MONITOR* AND *MERRIMAC*. Mar 9, 1862. Two ironclad ships, the Union's *Monitor* and the Confederacy's *Merrimac* (renamed *Virginia*), battled at Hampton Roads, VA. The battle ended in a draw. See also: "*Monitor* Sinking: Anniv" (Dec 30) and "*Merrimac* Destroyed: Anniv" (May 11).

BELIZE: BARON BLISS DAY. Mar 9. Official public holiday. Celebrated in honor of Sir Henry Edward Ernest Victor Bliss, a great benefactor of Belize.

CAMDEN DAFFODIL FESTIVAL. Mar 9-10. Camden, AR. 7th annual. A gardening festival. Acres of daffodils, crafters, antique car show, musical entertainment, Japanese garden, historic homes tour, children's activities, food vendors, private garden tours, antiques and collectibles show and scenic drives. Annually, the second weekend in March. Est attendance: 6,250. For info: Clara Freeland, PO Box 693, Camden, AR 71701. Phone: (870) 836-0023. Fax: (870) 836-0203. E-mail: Lucy2022 @cei.net.

CRAFTSMEN'S CLASSIC ARTS & CRAFTS FESTIVAL. Mar 9-11. Richmond Raceway Complex, Richmond, VA. Arts and crafts. Est attendance: 20,000. For info: Gilmore Enterprises, Inc, 1240 Oakland Ave, Greensboro, NC 27403. Phone: (336) 274-5550. Fax: (336) 274-1084.

"FAMILY" TV PREMIERE: 25th ANNIVERSARY. Mar 9, 1976. ABC drama about the Lawrence family living in Pasadena, CA, who stuck together through trials and triumphs. Cast members included Sada Thompson as Kate Lawrence, James Broderick as her husband Douglas, Elayne Heilveil and Meredith Baxter-Birney as their divorced daughter Nancy Maitland, Gary Frank as their son Willie and Kristy McNichol as youngest daughter Buddy (Letitia). The last episode aired on June 25, 1980.

GAGARIN, YURI ALEXSEYEVICH: BIRTH ANNIVERSARY. Mar 9, 1934. Russian cosmonaut Yuri Gagarin, the first person to travel in space, was born at Gzhatsk, USSR. The 27-year-old Soviet Air Force major made his flight Apr 12, 1961, lasting 108 minutes and orbiting Earth in a rocket-propelled, five-ton space capsule, 187 miles above the Earth's surface. Gagarin was killed in an airplane crash near Moscow, USSR, Mar 27, 1968. After his death the town in which he was born was renamed Gagarin, and the Gagarin Museum was established in the frame house where he spent his childhood.

GRANT COMMISSIONED COMMANDER OF ALL UNION ARMIES: ANNIVERSARY. Mar 9, 1864. At Washington, DC, Ulysses S. Grant accepted his commission as Lieutenant General, becoming the commander of all the Union armies.

INDIA: HOLI. Mar 9. In this spring festival people run through the streets smearing each other with brightly hued powders and colored water. This is observed by Indians without regard to caste. Huge bonfires are built on the eve of Holi. Because there is no one universally accepted Hindu calendar, this holiday may be celebrated on a different date in some parts of India but it always falls in February or March.

JULIA, RAUL: BIRTH ANNIVERSARY. Mar 9, 1940. Born at San Juan, Puerto Rico, Julia won acclaim and four Tony nominations for roles he played on Broadway ranging from Shakespeare's *Proteus* to *Mack the Knife.* Most widely known of his many film roles are Gomez in *The Addams Family* and Valentín in *Kiss of the Spider Woman.* Julia died Oct 24, 1994, at Manhasset, NY.

LONGHORN WORLD CHAMPIONSHIP RODEO. Mar 9–11. BI-LO Center, Greenville, SC. More than 200 cowboys and cowgirls compete in six professional contests ranging from bronc riding to bull riding for top prize money and world championship points. Featuring colorful opening pageantry and Big, Bad BONUS Bulls. 29th annual. Est attendance: 24,000. For info: W. Bruce Lehrke, Pres, Longhorn World Championship Rodeo, Inc, PO Box 70159, Nashville, TN 37207. Phone: (615) 876-1016. Fax: (615) 876-4685. E-mail: lhrodeo@idt.net. Web: www.long hornrodeo.com.

MIDNIGHT AT THE OASIS. Mar 9–11. Ray Kroc Complex/Desert Sun Stadium, Yuma, AZ. Stroll down memory lane at an incredible nostalgic festival featuring the cars and music of the '50s and '60s. Limited to 800 '72 and older American cars and trucks and foreign classics. Show & Shine, Rock 'n Roll Concert and Dance, vendors, activities and entertainment for the whole family. Est attendance: 50,000. For info: Caballeros de Yuma, PO Box 5987, Yuma, AZ 85366. Phone: (520) 343-1715. Fax: (520) 783-1609. Web: www.caballeros.org.

MOON PHASE: FULL MOON. Mar 9. Moon enters Full Moon phase at 12:23 PM, EST.

NCAA DIVISION I INDOOR TRACK CHAMPIONSHIPS. Mar 9–10. Fayetteville, AR. Annually, the second weekend in March. Est attendance: 7,000. For info: Natl Collegiate Athletic Assn, 700 W Washington Ave, PO Box 6222, Indianapolis, IN 46206-6222. Phone: (317) 917-6222. Fax: (317) 917-6888. Web: www.ncaa.org.

PANIC DAY. Mar 9. Run around all day in a panic, telling others you can't handle it anymore. [© 2000 by WH] For info: Tom or Ruth Roy, Wellcat Holidays, 2418 Long Ln, Lebanon, PA 17046. Phone: (717) 279-0184. E-mail: wellcat@supernet.com. Web: www .wellcat.com.

PEACE PRIZE FORUM 2001. Mar 9–10. Luther College, Decorah. IA. Held in cooperation with the Norwegian Nobel Institute in Oslo, the annual Peace Prize Forum offers an opportunity for Nobel Peace Prize laureates, diplomats, scholars, students and the general public to take part in a dialogue on the causes of conflict in society and the dynamics of peacemaking. The forum is hosted on a rotating basis by five Lutheran colleges of Norwegian heritage: Augsburg College, Augustana College, Concordia College, St. Olaf and Luther College , the host for 2001. This year's forum, "Striving for Peace: Crossing Borders—Challenging Boundaries," will honor Doctors Without Borders. Est attendance: 1,500. For info: Carol Birkland, Luther College, 700 College Dr, Decorah, IA 52101. Phone: (319) 387-1271. E-mail: birklaca @luther.edu. Web: www.luther.edu.

PHEASANT RUN ANTIQUE SHOW. Mar 9–11 (also Nov 3–5). St. Charles, IL. More than 150 dealers from Minnesota to Florida display their wares including jewelry, rare books, pottery, postcards, decorative lighting, glass and more. Parking is free and return passes are available throughout the weekend at no additional fee. Admission is $6. Est attendance: 7,000. For info: Laura Kennedy, Kennedy Productions, Inc, 1208 Lisle Place, Lisle, IL 60532. Phone: (630) 515-1160. Fax: (630) 515-1165.

PURIM. Mar 9. Hebrew calendar date: Adar 14, 5761. Feasts, gifts, charity and the reading of the Book of Esther mark this joyous commemoration of Queen Esther's intervention, in the 6th century BC, to save the Jews of ancient Persia. Haman's plot to exterminate the Jews was thwarted, and he was hanged on the very day he had set for execution of the Jews.

RATTLESNAKE ROUNDUP. Mar 9–11. Sweetwater, TX. Educational programs about rattlesnakes, flea market, gun, knife, and coin show, large cookoff, dances, numerous pounds of live rattlesnakes on display, snake meat available to eat and snake articles for sale. Snake hunts and bus tours available. Annually, the second weekend in March. Est attendance: 30,000. For info: Sweetwater Chamber of Commerce, PO Box 1148, Sweetwater, TX 79556. Phone: (915) 235-5488 or (800) 658-6757. Fax: (915) 235-1026. E-mail: swater@camalott.com. Web: camalott.com /~sweetwater.

SAINT FRANCES OF ROME: FEAST DAY. Mar 9. Patron of motorists and model for housewives and widows (1384–1440). After 40 years of marriage she was widowed in 1436 and later joined the community of Benedictine Oblates. Canonized in 1608.

SUGARLOAF'S SPRING SOMERSET CRAFT FESTIVAL. Mar 9–11. Garden State Exhibit Center, Somerset, NJ. This show, now in its 8th year, features 250 nationally recognized craft designers and fine artists displaying and selling their original creations. Craft demonstrations, hourly gift certificate drawings and more! Est attendance: 13,000. For info: Sugarloaf Mountain Works, Inc, 200 Orchard Ridge Dr, #215, Gaithersburg, MD 20878. Phone: (800) 210-9900. E-mail: smworks @sugarloafcrafts.com. Web: www.sugarloafcrafts.com.

TOKYO BLANKET BOMBING: ANNIVERSARY. Mar 9, 1945. The Japanese capital of Tokyo was bombed by 343 Superfortresses carrying all the incendiary bombs they could hold. Within the targeted areas of the city, population densities were four times greater than those of most American cities, and homes were made primarily of wood and paper. Carried by the wind, the fires leveled 16 sq miles. More than a quarter million buildings were destroyed, including 18% of the industrial area. The death toll was 83,000; 41,000 were injured. For the balance of WWII American strategic bombing followed this pattern.

VESPUCCI, AMERIGO: BIRTH ANNIVERSARY. Mar 9, 1451. Italian navigator, merchant and explorer for whom the Americas were named. Born at Florence, Italy. He participated in at least two expeditions between 1499 and 1502 which took him to the coast of South America, where he discovered the Amazon and Plata rivers. Vespucci's expeditions were of great importance because he believed that he had discovered a new continent, not just a new route to the Orient. Neither Vespucci nor his exploits achieved the fame of Columbus, but the New World was to be named for Amerigo Vespucci by an obscure German geographer and mapmaker, Martin Waldseemuller. Ironically, in his work as an outfitter of ships, Vespucci had been personally acquainted with Christopher Columbus. Vespucci died at Seville, Spain, Feb 22, 1512. See also: "Waldseemuller, Martin: Remembrance Day" (Apr 25).

VICTORIAN HOLMES WEEKEND. Mar 9–11. Cape May, NJ. A weekend of mystery and intrigue awaits amateur sleuths when Cape May celebrates the works of Sir Arthur Conan Doyle, creator of Sherlock Holmes. Est attendance: 200. For info: Mid-Atlantic Center for the Arts, 1048 Washington St, PO Box 340, Cape May, NJ 08204. Phone: (609) 884-5404. Fax: (609) 884-2006. E-mail: mac4arts@algorithms.com. Web: www.capemaymac.org.

BIRTHDAYS TODAY

Juliette Binoche, 37, actress (*The English Patient*), born Paris, France, Mar 9, 1964.

Linda Fiorentino, 41, actress (*Men in Black*), born Philadelphia, PA, Mar 9, 1960.

Robert James (Bobby) Fischer, 58, World Chess Champion (1972), born Chicago, IL, Mar 9, 1943.

Mickey Gilley, 65, singer, musician ("City Lights," "Stand by Me"), cousin of Jerry Lee Lewis, born Natchez, MS, Mar 9, 1936.

Marty Ingels, 65, actor ("I'm Dickens . . . He's Fenster," *A Guide for the Married Man*), born Brooklyn, NY, Mar 9, 1936.

David Hume Kennerly, 54, photographer, born Rosenburg, OR, Mar 9, 1947.

Emmanuel Lewis, 30, actor ("Webster"), born Brooklyn, NY, Mar 9, 1971.

Terence John (Terry) Mulholland, 38, baseball player, born St. Paul, MN, Mar 9, 1963.

Jeffrey Osborne, 53, musician, songwriter, born Providence, RI, Mar 9, 1948.

Benito Santiago, 36, baseball player, born Ponce, Puerto Rico, Mar 9, 1965.

Mickey Spillane (Frank Morrison), 83, author (*The Killing Man, Vengeance Is Mine*), born Brooklyn, NY, Mar 9, 1918.

Trish Van Devere, 58, actress (*Where's Poppa?, One Is a Lonely Number*), born Tenafly, NJ, Mar 9, 1943.

Joyce Van Patten, 67, actress (*Monkey Shines*, "The Goodbye Guys"), born Queens, NY, Mar 9, 1934.

MARCH 10 — SATURDAY
Day 69 — 296 Remaining

AMA GRAND NATIONAL KICKOFF DIRT TRACK. Mar 10. Daytona Beach Municipal Stadium, Daytona Beach, FL. 13th annual. For info: Daytona Intl Speedway, Box 2801, Daytona Beach, FL 32120-2801. Phone: (904) 947-6782. Fax: (904) 947-6791. Web: www.daytonausa.com.

BEACH PARTY. Mar 10. Deadwood, SD. 15th annual. Forget Ft Lauderdale for spring break! Head to the beach at the #10. Sand, hot tub, beach hats, music and limbo contests. Est attendance: 400. For info: Old Style Saloon #10, 657 Main St, Deadwood, SD 57732. Phone: (605) 578-3346 or (800) 952-9398. Fax: (605) 578-1944. E-mail: saloon10@deadwood.net. Web: www.saloon10.com.

BRUSH COUNTRY ANTIQUE SHOW & SALE. Mar 10–11. Kingsville, TX. An outstanding show and sale full of unique and antique collectibles, treasures and gifts. For info: Kingsville CVB, 1501 N Hwy 77, Kingsville, TX 78364-1562. Phone: (800) 333-5032. Fax: (361) 592-3227. E-mail: cvb@kingsvilletexas.com. Web: www.kingsvilletexas.com.

CANADIAN-AMERICAN DAYS FEST. Mar 10–18. Myrtle Beach, SC. Concerts, square dances, beach games and sports events. Est attendance: 100,000. For info: Holly T Fields, Mgr, Myrtle Beach Area Chamber of Commerce, PO Box 2115, Myr-

March 2001	S	M	T	W	T	F	S
					1	2	3
	4	5	6	7	8	9	10
	11	12	13	14	15	16	17
	18	19	20	21	22	23	24
	25	26	27	28	29	30	31

tle Beach, SC 29578. Phone: (843) 626-7444. Fax: (843) 626-0009. Web: www.myrtlebeachlive.com.

DAYTONA SUPERCROSS BY HONDA. Mar 10. Daytona International Speedway, Daytona Beach, FL. 31st annual. One of the most famous and toughest Supercross races in the world. Sponsor: Honda. For info: Daytona Intl Speedway, PO Box 2801, Daytona Beach, FL 32120-2801. Phone: (904) 947-6782. Fax: (904) 947-6791. Web: www.daytonausa.com.

GIRL SCOUT SABBATH. Mar 10. Girl Scouts of Jewish faith worship together in the temple of their choice. For info: Media Services, Girl Scouts of the USA, 420 Fifth Ave, New York, NY 10018. Phone: (212) 852-8000. Fax: (212) 852-6514. Web: www.gsusa.org.

HIGHLAND COUNTY MAPLE FESTIVAL. Mar 10–11 (also Mar 17–18). Highland County, VA. To welcome visitors to view the process of syrup making. Large craft shows. Est attendance: 60,000. For info: Highland County Chamber of Commerce, PO Box 223, Monterey, VA 24465. Phone: (540) 468-2550. Fax: (540) 468-2551. E-mail: highcc@cfw.com. Web: www.highlandcounty.org.

"THE INCREDIBLE HULK" TV PREMIERE: ANNIVERSARY. Mar 10, 1978. A wonderfully campy action series based on the popular Marvel comic books as well as a modern-day Jekyll and Hyde story. Bill Bixby played the erudite scientist, Dr. David Banner, who accidentally exposed himself to gamma radiation. When provoked, Banner metamorphosed into the shirt-shredding, body-baring, green-skinned, snarling neanderthal Hulk. The 6'5", 275-lb former Mr Universe, Lou Ferrigno, played the largely non-speaking part of the Hulk.

INDIANA FLOWER AND PATIO SHOW. Mar 10–18. Indiana State Fairgrounds Event Center, Indianapolis, IN. The oldest show of its kind in the Midwest, featuring 20 landscaped gardens and products and services for home, yard and patio. Est attendance: 100,000. For info: Debbie Bossi, Show Mgr, HSI Show Productions, Box 502797, Indianapolis, IN 46250. Phone: (317) 576-9933. Fax: (317) 576-9955.

JUPITER EFFECT: ANNIVERSARY. Mar 10, 1982. The much-talked-about and sometimes-feared planetary configuration of a semi-alignment of the planets on the same side of the sun occurred on this date without causing any of the disasters or unusual natural phenomena that some had predicted.

LUCE, CLARE BOOTHE: BIRTH ANNIVERSARY. Mar 10, 1903. Playwright and politician Clare Boothe Luce was born at New York City. Luce wrote for and edited *Vogue* and *Vanity Fair* as well as writing plays, three of which were later adapted into motion pictures—*The Women* (1936), *Kiss the Boys Goodbye* (1938) and *Margin of Error* (1939). She served in the US House of Representatives (1943–47) and as ambassador to Italy (1953–56)—the first woman appointed ambassador to a major country. Luce died Oct 9, 1987, at Washington, DC.

MALPIGHI, MARCELLO: BIRTH ANNIVERSARY. Mar 10, 1628. Italian physician, physiologist, author and teacher, called the "father of microscopic anatomy." Born near Bologna, Italy, Malpighi was a pioneer in the use of the microscope for biological and botanical study. Died at Rome, Italy, Nov 30, 1694.

MARIO DAY. Mar 10. A day for all persons named Mario. Using the abbreviation for the month of March, i.e., MAR, with the day, i.e., 10, you get the name spelled out: MAR10. Annually, Mar 10. For info: Mario Fascitelli, 6005 Osuna Rd, NE, Albuquerque, NM 87109. Phone: (505) 881-2414. Fax: (505) 889-8661. E-mail: C21Allied@aol.com.

NATIONAL SKI-JORING FINALS. Mar 10–11. Red Lodge Rodeo Grounds, Red Lodge, MT. Horsemen and skiers provide action entertainment. Derived from the Scandinavian sport of pulling a skier behind a horse, Ski-joring has evolved from a leisure winter diversion into lively, regulated competition. Annually, the second weekend in March. Est attendance: 4,000. For info: Red Lodge Chamber of Commerce, Box 988, Red Lodge,

MT 59068. Phone: (888) 281-0625. Fax: (406) 446-1718. E-mail: information@redlodge.com. Web: www.redlodge.com.

NETHERLANDS: EUROPEAN FINE ART FAIR. Mar 10–18. MECC, Maastricht. Old Master paintings, antiques, textile arts, modern paintings and sculptures, antiquities, books and prints. Annually, in March. Est attendance: 60,000. For info: The European Fine Art Fdtn, PO Box 1035, 5200 BA's Hertogenbosch, Netherlands. Phone: 00 31 73 6145165. E-mail: info@tefaf.com. Web: www.tefaf.com.

PREMIERE ANTIQUE SHOW. Mar 10–11. The American Club, Kohler, WI. Discerning collectors find a wide variety of antiques, furniture, silver, linens, laces and jewelry from some of the Midwest's finest antique dealers. With a variety of outstanding displays, often highlighted with rare items, the show covers more than 10,000 square feet of space in the American Club's Grand Hall of the Great Lakes conference level. Est attendance: 1,500. For info: The American Club, Highland Dr, Kohler, WI 53044. Phone: (800) 344-2838. Fax: (920) 457-0299. Web: www.americanclub.com.

SALVATION ARMY IN THE US: ANNIVERSARY. Mar 10, 1880. Commissioner George Scott Railton and seven women officers landed at New York to officially begin the work of the Salvation Army in the US.

TELEPHONE INVENTION: 125th ANNIVERSARY. Mar 10, 1876. Alexander Graham Bell transmitted the first telephone message to his assistant in the next room: "Mr Watson, come here, I want you," at Cambridge, MA. See also: "Bell, Alexander Graham: Birth Anniversary" (Mar 3).

TUBMAN, HARRIET: DEATH ANNIVERSARY. Mar 10, 1913. American abolitionist, Underground Railroad leader, born a slave at Bucktown, Dorchester County, MD, about 1820 or 1821. She escaped from a Maryland plantation in 1849 and later helped more than 300 slaves reach freedom. Died at Auburn, NY.

US PAPER MONEY ISSUED: ANNIVERSARY. Mar 10, 1862. The first paper money was issued in the US on this date. The denominations were $5 (Hamilton), $10 (Lincoln) and $20 (Liberty). They became legal tender by Act of Mar 17, 1862.

WALD, LILLIAN D.: BIRTH ANNIVERSARY. Mar 10, 1867. American sociologist, founder of the Henry Street Settlement at New York City and of the first nonsectarian public health nursing service. Born at Cincinnati, OH; died at Westport, CT, Sept 1, 1940, at age 73.

BIRTHDAYS TODAY

Edie Brickell, 35, folksinger (New Bohemians), born Oak Cliff, TX, Mar 10, 1966.

Heywood Hale Broun, 83, broadcaster, born New York, NY, Mar 10, 1918.

Kim Campbell, 54, first woman prime minister of Canada (for five months in 1993), born Vancouver Island, British Columbia, Canada, Mar 10, 1947.

Prince Edward, 37, son of Queen Elizabeth II, born London, England, Mar 10, 1964.

Bob Greene, 54, journalist, born Columbus, OH, Mar 10, 1947.

Jasmine Guy, 37, singer, actress ("A Different World"), born Boston, MA, Mar 10, 1964.

Shannon Miller, 24, gymnast, born Edmond, OK, Mar 10, 1977.

Chuck Norris, 61, actor (*Missing in Action*, "Walker, Texas Ranger"), born Ryan, OK, Mar 10, 1940.

David Rabe, 61, playwright, born Dubuque, IA, Mar 10, 1940.

Sharon Stone, 43, actress (*Basic Instinct, The Specialist, Casino*), born Meadville, PA, Mar 10, 1958.

Shannon Tweed, 44, actress ("Pacific Blue," *Detroit Rock City*), born St. John's, Newfoundland, Canada, Mar 10, 1957.

MARCH 11 — SUNDAY
Day 70 — 295 Remaining

BUREAU OF INDIAN AFFAIRS ESTABLISHED: ANNIVERSARY. Mar 11, 1824. The US War Department created the Bureau of Indian Affairs.

CAMPBELL, MALCOLM: BIRTH ANNIVERSARY. Mar 11, 1885. Record-making British auto racer, the first man to travel five miles a minute (300 mph) in an automobile. Born at Chislehurst, Kent, England, Mar 11, 1885. Died at his home at Surrey, England, Dec 31, 1948.

DAYTONA 200 AMA SUPERBIKE CLASSIC. Mar 11. Daytona International Speedway, Daytona Beach, FL. Motorcycle road race for superbikes. 60th annual. Sponsor: Arai Helmets. For info: Daytona Intl Speedway, PO Box 2801, Daytona Beach, FL 32120-2801. Phone: (904) 947-6782. Fax: (904) 947-6791. Web: www.daytonausa.com.

DREAM 2001 DAY. Mar 11. To focus attention on the new millennium so that 2001 is devoted by all humans, nations and institutions to unparalleled dreams for a better world and thinking, action, inspiration, determination and love to solve the remaining problems and to achieve a peaceful, united human family on Earth. Those words are from *My Dream 2000*, by Robert Muller, called the Millennium Man. Send for a copy of *My Dream 2000* in English, Russian, Spanish and several other languages. For info: Barbara Gaughen-Muller, Pres, Gaughen Global Public Relations, 7456 Evergreen Dr, Santa Barbara, CA 93117. Phone: (805) 968-8567. Fax: (805) 968-5747. E-mail: barbara@rain.org.

GIRL SCOUT SUNDAY. Mar 11. Girl Scouts worship together in the place of their choice. For info: Media Services, Girl Scouts of the USA, 420 Fifth Ave, New York, NY 10018. Phone: (212) 852-8000. Fax: (212) 852-6514. Web: www.gsusa.org.

GIRL SCOUT WEEK. Mar 11–17. To observe the anniversary of the founding of the Girl Scouts of the USA, the largest voluntary organization for girls and women in the world, which began Mar 12, 1912. Special observances include: Girl Scout Sabbath, Mar 11, Girl Scout Sunday, Mar 12, when Girl Scouts gather to attend religious services together, and Girl Scout Birthday, Mar 12. For info: Media Services, Girl Scouts of the USA, 420 Fifth Ave, New York, NY 10018. Phone: (212) 852-8000. Fax: (212) 852-6514. Web: www.gsusa.org.

JOHNNY APPLESEED DAY (JOHN CHAPMAN DEATH ANNIVERSARY). Mar 11, 1845. Anniversary of the death of John Chapman, better known as Johnny Appleseed, believed to have been born at Leominster, MA, Sept 26, 1774. The planter of orchards and friend of wild animals was regarded by the Indians as a great medicine man. He died at Allen County, IN. See also: "Johnny Appleseed: Birth Anniversary" (Sept 26).

LEND-LEASE PROGRAM BEGINS: 60th ANNIVERSARY. Mar 11, 1941. The Lend-Lease Bill, which enabled Britain to borrow money from the US to buy food and arms during World War II, went into effect.

LITHUANIA: RESTITUTION OF INDEPENDENCE DAY. Mar 11. National holiday. Commemorates independence from the Soviet Union in 1990. Lithuania had initially declared its independence in 1918 but lost it to the Soviet Union in 1940.

PAINE, ROBERT TREAT: BIRTH ANNIVERSARY. Mar 11, 1731. Jurist and signer of the Declaration of Independence. Born at Boston, MA; died there May 11, 1814.

PANDEMIC OF 1918 HITS US: ANNIVERSARY. Mar 11, 1918. The first cases of the "Spanish" influenza were reported in the US when 107 soldiers became sick at Fort Riley, KS. By the end of 1920 nearly 25 percent of the US population had had it. As many as 500,000 civilians died from the virus, exceeding the number of US troops killed abroad in WWI. Worldwide, more than 1 percent of the global population, or 22 million people, had died by 1920. The origin of the virus was never determined absolutely, though it was probably somewhere in Asia. The name "Spanish" influenza came from the relatively high number of cases in that country early in the epidemic. Due to the panic, cancellation of public events was common and many public service workers wore masks on the job. Emergency tent hospitals were set up in some locations due to overcrowding.

PEDIATRIC NURSE PRACTITIONER WEEK. Mar 11–17. The National Association of Pediatric Nurse Associates and Practitioners, an association of more than 5,600 pediatric nurse practitioners and specialty nurses in advanced practice providing primary health care to infants, children, adolescents and young adults, proclaims this week in honor of nearly 11,000 practitioners dedicated to improving children's health. For info: Joe Casey, Dir of Membership and Communications, NAPNAP, 1101 Kings Highway North, Ste 206, Cherry Hill, NJ 08034-1912. Phone: (856) 667-1773. Fax: (856) 667-7187. E-mail: napnap1@aol.com. Web: www.napnap.org.

PULMONARY REHABILITATION WEEK. Mar 11–17. For info: American Assn of Cardiovascular and Pulmonary Rehabilitation, 7611 Elmwood Ave, Ste 201, Middleton, WI 53562. Phone: (608) 831-6989. Fax: (608) 831-5122. E-mail: aacvpr@tmahq.com.

TASSO, TORQUATO: BIRTH ANNIVERSARY. Mar 11, 1544. Poet of the late Renaissance, born at Sorrento, Italy. His violent outbursts and acute sensitivity to criticism led to his imprisonment for seven years, during which the "misunderstood genius" continued his literary creativity. Died at Rome, Italy, Apr 25, 1595.

WELK, LAWRENCE: BIRTH ANNIVERSARY. Mar 11, 1903. Bandleader Lawrence Welk was born at Strasburg, ND. He learned to play the accordion and at 17 formed his first band. After playing all over the Midwest, he moved to Los Angeles where in 1955 his show began its nationwide television broadcast of "Champagne Music." The longest-running program in TV history, "The Lawrence Welk Show" played each Saturday on ABC from 1955 until 1971 when it was dropped because sponsors thought its audience was too old. Welk kept the show on a network of more than 250 independent stations for 11 more years and it still can be seen in reruns. Welk's entertainment empire included the purchase of royalty rights to songs, including the entire collection of songs by Jerome Kern. Welk died at Santa Monica, CA, May 17, 1992.

WILSON, HAROLD: 85th BIRTH ANNIVERSARY. Mar 11, 1916. British statesman and twice prime minister (1964–70 and 1974–76), leader of the Labor Party. Born at Huddersfield, Yorkshire. He died May 24, 1995, at London.

March 2001	S	M	T	W	T	F	S
					1	2	3
	4	5	6	7	8	9	10
	11	12	13	14	15	16	17
	18	19	20	21	22	23	24
	25	26	27	28	29	30	31

BIRTHDAYS TODAY

Douglas Adams, 49, author (*Hitchhiker's Guide to the Galaxy*), born Cambridge, England, Mar 11, 1952.
Roy Barnes, 53, Governor of Georgia (D), born Mableton, GA, Mar 11, 1948.
Curtis Brown, Jr, 45, astronaut, born Elizabethtown, NC, Mar 11, 1956.
Sam Donaldson, 67, journalist, born El Paso, TX, Mar 11, 1934.
Alex Kingston, 38, actress ("ER"), born London, England, Mar 11, 1963.
Bobby McFerrin, 51, jazz musician, singer, songwriter, born New York, NY, Mar 11, 1950.
Rupert Murdoch, 70, newspaper publisher (*New York Post, The Boston Herald*), born Melbourne, Australia, Mar 11, 1931.
Dominique Sanda, 50, actress (*The Garden of the Finzi-Continis, 1900*), born Paris, France, Mar 11, 1951.
Antonin Scalia, 65, Associate Justice of the US Supreme Court, born Trenton, NJ, Mar 11, 1936.
Jerry Zucker, 51, writer, (*Naked Gun* movies with brother David, producer *Airplane!*), born Milwaukee, WI, Mar 11, 1950.

MARCH 12 — MONDAY
Day 71 — 294 Remaining

AMERICAN BOWLING CONGRESS CONVENTION & HALL OF FAME INDUCTION CEREMONIES. Mar 12–17. Albuquerque, NM. Local, state and national bowling leaders gather to decide the rules of the game and the future of bowling in a democratic setting. The week features board of directors' meetings, special seminars, dinners honoring top leaders, Hall of Fame induction ceremonies (Mar 16) and workshops. Est attendance: 5,000. For info: Michael Deering, American Bowling Congress, 5301 S 76th St, Greendale, WI 53129-0500. Phone: (414) 423-3309. Fax: (414) 421-3013.

ATATÜRK, MUSTAFA KEMAL: BIRTH ANNIVERSARY. Mar 12, 1881. The founder of modern Turkey was born at Salonika, Greece (then part of the Ottoman Empire). After a distinguished army career, he led the Turkish revolution after World War I and was elected Turkey's first president. He died at Istanbul, Nov 10, 1938.

AUSTRIA INVADED BY NAZI GERMANY: ANNIVERSARY. Mar 12, 1938. As a test of its own war readiness and of the response of the other major powers, Germany occupied Austria. A year later Germany invaded Czechoslovakia and, in September, Poland, beginning World War II.

BERMUDA COLONIZED BY ENGLISH: ANNIVERSARY. Mar 12, 1609. The ship of Admiral Sir George Somers, taking settlers to Virginia, was wrecked on the reefs of Bermuda. The islands had been discovered in the early 1500s but were uninhabited until 1609.

BOYCOTT, CHARLES CUNNINGHAM: BIRTH ANNIVERSARY. Mar 12, 1832. Charles Cunningham Boycott, born at Norfolk, England, has been immortalized by having his name become part of the English language. In County Mayo, Ireland, the Tenants' "Land League" in 1880 asked Boycott, an estate agent, to reduce rents (because of poor harvest and dire economic conditions). Boycott responded by serving eviction notices on the tenants, who retaliated by refusing to have any dealings with him. Charles Stewart Parnell, then President of the National Land League and agrarian agitator, retaliated against Boycott by formulating and implementing the method of economic and social ostracism that came to be called a "boycott." Boycott died at Suffolk, England, June 19, 1897.

CAMP FIRE BOYS AND GIRLS BIRTHDAY WEEK. Mar 12–18. To celebrate the 91st anniversary of Camp Fire Boys and Girls (founded in 1910 as Camp Fire Girls). For info: Camp Fire Boys and Girls, 4601 Madison Ave, Kansas City, MO 64112. Phone: (816) 756-1950. Fax: (816) 756-0258. E-mail: info@campfire.org. Web: www.campfire.org.

CHURCH OF ENGLAND ORDAINS WOMEN PRIESTS: ANNIVERSARY. Mar 12, 1994. The Church of England for the first time ordained 32 women at Bristol Cathedral. About 700 male members of the clergy and unknown thousands of members indicated they would leave the Church of England and join the Roman Catholic Church. The Catholic Church responded to the ordination by saying that it "constitutes a profound obstacle to every hope of reunion between the Catholic Church and the Anglican Communion." This day's ordinations were not the first. In early 1994 about 1,380 women priests were ordained in churches of the Anglican Communion outside of Great Britain.

FDR'S FIRST FIRESIDE CHAT: ANNIVERSARY. Mar 12, 1933. President Franklin Delano Roosevelt made the first of his Sunday evening "fireside chats" to the American people on Mar 12, 1933. Speaking by radio from the White House, he reported rather informally on the economic problems of the nation and on his actions to deal with them.

GIRL SCOUTS OF THE USA FOUNDING: ANNIVERSARY. Mar 12, 1912. Juliet Low founded the Girl Scouts of the USA at Savannah, GA.

GREAT BLIZZARD OF '88: ANNIVERSARY. Mar 12, 1888. One of the most devastating blizzards to hit the northeastern US began in the early hours of Monday, Mar 12, 1888. A snowfall of 40–50 inches, accompanied by gale-force winds, left drifts as high as 30–40 feet. More than 400 persons died in the storm (200 at New York City alone). Some survivors of the storm, "The Blizzard Men of 1888," held annual meetings at New York City as late as 1941 to recount personal recollections of the event.

KEROUAC, JACK: BIRTH ANNIVERSARY. Mar 12, 1922. American poet and novelist Jack (Jean-Louis) Kerouac, leader and spokesman for the Beat movement, was born at Lowell, MA. Kerouac is best known for his novel *On the Road*, published in 1957, which celebrates the Beat ideal of nonconformity. Kerouac published *The Dharma Bums* in 1958, followed by *The Subterraneans* the same year, *Doctor Sax* and its sequel *Maggie Cassidy* in 1959, *Lonesome Traveler* in 1960, *Big Sur* in 1962 and *Desolation Angels* in 1965. Kerouac died at St. Petersburg, FL, at age 47, Oct 21, 1969. A previously unpublished part of *On the Road* called *Visions of Cody* was published posthumously in 1972.

LESOTHO: MOSHOESHOE'S DAY. Mar 12. National holiday. Commemorates the great leader, Chief Moshoeshoe I, who unified the Basotho people, beginning in 1820.

MAURITIUS: INDEPENDENCE DAY. Mar 12, 1968. National holiday commemorates attainment of independent nationhood (within the British Commonwealth) on Mar 12, 1968.

★NATIONAL OLDER WORKERS EMPLOYMENT WEEK. Mar 12–18. To encourage employers, when they hire new workers, to consider carefully the skills and other qualifications of men and women aged 55 and older.

NATIONAL ORGANIZE YOUR HOME OFFICE DAY. Mar 12. To set aside one day each year for the more than 34 million home office households to find files, purge papers and tackle to-do lists. Annually, the second Tuesday in March. For info: Lisa Kanarek, HomeOfficeLife.com, 660 Preston Forest Ctr, # 120, Dallas, TX 75230. Phone: (214) 361-0556. Web: www.homeofficelife.com.

NEWCOMB, SIMON: BIRTH ANNIVERSARY. Mar 12, 1835. Astronomer, born at Wallace, NS. Newcomb investigated the orbits of Uranus, Neptune and the inner planets and devised planetary tables that were used universally by observatories. Died at Washington, DC, July 11, 1909.

PIERCE, JANE MEANS APPLETON: BIRTH ANNIVERSARY. Mar 12, 1806. Wife of Franklin Pierce, 14th president of the US. Born at Hampton, NH. Died at Concord, NH, Dec 2, 1863.

SPAIN: FIESTA DE LAS FALLAS. Mar 12–19. Valencia, Spain. This festival of burning effigies and fireworks has been celebrated for more than 150 years.

SUN YAT-SEN: DEATH ANNIVERSARY. Mar 12, 1925. The heroic leader of China's 1911 revolution is remembered on the anniversary of his death at Peking, China. Observed as Arbor Day in Taiwan.

TURKEY VULTURES RETURN TO THE LIVING SIGN. Mar 12–17. Entire Canisteo Valley, Canisteo, NY. Traditionally turkey vultures return on St. Pat's Day to their roosting sites in and around the world-famous living sign. For info: Rick Roche, 4904 State Route 36, Canisteo, NY 14823. Phone: (607) 698-2134 after 4 PM EST.

UNITED KINGDOM: COMMONWEALTH DAY. Mar 12. Replaces Empire Day observance recognized until 1958. Observed on second Monday in March. Also observed in the British Virgin Islands, Gibraltar and Newfoundland, Canada.

BIRTHDAYS TODAY

Edward Albee, 73, playwright, born Washington, DC, Mar 12, 1928.

Rob Cohen, 52, producer (*Bird on a Wire*), director (*Dragonheart*), born Cornwall-on-Hudson, NY, Mar 12, 1949.

Kent Conrad, 53, US Senator (D, North Dakota), born Bismarck, ND, Mar 12, 1948.

Barbara Feldon, 60, actress ("Get Smart," *Smile*), born Pittsburgh, PA, Mar 12, 1941.

Marlon Jackson, 44, singer (Jackson 5), born Gary, IN, Mar 12, 1957.

Al (Alwin) Jarreau, 61, singer, songwriter, born Milwaukee, WI, Mar 12, 1940.

Liza Minnelli, 55, singer, actress (Oscar for *Cabaret; The Sterile Cuckoo, Arthur*), born Los Angeles, CA, Mar 12, 1946.

Raul Mondesi, 30, baseball player, born San Cristobal, Dominican Republic, Mar 12, 1971.

Dale Bryan Murphy, 45, former baseball player, born Portland, OR, Mar 12, 1956.

Wally Schirra, 78, former astronaut, born Hackensack, NJ, Mar 12, 1923.

Darryl Eugene Strawberry, 39, baseball player, born Los Angeles, CA, Mar 12, 1962.

James Taylor, 53, singer, musician ("You've Got a Friend," "Handy Man"), born Boston, MA, Mar 12, 1948.

Andrew Young, 69, civil rights leader, former mayor of Atlanta, GA, born New Orleans, LA, Mar 12, 1932.

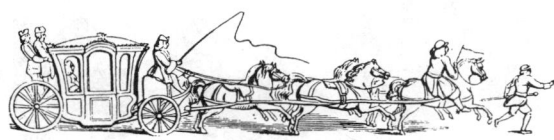

MARCH 13 — TUESDAY
Day 72 — 293 Remaining

ANN ARBOR FILM FESTIVAL. Mar 13–18. Ann Arbor, MI. Independent 16mm film festival in its 39th year. Genres represented include experimental, animation, documentary, narrative, avant-garde. No video for pre-entry. Entry deadline: Feb 1, 2001. $16,000 awarded in prizes. Est attendance: 5,000. For info: Vicki Honeyman, Festival Dir, Ann Arbor Film Festival, PO Box 8232, Ann Arbor, MI 48107. Phone: (734) 995-5356. Fax: (734) 995-5396. E-mail: vicki@honeyman.org. Web: aafilmfest.org.

ARAB OIL EMBARGO LIFTED: ANNIVERSARY. Mar 13, 1974. The oil-producing Arab countries agreed to lift their five-month embargo on petroleum sales to the US. During the embargo prices went up 300 percent and a ban was imposed on Sunday gasoline sales. The embargo was in retaliation for US support of Israel during the October 1973 Middle-East War.

CLARENCE DARROW DEATH COMMEMORATION.
Mar 13. Jackson Park, Chicago, IL. Annually, on the anniversary of his death, a wreath is tossed from the Jackson Park Clarence Darrow Bridge, named in honor of the famed lawyer and civil libertarian at 10 AM. At 11 AM a discussion follows in the Columbian Room of the Museum of Science and Industry. Est attendance: 100. For info: Herb Kraus, 875 N Michigan, Ste 2250, Chicago, IL 60611. Phone: (312) 266-7800 or (312) 640-6791. Fax: (312) 266-2874.

DEAF HISTORY MONTH. Mar 13–Apr 15. Observance of three of the most important anniversaries for deaf Americans: Apr 15, 1817, establishment of the first public school for the deaf in America, later known as The American School for the Deaf; Apr 8, 1864, charter signed by President Lincoln authorizing the Board of Directors of the Columbia Institution (now Gallaudet University) to grant college degrees to deaf students; Mar 13, 1988, the victory of the Deaf President Now movement at Gallaudet. For info: Library for Deaf Action, 2930 Craiglawn Rd, Silver Spring, MD 20904-1816. Phone: (301) 572-5168 (TTY). Fax: (301) 572-4134. E-mail: alhagemeyer@juno.com. Web: www.LibraryDeaf.com.

DELMONICO, LORENZO: BIRTH ANNIVERSARY. Mar 13, 1813. Famed restaurateur and gastronomic authority. Born at Marengo, Switzerland. Operated a number of restaurants at New York, NY, where he died, Sept 3, 1881.

EARMUFFS PATENTED: ANNIVERSARY. Mar 13, 1887. Chester Greenwood of Maine received a patent for earmuffs.

ENGLAND: CHELTENHAM HUNT FESTIVAL. Mar 13–15. Cheltenham Racecourse, Prestbury, Cheltenham, Gloucestershire. "The Olympics of steeplechasing." Cheltenham Gold Cup on March 15. Est attendance: 150,000. For info: Cheltenham Racecourse, Prestbury Park, Cheltenham, Gloucestershire, England GL50 4SH. Phone: (44) (1242) 513014. Fax: (44) (1242) 224227. Web: www.cheltenham.co.uk.

FILLMORE, ABIGAIL POWERS: BIRTH ANNIVERSARY. Mar 13, 1798. First wife of Millard Fillmore, 13th president of the US. Born at Stillwater, NY. It is said that the White House was without any books until Abigail Fillmore, formerly a teacher, made a room on the second floor into a library. Within a year, Congress appropriated $250 for the president to spend on books for the White House. Died at Washington, DC, Mar 30, 1853.

GOOD SAMARITAN INVOLVEMENT DAY. Mar 13. A day to emphasize the importance of unselfish aid to those who need it. Recognized on the anniversary of the killing of Catherine (Kitty) Genovese, Mar 13, 1964, in the Kew Gardens community, Queens, NY. Reportedly no fewer than 38 of her neighbors, not wanting "to get involved," witnessed and watched for nearly 30 minutes as the fleeing girl was pursued and repeatedly stabbed by her 29-year-old attacker.

HUBBARD, L. RON: 90th BIRTH ANNIVERSARY. Mar 13, 1911. Lafayette Ronald Hubbard, science fiction writer, recluse and founder of the Church of Scientology, was born at Tilden, NE. His best-known book was *Dianetics: The Modern Science of Mental Health*. Died at San Luis Obispo County, CA, Jan 24, 1986.

"THE LARRY KING SHOW" TV PREMIERE: ANNIVERSARY. Mar 13, 1983. Radio talk show host Larry King brought his topical interview program to syndicated TV in 1983. Using a telephone hook-up, viewers called in to speak to particular guests. King has been appearing on CNN since 1985 interviewing a variety of newsmakers and celebrities.

LOWELL, PERCIVAL: BIRTH ANNIVERSARY. Mar 13, 1855. American astronomer, founder of the Lowell Observatory at Flagstaff, AZ. Born at Boston, MA, he died at Flagstaff, Nov 12, 1916. Lowell was initiator of the search that resulted (25 years after the search began and 14 years after his death) in discovery of the planet Pluto. The discovery was announced on Lowell's birthday, Mar 13, 1930, by the Lowell Observatory.

NATIONAL OPEN AN UMBRELLA INDOORS DAY. Mar 13. The purpose of this day is for people to open umbrellas indoors and note whether they have any bad luck. To arrange for an interview, call 24 hours in advance. Annually, Mar 13. For info: Thomas Edward Knibb, 8819 Adventure Ave, Walkersville, MD 21793-7828. Phone: (301) 898-3009. E-mail: tomknibb@juno.com.

OPERATION FLASH: ANNIVERSARY. Mar 13, 1943. Disillusioned German officers planned to take the life of Adolf Hitler on this date. Hitler was to stop at Smolensk on his way to his headquarters and an officer who was not involved in the plot had been commissioned to deliver a package to Hitler's plane which he was told contained two bottles of liquor for a friend in Rastenburg. A bomb in the package was timed to go off over Minsk, but it reached Rastenburg without detonating. The package was later recovered and a defective detonator was found. See also: "Gersdorff Hitler Assassination Attempt" (Mar 21).

PLANET URANUS DISCOVERY: ANNIVERSARY. Mar 13, 1781. German-born English astronomer Sir William Herschel discovered the seventh planet from the sun, Uranus.

PRIESTLY, JOSEPH: BIRTH ANNIVERSARY. Mar 13, 1733 (OS). English clergyman and scientist, discoverer of oxygen, born at Fieldhead, England. He and his family narrowly escaped an angry mob attacking their home because of his religious and political views. They moved to the US in 1794. Died at Northumberland, PA, Feb 6, 1804.

SAINT AUBIN, HELEN "CALLAGHAN" CANDAELE: BIRTH ANNIVERSARY. Mar 13, 1929. Helen Candaele Saint Aubin, known as Helen Callaghan during her baseball days, was born at Vancouver, British Columbia, Canada. Saint Aubin and her sister, Margaret Maxwell, were recruited for the All-American Girls Professional Baseball League, which flourished in the 1940s when many major league players were off fighting WWII. She first played at age 15 for the Minneapolis Millerettes, an expansion team that moved to Indiana and became the Fort Wayne Daisies. For the 1945 season the left-handed outfielder led the league with a .299 average and 24 extra base hits. In 1946 she stole 114 bases in 111 games. Her son Kelly Candaele's documentary on the women's baseball league inspired the film *A League of Their Own*. Saint Aubin, who was known as the "Ted Williams of women's baseball," died Dec 8, 1992, at Santa Barbara, CA.

TAIWAN: BIRTHDAY OF KUAN YIN, GODDESS OF MERCY. Mar 13. Nineteenth day of Second Moon of the lunar calendar, celebrated at Taipei's Lungshan (Dragon Mountain) and other temples.

March 2001	S	M	T	W	T	F	S
					1	2	3
	4	5	6	7	8	9	10
	11	12	13	14	15	16	17
	18	19	20	21	22	23	24
	25	26	27	28	29	30	31

BIRTHDAYS TODAY

Walter Annenberg, 93, publisher, philanthropist, born Milwaukee, WI, Mar 13, 1908.

Thomas Andrew (Andy) Bean, 48, golfer, born Lafayette, GA, Mar 13, 1953.

Adam Clayton, 41, musician (U2), born Dublin, Ireland, Mar 13, 1960.

Dana Delany, 45, actress ("China Beach," *Moon Over Parador*), born New York, NY, Mar 13, 1956.

Glenne Headly, 44, actress (*The Purple Rose of Cairo, Dick Tracy, Mortal Thoughts*), born New London, CT, Mar 13, 1957.

William H. Macy, 51, actor (*Fargo*, "ER," "Sports Night"), born Miami, FL, Mar 13, 1950.

Deborah Raffin, 48, actress ("Foul Play"), born Los Angeles, CA, Mar 13, 1953.

Neil Sedaka, 62, singer, songwriter ("Breaking Up Is Hard to Do," with Howard Greenfield), born Brooklyn, NY, Mar 13, 1939.

MARCH 14 — WEDNESDAY

Day 73 — 292 Remaining

CARAY, HARRY: BIRTH ANNIVERSARY. Mar 14, 1914. Born Harry Christopher Carabini at St. Louis, MO (some sources say Mar 1, 1920). Caray began his baseball broadcasting career with the St. Louis Cardinals in 1945. He then was the announcer for the Oakland A's, the Chicago White Sox and finally the Chicago Cubs. He became a legend at Wrigley Field with his 7th-inning stretch "Take Me out to the Ball Game" and his quirky phrase "Holy Cow." Caray was inducted into the Broadcasters Hall of Fame in 1989. Died at Rancho Mirage, CA, Feb 18, 1998.

EDUCATION ADVOCACY WEEK. Mar 14–21. The Individuals with Disabilities in Education Act is the federal law of the land. How many people know what it is or what it does? How many people know that it guarantees a free appropropriate public education to children with handicaps so that they can learn and succeed? Learn the law and the skills needed to get what you are entitled to from the school system. Workshops, seminars and information all week long. For info: Action Advocacy Rights and Representation, 6753 El Cajon Blvd, San Diego, CA 92115. Phone: (619) 433-3323. Fax: (619) 460-0423. Web: www .hizhonor.com.

EINSTEIN, ALBERT: BIRTH ANNIVERSARY. Mar 14, 1879. Theoretical physicist best known for his theory of relativity. Born at Ulm, Germany, he won the Nobel Prize in 1921. Died at Princeton, NJ, Apr 18, 1955.

JONES, CASEY: BIRTH ANNIVERSARY. Mar 14, 1864. Railroad engineer and hero of ballad, whose real name was John Luther Jones. Born near Cayce, KY, he died in a railroad wreck near Vaughn, MS, Apr 30, 1900.

MARSHALL, THOMAS RILEY: BIRTH ANNIVERSARY. Mar 14, 1854. 28th vice president of the US (1913–21). Born at North Manchester, IN, he died at Washington, DC, June 1, 1925.

MOTH-ER DAY. Mar 14. A day set aside to honor moth collectors and specialists. Celebrated in museums or libraries with moth collections. For info: Bob Birch, Puns Corps Grand Punscorpion, Box 2364, Falls Church, VA 22042-0364. Phone: (703) 533-3668.

A MOUNTAIN QUILTFEST. Mar 14–18. Smoky Mountain Convention Center, Pigeon Forge, TN. The Piecemakers and the Sevier Valley Quilters join forces with some world-renowned instructors. Show free; fees for lessons. Est attendance: 9,000. For info: Pigeon Forge Dept of Tourism, 2450 Parkway, PO Box 1390, Pigeon Forge, TN 37868. Phone: (800) 251-9100 or (423) 429-7350. Fax: (423) 429-7362. Web: pigeon-forge.tn.us.

NAIA MEN'S DIVISION I NATIONAL BASKETBALL CHAMPIONSHIP. Mar 14–20. Tulsa, OK. 64th annual tournament. Est attendance: 35,000. For info: Natl Assn of Intercollegiate Athletics, 6120 S Yale Ave, Ste 1450, Tulsa, OK 74136. Phone: (918) 494-8828. Fax: (918) 494-8841. E-mail: kdee@naia .org. Web: www.naia.org.

NAIA WOMEN'S DIVISION I NATIONAL BASKETBALL CHAMPIONSHIP TOURNAMENT. Mar 14–20. Jackson, TN. 32-team field competes for the national championship. 21st annual competition. Est attendance: 38,000. For info: Natl Assn of Intercollegiate Athletics, 6120 S Yale Ave, Ste 1450, Tulsa, OK 74136. Phone: (918) 494-8828. Fax: (918) 494-8841. E-mail: ncronkhite@naia.org. Web: www.naia.org.

NATIONAL TOAD HOLLOW WEEK. Mar 14–21. A community outreach program encouraging people to nourish their imagination, pursue their dreams and practice old fashioned values in their relationships with others. For info: Ralph Morrison, Dir, Toad Hollow, PO Box 151, Fulton, MI 49052. Phone: (800) 574-8623.

RIO GRANDE VALLEY LIVESTOCK SHOW. Mar 14–18. Mercedes, TX. Rodeo, open cattle show and carnival. For the youth of the four counties in the valley to exhibit their projects. Est attendance: 150,000. For info: Jim Beale, Rio Grande Valley Livestock Show Inc, Box 867, Mercedes, TX 78570. Phone: (956) 565-2456. Fax: (956) 565-3005.

SAINT PATRICK'S DAY PARADE & FESTIVAL. Mar 14. Hollywood, FL. Traditional parade with pipes and drums, floats, etc, on downtown streets and festival in the park with entertainment stage, Irish food and wares. Est attendance: 15,000. For info: Roguey Doyle, City of Hollywood Dept of Parks, 1940 Harrison St, Ste 101, Hollywood, FL 33020. Phone: (954) 921-3404.

SEOUL RECAPTURED BY UN FORCES: 50th ANNIVERSARY. Mar 14, 1951. Seoul, Korea, which had fallen to Chinese forces in January 1951, was retaken by United Nations troops during the Korean War.

TAYLOR, LUCY HOBBS: BIRTH ANNIVERSARY. Mar 14, 1833. Lucy Beaman Hobbs, first woman in America to receive a degree in dentistry (Ohio College of Dental Surgery, 1866) and to be admitted to membership in a state dental association. Born at Franklin County, NY. In 1867 she married James M. Taylor, who also became a dentist (after she instructed him in the essentials). Active women's rights advocate. Died at Lawrence, KS, Oct 3, 1910.

"10 MOST WANTED" LIST DEBUTS: ANNIVERSARY. Mar 14, 1950. The Federal Bureau of Investigation instituted the "10 Most Wanted Fugitives" list in an effort to publicize particularly dangerous criminals who were at large. From 1950 to 1998, 454 fugitives appeared on the list; 130 were captured. Generally, the only way to get off the list is to die or be captured. The FBI cooperates with the producers of TV's "America's Most Wanted" to further publicize these fugitives.

BIRTHDAYS TODAY

Frank Borman, 73, former astronaut, airline executive, born Gary, IN, Mar 14, 1928.

Michael Caine (Maurice Joseph Micklewhite), 68, actor (*Alfie, The Ipcress File, Sleuth*), born London, England, Mar 14, 1933.

Billy Crystal, 54, actor ("Soap," *When Harry Met Sally . . ., City Slickers*), born Long Beach, NY, Mar 14, 1947.

Rick Dees, 50, disc jockey, comedian, born Jacksonville, FL, Mar 14, 1951.

Quincy Jones, 68, composer, producer ("We Are the World"), born Chicago, IL, Mar 14, 1933.

Hank Ketcham, 81, cartoonist ("Dennis the Menace"), born Seattle, WA, Mar 14, 1920.

Kirby Puckett, 40, former baseball player, born Chicago, IL, Mar 14, 1961.

Rita Tushingham, 59, actress (*Dr. Zhivago, A Taste of Honey*), born Liverpool, England, Mar 14, 1942.

MARCH 15 — THURSDAY
Day 74 — 291 Remaining

ABSOLUTELY INCREDIBLE KID DAY. Mar 15. Camp Fire Boys and Girls, one of the nation's oldest and largest youth development organizations, holds its third annual event to encourage adults to write letters to children telling them how special they are and how much they mean to them. Annually, the third Thursday in March. For info: Camp Fire Boys and Girls, 4601 Madison Ave, Kansas City, MO 64112. Phone: (816) 756-1950 or (888) 2KIDDAY. Fax: (816) 756-2650. E-mail: kidday@yahoo.com. Web: www.campfire.org.

"EIGHT IS ENOUGH" TV PREMIERE: ANNIVERSARY. Mar 15, 1977. This one-hour comedy-drama was set in Sacramento and starred Dick Van Patten as Tom Bradford, a columnist for a local paper and a widower with eight children. Diana Hyland played his wife Joan; she died from cancer after filming five shows. The children were played by Grant Goodeve, Lani O'Grady, Laurie Walters, Susan Richardson, Dianne Kay, Connie Needham, Willie Aames and Adam Rich. In the fall of 1977 Betty Buckley joined the cast as tutor Abby Abbott, who later married Tom. Most of the cast was reunited for Tom's 50th birthday on "Eight Is Enough: A Family Reunion" shown on Oct 18, 1987.

FLORIDA STATE BOAT AND SPORTS SHOW. Mar 15–18. Florida Expo Park, Tampa, FL. Sponsor: National Marine Manufacturers Association. Est attendance: 15,000. For info: Media Relations, Natl Marine Manufacturers Assn, 200 East Randolph Dr, Ste 5100, Chicago, IL 60601. Phone: (312) 946-6200. Fax: (312) 946-0388.

FORT WAYNE SPORTS, VACATION & BOAT SHOW. Mar 15–18. Allen County War Coliseum, Fort Wayne, IN. Est attendance: 30,000. For info: Kevin Renfro, VP, Renfro Productions & Management, Ste E-2, Corporate Square East, 2511 E 46th, Indianapolis, IN 46205. Phone: (317) 546-4344. Fax: (317) 546-3002. E-mail: insportshow@iquest.net. Web: www.renfrosportshow.com.

GRAND CENTER SPORT, FISHING AND TRAVEL SHOW. Mar 15–18. Grand Center, Grand Rapids, MI. This event brings together buyers and sellers of fishing boats and equipment, RVs, campers and their accessories, as well as other outdoor sporting goods. US and Canadian hunting and fishing trips and other vacation travel destinations are featured. All aspects of fishing, including tackle boats, seminars, demonstrations and displays are emphasized. Est attendance: 45,000. For info: Adam Starr, ShowSpan, Inc, 1400 28th St SW, Grand Rapids, MI 49509. Phone: (616) 530-1919. Fax: (616) 530-2122. Web: www.showspan.com.

HUNGARY: ANNIVERSARY OF THE 1848 REVOLUTION. Mar 15. National day.

IDES OF MARCH. Mar 15. In the Roman calendar the days of the month were not numbered sequentially. Instead, each month had three division days: kalends, nones and ides. Days were numbered from these divisions: e.g., IV Nones or III Ides. The ides occurred on the 15th of the month (or on the 13th in months that had less than 31 days). Julius Caesar was assassinated on this day in 44 BC. This system was used in Europe well into the Renaissance. When Shakespeare wrote "Beware the ides of March" in *Julius Caesar* his audience knew what he meant.

JACKSON, ANDREW: BIRTH ANNIVERSARY. Mar 15, 1767. 7th president of the US (Mar 4, 1829–Mar 3, 1837) was born in a log cabin at Waxhaw, SC. Jackson was the first president since George Washington who had not attended college. He was a military hero in the War of 1812. His presidency reflected his democratic and egalitarian values. Died at Nashville, TN, June 8, 1845. His birthday is observed as a holiday in Tennessee.

MAINE: ADMISSION DAY: ANNIVERSARY. Mar 15. Became 23rd state in 1820. Prior to this date, Maine had been part of Massachusetts.

"MR BELVEDERE" TV PREMIERE: ANNIVERSARY. Mar 15, 1985. A sitcom about a sarcastic, talented, wise British housekeeper and his love-hate relationship with a Pittsburgh family. It starred Christopher Hewett as Lynn Belvedere, former baseball player Bob Uecker as his employer/antagonist sportswriter George Owens, Ilene Graff as George's wife Marsha, a law student, Rob Stone as Kevin, Tracy Wells as Heather and Brice Beckham as mischievous Wesley. At the end of each episode, Mr Belvedere narrated the day's lesson as he wrote in his journal, and ended the show on a funny note. The last telecast aired July 8, 1990.

NATIONAL BRUTUS DAY. Mar 15. No matter where you work, you must admit there's as much intrigue, plotting and back-stabbing as was found in ancient Rome or is found today inside the Beltway. [© 2000 by WH]. For info: Thomas Roy, Wellcat Holidays, 2418 Long Ln, Lebanon, PA 17046. Phone: (717) 279-0184. E-mail: wellcat@supernet.com. Web: www.wellcat.com.

NCAA DIVISION I WOMEN'S SWIMMING AND DIVING CHAMPIONSHIPS. Mar 15–17. Goodwill Games Aquatic Center, Long Island, NY. Est attendance: 3,000. For info: NCAA, 700 W Washington Ave, PO Box 6222, Indianapolis, IN 46206-6222. Phone: (317) 917-6222. Fax: (317) 917-6888. Web: www.ncaa.org.

NCAA DIVISION I WRESTLING CHAMPIONSHIP. Mar 15–17. Iowa City, IA. For info: Natl Collegiate Athletic Assn, 700 W Washington Ave, PO Box 6222, Indianapolis, IN 46206-6222. Phone: (317) 917-6222. Web: www.ncaa.org.

NURSING CONFERENCE ON PEDIATRIC PRIMARY CARE. Mar 15–18. Phoenix, AZ. Offers continuing education on clinical practice, professional development and legislative issues relevant to the nursing profession. Est attendance: 1,200. For info: Natl Assn of Pediatric Nurse Associates and Practitioners, 1101 Kings Hwy N, Ste 206, Cherry Hill, NJ 08034. Phone: (856) 667-1773. Fax: (856) 667-7187. E-mail: napnap1@aol.com. Web: www.napnap.org.

"THREE'S COMPANY" TV PREMIERE: ANNIVERSARY. Mar 15, 1977. This half-hour comedy featured two girls and a guy sharing an apartment. In order for the landlord to go along with the living arrangements, Jack Tripper, played by John Ritter, had to pretend he was gay. Cast included Joyce DeWitt, Suzanne Somers, Norman Fell, Audra Findley, Richard Kline, Don Knotts and Priscilla Barnes. The last telecast aired on Sept 18, 1984.

VAN BROCKLIN, NORM: 75th BIRTH ANIVERSARY. Mar 15, 1926. Norman Van Brocklin, Pro Football Hall of Fame quarterback and coach, born at Eagle Butte, SD. Van Brocklin played college football at Oregon and then signed with the Los Angeles Rams. He helped the Rams win their only NFL title in 1951. After finishing his playing career with the Philadelphia Eagles, he coached the Minnesota Vikings and the Atlanta Falcons. Inducted into the Pro Football Hall of Fame in 1979. Died at Social Circle, GA, May 2, 1983.

WASHINGTON'S ADDRESS TO CONTINENTAL ARMY OFFICERS: ANNIVERSARY. Mar 15, 1783. George Washington addressed a meeting at Newburgh, NY, of Continental Army officers who were dissatisfied and rebellious for want of back pay, food, clothing and pensions. General Washington called for patience, opening his speech with the words: "I have grown grey in your service. . . ." Congress later acted to satisfy most of the demands.

"THE WONDER YEARS" TV PREMIERE: ANNIVERSARY. Mar 15, 1988. A coming-of-age tale set in suburbia in

	S	M	T	W	T	F	S
March					1	2	3
2001	4	5	6	7	8	9	10
	11	12	13	14	15	16	17
	18	19	20	21	22	23	24
	25	26	27	28	29	30	31

the 1960s and 1970s. This drama/comedy starred Fred Savage as Kevin Arnold, Josh Saviano as his best friend Paul and Danica McKellar as girlfriend Winnie. Kevin's dad was played by Dan Lauria, his homemaker mom by Alley Mills, his hippie sister by Olivia d'Abo and his bully brother by Jason Hervey. Narrator Daniel Stern was the voice of the grown-up Kevin. The last episode ran Sept 1, 1993 but it remains popular in syndication.

BIRTHDAYS TODAY

Harold Douglas Baines, 42, baseball player, born St. Michael's, MD, Mar 15, 1959.

Alan Bean, 69, former astronaut, born Wheeler, TX, Mar 15, 1932.

Robert Terrell (Terry) Cummings, 40, basketball player, born Chicago, IL, Mar 15, 1961.

Fabio, 40, model, born Fabio Lanzoni, Milan, Italy, Mar 15, 1961.

Ruth Bader Ginsburg, 68, Associate Justice of the US Supreme Court, born Brooklyn, NY, Mar 15, 1933.

Judd Hirsch, 66, actor (Emmy for "Taxi"; *Ordinary People*), born New York, NY, Mar 15, 1935.

Mike Love, 60, singer, musician (Beach Boys), born Los Angeles, CA, Mar 15, 1941.

Mark McGrath, 33, singer (Sugar Ray), born Newport Beach, CA Mar 15, 1968.

Park Overall, 44, actress ("Empty Nest," *Mississippi Burning*), born Nashville, TN, Mar 15, 1957.

Dee Snider, 46, singer (Twisted Sister), composer, born Massapequa, NY, Mar 15, 1955.

Sly Stone (Sylvester Stewart), 57, singer, musician (Sly & the Family Stone), born Dallas, TX, Mar 15, 1944.

Don Sundquist, 65, Governor of Tennessee (R), born Moline, IL, Mar 15, 1936.

Craig Wasson, 47, actor ("Phyllis," *Body Double, Malcolm X*), born Ontario, OR, Mar 15, 1954.

MARCH 16 — FRIDAY

Day 75 — 290 Remaining

AMERICAN CROSSWORD PUZZLE TOURNAMENT AND CONVENTION. Mar 16–18. Stamford Marriott Hotel, Stamford, CT. 350 solvers from the US and Canada compete on eight puzzles during this 24th annual event. Points are awarded for accuracy and speed. The final puzzle is played on giant white boards for everyone to watch. Prizes are awarded in 21 skill, age and geographical categories and the grand prize is $1,000. The weekend also includes group word games, guest speakers and appearances by celebrity crossword solvers. Solvers can compete at home for fun either on-line or by mail and receive a ranking in all their solving categories. Est attendance: 400. For info: Will Shortz, Dir, American Crossword Puzzle Tournament, 55 Great Oak Lane, Pleasantville, NY 10570. Phone: (732) 274-9848. Web: www.crosswordtournament.com.

BLACK PRESS DAY: ANNIVERSARY OF THE FIRST BLACK NEWSPAPER. Mar 16, 1827. Anniversary of the founding of the first black newspaper in the US, *Freedom's Journal*, on Varick Street at New York, NY.

BLUEGRASS MUSIC WEEKEND. Mar 16–18. Iowan Motor Lodge, Ft Madison, IA. Est attendance: 2,000. For info: Delbert Spray, RR1, Kahoka, MO 63445. Phone: (573) 853-4344 or (319) 752-9541.

BONHEUR, ROSA: BIRTH ANNIVERSARY. Mar 16, 1822. French painter and sculptor best known for her paintings of animals, Rosa (Marie-Rosalie) Bonheur was born at Bordeaux. With the income from the sale of her art she purchased the castle of By near Fontainebleau at Melun, France, where she died May 25, 1899. Bonheur's *The Horse Fair*, which she painted in 1849, was purchased by the American millionaire Cornelius Vanderbilt for $53,600, a record price at the time. In 1865 Bonheur was awarded the Grand Cross of the Légion d'Honneur, the first woman so honored. An early Bohemian and feminist, Bonheur defied female convention of the day by dressing in pants and smoking cigarettes.

CLYMER, GEORGE: BIRTH ANNIVERSARY. Mar 16, 1739. Signer of the Declaration of Independence and of the US Constitution. Born at Philadelphia, PA and died there Jan 24, 1813.

CURLEW DAY. Mar 16. Traditional arrival date for the long-billed curlew at the Umatilla (Oregon) National Wildlife Refuge. More than 500 of the long-billed curlews have been reported at this location during their nesting season.

ENGLAND: CHELSEA ANTIQUES FAIR. Mar 16–25 (also Sept 14–23). Chelsea Old Town Hall, King's Rd, London. Prestigious antiques fair with a wide range of pre-1830 furniture and other items with a pre-1860 dateline, for sale. Est attendance: 9,000. For info: Penman Antiques Fair, PO Box 114, Haywards Heath, West Sussex, England RH16 2YU. Phone: 441444482514. Fax: 441444483412. E-mail: info@penman-fairs.co.uk.

FREEDOM OF INFORMATION DAY. Mar 16. The American Library Association supports free and open access to government information created at taxpayer expense. On the birthday of James Madison, ALA urges libraries and librarians to join in celebrating the public's "right to know" by sponsoring activities to educate their communities about the importance of promoting and protecting freedom of information. Sponsored by the Freedom Forum and the American Library Association. For info: American Library Assn Washington Office, 1301 Pennsylvania Ave NW, Ste 403, Washington, DC 20004. Phone: (202) 628-8410. E-mail: alawash@alawash.org. Web: www.ala.org.

GODDARD DAY: 75th ANNIVERSARY. Mar 16, 1926. Commemorates first liquid-fuel-powered rocket flight launched by Robert Hutchings Goddard (1882–1945) at Auburn, MA.

"THE GUMBY SHOW" TV PREMIERE: ANNIVERSARY. Mar 16, 1957. This kids' show was a spin-off from "Howdy Doody," where the character of Gumby was first introduced in 1956. Gumby and his horse Pokey were clay figures whose adventures were filmed using the process of "claymation." "The Gumby Show," created by Art Clokey, was first hosted by Bobby Nicholson and later by Pinky Lee. It was syndicated in 1966 and again in 1988.

LONGHORN WORLD CHAMPIONSHIP RODEO. Mar 16–18. UTC Arena, Chattanooga, TN. More than 200 cowboys and cowgirls compete in six professional contests ranging from bronco riding to bull riding for top prize money and world championship points. Featuring colorful opening pageantry and Big, Bad BONUS Bulls. 19th annual. Est attendance: 15,000. For info: W. Bruce Lehrke, Pres, Longhorn World Championship Rodeo, Inc, PO Box 70159, Nashville, TN 37207. Phone: (615) 876-1016. Fax: (615) 876-4685. E-mail: lhrodeo@idt.net. Web: www.longhornrodeo.com.

MACON CHERRY BLOSSOM FESTIVAL. Mar 16–25. Macon, GA. 19th annual Cherry Blossom Festival features concerts, exhibits, parades, children's events, hot-air balloons, street party, fireworks, food, fun and family entertainment. 250,000 Yoshino cherry trees. Est attendance: 600,000. For info: Debbie Smith, Macon Cherry Blossom Fest, 794 Cherry St, Macon, GA 31201. Phone: (912) 751-7429. Fax: (912) 751-7408. Web: www.cherryblossom.com.

MADISON, JAMES: 250th BIRTH ANNIVERSARY.
Mar 16, 1751. 4th president of the US (Mar 4, 1809–Mar 3, 1817), born at Port Conway, VA. He was president when British forces invaded Washington, DC, requiring Madison and other high officials to flee while the British burned the Capitol, the president's residence and most other public buildings (Aug 24–25, 1814). Died at Montpelier, VA, June 28, 1836.

***MILWAUKEE JOURNAL SENTINEL* SPORTS SHOW.**
Mar 16–25. Milwaukee, WI. Travel and resort exhibits, hunting, fishing, boating, family travel, outdoor recreation. Largest outdoor show in Wisconsin. Est attendance: 150,000. For info: Great Outdoors, 420 Lake Cook Rd, Ste 108, Deerfield, IL 60015. Phone: (847) 914-0630. Fax: (847) 914-0333.

MOON PHASE: LAST QUARTER. Mar 16. Moon enters Last Quarter phase at 3:45 PM, EST.

MY LAI MASSACRE: ANNIVERSARY. Mar 16, 1968. Most-publicized atrocity of Vietnam War. According to findings of US Army's investigating team, approximately 300 noncombatant Vietnamese villagers (at My Lai and Mykhe, near the South China Sea) were killed by infantrymen of the American Division.

NIXON, THELMA CATHERINE PATRICIA ("PAT") RYAN: BIRTH ANNIVERSARY. Mar 16, 1912. Wife of Richard Milhous Nixon, 37th president of the US. Born at Ely, NV, she died at Park Ridge, NJ, June 22, 1993.

NORTHEAST GREAT OUTDOORS SHOW. Mar 16–18. Empire State Plaza, Albany, NY. 15th annual expo featuring fishing, hunting, boating, camping, adventure travel and much more. Attractions include informative seminars, fly casting pond, fully stocked trout pond, archery ranges for children and adults and live predatory animals. Annually, the third full weekend in March. Est attendance: 20,000. For info: Tara Sullivan, Dir, Consumer Shows and Special Events, Ed Lewi Assoc, 6 Chelsea Pl, Clifton Park, NY 12065. Phone: (518) 383-6183. Fax: (518) 383-6755.

POPE, JOHN: BIRTH ANNIVERSARY. Mar 16, 1822. Pope, a Union general in the Civil War, was born at Louisville, KY, graduated from West Point in 1842 and fought in the Mexican War. During the Civil War President Lincoln put Pope in charge of the Army of Virginia. He led the Union forces at the second Battle of Bull Run (August 1862) to a disastrous defeat, losing about 15,000 troops. He was immediately relieved of his command and sent to Minnesota to handle rioting Sioux Indians. Pope continued to deal with Indian matters until 1883 and eventually espoused the goal of assimilation into white culture. He died at Ohio, Sept 23, 1892.

SAINT PATRICK'S DAY CELEBRATION BEARD-GROWING CONTEST. Mar 16–18. Shamrock, TX. All men in town must either grow a beard or purchase a permit, and they must begin growing beard after Jan 1, 2001. Celebration also includes Miss Irish Rose Pageant, chuck wagon cookoff, rodeo events and dances. Est attendance: 10,000. For info: Connie Wilson, Chamber of Commerce, 207 N Main, Shamrock, TX 79079. Phone: (806) 256-2516 or (806) 256-2501. Fax: (806) 256-3739. E-mail: irishedb@pan-tex.net.

SAINT URHO'S DAY. Mar 16. Hood River, OR. Join the parade and party to honor the tongue-in-cheek patron saint (invented in 1956) who drove the grasshoppers out of the vineyards in Finland. Est attendance: 150. For info: Camille Hukari, 3009 Dethman Ridge, Hood River, OR 97031. Phone: (541) 386-5785. Fax: (541) 387-4657.

March 2001	S	M	T	W	T	F	S
					1	2	3
	4	5	6	7	8	9	10
	11	12	13	14	15	16	17
	18	19	20	21	22	23	24
	25	26	27	28	29	30	31

SPACE MILESTONE: *GEMINI 8* (US): 35th ANNIVERSARY. Mar 16, 1966. Executed (with *Agena*) first docking of orbiting spacecraft. Safe emergency landing after malfunction. Launched Mar 16, 1966.

SPRING POLKA FEST. Mar 16–18. Wisconsin Dells, WI. Popular Midwest polka bands playing song and dance favorites at Antigua Bay (formerly Holiday Inn). Food specialties. Est attendance: 1,500. For info: Antiqua Bay, PO Box 236, Wisconsin Dells, WI, 53965. Phone: (800) 54-DELLS. E-mail: reservations @antiquabay.com.

SUGARLOAF'S SPRING FORT WASHINGTON CRAFT FESTIVAL. Mar 16–18. Fort Washington Expo Center, Fort Washington, PA. Now in its 7th year, this show features 350 nationally recognized craft designers and fine artists displaying and selling their original creations. Demonstrations, hourly gift certificate drawings and more. Est attendance: 25,000. For info: Sugarloaf Mountain Works, Inc, 200 Orchard Ridge Dr, #215, Gaithersburg, MD 20878. Phone: (800) 210-9900. E-mail: smworks@sugarloafcrafts.com. Web: www.sugarloafcrafts.com.

WHOOPERS AND HOOPERS INVITATIONAL BASKETBALL TOURNAMENT. Mar 16–18. Hastings, NE. 20th annual tournament in which more than 120 teams and 1,200 invited basketball participants—former professional, collegiate and high school—compete five-on-five. Divided into seven divisions including A (semi-pro or AAU caliber), B (upper intermediate), C (intermediate), D1 & D2 (small-town teams) and women's A (AAU caliber) and B (all others). Est attendance: 3,000. For info: Whoopers and Hoopers, 606 West Fifth, Hastings, NE 68901. Phone: (402) 462-4159.

BIRTHDAYS TODAY

Bernardo Bertolucci, 60, filmmaker (Oscar for *The Last Emperor; Once Upon a Time in the West, Last Tango in Paris*), born Parma, Italy, Mar 16, 1941.

Erik Estrada, 52, actor ("CHiPS," *Honey Boy*), born New York, NY, Mar 16, 1949.

Isabelle Huppert, 46, actress (*Violette, Story of Women*), born Paris, France, Mar 16, 1955.

Jerry Lewis, 76, comedian, actor (*My Friend Irma*); director (*The Bellboy*), born Newark, NJ, Mar 16, 1925.

Leo McKern, 81, actor (*The Mouse That Roared, A Man for All Seasons, Help*, "Rumpole of the Bailey"), born New South Wales, Australia, Mar 16, 1920.

Daniel Patrick Moynihan, 74, US Senator (D, New York), born Tulsa, OK, Mar 16, 1927.

Kate Nelligan, 50, actress (*Eye of the Needle, Frankie and Johnny, The Prince of Tides*), born London, Ontario, Canada, Mar 16, 1951.

Chuck Woolery, 59, game-show host ("Love Connection," "Scrabble"), born Ashland, KY, Mar 16, 1942.

MARCH 17 — SATURDAY
Day 76 — 289 Remaining

BATTLE OF GUILFORD COURTHOUSE OBSERVANCE. Mar 17–18. Guilford Courthouse National Military Park, Greensboro, NC. A program to observe the 220th anniversary of the Battle of Guilford Courthouse, the largest Revolutionary War battle in North Carolina. Est attendance: 5,000. For info: Robert A. Vogel, Superintendent, Guilford Courthouse NMP, 2332 New Garden Rd, Greensboro, NC 27410-2355. Phone: (336) 288-1776. Fax: (336) 282-2296.

BERING SEA ICE GOLF CLASSIC. Mar 17. Nome, AK. A six-hole course played on the frozen Bering Sea. The object is to land the bright-orange ricocheting golf ball into the sunken, flagged coffee cans before losing it among the built-up chunks of ice. Starts promptly at 10 AM at the Breakers Bar. Approximately 60 golfers. Est attendance: 150. For info: Bering Sea Lions Club, Box 326, Nome, AK 99762. Phone: (907) 443-5904.

BRIDGER, JIM: BIRTH ANNIVERSARY. Mar 17, 1804. American fur trader, frontiersman and scout, born at Richmond, VA, and died July 17, 1881, near Kansas City, MO. Believed to be the first white man to visit (in 1824) the Great Salt Lake, he also established Fort Bridger in southwestern Wyoming as a fur-trading post and as a way station for pioneers heading west on the Oregon Trail. Bridger National Forest in western Wyoming is named for him.

CAMP FIRE BOYS AND GIRLS BIRTHDAY SAB-BATH. Mar 17. A day when Camp Fire Boys and Girls commemorate the organization's founding and worship together and participate in the services in their churches or temples. For info: Camp Fire Boys and Girls, 4601 Madison Ave, Kansas City, MO 64112. Phone: (816) 756-1950. Fax: (816) 756-2650. E-mail: info@campfire.org. Web: www.campfire.org.

CAMP FIRE BOYS AND GIRLS: ANNIVERSARY. Mar 17. To commemorate the anniversary of the founding of Camp Fire Boys and Girls and the service given to children and youth across the nation. Founded in 1910 as Camp Fire Girls. For info: Camp Fire Boys and Girls, 4601 Madison Ave, Kansas City, MO 64112. Phone: (816) 756-1950. Fax: (816) 756-2650. E-mail: info @campfire.org. Web: www.campfire.org.

CANADA: MAPLE FESTIVAL OF NOVA SCOTIA. Mar 17–Apr 14 (Saturdays only). Northern Nova Scotia. Promotion of the maple industry. Pancake suppers with entertainment, industry equipment displays and crafts displays. Est attendance: 5,000. For info: Lorna A. Crowe, RR1, Southampton, Cumberland County, NS, Canada B0M 1W0. Phone: (902) 546-2844.

COLE, NAT "KING" (NATHANIEL ADAMS COLE): BIRTH ANNIVERSARY. Mar 17, 1919. Nat "King" Cole was born at Montgomery, AL, and began his musical career at an early age, playing the piano at age four. His career included many highlights, among which was his role as the first black entertainer to host a national television show. His many songs included "The Christmas Song," "Nature Boy," "Mona Lisa," "Ramblin' Rose" and "Unforgettable." Although he was dogged by racial discrimination throughout his career, including the cancellation of his television show because opposition from southern white viewers decreased advertising revenue, Cole was criticized by prominent black newspapers for not joining other black entertainers in the civil rights struggle. Cole contributed more than $50,000 to civil rights organizations in response to the criticism. Nat "King" Cole died Feb 25, 1965, at Santa Monica, CA.

ENGLAND: HEAD OF THE RIVER RACE. Mar 17. Mortlake to Putney, River Thames, London. At 9:45 AM. Processional race for 420 eight-oared crews, starting at 10-second intervals. Est attendance: 7,000. For info: Mr A. Ruddle, 59 Berkeley Ct, Oaklands Dr, Weybridge, Surrey, UK KT13 9HY. Phone: (44) (1932) 220401.

EVACUATION DAY: 225th ANNIVERSARY. Mar 17, 1776. A public holiday at Boston and Suffolk County, MA, celebrates anniversary of the evacuation from Boston of British troops.

FEMALE RELIEF SOCIETY OF NAUVOO ORGANIZED: ANNIVERSARY. Mar 17, 1842. Twenty Mormon women formally initiated this organization at Nauvoo, IL, which is now known as the Relief Society and has grown to almost four million members. Information furnished by Church of Jesus Christ of Latter-day Saints, Public Affairs Department.

IRELAND: NATIONAL DAY. Mar 17. St. Patrick's Day is observed in the Republic of Ireland as a legal national holiday.

JONES, BOBBY: BIRTH ANNIVERSARY. Mar 17, 1902. Golfing great Robert Tyre Jones, Jr, first golfer to win the grand slam (the four major British and American tournaments in one year). Born at Atlanta, GA, he died there Dec 18, 1971.

MAPLE SYRUP SATURDAY. Mar 17. Gordon Bubolz Nature Preserve, Appleton, WI. Find out how to make maple syrup. Est attendance: 1,000. For info: Mike Brandel, Exec Dir, Gordon Bubolz Nature Preserve, 4815 N Lynndale Dr, Appleton, WI 54913. Phone: (920) 731-6041. Fax: (920) 731-9593. E-mail: Bubolz@dataex.com.

MILITARY THROUGH THE AGES. Mar 17–18. Jamestown Settlement, Williamsburg, VA. Reenactment groups depicting soldiers and military encounters throughout history join forces with modern-day veterans and active units to demonstrate camp life, tactics and weaponry. Est attendance: 4,000. For info: Media Relations, Jamestown-Yorktown Fdtn, Box 1607, Williamsburg, VA 23187. Phone: (757) 253-4838. Web: www.historyisfun.org.

NORTHERN IRELAND: SAINT PATRICK'S DAY HOLIDAY. Mar 17. National Holiday.

NUREYEV, RUDOLF HAMETOVICH: BIRTH ANNIVERSARY. Mar 17, 1938. Rudolf Nureyev, one of the most charismatic ballet stars of the 20th century, was born on a train in southeastern Siberia. Nureyev's defection from the Soviet Union on June 17, 1961, while on tour with the Kirov Ballet, made headlines worldwide. The dancer was known for his ability to combine passion with a high level of perfectionism. His long partnership with Dame Margot Fonteyn of the Royal Ballet was legendary, and he also performed frequently with the Martha Graham Dance Company. Nureyev also choreographed, restaged many classics and served as the Paris Opera Ballet's artistic director. He died Jan 6, 1993, at Levallois, France, a suburb of Paris.

PARKER, GEORGE: DEATH ANNIVERSARY. Mar 17, 1764. George Parker, the second Earl of Macclesfield, was born in 1697 (exact date unknown). The eminent English astronomer was president of the Royal Society from 1752 until his death. He was one of the principal authors of the Bill for Regulating the Commencement of the Year (British Calendar Act of 1751), which was introduced in Parliament by Lord Chesterfield. That act caused the adoption, in 1752, of the "New Style" Gregorian calendar, which is still in use today. Parker died at Shirburn Castle, England.

RAPPAHANNOCK RIVER WATERFOWL SHOW. Mar 17–18. White Stone, VA. Preview Night Gala, Mar 16, advance tickets required. 90 nationally recognized artists display their wildfowl art, including sculptures, paintings, photography, prints and carvings. Sponsored by the White Stone Volunteer Fire Dept. For info: William Bruce, Waterfowl Show, 151 Bruce Ln, White Stone, VA 22578. Phone: (804) 435-6355.

RUSTIN, BAYARD: BIRTH ANNIVERSARY. Mar 17, 1910. Black pacifist and civil rights leader, Bayard Rustin was an organizer and participant in many of the great social protest marches—for jobs, freedom and nuclear disarmament. He was arrested and imprisoned more than 20 times for his civil rights and pacifist activities. Born at West Chester, PA, Rustin died at New York, NY, Aug 24, 1987.

SAINT PATRICK'S DAY. Mar 17. Commemorates the patron saint of Ireland, Bishop Patrick (AD389–461) who, about AD 432, left his home in the Severn Valley, England, and introduced Christianity into Ireland. Feast Day in the Roman Catholic Church. A national holiday in Ireland and Northern Ireland.

SAINT PATRICK'S DAY CELEBRATION. Mar 17. McMenamins Edgefield, Troutdale, OR. Bagpipes, Celtic music, wandering storyteller, Irish coffees and special Irish menus in the pub and restaurant. Annual McMenamins tradition. Est attendance: 1,000. For info: McMenamins Edgefield, 2126 SW Halsey, Troutdale, OR 97060. Phone: (800) 669-8610. E-mail: edge @mcmenamins.com. Web: www.mcmenamins.com.

SAINT PATRICK'S DAY CELEBRATION. Mar 17. Huntington, WV. Live entertainment, music and dance appropriate for St. Patrick's Day. Food, games, beverages, concessions and parade. Est attendance: 3,500. For info: Rick Abel, Greater Huntington Parks & Recreation, PO Box 2985, Huntington, WV 25728. Phone: (304) 696-5954. Fax: (304) 696-5588. Web: www.ghprd.org.

SAINT PATRICK'S DAY PARADE. Mar 17. Downtown Hornell, NY. 14th annual. It's a "come as you are" line of march, open to anyone, with no entry fee, no judges, no prizes. Hornell's parade is designed as purely a fun affair, especially for those people who've always wanted to be in a parade but never had the opportunity. It has gotten larger and longer every year, with more and more "would-be Irish" strolling down Main Street. Annually, the Saturday before Saint Patrick's Day except when Saint Patrick's Day is a Thursday or Friday, then, the following Saturday. Est attendance: 4,000. For info: Wolf Berry, Bilbat Radio, Inc, PO Box 726, Hornell, NY 14843. Phone: (607) 324-2000. Fax: (607) 324-2001. E-mail: sales@wkpq.com. Web: www.wkpq.com.

SAINT PATRICK'S DAY PARADE. Mar 17. Fifth Avenue, New York, NY. Held since 1762, the parade of 125,000 begins the two-mile march at 11:30 AM and lasts about six hours. Starts on 42nd Street and 5th Avenue and ends at 86th Street and First Avenue. Est attendance: 1,000,000. For info: NY CVB, 810 7th Ave, 3rd Floor, New York, NY 10019. Phone: (800) NYC-VISIT or (212) 484-1222.

SAINT PATRICK'S DAY PARADE & CELTIC FESTIVAL. Mar 17. Roanoke, VA. Sponsors: The Roanoke Special Events Committee. Est attendance: 20,000. For info: Shauna Hudson, Special Events Coord, City of Roanoke, 210 Reserve Ave SW, Roanoke, VA 24016. Phone: (540) 853-2889. E-mail: shudson@ci.roanoke.va.us.

SAINT PATRICK'S DAY PARADE: "THE WEARIN' OF THE GREEN." Mar 17. Baton Rouge, LA. Headquarters: Zee Zee Gardens. Includes floats, marching bands, walking groups, bagpipers and more. Largest St. Patrick's Day celebration in area. Street celebration follows with live entertainment. Est attendance: 80,000. For info: Baton Rouge Irish Club, 6906 Moniteau Court, Baton Rouge, LA 70809. Phone: (225) 925-8295. Fax: (225) 925-8295.

SAVE THE FLORIDA PANTHER DAY. Mar 17. Florida. A ceremonial holiday on the third Saturday in March.

SOUTH AFRICAN WHITES VOTE TO END MINORITY RULE: ANNIVERSARY. Mar 17, 1992. A referendum proposing ending white minority rule through negotiations was supported by a whites-only ballot. The vote of 1,924,186 (68.6 percent) whites in support of President F.W. de Klerk's reform policies was greater than expected.

SPACE MILESTONE: *DISCOVERY* (US). Mar 17, 1989. Space shuttle *Discovery* landed at Edwards Air Force Base after carrying five astronauts on mission to put into orbit a $100 million tracking and data-relay satellite.

SPACE MILESTONE: *VANGUARD 1* (US). Mar 17, 1958. Established "pear shape" of Earth. At only three pounds it was the first solar-powered satellite.

SPRING CRAFT AND GIFT SHOW: INDOOR SHOW. Mar 17–18. Wisconsin State Fair Park, Milwaukee, WI. Show combined with commercial gift exhibitors and craftsmen. Est attendance: 20,000. For info: Dir, Spring Craft and Gift Show, 9312 W National Ave, Milwaukee, WI 53227-1542. Phone: (414) 321-2100. Web: www.CraftFairUSA.com.

TANEY, ROGER B.: BIRTH ANNIVERSARY. Mar 17, 1777. Fifth Chief Justice of the Supreme Court, born at Calvert County, MD. Served as Attorney General under President Andrew Jackson. Nominated as Secretary of the Treasury, he became the first presidential nominee to be rejected by the Senate. His rejection centered on his strong stance against the Bank of the United States as a central bank and his role in urging President Jackson to veto the congressional bill extending its charter. A year later, he was nominated to the Supreme Court as an associate justice by Jackson, but his nomination was stalled until the death of Chief Justice John Marshall July 6, 1835. Taney was nominated to fill Marshall's place on the bench and after much resistance he was sworn in as Chief Justice in March 1836. His tenure on the Supreme Court is most remembered for the Dred Scott decision. He died at Washington, DC, Oct 12, 1864.

A VICTORIAN EASTER. Mar 17–Apr 15. Belle Meade Plantation, Nashville, TN. Put on your Easter bonnet and tour this 1853 Southern mansion decorated for the holiday in the late 19th century. For info: Belle Meade Plantation, 5025 Harding Rd, Nashville, TN 37205. Phone: (800) 270-3991 or (615) 356-0501. Fax: (615) 356-2336. Web: www.bellemeadeplantation.com.

BIRTHDAYS TODAY

Daniel Ray (Danny) Ainge, 42, basketball coach, former basketball and baseball player, born Eugene, OR, Mar 17, 1959.

Susie Allanson, 49, singer ("Baby Don't Keep Me Hangin' On"), born Minneapolis, MN, Mar 17, 1952.

Lesley-Anne Down, 47, actress ("Upstairs, Downstairs," "Dallas," *The Pink Panther Strikes Again*), born London, England, Mar 17, 1954.

Patrick Duffy, 52, actor ("Step by Step," "Dallas"), born Townsend, MT, Mar 17, 1949.

Paul Horn, 71, composer, musician, born New York, NY, Mar 17, 1930.

Vicki Lewis, 35, actress ("NewsRadio," *Godzilla*), born Cincinnati, OH, Mar 17, 1966.

Rob Lowe, 37, actor (*St. Elmo's Fire, About Last Night . . .*), born Charlottesville, VA, Mar 17, 1964.

Mercedes McCambridge, 83, actress (voice of Satan in *The Exorcist*; Oscar for *All the King's Men*), born Joliet, IL, Mar 17, 1918.

Kurt Russell, 50, actor (*Backdraft, Elvis*), born Springfield, MA, Mar 17, 1951.

Gary Sinise, 46, stage and screen actor (*Forrest Gump, Apollo 13*), born Chicago, IL, Mar 17, 1955.

MARCH 18 — SUNDAY

Day 77 — 288 Remaining

ANONYMOUS GIVING WEEK. Mar 18–24. A time to celebrate the true spirit of giving. Experience the joy in random acts of kindness. Leave a legacy of anonymous contribution. Perfect for a onetime or all-week adventure designed to share time, talent and treasure. For info: Janna Krammer, Legacy Institute, 42747 Blackhawk Rd, Harris, MN 55032. Phone: (877) 646-9200. Fax: (651) 674-0228. E-mail: info@legacyinstitute.com.

ARUBA: FLAG DAY. Mar 18. Aruba national holiday. Display of flags, national music and folkloric events.

BUZZARD DAY. Mar 18. Hinckley, OH. Tradition says that on this day the buzzards (also known as turkey vultures or carrion crows) return to Hinckley, OH, from their winter quarters in the Great Smoky Mountains to rear their young. Pancake and sausage breakfast, crafters and exhibits. For info: Hinckley Chamber of Commerce, PO Box 354, Hinckley, OH 44233.

CALHOUN, JOHN CALDWELL: BIRTH ANNIVERSARY. Mar 18, 1782. American statesman and first vice president of the US to resign that office (Dec 28, 1832). Born at Abbeville District, SC, died at Washington, DC, Mar 31, 1850.

March 2001	S	M	T	W	T	F	S
					1	2	3
	4	5	6	7	8	9	10
	11	12	13	14	15	16	17
	18	19	20	21	22	23	24
	25	26	27	28	29	30	31

CAMP FIRE BOYS AND GIRLS BIRTHDAY SUNDAY.
Mar 18. A day when Camp Fire Boys and Girls commemorate the organization's founding and worship together and participate in the services of their churches or temples. For info: Camp Fire Boys and Girls, 4601 Madison Ave, Kansas City, MO 64112. Phone: (816) 756-1950. Fax: (816) 756-0258. E-mail: info@campfire.org. Web: www.campfire.org.

CANADA: WORLD FIGURE SKATING CHAMPION-SHIPS. Mar 18–25. Vancouver, BC. More than 200 of the world's best skaters from 55 countries will compete in the last World Championships to be held before the 2002 Winter Olympics in Salt Lake City. For info: Canadian Figure Skating Assn, 1600 James Naismith Dr, Gloucester, ON, Canada K1B 5N4. Phone: (613) 747-1007. Web: www.cfsa.ca/2001/index.htm.

CLEVELAND, GROVER: BIRTH ANNIVERSARY. Mar 18, 1837. The 22nd and 24th president of the US was born Stephen Grover Cleveland at Caldwell, NJ. Terms of office as president: Mar 4, 1885–Mar 3, 1889, and Mar 4, 1893–Mar 3, 1897. He ran for president for the intervening term and received a plurality of votes cast but failed to win electoral college victory for that term. Only president to serve two nonconsecutive terms. Also the only president to be married in the White House. He married 21-year-old Frances Folsom, his ward. Their daughter, Esther, was the first child of a president to be born in the White House. Died at Princeton, NJ, June 24, 1908.

FIRST ELECTRIC RAZOR MARKETED: 70th ANNI-VERSARY. Mar 18, 1931. The first electric razor was marketed by Schick, Inc.

GO NUTS OVER TEXAS PEANUTS WEEK. Mar 18–24. Everything's big in Texas, including the pride in its peanut industry! Texas is the nation's second largest peanut-producing state and is one of only two states that grow all four US peanut varieties: Runner, Spanish, Virginia and Valencia. Part of National Peanut Month, "Go Nuts Over Peanuts Week," celebrates America's favorite nut. Annually, the third full week of March. For info: Mary Webb, Texas Peanut Producers Board, PO Box 398, Gorman, TX 76454. Phone: (800) 734-0086. Fax: (254) 734-2017. Web: www.texaspeanutboard.com.

ISRAEL: JERUSALEM INTERNATIONAL BOOK FAIR. Mar 18–23. Jerusalem. 20th annual fair. For info: Jerusalem Intl Book Fair, PO Box 775, Jerusalem, Israel, 91007. Phone: 972 2 629-7922. Fax: 972 2 624-3144. E-mail: jer-fair@netvision.net.il. Web: www.jerusalembookfair.com.

JAPANESE SUICIDE WEAPON INTRODUCED: ANNI-VERSARY. Mar 18, 1945. The Japanese released mechanized flying bombs piloted by young Japanese men. These suicide bombs, directed against the US aircraft carrier fleet attacking the Japanese fleet in the Kure-Kobe area, inflicted serious damage on the *Enterprise, Intrepid* and *Wasp*.

JOBS FOR TEENS WEEK. Mar 18–24. To encourage young adults to better prepare themselves for their future career through practical experience in the workplace. Free information/resource kit available for teachers, librarians, counselors. Annually, the week containing the first day of Spring. For info: Highsmith Press, PO Box 800, Ft Atkinson, WI 53538-0800. Phone: (800) 558-2110 or 9205639571. Fax: (920) 563-4801. E-mail: hpress@highsmith.com. Web: www.hpress.highsmith.com/jobweek.htm.

JOHNSON, WILLIAM H.: 100th BIRTH ANNIVER-SARY. Mar 18, 1901. African American artist born at Florence, SC; died Apr 13, 1970, at Islip, NY. Johnson spent many years in Europe painting expressionist works. He was strongly influenced by the vivid styles and brushstrokes of Henry O. Tanner, Vincent van Gogh, Paul Gauguin, Edvard Munch and Otto Dix. He left Europe when Hitler began destroying art that had primitivist or African themes. Back in the US, Johnson developed a new, flatter style and delved into subjects of his own experience as well as historical African-American figures and events. *Going to Church* (1940–41) and *Mom and Dad* (1944) are examples of his later work.

JORDAN'S BACK!: ANNIVERSARY. Mar 18, 1995. Michael Jordan, considered one of the NBA's greatest all-time players, made history again when he announced that he was returning to professional play after a 17-month break. The 32-year-old star had retired just before the start of the 1993–94 season, following the murder of his father, James Jordan. Jordan, who averaged 32.3 points a game during regular season play, had led the Chicago Bulls to three successive NBA titles. While retired, he tried a baseball career, playing for the Chicago White Sox minor league team. On his return to the Bulls, he led them to three more NBA titles in 1996, 1997 and 1998. He announced his retirement again Jan 13, 1999, after the six-month NBA lock-out was resolved.

MICHIGAN'S GRANDPARENTS AND GRANDCHIL-DREN DAY. Mar 18. During this annual observance grandparents are invited into schools across Michigan to join with the children in special programs and events. For info: Luella Davison, Grandparents Anonymous, 900 N Cass Lake Rd, Waterford, MI 48328. Phone: (800) 4AC-hild.

NATIONAL AGRICULTURE WEEK. Mar 18–24. "America's Largest Classroom on Agriculture." To honor America's providers of food and fiber and to educate future generations about the US agricultural system. Annually, the week that includes the first day of spring. For info: Agriculture Council of America, 11020 King St, Ste 205, Overland Park, KS 66210. Phone: (913) 491-1895. Fax: (913) 491-6502. E-mail: info@agday.org. Web: www.agday.org.

NATIONAL POISON PREVENTION WEEK. Mar 18–24. To aid in encouraging the American people to learn of the dangers of accidental poisoning and to take preventive measures against it. Annually, the third full week in March. For info: Ken Giles, Secy, Poison Prevention Week Council, PO Box 1543, Washington, DC 20013. E-mail: kgiles@cpsc.gov. Web: www.cpsc.gov.

★**NATIONAL POISON PREVENTION WEEK.** Mar 18–24. Presidential Proclamation issued each year for the third week of March since 1962. (PL87–319 of Sept 26, 1961.)

SPACE MILESTONE: *VOSKHOD 2* (USSR). Mar 18, 1965. Colonel Leonov stepped out of the capsule for 20 minutes in a special space suit, the first man to leave a spaceship. It was two months prior to the first US space walk. See also: "Space Milestone: *Gemini 4* US" (June 3).

"TALES OF WELLS FARGO" TV PREMIERE: ANNI-VERSARY. Mar 18, 1957. This half-hour western starred Dale Robertson as Jim Hardie, agent for Wells Fargo transport company. In the fall of 1961, the show expanded to an hour. Hardie bought a ranch, and new cast members were added, including Jack Ging as Beau McCloud, another agent, Virginia Christine as Ovie, a widow owning a nearby ranch, Lory Patrick and Mary Jane Saunders as Ovie's daughters and William Demarest as Jeb, Hardie's ranch foreman. Jack Nicholson appeared in one of his first major TV roles in the episode "The Washburn Girl."

BIRTHDAYS TODAY

Bonnie Blair, 37, Olympic gold medal speed skater, born Cornwall, NY, Mar 18, 1964.

Irene Cara, 42, singer ("Fame," "The Dream"), actress (*Ain't Misbehavin'*), born The Bronx, NY, Mar 18, 1959.

Frederik Willem de Klerk, 65, former president of South Africa, born Johannesburg, South Africa, Mar 18, 1936.

Kevin Dobson, 57, actor ("Kojak," "Knots Landing"), born New York, NY, Mar 18, 1944.

Brad Dourif, 51, actor (*One Flew Over the Cuckoo's Nest, Blue Velvet, Jungle Fever*), born Huntington, WV, Mar 18, 1950.

Peter Graves, 75, actor ("Mission: Impossible," "The Winds of War"), born Minneapolis, MN, Mar 18, 1926.

George Kander, 74, composer (*Cabaret, Chicago*), born Kansas City, MO, Mar 18, 1927.

Shashi Kapoor, 63, actor (*Heat and Dust, Sammy and Rosie Get Laid*), born Calcutta, India, Mar 18, 1938.

Queen Latifah, 31, rap artist, actress (*Jungle Fever*, "Living Single"), born Dana Owens, East Orange, NJ, Mar 18, 1970.

Wilson Pickett, 60, singer, songwriter ("The Midnight Hour," "It's Too Late"), born Prattville, AL, Mar 18, 1941.

George Plimpton, 74, author (*Paper Lion, Shadow Box*), TV host, editor, born New York, NY, Mar 18, 1927.

Charley Pride, 63, singer, former minor league baseball player, born Sledge, MS, Mar 18, 1938.

John Updike, 69, author (*Rabbit Run, The Witches of Eastwick*), born Shillington, PA, Mar 18, 1932.

Vanessa Williams, 38, singer, actress (*Bye, Bye Birdie; Kiss of the Spider Woman*), born New York, NY, Mar 18, 1963.

MARCH 19 — MONDAY

Day 78 — 287 Remaining

AUSTRALIA: CANBERRA DAY. Mar 19. Australian Capital Territory. Public holiday the third Monday in March.

BRADFORD, WILLIAM: BIRTH ANNIVERSARY. Mar 19, 1589 (OS). Pilgrim father, governor of Plymouth Colony. Born at Yorkshire, England, and baptized Mar 19, 1589. Sailed from Southampton, England, on the *Mayflower* in 1620. Died at Plymouth, MA, May 9, 1657 (OS).

BRYAN, WILLIAM JENNINGS: BIRTH ANNIVERSARY. Mar 19, 1860. American political leader, member of Congress, Democratic presidential nominee (1896), "free silver" advocate, assisted in prosecution at Scopes trial, known as "the Silver-Tongued Orator." Born at Salem, IL, he died at Dayton, TN, July 26, 1925.

EARP, WYATT: BIRTH ANNIVERSARY. Mar 19, 1848. Born at Monmouth, IL, and died Jan 13, 1929, at Los Angeles, CA. A legendary figure of the Old West, Earp worked as a railroad hand, saloonkeeper, gambler, lawman, gunslinger, miner and real estate investor at various times. Best known for the gunfight at the OK Corral Oct 26, 1881, at Tombstone, AZ.

LIVINGSTONE, DAVID: BIRTH ANNIVERSARY. Mar 19, 1813. Scottish physician, missionary and explorer born at Blantyre, Scotland. Subject of a famous search by Henry M. Stanley, who found him at Ujiji, near Lake Tanganyika in Africa, on Nov 10, 1871. Dr. Livingstone died at Africa, May 1, 1873. See also: "Stanley, Henry Morton: Birth Anniversary" (Jan 28).

"THE MARY TYLER MOORE SHOW": THE FINAL EPISODE: ANNIVERSARY. Mar 19, 1977. "Mary Tyler Moore" was the first of a new wave of sitcoms to make it big in the early '70s. It combined good writing, an effective supporting cast and contemporary attitudes. The show centered around the two most important places in Mary Richards's (Mary Tyler Moore) life—the WJM-TV newsroom and her apartment at Minneapolis. At home she shared the ups and downs of life with her friend Rhoda Morgenstern (Valerie Harper) and the manager of her apartment building, Phyllis Lindstrom (Cloris Leachman). At work, as the associate producer (later producer) of "The Six O'Clock News," Mary struggled to function in a man's world. Figuring in her professional life were her irascible boss Lou Grant (Ed Asner), levelheaded and softhearted news writer Murray Slaughter (Gavin MacLeod) and self-obsessed, narcissistic anchorman Ted Baxter (Ted Knight). In the last episode the unthinkable happened—everyone in the WJM newsroom except the inept Ted was fired. (Premiered Sept 19, 1970, and ran for 168 episodes.)

McKEAN, THOMAS: BIRTH ANNIVERSARY. Mar 19, 1734. Signer of the Declaration of Independence and governor of Pennsylvania. Born at Chester County, PA, he died June 24, 1817.

NABISCO CHAMPIONSHIP. Mar 19–25. Mission Hills Country Club, Rancho Mirage, CA. Held since 1972, this tournament is often called the Master's of women's professional golf. For info: Nabisco Championship. Phone: (760) 324-4546. Web: www.nabiscodinahshore.com.

NATIONAL BUBBLE WEEK. Mar 19–25. A chance for Americans of all ages to celebrate the classic play and enhancement of bubbles, a favorite hobby in this country for the past 60 years. Annually, begins the Monday before the first day of spring. For info: Litzky Public Relations, 261 First St, Hoboken, NJ 07030. Phone: (201) 222-9118. Fax: (201) 222-9418.

NATIONAL CLUTTER AWARENESS WEEK. Mar 19–25. To provide a week of awareness of clutter accumulated over the summer, fall and winter months; to begin that Spring Cleaning purge. From the garage to the kitchen cabinets, the hall closet to the desk drawers, the piles of magazines, clothes that don't fit, junk drawers, purses, toys and tool chest, begin to make plans to purge, sort, recycle and organize all the piles of clutter. Let go of unused, worn-out, out-of-style stuff that takes up much-needed space and have time to enjoy summer. In the office, from the storeroom to the supply cabinets, the lunchroom, desks, computers, bulletin boards, file cabinets. Creating awareness of excess and unused items will help employees to take action to maintain more order and tidiness in their work areas. Annually, the last full week of March. For info: Gloria Schaaf, The Schaaf Organization, LLC, Gracie Station, PO Box 1166, New York, NY 10028. Phone: (212) 410-4937.

NATIONAL SECONDHAND SHOPPING WEEK. Mar 19–23. Spring is a great time to clean your closets. Bring your items into a consignment store or donate them to a thrift store which will benefit a worthy cause. For info: Carolyn Schneider, The Ultimate Consignment & Thriftstore Guide, 442 Route 202-206 N, Ste 274, Bedminster, NJ 07921. Phone: (908) 781-2589 or (800) 361-5171. Fax: (908) 781-8598. E-mail: carolyn@consignmentguide.com. Web: www.consignmentguide.com.

NATIONAL SPRING FEVER WEEK. Mar 19–25. Annually, including the first day of spring. Recognizing the special socialization rites single people face during this season of revitalization. For info: Robin Gorman Newman, 44 Somerset Dr N, Great Neck, NY 11020. Phone: (516) 773-0911. E-mail: rgnewman@aol.com.

ROGERS, EDITH NOURSE: BIRTH ANNIVERSARY. Mar 19, 1881. Edith Nourse Rogers was a YMCA and Red Cross volunteer in France during World War I. In 1925 she was elected to the US Congress to fill the vacancy left by the death of her husband. An able legislator, she was reelected to the House of Representatives 17 times and became the first woman to have her name attached to major legislation. She was a major force in the legislation creating the Women's Army Auxiliary Corps (May 14, 1942) during World War II. Rogers was born at Saco, ME, and died Sept 10, 1960, at Boston.

	S	M	T	W	T	F	S
March					1	2	3
2001	4	5	6	7	8	9	10
	11	12	13	14	15	16	17
	18	19	20	21	22	23	24
	25	26	27	28	29	30	31

RUSSELL, CHARLES M.: BIRTH ANNIVERSARY. Mar 19, 1864. Born at St. Louis, MO, Charles M. Russell moved to Montana at about age 16 and became a cowboy. Considered one of the greatest Western artists, he recorded the life of the cowboy in his artwork. He died Oct 26, 1926, at Great Falls, MT.

RYDER, ALBERT PINKHAM: BIRTH ANNIVERSARY. Mar 19, 1847. Painter Albert Pinkham Ryder was born at New Bedford, MA, where he gained a great love for the sea, the subject of many of his works. Ryder was a misanthrope and recluse. He dedicated himself to his painting, working slowly and piling layer after layer of paint on his canvases until he achieved the look he was after. In his lifetime Ryder created only 150 paintings. Three of his best-known works are *The Race Track, Toilers of the Sea* and *Siegfried and the Rhine Maidens*. Ryder died Mar 28, 1917, at Elmhurst, NY. Because of his method of painting, many of his works have deteriorated since their creation.

SIRICA, JOHN JOSEPH: BIRTH ANNIVERSARY. Mar 19, 1904. John Sirica, "the Watergate Judge," was born at Waterbury, CT. During two years of trials and hearings, Sirica relentlessly pushed for the names of those responsible for the June 17, 1972, burglary of the Democratic National Committee headquarters in Washington's Watergate Complex. His unwavering search for the truth ultimately resulted in the toppling of the Nixon administration. Judge John Sirica died Aug 15, 1992, at Washington, DC.

SWALLOWS RETURN TO SAN JUAN CAPISTRANO. Mar 19. Traditional date (St. Joseph's Day), since 1776, for swallows to return to old mission of San Juan Capistrano, CA. See also: "St. John of Capistrano: Death Anniversary" (Oct 23).

US STANDARD TIME ACT: ANNIVERSARY. Mar 19, 1918. Anniversary of passage by the Congress of the Standard Time Act, which authorized the Interstate Commerce Commission to establish standard time zones for the US. The Act also established "Daylight Saving Time," to save fuel and to promote other economies in a country at war. Daylight-Saving Time first went into operation on Easter Sunday, Mar 31, 1918. The Uniform Time Act of 1966, as amended in 1986, by Public Law 99–359, now governs standard time in the US. See also: "US: Daylight Saving Time Begins" (Apr 1).

VAN FLEET, JAMES ALWARD: BIRTH ANNIVERSARY. Mar 19, 1892. US Army four-star general James Alward Van Fleet was born at Coytesville, NJ. He served in World War I, World War II, the Korean War and consulted for the Defense Department during the Vietnam War. He was awarded the Distinguished Service Cross with three oak leaf clusters among numerous other decorations during his service. He died Sept 23, 1992, at Polk City, FL.

WARREN, EARL: BIRTH ANNIVERSARY. Mar 19, 1891. American jurist, 14th Chief Justice of the US Supreme Court. Born at Los Angeles, CA; died at Washington, DC, July 9, 1974.

BIRTHDAYS TODAY

Ursula Andress, 65, actress (*Dr. No, What's New Pussycat?*), born Bern, Switzerland, Mar 19, 1936.

Michael Bergin, 32, actor ("Baywatch"), born Naugatuck, CT, Mar 19, 1969.

Glenn Close, 54, actress (*The Big Chill, Fatal Attraction*; stage: *Sunset Boulevard*), born Greenwich, CT, Mar 19, 1947.

Ornette Coleman, 71, composer, saxophonist, born Fort Worth, TX, Mar 19, 1930.

Patrick McGoohan, 73, director, actor ("The Prisoner"), born New York, NY, Mar 19, 1928.

Philip Roth, 68, author (*The Great American Novel, Portnoy's Complaint*), born Newark, NJ, Mar 19, 1933.

Renee Taylor, 66, actress, writer (Emmy for "Acts of Love and Other Comedies"; "Mary Hartman, Mary Hartman," *The Producers, A New Leaf*), born New York, NY, Mar 19, 1935.

Bruce Willis, 46, actor ("Moonlighting," *In Country, Die Hard*), born Penn's Grove, NJ, Mar 19, 1955.

MARCH 20 — TUESDAY
Day 79 — 286 Remaining

GREAT AMERICAN MEATOUT. Mar 20. America's foremost celebration of meatless eating asks consumers to "kick the meat habit, at least for the day" at 2,000 events across the country. For info: Farm Animal Reform Movement, Box 30654, Bethesda, MD 20824. Phone: (301) 530-1737 or (800) MEATOUT. Fax: (301) 530-5747. E-mail: farm@farmusa.org. Web: www.meatout.com.

IBSEN, HENRIK: BIRTH ANNIVERSARY. Mar 20, 1828. Norwegian playwright born at Skien, Norway. Among his best-remembered plays: *Peer Gynt, The Pillars of Society, The Wild Duck, An Enemy of the People* and *Hedda Gabler*. Died at Oslo, Norway, May 23, 1906.

JAPAN: VERNAL EQUINOX DAY. Mar 20. National holiday in Japan. When it falls on a weekend, it is celebrated on the closest working day.

NATIONAL AGRICULTURE DAY. Mar 20. A day to honor America's providers of food and fiber and to educate the general public about the US agricultural system. Week of celebration: Mar 18–24. Annually, the first day of spring. For info: Agriculture Council of America, 11020 King St, Ste 205, Overland Park, KS 66210. Phone: (913) 491-1895. Fax: (913) 491-6502. E-mail: info@agday.org. Web: www.agday.org.

NERVE-GAS ATTACK ON JAPANESE SUBWAY: ANNIVERSARY. Mar 20, 1995. Twelve people were killed and 5,000 injured in a nerve gas attack on the Tokyo subway system during rush hour. Suspected in the attack was the Japanese religious sect Aum Shinrikyo, founded and led by Shoko Asahara (real name Chizuo Matsumoto). The group, which professes belief in a hybrid of Buddhist-Hindu teachings, predicts an apocalypse. In a raid conducted against the sect's main compound in Kamikuishiki on Mar 25, police seized literature that predicted 90 percent of the people in the world would be killed by poison gas. Also seized were two tons of chemicals for making sarin, the poison used in the Mar 20 attack. This cache was reported to contain enough materials to kill five million people. In a second raid, Asahara was arrested.

OMAHA HOME AND GARDEN EXPO. Mar 20–25. Omaha Civic Auditorium, Omaha, NE. Annually, in March. For info: Robert P. Mancuso, Pres, Mid-America Exposition, Inc, PO Box 24851, Omaha, NE 68124-0851. Phone: (402) 346-8003 or (800) 475-SHOW. Fax: (402) 346-5412. Web: www.showofficeonline.com.

"ORIGINAL" WESTERN MASSACHUSETTS HOME SHOW. Mar 20–25. West Springfield, MA. The largest home show in New England with more than 700 booths and a large outside area covering more than six acres of exhibits. Annually, third or fourth week of March. Est attendance: 87,500. For info: Richard B. Kramer, Exec Dir, Home Builders Assn of Western Massachusetts, 240 Cadwell Dr, Springfield, MA 01104. Phone: (413) 733-3126. Fax: (413) 781-8416. E-mail: rkramer@hbawm.com. Web: www.hbawm.com.

OSTARA. Mar 20. (Also called Alban Eilir.) One of the "Lesser Sabbats" during the Wiccan year, Ostara is a fire and fertility festival that marks the beginning of spring. Annually, on the spring equinox.

PIZZA EXPO 2001. Mar 20–22. Las Vegas Convention Center, Las Vegas, NV. This show provides an opportunity for independent, chain and franchise pizza operators to meet with manufacturers and service representatives from the pizza industry. Also includes Pizza Festiva™ recipe and Pizza World Games™ competitions. Est attendance: 6,000. For info: Natl Assn of Pizza Operators, PO Box 1347, New Albany, IN 47151. Phone: (812) 949-0909 or (800) 489-8324. Fax: (812) 941-9711. Web: www.pizzaexpo.com.

PROPOSAL DAY!®. Mar 20 (also Sept 22). Proposal Day is a holiday for singles who are seeking marriage. Both bachelors and bachelorettes are encouraged to propose marriage to their true love on Proposal Day; the days of the vernal and autumnal equinoxes. Singles not quite ready to propose can celebrate the holiday by sending a gift to the one they hope to marry someday. List released each equinox of the 10 most eligible celebrity singles. Annually, on the first day of spring (vernal equinox). For info: John Michael O'Loughlin, 1333 W Campbell, #125, Richardson, TX 75080. Phone: (972) 565-0781.

SKINNER, B.F.: BIRTH ANNIVERSARY. Mar 20, 1904. American psychologist Burrhus Frederic Skinner was born at Susquehanna, PA. He was a pioneer in behaviorism, and is best known for developing the "Skinner box" (an enclosed experimental environment). He died Aug 18, 1990, at Cambridge, MA.

SNOWMAN BURNING. Mar 20. Reading of poetry heralding the end of winter and the arrival of spring, followed by sacrifice in effigy, toasts and cheers. Annually, on or near the first day of spring. Est attendance: 300. For info: Public Relations Office, Lake Superior State Univ, Sault Ste. Marie, MI 49783. Phone: (906) 635-2315. Fax: (906) 635-2623. E-mail: tpink@gw.lssu.edu. Web: www.lssu.edu.

SPRING. Mar 20–June 21. In the Northern Hemisphere spring begins today with the vernal equinox, at 8:31 AM, EST. Note that in the Southern Hemisphere today is the beginning of autumn. Sun rises due east and sets due west everywhere on Earth (except near poles) and the daylight length (interval between sunrise and sunset) is virtually the same everywhere today: 12 hours, 8 minutes.

TUNISIA: INDEPENDENCE DAY: 45th ANNIVERSARY. Mar 20. Commemorates treaty in 1956 by which France recognized Tunisian autonomy.

BIRTHDAYS TODAY

Holly Hunter, 43, actress (Oscar for *The Piano*; *Broadcast News, The Firm*), born Conyers, GA, Mar 20, 1958.

William Hurt, 51, actor (*The Accidental Tourist, Broadcast News*), born Washington, DC, Mar 20, 1950.

Spike Lee, 44, director, producer, writer, actor (*She's Gotta Have It, Do the Right Thing, Mo' Better Blues, Jungle Fever, Malcolm X*), born Atlanta, GA, Mar 20, 1957.

Hal Linden (Harold Lipshitz), 70, actor ("Barney Miller," "Blacke's Magic"), born The Bronx, NY, Mar 20, 1931.

Marian McPartland, 81, jazz pianist (*After Hours, Personal Choice, In My Life*), born Slough, England, Mar 20, 1920.

Brian Mulroney, 62, Canadian statesman and 18th prime minister of Canada, born Baie Comeau, Quebec, Mar 20, 1939.

Robert Gordon (Bobby) Orr, 53, Hockey Hall of Fame defenseman, born Parry Sound, Ontario, Canada, Mar 20, 1948.

Jerry Reed (Jerry Hubbard), 64, singer, songwriter ("When You're Hot, You're Hot"), born Atlanta, GA, Mar 20, 1937.

March *2001*	S	M	T	W	T	F	S
					1	2	3
	4	5	6	7	8	9	10
	11	12	13	14	15	16	17
	18	19	20	21	22	23	24
	25	26	27	28	29	30	31

Carl Reiner, 79, actor ("The Dick Van Dyke Show," "Your Show of Shows"), writer, director, born The Bronx, NY, Mar 20, 1922.

Patrick James (Pat) Riley, 56, basketball coach and former player, born Schenectady, NY, Mar 20, 1945.

Fred Rogers, 73, producer, TV personality ("Mr Rogers' Neighborhood"), born Latrobe, PA, Mar 20, 1928.

Theresa Russell, 44, actress (*Straight Time, Black Widow*), born San Diego, CA, Mar 20, 1957.

Paul Junger Witt, 58, producer, director, born New York, NY, Mar 20, 1943.

MARCH 21 — WEDNESDAY
Day 80 — 285 Remaining

ARIES, THE RAM. Mar 21–Apr 19. In the astronomical/astrological zodiac, which divides the sun's apparent orbit into 12 segments, the period Mar 21–Apr 19 is identified, traditionally, as the sun sign of Aries, the Ram. The ruling planet is Mars.

BACH, JOHANN SEBASTIAN: BIRTH ANNIVERSARY. Mar 21, 1685 (OS). Organist and composer, one of the most influential composers in musical history. Born at Eisenach, Germany; he died at Leipzig, Germany, July 28, 1750.

C.M. RUSSELL AUCTION OF ORIGINAL WESTERN ART. Mar 21–24. Heritage Inn, Great Falls, MT. Western art event features auctions, free seminars, 102 free display/sale rooms with thousands of artworks for sale, entertainment, elegant receptions and the best of Montana hospitality. Annually, the third Wednesday–Saturday in March. Est attendance: 6,000. For info: Donna Madison, Exec Dir, Great Falls Adv Fed, PO Box 634, Great Falls, MT 59403-0634. Phone: (800) 803-3351 or (406) 761-6453. E-mail: gfaf@gfaf.com.

FIRST ROUND-THE-WORLD BALLOON FLIGHT: ANNIVERSARY. March 21, 1999. Swiss psychiatrist Bertrand Piccard and British copilot Brian Jones landed in the Egyptian desert on this date, having flown 29,056 miles nonstop around the world in a hot-air balloon. Leaving from Chateau d'Oex in the Swiss Alps on Mar 1, the trip took 19 days, 21 hours and 55 minutes. Piccard is the grandson of balloonist Auguste Piccard, who was the first to ascend into the stratosphere in a balloon. See also: "Piccard, Auguste: Birth Anniversary" (Jan 28).

FLOWER DAY. Mar 21. Citizens will give or display flowers or plants in their communities and neighborhoods, schools, hospitals, businesses, memorials, shopping malls, government agencies; each state will honor the state flower at its capital. Area florists will also advertise Flower Day. For info: Fifth Street Flower Shop, 739 S 5th St, Springfield, IL 62703.

GALLO, JULIO: BIRTH ANNIVERSARY. Mar 21, 1910. American vintner Julio Gallo was born at Oakland, CA. He is best known for his role in the Ernest and Julio Gallo Winery, of Modesto, CA, which at one time claimed about 26 percent of the US wine industry. He died May 2, 1993, near Tracy, CA.

GERSDORFF HITLER ASSASSINATION ATTEMPT: ANNIVERSARY. Mar 21, 1943. In a suicide/assassination attempt planned for this date, Major General Baron von Gersdorff was to carry a bomb in the pocket of his greatcoat to the

"Heroes Memorial Day" annual dedication to the dead of the First World War. Hitler was to attend this event to inspect some weaponry taken from captured Russian soldiers. The bomb was to go off within 10 minutes of Hitler's arrival at the event as he was not expected to be there for very long. The conspirators were unable to locate the necessary short time fuse and the attempt had to be called off. This was the second serious plan to assassinate Hitler in 1943.

IRANIAN NEW YEAR: NORUZ. Mar 21. National celebration for all Iranians, this is the traditional Persian New Year. (In Iran spring comes Mar 20 or 21.) It is a celebration of nature's rebirth. Every household spreads a special cover with symbols for the seven good angels on it. These symbols are sprouts, wheat germ, apples, hyacinth, fruit of the jujube, garlic and sumac heralding life, rebirth, health, happiness, prosperity, joy and beauty. A fishbowl is also customary, representing the end of the astrological year and wild rue is burnt to drive away evil and bring about a happy New Year. This pre-Islamic holiday, a legacy of Zoroastrianism, is also celebrated as Navruz, Nau-Roz or Noo Roz in Afghanistan, Albania, Azerbaijan, Kazakhstan, Kyrgyzstan, Tajikistan and Turkmenistan. For info: Mahvash Tafreshi, Librarian, Farmingdale Public Library, 116 Merritts Rd, Farmingdale, NY 11735. Phone: (516) 249-9090. Fax: (516) 694-9697 or Yassaman Djalali, Librarian, West Valley Branch Library, 1243 San Tomas Aquino Rd, San Jose, CA 95117. Phone: (408) 244-4766.

JUAREZ, BENITO: BIRTH ANNIVERSARY. Mar 21, 1806. A full-blooded Zapotec Indian, Benito Pablo Juarez was born at Oaxaca, Mexico and grew up to become the president of Mexico. He learned Spanish at age 12. Juarez became judge of the civil court in Oaxaca in 1842, a member of congress in 1846 and governor in 1847. In 1858, following a rebellion against the constitution, the presidency was passed to Juarez. He died at Mexico City, July 18, 1872. A symbol of liberation and of Mexican resistance to foreign intervention, his birthday is a public holiday in Mexico.

LESOTHO: NATIONAL TREE PLANTING DAY. Mar 21. Lesotho.

LEWIS, FRANCIS: BIRTH ANNIVERSARY. Mar 21, 1713. Signer of the Declaration of Independence, born at Wales. Died Dec 31, 1802, at Long Island, NY.

LUNSFORD, BASCOM LAMAR: BIRTH ANNIVERSARY. Mar 21, 1882. Folk song writer and folklorist who authored the folk song "Mountain Dew," Lunsford started the first folk music festival in 1928 at Asheville, NC. This event, which led to the formation of the National Clogging and Hoedown Council, is held to this day. He was known as the "father of clogging dance" and the "king of folk music." He recorded some 320 folk songs, tunes and stories for the Library of Congress. Born at Mars Hill, NC, Lunsford died Sept 4, 1973, at South Turkey Creek, NC.

MEMORY DAY. Mar 21. To encourage awareness of traditional memory system using pattern t,d = 1; n = 2; m = 3; r = 4; l = 5; j,ch = 6; k,q,g-hard = 7; f,v = 8; b,p = 9. Study historic examples of the use of the memory system in the writings of Milton, Thomas Gray, Longfellow, Lincoln and others. For info: Robert L. Birch, Coord, Puns Corps, Box 2364, Falls Church, VA 22042-0364. Phone: (703) 533-3668.

NAMIBIA: INDEPENDENCE DAY: ANNIVERSARY. Mar 21. National Day. Commemorates independence from South Africa in 1990.

NAW-RUZ. Mar 21. Baha'i New Year's Day. Astronomically fixed to commence the year. One of the nine days of the year when Baha'is suspend work. For info: Dir, Baha'is of the US, Office of Public Info, 866 UN Plaza, Ste 120, New York, NY 10017-1822. Phone: (212) 803-2500. Fax: (212) 803-2573. E-mail: usopiny@bic.org. Web: www.us.bahai.org.

NJCAA DIVISION II MEN'S BASKETBALL NATIONAL FINALS. Mar 21-24. Danville, IL. Junior College Division II national men's basketball finals tournament. Est attendance:

8,000. For info: Jeanie Cooke, Exec Dir, Danville Area Conv/Visitors Bureau, PO Box 992, Danville, IL 61834. Phone: (800) 383-4386.

POCAHONTAS (REBECCA ROLFE): DEATH ANNIVERSARY. Mar 21, 1617. Pocahontas, daughter of Powhatan, born about 1595, near Jamestown, VA, leader of the Indian union of Algonkin nations, helped to foster good will between the colonists of the Jamestown settlement and her people. Pocahontas converted to Christianity, was baptized with the name Rebecca and married John Rolfe Apr 5, 1614. In 1616, she accompanied Rolfe on a trip to his native England, where she was regarded as an overseas "ambassador." Pocahontas's stay in England drew so much attention to the Virginia Company's Jamestown settlement that lotteries were held to help support the colony. Shortly before she was scheduled to return to Jamestown, Pocahontas died at Gravesend, Kent, England, of either smallpox or pneumonia.

SECOND BATTLE OF SOMME: ANNIVERSARY. Mar 21–Apr 4, 1918. General Erich Ludendorff launched the Michael offensive, the biggest German offensive of 1918, on Mar 21 with a five-hour artillery barrage. The Central Powers objective was to drive a wedge between the British and French forces and drive the British to the sea. Although they did not accomplish this objective, in the south they captured Montdidier and advanced to a depth of 40 miles. They managed to create a bulge in the front south of Somme and end what had effectively been a stalemate. The Allies lost nearly 230,000 men and the Germans almost as many in the Battle of Somme.

SELMA CIVIL RIGHTS MARCH: ANNIVERSARY. Mar 21, 1965. More than 3,000 civil rights demonstrators led by Dr. Martin Luther King, Jr, began a four-day march from Selma, AL, to Montgomery, AL, to demand federal protection of voting rights. There were violent attempts by local police, using fire hoses and dogs, to suppress the march. A march two weeks before on Mar 7, 1965, was called "Bloody Sunday" because of the use of night sticks, chains and electric cattle prods against the marchers by the police.

SINGLE PARENTS DAY. Mar 21. Dedicated to recognizing and heightening awareness of Americans to the issues related to single-parent households. In 1984, Congress established Mar 21 as Single Parents Day. Each year the Coalition for Single Parents Day honors the Single Parent of the Year with an award. 2000 recipients: Candace Carpenter, CEO ivillage.com and Kimi O. Gray, national public housing advocate. For info: Janice S. Moglen, Coalition for Single Parents Day, PO Box 61014, Denver, CO 80206. Phone: (303) 899-4971. Fax: (303) 832-1667. E-mail: singleparents_day@yahoo.com. Web: www.singleparentsday.com.

SOUTH AFRICA: HUMAN RIGHTS DAY. Mar 21. National holiday. Commemorates the Mar 21, 1960 massacre at Sharpeville and all those who lost their lives in the struggle for equal rights as citizens of South Africa.

STRANG, JAMES JESSE (KING STRANG): BIRTH ANNIVERSARY. Mar 21, 1813. Perhaps America's only crowned king was born at Scipio, NY, and christened Jesse James Strang (which he later changed to James Jesse Strang). He was crowned king of Mormons at Beaver Island, MI, July 8, 1850, and ruled his kingdom until his death. Elected to Michigan legislature in 1852 and 1854. Wounded by assassins June 16, 1856, at Beaver Island, he died June 19, 1856, at Voree, WI.

UNITED NATIONS: INTERNATIONAL DAY FOR THE ELIMINATION OF RACIAL DISCRIMINATION. Mar 21. Initiated by the United Nations General Assembly in 1966 to be observed annually Mar 21, the anniversary of the killing of 69 African demonstrators at Sharpeville, South Africa, in 1960, as a day to remember "the victims of Sharpeville and those countless others in different parts of the world who have fallen victim to racial injustice" and to promote efforts to eradicate racial discrimination worldwide. Info from: United Nations, Dept of Public Info, New York, NY 10017.

UNITED NATIONS: WEEK OF SOLIDARITY WITH THE PEOPLES STRUGGLING AGAINST RACISM AND RACIAL DISCRIMINATION. Mar 21–27. Annual observance initiated by United Nations General Assembly as part of its program of the Decade for Action to Combat Racism and Racial Discrimination. Info from: United Nations, Dept of Public Info, New York, NY 10017.

BIRTHDAYS TODAY

Matthew Broderick, 39, actor (*War Games, The Freshman, Family Business*), born New York, NY, Mar 21, 1962.

Peter Brook, 76, theater director, born London, England, Mar 21, 1925.

Timothy Dalton, 55, actor (*Centennial*, as James Bond in *License to Kill*) , born Colwyn Bay, Wales, Mar 21, 1946.

Al Freeman, Jr, 67, actor (*A Patch of Blue; Roots: The Next Generations*), born San Antonio, TX, Mar 21, 1934.

Rosie O'Donnell, 39, actress (*A League of Their Own*), host ("The Rosie O'Donnell Show"), born Commack, NY, Mar 21, 1962.

Gary Oldman, 43, actor (*Sid and Nancy, JFK*), born South London, England, Mar 21, 1958.

MARCH 22 — THURSDAY

Day 81 — 284 Remaining

AS YOUNG AS YOU FEEL DAY. Mar 22. Now more than ever you are as young as you feel. So stop acting your chronological age and get out there and start feeling peppy! [© 2000 by WH] For info: Thomas Roy, Wellcat Holidays, 2418 Long Ln, Lebanon, PA 17046. Phone: (717) 279-0184. E-mail: wellcat @supernet.com. Web: www.wellcat.com.

EQUAL RIGHTS AMENDMENT SENT TO STATES FOR RATIFICATION: ANNIVERSARY. Mar 22, 1972. The Senate passed the 27th Amendment, prohibiting discrimination on the basis of sex, sending it to the states for ratification. Hawaii led the way as the first state to ratify and by the end of the year 22 of the required states had ratified it. On Oct 6, 1978, the deadline for ratification was extended to June 30, 1982, by Congress. The amendment still lacked three of the required 38 states for ratification. This was the first extension granted since Congress set seven years as the limit for ratification. The amendment failed to achieve ratification as the deadline came and passed and no additional states ratified the measure.

FIRST WOMEN'S COLLEGIATE BASKETBALL GAME: ANNIVERSARY. Mar 22, 1893. The first women's collegiate basketball game was played at Smith College at Northampton, MA. Senda Berenson, then Smith's director of physical education and "mother of women's basketball," supervised the game, in which Smith's sophomore team beat the freshman team 5–4. For info: Dir of Media Relations, Smith College, Office of College Relations, Northampton, MA 01063. Phone: (413) 585-2190. Fax: (413) 585-2174. E-mail: lfenlaso@smith.edu. Web: www .smith.edu.

INDIA: NEW YEAR'S DAY. Mar 22. This is the first day of the New Year on the Saka calendar adopted by India after independence from Great Britain. The Saka calendar is a solar calendar with the same Leap Year schedule as the Gregorian calendar. In Leap Years, the New Year falls on Mar 21.

INTERNATIONAL DAY OF THE SEAL. Mar 22. In 1982 Congress declared an International Day of the Seal to draw attention to the cruelty of seal hunts and the virtual inevitability of these creatures' extinction. Zoos and aquariums around the world observe this day with special programs and activities; contact your local affiliate for a schedule of activities.

LASER PATENTED: ANNIVERSARY. Mar 22, 1960. The first patent for a laser (light amplification by stimulated emission of radiation) granted to Arthur Schawlow and Charles Townes.

NCAA DIVISION I MEN'S SWIMMING AND DIVING CHAMPIONSHIPS. Mar 22–24. Texas A&M University, College Station, TX. For info: NCAA, 700 W Washington Ave, PO Box 6222, Indianapolis, IN 46206-6222. Phone: (317) 917-6222. Fax: (317) 917-6888. Web: www.ncaa.org.

PAGE, RUTH: BIRTH ANNIVERSARY. Mar 22, 1899. American dancer and choreographer Ruth Page was born at Indianapolis, IN. She was a leading figure in Chicago dance with the Lyric Opera of Chicago, the Chicago Opera Ballet and the Chicago Ballet. She died Apr 7, 1991, at Chicago, IL.

SPACE MILESTONE: RECORD TIME IN SPACE. Mar 22, 1995. A Russian cosmonaut returned to Earth after setting a record of 439 days in space aboard *Mir*. Previous records include three Soviet cosmonauts who spent 237 days in space at *Salyut 7* space station in 1984, a Soviet cosmonaut who spent 326 days aboard *Mir* in 1987 and two Soviets who spent 366 days aboard *Mir* in 1988. The longest stay in space by any US astronaut was Shannon Lucid's 188-day stay on *Mir* in 1996. This also set a record for women in space.

UNITED NATIONS: WORLD DAY FOR WATER. Mar 22. The General Assembly declared this observance (Res 47/193) to promote public awareness of how water resource development contributes to economic productivity and social well-being of all nations.

BIRTHDAYS TODAY

George Benson, 58, singer, guitarist ("On Broadway," "Give Me the Night"), born Pittsburgh, PA, Mar 22, 1943.

Robert Quinlan (Bob) Costas, 49, sportscaster, born New York, NY, Mar 22, 1952.

Bruno Ganz, 60, actor (*The American Friend, Wings of Desire, The Last Days of Chez Nous*), born Zurich, Switzerland, Mar 22, 1941.

Orrin Grant Hatch, 67, US Senator (R, Utah), born Pittsburgh, PA, Mar 22, 1934.

Werner Klemperer, 81, actor (Emmy for "Hogan's Heroes"; *Ship of Fools*), born Cologne, Germany, Mar 22, 1920.

Andrew Lloyd Webber, 53, composer (*Cats, Phantom of the Opera*), born London, England, Mar 22, 1948.

Karl Malden (Mladen Sekulovich), 87, actor (*A Streetcar Named Desire*, "The Streets of San Francisco"), born Gary, IN, Mar 22, 1914.

Marcel Marceau, 78, actor, pantomimist (had the only speaking part in *Silent Movie*), born Strasbourg, France, Mar 22, 1923.

Matthew Modine, 42, actor (*Married to the Mob*, "And the Band Played On"), born Loma Linda, CA, Mar 22, 1959.

Allen Neuharth, 77, founder of *USA Today*, born Eureka, SD, Mar 22, 1924.

Cristen Powell, 22, race car driver, born Portland, OR, Mar 22, 1979.

Pat (Marion Gordon) Robertson, 71, TV evangelist, born Lexington, VA, Mar 22, 1930.

William Shatner, 70, actor ("Star Trek," "TJ Hooker"), author (*Tek* novels), born Montreal, Quebec, Canada, Mar 22, 1931.

Stephen Sondheim, 71, composer (*A Little Night Music*), born New York, NY, Mar 22, 1930.

Elvis Stojko, 29, skater, born Newmarket, Ontario, Canada, Mar 22, 1972.

M. Emmet Walsh, 66, actor (*Serpico, Blood Simple, Raising Arizona*), born Ogdensburg, NY, Mar 22, 1935.

Reese Witherspoon, 25, actress (*Fear, Twilight*), born Nashville, TN, Mar 22, 1976.

March 2001

S	M	T	W	T	F	S
				1	2	3
4	5	6	7	8	9	10
11	12	13	14	15	16	17
18	19	20	21	22	23	24
25	26	27	28	29	30	31

MARCH 23 — FRIDAY
Day 82 — 283 Remaining

BATTLE OF KERNSTOWN: ANNIVERSARY. Mar 23, 1862. As General George McClellan began the Peninsular campaign to move on the Confederate capital of Richmond, VA, Confederate General Stonewall Jackson engaged a larger force of Union troops at Kernstown in the northern Shenandoah Valley of Virginia on Mar 23, 1862. Although he ultimately was forced to retreat, the Battle of Kernstown provided a diversion central to the South's military strategy. Northern troops were kept around Washington as part of its defense, leaving fewer troops available for the Peninsular campaign.

"BEAT THE CLOCK" TV PREMIERE: ANNIVERSARY. Mar 23, 1950. On this game show from the team of Mark Goodson and Bill Todman, couples performed stunts within a specified time period (usually under 60 seconds) with the winners being given a chance to try a special stunt to win a great prize. Special stunts were very difficult, and the same one was attempted every week until a couple got it right. In 1952, James Dean got his first TV job testing stunts and warming up the audience. Bud Collyer was the host, assisted by Roxanne (real name Dolores Rosedale). A 1969 syndicated version hosted by Jack Narz and then by Gene Wood had celebrities to help the contestants. A 1979 revival was hosted by Monty Hall.

"BIG BERTHA" PARIS GUN: ANNIVERSARY. Mar 23, 1918. Germany initiated use of a terrifying new weapon—the Paris Gun—so called because it was first used against that city. The great gun, with a 25-foot carriage, was first used in combat when it was fired from a wooded location near Laon on Mar 23, 1918. It took 176 seconds for a shell to reach the city from a distance of 75 miles. On that first day 15 shots killed 16 individuals. Ridiculing the designers and manufacturers of the weapon, Parisians nicknamed it "Big Bertha" after the wife of the head of the munitions corporation. On Good Friday, Mar 29, a shell from the armament struck the church of Saint Gervais, which was crowded with worshipers. The casualty toll was 88 dead and 68 injured.

BIG TEN MEN'S GYMNASTICS CHAMPIONSHIP. Mar 23–24. Penn State, State College, PA. For info: Sue Ryan, Big Ten Conference, 1500 W Higgins Rd, Park Ridge, IL 60068-6300. Phone: (847) 696-1010. Fax: (847) 696-1110. Web: www.bigten .org or www.bigtenchampionships.com.

"THE BOLD AND THE BEAUTIFUL" TV PREMIERE: ANNIVERSARY. Mar 23, 1987. A continuing daytime serial created by William Bell and Lee Phillip Bell to be "young and hip." It is set in the fashion industry of Los Angeles with two central families, the Logans and the Forresters. The cast has included, as the Forresters: John McCook, Susan Flannery, Clayton Norcross, Jeff Trachta, Ronn Moss, Teri Ann Linn, Colleen Dion and as the Logans: Robert Pine, Judith Baldwin, Nancy Burnette, Nancy Sloan, Carrie Mitchum (granddaughter of Robert), Ethan Wayne (son of John), Brian Patrick Clarke, Katherine Kelly Lang and Lesley Woods. Other cast members include Jeff Conaway, Tippi Hedren and Hunter Tylo.

CLARK, BARNEY: DEATH ANNIVERSARY. Mar 23, 1983. Barney Clark died after living almost 112 days with an artificial heart. The heart, made of polyurethane plastic and aluminum, was implanted in Clark at the University of Utah Medical Center, Salt Lake City, Dec 2, 1982. Clark was the first person ever to receive a permanent artificial heart. Born at Provo, UT, Jan 21, 1921, Clark was 62 when he died.

COLFAX, SCHUYLER: BIRTH ANNIVERSARY. Mar 23, 1823. 17th vice president of the US (1869–73). Born at New York, NY. Died Jan 13, 1885, at Mankato, MN.

CRAFTSMEN'S SPRING CLASSIC. Mar 23–25. Capital Expo Center, Chantilly, VA. Arts and crafts. Est attendance: 20,000. For info: Gilmore Enterprises, Inc, 1240 Oakland Ave, Greensboro, NC 27403. Phone: (336) 274-5550. Fax: (336) 274-1084.

CRAWFORD, JOAN: BIRTH ANNIVERSARY. Mar 23, 1904. Actress, born Lucille Fay LeSueur at San Antonio, TX. Crawford became a Hollywood star with her performance in *Our Dancing Daughters*. She won an Oscar in 1945 for her role in *Mildred Pierce*. Events of Crawford's life are chronicled in *Mommie Dearest*. Other films included *The Women, Whatever Happened to Baby Jane?* and *Twelve Miles Out*. She died at New York, NY, May 10, 1977.

DAYTONA BEACH SPRING CAR SHOW & SWAP MEET. Mar 23–25. Daytona International Speedway, Daytona Beach, FL. 13th annual car show of all makes and models of collector vehicles. Many car clubs make this their largest annual event. Show includes display of antiques, classics, sportscars, muscle cars, race cars, customs, street rods and special trucks on the speedway infield, with a large swap meet of auto parts and accessories. Collector car sales corral and crafts sale. Annually, the last or next to the last weekend in March. Est attendance: 30,000. For info: Rick D'Louhy, Exec Dir, Daytona Beach Racing and Recreational Facilities District, PO Box 1958, Daytona Beach, FL 32115-1958. Phone: (904) 255-7355. Web: www.carshows .org.

DICK CLARK RETIRES FROM "AMERICAN BANDSTAND": ANNIVERSARY. Mar 23, 1989. After 33 years, 59-year-old Dick Clark retired from hosting the television program "American Bandstand."

EDISTO INDIAN CULTURAL FESTIVAL. Mar 23–24. Summerville, SC. Craft competition, unrestricted dance competition, free camping. Annually, the fourth weekend in March. Est attendance: 3,000. For info: Matthew Creel, Chief, Edisto Tribal Council, 1125 Ridge Rd, Ridgeville, SC 29472. Phone: (803) 871-2126. Fax: (803) 871-8048.

KUROSAWA, AKIRA: BIRTH ANNIVERSARY. Mar 23, 1910. Filmmaker (*Rashomon, The Seven Samurai*), born at Tokyo, Japan. Died at Tokyo, Sept 6, 1998.

LIBERTY DAY: ANNIVERSARY. Mar 23, 1775. Anniversary of Patrick Henry's speech for arming the Virginia militia at St. Johns Church, Richmond, VA. "I know not what course others may take, but as for me, give me liberty or give me death."

NAIC INVEST FEST. Mar 23–25. Austin, TX. Focuses on NAIC's methods of successful investing for investors in a specific region of the US. Included are nationally known speakers, informative seminars, the corporate exhibit area, mini presentations and a computer demonstration area. For info: Jonathan Strong, Membership Dir, Natl Assn of Investors Corp, 711 W Thirteen Mile Rd, Madison Heights, MI 48071. Phone: (248) 583-6242. Fax: (248) 583-4880. Web: www.better-investing.org.

NEAR MISS DAY. Mar 23, 1989. A mountain-sized asteroid passed within 500,000 miles of Earth, a very close call according to NASA. Impact would have equaled the strength of 40,000 hydrogen bombs, created a crater the size of the District of Columbia and devastated everything for 100 miles in all directions.

NEW ZEALAND: OTAGO AND SOUTHLAND PROVINCIAL ANNIVERSARY. Mar 23. In addition to the statutory public holidays of New Zealand, there is in each provincial district a holiday for the provincial anniversary. This day is observed in Otago and Southland.

PAKISTAN: REPUBLIC DAY: ANNIVERSARY. Mar 23, 1940. National holiday. In 1940 the All-India-Muslim League adopted a resolution calling for a Muslim homeland. On the same day in 1956 Pakistan declared itself a republic.

PALMETTO SPORTSMEN'S CLASSIC. Mar 23–25. South Carolina State Fairgrounds, Columbia, SC. Largest family-oriented wildlife show in the Carolinas with information on natural resources education and conservation, hunting, fishing and outdoor recreation. You will find activities for kids and adults throughout the show. A 5K race is held on Saturday morning. Est attendance: 40,000. For info: Jim Goller or Mary Pugh, Palmetto Sportsmen's Classic, PO Box 167, Columbia, SC 29202. Phone: (803) 734-4008. E-mail: gollerj@scdnr.state.sc.us or maryp@scdnr .state.sc.u. Web: www.dnr.state.sc.us/etc/classic/classic.

PITTSBURGH ARTS & CRAFTS SPRING FEVER FESTIVAL. Mar 23–25. Expo Center at Greengate Mall, Greensburg, PA. Approximately 200 booths, including pottery, jewelry, quilts, furniture, tole and decorative painting, leather, toys and much more. Find that perfect gift. Est attendance: 14,000. For info: Debbie & Steve Stoner, PO Box 166, Irwin, PA 15642. Phone: (724) 863-4577. Fax: (724) 863-4577.

SHABBAT ACROSS AMERICA. Mar 23. More than 800 participating synagogues (Conservative, Orthodox, Reform and Reconstructionist) encourage Jews to observe the Sabbath on this Friday night. Est attendance: 75,000. For info: Natl Jewish Outreach Program, 485 5th Ave, New York, NY 10017-6104. Phone: (888) SHABBAT or (212) 986-7450. Web: www.njop.org/

UNITED NATIONS: WORLD METEOROLOGICAL DAY. Mar 23. An international day observed by meteorological services throughout the world and by the organizations of the UN system. Info from: United Nations, Dept of Public Info, New York, NY 10017.

BIRTHDAYS TODAY

Louie Anderson, 48, comedian, actor ("Life with Louie"), host ("Family Feud"), born Minneapolis, MN, Mar 23, 1953.

Dr. Roger Bannister, 72, distance runner, broke the 4-minute-mile record in 1954, born Harrow, Middlesex, England, Mar 23, 1929.

Richard Grieco, 36, actor (*Ultimate Deception, Blackheart*), born Watertown, NY, Mar 23, 1965.

Chaka Khan (Yvette Marie Stevens), 48, singer ("Tell Me Something Good," "You Got the Love"), born Chicago, IL, Mar 23, 1953.

Jason Kidd, 28, basketball player, born San Francisco, CA, Mar 23, 1973.

Moses Eugene Malone, 47, former basketball player, born Petersburg, VA, Mar 23, 1954.

Amanda Plummer, 44, actress (Tony for *Agnes of God; The Fisher King*), born New York, NY, Mar 23, 1957.

Keri Russell, 25, actress ("Felicity"), born Denver, CO, Mar 23, 1976.

	S	M	T	W	T	F	S
March					1	2	3
2001	4	5	6	7	8	9	10
	11	12	13	14	15	16	17
	18	19	20	21	22	23	24
	25	26	27	28	29	30	31

MARCH 24 — SATURDAY
Day 83 — 282 Remaining

ARTISTS' NATIONAL JURIED COMPETITION. Mar 24–Apr 14. Coastal Center for the Arts, St. Simons Island, GA. Artists nationwide submit work to be judged for entry and prizes. Deadline for entry is Feb 10, 2001. 48th annual exhibit opens the Saturday of the Annual Tour of Homes as a special event of the tour with official opening awards presentation. Leading floral designers interpret selected artworks. This show attracts artists from the US and abroad and is considered the premiere show of the region for the year. Est attendance: 2,000. For info: Coastal Center for the Arts, 2012 Demere Rd, St. Simons Island, GA 31522. Phone: (912) 634-0404.

ATLANTIQUE CITY ANTIQUES AND COLLECTIBLES SPRING MEGASHOW. Mar 24–25. Atlantic City Convention Center, Atlantic City, NJ. "World's largest" antiques and collectibles show, with more than 1,600 booths displaying and selling an array of memorabilia from Jack Benny's violin to a first-edition Superman comic book. Est attendance: 65,000. For info: Mark Soifer, PR, 1803 Clover Ave, Vineland, NJ 08361. Phone: (609) 691-7535. Fax: (609) 691-9458.

BIG TEN WOMEN'S GYMNASTICS CHAMPIONSHIP. Mar 24. Michigan State University, East Lansing, MI. For info: Sue Ryan, Big Ten Conference, 1500 W Higgins Rd, Park Ridge, IL 60068-6300. Phone: (847) 696-1010. Fax: (847) 696-1110. Web: www.bigten.org or www.bigtenchampionships.com.

BIG 12 WOMEN'S GYMNASTICS CHAMPIONSHIP. Mar 24. Norman, OK. Est attendance: 3,000. For info: Big 12 Conference, 2201 Stemmons Freeway, 28th Floor, Dallas, TX 75207. Phone: (214) 742-1212. Fax: (214) 742-2045. Web: www.big12sports.com.

CENTRAL FLORIDA BALLOON RALLY. Mar 24–25. DeLand Municipal Airport, DeLand, FL. The skies over DeLand will be filled with some of the most beautiful hot-air balloons ever created, during the 17th annual rally. The "Balloon Glow" begins at sunset Saturday as the balloons fire up their burners, creating a giant colorful lightbulb effect. Hot-air balloon rides are available for a nominal fee. For info: Doug Gantt, Coordinator, Central Florida Balloon Rally. Phone: (904) 736-1010.

DELAND OUTDOOR ART FESTIVAL. Mar 24–25. Earl Brown Park, DeLand, FL. In its 35th year, the festival features more than 250 artists and craftsmen from around the US. Among the works featured are oil and acrylic paintings, watercolors, photography, pottery, sculpture and jewelry. A variety of entertainment runs throughout the festival featuring everything from jazz to original Irish music, classical to folk, strolling musicians and more. For info: Flo Perro, Coordinator, DeLand Outdoor Art Festival. Phone: (904) 734-8333.

DULCIMER FESTIVAL. Mar 24. Lumpkin, GA. Appalachian dulcimer music, professional and amateur. Dulcimer-building workshop and teaching sessions available. Est attendance: 750. For info: Patty Cannington, PR, PO Box 1850, Lumpkin, GA 31815. Phone: (912) 838-6310. Web: www.westville.org.

EXXON VALDEZ OIL SPILL: ANNIVERSARY. Mar 24, 1989. The tanker *Exxon Valdez* ran aground at Prince William Sound, leaking 11 million gallons of oil into one of nature's richest habitats.

GUTHRIE ART WALK. Mar 24. Guthrie, OK. New works by guest artists are featured in a leisurely Saturday evening walkabout. For info: Guthrie Conv & Visitors Bureau, PO Box 995, Guthrie, OK 73044-0995. Phone: (405) 260-2345 or (800) 299-1889.

HOUDINI, HARRY: BIRTH ANNIVERSARY. Mar 24, 1874. Magician and escape artist. Born at Budapest, Hungary, died at Detroit, MI, Oct 31, 1926. Lecturer, athlete, author, expert on history of magic, exposer of fraudulent mediums and motion picture actor. Was best known for his ability to escape from locked restraints (handcuffs, straitjackets, coffins, boxes and milk cans).

Anniversary of his death (Halloween) has been the occasion for meetings of magicians and attempts at communication by mediums.

INTERNATIONAL DAY OF THE SEAL. Mar 24. Jenkinson's Aquarium, Point Pleasant Beach, NJ. Learn all about seals and help us celebrate our seals' birthdays! A special artifact cart and seal stories for children will be presented throughout the day. Seals are fed at 10 AM, 1 PM and 4 PM. Crafts and face painting 1–4 PM. Free seal buttons to the first 300 visitors. Est attendance: 600. For info: Liz Carletta, Education Coord, Jenkinson's Aquarium, 300 Ocean Ave, Point Pleasant Beach, NJ 08742. Phone: (732) 899-1212. Fax: (732) 899-1717. E-mail: aquarium @jenkinsons.com. Web: www.jenkinsons.com.

MELLON, ANDREW W.: BIRTH ANNIVERSARY. Mar 24, 1855. American financier, industrialist, government official (Secretary of the Treasury), art and book collector born at Pittsburgh, PA. Died Aug 27, 1937, at Southhampton, NY.

MOON PHASE: NEW MOON. Mar 24. Moon enters New Moon phase at 8:21 PM, EST.

MORRIS, WILLIAM: BIRTH ANNIVERSARY. Mar 24, 1834. English poet, artist and social reformer. Born at Walthamstow, England; died at Hammersmith, London, Oct 3, 1896.

MUSEUM OPEN HOUSE. Mar 24–25 (Also Nov 24–25). Clinton, MD. Annual open house at historic site features free tours, special gift shop sales. Est attendance: 500. For info: Surratt House and Tavern, PO Box 427, Clinton, MD 20735. Phone: (301) 868-1121. Fax: (301) 868-8177. Web: www.surratt.org.

NATCHEZ POWWOW. Mar 24–25. Natchez, MS. Native American dancing and crafts. Est attendance: 5,000. For info: Jim Barnett, Grand Village of the Natchez Indians, 400 Jefferson Davis Blvd, Natchez, MS 39120. Phone: (601) 446-6502. Fax: (601) 446-6503. E-mail: gvni@bkbank.com.

NATIONAL WEEK OF THE OCEAN FESTIVAL SEA–SON. Mar 24–June 10. Fort Lauderdale, FL. This 12-week celebration includes billfish tournament, sea chanty concerts, school marine fair, marine flea market, waterway cleanup, two seafood festivals, a regatta and Mother Ocean Day. Est attendance: 305,500. For info: Cynthia Hancock, Pres, Natl Week of the Ocean, Inc, PO Box 179, Ft Lauderdale, FL 33302. Phone: (954) 462-5573.

PHILIPPINE INDEPENDENCE: ANNIVERSARY. Mar 24, 1934. President Franklin Roosevelt signed a bill granting independence to the Philippines. The bill, which took effect July 4, 1946, brought to a close almost half a century of US control of the islands.

POWELL, JOHN WESLEY: BIRTH ANNIVERSARY. Mar 24, 1834. American geologist, explorer, ethnologist. He is best known for his explorations of the Grand Canyon by boat on the Colorado River. Born at Mount Morris, NY, he died at Haven, ME, Sept 23, 1902.

RHODE ISLAND VOTERS REJECT CONSTITUTION: ANNIVERSARY. Mar 24, 1788. In a popular referendum, Rhode Island rejected the new Constitution by a vote of 2,708 to 237. The state later ratified the Constitution (May 29, 1790) and the Bill of Rights (June 7, 1790).

SAINT GABRIEL FEAST DAY. Mar 24. Saint Gabriel the Archangel, patron saint of postal, telephone and telegraph workers.

SPRING CRAFT SHOW. Mar 24–25. St. Simons Island, GA. Annual show where 75 fine crafts artists exhibit and sell their creations. Est attendance: 10,000. For info: Glynn Art Assn, 319 Mallory St, St. Simons Island, GA 31522. Phone: (912) 638-8770. Fax: (912) 634-2787. Web: www.glynnart.org.

STRATTON, DOROTHY CONSTANCE: BIRTH ANNIVERSARY. Mar 24, 1898. Dorothy Constance Stratton, born at Brookfield, MO, was instrumental during WWII in organizing the SPARS, the women's branch of the US Coast Guard (authorized Nov 23, 1942). Under Lieutenant Commander Stratton's command some 10,000 women were trained for supportive non-combat roles in the Coast Guard. SPARS was dissolved in 1946 after the war had ended. Stratton worked with many women's organizations, including the Girl Scouts.

TRIPEX. Mar 24–25. LaVale Fire Hall, west of Cumberland, MD. A show for stamp collectors featuring eight or nine dealers, stamp exhibits, free information on collecting stamps, door prizes and the US Postal Service. Free admission and parking. Sponsored by the Tri-State Stamp Club. Annually, the last weekend in March unless Easter or Palm Sunday falls on that weekend. Est attendance: 200. For info: Ted Rissell, 365 Back Bay Rd, Swanton, MD 21561. Phone: (301) 387-6463. E-mail: tedriss@mail2.genet .net.

UNITED NATIONS: WORLD TUBERCULOSIS DAY. Mar 24. Commemorates the day in 1882 when the tuberculosis bacillus was discovered by German scientist Robert Koch.

WORLD TB DAY. Mar 24. Designed to promote awareness about the serious health consequences of tuberculosis in the US and throughout the world. For info: American Assn for World Health, 1825 K St NW, Ste 1208, Washington, DC 20006. Phone: (202) 466-5883. Fax: (202) 466-5896. E-mail: staff @aawhworldhealth.org. Web: www.aawhworldhealth.org.

BIRTHDAYS TODAY

Lara Flynn Boyle, 31, actress ("Twin Peaks," "The Practice," *Dead Poets Society*), born Davenport, IA, Mar 24, 1970.
R. Lee Ermey, 57, actor (*Full Metal Jacket, Mississippi Burning*), born Emporia, KS, Mar 24, 1944.
Lawrence Ferlinghetti, 82, "Beat" poet, author (*Coney Island of the Mind*), born Yonkers, NY, Mar 24, 1919.
Byron Janis, 73, pianist, born McKeesport, PA, Mar 24, 1928.
Bob Mackie, 61, costume and fashion designer, born Monterey Park, CA, Mar 24, 1940.
Peyton Manning, 25, football player, born New Orleans, LA, Mar 24, 1976.
Donna Pescow, 47, actress (*Saturday Night Fever*, "Angie"), born Brooklyn, NY, Mar 24, 1954.
Annabella Sciorra, 37, actress (*The Hand That Rocks the Cradle, Jungle Fever*), born Wethersville, CT, Mar 24, 1964.

MARCH 25 — SUNDAY
Day 84 — 281 Remaining

BARTOK, BELA: BIRTH ANNIVERSARY. Mar 25, 1881. Hungarian composer born at Nagyszentmiklos (now in Romania). Died at New York, NY, Sept 26, 1945.

BORGLUM, GUTZON: BIRTH ANNIVERSARY. Mar 25, 1871. American sculptor who created the huge sculpture of four American presidents (Washington, Jefferson, Lincoln and Theodore Roosevelt) at Mount Rushmore National Memorial in the Black Hills of South Dakota. Born John Gutzon de la Mothe Borglum at Bear Lake, ID, the son of Mormon pioneers, he worked the last 14 years of his life on the Mount Rushmore sculpture. He died at Chicago, IL, Mar 6, 1941.

"CAGNEY & LACEY" TV PREMIERE: ANNIVERSARY. Mar 25, 1982. "Cagney & Lacey" broke new ground as the first TV crime show in which the central characters were both female. The series was based on a made-for-TV movie that aired Oct 8, 1981, starring Loretta Swit and Tyne Daly. Meg Foster played Swit's character, Chris Cagney, but after one season she was replaced by Sharon Gless. Daly and Gless won six Emmys together for their roles. The last telecast aired on Aug 25, 1988.

CHERRY BLOSSOM FESTIVAL. Mar 25–Apr 8. Various sites in Washington, DC. See more than 6,000 Japanese cherry blossom trees. Festivities include the crowning of the Cherry Blossom Festival Queen, a 10-mile race, golf and rugby tournament, arts and craft show and the festival parade on Apr 7. For info: Washington, DC Conv & Visitors Assn, Washington, DC, 20006. Phone: (202) 789-7000 or (202) 547-1500.

CHURCHILL ENTERS GERMANY: ANNIVERSARY. Mar 25, 1945. Winston Churchill briefly crossed to the eastern bank of the Rhine, the first British leader to enter Germany since Chamberlain signed the Munich Pact in September 1938. Churchill later wrote to Montgomery, "The Rhine and all its fortress lines lie behind the 21st Group of Armies. A beaten army, not long ago Master of Europe, retreats before its pursuers."

COSELL, HOWARD: BIRTH ANNIVERSARY. Mar 25, 1918. Howard Cosell, broadcaster, born at New York, NY. After earning a law degree, Cosell began his broadcasting career as the host of "Howard Cosell Speaking of Sports." He achieved national prominence and a great deal of notoriety for his support of Muhammad Ali's stand against the Vietnam War and then as co-host of ABC's Monday Night Football. Died at New York, Apr 23, 1994.

COXEY'S ARMY MARCH ON WASHINGTON: ANNIVERSARY. Mar 25, 1894. Anniversary of a march on the nation's Capitol. Jacob S. Coxey, businessman, economic reformer, advocate of interest-free government bonds, left Massillon, OH, on foot with an "army" of about 100 followers. Arrived at Washington, DC, May 1. His hope to influence Congress was thwarted when he and part of his army were arrested for trespassing on government property. Fifty years later he spoke from the Capitol steps, reiterating his belief in non-interest-bearing government bonds.

ENGLAND: MOTHERING SUNDAY. Mar 25. Fourth Sunday of Lent, formerly occasion for attending services at Mother Church, family gatherings and visits to parents. Now popularly known as Mother's Day, and a time for visiting and taking gifts to mothers.

EUROPE: SUMMER DAYLIGHT SAVING TIME. Mar 25–Oct 28. All members of the European Union observe daylight-saving (summer) time from the last Sunday in March until the last Sunday in October.

FEAST OF ANNUNCIATION. Mar 25. Celebrated in the Roman Catholic Church in commemoration of the message of the Angel Gabriel to Mary that she was to be the Mother of Christ.

GREECE: INDEPENDENCE DAY. Mar 25. National holiday. Celebrates the beginning of the Greek revolt for independence from the Ottoman Empire, Mar 25, 1821 (OS). Greece attained independence in 1829.

★**GREEK INDEPENDENCE DAY: A NATIONAL DAY OF CELEBRATION OF GREEK AND AMERICAN DEMOCRACY.** Mar 25.

JAZZ AT THE PHILHARMONIC: 55th ANNIVERSARY. Mar 25, 1946. One of the most influential solos of jazz alto saxophonist Charlie ("Bird") Parker's career was his rendition of "Lady Be Good," performed at the Los Angeles Philharmonic Auditorium. Every aspect of the performance became part of the language of modern jazz.

LEAN, SIR DAVID: BIRTH ANNIVERSARY. Mar 25, 1908. British film director Sir David Lean was born at London. He directed 16 films and won 28 Academy Awards. His films include *Bridge on the River Kwai* (1957), *Lawrence of Arabia* (1962) and *Dr. Zhivago* (1965). He died Apr 16, 1991, at London.

LUXEMBOURG: BRETZELSONNDEG. Mar 25. The fourth Sunday in Lent is occasion for boys to give pretzel-shaped cakes to sweethearts who may respond, on Easter Sunday, with a gift of decorated egg or sweet.

	S	M	T	W	T	F	S
March					1	2	3
2001	4	5	6	7	8	9	10
	11	12	13	14	15	16	17
	18	19	20	21	22	23	24
	25	26	27	28	29	30	31

MARYLAND DAY. Mar 25. Commemorates arrival of Lord Baltimore's first settlers in Maryland in 1634.

MARYLAND DAY. Mar 25. Historic St. Mary's City, MD. Celebrate Mayland's 367th birthday with pageantry and ceremonies marking the founding of the state in 1634. Est attendance: 6,000. For info: Visitors Services, Historic St. Mary's City, PO Box 39, St. Mary's City, MD 20686. Phone: (301) 862-0990 or (800) SMC-1634. Fax: (301) 862-0968. Web: www.smcm.edu/hsmc/.

NATIONAL BOYS AND GIRLS CLUB WEEK. Mar 25–31. An annual event commemorating the founding of the first club 132 years ago. Every president since Herbert Hoover has served as Honorary Chairman of Boys and Girls Clubs of America. Today there are 1,700 clubs providing educational, arts and sports programs to 2.2 million young people in the US and the Virgin Islands. For info: Natl Boys and Girls Clubs of America, 1230 W Peachtree St NW, Atlanta, GA 30309. Phone: (404) 815-5700. Fax: (404) 815-5789.

NATIONAL CLEANING WEEK. Mar 25–31. Established by Monica Nassif, founder and president of The Caldrea Company, the manufacturer of upscale cleaning products and cleaning accessories, National Cleaning Week serves as a reminder to tackle spring cleaning. Each day will be dedicated to a specific chore. Annually, the last week in March. For info: Monica Nassif, The Caldrea Company, 1010 Minnehaha Pkwy, Minneapolis, MN 55419. Phone: (612) 825-5590. Fax: (612) 825-5609. E-mail: mnassif@uswest.net.

NATIONAL FAMILYDAY™. Mar 25. Created by KidsPeace and developed in cooperation with the National Tabletop and Giftware Association to honor the importance of families in raising emotionally healthy and physically safe kids. Focused on providing opportunities for families to foster better communications, establish and celebrate traditions (especially regular mealtimes), share values and build strong families because strong families give kids peace. The 106th Congress passed H. Con. Res #288 recognizing the goals and ideas of National FamilyDay. KidsPeace has been helping kids and families overcome crisis since 1882. For info: Paula Knouse, KidsPeace, 5300 KidsPeace Dr, Orefield, PA 18069-9101. Phone (610) 799-8325. Web: www.nationalfamilyday.net.

NATIONAL KITE MONTH. Mar 25–Apr 30. Celebrates kiting through several hundred events throughout the country including kite festivals, kitemaking classes for kids and adults, kitemaking classes in schools, kite displays in museums and public libraries and "fun flys" at local parks and beaches. For info: Jim M. Miller, Program Mgr, Kite Trade Assn, Intl, 442 E Club Dr, Palm Springs, CA 92262. Phone: (760) 322-4128. Fax: (760) 416-0837. E-mail: NationalKiteMonth@KiteTrade.org. Web: www.KiteTrade.org/NationalKiteMonth.

NATO FORCES ATTACK YUGOSLAVIA: ANNIVERSARY. Mar 25, 1999. After many weeks of unsuccessful negotiations with Serb leader Slobodan Milosevic over the treatment of ethnic Albanians by Serb forces in the Kosovo Province of Yugoslavia, NATO forces began bombing Serbia and Kosovo. In response, the Serb army forced hundreds of thousands of ethnic Albanians to flee Kosovo for neighboring Albania, Macedonia and Montenegro. On June 10, 1999, NATO and Yugoslav officials signed an agreement providing for withdrawal of Serb troops from Kosovo, the end of Allied air strikes and the return of Kosovo refugees.

"9 to 5" TV PREMIERE: ANNIVERSARY. Mar 25, 1982. This half-hour sitcom was based on the 1980 movie of the same name about three working women in dead-end jobs in a large corporation. The three women were played by Rita Moreno, Valerie Curtin and Rachel Dennison (in the role her sister Dolly Parton had played in the movie).

OLD NEW YEAR'S DAY. Mar 25. In Great Britain and its North American colonies this was the beginning of the new year up through 1751, when with the adoption of the Gregorian calendar the beginning of the year was changed to Jan 1.

PECAN DAY. Mar 25, 1775. Anniversary of the planting by George Washington of pecan trees (some of which still survive) at Mount Vernon. The trees were a gift to Washington from Thomas Jefferson, who had planted a few pecan trees from the southern US at Monticello, VA. The pecan, native to southern North America, is sometimes called "America's own nut." First cultivated by American Indians, it has been transplanted to other continents but has failed to achieve wide use or popularity outside the US.

ROME EXECUTIONS: ANNIVERSARY. Mar 25, 1944. Nazis occupying Rome during World War II executed 300 Italian priests, Jews, women and two 14-year-old boys in retaliation for the deaths of 33 German soldiers who had been killed by Italian partisans. Hitler demanded 50 Italian lives for each German life that had been taken, but German officials in Italy lowered the number.

SLAVE TRADE ABOLISHED BY ENGLAND: ANNIVERSARY. Mar 25, 1807. The English Parliament abolished the slave trade, after a long campaign against it.

TOSCANINI, ARTURO: BIRTH ANNIVERSARY. Mar 25, 1867. Italian opera and symphony conductor Arturo Toscanini was born at Parma, Italy. He had an all-encompassing repertoire but was famous primarily for the operas of Verdi and the symphonies of Beethoven. Toscanini died at New York City, Jan 16, 1957.

TRIANGLE SHIRTWAIST FIRE: 90th ANNIVERSARY. Mar 25, 1911. At about 4:30 PM, fire broke out at the Triangle Shirtwaist Company at New York, NY, minutes before the seamstresses were to go home. Some workers were fatally burned while others leaped to their deaths from the windows of the 10-story building. The fire lasted only 18 minutes but left 146 workers dead, most of them young immigrant women. Some of the deaths were a direct result of workers being trapped on the ninth floor by a locked door. Labor law forbade locking factory doors while employees were at work, and owners of the company were indicted on charges of first- and second-degree manslaughter. The tragic fire became a turning point in labor history, bringing about reforms in health and safety laws.

UNITED KINGDOM: SUMMER TIME. Mar 25–Oct 28. "Summer Time" (one hour in advance of Standard Time), similar to daylight-saving time, is observed from the last Sunday in March until the last Sunday in October.

Bonnie Bedelia, 55, actress (*My Sweet Charlie, Die Hard, Die Hard 2*), born New York, NY, Mar 25, 1946.

Anita Bryant, 61, singer ("The George Gobel Show"; hit song "Paper Roses"), Miss America ('58), born Barnsdall, OK, Mar 25, 1940.

Eileen Ford, 79, model agency executive, born New York, NY, Mar 25, 1922.

Aretha Franklin, 59, singer ("Respect," "Think"), born Memphis, TN, Mar 25, 1942.

Paul Michael Glaser, 58, actor ("Starsky and Hutch"), director (*Butterflies Are Free*), born Cambridge, MA, Mar 25, 1943.

Tom Glavine, 35, baseball player, born Concord, MA, Mar 25, 1966.

Cammi Granato, 30, hockey player, member of the 1998 Olympic team, born Maywood, IL, Mar 25, 1971.

Mary Gross, 48, comedienne, actress ("Saturday Night Live"), born Chicago, IL, Mar 25, 1953.

Elton John (Reginald Kenneth Dwight), 54, musician, singer, songwriter, born Pinner, England, Mar 25, 1947.

James Lovell, 73, astronaut, born Cleveland, OH, Mar 25, 1928.

Sarah Jessica Parker, 36, actress (*LA Story, Honeymoon in Vegas*), born Nelsonville, OH, Mar 25, 1965.

Gloria Steinem, 66, feminist (original publisher of *Ms* magazine), journalist, born Toledo, OH, Mar 25, 1935.

John Stockwell, 40, actor, writer, director (*Top Gun, Under Cover*), born Galveston, TX, Mar 25, 1961.

Sheryl Swoopes, 30, basketball player, US Olympic Basketball Team, born Brownfield, TX, Mar 25, 1971.

MARCH 26 — MONDAY
Day 85 — 280 Remaining

BANGLADESH: INDEPENDENCE DAY: 30th ANNIVERSARY. Mar 26. Commemorates East Pakistan's independence in 1971 as the state of Bangladesh. Celebrated with parades, youth festivals and symposia.

BELLAMY, EDWARD: BIRTH ANNIVERSARY. Mar 26, 1850. American author best remembered for his novel *Looking Backward* (1888). Born at Chicopee Falls, MA, he died there May 28, 1898.

BOWDITCH, NATHANIEL: BIRTH ANNIVERSARY. Mar 26, 1773. American mathematician and astronomer, author of the *New American Practical Navigator*. Born at Salem, MA, he died at Boston, MA, Mar 16, 1838.

CAMP DAVID ACCORD SIGNED: ANNIVERSARY. Mar 26, 1979. Israeli Prime Minister Menachem Begin and Egyptian President Anwar Sadat signed the Camp David peace treaty, ending 30 years of war between their two countries. The agreement was fostered by President Jimmy Carter.

DELANO, JANE: BIRTH ANNIVERSARY. Mar 26, 1858. Jane Arminda Delano, dedicated American nurse and teacher, superintendent of the US Army Nurse Corps, chairman of the American Red Cross Nursing Service and recipient (posthumously) of the Distinguished Service Medal of the US, was born near Townsend, NY. While on an official visit to review Red Cross activities, she died Apr 15, 1919, in an army hospital at Savenay, France. Her last words: "What about my work? I must get back to my work." Buried at Loire, France, her remains were reinterred at Arlington Cemetery in 1920.

FOCH TAKES COMMAND ON WESTERN FRONT: ANNIVERSARY. Mar 26, 1918. General Ferdinand Foch, Commander of the French Army at the Maine and the Somme, was appointed General-in-Chief of the joint Allied forces on the Western Front. In practice the national commanders (Haig, King Albert, Pershing) retained extensive control of the individual forces.

FROST, ROBERT LEE: BIRTH ANNIVERSARY. Mar 26, 1874. American poet who tried his hand at farming, teaching, shoemaking and editing before winning acclaim as a poet. Pulitzer Prize winner. Born at San Francisco, CA, he died at Boston, MA, Jan 29, 1963.

ISLAMIC NEW YEAR. Mar 26. Islamic calendar date: Muharram 1, 1422. The first day of the first month of the Islamic calendar. Different methods for "anticipating" the visibility of the new moon crescent at Mecca are used by different groups. US date may vary.

LEGAL ASSISTANTS DAY. Mar 26. A day recognizing the many contributions made to the legal profession by legal assistants. For info: Claudia A. Evart, 30 Park Ave, Ste 2-P, New York, NY 10016. Phone: (212) 779-2227.

MAKE UP YOUR OWN HOLIDAY DAY. Mar 26. This day is a day you may name for whatever you wish. Reach for the stars! Make up a holiday! Annually, Mar 26. [© 2000 by WH] For info: Thomas and Ruth Roy, Wellcat Holidays, 2418 Long Ln, Lebanon, PA 17046. Phone: (717) 279-0184. E-mail: wellcat @supernet.com. Web: www.wellcat.com.

NATIONAL SLEEP AWARENESS WEEK. Mar 26–Apr 1. All Americans are urged to recognize the dangers of untreated sleep disorders and the importance of proper sleep to their health, safety and productivity. For info: Natl Sleep Foundation, 1522 K St NW, Ste 500, Washington, DC 20005. Web: www .sleepfoundation.org.

NATIONAL VENTURE CAPITAL EDUCATION DAY. Mar 26. San Francisco, CA. A one-day event planned to promote entrepreneurship and venture capital by providing access to comprehensive historical background, expert commentary and educational resources. Annually, the last Monday in March. Est attendance: 1,000. For info: Wendy Malaspina, 991 Folsom St, San Francisco, CA 94107. Phone: (415) 348-1688. E-mail: wendy @mevc.com. Web: www.mevc.com.

PRINCE JONAH KUHIO KALANIANOLE DAY. Mar 26. Hawaii. Commemorates the man who, as Hawaii's delegate to the US Congress, introduced the first bill for statehood in 1919.

SEWARD'S DAY: ANNIVERSARY OF THE ACQUISITION OF ALASKA. Mar 26. Observed in Alaska near anniversary of its acquisition from Russia in 1867. The treaty of purchase was signed between the Russians and the Americans Mar 30, 1867, and ratified by the Senate May 28, 1867. The territory was formally transferred Oct 18, 1867. Annually, the last Monday in March.

SOVIET COSMONAUT RETURNS TO NEW COUNTRY: ANNIVERSARY. Mar 26, 1992. After spending 313 days in space in the Soviet *Mir* space station, cosmonaut Serge Krikalev returned to Earth and to what was for him a new country. He left Earth May 18, 1991, a citizen of the Soviet Union, but during his stay aboard the space station, the Soviet Union crumbled and became the Commonwealth of Independent States. Originally scheduled to return in October 1991, Krikalev's return was delayed by five months due to his country's disintegration and the ensuing monetary problems.

WILLIAMS, TENNESSEE: 90th BIRTH ANNIVERSARY. Mar 26, 1911. Tennessee Williams was born at Columbus, MS. He was one of America's most prolific playwrights, producing such works as *The Glass Menagerie; A Streetcar Named Desire*, which won a Pulitzer Prize; *Cat on a Hot Tin Roof*, which won a second Pulitzer; *Night of the Iguana, Summer and Smoke, The Rose Tattoo* and *Sweet Bird of Youth*, among others. Williams died at New York, NY, Feb 25, 1983.

March 2001	**S**	**M**	**T**	**W**	**T**	**F**	**S**
					1	2	3
	4	5	6	7	8	9	10
	11	12	13	14	15	16	17
	18	19	20	21	22	23	24
	25	26	27	28	29	30	31

"THE YOUNG AND THE RESTLESS" TV PREMIERE: ANNIVERSARY. Mar 26, 1973. This daytime serial is generally thought of as TV's most artistic soap and has won numerous Emmys for outstanding daytime drama series. Its original storylines revolved around the Brooks and Foster families, but by the early '80s most of them were gone and the Abbott and Williams families were highlighted. The serial's very large and changing cast has included now-famous actors David Hasselhoff, Tom Selleck, Wings Hauser, Deidre Hall and Michael Damian. In 1980, "Y&R" expanded from a half-hour to an hour. Its theme music is well known as "Nadia's Theme," as it was played during Nadia Comaneci's routine at the 1976 Olympics.

BIRTHDAYS TODAY

Marcus Allen, 41, former football player, TV commentator, born San Diego, CA, Mar 26, 1960.

Alan Arkin, 67, actor (*Catch-22*); director (*Little Murders*), born New York, NY, Mar 26, 1934.

Pierre Boulez, 76, composer, conductor, born Montbrison, France, Mar 26, 1925.

James Caan, 61, actor (*Rabbit Run, The Godfather*), director, born New York, NY, Mar 26, 1940.

Lincoln Chafee, 48, US Senator (R, Rhode Island), born Warwick, RI, Mar 26, 1953.

Leeza Gibbons, 44, TV hostess ("Entertainment Tonight"), born Hartsville, SC, Mar 26, 1957.

Jennifer Grey, 41, actress (*Dirty Dancing*, "It's Like, You Know . . ."), born New York, NY, Mar 26, 1960.

Erica Jong, 59, author, poet (*Fear of Flying, Becoming Light, How to Save Your Own Life*), born New York, NY, Mar 26, 1942.

Vicki Lawrence, 52, singer, actress ("The Carol Burnett Show," "Mama's Family"), born Inglewood, CA, Mar 26, 1949.

Leonard Nimoy, 70, actor ("Star Trek"), director (*Three Men and a Baby*), writer, born Boston, MA, Mar 26, 1931.

Sandra Day O'Connor, 71, Associate Justice of the US Supreme Court, born El Paso, TX, Mar 26, 1930.

Teddy Pendergrass, 51, singer, born Philadelphia, PA, Mar 26, 1950.

Diana Ross, 57, singer ("Keep Me Hangin' On," "Ain't No Mountain High Enough"); actress (*Lady Sings the Blues, The Wiz*), born Detroit, MI, Mar 26, 1944.

Martin Short, 51, actor (*The Three Amigos, Inner Space*), comedian ("SCTV Network 90," "Saturday Night Live"), born Hamilton, Ontario, Canada, Mar 26, 1950.

John Houston Stockton, 39, basketball player, born Spokane, WA, Mar 26, 1962.

Bob Woodward, 58, journalist (investigated Watergate with Carl Bernstein), born Geneva, IL, Mar 26, 1943.

MARCH 27 — TUESDAY

Day 86 — 279 Remaining

AMERICAN DIABETES ALERT. Mar 27. A one-day "wake-up call" for those six million Americans who have diabetes and don't even know it. During the Alert, local ADA offices use the diabetes risk test—a simple paper-and-pencil quiz—to communicate the risk factors and symptoms of the disease. Annually, the fourth Tuesday in March. For info: Phone: 800-DIABETES (342-2383). Web: www.diabetes.org

CANARY ISLANDS PLANE DISASTER: ANNIVERSARY. Mar 27, 1977. The worst accident in the history of civil aviation. Two Boeing 747s collided on the ground; 570 people lost their lives—249 on the KLM Airlines plane and 321 on the Pan Am plane.

EARTHQUAKE STRIKES ALASKA: ANNIVERSARY. Mar 27, 1964. The strongest earthquake in North American history (8.4 on the Richter scale) struck Alaska, east of Anchorage. 117 people were killed.

FUNKY WINKERBEAN: ANNIVERSARY. Mar 27, 1972. Anniversary of the nationally syndicated comic strip. For info: Tom Batiuk, Creator, 2750 Substation Rd, Medina, OH 44256. Phone: (330) 722-8755.

HILL, PATTY SMITH: BIRTH ANNIVERSARY. Mar 27, 1868. Patty Smith Hill, schoolteacher, author and education specialist, was born at Anchorage (suburb of Louisville), KY. She was author of the lyrics of the song "Good Morning to All," which later became known as "Happy Birthday to You." Her older sister, Mildred J. Hill, composed the melody for the song which was first published in 1893 as a classroom greeting in the book *Song Stories for the Sunday School.* A stanza beginning "Happy Birthday to You" was added in 1924, and the song became arguably the most frequently sung song in the world. Hill died at New York, NY, May 25, 1946. See also: "Happy Birthday to 'Happy Birthday to You' " (June 27).

LUXEMBOURG: OSWEILER. Mar 27. Blessing of horses, tractors and cars.

NATIONAL EXCHANGE CLUB: 90th BIRTHDAY. Mar 27, 1911. Anniversary of the day when the first Exchange Club was founded at Detroit, MI, by Charles A. Berkey. Celebrated annually by nearly 40,000 Exchangites in the US and Puerto Rico. For info: The Natl Exchange Club, 3050 Central Ave, Toledo, OH 43606-1700. Phone: (800) 924-2643. Fax: (419) 535-1989. E-mail: nechq@aol.com. Web: www.nationalexchangeclub.com.

NORTH SEA OIL RIG DISASTER: ANNIVERSARY. Mar 27, 1980. The Alexander L. Keilland Oil Rig capsized during a heavy storm in the Norwegian sector of the North Sea. The pentagon-type, French-built oil rig had about 200 persons aboard, and 123 lives were lost.

ROENTGEN, WILHELM KONRAD: BIRTH ANNIVERSARY. Mar 27, 1845. German scientist who discovered X-rays (1895) and won a Nobel Prize in 1901. Born at Lennep, Prussia, he died at Munich, Germany, Feb 10, 1923.

SMITH, THORNE: BIRTH ANNIVERSARY. Mar 27, 1892. Perhaps the most critically neglected popular author of the 20th century, he was born James Thorne Smith, Jr, at Annapolis, MD, educated at Dartmouth, and died at Florida, June 20, 1934. Author of numerous humorous supernatural fantasy novels, including *Rain in the Doorway, The Stray Lamb* and *Topper,* he was the master of the pointless conversation. The "Thorne Smith" touch has inspired several motion pictures and television series, including "Bewitched." For info: George H. Scheetz, Exec Secy, The Thorne Smith Soc, 310 S Prospect Ave, Champaign, IL 61820-4715. E-mail: scheetz@soltec.net.

SPACE MILESTONE: *VENERA 8* (USSR). Mar 27, 1972. Launched on this date, this unmanned probe made a soft landing on Venus July 22 and sent back radio transmissions of surface data.

STEICHEN, EDWARD: BIRTH ANNIVERSARY. Mar 27, 1879. Celebrated American photographer. Born at Luxembourg, Germany, and died Mar 25, 1973, at West Redding, CT.

SWANSON, GLORIA: BIRTH ANNIVERSARY. Mar 27, 1899. American film actress (*Sunset Boulevard*) and businesswoman. Born Gloria May Josephine Svensson at Chicago. Author of an autobiography, *Swanson on Swanson,* published in 1980. Died at New York, NY, Apr 4, 1983.

VAUGHAN, SARAH: BIRTH ANNIVERSARY. Mar 27, 1924. Legendary jazz singer, born at Newark, NJ, renowned for her melodic improvising, wide vocal range and extraordinary technique. She began her career by winning an amateur contest at New York's Apollo Theater in 1943. She was spotted and hired by Earl Hines to accompany his band as his relief pianist as well as singer. As her career took off, she was given the nickname "The Divine One" by Chicago disc jockey Dave Garroway, a moniker that would remain with her the rest of her life. Died at Los Angeles, CA, Apr 3, 1990.

Mariah Carey, 31, singer ("Vision of Love," "I'll Be There"), born Long Island, NY, Mar 27, 1970.
Randall Cunningham, 38, former football player, born Santa Barbara, CA, Mar 27, 1963.
Anthony Lewis, 74, journalist, author (*Gideon's Trumpet, Make No Law: The Sullivan Case and the First Amendment*), born New York, NY, Mar 27, 1927.
Austin Pendleton, 61, actor (*Mr and Mrs Bridge, Guarding Tess*), born Warren, OH, Mar 27, 1940.
Mstislav Leopoldovich Rostropovich, 74, musician, born Baku, USSR, Mar 27, 1927.
Maria Schneider, 49, actress (*Last Tango in Paris*), born Paris, France, Mar 27, 1952.
Quentin Tarantino, 38, actor, director (*Pulp Fiction, Jackie Brown*), born Knoxville, TN, Mar 27, 1963.
William Caleb (Cale) Yarborough, 61, former auto racer, born Timmonsville, SC, Mar 27, 1940.
Michael York, 59, actor (*Cabaret, The Three Musketeers*), born Fulmer, England, Mar 27, 1942.

MARCH 28 — WEDNESDAY
Day 87 — 278 Remaining

BARTHOLOMEW, FREDDIE: BIRTH ANNIVERSARY. Mar 28, 1924. Child star of the 1930s, Freddie Bartholomew was born Frederick Llewellyn at Great Britain. He appeared in 24 films and became the second-highest paid child star after Shirley Temple. He died Jan 23, 1992, at Sarasota, FL.

BATTLE OF LA GLORIETTA PASS: ANNIVERSARY. Mar 28, 1862. At Pigeon's Ranch, a stagecoach stop on the Santa Fe Trail (about 19 miles southeast of Santa Fe, NM), Confederate forces briefly prevailed over Union troops in what some have called the most important battle of the Civil War in the Southwest. It was feared that if Union troops failed to hold here, the Confederate forces would proceed to Fort Union and on to control of the rich gold fields of Colorado and California.

CHINA: QING MING FESTIVAL. Mar 28. Observed on the fourth or fifth day of the third month. This Confucian festival honors the dead. Families maintain ancestral graves and present food, wine and flowers; paper money is burned at graves to provide ancestors with funds in the afterworld. People picnic and gather for family meals. Also observed in Korea.

CZECH REPUBLIC: TEACHERS' DAY. Mar 28. Celebrates birth on this day of Jan Amos Komensky (Comenius), Moravian educational reformer (1592–1671).

"GREATEST SHOW ON EARTH" FORMED: ANNIVERSARY. Mar 28, 1881. P.T. Barnum and James A. Bailey merged their circuses to form the "Greatest Show on Earth."

HAIR BROADWAY OPENING: ANNIVERSARY. Mar 28, 1968. The controversial rock musical *Hair*, produced by Michael Butler, opened at the Biltmore Theatre at New York City, after playing off-Broadway. For those who opposed the Vietnam War and the "Establishment," this was a defining piece of work—as evidenced by some of its songs, such as "Aquarius," "Hair" and "Let the Sunshine In."

LAZAR, IRVING ("SWIFTY"): BIRTH ANNIVERSARY. Mar 28, 1907. Hollywood talent agent whose clients included Ernest Hemingway, Lillian Hellman, Cole Porter, Richard Nixon and Humphrey Bogart (who nicknamed him "Swifty" after Lazar met Bogart's challenge to make him five film deals in one day in 1955). He died Dec 30, 1993, at Beverly Hills, CA.

SAINT JOHN NEPOMUCENE NEUMANN: BIRTH ANNIVERSARY. Mar 28, 1811. First male saint of the US. Born at Prachatice, Bohemia, came to the US in 1836. As Bishop of Philadelphia, he was affectionately known as the "Little Bishop." Died at Philadelphia, PA, Jan 5, 1860. Beatified Oct 13, 1963. Canonized June 19, 1977.

SPACE MILESTONE: NOAA 8 (US). Mar 28, 1983. Search and Rescue Satellite (SARSAT) launched from Vandenburg Air Force Base, CA, to aid in locating ships and aircraft in distress. *Kosmos 1383*, launched July 1, 1982, by the USSR, in a cooperative rescue effort, is credited with saving more than 20 lives.

TEN BEST-CENSORED STORIES OF 2000. Mar 28. To announce the top 10 underreported news stories of 2000 as determined by a national panel of jurors. On Mar 28 a 250–300 page Sourcebook detailing the "Top 25 Censored Stories of 2000" will be released by Project Censored. For info: Peter Phillips, Dir, Project Censored, Sonoma State University, Rohnert Park, CA 94928. Phone: (707) 664-2500. Fax: (707) 664-2108.

THREE MILE ISLAND NUCLEAR POWER PLANT ACCIDENT: ANNIVERSARY. Mar 28, 1979. A series of accidents beginning at 4 AM, EST, at Three Mile Island on the Susquehanna River about 10 miles southeast of Harrisburg, PA, was responsible for extensive reevaluation of the safety of existing nuclear power generating operations. Equipment and other failures reportedly brought Three Mile Island close to a meltdown of the uranium core, threatening extensive radiation contamination.

VIETNAM MORATORIUM CONCERT: ANNIVERSARY. Mar 28, 1970. A seven-hour concert at Madison Square Garden at New York City featured many stars who donated their services for the antiwar cause. Among them were Jimi Hendrix; Dave Brubeck; Harry Belafonte; Peter, Paul and Mary; Judy Collins; the Rascals; Blood, Sweat and Tears and the Broadway cast of *Hair*.

BIRTHDAYS TODAY

Conchata Ferrell, 58, actress ("LA Law," "Hearts Afire," *Edward Scissorhands*), born Charleston, WV, Mar 28, 1943.

Ken Howard, 57, actor ("The White Shadow"), born El Centro, CA, Mar 28, 1944.

Reba McEntire, 47, singer ("For My Broken Heart"), born Chockie, OK, Mar 28, 1954.

Frank Hughes Murkowski, 68, US Senator (R, Alaska), born Seattle, WA, Mar 28, 1933.

Dianne Wiest, 53, actress (Oscars for *Hannah and Her Sisters* and *Bullets Over Broadway*), born Kansas City, MO, Mar 28, 1948.

	S	M	T	W	T	F	S
March					1	2	3
2001	4	5	6	7	8	9	10
	11	12	13	14	15	16	17
	18	19	20	21	22	23	24
	25	26	27	28	29	30	31

MARCH 29 — THURSDAY
Day 88 — 277 Remaining

"AMERICA'S SUBWAY" DAY: 25th ANNIVERSARY. Mar 29, 1976. 25 years ago, the Washington (DC) Metropolitan Area Transit Authority (WMATA) ran its first Metrorail passenger train. The Metro system consisted of only five stations and 4.6 miles on the Red Line Route. Metro now consists of 78 stations and 96 miles of service. In early 2001 the number of stations will increase to 83 stations and 103 miles. Passengers make more than 550,000 trips each weekday in the nation's capital and the greater Washington area. Many of these are made by tourists from across the country and around the world—hence the moniker "America's Subway." For info: Cheryl Johnson, WMATA, 600 Fifth St NW, Washington, DC 20001. Phone: (202) 962-1051. Fax: (202) 962-2897. Web: www.wmata.com.

BAILEY, PEARL MAE: BIRTH ANNIVERSARY. Mar 29, 1918. American singer and Broadway musical star Pearl Bailey was born at Newport News, VA. She began her career in vaudeville and won a special Tony Award in 1968 and the Presidential Medal of Freedom in 1988. Bailey died Aug 17, 1990, at Philadelphia, PA.

BIGGS, E. POWER: 95th BIRTH ANNIVERSARY. Mar 29, 1906. Baroque organist who helped establish the organ as a concert instrument. Biggs refused to perform on electronic organs, but sought out and recorded on organs surviving from the era of Johann Sebastian Bach and George Frederick Handel. After arthritis forced him to retire, he published early organ music. Biggs was born at Westcliff-on-Sea, Essex, England, and came to the US in 1930 at the age of 24. He died Mar 10, 1977, at Boston.

CANADA: BRITISH NORTH AMERICA ACT: ANNIVERSARY. Mar 29, 1867. This act of the British Parliament established the Dominion of Canada, uniting Ontario, Quebec, Nova Scotia and New Brunswick. The remaining colonies in Canada were still ruled directly by Great Britain until Manitoba joined the Dominion in 1870, British Columbia in 1871, Prince Edward Island in 1873, Alberta and Saskatchewan in 1905 and Newfoundland in 1949. Union was proclaimed July 1, 1867. See also: "Canada: Canada Day" (July 1).

COMMITTEE ON ASSASSINATIONS REPORT: ANNIVERSARY. Mar 29, 1979. The House Select Committee on Assassinations released the final report on its investigation into the assassinations of President John F. Kennedy, Martin Luther King, Jr, and Robert Kennedy on this day. Based on available evidence, the committee concluded that President Kennedy was assassinated as a result of a conspiracy, although no trail of a conspiracy could be established. They also concluded that on the basis of scientific acoustical evidence two gunmen fired at the President, although no second gunman could be identified. [Note: In December 1980, the FBI released a report discounting the two-gunman theory, stating that the distinguishable sounds of two separate guns were not proven scientifically.] In addition the committee concluded that the possibility of conspiracy did exist in the cases of Dr. King and Robert Kennedy, although no specific individuals or organizations could be pinpointed as being involved. See also: "Warren Commission Report: Anniversary" (Sept 27).

DOW-JONES TOPS 10,000: ANNIVERSARY. Mar 29, 1999. The Dow-Jones Index of 30 major industrial stocks topped the 10,000 mark for the first time.

HOOVER, LOU HENRY: BIRTH ANNIVERSARY. Mar 29, 1875. Wife of Herbert Clark Hoover, 31st president of the US. Born at Waterloo, IA, she died at Palo Alto, CA, Jan 7, 1944.

JOHN PARTRIDGE "DEATH" HOAX: ANNIVERSARY. Mar 29, 1708. English astrologer John Partridge (real name: John Hewson) so offended readers by his foolish predictions that he became the target of parodies and jokes, most serious of which was that of the satirist Jonathan Swift. Under the pseudonym Isaac Bickerstaff, Swift published his own almanac for the year 1708, in which he predicted that Partridge would die at 11 PM, Mar 29, 1708, "of a raging fever." Poor Partridge made the mistake of trying to prove he was still alive, only to find writers, citizens and even the court were more amused by continuing the fiction of his death.

KNIGHTS OF COLUMBUS FOUNDER'S DAY. Mar 29. The first Knights of Columbus charter was granted in 1882 by the state of Connecticut. This Catholic, family, fraternal, service organization has grown into a volunteer force of Knights and family members totaling nearly six million who annually donate tens of millions of dollars and volunteer hours to countless charitable projects. For info: Ronald J. Tracz, VP, Fraternal Services, Knights of Columbus, 1 Columbus Plaza, New Haven, CT 06510-3326.

MADAGASCAR: COMMEMORATION DAY. Mar 29. Commemoration Day for the victims of the rebellion in 1947 against French colonization.

NATIONAL MOM AND POP BUSINESS OWNERS DAY. Mar 29. A day recognizing those very special husband and wife business owner teams that work and commune together. Take this day to strike a balance between business and love. For info: Rick/Margie Segel, 1 Wheatland St, Burlington, MA 01803. Phone: (781) 272-9995. Fax: (781) 272-9996.

QUINLAN, KAREN ANN: BIRTH ANNIVERSARY. Mar 29, 1954. Born at Scranton, PA, Karen Ann Quinlan became the center of a legal, medical and ethical controversy over the right to die. She became irreversibly comatose on Apr 14, 1975. A petition filed by her adoptive parents in New Jersey's Superior Court, Sept 12, 1975, sought permission to discontinue use of a respirator, allowing her to die "with grace and dignity." In 1976 the petition was upheld by New Jersey's Supreme Court. Quinlan lived nearly a decade without the respirator, until June 11, 1985. Her plight brought into focus the ethical dilemmas of advancing medical technology—the need for a new understanding of life and death; the right to die; the role of judges, doctors and hospital committees in deciding when not to prolong life.

SCHMECKFEST. Mar 29–Apr 1. Freeman, SD. (Apr 1 matinee performance only.) Bratwurst and sauerkraut, kuchen and pluma moos. These are just a few of the dishes served at this German "festival of tasting" where visitors can also watch cooking and craft demonstrations and an evening musical. Est attendance: 3,000. For info: LaNae Waltner, Box 295, Freeman, SD 57029.

TAIWAN: YOUTH DAY. Mar 29.

TEXAS LOVE THE CHILDREN DAY. Mar 29. A day recognizing every child's right and need to be loved. Promoting the hope that one day all children will live in loving, safe environments and will be given proper health care and equal learning opportunities. Precedes the start of National Child Abuse Prevention Month (April). For info: Patty Murphy, 7713 Chasewood Dr, North Richland Hills, TX 76180. Phone: (817) 498-5840. E-mail: MURPH0@flash.net.

TWENTY-THIRD AMENDMENT TO US CONSTITUTION RATIFIED: 40th ANNIVERSARY. Mar 29, 1961. District of Columbia residents were given the right to vote in presidential elections under the 23rd Amendment.

TYLER, JOHN: BIRTH ANNIVERSARY. Mar 29, 1790. Tenth president of the US (Apr 6, 1841–Mar 3, 1845). Born at Charles City County, VA, Tyler succeeded to the presidency upon the death of William Henry Harrison. Tyler's first wife died while he was president, and he remarried before the end of his term in office, becoming the first president to marry while in office. Fifteen children were born of the two marriages. In 1861 he was elected to the Congress of the Confederate States but died at Richmond, VA, Jan 18, 1862, before being seated. His death received no official tribute from the US government.

WALTON, SAM: BIRTH ANNIVERSARY. Mar 29, 1918. Founder of Wal-Mart discount stores, born at Kingfisher, OK. One of the wealthiest men in America, he died at Little Rock, AR, Apr 5, 1992.

WASHINGTON FLOWER & GARDEN SHOW. Mar 29–Apr 1. Washington Convention Center, Washington, DC. Two and a half acres of full-size blooming gardens created by the area's best landscapers. The show also has demonstrations, lectures and a Spring Marketplace where visitors can purchase anything from orchids to garden tools. For info: Gail Stafford, Washington Flower & Garden Show, 6017 Tower Ct, Alexandria, VA 22304. Phone: (703) 823-7960.

YOUNG, DENTON TRUE (CY): BIRTH ANNIVERSARY. Mar 29, 1867. Baseball Hall of Fame pitcher born at Gilmore, OH. Young is baseball's all-time winningest pitcher, having accumulated 511 victories in his 22-year career. The Cy Young Award is given each year in his honor to major league's best pitcher. Inducted into the Hall of Fame in 1937. Died at Peoli, OH, Nov 4, 1955.

BIRTHDAYS TODAY

Earl Christian Campbell, 46, Pro Football Hall of Fame running back, born Tyler, TX, Mar 29, 1955.

Jennifer Capriati, 25, tennis player, born New York, NY, Mar 29, 1976.

Bud Cort, 51, actor (*Harold and Maude, Brewster McCloud*), born New Rochelle, NY, Mar 29, 1950.

Eric Idle, 58, actor ("Monty Python's Flying Circus," "Suddenly Susan"), author, born Durham, England, Mar 29, 1943.

Christopher Lambert, 44, actor (*Greystoke: The Legend of Tarzan, Lord of the Apes; To Kill a Priest*), born New York, NY, Mar 29, 1957.

Lucy Lawless, 33, actress ("Xena"), born Mount Albert, Auckland, New Zealand, Mar 29, 1968.

Elle Macpherson, 37, model, actress (*Sirens*), born Sydney, Australia, Mar 29, 1964.

John Major, 58, former British prime minister, born Brixton, England, Mar 29, 1943.

Eugene McCarthy, 85, former US Senator (anti-Vietnam War presidential hopeful in '68), born Watkins, MN, Mar 29, 1916.

John Joseph McLaughlin, 74, editor, columnist, TV host, born Providence, RI, Mar 29, 1927.

Kurt Thomas, 45, former gymnast, born Miami, FL, Mar 29, 1956.

MARCH 30 — FRIDAY

Day 89 — 276 Remaining

ANESTHETIC FIRST USED IN SURGERY: ANNIVERSARY. Mar 30, 1842. Dr. Crawford W. Long, having seen the use of nitrous oxide and sulfuric ether at "laughing gas" parties, observed that individuals under their influence felt no pain. On this date, he removed a tumor from the neck of a man who was under the influence of ether.

CHICAGO LATINO FILM FESTIVAL. Mar 30–Apr 11. Chicago, IL. Come celebrate films from countries around the world including Chile, Brazil, Spain, Mexico, Ecuador, Peru and others. Films are scheduled at various theatres throughout Chicago. 17th annual. For info: Intl Latino Cultural Center of Chicago, c/o Columbia College Chicago, 600 S Michigan Ave, Chicago, IL 60605-1996. Phone: (312) 431-1330. Fax: (312) 344-8030. E-mail: clc@popmail.colum.edu. Web: www.chicagolatinocinema.org.

CRAFTSMEN'S CLASSIC ARTS & CRAFTS FESTIVAL. Mar 30–Apr 1. Greensboro Coliseum, Greensboro, NC. Arts and crafts. Est attendance: 20,000. For info: Gilmore Enterprises, Inc, 1240 Oakland Ave, Greensboro, NC 27403. Phone: (336) 274-5550. Fax: (336) 274-1084.

DOCTORS' DAY. Mar 30. Traditional annual observance since 1933 to honor America's physicians on anniversary of occasion when Dr. Crawford W. Long became the first acclaimed physician to use ether as an anesthetic agent in a surgical technique, Mar 30, 1842. The red carnation has been designated the official flower of Doctors' Day.

GERMANY: HANDARBEIT + HOBBY: THE INTERNATIONAL TRADE FAIR FOR CRAFT AND HOBBY SUPPLIES. Mar 30–Apr 1. Dusseldorf. Largest European market dedicated to needlecrafts and crafts and hobbies. A trade-only event. Est attendance: 7,500. For info: Susan Danker, Dir of Mtgs and Expos, HIA, 319 E 54th St, Elmwood Park, NJ 07407. Phone: (201) 794-1133. Fax: (201) 797-0657. E-mail: sdanker@hobby.org. Web: www.hobby.org/hia.

GOYA, FRANCISCO JOSE de: BIRTH ANNIVERSARY. Mar 30, 1746. Spanish painter and etcher. It is estimated that he executed more than 1,800 paintings, drawings and lithographs during his lifetime. Born at Aragon, Spain; died at Bordeaux, France, Apr 16, 1828.

"I AM IN CONTROL" DAY: 20th ANNIVERSARY. Mar 30, 1981. Anniversary of former Secretary of State Alexander Haig's televised announcement (while President Ronald Reagan was undergoing surgery after being shot by a would-be assassin): "As of now, I am in control here in the White House. . . ." Haig continued to say: "Constitutionally, gentlemen, you have the president, the vice president and the secretary of state in that order. . . ."

INTERNATIONAL CONFERENCE ON THE POSITIVE POWER OF HUMOR & CREATIVITY. Mar 30–Apr 1. Saratoga Springs, NY. Participants will enjoy themselves while learning practical ideas they can apply both personally and on the job. Recent conferences have featured special appearances by Jay Leno, Victor Borge, Steve Allen, Sid Caesar, The Capitol Steps and The Smothers Brothers. More than 13,000 attendees from all 50 states and abroad. 16th annual conference. To receive a conference brochure and free humor info packet, send SASE (99 cents) to The Humor Project, 480 Broadway, Ste 210, Saratoga Springs, NY 12866-2288. Phone: (518) 587-8770. Fax: (518) 587-8771. E-mail: chase@HumorProject.com. Web: www.humorproject.com.

"JEOPARDY" TV PREMIERE: ANNIVERSARY. Mar 30, 1964. The "thinking person's" game show, "Jeopardy" has a reputation as an intelligent and classy program. Art Fleming was the original host of the show, in which three contestants won cash by attempting to give the correct question to an answer. Contestants go through two rounds and "final jeopardy," where they can wager up to all their earnings on one question. The series returned in 1984 with Alex Trebek as the popular host. The cable channel VH1 now hosts "Rock & Roll Jeopardy!"

JOSE CUERVO MARGARITA SEASON. Mar 30–Sept 29. Cuervo makes any occasion a party—whether hanging out with friends, watching a football game or going out on a Saturday night. Jose Cuervo invites you to celebrate Margarita season by raising a pitcher of the official fun-times beverage—the Jose Cuervo Margarita. Put down that beer and come play! Annually, the last Friday in March to the last Saturday in September. For info: Kris Krioeske, 5666 Sierra Dr, Irvine, TX 75039. Phone: (972) 830-2502. Fax: (972) 868-7671. E-mail: kkrioesk@bsmg.com. Web: www.cuervo.com.

LONGHORN WORLD CHAMPIONSHIP RODEO. Mar 30–Apr 1. Bossier City Arena, Bossier City, LA. More than 200 cowboys and cowgirls compete in six professional contests ranging from bronc riding to bull riding for top prize money and world championship points. Featuring colorful opening pageantry and Big, Bad BONUS Bulls. 1st annual. Est attendance: 15,000. For info: W. Bruce Lehrke, Pres, Longhorn World Chmpshp Rodeo, Inc, PO Box 70159, Nashville, TN 37207. Phone: (615) 876-1016. Fax: (615) 876-4685. Web: www.longhornrodeo.com.

March 2001	S	M	T	W	T	F	S
					1	2	3
	4	5	6	7	8	9	10
	11	12	13	14	15	16	17
	18	19	20	21	22	23	24
	25	26	27	28	29	30	31

NCAA DIVISION I WOMEN'S BASKETBALL CHAMPIONSHIP FINALS. Mar 30–Apr 1. Kiel Center, St. Louis, MO. Est attendance: 17,500. For info: Natl Collegiate Athletic Assn, 700 W Washington Ave, PO Box 6222, Indianapolis, IN 46206-6222. Phone: (317) 917-6222. Fax: (317) 917-6888. Web: www.ncaa.org.

NICKERSON, CAMILLE ("THE LOUISIANA LADY"): BIRTH ANNIVERSARY. Mar 30, 1888. Camille Nickerson, music arranger, composer, musician and educator, is remembered for her musical talent and her work as a music collector who gathered and transcribed Creole music. Born at the French Quarter, New Orleans. Of Creole extraction herself, Nickerson performed for a time in the US and Europe using the stage name "The Louisiana Lady." She died at Washington, DC, at age 94.

O'CASEY, SEAN: BIRTH ANNIVERSARY. Mar 30, 1880. Irish playwright (*Juno and the Paycock*). Born at Dublin, Ireland, he died at Torquay, England, Sept 18, 1964.

PENCIL PATENTED: ANNIVERSARY. Mar 30, 1858. First pencil with the eraser top was patented by Hyman Lipman.

REAGAN, RONALD: ASSASSINATION ATTEMPT: 20th ANNIVERSARY. Mar 30, 1981. President Ronald Reagan was shot in the chest by a 25-year-old gunman at Washington, DC. Three other persons were wounded. John W. Hinckley, Jr, the accused attacker, was arrested at the scene. On June 21, 1982, a federal jury in the District of Columbia found Hinckley not guilty by reason of insanity and he was committed to St. Elizabeth's Hospital at Washington, DC, for an indefinite time.

SAINT PETERSBURG FESTIVAL OF STATES (WITH NATIONAL BAND CHAMPIONSHIPS). Mar 30–Apr 8. To salute civic endeavors and highlight the 50 states. National band championships, art show, two parades, antique cars, blues festival, kids' art festival plus one more night of concert entertainment, x-games, 3-on-3 basketball, 5K run. Est attendance: 250,000. For info: St. Petersburg Festival of States, Box 1731, St. Petersburg, FL 33731. Phone: (813) 898-3654. Fax: (813) 821-2601. Web: festivalofstates.com.

TEMPE SPRING FESTIVAL OF THE ARTS. Mar 30–Apr 1. Downtown Tempe, AZ. Features 500 artists and craftspeople, continuous entertainment and children's activity area. Est attendance: 240,000. For info: Gary Sanders, Exec Dir, Mill Avenue Merchants Assn, PO Box 3084, Tempe, AZ 85281. Phone: (480) 967-4877. Fax: (480) 967-6638. E-mail: info@millavenue.org. Web: www.millavenue.org.

TRINIDAD AND TOBAGO: SPIRITUAL BAPTIST LIBERATION SHOUTER DAY. Mar 30. Public holiday. For info: Information Dept, Tourism Div, Tourism and Industrial Development Co, 10-14 Phillips St, Port of Spain, Trinidad, West Indies.

VAN GOGH, VINCENT: BIRTH ANNIVERSARY. Mar 30, 1853. Dutch post-Impressionist painter, especially known for his bold and powerful use of color. Born at Groot Zundert, Holland, he died at Auvers-sur-Oise, France, July 29, 1890.

BIRTHDAYS TODAY

John Astin, 71, actor ("The Addams Family"; stage: *The Three Penny Opera*), director, born Baltimore, MD, Mar 30, 1930.

Warren Beatty, 63, actor (*Bonnie and Clyde*); director (*Reds, Dick Tracy*), producer, born Richmond, VA, Mar 30, 1938.

Tracy Chapman, 37, singer ("Fast Car"), born Cleveland, OH, Mar 30, 1964.

Eric Clapton, 56, singer (with Yardbirds, Cream), songwriter ("Layla," with Jim Gordon), born Ripley, England, Mar 30, 1945.

Celine Dion, 33, pop singer, Grammy winner, born Charlemagne, Quebec, Canada, Mar 30, 1968.

Richard Dysart, 72, actor ("LA Law"), born Augusta, ME, Mar 30, 1929.

M.C. Hammer, 38, rapper, born Stanley Kirk Burrell, Oakland, CA, Mar 30, 1963.

Frankie Laine, 88, actor, singer ("Frankie Laine Time," *Viva Las Vegas*), born Chicago, IL, Mar 30, 1913.

Peter Marshall, 74, TV host, actor, born Huntington, WV, Mar 30, 1927.

Paul Reiser, 44, actor (*Diner*, "Mad About You"), born New York, NY, Mar 30, 1957.

Robert C. Smith, 60, US Senator (R, New Hampshire), born Tuftonboro, NH, Mar 30, 1941.

MARCH 31 — SATURDAY
Day 90 — 275 Remaining

BUNSEN BURNER DAY. Mar 31. A day to honor the inventor of the Bunsen burner, Robert Wilhelm Eberhard von Bunsen, who provided chemists and chemistry students with one of their most indispensable instruments. The Bunsen burner allows the user to regulate the proportions of flammable gas and air to create the most efficient flame. Bunsen was born at Gottingen, Germany, Mar 31, 1811, and was a professor of chemistry at the universities at Kassel, Marburg, Breslau and Heidelberg. He died at Heidelberg, Germany, Aug 16, 1899.

CHAVEZ, CESAR ESTRADA: BIRTH ANNIVERSARY. Mar 31, 1927. Labor leader who organized migrant farm workers in support of better working conditions. Chavez initiated the National Farm Workers Association in 1962, attracting attention to the migrant farm workers' plight by organizing boycotts of products including grapes and lettuce. He was born at Yuma, AZ, and died Apr 23, 1993, at San Luis, AZ. His birthday is a holiday in California.

CHESNUT, MARY BOYKIN MILLER: BIRTH ANNIVERSARY. Mar 31, 1823. Born at Pleasant Hill, SC, and died Nov 22, 1886, at Camden, SC. During the Civil War Chesnut accompanied her husband, a Confederate staff officer, on military missions. She kept a journal of her experiences and observations, which was published posthumously as *A Diary from Dixie*, a perceptive portrait of Confederate military and political leaders and insightful view of Southern life during the Civil War.

CHRYSLER OPENS DETROIT FACTORY: ANNIVERSARY. Mar 31, 1992. In an unorthodox move for recessionary times, the Chrysler Corporation opened a new plant on Jefferson Avenue at Detroit, MI. The opening came at a time when American automakers were scaling back and closing plants while Japanese competitors were opening facilities in mid-South rural locations to avoid unions and urban problems. Located across the street from the site of its 85-year-old predecessor that was torn down in 1991, the new plant produces Jeep Grand Cherokee utility vehicles.

DALAI LAMA FLEES TIBET: ANNIVERSARY. Mar 31, 1959. The Dalai Lama fled Chinese suppression and was granted political asylum in India. In 1950, Tibet had been invaded by China and in 1951 an agreement was signed under which Tibet became a "national autonomous region" of China. Tibetans suffered under China's persecution of Buddhism and after years of scattered protest a full-scale revolt broke out in 1959. The Dalai Lama fled and with the beginning of the Chinese Cultural Revolution the Chinese took brutal repressive measures against the Tibetans, with the practice of religion banned and thousands of monasteries destroyed. The ban was lifted in 1976 with the end of the Cultural Revolution. The Dalai Lama received the Nobel Peace Prize in 1989 for his commitment to the nonviolent liberation of his country.

DESCARTES, RENE: BIRTH ANNIVERSARY. Mar 31, 1596. French philosopher and mathematician, known as the "father of modern philosophy," born at La Haye, Touraine, France. Cartesian philosophical precepts are often remembered because of his famous proposition "I think, therefore I am" (*Cogito ergo sum . . .*). Died of pneumonia at Stockholm, Sweden, Feb 11, 1650.

EGGSIBIT. Mar 31–Apr 1. Firth Youth Center, Phillipsburg, NJ. 31st annual show to encourage the art of decorating eggshells. Annually, the weekend prior to Palm Sunday. Est attendance: 2,000. For info: Dawn Slifer, Firth Youth Center, 108 Anderson St, Phillipsburg, NJ 08865. Phone: (908) 454-7281.

EIFFEL TOWER: ANNIVERSARY. Mar 31, 1889. Built for the Paris Exhibition of 1889, the tower was named for its architect, Alexandre Gustave Eiffel, and is one of the world's best known landmarks.

FESTIVAL OF FLOWERS. Mar 31–Apr 29 (tentative). Biltmore Estate, Asheville, NC. A Victorian celebration of spring with floral displays filling each room of Biltmore House. Call for a schedule of events. Est attendance: 86,000. For info: Biltmore Estate, 1 N Pack Sq, Asheville, NC 28801. Phone: (800) 543-2961. Web: www.biltmore.com.

FITZGERALD, EDWARD: BIRTH ANNIVERSARY. Mar 31, 1809. English author, born at Bredfield, England, perhaps best known for his translation of Omar Khayyam's *Rubaiyat*. Died at Merton, Norfolk, June 14, 1883.

GOGOL, NIKOLAI VASILEVICH: BIRTH ANNIVERSARY. Mar 31, 1809. Russian author of plays, novels and short stories. Born at Sorochinsk, Russia, he died at Moscow, Russia, Mar 4, 1852. Gogol's most famous work was the novel *Dead Souls*.

GORE, ALBERT, JR.: BIRTHDAY. Mar 31, 1948. 45th US vice president, 2000 Democratic presidential candidate, born at Washington, DC.

HAYDN, FRANZ JOSEPH: BIRTH ANNIVERSARY. Mar 31, 1732. "Father of the symphony," born at Rohrau, Austria-Hungary. Composed about 120 symphonies, more than a hundred works for chamber groups, a dozen operas and hundreds of other musical works. Died at Vienna, Austria, May 31, 1809.

JOHNSON, JOHN (JACK) ARTHUR: BIRTH ANNIVERSARY. Mar 31, 1878. In 1908 Jack Johnson became the first black to win the heavyweight boxing championship when he defeated Tommy Burns at Sydney, Australia. Unable to accept a black man's triumph, the boxing world tried to find a white challenger. Jim Jeffries, former heavyweight title holder, was badgered out of retirement. On July 4, 1919, at Reno, NV, the "battle of the century" proved to be a farce when Johnson handily defeated Jeffries. Race riots swept the US, and plans to exhibit the film of the fight were canceled. Johnson was born at Galveston, TX, and died in an automobile accident June 10, 1946, at Raleigh, NC. He was inducted into the Boxing Hall of Fame in 1990. The film *The Great White Hope* is based on his life.

MARVELL, ANDREW: BIRTH ANNIVERSARY. Mar 31, 1621. English poet. Born at Winestead, Yorkshire, England. From his poem "To His Coy Mistress": "Had we but world enough and time/this coyness, lady, were no crime. . . . But at my back I always hear/time's winged chariot drawing near. . . ." Died at London, England, Aug 18, 1678.

MORGAN, HENRY: BIRTH ANNIVERSARY. Mar 31, 1915. Henry Lerner von Ost, Jr (Henry Morgan) was born at New York City. In 1933, at age 18, he became the youngest radio announcer in the US. His prickly quips and frequent antics quickly won him his own show. No one—politicians, radio executives or even his own sponsors—was spared his sharp tongue. From 1963 to 1977 he was a panelist on "I've Got a Secret," and he was a frequent guest on other television shows. Henry Morgan died May 19, 1994, at New York City.

NCAA DIVISION I MEN'S BASKETBALL CHAMPI-ONSHIPS. Mar 31–Apr 2. Minneapolis, MN. For info: Natl Collegiate Athletic Assn, 700 W Washington Ave, PO Box 6222, Indianapolis, IN 46206-6222. Phone: (317) 917-6222. Fax: (317) 917-6888. Web: www.ncaa,org.

PEARSE, RICHARD: FLIGHT ANNIVERSARY. Mar 31, 1903. Richard Pearse, a farmer and inventor, flew a monoplane of his own design several hundred yards along a road near Temuka, New Zealand, and then landed it on top of a 12-foot-high hedge. Pearse had built the craft, which consisted of a steerable tricycle undercarriage and an internal combustion engine. A Pearse commemorative medal was issued on Sept 19, 1971, by the Museum of Transport and Technology, Auckland, New Zealand.

PENNSYLVANIA MAPLE FESTIVAL. Mar 31–Apr 1 (also Apr 6–8). Meyersdale, PA. To celebrate the miracle of the maple. Est attendance: 25,000. For info: Pennsylvania Maple Festival, Box 222, Meyersdale, PA 15552. Phone: (814) 634-0213. Fax: (814) 634-0147. E-mail: maple@shol.com. Web: www .pamaplefestival.com.

SFCC SPRING ARTS FESTIVAL. Mar 31–Apr 1. Northeast 1st Street, Gainesville, FL. Artists and craftsmen from all areas of the US display their work. Also, Kids Art Jungle—a complete art fest for kids. Est attendance: 120,000. For info: Santa Fe Community College, Spring Arts Fest, 3000 NW 83rd St, Gainesville, FL 32606. Phone: (352) 395-5355. Fax: (352) 395-5918. E-mail: kathryn.lehman@santafe.cc.fl.us.

SOVIET GEORGIA VOTES FOR INDEPENDENCE: 10th ANNIVERSARY. Mar 31, 1991. On this date the Soviet Republic of Georgia voted to declare its independence from the Soviet Union. Georgia followed the Baltic States of Lithuania, Estonia and Latvia by becoming the fourth republic to reject Mikhail Gorbachev's new vision of the Soviet Union as espoused in a new Union Treaty. Totals revealed that 98.9 percent of those voting favored independence from Moscow. Hours after the election, troops were dispatched from Moscow to Georgia under a state of emergency.

SPRING STROLL. Mar 31–Apr 1 (also Apr 7–8). MainStrasse Village, Covington, KY. The Village welcomes spring with an Easter basket extravaganza! Drawing for two Easter baskets, brimming with delightful gifts for adults and children. No purchase necessary; entry forms available at all participating MainStrasse Village businesses. Saturday 10–6; Sunday noon–5. Est attendance: 1,000. For info: MainStrasse Village, 605 Philadelphia St, Covington, KY 41011. Phone: (859) 491-0458. Fax: (859) 655-7932. Web: www.state.ky.us.

SPRINGTIME TALLAHASSEE. Mar 31. Tallahassee, FL. This 33rd annual festival celebrates Florida's capital city, Tallahassee, "the city where spring begins!" Grand Parade and Jubilee on the streets of downtown Tallahassee. Est attendance: 250,000. For info: Greg Furnas, Exec Dir, Springtime Tallahassee, PO Box 1465, Tallahassee, FL 32302-1465. Phone: (904) 224-5012. Fax: (904) 224-0833.

SWITZERLAND: EASTER FESTIVAL LUCERNE. Mar 31–Apr 8. Lucerne. Easter festival of classical music including chamber music and concerts with sacred music, which will take place in two of the most splendid churches in Lucerne, the Jesuit and Franciscan churches. For info: Secretariat/Press Office, Easter Festival Lucerne, Hirschmattstrasse 13, PO Box CH-6002, Lucerne, Switzerland. Phone: (41) 226-4400. Fax: (41) 226-4460. E-mail: media@LucerneMusic.ch. Web:www.LucerneMusic.ch/

US AIR FORCE ACADEMY ESTABLISHED: ANNI-VERSARY. Mar 31, 1954. The US Air Force Academy was established at Colorado Springs, CO to train officers for the Air Force.

US VIRGIN ISLANDS: TRANSFER DAY. Mar 31. Commemorates transfer resulting from purchase of the Virgin Islands by the US from Denmark, Mar 31, 1917, for $25 million.

BIRTHDAYS TODAY

Herb Alpert, 66, musician (Tijuana Brass), born Los Angeles, CA, Mar 31, 1935.

Pavel Bure, 30, hockey player, born Moscow, USSR, Mar 31, 1971.

Richard Chamberlain, 66, actor ("Dr. Kildare," *Shogun*), born Los Angeles, CA, Mar 31, 1935.

Thomas Haden Church, 41, actor ("Wings," "Ned & Stacey"), born El Paso, TX, Mar 31, 1960.

Liz Claiborne, 72, fashion designer, born Brussels, Belgium, Mar 31, 1929.

William Daniels, 74, actor (Emmy for "St. Elsewhere"; "Boy Meets World"), born Brooklyn, NY, Mar 31, 1927.

Gordon (Gordie) Howe, 73, Hockey Hall of Fame right wing, born Floral, Saskatchewan, Canada, Mar 31, 1928.

John Jakes, 69, author (*California Gold, In the Big Country*), born Chicago, IL, Mar 31, 1932.

James Earl (Jimmy) Johnson, 63, Pro Football Hall of Fame defensive back, born Dallas, TX, Mar 31, 1938.

Shirley Jones, 67, singer, actress ("The Partridge Family," *Elmer Gantry, Oklahoma!*), born Smithton, PA, Mar 31, 1934.

Gabe Kaplan, 55, actor ("Welcome Back Kotter"), born Brooklyn, NY, Mar 31, 1946.

Angus King, Jr, 57, Governor of Maine (I), born Alexandria, VA, Mar 31, 1944.

Patrick J. Leahy, 61, US Senator (D, Vermont), born Montpelier, VT, Mar 31, 1940.

Edward Francis (Ed) Marinaro, 51, actor ("Hill Street Blues," "Sisters"), former football player, born New York, NY, Mar 31, 1950.

Marc McClure, 44, actor (*Freaky Friday, Back to the Future*), born San Mateo, CA, Mar 31, 1957.

Ewan McGregor, 30, actor (*Emma, The Serpent's Kiss*), born Crieff, Scotland, Mar 31, 1971.

Rhea Perlman, 53, actress ("Cheers" [three Emmy Awards]; *Carpool*), born Brooklyn, NY, Mar 31, 1948.

Steve Smith, 32, basketball player, born Highland Park, MI, Mar 31, 1969.

Christopher Walken, 58, actor (*The Deer Hunter, Batman Returns*), born Queens, NY, Mar 31, 1943.

April.

APRIL 1 — SUNDAY
Day 91 — 274 Remaining

ALCOHOL AWARENESS MONTH. Apr 1–30. To help raise awareness among community prevention leaders and citizens about the problem of underage drinking. Concentrates on community grassroots activities. For info: Public Info Dept, Natl Council on Alcoholism and Drug Dependence, Inc, 12 W 21st St, New York, NY 10010. Phone: (212) 206-6770. Fax: (212) 645-1690. Web: www.ncadd.org.

ANIMAL CRUELTY PREVENTION MONTH. Apr 1–30. The ASPCA sponsors this crucial month which is designed to prevent cruelty to animals by focusing on public awareness, advocacy and public education campaigns. For info: ASPCA Public Affairs Dept, 424 E 92nd St, New York, NY 10128. Phone: (212) 876-7700. E-mail: press@aspca.org. Web: www.aspca.org.

APRIL FOOLS' or ALL FOOLS' DAY. Apr 1. April Fool's Day seems to have begun in France in 1564. Apr 1 used to be New Year's day but the New Year was changed to Jan 1 that year. People who insisted on celebrating the "old" New Year became known as April fools and it became common to play jokes and tricks on them. The general concept of a feast of fools is, however, an ancient one. The Romans had such a day and medieval monasteries also had days when the abbot or bishop was replaced for a day by a common monk, who would order his superiors to do the most menial or ridiculous tasks. "The joke of the day is to deceive persons by sending them upon frivolous and nonsensical errands; to pretend they are wanted when they are not, or, in fact, any way to betray them into some supposed ludicrous situation, so as to enable you to call them 'An April Fool.' "—Brady's *Clavis Calendaria*, 1812.

ARCHITECTURAL FEATURE TOURS. Apr 1–Nov 4 (first Sunday of the month). Oak Park, IL. The Frank Lloyd Wright Preservation Trust sponsors walking tours that focus on architectural features and styles found in the Oak Park/River Forest community. Est attendance: 500. For info: Frank Lloyd Wright Preservation Trust, 951 Chicago Ave, Oak Park, IL 60302. Phone: (708) 848-1976. Web: www.wrightplus.org.

BATTLE OF OKINAWA BEGINS: ANNIVERSARY. Apr 1, 1945. On Easter Sunday, the US 10th Army began operation *Iceberg*, the invasion of the Ryukyu Islands of Okinawa. Ground troops numbering 180,000 plus 368,000 men in support services made a total of 548,000 troops involved—the biggest amphibious operation of the Pacific war.

BOOMER BONUS DAY. Apr 1. Aging Baby Boomers do not look forward to birthdays. This is a non-threatening (no extra years added) day to celebrate for the over-50 crowd only! On April 1 because the whole thing gets to be a joke—the body goes . . . but the mind still thinks it's 21! For info: Gaye Anderson, Davenport College Library, 8200 Georgia St, Merrillville, IN 46410. Phone: (219) 769-5556. Fax: (219) 756-8911.

BRIDGE OVER THE NEPONSET: ANNIVERSARY. Apr 1, 1634. The first bridge built in the US spanned the Neponset River between Milton and Dorchester, MA. The authority to build the bridge and an adjoining mill was issued to Israel Stoughton on this date by the Massachusetts General Court.

BULGARIA: SAINT LASARUS'S DAY. Apr 1. Ancient Slavic holiday of young girls, in honor of the goddess of spring and love.

CALIFORNIA EARTHQUAKE PREPAREDNESS MONTH. Apr 1–30. Earthquakes are a constant concern in California. For the Los Angeles area, television station KTLA has a "Care & Prepare" earthquake readiness campaign. For information, go to www.ktla.com. For info: Governor's Office of Emergency Services, 2800 Meadowview Rd, Sacramento, CA 95832. Phone: (916) 262-1843. Web: www.oes.ca.gov/cepm2000.nsf.

CANADA: NUNAVUT INDEPENDENCE: ANNIVERSARY. Apr 1, 1999. Nunavut became Canada's third independent territory. This self-governing territory with an Inuit majority was created from the eastern half of the Northwest Territories.

CANCER CONTROL MONTH. Apr 1–30. For info: American Cancer Soc, 1599 Clifton Rd NE, Atlanta, GA 30329-4251. Phone: (800) ACS-2345.

★**CANCER CONTROL MONTH.** Apr 1–30.

CHECK YOUR BATTERIES DAY. Apr 1. A day set aside for checking the batteries in your smoke detector, carbon monoxide detector, HVAC thermostat, audio/visual remote controls and other electronic devices. This could save your life! Annually, the first Sunday in April.

COMMUNITY SPIRIT DAYS. Apr 1–30. During the 30 days of April each community collects items at a central point for distribution to local charities, conducts special projects to help the local populace, congregates the town's nonprofit groups and businesses, thanks all participants and presents the community's Spirit of America Foundation Awards for outstanding volunteerism. For info: Jennifer Connolly, Spirit of America Foundation, PO Box 5637, Augusta, ME 04332. Phone: (207) 797-7326.

CONSIDER CHRISTIANITY WEEK. Apr 1–7. A week to encourage Christians to examine the evidence and reasons for their faith, and for non-Christians to take another look at the faith that has played such an important role in shaping the history and culture in which we live. Annually, beginning two Sundays before Easter. For info: Hanna Hushbeck, PR, Aletheia Publishing, 936 N Lincoln St, Redlands, CA 92374. Phone: (909) 794-8941. Fax: (909) 794-8941. E-mail: hanna@consider.org. Web: www.consider.org.

COUPLE APPRECIATION MONTH. Apr 1–30. To show thanks for each other's love and emotional support. Do something special to reinforce and celebrate your relationship. Annually, the month of April. For info: Donald Etkes, PhD, PMB 148, 112 Harvard Ave, Claremont, CA 91711. Phone: (909) 981-7333. Fax: (909) 985-8474.

DAYLIGHT SAVING TIME BEGINS. Apr 1–Oct 28. Daylight Saving Time begins at 2 AM in the US and Canada. The Uniform Time Act of 1966 (as amended in 1986 by Public Law 99–359), administered by the US Dept of Transportation, provides that Standard Time in each zone be advanced one hour from 2 AM on the first Sunday in April until 2 AM on the last Sunday in October (except where state legislatures provide exemption, as in Hawaii and parts of Arizona and Indiana). Prior to 1986, Daylight Saving time began on the last Sunday in April. Many use the popular rule "spring forward, fall back" to remember which way to turn their clocks. See also: "Standard Time" (Oct 28).

DEFEAT AT FIVE FORKS: ANNIVERSARY. Apr 1, 1865. After withdrawing to Five Forks, VA, Confederate troops under George Pickett were defeated and cut off by Union troops. This defeat, according to many military historians, sealed the immediate fate of Robert E. Lee's armies at Petersburg and Richmond. On Apr 2, Lee informed Confederate President Jefferson Davis that he would have to evacuate Richmond. Davis and his cabinet fled by train to Danville, VA.

"THE DOCTORS" TV PREMIERE: ANNIVERSARY.
Apr 1, 1963. "The Doctors" premiered on NBC on the same day as ABC's long-running soap "General Hospital," providing viewers with a double dose of medical drama. The show was set at Hope Memorial Hospital and began as an anthology series that was subsequently transformed into a serial in 1964. Created by Orin Tovrov, "The Doctors" ran for 19 years. Ellen Burstyn, Anna Stuart, Nancy Pinkerton, Jonathan Hogan, Julia Duffy and Alec Baldwin are some of its famous alums.

DOGWOOD ARTS FESTIVAL. Apr 1–30. Maryville, TN. To celebrate spring. Activities and events for all ages. Est attendance: 12,000. For info: Chamber of Commerce, Blount County Dogwood Arts Fest, 201 S Washington St, Maryville, TN 37804-5728. Phone: (865) 983-2241. Fax: (865) 984-1386. E-mail: foundtn@chamber.blount.tn.us. Web: chamber.blount.tn.us.

ENGLAND: CARE SUNDAY. Apr 1. The fifth Sunday of Lent, also known as Carling Sunday and Passion Sunday. First day of Passiontide, remembering the sorrow and passion of Christ.

EXCHANGE CLUB CHILD ABUSE PREVENTION MONTH. Apr 1–30. Nationwide effort to raise awareness of child abuse and how to prevent it. For info: The Natl Exchange Club Foundation, 3050 Central Ave, Toledo, OH 43606-1700. Phone: (419) 535-3232 or (800) 760-3413. Fax: (419) 535-1989. E-mail: info@preventchildabuse.com. Web: www.preventchildabuse.com.

FRESH FLORIDA TOMATO MONTH. Apr 1–30. To publicize the Florida tomato as a versatile, nutritious, flavorful food. For info: Anita Fial, Lewis & Neale, Inc, 49 E 21st St, 8th Flr, New York, NY 10010. Phone: (212) 420-8808. Fax: (212) 254-2452. E-mail: laneale@aol.com.

"GENERAL HOSPITAL" TV PREMIERE: ANNIVERSARY. Apr 1, 1963. "General Hospital," ABC's longest-running soap, revolves around the denizens of fictional Port Charles, NY. "GH" was created by Doris and Frank Hursley. John Beradino, who was with the show from the beginning until his death in May of 1996, played the role of Dr. Steve Hardy, director of medicine and pillar of the community. In the '80s, story lines became more unusual with plots involving international espionage, mob activity and aliens. The wedding of supercouple Luke and Laura (Anthony Geary and Genie Francis) was a ratings topper. By the '90s, stories moved away from high-powered action to more conventional romance. Many actors received their big break on the show: Demi Moore, Janine Turner, Jack Wagner, Richard Dean Anderson, Rick Springfield, John Stamos, Emma Samms, Mark Hamill, Finola Hughes and Tia Carrere.

GOLDEN RULE WEEK. Apr 1–7. The purpose of this week is to remind everyone of the importance of the Golden Rule in making this a better world in which we all may live. For a copy of the Golden Rule of 10 religions, send $4 to cover printing and postage. For info: Dr. S. J. Drake, Pres, Intl Society of Friendship and Goodwill, 8592 Roswell Rd, Ste 434, Atlanta, GA 30350-1870.

GRAND STRAND FISHING RODEO. Apr 1–Oct 31. Myrtle Beach, SC. Awards for surf, inlet, pier and deep-sea fish catches. Est attendance: 1,000. For info: Chamber of Commerce, PO Box 2115, Myrtle Beach, SC 29578. Phone: (843) 626-7444. Fax: (843) 626-0009. Web: www.myrtlebeachlive.com.

GREECE: DUMB WEEK. Apr 1–7. The week preceding Holy Week on the Orthodox calendar is known as Dumb Week, as no services are held in churches throughout this period except on Friday, eve of the Saturday of Lazarus.

	S	M	T	W	T	F	S
April	1	2	3	4	5	6	7
2001	8	9	10	11	12	13	14
	15	16	17	18	19	20	21
	22	23	24	25	26	27	28
	29	30					

HARVEY, WILLIAM: BIRTH ANNIVERSARY. Apr 1, 1578 (OS). Physician, born at Folkestone, England. The first to discover the mechanics of the circulation of the blood. Died at Roehampton, England, June 3, 1657 (OS).

HOLY HUMOR MONTH. Apr 1–30. To recognize the healing power of Christian joy, humor and celebration; to be "Fools for Christ" on April Fools' Day (Apr 1); to celebrate "Holy Humor Sunday," the Sunday after Easter (Apr 22). Churches and prayer groups nationwide participate. For info: George Goldtrap, The Fellowship of Merry Christians, Inc. PO Box 895, Portage, MI 49081-0895. Phone: (904) 441-8197. Fax: (616) 324-3984. E-mail: joyfulnz@aol.com. Web: www.joyfulnoiseletter.com.

HOME IMPROVEMENT SAFETY MONTH. Apr 1–30. Every year thousands of Americans injure themselves while taking on home improvement projects. This month is intended to encourage them to learn the how-tos of home improvement to avoid injury during the biggest home improvement season. For info: Heather Snavely, 80 S Washington St, Seattle, WA 98104. Phone: (206) 467-7978. E-mail: Heather_Snavely@edelman.com. Web: www.hardware.com.

HOME IMPROVEMENT TIME. Apr 1–Sept 30. To explain the investment advantages of spending disposable income for home improvement to create better family living and improved community environment. Editorial package includes approximately 100 camera-ready stories and photos free to editors. Also available on disk. (May is a promotion focal point.) For info: James A. Stewart, Jr, Home Improvement Time, PO Box 247, Oakdale, PA 15701-0247. Phone: (412) 787-2881. Fax: (412) 787-3233. E-mail: hitdirect@aol.com. Web: homeimprovementtime.com.

HOOSIER STATE GAMES: FINALS. Apr 1–Dec 31. State champions are crowned in 15 different sports during the Hoosier State Games, as athletes of all ages and skill levels compete in this statewide multi-sport competition. Since 1983 more than 250,000 athletes have competed in the Hoosier State Games. For info: Indiana Sports Corp, 201 S Capitol Ave, Ste 1200, Indianapolis, IN 46225. Phone: (800) HI-FIVES. Fax: (317) 237-5041. Web: www.indianasportscorp.com.

INDIAN DANCE FESTIVAL. Apr 1. DeSoto Caverns Park, Childersburg, AL. 26th annual festival. Est attendance: 12,000. For info: DeSoto Caverns Park, DeSoto Caverns Pkwy, Childersburg, AL 35044. Phone: (205) 378-7252 or (800) 933-2283. E-mail: fun@desotocavernspark.com. Web: www.desotocavernspark.com.

INFORMED WOMAN MONTH. Apr 1–30. You owe it to yourself to feel happy and fulfilled. To have confidence that you're in charge of your life and you're guiding it in the right direction. You can have whatever you want, but you need to determine what you need to know, where to go and whom to contact. Discover how to enjoy better living today and learn how to become a more informed and aware individual for the future. Send $2.75 for a sample copy of our newsletter "The Informed Women Files" with useful ideas, solutions, tips and examples that will help you accomplish anything you set your mind to. For info: Lorrie Walters Marsiglio, Lorimar Communications, PO Box 284-CC, Wasco, IL 60183-0284.

INTERNATIONAL AMATEUR RADIO MONTH. Apr 1–30. To disseminate information about the important part amateur radio operators or "hams" throughout the world are playing in promoting friendship, peace and good will. To obtain complete information about becoming an International Good Will Ambassador as well as a list of amateur radio operators in many countries, send $4 to cover expense of printing, handling and postage. Annually, the month of April. For info: Dr. Stanley Drake, Pres, Intl Soc of Friendship and Good Will, 8592 Roswell Rd, Ste 434, Atlanta, GA 30350-1870.

INTERNATIONAL BUILDING SAFETY WEEK. Apr 1–7. To make all Americans aware of the important health and life safety services available to them from their state and local professional building departments. Sponsors: International Conference of Building Officials, Southern Building Code Congress International and Building Officials and Code Administrators International. For info: NCSBCS, 505 Huntmar Park Dr, Ste 210, Herndon, VA 20170. Phone: (703) 437-0100. Fax: (703) 481-3596. Web: www.ncsbcs.org.

INTERNATIONAL CUSTOMER LOYALTY MONTH. Apr 1–30. We highlight this month to honor and generate customer loyalty! Even though building customer loyalty should be a year-round thing, not just a month, take this month to strategize on how you can improve on relationships with your customers through better service, higher quality, etc. For info: Shep Hyken, Shepard Presentations, 711 Old Ballas Rd, #215, St. Louis, MO 63141. Phone: (314) 696-2200. E-mail: Shep@hyken.com. Web: www.hyken.com.

INTERNATIONAL DAFFYNITIONS MONTH. Apr 1–30. Based on the book, *Daffynitions: A Dictionary for the Humor Impaired*, a celebration of creativity. It kicks off each year on April Fool's Day with the Daffynitions Creativity Festival. Author Joe Heuer will deliver 20 speeches throughout the country during the monthlong celebration as well as numerous radio and television interviews. For info: Joe Heuer, PO Box 170933, Milwaukee, WI 53217. Phone: (414) 964-0936 or (800) 492-3548. Fax: (414) 964-0932. E-mail: joe@daffynitions.com. Web: www.daffynitions.com.

INTERNATIONAL LEGACY MONTH. Apr 1–30. A month to focus on the legacy you are leaving for your family, friends, colleagues, career and community. What you have to remember depends on what you do today. Let this month be the opportunity you've been waiting for, inspire yourself and others to leave enduring gifts and create yesterdays worth remembering. For info: Janna Krammer, Legacy Institute, 42747 Blackhawk Rd, Harris, MN 55032. Phone: (877) 646-9100. Fax: (651) 674-0228. E-mail: info@legacyinstitute.com.

INTERNATIONAL TWIT AWARD MONTH. Apr 1–30. Any famous name (celebrity with the worst sense of humor) is eligible for most Tiresome Wit (TWIT) of 2001. For info: Lauren Barnett, Lone Star Publications of Humor, 8452 Fredericksburg Rd, Ste #103, San Antonio, TX 78229. E-mail: lspubs@aol.com. Web: members.aol.com/lspubs/lsindex.html.

INTERNATIONAL WORK LIFE ENRICHMENT MONTH. Apr 1–30. Take the next 30 days to focus on improving the quality of your life and work. Also, use this month to activate and celebrate improvements in your workplace. Individuals will gain more work satisfaction. Employers will gain more productive employees. For info: Gloria Dunn, Pres, Wiser Ways to Work®, PO Box 150869, San Rafael, CA 94915. Phone: (415) 459-4843. E-mail: gloriadunn@aol.com. Web: www.gloriadunn.com.

IRAN: ISLAMIC REPUBLIC DAY. Apr 1. National holiday. Commemorates the proclamation of the Islamic Republic of Iran in 1979.

KEEP AMERICA BEAUTIFUL MONTH. Apr 1–30. To educate Americans about their personal responsibility for litter prevention, proper waste disposal and environmental improvement through various community projects. Annually, the month of April. For info: Dir of Communications, Keep America Beautiful, Inc, Washington Square, 1010 Washington Blvd, Stamford, CT 06901. Phone: (203) 323-8987. Fax: (203) 325-9199. E-mail: info@kab.org. Web: www.keepamericabeautiful.org.

LUPUS ALERT DAY. Apr 1. Don't be fooled by lupus! To call attention to the confusing characteristics of this potentially fatal auto-immune disease that mimics other, less serious illnesses. For info: Duane Peters, Dir of Communications and Advocacy, Lupus Foundation of America, 1300 Piccard Dr, Ste 200, Rockville, MD 20850-4303. Phone: (301) 670-9292. Fax: (301) 670-9486. E-mail: lfanatl@aol.com. Web: www.lupus.org.

MATHEMATICS EDUCATION MONTH. Apr 1–30. An opportunity for students, teachers, parents and the community as a whole to focus on the importance of mathematics and the changes taking place in mathematics education. For info: Communications Manager, Natl Council of Teachers of Mathematics, 1906 Association Dr, Reston, VA 20191-1593. Phone: (703) 620-9840. Fax: (703) 476-2970. E-mail: infocentral@nctm.org. Web: www.nctm.org.

MONTH OF THE YOUNG CHILD®. Apr 1–30. Michigan. To promote awareness of the importance of young children and their specific needs in today's society. Many communities celebrate with special events for children and families. For info: Michigan Assn for Education of Young Children, Beacon Pl, Ste 1-D, 4572 S Hagadorn Rd, East Lansing, MI 48823-5385. Phone: (800) 336-6424 or (517) 336-9700. Fax: (517) 336-9790. E-mail: moyc@miaeyc.com. Web: www.miaeyc.com.

MOON PHASE: FIRST QUARTER. Apr 1. Moon enters First Quarter phase at 6:49 AM, EDT.

MOUNT HOOD RAILHOOD: A SEASON OF FUN. Apr 1–Dec 19. Hood River, OR. 94-year-old historic railroad offers 44-mile round-trip excursions through natural beauty of the northwest Columbia River Gorge and foothills of Mount Hood, Oregon's highest peak. Special holiday events, murder mystery, dinner trains and harrowing train robberies throughout the season. For info: Mt Hood Railroad, 110 Railroad Ave, Hood River, OR 97031. Phone: (800) TRAIN-61 or (541) 386-3556. Fax: (541) 386-2140. Web: www.mthoodrr.com.

NATIONAL AUTISM AWARENESS MONTH. Apr 1–30. A month filled with autism awareness events such as conferences, presentations, displays and media attention. This is a national celebration held every April. For info: Jennifer Stillitano, Coord of Mktg & PR, COSAC, 1450 Parkside Ave, Ste 22, Ewing, NJ 08638. Phone: (609) 863-8100. Fax: (609) 883-5509. E-mail: njautism@aol.com. Web: members.aol.com/njautism.

NATIONAL BLUE RIBBON WEEK. Apr 1–7. Wear a blue ribbon to show your concern about and objection to child abuse. Nationwide public awareness effort. For info: The Natl Exchange Club Foundation, 3050 Central Ave, Toledo, OH 43606-1700. Phone: (419) 535-3232 or (800) 924-2643. Fax: (419) 535-1989. E-mail: info@preventchildabuse.com. Web: www.preventchildabuse.com.

★NATIONAL CHILD ABUSE PREVENTION MONTH. Apr 1–30.

NATIONAL CHILD ABUSE PREVENTION MONTH. Apr 1–30. For info: Natl Committee to Prevent Child Abuse, 332 S Michigan Ave, Ste 1600, Chicago, IL 60604. Phone: (312) 663-3520. Web: www.preventchildabuse.org.

NATIONAL HUMOR MONTH. Apr 1–30. 25th anniversary. Focuses on the joy and therapeutic value of laughter and how it can reduce stress, improve job performance and enrich the quality of life. For info send 55 cent SASE to: Larry Wilde, Dir, The Carmel Institute of Humor, 25470 Canada Dr, Carmel, CA 93923-8926. Web: www.larrywilde.com.

NATIONAL KNUCKLES DOWN MONTH. Apr 1–30. To recognize and revive the American tradition of playing and collecting marbles and keep it rolling along. Please send SASE with inquiries. For info: Cathy C. Runyan-Svacina, The Marble Lady, 7812 NW Hampton Rd, Kansas City, MO 64152. Phone: (816) 587-8687. Fax: (816) 587-8687.

NATIONAL LAWN AND GARDEN MONTH. Apr 1–30. National celebration highlighting the benefits of landscape and lawn care in the new millennium. Annually, the month of April. For info: Bonnie Van Fleet, Associated Landscape Contractors of America (ALCA), 150 Elden St, Ste 270, Herndon, VA 20170. Phone: (703) 736-9666. Fax: (703) 736-9668. Web: www.alca.org.

NATIONAL LIBRARY WEEK. Apr 1–7. A nationwide observance sponsored by the American Library Association. Celebrates libraries and librarians, the pleasures and importance of reading and invites library use and support. For info: American Library Assn, Public Info Office, 50 E Huron St, Chicago, IL 60611. Phone: (312) 280-5044. Fax: (312) 944-8520. E-mail: pio@ala.org. Web: www.ala.org.

NATIONAL MEDICAL PATIENT ADVOCACY WEEK. Apr 1–7. As the medical community continues to grow and get more complicated, patients will require help in navigating through the sea of doctors and hospitals. This week is to bring attention to the fact that there is help available and that patients have the right to seek it out. Annually, the first week in April. For info: Mark S. Vass, 617 Keller Smithfield Rd, Keller, TX 76248-4229. Phone: (817) 379-5372. E-mail: mvass@gte.net. Web: www.txbenefit.com.

NATIONAL OCCUPATIONAL THERAPY MONTH. Apr 1–30. To recognize the services and accomplishments of occupational therapy practitioners and promote awareness of the benefits of occupational therapy. For info: The American Occupational Therapy Assn, Inc, 4720 Montgomery Ln, PO Box 31220, Bethesda, MD 20824-1220. Phone: (301) 652-2682 or (301) 652-6611 ext 2962. Fax: (301) 652-7711. TDD: (800) 377-8555. Consumer Line: (800) 668-8225. Web: www.aota.org.

NATIONAL PECAN MONTH. Apr 1–30. A celebration of the great taste, health benefits and versatility of pecans. This delicious tree nut native to North America adds unmistakable flavor, crunch and texture to just about any meal or snack. Pecans have proven cholesterol-lowering properties and contain more than 19 important vitamins and minerals. Almost 90 percent of the fats in pecans are of the heart-healthy, unsaturated variety. For info: Natl Pecan Shellers Assn, 5775 Peachtree-Dunwoody Rd, Ste 500, Bldg G, Atlanta, GA 30342. Phone: (404) 252-3663. Fax: (404) 252-0774. E-mail: npsa@assnhq.com. Web: www.ilovepecans.org.

NATIONAL PET FIRST AID AWARENESS MONTH. Apr 1–30. Sponsored by Pet Tech, Inc, the first national training center for Pet First Aid & Care. To help pet owners everywhere in understanding the importance of knowing the skills and techniques of Pet First Aid, CPR & Care for their pet. For info: Pet Tech, Inc, 5800 Severin Dr, La Mesa, CA 91942. Phone: (619) 589-7475. E-mail: info@pettech.net. Web: www.pettech.net.

NATIONAL POETRY MONTH. Apr 1–30. Annual observance to pay tribute to the great legacy and ongoing achievement of American poets and the vital place of poetry in American culture. In a proclamation issued in honor of the first observance, President Bill Clinton called it "a welcome opportunity to celebrate not only the unsurpassed body of literature produced by our poets in the past, but also the vitality and diversity of voices reflected in the works of today's American poets. . . . Their creativity and wealth of language enrich our culture and inspire a new generation of Americans to learn the power of reading and writing at its best." Spearheaded by the Academy of American Poets, this is the largest and most extensive celebration of poetry in American history. For info: Academy of American Poets, 584 Broadway, Ste 1208, New York, NY 10012-3250. Phone: (212) 274-0343. Web: www.poets.org.

NATIONAL REPOT YOUR PLANT DAY. Apr 1. The Scotts Company would like to remind people to repot their plants when they reset their clocks. When your prized plants starts to lose their vigor and color, the problem is usually due to growing pains below the surface. Over time, potting soil becomes tired and lacks essential nutrients and plants' roots continue to grow, taking up more space than the pots allow for, leaving plants root-bound. This combination of decomposing pot medium and cramped quarters inevitably leads to an unhealthy environment. Annually, on Daylight Saving Day. For info: Mr Aram Sabet, Dan Klores Associates, Inc, 386 Park Ave South, 10th Fl, New York, NY 10016. Phone: (212) 981-5244. Fax: (212) 981-5444. E-mail: aram.sabet @dkanews.com. Web: www.Scottsco.com.

NATIONAL SELF-PUBLISHING MONTH. Apr 1–30. A month recognizing the hard work and risk that many authors endure to see their work published. Annually, the month of April. For info: Offtime Press, 41 Sutter St. 1763, San Francisco, CA 94104. Phone: (415) 292-5230. E-mail: drdecastro@aol.com.

NATIONAL SEXUALLY TRANSMITTED DISEASES (STDs) EDUCATION AND AWARENESS MONTH. Apr 1–30. To educate consumers, patients, students and professionals about the prevention of sexually transmitted diseases. Kit of materials available for $15. For info: Frederick Mayer, Pharmacists Planning Service, Inc, 101 Lucas Valley Rd, #210, San Rafael, CA 94903. E-mail: ppsi@aol.com. Web: www.ppsinc.org.

April 2001	S	M	T	W	T	F	S
	1	2	3	4	5	6	7
	8	9	10	11	12	13	14
	15	16	17	18	19	20	21
	22	23	24	25	26	27	28
	29	30					

NATIONAL YOUTH SPORTS SAFETY MONTH. Apr 1–30. Bringing public attention to the prevalent problem of injuries in youth sports. This event promotes safety in sports activities and is supported by more than 60 national sports and medical organizations. Resource material available on website. For info: Michelle Klein, Exec Dir, Natl Youth Sports Safety Fdtn, 333 Longwood Ave, Ste 202, Boston, MA 02115. Phone: (617) 277-1171. Fax: (617) 277-2278. E-mail: NYSSF@aol.com. Web: www.nyssf.org.

150 YEARS OF ROBINSON FAMILY HATS: EXHIBIT. Apr 1–May 31. Granville Life-Style Museum, Granville, OH. 17th annual. Family members of the late Hubert and Oese Robinson saved their bonnets, hats, infant caps and headwear of all descriptions from the 1820s to the 1970s. All on exhibit. For info: Gina Hughes, Dir, Granville Life-Style Museum, H.D. Robinson House, 121 S Main St, Granville, OH 43023. Phone: (740) 587-0373.

PASSION WEEK. Apr 1–7. The week beginning on the fifth Sunday in Lent; the week before Holy Week.

PASSIONTIDE. Apr 1–14. The last two weeks of Lent (Passion Week and Holy Week), beginning with the fifth Sunday of Lent (Passion Sunday) and continuing through the day before Easter (Holy Saturday or Easter Even).

PREVENT INJURIES AMERICA!. Apr 1–30. Move Better, Play Better, Live Better. Learn about preventing orthopaedic injuries and conditions. Throughout the month, orthopaedic surgeons will provide injury prevention information on topics such as preventing playground and sports injuries, osteoporosis, workplace injuries, low back pain and proper shoewear tips. For info: American Academy of Orthopaedic Surgeons, 6300 N River Rd, Rosemont, IL 60018. Phone: (800) 824-BONES. Fax: (847) 823-8125. Web: www.aaos.org.

PRO-AM SNIPE EXCURSION AND HUNT. Apr 1. Moultrie, GA. Celebrating the time-honored custom of snipe hunting. The denim snipe has come back from the brink of extinction and will be honored at the 2001 event which will include a Snipe Parade, a Snipe Ball and festivities at the Denim Wing of the Snipe Museum at New Elm, GA. New Snipe-O-Rama racing oval open! Annually, Apr 1. For info: Beth Gay, PO Box 2828, Moultrie, GA 31776. Phone: (912) 985-6540.

RAM, JAGJIVAN: BIRTH ANNIVERSARY. Apr 1, 1908. Indian political leader and coworker with Mohandas K. Gandhi and Jawaharlal Nehru in the fight for Indian independence. Born into a family of "untouchables" at the village of Chandwa, Bihar, India, Ram was one of the first of that class to attend school and university. Known as the champion and spokesman for India's 100 million untouchables, he overcame most of the handicaps of caste. He served in a number of ministerial cabinet posts and twice was a candidate for prime minister. Ram died at New Delhi, India, July 6, 1986.

ROBERT THE HERMIT: DEATH ANNIVERSARY. Apr 1, 1832. One of the most famous hermits in American history died in his hermitage at Seekonk, MA. Robert was a bonded slave, the son of an African mother and probably an Anglo-Saxon father. After obtaining his freedom, he was swindled out of it and shipped to a foreign slave market, then later escaped to America. He was separated from his first wife by force and rejected by his second wife after a long sea voyage, before withdrawing from society.

SCHOOL LIBRARY MEDIA MONTH. Apr 1–30. Celebrates the work of school library media specialists in our nation's elementary and secondary schools. For info: American Assn of School Librarians, American Library Assn, 50 E Huron St, Chicago, IL 60611. Phone: (800) 545-2433. E-mail: AASL@ala.org. Web: www.ala.org/aasl.

SHEEP TO SHAWL. Apr 1. Jarrell Plantation, Juliette, GA. Hand shearing of sheep. Washing, dyeing, felting of wool. Carding, spinning and weaving of wool and cotton. Self-guided tour of plain-style plantation houses and mill complex. 10:30 AM–3:30 PM. Admission fee. Sponsor: Georgia Heartland Spinners and Weavers Guild. Est attendance: 300. For info: Jarrell Plantation State Historic Site, 711 Jarrell Plantation Rd, Juliette, GA 31046. Phone: (912) 986-5172.

SORRY CHARLIE DAY. Apr 1. To honor Charlie the Tuna, who has been rejected for 35 years and still keeps his spunk. A day to recognize anyone who has been rejected and lived through it. Join the "Sorry Charlie, No-Fan-Club-for-You Club." Please send SASE with inquiries. For info: Cathy Runyan-Svacina, 7812 NW Hampton Rd, Kansas City, MO 64152. Phone: (816) 587-8687. Fax: (816) 587-8687.

STRAW HAT MONTH. Apr 1–30. A month of celebration during which the felt hat is put aside in favor of the straw or fabric hat by both men and women. Local businesses and the media are encouraged to plan hat-related activities. Annually, coordinated with Easter. For info: Casey Bush, Exec Dir, Headwear Info Bureau, 302 W 12 St, PH-C, New York, NY 10014. Phone: (212) 627-8333. Fax: (212) 627-0067. E-mail: milicase@aol.com. Web: www.hatsny.com/hib.

STRESS AWARENESS MONTH. Apr 1–30. To promote public awareness of what stress is, what causes it to occur and what can be done about it. A monthlong focus on the dangers of stress, successful coping strategies and the myths about stress that are prevalent in our society. For info: Morton C. Orman, MD, Dir, The Health Resource Network, 2936 E Baltimore St, Baltimore, MD 21224. Phone: (410) 732-1900. Web: www.stresscure.com.

TOUR de CURE. Apr 1–June 30. Thousands of cyclists participate in the American Diabetes Association's annual cycling event to raise money to help find a cure for diabetes and to provide information and resources to improve the lives of all people affected by diabetes. Tours are held in communities across America, combining fun and fitness with the chance to help people with diabetes through April, May and June. Contact your local affiliate for the date in your area. For info: American Diabetes Assn, Natl HQ, 1660 Duke St, Alexandria, VA 22314. Phone: (800) TOUR-888. Web: www.diabetes.org.

US HOUSE OF REPRESENTATIVES ACHIEVES A QUORUM: ANNIVERSARY. Apr 1, 1789. First session of Congress was held Mar 4, 1789, but not enough representatives arrived to achieve a quorum until Apr 1.

WEEK OF THE YOUNG CHILD. Apr 1–7. To focus on the importance of quality early childhood education. For info: Natl Assn for the Educ of Young Children, 1509 16th St NW, Washington, DC 20036. Phone: (800) 424-2460. Fax: (202) 328-1846. E-mail: naeyc@naeyc.org. Web: www.naeyc.org.

WOMEN'S EYE HEALTH AND SAFETY MONTH. Apr 1–30. Women often manage family health concerns. Do you know how to protect your sight? Hormonal changes, age and even the sun can endanger sight. Information on women's and family eye-health issues will be provided. For info: Prevent Blindness America®, 500 E Remington Rd, Schaumburg, IL 60173. Phone: (800) 331-2020. Fax: (847) 843-8458. Web: www.preventblindness.org.

WORLD HABITAT AWARENESS MONTH. Apr 1–30. A worldwide observance of the need to protect the habitat of all Earth's creatures, to make a conscious effort to preserve nature's ecosystems. Annually, the entire month of April. For info: ARK (Animalkind Rescue Kids), PO Box 1271, San Luis Obispo, CA 93406. Phone: (805) 544-0984. Web: www.expage.com/page /ARKhome.

ZAM! ZOO AND AQUARIUM MONTH. Apr 1–30. A national celebration to focus public attention on the role of zoos and aquariums in wildlife education and conservation. Held at 184 AZA member institutions in the US and Canada. Sponsor: American Zoo and Aquarium Association. For information, contact your local zoo or aquarium. For info: Zoo and Aquarium Assn, 8403 Colesville Rd, Ste 710, Silver Spring, MD 20910. Phone: (301) 562-0777. Fax: (301) 562-0888. Web: www.aza.org.

BIRTHDAYS TODAY

David Eisenhower, 54, author (*Eisenhower at War*), lawyer, grandson of former president Dwight Eisenhower, born West Point, NY, Apr 1, 1947.

Ali MacGraw, 62, actress (*Goodbye, Columbus, Love Story*), born Pound Ridge, NY, Apr 1, 1939.

Annette O'Toole, 48, actress (*Smile, 48Hrs*), born Houston, TX, Apr 1, 1953.

Jane Powell (Suzanne Burce), 72, actress (*Seven Brides for Seven Brothers*), born Portland, OR, Apr 1, 1929.

Debbie Reynolds, 69, actress (*Singin' in the Rain, Mother*), born El Paso, TX, Apr 1, 1932.

Libby Riddles, 45, first woman to win the 1,135-mile Iditarod Alaskan dogsled race, born Madison, WI, Apr 1, 1956.

Glenn Edward ("Bo") Schembechler, Jr, 72, former baseball executive and football coach, born Barberton, OH, Apr 1, 1929.

Daniel Joseph ("Rusty") Staub, 57, former baseball player, born New Orleans, LA, Apr 1, 1944.

APRIL 2 — MONDAY
Day 92 — 273 Remaining

ANDERSEN, HANS CHRISTIAN: BIRTH ANNIVERSARY. Apr 2, 1805. Author chiefly remembered for his more than 150 fairy tales, many of which are regarded as classics of children's literature. Andersen was born at Odense, Denmark, and died at Copenhagen, Denmark, Aug 4, 1875.

"AS THE WORLD TURNS" TV PREMIERE: 45th ANNIVERSARY. Apr 2, 1956. One of the longest-running soaps currently on the air, "ATWT" premiered on CBS. The series is set in midwestern Oakdale and revolves around the Hughes family and their neighbors. Irna Phillips was the show's creator and head writer. Some of its cast members who made it big are: Meg Ryan, Julianne Moore, Michael Nader, Steven Weber and Swoosie Kurtz.

BARTHOLDI, FREDERIC AUGUSTE: BIRTH ANNIVERSARY. Apr 2, 1834. French sculptor who created *Liberty Enlightening the World* (better known as the Statue of Liberty), which stands at New York Harbor. Also remembered for the *Lion of Belfort* at Belfort, France. Born at Colman, at Alsace, France. Died at Paris, France, Oct 4, 1904.

BREAD RIOT AT RICHMOND: ANNIVERSARY. Apr 2, 1863. Indicative of conditions in the Confederate capital of Richmond, VA, an angry mob's demands for bread from a bakery wagon escalated into the destruction of nearby shops. Confederate president Jefferson Davis, in a bold move, stepped into the angry crowd and stated, "We do not desire to injure anyone, but this lawlessness must stop. I will give you five minutes to disperse, otherwise you will be fired upon." The mob dispersed without bloodshed.

CASANOVA, GIOVANNI GIACOMO GIROLAMO: BIRTH ANNIVERSARY. Apr 2, 1725. Celebrated Italian writer-librarian and, by his own account, philanderer, adventurer, rogue, seminarian, soldier and spy, was born at Venice, Italy. As the Chevalier de Seingalt, he died at Dux, Bohemia, June 4, 1798, while serving as librarian and working on his lively and frank *History of My Life*, a brilliant picture of 18th-century life.

	S	M	T	W	T	F	S
April		1	2	3	4	5	6	7
2001	8	9	10	11	12	13	14
	15	16	17	18	19	20	21
	22	23	24	25	26	27	28
	29	30					

"DALLAS" TV PREMIERE: ANNIVERSARY. Apr 2, 1978. Oil tycoons battled for money, power and prestige in this prime-time CBS drama that ran for nearly 13 years. The Ewings and Barneses were Texas's modern-day Hatfields and McCoys. Larry Hagman starred as the devious, scheming womanizer J.R. Ewing. When J.R. was shot in the 1980 season-ending cliffhanger, the revelation of the mystery shooter was the single-most watched episode of its time (it was Kristin, J.R.'s sister-in-law, played by Mary Crosby). Cast members included Jim Davis, Barbara Bel Geddes, Donna Reed, Ted Shackelford, Joan Van Ark (who, along with Shackelford, starred in the spin-off "Knots Landing"), Patrick Duffy, Linda Gray, Charlene Tilton, David Wayne, Keenan Wynn, Ken Kercheval, Victoria Principal and Steve Kanaly.

"THE EDGE OF NIGHT" TV PREMIERE: 45th ANNIVERSARY. Apr 2, 1956. "The Edge of Night" premiered on CBS along with "As The World Turns." Though the plots initially revolved around crime and courtroom drama, the serial's format soon developed along more conventional soap story lines of romance. The soap shifted to ABC in 1975 but was cancelled in 1984. Larry Hagman, Dixie Carter, Lori Loughlin, Willie Aames and Amanda Blake were some of the show's most prominent players.

FALKLAND ISLANDS WAR: ANNIVERSARY. Apr 2–June 15, 1982. Argentina, claiming sovereignty over the nearby Falkland Islands (called by them the Malvinas), invaded and occupied the British Crown Colony on Apr 2, 1982. British forces defeated the Argentinians on June 15, 1982. About 250 British and 600 Argentine lives were lost in the conflict. In 1986, three military officers, including General Leopoldo Galtieri (who was president of Argentina at the time of the invasion), were convicted and sentenced for the military crime of negligence. Commemorative ceremonies are observed on Apr 2 in Argentina and on June 15 in the Falkland Islands.

FIRST WHITE HOUSE EASTER EGG ROLL: ANNIVERSARY. Apr 2, 1877. The first White House Easter Egg Roll took place during the administration of Rutherford B. Hayes. The traditional event was discontinued by President Franklin D. Roosevelt in 1942 and reinstated Apr 6, 1953, by President Dwight D. Eisenhower.

INTERNATIONAL CHILDREN'S BOOK DAY. Apr 2. Commemorates the international aspects of children's literature and observes Hans Christian Andersen's birthday. Sponsor: International Board on Books for Young People, Nonnenweg 12, Postfach, CH-4003 Basel, Switzerland. For info: USBBY Secretariat, c/oIntl Reading Assn, Box 8139, Newark, DE 19714-8139. E-mail: usbby@reading.org.

NATIONAL PUBLIC HEALTH WEEK. Apr 2–8. Annually, the first full week in April. For info: American Public Health Assn, 1015 15th St NW, Washington, DC, 20005. Phone: (202) 789-5600.

NICKELODEON PREMIERE: ANNIVERSARY. Apr 2, 1979. Nickelodeon, the cable TV channel for kids owned by MTV Networks, debuted on this date.

PASCUA FLORIDA DAY. Apr 2. A legal holiday in Florida, designated as State Day. When it falls on a Saturday or Sunday, the governor may declare either the preceding Friday or the following Monday as State Day. Florida also observes Pascua Florida Week from Mar 27–Apr 2. Commemorates the sighting of Florida by Ponce de Leon in 1513. He named the land Pascua Florida because of its discovery at Easter, the "Feast of the Flowers."

PONCE DE LEON DISCOVERS FLORIDA: ANNIVERSARY. Apr 2, 1513. Juan Ponce de Leon discovered Florida, landing at the site that became the city of St. Augustine. He claimed the land for the King of Spain.

RECONCILIATION DAY. Apr 2. Columnist Ann Landers writes, "Since 1989, I have suggested that April 2 be set aside to write that letter or make that phone call and mend a broken relationship. Life is too short to hold grudges. To forgive can be enormously life-enhancing . . . ."

STROLF-STRETCH WEEK. Apr 2–6. A dynamic stretching, strengthening and conditioning program designed for golf and other rotational sports. To promote the benefits of stretching in maintaining body balance and wellness. For info: Body Works Rehab and Fitness Intl Ltd, 1118 Centre St, Thornhill, ON, Canada L4J 7R9. Phone: (905) 763-8811. Fax: (905) 763-9675. Web: www.STROLF.com.

TIN PAN SOUTH. Apr 2–7. Nashville, TN. Annual music festival sponsored by the Nashville Songwriters Association International (NSAI) celebrates songwriters and their craft. Highlights of the week include the Legendary Songwriter Concert at the historic Ryman Auditorium, related-songwriter events and golf tournament. During the rest of the week, the nation's top performing songwriters in gospel, rock and country will appear at local clubs around town. Est attendance: 5,000. For info: Tin Pan South, c/o NSAI, 1701 West End Ave, 3rd Fl, Nashville, TN 37203. Phone: (615) 256-3354. Fax: (615) 256-0034. E-mail: tinpansouth @nashvillesongwriters.com. Web: www.nashvillesongwriters.com.

US MINT: ANNIVERSARY. Apr 2, 1792. The first US Mint was established at Philadelphia, PA, as authorized by an act of Congress.

WHITE, CHARLES: BIRTH ANNIVERSARY. Apr 2, 1918. Renowned African-American artist, born at Chicago, IL; died Oct 3, 1979. Charles White began his professional career by painting murals for the WPA during the Depression. He was influenced by Mexican muralists Diego Rivera and David Alfaro Siquieros. Among his most notable creations are: *J'Accuse* (1966), a series of charcoal drawings depicting a variety of African-Americans from all ages and walks of life; the *Wanted* posters (c. 1969), a series of paintings based on old runaway slave posters; and *Homage to Langston Hughes* (1971).

ZOLA, EMILE: BIRTH ANNIVERSARY. Apr 2, 1840. Prolific French novelist of the naturalist school, remembered especially for his role in the Dreyfus case (resulting in retrial and vindication of Alfred Dreyfus). Emile Edouard Charles Antoine Zola was born at Paris, France. Defective venting of a stove flue in his bedroom (which some believed to be the work of political enemies) resulted in his death from carbon monoxide poisoning at Paris, Sept 28, 1902.

BIRTHDAYS TODAY

Buddy Ebsen, 93, actor ("The Beverly Hillbillies," "Barnaby Jones"), born Belleville, IL, Apr 2, 1908.

Sir Alec Guinness, 87, British actor (*Star Wars, A Passage to India*), born London, England, Apr 2, 1914.

Emmylou Harris, 54, singer ("Amarillo," "Till I Gain Control Again"), born Birmingham, AL, Apr 2, 1947.

Linda Hunt, 56, actress ("The Flying Nun"; Oscar for *The Year of Living Dangerously*), born Morristown, NJ, Apr 2, 1945.

Christopher Meloni, 40, actor (*Runaway Bride*, "Law & Order: Special Victims Unit"), born Washington, DC, Apr 2, 1961.

Camille Paglia, 54, literature professor and literary and cultural critic, born Endicott, NY, Apr 2, 1947.

Pamela Reed, 48, actress (*The Right Stuff, Bob Roberts*; stage: *Getting Out* [Drama Desk Award]), born Tacoma, WA, Apr 2, 1953.

Leon Russell, 60, musician, born Lawton, OK, Apr 2, 1941.

APRIL 3 — TUESDAY
Day 93 — 272 Remaining

ARMENIAN APPRECIATION DAY. Apr 3. Lighthearted look at the contribution of legendary Armenians such as Palboonian (Paul Bunyan) and Tontonian to American folklore, with special emphasis on studies of the relationship of the Smithsonian Institution Collection to the history of Armenian-American folklore. Annually, Apr 3. For info: Robert L. Birch, Puns Corps, Box 2364, Falls Church, VA 22042-0364. Phone: (703) 533-3668.

BIRMINGHAM RESISTANCE: ANNIVERSARY. Apr 3, 1962. In retaliation against a black boycott of downtown stores, the Birmingham, AL, City Commission voted not to pay the city's $45,000 share of a $100,000 county program which supplied surplus food to the needy. More than 90 percent of the recipients of aid were black. When the NAACP protested the Commission's decision, Birmingham Mayor Arthur J. Hanes dismissed their complaint as a "typical reaction from New York Socialist radicals."

BLACKS RULED ELIGIBLE TO VOTE: ANNIVERSARY. Apr 3, 1944. The US Supreme Court, in an 8–1 ruling, declared that blacks could not be barred from voting in the Texas Democratic primaries. The high court repudiated the contention that political parties are private associations and held that discrimination against blacks violated the 15th Amendment.

BOSTON PUBLIC LIBRARY: ANNIVERSARY. Apr 3, 1848. The Massachusetts legislature passed legislation enabling Boston to levy a tax for a public library. This created the funding model for all public libraries in the US. The Boston Public Library opened its doors in 1854.

BURROUGHS, JOHN: BIRTH ANNIVERSARY. Apr 3, 1837. American naturalist and author, born at Roxbury, NY. "Time does not become sacred to us until we have lived it," he wrote in 1877. Died en route from California to New York, Mar 29, 1921.

CHASE'S DEADLINE APPROACHING. Apr 3. Time to plan ahead. Schedule 2002 celebrations and observances and submit information to *Chase's 2002 Calendar of Events* by May 10, 2001. Sponsors/information suppliers of events in this book should have received confirmation/revision ("reup") forms for the 2002 edition by this time. To submit new entries for consideration, use a copy of the form on the last page of this book. Send to: Chase's Editor, Chase's Calendar of Events, NTC/Contemporary Publishing, 4255 W Touhy Ave, Lincolnwood, IL 60712-1975.

FALL OF RICHMOND: ANNIVERSARY. Apr 3, 1865. After the withdrawal of Robert E. Lee's troops, the Confederate capital of Richmond and nearby Petersburg surrendered to Union forces on this day. Richmond had survived four years of continuous threats from the North. On Apr 4, the city was toured by President Abraham Lincoln.

GRAHAM, CALVIN "BABY VET": BIRTH ANNIVERSARY. Apr 3, 1930. The man who became known as World War II's "baby vet," Calvin Graham was born at Canton, TX, and enlisted in the Navy at the age of 12. As a gunner on the USS *South Dakota*, he was struck by shrapnel during the battle of Guadalcanal in 1942 but still helped pull fellow crew members to safety. The navy gave Graham a dishonorable discharge, revoked his disability benefits and stripped him of his decorations, including a Purple Heart and Bronze Star, after discovering his age. Eventually, through congressional efforts, he was granted an honorable discharge and won back all but the Purple Heart. His benefits were restored in 1988. Graham died Nov 6, 1992, at Fort Worth, TX.

GUINEA: ANNIVERSARY OF THE SECOND REPUBLIC. Apr 3. National holiday. Commemorates the establishment of the Second Republic in 1984.

HOWARD, LESLIE: BIRTH ANNIVERSARY. Apr 3, 1893. During the return trip from a British government-sponsored tour of Spain, a plane transporting 50-year-old actor Leslie Howard was shot down by German raiders. Rumors that he was serving on a spy mission for his government circulated at the time. In her biography about her father (*A Quite Remarkable Father*) his daughter expressed doubt that her father was the sort to get involved in espionage. Howard's most-remembered film role is that of Ashley Wilkes in *Gone with the Wind*. Born at London, England; died at sea June 1, 1943.

INAUGURATION OF PONY EXPRESS: ANNIVERSARY. Apr 3, 1860. The Pony Express began when the first rider left St. Joseph, MO. The following day another rider headed east from Sacramento, CA. For $5 an ounce letters were delivered within 10 days. There were 190 way stations between 10 and 15 miles apart, and each rider had a "run" of between 75 and 100 miles. The Pony Express lasted less than two years, ceasing operation in October 1861, when the overland telegraph was completed.

IRVING, WASHINGTON: BIRTH ANNIVERSARY. Apr 3, 1783. American author, attorney and one-time US Minister to Spain, Irving was born at New York, NY. Creator of *Rip Van Winkle* and *The Legend of Sleepy Hollow*, he was also the author of many historical and biographical works, including *A History of the Life and Voyages of Christopher Columbus* and the *Life of Washington*. Died at Tarrytown, NY, Nov 28, 1859.

ISLE ROYALE NATIONAL PARK ESTABLISHED: ANNIVERSARY. Apr 3, 1940. Isle Royale is the largest of a group of more than 200 islands that make up this national park preserve. To preserve upper Michigan's flora and fauna, Congress authorized a national park in 1931 and it was established in 1940.

LUCE, HENRY: BIRTH ANNIVERSARY. Apr 3, 1898. American editor and publisher, born to missionary parents at Penglai, China. He built his publishing empire with *Time, Fortune, Life* and *Sports Illustrated*. Luce also was involved in broadcasting. Died at Phoenix, AZ, Feb 28, 1967.

MARSHALL PLAN: ANNIVERSARY. Apr 3, 1948. Suggested by Secretary of State George C. Marshall in a speech at Harvard, June 5, 1947, the legislation for the European Recovery Program, popularly known as the Marshall Plan, was signed by President Truman on Apr 3, 1948. After distributing more than $12 billion, the program ended in 1952.

RAINEY, MA (GERTRUDE BRIDGET): BIRTH ANNIVERSARY. Apr 3, 1888. Known as the "Mother of the Blues," Gertrude "Ma" Rainey was born at Columbus, GA. She made her stage debut at the Columbus Opera House in 1900 in a talent show called "The Bunch of Blackberries." After touring together as "Rainey and Rainey, the Assassinators of the Blues," she and her husband eventually separated and she toured on her own under the auspices of the Theater Owners Booking Association. She made her first recording in 1923 and her last on Dec 28, 1928, after being told that the rural southern blues she sang had gone out of style. She died Dec 22, 1939, at Columbus, GA.

RAND, SALLY: BIRTH ANNIVERSARY. Apr 3, 1904. American actress, ecdysiast and inventor of the fan dance, which gained fame at the 1933 Chicago World's Fair. Born Helen Gould Beck at Hickory County, MO. Died at Glendora, CA, Aug 31, 1979.

TWEED DAY: ANNIVERSARY. Apr 3, 1823. Day to consider the cost of political corruption. Birthday of William March Tweed, New York City political boss, whose "Tweed Ring" is said to have stolen $30 million to $200 million from the city. Born at New York, NY, Apr 3, 1823, he died in his cell at New York's Ludlow Street Jail, Apr 12, 1878. Cartoonist Thomas Nast deserves much credit for Tweed's arrests and convictions.

2001: A SPACE ODYSSEY PREMIERE: ANNIVERSARY. Apr 3, 1968. Directed by Stanley Kubrick, this influential film has elicited many different interpretations. Sci-fi novelist Arthur C. Clarke based the screenplay on his 1966 book which was prescient in several ways. Written before men had landed on the moon, Clarke describes an expedition launched to Jupiter to track a mysterious signal emanating from the moon. Clarke gave the world's population as six billion (achieved in 1999) and described a space station (the US is currently building one with Russia). During a flight, a character reads the news on his electronic newspad. The film starred Keir Dullea, William Sylvester, Gary Lockwood, Daniel Richter and HAL 9000, the creepy computer that had human emotions. The theme music was Richard Strauss's *Also Sprach Zarathrustra*. Warner Brothers re-released the film on New Year's Eve 2000.

WOMAN PRESIDES OVER US SUPREME COURT: ANNIVERSARY. Apr 3, 1995. Supreme Court Justice Sandra Day O'Connor became the first woman to preside over the US high court when she sat in for Chief Justice William H. Rehnquist and second in seniority Justice John Paul Stevens when both were out of town.

BIRTHDAYS TODAY

Alec Baldwin, 43, actor ("Knots Landing," *The Getaway, Miami Blues*), born Massapequa, NY, Apr 3, 1958.

Marlon Brando, 77, actor (Oscars for *On the Waterfront, The Godfather*; Emmy for *Roots: The Next Generations*), born Omaha, NE, Apr 3, 1924.

Doris Day (Doris Von Kappelhoff), 77, actress, singer ("Young at Heart," *The Man Who Knew Too Much, Pillow Talk*, "The Doris Day Show"), born Cincinnati, OH, Apr 3, 1924.

Max Frankel, 71, journalist, born Gera, Germany, Apr 3, 1930.

Jennie Garth, 29, actress ("Beverly Hills 90210"), born Champaign, IL, Apr 3, 1972.

Jane Goodall (Baroness Van Lawick-Goodall), 67, anthropologist known for study of chimpanzees, born London, England, Apr 3, 1934.

Jonathan Lynn, 58, writer, actor, director (*Into the Night, Nuns on the Run, My Cousin Vinny*), born Bath, England, Apr 3, 1943.

Marsha Mason, 59, actress (*The Goodbye Girl, Cinderella Liberty*), born St. Louis, MO, Apr 3, 1942.

Eddie Murphy, 40, comedian ("Saturday Night Live"), actor (*Trading Places, 48HRS, Beverly Hills Cop*), born Brooklyn, NY, Apr 3, 1961.

Wayne Newton, 59, singer ("Danke Schoen," "Daddy Don't You Walk So Fast"), born Norfolk, VA, Apr 3, 1942.

Michael Olowokandi, 26, basketball player, born Lagos, Nigeria, Apr 3, 1975.

Tony Orlando (Michael Orlando Cassivitis), 57, singer (Tony Orlando and Dawn, "Tie a Yellow Ribbon Round the Old Oak Tree"), born New York, NY, Apr 3, 1944.

David Hyde Pierce, 42, actor ("Frasier"), born Albany, NY, Apr 3, 1959.

Picabo Street, 30, Olympic skier, born Triumph, ID, Apr 3, 1971.

April *2001*	S	M	T	W	T	F	S
	1	2	3	4	5	6	7
	8	9	10	11	12	13	14
	15	16	17	18	19	20	21
	22	23	24	25	26	27	28
	29	30					

APRIL 4 — WEDNESDAY
Day 94 — 271 Remaining

ASHURA: TENTH DAY. Apr 4. Islamic calendar date: Muharram 10, 1422. Commemorates death of Muhammad's grandson and the Battle of Karbala. A time of fasting, reflection and meditation. Jews of Medina fasted on the tenth day in remembrance of their salvation from Pharoah. The Prophet Muhammad desired to fast two days instead of one in remembrance, but he died the next year. Different methods for "anticipating" the visibility of the new moon crescent at Mecca are used by different groups. US date may vary.

BONZA BOTTLER DAY™. Apr 4. To celebrate when the number of the day is the same as the number of the month. Bonza Bottler Day™ is an excuse to have a party at least once a month. For more information, see Jan 1. For info: Gail M. Berger, 109 Matthew Ave, Poca, WV 25159. Phone: (304) 776-7746. E-mail: gberger5@aol.com.

BRANSON FEST. Apr 4–8. Branson, MO. The Branson area's kick-off to a new season of great entertainment! The celebration of Ozarks food, arts and culture features some of Branson's best known performers and a taste of all the Branson area has to offer. For info: Branson/Lakes Area Chamber of Commerce, PO Box 1897, Branson, MO 65615. Phone: (800) 214-3661. Web: www.bransonchamber.com.

DIX, DOROTHEA LYNDE: BIRTH ANNIVERSARY. Apr 4, 1802. American social reformer and author, born at Hampden, ME. Left home at age 10, was teaching at age 14 and founded a home for girls at Boston while still in her teens. In spite of frail health, she was a vigorous crusader for humane conditions in insane asylums, jails and almshouses and for the establishment of state-supported institutions to serve those needs. Named superintendent of women nurses during the Civil War. Died at Trenton, NJ, July 17, 1887.

FLAG ACT OF 1818: ANNIVERSARY. Apr 4, 1818. Congress approved the first flag of the US.

GIAMATTI, ANGELO BARTLETT: BIRTH ANNIVERSARY. Apr 4, 1938. Baseball Commissioner and former president of Yale University. Born at Boston, MA, Giamatti was the youngest person to be named president of Yale, at the age of 39, in 1978. He became the president of Major League Baseball's National League in 1986 and served in that capacity until he was appointed Commissioner of Baseball Apr 1, 1989. An accomplished author, he moved freely between the worlds of literature and baseball, often linking the two in the many articles he wrote. One week prior to his death, he suspended Pete Rose for life for betting on baseball games. Giamatti died at Martha's Vineyard, MA, Sept 1, 1989.

HATE WEEK. Apr 4–10. Recognizes the day on which the fictional character Winston Smith started his secret diary and wrote the words "DOWN WITH BIG BROTHER," Wednesday, Apr 4, 1984. From George Orwell's anti-Utopian novel, *1984*, portraying the end of human privacy and the destruction of the individual in a totalitarian state (first published in 1949). "Hates" varied from the daily two-minute concentrated hate to the grand culmination observed during Hate Week.

KING, MARTIN LUTHER, JR: ASSASSINATION ANNIVERSARY. Apr 4, 1968. The Reverend Dr. Martin Luther King, Jr, was shot at Memphis, TN. James Earl Ray was serving a 99-year sentence for the crime at the time of his death in 1998. See also: "King, Martin Luther, Jr: Birth Anniversary" (Jan 15).

KING OPPOSES VIETNAM WAR: ANNIVERSARY. Apr 4, 1967. Speaking before the Overseas Press Club at New York City, Reverend Dr. Martin Luther King, Jr, announced his opposition to the Vietnam War. That same day, at the Riverside Church at Harlem, King suggested that those who saw the war as dishonorable and unjust should avoid military service. He proposed that the US take new initiatives to conclude the war.

LADY BE GOOD LOST: ANNIVERSARY. Apr 4, 1943. The nine-man crew of the World War II American Liberator bomber *Lady Be Good* bailed out 200 miles off course over the Sahara Desert and disappeared. They were returning to their base in Libya after a raid over southern Italy. On Nov 9, 1958, 15 years after the plane went down and more than 13 years after the war had ended, a pilot flying across the Sahara south of Tobruck sighted wreckage of an aircraft in the sand. Five skeletons and a diary describing the final days of the crew were recovered. The radio, guns and ammunition in the plane were in working order.

NORTH ATLANTIC TREATY RATIFIED: ANNIVERSARY. Apr 4, 1949. The North Atlantic Treaty Organization was created by this treaty, which was signed by 12 nations, including the US. (Other countries joined later.) The NATO member nations are united for common defense. The treaty went into effect Apr 24, 1949, and the first session of the North Atlantic Council was held Sept 17, 1949.

PERKINS, ANTHONY: BIRTH ANNIVERSARY. Apr 4, 1932. American actor Anthony Perkins was born at New York, NY. Best known for his movie role as homicidal innkeeper Norman Bates in the film *Psycho* (1960), Perkins appeared in many Broadway plays in addition to his numerous film roles. He received an Oscar nomination for his supporting role in *Friendly Persuasion* (1956). Perkins died Sept 12, 1992, at Hollywood, CA.

"POLICE STORY" TV PREMIERE: ANNIVERSARY. Apr 4, 1952. Produced by Jerome Robinson, directed by David Rich and narrated by Norman Rose, "Police Story" was an early anthology series on CBS depicting incidents from real-life police files.

SALTER ELECTED FIRST WOMAN MAYOR IN US: ANNIVERSARY. Apr 4, 1887. The first woman elected mayor in the US was Susanna Medora Salter, who was elected mayor of Argonia, KS. Her name had been submitted for election without her knowledge by the Women's Christian Temperance Union, and she did not know she was a candidate until she went to the polls to vote. She received a two-thirds majority vote and served one year for the salary of $1.

SENEGAL: INDEPENDENCE DAY: ANNIVERSARY. Apr 4. National holiday. Commemorates independence from France in 1960.

SMOTHERS BROTHERS FIRED: ANNIVERSARY. Apr 4, 1969. CBS canceled this popular comedy series on this date. The hour-long show strongly influenced television humor during the two years it aired. Tom and Dick, however, frequently found themselves at odds with the censors over material that would be considered tame today. Guests and cast members frequently knocked the Vietnam War and the Nixon Administration. Acts featuring antiwar protestors such as Harry Belafonte were often cut.

SPACE MILESTONE: *CHALLENGER* STS-6 (US). Apr 4, 1983. Shuttle *Challenger* launched from Kennedy Space Center, FL, with four astronauts (Paul Weitz, Karol Bobko, Storey Musgrave and Donald Peterson). Four-hour spacewalk by Musgrave and Peterson. Landed Edwards Air Force Base, CA, Apr 9.

THANK YOU, SCHOOL LIBRARIAN DAY. Apr 4. Recognizes the unique contribution made by school librarians who are resource people extraordinaire, supporting the myriad educational needs of faculty, staff, students and parents *all year long!* Three cheers to all the public, private and parochial school infomaniacs whose true love of reading and lifelong learning make them great role models for kids of all ages. To help celebrate, take your school librarian to lunch, donate a book in his/her honor to the library, tell your librarian what a difference he/she has made in your life. Sponsor: "Carpe Libris" (Seize the Book), a loosely knit group of underappreciated librarians. For info: Judyth Lessee, Organizer, Carpe Libris, PO Box 40503, Tucson, AZ 85717-0503. Phone: (520) 318-2954. E-mail: rinophyl@rtd.com.

VICTIMS OF VIOLENCE HOLY DAY. Apr 4. One of the three Emancipation Days of Respect that highlights the three key principles of the American Civil Rights Renaissance of the 1960s. Wearing black shows visible respect for slavery victims, present innocent victims, survivors of rape and missing children who are potential victims of violence. The Emancipation D.o.R. promote practice of unity, respect and remembrance and focuses awareness on the global economical impact of slavery and unjust laws of segregation. See also: "Humanitarian Day" (Jan 15) and "Emancipation Dream Day" (Aug 28). For info: Dee D. Smith Simmons, Global Committee Commemorating Emancipation Days of Respect, PO Box 21050, Chicago, IL 60621. Phone: (773) RESPECT (737-7328).

VITAMIN C ISOLATED: ANNIVERSARY. Apr 4, 1932. Vitamin C was first isolated by C.C. King at the University of Pittsburgh.

WATERS, MUDDY: BIRTH ANNIVERSARY. Apr 4, 1915. Born McKinley Morganfield at Rolling Fork, MS, American blues guitarist and singer Muddy Waters played a significant part in developing modern rhythm and blues that came to be known as Chicago or urban blues. It was predominately from this music that later forms such as rock and roll and soul sprang. Muddy Waters died at Westmont, IL, Apr 30, 1983.

YALE, LINUS: BIRTH ANNIVERSARY. Apr 4, 1821. American portrait painter and inventor of the lock that is named for him was born at Salisbury, NY. He was creator of the Yale Infallible Bank Lock and developer of the cylinder lock. Yale died at New York, NY, Dec 25, 1868.

YAMAMOTO, ISOROKU: BIRTH ANNIVERSARY. Apr 4, 1884. Considered Japan's greatest naval strategist, Admiral Isoroku Yamamoto, who planned the attack on Pearl Harbor, was born at Nagaoko, Honshu. Yamamoto also devised the complex attack on Midway Island which ended in defeat for the Japanese because the Allies had the key to the Imperial fleet code and were prepared for the June 4, 1942, attack. The US intercepted reports of Yamamoto's proposed 1943 tour of the Western Solomons and shot down his plane Apr 18, while he was touring Japanese installations in the area.

	S	M	T	W	T	F	S
April	1	2	3	4	5	6	7
2001	8	9	10	11	12	13	14
	15	16	17	18	19	20	21
	22	23	24	25	26	27	28
	29	30					

Maya Angelou, 73, poet, author (*I Know Why the Caged Bird Sings*), born St. Louis, MO, Apr 4, 1928.
Elmer Bernstein, 79, composer of dozens of movie soundtracks, born New York, NY, Apr 4, 1922.
Robert Downey, Jr, 36, actor (*Chaplin, Short Cuts, Natural Born Killers*), born New York, NY, Apr 4, 1965.
Kitty Kelley, 59, author (*Jackie Oh!, Nancy Reagan*), born Hartford, CT, Apr 4, 1942.
Christine Lahti, 51, actress ("The Harvey Korman Show," "Chicago Hope," *Swing Shift*), born Birmingham, MI, Apr 4, 1950.
Richard G. Lugar, 69, US Senator (R, Indiana), born Indianapolis, IN, Apr 4, 1932.
William Manchester, 79, author (*The Last Lion, A World Lit Only by Fire*), born Attleboro, MA, Apr 4, 1922.
Nancy McKeon, 35, actress ("The Facts of Life"), born Westbury, NY, Apr 4, 1966.
Craig T. Nelson, 55, actor ("Coach," *Private Benjamin, Poltergeist, The Killing Fields*), born Spokane, WA, Apr 4, 1946.
Michael Parks, 63, actor ("Then Came Bronson," "Twin Peaks," *The Happening*), born Corona, CA, Apr 4, 1938.
Barry Pepper, 31, actor (*Saving Private Ryan, Enemy of the State*), born Campbell River, British Columbia, Canada, Apr 4, 1970.
Scott Rolen, 26, baseball player, born Evansville, IN, Apr 4, 1975.
Elizabeth Wilson, 76, actress (*The Prisoner of Second Avenue, The Addams Family*; stage: *Taken in Marriage*), born Grand Rapids, MI, Apr 4, 1925.

APRIL 5 — THURSDAY
Day 95 — 270 Remaining

DAVIS, BETTE: BIRTH ANNIVERSARY. Apr 5, 1908. American actress Bette Davis was born Ruth Elizabeth Davis at Lowell, MA. In addition to acting in more than 80 films, earning 10 Academy Award nominations and winning the best actress Academy Award twice, for *Dangerous* (1935) and *Jezebel* (1938), Davis also claimed to have nicknamed the Academy Award "Oscar" after her first husband, Harmon Oscar Nelson, Jr. She died Oct 6, 1989, at Neuilly-sur-Seine, France.

DISCOTHEQUE BOMBING: 15th ANNIVERSARY. Apr 5, 1986. A bomb exploded at a popular discotheque in West Berlin, Germany, killing two American soldiers and a Turkish woman. Although three groups claimed responsibility for the bombing, American intelligence organizations attributed it to orders from Libyan head-of-state Muammar el-Qaddafi, and President Reagan ordered a retaliatory air strike on Libya. At 7 PM, EST, on Apr 14, 1986 (1 AM, Apr 15, Libyan time), American forces launched a bombing attack on the Libyan cities of Tripoli and Benghazi, reportedly killing 37 (including a daughter of Qaddafi) and wounding another 93. Nearly two years later, on Jan 11, 1988, West German authorities arrested 27-year-old Christine Gabriele Endrigkeit, charging her with the bombing, citing "clues" that it might have been ordered by Syrian agents.

ENGLAND: MARTELL GRAND NATIONAL FESTIVAL. Apr 5–7. Aintree Racecourse, Aintree, Liverpool. Britain's premier horse race and most famous steeplechase is run over 4.5 miles on this beautiful and legendary course. Est attendance: 100,000. For info: Racecourse Mgr, Aintree Racecourse, Liverpool, Merseyside, England L9 5AS. Phone: (44) (151) 523-2600. Fax: (44) (151) 530-1512. E-mail: aintree@rht.net. Web: www.aintree.co.uk.

"FIRESIDE THEATRE" TV PREMIERE: ANNIVERSARY. Apr 5, 1949. Gene Raymond and later Jane Wyman hosted this NBC anthology program consisting of 15- and 30-minute dramas. One of its most acclaimed presentations was "The Reign of Amelika Jo" on Oct 12, 1954. It was set in the South Pacific during World War II and had a mostly black and Asian cast.

FIRST US CHAMBER OF COMMERCE FOUNDED: ANNIVERSARY. Apr 5, 1768. The first Chamber of Commerce in the US was founded at New York City.

KINGSVILLE INTERNATIONAL YOUNG PERFORMERS' COMPETITIONS WITH THE ISABEL SCIONTI PIANO SOLO COMPETITIONS. Apr 5–7. Texas A&M University–Kingsville, TX. 20th annual international music competition for performers of classical music. Prodigies and aspiring concert artists under age 26 compete in separate contests for piano solo and orchestral instruments. Cash prizes total about $25,000. Performance awards with orchestra and in recital offered. All contest events—including string, woodwind and brass master classes given by concert artist–contest judges—are free and open to the public. Annual. Contestant's entry fee $30; deadline Jan 22, 2001. Sponsor: Music Club of Kingsville, Inc (affiliate of National Federation and Texas Federation of Music Clubs). Est attendance: 1,500. For info: Mary Tryer, 1222 W Lee, Kingsville, TX 78363. Phone: (361) 592-2374. Fax: (361) 592-9551. E-mail: youngperf@hotmail.com.

LISTER, JOSEPH: BIRTH ANNIVERSARY. Apr 5, 1827. English physician who was the founder of aseptic surgery, born at Upton, Essex, England. Died at Walmer, England, Feb 10, 1912.

"MARRIED . . . WITH CHILDREN" TV PREMIERE: ANNIVERSARY. Apr 5, 1987. This raunchy Fox TV show premiered as the antidote to Cosby-style family shows. Ed O'Neill starred as boorish, luckless shoe salesman Al Bundy, Katey Sagal portrayed Al's big-haired, spandex-clad, sex-starved wife Peggy, Christina Applegate played airheaded bombshell daughter Kelly and David Faustino played hormone-driven son Bud. The Bundys' neighbors were portrayed by Amanda Bearse as Marcy Rhoades, David Garrison as husband #1, Steve Rhoades and Ted McGinley as husband #2, Jefferson D'Arcy. The last episode aired Apr 20, 1997.

MULE DAY. Apr 5–8. Columbia, TN. Started in 1934 as Breeders Day when mules were brought into town to be sold and traded. Today this homecoming is celebrated with arts and crafts, flea market, knife show and a huge parade. Est attendance: 250,000. For info: Mule Day, PO Box 66, Columbia, TN 38402. Phone: (931) 381-9557.

NATIONAL ALCOHOL SCREENING DAY. Apr 5. To increase awareness of alcohol problems and connect people in need with treatment. Free, anonymous, nationwide. For info: Screening for Mental Health, One Washington St, Ste 304, Wellesley Hills, MA 02481-1706. Phone: (781) 239-0071. Fax: (781) 431-7447. Web: www.mentalhealthscreening.org.

NATIONAL ASSOCIATION OF COLLEGE STORES MEETING & CAMPUS MARKET EXPO. Apr 5–10. New Orleans, LA. The only national conference and trade exhibit designed exclusively for collegiate retailers. The NACS Annual Meeting/CAMEX brings college store managers and buyers together with publishing companies and other suppliers in this yearly exposition of the products to be seen on college campuses next fall. Est attendance: 8,000. For info: Laura Nakoneczny, Dir PR, Natl Assn of College Stores, 500 E Lorain St, Oberlin, OH 44074. Phone: (440) 775-7777. E-mail: lnakoneczny@nacs.org. Web: www.nacs.org.

★**NATIONAL EQUAL PAY DAY.** Apr 5. In 1998 this fell on the day on which the typical woman's 1998 earnings, when added to her 1997 wages, finally equaled what the typical man earned in 1997 alone.

NATIONAL FUN AT WORK DAY. Apr 5. Today and every day the workplace should be spiced with fun, laughter and a playful attitude. Morale will increase, productivity will soar and the bottom line will improve. For info: Matt Weinstein, Playfair, 2207 Oregon St, Berkeley, CA 94705. Phone: (510) 540-8768. Fax: (510) 540-7638. E-mail: playfair1@aol.com. Web: www.playfair .com.

NCAA DIVISION I MEN'S ICE HOCKEY CHAMPIONSHIP FINALS. Apr 5–7. Pepsi Arena, Albany, NY. Est attendance: 48,000. For info: NCAA, 700 W Washington Ave, PO Box 6222, Indianapolis, IN 46206-6222. Phone: (317) 917-6222. Fax: (317) 917-6888. Web: www.ncaa.org.

RESNIK, JUDITH A.: BIRTH ANNIVERSARY. Apr 5, 1949. Dr. Judith A. Resnik, the second American woman in space (1984), was born at Akron, OH. The 36-year-old electrical engineer was mission specialist on Space Shuttle *Challenger*. She perished with all others aboard when *Challenger* exploded Jan 28, 1986. See also: "*Challenger* Space Shuttle Explosion: Anniversary" (Jan 28).

ROBERT PRAGER MEMORIAL DAY: A GERMAN-AMERICAN DAY OF REMEMBRANCE. Apr 5. A day to commemorate the anti-German hysteria of the two World Wars, to pay tribute to German-American heritage and recognize its contribution to the American community and to remember all people who have suffered from prejudice and hate. Annually, Apr 5. For info: Dr. Don Heinrich Tolzmann, Dir, German-American Studies Program, Univ of Cincinnati, PO Box 20113, Cincinnati, OH 45221-0113. Phone: (513) 556-1955. Fax: (513) 556-1955.

"SECRET AGENT" TV PREMIERE: 40th ANNIVERSARY. Apr 5, 1961. Before Patrick McGoohan became "The Prisoner," he played the role of intelligence agent John Drake on this CBS adventure series. Produced in England by ATV, it also aired there as "Danger Man."

SWITZERLAND: NAFELS PILGRIMAGE. Apr 5. Canton Glarus. Commemoration of the Battle of Nafels, fought on Apr 9, 1388. Observed annually on first Thursday in April, with processions, prayers, sermon and a reading out of the names of those killed in the battle.

TAIWAN: NATIONAL TOMB-SWEEPING DAY. Apr 5. National holiday since 1972. According to Chinese custom, the tombs of ancestors are swept "clear and bright" and rites honoring ancestors are held. Tomb-Sweeping Day is observed Apr 5, except in leap years, when it falls Apr 4.

"THE TRACEY ULLMAN SHOW" TV PREMIERE: ANNIVERSARY. Apr 5, 1987. This Emmy award-winning comedy-variety show was one of the Fox network's early critical hits. Tracey Ullman starred with Julie Kavner, Dan Castellaneta, Joe Malone and Sam McMurray. The show, produced by James L. Brooks, contained sketches, songs and satire. Animated snippets in between segments introduced us to the Simpsons, executed by Matt Groening, creator of the "Life in Hell" comic strip. "The Simpsons" spun off from the show in 1990 with Castellaneta and Kavner speaking the voices of Homer and Marge Simpson.

WASHINGTON, BOOKER TALIAFERRO: BIRTH ANNIVERSARY. Apr 5, 1856. Black educator and leader born at Franklin County, VA. "No race can prosper," he wrote in *Up from Slavery*, "till it learns that there is as much dignity in tilling a field as in writing a poem." Died at Tuskegee, AL, Nov 14, 1915.

WAYNE STATE UNIVERSITY: FUNERAL FOR WINTER. Apr 5. Detroit, MI. Events include a New Orleans-style procession with jazz band playing Dixieland music. "Miss Spring" and a local TV personality conduct an irreverent burial ceremony. Est attendance: 1,000. For info: Pat Borninski, Public Relations Officer, Wayne State Univ, 3222 FAB, Detroit, MI 48202. Phone: (313) 577-2150. Fax: (313) 577-8154. E-mail: p.borninski@wayne.edu. Web: www.media.wayne.edu/

BIRTHDAYS TODAY

Jane Asher, 55, actress (*DreamChild, Brideshead Revisited*), born London, England, Apr 5, 1946.

Eric Burdon, 60, singer (*Eric Burdon Declares War, Black Man's Burdon*), songwriter, born Walker-on-Tyne, England, Apr 5, 1941.

Roger Corman, 75, filmmaker (king of B horror movies), born Detroit, MI, Apr 5, 1926.

Max Gail, 58, actor ("Barney Miller," *Pearl*), born Grosse Point, MI, Apr 5, 1943.

Arthur Hailey, 81, author (*Airport, The Final Diagnosis*), born Luton, England, Apr 5, 1920.

Nigel Hawthorne, 72, actor (*Young Winston, Gandhi*), born Coventry, England, Apr 5, 1929.

Michael Moriarty, 59, actor (*The Last Detail, Bang the Drum Slowly*, "Law & Order"), born Detroit, MI, Apr 5, 1942.

Gregory Peck, 85, actor (Oscar for *To Kill a Mockingbird; Roman Holiday, Gentleman's Agreement*), born La Jolla, CA, Apr 5, 1916.

Mitch Pileggi, 49, actor ("The X-Files"), born Portland, OR, Apr 5, 1952.

Colin Luther Powell, 64, general, former Chairman US Joint Chiefs of Staff, born New York, NY, Apr 5, 1937.

Gale Storm, 79, actress ("My Little Margie," "NBC Comedy Hour," "The Gale Storm Show"), born Bloomington, TX, Apr 5, 1922.

APRIL 6 — FRIDAY

Day 96 — 269 Remaining

ABRAHAM BALDWIN AGRICULTURAL COLLEGE HOMECOMING CELEBRATION. Apr 6–7. ABAC Campus, Tifton, GA. Class reunions, alumni awards banquet, dance. Est attendance: 500. For info: Nancy Coleman, Exec VP, ABAC Alumni Assn, ABAC 13, 2802 Moore Hwy, Tifton, GA 31794-2693. Phone: (912) 386-3321. Fax: (912) 386-7144. E-mail: alumni@abac.peachnet.edu.

AFRMA FANCY RAT & MOUSE DISPLAY AMERICA'S FAMILY PET EXPO. Apr 6–8. Pomona, CA. As urban sprawl continues to limit the space needed to keep dogs and cats as pets, rats and mice are gradually emerging as an ideal substitute. They provide all the pleasure and satisfaction of a warm, cuddly, intelligent and friendly pet companion. The American Fancy Rat and Mouse Association (AFRMA) was founded in 1983 to promote and encourage the breeding and exhibition of fancy rats and mice, to educate the public on their positive qualities as companion animals and to provide information on their proper care. For info: AFRMA (CAE), PO Box 2589, Winnetka, CA 91396-2589. Phone: (909) 685-2350. Fax: (818) 592-6590. E-mail: craigr@afrma.org. Web: www.afrma.org.

April	S	M	T	W	T	F	S
2001	1	2	3	4	5	6	7
	8	9	10	11	12	13	14
	15	16	17	18	19	20	21
	22	23	24	25	26	27	28
	29	30					

ALCOHOL-FREE WEEKEND. Apr 6–8. Observance to increase public awareness of the problems associated with drinking alcoholic beverages by asking Americans to refrain from drinking them for this weekend. For info: Public Info Office, Natl Council on Alcoholism and Drug Dependence, Inc, 12 W 21st St, New York, NY 10010. Phone: (212) 206-6770. Fax: (212) 645-1690. E-mail: national@ncadd.crg. Web: www.ncadd.org.

"BARNEY & FRIENDS" TV PREMIERE: ANNIVERSARY. Apr 6, 1992. Although most adults find it hopelessly saccharine, this PBS program is hugely popular with preschoolers. Purple dinosaur Barney, his pals, dinosaurs Baby Bop and B.J. and a multi-ethnic group of children sing, play games and learn simple lessons about getting along with one another.

BIG MUDDY FOLK MUSIC FESTIVAL. Apr 6–7. Thespian Hall, Boonville, MO. Performing folk festival with instructional workshop by artists appearing. Est attendance: 3,000. For info: Judy Shields, Admin, Friends of Historic Boonville, PO Box 1776, Boonville, MO 65233. Phone: (660) 882-7977. Fax: (660) 882-9194. E-mail: friendsart@mid-mo.net.

BRIGHAM YOUNG'S LAST MARRIAGE: ANNIVERSARY. Apr 6, 1868. Brigham Young, Mormon Church leader, married his 27th, and last, wife on this day.

CHURCH OF JESUS CHRIST OF LATTER-DAY SAINTS: ANNIVERSARY. Apr 6, 1830. Under the leadership of Joseph Smith, Jr, The Church of Jesus Christ of Latter-day Saints was founded with six members in a log cabin at Fayette, NY. For info: Church of Jesus Christ of Latter-day Saints, Public Affairs Dept, 15 E South Temple St, Salt Lake City, UT 84150. Phone: (801) 240-4395. Fax: (801) 240-1167.

DOGWOOD ARTS FESTIVAL. Apr 6–22. Knoxville, TN. A springtime celebration with more than 60 miles of dogwood trails and more than 100 events featuring arts, crafts, parades and musical performances. It's the "Best 17 Days of Spring in America." Est attendance: 350,000. For info: Dogwood Arts Festival, 111 N Central Ave, Knoxville, TN 37902. Phone: (865) 637-4561. Web: www.dogwoodarts.usit.com.

DOW-JONES TOPS 9,000: ANNIVERSARY. Apr 6, 1998. The Dow-Jones Index of 30 major industrial stocks topped the 9,000 mark for the first time.

FIRST MODERN OLYMPICS: ANNIVERSARY. Apr 6, 1896. The first modern Olympics formally opened at Athens, Greece, after a 1,500-year hiatus.

FIRST TONY AWARDS PRESENTED: ANNIVERSARY. Apr 6, 1947. The American Theatre Wing bestowed the first annual Tony awards for distinguished service to the theater.

FIRST US CREDIT UNION LAW: ANNIVERSARY. Apr 6, 1909. The St. Canadian credit union of Manchester, NH, was chartered with the help of Alphonse Desjardins, Canadian credit union pioneer.

JOYCE PAPERS RELEASED: ANNIVERSARY. Apr 6, 1992. After 51 years, many of the personal papers of James Joyce were put on display at the National Library of Ireland in Dublin. The papers were gathered by Joyce's secretary Paul Léon during the early days of World War II in Paris. Léon, who was eventually killed at Auschwitz, gave the papers to the Irish envoy in Paris to send to the National Library, with instructions not to allow their viewing until 50 years after Joyce's death. Some of the documents cannot be viewed until the year 2050.

MEDIEVAL FAIR. Apr 6–8. University of Oklahoma Brandt Park Duck Pond, Norman, OK. Arts and crafts and living history fair. The Middle Ages come alive with dancers, music, theater, jousting, knights in combat and a human chess match. Feasts and follies include games and food "fit for a king." Meet such characters as King Arthur, Sir Lancelot and Merlin. Admission is free. Annually, the second weekend in April (unless Easter weekend). Est attendance: 100,000. For info: Linda Linn, 1700 Asp, Norman, OK 73072. Phone: (405) 288-2536. Fax: (405) 325-7698. E-mail: llinn@cce.occe.ou.edu. Web: www.occe.ou.edu/medievalfair.

MENNONITE RELIEF SALE. Apr 6–7. Kansas State Fair Grounds, Hutchinson, KS. More than 70 Mennonite, Brethren in Christ and Amish congregations in Kansas sponsor this annual festival and benefit auction for the worldwide hunger relief and community aid programs of the Mennonite Central Committee. Auctions of quilts, grandfather clocks, furniture, tools and crafts. Great food and lots more. No vendors. Est attendance: 30,000. For info: Richard Ediger, Pres, Box 488, Buhler, KS 67522. Phone: (316) 543-2787. Web: www2.southwind.net/~davidg /relief-sale/

MULLIGAN, GERRY: BIRTH ANNIVERSARY. Apr 6, 1927. American jazz saxophonist Gerry Mulligan was born at New York, NY. He performed with many great jazz musicians including Miles Davis, Dave Brubeck, Chet Baker and Duke Ellington, and is credited with helping create the cool-jazz movement with Miles Davis. Mulligan died Jan 20, 1996, at Darien, CT.

NATIONAL GEOGRAPHY BEE, STATE LEVEL. Apr 6. Site is different in each state—many are in state capital. Winners of school-level competitions who scored in the top 100 in their state on a written test compete in the State Geography Bees. The winner of each state bee will go to Washington, DC, for the national level in May. Est attendance: 450. For info: Natl Geography Bee, Natl Geographic Soc, 1145 17th St NW, Washington, DC 20036. Phone: (202) 857-7001.

NORTH POLE DISCOVERED: ANNIVERSARY. Apr 6, 1909. Robert E. Peary reached the North Pole after several failed attempts. The team consisted of Peary, leader of the expedition; Matthew A. Henson, a black man who had served with Peary since 1886 as ship's cook, carpenter and blacksmith, and then as Peary's co-explorer and valuable assistant and four Eskimo guides—Coquesh, Ootah, Eginwah and Seegloo. They sailed July 17, 1908, on the ship *Roosevelt*, wintering on Ellesmere Island. After a grueling trek with dwindling food supplies, Henson and two of the Eskimos were first to reach the Pole. An exhausted Peary arrived 45 minutes later and confirmed their location.

OPERATION FLOATING CHRYSANTHEMUM: ANNIVERSARY. Apr 6, 1945. Two US destroyers, two ammunition ships and a tank-landing ship were sunk off the coast of Okinawa when the Japanese Air Force launched 355 Kamikaze (suicide) pilots against the Allied fleet in Operation Floating Chrysanthemum.

OZARK UFO CONFERENCE. Apr 6–8. Inn of the Ozarks Conference Center, Eureka Springs, AR. 13th annual meeting of researchers from various states and foreign countries to inform the public of the latest news concerning UFOs. Speakers include authors of books on the subject and people who have investigated UFO cases; program includes audiovisual presentations of UFO evidence. Est attendance: 500. For info: Lucius Farish, Ozark UFO Conference, #2 Caney Valley Drive, Plumerville, AR 72127-8725. Phone: (501) 354-2558. E-mail: ozarkufo@webtv .net.

POLKA FEST. Apr 6–8 (also Nov 2–4). Wisconsin Dells, WI. Popular Midwest polka bands playing song and dance favorites at Antigua Bay. Food specialties. Est attendance: 1,500. For info: Antiqua Bay, PO Box 236, Wisconsin Dells, WI 53965. Phone: (800) 54-DELLS. E-mail: reservations@antiquabay.com.

PORTLAND, OREGON: 150th BIRTHDAY. Apr 6, 1851. "The City of Roses" adds a year today.

POTEET STRAWBERRY FESTIVAL. Apr 6–8. Poteet, TX. One of the oldest and largest festivals in Texas established to promote Poteet's crop—strawberries. Great food and family entertainment. Est attendance: 115,000. For info: Nita Harvey, Festival Coord, Poteet Strawberry Festival Assn, PO Box 227, Poteet, TX 78065. Phone: (830) 742-8144. Fax: (830) 742-3608. E-mail: nharvey@texas.net. Web: www.strawberryfestival.com.

"PRIVATE BENJAMIN" TV PREMIERE: 20th ANNIVERSARY. Apr 6, 1981. The CBS sitcom was based on the Goldie Hawn movie about a pampered young woman enlisting in the army and going through the trials of basic training. Eileen Brennan and Hal Williams reprised their movie roles as Captain Doreen Lewis and drill instructor Sergeant Ted Ross. Lorna Patterson played Private Judy Benjamin.

RAPHAEL: BIRTH ANNIVERSARY. Apr 6, 1483. Raffaello Santi (Sanzio), Italian painter and architect. Probably born Apr 6, 1483, at Urbino, Italy. Died on his birthday, at Rome, Italy, Apr 6, 1520.

SCHNEIDERMAN, ROSE: BIRTH ANNIVERSARY. Apr 6, 1882. A pioneer in the battle to increase wages and improve working conditions for women, Rose Schneiderman was born at Saven, Poland, and her family immigrated to the US six years later. At age 16 she began factory work in New York City's garment district and quickly became a union organizer. Opposed to the open-shop policy, which permitted nonunion members to work in a unionized shop, Schneiderman organized a 1913 strike of 25,000 women shirtwaist makers. She worked as an organizer for the International Ladies Garment Workers Union (ILGWU) and for the Women's Trade Union League (WTUL), serving as president for more than 20 years. During the Great Depression President Roosevelt appointed her to his Labor Advisory Board—the only woman member. Died Aug 11, 1972, at New York, NY.

SCOTTSBORO TRIAL: 70th ANNIVERSARY. Apr 6, 1931. In what became a *cause célèbre*, nine black youths went on trial at Scottsboro, AL, accused of raping two white women on a freight train. All were convicted in a hasty trial, but by 1950 were free by parole, appeal or escape.

SKAGIT VALLEY TULIP FESTIVAL. Apr 6–22. Skagit County, La Conner, Mount Vernon, Burlington, WA. To celebrate and share the spectacular beauty of more than 1,500 acres of blooming daffodils and tulips that herald the arrival of spring in the Skagit Valley of Washington state. Est attendance: 1,000,000. For info: Audrey Smith, SVTF Exec Dir, PO Box 1784, Mt Vernon, WA 98273. Phone: (360) 428-5959. Fax: (360) 424-6237. E-mail: tulip@sos.net. Web: www.tulipfestival.org.

SPACE MILESTONE: ***CHALLENGER STS-11 (US).*** Apr 6, 1984. Shuttle *Challenger* launched with five astronauts (Robert Crippen, Francis Scobee, George Nelson, Terry Hart and James Van Hoften). Mission required recovery and repair of damaged satellite. Landed at Edwards Air Force Base, CA, on Apr 13.

STAMP EXPO. Apr 6–8. Wilshire Ebell Convention Complex, Los Angeles, CA. Est attendance: 4,000. For info: Intl Stamp Collectors Soc, PO Box 854, Van Nuys, CA 91408. Phone: (818) 997-6496. Fax: (818) 988-4337. E-mail: iibick@aol.com. Web: www.bick.net.

STUDENT GOVERNMENT DAY IN MASSACHUSETTS. Apr 6. Annually, the first Friday of April.

SUGARLOAF'S SPRING GAITHERSBURG CRAFT FESTIVAL. Apr 6–8. Montgomery County Fairgrounds, Gaithersburg, MD. This show, now in its 26th year, features 500 nationally recognized craft designers and fine artists displaying and selling their original creations. Craft demonstrations, children's entertainment, live music, hourly gift certificate drawings, large selection of delicious food and more. Est attendance: 28,000. For info: Sugarloaf Mountain Works, Inc, 200 Orchard Ridge Dr, #215, Gaithersburg, MD 20878. Phone: (800) 210-9900. E-mail: smworks@sugarloafcrafts.com. Web: www .sugarloafcrafts.com.

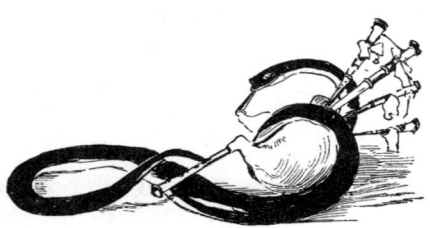

TARTAN DAY. Apr 6. Groups and societies throughout North America take the anniversary of the Declaration of Arbroath (1320) as the day to celebrate their Scottish roots. For more info: www.tartanday.com.

TEFLON INVENTED: ANNIVERSARY. Apr 6, 1938. Poly-tetraflouroethylene resin was invented by Roy J. Plunkett while he was employed by E.I. Du Pont de Nemours & Co. Commonly known as Teflon, it revolutionized the cookware industry. This substance or something similar coated three-quarters of the pots and pans in America at the time of Plunkett's death in 1994.

THAILAND: CHAKRI DAY. Apr 6. Commemorates foundation of present dynasty by King Rama I (1782–1809), who also established Bangkok as capital.

THOMAS, LOWELL: BIRTH ANNIVERSARY. Apr 6, 1892. World traveler, reporter, editor and radio newscaster, whose broadcasts spanned more than half a century, 1925–76. His radio sign-off, "So long until tomorrow," was known to millions of listeners and he is said to have been the first to broadcast from a ship, an airplane, a submarine and a coal mine. Born at Woodington, OH, he died at Pawling, NY, Aug 29, 1981.

TRAGEDY IN RWANDA: ANNIVERSARY. Apr 6, 1994. A plane carrying the presidents of Rwanda and Burundi was shot down near Kigali, the Rwandan capital, exacerbating a brutal ethnic war that led to the massacre of hundreds of thousands. Presidents Juvenal Habyarimana of Rwanda and Cyprien Ntaryamira of Burundi were returning from a summit in Tanzania where they discussed ways of ending the killing in their countries sparked by ethnic rivalries between the Hutu and Tutsi tribes. Following the attack on the two leaders, Rwanda descended into chaos as the two tribes began killing each other in a genocidal battle for power, leading to a mass exodus of civilians caught in the maelstrom.

US ENTERS WORLD WAR I: ANNIVERSARY. Apr 6, 1917. Congress approved a declaration of war against Germany and the US entered WWI, which had begun in 1914. The first US "doughboys" landed in France June 27, 1914.

US SENATE ACHIEVES A QUORUM: ANNIVERSARY. Apr 6, 1789. The US Senate was formally organized after achieving a quorum.

BIRTHDAYS TODAY

Candace Cameron Bure, 25, actress ("Full House"), born Canoga Park, CA, Apr 6, 1976.

Merle Haggard, 64, singer, songwriter ("Okie from Muskogee"), born Bakersfield, CA, Apr 6, 1937.

Marilu Henner, 49, actress ("Taxi," "Evening Shade"), born Chicago, IL, Apr 6, 1952.

Olaf Kolzig, 31, hockey player, born Johannesburg, South Africa, Apr 6, 1970.

Barry Levinson, 59, director, producer, writer, actor ("The Carol Burnett Show" [writer; Emmy Awards 1974, 1975], *Rain Man, Avalon, Bugsy*), born Baltimore, MD, Apr 6, 1942.

April 2001	S	M	T	W	T	F	S
		1	2	3	4	5	6	7
	8	9	10	11	12	13	14
	15	16	17	18	19	20	21
	22	23	24	25	26	27	28
	29	30					

Andre Previn, 72, composer, conductor, born Berlin, Germany, Apr 6, 1929.

John Ratzenberger, 54, actor ("Cheers"), born Bridgeport, CT, Apr 6, 1947.

Paul Rudd, 32, actor (*The Object of My Affection, Clueless*), born Passaic, NJ, Apr 6, 1969.

Roy Thinnes, 63, actor ("The Invaders," "The Outer Limits"), born Chicago, IL, Apr 6, 1938.

James Watson, 73, discoverer (with Francis Crick) of the structure of DNA, born Chicago, IL, Apr 6, 1928.

Billy Dee Williams, 64, actor (*Brian's Song, Lady Sings the Blues, Return of the Jedi*), born New York, NY, Apr 6, 1937.

APRIL 7 — SATURDAY
Day 97 — 268 Remaining

AZALEA FESTIVAL. Apr 7–28. Muskogee, OK. One of the oldest and most celebrated public parks in the southwest: 122 acres, 40 acres of manicured gardens with 30,000 azaleas of 625 varieties. Ranked in the top 100 events by the National Bus Association. Annually in April since 1967. Est attendance: 300,000. For info: Ervalene Jenkins, Muskogee Conv and Tourism, PO Box 2361, Muskogee, OK 74402. Phone: (888) 687-6137. Fax: (918) 684-6364. E-mail: tourism@ok.azalea.net.

BATTLE OF LYS RIVER: ANNIVERSARY. Apr 7, 1918. Having failed to break through Allied lines at Somme in March, General Erich Ludendorff made another attempt by attacking Flanders along the Lys River. On the hot, misty, sticky mornings of Apr 7 and 8, 1918, the Germans released mustard gas. On Apr 9 the Central Powers began a high explosive bombardment along the 12-mile front from LaBasse to Armentieres. The British managed to avoid a break in their line, and finally Ferdinand Foch sent nine French divisions to take over a portion of it. On Apr 30, realizing that "further attacks promised no success," Ludendorff ended the offensive. As a result of this battle the British were unable to initiate an offensive for three months. The Allies suffered 240,000 casualties while the German losses exceeded 348,000.

BENNETTSVILLE DOWNTOWN CHILDREN'S FESTIVAL. Apr 7. Bennettsville, SC. Free children's events on Murchinson School grounds. Annually, the first Saturday in April. Est attendance: 1,000. For info: Ken Harmon, PO Box 1036, Bennettsville, SC 29512. Phone: (843) 479-3869.

CALIFORNIA POPPY FESTIVAL. Apr 7–8. Lancaster, CA. Celebrating the golden poppy as the state flower of California, the California Poppy Festival features unique homemade crafts, a variety of musical entertainers, delicious food booths and a flower and garden market. Visitors can stop by the Poppy Pavilion to see dazzling displays of poppies or visit the Wildflower Information Center to get maps of the best poppy fields. Both kids and adults will enjoy the carnival, games and rides. Est attendance: 60,000. For info: Anne Aldrich, Public Information Officer, City of Lancaster, 44933 N Fern Ave, Lancaster, CA 93534. Phone: (661) 723-6053. Fax: (661) 723-6141. Web: city.lancaster.ca.us.

CAMP, WALTER: BIRTH ANNIVERSARY. Apr 7, 1859. Walter Chauncey Camp, college athlete, coach and administrator, born at New Britain, CT. Camp played football and several other sports at Yale, but he gained prominence for helping to reshape the rules of rugby football into American football. Among his innovations were reducing the number of players on a side from 15 to 11, introducing the scrimmage, giving one team definite possession of the ball and proposing the downs system. He served as a volunteer coach at Yale and became a national figure as a promoter of football. He selected an All-American team from 1889 to his death. Died at New York, NY, Mar 14, 1925.

CANADA: ELMIRA MAPLE SYRUP FESTIVAL. Apr 7. Elmira, ON. Tours of maple bush by hay wagon, sugaring-off shanty in operation, Pennsylvania Dutch cuisine, handcrafted goods, arts and crafts and antiques. Est attendance: 40,000. For

info: Elmira & Woolwich Chamber of Commerce, 5 First St E, Elmira, ON, Canada N3B 2E3. Phone: (519) 669-2605. Fax: (519) 669-8251. Web: www.elmiramaplesyrup.com.

CHANNING, WILLIAM ELLERY: BIRTH ANNIVERSARY. Apr 7, 1780. Well-known abolitionist and leader of the Unitarian movement in the US, born at Newport, RI. He stood for religious liberalism and influenced such people as Longfellow, Bryant, Emerson, Lowell and Holmes. Died at Bennington, VT, Oct 2, 1842.

CLEAR LAKE CRAWFISH FESTIVAL. Apr 7. Landolt Pavilion, Clear Lake Park, Seabrook, TX. 6th annual. The festival will have food, games, Easter Egg Hunt, crawfish-eating contests, silent auction and live zydeco and bluegrass music. Sponsored by the Clear Lake Area Chamber of Commerce. Proceeds fund the annual July 4th fireworks on Clear Lake. For info: Shari Sweeney, Clear Lake Area Chamber of Commerce, 1201 NASA Rd One, Houston, TX 77058. Phone: (281) 488-7676. Fax: (281) 488-8981.

DESOTO CAVERNS PARK'S INDIAN DANCE FEST. Apr 7-8. DeSoto Caverns Park, Childersburg, AL. Artists and craftspeople from across the US. Native American dancing includes hoop, traditional, fine, fancy and many more. 27th annual festival. Est attendance: 9,000. For info: DeSoto Caverns Park, 5181 DeSoto Caverns Pkwy, Childersburg, AL 35044. Phone: (800) 933-2282. E-mail: fun @desotocavernspark.com. Web: www.DeSotoCavernsPark.com.

EASTER BEACH RUN. Apr 7. Daytona Beach, FL. The 33rd annual beach run on "the world's most famous beach" includes a four-mile run for 28 age divisions and a two-mile run for youth 11 years old and younger. Est attendance: 1,500. For info: Easter Beach Run, Daytona Beach Leisure Services Dept, PO Box 2451, Daytona Beach, FL 32115-2451. Phone: (904) 258-3106. Fax: (904) 947-3062.

FAIRCHILD, DAVID GRANDISON: BIRTH ANNIVERSARY. Apr 7, 1869. American botanist, government official and explorer, born at East Lansing, MI. Noted for scientific studies on importation of tropical plant species such as avocados and mangoes. Died at Miami, FL, Aug 6, 1954.

HISTORIC PENDLETON SPRING JUBILEE. Apr 7-8. Pendleton, SC. Come and join the fun in historic Pendleton with arts and crafts displays, food booths, entertainment and much more. Annually, the first full weekend in April. Est attendance: 45,000. For info: Historic Pendleton Spring Jubilee, PO Box 565, Pendleton, SC 29670. Phone: (864) 646-3782. Fax: (864) 646-2506. E-mail: pendtour@innova.net.

HOLIDAY, BILLIE: BIRTH ANNIVERSARY. Apr 7, 1915. Billie Holiday (born Eleanora Fagan, nicknamed "Lady Day") is considered by many jazz critics to have been the greatest jazz singer ever recorded. In her 26-year career, despite having received no formal training, she demonstrated a unique style with sophisticated and dramatic phrasing. Among her best-known songs are "Lover Man," "God Bless the Child," "Don't Explain" and "Strange Fruit." Holiday was born at Philadelphia, PA. She died at New York, NY, July 17, 1959.

KING, WILLIAM RUFUS DEVANE: BIRTH ANNIVERSARY. Apr 7, 1786. 13th vice president of the US died on the 46th day after taking the Oath of Office, of tuberculosis, at Cahawba, AL, Apr 18, 1853. The Oath of Office had been administered to King at Havana, Cuba, as authorized by a special act of Congress (the only presidential or vice presidential oath to be administered outside the US). Born at Sampson County, NY, King was the only vice president who had served in both the House of Representatives and the Senate. Never married, King's term as vice president was Mar 4–Apr 18, 1853.

LONGWOOD GARDENS EASTER DISPLAY. Apr 7–20. Kennett Square, PA. Fragrant Easter lilies trumpet the season, while brilliant tulips, daffodils, freesias and other colorful plants fill four acres of indoor gardens. Est attendance: 40,000. For info: Longwood Gardens, PO Box 501, Kennett Square, PA 19348-0501. Phone: (610) 388-1000. Web: www.longwoodgardens.org.

MALINOWSKI, BRONISLAW: BIRTH ANNIVERSARY. Apr 7, 1884. Leading British anthropologist, author and teacher, born at Krakow, Poland. His pioneering anthropological fieldwork in Melanesia inspired his colleagues and students. In 1939 he became a visiting professor at Yale University. Died at New Haven, CT, May 16, 1942.

MAPLE SYRUP FESTIVAL. Apr 7–8. Bradys Run County Park, Fallston, PA. Demonstrates the maple-tree-tapping process and builds a 19th-century arts, crafts and educational festival around it. Est attendance: 40,000. For info: Beaver County Conservation District, 1000 Third St, Ste 202, Beaver, PA 15009-2026. Phone: (412) 774-7090. Fax: (412) 774-9421.

MCGRAW, JOHN: BIRTH ANNIVERSARY. Apr 7, 1873. John Joseph McGraw, Baseball Hall of Fame third baseman and manager, born at Truxton, NY. Generally regarded as the best manager ever or close to it, McGraw ran the New York Giants with an iron hand from 1902 to 1932. A scrappy ballplayer with the Baltimore Orioles in the 1890s, McGraw demanded and got total effort from his players. Inducted into the Hall of Fame in 1937. Died at New Rochelle, NY, Feb 25, 1934.

METRIC SYSTEM: ANNIVERSARY. Apr 7, 1795. The metric system was adopted in France, where it had been developed.

MOON PHASE: FULL MOON. Apr 7. Moon enters Full Moon phase at 11:22 PM, EDT.

MULTI-CULTURAL EASTER EGG DISPLAY. Apr 7–22. Belleville, IL. A multi-cultural exhibit of Easter eggs decorated in various ethnic and modern artistic styles and featuring daily demonstrations of individual techniques. No admission fee. Est attendance: 9,000. For info: Shrine of Our Lady of the Snows, 442 S DeMazenod Dr, Belleville, IL 62223-1094. Phone: (618) 397-6700. Fax: (618) 397-1210. Web: www.snows.org.

NATCHITOCHES JAZZ FESTIVAL. Apr 7. Natchitoches, LA. The event features numerous bands, continuous music from 11 AM til 9 PM. Annually, the first weekend of April. Est attendance: 25,000. For info: Calendar of Events, Natchitoches Parish Tourism Commission, 781 Front St, Natchitoches, LA 71457. Phone: (318) 352-8072 or (800) 259-1714. Fax: (318) 352-2415. Web: www.natchitoches.net.

NATIONAL HUG YOUR NEWSMAN DAY. Apr 7. To recognize those who deal with death, destruction and tragedy on an everyday basis to deliver local, state and national news. Annually, the first Saturday in April. For info: Mike Anthony or Patti Dee, PO Box 822, Rocky Mount, MO 65072. Phone: (573) 480-3861. E-mail: mapd@mail.advertisnet.com.

NEW ENGLAND CONFERENCE ON STORYTELLING FOR CHILDREN. Apr 7. Arts Center, Keene State College, Keene, NH. Warm, supportive one-day conference for teachers and others interested in learning about storytelling. Keynote speaker, plus two workshops and a performance. Children may attend if capable. Resources will be available. Est attendance: 100. For info: Mary Mayshark-Stavely, Keene State College, Keene, NH 03435-2503. Phone: (603) 358-2218. E-mail: mmayshar @keene.edu.

NEW YORK SLAVE REVOLT: ANNIVERSARY. Apr 7, 1712. Nine whites were killed in a slave revolt in New York City. Planned by 27 slaves, the rebellion was begun by setting fire to an outhouse; as whites came to put the fire out, they were shot. The state militia was called out to capture the rebels and the city of New York responded to the event by strengthening its slave codes. Twenty-one blacks were executed as participants, and six alleged participants committed suicide. New York outlawed slavery in 1799.

NO HOUSEWORK DAY. Apr 7. No trash. No dishes. No making of beds or washing of laundry. And no guilt. Give it a rest. [© 2000 by WH] For info: Tom or Ruth Roy, Wellcat Holidays, 2418 Long Ln, Lebanon, PA 17046. Phone: (717) 279-0184. E-mail: wellcat@supernet.com. Web: www.wellcat.com.

PASSOVER BEGINS AT SUNDOWN. Apr 7. See "Pesach" (Apr 8).

PRAIRIE DOG CHILI COOKOFF AND WORLD CHAMPIONSHIP OF PICKLED QUAIL-EGG EATING. Apr 7-8. Traders Village, Grand Prairie, TX. Tongue-in-cheek salute to the official state dish of Texas, chili con carne, or "Texas Red." World championship of pickled quail-egg eating featuring contestants devouring as many of these gourmet delights as possible in the 60-second time limit. Est attendance: 80,000. For info: Traders Village, Allan Hughes, 2602 Mayfield Rd, Grand Prairie, TX 75052-7246. Phone: (972) 647-2331.

PROSPECT PARK TRIPLE CHALLENGE & SAFETY RODEO. Apr 7. Prospect Park, Brooklyn, NY. Open to individuals and teams, the Triple Challenge is the only relay event of its kind in New York, New Jersey and Connecticut and is composed of in-line skating, running and cycling. The Safety Expo features safety exhibitions and informational booths providing info on athletic and recreational safety among Prospect Park road users. Est attendance: 2,500. For info: Development & Mktg, Prospect Park, 95 Prospect Park West, Brooklyn, NY 11215. Phone: (718) 965-8954. Fax: (718) 965-8972. E-mail: marketing @prospectpark.org. Web: www.prospectpark.org.

SCOTLAND: EDINBURGH INTERNATIONAL SCIENCE FESTIVAL. Apr 7-17. Edinburgh. More than 250 events at 35 venues. Includes workshops, talks, films and exhibitions. Est attendance: 200,000. For info: Pauline Mullin, Media and Info Officer, Edinburgh Intl Science Festival, 149 Rose St, Edinburgh, Scotland EH2 4LS. Phone: (44)1312203977. Fax: (44)1312203987. E-mail: esf@scifest.demon.co.uk. Web: www.edinburghfestivals.co.uk.

	S	M	T	W	T	F	S
April	1	2	3	4	5	6	7
2001	8	9	10	11	12	13	14
	15	16	17	18	19	20	21
	22	23	24	25	26	27	28
	29	30					

SPRING FLOWER SHOW. Apr 7-May 13. Garfield Park Conservatory and Lincoln Park Conservatory, Chicago, IL. Say good-bye to winter and hello to thousands of blooming lilies, hydrangeas, begonias, columbine, crocus, tulips and daffodils. Stroll the fragrant paths and enjoy the full breadth of spring's color and beauty in turn of the century glass houses. For info: Garfield Park Conservatory, 300 N Central Park Ave, Chicago, IL 60624. Phone: (312) 746-5100. Fax: (773) 638-1777. Web: www.garfield-conservatory.org. Lincoln Park Conservatory, 2400 N Stockton Dr, Chicago, IL 60614. Phone: (312) 742-7736.

SPRING SWING CITY ELECTRA-QUANAH WIDE GARAGE SALE. Apr 7. Electra, TX. Sales throughout the Electra area. 50 miles of garage sales. Chamber of Commerce will provide free coffee and maps at 7 AM; sales start at 8 AM. The Chamber of Commerce office will close at 8 AM so that we too may enjoy all of the bargains. Est attendance: 500. For info: Dawn Dunsmore, Electra Chamber of Commerce, 112 W Cleveland, Electra, TX 76360. Phone: (940) 495-3577. E-mail: ElectraCoC@aol.com. Web: www.electratexas.org.

UNITED NATIONS: WORLD HEALTH DAY. Apr 7. A United Nations observance commemorating the establishment of the World Health Organization in 1948. Info from: United Nations, Dept of Public Info, New York, NY 10017.

WINCHELL, WALTER: BIRTH ANNIVERSARY. Apr 7, 1897. Journalist, broadcaster, reporter and gossip columnist Walter Winchell was born at New York, NY, and died at Los Angeles, CA, Feb 20, 1972. He was admired for his way with turning a phrase. His show business columns were voraciously read by millions of Americans between 1924-63.

WORDSWORTH, WILLIAM: BIRTH ANNIVERSARY. Apr 7, 1770. English Lake Poet and philosopher born at Cumberland, England. "Poetry," he said, "is the spontaneous overflow of powerful feelings: it takes its origin from emotion recollected in tranquility." Wordsworth died Apr 23, 1850, at Rydal Mount, Westmorland.

WORLD HEALTH DAY. Apr 7. A worldwide focus on a health topic of international concern is explored in depth to raise public awareness and stimulate local, national and international action. For info: American Assn for World Health, 1825 K St NW, Ste 1208, Washington, DC 20006. Phone: (202) 466-5883. Fax: (202) 466-5896. E-mail: staff@aawhworldhealth.org. Web: www.aawhworldhealth.org.

WORLD HEALTH ORGANIZATION: ANNIVERSARY. Apr 7, 1948. This agency of the UN was founded to coordinate international health systems. It is headquartered at Geneva. Among its achievements is the elimination of smallpox.

YO-YO DAYS AND CONVENTION. Apr 7-8. Spinning Top Museum, Burlington, WI. Midwest yo-yo convention, Wisconsin State Yo-Yo Contest, classes, demonstrations, collections of yo-yos on exhibit and yo-yo shows for all generations. For info: Spinning Top Museum, 533 Milwaukee Ave (Hwy 36), Burlington, WI 53105. Phone: (262) 763-3946.

BIRTHDAYS TODAY

(William) Hodding Carter III, 66, television and newspaper journalist, born New Orleans, LA, Apr 7, 1935.

Jackie Chan, 47, actor (*Rumble in the Bronx*), born Hong Kong, Apr 7, 1954.

Francis Ford Coppola, 62, filmmaker (*Godfather* movies, *Apocalypse Now*), born Detroit, MI, Apr 7, 1939.

Russell Crowe, 37, actor (*LA Confidential, Gladiator*), born Auckland, New Zealand, Apr 7, 1964.

Anthony Drew (Tony) Dorsett, 47, Pro Football Hall of Fame running back, born Rochester, PA, Apr 7, 1954.

Daniel Ellsberg, 70, author (released the "Pentagon Papers" to *The New York Times*), born Chicago, IL, Apr 7, 1931.

David Frost, 62, entertainer ("That Was the Week That Was"), interviewer, born Tenterden, England, Apr 7, 1939.

James Garner (James Baumgardner), 73, actor (*The Americanization of Emily*, "Maverick," "The Rockford Files"), born Norman, OK, Apr 7, 1928.

John Oates, 53, singer ("Maneater" with Daryl Hall), songwriter, born New York, NY, Apr 7, 1948.

Wayne Rogers, 68, actor ("M*A*S*H," "House Calls"), born Birmingham, AL, Apr 7, 1933.

Gerhard Schröder, 57, chancellor of Germany, born Mossenberg, Germany, Apr 7, 1944.

APRIL 8 — SUNDAY
Day 98 — 267 Remaining

BIRTHDAY OF THE BUDDHA: BIRTH ANNIVERSARY. Apr 8. Among Buddhist holidays, this day is the most important as it commemorates the birthday of the Buddha. It is also known as the Day of Vesak. The founder of Buddhism had the given name Siddhartha, the family name Gautama and the clan name Shaka. He is commonly called the Buddha, meaning in Sanskrit "the enlightened one." He is thought to have lived in India from c. 563 BC to 483 BC. Some countries celebrate this holiday on the lunar calendar, so the date changes from year to year but it always occurs in either April or May. This day is a holiday in Indonesia, Korea, Singapore and Thailand

BLACK SENATE PAGE APPOINTED: ANNIVERSARY. Apr 8, 1965. Sixteen-year-old Lawrence Bradford of New York City was the first black page appointed to the US Senate.

CURTIS EASTER PAGEANT. Apr 8. Medicine Valley High School Auditorium, Curtis, NE. "Truly an unforgettable, inspirational, touching spiritual experience!" A choir, acting cast and supporting cast of more than 200 people depict the last week in the life of Christ through music and narration. Seventeen magnificent "Living Pictures." Curtis is Nebraska's official "Easter City." Annually, 3 PM Palm Sunday afternoon. Sponsor: Curtis Community. Est attendance: 2,000. For info: Chris Dodson, Easter Pageant Pres, Easter Pageant, 13853 E Wells Rd, Maywood, NE 68038. Phone: (308) 367-4449. E-mail: dodsquad@curtis-ne.com.

FEDERAL GOVERNMENT SEIZURE OF STEEL MILLS: ANNIVERSARY. Apr 8, 1952. On this date President Harry S. Truman seized control of the nation's steel mills by presidential order in an attempt to prevent a shutdown by strikers. On Apr 29, a US District Court declared the seizure unconstitutional and workers immediately walked out. Production dropped from 300,000 tons a day to less than 20,000. After 53 days the strike ended on July 24, with steelworkers receiving a 16¢ hourly wage raise plus a 5.4¢ hourly increase in fringe benefits.

FIRST INTERCOLLEGIATE RODEO: ANNIVERSARY. Apr 8, 1939. The first Intercollegiate Rodeo was held at historic Godshall Ranch, Apple Valley, CA. The student cowboys and cowgirls, who hailed from California and Arizona colleges and universities, were assisted by world champion professional cowboys including Harry Carey, Dick Foran, Curley Fletcher, Tex Ritter and Errol Flynn from Hollywood. Collegiate rodeos had been held since 1919 at Texas A&M University. College cowboys and cowgirls organized a national association in Texas in 1949 named National Intercollegiate Rodeo Association, which continues today as the only national college rodeo organization.

FISCUS, KATHY: DEATH ANNIVERSARY. Apr 8, 1949. While playing, three-year-old Kathy Fiscus of San Marino, CA, fell into an abandoned well pipe 14 inches wide and 120 feet deep. Rescue workers toiled for two days while national attention was focused on the tragedy. Her body was recovered Apr 10, 1949. An alarmed nation suddenly became attentive to other abandoned wells and similar hazards, and "Kathy Fiscus laws" were enacted in a number of places requiring new safety measures to prevent recurrence of such an accident.

GAINES-SHELTON, RUTH: BIRTH ANNIVERSARY. Apr 8, 1872. African-American playwright born at Glasgow, MO. Best known for prize-winning comedy *The Church Fight*, which was published in *Crisis* (a publication of the NAACP) in May 1926.

HENIE, SONJA: BIRTH ANNIVERSARY. Apr 8, 1912. Sonja Henie, Olympic gold medal figure skater, born at Oslo, Norway. Henie competed in the 1924 Winter Olympics when she was just 11, but finished last in ladies' singles. She won gold medals at the Winter Games of 1928, 1932 and 1936. She became a professional skater and an actress and lived quite extravagantly. Died Oct 13, 1969.

HISPANICFEST 2001. Apr 8. Hollywood, FL. Latin cultural festival with three entertainment stages featuring salsa and merengue bands, celebrity appearances and folkloric presentations. Latin food court, children's games. Est attendance: 20,000. For info: Judy Erickson, Project Marketing, City of Hollywood Dept of Parks, 1940 Harrison, Hollywood, FL 33020. Phone: (954) 922-9959.

HOLY WEEK. Apr 8–14. Christian observance dating from the fourth century, known also as Great Week. The seven days beginning on the sixth and final Sunday in Lent (Palm Sunday), consisting of: Palm Sunday, Monday of Holy Week, Tuesday of Holy Week, Spy Wednesday (or Wednesday of Holy Week), Maundy Thursday, Good Friday and Holy Saturday (or Great Sabbath or Easter Even). A time of solemn devotion to and memorializing of the suffering (passion), death and burial of Christ. Formerly a time of strict fasting.

HOME RUN RECORD SET BY HANK AARON: ANNIVERSARY. Apr 8, 1974. Henry ("Hammerin' Hank") Aaron hit the 715th home run of his career, breaking the record set by Babe Ruth in 1935. Playing for the Atlanta Braves, Aaron broke the record at Atlanta in a game against the Los Angeles Dodgers. He finished his career in 1976 with a total of 755 home runs. This record remains unbroken. At the time of his retirement, Aaron also held records for first in RBIs, second in at-bats and runs scored and third in base hits.

HUNTER, "CATFISH": BIRTH ANNIVERSARY. Apr 8, 1946. James Augustus ("Catfish") Hunter, Baseball Hall of Fame pitcher, born at Hertford, NC. Died Sept 9, 1999, at Hertford.

INTERNATIONAL FENG SHUI AWARENESS DAY. Apr 8. To foster a better understanding of the principles and benefits of feng shui, the oriental art of placement. This ancient art/science promotes better health, success and wellbeing on all levels through proper alignment and coordination of one's property, home, furniture, pathways with universal forms and flow patterns to the natural landforms, local plant/animal life, waterways and general vibration of the area. The overall goal of feng shui is to help blend human creations with those of nature to attain and maintain the inherent harmony of the universe. For info: Bob or Celeste Longacre. Phone: (603) 756-4152. Fax: (603) 756-3196. E-mail: bob@bobsfengshui.com. Web: www.bobsfengshui.com.

JAPAN: FLOWER FESTIVAL (HANA MATSURI). Apr 8. Commemorates Buddha's birthday. Ceremonies in all temples.

KNIGHT, O. RAYMOND: BIRTH ANNIVERSARY. Apr 8, 1872. The "Father of Canadian Rodeo," O. Raymond Knight was born at Payson, UT. His father, the Utah mining magnate Jesse Knight, founded the town of Raymond, Alberta, in 1901. In 1902 Raymond produced Canada's first rodeo, "Raymond Stampede." He also built rodeo's first grandstand and first chute in 1903. O. Raymond Knight died Feb 7, 1947.

McRAE, CARMEN: BIRTH ANNIVERSARY. Apr 8, 1920. After winning an amateur contest at Harlem's legendary Apollo Theatre in her hometown New York City, McRae went on to become a noted jazz singer, singing with the Earl Hines, Mercer Ellington and Benny Carter bands among others and recording more than 20 albums. She died Nov 10, 1994, at Beverly Hills, CA.

MORRIS, LEWIS: 275th BIRTH ANNIVERSARY. Apr 8, 1726. Signer of the Declaration of Independence, born at Westchester County, NY. Died Jan 22, 1798, at the Morrisania manor at NY.

NATIONAL GARDEN WEEK. Apr 8–14. To recognize and honor the 78 million Americans who eagerly garden each year. These American gardeners enhance and improve the environment with their efforts. Annually, the second full week of April. For info: Natl Garden Bureau, 1311 Butterfield Rd, Ste 310, Downers Grove, IL 60515.

NATIONAL WEEK OF THE OCEAN. Apr 8–14. A week focusing on humanity's interdependence with the ocean, asking each of us to appreciate, protect and use the ocean wisely. 18th annual. For info: Pres/Co-Founder, Cynthia Hancock, Natl Week of the Ocean, Inc, PO Box 179, Ft Lauderdale, FL 33302. Phone: (954) 462-5573.

NATIONAL WOMEN'S NUTRITION WEEK. Apr 8–14. To recognize the importance and value of health in all phases of a woman's life. A woman's biochemistry needs nutritional support when on the pill, during pregnancy, during lactation, when she is under stress and going through menopause. This week is designed to educate women about the importance of nutrition for their ongoing health and well-being. For info: Dr Lois M Vanderhoof, Applied Nutrition Concepts, 2828 W Parker Rd, #208, Plano, TX 75075. Phone: (972) 612-5505. E-mail: drlmv@appliednutrition.net. Web: www.appliednutrition.net.

NETWORK MARKETING PROFESSIONALS WEEK. Apr 8–14. Network marketing represents the largest movement of people in the history of our planet. In North America alone, more than 10 million people distribute more than $23 billion worth of products and services each year. This week celebrates and honors all those whose high-integrity business and professional practices make them a dynamic force for positive change. For a free report, "How Network Marketing Can Change Your Life," e-mail ChangeYourLife@sendfree.com. For info: Sheila Martin, 250 H St, Blaine, WA 98230. Phone: (604) 535-3636. E-mail: sheila@we-build-dreams.com. Web: www.we-build-dreams.com.

ORTHODOX PALM SUNDAY. Apr 8. Celebration of Christ's entry into Jerusalem, when His way was covered with palms by the multitudes. Beginning of Holy Week in the Orthodox Church.

PALM SUNDAY. Apr 8. Commemorates Christ's last entry into Jerusalem, when His way was covered with palms by the multitudes. Beginning of Holy (or Great) Week in Western Christian churches.

★**PAN AMERICAN WEEK.** Apr 8–14. Presidential Proclamation customarily issued as "Pan American Day and Pan American Week." Always issued for the week including Apr 14, except in 1965, from 1946 through 1948, 1955 through 1977, and 1979.

PESACH or PASSOVER. Apr 8–15. Hebrew calendar dates: Nisan 15–22, 5761. Apr 8, the first day of Passover, begins an eight-day celebration of the delivery of the Jews from slavery in Egypt. Unleavened bread (matzoh) is eaten at this time.

PHILIPPINES: HOLY WEEK. Apr 8–14. National observance. Flagellants in the streets, *cenaculos* (passion plays) and other colorful and solemn rituals mark the country's observance of Holy Week.

POLL TAX OUTLAWED: 35th ANNIVERSARY. Apr 8, 1966. In the last of a series of moves to abolish poll taxes, a three-judge federal court at Jackson, MS, outlawed Mississippi's $2 poll tax as a voting requirement for state and local elections.

	S	M	T	W	T	F	S
April		1	2	3	4	5	6	7
2001	8	9	10	11	12	13	14
	15	16	17	18	19	20	21
	22	23	24	25	26	27	28
	29	30					

PORTUGAL: HOLY WEEK FESTIVITIES. Apr 8–14. Braga, Ovar, Povoa de Varzim and other major cities. The Holy Week celebrations attain a great splendor in these places, especially in Braga, a bulwark of Christianity from early times. The most important events take place on Monday, Thursday and Good Friday when imposing parades march through the streets. For info: Dept of PR, Portuguese Natl Tourist Office, 590 Fifth Ave, New York, NY 10036. Phone: (212) 354-4403. Fax: (212) 764-6137.

SEVENTEENTH AMENDMENT TO US CONSTITUTION RATIFIED. Apr 8, 1913. Prior to the 17th Amendment, members of the Senate were elected by each state's respective legislature. The advent and popularity of primary elections during the last decade of the 19th century and the early 20th century and a string of senatorial scandals, most notably a scandal involving William Lorimer, an Illinois political boss in 1909, forced the Senate to end its resistance to a constitutional amendment requiring direct popular election of senators.

VOYAGEURS NATIONAL PARK ESTABLISHED: ANNIVERSARY. Apr 8, 1975. Minnesota's Voyageurs land was preserved by Congress on Jan 8, 1971. Four years later, it became the 36th US national park.

WHITE, RYAN: DEATH ANNIVERSARY. Apr 8, 1990. This young man, born Dec 6, 1971, at Kokomo, IN, put the face of a child on AIDS and helped promote greater understanding of the disease. Ryan, a hemophiliac, contracted AIDS from a blood transfusion. Banned from the public school system in Central Indiana in 1984 at the age of 10, he moved with his mother and sister to Cicero, IN, where he was accepted by students and faculty alike. Ryan once stated that he only wanted to be treated as a normal teenager, but that was not to be as media attention made him a celebrity. A few days after attending the Academy Awards in 1990, 18-year-old Ryan was hospitalized and on Palm Sunday lost his valiant fight at Indianapolis, IN. His funeral was attended by many celebrities.

WILLIAMS, WILLIAM: BIRTH ANNIVERSARY. Apr 8, 1731. Signer of the Declaration of Independence, born at Lebanon, CT. Died there Aug 2, 1811.

WSBA/WARM 103 SPRING CRAFT SHOW. Apr 8. York Fairgrounds, York, PA. More than 225 crafts, from country to contemporary, Victorian and southwestern, handcrafted furniture, wood carvings, dolls, jewelry, pottery, collectibles, quilts, baskets, garden needs and much more. Admission fee. Est attendance: 5,000. For info: Joe Alfano, Asst Promo Dir, PO Box 910, York, PA 17402-0910. Phone: (717) 764-1155. Fax: (717) 252-4708. E-mail: jalfano@suscom.com.

BIRTHDAYS TODAY

Kofi Annan, 63, UN Secretary General, born Kumasi, Ghana, Apr 8, 1938.

Patricia Arquette, 33, actress (*Lost Highway, Flirting with Disaster*), born Chicago, IL, Apr 8, 1968.

Gary Edmund Carter, 47, sportscaster, former baseball player, born Culver City, CA, Apr 8, 1954.

William D. Chase, 79, librarian and chronicler of contemporary civilization as cofounder and coeditor of *Chase's Annual Events*, born Lakeview, MI, Apr 8, 1922.

Betty (Elizabeth) Ford, 83, wife of Gerald Ford, 38th president of the US, born Chicago, IL, Apr 8, 1918.

Shecky Greene, 76, comedian, actor, born Chicago, IL, Apr 8, 1925.

John J. Havlicek, 61, Basketball Hall of Fame forward, born Lansing, OH, Apr 8, 1940.

Seymour Hersh, 64, journalist, born Chicago, IL, Apr 8, 1937.

Julian Lennon, 38, musician, singer, son of John Lennon, born Liverpool, England, Apr 8, 1963.

Stuart Pankin, 55, actor ("Not Necessarily the News," *Irreconcilable Differences, Arachnophobia*), born Philadelphia, PA, Apr 8, 1946.

Terry Porter, 38, basketball player, born Milwaukee, WI, Apr 8, 1963.

John Schneider, 47, actor ("Dukes of Hazzard," *Smokey and the Bandit*), born Mount Kisco, NY, Apr 8, 1954.

Taran Noah Smith, 17, actor ("Home Improvement"), born San Francisco, CA, Apr 8, 1984.

Robin Wright, 35, actress (*Message in a Bottle, Forrest Gump*), born Dallas, TX, Apr 8, 1966.

APRIL 9 — MONDAY
Day 99 — 266 Remaining

AFRICAN METHODIST EPISCOPAL CHURCH ORGANIZED: ANNIVERSARY. Apr 9, 1816. The first all-black US religious denomination, the AME church was organized at Philadelphia with Richard Allen, a former slave who had bought his freedom, as the first bishop.

BIRMINGHAM INTERNATIONAL FESTIVAL SALUTE TO HUNGARY. Apr 9–27. Birmingham, AL. A salute to the arts and culture of Hungary. This festival, now in its 51st year, celebrates the arts and culture of a different country each year. Features three-day Hungarian Street Festival Apr 20–22. Est attendance: 30,000. For info: Birmingham Intl Festival, 205 20th St N, Ste 423, Birmingham, AL 35203. Phone: (205) 252-7652. Fax: (205) 252-7656. E-mail: bifstaff@bellsouth.net. Web: www.bifsalutes.org.

BLACK PAGE APPOINTED TO US HOUSE OF REPRESENTATIVES: ANNIVERSARY. Apr 9, 1965. Fifteen-year-old Frank Mitchell of Springfield, IL, was the first black page appointed to the US House of Representatives.

CHICKEN LITTLE AWARDS. Apr 9. 11th annual awards to organizations and/or individuals "who have frightened the daylights out of large numbers of people" with scientifically dubious predictions, theories and statements. The Center monitors the media for "scare campaigns." For info: Alan Caruba, Natl Anxiety Center, PO Box 40, Maplewood, NJ 07040. Phone: (973) 763-6392. E-mail: acaruba@aol.com. Web: www.anxietycenter.com.

CIVIL RIGHTS BILL OF 1866: ANNIVERSARY. Apr 9, 1866. The Civil Rights Bill of 1866, passed by Congress over the veto of President Andrew Johnson, granted blacks the rights and privileges of American citizenship and formed the basis for the Fourteenth Amendment to the US Constitution.

CIVIL WAR ENDING: ANNIVERSARY. Apr 9, 1865. At 1:30 PM General Robert E. Lee, commander of the Army of Northern Virginia, surrendered to General Ulysses S. Grant, commander-in-chief of the Union Army, ending four years of civil war. The meeting took place in the house of Wilmer McLean at the village of Appomattox Court House, VA. Confederate soldiers were permitted to keep their horses and go free to their homes, while Confederate officers were allowed to retain their swords and side arms as well. Grant wrote the terms of surrender. Formal surrender took place at the Courthouse on Apr 12. Death toll for the Civil War is estimated at 500,000 men.

ECKERT, J(OHN) PRESPER, JR: BIRTH ANNIVERSARY. Apr 9, 1919. Co-inventor with John W. Mauchly of ENIAC (Electronic Numerical Integrator and Computer), which was first demonstrated at the Moore School of Electrical Engineering at the University of Pennsylvania at Philadelphia Feb 14, 1946. This is generally considered the birth of the computer age. Originally designed to process artillery calculations for the Army, ENIAC was also used in the Manhattan Project. Eckert and Mauchly formed Electronic Control Company, which later became Unisys Corporation. Eckert was born at Philadelphia and died at Bryn Mawr, PA, June 3, 1995.

FIELDS, W.C.: BIRTH ANNIVERSARY. Apr 9, 1879. Claude William Dukenfield (W.C. Fields), stage and motion picture actor and expert juggler. Born at Philadelphia, PA; died Dec 25, 1946, at Pasadena, CA. He wrote his own epitaph: "On the whole, I'd rather be in Philadelphia."

JENKINS'S EAR DAY: ANNIVERSARY. Apr 9, 1731. Spanish *guardacosta* boarded and plundered the British ship *Rebecca* off Jamaica, and, among other outrages, cut off the ear of English master mariner Robert Jenkins. Little notice was taken until seven years later, when Jenkins exhibited the detached ear and described the atrocity to a committee of the House of Commons. In consequence, Britain declared war on Spain in October 1739, a war that lasted until 1743 and is still known as the "War of Jenkins's Ear." Nothing else is known of him.

KING, FRANK: BIRTH ANNIVERSARY. Apr 9, 1883. Created by Frank King in 1919 as a comic strip about men's interest in autos, *Gasoline Alley* had a tremendous jump in popularity in 1921 when its main character Walt adopted a foundling called Skeezix. Devoid of melodrama, this strip sympathetically described the day-to-day lives of Walt, Skeezix and their friends and family, and it was the first American cartoon in which the characters actually aged. Frank King was born at Cashon, WI, and died at Winter Park, FL, June 24, 1969.

LUDENDORFF, ERICK: BIRTH ANNIVERSARY. Apr 9, 1865. German general who, during the last years of World War I, was chiefly responsible for military policy and strategy. Born near Pozen, Prussia, and died at Tutzing, Dec 20, 1937.

MARIAN ANDERSON EASTER CONCERT: ANNIVERSARY. Apr 9, 1939. On this Easter Sunday, black American contralto Marian Anderson sang an open-air concert from the steps of the Lincoln Memorial at Washington, DC, to an audience of 75,000, after having been denied use of the Daughters of the American Revolution (DAR) Constitution Hall. The event became an American antidiscrimination *cause célèbre* and led First Lady Eleanor Roosevelt to resign from the DAR.

MUYBRIDGE, EADWEARD: BIRTH ANNIVERSARY. Apr 9, 1830. English photographer famed for his studies of animals in motion. Born Edward James Muggeridge, at Kingston-on-Thames, England. Died there May 8, 1904.

★**NATIONAL FORMER PRISONER OF WAR RECOGNITION DAY.** Apr 9.

PHILIPPINES: ARAW NG KAGITINGAN. Apr 9, 1942. National observance to commemorate the fall of Bataan. The infamous "Death March" is reenacted at the Mount Samat Shrine, the Dambana ng Kagitingan.

ROBESON, PAUL BUSTILL: BIRTH ANNIVERSARY.
Apr 9, 1898. Paul Robeson, born at Princeton, NJ, was an All-American football player at Rutgers University and received his law degree from Columbia University in 1923. After being seen by Eugene O'Neill in an amateur stage production, he was offered a part in O'Neill's play *The Emperor Jones*. His performance in that play with the Provincetown Players established him as an actor. Without ever having taken a voice lesson, he also became a popular singer. His stage credits include *Show Boat, Porgy and Bess, The Hairy Ape* and *Othello*, which enjoyed the longest Broadway run of a Shakespeare play. In 1950 he was denied a passport by the US for refusing to sign an affidavit stating whether he was or ever had been a member of the Communist Party. The action was overturned by the Supreme Court in 1958. His film credits include *Emperor Jones, Show Boat, King Solomon's Mines* and *Song of Freedom*, among others. Robeson died at Philadelphia, PA, Jan 23, 1976.

SPACE MILESTONE: *SOYUZ 35* (USSR). Apr 9, 1980. Two cosmonauts (Valery Ryumin and Leonid Popov) were launched from Baikonur space center at Kazakhstan, USSR. Docked at *Salyut 6* Apr 10. Ryumin and Popov returned to Earth Oct 11, 1980, after setting a new space endurance record of 185 days.

TUNISIA: MARTYRS' DAY. Apr 9.

WINSTON CHURCHILL DAY. Apr 9. Anniversary of enactment of legislation in 1963 that made the late British statesman an honorary citizen of the US.

BIRTHDAYS TODAY

Severiano (Seve) Ballesteros, 44, golfer, born Pedrena, Spain, Apr 9, 1957.

Jean-Paul Belmondo, 68, actor (*The Man from Rio, Is Paris Burning?*), born Neuilly-sur-Seine, France, Apr 9, 1933.

Hugh Hefner, 75, founder of *Playboy*, born Chicago, IL, Apr 9, 1926.

Paul Krassner, 69, editor, journalist, born Brooklyn, NY, Apr 9, 1932.

Michael Learned, 62, actress (*The Waltons, Nurses*; stage: *The Sisters Rosenzweig*), born Washington, DC, Apr 9, 1939.

Tom Lehrer, 73, songwriter ("Vatican Rag," "New Math"), pianist, mathematician, born New York, NY, Apr 9, 1928.

Cynthia Nixon, 35, actress (*Tattoo, Amadeus*), born New York, NY, Apr 9, 1966.

Keshia Knight Pulliam, 22, actress ("The Cosby Show"), born Newark, NJ, Apr 9, 1979.

Dennis Quaid, 47, actor (*Everybody's All-American*), born Houston, TX, Apr 9, 1954.

Jacques Villeneuve, 30, race car driver, winner of 1995 Indianapolis 500, born St. Jean d'Iberville, Quebec, Canada, Apr 9, 1971.

April *2001*	S	M	T	W	T	F	S
	1	2	3	4	5	6	7
	8	9	10	11	12	13	14
	15	16	17	18	19	20	21
	22	23	24	25	26	27	28
	29	30					

APRIL 10 — TUESDAY
Day 100 — 265 Remaining

BATAAN DEATH MARCH: ANNIVERSARY. Apr 10, 1942. On this morning American and Filipino prisoners were herded together by Japanese soldiers on Mariveles Airfield on Bataan (in the Philippine islands) and began the Death March to Camp O'Donnell, near Cabanatuan. During the six-day march they were given only one bowl of rice. More than 5,200 Americans and many more Filipinos lost their lives in the course of the march.

BOOTH, WILLIAM: BIRTH ANNIVERSARY. Apr 10, 1829. General William Booth, founder of the movement that became known, in 1878, as the Salvation Army, was born at Nottingham, England. Apprenticed to a pawnbroker at the age of 13, Booth experienced firsthand the misery of poverty. He broke with conventional church religion and established a quasi-military religious organization with military uniforms and ranks. Recruiting from the poor, from converted criminals and from many other social outcasts, his organization grew rapidly and its influence spread from England to the US and to other countries. At revivals in slum areas the itinerant evangelist offered help for the poor, homes for the homeless, sobriety for alcoholics, rescue homes for women and girls, training centers and legal aid. Booth died at London, England, Aug 20, 1912. See also: "Salvation Army Founder's Day" (Apr 10).

BRAHMS "REQUIEM" PREMIERE: ANNIVERSARY. Apr 10, 1868. Composer Johannes Brahms fortified his reputation as one of the leading figures in 19th-century German Romantic music with the success of his *Requiem*, which premiered at Bremen Cathedral on this date. The peaceful choral piece, at turns both melancholy and exuberant, is one of the more recognized and often-sung funerary works in the musical canon.

CHILDREN'S DAY IN FLORIDA. Apr 10. A legal holiday in Florida commemorated on the second Tuesday in April.

COMMODORE PERRY DAY. Apr 10, 1794. Birthday of Matthew Calbraith Perry, commodore in the US Navy, negotiator of first treaty between US and Japan (Mar 31, 1854). Born at South Kingston, RI. Died Mar 4, 1858, at New York, NY.

CONNORS, CHUCK (KEVIN JOSEPH): 80th BIRTH ANNIVERSARY. Apr 10, 1921. "The Rifleman" of television fame, Chuck Connors played that role from 1958 to 1963. His portrayal of a slave owner in the miniseries *Roots* won him an Emmy nomination. Connors acted in more than 45 films and appeared on many TV series and specials. He played professional basketball and baseball before becoming an actor. Born at Brooklyn, NY; died Nov 10, 1992, at Los Angeles, CA.

FIRST PGA CHAMPIONSHIP: 85th ANNIVERSARY. Apr 10, 1916. The recently formed Professional Golfer's Association of America held its first championship at Siwanoy golf course at Bronxville, NY. The trophy and the lion's share of the $2,580 purse were won by British golfer Jim Barnes.

GROTIUS, HUGO: BIRTH ANNIVERSARY. Apr 10, 1583 (OS). Anniversary of the birth of Hugo Grotius, the Dutch theologian, attorney, scholar and statesman whose beliefs profoundly influenced American thinking, especially with regard to the conscience of humanity. Born at Delft, Holland, he died at Rostock, Germany, Aug 28, 1645 (OS).

NATIONAL SIBLINGS DAY. Apr 10. A commemorative day to honor all brothers and sisters who are living and memorialize those who have died. Created by Claudia A. Evart of New York City in memory of her sister Lisette and brother Alan; they both died from accidents early in their lives. Annually, Apr 10. For info: Claudia A. Evart, Siblings Day Foundation, Inc, 30 Park Ave, Ste 2-P, New York, NY 10016-3833. Phone: (212) 779-2227. E-mail: siblingsday@earthlink.net. Web: www.siblings-day.com.

ODESSA RETAKEN: ANNIVERSARY. Apr 10, 1944. The Red Army retook the Ukrainian city of Odessa, the port on the northwest coast of the Black Sea that had been in the hands of the Nazis since October 1941.

PERKINS, FRANCES: BIRTH ANNIVERSARY. Apr 10, 1880. First woman member of a US presidential cabinet. Born at Boston, MA, she was married in 1915 to Paul Caldwell Wilson, but used her maiden name in public life. She was appointed secretary of labor by President Franklin D. Roosevelt in 1933, a post in which she served until 1945. Died at New York, NY, May 14, 1965.

PULITZER, JOSEPH: BIRTH ANNIVERSARY. Apr 10, 1847. American journalist and newspaper publisher, founder of the Pulitzer Prizes, born at Budapest, Hungary. Died at Charleston, SC, Oct 29, 1911. Pulitzer Prizes awarded annually since 1917. Write for entry and deadline info. (Please specify Book, Journalism, Drama or Music Competition.) For info: Pulitzer Prize Bd, 709 Journalism, Columbia Univ, New York, NY 10027. Phone: (212) 854-3841. WWW: http://www.pulitzer.org

ROBERT GRAY BECOMES FIRST AMERICAN TO CIRCUMNAVIGATE THE EARTH: ANNIVERSARY. Apr 10, 1790. When Robert Gray docked the *Columbia* at Boston Harbor, he became the first American to circumnavigate the earth. He sailed from Boston, MA, in September 1787, to trade with Indians of the Pacific Northwest. From there he sailed to China and then continued around the world. His 42,000-mile journey opened trade between New England and the Pacific Northwest and helped the US establish claims to the Oregon Territory.

SAFETY PIN PATENTED: ANNIVERSARY. Apr 10, 1849. Walter Hunt of New York patented the first safety pin.

SALVATION ARMY FOUNDER'S DAY. Apr 10, 1829. Birth anniversary of William Booth, a Methodist minister who began an evangelical ministry in the East End of London in 1865 and established mission stations to feed and house the poor. In 1878 he changed the name of the organization to the Salvation Army. Booth was born at Nottingham, England; he died at London, Aug 20, 1912. See also: "Booth, William: Birth Anniversary" (Apr 10).

WOODWARD, ROBERT BURNS: BIRTH ANNIVERSARY. Apr 10, 1917. Nobel Prize—winning (1965) Harvard University science professor whose special field of study was molecular structure of complex organic compounds. Called "one of the most outstanding scientific minds of the century." Born at Boston, MA, he died at Cambridge, MA, July 8, 1979.

BIRTHDAYS TODAY

Kenneth ("Babyface") Edmonds, 44, pop performer and songwriter, born Indianapolis, IN, Apr 10, 1957.
David Halberstam, 67, author (*The Best and the Brightest, The Summer of Forty-Nine*), born New York, NY, Apr 10, 1934.
Dolores Huerta, 71, cofounder, with Cesar Chavez, of the United Farm Workers Union, born Dawson, NM, Apr 10, 1930.
Peter MacNicol, 47, actor ("Ally McBeal," *Ghostbusters II*), born Dallas, TX, Apr 10, 1954.
John Earl Madden, 65, sportscaster, former football coach, born Austin, MN, Apr 10, 1936.
Joe Don Meredith, 63, former sportscaster, actor and football player, born Mount Vernon, TX, Apr 10, 1938.
Harry Morgan (Harry Bratsburg), 86, actor (Emmy for "M*A*S*H"; "Dragnet"), born Detroit, MI, Apr 10, 1915.
Haley Joel Osment, 13, actor (*The Sixth Sense, Bogus*), born Los Angeles, CA, Apr 10, 1988.
Steven Seagal, 50, actor, producer (*Hard to Kill, On Deadly Ground*), born Lansing, MI, Apr 10, 1951.
Omar Sharif (Michael Shalhoub), 69, actor (*Lawrence of Arabia, Dr. Zhivago*), born Alexandria, Egypt, Apr 10, 1932.
Paul Edward Theroux, 60, author (*The Mosquito Coast, Millroy the Magician*), born Medford, MA, Apr 10, 1941.
Max Von Sydow, 72, actor (*The Seventh Seal, The Emigrants*), born Lund, Sweden, Apr 10, 1929.

APRIL 11 — WEDNESDAY
Day 101 — 264 Remaining

BARBERSHOP QUARTET DAY. Apr 11. Commemorates the gathering of some 26 persons at Tulsa, OK, Apr 11, 1938, and the founding there of the Society for the Preservation and Encouragement of Barbershop Quartet Singing in America.

BLISS, LIZZIE "LILLIE": BIRTH ANNIVERSARY. Apr 11, 1864. Lizzie "Lillie" Bliss was born at Boston, MA. She was one of the three founders (all women) of the Museum of Modern Art at New York City in 1929. She died Mar 12, 1931, at New York City.

BOLIN, JANE MATILDA: BIRTHDAY. Apr 11, 1908. Jane Matilda Bolin, born at Poughkeepsie, NY, was the first black woman to graduate from the Yale School of Law (1931) and went on to become the first black woman judge in the US. She served as assistant corporation counsel for the city of New York before being appointed to the city's Domestic Relations Court and the Family Court of the State of New York.

CIVIL RIGHTS ACT OF 1968: ANNIVERSARY. Apr 11, 1968. Exactly one week after the assassination of Martin Luther King, Jr, the Civil Rights Act of 1968 (protecting civil rights workers, expanding the rights of Native Americans and providing antidiscrimination measures in housing) was signed into law by President Lyndon B. Johnson, who said: " . . . the proudest moments of my presidency have been times such as this when I have signed into law the promises of a century."

EVERETT, EDWARD: BIRTH ANNIVERSARY. Apr 11, 1794. American statesman and orator, born at Dorchester, MA. It was Edward Everett who delivered the main address at the dedication of Gettysburg National Cemetery, Nov 19, 1863. President Abraham Lincoln also spoke at the dedication, and his brief speech (less than two minutes) has been called one of the most eloquent in the English language. Once a candidate for vice president of the US (1860), Everett died at Boston, MA, Jan 15, 1865.

FORT PULASKI: ANNIVERSARY. Apr 11, 1862. Fort Pulaski National Monument, Tybee Island, GA. Commemorates the siege and reduction of the fort in 1862. On this date the age of masonry fortification ended and the era of rifled artillery began, with the surrender of the Confederate garrison after a 30-hour siege.

HAROLD WASHINGTON ELECTED FIRST BLACK MAYOR OF CHICAGO: ANNIVERSARY. Apr 11, 1983. Harold Washington defeated Bernard Epton and became the first black mayor of Chicago. Of the city's 1.6 million voters a record 82 percent voted. Washington won 51 percent of the votes, which split along racial lines. He was reelected in April 1987, but died suddenly seven months later at his office, Nov 25, 1987.

HUGHES, CHARLES EVANS: BIRTH ANNIVERSARY. Apr 11, 1862. 11th chief justice of US Supreme Court. Born at Glens Falls, NY. Died at Osterville, MA, Aug 27, 1948.

JULIAN, PERCY: BIRTH ANNIVERSARY. Apr 11, 1899. Percy Julian, producer of a synthetic progesterone using soy beans, was born at Montgomery, AL. He also developed a cheaper method of producing cortisone, a drug to treat glaucoma and a chemical foam to fight petroleum fires. Julian died Apr 19, 1975, at Waukegan, IL.

LIBERATION OF BUCHENWALD CONCENTRATION CAMP: ANNIVERSARY. Apr 11, 1945. Buchenwald, north of Weimar, Germany, was entered by Allied troops. It was the first of the Nazi concentration camps to be liberated. It had been established in 1937, and about 56,000 people died there.

SPACE MILESTONE: *APOLLO 13* (US). Apr 11, 1970. Astronauts Lovell, Haise and Swigert endangered when oxygen tank ruptured. Planned moon landing canceled. Details of accident made public and world shared concern for crew who splashed down successfully in the Pacific Apr 17.

SPELMAN COLLEGE ESTABLISHED: ANNIVERSARY. Apr 11, 1881. Spelman College, with funding from the Rockefeller family, opened its doors for the first time with the purpose of educating young African-American women. The institution, located at Atlanta, GA, was dubbed "the Radcliffe for Negro women."

UGANDA: LIBERATION DAY: ANNIVERSARY. Apr 11. Republic of Uganda celebrates anniversary of overthrow of Idi Amin's dictatorship in 1979.

BIRTHDAYS TODAY

Tony Brown, 68, journalist, host of "Tony Brown," born Charleston, WV, Apr 11, 1933.

Oleg Cassini, 88, fashion designer, born Paris, France, Apr 11, 1913.

Ellen Goodman, 53, Pulitzer Prize–winning columnist, born Newton, MA, Apr 11, 1948.

Joel Grey (Joe Katz), 69, actor (Oscar for *Cabaret; The Seven Per Cent Solution*), born Cleveland, OH, Apr 11, 1932.

Bill Irwin, 51, actor, choreographer (*The Regard of Flight*), born Santa Monica, CA, Apr 11, 1950.

Ethel Kennedy, 73, widow of Robert Kennedy, born Greenwich, CT, Apr 11, 1928.

Louise Lasser, 62, actress ("Mary Hartman, Mary Hartman"), born New York, NY, Apr 11, 1939.

Peter Riegert, 54, actor (*Local Hero, Crossing Delancey*), born New York, NY, Apr 11, 1947.

Bret William Saberhagen, 37, baseball player, born Chicago Heights, IL, Apr 11, 1964.

Jean-Claude Servan-Schreiber, 83, journalist, author (*The Chosen and the Choice*), born Paris, France, Apr 11, 1918.

Meshach Taylor, 54, actor ("Dave's World," "Designing Women"), born Boston, MA, Apr 11, 1947.

APRIL 12 — THURSDAY

Day 102 — 263 Remaining

ANNIVERSARY OF THE BIG WIND. Apr 12, 1934. The highest-velocity natural wind ever recorded occurred in the morning at the Mount Washington, NH, Observatory. Three weather observers, Wendell Stephenson, Alexander McKenzie and Salvatore Pagliuca, observed and recorded the phenomenon in which gusts reached 231 miles per hour—"the strongest natural wind ever recorded on the earth's surface." The 50th anniversary was observed at the site in 1984, with the three original observers participating in the ceremony.

ATTACK ON FORT SUMTER: ANNIVERSARY. Apr 12, 1861. After months of escalating tension, Major Robert Anderson refused to evacuate Fort Sumter at Charleston, SC. Confederate troops under the command of General P.T. Beauregard opened fire on the harbor fort at 4:30 AM and continued until Major Anderson surrendered on Apr 13. No lives were lost despite the firing of some 40,000 shells in the first major engagement of the American Civil War.

BILLINGS, JOHN SHAW: BIRTH ANNIVERSARY. Apr 12, 1838. American medical librarian and army physician. Born at Switzerland County, IN. Died at New York, NY, Mar 11, 1913.

CLAY, HENRY: BIRTH ANNIVERSARY. Apr 12, 1777. Statesman, born at Hanover County, VA. Was the Speaker of the House of Representatives and later became the leader of the new Whig party. He was defeated for the presidency three times. Clay died at Washington, DC, June 29, 1852.

	S	M	T	W	T	F	S
April	1	2	3	4	5	6	7
2001	8	9	10	11	12	13	14
	15	16	17	18	19	20	21
	22	23	24	25	26	27	28
	29	30					

FDR COMMEMORATIVE CEREMONY. Apr 12. Little White House, Warm Springs, GA. Ceremony honoring Franklin Delano Roosevelt on the 56th anniversary of his death in Warm Springs. Keynote speaker; Marine color guard. Sponsor: Georgia Dept of Natural Resources. Est attendance: 1,000. For info: Mgr, Little White House, 401 Little White House Rd, Warm Springs, GA 31830. Phone: (706) 655-5870.

GRAND PRAIRIE SPIRIT OF THE WEST FESTIVAL. Apr 12–15. Grand Prairie, TX. Tribute to western heritage featuring AQHA-sanctioned trail ride, free pancake breakfasts, western art show, Thoroughbred horse racing, parade, chili cook off, C & W dance and other equestrian events. Est attendance: 25,000. For info: Doug Beich, City of Grand Prairie, 326 W Main St, Grand Prairie, TX 75053-4045. Phone: (972) 237-8112. Fax: (972) 237-8267.

HALIFAX INDEPENDENCE DAY: 225th ANNIVERSARY. Apr 12, 1776. North Carolina. Anniversary of the resolution adopted by the Provincial Congress of North Carolina at Halifax, NC, authorizing the delegates from North Carolina to the Continental Congress to vote for a Declaration of Independence.

HALL, LYMAN: BIRTH ANNIVERSARY. Apr 12, 1724. Signer of the Declaration of Independence. Born at Wallingford, CT, he died at Burke County, GA, Oct 19, 1790.

ITALY: PROCESSION OF THE ADDOLORATA AND PROCESSION OF THE MYSTERIES. Apr 12–13. Taranto. Procession of the Addolorata is held on Holy Thursday, while the Procession of the Mysteries takes place on Good Friday. Both processions have in common the very slow pace of the participants and their unusual costumes.

MAUNDY THURSDAY or HOLY THURSDAY. Apr 12. The Thursday before Easter, originally "dies mandate," celebrates Christ's injunction to love one another, "Mandatus novum do vobis. . . ." ("A new commandment I give to you. . . .")

NATIONAL MINORITY CANCER AWARENESS WEEK. Apr 12–18. For info: Natl Cancer Information Service, 550 N Broadway, Ste 300, Baltimore, MD 21205. Phone: (800) 4-CANCER.

PHILIPPINES: MORIONE'S FESTIVAL. Apr 12–15. Marinduque Island. Provincewide masquerade, Lenten plays and celebrations. Annually, Holy Thursday through Easter Sunday.

POLIO VACCINE: ANNIVERSARY. Apr 12, 1955. Anniversary of announcement that the polio vaccine developed by American physician Dr. Jonas E. Salk was "safe, potent and effective." Incidence of the dreaded infantile paralysis, or poliomyelitis, declined by 95 percent following introduction of preventive vaccines.

ROOSEVELT, FRANKLIN DELANO: DEATH ANNIVERSARY. Apr 12, 1945. With the end of WWII only months away, the nation and the world were stunned by the sudden death of the president shortly into his fourth term of office. Roosevelt, 32nd president of the US (Mar 4, 1933–Apr 12, 1945), was the only president to serve more than two terms—he was elected to four consecutive terms. He died at Warm Springs, GA.

SPACE MILESTONE: *COLUMBIA STS 1* (US) FIRST SHUTTLE FLIGHT: 20th ANNIVERSARY. Apr 12, 1981. First flight of shuttle *Columbia*. Two astronauts (John Young and Robert Crippen), on first manned US space mission since *Apollo-Soyuz* in July 1976, spent 54 hours in space (36 orbits of Earth) before landing at Edwards Air Force Base, CA, Apr 14.

SPACE MILESTONE: *DISCOVERY* (US). Apr 12, 1985. On its 16th mission (from Kennedy Space Center, FL) shuttle *Discovery* was launched carrying a US Senator (Jake Garn) as a member of its crew of seven.

SPACE MILESTONE: *VOSTOK I*, FIRST MAN IN SPACE: 40th ANNIVERSARY. Apr 12, 1961. Yuri Gagarin became the first man in space when he made a 108-minute voyage, orbiting Earth in a 10,395-lb vehicle, *Vostok I*, launched by the USSR.

SPRING BLUEGRASS FESTIVAL. Apr 12–15. Live Oak, FL. Four days of extraordinary bluegrass music in a beautiful outdoor setting. Est attendance: 10,000. For info: James Cornett, Spirit of the Suwannee Music Park, 3076 95th Dr, Live Oak, FL 32060. Phone: (904) 364-1683. Fax: (904) 364-2998. E-mail: spirit@musicliveshere.com. Web: www.musicliveshere.com.

TRUANCY LAW: ANNIVERSARY. Apr 12, 1853. The first truancy law was enacted at New York. A $50 fine was charged against parents whose children between the ages of five and 15 were absent from school.

"21 JUMP STREET" TV PREMIERE: ANNIVERSARY. Apr 12, 1987. Youthful big city cops busted crime in the local schools and colleges in this Fox police drama. Starred Johnny Depp as Tom Hanson, Holly Robinson Peete as Judy Hoffs, Dustin Nguyen as H.T. Ioki, Peter DeLuise as Doug Penhall, Frederic Forrest as Captain Jenko, Steven Williams as Captain Adam Fuller and Richard Grieco as Dennis Booker.

VOTE LAWYERS OUT OF OFFICE DAY. Apr 12. This is a day prior to tax deadlines when voters renew their pledge never to vote for a lawyer for public office. A cleansing effort. Annually, the second Thursday in April. Sponsor: Sharkbait Press. For info: Marcus P. Meleton, Jr, Sharkbait Press, PO Box 11300, Costa Mesa, CA 92627-0300. Phone: (949) 645-0139. E-mail: Sharkbaitp@aol.com. Web: www.sharkbaitpress.com.

"YOUR HIT PARADE" RADIO PREMIERE: ANNIVERSARY. Apr 12, 1935. This program debuted on radio in 1935 with its countdown of the week's top songs. In 1950 it became a TV program. See also: "Your Hit Parade TV Premiere: Anniversary" (Oct 7).

BIRTHDAYS TODAY

David Cassidy, 51, singer ("Cherish"), actor ("The Partridge Family"), born New York, NY, Apr 12, 1950.

Tom Clancy, 54, author (*The Hunt for Red October, Red Storm Rising*), born Baltimore, MD, Apr 12, 1947.

Beverly Cleary, 85, author (*Ramona* series for children; winner of the Newbery Medal for *Dear Mr Henshaw*), born McMinnville, OR, Apr 12, 1916.

Claire Danes, 22, actress (*The Rainmaker*), born New York, NY, Apr 12, 1979.

Shannen Doherty, 30, actress ("Beverly Hills 90210," *Night Shift, Heathers*), born Memphis, TN, Apr 12, 1971.

Andy Garcia, 45, actor (*The Untouchables; The Godfather, Part III*), born Havana, Cuba, Apr 12, 1956.

Lionel Hampton, 92, bandleader, born Louisville, KY, Apr 12, 1909.

Herbie Hancock, 61, musician, born Chicago, IL, Apr 12, 1940.

Dan Lauria, 54, actor ("The Wonder Years," *Stakeout*), born Brooklyn, NY, Apr 12, 1947.

David Letterman, 54, comedian, TV talk-show host ("Late Show with David Letterman"), born Indianapolis, IN, Apr 12, 1947.

Ann Miller (Lucille Ann Collier), 82, actress (*Sugar Babies, You Can't Take It with You, Easter Parade*), born Chireno, TX, Apr 12, 1919.

Ed O'Neill, 55, actor ("Married . . . With Children," *Deliverance, Wayne's World*), born Youngstown, OH, Apr 12, 1946.

Scott Turow, 52, writer (*Presumed Innocent, Burden of Proof*), born Chicago, IL, Apr 12, 1949.

APRIL 13 — FRIDAY
Day 103 — 262 Remaining

BECKETT, SAMUEL: 95th BIRTH ANNIVERSARY. Apr 13, 1906. Author, critic and playwright born at Foxrock, County Dublin, Ireland. Writing in both French and English, Samuel Beckett is best remembered for his plays, including *Waiting for Godot, Endgame, Krapp's Last Tape* and *Happy Days*. Beckett settled at Paris, France, in 1937 and served with an underground resistance group during the early years of World War II. In the years following the war he entered a period of intense creativity, producing among others the novels *Molloy, Malone Dies* and *The Unnamable* and two plays, *Eleutheria* and *Waiting for Godot*. *Waiting for Godot* received an acclaimed production at the Theatre de Babylone in Paris in Jan 1953, and with it Beckett achieved worldwide renown. He died Dec 22, 1989, at Paris, France.

BLAME SOMEONE ELSE DAY. Apr 13. To share the responsibility and the guilt for the mess we're in. Blame someone else! Annually, the first Friday the 13th of the year. For info: A.C. Moeller, Box 71, Clio, MI 48420-1042.

BUTTS, ALFRED M.: BIRTH ANNIVERSARY. Apr 13, 1899. Alfred Butts was a jobless architect in the Depression when he invented the board game Scrabble. The game was just a fad for Butts's friends until a Macy's executive saw the game being played at a resort in 1952, and the world's largest store began carrying it. Manufacturing of the game was turned over to Selchow & Righter when 35 workers were producing 6,000 sets a week. Butts received three cents per set for years. He said, "One-third went to taxes. I gave one-third away, and the other third enabled me to have an enjoyable life." Butts was born at Poughkeepsie, NY. He died Apr 4, 1993, at Rhinebeck, NY.

CASSIDY, BUTCH: BIRTH ANNIVERSARY. Apr 13, 1866. Born Robert Leroy Parker at Beaver, UT, son of Mormon pioneer Maximillian Parker, he became a notorious outlaw of the Old West and leader of The Wild Bunch gang. Some believed he died in a gun battle at Bolivia in 1909, while others are certain he returned and died in the USA.

DOLLY'S MUSIC ON PARADE. Apr 13. Pigeon Forge, TN. Dolly Parton serves as grand marshal in the 16th annual parade. Theme-based parade kicks off the spring season. Est attendance: 40,000. For info: Pigeon Forge Dept of Tourism, 2450 Parkway, PO Box 1390, Pigeon Forge, TN 37868. Phone: (800) 251-9100 or (423) 453-8574. Web: www.pigeon-forge.tn.us.

EASTER EGG HUNT. Apr 13. Shane Hill Nursing Home, Rockford, OH. Residents color 60 dozen Easter eggs to hide for children and grandchildren of nursing home employees. Est attendance: 70. For info: Brooke Reyman, Activities Dir, Shane Hill Nursing Home, 10731 State Rte 118, Rockford, OH 45882-0159.

EGGS, EGGS, EGGS. Apr 13–14. Burlington, WI. 22nd annual egg dyeing event from classic to modern styles. English pace methods to to racing stripes, take home awesome eggs. For info: Teacher Place & Parent Resources, 533 Milwaukee Ave (Hwy 36), Burlington, WI 53105. Phone: (262) 763-3946.

ENGLAND: DEVIZES TO WESTMINSTER INTERNATIONAL CANOE RACE. Apr 13–16. Starts from Wharf Car Park, Wharf St, Devizes, Wiltshire. Canoes race along 125 miles of the Kennet and Avon canals and the River Thames, ending at County Hall Steps, Westminster Bridge Rd, London. Annually, Good Friday to Easter Monday. Est attendance: 6,000. For info: Competition Sec, Boscombe Forge, Church Road, Bookham, Surrey, England KT23 3JG. Phone: (44) (171) 401-8266. E-mail: dw@mackinlay.demon.co.uk. Web: www.mackinlay.demon.co.uk/dw/

ENGLAND: HARROGATE INTERNATIONAL YOUTH MUSIC FESTIVAL. Apr 13–20. Harrogate, North Yorkshire. Noncompetitive festival that brings together youth (up to 25 years of age) in bands, choirs, orchestras and dance groups from all over the world. Est attendance: 7,000. For info: Perform Europe, Deepdene Lodge, Deepdene Ave, Doricing, Surrey, England R4S 4A2. Phone: (44) (130) 674-4360. Fax: (44) (130) 674-4361. E-mail: peurope@kuoni.co.uk.

ENGLAND: WEST SUSSEX INTERNATIONAL YOUTH MUSIC FESTIVAL. Apr 13–17. West Sussex. Noncompetitive festival that brings together youth (up to 25 years of age) in bands, choirs, orchestras and dance groups from all over the world. For info: Perform Europe, Deepdene Lodge, Deepdene Avenue, Surrey, England, R4S 4A2. Phone: (44) (130) 674-4360. Fax: (44) (130) 674-4361. E-mail: peurope@kuoni.co.uk.

FIRST BASEBALL STRIKE ENDS: ANNIVERSARY. Apr 13, 1972. Major league baseball players and owners agreed on a settlement in which owners added an additional $500,000 to the players' pension fund. This ended the first baseball strike, which had begun Apr 5 when the season opener was canceled.

FRIDAY THE THIRTEENTH. Apr 13. Variously believed to be a lucky or unlucky day. Every year has at least one Friday the 13th, but never more than three. Two Fridays in 2001 fall on the 13th day, in April and July. Fear of the number 13 is known as triskaidekaphobia.

GOOD EGG HUNT. Apr 13–14. Good Zoo, Oglebay, Wheeling, WV. Children receive a treasure map and Easter bucket to hold their treats. This is a non-competitive event, so children of all ages can fully participate. Est attendance: 2,000. For info: Good Zoo. Phone: (304) 243-4030. Fax: (304) 243-4110. Web: www.oglebay-resort.com.

GOOD FRIDAY. Apr 13. Observed in commemoration of the crucifixion. Oldest Christian celebration. Possible corruption of "God's Friday." Observed in some manner by most Christian sects and as a public holiday or part holiday in Canada and in Delaware, Florida, Hawaii, Illinois, Indiana, New Jersey, North Carolina, Pennsylvania and Tennessee.

GREAT CHICAGO FLOOD: ANNIVERSARY. Apr 13, 1992. On this morning Chicagoans awoke to one of the most unusual disasters of modern times: the Chicago River broke through a rupture in an old underground freight tunnel wall, sending millions of gallons of water flooding into the tunnel system beneath the downtown business district. The water began pouring into basements of buildings that previously had been con-nected to the tunnel system. The greater Loop area had to be evacuated as electricity was cut off ahead of the rising water. A hectic effort mounted to plug the leak in the river eventually succeeded. Once the flow of water had stopped, the city began the slow and expensive process of draining the water.

INDIA: BAISAKHI. Apr 13. Sikh holiday that commemorates the founding of the brotherhood of the Khalsa in 1699. A large fair is held at the Golden Temple at Amritsar, the central shrine of Sikhism. While the date may vary in different parts of India, this holiday always falls in April or May.

★**JEFFERSON, THOMAS: BIRTH ANNIVERSARY.** Apr 13. Presidential Proclamation 2276, of Mar 21, 1938, covers all succeeding years. (Pub Res No. 60 of Aug 16, 1937.)

JEFFERSON, THOMAS: BIRTH ANNIVERSARY. Apr 13, 1743. 3rd president of the US (Mar 4, 1801–Mar 3, 1809), born at Albermarle County, VA. Jefferson, who died at Charlottesville, VA, July 4, 1826, wrote his own epitaph: "Here was buried Thomas Jefferson, author of the Declaration of American Independence, of the statute of Virginia for religious freedom, and father of the University of Virginia." A holiday in Alabama and Oklahoma.

★**NATIONAL D.A.R.E. DAY.** Apr 13. The Drug Abuse Resistance Education (D.A.R.E.) Program, founded in 1983 by the Los Angeles Police Department and the Los Angeles Unified School District, helps give children in grades K–12 the skills they need to avoid involvement in drugs, gangs and violence. Nearly 75 percent of American school districts offer D.A.R.E. training.

PYRAMID FESTIVALS. Apr 13–14 (also June 9–11). Sacramento, CA. There is so much mystery about pyramid structures that are being discovered all over the world. We are in awe of these structures for the precision skills and focus of those who actually performed the work to design and build them. Let us meditate on the basic principle to accomplish any high goal. For info: Rev Margaret Allbritten, 2050 State University Dr East, PMB 182, Sacramento, CA 95819. Phone: (916) 466-8172. Fax: (916) 278-4502.

SILENT SPRING PUBLICATION: ANNIVERSARY. Apr 13, 1962. Rachel Carson's *Silent Spring* warned humankind that for the first time in history every person is subjected to contact with dangerous chemicals from conception until death. Carson painted a vivid picture of how chemicals—used in many ways but particularly in pesticides—have upset the balance of nature, undermining the survival of countless species. This enormously popular and influential book was a soft-spoken battle cry to protect our natural surroundings. Its publication signaled the beginning of the environmental movement.

SRI LANKA: SINHALA AND TAMIL NEW YEAR. April 13–14. This New Year festival includes traditional games, the wearing of new clothes in auspicious colors and special foods. Public holiday.

STOCK EXCHANGE HOLIDAY (GOOD FRIDAY). Apr 13. The holiday schedules for the various exchanges are subject to change if relevant rules, regulations or exchange policies are revised. If you have questions, phone: American Stock Exchange (212) 306-1000; Chicago Board of Trade (312) 435-3500; Chicago Board of Options Exchange (312) 786-5600; New York Stock Exchange (212) 656-2065; Pacific Stock Exchange (415) 393-4000; Philadelphia Stock Exchange (215) 496-5000.

THAILAND: SONGKRAN FESTIVAL. Apr 13–15. Public holiday. Thai water festival. To welcome the new year the image of Buddha is bathed with holy or fragrant water and lustral water is sprinkled on celebrants. Joyous event, especially observed at Buddhist temples.

UNITED KINGDOM: GOOD FRIDAY BANK HOLIDAY. Apr 13. Bank and public holiday in England, Wales, Scotland and Northern Ireland.

April *2001*	S	M	T	W	T	F	S
	1	2	3	4	5	6	7
	8	9	10	11	12	13	14
	15	16	17	18	19	20	21
	22	23	24	25	26	27	28
	29	30					

BIRTHDAYS TODAY

Peabo Bryson, 50, singer ("Just Another Day," "I Can Make It Better"), born Greenville, SC, Apr 13, 1951.

Ben Nighthorse Campbell, 68, US Senator (R, Colorado), born Auburn, CA, Apr 13, 1933.

Jack Casady, 57, musician, born Washington, DC, Apr 13, 1944.

Bill Conti, 59, composer (Oscar for *The Right Stuff*; "Falcon Crest," "Inside Edition"), born Providence, RI, Apr 13, 1942.

Tony Dow, 56, actor ("Leave It to Beaver"), born Hollywood, CA, Apr 13, 1945.

Edward Fox, 64, actor (*The Day of the Jackal, Gandhi, The Dresser*), born London, England, Apr 13, 1937.

Al Green, 55, singer ("Let's Stay Together," "You Ought to Be with Me"), born Forrest City, AR, Apr 13, 1946.

Howard Keel (Howard Leek), 82, actor (*Annie Get Your Gun, Seven Brides for Seven Brothers*), born Gillespie, IL, Apr 13, 1919.

Davis Love, III, 37, golfer, born Charlotte, NC, Apr 13, 1964.

Ron Perlman, 51, actor ("Beauty and the Beast," *The Name of the Rose*), born New York, NY, Apr 13, 1950.

Saundra Santiago, 44, actress ("Miami Vice"), born The Bronx, NY, Apr 13, 1957.

Rick Schroder, 31, actor ("Silver Spoons," "NYPD Blue," *The Champ*), born Staten Island, NY, Apr 13, 1970.

Paul Sorvino, 62, actor ("Law & Order"), born Brooklyn, NY, Apr 13, 1939.

Lyle Waggoner, 66, actor ("The Carol Burnett Show," "Wonder Woman," *Dead Women in Lingerie*), born Kansas City, KS, Apr 13, 1935.

Max M. Weinberg, 50, musician, bandleader ("Late Night with Conan O'Brien"), born South Orange, NJ, Apr 13, 1951.

Eudora Welty, 92, author (*Delta Wedding, Losing Battles*), born Jackson, MS, Apr 13, 1909.

APRIL 14 — SATURDAY
Day 104 — 261 Remaining

CAMPBELL BECOMES FIRST AMERICAN AIR ACE: ANNIVERSARY. Apr 14, 1918. Lieutenant Douglas Campbell became the first American pilot to achieve the designation of ACE when he shot down his fifth German aircraft.

CHINCOTEAGUE ISLAND EASTER DECOY SHOW. Apr 14–15. Chincoteague Island, VA. Wildfowl carving and wildlife art exhibits. Annually, Easter weekend. Est attendance: 3,200. For info: Jacklyn Russell, Chincoteague Chamber of Commerce, Box 258, Chincoteague Island, VA 23336. Phone: (757) 336-6161. Fax: (757) 336-1242. E-mail: pony@shore.intercom.net. Web: www.chincoteaguechamber.com.

CIMARRON TERRITORY CELEBRATION. Apr 14–21. Beaver, OK. Shoot-out, parade, talent show, Cow Chip Chili Cook-Off, Cow Chip Classic Races. 31st annual "World Cow Chip Throwing Championship®" Contest on Apr 20–22. Antiques, coins, guns and crafts show. Est attendance: 4,500. For info: Melodie Barnett, Secy, Beaver County Chamber of Commerce, PO Box 878, Beaver, OK 73932. Phone: (580) 625-4726.

CYPRUS: THE PROCESSION OF ICON OF SAINT LAZARUS. Apr 14. Larnaca, Cyprus. Annually, the day before the Orthodox Easter Sunday.

EASTER BUNNY BOP AND HOP. Apr 14. Aiken, SC. The Easter Bunny Bop and Hop is a noncompetitive Easter egg hunt with carnival rides and games at Virginia Acres Soccer Field. Annually, the Saturday before Easter. Est attendance: 700. For info: Easter Bunny Bop and Hop, City of Aiken Parks and Recreation, Odell Weeks Center, PO Box 1177, Aiken, SC 29803. Phone: (803) 642-7631. Fax: (803) 642-7639. E-mail: howeeks @aiken.net.

EASTER EVEN. Apr 14. The Saturday before Easter. Last day of Holy Week and of Lent.

FEAST OF THE RAMSON. Apr 14. Richwood, WV. A dinner dedicated to the ramp, a wild leek, which grows wild in the mountains. Arts and crafts; mountain song and dance. Est attendance: 2,000. For info: Richwood Area Chamber of Commerce, 50 Oakford Ave, Richwood, WV 26261. Phone: (304) 846-6790.

FIRST AMERICAN ABOLITION SOCIETY FOUNDED: ANNIVERSARY. Apr 14, 1775. The first abolition organization formed in the US was The Society for the Relief of Free Negroes Unlawfully Held in Bondage, founded at Philadelphia, PA.

FIRST DICTIONARY OF AMERICAN ENGLISH PUBLISHED: ANNIVERSARY. Apr 14, 1828. Noah Webster published his *American Dictionary of the English Language*.

GIELGUD, SIR JOHN: BIRTH ANNIVERSARY. Apr 14, 1904. Director and actor, born at London, England. He made his professional film debut in 1924 in *Who Is the Man?*. Other film credits include *Arthur, Murder on the Orient Express* and *Plenty*. He had played the role of Hamlet more than 500 times. He won the Tony Award for best director in 1961 for *Big Fish Little Fish*. He died at Buckinghamshire, England, May 21, 2000.

GRAPES OF WRATH PUBLISHED: ANNIVERSARY. Apr 14, 1939. John Steinbeck's novel of the Great Depression, *Grapes of Wrath*, won the 1940 Pulitzer Prize. It chronicled the mass migration to California of dispossessed farmers from the Dust Bowl region of the Great Plains.

GREAT EASTER EGG SCRAMBLE. Apr 14. Cincinnati, OH. Ramble to the Zoo's scramble and enjoy watching two separate egg hunts for children up to five years of age. Treat stations will be set up throughout the park for older children. Event also includes Easter Bunny photos, a puppet show and wagon rides. Est attendance: 6,000. For info: Events & Promo Dept, Cincinnati Zoo and Botanical Gardens, 3400 Vine St, Cincinnati, OH 45220. Phone: (513) 281-4701. Fax: (513) 559-7790. Web: circus.compuware.com.

GREAT EGG CAPER AT AUDUBON ACRES. Apr 14. Audubon Acres, Chattanooga, TN. Children color eggs with natural dyes, play egg games, hunt eggs along the trails and meadows of Audubon Acres, then stroll to the swinging bridge and observe the beauty of wildflowers. Sponsor: Chattanooga Audubon Society. Annually, the Saturday before Easter. Est attendance: 250. For info: Lynda Logan, Audubon Acres, 900 N Sanctuary Rd, Chattanooga, TN 37421. Phone: (423) 892-1499. Fax: (423) 892-1499. E-mail: caudubon@aol.com.

HONDURAS: DIA DE LAS AMERICAS. Apr 14. Honduras. Pan-American Day, a national holiday.

HUYGENS, CHRISTIAAN: BIRTH ANNIVERSARY. Apr 14, 1629. Scientist born at The Hague, Netherlands. He discovered the rings of Saturn and the wave or pulse theory of light. In 1656 he invented the pendulum clock. He died at The Hague, June 8, 1695.

INTERNATIONAL MOMENT OF LAUGHTER DAY. Apr 14. Laughter is a potent and powerful way to deal with the difficulties of modern living. Since the physical, emotional and spiritual benefits of laughter are widely accepted, this day is set aside for everyone to take the necessary time to experience the power of laughter. For info: Izzy Gesell, Head Honcho of Wide Angle Humor, PO Box 962, Northampton, MA 01061. Phone: (413) 586-2634. E-mail: izzy@izzyg.com. Web: www.izzyg.com.

INTERNATIONAL WILDLIFE FILM FESTIVAL. Apr 14–21. Missoula, MT. 24th annual. A juried international wildlife film festival. This eight-day gathering will involve the world's top wildlife filmmakers and producers sharing their ideas, techniques and products to interested members of the public and filmmaking profession. The festival provides films for viewing by people of all ages with special sections for children. Community celebrations such as a wildlife parade, workshops and panel discussions are also part of this annual festival. Festival venues are located at various locations in downtown Missoula. Est attendance: 12,000. For info: Randy Ammon, Exec Dir, Intl Wildlife Film Festival, 27 Fort Missoula Rd, Ste 2, Missoula, MT 59804. Phone: (406) 728-9380. Fax: (406) 728-2881. E-mail: iwff @wildlifefilms.org. Web: www.wildlifefilms.org.

JOHN WILKES BOOTH ESCAPE ROUTE TOUR. Apr 14 and 21. (also May 5 and 12, Sept 1 and 15, and Oct 6 and 13.) Clinton, MD. A 12-hour bus tour over the route used by Lincoln's assassin. Est attendance: 350. For info: Surratt House & Tavern, Box 427, Clinton, MD 20735. Phone: (301) 868-1121. Fax: (301) 868-8177. Web: www.surratt,org.

LIBERACE MUSEUM CELEBRATED. Apr 14. The Liberace Museum at Las Vegas, NV, houses "Mr Showmanship's" million-dollar stage wardrobe, rare antiques, classic cars and his collection of pianos. The museum is a key funding arm for the non-profit Liberace Foundation for the Performing and Creative Arts that provides scholarship grants for schools, colleges and universities across the nation. Annually, the Saturday nearest Apr 15. For info: Jamie G. James, James Agency, PR, 3630 Coldwater Canyon Ave, Studio City, CA 91604. Phone: (818) 508-4902. Fax: (818) 508-0562. E-mail: JJames@Liberace.org.

LINCOLN, ABRAHAM: ASSASSINATION ANNIVERSARY. Apr 14, 1865. President Abraham Lincoln was shot while watching a performance of *Our American Cousin* at Ford's Theatre, Washington, DC. He died the following day. Assassin was John Wilkes Booth, a young actor.

OUTDOOR SHOW. Apr 14–15 (tentative). Florence Event Center, Florence, OR. Features hunting and fishing demonstrations. Florence's abundant natural resources, recreational activities and related businesses, products and services are showcased. For info: Florence Event Center, 715 Quince St, Florence, OR 97439. Phone: (888) 968-4086. E-mail: mary@eventcenter.org. Web: www.eventcenter.org.

★**PAN AMERICAN DAY.** Apr 14. Presidential Proclamation 1912, of May 28, 1930, covers every Apr 14 (required by Governing Board of Pan American Union). Proclamation issued each year since 1948. Commemorates the first International Conference of American States in 1890.

PAN-AMERICAN DAY IN FLORIDA. Apr 14. A ceremonial day in Florida which is observed in the public schools as a day honoring the republics of Latin America. When Apr 14 does not fall on a school day, the Governor may designate the preceding Friday or the following Monday as Pan-American Day.

REMEMBRANCE DAY. Apr 14. A special day to remember a loved one who has died. A way to say "I still love you; I have not forgotten" by planting a tree, performing community service, saying a prayer, etc. Send an LSASE for info. Annually, the Saturday before Easter. For info: Chaplain Mike Miller, Happy Days Ministries, 35 Hilcreek Blvd, Charleston, SC 29412.

SEA LION SUDS FEST. Apr 14. Curry County Fairgrounds, Gold Beach, OR. Celebration of Oregon's micro-brewed suds with a slew of beers to sample. Fun games, craft booths, food from pizza to seafood and live music and dancing. Est attendance: 500. For info: Gold Beach Chamber of Commerce, 29279 S Ellensburg Ave, #3, Gold Beach, OR 97444. Phone: (800) 525-2334. Fax: (541) 247-0188. E-mail: goldbeach@harborside.com. Web: www.harborside.com/gb.

April 2001	S	M	T	W	T	F	S
	1	2	3	4	5	6	7
	8	9	10	11	12	13	14
	15	16	17	18	19	20	21
	22	23	24	25	26	27	28
	29	30					

STRAWBERRY HILL RACES. Apr 14. Fairgrounds on Strawberry Hill, Richmond, VA. Annual steeplechase featuring a week of festivities leading up to the event. Elegant, yet fun, pre-race party and tailgate competition on race day. $58,000 in purses. Sponsored by Atlantic Rural Exposition, Inc. Est attendance: 22,000. For info: Sue Mullins, Equine Dir, Strawberry Hill Races, PO Box 26805, Richmond, VA 23261. Phone: (804) 569-3238. Fax: (804) 569-3252. E-mail: equine@freeevents.com.

SULLIVAN, ANNE: BIRTH ANNIVERSARY. Apr 14, 1866. Anne Sullivan, born at Feeding Hills, MA, became well known for "working miracles" with Helen Keller, who was blind and deaf. Nearly blind herself, Sullivan used a manual alphabet communicated by the sense of touch to teach Keller to read, write and speak and then to help her go on to higher education. Anne Sullivan died Oct 20, 1936, at Forest Hills, NY.

TAFT OPENED BASEBALL SEASON: ANNIVERSARY. Apr 14, 1910. President William Howard Taft began a sports tradition by throwing out the first baseball of the season at an American League game between Washington and Philadelphia. Washington won 3–0.

TEXAS COASTAL BIRDING CELEBRATION AND COMPETITION. Apr 14–26. Kingsville, TX. For info: Kingsville CVB, 1501 N Hwy 77, Kingsville, TX 78363. Phone: (800) 333-5032. Fax: (361) 592-3227. Web: www.kingsvilletexas.com.

TOYNBEE, ARNOLD JOSEPH: BIRTH ANNIVERSARY. Apr 14, 1889. English historian, author of monumental *Study of History*. Born at London, England; died at York, England, Oct 22, 1975.

WICHITA WEST SPRING ARTS AND CRAFTS SHOW. Apr 14–15. Wichita Falls, TX. Artist/craftsmen from the area display and sell their quality arts and crafts. Free admission to the public. Est attendance: 2,500. For info: Wichita Falls CVB, 1000 5th St, Wichita Falls, TX 76301. Phone: (940) 716-5500 or (940) 691-2738. Fax: (940) 716-5509. E-mail: MPEC@wf.net. Web: www.viewscape.com or www.wf.net.

BIRTHDAYS TODAY

Julie Christie, 61, actress (*Dr. Zhivago, Petulia, Shampoo*), born Chukua, India, Apr 14, 1940.

Cynthia Cooper, 38, basketball player, born Chicago, IL, Apr 14, 1963.

Bradford Dillman, 71, actor (*Compulsion,* "Falcon Crest"), born San Francisco, CA, Apr 14, 1930.

Brad Garrett, 41, comedian, actor ("Everybody Loves Raymond"), born Woodland Hills, CA, Apr 14, 1960.

Sarah Michelle Gellar, 24, actress (*I Know What You Did Last Summer,* "Buffy the Vampire Slayer"), born New York, NY, Apr 14, 1977.

Anthony Michael Hall, 33, actor, comedian ("Saturday Night Live," *Sixteen Candles, The Breakfast Club*), born Boston, MA, Apr 14, 1968.

David Christopher Justice, 35, baseball player, born Cincinnati, OH, Apr 14, 1966.

Loretta Lynn, 66, singer/songwriter ("Coal Miner's Daughter," "The Pill"), born Butcher's Hollow, KY, Apr 14, 1935.

Gregory Alan (Greg) Maddux, 35, baseball player, born San Angelo, TX, Apr 14, 1966.

Peter Edward (Pete) Rose, 60, former baseball manager and player, born Cincinnati, OH, Apr 14, 1941.

Rod Steiger, 76, actor (*On the Waterfront, The Pawnbroker*; Oscar for *In the Heat of the Night*), born Westhampton, NY, Apr 14, 1925.

Emma Thompson, 42, actress (*Howard's End, Sense and Sensibility*), born London, England, Apr 14, 1959.

APRIL 15 — SUNDAY
Day 105 — 260 Remaining

ASTRONOMERS FIND NEW SOLAR SYSTEM: ANNIVERSARY. Apr 15, 1999. Astronomers from San Francisco State University working at an observatory in Arizona announced the discovery of the first multi-planet system ever found orbiting around a star other than our own. Three planets orbit the star Upsilon Andromedae, which can be seen with the naked eye. This suggests that the Milky Way probably teems with similar planetary systems.

AVOCADO FESTIVAL. Apr 15. Fallbrook, CA. Annually, the third Sunday in April. For info: Michelle Spelman, Communications Mgr, California Avocado Commission. Phone: (800) 344-4333. Web: www.avocado.org.

BENTON, THOMAS HART: BIRTH ANNIVERSARY. Apr 15, 1889. Thomas Hart Benton was an artist whose work was indicative of the American style of painting known as Regionalism. His works of life in the Midwest and South were not always flattering to their subjects, but his style became known as a truly American style of painting. He was born at Neosho, MO, and died at Kansas City, MO, Jan 19, 1975.

"BUCK ROGERS" TV PREMIERE: ANNIVERSARY. Apr 15, 1950. At first a radio show, "Buck Rogers" premiered on ABC with Kem Dibbs. Buck was an average American who woke up from a cave behind Niagara Falls to find himself in the year 2430. The show featured Lou Prentis as Lieutenant Wilma Deering; Harry Sothern as Dr. Huer and Harry Kingston as Black Barney Wade. Buck was later played by Robert Pastene.

CHINA: CANTON SPRING TRADE FAIR. Apr 15–May 15. The Guangzhou (Canton) Spring Trade Fair is held on the same dates each year.

EASTER PARADE. Apr 15. Atlantic City, NJ. Awards presented for best bonnet and best-dressed woman, couple, gentleman, senior citizen, girl and boy. Annually, Easter Sunday. Est attendance: 8,000. For info: Greater Atlantic City Conv and Visitors Authority, 2314 Pacific Ave, Atlantic City, NJ 08401. Phone: (609) 449-7130.

EASTER SUNDAY. Apr 15. Commemorates the Resurrection of Christ. Most joyous festival of the Christian year. The date of Easter, a movable feast, is derived from the lunar calendar: the first Sunday following the first ecclesiastical full moon on or after Mar 21—always between Mar 22 and Apr 25. The Council of Nicaea (AD 325) prescribed that Easter be celebrated on the Sunday after Passover, as that feast's date had been established in Jesus' time. After 1582, when Pope Gregory XIII introduced the Gregorian calendar, Orthodox Christians continued to use the Julian calendar, so Easter can sometimes be as much as five weeks apart in the Western and Eastern churches. However, this year Easter falls on the same date for both churches. Easter in 2002 will be Mar 31; in 2003 will be Apr 20; in 2004 will be Apr 11. Many other dates in the Christian year are derived from the date of Easter. See also: "Orthodox Easter Sunday or Pascha."

EASTER SUNRISE SERVICE. Apr 15. Chimney Rock Park, Chimney Rock, NC. Celebrate the glory of Easter at this 46th annual nondenominational community worship service overlooking beautiful Lake Lure. Gates open at 4:30 AM. No admission charge. Est attendance: 1,500. For info: Mary R. Ritter, PR, PO Box 39, Chimney Rock, NC 28720. Phone: (800) 277-9611 or (828) 625-9611. Fax: (828) 625-9610. E-mail: visit @chimneyrockpark.com. Web: www.chimneyrockpark.com.

FIRST MCDONALD'S OPENS: ANNIVERSARY. Apr 15, 1955. The first franchised McDonald's was opened at Des Plaines, IL, by Ray Kroc, who had gotten the idea from a hamburger joint at San Bernardino, CA, run by the McDonald brothers. On opening day a hamburger was 15 cents. The Big Mac was introduced in 1968 for 49 cents and the Quarter Pounder in 1971 for 53 cents. By the late 1990s, there were more than 25,000 McDonald's in 115 countries.

FIRST SCHOOL FOR DEAF FOUNDED: ANNIVERSARY. Apr 15, 1817. Thomas Hopkins Gallaudet and Laurent Clerc founded the first US public school for the deaf, Connecticut Asylum for the Education and Instruction of Deaf and Dumb Persons (now the American School for the Deaf), at Hartford, CT.

GOLDEN BUNNY EGG HUNT AND RACE. Apr 15. Winter Park Resort, Winter Park, CO. Winter Park Willie and the Easter Bunny give kids some holiday fun with an on-mountain egg hunt and traditional fun race for children 10 and under. Est attendance: 500. For info: Winter Park Resort, PO Box 36, Winter Park, CO 80482. Phone: (970) 726-1580. Fax: (970) 726-1572. E-mail: wpinfo@mail.skiwinterpark.com. Web: winterparkresort.com.

GRANGE WEEK. Apr 15–21. State and local recognition for Grange's contribution to rural/urban America. Celebrated at National Headquarters at Washington, DC, and in all states with local, county and state Granges. Begun in 1867, the National Grange is the oldest US rural community service, family-oriented organization with a special interest in agriculture. Annually, the third full week in April. For info: Kermit W. Richardson, Natl Master, The Natl Grange, 1616 H St NW, Washington, DC 20006. Phone: (202) 628-3507 or (888) 4-Grange. Fax: (202) 347-1091. Web: www.nationalgrange.org.

"IN LIVING COLOR" TV PREMIERE: ANNIVERSARY. Apr 15, 1990. Fox's sketch comedy series was modeled after "Saturday Night Live." The show was created by Keenen Ivory Wayans. Between skits, the Fly Girls would entertain the studio audience with hip dances (actress Rosie Perez choreographed the dances before breaking into movies). The show featured Wayans, his brothers Damon, Marlon and Shawn, his sister Kim, Tommy Davidson, David Alan Grier, T'Keyah "Crystal" Keymáh, Kelly Coffield, Kim Coles and Jim Carrey before he was Ace Ventura. Some of the most popular recurring characters were Homey, the embittered clown, the flammable Fire Marshall Bill and the effeminate movie critics of "Men on Film."

INCOME TAX PAY DAY—BUT NOT THIS YEAR. Apr 15. A day all Americans need to know—the day by which taxpayers are supposed to make their accounting of the previous year and pay their share of the cost of government. The US Internal Revenue Service provides free forms. But since Apr 15 is a Sunday in 2001, the deadline is extended to Apr 16.

ITALY: EXPLOSION OF THE CART. Apr 15. Florence. At noon on Easter Sunday in Piazza del Duomo a cart full of fireworks is exploded, perpetuating a ceremony of ancient origin and recalling the fire that used to be kindled during the *Gloria* at Easter mass, and was then distributed to all of Florence's households. The tradition is held to date back to the time of the First Crusade, when the valorous Pazzino dei Pazzi was awarded some pieces of flint from the Holy Sepulcher. After his return to Florence the holy fire was kindled with these flints, now preserved in the church of Santi Apostoli.

JAMES, HENRY: BIRTH ANNIVERSARY. Apr 15, 1843. Novelist and critic, born at New York, NY. Among his best-known works are *The Portrait of a Lady, Washington Square* and *The Ambassadors.* James died Feb 28, 1916, at London, England.

MARKSVILLE EASTER EGG KNOCKING CONTEST. Apr 15. Marksville, LA. Competition among owners of chicken and guinea eggs which have been boiled and dyed. Annually, on Easter Sunday 9 AM–noon. Est attendance: 300. For info: Chamber of Commerce, Box 767, Marksville, LA 71351. Phone: (318) 253-9222 or (318) 253-0284.

MERRIE MONARCH FESTIVAL (WITH WORLD'S LARGEST HULA COMPETITION). Apr 15–21. Hilo, HI. Cultural event honoring King David Kalakaua. Festival culminates with the world's largest hula competition. Hawaii's finest hula schools compete in ancient and modern divisions. Annually, beginning on Easter Sunday. Est attendance: 6,000. For info: Dorothy Thompson, Hawaii Naniloa Hotel, Merrie Monarch Office, 93 Banyan Dr, Hilo, HI 96720. Phone: (808) 935-9168.

MOON PHASE: LAST QUARTER. Apr 15. Moon enters Last Quarter phase at 11:31AM, EDT.

MORAVIAN EASTER RESURRECTION SERVICE. Apr 15. Winston-Salem, NC. Outdoor religious service featuring Moravian bands playing in streets to awaken sleepers. Service begins in Salem Square, and concludes in God's Acre, the Moravian Graveyard, at daybreak. Est attendance: 12,500. For info: Salem Congregation, 459 S Church St, Winston-Salem, NC 27101-5314. Phone: (336) 722-6504 ext 1006. Fax: (336) 723-1222. E-mail: jlineberger@mcsp.org.

NATIONAL COIN WEEK. Apr 15–21. To promote the history and lore of numismatics and the hobby of coin collecting. For info: Gail Baker, Dir of Educ, American Numismatic Assn, 818 N Cascade Ave, Colorado Springs, CO 80903. Phone: (719) 632-2646 or (800) 367-9723. Fax: (719) 634-4085. E-mail: anaedu@money.org. Web: www.money.org.

NATIONAL INFANT IMMUNIZATION WEEK. Apr 15–21. The level of eight vaccine-preventable diseases has dropped 97 percent since the introduction of vaccines. The US goal is to immunize at least 90 percent of children under the age of two. Promotion kits are available. For info: Centers for Disease Control and Prevention, 1600 Clifton RD NE, Atlanta, GA 30333. Phone: (404) 639-8375. Web: www.cdc.gov/nip/publications.niiw.

NATIONAL ORGAN AND TISSUE DONOR AWARENESS WEEK. Apr 15–21. To encourage Americans to consider organ and tissue donation and to sign donor cards when getting a driver's license. For info: Ellie Schlam, Natl Kidney Foundation, 30 E 33rd St, New York, NY 10016. Phone: (800) 622-9010 or (212) 889-2210. Web: www.kidney.org or www.organdonor.gov.

ORTHODOX EASTER SUNDAY OR PASCHA. Apr 15. Observed by Eastern Orthodox Churches on this date. Normally Easter falls on different Sundays in the Eastern and Western churches; however, this year Easter is on the same date in both. See also: "Easter Sunday" (Apr 15).

PEALE, CHARLES WILLSON: BIRTH ANNIVERSARY. Apr 15, 1741 (OS). American portrait painter (best known for his many portraits of colonial and American Revolutionary War figures) was born at Queen Anne County, MD. His children Raphael, Rembrandt, Titian and Sarah were also artists. Died at Philadelphia, PA, Feb 22, 1827.

	S	M	T	W	T	F	S
April	1	2	3	4	5	6	7
2001	8	9	10	11	12	13	14
	15	16	17	18	19	20	21
	22	23	24	25	26	27	28
	29	30					

READING IS FUN WEEK. Apr 15–21. To highlight the importance and fun of reading. Annually, the last full week of April. For info: Jill S. Colby, CMP, Special Events and Conference Coord, Reading Is Fundamental, Inc, 1825 Connecticut Ave NW, Ste 400, Washington, DC 20009. Phone: (202) 673-1613. Fax: (202) 287-3196. E-mail: jcolby@rif.org. Web: www.rif.org.

SIMMS, HILDA: BIRTH ANNIVERSARY. Apr 15, 1920. American stage and film actress born Hilda Moses at Minneapolis, MN. She joined the American Negro Theater at Harlem, NY, in 1943 and was given the title role in *Anna Lucasta.* When the production moved to Broadway in 1944, it became the first all-black production to be performed on Broadway without a racial theme. Simms was the creative arts director of New York State's human rights division, through which she was instrumental in bringing discrimination against black actors to public attention during the 1960s. She died at Buffalo, NY, Feb 6, 1994.

SINKING OF THE *TITANIC*: ANNIVERSARY. Apr 15, 1912. The "unsinkable" luxury liner *Titanic* on its maiden voyage from Southampton, England, to New York, NY, struck an iceberg just before midnight Apr 14, and sank at 2:27 AM, Apr 15. The *Titanic* had 2,224 persons aboard. Of these, more than 1,500 were lost. About 700 people were rescued from the icy waters off Newfoundland by the liner *Carpathia,* which reached the scene about two hours after the *Titanic* went down. The sunken *Titanic* was located and photographed in September 1985. In July 1986 an expedition aboard the *Atlantis II* descended to the deck of the *Titanic* in a submersible craft, *Alvin,* and guided a robot named Jason, Jr in a search of the ship. Two memorial bronze plaques were left on the deck of the sunken ship.

SMITH, BESSIE: BIRTH ANNIVERSARY. Apr 15, 1894. The "Empress of the Blues," Bessie Smith, was born at Chattanooga, TN (year varies as late as 1900). She was assisted in her efforts to break into show business by Ma Rainey, the first great blues singer. Her first recording was made in February 1923. Smith died of injuries she sustained in an automobile accident at Clarksdale, MS, Sept 26, 1937.

WASHINGTON, HAROLD: BIRTH ANNIVERSARY. Apr 15, 1922. Illinois legislator and Mayor of Chicago (1983–87). Born at Chicago, IL, and died there Nov 25, 1987. Harold Washington was one of the first African-Americans to head a major US city. He was instrumental in tearing down Chicago's famed Democratic machine, a holdover from the many decades of domination by the Richard J. Daley administration.

WORLD'S LARGEST EASTER EGG HUNT. Apr 15. Garrison Homes, Homer, GA. Approximately 150,000 hidden eggs and 100 prize eggs. Begins at 2 PM. Free and open to all—no age limit. Est attendance: 10,000. For info: Banks County Chamber of Commerce, PO Box 57, Homer, GA 30547. Phone: (706) 677-2108 or (800) 638-5004.

★**NATIONAL ORGAN AND TISSUE DONOR AWARENESS WEEK.** Apr 15–21.

BIRTHDAYS TODAY

Evelyn Ashford, 44, Olympic gold medal track athlete, born Shreveport, LA, Apr 15, 1957.

Linda Bloodworth-Thomason, 54, producer, writer ("Designing Women," "Evening Shade"), born Poplar Bluff, MO, Apr 15, 1947.

Claudia Cardinale, 63, actress (*The Pink Panther, Once Upon a Time in the West*), born Tunis, Italy, Apr 15, 1938.

Roy Clark, 68, singer and guitarist ("Yesterday, When I Was Young," regular on "Hee Haw"), born Meherrin, VA, Apr 15, 1933.

Heloise Cruse Evans, 50, newspaper columnist ("Hints from Heloise"), born Waco, TX, Apr 15, 1951.

Jason Sehorn, 30, football player, born Mt Shasta, CA, Apr 15, 1971.

Amy Wright, 51, actress (*Breaking Away, Wise Blood, The Accidental Tourist*), born Chicago, IL, Apr 15, 1950.

APRIL 16 — MONDAY
Day 106 — 259 Remaining

AMIS, KINGSLEY: BIRTH ANNIVERSARY. Apr 16, 1922. Author (*The Crime of the Century, Lucky Jim*), born at London, England, and died there Oct 22, 1995.

BOSTON MARATHON—105th RUNNING. Apr 16. Boston, MA. The marathon begins in the rural New England town of Hopkinton, winds through eight cities and towns and finishes near downtown Boston. 2001 will be the 105th year of this historic running event. 15,000 participants. Est attendance: 2,000,000. For info: Boston Athletic Assn, Boston Marathon, One Ash St, Hopkinton, MA 01748-1897. Phone: (508) 435-6905. E-mail: mile27@star.net. Web: www.baa.org.

CHAPLIN, CHARLES SPENCER: BIRTH ANNIVERSARY. Apr 16, 1889. Celebrated film comedian who portrayed "The Little Tramp" was born at London, England. Film debut in 1914. Knighted in 1975. Died at Vevey, Switzerland, Dec 25, 1977. In his autobiography Chaplin wrote: "There are more valid facts and details in works of art than there are in history books."

CONSUMER AWARENESS WEEK. Apr 16–20. Consumer advocate Bob O'Brien kicks off a weeklong event aimed at advising and helping consumers with their rights. For info: Bob O'Brien, Consumer Advocate, PO Box 2356, Secaucus, NJ 07096. Phone: (201) 860-1595. Fax: (201) 865-4775. E-mail: bob consumeradvocate@excite.com. Web: www.consumeradvocate obrien.com.

DENMARK: QUEEN MARGRETHE'S BIRTHDAY. Apr 16. Thousands of children gather to cheer the queen at Amalienborg Palace and the Royal Guard wears scarlet gala uniforms.

DIEGO, JOSE de: BIRTH ANNIVERSARY. Apr 16, 1866. Puerto Rican patriot and political leader Jose de Diego was born at Aguadilla, PR. His birthday is a holiday in Puerto Rico. He died July 16, 1918, at New York, NY.

EASTER MONDAY. Apr 16. Holiday or bank holiday in many places, including England, Northern Ireland, Wales, Canada and North Carolina in the US.

EGG SALAD WEEK. Apr 16–22. Dedicated to the many delicious uses for all of the Easter eggs that have been cooked, colored, hidden and found. Annually, the full week after Easter. For info: Linda Braun, Consumer Serv Dir, American Egg Bd, 1460 Renaissance Dr, Park Ridge, IL 60068. Web: www.aeb.org.

ENGLAND: HALLATON BOTTLE KICKING. Apr 16. Hallaton, Leicestershire. Ancient custom dating back at least 600 years. Annually, Easter Monday.

EXPLORE YOUR CAREER OPTIONS WEEK. Apr 16–22. Maybe you're aspiring to a new career or merely interested in more opportunities in your present career. Get a fresh start by taking stock of all available options. For info: Dorothy Zjawin, Dir, 61 W Colfax Ave, Roselle Park, NJ 07204. Phone: (908) 241-6241. Fax: (908) 241-6241.

FAMILIES LAUGHING THROUGH STORIES WEEK. Aug 16–22. Free through its website, or for a fee for mailed packets, Teachable Moments distributes educational information to family-oriented and storytelling agencies and organizations, teaching them how to encourage instruction that will enhance the telling of humorous family stories. This activity not only promotes the art of storytelling, but also leaves lasting, laughing memories for family participants. For info: Shirley Trout, Teachable Moments, PO Box 359, Waverly, NE 68462. Phone: (402) 786-3100. Fax: (402) 788-2131. E-mail: strout@teachable moments.com. Web: www.teachablemoments.com.

INCOME TAX PAY-DAY: THIS IS REALLY IT. Apr 16. Taxpayers get a temporary reprieve this year. Since Apr 15 fell on a Sunday, we all have had an extra day to procrastinate. But now it's time to face the music and pay the piper—get those returns in the mail by midnight!

LUXEMBOURG: EMAISHEN. Apr 16. Luxembourg (city). Popular traditional market and festival at the "Marche-aux-Poissons." Young lovers present each other with earthenware articles, sold only on this day. Annually, Easter Monday.

MANCINI, HENRY: BIRTH ANNIVERSARY. Apr 16, 1924. Born at Cleveland, OH, Mancini made his mark in Hollywood composing film scores and songs. He won 20 Grammy Awards and four Oscars (song "Moon River" and score for *Breakfast at Tiffany's*; song "Days of Wine and Roses" for the film; score for *Victor/Victoria*). He also composed *The Pink Panther*, "Peter Gunn" and "Mr Lucky" themes. Died June 14, 1994, at Beverly Hills, CA.

MASIH, IQBAL: DEATH ANNIVERSARY. Apr 16, 1995. Twelve-year-old Iqbal Masih, born at Pakistan in 1982, who reportedly had received death threats after speaking out against Pakistan's child labor practices, was shot to death, at Muridke Village, Punjab Province. Masih, who was sold into labor as a carpet weaver at the age of four, spent the next six years of his life shackled to a loom. He began speaking out against child labor after escaping from servitude at the age of 10. In November 1994 he spoke at an international labor conference in Sweden and he received a $15,000 Reebok Youth in Action Award a month later. There were reports after the shooting that Masih's death was arranged by a "carpet mafia."

★**NATIONAL CRIME VICTIMS' RIGHTS WEEK.** Apr 16–22.

★**NATIONAL ORGAN AND TISSUE DONOR AWARENESS WEEK.** Apr 16–22.

NATIONAL ORGANIZE YOUR FILES WEEK. Aug 16–22. To provide a week (after tax season and in conjunction with spring cleaning) for corporations, offices and home offices to annually review and organize their files and file systems. From purging, reorganizing and creating new systems to upgrading files and tabbing—creating more effective files will save time and money for every business, not to mention alleviate the frustration of not being able to retrieve files in a timely manner. Annually, third full week of April. For info: Gloria Schaaf, The Schaaf Organization, LLC, Gracie Station, PO Box 1166, New York, NY 10028. Phone: (212) 410-4937.

NATURAL BRIDGES NATIONAL MONUMENT: ANNIVERSARY. Apr 16, 1908. Utah. Natural Bridges National Monument was established on this date.

PATRIOT'S DAY IN MASSACHUSETTS AND MAINE. Apr 16. Commemorates Battles of Lexington and Concord, 1775. Annually, the third Monday in April.

QUARTERLY ESTIMATED FEDERAL INCOME TAX PAYERS' DUE DATE. Apr 16. For those individuals whose fiscal year is the calendar year and who make quarterly estimated federal income tax payments, today is one of the due dates (Jan 15, Apr 16, June 15 and Sept 17, 2001). Because April 15 is a Sunday, taxpayers have until Monday, Apr 16, to make their payment.

SELENA: BIRTH ANNIVERSARY. Apr 16, 1971. Tejana singer, born Selena Quintanilla at Lake Jackson, TX. Died Mar 31, 1995, at Corpus Christi, TX, murdered by the president of her fan club.

SLAVERY ABOLISHED IN DISTRICT OF COLUMBIA: ANNIVERSARY. Apr 16, 1862. Congress abolished slavery in the District of Columbia. One million dollars was appropriated to compensate owners of freed slaves, and $100,000 was set aside to pay district slaves who wished to emigrate to Haiti, Liberia or any other country outside the US.

SLOANE, HANS: BIRTH ANNIVERSARY. Apr 16, 1660. British medical doctor and naturalist whose personal collection became the nucleus of the British Museum, born at County Down, Ireland. Upon his death at Chelsea, England, Jan 11, 1753, his collections of books, manuscripts, medals and antiquities were bequeathed to Britain and accepted by an act of Parliament that incorporated the British Museum. It was opened to the public at London, England, Jan 15, 1759. It is the national museum of the United Kingdom.

SOUTH AFRICA: FAMILY DAY. Apr 16. National holiday. Annually, Easter Monday.

SPACE MILESTONE: *APOLLO 16* (US). Apr 16, 1972. Astronauts John W. Young, Charles M. Duke, Jr and Thomas K. Mattingly II (command module pilot) began an 11-day mission that included 71-hour exploration of moon (Apr 20–23). Landing module (LM) named *Orion*. Splashdown in Pacific Ocean within a mile of target, Apr 27.

SWITZERLAND: EGG RACES. Apr 16. Rural northwest Swiss Easter Monday custom. Race among competitors carrying large numbers of eggs while running to neighboring villages.

SYNGE, JOHN MILLINGTON: BIRTH ANNIVERSARY. Apr 16, 1871. Irish dramatist and poet, most of whose plays were written in the brief span of six years before his death at age 37 of lymphatic sarcoma. His best-known work was *The Playboy of the Western World* (1907), which caused protests and rioting at early performances. Synge (pronounced "Sing") was born near Dublin, Ireland, and died there Mar 24, 1909.

UNITED KINGDOM: EASTER MONDAY BANK HOLIDAY. Apr 16. Bank and public holiday in England, Wales and Northern Ireland. (Scotland not included.)

WHITE HOUSE EASTER EGG ROLL. Apr 16. Traditionally held at executive mansion's south lawn on Easter Monday. Custom said to have started at Capitol grounds about 1810. Transferred to White House lawn in 1870s.

WRIGHT, WILBUR: BIRTH ANNIVERSARY. Apr 16, 1867. Aviation pioneer born at Millville, IN. Died at Dayton, OH, May 30, 1912. See also: "Wright Brothers First Powered Flight" (Dec 17).

YOUNG PEOPLE'S POETRY WEEK. Apr 16–22. An annual event, sponsored by The Children's Book Council, that highlights poetry for children and young adults and encourages everyone to celebrate poetry—read it, enjoy it, write it—in their homes, child-care centers, classrooms, libraries and bookstores. The CBC is coordinating its promotional efforts with the Academy of American Poets, the sponsor of National Poetry Month in April, and The Center for the Book in the Library of Congress. For info: JoAnn Sabatino-Falkenstein, The Children's Book Council, PO Box 2640/JAF Station, New York, NY 10116-2640. Phone: (800) 999-2160. Fax: (888) 807-9355. E-mail: joanncbc@aol.com. Web: www.cbcbooks.org.

April *2001*	S	M	T	W	T	F	S
	1	2	3	4	5	6	7
	8	9	10	11	12	13	14
	15	16	17	18	19	20	21
	22	23	24	25	26	27	28
	29	30					

BIRTHDAYS TODAY

Kareem Abdul-Jabbar, 54, Basketball Hall of Fame center, born Lewis Ferdinand Alcindor, Jr, New York, NY, Apr 16, 1947.
Edie Adams (Elizabeth Edith Enke), 70, singer, actress, born Kingston, PA, Apr 16, 1931.
Ellen Barkin, 46, actress (*Tender Mercies, Diner*), born New York, NY, Apr 16, 1955.
Jon Cryer, 36, actor ("Partners," *Pretty in Pink, Hot Shots!*), born New York, NY, Apr 16, 1965.
Merce Cunningham, 82, dancer, choreographer, born Centralia, WA, Apr 16, 1919.
Lukas Haas, 25, actor (*Witness, Rambling Rose*), born West Hollywood, CA, Apr 16, 1976.
Martin Lawrence, 36, actor ("Martin," *Bad Boys*), born Frankfurt, Germany, Apr 16, 1965.
Barry Nelson, 78, actor (*Pete 'n Tillie, The Shining*), born San Francisco, CA, Apr 16, 1920.
Jay O. Sanders, 48, actor ("Crime Story," *Tucker: The Man and His Dream*), born Austin, TX, Apr 16, 1953.
Peter Ustinov, 80, actor (Oscars for *Spartacus, Topkapi*), born London, England, Apr 16, 1921.
Bobby Vinton, 66, singer ("Mr Lonely," "Roses Are Red [My Love]"), born Canonsburg, PA, Apr 16, 1935.

APRIL 17 — TUESDAY
Day 107 — 258 Remaining

AMERICAN SAMOA: FLAG DAY: ANNIVERSARY. Apr 17. National holiday commemorating first raising of American flag in what was formerly Eastern Samoa in 1900. Public holiday with singing, dancing, costumes and parades.

ANSON, CAP: BIRTH ANNIVERSARY. Apr 17, 1852. Adrian Constantine ("Cap") Anson, Baseball Hall of Fame player and manager, born at Marshalltown, IA. Anson played professional baseball from 1871 through 1897 and is considered one of the game's greatest first basemen. As a manager, he piloted the Chicago White Stockings (today's Cubs) to five National League pennants and a .575 winning percentage. Inducted into the Hall of Fame in 1939. Died at Chicago, IL, Apr 18, 1922.

BAY OF PIGS INVASION LAUNCHED: 40th ANNIVERSARY. Apr 17, 1961. More than 1,500 Cuban exiles invaded Cuba in an ill-fated attempt to overthrow Fidel Castro.

BLAH BLAH BLAH DAY. Apr 17. Today's the day to do any of the following, or whatever. Stop smoking, take out the trash, empty the cat litter, lose weight, pick up your clothes, put dirty dishes in the sink, get a job or quit your job. Annually, Apr 17. © 2000 WH. For info: Thomas and Ruth Roy, Wellcat Holidays, 2418 Long Ln, Lebanon, PA 17046. Phone: (717) 279-0184. E-mail: wellcat@supernet.com. Web: www.wellcat.com.

CAMBODIA FALLS TO THE KHMER ROUGE: ANNIVERSARY. Apr 17, 1975. Cambodia fell when its capital, Phnom Penh, was captured by the Khmer Rouge. The Pol Pot regime inaugurated "Year One," and the wholesale slaughter of intellectuals, political enemies and peasants began. As many as two million Cambodians perished. See also: "Pol Pot Overthrown: Anniversary" (Jan 7).

CHASE, SAMUEL: BIRTH ANNIVERSARY. Apr 17, 1741. Signer of the Declaration of Independence. Born at Somerset County, MD, he died June 19, 1811.

DOW-JONES TOPS 3,000: 10th ANNIVERSARY. Apr 17, 1991. The Dow-Jones Index of 30 major industrial stocks topped the 3,000 mark for the first time.

"THE FRED WARING SHOW" TV PREMIERE: ANNIVERSARY. Apr 17, 1949. Fred Waring was leader of the big band called the Pennsylvanians, which featured about 65 musicians and singers. The show aired on Sunday nights until 1954.

HOLDEN, WILLIAM: BIRTH ANNIVERSARY. Apr 17, 1918. William Holden's first starring role was in *Golden Boy*. The actor, born at O'Fallon, IL, won an Oscar for his role in *Stalag 17* in 1953. He was found dead at Los Angeles, CA, Nov 16, 1981.

MORGAN, JOHN PIERPONT: BIRTH ANNIVERSARY. Apr 17, 1837. American financier and corporation director born at Hartford, CT, Morgan died Mar 31, 1913, at Rome, Italy, leaving an estate valued at more than $70 million.

NATIONAL CATHOLIC EDUCATIONAL ASSOCIATION CONVENTION AND EXPOSITION. Apr 17–20. Midwest Express Center, Milwaukee, WI. Annual meeting for NCEA members and anyone working in, or interested in, the welfare of Catholic education. Est attendance: 10,000. For info: Sue Arvo, Conv Dir, Natl Catholic Educational Assn, 1077 30th St NW, Ste 100, Washington, DC 20007. Phone: (202) 337-6232. Fax: (202) 333-6706.

★**NATIONAL PARK WEEK.** Apr 17–23.

NATIONAL POSITIVE ALTERNATIVES FOR LIVING DAY. Apr 17. Each of us makes choices in our lives daily that can affect the overall happiness of ourselves and those around us. Today is a chance to make positive choices for life, such as choosing to live, not to smoke, respect others or doing something to help another. Make a positive choice today! Special programs available for youth organizations and schools, motivational presentations and media interviews. For info: Rhonda Patras, The Respect Lady, Empowering U™, 724 Irving Ave NW, Elk River, MN 55330. Phone: (763) 441-0197. Fax: (413) 208-4145. E-mail: info@empoweringu.net. Web: www.empoweringu.net.

NATIONAL STRESS AWARENESS DAY. Apr 17. To focus public awareness on one of the leading health problems in the world today. Health-related organizations throughout the country are encouraged to sponsor stress education programs and events. Annually, the first day after income taxes due. For info: Morton C. Orman, MD, Dir, The Health Resource Network, 2936 E Baltimore St, Baltimore, MD 21224. Phone: (410) 732-1900. Web: www.stresscure.com.

NEEDHAM, THERESA: BIRTH ANNIVERSARY. Apr 17, 1912. Owner of Chicago's legendary South Side blues bar, Theresa's Lounge, Theresa Needham was born at Meridian, MS. Especially memorable at the bar were "Blue Monday" all-day jams at which the city's top blues performers locked horns in musical battles. Needham, who was bartender, bouncer and talent agent, came to be known as "the Godmother of Chicago Blues." Died at Chicago, IL, Oct 16, 1992.

NETHERLANDS AND SCILLY ISLES PEACE: 15th ANNIVERSARY. Apr 17, 1986. The 335-year "state of war" that had existed between the Netherlands and the Scilly Isles came to an end on this date when Dutch ambassador Jonkheer Huydecoper flew to the Scilly Isles to deliver a proclamation terminating the war that had started in 1651. Though hostilities had ceased three centuries earlier, a standing joke in the islands was that no one had bothered to declare an end to the war.

REASONER, HARRY: BIRTH ANNIVERSARY. Apr 17, 1923. American television journalist Harry Reasoner was born at Dakota City, IA. In 1956 Reasoner joined CBS News, where he anchored the "CBS Sunday News" (1963–70) and was one of the two original anchors, along with Mike Wallace, of the news magazine show "60 Minutes." He was co-anchor of the "ABC Evening News" from 1970 until 1978, when he returned to CBS and "60 Minutes." He died Aug 6, 1991, at Norwalk, CT.

SOLIDARITY GRANTED LEGAL STATUS: ANNIVERSARY. Apr 17, 1989. After nearly a decade of struggle and suppression the Polish labor union Solidarity was granted legal status, clearing the way for the downfall of the Polish Communist Party. Solidarity and the Polish people surprised the government by winning 99 of the 100 parliamentary seats in the election. General Wojciech Jaruzelski was elected president on July 19 and nominated Czelaw Kiszczak prime minister, enraging the Lech Walesa–led Solidarity. On Aug 7 Walesa swayed the traditional allies of the Communist Party—the United Peasant and Democratic Parties—to switch sides. Kiszczak resigned as prime minister a week later after failing to form a government, forcing Jaruzelski to accept the principle of a government led by Solidarity.

SPACE MILESTONE: *COLUMBIA NEUROLAB (US)*. Apr 17, 1998. Seven astronauts and scientists were launched with 2,000 animals (crickets, mice, snails and fish) to study the nervous system in space.

SPACE MILESTONE: *SURVEYOR 3 (US)*. Apr 17, 1967. Launch date of lunar probe vehicle, which made soft landing on Moon on Apr 20 and with its digging apparatus established surface qualities.

SYRIAN ARAB REPUBLIC: INDEPENDENCE DAY: 55th ANNIVERSARY. Apr 17. Official holiday. Proclaimed independence from League of Nations mandate under French administration in 1946.

VERRAZANO DAY: ANNIVERSARY. Apr 17, 1524. Celebrates discovery of New York harbor by Giovanni Verrazano, Florentine navigator, 1485–1527.

WILDER, THORNTON: BIRTH ANNIVERSARY. Apr 17, 1897. Pulitzer Prize–winning American playwright (*Our Town*) and novelist, born at Madison, WI. Died at Hamden, CT, Dec 7, 1975.

BIRTHDAYS TODAY

Sean Bean, 43, actor (*Stormy Monday, The Field, Patriot Games*), born Sheffield, Yorkshire, England, Apr 17, 1958.

Norman Julius ("Boomer") Esiason, 40, broadcaster and former football player, born West Islip, NY, Apr 17, 1961.

Olivia Hussey, 50, actress (*Romeo and Juliet*), born Buenos Aires, Argentina, Apr 17, 1951.

Don Kirshner, 67, music publisher, promoter, born The Bronx, NY, Apr 17, 1934.

Cynthia Ozick, 73, feminist, writer, born New York, NY, Apr 17, 1928.

Lela Rochon, 35, actress (*Waiting to Exhale, Boomerang*), born Los Angeles, CA, Apr 17, 1966.

APRIL 18 — WEDNESDAY
Day 108 — 257 Remaining

CANADA: CONSTITUTION ACT OF 1982: ANNIVERSARY. Apr 18, 1982. Replacing the British North America Act of 1867, the Canadian Constitution Act of 1982 provides Canada with a new set of fundamental laws and civil rights. Signed by Queen Elizabeth II, at Parliament Hill, Ottawa, Canada, it went into effect at 12:01 AM, Sunday, Apr 19, 1982.

CRAWFORD, SAMUEL EARL "WAHOO SAM": BIRTH ANNIVERSARY. Apr 18, 1880. Major league baseball player with the Detroit Tigers, born at Wahoo, NE. Wahoo Sam played pro ball for 20 years, racking up a career batting average of .309. His record of 312 career triples still stands. He was inducted into the Baseball Hall of Fame in 1957. Crawford died June 15, 1968, at Hollywood, CA.

DARROW, CLARENCE SEWARD: BIRTH ANNIVERSARY. Apr 18, 1857. American attorney often associated with unpopular causes, from the Pullman strike in 1894 to the Scottsboro case in 1932, born at Kinsman, OH. At the Scopes trial, July 13, 1925, Darrow said: "I do not consider it an insult, but rather a compliment, to be called an agnostic. I do not pretend to know where many ignorant men are sure—that is all that agnosticism means." Darrow died at Chicago, IL, Mar 13, 1938.

THE HOUSE THAT RUTH BUILT: ANNIVERSARY. Apr 18, 1923. More than 74,000 fans attended Opening Day festivities as the New York Yankees inaugurated their new stadium. Babe Ruth christened it with a game-winning three-run homer into the right-field bleachers. In his coverage of the game for the *New York Evening Telegram* sportswriter Fred Lieb described Yankee Stadium as "The House That Ruth Built," and the name stuck.

JAPAN BOMBED: ANNIVERSARY. Apr 18, 1942. For the first time during WWII, the mainland of Japan was bombed. Brigade General James Doolittle led a squadron of B-25s from the US carrier *Hornet*. Cities bombed included Tokyo, Yokohama, Kobe and Nagoya. Doolittle said they flew so low that "one of our party observed a ball game in progress." The bombers did little damage, but the psychological victory was great.

PAUL REVERE'S RIDE: ANNIVERSARY. Apr 18, 1775. The "Midnight Ride" of Paul Revere and William Dawes started at about 10 PM, to warn American patriots between Boston, MA, and Concord, MA, of the approaching British.

PET OWNERS INDEPENDENCE DAY. Apr 18. Dog and cat owners take day off from work and the pets go to work in their place, since most pets are jobless, sleep all day and do not even take out the trash. [© 2000 by WH] For info: Tom or Ruth Roy, Wellcat Holidays, 2418 Long Ln, Lebanon, PA 17046. Phone: (717) 279-0184. E-mail: wellcat@supernet.com. Web: www.wellcat.com.

"REAL PEOPLE" TV PREMIERE: ANNIVERSARY. Apr 18, 1979. Real people do the darndest things—from making paintings out of lint to making houses out of aluminum cans. NBC developed the program to spotlight the achievements, funny inventions and extraordinary stunts of ordinary Americans. Hosts of the show included: Fred Willard, Sarah Purcell, John Barbour, Skip Stephenson, Byron Allen and Peter Billingsley.

SAN FRANCISCO 1906 EARTHQUAKE: 95th ANNIVERSARY. Apr 18, 1906. Business section of San Francisco, some 10,000 acres, destroyed by earthquake. First quake at 5:13 AM, followed by fire. Nearly 4,000 lives lost.

SCOTTSDALE CULINARY FESTIVAL™. Apr 18–22. Scottsdale, AZ. Ten spectacular culinary events including Wine Country Brunch; Le Tour Culinaire, a progressive black-tie dinner; Best of the Fest featuring 8 of the valley's best chefs; Mayor's Culinary Cup Appetizer Competition; Great Arizona Picnic featuring 50 of the Valley's best restaurants; and more. Proceeds benefit arts education programs for youth in the community. Est attendance: 64,000. For info: Scottsdale Culinary Festival, 7375 E 6th Ave, #9, Scottsdale, AZ 85251. Phone: (480) 945-7193. Fax: (480) 990-1889. E-mail: kiburz@aol.com.

SPACE MILESTONE: *TITAN 34-D* ROCKET FAILURE: 15th ANNIVERSARY. Apr 18, 1986. Launched from Vandenburg Air Force Base, CA, the $65 million *Titan* exploded when it was only a few hundred feet into flight, destroying the $500 million KH-11 reconnaissance satellite payload. Poisonous fumes were released by the explosion, causing concern for the safety of persons in nearby communities.

April 2001	S	M	T	W	T	F	S
		2	3	4	5	6	7
	1	9	10	11	12	13	14
	8	16	17	18	19	20	21
	15	23	24	25	26	27	28
	22	30					
	29						

SURRENDER AT DURHAM STATION: ANNIVERSARY. Apr 18, 1865. Union General William Tecumseh Sherman and Confederate General Joseph Johnston signed a broad political peace agreement at Durham Station, NC. The agreement promised a general amnesty for all Southerners and pledged federal recognition of all Southern state governments after their officials took an oath of allegiance to the US. Sherman was roundly criticized for his role in drawing up the agreement, although he based it on an earlier conversation with Lincoln and Grant. The agreement was rejected by President Andrew Johnson, and Sherman and Johnston were forced to reach a new agreement with terms virtually the same as those given Robert E. Lee.

"THIRD WORLD" DAY: ANNIVERSARY. Apr 18, 1955. Anniversary of the first use of the phrase "third world," which was by Indonesia's President Sukarno in his opening speech at the Bandung Conference. Representatives of nearly 30 African and Asian countries (2,000 attendees) heard Sukarno praise the American war of independence, "the first successful anticolonial war in history." More than half the world's population, he said, was represented at this "first intercontinental conference of the so-called colored peoples, in the history of mankind." The phrase and the idea of a "third world" rapidly gained currency, generally signifying the aggregate of nonaligned peoples and nations—the nonwhite and underdeveloped portion of the world.

WILLIAM INGE FESTIVAL. Apr 18–21. Independence Community College, Independence, KS. Seminars, presentations, lectures and banquet with nationally known playwrights honoring the Pulitzer Prize– and Academy Award–winning author of *Picnic* and *Splendor in the Grass*. Annually, the third Wednesday through Saturday of April. Est attendance: 5,000. For info: Jill Warford, Festival Dir, Independence Community College, PO Box 708, Independence, KS 67301. Phone: (800) 842-6063.

ZIMBABWE: INDEPENDENCE DAY: ANNIVERSARY. Apr 18. National holiday commemorates the recognition by Great Britain of Zimbabwean independence on this day in 1980. Prior to this, the country had been the British colony of Southern Rhodesia.

BIRTHDAYS TODAY

Ed Garvey, 61, lawyer, union official, labor negotiator, born Burlington, WI, Apr 18, 1940.

Melissa Joan Hart, 25, actress ("Clarissa Explains It All," "Sabrina the Teenage Witch"), born Long Island, NY, Apr 18, 1976.

Robert Hooks, 64, actor, director, producer (*Star Trek III: The Search for Spock*; stage: *Day of Absence, Where's Daddy?* [Theatre World Awards for both]), born Washington, DC, Apr 18, 1937.

John James, 45, actor ("Search for Tomorrow," "Dynasty"), born Minneapolis, MN, Apr 18, 1956.

Jane Leeves, 40, actress ("Murphy Brown," "Frasier"), born East Grinstead, England, Apr 18, 1961.

Dorothy Lyman, 54, actress ("All My Children," "Mama's Family"), director, born Minneapolis, MN, Apr 18, 1947.

Eric McCormack, 38, actor ("Lonesome Dove," "Will & Grace"), born Toronto, Ontario, Canada, Apr 18, 1963.

Hayley Mills, 55, actress (*Pollyana, The Parent Trap, The Moon Spinners*), born London, England, Apr 18, 1946.

Rick Moranis, 47, actor, writer (*Ghostbusters, Honey I Shrunk the Kids*), born Toronto, Ontario, Canada, Apr 18, 1954.

Conan O'Brien, 38, host ("Late Night with Conan O'Brien"), born Brookline, MA, Apr 18, 1963.

Eric Roberts, 45, actor (*Runaway Train, Star 80*), born Biloxi, MS, Apr 18, 1956.

James Woods, 54, actor (*Holocaust, The Onion Field*), born Vernal, UT, Apr 18, 1947.

APRIL 19 — THURSDAY

Day 109 — 256 Remaining

AMERICAN HERO COMMEMORATIVE STAMP. Apr 19. Teachers all across America are invited to have their students complete petitions to persuade the US Postal Service to issue a commemorative stamp honoring the volunteer nurse, Rebecca Anderson, who perished during the rescue effort in the Oklahoma City bombing, Apr 19, 1995. For info: Rich Bysina, 853 Lorlyn Dr, #3D, West Chicago, IL 60185. Phone: (630) 876-9615.

BATTLE OF LEXINGTON AND CONCORD: ANNIVERSARY. Apr 19, 1775. Massachusetts. Start of the American Revolution as the British fired the "shot heard 'round the world."

BRANCH DAVIDIAN FIRE AT WACO: ANNIVERSARY. Apr 19, 1993. After a 51-day standoff between the Branch Davidians and law-enforcement groups, the compound of the religious cult burned to the ground with 86 of its members inside, near Waco, TX, after federal agents began battering the compound with armored vehicles. Nine people escaped, but the 86 that perished included 17 children and the cult's leader, David Koresh.

BYRON, GEORGE GORDON: DEATH ANNIVERSARY. Apr 19, 1824. Romantic poet, born at London, England, Jan 22, 1788. Died of fever at Missolonghi, Greece, Apr 19, 1824, while fighting for Greek independence.

EIGHTY-NINER CELEBRATION. Apr 19–22. Guthrie, OK. In celebration of its heritage, this historically restored town features Old West gunfights, chuckwagon feed, professional rodeo and Oklahoma's largest parade of bands, floats and roundup clubs from across the state. Est attendance: 40,000. For info: American Legion, Post 58, 123 N 21st St, Guthrie, OK 73044. Phone: (405) 282-2589.

EXPLOSION ON THE USS *IOWA*: ANNIVERSARY. Apr 19, 1989. In one of the worst naval disasters since the war in Vietnam, a freak explosion rocked the battleship USS *Iowa*, killing 47 sailors. The explosion occurred in the No. 2 gun turret as the *Iowa* was participating in gunnery exercises about 300 miles northeast of Puerto Rico.

GARFIELD, LUCRETIA RUDOLPH: BIRTH ANNIVERSARY. Apr 19, 1832. Wife of James Abram Garfield, 20th president of the US, born at Hiram, OH. Died at Pasadena, CA, Mar 14, 1918.

ICELAND: "FIRST DAY OF SUMMER." Apr 19. A national public holiday, *Sumardagurinn fyrsti*, with general festivities, processions and much street dancing, especially at Reykjavik, greets the coming of summer. Flags are flown. Annually, the third Thursday in April.

INTERNATIONAL HOME FURNISHINGS MARKET. Apr 19–26 (also Oct 18–25). High Point and Thomasville, NC. The largest wholesale home furnishings market in the world. (Not open to the general public.) Est attendance: 80,000. For info: Intl Home Furnishings Mktg Assn, PO Box HP7, High Point, NC 27261. Phone: (336) 869-1000. Fax: (336) 889-7460. Web: www.furnituremarket.org.

INTERNATIONAL WHISTLERS CONVENTION. Apr 19–22. Louisburg, NC. Music festival. Assemblage and contest of professional and amateur whistlers and whistle collectors. Contests for children, teens and adults. Est attendance: 2,500. For info: Allen de Hart, Dir, Franklin County Arts Council, Inc, PO Box 758, Louisburg, NC 27549. Phone: (919) 496-4771. Fax: (919) 496-1191.

JOHN PARKER DAY. Apr 19. Remembering John Parker's order, at Lexington Green, Apr 19, 1775: "Stand your ground. Don't fire unless fired upon; but if they mean to have a war, let it begin here." Revolutionary soldier, captain of minutemen, born at Lexington, MA, July 13, 1729. Died Sept 17, 1775.

NCAA DIVISION I WOMEN'S GYMNASTICS. Apr 19–21. Athens, GA. For info: Natl Collegiate Athletic Assn, 700 W Washington Ave, PO Box 6222, Indianpolis, IN 46206-6222. Phone: (317) 917-6222. Fax: (317) 917-6888. Web: www.ncaa.org.

NETHERLANDS–US DIPLOMATIC RELATIONS: ANNIVERSARY. Apr 19, 1782. Anniversary of establishment of America's oldest continuously peaceful diplomatic relations. On this date, the States General of the Netherlands United Provinces admitted John Adams (later to become second president of the US) as minister plenipotentiary of the young American republic. This was the second diplomatic recognition of the US as an independent nation. Within six months Adams had succeeded in bringing about the signing of the first Treaty of Amity and Commerce between the two countries (Oct 8, 1782).

NICARAGUA: CIVIL WAR: ANNIVERSARY. Apr 19, 1990. The Contra guerrillas, the leftist Sandinistas and the incoming Chamorro government agreed to a truce, ending a nine-year civil war.

OKLAHOMA CITY BOMBING: ANNIVERSARY. Apr 19, 1995. A car bomb exploded outside the Alfred P. Murrah Federal Building at Oklahoma City, OK, at 9:02 AM, killing 168 people, 19 of them children at a day-care center; a nurse died of head injuries sustained while helping in rescue efforts. The bomb, estimated to have weighed 5,000 pounds, had been placed in a rented truck. The blast ripped off the north face of the nine-story building, leaving a 20-foot-wide crater and debris two stories high. Cost of the damage was estimated at $500 million. Structurally unsound and increasingly dangerous, the bombed building was razed May 23. Timothy J. McVeigh, a decorated Gulf War army vet who is alleged to have been deeply angered by the Bureau of Alcohol, Tobacco and Firearms (ATF) attack on the Branch Davidian compound at Waco, TX, exactly two years before, was convicted of the bombing. The ATF had offices in the OK federal building. Terry L. Nicholls, an army buddy of McVeigh, was convicted of lesser charges.

PATRIOT'S DAY IN FLORIDA. Apr 19. A ceremonial day to commemorate the first blood shed in the American Revolution at Lexington and Concord in 1775.

RICARDO, DAVID: BIRTH ANNIVERSARY. Apr 19, 1772. Economist David Ricardo, whose writings greatly influenced later economic theory, was born at London, England. He is recognized as the man who first systematized economics. In his best-known work, *Principles of Political Economy and Taxation* (1817), he discussed wages and rent and the economic relationships among landlords, workers and owners of capital. In 1819 Ricardo purchased his own seat in the House of Commons and became a member of Parliament. He was forced by illness to retire just four years later and died Sept 11, 1823, at Gatcombe Park, Gloucestershire.

SHERMAN, ROGER: BIRTH ANNIVERSARY. Apr 19, 1721 (OS). American statesman, member of the Continental Congress (1774–81 and 1783–84), signer of the Declaration of Independence and of the Constitution, was born at Newton, MA. He also calculated astronomical and calendar information for an almanac. Sherman died at New Haven, CT, July 23, 1793.

SIERRA LEONE: NATIONAL HOLIDAY. Apr 19. Sierra Leone became a republic in 1971.

SPACE MILESTONE: *SALYUT* (USSR): 30th ANNIVERSARY. Apr 19, 1971. The Soviet Union launched *Salyut*, the first manned orbiting space laboratory. It was replaced in 1986 by *Mir*, a manned space station and laboratory.

SPACE MILESTONE: *SALYUT 7* (USSR). Apr 19, 1982. New space station launched from Tyuratam, USSR, to replace the aging *Salyut 6.*

WARSAW GHETTO REVOLT: ANNIVERSARY. Apr 19, 1943. A prolonged revolt began at Warsaw, Poland, when German troops tried to resume deportation of Jewish residents of the Warsaw Ghetto to the Treblinka concentration camp. With only 17 rifles and handmade grenades, for almost a month 1,200 Jewish fighters resisted 2,100 German troops who were armed with machine guns. When the uprising ended on May 16, 300 Germans and 7,000 Jews had died and the Warsaw Ghetto lay in ruins.

BIRTHDAYS TODAY

Don Adams, 74, actor (Emmy for "Get Smart"), born New York, NY, Apr 19, 1927.

Tim Curry, 55, actor (*The Rocky Horror Picture Show*; stage: *Hair, Amadeus, My Favorite Year*), born Cheshire, England, Apr 19, 1946.

Elinor Donahue, 64, actress ("Father Knows Best," "The Andy Griffith Show"), born Tacoma, WA, Apr 19, 1937.

Kate Hudson, 22, actress (*200 Cigarettes*), born Los Angeles, CA, Apr 19, 1979.

Ashley Judd, 33, actress ("Sisters," *Double Jeopardy*), born Los Angeles, CA, Apr 19, 1968.

Dudley Moore, 66, actor (*Arthur, Bedazzled*), composer, born London, England, Apr 19, 1935.

Hugh O'Brian, 71, actor ("The Life and Legend of Wyatt Earp," *Broken Lance, Ten Little Indians*), born Rochester, NY, Apr 19, 1930.

Alan Price, 59, singer, songwriter, born Fairfield, England, Apr 19, 1942.

Al Unser, Jr, 39, auto racer, Indy Car national champion, born Albuquerque, NM, Apr 19, 1962.

APRIL 20 — FRIDAY
Day 110 — 255 Remaining

BIG 12 WOMEN'S GOLF CHAMPIONSHIP. Apr 20–22. Rhodes, IA. Est attendance: 1,000. For info: Big 12 Conference, 2201 Stemmons Freeway, 28th Fl, Dallas, TX 75207. Phone: (214) 742-1212. Fax: (214) 742-2046. Web: www.big12sports.com.

CANADA: MUSKOKA ARTS AND CRAFTS SPRING MEMBERS' SHOW. Apr 20–22. Bracebridge, ON. For info: Muskoka Arts and Crafts, Box 376, 15 King St, Bracebridge, ON, Canada P1L 1T7. Phone: (705) 645-5501. E-mail: mac@surenet.net. Web: www.muskokaartsandcrafts.com.

April 2001	S	M	T	W	T	F	S
	1	2	3	4	5	6	7
	8	9	10	11	12	13	14
	15	16	17	18	19	20	21
	22	23	24	25	26	27	28
	29	30					

COLUMBINE HIGH SCHOOL KILLINGS: ANNIVERSARY. Apr 20, 1999. At this high school at Littleton, CO, students Eric Harris and Dylan Klebold killed 12 other students, a teacher and then themselves.

DOGWOOD FESTIVAL. Apr 20–29. Lewiston, ID. Art show, arts and crafts fair, wine and beer tasting, concerts and plays. Many sports and recreational events. Est attendance: 40,000. For info: Dogwood Festival, 415 Main, Lewiston, ID 83501. Phone: (208) 799-2243. Fax: (208) 799-2850.

FRENCH, DANIEL CHESTER: BIRTH ANNIVERSARY. Apr 20, 1850. American sculptor born at Exeter, NH. One of the most important artists of the 19th and early 20th centuries as a sculptor of public monuments, French is best known for his 1875 "Minute Man" statue at Concord, MA, and his 1922 statue of the seated Abraham Lincoln in the Lincoln Memorial at Washington, DC. French died at Stockbridge, MA, Oct 7, 1931. His home and studio at Stockbridge, MA, were donated to the National Trust for Historic Preservation and are open to the public. For info: Chesterwood, PO Box 827, Stockbridge, MA 01262-0827.

FRENCH QUARTER FESTIVAL. Apr 20–22. New Orleans, LA. This festival focuses on all that makes the Quarter special—art, antiques, food, music, shopping, lifestyles and the people. Free concerts on 13 stages, historic patio tours, parade, children's activities, fireworks, 5K race and other family activities. Est attendance: 250,000. For info: Sandra Dartus, Exec Dir, 100 Conti St, New Orleans, LA 70130. Phone: (504) 522-5730. Fax: (504) 522-5711. E-mail: info@frenchquarterfestivals.org. Web: www.frenchquarterfestivals.org.

HISTORY MEETS THE ARTS. Apr 20–22. Gettysburg, PA. More than 75 historical artists, authors and artisans with original artwork, special tours, historical films, book and print signings. Annually, the third Friday through Sunday in April. For info: Gettysburg CVB, PO Box 4117, Gettysburg, PA 17325. Phone: (717) 334-6274. Fax: (717) 334-1166. Web: www.gettysburg.com.

HITLER, ADOLF: BIRTH ANNIVERSARY. Apr 20, 1889. German dictator, frustrated artist, obsessed with superiority of the "Aryan race" and the evil of Marxism (which he saw as a Jewish plot). Hitler was born at Braunau am Inn, Austria. Turning to politics, despite a five-year prison sentence (writing *Mein Kampf* during the nine months he served), his rise was predictable and, Aug 19, 1934, a German plebiscite vested sole executive power in Führer Adolf Hitler. Facing certain defeat by the Allied Forces, he shot himself, Apr 30, 1945, while his mistress, Eva Braun, took poison in a Berlin bunker where they had been hiding for more than three months.

HOLIDAY IN DIXIE. Apr 20–29. Shreveport and Bossier City, LA. Ten days in April celebrating the beginning of spring with more than 50 events including carnival, tournaments, a treasure hunt, parades; also Barksdale AFB Open House. Takes place throughout both cities. Est attendance: 300,000. For info: Kay Pierson, Exec Dir, Holiday in Dixie, 220 Carroll St, Ste C-2, Shreveport, LA 71105. Phone: (318) 865-5555. Web: www.holidayindixie.com.

HOLOCAUST DAY (YOM HASHOAH). Apr 20. Hebrew calendar date: Nisan 27, 5761. A day established by Israel's Knesset as a memorial to the Jewish dead of WWII. Anniversary in Jewish calendar of Nisan 27, 5705 (corresponding to Apr 10, 1945, in the Gregorian calendar), the day on which Allied troops liberated the first Nazi concentration camp, Buchenwald, north of Weimar, Germany, where about 56,000 prisoners, many of them Jewish, perished.

LUDLOW MINE INCIDENT: ANNIVERSARY. Apr 20, 1914. Miners struggling for recognition of their United Mine Workers Union were attacked at Ludlow, CO, by National Guard troops. The Guardsmen were paid by the mining company. A tent colony was destroyed, five men and one boy were killed by machine-gun fire and eleven children and two women were burned to death.

NATIONAL YOUTH SERVICE DAY. Apr 20–21. This 12th annual day offers thousands of volunteer opportunities in all 50 states for young people, kindergarten and up. More than three million young Americans will serve in 3,000 communities. This is the world's largest volunteer event. More than 40 organizations and 18 corporations serve as partners for this event. For info: Youth Service America, Dept P, Ste 200, 1101 15th St NW, Washington, DC 20005-5002. Phone: (202) 296-2992. Web: www.SERVEnet.org.

PUYALLUP SPRING FAIR. Apr 20–22. Puyallup Fairgrounds, Puyallup, WA. Fair to celebrate spring, including exhibits, animals, flowers, rides, demonstrations, gardening, recycling, lots of entertainment, food and much more. Est attendance: 90,000. For info: Puyallup Spring Fair, PO Box 430, Puyallup, WA 98371-0162. Phone: (253) 841-5045. Fax: (253) 841-5300. E-mail: info@thefair.com. Web: www.thefair.com.

SMITH, HOLLAND: BIRTH ANNIVERSARY. Apr 20, 1882. Considered the father of amphibious warfare, Holland "Howling Mad" Smith was born at Hatchechubie, AL. Smith developed techniques for amphibious assaults that involved coordination of land, sea and air forces. During WWII he led troops in assaults in the Marshall and Mariana Islands and also directed forces at Guam, Iwo Jima and Okinawa. Smith died Jan 12, 1967, at San Diego, CA.

STAMP EXPO: SOUTH. Apr 20–22. Radisson Hotel, Anaheim, CA. Est attendance: 4,000. For info: Intl Stamp Collectors Soc, PO Box 854, Van Nuys, CA 91408. Phone: (818) 997-6496. Fax: (818) 988-4337. E-mail: iibick@aol.com. Web: www.bick.net.

SUGARLOAF'S SPRING NOVI ART FAIR. Apr 20–22. Novi Expo Center, Novi, MI. This show, now in its 7th year, features 350 nationally recognized craft designers and fine artists displaying and selling their original creations. Craft demonstrations, hourly gift certificate drawings, and more. Est attendance: 21,000. For info: Sugarloaf Mountain Works, Inc, 200 Orchard Ridge Dr, #215, Gaithersburg, MD 20878. Phone: (800) 210-9900. E-mail: smworks@sugarloafcrafts.com. Web: www.sugarloafcrafts.com.

TAURUS, THE BULL. Apr 20–May 20. In the astronomical/astrological zodiac that divides the sun's apparent orbit into 12 segments, the period Apr 20–May 20 is identified, traditionally, as the sun sign of Taurus, the Bull. The ruling planet is Venus.

WORLD COW CHIP–THROWING CHAMPIONSHIP® CONTEST. Apr 20–22. Beaver, OK. 31st annual. A highly specialized international organic sporting event which draws dung flingers from around the world. A special division of this competition is held for politicians, who are known to be highly practiced in this area. Est attendance: 4,500. For info: Beth Elston, Secy, Beaver County Chamber of Commerce, PO Box 878, Beaver, OK 73932-0878. Phone: (580) 625-4726.

WORLD GRITS FESTIVAL. Apr 20–22. St. George, SC. Come join in the family fun at this unique festival. Plenty of food, entertainment, amusement rides, a parade, arts and crafts, merchandise exhibits, sports events and much more. Est attendance: 40,000. For info: World Grits Festival, PO Box 787, Saint George, SC 29477. Phone: (843) 563-4366.

WORLD'S LARGEST TRIVIA CONTEST. Apr 20–22. Stevens Point, WI. More than 12,000 players including more than 500 teams compete to answer eight questions every hour for 54 hours straight. Prize: Oscar-like trophy. Est attendance: 12,000. For info: Jim Oliva, University of Wisconsin, Rm 105 CAC, WWSP-Radio (89.9 FM), Stevens Point, WI 54481. Phone: (715) 346-3755. E-mail: theoz@coredcs.com. Web: www.easy-axcess.com/trivia.

BIRTHDAYS TODAY

Carmen Electra, 28, actress ("Baywatch," "Singled Out"), born Cincinnati, OH, Apr 20, 1973.

Nina Foch, 77, actress (*Scaramouche*), born Leyden, Holland, Apr 20, 1924.

Crispin Glover, 37, actor (*Back to the Future, The People vs. Larry Flynt*), born New York, NY, Apr 20, 1964.

Jessica Lange, 52, actress (Oscars for *Tootsie* and *Blue Skies*; *Frances, Sweet Dreams*), born Cloquet, MN, Apr 20, 1949.

Joey Lawrence, 25, actor ("Blossom," "Brotherly Love"), born Strawbridge, PA, Apr 20, 1976.

David Leland, 54, actor (*Time Bandits*); writer, director (*Wish You Were Here*), born Cambridge, England, Apr 20, 1947.

Donald Arthur (Don) Mattingly, 40, former baseball player, born Evansville, IN, Apr 20, 1961.

Ryan O'Neal, 60, actor ("Peyton Place," *Love Story, Paper Moon*), born Los Angeles, CA, Apr 20, 1941.

Pat Roberts, 65, US Senator (R, Kansas), born Topeka, KS, Apr 20, 1936.

Steve Spurrier, 56, football player and Heisman Trophy quarterback, born Miami Beach, FL, Apr 20, 1945.

John Paul Stevens, 81, Associate Justice of the US Supreme Court, born Chicago, IL, Apr 20, 1920.

Luther Vandross, 50, singer, songwriter ("Never Too Much"), born New York, NY, Apr 20, 1951.

APRIL 21 — SATURDAY
Day 111 — 254 Remaining

ART IN THE PARK PLUS. Apr 21. Oakland Park Library, Oakland Park, FL. Annual celebration of National Library Week, features a juried fine arts and crafts show with cash awards. Free activities for all ages, including "Create Your Own Book," professional storytelling, face painting and sidewalk chalk art contest for children, plant displays, used book sale, live music and more. Annually, the Saturday before or after National Library Week. For info: Joanne Fischer, Art In The Park Plus Coord, Oakland Park Library, 1298 NE 37 St, Oakland Park, FL 33334-4576. Phone: (954) 561-6289. Fax: (954) 561-6146. E-mail: joannef@oaklandparkfl.org.

BLOCK HOUSE STEEPLECHASE RACES. Apr 21. Foothills Equestrian Nature Center, Tryon, NC. 55th annual running of the Block House Steeplechase. Est attendance: 18,000. For info: Tryon Riding & Hunt Club, PO Box 1095, Tryon, NC 28782. Phone: (800) 438-3681. Fax: (828) 859-5598. E-mail: trhc@teleplex.net. Web: teleplex.net/trhc.

BRAZIL: TIRADENTES DAY. Apr 21. National holiday commemorating execution of national hero, dentist Jose da Silva Xavier, nicknamed Tiradentes (tooth-puller), a conspirator in revolt against the Portuguese in 1789.

BRONTE, CHARLOTTE: BIRTH ANNIVERSARY. Apr 21, 1816. English novelist born at Hartshead, Yorkshire, England. "Conventionality," she wrote in the preface to *Jane Eyre*, "is not morality. Self-righteousness is not religion. To attack the first is not to assail the last." She died Mar 31, 1855, at Haworth, Yorkshire, England.

CHARLOTTE OBSERVER RACE FESTIVAL. Apr 21. Charlotte, NC. Half marathon, 10K race, 10K walk and other fitness activities. For info: Observer Race Festival, Box 30294, Charlotte, NC 28230. Phone: (704) 358-5425. Fax: (704) 358-5430. E-mail: racefest@charlotteobserver.com.

CRAFT FAIR USA: INDOOR SHOW. Apr 21–22. Wisconsin State Fair Park, Milwaukee, WI. Sale of handcrafted items—jewelry, pottery, weaving, leather, wood, glass and sculpture. Est attendance: 10,000. For info: Dir, Craft Fair USA, 9312 W National Ave, Milwaukee, WI 53227-1542. Phone: (414) 321-2100. Web: www.craftfairusa.com.

DAFFODIL FESTIVAL PARADE. Apr 21. Tacoma, Puyallup, Sumner and Orting, WA. Annual parade, featuring a myriad of floats decorated with freshly cut flowers, primarily daffodils. Est attendance: 140,000. For info: Daffodil Fest, Inc, 741 St. Helens, Tacoma, WA 98402. Phone: (253) 627-6176.

EARLE M. HERBERT MEMORIAL SCHOLARSHIP OF ALPHA PHI OMEGA BANQUET. Apr 21. Los Angeles, CA. Earle Herbert was national president of Alpha Phi Omega National Service Fraternity 1982–86. In memory of Earle Herbert a scholarship was founded in 1995 by the Chaparral Alumni of Alpha Phi Omega to be awarded annually. Est attendance: 200. For info: Chaparral Alumni Assn of Alpha Phi Omega, Jeff Schwartz, Scholarship Trustee, PO Box 6056, Alhambra, CA 91802. Phone: (323) 964-1626.

EARTH DAY COMMUNITY FESTIVAL. Apr 21–22. St. Louis, MO. An educational event with hundreds of exhibitors related to environmental issues and their solutions. Est attendance: 50,000. For info: Jerry Klamon, Alliance for a Livable World, PO Box 63350, St. Louis, MO 63163. Phone: (314) 776-4442 or (314) 962-5838. E-mail: earthdystl@aol.com. Web: www.moenvfund.org.

EARTH DAY WEEKEND. Apr 21–22. Jenkinson's Aquarium, Point Pleasant Beach, NJ. Celebrate Earth Day in a positive way—learn what you can do to help the environment. Take part in environmental games and stop by for storytelling. Crafts and face painting 1–4 PM. Free Earth Day buttons to first 300 visitors. Est attendance: 1,200. For info: Liz Carletta, Education Coord, Jenkinson's Aquarium, 300 Ocean Ave, Point Pleasant Beach, NJ 08742. Phone: (732) 899-1212. Fax: (732) 899-1717. E-mail: aquarium@jenkinsons.com. Web: www.jenkinsons.com.

EARTH ENVIRONMENTAL ANGELS DAY. Apr 21. It is the ongoing responsibility of the Earth's population to be responsible stewards of our world and our resources. There are many who take this role seriously. They see the natural harmony in our environment vanishing because of pollution, excessive consumption and the abuse of our resources. They devote considerable effort to restoring the balance that is inherent in nature. This is the day to honor those who promote responsible use of our natural resources and the return to a healthy environment. Annually, the day before Earth Day. For info: Tom Kemper, Pres, Dolphin Blue, 1920 Abrams Pkwy, #416, Dallas, TX 75214-6218. Phone: (800) 932-7715. Fax: (214) 565-7835. E-mail: tdolphin@dolphinblue.com. Web: www.dolphinblue.com.

April *2001*	S	M	T	W	T	F	S
	1	2	3	4	5	6	7
	8	9	10	11	12	13	14
	15	16	17	18	19	20	21
	22	23	24	25	26	27	28
	29	30					

FESTIVAL OF RIDVAN. Apr 21–May 2. Annual Baha'i festival commemorating the 12 days (Apr 21–May 2, 1863) when Baha'u'llah, the prophet-founder of the Baha'i faith, resided in a garden called Ridvan (Paradise) in Baghdad, at which time He publicly proclaimed His mission as God's messenger for this age. The first, ninth (Apr 29) and twelfth days are celebrated as holy days and are three of the nine days of the year when Baha'is suspend work. For info: Dir, Baha'is of the US, Office of Public Information, 866 UN Plaza, Ste 120, New York, NY 10017-1822. Phone: (212) 803-2500. Fax: (212) 803-2573. E-mail: usopi-ny@bic.org. Web: www.us.bahai.org.

FROEBEL, FRIEDRICH: BIRTH ANNIVERSARY. Apr 21, 1782. German educator and author Friedrich Froebel, who believed that play is an important part of a child's education, was born at Oberwiessbach, Thuringia. Froebel invented the kindergarten, founding the first one at Blankenburg, Germany, in 1837. Froebel also invented a series of toys which he intended to stimulate learning. (The American architect Frank Lloyd Wright as a child received these toys [maplewood blocks] from his mother and spoke throughout his life of their value.) Froebel's ideas about the role of directed play, toys and music in children's education had a profound influence in England and the US, where the nursery school became a further extension of his ideas. Froebel died at Marienthal, Germany, June 21, 1852.

GARDEN EXPO. Apr 21–May 13 (weekends only). St. Louis, MO. Three days dedicated to fun and fascination of gardening in the Midwest. Lectures, exhibits, demonstrations and vendors—the Garden's expert staff will be on hand to answer questions. Est attendance: 15,000. For info: Missouri Botanical Garden, PO Box 299, St. Louis, MO 63166-0299. Phone: (800) 642-8842 or (314) 577-9400. Web: www.mobot.org.

HISTORIC GARDEN WEEK IN VIRGINIA. Apr 21–28. This annual statewide event, celebrating its 68th anniversary, is billed as "America's Largest Open House." Showcases more than 250 of Virginia's finest homes, gardens, plantations and landmark properties on more than 30 separate tours on different days of the week. Brochure available. A 200-page guidebook will be available in February 2001. Please mail a contribution of $5 to cover postage and handling. Est attendance: 50,000. For info: Garden Club of Virginia, 12 E Franklin St, Richmond, VA 23219. Phone: (804) 644-7776. Fax: (804) 644-7778. E-mail: gardenwk@erols.com or gdnweek@erols.com. Web: www.VAGardenweek.org.

INDONESIA: KARTINI DAY. Apr 21. Republic of Indonesia. Honors Raden Adjeng Kartini, pioneer in the emancipation of the women of Indonesia.

ITALY: BIRTHDAY OF ROME. Apr 21. Celebration of the founding of Rome, traditionally thought to be in 753 BC.

JUST PRAY NO: WORLDWIDE WEEKEND PRAYER. Apr 21–22. 11th annual. Churches throughout the world. Prayer breakfasts, lunches, street rallies and marches to gain media attention. Bible studies and sermons concerning alcoholism and drug abuse and revival meetings aimed at those bound by addiction. For info: "Just Pray No," Ltd, 2919 Bayview Ave, Baldwin, NY 11510-2444. Phone: (516) 377-6779.

KENDUSKEAG STREAM CANOE RACE. Apr 21. Bangor, ME. 16.5-mile whitewater open canoe race. Est attendance: 10,000. For info: Bangor Parks and Recreation Dept, 647 Main St, Bangor, ME 04401. Phone: (207) 947-1018. Fax: (207) 947-1605.

KENTUCKY DERBY FESTIVAL. Apr 21–May 6. Louisville, KY. Civic celebration as Louisville warms up for the Kentucky Derby. About 70 events, two-thirds of which are free to the public. Est attendance: 1,500,000. For info: Kentucky Derby Festival, Inc, 1001 S Third St, Louisville, KY 40203. Phone: (502) 584-6383. Fax: (502) 589-4674. E-mail: info@kdf.org. Web: www.kdf.org.

KINDERGARTEN DAY. Apr 21. A day to recognize the importance of play, games and "creative self-activity" in children's education and to note the history of the kindergarten. Observed on the anniversary of the birth of Friedrich Froebel, in 1782, who established the first kindergarten in 1837. German immigrants brought Froebel's ideas to the US in the 1840s. The first kindergarten in a public school in the US was started in 1873, at St. Louis, MO.

LIVINGSTON RAILROAD SWAP MEET. Apr 21. Northern Pacific Passenger Depot, Livingston, MT. Railroad hobby items and collectibles for sale at this 11th annual swap. Est attendance: 750. For info: Livingston Depot Center, Box 1319, Livingston, MT 59047. Phone: (406) 222-2300 or 2304.

LONGWOOD GARDENS ACRES OF SPRING. Apr 21–May 25. Kennett Square, PA. Thousands of spring bulbs, flowering shrubs and trees bloom throughout 1,050 acres of formal gardens, woodlands and meadows. Est attendance: 150,000. For info: Longwood Gardens, PO Box 501, Kennett Square, PA 19348-0501. Phone: (610) 388-1000. Web: www.longwood gardens.org.

MOSSY CREEK BARNYARD FESTIVAL. Apr 21–22 (also Oct 20–21). Warner Robins, GA. Arts and crafts chosen from best in the nation; heritage crafts, country and folk music and folk tales in relaxed atmosphere. Semiannually, the third weekend of April (usually) and of October. Est attendance: 25,000. For info: Carolyn Chester, Mossy Creek Barnyard Festival, Inc, 106 Anne Dr, Warner Robins, GA 31093. Phone: (912) 922-8265.

MUIR, JOHN: BIRTH ANNIVERSARY. Apr 21, 1838. American naturalist, explorer, conservationist and author for whom the 550-acre Muir Woods National Monument (near San Francisco, CA) is named. Muir, born at Dunbar, Scotland, emigrated to the US in 1849, where he urged establishment of national parks and profoundly influenced US forest conservation. Died at Los Angeles, CA, Dec 24, 1914.

NAB 2001/NATIONAL BROADCASTERS CONVENTION. Apr 21–26. Las Vegas, NV. World's largest convention of radio, television and other types of multimedia. The awards for the National Broadcasting Hall of Fame are also awarded at the convention. Exhibits from Apr 23–26. For info: Natl Assn of Broadcasters, 1771 N St NW, Washington, DC 20036-2891. Phone: (800) 342-2460 or (202) 429-4194. Fax: (202) 429-5343. E-mail: register@nab.org. Web: www.nab.org/conventions.

NATIONAL HEADACHE FOUNDATION FUNDRAISER. Apr 21. New York, NY. Annual black tie silent auction and dinner serves as the major fundraiser for the National Headache Foundation. Proceeds are used for research, education and service. Est attendance: 300. For info: Suzanne E. Simons, Exec Dir, Natl Headache Fdtn, 428 W St. James Place, 2nd Fl, Chicago, IL 60614-2750. Phone: (773) 388-6395. Fax: (773) 525-7357.

NORTHERN CALIFORNIA CHERRY BLOSSOM FESTIVAL. Apr 21–22 (also Apr 27–29). Japantown, San Francisco, CA. More than 2,000 Californians of Japanese descent and performers from Japan participate in this most elaborate offering of Japanese culture and customs this side of the Pacific, highlighted by colorful parade. Sponsors: Japanese-American communities of Northern California and several corporations. Est attendance: 150,000. For info: Cherry Blossom Festival, PO Box 15147, San Francisco, CA 94115-0147. Phone: (415) 563-2313. Fax: (415) 563-2307. Web: www.e-media.com/sakura.

RED BARON SHOT DOWN: ANNIVERSARY. Apr 21, 1918. German flying ace Baron Manfred von Richtofen was shot down and killed during the battle of the Somme. The "Red Baron," so named for the color of his Fokker triplane, was credited with 80 kills in less than two years. Royal Flying Corp pilots recovered his body and the Allies buried him with full military honors. Asked about his fighting philosophy he was quoted as saying, "I am a hunter. My brother Lothar is a butcher. When I have shot down an Englishman, my hunting passion is satisfied for a quarter of an hour."

SAINT LOUIS VARIETY CLUB TELETHON AND DINNER WITH THE STARS. Apr 21–22. Adam's Mark Hotel, St. Louis, MO. A 10-hour telethon to raise funds for disabled and disadvantaged children in the greater St. Louis area. Televised on 4 St. Louis KMOV, Channel 4 (CBS). Est attendance: 1,900. For info: St. Louis Variety Club, 2200 Westport Plaza Dr, St. Louis, MO 63146. Phone: (314) 453-0453. Fax: (314) 453-0488.

SAN JACINTO DAY. Apr 21. Texas. Commemorates Battle of San Jacinto in 1836, in which Texas won independence from Mexico. A 570-foot monument, dedicated on the 101st anniversary of the battle, marks the site on the banks of the San Jacinto River, about 20 miles from present city of Houston, TX, where General Sam Houston's Texans decisively defeated the Mexican forces led by Santa Ana in the final battle between Texas and Mexico.

SPACE MILESTONE: *COPERNICUS, OAO 4 (US).* Apr 21, 1972. Launch of Orbiting Astronomical Observer, named in honor of the Polish astronomer.

WISCONSIN SPRING GARDEN MARKET. Apr 21–22. The American Club, Kohler, WI. Spring plants, garden ornaments, herbs and unusual varieties of annuals and perennials fill the Grand Hall of the Great Lakes. Lending counsel and a helping hand with seminars, demonstrations and an array of products are more than 70 plant and gardening specialists, landscape designers and architects. Est attendance: 5,000. For info: The American Club, Highland Dr, Kohler, WI 53044. Phone: (800) 344-2838. Fax: (920) 457-0299. Web: www.americanclub.com.

WORLD CHAMPIONSHIP GOLD PANNING COMPETITION. Apr 21–22. Consolidated Gold Mine, Dahlonega, GA. Competitions for the quickest gold panner. Annually, the third weekend in April. For info: Dahlonega-Lumpkin Co Chamber of Commerce, 13 S Park St, Dahlonega, GA 30533. Phone: (706) 864-3513 or (800) 231-5543. Fax: (706) 864-7917. E-mail: dahlonegacoc@alltel.net. Web: www.dahlonega.org.

BIRTHDAYS TODAY

Tony Danza, 50, actor ("Taxi," "Who's the Boss?"), born Brooklyn, NY, Apr 21, 1951.

Queen Elizabeth II, 75, Queen of the United Kingdom, born London, England, Apr 21, 1926.

Charles Grodin, 66, actor (*Midnight Run, Beethoven*); director, host ("The Charles Grodin Show"), born Pittsburgh, PA, Apr 21, 1935.

Patti LuPone, 52, actress (*Evita*, "Life Goes On"), born Northport, NY, Apr 21, 1949.

Andie MacDowell, 43, actress (*sex, lies, and videotape* [Best Actress Award, LA Film Critics], *Groundhog Day*), born Gaffney, SC, Apr 21, 1958.

Elaine May, 69, actress, writer (comedy with Mike Nichols), director (*A New Leaf*), born Philadelphia, PA, Apr 21, 1932.

Iggy Pop, 54, singer, born Ann Arbor, MI, Apr 21, 1947.

Anthony Quinn, 85, actor (Oscars for *Viva Zapata, Lust for Life*), born Chihuahua, Mexico, Apr 21, 1916.

APRIL 22 — SUNDAY
Day 112 — 253 Remaining

ADMINISTRATIVE PROFESSIONALS WEEK. Apr 22–28. Acknowledgment of the contributions of all administrative professionals and their vital roles in business, industry, education and government. Annually, the last full week (from Sunday–Saturday) in April. Administrative Professionals Day is observed on Wednesday of this week (Apr 25 in 2001). For info: Rick Stroud, Communications Dir, Intl Assn of Administrative Professionals, 10502 NW Ambassador Dr, PO Box 20404, Kansas City, MO 64195-0404. Phone: (816) 891-6600 ext 239. Fax: (816) 891-9118. E-mail: rstroud@iaap-hq.org. Web: www.iaap-hq.org.

BABE'S PITCHING DEBUT: ANNIVERSARY. Apr 22, 1914. Babe Ruth made his professional pitching debut, playing for the Baltimore Orioles in his own hometown. Allowing just six hits and contributing two singles himself, Ruth shut out the Buffalo Bisons, 6–0.

BRAZIL: DISCOVERY OF BRAZIL DAY: ANNIVERSARY. Apr 22. Commemorates discovery by Pedro Alvarez Cabral in 1500.

COINS STAMPED "IN GOD WE TRUST": ANNIVERSARY. Apr 22, 1864. By Act of Congress, the phrase "In God We Trust" began to be stamped on all US coins.

EARTH DAY: ANNIVERSARY. Apr 22. Earth Day, first observed Apr 22, 1970, with message "New Energy for a New Era" and attention to accelerating the transition to renewable energy worldwide. Earth Day 1990 was a global event with more than 200 million participating in 142 countries. Annually, Apr 22. Note: Earth Day activities are held by many groups on various dates, often on the weekend before and after Apr 22. Search for events online. For info: Earth Day Network, PO Box 9827, San Diego, CA 92169. Phone: (619) 272-0347. Fax: (619) 272-2933. E-mail: earthday@earthdayweb.org.

EARTH FAIR. Apr 22. Balboa Park, San Diego, CA. A free public Earth Day event featuring more than 200 exhibitors representing nonprofit, for-profit and government organizations. Events foster public education and awareness of contemporary environmental issues. Included are seven stages of live entertainment, a special edition "Earth Times" newspaper, speakers, natural food and a popular Kids Area. Fair will be kicked off by the Earth Parade at 10:30 AM. Est attendance: 70,000. For info: San Diego EarthWorks, PO Box 9827, San Diego, CA 92169-9827. Phone: (858) 496-6666. Fax: (858) 272-2933. E-mail: earthday@earthdayweb.org. Web: www.earthdayweb.org.

FIRST SOLO TRIP TO NORTH POLE: ANNIVERSARY. Apr 22, 1994. Norwegian explorer Borge Ousland became the first person to make the trip to the North Pole alone. The trip took 52 days, during which he pulled a 265-pound sled. Departing from Cape Atkticheskiy at Siberia Mar 2, he averaged about 18½ miles per day over the 630-mile journey. Ousland had traveled to the Pole on skis with Erling Kagge in 1990.

HELENA RAILROAD FAIR. Apr 22. Civic Center, Helena, MT. Largest railroad hobby event in Montana features a mix of scale and tin-plate trains; railroad memorabilia and collectibles; real-life train watching at the MRL Helena depot. Est attendance: 3,000. For info: Helena Railroad Fair, PO Box 4914, Helena, MT 59604. Phone: (406) 443-0315. E-mail: rrfair@mt.net.

★**JEWISH HERITAGE WEEK.** Apr 22–29.

	S	M	T	W	T	F	S
April 2001	1	2	3	4	5	6	7
	8	9	10	11	12	13	14
	15	16	17	18	19	20	21
	22	23	24	25	26	27	28
	29	30					

JIMMY STEWART RELAY MARATHON. Apr 22. Griffith Park, Los Angeles, CA. Team relay with five people, each running 5.2 miles. Funds raised go to benefit the Saint John's Child and Family Development Center, 20th annual marathon. Est attendance: 15,000. For info: Jimmy Stewart Relay Marathon, St. John's Health Ctr, 1328 22nd St, Santa Monica, CA 90404. Phone: (310) 829-8968. Fax: (310) 315-6167.

LENIN, NIKOLAI: BIRTH ANNIVERSARY. Apr 22, 1870. Russian socialist and revolutionary leader (real name: Vladimir Ilyich Ulyanov), ideological follower of Karl Marx, born at Simbirst, on the Volga, Russia. Leader of the Great October Socialist Revolution of 1917. Died at Gorky, near Moscow, Jan 21, 1924. His embalmed body, in a glass coffin at the Lenin Mausoleum, has been viewed by millions of visitors to Moscow's Red Square. In 1999 the Russian government announced that his body would be buried.

NATIONAL KARAOKE WEEK. Apr 22–28. Karaoke has grown by leaps and bounds in the US. Once thought to be a fad, more and more people are recognizing the benefits of karaoke—increased self-esteem, confidence and stress release. Annually, the fourth week in April. For info: Visual Perspectives, 1083 W 124th Dr, Westminster, CO 80234-1757. Phone: (303) 452-5140. E-mail: shirai@uswest.net.

NATIONAL VOLUNTEER WEEK. Apr 22–28. National Volunteer Week honors those who reach out to others through volunteer community service and calls attention to the need for more community services for individuals, groups and families to help solve serious social problems that affect our communities. For info: Customer Information Center, Points of Light Foundation, 1400 I St NW, Ste 800, Washington, DC 20005. Phone: (202) 729-8000. Fax: (202) 729-8100. E-mail: volnet@aol.com. Web: www.pointsoflight.org.

★**NATIONAL VOLUNTEER WEEK.** Apr 22–28.

OCEAN SPRAY SPRING SPLASH. Apr 22. Winter Park Resort, Winter Park, CO. One of Winter Park's most anticipated events, the wet and wild Spring Splash celebrates the joy of spring skiing. Spectators cheer as skiers and snowboarders struggle through a hilarious and challenging obstacle course that includes skimming across a pond of icy water to cross the finish line. Est attendance: 2,000. For info: Winter Park Resort, PO Box 36, Winter Park, CO 80482. Phone: (970) 726-1580. Fax: (970) 726-1572. E-mail: wpinfo@mail.skiwinterpark.com. Web: winterparkresort.com.

OKLAHOMA DAY. Apr 22. Oklahoma.

OKLAHOMA LAND RUSH: ANNIVERSARY. Apr 22, 1889. At noon a gunshot signaled the start of the Oklahoma land rush as thousands of settlers rushed into the territory to claim land. Under pressure from cattlemen, the federal government opened 1,900,000 acres of central Oklahoma that had been bought from the Creek and Seminole tribes.

SKY AWARENESS WEEK. Apr 22–28. A celebration of the sky and an opportunity to appreciate its natural beauty, to understand sky and weather processes and to work together to protect the sky as a natural resource (it's the only one we have). Events are held at schools, nature centers, etc, all across the US. For info: Barbara G. Levine, How The Weatherworks, 301 Creek Valley Lane, Rockville, MD 20850. Phone: (301) 990-9324 or (301) 527-9339. Fax: (630) 563-1782. E-mail: skyweek@weatherworks.com. Web: www.weatherworks.com.

BIRTHDAYS TODAY

Eddie Albert (Edward Albert Heimberger), 93, actor ("Green Acres," *Roman Holiday*), born Rock Island, IL, Apr 22, 1908.

Byron Allen, 40, comedian, TV host ("Byron Allen Show," "Real People"), actor (*Case Closed*), born Detroit, MI, Apr 22, 1961.

Glen Campbell, 66, singer ("Gentle on My Mind," "By the Time I Get to Phoenix"), born Billstown, AR, Apr 22, 1935.

Peter Frampton, 51, singer ("Show Me the Way," "Do You Feel Like We Do"), born Beckenham, England, Apr 22, 1950.

Chris Makepeace, 37, actor (*My Bodyguard*), born Montreal, Quebec, Canada, Apr 22, 1964.

Jason Miller, 62, playwright (*That Championship Season* [Tony Award and Pulitzer Prize for Drama]); actor (*The Exorcist, The Ninth Configuration*), born Scranton, PA, Apr 22, 1939.

Jack Nicholson, 65, actor (Oscars for *One Flew Over the Cuckoo's Nest, Terms of Endearment* and *As Good as It Gets*), born Neptune, NJ, Apr 22, 1936.

Charlotte Rae, 75, actress ("Diff'rent Strokes," "Facts of Life"), born Milwaukee, WI, Apr 22, 1926.

Aaron Spelling, 73, writer, producer ("Fantasy Island," "Melrose Place"), born Dallas, TX, Apr 22, 1928.

Ryan Stiles, 42, actor ("The Drew Carey Show," "Whose Line Is It Anyway?"), born Seattle, WA, Apr 22, 1959.

John Waters, 55, filmmaker (*Pink Flamingoes*), born Baltimore, MD, Apr 22, 1946.

APRIL 23 — MONDAY
Day 113 — 252 Remaining

ASTRONOMY WEEK. Apr 23–29. To take astronomy to the people. Astronomy Week is observed during the calendar week in which Astronomy Day falls. See also: "Astronomy Day" (Apr 28).

"BAYWATCH" TV PREMIERE: ANNIVERSARY. Apr 23, 1989. Set on a California beach, this program stars David Hasselhoff and a changing cast of nubile young men and women who are lifeguards. The program airs in 148 countries.

BERMUDA: PEPPERCORN CEREMONY: ANNIVERSARY. Apr 23. St. George. Commemorates the payment of one peppercorn in 1816 to the governor of Bermuda for rental of Old State House by the Masonic Lodge.

BIG 12 MEN'S GOLF CHAMPIONSHIP. Apr 23–24. Prairie Dunes Golf Course, Hutchinson, KS. Est attendance: 1,000. For info: Big 12 Conference, 2201 Stemmons Freeway, 28th Fl, Dallas, TX 75207. Phone: (214) 742-1212. Fax: (214) 742-2046. Web: www.big12sports.com.

BUCHANAN, JAMES: BIRTH ANNIVERSARY. Apr 23, 1791. 15th president of the US, born at Cove Gap, PA, was the only president who never married. He served one term in office, Mar 4, 1857–Mar 3, 1861, and died at Lancaster, PA, June 1, 1868.

CANADA: NEWFOUNDLAND: SAINT GEORGE'S DAY. Apr 23. Holiday observed at Newfoundland on Monday nearest Feast Day (Apr 23) of Saint George.

CERVANTES SAAVEDRA, MIGUEL DE: DEATH ANNIVERSARY. Apr 23, 1616. Spanish poet, playwright and novelist died at Madrid, Spain. The exact date of Cervantes' birth at Alcala de Henares is unknown, but he was baptized Oct 9, 1547. As soldier and tax collector, Cervantes traveled widely. He spent more than five years in prisons in Spain, Italy and North Africa. His greatest creation was Don Quixote, the immortal Knight of La Mancha whose profession was chivalry. Riding his nag, Rozinante, and accompanied by Squire Sancho Panza, Don Quixote tilts at windmills of the mind in the world's best-known novel. Nearly a thousand editions of *Don Quixote* (a bestseller since its first appearance in 1605) have been published, and it has been translated into more languages than any other book except the Bible.

ENGLAND: BRITISH GRAND PRIX. Apr 23 (tentative). Silverstone Circuit, Towcester, Northamptonshire. Britain's only round of the FIA Formula One World Championship is the highlight of the motor racing calendar. For info: Silverstone Circuit Limited, Towcester, Northamptons, England NN12 8TN. Phone: (44) (132) 785-7273. Fax: (44) (132) 320-300. E-mail: info @silverstone-circuit.co.uk. Web: www.silverstone-circuit.co.uk.

FIRST MOVIE THEATER OPENS: ANNIVERSARY. Apr 23, 1896. The first movie was shown at Koster and Bials Music Hall at New York City. Up until this time, people saw films individually by looking into a Kinetoscope, a box-like "peep show." This was the first time in the US that an audience sat in a theater and watched a movie together.

FIRST PUBLIC SCHOOL IN AMERICA: ANNIVERSARY. Apr 23, 1635. The Boston Latin School opened and is America's oldest public school.

FORDYCE ON THE COTTON BELT FESTIVAL. Apr 23–28. Fordyce, AR. 21st annual railroad event includes arts and crafts, quilt show and sale, train rides, musical entertainment, rodeo, parade, railroad displays, beauty pageants, gospel singing and more. Est attendance: 10,000. For info: Chamber of Commerce, PO Box 588, Fordyce, AR 71742. Phone: (870) 352-5125. Fax: (870) 352-8090. E-mail: fordyce@ipa.net.

MOON PHASE: NEW MOON. Apr 23. Moon enters New Moon phase at 11:26 AM, EDT.

NATIONAL PLAYGROUND SAFETY WEEK. Apr 23–27. An opportunity for families, community parks, schools and childcare facilities to focus on preventing public playground-related injuries. Sponsored by the National Program for Playground Safety (NPPS), this event helps educate the public about the more than 200,000 children (that's one child every 2 ½ minutes) that require emergency-room treatment for playground-related injuries each year. For info: Natl Program for Playground Safety, School of HPELS, UNI, Cedar Falls, IA 50614-0618. Phone: (800) 554-PLAY. Fax: (319) 273-7308. Web: www.uni.edu/playground.

NATIONAL TV TURNOFF WEEK. Apr 23–29. Encourages Americans to voluntarily turn off their TVs for seven days in order to promote richer, healthier and more connected lives, families and communities. Organizer's kit available. For info: TV-Turnoff Network, 1611 Connecticut Ave, Ste 3A, Washington, DC 20009. Phone: (800) 939-6737. Web: www.tvturnoff.org.

NATIONAL YWCA WEEK. Apr 23–29. To promote the YWCA of the USA nationally. Annually, the last full week in April. For info: YWCA of the USA, Empire State Bldg, Ste 301, 350 Fifth Ave, New York, NY 10118. Phone: (212) 273-7800. Web: www .ywca.org.

PEARSON, LESTER B.: BIRTH ANNIVERSARY. Apr 23, 1897. 14th prime minister of Canada, born at Toronto, Canada. He was Canada's chief delegate at the San Francisco conference where the UN charter was drawn up and later served as president of the General Assembly. He wrote the proposal that resulted in the formation of the North Atlantic Treaty Organization (NATO). He was awarded the Nobel Peace Prize. Died at Rockcliffe, Canada, Dec 27, 1972.

PHYSICISTS DISCOVER TOP QUARK: ANNIVERSARY. Apr 23, 1994. Physicists at the Department of Energy's Fermi National Accelerator Laboratory found evidence for the existence of the subatomic particle called the top quark, the last undiscovered quark of the six predicted to exist by current scientific theory. The discovery provides strong support for the quark theory of the structure of matter. Quarks are subatomic particles that make up protons and neutrons found in the nuclei of atoms. The five other quark types that had already been proven to exist are the up quark, down quark, strange quark, charm quark and bottom quark. Further experimentation over many months confirmed the discovery and it was publicly announced Mar 2, 1995.

PLANCK, MAX: BIRTH ANNIVERSARY. Apr 23, 1858. Formulator of the quantum theory which revolutionized physics, born at Kiel, Germany. Einstein's application of quantum theory to light led to the theories of relativity. Planck died at Gottingen, Germany, Oct 3, 1947.

SAINT GEORGE FEAST DAY. Apr 23. Martyr and patron saint of England, who died Apr 23, AD 303. Hero of the George and the dragon legend. The story says that his faith helped him slay a vicious dragon that demanded daily sacrifice after the king's daughter became the intended victim.

SAINT GEORGE'S DAY CELEBRATION. Apr 23. New York, NY. Celebration of the birth of St. George, the patron saint of England, at an authentic British pub featuring coloring contests, prizes and appearances of St. George and the dragon. Est attendance: 200. For info: Deven Black, Genl Mgr, North Star Pub, 93 South St, New York, NY 10038. Phone: (212) 509-6757. Web: www.northstarpub.com.

SHAKESPEARE, WILLIAM: BIRTH AND DEATH ANNIVERSARY. Apr 23. England's most famous and most revered poet and playwright. He was born at Stratford-on-Avon, England, Apr 23, 1564 (OS), baptized there three days later and died there on his birthday, Apr 23, 1616 (OS). Author of at least 36 plays and 154 sonnets, Shakespeare created the most influential and lasting body of work in the English language, an extraordinary exploration of human nature. His epitaph: "Good frend for Jesus sake forbeare, To digg the dust enclosed heare. Blese be ye man that spares thes stones, And curst be he that moves my bones."

SPACE MILESTONE: *SOYUZ 10* (USSR): 30th ANNIVERSARY. Apr 23, 1971. Launch date of Soviet mission in which cosmonauts V.A. Shatalov, A.S. Yeliseyev and N.N. Rukavishnikov docked Apr 24 with *Salyut 1* orbital space station. The crew did not enter the space station. Return Earth landing at Kazakhstan, USSR, Apr 24.

SPAIN: BOOK DAY AND LOVER'S DAY. Apr 23. Barcelona. Saint George's Day and the anniversary of the death of Spanish writer Miguel de Cervantes have been observed with special ceremonies in the Palacio de la Disputacion and throughout the city since 1714. Book stands are set up in the plazas and on street corners. This is Spain's equivalent of Valentine's Day. Women give books to men; men give roses to women.

TURKEY: NATIONAL SOVEREIGNTY AND CHILDREN'S DAY. Apr 23, 1923. Commemorates Grand National Assembly's inauguration.

UNITED NATIONS: WORLD BOOK AND COPYRIGHT DAY. Apr 23. Observed throughout the United Nations system.

WOODS, GRANVILLE T.: BIRTH ANNIVERSARY. Apr 23, 1856. Granville T. Woods was born at Columbus, OH. He invented the Synchronous Multiplex Railway Telegraph which allowed communication between dispatchers and trains while the trains were in motion, which decreased the number of train accidents. In addition, Woods is credited with a number of other electrical inventions and was compared favorably to Thomas Edison. Died Jan 30, 1910, at New York, NY.

BIRTHDAYS TODAY

Valerie Bertinelli, 41, actress ("One Day at a Time," *Silent Witness*), born Wilmington, DE, Apr 23, 1960.
David Birney, 61, actor (*Summertree*; "Love Is a Many Splendored Thing," "Bridget Loves Bernie"), born Washington, DC, Apr 23, 1940.
Shirley Temple Black, 73, former ambassador to Ghana, child actress (*Heidi, Curly Top, Little Miss Marker*), TV hostess ("Shirley Temple's Storybook" and "Shirley Temple Theatre"), born Santa Monica, CA, Apr 23, 1928.
Judy Davis, 46, actress (*A Passage to India, Deconstructing Harry*), born Perth, Australia, Apr 23, 1955.
Sandra Dee (Alexandra Zuck), 59, actress (*Imitation of Life, A Summer Place, Gidget*), born Bayonne, NJ, Apr 23, 1942.
Joyce Dewitt, 52, actress ("Three's Company"), born Wheeling, WV, Apr 23, 1949.

April *2001*	S	M	T	W	T	F	S
		1	2	3	4	5	6	7
	8	9	10	11	12	13	14
	15	16	17	18	19	20	21
	22	23	24	25	26	27	28
	29	30					

Jan Hooks, 44, actress ("Saturday Night Live," "Designing Women"), born Atlanta, GA, Apr 23, 1957.
Andruw Jones, 24, baseball player, born Wellstad, Curacao, Netherlands Antilles, Apr 23, 1977.
Melina Kanakaredes, 34, actress ("Providence," "Guiding Light"), born Akron, OH, Apr 23, 1967.
Lee Majors, 61, actor ("The Six Million Dollar Man," "The Fall Guy"), born Wyandotte, MI, Apr 23, 1940.
Bernadette Devlin McAliskey, 54, political activist, born Cookstown, Northern Ireland, Apr 23, 1947.
Warren Edward Spahn, 80, Baseball Hall of Fame pitcher, born Buffalo, NY, Apr 23, 1921.
Narada Michael Walden, 49, drummer (with Mahavishnu Orchestra), singer, songwriter and record producer, born Kalamazoo, MI, Apr 23, 1952.

APRIL 24 — TUESDAY

Day 114 — 251 Remaining

ARMENIA: ARMENIAN MARTYRS DAY. Apr 24. Commemorates the massacre of Armenians under the Ottoman Turks in 1915. Deportations from Turkey began. Also called Armenian Genocide Memorial Day. Adolf Hitler, in a speech at Obersalzberg, Aug 22, 1939, is reported to have said, "Who today remembers the Armenian extermination?" in an apparent justification of the Nazis' use of genocide.

BASCOM, GEORGE N.: BIRTH ANNIVERSARY. Apr 24, 1836. West Point Graduate Lieutenant George N. Bascom was assigned to search out Apache chief Cochise, believed to be responsible for an 1861 raid on an Arizona ranch. He arrested Cochise at Apache Pass, but the chief escaped and declared war, launching a reign of terror known as the Apache Wars. Bascom was born at Owingsville, KY, and died the year following his Apache adventure when he became a casualty of the Civil War battle at Fort Craig, Valverde, NM, Feb 21, 1862.

CARTWRIGHT, EDMUND: BIRTH ANNIVERSARY. Apr 24, 1743. English cleric and inventor (developed the power loom and other weaving inventions) was born at Nottinghamshire, England. He died at Hastings, Sussex, England, Oct 30, 1823.

FORT MOORE ESTABLISHED: ANNIVERSARY. Apr 24, 1847. At the conclusion of the Mexican War, the Mormon Battalion of the Army of the West established Fort Moore overseeing the pueblo of Los Angeles. The fort was named in honor of their captain who had perished in the Battle of San Pascual.

FREDERICKSBURG DAY. Apr 24. Fredericksburg, VA. Spring tour of historic homes and gardens. To fund one historic garden restoration in Virginia per year. Est attendance: 2,000. For info: Visitor Center, 706 Caroline St, Fredericksburg, VA 22401. Phone: (800) 678-4748. Fax: (540) 372-6587. E-mail: fburg @illuminet.net.

IBM PERSONAL COMPUTER INTRODUCED: 20th ANNIVERSARY. April 24, 1981. IBM's first personal computer was released. Although IBM was one of the pioneers in making mainframe and other large computers, this was the company's first foray into the desktop computer market. Eventually, more IBM-compatible computers were manufactured by IBM's competitors than by IBM itself.

IRELAND: EASTER RISING: 85th ANNIVERSARY. Apr 24, 1916. Irish nationalists seized key buildings in Dublin and proclaimed an Irish republic. The rebellion collapsed, however, and it wasn't until 1922 that the Irish Free State, the predecessor of the Republic of Ireland, was established.

LIBRARY OF CONGRESS: ANNIVERSARY. Apr 24, 1800. Congress approved an act providing "for the purchase of such books as may be necessary for the use of Congress . . . and for fitting up a suitable apartment for containing them." Thus began one of the world's greatest libraries.

NATIONAL CONVENTION OF AMERICAN MOTHERS, INC (WITH MOTHER OF THE YEAR AWARD). Apr 24–29. Portland, OR. To announce the National Mother of the Year®. For info: Susan Hickenlooper, Exec Dir, American Mothers, Inc®, Waldorf-Astoria, 301 Park Ave, New York, NY 10022. Phone: (212) 755-2539 or (877) 242-4AMI. Fax: (212) 755-2539. E-mail: info@americanmothers.org.

SPACE MILESTONE: *CHINA 1* (PEOPLE'S REPUBLIC OF CHINA). Apr 24, 1970. China became the fifth nation to orbit a satellite with launch of its own rocket. Broadcast Chinese song "Tang Fang Hung" ("The East Is Red") and telemetric signals.

THOMAS, ROBERT BAILEY: BIRTH ANNIVERSARY. Apr 24, 1766. Founder and editor of *The Farmer's Almanac* (first issue for 1793) was born at Grafton, MA. Thomas died May 19, 1846, while working on the 1847 edition.

TROLLOPE, ANTHONY: BIRTH ANNIVERSARY. Apr 24, 1815. English novelist (*Barchester Towers*), born at London, England, and died there Dec 6, 1882. "Of the needs a book has," he wrote in his autobiography, "the chief need is that it be readable."

WARREN, ROBERT PENN: BIRTH ANNIVERSARY. Apr 24, 1905. American poet, novelist, essayist and critic. America's first official poet laureate, 1986–88, Robert Penn Warren was born at Guthrie, KY. Warren was awarded the Pulitzer Prize for his novel *All the King's Men*, as well as for his poetry in 1958 and 1979. He died of cancer Sept 15, 1989, at Stratton, VT.

BIRTHDAYS TODAY

Eric Balfour, 24, actor (*Rescue Me, No One Would Tell*), musician, born Los Angeles, CA, Apr 24, 1977.

Eric Bogosian, 48, actor (*Under Siege 2*), playwright, performance artist, born Boston, MA, Apr 24, 1953.

A. Paul Cellucci, 53, Governor of Massachusetts (R), born Hudson, MA, Apr 24, 1948.

Richard M. Daley, 58, mayor of Chicago, born Chicago, IL, Apr 24, 1943.

Jim Geringer, 57, Governor of Wyoming (R), born Wheatland, WY, Apr 24, 1944.

Sue Grafton, 61, author (*L Is for Lawless, M Is for Malice*), born Louisville, KY, Apr 24, 1940.

Chipper Jones, 29, baseball player, born DeLand, FL, Apr 24, 1972.

Stanley J. Kauffmann, 85, critic, born New York, NY, Apr 24, 1916.

Shirley MacLaine, 67, author, actress (Oscar for *Terms of Endearment; The Turning Point, Being There*), born Richmond, VA, Apr 24, 1934.

Michael O'Keefe, 46, actor (*The Great Santini, Caddyshack*; stage: *Mass Appeal*), born Larchmont, NY, Apr 24, 1955.

Barbra Streisand, 59, singer, actress (Oscar for *Funny Girl; The Way We Were, Yentl*); director (*Prince of Tides*), born New York, NY, Apr 24, 1942.

APRIL 25 — WEDNESDAY
Day 115 — 250 Remaining

ABORTION FIRST LEGALIZED: ANNIVERSARY. Apr 25, 1967. The first law legalizing abortion in the US was signed by Colorado Governor John Arthur Love. The law allowed therapeutic abortions in cases in which a three-doctor panel unanimously agreed.

ADMINISTRATIVE PROFESSIONALS DAY. Apr 25. Annually, the Wednesday of Administrative Professionals Week. For info: Rick Stroud, Communications Dir, Intl Assn of Administrative Professionals, 10502 NW Ambassador Dr, PO Box 20404, Kansas City, MO 64195-0404. Phone: (816) 891-6600 ext 239. E-mail: rstroud@iaap-hq.org. Web: www.iaap-hq.org.

AMERICAN QUILTER'S SOCIETY QUILT SHOW. Apr 25–28. Paducah, KY. More than 400 quilts are exhibited with $100,000 awarded in prizes. Seminars, workshops. Est attendance: 30,000. For info: American Quilter's Soc, PO Box 3290, Paducah, KY 42002. Phone: (502) 898-7903.

ANZAC DAY. Apr 25. Australia, New Zealand and Samoa. Memorial day and veterans' observance, especially to mark WWI Anzac landing at Gallipoli, Turkey, in 1915 (ANZAC: Australia and New Zealand Army Corps).

BATTLE OF GALLIPOLI: ANNIVERSARY. Apr 25, 1915–Jan, 1916. In the Gallipoli Expedition, or the Dardanelles Campaign, during World War I combined Allied naval and military forces tried to capture the Gallipoli peninsula in Turkey in order to effect an open route to Russia via the Black Sea. One French and four British divisions were forced back by a strong Turkish-German defense after almost nine months of fighting. The Australian-New Zealand Army Corps (ANZACS) took much of the brunt of the battle.

EAST MEETS WEST: ANNIVERSARY. Apr 25, 1945. US Army Lieutenant Albert Kotzebue encountered a single Soviet soldier near the German village of Lechwitz, 75 miles south of Berlin. Patrols of General Leonard Gerow's V Corps saluted the advance guard of Marshall Ivan Konev's Soviet 58th Guards Division. Soldiers of both nations embraced and exchanged toasts.

EGYPT: SINAI DAY. Apr 25. National holiday celebrating the liberation of Sinai in 1982 after the peace treaty between Egypt and Israel.

FARRAGUT CAPTURES NEW ORLEANS: ANNIVERSARY. Apr 25, 1862. Union forces under the command of Flag Officer David Farragut seized the city of New Orleans, LA, resulting in the surrender of several Confederate forts along the Mississippi in subsequent days. This action removed any Confederate resistance to Northern action on the Mississippi River as far north as New Orleans.

FIRST LICENSE PLATES: 100th ANNIVERSARY. Apr 25, 1901. New York began requiring license plates on automobiles, the first state to do so.

FITZGERALD, ELLA: BIRTH ANNIVERSARY. Apr 25, 1917. "First Lady of Song," born at Newport News, VA. Jazz singer known for her treatments of Gershwin, Cole Porter, Duke Ellington and Rogers and Hart. Fitzgerald died at Beverly Hills, CA, June 15, 1996.

ITALY: LIBERATION DAY: ANNIVERSARY. Apr 25. National holiday. Commemorates the liberation of Italy from German troops in 1945.

KGBX TYPEWRITER TOSS. Apr 25. KGBX FM Radio, Springfield, MO. Participating secretaries toss a "typewriter" (now a computer terminal) from a lift-truck 30 feet in the air. The "typewriter" landing closest to the bullseye of a 60-foot target wins an array of prizes, including the afternoon off from a staffing service. 12th annual toss. Est attendance: 300. For info: Teeg Stoufer, KGBX Radio, 1856 S Glenstone, Springfield, MO 65804. Phone: (417) 890-5555. Fax: (417) 890-5050. Web: www.kgbx.com.

LEWIS, ROBERT Q.: BIRTH ANNIVERSARY. Apr 25, 1920. American comedian Robert Q. Lewis was born at New York, NY. He is best known for his many appearances on television quiz shows such as "What's My Line," "To Tell the Truth" and "Call My Bluff." He died Dec 11, 1991, at Los Angeles, CA.

MARCONI, GUGLIELMO: BIRTH ANNIVERSARY. Apr 25, 1874. Inventor of wireless telegraphy (1895) born at Bologna, Italy. Died at Rome, Italy, July 20, 1937.

PORTUGAL: LIBERTY DAY. Apr 25. Portugal. Public holiday. Anniversary of the 1974 revolution.

SPACE MILESTONE: HUBBLE SPACE TELESCOPE DEPLOYED (US). Apr 25, 1990. Deployed by *Discovery*, the telescope is the largest on-orbit observatory to date and is capable of imaging objects up to 14 billion light-years away. The resolution of images was expected to be seven to ten times greater than images from Earth-based telescopes, since the Hubble Space Telescope is not hampered by Earth's atmospheric distortion. Launched Apr 12, 1990, from Kennedy Space Center, FL. Unfortunately, the telescope's lenses were defective, so the anticipated high quality of imaging was not possible. In 1993, however, the world watched as a shuttle crew successfully retrieved the Hubble from orbit, executed the needed repair and replacement work and released it into orbit once more. In December 1999 the space shuttle *Discovery* was launched to do extensive repairs on the telescope.

THEODORE ROOSEVELT NATIONAL PARK ESTABLISHED: ANNIVERSARY. Apr 25, 1947. Located in North Dakota, the Theodore Roosevelt National Park includes two sections of the Badlands on the Missouri River as well as Theodore Roosevelt's Elkhorn Ranch.

WALDSEEMULLER, MARTIN: REMEMBRANCE DAY. Apr 25, 1507. Little is known about the obscure scholar now called the "godfather of America," the German geographer and mapmaker Martin Waldseemuller, who gave America its name. In a book titled *Cosmographiae Introductio*, published Apr 25, 1507, Waldseemuller wrote: "Inasmuch as both Europe and Asia received their names from women, I see no reason why any one should justly object to calling this part Amerige, i.e., the land of Amerigo, or America, after Amerigo, its discoverer, a man of great ability." Believing it was the Italian navigator and merchant Amerigo Vespucci who had discovered the new continent, Waldseemuller sought to honor Vespucci by placing his name on his map of the world, published in 1507. First applied only to the South American continent, it soon was used for both the American continents. Waldseemuller did not learn about the voyage of Christopher Columbus until several years later. Of the thousand copies of his map that were printed, only one is known to have survived. Waldseemuller probably was born at Radolfzell, Germany, about 1470. He died at St. Die, France, about 1517–20. See also: "Vespucci, Amerigo: Birth Anniversary" (Mar 9).

BIRTHDAYS TODAY

Hank Azaria, 37, actor (*The Birdcage*, many voices on "The Simpsons"), born Forest Hills, NY, Apr 25, 1964.

Jeffrey DeMunn, 54, actor (*Ragtime, Frances*), born Buffalo, NY, Apr 25, 1947.

Tim Duncan, 25, basketball player, born St. Croix, Virgin Islands, Apr 25, 1976.

Jon Kyl, 59, US Senator (R, Arizona), born Oakland, NE, Apr 25, 1942.

Meadow George ("Meadowlark") Lemon III, 69, former basketball player, born Lexington, SC, Apr 25, 1932.

	S	M	T	W	T	F	S
April		1	2	3	4	5	6	7
2001	8	9	10	11	12	13	14
	15	16	17	18	19	20	21
	22	23	24	25	26	27	28
	29	30					

Paul Mazursky, 71, director (*Harry and Tonto, An Unmarried Woman, Scenes from a Mall*), born Brooklyn, NY, Apr 25, 1930.

Al Pacino, 61, actor (Oscar for *Scent of a Woman; Dog Day Afternoon, Godfather* movies), born East Harlem, NY, Apr 25, 1940.

Talia Shire, 55, actress (Connie in the *Godfather* movies, Adrian in the *Rocky* movies), born Jamaica, NY, Apr 25, 1946.

Renee Zellweger, 32, actress (*Jerry Maguire, Reality Bites*), born Katy, TX, Apr 25, 1969.

APRIL 26 — THURSDAY
Day 116 — 249 Remaining

AUDUBON, JOHN JAMES: BIRTH ANNIVERSARY. Apr 26, 1785. American artist and naturalist, best known for his *Birds of America*, born at Haiti. Died Jan 27, 1851, at New York, NY.

A(UGUSTA) BAKER'S DOZEN—A CELEBRATION OF STORIES. Apr 26–28. Columbia, SC. Annual event honors Augusta Baker and recognizes her distinguished career as librarian, storyteller, teacher and author. It features outstanding authors, illustrators and storytellers. Sponsors: Richland County Public Library and the College of Library and Information Science, Univ of South Carolina. Est attendance: 4,000. For info: Judy McClendon, PR Librarian, Richland County Public Library, 1431 Assembly St, Columbia, SC 29201. Phone: (803) 929-3440. Fax: (803) 929-3459.

BECKWOURTH, JIM: BIRTH ANNIVERSARY. Apr 26, 1798. Black American mountain man was born at Virginia and died in 1867(?) at Denver, Colorado Territory. Marrying a series of Indian women, Beckwourth lived with the Crow Indians for about six years. He went further west, establishing a route through the Sierras to the newly discovered gold fields of California, where he was immortalized by journalist Thomas Bonner. He later served as a guide and interpreter for US troops in the Cheyenne War of 1864. He died mysteriously during a return visit to the Crow.

BIG TEN MEN'S TENNIS CHAMPIONSHIP. Apr 26–29. University of Wisconsin, Madison, WI. For info: Sue Ryan, Big Ten Conference, 1500 W Higgins Rd, Park Ridge, IL 60068-6300. Phone: (847) 696-1010. Fax: (847) 696-1110. Web: www.bigten .org or www.bigtenchampionships.com.

BIG TEN WOMEN'S TENNIS CHAMPIONSHIP. Apr 26–29. Ohio State University, Columbus, OH. For info: Big Ten Conference, 1500 W Higgins Rd, Park Ridge, IL 60068-6300. Phone: (847) 696-1010. Fax: (847) 696-1150. Web: www.bigten .org.

BIG 12 MEN'S AND WOMEN'S TENNIS CHAMPIONSHIP. Apr 2–29. Waco, TX. Est attendance: 1,000. For info: Big 12 Conference, 2201 Stemmons Freeway, 28th Floor, Dallas, TX 75207. Phone: (214) 742-1212. Fax: (214) 742-2046. Web: www.big12sports.com.

BILL SHAKESPEARE'S BIRTHDAY CELEBRATION. Apr 26. Botanica, the Wichita Gardens, Wichita, KS. A celebration of Shakespeare's 437th birthday. The Birthday Boy is joined by more than 200 entertainers—musicians, actors, jugglers, duelers and members of the Royal Court. Annually, the closest Thursday to Shakespeare's birth. Est attendance: 2,500. For info: Jeanice Thomas, Arts and Humanities Council, 225 W Lewis, Wichita, KS 67202. Phone: (316) 337-9045. E-mail: cityarts .wichita@kscable.com. Web: www.cityartswichita.com.

CHERNOBYL NUCLEAR REACTOR DISASTER: 15th ANNIVERSARY. Apr 26, 1986. At 1:23 AM, local time, an explosion occurred at the Chernobyl atomic power station at Pripyat in the Ukraine. The resulting fire burned for days, sending radioactive material into the atmosphere. More than 100,000 persons were evacuated from a 300-square-mile area around the plant. Three months later 31 people were reported to have died and thousands exposed to dangerous levels of radiation. Estimates projected an additional 1,000 cancer cases in nations downwind of the radioactive discharge. The plant was encased in a concrete tomb in an effort to prevent the still-hot reactor from overheating again and to minimize further release of radiation.

"CHINA BEACH" TV PREMIERE: ANNIVERSARY. Apr 26, 1988. The stories of "China Beach" revolved around the lives of the women serving at a Da Nang armed forces hospital during the Vietnam War. The theme and background music of the series evoked plenty of nostalgia from the turbulent era. The ABC drama was created by William Boyles, Jr, and John Sacret Young. The cast featured Dana Delany, Michael Boatman, Nancy Giles, Jeff Kober, Robert Picardo, Concetta Tomei, Brian Wimmer, Marg Helgenberger, Chloe Webb, Nan Woods, Megan Gallagher, Ned Vaughn and Ricki Lake.

CIVIL WAR REENACTMENT. Apr 26–29. Rand Park, Keokuk, IA. Battle reenactment, military ball, theater production, historic encampment, ladies' tea and style show and military band concert. Est attendance: 25,000. For info: Kirk Brandenberger, Keokuk Area Conv and Tourism Bureau, 329 Main, Keokuk, IA 52632. Phone: (800) 383-1219 or (319) 524-5599. Fax: (319) 524-5016. E-mail: keokukia@interl.net. Web: www.keokuktourism.com.

CONFEDERATE MEMORIAL DAY IN FLORIDA AND GEORGIA. Apr 26. See also: Confederate Memorial Day entries for Apr 30, May 10 and May 28.

EIGHTEENTH-CENTURY MARKET FAIR AND RIFLE FROLIC. Apr 26–29 (tentative). Big Pool, MD. A gathering of the best 18th-century-style artisans and craftsmen amidst a historical encampment. Est attendance: 6,000. For info: Fort Frederick State Park, 11100 Fort Frederick Rd, Big Pool, MD 21711. Phone: (301) 842-2155. Fax: (301) 842-0028.

ENGLAND: HARROGATE SPRING FLOWER SHOW. Apr 26–29. Great Yorkshire Showground, Harrogate, North Yorkshire. Spectacular exhibits and displays at Britain's largest spring show. Est attendance: 60,000. For info: Roger Brownbridge, Show Dir, North of England Horticultural Soc, 4A South Park Rd, Harrogate, North Yorkshire, England HG1 4RQ. Phone: (44) (142) 356-1049. Fax: (44) (142) 353-6880. E-mail: info@flowershow.org.uk. Web: www.flowershow.org.uk.

FAUSET, JESSIE REDMON: BIRTH ANNIVERSARY. Apr 26, 1882. African-American poet, editor and novelist, born at Fredericksville, NJ, and died in 1961. Fauset, as literary editor of *Crisis* (a publication of the NAACP), was a patron to so many writers of the Harlem Renaissance that her efforts prompted Langston Hughes to dub her the "midwife of the so-called New Negro Literature." Along with W.E.B. Du Bois, Fauset also published and edited the children's magazine *The Brownie Book*. Her novels about the African-American middle-class experience dealt with issues of identity, autonomy and struggles for fulfillment. Her most recognized works include *The Chinaberry Tree* (1931) and *Comedy, American Style* (1933).

FIDDLER'S FROLICS. Apr 26–29. Knights of Columbus Hall, Hallettsville, TX. Competition to determine the Texas state champion fiddler and inductees to the Texas Fiddlers Hall of Fame. Est attendance: 15,000. For info: Kenneth Henneke, Co-chair, PO Box 46, Hallettsville, TX 77964. Phone: (361) 798-5934 or (361) 798-2311. Fax: (361) 798-4365. Web: www.kchall.com.

GUERNICA MASSACRE: ANNIVERSARY. Apr 26, 1937. Late in the afternoon, the ancient Basque town of Guernica, in northern Spain, was attacked without warning by German-made airplanes. Three hours of intensive bombing left the town in flames, and citizens who fled to the fields and ditches around Guernica were machine-gunned from the air. This atrocity inspired Pablo Picasso's mural *Guernica*. Responsibility for the bombing was never officially established, but the suffering and anger of the victims and their survivors are still evident at anniversary demonstrations. Intervention by Nazi Germany in the Spanish Civil War has been described as practice for WWII.

HESS, RUDOLF: BIRTH ANNIVERSARY. Apr 26, 1894. One of the most bizarre figures of World War II Germany, Walter Richard Rudolf Hess was born at Alexandria, Egypt. He was a close friend, confidant and personal secretary to Adolf Hitler who had dictated much of *Mein Kampf* to Hess while both were prisoners at Landsberg Prison. Third in command in Nazi Germany, Hess surprised the world on May 10, 1941, by flying alone to Scotland and parachuting from his plane on what he called a "mission of humanity": offering peace to Britain if she would join Germany in attacking the Soviet Union. He was immediately taken prisoner of war. At the Nuremberg Trials (1946), after questions about his sanity, he was convicted and sentenced to life imprisonment at Spandau Allied War Crimes Prison at Berlin, Germany. Outliving all other prisoners there, he was the only inmate from 1955 until he succeeded (in his fourth attempt) in committing suicide. He died at West Berlin, Germany, Aug 17, 1987.

HUG AN AUSTRALIAN DAY. Apr 26. To show our great appreciation for all the love and support the Aussies have given us over the years. Sponsored by Wellcat Holidays [© 2000 WH]. For info: Thomas or Ruth Roy, 2418 Long Ln, Lebanon, PA 17046. Phone: (717) 279-0184. E-mail: wellcat@supernet.com. Web: www.wellcat.com.

LOOS, ANITA: BIRTH ANNIVERSARY. Apr 26, 1893. American author and playwright, born at Sisson, CA. She is best remembered for her book *Gentlemen Prefer Blondes*, published in 1925. Loos, a brunette, died at New York, NY, Aug 18, 1981.

MONTGOMERY WARD SEIZED: ANNIVERSARY. Apr 26, 1944. Montgomery Ward Chairman Sewell Avery was physically removed from his office when federal troops seized Ward's Chicago offices after the company refused to obey President Franklin D. Roosevelt's order to recognize a CIO union. Government control ended May 9, shortly before the National Labor Relations Board announced the United Mail Order Warehouse and Retail Employees Union had won an election to represent the company's workers.

NATIONAL PLAYGROUND SAFETY DAY. Apr 26. An opportunity for families, community parks, schools and childcare facilities to focus on preventing public playground-related injuries. Sponsored by the National Program for Playground Safety (NPPS), this event helps educate the public about the more than 200,000 children (that's one child every 2 ½ minutes) that require emergency-room treatment for playground-related injuries each year. For info: Natl Program for Playground Safety, School of HPELS, UNI, Cedar Falls, IA 50614-0618. Phone: (800) 554-PLAY. Fax: (319) 273-7308. Web: www.uni.edu/playground.

NEW BEGINNING FESTIVAL. Apr 26–28. Coffeyville, KS. A multi-state arts and crafts festival, cheese festival, carnival, entertainment, 5K run, car show, kite festival. Est attendance: 15,000. For info: Chamber of Commerce, Box 457, Coffeyville, KS 67337. Phone: (316) 251-2550. Fax: (316) 251-5448. E-mail: chamber@coffeyville.com.

OLMSTED, FREDERICK LAW: BIRTH ANNIVERSARY. Apr 26, 1822. Known as the "father of landscape architecture in America," Olmsted participated in the designing of Yosemite National Park, New York City's Central Park and parks for Boston, Hartford and Louisville. Born at Hartford, CT, died at Waverly, MA, Aug 28, 1903. Olmsted's home and studio, Fairsted Estate outside of Boston, is now preserved as a National Historic Site and is open to the public: 99 Warren St, Brookline, MA 02146.

RICHTER SCALE DAY. Apr 26. A day to recognize the importance of Charles Francis Richter's research and his work in development of the earthquake magnitude scale that is known as the Richter scale. Richter, an American author, physicist and seismologist, was born Apr 26, 1900, near Hamilton, OH. Richter died at Pasadena, CA, Sept 30, 1985.

SIRK, DOUGLAS: BIRTH ANNIVERSARY. Apr 26, 1900. Film director Douglas Sirk was born Detlef Sierck at Hamburg, Germany. His films include *Magnificent Obsession* (1954), *Written on the Wind* (1956) and *Imitation of Life* (1959). He died Jan 14, 1987, at Lugano, Switzerland.

SOUTH AFRICAN MULTIRACIAL ELECTIONS: ANNIVERSARY. Apr 26–29, 1994. For the first time in the history of South Africa, the nation's approximately 18 million blacks voted in multiparty elections. This event marked the definitive end of apartheid, the system of racial separation that had kept blacks and other minorities out of the political process. The election resulted in Nelson Mandela of the African National Congress being elected president and F.W. de Klerk (incumbent president) of the National Party vice president.

TAKE OUR DAUGHTERS TO WORK DAY. Apr 26. A national public education campaign sponsored by the Ms Foundation for Women in which girls aged 9–15 go to work with adult hosts—parents, grandparents, cousins, aunts, uncles, friends. Take Our Daughters to Work Day has succeeded in mobilizing parents, educators, employers and other caring adults to take action to redress the inequalities in girls' lives and focus national attention on the concerns, hopes and dreams of girls. Annually, the fourth Thursday in April. For info: Take Our Daughters to Work Day, Ms. Foundation for Women, 120 Wall St, 33rd Fl, New York, NY 10005. Phone: (800) 676-7780. Fax: (212) 742-1531. E-mail: todtwcom@ms.foundation.org. Web: www.takeourdaughterstowork.org.

TANZANIA: UNION DAY. Apr 26. Celebrates union between mainland Tanzania (formerly Tanganyika) and the islands of Zanzibar and Pemba, in 1964.

A TASTE FOR KNOWLEDGE. Apr 26. Los Angeles County, CA. A massive county-wide collaboration among the region's finest restaurants and dining establishments to raise monies for public libraries in Los Angeles County. The Los Angeles Public Library Foundation will partner with a number of the region's restaurant chef/owners, food editors, restaurant reviewers, the Food Channel and renowned cookbook authors. Participating restaurants are asked to donate 10 percent of the day's gross revenues to the Foundation. Annually, the Wednesday or Thursday before the last weekend in April. Est attendance: 50,000. For info: Los Angeles County Public Library Foundation, 7400 E Imperial Hwy, Downey, CA 90241. Phone: (562) 434-1010. Fax: (562) 803-3032. E-mail: bizlinks@webtv.net.

US HOLOCAUST MUSEUM: ANNIVERSARY. Apr 26, 1993. Washington, DC. More than two million visitors toured the permanent exhibition during its first year of operation.

WASHINGTON STATE APPLE BLOSSOM FESTIVAL. Apr 26–May 7. Wenatchee, WA. To showcase the greater Wenatchee Valley, its people and heritage by producing an ongoing community celebration. Parades, arts and crafts, gem and mineral show, theatrical productions, Youth Day and carnival. More than 40 events. Annually, the last weekend in April through the first weekend in May. Est attendance: 100,000. For info: Washington State Apple Blossom Festival, Box 2836, Wenatchee, WA 98807. Phone: (509) 662-3616. Fax: (509) 665-0347.

April *2001*	S	M	T	W	T	F	S
		1	2	3	4	5	6	7
	8	9	10	11	12	13	14
	15	16	17	18	19	20	21
	22	23	24	25	26	27	28
	29	30					

BIRTHDAYS TODAY

Carol Burnett, 65, actress ("Garry Moore Show," "Carol Burnett Show," *The Four Seasons*), born San Antonio, TX, Apr 26, 1936.

Joan Chen, 40, actress ("Twin Peaks," "Golden Gates"), born Shanghai, China, Apr 26, 1961.

Michael Damian, 39, actor ("Young and the Restless"; stage: *Joseph and the Amazing Technicolor Dreamcoat*), born San Diego, CA, Apr 26, 1962.

Duane Eddy, 63, musician, born Corning, NY, Apr 26, 1938.

Giancarlo Esposito, 43, actor (*Do the Right Thing, Twilight*), born Copenhagen, Denmark, Apr 26, 1958.

Kevin James, 36, actor ("The King of Queens"), born Stony Brook, NY, Apr 26, 1965.

Boyd Matson, 54, TV journalist (host of "National Geographic Explorer"), born Oklahoma City, OK, Apr 26, 1947.

Bobby Rydell, 59, singer ("Wild One," "Volare"), born Philadelphia, PA, Apr 26, 1942.

Gary Wright, 58, musician, born Englewood, NJ, Apr 26, 1943.

APRIL 27 — FRIDAY
Day 117 — 248 Remaining

ARBOR DAY IN ARIZONA. Apr 27. The last Friday in April is proclaimed as Arbor Day in Arizona. It is not a legal holiday.

BABE RUTH DAY: ANNIVERSARY. Apr 27, 1947. Babe Ruth Day was celebrated in every ballpark in organized baseball in the US as well as Japan. Mortally ill with throat cancer, Ruth appeared at Yankee Stadium to thank his former club for the honor.

BEGINNING OF THE END OF THE CIVIL WAR: ANNIVERSARY. Apr 27, 1864. Union General Ulysses S. Grant issued orders to his armies that would lead to the end of the American Civil War. The plan called for Sherman to advance on Confederate forces through Georgia, Siegal to move through the Shenandoah Valley, Butler to advance up the James River toward Richmond and Meade to follow and engage the Army of Northern Virginia under Robert E. Lee.

BIG TEN WOMEN'S GOLF CHAMPIONSHIP. Apr 27–29. University of Minnesota, Minneapolis, MN. For info: Sue Ryan, Big Ten Conference, 1500 W Higgins Rd, Park Ridge, IL 60068-6300. Phone: (847) 696-1010. Fax: (847) 696-1110. Web: www.bigten.org or www.bigtenchampionships.com.

BIRDWATCHING WEEKEND. Apr 27–29. Madison, MN. More than 225 birdwatchers check out the birds at Salt Lake, a small saltwater lake just west and south of Madison where more than 150 species of birds have been spotted in past years. Sponsor: Minnesota Ornithologists' Union and the Prairie Woods Nature Society. Housing sponsored by Madison Ambassadors, Saturday evening meal sponsored by Sons of Norway in Madison. Continental breakfast and noon lunch on Saturday sponsored by American Legion Club of Marietta. Annually, the fourth weekend in April. Est attendance: 500. For info: Maynard Meyer, Chamber of Commerce, PO Box 70, Madison, MN 56256. Phone: (320) 598-7301. Fax: (320) 598-7955.

BLUEBERRY HILL OPEN DART TOURNAMENT. Apr 27–29. St. Louis, MO. America's oldest (29th annual) and largest pub dart tournament open to everyone. Est attendance: 500. For info: Joe Edwards, Blueberry Hill, 6504 Delmar, St. Louis, MO 63130. Phone: (314) 727-0880. Web: www.blueberryhill.com.

CONNECTICUT STORYTELLING FESTIVAL. Apr 27–29. Connecticut College, New London, CT. Annual festival features performances for families and adults, plus workshops and story-sharing by Connecticut and nationally renowned storytellers. Annually, in April. Est attendance: 500. For info: Ann Shapiro, Adm, Connecticut Storytelling Center, Connecticut College Box 5295, 270 Mohegan Ave, New London, CT 06320. Phone: (860) 439-2764. Fax: (860) 439-2895. E-mail: csc@conncoll.edu.

DAFFODIL FESTIVAL. Apr 27–29. Nantucket Island, MA. Daffodil show, shop window displays, antique car parade, tailgate picnic, flower show (Saturday and Sunday). Est attendance: 5,000. For info: Nantucket Island Chamber of Commerce, 48 Main St, Nantucket, MA 02554-3595. Phone: (508) 228-1700.

DENNIS, SANDY: BIRTH ANNIVERSARY. Apr 27, 1937. American actress Sandy Dennis was born Sandra Dale Dennis at Hastings, NE. In addition to two Tony Awards she won an Academy Award for her supporting role in *Who's Afraid of Virginia Woolf* (1966). She died Mar 2, 1992, at Westport, CT.

DISCOVERY WALK FESTIVAL. Apr 27–29. Red Lion Inn at the Quay, Vancouver, WA. International multi-day walking event, non-competitive. Sanctioned by the International Marching League and American Volkssport Association. Distances of 5K, 10K, 21K and 42K. Annually, the fourth weekend in April. Est attendance: 3,000. For info: William Byrd, PO Box 2009, Vancouver, WA 98668. Phone: (360) 892-6758. E-mail: bill@discoverywalk.org. Web: www.discoverywalk.org.

DOGWOOD ARTS AND CRAFTS FESTIVAL. Apr 27–29. Huntington Civic Arena, Huntington, WV. 31st annual. Craft and food booths plus live entertainment for all ages. Annually, the last full weekend in April. Est attendance: 15,000. For info: Cheryl Myers, Huntington Civic Arena, PO Box 2767, One Civic Center Plaza, Huntington, WV 25701. Phone: (304) 696-5990. Fax: (304) 696-4463. Web: www.hcarena.com.

DOGWOOD FESTIVAL. Apr 27–29. Camdenton, MO. This annual rite of spring features music, food, parade, arts and crafts, art exhibitions and more. For info: Bruce Mitchell, Exec Dir, Camdenton Area Chamber of Commerce, PO Box 1375, Camdenton, MO 65020. Phone: (573) 346-2227 or (800) 769-1004. Fax: (573) 346-3496.

FLOWERCRAFT. Apr 27–29. Wilson Lodge, Oglebay, Wheeling, WV. A unique arts and crafts show, featuring more than 75 artisans displaying spring garden floral themed handcrafts. Est attendance: 4,000. For info: John Morrison, Special Events Dir, Oglebay, Rt 88 N, Wheeling, WV 26003. Phone: (304) 243-4143. Fax: (304) 243-4045. Web: www.oglebay-resort.com.

GODWIN, MARY WOLLSTONECRAFT: BIRTH ANNIVERSARY. Apr 27, 1759. English writer whose best-known book was *Vindication of the Rights of Women*, published in 1792. Born at London, England, and died there Sept 10, 1797. Her daughter, Mary, was the wife of poet Percy Bysshe Shelley but is best remembered as the author of *Frankenstein*, published in 1818.

GRANT, ULYSSES SIMPSON: BIRTH ANNIVERSARY. Apr 27, 1822. 18th president of the US (Mar 4, 1869–Mar 3, 1877), born Hiram Ulysses Grant at Point Pleasant, OH. He graduated from the US Military Academy in 1843. President Lincoln promoted Grant to lieutenant general in command of all the Union armies Mar 9, 1864. On Apr 9, 1865, Grant received General Robert E. Lee's surrender, at Appomattox Court House, VA, which he announced to the Secretary of War as follows: "General Lee surrendered the Army of Northern Virginia this afternoon on terms proposed by myself. The accompanying additional correspondence will show the conditions fully." Nicknamed "Unconditional Surrender Grant," he died at Mount McGregor, NY, July 23, 1885, just four days after completing his memoirs. He was buried at Riverside Park, New York, NY, where Grant's Tomb was dedicated in 1897.

HUG A PROM SPONSOR DAY. Apr 27. A day honoring all the teachers across the US who successfully help to organize, promote and chaperone their high school's prom. Annually, the fourth Friday in April. For info: Shep Moyle, Pres, Stumps, One Party Place, South Whitley, IN 46787. Phone: (800) 22-Party. Fax: (219) 723-6976. Web: www.stumpsparty.com.

ISRAEL: YOM HA'ZIKKARON (REMEMBRANCE DAY). Apr 27. Hebrew calendar date: Iyar 4, 5761. Honors the more than 20,000 soldiers killed in battle since the start of the nation's war for independence in 1947.

LANTZ, WALTER: BIRTH ANNIVERSARY. Apr 27, 1900. Originator of Universal Studios' animated opening sequence for their first major musical film, *The King of Jazz*. Walter Lantz is best remembered as the creator of Woody Woodpecker, the bird with the wacky laugh and the taunting ways. Lantz received a lifetime achievement Academy Award for his animation in 1979. He was born at New Rochelle, NY, and died Mar 22, 1994, at Burbank, CA.

MAGELLAN, FERDINAND: DEATH ANNIVERSARY. Apr 27, 1521. Portuguese explorer Ferdinand Magellan was probably born near Oporto, Portugal, about 1480, but neither the place nor the date is certain. Usually thought of as the first man to circumnavigate the earth, he died before completing the voyage; thus his co-leader, Basque navigator Juan Sebastian de Elcano, became the world's circumnavigator. The westward, 'round-the-world expedition began Sept 20, 1519, with five ships and about 250 men. Magellan was killed by natives of the Philippine island of Mactan.

MARRIAGE ENRICHMENT WEEKEND. Apr 27–29 (also Nov 2–4). Belleville, IL. Join other couples as they gather to discuss, reflect, pray, relax and share their marriage journey. The weekend includes lodging at the Shrine Motel, meals, program materials and refreshments. Registration is limited. Est attendance: 60. For info: Shrine of Our Lady of the Snows, 442 S DeMazenod Dr, Belleville, IL 62223-1094. Phone: (618) 397-6700. Fax: (618) 397-1210. Web: www.snows.org.

MATANZAS MULE DAY. Apr 27, 1898. In one of the first naval actions of the Spanish-American War, US naval forces bombarded the Cuban village of Matanzas. It was widely reported that the only casualty of the bombardment was one mule. "The Matanzas Mule" became instantly famous and remains a footnote in the history of the Spanish-American War.

MORSE, SAMUEL FINLEY BREESE: BIRTH ANNIVERSARY. Apr 27, 1791. American artist and inventor, after whom the Morse code is named, was born at Charlestown, MA, and died at New York, NY, Apr 2, 1872. Graduating from Yale University in 1810, he went to the Royal Academy of London to study painting. After returning to America he achieved success as a portraitist. Morse conceived the idea of an electromagnetic telegraph while on shipboard, returning from art instruction in Europe in 1832, and he proceeded to develop his idea. With financial assistance approved by Congress, the first telegraph line in the US was constructed, between Washington, DC, and Baltimore, MD. The first message tapped out by Morse from the Supreme Court Chamber at the US Capitol building on May 24, 1844, was: "What hath God wrought?"

NATIONAL ARBOR DAY. Apr 27. The Committee for National Arbor Day has as its goal the observance of Arbor Day in all states on the same day, the last Friday in April. This unified Arbor Day date would provide our citizenry with the opportunity to better learn the importance of trees to our way of life. This date is a good planting date for many states throughout the country. First observance of Arbor Day was in Nebraska, Apr 10, 1872, where it is still a state holiday. Observed on different dates in some states. Internationally it is Dec 22. National Arbor Day has been observed in 1970, 1972, 1988, 1990, 1991 and 1993 by Presidential Proclamation. More than half the states now observe Arbor Day on the proposed April Friday. Sponsors include: International Society of Arboriculture, Society of Municipal Arborists, American Association of Nurserymen, National Arborist Association, National Recreation and Park Association and Arborists Association of New Jersey. For info: Committee for Natl Arbor Day, 63 Fitzrandolph Rd, West Orange, NJ 07052. Phone: (201) 731-0840. Fax: (201) 731-6020.

NATIONAL CHILD CARE PROFESSIONALS DAY. Apr 27. A day of recognition for child care providers. A day to increase the visibility of the role child care providers play in our society and celebrate the partnership between parents and caregivers to help children develop to their full potential. Sponsored by Scholastic Publishing. Annually, the last Friday in April. For info: Natl Assn of Child Care Research and Referral Agencies, 1319 F St NW, Ste 810, Washington, DC 20004-1106. Phone: (202) 393-5501. Web: www.naccrra.org.

NATIONAL DREAM HOTLINE®. Apr 27–29. Now in its 13th year, the National Dream Hotline is sponsored by the School of Metaphysics as an educational service to people throughout the world. Faculty and staff of the College and Schools of Metaphysics throughout the Midwest will offer the benefits of 30 years of research into the significance and meaning of dreams by manning the hotline phones from 6 PM, EDT, Friday until midnight Sunday. Annually, the last weekend in April. For info: Laurel Clark, Natl Advisor, School of Metaphysics, World Headquarters, Windyville, MO 65783. Phone: (417) 345-8411. Fax: (417) 345-6668. E-mail: som@som.org. Web: www.som.org.

NATIONAL HAIRBALL AWARENESS DAY. Apr 27. A day to recognize hairballs in cats—the inconvenience created for owners and the discomfort suffered by our feline friends—and offer solutions to the problem while raising awareness. Annually, the last Friday in April. For info: Blake Hawley, PO Box 148, Topeka, KS 66601-0148. Phone: (785) 368-5614. Fax: (785) 368-5566. E-mail: blake_hawley@hillspet.com. Web: www.hillspet.com.

NEW ORLEANS JAZZ & HERITAGE FESTIVAL. Apr 27–May 6. New Orleans, LA. A two-weekend festival with thousands of musicians playing. Evening concerts, outdoor daytime activities, Louisiana specialty foods and handmade crafts. Est attendance: 400,000. For info: New Orleans Jazz & Heritage Festival, 1205 N Rampart St, New Orleans, LA 70116. Phone: (504) 522-4786. Web: www.nojazzfest.com.

PANOPLY® 2001. Apr 27–29. Big Spring International Park, Huntsville, AL. Comprehensive arts festival celebrating the performing arts through a variety of music, theatre and dance. Visual arts are presented in a juried art show. Est attendance: 120,000. For info: The Arts Council, 700 Monroe St, Ste 2, Huntsville, AL 35801. Phone: (256) 519-ARTS. Fax: (256) 533-3811. Web: www.panoply.org.

POMPANO BEACH SEAFOOD FESTIVAL. Apr 27–29. Pompano Beach, FL. Fresh seafood prepared by Broward's finest restaurants plus live music and arts and crafts. Est attendance: 100,000. For info: Pompano Beach Chamber of Commerce, 2200 E Atlantic Blvd, Pompano Beach, FL 33062. Phone: (954) 941-2940.

RATTLESNAKE DERBY. Apr 27–29. Mangum, OK. Hunters stalk these wily reptiles and attempt to bring in the most snakes and the longest snake. Snakeskins and meat will be sold, and entertainment will include live music, a carnival and flea market. A herpetologist will be on hand to educate festival-goers. Annually, the last full weekend in April. Est attendance: 40,000. For info: Shortgrass Rattlesnake Assn. Phone: (580) 782-2434 or Chamber of Commerce, 222 W Jefferson, Mangum, OK 73554. Phone: (580) 782-2444.

April 2001	S	M	T	W	T	F	S
	1	2	3	4	5	6	7
	8	9	10	11	12	13	14
	15	16	17	18	19	20	21
	22	23	24	25	26	27	28
	29	30					

SIERRA LEONE: INDEPENDENCE DAY: 40th ANNIVERSARY. Apr 27. National Day. Commemorates independence from Britain in 1961.

SOUTH AFRICA: FREEDOM DAY. Apr 27. National holiday. Commemorates the day in 1994 when, for the first time, all South Africans had the opportunity to vote.

SOUTH CAROLINA FESTIVAL OF ROSES. Apr 27–29 (tentative). Edisto Memorial Gardens, Orangeburg, SC. To celebrate the beauty of the roses and the gardens. Est attendance: 35,000. For info: Lue Aiken, Orangeburg County Chamber of Commerce, PO Box 328, Orangeburg, SC 29116-0328. Phone: (803) 534-6821 or (800) 545-6153. Fax: (803) 531-9435. Web: www.orangeburgsc.net.

SPRING FESTIVAL. Apr 27–May 6. Cape May, NJ. Spring into the Victorian lifestyle with a weekend of tours and events celebrating the coming of spring in the nation's first seashore resort. Features a restoration house tour and exposition, brass band concert, authentic Victorian dinner and more. Annually, the third week in April. Est attendance: 6,500. For info: Mid-Atlantic Center for the Arts, 1048 Washington St, PO Box 340, Cape May, NJ 08204. Phone: (609) 884-5404. Fax: (609) 884-2006. Web: www.capemaymac.org.

SPRING FLING. Apr 27–29. Wichita Falls, TX. A celebration of the arts. Artists from all over the US display their art. Food booths, demonstrations and entertainment. Est attendance: 21,000. For info: Wichita Falls CVB, PO Box 1860, Wichita Falls, TX 76307. Phone: (940) 716-5500 or (940) 692-0923. Fax: (940) 716-5509.

SUGARLOAF'S SPRING TIMONIUM CRAFT FESTIVAL. Apr 27–29. Maryland State Fairgrounds, Timonium, MD. This show, now in its 24th year, features 380 nationally recognized craft designers and fine artists displaying and selling their original creations. Craft demonstrations, live music, children's entertainment, food, hourly gift certificate drawings and more. Est attendance: 23,000. For info: Sugarloaf Mountain Works, Inc, 200 Orchard Ridge Dr, #215, Gaithersburg, MD 20878. Phone: (800) 210-9900. E-mail: smworks@sugarloafcrafts.com. Web: www.sugarloafcrafts.com.

SULTANA STEAMSHIP EXPLOSION: ANNIVERSARY. Apr 27, 1865. Early in the morning on this day, America's worst steamship disaster occurred. The *Sultana*, heavily overloaded with an estimated 2,300 passengers, exploded in the Mississippi River, just north of Memphis, en route to Cairo, IL. Most of the passengers were Union soldiers who had been prisoners of war and were eagerly returning to their homes. Although there was never an accurate accounting of the dead, estimates range from 1,450 to nearly 2,000. Cause of the explosion was not determined, but the little-known event is unparalleled in US history.

TEXAS STATE CHAMPIONSHIP FIDDLERS FROLICS. Apr 27–29. Halletsville, TX. Old-time fiddling championship of Texas. The best-tasting sausage in Texas contest. Proceeds to various charities. Est attendance: 15,000. For info: Knights of Columbus, Box 46, Hallettsville, TX 77964. Phone: (512) 798-2311. Fax: (512) 798-4365. E-mail: arjo9286@cvtv.net. Web: www.hallettsville.com.

TOGO: INDEPENDENCE DAY: ANNIVERSARY. Apr 27. National holiday. In 1960 Togo gained its independence from French administration under a UN trusteeship.

WORLD'S LARGEST MATH EVENT. Apr 27. This will be a one-day event celebrating mathematics. Students will use mathematics to perform fascinating tasks and gain a greater understanding of mathematics and how it relates to the real world. For info: Natl Council of Teachers of Mathematics, 1906 Association Dr, Reston, VA 20191-9988. Phone: (703) 620-9840. Fax: (703) 476-2970. E-mail: infocentral@nctm.org. Web: www.nctm.org.

YUGOSLAVIA: NATIONAL DAY. Apr 27. Commemorates the formulation of Yugoslav Federation (consisting of Serbia and Montenegro) by the adoption of a constitution in 1992

BIRTHDAYS TODAY

Anouk Aimee, 67, actress (*A Man and a Woman, The Golden Salamander*), born Paris, France, Apr 27, 1934.

Sheena Easton (Sheena Shirley Orr), 42, singer ("Morning Train"), born Bellshill, Scotland, Apr 27, 1959.

Casey Kasem, 69, radio, TV host ("America's Top 40"), born Detroit, MI, Apr 27, 1932.

Coretta Scott King, 74, lecturer, writer, widow of Martin Luther King, Jr, born Marion, AL, Apr 27, 1927.

Jack Klugman, 79, actor ("The Odd Couple," "Quincy, ME"), born Philadelphia, PA, Apr 27, 1922.

APRIL 28 — SATURDAY

Day 118 — 247 Remaining

ANTIQUE AND COLLECTIBLE FLEA MARKET. Apr 28–29. Weston, MO. 19th annual flea market sponsored by the Weston Lions Club, with antiques, collectibles and food available. Est attendance: 2,000. For info: Weston Development, 502 Main, Weston, MO 64098. Phone: (816) 640-2909.

ASTRONOMY DAY. Apr 28. To take astronomy to the people. International Astronomy Day is observed on a Saturday near the first quarter moon between mid-April and mid-May. Co-sponsored by 15 astronomical organizations. See also "Astronomy Week" (Apr 23). For info: Gary E. Tomlinson, Coord, Astronomy Day Headquarters, c/o Chaffee Planetarium, 272 Pearl NW, Grand Rapids, MI 49504. Phone: (616) 456-3532. E-mail: gtomlins @triton.net. Web: www.astroleague.org.

BARRYMORE, LIONEL: BIRTH ANNIVERSARY. Apr 28, 1878. Famed American actor of celebrated acting family, Lionel Barrymore was born Lionel Blythe, at Philadelphia, PA. He died at Van Nuys, CA, Nov 15, 1954. US Postal Service stamp issued in 1982 honored Ethel, John and Lionel Barrymore.

BIG TEN WOMEN'S ROWING CHAMPIONSHIP. Apr 28. Michigan State University, East Lansing, MI. For info: Big Ten Conference, 1500 W Higgins Rd, Park Ridge, IL 60068-6300. Phone: (847) 696-1010. Fax: (847) 696-1150. Web: www.bigten .org.

BIOLOGICAL CLOCK GENE DISCOVERED: ANNIVERSARY. Apr 28, 1994. Northwestern University announced that the so-called biological clock, that gene governing the daily cycle of waking and sleeping called the circadian rhythm, had been found in mice. Never before pinpointed in a mammal, the biological clock gene was found on mouse chromosome #5.

CANADA: NATIONAL DAY OF MOURNING. Apr 28. A national day of mourning for workers killed or injured on the job in Canada. The Canadian Labour Congress first officially recognized the day in 1986. Pointing to the nearly one million workplace injuries each year in Canada, the CLC has called for stricter health and safety regulations and for annual recognition of this day throughout Canada. Federal legislation (Bill D–223) first recognized this day in 1991.

CHAUTAUQUA CELEBRATION. Apr 28. DeFuniak Springs, FL. Annually, the fourth Saturday in April. Est attendance: 7,000. For info: Florida Chautauqua, PO Box 847, DeFuniak Springs, FL 32435. Phone: (850) 892-9494. Fax: (850) 892-9622. Web: www.floridachautauqua.com.

CRACKER DAY. Apr 28. Volusia County Fairgrounds, DeLand, FL. A celebration of Florida heritage, this event began as a cattle roundup for regional families. A variety of adult and youth events are planned, including a full rodeo, a barbecue lunch and a Cracker dance. For info: Volusia County Cattleman's Assn. Phone: (904) 822-5778.

FIRST BLOOM FESTIVAL. Apr 28–May 6. American Rose Center, Shreveport, LA. Annual festival celebrating the first spring bloom of more than 20,000 roses, camellias, azaleas, daffodils and other flowering plants. Entertainment, mini-rose sale and refreshments. Est attendance: 10,000. For info: American Rose Center, PO Box 30000, Shreveport, LA 71130-0030. Phone: (318) 938-5402. Fax: (318) 938-5405. E-mail: ars@ars-hg.org. Web: www.ars.org.

FOX 16 3-ON-3 BASKETBALL CLASSIC. Apr 28–29. War Memorial Stadium, Little Rock, AR. For info: Karen Tobey, 11711 West Markham, Little Rock, AR 72211. Phone: (501) 225-0016. Fax: (501) 225-0428. E-mail: tobey@fox16.com. Web: www.fox16.cc.

GIBBS, MIFFLIN WISTER: BIRTH ANNIVERSARY. Apr 28, 1828. Mifflin Wister Gibbs was born at Philadelphia, PA. In 1873 he became the first black man to be elected a judge in the US, winning an election for City Judge at Little Rock, AR.

HOMER, LOUISE DILWORTH: BIRTH ANNIVERSARY. Apr 28, 1871. The mesmerizing Louise Dilworth Homer was one of the most formidable contraltos of her time. Her plum roles in *Aïda, Tristan und Isolde, Hänsel und Gretel* and *Samson et Dalilah* (with the legendary Caruso), brought her tremendous acclaim. She was born at Sewickley, PA, and died at Winter Park, FL, May 6, 1947.

INDIANA GENEALOGICAL SOCIETY ANNUAL MEETING & CONFERENCE. Apr 28. Kokomo, IN. All-day conference featuring lectures, exhibits and genealogical vendors. Open to all interested in family and local history. Est attendance: 250. For info: Public Relations, Indiana Genealogical Society, PO Box 10507, Fort Wayne, IN 46852-0507. Web: www .IndGenSoc.org.

ISRAEL: YOM HA'ATZMA'UT (INDEPENDENCE DAY): ANNIVERSARY. Apr 28. Hebrew calendar date: Iyar 5, 5761. Celebrates proclamation of independence from British mandatory rule by Palestinian Jews and establishment of the state of Israel and the provisional government May 14, 1948 (Hebrew calendar date: Iyar 5, 5708). Dates in the Hebrew calendar vary from their Gregorian equivalents from year to year, so, while Iyar 5 in 1948 was May 14, in 2001 it is Apr 28.

JAMES MONROE BIRTHDAY CELEBRATION. Apr 28. Ashlawn-Highland, home of James Monroe, Charlottesville, VA. Presentation in garden pavilion. Cookies prepared from Monroe family recipe. For info: Carolyn C. Holmes, Ashlawn-Highland, 1000 James Monroe Pkwy, Charlottesville, VA 22902. Phone: (804) 293-9539. Fax: (804) 293-8000. E-mail: ashlawnjm@aol .com.

KECHI'S REDBUD FESTIVAL AND ART SHOW. Apr 28. Kechi, KS. Juried art show, including painting, sculpture, ceramics, jewelry, photography, weaving and glass. Est attendance: 1,000. For info: Rick Eberhard, Kechi Area Chamber of Commerce, 205 Heritage Ct, Kechi, KS 67067-8710. Phone: (316) 744-1337. E-mail: kechichamber@domaindiner.com. Web: www.kechiksoc.com.

KISS-YOUR-MATE DAY. Apr 28. Show your mate how much you care. Share the pleasure of a kiss when he or she least expects it. Annually, Apr 28. For info: Alan W. Brue, 1317 London Way, Lithia Springs, GA 30122. E-mail: afn05660@afn.org.

MAIN STREET FESTIVAL. Apr 28–29. Downtown Franklin, TN. 18th annual festival features more than 220 of the South's leading craftspersons. Food, entertainment (blues, pop, country, classical and rock), children's area and carnival. Showcases historical downtown. Est attendance: 100,000. For info: Laura Bustetter, Main Street Festival, PO Box 807, Franklin, TN 37065. Phone: (615) 791-9924. Fax: (615) 791-0372. E-mail: lbustetter @historicfranklin.com. Web: www.historicfranklin.com.

MARYLAND CONSTITUTION RATIFICATION: ANNIVERSARY. Apr 28, 1788. Maryland became the seventh state to ratify the Constitution, by a vote of 63 to 11.

MAYMONT'S HERBS GALORE. Apr 28. Richmond, VA. Annual celebration of herbs at Maymont, Richmond's 100-acre Victorian estate. A variety of speakers, cooking demonstrations, garden walks and more than 40 plant and craft vendors. Est attendance: 5,000. For info: Maymont Foundation, 1700 Hampton St, Richmond, VA 23220. Phone: (804) 358-7166. Web: www .maymont.org.

MONROE, JAMES: BIRTH ANNIVERSARY. Apr 28, 1758. 5th president of the US was born at Westmoreland County, VA, and served two terms in that office (Mar 4, 1817–Mar 3, 1825). Monrovia, the capital city of Liberia, is named after him, as is the Monroe Doctrine, which he enunciated at Washington, DC, Dec 2, 1823. Last of three presidents to die on US Independence Day, Monroe died at New York, NY, July 4, 1831.

MUSSOLINI EXECUTED: ANNIVERSARY. Apr 28, 1945. Italian partisans shot Benito Mussolini near the lakeside village of Dongo. Leaders of the Fascist Party, several of his friends and his mistress Clara Petacci also were executed. The 23-year-long Fascist rule of Italy was ended.

MUTINY ON THE *BOUNTY*: ANNIVERSARY. Apr 28, 1789. The most famous of all naval mutinies occurred on board HMS *Bounty*. Captain of the *Bounty* was Lieutenant William Bligh, an able seaman and a mean-tempered disciplinarian. The ship, with a load of breadfruit tree plants from Tahiti, was bound for Jamaica. Fletcher Christian, leader of the mutiny, put Bligh and 18 of his loyal followers adrift in a 23-foot open boat. Miraculously Bligh and all of his supporters survived a 47-day voyage of more than 3,600 miles, before landing on the island of Timor, June 14, 1789. In the meantime, Christian had put all of the

remaining crew (excepting 8 men and himself) ashore at Tahiti where he picked up 18 Tahitians (6 men and 12 women) and set sail again. Landing at Pitcairn Island in 1790 (probably uninhabited at the time), they burned the *Bounty* and remained undiscovered for 18 years, when an American whaler, the *Topaz*, called at the island (1808) and found only one member of the mutinous crew surviving. However, the little colony had thrived and, when counted by the British in 1856, numbered 194 persons.

NATIONAL SENSE OF SMELL DAY. Apr 28. A day when museums and science centers across the country, supported by a grant from the Olfactory Research Fund, host a variety of interactive educational activities. This day was created to educate the public about this mysterious fifth sense and explore the many ways it can positively impact our quality of life. For info: Olfactory Research Fund, 145 E 32nd St, New York, NY 10016. Phone: (212) 725-2755. Web: www.olfactory.org.

NATIVE AMERICAN HERITAGE DAY. Apr 28. Stately Oaks Plantation, Jonesboro, GA. Native American folktales, food and crafts demonstrations. Visitors get a chance to learn Native American dances and can learn to shoot a blowgun. Est attendance: 1,000. For info: Historical Jonesboro, PO Box 922, Jonesboro, GA 30237. Phone: (770) 473-0197.

NORTH TEXAS ARTS & CRAFTS SHOW. Apr 28–29 (also June 2–3, Sept 1–2 and Dec 15–16). Multi-Purpose Events Center Exhibit Hall, Wichita Falls, TX. Come shop with some of America's finest artisans. Free admission. Est attendance: 4,500. For info: Wichita Falls CVB, 1000 5th St, Wichita Falls, TX 76301. Phone: (940) 716-5500. Fax: (940) 716-5509. E-mail: MPEC@wf .net. Web: www.viewscape.com or www.wf.net.

POLK COUNTY RAMP TRAMP FESTIVAL. Apr 28. Polk County 4-H Camp, Camp McCoy, near Benton, TN. A tribute to the ramp, a wild onionlike plant that grows only in the Appalachian Mountains. Bluegrass music and feast of the ramps. Est attendance: 1,000. For info: Wm Don Ledford, Extension Leader, Box 189, Benton, TN 37307. Phone: (423) 338-4503.

REDBUD TRAIL RENDEZVOUS. Apr 28–29. Rochester, IN. Reenactment of a pre-1840 gathering to trade furs on the Tippecanoe River, tepee village, traditional music and crafts, pioneer and Indian dances, foods cooked over wood fires. Museum, round barn and Living History Village at north end of grounds. For frontier fun, follow the redbuds blooming along the Tippecanoe River. Est attendance: 2,000. For info: Fulton County Historical Soc, 37 E 375 N, Rochester, IN 46975. Phone: (219) 223-4436. E-mail: wwillard@rtcol.com.

SHRIMPFEST. Apr 28. Salem Civic Center Fairgrounds, Salem, VA. 8th annual all-you-can-eat shrimp, baked beans, corn on the cob, slaw and dessert. Outdoors; tickets in advance $18. Also includes live music, shrimp-eating contest. Est attendance: 2,500. For info: Wendi Schultz, CFE Exec Dir, Roanoke Festival in the Park, PO Box 8276, Roanoke, VA 24014. Phone: (540) 342-2640.

SOUTHERN MARYLAND CELTIC FESTIVAL. Apr 28. Jefferson Patterson Park, St. Leonard, MD. Scottish fiddling championship, bagpipe competition, Scottish heptathlon, Highland dancing competition, Celtic marketplace and crafts, parade of clans and nations, Celtic harp workshop, Celtic folk music, demonstrations and Celtic foods. Annually, the last Saturday in April. Est attendance: 10,000. For info: Celtic Soc of Southern Maryland, PO Box 209, Prince Frederick, MD 20678. Phone: (410) 257-9003. E-mail: ArkhamAslm@aol.com.

WINE AND ROSES FESTIVAL. Apr 28. Bryan, TX. This event features the 18th annual Texas Artists' Competition. The winning painting becomes the focal point for next year's Private Reserve wine label. Team grape-stomping competition, dozens of food and craft booths, a petting zoo, vineyard hayrides and tours, classic and antique cars plus a variety of live music performances. Est attendance: 9,000. For info: Steve Wiley, Mktg Dir, Messina Hof Wine Cellars, 4545 Old Reliance Rd, Bryan, TX 77808. Phone: (409) 778-9463.

April 2001	S	M	T	W	T	F	S
	1	2	3	4	5	6	7
	8	9	10	11	12	13	14
	15	16	17	18	19	20	21
	22	23	24	25	26	27	28
	29	30					

BIRTHDAYS TODAY

Ann-Margret (Ann-Margaret Olsson), 60, actress (*Carnal Knowledge, Tommy*), born Stockholm, Sweden, Apr 28, 1941.

John Daly, 35, golfer, born Carmichael, CA, Apr 28, 1966.

Saddam Hussein, 64, Iraqi dictator, born Takrit, Iraq, Apr 28, 1937.

Bruno Kirby, 52, actor (*When Harry Met Sally. . ., City Slickers*), born New York, NY, Apr 28, 1949.

Barry Louis Larkin, 37, baseball player, born Cincinnati, OH, Apr 28, 1964.

Harper Lee (Nelle Harper), 75, author (*To Kill a Mockingbird*), born Monroeville, AL, Apr 28, 1926.

Jay Leno, 51, TV talk-show host ("The Tonight Show"), comedian, born New Rochelle, NY, Apr 28, 1950.

Marcia Strassman, 53, actress ("Welcome Back Kotter," *Honey, I Shrunk the Kids*), born New York, NY, Apr, 28, 1948.

Chris Young, 30, actor ("Falcon Crest," *The Great Outdoors*), born Chambersburg, PA, Apr 28, 1971.

APRIL 29 — SUNDAY

Day 119 — 246 Remaining

ELLINGTON, "DUKE" (EDWARD KENNEDY): BIRTH ANNIVERSARY. Apr 29, 1899. "Duke" Ellington, one of the most influential individuals in jazz history, was born at Washington, DC. Ellington's professional career began when he was 17, and by 1923 he was leading a small group of musicians at the Kentucky Club at New York City who became the core of his big band. Ellington is credited with being one of the founders of big band jazz. He used his band as an instrument for composition and orchestration to create big band pieces, film scores, operas, ballets, Broadway shows and religious music. Ellington was responsible for more than 1,000 musical pieces. He drew together instruments from different sections of the orchestra to develop unique and haunting sounds such as that of his famous "Mood Indigo." "Duke" Ellington died May 24, 1974, at New York City.

ELLSWORTH, OLIVER: BIRTH ANNIVERSARY. Apr 29, 1745 (OS). Third chief justice of the US Supreme Court, born at Windsor, CT. Died there, Nov 26, 1807.

EWELL, TOM: BIRTH ANNIVERSARY. Apr 29, 1909. Born Samuel Yewell Tompkins at Owensboro, KY, Ewell acted in many films and TV series. He won a Tony Award for his Broadway role as the husband in *The Seven Year Itch*, a role he reprised in the film version costarring with Marilyn Monroe. In the '60s he starred in his own TV show, "The Tom Ewell Show." He died Sept 12, 1994, at Woodland Hills, CA.

HEARST, WILLIAM RANDOLPH: BIRTH ANNIVERSARY. Apr 29, 1863. American newspaper editor and publisher, born at San Francisco, CA. Died at Beverly Hills, CA, Aug 14, 1951.

HIROHITO MICHI-NO-MIYA, EMPEROR: 100th BIRTH ANNIVERSARY. Apr 29, 1901. Former Emperor of Japan, born at Tokyo. Hirohito's death, Jan 7, 1989, ended the reign of the world's longest ruling monarch. He became the 124th in a line of monarchs when he ascended to the Chrysanthemum Throne in 1926. Hirohito presided over perhaps the most eventful years in the 2,500 years of recorded Japanese history, including the attempted military conquest of Asia; the attack on the US that brought that country into WWII, leading to Japan's ultimate defeat after the US dropped atomic bombs on Hiroshima and Nagasaki; and the amazing economic restoration following the war that led Japan to a preeminent position of economic strength. Although he opposed initiating hostilities with the US, he signed a declaration of war, allowing Japan's militarist Prime Minister, Hideki Tojo, to begin the fateful campaign. During the war's final days he overruled Tojo and advocated surrender. Hirohito broadcast a taped message to the Japanese people to stop fighting and "endure the unendurable." This radio message was the first time the emperor's voice had ever been heard outside the imperial household and inner circle of government. After the war, Hirohito was allowed to remain on his throne. He denounced his divinity in 1946, bestowed upon him by Japanese law, and became a "symbol of the state" in Japan's new parliamentary democracy. Hirohito turned his energies to his real passion, marine biology, becoming a recognized world authority in the field.

INDUSTRY DAY. Apr 29. Beatrice, NE. Features early industries of Gage County and their products. Antique gas engine demonstrations, exhibits of stationary engine equipment. Est attendance: 300. For info: Kent Wilson, Dir, Gage County Historical Soc, PO Box 793, Beatrice, NE 68310. Phone: (402) 228-1679. Web: www4.infoanalytic.com/h/beatrice.html#gage.

JAPAN: GREENERY DAY. Apr 29. National holiday.

KENNEDY CENTER IMAGINATION CELEBRATION. Apr 29–30. Colorado Springs, CO. A national festival program of the John F. Kennedy Center for the Performing Arts, this community-wide celebration has something for everyone: from hundreds of lively performances that delight the senses to friendly, small-town happenings that warm the heart. Most events are free; a nominal fee is charged for those that are not. Est attendance: 231,000. For info: Mary Mashburn, Coord, Pikes Peak Library District, 1515 N Academy Blvd, Ste 200, Colorado Springs, CO 80909. Phone: (719) 597-3344. Fax: (719) 597-3343. E-mail: mary@imaginationcelebration.org. Web: imaginecelebration.org.

LOS ANGELES RIOTS: ANNIVERSARY. Apr 29, 1992. A jury in Simi Valley, CA, failed to convict four Los Angeles police officers accused in the videotaped beating of Rodney King, providing the spark that set off rioting, looting and burning at South Central Los Angeles, CA, and other areas across the country. The anger unleashed during and after the violence was attributed to widespread racism, lack of job opportunities and the resulting hopelessness of inner-city poverty.

MOTHER, FATHER DEAF DAY. Apr 29. A day to honor deaf parents and recognize the gifts of culture and language they give to their hearing children. Annually, the last Sunday of April. Sponsored by Children of Deaf Adults International Inc (CODA). For info: Francine Stern, Deaf Awareness Events, 6605 Gaviota Ave, Van Nuys, CA 91406. Phone: (818) 786-8459. E-mail: ocodasister@earthlink.com.

NATIONAL PUPPETRY DAY. Apr 29. A day to celebrate the lively art of puppetry through performances, seminars, lectures and parades. Sponsored by Puppeteers of America, Inc. For info: Heather Loewenstein, 1820 McGee, Kansas City, MO 64108. E-mail: hlstoney@worldnet.att.net. Web: www.puppeteers.org.

NATIONAL SCIENCE AND TECHNOLOGY WEEK. Apr 29–May 5. National Science and Technology Week is sponsored by the Office of Legislative and Public Affairs of the National Science Foundation to promote awareness of science and technology to the general public and especially to children. Annually, in April. For info: Natl Science Fdtn, 4201 Wilson Blvd, Arlington, VA 22230. E-mail: nstw@nsf.gov. Web: www.nsf.gov/od/lpa/nstw/start.htm.

★NATIONAL SCIENCE AND TECHNOLOGY WEEK. Apr 29–May 5.

NEWSPAPER ASSOCIATION OF AMERICA ANNUAL CONFERENCE. Apr 29–May 2. Toronto, Ontario, Canada. For info: Newspaper Assn of America, 1921 Gallows Rd, Ste 600, Vienna, VA 22182. Phone: (703) 902-1600. Web: www.naa.org.

RAILROAD MEMORABILIA AND MODEL SHOW. Apr 29. National Farm Toy Museum, Dyersville, IA. Features railroad collectibles and all scales of model railroad equipment. Annually, the last Sunday in April. Est attendance: 800. For info: Dyersville Area Chamber of Commerce, PO Box 187, Dyersville, IA 52040. Phone: (319) 875-2311. Fax: (319) 875-8391. E-mail: farmtoys@juno.com. Web: www.rcww.com/dyersville.

SAINT CATHERINE OF SIENA: FEAST DAY. Apr 29, 1347. St. Catherine of Siena was born at Tuscany, Italy. Patron saint of Italy. She died Apr 29, 1380, at Rome, Italy.

SPACE MILESTONE: *CHALLENGER STS-51B* (US). Apr 29, 1985. *Challenger* launched from Kennedy Space Center, FL, with crew of seven and animal menagerie including monkeys and rats. Landed after 111 orbits of Earth on May 6, 1985, at Edwards Air Force Base, CA.

TAIWAN: CHENG CHENG KUNG LANDING DAY. Apr 29. Commemorates landing in Taiwan in 1661 of Ming Dynasty loyalist Cheng Cheng Kung (Koxinga), who ousted Dutch colonists who had occupied Taiwan for 37 years. Main ceremonies held at Tainan, in south Taiwan, where Dutch had their headquarters and where Cheng is buried. Cheng's birthday is also joyously celebrated, but according to the lunar calendar—on the 14th day of the seventh moon, Sept 1 in 2001.

ZIPPER PATENTED: ANNIVERSARY. Apr 29, 1913. Gideon Sundbach of Hoboken, NJ, received a patent for the zipper.

BIRTHDAYS TODAY

Andre Kirk Agassi, 31, tennis player, born Las Vegas, NV, Apr 29, 1970.
Daniel Day-Lewis, 44, actor (Oscar for *My Left Foot; The Unbearable Lightness of Being*), born London, England, Apr 29, 1957.
Nora Dunn, 49, actress (*Passion Fish*, "Saturday Night Live"), born Chicago, IL, Apr 29, 1952.
Dale Earnhardt, 49, auto racer, born Kannapolis, NC, Apr 29, 1952.
Robert Gottlieb, 70, editor, born New York, NY, Apr 29, 1931.
Celeste Holm, 82, actress (*All About Eve*; Oscar for *Gentleman's Agreement*), born New York, NY, Apr 29, 1919.
Rod McKuen, 68, poet, singer, born San Francisco, CA, Apr 29, 1933.
Zubin Mehta, 65, conductor, born Bombay, India, Apr 29, 1936.
Kate Mulgrew, 46, actress ("Star Trek: Voyager," "Ryan's Hope"), born Dubuque, IA, Apr 29, 1955.
Michelle Pfeiffer, 43, actress (*Batman Returns, Dangerous Liaisons, The Fabulous Baker Boys*), born Orange County, CA, Apr 29, 1958.
Eve Plumb, 43, actress ("The Brady Bunch," "Fudge"), born Burbank, CA, Apr 29, 1958.
Jerry Seinfeld, 47, comedian, actor ("Seinfeld"), born Brooklyn, NY, Apr 29, 1954.
Uma Thurman, 31, actress (*Henry and June, Pulp Fiction*), born Boston, MA, Apr 29, 1970.

APRIL 30 — MONDAY
Day 120 — 245 Remaining

BELTANE. Apr 30. (Also called Bealtaine, May Eve, Walpurgis Night, Cyntefyn, Roodmass and Cethsamhain.) One of the "Greater Sabbats" during the Wiccan year, it celebrates the union or marriage of the Goddess and God. In Scotland, Beltane was one of the quarter days or terms when rents were due and debts settled. On the eve of Beltane, two fires were built close together and cattle driven between them to ward off disease prior to putting them out to pasture for the new season. Annually, on Apr 30.

April 2001	S	M	T	W	T	F	S
	1	2	3	4	5	6	7
	8	9	10	11	12	13	14
	15	16	17	18	19	20	21
	22	23	24	25	26	27	28
	29	30					

CAMBODIA INVADED BY US: ANNIVERSARY. Apr 30, 1970. President Nixon announced the US was sending troops into Cambodia in an attempt to destroy the "sanctuaries" from which men and materiel were infiltrated into South Vietnam. This sparked widespread protests on the homefront, including a march on Washington and the closure of many American colleges and universities. See also: "Kent State Students' Memorial Day: Anniv" (May 4).

CONFEDERATE MEMORIAL DAY IN MISSISSIPPI. Apr 30. Annually, last Monday in April. Observed on other dates in some states: the fourth Monday in April in Alabama, Apr 26 in Florida and Georgia, May 10 in South Carolina, last Monday in May in Virginia and June 3 in Kentucky.

FIRST PRESIDENTIAL TELECAST: ANNIVERSARY. Apr 30, 1939. Franklin D. Roosevelt became the first president to appear on television when he was televised at the New York World's Fair. However, the appearance was only beamed to 200 TV sets in a 40-mile radius.

HAIRSTYLIST APPRECIATION DAY. Apr 30. The personalized service of hairstylists makes customers look great and feel great about themselves. Hairstyling is the art of creating a self-image to help boost self-esteem while lending an ear to customers' problems, thereby lessening their stress. For info: Anne Camilleri, 1220 Arroyo St, San Carlos, CA 94070. Phone: (415) 593-3733 or (415) 568-0565.

HARRISON, MARY SCOTT LORD DIMMICK: BIRTH ANNIVERSARY. Apr 30, 1858. Second wife of Benjamin Harrison, twenty-third president of the US, born at Honesdale, PA. Died at New York, NY, Jan 5, 1948.

INTERNATIONAL DARE TO LIVE DAY. Apr 30. Be all that you can be—we dare you! We dare you to enrich the lives of others by the richness of your own. Dare to live your life with all the passion and gusto you can muster. Contact us for information on how to begin. Seminars, keynote presentations, along with other products and services available to corporations, associations, schools and individuals. For info: Dare to Live, 1825 Wallace Ave, Marshalltown, IA 50158. Phone: (515) 474-2463. E-mail: info @daretolive.com. Web: www.daretolive.com.

INTERNATIONAL SCHOOL SPIRIT SEASON. Apr 30–Sept 30. To recognize everyone who has helped to make school spirit better and to provide time to plan improved spirit ideas for the coming school year. For info: Jim Hawkins, Chairman, Pepsters, Committee for More School Spirit, P.O. Box 122652, San Diego, CA 92112. Phone: (619) 280-0999.

INTERNATIONAL WALK DAYS. Apr 30 (also Dec 26). Today is the day to get primal, leave the car at home and whenever possible walk to your destination. Touted as the best exercise, walking is an undertaking that is not only aerobically correct, vital for workouts and a great method to pass the time, but it enables a person to get out and enjoy the weather and surroundings. [©1994] For info: Adrienne Sioux Koopersmith, 1437 W Rosemont, #1W, Chicago, IL 60660-1319. Phone: (773) 743-5341. Fax: (773) 743-5395. E-mail: adrienne@21stcentury.net.

LILLY, WILLIAM: BIRTH ANNIVERSARY. Apr 30, 1602 (OS). English astrologer, author and almanac compiler, born at Diseworth, Leicestershire. His almanacs were among the most popular in Britain from 1644 until his death, June 9, 1681 (OS), at Hersham, Surrey, England.

LOUISIANA: ADMISSION DAY: ANNIVERSARY. Apr 30. Became 18th state in 1812.

MUHAMMAD ALI STRIPPED OF TITLE: ANNIVERSARY. Apr 30, 1967. Muhammad Ali was stripped of his world heavyweight boxing championship when he refused to be inducted into military service. Said Ali, "I have searched my conscience, and I find I cannot be true to my belief in my religion by accepting such a call." He had claimed exemption as a minister of the Black Muslim religion. Convicted of violating the Selective Service Act but the Supreme Court reversed this decision in 1971.

NATIONAL HONESTY DAY (WITH HONEST ABE AWARDS). Apr 30. To celebrate honesty and those who are honest and honorable in their dealings with others. Nominations accepted for most honest people and companies. Winners to be awarded "Honest Abe" awards and given "Abies" on National Honesty Day. Also presented are dishonorable mentions for notables who have been less than honest. Annually, Apr 30. For info: M. Hirsh Goldberg, Author of *The Book of Lies*, 3103 Szold Dr, Baltimore, MD 21208. Phone: (410) 486-4150.

NETHERLANDS: QUEEN'S BIRTHDAY. Apr 30. A public holiday in celebration of the Queen's birthday and the Dutch National Day. The whole country parties as young and old participate in festivities such as markets, theater, music and games.

ORGANIZATION OF AMERICAN STATES FOUNDED: ANNIVERSARY. Apr 30, 1948. This regional alliance was founded by 21 nations of the Americas at Bogota, Colombia. Its purpose is to further economic development and integration among nations of the Western hemisphere, to promote representative democracy and to help overcome poverty. The Pan-American Union, with offices at Washington, DC, serves as the General Secretariat for the OAS.

SMITH, MICHAEL J.: BIRTH ANNIVERSARY. Apr 30, 1945. Michael J. Smith, 40-year-old pilot of the Space Shuttle *Challenger* on Jan 28, 1986. It was to have been Commander Smith's first space flight. Born at Beaufort, NC, Smith perished with all others on board when the Space Shuttle *Challenger* exploded on Jan 28, 1986. See also: "*Challenger* Space Shuttle Explosion Anniversary" (Jan 28).

SOUTH VIETNAM FALLS TO VIETCONG: ANNIVERSARY. Apr 30, 1975. The president of South Vietnam announced the country's unconditional surrender to the Vietcong. Communist troops moved into Saigon and 1,000 Americans in the city were hastily evacuated. Thousands of South Vietnamese also tried to flee. The surrender announcement came 21 years after the 1954 Geneva agreements divided Vietnam into North and South. The last American troops had left South Vietnam in March, 1973.

SPANK OUT DAY USA. Apr 30. A day on which all caretakers of children—parents, teachers and daycare workers—are asked not to use corporal punishment as discipline and to become aquainted with positive, effective disciplinary alternatives. For info: Nadine Block, EPOCH-USA, 155 W Main St, Ste 1603, Columbus, OH 43215. Phone: (614) 221-8829. E-mail: nblock@infinet.com. Web: www.stophitting.com.

SWEDEN: FEAST OF VALBORG. Apr 30. An evening celebration in which Sweden "sings in the spring" by listening to traditional hymns to the spring, often around community bonfires. Also known as Walpurgis Night, the Feast of Valborg occurs annually Apr 30.

TENNIS STAR SELES STABBED AT COURTSIDE: ANNIVERSARY. Apr 30, 1993. While resting at courtside during a match at Hamburg, Germany, 19-year-old Yugoslavian tennis player Monica Seles was stabbed between her shoulder blades with a five-inch steak knife by a 38-year-old German, Guenter P. (his last name was not identified under German privacy laws). Seles suffered a half-inch puncture wound and was released from the hospital on May 2.

THEATER IN NORTH AMERICA FIRST PERFORMANCE: ANNIVERSARY. Apr 30, 1598. On the banks of the Rio Grande, near present day El Paso, TX, the first North American theatrical performance was acted. The play was a Spanish commedia featuring an expedition of soldiers. On July 10 of the same year, the same group produced *Moros y Los Cristianos* (Moors and Christians), an anonymous play.

WALPURGIS NIGHT. Apr 30. The eve of May Day, which is the feast day of St. Walpurgis, the protectress against the magic arts. According to German legend, witches gather this night and celebrate their sabbath on the highest peak in the Harz Mountains. Celebrated particularly by university students in northern Europe.

WASHINGTON, GEORGE: PRESIDENTIAL INAUGURATION ANNIVERSARY. Apr 30, 1789. George Washington was inaugurated as the first president of the US under the new Constitution at New York, NY. Robert R. Livingston administered the oath of office to Washington on the balcony of Federal Hall, at the corner of Wall and Broad streets.

WILSON, ELLIS: BIRTH ANNIVERSARY. Apr 30, 1899. African-American artist born at Mayfield, KY, and died at New York, NY, Jan 1, 1977. Wilson painted realistic portrayals of African-Americans at work and at play. In 1944 he was awarded a Guggenheim fellowship. He then visited South Carolina, painting city scenes and fishing towns. *The Open Market at Charleston* was one of his favorite paintings of the period. In the 1950s, Wilson took a revelatory trip to Haiti which changed the way he painted. Unable to note any facial features on the Haitians he painted from a distance, Wilson began painting flat, stylized silhouettes. *Haitian Funeral Procession* (c 1950s) remains Wilson's most popular and accessible painting.

BIRTHDAYS TODAY

Jane Campion, 47, film director (*The Piano*), born Wellington, New Zealand, Apr 30, 1954.

Jill Clayburgh, 57, actress (*Fools Rush In, Luna*), born New York, NY, Apr 30, 1944.

Gary Collins, 63, actor, talk-show host, born Boston, MA, Apr 30, 1938.

Kirsten Dunst, 19, actress (*Little Women, Interview With the Vampire*), born Point Pleasant, NJ, Apr 30, 1982.

Johnny Galecki, 26, actor ("Roseanne," *Suicide Kings*), born Bree, Belgium, Apr 30, 1975.

Perry King, 53, actor (*Slaughterhouse Five, The Lords of Flatbush, Switch*), born Alliance, OH, Apr 30, 1948.

Cloris Leachman, 71, actress (Oscar for *The Last Picture Show*; "Phyllis,"), born Des Moines, IA, Apr 30, 1930.

Willie Nelson, 68, singer ("Always on My Mind," "Woman," "On the Road Again"); actor (*Honeysuckle Rose, The Electric Horseman*), born Abbott, TX, Apr 30, 1933.

Isiah Thomas, 40, former basketball player, born Chicago, IL, Apr 30, 1961.

Burt Young, 61, writer, actor (*Chinatown, Rocky, Once Upon a Time in America*), born New York, NY, Apr 30, 1940.

Maye.

MAY 1 — TUESDAY
Day 121 — 244 Remaining

ADDISON, JOSEPH: BIRTH ANNIVERSARY. May 1, 1672 (OS). English essayist born at Milston, Wiltshire, England. Died at London, June 17, 1719 (OS). "We are," he wrote in *The Spectator*, "always doing something for Posterity, but I would fain see Posterity do something for us."

AMTRAK: 30th ANNIVERSARY. May 1, 1971. Amtrak, the national rail service which combined the operations of 18 passenger railroads, went into service.

★ **ASIAN PACIFIC AMERICAN HERITAGE MONTH.** May 1–31. Presidential Proclamation issued honoring Asian Pacific Americans each year since 1979. Public Law 102-450 of Oct 28, 1992, designated the observance for the month of May each year.

BELGIUM: PLAY OF SAINT EVERMAAR. May 1. Annual performance (for more than 1,000 years) of a mystery play, in its original form, by the village inhabitants.

BETTER HEARING AND SPEECH MONTH. May 1–31. A nationwide public information campaign held each May to inform the 41 million Americans with hearing and speech problems that help is available. Annually, the month of May. For info: Janet Price, Dir of Deaf Activities, Natl Grange, 1616 H St NW, Washington, DC 20006. Phone: (202) 628-3507 or (740) 927-0690. Fax: (202) 347-1091. E-mail: grangedeaf@aol.com.

BETTER SLEEP MONTH. May 1–31. Emphasizes the importance of good sleep to good health and encourages Americans to reevaluate their bedtime habits and check bedding for signs of old age. Sponsor: The Better Sleep Council. For info: Erin Hill, Better Sleep Council, 1901 L St NW, Ste 300, Washington, DC 20036. Phone: (703) 683-8371. Fax: (703) 683-4503. E-mail: bsc @sleepproducts.org. Web: www.bettersleep.org/month.htm.

BREAD PUDDING RECIPE EXCHANGE. May 1–7. A week dedicated to the exchange of creative bread pudding recipes. For sample recipes send a SASE. For info: Bread Pudding Update, PO Box 416, Denver, CO 80201. Phone: (303) 575-5676.

CLARK, MARK: BIRTH ANNIVERSARY. May 1, 1896. US general who served in both World Wars, Mark Clark was born at Madison Barracks, NY. In November 1942, he commanded the US forces taking part in the invasion of North Africa, and in January 1943, he became commander of the US Fifth Army, which invaded Italy in September 1943, taking Rome in June of 1944. After the Germans capitulated in Italy, Clark was appointed commander of US occupation forces in Austria. He died at Charleston, SC, Apr 17, 1984.

COLUMBIAN EXPOSITION OPENING: ANNIVERSARY. May 1, 1893. At 12:08 PM President Grover Cleveland, in the presence of nearly a quarter of a million people, placed his finger on a golden key opening the Columbian Exposition at Chicago, IL. Amid the unfurling of thousands of flags, sounding of trumpets and booming of cannons, the key activated an electromagnetic valve, steam rushed into great cylinders and the immense pump began its enormous burden of pumping 15,000,000 gallons of water a day to supply the 685-acre fair and its visitors with an ample water supply.

CONTRABAND DAYS (PIRATE FESTIVAL). May 1–13. Lake Charles, LA. A major 13-day festival celebrating Jean Lafitte, "The Gentleman Pirate," and the contraband treasures he is supposed to have hidden along the shores of Lake Charles. Events include a mock invasion by pirates, a night boat parade, concerts, fireworks, water events, children's area. Est attendance: 250,000. For info: Marlene C. Hobbs, Exec Dir, Contraband Days, Inc, PO Box 679, Lake Charles, LA 70602. Phone: (337) 436-5508. Fax: (337) 436-1126. E-mail: contraband@usunwired.net.

CREATIVE BEGINNINGS MONTH. May 1–31. How are you creative? Have you tapped into your full potential? Enjoy the budding month of May while discovering something new about yourself. Enroll in a course, write a poem, plant a garden, coordinate a social event. While developing your gifts, encourage others to also cultivate their own creative beginnings. For info: Christina Bergenholtz, PO Box 301, Grafton, MA 01519. Phone: (508) 839-5139. Fax: (508) 887-9556. E-mail: chrismhb@aol.com.

DENMARK: TIVOLI GARDENS SEASON. May 1–Sept 16. Copenhagen. World famous for its variety of entertainment, symphony concerts, pantomime and ballet. Beautiful flower arrangements and excellent restaurants. Traditional season: May 1 until the third Sunday in September.

EXECUTIVE COACHING DAY. May 1. Workers deserve the best leaders they can get! Our sports stars have skill and strength coaches, our great actors have speech and movement coaches, our politicians have media coaches. Why don't more of our corporate and union executives who are responsible for effectively leading thousands of employees and members utilize the power of coaching? This is a day to applaud all organizational leaders who take their profession seriously enough to improve their skills through coaching. A day to raise awareness of those who do not utilize coaching as to its power to improve their capacity to effectively lead their organizations. For info: Ira Chaleff, Pres, Exec Coaching & Consulting Assoc. Phone: (301) 933-3752. Web: www.exe-coach.com.

FAMILY SUPPORT MONTH. May 1–31. The purpose of this observance is to support families with children during divorce, separation and custody issues. Promotes respect for mother/child relationships. Current projects include lobbying for law changes regarding divorce/custody. For info: Children Hurt in Legal Disputes (CHILD), PO Box 2373, Glenview, IL 60025. Phone: (847) 998-9950. Fax: (847) 998-9945. E-mail: proquestkq@aol.com.

FIBROMYALGIA EDUCATION AND AWARENESS MONTH. May 1–31. To promote education and awareness of the dangers of fibromyalgia which is also known as the fibromyalgia syndrome (FSM), fibrositis or chronic muscle pain syndrome. Fibromyalgia affects more than 10 million American women. Kit of materials available for $15. For info: Frederick S. Mayer, Pres, PPSI, 101 Lucas Valley Rd, San Rafael, CA 94903. Phone: (415) 479-8628. Fax: (415) 479-8608. E-mail: ppsi@aol.com. Web: www .ppsinc.org.

	S	M	T	W	T	F	S
May			1	2	3	4	5
2001	6	7	8	9	10	11	12
	13	14	15	16	17	18	19
	20	21	22	23	24	25	26
	27	28	29	30	31		

FIRST SKYSCRAPER: ANNIVERSARY. May 1, 1884. Construction was begun on the Home Insurance Company building on this date in Chicago. The 10-story building was completed in 1885. Designed by William Le Baron Jenney, it had a steel frame which carried the weight of the building. The walls provided no support but hung like curtains on the metal frame. This method of construction revolutionized American architecture and allowed architects to build taller and taller buildings.

FREEDOM RIDERS: 40th ANNIVERSARY. May 1, 1961. Militant students joined James Farmer of the Congress of Racial Equality (CORE) to conduct "freedom rides" on public transportation from Washington, DC, across the deep South to New Orleans. The trips were intended to test Supreme Court decisions and Interstate Commerce Commission regulations prohibiting discrimination in interstate travel. In several places riders were brutally beaten by local people and policemen. On May 14, members of the Ku Klux Klan attacked the Freedom Riders in Birmingham, AL, while local police watched. The rides were patterned after a similar challenge to segregation, the 1947 Journey of Reconciliation, which tested the US Supreme Court's June 3, 1946, ban against segregation in interstate bus travel.

GAZPACHO AFICIONADO TIME. May 1–Oct 31. A time to appreciate one of Spain's finest contributions to international cuisine: gazpacho, a nutritious cold soup made from fresh tomatoes and other vegetables. Observed while tomatoes are ripe.

GET CAUGHT READING MONTH. May 1–31. Celebrities appear in ads appealing to people of all ages to remind them of the joys of reading. Events will be held throughout the country to celebrate reading. For info: Assn of American Publishers, 71 Fifth Ave, New York, NY 10003. Phone: (212) 255-0200. Web: www.publishers.org or www.getcaughtreading.org.

GREAT BRITAIN FORMED: ANNIVERSARY. May 1, 1707 (OS). A union between England and Scotland resulted in the formation of Great Britain. (Wales had been part of England since the 1500s.) Today's United Kingdom consists of Great Britain and Northern Ireland.

INTERNATIONAL BUSINESS IMAGE IMPROVEMENT MONTH. May 1–31. The image of your business sets the tone to how successful your company will be. Just as we judge others within the first few seconds of meeting, we do the same for a business. Receive more information on how to improve your business image and a free business card evaluation. For info: Debbie Allen, Pres, Allen & Assn Consulting, Inc, 131 W Sunburst Ln, Tempe, AZ 85284. Phone: (800) 359-4544. Fax: (480) 831-8334. E-mail: debbie@debbieallen.com. Web: www.debbieallen.com.

ITALY: FESTIVAL OF SAINT EFISIO. May 1–4. Cagliari. Said to be one of the biggest and most colorful processions in the world. Several thousand pilgrims on foot, in carts and on horseback wearing costumes dating from the 17th century accompany the statue of the saint through the streets.

JONES, MARY HARRIS (MOTHER JONES): BIRTH ANNIVERSARY. May 1, 1830. Irish-born American labor leader. After the death of her husband and four children (during the Memphis yellow fever epidemic of 1867) and loss of her belongings in the Chicago Fire in 1871, Jones devoted her energies and her life to organizing and advancing the cause of labor. It seemed she was present wherever there were labor troubles. She gave her last speech on her 100th birthday. Born at Cork, Ireland, she died Nov 30, 1930, at Silver Spring, MD.

LABOR DAY. May 1. In 76 countries, May 1 is observed as a workers' holiday. When it falls on a Saturday or Sunday, the following Monday is observed as a holiday. Bermuda, Canada and the US are the only countries that observe Labor Day in September.

★**LAW DAY.** May 1. Presidential Proclamation issued each year for May 1 since 1958 at request. (PL87–20 of Apr 7, 1961.)

LAW ENFORCEMENT APPRECIATION MONTH IN FLORIDA. May 1–31. Law Enforcement Appreciation Day is May 15 in Florida, a ceremonial day.

LEI DAY. May 1. Hawaii. On this special day—the Hawaiian version of May Day—leis are made, worn, given, displayed and entered in lei-making contests. One of the most popular Lei Day celebrations takes place at Honolulu at Kapiolani Park at Waikiki. Includes the state's largest lei contest, the crowning of the Lei Day Queen, Hawaiian music, hula and flowers galore.

★**LOYALTY DAY.** May 1. Presidential Proclamation issued annually for May 1 since 1959 at request. (PL85–529 of July 18, 1958.) Note that an earlier proclamation was issued in 1955.

LUCY STONE MARRIED: ANNIVERSARY. May 1, 1855. When nationally known public speaker and feminist Lucy Stone married Henry Blackwell, a marriage contract written by the bride and groom was read at the wedding that disavowed the gross inequity married women suffered under American law, and the word "obey" was omitted from their marriage vows. A year after the ceremony the bride further shocked society by taking back her maiden name, which she kept for the rest of her life.

MARSHALL ISLANDS, REPUBLIC OF THE: CONSTITUTION DAY. May 1. National holiday.

MAY DAY. May 1. The first day of May has been observed as a holiday since ancient times. Spring festivals, maypoles and maying are still common, but the political importance of May Day has grown since the 1880s, when it became a workers' day in the US. Now widely observed in countries as a workers' holiday or as Labor Day. In most European countries, when May Day falls on Saturday or Sunday, the Monday following is observed as a holiday, with bank and store closings, parades and other festivities.

MAY IN MONTCLAIR. May 1–31. Montclair Township, NJ. 23rd annual month-long festival celebrating the wealth of cultural, artistic, historic and recreational opportunities in Montclair for residents, merchants and visitors. Est attendance: 4,000. For info: Jean H. Kidd, Chair, May in Montclair, 91 Central Ave, Montclair, NJ 07042. Phone: (201) 744-7660.

MELANOMA/SKIN CANCER DETECTION AND PREVENTION MONTH. May 1–31. For info: American Academy of Dermatology, 930 N Meacham Rd, Schaumburg, IL 60173. Phone: (847) 330-0230 or (888) 462-DERM. Web: www.aad.org.

MILESTONES: A MILES DAVIS RETROSPECTIVE EXHIBIT. May 1–July 31. Missouri History Museum, Forest Park, St. Louis, MO. The year 2001 marks the 75th anniversary of the birth of Miles Davis in the St. Louis area. In honor of the achievements of this jazz artist, the museum hosts a retrospective exhibit of music, artifacts and photographs. For info: Missouri Historical Society, PO Box 11940, St. Louis, MO 63112-0040. Phone: (314) 746-4599.

MORE THAN JUST A PRETTY FACE MONTH. May 1–31. Great skin begins from the scalp down to the soles of the feet. May is a perfect time to begin to prepare skin for the summer. A sun protection cream with a SPF of 15 or higher is to be applied all over the skin daily. Did you know that on average we receive approximately 24 hours a week of accidental sun? This is gathered via windshields, office windows, walking to and from the office or store. For tips on "saving face" and great skin ideas, ask for our free booklet. Annually, the month of May. For info: Susie Galvez, Face Works Day Spa, 8502 Patterson Ave, Richmond, VA 23229. Phone: (804) 740-5665. Fax: (804) 741-7203. Web: www.faceworksdayspa.com.

MOTHER GOOSE DAY. May 1. To re-appreciate the old nursery rhymes. Motto is "Either alone or in sharing, read childhood nursery favorites and feel the warmth of Mother Goose's embrace." Annually, May 1. For info: Gloria T. Delamar, Founder, Mother Goose Soc, 7303 Sharpless Rd, Melrose Park, PA 19027. Phone: (215) 782-1059. E-mail: Mother.Goose.Society@juno.com. Web: www.gbalc.org/MotherGooseSociety.

NATIONAL ALLERGY/ASTHMA AWARENESS MONTH. May 1–31. Kit of materials available for $15 from this nonprofit organization. For info: Frederick S. Mayer, Pres, Pharmacist Planning Services, Inc, c/o Allergy Council of America (ACA), 101 Lucas Valley Rd, #210, San Rafael, CA 94903. Phone: (415) 479-8628. Fax: (415) 479-8608. E-mail: ppsi@aol.com. Web: www.ppsinc.org.

NATIONAL ARTISAN GELATO MONTH. May 1–31. To celebrate America's new love of gelato, Italian ice cream, and the art of artisan gelato making. Gelato is a rich and creamy premium ice cream that is different from its American counterpart in many ways. It is largely considered more flavorful and creamier than American premium ice cream, but has less than half the fat content. Gelato does not have as much air pumped into it, so it is denser and more velvety. Unlike industrial gelato, artisan gelato is made fresh daily in small batches. For info: Daniel Sarno, Sarno's Gelato, Mall of America, 238 N Garden, Bloomington, MN 55425. Phone: (612) 831-3031. Fax: (612) 831-0368.

May	S	M	T	W	T	F	S
2001			1	2	3	4	5
	6	7	8	9	10	11	12
	13	14	15	16	17	18	19
	20	21	22	23	24	25	26
	27	28	29	30	31		

NATIONAL BARBECUE MONTH. May 1–31. To encourage people to start enjoying barbecuing early in the season when Daylight Saving Time lengthens the day. Annually, the month of May. Sponsor: Barbecue Industry Association. For info: NBM, DHM Group, Inc, PO Box 767, Dept CC, Holmdel, NJ 07733-0767. Fax: (732) 946-3343.

NATIONAL BIKE MONTH. May 1–31. 43rd annual celebration of bicycling for recreation and transportation. Local activities sponsored by bicycling organizations, environmental groups, PTAs, police departments, health organizations and civic groups. About five million participants nationwide. Annually, the month of May. For info: Patrick McCormick, Communications Dir, League of American Bicyclists, 1612 K St, Ste 401, Washington, DC 20006. Phone: (202) 822-1333. Fax: (202) 822-1334. E-mail: bikeleague@bikeleague.org. Web: www.bikeleague.org.

NATIONAL CONNECTING WEEK. May 1–7. A week recognizing the need to work on developing new relationships and trying new interests. Annually, the first week in May. For info: Offtime Press, 41 Sutter St, #1763, San Francisco, CA 94104. Phone: (415) 292-5230. E-mail: drdecastro@aol.com.

NATIONAL CORRECT POSTURE MONTH. May 1–31. For info: American Chiropractic Assn, 1701 Clarendon Blvd, Arlington, VA 22209. Phone: (800) 986-4636. E-mail: memberinfo@amerchiro.org. Web: www.amerchiro.org.

NATIONAL DIGESTIVE DISEASES AWARENESS MONTH. May 1–31. For info: Digestive Disease Natl Coalition, 507 Capitol Ct NE, Ste 200, Washington, DC 20002. Phone: (202) 544-7494.

NATIONAL EGG MONTH. May 1–31. Dedicated to the versatility, convenience, economy and good nutrition of The incredible edible egg{TM}. Annually, the month of May. For info: Linda Braun, Consumer Serv Dir, American Egg Board, 1460 Renaissance Dr, Park Ridge, IL 60068. Web: www.aeb.org.

NATIONAL "GET HAPPY" WEEK. May 1–8. A week dedicated to the 3 c's: caring, connection and community. Annually, the first week in May. For info: The Happy Company, 31055 Huntwood Ave, Hayward, CA 94544. Phone: (510) 476-5900. Web: www.thehappycompany.com.

NATIONAL GOMINGLE MONTH. May 1–31. A month recognizing the need for people to get out into the real world and mingle with new people while exploring similar interests. For info: Paul Santello, VP Mktg, GoMingle.com, 23 Grant St, 5th Fl, San Francisco, CA 94108. Phone: (415) 901-2456. Fax: (415) 901-2451. Web: www.gomingle.com.

NATIONAL GOOD CAR-KEEPING MONTH. May 1–31. To promote increased safety and value through good car maintenance. For info: Sander Allen, Good Car-Keeping Institute, 990 N Lake Shore Dr, Ste 11-A, Chicago, IL 60611.

NATIONAL HAMBURGER MONTH. May 1–31. Sponsored by White Castle, the original fast-food hamburger chain, founded in 1921, to pay tribute to one of America's favorite foods. With or without condiments, on or off a bun or bread, hamburgers have grown in popularity since the early 1920s and are now an American meal mainstay. For info: White Castle System, Inc, Marketing Dept, 555 W Goodale St, Columbus, OH 43215-1171. Phone: (614) 228-5781. Fax: (614) 228-8841. Web: www.whitecastle.com.

NATIONAL HEPATITIS AWARENESS MONTH. May 1–31. For info: Hepatitis Foundation Intl, 30 Sunrise Terr, Cedar Grove, NJ 07009. Phone: (800) 891-0707. E-mail: hfi@intac.com. Web: www.hepfi.org.

NATIONAL HIGH BLOOD PRESSURE EDUCATION MONTH. May 1–31. To promote the control and treatment of high blood pressure. Church Blood Pressure Sunday, May 6. Annually, the month of May. For info: Natl High Blood Pressure

Education Program Info Ctr, Natl Heart, Lung and Blood Institute, PO Box 30105, Bethesda, MD 20824-0105. Phone: (301) 251-1222. Fax: (301) 251-1223. E-mail: nhlbiic@dgsys.com. Web: www.nhlbi.nih.gov/nhlbi/nhlbi.htm.

NATIONAL MENTAL HEALTH MONTH. May 1–31. For info: Natl Mental Health Assn, 1021 Prince St, Alexandria, VA 22314-2971. Phone: (800) 969-6642 or (703) 684-7722. E-mail: nmhainfo@aol.com. Web: www.nmha.org.

NATIONAL NEUROFIBROMATOSIS AWARENESS MONTH. May 1–31. For info: Erica Mayer, Dir of Public Education, Natl Neurofibromatosis Foundation, 120 Wall St, 16th Fl, New York, NY 10005. Phone: (800) 323-7938 or (212) 344-6633. E-mail: NNFF@nf.org. Web: www.nf.org.

NATIONAL OSTEOPOROSIS PREVENTION MONTH. May 1–31. Osteoporosis is not a natural part of aging but is a preventable disease for most people. For info: Natl Osteoporosis Foundation, 1232 22nd St NW, Washington, DC 20037. Phone: (202) 223-2226. Fax: (202) 223-2237. E-mail: nofmail@nof.org. Web: www.nof.org.

NATIONAL PEACE OF MIND WEEK. May 1–7. Peace of mind is knowing that you are doing your best at any given time (otherwise you would do better); it is accepting yourself unconditionally—forgiving yourself and others, having faith and allowing love and joy into your heart. It means gaining "The Inside Advantage" and it is the most extraordinary accomplishment. For info: Cathy Lauro. Phone: (800) 215-3644. E-mail: mind@cwlauro.com. Web: www.cwlauro.com.

NATIONAL PHYSICAL FITNESS AND SPORTS MONTH. May 1–31. Encourages individuals and organizations to promote fitness activities and programs. For info: President's Council on Physical Fitness and Sports, HHH Building, 200 Independence Ave SW, Room 738H, Washington, DC 20201-0004. Phone: (202) 690-9000. Fax: (202) 690-5211.

NATIONAL PROM GRADUATION SAFETY MONTH. May 1–31. Comprehensive public awareness campaign providing information to high school students as well as parents, educators and other influencers of high school-aged children about the dangers of drinking and driving and the importance of making responsible decisions. For info: The Century Council, 1310 G St, NW, #600, Washington, DC 20005. Phone: (202) 637-0077. Fax: (202) 637-0079. Web: www.centurycouncil.org.

NATIONAL RECOMMITMENT MONTH. May 1–31. Each week of this month has been designated as a time for each of us to assess, alter and act on our commitments to our spiritual, personal, marital, family and work-related lives. Recommitment rejuvenates our goals, plans and strategies for maximizing these areas of our lives in a healthy, balanced way. Includes National Spiritual Recommitment Week (May 1–6), National Personal Recommitment Week (May 7–13), National Marital Recommitment Week (May 14–20), National Family Recommitment Week (May 21–27) and National Work Recommitment Week (May 28–31). For info: Dr. T. Marie Carson, Individual, Couple & Family Therapist, PO Box 412, Dayton, TX 77535. Phone: (936) 257-0222. E-mail: drtmariecarson@aol.com.

NATIONAL SALAD MONTH. May 1–31. Americans celebrate salads and their role in today's healthy lifestyle. Annually, the month of May. For info: The Assn for Dressings and Sauces, 5775-G Peachtree-Dunwoody Rd, Atlanta, GA 30342. Phone: (404) 252-3663. Fax: (404) 252-0774. E-mail: ads@assnhq.com. Web: www.dressings-sauces.org.

NATIONAL SALSA MONTH. May 1–31. Recognizing salsa as America's favorite way to add flavor to all kinds of food, such as eggs, burgers, chicken, tacos, chips, potatoes, rice and much more. Celebrates more than 50 years of picante sauce, a salsa created in 1947, and celebrates Cinco de Mayo, a major Mexican holiday now recognized across North America. For info: Pace Foods, PO Box 9200, Paris, TX 75461. Phone: (800) 433-PACE. Web: www.pacefoods.com.

NATIONAL SCHOLARSHIP MONTH. May 1–31. To applaud those organizations, businesses, individuals and communities that have helped and continue to help students with scholarships; to increase awareness of the need for more private sector aid for students; and to focus attention on the impact made by scholarships on students seeking postsecondary educational opportunities. An initiative of Citizens' Scholarship Foundation of America in partnership with America's Promise, the Points of Light Foundation, Sallie Mae, Kaplan, KPMG, American Council on Education, the United Parcel Service (UPS) and the Miss America Organization. For info: Office of Communications, Citizens' Scholarship Foundation of America, 1505 Riverview Rd, PO Box 297, St. Peter, MN 56082. Phone: (952) 830-7308. Fax: (952) 830-1929. E-mail: VPCOMMCSFA@aol.com. Web: www.csfa.org.

NATIONAL SIGHT-SAVING MONTH. May 1–31. Prevent Blindness America® annually devotes this observance to a different topic in the fields of vision health or vision safety. Each topic reflects the latest developments in the specific area of focus. For info: Prevent Blindness America®, 500 E Remington Rd, Schaumburg, IL 60173. Phone: (800) 331-2020 or (847) 843-2020.

NATIONAL STROKE AWARENESS MONTH. May 1–31. For info: Natl Stroke Assn, 9707 E Easter Ln, Englewood, CO 80112. Phone: (800) STROKES or (800) 787-6537. Web: www.stroke.org.

NATIONAL TEACHING AND JOY MONTH. May 1–31. A month of celebrating the joy of great teaching and great learning. Thank a teacher for creating an atmosphere of joy. Notice those students who demonstrate a love of learning. Call or write someone who helped you learn an important life skill. For info: Dr. Jim Scott, Jackson Community College, 2111 Emmons Rd, Jackson, MI 49201. Phone: (517) 796-8488. Fax: (517) 796-8631. E-mail: jim_scott@jackson.cc.mi.us.

NATIONAL TUBEROUS SCLEROSIS AWARENESS MONTH. May 1–31. A presidential proclamation in 1974 declared the month of May to be National Tuberous Sclerosis Awareness Month, and it has been observed as such annually. Tuberous sclerosis is a genetic disease that affects 1 in 5,500 Americans every year. Contact the National HQ for a listing of current activities. Events will be listed on the website. For info: Natl Tuberous Sclerosis Assn (NTSA), 8181 Professional Place, Ste 110, Landover, MD 20785. Phone: (800) 225-6872. Fax: (301) 459-0394. E-mail: ntsa@ntsa.org. Web: www.ntsa.org.

NEW HOMEOWNER'S DAY. May 1. You have faced all the challenges—now take the time as a new homeowner to stand back and reflect on your new home and savor the feeling. For info: Dorothy Zjawin, Dir, 61 W Colfax Ave, Roselle Park, NJ 07204. Phone: (908) 241-6241. Fax: (908) 241-6241.

★**OLDER AMERICANS MONTH.** May 1–31. Presidential Proclamation; from 1963 through 1973 this was called "Senior Citizens Month." In May 1974 it became Older Americans Month. In 1980 the title included Senior Citizens Day, which was observed May 8, 1980. Issued annually since 1963.

PEN-FRIENDS WEEK INTERNATIONAL. May 1–7. To encourage everyone to have one or more pen-friends not only in their own country but in other countries. For complete information on how to become a good pen-friend and information about how to write good letters, send $4 to cover expense of printing, handling and postage. Annually, May 1–7. For info: Dr. Stanley J. Drake, Pres, Intl Soc of Friendship and Good Will, 8592 Roswell Rd, Ste 434, Atlanta, GA 30350-1870.

PHILIPPINES: FEAST OF OUR LADY OF PEACE AND GOOD VOYAGE. May 1–31. Pilgrimage to the shrine of Nuestra Sra de la Paz y Buen Viaje at Antipolo, Rizal.

PHILIPPINES: SANTACRUZAN. May 1–31. Maytime pageant-procession that recalls the quest of Queen Helena and Prince Constantine for the Holy Cross.

REACT MONTH. May 1–31. Highlights safety education in the correct emergency use of CB radio by travelers. Recognizes the contributions of REACT volunteers to safety communications within their communities for public events or local emergencies. Encourages the public to join a REACT Team and further its safety communications initiatives in the community. For info: REACT International Inc, 5210 Auth Rd, # 403, Suitland, MD 20746. Phone: (301) 316-2900. E-mail: react@reactintl.org. Web: www.reactintl.org/.

REVISE YOUR WORK SCHEDULE MONTH. May 1–31. To increase awareness, exploration and implementation of non-traditional work schedules such as flextime, telecommuting, job sharing and compressed work weeks. Annually, the month of May. For info: Maggi Payment, Center for Worktime Options, 1286 University Ave, #192, San Diego, CA 92103-3312. Phone: (619) 232-0404. E-mail: info@worktimeoptions.com.

THE ROARING 20s. May 1–12. Mount Hope Estate, Manheim, PA. Mount Hope Mansion turns speakeasy as the Philadelphia Renaissance Faire's acting company lights the fires that made the 1920s roar. Wine served for medicinal purposes, of course. Est attendance: 7,000. For info: Thomas Roy, Mgr, Mount Hope Estate and Winery, PO Box 685, Cornwall, PA 17016. Phone: 7176657021, ext 127. Fax: (717) 664-3466. E-mail: TomRoy @parenaissancefaire.com. Web: www.parenfaire.co.

RUSSIA: INTERNATIONAL LABOR DAY. May 1–2. Public holiday in Russian Federation. "Official May Day demonstrations of working people."

SAINT TAMENEND'S DAY. May 1. Colonial American joyous May Day celebration, recently revived. Legendary American Indian sage, Chief Tamenend, canonized by fun-loving young colonists asserting independence from old-world patrons. Modern celebrants, tired of overly serious political observances, identify themselves by pinning dollar bills to their jackets. For info: Dr. Nicholas Varga, Dept of History, Loyola College, 4501 N Charles St, Baltimore, MD 21210-2699. Phone: (410) 617-2554.

SAVE THE RHINO DAY. May 1. A new century. An old problem. Rhinos still in danger! Help save the world's remaining rhinos on the verge of extinction! Get involved with local, national and international conservation efforts to stop the senseless slaughter of these gentle pachyderms. Call your local zoo or write Really, Rhinos! for a $5 information packet. For info: Judyth Lessee, Founder, Really, Rhinos!, PO Box 40503, Tucson, AZ 85717-0503. Phone: (520) 327-9048. E-mail: rinophyl@rtd.com.

		S	M	T	W	T	F	S
				1	2	3	4	5
May		6	7	8	9	10	11	12
2001		13	14	15	16	17	18	19
		20	21	22	23	24	25	26
		27	28	29	30	31		

SCHOOL PRINCIPALS' DAY. May 1. A day of recognition for all elementary, middle and high school principals for their leadership and dedication to providing the best education possible for their students. Annually, May 1. For info: Janet M. Dellaria, 202 N Bennett St, Geneva, IL 60134. Phone: (630) 232-0425.

SCOTLAND: PITLOCHRY FESTIVAL THEATRE SEASON. May 1–Oct 31. Pitlochry Festival Theatre, Pitlochry, Tayside. Annual festival of drama, music and the arts, with plays performed in repertory, plus concerts, exhibitions and fringe events. For info: Box Office, Pitlochry Festival Theatre, Pitlochry, Perthshire, Scotland PH16 5DR. Phone: (01796) 484620. Fax: (01796) 484616. E-mail: boxoffice@pitlochry.org.uk. Web: www.pitlochry.org.uk.

SENIOR CITIZENS MONTH. May 1–31. Massachusetts.

SIGHT-SAVING ULTRAVIOLET AWARENESS MONTH. May 1–31. While the damage ultraviolet (UV) causes to skin is obvious, the damage it can do to eyes may not be. Not enough attention is paid to the damage UV can do to the eyes. Exposure to UV can burn delicate eye tissue and raise the risk of developing cataracts and cancers of the eye. For info: Prevent Blindness America®, 500 E Remington Rd, Schaumburg, IL 60173. Phone: (800) 331-2020. Fax: (847) 843-8458. Web: www.preventblindness.org.

SMITH, KATE: BIRTH ANNIVERSARY. May 1, 1909. One of America's most popular singers. Kate Smith, who never took a formal music lesson, recorded more songs than any other performer (more than 3,000), made more than 15,000 radio broadcasts and received more than 25 million fan letters. On Nov 11, 1938, she introduced a new song during her regular radio broadcast, written especially for her by Irving Berlin: "God Bless America." It soon became the unofficial national anthem. Born Kathryn Elizabeth Smith at Greenville, VA, she began her radio career May 1, 1931, with "When the Moon Comes Over the Mountain," a song identified with her throughout her career. She died at Raleigh, NC, June 17, 1986.

SOWERBY, LEO: BIRTH ANNIVERSARY. May 1, 1895. Pulitzer prize–winning composer of more than 550 compositions, born at Grand Rapids, MI, and died July 7, 1968, at Port Clinton, OH.

STRIKE OUT STROKES MONTH. May 1–31. Dedicated to the prevention of strokes. Factors resulting from heredity or natural processes can't be changed but with proper medical treatment and healthful lifestyle adjustments, some risk factors can be eliminated. Kit materials available for $15. For info: Frederick S. Mayer, Pres, Pharmacy Council on Stroke Prevention, 101 Lucas Valley Rd, #210, San Rafael, CA 94903. Phone: (415) 479-8628. Fax: (415) 479-8608. E-mail: ppsi@aol.com. Web: www.ppsinc.org.

TEEN DAY. May 1. An annual event started in 1999 in West Hartford, CT, aimed at creating beneficial dialogue between teenagers and adults and establishing and celebrating positive aspects of teen life and their contributions to the community. Est attendance: 350. For info: Veronica Esposito, Teen Services Librarian, West Hartford Public Library, 20 S Main St, West Hartford, CT 06107. Phone: (860) 570-3777. E-mail: ronnie@connect.crlc.org.

TEILHARD DE CHARDIN, PIERRE: BIRTH ANNIVERSARY. May 1, 1881. French Jesuit author, paleontologist and philosopher, born at Sarcenat, France. He died at New York, NY, Apr 10, 1955.

USA TENNIS MONTH. May 1–31. More than 165 cities across the country will stage USA Tennis Free for All events—tennis festivals featuring free lessons for all ages. The USA Tennis Free for All events will introduce the public to a new step-by-step pathway into the game, supported by the entire tennis community. For info: Phone: (800) 884-USTA. Web: www.usta.com

U-2 INCIDENT: ANNIVERSARY. May 1, 1960. On the eve of a summit meeting between US President Dwight D. Eisenhower and Soviet Premier Nikita Khrushchev, a U-2 espionage plane was shot down over Sverdlovsk, in central USSR. The pilot, CIA agent Francis Gary Powers, survived the crash, as did large parts of the aircraft, a suicide kit and sophisticated surveillance equipment. The sensational event, which US officials described as a weather reconnaissance flight gone astray, resulted in cancellation of the summit meeting. Powers was tried, convicted and sentenced to 10 years in prison by a Moscow court. In 1962 he was returned to the US in exchange for an imprisoned Soviet spy. He died in a helicopter crash in 1977. See also: "Powers, Francis Gary: Birth Anniversary" (Aug 17).

VEGETARIAN RESOURCE GROUP'S ESSAY CONTEST FOR KIDS. May 1. Children ages 18 and under are encouraged to submit a two–three-page essay on topics related to vegetarianism. Essays accepted up to May 1. Winners announced Sept 15 and will receive a $50 savings bond. For info: The Vegetarian Resource Group, PO Box 1463, Baltimore, MD 21203. Phone: (410) 366-8343. E-mail: vrg@vrg.org. Web: www.vrg.org.

WILLIAMS, ARCHIE: BIRTH ANNIVERSARY. May 1, 1915. Archie Williams, along with Jesse Owens and others, debunked Hitler's theory of the superiority of Aryan athletes at the 1936 Berlin Olympics. As a black member of the US team Williams won a gold medal by running the 400-meter in 46.5 seconds (.4 second slower than his own record of earlier that year). Williams, who was born at Oakland, CA, earned a degree in mechanical engineering from the University of California–Berkeley in 1939 but had to dig ditches for a time because they weren't hiring black engineers. He became an airplane pilot and for 22 years trained Tuskegee Institute pilots, including the black air corp of WWII. When asked during a 1981 interview about his treatment by the Nazis during the 1936 Olympics, he replied, "Well, over there at least we didn't have to ride in the back of the bus." Archie Williams died June 24, 1993, at Fairfax, CA.

WOMEN'S HEALTH CARE MONTH. May 1–31. To initiate a public education campaign devoted to increasing awareness of the many health concerns unique to women. Focus will be on the prevention of the major causes of death and poor health among women—heart disease, cancer, arthritis, osteoporosis and bone fractures, as well as on depression and alcoholism in women. There is a $15 charge for kit materials. Annually, the month of May. For info: Pharmacists Planning Service, Inc, 101 Lucas Valley Rd, #210, San Rafael, CA 94903. Phone: (415) 479-8628. Fax: (415) 479-8608. E-mail: ppsi@aol.com. Web: www.ppsinc.org.

BIRTHDAYS TODAY

Charles (Chuck) Bednarik, 76, Pro Football Hall of Fame center and linebacker, born Bethlehem, PA, May 1, 1925.

Steve Cauthen, 41, former jockey, born Walton, KY, May 1, 1960.

Judy Collins, 62, singer ("Both Sides Now," "Chelsea Morning"), born Seattle, WA, May 1, 1939.

Rita Coolidge, 56, singer ("[Your Love Has Lifted Me] Higher and Higher," "We're All Alone"), born Nashville, TN, May 1, 1945.

Glenn Ford, 85, actor (*The Blackboard Jungle, The Fastest Gun Alive*, "The Family Holvak"), born Sainte-Christine, Quebec, Canada, May 1, 1916.

Sonny James (Jimmy Loden), 72, singer ("Young Love"), born Hackleburg, AL, May 1, 1929.

Curtis Martin, 28, football player, born Pittsburgh, PA, May 1, 1973.

Bobbie Ann Mason, 61, writer (*In Country, Spence and Lila*), born Mayfield, KY, May 1, 1940.

Tim McGraw, 34, country singer, born Delhi, LA, May 1, 1967.

Jack Paar, 84, early host of "The Tonight Show," born Canton, OH, May 1, 1917.

Charlie Schlatter, 35, actor ("Diagnosis Murder"), born Englewood, NJ, May 1, 1966.

MAY 2 — WEDNESDAY
Day 122 — 243 Remaining

CROSBY, HARRY LILLIS "BING": BIRTH ANNIVERSARY. May 2, 1904. Singer, composer and actor (*White Christmas, High Society*, various *Road* movies), born at Tacoma, WA. Died while playing golf near Madrid, Spain, Oct 14, 1977.

KING JAMES BIBLE PUBLISHED: ANNIVERSARY. May 2, 1611. King James I had appointed a committee of learned men to produce a new translation of the Bible in English. This version, popularly called the King James Version, is known in England as the Authorized Version.

LEE, PINKY (PINCUS LEFF): BIRTH ANNIVERSARY. May 2, 1907. Born at St. Paul, MN. When young, Leff had dreams of becoming an attorney, but abandoned the idea when classmates laughed at his lisp. His show business debut was in burlesque in the 1930s. He is best remembered for "The Pinky Lee Show" which telecast from Los Angeles in the early 1950s. Pinky Lee died Apr 3, 1993, at Mission Viejo, CA.

LEONARDO DA VINCI: DEATH ANNIVERSARY. May 2, 1519. Artist, scientist and inventor. Painter of the famed *Last Supper*, perhaps the first painting of the High Renaissance, and of the *Mona Lisa*. Inventor of the first parachute. Born at Vinci, Italy, in 1452 (date unknown), he died at Amboise, France.

NATIONAL ANXIETY DISORDERS SCREENING DAY. May 2. For info: NADSD, 308 Seaview Ave, Staten Island, NY 10305. Phone: (718) 351-1717 or (888) 442-2022 for screening locations. Fax: (718) 667-8893. E-mail: FFFNADSD@aol.com. Web: freedomfromfear.org.

RAY, SATYAJIT: 80th BIRTH ANNIVERSARY. May 2, 1921. Film director Satyajit Ray was born at Calcutta, India. Possibly India's best known film director, he made more than 30 films and won numerous international awards, including an Academy Award for lifetime achievement. His films include the trilogy *Pather Panchali* (1956), *Aparajito* (1956) and *The World of Apu* (1959). Ray died Apr 23, 1992, at Calcutta.

ROAD RUNNERS CLUB OF AMERICA NATIONAL CONVENTION. May 2–6. Albuquerque, NM. RRCA, the national association of more than 600 non-profit running clubs, will hold its national convention for club members, race directors and health and fitness enthusiasts. Over four days participants will attend workshops, fun runs, social events and run in the Lilac Bloomsday race. Est attendance: 450. For info: Conv Dir, RRCA, 1150 S Washington St, Ste 250, Alexandria, VA 22314. Phone: (703) 836-0558. Fax: (703) 836-4430. E-mail: convention@rrca.org. Web: www.rrca.org.

ROBERT'S RULES DAY. May 2, 1837. Anniversary of the birth of Henry M. Robert (General, US Army), author of *Robert's Rules of Order*, a standard parliamentary guide. Born at Robertville, SC. Died at Hornell, NY, May 11, 1923.

SIBLING APPRECIATION DAY. May 2. This is a day to let your brothers and sisters know you care. If you're not speaking to them, make an exception today. If they are mean and pick on you, tell them you love them anyway. If you think they already know you care, make sure by telling them how you feel and doing something extra nice. If you're lucky, you'll have them around for years to share your joys and sorrows with, to play practical jokes on and to remember when you were young. Annually, May. For info: Keri Mertens, 3115 Staten Ave, Lansing, MI 48910. E-mail: kerimert@worldnet.att.net. Web: www.gurlpages.com/other/kerim.

SPOCK, BENJAMIN: BIRTH ANNIVERSARY. May 2, 1903. Pediatrician and author, born at New Haven, CT. His book on childrearing, *Common Sense Book of Baby and Child Care* later called *Baby and Child Care*, has sold more than 30 million copies. In 1955 he became professor of child development at Western Reserve University at Cleveland, OH. He resigned from this position in 1967 to devote his time to the pacifist movement. Spock died at San Diego, CA, Mar 15, 1998.

SUNFEST. May 2–6. West Palm Beach, FL. Florida's largest music, art and waterfront festival features some of the best acts in jazz, pop, blues and more. Family-oriented event includes a juried art show, handmade crafts, fireworks, water and youth park activities and fabulous foods. Est attendance: 300,000. For info: SunFest of Palm Beach County, Inc, 525 Clematis St, West Palm Beach, FL 33401. Phone: (561) 659-5980. Fax: (561) 659-3567. E-mail: sunfest@sunfest.org. Web: www.sunfest.org.

BIRTHDAYS TODAY

Christine Baranski, 49, actress ("Cybill"), born Buffalo, NY, May 2, 1952.

Elizabeth Berridge, 39, actress ("The John Larroquette Show"), born Westchester, NY, May 2, 1962.

Theodore Bikel, 77, singer, actor (*Man On the Run, My Fair Lady*), born Vienna, Austria, May 2, 1924.

Larry Gatlin, 52, singer, songwriter ("Broken Lady," "All the Gold in California"), born Odessa, TX, May 2, 1949.

Lesley Gore, 55, singer ("I'll Cry If I Want To"), born Tenafly, NJ, May 2, 1946.

Bianca Jagger, 56, actress, political activist, ex-wife of Mick Jagger, born Managua, Nicaragua, May 2, 1945.

David Suchet, 55, actor ("Mystery"), born London, England, May 2, 1946.

Jenna Von Oy, 24, actress (*She Cried No*, "Blossom"), born Newtown, CT, May 2, 1977.

MAY 3 — THURSDAY
Day 123 — 242 Remaining

BIRDS & BLOSSOMS SPRING NATURE FESTIVAL. May 3–6. Norfolk Botanical Garden, Norfolk, VA. The Garden, in conjunction with the Commonwealth of Virginia's Department of Game and Inland Fisheries, is hosting this festival, the region's first birding festival. For beginning to experienced birders and naturalists of all ages. Special guests and keynote speakers: Don and Lillian Stokes. Activities include water fowl boat tours, sunrise birding walks, bird clinics, lectures, butterfly tours and nature walks. Est attendance: 6,000. For info: Norfolk Botanical Garden, 6700 Azalea Garden Rd, Norfolk, VA 23518-5337. Phone: (757) 441-5830. Fax: (757) 853-8294. Web: www.virginiagarden.org.

CANADA: OKANAGAN WINE FESTIVAL. May 3–6. (also Sept 28–Oct 7.) Penticton, Kelowna, Vernon, Osoyoos, BC. Both a spring and fall annual celebration surrounding the annual wine grape harvest: winemasters dinners, wine tastings, seminars, picnics, sports and family fun events throughout scenic Okanagan Valley. Est attendance: 18,000. For info: Okanagan Wine Fest Soc, 1527 Ellis St, Kelowna, BC, Canada V1Y 2A7. Phone: (250) 861-6654. Fax: (250) 861-3942. E-mail: info@owfs.com. Web: www.owfs.com.

"CBS EVENING NEWS" TV PREMIERE: ANNIVERSARY. May 3, 1948. The news program began as a 15-minute telecast with Douglas Edwards as anchor. Walter Cronkite succeeded him in 1962 and expanded the show to 30 minutes; Eric Sevareid served as commentator. Dan Rather anchored the newscasts upon Cronkite's retirement in 1981. At one point, to boost sagging ratings, Connie Chung was added to the newscast as Rather's co-anchor, but she left in 1995 in a well-publicized dispute. Rather remains solo, and, as Cronkite would say, " . . . that's the way it is."

		S	M	T	W	T	F	S
May				1	2	3	4	5
2001		6	7	8	9	10	11	12
		13	14	15	16	17	18	19
		20	21	22	23	24	25	26
		27	28	29	30	31		

DOW-JONES TOPS 11,000: ANNIVERSARY. May 3, 1999. The Dow-Jones Index of 30 major industrial stocks topped the 11,000 mark for the first time.

ENGLAND: MITSUBISHI MOTORS BADMINTON HORSE TRIALS. May 3–6 (tentative). Badminton, Glos. Famous international horse trials consisting of showjumping, cross country and dressage. Est attendance: 200,000. For info: Box Office, Badminton Horse Trials, Badminton, Avon, England GL9 1DF. Phone: (44) (1454) 21-8272. Fax: (44) (1454) 21-8596. E-mail: info@badminton-horse.co.uk.

FESTIVAL OF NATIONS. May 3–6. River Centre, St. Paul, MN. Celebration by 100 ethnic groups, each presenting food specialties, folk dances and folk arts to the public. Est attendance: 95,000. For info: Intl Institute of Minnesota, 1694 Como Ave, St. Paul, MN 55108. Phone: (651) 647-0191. Fax: (651) 647-9268. Web: www.festivalofnations.com.

JAPAN: CONSTITUTION MEMORIAL DAY. May 3. National holiday commemorating adoption of constitution in 1947.

JOSEY'S WORLD CHAMPION JUNIOR BARREL RACE. May 3–6. Josey's Ranch, Marshall, TX. Youth barrel-racing competition. Annually, the first weekend in May. Est attendance: 4,000. For info: Pam Whisenant, Dir of Conv and Visitor Development, Marshall Chamber of Commerce, PO Box 520, Marshall, TX 75671. Phone: (903) 935-7868. Fax: (903) 935-9982. E-mail: cvd@internetwork.net. Web: www.marshalltxchamber.com.

KANSAS BARBED WIRE SWAP/SELL. May 3–5. LaCrosse, KS. Barbed Wire Collectors Association show and meeting. Est attendance: 200. For info: Kansas Barbed Wire Collectors Assn, PO Box 578, LaCrosse, KS 67548. Phone: (785) 222-9900.

LIBRARY LEGISLATIVE DAY. May 3. Librarians go to Washington and to their state capitals to talk to legislators about important library issues. For info: Public Information Office, American Library Assn, 50 E Huron St, Chicago, IL 60611. Phone: (312) 944-6780. Web: ww.ala.org.

LOYALTY DAYS AND SEAFAIR FESTIVAL. May 3–6. Newport, OR. Celebration of loyalty to America. Parade, queen and court, sports car races, Navy ships in port and other activities. Est attendance: 5,000. For info: Chamber of Commerce, 555 SW Coast Hwy, Newport, OR 97365. Phone: (541) 265-8801 or (800) 262-7844. Fax: (541) 265-5589. E-mail: chamber@newport.com.

LUMPY RUG DAY. May 3. To encourage the custom of teasing bigots and trigots for shoving unwelcome facts under the rug. When many cans of worms have been shoved under the rug, the defenders of the status quo obtain a new rug high enough to cover the unwanted facts. For info: Robert L. Birch, Coord, Puns Corps, Box 2364, Falls Church, VA 22042-0364. Phone: (703) 533-3668.

MACHIAVELLI, NICCOLO: BIRTH ANNIVERSARY. May 3, 1469. Italian writer and statesman, born at Florence, Italy. Author of *The Prince*, a book of advice for a ruler that prescribes strong, absolute government. Died at Florence, June 22, 1527.

MARTIN Z. MOLLUSK DAY. May 3. Moorlyn Terrace Beach, Ocean City, NJ. If Martin Z. Mollusk, a hermit crab, sees his shadow at 11 AM, EST, summer comes a week early—if he doesn't, summer begins on time. Est attendance: 300. For info: Mark Soifer, City Hall, 9th St and Asbury Ave, Ocean City, NJ 08226. Phone: (609) 525-9300 or (609) 399-0272. Fax: (609) 399-0374. E-mail: MTSoifer@aol.com.

MEIR, GOLDA: BIRTH ANNIVERSARY. May 3, 1898. Born at Kiev, Russia, Meir was prime minister of Israel from 1969 to 1974. She died at Jerusalem, Dec 8, 1978.

MEXICO: DAY OF THE HOLY CROSS. May 3. Celebrated especially by construction workers and miners, a festive day during which anyone who is building must give a party for the workers. A flower-decorated cross is placed on every piece of new construction in the country.

★**NATIONAL DAY OF PRAYER.** May 3. Presidential Proclamation always issued for the first Thursday in May since 1981. (PL100–307 of May 5, 1988.) Beginning in 1957, a day in October was designated, except in 1972 and 1975 through 1977.

NATIONAL PUBLIC RADIO FIRST BROADCAST: 30th ANNIVERSARY. May 3, 1971. National noncommercial radio network, financed by Corporation for Public Broadcasting, began programming.

POLAND: CONSTITUTION DAY (SWIETO TRZE-CIEGO MAJO). May 3. National Day. Celebrates ratification of Poland's first constitution, 1791.

REOPENING OF THE 1743 PALATINE HOUSE MUSEUM. May 3. Schoharie, NY. Open Thursday through Monday 1–5 PM, May through October. The Palatine House is a living museum and is the oldest existing building in Schoharie County. Est attendance: 900. For info: Angela DeGroff, Program Dir, Schoharie Colonial Heritage Assn, PO Box 554, Schoharie, NY 12157. Phone: (518) 295-7505 or (518) 295-7585. E-mail: scha@midtel.net.

ROBINSON, SUGAR RAY: BIRTH ANNIVERSARY. May 3, 1921. Ray ("Sugar Ray") Robinson, boxer, born Walker Smith, Jr, at Detroit, MI. Generally considered "pound for pound the greatest boxer of all time," Robinson was a welterweight and middleweight champion who won 175 professional fights and lost only 19. A smooth and precise boxer, he fought until he was 45, dabbled in show business and established the Sugar Ray Robinson Youth Foundation to counter juvenile delinquency. To this day, his name connotes class, style and dignity. Died at Los Angeles, CA, Apr 12, 1989.

ROCK-A-THON. May 3. Senior citizens and their friends, family and local businesses commit to rocking in rocking chairs to raise money for area children's hospitals and charities. Money raised is often used by the neonatal and pediatrics units of these hospitals to purchase rocking chairs to be used to rock and comfort sick children. For info: Rock-A-Thon/Mktg Dept, Marriott Senior Living Services, 8550 Katy Freeway, Ste 201, Houston, TX 77024. Phone: (713) 464-4884. Fax: (713) 827-7693.

SIEGE OF YORKTOWN OUSTS REBELS: ANNIVERSARY. May 3, 1862. After nearly a month's siege, General Joseph Johnston's outnumbered Confederate forces evacuated Yorktown, VA, and moved back to Richmond. General McClellan's Army of the Potomac occupied Yorktown the following day. With the capture of Yorktown, President Abraham Lincoln left Washington, DC, for Fort Monroe, VA, to observe the ongoing Peninsula Campaign.

SPACE MILESTONE: *DELTA 3914* ROCKET FAILURE: 15th ANNIVERSARY. May 3, 1986. Launched from Cape Canaveral, FL, the rocket failed, flew out of control and was intentionally destroyed by explosives 90 seconds after launch to avoid the risk of having it land in a populated area.

TAX FREEDOM DAY. May 3. According to the Tax Freedom Foundation, the average American had to work until this day in 2000 to pay federal, state and local taxes. Because state and local taxes vary, this date can vary by almost a whole month depending on the state you live in, ranging from May 18 (Connecticut) to April 23 (Alabama, Alaska, Kentucky, Mississippi, Oklahoma, Tennessee).

UNITED NATIONS: WORLD PRESS FREEDOM DAY. May 3. A day to recognize that a free, pluralistic and independent press is an essential component of any democratic society and to promote press freedom in the world.

James Brown, 68, singer, songwriter ("Papa's Got a Brand New Bag"), born Augusta, GA, May 3, 1933.

Christopher Cross, 50, musician, songwriter, born Anston, TX, May 3, 1951.

Greg Gumbel, 55, TV personality, sportscaster, born New Orleans, LA, May 3, 1946.

Jeffrey John Hornacek, 38, basketball player, born Elmhurst, IL, May 3, 1963.

Engelbert Humperdinck (Gerry Dorsey), 65, singer ("Release Me," "After the Lovin' "), born Madras, India, May 3, 1936.

Pete Seeger, 82, folksinger, songwriter ("Where Have All the Flowers Gone?"), born New York, NY, May 3, 1919.

Frankie Valli, 64, singer ("Can't Take My Eyes Off You," "Grease"), born Newark, NJ, May 3, 1937.

Ron Wyden, 52, US Senator (D, Oregon), born Wichita, KS, May 3, 1949.

MAY 4 — FRIDAY
Day 124 — 241 Remaining

"ANOTHER WORLD" TV PREMIERE: ANNIVERSARY. May 4, 1964. Created by Irna Phillips and sponsored by P&G, this soap was set in fictional Bay City. It was the first soap to air for a full hour and the first to beget two spin-offs ("Somerset" and "Texas"). Charles Durning, Ted Shackelford, Eric Roberts, Ray Liotta, Kyra Sedgwick, Faith Ford, Morgan Freeman, Jackée Harry, Victoria Wyndham and Valarie Pettiford are some of its well-known alums. The show was cancelled in 1999 and the last episode aired June 25, 1999.

BREAUX BRIDGE CRAWFISH FESTIVAL. May 4–6. Breaux Bridge, LA. This festival includes live Cajun and Zydeco music on 3 stages, parade, contests, arts and crafts and thousands of pounds of crawfish cooked every way imaginable. Est attendance: 30,000. For info: BBCFA, PO Box 25, Breaux Bridge, LA 70517. Phone: (337) 332-6655. Fax: (337) 332-5917. E-mail: crawfest@iamerica.net. Web: www.bbcrawfest.com.

CHINA: YOUTH DAY. May 4. Annual public holiday "recalls the demonstration on May 4, 1919, by thousands of patriotic students in Beijing's Tiananmen Square to protest imperialist aggression in China."

CLAM CHOWDER FESTIVAL, SPRING FLOWER & ART SHOW. May 4–6. Gold Beach, OR. Curry County Fairgrounds. The Curry County Historical Society, Innominata Garden Club and Curry Arts Association put together a weekend of food, fun, flowers and fine art. Est attendance: 1,000. For info: Gold Beach Chamber of Commerce, 29279 Ellensburg Ave, #3, Gold Beach, OR 97444. Phone: (800) 525-2334. Fax: (541) 247-0188. E-mail: goldbeach@harborside.com. Web: www.goldbeach.org.

COSAC ANNUAL CONFERENCE: ISSUES IN AUTISM 2001. May 4–5. The NJ Center for Outreach & Services for the Autism Community (COSAC) holds its annual conference featuring educational workshops, exhibitions and an awards reception. For info: Jennifer Stillitano, Coord of Mktg & PR, COSAC, 1450 Parkside Ave, Ste 22, Ewing, NJ 08638. Phone: (609) 883-8100. Fax: (609) 883-5509. E-mail: njautism@aol.com. Web: members.aol.com/njautism.

CURACAO: MEMORIAL DAY. May 4. Victims of WWII are honored on this day. Military ceremonies at the War Monument. Not an official public holiday.

DANDELION MAY FEST. May 4–5. Der Marktplatz, Dover, OH. Old-fashioned festival includes finals in a nationwide dandelion recipe contest, live entertainment, slides and presentations about dandelions and food booths featuring dishes made from dandelions, including dandelion coffee ice cream, dandelion pizza, dandelion bread and dandelion omelettes. Also, dandelion wine and jelly tasting, family entertainment and 5K fun run. Festival includes 8th National Dandelion Cook-Off; for entry forms for cook-off call: (800) 697-4858. Est attendance: 15,000. For info: Anita Davis, Coord, Der Marktplatz-Breitenbach Wine Cellars, 5934 Old Route 39 NW, Dover, OH 44622. Phone: (330) 343-3603. Fax: (330) 343-8290. E-mail: amishwine@tusco.net. Web: www.breitenbachwine.com.

DISCOVERY OF JAMAICA BY CHRISTOPHER COLUMBUS: ANNIVERSARY. May 4, 1494. Christopher Columbus discovered Jamaica. The Arawak Indians were its first inhabitants.

EMMETT KELLY CLOWN FESTIVAL. May 4–5. Downtown Houston, MO. Carnival, clown school, parade on Saturday, arts & crafts, Big Top performances, book sales. Appearance by Emmett Kelly, Jr. Est attendance: 5,000. For info: Houston Area Chamber of Commerce, 111 W Main, Houston, MO 65483. Phone: (417) 967-2220. Fax: (417) 967-2178.

FASHION SHOW. May 4. Mount Mary College, Milwaukee, WI. Student designer fashion show. Est attendance: 1,500. For info: Mary Cain, Mount Mary College, 2900 N Menomonee River Parkway, Milwaukee, WI 53222-4597. Phone: (414) 256-1210. Fax: (414) 256-1239. E-mail: mktg@mtmary.edu. Web: www.mtmary.edu.

GARDEN TOUR. May 4–6. Gold Beach, OR. Tickets and maps available at the Chamber of Commerce. 10 AM–5 PM. Est attendance: 300. For info: Gold Beach Chamber of Commerce, 29279 Ellensburg Ave, Gold Beach, OR 97444. Phone: (800) 525-2334. Fax: (541) 247-0188. E-mail: goldbeach@harborside.com. Web: www.goldbeach.org.

GETAWAY GARDENS WEEKEND. May 4–6. Northeastern Connecticut. More than 30 shops offer special displays, discounts and demonstrations throughout the region. Annually, the first weekend in May. Est attendance: 1,000. For info: Northeast Connecticut Visitors District, PO Box 598, Putnam, CT 06260. Phone: (860) 928-1228. Fax: (860) 928-4720. E-mail: quietcorner @snet.net. Web: www.webtravels.com/quietcorner.

HARRY S TRUMAN AWARD FOR PUBLIC SERVICE. May 4 (tentative). Harry S Truman Library, Independence, MO. Each year the city of Independence honors Harry S Truman by presenting the Harry S Truman Award for Public Service to an individual who best typifies and possesses the qualities of dedication, ability, honesty and integrity that distinguished the former president. There was a departure from tradition in 2000 when the award was presented to the Truman Library and Truman Library Institute for its great service over the years to the citizens of Independence and visitors far beyond. Previous recipients include Senator Bill Bradley, former President Gerald Ford and Jane Alexander, former head of the National Endowment for the Arts. A reception follows immediately after the program. Est attendance: 500. For info: Sheila Saxton, Mayor's Office, Independence, MO 64050. Phone: (816) 325-7022. Web: www.trumanlibrary.org.

	May 2001		**S**	**M**	**T**	**W**	**T**	**F**	**S**
					1	2	3	4	5
			6	7	8	9	10	11	12
			13	14	15	16	17	18	19
			20	21	22	23	24	25	26
			27	28	29	30	31		

HAYMARKET SQUARE RIOT: ANNIVERSARY. May 4, 1886. Labor union unrest at Chicago led to violence when a crowd of unemployed men tried to enter the McCormick Reaper Works, where a strike was underway. Although no one was killed, anarchist groups called a mass meeting in Haymarket Square to avenge the "massacre." When the police advanced on the demonstrators, a bomb was thrown and several policemen were killed. Four leaders of the demonstration were hanged and another committed suicide in jail. Three others were given jail terms. The case aroused considerable controversy around the world. See also: "Haymarket Pardon: Anniversary (June 26)."

HEPBURN, AUDREY (EDDA VAN HEEMSTRA HEPBURN-RUSTEN): BIRTH ANNIVERSARY. May 4, 1929. Audrey Hepburn, whose first major movie role in *Roman Holiday* (1953) won her an Academy Award as best actress, was born near Brussels, Belgium. She made 26 movies during her career and received four additional Oscar nominations. During the latter years of her life Hepburn served as spokesperson for the United Nations Children's Fund, traveling worldwide raising money for the organization. Audrey Hepburn died Jan 20, 1993, at Tolochenaz, Switzerland.

HOT-AIR BALLOON CLASSIC. May 4–6. Live Oak, FL. Spectacular fun, color and music, along with a car and truck show. Est attendance: 10,000. For info: James Cornett, Spirit of the Suwannee Music Park, 3076 95th Dr, Live Oak, FL 32060. Phone: (904) 364-1683. Fax: (904) 364-2998. E-mail: spirit @musicliveshere.com. Web: www.musicliveshere.com.

INTERNATIONAL TUBA DAY. May 4. To recognize tubists in musical organizations around the world who have to go through the hassle of handling a tuba in order to make beautiful music. Annually, the first Friday in May. For info: Dr. Mark Sheridan-Rabideau, Music Dept, Millersville Univ, PO Box 1002, Millersville, PA 17551-0302. Phone: (717) 872-3439. Fax: (717) 871-2304.

ISLE OF EIGHT FLAGS SHRIMP FESTIVAL. May 4–6. Fernandina Beach, FL on beautiful Amelia Island. Commemorates Fernandina's role as the birthplace of the modern shrimping industry. Multi-event festival includes juried fine arts and crafts show, entertainment, antiques, pirates, fun zone and food. Est attendance: 150,000. For info: Isle of Eight Flags Shrimp Festival, PO Box 6146, Fernandina Beach, FL 32035. Phone: (904) 261-3248 or (800) 2AMELIA. Web: www.shrimpfestival.com.

JAPAN: GOLDEN WEEK HOLIDAY. May 4. National holiday.

KENT STATE STUDENTS' MEMORIAL DAY: ANNIVERSARY. May 4, 1970. Four students (Allison Krause, 19; Sandra Lee Scheuer, 20; Jeffrey Glenn Miller, 20 and William K. Schroeder, 19) were killed by the National Guard during demonstrations against the Vietnam War at Kent (Ohio) State University.

LANDON AZALEA GARDEN FESTIVAL AND ANTIQUE SHOW. May 4–6. Bethesda, MD. Garden stroll amid 15,000 blooming azaleas. Plant sale, flower show, historic farmhouse tour, lunch, musical entertainment and 90 craft and antique dealers. Annually. Est attendance: 30,000. For info: Landon School, 6101 Wilson Lane, Bethesda, MD 20817. Phone: (301) 320-3200. Fax: (301) 320-1133. E-mail: jeanne_hamrick @landon.net. Web: www.landon.net.

MANN, HORACE: BIRTH ANNIVERSARY. May 4, 1796. American educator, author, public servant, known as the "father of public education in the US," was born at Franklin, MA. Founder of Westfield (MA) State College and editor of the influential *Common School Journal*. Mann died at Yellow Springs, OH, Aug 2, 1859.

MAY DAY. May 4. Lumpkin, GA. Celebration of the planting season with traditional May Day activities and the May Pole Dance. Est attendance: 800. For info: Patty Cannington, PR Dir, Westville Village, PO Box 1850, Lumpkin, GA 31815. Phone: (912) 838-6310. Web: www.westville.org.

MAY FELLOWSHIP DAY. May 4. Theme: "For Such a Time As This: A Time to Eliminate Racism." Luncheon worship service that seeks a realistic response to violence and victims in our midst. An ecumenical event that responds to local community needs. Annually, the first Friday in May. Est attendance: 64,000. For info: Dir for Ecumenical Celebs, Church Women United, 475 Riverside Dr, 5th Fl, New York, NY 10115. Phone: (212) 870-3339. Fax: (212) 870-2338. E-mail: jzaragoza @churchwomen.org.

NATIONAL WEATHER OBSERVER'S DAY. May 4. For those people, amateurs and professionals alike, who love to follow the everyday phenomenon known as weather. Annually, May 4. For info: Alan W. Brue, 1317 London Way, Lithia Springs, GA 30122. E-mail: afn05660@afn.org.

RED RIVER QUILTERS QUILTFEST. May 4–6. Bossier Convention Center, Bossier City, LA. A new millennium starts with old favorites. Quilts, wearables, demonstrations, merchant mall, raffle quilt. Admission $5. Est attendance: 1,500. For info: Robin McNeil, Red River Quilters, PO Box 4811, Shreveport, LA 71134-0811. Phone: (318) 929-7492. E-mail: techmc@msn.comt.

RELATIONSHIP RENEWAL DAY. May 4. To salute and strengthen committed couples who value change and acceptance in the context of an ongoing relationship. Celebrants will mutually cite the challenges and changes met in the past year and offer each other well-deserved congratulations. For info: Peter Rosenzweig, PhD, Cheerleader, Nondisposable Relationships, 8 S Michigan Ave, Ste 1405, Chicago, IL 60601. Phone: (847) 677-3560.

RHODE ISLAND: INDEPENDENCE DAY: 225th ANNIVERSARY. May 4. Rhode Island abandoned allegiance to Great Britain in 1776.

ROAN MOUNTAIN SPRING NATURALISTS' RALLY. May 4–6. Roan Mountain State Park, Roan Mountain, TN. Wildflower and nature identification and inspiration. Est attendance: 1,500. For info: Jennifer Laughlin, Ranger Naturalist, Roan Mtn State Park, 1015 Hwy 143, Roan Mountain, TN 37687. Phone: (423) 772-0190 ext 108.

SEQUIM IRRIGATION FESTIVAL. May 4–13. Sequim, WA. Come and join the fun at this unique festival. Includes amusement rides, fireworks, a parade, arts and crafts displays, entertainment, food booths and much more. Est attendance: 20,000. For info: Sequim Chamber of Commerce, Sequim Irrigation Festival, PO Box 2073, Sequim, WA 98382. Phone: (360) 683-6197. Fax: (360) 683-6349. E-mail: sequimccr@olypen.com.

SPACE MILESTONE: *ATLANTIS* **(US).** May 4, 1989. First American planetary expedition in 11 years. Space shuttle *Atlantis* was launched, its major objective to deploy the *Magellan* spacecraft on its way to Venus to map the planet's surface. The shuttle was on its 65th orbit when it landed May 8, mission accomplished.

SUGARLOAF'S SPRING MANASSAS CRAFT FESTIVAL. May 4–6. Prince William County Fairgrounds, Manassas, VA. This show, now in its 6th year, features 250 nationally recognized craft designers and fine artists displaying and selling their original creations. Craft demonstrations, children's entertainment, live music, drawings, food, hourly gift certificate drawings and more. Est attendance: 15,000. For info: Sugarloaf Mountain Works, Inc, 200 Orchard Ridge Dr, #215, Gaithersburg, MD 20878. Phone: (800) 210-9900. E-mail: smworks@sugarloafcrafts.com. Web: www.sugarloafcrafts.com.

TYLER, JULIA GARDINER: BIRTH ANNIVERSARY. May 4, 1820. Second wife of John Tyler, tenth president of the US, born at Gardiners Island, NY. Died at Richmond, VA, July 10, 1889.

WADE-DAVIS RECONSTRUCTION BILL PASSES THE HOUSE: ANNIVERSARY. May 4, 1864. Over the objections of President Lincoln, the House of Representatives on this date passed the Wade-Davis Reconstruction bill, containing stiff punitive measures against the South that if put into law would have destroyed Lincoln's more moderate reconstruction aims. The bill was also adamantly opposed by Radical Republicans, led by Thaddeus Stevens for whom it was insufficiently severe in its treatment of the Southern rebels. Lincoln eventually killed the bill by using the pocket veto.

WILLA CATHER SPRING CONFERENCE. May 4–5. Red Cloud, NE. A 1½-day event devoted to noted American author Willa Cather. Includes church service, tour of Cather Country, lunch, panel discussion, banquet, entertainment and keynote speaker. Paper session and evening entertainment on Friday; main conference on Saturday. Annually, the first weekend in May. Est attendance: 250. For info: Willa Cather Pioneer Memorial & Educational Fdtn, 326 N Webster, Red Cloud, NE 68970. Phone: (402) 746-2653.

WORLD CHAMPIONSHIP CRIBBAGE TOURNAMENT. May 4–6. Plumas County Fairgrounds, Quincy, CA. 30th annual tournament. Founded in 1972, the country's oldest cribbage tournament now draws entrants from all over the country. Annually, the first weekend in May. Est attendance: 700. For info: Mike Taborski, Tournament Chair, PO Box B, Quincy, CA 95971. Phone: (530) 283-0800. Fax: (530) 283-3952. E-mail: featherpub@aol.com.

BIRTHDAYS TODAY

Nickolas Ashford, 59, singer, songwriter ("Ain't No Mountain High Enough"), born Fairfield, SC, May 4, 1942.

Maynard Ferguson, 73, bandleader, born Verdun, Quebec, Canada, May 4, 1928.

Ben Grieve, 25, baseball player, 1998 American League Rookie of the Year, born Arlington, TX, May 4, 1976.

David Guterson, 45, author (*Snow Falling on Cedars*), born Seattle, WA, May 4, 1956.

Jackie Jackson (Sigmund Esco Jackson), 50, singer (Jackson 5), born Gary, IN, May 4, 1951.

Roberta Peters, 71, opera singer (retired), born The Bronx, NY, May 4, 1930.

Dawn Staley, 31, basketball player, born Philadelphia, PA, May 4, 1970.

Randy Travis, 42, country and western musician ("Forever and Ever, Amen"), born Marshville, NC, May 4, 1959.

George F. Will, 60, editor, columnist, baseball executive, born Champaign, IL, May 4, 1941.

Pia Zadora, 45, actress, singer, dancer, born Hoboken, NJ, May 4, 1956.

MAY 5 — SATURDAY
Day 125 — 240 Remaining

AMERICAN MEDICAL ASSOCIATION FOUNDED: ANNIVERSARY. May 5, 1847. The American Medical Association was organized at a meeting at Philadelphia attended by 250 delegates. This was the first national medical convention in the US.

ANN ARBOR SPRING ART FAIR. May 5–6. Ann Arbor, MI. To give the public the opportunity to view and invest in the finest arts and crafts. 23rd annual. Est attendance: 15,000. For info: Audree Levy, 1809 Morning Glory, Carrollton, TX 75007. Phone: (972) 735-9898. Fax: (972) 735-9808. E-mail: audree @levyartfairs.com. Web: www.levyartfairs.com.

APPLE BLOSSOM FESTIVAL. May 5–6. Gettysburg, PA. An annual event held the first weekend in May at the South Mountain Fairgrounds. Est attendance: 25,000. For info: Gettysburg CVB, PO Box 4117, Gettysburg, PA 17325. Phone: (717) 334-6274. Fax: (717) 334-1166. Web: www.gettysburg.com.

BARK IN THE PARK. May 5. Lincoln Park, Chicago, IL. In recognition of Be Kind to Animals Week, thousands of paws and feet will hit the ground running or walking for this 5K event. Entrance fee. Est attendance: 3,500. For info: The Anti-Cruelty Society, 157 W Grand Ave, Chicago, IL 60610. Phone: (312) 644-8338. E-mail: info@anticruelty.org. Web: www.anticruelty .org.

BASEBALL'S FIRST PERFECT GAME: ANNIVERSARY. May 5, 1904. Denton T. "Cy" Young pitched baseball's first perfect game, not allowing a single opposing player to reach first base. Young's outstanding performance led the Boston Americans in a 3–0 victory over Philadelphia in the American League. The Cy Young Award for pitching was named in his honor.

BATTLE OF THE WILDERNESS: ANNIVERSARY. May 5, 1864. The Battle of the Wilderness began, the first major encounter between opposing troops under Robert E. Lee and Ulysses S. Grant. So named for the area of dense forest and underbrush of northern Virginia where the battle occurred, the fighting was especially fierce with opposing armies often fighting at point-blank range as the battle lines became obscured in the smoke-filled forest. Both sides suffered heavy casualties totaling more than 24,000, and after the fighting had ceased on the second day, more than 200 wounded Federal troops were trapped and killed by the flames of fires started by the battle.

		S	M	T	W	T	F	S
May				1	2	3	4	5
2001		6	7	8	9	10	11	12
		13	14	15	16	17	18	19
		20	21	22	23	24	25	26
		27	28	29	30	31		

BLY, NELLIE: BIRTH ANNIVERSARY. May 5, 1867. Born at Cochran's Mills, PA, Nellie Bly was the pseudonym used by pioneering American journalist Elizabeth Cochrane Seaman. Like her namesake in a Stephen Foster song, Nellie Bly was a social reformer and human rights advocate. As a journalist, she is best known for her exposé of conditions in what were then known as "insane asylums," where she posed as an "inmate." As an adventurer, she is best known for her 1889–90 tour around-the-world in 72 days, in which she bettered the time of Jules Verne's fictional character Phileas Fogg by eight days. She died at New York, NY, Jan 27, 1922.

BONZA BOTTLER DAY™. May 5. To celebrate when the number of the day is the same as the number of the month. Bonza Bottler Day™ is an excuse to have a party at least once a month. For more information, see Jan 1. For info: Gail M. Berger, 109 Matthew Ave, Poca, WV 25159. Phone: (304) 776-7746. E-mail: gberger5@aol.com.

CARTOONISTS DAY. May 5. To honor all cartoonists in the industry: animation, magazines, comic strips, etc. Designated by the National Cartoonists Society. For info: Ken Alvine, Creative Comic Syndicate, 1608 S Dakota Ave, Sioux Falls, SD 57105. Phone: (605) 336-9434. Fax: (605) 338-3501. E-mail: KAI1303567@aol.com.

COMMUNITY WIDE GARAGE SALE. May 5. Elgin, TX. Bargains abound in Elgin. More than 100 garage sales held on the same day. Downtown businesses have sidewalk sales. Visitors and locals can seek out treasures in an historic setting. Annually, the first Saturday in May. Est attendance: 3,000. For info: Aletha Krebs, 150 Evergreen, Elgin, TX 78621. Phone: (512) 281-4380. E-mail: economic@totalaccess.net. Web: www.elgintx.com.

COTTON PICKIN' FAIR. May 5–6 (also Oct 6–7). Gay, GA. At the old cotton gin complex, this award-winning festival features 300 exhibitors of antiques and arts and crafts, ongoing entertainment, great country cooking, children's activities and demonstrations by craftspeople. Biannually, the first weekend of May and October. Est attendance: 30,000. For info: Kris Price, Asst Dir, PO Box 1, Gay, GA 30218. Phone: (706) 538-6814. Web: www.cpfair.com.

DEPOT LANE SINGERS. May 5 (also Dec 1). Schoharie, NY. 75–100 singers celebrate the seasons in song. Est attendance: 700. For info: Frances Tripp, Dir, Schoharie Colonial Heritage Assn, PO Box 554, Schoharie, NY 12157. Phone: (518) 295-7168 or (518) 295-7505. E-mail: scha@midtel.net.

ENGLAND: BRIGHTON FESTIVAL. May 5–27. Various venues, Brighton, East Sussex. Annual international festival which includes all aspects of the performing arts. Annually, the first Saturday in May to the final Sunday in May. Est attendance: 150,000. For info: Brighton Festival, 12A Pavilion Bldgs, North Street, Brighton, East Sussex, England BN1 1EL. Phone: (44) (1273) 700747. Fax: (44) (1273) 707505. E-mail: info@brighton-festival .org.uk. Web: www.brighton-festival.org.uk.

FISHING CONTEST. May 5. Lake Shenandoah County Park, Lakewood, NJ. Catch the longest fish of a specific species. Novice or expert. Prizes awarded. Bait and Tackle Shop on premises. Picnic area. Rain or shine. Children $1, Adults $3. Est attendance: 500. For info: German Georgieff, Coord, Wells Mills County Park, 905 Wells Mills Rd, Waretown, NJ 08758. Phone: (609) 971-3085. Fax: (609) 971-9540.

FLEMINGTON SPEEDWAY RACING SEASON. May 5–Sept 9. Flemington Fairgrounds, Flemington, NJ. Racing by various types of stock cars and other vehicles. 6:30 PM starting time. Est attendance: 5,000. For info: Paul Kuhl, Flemington Fairgrounds, PO Box 293, Rt 31, Flemington, NJ 08822. Phone: (908) 782-2413. Fax: (908) 806-8432. Web: www .flemingtonspeedway.com.

GENEVA ON THE RIVER. May 5–6. Geneva, IL. Spring into the season. Bloom with ideas for your home and you. Relive the past with historic downtown tours and horse-drawn carriage rides. For info: Geneva Chamber of Commerce, 8 S Third St, PO Box 481, Geneva, IL 60134. Phone: (630) 232-6060. Fax: (630) 232-6083. E-mail: chamberinfo@genevachamber.com. Web: www.genevachamber.com.

HALFWAY POINT OF SPRING. May 5. On this day, 47 days of spring will have elapsed, and the equivalent will remain before June 21, 2001, which is the summer solstice and the beginning of summer.

HISTORY CONFERENCE. May 5. Washington, PA. Sponsored by Washington County, Pennsylvania Historical Society. 9 AM–4:30 PM. Est attendance: 150. For info: Washington County Historical Society, 49 E Maiden St, Washington, PA 15301. Phone: (724) 225-6740. Fax: (724) 225-8495. E-mail: info@wchspa.org. Web: www.wchspa.org.

INDIAN DAY. May 5–6. Russell Cave National Monument, Bridgeport, AL. Programs on Native American culture with demonstrations of how everyday things were done in the past. Activities may include flint knapping, pipe carving, bows, arrows, fire, pottery, finger weaving, petroglyphs and much more. Est attendance: 2,500. For info: Park Ranger, 3729 County Rd 98, Bridgeport, AL 35740. Phone: (205) 495-2672.

JAPAN: CHILDREN'S DAY. May 5. National holiday. Observed on the fifth day of the fifth month each year.

JOHNSON, AMY: FLIGHT ANNIVERSARY. May 5, 1930. Yorkshire-born Amy Johnson began the first successful solo flight by a woman from England to Australia. Leaving Croydon Airport in a de Havilland Tiger Moth named *Jason*, she flew 9,960 miles to Port Darwin, Australia, arriving May 28. The song "Amy, Wonderful Amy" celebrated the fame of this "wonder girl of the air," who became a legend in her own lifetime. Serving as an air ferry pilot during WWII, she was lost over the Thames Estuary in 1941.

KENTUCKY DERBY. May 5. Churchill Downs, Louisville, KY. The running of America's premier thoroughbred horse race, inaugurated in 1875. First jewel in the "Triple Crown," traditionally followed by the Preakness (the second Saturday after Derby) and the Belmont Stakes (the fifth Saturday after Derby). Annually, the first Saturday in May. Est attendance: 135,000. For info: Churchill Downs, 700 Central Ave, Louisville, KY 40208. Phone: (502) 636-4400. Web: kentuckyderby.com.

KOREA: CHILDREN'S DAY. May 5. A time for families to take their children on excursions. Parks and children's centers throughout the country are packed with excited and colorfully dressed children. A national holiday since 1975.

LEE-JACKSON LACROSSE CLASSIC. May 5. Virginia Military Institute, Lexington, VA. Community-wide event when the Washington and Lee lacrosse team meets the Virginia Military Institute team. 2 PM. For info: Lexington Visitors Bureau, 106 E Washington St, Lexington, VA 24450. Phone: (540) 463-3777. Fax: (540) 463-1105. E-mail: lexington@rockbridge.net.

LILAC TIME. May 5–20. Lilacia Park, Lombard, IL. The world-renowned Lilacia Park, an 8.5 acre horticulture showcase with 1,200 lilacs and 25,000 tulips, is the site of Lilac Time, Lombard's annual celebration of spring. The festival includes horticulture seminars, Lilacia Park tours, concerts, luncheons in the park, an art show, kids' activities, Lilac Queen Coronation, Lilac Ball and the annual Lilac Parade. Annually, the first two weeks in May. Est attendance: 18,000. For info: Lilac Time Hotline, Phone: (630) 953-6000 ext 27.

LONG GROVE CHOCOLATE FESTIVAL. May 5–6. Long Grove, IL. Restaurants and outdoor food booths serve up chocolate creations galore. Demonstrations by chocolate artists and chefs, contests, displays and free samples and tastings. Admission and parking free. 10 AM–6 PM. Est attendance: 30,000. For info: Long Grove Merchants Assn, 307 Old McHenry Rd, Long Grove, IL 60047. Phone: (847) 634-0888. Fax: (847) 634-6373.

LOW COUNTRY SHRIMP FESTIVAL. May 5. McClellanville, SC. Seafood, arts, crafts, civic display, entertainment and Blessing of the Fleet. Annually, the first Saturday in May. Est attendance: 8,000. For info: The Archibald Rutledge Academy, PO Box 520, McClellanville, SC 29458. Phone: (843) 887-3323.

MALTA: CARNIVAL. May 5–6. Valletta. Festival dates from 1535 when Knights of St. John introduced Carnival at Malta. Dancing, bands, decorated trucks and grotesque masks. Annually, the first weekend after May 1.

MARX, KARL: BIRTH ANNIVERSARY. May 5, 1818. German socialist, founder and father of modern communism, author of *Das Kapital* and (with Friedrich Engels) the *Communist Manifesto*. Born at Treves, Germany, he died at London, England, Mar 14, 1883, at age 64.

MAY DAY FAIRIE FESTIVAL. May 5 (raindate May 6). Spoutwood Farm, Glen Rock, PA. Family-oriented event celebrating springtime, fairies and nature spirits. Activities include maypole dancing, earth healing circle, face painting, fairie dust making, strolling performers, music, food, vendors and much more. Admission: $5. Annually, the first Saturday in May. Est attendance: 2,000. For info: Rob Wood, RD3 Box 66, Glen Rock, PA 17327. Phone: (717) 235-6610. Web: www.fairiefestival.net.

MEXICO: BATTLE OF PUEBLA: ANNIVERSARY. May 5, 1862. The Mexican Army defeated French troops at the city of Puebla. This day is commemorated as a national holiday in Mexico.

MEXICO: CINCO DE MAYO: ANNIVERSARY. May 5. Mexican national holiday recognizing the anniversary of the Battle of Puebla in 1862, in which Mexican troops under General Ignacio Zaragoza, outnumbered three to one, defeated invading French forces of Napoleon III. Anniversary is observed by Mexicans everywhere with parades, festivals, dances and speeches.

NATIONAL SAFE KIDS WEEK. May 5–12. Mission is to prevent the number one killer of children—unintentional injury. For info: National SAFE KIDS Campaign, 111 Michigan Ave NW, Washington, DC 20010-2970. Phone: (202) 662-0600. Web: www.safekids.org.

NATIONAL SCRAPBOOK DAY. May 5. Celebrate and preserve your memories through scrapbooking! Annually, the first Saturday in May. For info: *Creating Keepsakes* Scrapbook Magazine, 354 S Mountain Way Dr, Orem, UT 84058. Phone: (801) 224-8235. Fax: (801) 227-0059. E-mail: comments@creatingkeepsakes.com. Web: www.creatingkeepsakes.com.

NETHERLANDS: LIBERATION DAY: ANNIVERSARY. May 5. Marks liberation of the Netherlands from Nazi Germany in 1945.

POWER, TYRONE: BIRTH ANNIVERSARY. May 5, 1913. American actor, best known for his motion picture action-adventure roles, Tyrone Power was born at Cincinnati, OH. He died Nov 15, 1958, at Madrid, Spain.

RICHMOND'S MUSHROOM FESTIVAL. May 5–6. Richmond, MO. Parade, arts and crafts, carnival, bands and beer gardens. Est attendance: 5,000. For info: Exec Dir, Chamber of Commerce, 107 N Thornton, Richmond, MO 64085. Phone: (816) 776-6916. Fax: (816) 776-6917.

SOUTHERN APPALACHIAN DULCIMER FESTIVAL. May 5. Tannehill Historical State Park, McCalla, AL. Festival highlighting old-time dulcimer music. Est attendance: 2,000. For info: Vicki Gentry, Tannehill Historical State Park, 12632 Confederate Parkway, McCalla, AL 35111. Phone: (205) 477-5711. Fax: (205) 477-9400.

SPACE MILESTONE: *FREEDOM 7* (US): 40th ANNIVERSARY. May 5, 1961. First US astronaut in space, second man in space, Alan Shepard, Jr, projected 115 miles into space in suborbital flight reaching a speed of more than 5,000 miles per hour. This was the first piloted Mercury mission.

SPRING CORN FESTIVAL. May 5–6. Museum of Indian Culture, Allentown, PA. Welcome spring with a celebration of Native American cultures featuring arts, crafts, demonstrations, foods and family fun. Annually, the first Saturday and Sunday in May. Est attendance: 3,000. For info: Lenni Lenape Historical Soc, Museum of Indian Culture, 2825 Fish Hatchery Rd, Allentown, PA 18103-9801. Phone: (610) 797-2121. Fax: (610) 797-2801. Web: www.lenape.org.

SPRING GALA. May 5–6. Lovington, NM. Arts and crafts show at the Lea County Fairgrounds. For info: Andra Conner, Dir, Lovington Chamber of Commerce, 201 S Main St, Lovington, NM 88260. Phone: (505) 396-5311. Fax: (505) 396-2823. E-mail: visitus@leaconet.com. Web: visitus.leaco.net.

STOCK MARKET CRASH OF 1893: ANNIVERSARY. May 5, 1893. Wall Street stock prices took a sudden drop. By the end of the year 600 banks had closed. The Philadelphia and Reading, the Erie, the Northern Pacific, the Union Pacific and the Atchison, Topeka and Santa Fe railroads had gone into receivership; 15,000 other businesses went into bankruptcy. Other than the "Great Depression" of the 1930s, this was the worst economic crisis in US history; 15–20 percent of the workforce was unemployed.

"STOP THE MUSIC" TV PREMIERE: ANNIVERSARY. May 5, 1949. ABC's prime-time musical-game show hosted by Bert Parks. Featured the singing talents of Kay Armen, Jimmy Blaine, Betty Ann Grove, Estelle Loring, Jaye P. Morgan and June Valli, and the dancing numbers of Sonja and Courtney Van Horne. Harry Salter conducted the band.

STRAWBERRY, FLOWER & GARDEN FESTIVAL. May 5–6. Lahaska, PA. Craftspeople gather to show their wares and demonstrate their skills. Strawberries served up in various forms—dipped in chocolate, in assorted pastries and shortcake, in jams, in fritters, and fresh and unadorned. Exhibitors from area nurseries and environmental groups. Live entertainment and pie-eating contests add to the festivities of this traditional Spring celebration. Free admission. Est attendance: 18,000. For info: Peddler's Village, Routes 202 & 263, Lahaska, PA 18931. Phone: (215) 794-4000. Fax: (215) 794-4001. Web: www.peddlersvillage.com.

TENNESSEE RIVER FIDDLERS CONVENTION. May 5–6. McFarland Park, Florence, AL. The lazy Tennessse River will be the backdrop to the sounds of banjos, dobros, guitars and fiddles during this Bluegrass celebration. Musicians, both young and old, compete for more than $5,000 in prize money in 16 categories. Annually, the first full weekend in May. Est attendance: 5,000. For info: City of Florence, Park and Recreation Dept, 2500 Chisholm Rd, PO Box 2040, Florence, AL 35630. Phone: (205) 760-6416. Fax: (205) 760-6497. E-mail: RGres33403@aol.com.

THAILAND: CORONATION DAY. May 5. Thailand.

TOTALLY CHIPOTLE DAY. May 5. To help usher in what should prove to be one of the most popular flavors of the new millennium. Totally Chipotle Day helps familiarize the uninitiated with the gorgeously smoked chipotle pepper—and its somewhat difficult pronunciation. Celebrated alongside Cinco De Mayo to honor its Mexican-Indian heritage. For info: Martin Larkin, Pres, RRC Productions, 1924 W Montrose Ave, #117, Chicago, IL 60613. Phone: (877) 244-7085. E-mail: rnrchef@aol.com. Web: www.totallychipotle.com.

	S	M	T	W	T	F	S
May			1	2	3	4	5
2001	6	7	8	9	10	11	12
	13	14	15	16	17	18	19
	20	21	22	23	24	25	26
	27	28	29	30	31		

TOWSONTOWN SPRING FESTIVAL. May 5–6. Towson, MD. Six stages with continuous entertainment. 400 food, craft and display vendors on the street. Art and photography exhibit and antique auto display. Annually, the first Saturday and Sunday in May. Est attendance: 250,000. For info: Towsontown Spring Fest, PO Box 10115, Towson, MD 21285-0115. Phone: (410) 825-1144. Fax: (410) 832-5863.

VIRGINIA GOLD CUP. May 5. Great Meadow, The Plains, VA. Steeplechasing began in Ireland in 1762 when two horsemen held a cross-country match race to a far away church steeple. Great Meadow is the largest steeplechase course in the country with a spectacular hillside amphitheater. The $50,000 Virginia Gold Cup race is run over a challenging 4-mile post and rail course of 23 fences. Advance tickets only. Annually, the first Saturday in May. Est attendance: 45,000. For info: Virginia Gold Cup Assn, PO Box 840, Warrenton, VA 20188. Phone: (540) 347-2612. Fax: (540) 349-1829. Web: www.vagoldcup.com.

VIRGINIA STATE CHAMPIONSHIP CHILI COOK-OFF. May 5. Historic Market area, Roanoke, VA. Live entertainment, pepper eating contest, children's festival area and the best chili samples from across the US and the Commonwealth of Virginia. All compete for the state title. Annually, the first Saturday in May. Est attendance: 55,000. For info: Sandra Carroll, Greenvale School, 627 Westwood Blvd, Roanoke, VA 24017. Phone: (540) 342-4716. Fax: (540) 344-0876. E-mail: scgns@aol.com. Web: downtown.roanoke.org.

YWCA FESTIVAL OF RACES. May 5. Cedar Rapids, IA. A festival of family fun with an 8K and 5K run, a 5K health walk, two children's races and a carnival with entertainment for kids. Annually, the first Saturday in May. Est attendance: 3,000. For info: YWCA, 318 Fifth St SE, Cedar Rapids, IA 52401. Phone: (319) 365-1458. Fax: (319) 365-2263.

BIRTHDAYS TODAY

Pat Carroll, 74, actress (Emmy for "Caesar's Hour"; "The Ted Knight Show"), born Shreveport, LA, May 5, 1927.

Richard E. Grant, 44, actor (*Henry and June, LA Story, The Age of Innocence*), born Mbabane, Swaziland, May 5, 1957.

Lance Henriksen, 58, actor (*Dog Day Afternoon, The Terminator, Near Dark*), born New York, NY, May 5, 1943.

Jean-Pierre Leaud, 57, actor (Truffaut's *The 400 Blows, Love at 20, Stolen Kisses, Bed and Board, Love on the Run*), born Paris, France, May 5, 1944.

Michael Murphy, 63, actor (*Nashville, Manhattan, Salvador*), born Los Angeles, CA, May 5, 1938.

Ziggy Palffy, 29, hockey player, born Skalica, Czechoslovakia, May 5, 1972.

Michael Palin, 58, actor, comedian ("Monty Python's Flying Circus," *Life of Brian*), born Sheffield, Yorkshire, England, May 5, 1943.

Tina Yothers, 28, actress ("Family Ties"), born Whittier, CA, May 5, 1973.

MAY 6 — SUNDAY
Day 126 — 239 Remaining

BABE RUTH'S FIRST MAJOR LEAGUE HOME RUN: ANNIVERSARY. May 6, 1915. George Herman "Babe" Ruth of the Boston Red Sox hit his first major league home run in a game against the New York Yankees in New York.

BANNISTER BREAKS FOUR-MINUTE-MILE: ANNIVERSARY. May 6, 1954. Running for the British Amateur Athletic Association in a meet at Oxford University, Roger Bannister broke the four-minute barrier with a time of 3:59.4. Four minutes for a mile at the time was considered not only a physical barrier but also a psychological one.

EARLHAM COLLEGE GRADUATION. May 6. Richmond, IN. Congratulations to the Class of 2001! For info: Earlham College, 801 National Rd West, Richmond, IN 47374-4095. Phone: (765) 983-1200. Web: www.earlham.edu.

FLEXIBLE WORK ARRANGEMENTS WEEK. May 6–12. To promote experimentation with alternate work schedules and working at home. Annually, the week beginning with the first Sunday in May. For info: Maggi Payment, 1286 University Ave, #192, San Diego, CA 92103-3312. Phone: (619) 232-0404. E-mail: info @worktimeoptions.com.

FRANKENMUTH SKYFEST. May 6. Frankenmuth, MI. To encourage family participation in a healthy outdoor sport that adapts to all age groups. 20th annual. Annually, the first Sunday in May. Est attendance: 4,500. For info: Audrey Fischer, Kite Kraft, 576 S Main St, Frankenmuth, MI 48734. Phone: (517) 652-2961.

FREUD, SIGMUND: BIRTH ANNIVERSARY. May 6, 1856. Austrian physician, born at Freiberg, Moravia. Founder of psychoanalysis. Freud died at London, England, Sept 23, 1939.

GOODWILL INDUSTRIES WEEK. May 6–12. To call international attention to Goodwill Industries as a leader in job training and employment services for people with disabilities and other barriers to employment. Annually, the first full week in May. For info: Goodwill Industries Intl, Communications Dept, 9200 Rockville Pike, Bethesda, MD 20814-3896. Phone: (301) 530-6500. Fax: (301) 530-1516. Web: www.goodwill.org.

GOSPEL SING—BLACK AND WHITE/NOW AND THEN. May 6. Arrow Rock, MO. A celebration of gospel music with mid-Missouri choirs, quartets, duets and soloists performing music from black and spiritual traditions all the way to contemporary songs of praise. Recognizing the vast array of music written in praise of the same Lord. Est attendance: 200. For info: HARC, PO Box M, Arrow Rock, MO 65320. E-mail: tmcglaughlin@mid-mo.net.

HINDENBURG DISASTER: ANNIVERSARY. May 6, 1937. At 7:20 PM, the dirigible *Hindenburg* exploded as it approached the mooring mast at Lakehurst, NJ, after a trans-Atlantic voyage. Of its 97 passengers and crew, 36 died in the accident, which ended the dream of mass transportation via dirigible.

INTERNATIONAL UNMOTHERS DAY. May 6. A holiday to bring attention and acceptance to the millions of women worldwide who through circumstances or choice are child-free. We would like to dedicate this year to the women of journalism whose columns have meant so much to us and helped in the promotion of Unmothers International. Annually, the first Sunday in May. For info: Denise Marquardt, Pres, Unmothers Intl, 8678 Meade St, Montague, MI 49437-1350.

NATIONAL CLERGY DAY. May 6. Established in 1999 by Divine Word Missionaries Mission Office as a day of celebration for peoples of all faiths to show recognition and appreciation for the significant contributions of religious leaders. For info: Thomas A Krosnicki, SVD, Divine Word Missionaries, PO Box 6099, Techny, IL 60082. Phone: (847) 272-8572. E-mail: TAK6099@aol.com. Web: www.divinewordmissionaries.org.

NATIONAL FAMILY WEEK. May 6–12. Traditionally the first Sunday and the first full week in May are observed as National Family Week in many Christian churches.

NATIONAL NURSES DAY AND WEEK. May 6–12. A week to honor the outstanding efforts of nurses everywhere to strengthen the health of the nation. Annually, beginning May 6, National Nurses Day, and ending May 12, Florence Nightingale's birthday. Call or write for a free catalog. For info: American Nurses Assn, 600 Maryland Ave SW, Ste 100W, Washington, DC 20024. Phone: (800) 274-4262. Fax: (202) 651-7003. E-mail: jstanish@ana.org. Web: www.nursingworld.org.

NATIONAL PET WEEK. May 6–12. To promote responsible pet ownership and public awareness of veterinary medical service for animal health and care. Annually, the first full week in May. For info: The American Veterinary Medical Assn, 1931 N Meacham Rd, Schaumburg, IL 60173. Phone: (847) 925-8070. Fax: (847) 925-1329. Web: www.avma.org.

NATIONAL POSTCARD WEEK. May 6–12. To advertise use of picture postcards for correspondence and collecting. Annually, the first full week of May since 1984. For info: John H. McClintock, Founder, Postcard History Soc, Box 1765, Manassas, VA 22110. Phone: (703) 368-2757.

NATIONAL PTA TEACHER APPRECIATION WEEK. May 6–12. PTAs across the country conduct activities to strengthen respect and support for teachers and the teaching profession. For info: Natl PTA, 330 N Wabash Ave, Ste 2100, Chicago, IL 60611. Phone: (312) 670-6782. Fax: (312) 670-6783. E-mail: info@pta.org. Web: www.pta.org.

NATIONAL SUICIDE AWARENESS WEEK. May 6–12. For info: American Assn of Suicidology, 4201 Connecticut Ave NW, Ste 408, Washington, DC 20009. Phone: (202) 237-2280.

NATIONAL TOURISM WEEK. May 6–12. To promote and enhance awareness of travel and tourism's importance to the economic, social and cultural well-being of the US. Annually, beginning the first Sunday in May. For info: Travel Industry Assn of America, 1100 New York Ave NW, Ste 450, Washington, DC 20005-3934. Phone: (202) 408-8422. E-mail: ckeefe@tia.org. Web: www.tia.org.

NATIONAL WILDFLOWER WEEK. May 6–12. A week dedicated to encouraging observation, cultivation and study of native wildflowers as a way to deepen humankind's relationship and responsibility to creation and Creator. Annually, the first full week in May. Sponsor: Secular Franciscan Order, USA. For info: Charles Spencer, SFO, Natl Ecology Commission, 107 Jensen Circle, West Springfield, MA 01089-4451. Phone: (413) 737-7600. Fax (voice first): (413) 737-7600. E-mail: cspencer@mail.map.com. Web: www.francisanecology.com.

NO DIET DAY. May 6. Celebrates an understanding that it is time to stop dieting and trying to lose weight. Time to shift the focus toward good health and well-being, to self acceptance and respect toward others whatever their size. Find out the Top 10 reasons not to diet with the book *Women Afraid to Eat*. For info: Francie M. Berg, Healthy Weight Network, 402 S 14th St, Hettinger, ND 58639. Phone: (701) 567-2646. Fax: (701) 567-2602. E-mail: hwj@healthyweight.net. Web: www.healthyweight.net.

O. HENRY PUN-OFF (WORLD CHAMPIONSHIP). May 6. The O. Henry Museum, Austin, TX. Pundits and punographers match wits for a wordy cause in two separate pun-filled competitions (Punniest of Show and High Lies & Low Puns). Sponsors: The City of Austin Parks and Recreation Department, Friends of the O. Henry Museum and Punsters United Nearly Yearly (PUNY). Est attendance: 2,000. For info: Valerie Bennett, Curator, O. Henry Museum, 409 E Fifth St, Austin, TX 78701. Phone: (512) 453-4431 or (512) 472-1903. Fax: (512) 472-7102. Web: www.ci .austin.tx.us/parks/ohenry.htm.

PEARY, ROBERT E.: BIRTH ANNIVERSARY. May 6, 1856. Born at Cresson, PA. Peary served as a cartographic draftsman in the US Coast and Geodetic Survey for two years, then joined the US Navy's Corps of Civil Engineers in 1881. He first worked as an explorer in tropical climates as he served as subchief of the Inter-Ocean Canal Survey in Nicaragua. After reading of the inland ice of Greenland, Peary became attracted to the Arctic. He organized and led eight Arctic expeditions and is credited with the verification of Greenland's island formation, proving that the polar ice cap extended beyond 82° north latitude, and the discovery of the Melville meteorite on Melville Bay, in addition to his famous discovery of the North Pole, Apr 6, 1909. Peary died Feb 20, 1920, at Washington, DC.

PENN, JOHN: BIRTH ANNIVERSARY. May 6, 1740. Signer of the Declaration of Independence, born at Caroline County, VA. Died Sept 14, 1788.

SACK OF ROME: ANNIVERSARY. May 6, 1527. The Renaissance ended with the Sack of Rome which began on this date. As part of a series of wars between the Hapsburg Empire and the French monarchy, German troops killed some 4,000 inhabitants of Rome, looted works of art and libraries. Pope Clement VII, who supported the French, was imprisoned.

TAGORE, RABINDRANATH: BIRTH ANNIVERSARY. May 6, 1861. Hindu poet, mystic and musical composer was born at Calcutta, India. Received Nobel Prize (literature) in 1913. Died at Calcutta, Aug 7, 1941. His birthday is observed in Bangladesh on the 25th day of the Bengali month of Baishakha (second week of May), when the poet laureate is honored with songs, dances and discussions of his works.

TEACHER APPRECIATION WEEK. May 6–12. A day for elementary through high school students to show appreciation to their teachers. Students are urged to thank their teachers for their care and concerned effort, to be extra cooperative with them. For info: Connie Morris, Natl Education Assn, 1201 16th St, NW, Washington, DC 20036. Phone: (202) 822-7262. Fax: (202) 822-7292. Web: www.nea.org.

TRADITIONAL PLOWING MATCH. May 6. Woodstock, VT. This annual event features a horse- and oxen-drawn plowing competition as well as demonstrations of different plowing techniques. Est attendance: 1,050. For info: Susan Plump, Public Relations Asst, Billings Farm and Museum, PO Box 489, Woodstock, VT 05091. Phone: (802) 457-2355. Fax: (802) 457-4663. E-mail: billings.farm@valley.net.

VALENTINO, RUDOLPH: BIRTH ANNIVERSARY. May 6, 1895. Rodolpho Alfonzo Rafaello Pietro Filiberto Guglieimi Di Valentina D'Antonguolla, whose professional name was Rudolph Valentino, was born at Castellaneta, Italy. Popular cinema actor. For years press reports claimed that "at least one weeping veiled woman in black brought flowers to his tomb" (at Hollywood Memorial Park) every year on the anniversary of his death at New York, NY, Aug 23, 1926.

		S	M	T	W	T	F	S
May				1	2	3	4	5
2001		6	7	8	9	10	11	12
		13	14	15	16	17	18	19
		20	21	22	23	24	25	26
		27	28	29	30	31		

WELLES, ORSON: BIRTH ANNIVERSARY. May 6, 1915. Actor and director born at Kenosha, WI. *Citizen Kane*, which he directed and in which he played the title role, is one of the most influential films ever made. Other films in which he had a role include *The Third Man* and *The Magnificent Ambersons*. Welles died at Los Angeles, CA, Oct 10, 1985.

WINTERTHUR POINT-TO-POINT. May 6. Winterthur Museum, Garden & Library, Wilmington, DE. Steeplechase races, antique carriage parade, canine agility competition, kids' activities, tailgating plus much more! Call for pricing. Rain or shine event. Est attendance: 26,000. For info: Greater Wilmington CVB, 100 W 10th St, Ste 20, Wilmington, DE 19801-1661. Phone: (800) 422-1181 or (302) 652-4088. E-mail: info@wilmcvb.org. Web: www.wilmcvb.org.

BIRTHDAYS TODAY

Tony Blair, 48, British prime minister, born Edinburgh, Scotland, May 6, 1953.

George Clooney, 40, actor ("ER," *Batman and Robin, One Fine Day*), born Lexington, KY, May 6, 1961.

Roma Downey, 37, actress ("Touched By an Angel"), born Derry, Northern Ireland, May 6, 1964.

Ben Masters, 54, actor (*All That Jazz, Making Mr Right*), born Corvallis, OR, May 6, 1947.

Willie Howard Mays, 70, Baseball Hall of Fame outfielder, born Westfield, AL, May 6, 1931.

Bob Seger, 56, musician, singer ("Night Moves," "Travelin' Man"), born Ann Arbor, MI, May 6, 1945.

Richard C. Shelby, 67, US Senator (D, Alabama), born Birmingham, AL, May 6, 1934.

Lynn Whitfield, 48, actress (*Stepmom, Eve's Bayou*), born Baton Rouge, LA, May 6, 1953.

MAY 7 — MONDAY
Day 127 — 238 Remaining

BEAUFORT SCALE DAY (FRANCIS BEAUFORT BIRTH ANNIVERSARY). May 7, 1774. A day to honor the British naval officer, Sir Francis Beaufort, who devised in 1805 a scale of wind force from 0 (calm) to 12 (hurricane) that was based on observation, not requiring any special instruments. The scale was adopted for international use in 1874 and has since been enlarged and refined. Beaufort was born at Flower Hill, Meath, Ireland, and died at Brighton, England, Dec 17, 1857.

BEETHOVEN'S NINTH SYMPHONY PREMIERE: ANNIVERSARY. May 7, 1824. Beethoven's Ninth Symphony in D Minor was performed for the first time at Vienna, Austria. Known as the *Choral* because of his use of voices in symphonic form for the first time, the Ninth was his musical interpretation of Schiller's *Ode to Joy*. Beethoven was completely deaf when he composed it, and it was said a soloist had to tug on his sleeve when the performance was over to get him to turn around and see the enthusiastic response he could not hear.

BROWNING, ROBERT: BIRTH ANNIVERSARY. May 7, 1812. English poet and husband of poet Elizabeth Barrett Browning, born at Camberwell, near London. Known for his dramatic monologues. Died at Venice, Italy, Dec 12, 1889.

COOPER, GARY: 100th BIRTH ANNIVERSARY. May 7, 1901. Frank James Cooper was born at Helena, MT. He changed his name to Gary at the start of his movie career. He is best known by baseball fans for his portrayal of Lou Gehrig in *The Pride of the Yankees.* Other films included *Wings, The Virginian, The Plainsman, Beau Geste, Sergeant York* (for which he won his first Academy Award), *High Noon* (winning his second Oscar for best actor), *The Court Martial of Billy Mitchell* and *Friendly Persuasion.* He died May 13, 1961, at Hollywood, CA.

DIEN BIEN PHU FALLS: ANNIVERSARY. May 7, 1954. Vietnam's victory over France at Dien Bien Phu ended the Indochina War. This battle is considered one of the greatest victories won by a former colony over a colonial power.

FIRST PRESIDENTIAL INAUGURAL BALL: ANNIVERSARY. May 7, 1789. Celebrating the inauguration of George Washington, the first Presidential Inaugural Ball was held at New York, NY.

GERMANY: HAMBURG HARBOR BIRTHDAY. May 7, 1189. "Hafengeburtstag" celebrates establishment of Hamburg as a free city.

GERMANY'S FIRST SURRENDER: ANNIVERSARY. May 7, 1945. Russian, American, British and French ranking officers crowded into a second-floor recreation room of a small red-brick schoolhouse (which served as Eisenhower's headquarters) at Reims, Germany. Representing Germany, Field Marshall Alfred Jodl signed an unconditional surrender of all German fighting forces. After a signing that took almost 40 minutes, Jodl was ushered into Eisenhower's presence. The American general asked the German if he fully understood what he had signed and informed Jodl that he would be held personally responsible for any deviation from the terms of the surrender, including the requirement that German commanders sign a formal surrender to the USSR at a time and place determined by that government.

"KRAFT TELEVISION THEATRE" TV PREMIERE: ANNIVERSARY. May 7, 1947. Live theatrical programs appearing on both the NBC and ABC networks. The show was a gold mine for discovering new talent. Among the playwrights getting their big breaks were: Rod Serling, Paddy Chayefsky and Tad Mosel. Some of the show's most notable plays included: "The Easy Mark" (1951) with Jack Lemmon, "Double in Ivory" (1953) with Lee Remick, "To Live in Peace" (1953) with Anne Bancroft, "The Missing Years" (1954) with Anthony Perkins and Mary Astor, "Alice in Wonderland" (1954) with Robin Morgan, Art Carney, Edgar Bergen and Charlie McCarthy and "A Profile in Courage" (1956) with James Whitmore. The last play was based on a book by John F. Kennedy who also appeared on the program.

LUSITANIA SINKING: ANNIVERSARY. May 7, 1915. British passenger liner *Lusitania,* on its return trip from New York to Liverpool, carrying nearly 2,000 passengers, was torpedoed by a German submarine off the coast of Ireland, sinking within minutes; 1,198 lives were lost. US President Wilson sent note of protest to Berlin on May 13, but Germany, which had issued warning in advance, pointed to *Lusitania*'s cargo of ammunition for Britain. US maintained "neutrality," for the time being.

MacLEISH, ARCHIBALD: BIRTH ANNIVERSARY. May 7, 1892. American poet and Librarian of Congress (1939–44), born at Glencoe, IL. MacLeish, who was also a playwright, Pulitzer Prize winner, editor, lawyer, professor and farmer, died at Boston, MA, Apr 20, 1982.

MELANOMA MONDAY. May 7. Also known as National Self-Examination Day. People are encouraged to examine their skin for moles or other growths. For info: American Academy of Dermatology, 930 N Meacham Rd, Schaumburg, IL 60173. Phone: (847) 330-0230 or (888) 462-DERM. Web: www.aad.org.

MOON PHASE: FULL MOON. May 7. Moon enters Full Moon phase at 9:52 AM, EDT.

"STRIKE IT RICH" TV PREMIERE: 50th ANNIVERSARY. May 7, 1951. The downtrodden and the poverty-stricken showed up on this game show to tell their sob stories. Whoever received the most votes from the studio audience was declared the winner. The losers were able to receive help from sympathetic viewers through a telephone "heart line." Warren Hull hosted the program. The show got in trouble with the New York City Welfare Department in 1954 when 55 of the show's hopeful contestants remained in New York and went on welfare.

TCHAIKOVSKY, PETER ILICH: BIRTH ANNIVERSARY. May 7, 1840. Ranked among the outstanding composers of all time, Peter Ilich Tchaikovsky was born at Vatkinsk, Russia. His musical talent was not encouraged and he embarked upon a career in jurisprudence, not studying music seriously until 1861. Among his famous works are the three-act ballet *Sleeping Beauty,* two-act ballet *The Nutcracker* and the symphony *Pathetique.* Mystery surrounds Tchaikovsky's death. It was believed he had caught cholera from contaminated water, but 20th-century scholars believe he probably committed suicide to avoid his homosexuality being revealed. He died at St. Petersburg, Nov 6, 1893.

UNITED KINGDOM: MAY DAY BANK HOLIDAY. May 7. Bank and public holiday in England, Wales, Scotland and Northern Ireland. Annually, the first Monday in May.

BIRTHDAYS TODAY

Theresa Brewer, 70, singer ("[Open Up Your Heart and] Let the Sun Shine In"), born Toledo, OH, May 7, 1931.

Pete V. Domenici, 69, US Senator (R, New Mexico), born Albuquerque, NM, May 7, 1932.

Amy Heckerling, 47, filmmaker (*Fast Times at Ridgemont High, Look Who's Talking*), born New York, NY, May 7, 1954.

Darren McGavin, 79, actor (*The Man with the Golden Arm,* "Mickey Spillane's Mike Hammer"), born Spokane, WA, May 7, 1922.

Peter Reckell, 46, actor ("Days of Our Lives"), born Elkhart, IN, May 7, 1955.

Tim Russert, 51, TV news talk-show moderator ("Meet the Press"), born Buffalo, NY, May 7, 1950.

John Constantine (Johnny) Unitas, 68, Pro Football Hall of Fame quarterback, born Pittsburgh, PA, May 7, 1933.

MAY 8 — TUESDAY
Day 128 — 237 Remaining

BATTLE OF McDOWELL: ANNIVERSARY. May 8, 1862. In a major engagement in the Shenandoah Valley Campaign of the Civil War, General Stonewall Jackson's rebel forces repulsed an attack by Union forces at McDowell, VA.

BATTLE OF THE CORAL SEA: ANNIVERSARY. May 8, 1942. Beginning on this date, the Battle of the Coral Sea impeded Japanese expansion and introduced a new form of naval warfare. None of the surface vessels exchanged fire—the entire battle was waged by aircraft. The US lost a carrier, destroyer and tanker. The Japanese lost seven warships, including a carrier.

CZECH REPUBLIC: LIBERATION DAY: ANNIVERSARY. May 8. Commemorates the liberation of Czechoslovakia from the Germans in 1945.

DUNANT, JEAN HENRI: BIRTH ANNIVERSARY. May 8, 1828. Author and philanthropist, founder of the Red Cross Society, was born at Geneva, Switzerland. Nobel prize winner in 1901. Died at Heiden, Switzerland, Oct 30, 1910.

ENGLAND: HELSTON FURRY DANCE. May 8. The world-famous Helston Furry Dance is held each year on May 8 (except when the 8th is a Sunday or Monday, in which case it is held on the previous Saturday). Dancing around the streets of Helston, Cornwall, begins early in the morning and continues throughout the day. The "Furry" dance leaves Guildhall at the stroke of noon and winds its way in and out of many of the larger buildings.

FRANCE: VICTORY DAY. May 8. Commemorates the surrender of Germany to Allied forces and the cessation of hostilities in 1945.

GERMANY'S SECOND SURRENDER: ANNIVERSARY. May 8, 1945. Stalin refused to recognize the document of unconditional surrender signed at Reims the previous day, so a second signing was held at Berlin. The event was turned into an elaborate formal ceremony by the Soviets who had lost some 20 million lives during the war. As in the Reims document, the end of hostilities was set for 12:01 AM local time on May 9.

GOOD NEIGHBOR AWARD PRESENTATION. May 8. Independence, MO. The Good Neighbor Award Foundation honors an outstanding American each year at a luncheon in celebration of Truman's birthday. Past recipients include David McCullough, Tom Clancy, Nancy Kassebaum, Bill Mauldin and Arthur Schlesinger, Jr. The 2000 recipient of this prestigious award was General Norman Schwarzkopf. For info: Margaret McDonald. Phone: (816) 561-2008.

GOTTSCHALK, LOUIS MOREAU: BIRTH ANNIVERSARY. May 8, 1829. American pianist of international fame who toured the US during the Civil War. Gottschalk composed for the piano combining American and Creole folk themes and rhythms in his work. Born at New Orleans, LA, he died Dec 18, 1869, at Rio de Janeiro, Brazil.

JOHNSON, ROBERT: 90th BIRTH ANNIVERSARY. May 8, 1911. Born at Hazelhurst, MS, and murdered at age 27, Aug 16, 1938, at Greenwood, MS (poisoned by a jealous husband), in his short life Johnson was a master blues guitarist, a singer and songwriter of great influence. He developed a unique guitar style of such skill that it was said he acquired his ability by selling his soul to the Devil—the film *Crossroads* is based very loosely on this myth. Johnson's only two recording sessions captured for us the classics "Sweet Home Chicago," "Cross Road Blues," "Me and the Devil Blues" and others. Johnson was inducted posthumously into the Blues Hall of Fame in 1980 and the Rock & Roll Hall of Fame in 1986.

LAVOISIER, ANTOINE LAURENT: EXECUTION ANNIVERSARY. May 8, 1794. French chemist and the "father of modern chemistry." Especially noted for having first explained the real nature of combustion and for showing that matter is not destroyed in chemical reactions. Born at Paris, France, Aug 26, 1743, Lavoisier was guillotined at the Place de la Revolution for his former position as a tax collector. The Revolutionary Tribunal is reported to have responded to a plea to spare his life with the statement: "We need no more scientists in France."

LISTON, SONNY: BIRTH ANNIVERSARY. May 8, 1932. Charles ("Sonny") Liston, boxer born at St. Francis County, AR. Liston rose above a record of criminal activity to defeat Floyd Patterson for the heavyweight title on Sept 25, 1962. He defeated Patterson in a rematch but then lost the title to Cassius Clay, who later changed his name to Muhammad Ali. In a rematch Ali knocked out Liston with a punch few observers saw. Died at Las Vegas, NV, Dec 30, 1970.

		S	M	T	W	T	F	S
May				1	2	3	4	5
2001		6	7	8	9	10	11	12
		13	14	15	16	17	18	19
		20	21	22	23	24	25	26
		27	28	29	30	31		

NATIONAL TEACHER DAY. May 8. To pay tribute to American educators, sponsored by the National Education Association, Teacher Day falls during the National PTA's Teacher Appreciation Week. Local communities and organizations are encouraged to use this opportunity to honor those who influence and inspire the next generation through their work. Annually, the Tuesday of the first full week in May. For info: Natl Education Assn (NEA), 1201 16th St NW, Washington, DC 20036. Phone: (202) 833-4000. Web: www.nea.org.

NO SOCKS DAY. May 8. If we give up wearing socks for one day, it will mean a little less laundry, thereby contributing to the betterment of the environment. Besides, we will all feel a bit freer, at least for one day. Annually, May 8. [© 2000 by WH] For info: Thomas and Ruth Roy, Wellcat Holidays, 2418 Long Ln, Lebanon, PA 17046. Phone: (717) 279-0184. E-mail: wellcat @supernet.com. Web: www.wellcat.com.

OUIMET, FRANCIS DESALES: BIRTH ANNIVERSARY. May 8, 1893. American amateur golfer who is credited with establishing the popularity of golf in the US. Born at Brookline, MA, his golfing career began as a caddy. In 1913, at age 20, he generated national enthusiasm for the game when he became the first American and first amateur to win the US Open Golf Championship. He won the US Amateur Championship in 1914 and 1931, and was a member of the US Walker Cup team from its first tournament in 1922 until 1949, serving as its nonplaying captain for six of those years. In 1949, he established the Francis Ouimet Caddy Scholarship Fund, and in 1951, he became the first American to be elected Captain of the Royal and Ancient Golf Club of St. Andrews, Scotland. Ouimet died at Newton, MA, Sept 2, 1967.

PRESIDENTIAL WREATH LAYING. May 8. Harry S Truman Library, Independence, MO. Each year the US government marks President Truman's birthday anniversary with a Presidential wreath laying ceremony. If the current President is unable to participate, he appoints someone in his stead to place a wreath on President Truman's grave in a ceremony conducted by officers and color guard from the US Army Command and General Staff College. Est attendance: 250. For info: Rita Klepac, Harry S Truman Library, US Hwy 24 and Delaware St, Independence, MO 64050-1798. Phone: (816) 833-1400. Ext 236. Fax: (816) 833-4368. E-mail: library@truman.nara.gov. Web: www .trumanlibrary.org.

PRIMARY DAY: LIVE FROM DELAWARE STREET. May 8. Indianapolis, IN. Visit President Benjamin Harrison Home and listen to the conversations and gossip of the day as you enter each room and meet and speak with all the family members and household staff, whose roles are recreated by exceptional actors. Est attendance: 500. For info: PR Dept, President Benjamin Harrison Home, 1230 N Delaware St, Indianapolis, IN 46202. Phone: 316311888. Fax: (317) 632-5488.

SLOVAK REPUBLIC: LIBERATION DAY: ANNIVERSARY. May 8. Commemorates the liberation of Czechoslovakia from the Germans in 1945.

TRUMAN, HARRY S: BIRTH ANNIVERSARY. May 8, 1884. The 33rd president of the US, succeeded to that office upon the death of Franklin D. Roosevelt, Apr 12, 1945, and served until Jan 20, 1953. Born at Lamar, MO, Truman was the last of the nine US presidents who did not attend college. Affectionately nicknamed "Give 'em Hell Harry" by admirers. Truman died at Kansas City, MO, Dec 26, 1972. His birthday is a holiday in Missouri.

V-E DAY: ANNIVERSARY. May 8, 1945. Victory in Europe Day commemorates unconditional surrender of Germany to Allied Forces. The surrender document was signed by German representatives at General Dwight D. Eisenhower's headquarters at Reims to become effective, and hostilities to end, at one minute past midnight May 9, 1945, which was 9:01 PM EDT on May 8 in the US. President Harry S Truman May 8 declared May 9, 1945, to be "V-E Day," but it later came to be observed on May 8. A separate German surrender to the USSR was signed at Karlshorst, near Berlin, May 8. See also: "Russia: Victory Day: Anniversary" (May 9).

WORLD RED CROSS DAY. May 8. A day for commemorating the birth of Jean Henry Dunant, the Swiss founder of the International Red Cross Movement in 1863, and for recognizing the humanitarian work of the Red Cross around the world. For info on activities in your area, contact your local Red Cross chapter. For info: Media Associate, American Red Cross Natl Headquarters, 1621 N Kent St, Arlington, VA 22209. Phone: (703) 248-4219. Fax: (703) 248-4256.

BIRTHDAYS TODAY

David Attenborough, 75, author, naturalist (*Life on Earth, Trials of Life*), born London, England, May 8, 1926.

Peter Benchley, 61, author, journalist (*Rummies, Jaws*), born New York, NY, May 8, 1940.

Bill Cowher, 44, football coach and former player, born Pittsburgh, PA, May 8, 1957.

Melissa Gilbert, 37, actress ("Little House on the Prairie," *The Miracle Worker*), born Los Angeles, CA, May 8, 1964.

Enrique Iglesias, 26, singer, son of Julio Iglesias, born Madrid, Spain, May 8, 1975.

David Keith, 47, actor, director (*The Great Santini, An Officer and a Gentleman*), born Knoxville, TN, May 8, 1954.

Ronald Mandel (Ronnie) Lott, 42, former football player, born Albuquerque, NM, May 8, 1959.

Janet McTeer, 40, actress (*Tumbleweeds*, born Newcastle, England, May 8, 1961.

Thomas Pynchon, 64, writer (*V, Gravity's Rainbow*), born Glen Cove, NY, May 8, 1937.

Don Rickles, 75, comedian, actor (*Blazing Saddles*, "The Dean Martin Show"), born New York, NY, May 8, 1926.

Toni Tennille, 58, singer (with husband Daryl Dragon made up Captain and Tennille), born Montgomery, AL, May 8, 1943.

MAY 9 — WEDNESDAY

Day 129 — 236 Remaining

BIG 12 WOMEN'S SOFTBALL CHAMPIONSHIPS. May 9–12. Oklahoma City, OK. For info: Big 12 Conference, 2201 Stemmons Frwy, 28th Fl, Dallas, TX 75207. Phone: (214) 742-1212. Fax: (214) 753-0145. Web: www.big12sports.com.

BONNIE BLUE NATIONAL HORSE SHOW. May 9–12. Virginia Horse Center, Lexington, VA. Major all-breed event, "A"-rated show of the American Horse Show Association. For info: Lexington Visitors Bureau, 106 E Washington St, Lexington, VA 24450. Phone: (540) 463-3777. Fax: (540) 463-1105. E-mail: lexington@rockbridge.net.

BOYD, BELLE: BIRTH ANNIVERSARY. May 9, 1843. Notorious Confederate spy who later became an actress and lecturer was born at Martinsburg, VA. Author of the book *Belle Boyd in Camp and Prison*, she died June 11, 1900 at Kilbourne, WI.

BROWN, JOHN: BIRTH ANNIVERSARY. May 9, 1800. Abolitionist leader born at Torrington, CT, and hanged Dec 2, 1859, at Charles Town, WV. Leader of attack on Harpers Ferry, Oct 16, 1859, which was intended to give impetus to movement for escape and freedom for slaves. His aim was frustrated and in fact resulted in increased polarization and sectional animosity. Legendary martyr of the abolitionist movement.

ENGLAND: ROYAL WINDSOR HORSE SHOW. May 9–13. Home Park, Windsor, Berkshire. Major annual show jumping event with royal pageantry and color. Est attendance: 60,000. For info: Penelope Henderson, Sec'y, Royal Windsor Horse Show, The Royal Mews, Windsor Castle, Windsor, Berkshire, England SL4 1NG. Phone: (44) (175) 386-0633. Fax: (44) (175) 383-1074.

EUROPEAN UNION: ANNIVERSARY OBSERVANCE. May 9, 1950. Member countries of the European Union commemorate the announcement by French statesman Robert Schuman of the "Schuman Plan" for establishing a single authority for production of coal, iron and steel in France and Germany. The European Coal and Steel Community was founded in 1952. This organization was a forerunner of the European Economic Community, founded in 1958, which later became the European Union. At the European Summit at Milan in 1985, this day was proclaimed the Day of Europe.

GONZALES, PANCHO: BIRTH ANNIVERSARY. May 9, 1928. Richard Alonzo ("Pancho") Gonzales, tennis player born at Los Angeles, CA. A self-taught player, Gonzales won the 1948 US National Singles Championship and repeated in 1949. He turned pro and won the world's championship from 1954 through 1962. Gonzales was an aggressive, temperamental player who rarely trained. Died at Las Vegas, NV, July 3, 1995.

HUNTER FREES THE SLAVES: ANNIVERSARY. May 9, 1862. At Hilton Head, SC, General David Hunter, commander of the Department of the South, issued orders freeing slaves in South Carolina, Florida and Georgia. Not having congressional or presidential approval, the orders were countermanded by President Lincoln on May 19.

NATIONAL NIGHTSHIFT WORKERS DAY. May 9. To honor those workers who reverse their natural circadian rhythm to keep business running 24 hours a day. Annually, the second Wednesday of May. For info: Velcea Kae, 3 Chester Rd, Springfield, VT 05156.

NATIONAL RECEPTIONISTS DAY. May 9. Day of recognition for our nation's frontline personnel in business, because you only get one chance to make a good first impression. Receptionists may go by other names such as host/hostess, maitre d', front desk clerk, operator, customer service representative, information desk personnel or anyone responsible for creating or maintaining a favorable image for the company by greeting clients and guests. There are some 892,000 receptionists in the US. Annually, the second Wednesday in May. For info: Jennifer Alexander, Natl Receptionists Society, 740 Hobart St, Menlo Park, CA 94025. Phone: (650) 328-6060. E-mail: jennifer_alexander@music.com.

NATIONAL THIRD SHIFT WORKERS DAY. May 9. To show appreciation for and to honor those often-forgotten workers who toil through the night to keep countless companies and businesses running smoothly. Annually, the second Wednesday in May. For info: Jeff Corbett, PO Box 2, Statesville, NC 28687.

PENINSULA CAMPAIGN INTENSIFIED: ANNIVERSARY. May 9, 1862. Confederate forces at Norfolk, VA, evacuated the city in a costly move, leaving valuable materiel for the Union army. Norfolk and Portsmouth were occupied on May 10 and the naval yard at Gosport, VA, was burned. President Abraham Lincoln was personally involved in this action, supervising the Federal expeditionary force.

RENO, NEVADA: BIRTHDAY. May 9, 1868. First known as Fullers Crossing, then Lakes Crossing, on this date it officially became Reno, known today as "The Biggest Little City in the World." Its six-week residency requirement for divorce became law on May 1, 1931.

RUSSIA: VICTORY DAY: ANNIVERSARY. May 9. National holiday observed annually to commemorate the 1945 Allied Forces defeat of Nazi Germany in WWII and to honor the 20 million Soviet people who died in that war. Hostilities ceased and the German surrender became effective at one minute after midnight on May 9, 1945. See also: "V-E Day: Anniversary" (May 9).

UNIVERSAL FAMILY WEEK. May 9–15. To stress the importance of the fundamental role of good families in strengthening humankind. For complete info, send $4 to cover expense of printing, handling and postage. For info: Dr. Stanley Drake, Pres, Intl Soc of Friendship and Goodwill, 8592 Roswell Rd, Ste 434, Atlanta, GA 30350-1870.

"VAST WASTELAND" SPEECH: 40th ANNIVERSARY. May 9, 1961. Speaking before the bigwigs of network TV at the annual convention of the National Association of Broadcasters, Newton Minow, the new chairman of the Federal Communications Commission, exhorted those executives to sit through an entire day of their own programming. He suggested that they "will observe a vast wasteland." Further, he urged them to try for "imagination in programming, not sterility; creativity, not imitation; experimentation, not conformity; excellence, not mediocrity."

BIRTHDAYS TODAY

John Ashcroft, 59, US Senator (R, Missouri), born Springfield, MO, May 9, 1942.

Candice Bergen, 55, actress (*Starting Over, The Group,* "Murphy Brown"), daughter of ventriloquist Edgar Bergen, born Beverly Hills, CA, May 9, 1946.

James L. Brooks, 61, screenwriter, producer ("Taxi," "The Mary Tyler Moore Show"), born Brooklyn, NY, May 9, 1940.

Albert Finney, 65, actor (*Tom Jones, Shoot the Moon, Annie, The Dresser*), born Salford, England, May 9, 1936.

Anthony Keith (Tony) Gwynn, 41, baseball player, born Los Angeles, CA, May 9, 1960.

Glenda Jackson, 64, actress (Oscars for *Women in Love, Touch of Class*), born Cheshire, England, May 9, 1937.

Billy Joel, 52, singer, composer ("It's Still Rock and Roll to Me," "Just the Way You Are"), born Hicksville, NY, May 9, 1949.

Mike Wallace, 83, TV journalist ("60 Minutes"), born Brookline, MA, May 9, 1918.

Steve Yzerman, 36, hockey player, born Cranbrook, British Columbia, Canada, May 9, 1965.

MAY 10 — THURSDAY

Day 130 — 235 Remaining

ALBANY TULIP FESTIVAL. May 10–13. Washington Park, Albany, NY. A celebration of spring, the Tulip Festival features thousands of tulips abloom throughout the city and honors Albany's Dutch heritage. Events include crowning of a Tulip Queen, arts and crafts vendors, food vendors, entertainment on three stages, children's activities and Dutch dancers in costume. Est attendance: 80,000. For info: City of Albany Office of Special Events, Eagle Street, Albany, NY 12207. Phone: (518) 434-2032. Web: www.albanyevents.org.

ASTAIRE, FRED: BIRTH ANNIVERSARY. May 10, 1899. Actor, dancer and choreographer, born at Omaha, NE. Astaire began dancing with his sister Adele and in the mid-1930s began dancing with Ginger Rogers. His resume said, "Can't act. Slightly bald. Can dance a little." Despite this, Astaire starred in more than 40 films including *Holiday Inn, The Gay Divorcee, Silk Stockings* and *Easter Parade.* Died at Los Angeles, CA, June 22, 1987.

ASTOR PLACE RIOT: ANNIVERSARY. May 10, 1849. A riot erupted outside the Astor Place Opera House at New York, NY, where the British actor William Charles Macready was performing. Led by the American actor Edwin Forrest, angry crowds revolted against dress requirements for admission and against Macready's public statements on the vulgarity of American life.

		S	**M**	**T**	**W**	**T**	**F**	**S**
May				1	2	3	4	5
2001		6	7	8	9	10	11	12
		13	14	15	16	17	18	19
		20	21	22	23	24	25	26
		27	28	29	30	31		

On May 8, Macready's performance of *Macbeth* was stopped by Forrest's followers. Two days later, a mob led by Ned Buntline shattered the windows of the theater during a performance. Troops were summoned and they were ordered to fire, killing 22 and wounding 26.

CANADA: THUNDER BAY CHAMBER OF COMMERCE TRADE SHOW. May 10–12. Thunder Bay, Ontario, Canada. For info: Mary Ann Agostino, Thunder Bay Chamber of Commerce, 857 May St North, Thunder Bay, ON, Canada P7C 3S2. Phone: (807) 622-9642. Fax: (807) 622-7752. E-mail: chamber@tb-chamber.on.ca. Web: www.tb-chamber.on.ca.

CONFEDERATE MEMORIAL DAY IN SOUTH CAROLINA. May 10. See also Apr 26, Apr 30, May 28 and June 3 for Confederate Memorial Day observances in other southern states.

GOLDEN SPIKE DRIVING: ANNIVERSARY. May 10, 1869. Anniversary of the meeting of Union Pacific and Central Pacific railways, at Promontory Point, UT. On that day a golden spike was driven by Leland Stanford, president of the Central Pacific, to celebrate the linkage. The golden spike was promptly removed for preservation. Long called the final link in the ocean-to-ocean railroad, this event cannot be accurately described as completing the transcontinental railroad, but it did complete continuous rail tracks between Omaha and Sacramento. See also: "Transcontinental US Railway Completion: Anniversary" (Aug 15).

HOLLAND TULIP TIME FESTIVAL. May 10–19. Holland, MI. To promote the tulip and to preserve the Dutch cultural heritage in the city of Holland. Est attendance: 750,000. For info: Holland Tulip Time Festival, Inc, 171 Lincoln Ave, Holland, MI 49423. Phone: (616) 396-4221 or (800) 822-2770. Fax: (616) 396-4545. E-mail: tulip@tuliptime.org. Web: www.tuliptime.org.

MANDELA INAUGURATION: ANNIVERSARY. May 10, 1994. In a dramatic and historic exchange of power, former political prisoner Nelson Mandela was inaugurated as President of South Africa. Long the focal point of apartheid foes' attempts to end the enforced policy of discrimination in South Africa, Mandela handily won the first free election in South Africa despite many attempts by various political factions to either stop the electoral process or alter the outcome.

MICRONESIA, FEDERATED STATES OF: NATIONAL HOLIDAY. May 10. Proclamation of the Federated States of Micronesia in 1979.

NATIONAL SMALL BUSINESS DAY. May 10. To honor entrepreneurs and small businesses in the US. Tips for promoting your small business will be provided. For info: Nancy Michaels, Impression Impact, 60 Thoreau St, Ste 308, Concord, MA 01742. Phone: (978) 287-0718. Fax: (978) 287-0410. E-mail: NMichaels @impressionimpact.com.

PELLA TULIP TIME FESTIVAL. May 10–12. Pella, IA. To pay homage to the founders of this predominately Dutch community. Activities include coronation of queen, parades, flowers, Dutch singing and dancing. Est attendance: 100,000. For info: Pella Historical Soc, 507 Franklin, Pella, IA 50219. Phone: (515) 628-4311. Fax: (515) 628-9192. E-mail: pellatt@kdsi.net. Web: www.pellatuliptime.com.

THE READ IN!. May 10. A day-long online reading project for students throughout the world in grades K–12. They chat together online with 22 of the world's best children's and young adult literature authors. This day is a culmination of several weeks of online participation by teachers and students, during which they share descriptions of their schools and communities. For info: Jane Coffey, Program Dir, The Read In Foundation, 6043 Channel Dr, Riverbank, CA 95367. Phone: (209) 869-0713. E-mail: Thereadin@aol.com. Web: www.readin.org.

ROSS, GEORGE: BIRTH ANNIVERSARY. May 10, 1730. Signer of the Declaration of Independence. Born at New Castle, DE, he died July 14, 1779, at Philadelphia.

SINGAPORE: VESAK DAY. May 10. Public holiday. Monks commemorate their Lord Buddha's entry into Nirvana by chanting holy sutras and freeing captive birds.

TRUST YOUR INTUITION DAY. May 10. Today is the day we pay homage to the wonderful gift of sixth sense, "gut" feelings or that still small voice that is sometimes the only clue we have to go on in this ever-changing world. [©1994] For info: Adrienne Sioux Koopersmith, 1437 W Rosemont, #1W, Chicago, IL 60660-1319. Phone: (773) 743-5341. Fax: (773) 743-5395. E-mail: adrienne@21stcentury.net.

BIRTHDAYS TODAY

Bono, 41, singer (U2), born Dublin, Ireland, May 10, 1960.
T. Berry Brazleton, 83, pediatrician, author, born Waco, TX, May 10, 1918.
Jason Brooks, 35, actor ("Days of Our Lives"), born Colorado Springs, CO, May 10, 1966.
Judith Jamison, 57, dancer and choreographer, born Philadelphia, PA, May 10, 1944.
Dave Mason, 55, singer, musician, songwriter ("We Just Disagree," "So High"), born Worcester, England, May 10, 1946.
Gary Owens, 65, actor ("Rowan & Martin's Laugh-In," "The Gong Show"), born Mitchell, SD, May 10, 1936.
Ara Raoul Parseghian, 78, former football coach and sportscaster, born Akron, OH, May 10, 1923.
Marie-France Pisier, 57, actress (*Cousin Cousine, French Postcards*), born Daclat, Vietnam, May 10, 1944.
Rick Santorum, 43, US Senator (R, Pennsylvania), born Winchester, VA, May 10, 1949.
Ronald F. (Rony) Seikaly, 36, basketball player, born Beirut, Lebanon, May 10, 1965.

MAY 11 — FRIDAY
Day 131 — 234 Remaining

AUSTRIA: VIENNA FESTIVAL. May 11–June 17. Held since 1951, this festival features 1,000 events, including opera, dance, theater, chamber and symphonic music. For info: Wiener Festwochen, Lehargasse 11, A-1060 Vienna, Austria. Phone: (431) 589 22330. Fax: (431) 589-2249. E-mail: festwochen @festwochen.at. Web: www.festwochen.or.at.

BATTLE OF HAMBURGER HILL: ANNIVERSARY. May 11, 1969. Beginning of one of the most infamous battles that signified the growing frustration with America's involvement in the Vietnam war. Attempting to seize Dong Ap Bia mountain, American troops repeatedly scaled the hill over a 10-day period, often engaging in bloody hand-to-hand combat with the North Vietnamese. After finally securing the objective, American military decision makers chose to abandon it and the North Vietnamese retook it shortly thereafter. The heavy casualties in the struggle to take the hill inspired the name "Hamburger Hill."

BATTLE OF YELLOW TAVERN: ANNIVERSARY. May 11, 1864. Attempting to head off Union General Phil Sheridan's cavalry advance on Richmond, Confederate General J.E.B. Stuart's Confederate cavalry encountered the Federals at Yellow Tavern, VA. Stuart was mortally wounded in the battle and died the following day. The loss of one of its most colorful and effective cavalry leaders was a great blow to the South. The battle delayed the Federal advance long enough for the Confederates to strengthen the defenses at Richmond, and Sheridan was forced to change his plans.

BERLIN, IRVING: BIRTH ANNIVERSARY. May 11, 1888. Songwriter born Israel Isidore Baline at Tyumen, Russia. Irving Berlin moved to New York, NY, with his family when he was four years old. After the death of his father, he began singing in saloons and on street corners in order to help his family and worked as a singing waiter as a teenager. Berlin became one of America's most prolific songwriters, authoring such songs as "Alexander's Ragtime Band," "White Christmas," "God Bless America," "There's No Business Like Show Business," "Doin' What Comes Naturally," "Puttin' On the Ritz," "Blue Skies" and "Oh! How I Hate to Get Up in the Morning" among others. He could neither read nor write musical notation. Berlin died Sept 22, 1989, at New York, NY.

BIG TEN MEN'S GOLF CHAMPIONSHIP. May 11–13. University of Illinois. For info: Sue Ryan, Big Ten Conference, 1500 W Higgins Rd, Park Ridge, IL 60068-6300. Phone: (847) 696-1010. Fax: (847) 696-1110. Web: www.bigten.org or www .bigtenchampionships.com.

BIG TEN SOFTBALL TOURNAMENT. May 11–12. Site of conference champion. Est attendance: 1,500. For info: Dennis LaBissoniere, Big Ten Conference, 1500 W Higgins Rd, Park Ridge, IL 60068-6300. Phone: (847) 696-1010. Fax: (847) 696-1110. Web: www.bigten.org.

DALI, SALVADOR: BIRTH ANNIVERSARY. May 11, 1904. A leading painter in the Surrealist movement, Salvador Dali was equally well known for his baffling antics and attempts to shock his audiences. The largest collection of his works resides in the Salvador Dali Museum at St. Petersburg, FL. Born at Figueras, Spain, Dali died Jan 23, 1989, at his hometown of Figueras.

DENMARK: COMMON PRAYER DAY. May 11. Public holiday. The fourth Friday after Easter, known as "Store Bededag," is a day for prayer and festivity.

EAT WHAT YOU WANT DAY. May 11. Here's a day you may actually enjoy yourself. Ignore all those on-again/off-again warnings. [© 2000 by WH] For info: Tom and Ruth Roy, Wellcat Holidays, 2418 Long Ln, Lebanon, PA 17046. Phone: (717) 279-0184. E-mail: wellcat@supernet.com. Web: www.wellcat.com.

ELKIN, STANLEY: BIRTH ANNIVERSARY. May 11, 1930. Born at Brooklyn, NY, Stanley Elkin became a professor at Washington University at St. Louis, MO, where he lectured on fiction writing for more than 30 years. In addition to his teaching, Elkin was a novelist of particular acclaim. Author of 17 books, he was awarded the National Book Critics Circle Award in 1983 for his novel *George Mills*. Elkin died of a heart attack at St. Louis, MO, May 31, 1995.

FAIRBANKS, CHARLES WARREN: BIRTH ANNIVERSARY. May 11, 1852. 26th vice president of the US (1905–09) born at Unionville Center, OH. Died at Indianapolis, IN, June 4, 1918.

GLACIER NATIONAL PARK ESTABLISHED: ANNIVERSARY. May 11, 1910. Located in northwest Montana on the Canadian border. In 1932 Glacier and Waterton Lakes National Park in Alberta were joined together by the governments of the US and Canada as Waterton-Glacier International Peace Park.

GRAHAM, MARTHA: BIRTH ANNIVERSARY. May 11, 1894. Martha Graham was born at Allegheny, PA, and became one of the giants of the modern dance movement in the US. She began her dance career at the comparatively late age of 22 and joined the Greenwich Village Follies in 1923. Her new ideas began to surface in the late '20s and '30s, and by the mid-1930s she was incorporating the rituals of the southwestern American Indians in her work. She is credited with bringing a new psychological depth to modern dance by exploring primal emotions and ancient rituals in her work. She performed until the age of 75, and premiered in her 180th ballet, *The Maple Leaf Rag*, in the fall of 1990. Died Apr 1, 1991, at New York, NY.

HART, JOHN: DEATH ANNIVERSARY. May 11, 1779. Signer of the Declaration of Independence, farmer and legislator, born about 1711 (exact date unknown), at Stonington, CT, died at Hopewell, NJ.

INTERNATIONAL MIGRATORY BIRD CELEBRATION. May 11–13. Chincoteague, VA. Three days of walks, talks, workshops, boat tours, children's activities and an art celebration all conducted outdoors with the birds. Annually, Mother's Day weekend. Est attendance: 10,000. For info: Chincoteague Chamber of Commerce, PO Box 258, Chincoteague, VA 23336. Phone: (757) 336-6161. Fax: (757) 336-1242. E-mail: pony@shore.intercom.net. Web: www.chincoteaguechamber.com.

JAPAN: CORMORANT FISHING FESTIVAL. May 11–Oct 15. Cormorant fishing on the Nagara River, Gifu. "This ancient method of catching Ayu, a troutlike fish, with trained cormorants, takes place nightly under the light of blazing torches."

LAG B'OMER. May 11. Hebrew calendar date: Iyar 18, 5761. Literally, the 33rd day of the omer (harvest time), the 33rd day after the beginning of Passover. Traditionally a joyous day for weddings, picnics and outdoor activities.

MERRIMAC DESTROYED: ANNIVERSARY. May 11, 1862. After a standoff with the Union ironclad *Monitor* on Mar 9, the Confederate ironclad *Merrimac* was destroyed by the Confederate navy on May 11. In the wake of advancing Union troops in the Peninsular Campaign, the South was forced to destroy the valuable vessel to prevent its capture by Union forces. See also: "Battle of the *Monitor* and the *Merrimac*: Anniv" (Mar 9).

MINNESOTA: ADMISSION DAY: ANNIVERSARY. May 11. Became 32nd state in 1858.

SEATTLE BLACKOUT: ANNIVERSARY. May 11, 1942. Seattle, WA, became the first US city to institute outside blackout control during WWII. All outdoor lighting became subject to permit.

SPRING GARDENER'S MARKET AND PLANT SALE. May 11–13. Norfolk Botanical Garden, Norfolk, VA. Gardening enthusiasts can shop from more than 30 specialty growers, plant societies and wholesalers for the best selection of plants, garden art, accessories, furniture and wildlife supplies. Annually, Mother's Day weekend. Est attendance: 4,000. For info: Norfolk Botanical Garden, 6700 Azalea Garden Rd, Norfolk, VA 23518. Phone: (757) 441-5830. Fax: (757) 853-8294. Web: www.virginiagarden.org.

May 2001	S	M	T	W	T	F	S
			1	2	3	4	5
	6	7	8	9	10	11	12
	13	14	15	16	17	18	19
	20	21	22	23	24	25	26
	27	28	29	30	31		

MAY 12 — SATURDAY

Day 132 — 233 Remaining

BATTLE OF SPOTSYLVANIA: ANNIVERSARY. May 12, 1864. After the Battle of the Wilderness, Grant and Lee next engaged at the Battle of Spotsylvania (VA). Lee had positioned his troops in breastworks along a horseshoe formation utilizing the natural features of the landscape. During Grant's attack on this strong defensive position both sides suffered losses of more than 12,000 in what became known as "The Bloody Angle." Lee was forced to use every available man in order to protect the position and so ordered his troops to pull back during the night.

CELEBRATE!. May 12. Lawrence University, Appleton, WI. Five stages of entertainment. Children's area with activities and entertainment. Annually, the Saturday before Mother's Day. Est attendance: 40,000. For info: Campus Activities, Lawrence University, PO Box 599, Appleton, WI 54912.

DONIZETTI'S *L'ELISIR D'AMORE* PREMIERE: ANNIVERSARY. May 12, 1832. Italian composer Gaetano Donizetti's famed comic opera *L'Elisir d'amore* (*The Elixir of Love*) premiered on this date. With a libretto written by Felice Romani, the opera is about a poor peasant's attempts to woo a wealthy and spirited girl. It remains among Donizetti's best known works.

ELECTRA GOAT BBQ COOK-OFF & ARTS AND CRAFTS SHOW. May 12. Electra Goat Grounds, Electra, TX. Goat Brisket, Pork Ribs, Chicken Cook-Off, Cow Patty Drop, live band, Jackpot Steak & Beans Competition, tug-o-war, eating contest, children's games and crafts. Little Mr and Miss Goat Competition, Cool Ice Meltdown—100 lbs of ice melted by body heat only— radio station competition and Friday Night Cookie Toss. Dance 9 PM–1 AM after cook-off. Est attendance: 2,000. For info: Dawn Dunsmore, Electra Chamber of Commerce, 112 W Cleveland, Electra, TX 76360. Phone: (940) 495-3577. E-mail: ElectraCoC@aol.com. Web: www.electratexas.org.

GEORGE VI'S CORONATION: ANNIVERSARY. May 12, 1937. George VI was crowned at Westminster Abbey at London, following the abdication of his brother, Edward VIII. Born Dec 14, 1895, King George died Feb 6, 1952. He was succeeded by his daughter Elizabeth, the current reigning monarch.

GOODWILL EMBASSY TOUR. May 12. Washington, DC. Eight–ten embassies (ambassadors' residences) and chanceries (ambassadors' offices) open their doors to visitors on this self-guided tour. Experience each country's culture and history as each building contains native architecture, furnishings and fine arts. Tickets: $30 in advance, $35 on day of tour. Est attendance: 2,500. For info: Dir of Community Resources, Davis Memorial Goodwill Industries Inc, 2200 South Dakota Ave NE, Washington, DC 20018. Phone: (202) 636-4225. E-mail: DMGI@dcgoodwill.org. Web: www.dcgoodwill.org.

GUM TREE FESTIVAL. May 12–13. Tupelo, MS. A juried art show with arts, crafts and live entertainment. 10K run. Annually, the second weekend in May. Est attendance: 15,000. For info: Tupelo Conv and Visitors Bureau, PO Drawer 47, Tupelo, MS

38802. Phone: (800) 533-0611 or (662) 844-2787. Fax: (662) 844-2787.

IROQUOIS STEEPLECHASE. May 12. Percy Warner Park, Nashville, TN. Nashville's original "Rite of Spring." This event is the oldest continuously run, weight-for-age steeplechase in the US. The steeplechase has a seven-race card with the featured Iroquois Memorial. Annually, the second Saturday in May. Est attendance: 30,000. For info: Steeplechase Office, 2424 Garland Ave, Nashville, TN 37212. Phone: (615) 343-4231. Fax: (615) 322-6453.

JAMESTOWN FOUNDING DAY. May 12. Jamestown, VA. Anniversary of the founding of Jamestown, first permanent English colony in North America in 1607. Est attendance: 3,000. For info: Public Affairs Officer, Colonial Natl Historical Park, PO Box 210, Yorktown, VA 23690. Phone: (757) 229-1733. Web: www.nps.gov/colo.

JAMESTOWN LANDING DAY. May 12. Jamestown Settlement, Williamsburg, VA. Celebration of the anniversary of the establishment of America's first permanent English settlement at Jamestown, VA, in 1607. Militia presentations and sailing demonstrations. Est attendance: 1,200. For info: Media Relations, Jamestown-Yorktown Fdtn, PO Box 1607, Williamsburg, VA 23187. Phone: (757) 253-4838. Fax: (757) 253-5299. Web: www.historyisfun.org.

JUBILEE. May 12. Bennettsville, SC. Arts and crafts festival with entertainment, children's events and juried art show. Annually, the Saturday before Mother's Day. Est attendance: 6,000. For info: Ivy McLaurin, PO Box 765, Bennettsville, SC 29512. Phone: (843) 479-6982.

LEAR, EDWARD: BIRTH ANNIVERSARY. May 12, 1812. English artist and author, best remembered for his light verse and limericks. Lear was born at Highgate, England, and died at San Remo, Italy, Jan 29, 1888. See also: "Limerick Day" (May 12).

LIBERACE PLAY-A-LIKE COMPETITION. May 12. The Liberace Museum, Las Vegas, NV. Judges pianists on keyboard technique, costume and presentation in two divisions: professional and non-professional. Winners will receive specially inscribed Crystal Piano awards. Annually, the Saturday before May 16 (Liberace's birthday). Est attendance: 1,000. For info: Jamie G. James, The James Agency, 3630 Coldwater Canyon Ave, Studio City, CA 91604. Phone: (818) 508-4902. Fax: (818) 508-0562. E-mail: Jjames@Liberace.org.

LIMERICK DAY. May 12. Observed on the birthday of one of its champions, Edward Lear. The limerick, which dates from the early 18th century, has been described as the "only fixed verse form indigenous to the English language." It gained its greatest popularity following the publication of Edward Lear's *Book of Nonsense* (and its sequels). Write a limerick today! Example: There was a young poet named Lear/Who said, it is just as I fear/Five lines are enough/For this kind of stuff/Make a limerick each day of the year. See also: "Lear, Edward: Birth Anniversary" (May 12).

MARKET SQUARE FAIR. May 12. Fredericksburg, VA. To create an awareness of Fredericksburg's historic heritage. Arts, crafts, food and entertainment. Est attendance: 6,000. For info: Visitor Center, 706 Caroline St, Fredericksburg, VA 22401. Phone: (800) 678-4748. Fax: (540) 372-6587. E-mail: fburg@illuminet.net.

MOTHER'S DAY ANNUAL RHODODENDRON SHOW. May 12–13. Crystal Springs Rhododendron Gardens, Portland, OR. Spectacular display of rhododendron and azalea blooms and plant sale. Est attendance: 6,000. For info: Ted Van Veen, Garden Chair, American Rhododendron Soc, Portland Chapter, PO Box 86424, Portland, OR 97286. Phone: (503) 777-1734.

NATIVE AMERICAN ARTS FESTIVAL AND MOTHER'S DAY POW WOW. May 12–13. Riverside Park, Grants Pass, OR. Est attendance: 2,500. For info: American Indian Traditional Preservation Committee, 773 Hitching Post Rd, Grants Pass, OR 97526. Phone: (541) 474-6394 or (541) 839-6704.

NETHERLANDS: NATIONAL WINDMILL DAY. May 12. About 950 windmills still survive, and some 300 still are used occasionally and have been designated national monuments by the government. As many windmills as possible are in operation on National Windmill Day for the benefit of tourists. Annually, the second Saturday in May.

NIGHTINGALE, FLORENCE: BIRTH ANNIVERSARY. May 12, 1820. English nurse and public health activist who, through her unselfish devotion to nursing, contributed perhaps more than any other single person to the development of modern nursing procedures and dignity of nursing as a profession. Founder of the Nightingale training school for nurses. Author of *Notes on Nursing*. Born at Florence, Italy. Died at London, England, Aug 13, 1910.

OCCONEECHEE STATE PARK NATIVE AMERICAN FESTIVAL AND POW WOW. May 12. Clarksville, VA. Gates open at 10 AM, Grand Entry at 12 PM and continues until 8 PM. Native American artists and crafters show and sell their wares. Dancers, singers and drums perform intertribal songs and dances. A living history of Native American life prior to the European invasion is offered. Annually, the second weekend in May. Est attendance: 2,500. For info: Clarksville Lake Country Chamber of Commerce, PO Box 1017, Clarksville, VA 23927. Phone: (804) 374-2436. Fax: (804) 374-8174. E-mail: clarksville@kerrlake.com. Web: www.kerrlake.com/chamber.

ODOMETER INVENTED: ANNIVERSARY. May 12, 1847. Anniversary of the invention of the first odometer, invented by Mormon pioneer William Clayton while crossing the plains in a covered wagon. Previous to this, mileage was calculated by counting the revolutions of a rag tied to a spoke of a wagon wheel. For info: Museum of Church History and Art, 45 North West Temple, Salt Lake City, UT 84150. Phone: (801) 240-4604.

PORTUGAL: PILGRIMAGE TO FATIMA. May 12–13. Commemorates first appearance of the Virgin of the Rosary to little shepherd children May 13, 1917. Pilgrims come to Cova da Iria, religious center, candlelit procession, Mass of the sick, for annual observance.

PRATER'S MILL COUNTRY FAIR. May 12–13 (also Oct 6–7). Dalton, GA. Arts and crafts show in the atmosphere of an old-fashioned country fair. Est attendance: 25,000. For info: Judy Alderman, Prater's Mill Fdtn, Inc, PO Drawer H, Varnell, GA 30756. Phone: (706) 694-MILL or (800) 331-3258. Fax: (706) 694-8413. E-mail: pratersmill@daton.net.

SAVANNAH SCOTTISH GAMES AND HIGHLAND GATHERING. May 12. Old Fort Jackson, Savannah, GA. Clan tents, genealogical information, regimental pipe bands, Southeast Regional Highland Dancing Championship, single malt Scotch whisky tasting, entertainment by Scotland's finest musicians and children's games. Annually, the second Saturday in May. Est attendance: 6,000. For info: Savannah Scottish Games and Highland Gathering, PO Box 13435, Savannah, GA 31416. Phone: (912) 352-9959 or (912) 354-2129. Fax: (912) 234-0447.

TAOS SPRING ARTS FESTIVAL. May 12–29. Taos, NM. Featuring arts and crafts from all around New Mexico. Est attendance: 20,000. For info: Taos Spring Arts Festival, PO Drawer I, Taos, NM 87571. Phone: (800) 732-8267. Fax: (505) 758-3872. E-mail: taos@taoschamber.com.

BIRTHDAYS TODAY

MacKenzie Astin, 28, actor ("The Long Island Incident"), son of John Astin and Patty Duke, born Los Angeles, CA, May 12, 1973.

Burt Bacharach, 72, composer ("Walk On By," "Close to You," "Raindrops Keep Fallin' on My Head"); many film scores, born Kansas City, MO, May 12, 1929.

Stephen Baldwin, 35, actor (*The Usual Suspects*), born Massapequa, NY, May 12, 1966.

Lawrence Peter ("Yogi") Berra, 76, former baseball coach and manager, Baseball Hall of Fame catcher, born St. Louis, MO, May 12, 1925.

Bruce Boxleitner, 50, actor (*How the West Was Won*, "Scarecrow and Mrs King"), born Elgin, IL, May 12, 1951.

Gabriel Byrne, 51, actor (*The Usual Suspects*), born Dublin, Ireland, May 12, 1950.

Christian Campbell, 29, actor ("Malibu Shores," *Cold Hearts*), born Toronto, Ontario, Canada, May 12, 1972.

George Carlin, 64, comedian ("That Girl," "The George Carlin Show"), born New York, NY, May 12, 1937.

Lindsay Crouse, 53, actress (*Slap Shot, The Verdict, Places in the Heart*), born New York, NY, May 12, 1948.

Emilio Estevez, 39, actor (*Breakfast Club, Repo Man*), born New York, NY, May 12, 1962.

Kim Fields, 32, actress ("The Facts of Life," "Living Single"), born Los Angeles, CA, May 12, 1969.

Kim Greist, 43, actress (*Brazil, Throw Momma from the Train*), born Stamford, CT, May 12, 1958.

Katharine Hepburn, 94, actress (Oscars for *Morning Glory, Guess Who's Coming to Dinner, Lion in Winter, On Golden Pond*), born Hartford, CT, May 12, 1907. This is the date given by Hepburn in her autobiography; many other sources list Nov 8, 1909 as her birthdate.

Jaime Luner, 30, actress ("Melrose Place," "Profiler"), born Los Angeles, CA, May 12, 1971.

Millie Perkins, 63, actress ("Knots Landing," *The Diary of Anne Frank, Wall Street*), born Passaic, NJ, May 12, 1938.

Ving Rhames, 40, actor (*Pulp Fiction*), born New York, NY, May 12, 1961.

Howard K. Smith, 87, journalist, born Ferriday, LA, May 12, 1914.

Tom Snyder, 65, broadcast journalist, TV personality, born Milwaukee, WI, May 12, 1936.

Frank Stella, 65, artist (*Empress of India*), born Malden, MA, May 12, 1936.

Steve Winwood, 53, musician, singer, born Birmingham, England, May 12, 1948.

	S	M	T	W	T	F	S
May			1	2	3	4	5
2001	6	7	8	9	10	11	12
	13	14	15	16	17	18	19
	20	21	22	23	24	25	26
	27	28	29	30	31		

MAY 13 — SUNDAY

Day 133 — 232 Remaining

ATTEMPTED ASSASSINATION OF POPE JOHN PAUL II: 20th ANNIVERSARY. May 13, 1981. Pope John Paul II was shot twice at close range while riding in an open automobile at St. Peter's Square at Rome, Italy. Two other persons also were wounded. An escaped terrorist, Mehmet Ali Agca (already under sentence of death for the murder of a Turkish journalist), was arrested immediately and was convicted July 22, 1981, of attempted murder of the pope. After convalescence Pope John Paul II was pronounced recovered by his doctors Aug 14, 1981. In 2000 Agca was released from prison and extradited to Turkey.

COACH RECOGNITION WEEK. May 13–19. Coaches love to help people lead joyful, purposeful, successful lives. Whether the goals be to find love, pursue passions, embrace challenges, cultivate a career or achieve personal gratification, a coach's job is to empower, guide and inform. This week is a time to recognize the contributions coaches make to the well-being of society. For info: Robin Gorman Newman, 44 Somerset Dr N, Great Neck, NY 10020. Phone: (516) 773-0911. Fax: (516) 773-0173. E-mail: rgnewman@aol.com. Web: www.lovecoach.com.

DOUGLAS, VIRGINIA O'HANLON: 30th DEATH ANNIVERSARY. May 13, 1971. Virginia O'Hanlon Douglas lived a long and productive life as an educator and a loving mother. However, to the reading public she is re-introduced year after year at Christmas time, as the disheartened eight-year-old who asked the staff of *The New York Sun* whether Santa Claus exists. In a famous 1897 editorial Francis P. Church answered her question and re-assured Virginia that yes, indeed " . . . there is a Santa Claus." Douglas died at Valatie, NY, at the age of 81.

KITE DAY. May 13. Charlottesville, VA. Fly a kite at Ash Lawn-Highland. Est attendance: 300. For info: Ash Lawn-Highland, James Monroe Parkway, Charlottesville, VA 22902. Phone: (804) 293-9539. E-mail: ashlawnjm@aol.com. Web: monticello.avenue.gen.va.us/ashlawn/.

KIWANIS PRAYER WEEK. May 13–19. Encourages Kiwanis Clubs to promote religious activities throughout their communities and to recognize individuals for their contributions to spiritual welfare. Annually, the second full week in May. For info: Kiwanis Intl, Program Development Dept, 3636 Woodview Trace, Indianapolis, IN 46268. Web: www.kiwanis.org.

LIBERACE'S BIRTHDAY CELEBRATION. May 13. The Liberace Museum, Las Vegas, NV. To celebrate Liberace's birthday, the museum will share a giant piano-shaped birthday cake with museum guests. Annually, the Sunday following the Liberace "Play-A-Like" Competition. For info: Jamie G. James, The James Agency, 3630 Coldwater Canyon Ave, Studio City, CA 91604. Phone: (818) 508-4902. Fax: (818) 508-0562. E-mail: Jjames@Liberace.org.

LOUIS, JOE: BIRTH ANNIVERSARY. May 13, 1914. World heavyweight boxing champion, 1937–49, nicknamed the "Brown Bomber," Joseph Louis Barrow was born near Lafayette, AL. He died Apr 12, 1981, at Las Vegas, NV. Burial at Arlington National Cemetery. (Louis's burial there, by presidential waiver, was the 39th exception ever to the eligibility rules for burial in Arlington National Cemetery.)

MEXICAN WAR DECLARED: ANNIVERSARY. May 13, 1846. Although fighting had begun days earlier, Congress officially declared war on Mexico on this date. The struggle cost the lives of 11,300 American soldiers and resulted in the annexation by the US of land that became parts of Oklahoma, New Mexico, Arizona, Nevada, California, Utah and Colorado. The war ended in 1848. See also "Treaty of Guadalupe Hidalgo (Feb 2)."

MOTHER OCEAN DAY. May 13. To celebrate the wonder, the vastness and beauty of the ocean. Casting of roses into the sea from the beach and from the water. Annually, on Mother's Day. For info: Cynthia Hancock, Pres, Natl Week of the Ocean, Inc, PO Box 179, Ft Lauderdale, FL 33302. Phone: (954) 462-5573.

★MOTHER'S DAY. May 13. Presidential Proclamation always issued for the second Sunday in May. (Pub Res No. 2 of May 8, 1914.)

MOTHER'S DAY. May 13. Observed first in 1907 at the request of Anna Jarvis of Philadelphia, PA, who asked her church to hold service in memory of all mothers on the anniversary of her mother's death. Annually, the second Sunday in May.

MOTHER'S DAY CELEBRATION. May 13. Jenkinson's Aquarium, Point Pleasant Beach, NJ. Calling all kids! Bring your mom for a special day to learn about the roles of mothers in the marine environment. One mother admitted free with each paid child's admission. Est attendance: 600. For info: Liz Carletta, Education Coord, Jenkinson's Aquarium, 300 Ocean Ave, Point Pleasant Beach, NJ 08742. Phone: (732) 899-1212. Fax: (732) 899-1717. E-mail: aquarium@jenkinsons.com. Web: www.jenkinsons.com.

MOTHER'S DAY HOUSE AND GARDEN TOUR. May 13. The Museum District, Richmond, VA. An annual tour of beautiful houses and gardens located in one of Virginia's largest historic districts. Held annually on Mother's Day from 1–6 PM. The tour is a family affair and children are welcome. Tickets available in advance or the day of the tour. Est attendance: 1,000. For info: Historic West of the Boulevard Assn, 3300-A W Cary St, Box 131, Richmond, VA 23221. Phone: (804) 257-9622 ext 2. E-mail: housetour@westoftheboulevard.org.

MOTHER'S DAY HOUSEWALK. May 13. Evanston, IL. 26th annual tour of historic homes as a fund-raiser for the Evanston Historical Society. Annually, on Mother's Day. Est attendance: 2,000. For info: Evanston Historical Soc, 225 Greenwood St, Evanston, IL 60201. Phone: (847) 475-3410.

MUDDER'S DAY OFF ROAD CHALLENGE. May 13. Rhinelander, WI. 22K mountain bike race on the scenic Mudder's Day Trail at Holiday Acres Resort. Annually, on Mother's Day. Est attendance: 250. For info: Rhinelander Area Chamber of Commerce, Rhinelander, WI 54501. Phone: (800) 236-4386. Fax: (715) 365-7467. E-mail: info@rhinelanderchamber.com. Web: www.rhinelanderchamber.com.

NATIONAL ALCOHOL AND OTHER DRUG-RELATED BIRTH DEFECTS WEEK. May 13–19. For info: Natl Council on Alcoholism and Drug Dependence, 12 W 21st St, New York, NY 10010. Phone: (212) 206-6770.

NATIONAL EMPHYSEMA AWARENESS WEEK. May 13–19. To call attention to the plight of those suffering from lung disease. Annually, the second week in May. For info: Gary Bain, Emphysema Foundation, 7605 E 12th St, Kansas City, MO 64126. Phone: (816) 483-9166. E-mail: 1efforts@emphysema.net. Web: www.emphysema.net.

NATIONAL FAMILY MONTH®. May 13–June 17. A month-long national observance to celebrate and promote strong, supportive families. Sponsored by KidsPeace®, a private, not-for-profit organization that has been helping kids overcome crisis since 1882. Annually, Mother's Day through Father's Day. For info: Paula Knouse, Kids Peace, 5300 KidsPeace Dr, Orefield, PA 18069. Phone: (610) 799-8325. Web: www.familymonth.net.

NATIONAL HISTORIC PRESERVATION WEEK. May 13–19. To draw public attention to historic preservation including neighborhoods, districts, landmark buildings, open space and maritime heritage. Annually, the second full week in May. For info: Gary Kozel, Natl Trust for Historic Preservation, 1785 Massachusetts Ave NW, Washington, DC 20036. Phone: (202) 588-6141. Fax: (202) 588-6299. E-mail: pr@nthp.org. Web: www.nationaltrust.org.

NATIONAL NURSING HOME WEEK. May 13–19. A community outreach program designed to familiarize the public with long-term care facilities and the services they provide. Activities are conducted locally by individual long-term care facilities. Annually, Mother's Day through the following Saturday. For info: American Health Care Assn, Natl Nursing Home Week, 1201 L St NW, Washington, DC 20005. Phone: (202) 842-4444. Fax: (202) 842-3860.

NATIONAL POLICE WEEK. May 13–19. See also "Peace Officer Memorial Day" (May 15). For info: American Police Hall of Fame and Museum, 3801 Biscayne Blvd, Miami, FL 33137. Phone: (305) 573-0070.

NATIONAL RUNNING AND FITNESS WEEK. May 13–19. Educational campaign designed to introduce more Americans to the pleasures and benefits of participating in a regular exercise program. For info: Barbara Baldwin, American Running Assn, 4405 East-West Hwy, Ste 405, Bethesda, MD 20814. Phone: (800) 776-2732. Fax: (301) 913-9520. E-mail: run@americanrunning.org. Web: www.americanrunning.org.

NATIONAL STUTTERING AWARENESS WEEK. May 13–19. Annually, the second full week of May. For info: Stuttering Foundation of America, 3100 Walnut Grove Rd, Ste 603, Memphis, TN 38111-0749. Phone: (800) 992-9392 or (901) 452-7343. Web: www.stuttersfa.org.

★NATIONAL TRANSPORTATION WEEK. May 13–19. Presidential Proclamation issued for week including third Friday in May since 1960. (PL 86–475 of May 20, 1960, first requested; PL87–449 of May 14, 1962, requested an annual proclamation.)

NATIONAL VEAL BAN CAMPAIGN. May 13. (Mother's Day) To publicize the inhumane and unsanitary conditions under which "milk-fed veal" calves are raised. Local actions include picketing of veal restaurants, leafletting and information tables. For info: Farm Animal Reform Movement, Box 30654, Bethesda, MD 20824. Phone: (301) 530-1737. Fax: (301) 530-5747. E-mail: farm@farmusa.org. Web: www.farmusa.org.

PHILADELPHIA POLICE BOMBING: ANNIVERSARY. May 13, 1985. During the siege of the radical group MOVE at Philadelphia, PA, police in a helicopter reportedly dropped a bomb containing the powerful military plastic explosive C-4 on the building in which the group was housed. The bomb and the resulting fire left 11 persons dead (including four children) and destroyed 61 homes.

★POLICE WEEK. May 13–19. Presidential Proclamation 3537 of May 4, 1963, covers all succeeding years. (PL87–726 of Oct 1, 1962.) Always the week including May 15 since 1962.

RACE FOR THE CURE®. May 13. Pittsburgh, PA. 5K walk/run and one-mile fun walk to raise awareness of breast cancer and help fund research for a cure. One of 106 races around the country founded by the Susan G. Komen Breast Cancer Foundation.

Annually, on Mother's Day. For info: Race for the Cure®, 1620 Murray Ave, Pittsburgh, PA 15217. Phone: (412) 521-2873. Fax: (412) 421-1121. E-mail: race4cure@aol.com. Web: race4cure.lm .com.

SAINT LAWRENCE SEAWAY ACT: ANNIVERSARY. May 13, 1954. President Dwight D. Eisenhower signed legislation authorizing US–Canadian construction of a waterway that would make it possible for oceangoing ships to reach the Great Lakes.

SPACE MILESTONE: *ENDEAVOUR* (US). May 13, 1992. Three astronauts from the shuttle *Endeavour* simultaneously walked in space for the first time.

SULLIVAN, ARTHUR: BIRTH ANNIVERSARY. May 13, 1842. English composer best known for light operas (with Sir William Gilbert), born at London, England. Died there Nov 22, 1900.

TUNIS CAMPAIGN VICTORY: ANNIVERSARY. May 13, 1943. General Sir Harold Alexander telegraphed Winston Churchill, who was in Washington attending a conference, "It is my duty to report that the Tunis campaign is over. All enemy resistance has ceased. We are masters of the North African shores." About 250,000 Germans and Italians surrendered in the last few days of the campaign. This Allied victory in North Africa helped open Mediterranean shipping lines.

WELLS, MARY: BIRTH ANNIVERSARY. May 13, 1943. Motown's first big star, Mary Wells was born at Detroit, MI. She was known for such hits as "You Beat Me to the Punch," "Two Lovers" and her signature song, "My Guy." She was one of a group of black artists of the '60s who helped end musical segregation by being played on white radio stations. Mary Wells died July 26, 1992, at Los Angeles, CA.

★ **WORLD TRADE WEEK.** May 13–19. Presidential Proclamation has been issued each year since 1948 for the third week of May with three exceptions: 1949, 1955 and 1966.

BIRTHDAYS TODAY

Franklyn Ajaye, 52, actor ("Keep on Truckin'," *Car Wash*), born Brooklyn, NY, May 13, 1949.

Beatrice Arthur (Bernice Frankel), 75, actress (*Mame*, "Maude," "Golden Girls"), born New York, NY, May 13, 1926.

Frances Barber, 44, actress (*Sammy and Rosie Get Laid, We Think the World of You*), born Wolverhampton, England, May 13, 1957.

Clive Barnes, 74, critic, born London, England, May 13, 1927.

Harvey Keitel, 62, actor (*Mean Streets, Blue Collar, Bugsy, The Piano*), born Brooklyn, NY, May 13, 1939.

Julianne Phillips, 39, actress (*Allie & Me*, "Sisters"), born Lake Oswego, OR, May 13, 1962.

Tim Pigott-Smith, 55, actor ("The Jewel in the Crown," *Remains of the Day*), born Rugby, England, May 13, 1946.

Dennis Keith ("Worm") Rodman, 40, former basketball player, born Trenton, NJ, May 13, 1961.

Herbert Ross, 74, actor, choreographer, director (*The Turning Point*), born New York, NY, May 13, 1927.

Darius Rucker, 33, lead singer (Hootie and the Blowfish), born Charleston, SC, May 13, 1968.

Bobby Valentine, 51, baseball manager and former player, born Stamford, CT, May 13, 1950.

Stevie Wonder (Steveland Morris Hardaway), 50, singer, musician (16 Grammy Awards; "I Just Called to Say I Love You"), born Saginaw, MI, May 13, 1951.

	May **2001**	S	M	T	W	T	F	S
				1	2	3	4	5
		6	7	8	9	10	11	12
		13	14	15	16	17	18	19
		20	21	22	23	24	25	26
		27	28	29	30	31		

MAY 14 — MONDAY
Day 134 — 231 Remaining

BALANCHINE-GRAHAM COLLABORATION: ANNIVERSARY. May 14, 1959. In a melding of classical ballet and modern dance, George Balanchine's and Martha Graham's *Episodes* premiered. A new experience for ballet enthusiasts, half of the program was choreographed by Balanchine and the other half by Graham.

CARLSBAD CAVERNS NATIONAL PARK ESTABLISHED: ANNIVERSARY. May 14, 1930. Located in western New Mexico, Carlsbad Caverns was proclaimed a national monument, Oct 25, 1923 and later established as national park and preserve.

"ERNIE KOVACS" TV PREMIERE: 50th ANNIVERSARY. May 14, 1951. Comedian Ernie Kovacs first hosted "It's Time for Ernie," a 15-minute afternoon program on NBC in May of 1951 before replacing the "Kukla, Fran and Ollie Show" with "Ernie in Kovacsland." "The Ernie Kovacs Show" debuted on Dec 30, 1952. Kovacs also appeared on a variety of daytime and prime-time series and was a fill-in for Steve Allen on the "Tonight!" show. His early shows featured his wife, Edie Adams.

FAHRENHEIT, GABRIEL DANIEL: BIRTH ANNIVERSARY. May 14, 1686. German physicist whose name is attached to one of the major temperature measurement scales. He introduced the use of mercury in thermometers and greatly improved their accuracy. Born at Danzig, Germany, he died at Amsterdam, Holland, Sept 16, 1736.

FIRST REAL FEMALE HOUSE PAGE APPOINTMENT: ANNIVERSARY. May 14, 1973. The House of Representatives received formal approval of the appointment of female pages in 1972. On May 14, 1973, in the 93rd Congress, Felda Looper was appointed as the successor to Gene Cox who, for three hours, had served as the first female page 34 years earlier.

GAINSBOROUGH, THOMAS: BIRTH ANNIVERSARY. May 14, 1727 (OS). English landscape and portrait painter. Among his most remembered works: *The Blue Boy, The Watering Place* and *The Market Cart*. Born at Sudbury, Suffolk, England, he was baptized on May 14, 1727 (OS), and he died at London, Aug 2, 1788.

GIRLS INCORPORATED WEEK. May 14–20. To focus national and local attention on the goals of Girls Incorporated as an organization for the rights and needs of girls. For info: Communications, Girls Inc, 120 Wall St, 3rd Fl, New York, NY 10005. Phone: (212) 509-2000. Fax: (212) 509-8708. Web: www.girlsinc .org.

JAMESTOWN, VIRGINIA: FOUNDING ANNIVERSARY. May 14, 1607 (OS). The first permanent English settlement in what is now the US took place at Jamestown, VA (named for England's King James I), on this date. Captains John Smith and Christopher Newport were among the leaders of the group of royally chartered Virginia Company settlers who had traveled from Plymouth, England, in three small ships: *Susan Constant, Godspeed* and *Discovery*.

LEWIS AND CLARK EXPEDITION: ANNIVERSARY. May 14, 1804. Charged by President Thomas Jefferson with finding a route to the Pacific, Meriwether Lewis and Captain William Clark left St. Louis. They arrived at the Pacific coast of Oregon in November 1805 and returned to St. Louis, Sept 23, 1806.

MILLION MOM MARCH: ANNIVERSARY. May 14, 2000. Women rallied in Washington, DC, and 60 other US cities to urge Congress to "get serious about common sense gun legislation." For info: Million Mom March, PO Box 762, Washington, DC 20044-0762. Phone: (888) 989-MOMS. Web: www .millionmommarch.com.

NATIONAL ETIQUETTE WEEK. May 14–19. A national recognition of proper etiquette in all areas of American life (business, social, dining, international, wedding, computer, etc.). A self-assessment on the current status of civility in the US. Annually, the second week in May starting on Monday. For info: Sandra Morisset, Protocol Training Services, PO Box 4981, New York, NY 10185. Phone: (212) 802-9098. Fax: (209) 370-9844. Web: www.zyworld.com/etiquette.

NATIONAL GAMBLERS WEEK. May 14–18. Learn how to gamble wisely this week with acclaimed expert gambler, Fred Capitone from Cappy's Casino Corner. For info: Carolyn Schneider, CATS Publishing Inc, 442 Route 202-206 N, Ste 274, Bedminster, NJ 07921. Phone: (908) 781-2589. Fax: (908) 781-8598. E-mail: carolyn@net-lipix.com.

NORWAY: MIDNIGHT SUN AT NORTH CAPE. May 14–July 30. North Cape. First day of the season with around-the-clock sunshine. At North Cape, the sun never dips below the horizon from May 14 to July 30, but the night is bright long before and after these dates.

OWEN, ROBERT: BIRTH ANNIVERSARY. May 14, 1771. English progressive owner of spinning works, philanthropist, Utopian socialist, founder of New Harmony, IN, born at Newtown, Wales. Died there Nov 17, 1858.

PHILIPPINES: CARABAO FESTIVAL. May 14–15. Pulilan, Bulacan; Nueva Ecija; Angono, Rizal. Parade of farmers to honor their patron saint, San Isidro, with hundreds of "dressed up" carabaos participating.

SMALLPOX VACCINE DISCOVERED: ANNIVERSARY. May 14, 1796. In the 18th century, smallpox was a widespread and often fatal disease. Edward Jenner, a physician in rural England, heard reports of dairy farmers who apparently became immune to smallpox as a result of exposure to cowpox, a related but milder disease. After two decades of study Jenner injected cowpox into a healthy eight-year-old boy, who subsequently developed cowpox. Six weeks later, Jenner inoculated the boy with smallpox. He remained healthy. Jenner called this new procedure *vaccination*, from *vaccinia*, another term for cowpox. Within 18 months, 12,000 people in England had been vaccinated and the number of smallpox deaths dropped by two-thirds.

SPACE MILESTONE: SKYLAB (US). May 14, 1973. The US launched *Skylab*, its first manned orbiting laboratory.

"THE STARS AND STRIPES FOREVER" DAY: ANNIVERSARY. May 14, 1897. Anniversary of the first public performance of John Philip Sousa's march "The Stars and Stripes Forever," at Philadelphia, PA. The occasion was the unveiling of a statue of George Washington, and President William McKinley was present. In 1997 the US Postal Service issued a stamp commemorating the 100th anniversary of the premiere of the march.

UNDERGROUND AMERICA DAY. May 14. Underground America Day is one man's (Malcolm Wells) attempt to get others to think of designing and building structures underground. Mr Wells publishes illustrations and humorous suggestions for celebrating Underground America Day. 27th anniversary. Annually, May 14. For info: Malcolm Wells, 673 Satucket Rd, Brewster, MA 02631. Phone: (508) 896-6850. Fax: (508) 896-5116.

WAAC: ANNIVERSARY. May 14, 1942. During WWII women became eligible to enlist for noncombat duties in the Women's Auxiliary Army Corps (WAAC) by an act of Congress. Women also served as Women Appointed for Voluntary Emergency Service (WAVES), Women's Auxiliary Ferrying Squadron (WAFS), and Coast Guard or Semper Paratus Always Ready Service (SPARS), the Women's Reserve of the Marine Corp.

Cate Blanchett, 32, actress (*Elizabeth, Lord of the Rings*), born Melbourne, Australia, May 14, 1969.

David Byrne, 49, singer (Talking Heads), composer (songs, film scores), born Dumbarton, Scotland, May 14, 1952.

Byron L. Dorgan, 59, US Senator (D, North Dakota), born Dickinson, ND, May 14, 1942.

Meg Foster, 53, actress ("Cagney & Lacey," *The Emerald Forest, They Live*), born Reading, PA, May 14, 1948.

George Lucas, 57, filmmaker (*Star Wars* trilogy; director *American Graffiti*), born Modesto, CA, May 14, 1944.

Jose Dennis Martinez, 46, former baseball player, born Granada, Nicaragua, May 14, 1955.

Patrice Munsel, 76, opera singer, born Spokane, WA, May 14, 1925.

Ralph Neas, 55, Executive Director of the Leadership Conference on Civil Rights, born Brookline, MA, May 14, 1946.

Atanasio (Tony) Perez, 59, Baseball Hall of Fame player, born Camaguey, Cuba, May 14, 1942.

Tim Roth, 40, actor (*Pulp Fiction*), born London, England, May 14, 1961.

Valerie Still, 40, basketball player, born Lexington, KY, May 14, 1961.

Robert Zemeckis, 49, director (*Forest Gump, Back to the Future*), born Chicago, IL, May 14, 1952.

MAY 15 — TUESDAY
Day 135 — 230 Remaining

BAUM, LYMAN FRANK: BIRTH ANNIVERSARY. May 15, 1856. American newspaperman who wrote the Wizard of Oz stories was born at Chittenango, NY. Although *The Wonderful Wizard of Oz* is the most famous, Baum also wrote many other books for children, including more than a dozen about Oz. He died at Hollywood, CA, May 6, 1919.

COTTEN, JOSEPH: BIRTH ANNIVERSARY. May 15, 1905. Stage and screen star Joseph Cotten was born at Petersburg, VA. Among Cotten's movie credits were *Citizen Kane, The Magnificent Ambersons* and *The Third Man*. Among his most noted performances on Broadway were *The Philadelphia Story* and *Once More With Feeling*. Joseph Cotten died Feb 6, 1994, at Los Angeles.

EASTERN PACIFIC HURRICANE SEASON. May 15–Nov 30. Eastern Pacific defined as: Coast to 140 degrees west longitude. Info from: US Dept of Commerce, Natl Oceanic and Atmospheric Admin, Rockville, MD 20852.

FIRST FLIGHT ATTENDANT: ANNIVERSARY. May 15, 1930. Ellen Church became the first airline stewardess (today's flight attendant), flying on a United Airlines flight from San Francisco to Cheyenne, WY.

FRISCH, MAX: 90th BIRTH ANNIVERSARY. May 15, 1911. Max Frisch was one of Europe's leading post–World War II literary figures. His work includes the novels *Homo Faber, I'm Not Stiller, Juerg Reinhardt* and plays *The Firebugs, Andorra*. In addition to his writing, he was a controversial critic of his native Switzerland. Born at Zurich, Switzerland, he died there Apr 4, 1991.

GASOLINE RATIONING: ANNIVERSARY. May 15, 1942. Seventeen eastern states initiated gasoline rationing as part of the war effort. By Sept 25, rationing was nationwide. A limit of three gallons a week for nonessential purposes was set and a 35 mph speed limit was imposed.

GEORGE WALLACE SHOT: ANNIVERSARY. May 15, 1972. George Wallace, a former governor of Alabama and a symbol of segregation, was shot by Arthur Bremer while Wallace was at Laurel, MD, campaigning for the US presidency. For the remainder of his life, until he died in 1998, Wallace was paralyzed from the waist down. On Aug 4, 1972, Bremer was sentenced to 67 years in prison for the shooting.

HUG YOUR CAT DAY. May 15. Cats act like they don't want or need attention—but they do. Apricat, the pampered star of her own book series, has created a special day for humans to hug their cats without fear of scratches or hisses. For info: Marisa D'Vari, PO Box 413, Boston, MA 02116. Phone: (617) 351-2279. E-mail: mdvari@msn.com. Web: www.deg.com.

JAPAN: AOI MATSURI (HOLLYHOCK FESTIVAL). May 15. Kyoto. The festival features a pageant reproducing imperial processions of ancient times that paid homage to the shrine of Shimogamo and Kamigamo.

MEXICO: SAN ISIDRO DAY. May 15. Day of San Isidro Labrador celebrated widely in farming regions to honor St. Isidore, the Plowman. Livestock gaily decorated with flowers. Celebrations usually begin about May 13 and continue for about a week.

MOON PHASE: LAST QUARTER. May 15. Moon enters Last Quarter phase at 6:11 AM, EDT.

NAIA WOMEN'S GOLF NATIONAL CHAMPION-SHIPS. May 15–17. 7th annual. Est attendance: 300. For info: Natl Assn of Intercollegiate Athletics, 6120 S Yale Ave, Ste 1450, Tulsa, OK 74136. Phone: (918) 494-8828. Fax: (918) 494-8841. E-mail: kregister@naia.org. Web: www.naia.org.

NYLON STOCKINGS: ANNIVERSARY. May 15, 1940. Nylon hose went on sale at stores throughout the country. Competing producers bought their nylon yarn from E.J. du Pont de Nemours. W.H. Carothers of Du Pont developed nylon, called "Polymer 66," in 1935. It was the first totally man-made fiber and over time substituted for other materials and came to have widespread application.

OCONALUFTEE INDIAN VILLAGE. May 15–Oct 25. Cherokee Indian Reservation, Cherokee, NC. To portray the Cherokee lifestyle of the 1750 period. Also featuring *Unto These Hills* (mid-June–late-August), a drama portraying history of eastern band of Cherokees. Est attendance: 150,000. For info: Margie Douthit, PR, Cherokee Historical Assn, PO Box 398, Cherokee, NC 28719. Phone: (828) 497-2111. Fax: (828) 497-6987. Web: www.oconalufteevillage.com.

PARAGUAY: INDEPENDENCE DAY. May 15. Commemorates independence from Spain, attained 1811.

★**PEACE OFFICER MEMORIAL DAY.** May 15. Presidential Proclamation 3537, of May 4, 1963, covers all succeeding years. (PL87–726 of Oct 1, 1962.) Always May 15 of each year since 1963; however, first issued in 1962 for May 14.

May 2001	S	M	T	W	T	F	S
			1	2	3	4	5
	6	7	8	9	10	11	12
	13	14	15	16	17	18	19
	20	21	22	23	24	25	26
	27	28	29	30	31		

PEACE OFFICER MEMORIAL DAY. May 15. An event honored by some 21,000 police departments nationwide. Memorial ceremonies at 10 AM in American Police Hall of Fame and Museum, Miami, FL. See also: "National Police Week" (May 13–19). Sponsor: National Association of Chiefs of Police. Est attendance: 1,000. For info: American Police Hall of Fame and Museum, 3801 Biscayne Blvd, Miami, FL 33137. Phone: (305) 573-0070. Web: www.aphf.org.

PORTER, KATHERINE ANNE: BIRTH ANNIVERSARY. May 15, 1890. Porter was born at Indian Creek, TX. Her one long novel, *Ship of Fools* (1962), is considered by some to be one of the greatest allegorical works in English. She won the Pulitzer Prize and the National Book Award in 1965 for *Collected Short Stories*. Died Sept 18, 1980, at Silver Spring, MD.

SCHNITZLER, ARTHUR: BIRTH ANNIVERSARY. May 15, 1862. Austrian playwright, novelist and medical doctor, Arthur Schnitzler was born at Vienna. Noted for his psychoanalytical examination of Viennese society. Died at Vienna, Oct 21, 1931.

SPACE MILESTONE: *FAITH 7* (US). May 15, 1963. Launched with Major Gordon Leroy Cooper and orbited the Earth 22 times.

TRUE CONFESSIONS DAY. May 15. Confession is good for the soul. Go into work today and tell all. If you plan to stay home, make an appointment with your mirror. [© 2000 by WH] For info: Tom and Ruth Roy, Wellcat Holidays, 2418 Long Ln, Lebanon, PA 17046. Phone: (717) 279-0184. E-mail: wellcat@supernet.com. Web: www.wellcat.com.

UNITED NATIONS: INTERNATIONAL DAY OF FAMILIES. May 15. The general assembly (res 47/237) Sept 20, 1993, voted this as an annual observance beginning in 1994.

WILSON, ELLEN LOUISE AXSON: BIRTH ANNIVERSARY. May 15, 1860. First wife of Woodrow Wilson, 28th president of the US, born at Savannah, GA. Died at Washington, DC, Aug 6, 1914.

BIRTHDAYS TODAY

Anna Marie Alberghetti, 65, singer, actress (*Cinderfella, Carnival*), born Pesaro, Italy, May 15, 1936.

Madeleine Albright, 64, US Secretary of State (Clinton administration), born Prague, Czechoslovakia, May 15, 1937.

Eddy Arnold, 83, the "Tennessee Plowboy" singer ("Make the World Go Away"), born Henderson, TN, May 15, 1918.

Richard Avedon, 78, photographer, born New York, NY, May 15, 1923.

George Howard Brett, 48, baseball executive and Hall of Famer, born Glen Dale, WV, May 15, 1953.

David Charvet, 29, actor ("Melrose Place," "Baywatch"), born Lyon, France, May 15, 1972.

David Cronenberg, 58, filmmaker (*The Fly, Naked Lunch*), born Toronto, Ontario, Canada, May 15, 1943.

Brian Eno, 53, avant-garde musician, born Woodbridge, England, May 15, 1948.

Giselle Fernandez, 40, host ("Access Hollywood"), born Mexico City, Mexico, May 15, 1961.

Lee Horsley, 46, actor ("Nero Wolfe," "Matt Houston"), born Muleshoe, TN, May 15, 1955.

Jasper Johns, 71, artist (Neo-Dada Encaustic and collage composition *Flag*), born Augusta, GA, May 15, 1930.

Lainie Kazan, 59, singer, actress (*My Favorite Year, Beaches*), born New York, NY, May 15, 1942.

Trini Lopez, 64, actor, singer (*Marriage on the Rocks, The Dirty Dozen*), born Dallas, TX, May 15, 1937.

Chazz Palminteri, 50, actor (*Bullets Over Broadway*), playwright, screenwriter (*A Bronx Tale*), born The Bronx, NY, May 15, 1951.

Emmitt Smith, 32, football player, born Pensacola, FL, May 15, 1969.

John Smoltz, 34, baseball player, born Warren, MI, May 15, 1967.

Paul Zindel, 65, writer (*The Effect of Gamma Rays on Man-in-the-Moon Marigolds*), born New York, NY, May 15, 1936.

MAY 16 — WEDNESDAY

Day 136 — 229 Remaining

BATTLE OF CHAMPION'S HILL: ANNIVERSARY. May 16, 1863. After a standoff of nearly a year around the strategic Mississippi River city of Vicksburg, MS, Union forces under Ulysses S. Grant defeated Southern forces under General John Pemberton at Champion's Hill, MS, on this date. Pemberton's forces withdrew into Vicksburg, and the siege of Vicksburg began on May 19.

BIG 12 MEN'S BASEBALL CHAMPIONSHIP. May 16–20. Southwestern Bell Bricktown Ballpark, Oklahoma City, OK. Fifth annual Big 12 Baseball Tournament. Most successful conference championship in the USA. Est attendance: 100,000. For info: OK City All Sports Assn, 100 W Main, Ste 287, Oklahoma City, OK 73102. Phone: (405) 236-5000. Fax: (405) 236-5008. E-mail: info@okcallsports.org. Web: www.okcallsports.org.

BIOGRAPHERS DAY. May 16. Anniversary of the meeting, at London, England, May 16, 1763, of James Boswell and Samuel Johnson, beginning history's most famous biographer-biographee relationship. Boswell's *Journal of a Tour to the Hebrides* (1785) and his *Life of Samuel Johnson* (1791) are regarded as models of biographical writing. Thus, this day is recommended as one on which to start reading or writing a biography.

BUTLER ISSUES "WOMAN ORDER": ANNIVERSARY. May 16, 1862. General Benjamin Butler, military governor of New Orleans, issued what became known as the "Woman Order." The text of General Order Number 28 read, in part, "As the officers and soldiers of the United States have been subjected to repeated insults from women (calling themselves ladies) of New Orleans . . . when any female shall . . . show contempt for the United States, she shall be regarded as a woman of the town plying her avocation." This order typified Butler's attitude toward the captured city and its populace and, along with other controversial acts, set the stage for his dismissal as military governor in December of 1862.

FIRST ACADEMY AWARDS: ANNIVERSARY. May 16, 1929. About 270 people attended a dinner at the Hollywood Roosevelt Hotel at which the first Academy Awards were given in 12 categories. The silent film *Wings* won Best Picture. A committee of only 20 members selected the winners that year. By the third year, the entire membership of the Academy voted.

FONDA, HENRY: BIRTH ANNIVERSARY. May 16, 1905. American stage, TV and screen actor (*The Grapes of Wrath, Mister Roberts*), Academy Award winner, born Henry Jaynes Fonda at Grand Island, NE. Began his acting career at the Omaha (NE) Playhouse. Fonda died at Los Angeles, CA, Aug 12, 1982.

GWINNETT, BUTTON: DEATH ANNIVERSARY. May 16, 1777. Signer of the Declaration of Independence, born at Down Hatherley, Gloucestershire, England, about 1735 (exact date unknown). Died following a duel at St. Catherine's Island, off of Savannah, GA.

LIBERACE: BIRTH ANNIVERSARY. May 16, 1919. Wladziu Valentino Liberace, concert pianist who began with a piano, a candelabra, a brother named George and a huge engaging smile, threw in extravagant clothes and jewels and became a Las Vegas headliner and the winner of two Emmy Awards, six gold albums and two stars on the Hollywood Walk of Fame. Liberace was born at West Allis, WI, he died Feb 4, 1987, at Palm Springs, CA.

MARTIN, BILLY: BIRTH ANNIVERSARY. May 16, 1928. Baseball player and manager born at Berkeley, CA. Billy Martin's baseball career included managerial stints with five major league teams: the New York Yankees, Minnesota Twins, Detroit Tigers, Texas Rangers and the Oakland Athletics. After a successful playing career, he compiled a record of 1,258 victories to 1,018 losses in his 16 seasons as a manager. His combative style both on and off the field kept him in the headlines, and he will long be remembered for his on-again/off-again relationship with Yankees' owner George Steinbrenner, for whom he managed the Yankees five different times. Martin died in an auto accident near Fenton, NY, Dec 25, 1989.

MORTON, LEVI PARSONS: BIRTH ANNIVERSARY. May 16, 1824. 22nd vice president of the US (1889–93) born at Shoreham, VT. Died at Rhinebeck, NY, May 16, 1920.

NAIA SOFTBALL NATIONAL CHAMPIONSHIP. May 16–19. Location TBA. 21st annual competition. Est attendance: 2,000. For info: Natl Assn of Intercollegiate Athletics, 6120 S Yale Ave, Ste 1450, Tulsa, OK 74136. Phone: (918) 494-8828. Fax: (918) 494-8841. E-mail: ncronkhite@naia.org. Web: www.naia.org.

NATIONAL BE A MILLIONAIRE DAY. May 16. A global celebration of the joys of achieving millionaire status. This day launches a year-long series of activities to teach people the premier skills, habits, attitudes and strategies used by the 400 richest Americans. It motivates people to use their own unique talents to convert paycheck skills to wealth. Annually, the third Wednesday in May. For info: Dee Wright, 106 Long Pine Place, #3B, Baltimore, MD 21244.

NATIONAL EMPLOYEE HEALTH AND FITNESS DAY. May 16. To focus on the importance of fitness and healthy lifestyles at the worksite. Annually, the third Wednesday in May. For info: Natl Assn of Governor's Councils on Physical Fitness/Sports, 201 S Capitol Ave, Ste 560, Indianapolis, IN 46225-1072. Phone: (317) 237-5630. Fax: (317) 237-5632. E-mail: Govcouncil@aol.com. Web: www.physicalfitness.org.

NORTHERN IRELAND: ROYAL ULSTER AGRICULTURAL SOCIETY BALMORAL SHOW. May 16–18. The Showgrounds, Balmoral, Belfast. The premier agricultural show on Northern Ireland's calendar. Est attendance: 70,000. For info: Mr Rees, Royal Ulster Agricultural Society, Balmoral Showgrounds, Belfast, Northern Ireland BT9 6GW. Phone: (44) (123) 266-5225. Fax: (44) (123) 266-1264. E-mail: prees@kingshall.co.uk. Web: www.ruas.co.uk.

PEABODY, ELIZABETH PALMER: BIRTH ANNIVERSARY. May 16, 1804. Born at Billerica, MA, Peabody was an innovative educator, author and publisher. She opened her first school at Lancaster, MA, when only 16. In 1839 Peabody opened a bookstore that quickly became the intellectuals' hangout. With her own printing press Peabody became the first woman publisher of Boston and possibly the US. She published three of her brother-in-law Nathaniel Hawthorne's books. For two years she published and wrote for *The Dial*, the literary magazine and voice of the Transcendental movement. Peabody's enduring accomplishment was the establishment of the first kindergarten in the US, in 1860 at Boston. She created a magazine, *Kindergarten Messenger*, in 1873. Died Jan 3, 1894, at Jamaica Plain, MA.

RAF BOMBS RUHR DAMS: ANNIVERSARY. May 16–17, 1943. Over these two days, Royal Air Force Lancasters attacked three dams in the German Ruhr Valley. They dropped 4.5 ton bombs designed specifically for this mission. The Mohne and the Eder (the largest dam in Europe at the time) were both damaged. These two dams provided drinking water for four million people and supplied 75 percent of the electrical power for industry. Widespread flooding and many deaths resulted.

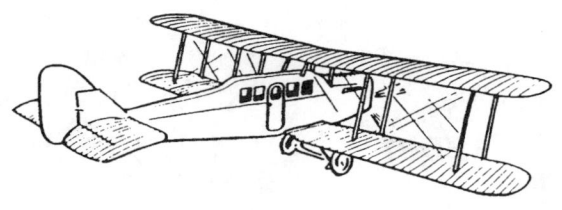

BIRTHDAYS TODAY

David Boreanaz, 30, actor ("Buffy the Vampire Slayer"), born Philadelphia, PA, May 16, 1971.

Pierce Brosnan, 49, actor ("Remington Steele," James Bond in *GoldenEye*), born County Meath, Ireland, May 16, 1952.

Tracey Gold, 32, actress ("Shirley," "Goodnight Beantown," "Growing Pains"), born New York, NY, May 16, 1969.

James B. Hunt, Jr, 64, Governor of North Carolina (D), born Greensboro, NC, May 16, 1937.

Janet Jackson, 35, singer ("What Have You Done for Me Lately"), born Gary, IN, May 16, 1966.

Olga Korbut, 46, Olympic gold medal gymnast, born Grodno, USSR, May 16, 1955.

John Scott (Jack) Morris, 46, former baseball player, born St. Paul, MN, May 16, 1955.

Gabriela Sabatini, 31, tennis player, born Buenos Aires, Argentina, May 16, 1970.

Joan (Benoit) Samuelson, 44, Olympic gold medal runner, born Cape Elizabeth, ME, May 16, 1957.

Bill Smitrovich, 54, actor ("Crime Story," *Splash, Manhunter*), born Bridgeport, CT, May 16, 1947.

Tori Spelling, 28, actress ("Beverly Hills 90210"), born Beverly Hills, CA, May 16, 1973.

Studs Terkel (Louis Terkel), 89, author, journalist (*Hard Times, Working*), born New York, NY, May 16, 1912.

Lowell P. Weicker, Jr, 70, former Governor of Connecticut (CP), born Paris, France, May 16, 1931.

Debra Winger, 46, actress (*Terms of Endearment, Shadowlands*), born Columbus, OH, May 16, 1955.

Mare Winningham, 42, actress (*The Thornbirds*), born Phoenix, AZ, May 16, 1959.

MAY 17 — THURSDAY

Day 137 — 228 Remaining

ASPENCASH MOTORCYCLE RALLY. May 17–20. Ruidoso, NM. $10,000 cash poker run, trade show, poker run pen. Est attendance: 10,000. For info: Golden Aspen Rally Assn, PO Box 1458, Ruidoso, NM 88355. Phone: (800) 452-8045. E-mail: Gara@usa.net. Web: www.motorcyclerally.com.

BELL, JAMES (COOL PAPA): BIRTH ANNIVERSARY. May 17, 1903. Negro League baseball player James "Cool Papa" Bell was born at Starkville, MS. He played 25 seasons from 1922 to 1946 (one year before Jackie Robinson broke the "color barrier" in major league baseball) with a career average of .338. Regarded as the fastest man ever to play the game—he could round the bases in 13 seconds—he was inducted into the Baseball Hall of Fame in 1974. Bell died Mar 7, 1991, at St. Louis, MO.

BIG TEN BASEBALL TOURNAMENT. May 17–20. Site of conference champion. Est attendance: 1,500. For info: Dennis LaBissoniere, Big Ten Conference, 1500 W Higgins Rd, Park Ridge, IL 60068-6300. Phone: (847) 696-1010. Fax: (847) 696-1110. Web: www.bigten.org.

BIG 12 MEN AND WOMEN'S OUTDOOR TRACK AND FIELD. May 17–20. College Station, TX. For info: Big 12 Conference, 2201 Stemmons Frwy, 28th flr, Dallas, TX 75207. Phone: (214) 742-1212. Fax: (214) 753-0145. Web: www.big12sports.com.

	S	**M**	**T**	**W**	**T**	**F**	**S**
May			1	2	3	4	5
2001	6	7	8	9	10	11	12
	13	14	15	16	17	18	19
	20	21	22	23	24	25	26
	27	28	29	30	31		

BROWN v BOARD OF EDUCATION DECISION: ANNIVERSARY. May 17, 1954. The US Supreme Court ruled unanimously that segregation of public schools "solely on the basis of race" denied black children "equal educational opportunity" even though "physical facilities and other 'tangible' factors may have been equal. Separate educational facilities are inherently unequal." The case was argued before the Court by Thurgood Marshall, who would go on to become the first black appointed to the Supreme Court.

FIRST KENTUCKY DERBY: ANNIVERSARY. May 17, 1875. The first running of the Kentucky Derby took place at Churchill Downs, Louisville, KY. Jockey Oliver Lewis rode the horse Aristides to a winning time of 2:37.25.

GATEWAY FARM EXPO. May 17–19. Buffalo County Fairgrounds, Kearney, NE. Est attendance: 6,000. For info: Kearney Area Chamber of Commerce, PO Box 607, Kearney, NE 68847. Phone: (800) 652-9435. Web: www.gatewayfarmexpo.org.

GETTYSBURG BLUEGRASS FESTIVAL. May 17–20. Gettysburg, PA. Granite Hill Campground on Rt 116. Est attendance: 5,000. For info: Gettysburg CVB, PO Box 4117, Gettysburg, PA 17325. Phone: (717) 334-6274. Fax: (717) 334-1166. Web: www.gettysburg.com.

JENNER, EDWARD: BIRTH ANNIVERSARY. May 17, 1749. English physician, born at Berkeley, England. He was the first to establish a scientific basis for vaccination with his work on smallpox. Jenner died at Berkeley, England, Jan 26, 1823.

LITTLE NORWAY FESTIVAL. May 17–20. Petersburg, AK. Celebration of Norwegian Constitution Day. The majestic natural beauty that gives Petersburg its nickname ("Little Norway"), the rich Norwegian traditions and spirit and the combination of visitors from near and far and friendly residents form the backdrop to the gala celebration. Food and craft booths, kids activities, dancing, melodrama, pageant, various food feasts. Est attendance: 3,000. For info: Petersburg Visitors' Info Center, Box 649, Petersburg, AK 99833. Phone: (907) 772-4636. Fax: (907) 772-3646. Web: www.petersburg.org.

MAGNOLIA BLOSSOM FESTIVAL. May 17–19. Magnolia, AR. 13th annual. The week's events include old-fashioned chicken supper, arts and crafts, entertainment and activities for all. World Championship Steak Cookoff (May 19) dinner served under fragrant magnolia trees. Est attendance: 40,000. For info: Magnolia-Columbia County Chamber of Commerce, 202 N Pine, PO Box 866, Magnolia, AR 71753. Phone: (800) 482-3330. E-mail: magcoc@arkansas.net. Web: www.magblossom.org.

NATIONAL ROAD FESTIVAL. May 17–20. Washington, Fayette and Somerset counties, PA. Wagon train encampments, food and entertainment. Festival celebrates the first national road commissioned by Thomas Jefferson. For info: Coordinator, National Road Festival, US Rt 40, c/o 3543 National Pike, Farmington, PA 15437. Phone: (724) 329-1560.

NCAA DIVISION I WOMEN'S TENNIS CHAMPIONSHOP. May 17–25. Location TBA. For info: Natl Collegiate Athletic Assn, 700 W Washington Ave, PO Box 6222, Indianapolis, IN 46206-6222. Phone: (317) 917-6222. Fax: (317) 917-6888. Web: www.ncaa.org.

NEW YORK STOCK EXCHANGE ESTABLISHED: ANNIVERSARY. May 17, 1792. Some two dozen merchants and brokers agreed to establish what is now known as the New York Stock Exchange. In fair weather they operated under a buttonwood tree on Wall Street, at New York, NY. In bad weather they moved to the shelter of a coffeehouse to conduct their business.

NORWAY: CONSTITUTION DAY OR INDEPENDENCE DAY. May 17. National holiday. Constitution signed and Norway separated from Denmark in 1814. Parades and children's festivities.

PHILIPPINES: FERTILITY RITES. May 17–19. Obando, Bulacan. A triple religious fete in honor of San Pascual, Santa Clara and the Virgin of Salambao marked by dancing of childless couples.

SANTA CRUZ BEACH BOARDWALK GIANT DIPPER: ANNIVERSARY. May 17, 1924. The Giant Dipper roller coaster opened at Santa Cruz Beach Boardwalk at Santa Cruz, CA, and quickly became the park's most popular ride. The Dipper was built by Arthur Looff, the son of master carousel-horse carver Charles I.D. Looff. In June 1987 the Giant Dipper and the Looff carousel were designated National Historic Landmarks by the US National Park Service.

UNITED NATIONS: WORLD TELECOMMUNICATION DAY. May 17. A day to draw attention to the necessity and importance of further development of telecommunications in the global community. Info from: United Nations, Dept of Public Info, New York, NY 10017.

USS *STARK* ATTACKED: ANNIVERSARY. May 17, 1987. The US Navy's guided missile frigate *Stark*, sailing off the Iranian coast in the Persian Gulf, was struck and set afire by two Exocet sea-skimming missiles fired from an Iraqi warplane at 2:10 PM, EDT. Also struck was a Cypriot flag tanker. At least 28 American naval personnel were killed. Only hours earlier a Soviet oil tanker in the Gulf had struck a mine.

BIRTHDAYS TODAY

Mia Hamm, 29, soccer player (US National Soccer Team), born Selma, AL, May 17, 1972.

Dennis Hopper, 65, actor (*Easy Rider, Giant, Rebel Without a Cause*), born Dodge City, KS, May 17, 1936.

Christian Lacroix, 51, French couturier, born Arles, France, May 17, 1950.

Ray Charles ("Sugar Ray") Leonard, 45, former boxer, born Washington, DC, May 17, 1956.

Daniel Ricardo (Danny) Manning, 35, basketball player, born Hattiesburg, MS, May 17, 1966.

Bill Paxton, 46, actor (*Aliens, One False Move, Twister*), born Fort Worth, TX, May 17, 1955.

Trent Reznor, 36, singer (Nine Inch Nails), born Mercer, PA, May 17, 1965.

Bob Saget, 45, actor ("Full House"), host ("America's Funniest Home Videos"), born Philadelphia, PA, May 17, 1956.

MAY 18 — FRIDAY

Day 138 — 227 Remaining

ALLIES CAPTURE MONTE CASSINO: ANNIVERSARY. May 18, 1944. Between Oct 12, 1943, and Jan 17, 1944, there were five Allied attempts to take the German position at the Benedictine abbey at Monte Cassino. Although the abbey had been reduced to rubble, it served as a bunker for the Germans. In the spring of 1944 Marshal Alphonse Pierre Juin devised an operation that crossed the mountainous regions behind the fortresslike structure, using Moroccan troops of the French Expeditionary Force. Specially trained for mountain operations, they climbed 4,850 feet to locate a pass. On May 15, 1944, they attacked the Germans from behind. On May 18, Polish troops attached to this force took Monte Cassino.

ART FAIR AND WINEFEST. May 18–20. Washington, MO. The largest Missouri wine tasting of state wines as well as a juried art show featuring 60 midwestern artists. Art fair is free. Admission to the wine pavilion includes a commemorative wine glass. For info: Downtown Washington Inc, PO Box 144, Washington, MO 63090. Phone: (636) 239-1743. Fax: (636) 239-4832. Web: downtownwashmo.com.

BIG TEN MEN'S/WOMEN'S OUTDOOR TRACK AND FIELD CHAMPIONSHIPS. May 18–20. Indiana University, Bloomington, IN. Est attendance: 1,500. For info: Sue Ryan, Asst Commissioner, Big Ten Conference, 1500 W Higgins Rd, Park Ridge, IL 60068-6300. Phone: (847) 696-1010. Fax: (847) 696-1110. Web: www.bigten.org and www.bigtenchampions.com.

BIRTHDAY OF MOTHER'S WHISTLER. May 18. To celebrate the birthday of the world's most melodious human whistler, who cannot only duplicate the songs of rare, exotic and extinct birds, but in many cases, do so better than the birds themselves. For info: Mother's Whistler, Warfield and Twin Silo Lanes, Huntingdon Valley, PA 19006. Phone: (215) 947-7007. E-mail: whistler _00_00@yahoo.com.

CALAVERAS COUNTY FAIR AND JUMPING FROG JUBILEE. May 18–20. Calaveras Fairgrounds, Angels Camp, CA. County fair and reenactment of Mark Twain's "Celebrated Jumping Frog of Calaveras County." This "Superbowl" of the sport of frog jumping attracts more than 3,000 frogs annually from around the world. Annually, the third full weekend in May. Est attendance: 45,000. For info: 39th District Agricultural Assn, S Highway 49, PO Box 489, Angels Camp, CA 95222. Phone: (209) 736-2561. Fax: (209) 736-2476. E-mail: info@frogtown.org. Web: www.frogtown.org.

CAPRA, FRANK: BIRTH ANNIVERSARY. May 18, 1897. The Academy Award–winning director whose movies were suffused with affectionate portrayals of the common man and the strengths and foibles of American democracy. Capra was born at Palermo, Sicily. He bluffed his way into silent movies in 1922 and, despite total ignorance of movie making, directed and produced a profitable one-reeler. He was the first to win three directorial Oscars—for *It Happened One Night* (1934), *Mr Deeds Goes to Town* (1936) and *You Can't Take It with You* (1938). The motion picture academy voted the first and third of these as best picture. Capra said his favorite of the films he made was *It's a Wonderful Life* (1946). He died at La Quinta, CA, Sept 3, 1991.

DERMOTT'S ANNUAL CRAWFISH FESTIVAL. May 18–19. Dermott, AR. 17th annual. To publicize and popularize crawfish as a delicacy, to promote the area and to raise funds for industrial expansion. Family fun, arts, crafts, exotic foods, carnival, live music and street dances. Annually, the third weekend in May. Est attendance: 20,000. For info: Dermott Area Chamber of Commerce, Box 147, Dermott, AR 71638. Phone: (870) 538-5656.

DUBUQUEFEST/VERY SPECIAL ARTS FESTIVAL. May 18–20. Dubuque, IA. A celebration of folk and fine arts. Dance, music, mime, arts, crafts, poetry, drama and old house tour. Annually, the third weekend in May, Friday–Sunday. Est attendance: 45,000. For info: DubuqueFest/Very Special Arts Festival, 434 Loras Blvd, Dubuque, IA 52001. Phone: (319) 557-9384. Fax: (319) 557-1905.

DULCIMER DAYS. May 18–20. Coshocton, OH. Dulcimer competition, workshops, exhibits, open stage, jam sessions, Saturday evening concert and more. Est attendance: 1,400. For info: Cheryl Oswald, Roscoe Village, 381 Hill St, Coshocton, OH 43812. Phone: (800) 877-1830 or (740) 622-9310. Fax: (740) 623-6555. E-mail: rvmarketing@coshocton.com. Web: www.roscoevillage .com.

FISHING HAS NO BOUNDARIES—HAYWARD EVENT. Mar 18–20. Lake Chippewa Campgrounds, Hayward, WI. A three-day fishing experience for disabled persons. Any disability, age, sex, race, etc, eligible. Fishing with experienced guides on one of the best fishing waters in Wisconsin, attended by 200 participants and 500 volunteers. Register by Mar 15. Est attendance: 2,400. For info: Fishing Has No Boundaries, PO Box 375, Hayward, WI 54843. Phone: (715) 634-3185. Fax: (715) 634-1305.

FONTEYN, MARGOT: BIRTH ANNIVERSARY. May 18, 1919. Born Margaret Hookman at Reigate, Surrey, England, Dame Margot Fonteyn thrilled ballet audiences for 45 years. She emerged from the Sadler's Wells company during the 1930s and 1940s as a solo artist and followed those successes by partnering with Soviet exile Rudolph Nureyev in the 1960s. She died Feb 21, 1991, at Panama City, Panama.

FREDERICK ART & CRAFT FESTIVAL. May 18–20. Frederick Fairgrounds, Frederick, MD. Enjoy displays of fine craftsmanship, including clothing, furniture, folk art, oils, watercolors and much more. Ranked as one of the top 100 juried craft shows in the country. 27th annual. Est attendance: 10,000. For info: Natl Crafts, Ltd, 4845 Rumler Rd, Chambersburg, PA 17201. Phone: (717) 369-4810. Fax: (717) 369-5001. E-mail: nclinc@cvn.net. Web: www.nationalcrafts.com.

GATLINBURG SCOTTISH FESTIVAL AND GAMES. May 18–20. Gatlinburg, TN. Celebration of Scotland, its people and traditions. Music, food and fun. Est attendance: 5,000. For info: Larry Dial, PO Box 1487, Gatlinburg, TN 37738. Phone: (865) 436-5346. Fax: (423) 436-3704. Web: www.gatlinburg.com.

HAITI: FLAG AND UNIVERSITY DAY. May 18. Public holiday.

INTERNATIONAL MUSEUM DAY. May 18. To pay tribute to museums of the world. "Museums are an important means of cultural exchange, enrichment of cultures and development of mutual understanding, cooperation and peace among people." Annually, May 18. Sponsor: International Council of Museums, Paris, France. For info: AAM/ICOM, 1575 Eye St NW, 4th Fl, Washington, DC 20005. Phone: (202) 289-9115. Fax: (202) 289-6578.

INTERNATIONAL PICKLE WEEK. May 18–28. To give national recognition to the world's most humorous vegetable. Sponsor: Pickle Packers International, Inc. For info: IPW, DHM Group, Inc, PO Box 767, Dept CC, Holmdel, NJ 07733-0767. Fax: (732) 946-3343.

LILAC FESTIVAL. May 18–27. Highland Park, Rochester, NY. Developed by renowned park designer Frederick Law Olmstead, Highland Park is the site of the Lilac Festival, the largest celebration of its kind in North America. In addition to the more than 500 varieties of lilacs in bloom, the festival provides free admission, free entertainment, free children's activities and entertainment, a free concert with the Rochester Philharmonic Orchestra, a parade, a 10K race, two juried art shows, a senior citizens day and music festivals. Est attendance: 500,000. For info: Nicole Mahoney, Exec Dir, Lilac Festival, 171 Reservoir Ave, Rochester, NY 14620. Phone: (716) 256-4960. Fax: (716) 256-4968. E-mail: lilacfest@aol.com. Web: www.roch.com/lilacfestival.

MAIFEST '01. May 18–20. MainStrasse Village, Covington, KY. MainStrasse celebrates the German tradition of welcoming the first spring wines and the beginning of the festival season. Artist and craftsman exhibits, food and drink, live music and entertainment. Est attendance: 300,000. For info: Promotions Coordinator, MainStrasse Village, 605 Philadelphia St, Covington, KY 41011. Phone: (859) 491-0458. Fax: (859) 655-7932.

	S	M	T	W	T	F	S
May			1	2	3	4	5
2001	6	7	8	9	10	11	12
	13	14	15	16	17	18	19
	20	21	22	23	24	25	26
	27	28	29	30	31		

MILES CITY BUCKING HORSE SALE. May 18–20. Miles City, MT. Miles City is real "Lonesome Dove" country and its annual bucking horse sale is where rodeo stock operators from around the nation and Canada come to purchase their bucking horses for the coming rodeo season. A festive event, the sale not only involves cowboys trying to ride some of the wildest horses in the country, but western artists displaying and creating works in a weekend art show, a gun and coin show, a western trade show featuring practical and gift items, a Saturday morning parade and Miles City's western attractions like the Range Riders Museum which chronicles the life of the cowboy on the northern Great Plains. (Miles City is the community featured in the novel and the two television miniseries about "Lonesome Dove.") Est attendance: 10,000. For info: Miles City Chamber of Commerce, 901 Main St, Miles City, MT 59301. Phone: (406) 232-2890.

MOREL MUSHROOM FESTIVAL. May 18–20. Muscoda, Wisconsin's "Morel Mushroom Capital," celebrates the end of the morel mushroom's two-week peak season. The 18th celebration includes a contest with mushrooms judged in four categories: heaviest, tallest, most on one stem (cluster) and oddest. Mushrooms available to sample and purchase. Huge parade Sunday. Arts and crafts. Photos of mushrooms contest. Many fun activities for the whole family. Annually, the weekend after Mother's Day. Est attendance: 2,000. For info: Muscoda Civic Pride Organization, Morel Mushroom Fest, PO Box 706, Muscoda, WI 53573. Phone: (608) 739-3770 or (608) 739-3152. Fax: (608) 739-3941. E-mail: glm@mwt.net.

MOUNT SAINT HELENS ERUPTION: ANNIVERSARY. May 18, 1980. A major eruption of Mount St. Helens volcano, in southwestern Washington, blew steam and ash more than 11 miles into the sky. First major eruption of Mount St. Helens since 1857, though Mar 26, 1980, there had been a warning eruption of smaller magnitude.

NATIONAL BIKE TO WORK DAY. May 18. At the state or local level, Bike to Work events are conducted by small and large businesses, city governments, bicycle clubs and environmental groups. About two million participants nationwide. Annually, the third Friday in May. For info: Patrick McCormick, Communications Dir, League of American Bicyclists, 1612 K St NW, Ste 401, Washington, DC 20006. Phone: (202) 822-1333. Fax: (202) 822-1334. E-mail: bikeleague@bikeleague.org. Web: www.bikeleague.org.

★**NATIONAL DEFENSE TRANSPORTATION DAY.** May 18. Presidential Proclamation customarily issued as "National Defense Transportation Day and National Transportation Week." Issued each year for the third Friday in May since 1957. (PL85–32 of May 16, 1957.)

PICKLEFEST. May 18–19. Atkins, AR (home of the fried dill pickle). Festivities include World's Champion Pickle Juice Drinking Contest, World's Champion Pickle Eating Contest, a pickle tasting booth, tours of the pickle plant, the Pickle Pageant and pickle contest, arts and crafts and live entertainment. Est attendance: 20,000. For info: Picklefest, People for a Better Atkins, PO Box 474, Atkins, AR 72823. Phone: (501) 641-7210.

POPE JOHN PAUL II: BIRTHDAY. May 18, 1920. Karol Wojtyla, 264th pope of the Roman Catholic Church, born at Wadowice, Poland. Elected pope Oct 16, 1978. He was the first non-Italian to be elected pope in 456 years (since the election of Pope Adrian VI, in 1522) and the first Polish pope.

RHODODENDRON FESTIVAL. May 18–20. Florence, OR. Abundance of springtime rhododendron blooms celebrated with a Grand Floral parade, arts and crafts show, dance, show & shine, car cruise and carnival. Est attendance: 35,000. For info: Chamber of Commerce, Box 26000, Florence, OR 97439. Phone: (541) 997-3128 or (800) 524-4864. Fax: (541) 997-4101. E-mail: florence@harborside.com. Web: www.florencechamber.com.

RHODODENDRON FESTIVAL. May 18–20 (also May 25–27). Georgia Mountain Fairgrounds, Hiawassee, GA. A weekend of country music with amateur talent. Open invitation to any single performer or band wishing to participate. Arts & crafts. Est attendance: 15,000. For info: Spring Music Festival, PO Box 444, Hiawassee, GA 30546. Phone: (706) 896-4191.

RHUBARB FESTIVAL. May 18–19. Intercourse, PA. A light-hearted celebration honoring rhubarb, which grows abundantly in the Pennsylvania Dutch country. Food, games and contests all featuring rhubarb—recipe contest, rhubarb derby, rhubarb pick-up sticks and more—plus entertainment. Est attendance: 10,000. For info: Lisa Horn, Kitchen Kettle Village, Box 380, Intercourse, PA 17534. Phone: (800) 732-3538 or (717) 768-8261. Web: www.kitchenkettle.com.

ST. LOUISE DE MARILLAC LOUISIANA BAR-B-Q FESTIVAL. May 18–20. St. Louise de Marillac Church, Arabi, LA. Festival includes live entertainment, booths, rides, raffle and home-cooked foods. Foods featured include Bar-B-Q chicken, ribs and sausage topped with our own homemade Bar-B-Q sauce, Crawfish Pizza, Muffulattas, Pasta Louise, Jambalaya, Shish ka-bobs and more. Est attendance: 7,000. For info: St. Louise de Marillac Church, 6800 Patricia St, Arabi, LA 70032.

SEDONA CHAMBER MUSIC FESTIVAL. May 18–27. Sedona, Flagstaff and Prescott, AZ. 17th annual festival with the Chicago String Quartet and national guest artists. For info: Chamber Music Sedona, PO Box 153, Sedona, AZ 86339-0153. Phone: (520) 204-2415. E-mail: SedonaCMS@aol.com. Web: www.chambermusicsedona.org.

SPACE MILESTONE: *APOLLO 10* (US). May 18, 1969. Launched with astronauts Colonel Thomas Stafford and Commander Eugene Cernan, who brought lunar module (LM) "Snoopy" within nine miles of the moon's surface on May 22. *Apollo 10* circled moon 31 times and returned to Earth May 26.

STAGECOACH DAYS. May 18–20. Marshall, TX. Arts and craft booths, Wild West shootouts, stagecoach rides, historic home tours, children's events, parade, Miss Loose Caboose Contest, live entertainment, lip synch contest, pet show, barbeque cook-off and Bull Plop contest. Annually, the third weekend in May. Est attendance: 30,000. For info: Pam Whisenant, Dir, Convention & Visitor Development, PO Box 520, Marshall, TX 75671. Phone: (903) 935-7868. Fax: (903) 935-9982. E-mail: cvd @internetwork.net. Web: www.marshalltxchamber.com.

STAMP EXPO. May 18–20. Radisson Hotel, Anaheim, CA. Annual Anaheim expo. Est attendance: 4,000. For info: Intl Stamp Collectors Soc, PO Box 854, Van Nuys, CA 91408. Phone: (818) 997-6496. Fax: (818) 988-4337. E-mail: iibick@aol.com. Web: www.bick.net.

TEACHER'S DAY IN FLORIDA. May 18. A ceremonial day on the third Friday in May.

TUSCARORA NATION POWWOW. May 18–20. Tribal Grounds (1½ miles NE of Maxton, NC, on Old Red Springs Rd). Crafts, camping, Iroquois dancing and singing, ticket raffles, original foods, powwow dancing and much more. Est attendance: 5,000. For info: Tuscarora Nation of North Carolina, 288 Tuscarora Nation Rd, Maxton, NC 28364. Phone: (910) 844-3352. Fax: (910) 844-3940.

VIKING FEST. May 18–20. Poulsbo, WA. Celebrating Poulsbo's Norwegian heritage, festival features Scandinavian luncheon, pancake breakfast, road race, food booths, parade, entertainment, crafts, outdoor concerts, flea market and carnival. Coincides with "Syttende Mai" (17th of May)—the Norwegian Constitution Day. Est attendance: 40,000. For info: Viking Fest, PO Box 1125, Poulsbo, WA 98370. Phone: (360) 779-4848. Fax: (360) 779-3115. Web: www.poulsbo.net.

VISIT YOUR RELATIVES DAY. May 18. A day to renew family ties and joys by visiting often-thought-of-seldom-seen relatives. Annually, May 18. For info: A.C. Moeller, Box 71, Clio, MI 48420-1042.

WILLAMETTE VALLEY FOLK FESTIVAL. May 18–20. Eugene, OR. 31st annual folk festival with multiple stages of musical performances, workshops, food and craft booths. Sponsor: EMU Cultural Forum. Free. Est attendance: 10,000. For info: Debby Martin, Program Mgr, EMU Cultural Forum, University of Oregon, Eugene, OR 97403. Phone: (541) 346-4373. Fax: (541) 346-4400. Web: darkwing.uoregon.edu/~cultural/.

WILLSON, MEREDITH: BIRTH ANNIVERSARY. May 18, 1902. American musician, playwright and composer best known for *The Music Man*. Born at Mason City, IA, Willson received Oscar nominations for *The Little Foxes* and *The Great Dictator*. Many of his songs, including "It's Beginning to Look a Lot Like Christmas," "Seventy-six Trombones" and "Till There Was You" have become standards. Willson died at Santa Monica, CA, June 15, 1984.

WOMAN INDUCTED INTO NATIONAL INVENTORS HALL OF FAME: 10th ANNIVERSARY. May 18, 1991. Gertrude Belle Elion, co-recipient of the 1988 Nobel Prize in Medicine, became the first woman inducted as a member of the National Inventors Hall of Fame. Elion's research led to the development of leukemia-fighting drugs and immunosuppressant Imuran which is used in kidney transplants.

BIRTHDAYS TODAY

Chow Yun-Fat, 46, actor (*Anna and the King, King's Ransom*), born Lamma Island, Hong Kong, May 18, 1955.

Perry Como (Pierino Como), 89, singer ("Catch a Falling Star"), actor, born Canonsburg, PA, May 18, 1912.

Reginald Martinez (Reggie) Jackson, 55, Baseball Hall of Fame outfielder, born Wyncote, PA, May 18, 1946.

Robert Morse, 70, actor (*The Loved One, A Guide for the Married Man*; stage: *How to Succeed in Business Without Really Trying* [Tony Award]), born Newton, MA, May 18, 1931.

Yannick Simone Camille Noah, 41, former tennis player, born Sedan, France, May 18, 1960.

Pope John Paul II (Karol Wojtyla), 81, Roman Catholic leader, born Wadowice, Poland, May 18, 1920.

Pernell Roberts, 73, actor (*Ride Lonesome*, "Bonanza," "Trapper John, MD"), born Waycross, GA, May 18, 1928.

Brooks Robinson, 64, Baseball Hall of Fame third baseman, born Little Rock, AR, May 18, 1937.

James Stephens, 50, actor ("The Paper Chase"), born Mount Kisco, NY, May 18, 1951.

George Strait, 49, country singer, musician, born Poteet, TX, May 18, 1952.

MAY 19 — SATURDAY

Day 139 — 226 Remaining

★**ARMED FORCES DAY.** May 19. Presidential Proclamation 5983, of May 17, 1989, covers the third Saturday in May in all succeeding years. Originally proclaimed as "Army Day" for Apr 6, beginning in 1936 (S.Con.Res. 30 of Apr 2, 1936). S.Con.Res. 5 of Mar 16, 1937, requested annual Apr 6 issuance, which was done through 1949. Always the third Saturday in May since 1950. Traditionally issued once by each Administration.

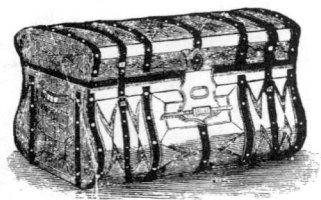

ARROW ROCK ANTIQUE SHOW & SALE. May 19–20. Arrow Rock, MO. Dealers from Mid-America under tent and indoors offering fine examples of 19th and 20th century antiques, collectibles and Americana. Est attendance: 3,000. For info: Karen Murray, Arrow Rock Antiques. Phone: (660) 837-3333.

AUTOMOTION. May 19–20. Noah's Ark Waterpark, Wisconsin Dells, WI. More than 700 cars on display, including street machines, classics and antiques. Event includes swap meet, live entertainment, "Car Cruise," car corral, four $500 cash drawings, four gateway packages valued at more than $400 each, sock hop, classic movie at Big Sky Drive-In Theatre and other activities. Est attendance: 30,000. For info: Angie Rizner, Wisc Dells Visitors Bureau, Box 390, Wisconsin Dells, WI 53965. Phone: (800) 223-3557. E-mail: info@wisdells.com. Web: www .wisdells.com.

BEVERLY HILLS: AFFAIRE IN THE GARDENS. May 19–20 (also Oct 20–21). Beverly Gardens Park at Rodeo Drive, Beverly Hills, CA. To foster an appreciation of arts in the community. Juried show; only fine arts and crafts considered. Garden setting. Biannually, the third weekends in May and October. Est attendance: 50,000. For info: Brad Meyerowitz, Sr Rec Supr, Beverly Hills Recreation and Parks Dept, 501 Doheny Rd, Beverly Hills, CA 90210. Phone: (310) 550-4796. Fax: (310) 858-9238.

BOYS' CLUBS FOUNDED: 95th ANNIVERSARY. May 19, 1906. The Federated Boys' Clubs, which later became the Boys' Clubs of America, was founded.

CALIFORNIA STRAWBERRY FESTIVAL. May 19–20. Strawberry Meadows of College Park, Oxnard, CA. This weekend event features a variety of gourmet strawberry foods, live musical entertainment, a 325-booth juried arts and crafts show. Strawberryland for children and the Strawberry Shortcake Eating Competition. Annually, the third weekend in May. Est attendance: 90,000. For info: Shelley Merrick, Festival Mgr, 1621 Pacific Ave, #127, Oxnard, CA 93033. Phone: (805) 385-7578.

CANADA: UPPER CANADA VILLAGE. May 19–Oct 8. Morrisburg, ON (9:30–5 daily). One of Canada's premier attractions. Visitors enter the world of the 1860s. Costumed interpreters bring history to life in this fully operational rural community as they perform period activities, entertain as townsfolk or as tradesmen apply their skills in restored buildings ranging from homes to trade shops. Many special events and programs offered throughout the season. Est attendance: 200,000. For info: Upper Canada Village, Parks of the St. Lawrence, RR 1, Morrisburg, ON, Canada K0C 1X0. Phone: (800) 437-2233 or (613) 543-3704. Web: www .uppercanadavillage.com.

CHEROKEE ROSE FESTIVAL. May 19–20. Gilmer, TX. Car show, arts and crafts, turtle race, children's games, ice cream crank-off, quilt show and much more. For info: Upshur County Chamber of Commerce, PO Box 854, Gilmer, TX 75644. Phone: (903) 843-2413 or (903) 843-3981. Fax: (903) 843-3759. E-mail: upchamber@aol.com.

	S	M	T	W	T	F	S
May			1	2	3	4	5
2001	6	7	8	9	10	11	12
	13	14	15	16	17	18	19
	20	21	22	23	24	25	26
	27	28	29	30	31		

DARK DAY IN NEW ENGLAND: ANNIVERSARY. May 19, 1780. At midday near-total darkness unaccountably descended on much of New England. Candles were lit, fowls went to roost and many fearful persons believed that doomsday had arrived. At New Haven, CT, Colonel Abraham Davenport opposed adjournment of the town council in these words: "I am against adjournment. The day of judgment is either approaching or it is not. If it is not, there is no cause for an adjournment. If it is, I choose to be found doing my duty. I wish therefore that candles may be brought." No scientifically verifiable cause for this widespread phenomenon was ever discovered.

A DAY IN OLD NEW CASTLE. May 19. New Castle, DE. Many historic homes and buildings of New Castle exhibit rare and beautiful pieces of colonial furniture and charming specimens of the builder's art. Annually, the third Saturday in May. Est attendance: 2,000. For info: A Day in Old New Castle, Box 166, New Castle, DE 19720. Phone: (877) 496-9498.

DO DAH DAY. May 19. Birmingham, AL. Free music, arts and crafts festival and more to raise funds for the Greater Birmingham Humane Society. A mile-long parade kicks off the event. Est attendance: 40,000. For info: Betsy Stout-Jones, Do Dah Day Committee, 900 Essex Rd, Birmingham, AL 35222. Phone: (205) 595-3771. Fax: (205) 592-3083. E-mail: dodah2001@aol.com. Web: www.dodahday.org.

EIGHTEENTH-CENTURY SPRING MARKET FAIR. May 19–20. McLean, VA. Learn 18th-century crafts, music and games. Period wares for sale. Est attendance: 4,000. For info: Publicist, Claude Moore Colonial Farm at Turkey Run, 6310 Georgetown Pike, McLean, VA 22101. Phone: (703) 442-7557. Fax: (703) 442-0714.

FISHING HAS NO BOUNDARIES—MONTICELLO. May 19–20. Freeman Lake, Monticello, IN. A two-day event for disabled persons to experience fishing on the lake. Any disability, sex, age, race, etc, are eligible. Expected attendance will be 50 participants and 130 volunteers. For info: FHNB, 7805 N Harrison, PO Box 325, Battle Ground, IN 47920. Phone: (765) 567-2567.

GETTYSBURG OUTDOOR ANTIQUE SHOW. May 19. Gettysburg, PA. Features 175 dealers in antiques with exhibits and displays. Annually, the third Saturday in May. Est attendance: 25,000. For info: Gettysburg CVB, PO Box 4117, Gettysburg, PA 17325. Phone: (717) 334-6274. Fax: (717) 334-1166. Web: www .gettysburg.com.

HANSBERRY, LORRAINE: BIRTH ANNIVERSARY. May 19, 1930. American playwright Lorraine Hansberry was born at Chicago, IL. For her now classic play *A Raisin in the Sun*, she became the youngest American and first black to win the Best Play Award from the New York Critics' Circle. The play, titled after the Langston Hughes poem, deals with issues such as racism, cultural pride and self-respect and was the first stage production written by a black woman to appear on Broadway (1959). *To Be Young, Gifted, and Black*, a book of excerpts from her journals, letters, speeches and plays, was published posthumously in 1969. Lorraine Hansberry died of cancer Jan 12, 1965, at New York, NY.

HO CHI MINH: BIRTH ANNIVERSARY. May 19, 1890. Vietnamese leader and first president of the Democratic Republic of Vietnam, born at Kim Lien, a central Vietnamese village (Nghe An Province), probably May 19, 1890. His original name was Nguyen That Thanh. Died at Hanoi, Vietnam, Sept 3, 1969.

HUMANATEE/ST. MARKS FESTIVAL. May 19. San Marcos de Apalache State Historic Site, St. Marks, FL. Celebrate and welcome manatees back to St. Marks and Wakulla Rivers. Food, displays, music, walk and much more. Annually, the third Saturday in May. Est attendance: 1,500. For info: HuManatee, PO Box 52, St. Marks, FL 32355. Phone: (850) 925-6412 or San Marcos Fort at (850) 925-6216.

KOREA: WORLD FESTIVAL FOR ISLAND CULTURES. May 19–June 17. Jeju, Republic of Korea. More than 30 islands will be represented at this meeting with the theme "From Islands to World!" on the island of Jeju, off the coast of South Korea. For info:. Web: www.wofic.or.kr.

LEWIS AND CLARK RENDEZVOUS. May 19–20. St. Charles, MO. Authentic reenactment of Lewis and Clark's encampment in 1804 prior to embarking on the exploration of the Louisiana Purchase. Activities include parades with fife and drum corps, church service and 19th-century crafts, food and demonstrations. Annually, the third weekend in May. Est attendance: 25,000. For info: St. Charles Conv and Visitors Bureau, 230 S Main, St. Charles, MO 63301. Phone: (800) 366-2427 or (636) 946-7776. Web: www.historicstcharles.com.

MALCOLM X: BIRTH ANNIVERSARY. May 19, 1925. Black nationalist and civil rights activist Malcolm X was born Malcolm Little at Omaha, NE. While serving a prison term he resolved to transform his life. On his release in 1952 he changed his name to Malcolm X and worked for the Nation of Islam until he was suspended by Black Muslim leader Elijah Muhammed Dec 4, 1963. Malcolm X later made the pilgrimage to Mecca and became an orthodox Muslim. He was assassinated as he spoke to a meeting at the Audubon Ballroom at New York, NY, Feb 21, 1965.

MAY RAY DAY. May 19. To celebrate the beginning of the warm outside days the sun gives us. Also, a day for people named Ray. Annually, May 19. For info: Richard Ankli, The Fifth Wheel Tavern, 639 Fifth St, Ann Arbor, MI 48103.

MAYFEST. May 19. Muskegon Community College, Muskegon, MI. Annual spring picnic and celebration of arts, music, children's activities and American exhibits. All activities and events are free. Annually, the third Saturday in May. Est attendance: 3,500. For info: Dr. Dennis Wilson, Sec/Treasurer, Muskegon Community College, 221 S Quarterland Rd, Muskegon, MI 49442. Phone: (616) 777-0255. E-mail: wilsond@muskegon.cc.mi.us.

MEET THE ARTISTS AND ARTISANS SHOW. May 19–20 (also Sept 29–30). Milford Green, CT. 39th annual. More than 200 juried, award-winning artists and crafters from throughout the nation. For info: Meet the Artists & Artisans Show, (203) 874-5672 or Greater New Haven Conv & Visitors Bureau, 59 Elm St, New Haven, CT 06510. Phone: (203) 777-8550 or (800) 332-STAY. Fax: (203) 782-7755. Web: www.newhavencvb.org.

MEMORY DAYS. May 19–27. Grayson, KY. Parade, art show and horse show. Est attendance: 10,000. For info: Robert L. Caummisar, Chamber of Commerce, 301 W Main St, Grayson, KY 41143. Phone: (606) 474-9522.

MIFFLIN-JUNIATA ARTS FESTIVAL. May 19–20. Lewistown Rec Park, Lewistown, PA. More than 75 juried arts and craft vendors; professional and amateur performances; free children's crafts and special exhibits. Admission free. Est attendance: 18,000. For info: Jenny Landis, Co-Chair, c/o Mifflin-Juniata Arts Council, PO Box 1126, Lewistown, PA 17044. Phone: (717) 248-8711. E-mail: jenny@acsworld.net.

NATIONAL RESTAURANT ASSOCIATION: RESTAURANT, HOTEL-MOTEL SHOW. May 19–22. McCormick Place, Chicago, IL. Est attendance: 100,000. For info: Richard Gaven, Natl Restaurant Assn, 150 N Michigan Ave, Ste 2000, Chicago, IL 60601. Phone: (312) 853-2525. Fax: (312) 853-2548. Web: www.restaurant.org.

NATIONAL SAFE BOATING WEEK. May 19–25. Brings boating safety to the public's attention, decreases the number of boating fatalities and makes the waterways safer for all boaters. Sponsor: US Coast Guard. For info: Jo Calkin, Commandant (G-OPB-2), US Coast Guard, 2100 Second St SW, Washington, DC 20593. Phone: (800) 368-5647.

★**NATIONAL SAFE BOATING WEEK.** May 19–25. Presidential Proclamation during May since 1995. From 1958 through 1977, issued for a week including July 4 (PL85–445 of June 4, 1958). From 1981 through 1994, issued for the first week in June (PL96–376 of Oct 3, 1980). From 1995, issued for a seven-day period ending on the Friday before Memorial Day. Not issued from 1978 through 1980.

NCAA DIVISION I MEN'S TENNIS CHAMPIONSHIP. May 19–27. Athens, GA. For info: Natl Collegiate Athletic Assn, 700 W Washington Ave, PO Box 6222, Indianapolis, IN 46206-6222. Phone: (317) 917-6222. Fax: (317) 917-6888. Web: www.ncaa.org.

OLD TOWNE FIESTA. May 19. Old Towne, Placentia, CA. Event features cultural entertainment, food, game booths and children's activities. 11 AM–7 PM. Est attendance: 10,000. For info: Steve Pischel, City of Placentia, 401 E Chapman Ave, Placentia, CA 92870. Phone: (714) 993-8184.

"PEC THING." May 19–20 (also Sept 15–16). Pecatonica, IL. Semi-annual antique show with more than 400 exhibitors. Est attendance: 15,000. For info: Lisa RosenKrans, Winnebago Country Fair Assn, PO Box 810, Pecatonica, IL 61063-0670. Phone: (815) 239-1641 or (800) 238-3587. Fax: (815) 239-1653. E-mail: pecthing@winnebagocountyfair.com.

POLE, PEDAL, PADDLE. May 19. Bend, OR. Five-stage ironman-type race for singles, teams and pairs; includes downhill skiing, nordic skiing, biking, canoeing and running. Annually, the third Saturday in May. Sponsors: US Bank, Pepsi, Bud Light, Teva, Cellular One, Z21TV. Est attendance: 10,000. For info: Mt Bachelor Ski Education Foundation, PO Box 388, Bend, OR 97709. Phone: (541) 388-0002. Fax: (541) 388-7848. E-mail: mbsef@bendnet.com. Web: www.bendnet.com/ppp.

POSTCARD SALE. May 19–20. Howard Johnson Hotel, Hagerstown, MD. 36 tables filled with antique and modern postcards. Est attendance: 200. For info: James Ward, Postcard History Society, 1795 Kleinfeltersville Rd, Stevens, PA 17578-9773. Phone: (717) 721-9273.

PREAKNESS STAKES. May 19. Pimlico Race Course, Baltimore, MD. Preakness Stakes, middle jewel in the Visa Triple Crown, was inaugurated in 1873. Annually, the third Saturday in May—two Saturdays after the Kentucky Derby—and followed, three Saturdays later, by the Belmont Stakes. Est attendance: 100,000. For info: Maryland Jockey Club, Pimlico Race Course, Baltimore, MD 21215. Phone: (410) 542-9400. Web: www.marylandracing.com.

RAGGEDY ANN & ANDY FESTIVAL. May 19–20. Arcola, IL. The whole town celebrates Raggedy Ann's 85th birthday with a parade, arts & crafts and antique shows, food and entertainment. For info: Arcola Chamber of Congress, Arcola, IL 61910. Phone: (800) 336-5456.

ROAD CHURCH MISSIONARY FAIR. May 19. Road Congregational Church, Pequot Trail, Stonington, CT. Bake sale, crafts, white elephants and more. Homemade luncheon available at noon. 10 AM–2 PM. For info: Libby Kennedy, 21 Roosevelt Ave, Mystic, CT 06355. Phone: (860) 536-1514.

SCOBEE, FRANCIS R.: BIRTH ANNIVERSARY. May 19, 1939. Commander of the ill-fated space shuttle *Challenger*, 46-year-old pilot Francis R. Scobee had been in the astronaut program since 1978 and had been pilot of the *Challenger* in 1984. Born at Cle Elum, WA, Scobee perished with all others on board when the *Challenger* exploded on Jan 28, 1986. See also: "*Challenger* Space Shuttle Explosion Anniversary" (Jan 28).

SEND A KID TO KAMP RADIOTHON. May 19. Masterson Station Park, Lexington, KY. Annually, the third Saturday in May. Est attendance: 15,000. For info: Dennis Smith, 770 AM, WCGW, 3270 Blazer Parkway, Ste 101, Lexington, KY 40509-1847. Phone: (606) 264-9700. Fax: (606) 264-9705. E-mail: info @kidtokamp.com. Web: www.kidtokamp.com.

SEQUANOTA'S HERITAGE FESTIVAL. May 19. Jennerstown, PA. Crafts, entertainment, children's booths, food booths, antique cars and quilt auction. Est attendance: 1,200. For info: Cecilia Williams, Sequanota's Heritage Festival, Box 245, Jennerstown, PA 15547. Phone: (814) 629-6627.

SIMPLON TUNNEL OPENING: 95th ANNIVERSARY. May 19, 1906. Tunnel from Brig, Switzerland to Iselle, Italy officially opened on this day. Construction started in 1898.

SPACE MILESTONE: *MARS 2* AND *MARS 3* (USSR): 30th ANNIVERSARY. May 19 and 28, 1971. Entered Martian orbits on Nov 27 and Dec 2, respectively. *Mars 3* sent down a TV-equipped capsule that soft-landed and transmitted pictures for 20 seconds. Launch dates: May 19 and 28, 1971.

STORYTELLING HISTORICAL WALK AROUND WASHINGTON. May 19–20. Washington, PA. Sponsored by Washington County, Pennsylvania Historical Society. Free admission. Est attendance: 180. For info: Washington County Historical Soc, 49 E Maiden St, Washington County, PA 15301. Phone: (724) 225-6740. Fax: (724) 225-8495. E-mail: info@wchspa.org. Web: www.wchspa.org.

TURKEY: YOUTH AND SPORTS DAY. May 19. Public holiday commemorating the beginning of a national movement for independence in 1919, led by Mustafa Kemal Ataturk.

TWENTY-SEVENTH AMENDMENT RATIFIED: ANNIVERSARY. May 19, 1992. The 27th amendment to the Constitution was ratified, prohibiting Congress from giving itself midterm pay raises.

VIRGINA WINE FESTIVAL. May 19–20. Ashlawn-Highland, Home of James Monroe, Charlottesville, VA. Ten wineries offering tastings and sales. Commemorative wine glasses as gifts, crafts for sale, children's games, food and picnicking, live entertainment and tours of Monroe house and grounds. Est attendance: 2,000. For info: Carolyn C. Holmes, Ashlawn-Highland, 1000 James Monroe Pkwy, Charlottesville, VA 22902. Phone: (804) 293-9539. Fax: (804) 293-8000. E-mail: ashlawnjm@aol.com.

WILDFLOWER FESTIVAL OF THE ARTS. May 19–20. Historic Square, Dahlonega, GA. Springtime in the North Georgia Mountains in a historic 1800s mining town. Visual and performing artists, programs and exhibits on wildflowers of the area, children's art area where children can create their own art. Annually, the third weekend in May. Est attendance: 25,000. For info: Dahlonega–Lumpkin County Chamber of Commerce, 13 S Park St, Dahlonega, GA 30533. Phone: (706) 864-3711. Fax: (706) 864-7917. E-mail: dahlonega@alltel.net. Web: www.dahlonega.org/festivals.

WORLD CHAMPIONSHIP STEAK COOKOFF. May 19. Magnolia, AR. Held on the last day of the Magnolia Blossom Fest. Teams prepare and grill more than 5,000 ribeye steaks to win $2,000 first place and Governor's Silver Cup. Cash prizes for best pit, parade and showmanship. Steak dinners sold to public. Annually, the third Saturday of May. Est attendance: 40,000. For info: Magnolia-Columbia County Chamber of Commerce, 202 N Pine, PO Box 866, Magnolia, AR 71754-0866. Phone: (800) 482-3330. Fax: (870) 234-7937. E-mail: magcoc@arkansas.net.

May 2001	S	M	T	W	T	F	S
			1	2	3	4	5
	6	7	8	9	10	11	12
	13	14	15	16	17	18	19
	20	21	22	23	24	25	26
	27	28	29	30	31		

WRIGHT PLUS. May 19. Oak Park, IL. The Frank Lloyd Wright Preservation Trust's annual housewalk features guided tours of the interiors of 10 buildings designed by Frank Lloyd Wright and his architectural contemporaries, including Wright's own home and studio. Reservations are required. Tickets limited. (Tickets available Mar 1.) Annually, third Saturday in May. Est attendance: 2,500. For info: Director of Public Relations, Frank Lloyd Wright Preservation Trust, 951 Chicago Ave, Oak Park, IL 60302. Phone: (708) 848-1976 or (708) 848-9518. Fax: (708) 848-1248. Web: www.wrightplus.org.

YOU GOTTA HAVE PARK. May 19–20. Prospect Park, Brooklyn, NY. This annual weekend-long celebration of Brooklyn's Prospect Park is dedicated to cleaning, greening and bringing the Park's neighbors and volunteers together. Annually, the third weekend in May. Est attendance: 20,000. For info: Prospect Park Alliance, Public Info Office, External Affairs, Litchfield Villa, 95 Prospect Park W, Brooklyn, NY 11215. Phone: (718) 965-8954 or (718) 965-8951. Fax: (718) 965-8972. E-mail: marketing @prospectpark.org. Web: www.prospectpark.org.

BIRTHDAYS TODAY

Nora Ephron, 60, writer (*Heartburn* [made into a movie]), born New York, NY, May 19, 1941.

James Fox, 62, actor (*A Passage to India, The Russia House, Patriot Games*), born London, England, May 19, 1939.

Kevin Garnett, 25, basketball player, born Mauldin, SC, May 19, 1976.

David Hartman, 64, actor (Emmy for "Good Morning America"; *Hello Dolly*), born Pawtucket, RI, May 19, 1937.

Grace Jones, 49, model, singer ("Sorry," "I Need a Man"), actress, born Spanishtown, Jamaica, May 19, 1952.

William (Bill) Laimbeer, Jr, 44, former basketball player, born Boston, MA, May 19, 1957.

James Lehrer, 67, journalist, anchor ("The Newshour with Jim Lehrer"), born Wichita, KS, May 19, 1934.

Eric Lloyd, 15, actor ("Jesse," *Dunston Checks In*), born Glendale, CA, May 19, 1986.

Pete Townshend, 56, musician (The Who, "Let My Love Open the Door"), born London, England, May 19, 1945.

MAY 20 — SUNDAY
Day 140 — 225 Remaining

AFRMA FANCY RAT & MOUSE DISPLAY. May 20. Wm. S. Hart Park, Newhall, CA. American Fancy Rat and Mouse Association exhibits rats and mice of "fancy" species that make good pets. For info: AFRMA, PO Box 2589, Winnetka, CA 91396-2589. Phone: (909) 685-2350 or (818) 992-5564. Fax: (818) 592-6590. E-mail: craigr@afrma.org. Web: www.afrma.org.

AMELIA EARHART ATLANTIC CROSSING: ANNIVERSARY. May 20, 1932. Leaving Harbor Grace, Newfoundland, Canada at 7 PM, Amelia Earhart landed near Londonderry, Ireland. The 2,026-mile flight took 13 hours and 30 minutes. She was the first woman to fly solo across the Atlantic. Earhart, along with her navigator Fred Noonan, disappeared on July 2, 1937, between Lae, New Guinea, and Howland Island while trying to fly her Lockheed twin-engine plane around the equator to gather scientific data.

BALZAC, HONORE DE: BIRTH ANNIVERSARY. May 20, 1799. French author of a huge cycle of stories and novels known as *The Human Comedy*, born at Tours, France. "It is easier," Balzac wrote in 1829, "to be a lover than a husband for the simple reason that it is more difficult to be witty every day than to say pretty things from time to time." Died at Paris, Aug 18, 1850.

CAMEROON: NATIONAL HOLIDAY. May 20. Republic of Cameroon. Commemorates adoption of constitution in 1972.

CAPE MAY MUSIC FESTIVAL. May 20–June 24. Cape May, NJ. A dazzling array of sounds and styles—from Vivaldi to Stravinski, from the Renaissance to the Jazz Era, from ethnic folk to world music and more. The world's finest chamber ensembles and special guest artists perform in the elegant Victorian setting of Cape May. Est attendance: 10,000. For info: Mid-Atlantic Center for the Arts, PO Box 340, Cape May, NJ 08204. Phone: (800) 275-4278 or (609) 884-5404. Web: www.capemaymac.org.

COUNCIL OF NICAEA I: ANNIVERSARY. May 20–Aug 25, 325. First ecumenical council of Christian Church, called by Constantine I, first Christian emperor of Roman Empire. Nearly 300 bishops are said to have attended this first of 21 ecumenical councils (latest, Vatican II, began Sept 11, 1962), which was held at Nicaea, in Asia Minor (today's Turkey). The council condemned Arianism (which denied divinity of Christ), formulated the Nicene Creed and fixed the day of Easter—always on a Sunday.

D.C. BOOTH DAY (WITH FISH CULTURE HALL OF FAME). May 20. D.C. Booth Historic Fish Hatchery, Spearfish, SD. Antique auto show, musical entertainment, free tours of the historic Booth home and installation of new members into the Fish Culture Hall of Fame. Est attendance: 1,200. For info: Molly Salcone, D.C. Booth Historic Fish Hatchery, 423 Hatchery Circle, Spearfish, SD 57783. Phone: (605) 642-7730.

ELIZA DOOLITTLE DAY. May 20. To honor Miss Doolittle (heroine of Bernard Shaw's *Pygmalion*) for demonstrating the importance and the advantage of speaking one's native language properly. For info: H.M. Chase, Doolittle Day Committee, 2460 Devonshire Rd, Ann Arbor, MI 48104-2706.

EXAMINER BAY TO BREAKERS RACE. May 20. San Francisco, CA. Largest footrace in the world attracts 80,000 runners each year, from world-class athletes to fun runners; post-race festival, live concert, food and beverages. Annually, the third Sunday in May. Est attendance: 75,000. For info: *Examiner* Bay to Breakers, PO Box 429200, San Francisco, CA 94142. Phone: (415) 808-5000 ext 2222. Web: www.baytobreakers.com.

HERZL, THEODOR: BIRTH ANNIVERSARY. May 20, 1860. Founder of the modern Zionist movement, born at Budapest, Hungary. Herzl died at Edlach, Austria, July 3, 1904.

HOMESTEAD ACT: ANNIVERSARY. May 20, 1862. President Lincoln signed the Homestead Act opening millions of acres of government-owned land in the West to settlers or "homesteaders," who had to reside on the land and cultivate it for five years.

INTERNATIONAL AIDS CANDLELIGHT MEMORIAL. May 20. The world's largest grassroots AIDS event has four goals: to commemorate those who have died of AIDS, to show support for those living with HIV/AIDS, to raise awareness of the disease's impact and of the opportunities to respond to HIV/AIDS. The 18th annual Memorial will be observed in more than 45 nations. For info: Global Health Council, 1701 K St NW, Ste 600, Washington, DC 20006-1503. Phone: (202) 833-5900. E-mail: ghc@globalhealth.org. Web: www.globalhealthcouncil.org.

LINDBERGH FLIGHT: ANNIVERSARY. May 20–21, 1927. Anniversary of the first solo trans-Atlantic flight. Captain Charles Augustus Lindbergh, 25-year-old aviator, departed from rainy, muddy Roosevelt Field, Long Island, NY, alone at 7:52 AM, May 20, 1927, in a Ryan monoplane named *Spirit of St. Louis*. He landed at Le Bourget airfield, Paris, at 10:24 PM Paris time (5:24 PM, NY time), May 21, winning a $25,000 prize offered by Raymond Orteig for the first nonstop flight between New York City and Paris, France (3,600 miles). The "flying fool" as he had been dubbed by some doubters became "Lucky Lindy," an instant world hero. See also: "Lindbergh, Charles Augustus: Birth Anniversary" (Feb 4).

LOCAL COLORS. May 20. Roanoke, VA. An international event celebrating the cultural richness of the Roanoke Valley and surrounding areas. The event begins with an international parade at noon and the celebration continues until 5 PM. Included in the day's activities are an international fashion show, storytelling, crafts and displays from more than 60 countries, entertainment on stage, games for children and ethnic foods from around the world. Est attendance: 25,000. For info: NCCJ/Roanoke Region, PO Box 1323, Roanoke, VA 24007. Phone: (540) 342-4540. Fax: (540) 342-4543. E-mail: CTIS@CTIS.org.

MADISON, DOLLY (DOROTHEA) DANDRIDGE PAYNE TODD: BIRTH ANNIVERSARY. May 20, 1768. Wife of James Madison, 4th president of the US, born at Guilford County, NC. Died at Washington, DC, July 12, 1849.

MECKLENBURG DAY. May 20. North Carolina. Commemorates claimed signing of a declaration of independence from England by citizens of Mecklenburg County on this day, 1775.

MOTOR VOTER BILL SIGNED: ANNIVERSARY. May 20, 1993. The latest effort to remove barriers to voter registration resulted in the passage of the Motor Voter Bill, which was signed into law by President William Clinton. This bill requires the states to allow voter registration by mail or when a citizen applies for or renews a driver's license.

NATIONAL EMERGENCY MEDICAL SERVICES (EMS) WEEK. May 20–26. Honoring EMS providers nationwide who provide life-saving care in a multitude of circumstances. Also a time for the public to learn about injury prevention, safety awareness and emergency preparedness. Theme: EMS—New Century, New Hope. Annually, the third full week in May. For info: American College of Emergency Physicians, PO Box 619911, Dallas, TX 75261-9911. Phone: (800) 748-1822. E-mail: emsweek@acep.org. Web: www.acep.org.

NATIONAL NEW FRIENDS, OLD FRIENDS WEEK. May 20–27. A week to celebrate old friends and new friends and remember how vital friends are for our emotional, physical and even professional or career success. Friendshifts® is the word coined by author and sociologist Jan Yager to denote the way our ideas about friendships as well as who our friends are change as we go through different stages of life. But at every stage, friendship is crucial, for children, for teenagers, for young adults, singles, couples, new mothers, the middle-aged and especially for those who are older, retired or widowed. For info: Jan Yager, PhD, PO Box 8038, Stamford, CT 06905-8038. Fax: (203) 968-0193. E-mail: jyager@aol.com. Web: www.JanYager.com/friendship.

NATIONAL SPORTING GOODS ASSOCIATION MANAGEMENT CONFERENCE. May 20–23. Loews Ventana Canyon Resort, Tucson, AZ. The premier educational and networking event for the sporting goods industry. Attracts leading retailers, dealers, manufacturers, agents, media and industry organizations. Est attendance: 350. For info: Larry Weindruch, Dir of Communications, Natl Sporting Goods Assn, 1601 Feehanville Dr, Ste 300, Mt Prospect, IL 60056-6035. Phone: (847) 296-NSGA. Fax: (847) 391-9827. E-mail: nsga1699@aol.com. Web: www.nsga.org.

NATIONAL STATIONERY SHOW. May 20–23. Javits Center, New York, NY. For info: George Little Management, 10 Bank St, White Plains, NY 10606. Phone: (914) 421-3200. Fax: (914) 948-6088. Web: www.glmshows.com or www.nationalstationery show.com.

NEIGHBOR DAY. May 20. A "Day of Special Observance" in Rhode Island, declared by the General Assembly. Annually, the Sunday prior to Memorial Day weekend. For info: Mary Jane DiMaio, Westerly Town Councilor, 15 Windward Dr, Westerly, RI 02891. Web: WatchHill.com.

NORMAN ROCKWELL'S FIRST *SATURDAY EVENING POST* COVER: ANNIVERSARY. May 20, 1916. Norman Rockwell's first cover for the *Post*, depicting a boy having to care for his infant sibling—pushing the baby carriage while his buddies set off to play ball—appeared on the May 20 edition. His last *Post* cover appeared in 1963.

PENNSYLVANIA AVENUE CLOSED: ANNIVERSARY. May 20, 1995. Barricades were erected to close off a two-block stretch of Pennsylvania Avenue, a six-lane street with a sidewalk that passes within 150 feet of the north face of the White House. A review of security procedures had been initiated after an attempt by an unemployed truck driver to land a small airplane on the South Lawn in September of 1994, but the closing was a direct response to the bombing of the Alfred P. Murrah Federal Building at Oklahoma City, OK, Apr 19, 1995.

ROGATION SUNDAY. May 20. The fifth Sunday after Easter is the beginning of Rogationtide (Rogation Sunday and the following three days before Ascension Day). Rogation Day rituals date from the 5th century.

ROUSSEAU, HENRI JULIEN FELIX: BIRTH ANNIVERSARY. May 20, 1844. Henri Rousseau, nicknamed Le Douanier because of his onetime post as customs toll-keeper, was a celebrated French painter born at Laval, Mayenne, France. Painted deceptively "primitive" pictures of exotic foliage, flowers and fruit of the jungle, with stilted human and animal figures. Died at Hospital Necker, Paris, Sept 4, 1910.

RURAL LIFE SUNDAY OR SOIL STEWARDSHIP SUNDAY. May 20. With an increase in ecological and environmental concerns, Rural Life Sunday emphasizes the concept that Earth belongs to God, who has granted humanity the use of it, along with the responsibility of caring for it wisely. At the suggestion of the International Association of Agricultural Missions, Rural Life Sunday was first observed in 1929. The day is observed annually by churches of many Christian denominations and includes pulpit exchanges by rural and urban pastors. Under the auspices of the National Association of Soil and Water Conservation Districts, the week beginning with Rural Life Sunday is now widely observed as Soil Stewardship Week, with the Sunday itself alternatively termed Soil Stewardship Sunday. Traditionally, Rural Life Sunday is Rogation Sunday, the Sunday preceding Ascension Day.

SAINT LOUIS WALK OF FAME INDUCTION CEREMONY. May 20. St. Louis, MO. Outdoor free-admission ceremony with ragtime band. Famous St. Louisans are honored. Nonprofit organization showcases for the cultural heritage of St. Louis. In addition to stars in the sidewalks are plaques describing the achievements and contributions each creative St. Louisan made to our country's culture (Chuck Berry, Miles Davis, Bob Costas, Betty Grable, Vincent Price, Tennessee Williams, Scott Joplin, Charles Lindbergh, John Goodman, etc). Annually, the third Sunday in May. Est attendance: 1,000. For info: Joe Edwards, Chair, St. Louis Walk of Fame, 6504 Delmar, St. Louis, MO 63130. Phone: (314) 727-STAR. Web: www.stlouiswalk offame.org.

SCHOOL SUPPORT STAFF WEEK. May 20–26. One way to show appreciation to instructional aides/assistants, custodial staff, maintenance workers and others who are many times overlooked for the jobs they do. They are vital to the running of the school and seldom get get any recognition for a job well done. All employees of a school system who come in contact with our children are important. They all have lessons to teach our children, whether it is cleaning the school, making repairs or giving a child the extra help they need to succeed in school. Annually, the fourth week in May. For info: Joyce G. Dunigan, 2950 Deercreek Trail, Powhatan, VA 23139. E-mail: Bloomy1999@aol.com.

SPACE MILESTONE: *PIONEER VENUS I (US).* May 20, 1978. Launched this date, became first Venus orbiter the following Dec 4.

STEWART, JIMMY: BIRTH ANNIVERSARY. May 20, 1908. Film actor born James Stewart at Indiana, PA. Best known for his roles in *Mr Smith Goes to Washington* and the Christmas classic, *It's a Wonderful Life*, he won an Oscar for *The Philadelphia Story*. Died July 2, 1997 at Beverly Hills, CA.

WEIGHTS AND MEASURES DAY: ANNIVERSARY. May 20. Anniversary of international treaty, signed May 20, 1875, providing for the establishment of an International Bureau of Weights and Measures. The bureau was founded on international territory at Sevres, France.

YOUTH AGAINST VIOLENCE. May 20. Westboro, MA. Youth raising awareness about domestic violence through education and an annual Walk Against Violence. Annually, the third Sunday in May. Est attendance: 100. For info: Westboro Youth & Family Services, Explorer Post 24, Town Hall, 34 W Main St, Westboro, MA 01581. Phone: (508) 366-3090. Fax: (508) 366-3047.

BIRTHDAYS TODAY

Cher (Cherilyn Sarkisian), 55, singer ("Half Breed," "Dark Lady"), actress (*Moonstruck*), born El Centro, CA, May 20, 1946.

Joe Cocker, 57, singer ("You Are So Beautiful"), born Sheffield, England, May 20, 1944.

Michael Crapo, 50, US Senator (R, Idaho), born Idaho Falls, ID, May 20, 1951.

Tony Goldwyn, 41, actor (*Ghost, Kiss the Girls*), born Los Angeles, CA, May 20, 1960.

Bronson Pinchot, 42, actor ("Perfect Strangers," "Step By Step"), born New York, NY, May 20, 1959.

Ronald Prescott Reagan, 43, dancer, talk-show host, son of former President Ronald Reagan, born Los Angeles, CA, May 20, 1958.

Anthony Zerbe, 65, actor ("Harry-O," *Cool Hand Luke, Papillon*), born Long Beach, CA, May 20, 1936.

MAY 21 — MONDAY
Day 141 — 224 Remaining

AMERICAN RED CROSS: FOUNDING ANNIVERSARY. May 21, 1881. Commemorates the founding of the American Red Cross by Clara Barton, its first president. The Red Cross had been founded in Switzerland in 1864 by representatives from 16 European nations. The organization is a voluntary, not-for-profit organization governed and directed by volunteers and provides disaster relief at home and abroad. 1.1 million volunteers are involved in community services such as collecting and distributing donated blood and blood products, teaching health and safety classes and acting as a medium for emergency communication between Americans and their armed forces.

BURR, RAYMOND WILLIAM STACY: BIRTH ANNIVERSARY. May 21, 1917. Stage, film and TV actor best known for the role of Perry Mason in the series of the same name. He was born at New Westminster, British Columbia, and died near Healdsburg, CA, Sept 12, 1993.

		S	M	T	W	T	F	S
May				1	2	3	4	5
2001		6	7	8	9	10	11	12
		13	14	15	16	17	18	19
		20	21	22	23	24	25	26
		27	28	29	30	31		

CANADA: VICTORIA DAY. May 21. Commemorates the birth of Queen Victoria May 24, 1819. Observed annually on the first Monday preceding May 25.

CHILE: BATTLE OF IQUIQUE DAY. May 21. Commemorates a naval battle in 1879, part of the War of the Pacific with Peru and Bolivia.

CURTISS, GLENN HAMMOND: BIRTH ANNIVERSARY. May 21, 1878. American inventor and aviator, born at Hammondsport, NY. The aviation pioneer died at Buffalo, NY, July 23, 1930.

DURER, ALBRECHT: BIRTH ANNIVERSARY. May 21, 1471. German painter and engraver, one of the greatest artists of the Renaissance, was born at Nuremberg, Germany, and died there Apr 6, 1528.

FRY, ELIZABETH GURNEY: BIRTH ANNIVERSARY. May 21, 1780. English reformer who dedicated her life to improving the condition of the poor and especially of women in prison, born at Earlham, Norfolk, England. Died at Ramsgate, Oct 12, 1845.

Gemini

GEMINI, THE TWINS. May 21–June 20. In the astronomical/astrological zodiac, which divides the sun's apparent orbit into 12 segments, the period May 21–June 20 is traditionally identified as the sun sign period of Gemini, the Twins. The ruling planet is Mercury.

HAMMER, ARMAND: BIRTH ANNIVERSARY. May 21, 1898. American industrialist Armand Hammer was born at New York, NY. He built the Occidental Petroleum Company into a $20 billion conglomerate after he invested $100,000 in it in 1956 and it was awarded two oil concessions in Libya. He was a trained physician who was sympathetic to the Soviet people and gave away millions of dollars through philanthropy to cancer research. Hammer died Dec 10, 1990, at Los Angeles, CA.

HUMMEL, SISTER MARIA INNOCENTIA: BIRTH ANNIVERSARY. May 21, 1909. Born at Massing, Bavaria, Sister Maria Innocentia Hummel cultivated an early interest in drawing and attended Munich's Academy of Fine Arts. She entered Siessen Convent run by the Sisters of the Third Order of St. Francis, a teaching order, and began teaching art to kindergarten children. In 1934 Franz Goebel obtained an exclusive license to translate her drawings into three-dimensional figurines. The first M.I. Hummel figurines were displayed at the Leipzig Trade Fair in 1935; they made their first appearance in the American market in May 1935. She died Nov 6, 1946, at Siessen, Germany. Many M.I. Hummel Clubs across the country commemorate her birthdate with special events and fundraisers for local charities.

INTERNATIONAL SALUTE TO PUBLIC RELATIONS WEEK. May 21–27. Recognition of the positive role public relations practitioners play in disseminating relevant information to the news media and the general public. The strategic counseling provided to companies is another invaluable component of the practice. Annually, the third full week of May. For info: Robin Gorman Newman, RGN Communications, 44 Somerset Dr, N, Great Neck, NY 11020. Phone: (516) 773-0911. E-mail: rgnewman@aol.com.

ISRAEL: YOM YERUSHALAYIM (JERUSALEM DAY). May 21. Hebrew calendar date: Iyar 28, 5761. Commemorates the liberation of the old city, June 7, 1967.

NAIA MEN'S TENNIS NATIONAL CHAMPIONSHIPS. May 21–25. Site to be determined. 50th annual. Est attendance: 1,500. For info: Natl Assn of Intercollegiate Athletics, 6120 S Yale Ave, Ste 1450, Tulsa, OK 74136. Phone: (918) 494-8828. Fax: (918) 494-8841. E-mail: jkehl@naia.org. Web: www.naia.org.

NAIA WOMEN'S TENNIS NATIONAL CHAMPIONSHIPS. May 21–25. Location. TBA. 21st annual tournament. Individuals compete for All-America honors, while teams compete for the national championship. Est attendance: 1,500. For info: Natl Assn of Intercollegiate Athletics, 6120 S Yale Ave, Ste 1450, Tulsa, OK 74136. Phone: (918) 494-8828. Fax: (918) 494-8841. E-mail: jkehl@naia.org. Web: www.naia.org.

NATIONAL BACKYARD GAMES WEEK. May 21–28. Observance to celebrate the unofficial start of summer by fostering social interaction and family togetherness through backyard games. Get outside and be both physically and mentally stimulated, playing classic games of the past while discovering and creating new ways to be active and interact with friends and neighbors. For info: Frank Beres, Patch Products, PO Box 268, Beloit, WI 53511. Phone: (608) 362-6896. Fax: (608) 362-8178. E-mail: patch@patchproducts.com. Web: www.patchproducts.com.

NATIONAL WAITSTAFF DAY. May 21. A day for restaurant managers and patrons to recognize and to express their appreciation for the many fine and dedicated waitresses and waiters. For info: Gaylord F. Ward, Promotion Dir, 1505 E Bristol Rd, Burton, MI 48529-2214.

PIETA ATTACKED: ANNIVERSARY. May 21, 1972. Lazlo Toth, a Hungarian native, attacked Michelangelo's centuries-old sculpture *The Pieta* while screaming, "I am Jesus Christ!" The Madonna's left arm was severed, her veil and nose were smashed and her left eye was disfigured.

POPE, ALEXANDER: BIRTH ANNIVERSARY. May 21, 1688 (OS). English poet born at London, England. "A man," Pope wrote in 1727, "should never be ashamed to own he has been in the wrong, which is but saying, in other words, that he is wiser today than he was yesterday." Died at Twickenham, May 30, 1744 (OS).

RAJIV GANDHI ASSASSINATED: 10th ANNIVERSARY. May 21, 1991. Former Indian Prime Minister Rajiv Gandhi was assassinated in the midst of a reelection campaign. He was killed when a bomb, hidden in a bouquet of flowers given by admirers, exploded as he approached a dais to begin a campaign rally. He had served as prime minister between 1984 and 1989 after succeeding his mother, Indira Gandhi, who was assassinated in 1984.

SAKHAROV, ANDREI DMITRIYEVICH: 80th BIRTH ANNIVERSARY. May 21, 1921. Soviet physicist, human rights activist and environmentalist Andrei Sakharov was born at Moscow, Russia. A collaborator in producing the first Soviet atomic bomb, and later the hydrogen bomb, Sakharov later denounced shortcomings of his country's government and was exiled to Gorky, Russia, 1980–86. He was a formulator of the reform and restructuring concept known as *perestroika* and of *glasnost* (freedom). He was named to the Soviet Congress of Peoples Deputies eight months before his death at Moscow on Dec 14, 1989. As a physicist, he was the developer of destructive weapons; as a humanitarian, he was courageous as a dissident from militarism and an advocate of human rights and conservation.

SWITZERLAND: PACING THE BOUNDS. May 21. Liestal. Citizens set off at 8 AM and march along boundaries to the beating of drums and firing of pistols and muskets. Occasion for fetes. Annually, the Monday before Ascension Day.

BIRTHDAYS TODAY

Bobby Cox, 60, baseball manager and former executive and player, born Tulsa, OK, May 21, 1941.

Robert Creeley, 75, author, poet (*Have a Heart, Windows*), born Arlington, MA, May 21, 1926.

Janet Dailey, 57, romance novelist (*Tangled Vines*), born Storm Lake, IA, May 21, 1944.

Al Franken, 50, comedian, writer (*Rush Limbaugh Is a Big Fat Idiot and Other Observations*), actor ("Saturday Night Live"), born New York, NY, May 21, 1951.

Heinz Holliger, 62, oboist, composer, conductor, born Langenthal, Switzerland, May 21, 1939.

William "Spike" O'Dell, 48, Chicago radio personality, born Moline, IL, May 21, 1953.

Judge Reinhold, 44, actor (*Beverly Hills Cop*), born Wilmington, DE, May 21, 1957.

Leo Sayer, 53, singer ("You Make Me Feel Like Dancing"), songwriter, born Shoreham, England, May 21, 1948.

Mr T (Lawrence Tero or Tureaud), 49, actor (*Rocky III*, "The A-Team"), born Chicago, IL, May 21, 1952.

MAY 22 — TUESDAY

Day 142 — 223 Remaining

CANADA: IMMIGRANTS' DAY. May 22. A day to celebrate and recognize the contributions made by immigrants to Canada and to discuss the Canadian Immigration policy and experience. For info: Sergio R. Karas, BA, LLB, Barrister and Solicitor, Karas & Assoc, 1 First Canadian Place, 100 King St W, Ste 2640, Toronto, ON, Canada M5X 1E4. Phone: (416) 506-1800. Fax: (416) 599-5582. E-mail: karas@karas.ca. Web: www.karas.ca.

CASSATT, MARY: BIRTH ANNIVERSARY. May 22, 1844. Leading American artist of the Impressionist school, Mary Cassatt was born May 22, 1844 (some sources give 1845), at Allegheny City, PA (now part of Pittsburgh). She settled in Paris in 1874 where she was influenced by Degas and the Impressionists. She was later instrumental in their works becoming well known in the US. The majority of her paintings and pastels were based on the theme of mother and child. After 1900 her eyesight began to fail, and by 1914 she was no longer able to paint. Cassatt died at Chateau de Beaufresne near Paris, June 14, 1926.

CRATER LAKE NATIONAL PARK ESTABLISHED: ANNIVERSARY. May 22, 1902. One of the world's deepest lakes, Crater Lake was first discovered in 1853. In 1885 William Gladstone Steele saw the lake and made it his personal goal to establish the lake and surrounding areas as a national park. His goal was attained 17 years later.

DOYLE, SIR ARTHUR CONAN: BIRTH ANNIVERSARY. May 22, 1859. English physician Sir Arthur Conan Doyle is best remembered as a detective story writer, especially for the creation of Sherlock Holmes and Dr. Watson. Doyle was born at Edinburgh, Scotland. He was deeply interested in and lectured on the subject of spiritualism. Died at Crowborough, Sussex, England, July 7, 1930.

ENGLAND: CHELSEA FLOWER SHOW. May 22–25. Royal Hospital, Chelsea, London. Britain's major flower show with specially designed gardens and spectacular flower displays. Est attendance: 170,000. For info: Shows Dept, Royal Horticultural Soc, Vincent Sq, London, England SW1P 2PE. Phone: (44) (171) 630-7422 or 24-hour info line (44) (171) 649-1885. Fax: (44) (171) 233-9525.

	S	**M**	**T**	**W**	**T**	**F**	**S**
May			1	2	3	4	5
2001	6	7	8	9	10	11	12
	13	14	15	16	17	18	19
	20	21	22	23	24	25	26
	27	28	29	30	31		

"MISTER ROGERS' NEIGHBORHOOD" TV PREMIERE: ANNIVERSARY. May 22, 1967. Presbyterian minister Fred Rogers hosts this long-running PBS children's program. Puppets and human characters interact in the neighborhood of make-believe. Rogers plays the voices of many of the puppets and educates young viewers on a variety of important subjects. The human cast members included: Betty Aberlin, Joe Negri, David Newell, Don Brockett, Francois Clemmons, Robert Trow, Audrey Roth, Elsie Neal and Yoshi Ito.

MOON PHASE: NEW MOON. May 22. Moon enters New Moon phase at 10:46 PM, EDT.

NAIA MEN'S GOLF NATIONAL CHAMPIONSHIPS. May 22–25. Site to be determined. 50th annual. Est attendance: 500. For info: Natl Assn of Intercollegiate Athletics, 6120 S Yale Ave, Ste 1450, Tulsa, OK 74136. Phone: (918) 494-8828. Fax: (918) 494-8841. E-mail: kdee@naia.org. Web: www.naia.org.

NATIONAL GEOGRAPHY BEE: NATIONAL FINALS. May 22–23. National Geographic Society Headquarters, Washington, DC. The first place winner from each state-level competition Apr 7 advances to the national level. Alex Trebek of "Jeopardy!" fame moderates the finals which are televised on PBS stations. They compete for scholarships and prizes totaling more than $50,000. Est attendance: 400. For info: Natl Geographic Bee, Natl Geographic Soc, 1145 17th St NW, Washington, DC 20036. Phone: (202) 857-7001.

NATIONAL MARITIME DAY. May 22. Anniversary of departure for first steamship crossing of Atlantic from Savannah, GA, to Liverpool, England, by steamship *Savannah* in 1819.

★**NATIONAL MARITIME DAY.** May 22. Presidential Proclamation always issued for May 22 since 1933. (Pub Res No. 7 of May 20, 1933.)

NIXON FIRST AMERICAN PRESIDENT TO VISIT MOSCOW: ANNIVERSARY. May 22, 1972. President Richard Nixon became the first American president to visit Moscow. Four days later on May 26, Nixon and Soviet leader Leonid Brezhnev signed a treaty on antiballistic missile systems and an interim agreement on limitation of strategic missiles.

OLIVIER, LAURENCE: BIRTH ANNIVERSARY. May 22, 1907. Actor, director and theater manager, born at Dorking, England. Thought by many to be the most influential actor of this century, Olivier's theatrical and film career shaped the art forms in which he participated. Honored with nine Academy Award nominations, three Oscars and five Emmy awards, his repertoire included most of the prime Shakespearean roles and roles in such films as *Rebecca, Pride and Prejudice, Marathon Man* and *Wuthering Heights*. Olivier was an innovative theater manager with London's Old Vic company and the National Theatre of Great Britain. The National Theatre's largest auditorium and Britain's equivalent of Broadway's Tony awards carry his name. He was knighted in 1947 and made a peer of the throne in 1970. Olivier died at Ashurst, England, July 11, 1989.

RA, SUN: BIRTH ANNIVERSARY. May 22, 1914. Born Herman (Sonny) Blount, Sun Ra was a pioneering and innovative jazz musician whose avant garde performances mixed elements of theater with his surreal composition and performance style. Ra was born at Birmingham, AL, and died there May 30, 1993.

SRI LANKA: NATIONAL HEROES DAY. May 22. Commemorates the struggle of the leaders of the National Independence Movement to liberate the country from colonial rule. Public holiday.

"THERE WENT JOHNNY!" NIGHT: ANNIVERSARY. May 22, 1992. After almost 30 years as host of the "Tonight" show, Johnny Carson hosted his last show. Carson became host of the late-night talk show, which began as a local New York program hosted by Steve Allen, Oct 1, 1962. Over the years Carson occasionally made headlines with such extravaganzas as the marriage of Tiny Tim and Miss Vicki. Johnny received Emmys for his work four years in a row, 1976–79. Ed McMahon, his sidekick of

30 years, and Doc Severinsen, longtime bandleader, left the show with Carson. Jay Leno, the show's exclusive guest host, became the new regular host.

TRUMAN DOCTRINE: ANNIVERSARY. May 22, 1947. In order to contain Communism after World War II, the US furnished aid to Greece and Turkey. Congress approved the Truman Doctrine on this day. A corollary of this doctrine was the Marshall Plan, which began sending aid to war-torn European countries in 1948.

WAGNER, RICHARD: BIRTH ANNIVERSARY. May 22, 1813. German composer born at Leipzig who made revolutionary changes in the structure of opera. Best known for his Ring Cycle (*Der Ring des Nibelungen*). Died at Italy, Feb 13, 1883.

YEMEN: NATIONAL DAY: ANNIVERSARY. May 22. Public holiday. Commemorates the reunification of Yemen in 1990.

BIRTHDAYS TODAY

Charles Aznavour, 77, singer, songwriter, actor (*Shoot the Piano Player, Candy, The Tin Drum*), born Paris, France, May 22, 1924.

Richard Benjamin, 63, actor (*Goodbye Columbus, Diary of a Mad Housewife*, "He & She"), born New York, NY, May 22, 1938.

Naomi Campbell, 31, model, born London, England, May 22, 1970.

Frank Converse, 63, actor ("Movin' On," *Hurry Sundown*), born St. Louis, MO, May 22, 1938.

Judith Crist, 79, critic, born New York, NY, May 22, 1922.

Thomas Edward (Tommy) John, 58, former baseball player, born Terre Haute, IN, May 22, 1943.

A.J. Langer, 27, actress ("My So-Called Life," "Brooklyn South"), born Columbus, OH, May 22, 1974.

Barbara Parkins, 58, actress ("Peyton Place," *Valley of the Dolls*), born Vancouver, British Columbia, Canada, May 22, 1943.

Michael Sarrazin, 61, actor (*The Flim Flam Man, The Reincarnation of Peter Proud*), born Quebec City, Quebec, Canada, May 22, 1940.

Garry Wills, 67, author (*John Wayne's America, Lincoln at Gettysburg*), born Atlanta, GA, May 22, 1934.

Paul Winfield, 61, actor (*Sounder, Star Trek II: The Wrath of Khan, Presumed Innocent*), born Los Angeles, CA, May 22, 1940.

MAY 23 — WEDNESDAY
Day 143 — 222 Remaining

DECLARATION OF THE BAB. May 23. Baha'i commemoration of May 23, 1844, when the Bab, the prophet-herald of the Baha'i Faith, announced in Shiraz, Persia, that he was the herald of a new messenger of God. One of the nine days of the year when Baha'is suspend work. For info: Dir, Baha'is of the US, Office of Public Information, 866 UN Plaza, Ste 120, New York, NY 10017-1822. Phone: (212) 803-2500. Fax: (212) 803-2573. E-mail: usopi-ny@bic.org. Web: www.us.bahai.org.

FAIRBANKS, DOUGLAS ELTON: BIRTH ANNIVERSARY. May 23, 1883. Douglas Fairbanks was born at Denver, CO. He made his professional debut as an actor at Richmond, VA, Sept 10, 1900, in *The Duke's Jester*. His theatrical career turned to Hollywood, and he became a movie idol appearing in such films as *The Mark of Zorro, The Three Musketeers, Robin Hood, The Thief of Bagdad, The Black Pirate* and *The Gaucho*. He married "America's Sweetheart," Mary Pickford, in 1918, and in 1919 he joined with D.W. Griffith and Charlie Chaplin to form the production company United Artists. He died at Santa Monica, CA, Dec 12, 1939.

FULLER, MARGARET: BIRTH ANNIVERSARY. May 23, 1810. Journalist and author Sarah Margaret Fuller, born at Cambridgeport, MA, began reading Virgil at age six. Her conversational powers won her the admiration of students at Harvard University, and she was befriended by Ralph Waldo Emerson. She shared editorial duties with Emerson on the Transcendentalist quarterly *The Dial*, and was hired by Horace Greeley as literary

critic for the *New York Tribune*. Her book *Women in the Nineteenth Century*, the first feminist statement by an American writer, brought her international acclaim. In 1846, as a foreign correspondent for the *Tribune*, she became caught up in the Italian revolutionary movement and secretly married a young Roman nobleman, the Marquis Giovanni Angelo Ossoli. En route to the US, Fuller and her husband and child died July 19, 1850, when their ship was wrecked off Fire Island near New York, NY.

MANSFIELD, ARABELLA: BIRTH ANNIVERSARY. May 23, 1846. Arabella Mansfield, born Belle Aurelia Babb near Burlington, IA, was the first woman admitted to the legal profession in the US. In 1869 while teaching at Iowa Wesleyan College, Mansfield was certified as an attorney and admitted to the Iowa bar. According to the examiners, "she gave the very best rebuke possible to the imputation that ladies cannot qualify for the practice of law." Mansfield never did practice law, however, continuing her career as an educator. She joined the faculty of DePauw University, at Greencastle, IN, where she became dean of the schools of art and music. One of the first woman college professors and administrators in the US, Mansfield was also instrumental in the founding of the Iowa Woman Suffrage Society in 1870. She died Aug 2, 1911, at Aurora, IL.

MESMER, FRIEDRICH ANTON: BIRTH ANNIVERSARY. May 23, 1734. German physician after whom Mesmerism was named. Magnetism and hypnotism were used by him in treating disease. Born at Iznang, Swabia, Germany. Died Mar 5, 1815, at Meersburg, Swabia, Germany.

MOROCCO: NATIONAL DAY. May 23. National holiday. Commemorates referendum on the majority of the king in 1980.

NCAA DIVISION I WOMEN'S GOLF CHAMPIONSHIPS. May 23–26. Mission Inn, Howey-in-the-Hills, FL. For info: NCAA, 700 W Washington Ave, PO Box 6222, Indianapolis, IN 46206-6222. Phone: (317) 917-6222. Fax: (317) 917-6888. Web: www.ncaa.org.

NEW YORK PUBLIC LIBRARY: ANNIVERSARY. May 23, 1895. New York's then-governor Samuel J. Tilden was the driving force that resulted in the combining of the private Astor and Lenox libraries with a $2 million endowment and 15,000 volumes from the Tilden Trust to become the New York Public Library. The main branch of the library opened to the public on this day in 1911.

PAYNE, JOHN: BIRTH ANNIVERSARY. May 23, 1912. American actor John Payne was born at Roanoke, VA. He is best known as the idealistic lawyer who helps Santa Claus in *Miracle on 34th Street* (1947). He died Dec 6, 1989, at Malibu, CA.

SLOVO, JOE: 75th BIRTH ANNIVERSARY. May 23, 1926. South African Communist Party leader Joe Slovo was a longtime friend and ally of Nelson Mandela. The first white to become a member of the African National Congress Executive Committee, Slovo was one of the most prominent white men involved in South Africa's antiapartheid movement. He lived in exile from 1963 to 1990, serving as head of the military arm of the ANC during that period. Born at Obelai, Lithuania, he died Jan 6, 1995, at Johannesburg.

SOUTH CAROLINA CONSTITUTION RATIFICATION: ANNIVERSARY. May 23, 1788. By a vote of 149 to 73, South Carolina became the eighth state to ratify the Constitution.

SUPREME COURT UPHOLDS BAN ON ABORTION COUNSELING: 10th ANNIVERSARY. May 23, 1991. In the case *Rust v Sullivan*, the Supreme Court, in a 5–4 ruling, upheld federal regulations that barred federally funded family planning clinics from providing any information about abortion.

SWEDEN: LINNAEUS DAY. May 23. Stenbrohult. Commemorates birth of Carolus Linnaeus (Carl von Linne), Swedish naturalist, born May 23, 1707 (OS) and who died at Uppsala, Sweden, Jan 10, 1778.

WEST VIRGINIA STRAWBERRY FESTIVAL. May 23–27. Buckhannon, WV. A family event with activities including 3 parades, carnival, strawberry auctions, band competitions, Party Gras, Concert, and special entertainment for all. Est attendance: 100,000. For info: Pres, WV Strawberry Festival, PO Box 117, Buckhannon, WV 26201. Phone: (304) 472-9036. E-mail: lively _a@wvwc.edu.

WILLIAM CARNEY RECEIVES CONGRESSIONAL MEDAL OF HONOR: ANNIVERSARY. May 23, 1900. Sergeant William H. Carney, of the 54th Massachusetts Colored Infantry, was the first black to win the Congressional Medal of Honor. He was cited for his efforts, although wounded twice, during the Battle of Fort Wagner, SC, June 18, 1863.

WORLD TURTLE DAY. May 23. An observance sponsored by American Tortoise Rescue to help people celebrate and protect turtles and tortoises, as well as their habitat around the world. For info: Susan Tellem, American Tortoise Rescue, 23852 Pacific Coast Highway, Malibu, CA 90265. Phone: (310) 589-6101. E-mail: turtleresq@aol.com. Web: www.tortoise.com.

BIRTHDAYS TODAY

Barbara Barrie, 70, actress ("Suddenly Susan," *One Potato, Two Potato; Breaking Away*), born Chicago, IL, May 23, 1931.
Drew Carey, 40, actor ("The Drew Carey Show"), born Cleveland, OH, May 23, 1961.
Rosemary Clooney, 73, singer ("The Rosemary Clooney Show"), actress (*White Christmas*), born Maysville, KY, May 23, 1928.

	S	M	T	W	T	F	S
May			1	2	3	4	5
2001	6	7	8	9	10	11	12
	13	14	15	16	17	18	19
	20	21	22	23	24	25	26
	27	28	29	30	31		

Joan Collins, 68, actress ("Dynasty"), born London, England, May 23, 1933.
Marvelous Marvin Hagler, 47, former boxer, born Newark, NJ, May 23, 1954.
Jewel, 27, singer, born Jewel Kilcher, Payson, UT, May 23, 1974.
Charles Kimbrough, 65, actor ("Murphy Brown"), born St. Paul, MN, May 23, 1936.
Robert Moog, 67, inventor of first commercially viable keyboard synthesizer, born Flushing, NY, May 23, 1934.
Artie Shaw, 91, musician, bandleader, born New York, NY, May 23, 1910.

MAY 24 — THURSDAY
Day 144 — 221 Remaining

ANTI-SALOON LEAGUE FOUNDED: ANNIVERSARY. May 24, 1893. Anti-Saloon League was founded by Howard H. Russell at Oberlin, OH. Efforts in that state were so successful the Anti-Saloon League of America was organized in 1895. The League's permanent home became Otterbein College at Westerville, OH, in 1909.

ASCENSION DAY. May 24. Commemorates Christ's ascension into heaven. Observed since AD 68. Ascension Day is the 40th day after the Resurrection, counting Easter as the first day.

BASEBALL FIRST PLAYED UNDER LIGHTS: ANNIVERSARY. May 24, 1935. The Cincinnati Reds defeated the Philadelphia Phillies by a score of 2–1, as more than 20,000 fans enjoyed the first night baseball game in the major leagues. The game was played at Crosley Field, Cincinnati, OH.

BELGIUM: PROCESSION OF THE HOLY BLOOD. May 24. Religious historical procession. Recalls adventurous crusaders, including Count Thierry of Alsace, who carried back relics of the Holy Blood. Always on Ascension Day.

BELIZE: COMMONWEALTH DAY. May 24. Public holiday.

BROOKLYN BRIDGE OPENED: ANNIVERSARY. May 24, 1883. Nearly 14 years in construction, the $16 million Brooklyn Bridge over the East River opened. Designed by John A. Roebling, the steel suspension bridge has a span of 1,595 feet.

BULGARIA: CULTURE DAY. May 24. National holiday festively celebrated by schoolchildren, students, people of science and art.

ERITREA: INDEPENDENCE DAY. May 24. National Day. Gained independence from Ethiopia in 1993 after 30-year civil war.

HERRINFESTA ITALIANA. May 24–28. Herrin Civic Center, Herrin, IL. Authentic Italian food, name Italian and American entertainers, bocce tournament, Midwest Pasta Sauce Contest, grape stomp, hot-air balloon races and more. Est attendance: 55,000. For info: Herrinfesta Italiana, PO Box 2005, Herrin, IL 62948. Phone: (800) ITF-ESTA. Web: www.herrinfesta.com.

KODIAK CRAB FESTIVAL. May 24–28. Kodiak, AK. A celebration of spring and the Emerald Isle. Featured are parades, carnival booths and midway, running events, a golf tournament, bicycle and survival suit races, a blessing of the fleet ceremony and memorial services. Annually, Memorial Day weekend. Est attendance: 15,000. For info: Kodiak Chamber of Commerce, Box 1485, Kodiak, AK 99615. Phone: (907) 486-5557. Fax: (907) 486-7605. E-mail: chamber@kodiak.org and eric@kodiak.org. Web: www.kodiak.org.

LEUTZE, EMANUEL: BIRTH ANNIVERSARY. May 24, 1816. Obscure itinerant painter, born at Wurttemberg, Germany, came to the US when he was nine years old, began painting by age 15. Painted some of the most famous of American works, such as *Washington Crossing the Delaware, Washington Rallying the Troops at Monmouth* and *Columbus Before the Queen*. Died July 18, 1868, at Washington, DC.

MANNOCK, "MICK" EDWARD: BIRTH ANNIVERSARY. May 24, 1887. Edward Mannock, British flying ace credited with 73 hits during World War I, was born at Preston Cavalry Barracks, Brighton, England. Mannock most likely would not have been considered eligible to fly due to an astigmatism in one eye, but probably memorized the chart prior to having his eyesight tested. Mannock died during a flight on July 26, 1918.

MORSE OPENS FIRST US TELEGRAPH LINE: ANNIVERSARY. May 24, 1844. The first US telegraph line was formally opened between Baltimore, MD, and Washington, DC. Samuel F.B. Morse sent the first officially telegraphed words "What hath God wrought?" from the Capitol building to Baltimore. Earlier messages had been sent along the historic line during testing, and one, sent May 1, contained the news that Henry Clay had been nominated as president by the Whig party, from a meeting in Baltimore. This message reached Washington one hour prior to a train carrying the same news.

MUDBUG MADNESS. May 24–27. Riverfront, Shreveport, LA. The state's delectable crustacean, the crawfish, and Cajun heritage are celebrated during this four-day festival. Est attendance: 200,000. For info: DSU, PO Box 235, Shreveport, LA 71162. Phone: (318) 222-7403.

NAIA MEN'S AND WOMEN'S OUTDOOR TRACK AND FIELD NATIONAL CHAMPIONSHIPS. May 24–26. Abbottsford, BC, Canada. 50th annual men's and 21st annual women's competition. Est attendance: 2,500. For info: Natl Assn of Intercollegiate Athletics, 6120 S Yale Ave, Ste 1450, Tulsa, OK 74136. Phone: (918) 494-8828. Fax: (918) 494-8841. E-mail: thasseltine@naia.org. Web: www.naia.org.

NCAA DIVISION I WOMEN'S SOFTBALL CHAMPIONSHIP. May 24–28. Oklahoma City, OK. For info: Natl Collegiate Athletic Assn, 700 W Washington Ave, PO Box 6222, Indianapolis, IN 46206-6222. Phone: (317) 917-6222. Fax: (317) 917-6888. Web: www.ncaa.org.

NCAA WOMEN'S COLLEGE WORLD SERIES. May 24–28. ASA Hall of Fame Stadium, Oklahoma City, OK. 20th annual championship for women's fast pitch featuring the nation's eight best universities in softball. Est attendance: 32,000. For info: Oklahoma City All Sports Assn, 100 W Main, Ste 287, Oklahoma City, OK 73102. Phone: (405) 236-5000. Fax: (405) 236-5008. E-mail: info@okcallsports.org. Web: www.okcallsports.org.

NEWHOUSE, SAMUEL I.: BIRTH ANNIVERSARY. May 24, 1895. Multimillionaire businessman who built family publishing and communications empire. Born to immigrant parents in a New York City tenement, Newhouse became "America's most profitable publisher." He accumulated 31 newspapers, seven magazines, six television stations, five radio stations and 20 cable television systems. He died at New York, NY, Aug 29, 1979.

ORTHODOX ASCENSION DAY. May 24. Observed by Eastern Orthodox Churches.

PALMER, LILLI: BIRTH ANNIVERSARY. May 24, 1914. Stage, screen and television actress Lilli Palmer was born Lillie Marie Peiser, at Poznan, Poland. She also painted and was the author of several novels and an autobiography titled *Change Lobsters—And Dance.* She died at Los Angeles, CA, Jan 27, 1986.

PEALE, JAMES: DEATH ANNIVERSARY. May 24, 1831. American portrait and miniature painter (painted portraits of George and Martha Washington and General Sir Thomas Shirley) was born at Chestertown, MD, in 1749 (exact date unknown). Died at Philadelphia, PA.

PGA SENIORS' CHAMPIONSHIP. May 24–27. Ridgewood Country Club, Paramus, NJ. 61st competition for the oldest major championship in senior golf. Conducted by the Professional Golfers' Association of America. For info: Jamie Roggero, Program Mgr, PGA, Box 109601, Palm Beach Gardens, FL 33410-9601. Phone: (561) 624-8400. Fax: (561) 624-8448. Web: www.pgaonline.com.

RABI' I: THE MONTH OF THE MIGRATION. May 24. Begins on Islamic calendar date Rabi' I 1, 1422. The third month of the Islamic calendar, the month of the migration of the Prophet Muhammad from Mecca to Medina in AD 622, the event that was used as the starting year of the Islamic lunar calendar. Different methods for "anticipating" the visibility of the new moon crescent at Mecca are used by different Muslim groups. US date may vary.

SIGHTS & SOUNDS WINE DOWN. May 24–Aug 30 (Thursday only). Historic Larimer Square, Denver, CO. Live jazz and casual art markets, three street closures with modern and performance art, Colorado wine and fine dining. Est attendance: 15,000. For info: Historic Larimer Square. Phone: (303) 534-2367. Fax: (303) 623-1041. Web: www.larimersquare.com.

SPACE MILESTONE: *AURORA 7* MERCURY SPACE CAPSULE (US). May 24, 1962. With this launch Scott Carpenter became second American to orbit Earth, circling it three times.

***VICTORIA* BOAT DISASTER: ANNIVERSARY.** May 24, 1881. One of Canada's worst marine disasters occurred on the Thames River (near London, Ontario). "The *Victoria,* a small, double-decked stern-wheeler, was conducting holiday excursion trips between London and Springbank Park. On a return trip to London the boat was dangerously overcrowded with more than 600 passengers. The crowd shifted from side to side, resulting in a precarious rocking motion of the boat. It finally keeled over and the boiler crashed through the bulwarks, bringing the upper deck and large awning down upon the struggling crowd. The *Victoria* sank immediately, and at least 182 people lost their lives.

BIRTHDAYS TODAY

Gary Burghoff, 58, actor (Emmy for "M*A*S*H"), born Bristol, CT, May 24, 1943.

Roger Caras, 73, nature writer, born Methuen, MA, May 24, 1928.

Tommy Chong, 63, actor (*Up in Smoke, The Corsican Brothers* [also wrote screenplay and directed]), born Edmonton, Alberta, Canada, May 24, 1938.

Joe Dumars III, 38, former basketball player, born Shreveport, LA, May 24, 1963.

Bob Dylan (Robert Zimmerman), 60, composer, singer, born Duluth, MN, May 24, 1941.

Patti LaBelle (Patricia Louise Holte), 57, singer ("Since I Don't Have You"), born Philadelphia, PA, May 24, 1944.

Alfred Molina, 48, actor (*Raiders of the Lost Ark, Letter to Brezhnev*), born London, England, May 24, 1953.

Frank Oz, 57, puppeteer, born Hereford, England, May 24, 1944.

Priscilla Beaulieu Presley, 56, actress ("Dallas," *Naked Gun* movies), ex-wife of Elvis, born Brooklyn, NY, May 24, 1945.

John Rowland, 44, Governor of Connecticut (R), born Waterbury, CT, May 24, 1957.

Kristin Scott Thomas, 41, actress (*The English Patient, The Horse Whisperer*), born Cornwall, England, May 24, 1960.

MAY 25 — FRIDAY
Day 145 — 220 Remaining

AFRICAN FREEDOM DAY: ANNIVERSARY. May 25. Public holiday in Chad, Zambia and some other African states. Members of the Organization for African Unity (formed May 25, 1963) commemorate their independence from colonial rule. Sports contests, political rallies and tribal dances.

ALMA HIGHLAND FESTIVAL AND GAMES. May 25–27. Alma College, Alma, MI. Old-world pageantry honoring Scottish traditions—Highland dancing, piping, drumming, athletic competitions, clan tents and grand parade. 34th annual festival. Annually, Memorial Day weekend. Est attendance: 60,000. For info: Alma Highland Festival, 110 W Superior St, PO Box 516, Alma, MI 48801. Phone: (517) 463-8979. E-mail: highland@mach7.com. Web: www.almahighlandfestival.com.

AMERICAN FLIGHT CRASHES AT O'HARE: ANNIVERSARY. May 25, 1979. An American Airlines DC-10 lost an engine upon takeoff and crashed seconds later, killing all 272 aboard and three people on the ground. This is the worst US air disaster in history.

ARGENTINA: REVOLUTION DAY. May 25. Commemoration of revolt against Spanish rule in 1810.

ARTHUR FIRST PUBLISHED: 25th ANNIVERSARY. May 25, 1976. Celebrate the 25th anniversary of Arthur—the star of one of the most successful children's books series and the Emmy Award-winning television show. Created by children's author and illustrator Marc Brown, the Arthur series of 75 books has sold more than 30 million copies. The Children's Museum of Manhattan will host the Arthur's World Exhibit from May–September 2001. Teachers, librarians and parents are invited to join in the festivities by creating their own birthday bash featuring lots of fun reading and writing-related activities. For ideas and materials: Web: www.pbskids.org/arthur.

BROOKINGS-HARBOR AZALEA FESTIVAL. May 25–28. Brookings, OR. Parade, street fair, art shows, seafood, 10K run, Bonsai exhibit, regional quilt show, crafts fair, Coast Guard demonstration, live music. 62nd festival. Annually, Memorial Day weekend. Est attendance: 12,000. For info: Brookings-Harbor Chamber of Commerce, PO Box 940, Brookings, OR 97415. Phone: (800) 535-9469. Fax: (541) 469-4094. E-mail: chamber@wave.net.

CANADA: GUELPH SPRING FESTIVAL. May 25–June 3. Guelph, ON. Classical music, theatre, dance, opera and jazz with celebrated performers. Est attendance: 21,000. For info: Guelph Spring Festival, Box 1718, Guelph, ON, Canada N1H 6Z9. Phone: (519) 821-3210. Fax: (519) 821-4403. E-mail: gsf@freespace.net. Web: www.freespace.net/~gsf.

CARVER, RAYMOND: BIRTH ANNIVERSARY. May 25, 1938. American poet and short story writer who chronicled the lives of America's working poor. Born at Clatskanie, OR, he died Aug 2, 1988, at his home at Port Angeles, WA, soon after finishing a book of poetry titled *A New Path to the Waterfall*.

CONSTITUTIONAL CONVENTION: ANNIVERSARY. May 25, 1787. At Philadelphia, PA, delegates from seven states, forming a quorum, opened the Constitutional Convention, which had been proposed by the Annapolis Convention Sept 11–14, 1786. Among those who were in attendance: George Washington, Benjamin Franklin, James Madison, Alexander Hamilton and Elbridge Gerry. See also: "Annapolis Convention: Anniversary" (Sept 11).

DAVIS, MILES: 75th BIRTH ANNIVERSARY. May 25, 1926. Jazz trumpeter Miles Davis was born at Alton, IL. He was influenced by the be-bop music style of Charlie Parker and Dizzy Gillespie and ended up leaving the Juilliard School of Music to join Parker's quintet in 1945 at the age of 19. He experimented with different styles throughout his career, exploring new voicings in jazz with arranger Gil Evans and musicians John Coltrane and Red Garland, delving into "modal" music with Tony Williams and Wayne Shorter and moving into a fusion sound in the '60s. His career was beset with bouts of drug addiction, but in the 1970s his return to the music scene found him creating a sound that melded his be-bop origins, modal chord progressions and driving rock rhythms. He died Sept 28, 1991, at Santa Monica, CA.

May 2001	S	M	T	W	T	F	S
			1	2	3	4	5
	6	7	8	9	10	11	12
	13	14	15	16	17	18	19
	20	21	22	23	24	25	26
	27	28	29	30	31		

DOWIE, JOHN ALEXANDER: BIRTH ANNIVERSARY. May 25, 1847. Evangelist and claimant of the title "Elijah the Restorer" was born at Edinburgh, Scotland. He established the Christian Catholic Church at Zion, IL, where some 5,000 followers created a unique community without pharmacies, physicians, theaters or dance halls and where smoking, drinking and the eating of pork were prohibited. Dowie's ostentatiously expensive personal lifestyle and his unsuccessful attempt to convert New York City were partially responsible for the falling away of his followers. He was expelled from the church in 1906 and died at Chicago, IL, Mar 9, 1907.

EMERSON, RALPH WALDO: BIRTH ANNIVERSARY. May 25, 1803. American author and philosopher born at Boston, MA, and died there Apr 27, 1882. It was Emerson who wrote (in his essay "Self-Reliance," 1841), "A foolish consistency is the hobgoblin of little minds, adored by little statesmen and philosophers and divines. With consistency a great soul has simply nothing to do."

ENGLAND: ENGLISH RIVIERA DANCE FESTIVAL. May 25–June 9. Torquay, Devon. Demonstrations by world champions and participatory events including Modern, Ballroom, Disco and Latin American dance styles. Est attendance: 2,000. For info: Philip Wylie, Ickenham, 73 Hoylake Crescent, Middlesex, England UB10 8JQ. Phone: (44) (189) 563-2143. Fax: (44) (189) 563-8015.

FARMINGTON INVITATIONAL BALLOON FESTIVAL. May 25–27. Farmington, NM. Hot-air balloons launch off the banks of Farmington Lake. Famous Splash and Dash and Hare and Hound races included in the two-day event. Est attendance: 2,000. For info: Farmington Conv and Visitors Bureau, 3041 E Main St, Farmington, NM 87402. Phone: (800) 448-1240 or (505) 326-7602. Fax: (505) 327-0577. E-mail: fmncvb@cyberport.com. Web: www.farmingtonnm.org.

FLORIDA FOLK FESTIVAL. May 25–27. Stephen Foster State Folk Culture Center, White Springs, FL. To celebrate Florida's folk heritage with music, song, dance and stories. Est attendance: 30,000. For info: Florida Dept of State, Div of Historical Resources, 500 S Bronough St, Tallahassee, FL 32399-0250. Phone: (850) 488-1484. Fax: (850) 921-2503.

GETTYSBURG SQUARE DANCE ROUND-UP. May 25–26. Gettysburg, PA. Annual event held at Gettysburg College with nationally known callers. For info: Gettysburg CVB, PO Box 4117, Gettysburg, PA 17325. Phone: (717) 334-6274. Fax: (717) 334-1166. Web: www.gettysburg.com.

GRUBSTAKE DAYS. May 25–28. Yucca Valley, CA. Includes parade, Monster Truck racing, Quad and Tough Truck racing, gold panning demonstration, carnival, dances, horseshoe tournament, food and community booths, arts and craft booths and breakfasts offered by local service organizations. Annually, Memorial Day weekend. Est attendance: 20,000. For info: Yucca Valley Chamber of Commerce, 55569 29 Palms Hwy, Yucca Valley, CA 92284. Phone: (760) 365-6323. Fax: (760) 365-0763. E-mail: chamber@yuccavalley.org. Web: www.yuccavalley.org.

GUTHRIE JAZZ BANJO FESTIVAL. May 25–27. Downtown Guthrie, OK. Jazz banjo bands and soloists from all over the US perform music from the gay '90s, as well as the roaring '20s and contemporary selections at various venues around historic Guthrie. Also antique autos on parade. Annually, on Memorial Day weekend. Sponsor: Mr Brady Hunt/Guthrie CVB. Est attendance: 10,000. For info: Chamber of Commerce, Guthrie Conv & Visitors Bureau, PO Box 995, Guthrie, OK 73044. Phone: (405) 282-1948 or (800) 299-1889 or (800) OK-BANJO. Fax: (405) 282-0061.

JORDAN: INDEPENDENCE DAY: 55th ANNIVERSARY. May 25. National holiday. Commemorates treaty in 1946, proclaiming independence from Britain and establishing monarchy.

MEMORIAL DAY BURLINGTON BLUEGRASS FESTIVAL. May 25–27. Burlington, IA. Annually, Memorial Day Weekend. Est attendance: 3,000. For info: Delbert Spray, RR1, Kahoka, MO 63445. Phone: (573) 853-4344.

MEMORIAL WEEKEND GETAWAY. May 25–28. Live Oak, FL. A great family weekend filled with activities. Est attendance: 3,000. For info: James Cornett, Spirit of the Suwannee Music Park, 3076 95th Dr, Live Oak, FL 32060. Phone: (904) 364-1683. Fax: (904) 364-2998. E-mail: spirit@musicliveshere.com. Web: www.musicliveshere.com.

MEMORIAL WEEKEND SALMON DERBY. May 25–28. Petersburg, AK. Four days of fishing with more than $30,000 in prizes awarded! Est attendance: 700. For info: Petersburg Visitors Information Center, PO Box 649, Petersburg, AK 99833. Phone: (907) 772-4636. Fax: (907) 772-3646. Web: www.petersburg.org.

MORNING RADIO WISE GUY DAY. May 25. To honor all morning radio disc jockeys who get your day started with humor, music and information. Annually, last Friday in May. For info: Rob and Mark, 98 KISC FM, 300 E Third, Spokane, WA 99202. Phone: (509) 459-9800. Fax: (509) 624-5957. E-mail: mholman@omnicast.net. Web: www.literockkiss.com.

MURRAY, PHILIP: BIRTH ANNIVERSARY. May 25, 1886. American labor leader and founder of the Congress of Industrial Organizations, also active in and a leader of the United Mine Workers, was born near Blantyre, Scotland. Murray died at San Francisco, CA, Nov 9, 1952.

NAIA BASEBALL WORLD SERIES. May 25–June 1. Lewiston, ID. 45th annual competition. Est attendance: 20,000. For info: Natl Assn of Intercollegiate Athletics, 6120 S Yale Ave, Ste 1450, Tulsa, OK 74136. Phone: (918) 494-8828. Fax: (918) 494-8841. E-mail: mchiarucci@naia.org. Web: www.naia.org.

NATIONAL MISSING CHILDREN'S DAY. May 25. To promote awareness of the problem of missing children, to offer a forum for change and to offer safety information for children in school and community. Annually, May 25. For info: Child Find of America, Inc, PO Box 277, New Paltz, NY 12561-0277. Phone: (914) 255-1848. Natl toll-free hotline phone numbers: (800) I-AM-LOST or (800) A-WAY-OUT.

NATIONAL TAP DANCE DAY. May 25. To celebrate this unique American art form that represents a fusion of African and European cultures and to transmit tap to succeeding generations through documentation and archival and performance support. Held on the anniversary of the birth of Bill "Bojangles" Robinson to honor his outstanding contribution to the art of tap dancing on stage and in films through the unification of diverse stylistic and racial elements.

NORTHWEST FOLKLIFE FESTIVAL. May 25–28. Seattle Center, Seattle, WA. Ethnic and traditional arts event celebrating world cultures in the Northwest Region. Includes music, dance, food, crafts, visual arts exhibits, children's programs, demonstrations, films and more. More than 6,000 performers. Annually, Friday–Monday of Memorial Day weekend. Est attendance: 225,000. For info: Northwest Folklife Fest, 305 Harrison St, Seattle, WA 98109-4645. Phone: (206) 684-7300. Fax: (206) 684-7190. E-mail: folklife@nwfolklife.org. Web: www.nwfolklife.org/folklife/

POETRY DAY IN FLORIDA. May 25. In 1947 the Legislature decreed this day to be "Poetry Day in all of the public schools of Florida."

RIVERFEST. May 25–27. Riverfront Park, Little Rock, AR. 24th annual outdoor festival of the visual and performing arts with 100 acts on six stages, food vendors, visual artists, kid stuff. Est attendance: 200,000. For info: Van Tilbury, PO Box 3232, Little Rock, AR 72203. Phone: (501) 255-FEST. Fax: (501) 255-3379. E-mail: info@riverfestarkansas.com. Web: www.riverfestarkansas.com.

ROANOKE FESTIVAL IN THE PARK. May 25–June 3. Roanoke, VA. 32nd annual celebration of life and the arts. Three-day juried fine art and craft show, children's activities, children's theatre, parade, river boat races, USCF bike races, USSSA softball tournament, youth art show, eclectic market, Senior Citizen Day, tennis tournament, 5K and 10K races, concerts, product and service area. Est attendance: 375,000. For info: Wendi Schultz, CFE Dir, Roanoke Festival in the Park, PO Box 8276, Roanoke, VA 24014. Phone: (540) 342-2640.

ROBINSON, BILL "BOJANGLES": BIRTH ANNIVERSARY. May 25, 1878. Born at Richmond, VA, the grandson of a slave, Robinson is considered one of the greatest tap dancers. He is best known for a routine in which he tap-danced up and down a staircase. He appeared in several films with Shirley Temple and taught Gene Kelly, Sammy Davis, Jr, Gregory Hines, and others. Died at New York City, Nov 25, 1949.

SACRAMENTO JAZZ JUBILEE. May 25–28. Sacramento, CA. More than 100 bands from the US, Canada and foreign countries perform American traditional jazz music in approximately 40 venues around Sacramento at the world's largest traditional jazz festival. Est attendance: 100,000. For info: Roger Krum, Exec Dir, Sacramento Traditional Jazz Society, 2787 Del Monte Blvd, Sacramento, CA 95691. Phone: (916) 372-5277. Fax: (916) 372-3429. E-mail: stjs@earthlink.net. Web: www.sacjazz.com.

SIKORSKY, IGOR: BIRTH ANNIVERSARY. May 25, 1889. Aeronautical engineer best remembered for his development of the first successful helicopter in 1939. Also pioneered in multi-engine airplanes and large flying boats that made transoceanic air transportation possible. Born at Kiev, Russia, and died Oct 26, 1972, at Easton, CT.

SOLZHENITSYN GOES HOME: ANNIVERSARY. May 25, 1994. After 20 years living in exile, mostly in the US, Russian author Alexander Solzhenitsyn returned to his homeland. The author had been expelled from the Soviet Union in 1974 after his three-volume work exposing the Soviet prison camp system, *The Gulag Archipelago*, was published in the West. After the collapse of the Soviet Union late in 1991, he announced his intention to go back.

SPACE MILESTONE: *SKYLAB 2* (US). May 25, 1973. Joseph P. Kerwin, Paul J. Weitz and Charles (Pete) Conrad, Jr, spent 28 days in experimentation on this space station which had been launched May 14. Pacific splashdown occurred June 22. Launched May 25, 1973.

SPOLETO FESTIVAL USA. May 25–June 10. Charleston, SC. Comprehensive arts festival with a mix of more than 100 performances of opera, dance, theater, chamber and symphonic music, jazz, literary and visual arts set in one of America's most beautiful and historic cities. For info: Spoleto Festival USA, PO Box 157, Charleston, SC 29402. Phone: (843) 722-2764. Web: www.spoletousa.org.

STAMP EXPO. May 25–27. Pasadena Convention Center, Pasadena, CA. Annual expo. Est attendance: 5,000. For info: Intl Stamp Collectors Society, Box 854, Van Nuys, CA 91408. Phone: (818) 997-6496. Fax: (818) 988-4337. E-mail: iibick@aol.com. Web: www.bick.net.

SUMMER CELEBRATION. May 25–27. Florence, AL. Four days filled with sporting events for the entire family. All events focus on summer fun and safety and include tennis, golf, frisbee golf tournament, 5K run, century bike ride, mountain bike race, waverunner races, BBQ cook-off and Veteran's Memorial Celebration complete with a fireworks show. Est attendance: 10,000. For info: Debbie Wilson, Florence/Lauderdale Tourism, One Hightower Place, Florence, AL 35630. Phone: (256) 740-4141 or (888) FLO-TOUR. Fax: (256) 740-4142. E-mail: dwilson@floweb.com. Web: www.flo-tour.org.

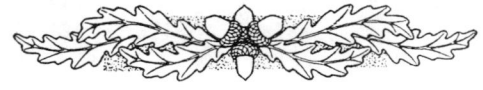

TITO (JOSIP BROZ): BIRTH ANNIVERSARY. May 25, 1892. Josip Broz, Yugoslavian soldier and political leader, born near Zagreb, Yugoslavia. Died May 4, 1980, at Ljubljana, Yugoslavia (now Slovenia), and was interred in the garden of his home at Belgrade. Tito, a Croat, had managed to keep the many nationalities and religions that made up Yugoslavia in one state but in the early 1990s the nation broke up as Croats, Serbs and others went to war against each other.

TUNNEY, JAMES JOSEPH (GENE): BIRTH ANNIVERSARY. May 25, 1898. Heavyweight boxing champion, business executive. The famous "long count" occurred in the seventh round of the Jack Dempsey–Gene Tunney world championship fight, Sept 22, 1927, at Soldier Field, Chicago, IL. Tunney was born at New York, NY, and died at Greenwich, CT, Nov 7, 1978.

UNITED NATIONS: WEEK OF SOLIDARITY WITH THE PEOPLE OF NON-SELF-GOVERNING TERRITORIES. May 25–31. On Dec 6, 1999 (res 54/91) the General Assembly requested the Special Committee on Decolonization to observe this week beginning on May 25, Africa Liberation Day. For info: United Nations, Dept of Public Info, New York, NY 10017. Web: www.un.org.

VEGASPEX. May 25–27 (also Dec 14–16). Anaheim, CA. Coin, stamp, antique watch, jewelry and collectibles expo. Est attendance: 10,000. For info: Intl Coin & Stamp Collectors Soc, PO Box 854, Van Nuys, CA 91408. Phone: (818) 997-6496. Fax: (818) 988-4337. E-mail: iibick@aol.com. Web: www.bick.net.

WALES: HAY-ON-WYE FESTIVAL OF LITERATURE. May 25–June 3. Hay-on-Wye, Powys. Largest annual festival of literature takes place in the beautiful market town of Hay-on-Wye in the Black Mountains of the Welsh Marches. Est attendance: 30,000. For info: The Hay Festival, Hay-on-Wye, Wales, UK HR3 5BX. Phone: (44) (149) 782-1299. Fax: (44) (149) 782-1066. E-mail: boxoffice@litfest.co.uk.

WORLD CHAMPIONSHIP OLD-TIME PIANO PLAYING CONTEST. May 25–28. Holiday Inn, Decatur, IL. Competition and festival of ragtime, honky-tonk and old-time music. Annually, Memorial Day weekend. Sponsor: Old-Time Music Preservation Association (OMPA) Inc. Est attendance: 1,000. For info: Judy Leschewski, PO Box 4714, Decatur, IL 62525. Phone: (217) 428-2403. Web: www.pianoctest.com.

BIRTHDAYS TODAY

Dixie Carter, 62, actress ("Designing Women"), born McLemoresville, TN, May 25, 1939.
Jessi Colter (Miriam Johnson), 54, singer, songwriter, born Phoenix, AZ, May 25, 1947.
Tom T. Hall, 65, singer ("P.S. I Love You"), songwriter ("Harper Valley PTA"), born Olive Hill, KY, May 25, 1936.
Anne Heche, 32, actress (*Volcano; Six Days, Seven Nights*), born Aurora, OH, May 25, 1969.
Justin Henry, 30, actor (*Kramer v Kramer, Sixteen Candles*), born Rye, NY, May 25, 1971.
Lauryn Hill, 26, singer, actress (*Sister Act 2*), born South Orange, NJ, May 25, 1975.
K.C. Jones, 69, former basketball coach and player, Basketball Hall of Famer, born Tyler, TX, May 25, 1932.
Robert Ludlum, 74, author (*The Aquitaine Progression, The Parsifal Mosaic*), born New York, NY, May 25, 1927.
Sir Ian McKellen, 62, actor (stage: *Amadeus* [Tony Award]; *Last Action Hero, Six Degrees of Separation*), born Burnley, England, May 25, 1939.

	S	M	T	W	T	F	S
May			1	2	3	4	5
2001	6	7	8	9	10	11	12
	13	14	15	16	17	18	19
	20	21	22	23	24	25	26
	27	28	29	30	31		

Mike Myers, 38, comedian, actor ("Saturday Night Live," *Wayne's World, Austin Powers: International Man of Mystery*), born Scarsborough, Ontario, Canada, May 25, 1963.
Connie Sellecca, 46, actress ("Hotel," *While My Pretty One Sleeps*), born The Bronx, NY, May 25, 1955.
Beverly Sills, 72, opera singer (retired), born Brooklyn, NY, May 25, 1929.
Gordon Smith, 49, US Senator (R, Oregon), born Pendleton, OR, May 25, 1952.
Leslie Uggams, 58, singer ("Sing Along with Mitch"), actress, born New York, NY, May 25, 1943.
Karen Valentine, 54, actress ("Room 222"), born Sebastopol, CA, May 25, 1947.

MAY 26 — SATURDAY
Day 146 — 219 Remaining

ALABAMA JUBILEE. May 26–28. Point Mallard, Decatur, AL. Hot-air balloon races, arts, crafts, antique cars, water and air shows. Annually, Memorial Day weekend. Est attendance: 100,000. For info: Jacklyn Bailey, Decatur Conv and Visitors Bureau, Box 2349, 719 6th Ave SE, Decatur, AL 35602. Phone: (256) 350-2028 or (800) 524-6181. E-mail: dcvb@hiwaay.net.

CATFISH DERBY. May 26–28. Huntington, OR. Annually, Memorial Day weekend. Est attendance: 400. For info: Baker County CVB, 490 Campbell St, Baker City, OR 97814. Phone: (800) 523-1235.

CHESTERTOWN TEA PARTY FESTIVAL. May 26–27. Chestertown, MD. Reenactment of 1774 tea dumping, crafts, music, food and games, 10 mile and 5K runs. Est attendance: 15,000. For info: Chestertown Tea Party Festival, Inc, Box 526, Chestertown, MD 21620. Phone: (410) 778-0416. Web: www.kentcounty.com.

CIVIL WAR WEEKEND. May 26–28. Yorktown Battlefield, Yorktown, VA. 100 reenactors present a recreated Civil War encampment, Confederate field hospital and military drills performed on the battlefield in Colonial National Historical Park. Est attendance: 3,000. For info: Public Affairs Officer, Colonial Natl Historical Park, PO Box 210, Yorktown, VA 23690. Phone: (757) 898-2410. Web: www.nps.gov/colo.

COLONIAL MICHILIMACKINAC HISTORICAL REENACTMENT PAGEANT. May 26–28. Mackinaw City, MI. 200 local residents come together and reenact actual events that occurred from 1715–1763, including the Indians' uprising and capturing of the British forts. The reenactment is at Colonial Michilimackinac and occurs one time each day through the weekend. Fireworks are shot over the bay of Lake Huron on Saturday night and a Memorial Day Parade is held to close the weekend. Est attendance: 8,500. For info: Mackinaw Area Tourist Bureau, PO Box 160, Mackinaw City, MI 49701. Phone: (800) 666-0160. Web: www.mackinawcity.com.

DAKOTA COWBOY POETRY GATHERING. May 26–27. Medora Community Center, Medora, ND. 15th annual. This cowboy event hosts some of the most colorful cowboy poets in North Dakota and Montana. There are also singers and songwriters who perform. Annually, the Memorial Day Weekend. Est attendance: 700. For info: Bill Lowman, HC01 Box 25, Sentinel Butte, ND 58654. Phone: (701) 872-4746.

DUNKIRK EVACUATED: ANNIVERSARY. May 26, 1940. The British Expeditionary Force had become trapped by advancing German armies near this port on the northern coast of France. On this date, the evacuation of 200,000 British and 140,000 French and Belgian soldiers began. Sailing on every kind of transport available, including fishing boats and recreational craft, these men were safely across the English Channel by June 2.

EAGLE CREEK RENDEZVOUS. May 26–28. Murphy's Landing, Shakopee, MN. Recreation of an early 1800s fur traders gathering. Visitors can witness black powder shooting contests, tomahawk and knife throwing events, flint and steel fire-starting demonstrations and other games of skill located within a period encampment. Antiques and replicas of the time period are available for sale. Annually, Saturday–Monday of Memorial Day weekend. Est attendance: 2,000. For info: Mktg Dept, Murphy's Landing, 2187 E Highway, Shakopee, MN 55379. Phone: (952) 445-6901. Web: www.murphyslanding.com.

1836 ENCAMPMENT. May 26–27. Westville-Lumpkin, GA. Reenactment of an encampment of soldiers who had been dispatched to protect local citizens against Indian attacks. An Indian camp will also be demonstrated. Est attendance: 1,500. For info: Patty Cannington, Westville, PO Box 1850, Lumpkin, GA 31815. Phone: (912) 838-6310 or (888) 733-1850. Web: www.westville.org.

ENGLAND: INTERNATIONAL TT MOTORCYCLE RACES. May 26–June 9. Isle of Man. World-famous motorcycle road races held over a 38-mile course. Est attendance: 40,000. For info: Auto Cycle Union, Road Race Dept, Wood St, Rugby, Warwickshire, England CV21 2YX. Phone: (44) (1788) 566400. Fax: (44) (1788) 573585. E-mail: admin@acu.org.uk. Web: www.acu.org.uk.

FAIRMOUNT ACADEMY 1800s FESTIVAL. May 26. Fairmount, MD. Rain date the following Saturday. Restored school, spelling bees, square dancing, quilt show, folk arts and crafts, music and plenty of good food. Annually, the last Saturday in May. Est attendance: 2,500. For info: Nevette Muir, Fairmount Academy Historical Assn, PO Box 134, Upper Fairmount, MD 21867. Phone: (410) 651-0351 or (410) 651-3945.

FEAST OF SAINT AUGUSTINE OF CANTERBURY. May 26. Pope Gregory sent Augustine to convert the pagan English. Augustine became the first archbishop of Canterbury. He died May 26, 604 AD.

FRENCH AND INDIAN WAR MUSTER. May 26–27. Fort Frederick State Park, Big Pool, MD. Reactivated 18th century military units portray life during the French and Indian War. Frontier and tactical skills are demonstrated as the units "rendezvous" for spring. Period wares will be sold by various sutlers. Est attendance: 2,000. For info: Fort Frederick State Park, 11100 Fort Frederick Rd, Big Pool, MD 21711. Phone: (301) 842-2155. Fax: (301) 842-0028.

GEORGIA: INDEPENDENCE RESTORATION DAY: 10th ANNIVERSARY. May 26. National Day. Commemorates independence from the Soviet Union in 1991.

GREAT FLOOD OF 1889 COMMEMORATIVE WEEKEND. May 26–31. Johnstown Flood Museum, Johnstown, PA. The Johnstown Flood Museum recreates the catastrophe in which 2,209 people died, tens of thousands were left homeless and a prospering city was left a wasteland. "The Johnstown Flood" documentary, winner of Best Documentary, Short Subject in 1989, is shown hourly. For info: Katherine A. Morris, Johnstown Flood Museum, PO Box 1889, Johnstown, PA 15907-1889. Phone: (814) 539-1889 or (888) 222-1889. Fax: (814) 533-4885. Web: www.ctcnet.net/jaha.

GREAT MISSISSIPPI RIVER ARTS AND CRAFTS FESTIVAL. May 26–27. Mark Twain Historic District, Hannibal, MO. 14th annual art fair featuring 80 exhibitors in the areas of fine art, fine crafts and traditional arts. Concession stands with fried catfish, bbq porkchop sandwiches and lemonade, a variety of entertainment groups and creative learning fun in the children's area. Est attendance: 15,000. For info: Hannibal Arts Council, PO Box 1202, Hannibal, MO 63401. Phone: (573) 221-6545. E-mail: arts@nemonet.com.

HALFWAY PARK DAYS. May 26–27. Martin L. (Marty) Snook Memorial Park, Hagerstown, MD. Family fun in the park with arts and crafts, free entertainment, food and children's rides. Annually, Memorial Day weekend. Est attendance: 9,000. For info: Lions Club of Halfway, 10923 Holly Terrace, Hagerstown, MD 21740-7804. Phone: (301) 739-3219.

HEAD-OF-THE-MON-RIVER HORSESHOE TOURNAMENT. May 26–28. Fairmont, WV. Open to horseshoe pitchers with a 2000 State/National Horseshoe Pitchers Association membership card. Est attendance: 300. For info: Tri-County Horseshoe Club Dir, Davis "Catfish" Woodward and Beverly Tiano, 1133 Sunset Dr, Fairmont, WV 26554. Phone: (304) 366-3819.

INTERNATIONAL JAZZ DAY. May 26. Jazz lovers worldwide celebrate jazz every May, on the Saturday of the Memorial Day weekend. Originated by the New Jersey Jazz Society, and sanctioned by the American Federation of Jazz Societies, the United Nations Jazz Society and the Sacramento Traditional Jazz Society. For info: D. Michael Denny, PO Box 303, East Hanover, NJ 07936. Fax: (973) 503-0126. E-mail: michaeldenny@earthlink.net. Web: www.geocities.com/BourbonStreet/4270.

JOLSON, AL: BIRTH ANNIVERSARY. May 26, 1886. Actor, singer, born Asa Yoelson at St. Petersburg, Russia. Died at San Francisco, CA, Oct 23, 1950.

LOBSTERFEST. May 26–28. Mystic Seaport, Mystic, CT. A New England lobster bake on the banks of the Mystic River over the Memorial Day weekend, put on by the Mystic Rotary Club. Est attendance: 10,000. For info: Mystic Seaport, 75 Greenmanville Ave, PO Box 6000, Mystic, CT 06355-0990. Phone: (860) 572-5315 or (888) 9SEAPORT. Web: www.mysticseaport.org.

LONGWOOD GARDENS FESTIVAL OF FOUNTAINS. May 26–Sept 1. Kennett Square, PA. A magical mixture of rainbow-hued fountains, alfresco concerts, fireworks and leisurely evenings in the Conservatory. Est attendance: 275,000. For info: Longwood Gardens, PO Box 501, Kennett Square, PA 19348-0501. Phone: (610) 388-1000. Web: www.longwoodgardens.org.

MEMORIAL WEEKEND PAGEANT. May 26–28. Mackinaw City, MI. 37th annual. Reenactment of the capture of Fort Michilimackinac by Indians with more than 200 residents participating. Weekend includes a colorful parade. For info: Mackinaw Area Tourist Bureau, PO Box 160, Mackinaw City, MI 49701. Phone: (616) 436-5574. E-mail: info@mackinawcity.com. Web: www.mackinawcity.com.

MONTAGU, LADY MARY WORTLEY: BAPTISM ANNIVERSARY. May 26, 1689. English author baptized on this date. Died Aug 21, 1762, at London, England.

MORLEY, ROBERT: BIRTH ANNIVERSARY. May 26, 1908. British actor Robert Morley was born at Semley, England. Among his best known film credits are *Major Barbara* (1939) and *The African Queen* (1951). He died June 3, 1992, at Reading, England.

RIDE, SALLY KRISTEN: 50th BIRTHDAY. May 26, 1951. Dr. Sally Ride, one of the first women in the US astronaut corps and the first American woman in space, was born at Encino, CA. Her flight aboard the space shuttle *Challenger* was launched from Cape Canaveral, FL, June 18 and landed at Edwards Air Force Base, CA, June 24, 1983. The six-day flight was termed "nearly a perfect mission."

SEASIDE FINE ART SHOW. May 26–27. Neptune Park, St. Simons Island, GA. Strictly juried fine art festival attracts top artists from all over the country. Prestigious judges, top prize money. Annually, Memorial Day weekend. Est attendance: 15,000. For info: The Glynn Art Assn, PO Box 20673, St. Simons Island, GA 31522. Phone: (912) 638-8770. Fax: (912) 634-ARTS.

TASTE OF CINCINNATI. May 26–28. Cincinnati, OH. Greater Cincinnati is famous for its fine food, from elegant five-star dining to five-way chili. This popular eating extravaganza presents a taste of the most delicious culinary delights available. Annually, Memorial Day weekend. Est attendance: 500,000. For info: Greater Cincinnati Chamber of Commerce, 441 Vine St, Ste 300, Cincinnati, OH 45202. Phone: (513) 579-3100. Fax: (513) 579-3100. E-mail: info@gccc.com. Web: www.gccc.com.

TIVOLI FEST. May 26–27. Elk Horn, IA. Annual Danish celebration with parade, Danish Folk Dancers, Danish foods, unique giftshops, historical tours and much more. Annually, Memorial Day weekend. Sponsors: Better Elk Horn Club. Est attendance: 5,000. For info: Lisa Riggs, Danish Windmill, PO Box 245, Elk Horn, IA 51531. Phone: (712) 764-7472 or (800) 451-7960. Fax: (712) 764-7475. Web: www.danishwindmill.com.

UTICA OLD-FASHIONED ICE CREAM FESTIVAL. May 26–28. Utica, OH. Saluting "America's favorite dessert," ice cream, with a weekend of fun and entertainment—parade, queen contest, arts and crafts, antique gas engines, sheep herding with border collies and plenty of delicious ice cream. Est attendance: 26,000. For info: Michael Dager, Utica Ice Cream Festival, PO Box 588, Utica, OH 43080. Phone: (740) 892-3921. Web: www.velvet-icecream.com.

VIETNAM AND US RESUME RELATIONS: ANNIVERSARY. May 26, 1994. Nearly 20 years after the end of the Vietnam War, the US and Vietnam agreed to resume diplomatic relations. In the early 1990s Vietnam had become one of the fastest growing economies in Asia after giving up Communist controls and allowing economic reform. Earlier in 1994 President Bill Clinton had lifted the American embargo that hindered Americans from doing business in Vietnam.

WAR OF JENKIN'S EAR: LIVING HISTORY. May 26. Wormsloe Historic Site, Savannah, GA. A colonial living history event focusing on the conflict between England and Spain. Features musket demonstrations, military drill, musket ball casting, tomahawk throwing and more. Est attendance: 500. For info: Wormsloe State Historic Site, 7601 Skidaway Rd, Savannah, GA 31406. Phone: (912) 353-3023.

WAYNE, JOHN: BIRTH ANNIVERSARY. May 26, 1907. American motion picture actor, born Marion Michael Morrison, at Winterset, IA. He died at Los Angeles, CA, June 11, 1979. "Talk low, talk slow and don't say too much" was his advice on acting.

WHIPPOORWILL MORGAN HORSE OPEN BARN. May 26–28. Old Lyme, CT. Visitors can pet newborn foals and watch stallions and mares perform. There will also be an informative and informal introduction to the Morgan Horse. Est attendance: 250. For info: McCulloch Farm, Whippoorwill Morgan, 100 Whippoorwill Rd, Old Lyme, CT 06371. Phone: (860) 434-7355.

		S	M	T	W	T	F	S
May				1	2	3	4	5
2001		6	7	8	9	10	11	12
		13	14	15	16	17	18	19
		20	21	22	23	24	25	26
		27	28	29	30	31		

MAY 27 — SUNDAY
Day 147 — 218 Remaining

ANCESTOR HONOR DAY. May 27. A national, commemorative observance to honor the nonmilitary contributions of the many nationalities and cultures that worked and died for freedom, justice and equality. This holiday was envisioned and proclaimed in 1998 by Ayo Handy Kendi, founder and director of the African American Holiday Association (AAHA). Annually, the day before Memorial Day. For info: African American Holiday Assn, 1305 Emerson St NW, Washington, DC 20011. Phone: (202) 310-1430. E-mail: aaha@aaha-info.org. Web: www.aaha-info.org.

BENNETT, ARNOLD: BIRTH ANNIVERSARY. May 27, 1867. English novelist, playwright and critic (Enoch) Arnold Bennett was born at Hanley, in the pottery-manufacturing district of North Staffordshire, England. Best known of his novels is *The Old Wives' Tale* (1908), and most harshly criticized (by the literati) of his books was the popular *How to Live on Twenty-Four Hours a Day* (1908). His *Journals* from 1896 until near the time of his death in 1931 provide insight into Bennett's thought. "The price of justice," Arnold wrote, "is eternal publicity." He contracted typhoid fever in France and died at London, May 27, 1931.

BLOOMER, AMELIA JENKS: BIRTH ANNIVERSARY. May 27, 1818. American social reformer and women's rights advocate, born at Homer, NY. Her name is remembered especially because of her work for more sensible dress for women and her recommendation of a costume that had been introduced about 1849 by Elizabeth Smith Miller but came to be known as the "Bloomer Costume" or "Bloomers." Amelia Bloomer died at Council Bluffs, IA, Dec 30, 1894.

CARSON, RACHEL (LOUISE): BIRTH ANNIVERSARY. May 27, 1907. American scientist and author, born at Springdale, PA. Author of *Silent Spring* (1962), a book that provoked widespread controversy over the use of pesticides. Died Apr 14, 1964, at Silver Spring, MD.

CELLOPHANE TAPE PATENTED: ANNIVERSARY. May 27, 1930. Richard Gurley Drew received a patent for his adhesive tape, later manufactured by 3M as Scotch tape.

COAL MINER DAYS. May 27–28. Downtown and fairgrounds. Novinger, MO. Turn-of-the-century coal mining boom town celebrates its heritage with old-time contests, music, dancing and displays. Est attendance: 3,000. For info: Glenna Daniels, Novinger Renewal Inc, Rt 3, Box 31, Novinger, MO 63559. Phone: (660) 488-5280. E-mail: ddaniels@nemr.net.

DUNCAN, ISADORA: BIRTH ANNIVERSARY. May 27, 1878. American-born interpretive dancer who revolutionized the entire concept of dance. Bare-footed, freedom-loving, liberated woman and rebel against tradition, she experienced worldwide professional success and profound personal tragedy (her two children drowned, her marriage failed and she met a bizarre death when the long scarf she was wearing caught in a wheel of the open car in which she was riding, strangling her). Born at San Francisco, CA; died at Nice, France, Sept 14, 1927.

ENGLAND: SALISBURY FESTIVAL. May 27–June 9 (tentative). Various venues, Salisbury, Wiltshire. Annual festival of arts featuring music, comedy, literature and the visual arts. Annually, the last week in May and the first week in June. For info: Festival Dir, Salisbury Festival, 75 New St, Salisbury, England SP1 2PH. Phone: (44) (172) 232-3888. Fax: (44) (172) 241-0552. E-mail: info@salisburyfestival.co.uk. Web: www.salisburyfestival .co.uk.

FIRST FLIGHT INTO THE STRATOSPHERE: ANNIVERSARY. May 27, 1931. In a balloon launched from Augsburg, Germany, Paul Kipfer and Auguste Piccard became the first to reach the stratosphere. In a pressurized cabin they rose almost ten miles during their flight.

FIRST RUNNING OF PREAKNESS: ANNIVERSARY. May 27, 1873. The first running of the Preakness Stakes at Pimlico, MD, was won by Survivor with a time of 2:43. The winning jockey was G. Barbee.

GOLDEN GATE BRIDGE OPENED: ANNIVERSARY. May 27, 1937. 200,000 people crossed San Francisco's Golden Gate Bridge on its first day open.

HAMMETT, (SAMUEL) DASHIELL: BIRTH ANNIVERSARY. May 27, 1894. The man who brought realism to the genre of mystery writing, Dashiell Hammett was born at St. Mary's County, MD. His first two novels, *Red Harvest* (1929) and *The Dain Curse* (1929), were based on his eight years spent as a Pinkerton detective. Hammett is recognized as the founder of the "hard-boiled" school of detective fiction. Three of his novels have been made into films: *The Maltese Falcon* (1930), considered by many to be his finest work; *The Thin Man* (1932), which provided the basis for a series of five movies starring William Powell and Myrna Loy; and *The Glass Key* (1931). Hammett was called to testify but refused to name members of an alleged subversive organization during House Un-American Activities Committee hearings. He died Jan 10, 1961, at New York City.

HICKOK, WILD BILL: BIRTH ANNIVERSARY. May 27, 1837. Born at Troy Grove, IL, and died Aug 2, 1876, at Deadwood, SD. American frontiersman, legendary marksman, lawman, army scout and gambler. Hickock's end came when he was shot dead at a poker table by a drunk in the Number Ten saloon.

HUMPHREY, HUBERT HORATIO: 90th BIRTH ANNIVERSARY. May 27, 1911. Born at Wallace, SD. The 38th vice president of the US. Died at Waverly, MN, Jan 13, 1978.

INDIANAPOLIS 500-MILE RACE. May 27. Indianapolis, IN. Recognized as the world's largest single-day sporting event. First race was in 1911. Annually, the Sunday of Memorial Day weekend. For info: Indianapolis Motor Speedway Corp, 4790 W 16th St, Indianapolis, IN 46222. Phone: (317) 481-8500. Web: www.indy500.com.

ITALY: PALIO DEI BALESTRIERI. May 27. Gubbio. The last Sunday in May is set aside for a medieval crossbow contest between Gubbio and Sansepolcro; medieval costumes, arms.

ITALY: WEDDING OF THE SEA. May 27. Venice. The feast of the Ascension is the occasion of the ceremony recalling the "Wedding of the Sea" performed by Venice's Doge, who cast his ring into the sea from the ceremonial ship known as the *Bucintoro* to symbolize eternal dominion. Annually, on the Sunday following Ascension.

MEMORIAL DAY CEREMONIES. May 27. Andersonville, GA. Ceremonies pay tribute to our country's men and women who paid for our freedom with their lives. Est attendance: 800. For info: Alan Marsh, Park Ranger, Andersonville Natl Historic Site, Rte 1, Box 800, Hwy 49 North, Andersonville, GA 31711. Phone: (912) 924-0343.

PRICE, VINCENT: 90th BIRTH ANNIVERSARY. May 27, 1911. Actor, best known for his portrayal of sinister villains in horror films and as host for the TV series "Mystery." Born at St. Louis, MO, and died at Los Angeles, CA, Oct 25, 1993.

RMS *QUEEN MARY* : MAIDEN VOYAGE: 65th ANNIVERSARY. May 27, 1936. Anniversary of the maiden voyage from Southampton, England, to New York Harbor.

SHAVUOT BEGINS AT SUNDOWN. May 27. Jewish Pentecost. See "Shavuot" (May 28).

SMITH VALLEY STRAWBERRY FESTIVAL. May 27. Wellington, NV. Strawberry shortcake fest and music. Annually, the fourth Sunday of May. For info: Mason Valley, Chamber of Commerce, 227 S Main St, Yerington, NV 89447. Phone: (775) 463-2245. Fax: (775) 463-3369. Web: www.tele-net.net/lyon.

BIRTHDAYS TODAY

Jeff Bagwell, 33, baseball player, born Boston, MA, May 27, 1968.
John Barth, 71, author (*Last Voyage of Somebody the Sailor, Letters*), born Cambridge, MD, May 27, 1930.
Todd Bridges, 36, actor ("Diff'rent Strokes"), born San Francisco, CA, May 27, 1965.
Pat Cash, 36, tennis player, born Melbourne, Australia, May 27, 1965.
Christopher J. Dodd, 57, US Senator (D, Connecticut), born Willimantic, CT, May 27, 1944.
Joseph Fiennes, 31, actor (*Shakespeare In Love*), born Salisbury, England, May 27, 1970.
Peri Gilpin, 40, actress ("Frasier"), born Waco, TX, May 27, 1961.
Louis Gossett, Jr, 65, actor (Emmy for "Roots"; Oscar for *An Officer and a Gentleman*), born Brooklyn, NY, May 27, 1936.
Henry Kissinger, 78, former secretary of state, author, born Fuerth, Germany, May 27, 1923.
Christopher Lee, 79, actor (*Dracula, The Mummy*), born London, England, May 27, 1922.
Ramsey Lewis, 66, jazz musician, winner of three Grammy awards, born Chicago, IL, May 27, 1935.
Lee Meriwether, 66, actress (Cat Woman on TV "Batman"), former Miss America ('55), born Los Angeles, CA, May 27, 1935.
Samuel Jackson (Sam) Snead, 89, golfer, born Hot Springs, VA, May 27, 1912.
Frank Thomas, 33, baseball player, born Columbus, GA, May 27, 1968.
Bruce Weitz, 58, actor ("Hill Street Blues," "Death of a Centerfold: The Dorothy Stratton Story"), born Norwalk, CT, May 27, 1943.
Herman Wouk, 86, writer (*Marjorie Morningstar, The Winds of War*), born New York, NY, May 27, 1915.

MAY 28 — MONDAY

Day 148 — 217 Remaining

AGASSIZ, LOUIS: BIRTH ANNIVERSARY. May 28, 1807. Professor of zoology and geology at Harvard, born at Motier, Switzerland. He was a major influence in spawning American interest in natural history and helped to establish the Harvard Museum of Comparative Zoology. "The eye of the trilobite," Agassiz wrote in 1870, "tells us that the sun shone on the old beach where he lived; for there is nothing in nature without a purpose, and when so complicated an organ was made to receive the light, there must have been light to enter it." Died at Cambridge, MA, Dec 14, 1873.

AMNESTY INTERNATIONAL FOUNDED: 40th ANNIVERSARY. May 28, 1961. This Nobel Prize—winning human rights organization was founded by London lawyer Peter Berenson when he read about the arrest of a group of students at Portugal. He launched a one-year campaign called Appeal for Amnesty. Today Amnesty International has more than one million members in 150 countries who work to free all prisoners of conscience (those imprisoned for their beliefs), abolish the use of torture and the death penalty and guarantee human rights for women. For info: Amnesty USA, 322 8th Ave, New York, NY 10001. Phone: (800) AMNESTY or (212) 807-8400. Web: www .amnesty-usa.org.

AZERBAIJAN: DAY OF THE REPUBLIC. May 28. Public holiday. Commemorates the declaration of the Azerbaijan Democratic Republic in 1918.

BOLDER BOULDER 10K. May 28. Boulder, CO. A 10K race of walkers, joggers and world-class runners through the streets of Boulder. Annually, on Memorial Day. Est attendance: 42,000. For info: Bolder Boulder, 4571 N Broadway, Boulder, CO 80304. Phone: (303) 444-7223. Fax: (303) 444-6411. E-mail: race @bolderboulder.com. Web: www.bolderboulder.com.

CONFEDERATE MEMORIAL DAY IN VIRGINIA. May 28. Annually, the last Monday in May.

DIONNE QUINTUPLETS: BIRTHDAY. May 28, 1934. Five daughters (Marie, Cecile, Yvonne, Emilie and Annette) were born to Oliva and Elzire Dionne, near Callander, Ontario, Canada. They were the first quints known to have lived for more than a few hours after birth. Emilie died in 1954, Marie in 1970. The other three sisters are still living.

ETHIOPIA: NATIONAL DAY. May 28. Commemorates the downfall of the Dergue, the military government that ruled Ethiopia from 1974 to 1991.

FLEMING, IAN: BIRTH ANNIVERSARY. May 28, 1908. English novelist, creator of the James Bond series. Born at London, died Aug 12, 1964, at Sandwich, England.

GUILLOTIN, JOSEPH IGNACE: BIRTH ANNIVERSARY. May 28, 1738. French physician and member of the Constituent Assembly who urged the use of a machine that was sometimes called the "Maiden" for the execution of death sentences—a less painful, more certain way of dispatching those sentenced to death. The guillotine was first used on Apr 25, 1792, for the execution of a highwayman, Nicolas Jacques Pelletier. Other machines for decapitation had been in use in other countries since the Middle Ages. Guillotin was born at Saintes, France and died at Paris, Mar 26, 1814.

		S	M	T	W	T	F	S
May				1	2	3	4	5
2001		6	7	8	9	10	11	12
		13	14	15	16	17	18	19
		20	21	22	23	24	25	26
		27	28	29	30	31		

MEMORIAL DAY. May 28. Legal public holiday. (PL90–363 sets Memorial Day on last Monday in May. Applicable to federal employees and District of Columbia.) Also known as Decoration Day because of the tradition of decorating the graves of servicemen. An occasion for honoring those who have died in battle. (Observance dates from Civil War years in US: first documented observance at Waterloo, NY, May 5, 1865.) See also: "Confederate Memorial Day" (Apr 26, Apr 30, May 10, May 28 and June 3).

MEMORIAL DAY PARADE AND CEREMONIES. May 28. Gettysburg National Cemetery, Gettysburg, PA. 2,000 schoolchildren scatter flowers over the unknown graves. Memorial services follow parade. For info: Gettysburg CVB, PO Box 4117, Gettysburg, PA 17325. Phone: (717) 334-6274. Fax: (717) 334-1166. Web: www.gettysburg.com.

★MEMORIAL DAY, PRAYER FOR PEACE. May 28. Presidential Proclamation issued each year since 1948. PL81–512 of May 11, 1950, asks President to proclaim annually this day as a day of prayer for permanent peace. PL90–363 of June 28, 1968, requires that beginning in 1971 it will be observed the last Monday in May. Often titled "Prayer for Peace Memorial Day," and traditionally requests the flying of the flag at half-staff "for the customary forenoon period."

PITT, WILLIAM: BIRTH ANNIVERSARY. May 28, 1759. British prime minister from 1783 to 1801 and from 1804 to 1806, Pitt was influenced by Adam Smith's economic theories and reduced England's large national debt caused by the American Revolution. Born at Hayes, Kent, England, he died Jan 23, 1806, at Putney. He was the son of William Pitt, first earl of Chatham, for whom the city of Pittsburgh was named.

POLAR BEAR SWIM. May 28. Nome, AK. Dozens of intrepid swimmers have plunged into the frigid Bering Sea on this day since 1975. The swim may be rescheduled if the ocean ice hasn't sufficiently broken up. For info: Leo B. Rasmussen, Nome Rotary Club, PO Box 275, Nome, AK 99762. Phone: (907) 443-2798.

SAINT BERNARD OF MONTJOUX FEAST DAY. May 28. Patron saint of mountain climbers, founder of Alpine hospices of the Great and Little St. Bernard, died at age 85, probably on May 28, 1081.

SAKHALIN ISLAND QUAKE: ANNIVERSARY. May 28, 1995. At 1:03 AM, the island of Sakhalin, off the east coast of Russia, was struck by an earthquake that measured 7.5 on the Richter scale. The town of Neftegorsk at the epicenter was almost completely flattened. More than 2,000 of the town's 3,200 citizens were buried in rubble while they slept. Although rescue efforts were severely hampered by frigid weather and the remoteness of the area, the Russian government nevertheless turned down offers of help from South Korea and Japan. It was determined that the city would not be rebuilt and survivors were relocated to southern Sakhalin.

SHAVUOT or FEAST OF WEEKS. May 28. Jewish Pentecost holy day. Hebrew date, Sivan 6, 5761. Celebrates giving of Torah (the Law) to Moses on Mount Sinai.

SIERRA CLUB FOUNDED: ANNIVERSARY. May 28, 1892. Founded by famed naturalist John Muir, the Sierra Club promotes conservation of the natural environment by influencing public policy. It has been especially important in the founding of and protection of our national parks. For info: Sierra Club, 85 Second St, 2nd Fl, San Francisco, CA 94105-3441. Phone: (415) 977-5500. Web: www.sierraclub.org.

SLUGS RETURN FROM CAPISTRANO DAY. May 28. It's a little known secret that slimy slugs spend their winters in lovely Capistrano and return to our patios and gardens on this date. Bare feet not a good idea now through first frost. [© 2000 by WH] For info: Tom or Ruth Roy, Wellcat Holidays, 2418 Long Ln, Lebanon, PA 17046. Phone: (717) 279-0184. E-mail: wellcat @supernet.com. Web: www.wellcat.com.

STAFF HOUSE MUSEUM OPENING/PIE SOCIAL. May 28. Staff House Museum, Kellogg, ID. Yearly opening of Staff House Museum where you will find scale models of Bunker Hill Mine, outdoor mining/smelting equipment exhibits, 1899 Nordberg air compressor, gift shop, metallurgical exhibits and numerous other mining memories as well as a pie social for all. Closes after Labor Day. Est attendance: 100. For info: Sharon Waldo, Mgr, Kellogg Chamber of Commerce, 608 Bunker Ave, Kellogg, ID 83837. Phone: (208) 786-4141.

STOCK EXCHANGE HOLIDAY (MEMORIAL DAY). May 28. The holiday schedules for the various exchanges are subject to change if relevant rules, regulations or exchange policies are revised. If you have questions, phone: American Stock Exchange (212) 306-1000; Chicago Board of Trade (312) 435-3500; Chicago Board of Options Exchange (312) 786-5600; New York Stock Exchange (215) 656-2065; Pacific Stock Exchange (415) 393-4000; Philadelphia Stock Exchange (215) 496-5000.

THORPE, JAMES FRANCIS (JIM): BIRTH ANNIVERSARY. May 28, 1888. Jim Thorpe, Pro Football Hall of Famer, distinguished Native American athlete, winner of pentathlon and decathlon events at the 1912 Olympic Games, professional baseball and football player. Born near Prague, OK, and died at Lomita, CA, Mar 28, 1953.

TOUR OF SOMERVILLE. May 28. Somerville, NJ. The oldest continuously run major bicycle race in America. 2001 marks the 58th running. Attracts more than 600 top amateur cyclists for seven events. Annually, on Memorial Day. Est attendance: 40,000. For info: Dan Puntillo, Admin, 98 Grove St, Somerville, NJ 08876. Phone: (908) 725-7223.

UNITED KINGDOM: SPRING BANK HOLIDAY. May 28. Bank and public holiday in England, Wales, Scotland and Northern Ireland. Annually, the last Monday in May.

USS *NORTH CAROLINA* MEMORIAL DAY OBSERVANCE. May 28. Wilmington, NC. Annual Memorial Day observance held at 5:45 PM. Est attendance: 450. For info: USS *North Carolina* Battleship Memorial, Susan Pope, Box 480, Wilmington, NC 28402. Phone: (910) 251-5797. Fax: (910) 251-5807. E-mail: ncbb55@aol.com. Web: www.city-info.com/ncbb55.html.

"ZOO PARADE" TV PREMIERE: ANNIVERSARY. May 28, 1950. NBC's half-hour program on animals and animal behavior was hosted by Marlin Perkins and Jim Hurlbut. Initially, it was broadcast from Lincoln Park Zoo in Chicago, but after 1955, the show was broadcast from other locales throughout the country. A successor program, "Mutual of Omaha's Wild Kingdom," was shot almost entirely in the wild and ran into the 1980s.

BIRTHDAYS TODAY

Carroll Baker, 70, actress (*Baby Doll, Harlow*), born Johnstown, PA, May 28, 1931.
Barry Commoner, 84, biologist, politician, born Brooklyn, NY, May 28, 1917.
Kirk Harold Gibson, 44, former baseball player, born Pontiac, MI, May 28, 1957.
Armon Louis Gilliam, 37, basketball player, born Pittsburgh, PA, May 28, 1964.
Rudolph Giuliani, 57, Mayor of New York City, born Brooklyn, NY, May 28, 1944.
Gladys Knight, 57, singer (and the Pips; "Neither One of Us," "If I Were Your Woman"), born Atlanta, GA, May 28, 1944.
Sondra Locke, 54, actress (*The Heart Is a Lonely Hunter, Bronco Billy*), director (*Ratboy*), born Shelbyville, TN, May 28, 1947.
Christa Miller, 37, actress ("The Drew Carey Show"), born New York, NY, May 28, 1964.
Glen Rice, 34, basketball player, born Flint, MI, May 28, 1967.

MAY 29 — TUESDAY
Day 149 — 216 Remaining

AMNESTY ISSUED FOR SOUTHERN REBELS: ANNIVERSARY. May 29, 1865. President Andrew Johnson issued a proclamation giving a general amnesty to all who participated in the rebellion against the US. High ranking members of the Confederate government and military and those who owned more than $20,000 worth of property were excepted and had to apply individually to the President for a pardon. Once an oath of allegiance was taken, all former property rights, except those in slaves, were returned to the former owners.

ASCENSION OF BAHA'U'LLAH: ANNIVERSARY. May 29. Baha'i observance of the anniversary of the death in exile of Baha'u'llah (the prophet-founder of the Baha'i Faith), May 29, 1892. One of the nine days of the year when Baha'is suspend work. For info: Baha'is of the US, Office of Public Information, 866 UN Plaza, Ste 120, New York, NY 10017-1822. Phone: (212) 803-2500. Fax: (212) 803-2573. E-mail: usopi-ny@bic.org. Web: www.us.bahai.org.

CHARLES II: RESTORATION AND BIRTH ANNIVERSARY. May 29, 1660. Restoration of Charles II to English throne. Also his birthday (May 29, 1630). English monarchy restored after Commonwealth period under Oliver Cromwell.

CHESTERTON, GILBERT KEITH: BIRTH ANNIVERSARY. May 29, 1874. English author and critic born at London, England. Died June 14, 1936, at Beaconsfield, Buckinghamshire, England.

CONSTANTINOPLE FALLS TO THE TURKS: ANNIVERSARY. May 29, 1453. The city of Constantinople was captured by the Turks, who eventually renamed it Istanbul. This conquest marked the end of the Byzantine Empire; the city became the capital of the Ottoman Empire.

HENRY, PATRICK: BIRTH ANNIVERSARY. May 29, 1736. American revolutionary leader and orator, born at Studley, VA, and died near Brookneal, VA, June 6, 1799. Especially remembered for his speech (Mar 23, 1775) for arming the Virginia militia, at St. Johns Church, Richmond, VA, when he declared: "I know not what course others may take, but as for me, give me liberty or give me death."

KENNEDY, JOHN FITZGERALD: BIRTH ANNIVERSARY. May 29, 1917. 35th president of the US (1961–63), born at Brookline, MA. Assassinated while riding in an open automobile, at Dallas, TX, Nov 22, 1963. (Accused assassin Lee Harvey Oswald was killed at the Dallas police station by a gunman, Jack Rubenstein [Ruby], two days later.) Kennedy was the youngest man ever elected to the presidency, the first Roman Catholic and the first president to have served in the US Navy. He was the fourth US president to be killed by an assassin, and the second to be buried at Arlington National Cemetery.

MOON PHASE: FIRST QUARTER. May 29. Moon enters First Quarter phase at 6:09 PM, EDT.

MOSCOW COMMUNIQUE: ANNIVERSARY. May 29, 1972. President Richard Nixon and Soviet Party leader Leonid Brezhnev released a joint communique after Nixon's week-long visit to Moscow. During the visit the two men acknowledged their major differences on the Vietnam War, signed a treaty on antiballistic missile systems as well as an interim agreement on limitation of strategic missiles and an agreement for a joint space flight in 1975. This was the first visit ever to Moscow by a US president (May 22–30, 1972).

MOUNT EVEREST SUMMIT REACHED: ANNIVERSARY. May 29, 1953. New Zealand explorer Sir Edmund Hillary and Tensing Norgay, a Sherpa guide, became the first team to reach the summit of Mount Everest, the world's highest mountain.

RHODE ISLAND: RATIFICATION DAY. May 29. The last of the 13 original states to ratify the Constitution in 1790.

SOCCER TRAGEDY: ANNIVERSARY. May 29, 1985. A riot at Heysel stadium at Brussels, Belgium, killed 39 people. Fans attending the European Cup Final, between Liverpool and Juventus of Turin, clashed before the match started. Some 400 people were injured in the riot. The incident was televised and viewed by millions throughout Europe. More than two years later, Sept 2, 1987, the British government announced that 26 British soccer fans (identified from television tapes) would be extradited to Belgium for trial. Hooliganism at soccer matches became the target of increased security measures for England's professional teams following the 1985 tragedy.

SPENGLER, OSWALD: BIRTH ANNIVERSARY. May 29, 1880. German historian, author of *The Decline of the West*, born at Blankenburg-am-Harz, Germany. Died at Munich, Germany, May 8, 1936.

VIRGINIA PLAN PROPOSED: ANNIVERSARY. May 29, 1787. Just five days after the Constitutional Convention met at Philadelphia, PA, the "Virginia Plan" was proposed. It called for establishment of a new governmental organization consisting of a legislature with two houses, an executive (chosen by the legislature) and a judicial branch.

WISCONSIN: ADMISSION DAY: ANNIVERSARY. May 29. Became 30th state in 1848.

BIRTHDAYS TODAY

Annette Bening, 43, actress (*The American President, Bugsy, The Grifters*), born Topeka, KS, May 29, 1958.

Melanie Janine Brown, 26, singer (Spice Girls), born Leeds, England, May 29, 1975.

Kevin Conway, 59, actor (*When You Comin' Back, Red Ryder?, Of Mice and Men, Other People's Money*), born New York, NY, May 29, 1942.

Eric Davis, 39, baseball player, born Los Angeles, CA, May 29, 1962.

Paul Ehrlich, 69, population biologist, born Philadelphia, PA, May 29, 1932.

Melissa Etheridge, 40, singer, guitarist, born Leavenworth, KS, May 29, 1961.

Rupert Everett, 42, actor (*My Best Friend's Wedding*), born Norfolk, England, May 29, 1959.

Anthony Geary, 53, actor ("General Hospital"), born Coalville, UT, May 29, 1948.

	S	M	T	W	T	F	S
May			1	2	3	4	5
2001	6	7	8	9	10	11	12
	13	14	15	16	17	18	19
	20	21	22	23	24	25	26
	27	28	29	30	31		

Bob Hope (Leslie Townes), 98, comedian ("Road" movies with Bing Crosby), born Eltham, England, May 29, 1903.

Adrian Paul, 42, actor ("Highlander" series), born London, England, May 29, 1959.

Felix Rohatyn, 73, US Ambassador to France, former investment banker (developed strategy to keep New York City solvent), born Vienna, Austria, May 29, 1928.

Alfred (Al) Unser, Sr, 62, former auto racer, born Albuquerque, NM, May 29, 1939.

Francis Thomas (Fay) Vincent, Jr, 63, former commissioner of baseball, born Waterbury, CT, May 29, 1938.

Lisa Whelchel, 38, actress ("Facts of Life"), born Fort Worth, TX, May 29, 1963.

MAY 30 — WEDNESDAY
Day 150 — 215 Remaining

BATTLE OF THE ALEUTIAN ISLANDS: ANNIVERSARY. May 30, 1943. The islands of Kiska and Attu in the Aleutian Islands off the coast of Alaska were retaken by the US 7th Infantry Division. The battle (Operation Landgrab) began when an American force of 11,000 landed on Attu May 12. In three weeks of fighting US casualties numbered 552 killed and 1,140 wounded. Only 28 wounded Japanese were taken prisoner. Their dead amounted to 2,352, of whom 500 committed suicide.

CANADA: ANNAPOLIS VALLEY APPLE BLOSSOM FESTIVAL. May 30–June 4. Windsor to Digby, NS. Annual festival with barbecues, sports events, art show, Princess Tea, coronation ceremonies, dances, concerts, fireworks, craft fair, children's parade, Grand Street Parade and "Sunday in the Park" (family entertainment). Annually, since 1933. Est attendance: 125,000. For info: Festival Office, 37 Cornwallis St, Kentville, NS, Canada B4N 2E2. Phone: (902) 678-8322. Fax: (902) 678-3710. E-mail: appleblossom@ns.sympatico.ca. Web: www.appleblossom.com.

CANADA: THE NATIONAL TOURNAMENT. May 30–June 3. Spruce Meadows, Calgary, AB. The National Tournament features the Canadian Show Jumping Championship, including the Canadian Pacific World Cup and the Shell Cup. Enjoy country atmosphere in the Agrium Country Fair on the Spruce Meadows Plaza. Live entertainment and activities daily. Est attendance: 85,000. For info: Spruce Meadows, RR #9, Calgary, AB, Canada T2J 5G5. Phone: (403) 974-4200. Fax: (403) 947-4270. E-mail: smeadows@telusplanet.net. Web: www.sprucemeadows.com.

CROATIA: STATEHOOD DAY. May 30. Public holiday commemorating attainment of statehood in 1990.

ENGLAND: ROYAL BATH AND WEST OF ENGLAND SHOW. May 30–June 2. Royal Bath and West Showground, Shepton Mallet, Somerset. One of the largest agricultural shows for the whole family in the country. Est attendance: 155,000. For info: Royal Bath and West of England Soc, The Showground, Shepton Mallet, Somerset, England BA4 6QN. Phone: (44) (174) 982-2200. Fax: (44) (174) 982-3169.

FIRST AMERICAN DAILY NEWSPAPER PUBLISHED: ANNIVERSARY. May 30, 1783. *The Pennsylvania Evening Post* became the first daily newspaper published in the US. The paper was published at Philadelphia, PA, by Benjamin Towne.

GERMANY: MARBURG UNIVERSITY FOUNDING: ANNIVERSARY. May 30, 1527. University of Marburg was founded on this date.

INDIANAPOLIS 500: 90th ANNIVERSARY. May 30, 1911. Ray Harroun won the first Indy 500, averaging 74.6 MPH. The race was created by Carl Fisher, who in 1909 replaced the stone surface of his 2.5-mile racetrack with a brick one—hence the nickname "The Brickyard."

LINCOLN MEMORIAL DEDICATION: ANNIVERSARY.
May 30, 1922. The memorial is made of marble from Colorado and Tennessee and limestone from Indiana. It stands in West Potomac Park at Washington, DC. The outside columns are Doric, the inside, Ionic. The Memorial was designed by architect Henry Bacon and its cornerstone was laid in 1915. A skylight lets light into the interiors where the compelling statue "Seated Lincoln," by sculptor Daniel Chester French, is situated.

LOOMIS DAY. May 30. To honor Mahlon Loomis, a Washington, DC dentist who received a US patent on wireless telegraphy in 1872 (before Marconi was born). Titled "An Improvement in Telegraphing," the patent described how to do without wires; this patent was backed up by experiment on the Massanutten Mountains of Virginia. For info: Robert L. Birch, Puns Corps, Box 2364, Falls Church, VA 22042-0364. Phone: (703) 533-3668.

MEMORIAL DAY (TRADITIONAL). May 30. This day honors the tradition of making memorial tributes to the dead, especially remembering those who have died in battle. Observed as a legal public holiday on the last Monday in May.

NATIONAL SENIOR HEALTH AND FITNESS DAY. May 30. Local sites in all 50 states. Eighth annual event to promote the value of fitness and exercise for older adults. During this day—as part of Older Americans Month activities—seniors across the country are involved in locally organized health promotion activities. Call the toll-free number for further info and a list of local sites. Annually, the last Wednesday in May. In 2000 more than 100,000 older adults participated in fitness activities at more than 1,000 sites nationwide. Est attendance: 125,000. For info: Tina Godin, Program Mgr, Mature Market Resource Center, 1850 W Winchester Rd, Ste 213, Libertyville, IL 60048. Phone: (800) 828-8225. Fax: (847) 816-8662. E-mail: seniorprograms@aol.com. Web: www.fitnessday.com.

NATIONAL SPELLING BEE FINALS. May 30–31. Washington, DC. Newspapers and other sponsors across the country send 240–250 youngsters to the finals at Washington, DC. Annually, Wednesday and Thursday of Memorial Day Week. Est attendance: 1,000. For info: Dir Natl Spelling Bee, Scripps-Howard, PO Box 371541, Pittsburgh, PA 15251-7541. Phone: (513) 977-3040. E-mail: bee@scripps.com. Web: www.spellingbee.com.

NCAA DIVISION I MEN'S AND WOMEN'S OUTDOOR TRACK CHAMPIONSHIPS. May 30–June 2. University of Oregon, Eugene, OR. Est attendance: 20,000. For info: NCAA, 700 W Washington Ave, PO Box 6222, Indianapolis, IN 46206-6222. Phone: (317) 917-6222. Fax: (317) 917-6888. Web: www.ncaa.org.

NCAA DIVISION I MEN'S GOLF CHAMPIONSHIP.
May 30–June 2. Duke University, Durham, NC. For info: NCAA, 700 W Washington Ave, PO Box 6222, Indianapolis, IN 46206-6222. Phone: (317) 917-6222. Fax: (317) 917-6888. Web: www.ncaa.org.

POPE NIXES ORDAINING OF WOMEN: ANNIVERSARY. May 30, 1994. Pope John Paul II, in a letter to Roman Catholic bishops, declared the debate on the ordination of women closed. He stated that, based on New Testament practices and tradition, the church could not ordain women to the priesthood. This announcement put the Roman Catholic church at odds with the Anglican Communion, which had ordained a group of women earlier in the year.

SAINT JOAN OF ARC: FEAST DAY. May 30. French heroine and martyr, known as the Maid of Orleans, led the French against the English invading army. Captured, found guilty of heresy and burned at the stake in 1431 (at age 19). Innocence declared in 1456. Canonized in 1920.

SPACE MILESTONE: *MARINER 9* (US): 30th ANNIVERSARY. May 30, 1971. Unmanned spacecraft was launched, entering Martian orbit the following Nov 13. The craft relayed temperature and gravitational field information and sent back spectacular photographs of both the surface of Mars and of her two moons. First spacecraft to orbit another planet.

TRINIDAD: INDIAN ARRIVAL DAY. May 30. Port of Spain, West Indies. Public holiday. For info: Info Dept, Tourism Div, Tourism and Industrial Development Co, Trinidad and Tobago Ltd, 10—14 Phillips St, West Indies. Phone: (800) 595-1868.

BIRTHDAYS TODAY

Blake Bashoff, 20, actor (*Bushwhacked, Big Bully*), born Philadelphia, PA, May 30, 1981.
Keir Dullea, 65, actor (*David and Lisa; 2001: A Space Odyssey*), born Cleveland, OH, May 30, 1936.
Bob Evans, 83, restaurant executive, born Sugar Ridge, OH, May 30, 1918.
Wynonna Judd, 37, singer ("Wynonna," "Tell Me Why"), winner of six Grammy awards, born Ashland, KY, May 30, 1964.
Ted McGinley, 43, actor ("Married . . . With Children," *Revenge of the Nerds*), born Newport Beach, CA, May 30, 1958.
Colm Meaney, 48, actor ("Star Trek: The Next Generation," *Last of the Mohicans*), born Dublin, Ireland, May 30, 1953.
Trey Parker, 29, director, creator ("South Park"), born Auburn, AL, May 30, 1972.
Michael J. Pollard, 62, actor (*Bonnie and Clyde*, "Leo & Liz in Beverly Hills"), born Passaic, NJ, May 30, 1939.
Manny Ramirez, 29, baseball player, born Santo Domingo, Dominican Republic, May 30, 1972.
Gale Eugene Sayers, 58, Pro Football Hall of Fame running back, born Wichita, KS, May 30, 1943.
Stephen Tobolowsky, 50, actor (*The Grifters, Groundhog Day*), born Dallas, TX, May 30, 1951.
Clint Walker, 74, actor (*The Dirty Dozen*, "Cheyenne"), born Hartford, IL, May 30, 1927.

MAY 31 — THURSDAY
Day 151 — 214 Remaining

AMECHE, DON: BIRTH ANNIVERSARY. May 31, 1908. Film, stage, radio and TV actor. Born Dominic Felix Amici at Kenosha, WI, and died Dec 6, 1993, at Scottsdale, AZ.

BATTLE OF SEVEN PINES: ANNIVERSARY. May 31, 1862. Confederate General Joseph Johnston's troops defeated McClellan's Army of the Potomac at the Battle of Seven Pines (or Fair Oaks, VA). Although the Confederates scored a major battlefield victory and McClellan's forces withdrew the next day, the effect of the battle did little to ease the pressure on the besieged Confederate capital of Richmond. During the battle Johnston was wounded, and Robert E. Lee was named commander of the Army of Northern Virginia.

CALIFORNIA SENIOR GAMES SACRAMENTO. May 31–June 3. Sacramento, CA. Athletic competition for men and women age 50 and older. Compete in five-year age divisions. 21 sports. Est attendance: 1,000. For info: Kitty Esposto, Coord, 6005 Folsom Blvd, Sacramento, CA 95819. Phone: (916) 277-6094. Fax: (916) 277-6155.

COPYRIGHT LAW PASSED: ANNIVERSARY. May 31, 1790. President George Washington signed the first US copyright law. It gave protection for 14 years to books written by US citizens. In 1891 the law was extended to cover books by foreign authors as well.

HARRIS, PATRICIA ROBERTS: BIRTH ANNIVERSARY. May 31, 1924. Born at Matoon, IL. The first African American woman to serve in an ambassadorial post, the first African American to hold a cabinet position (Secretary of Housing and Urban Development) and the first woman to serve as dean of a law school. Died Mar 23, 1985.

JOHNSTOWN FLOOD: ANNIVERSARY. May 31, 1889. Heavy rains caused the Connemaugh River Dam to burst. At nearby Johnstown, PA, the resulting flood killed more than 2,300 people and destroyed the homes of thousands more. Nearly 800 unidentified drowning victims were buried in a common grave at Johnstown's Grandview Cemetery. So devastating was the flood and so widespread the sorrow for its victims that "Johnstown Flood" entered the language as a phrase to describe a disastrous event. The valley city of Johnstown, in the Allegheny Mountains, has been damaged repeatedly by floods. Floods in 1936 (25 deaths) and 1977 (85 deaths) were the next most destructive.

MAINLY MOZART FESTIVAL. May 31–June 17. San Diego County and Baja, CA. David Atherton conducts world-class artists in a bi-national celebration of Mozart and his contemporaries in San Diego and Escondido, CA, and Tijuana, Rosarito and Tecate, Mexico. Chamber orchestra, chamber music and recitals are presented. Est attendance: 20,000. For info: Public Relations, Mainly Mozart, PO Box 124705, San Diego, CA 92112-4705. Phone: (619) 239-0100. Fax: (619) 233-4292. E-mail: admin @mainlymozart.com. Web: www.mainlymozart.org.

PEALE, NORMAN VINCENT: BIRTH ANNIVERSARY. May 31, 1898. American religious leader Norman Vincent Peale was born at Bowersville, OH. He is best known for his book *The Power of Positive Thinking* (1952), which combines religion and psychiatry. He was a minister at the Marble Collegiate Church at New York, NY. He died Dec 24, 1993, at Pawling, NY.

POPE PIUS XI: BIRTH ANNIVERSARY. May 31, 1857. Ambrogio Damiano Achille Ratti, 259th pope of the Roman Catholic Church, born at Desio, Italy. Elected pope Feb 6, 1922. Died Feb 10, 1939, at Rome, Italy.

PORTLAND ROSE FESTIVAL. May 31–June 24. Portland, OR. Celebration includes more than 70 events featuring grand floral parade, the Portland Art Festival, band festivals, auto and dragon boat races, carnival, air show and Navy ship visits. Est attendance: 2,000,000. For info: Portland Rose Festival Assn, 220 NW Second Ave, Portland, OR 97209. Phone: (503) 227-2681. Fax: (503) 227-6603. E-mail: info@rosefestival.org. Web: www.rosefestival.org.

SUGAR VALLEY RALLY AND WEEKEND. May 31–June 3. Scottsbluff/Gering, NE, and thru North Platte Valley. Sanctioned computerized rally for pre-1952 antique vehicles. Participants come from throughout the US and foreign countries to compete for $5,000+ in prizes. "Second largest event of this type in US (first is Great American Race)." Also, at Pioneer Park, Scottsbluff, Sugar Valley Arts & Crafts Festival with more than 100 craftsmen/artisans selling and demonstrating their work. Live entertainment and more. Annually, the first weekend in June. Est attendance: 5,500. For info: Sugar Valley Rally, PO Box 1350, Scottsbluff, NE 69363-1350. Phone: (308) 632-2133.

UNITED NATIONS: WORLD NO-TOBACCO DAY. May 31.

US WOMEN'S OPEN CHAMPIONSHIP. May 31–June 3. Pine Needles Lodge and Country Club, Southern Pines, NC. Est attendance: 40,000. For info: USGA, PO Box 708, Far Hills, NJ 07931-0708. Phone: (908) 234-2300. Fax: (908) 234-9687. Web: www.usga.org.

VIVA EL PASO. May 31–Aug 25 (Thursday–Saturday). McKelligon Canyon Amphitheater, El Paso, TX. Outdoor drama celebrating El Paso's cultural history through song, dance, narration and dramatic scenes about early Native American, Spanish, Mexican and Western American settlers. Dinner at 6:30 PM, showtime 8:30 PM. Est attendance: 67,000. For info: El Paso Assn for the Performing Arts, PO Box 31340, El Paso, TX 79931-0340. Phone: (915) 565-6900 or (800) 915-8482. Fax: (915) 565-6999. E-mail: epapa@htg.net. Web: www.viva-ep.org.

WHITMAN, WALT: BIRTH ANNIVERSARY. May 31, 1819. Poet and journalist, born at West Hills, Long Island, NY. Whitman's best known work, *Leaves of Grass* (1855), is a classic of American poetry. His poems celebrated all of modern life, including subjects that were considered taboo at the time. Died Mar 26, 1892, at Camden, NJ.

WORLD NO-TOBACCO DAY. May 31. Designed to publicize the proven dangers of tobacco and promote a way of life where tobacco is not the accepted norm. For info: American Assn for World Health, 1825 K St NW, Ste 1208, Washington, DC 20006. Phone: (202) 466-5883. Fax: (202) 466-5896. E-mail: staff@aawhworldhealth.org. Web: www.aawhworldhealth.org.

BIRTHDAYS TODAY

Tom Berenger, 51, actor (*Born on the Fourth of July, The Field, Gettysburg*), born Chicago, IL, May 31, 1950.

Clint Eastwood, 71, actor, director (Oscar for *Unforgiven*), former mayor of Carmel, CA, born San Francisco, CA, May 31, 1930.

Chris Elliott, 41, writer ("Late Night with David Letterman"), actor ("Get a Life"), born New York, NY, May 31, 1960.

Sharon Gless, 58, actress (Emmy for "Cagney & Lacey"), born Los Angeles, CA, May 31, 1943.

Gregory Harrison, 51, actor ("Logan's Run," "Trapper John, MD"), born Avalon, Catalina Island, CA, May 31, 1950.

Kenny Lofton, 34, baseball player, born East Chicago, IN, May 31, 1967.

Joseph William (Joe) Namath, 58, Pro Football Hall of Fame quarterback, former sportscaster, actor, born Beaver Falls, PA, May 31, 1943.

Johnny Paycheck (Don Lytle), 60, singer ("Take This Job and Shove It"), songwriter, born Greenfield, OH, May 31, 1941.

Kyle Secor, 43, actor ("Homicide: Life on the Streets"), born Tacoma, WA, May 31, 1958.

Brooke Shields, 36, actress (*Pretty Baby, The Blue Lagoon*, "Suddenly Susan"), born New York, NY, May 31, 1965.

Lea Thompson, 40, actress ("Caroline in the City," *Back to the Future, Howard the Duck*), born Rochester, MN, May 31, 1961.

Terry Waite, 62, Church of England special envoy, former hostage in Lebanon (1987–'91), born Bollington, Cheshire, England, May 31, 1939.

Peter Yarrow, 63, composer, singer (Peter, Paul and Mary), born New York, NY, May 31, 1938.

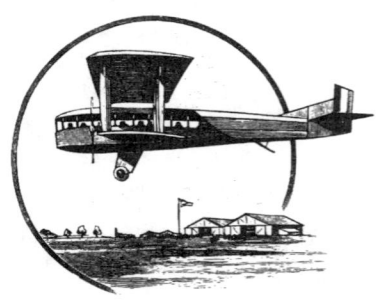

Iune.

JUNE 1 — FRIDAY
Day 152 — 213 Remaining

ADOPT-A-SHELTER CAT MONTH. June 1–30. To promote the adoption of cats from local shelters, the ASPCA sponsors this important observance. For info: ASPCA Public Affairs Dept, 424 E 92nd St, New York, NY 10128. Phone: (212) 876-7700. E-mail: press@aspca.org. Web: www.aspca.org.

ATLANTIC, CARIBBEAN AND GULF HURRICANE SEASON. June 1–Nov 30. For info: US Dept of Commerce, Natl Oceanic and Atmospheric Admin, Rockville, MD 20852.

BACK TO RATH'S TRAIL. June 1–3. Hamlin, TX. Historical event focusing on the period of the great buffalo hunts, in particular Rath City or Camp Reynolds (circa 1876–79), located just north of Hamlin. During its three-year lifespan, more than 1.1 million buffalo hides were shipped out of the old post. Event features tours of the site with interpretive living history camps, archaeological research, historical symposiums, artifacts exhibits, art show, frontier balls, parade, 5K fun run/walk, entertainment, poets and storytelling. Est attendance: 3,500. For info: Hamlin Chamber of Commerce, PO Box 402, Hamlin, TX 79520. Phone: (915) 576-3501. E-mail: hedc@camalott.com.

BAHAMAS: LABOR DAY. June 1. Public holiday. First Friday in June celebrated with parades, displays and picnics.

BOOKEXPO AMERICA TRADE EXHIBIT. June 1–3. McCormick Place, Chicago, IL. Publishers display fall titles for booksellers and all interested in reaching the retail bookseller. Book-related items also on display. For info: BookExpo America, 37–39 Fort Point St, E Norwalk, CT 06855. Phone: (800) 840-5614. Fax: (203) 855-9101. Web: bookexpo.reedexpo.com.

BUFFALO DAYS CELEBRATION (WITH BUFFALO CHIP THROWING). June 1–3. Luverne, MN. Parade, Arts in the Park, free barbecued buffalo burgers (while they last) and unique buffalo-chip throwing contest. Annually, the first weekend in June. Est attendance: 12,000. For info: Dave Smith, Exec Dir, Luverne Area Chamber of Commerce, 102 E Main, Luverne, MN 56156. Phone: (507) 283-4061. Fax: (507) 283-4061. Web: luvernemn.com.

CANADA: YUKON INTERNATIONAL STORYTELLING FESTIVAL. June 1–3. Whitehorse, YT. Storytellers from all over Canada and abroad. Est attendance: 5,000. For info: Yukon Intl Storytelling Fest, PO Box 5029, Whitehorse, YT, Canada Y1A 4S2. Phone: (867) 633-7550. Fax: (867) 633-3883. E-mail: yukonstory@yknet.yk.ca. Web: www.yukonalaska.com/storytelling.

CANCER FROM THE SUN MONTH. June 1–30. To promote education and awareness of the dangers of skin cancer from too much exposure to the sun. Kit of materials available for $15 from this nonprofit organization. For info: Frederick Mayer, Pres, Pharmacy Council on Dermatology (PCD), 101 Lucas Valley Rd, #210, San Rafael, CA 94903. Phone: (415) 479-8628. Fax: (415) 479-8608. E-mail: ppsi@aol.com. Web: www.ppsinc.org.

CANOE, CAPSTAN & CARGO. June 1–30. Jamestown Settlement, Williamsburg, VA and Yorktown Victory Center, Yorktown, VA. Discover maritime activities of 17th- and 18th-century Virginians who relied on waterways for transportation, food supply and commerce. For info: Jamestown-Yorktown Foundation, PO Box 1607, Williamsburg, VA 23187. Phone: (757) 253-4838 or (888) 593-4682. Fax: (757) 253-5299. Web: www.historyisfun.org.

CENTRAL PACIFIC HURRICANE SEASON. June 1–Oct 31. Central Pacific is defined as 140 West Longitude to the International Date Line (180 West Longitude). For info: Natl Dept of Commerce, Natl Oceanic and Atmospheric Admin, Rockville, MD 20852.

CHILDREN'S AWARENESS MONTH. June 1–30. A month-long celebration of America's children in our everyday lives and communities while lovingly remembering all of America's children that we have lost through violence. These could have been our children or grandchildren. We choose to remember the living during the month of June. For info: Judith Natale, CEO & Founder, Natl Children & Family Awareness of America, Administrative Headquarters, 3060 Rt 405 Hwy, Muncy, PA 17756-8808. Phone: (888) MAA-DESK. E-mail: ChildAware@aol.com. Web: hometown.aol.com/ChildAware/page1.html.

CHINA: INTERNATIONAL CHILDREN'S DAY. June 1. Shanghai.

CNN DEBUTED: ANNIVERSARY. June 1, 1980. The Cable News Network, TV's first all-news service, went on the air.

CURWOOD FESTIVAL. June 1–3. Owosso, MI. Homecoming celebration commemorating James Oliver Curwood, Owosso-born author and conservationist (June 12, 1878–Aug 13, 1927). The Curwood castle was built for a studio. Open to the public. 40 events including parades, races and music. Annually, the first full weekend in June. Est attendance: 75,000. For info: Owosso Curwood Festival, Box 461, Owosso, MI 48867. Phone: (517) 723-2161. E-mail: curwood@shianet.org.

DONUT DAY. June 1–2. Chicago, IL. Founded in 1938 by the Salvation Army for fundraising during the Great Depression, Donut Day is now an annual tradition. Recalling the donuts served to doughboys by the Salvation Army during World War I, symbolic paper "donuts" are given to contributors. Annually, the first Friday and Saturday in June. For info: Richard Grozik, Dir of Communications, The Salvation Army, Metro Div HQ, 5040 N Pulaski, Chicago, IL 60630. Phone: (773) 205-3546. Fax: (773) 725-2822.

ENTREPRENEURS 'DO IT YOURSELF' MARKETING MONTH. June 1–30. Want to stand out from your competition and get media attention, and more clients, while achieving your goals? Are you looking for better results from your marketing efforts? Would you like to become a new resource when the media calls? Remember, your success is a matter of choice, not chance. Discover and apply creative and effective problem-solving marketing ideas that will help you gain the competitive edge. For more information, get "101 Free Publicity, Marketing and Networking Ideas that Get Results." Send $5 to: Lorrie Walters Marsiglio, PO Box 284-CC, Wasco, IL 60183-0284. Phone: (630) 584-9368.

EVERETT SALTY SEA DAYS/BLUES BY THE BAY. June 1–4. Everett, WA. Four-day blues music festival with top regional bands. Funtastic Shows Carnival, food booths. Fireworks, grand parade, classic car show, limited hydro races and Hawaiian Outrigger Boat Races. Sponsors: City of Everett, Dwayne Lane's Family Auto Centers. Est attendance: 100,000. For info: Marion Pope, Exec Dir, Salty Sea Days Assn, 2520 Colby Ave, Ste 101, Everett, WA 98201. Phone: (425) 339-1113. Fax: (425) 259-0131. E-mail: saltysea@aol.com. Web: www.saltyseadays.org.

EXPERIENCE AIKEN CRAFT SHOW. June 1–2. Aiken, SC. Large craft show featuring 200 crafters from all over the southeast. Carnival rides, juggler, unicyclist and a puppet show. Annually, the first Friday and Saturday in June. Est attendance: 10,000. For info: Lisa J. Hall, Rec Prog Supervisor, City of Aiken Parks & Rec Dept, PO Box 1177, Aiken, SC 29802. Phone: (803) 642-7631. Fax: (803) 642-7639. E-mail: howeeks@aiken.net.

FARMINGTON COUNTRY DAYS. June 1–3. Farmington, MO. Three-day event featuring amusement rides, a free "oldies" concert and a Nashville country star concert, talent show and lots more fun for the whole family. Est attendance: 30,000. For info: Farmington Chamber of Commerce, PO Box 191, Farmington, MO 63640. Phone: (573) 756-3615. Fax: (573) 756-1003. E-mail: laura@fxnet.missouri.org. Web: fxnet.missouri.org/econdev.

FIREWORKS SAFETY MONTH. June 1–July 4. Activities during this month are designed to warn and educate parents and children about the dangers of playing with fireworks. Prevent Blindness America will offer suggestions for safer ways to celebrate the Fourth of July. For info: Prevent Blindness America®, 500 E Remington Rd, Schaumburg, IL 60173. Phone: (800) 331-2020. Fax: (847) 843-8458. Web: www.preventblindness.org.

FISHING HAS NO BOUNDARIES—EAGLE RIVER. June 1–3. Dock Park, Eagle River, WI. A three-day fishing experience for disabled persons on the Eagle River Chain of 28 beautiful lakes. Any disability, age, sex, race, etc, eligible. Attended by 100 participants and 200 volunteers. For info: Wil Campbell, Fishing Has No Boundaries, PO Box 2200, Eagle River, WI 54521. Phone: (715) 479-9309. Fax: (715) 479-4782. E-mail: wbc1@newnorth.net.

FREDERICKSBURG MUSIC FESTIVAL. June 1–13. Final date available after Apr 1. A series of concerts featuring some of the nation's top musicians with musical styles from Dixieland to symphony and jazz to chamber. Occasionally, dance performances are offered. Annually, around the first week of June. Est attendance: 4,500. For info: Fredericksburg Festival of the Arts, Inc, PO Box 7816, Fredericksburg, VA 22404. Phone: (540) 374-5040. Fax: (540) 368-1098.

FRONTIER DAYS. June 1–2. Culbertson, MT. Parades, rodeos, a barn dance, talent show and genuine Western hospitality. Annually, the first weekend in June. Est attendance: 2,000. For info: Ila Mae Forbregd, PO Box 639, Culbertson, MT 59218.

★**GAY AND LESBIAN PRIDE MONTH.** June 1–30. Observed this month because on June 28, 1969, the clientele of a gay bar at New York City rioted after the club was raided by the police. See also: "Stonewall Riot: Anniversary" (June 28).

GREAT WISCONSIN CHEESE FESTIVAL. June 1–3. Little Chute, WI. Festival features cheese breakfast, parade, cheese tasting, cheese-carving demo and cheesecake contest. Est attendance: 10,000. For info: Great Wisconsin Cheese Festival, 1940 Buchanan St, Little Chute, WI 54140-1414. Phone: (920) 788-7390. Fax: (920) 788-7820.

HAPPY WOMEN MONTH. June 1–30. Raise your level of attractiveness and spread a little joy by being happy this month. Compliment, appreciate and thank people, make phone calls to loved ones, spread some cheer, do someone a favor, leave a love note, flirt, send a friendship card, and, most importantly, smile and laugh as much as you can. Put complaining, negativity, competititon, PMS, nagging, put-downs and all forms of "ugliness" in the closet and get out there and have some fun. Go to www.AlluringYou.com to learn how. For info: Kara Oh. Phone: (877) 636-6233. E-mail: KaraOh@AlluringYou.com.

		S	M	T	W	T	F	S
June							1	2
2001		3	4	5	6	7	8	9
		10	11	12	13	14	15	16
		17	18	19	20	21	22	23
		24	25	26	27	28	29	30

HARBORFEST. June 1–3. Norfolk, VA. Live entertainment, sailboat races, water demonstrations, tall sailing ships from around the world, military displays, Chesapeake Bay seafood, special entertainment for children and a spectacular fireworks display. Annually, the first full weekend in June. Est attendance: 500,000. For info: Harborfest, 120 W Main St, Norfolk, VA 23510. Phone: (757) 441-2345. Fax: (757) 441-5198. Web: www.festevents va.org.

HARVARD MILK DAYS FESTIVAL. June 1–3. Harvard, IL. This salute to the dairy farmer includes a parade, evening entertainment, arts and crafts fair, Avenue of Display, milk drinking contest, farm tours, antique farm tractor display, carnival, fireworks, prince and princess contest, Milk Run/Walk (2-mile and 10K run), cattle show, talent show and Wee Farm. Est attendance: 125,000. For info: Harvard Milk Days Office, 201 W Front Street, PO Box 325, Harvard, IL 60033. Phone: (815) 943-4614. Fax: (815) 943-7404. E-mail: milkdays@avenew.com. Web: www.milk days.com.

INTERNATIONAL MEN'S MONTH. June 1–30. This program was initiated in 1996 to increase media and local community awareness of the many unique issues that impact men's lives and that are of concern to the people who love them. In an effort to promote positive changes in male roles and relationships, a different issue is addressed each day of the month during June and information and resources on that issue are provided on the website. This free information can be received automatically be signing up at www.onelist.com/community/Menstuff. For info: Gordon Clay, Exec Dir, National Men's Resource Center, PO Box 800, San Anselmo, CA 94979-0800. E-mail: menstuff@men stuff.org. Web: www.menstuff.org.

INTERNATIONAL PEOPLE SKILLS MONTH. June 1–30. Get a better job, improve the office atmosphere and increase rapport with your family. How? By understanding your personality and the personality of those you relate with on a daily basis. Contact the People Skills Institute for a People Skills Personality Indicator and information on resolving conflicts, gaining influence and encouraging others. For info: Karla Brandau, Dir, People Skills Institute, PO Box 450802, Atlanta, GA 31145-0802. Phone: (770) 923-0883. Fax: (770) 931-2530. E-mail: karla@karla speaks.com. Web: www.karlaspeaks.com.

INTERNATIONAL VOLUNTEERS WEEK. June 1–7. To honor men and women throughout the world who serve as volunteers, rendering valuable service without compensation to the communities in which they live and to honor nonprofit organizations dedicated to making the world a better place in which to live. For complete info, send $4 to cover expense of printing, handling and postage. Annually, the first seven days of June. For info: Dr. Stanley Drake, Pres, Intl Soc of Friendship and Good Will, 8592 Roswell Rd, Ste 434, Atlanta, GA 30350-1870.

JUNE DAIRY MONTH. June 1–30. Since 1937, the dairy industry has set aside June as a time to pay tribute to the vital role milk and dairy products play in the American diet and the outstanding contribution of America's dairy farmers.

JUNE IS TURKEY LOVERS' MONTH. June 1–30. Month-long campaign to promote awareness and increase turkey consumption at a nonholiday time. Annually, the month of June. For info: Natl Turkey Federation, 1225 New York Ave, NW, Ste 400, Washington, DC 20005. Phone: (202) 898-0100. Fax: (202) 898-0203. E-mail: info@turkeyfed.org. Web: www.eatturkey.com.

KENTUCKY: ADMISSION DAY: ANNIVERSARY. June 1. Became 15th state in 1792.

KENYA: MADARAKA DAY. June 1. Madaraka Day (Self-Rule Day) is observed as a national public holiday.

LEWIS AND CLARK DAYS. June 1–3. Washburn, ND. Rediscover the land that Lewis and Clark called home in 1804–05. Fur traders of the 1800s hold a rendezvous at Ft Mandan, while downtown Washburn celebrates with a parade, carnival, street dance, family fishing derby, plus many more fun activities. Est attendance: 4,500. For info: (701) 462-8535 or North Dakota Tourism, 604 E Boulevard, Bismarck, ND 58505. Phone: (701) 328-2525 or (800) 435-5663.

LITTLE, CLEAVON: BIRTH ANNIVERSARY. June 1, 1939. Best known for his role as the black sheriff who cleaned up a town of bumbling redneck toughs in the movie *Blazing Saddles*, Cleavon Little was born at Chickasha, OK. Little was the winner of a Tony award for the 1970 musical *Purlie* and an Emmy in 1989 for a guest appearance on the television series "Dear John." Died Oct 22, 1992, near Sherman Oaks, CA.

MARQUETTE, JACQUES: BIRTH ANNIVERSARY. June 1, 1637. Father Jacques Marquette (Père Marquette), Jesuit missionary-explorer of the Great Lakes region. Born at Laon, France. Died at Ludington, MI, May 18, 1675.

MEDORA MUSICAL. June 1–Sept 9. Medora, ND. Folks whoop it up at this Broadway-class variety show held nightly in a natural amphitheatre in the Badlands. Spectacular sunsets on painted buttes and ravines compete for attention with Western song and dance, all paying tribute to our Roughriding Conservation President, Theodore Roosevelt. Est attendance: 180,000. For info: (800) 633-6721 or Pat Hertz, Publications Asst, North Dakota Tourism, Liberty Memorial Bldg, State Capitol Grounds, Bismarck, ND 58505. Phone: (701) 328-2525. Web: www.ndtourism.com.

MIAMI/BAHAMAS GOOMBAY FESTIVAL. June 1–3. Miami, FL. 25th annual celebration of the black culture and heritage of Bahamian settlers in Miami's Coconut Grove area in the 1800s. Largest black heritage special event in the US. More than 400 vendor booths. Pre-festival events include golf tournament, beauty pageant, sailing regatta. Annually, the first full weekend in June. Est attendance: 600,000. For info: Susan Neuman, Miami/Bahamas Goombay Festival, 555 NE 15th St, #25-K, Miami, FL 33132. Phone: (305) 372-9966. Fax: (305) 372-9967. E-mail: susan_neuman@hotmail.com.

MONROE, MARILYN: 75th BIRTH ANNIVERSARY. June 1, 1926. American actress and sex symbol of the '50s, born at Los Angeles as Norma Jean Mortensen or Baker. She had an unstable childhood in a series of orphanages and foster homes. Her film career came to epitomize Hollywood glamour. In 1954 she wed Yankee legend "Jolting Joe" DiMaggio, but the marriage didn't last. Monroe remained fragile and insecure, tormented by the pressures of Hollywood life. Her death from an overdose Aug 5, 1962, at Los Angeles shocked the world. Among her films: *The Seven Year Itch, Bus Stop, Some Like It Hot, Gentlemen Prefer Blondes* and *The Misfits*.

NATIONAL ACCORDION AWARENESS MONTH. June 1–30. To increase public awareness of this multicultural instrument and its influence and popularity in today's music. For info: All Things Accordion, PO Box 475136, San Francisco, CA 94147-5136. Phone: (415) 440-0800. E-mail: bellows@ladyofspain.com.

NATIONAL ICED TEA MONTH. June 1–30. To celebrate one of the most widely consumed beverages in the world and one of nature's most perfect beverages, and to encourage Americans to refresh themselves with this all-natural, low-calorie, refreshing thirst-quencher. For info: Joseph P. Simrany, Pres, The Tea Council of the USA, 420 Lexington Ave, Ste 825, New York, NY 10170. Phone: (212) 986-6998. Fax: (212) 697-8658.

NATIONAL NEW YEAR'S RESOLUTION RECOMMITMENT DAY. June 1. Still haven't completed those New Year's resolutions? It's time to recommit. What you spend your time doing is a reflection of what you think about yourself; if you're stalling on doing what you know is best for you, then you lack self-respect. People who respect themselves do what maximizes themselves and their relationships. For info: Dr. T. Marie Carson, Individual, Couple & Family Therapist, PO Box 412, Dayton, TX 77535. Phone: (936) 257-0222. E-mail: drtmariecarson@aol.com.

NATIONAL RIVERS MONTH. June 1–30. Commemorated by local groups in many states.

NATIONAL ROSE MONTH. June 1–30. To recognize American-grown roses, our national floral emblem. America's favorite flower is grown in all 50 states and more than 1.2 billion fresh cut roses are sold at retail each year. For advance planning, please note the year 2002 will be designated the Year of the Rose. For info: Mktg Dir, Roses Inc, Box 99, Haslett, MI 48840. Phone: (517) 339-9544. Web: www.rosesinc.org.

NATIONAL SAFETY MONTH. June 1–30. For info: Laura Wilkinson, Natl Safety Council, 1121 Spring Lake Dr, Itasca, IL 60143-3201. Phone: (800) 621-7615, ext 2024. E-mail: wilkinsonl@nsc.org. Web: www.nsc.org.

NATIONAL SCLERODERMA AWARENESS MONTH. June 1–30. The Scleroderma Foundation is committed to providing educational and emotional support to persons with scleroderma and their familes; increasing awareness of this devastating disease; and raising essential research dollars to determine its cause, enhance treatment and find a cure. Call or write for more information, chapter and physician referrals, quarterly newsletter, annual conference and workshop and other info. Sponsor: Scleroderma Foundation, 89 Newbury St, Danvers, MA 01923. Phone: (800) 722-HOPE or (978) 750-4499. Fax: (978) 750-9902. E-mail: sclerofed@aol.com. Web: www.scleroderma.com.

NATIONAL SEAFOOD MONTH. June 1–30. To promote the taste, variety and nutrition of fish and shellfish. For info and recipes: Heather Rivenburg, Natl Fisheries Institute, 1901 N Ft Myer Dr, Ste 700, Arlington, VA 22209. Phone: (703) 524-8881. E-mail: fishery@ix.netcomm.com. Web: www.nfi.org.

NETHERLANDS: HOLLAND FESTIVAL. June 1–30. Holland. World famous festival of the performing arts, music, theatre, and dance in some of the finest theatrical venues. For info: Netherlands Board of Tourism, 355 Lexington Ave, New York, NY 10017. Phone: (800) GOHOLLAND. E-mail: info@holland.com. Web: www.holland.com.

NONGAME WILDLIFE WEEKEND. June 1–3. Blackwater Falls State Park, Davis, WV. Presentations by wildlife professionals regarding nongame wildlife and endangered species. Highlight on Saturday with morning workshops and afternoon field trips such as birdwatching, visiting a snake den, interpretive plant walks, caving, forest ecology, streamlife surveys and how to attract wildlife to the backyard. Annually, the first weekend in June. Est attendance: 300. For info: Jim Fregonara, WV Nongame Wildlife Program, WV Dept of Natural Resources, PO Box 67, Ward Rd, Elkins, WV 26241. Phone: (304) 637-0245. Fax: (304) 637-0250.

PHARMACISTS DECLARE WAR ON ALCOHOLISM.

June 1–30. To encourage pharmacists, healthcare professionals and consumers to better educate and counsel the public on alcoholism and other substance abuse illnesses. By promoting alcohol abuse awareness and education to healthcare professionals and the general public, PCAA strives to break the stereotype surrounding alcoholism that keeps millions of Americans from receiving proper treatment. There is a $15 charge for kit materials. For info: Pharmacists Planning Service, Inc, Pharmacy Council on Alcohol Abuse, 101 Lucas Valley Rd, #210, San Rafael, CA 94903. Phone: (415) 479-8628. Fax: (415) 479-8608. E-mail: ppsi@aol.com. Web: www.ppsinc.org.

PITTSBURGH THREE RIVERS ARTS FESTIVAL.

June 1–17. Gateway Plaza and Point State Park, Downtown Pittsburgh, PA. Arts, crafts and food are part of this 17-day festival where new exhibitors are introduced daily. Visitors can enjoy free performances and the artists' market. For info: Greater Pittsburgh Conv & Visitors Bureau, Regional Enterprise Tower, 30th Fl, 425 Sixth Ave, Pittsburgh, PA 15219-1834. Phone: (412) 281-7711. Fax: (412) 644-5512.

PLYMOUTH PLANTATION EARTHQUAKE: ANNIVERSARY.

June 1, 1638. The first earthquake in the US to have been recorded and described in writing occurred at Plymouth, MA, at 2 PM. Governor William Bradford described the event in his *History*: ." . . it was very terrible for ye time; and as ye men were set talking in ye house, some women and others were without ye doors, and ye earth shooke with ye violence as they could not stand without catching hold of ye posts . . . but ye violence lasted not long. And about halfe an hower, or less, came an other noyse & shaking, but neither so loud nor strong as ye former, but quickly passed over, and so it ceased."

"THE PRISONER" TV PREMIERE: ANNIVERSARY.

June 1, 1968. "The Prisoner" was one of the most imaginative shows on TV, regarded by some as the finest dramatic series in TV history. Patrick McGoohan, who produced and starred in the series, also wrote and directed some episodes. In the series, McGoohan found himself in a self-contained community known as "the village" where he was referred to, not by name, but as Number 6. Number 6 realized he was a prisoner, and spent most of the series trying to escape or to learn the identity of the leader, Number 1. In the last episode, he learned that he was Number 1.

REBUILD YOUR LIFE MONTH.

June 1–30. This is an opportunity for adults neglected and/or abused as children to celebrate their self-worth and discover inner power. They can learn to heal their lives and emotional pain by helping others. For info send SASE: Donald Etkes, PhD, PMB 148, 112 Harvard Ave, Claremont, CA 91711. Phone: (909) 981-7333.

ROSES INDOORS AND OUT.

June 1–July 31. Granville, OH. Granville Life-Style Museum. Robinson family possessions featuring rose motifs: embroidered tablecloths, linens, handpainted china, Rose Bowl Parade magazines, slides and phonographic records, greeting cards and other memorabilia and roses growing in Oese Robinson's garden. For info: Gina Hughes, Dir, Granville Life-Style Museum, H.D. Robinson House, 121 S Main St, Granville, OH 43023. Phone: (740) 587-0373.

SAMOA: INDEPENDENCE DAY.

June 1. The former Western Samoa changed its name in 1997.

		S	M	T	W	T	F	S
June							1	2
2001		3	4	5	6	7	8	9
		10	11	12	13	14	15	16
		17	18	19	20	21	22	23
		24	25	26	27	28	29	30

SITKA SUMMER MUSIC FESTIVAL.

June 1–22. (Tuesdays and Fridays, plus Saturdays June 9, 16.) Sitka, AK. Sitka hosts a highly acclaimed chamber music festival that attracts performers and spectators from all over the world. Est attendance: 4,000. For info: Sitka Summer Music Festival, PO Box 3333, Sitka, AK 99835. Phone: (907) 747-6774. Fax: (907) 747-6853. E-mail: director@sitkamusicfestival.org. Web: www.sitkamusicfestival.org.

SPRINT BILLY BOWLEGS PIRATE FESTIVAL.

June 1–9. Fort Walton Beach, FL. Captain Billy Bowlegs and his Krewe, portrayed by local businessmen, storm the city in the pirate ship *Blackhawk* for a week of fun and frolicking. Two treasure hunts for valuable prizes will take place during the festival. Fireworks on Friday night. Est attendance: 20,000. For info: Chamber of Commerce, PO Box 640, Ft Walton Beach, FL 32549-0640. Phone: (850) 244-8191. Fax: (850) 244-1935. E-mail: Roger@gnt.net. Web: www.fortwaltonbeachfl.org.

STAND FOR CHILDREN DAY.

June 1. Stand for Children is a national organization that encourages individuals to improve children's lives. Its mission is to identify, train and connect local children's activists engaging in advocacy, awareness-raising and service initiatives as part of Children's Action Teams. On this day each year a special issue, such as safer and healthier communities, is highlighted. For info: Children's Defense Fund, Stand for Children, 1834 Connecticut Ave NW, Washington, DC 20009. Phone: (800) 663-4032. Fax: (202) 234-0217. E-mail: tellstand @stand.org. Web: www.stand.org.

STEPPARENTS' WEEK.

June 1–7. The statistics on family life in the '90s are: 50 percent of all marriages end in divorce and 67 percent of all second marriages end in divorce. This week is in recognition of those brave souls who flaunt convention and plow forward despite the statistics. Annually, the first week in June. [©1996] For info: Adrienne Sioux Koopersmith, 1437 W Rosemont, #1W, Chicago, IL 60660-1319. Phone: (773) 743-5341. Fax: (773) 743-5395. E-mail: adrienne@21stcentury .net.

STUDENT SAFETY MONTH.

June 1–30. Heightening the awareness of safety and making sound decisions following graduations, parties, senior proms and other special events. The month encourages young people everywhere not to drink and drive and to use good judgment while celebrating throughout the month. For info: Carole Copeland Thomas, 400 W Cummings Pk, PMB 1725-154, Woburn, MA 01801. Phone: (617) 361-2044 or (800) 801-6599. Fax: (617) 361-1355. E-mail: carole@Tell Carole.com. Web: www.TellCarole.com.

SUN FUN FESTIVAL.

June 1–4 (tentative dates). Myrtle Beach, SC. Beauty contests, sporting events, live television shows, sandcastle-building contest, parade, greet visitors along the Grand Strand. Est attendance: 300,000. For info: Marilyn Chewning, Myrtle Beach Area Chamber of Commerce, PO Box 2115, Myrtle Beach, SC 29578. Phone: (843) 626-7444. Fax: (843) 626-0009. Web: www.myrtlebeachlive.com.

SWAP MEET AND TRACTOR SHOW. June 1–3. Washington, KS. The celebration includes swap meet, flea market, antique tractor and parts auction, antique tractor show, vehicle parade, car races, entertainment, children's games, etc. Est attendance: 5,000. For info: Dir, Washington County Economic Development, Court House, Washington, KS 66968. Phone: (785) 325-2116. Fax: (785) 325-2830. E-mail: washcoed@washington ks.net.

TASTE OF OMAHA. June 1–3. Heartland of America Park, Omaha, NE. Festival of great foods and live entertainment and fun rides for the kids. Est attendance: 40,000. For info: Robert P. Mancuso, Pres, Mid-America Expositions, Inc, PO Box 24851, Omaha, NE 68124-0851. Phone: (402) 346-8003. Fax: (402) 346-5412. Web: www.showofficeonline.com.

TENNESSEE: ADMISSION DAY: ANNIVERSARY. June 1. Became 16th state in 1796. Observed as a holiday in Tennessee.

VISION RESEARCH MONTH. June 1–30. Millions of Americans have healthy sight because of the work of medical and scientific researchers investigating vision-related problems. During this observance, Prevent Blindness America® encourages people to support vision-research letter-writing campaigns to Congress. Success in vision research is highlighted. Materials are available. For info: Prevent Blindness America®, 500 E Remington Rd, Schaumburg, IL 60173. Phone: (800) 331-2020. Fax: (847) 843-8458. Web: www.preventblindness.org.

WOLF POINT'S HOTTEST CHILI WEEKEND. June 1–2. Sherman Park, Stampede Ground, Wolf Point, MT. Carnival, demolition derby, chili cook-off. Est attendance: 1,500. For info: Wolf Point Optimist Club, PO Box 486, Wolf Point, MT 59201. Phone: (406) 653-3739 (evenings). E-mail: rboysun@midrivers .com or rab@wolfpoint.com. Web: www.wolfpoint.com/chili. htm.

YOUNG, BRIGHAM: 200th BIRTH ANNIVERSARY. June 1, 1801. Mormon church leader born at Whittingham, VT. Known as "the American Moses," having led thousands of religious followers across 1,000 miles of wilderness to settle more than 300 towns in the West. He died at Salt Lake City, UT, Aug 29, 1877, and was survived by 17 wives and 47 children. Utah observes, as a state holiday, the anniversary of his entrance into the Salt Lake Valley, July 24, 1847.

BIRTHDAYS TODAY

Rene Auberjonois, 61, actor (*M*A*S*H*, "Benson"; stage: *Coco* [Tony Award]), born New York, NY, June 1, 1940.

James Hadley Billington, 72, Librarian of Congress, born Bryn Mawr, PA, June 1, 1929.

Pat Boone, 67, singer, actor (*State Fair*), author, born Jacksonville, FL, June 1, 1934.

Pat Corley, 71, actor ("Bay City Blues," "Murphy Brown"), born Dallas, TX, June 1, 1930.

Mark Curry, 37, comedian, actor ("Hangin' With Mr Cooper"), born Oakland, CA, June 1, 1964.

Morgan Freeman, 64, stage and film actor (*Driving Miss Daisy*), born Memphis, TN, June 1, 1937.

Andy Griffith, 75, actor ("Matlock," "The Andy Griffith Show"), born Mount Airy, NC, June 1, 1926.

Lisa Hartman Black, 45, actress ("Tabitha," "Knots Landing"), born Houston, TX, June 1, 1956.

Alexi Lalas, 31, soccer player, born Detroit, MI, June 1, 1970.

Alanis Morissette, 27, singer, born, Ottawa, Ontario, Canada, June 1, 1974.

Jonathan Pryce, 54, actor (*The Age of Innocence, Glengarry Glen Ross*; stage: *Miss Saigon*; Tony Awards for *Comedians* and *Hamlet*), born Holywell, North Wales, June 1, 1947.

Frederica von Stade, 56, opera mezzo-soprano, born Somerville, NJ, June 1, 1945.

Ron Wood, 54, musician (guitarist with the Rolling Stones), born London, England, June 1, 1947.

Edward Woodward, 71, actor, singer ("The Equalizer," *Wicker Man, Breaker Morant*), born Croydon, England, June 1, 1930.

JUNE 2 — SATURDAY
Day 153 — 212 Remaining

BELGIUM: PROCESSION OF THE GOLDEN CHARIOT. June 2. Mons. Horse-drawn coach carrying a reliquary of St. Waudru circles the town of Mons. Procession commemorates delivery of Mons from the plague in 1349. In the town square, in afternoon, St. George fights the dragon.

BIGG'S KIDS' FEST. June 2–3. Central riverfront, Cincinnati, OH. Largest free event in the country for kids and their families. More than 100 free activities. Est attendance: 120,000. For info: Catherine Pleva, Event Producer, Clear Channel Communications, Inc, 1111 St. Gregory St, Cincinnati, OH 45202. Phone: (513) 852-1646. Fax: (513) 333-4269. E-mail: catherinepleva @clearchannel.com.

BULGARIA: HRISTO BOTEV DAY: 125th ANNIVERSARY. June 2. Poet and national hero Hristro Botev fell fighting Turks, 1876.

CAPITOL HILL PEOPLE'S FAIR. June 2–3. Civic Center Park, Denver, CO. More than 500 arts and crafts and other exhibit booths; live entertainment featuring local talent on six stages. Est attendance: 300,000. For info: Capitol Hill United Neighborhoods, 1490 Lafayette, #401, Denver, CO 80218. Phone: (303) 830-1651. Fax: (303) 830-1782. E-mail: TJKNORR@aol.com. Web: www.peoplesfair.com.

CHICKEN AND EGG FESTIVAL. June 2–3. Prescott, AR. Two days of athletic events, shows and entertainment for the entire family. Come and watch our famous Cackling and Crowing contest in Southwest Arkansas's friendliest city. Other activities include: 5-K run and walk, tennis tournament, softball, weight lifting, antique car show, Little Miss Hen and Little Mr Rooster Beauty Pageants and much more. Est attendance: 4,000. For info: Mary Godwin, PO Box 307, Prescott, AR 71857. Phone: (870) 887-2101. Fax: (870) 887-5317. E-mail: wdenton@pcfa.org. Web: partnership.pcfa.org/.

CMN CHAMPIONS. June 2–3. The largest televised fundraiser in history. More than $156 million was raised in 1998. Benefits 170 North American hospitals for children. For info: Children's Miracle Network, 4525 S 2300 E, Salt Lake City, UT 84117. Phone: (801) 278-8900. Web: www.cmn.org.

COUNTRYSIDE VILLAGE ART FAIR. June 2–3. Omaha, NE. Exhibits by 140 artists from 15 states. Juried fine arts show. 31st annual show. Est attendance: 10,000. For info: Judy Drawbaugh, Countryside Merchants Assn, 2336 S 138th St, Omaha, NE 68144. Phone: (402) 333-9629.

COWS ON THE CONCOURSE. June 2. Madison, WI. Pet a cow on the capitol square to celebrate June Dairy Month. Major breeds of cows will be on display. Ample samplings of all types of dairy products made in Wisconsin. Antique tractors, dairy-related crafts demonstrations and displays. Annually, the first Saturday in June. Est attendance: 20,000. For info: Rick Trinko, 3978 Schewe Rd, Middleton, WI 53562. Phone: (608) 829-3487.

DENMARK: EEL FESTIVAL. June 2–3. Jyllinge (near Roskilde). Festival celebrated since 1968. Every restaurant and pub in town serves delicious fried eel. Other entertainments include theater, sports, tattoo bands, sailing competitions, flea markets and fireworks. Annually, the first weekend in June.

DO-DAH PARADE. June 2. Kalamazoo, MI. "Salute to Silliness." Since 1981, offbeat entries have included a precision grill team (complete with spatulas) and a herbie curbie brigade. Annually, the first Saturday in June. Est attendance: 60,000. For info: Lisa Theisen, WKMI/WKFR Radio, 4154 Jennings Dr, Kalamazoo, MI 49005-0911. Phone: (616) 344-0111. Fax: (616) 344-4223. E-mail: LTheisen@wkfr.com. Web: www.wkfr.com.

FORT SISSETON HISTORICAL FESTIVAL. June 2–3. Fort Sisseton State Park, Lake City, SD. Fort Sisseton comes alive the first weekend in June every year. See life as it was in 1864 when the fort was established. Cavalry drills, military costume ball, Indian dancing, Dakota Dan's medicine show, wagon train, muzzle-loader shoot, rendezvous, draft-horse pulls, fiddlers, square dancing, melodramas and arts and crafts are popular features of the festival. Est attendance: 46,000. For info: Dave Daberkow, Fort Sisseton State Park, Dept of Game, Fish and Parks, 11545 Northside Dr, Lake City, SD 57247-6142. Phone: (605) 448-5701. Fax: (605) 448-5572. Web: www.state.sd.us/gfp/.

FREDERICK FESTIVAL OF THE ARTS. June 2–3. Carroll Creek Linear Park, Frederick, MD. A fine arts and fine craft juried arts market of 140 exhibitors. Two food courts, canoe and kayak rentals, children's interactive art center, art demos, literary activities, paved and tented booth sites and three stages of entertainment. Annually, the first weekend in June. Est attendance: 25,000. For info: Frederick Festival of the Arts, PO Box 3080, Frederick, MD 21705. Phone: (301) 694-9632. Fax: (301) 682-7378. E-mail: festarts@fred.net. Web: frederickarts.org.

GHOST TOURS. June 2. New Hope, PA. (Also every Saturday, June–August, and every Friday and Saturday, September–November.) Tours meet at 8 PM sharp at the Cannon on Main Street. No reservations required. Rain or shine. $8 per person. Private walks and gift certificates available. No tours July 4th weekend or Labor Day weekend. For info: Ghost Tours, PO Box 3354, Warminster, PA 18974. Phone: (215) 957-9988. E-mail: ghstofpa @aol.com.

GOVERNOR'S CUP. June 2. Helena, MT. Montana's premier running event. Includes a marathon, marathon relay, 20K, 10K and 5K. Corporate entries. Approximately 3,000 runners. Annually, the first Saturday in June. Sponsor: Blue Cross/Blue Shield. Est attendance: 7,000. For info: Tracy L. Koder, Race Dir, Blue Cross & Blue Shield, Box 451, Helena, MT 59624. Phone: (406) 447-3414. Fax: (406) 447-8607. Web: www.govcup.bcbsmt.com.

HEIRLOOM SEED DAY. June 2. Woodstock, VT. Learn about the importance of heirloom vegetables and the many seed varieties available. Take home a packet of select seeds saved from the museum's 19th-century garden. For info: Billings Farm & Museum, Box 489, Woodstock, VT 05091. Phone: (802) 457-2355. Fax: (802) 457-4663. E-mail: billings.farm@valley.net.

HORSERADISH FESTIVAL. June 2–3 (also June 8–9, 15–16). Collinsville, IL. Join in the fun at the horseradish capital of the world. Horseradish eating contest, root toss competition, races, food, music and more. For info: Collinsville Chamber of Commerce. Phone: (618) 344-2884.

ITALY: REPUBLIC DAY: 55th ANNIVERSARY. June 2. National holiday. Commemorates 1946 referendum in which republic status was selected instead of return to monarchy.

JUNE JUNQUE JAMBOREE. June 2. Lovington, NM. Townwide garage sale with merchants, clubs and individuals all participating. For info: Andra Conner, Lovington Chamber of Commerce, 201 S Main St, Lovington, NM 88260. Phone: (505) 396-5311. Fax: (505) 396-2823. E-mail: visitus@leaconet.com. Web: visitus.leaco.net.

	S	M	T	W	T	F	S
June						1	2
2001	3	4	5	6	7	8	9
	10	11	12	13	14	15	16
	17	18	19	20	21	22	23
	24	25	26	27	28	29	30

MAINE LAW: 150th ANNIVERSARY. June 2, 1851. America's first statewide statute prohibiting the sale of alcoholic beverages was enacted in the state of Maine, June 2, 1851. The following Independence Day the mayor of Bangor showed his support of the new law by smashing 10 kegs of confiscated booze.

MARBLE MEET AT AMANA. June 2–3. Holiday Inn, Amana, IA. Seminar, banquet and exhibits. Collectors buy, sell and trade marbles. Est attendance: 800. For info: Marble Collectors Unltd, Box 206, Northboro, MA 01532. Phone: (319) 642-3891 or (508) 393-2923. E-mail: marblesbev@aol.com.

MARQUIS DE SADE: BIRTH ANNIVERSARY. June 2, 1740. Donatien-Alphonse-François, Comte de Sade, was born at Paris, France. French military man, governor-general and author, who spent much of his life in prison because of his acts of cruelty and violence, outrageous behavior and debauchery. The word *sadism* was created from his name to describe gratification in inflicting pain. He died near Paris, at the Charenton lunatic asylum, Dec 2, 1814.

MISSISSIPPI BROILER FESTIVAL. June 2. Clark Park, Forest, MS. A variety of entertainment, arts, crafts. Also, tennis tournaments, youth league baseball tournament, coronation of Broiler Festival Queen, Mississippi Track Grand Prix Race, concert and fireworks. Est attendance: 5,000. For info: Patsy Nicholson, Forest Area Chamber of Commerce, PO Box 266, Forest, MS 39074. Phone: (601) 469-4332. Fax: (601) 469-3224.

MISSOURI STATE CHAMPIONSHIP RACKING HORSE SHOW. June 2. Stoddard County Fairgrounds, Dexter, MO. At this 24th annual event elegant showmanship by both horse and rider provides an afternoon and evening of spectator pleasure. Annually, the first Saturday in June. Est attendance: 500. For info: Missouri State Chmpshp Racking Horse Show, PO Box 21, Dexter, MO 63841. Phone: (573) 624-7458 or (800) 332-8857. Fax: (573) 624-7459.

NATIONAL FISHING WEEK. June 2–10. Annual celebration providing opportunities for youths to experience recreational fishing, learn about the environment firsthand and practice conservation ethics. We encourage all to take a friend fishing. Est attendance: 500,000. For info: Natl Fishing Week Steering Committee, 1033 N Fairfax St, Ste 200, Alexandria, VA 22314-1540. Phone: (703) 684-3201. E-mail: info@gofishing.org. Web: www.gofishing.org/.

NATIONAL HOMEOWNERSHIP WEEK. June 2–9. Sponsored by a public-private partnership that encourages homeownership. Partners include associations from the homebuilding and banking industries and nonprofits like Habitat for Humanity. For info: National Partners in Homeownership, Dept of Housing and Urban Development, 451 Seventh St SW, Washington, DC 20410. Phone: (800) 297-4183. Web: www.hud.gov/fha/sfh/nhs/partners.html.

NATIONAL TRAILS DAY. June 2. National Trails Day celebrates trails and the volunteers who maintain them. The first Saturday of every June more than 3,000 trail organizations, agencies, and businesses across the country host a variety of events including new trail dedications, workshops, educational exhibits, equestrian and mountain bike rides, boat paddling, rollerblading, trail maintenance projects, and, as always, hikes on backcountry trails in America's wild lands. For info: American Hiking Soc, PO Box 20160, Washington, DC 20041-2160. Phone: (301) 565-6704. E-mail: info@americanhiking.org. Web: www.americanhiking.org.

PEACHTREE JUNIOR. June 2. Atlanta, GA. A 3K noncompetitive run for children ages 7–12. Entries limited to 2,500. Online registration available. Send SASE for info: Atlanta Track Club, Peachtree Jr, 3097 E Shadowlawn Ave, Atlanta, GA 30305. Phone: (404) 231-9064. Web: www.atlantatrackclub.org.

PEDDLER'S VILLAGE FINE ART & CONTEMPORARY CRAFTS SHOW. June 2–3. Juried competition of paintings, prints, photography and more created by fine artists, plus contemporary crafts. Hands-on art activities for children. Shops offer various in-store exhibits and arts-related events. Live music, face painting and balloons. Free admission. Est attendance: 12,000. For info: Peddler's Village, Routes 202 & 263, Lahaska, PA 18931. Phone: (215) 794-4000. Fax: (215) 794-4001. Web: www.peddlersvillage.com.

PET PARADE. June 2. LaGrange, IL. Children and their pets parade through the streets of LaGrange in costume, accompanied by clowns, floats, celebrities and marching bands. Trophies awarded to the most original entries in 10 costume categories. Annually, the first Saturday in June. Est attendance: 10,000. For info: West Suburban Chamber of Commerce, PO Box 187, LaGrange, IL 60525. Phone: (708) 352-0494. Fax: (708) 352-0620. E-mail: wscc@megsinet.net. Web: www.westsuburban chamber.org.

PRINTERS ROW BOOK FAIR. June 2–3. South Dearborn Street between Congress and Polk at Chicago, IL. More than 170 booksellers and publishers from all over the US and Canada fill the streets with new, used, rare and antiquarian books for sale; demonstrations of paper making, paper marbling and book binding; author readings, panel discussions, poetry tent and an elaborate children's program are all part of the free programs. Food, music and much more at the largest book event in the Midwest. Est attendance: 75,000. For info: Mary Davis Fournier, Program Dir, Near South Planning Bd, 1727 S Indiana, Ste G02A, Chicago, IL 60616. Fax: (312) 987-9215. E-mail: prbookfair@ aol.com.

REOPENING OF THE SCHOHARIE VALLEY RAIL-ROADS MUSEUM. June 2. Depot Lane Complex, Schoharie, NY. Open each weekend, 1–5 PM, June through October. Also featuring Railroad Day, Sept 22. Est attendance: 500. For info: Schoharie Colonial Heritage Assn, PO Box 554, Schoharie, NY 12157. Phone: (518) 295-7505. E-mail: scha@midtel.net.

SAINT PIUS X: BIRTH ANNIVERSARY. June 2, 1835. Giuseppe Melchiorre Sarto, 257th pope of the Roman Catholic Church, born at Riese, Italy. Elected pope Aug 4, 1903. Died Aug 20, 1914, at Rome, Italy. Canonized May 29, 1954.

SMALL CRAFT WEEKEND. June 2–3. Mystic Seaport, Mystic, CT. The 32nd annual weekend when small-craft enthusiasts gather at the museum with their boats. Traditional small boats of every type sail from docks of Mystic Seaport on the Mystic River. Annually, first weekend in June. Est attendance: 4,000. For info: Mystic Seaport, 75 Greenmanville Ave, Box 6000, Mystic, CT 06355. Phone: (860) 572-5315 or (888) 9SEAPORT. Web: www.mysticseaport.org.

SOUTH JERSEY CANOE AND KAYAK CLASSIC. June 2. Ocean County Park, Rt 88, Lakewood, NJ. Canoe and Kayak vendors from around the country set up on the beach to show the public the thrill of water sports. You may test paddle the boats of your choice and attend a clinic about canoeing or kayaking throughout the day. Manufacturers, canoe clubs, accessories and more. Free rain or shine. Annually, the first Saturday in June. Est attendance: 3,000. For info: Michelle Urban, Coord, Wells Mills County Park, 905 Wells Mills Rd, Waretown, NJ 08758. Phone: (609) 971-3085. Fax: (609) 971-9540.

STORMIN' NORMAN POWOW. June 2. Memorial Courts, Kellog, ID. Sanctioned singles horseshoes. For info: Vicki McEnany, PO Box 770, Pinehurst, ID 83850-0770.

STRAWBERRY FESTIVAL. June 2. Vaile Mansion, Independence, MO. Outdoor Victorian-type festival featuring strawberry treats, crafts, antiques, children's activities, carriage rides, flea market and entertainment. Annually, first Saturday in June. For info: Stephanie Roush, Tourism Dir, 111 E Maple, Independence, MO 64050. Phone: (816) 252-9098.

TOPPENISH MURAL SOCIETY'S "MURAL-IN-A-DAY." June 2. Pioneer Park, Toppenish, WA. 12 professional artists paint a complete, historically authentic mural, 14′ × 48′, in eight hours. Starting at 9 AM they work until finished, usually until 4 PM. Accompanied by an arts and crafts show and an ethnic food fair. Annually, the first Saturday in June. Est attendance: 12,000. For info: Toppenish Mural Society, PO Box 1172, Toppenish, WA 98948. Phone: (509) 865-6516. E-mail: murals@ wolfenet.com. Web: www.wolfenet.com/~murals/.

TURTLE RACES. June 2. Knights of Columbus, Danville, IL. More than 100 turtles compete in 36th annual races throughout the day. Concessions available. Food and fun. Proceeds go to help people in the area with disabilities. Annually, the first Saturday in June. Est attendance: 3,000. For info: Nadine Schramm, Turtle Club, 2932 Batestown Rd, Oakwood, IL 61858. Phone: (217) 446-5327 or (800) 383-4386.

UNITED KINGDOM: CORONATION DAY. June 2. Commemorates the crowning of Queen Elizabeth II in 1953.

WEISSMULLER, JOHNNY: BIRTH ANNIVERSARY. June 2, 1904. Peter John (Johnny) Weissmuller, actor and Olympic gold medal swimmer, born at Windber, PA. Weissmuller won three gold medals at the 1924 Olympics and two more at the 1928 games. He set 24 world records and in 1950 was voted the best swimmer of the first half of the 20th century. After retiring from amateur competition, he appeared as Tarzan in a dozen movies and as "Jungle Jim" in the movies and on television. Died at Acapulco, Mexico, Jan 20, 1984.

YELL "FUDGE" AT THE COBRAS IN NORTH AMERICA DAY. June 2. Anywhere north of the Panama Canal. In order to keep poisonous cobra snakes out of North America, all citizens are asked to go outdoors at noon, local time, and yell "Fudge." Fudge makes cobras gag and the mere mention of it makes them skeedaddle. Annually, June 2. [© 2000 by WH] For info: Thomas or Ruth Roy, Wellcat Holidays, 2418 Long Ln, Lebanon, PA 17046. Phone: (717) 279-0184. E-mail: wellcat@super net.com. Web: www.wellcat.com.

ZOO BABIES. June 2–July 1. Cincinnati Zoo and Botanical Garden, Cincinnati, OH. The adorable new offspring are made easy to find with 8-ft storks placed at baby animal areas. Special weekend family entertainment. Est attendance: 180,000. For info: Events/Promo Dept, Cincinnati Zoo and Botanical Garden, 3400 Vine St, Cincinnati, OH 45220. Phone: (513)281-4701 ext 8316. Fax: (513) 559-7790. Web: www.cincyzoo.org.

BIRTHDAYS TODAY

Diana Canova, 48, actress ("Soap," "I'm a Big Girl Now"), born West Palm Beach, FL, June 2, 1953.

Dana Carvey, 46, comedian, actor (*Wayne's World*, "Saturday Night Live"), born Missoula, MT, June 2, 1955.

Gary Grimes, 46, actor (*Summer of '42, Class of '44*), born San Francisco, CA, June 2, 1955.

Charles Haid, 58, actor ("Hill Street Blues," "Delvecchio"), producer, born San Francisco, CA, June 2, 1943.

Marvin Hamlisch, 57, composer (Oscars for *The Sting, The Way We Were*; Tony for *A Chorus Line*), born New York, NY, June 2, 1944.

Stacy Keach, Jr, 60, actor (*Conduct Unbecoming*, "Mickey Spillane's Mike Hammer"), born Savannah, GA, June 2, 1941.

Sally Kellerman, 65, actress (*M*A*S*H, Back to School*), born Long Beach, CA, June 2, 1936.

Jerry Mathers, 53, actor ("Leave It to Beaver"), born Sioux City, IA, June 2, 1948.

Milo O'Shea, 75, actor (*The Purple Rose of Cairo*), born Dublin, Ireland, June 2, 1926.

Charlie Watts, 60, musician (drummer with the Rolling Stones), born Islington, England, June 2, 1941.

JUNE 3 — SUNDAY
Day 154 — 211 Remaining

BLACK HILLS PASSION PLAY—SOUTH DAKOTA. June 3–Aug 30. Passion Play Amphitheater, Spearfish, SD. Spectacular outdoor drama on a huge stage depicts the last seven days in the life of Christ. It features a cast of more than 200 and live animals. Annually, Sunday, Tuesday and Thursday evenings. Est attendance: 50,000. For info: Black Hills Passion Play—South Dakota, PO Box 489, Spearfish, SD 57783. Phone: (605) 642-2646 or (800) 457-0160. Fax: (941) 638-2037. E-mail: BHPP@blackhills.com. Web: www.blackhills.com/~BHPP.

BLACK SINGLE PARENTS' WEEK. June 3–9. This week is to honor all the black single parents who have successfully raised their sons and daughters depsite poor schools, crime and drug-infested neighborhoods to be responsible, self-sufficient (and sometimes famous) citizens. For info: Will Barnes, Exec Dir, The Black Single Parents' Network, 7732 S Cottage Grove, #431, Chicago, IL 60619. Phone: (773) 375-2214. Fax: (773) 375-6252. E-mail: enless@mailcity.com.

CHILDREN'S AWARENESS DAY. June 3. A day set aside each year to remember all of America's children who have died from violence. A day to bring flowers to the gravesite, have memorial services, spend time with or write a letter to a grieving parent or grandparent. A day to mourn and reach out with healing hands of love to those in need of support. Annually, the first Sunday in June. For info: Judith Natale, Natl Children & Family Awareness of America, 3060 Rt 405 Hwy, Muncy, PA 17756-8808. Phone: (888) MAA-DESK. E-mail: ChildAware@aol.com or MaaJudith@aol.com.

CHIMBORAZO DAY. June 3. To bring the shape of the earth into focus by publicizing the fact that Mount Chimborazo, Ecuador, near the equator, pokes farther out into space than any other mountain on earth, including Mount Everest. (The distance from sea level at the equator to the center of the earth is 13 miles greater than the radius to sea level at the north pole. This means that New Orleans is about six miles further from the center of the earth than is Lake Itasca at the headwaters of the Mississippi, so the Mississippi flows uphill.) For info: Robert L. Birch, Puns Corps, Box 2364, Falls Church, VA 22042-0364. Phone: (703) 533-3668.

June	S	M	T	W	T	F	S
2001						1	2
	3	4	5	6	7	8	9
	10	11	12	13	14	15	16
	17	18	19	20	21	22	23
	24	25	26	27	28	29	30

CRAZY HORSE MEMORIAL DEDICATED: ANNIVERSARY. June 3, 1998. The nine-story-high face of Crazy Horse was dedicated in South Dakota. When completed, the Crazy Horse Memorial will be the largest sculpture in the world. It will be 563 ft high and 641 ft long. The 22-story-high horse's head is the next major stage of the mountain carving in progress. Construction by sculptor Korczak Ziolkowski began in 1948. Since his death in 1982, work has been continued by his family. For info: Crazy Horse Memorial, Ave of the Chiefs, Crazy Horse, SD 57730-9506. Phone: (605) 673-4681.

DAVIS, JEFFERSON: BIRTH ANNIVERSARY. June 3, 1808. American statesman, US senator, only president of the Confederate States of America. Imprisoned May 10, 1865–May 13, 1867, but never brought to trial, deprived of rights of citizenship after the Civil War. Davis was born at Todd County, KY, and died at New Orleans, LA, Dec 6, 1889. His citizenship was restored, posthumously, Oct 17, 1978, when President Carter signed an Amnesty Bill. This bill, he said, "officially completes the long process of reconciliation that has reunited our people following the tragic conflict between the states." Davis's birth anniversary is observed in Florida, Kentucky and South Carolina on this day, in Alabama on the first Monday in June and in Mississippi on the last Monday in May. Davis's birth anniversary is observed as Confederate Memorial Day in Tennessee.

DEWHURST, COLLEEN: BIRTH ANNIVERSARY. June 3, 1924. Colleen Dewhurst was born at Quebec, Canada. Her 40-year career as an actress spanned stage, screen and television. After making her Broadway debut in Eugene O'Neill's *Desire Under the Elms* in 1952, she became the actress most associated with O'Neill's works in the later part of this century, also performing in *Long Day's Journey into Night, Mourning Becomes Electra, Ah, Wilderness!* and *A Moon for the Misbegotten,* for which she won her second Tony award. At the time of her death, she was president of Actor's Equity Association, the union for professional actors and stage managers. She won three Emmy awards, including one for her role as Murphy Brown's mother on the TV show "Murphy Brown" (1989). She died Aug 22, 1991, at South Salem, NY.

DREW, CHARLES RICHARD: BIRTH ANNIVERSARY. June 3, 1904. African American physician who discovered how to store blood plasma and who organized the blood bank system in the US and UK during WWII. Born at Washington, DC, he was killed in an automobile accident near Burlington, NC, Apr 1, 1950.

FIRST WOMAN RABBI IN US: ANNIVERSARY. June 3, 1972. Sally Jan Priesand was ordained the first woman rabbi in the US. She became assistant rabbi at the Stephen Wise Free Synagogue, New York City, Aug 1, 1972.

GINSBERG, ALLEN: 75th BIRTH ANNIVERSARY. June 3, 1926. Poet of the Beat Generation ("Howl"), born Newark, NJ. Died Apr 5, 1997, at New York, NY.

HOBART, GARRET AUGUSTUS: BIRTH ANNIVERSARY. June 3, 1844. 24th vice president of the US (1897–99), born at Long Branch, NJ. Died at Paterson, NJ, Nov 21, 1899.

HOCKHOCKING FOLK FESTIVAL. June 3. Robbins Crossing, Hocking College Campus, Nelsonville, OH. A celebration of music, culture and heritage set in an authentic pioneer village. Headline entertainment and other musicians. Visitors are encouraged to bring instruments for jam sessions, lawn chairs and blankets. Instrument building, make and take area, storytelling, dancing and food. For info: Ken Bowald, Hocking College, 3301 Hocking Pkwy, Nelsonville, OH 45764. Phone: (740) 753-3591, ext 2555. E-mail: bowald_k@hocking.edu.

HONE, WILLIAM: BIRTH ANNIVERSARY. June 3, 1780. English author and bookseller born at Bath, England; died at Tottenham, Nov 6, 1842. Compiler of *The Every-Day Book, or Everlasting Calendar of Popular Amusements* (1826). It was William Hone who said: "A good lather is half the shave."

INTERNATIONAL PBX TELECOMMUNICATORS WEEK. June 3–9. To honor the switchboard operators of private businesses, to acknowledge their dedicated professionalism and the vital role they play in the modern business world. Annually, the first full week in June. For info: Mary Bohl, Secretary, Intl PBX Telecommunicators Clubs, S 6145 Sundance Place, Eau Claire, WI 54701. Phone: (715) 839-6075. Fax: (715) 839-6015. E-mail: bohlrm@ecol.net.

ITALY: GIOCO DEL PONTE. June 3. Pisa. The first Sunday in June is set aside for the Battle of the Bridge, a medieval parade and a contest for possession of the bridge.

JACK JOUETT'S RIDE: ANNIVERSARY. June 3, 1781. Jack Jouett made a heroic 45-mile ride on horseback during the night of June 3–4, 1781, to warn Virginia Governor Thomas Jefferson and the legislature that the British were coming. Jouett rode from a tavern in Louisa County to Charlottesville, VA, in about 6½ hours, arriving at Jefferson's home at dawn on June 4. Lieutenant Colonel Tarleton's British forces raided Charlottesville, but Jouett's warning gave the Americans time to escape. Jouett was born at Albemarle County, VA, Dec 7, 1754, and died at Bath, KY, in 1822 (exact date unknown).

JAPAN: DAY OF THE RICE GOD. June 3. Chiyoda. Annual rice-transplanting festival observed on first Sunday in June. Centuries-old rural folk ritual revived in 1930s and celebrated with colorful costumes, parades, music, dancing and prayers to the Shinto rice god Wbai-sama.

KHOMEINI, AYATOLLAH RUHOLLAH: DEATH ANNIVERSARY. June 3, 1989. The Ayatollah Ruhollah Khomeini, leader of the Islamic Revolution, lifelong foe of the Shah of Iran, was arrested in 1963 after giving a speech accusing the Shah of seeking to destroy Islam. He was exiled to Turkey in 1964, following which he spent 13 years in Iraq and Paris, where he gained exposure to the world press for his cause. On Jan 16, 1979, the Shah of Iran left the country for a supposed vacation, setting the stage for Khomeini's triumphant return on Jan 31. The monarchy fell on Feb 11, 1979. Khomeini proceeded to reorganize the government based on Islamic principles. On Nov 11, 1979, a group of students loyal to Khomeini occupied the American Embassy in Teheran after the Shah was given admittance to the US for medical treatment, placing the Ayatollah at the center of a diplomatic crisis that consumed the presidency of Jimmy Carter. Khomeini focused attention on the US as the "Great Satan" and blamed many of his country's problems on imperialistic intervention.

MIGHTY CASEY HAS STRUCK OUT: ANNIVERSARY. June 3, 1888. The famous comic baseball ballad "Casey at the Bat" was printed in the Sunday *San Francisco Examiner*. Appearing anonymously, it was written by Ernest L. Thayer. Recitation of "Casey at the Bat" became part of the repertoire of actor William DeWolf Hopper. The recitation took 5 minutes and 40 seconds. Hopper claimed to have recited it more than 10,000 times, the first being at Wallack's Theater at New York, NY, in 1888. See also: "Thayer, Ernest Lawrence: Birth Anniversary" (Aug 14).

MISSION SAN CARLOS BORROMEO DE CARMELO: FOUNDING ANNIVERSARY. June 3, 1770. California mission to the Indians founded on this date.

NATIONAL CANCER SURVIVORS DAY. June 3. More than 700 communities nationwide honor survivors who are living with and beyond cancer. The 14th annual celebration of life. Annually, the first Sunday in June. For info: Natl Cancer Survivors Day Foundation, PO Box 682285, Franklin, TN 37068-2285. Phone: (615) 793-3006. Fax: (615) 794-0179. Web: www.ncsdf.org.

NATIONAL HEADACHE AWARENESS WEEK. June 3–9. Educating the public about the reality and severity of headache pain as a legitimate biological disease. Encouraging sufferers to consult with a physician for proper diagnosis and treatment, and to let sufferers know that there are new treatments available. For info: Suzanne E. Simons, Exec Dir, Natl Headache Foundation, 428 W St. James Place, 2nd Fl, Chicago, IL 60614-2750. Phone: (773) 388-6395. Fax: (773) 525-7357.

NATIONAL HUG HOLIDAY WEEK. June 3–9. Huggers of all ages are invited to make a difference one hug at a time for our elderly in support of the Hugs for Health movement. The Hugs for Health Foundation provides hug therapy and volunteer support services to the elderly residing in senior care and residential communities across the country. Send $5 for Holiday Hugger's package. For info: Hug Holiday Dept, Hugs for Health Foundation, PO Box 1704, Tustin, CA 92781. Web: www.hugs4health.org.

ORTHODOX PENTECOST. June 3. Observed by Eastern Orthodox churches.

PALATINE MUSEUM SPRING EVENT. June 3 (also Oct 7). Sheep shearing festival at Palatine House Museum, Schoharie, NY. This event is fun for the whole family. Oct 7 is Fall Harvest/Dye Day. Est attendance: 1,700. For info: Angela DeGroff, Program Dir, Schoharie Colonial Heritage Assn, Box 554, Schoharie, NY 12157. Phone: (518) 295-7505 or (518) 295-7585. E-mail: scha@midtel.net.

PENTECOST. June 3. The Christian feast of Pentecost commemorates descent of the Holy Spirit unto the Apostles, 50 days after Easter. Observed on the seventh Sunday after Easter. Recognized since the third century. See also: "Whitsunday" (below).

RED CLOUD INDIAN ART SHOW. June 3–Aug 12. Pine Ridge, SD. Encourages Native American artists and gives their artwork exposure to the general public. Juried Art Show with cash awards. Est attendance: 12,500. For info: Brother C.M. Simon, Red Cloud Indian School, Pine Ridge, SD 57770. Phone: (605) 867-5491. Fax: (605) 867-1291. Web: www.basec.net/~rcheritage.

★ **SMALL BUSINESS WEEK.** June 3–9. To honor the 22 million small businesses in the US. Annually, the first full week in June. For info: Small Business Administration, Info Services, 409 3rd St SW, 7th Fl, Washington, DC 20416. Phone: (202) 205-6606 or (202) 205-6531. Web: www.sba.gov.

SPACE MILESTONE: *GEMINI 4* (US). June 3, 1965. James McDivitt and Edward White made 66 orbits of Earth. White took the first space walk by an American and maneuvered 20 minutes outside the capsule.

SUNFLOWER MUSIC FESTIVAL. June 3–16. White Concert Hall, Washburn University, Topeka, KS. Nationally renowned chamber music students gather to perform a series of free concerts featuring ensembles and orchestras. No admission charge. For info: Washburn Univ Relations, 1700 SW College, Topeka, KS 66621. Phone: (785) 231-1010. Fax: (785) 231-1009. E-mail: zzdpmu@washburn.edu.

WHITSUNDAY. June 3. Whitsunday, the seventh Sunday after Easter, is a popular time for baptism. "White Sunday" is named for the white garments formerly worn by the candidates for baptism and occurs at the Christian feast of Pentecost. See also: "Pentecost" (above).

BIRTHDAYS TODAY

Chuck Barris, 72, TV producer ("Dating Game," "Newlywed Game," "Gong Show"), born Philadelphia, PA, June 3, 1929.
Tony Curtis (Bernard Schwartz), 76, actor ("Vega$," *Some Like It Hot*), born New York, NY, June 3, 1925.
Charles Hart, 40, lyricist, composer, born London, England, June 3, 1961.
Hale S. Irwin, 56, golfer, born Joplin, MO, June 3, 1945.
Scott Valentine, 43, actor ("Family Ties"), born Saratoga Springs, NY, June 3, 1958.
Deniece Williams, 50, singer ("Free," "It's Gonna Take a Miracle"), born Gary, IN, June 3, 1951.

JUNE 4 — MONDAY

Day 155 — 210 Remaining

ANGELA DAVIS ACQUITTAL: ANNIVERSARY. June 4, 1972. Angela Davis, black activist and professor, was found not guilty by an all-white jury of murder, kidnapping and conspiracy charges resulting from the Aug 7, 1970, fatal shooting of Judge Harold Haley during an attempted escape and kidnapping. While Davis was not present at the crime, the murder weapon had been purchased by her and she knew the perpetrators. Based upon these facts, she was arrested and charged. During her trial she told the court she bought guns to protect herself. "For a black person growing up in violence-filled Alabama," she said, "guns were a normal way of life."

BATTLE OF MIDWAY: ANNIVERSARY. June 4–6, 1942. A Japanese task force attempted to capture Midway Island in the Central Pacific. American bombers from Midway and from two nearby aircraft carriers sent the Japanese into retreat, having lost four carriers, two large cruisers and three destroyers. Midway was one of the most decisive naval battles of World War II. Japan never regained its margin in carrier strength and the Central Pacific was made safe for American troops.

"CAVALCADE OF STARS" TV PREMIERE: ANNIVERSARY. June 4, 1949. Although the Dumont network was not very successful, it was around long enough to launch this popular show. The one-hour variety show was hosted by Jack Carter (1949–50), Jackie Gleason (1950–52) and Larry Storch in the summer of 1952. It also served as a showcase for the soon-to-be immortal "The Honeymooners" with Gleason and Pert Kelton starring as the Kramdens.

CHINA: TIANANMEN SQUARE MASSACRE: ANNIVERSARY. June 4, 1989. After almost a month and a half of student demonstrations for democracy, the Chinese government ordered its troops to open fire on the unarmed protestors at Tiananmen Square at Beijing. The demonstrations began Apr 18 as several thousand students marched to mourn the death of Hu Yaobang, a pro-reform leader within the Chinese government. A ban was imposed on such demonstrations; Apr 22, 100,000 gathered in Tiananmen Square in defiance of the ban. On May 13, 2,000 of the students began a hunger strike, and on May 20 the government imposed martial law and began to bring in troops. On June 2 the demonstrators turned back an advance of unarmed troops in the first clash with the People's Army. Under the cover of darkness, early June 4, troops opened fire on the assembled crowds and armored personnel carriers rolled into the square crushing many of the students as they lay sleeping in their tents. Although the government claimed that few died in the attack, estimates range from several hundred to several thousand casualties. In the following months thousands of demonstrators were rounded up and jailed.

ENGLAND: DICING FOR BIBLES. June 4. An old Whitmonday ceremony at All Saints Church, St. Ives, Huntingdonshire. A bequest (in 1675) with the intent of providing Bibles for poor children of the parish required winning them at a dice game played in the church. In recent years the dicing has been moved from the altar to a "more suitable" place. Six Bibles are given on Whitmonday each year.

FINLAND: FLAG DAY. June 4, 1867. Finland's armed forces honor the birth anniversary of Carl Gustaf Mannerheim.

FIRST FREE FLIGHT BY A WOMAN: ANNIVERSARY. June 4, 1784. Marie Thible, of Lyons, France, accompanied by a pilot (Monsieur Fleurant), became the first woman in history to fly in a free balloon. She drifted across Lyons in a balloon named *Le Gustave* (for King Gustav III of Sweden, who was watching the ascent). The balloon reached a height of 8,500 feet in a flight that lasted about 45 minutes. The event occurred one day short of a year after the first flight in history by a man. See also: "First Balloon Flight: Anniversary" (June 5).

GEORGE III: BIRTH ANNIVERSARY. June 4, 1738. The English king against whom the American Revolution was directed. Born at London, England, died Jan 29, 1820, at Windsor Castle, near London.

GHANA: REVOLUTION DAY. June 4. National holiday.

MAWLID AL NABI: THE BIRTHDAY OF THE PROPHET MUHAMMAD. June 4. Mawlid al-Nabi (Birth of the Prophet Muhammad) is observed on Muslim calendar date Rabi al-Awal 12, 1422. Different methods for calculating the visibility of the new moon crescent at Mecca are used by different Muslim groups. US date may vary.

PULITZER PRIZES FIRST AWARDED: ANNIVERSARY. June 4, 1917. The first Pulitzer Prizes were awarded on this date: biography, *Julia Ward Howe* by Laura E. Richards and Maude H. Elliott assisted by Florence H. Hall; history, *With Americans of Past and Present Days* by Jean Jules Jusserand, the French ambassador to the US. Prizes were also awarded for journalistic achievement.

ROME LIBERATED: ANNIVERSARY. June 4, 1944. The US 9th Army, commanded by General Mark Clark, entered the southern suburbs of Rome as the last of the German rearguard retreated from Mussolini's former capital. Fearful of a last-ditch effort by the Germans to hold the city, the populace remained behind closed doors as Clark's forces entered the Eternal City.

SHUTTLE CAMP. June 4–Aug 3. Space Center, Alamogordo, NM. Annual series of week-long residential and day space science camps. Rocket building classes, field trips and astronomy classes. Est attendance: 940. For info: Jackie Diehl, Shuttle Camp Director, Space Center, PO Box 533, Alamogordo, NM 88311-0533. Phone: (800) 545-4021. Fax: (505) 437-7722. E-mail: space-ed @zianet.com. Web: www.spacefame.org/camp.html.

June 2001	S	M	T	W	T	F	S
						1	2
	3	4	5	6	7	8	9
	10	11	12	13	14	15	16
	17	18	19	20	21	22	23
	24	25	26	27	28	29	30

TONGA: EMANCIPATION DAY: ANNIVERSARY. June 4. National holiday. Commemorates independence from Britain in 1970.

UNITED NATIONS: INTERNATIONAL DAY OF INNOCENT CHILDREN VICTIMS OF AGGRESSION. June 4. On Aug 19, 1982, the General Assembly decided to commemorate June 4 of each year as the International Day of Innocent Children Victims of Aggression.

UPPERVILLE COLT AND HORSE SHOW. June 4–10. A week-long "A-rated" horse show involving hundreds of horse and rider combinations from 8- to 10-year-old children in the pony divisions to leading Olympic and World Cup riders and horses in the Hunter, Jumper and Grand Prix divisions. Sunday's highlight is the prestigious $50,000 Budweiser/Upperville Jumper Classic sponsored by Budweiser. Est attendance: 6,000. For info: Tommy L. Jones, Upperville Colt and Horse Show, PO Box 1288, Warrenton, VA 20188. Phone: (540) 592-3858. Fax: (540) 253-5761. Web: www.upperville.com.

WHITMONDAY. June 4. The day after Whitsunday is observed as a public holiday in some countries.

BIRTHDAYS TODAY

Gene Barry (Eugene Klass), 80, actor (*War of the Worlds*, "Bat Masterson"), born New York, NY, June 4, 1921.

Cecilia Bartoli, 35, mezzo-soprano, born Rome, Italy, June 4, 1966.

Keith David, 47, actor (*Platoon, Bird*), born New York, NY, June 4, 1954.

Eldra DeBarge, 40, singer, musician, lead singer (DeBarge), born Grand Rapids, MI, June 4, 1961.

Bruce Dern, 65, actor (*Coming Home, The Burbs*), born Chicago, IL, June 4, 1936.

Bettina Gregory, 55, journalist, born New York, NY, June 4, 1946.

Andrea Jaeger, 36, former tennis player, born Chicago, IL, June 4, 1965.

Angelina Jolie, 26, actress (Oscar for *Girl, Interrupted*), born Angelina Jolie Voight, Los Angeles, CA, June 4, 1975.

Robert Merrill, 84, singer, born New York, NY, June 4, 1917.

Michelle Phillips, 56, singer (with The Mamas and the Papas; "California Dreamin' "), actress ("Knots Landing"), born Long Beach, CA, June 4, 1945.

Parker Stevenson, 48, actor ("Falcon Crest," "Baywatch," *Lifeguard*), born Philadelphia, PA, June 4, 1953.

Dennis Weaver, 77, actor ("Gunsmoke," "McCloud"), born Joplin, MO, June 4, 1924.

Dr. Ruth Westheimer, 72, TV, radio host for shows on sexual relationships, born Frankfurt, Germany, June 4, 1929.

Scott Wolf, 33, actor ("Party of Five," *The Evening Star*), born Boston, MA, June 4, 1968.

Noah Wyle, 30, actor (*A Few Good Men*, "ER"), born Hollywood, CA, June 4, 1971.

JUNE 5 — TUESDAY
Day 156 — 209 Remaining

AMERICAN BAHA'I COMMUNITY: ANNIVERSARY. June 5, 1894. The first formal classes on the Baha'i were held at Chicago, IL.

APPLE II COMPUTER RELEASED: ANNIVERSARY. June 5, 1977. The Apple II computer, with 4K of memory, went on sale for $1,298. Its predecessor, the Apple I, was sold largely to electronic hobbyists the previous year. Apple released the Macintosh computer Jan 24, 1984.

BEEF EMPIRE DAYS. June 5–17. Finney County Fairgrounds, Garden City, KS. 33rd annual celebration of the beef industry. Live and carcass show; PRCA rodeo (three nights); parade; beef tasting for the public; cowboy poetry; Professional Western Art Show; feedlot roping and riding; walk/run; golf, softball and tennis tournaments; children's events. Annually, in June. Est attendance: 100,000. For info: Beef Empire Days, PO Box 1197, Garden City, KS 67846-1197. Phone: (316) 275-6807. Web: www.beefempiredays.com.

BOYD, WILLIAM: BIRTH ANNIVERSARY. June 5, 1895. Born at Hendrysburg, OH, Boyd went to Hollywood in 1919 and got a job as a film extra. His first major starring role was in *The Volga Boatman* (1926). In 1935 he got the role of Hopalong Cassidy in a series of popular westerns. He made 66 of these films between 1935 and 1948. Some of them were edited and shown on television; Boyd then made some episodes especially for TV. Died at Hollywood, CA, Sept 12, 1972. See also "Hopalong Cassidy TV Premiere (June 24)."

CLARK, CHARLES JOSEPH (JOE): BIRTHDAY. June 5, 1939. Canadian politician, born at High River, Alberta, Canada. Clark became Canada's 16th prime minister (and the youngest ever) on June 4, 1979, and served in that post until Mar 3, 1980.

DENMARK: CONSTITUTION DAY. June 5. National holiday. Commemorates Denmark's becoming a constitutional monarchy in 1849.

FIRST BALLOON FLIGHT: ANNIVERSARY. June 5, 1783. The first public demonstration of a hot-air balloon flight took place at Annonay, France, where the co-inventor brothers, Joseph and Jacques Montgolfier, succeeded in launching their 33-foot-diameter *globe aerostatique*. The unmanned balloon rose an estimated 1,500 feet and traveled, windborne, about 7,500 feet before landing after a 10-minute flight—the first sustained flight of any object achieved by man.

GERMANY: WALDCHESTAG. June 5. Frankfurt. Since the 19th century Frankfurters have spent the Tuesday after Whitsunday in their forest. See also: "Whitsunday" (June 3).

KENNEDY, ROBERT F.: ASSASSINATION ANNIVERSARY. June 5, 1968. Senator Kennedy was shot while campaigning for the Democratic presidential nomination at Los Angeles, CA; he died the following day. Sirhan Sirhan was convicted of his murder.

KEYNES, JOHN MAYNARD: BIRTH ANNIVERSARY. June 5, 1883. British economist born at Cambridge, England. Author of *Treatise on Money* and *The General Theory of Employment, Interest and Money* that focused on "expansionist" economic policy. Died at Firle, England, Apr 21, 1946.

MOON PHASE: FULL MOON. June 5. Moon enters Full Moon phase at 9:39 PM, EDT.

SCARRY, RICHARD McCLURE: BIRTH ANNIVERSARY. June 5, 1919. Author and illustrator of children's books was born at Boston, MA. Two widely known books of the more than 250 Scarry authored are *Richard Scarry's Best Word Book Ever* (1965) and *Richard Scarry's Please & Thank You* (1973). The pages are crowded with small animal characters who lived like humans. More than 100 million copies of his books sold worldwide. Died Apr 30, 1994, at Gstaad, Switzerland.

SMITH, ADAM: BIRTH ANNIVERSARY. June 5, 1723 (OS). Scottish economist and philosopher, author of *An Enquiry into the Nature and Causes of the Wealth of Nations* (published in 1776), born at Kirkcaldy, Fifeshire, Scotland. Died at Edinburgh, Scotland, July 17, 1790. "Consumption," he wrote, "is the sole end and purpose of production; and the interest of the producer ought to be attended to only so far as it may be necessary for promoting that of the consumer."

SPACE MILESTONE: *SOYUZ T-2* (USSR). June 5, 1980. Launched on this date, cosmonauts Yuri Malyshev and Vladimir Aksenov docked at *Salyut 6* on June 6 and returned to Earth June 9. First piloted flight of new T (Transport) spacecraft.

☆ ☆ ☆

UNITED NATIONS: WORLD ENVIRONMENT DAY.
June 5. Observed annually June 5, the anniversary of the opening of the UN Conference on the Human Environment held in Stockholm in 1972, which led to establishment of UN Environment Programme, based in Nairobi. The General Assembly has urged marking the day with activities reaffirming concern for the preservation and enhancement of the environment. For info: United Nations, Dept of Public Info, New York, NY 10017.

BIRTHDAYS TODAY

Chad Allen, 27, actor ("Dr. Quinn, Medicine Woman"), cartoon voice (Charlie Brown), born Cerritos, CA, June 5, 1974.

Bosin Blackbear, 80, artist, born Anadarko, OK, June 5, 1921.

Margaret Drabble, 62, Canadian novelist (*The Needle's Eye*), born Sheffield, Yorkshire, England, June 5, 1939.

Ken Follett, 52, British novelist (*The Eye of the Needle*), born Wales, UK, June 5, 1949.

Spalding Gray, 60, performance artist, actor, writer (*The Killing Fields, Swimming to Cambodia, Beyond Rangoon*), born Barrington, RI, June 5, 1941.

Bill Moyers, 67, journalist ("Bill Moyers' Journal"), born Hugo, OK, June 5, 1934.

Mark Wahlberg, 30, actor (*Boogie Nights*), also known as rapper Marky Mark (Marky Mark and the Funky Bunch, "Good Vibrations"), born Dorchester, MA, June 5, 1971.

JUNE 6 — WEDNESDAY
Day 157 — 208 Remaining

AMERICAN ROSE SOCIETY SPRING NATIONAL CONVENTION. June 6–10. Portland, OR. Amateur growers from all over the US display thousands of their roses in this major competition. Est attendance: 800. For info: American Rose Soc Publicity Committee, PO Box 30000, Shreveport, LA 71130-0030. Phone: (318) 637-6534. E-mail: ars@ars-hq.org. Web: www.ars.org.

"ARMSTRONG CIRCLE THEATER" TV PREMIERE: ANNIVERSARY. June 6, 1950. This half-hour weekly anthology series was commonly known as "Circle Theater" and specialized in dramatizations of actual events. In 1955 the format was extended to an hour and the program began running biweekly. Hosts of "ACT" included John Cameron Swayze, Douglas Edwards, Ron Cochran, Sandy Becker, Nelson Case, Joe Ripley, Bob Sherry and Henry Hamilton. Many stars had their first TV roles here, including John Cassavetes, Robert Duvall, Anne Jackson and Telly Savalas.

BONZA BOTTLER DAY™. June 6. To celebrate when the number of the day is the same as the number of the month. Bonza Bottler Day™ is an excuse to have a party at least once a month. For more information, see Jan 1. For info: Gail M. Berger, 109 Matthew Ave, Poca, WV 25159. Phone: (304) 776-7746. E-mail: gberger5@aol.com.

	S	M	T	W	T	F	S
June						1	2
2001	3	4	5	6	7	8	9
	10	11	12	13	14	15	16
	17	18	19	20	21	22	23
	24	25	26	27	28	29	30

D-DAY: ANNIVERSARY. June 6, 1944. In the early-morning hours Allied forces landed in Normandy on the north coast of France. In an operation that took months of planning, a fleet of 2,727 ships of every description converged from British ports from Wales to the North Sea. Operation *Overlord* involved 2,000,000 tons of war materials, including more than 50,000 tanks, armored cars, jeeps, trucks and half-tracks. The US alone sent 1,700,000 fighting men. The Germans believed the invasion would not take place under the adverse weather conditions of this early June day. But as the sun came up the village of Saint Mèere Eglise was liberated by American parachutists, and by nightfall the landing of 155,000 Allies attested to the success of D-Day. The long-awaited second front had at last materialized.

HALE, NATHAN: BIRTH ANNIVERSARY. June 6, 1755. American patriot Nathan Hale was born at Coventry, CT. During the battles for New York in the American Revolution, he volunteered to seek military intelligence behind enemy lines and was captured on the night of Sept 21, 1776. In an audience before General William Howe, Hale admitted he was an American officer and was ordered hanged the following morning. Although some question them, his dying words, "I only regret that I have but one life to lose for my country," have become a symbol of American patriotism. He was hanged Sept 22, 1776, at Manhattan, NY.

KHACHATURIAN, ARAM (ILICH): BIRTH ANNIVERSARY. June 6, 1903. Armenian musician and composer, noted for compositions based on folk music and legend, born at Tbilisi, Georgia, USSR. Died May 1, 1978.

KOREA: MEMORIAL DAY. June 6. Nation pays tribute to the war dead and memorial services are held at the National Cemetery in Seoul. Legally recognized Korean holiday.

NATIONAL TAILORS DAY. June 6. To honor tailors across the US. Our company, Tom James Clothiers, sells clothing to individuals in their office or home. Without our clothing tailors, we wouldn't be able to perform our jobs! Annually, the first Wednesday in June. For info: Doug Foley, Tom James Clothiers, 9302 N Meridian, Indianapolis, IN 46260. Phone: (317) 843-0696. E-mail: d.foley@tjm068.com. Web: www.tomjames.com.

PROPOSITION 13: ANNIVERSARY. June 6, 1978. California voters (65 percent of them) supported a primary election ballot initiative to cut property taxes 57 percent. Regarded as a possible omen of things to come across the country—a taxpayer's revolt against high taxes and government spending.

PUSHKIN, ALEXANDER: BIRTH ANNIVERSARY. June 6, 1799. Russian poet (*Eugene Onegin*, a novel in verse), born at Moscow. Died Feb 10, 1837 at St. Petersburg as the result of a duel.

RAVINIA FESTIVAL. June 6–Sept 8 (tentative). Highland Park, IL. Summer home of the Chicago Symphony Orchestra. This 63rd annual season also includes chamber music, jazz, pop, kids' concerts and dance. For info: Ravinia Festival, PO Box 896, Highland Park, IL 60035. Phone: (847) 266-5100. Fax: (847) 266-0641. Web: www.ravinia.org.

RED RIVER RODEO. June 6–9. Wichita Falls, TX. Professional circuit rodeo held at the Wichita County Mounted Patrol Arena, this event features all of the traditional rodeo attractions as well as a dance. Est attendance: 20,000. For info: Wichita Falls Conv & Visitors Bureau, 1000 5th St, Wichita Falls, TX 76301. Phone: (940) 716-5500. Fax: (940) 716-5509.

SECURITIES AND EXCHANGE COMMISSION CREATED: ANNIVERSARY. June 6, 1934. President Franklin D. Roosevelt signed the Securities Exchange Act that established the SEC. Wall Street had operated almost unfettered since the end of the eighteenth century. However, the stock market crash of 1929 necessitated regulation of the exchanges. The Securities and Exchange Commission is composed of five members appointed by the president of the US.

SPACE MILESTONE: *SOYUZ 11* (USSR): 30th ANNIVERSARY. June 6, 1971. Launched with cosmonauts G.T. Dobrovolsky, V.N. Volkov and V.I. Patsayev, who died during the return landing June 30, 1971, after a 24-day space flight. *Soyuz 11* had docked at *Salyut* orbital space station June 7–29; the cosmonauts entered the space station for the first time and conducted scientific experiments. First humans to die in space.

SURRENDER OF MEMPHIS: ANNIVERSARY. June 6, 1862. Confederate gunboats engaged a Union flotilla near Memphis, TN. As crowds of spectators watched from the riverbanks, the outgunned Confederates were defeated. The city of Memphis surrendered shortly before noon of that day, effectively opening up the Mississippi region.

SUSAN B. ANTHONY FINED FOR VOTING: ANNIVERSARY. June 6, 1872. Seeking to test for women the citizenship and voting rights extended to black males under the 14th and 15th Amendments, Susan B. Anthony led a group of women who registered and voted at a Rochester, NY, election. She was arrested, tried and sentenced to pay a fine. She refused to do so and was allowed to go free by a judge who feared she would appeal to a higher court.

SWEDEN: FLAG DAY. June 6. Commemorates the day upon which Gustavus I (Gustavus Vasa) ascended the throne of Sweden in 1523.

"20/20" TV PREMIERE: ANNIVERSARY. June 6, 1978. An hourly newsmagazine developed by ABC to compete with CBS's "60 Minutes." Its original hosts, Harold Hayes and Robert Hughes, were cut after the first show and replaced by Hugh Downs. Barbara Walters became co-anchor in 1984. The show consisted of investigative and background reports. Contributors to the show have included Tom Jarriel, Sylvia Chase, Geraldo Rivera, Thomas Hoving, John Stossel, Lynn Sherr and Stone Phillips.

US INTERNATIONAL FILM AND VIDEO FESTIVAL AWARDS PRESENTATIONS. June 6–7. Chicago, IL. World's largest awards competition honoring business, television, documentary, informational and industrial productions. Founded in 1968. Est attendance: 300. For info: J.W. Anderson, Chairman, US Intl Film and Video Festival, 841 N Addison Ave, Elmhurst, IL 60126-1291. Phone: (630) 834-7773. Fax: (630) 834-5565. E-mail: filmfestinfo@filmfestawards.com. Web: www.filmfestawards.com.

BIRTHDAYS TODAY

Sandra Bernhard, 46, comedienne, actress ("Roseanne"), born Flint, MI, June 6, 1955.

Gary U.S. Bonds (Gary Anderson), 62, singer ("Quarter to Three"), songwriter, born Jacksonville, FL, June 6, 1939.

Bjorn Rune Borg, 45, former tennis player, born Sodertalje, Sweden, June 6, 1956.

Dalai Lama, 66, Tibet's spiritual leader and Nobel Peace Prize winner, born Taktser, China, June 6, 1935.

David Dukes, 56, actor ("Sisters," *The Handmaid's Tale*), born San Francisco, CA, June 6, 1945.

Marian Wright Edelman, 62, president of Children's Defense Fund, civil rights activist, born Bennettsville, SC, June 6, 1939.

Harvey Fierstein, 47, playwright (Tony Awards for *Torch Song Trilogy*; *Tidy Endings*), born Brooklyn, NY, June 6, 1954.

Kenny G, 45, sax player, born Kenny Gorelick, Seattle, WA, June 6, 1956.

Amanda Pays, 42, actress ("Max Headroom," *Exposure*), born Berkshire, England, June 6, 1959.

Billie Whitelaw, 69, actress (*The Dressmaker*, "Masterpiece Theater"), born Coventry, England, June 6, 1932.

JUNE 7 — THURSDAY
Day 158 — 207 Remaining

ALBANY ALIVE AT FIVE. June 7 (also June 14, 21, 28, July 12, 19. 26 and Aug 2). Corning Preserve Riverfront Park, Albany, NY. A free eight-week summer concert series on Thursday evenings from 5–8 PM. A different theme of music each week, food and refreshment vendors. Est attendance: 75,000. For info: City of Albany Office of Special Events, Eagle Street, City Hall, 4th Fl, Albany, NY 12207. Phone: (518) 434-2032. Web: www.albanyevents.org.

APGAR, VIRGINIA: BIRTH ANNIVERSARY. June 7, 1909. Dr. Apgar developed the simple assessment method that permits doctors and nurses to evaluate newborns while they are still in the delivery room to identify those in need of immediate medical care. The Apgar score was first published in 1953, and the Perinatal Section of the American Academy of Pediatrics is named for Dr. Apgar. Born at Westfield, NJ, Apgar died Aug 7, 1974, at New York, NY.

BOONE DAY. June 7. Each year on June 7, the Kentucky Historical Society celebrates the anniversary of the day in 1767 when Daniel Boone, America's most famous frontiersman, reportedly first sighted the land that would become Kentucky. The June 7 date is taken from the book *The Discovery, Settlement and Present State of Kentucky*, by John Filson, published in 1784, with an appendix titled "The Adventures of Colonel Daniel Boone." The information in the appendix supposedly originated with Boone, although Filson is the actual author. The work is not considered completely reliable by historians.

BRUMMELL, GEORGE BRYAN "BEAU": BIRTH ANNIVERSARY. June 7, 1778. Born at London, England, Beau Brummell was, early in his life, a popular English men's fashion leader, the "arbiter elegantarium" of taste in dress. His extravagance and lack of tact (it was he who reportedly said—indicating the Prince of Wales, later George IV—"Who's your fat friend?") led him from wealth and popularity to poverty and disrepute. Once imprisoned for debt, he became careless of dress and personal appearance. He died in a charitable asylum at Caen, France, Mar 30, 1840.

CANADA: SHELBURNE COUNTY LOBSTER FESTIVAL. June 7–10. Shelburne County, NS. Four days of activities in celebration of the lobster-fishing industry. Local community groups and businesses throughout the county host lobster suppers, sporting events, craft shows, yacht, boat and dorey races and much more. "Shelburne County—The Lobster Capital of Canada." Annually, the first full weekend in June. Est attendance: 10,000. For info: Marilyn Johnston, Lobster Fest Sec'y, PO Box 280, Shelburne, NS, Canada 80T 1W0. Phone: (902) 875-3544. Fax: (902) 875-1278. E-mail: munshel@atcon.com.

COWBOY STATE SUMMER GAMES. June 7–10. Casper, WY. The Summer Games feature more than 30 different events including everything from archery to wrestling, basketball to volleyball. Participation is open to Wyoming's amateur athletes of all ages. Est attendance: 3,000. For info: Eileen Ford, Cowboy State Games, PO Box 3485, Casper, WY 82602. Phone: (307) 577-1125. Fax: (307) 577-8111. E-mail: csg@trib.com.

DISCOVERYLAND'S OKLAHOMA! June 7–Aug 18 (nightly except Sundays). Tulsa, OK. Discoveryland was proclaimed the "National Home of Rodgers and Hammerstein's *Oklahoma!*" by the children of that duo. Discoveryland presents the state's favorite musical in a beautiful 2,000-seat amphitheatre complex, complete with horses, wagons and a real surrey with a fringe on top. Barbecue dinner, Indian dancing, gift shops and ice cream parlor top the evening for the whole family. Est attendance: 75,000. For info: Bill Jeffers, Managing Dir, Discoveryland! Business Office, 5529 S Lewis, Tulsa, OK 74105. Phone: (918) 245-OKLA (for tickets) or (918) 742-5255 (business office).

FESTIVAL OF THE BLUEGRASS. June 7–10. Lexington, KY. Up to 25 bands perform bluegrass music in an outdoor setting. Est attendance: 20,000. For info: James Cornett, Spirit of the Suwannee Music Park, 3076 95th Dr, Live Oak, FL 32060. Phone: (904) 364-1683. Fax: (904) 364-2998.

GAUGUIN, (EUGENE HENRI) PAUL: BIRTH ANNIVERSARY. June 7, 1848. French painter born at Paris, France. Formerly a stockbroker, he became a painter in his middle age and three years later renounced his life at Paris to move to Tahiti. He is remembered best for his broad, flat tones and bold colors. Gauguin died May 8, 1903, at Atoana on the island of Hiva Oa in the Marquesas.

GLENN MILLER BIRTHPLACE SOCIETY FESTIVAL. June 7–10. Clarinda, IA. To commemorate Glenn Miller's contribution to big band music through exhibits, concerts, films, performances by winners of Glenn Miller scholarships and a big band dance. Annually, the second weekend in June. Est attendance: 3,500. For info: Glenn Miller Birthplace Soc, PO Box 61, Clarinda, IA 51632. Phone: (712) 542-2461. Fax: (712) 542-2461. E-mail: gmbs@clarinda.heartland.net. Web: www.glennmiller.org.

IDAHO SHAKESPEARE FESTIVAL. June 7–Sept 22. Boise, ID. Idaho's renowned professional repertory theater company presents a full summer season of The Bard, plus other classical playwrights, in its outdoor amphitheater along the Boise River. Bring your picnic dinner and enjoy "Shakespeare Under the Stars." Est attendance: 45,000. For info: Idaho Shakespeare Festival, PO Box 9365, Boise, ID 83707. Phone: (208) 429-9908. Fax: (208) 429-8798. E-mail: info@idahoshakespeare.org. Web: www.idahoshakespeare.org.

MALTA: NATIONAL DAY. June 7. National day or (in Maltese) Sette Giugno.

MINIATURES INTERNATIONAL. June 7–July 7. St. Simons Island, GA. A juried show of two- and three-dimensional miniature art created to provide exposure of quality miniature artwork to a large and knowledgeable audience in a recognized arts facility at the height of the visitor season. Deadline: May 22. For info: Coastal Center For The Arts, 2012 Demere Rd, St. Simons Island, GA 31522. Phone: (912) 634-0404.

NURSING ASSISTANTS DAY AND WEEK. June 7–14. Recognizes those nursing assistants who provide care to all ill, elderly and long-term residents in nursing homes and other long-term nursing care centers. Begins on Career Nurse Assistants' Day, June 7. 2001 focus is: "Care Sense." For info: Genevieve Gipson, RN M Ed, Dir, Career Nurse Assistant Programs Inc, 3577 Easton Rd, Norton, OH 44203. Phone: (330) 825-9342. E-mail: cnajeni@aol.com.

SEA MUSIC FESTIVAL. June 7–10. Mystic, CT. World-famous folksingers and musicians performing from Mystic Seaport's tall ships or in formal concert. Est attendance: 6,000. For info: Mystic Seaport, 75 Greenmanville Ave, Box 6000, Mystic, CT 06355. Phone: (860) 572-5315 or (888) 9-SEAPORT. Web: www.mystic seaport.org.

"THE $64,000 QUESTION" TV PREMIERE: ANNIVERSARY. June 7, 1955. This game show was a big hit, and the first of prime-time's big money shows. Contestants, each an expert in one area, answered questions; each time a question was answered correctly, contestants doubled their money and the questions became harder. Players, if successful, could come back the following week. For the $64,000 question, a player could bring along an expert, but if neither got the correct answer, the player left with $4,000. The host was Hal March, assisted by Lynn Dollar and later Pat Donovan, and questions were compiled by Dr. Bergen Evans. Some famous contestants were Dr. Joyce Brothers, Barbara Feldon and Jack Benny (as a joke). The show was dropped in 1958 amid the game show scandals.

SUPERMAN CELEBRATION. June 7–10. Metropolis, IL. Weekend full of Super activities. See 15-ft Superman Statue, live entertainment, super museum, road race, carnival, tennis tourney, Supertrek bicycle ride, super car show, children's games and food fair. Est attendance: 30,000. For info: Metropolis Area Chamber of Commerce, Tourism & Economic Development, PO Box 188, Metropolis, IL 62960. Phone: (618) 524-2714 or (800) 949-5740. Fax: (618) 524-4780. E-mail: metrochamber@hcis.net. Web: www.metropolischamber.com.

SUPREME COURT STRIKES DOWN CONNECTICUT LAW BANNING CONTRACEPTION: ANNIVERSARY. June 7, 1965. In Griswold v Connecticut, the Supreme Court guaranteed the right to privacy, including the freedom from government intrusion into matters of birth control.

TEXAS FOLKLIFE FESTIVAL. June 7–10. San Antonio, TX. Provides an entertaining and historic understanding of the crafts, art, food, music, history and heritage of the more than 40 different cultures and ethnic groups that settled and developed the state of Texas. Est attendance: 70,000. For info: Patty Burrus, PR Mgr, Institute of Texan Cultures, 801 S Bowie St, San Antonio, TX 78205-3296. Phone: (210) 458-2244. Fax: (210) 458-2380. E-mail: pburrus@utsa.edu. Web: www.texancultures.utsa.edu.

VCR INTRODUCED: ANNIVERSARY. June 7, 1975. The Sony Corporation released its videocassette recorder, the Betamax, which sold for $995 (more than $2,000 in today's dollars). Eventually, another VCR format, VHS, proved more successful and Sony stopped making the Betamax.

WILL ROGERS STAMPEDE SUMMER CELEBRATION. June 7–9. Claremore, OK. For info: Claremore Chamber of Commerce, Will Rogers Stampede Summer Celebration, 419 W Will Rogers Blvd, Claremore, OK 74017. Phone: (918) 341-2818. Fax: (918) 342-0663. Or Bob Morton. Phone: (918) 341-8699.

WORLD PORK EXPO. June 7–9. Iowa State Fairgrounds, Des Moines, IA. This is the world's largest pork-specific event, featuring free pork barbecue and musical entertainment, hog shows and sales, educational seminars and a trade show with more than 500 companies represented. Some of the nation's best barbecuers compete in the Great Pork BarbeQlossal™. Est attendance: 50,000. For info: Cindy Cunningham, Asst Vice President, Communications, Natl Pork Producers Council, PO Box 10383, Des Moines, IA 50306. Phone: (515) 223-2600. Fax: (515) 223-2646. Web: www.nppc.org/

BIRTHDAYS TODAY

Gwendolyn Brooks, 84, poet, author (Pulitzer for *Annie Allen*), born Topeka, KS, June 7, 1917.

Louise Erdrich, 47, author (*Love Medicine*, *The Beet Queen*), born Little Falls, MN, June 7, 1954.

Allen Iverson, 26, basketball player, born Hampton, VA, June 7, 1975.

Jenny Jones, 55, talk-show host, born London, Ontario, Canada, June 7, 1946.

Tom Jones (Thomas Woodward), 61, singer ("It's Not Unusual"), born Pontypridd, Wales, UK, June 7, 1940.

Anna Kournikova, 20, tennis player, born Moscow, Russia, June 7, 1981.

Bill Kreutzmann, Jr, 55, drummer, singer, cofounder of The Grateful Dead, born Palo Alto, CA, June 7, 1946.

Mike Modano, 31, hockey player, born Livonia, MI, June 7, 1970.

Liam Neeson, 49, actor (*Excalibur*, *Ethan Frome*, *Schindler's List*), born Ballymena, Northern Ireland, June 7, 1952.

Prince (Prince Rogers Nelson), 43, musician, singer, born Minneapolis, MN, June 7, 1958.

John Napier Turner, 72, Canada's 17th prime minister (served June 30, 1984–Sept 17, 1984), born Richmond, Surrey, England, June 7, 1929.

June 2001	S	M	T	W	T	F	S
						1	2
	3	4	5	6	7	8	9
	10	11	12	13	14	15	16
	17	18	19	20	21	22	23
	24	25	26	27	28	29	30

JUNE 8 — FRIDAY

Day 159 — 206 Remaining

AMERICAN HEROINE REWARDED: ANNIVERSARY. June 8, 1697. On Mar 16, 1697, in an attack on Haverhill, MA, Indians captured Hannah Duston and killed her baby, killing or capturing 39 others in addition. After being taken to an Indian camp, she escaped on Apr 29 after killing 10 Indians with a tomahawk and scalping them as proof of her deed. On June 8 her husband was awarded, on her behalf, the sum of 25 pounds for her heroic efforts, the first public award to a woman in America.

ATTACK ON THE USS *LIBERTY*: ANNIVERSARY. June 8, 1967. At 2 PM local time, the unescorted US intelligence ship USS *Liberty*, sailing in international waters off the Egyptian coast, was attacked without warning by Israeli jet planes and three Israeli torpedo boats. She was strafed and hit repeatedly by rockets, cannon, napalm and finally a torpedo. Casualties: out of a crew of 294 Americans, there were 34 dead and 171 wounded. Israel apologized, claiming mistaken identity, but surviving crew members charged deliberate attack by Israel and cover-up by US authorities.

BADGER STATE SUMMER GAMES REGIONALS AND FINALS. June 8–10. (Finals June 21–24.) Regional competition in seven Wisconsin communities, finals in Madison. 17th annual Olympic-style competition for Wisconsin residents of all ages and abilities, featuring 27 sports and opening ceremonies. Major sponsors: AT&T, Ameritech, American Family Insurance, Wisconsin Milk Marketing Board and Ministry Health Care. Member of the National Congress of State Games. 20,000 participants. Est attendance: 60,000. For info: Badger State Games, PO Box 7788, Madison, WI 53707-7788. Phone: (608) 226-4780. Fax: (608) 226-9550. E-mail: badger@badgerstategames.org. Web: www.badgerstategames.org.

BATTLE CREEK FESTIVAL/WORLD'S LARGEST BREAKFAST TABLE. June 8–10. Battle Creek, MI. Friday—Festival parade, downtown from 6 to 9 PM. Saturday events include arts and crafts, 5K and 10K races, family fun walk, food bank fundraiser, farmer's market and children's games. The World's Largest Breakfast Table will be on Saturday 8 AM–noon. Annually, the second weekend in June. Est attendance: 60,000. For info: Battle Creek Cereal Festival, Greater Battle Creek Visitor and Conv Bureau, 77 E Michigan Ave, Battle Creek, MI 49015. Phone: (616) 962-2240 or (800) 397-2240.

BILL OF RIGHTS PROPOSAL: ANNIVERSARY. June 8, 1789. The Bill of Rights, which led to the first 10 amendments to the US Constitution, was first proposed by James Madison.

BOLIVIAN EARTHQUAKE: ANNIVERSARY. June 8, 1994. A "deep focus" earthquake registering 8.2 on the Richter scale erupted 400 miles beneath the earth's surface in a remote area of Bolivia. The quake is believed to be the largest ever recorded in the Bolivian area. It was felt as far north as Minneapolis, MN.

CARSON CITY RENDEZVOUS. June 8–10. Mills Park, Carson City, NV. A living history event with something for every member of the family. Mountain Men in encampment demonstrate black powder shooting and tomahawk and knife throwing. Families can participate in pioneer crafts such as doll making and rope braiding. Visits by President Lincoln and Generals Grant and Lee. Annually, the second weekend in June. Est attendance: 25,000. For info: Joy Evans or Candy Duncan, Carson City CVB, 1900 S Carson St, Ste 200, Carson City, NV 89701. Phone: (775) 687-7410 or (800) NEVADA-1. Fax: (775) 687-7416. E-mail: cccvb@pyramid.net. Web: www.carson-city.org.

CENTER OF THE NATION ALL-CAR RALLY. June 8–10. Belle Fourche, SD. This three-day event includes Friday evening "Cruise Night"; Saturday's big "Show 'n Shine," held all day in Hermann Park, plus food booths, vendors, live '50's and '60's music; on Sunday, poker run and demolition derby. Annually, the second weekend in June. Est attendance: 5,000. For info: Belle Fourche Chamber of Commerce, 415 5th Ave, Belle Fourche, SD 57717. Phone: (605) 892-2676. Fax: (605) 892-4633. E-mail: chamber@bellefourche.org.

COCHISE: DEATH ANNIVERSARY. June 8, 1874. Born around 1810 in the Chiricahua Mountains of Arizona, Cochise became a fierce and courageous leader of the Apache. After his arrest in 1861, he escaped and launched the Apache Wars, which lasted for 25 years. He died 13 years later near his stronghold in southeastern Arizona.

CONNECTICUT EARLY MUSIC FESTIVAL. June 8–24. New London, CT. Concert Series of 17th and 18th century music performed on period instruments in historically informed styles. Annually, the last three weekends in June. Est attendance: 3,000. For info: Connecticut Early Music Festival, PO Box 329, New London, CT 06320. Phone: (860) 444-2419. Web: www.cemf.org.

CRAWFORDSVILLE STRAWBERRY FESTIVAL. June 8–10. Crawfordsville, IN. Festival at historic Lane Place includes 3 days of arts and crafts, food, music and children's activities. Great music, classic car show (Sunday), softball and tennis tournaments, bike tour, antique tractor exhibits and 4-mile run. All city museums open. Est attendance: 20,000. For info: Montgomery County Visitors & Conv Bureau, Inc, 412 E Main St, Crawfordsville, IN 47933. Phone: (800) 866-3973. Fax: (317) 362-5215. E-mail: mcvcb@tctc.com. Web: www.crawfordsville.org.

DAKOTA SOAP BOX DERBY. June 8–9. Valley City, ND. 6th annual. Two-day stock and super stock gravity pulled racers in downtown Valley City. Annually, the second weekend in June. Est attendance: 2,000. For info: Curt Brown, EVP, VCACC, PO Box 724, Valley City, ND 58072. Phone: (701) 845-1891. Fax: (701) 845-1892. E-mail: vccofc@ictc.com. Web: www.hellovalley.com.

DOWNTOWN ALIVE!. June 8. (also June 22 & 29, July 13 & 20 and Aug 3, 10, 17, 24 & 31). Downer Place, Aurora, IL. A summer series of events on Friday nights, each having a different theme: Let's Dance. The Fabulous 50s, Cajun Fest, Celtic Fest, Motown Memories, Rock on the Fox, Tropical Paradise, West Fest, That 70s Night and Aug-toberfest. Free carriage rides, inflatable games and admission to various museums. Specialty food and beverages available. For info: Gina Moga, Downtown Events Coord, City of Aurora, 43 E Downer Place, Aurora, IL 60507. Phone: (630) 844-3640. Fax: (630) 906-7068.

GREAT PLAINS BALLOON RACE. June 8–10. Tea, SD. Approximately 50 hot-air balloons from five states (Iowa, Minnesota, Nebraska, North and South Dakota) take to the sky. The event features skydivers, display of stunt planes and other fun activities. Est attendance: 20,000. For info: Aerostar, PO Box 5057, Sioux Falls, SD 57117-5057. Phone: (605) 331-3500.

ICELAND: LAKI VOLCANO ERUPTION: ANNIVERSARY. June 8, 1783. One of the most violent and important volcanic eruptions of recorded history began on this date. Laki, or Skafta, volcano in southern Iceland continued erupting for eight months, expelling an estimated 4½ cubic miles of lava, ultimately causing a famine and the deaths of nearly 10,000 persons. Acid rain reached western Europe, and other climatic and atmospheric changes were worldwide. English naturalist Gilbert White described some of the "horrible phenomena" of the summer of 1783, including the "peculiar haze, or smokey fog . . . unlike anything known within the memory of man." The effects of this volcanic eruption and its possible long-term consequences are still being studied by scientists. See also: "White, Gilbert: Birth Anniversary" (July 18).

INTERNATIONAL OLD-TIME FIDDLERS CONTEST. June 8–9. International Peace Garden, Dunseith, ND. The International Old Time Fiddlers Contest draws young and old fiddlers alike from both Canada and the US. Contestants compete for two days performing a required list of fiddle music in pursuit of cash prizes and trophies. Est attendance: 1,500. For info: Joseph T. Alme, 1725 11th St SW, Minot, ND 58701. Phone: (701) 838-8472. Fax: (701) 838-8472. E-mail: imc@minot.com.

LILAC FESTIVAL. June 8–15. Mackinac Island, MI. This summer festival provides an excellent chance to see the various lilacs on Mackinac Island. Includes a parade and entertainment. Est attendance: 30,000. For info: Mackinac Island Chamber of Commerce, PO Box 451, Mackinac Island, MI 49757. Phone: (906) 847-6418 or (800) 4LILACS. Fax: (906) 847-3571.

LOUISIANA PEACH FESTIVAL. June 8–17. Ruston, LA. The 51st annual Peach Festival will feature rodeo, parade, concerts, cooking contests, sporting events, arts & crafts and more. Est attendance: 50,000. For info: Ruston/Lincoln Chamber of Commerce, Becky O'Nan, PO Box 1383, Ruston, LA 71273-1383. Phone: (800) 392-9032.

MARKET SQUARE DAYS CELEBRATION. June 8–9. Portsmouth, NH. Historic tours, arts and crafts, a 10K road race, open-air concerts and fireworks are all part of the festivities. One of the biggest celebrations held each June on New Hampshire's picturesque seacoast. Free admission. Est attendance: 100,000. For info: Pro Portsmouth, 236 Union St, Portsmouth, NH 03801-4348. Phone: (603) 431-5388. Fax: (603) 431-3415.

McKINLEY, IDA SAXTON: BIRTH ANNIVERSARY. June 8, 1847. Wife of William McKinley, 25th president of the US, born at Canton, OH. Died at Canton, OH, May 26, 1907.

MILLIGAN JUNE JUBILEE. June 8–10. Milligan, NE. Music all weekend in Nebraska's largest beer garden, classic rock & roll and polka music. Carnival, tournament games, antique tractor pull on Saturday and parade on Sunday. Est attendance: 10,000. For info: Scott Oliva, PO Box 218, Milligan, NE 68406. Phone: (402) 629-4446. Fax: (402) 629-4446.

NCAA DIVISION I MEN'S BASEBALL CHAMPIONSHIP. June 8–16. Omaha, NE. For info: Natl Collegiate Athletic Assn, 700 W Washington Ave, PO Box 6222, Indianapolis, IN 46206-6222. Phone: (317) 917-6222. Fax: (317) 917-6888. Web: www.ncaa.org.

NEBRASKALAND DAYS AND PRCA BUFFALO BILL RODEO. June 8–19. North Platte, NE. To relive the Old West. Parades, contests, shoot-outs, art shows, frontier revue, top country-western stars. Est attendance: 100,000. For info: Sharon Hambek, Exec Dir, Nebraskaland Days, Box 706, North Platte, NE 69103. Phone: (308) 532-7939. Fax: (308) 532-3789. E-mail: nld@nebraskalanddays.com. Web: www.nebraskalanddays.com.

		S	M	T	W	T	F	S
June							1	2
2001		3	4	5	6	7	8	9
		10	11	12	13	14	15	16
		17	18	19	20	21	22	23
		24	25	26	27	28	29	30

OK MOZART INTERNATIONAL FESTIVAL. June 8–16. Bartlesville, OK. Festival features world-class artists performing with Solisti New York Orchestra, Ransom Wilson conducting. Est attendance: 40,000. For info: Jeanette Swindell, Public Relations, OK Mozart Intl Festival, Box 2344, Bartlesville, OK 74005. Phone: (918) 336-9900. Fax: (918) 336-9525. Web: www.webtek.com/okmozart.

OLDSMOBILE BALLOON CLASSIC. June 8–10. Vermilion County Airport, Danville, IL. More than 100 hot-air balloons in five morning and evening races, continuous entertainment, familyland, Balloon Glo and activities all day long. Annually, the second weekend in June. Sponsor: Oldsmobile. Est attendance: 100,000. For info: Jeanie Cooke, Exec Dir, Danville Area Conv & Visitors Bureau, 100 W Main St, Rm 146, PO Box 992, Danville, IL 61832. Phone: (217) 442-2096.

OUR LOVELADIES FAIR. June 8–10. Loveladies, NJ. 12th annual preseason introduction to Island and mainland merchants. Sponsored by Long Beach Island Foundation of Arts & Sciences. Est attendance: 1,200. For info: Long Beach Island Foundation of Arts & Sciences, 120 Long Beach Blvd, Loveladies, NJ 08008. Phone: (609) 494-1241. Fax: (609) 494-0662.

SCOTLAND: ROYAL SCOTTISH AUTOMOBILE CLUB INTERNATIONAL SCOTTISH RALLY. June 8–10 (tentative). Throughout Scotland with base at Dumfries. Scotland's only international rally that attracts many of the world's leading drivers. Est attendance: 200,000. For info: Jonathan Lord, Royal Scottish Automobile Club (Motor Sport) Ltd, 11 Blythswood Sq, Glasgow, Scotland G2 4AG. Phone: (44) (141) 204-4999. Web: www.motorsport.co.uk.

SPACE MILESTONE: *VENERA 9* AND 10 (USSR). June 8 and 14, 1975. Launched on this date, unmanned exploration vehicles landed on Venus Oct 22 and 25. Sent first pictures ever transmitted from Venus, atmospheric analysis and other data.

SUMMER FARM TOY SHOW. June 8–10. Beckman HS and National Farm Toy Museum, Dyersville, IA. Features tractor parade, tractor pull, citywide garage sales, live entertainment, antique tractors and farm machinery and indoor/outdoor farm toy show. Annually, the second full weekend in June. Est attendance: 9,000. For info: Dyersville Area Chamber of Commerce, 1100 16th Ave Ct SE, Dyersville, IA 52040. Phone: (319) 875-2311. Fax: (319) 875-8391. E-mail: dyersvillechamber@dyersville.org. Web: www.dyersville.org.

TECUMSEH!: THE EPIC OUTDOOR DRAMA. June 8–Sept 1. Chillicothe, OH. Witness the spectacular reenactment of the life and death of the great Shawnee leader Tecumseh. Held in the large, tiered amphitheater nestled in the hardwood forest of Sugarloaf Mountain. Take a backstage tour, visit the Prehistoric Museum, dine in the open-air Tecumseh Restaurant Terrace. Est attendance: 80,000. For info: Tecumseh!, PO Box 73, Chillicothe, OH 45601-0073. Phone: (740) 775-0700. Fax: (740) 775-4349. E-mail: tecumseh@bright.net. Web: www.tecumsehdrama.com.

WHITE, BYRON RAYMOND: BIRTHDAY. June 8, 1917. Retired associate justice of the Supreme Court of the US, nominated by President Kennedy Apr 3, 1962. (Oath of office, Apr 16, 1962.) Justice White was born at Fort Collins, CO.

WRIGHT, FRANK LLOYD: BIRTH ANNIVERSARY. June 8, 1867. American architect born at Richland Center, WI. In his autobiography Wright wrote: "No house should ever be *on* any hill or on anything. It should be *of* the hill, belonging to it, so hill and house could live together each the happier for the other." Wright died at Phoenix, AZ, Apr 9, 1959.

WYTHE, GEORGE: DEATH ANNIVERSARY. June 8, 1806. Signer of the Declaration of Independence. Born at Elizabeth County, VA, about 1726 (exact date unknown). Died at Richmond, VA.

BIRTHDAYS TODAY

Scott Adams, 44, cartoonist ("Dilbert"), born Windham, NY, June 8, 1957.

Kathy Baker, 51, actress ("Picket Fences," *The Right Stuff*), born Midland, TX, June 8, 1950.

Tim Berners-Lee, 46, inventor of the World Wide Web, born London, England, June 8, 1955.

Barbara Pierce Bush, 76, former First Lady, born Rye, NY, June 8, 1925.

Bernie Casey, 62, former football player, actor (*I'm Gonna Git You Sucka, Bill & Ted's Excellent Adventure, Roots: The Next Generations*), born Wyco, WV, June 8, 1939.

Francis Crick, 85, discoverer (with James Watson) of the structure of DNA, born Northhampton, England, June 8, 1916.

James Darren, 65, singer ("Goodbye Cruel World"), actor (*Gidget*), born Philadelphia, PA, June 8, 1936.

Lindsay Davenport, 25, tennis player, born Palos Verdes, CA, June 8, 1976.

Griffin Dunne, 46, actor (*Straight Talk*), producer, born New York, NY, June 8, 1955.

Don Grady, 57, actor ("My Three Sons," "Mickey Mouse Club"), born San Diego, CA, June 8, 1944.

Juliana Margulies, 35, actress ("ER"), born Spring Valley, NY, June 8, 1966.

Sara Paretsky, 54, writer (*Killing Orders, Burn Marks*), born Ames, IA, June 8, 1947.

Joan Rivers, 64, comedienne, talk-show host, born New York, NY, June 8, 1937.

Boz Scaggs, 57, singer, musician, songwriter (*Silk Degress, Middle Man*), born Dallas, TX, June 8, 1944.

Nancy Sinatra, 61, singer ("These Boots Are Made for Walkin'," "Something Stupid"), born Jersey City, NJ, June 8, 1940.

Jerry Stiller, 72, comedian, actor (*Hairspray*, "Seinfeld," "The King of Queens"), born Brooklyn, NY, June 8, 1929.

Keenen Ivory Wayans, 43, actor ("In Living Color"), born New York, NY, June 8, 1958.

Andrew Weil, MD, 59, physician and writer on natural healing, born Philadelphia, PA, June 8, 1942.

JUNE 9 — SATURDAY

Day 160 — 205 Remaining

ANTIQUES ON THE DIAMOND. June 9 (also Aug 25). Ligonier, PA. 70 quality antique dealers from six states set up their products along the Diamond. Est attendance: 10,000. For info: Ligonier Chamber of Commerce, 120 E Main St, Ligonier, PA 15658. Phone: (724) 238-4200. Fax: (724) 238-4610. E-mail: ligonier@ligonier.com. Web: www.ligonier.com.

ART FAIR ON THE COURTHOUSE LAWN. June 9. Rhinelander, WI. Original artwork and crafts, food, music and refreshments on the Oneida County Courthouse lawn. Annually, the second Saturday in June. Est attendance: 10,000. For info: Rhinelander Area Chamber of Commerce, PO Box 795, Rhinelander, WI 54501. Phone: (800) 236-4386. Fax: (715) 365-7467. E-mail: info@rhinelanderchamber.com. Web: www.rhinelanderchamber.com.

ART IN THE PARK. June 9 (raindate June 10). Bay Head, NJ. Juried outdoor art show. Annually, the second Saturday in June. Est attendance: 300. For info: Anne Neff, Chair, Anchor and Palette Gallery, 45 Mount St, PO Box 96, Bay Head, NJ 08742. Phone: (732) 892-7776 or (800) 4-BAYHED. E-mail: anne@flat disk.com. Web: www.bayhead.org.

BELMONT STAKES. June 9. Belmont Park, NY. Final race of the "Triple Crown" was inaugurated in 1867. Traditionally run on the fifth Saturday after Kentucky Derby (third Saturday after Preakness). Est attendance: 60,000. For info: Press Office, New York Racing Assn, PO Box 90, Jamaica, NY 11417. Phone: (718) 641-4700. Web: www.nyracing.com.

BETTY PICNIC. June 9. Tom Pierce Park, Grants Pass, OR. To celebrate the Bettys of this world for their vivacity, impulsiveness and similarities. Annually, the second Saturday in June. Send SASE since this is a nonprofit organization. Est attendance: 55. For info: Betty Wilder and Betty Patterson, c/o Betty Picnic, 1012 NE Madrone, Grants Pass, OR 97526. Phone: (541) 476-4104.

"BIG MAC" SHORELINE SPRING SCENIC TOUR. June 9–10 (also Sept 15–16). Mackinaw City and Harbor Springs, MI. Bike tours of 25-, 50-, 75- and 100-mile routes between the two cities. Each scenic tour will take you along the Lake Michigan shoreline past sparkling water, windswept dunes, through the renowned "Tunnel of Trees," over rolling hills and through quaint resort towns and old Native American villages steeped in legend and charm. Saturday evening dinner cruise on the Straits of Mackinac and a Sunday morning bike ride across the Mighty Mackinac Bridge. Est attendance: 4,000. For info: Mackinaw Area Tourist Bureau, PO Box 160, Mackinaw City, MI 49701. Phone: (800) 666-0160. Web: www.mackinawcity.com.

BUZZARD DAYS FESTIVAL. June 9. Makoshika State Park, Glendive, MT. Just as the swallows return to Capistrano each year, so do the turkey vultures come back to Makoshika. Festival activities include 10K, 5K and 1-mile runs, pancake breakfast, kids fun fest and bike rodeo, bird walks, FOLF (frisbee golf) tournament and lots more. For info: Makoshika State Park, Box 1242, Glendive, MT 59330. Phone: (406) 365-6256. Fax: (406) 365-8043. E-mail: makoshikapark@mcn.net.

CARS IN THE PARK. June 9. Dexter, MO. 17th annual. Experience the pleasure of a walk in the park among mint-condition vintage cars. Annually, the second Saturday in June. Est attendance: 1,400. For info: Annual Cars in the Park, 1 Corporate Dr, Dexter, MO 63841. Phone: (573) 624-8588 or (800) 332-8857.

CUMMINGS, ROBERT: BIRTH ANNIVERSARY. June 9, 1908. American actor Robert Cummings was born Charles Clarence Robert Orville Cummings at Joplin, MO. His best-known role was in the film *Dial M for Murder* (1954). He won an Emmy for his role in the television version of *Twelve Angry Men* (1954) and starred in the popular comedy "The Bob Cummings Show" (1955–59). He died Dec 2, 1990, at Woodland Hills, CA.

DONALD DUCK: BIRTHDAY. June 9, 1934. Donald Duck was "born."

ENGLAND: THE DERBY. June 9. Epsom Downs. Horse races. Annually, the Saturday after the first Wednesday in June.

FOUNDERS' DAY—THE GOOD LIFE. June 9 (rain date June 10). Toms River, NJ. Street fair for local non-profit organizations with a parade, entertainment, prizes, food, literature, games and a "Crafters Corner." Est attendance: 30,000. For info: Toms River-Ocean County Chamber of Commerce, 1200 Hooper Ave, Toms River, NJ 08753. Phone: (732) 349-0220. Fax: (732) 349-1252. Web: www.oc-chamber.com.

HERITAGE DAY CELEBRATION. June 9. Downtown Wisconsin Dells, WI. A return to the past featuring a craft fair, old-fashioned exhibits and displays, music, pancake breakfast, ice cream social and food stands. Annually, the second weekend following Memorial Day. Est attendance: 2,500. For info: Angie Rizner, Wisc Dells Visitors Bureau, PO Box 390, Wisconsin Dells, WI 53965. Phone: (800) 223-3557. E-mail: info@wisdells.com. Web: www.wisdells.com.

HERITAGE DAYS FESTIVAL. June 9–10. Cumberland, MD. 33rd annual. Held in historic downtown Cumberland, the festival showcases more than 300 arts and crafts booths. Also, music, entertainment, children's activities, carnivals, tours of historic homes and buildings as well as historic reenactments. Annually, the second weekend in June. Est attendance: 25,000. For info: Allegany Arts Council, 74 Baltimore St, Cumberland, MD 21502. Phone: (301) 777-2787.

HONG KONG: LEASE SIGNING ANNIVERSARY. June 9, 1898. Hong Kong, consisting of about 400 square miles (islands and mainland) with more than five million persons, was administered as a British Crown Colony after a 99-year lease was signed on June 9, 1898. In 1997 Hong Kong's sovereignty reverted to the People's Republic of China.

KUTNER, LUIS: BIRTH ANNIVERSARY. June 9, 1908. Human rights attorney Luis Kutner was born at Chicago, IL. Responsible for the release of many unjustly confined prisoners, he came to be known as "The Springman." He helped free Hungarian Cardinal Josef Mindszenty, poet Ezra Pound and former Congo President Moise Tshombe. He was the author of the living will and founded the World Habeas Corpus. Kutner was nominated nine times for the Nobel Peace Prize. He died Mar 1, 1993, at Chicago, IL.

LOLOMA, CHARLES: BIRTH ANNIVERSARY. June 9, 1921. Charles Loloma was a major influence on modern Indian art and was famous for changing the look of American Indian jewelry. A painter, sculptor and potter, he was best known for his jewelry, which broke tradition with previous Indian styles using materials such as coral, fossilized ivory, pearls and diamonds. Loloma was born at Hotevilla on the Hopi Indian Reservation and died June 9, 1991, at Scottsdale, AZ.

MELROSE PLANTATION ARTS AND CRAFTS FESTIVAL. June 9–10. Melrose, LA. Held on the grounds of Historic Melrose Plantation, this event features quality handcrafted items from more than 150 juried exhibitors. Food, including the famous meat pies and soft drinks will be available. Annually, the second full weekend in June. Est attendance: 20,000. For info: Calendar of Events, Natchitoches Parish Tourist Commission, 781 Front St, Natchitoches, LA 71457. Phone: (318) 352-8072 or (800) 259-1714. Fax: (318) 352-2415. Web: www.natchitoches .net.

OPERATION YOUTH. June 9–16. Xavier University, Cincinnati, OH. To provide a hands-on exercise in democracy for teenagers. Students elect, from their ranks, city officials who join their real counterparts in a Cincinnati council meeting. Speakers from education, industry and government. Est attendance: 100. For info: William Smith, CPA, Prof of Accounting, Dir of Operation Youth, Xavier University, 3800 Victory Pkwy, Cincinnati, OH 45207-5161. Phone: (513) 745-3504. Fax: (513) 745-4383.

PAYNE, JOHN HOWARD: BIRTH ANNIVERSARY. June 9, 1791. American author, actor, diplomat, born at New York, NY. Died at Tunis, Apr 9, 1852. Author of opera libretto (*Clari, or The Maid of Milan*), which contained the song "Home, Sweet Home."

PORTER, COLE: BIRTH ANNIVERSARY. June 9, 1891. Cole Porter published his first song, "The Bobolink Waltz," at the age of 10. His career as a composer and lyricist for Broadway was launched in 1928 when five of his songs were used in the musical play *Let's Do It*. His prolific contributions to the Broadway stage include *Fifty Million Frenchmen, Wake Up and Dream, The Gay Divorcée, Anything Goes, Leave It to Me, Du Barry Was a Lady, Something for the Boys, Kiss Me Kate, Can Can* and *Silk Stockings*. Porter was born at Peru, IN, and died at Santa Monica, CA, Oct 15, 1964.

POTOMAC CELTIC FESTIVAL. June 9–10. Morven Park Equestrian Center, Leesburg, VA. Featuring Brittany (France) in 2000, the Festival celebrates all seven Celtic nations: Scotland, Wales, Cornwall, the Isle of Man, Ireland, Brittany (France) and Galicia (Spain). Five stages of live music, dance stage, storytelling, drama, poetry, children's entertainment, workshops, crafts, sports and food. For info: Barnaby Council for Celtic Studies, PO Box 11160, Burke, VA 22009-1160. Phone: (703) 451-4492. E-mail: prez@pobox.com. Web: www.PotomacCelticFest.org.

RENDEZVOUS FESTIVAL. June 9–10. Icelandic State Park, Cavalier, ND. A festival of culture and art celebrating the history of North Dakota's Rendezvous Region. Activities include a muzzleloader's shoot, ethnic singers, dancers and performers, pioneer demonstrations and trades. There will also be a buckskinner's encampment, ceremonies and a Chautauqua. Est attendance: 2,500. For info: (701) 265-4561 or North Dakota Tourism, 604 East Boulevard, Bismarck, ND 58505. Phone: (701) 328-2525 or (800) 435-5663.

ROUND BARN RENDEZVOUS AND MARKET. June 9–10. Rochester, IN. Living history village called Loyal depicts life in 1900–25. Also 5K run, restored round barn with old-time farm tools, historic crafts and antiques, food, music, farm demonstrations in round barn and antique tractors and railcars. Est attendance: 1,000. For info: Fulton County Historical Society, 37 East 375 N, Rochester, IN 46975. Phone: (219) 223-4436. E-mail: wwillard@rtcol.com.

SEASPACE. June 9–10. Hyatt Regency Downtown Hotel, Houston, TX. Scuba diving convention featuring seminars, photo and video courses, workshops, photo contest and exhibit, film festivals, halls of exhibits, special kids talk, environmental awareness area, free intro to scuba and snorkeling and receptions. Sponsor: Houston Underwater Club. For more info send SASE. Est attendance: 10,000. For info: Seaspace, PO Box 3753, Houston, TX 77253-3753. Phone: (713) 467-6675. Web: www.seaspace.org.

SPECIAL LIBRARIES ASSOCIATION ANNUAL CONFERENCE. June 9–14. San Antonio, TX. Networking, educational activities, annual board meeting; exhibits for librarians at companies, government agencies, academic institutions, etc. 92nd annual. Theme: "2001, An Information Odyssey: Seizing the Competitive Advantage." Est attendance: 6,000. For info: SLA, 1700 18th St NW, Washington, DC 20009-2514. Phone: (202) 234-4700. Fax: (202) 265-9317. E-mail: sla@sla.org. Web: www.sla.org.

STEPHENSON, GEORGE: BIRTH ANNIVERSARY. June 9, 1781. English inventor, developer of the steam locomotive, born near Newcastle, England. Died near Chesterfield, England, Aug 12, 1848.

	S	M	T	W	T	F	S
June						1	2
2001	3	4	5	6	7	8	9
	10	11	12	13	14	15	16
	17	18	19	20	21	22	23
	24	25	26	27	28	29	30

SUMMER TROPICAL SHOW. June 9–Sept 2. Garfield Park Conservatory and Lincoln Park Conservatory, Chicago, IL. Experience the sights and smells of the tropics—without leaving Chicago. Exotic tropical plants with colorful flowers and foliage showcased in the recently renovated Horticulture Hall and the beautiful Show Room. For info: Garfield Park Conservatory, 300 N Central Park Ave, Chicago, IL 60624. Phone: (312) 746-5102. Fax: (773) 638-1777. Web: www.garfield-conservatory.org or Lincoln Park Conservatory, 2400 N Stockton, Chicago, IL 60614. Phone: (312) 746-7736.

TAKE A KID FISHING WEEKEND. June 9–10. St. Paul, MN. Resident adults may fish without a license on these days when fishing with a child under age 16. For info: Ron Payer, Fisheries Chief, DNR, Box 12, 500 Lafayette Rd, St. Paul, MN 55155. Phone: (651) 296-0792 or (651) 296-3325. Fax: (651) 297-4916. Web: www.dnr.state.mn.us/

THAYER, SYLVANUS: BIRTH ANNIVERSARY. June 9, 1785. A military engineer and educator, born at Braintree, MA. He was appointed superintendent of West Point at 32 and became known as the "Father of the Military Academy." Thayer died at Braintree, MA, Sept 7, 1872.

UNITED KINGDOM: TROOPING THE COLOUR—QUEEN'S OFFICIAL BIRTHDAY PARADE. June 9 (tentative). National holiday in the United Kingdom. Horse Guards Parade, Whitehall, London. Colorful ceremony with music and pageantry during which Her Majesty The Queen takes the salute. Starts at 11 AM. When requesting info, send stamped, self-addressed envelope. [Final date not set at press time.] Trooping the Colour is always the second or third Saturday in June; the Queen's real birthday is Apr 21. Est attendance: 10,000. For info: The Ticket Office, HQ Household Division, 1 Chelsea Barracks, London, England SW1H 8RF. Phone: (44) (171) 414-2357.

WYATT EARP BIRTHDAY CELEBRATION. June 9. Monmouth, IL. OK Corral reenactments, 2 PM & 3 PM. Tours of birthplace home listed on National Register of Historic Places. Visit Pioneer Cemetery where Earp's grandparents are buried and other Earp sites 1 PM to 4 PM. Annually, the second Saturday in June. Est attendance: 150. For info: Wyatt Earp Birthplace, Historic House Museum, Office: 1020 E Detroit Ave, Monmouth, IL 61462. Phone: (309) 734-6419 or Chamber of Commerce (309) 734-3181. Fax: (309) 734-6419.

BIRTHDAYS TODAY

George Axelrod, 79, writer (screenplays *Bus Stop, Breakfast at Tiffany's*), born New York, NY, June 9, 1922.

Patricia Cornwell, 45, best-selling mystery writer, born Miami, FL, June 9, 1956.

Johnny Depp, 38, actor ("21 Jump Street," *Edward Scissorhands, Ed Wood*), born Owensboro, KY, June 9, 1963.

Michael J. Fox, 40, actor ("Family Ties," "Spin City," *Back to the Future* films), born Edmonton, Alberta, Canada, June 9, 1961.

Marvin Kalb, 71, educator, journalist, born New York, NY, June 9, 1930.

Jackie Mason (Yacov Moshe Maza), 67, comedian ("Chicken Soup," *The World According to Me*), born Sheboygan, WI, June 9, 1934.

Robert S. McNamara, 85, banker, former cabinet member, born San Francisco, CA, June 9, 1916.

David Gene (Dave) Parker, 50, former baseball player, born Calhoun, MS, June 9, 1951.

Les Paul, 86, musician, singer (with the late Mary Ford; "Hummingbird"), born Waukesha, WI, June 9, 1915.

Natalie Portman, 20, actress (*Star Wars: Episode I—The Phantom Menace*), born Jerusalem, June 9, 1981.

Gloria Reuben, 37, actress ("ER"), born Toronto, Ontario, Canada, June 9, 1964.

Dick Vitale, 62, sportscaster, ESPN and ABC analyst, born East Rutherford, NJ, June 9, 1939.

JUNE 10 — SUNDAY
Day 161 — 204 Remaining

ABUSED WOMEN AND CHILDREN'S AWARENESS DAY. June 10. A day to reflect on how we can help stop the violence in America that is destroying the lives and well-being of women and children. A day to prayerfully put an end to violent behavior in American homes, schools, workplaces and communities. Annually, the second Sunday in June. For info: Judith Natale, CEO & Founder, Natl Children & Family Awareness of America, Administrative Headquarters, 3060 Rt 405 Hwy, Muncy, PA 17756-8808. Phone: (888) MAA-DESK. E-mail: MaaJudith@aol.com.

ALCOHOLICS ANONYMOUS: FOUNDING ANNIVERSARY. June 10, 1935. On this day at Akron, OH, Dr. Robert Smith completed his first day of permanent sobriety. "Doctor Bob" and William G. Wilson are considered to have founded Alcoholics Anonymous on that day.

BALL-POINT PEN PATENTED: ANNIVERSARY. June 10, 1943. Hungarian Laszlo Biro patented the ball-point pen, which he had been developing since the 1930s. He was living at Argentina, where he had gone to escape the Nazis. In many languages, the word for ball-point pen is "biro."

BELGIUM: MILITARY MUSIC FESTIVAL. June 10. Tournai. Traditional cultural observance. Annually, the second Sunday in June.

CHILDREN'S DAY IN MASSACHUSETTS. June 10. Annually, the second Sunday in June. The Governor proclaims this day each year.

CHILDREN'S SUNDAY. June 10. Traditionally the second Sunday in June is observed as Children's Sunday in many Christian churches.

CZECHOSLOVAKIA: RAPE OF LIDICE: ANNIVERSARY. June 10, 1942. Nazi German troops executed, by shooting, all male inhabitants of the Czechoslovakian village of Lidice (total population about 500 persons), burned every house and deported the women and children to Germany for "re-education." One of the most-remembered atrocities of World War II. June 10, Lidice Memorial Day, is observed in New Jersey.

GARLAND, JUDY: BIRTH ANNIVERSARY. June 10, 1922. American actress and singer born Frances Gumm at Grand Rapids, MN. While Garland played in many films and toured widely as a singer, she is probably most remembered for her portrayal of Dorothy Gale in the now-classic *The Wizard of Oz.* Died June 22, 1969, at London, England.

GERMANFEST. June 10–16. Fort Wayne, IN. A celebration of German heritage with folk music, folk dancing, beer tents, German food, beer and wine tastings, Männerchor (men's choir) singing, Gottesdienste (masses), genealogy workshops, classical organ music, Family Fest, German films, lectures and demonstrations. Est attendance: 80,000. For info: Germanfest Committee, PO Box 10971, Fort Wayne, IN 46855. Phone: (800) 767-7752. Fax: (219) 449-7495. E-mail: kscheib@mail.fwi.com. Web: www.fwi.com/germanfest.

GRANT WOOD ART FESTIVAL. June 10. Stone City–Anamosa, IA. Juried art exhibits, demonstrations, stage entertainment, tours of historic Stone City and more. Annually, the second Sunday in June. Est attendance: 8,000. For info: Marguerite Stoll, Media Coordinator, Grant Wood Art Festival, Inc, 124 E Main St, Anamosa, IA 52205. Phone: (319) 462-4267 or (319) 462-3988.

JOHN HULL OPENS FIRST MINT IN AMERICA: ANNIVERSARY. June 10, 1652. In defiance of English colonial law, John Hull, a silversmith, established the first mint in America. The first coin issued was the Pine Tree Shilling, designed by Hull.

JORDAN: GREAT ARAB REVOLT AND ARMY DAY: 85th ANNIVERSARY. June 10. Commemorates the beginning of the Great Arab Revolt in 1916. National holiday.

McDANIEL, HATTIE: BIRTH ANNIVERSARY. June 10, 1889. Hattie McDaniel was the first African-American to win an Academy Award. She won it in 1940 for her role in the 1939 film *Gone With the Wind*. Her career spanned radio and vaudeville in addition to her screen roles in *Judge Priest, The Little Colonel, Showboat* and *Saratoga*, among others. She was born at Wichita, KS, and died Oct 26, 1952, at Los Angeles, CA.

★**NATIONAL FLAG WEEK.** June 10–16. Presidential Proclamation issued each year since 1966 for the week including June 14. (PL89–443 of June 9, 1966.) In addition, the president often calls upon the American people to participate in public ceremonies in which the Pledge of Allegiance is recited.

ORTHODOX FESTIVAL OF ALL SAINTS. June 10. Observed by Eastern Orthodox churches on the Sunday following Orthodox Pentecost (June 3 in 2001). Marks the end of the 18-week Triodion cycle.

PORTUGAL: DAY OF PORTUGAL. June 10. National holiday. Anniversary of the death in 1580 of Portugal's national poet, Luis Vas de Camoes (Camoens), born in 1524 (exact date unknown) at either Lisbon or Coimbra. Died at Lisbon, Portugal.

RACE UNITY DAY. June 10. Baha'i-sponsored observance promoting racial harmony and understanding and the essential unity of humanity. Annually, the second Sunday in June. Established in 1957 by the Baha'is of the US. For info: Baha'is of the US, Office of Public Information, 866 UN Plaza, Ste 120, New York, NY 10017-1822. Phone: (212) 803-2500. Fax: (212) 803-2573. E-mail: usopi-ny@bic.org. Web: www.us.bahai.org.

ROCK CREEK PARK NATIONALIZED: ANNIVERSARY. June 10, 1933. Rock Creek Park, authorized Sept 27, 1890, was transferred to the National Park Service. For further park info: Rock Creek Park, 5000 Glover Rd NW, Washington, DC 20015.

TAG SALE ON THE GREEN. June 10. The Colchester Green, Colchester, CT. Largest tag sale event in the state, with more than 200 vendors. Free to the public. Open 9 AM–4 PM. Est attendance: 10,000. For info: Colchester Business Assn, PO Box 453, Colchester, CT 06415. Phone: (860) 537-0340.

TEENS' DIG FOR DINOSAURS. June 10–11 (also Aug 14–15). Thermopolis, WY. Work on actual dinosaur dig site with professionals. Includes guided tours of Wyoming Dinosaur Center museum, how to prepare bones and cast fossils plus other activities for ages 13–15. For info: Shawna Creamer, Big Horn Basin Foundation, Box 71, Thermopolis, WY 82443. Phone: (307) 864-2259. Fax: (307) 864-5762. E-mail: shawna@wyodino .org. Web: www.thermopwy.net/bhbf/.

June 2001	S	M	T	W	T	F	S
						1	2
	3	4	5	6	7	8	9
	10	11	12	13	14	15	16
	17	18	19	20	21	22	23
	24	25	26	27	28	29	30

TRINITY SUNDAY. June 10. Christian Holy Day on the Sunday after Pentecost commemorates the Holy Trinity, the three divine persons—Father, Son and Holy Spirit—in one God. See also: "Pentecost" (June 3).

BIRTHDAYS TODAY

F. Lee Bailey, 68, lawyer, born Waltham, MA, June 10, 1933.

John Edwards, 48, US Senator (D, North Carolina), born Seneca, SC, June 10, 1953.

Linda Evangelista, 36, model, born St. Catharines, Ontario, Canada, June 10, 1965.

Jeff Greenfield, 58, author, journalist, born New York, NY, June 10, 1943.

Nat Hentoff, 76, music critic, journalist, born Boston, MA, June 10, 1925.

Elizabeth Hurley, 36, model, actress (*Austin Powers: International Man of Mystery*), born Basingstoke, England, June 10, 1965.

Tara Lipinski, 19, figure skater, born Philadelphia, PA, June 10, 1982.

Doug McKeon, 35, actor (*On Golden Pond*), born Pomptain Plains, NJ, June 10, 1966.

Prince Philip, 80, Duke of Edinburgh, husband of Queen Elizabeth II, born Corfu, Greece, June 10, 1921.

Maurice Sendak, 73, author, illustrator (*Chicken Soup with Rice, Where the Wild Things Are*), born Brooklyn, NY, June 10, 1928.

Leelee Sobieski, 19, actress (*A Soldier's Daughter Never Cries*), born New York, NY, June 10, 1982.

JUNE 11 — MONDAY
Day 162 — 203 Remaining

AUSTRALIA: QUEEN'S BIRTHDAY. June 11. This is a holiday in all of Australia except Western Australia. It commemorates the Queen's "official" birthday, not the day she was actually born.

CONSTABLE, JOHN: 225th BIRTH ANNIVERSARY. June 11, 1776. English landscape painter. Born at East Bergholt, Suffolk, England, he died at London, Mar 31, 1837.

COUSTEAU, JACQUES: BIRTH ANNIVERSARY. June 11, 1910. French undersea explorer, writer and filmmaker born at St. Andre-de-Cubzac, France. He invented the Aqualung, which allowed him and his colleagues to produce more than 80 documentary films about undersea life, two of which won Oscars. This scientist and explorer was awarded the French Legion of Honor for his work in the Resistance in WWII. He died June 25, 1997, at Paris, France.

JONSON, BEN: BIRTH ANNIVERSARY. June 11, 1572 (OS). English playwright and poet. "Talking and eloquence," he wrote, "are not the same: to speak and to speak well, are two things." Born at London, England, he died there Aug 6, 1637 (OS). The epitaph written on his tombstone in Westminster Abbey: "O rare Ben Jonson."

KING KAMEHAMEHA I DAY. June 11. Designated state holiday in Hawaii honors memory of Hawaiian monarch (1737–1819). Governor appoints state commission to plan annual celebration.

LOMBARDI, VINCE: BIRTH ANNIVERSARY. June 11, 1913. Vincent Thomas (Vince) Lombardi, Pro Football Hall of Fame coach, born at New York, NY. Lombardi played football for Fordham's famed "Seven Blocks of Granite" line in the mid-1930s, became a teacher and began to coach high school football. He became offensive line coach at West Point in 1949 and moved to the New York Giants in 1954. Five years later, he was named head coach of the Green Bay Packers. His Packers won five NFL titles and two Super Bowls in nine years, and Lombardi was generally regarded as the greatest coach and the finest motivator in pro football history. He retired in 1968, but was lured back to coach the Washington Redskins a year later. Inducted into the Pro Football Hall of Fame in 1971. Died at Washington, DC, Sept 3, 1970.

MEET A MATE WEEK. June 11–17. To inspire singles seeking a mate to take advantage of summer by pursuing warm weather meeting opportunities. Options include singles travel, sports activities, New Blood parties and volunteer work. For info: Robin Gorman Newman, 44 Somerset Dr N, Great Neck, NY 11020. Phone: (516) 773-0911. E-mail: rgnewman@aol.com.

MOUNT PINATUBO ERUPTS IN PHILIPPINES: 10th ANNIVERSARY. June 11, 1991. Long-dormant volcano Mount Pinatubo erupted with a violent explosion, spewing ash and gases that could be seen for more than 60 miles, into the air. The surrounding areas were covered with ash and mud created by rainstorms. US Military bases Clark and Subic Bay were also damaged. On July 6, 1992, Ellsworth Dutton of the National Oceanic and Atmospheric Administration's Climate Monitoring and Diagnostics Laboratory announced that a layer of sulfuric acid droplets released into the Earth's atmosphere by the eruption had cooled the planet's average temperature by about 1 degree Fahrenheit. The greatest difference was noted in the Northern Hemisphere with a drop of 1.5 degrees. Although the temperature drop was temporary, the climate trend made determining the effect of greenhouse warming on the Earth more difficult.

NATIONAL E-MAIL WEEK. June 11–17. Sponsored by MiracleMail.com, this week is meant to draw awareness to the power of e-mail as a medium to communicate and influence change. Contact MiracleMail.com for a media kit. For info: Linda C. Richards, MiracleMail.com, 5 Wellwood Ave, Farmingdale, NY 11735. Phone: (631) 420-0200. Fax: (631) 420-4264. E-mail: info@miraclemail.com. Web: www.miraclemail.com.

★**NATIONAL LITTLE LEAGUE BASEBALL WEEK.** June 11–17. Presidential Proclamation 3296, of June 4, 1959, covers all succeeding years. Always the week beginning with the second Monday in June. (H.Con.Res. 17 of June 1, 1959.)

NATIONAL MEN'S HEALTH WEEK. June 11–17. For info: Natl Men's Health Week Foundation, 154-182 E Minor St, Emmaus, PA 18098. Phone: (610) 967-8620. Web: www.nmhw.org.

OLD TIME SCHOOL. June 11–July 13. West Riverside Historic Site, Cambridge, MN. Children attend school in a one-room school house from 1898. They dress in the style of Laura Ingalls Wilder, carry their lunch in a pail, play games and learn lessons from the year 1900, do art projects, give a program for parents and actually have homework. There are five one-week sessions beginning in mid-June. Student in grades 1–8 may apply. $30 fee. Est attendance: 300. For info: Valorie Arrowsmith, Isanti County Historical Soc, PO Box 525, Cambridge, MN 55008. Phone: (763) 689-4229. Fax: (763) 689-4229. E-mail: varrow2@ecenet.com.

QUEEN'S OFFICIAL BIRTHDAY. June 11. A holiday in Australia, Belize, Cayman Islands, Fiji and Papua New Guinea on the second Monday in June. In New Zealand and Tuvalu it is commemorated on the first Monday in June. Celebrating Queen Elizabeth II's birthday, which actually falls on Apr 21.

RANKIN, JEANNETTE: BIRTH ANNIVERSARY. June 11, 1880. First woman elected to the US Congress, a reformer, feminist and pacifist, was born at Missoula, MT. She was the only member of Congress to vote against a declaration of war against Japan in December 1941. Died May 18, 1973, at Carmel, CA.

RED ARMY DEPARTS BERLIN: ANNIVERSARY. June 11, 1994. After 49 years, the Russian military occupation of the region once called East Germany ended. At one time there had been 337,800 Soviet troops stationed in Germany. The departure was celebrated with a parade in Wupnsdorf south of Berlin, which was the Soviet Union's military headquarters in the former German Democratic Republic.

"SPACE ODDITY" SONG RELEASE: ANNIVERSARY. June 11, 1969. This single recorded by David Bowie was released to coincide with the *Apollo 11*'s trip to the moon, during which Neil Armstrong and Edwin Aldrin, Jr, landed and walked on the surface of the moon.

STRAUSS, RICHARD GEORG: BIRTH ANNIVERSARY. June 11, 1864. German composer, musician and conductor whose best-remembered works are *Till Eulenspiegel* (1895), *Also Sprach Zarathustra* (1896) and *Don Quixote* (1898). Born at Munich, he died at Garmisch-Partenkirchen, Germany, after a heart attack Sept 8, 1949, at age 85.

BIRTHDAYS TODAY

Adrienne Barbeau, 56, actress ("Maude"), born Sacramento, CA, June 11, 1945.
Chad Everett (Raymond Cramton), 65, actor ("The Dakotas," "Medical Center"), born South Bend, IN, June 11, 1936.
Parris Glendening, 59, Governor of Maryland (D), born The Bronx, NY, June 11, 1942.
Joshua Jackson, 23, actor ("Dawson's Creek," *Scream 2*), born Vancouver, British Columbia, Canada, June 11, 1978.
Joseph C. (Joe) Montana, Jr, 45, former sportscaster and football player, born New Eagle, PA, June 11, 1956.
Jackie Stewart, 62, former auto racer, born Dunbartonshire, Scotland, June 11, 1939.
William Styron, 76, author (*The Confessions of Nat Turner, Sophie's Choice*), born Newport News, VA, June 11, 1925.
Gene Wilder, 62, actor (*The Producers, Willy Wonka & the Chocolate Factory, Blazing Saddles, Young Frankenstein*), director, born Milwaukee, WI, June 11, 1939.

JUNE 12 — TUESDAY
Day 163 — 202 Remaining

BIG BEND NATIONAL PARK ESTABLISHED: ANNIVERSARY. June 12, 1944. Area on the "big bend" of the Rio Grande River in western Texas along the Mexican border, authorized June 20, 1935, was established as a national park. For further park info: Big Bend Natl Park, Big Bend Natl Park, TX 79834.

BURLINGTON STEAMBOAT DAYS/AMERICAN MUSIC FESTIVAL. June 12–17 (tentative). Mississippi Riverfront at Port of Burlington, IA. 39th annual. Week-long event offers community and visitors a chance to enjoy top-name entertainment and a carnival setting. Est attendance: 100,000. For info: Steamboat Days, PO Box 271, Burlington, IA 52601. Phone: (319) 754-4334. Fax: (319) 752-1299. Web: www.steamboatdays.com.

BUSH, GEORGE HERBERT WALKER: BIRTHDAY. June 12, 1924. Forty-first US president (1989–93), born at Milton, MA.

CHUY'S NATIONAL TACO DAY™. June 12. TX. To honor and celebrate the taco, one of our most versatile and convenient foods. The taco is a small meal made by simply rolling up your favorite ingredient in a fresh tortilla. Celebration festivities include cheap tacos and fun giveaways. Annually, the second Tuesday in June. For info: Page Nordstrom, Chuy's, 1623 Toomey Rd, Austin, TX 78704. Phone: (888) HEY-CHUY, ext 13. Web: www.chuys.com.

FIRST MAN-POWERED FLIGHT ACROSS ENGLISH CHANNEL: ANNIVERSARY. June 12, 1979. Bryan Allen, 26-year-old Californian, pedaled the 70-pound *Gossamer Albatross* 22 miles across the English Channel, from Folkestone, England, to Cape Gris-Nez, France, in 2 hours, 49 minutes, winning (with the craft's designer, Paul MacCready of Pasadena, CA) the £100,000 prize offered by British industrialist Henry Kremer for the first man-powered flight across the English Channel.

FRANK, ANNE: BIRTH ANNIVERSARY. June 12, 1929. Born at Frankfurt, Germany. Anne Frank's family moved to Amsterdam to escape the Nazis but after Holland was invaded by Germany, they had to go into hiding. In 1942 Anne began to keep a diary. She died at Bergen-Belsen concentration camp in 1945. After the war, her father published her diary, on which a stage play and movie were later based. See also "Diary of Anne Frank: Last Entry" (Aug 1).

KIDS' DIG FOR DINOSAURS. June 12-13 (also July 3-4 and Aug 7-8). Warm Springs Ranch, Thermopolis, WY. Work on actual dinosaur dig site with professionals. Includes guided tours of Wyoming Dinosaur Center museum, other dino-related activities for ages 8-12. For info: Shawna Creamer, The Wyoming Dinosaur Center, Big Horn Basin Foundation, PO Box 71, Thermopolis, WY 82443. Phone: (307) 864-2259. Fax: (307) 864-5762. E-mail: shawna@wyodino.org. Web: www.thermopwy.net/bhbf/.

LOVING *v* VIRGINIA: ANNIVERSARY. June 12, 1967. The US Supreme Court decision in *Loving v Virginia* swept away all 16 remaining state laws prohibiting interracial marriages.

NATIONAL BASEBALL HALL OF FAME: ANNIVERSARY. June 12, 1939. The National Baseball Hall of Fame and Museum, Inc, was dedicated at Cooperstown, NY. More than 200 individuals have been honored for their contributions to the game of baseball by induction into the Baseball Hall of Fame. The first players chosen for membership (1936) were Ty Cobb, Honus Wagner, Babe Ruth, Christy Mathewson and Walter Johnson. Relics and memorabilia from the history of baseball are housed at this shrine of America's national sport.

PARAGUAY: PEACE WITH BOLIVIA DAY. June 12. Commemorates the end of the Chaco War in 1935.

PETIT JEAN ANTIQUE AUTO SHOW AND SWAP MEET. June 12-16. Petit Jean Mountain, Morrilton, AR. 43rd annual show and meet with more than 100 antique and classic cars competing for awards, from turn-of-the-century to 1972 models. More than 1,500 vendor spaces filled with antique cars, parts and related items. Also, arts and crafts. Est attendance: 85,000. For info: Buddy Hoelzeman, Museum of Automobiles, 8 Jones Lane, Morrilton, AR 72110. Phone: (501) 727-5427. Fax: (501) 727-6482.

PHILIPPINES: INDEPENDENCE DAY. June 12. National holiday. Declared independence from Spain in 1898.

RUSSIA: INDEPENDENCE DAY: 10th ANNIVERSARY. June 12. National holiday. Commemorates the election in 1991 of the first popularly elected leader (Gorbachev) in the 1,000-year history of the Russian state.

SPACE MILESTONE: *VENERA 4* (USSR). June 12, 1967. Launched on this date, this instrumental capsule landed on Venus by parachute on Oct 18 and reported a temperature of 536°F.

		S	M	T	W	T	F	S
June							1	2
2001		3	4	5	6	7	8	9
		10	11	12	13	14	15	16
		17	18	19	20	21	22	23
		24	25	26	27	28	29	30

STUART'S FIRST RIDE AROUND McCLELLAN: ANNIVERSARY. June 12, 1862. In a flamboyant move Confederate J.E.B. "Beauty" Stuart led a force of cavalry and artillery to reconnoiter Federal positions on the Peninsula. Stuart and his men completely encircled McClellan's forces, disrupting communications and supply lines and leading the Union forces to believe they were threatened by a much larger force. The large boost to Confederate morale was strengthened when Stonewall Jackson's forces were reinforced under orders by Robert E. Lee.

BIRTHDAYS TODAY

Spencer Abraham, 49, US Senator (R, Michigan), born Lansing, MI, June 12, 1952.

Marv Albert (born Marvin Philip Aufrichtig), 58, sportscaster, born New York, NY, June 12, 1943.

Timothy Busfield, 44, actor ("thirtysomething," *Field of Dreams*), born Lansing, MI, June 12, 1957.

George Herbert Walker Bush, 77, 41st US president, born Milton, MA, June 12, 1924.

Chick Corea, 60, musician, born Chelsea, MA, June 12, 1941.

Vic Damone (Vito Farinola), 73, singer ("On the Street Where You Live"), born New York, NY, June 12, 1928.

Jim Nabors, 69, actor ("The Andy Griffith Show," "Gomer Pyle, U.S.M.C."), born Sylacauga, AL, June 12, 1932.

David Rockefeller, 86, banker, born New York, NY, June 12, 1915.

Sherry Stringfield, 34, actress ("NYPD Blue," "ER"), born Colorado Springs, CO, June 12, 1967.

JUNE 13 — WEDNESDAY
Day 164 — 201 Remaining

BOLLES, DON: 25th DEATH ANNIVERSARY. June 13, 1976. Don Bolles, investigative reporter for *The Arizona Republic*, died as a result of injuries received when a bomb exploded in his automobile, June 2, 1976, while he was engaged in journalistic investigation of an alleged Mafia story. Bolles was awarded, posthumously, the University of Arizona's John Peter Zenger Award, Dec 9, 1976.

EVERS, MEDGAR: ASSASSINATION ANNIVERSARY. June 13, 1963. Civil rights leader Medgar Wiley Evers was active in seeking integration of schools and voter registration. He was assassinated by Byron de la Beckwith. The public outrage following his death was one of the factors that led President John F. Kennedy to propose a comprehensive civil rights law.

GRANGE, RED: BIRTH ANNIVERSARY. June 13, 1903. Harold Edward ("Red") Grange, Pro Football Hall of Fame halfback and broadcaster, born at Forskville, PA. Perhaps the most famous football player of all time, Grange had a spectacular college career at the University of Illinois, being named an All-American in 1923, 1924 and 1925. When Illinois dedicated its Memorial Stadium on Oct 18, 1924, Grange scored four touchdowns in the game's first 12 minutes. Known as the "Galloping Ghost," Grange joined the Chicago Bears in 1925 for what amounted to a barnstorming tour, the start of a professional career dictated by Grange and his manager, Charles C. ("Cash and Carry") Pyle. He retired in 1934 following a knee injury, having put pro football on the sports map. Grange entered business and did announcing work on radio and television. In retirement, he lived quietly and humbly. Inducted into the Hall of Fame as a charter member in 1963. Died at Lake Wales, FL, Jan 28, 1991.

HOME OWNERS LOAN ACT: ANNIVERSARY. June 13, 1933. The Federal Savings and Loan Association was authorized with the passage of the Home Owners Loan Act. The purpose of the legislation was to provide a convenient place for investment and to lend money on first mortgages. The first association was the First Federal Savings and Loan Association of Miami, FL, which was chartered on Aug 8, 1933.

MIRANDA DECISION: 35th ANNIVERSARY. June 13, 1966. The US Supreme Court rendered a 5–4 decision in the case of *Miranda v Arizona*, holding that the Fifth Amendment of the Constitution "required warnings before valid statements could be taken by police." The decision has been described as "providing basic legal protections to persons who might otherwise not be aware of their rights." Ernesto Miranda, the 23-year-old whose name became nationally known, was retried after the Miranda Decision, convicted and sent back to prison. Miranda was stabbed to death in a card game dispute at Phoenix, AZ, in 1976. A suspect in the killing was released by police after he had been read his "Miranda rights." Police procedures now routinely require the reading of a prisoner's constitutional rights ("Miranda") before questioning.

MISSION SAN LUIS REY DE FRANCIA: FOUNDING ANNIVERSARY. June 13, 1798. California mission to the Indians founded on this date. Abandoned by 1846; restoration begun in 1892.

MOON PHASE: LAST QUARTER. June 13. Moon enters Last Quarter phase at 11:28 PM, EDT.

NATIONAL HERMIT WEEK. June 13–20. This week take an adventure in solitude. Discover yourself by journeying within or going off-the-grid. Celebrate the contributions of others who indulged their need to hermit. Whether you seek inner peace, spiritual release or a moment's peace this week is for you. Annually, beginning the 13th of June. For info: The Hermit Project, PO Box 5192, Fredericksburg, VA 22403-0192. Phone: (888) 222-5170.

SAINT ANTHONY OF PADUA: FEAST DAY: DEATH ANNIVERSARY. June 13. Born at Lisbon, Portugal, Aug 15, 1195, St. Anthony is patron of the illiterate and the poor. Died at Padua, June 13, 1231. Public holiday, Lisbon.

SCOTT, WINFIELD: BIRTH ANNIVERSARY. June 13, 1786. American army general, negotiator of peace treaties with Indians and twice nominated for president (1848 and 1852). Leader of brilliant military campaign in Mexico in 1847. Scott was born at Petersburg, VA and died at West Point, NY, May 29, 1866.

SPRING SUWANNEE RIVER GOSPEL JUBILEE. June 13–16. Live Oak, FL. A weekend filled with great gospel music groups at the beautiful amphitheater. Est attendance: 10,000. For info: James Cornett, Spirit of the Suwannee Music Park, 3076 95th Dr, Live Oak, FL 32060. Phone: (904) 364-1683. Fax: (904) 364-2998. E-mail: spirit@musicliveshere.com. Web: www.music liveshere.com.

VIEIRA DA SILVA, MARIA-HELENA: BIRTH ANNIVERSARY. June 13, 1908. Portuguese-born painter Maria Helena Vieira da Silva was born at Lisbon. Although a French citizen, she was considered by many as Portugal's greatest contemporary artist. Her work spanned the Parisian School and Abstract Expressionism. She died Mar 6, 1992, at Paris, France.

YEATS, WILLIAM BUTLER: BIRTH ANNIVERSARY. June 13, 1865. Nobel prize-winning Irish poet and dramatist, born at Dublin, Ireland. He once wrote: "If a poet interprets a poem of his own he limits its suggestility." Yeats died at France, Jan 28, 1939. After World War II his body was returned, as he had wished, for reburial in a churchyard at Drumcliff, Ireland.

BIRTHDAYS TODAY

Tim Allen, 48, comedian, actor ("Home Improvement", *Galaxy Quest*), born Denver, CO, June 13, 1953.

Christo (Christo Javacheff), 66, conceptual artist (*Running Fence, Valley Curtain*), born Babrovo, Bulgaria, June 13, 1935.

Malcolm McDowell, 58, actor (*A Clockwork Orange, O Lucky Man*), born Leeds, England, June 13, 1943.

Ashley Olsen, 15, actress ("Full House," "Two of a Kind"), born Los Angeles, CA, June 13, 1986.

Mary-Kate Olsen, 15, actress ("Full House," "Two of a Kind"), born Los Angeles, CA, June 13, 1986.

Ally (Alexandra Elizabeth) Sheedy, 39, actress (*St. Elmo's Fire, The Breakfast Club*), born New York, NY, June 13, 1962.

Richard Thomas, 50, actor ("The Waltons," *Roots: The Next Generations*), born New York, NY, June 13, 1951.

JUNE 14 — THURSDAY
Day 165 — 200 Remaining

ALZHEIMER, ALOIS: BIRTH ANNIVERSARY. June 14, 1864. The German psychiatrist and pathologist Alois Alzheimer was born at Markbreit am Mainz, Germany. In 1907 an article by Alzheimer appeared in *Allgemeine Zeitschrift für Psychiatrie*, first describing the disease that was named for him. It was thought of as a kind of presenile dementia, usually beginning at age 40–60. Alzheimer died Dec 19, 1915, at Breslau, Germany.

AMERICAN LIBRARY ASSOCIATION ANNUAL CONFERENCE. June 14–20. San Francisco, CA. Est attendance: 10,000. For info: Public Information Office, American Library Assn, 50 E Huron St, Chicago, IL 60611. Phone: (312) 280-5044. Fax: (312) 944-8520. E-mail: pio@ala.org. Web: www.ala.org

BARTLETT, JOHN: BIRTH ANNIVERSARY. June 14, 1820. American editor and compiler (Bartlett's *Familiar Quotations* [1855]) was born at Plymouth, MA. Though he had little formal education, he created one of the most-used reference works of the English language. No quotation of his own is among the more than 22,000 listed today, but in the preface to the first edition he wrote that the object of this work "originally made without any view of publication" was to show "the obligation our language owes to various authors for numerous phrases and familiar quotations which have become 'household words.' " Bartlett died at Cambridge, MA, Dec 3, 1905.

BOARDWALK ART SHOW. June 14–17. Virginia Beach, VA. 46th annual. The works of approximately 335 artists are displayed along the boardwalk in this nationally ranked fine art and crafts show and sale. High quality evening performances. Annually, on Father's Day weekend. Est attendance: 350,000. For info: Contemporary Art Center of Virginia, 2200 Parks Ave, Virginia Beach, VA 23451. Phone: (757) 425-0000. Fax: (757) 425-8186. Web: www.cacv.org.

BOURKE-WHITE, MARGARET: 95th BIRTH ANNIVERSARY. June 14, 1906. Margaret Bourke was born at New York City. One of the original photojournalists, she developed her personal style while photographing the Krupp Iron Works in Germany and the Soviet Union during the first Five-Year Plan. Bourke-White was one of the four original staff photographers for *Life* magazine in 1936. The first woman attached to the US armed forces during World War II, she covered the Italian campaign, the siege of Moscow and the American soldiers' crossing of the Rhine into Germany, and she shocked the world with her photographs of the concentration camps. Bourke-White photographed Mahatma Gandhi and covered the migration of millions of people after the Indian subcontinent was divided into Hindu India and Muslim Pakistan. She served as a war correspondent during the Korean War. Among her several books, the most famous was her collaboration with her second husband, novelist Erskine Caldwell, a study of rural poverty in the American South called *You Have Seen Their Faces*. She died Aug 27, 1971, at Stamford, CT.

CANADA: SAM STEELE DAYS. June 14–17. Cranbrook, BC. Parade, Sweetheart Pageant, banquet and ball, tug-of-war, railway museum tours, indoor bull-o-rama, bocce tournament, wild west show. Est attendance: 19,000. For info: Sam Steele Soc, PO Box 115, Cranbrook, BC, Canada V1C 4H6. Phone: (250) 426-4161. Fax: (250) 426-3873. E-mail: cbkchamber@cyberlink.bc.ca.

CHICAGO BULLS WIN THIRD STRAIGHT TITLE FOR THE SECOND TIME: ANNIVERSARY. June 14, 1998. The Chicago Bulls defeated the Utah Jazz to win their third consecutive NBA championship. This was their second "three-peat." They had accomplished this feat the first time with wins in 1991, 1992 and 1993.

CORPUS CHRISTI. June 14. Roman Catholic festival celebrated in honor of the Eucharist. A solemnity observed on the Thursday following Trinity Sunday since 1246. In the US Corpus Christi is celebrated on the Sunday following Trinity Sunday. See also: "Corpus Christi (US Observance)" (June 17).

FAMILY HISTORY DAY. June 14. Every summer family reunions are so busy with games and activities that most of us forget the true purpose: to share the folklore, legends and myths that bind us together. Each participant should share at least one good recollection (fact or fiction). Don't forget the hot dogs and lemonade. [© 2000 by WH] For info: Tom or Ruth Roy, Wellcat Holidays, 2418 Long Ln, Lebanon, PA 17046. Phone: (717) 279-0184. E-mail: wellcat@aupernet.com. Web: www.wellcat.com.

FIRST NONSTOP TRANSATLANTIC FLIGHT: ANNIVERSARY. June 14–15, 1919. Captain John Alcock and Lieutenant Arthur W. Brown flew a Vickers Vimy bomber 1,900 miles nonstop from St. Johns, Newfoundland, to Clifden, County Galway, Ireland. In spite of their crash landing in an Irish peat bog, their flight inspired public interest in aviation. See also: "Lindbergh Flight: Anniversary" (May 20).

FIRST US BREACH OF PROMISE SUIT: ANNIVERSARY. June 14, 1623. The first breach of promise suit in the US was filed in the Virginia Council of State, at Charles City, VA. Reverend Greville Pooley brought suit against Cicely Jordan, who had jilted him in favor of another man.

	S	M	T	W	T	F	S
June						1	2
2001	3	4	5	6	7	8	9
	10	11	12	13	14	15	16
	17	18	19	20	21	22	23
	24	25	26	27	28	29	30

★**FLAG DAY.** June 14. Presidential Proclamation issued each year for June 14. Proclamation 1335, of May 30, 1916, covers all succeeding years. Has been issued annually since 1941. (PL81–203 of Aug 3, 1949.) Customarily issued as "Flag Day and National Flag Week," as in 1986; the president usually mentions "a time to honor America," Flag Day to Independence Day (89 Stat. 211). See also: "National Flag Day USA: Pause for the Pledge" (this date).

FLAG DAY CEREMONIES. June 14. Betsy Ross House, Philadelphia, PA. Noon program. Est attendance: 200. For info: Betsy Ross House, 239 Arch St, Philadelphia, PA 19106. Phone: (215) 627-5343. Fax: (215) 627-0591.

FLAG DAY: ANNIVERSARY OF THE STARS AND STRIPES. June 14, 1777. John Adams introduced the following resolution before the Continental Congress, meeting at Philadelphia, PA: "Resolved, That the flag of the thirteen United States shall be thirteen stripes, alternate red and white; that the union be thirteen stars, white on a blue field, representing a new constellation." Legal holiday in Pennsylvania.

FORT UNION TRADING POST RENDEZVOUS. June 14–17. 25 miles SW of Williston, ND. Recreation of the fur trade era. Fur trade fair, music, blacksmith and craft demonstrations. Sponsor: National Park Service, Fort Union Trading Post National Historic Site. Est attendance: 5,000. For info: Fort Union Trading Post NHS, 15550 Hwy 1804, Williston, ND 58801. Phone: (701) 572-9083. Fax: (701) 572-7321. Web: www.nps.gov/fous.

"THE GONG SHOW" TV PREMIERE: 25th ANNIVERSARY. June 14, 1976. This popular show featured a panel of three celebrities judging amateur and professional acts, from the ordinary to the unusual. At any time, a judge could bang a gong to end the act; this was often done with gusto. Completed acts were then rated and the winner received a cash prize. Chuck Barris created (along with Chris Bearde) and hosted the show for all seasons and in syndication with the exception of one syndicated season hosted by Gary Owens. Celebrities who frequently appeared were Jaye P. Morgan, Rex Reed, Arte Johnson, Phyllis Diller and Jamie Farr.

IVES, BURL: BIRTH ANNIVERSARY. June 14, 1909. American singer and actor Burl Icle Ivanhoe Ives was born at Hunt, IL. He helped to reintroduce Anglo-American folk music in the '40s and '50s. Ives won an Academy Award for his supporting role in *The Big Country* (1958), and he is well known for his role as Big Daddy in both the film and Broadway productions of *Cat On a Hot Tin Roof*. He died Apr 14, 1995, at Anacortes, WA.

JAPAN: RICE PLANTING FESTIVAL. June 14. Osaka. Ceremonial transplanting of rice seedlings in paddy field at Sumiyashi Shrine, Osaka.

LUDINGTON HARBOR FESTIVAL. June 14–17. Ludington, MI. Nautical festival celebrating proud past and prosperous future of Ludington's Harbor. Featuring historical tours, loggers show, arts & crafts show, Coast Guard Open House, Old Time baseball, entertainment. Est attendance: 30,000. For info: Ludington Area Chamber of Commerce, 5827 W US 10, Ludington, MI 49431. Phone: (800) 542-4600. Fax: (231) 845-6857. E-mail: visitlud@carrinter.net. Web: www.ludingtoncvb.com.

MISS LOUISIANA PAGEANT. June 14–16. Monroe Civic Center, Monroe, LA. Preliminaries followed by the main event of crowning the new Miss Louisiana. Est attendance: 5,500. For info: Miss Louisiana Organization, PO Box 6003, Monroe, LA 71211. Phone: (318) 343-9034. Fax: (318) 343-4991. E-mail: hoogdot@aol.com. Web: www.bayou.com/misslouisiana.

NATIONAL FLAG DAY USA: PAUSE FOR THE PLEDGE. June 14. Held simultaneously across the country at 7 PM, EDT. Public law 99–54 recognizes the Pause for the Pledge as part of National Flag Day ceremonies. The concept of the Pause for the Pledge of Allegiance was conceived as a way for all citizens to share a patriotic moment. National ceremony at Fort McHenry National Monument and Historic Shrine.

PRAIRIE VILLA RENDEZVOUS. June 14–17. Prairie du Chien, WI. Rendezvous with history and learn about life during the fur trading days and experience the fur trader lifestyle first-hand. Many participants come from around the country to display furs, others demonstrate the cumbersome process of loading a rifle with gunpowder and some prepare Indian fry bread and buffalo burgers. Workshops offer information on a variety of subjects including plants and medicines, basket weaving and bead-working. With more than 600 lodges and teepees, this is one of the largest Midwest trading rendezvous. Est attendance: 25,000. For info: Prairie Du Chien Tourism Council, PO Box 326, Prairie du Chien, WI 53821. Phone: (800) 732-1673.

SMACKOVER OIL TOWN FESTIVAL. June 14–16 (tentative). Smackover, AR. A celebration of the impact the oil industry has had on Smackover and the surrounding area. Included is an oil run, bass fishing tournament, arts and crafts, music, an ice cream social and events for all ages. Est attendance: 8,000. For info: Smackover Chamber of Commerce, PO Box 275, Smackover, AR 71762. Phone: (870) 725-3521. Fax: (870) 725-3521. E-mail: schamber@ipa.net.

SPACE MILESTONE: *MARINER 5* (US). June 14, 1967. Launched on this date, interplanetary probe of Venus established that 72½–87½ percent of its atmosphere is carbon dioxide on Oct 18 flyby of planet.

STOWE, HARRIET BEECHER: BIRTH ANNIVERSARY. June 14, 1811. American writer Harriet Beecher Stowe, daughter of the Reverend Lyman Beecher and sister of Henry Ward Beecher. Author of *Uncle Tom's Cabin*, an antislavery novel that provoked a storm of protest and resulted in fame for its author. Two characters in the novel attained such importance that their names became part of the English language—the Negro slave, Uncle Tom, and the villainous slaveowner, Simon Legree. The reaction to *Uncle Tom's Cabin* and its profound political impact are without parallel in American literature. It is said that during the Civil War, when Harriet Beecher Stowe was introduced to President Abraham Lincoln, his words to her were, "So you're the little woman who wrote the book that made this great war." Stowe was born at Litchfield, CT and died at Hartford, CT, July 1, 1896.

UNIVAC COMPUTER: 50th ANNIVERSARY. June 14, 1951. Univac 1, the world's first commercial computer, designed for the US Bureau of the Census, was unveiled, demonstrated and dedicated at Philadelphia, PA. Though this milestone of the computer age was the first commercial electronic computer, it had been preceded by ENIAC (Electronic Numeric Integrator and Computer), completed under the supervision of J. Presper Eckert, Jr and John W. Mauchly, at the University of Pennsylvania in 1946.

US ARMY ESTABLISHED BY CONGRESS: ANNIVERSARY. June 14, 1775. Anniversary of Resolution of the Continental Congress establishing the army as the first US military service.

US OPEN (GOLF) CHAMPIONSHIP. June 14–17. Southern Hills Country Club, Tulsa, OK. For info: US Golf Assn, Golf House, PO Box 708, Championship Dept, Far Hills, NJ 07931. Phone: (908) 234-2300. Fax: (908) 234-9687. E-mail: usga@ix.netcom.com. Web: www.usga.org.

WARREN G. HARDING BECOMES FIRST PRESIDENT TO BROADCAST ON RADIO: ANNIVERSARY. June 14, 1922. Warren G. Harding became the first president to broadcast a message over the radio. The event was the dedication of the Francis Scott Key Memorial at Baltimore, MD. The first official government message was broadcast Dec 6, 1923.

WEST ALLIS WESTERN DAYS PARADE. June 14–17. West Allis, WI. Billed as "the World's Largest Non-Motorized Parade" or "North America's Largest Horse Drawn Parade," this annual procession steps off from the Wisconsin State Fair Park at 7 PM, part of the West Allis Western Days festivities. Est attendance: 150,000. For info: Publicity, West Allis Western Days, PO Box 14544, West Allis, WI 53214. Phone: (262) 821-7816. Web: www.badger.state.wi.us.

BIRTHDAYS TODAY

Yasmine Bleeth, 33, actress ("Baywatch," "Nash Bridges"), born New York, NY, June 14, 1968.

Boy George (George Alan O'Dowd), 40, lead singer (Culture Club), born London, England, June 14, 1961.

Marla Gibbs, 55, actress ("227," "The Jeffersons"), born Chicago, IL, June 14, 1946.

Stephanie Maria (Steffi) Graf, 32, former tennis player, born Bruhl, West Germany, June 14, 1969.

Eric Arthur Heiden, 43, Olympic gold medal speed skater, born Madison, WI, June 14, 1958.

Traylor Howard, 35, actress ("Two Guys and a Girl"), born Orlando, FL, June 14, 1966.

Dorothy McGuire, 83, actress (*A Tree Grows in Brooklyn, Gentlemen's Agreement*, "Rich Man, Poor Man"), born Omaha, NE, June 14, 1918.

Eddie Mekka, 49, actor ("Laverne and Shirley"), born Worcester, MA, June 14, 1952.

Will Patton, 47, actor (*Silkwood, Desperately Seeking Susan*; stage: *Tourists and Refugees #2* [Obie Award]), born Charleston, SC, June 14, 1954.

Samuel Bruce (Sam) Perkins, 40, basketball player, born New York, NY, June 14, 1961.

Patricia (Pat) Summitt, 49, college basketball coach and former player, born Clarksville, TN, June 14, 1952.

Donald Trump, 55, real estate mogul, born New York, NY, June 14, 1946.

JUNE 15 — FRIDAY
Day 166 — 199 Remaining

ARKANSAS: ADMISSION DAY: ANNIVERSARY. June 15. Became 25th state in 1836.

CHISHOLM TRAIL ROUND-UP FESTIVAL. June 15–16. Fort Worth, TX. Events include trail ride, Quanah Parker Comanche Indian Powwow and Honor Dance. Street fair, barbecue cook-off, chuckwagon cooks' races, gunfighters, parade, children's area with Western-theme carnival rides and three live stages with music. Est attendance: 40,000. For info: Chisholm Trail Round-Up, PO Box 4815, Fort Worth, TX 76164-0815. Phone: (817) 625-7005. Fax: (817) 625-4036. E-mail: ctstaff@chisholmtrail.org. Web: www.chisholmtrail.org.

CITY STAGES MUSIC FESTIVAL. June 15–17. Linn Park, Birmingham, AL. Music and heritage festival featuring local and nationally known talent on 15 stages, folklife festival, children's festival, jazz camp and classical music oasis. Annually, Father's Day weekend. Est attendance: 265,000. For info: City Stages, PO Box 2266, Birmingham, AL 35201. Phone: (205) 251-1272. Fax: (205) 323-7074. E-mail: jennifer@citystages.org. Web: www.citystages.org.

CZECH DAYS. June 15–16. Tabor, SD. Czechs dressed in their festive costumes gather with people from all parts of the world in this gala celebration. Fine Czech foods, dancing, music and entertainment. 53rd annual Czech Days celebration. Est attendance: 15,000. For info: Tabor Area Chamber of Commerce, Inc, Box 21, Tabor, SD 57063. Phone: (605) 463-2476. E-mail: czechdays@yahoo.com. Web: www.byelectric.com/~tabor.

DELMARVA CHICKEN FESTIVAL. June 15–16. Pocomoke City, MD. 53rd annual. A family event focusing on chicken, the leading agricultural enterprise on the Delmarva Peninsula. Food, entertainment and consumer information are featured. Est attendance: 25,000. For info: Connie Parvis, Delmarva Poultry Industry, Inc, RD 6, Box 47, Georgetown, DE 19947-9575. Phone: (302) 856-9037.

FIRST FATAL AVIATION ACCIDENT: ANNIVERSARY.
June 15, 1785. Two French aeronauts, Jean François Pilatre de Rozier and P.A. de Romain, attempting to cross the English Channel from France to England in a balloon, were killed when their balloon caught fire and crashed to the ground. Pilatre de Rozier, the first man to fly, thus became a fatality in the first fatal accident in aviation history.

GREAT SMOKY MOUNTAINS NATIONAL PARK ESTABLISHED: ANNIVERSARY. June 15, 1934. Area along southern section of Tennessee–North Carolina boundary was authorized May 22, 1926, established for administration and protection only Feb 6, 1930 and finally established for full development as a national park in 1934. For further park info: Great Smoky Mountains Natl Park, Gatlinburg, TN 37738.

GRIEG, EDVARD: BIRTH ANNIVERSARY. June 15, 1843. Pianist, composer, conductor and teacher, the first Scandinavian to compose nationalistic music. Born at Bergen, Norway, and died there Sept 4, 1907.

"HEE HAW" TV PREMIERE: ANNIVERSARY. June 15, 1969. "Hee Haw" has been described as a country-western version of "Laugh-In," composed of fast-paced sketches, silly jokes and songs. Though critics didn't like it, it had popular appeal and did well as a syndicated show. It was cohosted by Buck Owens and Roy Clark, alternating with guest hosts. Regular performers included Louis M. "Grandpa" Jones, Junior Samples, Jeannine Riley, Lulu Roman, David "Stringbean" Akeman, Sheb Wooley, Marianne Gordon, Minnie Pearl and Gordie Tapp.

HUCKFINN JUBILEE. June 15–17. Mojave Narrows Regional Park, Victorville, CA. A Huckfinn celebration with river raft building, country and bluegrass music, hay rides, old time tent circus, crafts and food, plus Route 66 car show and the California Arm Wrestling Championships. Annually, on Father's Day weekend. Est attendance: 15,000. For info: Don or Barbara Tucker, PO Box 56419, Riverside, CA 92517. Phone: (909) 780-8810. Fax: (909) 780-3765. E-mail: huckfinn@huckfinn.com. Web: www.huckfinn.com.

INTERNATIONAL FESTIVAL OF ARTS AND IDEAS. June 15–30. New Haven Green, New Haven, CT. Enjoy performing and visual arts from around the world at the annual festival. Experience international theater, classical, jazz and popular music, interactive activities for children, visual arts, poetry, street theatre, tours of historic spaces, dance. Literature, a street festival and conferences and discussions. Est attendance: 250,000. For info: Intl Festival of Arts & Ideas, (888) ART-IDEA or Greater New Haven Conv & Visitors Bureau, 59 Elm St, New Haven, CT 06510. Phone: (203) 777-8550 or (800) 332-STAY. Fax: (203) 782-7755. Web: www.newhavencvb.org or www.artidea.org.

JACKSON, RACHEL DONELSON ROBARDS: BIRTH ANNIVERSARY. June 15, 1767. Wife of Andrew Jackson, 7th president of the US, born at Halifax County, NC. Died at Nashville, TN, Dec 22, 1828.

KIAMICHI OWA-CHITO FESTIVAL OF THE FOREST. June 15–17. Beavers Bend State Park, Broken Bow, OK. A celebration of American Indian culture and of the forest industry. Compete in ax throwing, cross-buck sawing, pole climbing, pole filling and logging to become the "Bull of the Woods." Also kids' games, food booths, Miss Owa-Chito contest, photography contest, golf tournament, canoe races, archery contest, turkey-calling contest, 5K road race, talent contest and more. Est attendance: 50,000. For info: Chamber of Commerce, 113 W Martin Luther King, Broken Bow, OK 74728. Phone: (580) 584-3393. Fax: (580) 584-7698. E-mail: bbchamber@pine-net.com.

	S	M	T	W	T	F	S
June						1	2
2001	3	4	5	6	7	8	9
	10	11	12	13	14	15	16
	17	18	19	20	21	22	23
	24	25	26	27	28	29	30

LOCKPORT OLD CANAL DAYS. June 15–17. Lockport, IL. Festival in historic canal community. Crafts, parade. Annually, the third weekend in June. Est attendance: 20,000. For info: Lockport Old Canal Days, PO Box 31, Lockport, IL 60441. Phone: (815) 838-4744.

MACKINAW CITY KITE FESTIVAL. June 15–16. Mackinaw City, MI. The skies will be filled with brilliant colors as Mackinaw hosts the exciting and unique event that pays tribute to the Kite that comes in many shapes, sizes and colors. Est attendance: 3,000. For info: Mackinaw Area Tourist Bureau, PO Box 160, Mackinaw City, MI 49701. Phone: (800) 666-0160. Web: www.mackinawcity.com.

MAGNA CARTA DAY: ANNIVERSARY. June 15. Anniversary of King John's sealing, in 1215, of the Magna Carta "in the meadow called Ronimed between Windsor and Staines on the fifteenth day of June in the seventeenth year of our reign." This document is regarded as the first charter of English liberties and one of the most important documents in the history of political and human freedom. Four original copies of the 1215 charter survive.

MEEKER DAYS FESTIVAL. June 15–17. Downtown Puyallup, WA. Largest street fair in Pierce County features a main, acoustic, kids and community stage, arts and crafts show, Pontiac/Buick classic car show, farmer's market, children's activities, microbrew garden, antique tractors and farm engines and much more! Annually, the third weekend in June. Est attendance: 125,000. For info: Diane Picha, Meeker Days, PO Box 476, Puyallup, WA 98371. Phone: (206) 840-2631. Fax: (206) 840-2943.

"MY LITTLE MARGIE" TV PREMIERE: ANNIVERSARY. June 15, 1952. "My Little Margie" was a half-hour sitcom about a "womanizing widower and his meddlesome daughter." Margie was played by Gale Storm and Charles Farrell played her father, Vern Albright.

NORWAY: CELEBRATION OF EDVARD GRIEG'S BIRTH ANNIVERSARY. June 15. Special celebrations at Lofthus on the Hardanger fjord where Grieg's cabin still stands. Born June 15, 1843, at Bergen, Norway; died there Sept 4, 1907.

QUARTERLY ESTIMATED FEDERAL INCOME TAX PAYERS' DUE DATE. June 15. For those individuals whose fiscal year is the calendar year and who make quarterly estimated federal income tax payments, today is one of the due dates. (Jan 15, Apr 16, June 15 and Sept 17, 2001.)

RED RIVER VALLEY FAIR. June 15–24. Fargo, ND. One of the largest fairs in the state with 4-H and commercial exhibits, horse shows, car shows, large carnival midway, free entertainment. Big-name country western and rock entertainers perform all seven days. Est attendance: 30,000. For info: (701) 282-2200 or North Dakota Tourism, 604 East Boulevard, Bismarck, ND 58505. Phone: (701) 328-2525 or (800) 435-5663.

SPLINTERFEST. June 15–17. Amana, IA. A woodcraft show with displays, products, demonstrations, equipment, supplies, entertainment and food. Annually, the third weekend in June. Est attendance: 6,000. For info: Tammy Meyer, Splinterfest/Holzfest, PO Box 215, Dyersville, IA 52040. Phone: (319) 875-7017. Fax: (319) 875-9607. E-mail: dww@mwci.net.

TWELFTH AMENDMENT TO US CONSTITUTION RATIFIED: ANNIVERSARY. June 15, 1804. The 12th Amendment to the Constitution was ratified. It changed the method of electing the president and vice president after a tie in the electoral college during the election of 1800. Rather than each elector voting for two candidates with the candidate receiving the most votes elected president and the second-place candidate elected vice president, each elector was now required to designate his choice for president and vice president, respectively.

US LANDING ON SAIPAN: ANNIVERSARY. June 15, 1944. In a continued effort to penetrate the Japanese inner defenses, US amphibious forces invaded the Mariana Islands. A huge fleet of 800 ships from Guadalcanal and Hawaii carried the 2nd and 4th Marine Divisions, consisting of 162,000 men. By the end of the day 20,000 of these men had established a 5½-mile-long beachhead on the island of Saipan. Though the American forces suffered heavy losses during an overnight counterattack, on the morning of June 16 the Marines still held the area they had taken the day before.

WONAGO WORLD CHAMPIONSHIP RODEO. June 15–17. State Fair Coliseum, Milwaukee, WI. More than 200 cowboys and cowgirls compete in six professional contests ranging from bronc riding to bull riding for top prize and world championship points. Featuring colorful opening pageantry and Big, Bad BONUS Bulls. Held in conjunction with West Allis Western Days and North America's Largest Horse Drawn Parade on June 14. 44th annual. Est attendance: 10,000. For info: W. Bruce Lehrke, Pres, Longhorn World Chmpshp Rodeo Inc, Natl HQ, PO Box 70159, Nashville, TN 37207. Phone: (615) 876-1016. Fax: (615) 876-4685. Web: www.longhornrodeo.com.

BIRTHDAYS TODAY

Courteney Cox Arquette, 37, actress ("Family Ties," "Friends"), born Birmingham, AL, June 15, 1964.

Jim Belushi, 47, actor ("Saturday Night Live," *Men at Work*), born Chicago, IL, June 15, 1954.

Wade Anthony Boggs, 43, baseball player, born Omaha, NE, June 15, 1958.

Simon Callow, 52, actor (*A Room with a View, Mr and Mrs Bridge, Howards End*); author (*Orson Welles*), born London, England, June 15, 1949.

Mario M. Cuomo, 69, former governor of New York (D), born New York, NY, June 15, 1932.

Julie Hagerty, 46, actress (*Airplane!, Lost in America, Reversal of Fortune*; stage: *The House of Blue Leaves* [Theatre World Award]), born Cincinnati, OH, June 15, 1955.

Neil Patrick Harris, 28, actor ("Doogie Howser, MD," "Stark Raving Mad," *Clara's Heart*), born Albuquerque, NM, June 15, 1973.

Mike Holmgren, 53, football coach, born San Francisco, CA, June 15, 1948.

Helen Hunt, 38, actress ("Mad About You," *Twister*, Oscar for *As Good As It Gets*), born Los Angeles, CA, June 15, 1963.

Waylon Jennings, 64, singer ("Amanda," "Luckenbach, Texas"), born Littlefield, TX, June 15, 1937.

Justin Leonard, 29, golfer, born Dallas, TX, June 15, 1972.

Nicola Pagett, 56, actress ("Upstairs Downstairs," *There's a Girl in My Soup*), born Cairo, Egypt, June 15, 1945.

Leah Remini, 31, actress ("The King of Queens," "Saved By the Bell"), born Brooklyn, NY, June 15, 1970.

JUNE 16 — SATURDAY
Day 167 — 198 Remaining

AMERICAN BOWLING CONGRESS SENIORS TOURNAMENT. June 16–17. Albuquerque, NM. State and provincial senior champions compete for titles in four divisions at the American Bowling Congress Tournament site. For info: Michael Deering, ABC, 5301 S 76th St, Greendale, WI 53129. Phone: (414) 423-3309. Fax: (414) 421-3013.

BLOOMSDAY: ANNIVERSARY. June 16, 1904. Anniversary of events in Dublin recorded in James Joyce's *Ulysses*, whose central character is Leopold Bloom.

COYOTE CHASE. June 16. Wellington, NV. Annual Beta Sigma Phi 10K and 5K runs and a two-mile walk. Pancake breakfast, art, crafts and more. Annually, the third Saturday in June. For info: Mason Valley, Chamber of Commerce, 227 S Main St, Yerington, NV 89447. Phone: (775) 463-2245. Fax: (775) 463-3369. Web: www.tele-net.net/lyon.

ENGLAND: BROADSTAIRS DICKENS FESTIVAL. June 16–24. Broadstairs, Kent. Commemorates the association of the famous novelist Charles Dickens to the town of Broadstairs. For info: Dickens Festival Organiser, Kingscote, 8 Stone Rd, Broadstairs, Kent, England CT10 1DZ. Phone: (44) (184) 360-1364. Web: www.broadstairs.gov/uk/DickensSociety.html.

FRONTIER ARMY DAYS. June 16–17. Fort Abraham Lincoln State Park, Mandan, ND. Frontier Army re-creation groups reenact frontier military life with demonstrations and living history by infantry, cavalry and "Old Scouts" groups, along with others who populated the fort. Est attendance: 3,000. For info: Chuck Erickson, Park Mgr, Fort Abraham Lincoln State Park, 4480 Fort Lincoln Rd, Mandan, ND 58554. Phone: (701) 663-1464. Fax: (701) 663-9234.

GETTYSBURG BRASS BAND FESTIVAL. June 16. Gettysburg, PA. Brass bands, ensembles, drum and bugle corps converge on Gettysburg for many musical events along Gettysburg's "Historical Pathways." Workshops, concerts and performances culminate in one grand finale at the Gettysburg College Stadium on Saturday evening. For info: Gettysburg CVB, PO Box 4117, Gettysburg, PA 17325. Phone: (717) 334-6274. Fax: (717) 334-1166. Web: www.gettysburg.com.

GRIFFIN, JOHN HOWARD: BIRTH ANNIVERSARY. June 16, 1920. American author and photographer deeply concerned about racial problems in US. To better understand blacks in the American South, Griffin blackened his skin by the use of chemicals and ultraviolet light, keeping a journal as he traveled through the South, resulting in his best-known book, *Black Like Me*. Born at Dallas, TX. Died at Fort Worth, TX, Sept 9, 1980.

JOIN HANDS DAY. June 16 (tentative). A day designed to unite older and younger people on neighborhood volunteer projects. Sponsored by the Points of Light Foundation and America's Fraternal Benefits Societies. For info:. Phone: (877) OUR-1DAY. Web: www.joinhandsday.org.

KCQ COUNTRY MUSIC FEST. June 16. Saginaw, MI. Country music's hottest artists perform on stage on Ojibway Island. Coupled with a classic car show, art fair and great food make this mid-Michigan's hottest summer attraction. Free admission. Call to receive a free program of this year's performers. Est attendance: 70,000. For info: WKCQ, Box 1776, Saginaw, MI 48605. Phone: (517) 752-8161. Fax: (517) 752-8102. Web: www.98FM KCQ.com.

LADIES' DAY INITIATED IN BASEBALL: ANNIVERSARY. June 16, 1883. The New York Giants hosted the first Ladies' Day baseball game. Both escorted and unescorted ladies were admitted to the game free.

LAKESTRIDE HALF-MARATHON. June 16. Ludington, MI. Half-marathon race that begins at Lakeshore Drive and Tinkham (by the beach) takes runners along a scenic course through the wooded trails and sand dunes of Lake Michigan at Ludington State Park. Annually, the third Saturday in June. Est attendance:

10,000. For info: Ludington Area CVB, 5827 W US 10, Ludington, MI 49431. Phone: (800) 542-4600. Fax: (231) 845-6857. E-mail: visitlud@carrinter.net. Web: www.ludingtoncvb.com.

LAST DUSKY SEASIDE SPARROW: DEATH ANNIVERSARY. June 16, 1987. The last survivor of dusky seaside sparrows, whose habitat was a 10-mile stretch of marshland on Florida's east coast (near Titusville), died at age 12. The last specimen, named "Orange Band," lived its last days in a cage at Walt Disney World. For possible experimental cloning its heart and lungs were frozen and preserved.

LAUREL, STAN: BIRTH ANNIVERSARY. June 16, 1890. Worked with Oliver Hardy as the comedy team of Laurel & Hardy for more than 30 years. Born at Ulverston, England, Laurel died Feb 23, 1965 at Santa Monica, CA.

MACKINAW CITY FUDGE CLASSIC. June 16–17. Mackinaw City, MI. 11th annual fun run and jog. Starts at Mackinaw City high school. Sunday morning jog across the Mackinac Bridge for 5K or 10K for qualified runners. For info: Mackinaw City Chamber of Commerce, PO Box 856, Mackinaw City, MI 49701. Phone: (616) 436-5574. Web: www.mackinawcity.com.

NEW OXFORD OUTDOOR ANTIQUE SHOW. June 16. New Oxford, PA. Arts, crafts, antiques and flea market. Annually, the third Saturday in June. Est attendance: 20,000. For info: Gettysburg CVB, PO Box 4117, Gettysburg, PA 17325-1899. Phone: (717) 334-6274. Fax: (717) 334-1166. Web: www.gettysburg.com.

OLD WEST EXTRAVAGANZA. June 16–17. Shakopee, MN. The Old West rides again at historic Murphy's Landing. Meet famous Western heroes, witness shoot-outs, whip crackin' and rope twirling demonstrations. Also, great grub. Est attendance: 5,000. For info: Mktg Dept, Murphy's Landing, 2817 Hwy 101, Shakopee, MN 55379. Phone: (952) 445-6901. Web: www.murphyslanding.com.

RENO RODEO. June 16–24. Reno, NV. 82nd annual. Top professional cowboys ride in one of the west's richest rodeos. Est attendance: 120,000. For info: Reno Rodeo Assn, Box 12335, Reno, NV 89510. Phone: (702) 329-3877 or for tickets: (800) 842-7633.

ROCHESTERFEST. June 16–24. Rochester, MN. This community festival includes Midwestern lumberjack championships, cultural diversity, children's and senior events, gigantic street parade, street vendors with exotic foods, country night, rock and roll night, street dance and breakfast on the farm. Est attendance: 100,000. For info: Carole Brown, Exec Dir, Box 007, Rochester, MN 55903. Phone: (507) 285-8769. Fax: (507) 285-8718.

ROGUE RIVER JET BOAT MARATHON. June 16–17. Gold Beach, OR. Watch jet boats ply the twisted, rushing whitewater rapids of the mighty Rogue at speeds faster than your eyes can focus, starting from Jot's Resort at the mouth of the Rogue in Gold Beach, about 40 miles upriver to Foster Bar, and back again. Est attendance: 4,000. For info: Gold Beach Chamber of Commerce, 29279 Ellensburg Ave, #3, Gold Beach, OR 97444. Phone: (800) 525-2334. Fax: (541) 247-0188. E-mail: goldbeach @harborside.com. Web: www.harborside.com/gb.

SOUTH AFRICA: YOUTH DAY. June 16. National holiday. Commemorates a student uprising in Soweto against "Bantu Education" and the enforced teaching of Afrikaans in 1976.

SOUTHWEST REGIONAL SPORT LAUNCH. June 16–17. American Legion Post 345 Veterans Memorial Park, Alamogordo, NM. Launch model and high power rockets from 8 AM–2 PM, on both days. Est attendance: 150. For info: Bob Turner, Curator,

	S	M	T	W	T	F	S
June						1	2
2001	3	4	5	6	7	8	9
	10	11	12	13	14	15	16
	17	18	19	20	21	22	23
	24	25	26	27	28	29	30

The Space Center, PO Box 533, Alamogordo, NM 88311-0533. Phone: (877) 333-6589. Fax: (505) 434-2245. E-mail: space-cur@zianet.com.

SPACE MILESTONE: FIRST WOMAN IN SPACE, VOSTOK 6 (USSR). June 16, 1963. Valentina Tereshkova, 26, former cotton-mill worker, born on collective farm near Yaroslavl, USSR, became the first woman in space when her spacecraft, *Vostok 6*, took off from the Tyuratam launch site. She manually controlled *Vostok 6* during the 70.8-hour flight through 48 orbits of Earth and landed by parachute (separate from her cabin) June 19, 1963. In November 1963 she married cosmonaut Andrian Nikolayev, who had piloted *Vostok 3* through 64 earth orbits, Aug 11–15, 1962. Their child Yelena (1964) was the first born to space-traveler parents.

STEWART'S ROOT BEER DAY. June 16. Celebrate a truly American tradition today and enjoy a cold, frothy Stewart's root beer! Drink it straight or pour over your favorite ice cream for a delicious, old-fashioned root beer float. For info: Stewart's Beverages, Inc, 555 17th St, Ste 3550, Denver, CO 80202-3935. Phone: (303) 298-9038.

STONE MOUNTAIN VILLAGE ARTS AND CRAFTS FESTIVAL. June 16–17. Stone Mountain Village, GA. 29th annual juried arts and crafts show featuring more than 100 of the southeast's finest artists and crafters. With down-home entertainment and the best country cooking around. Est attendance: 8,000. For info: Dir, Village Festivals, PO Box 667, Stone Mountain Village, GA 30086. Phone: (770) 498-2097. Web: www.stonemountainvillage.com.

TRADITIONAL SMALL BOAT FESTIVAL. June 16. Berkley Island County Park, Berkley Township, NJ. Focuses on preserving the tradition of small boats of local design such as a sneakbox, catboat, garvey, etc, or non-local such as an Adirondack Guide Boat, Whitehall or sea kayak. Trailer your boat, sail or motor it into the park. Test other boats and allow people to test yours. Est attendance: 2,000. For info: German Georgieff, Coord, Wells Mills County Park, 905 Wells Mills Rd, Waretown, NJ 08758. Phone: (609) 971-3085. Fax: (609) 971-9540.

BIRTHDAYS TODAY

Lincoln Almond, 65, Governor of Rhode Island (R), born Central Falls, RI, June 16, 1936.

Billy "Crash" Craddock, 62, singer ("Don't Destroy Me," "Ruby, Baby"), born Greensboro, NC, June 16, 1939.

Roberto Duran, 50, boxer, born Chorillo, Panama, June 16, 1951.

Katharine Graham, 84, newspaper executive (*The Washington Post*), born New York, NY, June 16, 1917.

Cobi Jones, 31, soccer player, played in 1994 World Cup, born Westlake Village, CA, June 16, 1970.

Laurie Metcalf, 46, actress (Emmy for "Roseanne"; "The Norm Show"), born Edwardsville, IL, June 16, 1955.

Phil Mickelson, 31, golfer, born San Diego, CA, June 16, 1970.

Joyce Carol Oates, 63, writer (*Triumph of the Spider Monkey, The Time Traveler*), born Lockport, NY, June 16, 1938.

Irving Penn, 84, photographer, born Plainfield, PA, June 16, 1917.

Erich Segal, 64, author (*Acts of Faith, Love Story*), born Brooklyn, NY, June 16, 1937.

Joan Van Ark, 58, actress ("Knots Landing"), born New York, NY, June 16, 1943.

Kerry Wood, 24, baseball player, born Irving, TX, June 16, 1977.

JUNE 17 — SUNDAY

Day 168 — 197 Remaining

AMATEUR RADIO WEEK. June 17–24. To bring amateur radio to the attention of the public and test capabilities in preparation for emergencies. Annually, the week culminating in the fourth weekend of June. For info: PR Coord, American Radio Relay League, 225 Main St, Newington, CT 06111. Phone: (860) 594-0328. E-mail: jhagy@arrl.org. Web: www.arrl.org.

BELLAMY, RALPH: BIRTH ANNIVERSARY. June 17, 1904. American actor Ralph Rexford Bellamy was born at Chicago, IL. He appeared in more than 100 films and was best known for his stage and film portrayals of President Franklin D. Roosevelt. He was a founder of the Screen Actors' Guild and president of Actors' Equity. Bellamy was awarded an honorary Academy Award in 1987. He died Nov 29, 1991, at Los Angeles, CA.

BUNKER HILL DAY. June 17. Suffolk County, MA. Legal holiday in the county in commemoration of the Battle of Bunker Hill that took place in 1775.

CORPUS CHRISTI (US OBSERVANCE). June 17. A movable Roman Catholic celebration commemorating the institution of the Holy Eucharist. The solemnity has been observed on the Thursday following Trinity Sunday since 1246, except in the US, where it is observed on the Sunday following Trinity Sunday.

DONNA REED FESTIVAL FOR THE PERFORMING ARTS. June 17–23. Denison, IA. Performing arts festival in Donna Reed's hometown. Focus of the festival is educational workshops in various areas of the performing arts taught by Hollywood and New York professionals. Also included are celebrity golf tournament, auction, big band dance, parade, lunch with the stars, 10K run and theatrical performances for the general public. Annually, a week in June. Est attendance: 10,000. For info: Sandra Bailen-Scott, Dir, Donna Reed Foundation, 1305 Broadway, Denison, IA 51442. Phone: (712) 263-3334. Fax: (712) 263-8026. E-mail: info@donnareed.org. Web: www.donnareed.org.

EIGHTEENTH-CENTURY WHEAT HARVEST. June 17. The Claude Moore Colonial Farm at Turkey Run, McLean, VA. Help the colonial farm family cut and bind wheat, the farmer's second most important cash crop. Light refreshments and 18th-century games. Annually, the third Sunday in June. Est attendance: 500. For info: Gretchen Brodtman, The Claude Moore Colonial Farm, Turkey Run, 6310 Georgetown Pike, McLean, VA 22101. Phone: (703) 442-7557. Fax: (703) 442-0714.

FAIN, SAMMY: BIRTH ANNIVERSARY. June 17, 1902. American composer Sammy Fain was born Samuel Feinberg at New York, NY. He won an Academy Award for his song "Secret Love" from *Calamity Jane* (1953) and for "Love Is a Many-Splendored Thing" from the film of the same name (1955). He died Dec 6, 1989, at Los Angeles, CA.

FAMILY AWARENESS DAY. June 17. A day to reflect on the important role of fathers in the American family. "Remembering always that every kid needs a Dad." A day and time to reestablish and re-affirm every man's place in our culture. Annually, third Sunday in June. For info: Judith Natale, CEO & Founder, Natl Children & Family Awareness of America, Administrative Headquarters, 3060 Rt 405 Hwy, Muncy, PA 17756-8808. Phone: (888) MAA-DESK. E-mail: MaaJudith@aol.com or FamAware@aol.com. Web: hometown.aol.com/FamAware/page1.html.

FATHER'S DAY. June 17. Recognition of the third Sunday in June as Father's Day occurred first at the request of Mrs John B. Dodd of Spokane, WA, on June 19, 1910. It was proclaimed for that date by the mayor of Spokane and recognized by the governor of Washington. The idea was publicly supported by President Calvin Coolidge in 1924, but not presidentially proclaimed until 1966. It was assured of annual recognition by Public Law 92-278 of April 1972. Also celebrated on this day in Britain.

★**FATHER'S DAY.** June 17. Presidential Proclamation issued for third Sunday in June in 1966 and annually since 1971. (PL 92–278 of Apr 24, 1972.)

FATHER'S DAY CELEBRATION. June 17. Jenkinson's Aquarium, Point Pleasant Beach, NJ. Calling all kids! Bring your dad for a special day together to learn about the roles of fathers in the marine environment. One father admitted free with each paid child's admission. Est attendance: 600. For info: Liz Carletta, Education Coord, Jenkinson's Aquarium, 300 Ocean Ave, Point Pleasant Beach, NJ 08742. Phone: (732) 899-1212. Fax: (732) 899-1717. E-mail: aquarium@jenkinsons.com. Web: www.jenkinsons.com.

HERSEY, JOHN: BIRTH ANNIVERSARY. June 17, 1914. American novelist, born at Tientsin, China, who wrote *A Bell for Adano*, which won the Pulitzer Prize in 1945. *The Wall* and *Hiroshima* are both based on fact and set in Poland and Japan respectively in World War II. Died at Key West, FL, Mar 24, 1993.

HOOPER, WILLIAM: BIRTH ANNIVERSARY. June 17, 1742. Signer of the Declaration of Independence, born at Boston, MA. Died Oct 14, 1790, at Hillsboro, NC.

ICELAND: INDEPENDENCE DAY. June 17. Anniversary of founding of republic and independence from Denmark in 1944 is major festival, especially in Reykjavik. Parades, competitions, street dancing.

MARTIN, DEAN: BIRTH ANNIVERSARY. June 17, 1917. Actor/singer Dean Martin was born Dino Paul Crocetti, at Steubenville, OH. Martin's career was barely moving in 1946, when he met Jerry Lewis. Together they formed an unforgettable comedy act that carried them to dizzying heights of success. When the team broke up, Martin found continued success as a singer as well as a Hollywood film star. He died Dec 25, 1995, at Beverly Hills, CA.

NATIONAL FORGIVENESS WEEK. June 17–23. A celebration of the people, by the people and for the people of the US. Sponsored by Positive People Partners, the weeklong observance asks people to forgive themselves on Sunday, spouses on Monday, children on Tuesday, family on Wednesday, friends on Thursday, neighbors on Friday and enemies on Saturday. Annually, starting on Father's Day each year. For info: Bob Moyers, Exec Dir, Positive People Partners, 605 Orchard View Dr, Maumee, OH 43551. Phone: (419) 897-9914. E-mail: bobmoy@wcnet.org.

SOCCER'S WORLD CUP HELD IN US: ANNIVERSARY. June 17–July 17, 1994. The World Cup soccer games were played in the US for the first time. The international championship is held every four years. The 1994 games began at Chicago on June 17 with a match between Germany and Bolivia and ended at Los Angeles with a final between Brazil and Italy on July 17 with Brazil taking the Cup. Soccer, generally known as football outside the US, is the most popular spectator sport in the world, though it has never achieved great status in the US above the amateur level. The games were watched on television by billions of fans around the world.

SOUTH AFRICA REPEALS LAST APARTHEID LAW: 10th ANNIVERSARY. June 17, 1991. The Parliament of South Africa repealed the Population Registration Act, removing the law that was the foundation of apartheid. The law, first enacted in 1950, required the classification by race of all South Africans at birth. It established four compulsory racial categories: white, mixed race, Asian and black. Although this marked the removal of the last of the apartheid laws, blacks in South Africa still could not vote.

STRAVINSKY, IGOR FYODOROVICH: BIRTH ANNIVERSARY. June 17, 1882. Russian composer and author, born at Oranienbaum (near Leningrad). Among his best-known music: the ballets *The Firebird, Petrushka* and *The Rite of Spring*; the choral work *Symphony of Psalms*; and *Abraham and Isaac, A Sacred Ballet*. Died at New York, NY, Apr 6, 1971.

UNITED NATIONS: WORLD DAY TO COMBAT DESERTIFICATION AND DROUGHT. June 17. Proclaimed by the General Assembly Dec 19, 1994 (Res 49/115). States were invited to devote the World Day to promoting public awareness of the need for international cooperation to combat desertification and the effects of drought, and on the implementation of the UN Convention to Combat Desertification. For info: United Nations, Dept of Public Info, New York, NY 10017.

UNIVERSAL FATHER'S WEEK. June 17–23. The purpose of this week, which is celebrated throughout the world the third full week in June, is to stress the importance of fatherhood in family life. For complete info and quotations about the importance of the father, send $4 to cover expense of printing, handling and postage. For info: Dr Stanley Drake, Pres, Intl Society of Friendship and Goodwill, 8592 Roswell Rd, Ste 434, Atlanta, GA 30350-1870.

WATERGATE DAY. June 17, 1972. Anniversary of arrests at Democratic Party Headquarters (in Watergate complex, Washington, DC) that led to revelations of political espionage, threats of imminent impeachment of the president and, on Aug 9, 1974, the resignation of President Richard M. Nixon.

WESLEY, JOHN: BIRTH ANNIVERSARY. June 17, 1703. Born at Epworth, England. Wesley, along with his younger brother Charles, was the founder of Methodism. John Wesley died Mar 2, 1791.

	S	M	T	W	T	F	S
June						1	2
2001	3	4	5	6	7	8	9
	10	11	12	13	14	15	16
	17	18	19	20	21	22	23
	24	25	26	27	28	29	30

BIRTHDAYS TODAY

Dermontti Dawson, 36, football player, born Lexington, KY, June 17, 1965.

Elroy Leon ("Crazylegs") Hirsch, 78, Pro Football Hall of Fame end/halfback, born Wausau, WI, June 17, 1923.

Dan Jansen, 36, speedskater, sportscaster, born West Allis, WI, June 17, 1965.

Greg Kinnear, 38, actor (*Sabrina, As Good As It Gets*), born Logansport, IN, June 17, 1963.

Mark Linn-Baker, 48, actor ("Perfect Strangers," *My Favorite Year*), born St. Louis, MO, June 17, 1953.

Barry Manilow, 55, singer ("Mandy," "I Write the Songs"), songwriter, born Brooklyn, NY, June 17, 1946.

Joe Piscopo, 50, comedian (former "Saturday Night Live" regular), born Passaic, NJ, June 17, 1951.

Venus Williams, 21, tennis player, born Lynwood, CA, June 17, 1980.

JUNE 18 — MONDAY
Day 169 — 196 Remaining

ASPEN MUSIC FESTIVAL. June 18–Aug 19. Aspen, CO. Nine weeks of concerts performed by highly acclaimed artists. Est attendance: 100,000. For info: Aspen Music Festival, 2 Music School Rd, Aspen, CO 81611. Phone: (970) 925-3254. Fax: (970) 920-1643. E-mail: festival@aspenmusic.org. Web: www.aspenmusicfestival.com.

BATTLE OF WATERLOO: ANNIVERSARY. June 18, 1815. Date of the decisive defeat of Napoleon by Wellington and Blucher, near Waterloo in central Belgium.

CAHN, SAMMY: BIRTH ANNIVERSARY. June 18, 1913. Tin Pan Alley legend Sammy Cahn was born Samuel Cohen at New York City. He was nominated for 26 Academy Awards and won four times for "Three Coins in the Fountain" (1954), "All the Way" (1957), "High Hopes" (1959) and "Call Me Irresponsible" (1963). In the late 1940s he began working with composer Jimmy Van Heusen, and the two in essence were the personal songwriting team for Frank Sinatra. Cahn wrote the greatest number of Sinatra hits, including "Love and Marriage," "The Second Time Around," "High Hopes" and "The Tender Trap." Sammy Cahn died Jan 15, 1993, at Los Angeles, CA.

EGYPT: EVACUATION DAY. June 18. Public holiday celebrating the anniversary of the withdrawal of the British Army from the Suez Canal area of Egypt in 1954.

FIRST AMERICAN WOMAN IN SPACE: ANNIVERSARY. June 18, 1983. Dr. Sally Ride, 32-year-old physicist and pilot, functioned as a "mission specialist" and became the first American woman in space when she began a six-day mission aboard the space shuttle *Challenger*. The "near-perfect" mission was launched from Cape Canaveral, FL, and landed, June 24, 1983, at Edwards Air Force Base, CA. See also: "Ride, Sally Kristen: Birthday" (May 26) and "Space Milestone: First Woman in Space" (June 16).

FOLGER, HENRY CLAY, JR: BIRTH ANNIVERSARY. June 18, 1857. American businessman and industrialist who developed one of the finest collections of Shakespeareana in the world and bequeathed it (The Folger Shakespeare Library, Washington, DC) to the American people. Born at New York, NY. Died June 11, 1930, at Brooklyn, NY.

KYSER, KAY: 95th BIRTH ANNIVERSARY. June 18, 1906. American bandleader whose band, "Kay Kyser's Kollege of Musical Knowledge," enjoyed immense popularity in the swing era. He was born James King Kern Kyser at Rocky Mount, NC. A shrewd showman and performer, he said he never learned to read music or play an instrument. Among his hit recordings were "Three Little Fishes" and "Praise the Lord and Pass the Ammunition," a World War II favorite. Kyser retired from show business in 1951 and died at Chapel Hill, NC, July 23, 1985.

MALLORY, GEORGE LEIGH: BIRTH ANNIVERSARY.

June 18, 1886. English explorer and mountain climber born at Mobberley, Cheshire, England. Last seen climbing through the mists toward the summit of the highest mountain in the world, Mount Everest, on the morning of June 8, 1924. Best remembered for his answer when asked why he wanted to climb Mount Everest: "Because it is there."

NATIONAL OLD-TIME FIDDLERS' CONTEST AND FESTIVAL.

June 18–23. Weiser, ID. Largest fiddling event in the world to help perpetuate the old-time fiddling of pioneer America. Annually, the third full week in June. Est attendance: 15,000. For info: Chamber of Commerce, 8 E Idaho St, Weiser, ID 83672. Phone: (800) 437-1280. E-mail: notfc@ruralnetwork.net. Web: www.fiddlecontest.com.

NATIONAL SPLURGE DAY.

June 18. Today is the day to go out and do something indulgent. Have fun! [©1994] For info: Adrienne Sioux Koopersmith, 1437 W Rosemont, #1W, Chicago, IL 60660-1319. Phone: (773) 743-5341. Fax: (773) 743-5395. E-mail: adrienne@21stcentury.net.

PORTER, SYLVIA: BIRTH ANNIVERSARY.

June 18, 1913. American financial journalist Sylvia Feldman Porter was born at Patchogue, NY. Her column was syndicated by the *Los Angeles Times*, reaching 450 newspapers worldwide. She also wrote more than 20 books and was noted for her ability to turn complex economic language into readable prose. Porter died June 5, 1991, at Pound Ridge, NY.

ROANOKE VALLEY HORSE SHOW.

June 18–23. Salem Civic Center, Salem, VA. Multibreed horse show. Est attendance: 30,000. For info: Salem Civic Ctr, John Saunders, Box 886, Salem, VA 24153. Phone: (540) 375-3004.

SEYCHELLES: CONSTITUTION DAY.

June 18. National holiday commemorating adoption of constitution in 1993.

SPACE MILESTONE: *CHALLENGER STS-7 (US)*.

June 18, 1983. Shuttle *Challenger* launched from Kennedy Space Center, FL, with crew of five, including Sally K. Ride (first American woman in space), Robert Crippen, Norman Thagard, John Fabian and Frederick Houck. Landed at Edwards Air Force Base, CA, on June 24 after near-perfect six-day mission.

TAKE YOUR PET TO WORK WEEK.

June 18–22. To increase awareness of how to safely bring pets to the workplace. Additionally, to educate pet owners and businesses in the benefits of a "Bring Your Pet to Work" policy. For info send SASE: Pet Tech, Inc, 5800 Severin Dr, La Mesa, CA 91942. Phone: (619) 589-7475. E-mail: info@pettech.net. Web: www.pettech.net.

US VIRGIN ISLANDS: ORGANIC ACT DAY: ANNIVERSARY.

June 18. Commemorates the enactment by the US Congress, July 22, 1954, of the Revised Organic Act, under which the government of the Virgin Islands is organized. Observed annually on the third Monday in June.

WAR OF 1812: DECLARATION ANNIVERSARY.

June 18, 1812. After much debate in Congress between "hawks" such as Henry Clay and John Calhoun, and "doves" such as John Randolph, Congress issued a declaration of war on Great Britain. The action was prompted primarily by Britain's violation of America's rights on the high seas and British incitement of Indian warfare on the frontier. War was seen by some as a way to acquire Florida and Canada. The hostilities ended with the signing of the Treaty of Ghent on Dec 24, 1814, at Ghent, Belgium.

BIRTHDAYS TODAY

Lou Brock, 62, Baseball Hall of Fame outfielder, born El Dorado, AR, June 18, 1939.

Eddie Cibrian, 28, actor ("Third Watch"), born Burbank, CA, June 18, 1973.

Roger Joseph Ebert, 59, film critic ("Siskel and Ebert"), born Urbana, IL, June 18, 1942.

Carol Kane, 49, actress (*Hester Street, The Princess Bride*, "Taxi"), born Cleveland, OH, June 18, 1952.

Donald Keene, 79, literary critic, translator, educator, born New York, NY, June 18, 1922.

Paul McCartney, 59, singer, songwriter (The Beatles, Wings), born Liverpool, England, June 18, 1942.

John D. Rockefeller IV, 64, US Senator (D, West Virginia), born New York, NY, June 18, 1937.

Isabella Rossellini, 49, model, actress (*Blue Velvet, Cousins*), born Rome, Italy, June 18, 1952.

Tom Wicker, 75, journalist, author (*One of Us: Richard Nixon & the American Dream*), born Hamlet, NC, June 18, 1926.

JUNE 19 — TUESDAY
Day 170 — 195 Remaining

BASCOM, EARL W.: 95th BIRTH ANNIVERSARY.

June 19, 1906. Rodeo showman and pioneer, Earl W. Bascom was born at Vernal, UT. During his career he developed the first side-delivery rodeo chute (1916), the first hornless bronc saddle (1922) and the first one-handed bareback rigging (1924). He produced the first rodeo in Mississippi and also produced the first rodeo performed at night under electric lights (1935). Bascom died Aug 28, 1995, at Victorville, CA.

BATTLE OF PHILIPPINE SEA: ANNIVERSARY.

June 19–20, 1944. Determined to prevent any further advancement by the Allies in Japan's area of inner defense, Vice-Admiral Jisaburo Ozawa ordered the Imperial fleet to the Mariana Islands. Admiral Raymond Spruance, possibly the US's greatest and most successful naval commander, ordered a strike force against the Japanese fleet in the Philippine Sea. A furious battle developed in the skies between US carrier-borne aircraft and Japanese aircraft from their carriers and land bases on the Marianas. The Japanese lost three aircraft carriers (*Shokaku, Taiho* and *Hiyo*), two destroyers and one tanker. Three carriers, one battleship, three cruisers, one destroyer and three tankers were seriously damaged. The Japanese lost at least 400 aircraft, the Americans 130.

EMANCIPATION DAY IN TEXAS.

June 19, 1865. In honor of the emancipation of the slaves in Texas. See also: "Juneteenth" (below).

ENGLAND: ROYAL ASCOT.

June 19–22. Ascot, Berkshire. Horse races. Annually, the third Tuesday to Friday in June.

FIRST RUNNING OF THE BELMONT STAKES: ANNIVERSARY.

June 19, 1867. The first running of the Belmont Stakes took place at Jerome Park, NY. The team of jockey J. Gilpatrick and his horse Ruthless finished in a time of 3:05. The Belmont Stakes continued at Jerome Park until 1889, then moved to Morris Park, NY, between 1890–1905, and in 1906 settled at Belmont Park, NY, where it has continued to the present day. The Belmont Stakes is the oldest event of horse racing's Triple Crown.

FORTAS, ABE: BIRTH ANNIVERSARY.

June 19, 1910. Abe Fortas was born at Memphis, TN. He was appointed to the Supreme Court by President Lyndon Johnson in 1965. Prior to his appointment he was known as a civil libertarian, having argued cases for government employees and other individuals accused by Senator Joe McCarthy of having communist affiliations. He argued the 1963 landmark Supreme Court case of *Gideon v Wainright*, which established the right of indigent defendants to free legal aid in criminal prosecutions. In 1968, he was nominated by Johnson to succeed Chief Justice Earl Warren, but his nomination was withdrawn after much conservative opposition in the Senate. In 1969 Fortas became the first Supreme Court Justice to be forced to resign after revelations about questionable financial dealings were made public. He died Apr 5, 1982, at Washington, DC.

GARFIELD: BIRTHDAY. June 19, 1978. America's favorite lasagna-loving cat celebrates his birthday. "Garfield," a modern classic comic strip created by Jim Davis, first appeared in 1978, and has brought laughter to millions. For info: Kim Campbell, Paws, Inc, 5440 E Co Rd 450 N, Albany, IN 47320. Web: www.garfield.com.

GEHRIG, LOU: BIRTH ANNIVERSARY. June 19, 1903. Baseball great Henry Louis Gehrig (lifetime batting average of .341), who played in seven World Series, was born at New York, NY, and died there June 2, 1941, from the degenerative muscle disease amyotropic lateral sclerosis, which has become known as Lou Gehrig's disease.

HOWARD, MOE: BIRTH ANNIVERSARY. June 19, 1897. The head stooge in the Three Stooges, Moe Howard was born Moses Horwitz at Bensonhurst, NY. He died May 4, 1975, at Hollywood, CA. Howard began his show business career at age 12 by running errands at Vitagraph studios. He worked with Ted Healy in various comedy and singing acts, and together they teamed with Shemp Howard and Larry Fine in the mid-1920s for an early Stooges act. In 1930 the Stooges made their film debut in *Soup to Nuts*. Although the members of the Three Stooges changed over the years, Moe Howard was one of the constants. Howard appeared in four feature films without the other Stooges, including *Doctor Death, Seeker of Souls*.

HUBBARD, ELBERT: BIRTH ANNIVERSARY. June 19, 1856. Born at Bloomington, IL, Elbert Green Hubbard, American author and craftsman, founded the Roycroft Press at East Aurora, NY. Best known of his writings were *A Message to Garcia* and a series of essays titled *Little Journeys*. He also became famous for his furniture designs. Hubbard lost his life with the sinking of the *Lusitania*, May 7, 1915.

"I'VE GOT A SECRET" TV PREMIERE: ANNIVERSARY. June 19, 1952. Celebrity panelists tried to guess the guests' secrets on this popular game show; celebrity guests also came on to baffle the panel. Guests whispered their secret to the host and the audience saw it on the screen. Garry Moore hosted the show, followed by Steve Allen and Bill Cullen. Allen Sherman ("My Son the Folk Singer") created the show and most of the celebrity "secrets." Celebrity panelists included Bill Cullen, Betsy Palmer, Henry Morgan, Bess Myerson, Steve Allen and Jayne Meadows.

JUNETEENTH. June 19. Celebrated in Texas to commemorate the day in 1865 when Union General Granger proclaimed the slaves of Texas free. Also proclaimed as Emancipation Day by the Florida legislature. Juneteenth has become an occasion for commemoration by African Americans in many parts of the US.

MARCHAND, NANCY: BIRTH ANNIVERSARY. June 19, 1928. Actress ("Lou Grant," "The Sopranos") born at Buffalo, NY. Died June 18, 2000, at Stratford, CT.

PASCAL, BLAISE: BIRTH ANNIVERSARY. June 19, 1623. French philosopher, physicist and mathematician born at Clermont-Ferrand and died at Paris, Aug 19, 1662. It was Pascal who said, "Had Cleopatra's nose been shorter, the whole history of the world would have been different." And, in his *Provincial Letters*, he wrote, "I have made this letter longer than usual because I lack the time to make it short."

	S	M	T	W	T	F	S
June						1	2
2001	3	4	5	6	7	8	9
	10	11	12	13	14	15	16
	17	18	19	20	21	22	23
	24	25	26	27	28	29	30

ROSENBERG EXECUTION: ANNIVERSARY. June 19, 1953. Anniversary of the electrocution of the only married couple ever executed together in the US. Julius (35) and Ethel (37) Rosenberg were executed for espionage at Sing Sing Prison, Ossining, NY. Time for the execution was advanced several hours to avoid conflict with the Jewish Sabbath. Their conviction has been a subject of controversy over the years.

SPACE MILESTONE: *ARIANE* **(ESA): 20th ANNIVERSARY.** June 19, 1981. Launched from Kourou, French Guiana by the European Space Administration, *Ariane* carried two satellites into orbit: *Meteostat 2*, an ESA weather satellite, and *Apple*, a geostationary communications satellite for India, to be stationed over Sumatra.

STILL NEED TO DO DAY. June 19. Time runs out! All those dreams you've had, all those fantasies? It's time, friend. Do it! Annually, June 19. ©1999 Wellcat Herbs & Holidays. For info: Thomas Roy, 2418 Long Ln, Lebanon, PA 17046. Phone: (230) 332-4886. E-mail: wellcat@supernet.com. Web: www.wellcat.com.

SULLY, THOMAS: BIRTH ANNIVERSARY. June 19, 1783. Artist born at Horncastle, Lincolnshire, England; died at Philadelphia, PA, Nov 5, 1872. He is best known as a painter of nearly 2,000 portraits. Sully studied art first with his brother, a miniaturist, and then with Gilbert Stuart, Benjamin West and others. Among the people Sully painted were Queen Victoria, the Marquis de Lafayette and presidents Thomas Jefferson, James Madison and Andrew Jackson.

SWEDISH DAYS FESTIVAL. June 19–24. Geneva, IL. Geneva celebrates its Swedish heritage with this midsummer festival. Six days of craft, art, rosemailing display, music competitions, entertainment, carnival, Kids' Day activities and parade provide unlimited opportunities. Annually, begins the Tuesday after Father's Day. Est attendance: 250,000. For info: Geneva Chamber of Commerce, 8 S Third St., PO Box 481, Geneva, IL 60134. Phone: (630) 232-6060. Fax: (630) 232-6083. Web: www.genevachamber.com.

US WOMEN'S AMATEUR PUBLIC LINKS (GOLF) CHAMPIONSHIP. June 19–24. Kemper Lakes Golf Club, Long Grove, IL. For info: US Golf Assn, Golf House, PO Box 708, Championship Dept, Far Hills, NJ 07931. Phone: (908) 234-2300. Fax: (908) 234-9687. Web: www.usga.org.

WORLD SAUNTERING DAY. June 19. A day to revive the lost art of Victorian sauntering and to discourage jogging, lollygagging, sashaying, fast walking and trotting. [Originated by the late W.T. Rabe of Saulte Ste. Marie, MI.]

BIRTHDAYS TODAY

Paula Abdul, 39, singer ("Forever Your Girl"), dancer, choreographer, born Los Angeles, CA, June 19, 1962.

Aung San Suu Kyi, 56, Nobel Peace Prize winner, born Rangoon, Burma, June 19, 1945.

Charles Gwathmey, 63, architect, born Charlotte, NC, June 19, 1938.

Pauline Kael, 82, film critic, born Petaluma, CA, June 19, 1919.

Andy Lauer, 36, actor ("Caroline in the City," *I'll Be Home for Christmas*), born Santa Monica, CA, June 19, 1965.

Brian McBride, 29, soccer player, born Arlington Heights, IL, June 19, 1972.

Marisa Pavan, 69, actress (*The Diary of Anne Frank*), born Cagliari, Sardinia, June 19, 1932.

Phylicia Rashad, 53, actress ("The Cosby Show"), born Houston, TX, June 19, 1948.

Gena Rowlands, 65, actress ("Peyton Place," *A Woman Under the Influence*), born Cambria, WI, June 19, 1936.

Salman Rushdie, 54, author (*The Jaguar Smile, Satanic Verses, Midnight's Children*), born Bombay, India, June 19, 1947.

Kathleen Turner, 47, actress (*Body Heat, Peggy Sue Got Married, Romancing the Stone*), born Springfield, MO, June 19, 1954.

Ann Wilson, 50, musician, lead singer (Heart), born San Diego, CA, June 19, 1951.

JUNE 20 — WEDNESDAY

Day 171 — 194 Remaining

AEBLESKIVER DAYS. June 20–22. Tyler, MN. A celebration of the city's Danish heritage with Danish food, crafts and folk dancing. Est attendance: 3,000. For info: Tyler Area Chamber of Commerce, Box Q, Tyler, MN 56178. Phone: (507) 247-3905. Fax: (507) 247-5502. E-mail: tribute@tylertribute.com.

CHESNUTT, CHARLES W.: BIRTH ANNIVERSARY. June 20, 1858. Born at Cleveland, OH, Chesnutt was considered by many as the first important black novelist. His collections of short stories included *The Conjure Woman* (1899) and *The Wife of His Youth and Other Stories of the Color Line* (1899). *The Colonel's Dream* (1905) dealt with the struggles of the freed slave. His work has been compared to later writers such as William Faulkner, Richard Wright and James Baldwin. He died Nov 15, 1932, at Cleveland.

CHICAGO BULLS WIN THIRD STRAIGHT TITLE FOR THE FIRST TIME: ANNIVERSARY. June 20, 1993. With a four-games-to-two victory over the Phoenix Suns in the National Basketball Association (NBA) finals the Chicago Bulls earned their third straight NBA title. The Bulls became the first team to win three in a row since 1966, when the Boston Celtics won their eighth in a row. In 1996 the Bulls won the NBA title for a fourth time, in 1997 for a fifth and in 1998 for a sixth, for another three-in-a-row sweep.

DICK TRACY DAYS. June 20–24. Woodstock, IL. A hometown 5-day celebration including a band concert, family-oriented block party on Main Street, entertainment, water fights, dance, parade, drum and bugle corps and pageant. For info: Woodstock Chamber of Commerce, 136 Cass St, Woodstock, IL 60098. Phone: (815) 338-2436. Fax: (815) 338-2927. E-mail: chamber@stans.com.

"THE ED SULLIVAN SHOW" ("TOAST OF THE TOWN") TV PREMIERE: ANNIVERSARY. June 20, 1948. "The Ed Sullivan Show" was officially titled "Toast of the Town" until 1955. It was the longest-running variety show (through 1971) and the most popular for decades. Ed Sullivan, the host, signed all types of acts, both well known and new, trying to have something to please everyone. Thousands of performers appeared, many making their television debut, such as Irving Berlin, Victor Borge, Hedy Lamarr, Walt Disney, Fred Astaire and Jane Powell. Two acts attracted the largest audience of the time: Elvis Presley and the Beatles.

FIRST BALLOON HONEYMOON: ANNIVERSARY. June 20, 1909. Roger Burnham and Eleanor Waring took the first balloon honeymoon, ascending at 12:40 PM in the balloon *Pittsfield*. They began their trip at Woods Hole, Cape Cod, MA, and landed at 4:30 PM in an orchard at Holbrook, MA.

FIRST DOCTOR OF SCIENCE DEGREE EARNED BY A WOMAN: ANNIVERSARY. June 20, 1895. Caroline Willard Baldwin became the first woman to earn a doctor of science degree at Cornell University, Ithaca, NY.

LIZZIE BORDEN VERDICT: ANNIVERSARY. June 20, 1893. Spectators at her trial cheered when the "not guilty" verdict was read by the jury foreman in the murder trial of Lizzy Borden on this date. Elizabeth Borden had been accused of and tried for the hacking to death of her father and stepmother in their Fall River, MA, home, Aug 4, 1892.

MURPHY, AUDIE: BIRTH ANNIVERSARY. June 20, 1924. Born at Kingston, TX, Murphy was the most decorated soldier in World War II and later became an actor in western and war movies. He died May 28, 1971, in a plane crash near Roanoke, VA.

OUTDOOR SUMMER THEATER. June 20–Aug 11. Farmington, NM. Featuring *Black River Traders*. Performances are held in a natural sandstone amphitheater at the Lion's Wilderness park, with an optional southwest-style dinner served prior to each performance at 6:30 PM. Performances Wednesday through Saturday at 8 PM. Est attendance: 9,000. For info: Farmington Conv and Visitors Bureau, 3041 E Main St, Farmington, NM 87402. Phone: (800) 448-1240 or (505) 326-7602. Fax: (505) 327-0577. E-mail: fmncub@cyberport.com. Web: www.farmingtonnm.org.

SONOMA-MARIN FAIR. June 20–24. Petaluma Fairgrounds, Petaluma, CA. Annual country fair with livestock exhibitions, flowers, carnival and entertainment. Est attendance: 68,000. For info: Sonoma-Marin Fair, 175 Fairgrounds Dr, Petaluma, CA 94952. Phone: (707) 283-FAIR. Fax: (707) 283-3250. E-mail: info@sonoma-marinfair.org. Web: www.sonoma-marinfair.org.

SPANISH-AMERICAN WAR SURRENDER OF GUAM TO US: ANNIVERSARY. June 20, 1898. Having not known that a war was in progress and having no ammunition on the island, the Spanish commander of Guam surrendered to Captain Glass of the USS *Charleston*.

TOAD HOLLOW DAY OF THANK YOU. June 20. A day to say or write a thank you to the people who have helped us along the way. For info: Ralph Morrison, Toad Hollow, PO Box 151, Fulton, MI 49052. Phone: (800) 574-8623.

WEST VIRGINIA: ADMISSION DAY: ANNIVERSARY. June 20, 1863. Became 35th state in 1863. Observed as a holiday in West Virginia. The state of West Virginia is a product of the Civil War. Originally part of Virginia, West Virginia became a separate state when Virginia seceded from the Union.

WHITEWATER WEDNESDAY. June 20. Kernville, CA. One-hour and two-hour raft trips on the "Wild and Scenic" Kern River. BBQ lunch included. Fill out reservation form at www.kernvillechamber.org. Est attendance: 800. For info: Kernville Chamber of Commerce, PO Box 397, Kernville, CA 93238. Phone: (760) 376-2629. Fax: (760) 376-4371. E-mail: kernvillechamber@lightspeed.net.

WOMAN RUNS THE HOUSE: ANNIVERSARY. June 20, 1921. Miss Alice Robertson of Oklahoma became the first woman to preside in the US House of Representatives. Miss Robertson presided for half an hour.

WORLD JUGGLING DAY. June 20. Juggling clubs all over the world hold local festivals to demonstrate, teach and celebrate their art. For info: Intl Jugglers' Assn, PO Box 218, Montague, MA 01351. Phone: (413) 367-2401. Fax: (413) 367-0259. E-mail: secretary@juggle.org. Web: www.juggle.org/wjd/.

BIRTHDAYS TODAY

Danny Aiello, Jr, 68, actor ("Lady Blue," *Do the Right Thing*), born New York, NY, June 20, 1933.

Olympia Dukakis, 70, actress, theatrical director (Oscar for *Moonstruck; Steel Magnolias*), born Lowell, MA, June 20, 1931.

John Goodman, 49, actor ("Roseanne," *The Flintstones*), born Afton, MO, June 20, 1952.

Nicole Kidman, 34, actress (*The Portrait of a Lady, Eyes Wide Shut*), born Honolulu, HI, June 20, 1967.

Martin Landau, 70, actor (*Tucker: The Man and His Dream; Crimes and Misdemeanors*; Oscar for *Ed Wood*), born Brooklyn, NY, June 20, 1931.

Michael Landon, Jr, 37, actor ("Bonanza: The Return," "Bonanza: The Ghosts"), born Encino, CA, June 20, 1964.

Cyndi Lauper, 48, singer ("Girls Just Want to Have Fun"), born Brooklyn, NY, June 20, 1953.

John Mahoney, 61, actor ("Frasier"), born Manchester, England, June 20, 1940.

Anne Murray, 56, singer (*Country*, "Snowbird," "Could I Have This Dance"), born Springhill, Nova Scotia, Canada, June 20, 1945.

Lionel Richie, 52, singer ("Truly"), songwriter, born Tuskegee, AL, June 20, 1949.

James Tolkan, 70, actor (*Serpico, Back to the Future, Dick Tracy*), born Calumet, MI, June 20, 1931.

Bob Vila, 55, handyman, TV show host, born Miami, FL, June 20, 1946.

Andre Watts, 55, pianist, born Nuremburg, Germany, June 20, 1946.

Brian Wilson, 59, singer (The Beach Boys), songwriter, born Hawthorne, CA, June 20, 1942.

JUNE 21 — THURSDAY

Day 172 — 193 Remaining

BABY BOOMERS RECOGNITION DAY. June 21. As baby boomers, we'll never forget the Beatles, Vietnam War and other sixties events. However, many of us accomplished a great deal, becoming successful in business, education, medicine and other fields. This special day commemorates our contributions. Annually, June 21. For info: Dorothy Zjawin, 61 W Colfax Ave, Roselle Park, NJ 07204. Phone: (908) 241-6241. Fax: (908) 241-6241.

BATTLE OF OKINAWA ENDS: ANNIVERSARY. June 21, 1945. With American grenades exploding in the background, inside the Japanese command cave at Mabuni the battle for Okinawa was ended when Major General Isamu Cho and Lieutenant General Mitsuru Ushijima killed themselves in the ceremonial rite of hara-kiri. In the long battle that had begun Apr 1, the American death toll reached enormous proportions by Pacific battle standards—7,613 died on land and 4,907 in the air or from kamikaze attacks. A total of 36 US warships were sunk. More than 70,000 Japanese and 80,000 civilian Okinawans died in the course of the battle.

BOISE RIVER FESTIVAL. June 21–24. Boise, ID. "America's Finest Family Festival" is an international award-winning citywide celebration of families and the people of Boise. Features more than 300 events including entertainment, children's activities, sporting competitions, food and specialty events (parades, balloon rally, craft fair, international exchange, airshow, fireworks, etc). Est attendance: 1,000,000. For info: Steven Wood Schmader, CFE, Pres, Boise River Festival, 7032 S Eisenman Rd, Boise, ID 83716. Phone: (208) 338-8887. Fax: (208) 338-3833. E-mail: info@boiseriverfestival.org. Web: www.boiseriverfestival.org.

	S	M	T	W	T	F	S
June 2001						1	2
	3	4	5	6	7	8	9
	10	11	12	13	14	15	16
	17	18	19	20	21	22	23
	24	25	26	27	28	29	30

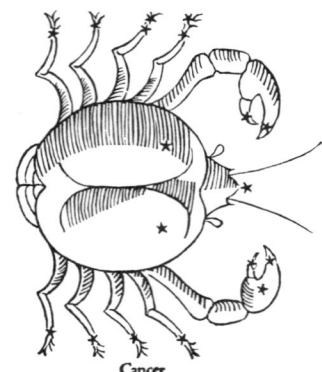

Cancer

CANCER, THE CRAB. June 21–July 22. In the astronomical/astrological zodiac, which divides the sun's apparent orbit into 12 segments, the period June 21–July 22 is identified, traditionally, as the sun sign of Cancer, the Crab. The ruling planet is the moon.

CIVIL RIGHTS WORKERS DISAPPEAR: ANNIVERSARY. June 21, 1964. James Chaney, Andrew Goodman and Michael Schwerner left Meridian, MS, at 9 AM to investigate a church burning at Philadelphia, MS. They were expected back by 4 PM. When they failed to return, a search was begun. Their murdered bodies were found on Aug 4.

CLARKSON CZECH FESTIVAL. June 21–24. Main St, Clarkson, NE. Czech food, entertainment, music, polkas, cooking, demonstrations, carnival, rodeo, arts and crafts. Annually, the fourth full weekend in June. Sponsor: Clarkson Commercial Club. Est attendance: 10,000. For info: Robert Brabec, 515 Elm St, Clarkson, NE 68629. Phone: (402) 892-3331 or (402) 892-3561. Fax: (402) 892-3318.

CUSTER'S LAST STAND REENACTMENT. June 21–24 (tentative). Hardin, MT. Reenactment of the Battle of the Little Bighorn based on an historical outline by Joe Medicine Crow, anthropologist and historian of the Crow Indian tribe. Reenacted by more than 200 Indian and cavalry riders in an outdoor arena near the site of the original battle. Est attendance: 10,000. For info: Amber Hope, Hardin Area Chamber of Commerce & Agriculture, 21 E 4th St, Hardin, MT 59034. Phone: (406) 665-1672. Fax: (406) 665-2917.

HOMESTEAD DAYS. June 21–24. Beatrice, NE. This community-wide celebration recognizes the importance of the Homestead Act of 1862 to the settlement of Nebraska. Entertainment and special museum exhibits. Est attendance: 10,000. For info: Kent Wilson, Dir, Gage County Historical Soc, PO Box 793, Beatrice, NE 68310. Phone: (402) 228-1679.

HURRICANE AGNES: ANNIVERSARY. June 21–26, 1972. Hurricane Agnes hit the eastern seaboard wreaking havoc across seven Atlantic Coast states. Casualties included 118 lives and 116,000 homes, leaving more than 200,000 homeless after Agnes dumped 28.1 trillion gallons of water over 5,000 square miles.

JUDY GARLAND FESTIVAL. June 21–23. Citywide, Grand Rapids, MN. 26th annual Judy Garland Festival. Celebrity Headliner each year. *The Wizard of Oz* and other movies shown on the big screen. Original Munchkins greet visitors each year. Saturday is Children's Day at the Garland Birthplace with free hands-on activities, walkway drawing, Ozercise and more. Seminars throughout the weekend. Plus Garland/Oz Collector's Exchange. Annually, the fourth weekend in June. Est attendance: 3,000. For info: Judy Garland Children's Museum and Birthplace, PO Box 724, Grand Rapids, MN 55744. Phone: (218) 327-9276 or (800) 664-JUDY. Fax: (218) 326-1934. E-mail: jgarland@uslink.net. Web: www.judygarlandmuseum.com.

LITTLE BIGHORN DAYS. June 21–24. Hardin, MT. To celebrate the history of the Old West. This annual celebration commemorates the anniversary of Custer's Last Stand (June 25).

Activities include carnival, Custer's Last Stand reenactment, parade, rodeo, shows, Military Ball and dances. Est attendance: 11,000. For info: Promotions, Hardin Area Chamber of Commerce, 21 E 4th St, Hardin, MT 59034. Phone: (406) 665-1672 or (888) 450-3577. E-mail: hardinchamber@juno.com. Web: mcn.net/~custerfight/.

MIDSUMMER. June 21. One of the "Lesser Sabbats" during the Wiccan year, celebrating the peak of the Sun God in his annual cycle. Annually, on the summer solstice.

MONTANA TRADITIONAL JAZZ FESTIVAL. June 21–24. Missoula, MT. Top-name Dixieland jazz bands from all over the nation fill the Clark Fork Valley with sweet sounds of jazz. Features concerts, a jazz mass, big bands, youth bands and food fair. Est attendance: 6,500. For info: Don West, PO Box 956, Great Falls, MT 59403. Phone: (800) 385-0194. E-mail: dkwest@montana.com. Web: www.montanatradjazz.com.

MOON PHASE: NEW MOON. June 21. Moon enters New Moon phase at 7:58 AM, EDT.

NEW HAMPSHIRE RATIFIES CONSTITUTION: ANNIVERSARY. June 21, 1788. By a vote of 57 to 47, New Hampshire became the ninth state to ratify the Constitution. With this ratification, the Constitution became effective for all ratifying states, as the approval of nine states was required for the Constitution to go into effect.

SARTRE, JEAN-PAUL: BIRTH ANNIVERSARY. June 21, 1905. French philosopher, "father of existentialism," born at Paris, France. In 1964 Sartre rejected the Nobel Prize for Literature when it was awarded to him. He died at Paris, Apr 15, 1980. In *Being and Nothingness*, he wrote: "Man can will nothing unless he has first understood that he must count on no one but himself; that he is alone, abandoned on earth in the midst of his infinite responsibilities, without help, with no other aim than the one he sets for himself, with no other destiny than the one he forges for himself on this earth."

SHAKESPEARE ON THE GREEN. June 21–24 (also June 28–July 1 and July 5–8). Elmwood Park, Univ of Nebraska, Omaha, NE. Nonprofit professional presentations of the works of William Shakespeare in a beautiful outdoor setting for the families of the Great Plains region. One of a handful of "free" festivals across the country. Includes pre-show seminars and workshops. Picnic area and concessions, Elizabethan entertainment featuring music, dancing, singing, juggling and acrobatics. Est attendance: 32,000. For info: Michael Markey, Managing Dir, Nebraska Shakespeare Festival, Dept of Fine Arts, Creighton Univ, Omaha, NE 68178. Phone: (402) 280-2391. E-mail: neshakes@creighton.edu.

SOLAR ECLIPSE. June 21. Total eclipse of the sun. Eclipse begins at 5:32 AM, EDT, reaches greatest eclipse at 7:57 AM and ends at 10:34 AM. Visible in South Atlantic Ocean, Angola, Zambia, Zimbabwe, Mozambique, Madagascar, Indian Ocean.

SUMMER. June 21–Sept 22. In the Northern Hemisphere summer begins today with the summer solstice, at 3:38 AM EDT. Note that in the Southern Hemisphere today is the beginning of winter. Anywhere between the Equator and the Arctic Circle, the sun rises and sets farthest north on the horizon for the year and length of daylight is maximum (12 hours, 8 minutes at equator, increasing to 24 hours at the Arctic Circle).

TANNER, HENRY OSSAWA: BIRTH ANNIVERSARY. June 21, 1859. Henry Ossawa Tanner was one of the first black artists to be exhibited in galleries in the US. He was born at Pittsburgh, PA. He died May 25, 1937, at Paris.

TOMPKINS, DANIEL D.: BIRTH ANNIVERSARY. June 21, 1774. 6th vice president of the US (1817–25), born at Fox Meadows, NY. Died at Staten Island, NY, June 11, 1825.

VIOLA GOPHER COUNT. June 21. Viola, MN. 127th anniversary of this community festival dating back to 1874. Parade, games, King & Queen, pie eating contest, ladies nail driving contest, dances and carnival. One of the oldest continuing Minnesota festivals. Annually, the third Thursday in June. Est attendance: 3,000. For info: Marilyn Shea, 10240 Viola Rd NE, Viola, MN 55934. Phone: (507) 876-2439.

WASHINGTON, MARTHA DANDRIDGE CUSTIS: BIRTH ANNIVERSARY. June 21, 1731. Wife of George Washington, first president of the US, born at New Kent County, VA. Died at Mount Vernon, VA, May 22, 1802.

WATERMELON THUMP (WITH WORLD CHAMPION SEED-SPITTING CONTEST). June 21–24. Luling, TX. Features World Champion Seed-Spitting Contest, street dance each night, giant parade on Saturday, free live entertainment in the Beer Garden, car rally, champion melon auction, arts and crafts exhibit and sales, food, games, fun run and rides. Annually, the last weekend in June (Thursday–Sunday). Est attendance: 35,000. For info: Susan H. Ward, Secretary, Luling Watermelon Thump Assn, Box 710, Luling, TX 78648. Phone: (830) 875-3214. Fax: (830) 875-2082. E-mail: thump@bcsnet.net. Web: www.bcsnet.net/lulingcc/thump.html.

BIRTHDAYS TODAY

Meredith Baxter, 54, actress ("Bridget Loves Bernie," "Family," "Family Ties"), born Los Angeles, CA, June 21, 1947.

Benazir Bhutto, 48, Pakistani political leader, born Karachi, Pakistan, June 21, 1953.

Berke Breathed, 44, cartoonist ("Bloom County"), born Croatia, June 21, 1957.

Thomas Doane (Tom) Chambers, 42, former basketball player, born Ogden, UT, June 21, 1959.

Derrick D. Coleman, 34, basketball player, born Mobile, AL, June 21, 1967.

Sammi Davis-Voss, 37, actress ("Homefront," *Hope and Glory*), born Kidderminster, Worcestershire, England, June 21, 1964.

Joe Flaherty, 61, writer, actor ("Second City TV," "SCTV Network 90"), born Pittsburgh, PA, June 21, 1940.

Michael Gross, 54, actor ("Family Ties"), born Chicago, IL, June 21, 1947.

Mariette Hartley, 60, actress ("Peyton Place"), born New York, NY, June 21, 1941.

Bernie Kopell, 68, actor ("Get Smart," "The Love Boat," "When Things Were Rotten"), born New York, NY, June 21, 1933.

Juliette Lewis, 28, actress (*The Other Sister, The Evening Star*), born Los Angeles, CA, June 21, 1973.

Nils Lofgren, 50, musician, singer, songwriter, born Chicago, IL, June 21, 1951.

Monte Markham, 63, actor ("Mr Deeds Goes to Town," "Dallas"), born Manatee, FL, June 21, 1938.

Robert Pastorelli, 47, actor (*Dances with Wolves, Michael*), born New Brunswick, NJ, June 21, 1954.

Jane Russell, 80, actress (*The Outlaw, Gentlemen Prefer Blondes*), born Bemidji, MN, June 21, 1921.

Maureen Stapleton, 76, actress (Oscar for *Reds*; stage: *The Little Foxes*), born Troy, NY, June 21, 1925.

Rick Sutcliffe, 45, former baseball player, born Independence, MO, June 21, 1956.

Togo D. West, 59, US Secretary of Veterans Affairs (Clinton administration), born Winston-Salem, NC, June 21, 1942.

Prince William (William Arthur Philip Louis), 19, son of Prince Charles and Princess Diana, born London, England, June 21, 1982.

JUNE 22 — FRIDAY
Day 173 — 192 Remaining

AFRMA FANCY RAT & MOUSE DISPLAY & SHOW.
June 22–23. Hosted by the West Coast Model Horse Collector's Jamboree, Pomona, CA. For info: AFRMA, PO Box 2589, Winnetka, CA 91396-2589. Phone: (818) 992-5564 or (909) 685-2350. Fax: (818) 592-6590. E-mail: craigr@afrma.org. Web: www.afrma.org.

ANTIQUES BY THE BAY. June 22–23. St. Ignace, MI. 5th annual show and swap meet for antique and classic original vehicles 25 years or older. Special tours and awards plus auto world celebrities. For info: Nostalgia Productions, Inc, 268 Hillcrest Blvd, St. Ignace, MI 49781. Phone: (906) 643-8087. Fax: (906) 643-9784. E-mail: edreavie@nostalgia-prod.com. Web: www.nostalgia-prod.com or www.auto-shows.com.

ART ESCAPE. June 22–24. Guthrie, OK. Indoor juried art show focusing on fine art. More than 30 artists will present their works for sale and judging. Food, entertainment and much more. Est attendance: 10,000. For info: Cherie Gorden, Art Escape, PO Box 1611, Guthrie, OK 73044. Phone: (405) 260-2345.

BAYOU BOOGALOO AND CAJUN FOOD FESTIVAL.
June 22–24. Town Point Park, Norfolk, VA. Town Point Park transforms itself into the big bayou complete with hot cajun and zydeco music, spicy foods and even hotter dancing and entertainment. Est attendance: 50,000. For info: Mktg Dir, Festevents, 120 W Main St, Norfolk, VA 23510. Phone: (757) 441-2345. Fax: (757) 441-5198. Web: www.festeventsva.org.

BLACK HILLS BLUEGRASS & ACOUSTIC MUSIC FESTIVAL. June 22–24. Mystery Mountain Resort, Rapid City, SD. This family event features concerts, open stage, workshops, jam sessions and Sunday morning gospel show. Camping with hookups available. Annually, the last weekend in June. Sponsor: Rapid City Art Council. Est attendance: 800. For info: Dahl Arts Center, 713 7th St, Rapid City, SD 57701. Phone: (605) 394-4101.

BUSKERFEST. June 22–24. Denver, CO. The 9th annual US WEST Buskerfest will bring more than 35 of the world's premier street performers to Downtown Denver. It's a free, family-oriented event featuring percussionists, jugglers, stilt walkers, magicians, fire-eaters, puppeteers, comedians, unicyclists and tightrope walkers from across the US and the world. Friday and Saturday, 11 AM–8 PM; Sunday 11 AM–5 PM. Est attendance: 150,000. For info: Susan Rogers Kark, Sr Dir, Mktg & Events, Downtown Partnership, Inc, 511 16th St, Ste 200, Denver, CO 80202-4250. Phone: (303) 534-6161. Fax: (303) 534-2803. Web: www.downtowndenver.com.

June 2001	S	M	T	W	T	F	S
						1	2
	3	4	5	6	7	8	9
	10	11	12	13	14	15	16
	17	18	19	20	21	22	23
	24	25	26	27	28	29	30

CANADA: JAZZ CITY INTERNATIONAL MUSIC FESTIVAL. June 22–July 1. Edmonton, AB. The Jazz City Festival is an annual 10-day celebration of jazz, blues and world-beat music featuring local, national and international artists. Est attendance: 125,000. For info: Jazz City Festival Soc, 10516 77 Ave NW, Edmonton, AB T6E 1N1, Canada. Phone: (403) 432-7166. Fax: (403) 433-3779. E-mail: jazzcity@planet.eon.net. Web: www.discoveredmonton.com/jazzcity/.

CHESAPEAKE-LEOPARD AFFAIR: ANNIVERSARY.
June 22, 1807. One of the events leading to the War of 1812 occurred about 40 miles east of Chesapeake Bay. The US frigate *Chesapeake* was fired upon and boarded by the crew of the British man-of-war *Leopard*. The *Chesapeake*'s commander, James Barron, was court-martialed and convicted of not being prepared for action. Later Barron killed one of the judges (Stephen Decatur) in a duel fought at Bladensburg, MD, Mar 22, 1820.

CIRCUS TRAIN WRECK: ANNIVERSARY. June 22, 1918. A Michigan Central Railroad troop train, after several days shuttling soldiers to New York from Chicago, was deadheading back to the Midwest when it struck the rear of the Hagenbeck–Wallace Circus train. The circus train had stopped to have its brake box overhauled at Ivanhoe, IN. Fifty-three circus performers were killed. Of the circus animals not killed outright, many that were crippled and maimed had to be destroyed by police officers. The performers, of whom only three could be identified, were buried in a mass grave. The engineer, A.K. Sargent, who was accused of falling asleep at the throttle, was tried and acquitted.

DALESBURG MIDSUMMER FESTIVAL. June 22. Dalesburg Lutheran Church, rural Vermillion, SD. Celebration of Scandinavian and rural heritage. Dances to raise the Midsummer Pole, a smorgasbord, arts and crafts area, band concert and more. Est attendance: 800. For info: Ronald Johnson, Midsummer Committee, Dalesburg Midsummer Festival, 30595 University Rd, Vermillion, SD 57069-6507. Phone: (605) 253-2575.

DENMARK: VIKING FESTIVAL. June 22–July 1. Frederiksund (about 25 miles northwest of Copenhagen). Famous outdoor plays based on Danish legends. Annually, the next-to-last Friday in June through the first Sunday in July.

GETTYSBURG CIVIL WAR BOOK FAIR. June 22–23. Gettysburg, PA. More than 60 major Civil War book dealers selling new, used, out-of-print and rare books, documents, prints and photographs. Est attendance: 1,000. For info: GBPA, PO Box 4087, Gettysburg, PA 17325-1899. Phone: (717) 337-0031.

GETTYSBURG CIVIL WAR HERITAGE DAYS. June 22–24 and June 29–July 8. Gettysburg, PA. Commemorates the Battle of Gettysburg. Living history encampment with both Union and Confederate army campsites, concerts, Civil War lecture series, a battle of Gettysburg reenactment, firefighter's festival, encampment church service and Civil War book fair. Est attendance: 37,500. For info: Gettysburg CVB, PO Box 4117, Gettysburg, PA 17325. Phone: (717) 334-6274. Fax: (717) 334-1166. Web: www.gettysburg.com.

GRANTSVILLE DAYS. June 22–24. Grantsville Park, Grantsville, MD. Three-day annual homecoming weekend. Free entertainment Friday 7:15 PM– Sunday 5 PM. Lion's chicken BBQ, local non-commercial food booths, children's games, tennis, horse pulling and tractor pulling contests, talent exhibition, fireworks Friday and Saturday nights. Annually, the last weekend in June. Est attendance: 15,000. For info: Gerry Beachy. Fax: (301) 895-3623. E-mail: gbeachy@garrett.ncin.com.

HELEN KELLER FESTIVAL. June 22–24. Tuscumbia, AL. Commemorates the remarkable life of Helen Keller with stage shows for all ages, arts and crafts fair, free musical entertainment, races, historic tours of Helen Keller's Birthplace and other beautiful homes and much more. *The Miracle Worker* play performed evenings during festival and for five weekends following. Annually, the last weekend in June. Est attendance: 105,000. For info: Debbie Wilson, Dir, Florence/Lauderdale Tourism, One Hightower Pl, Florence, AL 35630. Phone: (256) 740-4141 or (888) FLO-TOUR. Fax: (256) 740-4142. E-mail: dwilson@floweb.com. Web: www.flo-tour.org.

JOE LOUIS v BRADDOCK/SCHMELING FIGHT ANNIVERSARIES. June 22, 1937. At Chicago's Comiskey Park Joe Louis won the World Heavyweight Championship title by knocking out James J. Braddock (eighth round). Louis retained the title until his retirement in 1949. Exactly one year after the Braddock fight, on June 22, 1938, Louis met Germany's Max Schmeling, at New York City's Yankee Stadium. Louis knocked out Schmeling in the first round.

KLAMATH KRUISE & VINTAGE CAR SHOW. June 22–24. Klamath Falls, OR. Includes Saturday night cruise on Main St, show 'n shine, poker run, sock hop and more. Est attendance: 40,000. For info: Klamath Kruisers, PO Box 7363, Klamath Falls, OR 97602. Phone: (541) 884-0452.

KUSTOM KEMPS OF AMERICA CAR SHOW. June 22–24. Oakside Community Park, Biglerville, PA. Est attendance: 3,500. For info: Gettysburg CVB, PO Box 4117, Gettysburg, PA 17325. Phone: (717) 637-5229.

LINDBERGH, ANNE MORROW: BIRTHDAY. June 22, 1907. American author and aviator, born at Englewood, NJ. In *Gift from the Sea*, she wrote: "By and large, mothers and housewives are the only workers who do not have regular time off. They are the great vacationless class."

LONG GROVE STRAWBERRY FESTIVAL. June 22–24. Long Grove, IL. Country village of nearly 100 specialty shops and restaurants celebrates summer with strawberries in every form, outdoor food booths, free music and family entertainment. Admission and parking free. Annually, the weekend after Father's Day. Est attendance: 50,000. For info: Long Grove Merchants Assn, 307 Old McHenry Rd, Long Grove, IL 60047. Phone: (847) 634-0888. Fax: (847) 634-3673.

MALTA: MNARJA. June 22–23. Buskett Gardens. A folk-cum-harvest festival. An all-night traditional Maltese "festa" with folk music, dancing and impromptu Maltese folk singing (ghana). This festival originated in the Middle Ages, and the word *Mnarja* is derived from *luminarja* because the countryside and the bastions around Mdina, Malta's ancient capital, used to be illuminated by "Fjakkoli" (torches made of sand mixed with oil and animal fat) on the eve of and on the feast day itself.

MIDNIGHT SUN BASEBALL GAME. June 22. Fairbanks, AK. To celebrate the summer solstice. Game is played without artificial lights at 10:35 PM. Est attendance: 4,000. For info: Alaska Goldpanners, Box 71154, Fairbanks, AK 99707. Phone: (907) 451-0095.

OREGON BACH FESTIVAL. June 22–July 8. Hult Center for the Performing Arts and the University of Oregon, Eugene, OR. Artistic Director and conductor Helmuth Rilling leads an international gathering of musicians in choral-orchestral masterworks, intimate concerts and chamber music, informal free concerts and family events, adult education programs and master classes for conductors and composers. Emphasis is on J.S. Bach and his influence succeeding generations of composers. Est attendance: 30,000. For info: George Evano, Oregon Bach Fest, 1257 University of Oregon, Eugene, OR 97403. Phone: (800) 457-1486 or (541) 346-5666. Fax: (541) 346-5669. Web: bachfest.uoregon.edu.

PAPP, JOSEPH: BIRTH ANNIVERSARY. June 22, 1921. Born Yosl Papirofsky at Brooklyn, NY, Joe Papp became one of the leading figures in American theatre. At the helm of the New York Public Theatre, Papp produced a wide range of work from the classical to that of the newest American dramatists, including *Hair, Two Gentlemen of Verona, The Pirates of Penzance, The Mystery of Edwin Drood, That Championship Season* and *A Chorus Line*. He began in 1954 with the Shakespeare Theatre Workshop, taking touring productions around the city on a flatbed truck. When the truck broke down in Central Park, Papp turned his touring company into Shakespeare-in-the-Park. Producing and directing more than 400 productions, Papp garnered three Pulitzer Prizes, six New York Critics Circle Awards and 28 Tonys. He died Oct 31, 1991, at New York, NY.

PENNSYLVANIA ARTS & CRAFTS COUNTRY FESTIVAL. June 22–24. Fayette County Fairgrounds, Uniontown, PA. More than 150 arts and craft exhibits from 14 different states. Crafts include woodworking, pottery, jewelry, glass, quilts and folk art. Food, children's entertainment and live demonstrations. Est attendance: 12,000. For info: Debbie or Dave Stoner, Family Festivals Assn, Inc, PO Box 166, Irwin, PA 15642. Phone: (724) 863-4577. Fax: (724) 863-4577.

SOUTH CAROLINA FESTIVAL OF FLOWERS. June 22–24. Greenwood, SC. Come and see the beautiful flowers of South Carolina. Includes arts and crafts displays, entertainment, sports events and more. Est attendance: 25,000. For info: Greenwood Chamber of Commerce, SC Festival of Flowers, PO Box 980, Greenwood, SC 29648. Phone: (864) 223-8411. Fax: (864) 229-9785. E-mail: frankcc@greenwood.net. Web: www.scfestivalofflowers.org.

SOVIET UNION INVADED: 60th ANNIVERSARY. June 22, 1941. German troops invaded the Soviet Union, beginning a conflict that left 27 million Soviet citizens dead. Ceremonies are held this day in Russia, Belarus and Ukraine, the areas of the former Soviet Union which bore the brunt of the initial invasion.

STAMP EXPO. June 22–24. Radisson Hotel, Sherman Oaks, CA. Est attendance: 5,000. For info: Intl Stamp Collectors Soc, PO Box 854, Van Nuys, CA 91408. Phone: (818) 997-6496. Fax: (818) 988-4337. E-mail: iibick@aol.com. Web: www.bick.net.

STERNWHEELER DAYS. June 22–24. Port Marina Park, Cascade Locks, OR. Return of the 599-passenger sternwheeler *Columbia Gorge* to home port for the summer. Salmon Bake, Mountain Men Encampment, bingo, children's rides, parade, food, crafts, live bluegrass music, RV parking. Annually, the fourth weekend in June. Est attendance: 6,000. For info: Columbia Gorge Lions, PO Box 522, Cascade Locks, OR 97014. Phone: (541) 374-8313.

SWITZERLAND: MORAT BATTLE ANNIVERSARY. June 22, 1476. The little, walled town of Morat played a decisive part in Swiss history. There, the Confederates were victorious over Charles the Bold of Burgundy, laying the basis for French-speaking areas to become Swiss. Now an annual children's festival.

US DEPARTMENT OF JUSTICE: ANNIVERSARY. June 22. Established by an act of Congress, the Department of Justice is headed by the attorney general. Prior to 1870, the attorney general (whose office had been created Sept 24, 1789) had been a member of the president's cabinet but had not been the head of a department.

V-MAIL DELIVERY: ANNIVERSARY. June 22, 1942. The first V-Mail (V for victory) was dispatched from New York on this date. The system was devised during WWII to conserve cargo space for war materials and supplies. Special paper was used for writing the letters. At post offices, the letters were opened, censored and photographed in reduced proportions. The film was then transported overseas. A complete roll of film contained 1,600 letters.

VANCOUVER, GEORGE: BIRTH ANNIVERSARY. June 22, 1757. English navigator, explorer and author for whom Vancouver Island and the cities of Vancouver (British Columbia and Washington) are named was born at Norfolk, England and joined the navy at the age of 13. He surveyed the coasts of Australia, New Zealand and western North America and sailed with Captain James Cook to the Arctic in 1780. Vancouver died at Petersham, Surrey, England, May 10, 1798, just as he was correcting the final pages of his *Journal*, which was published at London later that year.

BIRTHDAYS TODAY

Darrell Armstrong, 33, basketball player, born Gastonia, NC, June 22, 1968.

Bill Blass, 79, fashion designer, born Fort Wayne, IN, June 22, 1922.

Ed Bradley, 60, broadcast journalist ("60 Minutes"), born Philadelphia, PA, June 22, 1941.

Klaus Maria Brandauer, 57, actor (*Out of Africa, White Fang*), born Altausse, Austria, June 22, 1944.

Clyde Austin Drexler, 39, basketball coach and former player, born Houston, TX, June 22, 1962.

Diane Feinstein, 68, US Senator (D, California), born San Francisco, CA, June 22, 1933.

Kris Kristofferson, 65, singer, actor (*Alice Doesn't Live Here Anymore, A Star Is Born*), born Brownsville, TX, June 22, 1936.

Michael Lerner, 60, actor (*The Candidate, Eight Men Out, Barton Fink*), born Brooklyn, NY, June 22, 1941.

Tracy Pollan, 41, actress ("Family Ties," *Bright Lights, Big City*), born New York, NY, June 22, 1960.

Todd Rundgren, 53, singer (*Something/Anything*), producer, born Upper Darby, PA, June 22, 1948.

Meryl Streep, 52, actress (Oscars for *Kramer v Kramer* and *Sophie's Choice*), born Summit, NJ, June 22, 1949.

Kurt Wagner, 30, football player, born Burlington, IA, June 22, 1971.

Lindsay Wagner, 52, actress ("The Bionic Woman," *The Paper Chase*), born Los Angeles, CA, June 22, 1949.

☆　☆　☆

JUNE 23 — SATURDAY

Day 174 — 191 Remaining

AMERICAN RED CROSS FAT TIRE CLASSIC. June 23–24. Winter Park Resort, Winter Park, CO. 11th annual. A two-day pledge ride/walk to benefit the Mile High Chapter of the American Red Cross. Participants choose from one of three different routes geared toward different ability levels. The festival offers entertainment, food, seminars and product demonstrations. Est attendance: 1,000. For info: Winter Park Resort, PO Box 36, Winter Park, CO 80482. Phone: (970) 726-1580. Fax: (970) 726-1572. E-mail: wpinfo@mail.skiwinterpark.com. Web: winterparkresort.com.

A BLAST FROM THE PAST. June 23–24. Mount Hope Estate & Winery, Manheim, PA. Relive those happy days with music, dance, record swaps, dance contests, classic cars and an end-of-the-day concert by the original performers of some of your favorite rock-n-roll. Est attendance: 15,000. For info: Thomas Roy, PRF, PO Box 685, Cornwall, PA 17016. Phone: (717) 665-7021 ext 127. Fax: (717) 664-3466. E-mail: TomRoy@parenaissancefaire.com. Web: www.parenfaire.com.

 *June* 2001	S	M	T	W	T	F	S
						1	2
	3	4	5	6	7	8	9
	10	11	12	13	14	15	16
	17	18	19	20	21	22	23
	24	25	26	27	28	29	30

"THE BREAKFAST CLUB" RADIO PREMIERE: ANNIVERSARY. June 23, 1933. It was corny, but it was loved. "The Breakfast Club with Don McNeil," which hit radio airwaves on this date, had a 35-year run. It was carried by 400 affiliates and tickets became as sought-after as those for a taping of "The Tonight Show" are today. The hour-long show included celebrities such as Fran Allison of "Kukla, Fran and Ollie" fame. Its popularity, however, stemmed mainly from regular features such as "Memory Time," when McNeil read poems and letters from listeners. During World War II "Prayer Time" was started. McNeil's "Call to Breakfast," which was announced every 15 minutes, invited listeners to get up and march around the breakfast table. McNeil died in 1996.

BULLWHACKER DAYS. June 23–24. Mahaffie Stagecoach Stop and Farm, Olathe, KS. A celebration of Olathe's Santa Fe Trail heritage with 1800s-period demonstrations, music, children's games and stagecoach rides. The Mahaffie Farmstead on the Santa Fe Trail near the Oregon Trail served warm meals for travelers as a stagecoach stop from 1863 to 1869. "Bullwhackers" were the men who drove teams of oxen. Annually, the fourth weekend in June. Est attendance: 10,000. For info: Mktg Dept, Bullwhacker Days, 1100 Kansas City Rd, Olathe, KS 66061. Phone: (913) 782-6972.

CANADA: NOVA SCOTIA MULTICULTURAL FESTIVAL. June 23–25. Dartmouth, NS. Cultural events include five tents housing exhibits, food booths, children's tent, performances, beer tent with live bands and fashion show. 16th annual. Annually, the fourth full weekend in June. Est attendance: 45,000. For info: Barbara Campbell, Exec Dir, Multicultural Assn of Nova Scotia, 1113 Marginal Rd, Halifax, NS, Canada B3H 4P7. Phone: (902) 423-6534. Fax: (902) 422-0881. E-mail: multicul@fox.nstn.ca. Web: Fox.NSTN.Ca/~multicul/.

CHILE CHALLENGE OFF-ROAD BIKE RACE. June 23–24. Angel Fire, NM. Annual bike race held on the ski mountain in this beautiful alpine setting. All skill levels. Est attendance: 400. For info: Angel Fire Resort, Attn: Special Events, PO Drawer B, Angel Fire, NM 87710. Phone: (800) 633-7463 or (505) 377-4237. Fax: (505) 377-4395. E-mail: events@angelfireresort.com. Web: www.angelfireresort.com.

DENMARK: MIDSUMMER EVE. June 23. Celebrated all over the country with bonfires and merrymaking.

EASTERN MUSIC FESTIVAL. June 23–Aug 4. Guilford College, Greensboro, NC. 40th annual summer festival of classical concerts and recitals performed by resident professionals and a corps of talented young students from the US and abroad. Est attendance: 63,000. For info: Evelyn Cottam, Mktg Dir, Eastern Music Festival, PO Box 22026, Greensboro, NC 27420. Phone: (336) 333-7450. Fax: (336) 333-7454. E-mail: easternmusicfestival@worldnet.att.net. Web: www.easternmusicfestival.com.

FIRST TYPEWRITER: ANNIVERSARY. June 23, 1868. First US typewriter was patented by Luther Sholes.

FISHING HAS NO BOUNDARIES—BEMIDJI. June 23–24. Lake Bemidji, Bemidji, MN. A two-day fishing experience for disabled persons. Any disability, age, sex, race, etc, eligible. Fishing with experienced guides; attended by 75 participants and 130 volunteers. For info: Carol Olson, Bemidji Chamber of Commerce, Fishing Has No Boundaries, 300 Bemidji Ave, PO Box 850, Bemidji, MN 56619-0850. Phone: (800) 458-2223. Fax: (218) 759-0810. Web: www.paulbunyan.net/FHNB.

FORT SEWARD WAGON TRAIL. June 23–30. Jamestown, ND. Relive an important part of western history as you travel in a covered wagon across the great prairies region of North Dakota. This year's ride is called the "Prairie Rose Trail" and follows a historic route. Enjoy fresh air, good campfire cooking and sleep under the stars in the great North Dakota sky. For info: (701) 252-6844 or North Dakota Tourism, 604 East Boulevard, Bismarck, ND 58505. Phone: (701) 328-2525 or (800) 435-5663.

FOSSE, ROBERT LOUIS (BOB): BIRTH ANNIVERSARY. June 23, 1927. Bob Fosse was born at Chicago, IL. The son of a vaudeville singer, he began his show business career at the age of 13. He was the only director in history to win an Oscar, an Emmy and a Tony for his work. As a choreographer he was known for his unique dance style that focused on explosive angularity of the human body in its movement. His body of work included the plays *Pippin, Sweet Charity, Pajama Game, Chicago, Dancin', Redhead* and *Damn Yankees.* His films included *Cabaret, Lenny* and the autobiographical *All That Jazz.* Fosse died Sept 23, 1987, at Washington, DC.

GALESBURG RAILROAD DAYS. June 23–24. Galesburg, IL. 24th annual festival celebrating the city's railroad heritage that dates back to 1854. Carnival, street fair, railroad exhibits and displays, railyard tours, 5K run, concerts and basketball. Includes more than 40 events. Annually, the fourth weekend in June. Est attendance: 55,000. For info: Galesburg Area CVB, PO Box 60, Galesburg, IL 61402-0060. Phone: (309) 343-2485. Fax: (309) 343-2521. E-mail: visitors@galesburg.org. Web: www.galesburg .org/visitors.

GETTYSBURG CIVIL WAR RELIC AND COLLECTOR'S SHOW. June 23–24. Gettysburg, PA. 27th annual. Accoutrements, weapons, uniforms and personal effects from American military history, 1865 and earlier. Leading collectors and dealers of Civil War material. Est attendance: 2,000. For info: Gettysburg CVB, PO Box 4117, Gettysburg, PA 17325. Phone: (717) 334-6274. Fax: (717) 334-1166. Web: www.gettysburg.com.

KIWANIS INTERNATIONAL CONVENTION. June 23–27. Taipei, Taiwan. Est attendance: 13,000. For info: Conv Dept, Kiwanis Intl, 3636 Woodview Trace, Indianapolis, IN 46268-3196. Phone: (317) 875-8755. Fax: (317) 879-0204. E-mail: kiwanismail@kiwanis.org. Web: www.kiwanis.org.

LAST FORMAL SURRENDER OF CONFEDERATE TROOPS: ANNIVERSARY. June 23, 1865. The last formal surrender of Confederate troops took place in the Oklahoma Territory. Cherokee leader and Confederate Brigadier General Waite surrendered his command of a battalion formed by Indians.

LAST GREAT BUFFALO HUNT: ANNIVERSARY. June 23–24. By 1882 most of the estimated 60–75 million buffalo had been killed by white hide hunters, the meat left to rot. Buffalo numbered only about 50,000 when "The Last Great Buffalo Hunt" took place on Indian reservation lands near Hettinger, ND. Some 2,000 Teton Sioux Indians in full hunting regalia killed about 5,000 buffalo. The occasion is also referred to as "The Last Stand of the American Buffalo" as within 16 months the last of the free-ranging buffalo were gone. For info: Wendy Hehn, Dir Community Promotions, Box 1323, Hettinger, ND 58639. Phone: (701) 567-2531. Fax: (701) 567-2690. E-mail: adamsdv@hettinger.ctctel .com. Web: hettingernd.com.

LET IT GO DAY. June 23. Whatever it is that's bugging you, drop it! It's only eating away at you and providing nothing positive. ©2000 Wellcat Herbs & Holidays. For info: Thomas & Ruth Roy, 2418 Long Ln, Lebanon, PA 17046-1708. Phone: (230) 332-4886. E-mail: wellcat@supernet.com. Web: www.wellcat.com.

LIGHT THE NIGHT FOR SIGHT. June 23–July 2. Celebrate sight and safety with this national walkathon organized to raise awareness of consumer fireworks dangers and to celebrate the gift of sight. Safe celebrations will be promoted. For info: Prevent Blindness America®, 500 E Remington Rd, Schaumburg, IL 60173. Phone: (800) 331-2020. Fax: (847) 843-8458. Web: www.preventblindness.org.

LONGEST DAM RUN. June 23. Glasgow, MT. This is a sanctioned 5K and 10K run. There are also 5K and one-mile walks. It crosses 1.8 miles of Fort Peck Dam. After two miles into the 10K race, the course rises in elevation from the low point at starting some 350 feet over a distance of approximately two miles. The 5K is flat. Both distances finish running downhill grade from the top of the dam. Annually, the fourth weekend in June. Est attendance: 550. For info: Glasgow Chamber of Commerce and Agriculture, Box 832, Glasgow, MT 59230. Phone: (406) 228-2222. Fax: (406) 228-2244. E-mail: chamber@nemontel.net.

LUXEMBOURG: NATIONAL HOLIDAY. June 23. Official birthday of His Royal Highness Grand Duke Jean in 1921. Also, Luxembourg's independence is celebrated June 23.

MIDNIGHT SUN FESTIVAL. June 23–24. Nome, AK. A celebration of the summer solstice, which is when Nome experiences the midnight sun with more than 22 hours of direct sunlight. The festival usually includes a parade, raft race and barbecue. Annually, on the Saturday and Sunday closest to the summer solstice. Est attendance: 500. For info: Nome Conv & Visitors Bureau, PO Box 240, Nome, AK 99762. Phone: (907) 443-6624. Fax: (907) 443-5832. Web: www.nomealaska.org.

MIDSUMMER DAY/EVE CELEBRATIONS. June 23. Celebrates the beginning of summer with maypoles, music, dancing and bonfires. Observed mainly in northern Europe, including Finland, Latvia and Sweden. Day of observance is sometimes St. John's Day (June 24), with celebration on St. John's Eve (June 23) as well, or June 19. Time approximates the summer solstice. See also: "Summer" (June 21).

NORSKEDALEN'S MIDSUMMER FEST. June 23–24. Norskedalen Nature and Heritage Center, Coon Valley, WI. Celebrate the summer solstice and Sankt Hans Dag (Saint John's Day) in Scandinavian style. Pioneer crafts and demonstrations; children's activities, entertainment, food and raffle; nature hikes, animal presentations and horse-drawn wagon rides. Woodcarving show and competition, open air museum; artisans demonstrating and selling their works. Est attendance: 1,500. For info: Nature and Heritage Center, Inc, Norskedalen, PO Box 235, Coon Valley, WI 54623. Phone: (608) 452-3424. Fax: (608) 452-3157. E-mail: info@norskedalen.org. Web: www.norskedalen .org.

OIL BOWL FOOTBALL CLASSIC. June 23. Memorial Stadium, Wichita Falls, TX. 63rd annual. For more than 60 years, high school all-stars from Texas and Oklahoma tangle in Memorial Stadium, to benefit disadvantaged children. Est attendance: 14,000. For info: Wichita Falls CVB, 1000 5th St, Wichita Falls, TX 76301. Phone: (940) 716-5500. Fax: (940) 716-5509. E-mail: MPEC@wf.net. Web: www.viewscape.com or www.wf.net.

PRE-OPERA LECTURE SERIES. June 23–24 (also June 30–July 1, July 7–8 and 14–15). Ash Lawn–Highland Summer Festival, Charlottesville, VA. Scholars present lectures during the opera season on the season's productions. Annually, the last Saturday and Sunday of June and every Saturday and Sunday in July. Est attendance: 17,000. For info: Judith H. Walker, General Dir, 1941 James Monroe Pkwy, Charlottesville, VA 22902. Phone: (804) 293-4500 or (804) 979-0122. Fax: (804) 293-0736. E-mail: summerfestival@avenue.org. Web: www.avenue.org/summer festival.

RUDOLPH, WILMA: BIRTH ANNIVERSARY. June 23, 1940. Olympic gold medal sprinter, born at Bethlehem, TN. She won the 100 meters, the 200 meters and the 400-meter relay at the 1960 Rome games, thus becoming the first woman to win three gold medals at the same Olympics. She overcame polio as a child and went on to Tennessee State University to become an athlete. Rudolph won the Sullivan Award in 1961. Died at Brentwood, TN, Nov 12, 1994.

SNAKE HUNT. June 23–24. Cross Fork, PA. To raise funds for the fire company. Est attendance: 5,000. For info: Barry Gipe, Chmn, Kettle Creek Hose Co #1, Box 264, Cross Fork, PA 17729. Phone: (570) 923-0848.

SOUTHERN CALIFORNIA CAJUN AND ZYDECO FESTIVAL. June 23–24. Rainbow Lagoon, Long Beach, CA. 15th annual. To celebrate Cajun and Creole cultures. Est attendance: 4,000. For info: Franklin Zawacki, 915 Sanchez St, San Francisco, CA 94114. Phone: (415) 643-9336.

SWEDEN: MIDSUMMER. June 23–24. Celebrated throughout Sweden. Maypole dancing, games and folk music.

YOUTH SING PRAISE PERFORMANCE. June 23. Belleville, IL. Talented high school students from all over the country gather at the Shrine to perform a musical in the outdoor amphitheatre. Saturday, 7 PM. Est attendance: 3,000. For info: Shrine of Our Lady of the Snows, 442 S De Mazenod Dr, Belleville, IL 62223-1094. Phone: (618) 397-6700. Fax: (618) 397-1210. Web: www.youthsingpraise.org.

BIRTHDAYS TODAY

Bryan Brown, 54, actor (*A Town Like Alice, Breaker Morant, F/X*), born Sydney, Australia, June 23, 1947.

June Carter Cash, 72, singer (Grammy with husband Johnny for "Jackson"), born Maces Spring, VA, June 23, 1929.

James Levine, 58, American conductor and pianist, Metropolitan Opera of New York City, born Cincinnati, OH, June 23, 1943.

Frances McDormand, 44, actress (*Fargo, Mississippi Burning*), born Chicago, IL, June 23, 1957.

Ted Shackelford, 55, actor ("Knots Landing," "Dallas"), born Oklahoma City, OK, June 23, 1946.

Clarence Thomas, 53, Supreme Court Associate Justice, born Pinpoint, GA, June 23, 1948.

JUNE 24 — SUNDAY
Day 175 — 190 Remaining

AMERICA'S KIDS DAY. June 24. A day set aside to reach out and teach our children in America the value of life, liberty and the pursuit of happiness. A time to help our kids to learn about the great nation that they live in and to help by demonstrating what it means to be an American. A time to teach them the historical value of their heritage as America's kids. Annually, the fourth Sunday in June. For info: Judith Natale, Natl Children & Family Awareness of America, Administrative Headquarters, 3060 Rt 405 Hwy, Muncy, PA 17756-8808. Phone: (888) MAA-DESK. E-mail: MaaJudith@aol.com or ChildAware@aol.com.

June 2001	S	M	T	W	T	F	S
						1	2
	3	4	5	6	7	8	9
	10	11	12	13	14	15	16
	17	18	19	20	21	22	23
	24	25	26	27	28	29	30

BEECHER, HENRY WARD: BIRTH ANNIVERSARY. June 24, 1813. Famous American clergyman and orator was born at Litchfield, CT. Died Mar 8, 1887, at Brooklyn, NY. His dying words were "Now comes the mystery."

BERLIN AIRLIFT: ANNIVERSARY. June 24, 1948. In the early days of the Cold War the Soviet Union challenged the West's right of access to Berlin. The Soviets created a blockade and an airlift to supply some 2,250,000 people resulted. The airlift lasted a total of 321 days and brought into Berlin 1,592,787 tons of supplies. Joseph Stalin finally backed down and the blockade ended May 12, 1949.

CANADA: NEWFOUNDLAND DISCOVERY DAY. June 24. Commemorates the discovery of Newfoundland by John Cabot in 1497.

CANADA: ST. JEAN-BAPTISTE DAY. June 24. Public holiday in Quebec.

CARPENTER ANT AWARENESS WEEK. June 24–30. Wood-destroying organisms cause Americans to spend $3.5 billion annually. This week will focus attention on the identification, biology and habits of carpenter ants, and provide consumers with information on the elimination of these costly pests. Annually, the last full week of June. For info: Jerry Batzner, Pres, Batzner Pest Management, Inc, 16700 W Victor Rd, New Berlin, WI 53151. Phone: (262) 797-4160. Fax: (262) 797-4166. E-mail: JerryB@batzner.com.

CELEBRATION OF THE SENSES. June 24. Treat yourself to a stimulation of the five senses—taste, touch, scent, sight and sound—and you may experience the elevation known to many mystics as the elusive sixth sense. [© 2000 by WH] For info: Tom or Ruth Roy, Wellcat Holidays, 2418 Long Ln, Lebanon, PA 17046. Phone: (717) 279-0184. E-mail: wellcat@supernet.com. Web: www.wellcat.com.

CIARDI, JOHN: 85th BIRTH ANNIVERSARY. June 24, 1916. American poet, critic, translator, teacher, etymologist and author of children's books, born at Boston, MA. John Anthony Ciardi's criticism and other writings were often described as honest and sometimes as harsh. Died at Edison, NJ, Mar 30, 1986.

DEMPSEY, JACK: BIRTH ANNIVERSARY. June 24, 1895. William Harrison Dempsey, known as "The Manassa Mauler," was world heavyweight boxing champion from 1919 to 1926. Following his boxing career Dempsey became a successful New York restaurant operator. Born at Manassa, CO, Dempsey died May 31, 1983, at New York, NY.

GAY AND LESBIAN PRIDE PARADE AND RALLY. June 24. Chicago, IL. Chicago's 32nd annual parade begins at 2 PM; the rally begins at 4:30 PM. Est attendance: 300,000. For info: Gay and Lesbian Pride Parade, 3712 N Broadway, PMB #544, Chicago, IL 60613. Phone: (773) 348-8243. E-mail: PrideChgo@aol.com. Web: www.chicagopridecalendar.org.

HELEN KELLER DEAF-BLINDNESS AWARENESS WEEK. June 24–30. Presidential proclamation since 1984. A week to observe the birth anniversary of Helen Keller who was born June 27, 1880. Annually, the full week that includes Helen Keller's birthday. For info: Library for Deaf Action, 2930 Craiglawn Rd, Silver Spring, MD 20904-1816. Phone: (301) 572-5168 (TTY). Fax: (301) 572-4134. E-mail: alhagemeyer@juno.com. Web: www.LibraryDeaf.com.

"HOPALONG CASSIDY" TV PREMIERE: ANNIVERSARY. June 24, 1949. A western series starring William Boyd in the title role as a hero who wore black and rode a white horse. The original episodes were segments edited from 66 movie features of Hopalong Cassidy and his sidekick, Red Connors (Edgar Buchanan). The films were so popular that Boyd produced episodes especially for TV.

INTERNATIONAL SIT-ON-THE-FRONT-PEW SUNDAY. June 24. An event that can be fun for the whole family, designed to fill churches from the front pew back so that clergy will feel encouraged that their people really do care and do want to see and hear them. Annually, the fourth Sunday in June. For info:

Don Hughes, General Manager, KJIL—Great Plains Christian Radio, PO Box 991, Meade, KS 67864. Phone: (316) 873-2991. Fax: (316) 873-2755. E-mail: kjil@kjil.com. Web: www.kjil.com.

ITALY: CALCIO FIORENTINO. June 24–28. Florence. Revival of a 16th-century football match in medieval costumes. Fireworks also June 24.

LATVIA: JOHN'S DAY (MIDSUMMER NIGHT DAY). June 24. The festival of Jani, which commemorates the summer solstice and the name day of (Janis) John, is one of Latvia's most ancient as well as joyous rituals. This festival is traditionally celebrated in the countryside, as it emphasizes fertility and the beginning of summer. Festivities begin June 23.

LEVITT PAVILION PERFORMING ARTS/MUSIC FESTIVAL. June 24–Aug 26. Levitt Pavilion, Westport, CT. 28th annual. Performing Arts/Music Festival conducts more than 50 nights of high-quality entertainment offered free to the general public. In addition, a few concerts are presented and a nominal admission is charged to raise money to underwrite the free nights of the festival. Est attendance: 60,000. For info: Freda Welsh, Exec Dir, Levitt Pavilion, 260 S Compo Rd, Westport, CT 06880. Phone: (203) 226-7600. Fax: (203) 226-2330. E-mail: levitt@ci.westport.ct.us. Web: www.levittpavilion.com.

LOG CABIN DAY. June 24. Michigan. Commemorates log cabins with tours, open houses and special festivities throughout the state. Est attendance: 4,000. For info: Virginia Handy, Sec/Treas, Log Cabin Soc of Michigan, 3503 Edwards Rd, Sodus, MI 49126. Phone: (616) 925-3836. E-mail: logcabincrafts@qtm.net. Web: www.qtm.net/logcabincrafts.

MACAU: MACAU DAY. June 24. Celebrates defeat of the Dutch invasion forces of 1622 and pays homage to patron saint of Macau, Saint John the Baptist.

NOME RIVER RAFT RACE. June 24. Nome, AK. Homemade rafts are paddled way down the 1–2 mile course on the Nome River. The victorious team claims first place recognition and the ownership of the fur-lined Honey-Bucket which is handed down from year to year. This event draws the entire town out for a fun afternoon at Nome's largest summer event. Annually, Sunday closest to summer solstice. Est attendance: 300. For info: Bering Sea Lions Club, Box 326, Nome, AK 99762. Phone: (907) 443-5904.

OLD TIME GERMAN SOCIAL. June 24. St. John's Lutheran Church, Isanti, MN. A German potluck with folk dancing or German games. Held at a German Lutheran Church now on the National Register of Historic Places. Annually, the fourth Sunday in June. For info: Valorie Arrowsmith, Isanti County Historical Soc, PO Box 525, Cambridge, MN 55008. Phone: (763) 689-4229. Fax: (763) 689-4229. E-mail: varrow2@ecenet.com.

ONIZUKA, ELLISON S.: 55th BIRTH ANNIVERSARY. June 24, 1946. Lieutenant Colonel Ellison S. Onizuka, 39-year-old aerospace engineer, was mission specialist aboard the Space Shuttle *Challenger* when it exploded Jan 28, 1986 (killing all aboard). Onizuka was born at Kealakekua, Kona, HI. See also: "*Challenger* Space Shuttle Explosion Anniversary" (Jan 28).

OPERA FESTIVAL OF NEW JERSEY. June 24–July 30. McCarter Theatre Center for the Performing Arts, Princeton, NJ. A professional organization founded in 1984 to present opera productions that are accessible to audiences of all ages and backgrounds. New Jersey's leading producer of professional opera, known for creating artistically focused new productions of opera that feature young American artists of excellence. Est attendance: 11,000. For info: Opera Festival of New Jersey, 228 Alexander St, Princeton, NJ 08540. Phone: (609) 279-1750. Fax: (609) 279-1832. E-mail: adminop@operafest.org. Web: www.operafest.org/nj.

PERU: COUNTRYMAN'S DAY. June 24. Half-day public holiday.

SAINT JOHN THE BAPTIST DAY. June 24. Celebrates the birth of the saint.

SINGING ON THE MOUNTAIN. June 24. Grandfather Mountain, Linville, NC. Modern and traditional gospel music featuring top groups and nationally known speakers. 77th annual sing. Annually, the fourth Sunday in June. Free admission. Est attendance: 12,000. For info: Grandfather Mountain, US Highway 221 N, PO Box 129, Linville, NC 28646. Phone: (828) 733-4337. Web: www.grandfather.com.

THORNTON, MATTHEW: DEATH ANNIVERSARY. June 24, 1803. Signer of the Declaration of Independence. Born at Ireland about 1714, he died at Newburyport, MA.

BIRTHDAYS TODAY

Nancy Allen, 51, actress (*Carrie, Blow Out, Robocop*), born New York, NY, June 24, 1950.

Claude Chabrol, 71, filmmaker (*La Femme Infidèle, The Cousins*), born Sardent, France, June 24, 1930.

Mick Fleetwood, 59, musician (drummer with Fleetwood Mac, "Dreams," "Don't Stop"), born Cornwall, England, June 24, 1942.

Phyllis George, 52, former sportscaster, former Miss America, born Denton, TX, June 24, 1949.

Juli Inkster, 41, golfer, born Santa Cruz, CA, June 24, 1960.

Michele Lee, 59, actress ("Knots Landing"), born Los Angeles, CA, June 24, 1942.

George Pataki, 56, Governor of New York (R), born Peekskill, NY, June 24, 1945.

Predrag "Preki" Radosavljevic, 38, soccer player, born Belgrade, Yugoslavia, June 24, 1963.

Peter Weller, 54, actor (*Robocop, Naked Lunch*), born Stevens Point, WI, June 24, 1947.

JUNE 25 — MONDAY

Day 176 — 189 Remaining

ARNOLD, HENRY H. "HAP": BIRTH ANNIVERSARY. June 25, 1886. US general and commander of the Army Air Force in all theaters throughout WWII, Arnold was born at Gladwyne, PA. Although no funds were made available, as early as 1938 Arnold was persuading the US aviation industry to step up manufacturing of airplanes. Production grew from 6,000 to 262,000 per year from 1940–44. He supervised pilot training and by 1944 Air Force personnel strength had grown to two million from a prewar high of 21,000. Made a full general in 1944, he became the US Air Force's first five-star general when the Air Force was made a separate military branch equal to the Army and Navy. Arnold died Jan 15, 1950, at Sonoma, CA.

BATTLE OF LITTLE BIGHORN: 125th ANNIVERSARY. June 25, 1876. Lieutenant Colonel George Armstrong Custer, leading military forces of more than 200 men, attacked an encampment of Sioux Indians led by Chiefs Sitting Bull and

Crazy Horse near Little Bighorn River, MT. Custer and all men in his immediate command were killed in the brief battle (about two hours) of Little Bighorn. One horse, named Comanche, is said to have been the only survivor among Custer's forces.

BHUTAN: NATIONAL DAY. June 25. National holiday observed.

CBS SENDS FIRST COLOR TV BROADCAST OVER THE AIR: 50th ANNIVERSARY. June 25, 1951. Columbia Broadcast System broadcast the first color television program. The four-hour program was carried by stations at New York City, Baltimore, Philadelphia, Boston and Washington, DC, although no color sets were owned by the public. At the time CBS, itself, owned fewer than 40 color receivers.

CENTRAL CHINA FLOOD: 10th ANNIVERSARY. June 25, 1991. The Huai River flooded its banks and ravaged major portions of the central Chinese province of Anhui. The poor agricultural region was devastated and approximately 3,000 people were killed. The Anhui region sustained enormous damages when the government ordered dikes broken and sluice gates opened in the rural area to prevent flooding of economically important rivers farther downstream.

CHINA: DRAGON BOAT FESTIVAL. June 25. An important Chinese observance, the Dragon Boat Festival commemorates a hero of ancient China, poet Qu Yuan, who drowned himself in protest against injustice and corruption. It is said that rice dumplings were cast into the water to lure fish away from the body of the martyr, and this is remembered by the eating of zhong zi, glutinous rice dumplings filled with meat and wrapped in bamboo leaves. Dragon boat races are held on rivers. The Dragon Boat Festival is observed in many countries by their Chinese populations. Also called Fifth Month Festival or Summer Festival. Annually, the fifth day of the fifth lunar month.

CIVIL WAR IN YUGOSLAVIA: 10th ANNIVERSARY. June 25, 1991. In an Eastern Europe freed from the iron rule of communism and the USSR, separatist and nationalist tensions suppressed for decades rose to a violent boiling point. The republics of Croatia and Slovenia declared their independence, sparking a fractious and bitter war that spread throughout what was formerly Yugoslavia. Ethnic rivalries between Serbians and Croatians began the military conflicts that spread to Slovenia, and in 1992 fighting began in Bosnia-Herzegovina between Serbians and ethnic Muslims. Although the new republics were recognized by the UN and sanctions passed to stop the fighting, it raged on through 1995 despite the efforts of UN peacekeeping forces.

ENGLAND: LAWN TENNIS CHAMPIONSHIPS AT WIMBLEDON. June 25–July 8. Wimbledon, London. World famous men's and women's singles and doubles championships for the most coveted titles in tennis. Advanced booking required—application forms for ticket lottery due by December. For info: All England Lawn Tennis and Croquet Club, Church Rd, Wimbledon, London, England SW19 5AE. Phone: (44) (181) 946-9122. Fax: (44) (181) 947-8752.

GILLARS, MILDRED "AXIS SALLY" E.: DEATH ANNIVERSARY. June 25, 1988. Mildred E. Gillars received the nickname "Axis Sally" during World War II, when she broadcast Nazi propaganda to US troops in Europe. An American citizen, born about 1900 at Portland, ME, she was arrested after the war and tried and convicted of treason. She was sentenced to 10 to 30 years in prison and fined $10,000. She was released after 12 years and later taught music in a convent school at Columbus, OH. She died June 25, 1988, at Columbus, OH.

	S	**M**	**T**	**W**	**T**	**F**	**S**
June						1	2
2001	3	4	5	6	7	8	9
	10	11	12	13	14	15	16
	17	18	19	20	21	22	23
	24	25	26	27	28	29	30

KIM CAMPBELL SWORN IN AS CANADIAN PRIME MINISTER: ANNIVERSARY. June 25, 1993. After winning the June 13 election to the leadership of the ruling Progressive-Conservative Party, Kim Campbell became Canada's 19th prime minister and its first woman prime minister. However, in the general election held Oct 25, 1993, the Liberal Party routed the Progressive-Conservatives in the worst defeat for a governing political party in Canada's 126-year history, reducing the former government's seats in the House of Commons from 154 to 2. Campbell was among those who lost their seats.

KOREA: TANO DAY. June 25. Fifth day of fifth lunar month. Summer food offered at the household shrine of the ancestors. Also known as Swing Day, since girls, dressed in their prettiest clothes, often compete in swinging matches. The Tano Festival usually lasts from the third through eighth day of the fifth lunar month: June 23–28.

KOREAN WAR BEGAN: ANNIVERSARY. June 25, 1950. Forces from northern Korea invaded southern Korea, beginning a civil war. US ground forces entered the conflict June 30. An armistice was signed at Panmunjom July 27, 1953, formally dividing the country into two—North Korea and South Korea.

MONTSERRAT: VOLCANO ERUPTS: ANNIVERSARY. June 25, 1997. After lying dormant for 400 years, the Soufriere Hills volcano began to come to life in July 1995. It finally erupted, wiping out the capital city of Plymouth and two-thirds of the rest of this lush Carribean island June 25, 1997. Two-thirds of the population relocated to other islands or to Great Britain.

MOZAMBIQUE: INDEPENDENCE DAY: ANNIVERSARY. June 25. National holiday. Commemorates independence from Portugal in 1975.

O'NEILL, ROSE CECIL: BIRTH ANNIVERSARY. June 25, 1874. Rose O'Neill was born at Wilkes-Barre, PA. Her career included work as an illustrator, author and doll designer, the latter gaining her commercial success with the Kewpie Doll. In 1910 *The Ladies Home Journal* devoted a full page to her Kewpie Doll designs, which were a marketing phenomenon for three decades. Died at Springfield, MO, Apr 6, 1944.

ORWELL, GEORGE: BIRTH ANNIVERSARY. June 25, 1903. English satirist, author of *Animal Farm, 1984* and other works, was born at Motihari, Bengal. George Orwell was the pseudonym of Eric Arthur Blair. Died at London, England, Jan 21, 1950.

PIONEER WEEK. June 25–29. Historic Jefferson College, Washington, MS. A hands-on program for children to learn through talks, demonstrations and activities how children lived 200 years ago (fee $25). Annually, in June. Est attendance: 20. For info: Anne L. Gray, Historian, Historic Jefferson College, PO Box 700, Washington, MS 39190. Phone: (601) 442-2901.

REVERE, ANNE: BIRTH ANNIVERSARY. June 25, 1903. American actress Anne Revere was born at New York, NY. She won an Academy Award for her supporting role in *National Velvet* (1944), but was barred from films for 20 years after she refused to testify before the House Committee on Un-American Activities in the 1950s. In 1960 she won a Tony Award for her role in *Toys in the Attic*. Revere died Dec 18, 1990, at Locust Valley, NY.

SEVEN DAYS CAMPAIGN BEGINS: ANNIVERSARY. June 25, 1862. In an effort to prevent an attack on Richmond, VA, Confederate General Robert E. Lee launched a series of engagements on this date that became known as the Seven Days Campaign. Battles at Oak Grove, Gaine's Mills, Garnett's Farm, Golding's Farm, Savage's Station, White Oak Swamp and finally Malvern Hill left more than 36,000 casualties on both sides. Despite losing the final assault at Malvern Hill, the Confederates succeeded in preventing the Union army from taking Richmond.

SLOVENIA: NATIONAL DAY: 10th ANNIVERSARY. June 25. Public holiday. Commemorates independence from the former Yugoslavia in 1991.

SUPREME COURT ABORTION NOTIFICATION RULING: ANNIVERSARY. June 25, 1990. The Supreme Court ruled, in a 5–4 decision, that it was unconstitutional for a state to require, without providing other options, that a minor notify both her parents before obtaining an abortion.

SUPREME COURT BANS SCHOOL PRAYER: ANNIVERSARY. June 25, 1962. The US Supreme Court ruled that a prayer read aloud in public schools violated the 1st Amendment's separation of church and state. The court again struck down a law pertaining to the First Amendment when it disallowed an Alabama law that permitted a daily one-minute period of silent meditation or prayer in public schools June 1, 1985. (Vote 6–3.)

SUPREME COURT UPHOLDS RIGHT TO DIE: ANNIVERSARY. June 25, 1990. In the case *Cruzan v Missouri*, the Supreme Court, in a 5–4 ruling, upheld the constitutional right of a person whose wishes are clearly known to refuse life-sustaining medical treatment.

TEXAS–OKLAHOMA JUNIOR GOLF TOURNAMENT. June 25–29. Wichita Falls, TX. More than 1,000 golfers 18 years old and under from 33 states and several foreign countries participate each year. Est attendance: 2,400. For info: Wichita Falls Conv & Visitors Bureau, 1000 5th St, Wichita Falls, TX 76301. Phone: (940) 716-5500. Fax: (940) 716-5509.

TWO YUGOSLAV REPUBLICS DECLARE INDEPENDENCE: 10th ANNIVERSARY. June 25, 1991. The republics of Slovenia and Croatia formally declared independence from Yugoslavia. The two northwestern republics did not, however, secede outright.

VIRGINIA: RATIFICATION DAY. June 25. 10th state to ratify the Constitution in 1788.

BIRTHDAYS TODAY

June Lockhart, 76, actress (mom in second "Lassie" series, "Lost in Space"), born New York, NY, June 25, 1925.

Sidney Lumet, 77, director (*12 Angry Men, Serpico, Dog Day Afternoon, Network*), born Philadelphia, PA, June 25, 1924.

George Michael, 38, singer (Wham!, "Wake Me Up Before You Go-Go," "Faith"), born Radlett, England, June 25, 1963.

Dikembe Mutombo, 35, basketball player, born Kinshasa, Zaire, June 25, 1966.

Willis Reed Jr, 59, basketball executive and former coach, Basketball Hall of Fame center, born Hico, LA, June 25, 1942.

Carly Simon, 56, singer ("You're So Vain," "Nobody Does It Better"), songwriter, born New York, NY, June 25, 1945.

Billy Wagner, 30, baseball player, born Tannersville, VA, June 25, 1971.

Jimmie Walker, 53, actor, comedian ("Good Times," "B.A.D. Cats"), born New York, NY, June 25, 1948.

JUNE 26 — TUESDAY
Day 177 — 188 Remaining

BAR CODE INTRODUCED: ANNIVERSARY. June 26, 1974. A committee formed in 1970 by US grocers and food manufacturers recommended in 1973 a Universal Product Code (i.e., a bar code) for supermarket items that would allow electronic scanning of prices. On this day in 1974 a pack of Wrigley's gum was swiped across the first checkout scanner at a supermarket in Troy, OH. Today bar codes are used to keep track of everything from freight cars to cattle.

BORDEN, SIR ROBERT LAIRD: BIRTH ANNIVERSARY. June 26, 1854. Canadian statesman and prime minister, born at Grand Pre, Nova Scotia. Died at Ottawa, June 10, 1937.

BUCK, PEARL SYDENSTRICKER: BIRTH ANNIVERSARY. June 26, 1892. American author (*The Good Earth*), noted authority on China, and humanitarian. Nobel Prize winner. Born at Hillsboro, WV. Died Mar 6, 1973, at Danby, VT.

CN TOWER: 25th OPENING ANNIVERSARY. June 26, 1976. Birthday of the world's tallest building and freestanding structure, the CN Tower, 1,815 feet, 5 inches high, at Toronto, Ontario, Canada. For info: CN Tower, 301 Front St W, Toronto, ON, Canada M5V 2T6. Phone: (416) 360-8500. Fax: (416) 601-4713.

DOUBLEDAY, ABNER: BIRTH ANNIVERSARY. June 26, 1819. Abner Doubleday served in the US Army during the Mexican War and the Seminole War in Florida prior to his service in the American Civil War. He was stationed at Charleston, SC, where he manned the first of Fort Sumter's guns to fire back at the Confederates. His service found him at the battle of Second Bull Run, Antietam, Fredricksburg and as a major general commanding a division at Gettysburg. A commission set up to investigate the origins of baseball by sporting goods manufacturer Albert Spalding credited Doubleday with inventing the game in the year 1839. Subsequent research has debunked the commission's finding. Abner Doubleday was born at Ballston Spa, NY, and died at Mendham, NJ, Jan 26, 1893.

ENGLAND: CITY OF LONDON FESTIVAL. June 26–July 19. London. Annual multi-arts festival held in some of the City's most historically interesting buildings, including St. Paul's Cathedral and the Tower of London. For info: City of London Festival, Bishopsgate Hall, 230 Bishopsgate, London, England EC2M 4HW. Phone: (44) 20 7377 0540. Fax: (44) 20 7377 1972. Web: www.colf.org.

FEDERAL CREDIT UNION ACT: ANNIVERSARY. June 26, 1934. Commemorates signing by President Franklin Delano Roosevelt of the Federal Credit Union Act, thus enabling the formation of credit unions anywhere in the US.

FLAG AMENDMENT DEFEATED: ANNIVERSARY. June 26, 1990. The Senate rejected a proposed constitutional amendment that would have permitted states to prosecute those who destroyed or desecrated American flags. Similar legislation continues to be introduced in Congress.

"THE GARRY MOORE SHOW" TV PREMIERE: ANNIVERSARY. June 26, 1950. Garry Moore hosted many programs which aired at various times; this daytime show proved longest lasting. Moore was the host, with his sidekick Durward Kirby, of a show blending singing, joking and talking with guests and regulars. Regulars included Ken Carson and Denise Lor. Guest performers included Don Adams, George Gobel, Don Knotts, Jonathan Winters, Leslie Uggams and Carol Burnett. Animals also appeared on the show.

"GUIDING LIGHT" TV PREMIERE: ANNIVERSARY. June 26, 1952. "Guiding Light," previously on radio, holds the title of longest-lasting daytime show and longest-lasting series. The Bauer family members were played by Charita Bauer as Bertha (Bert) Bauer, Theo Goetz as Papa Bauer and Lyle Sudrow as Bill Bauer. The Grants were Susan Douglas as Kathy Grant, James Lipton as Dr. Richard Grant and Alice Yourman as Laura Grant.

HAYMARKET PARDON: ANNIVERSARY. June 26, 1893. Illinois Governor John Peter Altgeld pardoned Samuel Fielden, Michael Schwab and Oscar Neebe, three of the anarchists who had been convicted in the violence connected with the Haymarket Riot on May 4, 1886. At a protest meeting at Haymarket Square an unknown individual threw a bomb which caused the death of several policemen. Eight anarchists were tried and convicted of the bombing. Of those one committed suicide the day before he was to be hanged; three were hanged; and Fielden, Schwab and Neebe were imprisoned. In 1893 the newly elected Altgeld, at the urging of Clarence Darrow, reviewed the transcripts of the trial of these men and concluded that they had been railroaded. The pardon was widely criticized. It was an act of political suicide for Altgeld.

MADAGASCAR: INDEPENDENCE DAY: ANNIVERSARY. June 26. National holiday. Commemorates independence from France in 1960.

MIDDLETON, ARTHUR: BIRTH ANNIVERSARY. June 26, 1742. American Revolutionary leader and signer of the Declaration of Independence, born near Charleston, SC. Died at Goose Creek, SC, Jan 1, 1787.

NATIONAL COLUMNIST'S DAY. June 26. Newspaper columnists, who bring you joy all year long, deserve to be celebrated by their readers at least once a year. Now you can send your favorite columnists, local or nationally syndicated, your own wishes for a Happy Columnist's Day and make him or her feel wonderful. Annually, the fourth Tuesday in June. For info: Jim Six, Columnist, *The Gloucester County Times*, 309 S Broad St, Woodbury, NJ 08096. Phone: (856) 845-3300. Fax: (856) 845-5480. E-mail: jimsix@reporters.net.

PIZARRO, FRANCESCO: DEATH ANNIVERSARY. June 26, 1541. Spanish conqueror of Peru, born at Extremadura, Spain, ca 1471. Pizarro died at Lima, Peru.

SAINT LAWRENCE SEAWAY DEDICATION: ANNIVERSARY. June 26, 1959. President Dwight D. Eisenhower and Queen Elizabeth II jointly dedicated the St. Lawrence Seaway in formal ceremonies held at St. Lambert, Quebec, Canada.

June 2001	S	M	T	W	T	F	S
						1	2
	3	4	5	6	7	8	9
	10	11	12	13	14	15	16
	17	18	19	20	21	22	23
	24	25	26	27	28	29	30

A project undertaken jointly by Canada and the US, the waterway (which provides access between the Atlantic Ocean and the Great Lakes) had been opened to traffic Apr 25, 1959.

UNITED NATIONS CHARTER SIGNED: ANNIVERSARY. June 26, 1945. The UN Charter was signed at San Francisco by representatives of 50 nations.

UNITED NATIONS: INTERNATIONAL DAY AGAINST DRUG ABUSE AND ILLICIT TRAFFICKING. June 26. Following a recommendation of the 1987 International Conference on Drug Abuse and Illicit Trafficking, the United Nations General Assembly (Res 42/112), expressed its determination to strengthen action and cooperation for an international society free of drug abuse and proclaimed June 26 as an annual observance to raise public awareness. For info: UN, Dept of Public Info, Public Inquiries Unit, RM GA-57, New York, NY 10017. Phone: (212) 963-4475. E-mail: inquiries@un.org.

UNITED NATIONS: INTERNATIONAL DAY IN SUPPORT OF VICTIMS OF TORTURE. June 26. For info: United Nations, Dept of Public Info, New York, NY 10017. Web: www.un.org.

WINDJAMMER DAYS. June 26–27. Boothbay Harbor, ME. Windjammer Days, the premier maritime event along the coast of Maine. Parades, concerts, waterfront food, interactive children's activities, arts showcase, live music, fireworks, visiting military vessels, windjammers sailing into harbor under full sail and much more. Fun for the whole family. Est attendance: 20,000. For info: Boothbay Harbor Chamber of Commerce, PO Box 356, Boothbay Harbor, ME 04538. Phone: (207) 633-2353. Fax: (207) 633-7448. E-mail: seamaine@boothbayharbor.com. Web: www.boothbayharbor.com.

ZAHARIAS, MILDRED "BABE" DIDRIKSON: BIRTH ANNIVERSARY. June 26, 1914. Born Mildred Ella Didrikson at Port Arthur, TX, the great athlete was nicknamed "Babe" after legendary baseball player Babe Ruth. She was named to the women's All-America basketball team when she was 16. At the 1932 Olympic Games, she won two gold medals and also set world records in the javelin throw and the 80-meter high hurdles; only a technicality prevented her from obtaining the gold in the high jump. Didrikson married professional wrestler George Zaharias in 1938, six years after she began playing golf casually. In 1946 Babe won the US Women's Amateur tournament, and in 1947 she won 17 straight golf championships and became the first American winner of the British Ladies' Amateur Tournament. Turning professional in 1948, she won the US Women's Open in 1950 and 1954, the same year she won the All-American Open. Babe also excelled in softball, baseball, swimming, figure skating, billiards—even football. In a 1950 Associated Press poll she was named the woman athlete of the first half of the 20th century. She died of cancer, Sept 27, 1956, at Galveston, TX.

BIRTHDAYS TODAY

Claudio Abbado, 68, conductor, born Milan, Italy, June 26, 1933.

Sean P. Hayes, 31, actor ("Will & Grace"), born Glen Ellyn, IL, June 26, 1970.

Chris Isaak, 45, actor (*That Thing You Do!*), born Stockton, CA, June 26, 1956.

Derek Jeter, 27, baseball player, born Pequannock, NJ, June 26, 1974.

Greg LeMond, 40, former cyclist, born Lakewood, CA, June 26, 1961.

Chris O'Donnell, 31, actor (*Dead Poet's Society, Scent of a Woman*), born Winnetka, IL, June 26, 1970.

Eleanor Parker, 79, actress (*The Sound of Music*), born Cedarsville, OH, June 26, 1922.

Charles Robb, 62, US senator (D, Virginia), married Lynda Bird Johnson (1967), born Phoenix, AZ, June 26, 1939.

Jason Schwartzman, 21, actor (*Rushmore*), born Los Angeles, CA, June 26, 1980.

Charlotte Zolotow, 86, author (*The Moon Was the Best, Peter and the Pigeons*), born Norfolk, VA, June 26, 1915.

JUNE 27 — WEDNESDAY
Day 178 — 187 Remaining

"CAPTAIN VIDEO AND HIS VIDEO RANGERS" TV PREMIERE: ANNIVERSARY. June 27, 1949. "Captain Video" was the first of several TV space shows. The show was set in the 22nd century and starred Richard Coogan as Captain Video, a human who led a squad of agents (the Video Rangers) fighting villains from their own and other worlds. Al Hodge later replaced Coogan. Also featured were Don Hastings and Hal Conklin, with Ernest Borgnine, Jack Klugman and Tony Randall as guest villains. A second series, "The Secret Files of Captain Video," began in 1953 but was dropped in 1955.

"DARK SHADOWS" TV PREMIERE: 35th ANNIVERSARY. June 27, 1966. This soap opera was completely different from all others because it featured vampires as main characters and had a dark, Gothic feel to it. The show focused on the Collins family living at Collinsport, ME, mainly Barnabas Collins (Jonathan Frid), a 200-year-old vampire. Other cast members included David Selby, Kate Jackson, Lara Parker and Jerry Lacy. Action shifted between the 1800s and the 1960s. This show was very popular with teenagers, and was remade as a short-lived series in 1991.

DECIDE TO BE MARRIED DAY. June 27. To focus attention on the joy of deciding to get married based on my poem *Decide to Be Married*, which I wrote to my husband the day we were married. "It's in the deciding to be united in love, to express your joyful oneness to every person you meet, and in every action you take and together a perfect marriage you'll make." For a copy of the poem: Barbara Gaughen-Muller, Pres, Gaughen Global Public Relations, 7456 Evergreen Dr, Santa Barbara, CA 93117. Phone: (805) 968-8567. Fax: (805) 968-5747. E-mail: barbara@rain.org.

DJIBOUTI: INDEPENDENCE DAY. June 27. National day. Commemorates independence from France in 1977.

FINLAND: KUOPIO DANCE AND MUSIC FESTIVAL. June 27–July 3. Kuopio, Finland. Some 70 events centering on classical ballet, dance theatre and jazz dance, plus other types depending on the theme for the festival. World-renowned dance and music companies; seminars, lectures, exhibits and films; selection of dance courses with internationally known dance teachers. Est attendance: 45,000. For info: Finnish Tourist Board, 655 Third Ave, New York, NY 10017. Phone: (212) 885-9700 or (358) (17) 261-8103. Fax: (358) (17) 261-1990. E-mail: dance.festival@kolumbus.fi. Web: www.kuopiodancefestival.fi.

HAPPY BIRTHDAY TO "HAPPY BIRTHDAY TO YOU." June 27, 1859. The melody of probably the most often sung song in the world, "Happy Birthday to You," was composed by Mildred J. Hill, a schoolteacher born at Louisville, KY, on this date. Her younger sister, Patty Smith Hill, was the author of the lyrics which were first published in 1893 as "Good Morning to All," a classroom greeting published in the book *Song Stories for the Sunday School*. The lyrics were amended in 1924 to include a stanza beginning "Happy Birthday to You." Now it is sung somewhere in the world every minute of the day. Although the authors are believed to have earned very little from the song, reportedly it later generated about $1 million a year for its copyright owner. The song is expected to enter public domain upon expiration of copyright in 2010. Mildred Hill died at Chicago, IL, June 5, 1916 without knowing that her melody would become the world's most popular song. See also: "Hill, Patty Smith: Birth Anniversary" (Mar 27).

HEARN, LAFCADIO: BIRTH ANNIVERSARY. June 27, 1850. Author, born on the Greek island of Santa Maura. Hearn, who had been a newspaper reporter at Cincinnati, OH, and at New Orleans, LA, went to Japan in 1890 as a magazine writer. Deeply attracted to the country and to the Japanese people, he stayed there as a writer and teacher until his death at Okubo, Japan, Sept 26, 1904. Though his writings are little remembered in America, he remains a popular figure in Japan, where his books are still used, especially in language classes. His home at Matsue is a tourist shrine.

KELLER, HELEN: BIRTH ANNIVERSARY. June 27, 1880. Born at Tuscumbia, AL, Helen Keller was left deaf and blind by a disease she contracted at 18 months of age. With the help of her teacher, Anne Sullivan, she graduated from college and had a career as an author and lecturer. She died June 1, 1968, at Westport, CT.

"LOVING" TV PREMIERE: ANNIVERSARY. June 27, 1983. This half-hour daytime serial was first introduced in prime time as a two-hour movie the day before its daytime premiere. The show takes place at Alden University in the town of Corinth. Famous alumni include Randolph Mantooth and Luke Perry. The show was renamed "The City" in 1996 and shifted locale to Soho in New York City.

MOON PHASE: FIRST QUARTER. June 27. Moon enters First Quarter phase at 11:19 PM, EDT.

NATIONAL HIV TESTING DAY. June 27. To help people to be more in control of their health. For info: Natl Assn of People with AIDS, 1413 K St NW, 7th Fl, Washington, DC 20005. Phone: 202-898-0414. E-mail: napwa@napwa.org. Web: www.napwa.org.

NATIONAL SQUARE DANCE CONVENTION. June 27–30. Anaheim Convention Center, Anaheim, CA. 50th annual convention. For info:. Phone: (562) 988-2275. Fax: (562) 988-2275. Web: home.earthlink.net/~zebrow/NSDC_50th/.

PARNELL, CHARLES STEWART: BIRTH ANNIVERSARY. June 27, 1846. Irish nationalist leader and home-rule advocate born at Avondale, County Wicklow, Ireland. Politically ruined as a result of an affair with Katherine O'Shea, the estranged wife of a member of Parliament. She was divorced by her husband (who named Parnell correspondent), and on June 25, 1891, she married Parnell. Less than a month later Parnell was defeated in a by-election. He made his last public speech Sept 27, 1891, and died in the arms of his wife, at Brighton, Oct 6, 1891. Reportedly he was given "a magnificent funeral" by the city of Dublin, where he was buried. The anniversary of Parnell's death is observed by some as Ivy Day when a sprig of ivy is worn on the lapel to remember him. See also: "Ivy Day" (Oct 6).

SMITH, JOSEPH, JR, AND HYRUM: DEATH ANNIVERSARY. June 27, 1844. The founding prophet of The Church of Jesus Christ of Latter-day Saints and his brother Hyrum were shot to death by an armed mob in Carthage, IL. At the time, Joseph Smith was the presidential candidate of the National Reform Party, the first US presidential candidate to be assassinated. Joseph Smith was born at Sharon, VT, Dec 3, 1805; Hyrum Smith was born at Sharon, VT,

SMITHSON, JAMES: DEATH ANNIVERSARY. June 27, 1829. Scientist and founder of the Smithsonian Institution, James Smithson was born at Paris, France in 1765 (exact date unknown). His will, dated Oct 23, 1826, bequeathed his great wealth to a nation he had never visited, to found "at Washington under the name of the Smithsonian Institution, establishment for the increase and diffusion of knowledge among men." In spite of opposition, the Congress approved, on Aug 10, 1846, an act to establish the Smithsonian Institution. Most of Smithson's personal documents, books and collections were destroyed by fire in 1865. Smithson died at Genoa, Italy, his remains were removed from there to Washington, DC, in 1904.

SPACE MILESTONE: *COLUMBIA STS-4* (US). June 27, 1982. Shuttle *Columbia* launched from Kennedy Space Center, FL, with astronauts K. Mattingly and Henry Hartsfield along with 22,000 lbs of cargo, landed at Edwards Air Force Base, California, on July 4.

SPECIAL RECREATION FOR DISABLED DAY. June 27. To focus attention on the recreation abilities, aspirations, needs and rights of people with disabilities—see Special Recreation Week (June 27–July 4). For info: John A. Nesbitt, EdD, Pres, SRDI-Special Recreation for disABLED Intl, 362 Koser Ave, Iowa City, IA 52246-3038. Phone: (319) 337-7578. E-mail: john-nesbitt@uiowa.edu.

SPECIAL RECREATION WEEK. June 27–July 4. To focus attention on the recreation rights, needs, aspirations and abilities of people with disabilities—infants, children, youth, young adults, adults and seniors; living in the community, in residential services and in institutions; in 40 types of play, recreation and leisure pursuits. (Special Recreation Day: June 27.) For info: John A. Nesbitt, Pres, SRDI-Special Recreation for disABLED Intl, 362 Koser Ave, Iowa City, IA 52246-3038. Phone: (319) 337-7578. E-mail: john-nesbitt@uiowa.edu.

THURGOOD MARSHALL RESIGNS FROM SUPREME COURT: 10th ANNIVERSARY. June 27, 1991. Signaling an end to the era of a liberal Supreme Court, Associate Justice Thurgood Marshall announced his resignation from the United States Supreme Court, effective once his successor was confirmed by the US Senate. Marshall was a pioneering civil rights lawyer who helped lead the fight to end racial segregation and served as US Solicitor General prior to his appointment to the high court by President Lyndon Johnson in 1967 as the first black ever to sit on the Supreme Court. As an attorney for the NAACP, he successfully argued the case of *Brown v Board of Education* before the Supreme Court, ending the doctrine of "separate but equal." Marshall's 24-year tenure on the bench was marked by his strong liberal voice championing the rights of criminal defendants and defending abortion rights, his opposition to the death penalty and his commitment to civil rights. On July 1, 1991, President George Bush selected Clarence Thomas, a conservative black jurist, to succeed Marshall. See also: "Marshall, Thurgood: Birth Anniversary" (July 2).

BIRTHDAYS TODAY

Isabelle Adjani, 46, actress (*The Story of Adele H., Camille Claudel*), born Paris, France, June 27, 1955.

Bruce Babbitt, 63, US Secretary of the Interior (Clinton administration), born Los Angeles, CA, June 27, 1938.

Julia Duffy, 50, actress ("Newhart," "Designing Women"), born St. Paul, MN, June 27, 1951.

Shirley-Anne Field, 63, actress (*Alfie, My Beautiful Laundrette, Getting It Right*), born London, England, June 27, 1938.

Norma Kamali, 56, fashion designer, born New York, NY, June 27, 1945.

Captain Kangaroo (Bob Keeshan), 74, TV personality, born Lynbrook, NY, June 27, 1927.

Tobey Maguire, 26, actor (*Pleasantville, The Cider House Rules*), born Santa Monica, CA, June 27, 1975.

Anna Moffo, 67, opera singer, born Wayne, PA, June 27, 1934.

Jason Patric, 35, actor (*Speed 2, Sleepers*), born Queens, NY, June 27, 1966.

H. Ross Perot, 71, philanthropist, businessman, 1992 and 1996 presidential candidate, born Texarkana, TX, June 27, 1930.

Chuck Connors Person, 37, basketball player, born Brantley, AL, June 27, 1964.

June *2001*	S	M	T	W	T	F	S
						1	2
	3	4	5	6	7	8	9
	10	11	12	13	14	15	16
	17	18	19	20	21	22	23
	24	25	26	27	28	29	30

JUNE 28 — THURSDAY
Day 179 — 186 Remaining

"AMOS 'N' ANDY" TV PREMIERE: 50th ANNIVERSARY. June 28, 1951. This show was based on the popular radio show about black characters played by white dialecticians Freeman Gosden and Charles Correll. In fact, it was the first dramatic series with an all-black cast. The cast included Tim Moore, Spencer Williams, Alvin Childress, Ernestine Wade, Amanda Randolph, Johnny Lee, Nick O'Demus and Jester Hairston. The series was widely syndicated until pressure from civil rights groups, who claimed the show was stereotypical and prejudicial, caused CBS to withdraw it from syndication.

BISCAYNE NATIONAL PARK ESTABLISHED: ANNIVERSARY. June 28, 1980. Including the coral reefs and waters of Biscayne Bay and the area of the Atlantic Ocean which surrounds the northernmost Florida Keys, Biscayne National Monumnet was authorized Oct 18, 1968. It became a national park in 1980.

BOSTON HARBORFEST. June 28–July 4. Boston, MA. Waterfront festival with fireworks, concerts, chowder competition, Children's Day and much more. Est attendance: 2,000,000. For info: Boston Harborfest, 45 School St, Boston, MA 02108. Phone: (617) 227-1528. Fax: (617) 227-1886. Web: www.bostonharborfest.com.

COLORADO SHAKESPEARE FESTIVAL. June 28–Aug 20 (Vail Performances Aug 24–26). Boulder, CO. One of top Shakespeare festivals in the country. Est attendance: 43,000. For info: Richard Devin, Producing Artistic Dir, Colorado Shakespeare Festival Admin Office, University of Colorado, Campus Box 277, Boulder, CO 80309-0277. Phone: (303) 492-1527. Fax: (303) 492-6121. E-mail: shakes@colorado.edu. Web: www.coloshakes.org.

COMECON AND WARSAW PACT DISBAND: 10th ANNIVERSARY. June 28, 1991. The last vestiges of the Cold War–era Soviet bloc, the Council for Mutual Economic Assistance (COMECON) and the Warsaw Pact, formally disbanded on June 28 and July 1, 1991, respectively.

CYPRUS: SAINT PAUL'S FEAST. June 28–29. Kato Paphos, Cyprus. Religious festivities at Kato Paphos at which the archbishop officiates. Procession of the icon of Saint Paul through the streets.

HUTCHFEST. June 28–July 4. Hutchinson, KS. Family festival with free entertainment, games, activities, arts and crafts, prairie heritage and "name entertainment." Est attendance: 60,000. For info: Dan Popp. Phone: (316) 665-6651. Web: www.hutchchamber.com.

JUSTICE BYRON R. WHITE RETIRES: ANNIVERSARY. June 28, 1993. After 31 years of serving on the Supreme Court, Justice Byron R. White retired from the Supreme Court. President William Clinton nominated Ruth Bader Ginsburg to fill the vacated seat.

MAASS, CLARA: 125th BIRTH ANNIVERSARY. June 28, 1876. Commemorates the birth in 1876 of Clara Louise Maass, the heroic nurse who gave her life in the yellow fever experiments of 1901. Created by the Clara Maass Foundation. Maass died at Havana, Cuba, Aug 24, 1901.

MANISTEE NATIONAL FOREST FESTIVAL. June 28–July 2. Manistee, MI. Grand Parade, a Venetian boat parade, fireworks over Lake Michigan and children's parade. Tours of historic buildings, Lake Bluff Audubon Center, the Big Manistee River by canoe, North Country Trail and other local attractions. Juried arts and crafts show, band concerts, entertainment, flea market, races, sports tournament and many other special events. Annually, on a weekend near the Fourth of July. Est attendance: 40,000. For info: Manistee Area Chamber of Commerce, 50 Filer St, Ste 224, Manistee, MI 49660. Phone: (231) 723-2575 or (800) 288-2286. E-mail: chamber@manistee.com. Web: www.manistee.com/~edo/chamber/

MAYER, MARIA GOEPPERT: 95th BIRTH ANNIVERSARY. June 28, 1906. German-American physicist Maria Goeppert Mayer was born at Kattowitz, Germany. A participant in the Manhattan Project, she worked on the separation of uranium isotopes for the atomic bomb. Mayer became the first American woman to win the Nobel Prize when she shared the 1963 prize for physics with J. Hans Daniel Jensen and Eugene P. Wigner for their explanation of the atomic nucleus, known as the nuclear shell theory. Mayer died Feb 20, 1972, at San Diego, CA.

MERAMEC COMMUNITY FAIR. June 28–30. Fairgrounds, Sullivan, MO. 15th annual. Ticket price includes big-name entertainment, huge carnival, truck and tractor pulls, arts and crafts, motorcross, kid's games, FFA-4H displays, pageants, demo derby and commercial booths. Est attendance: 40,000. For info: Meramec Community Fair, PO Box 386, Sullivan, MO 63080. Phone: (573) 860-2861.

MONDAY HOLIDAY LAW: ANNIVERSARY. June 28, 1968. President Lyndon B. Johnson approved Public Law 90–363, which amended section 6103(a) of title 5, United States Code, establishing Monday observance of Washington's Birthday, Memorial Day, Labor Day, Columbus Day and Veterans Day. The new holiday law took effect Jan 1, 1971. Veterans Day observance subsequently reverted to its former observance date, Nov 11. See individual holidays for further details.

RADNER, GILDA: 55th BIRTH ANNIVERSARY. June 28, 1946. Actress, comedian ("Saturday Night Live," *Hanky Panky*), born at Detroit, MI. Died May 20, 1989, at Los Angeles, CA.

ROUSSEAU, JEAN-JACQUES: BIRTH ANNIVERSARY. June 28, 1712. Philosopher, born at Geneva, Switzerland. Died July 2, 1778, at Ermenonville, France. "Man is born free," he wrote in *The Social Contract*, "and everywhere he is in chains."

RUBENS, PETER PAUL: BIRTH ANNIVERSARY. June 28, 1577. Flemish painter and diplomat born at Siegen, Westphalia. Died of gout at Antwerp, Belgium, May 30, 1640.

SIEGE OF VICKSBURG: ANNIVERSARY. June 28, 1862. The siege of the Confederate city of Vicksburg, MS, began in earnest when Admiral David Farragut succeeded in taking a fleet past the Mississippi River stronghold on this date. The siege continued for over a year.

ST. IGNACE AUTO SHOW. June 28–30. St. Ignace, MI. 26th anniversary. Parade, cruise night and swap meet. Entries from 25 states and Canada. Est attendance: 107,000. For info: Edward K. Reavie, 268 Hillcrest Blvd, St. Ignace, MI 49781. Phone: (906) 643-8087 or (906) 643-1USA. Fax: (906) 643-9784. E-mail: edreavie@nostalgia-prod.com. Web: www.nostalgia-prod.com or www.auto-shows.com.

STONEWALL RIOT: ANNIVERSARY. June 28, 1969. Early in the morning of June 28, 1969, the clientele of a gay bar, the Stonewall Inn at New York City, rioted after the club was raided by police. The riot was followed by several days of demonstrations. Stonewall is now recognized as the start of the gay liberation movement.

SUMMERFEST. June 28–July 8. Milwaukee, WI. Music festival. Est attendance: 900,000. For info: Mktg Dir, Summerfest, 200 N Harbor Dr, Milwaukee, WI 53202. Phone: (800) 273-3378 or (414) 273-2680. Web: www.summerfest.com.

TREATY OF VERSAILLES: ANNIVERSARY. June 28, 1919. The signing of the Treaty of Versailles at Versailles, France, formally ended WWI.

US SENIOR OPEN (GOLF) CHAMPIONSHIP. June 28–July 1. Salem Country Club, Peabody, MA. For info: US Golf Assn, Golf House, PO Box 708, Championship Dept, Far Hills, NJ 07931. Phone: (908) 234-2300. Fax: (908) 234-9687. E-mail: usga@ix.netcom.com. Web: www.usga.org.

BIRTHDAYS TODAY

Kathy Bates, 53, actress (Oscar for *Misery; Fried Green Tomatoes*), born Memphis, TN, June 28, 1948.

Donald Edward (Don) Baylor, 52, baseball manager, former player, born Austin, TX, June 28, 1949.

Danielle Brisebois, 32, actress ("All in the Family," "Knots Landing"), born Brooklyn, NY, June 28, 1969.

Mel Brooks (Melvyn Kaminsky), 73, actor, director (*The Producers, Blazing Saddles*), born New York, NY, June 28, 1928.

John Cusack, 35, actor (*Say Anything, The Grifters, Bullets Over Broadway*), born Chicago, IL, June 28, 1966.

Bruce Davison, 55, actor (*Ulzana's Raid, Longtime Companion, Six Degrees of Separation*), born Philadelphia, PA, June 28, 1946.

John Albert Elway, 41, former football player, born Port Angeles, WA, June 28, 1960.

Mark Eugene Grace, 37, baseball player, born Winston-Salem, NC, June 28, 1964.

Alice Krige, 47, actress (*Chariots of Fire, Barfly*), born Upington, South Africa, June 28, 1954.

Carl Levin, 67, US Senator (D, Michigan), born Detroit, MI, June 28, 1934.

Mary Stuart Masterson, 35, actress (*Fried Green Tomatoes, Benny & Joon*), born New York, NY, June 28, 1966.

JUNE 29 — FRIDAY
Day 180 — 185 Remaining

BLACK HILLS HERITAGE FESTIVAL. June 29–July 3. Memorial Park, Rapid City, SD. Umbrella festival with Arts Fair, Folk Art Fest, free entertainment, Literature Fest, food concessions, history tent. Annually, fourth of July weekend or weekend closest to the fourth. Est attendance: 35,000. For info: Laura Neubert, Heritage Festival, 1327 State St, Rapid City, SD 57702. Phone: (605) 341-5714.

CANADA: NOVA SCOTIA INTERNATIONAL TATTOO. June 29–July 7. Halifax, NS. The Tattoo combines more than 2,000 international military and civilian performers in bands, singing, dancing, marching, gymnastics and comedy. Annually, June 29–July 7. Est attendance: 60,000. For info: The Nova Scotia Intl Tattoo, PO Box 3233 South, Halifax, NS, Canada B3J 3H5. Phone: (902) 420-1114. Fax: (902) 423-6629. E-mail: info@nstattoo.ca. Web: www.nstattoo.ca.

COMPUFEST®. June 29–July 1. Orlando, FL. Annual gathering of investors who are interested in the NAIC way of investing. Seminars and computer labs are available. Windows and Macintosh programs are offered. For info: Natl Assn of Investors Corp, 711 W Thirteen Mile Rd, Madison Heights, MI 48071. Phone: (877) ASK-NAIC. Fax: (248) 583-4880. Web: www.better-investing.org.

DEATH PENALTY BANNED: ANNIVERSARY. June 29, 1972. In a decision that spared the lives of 600 individuals then sitting on death row, the US Supreme Court, in a 5–4 vote, found capital punishment a violation of the Eighth Amendment, which prohibits "cruel and unusual punishment." Overruling themselves, the court determined on July 2, 1976, that the death penalty was not cruel and unusual punishment and on Oct 4, 1976, lifted the ban on the death penalty in murder cases. On Jan 15, 1977, Gary Gilmore became first individual executed in the US in more than 10 years.

ELVIS PRESLEY BOULEVARD NAMED: 30th ANNIVERSARY. June 29, 1971. The City of Memphis, TN, voted to name a road in honor of Elvis—a 12-mile portion of the highway that passes Graceland.

ENGLAND: EXETER FESTIVAL. June 29–July 15. Various venues, Exeter, Devon. Major annual music and arts festival featuring the best of British arts and culture. Est attendance: 37,000. For info: Lesley Maynard, Fest Organizer, Exeter City Council, Festival Office, Paris Street, Exeter, England EX1 1JJ. Phone: (44) (139) 226-5200. Fax: (44) (139) 226-5265. Web: www.thisis exeter.com.

June 2001	S	M	T	W	T	F	S
						1	2
	3	4	5	6	7	8	9
	10	11	12	13	14	15	16
	17	18	19	20	21	22	23
	24	25	26	27	28	29	30

ENGLAND: SHREWSBURY INTERNATIONAL MUSIC FESTIVAL. June 29–July 6. Shrewsbury, Shropshire. Noncompetitive festival that brings together music and dance groups from all over the world. Est attendance: 2,700. For info: Nichola Stokes, Fest Mgr, Festival Office, Victoria Court, Ste 3, Bexton Rd, Knutsford, Cheshire, England WA16 OPF. Phone: (44) (156) 565-2667. Fax: (44) (156) 565-2062. E-mail: WSconcerts@ aol.com. Web: www.quikpage.com/C/concerttours.

GOETHALS, GEORGE WASHINGTON: BIRTH ANNIVERSARY. June 29, 1858. American engineer and army officer, chief engineer of the Panama Canal and first civil governor of the Canal Zone, born at Brooklyn, NY. Died at New York, NY, Jan 21, 1928.

ILLINOIS SHAKESPEARE FESTIVAL. June 29–Aug 12 (tentative). Ewing Manor, Bloomington, IL. Productions of three Shakespeare plays presented under the stars on alternating nights. Est attendance: 12,500. For info: Illinois Shakespeare Festival, Campus Box 5700, Normal, IL 61790-5700. Phone: (309) 438-2535. E-mail: theatre@oratmail.cfa.ilstu.edu. Web: www.orat .ilstu.edu/shakespeare.

INTERSTATE HIGHWAY SYSTEM BORN: ANNIVERSARY. June 29, 1956. President Dwight Eisenhower signed a bill providing $33.5 billion for highway construction. It was the biggest public works program in history.

LATHROP, JULIA C.: BIRTH ANNIVERSARY. June 29, 1858. A pioneer in the battle to establish child-labor laws, Julia C. Lathrop was the first woman member of the Illinois State Board of Charities and in 1900 was instrumental in establishing the first juvenile court in the US. In 1912 President Taft named Lathrop chief of the newly created Children's Bureau, then part of the US Dept of Commerce and Labor. In 1925 she became a member of the Child Welfare Committee of the League of Nations. Born at Rockford, IL, died there Apr 15, 1932.

LAURA INGALLS WILDER PAGEANT. June 29–July 1. (also July 6–8 and 13–15) De Smet, SD. An outdoor pageant on the natural prairie stage depicting "Medley of Memories," historically based on Laura Ingalls Wilder's life. Est attendance: 10,000. For info: The Laura Ingalls Wilder Pageant, PO Box 154, De Smet, SD 57231. Phone: (605) 692-2108.

MAYO, WILLIAM JAMES: BIRTH ANNIVERSARY. June 29, 1861. American surgeon, one of the Mayo brothers, establishers of the Mayo Foundation, born at LeSeuer, MN. Died July 28, 1939, at Rochester, MN.

MESA VERDE NATIONAL PARK ESTABLISHED: 95th ANNIVERSARY. June 29, 1906. Area of southwest Colorado established as a national park. For further park info: Mesa Verde Natl Park, Mesa Verde Natl Park, CO 81330.

OLYMPIC NATIONAL PARK ESTABLISHED: ANNIVERSARY. June 29, 1938. Washington's Mount Olympus National Monument, proclaimed Mar 2, 1909, was transferred from the US Dept of Agriculture's Forest Service to the National Park Service Aug 10, 1933, then established as Olympic National Park five years later. For further park info: Olympic Natl Park, 600 E Park Ave, Port Angeles, WA 98362.

PENNSYLVANIA DUTCH KUTZTOWN FOLK FESTIVAL. June 29–July 8. Summit Station, PA. To perpetuate the life and customs of the Pennsylvania Dutch people. Working craftspeople, special events and 800 handmade quilts. Est attendance: 75,000. For info: Festival Associates, 3760 Layfield Rd, Pennsburg, PA 18073. Phone: (215) 679-9610.

PETER AND PAUL DAY. June 29. Feast day for Saint Peter and Saint Paul. Commemorates dual martyrdom of Christian apostles Peter (by crucifixion) and Paul (by beheading) during persecution by Roman Emperor Nero. Observed since third century.

SAINT PETER'S DAY. June 29. Antakya, Turkey. Peter first preached Christianity at this place. Ceremonies at Saint Peter's Grotto, early Christian cave near Antakya.

SALEM FAIR AND EXPOSITION. June 29–July 8. Salem Civic Center Complex, Salem, VA. Fastest-growing and second largest state fair in Virginia. Wholesome family fun. Featuring agricultural exhibits, crafts, food, games and carnival rides. Est attendance: 300,000. For info: John Saunders, Salem Civic Center, Box 886, Salem, VA 24153. Phone: (540) 375-3004 or (540) 375-4013. Fax: (540) 375-4011. Web: www.salem-va.com.

SEYCHELLES: INDEPENDENCE DAY. June 29. National holiday. Gained independence from Great Britain in 1976.

SHOW-ME STATE CHAMPIONSHIP BBQ COOKOFF. June 29–30. Delta Fairgrounds, Kennett, MO. Event features live music, a carnival, demolition derby and is highlighted by a tasty barbeque. Annually, the last weekend in June. Est attendance: 1,000. For info: Kennett Jaycees, PO Box 165, Kennett, MO 63857. Phone: (573) 888-3808.

TRUMBULL DAYS. June 29–30. Hillcrest Middle School and Trumbull High School, New Haven, CT. 150 vendors, rides, puppet and magic shows for the children. Annually, the last Friday and Saturday in June. For info: Trumbull Days, (203) 377-2858 or Greater New Haven Conv & Visitors Bureau, 59 Elm St, New Haven, CT 06510. Phone: (203) 777-8550 or (800) 332-STAY. Fax: (203) 782-7755. Web: www.newhavencvb.org or www.trumbullct.com.

BIRTHDAYS TODAY

Gary Busey, 57, musician, actor ("The Texas Wheelers," *The Buddy Holly Story*), born Goose Creek, TX, June 29, 1944.

Theo Fleury, 33, hockey player, born Oxbow, Saskatchewan, Canada, June 29, 1968.

Fred Grandy, 53, former congressman (R, Iowa), former actor ("Love Boat"), born Sioux City, IA, June 29, 1948.

Harmon Clayton Killebrew, 65, Baseball Hall of Fame third baseman, born Payette, ID, June 29, 1936.

Sharon Lawrence, 39, actress ("Fired Up," "NYPD Blue"), born Charlotte, NC, June 29, 1962.

Ruth Warrick, 86, actress (*Citizen Kane*, "All My Children"), born St. Louis, MO, June 29, 1915.

JUNE 30 — SATURDAY

Day 181 — 184 Remaining

BEARTOOTH RUN. June 30. Red Lodge, MT. 8.2-mile or 4.4-mile foot race up scenic Beartooth Pass. Race will start at 7,000 feet and finish at 9,000 feet. Annually, last Saturday in June. Est attendance: 350. For info: Joan Cline, Box 988, Red Lodge, MT 59068. Phone: (406) 446-1718. E-mail: information@redlodge.com. Web: www.redlodge.com.

CHARLES BLONDIN'S CONQUEST OF NIAGARA FALLS: ANNIVERSARY. June 30, 1859. Charles Blondin, a French acrobat and aerialist (whose real name was Jean François Gravelet), in view of a crowd estimated at more than 25,000 persons, walked across Niagara Falls on a tightrope. The walk required only about five minutes. On separate occasions he crossed blindfolded, pushing a wheelbarrow, carrying a man on his back and even on stilts. Blondin was born Feb 28, 1824, at St. Omer, France, and died at London, England, Feb 19, 1897.

CONGO (KINSHASA): INDEPENDENCE DAY: ANNIVERSARY. June 30. National holiday. The Democratic Republic of Congo was previously known as Zaire. Commemorates independence from Belgium in 1960.

THE DAM EXPERIENCE. June 30 (tentative, rain date July 1). Truman Dam, Warsaw, MO. Gigantic fireworks display viewed from land and boat. Est attendance: 10,000. For info: Warsaw Area Chamber of Commerce, PO Box 264, Warsaw, MO 65355. Phone: (800) WARSAW-4. E-mail: warsawcc@iland.net. Web: www.warsawmo.org.

DESCENDANTS DAY. June 30. The day in each year when all the world's citizens take an accounting of their activities during the preceding year which will impact our descendants and our neighbors across time. Annually, last Sunday in June. For info: Charles A. Howell, Trust for the Future, 2704 12th Ave S, Nashville, TN 37204. Phone: (615) 297-2269. Fax: (615) 298-1611. E-mail: chowell@edge.net. Web: trustforthefuture.org/.

ENGLAND: CHELTENHAM INTERNATIONAL FESTIVAL OF MUSIC. June 30–July 15. Cheltenham, Gloucestershire. The best of contemporary British music including symphony and chamber music, opera, dance, and jazz. Est attendance: 32,000. For info: Mr Toby Smith, Festival Organiser, Town Hall, Imperial Square, Cheltenham, Gloucestershire, England GL50 1QA. Phone: (44) (1242) 52-1621. Fax: (44) (1242) 57-3902. E-mail: townhall@cheltenham.gov.uk. Web: www.cheltenhamfestivals.co.uk.

FIREFALL. June 30. Springfield/Branson Regional Airport, Springfield, MO. The Springfield Symphony provides live music choreographed to fireworks. Also other live entertainment and concert performances. Est attendance: 60,000. For info: Springfield Convention & Visitors Bureau, 3315 E Battlefield Rd, Springfield, MO 65804. Phone: (417) 881-5300 or (800) 678-8767. Web: www.springfieldmo.org.

FREEDOM DAYS. June 30–July 4. Farmington, NM. Celebration with a variety of special events, including spectacular fireworks, food fair, auction, gem and mineral show, parade, triathlon. Est attendance: 65,000. For info: Farmington Conv and Visitors Bureau, 3041 E Main St, Farmington, NM 87402. Phone: (800) 448-1240 or (505) 326-7602. Fax: (505) 327-0577. E-mail: fmncvb@cyberport.com. Web: www.farmingtonnm.org.

GUATEMALA: ARMED FORCES DAY. June 30. Guatemala observes public holiday.

INDEPENDENCE DAY CELEBRATION. June 30–July 1. Suwannee Music Park, Live Oak, FL. Mixture of fun, music and fireworks. Est attendance: 8,000. For info: James Cornett, Spirit of the Suwannee Music Park, 3076 95th Dr, Live Oak, FL 32060. Phone: (904) 364-1683. Fax: (904) 364-2998. E-mail: spirit@musicliveshere.com. Web: www.musicliveshere.com.

LAST HURRAH FOR BRITISH HONG KONG: ANNIVERSARY. June 30, 1997. The crested flag of the British Crown Colony was officially lowered at midnight and replaced by a new flag (marked by the bauhinia flower) representing China's sovereignty and the official transfer of power. Though Britain owned Hong Kong in perpetuity, the land areas surrounding the city were leased from China and the lease expired July 1, 1997. Rather than renegotiate a new lease, Britain ceded its claim to Hong Kong.

LEAP SECOND ADJUSTMENT TIME. June 30. June 30 is one of the times that has been favored for the addition or subtraction of a second from our clock time (to coordinate atomic and astronomical time). The determination to adjust is made by the International Earth Rotation Service of the International Bureau of Weights and Measures, at Paris, France. See also: "Note about Leap Seconds" (see Contents).

MONROE, ELIZABETH KORTRIGHT: BIRTH ANNIVERSARY. June 30, 1768. Wife of James Monroe, fifth president of the US, born at New York, NY. Died at their Oak Hill estate at Loudon County, VA, Sept 23, 1830.

MUSCLECAR MANIA. June 30. Cheboygan, MI. 6th annual event at the Kewadin Casino (tentative) after the St. Ignace car show. Flame throwers, burnout contests, neon, hopper and muffler rapping competition. For info: Nostalgia Productions, Inc, 268 Hillcrest Blvd, St. Ignace, MI 49781. Phone: (906) 643-8087. Fax: (906) 643-9784. E-mail: edreavie@nostalgia-prod.com. Web: www.nostalgia-prod.com or www.auto-shows.com.

NORFOLK CHAMBER MUSIC FESTIVAL. June 30–Aug 25. Norfolk, CT. Concerts by world-class artists in the historic Music Shed on an elegant old estate nestled in the Litchfield Hills. Performances are given each week on Thursday, Friday, Saturday and Sunday. *The New York Times* said that "no concert site is more beautiful than Norfolk, Connecticut." Arrive early and picnic or stroll the estate grounds. Est attendance: 20,000. For info: Norfolk Chamber Music Festival, Ellen Battell Stoeckel Estate, Rts 44 & 272, PO Box 545, Norfolk, CT 06058. Phone: (860) 542-3000. Web: www.yale.edu/norfolk.

NOW FOUNDED: 35th ANNIVERSARY. June 30, 1966. The National Organization for Women was founded at Washington, DC, by people attending the Third National Conference on the Commission on the Status of Women. NOW's purpose is to take action to take women into full partnership in the mainstream of American society, exercising all privileges and responsibilities in equal partnership with men. For info: Natl Organization for Women, 1000 16th St NW, Washington, DC 20036. Phone: (202) 331-0066. Web: www.now.org.

SALMON RIVER DAYS. June 30–July 4. Salmon, ID. Fourth of July celebration with a parade, boat races, auction, family reunions, rodeo and arts and crafts festival. Est attendance: 20,000. For info: Salmon Valley Chamber of Commerce, 200 Main, Ste 1, Salmon, ID 83467. Phone: (208) 756-2100.

SIBERIAN EXPLOSION: ANNIVERSARY. June 30, 1908. Early in the morning, a spectacular explosion occurred over central Siberia. The seismic shock, firestorm, ensuing "black rain" and the illumination that was reportedly visible for hundreds of miles led to speculation that a meteorite was the cause. Said to have been the most powerful explosion in history.

STRAIGHT LACED AND LOOSE WOMEN. June 30–Sept 16. Belle Meade Plantation, Nashville, TN. "The Foundations of Fashions." Explore how women's undergarments created the *Shape* of fashion, 1770–1900. Est attendance: 15,000. For info: Belle Meade Plantation, 5025 Harding Rd, Nashville, TN 37205. Phone: (615) 356-0501 or (800) 270-3991. Fax: (615) 356-2336. Web: www.bellemeadeplantation.com.

TWENTY-SIXTH AMENDMENT RATIFIED: 30th ANNIVERSARY. June 30, 1971. The 26th Amendment to the Constitution granted the right to vote in all federal, state and local elections to all persons 18 years or older. On the date of ratification the US gained an additional 11 million voters. Up until this time, the minimum voting age was set by the states; in most states it was 21.

TWINS FOUNDATION FOUNDING: ANNIVERSARY. June 30, 1983. The Twins Foundation is the country's primary research information center on the subject of twins. An international nonprofit membership organization, it was established by a group of prominent twins at New York City. The Foundation serves twins, their families, the media, medical and social scientists and the general public through its publications, its National Twins Registry and its multimedia resource center. For info: The Twins Foundation, PO Box 6043, Providence, RI 02940-6043. Phone: (401) 729-1000. Fax: (401) 751-4642. E-mail: twins@twinsfoundation.com. Web: www.twinsfoundation.com.

WHEELER, WILLIAM ALMON: BIRTH ANNIVERSARY. June 30, 1819. 19th vice president of the US (1877–81), born at Malone, NY. Died there June 4, 1887.

WORLD CHAMPIONSHIP ROTARY TILLER RACE AND PURPLEHULL PEA FESTIVAL. June 30. Emerson, AR. Domino tournaments, concessions, arts, crafts, entertainment, children's games, Queen's pageant (various ages), 3-on-3 basketball. 12th annual festival. Est attendance: 10,000. For info: Publicity, Purplehull Pea Fest, PO Box 1, Emerson, AR 71740. Phone: (501) 315-7373. E-mail: purplehull@juno.com. Web: wwww.purplehull.com.

BIRTHDAYS TODAY

William Atherton, 54, actor (*The Day of the Locust, Ghostbusters, Die Hard, Die Hard 2*), born New Haven, CT, June 30, 1947.

Nancy Dussault, 65, actress ("Too Close for Comfort," "The Ted Knight Show"), born Pensacola, FL, June 30, 1936.

Rupert Graves, 38, actor (*A Room with a View, Maurice*), born Weston-Super-Mare, England, June 30, 1963.

David Alan Grier, 46, actor (*A Soldier's Story, I'm Gonna Git You Sucka*), born Detroit, MI, June 30, 1955.

Lena Horne, 84, singer, actress (*Stormy Weather, Jamaica, Death of a Gunfighter, The Wiz*), born Brooklyn, NY, June 30, 1917.

Mitchell James (Mitch) Richmond, 36, basketball player, born Ft Lauderdale, FL, June 30, 1965.

Patricia Schroeder, 61, former member of Congress from Colorado, executive director of the American Booksellers Association, born Portland, OR, June 30, 1940.

Michael Gerard (Mike) Tyson, 35, former heavyweight champion boxer, born New York, NY, June 30, 1966.

Iulye.

JULY 1 — SUNDAY
Day 182 — 183 Remaining

ALL-AMERICAN BIRTHDAY PARTY. July 1 (tentative). Central Riverfront, Cincinnati, OH. "Traditional" Fourth of July celebration, musical talent and fireworks. Est attendance: 200,000. For info: Catherine Pleva, Event Producer, Clear Channel Communications, Inc, 1111 St Gregory St, Cincinnati, OH 45202. Phone: (513) 852-1646. Fax: (513) 333-4269. E-mail: catherinepleva@clearchannel.com.

ANTI-BOREDOM MONTH. July 1–31. 16th annual sponsorship of a "self-awareness" event to encourage people to examine whether they, co-workers, family or friends are experiencing "an extended period of boredom" in their lives. The Boring Institute identifies this as "a warning sign" of problems that include depression, self-destructive behavior and even suicide. Advice is offered on how to avoid and overcome boredom. For info: The Boring Institute, Alan Caruba, Founder, Box 40, Maplewood, NJ 07040. Phone: (973) 763-6392. E-mail: acaruba@aol.com. Web: www.boringinstitute.com.

ARAFAT RETURNS TO PALESTINE: ANNIVERSARY. July 1, 1994. Yasser Arafat, head of the Palestine Liberation Organization (PLO), returned to Palestine for the first time in 33 years. Israel's control of Palestine had prevented his visiting the region because he was a sworn enemy of the State of Israel and was regarded by Israelis as a terrorist. The agreement between Israel and the PLO, signed in September 1993, made possible Arafat's return. He went first to Gaza City in the Gaza Strip, where he was welcomed by a crowd estimated at 200,000. Three days later he flew by helicopter to the city of Jericho. Both areas were granted Palestinian rule by the treaty.

BATTLE OF GETTYSBURG: ANNIVERSARY. July 1, 1863. After the Southern success at Chancellorsville, VA, Confederate General Robert E. Lee led his forces on an invasion of the North, initially targeting Harrisburg, PA. As Union forces moved to counter the invasion, the battle lines were eventually formed at Gettysburg, PA, in one of the Civil War's most crucial battles. On the climactic third day of the battle (July 3), Lee ordered an attack on the center of the Union line, later to be known as Pickett's Charge. The 15,000 rebels were repulsed, ending the Battle of Gettysburg. After the defeat, Lee's forces retreated back to Virginia, listing more than one-third of the troops as casualties in the failed invasion. Union General George Meade initially failed to pursue the retreating rebels, allowing Lee's army to escape across the rain-swollen Potomac River.

BE NICE TO NEW JERSEY WEEK. July 1–7. A time to recognize the assets of the state most maligned by American comedians. Annually, the first full week of July. For info: Lauren Barnett, Lone Star Publications of Humor, 8452 Fredericksburg Rd, Ste 103, San Antonio, TX 78229. E-mail: lspubs@aol.com. Web: members.aol.com/lspubs/lsindex.html.

"BIG TOP" TV PREMIERE: ANNIVERSARY. July 1, 1950. Charles Vanda produced this CBS kiddie circus program that broadcast weekly for seven years from Camden, NJ. Jack Sterling played ringmaster. The show also featured Dan Lurie and Ed McMahon (as a clown, in his first TV appearance).

BLERIOT, LOUIS: BIRTH ANNIVERSARY. July 1, 1872. Louis Bleriot, aviation pioneer and first man to fly an airplane across the English Channel (July 25, 1909), was born at Cambrai, France. He died at Paris, Aug 2, 1936.

BUREAU OF INTERNAL REVENUE ESTABLISHED: ANNIVERSARY. July 1, 1862. The Bureau of Internal Revenue was established by an act of Congress.

BURUNDI: INDEPENDENCE DAY. July 1. National holiday. Anniversary of establishment of independence from Belgian administration in 1962. Had been part of Ruanda-Urundi.

CANADA: CANADA DAY. July 1. National holiday. Canada's national day, formerly known as Dominion Day. Observed on following day when July 1 is a Sunday (July 2 in 2001). Commemorates the confederation of Upper and Lower Canada and some of the Maritime Provinces into the Dominion of Canada in 1867.

CANADA: CANADA DAY CELEBRATIONS. July 1. Squamish, BC. Celebrate Canada's birthday with cake, games and entertainment. For info: Chamber of Commerce—Squamish Britannia and Furry Creek, PO Box 1009, Squamish, BC, Canada V0N 3G0. Phone: (604) 892-9244. Fax: (604) 892-2034. E-mail: cocsqhs@mountain-inter.net.

CANADA: CANADA DAY PARTY IN THE PARK. July 1. Bancroft, ON. Canada Day fireworks. Craft show, kids' games and local musicians. Est attendance: 5,000. For info: Bancroft and Dist Chmbr of Commerce, PO Box 539, Bancroft, ON, Canada K0L 1C0. Phone: (613) 332-1513. Fax: (613) 332-2119. E-mail: chamber@commerce.bancroft.on.ca. Web: www.commerce.bancroft.on.ca.

CANADA: YUKON GOLD PANNING CHAMPIONSHIPS. July 1. Dawson City, YT. Yukon residents compete for the honor of Territorial Champion Gold Panner. Dawson visitors can join in and compete for the Cheechako Award. Annually, July 1, Canada Day. Est attendance: 500. For info: Klondike Visitors Assn, PO Box 389, Dawson City, YT, Canada Y0B 1G0. Phone: (867) 993-5575. Fax: (867) 993-6415. E-mail: kva@dawson.net. Web: www.dawsoncity.com.

CLEMSON, THOMAS GREEN: BIRTH ANNIVERSARY. July 1, 1807. The man for whom Clemson University was named was born at Philadelphia, PA. The mining engineer and agriculturist married John C. Calhoun's daughter, Anna. Clemson bequeathed the old Calhoun plantation to South Carolina, and Clemson Agricultural College (now Clemson University) was founded there in 1889. Clemson died at Clemson, SC, Apr 6, 1888.

CLEVELAND'S SECRET SURGERY: ANNIVERSARY. July 1, 1893. President Grover Cleveland boarded the yacht *Oneida* for surgery to be performed in secret on a cancerous growth in his mouth. As this was during the 1893 depression, secrecy was thought desirable to avoid further panic by the public. The whole left side of Cleveland's jaw was removed as well as a small portion of his soft palate. A second, less extensive operation was performed July 17. He was later fitted with a prosthesis of vulcanized rubber that he wore until his death June 24, 1908. A single leak of the secret was plugged by Cleveland's Secretary of War, Daniel Lamont, the only member of the administration to know about the surgery. The illness did not become public knowledge until an article appeared Sept 22, 1917, in the *Saturday Evening Post*, written by William W. Keen, who assisted in the surgery.

COURT TV DEBUT: 10th ANNIVERSARY. July 1, 1991. The continuing evolution of home television entertainment brought on by the advent of cable television added another twist on July 1, 1991, with the debut of Court TV. Trials are broadcast in their entirety, with occasional commentary from the channel's anchor desk and switching between several trials in progress. Trials with immense popular interest, such as the William Kennedy Smith rape trial, the sentencing hearing of Marlon Brando's son and the Jeffrey Dahmer and O.J. Simpson trials, are broadcast along with more low-profile cases.

DIANA, PRINCESS OF WALES: 40th BIRTH ANNIVERSARY. July 1, 1961. Former wife of Charles, Prince of Wales, and mother of Prince William and Prince Harry. Born Lady Diana Spencer at Sandringham, England, she died in an automobile accident at Paris, France, Aug 31, 1997.

DIXON, WILLIE: BIRTH ANNIVERSARY. July 1, 1915. Blues legend Willie Dixon was born at Vicksburg, MI. He moved to Chicago in 1936 and began his career as a musician with the Big Three Trio. With the advent of instrument amplification Dixon migrated away from his acoustic upright bass into producing and songwriting with Chess Studios, where he became one of the primary architects of the classic Chicago sound in the 1950s. His songs were performed by Elvis Presley, the Everly Brothers, the Rolling Stones, Led Zeppelin, the Doors, Cream, the Yardbirds, Aerosmith, Jimi Hendrix and the Allman Brothers, among others. Dixon died Jan 29, 1992, at Burbank, CA.

DORSEY, THOMAS A.: BIRTH ANNIVERSARY. July 1, 1899. Thomas A. Dorsey, the father of gospel music, was born at Villa Rica, GA. Originally a blues composer, Dorsey eventually combined blues and sacred music to develop gospel music. It was Dorsey's composition "Take My Hand, Precious Lord" that Reverend Dr. Martin Luther King, Jr, had asked to have performed just moments before his assassination. Dorsey, who composed more than 1,000 gospel songs and hundreds of blues songs in his lifetime, died Jan 23, 1993, at Chicago, IL.

DUCKTONA 500. July 1. Riverview Park, Sheboygan Falls, WI. Plastic duck race in the park lagoon. dunk tank, antique car show, games for children, five-mile run and live bands. Pancake breakfast, burgers, brats, beverages. Annually, the first Sunday in July. Est attendance: 3,000. For info: Nancy Verstrate, Exec Dir, Sheboygan Falls Chamber Main St Office, 641 Monroe, Ste 108, Sheboygan Falls, WI 53085. Phone: (920) 467-6206. Fax: (920) 467-9571.

EASTPORT FOURTH OF JULY AND "OLD HOME WEEK CELEBRATION." July 1–5. Eastport, ME. Weekend-long event features a flea market, craft fair, theater, music, dance, demonstrations and exhibits, fireworks display, public entertainment July 3–4, US naval ship in port and a variety of contests. Est attendance: 10,000. For info: Eastport 4th of July Committee Inc, PO Box 187, Eastport, ME 04631. Phone: (207) 853-2930.

FIRST SCHEDULED TELEVISION BROADCAST: ANNIVERSARY. July 1, 1941. The National Broadcasting Company (NBC) began broadcasting from the Empire State Building on this day. The Federal Communications Commission had granted the first commercial TV licenses to ten stations on May 2, 1941.

FIRST US POSTAGE STAMPS ISSUED: ANNIVERSARY. July 1, 1847. The first US postage stamps were issued by the US Postal Service, a 5¢ stamp picturing Benjamin Franklin and a 10¢ stamp honoring George Washington. Stamps had been issued by private postal services in the US prior to this date.

FIRST US ZOO: ANNIVERSARY. July 1, 1874. The Philadelphia Zoological Society, the first US zoo, opened. Three thousand visitors traveled by foot, horse and carriage and steamboat to visit the exhibits. Price of admission was 25¢ for adults and 10¢ for children. There were 1,000 animals in the zoo when it opened.

FOURTH OF JULY EXTRAVAGANZA. July 1–4. Hettinger, ND. Parade, free noon meal, events happening all week long and dances, food, booths and the largest fireworks display in SW North Dakota. For info: Wendy Hehn, Community Promotions Office, Box 1031, Hettinger, ND 58639. Phone: (701) 567-2531. Fax: (701) 567-2690. E-mail: adamsdv@hettinger.ctctel.com. Web: hettingernd.com.

GHANA: REPUBLIC DAY: ANNIVERSARY. July 1. National holiday. Commemorates the inauguration of the Republic in 1960.

GUATEMALA: BANKER'S DAY. July 1. Bank holiday.

HEMOCHROMATOSIS SCREENING AWARENESS MONTH. July 1–31. To promote awareness, encourage routine screening, early diagnosis and treatment of the disorder of iron metabolism characterized by iron absorption and gradual iron accumulation in vital organs and joints. Treatment can prevent or reverse organ damage if not advanced. For info: Hemochromatosis Foundation, PO Box 8569, Albany, NY 12208. Phone: (518) 489-0972.

INTERNATIONAL JOKE DAY. July 1. International Joke Day marks the first day of the International Joke Contest, which runs through Oct 1. Participants can mail or fax their best jokes. Prizes are awarded in three categories: funniest, most original and largest collection (please mail). For info: Wayne Reinagel, Pres, Knightraven Books, PO Box 100, Collinsville, IL 62234-0100. Phone: (618) 345-7436.

KILLDEER MOUNTAIN ROUNDUP RODEO DAYS. July 1–4. Killdeer, ND. More than a rodeo, the western celebration features many events, including parades, contests, dances, musical entertainment, western art show, animal shows, historical reenactments of the Old West, cultural foods, Native American demonstrations, fireworks and two performances of great rodeo action. Est attendance: 5,000. For info: (701) 764-5328 or North Dakota Tourism, 604 E Boulevard, Bismarck, ND 58505. Phone: (701) 328-2525 or (800) 435-5663.

LAVALLETTE INDEPENDENCE EXTRAVAGANZA. July 1. Lavallette, NJ. 45-piece orchestra plays patriotic music during an outstanding fireworks display on the bay. Very suitable for boaters to watch from the water. Annually, the first Sunday in July. Est attendance: 30,000. For info: Lavallette Heritage Committee, Inc, Ocean County Public Affairs, PO Box 2191, Toms River, NJ 08754. Phone: (732) 793-3652. Fax: (732) 854-9038. E-mail: tgroskol@juno.com.

July 2001	S	M	T	W	T	F	S
	1	2	3	4	5	6	7
	8	9	10	11	12	13	14
	15	16	17	18	19	20	21
	22	23	24	25	26	27	28
	29	30	31				

"THE LIBERACE SHOW" TV PREMIERE: ANNIVERSARY. July 1, 1952. A pianist known for his outrageous style and a candelabra on his piano, Liberace hosted popular shows in the '50s and '60s. The first premiered on KLAC-TV in Los Angeles and went national in 1953. That did so well that he began a half-hour syndicated series which featured his brother George as violinist and orchestra leader. After a brief leave, he returned to TV in 1958 with a half-hour show that featured Joan O'Brien, Erin O'Brien, Dick Roman, Steve Dunne and the Gordon Robinson Orchestra. Liberace also hosted a British series and a summer series produced in London.

LINCOLN SIGNS INCOME TAX: ANNIVERSARY. July 1, 1862. President Abraham Lincoln signed into law a bill levying a 3 percent income tax on annual incomes of $600–$10,000, and 5 percent on incomes of more than $10,000. The revenues were to help pay for the Civil War. This tax law actually went into effect, unlike an earlier law passed August 5, 1861, making it the first income tax levied by the US. It was rescinded in 1872.

"MAMA" TV PREMIERE: ANNIVERSARY. July 1, 1949. One of TV's first popular sitcoms, "Mama" told the story of a Norwegian family living in San Francisco in 1917. The show aired live through 1956; after it was cancelled, a second, filmed version lasted only 13 weeks. Cast members included Peggy Wood, Judson Laire, Rosemary Rice, Dick Van Patten, Iris Mann, Robin Morgan, Ruth Gates, Malcolm Keen, Carl Frank, Alice Frost, Patty McCormack and Kevin Coughlin.

MAMMOTH CAVE NATIONAL PARK ESTABLISHED: 60th ANNIVERSARY. July 1, 1941. Area of central Kentucky, originally authorized May 25, 1926, was established as a national park. For more info: Mammoth Cave Natl Park, Mammoth Cave, KY 42259.

MANDAN JAYCEE RODEO DAYS. July 1–4. Mandan, ND. Watch the region's top cowboys and cowgirls compete. In addition to the parade and the carnival midway, wander through local arts and crafts exhibits at Art in the Park. Est attendance: 50,000. For info: Bismarck/Mandan Conv & Visitors Bureau, Box 2274, Bismarck, ND 58502. Phone: (800) 767-3555 or (701) 222-4308. Fax: (701) 222-0647.

MARYLAND SYMPHONY AT ANTIETAM. July 1. Antietam National Battlefield, Sharpsburg, MD. A glorious tribute to our country's independence on one of history's most legendary battlefields, featuring light classical and patriotic music and a spectacular fireworks finale. This free outdoor event is a regional favorite! Annually, the Sunday closest to July 4. Est attendance: 35,000. For info: Maryland Symphony Orchestra, 13 S Potomac St, Hagerstown, MD 21740-5512. Phone: (301) 797-4000. Fax: (301) 797-2314. Web: www.mdsymphony.com or www.culturefinder.com.

MEDICARE: ANNIVERSARY. July 1, 1968. Medicare, the US health insurance program for senior citizens, went into effect. The legislation authorizing the program had been signed by President Lyndon Johnson July 30, 1965.

MORRILL LAND GRANT ACT PASSED: ANNIVERSARY. July 1, 1862. This federal legislation led to the creation of the Land Grant universities and Agricultural Experiment Stations in each state.

NATIONAL BAKED BEAN MONTH. July 1–31. To pay tribute to one of America's favorite and most healthful and nutritious foods, baked beans, made with dry or canned beans. For info: Therese Schueneman, Bean Education & Awareness Network, 303 E Wacker Dr, Ste 440, Chicago, IL 60601. Phone: (312) 861-5200. Fax: (312) 861-5252. Web: www.americanbean.org.

NATIONAL FINANCIAL FREEDOM DAY. July 1. Don't gamble with your financial future by leaving your finances to chance. A day dedicated to starting on the path to being debt free and finding ways to build your personal wealth. For info: Jamie K. Urick, Debt Free Intl, Inc, PO Box 705, Frankfort, IL 60423. Phone: (815) 469-7662. Fax: (815) 469-7664. E-mail: urickdfi@aol.com.

NATIONAL FOREIGN LANGUAGE MONTH. July 1–31. Attempt to learn a foreign language this month. Experience life outside your country while staying home. For info: Jonathan Earling, 2072 W Palatine Rd, Inverness, IL 60067. Phone: (847) 963-0570.

NATIONAL JULY BELONGS TO BLUEBERRIES MONTH. July 1–31. To make the public aware that this is the peak month for fresh blueberries. For info: North American Blueberry Council, 4995 Golden Foothill Parkway, Ste #2, El Dorado Hills, CA 95762. E-mail: ddnabc@compuserve.com. Web: www.blueberry.org.

NATIONAL PURPOSEFUL PARENTING MONTH. July 1–31. Encourages parents to incorporate "purpose" in their parenting. Designed to elevate the level of parental effectiveness by building awareness and providing interested participants with tips for positive, conscientious parenting. For info send SASE to: Teresa Langston, Dir, Parenting Without Pressure (PWOP), 1330 Boyer St, Longwood, FL 32750-6311. Phone: (407) 767-2524.

NATIONAL RECREATION AND PARKS MONTH. July 1–31. To showcase and invite community participation in quality leisure activities for all segments of the population. For info: Information Resources, Natl Recreation and Park Assn, 22377 Belmont Ridge Rd, Ashburn, VA 20148. Phone: (703) 858-2170. Fax: (703) 858-0794. E-mail: info@nrpa.org. Web: www.nrpa.org.

NEBRASKA BIG RENDEZVOUS AND HISTORICAL FESTIVAL. July 1–4. Burwell, NE. Camp site near Calamus Lake. Reenactment of early 1800s fur trade encampment. Historical craft demos, period shelters and costumes. Early American frontier crafts and foods for sale. Blackpowder contest. Public welcome 9 AM to 7 PM daily. Admission charge. Est attendance: 1,000. For info: Peggy Haskell, Nebraska Big Rendezvous, PO Box 747, Burwell, NE 68823. Phone: (308) 346-5210. Web: www.BurwellNebr.com.

NICK AT NITE PREMIERE: ANNIVERSARY. July 1, 1985. The first broadcast of Nick at Nite, the creation of the kids' network Nickelodeon, occurred. Owned and operated by MTV Networks, Nick at Nite presents many of the old classic television series.

OLD-FASHIONED FOURTH OF JULY. July 1–4. Pioneer Village, Worthington, MN. Open to the general public. Children under 12 are admitted if accompanied by an adult. Events which emphasize the heritage of Southwest Minnesota are on display. Refreshments available and there are performances of a melodrama and shows in the Red Garter Saloon throughout the day. Est attendance: 700. For info: Nobles County Historical Soc, 407 12th St, Ste 2, Worthington, MN 56187. Phone: (507) 376-4011 or (507) 376-4431.

ROUGHRIDER DAYS. July 1–4. Dickinson, ND. Classic western celebration featuring rodeo performances, a parade, demolition derby, concerts, dances, displays and the Fourth of July fireworks show. Est attendance: 3,500. For info: (701) 225-5115 or North Dakota Tourism, 604 East Boulevard, Bismarck, ND 58505. Phone: (701) 328-2525 or (800) 435-5663.

RUSSIAN RUBLE BECOMES CONVERTIBLE: ANNIVERSARY. July 1, 1992. The Russian ruble became convertible with other currencies worldwide. Convertibility had long been held to be an important first move toward bringing the Russian economy into the mainstream of the world's economy. The official rate on July 1 was approximately 125 rubles to the dollar, and authorities hoped that it would eventually stabilize at approximately 80 rubles to the dollar. Previously it was illegal to convert rubles, although they traded briskly on the black market.

RWANDESE REPUBLIC: INDEPENDENCE DAY. July 1. National holiday. Commemorates independence from Belgium in 1962.

SAND, GEORGE: BIRTH ANNIVERSARY. July 1, 1804. French novelist, author of more than 100 volumes, whose real name was Amandine Aurore Lucile (Dupin) Dudevant, was born at Paris, France. Died at Nohant, France, June 8, 1876. She is better remembered for having been a liberated woman during a romantic epoch than for her literary works.

SOCIETY FOR THE PRESERVATION & ENCOURAGEMENT OF BARBER SHOP QUARTET SINGING IN AMERICA (SPEBSQSA) INTERNATIONAL CONVENTION. July 1–8. Nashville, TN. More than 10,000 members attend a week of shows, meetings, chorus and quartet contests. Est attendance: 10,000. For info: Crystal Miller, Mktg & Public Relations Coord, 6315 Third Ave, Kenosha, WI 53143. Phone: (800) 876-SING. E-mail: cmiller@spebsqsa.org. Web: www .spebsqsa.org.

SPACE MILESTONE: *KOSMOS 1383* (USSR). July 1, 1982. First search and rescue satellite—equipped to hear distress calls from aircraft and ships—launched in cooperative project with the US and France.

SUNDAYS IN THE GARDEN. July 1–29. Hamilton House, Vaughan's Lane, South Berwick, ME. Concerts in the formal gardens overlooking 1785 Georgian mansion and Salmon Falls River. Lawn chairs available, families welcome, but no dogs, please. Admission $6. Annually, Sundays in July, 4–5:30 PM. Est attendance: 400. For info: Soc for Preservation of New England Antiquities, 5 Portland St, South Berwick, ME 03908. Phone: (207) 384-2454. Fax: (207) 384-8192.

SUNSHINE FESTIVAL. July 1–4. Neptune Park on St. Simons Island, GA. Festival includes exhibits by more than 100 fine arts and crafts artists, rides, entertainment, food booths and a fireworks display. Annually, the three or four days around July 4th. Est attendance: 30,000. For info: Glynn Art Assn, 319 Mallory St, PO Box 20673, St. Simons Island, GA 31522. Phone: (912) 638-8770. Fax: (912) 634-ARTS. Web: www.glynnart.org.

UPTOWN, DOWNTOWN, ARTOWN. July 1–31. Reno, NV. More than 200 arts-related events including dance, plays, concerts, fine arts exhibits and demonstrations, hands-on programs for children and film. For info: Phone: (775) 329-2787.

WALKMAN DEBUTS: ANNIVERSARY. July 1, 1979. This month Sony introduced the Walkman under the name Soundabout, selling for $200. It had been released in Japan six months earlier. More than 185 million have been sold.

ZIP CODES INAUGURATED: ANNIVERSARY. July 1, 1963. The US Postal Service introduced the five-digit zip code on this day.

July		S	M	T	W	T	F	S
2001		1	2	3	4	5	6	7
		8	9	10	11	12	13	14
		15	16	17	18	19	20	21
		22	23	24	25	26	27	28
		29	30	31				

BIRTHDAYS TODAY

Pamela Anderson, 34, model, actress ("Baywatch," "Home Improvement"), born Ladysmith, British Columbia, Canada, July 1, 1967.

Dan Aykroyd, 49, actor (*The Blues Brothers, Dragnet, Ghostbusters*, "Saturday Night Live"), born Ottawa, Ontario, Canada, July 1, 1952.

Karen Black, 59, actress (*Five Easy Pieces, Nashville*), born Park Ridge, IL, July 1, 1942.

Andre Braugher, 39, actor ("Homicide," *City of Angels*), born Chicago, IL, July 1, 1962.

Genevieve Bujold, 59, actress (*Choose Me, Trouble in Mind, Dead Ringers*), born Montreal, Quebec, Canada, July 1, 1942.

Leslie Caron, 70, actress (*Gigi, An American in Paris*), dancer, born Paris, France, July 1, 1931.

Olivia De Havilland, 85, actress (Oscar for *To Each His Own* and *The Heiress*; *Gone with the Wind*), born Tokyo, Japan, July 1, 1916.

Jamie Farr (Jameel Farah), 65, actor ("M*A*S*H," *The Blackboard Jungle*), born Toledo, OH, July 1, 1936.

Estee Lauder, 93, cosmetics executive, born New York, NY, July 1, 1908.

Frederick Carlton (Carl) Lewis, 40, Olympic gold medal track athlete, born Birmingham, AL, July 1, 1961.

Jean Marsh, 67, writer, actress (*Upstairs, Downstairs*), born Stoke Newington, England, July 1, 1934.

Sydney Pollack, 67, filmmaker (*Tootsie, The Way We Were, The Fabulous Baker Boys*), born Lafayette, IN, July 1, 1934.

Alan Ruck, 41, actor ("Spin City," *Ferris Bueller's Day Off*), born Cleveland, OH, July 1, 1960.

Twyla Tharp, 60, dancer, choreographer, born Portland, IN, July 1, 1941.

Liv Tyler, 24, actress (*That Thing You Do, Armageddon*), born Portland, ME, July 1, 1977.

JULY 2 — MONDAY
Day 183 — 182 Remaining

"THE ANDY WILLIAMS SHOW" TV PREMIERE: ANNIVERSARY. July 2, 1957. Singer Andy Williams hosted many variety shows, including "The Andy Williams–June Valli Show," "The Chevy Showroom" and "The Andy Williams Show." His shows featured Dick Van Dyke and the Bob Hamilton Trio, the New Christy Minstrels, the Osmond Brothers, Charlie Callas, Irwin Corey and Janos Prohaska. In 1976 Williams hosted "Andy," a syndicated show.

BLACK HILLS ROUNDUP. July 2–4. Roundup Grounds, Belle Fourche, SD. This 80th annual Independence Day celebration includes an exciting PRCA rodeo each day, the Miss Rodeo South Dakota pageant, western South Dakota's largest fireworks display at dusk on the shore of Orman Dam, a big Fourth of July parade downtown at 10 AM and a thrilling carnival and midway. Est attendance: 10,000. For info: Belle Fourche Chamber of Commerce, 415 Fifth Ave, Belle Fourche, SD 57717. Phone: (605) 892-2676. Fax: (605) 892-4633. E-mail: chamber@bellefourche.org.

CARIBBEAN OR CARICOM DAY. July 2. The anniversary of the treaty establishing the Caribbean Community (also called the Treaty of Chaguaramas), signed by the prime ministers of Barbados, Guyana, Jamaica and Trinidad and Tobago July 4, 1973. Observed as a public holiday by the participating nations. Annually, the first Monday in July.

CIVIL RIGHTS ACT OF 1964: ANNIVERSARY. July 2, 1964. President Lyndon Johnson signed the Voting Rights Act of 1964 into law, prohibiting discrimination on the basis of race in public accommodations, in publicly owned or operated facilities, in employment and union membership and in the registration of voters. The bill included Title VI, which allowed for the cutoff of federal funding in areas where discrimination persisted.

CONSTITUTION OF THE US TAKES EFFECT: ANNIVERSARY. July 2, 1788. Cyrus Griffin of Virginia, the president of the Congress, announced that the Constitution had been ratified by the required nine states (the ninth being New Hampshire June 21, 1788), and a committee was appointed to make preparations for the change of government.

CRANMER, THOMAS: BIRTH ANNIVERSARY. July 2, 1489. English clergyman, reformer and martyr, born at Aslacton, Nottinghamshire, England. One of the principal authors of *The English Book of Common Prayer.* Archbishop of Canterbury. Tried for treason and burned at the stake at Oxford, England, Mar 21, 1556.

DECLARATION OF INDEPENDENCE RESOLUTION: 225th ANNIVERSARY. July 2, 1776. Anniversary of adoption by the Continental Congress, Philadelphia, PA, of a resolution introduced June 7, 1776, by Richard Henry Lee of Virginia: "Resolved, That these United Colonies are, and of right ought to be, free and independent States, that they are absolved from all allegiance to the British Crown, and that all political connection between them and the State of Great Britain is, and ought to be, totally dissolved. That it is expedient forthwith to take the most effectual measures for forming foreign Alliances. That a plan of confederation be prepared and transmitted to the respective Colonies for their consideration and approbation." This resolution prepared the way for adoption, July 4, 1776, of the Declaration of Independence. See also: "Declaration of Independence: Anniversary" (July 4).

DENMARK: AALBORG AND REBILD FESTIVAL (AMERICAN INDEPENDENCE DAY CELEBRATION). July 2–4. Aalborg. This celebration of the American Independence Day, at the Rebild National Park, Aalborg, Denmark, is described as "the largest single gathering for this occasion in the world." Guest speakers and Danish and American entertainment. Est attendance: 10,000. For info: 4 July Committee, Aalborg Tourist and Conv Bureau, PO Box 1862, Oesteraagade 8, DK-9100 Aalborg, Denmark. Phone: (45) (98) 12-6022. Fax: (45) (98) 16-6922. E-mail: info@aalborg-tourist.dk. Web: www.aalborg-tourist.dk.

GARFIELD, JAMES ABRAM: ASSASSINATION ANNIVERSARY. July 2, 1881. President James A. Garfield was shot as he entered the railway station at Washington, DC. He died Sept 19, 1881, never having recovered from the wound. The assassin, Charles J. Guiteau, was hanged June 30, 1882.

HALFWAY POINT OF 2001. July 2. At noon, July 2, 2001, 182½ days of the year will have elapsed and 182½ will remain before Jan 1, 2002.

I FORGOT DAY. July 2. A day to make up for all the birthdays, anniversaries, new births, graduations, etc, that you forgot to acknowledge with a greeting or gift. Annually, the 183rd day of the year—exact center (except for Leap Year). For info: Gaye Andersen, Davenport College, 8200 Georgia St, Merrillville, IN 46410. Phone: (219) 769-5556. Fax: (219) 756-8911. E-mail: mvganderse@davenport.edu.

INTERNATIONAL CARILLON FESTIVAL. July 2–7. Springfield, IL. A week of recitals by the world's best carillonneurs on Washington Park's carillon of 67 bronze bells. Since it began in 1961, this has become the world's best-known carillon festival. Est attendance: 21,000. For info: Karl Keldermans, Springfield Park District, PO Box 5052, Springfield, IL 62705. Phone: (217) 753-6219. E-mail: kkrees@fgi.net.

ITALY: PALIO. July 2 (also Aug 16). Siena. Colorful medieval horse race, competing for the banner (Palio).

"THE LAWRENCE WELK SHOW" TV PREMIERE: ANNIVERSARY. July 2, 1955. This musical series, hosted by accordionist and bandleader Lawrence Welk, lasted for almost three decades. In its early years it was known as "The Dodge Dancing Party." Regulars included the Lennon Sisters, Alice Lon, Norma Zimmer, Tanya Falan, Arthur Duncan, Joe Feeney, Guy Hovis, Jim Roberts, Ralna English, Larry Hooper, Jerry Burke and Bobby Burgess. From 1956–59, this show was on concurrently with either "Lawrence Welk's Top Tunes and New Talent" or "The Plymouth Show Starring Lawrence Welk (Lawrence Welk's Little Band)."

LIVINGSTON ROUNDUP. July 2–4. Park County Fairgrounds, Livingston, MT. Livingston is the trout capital of the world and the Gateway to Yellowstone National Park. Parade on July 2 at 4 PM. Rodeo held nightly followed by a fireworks display. Performances begin at 8 PM each evening. Est attendance: 10,500. For info: Bruce Becker, Pres of Livingston Roundup, PO Box 800, Livingston, MT 59047. Phone: (406) 222-2905. Fax: (406) 222-7725. For tickets: Cathy Bosley, Phone: (406) 222-7435. E-mail: bosley1@mcn.net.

MARSHALL, THURGOOD: BIRTH ANNIVERSARY. July 2, 1908. Thurgood Marshall, the first African American on the US Supreme Court, was born at Baltimore, MD. For more than 20 years, he served as director-counsel of the NAACP Legal Defense and Educational Fund. His greatest legal victory was on May 17, 1954, when the Supreme Court decision on *Brown v Board of Education* declared an end to the "separate but equal" system of racial segregation in public schools. Marshall argued 32 cases before the Supreme Court, winning 29 of them, before becoming a member of the high court himself. Nominated by President Lyndon Johnson, he began his 24-year career on the high court Oct 2, 1967, becoming a voice of dissent in an increasingly conservative court. Marshall announced his retirement June 27, 1991, and he died Jan 24, 1993, at Washington, DC.

NATIONAL EDUCATION ASSOCIATION MEETING. July 2–7. Los Angeles, CA. Representative Assembly. For info: Natl Education Assn, 1201 16th St NW, Washington, DC 20036-3290. Phone: (202) 822-7769. Web: www.nea.org.

RED LODGE HOME OF CHAMPIONS RODEO AND PARADE. July 2–4. Red Lodge, MT. This rodeo is part of the Professional Rodeo Cowboys Association circuit and brings nearly all of the national champions to Red Lodge each year. At noon each day the Home of Champions Parade struts its way through downtown Red Lodge with colorful floats, antique cars, horses, dancing girls, wagons and more. Annually, July 2–4. Sponsor: Red Lodge Rodeo Association. Est attendance: 15,000. For info: Red Lodge Area Chamber of Commerce, Box 988, Red Lodge, MT 59068. Phone: (888) 281-0625. Fax: (406) 446-1718. E-mail: info@redlodge.com.

SAINT LOUIS RACE RIOTS: ANNIVERSARY. July 2, 1917. Between 20 and 75 blacks were killed in a race riot in St. Louis, MO; hundreds more were injured. To protest this violence against blacks, W.E.B. DuBois and James Weldon Johnson, of the NAACP, led a silent march down Fifth Avenue at New York City.

SAUK TRAIL HERITAGE DAYS POWWOW RENDEZVOUS. July 2–4. Johnson's Sauk Trail State Park, Kewanee, IL. Three-day event features artifact display, powwow, Native American crafts, circa 1800 fur traders rendezvous, voyager canoe rides and tours of the Ryan Round Barn, one of the largest in the state of Illinois. Est attendance: 20,000. For info: Mark Mikenas, Exec VP, Kewanee Chamber of Commerce, 113 E 2nd St, Kewanee, IL 61443. Phone: (309) 852-2175. Fax: (309) 852-2176. E-mail: chamber@kewanee-il.com.

VESEY, DENMARK: DEATH ANNIVERSARY. July 2, 1822. Planner of what would have been the biggest slave revolt in US history, Denmark Vesey was executed at Charleston, SC. He had been born around 1767, probably in the West Indies, where he was sold at around age 14 to Joseph Vesey, captain of a slave ship. He purchased his freedom in 1800. In 1818 Vesey and others began to plot an uprising; he held secret meetings, collected disguises and firearms and chose a date in June 1822. But authorities were warned, and police and the military were out in full force. Over the next two months 130 blacks were taken into custody; 35, including Vesey, were hanged and 31 were exiled. As a result of the plot Southern legislatures passed more rigorous slave codes.

WALES: LLANGOLLEN INTERNATIONAL MUSICAL EISTEDDFOD. July 2–8. Eisteddfod Field, Llangollen, Clwyd. 55th annual. Thousands of singers and folk dancers from more than 30 countries take part in this annual international music festival. Friendly rivalry among amateur groups performing amid the Welsh rivers and mountains. Est attendance: 120,000. For info: Maureen A. Jones, Mktg Dir, Llangollen Intl Musical Eisteddfod, Llangollen, North Wales, UK LL20 8NG. Phone: (44) (1978) 8620236. Fax: (44) (1978) 861300. E-mail: info @international-eisteddfod.co.uk. Web: www.international-eisteddfod.co.uk.

ZAMBIA: HEROES DAY. July 2. First Monday in July is Zambian national holiday—memorial day for Zambians who died in the struggle for independence. Political rallies stress solidarity.

BIRTHDAYS TODAY

Jose Canseco, Jr, 37, baseball player, born Havana, Cuba, July 2, 1964.

Sean Casey, 27, baseball player, born Willingsboro, NJ, July 2, 1974.

Polly Holliday, 64, actress ("Alice," "Home Improvement"), born Jasper, AL, July 2, 1937.

Cheryl Ladd, 49, actress ("Charlie's Angels," "Grace Kelly"), born Huron, SD, July 2, 1952.

Jimmy McNichol, 40, actor ("The Fitzpatricks," "California Fever"), born Los Angeles, CA, July 2, 1961.

Richard Petty, 64, former auto racer, born Randleman, NC, July 2, 1937.

Ron Silver, 55, actor, director (*Silkwood, Enemies: A Love Story*; stage: *Speed-the-Plow*), born New York, NY, July 2, 1946.

Dave Thomas, 69, founder of Wendy's, Horatio Alger Award winner, adoption advocate, born Camden, NJ, July 2, 1932.

JULY 3 — TUESDAY

Day 184 — 181 Remaining

AIR CONDITIONING APPRECIATION DAYS. July 3–Aug 15. Northern Hemisphere. During Dog Days, the hottest time of the year in the Northern Hemisphere, to acknowledge the contribution of air conditioning to a better way of life. Annually, July 3–Aug 15. For info: Air-Conditioning and Refrig Institute, 4301 N Fairfax Dr, Ste 425, Arlington, VA 22203. Phone: (703) 524-8800. Fax: (703) 528-3816. E-mail: ari@ari.org. Web: www .ari.org.

BELARUS: INDEPENDENCE DAY. July 3. National holiday commemorating sovereignty in 1990.

BENNETT, RICHARD BEDFORD: BIRTH ANNIVERSARY. July 3, 1870. Former Canadian prime minister, born at Hopewell Hill, NB. Died at Mickelham, England, June 26, 1947.

CANADA: MINERAL COLLECTING FIELD TRIPS. July 3–Aug 30. Bancroft, ON. Geologist-led mineral collecting field trips visit nearby rock dumps, abandoned mines and collecting sites. Participants are educated about mineral identification, collecting techniques and earth sciences. Annually, every Tuesday, Thursday and Saturday in July and August. Est attendance: 2,000. For info: Bancroft and Dist Chamber of Commerce, PO Box 539, Bancroft, ON, Canada K0L 1C0. Phone: (613) 332-1513. Fax: (613) 332-2119. E-mail: chamber@commerce.bancroft.on.ca. Web: www.commerce.bancroft.on.ca.

	S	M	T	W	T	F	S
July	1	2	3	4	5	6	7
2001	8	9	10	11	12	13	14
	15	16	17	18	19	20	21
	22	23	24	25	26	27	28
	29	30	31				

COMPLIMENT-YOUR-MIRROR DAY. July 3. Participation consists of complimenting your mirror on having such a wonderful owner and keeping track of whether other mirrors you meet during the day smile at you. For info: Bob Birch, Grand Punscorpion, Puns Corps, Box 2364, Falls Church, VA 22042-0364. Phone: (703) 533-3668.

DOG DAYS. July 3–Aug 11. Hottest days of the year in Northern Hemisphere. Usually about 40 days, but variously reckoned at 30–54 days. Popularly believed to be an evil time "when the sea boiled, wine turned sour, dogs grew mad, and all creatures became languid, causing to man burning fevers, hysterics and phrensies" (from Brady's *Clavis Calendarium*, 1813). Originally the days when Sirius, the Dog Star, rose just before or at about the same time as sunrise (no longer true owing to precession of the equinoxes). Ancients sacrificed a brown dog at beginning of Dog Days to appease the rage of Sirius, believing that star was the cause of the hot, sultry weather.

ENNIS RODEO AND PARADE. July 3–4. Ennis, MT. Billed as the fastest two-day rodeo in Montana, this is a non-stop weekend of excitement. Parade with clowns, bucking broncos and everything imaginable. Annually, July 3–4. Est attendance: 4,000. For info: Pat Hamilton, PR, Ennis Rodeo Club, PO Box 236, Ennis, MT 59729. Phone: (406) 682-4700.

FIREWORKS ON THE FJORD. July 3. Waterfront, Poulsbo, WA. Family event featuring displays, food booths, entertainment and a giant fireworks display on picturesque Liberty Bay. Voted "Best in the West Sound (Puget)"; only fireworks display on July 3rd in the Puget Sound area, it's a great way to celebrate Independence Day early! Est attendance: 25,000. For info: Fireworks on the Fjord, Community Events Productions, PO Box 1976, Poulsbo, WA 98370. Phone: (360) 779-8018.

GEORGE WASHINGTON TAKES COMMAND OF THE CONTINENTAL ARMY: ANNIVERSARY. July 3, 1775. George Washington took command of the Continental Army at Cambridge, MA.

HAINES STAMPEDE AND RODEO. July 3–4. Baker City, OR. Fourth of July celebration with rodeo, fireworks, parade, food, entertainment and more. Est attendance: 500. For info: Baker County VCB, 490 Campbell St, Baker City, OR 97814. Phone: (800) 523-1235.

HUNTINGTON, SAMUEL: BIRTH ANNIVERSARY. July 3, 1731. President of the Continental Congress, Governor of Connecticut, signer of the Declaration of Independence, born at Windham, CT, died at Norwich, CT, Jan 5, 1796.

ICE CREAM DAYS. July 3–4. Le Mars, IA. Saturday parade, children's games, art fair, flea market, historic toys, food and souvenirs from the "Ice Cream Capital of the World," home of Wells' Blue Bunny. Est attendance: 10,000. For info: Sue Butcher, Operations Mgr, Le Mars Area Chamber of Commerce, 50 Central Ave, SE, Le Mars, IA 51031. Phone: (712) 546-8821. Fax: (712) 546-7218. Web: www.lemarsiowa.com.

IDAHO: ADMISSION DAY: ANNIVERSARY. July 3. Became 43rd state in 1890.

IRAN AIR FLIGHT 655 DISASTER: ANNIVERSARY. July 3, 1988. At 10:54 AM in the Persian Gulf, the US Navy warship *Vincennes* fired two surface-to-air missiles at Iran Air Flight 655 which destroyed the airbus, killing all 290 passengers aboard. The *Vincennes*, boasting the world's most sophisticated radar detection equipment, reportedly misread location, speed, direction, altitude, dimensions and radio signals of the airbus, mistaking it for a hostile F-14 fighter plane. A self-conducted military inquiry blamed human failure—stress on the tense crew rather than equipment malfunction—for the disaster. In the summer of 1992 the public learned that the ship had been in Iranian waters at the time in the course of an operation aimed at preventing Iranian boats from laying mines.

"MR PEEPERS" TV PREMIERE: ANNIVERSARY. July 3, 1952. This sitcom was broadcast live and focused on mild-mannered junior high school science teacher, Robinson J. Peepers

(Wally Cox). The cast also included Tony Randall, Georgann Johnson, Marion Lorne, Reta Shaw, Jack Warden and Ernest Truex. This half-hour series was a summer replacement, but it earned such positive reviews that it was brought back as a regular series. In 1954 TV Guide wrote that "Mr Peepers . . . comes close to being the perfect TV show."

MOUNT RUSHMORE FOURTH OF JULY CELEBRATION. July 3–5. Mount Rushmore National Memorial, SD. Fireworks July 3 and musical performances all three days. Est attendance: 8,000. For info: Mt Rushmore Natl Memorial, PO Box 268, Keystone, SD 57751. Phone: (605) 574-2523. Fax: (605) 574-2307.

RAID ON ENTEBBE: 25th ANNIVERSARY. July 3, 1976. An Israeli commando unit staged a raid on Entebbe airport in Uganda and rescued 103 hostages on a hijacked Air France airliner. Three of the hostages, seven hijackers and 20 Ugandan soldiers were killed in the raid. The plane had been en route from Tel Aviv to Paris when taken over by the pro-Palestinian guerrillas.

RED, WHITE & BOOM. July 3. Columbus, OH. Central Ohio's Independence Day celebration features one of the largest fireworks displays in the Midwest. Est attendance: 500,000. For info: Michael L. Collins, Exec Dir, Red, White & Boom, Inc, 833 Eastwind Dr, Westerville, OH 43081. Phone: (614) 891-BOOM. Fax: (614) 823-7152. Web: www.red-white-boom.com.

STAY OUT OF THE SUN DAY. July 3. For health's sake, give your skin a break today. [© 2000 by WH] For info: Tom and Ruth Roy, Wellcat Holidays, 2418 Long Ln, Lebanon, PA 17046. Phone: (717) 279-0184. E-mail: wellcat@supernet.com. Web: www.wellcat.com.

SUNDOWN SALUTE. July 3–4. Junction City, KS, with fireworks over Milford Lake. Free Independence Day Celebration includes Coors 10K Freedom Run, parade, Veterans Ceremony, family activities, music, crafts and much more. Sundown Salute is a nonprofit organization made up of citizens in the interest of freedom. The Celebration is run completely from corporate, private and individual donations. Est attendance: 35,000. For info: Connie Hall, Executive Dir, Geary County Conv & Visitors Bureau, 425 N Washington, PO Box 1846, Junction City, KS 66441-1846. Phone: (800) 528-2489 or (785) 238-2885. Fax: (785) 238-2313. E-mail: jccvb@flinthills.com.

TAIWAN: BIRTHDAY OF CHENG HUANG. July 3. Thirteenth day of fifth moon. Celebrated with a procession of actors on stilts doing dragon and lion dances.

"TONY ORLANDO AND DAWN" TV PREMIERE: ANNIVERSARY. July 3, 1974. Tony Orlando and Dawn (Telma Hopkins and Joyce Vincent Wilson) were a recording trio in the early '70s who hosted a summer replacement for "The Sonny and Cher Show" and then a series. Regulars during the 1975–76 season included Alice Nunn, Lonnie Schorr and Lynn Stuart. In fall of 1976 the show was renamed "Tony Orlando and Dawn Rainbow Hour" and included George Carlin, Edie McClurg and Susan Lanier.

US VIRGIN ISLANDS: DANISH WEST INDIES EMANCIPATION DAY: ANNIVERSARY. July 3, 1848. Commemorates freeing of slaves in the Danish West Indies. Ceremony at Frederiksted, St. Croix, where actual proclamation was first read by Governor-General Peter Von Scholten.

VICKSBURG SURRENDERS: ANNIVERSARY. July 3, 1863. After weeks of immediate siege at the end of a year-long campaign, Vicksburg, MS, surrendered to General Ulysses S. Grant. Formal surrender was consummated on July 4, and on July 8 the besieged city of Port Hudson also surrendered, giving the Union complete control of the Mississippi River.

ZAMBIA: UNITY DAY. July 3. Memorial day for Zambians who died in the struggle for independence. Political rallies stressing solidarity throughout country. Annually, the first Tuesday in July.

BIRTHDAYS TODAY

Lamar Alexander, 61, former US Secretary of Education (Bush administration), born Knoxville, TN, July 3, 1940.

Moises Alou, 35, baseball player, born Atlanta, GA, July 3, 1966.

Dave Barry, 54, humorist, author, born Brooklyn, NY, July 3, 1947.

Laura Branigan, 44, singer ("Gloria," "How Am I Supposed to Live Without You"), born Brewster, NY, July 3, 1957.

Betty Buckley, 54, actress (*Cats, Sunset Boulevard*, "Eight Is Enough"), born Big Springs, TX, July 3, 1947.

Tom Cruise, 39, actor (*Eyes Wide Shut, The Color of Money, Born on the Fourth of July*), born Syracuse, NY, July 3, 1962.

Pete Fountain, 71, jazz musician, born New Orleans, LA, July 3, 1930.

Thomas Gibson, 39, actor ("Dharma & Greg"), born Charleston, SC, July 3, 1962.

Teemu Selanne, 31, hockey player, born Helsinki, Finland, July 3, 1970.

Kurtwood Smith, 59, actor (*Robocop, Dead Poets Society*), born New Lisbon, WI, July 3, 1942.

Tom Stoppard, 64, playwright (*Travesties, On the Razzle, The Real Thing, Arcadia*), born Zlin, Czechoslovakia, July 3, 1937.

Montel Williams, 45, talk-show host ("The Montel Williams Show"), born Baltimore, MD, July 3, 1956.

JULY 4 — WEDNESDAY
Day 185 — 180 Remaining

AIR SHOW AND FIREWORKS DISPLAY. July 4. Aransas County Airport, Rockport, TX. A display of military, antique and aerobatic planes on display at the Aransas County Airport and a dazzling show of aerobatic flying over the airport. In the evening a beautiful fireworks show will be reflected off the serene waters at Beach Park. Est attendance: 26,000. For info: Dunny Dunsworth, PO Box 927, Rockport, TX 78381. Phone: (361) 729-6201. Web: www.rockport-fulton.org.

AMERICA THE BEAUTIFUL PUBLISHED: ANNIVERSARY. July 4, 1895. The poem "America the Beautiful" by Katherine Lee Bates, a Wellesley College professor, was first published in the *Congregationalist*, a church publication.

AMERICAN REDNECK DAY. July 4. To celebrate the work-hard, play-hard, independent spirit of the rural working class. For info: Ed Mason, Natl Dir, American Redneck Trading Post, 317 Fogwell Rd, Centreville, MD 21617. Phone: (410) 758-0777.

ANVIL MOUNTAIN RUN. July 4. Nome, AK. At 8 AM the 17K run up 1,134-ft Anvil Mountain and return to the city of Nome starts the day's activities. Record time: 1 hr, 11 min, 23 sec. 23rd running. Annually, July 4. Est attendance: 1,500. For info: Rasmussen's Music Mart, PO Box 2, Nome, AK 99762-0002. Phone: (907) 443-2798. Fax: (907) 443-5777.

ARMSTRONG, LOUIS: NOT BORN THIS DAY. July 4. Although he often said he was born on the 4th of July, according to personnel at the Louis Armstrong Archives of Queens College, Flushing, NY, documents in their collection indicate that Armstrong was actually born Aug 4, 1900 or 1901.

BOOM BOX PARADE. July 4. Main St, Willimantic, CT. Connecticut's unique people's parade. Anyone can march, enter a float or watch; only requirement—bring a radio. No "real" bands allowed. (Marching music broadcast on WILI-AM Radio and played by "boom boxes" along the parade route.) 11 AM. Est attendance: 10,000. For info: Wayne Norman, Prog Dir, WILI-AM, 720 Main St, Willimantic, CT 06226. Phone: (860) 456-1111. Fax: (860) 456-9501. E-mail: wayne@wili.com. Web: www.wili .com/am.

BRISTOL CIVIC, MILITARY AND FIREMEN'S PARADE. July 4. Bristol, RI. The nation's oldest 4th of July parade. Features floats, bands, veteran and patriotic organizations and military units. Patriotic exercises, a tradition dating to 1785, are held prior to the parade. Annually, July 4 except when July 4 is a Sunday, then the parade is held Monday, July 5. Est attendance: 175,000. For info: Chamber of Commerce, 654 Metacom Ave, Warren, RI 02885. Phone: (401) 245-0750. Web: www.eastbaychamberri.org.

CALITHUMPIAN PARADE. July 4. Biwabik, MN. Funny parade, clowns and bands; Biwabik's population of 1,000 jumps to more than 15,000 for a day. Annually, on the Fourth of July. For info: Darlene Jackson, Committee Co-Chair, Biwabik Area Civic Assn, Box 309, Biwabik, MN 55708. Phone: (218) 865-4183 or (218) 865-6033.

CANADA: THE NORTH AMERICAN TOURNAMENT. July 4–8. Spruce Meadows, Calgary, AB. Show jumping tournament featuring the North American Show Jumping Championships. Sunlife Days at Fort Meadows will offer a great variety of entertainment and food kiosks for your enjoyment. Est attendance: 97,000. For info: Spruce Meadows, RR #9, Calgary, AB, Canada T2J 5G5. Phone: (403) 974-4200. Fax: (403) 974-4270. E-mail: smeadows@telusplanet.net. Web: www.sprucemeadows.com.

CANADA: WOODLAND DISCOVERY TOURS. July 4–Aug 22. Bancroft, ON. A registered professional forester leads tours through local forests, identifying species, describing forestry practices and the forestry industry. Trips include tours of sawmill or fiberboard plant. Annually, every Wednesday in July and August. For info: Bancroft and District Chamber of Commerce, PO Box 539, Bancroft, ON, Canada K0L 1C0. Phone: (613) 332-1513. Fax: (613) 332-2119. E-mail: chamber@commerce.bancroft.on.ca. Web: www.commerce.bancroft.on.ca.

CATONSVILLE INDEPENDENCE DAY CELEBRATION. July 4. Catonsville, MD. Children's games and races, concerts, parade and fireworks display. One of the largest parade and fireworks in Maryland. 55th annual. Est attendance: 60,000. For info: Catonsville Celebrations Committee, PO Box 21074, Catonsville, MD 21228.

CELEBRATE NEW HAVEN 4TH. July 4. Long Wharf Park, New Haven, CT. Music and fireworks over New Haven harbor. For info: Cultural Affairs, (203) 946-7821 or Greater New Haven Conv & Visitors Bureau, 59 Elm St, New Haven, CT 06510. Phone: (203) 777-8550 or (800) 332-STAY. Fax: (203) 782-7755. Web: www.newhavencvb.org.

CELEBRATION ON THE CANE: AN OLD FASHIONED FOURTH OF JULY. July 4. Natchitoches, LA. Featuring hot dogs, apple pie, lemonade and a variety of traditional Fourth of July fare. Musical entertainment including string bands, brass bands, Sousa marches and patriotic choir presentations. Est attendance: 10,000. For info: Calendar of Events, Natchitoches Parish Tourist Commission, 781 Front St, Natchitoches, LA 71457. Phone: (318) 352-8072 or (800) 259-1714. Fax: (318) 352-2415.

COOLIDGE, CALVIN: BIRTH ANNIVERSARY. July 4, 1872. The 30th President of the US was born John Calvin Coolidge at Plymouth, VT. He succeeded to the presidency Aug 3, 1923, following the death of Warren G. Harding. Coolidge was elected president once, in 1924, but did "not choose to run for president in 1928." Nicknamed Silent Cal, he is reported to have said, "If you don't say anything, you won't be called on to repeat it." Coolidge died at Northampton, MA, Jan 5, 1933.

DECLARATION OF INDEPENDENCE APPROVAL AND SIGNING: 225th ANNIVERSARY. July 4, 1776. The Declaration of Independence was approved by the Continental Congress: "Signed by Order and in Behalf of the Congress, John Hancock, President, Attest, Charles Thomson, Secretary." The official signing occurred Aug 2, 1776. The manuscript journals of the Congress for that date state: "The declaration of independence being engrossed and compared at the table was signed by the members."

EARTH AT APHELION. July 4. At approximately 10 AM, EDT, planet Earth will reach aphelion, that point in its orbit when it is farthest from the sun (about 94,510,000 miles). The Earth's mean distance from the sun (mean radius of its orbit) is reached early in the months of April and October. Note that Earth is farthest from the sun during Northern Hemisphere summer. See also: "Earth at Perihelion" (Jan 4).

ENGLAND: HENLEY ROYAL REGATTA. July 4–8. Henley-on-Thames, Oxfordshire. International rowing event that is one of the big social events of the year. Est attendance: 100,000. For info: The Secretary, Henley Royal Regatta, Regatta Headquarters, Henley-on-Thames, Oxfordshire, England RG9 2LY. Phone: (44) (149) 157-2153. Fax: (44) (149) 157-5509. Web: www.hrr.co.uk.

FAMILY DAY/INDEPENDENCE DAY CELEBRATION. July 4. Historic Square, Dahlonega, GA. Voted as "Top 20 Event" by the Southeast Tourism Society. Craft booths of all kinds, continuous music all day, food booths, kids' fun booths with prizes, clogging and buckdancing. Est attendance: 18,000. For info: Dahlonega-Lumpkin Chamber of Commerce, 13 S Park St, Dahlonega, GA 30533. Phone: (706) 864-3711. Fax: (706) 864-7917. E-mail: dahloneg@alltel.net. Web: www.dahlonega.org.

FIRESTORM 2001. July 4. Lakemont Park, Altoona, PA. The region's largest Fourth of July celebration with live entertainment on stage all day and a spectacular fireworks show. For info: Melissa Vyborny, Lakemont Park, I-99 Frankstown Rd. Exit, Altoona, PA 16602. Phone: (814) 949-7275 or (800) 434-8006. Fax: (814) 949-9207. E-mail: Lakemont99@aol.com. Web: www .lakemontparkfun.com.

July 2001	S	M	T	W	T	F	S
	1	2	3	4	5	6	7
	8	9	10	11	12	13	14
	15	16	17	18	19	20	21
	22	23	24	25	26	27	28
	29	30	31				

FIREWORKS CELEBRATION. July 4. Demopolis, AL. Each year the Demopolis Area Chamber of Commerce presents a spectacular array of fireworks in celebration of Independence Day. The fireworks celebration is held at the Demopolis City Landing and begins at 9 PM. Est attendance: 10,000. For info: Kathy Leverett, Pres, Demopolis Area Chamber of Commerce, Box 667, Demopolis, AL 36732. Phone: (334) 289-0270. Fax: (334) 289-1382. Web: www.chamber.dempolis.us.

FOSTER, STEPHEN: 175th BIRTH ANNIVERSARY. July 4, 1826. Stephen Collins Foster, one of America's most famous and best-loved songwriters, was born at Lawrenceville, PA. Among his nearly 200 songs: "Oh! Susanna," "Camptown Races," "Old Folks at Home" ("Swanee River"), "Jeanie with the Light Brown Hair," "Old Black Joe" and "Beautiful Dreamer." Foster died in poverty at Bellevue Hospital at New York, NY, Jan 13, 1864. The anniversary of his death has been observed as Stephen Foster Memorial Day by Presidential Proclamation since 1952.

FOURTH OF JULY TORCHLIGHT PROCESSION. July 4. Winston-Salem, NC. Craft demonstrations, re-enactments of events in early Salem and other special activities. Torchlight procession: Reenactment of state's first 4th of July celebration by legislative proclamation (1783). 200 costumed participants, narration and music. Sponsor: Old Salem, Inc. Est attendance: 5,000. For info: Bill Cissna, Box F, Salem Station, Winston-Salem, NC 27108. Phone: (888) OLD-SALEM.

FREDERICKSBURG HERITAGE FESTIVAL. July 4. Fredericksburg, VA. To create an awareness of Fredericksburg's historic heritage. Parade, raft race, street festival, country music, jazz, rock and roll, fireworks and Civil War battle reenactment. Est attendance: 15,000. For info: Visitor Center, 706 Caroline St, Fredericksburg, VA 22401. Phone: (800) 678-4748. Fax: (540) 372-6587. E-mail: fburg@illuminet.net.

FREEDOM FEST. July 4 (rain date July 5). Lake of the Woods, Mahomet, IL. Annual celebration of patriotism. Family activities capped off by a spectacular fireworks display. Admission charged. Est attendance: 7,000. For info: Andee Chestnut, PR Coord, Champaign Co Forest Preserve District, PO Box 1040, Mahomet, IL 61853. Phone: (217) 586-3360. Fax: (217) 586-5724. E-mail: HQ@ccfpd.org. Web: www.ccfpd.org.

FREEDOM WEEK. July 4–10. To disseminate throughout the world information about freedom and liberty. For complete info and many famous quotations about freedom and liberty, send $4 to cover expense of printing, handling and postage. Annually, July 4–10. For info: Dr. Stanley Drake, Pres, Intl Soc of Friendship and Good Will, 8592 Roswell Rd, Ste 434, Atlanta, GA 30350-1870.

FREEDOM FROM FEAR OF SPEAKING DAY. July 4. This day is dedicated to stamping out the fear monster of public speaking. Priscilla Richardson, President of Write & Speak for Success!, has had to tame her own fear monster of public speaking to get her own speaking freedom. For info: Priscilla Richardson, Pres, Write & Speak for Success!, PO Box 275, Cloverdale, VA 24077-0275. Phone: (540) 992-1279. E-mail: Wrisuccess@aol.com.

GOLDBERG, RUBE: BIRTH ANNIVERSARY. July 4, 1883. The cartoonist with an engineering degree who put his education to work inventing elaborate machines with involved steps to accomplish ludicrously simple tasks. He is best remembered for the creative inventions of his cartoon character Lucifer Gorgonzola Butts. Born at San Francisco, Goldberg died Dec 7, 1970, at New York City.

GRAND TETON MUSIC FESTIVAL. July 4–Aug 25. Walk Festival Hall, Teton Village, WY. Eiji Oue, Music Director. Full symphony orchestra concerts on Friday and Saturday evenings, chamber music Tuesday through Thursday, performed by professional musicians from America's finest symphony orchestras with internationally acclaimed guest soloists and conductors 8 PM each night. Est attendance: 22,000. For info: Grand Teton Music Festival, Box 490, Teton Village, WY 83025. Phone: (307) 733-1128. Fax: (307) 739-9043. E-mail: gtmf@gtmf.org. Web: www.gtmf.org.

GREAT CARDBOARD BOAT REGATTA. July 4. Rotary Riverview Park, Sheboygan, WI. The most spectacular and hilarious races of somewhat seaworthy craft ever launched in Wisconsin. Person-powered cardboard boats compete in various classes for prizes. Awards for the most spirited team, the most beautiful boats, boats following a theme and the most spectacular sinking (Titanic Award). Prizes for top finishers in three boat classes: propelled by oars or paddles; propelled by mechanical means such as paddle wheels or propellers; and "Instant Boats" made from "Secret Kits" by spectators-turned-participants. Est attendance: 16,000. For info: John Michael Kohler Arts Center, 608 New York Ave, PO Box 489, Sheboygan, WI 53082-0489. Phone: (920) 458-6144. Fax: (920) 458-4473. Web: www.jmkac.org.

GREAT SEAL OF THE US PROPOSED: 225th ANNIVERSARY. July 4, 1776. The Continental Congress, meeting at Philadelphia, PA, after voting to adopt the Declaration of Independence, went on to approve the following: "Resolved, that Dr. Franklin, Mr J. Adams and Mr Jefferson, be a committee, to bring in a device for a seal for the United States of America," thus beginning the history of the Great Seal of the US on the first day of independence. The seal wasn't designed and used until 1782.

HAWTHORNE, NATHANIEL: BIRTH ANNIVERSARY. July 4, 1804. Novelist and short-story writer, born at Salem, MA. Works included *The Scarlet Letter*, *The House of the Seven Gables* and *The Blithedale Romance*. Hawthorne died at Plymouth, NH, May 19, 1864.

ICE CREAM SOCIAL. July 4. Indianapolis, IN. Independence Day celebration. Music, lawn games and living history. Est attendance: 1,000. For info: President Benjamin Harrison Home, PR Dept, 1230 N Delaware St, Indianapolis, IN 46202. Phone: (317) 631-1898.

INDEPENDENCE DAY (FOURTH OF JULY): 225th ANNIVERSARY. July 4, 1776. The US commemorates adoption of the Declaration of Independence by the Continental Congress. The nation's birthday. Legal holiday in all states and territories.

INDEPENDENCE DAY SYMPHONY CONCERT AND FIREWORKS. July 4. Wheeling, WV. Independence Day celebration on the Wheeling waterfront. Est attendance: 30,000. For info: Wheeling Conv and Visitors Bureau, 1401 Main, Wheeling, WV 26003. Phone: (800) 828-3097 or (304) 233-7709. Web: www.wheelingcvb.com/calendar.

INDEPENDENCE–FROM–MEAT DAY. July 4. Don't be a slave to tradition. Declare your freedom from flesh foods. Your fiery Fourth will be fantastic with a good-for-you vegetarian barbecue. Why not fix a freedom feast featuring veggie burgers and veggie dogs for your family and friends? It will be fun for you and your animal friends too! For info: Vegetarian Awareness Network, Communications Center, PO Box 321, Knoxville, TN 37901-0321. Phone: (800) USA-VEGE.

JULY 4th FAMILY CELEBRATION. July 4. Fort Lauderdale, FL. Featuring live music, fireworks and food. 6 PM–4:30 PM. Annually, July 4. Est attendance: 300,000. For info: Greater Fort Lauderdale Conv & Visitors Bureau, 1850 Eller Dr, Ste 303, Ft Lauderdale, FL 33316. Phone: (954) 489-3255.

JULY 4th FIREWORKS FESTIVAL. July 4. Hartsville, SC. An afternoon of family games, picnic, music and fireworks at dark. Est attendance: 8,000. For info: Tina Kissiah, Admin Asst, Greater Hartsville Chamber of Commerce, PO Box 578, Hartsville, SC 29551. Phone: (803) 332-6401.

LEWISTOWN 4th PARADE AND CELEBRATION. July 4. Lewistown, MT. Parade, breakfast, barbecue, baseball and games. The Shrine Circus (two performances), fireworks. Est attendance: 2,000. For info: Lewistown Chamber of Commerce, PO Box 818, Lewistown, MT 59457. Phone: (406) 538-5436. Fax: (406) 538-5437. E-mail: lewchamb@lewistown.net. Web: www.lewistownchamber.com.

LIGHT UP THE SKY—FOURTH OF JULY. July 4. St. Charles, MO. Traditional Independence Day celebration includes fireworks, craft and food booths, parade, entertainment and children's area. Est attendance: 35,000. For info: St. Charles CVB, 230 S Main St, St. Charles, MO 63301. Phone: (800) 366-2427 or (636) 946-7776. Web: www.historicstcharles.com.

MACKINAW CITY'S FOURTH OF JULY FIREWORKS. July 4. State Dock on South Huron Ave, Mackinaw City, MI. Starting at 1:30 PM on the marina lawn, there will be fun and games for all ages. One of the largest fireworks displays in the north will be shot off over the harbor at dusk. For info: Mackinaw City Chamber of Commerce, PO Box 856, Mackinaw City, MI 49701. Phone: (616) 436-5574. Web: www.mackinawcity.com.

MISSISSIPPI DEEP SEA FISHING TOURNAMENT RODEO. July 4–8. Gulfport, MS. Annual celebration, featuring fishing events, entertainment, rides, games and family fun. Sponsor: MS Deep Sea Rodeo, Inc. Est attendance: 150,000. For info: Chuck Dedeaux, MS Deep Sea Rodeo, Box 1289, Gulfport, MS 39502. Phone: (228) 863-2713.

MONETT OLD-FASHIONED FOURTH OF JULY CELEBRATION. July 4. Monett, MO. Parade, games, children's carnival, bands, gospel music, steam engine display, hot-air balloon rides, air stunts, skydivers, National Guard helicopter and vehicle display, food and a fireworks display. Annually, the Fourth of July. Est attendance: 5,000. For info: Deborah Schoen, 1304 Hemingway Dr, Monett, MO 65708.

		S	M	T	W	T	F	S
July		1	2	3	4	5	6	7
2001		8	9	10	11	12	13	14
		15	16	17	18	19	20	21
		22	23	24	25	26	27	28
		29	30	31				

MOUNT MARATHON RACE. July 4. Seward, AK. Grueling footrace begins in downtown Seward, then ascends and descends 3,022-ft Mt Marathon. Race began as a wager between two sourdoughs. 74th running. Est attendance: 20,000. For info: Seward Chamber of Commerce, PO Box 749, Seward, AK 99664. Phone: (907) 224-8051. Fax: (907) 224-5353. Web: www.sewardak.org.

MYSTIC SEAPORT INDEPENDENCE DAY CELEBRATION. July 4. Mystic Seaport, Mystic, CT. Visitors can participate in a recreation of an 1870s Fourth of July with costumed staff. There are patriotic ceremonies and a parade of the "Antiques and Horribles." Kids, old-fashioned spelling bee. Est attendance: 3,500. For info: Mystic Seaport, 75 Greenmanville Ave, Box 6000, Mystic, CT 06355. Phone: (860) 572-5315 or (888) 9-SEAPORT. Web: www.mystic.org.

NATIONAL TOM SAWYER DAYS (WITH FENCE PAINTING CONTEST). July 4–7. Hannibal, MO. Frog jumping, mud volleyball, Tom and Becky Contest, parade, Tomboy Sawyer Contest, 10K run, arts & crafts show and fireworks launched from the banks of the Mississippi River. Highlight is the National Fence Painting Contest. Sponsor: Hannibal Jaycees. Est attendance: 100,000. For info: Hannibal Visitors Bureau, 505 N 3rd St, Hannibal, MO 63401. Phone: (573) 221-2477.

OATMAN SIDEWALK EGG FRYING CONTEST. July 4. Oatman, AZ. Contest held at high noon on the downtown streets of old Rt 66. Also, Old West gun fights, wild burros roaming the streets, food, entertainment and more. Note: Only solar heat may be used to fry the eggs. 15-minute time limit. Annually, July 4. Est attendance: 2,500. For info: Spirit Mountain Productions, 1255 Hancock Rd, Bullhead City, AZ 86442. Phone: (520) 763-5885. Fax: (520) 763-3545.

OLD GLORY JUBILEE. July 4. Elsberry, MO. Old-time picnic, parade, entertainment, games, crafts and lots of food. Est attendance: 1,000. For info: Elsberry City Hall, 201 Broadway, Elsberry, MO 63343. Phone: (573) 898-5588. Fax: (573) 898-2249.

OLD VERMONT FOURTH. July 4. Woodstock, VT. A traditional Fourth of July with patriotic speeches and debates, making "1890" flags, a spelling bee for adults, ice cream making, sack race and more. Est attendance: 750. For info: Deborah Bullissa, Exec Asst, Billings Farm and Museum, PO Box 489, Woodstock, VT 05091. Phone: (802) 457-2355. Fax: (802) 457-4663. E-mail: billings.farm@valley.net.

PEACHTREE ROAD RACE. July 4. Atlanta, GA. 10K run. 50,000-runner limit; advance registration only. Send self-addressed stamped envelope by Mar 1, 2001. 45,000 entrants on first-come basis and 10,000 selected by lottery from other entries postmarked in March 2001. Est attendance: 55,000. For info: Atlanta Track Club, 3097 E Shadowlawn Ave, Atlanta, GA 30305. Phone: (404) 231-9064. Web: www.atlantatrackclub.org.

PHILIPPINES: FIL-AMERICAN FRIENDSHIP DAY. July 4. Formerly National Independence Day, when the Philippines were a colony of the US, now celebrated as Fil-American Friendship Day.

PRAIRIE PIONEER DAYS. July 4. Arapahoe, NE. Parade, games for kids, food booths, free swimming, watermelon bust, quilt show, horseshoe pitching, model airplane event, baseball games, fireworks and more. For info: Tammie Middagh, Secy, Arapahoe Chamber of Commerce, PO Box 624, Arapahoe, NE 68922.

RIVERFEST. July 4–8. Riverside Park, LaCrosse, WI. 19th annual Riverfest—the city's premier summer event! Top-name entertainers, river activities and continuous musical entertainment highlight this free fest. A food fair, beverage tent, clowns, children's activities and various athletic events held daily. Est attendance: 40,000. For info: Riverfest, Inc, PO Box 1745, LaCrosse, WI 54602. Phone: (608) 782-6000. Fax: (608) 784-1580.

"THE SOUPY SALES SHOW" TV PREMIERE: ANNIVERSARY. July 4, 1955. Soupy Sales hosted a number of national and local children's shows from 1955 to 1979. All of his programs included some of these features: jokes, puns, songs, sketches, puppets, silent films and pies in the face. Sales's humor occasionally went over the edge and got him in trouble; for example, in 1965 his show was suspended for a week because he asked his viewers to send him the green paper in their parents' wallets!

SPACE MILESTONE: *MARS PATHFINDER* (US). July 4, 1997. Unmanned spacecraft landed on Mars after a seven-month flight. Carried *Sojourner*, a roving robotic explorer that sent back photographs of the landscape. One of its missions was to find if life ever existed on Mars. See also: "Space Milestone: *Mars Global Surveyor*" (Sept 11).

SPACE MILESTONE: *NOZOMI* (JAPAN). July 4, 1998. Japan launched this mission to Mars, making it the third country (after the US and Russia) to attempt an interplanetary space mission. *Nozomi*, which means "Hope," is to orbit 84 miles above Mars and beam images back to Earth.

SPAM TOWN USA FESTIVAL. July 4–8. Austin, MN. Annual festival includes family activities, street dancing, stage entertainment, beer garden, running races, bike races, food and much more. Sunday features performance of the Austin Symphony Orchestra and fireworks. Est attendance: 15,000. For info: Spam Town USA Festival, 329 N Main St, Ste 102, Austin, MN 55912. Phone: (507) 437-3448.

SPIRIT OF FREEDOM CELEBRATION. July 4. Florence, AL. Celebrate America's birthday on the banks of the beautiful Tennessee River at McFarland Park. Enjoy sunning, swimming, bicycling, golf and entertainment. Playground, picnic tables and campground available. Annually, on July 4. Est attendance: 60,000. For info: Florence/Lauderdale Tourism, One Hightower Place, Florence, AL 35630. Phone: (256) 740-4141 or (888) FLO-TOUR. Fax: (256) 740-4142. E-mail: dwilson@floweb.com. Web: www.flo-tour.org.

STOCK EXCHANGE HOLIDAY (INDEPENDENCE DAY). July 4. The holiday schedules for the various exchanges are subject to change if relevant rules, regulations or exchange policies are revised. If you have questions, phone: American Stock Exchange (212) 306-1000; Chicago Board of Trade (312) 435-3500; Chicago Board of Options Exchange (312) 786-5600; New York Stock Exchange (212) 656-2065; Pacific Stock Exchange (415) 393-4000; Philadelphia Stock Exchange (215) 496-5000.

SULLIVAN FREEDOM FESTIVAL. July 4. Sullivan Fairgrounds, Sullivan, MO. Festival open 6 PM–10 PM. Features children's activities, contests, games, entertainment, food and fireworks. Est attendance: 5,000. For info: Sullivan Chamber of Commerce, PO Box 536, Sullivan, MO 63080. Phone: (573) 468-3314. E-mail: chamber@sullivanmo.com. Web: www.sullivanmo.com.

TEN THOUSAND CRESTONIANS. July 4. Downtown and McKinley Park, Creston, IA. Parade, fireworks, flea market, talent show, historical village, carnival and food. All to celebrate US founding. Est attendance: 8,000. For info: Creston Chamber of Commerce, PO Box 471, Creston, IA 50801. Phone: (515) 641-7021. E-mail: chamber@mddc.com. Web: www.mdcc.com/chamber.

TRADITIONAL SOUSA CONCERT. July 4. The American Club, Kohler, WI. Kohler Village Concert Series presents the Kiel Municipal Band featuring the distinctive swing and vigor that marks the work of the "March King," John Philip Sousa. Entertaining with a selection of marches, show tunes and contemporary favorites, this nationally recognized community concert ensemble has been awarded the Sudler Scroll for musical excellence by the Sousa Foundation. Est attendance: 1,000. For info: The American Club, Highland Dr, Kohler, WI 53044. Phone: (800) 344-2838. Fax: (920) 457-0299. Web: www.americanclub.com.

TUSKEGEE INSTITUTE OPENING: ANNIVERSARY. July 4, 1881. Booker T. Washington's famed agricultural-industrial institution was built from the ground up by dedicated students seeking academic and vocational training. The institute started in a shanty before Washington purchased an abandoned plantation at Tuskegee, AL. The students built the dormitories, classrooms and chapel from bricks out of their own kiln.

WESTON JAYCEE'S ANNUAL JULY 4TH CELEBRATION. July 4. Weston, MO. The evening begins with an ice cream social and a presentation by the Missouri Valley Skydivers with fireworks beginning at 9 PM. For info: Weston Development Co, 502 Main St, Weston, MO 64098. Phone: (816) 640-2909.

WORLD'S GREATEST LIZARD RACE. July 4. Chaparral Park, Lovington, NM. Participants and observers cheer as their lizards and iguanas race down a 16-ft ramp; winners are awarded trophies. Many other lizard events will be held throughout the day. Entertainment and other games are also featured. Annually, July 4. For info: Lovington Chamber of Commerce, 201 S Main St, Lovington, NM 88260. Phone: (505) 396-5311. Fax: (505) 396-2823. E-mail: visitus@leaconet.com. Web: visitus.leaco.net.

WSB-TV SALUTE 2 AMERICA PARADE. July 4. Atlanta, GA. One of the largest 4th of July parades in the US. 41st annual parade steps off at 1 PM. Est attendance: 300,000. For info: WSB-TV Salute 2 America Parade, 1601 W Peachtree St NE, Atlanta, GA 30309. Phone: (404) 897-7385. Fax: (404) 897-6236.

ZOOBALEE. July 4. Lee Richardson Zoo, Garden City, KS. Old-fashioned Independence Day celebration featuring duck races, dunk tank, ethnic foods, dart throw, moon walk and more. Est attendance: 5,000. For info: Heather Salyer, Dvmt Dir, Friends of Lee Richardson Zoo, Box 1638, Garden City, KS 67846. Phone: (316) 276-6243. Fax: (316) 276-0910.

BIRTHDAYS TODAY

Signy Coleman, 41, actress ("The Young and the Restless"), born Marin County, CA, July 4, 1960.

Allen (Al) Davis, 72, Pro Football Hall of Famer, football executive, born Brockton, MA, July 4, 1929.

Harvey Grant, 36, basketball player, born Augusta, GA, July 4, 1965.

Horace Grant, 36, basketball player, born Augusta, GA, July 4, 1965.

Leona Helmsley, 81, former hotel executive, born Brooklyn, NY, July 4, 1920.

Ann Landers (Esther Pauline Friedman), 83, advice columnist, born Sioux City, IA, July 4, 1918.

Gina Lollobrigida, 73, actress, photographer (*Belles de Nuit, Bread, Love and Dreams*), born Auviaco, Italy, July 4, 1928.

Geraldo Rivera, 58, journalist, talk-show host ("Geraldo," *Exposing Myself*), born New York, NY, July 4, 1943.

Eva Marie Saint, 77, actress (Oscar for *On the Waterfront; North by Northwest, Exodus*), born Newark, NJ, July 4, 1924.

Pamela Howard (Pam) Shriver, 39, broadcaster and former tennis player, born Baltimore, MD, July 4, 1962.

Neil Simon, 74, playwright (*The Odd Couple, Barefoot in the Park*), born New York, NY, July 4, 1927.

George Michael Steinbrenner III, 71, baseball executive, born Rocky River, OH, July 4, 1930.

Abigail Van Buren (Pauline Esther Friedman), 83, advice columnist, born Sioux City, IA, July 4, 1918.

JULY 5 — THURSDAY
Day 186 — 179 Remaining

ALGERIA: INDEPENDENCE DAY. July 5. National holiday. Commemorates the day in 1962 when Algeria gained independence from France.

BARNUM, PHINEAS TAYLOR: BIRTH ANNIVERSARY. July 5, 1810. Promoter of the bizarre and unusual. Barnum's American Museum opened in 1842, promoting unusual acts including the Feejee Mermaid, Chang and Eng (the original Siamese Twins) and General Tom Thumb. In 1850 he began his promotion of Jenny Lind, "The Swedish Nightingale," and parlayed her singing talents into a major financial success. Barnum also cultivated a keen interest in politics. A founder of the newspaper *Herald of Freedom*, he wrote outspoken editorials that resulted not only in lawsuits but also in at least one jail sentence. In 1852 he declined the Democratic nomination for governor of Connecticut but did serve two terms in the Connecticut legislature beginning in 1865. He was defeated in a bid for US Congress in 1866 but served as mayor of Bridgeport, CT, from 1875 to 1876. In 1871 "The Greatest Show on Earth" opened at Brooklyn, NY; Barnum merged with his rival J.A. Bailey in 1881 to form the Barnum and Bailey Circus. P.T. Barnum was born at Bethel, CT, and died at Bridgeport, CT, Apr 7, 1891.

BELGIUM: OMMEGANG PAGEANT. July 5. Splendid historic festival of medieval pageantry at the illuminated Grand-Palace in Brussels. The annual event (first Thursday in July) re-creates an entertainment given in honor of Charles V and his court.

FARRAGUT, DAVID: 200th BIRTH ANNIVERSARY. July 5, 1801. Born near Knoxville, TN, and died Aug 14, 1870, at Portsmouth, NH. Admiral in the American Civil War who was famous for his naval victories. At Mobile Bay, AL, in a disastrous attack on his entire fleet by the Confederates' Fort Morgan, Farragut proclaimed the famous cry, "Damn the torpedoes, full speed ahead!" They escaped the attack and Mobile Bay surrendered.

FINLAND: TIME OF MUSIC. July 5–11. Viitasaari. Festival in a town of 300 lakes focuses on contemporary music with top international and Finnish artists performing more than 100 works from some of the most interesting composers of our time, many being performed for the first time ever. Est attendance: 8,000. For info: Finnish Tourist Board, 655 Third Ave, New York, NY 10017. Phone: (212) 885-9700 or Time of Music, Kesleitie 10, Finland 44500 Viitasaari. Phone: (358) (14) 573195 or Fax: (358) (14) 5793515. E-mail: time.music@festivals.fi. Web: www.viitasaari.fi/tom/

ISLE OF MAN: TYNWALD DAY. July 5. Tynwald Hill at St. John's. Traditionally, on July 5, Old Midsummer Day, the island's parliament of Tynwald assembles at the meeting place of the Vikings to promulgate new laws.

	S	M	T	W	T	F	S
July		1	2	3	4	5	6	7
2001	8	9	10	11	12	13	14
	15	16	17	18	19	20	21
	22	23	24	25	26	27	28
	29	30	31				

LUNAR ECLIPSE. July 5. Partial eclipse of the moon. Moon enters penumbra at 8:10 AM, EDT, reaches middle of eclipse at 10:55 AM and leaves penumbra at 1:39 PM. Visible in Antarctica, New Zealand, Australia, eastern and central Asia, East Africa, Hawaiian Islands, Central Pacific Ocean.

MOON PHASE: FULL MOON. July 5. Moon enters Full Moon phase at 11:04 AM, EDT.

NATIONAL LABOR RELATIONS ACT (THE WAGNER ACT): ANNIVERSARY. July 5, 1935. This bill guaranteed workers the right to organize and bargain collectively with their employers. It also prohibited the formation of company unions. An enforcement agency, the National Labor Relations Board, was created by the Act.

RAFFLES, STAMFORD: BIRTH ANNIVERSARY. July 5, 1781. Sir Stamford Raffles, English colonial official, founder of Singapore, where he is supposed to have landed Jan 29, 1819, was born at sea, off Jamaica. He discovered with Joseph Arnold an East Indian fungus that is named after them, *Rafflesia Arnoldi*. Raffles died near London, England, on his birthday, July 5, 1826.

RHODES, CECIL JOHN: BIRTH ANNIVERSARY. July 5, 1853. English-born, South African millionaire politician. Said to have controlled at one time 90 percent of the world's diamond production. His will founded the Rhodes Scholarships at Oxford University for superior scholastic achievers. Rhodesia (now Zimbabwe) was named for him. Born at Bishop's Stortford, Hertfordshire, Rhodes died Mar 26, 1902, at Cape Town, South Africa.

SLOVAKIA: SAINT CYRIL AND METHODIUS DAY. July 5. This day is dedicated to the Greek priests and scholars from Thessalonniki, who were invited by Prince Rastislav of Great Moravia to introduce Christianity and the first Slavic alphabet to the pagan people of the kingdom in AD 863.

VENEZUELA: INDEPENDENCE DAY. July 5. National holiday. Commemorates Proclamation of Independence from Spain in 1811. Independence was not achieved until 1821.

WESTMORELAND ARTS & HERITAGE FESTIVAL. July 5–8. Twin Lakes Park, Greensburg, PA. Celebrating 27 years of arts and humanities. Multi-cultural celebration including food booths, ethnic area, children's area, crafts, fine art exhibition, continuous entertainment on five stages. Est attendance: 130,000. For info: John Vogt, RR 2, Box 355 A, Latrobe, PA 15650. Phone: (724) 834-7474. E-mail: festival@westol.com. Web: www.westol.com/wahf.

WOOD PELLET BBQ INTRODUCTION DAY. July 5. Commemorating the introduction of the revolutionary Wood Pellet BBQ Grill, invented by Joseph P. Traeger of Mt Angel, Oregon. The BBQ grill is sold around the world and is now the most revolutionary bio-mass cooking appliance ever invented in America. For info: Bruce Bjorkman, Traeger Industries, PO Box 829, Mt Angel, OR 97362. Phone: (503) 845-6366. E-mail: traeger@traegerindustries.com. Web: www.traegerindustries.com.

ZETKIN, CLARA: BIRTH ANNIVERSARY. July 5, 1857. Women's rights advocate, born at Wiederau, Germany. Zetkin has been credited with being the initiator of International Women's Day, which has been observed on Mar 8 at least since 1910. She died at Arkhangelskoe, Russia, June 20, 1933. See also: "International (Working) Women's Day" (Mar 8).

BIRTHDAYS TODAY

Eliot Feld, 59, dancer, born Brooklyn, NY, July 5, 1942.

Richard Michael ("Goose") Gossage, 50, former baseball player, born Colorado Springs, CO, July 5, 1951.

Chris Gratton, 26, hockey player, born Brantford, Ontario, Canada, July 5, 1975.

Katherine Helmond, 67, actress (stage: *The House of Blue Leaves*; "Soap," "Who's the Boss?"), born Galveston, TX, July 5, 1934.

Shirley Knight, 65, actress (stage: *Kennedy's Children* [Tony Award, 1976]; *The Dark at the Top of the Stairs, Sweet Bird of Youth, Petulia*), born Goessell, KS, July 5, 1936.

Huey Lewis (Hugh Anthony Cregg III), 50, singer (Huey Lewis and the News), born San Francisco, CA, July 5, 1951.

James David Lofton, 45, former football player, born Fort Ord, CA, July 5, 1956.

Robbie Robertson, 57, musician (guitarist with The Band), born Toronto, Ontario, Canada, July 5, 1944.

Janos Starker, 77, musician, born Budapest, Hungary, July 5, 1924.

JULY 6 — FRIDAY

Day 187 — 178 Remaining

CANADA: ABBOTSFORD BERRY FESTIVAL. July 6–7. Abbotsford, BC. July heralds the height of the Raspberry Capital of Canada's berry season. Sample delicious local berries and berry products. Linger to cheer the musicians, magicians and clowns; play bingo; take the kids on fun rides and browse through local craft and market-style food stands. Est attendance: 25,000. For info: Abbotsford Downtown Business Assn, 33780 Hazel St, Abbotsford, BC, Canada V2S 2M6. Phone: (604) 850-6547. Fax: (604) 850-6547. E-mail: adba@bia.bc.ca. Web: www.abbotsford downtownbia.bc.ca.

CANADA: EDMONTON INTERNATIONAL STREET PERFORMERS FESTIVAL. July 6–15. Sir Winston Churchill Square, Edmonton, AB. Family-oriented busking festival. More than 50 acts from around the world. Est attendance: 200,000. For info: Shelley Switzer, Producer, #650 7 Sir Winston Churchill Square, Edmonton, AB, Canada T5J 2V5. Phone: (780) 425-5162. Fax: (780) 426-0853. E-mail: street@connect.ab.ca.

CELEBRITY GOLF CHAMPIONSHIP. July 6–8. Stateline, NV. Sports and entertainment stars compete in a tournament at Edgewood Tahoe Golf Course. For info: Phone: (530) 544-5050.

COMOROS: INDEPENDENCE DAY: ANNIVERSARY. July 6. Federal and Islamic Republic of Comoros commemorates declaration of independence from France in 1975.

CZECH REPUBLIC: COMMEMORATION DAY OF BURNING OF JOHN HUS. July 6. In honor of Bohemian religious reformer John Hus, who was condemned as a heretic and burned at the stake in 1415.

ENGLAND: WAYS WITH WORDS LITERATURE FESTIVAL. July 6–16. Dartington Hall, Dartington, Devon. Some 200 writers give lectures, seminars, interviews, discussions and readings. Book stalls, workshops and plays are also included. Est attendance: 6,500. For info: Steven Bristow, Dir, Ways With Words Literature Festival, Droridge Farm, Dartington, Totnes, Devon, England TQ9 6JQ. Phone: (180) 386-7373. Fax: (180) 386-3688. E-mail: wwwords@globalnet.co.uk. Web: www.ways withwords.co.uk.

FIRST AIRSHIP CROSSING OF ATLANTIC: ANNIVERSARY. July 6, 1919. The first airship crossing of the Atlantic was completed as a British dirigible landed at New York's Roosevelt Field.

FIRST BLACK US STATE'S ATTORNEY: 40th ANNIVERSARY. July 6, 1961. Cecil Francis Poole became the first black US state's attorney when he was sworn in as US attorney for the Northern District of California. He served until his retirement on Feb 3, 1970.

FIRST SUCCESSFUL ANTIRABIES INOCULATION: ANNIVERSARY. July 6, 1885. Louis Pasteur gave the first successful antirabies inoculation to a boy who had been bitten by an infected dog.

JONES, JOHN PAUL: BIRTH ANNIVERSARY. July 6, 1747 (OS). American naval officer born at Kirkbean, Scotland. Remembered for his victory in the battle of his ship, the *Bonhomme Richard*, with the British frigate *Serapis*, Sept 23, 1779. When Jones was queried: "Do you ask for quarter?" he made his famous reply: "I have not yet begun to fight!" Jones was victorious, but the *Bonhomme Richard*, badly damaged, sank two days later. Jones died at Paris, France, July 18, 1792.

LUXEMBOURG: ETTELBRUCK REMEMBRANCE DAY: ANNIVERSARY. July 6. In honor of US General George Patton, Jr, liberator of the Grand-Duchy of Luxembourg in 1945, who is buried at the American Military Cemetery at Hamm, Germany, among 5,100 soldiers of his famous Third Army.

MAJOR LEAGUE BASEBALL HOLDS FIRST ALL-STAR GAME: ANNIVERSARY. July 6, 1933. The first midsummer All-Star Game was held at Comiskey Park, Chicago, IL. Babe Ruth led the American League with a home run, as they defeated the National League 4–2. Prior to the summer of 1933, All-Star contests consisted of pre- and postseason exhibitions that often found teams made up of a few stars playing beside journeymen and even minor leaguers.

MALAWI: REPUBLIC DAY: 35th ANNIVERSARY. July 6. National holiday. Commemorates attainment of independence from Britain in 1964 and Malawi's becoming a republic in 1966. Malawi was formerly known as Nyasaland.

"NAME THAT TUNE" TV PREMIERE: ANNIVERSARY. July 6, 1953. "Name That Tune" was a musical identification show that appeared in different formats in the '50s and the '70s. Red Benson was the host of the NBC series and Bill Cullen (and later George DeWitt) was the CBS host. Two contestants listened while an orchestra played a musical selection, and the first contestant who could identify it raced across the stage to ring a bell. The winner of the round then tried to identify a number of tunes within a specific time period. After 11 years, the show was brought back with Richard Hayes as host. In 1974 new network and syndicated versions appeared.

OLD-TIME FIDDLER'S JAMBOREE AND CRAFTS FESTIVAL. July 6–7. Smithville, TN. Thirty-one categories of old-time bluegrass including clogging, buck dancing, old-time fiddle band, five-string banjo, dulcimer, dobro, flat-top guitar and fiddle-off to decide the Grand Champion Fiddler. Annually, the weekend nearest July 4. Est attendance: 110,000. For info: Smithville Fiddlers' Jamboree, PO Box 83, Smithville, TN 37166. Phone: (615) 597-8500. Web: www.dekalbtn.com/jamboree or Dekalb Chamber of Commerce. Phone: (615) 597-4163.

OPERATION OVERCAST: ANNIVERSARY. July 6, 1945. As the end of the war approached, the US Army had begun to move German scientists and scientific equipment from the German territory designated for Russian occupation. On this date, the American Joint Chiefs of Staff authorized Operation Overcast, under which 350 German and Austrian scientists were transported to the US in a matter of months.

PROSPECT PARK FISHING CONTEST. July 6–14. Prospect Park, Brooklyn, NY. A contest for young anglers, 15 and under, with prizes for the largest or most fish. At the Rustic Shelter Lakeside near the Kate Wollman Rink parking lot. Groups must register ahead of time. Est attendance: 3,000. For info: Public Info Mgr, Public Info Office—Litchfield Villa, 95 Prospect Park W, Prospect Park, Brooklyn, NY 11215. Phone: (718) 965-8954. Fax: (718) 965-8972. E-mail: marketing@prospectpark.org. Web: www.prospectpark.org.

"THE QUIZ KIDS" TV PREMIERE: ANNIVERSARY. July 6, 1949. This show began on radio and continued on TV with the original host, Joe Kelly, and later with Clifton Fadiman.

The format was a panel of five child prodigies who answered questions sent in by viewers. Four were regulars, staying for weeks or months, while the fifth was a "guest child." The ages of the panelists varied from 6 to 16.

REPUBLICAN PARTY FORMED: ANNIVERSARY. July 6, 1854. The Republican Party formally originated at a convention at Ripon, WI.

SHRINE MUSICAL. July 6–8. Belleville, IL. A musical celebrating the first 2000 years of Christianity. Characters include the archangels, the evangelists, the saints and historical figures: Joan of Arc, St. Francis, St. Augustine, John of the Cross, John XXIII and Dorothy Day. Est attendance: 1,500. For info: Shrine of our Lady of the Snows, 442 S DeMazenod Dr, Belleville, IL 62223-1094. Phone: (618) 397-6700. Fax: (618) 397-1210. Web: www .snows.org.

SLOW PITCH SOFTBALL TOURNAMENT. July 6–8. Elm Park, Williamsport, PA. 28th annual charitable tournament with 64 teams. Sponsor: Miller Lite. Annually, the first weekend after July 4. Est attendance: 8,500. For info: Don Phillips, Mid-State Beverage Co, 532 Sylvan Dr, South Williamsport, PA 17702. Phone: (570) 322-3331.

SPACE MILESTONE: *SOYUZ 21* (USSR): 25th ANNIVERSARY. July 6, 1976. Launched this date. Two cosmonauts, Colonel B. Volynov and Lieutenant Colonel V. Zholobov, traveled to *Salyut 5* space station (launched June 22, 1976) to study Earth's surface and conduct zoological-botanical experiments. Forty-eight-day stay on space station. Return landing on Aug 24.

STAMP EXPO. July 6–8. Elks Lodge, Pasadena, CA. Est attendance: 4,000. For info: Intl Stamp Collectors Soc, Box 854, Van Nuys, CA 91408. Phone: (818) 997-6496. Fax: (818) 988-4337. E-mail: iibick@aol.com. Web: www.bick.net.

STATE GAMES OF OREGON. July 6–8. Portland, OR. Oregon's Olympic-style amateur sports festival. Normally, the first weekend after July 4th. Est attendance: 17,500. For info: Kerry Duffy, Exec Dir, 4840 SW Western Ave, Ste 900, Beaverton, OR 97005. Phone: (503) 520-1319. Fax: (503) 520-9747.

BIRTHDAYS TODAY

Allyce Beasley, 47, actress ("Moonlighting"), born Brooklyn, NY, July 6, 1954.
Ned Beatty, 64, actor (*Deliverance*, "Homicide," *Hear My Song*), born Lexington, KY, July 6, 1937.
George W. Bush, 55, Governor of Texas (R), 2000 Republican presidential candidate, born Midland, TX, July 6, 1946.
Donal Donnelly, 70, actor (*The Knack, The Dead, Godfather Part III*), born Bradford, England, July 6, 1931.
Grant Goodeve, 49, actor ("Eight Is Enough," "Dynasty"), born New Haven, CT, July 6, 1952.
Merv Griffin, 76, TV host, business executive, born San Mateo, CA, July 6, 1925.
Janet Leigh, 74, actress (*That Forsyte Woman, Psycho*), born Merced, CA, July 6, 1927.
Nancy Davis Reagan, 80, former First Lady, born New York, NY, July 6, 1921.
Della Reese (Deloreese Patricia Early), 69, singer ("Don't You Know," "And That Reminds Me"), actress ("Touched by an Angel"), born Detroit, MI, July 6, 1932.
Sylvester Stallone, 55, actor (*Rocky* films, *Cliffhanger, Rambo* films) director, born New York, NY, July 6, 1946.
Burt Ward, 56, actor ("Batman"), born Los Angeles, CA, July 6, 1945.

July *2001*	S	M	T	W	T	F	S
	1	2	3	4	5	6	7
	8	9	10	11	12	13	14
	15	16	17	18	19	20	21
	22	23	24	25	26	27	28
	29	30	31				

JULY 7 — SATURDAY
Day 188 — 177 Remaining

BARN DAY. July 7–8. Two miles south of Filley, NE. Threshing demonstration, antique farm equipment, entertainment. The barn is on the National Register of Historic Sites and is the largest limestone barn in Nebraska. Est attendance: 700. For info: Kent Wilson, Dir, Gage County Historical Soc, PO Box 793, Beatrice, NE 68310. Phone: (402) 228-1679. Web: www.infoanalytic.com /h/beatrice.html#gage.

BONZA BOTTLER DAY™. July 7. To celebrate when the number of the day is the same as the number of the month. Bonza Bottler Day™ is an excuse to have a party at least once a month. For more information, see Jan 1. For info: Gail M. Berger, 109 Matthew Ave, Poca, WV 25159. Phone: (304) 776-7746. E-mail: gberger5@aol.com.

CANADA: BUSINESS AND PROFESSIONAL WOMEN'S FLEA MARKET AND CRAFT SALE. July 7. Bracebridge, ON. Est attendance: 2,000. For info: Bracebridge Chamber of Commerce, 1-1 Manitoba St, Bracebridge, ON, Canada P1L 2A8. Phone: (705) 645-4600.

CANADA: HARRISON FESTIVAL OF THE ARTS. July 7–15. Harrison Hot Springs, BC. A celebration of world music, dance, theatre and visual art including a large outdoor art market. Various venues throughout the village. Variety of activities for the entire family. Est attendance: 12,000. For info: Ed Stenson, Gen Mgr, Harrison Fest, Box 399, Harrison Hot Springs, BC, Canada V0M 1K0. Phone: (604) 796-3664. Fax: (604) 796-3694. E-mail: harrfest@uniserve.com. Web: www.echoisland.com/harrfest.

CELTIC FLING. July 7–8. Mount Hope Estate & Winery, Manheim, PA. 'Tis but a wee journey to the Scottish Highlands or the Emerald Isle when you dance a jig through the gates of the Pennsylvania Renaissance Faire's annual "Celtic Fling." It's 35 acres of authentic Celtic arts and crafts, music and dance, concerts by nationally acclaimed Celtic recording artists and, of course, beer and bagpipes. For info: Thomas Roy, PRF, PO Box 685, Cornwall, PA 17016. Phone: (717) 665-7021 ext 127. Fax: (717) 664-3466. E-mail: TomRoy@parenaissancefaire.com. Web: www.parenfaire.com.

CRAFT DAY BY THE BAY. July 7. Harvey Cedars, NJ. More than 100 crafters and artists displaying and selling their handcrafted goods. Est attendance: 2,000. For info: Harvey Cedars Activity Committee, PO Box 3185, Harvey Cedars, NJ 08008. Phone: (609) 361-7990. Fax: (609) 494-8343. E-mail: hcboro @cybercomm.net. Web: www.cybercomm.net/~hcboro.

FATHER-DAUGHTER TAKE A WALK TOGETHER DAY. July 7. A special time in the summer for fathers and daughters of all ages to spend time together in the beautiful weather. Annually, July 7. For info: Janet Dellaria, 202 N Bennett St, Geneva, IL 60134. Phone: (630) 232-0425.

FINLAND: SAVONLINNA OPERA FESTIVAL. July 7–Aug 5. Savonlinna. Staged in the magnificent 15th-century Olavinlinna Castle in the beautiful lake district of Finland. Music includes Verdi, Mozart and performances by the Los Angeles Opera. Est attendance: 55,000. For info: Savonlinna Opera Festival, Olavinkatu 27, Savonlinna, Finland 57130. Phone: (358) 15-476750. Fax: (358) 15-4767540. E-mail: info@operafestival.fi. Web: www.operafestival.fi.

HAWAII ANNEXED BY US: ANNIVERSARY. July 7, 1898. President William McKinley signed a resolution annexing Hawaii. No change in government took place until 1900, when Congress passed an act making Hawaii an "incorporated" territory of the US. This act remained in effect until Hawaii became a state in 1959.

INTERNATIONAL CHERRY PIT SPITTING CONTEST. July 7. Tree-Mendus Fruit Farm, Eau Claire, MI. A nutritious sport—is there a better way to dispose of the pits once you have eaten the cherry? Entrants eat a cherry and then spit the pit as far as possible on a blacktop surface. The entrant who spits the pit the farthest including the roll is the champ. Annually, the first Saturday in July. Est attendance: 1,000. For info: Lynn Sage, Adv and Promo Mgr, Tree-Mendus Fruit Farm, 9351 E Eureka Rd, Eau Claire, MI 49111. Phone: (517) 782-7101. Fax: (517) 625-5588. E-mail: treemendus@aol.com. Web: www.treemendus-fruit.com.

JAPAN: TANABATA (STAR FESTIVAL). July 7. As an offering to the stars, children set up bamboo branches to which colorful strips of paper bearing poems are tied.

JIMMY AND ROSALYNN CARTER WEDDING: 55th ANNIVERSARY. July 7, 1946. Plains Methodist Church, Plains, GA. James Earl Carter, Jr, was 21 and Eleanor Rosalynn Smith was 18. They have four children: John William "Jack" Carter was born in 1947, James Carl "Chip" Carter, 1950, Donnell Jeffrey Carter, 1952, and Amy Lynn Carter, 1968.

KBCO WORLD CLASS ROCK FESTIVAL. July 7–8. Winter Park Resort, Winter Park, CO. Music lovers have the opportunity to catch major national rock acts as well as up and coming regional performers within an ideal concert setting. Concert-goers set up blankets and coolers on Parkway trail for a great view of the stage amid a natural amphitheater. Est attendance: 16,000. For info: Winter Park Resort, PO Box 36, Winter Park, CO 80482. Phone: (970) 726-1580. Fax: (970) 726-1572. E-mail: wpinfo@mail.skiwinterpark.com. Web: winterparkresort.com.

KUNSTLER, WILLIAM: BIRTH ANNIVERSARY. July 7, 1919. Radical attorney, defense lawyer for the Chicago Seven, born at New York, NY. Died Sept 4, 1995, at New York, NY.

LINCOLN ASSASSINATION CONSPIRATORS: HANGING ANNIVERSARY. July 7, 1865. Four persons convicted of complicity with John Wilkes Booth in the assassination of President Abraham Lincoln on Apr 14, 1865 were hanged at Washington, DC. The four: Mary E. Surratt, Lewis Payne, David E. Harold and George A. Atzerodt.

MOTHER FRANCES XAVIER CABRINI CANONIZED: 55th ANNIVERSARY. July 7, 1946. Pope Pius XII presided over the canonization ceremonies for Mother Frances Xavier Cabrini, as she became the first American to be canonized. She was the founder of the Missionary Sisters of the Sacred Heart of Jesus, and her principal shrine is at Mother Cabrini High School, New York, NY. Cabrini was born at Lombardy, Italy, July 15, 1850 and died at Chicago, IL, Dec 22, 1917. Her feast day is celebrated on Dec 22.

NATIONAL CHERRY FESTIVAL. July 7–14. Traverse City, MI. Festival is an eight-day celebration of the cherry industry with dozens of events for the entire family, including air shows, parades, music concerts, arts and crafts, sporting events and more. Est attendance: 500,000. For info: Natl Cherry Festival, 108 W Grandview Parkway, Traverse City, MI 49684. Phone: (800) 968-3380 or (231) 947-4230. Fax: (231) 947-7435. E-mail: ncf@traverse.com. Web: www.traverse.com/cherry/festival.html.

NEW ENGLAND ARTS & CRAFTS FESTIVAL. July 7–8. Milford Green, Milford, CT. Features more than 150 juried artists and crafters. Food court and entertainment. Annually, the weekend following July 4. For info: New England Arts & Crafts Festival, (203) 878-6647 or Greater New Haven CVB, 59 Elm St, New Haven, CT 06510. Phone: (203) 777-8550 or (800) 332-STAY. Fax: (203) 782-7755. Web: www.newhavencvb.org.

OLD-FASHIONED ICE CREAM FESTIVAL. July 7–8. Rockwood Museum, Wilmington, DE. Old-fashioned ice cream social. Hot-air balloons, craft show, antique show, Victorian fashion show, old-time music, high-wheeled bicycles, games and homemade ice cream. Est attendance: 30,000. For info: Rockwood Museum, 610 Shipley Rd, Wilmington, DE 19809. Phone: (302) 761-4340. Fax: (302) 764-4570. E-mail: info@rockwood.org. Web: www.rockwood.org.

PAIGE, LEROY ROBERT (SATCHEL): 95th BIRTH ANNIVERSARY. July 7, 1906. Baseball Hall of Fame pitcher born at Mobile, AL. Paige was the greatest attraction in the Negro Leagues and was also, at age 42, the first black pitcher in the American League. Inducted into the Hall of Fame in 1971. Died at Kansas City, MO, June 8, 1982.

PEPSI 400. July 7. Daytona International Speedway, Daytona Beach, FL. 42nd running of NASCAR Winston Cup's "Mid-Summer Classic." Sponsor: Pepsi. For info: Daytona Intl Speedway, PO Box 28014, Daytona Beach, FL 32120-2801. Phone: (904) 947-6782. Fax: (904) 947-6791. Web: www.daytonausa.com.

PLANTATION DAYS AT HIGHLAND. July 7–8. Ash Lawn–Highland, Charlottesville, VA. An Independence Day celebration with 18th-century crafts, living history, music, dance, food and games. Est attendance: 2,000. For info: Ash Lawn-Highland, James Monroe Parkway, Charlottesville, VA 22902. Phone: (804) 293-9539. Fax: (804) 293-8000. E-mail: ashlawnjm@aol.com. Web: avenue.org/ashlawn.

ROCKPORT ART FESTIVAL. July 7–8. Rockport Festival Grounds, Rockport, TX. The work of top artists from across the southwestern US lines the waterfront for two days. Jazz and plenty of good food. Est attendance: 25,000. For info: Rockport Center for the Arts, 902 Navigation Circle, Rockport, TX 78382. Phone: (361) 729-5519. Fax: (361) 729-3551. Web: www.rockport-fulton.org.

"RYAN'S HOPE" TV PREMIERE: ANNIVERSARY. July 7, 1975. This ABC soap ran until 1989 and was set mostly at the fictional Ryan's Tavern or Riverside Hospital at New York City. The show depicted the lives of the ardently Irish Ryan family. "Ryan's Hope" won a Daytime Emmy for Outstanding Drama Series in 1979. Claire Labine and Paul Avila Mayer created the show. The original cast included Faith Catlin, Justin Deas, Bernard Barrow, Helen Gallagher, Michael Hawkins, Ilene Kristen, Malcom Groome and Kate Mulgrew as members of the Ryan family. Marg Helgenberger, Nell Carter, Yasmine Bleeth, Gloria DeHaven, Corbin Bernsen and Grant Show have been among the show's other regulars.

SEAFAIR. July 7–Aug 5 (tentative). Seattle, WA. SEAFAIR will celebrate its anniversary as the northwest's largest summer festival. More than 40 events in all highlighted by the Milk Carton Derby, Torchlight Run and Torchlight Parade, Unlimited Hydroplane Race and Air Show. Also dozens of community parades and events. Est attendance: 1,000,000. For info: Seafair, 2200 6th Ave, Ste 400, Seattle, WA 98121. Phone: (206) 728-0123. Fax: (206) 728-9506. Web: www.seafair.com.

SOLOMON ISLANDS: INDEPENDENCE DAY. July 7. National holiday. Commemorates independence from Britain in 1978.

SOUTH AFRICA: ROTHMANS JULY. July 7. Durban. Premier horse racing event in South Africa with stakes of one million rand. Annually, the first Saturday in July. Est attendance: 40,000. For info: Durban Turf Club, PO Box 924, Durban, 4000, South Africa. Phone: (27) (31) 309-4545. Fax: (27) (31) 309-2553. E-mail: durbturf@global.co.za. Web: www.tabkzn.co.za/greyville.

SPAIN: RUNNING OF THE BULLS. July 7–14. Pamplona, Spain. Event made famous by Hemingway in his novel *The Sun Also Rises*, in which young men run through the streets of Pamplona chased by bulls from the bull ring. Part of the festival of San Fermin.

STERLING RENAISSANCE FESTIVAL. July 7–Aug 19 (Saturdays and Sundays only). Sterling, NY. 25th annual re-creation of an English village set in the time period of Queen Elizabeth I. The festival features authentic jousting, more than 80 stage and street performances, music and dance of the period, beautiful arts and handcrafts, unique and delicious foods and drink and much more. Est attendance: 100,000. For info: Festival Office, Sterling Renaissance Festival, 15385 Farden Rd, Sterling, NY 13156. Phone: (800) 879-4446. Web: sterlingfestival.com.

"THE STORK CLUB" TV PREMIERE: ANNIVERSARY. July 7, 1950. "The Stork Club" ran for four years on CBS and for one year on ABC. Sherman Billingsley served as host and producer of this variety show which was set in his famous night club.

SUMMERFEST. July 7. Monmouth, IL. A day of fun, crafts, shopping and special promotions in downtown Monmouth. Special sidewalk sales, crafts show and vendors. Est attendance: 2,500. For info: Monmouth Chamber of Commerce, PO Box 857, 68 Public Square, Monmouth, IL 61462. Phone: (309) 734-3181. Fax: (309) 734-6595.

SUMMER TYME. July 7–8 or July 14–15 (tentative). Franklin, CT. Collections, exhibits and demonstrations of 18th and 19th century agricultural and home implements. Children's activities.

July 2001	S	M	T	W	T	F	S
							1
	2	3	4	5	6	7	8
	9	10	11	12	13	14	15
	16	17	18	19	20	21	22
	23	24	25	26	27	28	29
	30	31					

Wagon rides. Reenactors. Refreshments available. Est attendance: 2,000. For info: Blue Slope Country Museum, 138 Blue Hill Rd, Franklin, CT 06254. Phone: (860) 642-6413. Fax: (860) 642-4424.

SURRATT, MARY: EXECUTION ANNIVERSARY. July 7, 1865. Mary E. Surratt, who had been convicted by a military commission of conspiracy in the assassination of President Abraham Lincoln, was hanged, becoming the first woman executed for a crime in the US. Her conviction was and is a subject of controversy, as the only crime she appeared to have committed was to own the boarding house where John Wilkes Booth planned the assassination.

TANZANIA: SABA SABA DAY. July 7. Tanzania's mainland ruling party, TANU, was formed in 1954.

TIVOLI—VIKING DAYS AT THE NORDIC HERITAGE MUSEUM. July 7–8. Nordic Heritage Museum, Seattle, WA. A two-day outdoor Scandinavian festival featuring crafts, foods, entertainment and children's activities. Swedish pancake breakfast Saturday morning, Sunday barbecued salmon in afternoon, roast pig and cafe Sunday morning and food booths throughout both days. Viking crafts and demonstrations. Est attendance: 3,500. For info: Marianne Forssblad, Dir, Nordic Heritage Museum, 3014 NW 67th St, Seattle, WA 98117. Phone: (206) 789-5707. Fax: (206) 789-3271.

UNITED NATIONS: INTERNATIONAL DAY OF COOPERATIVES. July 7. On Dec 16, 1992, the General Assembly proclaimed this observance for the first Saturday of July 1995 (Res 47/60). On Dec 23, 1994, recognizing that cooperatives are becoming an indispensable factor of economic and social development, the Assembly invited governments, international organizations, specialized agencies and national and international cooperative organizations to observe this day annually (Res 49/155). For info: United Nations, Dept of Public Info, New York, NY 10017.

WHITEFISH ART FESTIVAL. July 7–8. Whitefish, MT. Juried arts and crafts show and sale. Ninety artists, food booths and entertainment for all ages. One of the valley's finest presentations of art. Proceeds go to Cross Currents Christian School. Est attendance: 8,000. For info: Cross Currents Christian School, PO Box 131, Whitefish, MT 59937. Phone: (406) 862-5910 or (406) 862-5875.

WORLD FOLKFEST. July 7–14. Springville, UT. Large international folk dance event. No dance performances on the 8th or 11th. Est attendance: 30,000. For info: Springville World Folkfest, PO Box 306, 50 S Main, Springville, UT 84663. Phone: (801) 489-2726 or (801) 489-3657. Fax: (801) 489-2709. Web: www.AVPRO.com/folkfest.

BIRTHDAYS TODAY

Bill Campbell, 42, actor ("Once and Again"), born Charlottesville, VA. July 7, 1959.

Pierre Cardin, 79, fashion designer, born Venice, Italy, July 7, 1922.

Shelley Duvall, 52, actress (*Popeye, Nashville, Roxanne*), born Houston, TX, July 7, 1949.

Michelle Kwan, 21, figure skater, born Torrance, CA, July 7, 1980.

Lisa Leslie, 29, WNBA player, 1996 Women's Olympic Basketball team player, born Inglewood, CA, July 7, 1972.

Gian Carlo Menotti, 90, composer, born Cadigliano, Italy, July 7, 1911.

Joe Sakic, 32, hockey player, born Burnaby, British Columbia, Canada, July 7, 1969.

Ralph Lee Sampson, 41, former basketball player, born Harrisonburg, VA, July 7, 1960.

Doc Severinsen, 74, composer, conductor, musician (bandleader on "The Tonight Show"), born Arlington, OR, July 7, 1927.

Ringo Starr (Richard Starkey), 61, singer, musician (The Beatles), born Liverpool, England, July 7, 1940.

JULY 8 — SUNDAY

Day 189 — 176 Remaining

ASPINWALL CROSSES US ON HORSEBACK: 90th ANNIVERSARY. July 8, 1911. Nan Jane Aspinwall rode into New York City carrying a letter to Mayor William Jay Gaynor from San Francisco Mayor Patrick Henry McCarthy, becoming the first woman to cross the US on horseback. She began her trip in San Francisco on Sept 1, 1910, and covered 4,500 miles in 301 days.

DECLARATION OF INDEPENDENCE FIRST PUBLIC READING: 225th ANNIVERSARY. July 8, 1776. Colonel John Nixon read the Declaration of Independence to the assembled residents at Philadelphia's Independence Square.

ECKSTINE, BILLY: BIRTH ANNIVERSARY. July 8, 1914. Bandleader and bass-baritone singer Billy Eckstine was born William Clarence Eckstein at Pittsburgh, PA. After performing with the Earl Hines band for almost 20 years, Eckstine formed his own band in 1944. At one time or another the band's ranks included Charlie Parker, Dizzy Gillespie, Miles Davis, Fats Navarro, Dexter Gordon, Gene Ammons, Art Blakey and vocalist Sarah Vaughan—some of the greatest bebop musicians of all time. Among Eckstine's hits were "Fools Rush In," "Everything I Have Is Yours," "My Foolish Heart," "Blue Moon" and "Body and Soul." Billy Eckstine died Mar 8, 1993, at Pittsburgh, PA.

FAMILY, CAREER AND COMMUNITY LEADERS OF AMERICA NATIONAL LEADERSHIP MEETING. July 8–12. Anaheim, CA. This meeting is a unique opportunity to gain a national perspective on FCCLA activities and issues, elect officers, receive specialized leadership training and enhance chapter activities. Est attendance: 5,500. For info: Beth Carpenter, Family, Career and Community Leaders of America, Inc, 1910 Association Dr, Reston, VA 20191. Phone: (703) 476-4900. Fax: (703) 860-2713. E-mail: natlhdqtrs@fcclainc. Web: www.fcclainc.org.

FAST OF TAMMUZ. July 8. Jewish holiday. Hebrew calendar date: Tammuz 17, 5761. Shiva Asar B'Tammuz begins at first light of day and commemorates the first-century Roman siege that breached the walls of Jerusalem. Begins a three-week time of mourning.

GREAT SPANGLED BUTTERFLY DAYS. July 8–14. A weeklong event to celebrate the diversity of Michigan's butterflies. Est attendance: 10,000. For info: P.J. Hoffmaster State Park, Gillette Visitor Center, 6585 Lake Harbor Rd, Muskegon, MI 49441. Phone: (616) 798-3573. Fax: (616) 798-4336.

KIM IL SUNG: DEATH ANNIVERSARY. July 8, 1994. President Kim Il Sung, the only leader in the history of North Korea, died just a few weeks before an historic summit with the president of South Korea was to take place, at Pyongyang, North Korea. A Stalinist-styled dictator, born at Man'gyandae, Korea, Apr 15, 1912, Kim had created a godlike personality cult surrounding himself and his son and presumed heir apparent Kim Jong Il. His death came at a crucial time in world politics. North Korea and the US had recently cooled rhetoric regarding North Korea's nuclear program and had begun further talks just hours prior to the announcement of Kim's death. The North–South Summit and the US–North Korean talks were postponed.

MOULIN, JEAN: DEATH ANNIVERSARY. July 8, 1943. Jean Moulin, a Free French representative, born at Beziers, France, June 20, 1899, was parachuted into occupied France on Jan 1, 1942, with the task of uniting the underground resistance. Moulin had with him (in the false bottom of a matchbox) a personal message of admiration for the resistance from General Charles DeGaulle. On May 27, 1943, the underground agreed to the creation of a National Resistance Council with Moulin as president. A month later he was arrested at Lyon by the Gestapo. He was tortured for 11 days but betrayed no one. Moulin died on a train while being transferred by the Nazis to a concentration camp.

NATIONAL LAUNDRY WORKERS' WEEK. July 8–14. To promote public awareness of the importance of the laundry worker. Annually, the second full week in July. For info: Nemaha County Good Samaritan Center, Rt 1, Box 4, Auburn, NE 68305.

NATIONAL THERAPEUTIC RECREATION WEEK. July 8–14. To increase awareness of therapeutic recreation programs and services, and to expand leisure opportunities for individuals with disabilities in their local communities. Annually, the second full week in July. For info: Natl Therapeutic Recreation Soc, Ahren's NRPA Institute, 22377 Belmont Ridge Rd, Ashburn, VA 20148. Phone: (703) 858-2153. E-mail: NTRSNRPA@aol.com. Web: www.nrpa.org/branches/ntrs.htm.

OLD MISSION HISTORIC SKILLS FAIR. July 8. Old Mission State Park, Cataldo, ID. An event featuring old-fashioned skills such as spinning, quilting and black powder shooting. Annually, the second Sunday of July. Est attendance: 2,000. For info: Bill Scudder, Park Mgr, Old Mission State Park, PO Box 30, Cataldo, ID 83810-0030. Phone: (208) 682-3814. Fax: (208) 682-4032. E-mail: old@idpr.state.id.us.

OLIVE BRANCH PETITION: ANNIVERSARY. July 8, 1775. Representatives of New Hampshire, Massachusetts Bay, Rhode Island, Providence, Connecticut, New York, New Jersey, Pennsylvania, Delaware, Maryland, Virginia, North Carolina and South Carolina signed a petition from the Congress to the King (George III), a final attempt by moderates in the Second Continental Congress to avoid a complete break with England.

ROCKEFELLER, NELSON ALDRICH: BIRTH ANNIVERSARY. July 8, 1908. Born at Bar Harbor, ME. Governor of New York state (1958–73). Nominated as vice president by President Ford, Aug 20, 1974, under provisions of the 25th Amendment. Sworn in Dec 19, 1974, after confirmation by the Senate and served until Jan 20, 1977. Died at New York, NY, Jan 26, 1979. Rockefeller was the second person to become vice president without having been elected (Gerald R. Ford was the first).

TAKE CHARGE OF CHANGE WEEK. July 8–14. To increase awareness of the individual's power to control his own destiny, ChangeWorks will sponsor a series of events demonstrating the principles of taking charge of the changes that affect each of us. You can reduce stress and improve the quality of your life when you put yourself in the driver's seat. Learn how to accept the change you cannot control, manage the change you can and make change a positive force in your life. Free articles for publishers and webmasters at IdeaLady.com/content.htm. For info: Cathy Stucker, ChangeWorks, 4646 Hwy 6, PMB 123, Sugar Land, TX 77478. Phone: (281) 265-7342. Fax: (281) 265-9727. E-mail: cathy@idealady.com. Web: www.idealady.com.

BIRTHDAYS TODAY

Roone Arledge, 70, TV executive, born Forest Hills, NY, July 8, 1931.

Kevin Bacon, 43, actor (stage: *Forty Deuce* [Obie Award]; *A Few Good Men, Apollo 13*), born Philadelphia, PA, July 8, 1958.

Raffi Cavoukian, 53, children's singer and songwriter, born Cairo, Egypt, July 8, 1948.

Billy Crudup, 33, actor (*Sleepers*), born Manhasset, NY, July 8, 1968.

Kim Darby, 53, actress ("Rich Man, Poor Man," *True Grit*), born Los Angeles, CA, July 8, 1948.

Phil Gramm, 59, US Senator (R, Texas), born Fort Benning, GA, July 8, 1942.

Cynthia Gregory, 55, ballerina, born Los Angeles, CA, July 8, 1946.

Anjelica Huston, 50, actress (Oscar for *Prizzi's Honor; The Addams Family*), born Los Angeles, CA, July 8, 1951.

Steve Lawrence (Sidney Liebowitz), 66, singer ("Party Doll," "Go Away Little Girl"), born New York, NY, July 8, 1935.

Sarah Newcomb McClendon, 91, journalist (50+ years with White House press corps), columnist, born Tyler, TX, July 8, 1910.

Jeffrey Tambor, 57, actor ("Hill Street Blues," "The Larry Sanders Show," *City Slickers*), born San Francisco, CA, July 8, 1944.

Alyce Faye Wattleton, 58, former executive director of Planned Parenthood Federation, born St. Louis, MO, July 8, 1943.

JULY 9 — MONDAY

Day 190 — 175 Remaining

ALASKA FLAG DAY CELEBRATION. July 9. This day celebrates the first time Alaska's flag was unfurled over the Jesse Lee Home at Seward, AK, July 9, 1927. In 1927 Territorial Governor George Parks announced a contest in which children all over Alaska in grades 7–12 were encouraged to design Alaska's flag. The winning flag was designed by John Ben (Benny) Benson, a resident of the Jesse Lee Home, an orphanage. He was the only child in the US to design a state flag. Each year this day is celebrated at Alaska Children's Services (formerly the Jesse Lee Home). Est attendance: 750. For info: Alaska Children's Services, 4600 Abbott Rd, Anchorage, AK 99507-4314. Phone: (907) 346-2101.

ARGENTINA: INDEPENDENCE DAY. July 9. Anniversary of establishment of independent republic, with the declaration of independence from Spain in 1816.

EDWARDS, VINCE: BIRTH ANNIVERSARY. July 9, 1928. As Dr. Ben Casey on the 1961 television show "Ben Casey," Edwards's muscular, brooding charm made him an overnight sex symbol. Medical school enrollment increased while he was on the air. After conquering a gambling addiction, he became a real-life hero. Born at Brooklyn, NY, he died at Los Angeles, CA, Mar 11, 1996.

FIRST OPEN-HEART SURGERY: ANNIVERSARY. July 9, 1893. In Provident Hospital on Chicago's south side, black surgeon Dr. Daniel Hale Williams performed the first successful open-heart surgery.

FOURTEENTH AMENDMENT TO US CONSTITUTION RATIFIED: ANNIVERSARY. July 9, 1868. The 14th Amendment defined US citizenship and provided that no State shall have the right to abridge the rights of any citizen without due process and equal protection under the law. Coming three years after the Civil War, the 14th Amendment also included provisions for barring individuals who assisted in any rebellion or insurrection against the US from holding public office, and releasing federal and state governments from any financial liability incurred in the assistance of rebellion or insurrection against the US.

GERMAN ARMY GROUP CENTER CUT OFF IN BALTIC: ANNIVERSARY. July 9, 1944. German Army Group Center was taken by surprise when the Soviets began an offensive between the Baltic Sea and the Carpathian Mountains. The Germans had expected an attack farther south, where the Red Army had already penetrated deep into Poland. When Hitler refused to allow a German retreat, the Soviets easily broke through the German lines, and the Reich's forces were isolated in the Baltic states. Within a week Army Group Center was virtually annihilated, with a loss of 200,000 men.

HOWE, ELIAS: BIRTH ANNIVERSARY. July 9, 1819. American inventor of the sewing machine. Born at Spencer, MA, he died Oct 3, 1867, at Brooklyn, NY.

MARTYRDOM OF THE BAB. July 9. Baha'i observance of the anniversary of the execution by a firing squad, July 9, 1850, at Tabriz, Persia, of the 30-year-old Siyyid Ali Muhammed, the Bab (prophet-herald of the Baha'i Faith). One of the nine days of the year when Baha'is suspend work. For info: Baha'is of the US, Office of Public Information, 866 UN Plaza, Ste 120, New York, NY 10017-1822. Phone: (212) 803-2500. Fax: (212) 803-2573. E-mail: usopi-ny@bic.org. Web: www.us.bahai.org.

NUDE RECREATION WEEK. July 9–15. To promote acceptance of the body and understanding of the nude recreation movement with special events at clothes-optional beaches and resorts throughout North America. For info: The Naturist Society, Box 132, Oshkosh, WI 54902. Phone: (920) 231-9950. Fax: (920) 426-5184. E-mail: naturist@naturist.com. Web: www.naturist.com.

RADCLIFFE, ANN WARD: BIRTH ANNIVERSARY. July 9, 1764. English novelist famous for her gothic novels (fiction works especially popular in the late 18th and early 19th centuries). Among her works are *The Romance of the Forest, The Mysteries of Udolpho* and *The Italian*. She was born at London, England, and died there Feb 7, 1823.

RESPIGHI, OTTORINO: BIRTH ANNIVERSARY. July 9, 1879. Italian composer (*The Fountains of Rome*) born at Bologna, Italy. He died at Rome, Italy, Apr 18, 1936.

SWITZERLAND: SEMPACH BATTLE COMMEMORATION. July 9. On the morning of the first Monday after July 4, the Lucerne government, military and student delegations and historical groups make their way in solemn procession to the battlefield of 1386. Commemorative address, battle report and solemn service in the chapel. Also an evening procession.

US AMATEUR PUBLIC LINKS (GOLF) CHAMPIONSHIP. July 9–14. Pecan Valley Golf Club, San Antonio, TX. For info: US Golf Assn, Golf House, PO Box 708, Championship Dept, Far Hills, NJ 07931. Phone: (908) 234-2300. Fax: (908) 234-9687. Web: www.usga.org.

July 2001	S	M	T	W	T	F	S
	1	2	3	4	5	6	7
	8	9	10	11	12	13	14
	15	16	17	18	19	20	21
	22	23	24	25	26	27	28
	29	30	31				

BIRTHDAYS TODAY

Brian Dennehy, 63, actor ("Star of the Family," *Tommy Boy*), born Bridgeport, CT, July 9, 1938.

Margaret Gillis, 48, dancer, choreographer, born Montreal, Quebec, Canada, July 9, 1953.

James Hampton, 65, actor ("F Troop," "Love, American Style"), born Oklahoma City, OK, July 9, 1936.

Tom Hanks, 45, actor (*Big, Sleepless in Seattle, Saving Private Ryan*; Oscars for *Philadelphia, Forrest Gump*), born Concord, CA, July 9, 1956.

David Hockney, 64, artist, born Bradford, England, July 9, 1937.

Mathilde Krim, 75, geneticist, philanthropist, born Como, Italy, July 9, 1926.

Courtney Love, 36, singer ("Live Through This"), actress (*The People v Larry Flynt*), born San Francisco, CA, July 9, 1965.

Kelly McGillis, 44, actress (*Witness, Top Gun, The Accused*), born Newport Beach, CA, July 9, 1957.

Fred Savage, 25, actor ("The Wonder Years," "Working," *The Princess Bride*), born Highland Park, IL, July 9, 1976.

Orenthal James (O.J.) Simpson, 54, former sportscaster and actor, Pro Football Hall of Fame running back, born San Francisco, CA, July 9, 1947.

Jimmy Smits, 43, actor (*Glitz*, "LA Law," "NYPD Blue"), born New York, NY, July 9, 1958.

John Tesh, 49, TV host ("Entertainment Tonight"), born Garden City, NY, July 9, 1952.

JULY 10 — TUESDAY

Day 191 — 174 Remaining

ALLIED INVASION OF SICILY: ANNIVERSARY. July 10, 1943. Operation Husky, the Allied infantry attack on Italy, began on the island of Sicily. The British entry into Syracuse was the first Allied success in Europe. General Dwight D. Eisenhower, the Allied Commander-in-Chief, described the invasion as "the first page in the liberation of the European Continent."

ASHE, ARTHUR: BIRTH ANNIVERSARY. July 10, 1943. Born at Richmond, VA, Arthur Ashe became a legend for his list of firsts as a black tennis player. Ashe was chosen for the US Davis Cup team in 1963 and became captain in 1980. He won the US men's singles championship and US Open in 1968 and in 1975 the men's singles at Wimbledon. Ashe won a total of 33 career titles. In 1985 he was inducted into the International Tennis Hall of Fame. A social activist, Ashe worked to eliminate racism and stereotyping. He helped create inner-city tennis programs for youth and wrote the three-volume *A Hard Road to Glory: A History of the African-American Athlete*. Aware that *USA Today* intended to publish an article revealing that he was infected with the AIDS virus, Ashe announced Apr 8, 1992, that he probably contracted HIV through a transfusion during bypass surgery in 1983. In September of 1992 he began a $5 million fund-raising effort on behalf of the Arthur Ashe Foundation for the Defeat of AIDS and during his last year campaigned for public awareness regarding the AIDS epidemic. He died at New York, NY, Feb 6, 1993, from pneumonia.

BAHAMAS: INDEPENDENCE DAY. July 10. Public holiday. At 12:01 AM in 1973 the Bahamas gained their independence after 250 years as a British Crown Colony.

BETHUNE, MARY McLEOD: BIRTH ANNIVERSARY. July 10, 1875. Mary Jane McLeod Bethune was born at Mayesville, SC, the first in her family to be born free. Bethune became a teacher and in 1904 founded her own school in Florida, the Daytona Normal and Industrial School for Negro Girls. In 1931 the school merged with a local men's college, Cookman Institute, and was renamed Bethune-Cookman College. An adviser on minority affairs under President Franklin D. Roosevelt, she directed the Division of Negro Affairs of the National Youth Administration. She died May 18, 1955, at Daytona Beach, FL.

BORIS YELTSIN INAUGURATED AS RUSSIAN PRESIDENT: 10th ANNIVERSARY. July 10, 1991. Boris Yeltsin took the oath of office as the first popularly elected president in Russia's 1,000-year history. He defeated the Communist Party candidate resoundingly, establishing himself as a powerful political counterpoint to Mikhail Gorbachev, the president of the Soviet Union, of which Russia was the largest republic. Yeltsin had been dismissed from the Politburo in 1987 and resigned from the Communist Party in 1989. His popularity forced Gorbachev to make concessions to the republics in the new union treaty forming the Confederation of Independent States. Suffering from poor health, Yeltsin resigned as president at the end of 1999.

CALVIN, JOHN: BIRTH ANNIVERSARY. July 10, 1509. Theologian, born at Noyon, France. Reformer and founder of Presbyterianism. Calvin died at Geneva, Switzerland, May 27, 1564.

CLERIHEW DAY. July 10. A day recognized in remembrance of Edmund Clerihew Bentley, journalist and author of the celebrated detective thriller *Trent's Last Case* (1912), but perhaps best known for his invention of a popular humorous verse form, the clerihew, consisting of two rhymed couplets of unequal length:/Edmund's middle name was Clerihew/A name possessed by very few,/But verses by Mr Bentley/Succeeded eminently./ Bentley was born at London, July 10, 1875, and died there, Mar 30, 1956.

DALLAS, GEORGE MIFFLIN: BIRTH ANNIVERSARY. July 10, 1792. 11th vice president of the US (1845–49), born at Philadelphia, PA. Died there, Dec 31, 1864.

DON'T STEP ON A BEE DAY. July 10. Ten-year-old Michael Roy of the Wellness Permission League reminds kids and grown-ups that now is the time of year when going barefoot can mean getting stung by a bee. If you get stung tell Mom. [© 2000 by WH] For info: Michael Roy, Wellcat Holidays, 2418 Long Ln, Lebanon, PA 17046. Phone: (717) 279-0184. E-mail: wellcat@supernet.com. Web: www.wellcat.com.

ELEPHANT STAMPEDE: ANNIVERSARY. July 10, 1972. Due to drought and a massive heat wave, herds of thirst-crazed wild elephants went on a rampage through five villages near the Chandka Forest of India killing 24 people.

FINLAND: JYVASKYLA ARTS FESTIVAL. July 10–15 (tentative). Jyvaskyla. Annual festival begun in 1955 for the purpose of stimulating discussion of contemporary philosophical and social concerns and building a bridge between different national and ethnic traditions. About 50 events including seminars, music, visual arts and film. Est attendance: 10,000. For info: Finnish Tourist Board, 655 Third Ave, New York, NY 10017. Phone: (212) 885-9700 or (358) (14) 624385. Fax: (358) (14) 214808. E-mail: tanja.rasi@jkl.fi. Web: www.jkl.fi/festivaalit/kesa/

GILBERT, JOHN: BIRTH ANNIVERSARY. July 10, 1897. Silent film star John Gilbert was born John Pringle at Logan, UT. In 1916 he had his billed screen debut in *Bullets and Brown Eyes*. In the early 1920s Gilbert contracted with Fox and then with MGM and had leading roles in several films, such as *The Merry Widow* and *The Big Parade*. Although he was a popular leading man, he was unable to succeed when sound came to movies and MGM released him from his contract in 1934. He died Jan 9, 1936, at Los Angeles, CA.

GREAT CIRCUS PARADE WEEK. July 10-15 (tentative). Baraboo/Milwaukee, WI. Circus wagons make their annual journey to Milwaukee from Baraboo, home of the nation's largest collection of antique circus wagons. Visit the parade showgrounds off the shores of Lake Michigan, July 10-14, for a free viewing of a 40-tent display of circus wagons and performances under the Big Top. The Great Circus Parade, winding its way through the streets of Milwaukee on Sunday, July 15, is the only parade of its kind in the world—an authentic recreation of a 19th-century parade complete with 65 restored circus wagons, 750 horses, clowns, animals and marching bands. Est attendance: 500,000. For info: Great Circus Parade, Circus World Museum, 550 Water St, Baraboo, WI 53913. Phone: (608) 356-8341. Web: www.circusworldmuseum.com.

GWYNNE, FREDERICK HUBBARD: 75th BIRTH ANNIVERSARY. July 10, 1926. Stage, screen and TV actor, best known for the TV roles Herman Munster in "The Munsters" and Officer Muldoon in "Car 54, Where Are You?" Gwynne was born at New York, NY, and died at Taneytown, MD, July 2, 1993.

HOGG, IMA: BIRTH ANNIVERSARY. July 10, 1882. American collector and philanthropist Ima Hogg was born at Mineola, TX. She founded the Houston Symphony and created the Bayou Bend Collection of the Museum of Fine Arts. She was the only daughter of Texas Governor (1891-95) James Stephen Hogg who, some have suggested, deliberately named his daughter "Ima" for political attention. Contrary to folklore, she did not have a sister named Ura Hogg. She died at age 93, Aug 19, 1975, following an auto accident at London, England.

PROUST, MARCEL: BIRTH ANNIVERSARY. July 10, 1871. Famed French author, born at Auteuil, France. He gained an international reputation for his 13-volume masterpiece, *A la Recherche du Temps Perdu* (*Remembrance of Things Past*). "Happiness," he wrote in *The Past Recaptured*, "is beneficial for the body but it is grief that develops the powers of the mind." Proust died Nov 19, 1922, at Paris, France.

RAINBOW WARRIOR SINKING: ANNIVERSARY. July 10, 1985. The 160-ft ship, the *Rainbow Warrior*, operated by Greenpeace, an environmental organization, was sunk and a photographer aboard was killed while the ship was at Auckland, New Zealand. Reportedly a bomb was attached to the underside of the ship by saboteurs. The ship had been scheduled for use in a protest against nuclear tests in the South Pacific Ocean by the French government.

SPACE MILESTONE: *TELSTAR* (US). July 10, 1962. First privately owned satellite (American Telephone and Telegraph Company) and first satellite to relay live TV pictures across the Atlantic was launched.

	S	M	T	W	T	F	S
July	1	2	3	4	5	6	7
2001	8	9	10	11	12	13	14
	15	16	17	18	19	20	21
	22	23	24	25	26	27	28
	29	30	31				

US LIFTS SANCTIONS AGAINST SOUTH AFRICA: 10th ANNIVERSARY. July 10, 1991. President George Bush lifted US trade and investment sanctions against South Africa. The sanctions had been imposed through the Comprehensive Anti-Apartheid Act of 1986, which Congress had passed to punish South Africa for policies of racial separation.

WHISTLER, JAMES ABBOTT McNEILL: BIRTH ANNIVERSARY. July 10, 1834. American painter (especially known for painting of his mother) born at Lowell, MA. Died at London, England, July 17, 1903. When a woman declared that a landscape reminded her of Whistler's paintings, he reportedly said, "Yes, madam, Nature is creeping up."

WYOMING: ADMISSION DAY: ANNIVERSARY. July 10. Became 44th state in 1890.

BIRTHDAYS TODAY

Saul Bellow, 86, author (*Herzog, The Bellarosa Connection*), born Lachine, Quebec, Canada, July 10, 1915.

David Brinkley, 81, TV journalist, born Wilmington, NC, July 10, 1920.

Andre Nolan Dawson, 47, former baseball player, born Miami, FL, July 10, 1954.

David Norman Dinkins, 74, former and first black Mayor of New York City (D), born Trenton, NJ, July 10, 1927.

Ron Glass, 56, actor ("Barney Miller," voice on "Rugrats"), born Evansville, IN, July 10, 1945.

Arlo Guthrie, 54, singer ("The City of New Orleans," "Alice's Restaurant"), Woody Guthrie's son, born Brooklyn, NY, July 10, 1947.

Jerry Herman, 68, composer, lyricist, born New York, NY, July 10, 1933.

Jean Kerr, 78, author (*Finishing Touches, Please Don't Eat the Daisies*), born Scranton, PA, July 10, 1923.

Sue Lyon, 55, actress (*Lolita, The Flim Flam Man*), born Davenport, IA, July 10, 1946.

Lawrence Pressman, 62, actor ("Doogie Howser MD," *The Hanoi Hilton*), born Cynthiana, NY, July 10, 1939.

Eunice Mary Kennedy Shriver, 80, founder of the Special Olympics, born Brookline, MA, July 10, 1921.

Virginia Wade, 56, former tennis player, born Bournemouth, England, July 10, 1945.

JULY 11 — WEDNESDAY

Day 192 — 173 Remaining

ADAMS, JOHN QUINCY: BIRTH ANNIVERSARY. July 11, 1767. Sixth president of the US and the son of the second president, John Quincy Adams was born at Braintree, MA. After his single term as president, he served 17 years as a member of Congress from Plymouth, MA. He died Feb 23, 1848, at the House of Representatives (in the same room in which he had taken the presidential Oath of Office Mar 4, 1825). John Quincy Adams was the only president whose father had also been president of the US.

BABE'S DEBUT IN THE MAJORS: ANNIVERSARY. July 11, 1914. Babe Ruth made his debut in major league baseball when he took the mound in Fenway Park for the Boston Red Sox against the Cleveland Indians. Ruth was relieved for the last two innings but was the winning pitcher in a 4-3 game.

BOCA GRANDE TARPON TOURNAMENT ("WORLD'S RICHEST"). July 11-12. Boca Grande Pass, Boca Grande, FL. Tarpon fishing; field limited to 60 boats; entry fee $3,500 per boat. With 60 entries, first place (largest tarpon) pays off $100,000. Annually, the week after the Fourth of July. Est attendance: 1,000. For info: Boca Grande Chamber of Commerce, PO Box 704, Boca Grande, FL 33921. Phone: (941) 964-0568. Fax: (941) 964-0620. E-mail: bgcc@ewol.com. Web: www.bocagrandechamber.com.

BOWDLER'S DAY. July 11. A day to remember the prudish medical doctor, Thomas Bowdler, born near Bath, England, on July 11, 1754. He gave up the practice of medicine and undertook the cleansing of the works of Shakespeare by removing all the words and expressions he considered to be indecent or impious. His *Family Shakespeare*, in 10 volumes, omitted all those words "which cannot with propriety be read aloud in a family." He also "purified" Edward Gibbon's *History of the Decline and Fall of the Roman Empire* and selections from the Old Testament. His name became synonymous with self-righteous expurgation, and the word *bowdlerize* has become part of the English language. Bowdler died at Rhyddings, in South Wales, Feb 24, 1825.

CENTRAL PENNSYLVANIA FESTIVAL OF THE ARTS. July 11–15. State College, PA. A celebration of the arts—visual, performing—with 335 artists on hand. Est attendance: 100,000. For info: Central Pennsylvania Festival of the Arts, Box 1023, State College, PA 16804-1023. Phone: (814) 237-3682. Fax: (814) 237-0708. E-mail: office@arts-festival.com. Web: www.arts-festival.com.

CHOCTAW INDIAN FAIR. July 11–14. Philadelphia, MS. The fair presents cultural programs demonstrating native arts, crafts, social dancing, stickball, archery, blowgun and rabbit stick competition. Also native foods are prepared and served on the reservation. Annually, the second Wednesday through Saturday after July 4. Est attendance: 60,000. For info: Connie Sampsell, Dir, Philadelphia–Neshoba County Chamber of Commerce, PO Box 51, Philadelphia, MS 39350. Phone: (601) 656-1742.

DAY OF THE FIVE BILLION: ANNIVERSARY. July 11, 1987. An eight-pound baby boy, Matej Gaspar, born at 1:35 AM, EST, at Zagreb, Yugoslavia, was proclaimed the five billionth inhabitant of Earth. The United Nations Fund for Population Activities, hoping to draw attention to population growth, proclaimed July 11 as "Day of the Five Billion," noting that 150 babies are born each minute. See also: "World Population Six Billion: Anniversary" (Oct 12).

DINOSAUR ROUNDUP RODEO. July 11–14. Vernal, UT. 51st annual presentation of one of the top PRCA rodeos, plus wrangler bull fights and fun for the entire family. Annually, the second weekend in July. Est attendance: 28,000. For info: Vernal Chamber of Commerce, 134 W Main St, Vernal, UT 84078. Phone: (800) 421-9635 or (435) 789-1352.

MONGOLIA: NAADAM NATIONAL HOLIDAY: 80th ANNIVERSARY. July 11. Public holiday. Commemorates overthrow of the feudal monarch in 1921.

NAPALM USED: ANNIVERSARY. July 11, 1945. The US dropped several thousand pounds of the recently developed weapon napalm on Japanese forces still holed up on Luzon in the Philippines. Napalm, which was later used heavily as a defoliant in Vietnam, was a thickener consisting of a mixture of aluminum soaps used to jell gasoline.

"THE NEWLYWED GAME" TV PREMIERE: 35th ANNIVERSARY. July 11, 1966. Four newly married couples competed for prizes on this game show created by the inimitable Chuck Barris (mastermind of "The Gong Show"). The winners were determined by the couple that could best predict the responses of their respective spouses. Barris, Bob Eubanks and Paul Rodriguez have served as hosts.

SMITH, JAMES: DEATH ANNIVERSARY. July 11, 1806. Signer of the Declaration of Independence, born at Ireland about 1719 (exact date unknown). Died at York, PA.

SPACE MILESTONE: *SKYLAB* (US): FALLS TO EARTH. July 11, 1979. The 82-ton spacecraft launched May 14, 1973, re-entered Earth's atmosphere. Expectation was that 20–25 tons probably would survive to hit Earth, including one piece of about 5,000 pounds. This generated intense international public interest in where it would fall. The chance that some person would be hit by a piece of *Skylab* was calculated at one in 152. Targets were drawn and *Skylab* parties were held but *Skylab* broke up and fell to Earth in a shower of pieces over the Indian Ocean and Australia, with no known casualties.

UNITED NATIONS: WORLD POPULATION DAY. July 11. In June 1989 the Governing Council of the United Nations Development Programme recommended that July 11 be observed by the international community as World Population Day. An outgrowth of the Day of Five Billion (July 11, 1987), the Day seeks to focus public attention on the urgency and importance of population issues, particularly in the context of overall development plans and programs and the need to create solutions to these problems. For info: United Nations, Dept of Public Info, Public Inquiries Unit, RM GA-57, New York, NY 10017. Phone: (212) 963-4475. E-mail: inquiries@un.org.

WHITE, E.B.: BIRTH ANNIVERSARY. July 11, 1899. Versatile author of books for adults and children (*Charlotte's Web*) and *New Yorker* editor. Born at Mount Vernon, NY, White died at North Brooklyn, ME, Oct 1, 1985.

WYANDOTTE STREET ART FAIR. July 11–14. Downtown Wyandotte, MI. More than 350 artists and craftspeople display and sell their wares. Also, music, street entertainers, Children's Emporium and sidewalk sales. Sponsored by Anheuser Busch. Est attendance: 250,000. For info: Leslie Lupo, Dir, 3131 Biddle Ave, Wyandotte, MI 48192. Phone: (734) 324-4506. Fax: (734) 324-4552.

BIRTHDAYS TODAY

Giorgio Armani, 65, fashion designer, born Romagna, Italy, July 11, 1936.

Harold Bloom, 71, literary critic, born New York, NY, July 11, 1930.

Mike Foster, 71, Governor of Louisiana (R), born Shreveport, LA, July 11, 1930.

Debbie Harry, 56, lead singer (Blondie, "The Tide Is High"), born Miami, FL, July 11, 1945.

John Henson, 34, TV talk-show host ("Talk Soup"), born Stamford, CT, July 11, 1967.

Tab Hunter (Arthur Gelien), 70, actor (*Damn Yankees, Judge Roy Bean*, "The Tab Hunter Show"), born New York, NY, July 11, 1931.

Stephen Lang, 49, actor (*Last Exit to Brooklyn, Tombstone*), born Queens, NY, July 11, 1952.

Mark Lester, 43, actor (*Fahrenheit 451, Oliver*), born Oxford, England, July 11, 1958.

Al MacInnis, 38, hockey player, born Inverness, Nova Scotia, Canada, July 11, 1963.

Theodore Maiman, 74, physicist, developed first working laser, born Los Angeles, CA, July 11, 1927.

Bonnie Pointer, 50, singer (Pointer Sisters, "Steam Heat"), born East Oakland, CA, July 11, 1951.

Richie Sambora, 41, musician (Bon Jovi), born Amboy, NJ, July 11, 1960.

Leon Spinks, 48, former boxer, born St. Louis, MO, July 11, 1953.

Rod Strickland, 35, basketball player, born The Bronx, NY, July 11, 1966.

Beverly Todd, 55, actress, director, producer (*Baby Boom, Clara's Heart*), born Chicago, IL, July 11, 1946.

Suzanne Vega, 42, singer ("Luka"), born Santa Monica, CA, July 11, 1959.

Sela Ward, 45, actress ("Sisters," "Once and Again"), born Meridian, MS, July 11, 1956.

JULY 12 — THURSDAY
Day 193 — 172 Remaining

BASTILLE DAYS FESTIVAL. July 12–15. Milwaukee, WI. Celebrated "on the streets" of East Town in the heart of downtown Milwaukee. "Storm the Bastille" 5K run, sidewalk cafes, bicycle races, French marketplace, continuous entertainment on four stages, waiters'/waitresses' race, children's programs, dancing in the streets. Admission is free. Est attendance: 200,000. For info: East Town Assn, 770 N Jefferson, Milwaukee, WI 53202. Phone: (414) 271-1416. Fax: (414) 271-6401. Web: www.easttown.com.

BATTLE OF KURSK: ANNIVERSARY. July 12, 1943. The largest tank battle in history took place outside the small village of Prohorovka, Russia. Nine hundred Russian tanks attacked an equal number of German Panther and Porsche tanks. Though the German equipment was larger, that advantage was lost in a close range battle where they lacked maneuverability. When Hitler ordered a cease-fire, 300 German tanks remained strewn over the field.

DeRITA, JOE: BIRTH ANNIVERSARY. July 12, 1909. American comedian Curly Joe DeRita was the last surviving member of the Three Stooges comedy team. He joined the team in 1959 after Joe Besser left. He appeared in *Have Rocket, Will Travel* (1959), *Snow White and the Three Stooges* (1961) and *The Outlaw is Coming* (1965). Born at Philadelphia, PA, DeRita died July 3, 1993, at Los Angeles, CA.

"EVENING AT POPS" TV PREMIERE: ANNIVERSARY. July 12, 1970. PBS's popular concert series premiered with conductor Arthur Fiedler heading the Boston Pops Orchestra. Conductor/composer John Williams took over the post upon Fiedler's death in 1979; Keith Lockhart is the current conductor.

"FAMILY FEUD" TV PREMIERE: 25th ANNIVERSARY. July 12, 1976. From the production team of Mark Goodson and Bill Todman, this game show set two families against each other to raise the greater number of points. The contestants had to predict the most common answers to a given survey question. Richard Dawson, TV's famous kissing host, and the late Ray Combs served as hosts of the show. Another version of the show appeared in 1999 with Louie Anderson as host.

FULLER, BUCKMINSTER: ANNIVERSARY. July 12, 1895. Architect, inventor, engineer and philosopher, born Richard Buckminster Fuller at Milton, MA. His geodesic dome is one of the most important structural innovations of the 20th century. He died July 1, 1983, at Los Angeles, CA.

GERMANY ENDS MILITARY BAN: ANNIVERSARY. July 12, 1994. Germany's Constitutional Court ended the ban on sending German troops to fight outside the country. The ban had been in effect since shortly after World War II, when Germany was disarmed. (Japan has a similar ban.) The ruling would allow German troops to join in peacekeeping missions of the United Nations or the North Atlantic Treaty Organization (NATO). As if to signal the change in status, German military units marched in the Bastille Day celebration at Paris on July 14, the first time German troops had appeared in France since the German occupation ended in 1945.

HODAG COUNTRY FESTIVAL. July 12–15. Hodag "50" Track, Rhinelander, WI. 24th anniversary country music festival, one of the oldest open-air festivals in the Midwest. Annually, the second full weekend in July. Est attendance: 70,000. For info: Bernie or Diane Eckert, Hodag Country Fest, PO Box 1184, Rhinelander, WI 54501-1184. Phone: (715) 369-1300. Fax: (715) 362-3919. Web: www.hodag.com.

July *2001*	S	M	T	W	T	F	S
							7
	1	2	3	4	5	6	
	8	9	10	11	12	13	14
	15	16	17	18	19	20	21
	22	23	24	25	26	27	28
	29	30	31				

HOT DOG NIGHT. July 12. Luverne, MN. More than 12,000 hot dogs are served free of charge, free drink is also provided. Various demonstrations. Est attendance: 5,000. For info: Dave Smith, Exec Dir, Luverne Area Chamber of Commerce, 102 E Main, Luverne, MN 56156. Phone: (507) 283-4061. Fax: (507) 283-4061. Web: luvernemn.com.

ITALY: STRESA MUSIC WEEKS. July 12–15 (also Aug 24–Sept 28). Stresa. International festival includes concerts by symphonic orchestras, chamber music, recitals and a series by young winners of international musical contests. 40th annual festival. For info: Settimane Musicali di Stresae del Lago Maggiore, Via Canonica, 6, Stresa (Lago Maggiore), Italy 28838. Phone: (39) (0323) 31095 or (39) (0323) 30459. Fax: (39) (0323) 33006.

KIRIBATI: INDEPENDENCE DAY. July 12. Republic of Kiribati attained independence from Britain in 1979. Formerly known as the Gilbert Islands.

LOGGER DAYS. July 12–15 (tentative). Libby, MT. Celebration of logging heritage. Est attendance: 5,000. For info: Libby Chamber of Commerce, PO Box 704, Libby, MT 59923. Phone: (406) 293-4167. Fax: (406) 293-3222. E-mail: libbyacc@libby.org. Web: www.libby.org/libbyacc/.

MARION COUNTY FAIR. July 12–15. State Fairgrounds, Salem, OR. Exceptional food and entertainment, carnival, talent show, commercial exhibits, open class exhibits, horse and llama shows and livestock. Est attendance: 35,000. For info: Mary Boedigheimer, Coord, PO Box 703, Salem, OR 97308. Phone: (503) 585-9998. Fax: (503) 588-1659.

MICHIGAN STORYTELLERS FESTIVAL. July 12–14. Flint, MI. Storytelling performances, workshops and swaps come together for family fun and professional support at this 21st annual event. Est attendance: 1,500. For info: Cynthia Stilley, Flint Public Library, 1026 E Kearsley, Flint, MI 48502. Phone: (810) 232-7111. Fax: (810) 249-2635. E-mail: cstilley@flint.lib.mi.us.

MONTANA GOVERNOR'S CUP WALLEYE TOURNAMENT. July 12–14. Fort Peck, MT. Two-person team event, limited to 200 teams. First place award of $10,000. There is an 80 percent payback of $300 entry fee. Kids' fishing event also. Annually, the second weekend in July. Est attendance: 2,000. For info: Glasgow Area Chamber of Commerce & Agriculture, Box 832, Glasgow, MT 59230. Phone: (406) 228-2222 or (887) 228-2223. Fax: (406) 228-2244. E-mail: chamber@nemontel.net.

"NORTHERN EXPOSURE" TV PREMIERE: ANNIVERSARY. July 12, 1990. CBS's comedy-drama was essentially a fish-out-of-water (or rather a New Yorker out of Manhattan) series. Dr. Joel Fleischman (Rob Morrow) was forced to practice medicine in remote Cicely, Alaska, to pay off his student loans. He gradually accepted his lot through the help of the town's quirky citizens who needed him because he was the only doctor in town. The show's principal cast featured Barry Corbin as Maurice Minnefield, a former NASA astronaut and Cicely's most prominent businessman, Janine Turner as bush pilot Maggie O'Connell, Elaine Miles as Joel's assistant/receptionist Marilyn, Darren E. Burrows as Ed Chigliak, a half-Indian aspiring filmmaker, John Cullum as Cicely's mayor and tavern owner Holling Vincoeur, Cynthia Geary as Holling's girlfriend and waitress Shelley Tambo, Peg Phillips as store proprietor Ruth-Anne and John Corbett as deejay and philosopher Chris Stevens.

NORTHERN IRELAND: ORANGEMEN'S DAY. July 12. National holiday commemorates Battle of Boyne, July 1 (Old Style), 1690, in which the forces of King William III of England, Prince of Orange, defeated those of James II, at Boyne River in Ireland. Ordinarily observed July 12. If July 12 is a Saturday or a Sunday the holiday observance is on the following Monday.

OSLER, SIR WILLIAM: BIRTH ANNIVERSARY. July 12, 1849. Physician, teacher and author of *Principles and Practice of Medicine*, born at Tecumseh, Ontario, Canada. Osler died at Oxford, England, Dec 29, 1919.

SAO TOME AND PRINCIPE: INDEPENDENCE DAY: ANNIVERSARY. July 12. National holiday observed. Gained independence from Portugal in 1975.

SPACE MILESTONE: *PHOBOS 2* (USSR). July 12, 1988. Sent back the first close-up photos of Phobos, one of two small moons of Mars. Launched from Soviet space probe in central Asia on July 12, 1988.

THOREAU, HENRY DAVID: BIRTH ANNIVERSARY. July 12, 1817. American author and philosopher, born at Concord, MA. Died there May 6, 1862. In *Walden* he wrote, "I frequently tramped eight or ten miles through the deepest snow to keep an appointment with a beechtree, or a yellow birch, or an old acquaintance among the pines."

TURKEY RAMA. July 12-14. McMinnville, OR. This annual event at McMinnville, once known as the Turkey Capital of the world, continues to include Famous Turkey BBQ, Biggest Turkey contest, vendor street sales, 8K fun run, carnival, car show, entertainment. Est attendance: 25,000. For info: Greater McMinnville Chamber of Commerce, 417 NW Adams, McMinnville, OR 97128. Phone: (503) 472-6196. Fax: (503) 472-6198.

TURNER'S FRONTIER ADDRESS: ANNIVERSARY. July 12, 1893. Historian Frederick Jackson Turner delivered his paper,"The Significance of the Frontier in American History," at a meeting of the American Historical Association at Chicago during the Columbian Exposition. Stating that the frontier was a spawning ground for many of the social and intellectual traits that made Americans different from Europeans, Turner saw the end of the frontier as a major break in the psychology of the nation. Turner's formalization of this idea came in part from his reading the *Extra Census Bulletin No. 2: Distribution of Population According to Density: 1890* which said that, "Up to and including 1890 the country had a frontier of settlement, but at present the unsettled area has been so broken into by isolated bodies of settlement that there can hardly be said to be a frontier line."

WEDGWOOD, JOSIAH: BIRTH ANNIVERSARY. July 12, 1730. Famed English pottery designer and manufacturer, born at Burslem, Staffordshire, England. Died at Etruria, Staffordshire, England, Jan 3, 1795.

WILD ABOUT WILDLIFE. July 12-Aug 4. Coastal Center for the Arts, St. Simons Island, GA. A juried exhibit designed to give opportunity for focus on one of the most popular subjects for all ages—wildlife. Two- and three-dimensional. Deadline: June 5. For info: Coastal Center for the Arts, 2012 Demere Rd, St. Simons Island, GA 31522. Phone: (912) 634-0404.

BIRTHDAYS TODAY

Lisa Nicole Carson, 32, actress ("ER," "Ally McBeal"), born Brooklyn, NY, July 12, 1969.

Van Cliburn (Harvey Lavan, Jr), 67, pianist, born Shreveport, LA, July 12, 1934.

Bill Cosby, 63, comedian, actor (Emmys for "I Spy," "The Cosby Show"), born Philadelphia, PA, July 12, 1938.

Mel Harris, 44, actress ("Something So Right," "thirtysomething"), born Bethlehem, PA, July 12, 1957.

Christine McVie, 58, singer, musician (Fleetwood Mac, "Got a Hold On Me"), born Birmingham, England, July 12, 1943.

Denise Nicholas, 56, actress ("Room 222," "In the Heat of the Night," *Let's Do It Again*), born Detroit, MI, July 12, 1945.

Jamey Sheridan, 50, actor ("Shannon's Deal," *The House on Carroll Street*), born Pasadena, CA, July 12, 1951.

Richard Simmons, 53, TV personality, weight loss guru, author, born New Orleans, LA, July 12, 1948.

Roger Smith, 76, former chair of General Motors, born Columbus, OH, July 12, 1925.

Rolonda Watts, 42, talk-show host ("Rolonda"), born Winston-Salem, NC, July 12, 1959.

Kristi Tsuya Yamaguchi, 30, Olympic gold medal figure skater, born Hayward, CA, July 12, 1971.

JULY 13 — FRIDAY
Day 194 — 171 Remaining

AFRMA FANCY RAT & MOUSE DISPLAY ORANGE COUNTY FAIR. July 13-29. Costa Mesa, CA. American Fancy Rat and Mouse Association exhibits rats and mice of "fancy" species that make good pets. For info: AFRMA, PO Box 2589, Winnetka, CA 91396-2589. Phone: (818) 992-5564 or (909) 685-2350. Fax: (818) 592-6590. E-mail: craigr@afrma.org. Web: www.afrma.org.

BEREA CRAFT FESTIVAL. July 13-15. Berea, KY. Craftspeople from 20 states gather to exhibit, demonstrate and sell their work. Est attendance: 12,000. For info: Sandy Chowning, Berea Craft Enterprises, Box 128, Berea, KY 40403. Phone: (606) 986-2818.

BIG SKY STATE GAMES. July 13-15. Billings, MT. An Olympic-styled festival for Montana citizens. This statewide multisport program is designed to inspire people of all ages and skill levels to develop their physical and competitive abilities to the height of their potential through participation in fitness activities. Est attendance: 30,000. For info: Big Sky State Games, Box 7136, Billings, MT 59103-7136. Phone: (406) 254-7426. Fax: (406) 254-7439. E-mail: info@bigskygames.org. Web: www.bigskygames.org.

BLISSFEST. July 13-15. Cross Village, MI. Traditional, acoustic and folk music, two stages, workshops, camping, kids' area and activities. Music styles from jazz to bluegrass. Est attendance: 10,000. For info: Blissfest, Box 441, Harbor Springs, MI 49740. Phone: (231) 348-2815. Web: www.blissfest.org.

CANADA: CANADIAN TURTLE DERBY. July 13-15. Boissevain, MB. A fun-filled family weekend, adjacent to the famous International Peace Garden. Live turtle races. Curling Bonspiel, ball and volleyball tourneys, mini-triathlon, golf tournament, fireworks and children's entertainment. Outdoor Art Gallery with more than 24 murals! Ample camping available. 30th annual derby. Est attendance: 5,000. For info: Ivan Strain, Canadian Turtle Derby, PO Box 122, Boissevain, MB, Canada R0K 0E0. Phone: (204) 534-6000. Fax: (204) 534-6825.

FORREST, NATHAN BEDFORD: BIRTH ANNIVERSARY. July 13, 1821. Confederate cavalry commander whose birthday is observed in Tennessee, Forrest was one of the founders of the short-lived original Ku Klux Klan. Born at Bedford County, TN; died Oct 29, 1877, at Memphis, TN.

FRANCE: NIGHT WATCH or LA RETRAITE AUX FLAMBEAUX. July 13. Celebrates eve of the Bastille's fall.

HERITAGEFEST. July 13-15 (also 20-22). New Ulm, MN. This unique Old World celebration features continuous entertainment on five stages, including showbands direct from Europe along with storytellers, jugglers and mimes. Ethnic food and beverages. Arts and crafts and a unique Bavarian gift shop. Est attendance: 36,000. For info: Heritagefest, PO Box 461, New Ulm, MN 56073-0461. Phone: (507) 354-8850. E-mail: hfest@newulmtel.net. Web: www.heritagefest.net.

JAPAN: BON FESTIVAL (FEAST OF LANTERNS). July 13-15. Religious rites throughout Japan in memory of the dead, who, according to Buddhist belief, revisit Earth during this period. Lanterns are lighted for the souls. Spectacular bonfires in the shape of the character *dai* are burned on hillsides on the last day of the Bon or O-Bon Festival, bidding farewell to the spirits of the dead.

LAURA INGALLS WILDER PAGEANT. July 13–15. Walnut Grove, MN. Also July 20–22 and 27–29. Performed three weekends in July, the pageant attempts to catch the spirit of pioneer life as told in *On the Banks of Plum Creek* by Laura Ingalls Wilder. The live production tells the story of the Charles Ingalls family at Walnut Grove in the 1870s. Est attendance: 9,000. For info: Wilder Pageant Committee, Box 313, Walnut Grove, MN 56180. Phone: (888) 859-3102. E-mail: wpageant@rconnect.com. Web: www.walnutgrove.org.

LITCHFIELD OPEN HOUSE TOUR. July 13–14. Litchfield, CT. Preview tour and cocktail reception on Friday. Open house tour features an assortment of homes as well as additional attractions of historical and architectural significance. Annually, the second weekend in July. Est attendance: 1,800. For info: Connecticut Junior Republic, PO Box 161, Goshen Road, Litchfield, CT 06759. Phone: (860) 567-9423. Fax: (860) 567-9792.

"LIVE AID" CONCERTS: ANNIVERSARY. July 13, 1985. Concerts at Philadelphia, PA, and London, England (Kennedy and Wembley stadiums) were seen by 162,000 attendees and an estimated 1.5 billion television viewers. Organized to raise funds for African famine relief; the musicians performed without a fee, and nearly $100 million was pledged toward aid to the hungry.

MOON PHASE: LAST QUARTER. July 13. Moon enters Last Quarter phase at 2:45 PM, EDT.

NETHERLANDS: NORTH SEA JAZZ FESTIVAL. July 13–15. Nederlands Congresgebouw (Dutch Congress Building), The Hague. Live jazz festival with top-name entertainment. Annually, the second full weekend in July. Est attendance: 70,000. For info: North Sea Jazz Fest, PO Box 3325, 2601 DH Delft, Netherlands. Phone: (31) (15) 215-7756 or for tickets: (31) (10) 591-9000. Fax: (31) (10) 592-6130. E-mail: tejo@northseajazz.nl. Web: www.northseajazz.nl.

NEWPORT MUSIC FESTIVAL. July 13–29. Newport, RI. Unique chamber music programs, American debuts and international artists with special guest artists from the Festival's 33-year history. Three concerts daily held in Newport's fabled mansions. Est attendance: 25,000. For info: Dr. Mark P. Malkovich III, Gen Dir, The Newport Music Festival, PO Box 3300, Newport, RI 02840-0992. Phone: (401) 846-1133 or (401) 849-0700. Fax: (401) 849-1857. E-mail: staff@newportmusic.org. Web: www.newportmusic.org.

NORTHWEST ORDINANCE: ANNIVERSARY. July 13, 1787. The Northwest Ordinance, providing for government of the territory north of the Ohio River, became law. The ordinance guaranteed freedom of worship and the right to trial by jury, and it prohibited slavery.

SANTA FE CHAMBER MUSIC FESTIVAL. July 13–Aug 20. St. Francis Auditorium, Museum of Fine Arts, Santa Fe, NM. Highly acclaimed chamber music festival celebrates its 29th season. Draws on international talent, featuring works from the baroque, romantic and classical periods, as well as contemporary works, including world premiere performances. Est attendance: 15,000. For info: Santa Fe Chamber Music Fest, PO Box 853, Santa Fe, NM 87504. Phone: (505) 983-2075. Fax: (505) 986-0251. E-mail: info@santafechambermusic.org. Web: www.santafechambermusic.org.

SCHOONER DAYS. July 13–15. Harbor Park, Rockland, ME. Celebrates historic and landmark schooners engaged in the windjammer trade. Featuring the Tall Ships Parade of Sail, fireworks, Maine arts and crafts, maritime displays and demonstrations, entertainment and more. Est attendance: 20,000. For info: Susan MacMillan, Rockland Tomaston Area Chamber of Commerce, PO Box 508, Rockland, ME 04841. Phone: (207) 596-0376. Fax: (207) 596-6549. E-mail: rtacc@midcoast.com. Web: www.midcoast.com/~rtacc.

SKEPTICS' DAY. July 13. National celebration of skepticism. During this day examine those issues which you are most skeptical about. A day to collectively put these issues under a microscope and cut away those attachments that stand in your way of gaining greater success and freedom. Annually, on Friday the 13th. [©1996] For info: Adrienne Sioux Koopersmith, 1437 W Rosemont, #1W, Chicago, IL 60660-1319. Phone: (773) 743-5341. Fax: (773) 743-5395. E-mail: adrienne@21stcentury.net.

SYRACUSE ARTS & CRAFTS FESTIVAL. July 13–15. Syracuse, NY. Features a plethora of fine art and craft displays, food booths, family entertainment. Fun for the whole family. Est attendance: 70,000. For info: Syracuse Arts & Crafts Festival, 1900 State Tower Bldg, Syracuse, NY 13202. Phone: (315) 422-8284. Fax: (315) 471-4503. E-mail: downsyracuse@traknet.com. Web: www.downtownsyracuse.com.

THREE RIVERS FESTIVAL. July 13–22. Fort Wayne, IN. A citywide extravaganza of more than 200 events including parades, food, juried art show, concerts, children's events and fireworks. Est attendance: 500,000. For info: Three Rivers Festival, 102 Three Rivers North, Ft Wayne, IN 46802. Phone: (219) 426-5556. Fax: (219) 420-8611.

WAYNE CHICKEN SHOW. July 13–14. Wayne, NE. To allow humankind to pay tribute to chickenkind (without laying the proverbial egg). Parade, National Cluck-off, craft show and entertainment. Est attendance: 10,000. For info: Wayne Area Chamber of Commerce, 108 W Third St, Wayne, NE 68787. Phone: (402) 375-2240. E-mail: chamber@bloomnet.com. Web: www.chickenshow.com.

WILD HORSE STAMPEDE. July 13–15. Wolf Point, MT. The "Granddaddy" of all Montana rodeos features a wild-horse race, three rodeos, three parades and Native American culture. This is the oldest PRCA rodeo in Montana. Est attendance: 12,000. For info: Chairman, Wolf Point Chamber of Commerce, 218 3rd Ave S, Ste B, Wolf Point, MT 59201. Phone: (406) 653-2012. E-mail: wpchmber@nemontel.net.

WOOLLEY, MARY E.: BIRTH ANNIVERSARY. July 13, 1863. Mary Woolley was born at South Norwalk, CT. The first woman to graduate from Brown University (1894), Woolley pursued a career in education, serving on the faculty of Wellesley College. In 1901 she was named president of Mount Holyoke College, where she not only upgraded the school's faculty and curriculum but also raised the funds to add 16 major buildings to the campus. In 1932 she became the first female representative of the US at a major diplomatic conference, serving as a delegate to the Conference on Reduction and Limitation of Armaments. Woolley died Sept 5, 1947, at Westport, CT.

WORLD CUP INAUGURATED: ANNIVERSARY. July 13, 1930. The first World Cup soccer competition was held at Montevideo, Uruguay, with 14 countries participating. The host country had the winning team.

July 2001	S	M	T	W	T	F	S
		1	2	3	4	5	6	7
	8	9	10	11	12	13	14
	15	16	17	18	19	20	21
	22	23	24	25	26	27	28
	29	30	31				

BIRTHDAYS TODAY

Harrison Ford, 59, actor (*American Graffiti, Star Wars* films, *Indiana Jones* films), born Chicago, IL, July 13, 1942.

Robert Forster, 60, actor ("Banyon," *Reflections in a Golden Eye*), born Rochester, NY, July 13, 1941.

John French (Jack) Kemp, 66, former US Secretary of Housing and Urban Development, former football player, born Los Angeles, CA, July 13, 1935.

Louise Mandrell, 47, country western singer, born Corpus Christi, TX, July 13, 1954.

Cheech Marin, 55, writer (*My Name Is Cheech the School Bus Driver*), actor (Cheech and Chong films, "Nash Bridges"), born Los Angeles, CA, July 13, 1946.

Roger McGuinn (James Joseph McGuinn), 59, musician (The Byrds), born Chicago, IL, July 13, 1942.

Erno Rubik, 57, inventor of the Rubik's Cube, born in a hospital air raid shelter at Budapest, Hungary, July 13, 1944.

Wole Soyinka, 67, Nobel Prize–winning author (*The Lion and the Jewel, The Strong Breed*), born Abeokuta, Nigeria, July 13, 1934.

Michael Spinks, 45, former boxer, born St. Louis, MO, July 13, 1956.

Patrick Stewart, 61, actor ("Star Trek: The Next Generation," *Excalibur, LA Story*), born Mirfield, England, July 13, 1940.

David Storey, 68, author, playwright (*The Performance of Small Firms*), born Wakefield, England, July 13, 1933.

Anthony Jerome ("Spud") Webb, 38, basketball player, born Dallas, TX, July 13, 1963.

JULY 14 — SATURDAY

Day 195 — 170 Remaining

BASCOM, FLORENCE: BIRTH ANNIVERSARY. July 14, 1862. After receiving her third bachelor's degree from the University of Wisconsin in 1884 and a master's degree in 1887, Florence Bascom entered Johns Hopkins University and became the first woman to receive a doctorate in 1893. She taught at Ohio State and became a professor at Bryn Mawr. She also was the first woman appointed a geologist with the US Geological Survey, was Associate Editor of "American Geologist" (1890–1905) and became the first woman elected a Fellow of the Geological Society of America. Born at Williamstown, MA; died at Northampton, MA, June 18, 1945.

BASTILLE DAY CELEBRATION. July 14. Boston, MA. A street celebration with typical Parisian joie de vivre; dining and dancing under the stars. Est attendance: 3,000. For info: The French Library and Cultural Center, 53 Marlborough St, Boston, MA 02116-2099. Phone: (617) 266-4351. Fax: (617) 266-1780. E-mail: info@frenchlib.org. Web: www.frenchlib.org.

BON ODORI "FESTIVAL OF THE LANTERNS." July 14. Chicago, IL. 500 performers, most clad in colorful kimonos, dance in celebration to music of different prefectures of Japan. The beat of the huge *taiko* (drum) helps keep tempo. Dances are performed outdoors, and public participation is encouraged. 8 PM. Est attendance: 750. For info: Office Secretary, Midwest Buddhist Temple, 435 W Menomonee St, Chicago, IL 60614. Phone: (312) 943-7801. Fax: (312) 943-8069.

CANADA: GREAT RENDEZVOUS. July 14–17. Old Fort William, Thunder Bay, ON. Join hundreds of re-enactors as they celebrate the arrival of the partners, clerks and voyageurs to the inland headquarters of the North West Company. Take part in Rendezvous games and activities with colorful fur trade characters! Annually, mid-July. Est attendance: 4,000. For info: Marty Mascarin, Communications Officer, Vickers Heights Post Office, Thunder Bay, ON, Canada P0T 2Z0. Phone: (807) 473-2326 or (807) 577-8461. Fax: (807) 473-2327. Web: www.oldfortwilliam.on.ca.

CANADA: JEUX DE LA FRANCOPHONIE. July 14–24. Ottawa, ON and Hull, QC. More than 2,600 artists and athletes from 50 French-speaking countries will meet for the Games of the Francophone. This meeting of the worldwide French-speaking community is held every four years. The first games were held in Morocco in 1989. Later meetings were in Paris and Madagascar. The 2005 games will be in Niger. For info: Jeux de la Francophonie. Phone: (613) 749-5389. Fax: (613) 741-9906. E-mail: rheal@leroux.ca. Web: www.jeux2001.ca/.

CHANCELLOR, JOHN: BIRTH ANNIVERSARY. July 14, 1927. Television broadcast journalist John Chancellor was born at Chicago, IL. He rose through the ranks at the *Chicago Sun-Times*, from copy boy to feature writer. Chancellor spent more than four decades with the NBC network, beginning in 1950. During that time, he took a two-year respite from journalism to serve President Lyndon Johnson as director of the Voice of America. Chancellor retired in 1993, but his distinctive, familiar voice was still heard, for example, when he narrated a PBS documentary in 1996. He died July 12, 1996, at Princeton, NJ.

CHILDREN'S CELEBRATION. July 14. Island Park, Springfield, OR. Bring your family for a fun-filled day of activity and excitement. Island Park will be transformed into a child's world of life-size characters, creative craft booths, magnificent music, on-stage entertainment and demonstrations and fantastic foods. The dozens of booths and activities range from a petting zoo to exploring the universe. Annually, the second Saturday in July. For info: Willamalane Park and Recreation District, 765 A St, Springfield, OR 97477. Phone: (541) 736-4544. Fax: (541) 736-4529. Web: www.willamalane.org.

CHILDREN'S DAY. July 14. New Hampshire Farm Museum, Rte 125, Milton, NH. Hands-on activities for the children, small animals for petting, rides, games, face painting, wood-working table. Annually, the second Saturday in July. Sponsor: New Hampshire Farm Museum. Est attendance: 700. For info: Susann Brown, Admin Asst, PO Box 644, Milton, NH 03851. Phone: (603) 652-7840.

CHILDREN'S PARTY AT GREEN ANIMALS. July 14. Green Animals Topiary Garden, Portsmouth, RI. Annual party for children and adults at Green Animals, a delightful topiary garden and children's toy museum. Party includes pony rides, merry-go-round, games, clowns, refreshments, hot dogs, hamburgers and more. Annually, July 14. Est attendance: 800. For info: The Preservation Soc of Newport County, 424 Bellevue Ave, Newport, RI 02840. Phone: (401) 847-1000. Web: www.NewportMansions.org.

CIRCUS CITY FESTIVAL. July 14–21. Peru, IN. Youth amateur circus performed by children 7 to 21 years of age helping to preserve the circus heritage of Miami County, IN. Circus parade, July 21, 10 AM. Annually, beginning the Saturday before and ending the Saturday after the third Wednesday of July. Est attendance: 75,000. For info: Circus City Festival Inc, 154 N Broadway, Peru, IN 46970. Phone: (765) 472-3918. Fax: (765) 472-2826. Web: www.perucircus.com.

COW APPRECIATION DAY. July 14. Woodstock, VT. A "cowledge bowl" competition, dairy education programs, butter and ice cream making and more. Est attendance: 300. For info: Billings Farm & Museum, Box 489, Woodstock, VT 05091. Phone: (802) 457-2355. Fax: (802) 457-4663. E-mail: billings.farm@valley.net.

EDWARDS, DOUGLAS: BIRTH ANNIVERSARY. July 14, 1917. American television journalist Douglas Edwards was born at Ada, OK. He began his career in radio, but in 1947 he became the first major announcer to move to television. He was anchor for CBS's first nightly news program, "Douglas Edwards with the News" (1948–62), where he gave memorable on-scene coverage of such events as the sinking of the *Andrea Doria* in 1956. Edwards worked for CBS until his retirement two years before he died Oct 13, 1990, at Sarasota, FL.

ENGLAND: BIRMINGHAM RIOT: ANNIVERSARY. July 14, 1791. Following a dinner celebrating the second anniversary of the fall of the Bastille, an angry mob rioted at Birmingham, England. The main target of their wrath was the home of scientist (discoverer of oxygen) Joseph Priestley, who was unpopular because of his religious views and his approval of the American and French revolutionary causes. The mob ruled Birmingham for three days, burning Priestly's home and laboratory as well as the homes of his friends. Priestly, in disguise, and his family narrowly escaped with their lives. They lived for a time at London before moving in 1794 to America. See also: "Priestley, Joseph: Birth Anniversary" (Mar 13).

FINLAND: INTERNATIONAL JAZZ FESTIVAL. July 14–22. Pori. 36th international festival presenting the jazz music of today with top-name performances. 12 different venues; some go on all night. Est attendance: 150,000. For info: Finnish Tourist Board, 655 Third Ave, New York, NY 10017. Phone: (212) 885-9700 or (358) (2) 626-2200. Fax: (358) (2) 626-2225. E-mail: festival@porijazz.fi. Web: www.porijazz.fi.

FINLAND: KAUSTINEN FOLK MUSIC FESTIVAL. July 14–22. Kaustinen. Scandinavia's largest annual international festival of folk music and dance. Thousands of Finnish and hundreds of foreign artists perform. Every visitor has the opportunity to join in the music, dance and song. First organized in 1968. Est attendance: 100,000. For info: Finnish Tourist Board, 655 Third Ave, New York, NY 10017. Phone: (212) 885-9700 or (358) (6) 860-4111. Fax: (358) (6) 860-4222. E-mail: folk.fest@kaustinen.fi.

FORD, GERALD RUDOLPH: BIRTHDAY. July 14, 1913. Thirty-eighth president of the US (1974–77). Born Leslie King at Omaha, NE, Ford became forty-first vice president of the US on Dec 6, 1973, by appointment, following the resignation of Spiro T. Agnew from that office on Oct 10, 1973. Ford became president on Aug 9, 1974, following the resignation from that office on that day of Richard M. Nixon. He was the first nonelected vice president and president of the US.

FRANCE: BASTILLE DAY OR FETE NATIONAL. July 14. Public holiday commemorating the fall of the Bastille at the beginning of the French Revolution, July 14, 1789. Also celebrated or observed in many other countries.

FRONTIER DAYS. July 14–15. Old Cowtown Museum, Wichita, KS. Focusing on the white settlement of the Southern Plains, reenactors from Kansas, Oklahoma and Missouri will portray 1870s drovers, buffalo hunters, soldiers, traders and a Southern Cheyenne village. Lectures, clinics and demonstrations will be topped off by mounted shooting demonstrations on Sunday. Annually, mid-July. Est attendance: 1,000. For info: Gloria G. Campbell, Dir, Old Cowtown Museum, 1871 Sim Park Dr, Wichita, KS 67203. Phone: (316) 264-0671. Fax: (316) 264-2937.

GREATER PHILADELPHIA MID-SUMMER SCOTTISH AND IRISH MUSIC FESTIVAL AND FAIR. July 14–15. Valley Forge Convention Center, King of Prussia, PA. Music, dance, spectacle and song celebrate Ireland and Scotland. All-star lineup of entertainment and a host of ethnic activities, foods and products. Est attendance: 9,000. For info: Wm M. Reid, Jr, Scottish & Irish Festival, PO Box 102, Plymouth Meeting, PA 19462. Phone: (610) 825-7268. Fax: (610) 825-8745. E-mail: eohebrides@aol.com.

July *2001*	S	M	T	W	T	F	S
		1	2	3	4	5	6	7
	8	9	10	11	12	13	14
	15	16	17	18	19	20	21
	22	23	24	25	26	27	28
	29	30	31				

GUTHRIE, WOODROW WILSON "WOODY": BIRTH ANNIVERSARY. July 14, 1912. American folksinger, songwriter ("This Land Is Your Land," "Union Maid," "Hard Traveling"), born at Okemah, OK. Traveled the country by freight train, singing and listening. Became a strong union supporter. Died Oct 3, 1967, at New York, NY. Father of Arlo Guthrie.

HOMEFEST. July 14. Bald Knob, AR. School reunions, homecomings, sports events, 5K run-walk, basketball, horseshoe pitching, checkers, antique autos, crafts, street dance, parade, beauty pageant and more. Est attendance: 3,000. For info: Bald Knob Area Chamber of Commerce, PO Box 338, Bald Knob, AR 72010. Phone: (501) 724-3140.

JVC WINTER PARK JAZZ FESTIVAL. July 14–15. Winter Park Resort, Winter Park, CO. A two-day smooth jazz festival located on the slopes of Winter Park Resort. Loyal fans come equipped with lawn chairs, blankets and sunscreen to hear national jazz performers. Est attendance: 2,000. For info: Winter Park Resort, PO Box 36, Winter Park, CO 80482. Phone: (970) 726-1580. Fax: (970) 726-1572. E-mail: wpinfo@mail.skiwinterpark.com. Web: winterparkresort.com.

MAINE POTATO BLOSSOM FESTIVAL. July 14–22. Fort Fairfield, ME. 54th annual. Promotes and observes the importance of Maine's prime agricultural product. Est attendance: 35,000. For info: Fort Fairfield Chamber of Commerce, 128 Main St, Fort Fairfield, ME 04742. Phone: (207) 472-3802. Fax: (207) 472-3886. E-mail: ffcc@mfx.net. Web: www.fortfairfield.org.

"MASQUERADE PARTY" TV PREMIERE: ANNIVERSARY. July 14, 1952. Variations of this game show have appeared all over the TV schedule on NBC, CBS, ABC and in syndication. A panel of celebrities tried to guess the identity of a guest celebrity, who usually appeared in costume or under heavy makeup. Hosts of the show included: Bud Collyer, Douglas Edwards, Peter Donald, Eddie Bracken, Robert Q. Lewis, Bert Parks and Richard Dawson.

MISSION SAN ANTONIO DE PADUA: ANNIVERSARY. July 14. California. Mission to the Indians founded July 14, 1771.

MURRAY, KEN: BIRTH ANNIVERSARY. July 14, 1903. American comedian Ken Murray was born at New York, NY. He began in vaudeville, then moved to films and television. He died Oct 12, 1988, at Beverly Hills, CA.

OREGON COAST MUSIC FESTIVAL. July 14–28. Coos Bay, OR. Musical celebration features regional, national and international artists performing symphonic, choral and chamber music, plus jazz and world music. Est attendance: 15,000. For info: Oregon Coast Music Festival, PO Box 663, Coos Bay, OR 97420. Phone/Fax: (541) 267-0938. Web: www.coosnet.com/music.

PEDDLER'S VILLAGE TEDDY BEAR'S PICNIC. July 14–15. Lahaska, PA. Bring your teddy bear for the festivities: competitions, teddy bear craftspeople from across the country, puppet shows, parades, a backyard circus, live entertainment. Est attendance: 14,000. For info: Peddler's Village, Routes 202 &263, Lahaska, PA 18931. Phone: (215) 794-4000. Fax: (215) 794-4001. Web: www.peddlersvillage.com.

RENAISSANCE FAIRE. July 14–15. University of Great Falls, Great Falls, MT. Enter a world of the sights, sounds, tastes and activities of 16th-century Europe. Costumed village folk greet and entertain you. The Royal Retinue proceeds through the Faire, welcoming one and all to enjoy the sounds of madrigals, folk songs, dancers, minstrels, crafters and artisans demonstrating their skills. To add to the ambience the streets are filled with banners, pennants and coats of arms. Est attendance: 2,000. For info: Lana Furdell, Faire Dir, University of Great Falls, 1301 20th St South, Great Falls, MT 59405. Phone: (406) 791-5255. Fax: (406) 791-5393. E-mail: lfurdell@ugf.edu.

ROUTE 66 SUMMERFEST. July 14. Rolla, MO. 7th annual town-wide celebration including sporting events, car shows, crafts, entertainment and food. Annually, the second Saturday in July. Est attendance: 10,000. For info: Rolla Chamber of Commerce, 1301 Kingshighway, Rolla, MO 65401-2926. Phone: (573) 364-3577.

SARTO, ANDREA DEL: BIRTH ANNIVERSARY. July 14, 1486. Celebrated Italian painter was born near Florence, Italy. "Sarto," a nickname referring to his father's trade as a tailor, was the name he chose during his lifetime, though the real surname was probably either Vanucchi or di Francesco. One of the most renowned artists of his time, his paintings hang in the great galleries of the world. He died at Florence, Jan 22, 1531.

SHARK AWARENESS DAY. July 14. Jenkinson's Aquarium, Point Pleasant Beach, NJ. 10 AM–10 PM. Are sharks dangerous? Learn all about sharks and what you can do to protect them. A special artifact cart and shark stories for children will be presented throuhout the day. You can even touch a live shark in our touch tank. Sharks are fed at 9 PM. Crafts and face painting for children between 1 PM–4 PM. Free buttons to the first 300 visitors. Est attendance: 600. For info: Liz Carletta, Education Coord, Jenkinson's Aquarium, 300 Ocean Ave, Point Pleasant Beach, NJ 08742. Phone: (732) 899-1212. Fax: (732) 899-1717. E-mail: aquarium@jenkinsons.com. Web: www.jenkinsons.com.

SODBUSTER DAYS. July 14–15. Fort Ransom State Park, Fort Ransom, ND. Remember the way things were done in rural North Dakota during the early 1920s with shelling corn by hand, rope weaving, horse-drawn plowing and haying. Ladies' demonstrations, kids games, live music. Est attendance: 4,000. For info: Fort Ransom State Park, 5981 Walt Hjelle Parkway, Ft Ransom, ND 58033-9712. Phone: (701) 973-4331. Fax: (701) 973-4271.

STONE HOUSE DAY. July 14. Hurley, NY. Tour six to nine privately-owned, 250-plus year-old stone houses. Annually, the second Saturday in July. Est attendance: 800. For info: Stone House Day, Hurley Reformed Church, PO Box 328, Hurley, NY 12443. Phone: (914) 331-4121.

TALKEETNA MOOSE-DROPPING FESTIVAL (WITH MOOSE-DROPPING TOSS GAME). July 14–15. Talkeetna, AK. Parade, booths, entertainment, 5K fun run, Mountain Mother contest and the famous moose dropping toss game. Est attendance: 6,500. For info: Alice Johannewes, Talkeetna Historical Soc, PO Box 76, Talkeetna, AK 99676. Phone: (907) 733-2487. Fax: (907) 733-2484. E-mail: ths@matnet.com. Web: www.moosedrop.com.

TUPPER LAKE WOODSMEN'S DAYS (WITH CHAINSAW SCULPTURING CONTEST). July 14–15. Tupper Lake, NY. Competitions for woodsmen and lumberjacks. Includes the annual Northeast Regional Chainsaw Sculpturing Contest. Annually, the second weekend in July. Est attendance: 2,500. For info: Tupper Lake Woodsmen's Assn, PO Box 759, 19 Front St, Tupper Lake, NY 12986. Phone: (518) 359-9444. Fax: (518) 359-8244.

WOMEN'S RIGHTS CONVENTION CALLED: ANNIVERSARY. July 14, 1848. An announcement placed by Elizabeth Cady Stanton and Lucretia Mott appeared in the *Seneca Falls Courier.* The notice concerned a women's rights convention to be held at the Wesleyan Chapel, Seneca Falls, NY, July 19–20.

Polly Bergen, 71, actress ("To Tell the Truth," *The Winds of War*), singer, born Knoxville, TN, July 14, 1930.

Ingmar Bergman, 83, filmmaker (*The Seventh Seal, Wild Strawberries, Cries and Whispers*), born Uppsala, Sweden, July 14, 1918.

Gerald Rudolph Ford (born Leslie King), 88, 38th US President, born Omaha, NE, July 14, 1913.

Matthew Fox, 35, actor ("Party of Five"), born Crowheart, WY, July 14, 1966.

Missy Gold, 31, actress ("Benson"), born Great Falls, MT, July 14, 1970.

Roosevelt (Rosey) Grier, 69, actor, former football player, born Cuthbert, GA, July 14, 1932.

Joel Silver, 49, producer (*Lethal Weapon, Die Hard*), born South Orange, NJ, July 14, 1952.

Harry Dean Stanton, 75, actor (*Repo Man; Paris, Texas; Wild at Heart*), born West Irvine, KY, July 14, 1926.

Steven Michael (Steve) Stone, 54, sportscaster, former baseball player, born Euclid, OH, July 14, 1947.

Robin Ventura, 34, baseball player, born Santa Maria, CA, July 14, 1967.

JULY 15 — SUNDAY
Day 196 — 169 Remaining

ADMINISTRATIVE PROFESSIONALS INTERNATIONAL ANNUAL CONVENTION AND EDUCATION FORUM. July 15–18. Toronto, Ontario, Canada. Est attendance: 2,000. For info: Intl Assn for Administrative Professionals, 10502 NW Ambassador Dr, PO Box 20404, Kansas City, MO 64195-0404. Phone: (816) 891-6600, ext 223. Fax: (816) 891-9118. E-mail: service@iaap-hq.org. Web: www.iaap-hq.org.

BATTLE OF THE MARNE: ANNIVERSARY. July 15, 1918. General Erich Ludendorff launched Germany's fifth, and last, offensive to break through the Chateau-Thierry salient. This all-out effort involved three armies branching out from Rheims to cross the Marne River. The Germans were successful in crossing the Marne near Chateau-Thierry before American, British and Italian divisions stopped their progress. On July 18 General Foch, Commander-in-Chief of the Allied troops, launched a massive counteroffensive that resulted in a German retreat that continued for four months until they sued for peace in November.

CANADA: SAINT SWITHUN'S SOCIETY ANNUAL CELEBRATION. July 15. Toronto, ON. Goals include the promotion of feelings of goodwill and the patterning of members' lives after the example of our Patron. Affiliated with the Friends of Winchester Cathedral. Publishes "The Water Spout" newsletter, free upon request. Annually, July 15. Est attendance: 100. For info: Norman A. McMullen, Pres, St. Swithun's Soc, 427 Lynett Crescent, Richmond Hill, ON, Canada L4C 2V6. Phone: (905) 883-0984.

★**CAPTIVE NATIONS WEEK.** July 15–21. Presidential proclamation issued each year since 1959 for the third week of July. (PL86–90 of July 17, 1959.)

COMMERCIAL AIR FLIGHT BETWEEN THE US AND USSR BEGINS: ANNIVERSARY. July 15, 1968. A Soviet Aeroflot jet landed at Kennedy Airport at New York, NY, marking the start of direct commercial air flight between the US and the then USSR.

CONCOURS D'ELEGANCE. July 15. Forest Grove, OR. Set among the beauty of the Pacific University Campus, this is one of the premier car shows on the West Coast with dozens of beautifully restored vintage autos. A great family event. Annually, the third Sunday in July. Est attendance: 10,000. For info: Forest Grove Rotary Club, PO Box 387, Forest Grove, OR 97116. Phone: (503) 357-2300. Web: www.forestgroveconcours.org.

ITALY: FEAST OF THE REDEEMER. July 15. Venice. Procession of gondolas and other craft commemorating the end of the epidemic of 1575. Annually, the third Sunday in July.

LEGAL REVOLUTION WEEK. July 15–21. Have you ever been treated unfairly? Have you ever signed a contract you didn't understand? Can you afford to pay $150 to $300 an hour for expert legal advice? If not, join us in celebrating with hundreds of thousands of consumers who have banded together as members of prepaid legal service plans, and enjoy affordable access to attorneys. E-mail to legalrevolution@sendfree.com for a free report on how you can join the Legal Revolution. For info: Sheila Martin, 250 H St, Blaine, WA 98230. Phone: (604) 535-3636. E-mail: smartin@prepaidlegal.com. Web: www.legalhelpnet.com/martin.

LUXEMBOURG: BEER FESTIVAL. July 15. At Diekirch an annual beer festival is held on the third Sunday in July.

MOORE, CLEMENT CLARKE: BIRTH ANNIVERSARY. July 15, 1779. American author and teacher, best remembered for his popular verse "A Visit from Saint Nicholas" (" 'Twas the Night Before Christmas"), which was first published anonymously and without Moore's knowledge in a newspaper, Dec 23, 1823. Moore was born at New York, NY, and died at Newport, RI, July 10, 1863.

NATIONAL ICE CREAM DAY. July 15. To promote America's favorite dessert, ice cream, on "Sundae Sunday." Annually, the third Sunday in July.

NATIONAL PLAN TO PROMOTE YOUR BUSINESS WEEK. July 15–21. To encourage the more than 22 million small business owners in the US to actively plan to promote their businesses. Annually, the third week in July. For info: Rebecca Hart, APR, 13245 Atlantic Blvd, Ste 4-234, Jacksonville, FL 32246. Phone: (904) 220-4756. Fax: (904) 220-7648. E-mail: rebhart@mediaone.net. Web: www.simplyPR.com.

July *2001*	S	M	T	W	T	F	S
	1	2	3	4	5	6	7
	8	9	10	11	12	13	14
	15	16	17	18	19	20	21
	22	23	24	25	26	27	28
	29	30	31				

"ONE LIFE TO LIVE" TV PREMIERE: ANNIVERSARY. July 15, 1968. Set in the fictional Pennsylvania town of Llanview, the show was created by Agnes Nixon to depict the class and ethnic struggles of the town's denizens. The initial cast featured many Jewish, Polish and African American characters. The show departed from inter-ethnic storytelling in the 1980s for far more fantastic adventures set in locales such as heaven, the old west and a futuristic mountain silo called Eternia. Since then, the show has returned to its strengths of traditional storytelling by featuring Latino and African American actors as integral characters in new storylines. Award-winning actress Erika Slezak heads the cast as the venerable Viki Lord Riley Buchanan Carpenter, the town's matron with five alternate personalities. Among those who have appeared on "OLTL" are Tom Berenger, Judith Light, Robert Desiderio, Tommy Lee Jones, Laurence Fishburne, Jameson Parker, Phylicia Rashad, Christine Ebersole, Richard Grieco, Blair Underwood, Joe Lando, Audrey Landers, Christian Slater and Yasmine Bleeth.

REMBRANDT: BIRTH ANNIVERSARY. July 15, 1606. Dutch painter and etcher, born at Leiden, Holland. One of the undisputed giants of western art. Known for *The Night Watch* and many portraits and self-portraits, died at Amsterdam, Holland, Oct 4, 1669.

SAINT CYRIL'S PARISH FESTIVAL. July 15. Kiwanis Park, Sheboygan, WI. Slovenian foods, music, games, raffle 10:30 AM–7 PM. Polka Mass at 10:30 AM, $3,000 bingo at 1 PM under the Big Top tent. Est attendance: 5,000. For info: St. Cyril & Methodius Parish, 822 New Jersey Ave, Sheboygan, WI 53081. Phone: (414) 457-7110.

SAINT FRANCES XAVIER CABRINI: BIRTH ANNIVERSARY. July 15, 1850. First American saint, founder of schools, orphanages, convents and hospitals, born at Lombardy, Italy. Died of malaria at Chicago, IL, Dec 22, 1917. Canonized July 7, 1946.

SAINT SWITHIN'S DAY. July 15. Swithun (Swithin), Bishop of Winchester (AD 852–862), died July 2, 862. Little is known of his life, but his relics were transferred into Winchester Cathedral July 15, 971, a day on which there was a heavy rainfall. According to old English belief, it will rain for 40 days thereafter when it rains on this day. "St. Swithin's Day, if thou dost rain, for 40 days it will remain; St. Swithin's Day, if thou be fair, for 40 days, will rain nea mair."

TOBAGO: TOBAGO HERITAGE FESTIVAL. July 15–31 (tentative). A two-week festival celebrating indigenous cultural art forms features a different village each day depicting or reenacting an event related to that area. A variety of activities, from the "ole time" wedding and Belmana Riots to the pulsating rhythms of the music and dance as well as sea festival, folk tales, superstitions and Heritage queen competition. Annually, the last two weeks of July. For info: Tobago Heritage Festival Committee, Market Square, Scarborough, Tobago, West Indies. Phone: (809) 639-4441.

WOODSTOCK FOLK FESTIVAL. July 15. Woodstock, IL. Folk, blues, storytelling and fiddle tunes will ring out at the 16th annual festival and musicians will fill the square with the sounds of guitars and singing, banjo and fiddle. Hammered dulcimer and harmonica. 12:30 PM–6:30 PM. For info: Woodstock Chamber of Commerce, 136 Cass St, Woodstock, IL 60098. Phone: (815) 338-2436. Fax: (815) 338-2927. E-mail: chamber@stans.com.

BIRTHDAYS TODAY

Willie Aames, 41, actor ("Eight Is Enough," "Charles in Charge"), born Newport Beach, CA, July 15, 1960.
Kim Alexis, 41, model, born Lockport, NY, July 15, 1960.
Julian Bream, 68, musician (classical guitar, lute), born London, England, July 15, 1933.
Lolita Davidovich, 40, actress (*Indictment, Cobb*), born London, Ontario, Canada, July 15, 1961.

Brian Austin Green, 28, actor ("Beverly Hills 90210"), singer, born Van Nuys, CA, July 15, 1973.

Irene Jacob, 35, actress (*Red, Othello*), born Paris, France, July 15, 1966.

Alex George Karras, 66, former football player, actor ("Webster," *Babe, Victor/Victoria*), born Gary, IN, July 15, 1935.

Ken Kercheval, 66, actor ("Dallas," "Search for Tomorrow"), born Wolcottville, IN, July 15, 1935.

Linda Ronstadt, 55, singer ("Heart Like a Wheel," "Simple Dreams"), songwriter, born Tucson, AZ, July 15, 1946.

Jesse Ventura, 50, Governor of Minnesota (I), born Minneapolis, MN, July 15, 1951.

Jan-Michael Vincent, 57, actor ("The Winds of War," "Airwolf"), born Denver, CO, July 15, 1944.

George V. Voinovich, 65, US Senator (R, Ohio), born Cleveland, OH, July 15, 1936.

Forest Whitaker, 40, actor (*Platoon, Bird, The Crying Game*); director (*Waiting to Exhale*), born Longview, TX, July 15, 1961.

JULY 16 — MONDAY
Day 197 — 168 Remaining

AMUNDSEN, ROALD: BIRTH ANNIVERSARY. July 16, 1872. Norwegian explorer born near Oslo, Roald Amundsen was the first man to sail from the Atlantic to the Pacific Ocean via the Northwest Passage (1903–05). He discovered the South Pole (Dec 14, 1911) and flew over the North Pole in a dirigible in 1926. He flew, with five companions, from Norway, June 18, 1928, in a daring effort to rescue survivors of an Italian Arctic expedition. No trace of the rescue party or the airplane was ever located. See also: "South Pole: Discovery Anniversary" (Dec 14).

ATOMIC BOMB TESTED: ANNIVERSARY. July 16, 1945. In the New Mexican desert at Alamogordo Air Base, 125 miles southeast of Albuquerque, the experimental atomic bomb was set off at 5:30 AM. Dubbed "Fat Boy" by its creator, the plutonium bomb vaporized the steel scaffolding holding it as the immense fireball rose 8,000 ft in a fraction of a second—ultimately creating a mushroom cloud to a height of 41,000 ft. At ground zero the bomb emitted heat three times the temperature of the interior of the sun. All plant and animal life for a mile around ceased to exist. When informed by President Truman at Potsdam of the successful experiment, Winston Churchill responded, "It's the Second Coming in wrath!"

BOLIVIA: LA PAZ DAY: ANNIVERSARY. July 16, 1548. Founding of city, now capital of Bolivia, on this day, 1548.

COMET CRASHES INTO JUPITER: ANNIVERSARY. July 16, 1994. The first fragment of the comet Shoemaker-Levy crashed into the planet Jupiter, beginning a series of spectacular collisions, each unleashing more energy than the combined effect of an explosion of all our world's nuclear arsenal. Video imagery from earthbound telescopes as well as the Hubble telescope provided vivid records of the explosions and their aftereffects. In 1993 the comet had shattered into a series of about a dozen large chunks that resembled "pearls on a string" after its orbit brought it within the gravitational effects of our solar system's largest planet.

DISTRICT OF COLUMBIA: ESTABLISHING LEGISLATION ANNIVERSARY. July 16, 1790. George Washington signed legislation that selected the District of Columbia as the permanent capital of the US. Boundaries of the district were established in 1792. Plans called for the government to remain housed at Philadelphia, PA, until 1800, when the new national capital would be ready for occupancy.

DOW-JONES TOPS 8,000: ANNIVERSARY. July 16, 1997. The Dow-Jones Index of 30 major industrial stocks topped the 8,000 mark for the first time.

EARTHQUAKE JOLTS PHILIPPINES: ANNIVERSARY. July 16, 1990. An earthquake measuring 7.7 on the Richter scale struck the Philippines, killing an estimated 1,621 persons and leaving approximately 1,000 missing. The quake struck in an area north of Manila, and heavy damage was reported at Cabanatuan, Baguio and on Luzon island. The quake was the worst in the Philippines in 14 years.

EDDY, MARY BAKER: BIRTH ANNIVERSARY. July 16, 1821. Founder of Christian Science; born near Concord, NH, she died at Chestnut Hill, MA, Dec 3, 1910.

INTERNATIONAL TOWN CRIERS DAY. July 16. A day recognizing the ancient and honorable art and tradition of town crying and the significant contribution town criers make to promoting their respective towns and cities. Annually, a Monday in July. For info: David Phillips, Official Town Crier, Box 58, Dutton, ON, Canada N0L IJ0. E-mail: tcrier@hotmail.com.

ISRAEL: WORLD MACCABIAH GAMES. July 16–26. Israel. Held every four years, these games will be the 16th World Maccabiah Games. More than 5,600 athletes from around the world will compete. For info: Maccabi USA, 1926 Arch St, 4R, Philadelphia, PA 19103. Phone: (215) 561-6900. E-mail: maccabi@maccabiusa.com. Web: www.maccabiusa.com or www.maccabiah.org.

MISSION SAN DIEGO DE ALCALA: FOUNDING ANNIVERSARY. July 16, 1769. First of 21 California missions to the Indians.

NATIONAL GET OUT OF THE DOGHOUSE DAY. July 16. In trouble with someone you know and care about? This is the day when anyone can "Get out of the doghouse!" Annually, the third Monday in July. For info: Heidi Richards, Eden Florists and Gift Baskets, Miramar, FL 33023. Phone: (954) 964-3135. E-mail: wunspirit@aol.com or flowers@edenflorist.com.

ORGANIZATION DEVELOPMENT WORLD CONGRESS. July 16–21. Vienna, Austria. 21st annual. Organization development professionals exchange ideas on changes and new developments in the field. Est attendance: 100. For info: Dr. Donald W. Cole, RODC, Organization Development Institute, 11234 Walnut Ridge Rd, Chesterland, OH 44026. Phone: (440) 729-7419. Fax: (440) 729-9319. E-mail: DonWCole@aol.com. Web: members.aol.com/odinst.

REYNOLDS, JOSHUA: BIRTH ANNIVERSARY. July 16, 1723 (OS). English portrait painter whose paintings of 18th-century English notables are among the best of the time. Born at Plympton, Devon, England, Sir Joshua died at London, Feb 23, 1792, at age 68. "He who resolves never to ransack any mind but his own," Reynolds told students of the Royal Academy in 1774, "will be soon reduced, from mere barrenness, to the poorest of all imitations; he will be obliged to imitate himself, and to repeat what he has before often repeated."

ROGERS, GINGER: 90th BIRTH ANNIVERSARY. July 16, 1911. Ginger Rogers is best remembered as Fred Astaire's dance partner in a series of romantic musicals. She appeared in 70 films during her six-decade career, winning an Oscar for her leading role in the 1940 film *Kitty Foyle*. Rogers was born at Independence, MO, and died Apr 25, 1995, at Rancho Mirage, CA.

SPACE MILESTONE: *APOLLO 11* (US): MAN SENT TO THE MOON. July 16, 1969. This launch resulted in man's first moon landing, the first landing on any extraterrestrial body. See also: "Space Milestone: Moon Day" (July 20).

STANWYCK, BARBARA: BIRTH ANNIVERSARY. July 16, 1907. Actress Barbara Stanwyck was born Ruby Stevens at the Flatbush section of Brooklyn, NY. At the age of 18 she won a leading role in the Broadway melodrama *Noose*, appearing for the first time as Barbara Stanwyck. She appeared in 82 films including *Stella Dallas; Double Indemnity; Sorry, Wrong Number; The Lady Eve* and the television series "The Big Valley." In 1944, the government listed her as the nation's highest paid woman, earning $400,000 per year. Stanwyck died at Santa Monica, CA, Jan 21, 1990.

WELLS, IDA B.: BIRTH ANNIVERSARY. July 16, 1862. African American journalist and anti-lynching crusader Ida B. Wells was born the daughter of slaves at Holly Springs, MS, and grew up as Jim Crow and lynching were becoming prevalent. Wells argued that lynchings occurred not to defend white women but because of whites' fear of economic competition from blacks. She traveled extensively, founding anti-lynching societies and black women's clubs. Wells's *Red Record* (1895) was one of the first accounts of lynchings in the South. She died Mar 25, 1931, at Chicago, IL.

BIRTHDAYS TODAY

Ruben Blades, 53, singer (two Grammy Awards), actor (*Crossover Dreams, The Milagro Beanfield War*), born Panama City, Panama, July 16, 1948.

Richard H. Bryan, 64, US Senator (D, Nevada), born Washington, DC, July 16, 1937.

Phoebe Cates, 38, actress (*Fast Times at Ridgemont High, Gremlins*), born New York, NY, July 16, 1965.

Stewart Copeland, 49, musician (drummer with the Police), songwriter, born McLean, VA, July 16, 1952.

Corey Feldman, 30, actor (*Stand By Me, The Lost Boys*), born Reseda, CA, July 16, 1971.

Michael Flatley, 43, dancer (*Lord of the Dance*), born Chicago, IL, July 16, 1958.

Alexis Herman, 54, Secretary of Labor (Clinton administration), born Mobile, AL, July 16, 1947.

Barnard Hughes, 86, actor (*Sisters*, "Doc"), born Bedford Hills, NY, July 16, 1915.

Bess Myerson, 77, former Miss America ('45), former government official, born New York, NY, July 16, 1924.

Barry Sanders, 33, former football player, born Wichita, KS, July 16, 1968.

Pinchas Zukerman, 53, violinist, born Tel Aviv, Israel, July 16, 1948.

JULY 17 — TUESDAY

Day 198 — 167 Remaining

ABBOTT, BERENICE: BIRTH ANNIVERSARY. July 17, 1898. Berenice Abbott was born at Springfield, OH, and went on to become a pioneer of American photography. She is best remembered for her black and white photographs of New York City in the 1930s, many of which appeared in the book *Changing New York*. After publishing this collection she began photographing scientific experiments that illustrated the laws and processes of physics. She died at Monson, ME, Dec 11, 1991.

CZAR NICHOLAS II AND FAMILY EXECUTED: ANNIVERSARY. July 17, 1918. Russian Czar Nicholas II; his wife Alexandra; son and heir Alexis; and daughters Anastasia, Tatiana, Olga and Marie were executed by firing squad on this date. The murder of the last of the 300-year-old Romanov dynasty occurred at Yekaterinburg, in the Ural mountains of Siberia where Nicholas had been imprisoned since his abdication in 1917. Local Soviet officials, concerned about advancing pro-monarchist forces, executed the royal family rather than have them serve as a rallying point for the White Russians. In 1992 two of nine skeletons dug up the previous summer from a pit at Yekaterinburg (formerly Sverdlovsk) were identified as the remains of the czar and czarina.

DISNEYLAND OPENED: ANNIVERSARY. July 17, 1955. Disneyland, America's first theme park, opened at Anaheim, CA.

July 2001	S	M	T	W	T	F	S
							1
	2	3	4	5	6	7	8
	9	10	11	12	13	14	15
	16	17	18	19	20	21	22
	23	24	25	26	27	28	29
	30	31					

FOLKMOOT USA: THE NORTH CAROLINA INTERNATIONAL FOLK FESTIVAL. July 17–29. Waynesville, NC. A festival of international folk dance featuring groups from 10 countries. Est attendance: 75,000. For info: Folkmoot USA, PO Box 658, Waynesville, NC 28786. Phone: (828) 452-2997 or (877) FOLK-USA. Fax: (828) 452-5762. E-mail: folkmoot@pobox.com. Web: www.folkmoot.com.

GARDNER, ERLE STANLEY: BIRTH ANNIVERSARY. July 17, 1889. American author of detective fiction, born at Malden, MA. Best remembered for his series about lawyer-detective Perry Mason, Gardner also wrote novels under the pen name A.A. Fair. Gardner died at Temecula, CA, Mar 11, 1970.

GERRY, ELBRIDGE: BIRTH ANNIVERSARY. July 17, 1744. Fifth vice president of the US (1813–14), born at Marblehead, MA. Died at Washington, DC, Nov 23, 1814. His name became part of the language (gerrymander) after he signed a redistricting bill favoring his party while governor of Massachusetts in 1812.

IRAQ: NATIONAL DAY. July 17. National holiday commemorating anniversary of revolution of 1968.

KANSAS CITY HOTEL DISASTER: 20th ANNIVERSARY. July 17, 1981. Anniversary of the collapse of aerial walkways at the Hyatt Regency Hotel at Kansas City, MO. About 1,500 people were attending the popular weekly tea dance when, at about 7 PM, two concrete and steel skywalks that were suspended from the ceiling of the hotel's atrium broke loose and fell on guests in the crowded lobby, killing 114 people. In 1986 a state board revoked the licenses of two engineers convicted of gross negligence for their part in designing the hotel.

KOREA: CONSTITUTION DAY: ANNIVERSARY. July 17, 1948. Legal national holiday. Commemorates the proclamation of the constitution of the republic of Korea in 1948. Ceremonies at Seoul's capitol plaza and all major cities.

PUERTO RICO: MUÑOZ-RIVERA DAY. July 17. Public holiday on the anniversary of the birth of Luis Muñoz-Rivera. The Puerto Rican patriot, poet and journalist was born at Barranquitas, Puerto Rico in 1859. He died at Santurce, a suburb of San Juan, Puerto Rico, Nov 15, 1916.

SAINT ANN'S SOLEMN NOVENA. July 17–26. Scranton, PA. Religious festival in honor of Saint Ann, the mother of the Virgin Mary, the grandmother of Jesus. Some 10,000 people come to Saint Ann's shrine each day of the Solemn Novena. Mass is televised each day on national cable network (The Faith and Values Channel). Annually, July 17–26. Est attendance: 150,000. For info: Rev Peter Grace, Dir Media, Box 111, Scranton, PA 18504-0111. Phone: (800) THE-MASS or (717) 941-0185. Fax: (717) 941-0185. E-mail: frpeter@themass.org. Web: www.themass.org.

SNAKE RIVER STAMPEDE. July 17–21. Nampa, ID. In its 86th year this is one of the top 20 professional rodeo events in the nation featuring the world's top cowboys and cowgirls in action. Events include bareback bronc riding, saddle bronc riding, bull riding, calf roping, team roping, steer wrestling, barrel racing and the Wrangler bull fight. Est attendance: 40,000. For info: Jimmy Hurley, Snake River Stampede, PO Box 231, Nampa, ID 83653. Phone: (208) 466-8497. Fax: (208) 465-4438. E-mail: sstampede@earthlink.net.

SPACE MILESTONE: *APOLLO-SOYUZ TEST PROJECT (US, USSR).* July 17, 1975. After three years of planning, negotiation and preparation, the first US–USSR joint space project reached fruition with the linkup in space of *Apollo 18* (crew: T. Stafford, V. Brand, D. Slayton; landed in Pacific Ocean July 24, during 136th orbit) and *Soyuz 19* (crew: A.A. Leonov, V.N. Kubasov; landed July 21, after 96 orbits). *Apollo 18* and *Soyuz 19* were linked for 47 hours (July 17–19) while joint experiments and transfer of personnel and materials back and forth between craft took place. Launch date was July 15, 1975.

SPACE MILESTONE: *SOYUZ T-12* (USSR). July 17, 1984. Cosmonaut Svetlana Savitskaya became the first woman to walk in space (July 25) and the first woman to make more than one space voyage. With cosmonauts V. Dzhanibekov and I. Volk. Docked at *Salyut 7* July 18 and returned to Earth July 29.

SPAIN: CIVIL WAR BEGINS: 65th ANNIVERSARY. July 17, 1936. General Francisco Franco led an uprising of army troops based in North Africa against the elected government of the Spanish Republic. Spain was quickly divided into a Nationalist and a Republican zone. Franco's Nationalists drew support from Fascist Italy and Nazi Germany. On Apr 1, 1939, the Nationalists won a complete victory when they entered Madrid. Franco ruled as dictator in Spain until his death in 1975.

STEALTH BOMBER FLIGHT: ANNIVERSARY. July 17, 1989. The B-2 Stealth bomber airplane was flown successfully over the desert near Palmdale, CA, for almost two hours. A decade of work and $22 billion reportedly were spent on the project prior to the first flight. Designed to penetrate Soviet radar, the B-2 Stealth bomber was said to be capable of delivering up to 25 tons of nuclear or other bombs. Average cost of each of the 132 bombers requested by the Air Force was estimated to be $530 million. On this first test flight the plane flew at speeds of up to 180 knots (200 mph) and was put through several types of turns. Higher speeds and retraction of the landing gear were left for subsequent test flights.

"WRONG WAY" CORRIGAN DAY. July 17, 1938. Douglas Groce Corrigan, an unemployed airplane mechanic, left Brooklyn, NY's Floyd Bennett field, ostensibly headed for Los Angeles, CA, in a 1929 Curtiss Robin monoplane. He landed 28 hours, 13 minutes later at Dublin, Ireland's Baldonnell airport after a 3,150-mile nonstop flight without radio or special navigation equipment and in violation of American and Irish flight regulations. Born at Galveston, TX, Jan 22, 1907, Corrigan received a hero's welcome home; he was nicknamed "Wrong Way" Corrigan because he claimed he accidentally followed the wrong end of his compass needle. Died at New York, NY, Dec 9, 1995.

BIRTHDAYS TODAY

Lucie Arnaz, 50, actress ("Here's Lucy," "The Lucie Arnaz Show," *Lost in Yonkers*), born Los Angeles, CA, July 17, 1951.
Diahann Carroll (Carol Diahann Johnson), 66, singer, actress ("Julia," "Dynasty"), born New York, NY, July 17, 1935.
Phyllis Diller (Phyllis Driver), 84, actress ("The Beautiful Phyllis Diller Show," *Boy, Did I Get a Wrong Number!*), born Lima, OH, July 17, 1917.

David Hasselhoff, 49, actor ("Knight Rider," "Baywatch"), born Baltimore, MD, July 17, 1952.
Aaron Lansky, 46, founder of National Yiddish Book Center, born New Bedford, MA, July 17, 1955.
Pat McCormick, 67, writer ("Jack Paar Show," "The Tonight Show"), actor, (*Buffalo Bill and the Indians*), born July 17, 1934.
Phoebe Snow, 49, singer ("Poetry Man"), born New York, NY, July 17, 1952.
Donald Sutherland, 66, actor (*M*A*S*H, Klute, Backdraft*), born St. John, New Brunswick, Canada, July 17, 1935.
Alex Winter, 36, actor (*Bill & Ted's Excellent Adventure*), born London, England, July 17, 1965.

JULY 18 — WEDNESDAY
Day 199 — 166 Remaining

ANN ARBOR SUMMER ART FAIR®. July 18–21. Ann Arbor, MI. Juried art fair with more than 540 of the nation's finest artists and contemporary craftspeople. Free family art activity area, performance areas, specialty shops and restaurants. For Street Fair Info: Ann Arbor Street Art Fair, Inc, Box 1352, Ann Arbor, MI 48106. Est attendance: 500,000. For info: John Yanchula, Art Fair Dir, Michigan Guild of Artists and Artisans, 118 N Fourth Ave, Ann Arbor, MI 48104-1402. Phone: (734) 662-3382. Fax: (734) 662-0339. Web: www.artfair.org.

CHICAGO GOLF CLUB: ANNIVERSARY. July 18, 1893. The first 18-hole golf course in America, laid out by Charles Blair MacDonald, was incorporated at Wheaton, IL. MacDonald was the architect of many of the early US courses which he attempted to model on the best in Scotland and England. It was his belief that at each tee a golfer should face a hazard at the average distance of his shot.

EVANS, CHICK: BIRTH ANNIVERSARY. July 18, 1890. Charles (Chick) Evans, Jr, golfer born at Indianapolis, IN. Evans competed as an amateur against the best professionals in the early 20th century, winning the US Open in 1916. In the 1920s he established the Chick Evans Caddie Foundation, later called the Evans Scholarship Fund, that has helped send more than 4,000 people to college. Died at Chicago, IL, Nov 6, 1979.

FULLER, BOBBY: 35th DEATH ANNIVERSARY. July 18, 1966. Bobby Fuller, leader of the rock group Bobby Fuller Four, was found dead in his car at Los Angeles, CA. No definite cause of death was ever proven. The Bobby Fuller Four is best remembered for their 1966 hit song "I Fought the Law," which was written by Sonny Curtis, a member of Buddy Holly's Crickets. Fuller was born Oct 22, 1942, at Baytown, TX.

HAYAKAWA, SAMUEL ICHIYE: 95th BIRTH ANNIVERSARY. July 18, 1906. S. I. Hayakawa was born at Vancouver, BC, and came to the US in 1927. An academic, in 1968 he was appointed acting president of San Francisco State College. During student demonstrations on his first day in office he climbed atop a sound truck and disconnected the wires, silencing the demonstrators. His actions gained him enormous popularity among conservatives and he was promoted to permanent president by Governor Ronald Reagan. As his popularity grew he switched from the Democratic to the Republican party and in 1976 was elected to the US Senate. He led the successful California initiative to declare English the state's official language in 1986. Hayakawa wrote nine textbooks on language and semantics. He died Feb 27, 1992, at Greenbrae, CA.

JAPAN'S RULING PARTY SINCE 1955 LOSES PARLIAMENT MAJORITY: ANNIVERSARY. July 18, 1993. Japan's Liberal Democratic Party, the ruling conservative branch of the government, lost the majority in the general elections. They won only 223 seats in the 511-seat lower house, the more powerful of Japan's two houses. The party had held the majority since its inception in 1955. On July 22 Premier Kiichi Miyazawa resigned.

MANDELA, NELSON: BIRTHDAY. July 18, 1918. Former South African President Nelson Rolihlahla Mandela was born the son of a Tembu tribal chieftain at Qunu, near Umtata, in the Transkei territory of South Africa. Giving up his hereditary rights, Mandela chose to become a lawyer and earned his degree at the University of South Africa. He joined the African National Congress (ANC) in 1944, eventually becoming deputy national president in 1952. His activities in the struggle against apartheid resulted in his conviction for sabotage in 1964. During his 28 years in jail, Mandela remained a symbol of hope to South Africa's nonwhite majority, the demand for his release a rallying cry for civil rights activists. That release finally came Feb 11, 1990, as millions watched via satellite television. In 1994 Mandela was elected President of South Africa in the first all-race election there. See also: "Mandela, Nelson: Prison Release Anniversary " (Feb 11).

ODETS, CLIFFORD: 95th BIRTH ANNIVERSARY. July 18, 1906. Clifford Odets began his writing career as a poet before turning to acting. He helped found the Group Theatre in 1931. In 1935 he returned to writing with works for the Group Theatre such as *Waiting for Lefty, Awake and Sing!* and *Golden Boy.* His proletarian views helped make him a popular playwright during the Depression years. Odets was born at Philadelphia, PA, and died at Los Angeles, CA, Aug 15, 1963.

OSCAR MAYER WIENERMOBILE: 65th ANNIVER-SARY. July 18, 1936. Invented in 1936 by Carl Mayer, nephew of Oscar Mayer, the Oscar Mayer Wienermobile was built by General Body Company at Chicago, IL. Today a fleet of six Wienermobiles tours the country. For info: Hotdogger Advisor, PO Box 7188, Madison, WI 53707. Phone: (608) 285-6793 or (608) 285-3204. Fax: (608) 242-6108. E-mail: ksuto@kraft.com. Web: www .oscar-mayer.com.

PRESIDENTIAL SUCCESSION ACT: ANNIVERSARY. July 18, 1947. President Harry S Truman signed an Executive Order determining the line of succession should the president be temporarily incapacitated or die in office. The speaker of the house and president pro tem of the senate are next in succession after the vice president. This line of succession became the 25th Amendment to the Constitution, which was ratified Feb 10, 1967.

RUTLEDGE, JOHN: DEATH ANNIVERSARY. July 18, 1800. American statesman, associate justice on the Supreme Court, born at Charleston, SC, in September 1739. Nominated second Chief Justice of the Supreme Court to succeed John Jay and served as Acting Chief Justice until his confirmation was denied because of his opposition to the Jay Treaty. He died at Charleston, SC.

	S	M	T	W	T	F	S
July 2001	1	2	3	4	5	6	7
	8	9	10	11	12	13	14
	15	16	17	18	19	20	21
	22	23	24	25	26	27	28
	29	30	31				

SINCLAIR LEWIS DAYS. July 18-22. Sauk Centre, MN. Parade, park activities, street dance, fireworks, Miss Sauk Centre pageant, Fun Golf Tournament, flea market, craft sale, Heart of Lakes Bike Tour, softball tournament and kiddie caravan in Sinclair Lewis's hometown. Est attendance: 10,000. For info: Barb Borgerding, Mgr, Sauk Centre Chamber of Commerce, PO Box 222, Sauk Centre, MN 56378. Phone: (320) 352-5201. Web: www.saukcentre.com.

SPACE MILESTONE: *ROHINI 1* (INDIA). July 18, 1980. First successful launch from India, orbited 77-lb satellite.

THACKERAY, WILLIAM MAKEPEACE: BIRTH ANNI-VERSARY. July 18, 1811. English author, best remembered for his novels *Pendennis* and *Vanity Fair*, was born at Calcutta, India, and died at London, England, Dec 23, 1863.

WHITE, GILBERT: BIRTH ANNIVERSARY. July 18, 1720. Born at Selborne, Hampshire, England, Gilbert White has been called the "father of British naturalists." His book *The Natural History of Selborne*, published in 1788, enjoyed immediate success and is said never to have been out of print. White died near his birthplace, June 26, 1793. His home survives as a museum.

BIRTHDAYS TODAY

James Brolin, 60, actor (Emmy for "Marcus Welby, MD"; "Hotel"), born Los Angeles, CA, July 18, 1941.

Richard Totten (Dick) Button, 72, sportscaster, Olympic gold medal figure skater, born Englewood, NJ, July 18, 1929.

Hume Cronyn, 90, actor (*The Seventh Cross, Sunrise at Campobello, Cocoon*), born London, Ontario, Canada, July 18, 1911.

Dion DiMucci, 62, singer (Dion and the Belmonts), born The Bronx, NY, July 18, 1939.

Nick Faldo, 44, golfer, born Welwyn Garden City, England, July 18, 1957.

Steve Forbes, 54, publisher, chairman, Forbes Newspapers, born Morristown, NJ, July 18, 1947.

John Glenn, 80, astronaut, first American to orbit Earth, former US Senator (D, Ohio), born Cambridge, OH, July 18, 1921.

Anfernee "Penny" Hardaway, 29, basketball player, born Memphis, TN, July 18, 1972.

Elizabeth McGovern, 40, actress (*Ordinary People, Racing with the Moon*), born Evanston, IL, July 18, 1961.

Calvin Peete, 58, golfer, born Detroit, MI, July 18, 1943.

Martha Reeves, 60, lead singer (Martha & the Vandellas, "Power of Love"), born Detroit, MI, July 18, 1941.

Ricky Skaggs, 47, musician (bluegrass guitar), singer ("I Don't Care"), born Cordell, KY, July 18, 1954.

Hunter S. Thompson, 62, journalist, author (*Fear and Loathing on the Campaign Trail*), born Louisville, KY, July 18, 1939.

Joe Torre, 61, baseball manager and former player, born New York, NY, July 18, 1940.

Yevgeny Aleksandrovich Yevtushenko, 68, poet, born Zima, USSR, July 18, 1933.

JULY 19 — THURSDAY
Day 200 — 165 Remaining

ATTACK ON FORT WAGNER: ANNIVERSARY. July 19, 1863. In a second attempt to capture Fort Wagner, outside Charleston, SC, Federal troops were repulsed after losing 1,515 men as opposed to Southern losses of only 174. The attack was led by the 54th Massachusetts Colored Infantry, commanded by Colonel Robert Gould Shaw, who was killed in the action. This was the first use of black troops in the war. The film *Glory* was based on the Massachusetts 54th, and this was the attack featured in the film. Fort Wagner was never taken by the Union.

BIX BEIDERBECKE MEMORIAL JAZZ FESTIVAL. July 19-22. Davenport, IA. Four venues. Est attendance: 12,000. For info: Bix Beiderbecke Memorial Society, PO Box 3688, Davenport, IA 52808. Phone: (319) 324-7170. Fax: (319) 326-1732. Web: www.bixsociety.org.

CANADA: EDMONTON'S KLONDIKE DAYS EXPOSITION. July 19–28. Edmonton, AB. Commemorates the legendary Klondike Goldrush that brought great prosperity to the frontier community of Edmonton. The annual Klondike Days Parade kicks off this 10-day celebration which features an international consumer show, non-stop entertainment, professional chuckwagon racing, a casino, intriguing exhibits, gold panning and North America's largest travelling midway. Est attendance: 700,000. For info: Kate Rogers, Marketing Coord, Northlands Park, Box 1480, Edmonton, AB, Canada T5J 2N5. Phone: (780) 471-7210. Fax: (780) 471-8176. E-mail: krogers@northlands.com. Web: www.northlands.com.

CANADA: JUST FOR LAUGHS: THE MONTREAL INTERNATIONAL COMEDY FESTIVAL. July 19–29. Montreal, QC. Make the trip to the worldwide capital of comedy! More than 800 artists from 15 countries play in more than 2,000 shows and performances at indoor and outdoor venues that blanket the entire city. In the past, the Just for Laughs bilingual comedy marathon has featured some of the world's most impressive talent including Tim Allen, Jerry Seinfeld, Drew Carey, Kelsey Grammer, Rowan "Mr Bean" Atkinson, Jim Carrey and David Hyde Pierce, to name but a few. Est attendance: 1,200,000. For info: Suzanne Hinks, Just for Laughs Comedy Festival, 2102 St-Laurent Blvd, Montreal, QC, Canada H2X 2T5. Phone: (514) 845-3155. Fax: (514) 845-4140. Web: www.hahaha.com.

CANADA: WINNIPEG FRINGE THEATRE FESTIVAL. July 19–29. Winnipeg, MB. An 11-day, noon-to-midnight, non-stop theatrical smorgasbord with more than 100 theatre companies from around the world. The Winnipeg Fringe Festival: Pushing the envelope in theatrical entertainment since 1988. Est attendance: 100,000. For info: The Winnipeg Fringe Festival, 174 Market Ave, Winnipeg, MB, Canada R3B 0P8. Fax: (204) 947-3741. E-mail: fringe@mtc.mb.ca. Web: www.mtc.mb.ca.

CRAFT FAIR OF THE SOUTHERN HIGHLANDS. July 19–22. (Also Oct 18–21) Asheville Civic Center, Asheville, NC. In 1948 this fair started the crafts revival so evident today. More than a craft fair, this event includes demonstrations and traditional mountain music—all in addition to the 160+ craftspeople representing the finest crafts in a nine-state mountain region. Est attendance: 12,000. For info: Katherine Caldwell, PR, Southern Highland Craft Guild, PO Box 9545, Asheville, NC 28815. Phone: (828) 298-7928. Fax: (828) 298-7962.

DEGAS, EDGAR: BIRTH ANNIVERSARY. July 19, 1834. French Impressionist painter, especially noted for his paintings of dancers in motion, was born at Paris, France, and died there Sept 26, 1917.

DELAWARE STATE FAIR. July 19–28. Harrington, DE. Fireworks, country, rock and pop talent, rodeos, demolition derby, amusement rides and harness racing. Plenty of food and entertainment. Est attendance: 250,000. For info: Delaware State Fair, PO Box 28, Harrington, DE 19952. Phone: (302) 398-3269. Fax: (302) 398-5030. E-mail: fair@delawarestatefair.com. Web: www.delawarestatefair.com.

FIRST WOMAN VICE-PRESIDENTIAL CANDIDATE: ANNIVERSARY. July 19, 1984. Congresswoman Geraldine Ferraro was nominated to run with presidential candidate Walter Mondale on the Democratic ticket. They were defeated by the Republican ticket headed by Ronald Reagan.

GREY FOX BLUEGRASS FESTIVAL. July 19–22. Ancramdale, NY. Enjoy this legendary bluegrass festival with family entertainment and children's events in the picturesque New York Berkshires at Rothvoss Farm. For info: Columbia County Tourism Dept, 401 State St, Hudson, NY 12534. Phone: (888) 946-8495.

HEMINGWAY DAYS FESTIVAL. July 19–23. Key West, FL. Since its inception 18 years ago, this festival has included writing workshops, fly fishing clinics, readings and competitions, entertainment and fun honoring Ernest Hemingway as a literary icon and celebrating the lifestyle he enjoyed during his 10-year residence in Key West. For info send SASE: Hemingway Days, PO Box 4045, Key West, FL 33041. Web: www.hemingwaydays.com.

JAMBOREE IN THE HILLS. July 19–22. St. Clairsville, OH. 25th anniversary. Billed as the "Super Bowl of Country Music," this festival is a four-day outdoor country music show featuring the top names in country music today. Sponsors: Jamboree USA, WWVA Radio and WOVK Radio. Annually, the third weekend in July. Est attendance: 100,000. For info: Terri A. Phillips, Publicity Dir, Jamboree In The Hills, 1015 Main St, Wheeling, WV 26003. Phone: (800) 624-5456. Fax: (304) 234-0067. Web: www.jamboreeinthehills.com.

MANILA FLOODS: ANNIVERSARY. July 19, 1972. A 30-hour rainfall flooded much of the Philippine Archipelago leaving as many as 289 dead and thousands without shelter, 45,000 in one province alone. Starvation in highly populated areas like Manila caused President Ferdinand Marcos to send troops after profiteers who were stockpiling food.

MARILYN MONROE'S FIRST SCREEN TEST: 55th ANNIVERSARY. July 19, 1946. Marilyn Monroe was given her first screen test at Twentieth Century-Fox Studios. Even with no sound, this test was all they needed to sign her first contract. Beginning with *Scudda-Hoo! Scudda-Hay!* in 1948 and ending with *The Misfits* in 1961, Monroe made a total of 29 films during her short career.

MAYO, CHARLES HORACE: BIRTH ANNIVERSARY. July 19. 1865. American surgeon, one of the Mayo brothers, founders of the Mayo Clinic and Mayo Foundation, born at Rochester, MN. Died at Chicago, IL, May 26, 1939.

MERRIAM, EVE: 85th BIRTH ANNIVERSARY. July 19, 1916. A poet, playwright and author of more than 50 books for both adults and children. Merriam's works, which often focused on feminism, include *It Doesn't Always Have to Rhyme; After Nora Slammed the Door: The Women's Unfinished Revolution; Mommies at Work* and a book of poems attacked by authorities as glamorizing crime, *The Urban Mother Goose*. Her play *Out of Our Father's House*, portraying the lives of American women, was presented on public television's "Great Performances" series. She also wrote the first documentary on women's rights for network TV, *We the Women*. Born at Philadelphia, PA, she died at New York, NY, Apr 11, 1992.

NICARAGUA: NATIONAL LIBERATION DAY. July 19. Following the National Day of Joy (July 17—anniversary of date in 1979 when dictator Anastasio Somoza Debayle fled Nicaragua) is annual July 19 observance of National Liberation Day, anniversary of day the National Liberation Army claimed victory over the Somoza dictatorship.

RED RIVER STREET FAIR. July 19–21. Fargo, ND. Experience the warm friendly feeling of historic downtown Fargo—especially the fair with more than 300 exhibiting artists. Three days of unique arts and crafts, incredible food and free entertainment. Est attendance: 4,000. For info: (701) 282-2200 or North Dakota Tourism, 604 East Boulevard, Bismarck, ND 58505. Phone: (701) 328-2525 or (800) 435-5663.

SAINT VINCENT DE PAUL: OLD FEAST DAY. July 19. A day remembering the founder of the Vincentian Congregation and the Sisters of Charity, born at Pouy, France, Apr 24, 1581. He died Sept 27, 1660, at Paris, France. His Feast Day was formerly observed on July 19 but is now observed on the anniversary of his death, Sept 27.

WOMEN'S RIGHTS CONVENTION AT SENECA FALLS: ANNIVERSARY. July 19, 1848. A convention concerning the rights of women, called by Lucretia Mott and Elizabeth Cady Stanton, was held at Seneca Falls, NY, July 19–20, 1848. The issues discussed included voting, property rights and divorce. The convention drafted a "Declaration of Sentiments" that paraphrased the Declaration of Independence, addressing man instead of King George, and called for women's "immediate admission to all the rights and privileges which belong to them as citizens of the United States." This convention was the beginning of an organized women's rights movement in the US. The most controversial issue was Stanton's demand for women's right to vote.

YALOW, ROSALYN: 80th BIRTHDAY. July 19, 1921. Medical physicist Rosalyn Yalow was born at New York City. Along with Andrew V. Schally and Roger Guillemin, in 1977 Yalow was awarded the Nobel Prize for Physiology or Medicine. Through her research on medical applications of radioactive isotopes, Yalow developed RIA, a sensitive and simple technique used to measure minute concentrations of hormones and other substances in blood or other body fluids. First applied to the study of insulin concentration in the blood of diabetics, RIA was soon used in hundreds of other applications.

BIRTHDAYS TODAY

Philip Agee, 66, former CIA agent, author (*Inside the Company: CIA Diary*), born Tacoma Park, FL, July 19, 1935.

Vikki Carr (Florencia Bisenta deCasilla), 60, singer ("It Must Be Him," "With Pen in Hand"), born El Paso, TX, July 19, 1941.

Anthony Edwards, 39, actor ("ER," *Fast Times at Ridgemont High, Top Gun*), born Santa Barbara, CA, July 19, 1962.

Clea Lewis, 36, actress ("Ellen," *The Rich Man's Wife*), born Cleveland Heights, OH, July 19, 1965.

George Stanley McGovern, 79, former US senator and '72 Democratic presidential nominee, born Avon, SD, July 19, 1922.

Ilie Nastase, 55, former tennis player, born Bucharest, Romania, July 19, 1946.

Campbell Scott, 39, actor (*The Daytrippers, Hi-Life*), born Westchester County, NY, July 19, 1962.

JULY 20 — FRIDAY
Day 201 — 164 Remaining

"ARTHUR MURRAY PARTY" TV PREMIERE: ANNIVERSARY. July 20, 1950. This ballroom dancing show appeared on all four networks (ABC, Dumont, CBS and NBC) and was hosted by Kathryn Murray, wife of famed dance school founder Arthur Murray.

ARTS IN THE PARK. July 20–22. Kalispell, MT. Annual juried arts and crafts show and fair, food and entertainment. Est attendance: 12,000. For info: PR Dept, Hockaday Museum of Art, 302 Second Ave E, Kalispell, MT 59901. Phone: (406) 755-5268. Fax: (406) 755-2023. E-mail: hockaday@bigsky.net. Web: www.hockadaymuseum.org.

July 2001	S	M	T	W	T	F	S
							1	2	3	4	5	6	7
	8	9	10	11	12	13	14
	15	16	17	18	19	20	21
	22	23	24	25	26	27	28
	29	30	31				

ATTEMPT ON HITLER'S LIFE: ANNIVERSARY. July 20, 1944. During the daily staff meeting at German Headquarters at Rastenburg, an attempt was made to assassinate Adolf Hitler. Count Claus Schenk von Stauffenberg, chosen from a group of German military and civil servants involved in the plot, left a briefcase containing a bomb only six feet from Hitler under the staff table in the briefing room. Four people were killed in the blast, but Hitler's life was saved probably because Colonel Heinz Brandt (who was among those killed) found the briefcase in his way and moved it further from the German dictator.

BASEBALL DECLARED NON-ESSENTIAL OCCUPATION: ANNIVERSARY. July 20, 1918. Secretary of War Newton D. Baker ruled that baseball was a non-essential occupation. He stated that all players of draft age should seek "employment to aid successful prosecution of the war or shoulder guns and fight." On July 26, Baker allowed baseball to continue until Sept 1. Nearly 250 ballplayers entered the armed services.

CANADA: COUNTRY GOOD TIMES. July 20–22. Wilberforce, ON. Family fun celebrating music and local musicians featuring amateur contest, flea market, carnival midway, vendors and bingo. Annually, the third weekend in July. Est attendance: 5,000. For info: Bancroft and Dist Chamber of Commerce, PO Box 539, Bancroft, ON, Canada K0L 1C0. Phone: (613) 332-1513. Fax: (613) 332-2119. E-mail: chamber@commerce.bancroft.on.ca. Web: www.commerce.bancroft.on.ca.

CANADA: MUSKOKA ARTS AND CRAFTS SUMMER SHOW. July 20–22. Annie Williams Memorial Park, Bracebridge, ON. Est attendance: 35,000. For info: Muskoka Arts and Crafts, Box 376, Bracebridge, ON, Canada P1L 1T7. Phone: (705) 645-5501. E-mail: mac@surenet.net. Web: www.muskoka artsandcrafts.com.

CHEYENNE FRONTIER DAYS. July 20–29. Frontier Park, Cheyenne, WY. Held annually since 1897 the world's largest outdoor rodeo is the "Daddy of 'em All" with nine rodeos, nine night shows, three free pancake breakfasts, four parades, chuckwagon racing, carnival midway and exhibitors. Annually, the last full week in July. Est attendance: 210,000. For info: Cheyenne Frontier Days, PO Box 2477, Cheyenne, WY 82003. Phone: (800) 227-6336.

COLOMBIA: INDEPENDENCE DAY. July 20. National holiday. Commemorates the beginning of the independence movement with an uprising against Spanish officials in 1810 at Bogota. Colombia gained independence from Spain in 1819 when Simon Bolivar decisively defeated the Spanish.

DECOY AND WILDLIFE ART SHOW. July 20–22. Clayton Recreation Park Arena, Clayton, NY. 33rd annual juried show. World championship wildlife carvers, artists, taxidermists, collectors and dealers. Events include hunting decoy contest, gunning rig contest, vintage decoy contest and auction. Displays of handcrafted wildlife from wood, silver, gold and pewter. Annually, the third weekend in July. Est attendance: 5,000. For info: Thousand Islands Museum, 403 Riverside Dr, Clayton, NY 13624. Phone: (315) 686-5794. Fax: (315) 686-4867. E-mail: timuseum@gisco .net. Web: www.thousandislands.com/timuseum.

DETROIT 300 FESTIVAL. July 20–22. Hart Plaza, Detroit, MI and Dieppe Park, Canada. On July 24, 1701, Antoine de la Mothe Cadillac landed on the shores of the Detroit River and founded a fort and trading post. Three hundred years later, on July 24, 2001, 30 two-foot canoes will once again paddle down the Detroit River to Hart Plaza in an authentic re-enactment of Cadillac's landing. Also boat tours, entertainment, Celebrity Homecoming on Saturday and much more. For info: Detroit 300, Albert Kahn Bldg, Ste 300, 7430 Second Ave, Detroit, MI 48202. Phone: (313) 871-1303 or (877) 338-2001. Web: www.detroit 300.org.

ENGLAND: BBC HENRY WOOD PROMENADE CONCERTS. July 20–Sept 15. London. 107th season. "The BBC Proms" consists of more than 70 concerts at the Royal Albert Hall, including symphonic and chamber music, choral music, opera, world music and jazz. For info: BBC Henry Wood Promenade Concerts, Rm 4088, Broadcasting House, London, England W1A 1AA. Phone: (44) (171) 765-5575. Fax: (44) (171) 765-0619. E-mail: proms@bbc.co.uk. Web: www.bbc.co.uk /proms/

FALLON ALL-INDIAN RODEO AND POWOW. July 20–22. Fallon, NV. Colorful Native American dancers, handgames, dance, parade, traditional foods and arts and crafts. For info: Phone: (775) 423-2544.

FIRST SPECIAL OLYMPICS: ANNIVERSARY. July 20, 1968. One thousand mentally retarded athletes from the US and Canada competed in the first Special Olympics, held at Soldier Field at Chicago, IL. Today more than one million athletes from 146 countries compete in local, national and international games.

GENEVA ACCORDS: ANNIVERSARY. July 20, 1954. An agreement covering cessation of hostilities in Vietnam, signed at Geneva, Switzerland, on behalf of the commanders-in-chief of French forces at Vietnam and the People's Army of Vietnam. A further declaration of the Geneva Conference was released July 21, 1954. Partition, foreign troop withdrawal and elections for a unified government, within two years, were among provisions.

HILLARY, SIR EDMUND PERCIVAL: BIRTHDAY. July 20, 1919. Explorer, mountaineer born at Auckland, New Zealand. With Tenzing Norgay, a Sherpa guide, became first to ascend summit of highest mountain in the world, Mt Everest (29,028 ft), at 11:30 AM, May 29, 1953. "We climbed because nobody climbed it before," he said.

JAPAN: MARINE DAY. July 20. National holiday.

KANSAS CITY BLUES AND JAZZ FESTIVAL. July 20–22. Penn Valley Park, Kansas City, MO. The largest music festival in the region representing one of four world-renowned blues and jazz cities. During the 1920s and 1930s Kansas City was known for its blues-based, riff-oriented sound and was at the top of the jazz world. Annually, the third weekend in July. Est attendance: 50,000. For info: Greg Patterson, Exec Dir, Kansas City Blues and Jazz Festival, 4200 Pennsylvania Ave, Ste 230, Kansas City, MO 64111. Phone: (800) 530-KCMO. Fax: (816) 531-2583. E-mail: kcbluesjazz@kcbluesjazz.org. Web: www.kcblues jazz.org.

KENTUCKY STATE CHAMPIONSHIP OLD-TIME FIDDLER'S CONTEST. July 20–21. Rough River Dam State Resort Park, Falls of Rough, KY. Old-time and bluegrass music competition; Governor's cup trophy is awarded to the champion fiddler. More than $5,000 in prize money. Annually, the third Friday and Saturday in July. Est attendance: 4,000. For info: Brent L. Miller, PO Box 4042, Leitchfield, KY 42755. Phone: (270) 259-3578. Fax: (270) 259-5221.

MIDSUMMER NIGHTS' FAIR. July 20–21. Lions Park, Norman, OK. Juried and invited artists and craftspeople display their work for show and sale in booths under the stars. A pottery auction, Dalmatian mascot contest, festival foods, free entertainment and free art activities for the whole family are set for this 23rd annual event, 6 PM–midnight. Est attendance: 8,000. For info: Asst Dir, Firehouse Art Center, 444 S Flood, Norman, OK 73069. Phone: (405) 329-4523.

MINERS JUBILEE. July 20–22. Baker City, OR. Est attendance: 5,000. For info: Baker County VCB, 490 Campbell St, Baker City, OR 97814. Phone: (800) 523-1235 or (541) 523-5855.

MOON PHASE: NEW MOON. July 20. Moon enters New Moon phase at 3:44 PM, EDT.

MOZART FESTIVAL. July 20–Aug 5. San Luis Obispo, CA. Concerts celebrating the spirit of Wolfgang Amadeus Mozart. Est attendance: 15,000. For info: Mozart Festival, PO Box 311, San Luis Obispo, CA 93406. Phone: (805) 781-3008. Fax: (805) 781-3011. E-mail: slo@mozartfestival.com. Web: www.mozart festival.com.

NATCHITOCHES/NORTHWESTERN STATE UNIVERSITY FOLK FESTIVAL. July 20–21. Northwestern State University, Natchitoches, LA. The festival is a "purist" folk festival in that folk artists who are reviving a traditional Louisiana folk art or still working a Louisiana tradition are invited. Music, food, crafts and storytellers. Annually, the third weekend in July. Est attendance: 24,000. For info: Dr. Lisa Abney, Louisiana Folklife Center, Natchitoches/NSU Folk Fest, NSU PO Box 3663, Natchitoches, LA 71497. Phone: (318) 357-4332. Fax: (318) 357-4331. E-mail: folklife@alpha.nsula.edu. Web: www.liberalarts.nsula.edu /folklife.

NATIONAL ZIPPO DAY. July 20. Zippo/Case Visitors Center, Bradford, PA. Annual gathering of fans and collectors of Zippo windproof lighters and Case knives. Hosted by Zippo Manufacturing Company and its subsidiary W.R. Case & Sons Cutlery. Est attendance: 2,000. For info: Communications Coord, Zippo Manufacturing Co, 33 Barbour St, Bradford, PA 16701. Phone: (814) 368-2836. Fax: (814) 368-2874. Web: www.zippomfg.com.

NESHOBA COUNTY FAIR. July 20–27. Philadelphia, MS. Billed as "Mississippi's Giant Houseparty," this is one of the nation's last Campground Fairs. At this 111th annual fair, harness racing, state and national political speaking, crafts, music and amusement are the order each day. Est attendance: 175,000. For info: Connie Sampsell, Exec Dir, Philadelphia–Neshoba Co Chamber of Comm, PO Box 51, Philadelphia, MS 39350. Phone: (601) 656-1742.

NORTH DAKOTA STATE FAIR. July 20–28. Minot, ND. For nine days the State Fair features the best in big-name entertainment, farm and home exhibits, displays, the Midway and NPRA rodeo. Est attendance: 250,000. For info: North Dakota State Fair, Box 1796, Minot, ND 58702. Phone: (701) 857-7620. Fax: (701) 857-7622. E-mail: ndsf@minot.com

RIOT ACT: ANNIVERSARY. July 20. To "read the riot act" now usually means telling children to be quiet or less boisterous, but in 18th-century England reading the riot act was a more serious matter. On July 20, 1715, the Riot Act took effect. By law in England, if 12 or more persons were unlawfully assembled to the disturbance of the public peace an authority was required "with a loud voice" to command silence and read the riot act proclamation: "Our sovereign lord the king chargeth and commandeth all persons, being assembled, immediately to disperse themselves, and peaceably to depart to their habitations, or to their lawful business, upon the pains contained in the act made in the first year of King George, for preventing tumults and riotous assemblies. God save the king." Any persons who failed to obey within one hour were to be seized, apprehended and carried before a justice of the peace.

SAINT ANN'S ITALIAN STREET FESTIVAL. July 20–26. Hoboken, NJ. 91st annual festival features live entertainment nightly with top stars. Also, rides, games of chance, international foods, crafts and much more. Est attendance: 150,000. For info: Church of St. Ann's, 704 Jefferson St, Hoboken, NJ 07030-2010. Phone: (201) 659-1114. Fax: (201) 659-1416.

SALEM ART FAIR AND FESTIVAL. July 20–22. Bush's Pasture Park, Salem, OR. A celebration of the arts with 200 arts/crafts booths, continuous performing arts, food, children's parade and art activities, historic Bush House Museum and living history performances, special art exhibition, 5K walk and run for the arts. Annually, the third full weekend in July. Est attendance: 110,000. For info: Salem Art Assn, 600 Mission St SE, Salem, OR 97302. Phone: (503) 581-2228. Web: www.salemart festival.org.

SHOW ME STATE GAMES. July 20–22 (also July 27–29 and Aug 3–5). Columbia, MO. An Olympic-style athletic festival for Missouri citizens. This statewide multisport program is designed to inspire Missourians of every age and skill level to develop their physical and competitive abilities to the height of their potential through participation in fitness activities. Est attendance: 40,000. For info: Gary Filbert, Exec Dir, Show Me State Games, 1105 Carrie Francke Dr, Columbia, MO 65211. Phone: (573) 882-2101. Fax: (573) 884-4004. E-mail: show4games@aol.com. Web: www .smsg.org.

SONG OF HIAWATHA PAGEANT. July 20–22 (also July 27–29 and Aug 3–5). Pipestone, MN. 53rd annual presentation of pageant based on Longfellow's poem, held in a natural outdoor amphitheater. Elaborate lighting, lovely costumes and cast of 200 help make an unforgettable event. Annually, last two weekends in July and first weekend in August. Sponsor: The Hiawatha Club. Est attendance: 15,000. For info: Mick Myers, Exec Dir, Pipestone Chmbr Comm, PO Box 8 CAE, Pipestone, MN 56164. Phone: (507) 825-3316. Fax: (507) 825-3317. E-mail: pipecham @rconnect.com. Web: www.pipestoneminnesota.com.

SPACE MILESTONE: MOON DAY. July 20, 1969. Anniversary of man's first landing on moon. Two US astronauts (Neil Alden Armstrong and Edwin Eugene Aldrin, Jr) landed lunar module *Eagle* at 4:17 PM, EDT and remained on lunar surface 21 hours, 36 minutes and 16 seconds. The landing was made from the *Apollo XI*'s orbiting command and service module, code named *Columbia*, whose pilot, Michael Collins, remained aboard. Armstrong was first to set foot on the moon. Armstrong and Aldrin were outside the spacecraft, walking on the moon's surface, approximately 2¼ hours. The astronauts returned to Earth July 24, bringing photograph and rock samples.

UKRAINIAN FESTIVAL. July 20–22. Dickinson, ND. This three-day festival features Ukrainian food, arts and crafts, music and the talented Stepoui Dity dancers. If you are of Ukrainian culture you don't want to miss this. Est attendance: 2,000. For info: Agnes Palanuk, Ukrainian Cultural Institute, 1221 W Villard, Dickinson, ND 58601. Phone: (701) 225-1286. Fax: (701) 225-4366. Web: www.dickinsoncvb.com.

VIRGINIA LAKE FESTIVAL. July 20–22. Clarksville, VA. Fun-filled weekend with Pig Pickin, opening ceremonies on Friday; arts and crafts show, flea market, balloons, five-mile run, fish fry, live entertainment for children and adults and fireworks on Saturday; beach music festival on Sunday. Annually, the third weekend in July (Friday–Sunday). Est attendance: 50,000. For info: Clarksville Lake Country Chamber of Commerce, 105 2nd St, Box 1017, Clarksville, VA 23927. Phone: (804) 374-2436 or (800) 557-5582. Fax: (804) 374-8174. E-mail: clarksville@kerrlake.com. Web: www.kerrlake.com/chamber.

July *2001*	S	M	T	W	T	F	S
		1	2	3	4	5	6	7
	8	9	10	11	12	13	14
	15	16	17	18	19	20	21
	22	23	24	25	26	27	28
	29	30	31				

WESTERN DAYS. July 20–22. Elgin, TX. Events include a parade; Miss Western Days contest; cooking, sewing and quilting contests; live music; arts and crafts; rodeo and a carnival. Est attendance: 10,000. For info: Jamie Lundgren, Elgin Chamber of Commerce, PO Box 408, Elgin, TX 78621. Phone: (512) 285-4515.

YARMOUTH CLAM FESTIVAL. July 20–22. Yarmouth, ME. 36th annual. Family-oriented festival featuring clams and more. Annually, starts the third Friday in July. Est attendance: 150,000. For info: Yarmouth Chamber of Commerce, Carolyn Schuster, 158 Main St, Yarmouth, ME 04096. Phone: (207) 846-3984. Fax: (207) 846-5419. E-mail: yarmouth@yarmouthmaine.org. Web: www.yarmouthmaine.org.

BIRTHDAYS TODAY

Kim Carnes, 55, singer ("Bette Davis Eyes"), songwriter (cowrote score *Flashdance*), born Hollywood, CA, July 20, 1946.

Judy Chicago (Judy Cohen), 62, artist, feminist, born Chicago, IL, July 20, 1939.

Larry E. Craig, 56, US Senator (R, Idaho), born Council, ID, July 20, 1945.

John Daley, 16, actor ("Freaks and Geeks"), born Wheeling, IL, July 20, 1985.

Charles Joseph (Chuck) Daly, 71, Basketball Hall of Fame coach, sportscaster, born St. Mary's, PA, July 20, 1930.

Donna Dixon, 44, actress ("Bosom Buddies," *Dr. Detroit*), born Alexandria, VA, July 20, 1957.

Nelson Doubleday, 68, baseball executive, publisher, born Long Island, NY, July 20, 1933.

Peter Forsberg, 28, hockey player, born Ornskoldvik, Sweden, July 20, 1973.

Sir Edmund Hillary, 82, explorer (first to climb Mount Everest), born Auckland, New Zealand, July 20, 1919.

Sally Ann Howes, 67, actress (*Dead of Night, The History of Mr Polly*), singer, born London, England, July 20, 1934.

Michael Ilitch, 72, sports executive, former minor league baseball player, born Detroit, MI, July 20, 1929.

Barbara Ann Mikulski, 65, US Senator (D, Maryland), born Baltimore, MD, July 20, 1936.

Diana Rigg, 63, actress (Tony for *Medea; King Lear, Witness for the Prosecution*), "The Avengers"), born Doncaster, Yorkshire, England, July 20, 1938.

Carlos Santana, 54, musician, born Autlan, Mexico, July 20, 1947.

JULY 21 — SATURDAY
Day 202 — 163 Remaining

ALBANY RIVERFEST. July 21. Corning Preserve Riverfront Park, Albany, NY. A free festival encompassing an array of regional and national entertainment, taste temptations, arts and crafts, children's activities, games, water sports exhibitions and nautical displays, all brought to a fantastic finale via fireworks over the Hudson. Est attendance: 30,000. For info: City of Albany Office of Special Events, Eagle Street, Albany, NY 12207. Phone: (518) 434-2032. Web: www.albanyevents.org.

ANTIQUE AND CLASSIC BOAT RENDEZVOUS. July 21–22. Mystic Seaport, Mystic, CT. Pre-1952 power and sailing yachts on view for Mystic Seaport visitors. Mystic River parade on Sunday. Est attendance: 4,000. For info: Mystic Seaport, 75 Greenmanville Ave, Box 6000, Mystic, CT 06355. Phone: (860) 527-5315 or (888) 9-SEAPORT. Web: www.mysticseaport.org.

BANNACK DAYS. July 21–22. Bannack, MT. Montana's first territorial capital, now a living ghost town, comes to life with a celebration of Montana's mining, ranching and farming history. Stage coach rides, main street gunfights, old-time dancing, lots of music and fun are provided during this two-day celebration along Grasshopper Creek each year. Operated as a state park, Bannack features a town from the mid-1800s now held in a state of "arrested decay." It is open year 'round to the public. Est attendance: 5,200. For info: Cindy Staszak, Montana Fish, Wildlife and Parks, 4200 Bannack Rd, Dillon, MT 59725. Phone: (406) 834-3413.

BELGIUM: NATIONAL HOLIDAY. July 21. Marks accession of first Belgian king, Leopold I in 1831, after independence from Netherlands.

CARVER DAY COMMEMORATIVE CELEBRATION. July 21. Diamond, MO. Family-oriented educational programs, gospel singing, storytelling, environmental education and guided historic tours at the George Washington Carver National Monument. Est attendance: 1,300. For info: George Washington Carver Natl Monument, 5646 Carver Rd, Diamond, MO 64840. Phone: (417) 325-4151. Fax: (417) 325-4231.

CHURCH AND SYNAGOGUE LIBRARY ASSOCIATION CONFERENCE. July 21–24. Atlanta, GA. Est attendance: 200. For info: Judith Janzen, Administrator, Church and Synagogue Library Assn, Box 19357, Portland, OR 97280-0357. Phone: (503) 244-6919. Fax: (503) 977-3734. E-mail: csla@worldaccessnet.com. Web: www.worldaccessnet.com/~csla.

CLEVELAND, FRANCES FOLSOM: BIRTH ANNIVERSARY. July 21, 1864. Wife of Grover Cleveland, 22nd and 24th president of the US, born at Buffalo, NY. She was the youngest First Lady at age 22, and the first to marry a president in the White House. Died at Princeton, NJ, Oct 29, 1947.

COLTON COUNTRY DAY. July 21. Main St, Colton, NY. Annual flea market, live entertainment, museum exhibits. Special programs. Annually, the third weekend in July. Sponsor: Colton Historical Society. Est attendance: 1,500. For info: Dennis Eickhoff, Town Historian, PO Box 109, Colton, NY 13625-0109. Phone: (315) 262-2800. E-mail: eickhoff@northnet.org.

EIGHTEENTH-CENTURY SUMMER MARKET FAIR. July 21–22. McLean, VA. 18th-century games, music and crafts. Militia will drill. Est attendance: 5,000. For info: Publicist, Claude Moore Colonial Farm at Turkey Run, 6310 Georgetown Pike, McLean, VA 22101. Phone: (703) 442-7557. Fax: (703) 442-0714.

EVANSTON ETHNIC ARTS FESTIVAL. July 21–22. Evanston, IL. A lakefront festival of art, music, poetry, dance and ethnic foods. For info: Evanston Arts Council, 927 Noyes St, Evanston, IL 60201. Phone: (847) 448-8260.

FIRST ROBOT HOMICIDE: ANNIVERSARY. July 21, 1984. The first reported killing of a human by a robot occurred at Jackson, MI. A robot turned and caught a 34-year-old worker between it and a safety bar, crushing him. He died of the injuries July 26, 1984. According to the National Institute for Occupational Safety and Health, it was "the first documented case of a robot-related fatality in the US."

FLEA MARKET/CRAFT/COLLECTIONS SALE. July 21. Sauk Centre, MN. 30th year for this sale, sponsored by St. Michael's Auxiliary in conjunction with Sinclair Lewis Days. Sale features 90 exhibitors. The Auxiliary offers lunches at their food stand for a fee, also bake sale and raffle. Annually, the third Saturday in July. Est attendance: 2,000. For info: Joyce C. Lyng, St. Michael's Auxiliary, 1725 Sinclair Lewis Ave, Sauk Centre, MN 56378. Phone: (320) 352-2624.

FRIENDSVILLE FIDDLE AND BANJO CONTEST. July 21. Friendsville, MD. Fiddlers from Garrett County and surrounding region participate in event. Old-time bluegrass entertainment. Cloggers welcome. Est attendance: 300. For info: Friendsville Fiddle and Banjo Contest, 133 Claude Fike Rd, Accident, MD 21520.

GUAM: LIBERATION DAY. July 21. US forces returned to Guam in 1944.

HARVEST WEEKENDS. July 21–22. (also Aug 4–5, 11–12 and 18–19) Bryan, TX. Step into the romance of winemaking by joining the Harvest Pickers Club and participate in hand-harvesting. A typical harvest weekend begins with a walk through the vines followed by the leisurely hand-harvesting of grapes. Afterward, you're invited to attend a classic European-style harvest luncheon which is followed by a wine and food pairing seminar. Annually, late-July to mid-August to coincide with the grape harvest. For info: Steve Wiley, Mktg Dir, Messina Hof Wine Cellars, 4545 Old Reliance Rd, Bryan, TX 77808. Phone: (409) 778-9463. Fax: (409) 778-1729.

HEMINGWAY, ERNEST: BIRTH ANNIVERSARY. July 21, 1899. American short story writer and novelist born at Oak Park, IL. Made his name with such works as *The Sun Also Rises* (1926), *A Farewell to Arms* (1929), *For Whom the Bell Tolls* (1940) and *The Old Man and the Sea* (1952). He was awarded the Nobel Prize in 1954 and wrote little thereafter; he shot himself July 2, 1961, at Ketchum, ID, having been seriously ill for some time.

JOHN MICHAEL KOHLER ARTS CENTER'S OUTDOOR ARTS FESTIVAL. July 21–22. Sheboygan, WI. A multiarts extravaganza featuring the works of 130 artists, demonstrations, live entertainment, children's workshops and exhibition tours. Est attendance: 16,000. For info: John Michael Kohler Arts Center, 608 New York Ave, PO Box 489, Sheboygan, WI 53082-0489. Phone: (920) 458-6144. Fax: (920) 458-4473. Web: www.jmkac.org.

McLUHAN, MARSHALL: 90th BIRTH ANNIVERSARY. July 21, 1911. (Herbert) Marshall McLuhan, university professor and author, called "the Canadian sage of the electronic age," was born at Edmonton, Alberta, Canada. *Understanding Media* and *The Medium Is the Massage* (not to be confused with his widely quoted aphorism: "The medium is the message"), among other books, were widely acclaimed for their fresh view of communication. McLuhan is reported to have said: "Most people are alive in an earlier time, but you must be alive in our own time." He died at Toronto, Ontario, Dec 31, 1980.

NATIONAL WOMEN'S HALL OF FAME: ANNIVERSARY. July 21, 1979. Seneca Falls, NY. Founded to honor American women whose contributions "have been of the greatest value in the development of their country" and located in the community known as the "birthplace of women's rights," where the first Women's Suffrage Movement convention was held in 1848, the Hall of Fame was dedicated with 23 inductees. Earlier National Women's Hall of Fame, honoring "Twenty Outstanding Women of the Twentieth Century," was dedicated at New York World's Fair, on May 27, 1965.

SHERWOOD ROBIN HOOD FESTIVAL. July 21–22. Sherwood, OR. Parade, archery contest, dance, music, beer garden, game booths, food and arts and crafts. Annually, the third weekend in July. Est attendance: 5,000. For info: Robin Hood Festival Assn, PO Box 496, Sherwood, OR 97140. Phone: (503) 625-6873.

SUMMERSWAP. July 21. Heritage Park, Frankenmuth, MI. A beer can collectors and breweriana trade show. Breweriana is the collection of brewery memorabilia, including steins, signs, coasters, mirrors, neon signs, etc. The show is attended by collectors from a 10–12-state area and Canada. Annually, the third Saturday in July. Est attendance: 350. For info: Dave Van Hine, Show Chairman, Beer Can Collectors of America, Mid-Michigan Chapter, 357 N Harvest Lane, Frankenmuth, MI 48734. Phone: (989) 652-9818. E-mail: davevanh@aol.com.

TWIN-O-RAMA. July 21–23. Cassville, WI. Celebration honoring twin and other multiple births. Est attendance: 1,500. For info: Twin-O-Rama, Inc, PO Box 545, Cassville, WI 53806. Phone: (608) 725-5180 or (608) 725-5121. Web: www.cassville.org.

WOODCRAFT FESTIVAL. July 21–22. Grand Rapids, MN. Northern Minnesota woodcrafters demonstrate traditional woodcrafting techniques, discussions with artisans and hands-on activities. Est attendance: 1,000. For info: Robert Drake, Forest History Center, 2609 Cnty Rd 76, Grand Rapids, MN 55744. Phone: (218) 327-4482. Fax: (218) 327-4483.

BIRTHDAYS TODAY

Brandi Chastain, 33, soccer player, born San Jose, CA, July 21, 1968.

Lance Guest, 41, actor ("Lou Grant," *The Last Starfighter*), born Saratoga, CA, July 21, 1960.

Edward Herrmann, 58, actor (*The Paper Chase, Eleanor and Franklin*), born Washington, DC, July 21, 1943.

Norman Jewison, 75, producer, director (*Moonstruck, Fiddler on the Roof*), born Toronto, Ontario, Canada, July 21, 1926.

Don Knotts, 77, actor, comedian ("The Andy Griffith Show," *The Ghost and Mr Chicken*), born Morgantown, WV, July 21, 1924.

Jon Lovitz, 44, actor (*A League of Their Own*, "NewsRadio"), born Tarzana, CA, July 21, 1957.

Matt Mulhern, 41, actor ("Major Dad," *Biloxi Blues*), born Philadelphia, PA, July 21, 1960.

Janet Reno, 63, US Attorney General (Clinton administration), born Miami, FL, July 21, 1938.

Isaac Stern, 81, violinist, born Kreminiecz, Belarus, July 21, 1920.

Cat Stevens (Stephen Demetri Georgiou, chosen Muslim name is Yusuf Islam), 53, singer, songwriter, born London, England, July 21, 1948.

Billy Taylor, 80, jazz musician, born Greenville, NC, July 21, 1921.

Garry Trudeau, 52, political cartoonist ("Doonesbury"), born New York, NY, July 21, 1949.

Paul D. Wellstone, 57, US Senator (D, Minnesota), born Washington, DC, July 21, 1944.

Robin Williams, 49, actor ("Mork and Mindy," *Mrs Doubtfire, Dead Poets Society, Good Will Hunting*), born Chicago, IL, July 21, 1952.

JULY 22 — SUNDAY
Day 203 — 162 Remaining

ALLIES TAKE PALERMO: ANNIVERSARY. July 22, 1943. Two weeks after the July 10 Allied invasion of Sicily, the principal northern town of Palermo was captured. Americans had cut off 50,000 Italian troops in the west, but Germans were escaping to the northeastern corner of the island. After 39 days, on Aug 17, 1943, the entire island of Sicily was under the control of Allied forces. The official total of Germans and Italians captured was put at 130,000. The Germans, however, managed to transfer 60,000 of their 90,000 men back to the Italian mainland.

DIETARY MANAGERS ASSOCIATION ANNUAL MEETING AND EXPO. July 22–26. Hilton Riverside, New Orleans, LA. 41st annual meeting. Est attendance: 800. For info: Dennis Leopold, VP, Dietary Mgrs Assn, 406 Surrey Woods Dr, St. Charles, IL 60174-2386. Phone: (630) 587-6336. Fax: (630) 587-6308.

DILLINGER, JOHN: DEATH ANNIVERSARY. July 22, 1934. Bank robber, murderer, prison escapee and the first person to receive the FBI's appellation "Public Enemy No. 1" (July 1934). After nine years in prison (1924–33), Dillinger traveled through Indiana, Illinois, Ohio, Wisconsin, Minnesota and Iowa, leaving a path of violent crimes. Reportedly betrayed by the "Lady in Red," he was killed by FBI agents as he left Chicago's Biograph movie theater (where he had watched *Manhattan Melodrama*, starring Clark Gable and Myrna Loy), July 22, 1934. He was born at Indianapolis, IN, June 28, 1902.

HUMOR AND STRESS MANAGEMENT ANNUAL INTERNATIONAL WORKSHOP. July 22–27. Raquette Lake, New York. 25th annual. This workshop, which draws participants from around the world, is designed to help you tackle stress before it tackles you. Led by Margie Ingram and Joel Goodman, this program is fun but not for fun. Attendees laugh while learning practical ideas and skills they can use both personally as well as on the job. For a free information packet on the positive power of humor send SASE (99 cents). For info: Dr. Joel Goodman, The HUMOR Project, Inc, 480 Broadway, Ste 210-C, Saratoga Springs, NY 12866-2288. Phone: (518) 587-8770. Fax: (518) 587-8771. E-mail: Chase@HumorProject.com. Web: www.HumorProject.com.

MENDEL, GREGOR JOHANN: BIRTH ANNIVERSARY. July 22, 1822. Botanist Gregor Mendel was born of peasant parents at Heinzendorf, Austria. His pioneering work in genetics became the basis for the modern science of genetics and heredity. Around 1856 Mendel began experiments in the small monastery garden, crossing different varieties of the garden pea. The import of Mendel's work was not seen until many years after his death, Jan 6, 1884, at Brünn. In 1900 other European botanists discovered his papers and confirmed and extended his theories, which formed the basis of the study of heredity and genetics.

MENNINGER, KARL: BIRTH ANNIVERSARY. July 22, 1893. American psychiatrist Karl Augustus Menninger was born at Topeka, KS. Along with his father and brother, he founded the Menninger Clinic and Foundation at Topeka in the 1920s. He died July 18, 1990, at Topeka.

PIED PIPER OF HAMELIN: ANNIVERSARY—MAYBE. July 22, 1376. According to legend, the German town of Hamelin, plagued with rats, bargained with a piper who promised to, and did, pipe the rats out of town and into the Weser River. Refused payment for his work, the piper then piped the children out of town and into a hole in a hill, never to be seen again. More recent historians suggest that the event occurred in 1284 when young men of Hamelin left the city on colonizing adventures.

July 2001	S	M	T	W	T	F	S
		1	2	3	4	5	6	7
	8	9	10	11	12	13	14
	15	16	17	18	19	20	21
	22	23	24	25	26	27	28
	29	30	31				

RAT-CATCHERS DAY. July 22. A day to recognize the rat-catchers who labor to exterminate members of the genus *Rattus*, disease-carrying rodents that infest most of the "civilized" world. Observed on anniversary of the legendary feat of the Pied Piper of Hamelin on July 22, 1376 (according to 16th-century chronicler Richard Rowland Verstegen).

REGISTER'S ANNUAL GREAT BICYCLE RIDE ACROSS IOWA. July 22–28. A week-long bicycle ride across Iowa with 7,500 riders from across the country (and around the world). Annually, the last full week of July. After Nov 1 and before Mar 1 send a business-size SASE (two stamps) to the address below. Sponsor: *Des Moines Register*. Est attendance: 7,500. For info: RAGBRAI Coordinator, PO Box 622, Des Moines, IA 50303-0622. Phone: (800) 474-3342. Fax: (515) 284-8138. E-mail: jimg@ragbrai.org. Web: www.ragbrai.org.

RILEY, JAMES WHITCOMB: 85th DEATH ANNIVERSARY. July 22, 1916. American "Hoosier" poet, born at Greenfield, IN, Oct 7 probably in 1853, but possibly several years earlier. Riley died at Indianapolis, IN.

SPACE MILESTONE: *SOYUZ TM-3 (USSR).* July 22, 1987. Two Soviet cosmonauts, Aleksandr Viktorenko and Aleksandr Aleksandrov, along with the first Syrian space traveler, Mohammed Faris, were launched on a projected 10-day mission. Launched from the Baikonur base in Central Asia, the spacecraft orbited Earth for two days before linking with Soviet space station *Mir*. The *Soyuz TM* spacecraft was used as a shuttle to *Mir* into the 1990s.

SPOONER'S DAY *(WILLIAM SPOONER BIRTH ANNIVERSARY).* July 22. A day named for the Reverend William Archibald Spooner (born at London, England, July 22, 1844, warden of New College, Oxford, 1903–24, died at Oxford, England, Aug 29, 1930), whose frequent slips of the tongue led to coinage of the term *spoonerism* to describe them. A day to remember the scholarly man whose accidental transpositions gave us blushing crow (for crushing blow), tons of soil (for sons of toil), queer old dean (for dear old queen), swell foop (for fell swoop) and half-warmed fish (for half-formed wish).

SWITZERLAND: DORNACH BATTLE COMMEMORATION. July 22. The victory at Dornach in 1499 is remembered on the battlefield and in the city of Solothurn on the Sunday nearest to July 22. Dornach observes commemorative festival every five years.

BIRTHDAYS TODAY

Orson Bean (Dallas Frederick Burroughs), 73, actor ("To Tell the Truth," "Mary Hartman, Mary Hartman"), born Burlington, VT, July 22, 1928.

Irene Bedard, 34, actress ("Grand Avenue," "Crazy Horse," *Squanto: A Warrior's Tale*; voice of Pocahontas in the Disney film), born Anchorage, AK, July 22, 1967.

Albert Brooks (Albert Einstein), 54, comedian, director, actor (*Broadcast News, Mother*), born Los Angeles, CA, July 22, 1947.

Willem Dafoe, 46, actor (*Platoon, Mississippi Burning*), born Appleton, WI, July 22, 1955.

Oscar De La Renta, 69, fashion designer, born Santo Domingo, Dominican Republic, July 22, 1932.

Robert J. Dole, 78, former US Senator (R, Kansas), born Russell, KS, July 22, 1923.

Rob Estes, 38, actor ("Melrose Place," "Silk Stalkings"), born Norfolk, VA, July 22, 1963.

Danny Glover, 54, actor ("Chiefs," *Lethal Weapon, The Color Purple*), born San Francisco, CA, July 22, 1947.

Don Henley, 54, musician (The Eagles), songwriter (cowrote "The Boys of Summer"), born Linden, TX, July 22, 1947.

Kay Bailey Hutchison, 58, US Senator (R, Texas), born Galveston, TX, July 22, 1943.

Keyshawn Johnson, 29, football player, born Los Angeles, CA, July 22, 1972.

John Leguizamo, 36, actor (*Carlito's Way*; stage: *Mambo Mouth* [also writer; Obie Award], *Spic-O-Rama* [also writer; Theatre World Award]), born Bogota, Colombia, July 22, 1965.

Alan Menken, 52, film score composer (*Pocahontas, Aladdin*), born New Rochelle, NY, July 22, 1949.

William V. Roth, Jr, 80, US Senator (R, Delaware), born Great Falls, MT, July 22, 1921.

Bobby Sherman, 56, singer, actor, born Santa Monica, CA, July 22, 1945.

David Spade, 36, actor ("Saturday Night Live," "Just Shoot Me," *Black Sheep*), born Birmingham, MI, July 22, 1965.

Terence Stamp, 62, actor (*Superman, Wall Street, Alien Nation*), born London, England, July 22, 1939.

Keith Sweat, 70, R&B singer, born New York, NY, July 22, 1931.

Alex Trebek, 61, game-show host ("Concentration," "Jeopardy"), born Sudbury, Ontario, Canada, July 22, 1940.

Margaret Whiting, 77, singer ("The Money Tree," "The Wheel of Hurt"), born Detroit, MI, July 22, 1924.

JULY 23 — MONDAY
Day 204 — 161 Remaining

BROWNE, CORAL: BIRTH ANNIVERSARY. July 23, 1913. British actress Coral Edith Browne was born at Melbourne, Australia. In the 1950s she worked with the Old Vic theater at London. Her films include *Auntie Mame* (1958). She was married to actor Vincent Price. Browne died May 29, 1991, at Los Angeles, CA.

DRYSDALE, DON: 65th BIRTH ANNIVERSARY. July 23, 1936. Elected to the Baseball Hall of Fame in 1984, Don Drysdale was a pitcher for the Brooklyn and Los Angeles Dodgers from 1956 to 1969, compiling a won-lost record of 209–166 with a career ERA of 2.95. Following his playing career he became a successful and popular broadcast announcer for the Chicago White Sox and then for the Los Angeles Dodgers. He was born at Van Nuys, CA, and died at Montreal, Canada, July 3, 1993.

EGYPT, ARAB REPUBLIC OF: NATIONAL DAY. July 23, 1952. Anniversary of the Revolution in 1952, which was launched by army officers and changed Egypt from a monarchy to a republic.

FIRST US SWIMMING SCHOOL: OPENING ANNIVERSARY. July 23, 1827. The first swimming school in the US opened at Boston, MA. Its pupils included John Quincy Adams and James Audubon.

"THE GENE AUTRY SHOW" TV PREMIERE: ANNIVERSARY. July 23, 1950. Popular CBS western ran for six years starring movie actor Gene Autry. Along with sidekick Pat Buttram, Autry helped bring criminals to justice.

HOT ENOUGH FOR YA DAY. July 23. We are permitted today to utter the words that suffice when nothing of intelligence comes to mind. "Is is hot enough for ya?" Annually, July 23. ©1999 Wellcat Herbs & Holidays For info: Thomas & Ruth Roy, 2418 Long Ln, Lebanon, PA 17046-1708. Phone: (230) 332-4886. E-mail: wellcat@supernet.com. Web: www.wellcat.com.

JAPAN: SOMA NO UMAOI (WILD HORSE CHASING). July 23–25. Hibarigahara, Haramachi, Fukushima Prefecture, Japan. 1,000 horsemen clad in ancient armor compete for possession of three shrine flags shot aloft on Hibarigahara Plain, and men in white costumes attempt to catch wild horses corralled by the horsemen.

LEO, THE LION. July 23–Aug 22. In the astronomical/astrological zodiac, which divides the sun's apparent orbit into 12 segments, the period July 23–Aug 22 is identified, traditionally, as the sun sign of Leo, the Lion. The ruling planet is the sun.

PONY GIRLS SOFTBALL NATIONAL CHAMPIONSHIPS. July 23–28 (tentative). Site TBA. Slow- and fast-pitch National Championships for girls ages 7–18. Est attendance: 11,000. For info: PONY Baseball and Softball, PO Box 225, Washington, PA 15301. Phone: (724) 225-1060. Fax: (724) 225-9852. E-mail: pony@pulsenet.com. Web: www.pony.org.

REESE, HAROLD HENRY ("PEE WEE"): BIRTH ANNIVERSARY. July 23, 1918. Hall of Fame shortstop, born at Ekron, KY. Died Aug 14, 1999, at Louisville, KY.

SAINT APOLLINARIS: FEAST DAY. July 23. First bishop of Ravenna, and a martyr, of unknown date. Observed July 23.

SPACE MILESTONE: *COLUMBIA* (US): FIRST FEMALE COMMANDER. July 23, 1999. Colonel Eileen Collins lead a shuttle mission to deploy a $1.5 billion X-ray telescope, the Chandra observatory, into space. It is a sister satellite to the Hubble Space Telescope. The observatory is named after Nobel prizewinner Subrahamyar Chandrasekhar.

SPACE MILESTONE: *SOYUZ 37* (USSR). July 23, 1980. Cosmonauts Viktor Gorbatko and, the first non-Caucasian in space, Lieutenant Colonel Pham Tuan (Vietnam), docked at *Salyut 6* July 24. Returned to Earth July 31.

VIRGIN ISLANDS: HURRICANE SUPPLICATION DAY. July 23. Legal holiday. Population attends churches to pray for protection from hurricanes. Annually, the fourth Monday in July.

WALES: ROYAL WELSH SHOW. July 23–26. Royal Welsh Showground, Llanelwedd, Builth Wells, Powys. National agricultural show incorporating exhibitions of livestock, farm machinery, horticulture and forestry displays. Est attendance: 230,000. For info: The Secretary, Royal Welsh Agricultural Soc, Llanelwedd, Builth Wells, Powys, Wales, UK LD2 3SY. Phone: (01) (982) 553683. Fax: (01) (982) 553563. E-mail: info@rwas.co.uk. Web: www.rwas.co.uk.

BIRTHDAYS TODAY

Ronny Cox, 63, actor (*Deliverance, Bound for Glory, Total Recall*), born Cloudcroft, NM, July 23, 1938.
Gloria DeHaven, 76, actress (*Two Girls and a Sailor*, "Nakia"), born Los Angeles, CA, July 23, 1925.
Nicholas Gage, 62, journalist, film producer, writer (*Eleni*), born Lia, Greece, July 23, 1939.
Nomar Garciaparra, 28, baseball player, born Whittier, CA, July 23, 1973.

July 2001	S	M	T	W	T	F	S
	1	2	3	4	5	6	7
	8	9	10	11	12	13	14
	15	16	17	18	19	20	21
	22	23	24	25	26	27	28
	29	30	31				

Woody Harrelson, 40, actor (Emmy for "Cheers"; *White Men Can't Jump, Natural Born Killers*), born Midland, TX, July 23, 1961.
Don Imus, 61, radio talk-show host, media icon and author, born Riverside, CA, July 23, 1940.
Arata Isozaki, 70, architect, born Oita, Japan, July 23, 1931.
Anthony M. Kennedy, 65, Supreme Court Associate Justice, born Sacramento, CA, July 23, 1936.
Eriq La Salle, 39, actor ("ER," *]Coming to America*), born Hartford, CT, July 23, 1962.
Edie McClurg, 50, actress ("WKRP in Cincinnati," *Eating Raoul, A River Runs Through It*), born Kansas City, MO, July 23, 1951.
Belinda Montgomery, 51, actress ("Man From Atlantis"), born Winnipeg, Manitoba, Canada, July 23, 1950.
Gary Dwayne Payton, 33, basketball player, born Oakland, CA, July 23, 1968.

JULY 24 — TUESDAY

Day 205 — 160 Remaining

BOLIVAR, SIMON: BIRTH ANNIVERSARY. July 24, 1783. "The Liberator," born at Caracas, Venezuela. Commemorated in Venezuela and other Latin American countries. Died Dec 17, 1830, at Santa Marta, Colombia. Bolivia is named after him.

BRIGHAM YOUNG ENTERS SALT LAKE VALLEY: ANNIVERSARY. July 24, 1847. Utah state holiday commemorating this event.

BROOME COUNTY FAIR. July 24–29. Whitney Point, NY. County agricultural fair. Est attendance: 39,000. For info: Charles Franklin, Broome County Fair, PO Box 747, Whitney Point, NY 13862. Phone: (607) 692-4149.

CALIFORNIA WINE TASTING CHAMPIONSHIPS. July 24–25. Greenwood Ridge Winery, Philo, CA. A fun educational event popular with wine neophytes and wine maniacs. Live music, cheese and chocolate tasting and olive oil samples too. Est attendance: 800. For info: Allan Green, Greenwood Ridge Winery. Phone: (707) 895-2002. Fax: (707) 895-2001.

COUSINS DAY. July 24. A day to celebrate, honor and appreciate our cousins. For info: Claudia A. Evart, 30 Park Ave, Ste 2P, New York, NY 10016-3833. Phone: (212) 779-2227. E-mail: siblingsday@earthlink.net.

DETROIT: 300th ANNIVERSARY. July 24, 1701. Anniversary of the landing at the site of Detroit by Antoine de la Mothe Cadillac in the service of Louis XIV of France. Fort Pontchartrain du Detroit was first settlement on site.

DUMAS, ALEXANDRE: BIRTH ANNIVERSARY. July 24, 1802. French playwright and novelist, born at Villers-Cotterets, France. He is said to have written more than 300 volumes, including *The Count of Monte Cristo* and *The Three Musketeers*. Father of Alexandre Dumas (Dumas fils), also a novelist and playwright (1824–95). Dumas died near Dieppe, France, Dec 5, 1870.

EARHART, AMELIA: BIRTH ANNIVERSARY. July 24, 1898. American aviatrix lost on flight from New Guinea to Howland Island, in the Pacific Ocean, July 3, 1937. First woman to cross the Atlantic solo and fly solo across the Pacific from Hawaii to California. Born at Atchison, KS.

GARFIELD COUNTY FAIR. July 24–28. Burwell, NE. County fair, carnival, rodeo and commercial and craft concessions. Est attendance: 10,000. For info: Peggy Haskell, Garfield County Frontier Fair Assn, Box 747, Burwell, NE 68823. Phone: (308) 346-5210. Web: www.BurwellNebr.com.

HEALTH AND HAPPINESS WITH HYPNOSIS DAY. July 24. Participating members of the International Registry of Professional Hypnotherapists offer free seminars, free introductory hypnotherapy sessions, media appearances to publicize how hypnosis can help people be healthier and happier. Also, the launch of the updated edition of *Health and Happiness with Hypnosis*. Annually, the fourth Tuesday in July. For info: Dr. Bryan Knight, Intl Registry of Professional Hypnotherapists, 7306 Sherbrooke St West, Montreal, Quebec, Canada H4B 1R7. Phone: (514) 489-6733. Fax: (514) 485-3828. E-mail: drknight@hypnosis.org. Web: www.hypnosis.org.

NATIONAL BABY FOOD FESTIVAL. July 24–28 (tentative). Fremont, MI. Baby yourself at this 11th annual festival in the hometown of Gerber Products. Adults face off in the baby-food-eating contest and tots crawl in races. Top entertainers, two parades, arts and crafts, and car shows round out the fun. Est attendance: 100,000. For info: Natl Baby Food Festival, 9 E Main St, Fremont, MI 49412. Phone: (800) 592-BABY.

PIONEER DAY: ANNIVERSARY. July 24. Utah. Commemorates first settlement in 1847, by Brigham Young.

POTSDAM DECLARATION: ANNIVERSARY. July 24, 1945. As the Potsdam Conference came to a close in Germany, Churchill, Truman and China's representatives fashioned a communique to Japan offering it an opportunity to end the war. It demanded that Japan completely disarm, allowed them sovereignty to the four main islands and to minor islands to be determined by the Allies, and insisted that all Japanese citizens be given immediate and complete freedom of speech, religion and thought. The Japanese would be allowed to continue enough industry to maintain their economy. The communique concluded with a demand for unconditional surrender. Unaware these demands were backed up by an atomic bomb, on July 26 Japanese Prime Minister Admiral Kantaro Suzuki rejected the Potsdam Declaration.

RAF JAMS NAZI RADAR IN OPERATION GOMORRAH: ANNIVERSARY. July 24, 1943. On the first of the Royal Air Force Operation Gomorrah raids on Hamburg, Germany, "windows" (bales of 10 ½" strips of aluminum foil) were pushed out of the bombers causing the German radar screens to see a snowstorm of false echo "aircraft" on their screens. As a result only 12 of the 791 bombers sent on the mission were shot down.

ROCKBRIDGE REGIONAL FAIR. July 24–28. Lexington, VA. Held at the Virginia Horse Center. 4-H Show, rodeo, carnival, exhibits (commercial and crafts), activities of all kinds. For info: Lexington Visitors Bureau, 106 E Washington St, Lexington, VA 24450. Phone: (540) 463-3777. Fax: (540) 463-1105. E-mail: lexington@rockbridge.net.

US JUNIOR AMATEUR (GOLF) CHAMPIONSHIP. July 24–28. Oak Hills Country Club, San Antonio, TX. For info: US Golf Assn, Golf House, PO Box 708, Championship Dept, Far Hills, NJ 07931. Phone: (908) 234-2300. Fax: (908) 234-9687. Web: www.usga.org.

BIRTHDAYS TODAY

Barry Bonds, 37, baseball player, six-time All-Star, three-time National League MVP, born Riverside, CA, July 24, 1964.

Ruth Buzzi, 65, comedienne, actress ("Rowan & Martin's Laugh-In," "Sesame Street"), born Westerly, RI, July 24, 1936.

Lynda Carter, 50, actress ("Wonder Woman," "Partners in Crime") former Miss World–USA, singer, born Phoenix, AZ, July 24, 1951.

Kadeem Hardison, 36, actor ("A Different World," "The Sixth Man"), born New York, NY, July 24, 1965.

Robert Hays, 54, actor (*Airplane!*, "Starman"), born Bethesda, MD, July 24, 1947.

Julie A. Krone, 38, former jockey, born Benton Harbor, MI, July 24, 1963.

Jennifer Lopez, 31, actress (*Selena, Blood and Wine*), born The Bronx, NY, July 24, 1970.

Karl Malone, 38, basketball player, born Summerfield, LA, July 24, 1963.

Pat Oliphant, 66, cartoonist, born Adelaide, Australia, July 24, 1935.

Anna Paquin, 19, actress (*The Piano, Fly Away Home*), born Wellington, New Zealand, July 24, 1982.

Marc Racicot, 53, Governor of Montana (R), born Thompson Falls, MT, July 24, 1948.

Chris Sarandon, 59, actor (*Dog Day Afternoon, The Princess Bride*), born Beckley, WV, July 24, 1942.

Peter Serkin, 54, musician, born New York, NY, July 24, 1947.

JULY 25 — WEDNESDAY
Day 206 — 159 Remaining

ANDREA DORIA SINKS: 45th ANNIVERSARY. July 25, 1956. The Italian luxury liner collided with the *Stockholm*, a Swedish liner, on its way to New York. Other ships in the area came to the rescue of the *Andrea Doria*. 1,634 people were rescued during the ordeal, including the captain and the crew.

CHINCOTEAGUE PONY PENNING. July 25–26. Chincoteague Island, VA. To round up the 150 wild ponies living on Assateague Island and swim them across the inlet to Chincoteague, where about 75–85 of them are sold. Annually, the last Wednesday and Thursday of July. Est attendance: 50,000. For info: Jacklyn Russell, Chamber of Commerce, Box 258, Chincoteague, VA 23336. Phone: (757) 336-6161. Fax: (757) 336-1242. E-mail: pony@shore.intercom.net. Web: www.chincoteaguechamber.com.

EAA AIRVENTURE OSHKOSH. July 25–31. Wittman Regional Airport, Oshkosh, WI. World's largest sport aviation event. More than 12,000 airplanes annually fly in for this Experimental Aircraft Association event. Daily air shows, special programs, more than 500 forums, workshops and seminars. Est attendance: 800,000. For info: Dick Knapinski, Corporate Communications, Experimental Aircraft Assn, PO Box 3086, Oshkosh, WI 54903-3086. Phone: (920) 426-4800. Web: www.eaa.org.

FAIRFEST. July 25–29. Adams County Fairgrounds, Hastings, NE. Annual county fair featuring midway; open-class competitions in culinary arts, needlework, floral culture, woodworking and the visual arts; Adams County 4-H competition, livestock show; and live entertainment in the Grand Stand. Est attendance: 85,000. For info: Sandy Himmelberg, Genl Mgr, 947 S Baltimore, Hastings, NE 68901. Phone: (402) 462-3247. Fax: (402) 462-4731. Web: www.adamscountyfairgrounds.com.

FARMERS' FESTIVAL. July 25–29. Pigeon, MI. To recognize and honor farmers for their unique contribution to rural life in Michigan's "Thumb area." Features parades, barbecues, stage shows, crafts and sidewalk sales. Sponsor: Pigeon Chamber of Commerce. Est attendance: 10,000. For info: Linda Clabuesch, Chairman, 58 S Caseville Rd, Pigeon, MI 48755. Phone: (517) 453-2330.

FIRST AIRPLANE CROSSING OF ENGLISH CHANNEL: ANNIVERSARY. July 25, 1909. Louis Bleriot, after asking from the cockpit, "Where is England?" took off from Les Baraques (near Calais), France, and landed on English soil at Northfall Meadow, near Dover, where he was greeted first by English police and customs officers. This, the world's first international overseas airplane flight, was accomplished in a 28-hp monoplane with a wingspan of 23 ft. See also: "Bleriot, Louis: Birth Anniversary" (July 1).

GILFORD, JACK: BIRTH ANNIVERSARY. July 25, 1907. American actor Jack Gilford was born Jacob Gellman at New York, NY. Though he was blacklisted for 10 years following refusal to answer questions before the House Un-American Activities Committee in the 1950s, he appeared in many films, stage productions and television programs including an Academy Award-nominated role opposite Jack Lemmon in *Save the Tiger* (1973) and his best-known role as Hysterium in the stage and film versions of *A Funny Thing Happened on the Way to the Forum*. He died June 4, 1990, at New York, NY.

HARRISON, ANNA SYMMES: BIRTH ANNIVERSARY. July 25, 1775. Wife of William Henry Harrison, ninth president of the US, born at Morristown, NJ. Died at North Bend, IN, Feb 25, 1864.

HOOD RIVER COUNTY FAIR. July 25–28. Hood River, OR. From 4-H activities to the excitement of the carnival, this annual old-fashioned country fair is bustling with things to do! Est attendance: 23,000. For info: Hood River County Fair, Box 385, Odell, OR 97044. Phone: (541) 354-2865. Fax: (541) 354-2875.

MUSSOLINI OUSTED: ANNIVERSARY. July 25, 1943. Two weeks after the Allied attack on Sicily began, the Fascist Grand Council met for the first time since December of 1939 and took a confidence vote resulting in Mussolini's being removed from office and placed under arrest. Italy's King Victor Emmanuel ordered Marshal Pietro Badoglio to form a new government.

NATIONAL SALAD WEEK. July 25–31. A week to educate consumers of the importance of incorporating more raw vegetables in their diet. Entrèe salads are full healthy meals when served with breads. They can be made with or without grilled meats, tossed with tasty homemade dressings and garnished with fruits, nuts or raisins. Annually, the last week in July. For info: Karen Gunvalson, Restaurant Mgr, The Terrace Restaurant of Lawsonia Golf Courses, State Hwy 23, Green Lake, WI 54941. Phone: (800) 529-4453, ext 105. E-mail: kkgunv@maqs.net.

PUERTO RICO: CONSTITUTION DAY ANNIVERSARY. July 25. Also called Commonwealth Day or Occupation Day. Commemorates proclamation of constitution in 1952.

PUERTO RICO: LOIZA ALDEA FIESTA. July 25–28. Best known of Puerto Rico's patron saint festivities. Villagers of Loiza Aldea, 20 miles east of San Juan, don devil masks and colorful costumes for a variety of traditional activities.

SPAIN: SAINT JAMES DAY. July 25. Holy day of the patron saint of Spain. When this day falls on a Sunday it is a holy year and pilgrims make the pilgrimage to Santiago de Compostela, the site of the saint's tomb. The next holy year is in 2004.

TEST-TUBE BABY: BIRTHDAY. July 25, 1978. Anniversary of the birth of Louise Brown at Oldham, England. First documented birth of a baby conceived outside the body of a woman. Parents: Gilbert John and Lesley Brown, of Bristol, England. Physicians: Patrick Christopher Steptoe and Robert Geoffrey Edwards.

BIRTHDAYS TODAY

Louise Joy Brown, 23, first test-tube baby, born Oldham, England, July 25, 1978.
Midge Decter, 74, journalist, born St. Paul, MN, July 25, 1927.
Illeana Douglas, 36, actress (*Message in a Bottle, Can't Stop Dancing*), born Boston, MA, July 25, 1965.
Estelle Getty, 77, actress ("Golden Girls"), born New York, NY, July 25, 1924.
Iman (Iman Mohamed Abdulmajid), 46, model, actress (*Star Trek VI*), born Mogadishu, Somalia, July 25, 1955.
Matt LeBlanc, 34, actor ("Friends"), born Newton, MA, July 25, 1967.
Brad Renfro, 19, actor (*Telling Lies in America, Tom and Huck*), born Knoxville, TN, July 25, 1982.
Nathaniel (Nate) Thurmond, 60, Basketball Hall of Fame center, born Akron, OH, July 25, 1941.

	S	**M**	**T**	**W**	**T**	**F**	**S**
July	1	2	3	4	5	6	7
2001	8	9	10	11	12	13	14
	15	16	17	18	19	20	21
	22	23	24	25	26	27	28
	29	30	31				

JULY 26 — THURSDAY
Day 207 — 158 Remaining

AMERICANS WITH DISABILITIES ACT SIGNED: ANNIVERSARY. July 26, 1990. President Bush signed the Americans with Disabilities Act, which went into effect two years later. It required that public facilities be made accessible to the disabled.

ARMED FORCES UNIFIED: ANNIVERSARY. July 26, 1947. President Truman signed legislation unifying the two branches of the armed forces into the Department of Defense. The branches merged were the War Department (Army) and the Navy. The Air Force was separated from the Army at the same time. Truman nominated James Forrestal to be the first Secretary of Defense. The legislation also provided for the National Security Council, the Central Intelligence Agency and the Joint Chiefs of Staff.

ATOMIC BOMB DELIVERED: ANNIVERSARY. July 26, 1945. The US cruiser *Indianapolis* arrived at Tinian Island in the Marianas with a deadly cargo. Aboard were the makings of the atomic bomb. On the island waited scientists prepared to complete the assembly.

CANADA: CALGARY FOLK MUSIC FESTIVAL. July 26–29. Calgary, AB. Celebration of local, national and international folk music. Est attendance: 40,000. For info: Kerry Clarke, Assoc Producer, Folk Festival Soc of Calgary, PO Box 2897 Station M, Calgary, AB, Canada T2P 3C3. Phone: (403) 233-0904. E-mail: folkfest@canuck.com. Web: www.canuck.com/folkfest.

CATLIN, GEORGE: BIRTH ANNIVERSARY. July 26, 1796. American artist famous for his paintings of Native American life, born at Wilkes-Barre, PA. In 1832 he toured North and South American tribes, recording their lives in his work. He died Dec 23, 1872, at Jersey City, NJ.

CENTRAL MONTANA FAIR. July 26–28. Lewistown, MT. Draft and open-to-all-class horseshow, three sessions of rodeo, carnival, 4-H and open exhibits, night shows and AMX auto-motocross race. Annually, last full week in July. Est attendance: 25,000. For info: Central Montana Fair, PO Box 1098, Lewistown, MT 59457. Phone: (406) 538-8841. Fax: (406) 538-4060. Web: centralmontanafair.com.

CLINTON, GEORGE: BIRTH ANNIVERSARY. July 26, 1739 (OS). Fourth vice president of the US (1805–12), born at Little Britain, NY. Died at Washington, DC, Apr 20, 1812.

CUBA: NATIONAL HOLIDAY: ANNIVERSARY OF REVOLUTION. July 26. Anniversary of 1953 beginning of Fidel Castro's revolutionary "26th of July Movement."

CURACAO: CURACAO DAY. July 26. "Although not officially recognized by the government as a holiday, various social entities commemorate the fact that on this day Alonso de Ojeda, a companion of Christopher Columbus, discovered the Island of Curaçao in 1499, sailing into Santa Ana Bay, the entrance of the harbor of Willemstad." Festivities on this day.

CURRY COUNTY FAIR. July 26–29. Curry County Fairgrounds, Gold Beach, OR. A traditional, family-style celebration of food, fun and frolic, including a rodeo. For 12 consecutive years, it has been awarded the Gold Medal Medallion by Oregon's State Fair Association and rated the #1 Small County Fair on numerous occasions. Est attendance: 15,000. For info: Gold Beach Chamber of Commerce, 29279 Ellensburg Ave, #3, Gold Beach, OR 97444. Phone: (800) 525-2334. Fax: (541) 247-0188. E-mail: goldbeach@harborside.com. Web: www.goldenbeach.org.

GOLD DISCOVERY DAYS. July 26–29. Custer, SD. Parade, historic "Pageant of Paha Sapa," park festival, carnival, pancake breakfast, bed races, boat regatta, fun run, volksmarch and hot-air balloon rally. Est attendance: 6,000. For info: Jacki Conlon, Gold Discovery Days Committee, 615 Washington St, Custer, SD 57730. Phone: (605) 673-2244 or 8009929818. E-mail: custer chamber@gwtc.net. Web: www.custersd.com.

GREAT TEXAS MOSQUITO FESTIVAL. July 26–28. Clute, TX. More than 100 booths: arts and crafts, food, entertainment, novelty-games and carnival. Meet "Willie Man Chew," a 25-ft inflatable mosquito dressed in cowboy boots and hat. Annually, the last Thursday–Saturday in July. Est attendance: 23,000. For info: City of Clute Pks and Rec Dept, PO Box 997, Clute, TX 77531. Phone: (979) 265-8392 or (800) 371-2971. Fax: (979) 265-8767.

HUXLEY, ALDOUS: BIRTH ANNIVERSARY. July 26, 1894. English author, satirist, mystic and philosopher, Aldous Leonard Huxley was born at Godalming, Surrey, England. Best known of his works are *Brave New World* and *Point Counter Point.* Huxley died at Los Angeles, CA, Nov 22, 1963.

JOHN HUNT MORGAN CAPTURED: ANNIVERSARY. July 26, 1863. After harassing Union forces in Tennessee and Ohio throughout the Civil War, Confederate raider John Hunt Morgan was captured at New Lisbon, OH. He was imprisoned in the Ohio Penitentiary, from which he later escaped.

KUBRICK, STANLEY: BIRTH ANNIVERSARY. July 26, 1928. American film writer and producer, born at Bronx, NY. Kubrick started out in photography at the age of 16 with *Look* magazine. His first film, *Day of the Fight,* produced in 1950, was a documentary of his photo series about fighter Walter Cartier. His film credits include *Dr. Strangelove, Full Metal Jacket* and *2001: A Space Odyssey. Eyes Wide Shut,* Kubrick's final film, was released posthumously in the summer of 1999. He died at London, England, Mar 7, 1999.

LAST CHANCE STAMPEDE AND FAIR. July 26–29. Fairgrounds, Helena, MT. Fast-paced Montana rodeo action along with exhibits, carnival rides, 4-H animal judging and Demo-Derby. Annually, the last full weekend in July. Est attendance: 50,000. For info: Loren Davis, 1429 Helena Ave, Helena, MT 59601. Phone: (406) 442-1098. Web: travel.mt.gov.

LIBERIA: INDEPENDENCE DAY. July 26. National holiday. Became republic in 1847, under aegis of the US societies for repatriating former slaves in Africa.

MALDIVES: INDEPENDENCE DAY: ANNIVERSARY. July 26. National holiday. Commemorates independence from Britain in 1965.

NEBRASKA'S BIG RODEO. July 26–28. Fairgrounds, Burwell, NE. Professional rodeo. Contestants compete in four exciting performances in historic, outdoor rodeo arena. Added thrills—chuckwagon races, wild horse races, Dinnerbell Derby, bull fighting Burwell-style, quilt and art shows, parade, flea market, beef and longhorn cattle show, country and western music and dancing and Miss Burwell Rodeo Pageant. Est attendance: 10,000. For info: Peggy Haskell, Garfield County Frontier Fair Assn, Box 747, Burwell, NE 68823. Phone: (308) 346-5210 or (308) 346-5010 July 9–28. Web: www.BurwellNebr.com.

NEW YORK RATIFICATION DAY. July 26, 1788. 11th state to ratify Constitution in 1788.

PUBLICATION OF FIRST ESPERANTO BOOK: ANNIVERSARY. July 26, 1887. To commemorate the anniversary of the publication of Dr. Zamenhof's first textbook about the international language Esperanto. For complete information about Esperanto and this worldwide organization, please send $4 to cover expense of printing and postage. For info: Dr. Stanley J. Drake, Intl Soc of Friendship and Good Will, 8592 Roswell Rd, Ste 434, Atlanta, GA 30350-1870.

RUMSEY REGATTA. July 26–29. Historic Shepherdstown, WV. Featuring events for the whole family including golf tournament, canoe races, river to ridge relay race, Taste of the Town, parade, street dance, hot-air balloon rides and concert in the park. Est attendance: 20,000. For info: Rumsey Regatta, 17 Lowe Dr, Shepherdstown, WV 25443. Phone: (304) 876-7000 or (304) 876-8475.

SENTRY FOODS RIVERFEST. July 26–29. Frame Park, Waukesha, WI. 7th annual. Family festival featuring entertainment, ethnic and traditional food, children's entertainment, arts and crafts marketplace, river activities, carnival midway and more. Est attendance: 55,000. For info: Phone: (262) 542-0330. E-mail: laura@rspr.com.

SHAW, GEORGE BERNARD: BIRTH ANNIVERSARY. July 26, 1856. Irish playwright, essayist, vegetarian, socialist, antivivisectionist and, he said, ." . . one of the hundred best playwrights in the world." Born at Dublin, Ireland. Died at Ayot St. Lawrence, England, Nov 2, 1950.

SPACE MILESTONE: *APOLLO 15* (US): 30th ANNIVERSARY. July 26, 1971. Launched this date. Astronauts David R. Scott and James B. Irwin landed on moon (lunar module *Falcon*) while Alfred M. Worden piloted command module *Endeavor. Rover 1*, a four-wheel vehicle, was used for further exploration. Departed moon Aug 2, after nearly three days. Pacific landing Aug 7.

TOPS INTERNATIONAL RECOGNITION DAYS. July 26–28. Seattle, WA. TOPS (Take Off Pounds Sensibly), the leading non-profit international weight management group, will draw thousands of people throughout the world to celebrate weight-loss support and success. Features include numerous group seminars and workshops, celebration activities and ceremonial events honoring members' weight-loss successes. Est attendance: 4,000. For info: Susan Trones, TOPS Club, Inc, 4575 S Fifth St, Milwaukee, WI 53207. Phone: (414) 482-4620. Web: www.tops.org.

US ARMY FIRST DESEGREGATION: ANNIVERSARY. July 26, 1944. During WWII the US Army ordered desegregation of its training camp facilities. Later the same year black platoons were assigned to white companies in a tentative step toward integration of the battlefield. However, it was not until after the War—July 26, 1948—that President Harry Truman signed an order officially integrating the armed forces.

BIRTHDAYS TODAY

Sandra Bullock, 37, actress (*Speed, While You Were Sleeping*), born Arlington, VA, July 26, 1964.

Blake Edwards, 79, producer, writer, director (*Victor/Victoria, The Pink Panther*), born Tulsa, OK, July 26, 1922.

Susan George, 51, actress (*Straw Dogs*), born London, England, July 26, 1950.

Mick (Michael Philip) Jagger, 58, musician, lead singer (Rolling Stones), born Dartford, England, July 26, 1943.

Helen Mirren, 55, actress ("Prime Suspect"; *The Cook, The Thief, His Wife and Her Lover*), born London, England, July 26, 1946.

Jeremy Piven, 37, actor ("Ellen," *Grosse Pointe Blank*), born Manhattan, NY, July 26, 1964.

Jason Robards, 79, actor (*All the President's Men, Julia, Quick Change*; stage: *The Iceman Cometh, Long Day's Journey into Night*), born Chicago, IL, July 26, 1922.

Kevin Spacey, 42, actor (Oscar for *American Beauty; The Usual Suspects, Working Girl*; stage: *Lost in Yonkers*), born South Orange, NJ, July 26, 1959.

JULY 27 — FRIDAY
Day 208 — 157 Remaining

AIDS NAMED: ANNIVERSARY. July 27, 1982. The Centers for Disease Control adopted Acquired Immune Deficiency Syndrome as the official name for a new disease that was first described in a CDC newsletter on June 5, 1981. The virus that causes AIDS was identified in 1983 and in May 1985 was named Human Immunodeficiency Virus (HIV) by the International Committee on the Taxonomy of Viruses. The first person killed by this disease in the developed world died in 1959. More than 400,000 Americans have died of AIDS. Worldwide, more than 19 million people have died of AIDS.

ARCADIA DAZE. July 27–29. Arcadia, MI. The scenic village of Arcadia is the setting for this midsummer event. Activities include a parade on Sunday at 1:30 PM on Lake Street. An art fair, steak fry, fishing contest, games for the children, pancake breakfast, 5K running race on Saturday and a street dance on Friday and Saturday. An old-fashioned good time for the whole family. Annually, the fourth weekend in July. Sponsor: Arcadia Lion's Club. Est attendance: 2,500. For info: Wesley Hull, Arcadia Daze, 3269 Lake St, Arcadia, MI 49613. Phone: (231) 889-5555.

ATLANTIC TELEGRAPH CABLE LAID: ANNIVERSARY. July 27, 1866. Cable laying successfully completed.

BARBOSA, JOSÉ CELSO: BIRTH ANNIVERSARY. July 27, 1857. Puerto Rican physician and patriot, born at Bayamon, Puerto Rico. His birthday is a holiday in Puerto Rico. He died at San Juan, Puerto Rico, Sept 21, 1921.

BELE CHERE. July 27–29. Asheville, NC. A community celebration featuring a variety of food, music, children's activities and events. The largest free outdoor festival in the Southeast. Annually, the last full weekend in July. Est attendance: 350,000. For info: Paul Clarke, Events Mgr, Asheville Parks & Rec/Festival Division, PO Box 7148, Asheville, NC 28802. Phone: (828) 259-5800. Web: www.belechere.com.

BERNE SWISS DAYS. July 27–28. Berne, IN. Discover Switzerland in Indiana with Swiss food, dancing, yodeling and a parade. See quilt show, art show, "steintoss" contest, polka bands, old-fashioned horse pull, musical, factory tours and more. Est attendance: 75,000. For info: Berne Chamber of Commerce, PO Box 85, Berne, IN 46711. Phone: (219) 589-8080.

CANADA: NOVA SCOTIA BLUEGRASS AND OLD-TIME MUSIC FESTIVAL. July 27–29. Mt Denson, NS. 30th annual family event featuring acoustic music by groups from the US and Canada's Atlantic area. Annually, the last full weekend in July. Est attendance: 3,000. For info: Jerry Murphy, Dir, Downeast Bluegrass Oldtime Music Soc, PO Box 546, Elmsdale, NS, Canada B0N 1M0. Phone: (902) 883-7189. E-mail: MurphJ@chebucto.ns.ca.

CEDAR GROVE HOLLAND FEST. July 27–28. Cedar Grove, WI. Residents celebrate with street scrubbing, klompen dansing, films, wooden shoe races for children, parade, art fair and traditional Dutch foods. The Holland Fest Players perform each evening. Also Holland Festival Run/Walk. Annually, the last Friday and Saturday in July. Est attendance: 10,000. For info: Cedar Grove Holland Fest, PO Box 143, Cedar Grove, WI 53013. Phone: (920) 668-6523. Web: www.hollandfest.com.

CENTRAL NEBRASKA ETHNIC FESTIVAL. July 27–29. Downtown Grand Island, NE. The streets come alive with color, music and foods from all ethnic cultures in the Central Nebraska area. Singing, dancing, eating, laughter and enjoyment for the whole family. Annually, the fourth weekend in July. Est atten-

dance: 40,000. For info: Dianne Kelley, Downtown Dvmt Dir, PO Box 1968, Grand Island, NE 68802. Phone: (308) 385-5444 ext 230. Fax: (308) 385-5423.

DODGE CITY DAYS. July 27–Aug 5. Dodge City, KS. Western heritage celebration with concerts, arts and crafts, parades, PRCA rodeo, street dances, cookouts, art show, antique car show. Est attendance: 75,000. For info: Dodge City Conv & Visitors Bureau, Third & W Wyatt Earp, PO Box 1474, Dodge City, KS 67801. Phone: (800) OLD-WEST. Fax: (316) 225-8268. E-mail: dcvb@pld.com. Web: www.dodgecity.org.

DUMAS, ALEXANDRE (DUMAS FILS): BIRTH ANNIVERSARY. July 27, 1824. French novelist and playwright, as was his father. Author of *La Dame aux Camélias*. Dumas fils was born at Paris, France, and died at Marly-le-Roi, France, Nov 27, 1895.

DUROCHER, LEO: BIRTH ANNIVERSARY. July 27, 1905. Leo Durocher was born at West Springfield, MA. He began his major league baseball career with the New York Yankees in 1925. He also played for the St. Louis Cardinals' "Gashouse Gang" and the Brooklyn Dodgers, where he first served as player-manager in 1939. It was during that season that he used the phrase "Nice guys finish last," which would become his trademark. As a manager, he guided the New York Giants into two World Series. Following a five-year period away from baseball, he resurfaced as a coach with the Los Angeles Dodgers in 1961. In 1966 he signed with the Chicago Cubs as manager. After leaving the Cubs, he spent one season with the Houston Astros, then retired from baseball in 1973. He died Oct 7, 1991, at Palm Springs, CA.

FAIRBANKS SUMMER ARTS FESTIVAL. July 27–Aug 12. University of Alaska, Fairbanks, AK. Two weeks of workshops and concerts involving music, dance, theater, opera theater, figure skating and the visual arts. More than 70 guest artists and instructors from across the nation are featured. Est attendance: 12,500. For info: Jo Ryman Scott, Fairbanks Summer Arts Fest, Box 80845, Fairbanks, AK 99708. Phone: (907) 474-8869. Fax: (907) 479-4329. Web: www.fsaf.org.

FALCON RIDGE FOLK FESTIVAL. July 27–29. Hillsdale, NY. Mainstage concerts, all day and into the night dancing, camping, crafts and workshops. Plenty of activities for everyone in the family to enjoy at Long Hill Farm. For info: Columbia County Tourism Dept, 401 State St, Hudson, NY 12534. Phone: (860) 350-7472 or (860) 364-0366.

	S	M	T	W	T	F	S
July		1	2	3	4	5	6	7
2001	8	9	10	11	12	13	14
	15	16	17	18	19	20	21
	22	23	24	25	26	27	28
	29	30	31				

GERMAN FEST—GEMÜTLICHKEIT. July 27–29. Milwaukee, WI. The largest three-day German festival in the country, featuring a variety of authentic German food specialties, continuous German music and entertainment, German folk dancing, culture exhibits representing all the many regions of Germany, live glockenspiel and spectacular fireworks nightly. Simply Wunderbar! Est attendance: 100,000. For info: German Fest Milwaukee Inc, 8229 W Capitol Dr, Milwaukee, WI 53222. Phone: (414) 464-9444. Fax: (414) 464-3164. Web: www.germanfest.com.

GILROY GARLIC FESTIVAL. July 27–29. Gilroy, CA. Midsummer harvest celebration in the "Garlic Capital of the World." Great garlic recipe contest/cookoff. Ethnic foods, continuous entertainment on three stages, arts, crafts and children's area. Est attendance: 130,000. For info: Gilroy Garlic Festival Assn, PO Box 2311, Gilroy, CA 95021. Phone: (408) 842-1625. Web: www.gilroygarlicfestival.com.

INSULIN FIRST ISOLATED: 80th ANNIVERSARY. July 27, 1921. Dr. Frederick Banting and his assistant at the University of Toronto Medical School, Charles Best, gave insulin to a dog whose pancreas had been removed. In 1922 insulin was first administered to a diabetic, a 14-year-old boy.

IOWA STORYTELLING FESTIVAL. July 27–28. City Park, Clear Lake, IA. This 12th annual storytelling event is held in a scenic lakeside setting. Friday evening "Stories After Dark." Two performances Saturday plus story exchange for novice tellers. Annually, the last Friday and Saturday in July. Est attendance: 800. For info: Jean Casey, Dir, Clear Lake Public Library, 200 N 4th St, Clear Lake, IA 50428. Phone: (515) 357-6133. Fax: (515) 357-4645.

KALAMAZOO COUNTY FLOWERFEST. July 27–29. Bronson Park, Library Lane, Kalamazoo and Portage, MI. Celebration of color and beauty, highlighting the Kalamazoo County bedding plant industry, the largest producer of bedding plants in the nation. Three-dimensional sculptures, floral mounds, flower show, landscape seminars and entertainment. Annually, the fourth weekend in July. Est attendance: 5,000. For info: Kalamazoo County Flowerfest, Inc, PO Box 986, Portage, MI 49081-0986. Phone: (616) 381-3597.

KOREAN WAR ARMISTICE: ANNIVERSARY. July 27, 1953. Armistice agreement ending war that had lasted three years and 32 days was signed at Panmunjom, Korea (July 26, US time) by US and North Korean delegates. Both sides claimed victory at conclusion of two years, 17 days of truce negotiations.

MID AMERICA ALL-INDIAN CENTER POWWOW. July 27–29. Wichita, KS. Each year different tribes of Indians from all over the US come to Wichita to hold ceremonies celebrating their heritage. Authentic arts, crafts and food are available. Traditional dances are performed. Everyone is welcome. Annually, the last full weekend in July. Est attendance: 30,000. For info: Mid America All-Indian Center, 650 N Seneca, Wichita, KS 67203. Phone: (316) 262-5221. Web: www.theindiancenter.com.

MOON PHASE: FIRST QUARTER. July 27. Moon enters First Quarter phase at 6:08 AM, EDT.

MOUNTAIN MAN RENDEZVOUS. July 27–Aug 5. Red Lodge, MT. Montana's fur trapping era is re-created at an authentic mountain men rendezvous camp outside of Red Lodge. The camp residents are from around the country and they offer historical goods and crafts for sale as well as provide an opportunity for visitors to join in their rendezvous celebrations. There is music, dancing, games and food. Est attendance: 8,000. For info: Joan Cline, Red Lodge Chamber of Commerce, PO Box 988, Red Lodge, MT 59068. Phone: (888) 281-0265. Fax: (406) 446-1718. E-mail: information@redlodge.com. Web: www.red lodge.com.

★**NATIONAL KOREAN WAR VETERANS ARMISTICE DAY.** July 27.

OREGON BREWERS FESTIVAL. July 27–29. Tom McCall Waterfront Park, Portland, OR. 72 microbreweries from across the country showcase their handcrafted brews to beer lovers. Annually, the last full weekend in July. Est attendance: 90,000. For info: Chris Crabb, Campbell Productions, PR, 2274 Raleigh St, Portland, OR 97210. Phone: (503) 274-0019. Web: www.oregonbrewfest.com.

OZARK EMPIRE FAIR. July 27–Aug 5. Springfield, MO. Regional fair with carnival, exhibits, livestock and entertainment. Est attendance: 230,000. For info: Ozark Empire Fair, PO Box 630, Springfield, MO 65801. Phone: (417) 833-2660. Fax: (417) 833-3769. Web: www.ozarkempirefair.com.

SNOWBIRD, UTAH JAZZ & BLUES FESTIVAL. July 27–28. Snowbird, UT. Come and join the fun with plenty of jazz and blues music. Festival also includes food booths and much more. Annually, the last weekend in July. Est attendance: 6,000. For info: Snowbird & Ski Summer Resort, Snowbird, UT 84092. Phone: (801) 742-2222. Fax: (801) 933-2298.

STATE CRAFT FAIR. July 27–29. Franklin & Marshall College, Lancaster, PA. Est attendance: 25,000. For info: Pennsylvania Designer Craftsmen, 10 Stable Mill Trail, Richboro, PA 18954. Phone: (800) 684-7440. Web: www.pennsylvaniacrafts.com.

TAKE YOUR HOUSEPLANTS FOR A WALK DAY. July 27. Walking your plants around the neighborhood enables them to know their environment, thereby providing them with a sense of knowing, bringing on wellness. Sponsored by Wellcat Holidays (© 2000 WH) For info: Thomas or Ruth Roy, 2418 Long Ln, Lebanon, PA 17046. Phone: (717) 279-0184. E-mail: wellcat @supernet.com. Web: www.wellcat.com.

TAYLOR HORSEFEST. July 27–28. Taylor, ND. This annual celebration is highlighted by a parade of horses and horse-drawn equipment, ethnic food fest, craft vendors, exhibits, demonstrations, music and cowboy poetry. Horse drawn taxis provide transportation throughout the town during the day. Est attendance: 3,500. For info: (701) 974-2355 or North Dakota Tourism, 604 East Boulevard, Bismarck, ND 58505. Phone: (701) 328-2525 or (800) 435-5663.

THAT FAMOUS PRESTON NIGHT RODEO. July 27–29. Preston, ID. The second under-the-lights rodeo in America, this RCA-approved rodeo has top national cowboys. Est attendance: 16,000. For info: Preston Chamber of Commerce, 23 N State, Preston, ID 83263. Phone: (208) 852-2703. E-mail: pacc@ida com.net.

US DEPARTMENT OF STATE FOUNDED: ANNIVERSARY. July 27, 1789. The first presidential cabinet department, called the Department of Foreign Affairs, was established by the Congress. Later the name was changed to Department of State.

WOMEN ENGINEERS IN TELECOM DAY. July 27. Women engineers in telecom are an extreme minority. They continually come up against men who do not believe they can do the job. These women deserve a day to acknowledge their achievements and commitments. For info: Sandy Van Bemmel, 4001 Main St, Vancouver, WA 98663. Phone: (360) 883-8608. E-mail: sandy _vanbemmel@gstworld.net.

BIRTHDAYS TODAY

Peggy Gale Fleming, 53, Olympic gold medal figure skater, sportscaster, born San Jose, CA, July 27, 1948.

Bobbie Gentry (Roberta Streeter), 59, singer, songwriter ("Ode to Billie Joe"), born Chicasaw County, MS, July 27, 1942.

Norman Lear, 79, TV scriptwriter, producer ("All in the Family," "Maude"), born New Haven, CT, July 27, 1922.

Maureen McGovern, 52, singer ("The Morning After"), actress, born Youngstown, OH, July 27, 1949.

Alex Rodriguez, 26, baseball player, born New York, NY, July 27, 1975.

Betty Thomas, 53, director, actress ("Hill Street Blues"), born St. Louis, MO, July 27, 1948.

Jerry Van Dyke, 70, actor ("Coach," "Teen Angel"), born Danville, IL, July 27, 1931.

James Victor, 62, actor (*Fuzz, Stand and Deliver*), born Santiago, Dominican Republic, July 27, 1939.

JULY 28 — SATURDAY
Day 209 — 156 Remaining

AG DAYS—DOWN ON THE FARM. July 28–29. Old Cowtown Museum, Wichita, KS. Visitors will experience hands-on activities highlighting typical 1880s Sedgwick County farming. Horse-powered threshing, grain cleaning, rendering, canning and more is featured. Modern-day equipment display will contrast the 19th-century equipment. Annually, the last weekend in July. Est attendance: 1,000. For info: Gloria G. Campbell, Dir, Old Cowtown Museum, 1871 Sim Park Dr, Wichita, KS 67203. Phone: (316) 264-0671. Fax: (316) 264-2937.

ALL-AMERICAN SOAP BOX DERBY. July 28. Derby Downs, Akron, OH. A weeklong festival culminating in world championship race by regional champs from US, Canada, Germany, Venezuela and the Philippines. 64th annual derby. Est attendance: 20,000. For info: Jeff Iula, Genl Mgr, Intl Soap Box Derby, Inc, PO Box 7225, Derby Downs, Akron, OH 44306. Phone: (330) 733-8723. Fax: (330) 733-1370. E-mail: 2077607 @mcimail.com. Web: pages.prodigy.com/soapbox.

ALLEGANY COUNTY INVITATIONAL DRUM AND BUGLE CORPS CHAMPIONSHIPS. July 28. Cumberland, MD. Eastern Regional Senior Drum and Bugle Corps Championship featuring 10 drum and bugle corps competing for top honors. Annually, the last Saturday in July. Est attendance: 7,000. For info: Drumfest, PO Box 3571, LaVale, MD 21504. Phone: (301) 777-8325.

July 2001	S	M	T	W	T	F	S
	1	2	3	4	5	6	7
	8	9	10	11	12	13	14
	15	16	17	18	19	20	21
	22	23	24	25	26	27	28
	29	30	31				

BLACK HILLS JAZZ AND BLUES FESTIVAL. July 28. Memorial Park, Rapid City, SD. Outdoor music festival features national recording jazz and blues musicians and bands in a beautiful park setting. Est attendance: 2,500. For info: Rapid City Arts Council, 713 Seventh St, Rapid City, SD 57701. Phone: (605) 394-4101. E-mail: rcacaafd@rapidnet.com.

BLUE RIDGE DRAFT HORSE AND MULE SHOW. July 28. Ferrum, VA. One of the largest shows in the mid-Atlantic region, the event features 52 competitive classes for horses and mules. Show features major breeds of draft horses, more than 100 horses and mules from five states as well as crafts, music and food. Annually, the fourth Saturday in July. Est attendance: 1,500. For info: Blue Ridge Institute, c/o Ferrum College, Rt 40 West, Ferrum, VA 24088. Phone: (540) 365-4416.

CELEBRATION OF OUR LADY OF THE SNOWS. July 28–Aug 5. Belleville, IL. Eucharistic Celebration invites the public to celebrate the patroness of the Shrine at the Outdoor Amphitheatre. A candlelight procession will close the services. Est attendance: 7,500. For info: Shrine of Our Lady of the Snows, 442 S DeMazenod Dr, Belleville, IL 62223-1094. Phone: (618) 397-6700. Fax: (618) 397-1210. Web: www.snows.org.

FIRST ASSEMBLY DAY. July 28–29. Jamestown, Colonial National Historical Park, Yorktown, VA. Living history interpreters commemorate the beginning of representative government in the new world. Est attendance: 2,000. For info: Public Affairs Officer, Colonial Natl Historical Park, PO Box 210, Yorktown, VA 23690. Phone: (757) 229-1733. Web: www.nps.gov/colo.

HAMBURG FIRESTORM: ANNIVERSARY. July 28, 1943. More than 42,000 civilians were killed when 2,326 tons of bombs, predominantly incendiaries, were dropped on Hamburg, Germany, by the Allies on this date. At the center of the firestorm the winds uprooted trees, and flames burned eight square miles in the eight hours the fire lasted. A firestorm occurs when the fires in a given area become so intense they devour all the oxygen nearby and suck more into themselves creating hurricane-force winds which feed the fires and move them at great speeds.

HANOVER DUTCH FESTIVAL. July 28. Hanover, PA. Handmade crafts, ethnic foods, music, entertainment, children's carnival, petting zoo, antique car show. Est attendance: 10,000. For info: Hanover Area Chamber of Commerce, 146 Carlisle St, Hanover, PA 17331. Phone: (717) 637-6130.

HEYWARD, THOMAS: BIRTH ANNIVERSARY. July 28, 1746. American Revolutionary soldier, signer of the Declaration of Independence. Died Mar 6, 1809.

HOT AUGUST NIGHTS. July 28–Aug 5. Reno and Sparks, NV. Celebration of the music and hot rods of the '50s and '60s features show and shine, parade, cruises, proms and concerts by the entertainers of the era. For info: Phone: (775) 356-1956.

MID-SUMMER ANTIQUES AND COLLECTIBLES SHOW AND SALE. July 28–29. Millville, NJ. Rain or shine. Est attendance: 2,000. For info: Wheaton Village, 1501 Glasstown Rd, Millville, NJ 08332. Phone: (856) 825-6800 or (800) 998-4552. Fax: (856) 825-2410. E-mail: mail@wheatonvillage.org. Web: www.wheatonvillage.org.

MONTANA STATE FAIR. July 28–Aug 4. Great Falls, MT. Horse racing, petting zoo, carnival, discount days, nightly entertainment and plenty of food. Est attendance: 200,000. For info: Kelly Michel, State Fair, Box 1888, Great Falls, MT 59403. Phone: (406) 727-8900. Fax: (406) 452-8955.

NATHAN HALE ANCIENT FIFES AND DRUMS COLONIAL ENCAMPMENT AND MUSTER. July 28–29. Nathan Hale Homestead, Coventry, CT. Colonial battle reenactments, camplife demonstrations, colonial fashion show, open-hearth cooking and colonial crafts are highlights on Saturday. On Sunday, in addition to the above there is also a battle of colonial bands when fife and drum corps amass for a muster. Annually, the last weekend in July. Est attendance: 5,000. For info: The Nathan Hale Homestead, 2299 South St, Coventry, CT 06238. Phone: (860) 742-6917.

ONASSIS, JACQUELINE LEE BOUVIER KENNEDY: BIRTH ANNIVERSARY. July 28, 1929. Editor, widow of John Fitzgerald Kennedy (35th president of the US), born at Southampton, NY. Later married (Oct 20, 1968) Greek shipping magnate Aristotle Socrates Onassis, who died Mar 15, 1975. The widely admired and respected former First Lady died May 19, 1994, at New York City.

PERU: INDEPENDENCE DAY. July 28. San Martin declared independence in 1821. After the final defeat of Spanish troops by Simon Bolivar in 1824, Spanish rule ended.

POTTER, (HELEN) BEATRIX: BIRTH ANNIVERSARY. July 28, 1866. Author and illustrator of the Peter Rabbit stories for children, born at London, England. Died at Sawrey, Lancashire, Dec 22, 1943.

QUILT SHOW. July 28–Aug 22. Woodstock, VT. A juried showing of quilts made by Windsor County quilters, displayed with selected 19th-century Vermont quilts. Daily quilting demonstrations and activities. Est attendance: 9,700. For info: Billings Farm and Museum, PO Box 489, Woodstock, VT 05091. Phone: (802) 457-2355. Fax: (802) 457-4663. E-mail: billings.farm@valley.net.

"THE SAMMY KAYE SHOW" TV PREMIERE: 50th ANNIVERSARY. July 28, 1951. CBS's musical program hosted by bandleader Sammy Kaye swayed audiences to swinging tunes on Saturday nights.

SINGING TELEGRAM: ANNIVERSARY. July 28, 1933. Anniversary of the first singing telegram, said to have been delivered to singer Rudy Vallee on his 32nd birthday. Early singing telegrams often were delivered in person by uniformed messengers on bicycle. Later they were usually sung over the telephone.

SPACE MILESTONE: *RANGER 7* (US). July 28, 1964. Unmanned moon probe transmitted back to Earth 4,308 close-up photographs of moon.

SPACE MILESTONE: *SKYLAB 3* (US). July 28, 1973. Alan L. Bean, Owen K. Garriott and Jack R. Lousma started 59-day mission in the space station to test man's space flight endurance. Pacific splashdown Sept 25.

TERRY FOX DAY: BIRTH ANNIVERSARY. July 28, 1958. With cancer requiring amputation of his right leg at age 18, Fox was determined to devote his life to a fight against the disease. His "Marathon of Hope," a planned 5,200-mile run westward across Canada, started Apr 12, 1980, at St. John's, Newfoundland, and continued 3,328 miles to Thunder Bay, Ontario, Sept 1, 1980, when he was forced to stop by spread of the disease. During the run (on an artificial leg) he raised $24 million for cancer research and inspired millions with his courage. Terry Fox was born at Winnipeg, Manitoba, and died at New Westminster (near Vancouver), British Columbia, Canada, June 28, 1981.

TIDEWATER ARCHAEOLOGY DIG. July 28–29. St. Mary's City, MD. Hands-on opportunity to dig at an archaeology site at Maryland's first capital. Special behind-the-scenes tours. Annually, usually the last weekend in July. Est attendance: 1,000. For info: Visitors Services, Historic St. Mary's City, PO Box 39, St. Mary's City, MD 20686. Phone: (301) 862-0990 or (800) SMC-1634. Fax: (301) 862-0968. Web: www.smcm.edu/hsmc/.

VALLEE, RUDY: 100th BIRTH ANNIVERSARY. July 28, 1901. American singer, saxophone player and radio idol of millions during the 1930s. Born Hubert Prior Vallee, at Island Pond, VT, the crooner used a megaphone to amplify his voice and introduced his performances with the salutation, "Heigh-ho-everybody!" Vallee appeared in a number of movies, including *How to Succeed in Business Without Really Trying*. Among his best-remembered songs are "I'm Just a Vagabond Lover," "Cheerful Little Earful," "Say It Isn't So" and his signature song, "My Time Is Your Time." Vallee died at age 84 at North Hollywood, CA, July 3, 1986.

VETERANS BONUS ARMY EVICTION: ANNIVERSARY. July 28, 1932. Some 15,000 unemployed veterans of World War I marched on Washington, DC, in the summer of 1932, demanding payment of a war bonus. After two months' encampment in Washington's Anacostia Flats, eviction of the bonus marchers by the US Army was ordered by President Herbert Hoover. Under the leadership of General Douglas MacArthur, Major Dwight D. Eisenhower and Major George S. Patton, Jr (among others), cavalry, tanks and infantry attacked. Fixed bayonets, tear gas and the burning of the veterans' tents hastened the end of the confrontation. One death was reported.

WORLD WAR I BEGINS: ANNIVERSARY. July 28, 1914. Archduke Francis Ferdinand of Austria-Hungary and his wife were assassinated at Sarajevo, Bosnia, by a Serbian nationalist June 28, 1914, touching off the conflict that became WWI. Austria-Hungary declared war on Serbia July 28, the formal beginning of the war. Within weeks, Germany entered the war on the side of Austria-Hungary and Russia, France and Great Britain on the side of Serbia.

BIRTHDAYS TODAY

William Warren (Bill) Bradley, 58, former US senator, Basketball Hall of Fame forward, born Crystal City, MO, July 28, 1943.

Jim Davis, 56, cartoonist ("Garfield"), born Marion, IN, July 28, 1945.

Alberto Fujimori, 63, president of Peru, born Lima, Peru, July 28, 1938.

Darryl Hickman, 70, actor ("The Many Loves of Dobie Gillis," "The Americans"), born Los Angeles, CA, July 28, 1931.

Linda Kelsey, 55, actress ("Lou Grant"), born Minneapolis, MN, July 28, 1946.

Lori Loughlin, 37, actress ("Full House," *Back to the Beach*), born Long Island, NY, July 28, 1964.

Jacques Piccard, 79, inventor, explorer, born Brussels, Belgium, July 28, 1922.

Sally Struthers, 53, actress ("All in the Family"), born Portland, OR, July 28, 1948.

Rick Wright, 56, singer, musician (keyboard player with Pink Floyd), born London, England, July 28, 1945.

JULY 29 — SUNDAY

Day 210 — 155 Remaining

INDIANAPOLIS SUNK: ANNIVERSARY. July 29, 1945. After delivering the atomic bomb to Tinian Island, the American cruiser *Indianapolis* was headed for Okinawa to train for the invasion of Japan when it was torpedoed by a Japanese submarine. Of 1,196 crew members, more than 350 were immediately killed in the explosion or went down with the ship. There were no rescue ships nearby, and those fortunate enough to survive endured the next 84 hours in ocean waters. By the time they were spotted by air on Aug 2, only 318 sailors remained alive, the others either having drowned or been eaten by sharks. This is the US Navy's worst loss at sea.

LAVALLETTE HERITAGE ARTS AND CRAFTS SHOW.
July 29. Lavallette, NJ. Juried arts, crafts and antiques show. Only the best of the best welcome to exhibit. One of the best shows on the eastern seaboard. 3 PM to dark. Annually, the last Sunday in July. Est attendance: 20,000. For info: Joy Grosko, Heritage Committee of Lavallette, 13 Camden Ave, Lavallette, NJ 08735. Phone: (732) 793-3652.

MUSSOLINI, BENITO: BIRTH ANNIVERSARY. July 29, 1883. Italian Fascist leader, born at Dovia, Italy. Self-styled "Il Duce" (the leader), Mussolini governed Italy, first as prime minister and later as absolute dictator, 1922–43. Reportedly, under his regime "the trains ran on time." It was Mussolini who said: "War alone . . . puts the stamp of nobility upon the peoples who have the courage to face it." But military defeat of Italy in World War II was Mussolini's downfall. Repudiated and arrested by the Italian government, he was temporarily rescued by German paratroops in 1943. Later, as they attempted to flee in disguise to Switzerland, he and his mistress, Clara Petacci, were killed by Italian partisans near Lake Como, Italy, Apr 28, 1945.

NASA ESTABLISHED: ANNIVERSARY. July 29, 1958. President Eisenhower signed a bill creating the National Aeronautics and Space Administration to direct US space policy.

NORWAY: OLSOK EVE. July 29. Commemorates Norway's Viking king St. Olav, who fell in battle at Stiklestad near Trondheim, Norway, July 29, 1030. Bonfires, historical pageants.

★ **PARENTS' DAY.** July 29. To pay tribute to the men and women across our country whose devotion as parents strengthens our society and forms the foundation for a bright future for America. Public Law 103-362. Annually, the fourth Sunday in July.

RAIN DAY AT WAYNESBURG, PENNSYLVANIA. July 29. Legend has it that rain will fall at Waynesburg, PA, on July 29 as it has most years for the last century, according to local records in this community, which was laid out in 1796 and incorporated in 1816.

ROOSEVELT, ALICE HATHAWAY LEE: BIRTH ANNIVERSARY. July 29, 1861. First wife of Theodore Roosevelt, 26th President of the US, whom she married in 1880. Born at Chestnut Hill, MA, she died at New York, NY, Feb 14, 1884.

TARKINGTON, BOOTH: BIRTH ANNIVERSARY. July 29, 1869. American novelist (*The Magnificent Ambersons*), born at Indianapolis, IN. Died there May 19, 1946.

TISHA B'AV OR FAST OF AB. July 29. Hebrew calendar date: Ab 9, 5761. Commemorates and mourns the destruction of the first and second Temples in Jerusalem (586 BC and AD 70).

W.C. HANDY MUSIC FESTIVAL. July 29–Aug 4. Florence, AL. A weeklong street-strutting, toe-tapping and hand-clapping celebration of the musical heritage of Florence native W.C. Handy—"the father of the blues"—culminating in a spectacular Saturday-evening concert. Also includes athletic events. Est attendance: 150,000. For info: Nancy Gonce, Exec Dir, Music Preservation Soc, PO Box 1827, Florence, AL 35631. Phone: (256) 766-7642 or (800) 47-BLUES. Fax: (256) 766-7549. Web: www.wchandyfest.org.

WORLD FUTURE SOCIETY ANNUAL CONFERENCE. July 29–31. Minneapolis Hilton & Towers Hotel, Minneapolis, MN. For info: World Future Society, 7910 Woodmont Ave, Ste 450, Bethesda, MD 20814. Phone: (800) 989-8274. Fax: (301) 951-0394. Web: www.wfs.org.

July 2001	S	M	T	W	T	F	S
	1	2	3	4	5	6	7
	8	9	10	11	12	13	14
	15	16	17	18	19	20	21
	22	23	24	25	26	27	28
	29	30	31				

WSBA/WARM 103 SUMMER CRAFT SHOW/CHRISTMAS IN JULY. July 29. York Fairgrounds, York, PA. More than 150 crafts, from country to contemporary, Victorian and southwestern, handcrafted furniture, wood carvings, dolls, jewelry, pottery, collectibles, quilts, baskets and much more. Admission fee. Est attendance: 5,000. For info: Joe Alfano, Asst Promo Dir, PO Box 910, York, PA 17402-0910. Phone: (717) 764-1155. Fax: (717) 252-4708. E-mail: jalfano@suscom.com.

ZAMBIA: MUTOMBOKO CEREMONY. July 29. Ancient annual ceremony to honor Senior Chief, the traditional leader of the Luunda peoples of the Luapula Province in north-central Zambia. Joyous communal party and cultural get-together.

BIRTHDAYS TODAY

Debbie Black, 35, basketball player, born Philadelphia, PA, July 29, 1966.

Ken Burns, 48, documentary filmmaker ("Civil War" series), born New York, NY, July 29, 1953.

Elizabeth Hanford Dole, 65, former president, American Red Cross, former secretary of transportation and secretary of labor, born Salisbury, NC, July 29, 1936.

Peter Jennings, 63, journalist (anchorman for "ABC Evening News"), born Toronto, Ontario, Canada, July 29, 1938.

Martina McBride, 35, country singer, born Medicine Lodge, KS, July 29, 1966.

Ronnie Musgrove, 45, Governor of Mississippi (R), born David Ronald Musgrove, Panola County, MS, July 29, 1956.

Alexandra Paul, 38, actress ("Baywatch," *Dragnet*), born New York, NY, July 29, 1963.

Marilyn Tucker Quayle, 52, former Second Lady, born Indianapolis, IN, July 29, 1949.

Patty Scialfa, 45, singer, born Deal, NJ, July 29, 1956.

Paul Taylor, 71, dancer, choreographer, born Allegheny, NY, July 29, 1930.

David Warner, 60, actor ("Holocaust," *Tron*), born Manchester, England, July 29, 1941.

Wil Wheaton, 29, actor ("Star Trek: The Next Generation," *Stand by Me*), born Burbank, CA, July 29, 1972.

JULY 30 — MONDAY
Day 211 — 154 Remaining

BRONTE, EMILY: BIRTH ANNIVERSARY. July 30, 1818. English novelist, one of the Brontë sisters, best known for *Wuthering Heights*. Born at Thornton, Yorkshire, England. Died Dec 19, 1848, at Haworth, Yorkshire, England.

FINLAND: LAHTI ORGAN FESTIVAL. July 30–Aug 5. Lahti. Annual festival emphasizing organ music. Also, choirs, orchestras, instrumental groups and solo artists. Plus master classes, seminars and panel discussions. Est attendance: 15,000. For info: Finnish Tourist Board, 655 Third Ave, New York, NY 10017. Phone: (212) 885-9700 or (358) (3) 782-3184. Fax: (358) (3) 783-2190 or Lahti Organ Festival, Kirkkokatu 5, 15110 Lahti, Finland. Fax: 358-3-783 2190. E-mail: lof@pp.phnet.fi.

FORD, HENRY: BIRTH ANNIVERSARY. July 30, 1863. Industrialist Henry Ford, whose assembly-line method of automobile production revolutionized the industry, was born at Wayne County, MI, on the family farm. His Model T made up half of the world's output of cars during its years of production. Ford built racing cars until, in 1903, he and his partners formed the Ford Motor Company. In 1908 the company presented the Model T, which was produced until 1927, and in 1913 Ford introduced the assembly line and mass production. This innovation reduced the time it took to build each car from 12½ hours to only 1½. This enabled Ford to sell cars for $500, making automobile ownership a possibility for an unprecedented percentage of the population. He is also remembered for introducing a $5-a-day wage for automotive workers and for his statement: "History is bunk." Died Apr 7, 1947 at age 83 at Dearborn, MI, where his manufacturing complex was located.

HILL, ANITA FAYE: 45th BIRTHDAY. July 30, 1956. Law professor Anita Hill, born on an Oklahoma farm, forever changed public attitudes about sexual harassment of women. In her nationally televised testimony in October 1991 during the Senate Judiciary Committee's confirmation hearings on the nomination of Clarence Thomas to the Supreme Court, she accused Thomas of sexual harassment. From a rural upbringing as the youngest of 13 children, this Yale graduate became one of the nation's best-known and most-admired women.

HOFFA, JAMES: DISAPPEARANCE ANNIVERSARY. July 30, 1975. Former Teamsters Union leader, 62-year-old James Riddle Hoffa was last seen on this date outside a restaurant in Bloomfield Township, near Detroit, MI. His 13-year federal prison sentence had been commuted by former President Richard M. Nixon in 1971. On Dec 8, 1982, seven years and 131 days after his disappearance, an Oakland County judge declared Hoffa officially dead as of July 30, 1982.

MOORE, HENRY: BIRTH ANNIVERSARY. July 30, 1898. English sculptor born at Castleford, Yorkshire. Died at Hertfordshire, Aug 31, 1986.

PAPERBACK BOOKS INTRODUCED: ANNIVERSARY. July 30, 1935. Although books bound in soft covers were first introduced in 1841 at Leipzig, Germany, by Christian Bernhard Tauchnitz, the modern paperback revolution dates to the publication of the first Penguin paperback by Sir Allen Lane at London in 1935. Penguin Number 1 was *Ariel*, a life of Shelley by Andre Maurois.

SOUTH DAKOTA STATE FAIR. July 30–Aug 5. Huron, SD. Grandstand entertainment nightly, 10 free stages with multiple shows daily, hundreds of commercial exhibits and thousands of livestock exhibits. One of the largest agricultural fairs in the US. Est attendance: 250,000. For info: Craig Atkins, Mgr, South Dakota State Fair, PO Box 1275, Huron, SD 57350-1275. Phone: (605) 353-7340 or (800) 529-0900. Fax: (605) 353-7348. E-mail: statefair@state.sd.us.

STENGEL, CHARLES DILLON (CASEY): BIRTH ANNIVERSARY. July 30, 1890. Baseball Hall of Fame outfielder and manager born at Kansas City, MO. His success as manager of the New York Yankees (10 pennants and 7 World Series titles in 12 years) made him one of the game's enduring stars. Inducted into the Hall of Fame in 1966. Died at Glendale, CA, Sept 29, 1975.

"TIC TAC DOUGH" TV PREMIERE: 45th ANNIVERSARY. July 30, 1956. Game show premiered on CBS with Jay Jackson, Jack Barry, Gene Rayburn and Bill Wendell serving as hosts during its three-year run. Two contestants play tic-tac-toe by answering questions in a selected category. The show was resurrected in 1978 with Wink Martindale as host.

US WOMEN'S AMATEUR (GOLF) CHAMPIONSHIP. July 30–Aug 4. Flint Hills National Golf Club, Andover, KS. For info: US Golf Assn, Golf House, PO Box 708, Championship Dept, Far Hills, NJ 07931. Phone: (908) 234-2300. Fax: (908) 234-9687. Web: www.usga.org.

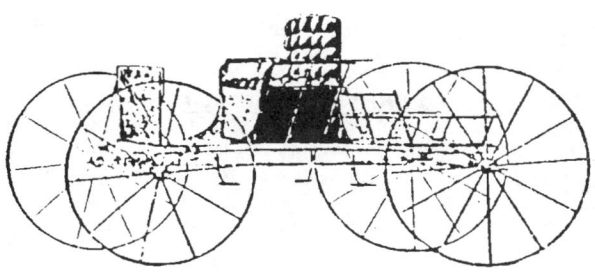

VANUATU: INDEPENDENCE DAY: ANNIVERSARY. July 30. Vanuatu became an independent republic in 1980 (from France and the UK) and observes its national holiday.

VEBLEN, THORSTEIN: BIRTH ANNIVERSARY. July 30, 1857. American economist, born at Valders, WI, and died at Menlo Park, CA, Aug 3, 1929. "Conspicuous consumption," he wrote in *The Theory of the Leisure Class*, "of valuable goods is a means of reputability to the gentleman of leisure."

WORLD FOOTBAG CHAMPIONSHIPS. July 30–Aug 5. Denver, CO. Seven-day sports event spotlights competition of footskills—the Super Bowl of footbag (also known as Hacky Sack ®)! Now in its 22nd year, it attracts the world's top footbag competitors from the US and six other countries. Prize money exceeds $10,000. Sponsors: Wham-O, Sipa Sipa Footbags and The World Footbag Association. Est attendance: 5,000. For info: Bruce Guettich, Dir, World Footbag Assn, PO Box 775208, Steamboat Springs, CO 80477. Phone: (800) 878-8797. Fax: (970) 870-2846. E-mail: wfa@worldfootbag.com. Web: www.worldfootbag.com.

BIRTHDAYS TODAY

Paul Anka, 60, singer, songwriter ("Diana," "My Way" for Frank Sinatra), born Ottawa, Ontario, Canada, July 30, 1941.

Peter Bogdanovich, 62, producer, director (*The Last Picture Show, Paper Moon*), born Kingston, NY, July 30, 1939.

Delta Burke, 45, actress ("Designing Women"), former Miss Florida, born Orlando, FL, July 30, 1956.

Kate Bush, 43, singer ("The Man with the Child in His Eyes"), songwriter, born Lewisham, England, July 30, 1958.

Edd Byrnes, 68, actor ("77 Sunset Strip," *Darby's Rangers*), born New York, NY, July 30, 1933.

Laurence Fishburne, 40, actor (*Boyz N the Hood, What's Love Got to Do with It, Higher Learning*; stage: *Two Trains Running* [Tony Award]), born Augusta, GA, July 30, 1961.

Anita Faye Hill, 45, law professor, born on an Oklahoma farm, July 30, 1956.

Lisa Kudrow, 38, actress ("Friends," *Romy and Michele's High School Reunion*), born Encino, CA, July 30, 1963.

Christopher Paul (Chris) Mullin, 38, basketball player, born New York, NY, July 30, 1963.

Ken Olin, 47, actor ("LA Doctors," "thirtysomething"), born Chicago, IL, July 30, 1954.

David Sanborn, 56, saxophonist, composer, born Tampa, FL, July 30, 1945.

Arnold Schwarzenegger, 54, bodybuilder, actor (*The Terminator, Twins, True Lies*), born Graz, Austria, July 30, 1947.

Allan Huber "Bud" Selig, 67, Commissioner of Baseball, born Milwaukee, WI, July 30, 1934.

Eleanor Marie Cutri Smeal, 62, feminist (former president of NOW), born Ashtabula, OH, July 30, 1939.

Hilary Swank, 27, actress (Oscar for *Boys Don't Cry*), born Lincoln, NE, July 30, 1974.

JULY 31 — TUESDAY
Day 212 — 153 Remaining

FEAST OF SAINT IGNATIUS OF LOYOLA. July 31. 1491–1556. Founder of the Society of Jesus and Jesuits. Canonized in 1622.

FIRST US GOVERNMENT BUILDING: ANNIVERSARY. July 31, 1792. The cornerstone of the Philadelphia Mint, the first US government building, was laid on this day.

KENNEDY-CHENG UNITED NATIONS MEMBERSHIP SUMMIT: 40th ANNIVERSARY. July 31, 1961. President John F. Kennedy agreed during talks held with General Chen Cheng July 31–Aug 1, 1961, to support Nationalist China in its bid for UN membership and oppose the admission of Communist China to the United Nations.

KENNEDY INTERNATIONAL AIRPORT DEDICATION: ANNIVERSARY. July 31, 1948. New York's International Airport at Idlewild Field was dedicated by President Harry S Truman. It was later renamed John F. Kennedy International Airport.

MELVILLE MARATHON. July 31–Aug 1. Mystic Seaport, Mystic, CT. Marathon reading of the classic *Moby-Dick* in celebration of Herman Melville's birthday. Reading takes place on deck and in foc's'le of the last wooden whaler, *Charles W. Morgan.* Annually, 24-hour reading from noon July 31 to noon Aug 1. Est attendance: 6,000. For info: Mystic Seaport, 75 Greenmanville Ave, PO Box 6000, Mystic, CT 06355-0990. Phone: (860) 572-5315 or (888) 9-SEAPORT. Web: www.mysticseaport.org.

SALVADOR, FRANCIS: 225th DEATH ANNIVERSARY. July 31, 1776. The first Jew to die in the American Revolution, Salvador was also the first Jew elected to office in colonial America. He was voted a member of the South Carolina Provincial Congress in January 1775.

TEXAS COUNTY FAIR/OLD SETTLERS REUNION. July 31–Aug 4 (tentative). Fair Grounds, Houston, MO. A fun festival with arts and crafts, carnival midway, gospel music concert, country bands and demolition derby. Est attendance: 8,000. For info: Texas County Fair/Old Settlers Reunion, 111 W Main, Houston, MO 65483. Phone: (417) 967-2220. Fax: (417) 967-2178.

TRINIDAD: SIGHTED BY COLUMBUS: ANNIVERSARY. July 31, 1498. Christopher Columbus first sighted the island that he called La Trinidad. The island was inhabited by two tribes of "Indians," the Arawaks, who were peaceful fishermen and farmers, and the more belligerent Caribs. Upon his return to Spain, Columbus described the islands to the King as very lush and pleasant, and soon the Spaniards began to colonize them. Trinidad and Tobago remained under Spanish rule from 1498 until Feb 18, 1797, when the Spanish Governor, Chacon, surrendered the islands to the British Navy. British rule continued until 1962 when Trinidad and Tobago gained their independence, after having been self-governing since 1956. (Info provided by the Trinidad and Tobago Tourism Development Authority.)

US PATENT OFFICE OPENS: ANNIVERSARY. July 31, 1790. The first US Patent Office opened its doors and the first US patent was issued to Samuel Hopkins of Vermont for a new method of making pearlash and potash. The patent was signed by George Washington and Thomas Jefferson.

ZIMBABWE: INTERNATIONAL BOOK FAIR. July 31–Aug 4. Open to the public Aug 3–4. Celebrate literature and reading, meet publishers, librarians and booksellers. For info: David Brine, Zimbabwe International Book Fair Limited, PO Box 21303, London, England. Phone: (44) (171) 836-8501. Fax: Same as Phone. E-mail: zibf.kingstreet@dial.pipex.com. Web: www.mediazw.com/zibf.

BIRTHDAYS TODAY

Dean Cain, 35, actor ("Lois & Clark: The New Adventures of Superman"), born Mount Clemens, MI, July 31, 1966.

Geraldine Chaplin, 57, actress (*Nashville, Roseland, Chaplin*), born Santa Monica, CA, July 31, 1944.

Milton Friedman, 89, economist, journalist, born Brooklyn, NY, July 31, 1912.

Evonne Goolagong, 50, former tennis player, born Griffith, Australia, July 31, 1951.

Irv Kupcinet, 89, former TV talk-show host, columnist, born Chicago, IL, July 31, 1912.

Sherry Lansing, 57, producer (*Fatal Attraction, The Accused*), born Chicago, IL, July 31, 1944.

Gary Lewis, 55, singer ("This Diamond Ring"), born New York, NY, July 31, 1946.

Don Murray, 72, actor (*Bus Stop*, "Knots Landing"), born Hollywood, CA, July 31, 1929.

France Nuyen, 62, actress ("St. Elsewhere"), born Marseilles, France, July 31, 1939.

J.K. Rowling, 36, author (the Harry Potter series), born Joanne Rowling, Bristol, England, July 31, 1965.

Wesley Snipes, 39, actor (*Jungle Fever, White Men Can't Jump, Rising Sun*), born Orlando, FL, July 31, 1962.

August.

AUGUST 1 — WEDNESDAY
Day 213 — 152 Remaining

ABBOTT'S MAGIC GET-TOGETHER (WITH TALENT CONTESTS). Aug 1–4. Colon, MI. Magic convention. Est attendance: 3,000. For info: Abbott's Magic Co, 124 St. Joseph St, Colon, MI 49040. Phone: (616) 432-3235. Fax: (616) 432-3357. E-mail: amagic@net-link.net. Web: www.abbott-magic.com.

ADMIT YOU'RE HAPPY MONTH. Aug 1–31. This month encourages people to express happiness and discourages parade-raining. Visit our website to find out about activities. For info: Pam Johnson, 5330 N MacArthur Blvd, 148-215, Irving, TX 75038. Phone: (972) 471-1485. E-mail: pjohnson@sohp.com. Web: www.sohp.com.

AMERICAN HISTORY ESSAY CONTEST. Aug 1–Dec 15. American History Committee activities are promoted throughout the year with the essay contest conducted in grades 5–8 beginning in August. Essays are submitted for judging by Dec 15, with the winners announced in April at the Daughters of the American Revolution Continental Congress. Events vary, but include programs, displays, spot announcements and recognition of essay writers. Essay topic can be obtained from DAR Headquarters. For info: Natl Soc Daughters of the American Revolution, Office of the Historian-General, Admin Bldg, 1776 D St NW, Washington, DC 20006-5392. Phone: (202) 628-1776.

BENIN, PEOPLE'S REPUBLIC OF: NATIONAL DAY: ANNIVERSARY. Aug 1. Public holiday. Commemorates independence from France in 1960. Benin at that time was known as Dahomey.

BROWN, RONALD H.: 60th BIRTH ANNIVERSARY. Aug 1, 1941. Born at Washington, DC, Ronald H. Brown grew up in Harlem and studied at Middlebury College in Vermont. After graduating from St. John's University law school, Brown served as chief council for the Senate Judiciary Committee. He went on to become the first African-American partner at the law firm of Patton Boggs & Blow, the first African-American leader of the Democratic National Committee and later served as the US Secretary of Commerce during the Clinton administration. Brown died in a plane crash at Dubrovnik, Croatia, Apr 3, 1996, while on government business.

BROWNIES AT BRUNCH. Aug 1–31. Decatur, IL. Celebrate 100+ years of the American brownie. Exotic flavors, served with seasonal berries, juice bar, New Salem cider. For info: Chocolate Research Library, 202 E North St, Decatur, IL 62523. Phone: (217) 422-7933.

BURK, MARTHA (CALAMITY JANE): DEATH ANNIVERSARY. Aug 1, 1903. Known as a frontierswoman and companion to Wild Bill Hickock, Calamity Jane Burk was born Martha Jane Canary at Princeton, MO, in May 1852. As a young girl living in Montana, she became an excellent markswoman. She went to the Black Hills of South Dakota as a scout for a geological expedition in 1875. Several opposing traditions account for her nickname, one springing from her kindness to the less fortunate, while another attributes it to the harsh warnings she would give men who would offend her. She died Aug 1, 1903, at Terry, SD, and was buried at Deadwood, SD, next to Wild Bill Hickock.

CANADA: MUSKOKA DISTRICT KENNEL CLUB CHAMPIONSHIP SHOW. Aug 1–3. Bracebridge Fairgrounds, Bracebridge, ON. For info: Muskoka Dist Kennel Club, Bracebridge C of C, 1-1 Manitoba St, Bracebridge, ON, Canada P1L-1S4. Phone: (705) 645-5801. E-mail: bracecha@muskoka.com.

CANADA: SAINT JOHN'S REGATTA. Aug 1. St. John's, NF. "North America's oldest sporting event." Rowing competition held on Quidi Vidi Lake. Est attendance: 40,000. For info: Coord of Research and Info, Dept of Tourism and Culture, Box 8700, St. John's, NF, Canada A1B 4J6. Phone: (800) 563-6353.

CHILDREN'S VISION AND LEARNING MONTH. Aug 1–31. A month-long campaign encouraging parents to have their children's vision examined by an eye-care professional prior to the start of the new school year. For info: Mike Smith, Exec Dir, American Foundation for Vision Awareness (AFVA), 243 N Lindbergh Blvd, St. Louis, MO 63141. Phone: (800) 927-AFVA. Fax: (314) 991-4101. E-mail: afva@aol.com. Web: www.afva.org.

COLORADO: ADMISSION DAY: 125th ANNIVERSARY. Aug 1, 1876. Colorado admitted to the Union as the 38th state. The first Monday in August is celebrated as Colorado Day.

DIARY OF ANNE FRANK: THE LAST ENTRY: ANNIVERSARY. Aug 1, 1944. To escape deportation to concentration camps, the Jewish family of Otto Frank hid for two years in the warehouse of his food products business at Amsterdam. Gentile friends smuggled in food and other supplies during their confinement. Thirteen-year-old Anne Frank, who kept a journal during the time of their hiding, penned her last entry in the diary Aug 1, 1944: "[I] keep on trying to find a way of becoming what I would like to be, and what I could be, if . . . there weren't any other people living in the world." Three days later (Aug 4, 1944) Grüne Polizei raided the "Secret Annex" where the Frank family was hidden. Anne and her sister were sent to Bergen-Belsen concentration camp where Anne died at age 15, two months before the liberation of Holland. Young Anne's diary, later found in the family's hiding place, has been translated into 30 languages and has become a symbol of the indomitable strength of the human spirit. See also: "Frank, Anne: Birth Anniversary" (June 12).

EMANCIPATION OF 500: ANNIVERSARY. Aug 1, 1791. Virginia planter Robert Carter III confounded his family and friends by filing a deed of emancipation for his 500 slaves. One of the wealthiest men in the state, Carter owned 60,000 acres over 18 plantations. The deed included the following words: "I have for some time past been convinced that to retain them in Slavery is contrary to the true principles of Religion and Justice and therefore it is my duty to manumit them." The document established a schedule by which 15 slaves would be freed each Jan 1, over a 21-year period, plus slave children would be freed at age 18 for females and 21 for males. It is believed this was the largest act of emancipation in US history and predated the Emancipation Proclamation by 70 years.

FAMILYFUN MONTH. Aug 1–31. Celebrate being a family this month with quick-and-easy, funfilled activities that bring everyone closer together. Try creative conversation-starters, backyard games, group art projects—all the activities that create family memories and start new family traditions. Sponsored by FamilyFun Magazine. For ideas and information visit our website at www.FamilyFun.com. For info: Cindy Littlefield, Assoc Editor, FamilyFun Magazine, 244 Main St, Northampton, MA 01060.

FIRST US CENSUS: ANNIVERSARY. Aug 1, 1790. The first census revealed that there were 3,939,326 citizens in the 16 states and the Ohio Territory. The US has taken a census every 10 years since 1790. The next one will be in 2010.

GARCIA, JERRY: BIRTH ANNIVERSARY. Aug 1, 1942. Jerome John Garcia was born at San Francisco, CA. Country, bluegrass and folk musician, a guitar player of remarkable ability, Garcia was the leading force behind the legendary Grateful Dead, the band that sustained a veritable industry for its legion of followers. He died Aug 9, 1995, at Forest Knolls, CA, ending a musical career that spanned more than three decades.

GEORGIA MOUNTAIN FAIR. Aug 1–12. Georgia Mountain Fairgrounds, Hiawassee, GA. Authentic mountain demonstrations including corn millin', board splittin', soap and hominy makin' and others. Pioneer village with re-created one-room school, log cabin, barn and corncrib. Nashville talent, clogging, midway, arts and crafts and much more. Est attendance: 130,000. For info: Georgia Mountain Fair, PO Box 444, Hiawassee, GA 30546. Phone: (706) 896-4191.

HAWAII VOLCANOES NATIONAL PARK ESTABLISHED: 85th ANNIVERSARY. Aug 1, 1916. Area of Hawaii's Hawaii Island, including active volcanoes Kilauea and Manua Loa, was established as Hawaii National Park in 1916 but its name was changed to Hawaii Volcanoes National Park in 1961. For further park info: Hawaii Volcanoes Natl Park, Hawaii Natl Park, HI 96718.

HILL, JAMES: 85th BIRTH ANNIVERSARY. Aug 1, 1916. British film director James Hill was born at Jeffersonville, IN. He is best known for his film *Born Free* (1966), but he also won an Academy Award for *Giuseppina* (1961). He died Oct 9, 1994, at London, England.

JAMAICA: ABOLITION OF SLAVERY. Aug 1, 1838. National day. Spanish settlers introduced the slave trade into Jamaica in 1509 and sugar cane in 1640. Slavery continued until Aug 1, 1838, when it was abolished by the British.

KEY, FRANCIS SCOTT: BIRTH ANNIVERSARY. Aug 1, 1779. American attorney, social worker, poet and author of the US national anthem. Key was on shipboard off Baltimore during the British bombardment of Fort McHenry on the night of Sept 13–14, 1814. Thrilled to see the American flag still flying over the fort at daybreak, Key wrote the poem "The Star-Spangled Banner." Born at Frederick County, MD, he died at Baltimore, MD, Jan 11, 1843.

LUGHNASADH. Aug 1. (Also called August Eve, Lammas Eve, Lady Day Eve and Feast of Bread.) One of the "Greater Sabbats" during the Wiccan year, Lughnasadh marks the first harvest. Annually, Aug 1.

MAINE LOBSTER FESTIVAL. Aug 1–5. Harbor Park, Public Landing, Rockland, ME. Annual celebration and promotion of the lobster industry featuring lobster dinners, arts, crafts, exhibits, live entertainment, parade, contests and a road race. Est attendance: 80,000. For info: Rockland Thomaston Area Chamber of Commerce, PO Box 508, Harbor Park Public Landing, Rockland, ME 04841. Phone: (207) 596-0376. Fax: (207) 596-6549. E-mail: rtacc@midcoast.com. Web: www.midcoast.com/~rtacc.

MCHENRY COUNTY FAIR. Aug 1–5. Woodstock, IL. Rides, food, entertainment, animal and antique competitions, talent and queen contests, demolition derby, exhibits, livestock judging and more. Est attendance: 125,000. For info: Woodstock Chamber of Commerce, 136 Cass St, Woodstock, IL 60098. Phone: (815) 338-2436. Fax: (815) 338-2927. E-mail: chamber@stans.com.

MELVILLE, HERMAN: BIRTH ANNIVERSARY. Aug 1, 1819. American author, best known for his novel *Moby Dick*, born at New York, NY and died there Sept 28, 1891.

August 2001	S	M	T	W	T	F	S
				1	2	3	4
	5	6	7	8	9	10	11
	12	13	14	15	16	17	18
	19	20	21	22	23	24	25
	26	27	28	29	30	31	

MISS CRUSTACEAN USA BEAUTY PAGEANT AND OCEAN CITY CREEP. Aug 1. 6th Street Beach, Ocean City, NJ. Participants are hermit tree crabs. To determine most beautiful tree crab and fastest tree crab on earth. Begins at 1 PM, EST. Est attendance: 500. For info: Mark Soifer, PR Dir, City of Ocean City, City Hall, Ocean City, NJ 08226. Phone: (609) 525-9300. Fax: (609) 399-0374. E-mail: MTSoifer@aol.com.

MITCHELL, MARIA: BIRTH ANNIVERSARY. Aug 1, 1818. An interest in her father's hobby and an ability for mathematics resulted in Maria Mitchell's becoming the first female professional astronomer. In 1847, while assisting her father in a survey of the sky for the US Coast Guard, Mitchell discovered a new comet and determined its orbit. She received many honors because of this, including being elected to the American Academy of Arts and Sciences—its first woman. Mitchell joined the staff at Vassar Female College in 1865—the first US female professor of astronomy—and in 1873 was a cofounder of the Association for the Advancement of Women. Born at Nantucket, MA, Mitchell died June 28, 1889, at Lynn, MA.

MTV PREMIERE: 20th ANNIVERSARY. Aug 1, 1981. The all-music-video channel debuted on this date. VH1, another music channel owned by MTV Networks that is aimed at older pop music fans, premiered in 1985.

MUSTANG LEAGUE WORLD SERIES. Aug 1–4. Irving, TX. International youth baseball World Series for players of league ages 9 and 10. Est attendance: 3,000. For info: PONY Baseball, Inc, PO Box 225, Washington, PA 15301. Phone: (724) 225-1060. Fax: (724) 225-9852. E-mail: pony@pulsenet.com. Web: www.pony.org.

NATIONAL INVENTORS' MONTH. Aug 1–31. To educate the American public about the value of creativity and inventiveness and the importance of inventions and inventors to the quality of our lives. This will be accomplished through the placement of media stories about living inventors in most of the top national, local and trade publications, as well as through the electronic media. Sponsored by the United Inventors Association of the USA (UIA-USA), the Academy of Applied Science and *Inventors' Digest*. For info: Joanne Hayes-Rines, Inventors' Digest. Phone: (617) 367-4540. Fax: (617) 723-6988. E-mail: inventorsd@aol.com. Web: www.inventorsdigest.com/

NATIONAL WIN WITH CIVILITY MONTH. Aug 1–31. When we are civil to each other we confirm our worth and acknowledge the worth of others. We can move in and out of all levels of society confident that we are always doing the "right thing." We gain recognition for civility and we secure the respect of our fellow human beings. For info: Thomas Danaher, PO Box 85147, Las Vegas, NV 89185. Web: americansforcivility.com.

NORTH CENTRAL MISSOURI FAIR. Aug 1–5. Trenton, MO. Country fair featuring livestock shows, carnival rides, demo derby, tractor pull and gospel show. Est attendance: 8,000. For info: Carol Ausberger, 559 NW 5th Ave, Trenton, MO 64683. Phone: (660) 485-6536.

OAK RIDGE ATOMIC PLANT BEGUN: ANNIVERSARY. Aug 1, 1943. Ground was broken at Oak Ridge, TN, for the first plant built to manufacture the uranium 235 needed to build an atomic bomb. The plant was largely completed by July of 1944 at a final cost of $280 million. By August 1945 the total cost for development of the A-bomb ran to $1 billion.

PRESIDENT'S ENVIRONMENTAL YOUTH AWARD NATIONAL COMPETITION. Aug 1–July 31, 2002. Young people in all 50 states are invited to participate in the President's Environmental Youth Awards program, which offers them, individually and collectively, an opportunity to be recognized for environmental efforts in their community. The program encourages individuals, school classes, schools, summer camps and youth organizations to promote local environmental awareness and positive community involvement. For info: Doris Gillispie, Environmental Education Coord, US Environmental Protection Agency, 401 M St, #1707, Washington, DC 20460. Phone: (202) 260-2744. Fax: (202) 260-0790.

ROUNDS RESOUNDING DAY. Aug 1. To sing rounds, catches and canons in folk contrapuntal tradition. Motto: "As rounds re-sound and resound, all the world's joined in a circle of harmony." Annually, Aug 1. For info: Gloria T. Delamar, Founder, Rounds Resounding Soc. Phone: (215) 782-1059. E-mail: Rounds.Resounding.Society@juno.com.

SCOTLAND: ABERDEEN INTERNATIONAL YOUTH FESTIVAL. Aug 1–11. Aberdeen, Scotland. Talented young people from all areas of the performing arts come from around the world to participate in this festival. Est attendance: 30,000. For info: Nicola Wallis, 3 Nutborn House, Clifton Rd, London, England SW19 4QT. Phone: (44) (20) 8946 2995. Fax: (44) (20) 8944 6507. E-mail: info@aberdeen-youth-fest.org.

SEASHORE OPEN HOUSE TOUR. Aug 1. Loveladies, NJ. 35th annual. Come and enjoy the fabulous shoreline houses. Est attendance: 8,000. For info: Long Beach Island Foundation of the Arts and Sciences, 120 Long Beach Blvd, Loveladies, NJ 08008. Phone: (609) 494-1241. Fax: (609) 494-0662.

SIMPLIFY YOUR LIFE WEEK. Aug 1–7. A week to encourage people to simplify their lives and reduce clutter, thereby reducing stress and acquiring a happier and more peaceful lifestyle. For information about this worldwide organization and 100 ways to simplify one's life, send $4 to cover expenses of printing, handling and postage. For info: Dr. Stanley Drake, Pres, Intl Soc of Friendship and Good Will, 8592 Roswell Rd, Ste 434, Atlanta, GA 30350-1870.

SPINAL MUSCULAR ATROPHY AWARENESS MONTH. Aug 1–31. To promote awareness of this congenital disease. For info: Families of Spinal Muscular Atrophy, PO Box 196, Libertyville, IL 60048. Phone: (800) 886-1762 or (847) 367-7620.

SWITZERLAND: NATIONAL DAY. Aug 1. Anniversary of the founding of the Swiss Confederation. Commemorates a pact made in 1291. Parades, patriotic gatherings, bonfires and fireworks. Young citizens' coming-of-age ceremonies. Observed since 600th anniversary of Swiss Confederation was celebrated in 1891.

TRINIDAD AND TOBAGO: EMANCIPATION DAY. Aug 1. Public holiday. Slavery was abolished in all British colonies on this day in 1834.

US CUSTOMS: ANNIVERSARY. Aug 1, 1789. "The first US customs officers began to collect the revenue and enforce the Tariff Act of July 4, 1789, on this date. Since then, the customhouse and the customs officer have stood as symbols of national pride and sovereignty at ports of entry along the land and sea borders of our country." (From Presidential Proclamation 4306.)

WARSAW UPRISING: ANNIVERSARY. Aug 1, 1944. Having received radio reports from Moscow promising aid from the Red Army, the Polish Home Army rose up against the Nazi oppressors. At 5 PM thousands of windows were thrown open and Polish patriots, 40,000 strong, began shooting at German soldiers in the streets. The Germans responded by throwing eight divisions into the battle. Despite appeals from the London-based Polish government-in-exile, no assistance was forthcoming from the Allies, and after two months of horrific fighting the rebellion was quashed.

WEAR WHAT THEY WORE. Aug 1–31. Jamestown Settlement, Williamsburg, VA and Yorktown Victory Center, Yorktown, VA. Clothing, from the single thread to the whole garment, is the focus of interpretive programs throughout the month. Try on garments like those worn by 17th-century English sailors and settlers, Powhatan Indians, Continental Army soldiers and 18th-century Virginia farmers. For info: Jamestown-Yorktown Foundation, PO Box 1607, Williamsburg, VA 23187. Phone: (757) 253-4838 or (888) 593-4682. Fax: (757) 253-5299. Web: www.historyisfun.org.

WISH YOU WERE HERE. Aug 1–Nov 16. Granville, OH. Group tours during the week by appointment only. An early 1900s to 1950s postcard exhibit in nine rooms of the "home" museum. Postcards include vacation, travel, season greetings, cartoons and local note-sending—all imply "Wish you were here." For info: Gina Hughes, Dir, Granville Life-Style Museum, 121 S Main St, Granville, OH 43023. Phone: (740) 587-0373.

WORLD BREASTFEEDING WEEK. Aug 1–7. Commemoration of signing of Innocenti Declaration. Includes a World Walk for Breastfeeding. Breastfeeding advocates, health care professionals and social service agencies focus attention on the importance and benefits of breastfeeding. Fairs, picnics, fund-raising and government proclamations highlight the week. Annually, the first week of August. For info: La Leche League Intl, 1400 N Meacham, Schaumburg, IL 60168-4079. Phone: (847) 519-7730 or (800) LA LECHE. Fax: (847) 519-0035. Web: www.lalecheleague.org/.

WORLD WIDE WEB: ANNIVERSARY. Aug 1, 1990. The creation of what would become the World Wide Web was suggested this month in 1990 by Tim Berners-Lee and Robert Cailliau at CERN, the European Laboratory for Particle Physics at Switzerland. By October, they had designed a prototype Web browser. They also introduced HTML (Hypertext Markup Language) and the URL (Universal Resource Locator). Mosaic, the first graphical Web browser, was designed by Marc Andreessen and released in 1993. By early 1993, there were 50 Web servers worldwide.

BIRTHDAYS TODAY

Tempestt Bledsoe, 28, talk-show host, actress ("Tempestt," "The Cosby Show"), born Chicago, IL, Aug 1, 1973.

Robert Cray, 48, singer, guitarist, songwriter, born Columbus, GA, Aug 1, 1953.

Dom DeLuise, 68, comedian, actor (*Cannonball Run*), born Brooklyn, NY, Aug 1, 1933.

Giancarlo Giannini, 59, actor (*Swept Away . . . , Seven Beauties*), born Spezia, Italy, Aug 1, 1942.

Arthur Hill, 79, actor (*Harper, The Andromeda Strain,* "Owen Marshall"), born Melfort, Saskatchewan, Canada, Aug 1, 1922.

Yves Saint Laurent, 65, fashion designer, born Oran, Algeria, Aug 1, 1936.

Tom Wilson, 70, cartoonist ("Ziggy"), born Grant Town, WV, Aug 1, 1931.

AUGUST 2 — THURSDAY
Day 214 — 151 Remaining

ALBERT EINSTEIN'S ATOMIC BOMB LETTER: ANNIVERSARY. Aug 2, 1939. Albert Einstein, world-famous scientist, a refugee from Nazi Germany, wrote a letter to US President Franklin D. Roosevelt, first mentioning a possible "new phenomenon . . . chain reactions . . . vast amounts of power." "A single bomb of this type," he wrote, "carried by boat and exploded in a port, might very well destroy the whole port together with some of the surrounding territory." Six years and four days later, Aug 6, 1945, the Japanese port of Hiroshima was destroyed by the first atomic bombing of a populated place.

BALDWIN, JAMES ARTHUR: BIRTH ANNIVERSARY. Aug 2, 1924. Black American author noted for descriptions of black life in the US. Born at New York, NY. His best-known work, *Go Tell It on the Mountain*, was published in 1953. Died at Saint Paul-de-Vence, France, Nov 30, 1987.

BRONCO LEAGUE WORLD SERIES. Aug 2–8. Monterey, CA. International youth baseball World Series for players of league ages 11 and 12. Est attendance: 4,350. For info: PONY Baseball, PO Box 225, Washington, PA 15301. Phone: (724) 225-1060. Fax: (724) 225-9852. E-mail: pony@pulsenet.com. Web: www.pony.org.

CANADA: AGRIFAIR. Aug 2–6. Abbotsford, BC. Fun for everyone with attractions like draft horses, dairy, beef, llama and poultry; hands-on milking display; motor sports; my marketplace trade show; antique farm display bursting with antique toys; midway; plus everything from national and international stage entertainment to a Pro rodeo and fireworks. Est attendance: 57,000. For info: Harvey Carroll, Abbotsford Agrifair, PO Box 2334, Abbotsford, BC, Canada V2T 4X2. Phone: (604) 852-6674. Fax: (604) 852-6631.

CANADA: BIG VALLEY JAMBOREE. Aug 2–5. Camrose, AB. Canada's premiere country music festival, featuring top-name entertainers and more than 25 acts. Beer gardens, trade shows, unserviced camping and parking. Est attendance: 60,000. For info: Glen Vinet, PO Box 1418, Camrose, AB, Canada T4V 1X3. Phone: (780) 672-0224 or (888) 404-1234. Fax: (780) 672-9530. E-mail: bvj@ccinet.ab.ca. Web: www.bigvalleyjamboree.com.

CANADA: ROCKHOUND GEMBOREE. Aug 2–5. Bancroft, ON. Daily expeditions to prime mineral locations; dealers, demonstrations and displays, swapping. Est attendance: 14,000. For info: Bancroft and District Chamber of Commerce, PO Box 539, Bancroft, ON, Canada K0L 1C0. Phone: (613) 332-1513. Fax: (613) 332-2119. E-mail: chamber@commerce.bancroft.on.ca. Web: www.commerce.bancroft.on.ca.

August *2001*	S	M	T	W	T	F	S
				1	2	3	4
	5	6	7	8	9	10	11
	12	13	14	15	16	17	18
	19	20	21	22	23	24	25
	26	27	28	29	30	31	

DECLARATION OF INDEPENDENCE: OFFICIAL SIGNING: 225th ANNIVERSARY. Aug 2, 1776. Contrary to widespread misconceptions, the 56 signers did not sign as a group and did not do so July 4, 1776. John Hancock and Charles Thomson signed only draft copies that day, the official day the Declaration was adopted by Congress. The signing of the official declaration occurred Aug 2, 1776, when 50 men probably took part. Later that year, five more apparently signed separately and one added his name in a subsequent year. (From "Signers of the Declaration . . ." US Dept of the Interior, 1975.) See also: "Declaration of Independence Approval and Signing: Anniversary" (July 4).

FRIENDSHIP DAY. Aug 2. A day to heed the advice of 18th-century English philosopher Samuel Johnson: "A man should keep his friendships in constant repair." A time to acknowledge old friends and celebrate new ones. Please enclose a SASE if you write. For info send SASE to: Linda Gorin, The Best To You, Elegant Gift Baskets, 8504 Commerce Ave, Ste A, San Diego, CA 92121. Web: www.thebesttoyou.com.

GREAT ARKANSAS PIG-OUT. Aug 2–4. Morrilton, AR. Focus is on food of all kinds: barbecue, chicken-on-a-stick, funnel cakes, hamburgers, spaghetti dinners. Activities include pig chase, hog calling, children's pig-tail park, arts, crafts, games, entertainment, Tour de Oink, 5K fun run, gospel singing. 13th annual pig-out. Est attendance: 30,000. For info: Chamber of Commerce, 120 N Division, Morrilton, AR 72110. Phone: (501) 354-2393. Fax: (501) 354-8642. E-mail: mcc@mev.net.

IRAQ INVADES KUWAIT: ANNIVERSARY. Aug 2, 1990. On President Saddam Hussein's orders, the Iraqi army invaded Kuwait. Hussein claimed that Kuwait presented a serious threat to Iraq's economic existence by overproducing oil and driving prices down on the world market. After conquering the capital, Kuwait City, Hussein installed a military government in Kuwait, prior to annexing it to Iraq on the claim that Kuwait was historically part of Iraq. The US and most other nations immediately condemned the aggression and the UN passed measures calling for broad economic sanctions against Iraq. As Iraqi forces began to mass along the border with Saudi Arabia, the US and other nations sent troops to Saudi Arabia to protect that country from invasion with an operation named Desert Shield. The multinational force included troops from other Arab countries such as Egypt, Syria and Morocco in addition to forces from Western governments with large economic interests in the region. Approximately 21,000 foreign nationals from several countries were detained by Iraq and were transported to various strategic locations to deter possible retaliatory attacks. The US military action was the largest mobilization of forces since the Vietnam War. The following January Desert Shield became Operation Desert Storm as the Allied forces went to war against Iraq.

L'ENFANT, PIERRE CHARLES: BIRTH ANNIVERSARY. Aug 2, 1754. The architect, engineer and Revolutionary War officer who designed the plan for the city of Washington, DC, L'Enfant was born at Paris, France. He died at Prince Georges County, MD, June 14, 1825.

LOY, MYRNA (WILLIAMS): BIRTH ANNIVERSARY. Aug 2, 1905. Actress known for her film roles in the "Thin Man" series. Born near Helena, MT, and died at New York, NY, Dec 14, 1993.

MACEDONIA, FORMER YUGOSLAV REPUBLIC OF: NATIONAL DAY. Aug 2. Commemorates the nationalist uprising against the Ottoman Empire in 1903.

PITTSBURGH THREE RIVERS REGATTA. Aug 2–5. Point State Park, Downtown Pittsburgh, PA. Pittsburgh's rivers and shores play host to the world's largest inland regatta. A family-oriented weekend full of thrilling air shows and on-land events as well as Formula One powerboat races, hot-air balloon races, fireworks and water skiing demonstrations. For info: Greater Pittsburgh Conv & Visitors Bureau, Regional Enterprise Tower, 30th Fl, 425 Sixth Ave, Pittsburgh, PA 15219-1834. Phone: (412) 281-7711. Fax: (412) 644-5512.

RIBFEST. Aug 2–4. Kalamazoo, MI. Features the smell of sizzling ribs as rib-burners from throughout the US tantalize the taste buds of West Michigan. Festival will feature live entertainment, family-oriented events, food booths and the "Sponsors Choice Award" for best ribs. Est attendance: 24,000. For info: Deborah Droppers, Community Advocates for Persons with Developmental Disabilities, 814 S Westnedge St, Kalamazoo, MI 49008-1162. Phone: (616) 373-4034. E-mail: eventkzoo@aol.com.

SAINT ELIAS DAY (ILLINDEN): ANNIVERSARY OF MACEDONIAN UPRISING. Aug 2, 1903. Most sacred, honored and celebrated day of the Macedonian people. Anniversary of the uprising of Macedonians against the Ottoman Empire. Turkish reprisals against the insurgents were ruthless, including the destruction of 105 villages and the execution of more than 1,700 noncombatants.

VIRGIN ISLANDS NATIONAL PARK ESTABLISHED: ANNIVERSARY. Aug 2, 1956. The Virgin Islands, including areas on St. John and St. Thomas, were established as a national park and preserve. On Oct 5, 1962, it was established that Virgin Islands National Park be enlarged to include offshore areas, including coral reefs, shorelines and sea grass beds.

BIRTHDAYS TODAY

Joanna Cassidy, 57, actress ("Buffalo Bill," *Under Fire*), born Camden, NJ, Aug 2, 1944.

Wes Craven, 62, writer, director (*The Nightmare on Elm Street, Scream*), born Cleveland, OH, Aug 2, 1939.

James Fallows, 52, journalist, former editor (*US News & World Report*), born Philadelphia, PA, Aug 2, 1949.

Edward Furlong, 24, actor (*Before and After, Terminator 2*), born Glendale, CA, Aug 2, 1977.

Kathryn Harrold, 51, actress ("I'll Fly Away," "The Larry Sanders Show," *Modern Romance*), born Tazewell, VA, Aug 2, 1950.

Lamar Hunt, 69, Pro Football Hall of Fame executive, born El Dorado, AR, Aug 2, 1932.

Carroll O'Connor, 77, actor (*Marlowe*, "All in the Family," "In the Heat of the Night"), born New York, NY, Aug 2, 1924.

Peter O'Toole, 68, actor (*Lawrence of Arabia, Becket*), born Connemara, Ireland, Aug 2, 1933.

Beatrice Straight, 83, actress (Oscar for *Network*), born Old Westbury, NY, Aug 2, 1918.

AUGUST 3 — FRIDAY
Day 215 — 150 Remaining

AMERICAN HERITAGE CRAFT FESTIVAL. Aug 3–5. Oglebay, Wheeling, WV. A grand gathering of the best craft artisans from a three-state area in the beautiful outdoors with food and entertainment. Annually, the first weekend in August. Sponsored by the Wheeling Park Commission (Oglebay). Est attendance: 9,000. For info: Barbara Palmer, Special Events Coord, Oglebay, Wheeling, WV 26003. Phone: (304) 243-4010. Fax: (304) 243-4110.

AMERICOVER 2001. Aug 3–5. Denver Marriott Tech Center, Denver, CO. 46th annual convention and exhibition. The AFDCS is the only not-for-profit, noncommercial, international philatelic (stamp collector) society devoted exclusively to First Day Covers and First Day Cover collecting. AMERICOVER will be the largest single philatelic event (stamp show and sale) this year dealing primarily with First Day Covers, their collectors, cachetmakers and dealers. Many activities require advance registration. Most events are free! Est attendance: 1,500. For info: American First Day Cover Soc, PO Box 1335, Maplewood, NJ 07040-0456. Phone: (973) 762-2012. Fax: (973) 762-7916. E-mail: americover@aol.com.

ARMY NURSES PAY RAISE: ANNIVERSARY. Aug 3, 1861. Although it had been known from the time the Second Continental Congress authorized the Continental Army (June 14, 1775) that " . . . the sick suffered much for want of good female nurses" (General Washington having asked the Congress to authorize a matron and nurses), progress was slow. The pay of a nurse, originally $2 per month and one ration per day, was increased to $8 per month and one ration per day on Apr 7, 1777. Congress, 84 years later, authorized the Surgeon General to employ women as nurses for army hospitals at a salary of $12 per month plus one ration per day.

BLUEBERRY FESTIVAL. Aug 3–4. Library Lawn and Village Green, Montrose, PA. 22nd annual fund-raiser for the Susquehanna County Library and Historical Society. Two days filled with food, fun and festivity. Raffles, book sale, children's games, silent auction, handstitched quilt, commemorative items and more. Annually, the first Friday and Saturday in August. Est attendance: 5,000. For info: Hilary Caws-Elwitt, Susquehanna Co Historical Soc & Free Library Assn, 2 Monument Sq, Montrose, PA 18801. Phone: (570) 278-1881. Fax: (570) 278-9336. E-mail: suspulib@epix.net. Web: www.epix.net/~suspulib.

BOOM DAYS. Aug 3–5. Leadville, CO. The city's oldest annual celebration features a large parade, street races, mining events, pack burro race and arts and crafts. Fun for the whole family. Est attendance: 35,000. For info: Chamber of Commerce, PO Box 861, Leadville, CO 80461. Phone: (719) 486-3900 or (888) 264-5344. Fax: (719) 486-8478. E-mail: leadville@leadvilleusa.com. Web: www.leadvilleusa.com.

BRAHAM PIE DAY. Aug 3. Freedom Park, Braham, MN. Celebrate Braham's status as "Homemade Pie Capital of Minnesota" during this one-day festival. Visitors will find homemade pies, craft displays, pie-eating contests, a pie auction, a pie race and performing artists in Braham's main street park. Activities also include an exotic pie-eating contest, a pi R squared contest, a pie art show and the "Pie-alluia" chorus. Est attendance: 5,000. For info: Valorie Arrowsmith, Isanti County Historical Soc, PO Box 525, Cambridge, MN 55008. Phone: (763) 689-4229. Fax: (763) 689-4229. E-mail: varrow2@ecenet.com. Web: www.braham.com.

BRATWURST DAYS. Aug 3–4. Sheboygan, WI. Sheboygan celebrates bratwurst at Kiwanis Park with music, national entertainment, Bratxotic (food court), parade, flea market and, of course, bratwurst-eating contest. Since 1953. Est attendance: 40,000. For info: Sheboygan Jaycees, PO Box 561, Sheboygan, WI 53081. Phone: (920) 803-8980. Fax: (920) 458-5922. Web: www.sheboyganjaycees.com.

CANADA: CANADA'S NATIONAL UKRAINIAN FESTIVAL. Aug 3–5. Dauphin, MB. Experience the richness and flavours of Ukrainian culture. From the colorful, energized dancers to the powerful folk songs of Ukraine, there is something for everyone to enjoy. Est attendance: 10,000. For info: Robert Michasiw, Canada's National Ukrainian Festival, 119 Main St, Dauphin, MB, Canada R7N 1K4. Phone: (204) 622-4600. Fax: (204) 622-4606. E-mail: CNUF@mb.sympatico.ca. Web: www.mb.sympatico.ca.

CANADA: IAAF WORLD CHAMPIONSHIPS IN ATHLETICS. Aug 3–12. Edmonton, AB. With 3,000 athletes from 200 countries, this is the third largest athletic event in the world, after the Olympics and World Cup Soccer. There will be 24 men's and 22 women's events in track and field and an anticipated viewing audience of 4 billion people. Held every two years, this is the eighth world championships sponsored by the International Amateur Athletic Federation. For info: 2001 Edmonton, PO Bag 2001, Station Main, Edmonton, AB, Canada, T5J 5A5. Phone: (780) 821-2001. Web: www.2001.edmonton.com.

COLUMBUS SAILS FOR THE NEW WORLD: ANNIVERSARY. Aug 3, 1492. Christopher Columbus, "Admiral of the Ocean Sea," set sail half an hour before sunrise from Palos, Spain, Aug 3, 1492. With three ships, *Niña*, *Pinta* and *Santa Maria*, and a crew of 90, he sailed "for Cathay" but found instead a New World of the Americas, first landing at Guanahani (San Salvador Island in the Bahamas) Oct 12. See also: "Columbus Day" (Oct 12).

DECATUR CELEBRATION. Aug 3–5. Decatur, IL. Illinois' largest free family street festival within 22 city blocks of fun with 13 entertainment stages; 96 arts and crafts and 44 commercial vendors; 66 one-of-a-kind food vendors. Est attendance: 300,000. For info: Decatur Celebration, 132 S Water, Ste 418, Decatur, IL 62521. Phone: (217) 423-4222. Fax: (217) 423-4271.

FOX ROX FESTIVAL. Aug 3–5. St. Charles, IL. Downtown will rock with exciting tent sales, craft show, live outdoor music, Bluesfest Saturday and Sunday, family activities and more. For info: St. Charles Convention and Visitor Bureau, 311 N Second St, Ste 100, St. Charles, IL 60174. Phone: (800) 777-4373 or (630) 377-6161. Web: www.dtown.org.

GUINEA-BISSAU: COLONIZATION MARTYR'S DAY. Aug 3. National holiday is observed.

KUHN, MARGARET (MAGGIE): BIRTH ANNIVERSARY. Aug 3, 1905. When she was forced into retirement because she'd reached the age of 65, Maggie Kuhn founded the Gray Panthers organization to fight age discrimination. Subsequently she waged a battle that resulted in mandatory retirement being banned. Born at Buffalo, NY, Kuhn died Apr 22, 1995, at Philadelphia, PA.

MAINE FESTIVAL. Aug 3–5. Thomas Point Beach, Brunswick, ME. Maine's premier art and cultural event, with more than 1,000 artists and craftspersons on site. Features seven stages of country, traditional and contemporary music, dance, theater and literary presentations. A juried art/craft market, giant paintings and art installations, a Maine products show, art workshops for all ages, musical instrument builders, fine woodworking, a microbrew festival, traditional Maine seafood and ethnic foods. Est attendance: 24,000. For info: Maine Arts, Inc, 582 Congress St, Portland, ME 04101. Phone: (207) 772-9012. Fax: (207) 772-3995. E-mail: mainearts@mainearts.org. Web: www.maine arts.org.

August 2001	S	M	T	W	T	F	S
				1	2	3	4
	5	6	7	8	9	10	11
	12	13	14	15	16	17	18
	19	20	21	22	23	24	25
	26	27	28	29	30	31	

MUSIKFEST. Aug 3–12. Bethlehem, PA. Entertainment, ethnic foods and music—more than 600 live performances from Bach to bluegrass to rock. Fifteen outdoor and five indoor stages. Est attendance: 1,000,000. For info: Bethlehem Musikfest Assn, 25 W Third St, Bethlehem, PA 18015-1238. Phone: (610) 861-0678. Fax: (610) 861-2644. E-mail: info@fest.org. Web: www.musikfest.org.

NATIONAL BALLOON CLASSIC. Aug 3–11. Indianola, IA. A spectator-oriented balloon extravaganza involving fun events utilizing up to 100 balloons. It is held on the Classic's specially designed balloon field with a natural amphitheater for perfect viewing. Balloons fly morning and evening, weather permitting. The Classic stage features live local & regional entertainment. Est attendance: 75,000. For info: Gerald Knoll, PO Box 346, Indianola, IA 50125. Phone: (800) FLY-IOWA or (515) 961-8415. Fax: (515) 961-8415. E-mail: classicgk@aol.com. Web: www.nationalballoonclassic.com.

NEWPORT FOLK FESTIVAL. Aug 3–5. Ft Adams State Park, Newport, RI. Nationally-known and up-and-coming performers. For info: Newport County CVB, 23 America's Cup Ave, Newport, RI 02840. Phone: (800) 326-6030. Fax: (401) 849-0291.

NIGER: INDEPENDENCE DAY: ANNIVERSARY. Aug 3. Niger gained its independence from France on this day in 1960.

OHIO STATE FAIR. Aug 3–19. Columbus, OH. Family fun, amusement rides, games, food booths, parades, entertainment, rodeos, circus, auto thrill show and tractor pulls. Est attendance: 900,000. For info: Ohio State Fair, 717 E 17th Ave, Columbus, OH 43211. Phone: (614) 644-4000. Fax: (614) 644-4031. Web: www.ohiostatefair.com.

"PRIMETIME LIVE" TV PREMIERE: ANNIVERSARY. Aug 3, 1989. Sam Donaldson and Diane Sawyer host this magazine show that features investigative and consumer reports as well as human interest stories.

PYLE, ERNEST TAYLOR: BIRTH ANNIVERSARY. Aug 3, 1900. Ernie Pyle was born at Dana, IN, and began his career in journalism in 1923. After serving as managing editor of the Washington *Daily News*, he returned to his first journalistic love of working as a roving reporter in 1935. His column was syndicated by nearly 200 newspapers and often focused on figures behind the news. His reports of the bombing of London in 1940 and subsequent reports from Africa, Sicily, Italy and France earned him a Pulitzer Prize in 1944. He was killed by machine-gun fire at the Pacific island of Ie Shima, Apr 18, 1945.

SANTA CRUZ BEACH BOARDWALK LOOFF CAROUSEL: 90th ANNIVERSARY. Aug 3, 1911. Danish woodcarver Charles I.D. Looff delivered the classic carousel on Aug 3, 1911. A furniture-maker by trade, Looff began carving carousel animals as a hobby after immigrating to America. His first carousel was installed at Coney Island in New York in 1875. The Boardwalk carousel features jeweled horses and a 342-pipe Ruth band organ built in 1894. The carousel and the park's Giant Dipper roller coaster were designated National Historic Landmarks by the US National Park Service in June of 1987.

SCOPES, JOHN T.: BIRTH ANNIVERSARY. Aug 3, 1900. Central figure in a cause célèbre (the "Scopes Trial" or the "Monkey Trial"), John Thomas Scopes was born at Paducah, KY. An obscure 24-year-old schoolteacher at the Dayton, TN, high school in 1925, he became the focus of world attention. Scopes never uttered a word at his trial, which was a contest between two of America's best-known lawyers, William Jennings Bryan and Clarence Darrow. The trial, July 10–21, 1925, resulted in Scopes's conviction. He was fined $100 "for teaching evolution" in Tennessee. The verdict was upset on a technicality and the statute he was accused of breaching was repealed in 1967. Scopes died at Shreveport, LA, Oct 21, 1970.

SCOTLAND: EDINBURGH MILITARY TATTOO: THE MAIN EVENT. Aug 3–25. Edinburgh Castle, Edinburgh, Lothian. Display of military color and pageantry held at night on the floodlit esplanade of Edinburgh Castle. A unique blend of music, ceremony, entertainment and theater. Est attendance: 200,000. For info: The Edinburgh Military Tattoo, The Tattoo Office, 32 Market St, Edinburgh, Scotland EH1 1QB. Phone: (44) (131) 225-1188. Fax: (44) (131) 225-8627. Web: www.edintattoo.co.uk/

SQUARE FAIR. Aug 3-5. Lima Town Square, Lima, OH. Outdoor performing and visual arts festival. Est attendance: 50,000. For info: Bart Mills, Exec Dir, Council for the Arts of Greater Lima, Box 1124, Lima, OH 45802. Phone: (419) 222-1096. Fax: (419) 222-3871. E-mail: bart@limaartscouncil.org.

SUSSEX COUNTY FARM AND HORSE SHOW/NEW JERSEY STATE FAIR. Aug 3-12. Augusta, NJ. The state's largest livestock and horse show also includes educational exhibits, amusements, commercial exhibits and entertainment. Located off Rt 206 Plains Rd. Gate opens 1 PM Friday and closes 7 PM Sunday. Est attendance: 220,000. For info: Howard Worts, Mgr, PO Box 2456, Branchville, NJ 07826. Phone: (973) 948-5500. Fax: (973) 948-0147. E-mail: thefair@ptd.net. Web: www.new jerseystatefair.org.

TELLURIDE JAZZ CELEBRATION. Aug 3-5 (tentative). Telluride, CO. Some of jazz's hottest rising stars and most accomplished musicians team up in the town park by day and in intimate nightclubs at night. Annually, the first weekend in August. Est attendance: 1,500. For info: Telluride Mountain Village Visitor Services, 700 W Colorado Ave, PO Box 653, Telluride, CO 81435. Phone: (888) 783-0257. Fax: (970) 728-6475. E-mail: info.tmvs@visit-telluride.org. Web: www.gotelluride.org.

TWINS DAY FESTIVAL. Aug 3-5. Twinsburg, OH. According to *Guinness Book of World Records*, this is the world's largest gathering of twins. Annually, the first weekend in August. For info: Twins Day Festival Committee, PO Box 29, Twinsburg, OH 44087. Phone: (330) 425-3652. E-mail: info@twinsday.org. Web: www.twinsday.org.

UPTOWN ART FAIR. Aug 3-5. Minneapolis, MN. The midwest's largest outdoor juried arts and crafts festival featuring 525 national artists, food and beverage booths, a children's art activities booth and entertainment. Est attendance: 350,000. For info: Uptown Art Fair, 3013 Holmes Ave South, Minneapolis, MN 55408. Phone: (612) 823-4581.

WEST VIRGINIA SQUARE AND ROUND DANCE CONVENTION. Aug 3-5. Buckhannon, WV. Promotes the fun and fellowship of western-style square dancing, rounds, contra, country western and clogging. Annually, the first full weekend in August. Sponsor: West Virginia Square and Round Dance Federation. Est attendance: 1,000. For info: Frank and Sheila Landis, 175 Fairmor Dr, Westover, WV 26501.

WINTERHAWK BLUEGRASS FESTIVAL. Aug 3-5. Hillsdale, NY. Mainstage concerts, all day and into the night dancing, camping and workshops. Plenty of activities for everyone in the family to enjoy. For info: Columbia County Tourism Dept, 401 State St, Hudson, NY 12534. Phone: (860) 364-9396.

WISCONSIN STATE FAIR. Aug 3-13. State Fair Park, Milwaukee, WI. Wisconsin celebrates its rural heritage at the state's most popular and most historic annual event. Features giant midway, 26 free stages, livestock, food and flower judging and top-name entertainment. [Call 24-hour recorded information line at 1-800-884-FAIR for performance times and dates.] Est attendance: 910,000. For info: PR Dept, Wisconsin State Fair Park, PO Box 14990, West Allis, WI 53214-0990. Fax: (414) 266-7007. E-mail: wsfp@sfp.state.wi.us. Web: www.wistatefair.com.

WORLD FREEFALL CONVENTION. Aug 3-11. Quincy, IL. More than 5,400 skydivers converge in Quincy and fill the skies with their brilliant-colored parachutes. Spectators can enjoy the sights and take part in helicopter rides and hot-air balloon rides. Those wishing to skydive may purchase a tandem skydive or take lessons and skydive on their own. Est attendance: 60,000. For info: World Freefall Convention, RR 1, Box 123, Quincy, IL 62301. Phone: (217) 222-5867. Fax: (217) 221-9999. E-mail: wffc@freefall.com.

BIRTHDAYS TODAY

Tony Bennett (Anthony Dominick Benedetto), 75, singer ("I Left My Heart in San Francisco"), born New York, NY, Aug 3, 1926.

Steven Berkoff, 64, actor, director, writer (*A Clockwork Orange, Beverly Hills Cop*), born London, England, Aug 3, 1937.

Victoria Jackson, 43, actress ("Saturday Night Live," *I Love You to Death*), born Miami, FL, Aug 3, 1958.

P. D. (Phyllis Dorothy) James, 81, mystery novelist (*Devices and Desires, Innocent Blood*), born Oxford, England, Aug 3, 1920.

John McGinley, 42, actor (*Platoon, Born on the Fourth of July*), born New York, NY, Aug 3, 1959.

Martin Sheen (Ramon Estevez), 61, actor (*Badlands, Apocalypse Now*), born Dayton, OH, Aug 3, 1940.

Martha Stewart, 60, lifestyle consultant, TV personality, writer, born Nutley, NJ, Aug 3, 1941.

Leon Uris, 77, author (*Mitla Pass, Exodus*), born Baltimore, MD, Aug 3, 1924.

AUGUST 4 — SATURDAY
Day 216 — 149 Remaining

AMHERST'S TEDDY BEAR RALLY. Aug 4. Amherst, MA. Teddy bear parade, official bear appraiser, coloring event, Teddy Bear Hospital, UMass Oompah Band, Winnie-the-Pooh readings and more than 165 teddy bear dealers and exhibits. Entertainment free; refreshments available. 19th annual rally. Est attendance: 25,000. For info: Amherst Rotary Club, Teddy Bear Rally Committee, PO Box 542, Amherst, MA 01004. Phone: (413) 545-3089.

ARMSTRONG, LOUIS: BIRTH ANNIVERSARY. Aug 4, 1900. (or 1901). Jazz musician extraordinaire born at New Orleans, LA. Died at New York, NY, July 6, 1971. Asked to define jazz, Armstrong reportedly replied, "Man, if you gotta ask, you'll never know." The trumpet player was also known as Satchmo. He appeared in many films. Popular singles included "What a Wonderful World" and "Hello, Dolly" (with Barbra Streisand).

ARTS AND CRAFTS FESTIVAL. Aug 4-5. Loveladies, NJ. Featuring arts and crafts displays, entertainment, food and more. For info: Long Beach Island Foundation of the Arts and Sciences, 120 Long Beach Blvd, Loveladies, NJ 08008. Phone: (609) 494-1241. Fax: (609) 494-0662.

BATTLE OF BUSHY RUN REENACTMENT. Aug 4-5. Harrison City, PA. This reenactment commemorates the decisive battle of Pontiac's War on Aug 5 and 6, 1763. Event includes a guided tour through the battle's historic camps and demonstrations of military crafts. Est attendance: 2,000. For info: John Giblin, PO Box 468, Harrison City, PA 15636-0468. Phone: (724) 527-5584. E-mail: jgiblin@phmc.state.pa.us.

BAY HARBOR SUMMER ART FAIR. Aug 4–5. Bay Harbor, MI. 2nd annual fine art and fine craft show, located in the Marina District, near Charlevoix and Petosky. Est attendance: 7,000. For info: Audree Levy, 1809 Morning Glory, Carrollton, TX 75007. Phone: (972) 735-9898. Fax: (972) 735-9808. E-mail: audree@levyartfairs.com. Web: www.levyartfairs.com.

BLUEBERRY ARTS FESTIVAL. Aug 4. State Office Building, Methodist Church and Main Street Gallery and Theatre, Ketchikan, AK. A street fair featuring arts and crafts, food, games and contests for all ages, performing arts events and poetry and prose reading. Annually, the first Saturday in August. Est attendance: 5,000. For info: Ketchikan Area Arts and Humanities Council, 338 Main St, Ketchikan, AK 99901. Phone: (907) 225-2211. Fax: (907) 225-4330.

CALIFORNIA DRY BEAN FESTIVAL. Aug 4–5. Tracy, CA. 15th annual. To promote the California dry bean industry, to raise funds for nonprofit organizations and to highlight the City of Tracy. Est attendance: 60,000. For info: Paula Marsh, Events Mgr, Tracy Chamber of Commerce, 223 E 10th St, Tracy, CA 95376. Phone: (209) 835-2131. Fax: (209) 833-9526. E-mail: pmarsh@tracychamber.org. Web: www.tracychamber.org.

CANADA: CANMORE FOLK MUSIC FESTIVAL. Aug 4–6. Centennial Park, Canmore, AB. 24th annual. Alberta's longest-running folk festival. Featuring food booths, entertainment, workshops and pancake breakfast on Monday. Est attendance: 10,000. For info: Canmore Folk Music Festival, PO Box 8098, Canmore, AB, Canada T1W 2T8. Phone: (403) 678-2524. Fax: (403) 678-2524. E-mail: canmorefolkfest@banff.net. Web: www.banff.net/users/canmorefolkfest.

CAPITOL AF'AIR. Aug 4–5. Bismarck, ND. The state capitol grounds provide the backdrop for this capital arts and crafts show. More than 90 exceptional artisans display and sell their artwork on the great mall of the capitol grounds. Other highlights include music and dance performances, children's activities and several food booths. For info: (701) 223-5986 or Bismarck Conv & Visitors Bureau, PO Box 2274, Bismarck, ND 58501. Phone: (701) 222-4308 or (800) 767-3555. Fax: (701) 222-0647.

CHEROKEE DAYS OF RECOGNITION. Aug 4–5. Red Clay State Park, Cleveland, TN. Traditional and contemporary Cherokee dances, storytelling, Native American food, Cherokee arts and crafts and the annual blowgun contest are featured. Annually, the first weekend in August. Sponsor: Tennessee Dept of Environment and Conservation. Est attendance: 15,000. For info: Lois I. Osborne, Park Mgr, Red Clay State Hist Park, 1140 Red Clay Park Rd SW, Cleveland, TN 37311. Phone: (423) 478-0339.

CHILDREN'S WEEKEND. Aug 4–5. Old Cowtown Museum, Wichita, KS. Children and parents go back in time to experience work and play the old-fashioned way; games, races, crafts and chores provide participants with a glimpse of life long ago. Annually, the first full weekend in August. Est attendance: 1,000. For info: Gloria G. Campbell, Dir, Old Cowtown Museum, 1871 Sim Park Dr, Wichita, KS 67203. Phone: (316) 264-0671. Fax: (316) 264-2937.

CIRCLE K INTERNATIONAL CONVENTION. Aug 4–8. Buffalo, NY. Est attendance: 1,200. For info: Circle K Intl, 3636 Woodview Trace, Indianapolis, IN 46268-3196. Phone: (317) 875-8755. Fax: (317) 879-0204. E-mail: cki@kiwanis.org. Web: www.circlek.org.

	S	**M**	**T**	**W**	**T**	**F**	**S**
August				1	2	3	4
2001	5	6	7	8	9	10	11
	12	13	14	15	16	17	18
	19	20	21	22	23	24	25
	26	27	28	29	30	31	

CIVIL RIGHTS WORKERS FOUND SLAIN: ANNIVERSARY. Aug 4, 1964. After disappearing on June 21, three civil rights workers were found murdered and buried in an earthen dam outside Philadelphia, MS. The three young men were workers on the Mississippi Summer Project organized by the Student Nonviolent Coordinating Committee (SNCC) to increase black voter registration. Prior to their disappearance, James Chaney, Andrew Goodman and Michael Schwerner were detained by Neshoba County police on charges of speeding. When their car was found, burned, on June 23, President Johnson ordered an FBI search for the men.

COAST GUARD DAY. Aug 4. Celebrates anniversary of founding of the US Coast Guard in 1790.

CUNNINGHAM, GLENN: BIRTH ANNIVERSARY. Aug 4, 1909. Glenn Clarence Cunningham, the "Kansas Ironman," American track athlete and 1934–37 world record holder for the mile, member of the US Olympic teams in 1932 and 1936, was born at Atlanta, KS. On June 16, 1934, at Princeton, NJ, Cunningham set a world record for the mile (4:06.7 min). Cunningham died at Menifee, AR, Mar 10, 1988.

ENGLAND: SKANDIA LIFE COWES WEEK. Aug 4–11. Cowes, Isle of Wight. Yachting festival covering all classes of yacht racing. Est attendance: 14,000. For info: Cowes Week Organizers, 18 Bath Rd, Cowes, Isle of Wight, England PO31 7QN. Phone: (44) 198 329-5744. Fax: (44) 198 329-5329. E-mail: ccc@cowesweek.co.uk. Web: www.cowesweek.co.uk.

E.P. "TOM" SAWYER STATE PARK/LOUISVILLE LANDSHARKS TRIATHLON XIX. Aug 4. Tom Sawyer State Park, Louisville, KY. Participants swim ½ mile, bicycle 16 miles and run 5K cross-country. Est attendance: 500. For info: Chris Head, Recreation Leader, E.P. "Tom" Sawyer Park, 3000 Freys Hill Rd, Louisville, KY 40241-2172. Phone: (502) 426-8950.

FARM SANCTUARY HOEDOWN. Aug 4–5. Farm Sanctuary, Watkins Glen, NY. America's shelter for farm animals hosts a fun and educational weekend of farm tours, hayrides, lectures, exhibits, music, food and more, all located on a beautiful 175-acre working farm with hundreds of cows, pigs, turkeys and other animals. Est attendance: 150. For info: Education Coord, Farm Sanctuary, PO Box 150, Watkins Glen, NY 14891. Phone: (607) 583-2225. Fax: (607) 583-2041.

FESTIVAL OF NATIONS. Aug 4–11. Red Lodge, MT. A nine-day extravaganza. All events are free, following the philosophy of festival founders that the festival should be a fun, educational experience including information on cooking, crafts, customs, dances and languages. Est attendance: 16,000. For info: Joan Cline, Exec Secy, Red Lodge Chamber of Commerce, PO Box 988, Red Lodge, MT 59068. Phone: (888) 281-0625. Fax: (406) 446-1718. E-mail: information@redlodge.com. Web: www.redlodge.com.

GEM, MINERAL AND JEWELRY SHOW AND SALE. Aug 4–5. Clayton Recreation Park Arena, Clayton, NY. Show includes fluorescent mineral light show, jewelry, dealers' supplies, crystals, beads, fossils, mineral specimens, gemstones and craft books. Archaeology clubs and lapidary societies will also be present. The clubs will be doing slide shows, giving out information and selling items. Annually, the first weekend in August. Est attendance: 1,000. For info: Thousand Islands Museum, 403 Riverside Dr, Clayton, NY 13624. Phone: (315) 686-5794. Fax: (315) 686-4867. E-mail: timuseum@gisco.net. Web: www.thousandislands.com/timuseum.

GIFT OF THE WATERS PAGEANT & ART FESTIVAL IN THE PARK. Aug 4–5. Hot Springs State Park, Thermopolis, WY. Indian dance demonstrations and pageant, pow-wow, arts & crafts festival, craft demonstrations. Est attendance: 2,000. For info: Toddi Darlington, Thermopolis Chamber of Commerce, 700 Broadway, Thermopolis, WY 82443. Phone: (307) 864-3192. E-mail: thercc@trib.com. Web: www.thermopolis.com.

HOME OF THE HAMBURGER CELEBRATION. Aug 4. Seymour, WI. Giant parade, live music, kids' games and entertainment, Hamburger Meet, lots of hamburgers to eat. Annually, first Saturday in August. Est attendance: 10,000. For info: Home of the Hamburger, Inc, PO Box 173, Seymour, WI 54165. Phone: (920) 833-9522 or (920) 833-2663. Fax: (920) 833-7414.

INDIAN ARTIFACT SHOW. Aug 4–5. Bowling Green, KY. To promote the art and culture of prehistoric Indians and to display outstanding collections of relics; buying, selling and trading. Est attendance: 3,000. For info: Kathy Pohl, Box 93, Cannelton, IN 47520-0093. Phone: (812) 547-3255. Fax: (812) 547-2525. E-mail: kpohl@psci.net.

JONATHAN HAGER FRONTIER CRAFT DAYS. Aug 4–5. Jonathan Hager House, City Park, Hagerstown, MD. Featuring dozens of demonstrating craftsmen, great bluegrass music and great food. Annually, the first weekend in August. Est attendance: 10,000. For info: John Nelson, Jonathan Hager House and Museum, 110 Key St, Hagerstown, MD 21740. Phone: (301) 739-8393.

KRXL CAR CRUISE. Aug 4. Kirksville, MO. Motorcycles, cars, antiques, hot rods, classics, originals and street rods. Est attendance: 1,000. For info: Steve Lloyd, General Mgr, KRXL, PO Box 130, Kirksville, MO 63501. Phone: (660) 665-9841.

MANDELA, NELSON: ARREST ANNIVERSARY. Aug 4, 1962. Nelson Rolihlahla Mandela, charismatic black South African leader, was born in 1918, the son of the Tembu tribal chief, at Umtata, Transkei territory of South Africa. A lawyer and political activist, Mandela, who in 1952 established the first black law partnership in South Africa, had been in conflict with the white government there much of his life. Acquitted of a treason charge after a trial that lasted from 1956 to 1961, he was apprehended again by security police Aug 4, 1962. The subsequent trial, widely viewed as an indictment of white domination, resulted in Mandela's being sentenced to five years in prison. In 1963 he was taken from the Pretoria prison to face a new trial—for sabotage, high treason and conspiracy to overthrow the government—and in June 1964 he was sentenced to life in prison. See also: "Mandela, Nelson: Prison Release Anniversary" (Feb 11).

MOON PHASE: FULL MOON. Aug 4. Moon enters Full Moon phase at 1:56 AM, EDT.

NATIONAL MUSTARD DAY. Aug 4. Mustard lovers across the nation pay tribute to the king of condiments by slathering their favorite mustard on hot dogs, pretzels, licorice and even ice cream (an acquired taste)! The Mount Horeb Mustard Museum contains the world's largest collection of prepared mustards and mustard memorabilia. Celebration festivities include free hot dogs, mustard games and mustard squirting. Annually, the first Saturday in August. Est attendance: 1,000. For info: Barry M. Levenson, Curator, The Mount Horeb Mustard Museum, 109 E Main St, Mount Horeb, WI 53572. Phone: (608) 437-3986. Fax: (608) 437-4018. E-mail: curator@mustardmuseum.com. Web: www.mustardmuseum.com.

SCALIGER, JOSEPH JUSTUS: BIRTH ANNIVERSARY. Aug 4, 1540 (OS). French scholar who has been called the founder of scientific chronology. Born at Agen, France, the son of classical scholar Julius Caesar Scaliger. In 1582 he suggested a new system for measuring time and numbering years. His "Julian Period" (named for his father), which consisted of 7,980 consecutive years (beginning Jan 1, 4713 BC), is still in use by astronomers. He died at Leiden, Netherlands, Jan 21, 1609 (OS).

SCHUMAN, WILLIAM HOWARD: BIRTH ANNIVERSARY. Aug 4, 1910. American composer who won the first Pulitzer Prize for composition and founded the Juilliard School of Music, born at New York. His compositions include *American Festival Overture, New England Triptych*, the baseball opera *The Mighty Casey* and *On Freedom's Ground*, written for the centennial of the Statue of Liberty in 1986. He was instrumental in the conception of the Lincoln Center for the Performing Arts and served as its first president. In 1985 he was awarded a special Pulitzer Prize for his contributions. He also received a National Medal of Arts in 1985 and a Kennedy Center Honor in 1989. Schuman died at New York City, Feb 15, 1992.

SHARON ON THE GREEN ARTS AND CRAFTS FAIR. Aug 4. Sharon, CT. A high-quality, juried art show with 140 regional artists and crafters offering a broad range of unique handmade items of glass, ceramics, pewter, jewelry, quilts, woodcrafts, photos, paintings, art-to-wear and gourmet items. Est attendance: 1,500. For info: Sharon, Rec/Youth, PO Box 385, Sharon, CT 06069. Phone: (860) 364-1400.

SHELLEY, PERCY BYSSHE: BIRTH ANNIVERSARY. Aug 4, 1792. Poet Percy Bysshe Shelley, one of the leading English Romantic poets and embodiment of a free spirit was born at Warnham, Sussex. He lived abroad in Italy until his death at sea off the coast of Viareggio, just a month before his 30th birthday, July 8, 1822. Shelley's important works include "Ozymandias" published in 1818; "Ode to the West Wind," "The Cloud," "To a Skylark" and *Prometheus Unbound* in 1819; and *Adonais* (an elegy for John Keats) in 1821.

TALL TIMBER DAYS FESTIVAL. Aug 4–5. Grand Rapids, MN. Festival features the Sheer Brothers Lumberjack Show, chainsaw carvers, arts and crafts, Applecords Quartet, competitions, YMCA run, canoeing and bed racing. Families welcome. Annually, the first full weekend in August. Est attendance: 30,000. For info: Tall Timber Days, PO Box 134, Grand Rapids, MN 55744. Phone: (218) 326-5618. E-mail: mojo@uslink.net.

TAWAS BAY WATERFRONT FINE ART SHOW. Aug 4–5. Tawas City Park, Tawas City, MI. Est attendance: 9,000. For info: Chamber of Commerce, Box 608, Tawas City, MI 48764-0608. Phone: (800) 55-TAWAS. Fax: (517) 362-7880.

WALES: ROYAL NATIONAL EISTEDDFOD. Aug 4–11. Denbigh. A cultural event with competitive festivals of music, drama, literature, arts and crafts. All events conducted in Welsh with simultaneous translation into English available. Est attendance: 160,000. For info: Royal Natl Eisteddfod, 40 Parc Ty Glas, Llanishen, Cardiff, Wales, UK CF4 5WU. Phone: (44) (1222) 763777. Fax: (44) (1222) 763737. Web: www.eisteddfod.org.uk.

WESTON SUMMER GLOW. Aug 4. Weston, MO. An evening of fun and shopping. Stores stay open until 8 PM. Outdoor activities include fresh vegetable market, kettlecorn, carriage rides and much more. For info: Weston Development Co, 502 Main, Weston, MO 64098. Phone: (816) 640-2909.

WHITE OAK RENDEZVOUS. Aug 4–5. Deer River, MN. Voted one of the top 25 Festivals by the Minnesota Office of Tourism. One big weekend for reenactment of fur trade history in a setting of 80 acres of pasture and wilderness. 200 tipis and white canvas lodges placed around a North West Company Fur Post from 1798. Blacksmith shop, root cellar, clerk's quarters and store, birchbark canoe–building shed, Ojibwe village. Country, bluegrass and old-time music, dance, puppetry and nature trail with plants labeled to explain their use in 1798 for medicine, shelter or food. 18th-century craft demonstrations and sales. Also, specialty foods from the fur trade period. RV and tent campground available. Est attendance: 8,000. For info: Perry Vining, White Oak Society, 33155 State Highway 6, Deer River, MN 56636. Phone: (218) 246-9393. Fax: (218) 246-9393. E-mail: pvining@ paulbunyan.net. Web: www.whiteoak.org.

WYATT EARP WESTERN DAY. Aug 4. Monmouth, IL. "OK Corral Reenactments" show at 2 PM and 3 PM. Birthplace home, listed on the National Register of Historic Places, open 1 PM to 4 PM. Annually, first Saturday in August. Est attendance: 200. For info: Wyatt Earp Birthplace, Historic House Museum, Office: 1020 E Detroit Ave, Monmouth, IL 61462. Phone: (309) 734-6419 or Chamber of Commerce (309) 734-3181. Fax: (309) 734-6419.

BIRTHDAYS TODAY

Yasser Arafat, 72, president of the Palestinian National Authority, chairman of the Executive Committee of the PLO, born Jerusalem, Aug 4, 1929.

Richard Belzer, 57, comedian, actor (*Mad Dog and Glory*, "Homicide: Life on the Street"), born Bridgeport, CT, Aug 4, 1944.

William Roger Clemens, 39, baseball player, born Dayton, OH, Aug 4, 1962.

Elizabeth, the Queen Mother (Elizabeth Angela Marguerite), 101, born Hertfordshire, England, Aug 4, 1900.

Jeff Gordon, 30, race car driver, born Pittsboro, IN, Aug 4, 1971.

Kristoffer Tabori, 49, actor ("Seventh Avenue," "Chicago Story"), born Los Angeles, CA, Aug 4, 1952.

Helen Thomas, 81, journalist (long-time White House correspondent), born Winchester, KY, Aug 4, 1920.

Billy Bob Thornton, 46, actor (*A Simple Plan*), born Little Rock, AR, Aug 4, 1955.

AUGUST 5 — SUNDAY
Day 217 — 148 Remaining

AIKEN, CONRAD: BIRTH ANNIVERSARY. Aug 5, 1899. American poet, short-story writer, critic and Pulitzer Prize winner (poetry, 1930). He was born at Savannah, GA, and died there Aug 17, 1973.

"AMERICAN BANDSTAND" TV PREMIERE: ANNIVERSARY. Aug 5, 1957. "American Bandstand" and Dick Clark are synonyomous; he hosted the show for more than 30 years. "AB" started out as a local show at Philadelphia in 1952. Clark, then a disk jockey, took over as host at the age of 26. The format was simple: teens dancing, performers doing their latest hits, Clark introducing songs and listing the top 10 songs each week. This hour-long show was not only TV's longest-running musical series, but also the first one devoted exclusively to rock and roll. The show was cancelled six months after Clark turned over the hosting duties to David Hirsch in 1989.

August 2001	S	M	T	W	T	F	S
				1	2	3	4
	5	6	7	8	9	10	11
	12	13	14	15	16	17	18
	19	20	21	22	23	24	25
	26	27	28	29	30	31	

AMERICAN FAMILY DAY IN ARIZONA. Aug 5. Observed in Arizona on the first Sunday in August. The observance date is designated by statute.

BATTLE OF MOBILE BAY: ANNIVERSARY. Aug 5, 1864. A Union fleet under Admiral David Farragut attempted to run past three Confederate forts into Mobile Bay, AL. After coming under fire, the Union fleet headed into a maze of underwater mines, known at that time as torpedos. The ironclad *Tecumseh* was sunk by a torpedo, after which Farragut is said to have exclaimed, "Damn the torpedos, full steam ahead." The Union fleet was successful and Mobile Bay was secured.

BEARD, MARY R.: 125th BIRTH ANNIVERSARY. Aug 5, 1876. American historian Mary Ritter Beard was born at Indianapolis, IN. Many of her books were written in collaboration with her husband, Charles A. Beard. She died at Phoenix, AZ, Aug 14, 1958.

BURKINA FASO: REPUBLIC DAY: ANNIVERSARY. Aug 5. Burkina Faso (formerly Upper Volta) gained autonomy from France in 1960.

BURRO RACE. Aug 5. Leadville, CO. International Pack Burro Race leaves from Main Street up Mosquito Pass and back. Est attendance: 35,000. For info: Chamber of Commerce, Box 861, Leadville, CO 80461. Phone: (719) 486-3900 or (888) 264-5344. Fax: (719) 486-8478. E-mail: leadville@leadvilleusa.com. Web: www.leadvilleusa.com.

CANADA: FOLKLORAMA—CANADA'S CULTURAL CELEBRATION. Aug 5–18. 32nd festival. Winnipeg, MB. More than 40 pavilions representing various cultures offer traditionally prepared cuisine, exhilarating entertainment and captivating cultural displays for 14 prairie summer nights. Folklorama is the largest multicultural celebration of its kind in the world and has been named the Internationally Known Super Event by the American Bus Association. Est attendance: 420,000. For info: Judy Murphy, Exec Dir, Folklorama, 183 Kennedy St, 2nd Fl, Winnipeg, MB, Canada R3C 1S6. Phone: (204) 982-6210 or (800) 665-0234. Fax: (204) 943-1956. E-mail: folkarts@mts.net. Web: www.folklorama.ca.

COLUMBUS SAILING ON THE SANTA MARIA: ANNIVERSARY. Aug 5. Battelle Park, Columbus, OH. Special observances for the anniversary of Christopher Columbus sailing from Spain in search of India held aboard the *Santa Maria*, the only full-size replica of Columbus's flagship on permanent display in North America. Est attendance: 400. For info: Columbus Santa Maria, 90 W Broad St, 1st Fl, Columbus, OH 43215-9019. Phone: (614) 645-8760. Fax: (614) 645-8748. Web: www.SantaMaria.org.

ELIOT, JOHN: BIRTH ANNIVERSARY. Aug 5, 1604 (OS). American "Apostle to the Indians," translator of the Bible into an Indian tongue (the first Bible to be printed in America), was born at Hertfordshire, England. He died at Roxbury, MA, May 21, 1690 (OS).

FIRST ENGLISH COLONY IN NORTH AMERICA: FOUNDING ANNIVERSARY. Aug 5, 1583. Sir Humphrey Gilbert, English navigator and explorer, aboard his sailing ship, the *Squirrel*, sighted the Newfoundland coast and took possession of the area around St. John's harbor in the name of the Queen, thus establishing the first English colony in North America. Gilbert was lost at sea, in a storm off the Azores, on his return trip to England.

INTERNATIONAL FESTIVAL. Aug 5–12. Calais, ME, and St. Stephen, NB, Canada. Festival of international cooperation between St. Stephen and Calais with the theme "The Spirit of International Friendship and Goodwill." Celebrating the friendship of two countries joining as one. Est attendance: 14,000. For info: Keith Guttormsen, Exec Chamber Dir, International Fest Committee, PO Box 368, Calais, ME 04619. Phone: (207) 454-2308 or (800) 377-9748. Web: www.calaismaine.com.

ITALY: JOUST OF THE QUINTANA. Aug 5. Ascoli/Piceno. The first Sunday in August is set aside for the Torneo della Quintana, an historical pageant with 15th-century costumes.

LYNCH, THOMAS: BIRTH ANNIVERSARY. Aug 5, 1749. Signer, Declaration of Independence, born Prince George's Parish, SC. Died 1779 (lost at sea, exact date of death unknown).

MONROE, MARILYN: DEATH ANNIVERSARY. Aug 5, 1962. The world fell in love with Monroe's unique combination of sensuality and approachability. She was the epitome of Hollywood glamour, making 29 films in her career. Her tragic death at age 36, at Los Angeles, from an overdose of sleeping pills, is shrouded in controversy. She was born June 1, 1926, at Los Angeles.

PYROTECHNICS GUILD INTERNATIONAL FIRE-WORKS CONVENTION. Aug 5–10. Appleton, WI. The world's finest fireworks are displayed and members compete for the title of Grand Master during this annual international pyrotechnic convention. The Pyrotechnics Guild promotes the design, construction and safe display of the highest-quality pyrotechnics. Est attendance: 50,000. For info: Mark Wray, Pyrotechnics Guild Intl, Inc, 11144 Claire Ave, Northridge, CA 91326-2333. Phone: (818) 363-6277. E-mail: mlwray@aol.com. Web: www.pgi.org/.

SCOTLAND: EDINBURGH FESTIVAL FRINGE. Aug 5–27 (tentative). Edinburgh. Three weeks of non-stop entertainment with more than 1,000 different events in 200 venues around the City, including theater, comedy, dance, music and children's shows. Coincides with Edinburgh's International Festival. Est attendance: 750,000. For info: Edinburgh Festival Fringe Society, 180 High St, Edinburgh, Scotland EH1 1QS. Phone: (44 131) 226-5257. Fax: (44 131) 220-4205. E-mail: admin@edfringe.com. Web: www.edfringe.com.

SISTERS' DAY. Aug 5. Celebrating the spirit of sisterhood—sisters nationwide show appreciation and give recognition to one another for the special relationship they share. Send a card, make a phone call, share memories, photos, flowers, candy, etc. Sisters may include biological sisters, sorority sisters, sisterly friends, etc. Annually, the first Sunday in August each year. For info: Tricia Eleogram, 666 Hawthorne, Memphis, TN 38107. Phone: (901) 725-5190 or (901) 755-0751. Fax: (901) 754-9923. E-mail: sisters day@aol.com.

VOLKSFEST. Aug 5. New Glarus, WI. Celebration of Swiss Independence Day. Annually, the first Sunday in August. Est attendance: 2,000. For info: Volksfest, Box 713, New Glarus, WI 53574. Phone: (608) 527-2095 or (800) 527-6838. E-mail: information@newglarus.com. Web: www.newglarus-wi.com.

WALLENBERG, RAOUL: BIRTH ANNIVERSARY. Aug 5, 1912. Swedish architect Raoul Gustaf Wallenberg was born at Stockholm, Sweden. He was the second person in history (Winston Churchill was the first) to be voted honorary American citizenship (US House of Representatives 396–2, Sept 22, 1981). He is credited with saving 100,000 Jews from almost certain death at the hands of the Nazis during WWII. Wallenberg was arrested by Soviet troops at Budapest, Hungary, Jan 17, 1945, and, according to the official Soviet press agency Tass, died in prison at Moscow, July 17, 1947.

WORLD SCRABBLE CHAMPIONSHIP. Aug 5–10 (tentative). Players compete for the world championship in the popular game invented by unemployed architect Alfred Butts in 1931. Est attendance: 125. For info: Kathy Hummel, Natl Scrabble Assn, Box 700, Front St Garden, Greenport, NY 11944. Phone: (516) 477-0033. Fax: (516) 477-0294. E-mail: info@scrabble-assoc.com.

BIRTHDAYS TODAY

Loni Anderson, 55, actress ("WKRP in Cincinnati," *The Jayne Mansfield Story*), born St. Paul, MN, Aug 5, 1946.

Neil Alden Armstrong, 71, former astronaut (first man to walk on moon), born Wapakoneta, OH, Aug 5, 1930.

Josie Bissett, 31, actress ("Melrose Place"), born Seattle, WA, Aug 5, 1970.

Ja'net DuBois, 63, actress ("Good Times," "Beverly Hills 90210"), born Philadelphia, PA, Aug 5, 1938.

Patrick Aloysius Ewing, 39, basketball player, born Kingston, Jamaica, Aug 5, 1962.

John Olerud, 33, baseball player, born Seattle, WA, Aug 5, 1968.

Samantha Sang, 48, singer ("Emotion"), born Melbourne, Australia, Aug 5, 1953.

John Saxon, 65, actor ("Falcon Crest," *Enter the Dragon, Nightmare on Elm Street*), born Brooklyn, NY, Aug 5, 1936.

Jonathan Silverman, 35, actor ("The Single Guy," *Weekend at Bernie's*), born Los Angeles, CA, Aug 5, 1966.

Erika Slezak, 55, actress ("One Life to Live"), born Los Angeles, CA, Aug 5, 1946.

Sammi Smith, 58, singer ("Help Me Make It Through the Night"), born Orange, CA, Aug 5, 1943.

AUGUST 6 — MONDAY

Day 218 — 147 Remaining

ANTIGUA AND BARBUDA: AUGUST MONDAY. Aug 6–7. The first Monday in August and the day following form the August Monday Public Holiday.

ATOMIC BOMB DROPPED ON HIROSHIMA: ANNIVERSARY. Aug 6, 1945. At 8:15 AM, local time, an American B-29 bomber, the *Enola Gay*, dropped an atomic bomb named "Little Boy" over the center of the city of Hiroshima, Japan. The bomb exploded about 1,800 ft above the ground, killing more than 105,000 civilians and destroying the city. It is estimated that another 100,000 persons were injured and died subsequently as a direct result of the bomb and the radiation it produced. This was the first time in history that such a devastating weapon had been used by any nation.

AUSTRALIA: PICNIC DAY. Aug 6. The first Monday in August is a bank holiday in New South Wales and Picnic Day in Northern Territory, Australia.

BAHAMAS: EMANCIPATION DAY. Aug 6. Public holiday in Bahamas. Annually, the first Monday in August. Commemorates the emancipation of slaves by the British in 1838.

BALL, LUCILLE: 90th BIRTH ANNIVERSARY. Aug 6, 1911. Film and television pioneer and comedian born at Butte, MT. In addition to her many other film and television credits, Lucille Ball always will be remembered for her role in the 1950s CBS sitcom *I Love Lucy*. As Lucy Riccardo, the wife of bandleader Ricky Riccardo (her real-life husband, Desi Arnaz), her comedic style became a trademark of early television comedy. She was instrumental in many pioneering innovations in TV production. Desilu Productions, the company founded by Ball and Arnaz, insisted on filming in Hollywood instead of New York. This move is largely credited with creating a shift in TV production to the west coast. In addition, theirs was the first TV show to use 35mm film to increase the clarity of the final image, the first to use three cameras instead of one and the first to be filmed in front of a live audience. On Apr 1, 1958, the final episode was broadcast, but *I Love Lucy* now is seen worldwide in syndication. Ball continued her involvement both before and behind the camera, appearing in three additional sitcoms. She became the first woman to head a major motion picture and TV studio when she purchased Arnaz's share of Desilu Productions. Ball and Arnaz were divorced in 1960; she later married Gary Morton. She died Apr 26, 1989, at Los Angeles, CA.

BOLIVIA: INDEPENDENCE DAY: ANNIVERSARY. Aug 6. National holiday. Gained freedom from Spain in 1825. Named after Simon Bolivar.

CANADA: CHOCOLATE FESTIVAL. Aug 6–11. St. Stephen, NB. Events include chocolate meals, chocolate teas, chocolate-eating contests, "Choctail hour" and the ever-popular Ganong Chocolate Factory tours. (Tours must be booked in advance.) Est attendance: 7,000. For info: Mr Derek O'Brien, Chair, Chocolate Fest Committee, PO Box 5002, St. Stephen, NB, Canada E3L 2X5. Phone: (506) 465-5616. Fax: (506) 465-5610. E-mail: ChocolateFest@ganong.com.

CANADA: CIVIC HOLIDAY. Aug 6. The first Monday in August is observed as a holiday in seven of Canada's 10 provinces. Civic holiday in Manitoba, New Brunswick, Northwest Territories, Ontario and Saskatchewan, British Columbia Day in British Columbia and Heritage Day in Alberta.

		S	M	T	W	T	F	S
August					1	2	3	4
2001		5	6	7	8	9	10	11
		12	13	14	15	16	17	18
		19	20	21	22	23	24	25
		26	27	28	29	30	31	

COLORADO DAY. Aug 6. Colorado. Annually, the first Monday in August. Commemorates Admission Day, Aug 1, 1876, when Colorado became the 38th state.

ELECTROCUTION FIRST USED TO CARRY OUT DEATH PENALTY: ANNIVERSARY. Aug 6, 1890. At Auburn Prison, Auburn, NY, William Kemmler of Buffalo, NY, became the first man to be executed by electrocution. He had been convicted of the hatchet murder of his common-law wife, Matilde Ziegler, on Mar 28, 1889. This first attempt at using electrocution to carry out the death penalty was a botched affair. As reported by George Westinghouse, Jr, "It has been a brutal affair. They could have done better with an axe."

FIRST WOMAN SWIMS THE ENGLISH CHANNEL: 75th ANNIVERSARY. Aug 6, 1926. The first woman to swim the English Channel was 19-year-old Gertrude Ederle of New York, NY. Her swim was completed in 14 hours and 31 minutes.

FLEMING, ALEXANDER: BIRTH ANNIVERSARY. Aug 6, 1881. Sir Alexander Fleming, Scottish bacteriologist, discoverer of penicillin and 1954 Nobel Prize recipient, was born at Lochfield, Scotland. He died at London, England, Mar 11, 1955.

"GREAT DEBATE": ANNIVERSARY. Aug 6–Sept 10, 1787. The Constitutional Convention engaged in the "Great Debate" over the draft constitution, during which it determined that Congress should have the right to regulate foreign trade and interstate commerce, established a four-year term of office for the president and appointed a five-man committee to prepare a final draft of the Constitution.

GRENADA: EMANCIPATION DAY. Aug 6. Grenada observes public holiday annually on the first Monday in August. Commemorates the emancipation of slaves by the British in 1834.

HALFWAY POINT OF SUMMER. Aug 6. On this day, 47 days will have elapsed and the equivalent will remain before Sept 22, 2001, the autumnal equinox and the beginning of autumn.

HIROSHIMA DAY: ANNIVERSARY. Aug 6. Memorial observances in many places for victims of the first atomic bombing of a populated place, which occurred at Hiroshima, Japan in 1945, when an American B-29 bomber dropped an atomic bomb over the center of the city. More than 205,000 civilians died either immediately in the explosion or subsequently of radiation.

ICELAND: SHOP AND OFFICE WORKERS' HOLIDAY. Aug 6. In Iceland an annual holiday for shop and office workers is observed on the first Monday in August.

JAMAICA: INDEPENDENCE DAY. Aug 6. National holiday observing achievement of Jamaican independence from Britain Aug 6, 1962. Annually, the first Monday in August.

JAPAN: PEACE FESTIVAL. Aug 6. Hiroshima, Japan. The festival held annually at Peace Memorial Park is observed in memory of the victims of the Aug 6, 1945, atomic bomb explosion there.

JUDGE CRATER DAY: ANNIVERSARY. Aug 6. Anniversary of mysterious disappearance at age 41, on Aug 6, 1930, of Joseph Force Crater, justice of the New York State Supreme Court. Never seen or heard from after disappearance on this date. Declared legally dead in 1939.

MITCHUM, ROBERT: BIRTH ANNIVERSARY. Aug 6, 1917. Film actor (*The Night of the Hunter, The Story of GI Joe*), born at Bridgeport, CT. Died July 1, 1997 at Santa Barbara County, CA.

NATIONAL FRESH BREATH DAY. Aug 6. The day is designed to bring attention to the importance of fresh breath as an integral part of your overall health and wellness, as well as the impact it has on your personal and professional image. For info: Carol Meyer, Personal Breath Consultants, PO Box 65, Westhampton Beach, NY 11978-0065. Phone: (631) 288-7285. E-mail: Breathlady@aol.com.

NATIONAL SMILE WEEK. Aug 6–12. "Share a smile and it will come back to you, bringing happiness to you and the giver." Annually, the first Monday in August through the following Sunday. For info: Heloise, Newspaper Columnist, Box 795000, San Antonio, TX 78279. Fax: (210) 435-6473. E-mail: heloise@compuserve.com. Web: www.heloise.com.

NEARING, SCOTT: BIRTH ANNIVERSARY. Aug 6, 1883. American sociologist, antiwar crusader, back-to-the-land advocate and author, with his wife Helen, of *Living the Good Life* (1954). He was born at Morris Run, PA, and died a century later at his farm at Harborside, ME, Aug 24, 1983.

O'CONNELL, DANIEL: BIRTH ANNIVERSARY. Aug 6, 1775. Irish Catholic political leader Daniel O'Connell, known as "the Liberator" for his role in achieving the right of Catholics to sit in Parliament, was born near Cahirciveen, County Kerry. He died at age 81, May 15, 1847, at Genoa, Italy.

OLD FIDDLERS' CONVENTION. Aug 6–11. Galax, VA. 66th annual event features dance, folk songs, old-time and bluegrass music competition. Est attendance: 25,000. For info: Edward F. Carico, Box 655, Galax, VA 24333. Phone: (540) 236-8541. Fax: (540) 236-8681.

PSYCHIC WEEK. Aug 6–10. To utilize the power of the psyche to bring peace, find lost individuals and concentrate "psychic power" on beneficial causes. Annually, the first week in August (Monday–Friday). [Created by the late Richard R. Falk.]

ROOSEVELT, EDITH KERMIT CAROW: BIRTH ANNIVERSARY. Aug 6, 1861. Second wife of Theodore Roosevelt, 26th president of the US, whom she married in 1886. Born at Norwich, CT, she died at Long Island, NY, Sept 30, 1948.

SPACE MILESTONE: *VOSTOK 2* (USSR): 40th ANNIVERSARY. Aug 6, 1961. Launched on Aug 6, 1961, Gherman Titov orbited Earth 17 times over period of 25 hours, 18 minutes. Titov broadcast messages in passage over countries, controlled spaceship manually for two hours.

STURGIS RALLY AND RACES. Aug 6–12. Sturgis, SD. The granddaddy of all motorcycle rallies and races. For 59 years the small community of Sturgis has welcomed motorcycle enthusiasts from around the world to a week of varied cycle racing, tours of the beautiful Black Hills, old and new cycles at the National Motorcycle Museum, trade shows and thousands of bikes on display. Annually, beginning the Monday after the first full weekend in August. Est attendance: 215,000. For info: Sturgis Rally & Races, Inc, PO Box 189, Sturgis, SD 57785. Phone: (605) 347-6570. Fax: (605) 347-3245. E-mail: srr@rally.sturgis.sd.us. Web: rally.sturgis.sd.us.

TENNYSON, ALFRED, LORD: BIRTH ANNIVERSARY. Aug 6, 1808. English poet born at Somersby, Lincolnshire, England. His most celebrated works include the poems "The Lady of Shalott" and "The Lotos-Eaters" and the verse novelettes *Maud, Enoch Arden, In Memoriam, Locksley Hall Sixty Years After* and *The Idylls of the King.* Appointed English poet laureate in 1850 in succession to William Wordsworth and made a peer in 1884. Died at Aldworth, England, Oct 6, 1892.

VOTING RIGHTS ACT OF 1965 SIGNED: ANNIVERSARY. Aug 6, 1965. Signed into law by President Lyndon Johnson, the Voting Rights Act of 1965 was designed to thwart attempts to discriminate against minorities at the polls. The act suspended literacy and other disqualifying tests, authorized appointment of federal voting examiners and provided for judicial relief on the federal level to bar discriminatory poll taxes. Congress voted to extend the Act in 1975, 1984 and 1991.

ZAMBIA: YOUTH DAY. Aug 6. National holiday. Youth activities are order of the day. Focal point is Lusaka's Independence Stadium. Annually, the first Monday in August.

Peter Bonerz, 63, actor ("The Bob Newhart Show," "9 to 5"), director, born Portsmouth, NH, Aug 6, 1938.

Soleil Moon Frye, 25, actress ("Punky Brewster"), born Glendora, CA, Aug 6, 1976.

Dorian Harewood, 51, actor (*The Falcon and the Snowman, Full Metal Jacket*), born Dayton, OH, Aug 6, 1950.

Catherine Hicks, 50, actress (*Marilyn, Peggy Sue Got Married*), born Scottsdale, AZ, Aug 6, 1951.

Shirley Ann Jackson, 55, first woman to chair US Nuclear Regulatory Commission, born Washington, DC, Aug 6, 1946.

Freddie Laker, 79, former airline executive, born Kent, England, Aug 6, 1922.

David Maurice Robinson, 36, basketball player, born Key West, FL, Aug 6, 1965.

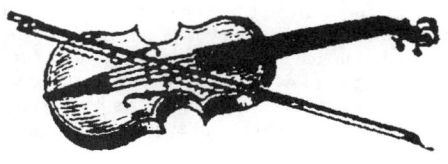

AUGUST 7 — TUESDAY
Day 219 — 146 Remaining

BUNCHE, RALPH JOHNSON: BIRTH ANNIVERSARY. Aug 7, 1904. American statesman, UN official, Nobel Peace Prize recipient (the first black to win the award), born at Detroit, MI. Died Dec 9, 1971, at New York, NY.

COTE D'IVOIRE: NATIONAL DAY: ANNIVERSARY. Aug 7. Commemorates the independence of the Ivory Coast from France in 1960.

DESERT SHIELD: ANNIVERSARY. Aug 7, 1990. Five days after the Iraqi invasion of Kuwait, US President George Bush ordered the military buildup that would become known as Desert Shield to prevent further Iraqi advances.

FIRST PICTURE OF EARTH FROM SPACE: ANNIVERSARY. Aug 7, 1959. US satellite *Explorer VI* transmitted the first picture of Earth from space. For the first time we had a likeness of our planet based on more than projections and conjectures.

GREENE, NATHANIEL: BIRTH ANNIVERSARY. Aug 7, 1742 (OS). Born at Patowomut, RI, American Revolutionary War General Nathaniel Greene was described as the "ablest military officer of the Revolution under Washington." Greene died at Savannah, GA, June 19, 1786.

GULF OF TONKIN RESOLUTION: ANNIVERSARY. Aug 7, 1964. Congress approved the "Gulf of Tonkin Resolution," pertaining to the war in Vietnam, which gave President Lyndon Johnson authority "to take all necessary measures to repel any armed attack against the forces of the United States and to prevent further aggression."

ISING, RUDOLF C.: BIRTH ANNIVERSARY. Aug 7, 1903. Rudolf C. Ising, co-creator with Hugh Harmon of "Looney Tunes" and "Merrie Melodies," was born at Kansas City, MO. Ising and Harmon's initial production, *Bosko the Talk-Ink Kid* (1929), was the first talkie cartoon synchronizing dialogue on the soundtrack with the action on screen. Ising received an Academy Award in 1948 for *Milky Way*, a cartoon about three kittens. During WWII he headed the animation division for the Army Air Forces movie unit developing training films. Rudolf Ising died July 18, 1992, at Newport Beach, CA.

MATA HARI: 125th BIRTH ANNIVERSARY. Aug 7, 1876. Mata Hari (child of the dawn) was born Margaret Gertrude Zelle at Leewarden, Netherlands. Her spectacular career as a dancer, courtesan and spy made her known around the world. Probably an ineffective double agent, she nevertheless fascinated royalty and high officials of several countries. Arrested as a German spy (Agent H-21) in a Paris hotel, Feb 13, 1917, she was tried, convicted and sentenced to death. The greatest of her many roles was the final one—when she refused a blindfold and threw a kiss to the firing squad at Vincennes, France, Oct 15, 1917. See also: "Mata Hari: Execution Anniversary" (Oct 15).

NATIONAL NIGHT OUT. Aug 7. Designed to heighten crime prevention awareness and to promote police-community partnerships. Annually, the first Tuesday in August. For info: Matt A. Peskin, Dir, Natl Assn of Town Watch, PO Box 303, Wynnewood, PA 19096. Phone: (610) 649-7055 or (800) 648-3688. Fax: (610) 649-5456. Web: www.natw.org.

PURPLE HEART: ANNIVERSARY. Aug 7, 1782. At Newburgh, NY, General George Washington ordered the creation of a Badge of Military Merit. The badge consisted of a purple cloth heart with silver braided edge. Only three are known to have been awarded during the Revolutionary War. The award was reinstituted on the bicentennial of Washington's birth, Feb 22, 1932, and recognizes those wounded in action.

SIOUX EMPIRE FAIR. Aug 7–12. Sioux Falls, SD. Grandstand concerts, free entertainment, livestock exhibits, 4-H activities, flower and vegetable displays and craft exhibits. Est attendance: 243,000. For info: Sioux Empire Fair, W.H. Lyon Fairgrounds, 4000 W 12th St, Sioux Falls, SD 57107. Phone: (605) 367-7178. Fax: (605) 367-7886. Web: www.siouxempirefair.com.

US WAR DEPARTMENT ESTABLISHED: ANNIVERSARY. Aug 7, 1789. The second presidential cabinet department, the War Department, was established by Congress.

BIRTHDAYS TODAY

Lana Cantrell, 58, singer, actress, born Sydney, Australia, Aug 7, 1943.

David Duchovny, 41, actor ("The X-Files"), born New York, NY, Aug 7, 1960.

Stan Freberg, 75, satirist, born Pasadena, CA, Aug 7, 1926.

John Glover, 57, actor (stage: *Great God Brown; Julia, Melvin and Howard*), born Kingston, NY, Aug 7, 1944.

Garrison Keillor, 59, humorist, producer (host "The Prairie Home Companion"), writer (*Lake Wobegon Days*), born Anoka, MN, Aug 7, 1942.

DeLane Matthews, 40, actress ("Dave's World"), born Rockledge, FL, Aug 7, 1961.

Alberto Salazar, 44, marathon runner, born Havana, Cuba, Aug 7, 1957.

B.J. Thomas (Billy Joe Thomas), 59, singer ("Raindrops Keep Falling on My Head"), born Houston, TX, Aug 7, 1942.

	S	**M**	**T**	**W**	**T**	**F**	**S**
August				1	2	3	4
2001	5	6	7	8	9	10	11
	12	13	14	15	16	17	18
	19	20	21	22	23	24	25
	26	27	28	29	30	31	

AUGUST 8 — WEDNESDAY
Day 220 — 145 Remaining

ADMIT YOU'RE HAPPY DAY. Aug 8. This day celebrates the birthday of the Secret Society of Happy People by encouraging the expression of happiness and discouraging parade-raining. For info: Pam Johnson, 5330 N MacArthur Blvd, 148-215, Irving, TX 75038. Phone: (972) 471-1485. E-mail: pjohnson@sohp.com. Web: www.sohp.com.

BONZA BOTTLER DAY™. Aug 8. To celebrate when the number of the day is the same as the number of the month. Bonza Bottler Day™ is an excuse to have a party at least once a month. For more information, see Jan 1. For info: Gail M. Berger, 109 Matthew Ave, Poca, WV 25159. Phone: (304) 776-7746. E-mail: gberger5@aol.com.

CANADA: DIGBY SCALLOP DAYS FESTIVAL. Aug 8–12. Digby, NS. A celebration of our seafaring heritage, honoring the fishermen of the world-famous Digby Scallop Fleet. Savor the marvelous mollusks of the deep. Cheer the scallop shuckers in competition. Enjoy local talent. Take in our grand street parade and children's events. Est attendance: 12,000. For info: Digby Scallop Days Assn, PO Box 983, Digby, NS, Canada B0V 1A0. Phone: (877) NS-DIGBY. Fax: (902) 245-2121. Web: www.valleyweb.com/digby/scallop.html.

THE DATE TO CREATE. Aug 8. All of us have creative potential, but may not realize it. Creativity may mean building on others' ideas, as Thomas Edison successfully did with his lightbulb invention. Using brainstorming techniques increases confidence and can unleash creativity. Discover your creative spark by expanding your view of the world. Annually, Aug 8. For info: Diane Decker, Quality Transitions. Phone: (847) 394-0994. E-mail: dcdecker@msn.com.

HENSON, MATTHEW A.: BIRTH ANNIVERSARY. Aug 8, 1866. American black explorer, born at Charles County, MD. He met Robert E. Peary while working in a Washington, DC, store in 1888 and was hired to be Peary's valet. He accompanied Peary on his seven subsequent Arctic expeditions. During the successful 1908–09 expedition to the North Pole, Henson and two of the four Eskimo guides reached their destination Apr 6, 1909. Peary arrived minutes later and verified the location. Henson's account of the expedition, *A Negro Explorer at the North Pole*, was published in 1912. In addition to the Congressional medal awarded all members of the North Pole expedition, Henson received the Gold Medal of the Geographical Society of Chicago and, at 81, was made an honorary member of the Explorers Club at New York, NY. Died Mar 9, 1955, at New York, NY.

INDIANA STATE FAIR. Aug 8–19. Indiana State Fairgrounds Event Center, Indianapolis, IN. Top-rated livestock exhibition, world-class harness racing, top country music, giant midway and Pioneer Village. Est attendance: 725,000. For info: Jeff Fites, Media Relations Dir, Indiana State Fair, 1202 E 38th St, Indianapolis, IN 46205-2869. Phone: (317) 927-7500. Fax: (317) 927-7578. Web: www.iquest.net/statefair.

INTERTRIBAL INDIAN CEREMONIAL. Aug 8–12. Red Rock State Park, Gallup, NM. A major Indian festival with more than 50 tribes from the US and Mexico. Parades, Indian dances, rodeos, arts and crafts and foods. Est attendance: 32,500. For info: Intertribal Indian Ceremonial Assn, 226 W Coal Ave, Gallup, NM 87301. Phone: (800) 233-4528 or (505) 863-3896. Fax: (505) 722-5158.

MARCH, FREDRIC: BIRTH ANNIVERSARY. Aug 8, 1897. Academy and Tony Award–winning actor Fredric March was born Frederick McIntyre Bickel at Racine, WI. Over the course of his long and distinguished career, March performed on both the stage and screen. He made more than 65 movies and was nominated for five Academy Awards, winning in 1932 for his role in *Dr. Jekyll and Mr Hyde* and in 1947 for *The Best Years of Our Lives*. In 1956 he appeared on stage in the world premiere of Eugene O'Neill's *Long Day's Journey into Night*. He received the Tony Award for that performance. He died Apr 14, 1975, at Los Angeles, CA.

MARKERT, RUSSELL: BIRTH ANNIVERSARY. Aug 8, 1899. American choreographer Russell Markert was born at Jersey City, NJ. He founded and directed the Radio City Music Hall Rockettes from 1932 to 1971. He died Dec 1, 1990, at Waterbury, CT.

MORRIS, ESTHER HOBART McQUIGG: BIRTH ANNIVERSARY. Aug 8, 1814. Esther Hobart McQuigg Morris was born at Tioga County, NY, but eventually moved to Wyoming Territory, where she worked in the women's rights movement and had a key role in getting a women's suffrage bill passed. Morris became justice of the peace of South Pass City, WY, in 1870, one of the first times a woman held public office in the US. She represented Wyoming at the national suffrage convention in 1895. She died Apr 2, 1902, at Cheyenne, WY.

ODIE: BIRTHDAY. Aug 8, 1978. Commemorates the birthday of Odie, Garfield's sidekick, who first appeared in the Garfield comic strip Aug 8, 1978. For info: Kim Campbell, Paws, Inc, 5440 E Co Rd, 450 N, Albany, IN 47320. Web: www.garfield.com.

RAWLINGS, MARJORIE KINNAN: BIRTH ANNIVERSARY. Aug 8, 1896. American short story writer and novelist (*The Yearling*), born at Washington, DC. Rawlings died at St. Augustine, FL, Dec 14, 1953.

ROOSEVELT COUNTY FAIR. Aug 8–11. Culbertson, MT. Exhibits, petting zoo, free meals, livestock auction and Bull-A-Rama. For info: Ida Mae Forbregd, PO Box 639, Culbertson, MT 59218.

SECOND BATTLE OF AMIENS: ANNIVERSARY. Aug 8, 1918. Two days after the Battle of Marne ended, the British Fourth Army mounted an offensive at Amiens with the objective of freeing the Amiens-Paris railway from bombardment by the German Second and Eighteenth Armies. More than 16,000 German prisoners were taken in two hours of fighting the first day. The German forces were forced back to the Hindenburg line by Sept 3. This battle is considered a turning point by many historians because of its impact on the psyche of Germany. Aug 8 was described by General Erich Ludendorff as a "Black Day" for Germany.

SHILTS, RANDY: 50th BIRTH ANNIVERSARY. Aug 8, 1951. Journalist known for his reporting on the AIDS epidemic. One of the first openly homosexual journalists to work for a mainstream newspaper and the author of *And the Band Played On: Politics, People and the AIDS Epidemic.* Born at Davenport, IA, and died at Guerneville, CA, Feb 17, 1994.

SNEAK SOME ZUCCHINI ONTO YOUR NEIGHBORS' PORCH NIGHT. Aug 8. Due to overzealous planting of zucchini, citizens are asked to drop off baskets of the squash on neighbors' doorsteps. Annually, Aug 8. [© 2000 by WH] For info: Tom or Ruth Roy, Wellcat Holidays, 2418 Long Ln, Lebanon, PA 17046. Phone: (717) 279-0184. E-mail: wellcat@supernet.com. Web: www.wellcat.com.

SPACE MILESTONE: *PIONEER VENUS* MULTIPROBE (US). Aug 8, 1978. Second craft in *Pioneer Venus* program. Split into five and probed Venus atmosphere Dec 9. Launched on Aug 8, 1978.

SWEDEN: CRAYFISH PREMIERE. Aug 8. Crayfish may be sold and served in restaurants the following day after the season opens. Annually, the second Wednesday in August.

BIRTHDAYS TODAY

Keith Carradine, 51, actor (*Nashville, Will Rogers Follies*), singer, born San Mateo, CA, Aug 8, 1950.

Benny Carter, 94, jazz musician, composer, born New York, NY, Aug 8, 1907.

Dino DeLaurentiis, 82, producer, born Torre Annunziata, Italy, Aug 8, 1919.

The Edge (David Evans), 40, musician (U2), born Dublin, Ireland, Aug 8, 1961.

Dustin Hoffman, 64, actor (Oscars for *Rain Man and Kramer v Kramer; The Graduate, Midnight Cowboy, Outbreak*), born Los Angeles, CA, Aug 8, 1937.

Jane Dee Hull, 66, Governor of Arizona (R), born Kansas City, MO, Aug 8, 1935.

Joan Adams Mondale, 71, wife of the 42nd vice president of the US, Walter F. Mondale, born Eugene, OR, Aug 8, 1930.

Deborah Norville, 43, TV hostess ("Today Show"), born Dalton, GA, Aug 8, 1958.

Roberta Cooper Ramo, 59, first woman president of the American Bar Association, born Denver, CO, Aug 8, 1942.

Edward T. Schafer, 55, Governor of North Dakota (R), born Bismarck, ND, Aug 8, 1946.

Connie Stevens, 63, actress ("Hawaiian Eye"), born Brooklyn, NY, Aug 8, 1938.

Mel Tillis, 69, singer, songwriter, born Pahokee, FL, Aug 8, 1932.

Esther Williams, 78, swimmer, actress (*Take Me Out to the Ball Game, Dangerous When Wet*), born Los Angeles, CA, Aug 8, 1923.

AUGUST 9 — THURSDAY

Day 221 — 144 Remaining

AMISH ACRES ARTS & CRAFTS FESTIVAL. Aug 9–12. Nappanee, IN. Displays of traditional arts and crafts including furniture and other objects. Also features a variety of entertainment. Est attendance: 60,000. For info: Amish Acres Arts & Crafts Festival, 1600 W Market St, Nappanee, IN 46550. Phone: (219) 773-4188 ext 215. Fax: (219) 773-4180. E-mail: Jennipletcher@ AmishAcres.com. Web: www.amishacres.com.

ATOMIC BOMB DROPPED ON NAGASAKI: ANNIVERSARY. Aug 9, 1945. Three days after the atomic bombing of Hiroshima, an American B-29 bomber named *Bock's Car* left its base on Tinian Island carrying a plutonium bomb nicknamed "Fat Man." Its target was the Japanese city of Kokura, but because of clouds and poor visibility the bomber headed for a secondary target, Nagasaki, where at 11:02 AM, local time, it dropped the bomb, killing an estimated 70,000 persons and destroying about half the city. Memorial services are held annually at Nagasaki and also at Kokura, where those who were spared because of the bad weather also grieve for those at Nagasaki who suffered in their stead.

COCHRAN, JACQUELINE: DEATH ANNIVERSARY.
Aug 9, 1980. American pilot Jacqueline Cochran was born at Pensacola, FL, about 1910. She began flying in 1932 and by the time of her death she had set more distance, speed and altitude records than any other pilot, male or female. She was founder and head of the WASPs (Women's Air Force Service Pilots) during WWII; she won the Distinguished Service Medal in 1945 and the US Air Force Distinguished Flying Cross in 1969. She died at Indio, CA.

ENGLAND: JERSEY BATTLE OF FLOWERS. Aug 9. St. Lawrence, Jersey Channel Islands. Colorful parade of floats decorated with hundreds of flowers. First held in 1902 to mark the coronation of Edward VII and Queen Alexandra. Annually, the second Thursday in August. Est attendance: 27,500. For info: The Jersey Battle of Flowers Assn, La Rue des Pres Sorsoliel, St. Lawrence, Jersey, Channel Islands, England JE3 1EE. Phone: (44) (153) 463-9000. Web: www.jtourism.com/index2.html.

FESTIVAL OF NORTH AMERICAN LIGHTHOUSES.
Aug 9–12. Mackinaw City, MI. Event is focused on the numerous lighthouses in the Great Lakes Region. Cruises to various lighthouses will be available. For info: Mackinaw City Tourist Bureau, PO Box 160, 708 S Huron, Mackinaw City, MI 49701. Phone: (800) 666-0160. Web: www.mackinawcity.com.

HOPE WATERMELON FESTIVAL. Aug 9–12. Hope, AR. An event in which the entire family can participate while promoting the city of Hope and having fun. Hope is the birthplace of 42nd President of the US Bill Clinton. Annually, in August. Est attendance: 50,000. For info: Mktg Dept, Hope–Hempstead County Chamber of Commerce, 108 W 3rd, PO Box 250, Hope, AR 71802-0250. Phone: (870) 777-3640. Fax: (870) 722-6154. E-mail: hopeark@arkansas.net. Web: www.hopemelonfest.com.

IOWA STATE FAIR. Aug 9–19. Iowa State Fairgrounds, Des Moines, IA. One of America's oldest and largest state fairs with one of the world's largest livestock shows. Ten-acre carnival, superstar grandstand stage shows, track events, spectacular free entertainment. 160-acre campgrounds. Est attendance: 970,000. For info: Kathie Swift, Mktg Dir, Iowa State Fair, 400 E 14th St, Des Moines, IA 50319-0210. Phone: (515) 262-3111. Fax: (515) 262-6906. Web: iowastatefair.org.

JAPAN: MOMENT OF SILENCE. Aug 9. Nagasaki. Memorial observance held at Peace Memorial Park for victims of second atomic bomb, which was dropped on Nagasaki by an American bomber Aug 9, 1945.

LASSEN VOLCANIC NATIONAL PARK ESTABLISHED: 85th ANNIVERSARY. Aug 9, 1916. California's Lassen Peak and Cinder Cone National Monument, proclaimed May 6, 1907, and other wilderness land were combined and established as a national park. For further park info: Lassen Volcanic Natl Park, Mineral, CA 96063.

MISSOURI RIVER FESTIVAL OF THE ARTS. Aug 9–11. Thespian Hall, Boonville, MO. Performing arts festival with major symphony, jazz, children's program, Broadway music, dance and contemporary music. Est attendance: 5,000. For info: Judy Shields, Admin, Friends of Historic Boonville, PO Box 1776, Boonville, MO 65233. Phone: (660) 882-7977. Fax: (660) 882-9194. E-mail: friendsart@mid-mo.net.

August 2001	S	M	T	W	T	F	S
				1	2	3	4
	5	6	7	8	9	10	11
	12	13	14	15	16	17	18
	19	20	21	22	23	24	25
	26	27	28	29	30	31	

MISSOURI STATE FAIR. Aug 9–19. Sedalia, MO. Livestock shows, commercial and competitive exhibits, horse show, car races, tractor pulls, carnival and headline musical entertainment. Economical family entertainment. Est attendance: 350,000. For info: Kimberly Allen, PR Dir, Missouri State Fair, 2503 W 16th, Sedalia, MO 65301. Phone: (816) 530-5600. Fax: (816) 530-5609. Web: www.mostatefair.com.

MORTON, WILLIAM THOMAS GREEN: BIRTH ANNIVERSARY. Aug 9, 1819. Dentist, born at Charlton, MA. Morton was the first to use ether as a general anesthetic. Died at New York, NY, July 15, 1868.

NATIONAL BLUEBERRY FESTIVAL. Aug 9–12. South Haven, MI. At the World's Highbush Blueberry Capital, enjoy events such as a sand-sculpting contest and beach volleyball on the shores of Lake Michigan. Est attendance: 50,000. For info: South Haven Chamber of Commerce, 300 Broadway, South Haven, MI 49090. Phone: (616) 637-5171. E-mail: cofc@south havenmi.com.

NIXON RESIGNS: ANNIVERSARY. Aug 9, 1974. Richard Milhous Nixon's resignation from the presidency of the US, which he had announced in a speech to the American people Thursday evening, Aug 8, became effective at noon. Nixon, under threat of impeachment as a result of the Watergate scandal, became the first person to resign the presidency. He was succeeded by Vice President Gerald Rudolph Ford, the first person to serve as vice president and president without having been elected to either office. Ford granted Nixon "full, free and absolute pardon" Sept 8, 1974. Although Nixon was the first US president to resign, two vice presidents had resigned: John C. Calhoun, Dec 18, 1832, and Spiro T. Agnew, Oct 10, 1973.

PERSEID METEOR SHOWERS. Aug 9–13. Among the best-known and most spectacular meteor showers are the Perseids, peaking about Aug 10–12. As many as 50–100 may be seen in a single night. Wish upon a "falling star"!

SINGAPORE: INDEPENDENCE DAY: ANNIVERSARY.
Aug 9, 1965. Most festivals in Singapore are Chinese, Indian or Malay, but celebration of national day is shared by all to commemorate the withdrawal of Singapore from Malaysia and its becoming an independent state in 1965. Music, parades, dancing.

SKOWHEGAN STATE FAIR. Aug 9–18. Fairgrounds, Skowhegan, ME. 183rd annual. Huge fair with horse pulling, tractor pulls, harness racing, carnival midway, exhibits, flower show, grandstand shows, coliseum events, truck pulls, demolition derby and much more. Annually, beginning three weeks before Labor Day. Est attendance: 100,000. For info: Skowhegan State Fair Assn, PO Box 39, Skowhegan, ME 04976. Phone: (207) 474-2947.

SOUTH AFRICA: NATIONAL WOMEN'S DAY: 45th ANNIVERSARY. Aug 9. National holiday. Commemorates the march of women in Pretoria to protest the pass laws in 1956.

UNITED NATIONS: INTERNATIONAL DAY OF THE WORLD'S INDIGENOUS PEOPLE. Aug 9. On Dec 23, 1994, the General Assembly decided that the International Day of the World's Indigenous People shall be observed Aug 9 every year during the International Decade of the World's Indigenous People (1994–2004) (Res 49/214). The date marks the anniversary of the first day of the meeting in 1992 of the Working Group on Indigenous Populations of the Subcommission on Prevention of Discrimination and Protection of Minorities. For info: United Nations, Dept of Public Info, Public Inquiries Unit, RM GA-57, New York, NY 10017. Phone: (212) 963-4475. E-mail: inquiries@un.org.

VEEP DAY. Aug 9. Commemorates the day in 1974 when Richard Nixon's resignation let Gerald Ford succeed to the presidency of the US. This was the first time the new Constitutional provisions for presidential succession took effect. For info: c/o Bob Birch, The Puns Corps, PO Box 2364, Falls Church, VA 22042-0364. Phone: (703) 533-3668.

WALTON, IZAAK: BIRTH ANNIVERSARY. Aug 9, 1593 (OS). English author of classic treatise on fishing, *The Compleat Angler*, published in 1653, was born at Stafford, England. Died at Winchester, England, Dec 15, 1683 (OS). "Angling," Walton wrote, "may be said to be so like the mathematics, that it can never be fully learnt."

WEBSTER-ASHBURTON TREATY SIGNED: ANNIVERSARY. Aug 9, 1842. The treaty delimiting the eastern section of the Canadian-American border was negotiated by the US Secretary of State, Daniel Webster, and Alexander Baring, president of the British Board of Trade. The treaty established the boundaries between the St. Croix and Connecticut rivers, between Lake Superior and the Lake of the Woods and between Lakes Huron and Superior. The treaty was signed at Washington, DC.

BIRTHDAYS TODAY

Gillian Anderson, 33, actress ("The X-Files"), born Chicago, IL, Aug 9, 1968.

Amanda Bearse, 43, actress ("Married . . . With Children"), born Atlanta, GA, Aug 9, 1958.

Robert Joseph (Bob) Cousy, 73, former coach and Basketball Hall of Fame guard, born New York, NY, Aug 9, 1928.

William Daley, 53, former US Secretary of Commerce (Clinton administration), born Chicago, IL, Aug 9, 1948.

Sam Elliott, 57, actor ("Mission Impossible," *Gettysburg*), born Sacramento, CA, Aug 9, 1944.

Melanie Griffith, 44, actress (*Working Girl, Something Wild, Milk Money*), born New York, NY, Aug 9, 1957.

Chamique Holdsclaw, 24, basketball player, born Astoria, NY, Aug 9, 1977.

Whitney Houston, 38, singer ("And I Will Always Love You"), actress (*Waiting to Exhale*), born Newark, NJ, Aug 9, 1963.

Brett Hull, 37, hockey player, born Belleville, Ontario, Canada, Aug 9, 1964.

Rodney George (Rod) Laver, 63, former tennis player, born Rockhampton, Australia, Aug 9, 1938.

Kenneth Howard (Ken) Norton, Sr, 56, former boxer, born Jacksonville, IL, Aug 9, 1945.

Deion Sanders, 34, football player, born Fort Myers, FL, Aug 9, 1967.

David Steinberg, 59, comedian ("The David Steinberg Show"), born Winnipeg, Manitoba, Canada, Aug 9, 1942.

AUGUST 10 — FRIDAY
Day 222 — 143 Remaining

BLUEGRASS FESTIVAL. Aug 10–12. Grand Targhee Ski and Summer Resort, Alta, WY. 14th annual. Set in a beautiful outdoor venue on a pristine mountainside on the gorgeous western slopes of the Grand Teton Mountains, this festival is three days of incredible bluegrass music featuring national, regional and local talent such as Alison Krauss, Del McCoury Band, Peter Rown and David Grisman. Also, arts and crafts, food and beverages. Est attendance: 7,000. For info: Grand Targhee Ski & Summer Resort, PO Box SKI, Alta, WY 83422. Phone: (800) TAR-GHEE. Fax: (307) 353-8148. E-mail: info@targhee.com. Web: www.grand targhee.com.

CAMPBELL, ANGUS: BIRTH ANNIVERSARY. Aug 10, 1910. Professor of psychology and sociology, author and director of the Institute for Social Research at the University of Michigan, called a "man with a scientist's mind and a humanist's heart," born at Leiters, IN. He was one of the principal researchers in studies of social and racial problems and attitudes. Campbell died Dec 15, 1980, at Ann Arbor, MI.

"CANDID CAMERA" TV PREMIERE: ANNIVERSARY. Aug 10, 1948. This show—which appeared at various times on the big three networks and in syndication—was created and hosted by Allen Funt. The show was initially an Armed Forces Radio program based on Funt's success in recording and broadcasting soldiers' gripes. The show's modus operandi was to catch people unawares on camera—either as part of a practical joke or just being themselves. It spawned numerous imitators such as "Totally Hidden Video," "People Do the Craziest Things" and "America's Funniest Home Videos."

CATFISH DAYS. Aug 10–12 (tentative). East Grand Forks, MN. The catfish tournament is held on the Red and Red Lake rivers. 150 teams from all over the US participate. Other weekend events held on the riverbank include a bike race, canoe workshop, fishing seminars, 10K run, live animal demonstrations and volleyball. Evening entertainment includes live music by various bands. Est attendance: 3,000. For info: Pamela Solga, Office Mgr, EGF Chamber of Commerce, 218 4th St NW, East Grand Forks, MN 56721. Phone: (218) 773-7481. Fax: (218) 773-7482.

COLT LEAGUE WORLD SERIES. Aug 10–17 (tentative). Lafayette, IN. International amateur baseball World Series for players of league ages 15 and 16. Est attendance: 2,500. For info: PONY Baseball, PO Box 225, Washington, PA 15301. Phone: (724) 225-1060. Fax: (724) 225-9852. E-mail: pony@pulsenet .com. Web: www.pony.org.

ECUADOR: INDEPENDENCE DAY. Aug 10. National holiday. Celebrates declaration of independence in 1809. Freedom from Spain was attained May 24, 1822.

ELVIS WEEK. Aug 10–16. Memphis, TN. Each year Elvis fans from around the world visit Memphis as Aug 16 marks the anniversary of Elvis Presley's death (Aug 16, 1977) at his beloved home, Graceland Mansion. More than 35 events occur throughout the city with special events sponsored by Graceland. Est attendance: 40,000. For info: Graceland, 3734 Elvis Presley Blvd, Memphis, TN 38116. Phone: (800) 238-2000. Web: www.elvis presley.com.

FINLAND: TURKU MUSIC FESTIVAL. Aug 10–19. Turku. One of Finland's oldest music festivals in its oldest city. Music ranges from the medieval era to present day, performed by world-famous artists and groups in halls with fine acoustics, churches and even museums. Est attendance: 15,000. For info: Finnish Tourist Board, 655 Third Ave, New York, NY 10017. Phone: (212) 885-9700. Or Turku Music Festival, Kauppiaskatu 11E40, 20100 Turku, Finland. E-mail: info@turkumusicfestival.fi. Web: www.turkumusicfestival.fi.

FIVE STATE FREE FAIR. Aug 10–19. Fairgrounds, Liberal, KS. Because Kansas, Oklahoma, New Mexico, Texas and Colorado are so close together, residents of each state enjoy one big fair. KRCA Finals Rodeo, Aug 19–21. Country-western entertainment, a carnival, kid's day and stock car races also featured. Annually, the third full week of August. Est attendance: 30,000. For info: Debra Huddleston, Box 420, Liberal, KS 67905. Phone: (316) 624-3712.

GOLD COAST ART FAIR. Aug 10–12. Chicago, IL. Features the work of 600 artists of painting and sculpture in a large outdoor exhibit. Est attendance: 800,000. For info: Gold Coast Art Fair, c/o *Near North News*, 222 W Ontario, Ste 502, Chicago, IL 60610-3695.

GREAT SALMON VALLEY BALLOONFEST. Aug 10–12. City Park, Salmon, ID. Arts and crafts, sidewalk sales, tethered rides, BBQs, Dutch oven tailgate brunch, whitewater float trips, fun flights and much more. Est attendance: 12,000. For info: Salmon Chamber of Commerce, 200 Main St, Ste 1, Salmon, ID 83467. Phone: (208) 756-2100.

HOOVER, HERBERT CLARK: BIRTH ANNIVERSARY. Aug 10, 1874. The 31st president of the US (1929–33) was born at West Branch, IA. Hoover was the first president born west of the Mississippi River and the first to have a telephone on his desk (installed Mar 27, 1929). "Older men declare war. But it is youth that must fight and die," he said at Chicago, IL, at the Republican National Convention, June 27, 1944. Hoover died at New York, NY, Oct 20, 1964. The Sunday nearest Aug 10th is observed in Iowa as Herbert Hoover Day.

ILLINOIS STATE FAIR. Aug 10–19. Springfield, IL. Amusement rides, food booths, parade, various types of entertainment, rodeos and tractor pulls. For info: Joe Saputo, Illinois State Fair, PO Box 19427, Springfield, IL 62794. Phone: (217) 782-6661. Fax: (217) 782-9115. Web: www.state.il.us/fair/.

JAPAN'S UNCONDITIONAL SURRENDER: ANNIVERSARY. Aug 10, 1945. Less than 24 hours after a meeting to discuss the acceptance of the Potsdam Declaration ended in stalemate, another gathering to discuss the surrender terms took place in Emperor Hirohito's bomb shelter. As on the previous day, the participants were stalemated. War General Anami continued to express the belief that "we may be able to reverse the situation in our favor, pulling victory out of defeat." Hirohito came down on the side of Suzuki and Togo. He believed continuation of the war would only result in further loss of Japanese lives. A message was transmitted from Tokyo to Japanese ambassadors in Switzerland and Sweden to accept the terms issued at Potsdam July 26, 1945, except that the prerogative of the Japanese emperor's sovereign rule must be maintained. The Allies devised a plan under which the emperor and the Japanese government would administer under the rule of the Supreme Commander of the Allied Powers and the Japanese surrendered.

"LIL" MARGARET'S BLUEGRASS AND OLD-TIME MUSIC FESTIVAL. Aug 10–12. Leonardtown, MD. Bluegrass music, crafts, old-time cars and tractors, plenty of home-cooked meals and lots of fun. Annually, the second weekend in August. Est attendance: 1,000. For info: Joseph H. Goddard, Lil Margaret's Bluegrass, 20529 White Point Rd, Leonardtown, MD 20650. Phone: (301) 475-8191. Web: www.gotech.com/

MISSOURI: ADMISSION DAY: ANNIVERSARY. Aug 10. Became 24th state in 1821.

MONTGOMERY COUNTY AGRICULTURAL FAIR. Aug 10–18. Gaithersburg, MD. Maryland's largest county fair, family-oriented entertainment, farm animals, arts and crafts exhibits of all types, many contests, carnival rides, grandstand entertainment to include demolition derby, horse events, musical performances, tractor pulls. Est attendance: 250,000. For info: Montgomery County Agricultural Fair, 16 Chestnut St, Gaithersburg, MD 20877. Phone: (301) 926-3100. Fax: (301) 926-1532. Web: www.mcagfair.com.

PALOMINO LEAGUE WORLD SERIES. Aug 10–13. Santa Clara, CA. International young adult baseball World Series for players of league ages 17 and 18. Est attendance: 6,650. For info: PONY Baseball, Inc, Box 225, Washington, PA 15301. Phone: (724) 225-1060. Fax: (724) 225-9852. E-mail: pony@pulse.net .com. Web: www.pony.org.

August *2001*	S	M	T	W	T	F	S
				1	2	3	4
	5	6	7	8	9	10	11
	12	13	14	15	16	17	18
	19	20	21	22	23	24	25
	26	27	28	29	30	31	

SAINT JOHNS MINT FESTIVAL. Aug 10–12. St. Johns, MI. To honor area mint farmers. Est attendance: 70,000. For info: St. Johns Area Chamber of Commerce, 201 E State St, Box 61, St. Johns, MI 48879. Phone: (517) 224-7248 or (517) 224-7667.

SHANTY DAYS: CELEBRATION OF THE LAKE. Aug 10–12. Legion Park, Algoma, WI. Three-day festival to celebrate lakeshore heritage. Entertainment, ethnic food, arts and crafts, street fair, 5K walk/run, fishing contest, kids' area, book sale, community parade, photo contest and fireworks finale. Est attendance: 23,000. For info: Pam Ritchie, Algoma Area Chamber of Commerce, 1226 Lake St, Algoma, WI 54201. Phone: (920) 487-2041 or (800) 498-4888. Fax: (920) 487-5519. E-mail: aacofc@ufw2.com. Web: www.algoma.org.

SMITHSONIAN INSTITUTION FOUNDED: ANNIVERSARY. Aug 10, 1846. Founding of the Smithsonian Institution at Washington, DC. For info: Smithsonian Institution, 900 Jefferson Dr SW, Washington, DC 20560. Phone: (202) 357-2700.

TETONKAHA RENDEZVOUS. Aug 10–12. Hole in the Mountain County Park, Lake Benton, MN. Presents the fur-trading atmosphere of the 1840s. Muzzle-loader contest, tomahawk and knife throw, log sawing, canoe races, kids' games. Est attendance: 300. For info: Dave Huebner, Brookings Renegade Muzzle Loaders, 47826 Main St, Bushnell, SD 57276. Phone: (605) 693-4589. Web: www.state.sd.us.

WYANDOTTE WATERFEST. Aug 10–12. Bishop Park, Wyandotte, MI. Outdoor boat show, fireworks, parade of boats, boat rides, chili cookoff and professional bands. Est attendance: 35,000. For info: Leslie Lupo, Dir, 3131 Biddle Ave, Wyandotte, MI 48192. Phone: (734) 324-4505. Fax: (734) 324-4506.

Leo

BIRTHDAYS TODAY

Ian Anderson, 54, musician, lead singer (Jethro Tull, "Bungle in the Jungle"), born Blackpool, England, Aug 10, 1947.

Rosanna Arquette, 42, actress (*Desperately Seeking Susan, New York Stories*), born New York, NY, Aug 10, 1959.

Antonio Banderas, 41, actor (*Too Much, Four Rooms*), born Malaga, Spain, Aug 10, 1960.

Riddick Bowe, 34, boxer, born Brooklyn, NY, Aug 10, 1967.

Jimmy Dean (Seth Ward), 73, singer ("Big Bad John," "P.T. 109"), born Plainview, TX, Aug 10, 1928.

Eddie Fisher, 73, singer ("Heart," "Cindy, Oh Cindy"), born Philadelphia, PA, Aug 10, 1928.

Rhonda Fleming (Marilyn Lewis), 78, actress ("Stage Door," *The Best of Broadway*), born Los Angeles, CA, Aug 10, 1923.

Angie Harmon, 29, actress ("Law & Order," "Baywatch Nights"), born Dallas, TX, Aug 10, 1972.

Betsy Johnson, 59, fashion designer, born Wethersfield, CT, Aug 10, 1942.

AUGUST 11 — SATURDAY

Day 223 — 142 Remaining

AMERICAN SOCIETY OF ASSOCIATION EXECUTIVES ANNUAL MEETING AND EXPOSITION. Aug 11–14. Washington, DC. Major meeting for ASAE members, non-members and suppliers including education sessions, trade show, speakers and networking events. Est attendance: 5,000. For info: Ken Sommer, American Soc of Assn Executives, 1575 I St NW, Washington, DC 20005-1168. Phone: (202) 626-2733. Fax: (202) 408-9633. E-mail: pr@asaenet.org. Web: www.asaenet.org.

ANTIQUE SHOW. Aug 11. Somerset, PA. 31st annual. More than 100 vendors dealing in quality antiques and collectibles. For info: Sandy Berkebile, Somerset County Chamber of Commerce, 601 N Center Ave, Somerset, PA 15501. Phone: (814) 445-6431. E-mail: somchmbr@shol.com.

ATCHISON, DAVID R.: BIRTH ANNIVERSARY. Aug 11, 1807. Missouri legislator who was president of the US for one day. Born at Frogtown, KY, Atchison's strong pro-slavery opinions made his name prominent in legislative debates. He served as president pro tempore of the Senate a number of times, and he became president of the US for one day—Sunday, Mar 4, 1849—pending the swearing in of President-elect Zachary Taylor on Monday, Mar 5, 1849. The city of Atchison, KS, and the county of Atchison, MO, are named for him. He died at Gower, MO, Jan 26, 1886.

BEATLES' NATIONAL APPLE WEEK: ANNIVERSARY. Aug 11–18. The Beatles proclaimed this week to be "National Apple Week" in 1965, when they launched their Apple recording label. Presentation boxes of "Our First Four" releases were sent to the Queen, the Queen Mother and Princess Margaret.

BOND, CARRIE JACOBS: BIRTH ANNIVERSARY. Aug 11, 1862. American composer of well-known songs, including "I Love You Truly" and "A Perfect Day," and of scores for motion pictures, Carrie Jacobs Bond was born at Janesville, WI. She died at Hollywood, CA, at age 84, Dec 28, 1946.

BUD BILLIKEN PARADE. Aug 11. Chicago, IL. A parade especially for children begun in 1929 by Robert S. Abbott. The second largest parade in the US, it features bands, floats, drill teams and celebrities. Annually, the second Saturday in August. For info: Michael Brown, PR Dir, Chicago Defender Charities, 2400 S Michigan, Chicago, IL 60616. Phone: (312) 225-2400. Fax: (312) 255-9231.

CHAD: INDEPENDENCE DAY: ANNIVERSARY. Aug 11. National holiday. Commemorates independence from France in 1960.

CHESTER COUNTY OLD FIDDLERS' PICNIC. Aug 11. Hibernia County Park, Coatesville, PA. Old-time musicians gather to make their traditional music. Annually, the second Saturday in August. Est attendance: 7,000. For info: Chester County Parks and Recreation Dept, PO Box 2747, 601 Westtown Rd, Ste 160, West Chester, PA 19380-0990. Phone: (610) 344-6415. Web: www.chesco.org/ccparks.

CRATER LAKE RIM RUNS AND MARATHON. Aug 11. Crater Lake National Park, OR. One of the toughest and most spectacular races you'll ever run! Race routes are around Crater Lake, the deepest lake in the US. Included are a 6.7-mile, a 13-mile and a full marathon. Est attendance: 500. For info: Crater Lake Rim Runs, 5830 Mack Ave, Klamath Falls, OR 97603. Phone: (541) 884-6939.

ELVIS PRESLEY REMEMBERED. Aug 11. St. Louis, MO. Singer Elvis Presley, his entire family and Colonel Tom Parker are impersonated in a live display titled "From Tupelo to Graceland" to mark the anniversary week of his death. Later a two-hour live music show featuring Steve Davis and the TCB Band will be held in the Duck Room at Blueberry Hill. Est attendance: 800. For info: Blueberry Hill, 6504 Delmar, St. Louis, MO 63130. Phone: (314) 727-0880 or 3147270110. Web: www.blueberry hill.com.

FIRST FOREIGN-BORN OFFICER APPOINTED CHAIR OF JOINT CHIEFS: ANNIVERSARY. Aug 11, 1993. President Bill Clinton appointed Army General John Shalikashvili to succeed Colin Powell as Chairman of the Joint Chiefs of Staff. Shalikashvili was born at Poland, but his family fled to Germany in 1944 to escape advancing Soviet troops. After moving to the US, his family lived at Peoria, IL. "General Shali" has a distinguished military record and is a Vietnam war veteran.

FREDERICK DOUGLASS SPEAKS: ANNIVERSARY. Aug 11, 1841. Having escaped from slavery only three years earlier, Frederick Douglass was legally a fugitive when he first spoke before an audience. At an antislavery convention on Nantucket Island, Douglass spoke simply but eloquently about his life as a slave. His words were so moving that he was asked to become a full-time lecturer for the Massachusetts Anti-Slavery Society. Douglass became a brilliant orator, writer and abolitionist who championed the rights of blacks as well as the rights of all humankind.

HALEY, ALEX PALMER: 80th BIRTH ANNIVERSARY. Aug 11, 1921. Born at Ithaca, NY, Alex Palmer Haley was raised by his grandmother at Henning, TN. In 1939 he entered the US Coast Guard and served as a cook, but eventually he became a writer and college professor. His interview with Malcolm X for *Playboy* led to his first book, *The Autobiography of Malcolm X*, which sold six million copies and was translated into eight languages. *Roots*, his Pulitzer Prize–winning novel published in 1976, sold millions, was translated into 37 languages and was made into an eight-part TV miniseries in 1977. The story generated an enormous interest in family ancestry. Haley died at Seattle, WA, Feb 13, 1992.

INGERSOLL, ROBERT GREEN: BIRTH ANNIVERSARY. Aug 11, 1833. American author, orator, lawyer, politician and agnostic was born at Dresden, NY, and died at Dobbs Ferry, NY, July 21, 1899. "An honest God," he wrote, "is the noblest work of man."

INTER-STATE FAIR AND RODEO. Aug 11–19. Coffeyville, KS. "Largest outdoor fair and rodeo event in southeast Kansas and northeast Oklahoma." Includes concerts, demo derby, four nights of PRCA rodeo and livestock shows. Est attendance: 75,000. For info: Montgomery County Fair Assn, Box 457, Coffeyville, KS 67337. Phone: (316) 251-2550. Fax: (316) 251-5448. E-mail: fair_rodeo@coffeyville.com. Web: www.coffeyville.com.

JOURS DE FÊTE (DAYS OF CELEBRATION). Aug 11–12. Ste. Genevieve, MO. Celebration of town's French heritage. Tours of historic homes dating to the 1700s that exemplify some of the finest French Creole architecture. Also more than 600 arts and crafts booths and colonial crafts demonstrations by authentically costumed crafters. Est attendance: 40,000. For info: Ste. Genevieve Tourist Info Center, 66 S Main, Ste. Genevieve, MO 63670. Phone: (573) 883-7097 or (800) 373-7007.

KNIGHTS OF COLUMBUS FAMILY WEEK. Aug 11–18. Held annually in August as a celebration of the importance of the family. Local councils throughout the countries in which the K of C is present hold family-oriented activities throughout this observance. The birth (Aug 12) and death (Aug 14) anniversaries of Father Michael J. McGivney, founder of the Knights of Columbus, fall during this event. For info: Ronald J. Tracz, VP, Fraternal Services, Knights of Columbus, 1 Columbus Plaza, New Haven, CT 06510-3326.

KOOL-AID DAYS. Aug 11. Hastings, NE. Family festival in the town where Kool-Aid was invented. Carnival games, chili cook-off, collectibles marketplace, dunk tank, commemoratives, crafts for kids. Purchase a mug and receive free Kool-Aid all day from the world's largest Kool-Aid stand where we pour more than a gallon a minute of a dozen flavors. Annually, the second weekend in August. Est attendance: 8,000. For info: Adams County CVB, PO Box 941, Hastings, NE 68902-0941. Phone: (800) 967-2189. Fax: (402) 461-7273. E-mail: hastingsne-visit@tcgcs.com. Web: www.hastingsnet.com/visitors/.

LEADVILLE TRAIL 100 BIKE RACE. Aug 11. Leadville, CO. Some 600 cyclists compete in this 100-mile off-road bike race over Colorado's high peaks—out 50 miles to a peak above Twin Lakes and back to Leadville. Sponsor: Leadville Trail 100, Inc. Est attendance: 1,000. For info: Greater Leadville Area Chamb of Comm, PO Box 861, Leadville, CO 80461. Phone: (719) 486-3900 or (800) 933-3901. Fax: (719) 486-8478. E-mail: leadville@leadvilleusa.com. Web: www.leadvilleusa.com.

LEITERSBURG PEACH FESTIVAL. Aug 11–12. Leitersburg Ruritan Community Park, Leitersburg, MD. This peach-oriented event features crafts, pony rides, bluegrass and country music and a quilt raffle. Annually, the second weekend in August. Est attendance: 10,000. For info: Leitersburg Ruritan Club, 21378 Leiters Mill Rd, Hagerstown, MD 21742-1633. Phone: (301) 797-6387.

August 2001	S	M	T	W	T	F	S
				1	2	3	4
	5	6	7	8	9	10	11
	12	13	14	15	16	17	18
	19	20	21	22	23	24	25
	26	27	28	29	30	31	

MICHIGAN RENAISSANCE FESTIVAL. Aug 11–23. Holly, MI. Continuous entertainment on 15 stages featuring comedy, drama, bawdy and classical music and folk dance at this re-creation of a 16th-century village harvest festival. More than 400 costumed participants join in theater, games and equestrian events. Also, more than 150 crafts booths. Est attendance: 250,000. For info: PR Dir, Michigan Renaissance Fest, 12600 Dixie Hwy, Holly, MI 48034. Phone: (800) 601-4848 or (248) 634-5552. E-mail: renfestmi@aol.com.

MONTANAFAIR. Aug 11–18. MetraPark, Billings, MT. Montana's biggest event featuring exhibits, livestock events, carnival, rodeo and entertainment. Est attendance: 240,000. For info: MetraPark, PO Box 2514, Billings, MT 59103. Phone: (406) 256-2400.

POLISH AMERICAN WEEKEND. Aug 11–12. Penn's Landing, Philadelphia, PA. Two-day festival of Polish food, music and dance. For info: Polish American Congress, Eastern Pennsylvania District, 308 Walnut St, Philadelphia, PA 19106. Phone: (215) 739-3408. Fax: (215) 922-1518. Web: www.polishamericancongress.com.

PRESIDENTIAL JOKE DAY: ANNIVERSARY. Aug 11, 1984. Anniversary of President Ronald Reagan's voice-test joke. In preparation for a radio broadcast, during a thought-to-be-off-the-record voice level test, instead of counting "one, two, three . . ." the president said: "My fellow Americans, I am pleased to tell you I just signed legislation which outlaws Russia forever. The bombing begins in five minutes." The statement was picked up by live television cameras and was heard by millions worldwide. The incident provoked national and international reactions, including a news network proposal of new ground rules concerning the use of "off-the-record" remarks.

RIVER REGALIA. Aug 11. Hot Springs State Park, Thermopolis, WY. River-floating parade. Decorate any legal flotation device, including inner tube, raft and canoe, and join the floating fun. Est attendance: 800. For info: Toddi Darlington, Thermopolis Chamber of Commerce, 700 Broadway, Thermopolis, WY 82443. Phone: (307) 864-3192. E-mail: thercc@trib.com. Web: www.thermopolis.com.

SAINT CLARE OF ASSISI: FEAST DAY. Aug 11, 1253. Chiara Favorone di Offreduccio, a religious leader inspired by St. Francis of Assisi, was the first woman to write her own religious order rule. Born at Assisi, Italy, July 16, 1194, she died there Aug 11, 1253. A "Privilege of Poverty" freed her order from any constraint to accept material security, making the "Poor Clares" totally dependent on God.

SCOTLAND: EDINBURGH INTERNATIONAL BOOK FESTIVAL. Aug 11–27. Charlotte Square Gardens, Edinburgh, Lothian. Europe's biggest book event for the public—with more than 250 international authors, an extensive program for children, plus thousands of books to buy. Est attendance: 80,000. For info: Edinburgh Intl Book Festival, Scottish Book Centre, 137 Dundee St, Edinburgh, Scotland EH1 11BG. Phone: (44) (131) 228-5444. E-mail: admin@edbookfest.co.uk. Web: www.edinburghfestivals.co.uk.

SEWARD SILVER SALMON DERBY. Aug 11–19. Seward, AK. Alaska's largest salmon derby. Fishermen vie for cash prizes, including tagged fish, daily top fish awards and sweepstakes drawing. 46th annual. Est attendance: 10,000. For info: Seward Chamber of Commerce, PO Box 749, Seward, AK 99664. Phone: (907) 224-8051. Fax: (907) 224-5353. E-mail: chamber@seward.net. Web: www.sewardak.org.

SILVER VALLEY CLASSIC HORSESHOE TOURNAMENT. Aug 11–12. Kellogg, ID. Annually, the second weekend of August. Saturday, sanctioned National Horseshoe Association singles tournament. Sunday, doubles fun tournament. Est attendance: 120. For info: Vicki McEnany, PO Box 770, Pinehurst, ID 83850-0770.

SPACE MILESTONE: *VOSTOK 3* (USSR). Aug 11, 1962. Launched on this date, Andrian Nikolayev orbited Earth 64 times over a period of 94 hours, 25 minutes, covering a distance of 1,242,500 miles. Achieved radio communication with *Vostok 4* and telecast from spacecraft.

STREETSCENE. Aug 11. Covington, VA. Car Show, open to all types of vehicles! 10–4. Entertainment throughout the day. Annually, the second Saturday in August. Est attendance: 12,500. For info: Kars Unlimited, Inc, PO Box 851, Covington, VA 24426. Phone: (540) 962-3642.

UNITY IN DIVERSITY DAY (UIDD). Aug 11. A national commemorative holiday to spiritually connect and celebrate the human race. This holiday was envisioned and proclaimed in 1998 by Ayo Handy Kendi, founder and director of the African American Holiday Association as a day to focus attention on the need for respect of people's differences and appreciation of all that they have in common. For info: African American Holiday Assn, 1305 Emerson St NW, Washington, DC 20011. Phone: (202) 310-1430. E-mail: aaha@aaha-info.org. Web: www.aaha-info.org.

WATERMELON FESTIVAL. Aug 11. Rush Springs, OK. Beginning with watermelon judging and ending with the crowning of the festival queen, the highlight of the celebration is the serving of 50,000 pounds of free watermelon at Jeff Davis Park. Est attendance: 20,000. For info: Chamber of Commerce, Box 298, Rush Springs, OK 73082. Phone: (580) 476-3277.

WATTS RIOT: ANNIVERSARY. Aug 11, 1965. A minor clash between the California Highway Patrol and two young blacks set off six days of riots in the Watts area of Los Angeles. Thirty-four deaths were reported and more than 3,000 people were arrested. Damage to property was listed at $40 million. The less-immediate cause of the disturbance and the others that followed was racial tension between whites and blacks in American society.

WORLDWIDE TOP COLLECTORS CONVENTION. Aug 11–12. Burlington, WI. Visit the world's only Spinning Top Museum. Collector's show-and-tell, demonstrations and research exchange. Also Wisconsin State Gyroscope Contest. For info: Spinning Top Museum, 533 Milwaukee Ave, Burlington, WI 53105. Phone: (262) 763-3946.

BIRTHDAYS TODAY

Joanna Coles, 57, children's author, born Newark, NJ, Aug 11, 1944.
Arlene Dahl, 73, actress ("One Life to Live," "Fantasy Island"), born Minneapolis, MN, Aug 11, 1928.
Mike Douglas (Michael Delaney Dowd, Jr), 76, TV host, singer, born Chicago, IL, Aug 11, 1925.
Jerry Falwell, 68, clergyman (head of Moral Majority PAC), born Lynchburg, VA, Aug 11, 1933.
Will Friedle, 25, actor ("Boy Meets World"), born Hartford, CT, Aug 11, 1976.
Hulk Hogan, 48, wrestler, actor, born Terry Gene Bollea, Augusta, GA, Aug 11, 1953.
Tim Hutchinson, 52, US Senator (R, Arkansas), born Gravette, AR, Aug 11, 1949.
Joe Jackson, 46, musician, songwriter, born Burton-on-Trent, England, Aug 11, 1955.
Anna Massey, 64, actress (*Bunny Lake Is Missing, A Doll's House*), born Thankeham, England, Aug 11, 1937.
Carl Rowan, 76, journalist, author (*Breaking Barriers*), born Ravenscraft, TN, Aug 11, 1925.
Marilyn vos Savant, 55, columnist ("Ask Marilyn"), claims world's highest IQ, born St. Louis, MO, Aug 11, 1946.
Stephen Wozniak, 51, Apple computer cofounder, born Sunnyvale, CA, Aug 11, 1950.

AUGUST 12 — SUNDAY
Day 224 — 141 Remaining

BEWICK, THOMAS: BIRTH ANNIVERSARY. Aug 12, 1753. English artist, wood engraver and author, remembered especially for his book illustrations in *History of Quadrupeds, British Birds* and *Fables of Aesop*. Born at Cherryburn, Northumberland, and died at Gateshead, Durham, England, Nov 8, 1828.

CANTINFLAS: 90th BIRTH ANNIVERSARY. Aug 12, 1911. Mexico's most famous comic actor, Cantinflas, was born at Mexico City as Mario Moreno Reyes. Particularly popular with the poor of Mexico because he most often portrayed the underdog, Cantinflas got his start in Mexico City *carpas*, the equivalent of vaudeville. He became internationally known for his role in *Around the World in 80 Days*. The name Cantinflas was invented by the comic to prevent his parents from learning he was in show business, which they considered a shameful endeavor. Died Apr 20, 1993, at Mexico City.

COUNTRY JAMBOREE. Aug 12. Trollwood Park, Fargo, ND. A full day of country music featuring the region's finest country music performers. Sponsor: Froggy 99.9 FM. Est attendance: 4,000. For info: Carolyn Boutain, Dir, Trollwood Park, 701 Main Ave, Fargo, ND 58103. Phone: (701) 241-8160. Fax: (701) 241-8266. Web: www.fargoparks.com.

DeMILLE, CECIL B.: BIRTH ANNIVERSARY. Aug 12, 1881. Film pioneer, born at Ashfield, MA. Cecil Blount DeMille was a film showman extraordinaire known for lavish screen spectacles. He produced more than 70 major films which were noted more for their large scale than for their subtle artistry. He produced one of the earliest four-reel films, *The Squaw Man*, in 1913, which boasted the first use of indoor lighting on an actor and was the first film to publicize the names of its stars. His other innovations included the sneak preview and the idea of producing different versions of a popular film. His films include *The Crusades, The Sign of the Cross, King of Kings, Cleopatra, The Plainsman, The Buccaneer, Reap the Wild Wind* and *The Ten Commandments*, which was made in 1923 and then in a new version in 1956. De Mille was awarded an Oscar for *The Greatest Show on Earth* in 1953. He died Jan 21, 1959, at Hollywood, CA.

FLOOD VICTIMS RECEIVE $6.2 BILLION: ANNIVERSARY. Aug 12, 1993. President Bill Clinton signed a bill Aug 12, 1993, providing $6.2 billion in federal relief to victims of floods in July and August for nine states from North Dakota to Missouri. Due to the record rains in the spring of up to 200 percent above average, the Midwest suffered 50 deaths, 70,000 left homeless and an estimated $12 billion in damage as of Aug 9, 1993.

HERBERT HOOVER DAY. Aug 12. Iowa. Annually, the Sunday nearest Aug 10th, the birthday of Herbert Hoover.

HOLLYWOOD BEACH LATIN FESTIVAL. Aug 12. Hollywood, FL. 8th annual. Weekend festival features Latin entertainment, food, arts and crafts and health court. Est attendance: 35,000. For info: Roguey Doyle, City of Hollywood, Dept of Parks, Recreation & Cultural Arts, 1940 Harrison St, Ste 101, Hollywood, FL 33020. Phone: (954) 921-3404.

ITALY: PALIO DEL GOLFO. Aug 12. La Spezia. A rowing contest over a 2,000-meter course is held on the second Sunday in August.

KING PHILIP ASSASSINATION: 325th ANNIVERSARY. Aug 12, 1676. Native American, Philip, son of Massasoit, chief of the Wampanog tribe, was killed near Mt Hope, RI, by a renegade Indian of his own tribe, bringing to an end the first and bloodiest war between American Indians and white settlers of New England, a war that had raged for nearly two years and was known as King Philip's War.

MATHEWSON, CHRISTY: BIRTH ANNIVERSARY. Aug 12, 1880. Famed American baseball player Christopher (Christy) Mathewson, one of the first players named to Baseball's Hall of Fame, was born at Factoryville, PA. Died at Saranac Lake, NY, Oct 7, 1925. He pitched three complete games during the 1905 World Series without allowing opponents to score a run. In 17 years he won 372 games while losing 188 and striking out 2,499 players.

MOON PHASE: LAST QUARTER. Aug 12. Moon enters Last Quarter phase at 3:53 PM, EDT.

MOUNT OGURA PLANE CRASH: ANNIVERSARY. Aug 12, 1985. A Japan Airlines plane crashed into the side of Mount Ogura, Japan, claiming 520 lives. The worst air disaster involving a single plane.

ROASTING EARS OF CORN FOOD FEST. Aug 12. The Museum of Indian Culture, Allentown, PA. Traditional American Indian event featuring traditional Native foods prepared with a contemporary flair and interactive activities for the whole family. Annually, the second Sunday in August. Est attendance: 3,000. For info: Lenni Lenape Historical Soc, 2825 Fish Hatchery Rd, Allentown, PA 18103-9801. Phone: (610) 797-2121. Fax: (610) 797-2801. Web: www.lenape.org.

SCOTLAND: EDINBURGH INTERNATIONAL FESTIVAL. Aug 12–Sept 1. Edinburgh, Lothian. One of the world's largest arts festivals, attracting many international stars. Now in its 55th year, the festival includes symphonic music, opera, theater and dance. Est attendance: 420,000. For info: Edinburgh Festival Soc, The Hub, Castlehill, The Royal Mile, Edinburgh, Scotland EH1 2NE. Phone: (44) (131) 473- 2001. Fax: (44) (131) 473-2002. Web: www.go-edinburgh.co.uk.

SCOTLAND: EDINBURGH INTERNATIONAL FILM FESTIVAL. Aug 12–26 (tentative). Edinburgh. Festival includes documentaries, world premieres, special events and lectures. Est attendance: 50,000. For info: Mktg Mgr, Edinburgh Intl Film Festival, 88 Lothian Rd, Filmhouse, Edinburgh, Scotland EH3 9BZ. Phone: (44) (131) 228-4051. Fax: (44) (131) 229-5501. E-mail: info@edfilmfest.org.uk. Web: www.edfilmfest.org.uk.

SEWING MACHINE INVENTED: 150th ANNIVERSARY. Aug 12, 1851. Isaac Singer developed the sewing machine for use in homes.

SPACE MILESTONE: *ECHO I (US).* Aug 12, 1960. First successful communications satellite in Earth's orbit to relay voice and TV signals from one ground station to another was launched.

SPACE MILESTONE: *ENTERPRISE (US).* Aug 12, 1977. Reusable orbiting vehicle (space shuttle) makes first successful flight on its own within Earth's atmosphere. Launched from Boeing 747 on Aug 12, 1977.

THAILAND: BIRTHDAY OF THE QUEEN. Aug 12. The entire kingdom of Thailand celebrates the birthday of Queen Sirikit.

THANKS FOR ALL THE GIFTS WEEK. Aug 12–18. A time to catch up on all the thank-you notes and cards for birthdays, graduations, weddings, etc, that you forgot to send. Annually, the third week in August. For info: Eva Rosenberg, Giftech Corp, 2961 Industrial Rd, Ste 731, Las Vegas, NV 89109. Phone: (888) 443-8547. Web: www.giftsurf.com.

UNITED NATIONS: INTERNATIONAL YOUTH DAY. Aug 12. For info: United Nations, Dept of Public Info, New York, NY 10017. Web: www.un.org.

August 2001	S	M	T	W	T	F	S
				1	2	3	4
	5	6	7	8	9	10	11
	12	13	14	15	16	17	18
	19	20	21	22	23	24	25
	26	27	28	29	30	31	

VOLVO CARS OF NORTH AMERICA'S NATIONAL BUCKLE UP WEEK. Aug 12–18. In honor of Nils Bohlin, inventor of the three-point safety belt and one time Volvo engineer. Throughout "Buckle Up Week" Volvo Cars of North America will educate Americans about the importance of using a seatbelt. Bohlin's invention was introduced in 1959 in the Volvo 544 Sedan. Since then the seatbelt has become so important that 49 states have instituted laws mandating that car passengers buckle up. Today the seatbelt is considered to be the most effective occupant restraint in all types of automobile accidents. Annually, the third week in August. For info: Jeannine Fallon, Media Relations Mgr, Volvo Cars of North America, 7 Volvo Dr, Rockleigh, NJ 07647. Phone: (201) 768-7300. Fax: (201) 767-4747. E-mail: fallonj@mail.volvo.com.

BIRTHDAYS TODAY

William Goldman, 70, writer (*The Princess Bride, Marathon Man*), born Chicago, IL, Aug 12, 1931.

George Hamilton, 62, actor (*Love at First Bite, Act One*, "The Survivors"), born Memphis, TN, Aug 12, 1939.

Sam J. Jones, 47, actor (*Flash Gordon, 10*), born Chicago, IL, Aug 12, 1954.

Michael Kidd (Milton Greenwald), 82, choreographer, born Brooklyn, NY, Aug 12, 1919.

Peter Krause, 36, actor ("Sports Night"), born Minneapolis, MN, Aug 12, 1965.

Ann Martin, 46, author (The Baby-Sitter's Club series), born Princeton, NJ, Aug 12, 1955.

Pat Metheny, 47, jazz guitarist ("Song X," "Letter from Home"), born Lee's Summit, MO, Aug 12, 1954.

"Buck" (Alvis Edgar) Owens, 72, singer ("Hee Haw," "Act Naturally"), songwriter, born Sherman, TX, Aug 12, 1929.

Pete Sampras, 30, tennis player, born Washington, DC, Aug 12, 1971.

George Soros, 71, billionaire, financier, philanthropist in Eastern Europe and the US, born Budapest, Hungary, Aug 12, 1930.

Porter Wagoner, 71, singer ("The Carroll County Accident"), born West Plains, MO, Aug 12, 1930.

Antoine Walker, 25, basketball player, born Chicago, IL, Aug 12, 1976.

Jane Wyatt, 88, actress ("Father Knows Best," "Star Trek"), born New York, NY, Aug 12, 1913.

AUGUST 13 — MONDAY

Day 225 — 140 Remaining

BERLIN WALL ERECTED: 40th ANNIVERSARY. Aug 13, 1961. Early in the morning, the East German government closed the border between east and west sectors of Berlin with barbed wire fence to discourage further population movement to the west. Telephone and postal services were interrupted, and, later in the week, a concrete wall was built to strengthen the barrier between official crossing points. The dismantling of the wall began Nov 9, 1989. See also: "Berlin Wall: Dismantling Anniversary" (Nov 9).

CANADA: YUKON DISCOVERY DAY: ANNIVERSARY. Aug 13. In the Klondike region of the Yukon, at Bonanza Creek (formerly known as Rabbit Creek), George Washington Carmack discovered gold Aug 16 or 17, 1896. During the following year more than 30,000 people joined the gold rush to the area. Anniversary is celebrated as a holiday (Discovery Day) in the Yukon, on nearest Monday.

CAXTON, WILLIAM: BIRTH ANNIVERSARY. Aug 13, 1422. First English printer, born at Kent, England. Died at London, England, 1491. Caxton produced his first book printed in English (while he was still at Bruges), the *Recuyell of the Histories of Troy*, in 1476, and in the autumn of 1476 set up a print shop at Westminster, becoming the first printer in England.

CENTRAL AFRICAN REPUBLIC: INDEPENDENCE DAY: ANNIVERSARY. Aug 13. Commemorates Proclamation of Independence from France in 1960.

HITCHCOCK, ALFRED (JOSEPH): BIRTH ANNIVERSARY. Aug 13, 1899. English film director and master of suspense born at London. Hitchcock's career as a filmmaker dates back to the silent film era when he made *The Lodger* in 1926, based on the tale of Jack the Ripper. American audiences were introduced to the Hitchcock style in 1935 with *The Thirty-Nine Steps* and *The Lady Vanishes* in 1938, after which he went to Hollywood. There he produced a string of classics including *Rebecca, Suspicion, Notorious, Rear Window, To Catch a Thief, The Birds, Psycho* and *Frenzy*, in addition to his TV series "Alfred Hitchcock Presents." He died Apr 29, 1980, at Beverly Hills, CA.

HOGAN, BEN: BIRTH ANNIVERSARY. Aug 13, 1912. Golfer born at Dublin, TX. Hogan was one of only four players to win all four major professional championships, and his 63 career victories rank him third after Sam Snead and Jack Nicklaus. Died at Ft Worth, TX, July 25, 1997.

NATIONAL AVIATION WEEK. Aug 13–19. A celebration of flight designed to increase public awareness, knowledge and appreciation of aviation. Annually, the week of Orville Wright's birthday, Aug 19. For info: Lafayette Natural History Museum and Planetarium, 637 Girard Park Dr, Lafayette, LA 70503. Phone: (337) 291-5544. Fax: (337) 291-5464.

OAKLEY, ANNIE: BIRTH ANNIVERSARY. Aug 13, 1860. Annie Oakley was born at Darke County, OH. She developed an eye as a markswoman early as a child, becoming so proficient that she was able to pay off the mortgage on her family farm by selling the game she killed. A few years after defeating vaudeville marksman Frank Butler in a shooting match, she married him and they toured as a team until joining Buffalo Bill's Wild West Show in 1885. She was one of the star attractions for 17 years. She died Nov 3, 1926, at Greenville, OH.

PGA CHAMPIONSHIP. Aug 13–19. Atlanta Athletic Club, Duluth, GA. The 83rd championship conducted by the Professional Golfers' Association of America. Est attendance: 150,000. For info: Kerry Haigh, Senior Dir of Tournaments, PGA of America, Box 109601, Palm Beach Gardens, FL 33410-9601. Phone: (561) 624-8495. Fax: (561) 624-8429. Web: www.pga.com.

SCOTTS BLUFF COUNTY FAIR. Aug 13–20. County Fairgrounds, Mitchell, NE. County fair including stock displays and shows, special events such as large-name country and western concert, largest amateur rodeo in Nebraska, tractor pull, free stage

acts, grounds act, rubber-check races, demolition derby. Beef sale on Monday, Aug 20. Est attendance: 40,000. For info: Diane Wurdeman, Operations Mgr, Scotts Bluff County Fair, Box 157, Mitchell, NE 69357. Phone: (308) 623-1828. Fax: (308) 623-1328. E-mail: sbcofair@scottsbluff.net.

STONE, LUCY: BIRTH ANNIVERSARY. Aug 13, 1818. American women's rights pioneer, born near West Brookfield, MA, Lucy Stone dedicated her life to the abolition of slavery and the emancipation of women. Although she graduated from Oberlin College, she had to finance her education by teaching for nine years because her father did not favor college education for women. An eloquent speaker for her causes, she headed the list of 89 men and women who signed the call to the first national Woman's Rights Convention, held at Worcester, MA, October 1850. On May 1, 1855, she married Henry Blackwell. She and her husband aided in the founding of the American Suffrage Association, taking part in numerous referendum campaigns to win suffrage amendments to state constitutions. She died Oct 18, 1893, at Dorchester, MA.

TUNISIA: WOMEN'S DAY. Aug 13. General holiday. Celebration of independence of women.

VICTORY DAY. Aug 13. Rhode Island. State holiday commemorating President Truman's announcement of the surrender of the Japanese to the Allies on Aug 14, 1945. Annually, the second Monday in August.

WEIRD CONTEST WEEK. Aug 13–17. Music Pier, Boardwalk and Moorlyn Terr, Ocean City, NJ. One contest daily. Contests include artistic pie eating (chewing something meaningful out of a TastyKake Pie), saltwater taffy sculpting, french fry sculpting, wet T-shirt throwing, animal and celebrity impersonation, putrid puns and Miss Miscellaneous Contest. 11 AM. Annually, the third week in August. Sponsors: The City of Ocean City, TastyKake Baking Company, Shriver's Saltwater Taffy. Est attendance: 4,500. For info: Mark Soifer, PR Dir, City of Ocean City, City Hall, 9th Asbury Ave, Ocean City, NJ 08226. Phone: (609) 525-9300. Fax: (609) 399-0374. E-mail: MTSoifer@aol.com.

BIRTHDAYS TODAY

Kathleen Battle, 53, opera soprano, born Portsmouth, OH, Aug 13, 1948.

Danny Bonaduce, 42, actor ("The Partridge Family"), born Broomall, PA, Aug 13, 1959.

Fidel Castro, 74, President of Cuba, former amateur baseball player, born Mayari, Oriente Province, Cuba, Aug 13, 1927.

Quinn Cummings, 34, actress (*The Goodbye Girl,* "Family"), born Los Angeles, CA, Aug 13, 1967.

Dan Fogelberg, 50, composer, singer ("Same Old Lang Syne," "Leader of the Band"), born Peoria, IL, Aug 13, 1951.

Pat Harrington, Jr, 72, actor, comedian ("The Jack Paar Show," "One Day at a Time"), born New York, NY, Aug 13, 1929.

Don Ho, 71, singer ("Tiny Bubbles"), born Kakaako, HI, Aug 13, 1930.

Kevin Tighe, 57, actor ("Emergency," *The Graduate, What's Eating Gilbert Grape?*), born Los Angeles, CA, Aug 13, 1944.

AUGUST 14 — TUESDAY
Day 226 — 139 Remaining

ATLANTIC CHARTER SIGNING: 60th ANNIVERSARY. Aug 14, 1941. The eight-point agreement was signed by US President Franklin D. Roosevelt and British Prime Minister Winston S. Churchill. The charter grew out of a three-day conference aboard ship in the Atlantic Ocean, off the Newfoundland coast, and stated policies and hopes for the future agreed to by the two nations.

BAHAMAS: FOX HILL DAY. Aug 14. Nassau. Annually, the second Tuesday in August.

COLOGNE CATHEDRAL: COMPLETION ANNIVERSARY. Aug 14, 1880. The largest Gothic church in northern Europe, the Cologne Cathedral at Cologne, Germany, was completed Aug 14, 1880, just 632 years after rebuilding began on Aug 14, 1248. In fact, there had been a church on its site since 873, but a fire in 1248 made rebuilding necessary. The cathedral was again damaged, by bombing, during World War II.

FINLAND: TAMPERE INTERNATIONAL THEATRE FESTIVAL. Aug 14–19. Tampere. Annual festival includes approximately 60 productions from abroad and Finland in about 200 performances, plus about 150 other events. Seminars, OFF Tampere, festival club's exhibitions, etc. Est attendance: 100,000. For info: Raija-Liisa Seilo, Exec Dir, Tampere Intl Theatre Festival Office, Tullikamarinaukio 2, Tampere, Finland FIN-33100. Phone: (358) (3) 222-8536. Fax: (358) (3) 223-0121. E-mail: theatre.festival@tt.tampere.fi. Web: www.tampere.fi/festival/theatre.

JUST, ERNEST E.: BIRTH ANNIVERSARY. Aug 14, 1883. American marine biologist Ernest E. Just was born at Charleston, SC. He was the first recipient of the NAACP's Spingarn Medal and was a professor at Howard University from 1907 to 1941, where he was head of physiology at the medical school (1912–20) and head of zoology (1912–41). He died Oct 27, 1941, at Washington, DC.

NATIONAL FINANCIAL AWARENESS DAY. Aug 14. To educate the public in the basic financial guidelines to form the foundations for financially sound practices from early adulthood through retirement. For info: Jamie K. Urick, Debt Free Intl, Inc, PO Box 705, Frankfort, IL 60423. Phone: (815) 469-7662. Fax: (815) 469-7664. E-mail: urickdfi@aol.com.

PAKISTAN: INDEPENDENCE DAY. Aug 14. Gained independence from Britain in 1947.

PENN STATE'S AGRI PROGRESS DAYS. Aug 14–16. The Larson Agricultural Research Center, Rock Springs, PA. To provide the public with the latest information on agricultural industries and developments Penn State has made in the field of agriculture. More than 300 commercial exhibitors. Est attendance: 50,000. For info: Robert Oberheim, Penn State Univ, 420 Agricultural Admin Bldg, University Park, PA 16802. Phone: (814) 865-2081. Fax: (814) 865-1677. Web: apd.cas.psu.edu.

SOCIAL SECURITY ACT: ANNIVERSARY. Aug 14, 1935. The Congress approved the Social Security Act, which contained provisions for the establishment of a Social Security Board to administer federal old-age and survivors' insurance in the US. By signing the bill into law, President Franklin D. Roosevelt was fulfilling a 1932 campaign promise.

THAYER, ERNEST LAWRENCE: BIRTH ANNIVERSARY. Aug 14, 1863. The man who wrote the famous comic baseball ballad "Casey at the Bat" was born at Lawrence, MA. He wrote a series of comic poems for the *San Francisco Examiner*, of which "Casey at the Bat" was the last. It was published Sunday, June 3, 1888, and Thayer received $5 in payment for it. Thayer, who regarded the poem's fame as a nuisance and whose other writings are widely forgotten, died at Santa Barbara, CA, Aug 21, 1940.

365-INNING SOFTBALL GAME: 25th ANNIVERSARY. Aug 14–15, 1976. The Gager's Diner softball team played the Bend'n Elbow Tavern in a 365-inning softball game. Starting at 10 AM Aug 14, the game was called because of rain and fog at 4 PM, Aug 15. The 70 players, including 20 women, raised $4,000 for construction of a new softball field and for the Monticello, NY, Community General Hospital. The Gagers beat the Elbows 491–467. To date, this remains the longest softball game on record.

TONTITOWN GRAPE FESTIVAL. Aug 14–18 (tentative). Tontitown, AR. 102nd annual festival features more than 100 crafts exhibitors, a carnival and more than 6,000 lbs of homemade pasta and sauce served at Italian spaghetti dinners, plus used book sale. Est attendance: 25,000. For info: Tontitown Grape Festival, PO Box 39, Tontitown, AR 72770. Phone: (501) 361-2612.

V-J DAY: ANNIVERSARY. Aug 14, 1945. Anniversary of President Truman's announcement that Japan had surrendered to the Allies, setting off celebrations across the nation. Official ratification of surrender occurred aboard the USS *Missouri* at Tokyo Bay, Sept 2 (Far Eastern time).

BIRTHDAYS TODAY

Russell Baker, 76, journalist, author, TV host ("Masterpiece Theatre"), born Loudoun County, VA, Aug 14, 1925.

Catherine Bell, 33, actress ("JAG"), born London, England, Aug 14, 1968.

Halle Berry, 33, actress (*Living Dolls, Boomerang*), born Cleveland, OH, Aug 14, 1968.

David Crosby, 60, singer (Crosby, Stills & Nash), songwriter, born Los Angeles, CA, Aug 14, 1941.

Antonio Fargas, 55, actor (*Shaft, I'm Gonna Git You Sucka!, Car Wash*), born The Bronx, NY, Aug 14, 1946.

Alice Ghostley, 75, actress ("Designing Women," "Bewitched"), born Eve, MO, Aug 14, 1926.

Buddy Greco, 75, singer ("Mr Lonely"), composer, musician, born Philadelphia, PA, Aug 14, 1926.

Earvin ("Magic") Johnson, Jr, 42, former basketball player, born Lansing, MI, Aug 14, 1959.

Arthur Betz Laffer, 61, economist (The Laffer Curve), born Youngstown, OH, Aug 14, 1940.

Gary Larson, 51, cartoonist ("The Far Side"), born Tacoma, WA, Aug 14, 1950.

Steve Martin, 56, comedian, actor ("Saturday Night Live," *LA Story, Roxanne, Parenthood*), born Waco, TX, Aug 14, 1945.

Susan Saint James, 55, actress ("MacMillan and Wife," "Kate and Allie"), born Long Beach, CA, Aug 14, 1946.

Danielle Steel, 54, author (*Vanished, Wanderlust*), born New York, NY, Aug 14, 1947.

Rusty Wallace, 45, auto racer, born St. Louis, MO, Aug 14, 1956.

August 2001	S	M	T	W	T	F	S
				1	2	3	4
	5	6	7	8	9	10	11
	12	13	14	15	16	17	18
	19	20	21	22	23	24	25
	26	27	28	29	30	31	

AUGUST 15 — WEDNESDAY

Day 227 — 138 Remaining

ALLIED LANDINGS IN SOUTH OF FRANCE: ANNIVERSARY. Aug 15, 1944. After several postponements, Allied forces began Operation *Dragoon*, the landing on the south coast of France. More than 2,000 transports and landing craft transported 94,000 men to an area between Toulon and Cannes, with only 183 Allied losses. They encountered minimal opposition, and by the end of August the French coast from the mouth of the Rhone to Nice was in Allied hands.

ARTISTS IN THE PARK. Aug 15. Cate Park, Wolfeboro, NH. 22nd annual juried exhibit and sale including 41 artists and craftspeople, demonstrations throughout the day and family entertainment. Held rain or shine, 10 AM–5 PM. Sponsors: Governor Wentworth Arts Council. Est attendance: 4,000. For info: Deborah Hopkins, Chair, PO Box 1379, Wolfeboro, NH 03894. Phone: (603) 569-4994.

ASSUMPTION OF THE VIRGIN MARY. Aug 15. Greek and Roman Catholic churches celebrate Mary's ascent to Heaven.

BARRYMORE, ETHEL: BIRTH ANNIVERSARY. Aug 15, 1879. Celebrated award-winning actress of stage, screen and television, born Ethel Blythe at Philadelphia, PA. Died at Beverly Hills, CA, June 18, 1959. US Postal Service stamp was issued in 1982 featuring Ethel, John and Lionel Barrymore.

BONAPARTE, NAPOLEON: BIRTH ANNIVERSARY. Aug 15, 1769. Anniversary of birth of French emperor Napoleon Bonaparte on the island of Corsica. He died in exile at 5:49 PM, May 5, 1821, on the island of St. Helena. Public holiday at Corsica, France.

CANADA: NMI MOBILITY YUKON RIVER BATHTUB RACE. Aug 15–20. Beginning in Whitehorse, YT. 10th annual 462-mile bathtub race from Whitehorse to Dawson. Est attendance: 1,500. For info: Yukon Sourdough Rendezvous Soc, Box 5108, Whitehorse, YT, Canada Y1A 4S3. Phone: (867) 667-2148. Fax: (867) 668-6755. E-mail: ysr@hypertech.yk.ca. Web: rendez vous.yukon.net/.

CAPE VERDE: NATIONAL DAY: ANNIVERSARY. Aug 15. Commemorates independence from Portugal in 1975.

CHAUVIN DAY. Aug 15. A day named for Nicholas Chauvin, French soldier from Rochefort, France, who idolized Napoleon and who eventually became a subject of ridicule because of his blind loyalty and dedication to anything French. Originally referring to bellicose patriotism, chauvinism has come to mean blind or absurdly intense attachment to any cause. Observed on Napoleon's birth anniversary because Chauvin's birth date is unknown.

COEUR D'ALENE TRIBAL PILGRIMAGE. Aug 15. Old Mission State Park, Cataldo, ID. The annual Feast of the Assumption pilgrimage by the Coeur d'Alene Indians. Annually, Aug 15. Est attendance: 1,800. For info: Bill Scudder, Park Mgr, Old Mission State Park, PO Box 30, Cataldo, ID 83810-0030. Phone: (208) 682-3814. Fax: (208) 682-4032. E-mail: old@ idpr.state.id.us.

CONGO (BRAZZAVILLE): NATIONAL DAY: ANNIVERSARY. Aug 15. National day of the People's Republic of the Congo. Commemorates independence from France in 1960.

FERBER, EDNA: BIRTH ANNIVERSARY. Aug 15, 1887. Edna Ferber was born at Kalamazoo, MI. She wrote her first novel, *Dawn O'Hara*, in 1911 and became a prolific writer, producing many popular magazine stories. Her novel *So Big* brought her commercial success in 1924 as well as a Pulitzer Prize. Her other novels include *Show Boat, Cimarron, Saratoga Trunk, Giant* and *Ice Palace*, all of which were made into successful films. Ferber collaborated with George Kaufman in writing for the stage on *The Royal Family, Dinner at Eight, Stage Door* and *Bravo*. Ferber died at New York, NY, Apr 16, 1968.

HARDING, FLORENCE KLING DeWOLFE: BIRTH ANNIVERSARY. Aug 15. Wife of Warren Gamaliel Harding, 29th president of the US, born at Marion, OH, Aug 15, 1860. Died at Marion, OH, Nov 21, 1924.

INDIA: INDEPENDENCE DAY. Aug 15. National holiday. Anniversary of Indian independence from Britain in 1947.

KOREA: LIBERATION DAY: ANNIVERSARY. Aug 15. National holiday commemorates acceptance by Japan of Allied terms of surrender in 1945, thereby freeing Korea from 36 years of Japanese domination. Also marks formal proclamation of the Republic of Korea in 1948. Military parades and ceremonies throughout country.

LIECHTENSTEIN: NATIONAL DAY. Aug 15. Public holiday on Assumption Day.

NATIONAL RELAXATION DAY. Aug 15. An excuse for every overworked and underpaid individual to do what they would rather be doing. Annually, Aug 15. For info: Sean M. Moeller, PO Box 71, Clio, MI 48420-1042. E-mail: relax15@yahoo.com.

PANAMA: PANAMA CITY FOUNDATION DAY. Aug 15. Traditional annual cultural observance recognizes foundation of Panama City.

SCOTT, SIR WALTER: BIRTH ANNIVERSARY. Aug 15, 1771. Born at Edinburgh, Scotland. Famed poet and novelist. "But no one shall find me rowing against the stream," he wrote in the introduction to *The Fortunes of Nigel*; "I care not who knows it—I write for the general amusement." Died at Abbotsford, Scotland, Sept 21, 1832.

TRANSCONTINENTAL US RAILWAY COMPLETION: ANNIVERSARY. Aug 15, 1870. The Golden Spike ceremony at Promontory Point, UT, May 10, 1869, was long regarded as the final link in a transcontinental railroad track reaching from an Atlantic port to a Pacific port. In fact, that link occurred unceremoniously on another date in another state. Diaries of engineers working at the site establish "the completion of a transcontinental track at a point 928 feet east of today's milepost 602, or 3,812 feet east of the present Union Pacific depot building at Strasburg (formerly Comanche)," CO. The final link was made at 2:53 PM, Aug 15, 1870. Annual celebration at Strasburg, CO, on a weekend in August. See also: "Golden Spike Driving: Anniversary" (May 10).

WEDDING OF THE SEA. Aug 15. Convention Center, Atlantic City, NJ. Begins with mass and interdenominational service; participants proceed to the beach and into the ocean for the blessing of all sea vessels including the lifeguard boats. Annually, Aug 15. For info: Visitor Info, Atlantic City Conv and Visitors Authority, 2314 Pacific Ave, Atlantic City, NJ 08401. Phone: (609) 347-2074 or (609) 344-8536. Fax: (609) 345-3685. E-mail: cdolan@accva.com. Web: www.atlanticcitynj.com.

WOODSTOCK: ANNIVERSARY. Aug 15, 1969. The Woodstock Music and Art Fair opened on this day on an alfalfa field on or near Yasgur's Farm at Bethel, NY. The three-day rock concert featured 24 bands and drew a crowd of more than 400,000 people.

BIRTHDAYS TODAY

Ben Affleck, 29, actor (*Good Will Hunting, Forces of Nature*), born Berkeley, CA, Aug 15, 1972.

Princess Anne, 51, Princess Royal of the UK, horsewoman, born London, England, Aug 15, 1950.

Stephen G. Breyer, 63, US Supreme Court justice, born San Francisco, CA, Aug 15, 1938.

Julia Child, 89, food authority, author (*The French Chef*), born Pasadena, CA, Aug 15, 1912.

Mike Connors (Krekor Ohanian), 76, actor ("Mannix"), born Fresno, CA, Aug 15, 1925.

Linda Ellerbee, 57, journalist, born Bryan, TX, Aug 15, 1944.

Vernon Jordan, Jr, 66, civil rights leader, born Atlanta, GA, Aug 15, 1935.

Debra Messing, 33, actress ("Ned and Stacey," "Will & Grace"), born Brooklyn, NY, Aug 15, 1968.

Phyllis Stewart Schlafly, 77, antifeminist, author, born St. Louis, MO, Aug 15, 1924.

Eugene (Gene) Upshaw, 56, union executive and former football player, Pro Football Hall of Famer, born Robstown, TX, Aug 15, 1945.

Kathryn Whitmire, 55, first woman mayor of Houston, Texas, born Houston, TX, Aug 15, 1946.

AUGUST 16 — THURSDAY
Day 228 — 137 Remaining

BABE RUTH: DEATH ANNIVERSARY. Aug 16, 1948. Baseball fans of all ages and all walks of life mourned when the great Bambino died of cancer at New York City at the age of 53. Born Feb 6, 1895, at Baltimore, MD, the left-handed pitcher and "Sultan of Swat" hit 714 home runs in 22 major league seasons of play and played in 10 World Series. His body lay in state at the main entrance of Yankee Stadium where people waited in line for hours to march past the coffin. On Aug 19, countless people surrounded St. Patrick's Cathedral for the funeral mass and lined the streets along the route to the cemetery as America bade farewell to one of baseball's greatest legends.

BATTLE OF CAMDEN: ANNIVERSARY. Aug 16, 1780. Revolutionary War battle fought near Camden, SC. American troops led by General Horatio Gates suffered disastrous losses. Nearly 1,000 Americans killed and another 1,000 captured by the British. British losses about 325. One of America's worst defeats in the war.

August 2001	S	M	T	W	T	F	S
				1	2	3	4
	5	6	7	8	9	10	11
	12	13	14	15	16	17	18
	19	20	21	22	23	24	25
	26	27	28	29	30	31	

BEGIN, MENACHEM: BIRTH ANNIVERSARY. Aug 16, 1913. Born at Brest-Litovsk, Poland. A militant Zionist and anti-communist, he fled to Russia in 1939 ahead of the advancing Nazis; he was soon arrested and sent to Siberia. Freed in 1941, he went to Palestine and became a leader in the Jewish underground, fighting for Israel's independence; by 1943 he headed the national military organization. Elected Prime Minister of Israel in 1977, he signed the historic peace treaty between Israel and Egypt with President Anwar el Sadat of Egypt and US president Jimmy Carter at Camp David in 1979. He died Mar 9, 1992, at Tel Aviv, Israel.

BENNINGTON BATTLE DAY: ANNIVERSARY. Aug 16, 1777. Anniversary of battle is legal holiday in Vermont.

THE CIDER MILL. Aug 16–Dec 1. The Cider Mill, Endicott, NY. A working cider mill—fresh cider is pressed and pasteurized for public viewing. Also, view our doughnut bakery where delicious doughnuts are being made fresh throughout the day. Fresh cider samples are always available. Est attendance: 270,000. For info: The Cider Mill, 2 S Nanticoke Ave, Endicott, NY 13760. Phone: (607) 754-0962.

COBBLESTONE FESTIVAL. Aug 16–19. Falls City, NE. Includes games, sporting events, contests, carnival rides, flea market, food concessions, car show, demolition derby, tractor pull, picnic, dance, fishing contest, parade, craft demos, motorcycle show and more. Est attendance: 5,000. For info: Chamber of Commerce, 107 E 17th, PO Box 146, Falls City, NE 68355. Phone: (402) 245-4228. Fax: (402) 245-4254.

COLUMBUS DAYS. Aug 16–19. Columbus, NE. Citywide. Concerts, prayer breakfast, coronation ball, baby show, arts and crafts, horseshoes, lip-sync, talent show, quilt show, book sale, pet show, fly-in breakfast, parades, senior activities, tractor pull, historic tours, biathlon, children's carnival and big-wheel races. Est attendance: 20,000. For info: Doris Chohon, Events Planner, Columbus Area Chamber of Commerce, PO Box 515, Columbus, NE 68602-0515. Phone: (402) 564-2769. Fax: (402) 564-2026. E-mail: chamber@megavision.com. Web: www.ci.columbus.ne.us/columbusdays.htm.

DOMINICAN REPUBLIC: RESTORATION OF THE REPUBLIC. Aug 16. The anniversary of the Restoration of the Republic is celebrated as an official public holiday.

ELWOOD GLASS FESTIVAL. Aug 16–18. Elwood, IN. Glass factory tours, parade, craft market, flea market, quilt show. Est attendance: 30,000. For info: Bill McQuitty or Pam Coryall, Chamber of Commerce, 108 S Anderson St, Elwood, IN 46036. Phone: (765) 552-0180.

ENGLAND: MANCHESTER MASSACRE or BATTLE OF PETERLOO: ANNIVERSARY. Aug 16, 1819. Anniversary of demonstration by more than 50,000 persons protesting unemployment, starvation wages, overcrowding, high costs and British government policies. The mass meeting was held at St. Peter's Fields, Manchester. Police and cavalry charged the unarmed crowd with sabres. Casualty estimates for the 10-minute battle varied widely, but several deaths and up to 500 injuries were claimed.

450-MILE OUTDOOR FESTIVAL. Aug 16–19. The World's Largest Outdoor Sale Festival. 1-27-corridor outdoor sale festival stretches from Covington, KY, covering 450 miles and ending at Gadsden, AL. The road comes alive as 35,000 cars bring people in search of antique cars, quilts, primitive furniture, arts and crafts and musical entertainment. Sponsor: Fentress County. Est attendance: 100,000. For info: Fentress County Chamber of Commerce, PO Box 1294, Jamestown, TN 38556. Phone: (800) 327-3945. E-mail: fccc@infoave.net. Web: www.127sale.com.

HARMONIC CONVERGENCE: ANNIVERSARY. Aug 16, 1987. At about 20 designated "sacred sites" around the world (including Lake Titicaca, Bolivia; Boulder, CO; Niagara Falls and the Grand Canyon in the US) believers gathered to meditate about peace and to ward off any impending doom. The harmonic convergence, projected from ancient Mayan and Aztec calendars to begin on this date, was said to signal the beginning of a period of cleansing that would last until 1992, in preparation for alien intelligence to be confronted in the next century.

INTERNATIONAL FEDERATION OF LIBRARY ASSOCIATIONS ANNUAL CONFERENCE. Aug 16–25. Boston, MA. "Libraries and Librarians: Making a Difference in the Knowledge Age." The 67th annual conference. For info: Intl Federation of Library Associations, The Royal Library, PO Box 95312, The Hague Netherlands. Web: www.ifla2001.org.

JOE MILLER'S JOKE DAY. Aug 16. A day to tell a joke in honor of the English comic actor Joseph (or Josias) Miller, who was born in 1684 (exact date unknown). Miller acted at the Drury Lane Theatre at London and was a popular favorite. A book with which Miller had no direct connection, *Joe Miller's Jests*, was compiled by John Mottley and first published in 1739. It consisted of 70 pages, containing 247 jokes. Revised and expanded hundreds of times, it contained more than 1,500 jokes in the ensuing two centuries. From *Joe Miller's Jests*, London, 1739: "A melting Sermon being preached in a country Church, all fell a weeping but one Man, who being asked, why he did not weep with the rest? O! said he. I belong to another Parish." He died at London, Aug 16, 1738.

KENTUCKY STATE FAIR (WITH WORLD CHAMPIONSHIP HORSE SHOW). Aug 16–26. Kentucky Fair and Expo Center, Louisville, KY. Midway, concerts by nationally known artists and the World's Championship Horse Show. Est attendance: 700,000. For info: Marketing Dept, KY Fair and Expo Ctr, Box 37130, Louisville, KY 40233. Phone: (502) 367-5000 or (502) 367-5291. Web: www.kyfairexpo.org.

KLONDIKE GOLD DISCOVERY: ANNIVERSARY. Aug 16, 1896. According to the oral tradition of the Tagish First Nations People, Skookum Jim, Dawson Charlie and George Carmack found gold in Rabbit Creek, a tributary of the Klondike River, lying "thick between the flaky slabs like cheese sandwiches." This event that led to the great Klondike Gold Rush is celebrated in the Yukon each year with a public holiday, Discovery Day, observed on the nearest Monday (see Aug 16).

LAWRENCE (OF ARABIA), T. E.: BIRTH ANNIVERSARY. Aug 16, 1888. British soldier, archaeologist and writer, born at Tremadoc, North Wales. During WWI, led the Arab revolt against the Turks and served as a spy for the British. His book, *Seven Pillars of Wisdom*, is a personal account of the Arab revolt. He was killed in a motorcycle accident at Dorset, England, May 19, 1935.

MacFADDEN, BERNARR: BIRTH ANNIVERSARY. Aug 16, 1868. Physical culture enthusiast and publisher, born at Mill Springs, MO. He was publisher of *Physical Culture Magazine, True Story Magazine, True Romances, True Detective Mysteries Magazine* and many others. MacFadden made parachute jumps on his 81st, 83rd and 84th birthdays. He died at Jersey City, NJ, of jaundice, following a three-day fast, Oct 12, 1955.

MEANY, GEORGE: BIRTH ANNIVERSARY. Aug 16, 1894. American labor leader George Meany was born at New York, NY. A plumber by trade, he became president of the AFL (American Federation of Labor) in 1952, and when he merged the AFL with the CIO (Congress of Industrial Organizations) he became the leading labor spokesperson in the US. In 1957 he expelled Jimmy Hoffa's Teamsters Union from the AFL-CIO and lost the United Auto Workers in 1967. His tenure as president lasted until 1979. He died Jan 10, 1980, at Washington, DC.

MICHIGAN FIBER FESTIVAL. Aug 16–19. Allegan County Fairgrounds, Allegan, MI. A unique opportunity to see and learn about natural fibers and the animals and plants that produce them. Includes classes and displays of fiber animals and processes of fiber into garments or décor. Est attendance: 8,000. For info: Michigan Fiber Festival, PO Box 310, Hastings, MI 49058. Phone: (616) 948-2497. Fax: (616) 945-4883. E-mail: mff@mvcc.com. Web: www.mvcc.com/non/mff.

MILWAUKEE IRISH FEST. Aug 16–19. Milwaukee, WI. World's largest and most comprehensive Irish music and cultural event, featuring 15 stages of Irish and Irish-American music, dance and theater. Activities include sports, contests, parades, displays, food, marketplace, dance and children's activities. Week-long summer school precedes the festival with lectures and demonstrations in Irish music, dance and culture. Annually, the third weekend in August. Est attendance: 100,000. For info: Milwaukee Irish Fest, 1532 Wauwatosa Ave, Milwaukee, WI 53213. Phone: (414) 476-3378. Fax: (414) 476-7712. E-mail: ifest@execpc.com. Web: www.irishfest.com.

NEWSPAPERS TAKEN TO COURT FOR PRO-CONFEDERATE SYMPATHIES: ANNIVERSARY. Aug 16, 1861. Beginning on Aug 16, several newspapers in Union states were brought to court for alleged pro-Confederate sympathies, including the Brooklyn *Eagle*, the New York *Journal of Commerce* and the New York *Daily News*. On Aug 19, an editor for the *Essex County Democrat*, at Haverhill, MA, was tarred and feathered for his Southern leanings expressed in the newspaper.

PRESLEY, ELVIS: DEATH ANNIVERSARY. Aug 16, 1977. One of America's most popular singers, Elvis Presley was pronounced dead at the Memphis Baptist Hospital at 3:30 PM, Aug 16, 1977, at age 42. The anniversary of his death is an occasion for pilgrimages by admirers to Graceland, his home and gravesite at Memphis, TN. See also: "Presley, Elvis: Birth Anniversary" (Jan 8).

RIVERFRONT RIBFEST. Aug 16–19. Harris Riverfront Park, Huntington, WV. World-class ribs cooked by rib vendors from around the country, competing for more than $4,000 in prizes. Continuous entertainment for all ages. Annually, the third weekend in August. Est attendance: 15,000. For info: Cheryl Myers, Huntington Civic Arena/Ogden Entertainment, PO Box 2767, Huntington, WV 25727. Phone: (304) 696-5990. Fax: (304) 696-4463. Web: www.hcarena.com.

SOLDIERS' REUNION CELEBRATION. Aug 16. Newton, NC. Parade climaxes the 112th annual soldiers' reunion celebration—"oldest patriotic event of its kind in the US, honoring all veterans." Annually, the third Thursday in August. Concerts, arts, crafts, food and games. Est attendance: 28,000. For info: Soldiers' Reunion Committee, Box 267, Newton, NC 28658. Phone: (828) 464-2383.

STAGG, AMOS ALONZO: BIRTH ANNIVERSARY. Aug 16, 1862. Amos Alonzo Stagg, football player and coach born at West Orange, NJ. Stagg played baseball and football at Yale and then forsook the ministry for physical education. He built the football program at the University of Chicago as an integral part of William Rainey Harper's plan to build a great university. Over 40 years at Chicago, he became the game's greatest innovator and master strategist. When Chicago de-emphasized football, he moved to the College of the Pacific, finishing his career with a record of 314-181-15. In 1959 he was inducted into the Basketball Hall of Fame as a contributor. Died at Stockton, CA, Mar 17, 1965.

SUN PRAIRIE'S SWEET CORN FESTIVAL. Aug 16–19. Sun Prairie, WI. Family-oriented fun. Carnival, midget auto races, parade, beer, brats, food, exhibits and tons of hot, buttered sweet corn. Est attendance: 100,000. For info: Chamber of Commerce, 109 E Main, Sun Prairie, WI 53590. Phone: (608) 837-4547. Fax: (608) 837-8765. E-mail: sprairie@merr.com.

SWEDEN: SOUR HERRING PREMIERE. Aug 16. By ordinance, the year's supply of sour herring may begin to be sold on the third Thursday in August.

SWITZERLAND: INTERNATIONAL FESTIVAL OF MUSIC. Aug 16–Sept 15. Lucerne. A classical music festival considered to have the most spectacular scenery of any music festival in Europe. Features more than 80 events including symphony concerts, chamber music, concerts presenting young artists and contemporary music. Annually, in August and September. Est attendance: 55,000. For info: H. Elisabeth Mlasko, Communications/Marketing, Intl Festival of Music, PO Box CH-6002,

Lucerne, Switzerland. Phone: (41) (41) 226-4400. Fax: (41) (41) 226-4460. E-mail: media@LucerneMusic.ch.

WE LOVE ERIE DAYS!. Aug 16–19. Erie, PA. Downtown Erie is the setting for Erie's largest celebration. Activities include continuous live onstage entertainment, rides, food, boat races and ship tours. Est attendance: 300,000. For info: C. Markiewicz, 626 State, Rm 507, Erie, PA 16501. Phone: (814) 870-1253. Fax: (814) 870-1415. E-mail: erie-tourism@erie.net. Web: www.eriepa.com.

BIRTHDAYS TODAY

Angela Bassett, 43, actress (*Malcolm X, What's Love Got to Do with It, Waiting to Exhale*), born New York, NY, Aug 16, 1958.

James Cameron, 47, director (*Titanic, True Lies*), born Kapuskasing, Ontario, Canada, Aug 16, 1954.

Robert Culp, 71, actor ("I Spy," *Bob and Carol and Ted and Alice*), born Berkeley, CA, Aug 16, 1930.

Frank Newton Gifford, 71, sportscaster, Pro Football Hall of Fame halfback/end, born Santa Monica, CA, Aug 16, 1930.

Kathie Lee Gifford, 48, TV personality, singer, married to football legend Frank Gifford, born Paris, France, Aug 16, 1953.

Eydie Gorme (Edith Gormezano), 69, singer ("Blame It on the Bossa Nova"), born New York, NY, Aug 16, 1932.

Timothy Hutton, 41, actor (*Taps, Made in Heaven*), born Malibu, CA, Aug 16, 1960.

Laura Innes, 41, actress ("ER," "Wings"), born Pontiac, MI, Aug 16, 1960.

Madonna (Madonna Louise Veronica Ciccone), 43, singer ("Material Girl"), actress (*Desperately Seeking Susan, A League of Their Own, Evita*), born Bay City, MI, Aug 16, 1958.

Julie Newmar, 66, actress (Cat Woman on TV's "Batman," *Li'l Abner*), born Hollywood, CA, Aug 16, 1935.

Fess Parker, 74, actor ("Daniel Boone," *Davy Crockett*), born Fort Worth, TX, Aug 16, 1927.

Jeff Perry, 46, actor ("Nash Bridges"), founder of Chicago's Steppenwolf Theater, born Highland Park, IL, Aug 16, 1955.

Seth Peterson, 31, actor ("Providence"), born The Bronx, NY, Aug 16, 1970.

Reginald VelJohnson, 49, actor (*Ghostbusters, Die Hard, Die Hard 2*), born Queens, NY, Aug 16, 1952.

Lesley Ann Warren, 55, actress (*Victor/Victoria, Choose Me*, "Cinderella"), born New York, NY, Aug 16, 1946.

AUGUST 17 — FRIDAY
Day 229 — 136 Remaining

ALABAMA PRO NATIONAL TRUCK AND TRACTOR PULL. Aug 17–18. Lexington, AL. Six different classes compete: Pro National 7500 Superstock, Pro National 6200 2-Wheel Drive Trucks, Pro National 7200 Modified Tractors (multiengine), State Level 6200 4-Wheel Drive Truck, Local Level 4×4 Street Class and Local Level 15,200 Farm Class. Est attendance: 25,000. For info: Debbie Wilson, Dir, Florence/Lauderdale Tourism, One Hightower Pl, Florence, AL 35630. Phone: (256) 740-4141 or (888) FLO-TOUR. Fax: (256) 740-4142. Web: www.flo-tour.org.

BALLOON CROSSING OF ATLANTIC OCEAN: ANNIVERSARY. Aug 17, 1978. Three Americans—Maxie Anderson, 44, Ben Abruzzo, 48, and Larry Newman, 31—all of Albuquerque, NM, became first to complete transatlantic trip in a balloon. Starting from Presque Isle, ME, Aug 11, they traveled some 3,200 miles in 137 hours, 18 minutes, landing at Miserey, France (about 60 miles west of Paris), in their craft, named the *Double Eagle II*.

August 2001	S	M	T	W	T	F	S
				1	2	3	4
	5	6	7	8	9	10	11
	12	13	14	15	16	17	18
	19	20	21	22	23	24	25
	26	27	28	29	30	31	

BATTLE OF BLUE LICKS CELEBRATION. Aug 17–18. Blue Licks Battlefield State Park, Mount Olivet, KY. Commemorates the anniversary of Revolutionary War Battle of Blue Licks (which involved Daniel Boone). Living-history demonstrations, arts, crafts, games, competitions and battle reenactment. Annually, the third weekend in August. Est attendance: 3,000. For info: Doug Price, Park Mgr, Blue Licks Battlefield State Pk, PO Box 66, Mt Olivet, KY 41064-0066. Phone: (606) 289-5507. Fax: (606) 289-5409. Web: www.state.ky.us/agencies/parks/bluelick.htm.

BLACK HILLS STEAM AND GAS THRESHING BEE. Aug 17–19. Sturgis, SD. Held annually one mile east of the Sturgis Airport. The pioneer heritage of our country comes alive with old steam and gas tractors, threshing machine demonstrations, flea market, parade, antique automobiles and dozens of other demonstrations related to yesteryear. Est attendance: 4,000. For info: Clif Roemmich. Phone: (605) 787-4647.

CALIFORNIA STATE FAIR. Aug 17–Sept 3. Sacramento, CA. Top-name entertainment, fireworks, California counties exhibits, livestock nursery, culinary delights, carnival rides, demolition derbies and award-winning wines and microbrews. For info: Cal Expo, PO Box 15649, Sacramento, CA 95852. Phone: (916) 263-3000. E-mail: SallyCSF@aol.com.

CANADA: NOVA SCOTIA'S GEM AND MINERAL SHOW. Aug 17–19. Parrsboro, NS. Geological tours by foot, rock collectors workshops and demonstrations, lectures about Nova Scotia. Est attendance: 2,000. For info: Marylynn Goguen, Box 640, 162 Two Island Rd, Parrsboro, NS, Canada B0M 1S0. Phone: (902) 254-3814. Fax: (902) 254-3666. Web: nova-scotia.com/fundygeomuseum.

CHASE, HARRISON V.: BIRTH ANNIVERSARY. Aug 17, 1913. Cofounder and coeditor of *Chase's Annual Events*, professor at Florida State University, born at Big Rapids, MI. Died Feb 6, 2000, at Tallahassee, FL.

COSHOCTON CANAL FESTIVAL. Aug 17–19. Coshocton, OH. Celebrates the arrival of first canal boat at Port Roscoe. Crafts, demonstrations and live entertainment. Annually, the third weekend in August. Est attendance: 14,000. For info: Roscoe Village Fdtn, 381 Hill St, Coshocton, OH 43812. Phone: (800) 877-1830 or (740) 622-9310. Fax: (740) 623-6555. E-mail: rvmarketing@coshocton.com. Web: www.roscoevillage.com.

CROCKETT, DAVID "DAVY": BIRTH ANNIVERSARY. Aug 17, 1786. American frontiersman, adventurer and soldier, born at Hawkins County, TN. Died during final heroic defense of the Alamo, Mar 6, 1836, at San Antonio, TX. In his *Autobiography* (1834), Crockett wrote, "I leave this rule for others when I'm dead, Be always sure you're right—then go ahead."

FESTIVAL OF THE LITTLE HILLS. Aug 17–19. Frontier Park and South Main, St. Charles, MO. The largest festival of the year; activities include demonstrations by craftspeople and artisans. Annually, the third weekend in August. Est attendance: 300,000. For info: St. Charles Conv and Visitors Bureau, 230 S Main, St. Charles, MO 63301. Phone: (800) 366-2427 or (636) 946-7776. Web: www.historicstcharles.com.

FORT SUMTER SHELLED BY NORTHERN FORCES: ANNIVERSARY. Aug 17, 1863. In what would become a long siege, Union forces began shelling Fort Sumter at Charleston, SC. The site of the first shots fired during the Civil War on Apr 12, 1861, Sumter endured the siege for a year and a half before being returned to Union hands.

FULTON SAILS STEAMBOAT: ANNIVERSARY. Aug 17, 1807. Robert Fulton began the first American steamboat trip between Albany and New York, NY, on a boat later called the *Clermont*. After years of promoting submarine warfare, Fulton engaged in a partnership with Robert R. Livingston, the US minister to France, allowing Fulton to design and construct a steamboat. His first success came in August 1803 when he launched a steam-powered vessel on the Seine. That same year the US Congress granted Livingston and Fulton exclusive rights to operate steamboats on New York waters during the next 20 years. The first Albany-to-New York trip took 32 hours to travel the 150-mile course. Although his efforts were labeled "Fulton's Folly" by his detractors, his success allowed the partnership to begin commercial service the next year, Sept 4, 1808.

GABON: NATIONAL DAY: ANNIVERSARY. Aug 17. National holiday. Commemorates independence from France in 1960.

GINZA HOLIDAY: JAPANESE CULTURAL FESTIVAL. Aug 17–19. Midwest Buddhist Temple, Chicago, IL. Experience the Waza (National Treasures tradition) by viewing 300 years of Edo craft tradition and seeing it come alive as master craftsmen from Tokyo demonstrate their arts. Japanese folk and classical dancing, martial arts, taiko (drums), flower arrangements and cultural displays. Chicken teriyaki, sushi, udon, shaved ice, corn on the cob and refreshments. Annually, the third weekend in August. Est attendance: 5,000. For info: Office Secretary, Midwest Buddhist Temple, 435 W Menomonee St, Chicago, IL 60614. Phone: (312) 943-7801. Fax: (312) 943-8069.

GOLDWYN, SAMUEL: BIRTH ANNIVERSARY. Aug 17, 1882. Motion picture producer and industry pioneer, born Samuel Goldfish, at Warsaw, Poland. Goldwyn died at Los Angeles, CA, Jan 31, 1974. Attributed to Goldwyn is the observation: "Anybody who goes to see a psychiatrist ought to have his head examined."

HAWAII ADMISSION DAY HOLIDAY. Aug 17. The third Friday in August is observed as a state holiday each year, recognizing the anniversary of Hawaii's statehood. Hawaii became the 50th state Aug 21, 1959.

HOLZFEST. Aug 17–19. Amana, IA. A woodcraft show with displays, products, demonstrations, equipment, supplies, entertainment and food. Annually, the third weekend in August. Est attendance: 10,000. For info: Tammy Meyer, Splinterfest/Holzfest, PO Box 215, Dyersville, IA 52040. Phone: (319) 875-7017. Fax: (319) 875-9607. E-mail: dww@mwci.net.

INDONESIA: INDEPENDENCE DAY: ANNIVERSARY. Aug 17. National holiday. Republic proclaimed in 1945. It was only after several years of fighting, however, that Indonesia was formally granted its independence by the Netherlands, Dec 27, 1949.

INTERNATIONAL IRONWORKERS FESTIVAL. Aug 17–19. Mackinaw City, MI. Meet the men who built the Mackinac Bridge. Weekend activities range from sports competitions to the annual Ironworkers parade through Mackinaw City. Est attendance: 6,000. For info: Macinaw Area Tourist Bureau, PO Box 160, Mackinaw City, MI 49701. Phone: (800) 666-0160. Web: www.mackinawcity.com.

KAHOKA FESTIVAL OF BLUEGRASS MUSIC. Aug 17–20. Kahoka, MO. Top bluegrass bands, clogging workshops and shows, Fiddlers Frolic, jam sessions, Miss Kahoka pageant, clogging contest. 29th annual festival. Est attendance: 4,000. For info: Delbert Spray, Program Dir, RR 1, Kahoka, MO 63445. Phone: (573) 853-4344.

LITTLE LEAGUE BASEBALL WORLD SERIES. Aug 17–25. Williamsport, PA. Sixteen teams from the US and foreign countries compete for the World Championship. Est attendance: 200,000. For info: Little League Baseball HQ, Box 3485, Williamsport, PA 17701. Phone: (570) 326-1921. Web: www.littleleague.org.

MACHIAS WILD BLUEBERRY FESTIVAL. Aug 17–19. Machias, ME. Harvest festival includes crafts sale, lobster boil, five-mile race, entertainment, children's parade, blueberry foods and a wild blueberry pie-eating contest. Annually, the third weekend in August. Est attendance: 15,000. For info: Machias Wild Blueberry Festival, PO Box 265, Machias, ME 04654. Phone: (207) 255-6665. Web: www.nemaine.com/blueberry.

MOUNTAIN MAN RENDEZVOUS. Aug 17–19. Old Mission State Park, Cataldo, ID. 1800s fur trappers and traders, in period clothing. Est attendance: 2,500. For info: Roger Howard, Old Mission State Park, PO Box 30, Cataldo, ID 83810-0030. Phone: (208) 682-3814. Fax: (208) 682-4032. E-mail: old@idpr.state.id.us.

MUDDY FROGWATER COUNTRY CLASSIC FESTIVAL. Aug 17–19. Yantis Park, Milton-Freewater, OR. Arts, crafts, food, bluegrass and country music, frog jumping contest, book sale, square dancing, bed races, firefighters' water fight, 3-on-3 basketball tournament. Annually, the third weekend in August. Est attendance: 5,000. For info: Milton-Freewater Area Chamber of Commerce, 505 N Ward St, Milton-Freewater, OR 97862. Phone: (541) 938-5563. Fax: (541) 938-5564.

PENNSYLVANIA RENAISSANCE FAIRE. Aug 17–Oct 14. Manheim, PA. Re-creation of 16th-century Elizabethan village. Lords and ladies, mongers, merchants, jousting, human chess match, medieval foods and crafts. Fair takes place Saturday–Monday from Aug 17 until Labor Day; Saturdays and Sundays only thereafter. Est attendance: 100,000. For info: Thomas Roy, Mount Hope Estate and Winery, PO Box 685, Cornwall, PA 17016. Phone: (717) 665-7021 ext 127. Fax: (717) 664-3466. E-mail: TomRoy@parenaissancefaire.com. Web: www.parenfaire.com.

PILOT PEN TENNIS PRESENTED BY MICHELOB LIGHT. Aug 17–25. CT Tennis Center, Yale University, New Haven, CT. A one week women's professional tennis event featuring many of the top players in the world. Singles Main Draw includes 28 players and Doubles Main Draw includes 16 teams. Event also features many special events weeklong like Kids Day, live music, sponsor give-aways and much more! For info: CT Tennis Center (888) 99-PILOT or Greater New Haven CVB, 59 Elm St, New Haven, CT 06510. Phone: (203) 777-8550 or (800) 332-STAY. Fax: (203) 782-7755.

POWERS, FRANCIS GARY: BIRTH ANNIVERSARY. Aug 17, 1929. One of America's most famous aviators, Francis Gary Powers was born at Jenkins, KY. The CIA agent, pilot of a U-2 overflight across the Soviet Union, was shot down May 1, 1960, near Sverdlovsk, USSR. He was tried, convicted and sentenced to 10 years' imprisonment, at Moscow, USSR, in August 1960. Returned to the US in 1962, in exchange for an imprisoned Soviet spy (Colonel Rudolf Abel), he found an unwelcoming homeland. Powers died in a helicopter crash near Los Angeles, CA, Aug 2, 1977.

TEXAS RANCH ROUNDUP. Aug 17–18. Wichita Falls, TX. Cowboys from prestigious ranches in Texas compete in the events that make up their daily work. Cattle roping and penning and other rodeo-type events plus ranch cooking contests, ranch talent contests. Est attendance: 18,000. For info: Wichita Falls Conv and Visitors Bureau, 1000 5th St, Wichita Falls, TX 76301. Phone: (800) 799-6732 or (940) 716-5500. Fax: (940) 716-5509.

TRAILS WEST!®. Aug 17–19. Civic Center Park, St. Joseph, MO. Arts festival celebrating St. Joseph's unique cultural heritage. Fine arts, crafts and heritage folk art, wide variety of taste-tempting food, beer saloon and wine garden, children's games, re-enactors and big-name entertainment. Annually, the third weekend in August. Est attendance: 90,000. For info: Program Aide, Allied Arts Council, 118 S 8th, St. Joseph, MO 64501. Phone: (800) 216-7080 or (816) 233-0231. Fax: (816) 233-6704. E-mail: artstaff@stjoearts.org. Web: stjoearts.org.

TURKISH EARTHQUAKE: ANNIVERSARY. Aug 17, 1999. A quake with a magnitude of 7.4 struck northwestern Turkey where 45 percent of the population lives. More than 17,000 died and thousands more remained missing. Many of the deaths were due to the shoddy construction of apartment houses. Aftershocks in the region through September 1999 resulted in more deaths. On Nov 12, 1999, a magnitude 7.2 earthquake struck Turkey, killing more than 800 people. Also in 1999 there were earthquakes in Greece (139 dead) and Taiwan (2,200 dead and many missing).

WORLD'S OLDEST CONTINUOUS PRCA RODEO. Aug 17–19. Payson Rodeo Grounds, Payson, AZ. The Payson Rodeo has been held continuously since 1884. Named number one small outdoor rodeo in America! Est attendance: 20,000. For info: Rim Country Regional Chamber of Commerce, Box 1380, Payson, AZ 85547. Phone: (800) 672-9766. Fax: (520) 474-8812. E-mail: pcoc@netzone.com.

BIRTHDAYS TODAY

Belinda Carlisle, 43, singer ("Mad About You"), born Hollywood, CA, Aug 17, 1958.
Robert De Niro, 58, actor (Oscars for *Raging Bull, The Godfather II; Taxi Driver*), born New York, NY, Aug 17, 1943.
Robert Joy, 50, actor (*Atlantic City, Desperately Seeking Susan, Longtime Companion*), born Montreal, Quebec, Canada, Aug 17, 1951.
Christian Laettner, 32, NBA forward, member of the Dream Team in the 1992 Olympics, born Angola, NY, Aug 17, 1969.
Maureen O'Hara, 81, actress (*Miracle on 34th Street, The Hunchback of Notre Dame*), born Dublin, Ireland, Aug 17, 1920.
Sean Penn, 41, actor (*Fast Times at Ridgemont High, Dead Man Walking*), born Santa Monica, CA, Aug 17, 1960.
Nelson Piquet, 49, former auto racer, born Brasilia, Brazil, Aug 17, 1952.
Larry Rivers, 78, artist, born New York, NY, Aug 17, 1923.
Guillermo Vilas, 49, former tennis player, born Mar del Plata, Argentina, Aug 17, 1952.

	S	M	T	W	T	F	S
August				1	2	3	4
2001	5	6	7	8	9	10	11
	12	13	14	15	16	17	18
	19	20	21	22	23	24	25
	26	27	28	29	30	31	

AUGUST 18 — SATURDAY
Day 230 — 135 Remaining

AMERICAN NEUTRALITY APPEAL: ANNIVERSARY. Aug 18, 1914. President Woodrow Wilson followed his Aug 4th Proclamation of Neutrality with an appeal to the American people to remain impartial in thought and deed with respect to the war that was raging in Europe (World War I).

ANTIQUE MARINE ENGINE EXPOSITION. Aug 18–19. Mystic Seaport, Mystic, CT. Collectors from across the US and Canada gather for the 10th annual exposition of pre-World War II marine engines and engine models. Unique engines power watercraft in a boat parade on the Mystic River. For info: Mystic Seaport, 75 Greenmanville Ave, PO Box 6000, Mystic, CT 06355-0990. Phone: (860) 572-5315 or (888) 9SEAPORT. Web: www.mysticseaport.org.

BAD POETRY DAY. Aug 18. After all the "good" poetry you were forced to study in school, here's a chance for a payback. Invite some friends over, compose some really rotten verse and send it to your old high school English teacher. [© 2000 by WH] For info: Tom or Ruth Roy, Wellcat Holidays, 2418 Long Ln, Lebanon, PA 17046. Phone: (717) 279-0184. E-mail: wellcat@supernet.com. Web: www.wellcat.com.

BIKE VAN BUREN XIV. Aug 18–19. Van Buren County, IA. A laid-back bicycle tour of the villages, landmarks and landscape of this rural Iowa county. The "red carpet of hospitality" is rolled out for the bikers as they pass through. Annually, the third weekend in August. Est attendance: 600. For info: Stacey Glandon, Exec Dir, Villages of Van Buren, Inc, PO Box 9, Keosauqua, IA 52565. Phone: (800) TOUR-VBC. Fax: (319) 293-7116. Web: www.800-tourvbc.com.

BIRTH CONTROL PILLS SOLD: ANNIVERSARY. Aug 18, 1960. The first commercially produced oral contraceptives were marketed by the G.D. Searle Company of Illinois. The pill, developed by Gregory Pincus, had been undergoing clinical trials since 1954.

BLUE CLAW CRAB CRAFT SHOW & CRAB RACE. Aug 18. Harvey Cedars, NJ. Crafters displaying their goods at Sunset Park. Crab race determines fastest crab on Long Beach Island. For info: Harvey Cedars Activity Committee, PO Box 3185, Harvey Cedars, NJ 08008. Phone: (609) 361-7990. Fax: (609) 494-2335. E-mail: hcboro@cybercomm.net.

BONANZAVILLE USA PIONEER DAYS. Aug 18–19. Bonanzaville USA, West Fargo, ND. The 43 buildings in the Victorian-era pioneer village come to life. Ice cream and lemonade are sold at the drugstore, log cabin residents turn out lefse and jellies for sample and sale, a country market sells garden produce, threshing machines crank up, church services are performed in both German and Norwegian, and the highlights of the weekend are the old-time vehicle parades. Est attendance: 10,000. For info: Bonanzaville USA, PO Box 719, West Fargo, ND 58078. Phone: (701) 282-2822 or (800) 700-5317. E-mail: bonanzaville@fargocity.com. Web: www.fargocity.com/bonanzaville.

CANADA: OJIBWA KEESHIGUN. Aug 18–19. Old Fort William, Thunder Bay, ON. A celebration of Old Fort William's native culture. Taste historic foods, enjoy unique demonstrations and join in crafts and games. Experience the atmosphere with traditional singing and dancing. Annually, late August. Est attendance: 3,000. For info: Marty Mascarin, Communications Officer, Vickers Heights PO, Thunder Bay, ON, Canada P0T 2Z0. Phone: (807) 473-2326 or (807) 577-8461. Fax: (807) 473-2327.

CANADA: PAINT THE TOWN©. Aug 18–19. Annapolis Royal, NS. 50 artists from across the province "paint the town," sketching at designated sites in Annapolis Royal. Work is auctioned off each evening. Entertainment. Est attendance: 900. For info: Susan Tileston, Exec Dir, ARCAC, Box 534, Annapolis Royal, NS, Canada B0S 1A0. Phone: (902) 532-7069. Fax: (902) 532-7357. E-mail: arcac@ns.sympatico.ca. Web: www.arcac.ns.ca.

CLEMENTE, ROBERTO: BIRTH ANNIVERSARY. Aug 18, 1934. National League baseball player, born at Carolina, Puerto Rico. Drafted by the Pittsburgh Pirates in 1954, he played his entire major league career with them. Clemente died in a plane crash Dec 31, 1972, while on a mission of mercy to Nicaragua to deliver supplies he had collected for survivors of an earthquake. He was elected to the Baseball Hall of Fame in 1973.

DARE, VIRGINIA: BIRTH ANNIVERSARY. Aug 18, 1587 (OS). Virginia Dare, the first child of English parents to be born in the New World, was born to Ellinor and Ananias Dare, at Roanoke Island, NC, Aug 18, 1587. When a ship arrived to replenish their supplies in 1591, the settlers (including Virginia Dare) had vanished, without leaving a trace of the settlement.

ENGLAND: THREE CHOIRS FESTIVAL. Aug 18–25. Gloucester Cathedral, Gloucester. Europe's oldest music festival, with performances by the three cathedral choirs and Festival choruses of Hereford, Worcester and Gloucester. Extensive Fringe. Est attendance: 20,000. For info: William Armiger, Three Choirs Festival Office, Community House, College Green, Gloucester, England GL1 2LZ. Phone: (44) 1452 529819. Fax: (44) 1452 502854.

GREATER PITTSBURGH RENAISSANCE FESTIVAL. Aug 18–19. (also Aug 25–26, Sept 1–3, 8–9, 15–16 and 22–23) West Newton, PA. A re-creation of a 16th-century marketplace where the king and queen come on holiday. Featured are more than 100 craft shops, five themed stages, games, food and armoured contact jousting. Est attendance: 60,000. For info: Lori Hughes, Greater Pittsburgh Renaissance Festival, PO Box 1670, Greensburg, PA 15601-7670. Phone: (724) 872-1670.

HOMETOWN DAYS. Aug 18–19. Strasburg, CO. To remind people of the first continuous chain of rails from an Atlantic to a Pacific port. The rails were joined Aug 15, 1870, at Comanche, which was later renamed Strasburg. Annually, the third weekend in August. Est attendance: 1,000. For info: Sandy Miller, Curator-Comanche Crossing Museum, 7433 S Rd 157, Strasburg, CO 80136. Phone: (303) 622-4690.

LEADVILLE TRAIL 100 ULTRAMARATHON. Aug 18–19 (tentative). Leadville, CO. One of the toughest 100-mile foot races in the country, the course goes through the Rocky Mountains 50 miles to the ghost town of Winfield and back. Runners begin at 4 AM and must complete the race in 30 hours. All race applications mailed by Jan 2. Race fills within two weeks. Sponsor: Leadville Trail 100, Inc. Est attendance: 2,000. For info: Greater Leadville Chamber of Commerce, PO Box 861, Leadville, CO 80461. Phone: (719) 486-3900 or (800) 933-3901. Fax: (719) 486-8478. E-mail: leadville@leadvilleusa.com. Web: www.leadville usa.com.

LEWIS, MERIWETHER: BIRTH ANNIVERSARY. Aug 18, 1774. American explorer (of Lewis and Clark expedition), born at Albemarle County, VA. Died Oct 11, 1809, near Nashville, TN.

MAIL-ORDER CATALOG: ANNIVERSARY. Aug 18, 1872. The first mail-order catalog was published by Montgomery Ward. It was only a single sheet of paper. By 1904 the Montgomery Ward catalog weighed four pounds.

MAINE HIGHLAND GAMES. Aug 18. Thomas Point Beach, Brunswick, ME. Presented by the Saint Andrew's Society of Maine. Bagpipe bands, Highland and Scottish dancing, Scottish arts and crafts fair, folksingers, Scottish fiddling, children's games, adult athletics including tossing of the caber, wheat sheaf toss and putting of the stone, border collie herding demonstrations, Highland cattle and individual piping contests. American and Scottish foods galore. The only Scottish event of its kind held in Maine! Scots and non-Scots will enjoy the color, pageantry and friendly atmosphere. 23rd annual. Est attendance: 8,000. For info: Thomas Point Beach, 29 Meadow Rd, Brunswick, ME 04011. Phone: (207) 725-6009. Web: www.thomaspointbeach.com.

MILFORD OYSTER FESTIVAL. Aug 18. Downtown Milford and Fowler Field, Milford, CT. 250 arts and crafts, headline entertainment, classic car show, canoe race, harbor activities, health fair, corporate row and food court. Annually, the third Saturday in August. For info: Milford Oyster Festival, (203) 878-5363 or Greater New Haven Conv & Visitors Bureau, 59 Elm St, New Haven, CT 06510. Phone: (203) 777-8550 or (800) 332-STAY. Fax: (203) 782-7755. Web: www.newhavencvb.org.

MINNESOTA RENAISSANCE FESTIVAL. Aug 18–Sept 30 (weekends and Labor Day only). Shakopee, MN. A celebration of 16th-century Renaissance Europe with entertainment on 11 lively stages, food, arts and crafts, games and live jousting. Est attendance: 350,000. For info: Minnesota Renaissance Festival, 1244 S Canterbury Rd, Ste 306, Shakopee, MN 55379. Phone: (800) 966-8215 or (952) 445-7361. Fax: (952) 445-7380. Web: www.renaissancefest.com.

MOON PHASE: NEW MOON. Aug 18. Moon enters New Moon phase at 10:55 PM, EDT.

NATIONAL HOMELESS ANIMALS DAY AND CANDLELIGHT VIGILS. Aug 18. A day to call attention to the fact that 12–17 million healthy dogs and cats are killed each year in the US in animal shelters because of overpopulation—a problem that has a solution: Spay/Neuter! It Stops the Killing! The vigils memorialize the animals killed in the preceding year and sympathize with the caring shelter personnel who must take the lives of the animals. Vigils will be held throughout the US and beyond. For info: Intl Soc for Animal Rights, Inc, Susan Altieri, Pres, 965 Griffin Pond Rd, Clarks Summit, PA 18411-1015. Phone: (570) 586-2200. Fax: (570) 586-9580. E-mail: isar@aol.com.

NINETEENTH AMENDMENT TO US CONSTITUTION RATIFIED: ANNIVERSARY. Aug 18, 1920. The 19th Amendment extended the right to vote to women.

NORTHEASTERN WISCONSIN ANTIQUE POWER AND MACHINERY SHOW THRESHEREE. Aug 18–19. Sturgeon Bay, WI. Continuous display of operating antique machinery, antique tractor pull, barefoot horsepull, crafts, games for kids, food and refreshments. Annually, the third weekend in August. Est attendance: 3,000. For info: Josephine Bochek, Northeastern Wisconsin Antique Power Assn, 4376 Rudy Rd, Sturgeon Bay, WI 54235. Phone: (920) 743-5251. E-mail: coldcomfortfarms@hotmail.com or Bernie Geisel (920) 743-4859.

PERIGEAN SPRING TIDES. Aug 18. Spring tides, the highest possible tides, which occur when New Moon or Full Moon takes place within 24 hours of the moment the Moon is nearest Earth (perigee) in its monthly orbit at 11 PM, EDT. These tides are not named for the season of spring but for the German *springen*, "to leap up."

PONY LEAGUE WORLD SERIES. Aug 18–25. Washington, PA. International youth baseball World Series for teams of players ages 13 and 14. Est attendance: 16,500. For info: PONY Baseball, PO Box 225, Washington, PA 15301. Phone: (724) 225-1060. Fax: (724) 225-9852. E-mail: pony@pulsenet.com. Web: www.pony.org.

WATERMELON DAY. Aug 18. Vining, MN. "The Biggest Small Town Celebration in Ottertail County." There is a large arts and crafts show (at least 90 vendors). Old-time musical jamboree, kids' games. Crowning of King and Queen. Evening features a large parade at 7 PM followed by a substance-free teen dance and drawings for prizes. Annually, the third Saturday in August. Est attendance: 4,500. For info: Watermelon Day Committee, PO Box 105, Vining, MN 56588-0105. Phone: (218) 769-4168.

BIRTHDAYS TODAY

Elayne Boosler, 49, comedienne, born Brooklyn, NY, Aug 18, 1952.

Rosalynn (Eleanor) Smith Carter, 74, former First Lady, wife of President Jimmy Carter, born Plains, GA, Aug 18, 1927.

Bobby Higginson, 31, baseball player, born Philadelphia, PA, Aug 18, 1970.

Mike Johanns, 51, Governor of Nebraska (R), born Osage, IA, Aug 18, 1950.

Luc Montagnier, 69, virologist, born Chabris, France, Aug 18, 1932.

Martin Mull, 58, actor, comedian ("Sabrina, the Teenage Witch," "Roseanne"), born Chicago, IL, Aug 18, 1943.

Roman Polanski, 68, filmmaker (*Rosemary's Baby, Macbeth, Chinatown*), born Paris, France, Aug 18, 1933.

Robert Redford, 64, actor (*Butch Cassidy and the Sundance Kid, The Sting, The Natural*), director (*A River Runs Through It*, Oscar for *Ordinary People*), born Santa Monica, CA, Aug 18, 1937.

Christian Slater, 32, actor (*Heathers, Broken Arrow, Pump Up the Volume*), born New York, NY, Aug 18, 1969.

Madeleine Stowe, 43, actress (*The Last of the Mohicans, Short Cuts*), born Los Angeles, CA, Aug 18, 1958.

Patrick Swayze, 47, dancer, actor ("North and South," *Dirty Dancing*), born Houston, TX, Aug 18, 1954.

Malcolm-Jamal Warner, 31, actor ("The Cosby Show"), born Jersey City, NJ, Aug 18, 1970.

Shelley Winters (Shelly Schrift), 79, actress (Oscars for *A Patch of Blue, The Diary of Anne Frank*), born St. Louis, MO, Aug 18, 1922.

AUGUST 19 — SUNDAY

Day 231 — 134 Remaining

AFGHANISTAN: INDEPENDENCE DAY. Aug 19. National day. Gained independence from British control, Treaty of Rawalpindi in 1919.

ANTIQUE FIRE APPARATUS MUSTER AND SHOW. Aug 19. Wheaton Village, Millville, NJ. Sponsored by the Glasstown Antique Fire Brigade. Held rain or shine. Est attendance: 2,000. For info: Wheaton Village, 1501 Glasstown Rd, Millville, NJ 08332. Phone: (856) 825-6800 or (800) 998-4552. Fax: (856) 825-2410. E-mail: mail@wheatonvillage.org. Web: www.wheatonvillage.org.

August 2001	S	M	T	W	T	F	S
				1	2	3	4
	5	6	7	8	9	10	11
	12	13	14	15	16	17	18
	19	20	21	22	23	24	25
	26	27	28	29	30	31	

"BLACK COW" CREATED: ANNIVERSARY. Aug 19, 1893. Frank J. Wisner, owner of Cripple Creek Brewing, served the first "Black Cow" root beer float in Cripple Creek, CO. Inspired by the moon-lit view of the snow-capped Cow Mountain which reminded him of vanilla ice cream floating on top of the pitch-black mountain, he added a scoop of ice cream to his Myers Avenue Red root beer and began serving it as the "Black Cow Mountain Ice Cream Root Beer Float." Kids loved it and shortened the name to "Black Cow." Cripple Creek Brewing, now located in Warrenville, IL, celebrating its 107th anniversary, sells beverages based on the original formulas, including Myers Avenue Red root beer. For info: Michael Lynn, Cripple Creek Brewing, Warrenville, IL 60555. Phone: (630) 393-2323. E-mail: lbartl6415@aol.com. Web: www.cripplecreekbrewing.com.

CLINTON, WILLIAM JEFFERSON (BILL): 55th BIRTHDAY. Aug 19, 1946. The 42nd US President (1993–2001), born at Hope, AR. Re-elected to a second term in 1996.

COUP ATTEMPT IN THE SOVIET UNION: 10th ANNIVERSARY. Aug 19. On Aug 19, 1991, a Soviet coalition of hard-line communists staged a coup d'état, removing Soviet President Mikhail Gorbachev from power. The hard-liners, who included Vice President Gennady Yanayev, the Soviet Defense Minister, the head of the KGB and the Soviet Interior Minister, claimed that Gorbachev was removed because of his ill health. Yanayev was installed as president and a six-month state of emergency was declared. Tanks rolled into the streets of Moscow but were met by thousands of citizens who urged the soldiers to lay down their arms. Russian President Boris Yeltsin asked the people to support him as leader of Russia and the troops to withdraw. Several companies of soldiers, including tanks in support of Yeltsin, arrayed themselves in defensive positions in front of the Russian Federation's parliament building in Moscow facing the troops loyal to the coup leaders. Gorbachev had been on vacation in the Crimea and was due to return to Moscow the next day to sign the historic union treaty that would have taken much of the power away from the Central USSR government and given it to the republics signing the treaty. On the third day, Aug 21, in the face of the massive public resistance, the conspirators gave up, flew to the Crimea hoping to negotiate with Gorbachev and were taken into custody. A shaken and chastened Gorbachev returned to Moscow in an extremely weakened position. Four persons died in the refusal to give up their fledgling democracy. The coup began a chain reaction of events involving the independence of the republics, the dissolution of the Soviet Union, the loss of power by Gorbachev and the formation of the Commonwealth of Independent States.

DOG DAY ROAD RACE. Aug 19. Harvey Cedars, NJ. 23rd annual. More than 800 runners will participate in this five-mile run. Sponsored by the High Point Volunteer Fire Department. For info: Dog Day Race, High Point Fire Co, 80th and Compass Ave, Harvey Cedars, NJ 08008. Phone: (609) 361-9364.

FORBES, MALCOLM: BIRTH ANNIVERSARY. Aug 19, 1919. Publisher, born at New York, NY. Malcolm Forbes was an unabashed proponent of capitalism, and his beliefs led to his colorful and successful climb to the top of the magazine-publishing industry. Known as much for his lavish lifestyle as his publishing acumen, Forbes was also an avid motorcyclist and hot-air balloonist. He died Feb 24, 1990, at Far Hills, NJ.

GERMAN PLEBISCITE: ANNIVERSARY. Aug 19, 1934. In a plebiscite, 89.9 percent of German voters approved giving Chancellor Adolf Hitler the additional office of president, placing the Führer in uncontestable supreme command of that country's destiny.

GORE, TIPPER (MARY ELIZABETH): BIRTHDAY. Aug 19, 1948. Second Lady, wife of Vice-President Al Gore, was born Mary Elizabeth Aitcheson at Washington, DC.

LUXEMBOURG: OUR LADY OF GIRSTERKLAUS PROCESSION. Aug 19. Rosport. Tradition since 1328. Annually, the Sunday after Aug 15.

LUXEMBOURG: SCHUEBERMESS SHEPHERD'S FAIR. Aug 19–Sept 1. Fair dates from 1340. (Two weeks beginning on the next to last Sunday of August.)

NASH, OGDEN: BIRTH ANNIVERSARY. Aug 19, 1902. American writer, best remembered for his humorous verse. Born at Rye, NY; died May 19, 1971, at Baltimore, MD. "Undeniably brash/Was young Ogden Nash/Whose notable verse/Was admirably terse/And written with panache."

★**NATIONAL AVIATION DAY.** Aug 19. Presidential Proclamation 2343, of July 25, 1939, covers all succeeding years. Always Aug 19 of each year since 1939. Observed annually on anniversary of birth of Orville Wright, who piloted "first self-powered flight in history," Dec 17, 1903. First proclaimed by President Franklin D. Roosevelt.

NATIONAL FRIENDSHIP WEEK. Aug 19–25. A celebration of the people, by the people and for the people. Sponsored by the Positive People Partners, this week-long observance asks people to focus on friendship with their self on Sunday, spouses on Monday, children on Tuesday, family on Wednesday, friends on Thursday, workers on Friday and neighbors on Saturday. For info: Bob Moyers, Positive People Partners, 605 Orchard View Dr, Maumee, OH 43537. Phone: (419) 897-9914. E-mail: bobmoy@wcnet.org.

NATIONAL HAWAIIAN SHAVE ICE WEEK. Aug 19–25. Honolulu, HI. Events to celebrate cold, refreshing, tasty Hawaiian Shave Ice. For info: Dan Endsley, 901 Gulick Ave, Honolulu, HI 96819. Phone: (800) 878-3538. E-mail: endmark@primenet.com.

NATIONAL RELIGIOUS SOFTWARE WEEK. Aug 19–25. To celebrate the increasing role computer software, such as The NIV Study Bible Complete Library® and Expositor's Bible Commentary for Macintosh®, is playing in biblical studies. Annually, the last full week of August. For info: Public Relations, Zondervan Publishing House, 5300 Patterson Ave SE, Grand Rapids, MI 49530. Phone: (616) 698-6900 or (800) 9-BOOK IT. Fax: (616) 698-3223. E-mail: public.relations@zph.com. Web: www.zondervansoftware.com.

RODDENBERRY, GENE: 80th BIRTH ANNIVERSARY. Aug 19, 1921. The creator of the popular TV series "Star Trek," Gene Roddenberry was born at El Paso, TX. Turning from his first career as an airline pilot to writing, he created one of the most successful TV science fiction series ever. The original series, which ended its run in 1969, lives on in reruns, and the "Star Trek: The Next Generation," "Star Trek: Deep Space Nine" and "Star Trek: Voyager" series have continuing popularity. Eight films also have been spawned from the original concept. Roddenberry died Oct 24, 1991, at Santa Monica, CA.

SPACE MILESTONE: *SOYUZ T-7* (USSR). Aug 19, 1982. Launched from Tyuratam, USSR, with second woman in space (test pilot Svetlana Savitskaya) and two other cosmonauts. Docked at *Salyut 7* and visited the cosmonauts who had been in residence there for the three previous months before returning to Earth on Aug 27 in the *Soyuz T-5* vehicle that had been docked there. The *Soyuz T-7* returned to Earth Dec 10 with the remaining two cosmonauts.

SPACE MILESTONE: *SPUTNIK 5* (USSR). Aug 19, 1960. Space menagerie satellite with dogs Belka and Strelka, mice, rats, houseflies and plants launched. These passengers became first living organisms recovered from orbit when the satellite returned safely to Earth the next day.

TOBACCO HARVEST. Aug 19. McLean, VA. Help cut and hang tobacco to dry. Enjoy 18th-century games and light refreshment afterward. Est attendance: 400. For info: Claude Moore Colonial Farm at Turkey Run, 6310 Georgetown Pike, McLean, VA 22101. Phone: (703) 442-7557. Fax: (703) 442-0714.

WEST MICHIGAN FAIR. Aug 19–25. West Michigan Fairgrounds, Ludington, MI. Traditional county fair, complete with carnival rides and games, livestock judging, 4-H exhibits, live entertainment and food. Annually, the third week in August. Est attendance: 20,000. For info: Ludington Area CVB, 5827 W US 10, Ludington, MI 49431. Phone: (800) 542-4600. Web: www.ludingtoncvb.com.

WRIGHT, ORVILLE: BIRTH ANNIVERSARY. Aug 19, 1871. Aviation pioneer born at Dayton, OH, and died there Jan 30, 1948. See also: "Wright Brothers First Powered Flight" (Dec 17).

BIRTHDAYS TODAY

Adam Arkin, 45, actor ("Chicago Hope," "Northern Exposure"), born Brooklyn, NY, Aug 19, 1956.
Kevin Dillon, 36, actor (*Platoon, The Doors*), born Mamaroneck, NY, Aug 19, 1965.
Peter Gallagher, 46, actor (*sex, lies and videotape, Short Cuts, The Hudsucker Proxy*), born New York, NY, Aug 19, 1955.
Ring Lardner, Jr, 86, screenwriter and member of blacklisted Hollywood Ten (Oscar for *Woman of the Year*; *M*A*S*H*), born Chicago, IL, Aug 19, 1915.
Gerald McRaney, 53, actor ("Simon & Simon," "Major Dad"), born Collins, MS, Aug 19, 1948.
Diana Muldaur, 63, actress ("Star Trek: The Next Generation," "LA Law," *The Swimmer*), born New York, NY, Aug 19, 1938.
(Franklin) Storey Musgrave, 66, astronaut, born Boston, MA, Aug 19, 1935.
Cindy Nelson, 46, former alpine skier, born Lutsen, MN, Aug 19, 1955.
Matthew Perry, 32, actor ("Friends," *Fools Rush In*), born Williamstown, MA, Aug 19, 1969.
Jill St. John (Jill Oppenheim), 61, actress (*Diamonds Are Forever*), born Los Angeles, CA, Aug 19, 1940.
Kyra Sedgwick, 36, actress (*Born on the Fourth of July*), born New York, NY, Aug 19, 1965.
William Lee (Willie) Shoemaker, 70, former jockey, born Fabens, TX, Aug 19, 1931.
John Stamos, 38, actor ("General Hospital," "Full House"), born Los Angeles, CA, Aug 19, 1963.
Fred Thompson, 59, US Senator (R, Tennessee), actor (*In the Line of Fire*), born Sheffield, AL, Aug 19, 1942.

AUGUST 20 — MONDAY

Day 232 — 133 Remaining

"ANDY'S GANG" TV PREMIERE: ANNIVERSARY. Aug 20, 1955. This children's program was originally known as "Smilin' Ed's Gang," which ran for five years until host Ed McConnell's death in 1955. Andy Devine took over the show which was retitled "Andy's Gang." The gangs of both shows included Midnight the Cat, Squeaky the Mouse, Froggy the Gremlin and Gunga Ram, the Indian boy.

GUEST, EDGAR ALBERT: BIRTH ANNIVERSARY. Aug 20, 1881. Newspaperman and author of folksy, homespun verse that enjoyed great popularity and was syndicated in more than 100 newspapers. Born at Birmingham, England; died at Detroit, MI, Aug 5, 1959. "Eddie Guest Day" usually proclaimed on birth anniversary in Detroit.

HARRISON, BENJAMIN: BIRTH ANNIVERSARY. Aug 20, 1833. The 23rd president of the US, born at North Bend, OH. He was the grandson of William Henry Harrison, 9th president of the US. His term of office, Mar 4, 1889–Mar 3, 1893, was preceded and followed by the presidential terms of Grover Cleveland (who thus became the 22nd and 24th president of the US). Harrison died at Indianapolis, IN, Mar 13, 1901.

HUNGARY: ST. STEPHEN'S DAY. Aug 20. National holiday. Commemorates the canonization of St. Stephen in 1083. Under the Communists commemorated as Constitution Day.

LOVECRAFT, H.P.: BIRTH ANNIVERSARY. Aug 20, 1890. Howard Phillips Lovecraft, American author of horror tales of the supernatural, a pioneering science fiction writer and a notable epistolarian, was born at Providence, RI and died there Mar 15, 1937.

MOROCCO: REVOLUTION OF THE KING AND THE PEOPLE. Aug 20. National holiday. Commemorates the response of the people to Sultan (later King) Sidi Muhammed being sent into exile in 1953 by the French.

O'HIGGINS, BERNARDO: BIRTH ANNIVERSARY. Aug 20, 1778. First ruler of Chile after its declaration of independence. Called the "Liberator of Chile." Born at Chillan, Chile. Died at Lima, Peru, Oct 24, 1842.

PERRY, OLIVER HAZARD: BIRTH ANNIVERSARY. Aug 20, 1785. American naval hero, born at South Kingston, RI. Died Aug 23, 1819, at sea. Best remembered is his announcement of victory at the Battle of Lake Erie, Sept 10, 1813: "We have met the enemy, and they are ours."

PLUTONIUM FIRST WEIGHED: ANNIVERSARY. Aug 20, 1942. University of Chicago scientist Glen Seaborg and his colleagues first weighed plutonium, the first man-made element.

PRESIDENT BENJAMIN HARRISON'S BIRTHDAY CELEBRATION. Aug 20 (tentative date). Indianapolis, IN, Harrison's hometown. Also free tours of the Victorian mansion. Est attendance: 500. For info: PR Dept, President Benjamin Harrison Home, 1230 N Delaware St, Indianapolis, IN 46202. Phone: (317) 631-1898. Fax: (317) 236-1688.

REEVES, JIM: BIRTH ANNIVERSARY. Aug 20, 1924. Country music star Jim Reeves was born at Galloway, Panola County, TX and died at Nashville, TN, July 31, 1964, when the single-engine plane in which he was traveling crashed in a dense fog. Reeves's biggest hit was "He'll Have to Go" (1959), and he was inducted into the Country Music Hall of Fame in 1967.

August 2001	S	M	T	W	T	F	S
				1	2	3	4
	5	6	7	8	9	10	11
	12	13	14	15	16	17	18
	19	20	21	22	23	24	25
	26	27	28	29	30	31	

SAARINEN, (GOTTLIEB) ELIEL: BIRTH ANNIVERSARY. Aug 20, 1873 (OS). Famed architect. Born at Helsinki, Finland. Died at Bloomfield Hills, MI, July 1, 1950.

SPACE MILESTONE: *VIKING 1* AND *2* (US). Aug 20 and Sept 9, 1975. Sister ships launched toward Mars from Cape Canaveral, FL, on Aug 20 and Sept 9, 1975. *Viking 1*'s lander touched down on Mars July 20, 1976, and *Viking 2*'s lander on Sept 3, 1976. Sent back to Earth high-quality photographs, analysis of atmosphere, weather information and results of sophisticated experiments intended to determine whether life may be present on Mars.

SPACE MILESTONE: *VOYAGER 2* (US). Aug 20, 1977. This unmanned spacecraft journeyed past Jupiter in 1979, Saturn in 1981, Uranus in 1986 and Neptune in 1989, sending photographs and data back to scientists on Earth.

24 HOURS OF ADRENALIN. Aug 20. Winter Park Resort, Winter Park, CO. Mountain bike enthusiasts "ride around the clock" during this ultimate rush of a race and festival at Winter Park Resort. Event involves teams of 2–10 people and solo riders competing for the most number of laps within the 24-hour time period, 12 PM Saturday–12 PM Sunday. Est attendance: 1,500. For info: Winter Park Resort, PO Box 36, Winter Park, CO 80482. Phone: (970) 726-1580. Fax: (970) 726-1572. E-mail: wpinfo@mail.skiwinterpark.com. Web: winterparkresort.com.

US AMATEUR (GOLF) CHAMPIONSHIP. Aug 20–26. East Lake Country Club, Atlanta, GA. For info: US Golf Assn, Golf House, PO Box 708, Championship Dept, Far Hills, NJ 07931. Phone: (908) 234-2300. Fax: (908) 234-9687. Web: www.usga .org.

XEROX 914 DONATED TO SMITHSONIAN: ANNIVERSARY. Aug 20, 1985. The original Xerox 914 copying machine (which had been introduced to the public 25 years earlier—in March 1960) was formally presented to the Smithsonian Institution's National Museum of American History at Washington, DC. Invented by Chester Carlson, a patent lawyer, the quick and easy copying of documents by machine revolutionized the world's offices.

BIRTHDAYS TODAY

Joan Allen, 45, actress (*Searching for Bobby Fischer, Nixon*), born Rochelle, IL, Aug 20, 1956.

Andy Benes, 34, baseball player, born Evansville, IN, Aug 20, 1967.

Connie Chung (Constance Yu-Hwa), 55, journalist, born Washington, DC, Aug 20, 1946.

Isaac Hayes, 59, musician, singer, songwriter, born Covington, TN, Aug 20, 1942.

Michael Jeter, 49, actor (Emmy for "Evening Shade"; *Miller's Crossing, The Fisher King*), born Lawrenceberg, TN, Aug 20, 1952.

Donald (Don) King, 70, boxing promoter, born Cleveland, OH, Aug 20, 1931.

Mark Edward Langston, 41, baseball player, born San Diego, CA, Aug 20, 1960.

Alfonso Raymond (Al) Lopez, 93, Baseball Hall of Fame manager and catcher, born Tampa, FL, Aug 20, 1908.

Robert Plant, 53, singer, born Bromwich, England, Aug 20, 1948.

Al Roker, 47, meteorologist ("Today Show"), born Brooklyn, NY, Aug 20, 1954.

Theresa Saldana, 46, actress ("The Commish"), born Brooklyn, NY, Aug 20, 1955.

AUGUST 21 — TUESDAY

Day 233 — 132 Remaining

AMERICAN BAR ASSOCIATION FOUNDING: ANNIVERSARY. Aug 21, 1878. Organized at Saratoga, NY.

AQUINO, BENIGNO: ASSASSINATION ANNIVERSARY. Aug 21, 1983. Filipino opposition leader Benigno S. Aquino, Jr, was shot and killed at the Manila airport on his return to the Philippines on Aug 21, 1983. The killing precipitated greater anti-Marcos feeling and figured significantly in the Feb 7, 1986, election that brought about the collapse of the government administration of Ferdinand E. Marcos and the inauguration of Corazon C. Aquino, widow of the slain man, as president.

BEARDSLEY, AUBREY VINCENT: BIRTH ANNIVERSARY. Aug 21, 1872. English artist and illustrator born at Brighton. Died at Menton, France, Mar 16, 1898.

HAWAII: ADMISSION DAY: ANNIVERSARY. Aug 21, 1959. President Dwight Eisenhower signed a proclamation admitting Hawaii to the Union. The statehood bill had passed the previous March with a stipulation that statehood should be approved by a vote of Hawaiian residents. The referendum passed by a huge margin in June and Eisenhower proclaimed Hawaii the 50th state on Aug 21.

MICHIGAN STATE FAIR. Aug 21–Sept 3. State Fairgrounds, Detroit, MI. Est attendance: 400,000. For info: State of Michigan, Dept of Agriculture, 1120 W State Fair Ave, Detroit, MI 48203. Phone: (313) 369-8250.

QUANTRILL'S RAID ON LAWRENCE, KANSAS: ANNIVERSARY. Aug 21, 1863. Confederate raider William Clarke Quantrill launched a predawn terrorist raid on Lawrence, KS, leaving 150 civilians dead and much of the town ruined. Quantrill had been denied a commission in the Southern army for his barbaric approach to war.

SEMINOLE TRIBE OF FLORIDA: ANNIVERSARY. Aug 21, 1957. In 1953 Congress adopted a proposal to terminate assistance to non-recognized Indian tribes. Seminole leaders and tribal members began to fight the proposal by drafting a constitution and charter for the Seminole Tribe. These were later approved by the Secretary of the Interior. On this date, a majority of tribal members voted to establish the Seminole Tribe of Florida. Today, 2,200 Seminoles live on five reservations in Florida.

SOUTH MOUNTAIN FAIR. Aug 21–25. Gettysburg, PA. Display of agricultural products, arts, crafts and industrial and agricultural exhibits. Est attendance: 12,500. For info: Gettysburg CVB, PO Box 4117, Gettysburg, PA 17325. Phone: (717) 334-6274. Fax: (717) 334-1166. Web: www.gettysburg.com.

SOUTHERN HEMISPHERE HOODIE-HOO DAY. Aug 21. Long awaited by our Southern-half friends, this is the day to go outdoors at high noon and yell "Hoodie-Hoo" to chase winter and make ready for spring. Sponsored by Wellcat Holidays (© 2000 WH). For info: Thomas or Ruth Roy, 2418 Long Ln, Lebanon, PA 17046. Phone: (717) 279-0184. E-mail: wellcat@supernet.com. Web: www.wellcat.com.

SPACE MILESTONE: *GEMINI 5 (US).* Aug 21, 1965. Launched on this date, this craft carrying astronauts Lieutenant Colonel Cooper and Lieutenant Commander Conrad orbited Earth 128 times for new international record of eight days.

BIRTHDAYS TODAY

Steve Case, 43, founder of America Online, born Oahu, HI, Aug 21, 1958.

Kim Cattrall, 45, actress (*Police Academy, Bonfire of the Vanities*), born Liverpool, England, Aug 21, 1956.

Jackie DeShannon, 57, singer, songwriter ("Put a Little Love in Your Heart"), born Hazel, KY, Aug 21, 1944.

Princess Margaret, 71, Countess of Snowdon, sister of Queen Elizabeth II, born Glamis, Scotland, Aug 21, 1930.

James Robert (Jim) McMahon, 42, former football player, born Jersey City, NJ, Aug 21, 1959.

Kenny Rogers, 63, singer ("Lucille," "Lady"), born Houston, TX, Aug 21, 1938.

Melvin Van Peebles, 69, playwright (*Ain't Supposed to Die a Natural Death*), born Chicago, IL, Aug 21, 1932.

Peter Weir, 57, director (*Dead Poets Society, Gallipoli, The Truman Show*), born Sydney, Australia, Aug 21, 1944.

Clarence Williams III, 62, actor ("The Mod Squad," *Purple Rain*), born New York, NY, Aug 21, 1939.

Alicia Witt, 26, actress ("Cybill") born Worcester, MA, Aug 21, 1975.

AUGUST 22 — WEDNESDAY

Day 234 — 131 Remaining

BE AN ANGEL DAY. Aug 22. A day to do "one small act of service for someone. Be a blessing in someone's life." Annually, Aug 22. For info: Angel Heights Healing Center, Rev Jayne M. Howard, PO Box 95, Upperco, MD 21155. Phone: (410) 833-6912. E-mail: blessing@erols.com. Web: drwnet.com/angel.

CAMEROON: VOLCANIC ERUPTION: 15th ANNIVERSARY. Aug 22, 1986. Deadly fumes from a presumed volcanic eruption under Lake Nios at Cameroon killed more than 1,500 persons. A similar occurrence two years earlier had killed 37 persons.

DEBUSSY, CLAUDE: BIRTH ANNIVERSARY. Aug 22, 1862. (Achille) Claude Debussy, French musician and composer, especially remembered for his impressionistic "tone poems," was born at St. Germain-en-Laye, France. He died at Paris, France, Mar 25, 1918.

HERRIMAN, GEORGE: BIRTH ANNIVERSARY. Aug 22, 1880. In 1910 when George Herriman introduced a cat and mouse as subplot characters to his comic strip "The Dingbat Family," their non-sequitur dialogue gained enough attention to result in a spin-off strip of their own. The superbly drafted "Krazy Kat and Ignatz" had as its central theme unrequited love. Kat loved Ignatz, but the malevolent mouse took every opportunity to throw bricks at the devoted cat. "Krazy Kat" was popular with a mass audience as well as artists and intellectuals, and it remained enormously popular after Herriman's death. Born at New Orleans, LA, he died at Hollywood, CA, Apr 25, 1944.

INTERNATIONAL YACHT RACE: 150th ANNIVERSARY. Aug 22, 1851. A silver trophy (then known as the "Hundred Guinea Cup," and offered by the Royal Yacht Squadron) was won in a race around the Isle of Wight by the US yacht *America*. The trophy, later turned over to the New York Yacht Club, became known as the America's Cup.

KGB FOUNDER STATUE DISMANTLED: 10th ANNIVERSARY. Aug 22, 1991. In the wake of the popular revolt that smashed the right-wing Soviet coup, a crowd of 10,000 Muscovites watched as cranes dismantled a 14-ton statue of Felix Dzerzhinsky, a Polish intellectual tapped by Vladimir Lenin to organize the fledgling Soviet Union's secret police. After trucks had hauled away the massive likeness of Dzerzhinsky, Moscow residents adorned the statue's pedestal and the nearby KGB headquarters with graffiti.

LANGLEY, SAMUEL PIERPONT: BIRTH ANNIVERSARY. Aug 22, 1834. American astronomer, physicist and aviation pioneer for whom Langley Air Force Base, VA, is named. Born at Roxbury, MA, Langley died at Aiken, SC, Feb 27, 1906.

MORMON CHOIR FIRST PERFORMANCE: ANNIVERSARY. Aug 22, 1847. What would later become the world-famous Mormon Tabernacle Choir gave its first public performance at Salt Lake City, UT, for an outdoor meeting of The Church of Jesus Christ of Latter-day Saints. Widely known for its concert tours, recordings and weekly radio and television broadcasts from Temple Square, the choir's radio program "Music and the Spoken Word" is the longest continuously running radio program in network history, dating back to 1929.

NATIONAL SAVE YOUR SMILE WEEK. Aug 22–29. A week dedicated to the prevention of adult tooth loss. Seeing the mouth as part of the whole body, correct selection of dental professionals and most important reversing gum disease naturally. For info: S. Senzon, RDH, 32 Bridies Path, Southampton, NY 11968. Phone: (516) 287-6671. Fax: (516) 287-9737. E-mail: S.Senzon961@aol.com. Web: www.tooth.qpg.com.

NATIONAL TOOTH FAIRY DAY. Aug 22. A playful educational program to help young adults develop good oral hygiene habits and prevent adult tooth loss. Annually, Aug 22. For info: Sandra Senzon, RDH, 32 Bridies Path, Southampton, NY 11968. Phone: (516) 287-6671. Web: www.tooth.qpg.com.

NEVADA STATE FAIR. Aug 22–26. Reno Livestock Events Center, Reno, NV. State entertainment and carnival, with creative living, agriculture and commercial exhibits. Est attendance: 73,000. For info: Gary Lubra, CEO, Nevada State Fair, 1350-A N Wells Ave, Reno, NV 89512. Phone: (775) 688-5767. Fax: (775) 688-5763. E-mail: nvstatefair@inetworld.com. Web: www.nevada statefair.org.

STONE, MELVILLE ELIJAH: BIRTH ANNIVERSARY. Aug 22, 1848. Influential American journalist Melville Stone was born at Hudson, IL, and died at New York, NY, Feb 15, 1929. His autobiography, *Fifty Years a Journalist*, was published in 1921.

VIETNAM CONFLICT BEGINS: ANNIVERSARY. Aug 22, 1945. Less than a week after the Japanese surrender ended WWII, a team of Free French parachuted into southern Indochina in response to a successful coup by a Communist guerrilla named Ho Chi Minh in the French colony.

WILLARD, ARCHIBALD M.: BIRTH ANNIVERSARY. Aug 22, 1836. American artist, best known for his painting *The Spirit of '76*, was born at Bedford, OH. Willard died at Cleveland, OH, Oct 11, 1918.

		S	M	T	W	T	F	S
August					1	2	3	4
2001		5	6	7	8	9	10	11
		12	13	14	15	16	17	18
		19	20	21	22	23	24	25
		26	27	28	29	30	31	

BIRTHDAYS TODAY

Tori Amos, 38, musician, singer, songwriter, born Newton, NC, Aug 22, 1963.

Ray Bradbury, 81, author (*The Toynbee Convector, Fahrenheit 451*), born Waukegan, IL, Aug 22, 1920.

Gerald Paul Carr, 69, former astronaut, born Denver, CO, Aug 22, 1932.

Henri Cartier-Bresson, 93, photographer, born Chanteloup, France, Aug 22, 1908.

Valerie Harper, 60, actress ("The Mary Tyler Moore Show," "Rhoda"), born Suffern, NY, Aug 22, 1941.

John Lee Hooker, 84, singer ("Boom, Boom"), born Clarksdale, MS, Aug 22, 1917.

Steve Kroft, 56, coeditor, correspondent ("60 Minutes"), born Kokomo, IN, Aug 22, 1945.

Paul Leo Molitor, 45, baseball player, born St. Paul, MN, Aug 22, 1956.

Duane Charles (Bill) Parcells, 60, football coach, born Englewood, NJ, Aug 22, 1941.

Norman H. Schwarzkopf, 67, retired army general, born Trenton, NJ, Aug 22, 1934.

Cindy Williams, 53, actress (*American Graffiti*, "Laverne & Shirley"), born Van Nuys, CA, Aug 22, 1948.

Carl Michael Yastrzemski, 62, Baseball Hall of Fame outfielder, born Southampton, NY, Aug 22, 1939.

AUGUST 23 — THURSDAY
Day 235 — 130 Remaining

ACTON FAIR. Aug 23–26. Acton, ME. A country fair featuring horse and ox pulls, antique tractor pull, firemen's muster, 4-H projects, flowers, arts and crafts, stage shows and handicraft. Vendors call Douglas Roberts at (207) 324-1250. Est attendance: 20,000. For info: Lista C. Staples, Secy, 178 Nason Rd, Shapleigh, ME 04076. Phone: (207) 636-2026.

BROOKLYN FAIR. Aug 23–26. Brooklyn County Fairgrounds, Rte 169, Brooklyn, CT. The nation's oldest continuously active agricultural fair offers a large variety of animals, contests, displays, crafts, working crafts, exhibits, entertainment and audience participation—from horse, pony, oxen and tractor pulls to cattle, sheep, pig and horsemanship shows and a whole lot more. Only fair in Connecticut having harness racing (Sulky-Horse). Est attendance: 60,000. For info: Roger Poitras, VP, Windham County Agricultural Fair, 80 Elmwood Ln, Danielson, CT 06239. Phone: (860) 774-3644. E-mail: rpoitras@snet.net.

EAST COAST SURFING CHAMPIONSHIPS AND SPORTS FESTIVAL. Aug 23–26. Virginia Beach, VA. 39th annual championship. Pro and amateur surfing and volleyball, 5K run, skimboarding, outrigger canoe racing, bands, food. Est attendance: 100,000. For info: Virginia Beach Jaycees, PO Box 62041, Virginia Beach, VA 23466. Phone: (800) 861-7873 or (757) 499-8822. Web: www.surfecsc.com.

FIRST MAN-POWERED FLIGHT: ANNIVERSARY. Aug 23, 1977. At Schafter, CA, Bryan Allen pedaled the '70-lb *Gossamer Condor* for a mile at a "minimal altitude of two pylons" in a flight certified by the Royal Aeronautical Society of Britain, winning a £50,000 prize offered by British industrialist Henry Kremer. See also: "First Man-Powered Flight Across English Channel: Anniversary" (June 12).

HOTTER 'N HELL HUNDRED BIKE RACE/FESTIVAL. Aug 23–26. Wichita Falls, TX. Cyclists of all ages participate in the largest sanctioned century ride in the US. Treks of 100, 50 or 25 miles. Est attendance: 10,000. For info: Wichita Falls CVB, 1000 5th St, Wichita Falls, TX 76301. Phone: (940) 716-5500. Fax: (940) 716-5509.

KELLY, GENE: BIRTH ANNIVERSARY. Aug 23, 1912. Actor, dancer born at Pittsburgh, PA. His movies included *Singin' in the Rain* and *An American in Paris*. Kelly died at Beverly Hills, CA, Feb 2, 1996.

MASTERS, EDGAR LEE: BIRTH ANNIVERSARY. Aug 23, 1869. American poet, author of the *Spoon River Anthology*, was born at Garnett, KS. He died at Melrose Park, PA, Mar 5, 1950.

MINNESOTA STATE FAIR. Aug 23–Sept 3. St. Paul, MN. Major entertainers, agricultural displays, arts, crafts, food, carnival rides, animal judging and performances. Est attendance: 1,700,000. For info: Minnesota State Fair, 1265 Snelling Ave N, St. Paul, MN 55108-3099. Phone: (651) 642-2200. E-mail: fair info@mnstatefair.org.

NEW YORK STATE FAIR. Aug 23–Sept 3. Empire Expo Center, Syracuse, NY. Agricultural and livestock competitions, top-name entertainment, the International Horse Show, business and industrial exhibits, the midway and ethnic presentations. Est attendance: 900,000. For info: Joseph LaGuardia, Dir of Mktg, NY State Fair, Empire Expo Ctr, Syracuse, NY 13209. Phone: (315) 487-7711. Fax: (315) 487-9260.

OHIO TOBACCO FESTIVAL (WITH TOBACCO WORM RACE). Aug 23–26. Ripley, OH. Bring your family to meet ours for continuous entertainment, craft show, flea market, commercial exhibits, more than 40 food booths. Unusual contests include tobacco worm race, bed races, garden tractor obstacle, cow chip throw, hand-tied tobacco stripping. Plus quilt show, clogging championships, arm wrestling, talent show, baby show, antique car show and parade. 20th annual festival. Est attendance: 75,000. For info: Ohio Tobacco Festival, PO Box 91, Ripley, OH 45167. Phone: (937) 392-4369 or (937) 377-6555.

OREGON STATE FAIR. Aug 23–Sept 3. Salem, OR. Exhibits, products and displays illustrate Oregon's role as one of the nation's major agricultural and recreational states. Floral gardens, carnival, big-name entertainment, horse show and food. Annually, 12 days ending on Labor Day. Est attendance: 700,000. For info: Oregon State Fair, 2330 17th St NE, Salem, OR 97303-3201. Phone: (503) 947-3247.

ROMANIA SURRENDER TO USSR: ANNIVERSARY. Aug 23, 1944. Romanian King Michael I removed pro-German Premier Jon Antonescue from his position, dismissed his entire government and broadcast to the people of Romania that all hostilities had ceased and that he had accepted all peace terms demanded by the Allies. Most important, the Ploesti oil fields would be secured by the Allies.

SACCO-VANZETTI MEMORIAL DAY: ANNIVERSARY. Aug 23, 1927. Nicola Sacco and Bartolomeo Vanzetti were electrocuted at the Charlestown, MA, prison on this date. Convicted of a shoe factory payroll robbery during which a guard had been killed, Sacco and Vanzetti maintained their innocence to the end. Six years of appeals marked this American cause célèbre during which substantial evidence was presented to show that both men were elsewhere at the time of the crime. However, on the 50th anniversary of their execution, Massachusetts governor Michael S. Dukakis proclaimed Aug 23, 1977, a memorial day, noting that the 1921 trial had been "permeated by prejudice."

SPACE MILESTONE: *INTELSAT-4 F-7* (US). Aug 23, 1973. International Communications Satellite Consortium's *Intelsat* launched Aug 23, 1973, to relay communications from North and South America to Europe and Africa.

TELLURIDE MUSHROOM FESTIVAL. Aug 23–26. Telluride, CO. To educate people about the types of wild mushrooms—edible, poisonous, psychoactive—and their cultivation. Est attendance: 250. For info: Fungophile, Inc, Box 480503, Denver, CO 80248-0503. Phone: (303) 296-9359. Fax: (303) 296-9359. E-mail: ladomyco@dnvr.uswest.net. Web: www.telluride mm.com.

TENNESSEE WALKING HORSE NATIONAL CELEBRATION. Aug 23–Sept 1. Celebration Grounds, Shelbyville, TN. More than 3,800 entries compete for more than $650,000 in prizes and awards—and the World Grand Championship titles. A 10-day festival for the whole family, plus trade show. Est attendance: 250,000. For info: Barbara Simmon, Public Relations Dir, Tennessee Walking Horse Natl Celebration, Calhoun and Evans, PO Box 1010, Shelbyville, TN 37162. Phone: (931) 684-5915. Fax: (931) 684-5949.

UNITED NATIONS: INTERNATIONAL DAY FOR THE REMEMBRANCE OF THE SLAVE TRADE AND ITS ABOLITION. Aug 23. For info: United Nations, Dept of Public Info, New York, NY. Web: www.un.org.

VIRGO, THE VIRGIN. Aug 23–Sept 22. In the astronomical/astrological zodiac, which divides the sun's apparent orbit into 12 segments, the period Aug 23–Sept 22 is identified, traditionally, as the sun sign of Virgo, the Virgin. The ruling planet is Mercury.

BIRTHDAYS TODAY

Tony Bill, 61, actor (*You're a Big Boy Now*), director (*My Bodyguard*), born San Diego, CA, Aug 23, 1940.

Kobe Bryant, 23, basketball player, born Philadelphia, PA, Aug 23, 1978.

Barbara Eden (Barbara Huffman), 67, actress ("I Dream of Jeannie," *The Wonderful World of the Brothers Grimm*), born Tucson, AZ, Aug 23, 1934.

Sonny Jurgensen, 67, Pro Football Hall of Fame quarterback, born Wilmington, NC, Aug 23, 1934.

Cortez Kennedy, 33, football player, born Osceola, AR, Aug 23, 1968.

Shelley Long, 52, actress ("Cheers," *Irreconcilable Differences*), born Fort Wayne, IN, Aug 23, 1949.

Patricia McBride, 59, dancer, born Teaneck, NJ, Aug 23, 1942.

Vera Miles, 71, actress (*The Wrong Man, Psycho*), born Boise City, OK, Aug 23, 1930.

Jay Mohr, 31, actor ("Saturday Night Live," *Action*), born Verona, NJ, Aug 23, 1970.

Antonia Novello, 57, first woman and first Hispanic US Surgeon General (1990–1993), born Fajardo, Puerto Rico, Aug 23, 1944.

Mark Russell (Mark Ruslander), 69, political comedian ("Real People"), born Buffalo, NY, Aug 23, 1932.

Richard Sanders, 61, actor ("WKRP in Cincinnati," "Berrengers"), born Harrisburg, PA, Aug 23, 1940.

Rik Smits, 35, basketball player, born Eindhoven, Netherlands, Aug 23, 1966.

Rick Springfield, 52, singer, actor, born Sydney, Australia, Aug 23, 1949.

AUGUST 24 — FRIDAY
Day 236 — 129 Remaining

ALASKA STATE FAIR. Aug 24–Sept 3. Palmer, AK. Cows and critters, music and dancing, rides, excitement and family fun at the state's largest summer extravaganza. See 100-lb cabbages, native art, more than 500 events including demonstrations, high-caliber entertainment, rodeos, horse shows, crafts and agricultural exhibits. Est attendance: 280,000. For info: Alaska State Fair, Inc, 2075 Glenn Hwy, Palmer, AK 99645. Phone: (907) 745-4827 or (800) 850-FAIR. Fax: (907) 746-2699. Web: www.alaskastatefair.org.

AMERICAN PSYCHOLOGICAL ASSOCIATION ANNUAL MEETING. Aug 24–28. San Francisco, CA. For info: Convention Office, American Psychological Assn, 750 First St NE, Washington, DC 20002-4242. Phone: (202) 336-6020. E-mail: convention.office@apa.org. Web: www.apa.org.

BALLUNAR LIFTOFF FESTIVAL. Aug 24–26. NASA/Johnson Space Center, Clear Lake Area, Houston, TX. Featuring more than 100 hot-air balloons, sky diving competitions, arts and crafts, midway game area, food, music and other entertainment. Sponsored by NASA/Johnson Space Center, Clear Lake Area Chamber of Commerce, ReMax and Space Center Houston. For info: Clear Lake Area Chamber of Commerce, 1201 NASA Rd One, Houston, TX 77058. Phone: (281) 488-7676. Fax: (281) 488-8981.

CANADA: COE HILL AGRICULTURAL FAIR. Aug 24–25. Coe Hill, ON. Competitions for best vegetables and animals, along with kids' games, Hell Driver's auto demonstration and music. Annually, the last weekend in August. Est attendance: 5,000. For info: Bancroft and District Chamber of Commerce, PO Box 539, Bancroft, ON, Canada K0L 1C0. Phone: (613) 332-1513. Fax: (613) 332-2119. E-mail: chamber@commerce.bancroft.on.ca. Web: www.commerce.bancroft.on.ca.

CANADA: MORDEN CORN AND APPLE FESTIVAL. Aug 24–26. Morden, MB. It's fun and it's free! Est attendance: 35,000. For info: Morden Chamber of Commerce, 102-195 Stephen St, Morden, MB, Canada R6M 1V3. Phone: (204) 822-5630. Fax: (204) 822-2041.

CAR SHOW. Aug 24–26. Site One, Oglebay, Wheeling, WV. Car enthusiasts can view a wide assortment of antique, sports and specialty cars and motorcycles at this event sponsored by the Good Zoo and the Ohio Valley Street Survivor's Car Club. Est attendance: 5,000. For info: John Hargleroad, Operations Dir, Good Zoo, Oglebay, Rt 88 N, Wheeling, WV 26003. Phone: (304) 243-4028. Fax: (304) 243-4045. Web: www.oglebay-resort.com.

CORVETTE SHOW. Aug 24–25. State Dock, Mackinaw City, MI. Parade of Corvettes on Friday at 7 PM. Show and visitor viewing, awards and Sunset Boat Cruise on Saturday. Est attendance: 4,000. For info: Corvette Show, 708 S Huron, Mackinaw City, MI 49701. Phone: (231) 436-5664.

August 2001	S	M	T	W	T	F	S
				1	2	3	4
	5	6	7	8	9	10	11
	12	13	14	15	16	17	18
	19	20	21	22	23	24	25
	26	27	28	29	30	31	

DUFF, HOWARD: BIRTH ANNIVERSARY. Aug 24, 1913. American actor Howard Duff was born at WA. He played detective Sam Spade on radio in the 1940s and then went on to films and television. He died July 9, 1990, at Santa Barbara, CA.

ENGLAND: ARUNDEL FESTIVAL. Aug 24–Sept 2. Arundel, West Sussex. Festival of the arts with some open air performances of Shakespeare and opera in the beautiful setting of Arundel Castle. Est attendance: 20,000. For info: Vicky Moles, Arundel Festival, The Mary Gate, Arundel, West Sussex, England BN18 9AT. Fax: (01) (903) 884243. E-mail: arundel.festival@argonet.co.uk. Web: www.argonet.co.uk/arundel.festival.

"THE FACTS OF LIFE" TV PREMIERE: ANNIVERSARY. Aug 24, 1979. This NBC sitcom was spun off from "Diff'rent Strokes" with Drummond family housekeeper Edna Garrett (Charlotte Rae) moving to Peekskill, NY, to take over as housemother at Eastland, a boarding school for girls. During the first season, the cast included John Lawlor as Headmaster Steven Bradley, Jenny O'Hara as Miss Mahoney, Lisa Whelchel as Blair Warner, Mindy Cohn as Natalie Green, Kim Fields as Dorothy "Tootie" Ramsey, Felice Schachter as Nancy Olson, Julie Piekarski as Sue Ann Weaver, Julie Anne Haddock as Cindy Webster and Molly Ringwald as Molly Parker.

HUSTLERFEST. Aug 24–26. Juneau County, WI. Demonstrations, arts and crafts, tractor pulls, bands, fair, parade, ceramics, soap making, fretwork, intarsia, great food, carnival and more. Held in conjunction with the Wisconsin Scroll Saw Picnic. Annually, the last full weekend in August. Est attendance: 3,000. For info: Hustlerfest, PO Box 155, Hustler, WI 54637-0155.

ITALY: VESUVIUS DAY. Aug 24, AD 79. Anniversary of the eruption of Vesuvius, an active volcano in southern Italy, which destroyed the cities of Pompeii, Stabiae and Herculaneum.

JARVIS, GREGORY B.: BIRTH ANNIVERSARY. Aug 24, 1944. Gregory B. Jarvis, a civilian engineer with Hughes Aircraft Co, was born at Detroit, MI. He was the 41-year-old payload specialist who perished with other crew members and Christa McAuliffe in the Space Shuttle *Challenger* explosion on Jan 28, 1986. See also: "*Challenger* Space Shuttle Explosion: Anniversary" (Jan 28).

MARYLAND STATE FAIR. Aug 24–Sept 3. Timonium, MD. Home arts, agricultural and livestock presentations, midway rides, live entertainment and thoroughbred horse racing. Est attendance: 500,000. For info: Max Mosner, State Fairgrounds, PO Box 188, Timonium, MD 21094. Phone: (410) 252-0200.

MEXICAN FIESTA. Aug 24–26. Milwaukee, WI. Mexican Fiesta brings the sound and taste of Mexico to Milwaukee's lakefront. Three days of fun, food, Mariachi and fiesta for everyone. Plus the traditional jalapeño-eating contest, national and international entertainment and the best Mexican cuisine. Est attendance: 20,000. For info: Mexican Fiesta, 1030 W Mitchell St, Milwaukee, WI 53204. Phone: (414) 383-7066. Fax: (414) 383-6677. E-mail: mexicanf@aol.com. Web: www.mexican-fiesta.com.

NEBRASKA STATE FAIR. Aug 24–Sept 3. Lincoln, NE. Food booths, variety of entertainment, rodeos, amusement rides, concerts, car racing, livestock shows and tractor pulls. Est attendance: 367,000. For info: Nebraska State Fair, PO Box 81223, Lincoln, NE 68501. Phone: (402) 474-5371. Fax: (402) 473-4114. E-mail: nestatefair@statefair.org.

NORTHERN PLAINS HERITAGE FESTIVAL. Aug 24–25. Dickinson, ND. Celebrate the Russian, German and Scandinavian heritage of our local homesteaders at this annual event. Ethnic foods, dress, music, demonstrations and displays round it out. Est attendance: 3,000. For info: Northern Plains Heritage Festival, 72 Museum Dr, Dickinson, ND 58602. Phone: (800) 279-7391 or (701) 483-4988. Fax: (701) 483-9261. Web: www.dickinsoncvb.com.

PRAIRIE VILLAGE JAMBOREE. Aug 24–26. Prairie Village, Madison, SD. Come and join the fun with arts and crafts displays, a parade, entertainment, tractor pulls, steam threshing, horse power and much more. Est attendance: 35,000. For info:

Prairie Village Jamboree, PO Box 256, Madison, SD 57042. Phone: (605) 256-3644.

ROCKY MOUNTAIN BALLOON FESTIVAL. Aug 24–26. Chatfield State Park, Denver, CO. Hot-air balloon festival and celebrate outdoors expo. Fun, free, family event with dawn balloon ascensions and Saturday sunset "Lites in the Nite" mass balloon illumination. Annually, the last weekend in August. Est attendance: 30,000. For info: Debby Pfauntsch. Phone: (303) 660-8025. Fax: (303) 814-1266. E-mail: rockymtnballoonfestival@uswest.net. Web: www.balloonevent.net.

SAINT BARTHELEMY: PATRON SAINT DAY. Aug 24. The festival of St. Barthelemy is celebrated for several days, beginning on Aug 24. The "look and feeling of a French country fair."

SAINT BARTHOLOMEW'S DAY MASSACRE: ANNIVERSARY. Aug 24, 1572. Anniversary of the massacre in Paris and throughout France of thousands of Protestant Huguenots. The massacre began when the church bells tolled at dawn on St. Bartholomew's Day, Aug 24, 1572, and continued for several days. Pope Gregory XIII ordered a medal struck to commemorate the event, but Protestant countries abhorred the killings, estimated at 2,000 to 70,000.

SOUTHERN CYCLONE: ANNIVERSARY. Aug 24, 1893. A hurricane hit Savannah, GA, and Charleston, SC, killing between 1,000 and 2,000 people.

SPACE MILESTONE: *VOYAGER 2* (US). Aug 24, 1989. Launched in 1977, *Voyager 2* had its first close encounter with Neptune.

SPIRIT OF WOVOKA DAYS POWWOW. Aug 24–26. Yerington, NV. Powwow held in honor of Wovoka, sponsored by the Mason Valley Wind Spirit dancers. For local info: Chamber of Commerce, 227 S Main St, Yerington, NV 89447. Phone: (775) 463-2350. Fax: (775) 463-3369. Web: www.tele-net.net/lyon.

UKRAINE: INDEPENDENCE DAY: 10th ANNIVERSARY. Aug 24. National day. Commemorates independence from the former Soviet Union in 1991.

WARNER WEATHER QUOTATION: ANNIVERSARY. Aug 24, 1897. Charles Dudley Warner, American newspaper editor for the *Hartford Courant*, published this now-famous and oft-quoted sentence, "Everybody talks about the weather, but nobody does anything about it." The quotation is often mistakenly attributed to his friend and colleague Mark Twain. Warner and Twain were part of the most notable American literary circle during the late 19th century. Warner was a journalist, essayist, novelist, biographer and author who collaborated with Mark Twain in writing *The Gilded Age* in 1873.

WASHINGTON, DC: INVASION ANNIVERSARY. Aug 24–25, 1814. British forces briefly invaded and raided Washington, DC, burning the Capitol, the president's house and most other public buildings. President James Madison and other high US government officials fled to safety until British troops (not knowing the strength of their position) departed the city two days later.

Max Cleland, 59, US Senator (D, Georgia), born Atlanta, GA, Aug 24, 1942.

Gerry Cooney, 45, former boxer, born New York, NY, Aug 24, 1956.

Stephen Fry, 44, actor ("Jeeves and Wooster"), born Hampstead, London, England, Aug 24, 1957.

Steve Guttenberg, 43, actor ("Billy," *Three Men and a Baby*), born Brooklyn, NY, Aug 24, 1958.

Mike Huckabee, 46, Governor of Arkansas (R), born Hope, AR, Aug 24, 1955.

Craig Kilborn, 39, TV host ("The Late Late Show"), born Hastings, MN, Aug 24, 1962.

Marlee Matlin, 36, actress (Oscar for *Children of a Lesser God*), born Morton Grove, IL, Aug 24, 1965.

Reginald Wayne (Reggie) Miller, 36, basketball player, born Riverside, CA, Aug 24, 1965.

Kenny Quinn, 65, Governor of Nevada (R), born Garland, AR, Aug 24, 1936.

Michael Richards, 51, actor ("Seinfeld," *Trial and Error*), born Culver City, CA, Aug 24, 1950.

Calvin Edward (Cal) Ripken, Jr, 41, baseball player, born Havre de Grace, MD, Aug 24, 1960.

Louis Teicher, 77, pianist (Ferrante and Teicher), composer, born Wilkes-Barre, PA, Aug 24, 1924.

Mason Williams, 63, composer, born Abilene, TX, Aug 24, 1938.

AUGUST 25 — SATURDAY
Day 237 — 128 Remaining

BE KIND TO HUMANKIND WEEK. Aug 25–31. All of the negative news that you read about in the paper each day and hear on your local news station is disheartening—but the truth is the "positive" stories outweigh the negative stories by a long shot! We just don't hear about them as often. Take heart . . .most people are caring individuals! Show you care by being kind. Daily affirmations: Motorist Consideration Monday. Touch-a-Heart Tuesday. Willing to Lend a Hand Wednesday. Thoughtful Thursday. Forgive Your Foe Friday. Speak Kind Words Saturday. Sacrifice Our Wants for Others Needs Sunday. For info: Lorraine Jara, PO Box 586, Island Heights, NJ 08732-0586. Web: www.bkhk.org.

BERNSTEIN, LEONARD: BIRTH ANNIVERSARY. Aug 25, 1918. American conductor and composer Leonard Bernstein was born at Lawrence, MA. One of the greatest conductors in American music history, he first conducted the New York Philharmonic Orchestra at age 25 and was its director from 1959 to 1969. His musicals include *West Side Story* and *On the Town*, and his operas and operettas include *Candide*. He died five days after his retirement Oct 14, 1990, at New York, NY.

CALVERT COUNTY JOUSTING TOURNAMENT. Aug 25. Christ Church grounds, Port Republic, MD. The 135th annual tournament of Maryland's official state sport, steeped in colorful pageantry. Country supper, bazaar, organ recitals, children's activities, one-room schoolhouse, colonial church. Admission fee. Annually, the last Saturday in August. Est attendance: 1,500. For info: Christ Church, 3100 Broomes Island Rd, Port Republic, MD 20676. Phone: (410) 586-0565.

CHAMPLAIN VALLEY FAIR. Aug 25–Sept 3. Essex Junction, VT. Vermont's largest fair. Agricultural exhibits and competitions, variety of entertainment, arts and crafts, midway rides, commercial exhibits, great food and much more. Est attendance: 300,000. For info: George Rousseau, Dir of Sales and Mktg, PO Box 209, Essex Junction, VT 05453. Phone: (802) 878-5545. Fax: (802) 879-5404. E-mail: cvfair@aol.com. Web: www.cvfair.com.

CHILDREN'S DAY. Aug 25. Woodstock, VT. Traditional farm activities from corn shelling to sawing firewood—19th-century games, traditional spelling bee, ice cream and butter making, wagon rides. Children ages 12 and under and accompanied by an adult are admitted free. For info: Billings Farm Museum, PO Box 489, Woodstock, VT 05091. Phone: (802) 457-2355. Fax: (802) 457-4663. E-mail: billings.farm@valley.net.

CHRISTMAS BAZAAR. Aug 25–26. Island Park, Fargo, ND. A two-day arts and crafts festival featuring more than 300 booths. All items handmade. Concessions available. Strolling and staged entertainment is also scheduled. Est attendance: 55,000. For info: Pat Jorgensen, Program Coord, 701 Main Ave, Fargo, ND 58103. Phone: (701) 241-8160. Fax: (701) 241-8266.

COUNTRY FEST AND AUCTION. Aug 25. Garrett County Fairgrounds, Deep Creek Lake, MD. Family-oriented activities, demonstrations, crafts, baked goods, gospel music, horse and buggy rides and an auction featuring wood furniture, collectibles and locally made hand-quilted quilts. Event Sponsored by the Dry Run Mennonite Church. Annually, the fourth Saturday in August. Est attendance: 2,400. For info: Country Fest & Auction, 1705 Foy Rd, Accident, MD 21520. Phone: (301) 895-3268 or (301) 746-8429. E-mail: countryfest@juno.com.

DANKFEST. Aug 25–26. Harmony Museum, Harmony, PA. Pioneer crafts, historic-district tours, food and entertainment. Est attendance: 3,000. For info: Kathy Luek, Administrator, Historic Harmony, 218 Mercer St, PO Box 524, Harmony, PA 16037. Phone: (724) 452-7341. Web: members.tripod.com/harmony museum.

DeFORE, DON: BIRTH ANNIVERSARY. Aug 25, 1913. American actor Don DeFore was born at Cedar Rapids, IA. He is best known for his roles on "The Adventures of Ozzie and Harriet" (1952–58) and "Hazel" (1961–65). He was president of the National Academy of Television Arts and Sciences in 1954. He died at Santa Monica, CA, Dec 22, 1993.

DENMARK: HO SHEEP MARKET. Aug 25. The village of Ho, near Esbjerg, holds its annual sheep market on the last Saturday in August, when some 50,000 people visit the fair.

GIANTS RIDGE MOUNTAIN BIKE FESTIVAL. Aug 25. Biwabik, MN. Trail rides, uphill-downhill, cross-country races. Est attendance: 400. For info: John Filander, Dir of Ski Programs, PO Box 190, Biwabik, MN 55708. Phone: (800) 688-7669. Fax: (218) 865-4733. E-mail: www.giantsridge.com.

HARTE, BRET: BIRTH ANNIVERSARY. Aug 25, 1836. Francis Bret(t) Harte, journalist, poet, printer, teacher and novelist, especially remembered for his early stories of California ("The Luck of Roaring Camp," "The Outcasts of Poker Flat" and "How Santa Claus Came to Simpson's Bar"), was born at Albany, NY. He died at London, England, May 5, 1902.

KELLY, WALT: BIRTH ANNIVERSARY. Aug 25, 1913. American cartoonist and creator of the comic strip "Pogo" was born at Philadelphia, PA. It was Kelly's character Pogo who paraphrased Oliver Hazard Perry to say, "We has met the enemy, and it is us." Kelly died at Hollywood, CA, Oct 18, 1973. See also: "Perry, Oliver Hazard: Birth Anniversary" (Aug 20).

KISS-AND-MAKE-UP-DAY. Aug 25. A day to make amends and for relationships that need mending! For info: Jacqueline V. Milgate, Media Dept, Jay Inc, 150 Linden Oaks Dr, Rochester, NY 14625.

MACKINAW CITY ART FAIR. Aug 25–26. Mackinaw City, MI. Juried art show that features some of Northern Michigan's premiere artists. Est attendance: 3,000. For info: Mackinaw Area Tourist Bureau, PO Box 160, Mackinaw City, MI 49701. Phone: (800) 666-0160. Web: www.mackinawcity.com.

August **2001**	S	M	T	W	T	F	S
				1	2	3	4
	5	6	7	8	9	10	11
	12	13	14	15	16	17	18
	19	20	21	22	23	24	25
	26	27	28	29	30	31	

MARYLAND RENAISSANCE FESTIVAL. Aug 25–Oct 21 (Saturdays, Sundays and Labor Day). Annapolis, MD. A 16th-century English festival with Henry VIII, sword swallowers, magicians, authentic jousting, juggling, music, theater, games, food and crafts. Est attendance: 230,000. For info: Jules Smith, Maryland Renaissance Festival, PO Box 315, Crownsville, MD 21032. Phone: (410) 266-7304 or (410) 573-1509. Fax: (410) 573-1508. E-mail: rennfest@erols.com. Web: www.rennfest.com.

MOON PHASE: FIRST QUARTER. Aug 25. Moon enters First Quarter phase at 3:55 PM, EDT.

NATIONAL PARK SERVICE ANNIVERSARY OBSERVANCE. Aug 25. Colonial National Historical Park, Jamestown and Yorktown, VA. Est attendance: 1,700. For info: Public Affairs Officer, Colonial Natl Historical Park, PO Box 210, Yorktown, VA 23690. Phone: (757) 898-2409. Web: www.nps.gov/colo.

PARIS LIBERATED: ANNIVERSARY. Aug 25, 1944. As dawn broke, the men of the 2nd French Armored Division entered Paris, ending the long German occupation of the City of Light. That afternoon General Charles de Gaulle led a parade down the Champs Elysées. Though Hitler had ordered the destruction of Paris, German occupying-officer General Dietrich von Choltitz refused that order and instead surrendered to French Major General Jacques Le Clerc.

PINKERTON, ALLAN: BIRTH ANNIVERSARY. Aug 25, 1819. Scottish-born American detective, founder of detective agency at Chicago, IL, in 1850, first chief of US Army's secret service, remembered now because of his strike-breaking and his lack of sympathy for working people. Pinkerton was born at Glasgow, Scotland, and died at Chicago, IL, July 1, 1884.

ROCKBRIDGE COMMUNITY FESTIVAL. Aug 25. Lexington, VA. Fun for all ages—crafts, exhibits, live music, food and games. For info: Lexington Visitors Bureau, 106 E Washington St, Lexington, VA 24450. Phone: (540) 463-3777. Fax: (540) 463-1105. E-mail: lexington@rockbridge.net.

SMITH, SAMANTHA: DEATH ANNIVERSARY. Aug 25, 1985. American schoolgirl whose interest in world peace drew praise and affection from people around the world. In 1982 the 10-year-old wrote a letter to Soviet leader Yuri Andropov asking him, "Why do you want to conquer the whole world, or at least our country?" The letter was widely publicized in the USSR and Andropov replied personally to her. Samantha Smith was invited to visit the Soviet Union. On Aug 25, 1985, the airplane on which she was riding crashed in Maine, killing all aboard. In 1986 minor planet No 3147, an asteroid between Mars and Jupiter, was named Samantha Smith in her memory.

URUGUAY: INDEPENDENCE DAY: ANNIVERSARY. Aug 25. National holiday. Declared independence from Brazil in 1825.

BIRTHDAYS TODAY

Anne Archer, 54, actress ("Falcon Crest"; stage: *A Couple of White Chicks Sitting Around Talking*), born Los Angeles, CA, Aug 25, 1947.

Albert Jojuan Belle, 35, baseball player, born Shreveport, LA, Aug 25, 1966.

Cornelius O'Landa Bennett, 35, football player, born Birmingham, AL, Aug 25, 1966.

Tim Burton, 43, director (*Edward Scissorhands*, *The Nightmare Before Christmas*), born Burbank, CA, Aug 25, 1958.

Sean Connery, 71, actor (James Bond movies; *The Man Who Would Be King*), born Edinburgh, Scotland, Aug 25, 1930.

Elvis Costello, 47, musician, songwriter ("Oliver's Army"), born London, England, Aug 25, 1954.

Billy Ray Cyrus, 40, country singer ("Achy Breaky Heart"), born Flatwoods, KY, Aug 25, 1961.

Mel Ferrer, 84, actor (*Scaramouche*, *The Sun Also Rises*), born Elberon, NJ, Aug 25, 1917.

Frederick Forsyth, 63, author (*The Day of the Jackal*), born Ashford, Kent, Aug 25, 1938.

Althea Gibson, 74, former tennis player, born Silver, SC, Aug 25, 1927.

Monty Hall, 78, former TV host ("Let's Make a Deal"), born Winnipeg, Manitoba, Canada, Aug 25, 1923.

Anthony Heald, 57, actor (*The Silence of the Lambs*, *Searching for Bobby Fischer*), born New Rochelle, NY, Aug 25, 1944.

Regis Philbin, 68, talk-show host ("Live with Regis and Kathie Lee," "Who Wants to Be a Millionaire?"), born New York, NY, Aug 25, 1933.

John Savage, 52, actor (*The Deer Hunter, Hair*), born Long Island, NY, Aug 25, 1949.

Claudia Schiffer, 31, model, born Rheinberg, Germany, Aug 25, 1970.

Wayne Shorter, 68, jazz musician ("High Life"), born Newark, NJ, Aug 25, 1933.

Tom Skerritt, 68, actor ("Picket Fences," *Steel Magnolias*), born Detroit, MI, Aug 25, 1933.

Blair Underwood, 37, actor ("One Life to Live," "LA Law"), born Tacoma, WA, Aug 25, 1964.

Ally Walker, 40, actress ("The Profiler"), born Tullahoma, TN, Aug 25, 1961.

Joanne Whalley, 37, actress ("The Singing Detective"; stage: *What the Butler Saw*) born Manchester, England, Aug 25, 1964.

AUGUST 26 — SUNDAY

Day 238 — 127 Remaining

BARNEGAT BAY CRAB RACE AND FESTIVAL. Aug 26. Seaside Heights, NJ. Crab race, festival and craft fair. Est attendance: 5,000. For info: Lucy Greene, Pres, Barbara Morgan, Admin Asst, Toms River–Ocean Co Chmbr of Com, 1200 Hooper Ave, Toms River, NJ 08753. Phone: (732) 349-0220. Fax: (732) 349-1252. Web: www.oc-chamber.com.

BELGIUM: WEDDING OF THE GIANTS. Aug 26. Traditional cultural observance. Annually, the fourth Sunday in August.

De FOREST, LEE: BIRTH ANNIVERSARY. Aug 26, 1873. American inventor of the electron tube, radio knife for surgery and the photoelectric cell and a pioneer in the creation of talking pictures and television. Born at Council Bluffs, IA, De Forest was holder of hundreds of patents but perhaps best remembered by the moniker he gave himself in the title of his autobiography, *Father of Radio*, published in 1950. So unbelievable was the idea of wireless radio broadcasting that De Forest was accused of fraud and arrested for selling stock to underwrite the invention that later was to become an essential part of daily life. De Forest died at Hollywood, CA, June 30, 1961.

DELICATO CHARITY GRAPE STOMP. Aug 26. Delicato Vineyards, Manteca, CA. Wine, food and entertainment. Est attendance: 5,000. For info: Dorothy Indelicato, Delicato Vineyards, 12001 S Hwy 99, Manteca, CA 95336-9209. Phone: (209) 824-3505. Fax: (209) 824-3510. E-mail: wine@delicato.com. Web: www.delicato.com.

FAMILY DAY IN TENNESSEE. Aug 26. Observed annually on the last Sunday in August.

FIRST BASEBALL GAMES TELEVISED: ANNIVERSARY. Aug 26, 1939. WXBS television, at New York City, broadcast the first major league baseball games—a doubleheader between the Cincinnati Reds and the Brooklyn Dodgers at Ebbets Field. Announcer Red Barber interviewed Leo Durocher, manager of the Dodgers, and William McKechnie, manager of the Reds, between games.

ISHERWOOD, CHRISTOPHER: BIRTH ANNIVERSARY. Aug 26, 1904. Author of short stories, plays and novels, Christopher William Isherwood was born at High Lane, Cheshire, England. The play and motion picture *I Am a Camera* and the musical *Cabaret* were based on the short story "Sally Bowles" in his collection from the 1930s titled *Goodbye to Berlin*, which contained the line "I am a camera with its shutter open, quite passive, recording, not thinking." Isherwood died at Santa Monica, CA, Jan 4, 1986.

KRAKATOA ERUPTION: ANNIVERSARY. Aug 26, 1883. Anniversary of the biggest explosion in historic times. The eruption of the Indonesian volcanic island, Krakatoa (Krakatau) was heard 3,000 miles away, created tidal waves 120 ft high (killing 36,000 persons), hurled five cubic miles of earth fragments into the air (some to a height of 50 miles) and affected the oceans and the atmosphere for years.

LIBERACE SCHOLARS FESTIVAL OF THE ARTS. Aug 26. Clark County Library Theater, Las Vegas, NV. 3rd annual. The event, free to the public, will feature performances by Liberace Scholars from the Las Vegas Music Festival, Nevada Ballet Theater, the UNLV Liberace String Quartet and the Nevada School for the Arts Suzuki violinists. Since 1976, the non-profit Liberace Foundation for the Performing and Creative Arts has granted almost $4 million in scholarship grants to students at 100 institutions nationwide. The Liberace Museum is a key funding arm of the Foundation. Annually, the last Sunday in August. For info: Jamie G. James, James Agency, PR, 3630 Coldwater Canyon Ave, Studio City, CA 91604. Phone: (818) 508-4902. Fax: (818) 508-0562. E-mail: Jjames@liberace.org.

MAKE YOUR OWN LUCK DAY. Aug 26. A day to take affirmative actions in your life to direct events and take control of your destiny for a happier, more productive and successful life by making your own luck and creating opportunities. Remember, the welcome mat is always out at the door to opportunity. For info: J. Richard Falls, PO Box 165090, Irving, TX 75016-5090.

MONTGOLFIER, JOSEPH MICHEL: BIRTH ANNIVERSARY. Aug 26, 1740. French merchant and inventor, born at Vidalonlez-Annonay, France, who, with his brother Jacques Etienne in November 1782, conducted experiments with paper and fabric bags filled with smoke and hot air, which led to invention of the hot-air balloon and man's first flight. Died at Balaruc-les-Bains, France, June 26, 1810. See also: "Montgolfier, Jacques Etienne: Birth Anniversary" (Jan 7), "First Balloon Flight: Anniversary" (June 5) and "Aviation History Month" (Nov 1).

PONY EXPRESS FESTIVAL. Aug 26. Hollenberg Pony Express Station, State Historic Site, Hanover, KS. Reenactment of Pony Express ride with mochila exchange, pioneer living-history demonstrations, 1860s historic dress group, circuit-rider church service and a noon meal on the grounds. Annually, the last Sunday in August. Sponsor: Kansas State Historical Society, Friends of Hollenberg Station. Est attendance: 5,000. For info: Duane Durst, Curator, Hollenberg Pony Express Station, State Historic Site, RR1, 2889, 23rd Rd, Hanover, KS 66945. Phone: (785) 337-2635.

SABIN, ALBERT BRUCE: 95th BIRTH ANNIVERSARY. Aug 26, 1906. American medical researcher Albert Bruce Sabin was born at Bialystok, Poland. He is most noted for his oral vaccine for polio, which replaced Jonas Salk's injected vaccine because Sabin's provided lifetime protection. He was awarded the US National Medal of Science in 1971. Sabin died Mar 3, 1993, at Washington, DC.

SPACE MILESTONE: *SOYUZ 31* (USSR). Aug 26, 1978. Launched on Aug 26, Valery Bykovsky and Sigmund Jaehn docked at *Salyut 6* on Aug 27, stayed for a week, then returned to Earth in *Soyuz 29* vehicle, leaving their *Soyuz 31* docked at space station. Earth landing on Sept 3.

★**WOMEN'S EQUALITY DAY.** Aug 26. Presidential Proclamation issued in 1973 and 1974 at request and since 1975 without request.

WOMEN'S EQUALITY DAY. Aug 26. Anniversary of certification as part of US Constitution, in 1920, of the 19th Amendment, prohibiting discrimination on the basis of sex with regard to voting. Congresswoman Bella Abzug's bill to designate Aug 26 of each year as "Women's Equality Day" in August 1974 became Public Law 93–382.

BIRTHDAYS TODAY

Benjamin Crowninshield Bradlee, 80, journalist, editor, born Boston, MA, Aug 26, 1921.
Christopher Burke, 36, actor ("Life Goes On"), host of Zoom Express/BMG Kidz, born New York, NY, Aug 26, 1965.
Macaulay Culkin, 21, actor (*Home Alone, My Girl*), born New York, NY, Aug 26, 1980.
Geraldine Ferraro, 66, first woman vice-presidential candidate, born Newburgh, NY, Aug 26, 1935.
Irving R. Levine, 79, broadcast journalist, born Pawtucket, RI, Aug 26, 1922.
Branford Marsalis, 41, musician, born New Orleans, LA, Aug 26, 1960.
Thomas J. Ridge, 56, Governor of Pennsylvania (R), born Munhall, PA, Aug 26, 1945.
Robert G. Torricelli, 50, US Senator (D, New Jersey), born Paterson, NJ, Aug 26, 1951.

AUGUST 27 — MONDAY
Day 239 — 126 Remaining

BURNING MAN 2001. Aug 27–Sept 3. Black Rock Desert, NV. A temporary art community in the desert. On the Saturday of this 17th annual experiment in radical self-expression, a 50′ statue will be burned. Participants must bring all necessities for survival, including food, water and shelter. Est attendance: 15,000. For info: Burning Man 2000, PO Box 420572, San Francisco, CA 94142-0572. Phone: (415) TOF-LAME. E-mail: questions@ burningman.com. Web: www.burningman.com.

		S	M	T	W	T	F	S
August					1	2	3	4
2001		5	6	7	8	9	10	11
		12	13	14	15	16	17	18
		19	20	21	22	23	24	25
		26	27	28	29	30	31	

DAWES, CHARLES GATES: BIRTH ANNIVERSARY. Aug 27, 1865. Thirtieth vice president of the US (1925–1929), born at Marietta, OH. Won the Nobel Peace Prize in 1925 for the Dawes Plan for German reparations. Died at Evanston, IL, Apr 23, 1951.

DREISER, THEODORE: BIRTH ANNIVERSARY. Aug 27, 1871. American novelist Theodore Dreiser was born at Terre Haute, IN. As part of the Chicago group he was an exponent of American naturalism in literature. His first novel, *Sister Carrie* (1900), was suppressed by his publisher on moral grounds. Dreiser's finest achievement is widely considered to be his novel *An American Tragedy* (1925). He died Dec 28, 1945, at Hollywood, CA.

"THE DUCHESS" WHO WASN'T DAY. Aug 27. At least once on Aug 27 (her birthdate in 1850), repeat the following quotation from the novel *Molly Bawn*, which has passed into the English language: "Beauty is in the eye of the beholder." Margaret Wolfe Hungerford often wrote under the pseudonym "The Duchess," which was the title of her most popular novel—hence the name of this event. A popular romance novelist with about 40 books published, Hungerford was born at Rosscarbery, County Cork, Ireland, on Aug 27, 1850; she died at Bandon, County Cork, in 1897. For info: Peggy Shirley, 3800 Treyburn Dr, #4402, Williamsburg, VA 23185. Phone: (757) 220-6870.

FIRST COMMERCIAL OIL WELL: ANNIVERSARY. Aug 27, 1859. W.A. "Uncle Billy" Smith discovered oil in a shaft being sunk by Colonel E.L. Drake at Titusville, in western Pennsylvania. Drilling had reached 69 ft, 6 inches when Smith saw a dark film floating on the water below the derrick floor. Soon 20 barrels of crude were being pumped each day. The first oil was refined to make kerosene for lighting, replacing whale oil. Later it was refined to make gasoline for cars. The first gas station opened in 1907.

FIRST PLAY PRESENTED IN NORTH AMERICAN COLONIES: ANNIVERSARY. Aug 27, 1655. Acomac, VA, was the site of the first play presented in the North American colonies. The play was *Ye Bare and Ye Cubb*, by Phillip Alexander Bruce. Three local residents were arrested and fined for acting in the play. At the time, most colonies had laws prohibiting public performances; Virginia, however, had no such ordinance.

HAMLIN, HANNIBAL: BIRTH ANNIVERSARY. Aug 27, 1809. Fifteenth vice president of the US (1861–1865) born at Paris, ME. Died at Bangor, ME, July 4, 1891.

HONG KONG: LIBERATION DAY. Aug 27. Public holiday to celebrate liberation from the Japanese in 1945. Annually, the last Monday in August.

JOHNSON, LYNDON BAINES: BIRTH ANNIVERSARY. Aug 27, 1908. The 36th president of the US succeeded to the presidency following the assassination of John F. Kennedy. Johnson's term of office: Nov 22, 1963–Jan 20, 1969. In 1964, he said: "The challenge of the next half-century is whether we have the wisdom to use [our] wealth to enrich and elevate our national life—and to advance the quality of American civilization." Johnson was born near Stonewall, TX, and died at San Antonio, TX, Jan 22, 1973. His birthday is observed as a holiday in Texas.

MOLDOVA: INDEPENDENCE DAY: 10th ANNIVERSARY. Aug 27. Republic of Moldova. Moldova declared its independence from the Soviet Union in 1991.

MOTHER TERESA: BIRTH ANNIVERSARY. Aug 27, 1910. Albanian Roman Catholic nun born Agnes Gonxha Bojaxhiu at Skopje, Macedonia. She founded the Order of the Missionaries of Charity, which cared for the destitute of Calcutta, India. She won the Nobel Peace Prize in 1979. She died at Calcutta, Sept 5, 1997.

NATIONAL OLD-TIME COUNTRY MUSIC CONTEST, FESTIVAL & EXPO.
Aug 27–Sept 2. Pottowattamie County Fairgrounds, Avoca, IA. Country music fans come from all around to hear their favorites. Also arts and crafts displays, other musical entertainment and food booths. Est attendance: 50,000. For info: Natl Old-Time Country Music Contest, Fest & Expo, PO Box 492, Anita, IA 50020. Phone: (712) 784-3001. E-mail: bobeverhart@yahoo.com.

RAYE, MARTHA: 85th BIRTH ANNIVERSARY.
Aug 27, 1916. Born at Butte, MT, Martha Raye began singing when she was three. Raye performed for American servicemen during three wars and received the Jean Hersholt Humanitarian Award from the Academy of Motion Picture Arts and Sciences (1969) for that service. She appeared in her first film, *Rhythm on the Range*, in 1936. She had several TV shows, including "The Martha Raye Show" (1955–56). In 1993 Raye was awarded the Presidential Medal of Freedom. Martha Raye died Oct 19, 1994, at Los Angeles, CA.

SWEDISH LANGUAGE AND CULTURE DAY CAMP.
Aug 27–31. West Riverside Historic Site, Cambridge, MN. Children learn to speak Swedish and understand Swedish culture through songs, games, language classes and craft classes. Families can see what the children have learned through a program at the end of the week. Annually, the last full week in August. For info: Valorie Arrowsmith, Isanti County Historical Soc, PO Box 525, Cambridge, MN 55008. Phone: (763) 689-4291. Fax: (763) 689-4229. E-mail: varrow2@ecenet.com.

UNITED KINGDOM: SUMMER BANK HOLIDAY.
Aug 27. Bank and public holiday in England, Wales and Northern Ireland. (Scotland not included.) Annually, the last Monday in August.

BIRTHDAYS TODAY

Sarah Chalke, 25, actress ("Roseanne"), born Ottawa, Ontario, Canada, Aug 27, 1976.

Daryl Dragon, 59, musician (Captain and Tennille), songwriter, born Studio City, CA, Aug 27, 1942.

J. Robert Kerrey, 58, US Senator (D, Nebraska), born Lincoln, NE, Aug 27, 1943.

Carlos Moya, 25, tennis player, born Palma, Mallorca, Aug 27, 1976.

Paul Rubens (Pee-wee Herman), 49, actor, writer ("Pee-wee's Playhouse," *Pee-wee's Big Adventure*), born Peekskill, NY, Aug 27, 1952.

Tommy Sands, 64, singer ("Teen-Age Crush," "Goin' Steady"), born Chicago, IL, Aug 27, 1937.

Jim Thome, 31, baseball player, born Peoria, IL, Aug 27, 1970.

Tuesday Weld (Susan Kerr), 58, actress ("The Many Loves of Dobie Gillis," *Looking for Mr Goodbar*), born New York, NY, Aug 27, 1943.

AUGUST 28 — TUESDAY
Day 240 — 125 Remaining

BOYER, CHARLES: BIRTH ANNIVERSARY.
Aug 28, 1889. Film star (*Mayerling, Gaslight*), born at Figeac, France. Died at Scottsdale, AZ, Aug 26, 1978.

EMANCIPATION DREAM DAY.
Aug 28. One of the three Emancipation Days of Respect that highlights the three key principles of the American Civil Rights Renaissance of the 1960s. Wearing black and white shows respect for Peoplehood in the Spirit of WAO (WeAreOne) on the anniversaries of three historic events: the Aug 28, 1955, kidnapping/lynching of 14-year-old Chicagoan Emmett Till that prompted the first March on Washington after 600,000 viewed his remains and ignited the Civil Rights Renaissance of the 60s; the Aug 28, 1963, March on Washington led by Rev. Dr. Martin Luther King, Jr, that prompted the passage of the Civil Rights Bill of 1964; and the Aug 28, 1818, death of Chicago's under acclaimed Black Founding Father, Jean Baptiste Pointe DuSable. See also: "Humanitarian Day" (Jan 15) and "Victims of Violence Holy Day" (Apr 4). For info: Dee D. Smith Simmons, Global Committee Commemorating Emancipation Days of Respect, PO Box 21050, Chicago, IL 60621. Phone: (773) RES-PECT.

FEAST OF SAINT AUGUSTINE.
Aug 28. Bishop of Hippo, author of *Confessions* and *The City of God*, born Nov 13, 354, at Tagaste, in what is now Algeria. Died Aug 28, 430, at Hippo, also in North Africa.

GOETHE, JOHANN WOLFGANG von: BIRTH ANNIVERSARY.
Aug 28, 1749. German author, poet, dramatist and philosopher, born at Frankfurt. Died Mar 22, 1832, at Weimar, Germany. Best known for the novels *The Sorrows of Young Werther* and *Wilhelm Meister* and the play *Faust*.

HAYES, LUCY WARE WEBB: BIRTH ANNIVERSARY.
Aug 28, 1831. Wife of Rutherford Birchard Hayes, nineteenth president of the US, born at Chillicothe, OH. Died at Fremont, OH, June 25, 1889. She was nicknamed "Lemonade Lucy" because she and the president, both abstainers, served no alcoholic beverages at White House receptions.

MARCH ON WASHINGTON: ANNIVERSARY.
Aug 28, 1963. More than 250,000 people attended this Civil Rights rally at Washington, DC, at which Reverend Dr. Martin Luther King, Jr, made his famous "I have a dream" speech.

NATIONAL SOBRIETY CHECKPOINT WEEK.
Aug 28–Sept 3. For info: Mothers Against Drunk Driving (MADD), PO Box 541688, Dallas, TX 75354-1688. Web: www.madd.org.

PETERSON, ROGER TORY: BIRTH ANNIVERSARY.
Aug 28, 1908. Naturalist, author of *A Field Guide to Birds*, born at Jamestown, NY. Peterson died at Old Lyme, CT, July 28, 1996.

PORT ROYAL HURRICANE: ANNIVERSARY.
Aug 28, 1722. The hapless Jamaican town of Port Royal was devastated twice within a 30-year span by two natural disasters—an earthquake in 1692 and a hurricane in 1722. The hurricane killed 400 townspeople and sunk 26 merchant ships.

RACE YOUR MOUSE AROUND THE ICONS DAY.
Aug 28. While you're waiting for any number of endless items to finally come up on your screen, don't just sit there. Race your mouse in and around the icons! You'll feel peppy for doing it. [© 2000 WH] For info: Thomas Roy, Wellcat Holidays, 2418 Long Ln, Lebanon, PA 17046. Phone: (717) 279-0184. E-mail: wellcat@supercat.com. Web: www.wellcat.com.

RADIO COMMERCIALS: ANNIVERSARY.
Aug 28, 1922. Broadcasters realized radio could earn profits from the sale of advertising time. WEAF in New York ran a commercial "spot," which was sponsored by the Queensboro Realty Corporation of Jackson Heights to promote Hawthorne Court, a group of apartment buildings at Queens. The commercial rate was $100 for 10 minutes.

SETON, ELIZABETH ANN BAYLEY: BIRTH ANNIVERSARY. Aug 28, 1774. First American-born saint was born at New York, NY. Seton died Jan 4, 1821, at Emmitsburg, MD. See also: "Seton, Elizabeth Ann Bayley: Feast Day" (Jan 4).

BIRTHDAYS TODAY

William S. Cohen, 61, US Secretary of Defense (Clinton administration), born Bangor, ME, Aug 28, 1940.

Ben Gazzara, 71, actor (*Anatomy of a Murder*, "Run for Your Life"), born New York, NY, Aug 28, 1930.

Ronald Ames (Ron) Guidry, 51, former baseball player, born Lafayette, LA, Aug 28, 1950.

Scott Hamilton, 43, Olympic gold medal figure skater, born Toledo, OH, Aug 28, 1958.

Noriyuki "Pat" Morita, 69, actor ("Sanford and Son," "Happy Days," *The Karate Kid*), born Isleton, CA, Aug 28, 1932.

Donald O'Connor, 76, actor, dancer ("Donald O'Connor Texaco Show," *Singin' in the Rain*), born Houston, TX, Aug 28, 1925.

Lou Piniella, 58, baseball manager and former player, born Tampa, FL, Aug 28, 1943.

Jason Priestley, 32, actor ("Beverly Hills 90210," *Tombstone*), born Vancouver, British Columbia, Canada, Aug 28, 1969.

LeAnn Rimes, 19, country and western singer, born Jackson, MS, Aug 28, 1982.

Rick Rossovich, 44, actor (*The Terminator, Roxanne*), born Palo Alto, CA, Aug 28, 1957.

Emma Samms (Emma Samuelson), 41, actress ("General Hospital," "Dynasty"), born London, England, Aug 28, 1960.

David Soul, 55, actor ("Starsky and Hutch," *Salem's Lot*), born Chicago, IL, Aug 28, 1946.

Daniel Stern, 44, actor (*City Slickers, Home Alone*), born Bethesda, MD, Aug 28, 1957.

Shania Twain, 36, country singer, born Eileen Twain, Windsor, Ontario, Canada, Aug 28, 1965.

AUGUST 29 — WEDNESDAY

Day 241 — 124 Remaining

AMISTAD SEIZED: ANNIVERSARY. Aug 29, 1839. In January 1839, 53 Africans were seized near modern-day Sierra Leone, taken to Cuba and sold as slaves. While being transferred to another part of the island on the ship *Amistad*, led by the African, Cinque, they seized control of the ship, telling the crew to take them back to Africa. However, the crew secretly changed course and the ship landed at Long Island, NY, where it and its "cargo" were seized as salvage. The *Amistad* was towed to New Haven, CT where the Africans were imprisoned and a lengthy legal battle began to determine if they were property to be returned to Cuba or free men. John Quincy Adams took their case all the way to the Supreme Court, where on Mar 9, 1841, it was determined that they were free and could return to Africa.

AUSTRALIA: GOODWILL GAMES. Aug 29–Sept 9. Brisbane, Queensland, Australia. The 5th Goodwill Games will feature 14 sports and more than 1,300 of the finest athletes in the world. For info: 2001 Goodwill Games, GPO Box 2110, Brisbane, Queensland, Australia, 4121. Phone: 61 7 3233 2001. Fax: 61 7 3233 2000. E-mail: info@goodwillgames.com. Web: www.good willgames.com.

BERGMAN, INGRID: BIRTH ANNIVERSARY. Aug 29, 1915. One of cinema's greatest actresses. Bergman was born at Stockholm, Sweden, and died at London, England, on her 67th birthday, Aug 29, 1982. Three-time Academy Award winner for *Gaslight, Anastasia, Murder on the Orient Express*. Controversy over her personal life made her and her films unpopular to American audiences during an interval of several years between periods of awards and adulation.

CARROLL, ANNA ELLA: BIRTH ANNIVERSARY. Aug 29, 1815. American writer and publicist for the Union cause during the Civil War, she was born at Somerset County, MD. Her actions in the Civil War were the subject of several books. She died at Washington, DC, Feb 18, 1894.

HOLMES, OLIVER WENDELL: BIRTH ANNIVERSARY. Aug 29, 1809. Physician and author, father of Supreme Court justice Oliver Wendell Holmes, born at Cambridge, MA. Died at Boston, MA, Oct 7, 1894. "A moment's insight," he wrote, "is sometimes worth a life's experience."

LOCKE, JOHN: BIRTH ANNIVERSARY. Aug 29, 1632 (OS). English philosopher, founder of philosophical liberalism, born at Wrington, England. His ideas influenced the American colonists and were enshrined in the Constitution. Locke died at Essex, England, Oct 28, 1704 (OS).

MORE HERBS, LESS SALT DAY. Aug 29. It's healthier, zestier and lustier! [© 2000 by WH] For info: Tom or Ruth Roy, Wellcat Holidays, 2418 Long Ln, Lebanon, PA 17046. Phone: (717) 279-0184. E-mail: wellcat@supernet.com. Web: www.wellcat.com.

PARKER, CHARLIE: BIRTH ANNIVERSARY. Aug 29, 1920. Jazz saxophonist Charlie Parker was born at Kansas City, KS. He earned the nickname "Yardbird" (later "Bird") from his habit of sitting in the backyard of speakeasies, fingering his saxophone. His career as a jazz saxophonist took him from jam sessions in Kansas City to New York, where he met Dizzy Gillespie and others who were creating a style of music that would become known as bop or bebop. Although Parker's musical genius was unquestioned, Parker's addiction to heroin haunted his life. He died at Rochester, NY, Mar 12, 1955, at the age of 34.

ROYAL GEORGE SINKS: ANNIVERSARY. Aug 29, 1792. Prized British battleship *Royal George* sank due to fatal human error in one of the worst maritime disasters in history. While the ship was being repaired at Spithead, the port side was tilted too close to the waterline. A gust of wind lowered the ship even further, allowing tons of water to flood into its open gunports. The ship sank within minutes before many of the 1,300 on board realized what was happening and more than 900 people drowned.

SHAYS REBELLION: ANNIVERSARY. Aug 29, 1786. Daniel Shays, veteran of the battles of Lexington, Bunker Hill, Ticonderoga and Saratoga, was one of the leaders of more than 1,000 rebels who sought redress of grievances during the depression days of 1786–87. They prevented general court sessions and on Sept 26 they prevented Supreme Court sessions at Springfield, MA. On Jan 25, 1787, they attacked the federal arsenal at Springfield; Feb 2, Shays's troops were routed and fled. Shays was sentenced to death but pardoned June 13, 1788. Later he received a small pension for services in the American Revolution.

	S	M	T	W	T	F	S
August				1	2	3	4
2001	5	6	7	8	9	10	11
	12	13	14	15	16	17	18
	19	20	21	22	23	24	25
	26	27	28	29	30	31	

SLOVAK REPUBLIC: NATIONAL DAY. Aug 29. National day commemorating national uprising in 1848.

SOVIET COMMUNIST PARTY SUSPENDED: 10th ANNIVERSARY. Aug 29, 1991. The Supreme Soviet, the parliament of the USSR, suspended all activities of the Communist Party, seizing its property and bringing to an end the institution that ruled the Soviet Union for nearly 75 years. The action followed an unsuccessful coup Aug 19–21 that sought to overthrow the government of Soviet President Mikhail Gorbachev but instead prompted a sweeping wave of democratic change. Gorbachev quit as party leader Aug 24.

SWEET CORN FESTIVAL. Aug 29–Sept 1. Millersport, OH. All concessions are operated by more than 80 non-profit charitable organizations. Wide variety of food, four entertainment stages, giant midway, exhibits, numerous contests and games. For info: Sweet Corn Festival Inc, Po Box 337, Millersport, OH 43046. Phone: (740) 467-3943. E-mail: query@sweetcornfest.com. Web: www.sweetcornfest.com.

BIRTHDAYS TODAY

Sir Richard Attenborough, 78, filmmaker (*In Which We Serve, The Great Escape*), born Cambridge, England, Aug 29, 1923.
Rebecca De Mornay, 39, actress (*Risky Business, The Hand That Rocks the Cradle*), born Santa Rosa, CA, Aug 29, 1962.
William Friedkin, 62, filmmaker (Oscar for *The French Connection; The Exorcist*), born Chicago, IL, Aug 29, 1939.
Richard Gere, 52, actor (*An Officer and a Gentleman, Pretty Woman*), born Philadelphia, PA, Aug 29, 1949.
Elliott Gould (Elliott Goldstein), 63, actor (*M*A*S*H, The Long Goodbye*), born Brooklyn, NY, Aug 29, 1938.
Michael Jackson, 43, singer, songwriter ("We Are the World," *Bad, Thriller, Beat It*), born Gary, IN, Aug 29, 1958.
Robin Leach, 60, TV host ("Lifestyles of the Rich and Famous"), born London, England, Aug 29, 1941.
John Sidney McCain III, 65, US Senator (R, Arizona), born Panama Canal Zone, Aug 29, 1936.
Mark Morris, 45, choreographer, dancer, born Seattle, WA, Aug 29, 1956.
William Edward (Will) Perdue III, 36, basketball player, born Melbourne, FL, Aug 29, 1965.
Pierre Turgeon, 32, hockey player, born Rouyn, Quebec, Canada, Aug 29, 1969.

AUGUST 30 — THURSDAY

Day 242 — 123 Remaining

ARTHUR, ELLEN LEWIS HERNDON: BIRTH ANNIVERSARY. Aug 30, 1837. Wife of Chester Alan Arthur, 21st president of the US, born at Fredericksburg, VA. Died at New York, Jan 12, 1880.

AUBURN CORD DUESENBERG FESTIVAL. Aug 30–Sept 5. Auburn, IN. Classic car parade, antiques show, decorators showcase, children's carnival, quilt show and classic car auction. Est attendance: 300,000. For info: Auburn Cord Duesenberg Festival, Box 6019, Auburn, IN 46706. Phone: (219) 925-3600. Fax: (219) 927-7200. Web: www.acdfestival.org.

BLUE HILL FAIR. Aug 30–Sept 3. Blue Hill, ME. A "down-to-earth" country fair. Annually, Labor Day weekend. Est attendance: 35,000. For info: Blue Hill Fair, PO Box 390, Blue Hill, ME 04614. Phone: (207) 374-3701. Fax: (207) 374-3702.

BOOTH, SHIRLEY: BIRTH ANNIVERSARY. Aug 30, 1898. American actress Shirley Booth was born Thelma Booth Ford at New York, NY. She won a Tony Award and an Oscar for her roles in the stage (1950) and film (1952) productions of *Come Back, Little Sheba*, but she is best known for her title role in the television program "Hazel" (1961–66). She died at Chatham, MS, Oct 16, 1992.

COLUMBIA COUNTY FAIR. Aug 30–Sept 3. Chatham, NY. Midway and agricultural exhibits for the family to enjoy. 161st annual fair. For info: Columbia County Tourism Dept, 401 State St, Hudson, NY 12534. Phone: (800) 724-1846.

FIRST WHITE HOUSE PRESIDENTIAL BABY: BIRTH ANNIVERSARY. Aug 30, 1893. Frances Folsom Cleveland (Mrs Grover Cleveland) was the first presidential wife to have a baby at the White House when she gave birth to a baby girl (Esther). The first child ever born in the White House was a granddaughter to Thomas Jefferson in 1806.

HUEY P. LONG DAY. Aug 30. A legal holiday in Louisiana.

LOUISIANA SHRIMP AND PETROLEUM FESTIVAL AND FAIR. Aug 30–Sept 3. Morgan City, LA. Free admission to this event that recognizes and celebrates the importance of the shrimp and oil industry to the area. Arts, crafts, water and street parades, Cajun culinary classic, antique show, shrimp cook-off, music in the park, unique children's village (a magical adventureland), gospel tent, coronation pageant and ball, carnival, blessing of the fleet. American Bus Association's "Top 100 Event." Est attendance: 150,000. For info: Louisiana Shrimp and Petroleum Festival and Fair Assn, Box 103, Morgan City, LA 70381. Phone: (504) 385-0703. Fax: (504) 384-4628. E-mail: info@shrimp-petrofest.org.

MacMURRAY, FRED: BIRTH ANNIVERSARY. Aug 30, 1908. Fred MacMurray was born at Kankakee, IL. His film and television career included a wide variety of roles, ranging from comedy (*The Absent-Minded Professor, Son of Flubber, The Shaggy Dog, The Happiest Millionaire*) to serious drama (*The Caine Mutiny, The Miracle of the Bells, Fair Wind to Java, Double Indemnity*). During 1960–72 he portrayed the father on "My Three Sons," which was second only to "Ozzie and Harriet" as network TV's longest running family sitcom. He died Nov 5, 1991, at Santa Monica, CA.

MILLENNIUM PHILCON. Aug 30–Sept 3. Philadelphia, PA. The 59th annual World Science Fiction Convention will promote the educational, creative and innovative aspects of all forms of science fiction and fantasy in literature and the arts. For info: Millennium Philcon, PO Box 310, Huntingdon Valley, PA 19006-0310. E-mail: phil2001@netaxs.com. Web: www.netaxs.com/~phil2001.

ON THE WATERFRONT. Aug 30–Sept 2. Rockford, IL. Largest street food and music festival in the region. Ten music stages, more than 50 specialty foods, dozens of special events. Est attendance: 350,000. For info: On the Waterfront, Inc, 308 W State St, Ste 115, Rockford, IL 61101. Phone: (815) 964-4388 or (815) 963-4FUN. E-mail: 4fun@OnTheWaterfront. Web: www.onthewaterfront.com.

PERU: SAINT ROSE OF LIMA DAY. Aug 30. Saint Rose of Lima was the first saint of the western hemisphere. She lived at the time of the colonization by Spain in the 16th century. Patron saint of the Americas and the Philippines. Public holiday in Peru.

RUTHERFORD, ERNEST: BIRTH ANNIVERSARY. Aug 30, 1871. Physicist, born at Nelson, New Zealand. He established the nuclear nature of the atom, the electrical structure of matter and achieved the transmutation of elements, research which later resulted in the atomic bomb. Rutherford died at Cambridge, England, Oct 19, 1937.

SHELLEY, MARY WOLLSTONECRAFT: BIRTH ANNIVERSARY. Aug 30, 1797. English novelist Mary Shelley, daughter of the philosopher William Godwin and the feminist Mary Wollstonecraft and wife of the poet Percy Bysshe Shelley, was born at London and died there Feb 1, 1851. In addition to being the author of the famous novel *Frankenstein*, Shelley is important in literary history for her work in the editing and publishing of her husband's unpublished work after his early death.

SPACE MILESTONE: *CHALLENGER STS-8* (US). Aug 30, 1983. Shuttle *Challenger* with five astronauts (Richard Truly, Daniel Brandenstein, Guion Bluford, Jr, Dale Garner and William Thornton) was launched from Kennedy Space Center, FL, on this date. Return landing six days later on Sept 5 at Edwards Air Force Base, CA.

SPACE MILESTONE: *DISCOVERY* (US). Aug 30, 1984. Space shuttle *Discovery* was launched from Kennedy Space Center, FL, for its maiden flight with six-member crew. During the flight the crew deployed three satellites and used a robot arm before landing at Edwards Air Force Base, CA, Sept 5.

STRAITH, CLAIRE, MD: BIRTH ANNIVERSARY. Aug 30, 1891. Innovator in plastic and cosmetic surgery, born at Southfield, MI. After attending an international meeting at Paris, France, at the end of World War I to discuss and share information regarding reconstructive surgical techniques used on the battlefield, Dr. Claire Straith dedicated his career to the new field of plastic surgery. He developed many of the techniques used in plastic and cosmetic surgery, designed new surgical instruments and led a campaign that convinced automakers, in 1930, to use safety glass and remove dangerous projections from the interior of cars. Dr. Straith died July 13, 1958.

THOMAS POINT BEACH BLUEGRASS FESTIVAL. Aug 30–Sept 2. Brunswick, ME. Featuring world-class bluegrass musicians on the southern coast of Maine. Swimming, playground, picnic area, snack bar, free camping, Sunday-morning worship service on the beach. Fun for the whole family! 24th annual festival. Enjoy an end-of-summer family outing and terrific bluegrass music. Est attendance: 4,000. For tickets and info: Thomas Point Beach, 29 Meadow Rd, Brunswick, ME 04011. Phone: (207) 725-6009 or (877) TPB-4321. Web: www.thomaspointbeach.com.

TURKEY: VICTORY DAY. Aug 30. Commemorates victory in War of Independence in 1922. Military parades, performing of the Mehtar band (the world's oldest military band), fireworks.

WILKINS, ROY: 100th BIRTH ANNIVERSARY. Aug 30, 1901. Roy Wilkins, grandson of a Mississippi slave, civil rights leader, active in the National Association for the Advancement of Colored People (NAACP), retired as its executive director in 1977. Born at St. Louis, MO. Died at New York, NY, Sept 8, 1981.

BIRTHDAYS TODAY

Elizabeth Ashley (Elizabeth Ann Cole), 60, actress (*Agnes of God, Cat on a Hot Tin Roof*, "Evening Shade"), born Ocala, FL, Aug 30, 1941.
Timothy Bottoms, 50, actor (*The Last Picture Show, The Paper Chase*), born Santa Barbara, CA, Aug 30, 1951.
Michael Chiklis, 38, actor ("The Commish"), born Lowell, MA, Aug 30, 1963.
Cameron Diaz, 29, actress (*My Best Friend's Wedding, There's Something about Mary*), born San Diego, CA, Aug 30, 1972.
Jean-Claude Killy, 58, Olympic gold medal alpine skier, born Saint Cloud, France, Aug 30, 1943.

August 2001	S	M	T	W	T	F	S
				1	2	3	4
	5	6	7	8	9	10	11
	12	13	14	15	16	17	18
	19	20	21	22	23	24	25
	26	27	28	29	30	31	

Peggy Lipton, 54, actress (Golden Globe Award for "The Mod Squad"; "Twin Peaks"), born New York, NY, Aug 30, 1947.
Michael Michele, 35, actress ("Homicide: Life on the Street," "ER"), born Evansville, IN, Aug 30, 1966.
Robert Lee Parish, 48, former basketball player, born Shreveport, LA, Aug 30, 1953.
David Paymer, 47, actor (*City Slickers, Mr Saturday Night*), born Long Island, NY, Aug 30, 1954.
Kitty Wells (Muriel Deason), 82, singer ("Jealousy"), born Nashville, TN, Aug 30, 1919.
Theodore Samuel (Ted) Williams, 83, Baseball Hall of Fame outfielder, born San Diego, CA, Aug 30, 1918.

AUGUST 31 — FRIDAY
Day 243 — 122 Remaining

"ALICE" TV PREMIERE: 25th ANNIVERSARY. Aug 31, 1976. Linda Lavin played the title role in this CBS comedy that was based on the 1975 film *Alice Doesn't Live Here Anymore*. Alice Hyatt was the new girl in town—a widow raising her son while trying to make ends meet by waitressing at a diner. She also had dreams of making it big as a singer. Nine years later, Alice was able to leave her "temp" job for a gig. Lavin's co-stars were: Vic Tayback as diner owner Mel Sharples, Philip McKeon as Alice's son Tommy, Beth Howland as waitress Vera Gorman, Polly Holliday as sassy waitress Flo Castleberry, Diane Ladd as Flo's replacement Belle Dupree, Celia Weston as waitress Jolene Hunnicutt, Martha Raye as Mel's mother Carrie and Marvin Kaplan as customer Henry Beesmyer. The last telecast aired on July 2, 1985.

BENTON NEIGHBOR DAY. Aug 31–Sept 1. Benton, MO. Large festival that includes exhibits, greased pole climb, indoor dance, amusement park, Little Mr and Miss contest, greased pig contest, live bands, antique car show, horseshoe tournament, sky divers, queen contest, kid tractor pull, parade and talent show. Annually, the Friday and Saturday before Labor Day. Est attendance: 3,000. For info: Benton Chamber of Commerce, PO Box 477, Benton, MO 63736. Phone: (573) 545-3125.

BEST IN THE WEST NUGGET RIB COOK-OFF. Aug 31–Sept 3. Victorian Square, Sparks, NV. Rib cookers from across the country compete for the title of Nugget Best in the West Rib Cooker. Competing cookers sell ribs to the crowd over the four-day Labor Day weekend. Free concerts nightly feature groups like BTO, War and Terri Clark. Other music groups presented throughout the day—all free. Hundreds of craft booths and activities for the whole family. Est attendance: 200,000. For info: John Ascuaga's Nugget, 1100 Nugget Ave, Sparks, NV 89431. Phone: (800) 648-1177. Web: www.janugget.com.

BOX CAR DAYS. Aug 31–Sept 3. Tracy, MN. Celebrates the city's heritage as a railroad community. Annually, Labor Day weekend. Est attendance: 10,000. For info: Chamber of Commerce, 372 Morgan St, Tracy, MN 56175. Phone: (507) 629-4021. E-mail: tracyacc@rconnect.com. Web: www.tracymn.com.

BRITT DRAFT HORSE SHOW. Aug 31–Sept 2. Hancock County Fairgrounds, Britt, IA. One of the largest draft horse hitch shows in North America, featuring 16 six-horse hitches from the US and Canada representing the very best of the Belgian, Percheron and Clydesdale performance horses. Annually, Labor Day weekend. Est attendance: 10,000. For info: Randel or Melodie Hiscocks, Britt Draft Horse Assn, PO Box 312, Britt, IA 50423. Phone: (515) 843-4181.

BUMBERSHOOT, THE SEATTLE ARTS FESTIVAL. Aug 31–Sept 3. Seattle Center, Seattle, WA. Celebrates the arts in every genre; includes kids' activities. Annually, Labor Day weekend. Est attendance: 250,000. For info: One Reel, PO Box 9750, Seattle, WA 98109. Phone: (206) 281-8111. Web: www.bumbershoot.org.

CANADA: CLASSIC BOAT FESTIVAL. Aug 31–Sept 2. Victoria, BC. 24th annual. Classic sail and power vessels from all over the west coast of the US, Canada and beyond gather in Victoria's Inner Harbour. View these lovingly restored and maintained boats with their polished brass fittings and rich teak and oak decks and hulls. Schooner races, sailpast, steamboat parade. Sponsored by Victoria Real Estate Board and Times Colonist. For info: Classic Boat Festival, 3035 Nanaimo St, Victoria, BC, Canada V8T 4W2. Phone: (604) 385-7766. Fax: (604) 385-8773. E-mail: msampson@vreb.org.

CHARLESTON EARTHQUAKE: ANNIVERSARY. Aug 31, 1886. Charleston, SC. The first major earthquake in the recorded history of the eastern US occurred on this date. It is believed that about 100 persons perished in the quake, centered near Charleston but felt up to 800 miles away. Though a number of smaller eastern US quakes had been described and recorded since 1638, this affected persons living in an area of some 2 million square miles.

"CRANKSHAFT": ANNIVERSARY. Aug 31. Celebrating the anniversary of the nationally syndicated comic strip. For info: Tom Batiuk, 2750 Substation Rd, Medina, OH 44256. Phone: (330) 722-8755.

ENGLAND: BLACKPOOL ILLUMINATIONS. Aug 31–Nov 4. The Promenade, Blackpool, Lancashire. "A five-mile spectacle of lighting." Est attendance: 8,000,000. For info: Tourism and Services Dept, 1 Clifton St, Blackpool, Lancashire, England FY1 1LY. Phone: (44) 1253 477477. Fax: (44) 1253 478210. E-mail: tourism@blackpool.gov.uk. Web: www.blackpool.gov.uk.

FESTIVAL OF MOUNTAIN AND PLAIN . . . A TASTE OF COLORADO. Aug 31–Sept 3. Denver, CO. The Rocky Mountain region's largest free outdoor festival, this four-day food and entertainment extravaganza over Labor Day weekend features 50 of Colorado's best restaurants. Musical entertainment on six outdoor stages, gourmet cooking demonstrations, 200 arts and crafts vendors and children's music and activities. Friday, Saturday and Sunday 11 AM–10:30 PM. Monday 11 AM–8:30 PM. Est attendance: 350,000. For info: Susan Rogers Kark, Sr Dir, Mktg & Events, Downtown Denver Partnership, Inc, 511 16th St, Ste 200, Denver, CO 80202. Phone: (303) 534-6161. Fax: (303) 534-2803. Web: www.downtowndenver.com.

FORT BRIDGER RENDEZVOUS. Aug 31–Sept 3. Fort Bridger, WY. Come and join in the family fun with entertainment, food booths, merchandise exhibits and much more. Est attendance: 30,000. For info: Debbie Devish, Fort Bridger Rendezvous, PO Box 198, Ft Bridger, WY 82933. Phone: (307) 782-6572. Fax: (307) 782-7888.

HOG CAPITAL OF THE WORLD FESTIVAL. Aug 31–Sept 3. Kewanee, IL. World's largest pork chop BBQ. Also features professional entertainment, carnival, flea market, Model T races, parade, four-mile-run (Hog Stampede) and the Hogatta Regatta. Annually, Labor Day weekend. Est attendance: 60,000. For info: Mark Mikenas, Exec VP, Kewanee Chamber of Commerce, 113 E 2nd St, Kewanee, IL 61443. Phone: (309) 852-2175. Fax: (309) 852-2176. E-mail: chamber@kewanee-il.com.

HOISINGTON CELEBRATION. Aug 31–Sept 3. Bicentennial Park, Hoisington, KS. Annual event includes dances, demolition derby, parade, car show, carnival, kiddie events, baby contest, float contest. Annually, Labor Day weekend. Est attendance: 35,000. For info: Hoisington Labor Day Committee, 123 N Main, Hoisington, KS 67544. Phone: (316) 653-4311.

IRA DECLARES TRUCE: ANNIVERSARY. Aug 31, 1994. The Irish Republican Army (IRA) announced a cease-fire in its 25-year-old war against British control of Northern Ireland. The conflict, which had taken 3,167 lives, started with Roman Catholic protests against discrimination by the Protestant majority in the country. British authorities sent in heavily armed troops to patrol the country, especially its capital, Belfast. The Catholic goal was reunification with the predominately Catholic Republic of Ireland, while the Protestant majority in Northern Ireland steadfastly opposed such a reunion. The IRA gave no timetable for the duration of the cease-fire, nor were any weapons turned in. Two earlier cease-fires, in 1972 and 1975, both failed to last.

ITALIAN STREET FAIR. Aug 31–Sept 3. Centennial Park, midtown Nashville, TN. Benefits the Nashville Symphony Orchestra. Annually, Labor Day weekend. Est attendance: 100,000. For info: Nashville Symphony Guild, 209 Tenth Ave S, Nashville, TN 37203. Phone: (615) 252-4601. E-mail: nashsymphguild@mindspring.com. Web: www.italianstreetfair.com.

JOHNSON CITY FIELD DAYS. Aug 31–Sept 3. Northside Park, Johnson City, NY. Amusement rides, game booths, live entertainment, food concessions, area's largest fireworks display. The annual celebration benefits many non-profit organizations in Johnson City. Annually, Labor Day weekend. For info: Johnson City Celebration Committee, 124 Brown St, Johnson City, NY 13790. Phone: (607) 797-9098. Fax: (607) 798-9553. E-mail: jcplan@pronetisp.net.

JOHNSTOWN FOLKFEST. Aug 31–Sept 2. Johnstown, PA. A three-day heritage festival held over Labor Day weekend, incorporates five performance stages featuring Grammy-winning entertainers, more than 50 ethnic food vendors, children's entertainment and tours of the magnificent churches that surround the festival grounds. Est attendance: 120,000. For info: Juli Gardill, Johnstown Area Heritage Assn, PO Box 1889, Johnstown, PA 15907-1889. Phone: (814) 539-1889.

KLONDIKE ELDORADO GOLD DISCOVERY: ANNIVERSARY. Aug 31, 1896. Two weeks after the Rabbit/Bonanza Creek claim was filed, gold was discovered on Eldorado Creek, a tributary of Bonanza. More than $30 million worth of gold (worth some $600–$700 million in today's dollars) was mined from the Eldorado Claim in 1896.

KYRGYZSTAN: INDEPENDENCE DAY: 10th ANNIVERSARY. Aug 31, 1991. National holiday. Commemorates independence from the former Soviet Union in 1991.

MALAYSIA: NATIONAL DAY. Aug 31. National holiday. Commemorates independence from Britain in 1957.

MARSHALL COUNTY BLUEBERRY FESTIVAL. Aug 31–Sept 3. Plymouth, IN. More than 600 craft and commercial booths, parade, circus, fireworks, 15K run, antique car show, horse pull and luscious blueberry treats. Est attendance: 500,000. For info: Marshall County Blueberry Festival, 220 N Center St, PO Box 639, Plymouth, IN 46563-0639. Phone: (219) 936-5020 or (888) 936-5020. Fax: (219) 936-9845.

MONTESSORI, MARIA: BIRTH ANNIVERSARY. Aug 31, 1870. Italian physician and educator, born at Chiaraville, Italy. Founder of the Montessori method of teaching children. Montessori died at Noordwijk, Holland, May 6, 1952.

NATIONAL CHAMPIONSHIP CHUCKWAGON RACES. Aug 31–Sept 2. Clinton, AR. Five divisions of chuckwagon races, bronc fanning, Snowy River race, live entertainment, trail rides, barn dance, western show, western art, saddles, tack-clothing vendors. Annually, Labor Day weekend. 16th annual. Est attendance: 20,000. For info: Dan Eoff, Rt 6, Box 187-1, Clinton, AR 72031. Phone: (501) 745-8407. Fax: (501) 745-4416. E-mail: chuckwag@artelco.com. Web: www.chuckwagonraces.com.

NATIONAL SWEETCORN FESTIVAL. Aug 31–Sept 3. McFerron Park, Hoopeston, IL. Annual festival includes 29 tons of free corn on the cob, nationally sanctioned beauty pageant, carnival, flea market, horse show, demolition derby, bands and talent shows. Est attendance: 50,000. For info: Jeanie Cooke, Exec Dir, Danville Area Conv/Visitors Bureau, PO Box 992, Danville, IL 61834. Phone: (217) 442-2096.

NORTH CAROLINA APPLE FESTIVAL. Aug 31–Sept 3. Hendersonville, NC. Festival includes arts and crafts displays, entertainment, food booths, sports events and much more. Est attendance: 200,000. For info: North Carolina Apple Festival, PO Box 886, Hendersonville, NC 28793. Phone: (828) 697-4557.

OATMEAL FESTIVAL. Aug 31–Sept 1. Bertram/Oatmeal, TX. Annual festival to honor Oatmeal, the community and the cereal, and to have a weekend of family fun, good food and a whole lot of foolishness. Observed Labor Day weekend. Est attendance: 7,000. For info: Oatmeal Fest, PO Box 70, Bertram/Oatmeal, TX 78605. Phone: (512) 355-2197. Fax: (512) 355-3182.

PAYSON GOLDEN ONION DAYS. Aug 31–Sept 3. Payson, UT. This unique festival includes amusement rides, fireworks, a parade, arts and crafts displays, entertainment, food booths, a demolition derby and much more. Annually, Labor Day weekend. Est attendance: 13,000. For info: Payson Chamber of Commerce, 439 W Utah Ave, Payson, UT 84651. Phone: (801) 465-2634. Fax: (801) 465-5208.

PENNSYLVANIA ARTS & CRAFTS COLONIAL FESTIVAL. Aug 31–Sept 3. Westmoreland Fairgrounds, Greensburg, PA. Step back to colonial times with more than 200 exhibits of handcrafted furniture, floral arrangements, ceramics, tole, decorative paintings and wrought iron. Civil War encampment, fife and drum music and food booths. Est attendance: 30,000. For info: Debbie or Dave Stoner, Family Festivals Assn, Inc, PO Box 166, Irwin, PA 15642. Phone: (724) 863-4577. Fax: (724) 863-4577.

August	S	M	T	W	T	F	S
2001				1	2	3	4
	5	6	7	8	9	10	11
	12	13	14	15	16	17	18
	19	20	21	22	23	24	25
	26	27	28	29	30	31	

POLAND: SOLIDARITY FOUNDED: ANNIVERSARY. Aug 31, 1980. The Polish trade union Solidarity was formed at the Baltic Sea port of Gdansk, Poland. Outlawed by the government, many of its leaders were arrested. Led by Lech Walesa, Solidarity persisted in its opposition to the Communist-controlled government, and Aug 19, 1989, Polish president Wojcieck Jaruzelski astonished the world by nominating for the post of prime minister Tadeusz Mazowiecki, a deputy in the Polish Assembly, 1961–72, and editor-in-chief of Solidarity's weekly newspaper, bringing to an end 42 years of Communist Party domination.

SANTA-CALI-GON DAYS FESTIVAL. Aug 31–Sept 3. Historic Square, Independence, MO. Regional celebration for the three trails—Santa Fe, California, Oregon—which all started in Independence. Huge arts and crafts show, live Nashville performers, large carnival midway and free admission. Largest Labor Day weekend event in Kansas City metropolitan area. Est attendance: 225,000. For info: Santa-Cali-Gon Days, 210 W Truman Rd, Independence, MO 64051. Phone: (816) 252-4745. Web: www.independencechamber.com.

SAROYAN, WILLIAM: BIRTH ANNIVERSARY. Aug 31, 1908. American writer of Armenian descent, author of *The Human Comedy* and of the Pulitzer Prize–winning play *The Time of Your Life*, was born at Fresno, CA, and died there May 18, 1981. In April 1981 he gave reporters a final statement for publication after his death: "Everybody has got to die, but I have always believed an exception would be made in my case. Now what?"

SHAWN, WILLIAM: BIRTH ANNIVERSARY. Aug 31, 1907. William Shawn, editor of *The New Yorker* for 35 years, was born at Chicago, IL. He was virtual dictator of editorial policy for the magazine, which in turn had an impact on the literary and reportorial styles of writers throughout the country. Nonfiction pieces in *The New Yorker* contributed to public opinion on important issues during Shawn's tenure. Shawn died Dec 8, 1992, at New York, NY.

STONEWALL JACKSON HERITAGE ARTS AND CRAFTS JUBILEE. Aug 31–Sept 3. Jackson's Mill 4-H Camp, Weston, WV. Historic and contemporary celebration of Appalachian heritage with music, dancing, arts and crafts, photo and quilt shows, Civil War reenactment, living history on the site of Stonewall Jackson's childhood home. Est attendance: 45,000. For info: Stonewall Jackson Heritage Arts and Crafts Jubilee, PO Box 956, Weston, WV 26452. Phone: (304) 269-1863 or (800) 296-1863.

TELLURIDE FILM FESTIVAL. Aug 31–Sept 3. Telluride, CO. 27th film festival attracts film lovers, artists and scholars from all over the globe. National and international premiers, world archive treasures, innovative or experimental filmmaking and retrospectives. Annually, Labor Day weekend. Est attendance: 5,000. For info: The Natl Film Preserve, 379 State St, Portsmouth, NH 03801. Phone: (603) 433-9202. Fax: (603) 433-9206. E-mail: tellufilm@aol.com. Web: www.telluridefilmfestival.com.

TOPEKA RAILROAD DAYS FESTIVAL. Aug 31–Sept 3. Topeka, KS. A celebration of Topeka's railroad heritage with exhibits, arts and crafts, entertainment, carnival and excursion-train trips. Annually, Labor Day weekend. Est attendance: 86,000. For info: Topeka Railroad Days, Inc, 824 N Kansas Ave, Topeka, KS 66608. Phone: (785) 232-5533. Fax: (785) 232-6259. E-mail: rrdays@cjnetworks.com.

TOTAH FESTIVAL. Aug 31–Sept 2. Farmington, NM. Native American arts and crafts show and marketplace—highlighted by an Indian rug auction. Est attendance: 10,000. For info: Farmington Conv and Visitors Bureau, 3041 E Main St, Farmington, NM 87402. Phone: (800) 448-1240 or (505) 326-7602. Fax: (505) 327-0577. E-mail: fmncvb@cyberport.com. Web: farmingtonnm.org.

TRINIDAD AND TOBAGO: INDEPENDENCE DAY. Aug 31. National holiday. Became an independent nation within the British Commonwealth on this day in 1962. Trinidad became a republic, Sept 24, 1976.

VERMONT STATE FAIR. Aug 31–Sept 9. Fairgrounds, Rutland, VT. Est attendance: 100,000. For info: Vermont State Fair, 175 S Main St, Rutland, VT 05701. Phone: (802) 775-5200.

WEST VIRGINIA ITALIAN HERITAGE FESTIVAL. Aug 31–Sept 2. Clarksburg, WV. Includes Pasta Cookoff—participants cook a pasta dish to compete for prizes. Est attendance: 150,000. For info: West Virgina Italian Heritage Festival Office, PO Box 1632, Clarksburg, WV 26302. Phone: (304) 622-7314. Fax: (304) 622-5727. E-mail: wvihf@wvonline.com. Web: www.wvonline.com/wvihf.

WISCONSIN STATE COW-CHIP THROW. Aug 31–Sept 1. Prairie du Sac, WI. Cow-Chip Throw, 5K and 10K runs, arts and crafts fair, live music, parade, Cow-Pie Eating Contest. Annually, the Friday night and Saturday of Labor Day weekend. Est attendance: 50,000. For info: Wisconsin State Cow-Chip Throw, PO Box 3, Prairie du Sac, WI 53578. Phone: (608) 643-4317. Fax: (608) 643-5421. E-mail: toolsmkt@bankpds.com.

WOODSTOCK FAIR. Aug 31–Sept 3. Woodstock, CT. Annually, Labor Day weekend. Est attendance: 250,000. For info: Woodstock Fair, PO Box 1, South Woodstock, CT 06267. Phone: (860) 928-3246.

BIRTHDAYS TODAY

Jennifer Azzi, 33, basketball player, born Oak Ridge, TN, Aug 31, 1968.

James Coburn, 73, actor (*Our Man Flint, The President's Analyst*), born Laurel, NE, Aug 31, 1928.

Debbie Gibson, 31, singer ("Only in My Dreams," "Foolish Beat"), born Brooklyn, NY, Aug 31, 1970.

Buddy Hackett (Leonard Hacker), 77, comedian, actor (*The Love Bug, The Music Man*), born New York, NY, Aug 31, 1924.

Van Morrison, 56, singer, songwriter ("Brown Eyed Girl," "Domino"), born Belfast, Northern Ireland, Aug 31, 1945.

Edwin Corley Moses, 46, Olympic gold medal track athlete, born Dayton, OH, Aug 31, 1955.

Hideo Nomo, 33, baseball player, born Osaka, Japan, Aug 31, 1968.

Itzhak Perlman, 56, violinist, born Tel Aviv, Israel, Aug 31, 1945.

Frank Robinson, 66, former baseball executive and manager, Baseball Hall of Fame outfielder, born Beaumont, TX, Aug 31, 1935.

Daniel Schorr, 85, journalist, born New York, NY, Aug 31, 1916.

G.D. Spradlin, 81, actor (*The Godfather Part II, North Dallas Forty, The War of the Roses*), born Garvin County, OK, Aug 31, 1920.

Jack Thompson, 61, actor (*The Chant of Jimmie Blacksmith, Breaker Morant*), born Sydney, Australia, Aug 31, 1940.

Glenn Tilbrook, 44, singer, musician, born London, England, Aug 31, 1957.

Noble Willingham, 70, actor (*Ace Ventura: Pet Detective, Up Close and Personal*), born Mineola, TX, Aug 31, 1931.

September.

SEPTEMBER 1 — SATURDAY
Day 244 — 121 Remaining

"ART LINKLETTER'S HOUSE PARTY" TV PRE-MIERE: ANNIVERSARY. Sept 1, 1952. Television's longest-running daytime variety show was hosted by Art Linkletter. This blend of talk and audience participation started on radio. In 1968 the show was renamed "The Linkletter Show." The series was well known for its daily interview with four schoolchildren.

BABY SAFETY MONTH. Sept 1–30. The Juvenile Products Manufacturers Association, Inc (JPMA), a national trade organization of juvenile product manufacturers devoted to helping parents keep baby safe, is disseminating information to parents, grandparents and other child caregivers about baby safety. The information from JPMA pertains to safe selection of juvenile products through the Association's Safety Certification Program and tips on correct use of products such as cribs, car seats, infant carriers and decorative accessories. For a free copy of JPMA's brochure "Safe and Sound for Baby," write to the address below and mark ATTN: JPMA Safety Brochure. Enclose a self-addressed stamped envelope and specify whether you want the brochure in English or Spanish. For info: JPMA, PR Dept, 236 Rte 38-W, Ste 100, Moorestown, NJ 08057.

BE KIND TO EDITORS AND WRITERS MONTH. Sept 1–30. A time for editors and writers to show uncommon courtesy toward each other. For info: Lauren Barnett, Lone Star Publications of Humor, 8452 Fredericksburg Rd, Ste 103, San Antonio, TX 78229. E-mail: lspubs@aol.com. Web: members.aol.com/lspubs/lsindex.html.

BRAZIL: INDEPENDENCE WEEK. Sept 1–7. The independence of Brazil from Portugal in 1822 is commemorated with civic and cultural ceremonies promoted by federal, state and municipal authorities. On Sept 7, a grand military parade takes place and the National Defense League organizes the Running Race in Honor of the Symbolic Torch of the Brazilian Nation.

BURROUGHS, EDGAR RICE: BIRTH ANNIVERSARY. Sept 1, 1875. US novelist (*Tarzan of the Apes*), born at Chicago, IL. Correspondent for the *Los Angeles Times*, died at Encino, CA, Mar 19, 1950.

CAL FARLEY'S BOYS RANCH RODEO. Sept 1–2. Boys Ranch, TX. From young stick-horse riders to more experienced bareback bronc riders, the two-day event provides recognition and rewards for children living at Boys Ranch, Girlstown, USA and Cal Farley's Family Program. Winners in each event are presented with rodeo belt buckles. Special awards are given to the

		S	M	T	W	T	F	S
September								1
2001		2	3	4	5	6	7	8
		9	10	11	12	13	14	15
		16	17	18	19	20	21	22
		23	24	25	26	27	28	29
		30						

All-Around Cowboy, the All-Around Cowgirl and the Junior All-Around Cowboy. Annually, Labor Day weekend. Est attendance: 10,000. For info: Jennifer Herber, PO Box 1890, Amarillo, TX 79174. Phone: (806) 372-2341. Fax: (806) 372-6638. E-mail: jherber@nts-online.net. Web: www.calfarleysboysranch.org.

CANADA: MAYNOOTH MADNESS AND LOGGERS GAMES. Sept 1–2. Maynooth, ON. An exciting, fun-filled weekend for the whole family, with loggers' games and parade, children's activities, petting zoo, pony rides and a craft show featuring original arts and crafts. Est attendance: 7,000. For info: Bancroft and District Chamber of Commerce, PO Box 539, Bancroft, ON, Canada K0L 1C0. Phone: (613) 332-1513. Fax: (613) 332-2119. E-mail: chamber@commerce.bancroft.on.ca. Web: www.commerce.bancroft.on.ca.

CARTIER, JACQUES: DEATH ANNIVERSARY. Sept 1, 1557. French navigator and explorer who sailed from St. Malo, France, Apr 20, 1534, in search of a northwest passage to the Orient. Instead, he discovered the St. Lawrence River, explored Canada's coastal regions and took possession of the country for France. Cartier was born at St. Malo, about 1491 (exact date unknown) and died there.

CHARLESTON DISTANCE RUN. Sept 1. Charleston, WV. Amateur 15-mile race of professional quality for residents and visitors. A 5K (3.1 miles) race also will be held. Est attendance: 1,500. For info: Danny Wells, Race Dir, Charleston Festival Commission, Inc, PO Box 11595, Charleston, WV 25339. Phone: (304) 348-6464 or (304) 348-5122. Fax: (304) 348-8034.

CHICKEN BOY'S BIRTHDAY. Sept 1. Chicken Boy is a 22-ft statue of a boy with a chicken's head, holding a bucket of chicken. Formerly the signage for the restaurant for which he is named, he was rescued from destruction when the restaurant went out of business by Future Studio of Los Angeles, a graphic design studio. Chicken Boy has since become a pop culture icon. (Some call him the Statue of Liberty of Los Angeles.) For info: Amy Inouye, Owner of Future Studio, PO Box 292000, Los Angeles, CA 90029. Phone: (323) 660-0620. Fax: (323) 660-2571.

CHILDREN'S EYE HEALTH AND SAFETY MONTH. Sept 1–30. Prevent Blindness America® directs its educational efforts to common causes of eye injuries and common eye problems among children. Materials that can easily be posted or distributed to the community will be provided. For info: Prevent Blindness America®, 500 E Remington Rd, Schaumburg, IL 60173. Phone: (800) 331-2020. Fax: (847) 843-8458. Web: www.preventblindness.org.

CHILDREN'S GOOD MANNERS MONTH. Sept 1–30. Starts the school year with a national program of teachers and parents encouraging good manners in children. The year-long program includes monthly objectives that work in conjunction with a reinforcing home program. For info: "Dr. Manners," Fleming Allaire, PhD, 35 Eastfield St, Manchester, CT 06040. Phone: (860) 643-0051.

CHILE: NATIONAL MONTH. Sept 1–30. A month of special significance in Chile: arrival of spring, a Day of Unity on the first Monday in September, Independence of Chile anniversary (proclaimed Sept 18, 1810) and celebration of the 1980 Constitution and Army Day, Sept 19.

CHRISTMAS SEAL CAMPAIGN®. Sept 1–Dec 31. An American tradition dating back to 1907 when the first Christmas Seals® were made available in the US, the annual campaign is a major support of American Lung Association programs dedicated to fighting lung diseases such as asthma, emphysema, tuberculosis and lung cancer, as well as their causes. For info: American Lung Assn, Media Relations, 1740 Broadway, New York, NY 10019-4374. Phone: (800) LUNG-USA or (212) 315-6473. Web: www.lungusa.org.

CLASSIC LABOR DAY WEEKEND. Sept 1–3. Steamboat Springs, CO. Vintage airplanes, pro bull riding, music and more. Est attendance: 15,000. For info: John Waldman, Special Events Coord, Steamboat Springs Chamber Resort Assn, PO Box

774408, Steamboat Springs, CO 80477. Phone: (970) 879-0880. Fax: (970) 879-2543. E-mail: info@steamboat-chamber.com. Web: www.steamboat-chamber.com.

CLEVELAND NATIONAL AIR SHOW. Sept 1–3. Burke Lakefront Airport, Cleveland, OH. Country's oldest air show, featuring extensive military and foreign aircraft participation. Est attendance: 80,000. For info: Cleveland Natl Air Show, Burke Lakefront Airport, Cleveland, OH 44114. Phone: (216) 781-0747. Fax: (216) 781-7810. E-mail: cknacle@aol.com. Web: www.clevelandairshow.com.

CLOTHESLINE FAIR. Sept 1–3. Prairie Grove Battlefield State Park, Prairie Grove, AR. 50th annual fair with more than 200 arts and crafts exhibitors; parade; folk, bluegrass, gospel and country music; square-dancing exhibitions and competitions; living history programs and tours. Annually, Labor Day weekend. Est attendance: 45,000. For info: Rhonda Escobedo, Prairie Grove Battlefield State Park, PO Box 306, Prairie Grove, AR 72753. Phone: (501) 846-2990. Fax: (501) 846-4035.

COLLEGE SAVINGS MONTH. Sept 1–30. Encourages families to plan ahead for the cost of college attendance. College savings programs make it easy and affordable for the average family to save and are available in most states. The programs offer affordable, flexible and tax-advantaged savings options that deliver the dream of education to our most precious resources—the children of America. Sponsored by the College Savings Plan Network of the National Association of State Treasurers. For info: College Savings Plan Network, PO Box 11910, Lexington, KY 40578-1910. Phone: (859) 244-8175. Fax: (859) 244-8053. E-mail: cspn@csg.org. Web: www.collegesavings.org.

COMMONWHEEL LABOR DAY WEEKEND ARTS AND CRAFTS FESTIVAL. Sept 1–3. Memorial Park, Manitou Springs, CO. 27th annual juried arts and crafts festival, featuring 100 fine artists and craftsmen and a variety of foods with continuous live entertainment ranging from Celtic harp music to jazz to mime. Est attendance: 20,000. For info: Commonwheel Artists Fair, PO Box 42, Manitou Springs, CO 80829. Phone: (719) 577-7700.

CULBERTSON WAGON TRAIN. Sept 1–2. Culbertson, MT. Hundreds arrive to live outdoors for two days and nights. Ride horseback or in covered wagon for miles over the open prairie. For info: Ida Mae Forbregd, PO Box 639, Culbertson, MT 59218.

DENMARK: AARHUS FESTIVAL WEEK. Sept 1–10. Observed from the first Saturday in September and for nine days after since 1965, with theater, ballet, opera, sports, exhibitions and special programs for children.

EASTERN IDAHO STATE FAIR. Sept 1–8. Blackfoot, ID. Family fun, amusement rides, food booths, entertainment, tractor pulls and more. Est attendance: 212,000. For info: Manager, Eastern Idaho State Fair, PO Box 250, Blackfoot, ID 83221. Phone: (208) 785-2480. Fax: (208) 785-2483. E-mail: theFair@ida.net. Web: www.Fair.ida.net.

EMMA M. NUTT DAY. Sept 1. A day to honor the first woman telephone operator, Emma M. Nutt, who reportedly began her professional career at Boston, MA, Sept 1, 1878, and continued working as a telephone operator for some 33 years.

EVERLY BROTHERS HOMECOMING. Sept 1. Central City, KY. The homecoming celebration features top artists. Est attendance: 20,000. For info: Everly Brothers Foundation, PO Box 309, Central City, KY 42330. Phone: (270) 754-2360. Fax: (270) 754-5745. Web: www.centralcityky.com.

FAIR AT NEW BOSTON. Sept 1–2. George Rogers Clark Park, Springfield, OH. An authentic re-creation of an 18th-century trades fair with period crafts, military encampments, food and entertainment. Annually, the Saturday and Sunday of Labor Day weekend. Est attendance: 12,000. For info: Fairmaster, George Rogers Clark Heritage Assn, PO Box 1251, Springfield, OH 45501. Phone: (937) 882-9216 or (937) 864-2526. E-mail: ruthrbp@aol.com.

FALL HAT MONTH. Sept 1–30. A month of celebration during which the straw hat is put aside in favor of the felt or fabric hat by both men and women. Local businesses and the media are encouraged to plan hat-related activities. For info: Casey Bush, Exec Dir, Headwear Info Bureau, 302 W 12 St, PH-C, New York, NY 10014. Phone: (212) 627-8333. Fax: (212) 627-0067. E-mail: milicase@aol.com. Web: www.hatsny.com/hib.

FRANKFORT FALL FESTIVAL. Sept 1–3. Frankfort, IL. One of the largest fine arts and crafts festivals in the Midwest. Annually, on Labor Day weekend. Est attendance: 200,000. For info: Lynne Doogan, Exec Dir, Frankfort Chamber of Commerce, 123 Kansas St, Frankfort, IL 60423. Phone: (877) 469-3356. Fax: (815) 469-4352. E-mail: Lynne@frankfortchamber.com. Web: www.frankfortchamber.com.

GERMANY: CAPITAL RETURNS TO BERLIN: ANNIVERSARY. Sept 1, 1999. In July the monthlong process of moving the German government from Bonn to Berlin began, eight years after Parliament had voted to return to its prewar seat. Berlin officially became the capital of Germany on Sept 1, 1999, and Parliament reconvened at the newly restored Reichstag on Sept 7, 1999.

HUG A TEXAS CHEF MONTH. Sept 1–30. Everybody knows when Texans set out to do something, they do it in a BIG, BIG way. This month shows a Texas-sized thanks to chefs across the Lone Star State. How? Simply lasso your favorite Texas chef with a heart-warming hug that says thanks for the vittles so good they make you want to throw down your hat and holler! For info: Texas Chefs Assn, 320 Kitty Hawk Rd, Ste 103, Universal City, TX 78148. Phone: (210) 566-5003. E-mail: TCA@texchef.org. Web: www.texchef.org.

INTERNATIONAL SELF AWARENESS MONTH. Sept 1–30. Cathcart Institute of La Jolla, CA, hosts this month each year to draw attention to the value of knowing oneself. Taking Socrates' advice "Know Thyself," this effort is targeted to identify, highlight and explore all the various means and models people use for improved understanding. Jim Cathcart, founder, is the author of *The Acorn Principle (Know Yourself–Grow Yourself)* and one of the premier professional speakers on self-awareness. For info: Jim Cathcart, Cathcart Institute, PO Box 9075, La Jolla, CA 92038-9075. Phone: (800) 222-4883. Fax: (858) 456-7218. E-mail: info@cathcart.com. Web: www.cathcart.com.

INTERNET SAFETY MONTH. Sept 1–30. Dedicated to the ideal of keeping children safe from harmful sites and information on the Internet. It is a month for parents to become more connected with their children through safe family surfing and visits to educational sites on the Internet. The first month of the school year is a good time for parents to show kids that the Internet can be fun without going to sites designated as "off limits." For info: Jessica R. Hart, Acct Exec, DindyCo Public Relations and Marketing, 139 NE 40th St, Ste 202, Miami, FL 33137.

JAPAN: KANTO EARTHQUAKE MEMORIAL DAY. Sept 1, 1923. A day to remember the 57,000 people who died during Japan's greatest earthquake.

JAPANESE FESTIVAL. Sept 1–3. Missouri Botanical Garden, St. Louis, MO. Japanese cultural activities including taiko (drumming), kabuki, bon odori festival dancing, bonsai demonstrations, martial arts, tea ceremonies, cooking demonstrations, contemporary clay works, craft demos, ikebana, karaoke, kimono fashion show, zen lectures and much more. Est attendance: 31,000. For info: Missouri Botanical Garden, 4344 Shaw Blvd, PO Box 299, St. Louis, MO 63166-0299. Phone: (314) 577-9400 or (800) 642-8842. Web: www.mobot.org.

JUBILEE DAYS FESTIVAL. Sept 1–3. Zion, IL. 52nd annual communitywide festival featuring arts and crafts, Queen's Pageant, Illinois's largest Labor Day parade and fireworks. Annually, Labor Day weekend. Est attendance: 10,000. For info: Jubilee Days Fest, Inc, Richard Walker, Exec Dir, PO Box 23, Zion, IL 60099. Phone: (847) 746-5500.

KANSAS CITY RENAISSANCE FESTIVAL. Sept 1–Oct 14. Bonner Springs, KS. Recreation of a 16th-century harvest fair featuring more than 160 artisans selling handcrafted wares and continuous entertainment on 12 stages. Food, special events and the Children's Realm are highlights. Est attendance: 200,000. For info: Director of PR, The Kansas City Renaissance Festival, PO Box 32667, Kansas City, MO 64171. Phone: (800) 373-0357. Fax: (816) 561-6493. E-mail: renfest@kcrenfest.com. Web: www.kcrenfest.com.

KOREAN AIR LINES FLIGHT 007 DISASTER: ANNIVERSARY. Sept 1, 1983. Korean Air Lines Flight 007, en route from New York, NY, to Seoul, Korea, reportedly strayed more than 100 miles off course, flying over secret Soviet military installations on the Kamchatka Peninsula and Sakhalin Island. Two and one half hours after it was said to have entered Soviet airspace, a Soviet interceptor plane destroyed the Boeing 747 with 269 persons on board which then crashed in the Sea of Japan. There were no survivors. President Reagan, in Proclamation 5093, named Sunday, Sept 11, 1983, as a National Day of Mourning as "homage to the memory of those who died."

LIBRARY CARD SIGN-UP MONTH. Sept 1–30. National effort to sign up every child for a library card. Annually, the month of September. For info: American Library Assn, Public Information Office, 50 E Huron St, Chicago, IL 60611. Phone: (312) 280-5043 or (312) 280-5042. E-mail: pio@ala.org. Web: www.ala.org.

LIBYA: REVOLUTION DAY. Sept 1. Commemorates the revolution in 1969 when King Idris I was overthrown by Colonel Qaddafi. National holiday.

LITTLE BALKANS DAYS/PAACA LITTLE BALKANS FOLKLIFE FESTIVAL. Sept 1–3. Pittsburg, KS. This event attracts more than 100 arts and crafts booths, is spread all over Pittsburg from the mall on the south to the Historical Museum on the north and in the parks in between. Contests, tournaments, food, live entertainment, street dances, displays and much more. Annually, Labor Day weekend. Est attendance: 40,000. For info: Little Balkans Festival Assn, PO Box 1115, Pittsburg, KS 66762. Phone: (316) 231-1000 or (800) 879-1212. Fax: (316) 231-3178. E-mail: cvb@pitton.com.

MARCIANO, ROCKY: BIRTH ANNIVERSARY. Sept 1, 1923. Rocky Marciano, boxer born Rocco Francis Marchegiano at Brockton, MA. Marciano used superb conditioning to fashion an impressive record that propelled him to fight against Jersey

Joe Walcott for the heavyweight title on Sept 23, 1952. Marciano knocked Walcott out and in 1956 he retired as the only undefeated heavyweight champion. Died in a plane crash at Newton, IA, Aug 31, 1969. The film *Somebody Up There Likes Me* recounts his life story.

MISSION SAN LUIS OBISPO DE TOLOSA: FOUNDING ANNIVERSARY. Sept 1, 1772. California mission to the Indians.

MISSOURI RIVER BLUEGRASS AND OLD-TIME MUSIC FESTIVAL. Sept 1–2. Cross Ranch State Park, Cross Ranch, ND. The location of this primitive state park along the Missouri River offers a perfect setting for a picking and fiddling get-together for local, regional and national bluegrass groups. Other activities include a children's fest with games and entertainment, gospel concerts and a Sunday church service. Est attendance: 3,000. For info: (701) 794-3731 or North Dakota Tourism, 604 East Boulevard, Bismarck, ND 58505. Phone: (701) 328-2525 or (800) 435-5663.

NATIONAL BISCUIT MONTH. Sept 1–30. To promote usage of biscuits in restaurants and other foodservice outlets. Biscuits are a classic American food, good at any time of day—morning, noon or night. They're great alone and make a perfect partner to all sorts of dishes. For info: Tom O'Brien, Bakery Chef, Inc. Phone: (312) 372-6142.

NATIONAL CHICKEN MONTH. Sept 1–30. Focuses consumer attention on chicken as the most nutritious, convenient, economical and versatile food available; in short, "America's favorite." For info: Bill Roenigk, Sr VP, Natl Chicken Council, 1015 15th St NW, Ste 930, Washington, DC 20005. Phone: (202) 296-2622. Fax: (202) 293-4005. E-mail: WRoenigk@chickenUSA.org.

NATIONAL CHILDHOOD INJURY PREVENTION WEEK. Sept 1–7. To stress the importance of community involvement in protecting the nation's children from harm. Accidental injuries are the #1 killer of children in the US. More alarming . . . most of these accidents are preventable. Organized by The As Safe As Possible Campaign, a not-for-profit organization, and sponsored by Safety By Design®, our program reflects the belief that the foundation for broad-based participation must be built at the community level. The program has both a national and a regional focus. With the primary purpose of raising the awareness of parents, grandparents and caregivers, our campaign is energized by the belief that you can do well by doing good. Assistance is available for devising a program to reflect each participant's individual tie-in with the promotion of child safety. For info: The Safe As Possible Campaign, PO Box 4312, Great Neck, NY 11023. E-mail: KidzSafT@aol.com or noboohoos@aol.com. Web: www.AsSafeAsPossible.com.

NATIONAL CHOLESTEROL EDUCATION MONTH. Sept 1–30. Promoting education about and treatment of high blood cholesterol. Annually, the month of September. For info: Info Center Mgr, Natl Heart, Lung and Blood Institute, Natl Cholesterol Education Program, PO Box 30105, Bethesda, MD 20824-0105. Phone: (301) 592-8573. Fax: (301) 592-8563. E-mail: NHLBIinfo@rover.nhlbi.nih.gov. Web: www.nhlbi.nih.gov/nhlbi/nhlbi.htm.

September 2001	S	M	T	W	T	F	S
							1
	2	3	4	5	6	7	8
	9	10	11	12	13	14	15
	16	17	18	19	20	21	22
	23	24	25	26	27	28	29
	30						

NATIONAL COUPON MONTH. Sept 1–30. Sponsored by the Coupon Council of the Promotional Marketing Association and celebrates the nearly four billion dollar savings American consumers receive each year by redeeming coupons for their favorite brands. Contests and fun activities are planned on a national level to raise the awareness of coupons and their redemption value. For info: Lynn Liddle, Valassis Communications, 19775 Victor Parkway, Livonia, MI 47152. Phone: (734) 591-7374. Fax: (734) 591-4503. E-mail: lliddle@valassis.com. Web: www.couponmonth.com.

NATIONAL HONEY MONTH. Sept 1–30. To honor the US's 211,600 beekeepers and 2.63 million colonies of honeybees, which produce more than 220 million pounds of honey each year. For info: Natl Honey Bd, 390 Lashley St, Longmont, CO 80501-6045. Phone: (303) 776-2337. Web: www.honey.com.

NATIONAL LITTLE LEAGUE MONTH. Sept 1–30. Celebrate the lessons learned in Little League: what to do when: (1) life is not fair, (2) the umpire makes a bad call or (3) you have to sit on the bench. Use this month to encourage Little Leaguers and reinforce the life skills that are there to be acquired. For info: Karla Brandau, Life Power Dynamics, 4985 Chartley Circle, Lilburn, GA 30047. Phone: (770) 923-0883. Fax: (770) 931-2530. E-mail: karla@karlaspeaks.com. Web: www.karlaspeaks.com.

NATIONAL MUSHROOM MONTH. Sept 1–30. To promote the greater appreciation and use of cultivated mushrooms. For info: Ruth Lowenberg, Lewis & Neale, Inc, 49 E 21st St, New York, NY 10010. Phone: (212) 420-8808. Fax: (212) 254-2452. E-mail: laneale@aol.com. Web: www.mushroomcouncil.com.

NATIONAL ORGANIC HARVEST MONTH. Sept 1–30. National celebration to educate all ages about organic agriculture and products sponsored by Organic Trade Association. Local and regional events organized by retailers, manufacturers, distributors and consumer groups include food fairs, tastings, farm tours, cooking demonstrations and meet-the-farmer days. Annually, the month of September. For info: Holly Givens, Organic Trade Assn, PO Box 547, Greenfield, MA 01302. Phone: (413) 774-7511. Fax: (413) 774-6432. E-mail: info@ota.com.

NATIONAL PIANO MONTH. Sept 1–30. Recognizes America's most popular instrument and its more than 20 million players; also encourages piano study by people of all ages. For info: Donald W. Dillon, Exec Dir, Natl Piano Foundation, 4020 McEwen, Ste 105, Dallas, TX 75244-5019. Phone: (972) 233-9107. Fax: (972) 490-4219. E-mail: don@dondillon.com. Web: www.pianonet.com.

NATIONAL RICE MONTH. Sept 1–30. To focus attention on the importance of rice to the American diet and to salute the US rice industry. For info: Molly Johnson, Mgr Retail Trade Development, USA Rice Federation, PO Box 740123, Houston, TX 77274. Phone: (713) 270-6699. Fax: (713) 270-9021. Web: www.usarice.com.

NATIONAL SCHOOL SUCCESS MONTH. Sept 1–30. Today's young people have many distractions from school and are sometimes overwhelmed when it comes to academics. Parents are often unskilled at effectively redirecting the attention of their children, especially their teenagers. This observance is to recognize parents who want to support and encourage their children to succeed in school and to explore ways to do that. Annually, the month of September. For info send SASE to: Teresa Langston, Dir, Parenting Without Pressure, 1330 Boyer St, Longwood, FL 32750-6311. Phone: (407) 767-2524.

NATIONAL SEWING MONTH. Sept 1–30. Celebrates the art, craft and hobby of sewing. The month-long celebration includes special sales, promotions and education programs directed at increased awareness for sewing. For info: Home Sewing Assn, 1350 Broadway, Ste 1601, New York, NY 10018. Phone: (212) 714-1633. E-mail: ccampbell@sewing.org. Web: www.sewing.org.

NATIONAL SICKLE CELL MONTH. Sept 1–30. For info: Ralph D. Sutton, Deputy Dir, Sickle Cell Disease Assn of America (SCDAA), 200 Corporate Pointe, Ste 495, Culver City, CA 90230-7633. Phone: (800) 421-8453 or (310) 216-6363. Web: www.SickleCellDisease.org.

NATIONAL STORYTELLER OF THE YEAR CONTEST. Sept 1. Millersport, OH. Official Storyteller of the Year named at this event. Sponsored by the Creative Arts Institute, Inc, Adventures in Storytelling Magazine and the Ohio Arts Council. Annually, the Saturday before Labor Day. Est attendance: 500. For info: Donna Foster, Creative Arts, 8021 Kennedy Rd, Blacklick, OH 43004. Phone: (614) 759-9407. Fax: (614) 759-8480. E-mail: dfoster@gcfn.org.

NATIONAL YOUTH PASTORS APPRECIATION MONTH. Sept 1–30. To celebrate and honor the significant role of the youth pastor and youth worker in local churches across the country. Sponsored by Youth Specialties and Zondervan Publishing House. For info: Public Relations, Zondervan Publishing House, 5300 Patterson Ave SE, Grand Rapids, MI 49530. Phone: (616) 698-6900 or (800) 9-BOOK IT. Fax: (616) 698-3223. E-mail: public.relations@zph.com. Web: www.zondervan.com/ or www.youthspecialties.com.

ODYSSEY—A GREEK FESTIVAL. Sept 1–4. Orange, CT. An indoor/outdoor festival celebrating Greek culture, featuring authentic Greek cuisine, live music and marketplace. For info: St. Barbara Greek Orthodox Church, 480 Racebrook Rd, Orange, CT 06477. Phone: (203) 795-1347 or Greater New Haven Conv & Visitors Bureau, One Long Wharf Dr, New Haven, CT, 06511. Phone: (203) 777-8550 or (800) 332-STAY. Fax: (203) 782-7755.

OLDE-TIME ANTIQUES AND COLLECTIBLES FAIRE. Sept 1. Toms River, NJ. More than 100 dealers, appraisals, glass repair, displays and demonstrations and museum exhibits. Free admission. 17th annual. Est attendance: 5,000. For info: Ocean County Historical Soc, PO Box 2191, 26 Hadley Ave, Toms River, NJ 08754-2191. Phone: (732) 341-1880. Fax: (732) 341-4372.

OREGON TRAIL RODEO. Sept 1–3. Hastings, NE. PRCA-sponsored rodeo. Annually, Saturday–Monday of Labor Day weekend. Est attendance: 6,500. For info: Sandy Himmelberg, Genl Mgr, Oregon Trail Rodeo, 947 S Baltimore, Hastings, NE 68901. Phone: (402) 462-3247. Fax: (402) 462-4731. Web: www.adamscountyfairgrounds.com.

OVARIAN CANCER AWARENESS MONTH. Sept 1–30. For info: Natl Ovarian Cancer Coalition, PO Box 4472, Boca Raton, FL 33429-4472. Phone: (888) OVARIÁN.

PICATINNY PEAK FALL HAWKWATCH. Sept 1–Dec 1. Picatinny Arsenal, Dover, NJ. Fall hawkwatch to count migrating raptors. Between 9,000 and 12,000 raptors per year are counted. Member site of Hawk Migration Association of North America (HMANA). Annually, Sept 1 through Dec 1. For info: John J. Reed, 31 Croft Rd, Lake Hopatcong, NJ 07849-1023. Phone: (201) 724-2703. E-mail: eagle76@bellatlantic.net.

PLEASURE YOUR MATE MONTH. Sept 1–30. To promote love and show appreciation to your mate. Look for new ways to create happiness together. Use this event to establish a lifelong habit of sharing pleasure. Annually, the month of September. For info: Donald Etkes, PhD, PMB 148, 112 Harvard Ave, Claremont, CA 91711. Phone: (909) 981-7333.

POWERS' CROSSROADS COUNTRY FAIR AND ART FESTIVAL. Sept 1–3. Newnan, GA. 300 top US and Canadian artists and craftsmen. Old plantation skills revived including using a gristmill, entertainment, country music and down-home country cooking. Est attendance: 60,000. For info: Coweta Festivals, Inc, 4766 W Hwy 34, Newnan, GA 30263. Phone: (770) 253-2011. Fax: (770) 253-8180.

REUTHER, WALTER PHILIP: BIRTH ANNIVERSARY. Sept 1, 1907. American labor leader who began work in a steel factory at age 16 and later became president of the United Automobile Workers (UAW) and the Congress of Industrial Organizations (CIO). Born at Wheeling, WV, Reuther worked for two years in a Russian automobile factory. Often at the center of controversy, he was the target of an assassin in 1948. Reuther and his wife died in an airplane crash May 9, 1970, at Black Lake, MI. The UAW Family Education Center, a project which he had cherished, was later named for Walter and May Reuther.

RIVERWALK FESTIVAL. Sept 1. Riverwalk Plaza, Lowell, MI. A fun-filled family day with arts and crafts, parade, food booths, live entertainment all day long, children's area and a duck race on the Flat River. 10 AM–5 PM. Est attendance: 7,000. For info: Liz Baker, Lowell Area Chamber of Commerce, PO Box 224, Lowell, MI 49331. Phone: (616) 897-9161. Fax: (616) 897-9101.

SCOTLAND: BRAEMAR ROYAL HIGHLAND GATHERING. Sept 1. Princess Royal and Duke of Fife Memorial Park, Braemar, Grampian. Kilted clansmen from all over the world gather. Traditional activities including tossing cabers, dancing and playing bagpipes. Est attendance: 18,000. For info: Mr W.A. Meston, Coilacriech, Ballater, Aberdeenshire, Scotland AB35 5UH. Phone: (44) (133) 975-5377.

SEA CADET MONTH. Sept 1–30. Nationwide year-round youth program for boys and girls 11–17 teaches leadership and self-discipline with emphasis on nautically oriented training without military obligation. Est attendance: 9,000. For info: US Naval Sea Cadet Corps, 2300 Wilson Blvd, Arlington, VA 22201. Phone: (703) 243-6910. Fax: (703) 243-3985. E-mail: mford@NAVY LEAGUE.org. Web: www.seacadets.org.

SELF-IMPROVEMENT MONTH. Sept 1–30. To disseminate information about the importance of lifelong learning and self-improvement. For complete information and lists of books, materials and cassettes, send $4 to cover expense of printing, handling and postage. Annually, the month of September. For info: Dr. Stanley Drake, Pres, Intl Soc of Friendship and Good Will, 8592 Roswell Rd, Ste 434, Atlanta, GA 30350-1870.

SELF-UNIVERSITY WEEK. Sept 1–7. Reminds adults (in or out of school) that each of us has a responsibility to help shape the future by pursuing life-long learning. Committed to self-education as the lifeblood of democracy and the key to living life to its fullest. Dedicated to furthering education not as something you get but as something you take. We assert that America's greatest treasures are found not in our shopping malls but in our libraries. Annually, the first seven days of September. For info: Charles Hayes, Publisher, Autodidactic Press, PO Box 872749, Wasilla, AK 99687. Phone: (907) 376-2932. Fax: (907) 376-2932. E-mail: autpress@alaska.net. Web: www.autodidactic.com.

SHAMELESS PROMOTION MONTH. Sept 1–30. This is the month for you to go out and promote yourself, your business, your book or your product shamelessly. For outrageous tips, visit our website. For info: Marisa D'Vari, PO Box 413, Boston, MA 02117. Phone: (617) 351-2279. E-mail: mdvari@msn.com. Web: www.deg.com.

SIGOURNEY, LYDIA: BIRTH ANNIVERSARY. Sept 1, 1791. Prolific American author, Lydia Howard Huntley Sigourney was born at Norwich, CT. Her writings, mainly moral and religious works, included such titles as *How to Be Happy, Letters to Young Ladies* and *Pleasant Memories of Pleasant Lands*. She wrote more than 65 books before her death June 10, 1865, at Hartford, CT.

SLOVAKIA: NATIONAL DAY. Sept 1. Anniversary of the adoption of the Constitution of the Slovak Republic in 1992.

SNOWBIRD OKTOBERFEST. Sept 1–3. Snowbird, UT. (Also Sept 8–9, Sept 15–16, Sept 22–23, Sept 29–30, Oct 6–7) Festival includes traditional European music, shopping, dancing and food. For info: Snowbird & Ski Summer Resort, Snowbird, UT 84092. Phone: (801) 742-2222. Fax: (801) 933-2298.

SOUTHERN GOSPEL MUSIC MONTH. Sept 1–30. To promote the growth, enjoyment and awareness nationwide of Southern Gospel music, a cherished American art form, by promoting radio airplay, concert attendance and retail awareness. For info: Southern Gospel Music Guild, PO Box 1372, Lancaster, PA 17608-1372. Phone: (717) 898-6806. Fax: (717) 898-6600. E-mail: SGMGuild@aol.com.

STA-BIL NATIONALS CHAMPIONSHIP LAWN MOWER RACE. Sept 1. Greenfield, IN. Five classes of races for winners of regional races held across the US. Mowers will travel at speeds ranging from 10 mph to more than 50 mph. Est attendance: 2,000. For info: US Lawn Mower Racing Assn, 1812 Glenview Rd, Glenview, IL 60025. Phone: (847) 729-7363. E-mail: letsmow@aol.com. Web: www.letsmow.com/

SUBLIMINAL MARKETING MONTH. Sept 1–30. Not getting the results you want? Make a change for the positive and learn how to maximize your effectiveness. Uncover "hidden profits and opportunities." Turn your goals into realities. Learn how to put to use your entrepreneurial thinking to achieve your goals and increase your visibility socially or in the corporate world. Recognize and apply prosperity-building opportunities for increasing your networking, marketing and publicity goals through the use of color, scents and language. For info send a LSASE to: Lorrie Walters Marsiglio, Lorimar Communications, PO Box 284-CC, Wasco, IL 60183-0284. Phone: (630) 584-9368.

TAIWAN: CHENG CHENG KUNG BIRTH ANNIVERSARY. Sept 1. Joyous celebration of birth of Cheng Cheng Kung (Koxinga), born at Hirado, Japan, the Ming Dynasty loyalist who ousted the Dutch colonists from Taiwan in 1661. Dutch landing is commemorated annually Apr 29, but Cheng's birthday is honored on the 14th day of the seventh moon according to the Chinese lunar calendar. Cheng Cheng Kung died June 23, 1662, at Taiwan. See also: "Taiwan: Cheng Cheng Kung Landing Day" (Apr 29).

	S	M	T	W	T	F	S
September							1
2001	2	3	4	5	6	7	8
	9	10	11	12	13	14	15
	16	17	18	19	20	21	22
	23	24	25	26	27	28	29
	30						

TASTE OF MADISON. Sept 1–2. Capitol Concourse, Madison, WI. Food and entertainment fest, including booths from more than 60 restaurants, five stages, waiters' race and Kiddie Korner. Est attendance: 175,000. For info: Madison Festivals, Inc, 7818 Big Sky Dr, Ste 205, Madison, WI 53719. Phone: (608) 831-1725. Fax: (608) 831-1727. Web: www.madfest.org.

TOOLS AND SKILLS THAT BUILT THE COLONY. Sept 1. Wormsloe Historic Site, Savannah, GA. Living history demonstrations relating to the tools and skills that were used to build the colony. These will include woodworking, blacksmithing, spinning, candlemaking and more. Museum, film and trails. 11–4. Est attendance: 500. For info: Wormsloe State Historic Site, 7601 Skidaway Rd, Savannah, GA 31406. Phone: (912) 353-3023.

TOOLS OF THE TRADE. Sept 1–30. Jamestown Settlement, Williamsburg, VA and Yorktown Victory Center, Yorktown, VA. Discover tools and technology of the 17th and 18th centuries, from the navigation instruments that led English colonists to the New World to the medical instruments used to treat injured soldiers in the Revolutionary War. For info: Jamestown-Yorktown Foundation, PO Box 1607, Williamsburg, VA 23187. Phone: (757) 253-4838 or (888) 593-4682. Web: www.historyisfun.org.

TWITTY, CONWAY: BIRTH ANNIVERSARY. Sept 1, 1933. Country and western music star who began his career as a rock 'n'roll performer in the style of Elvis Presley, born at Friars Point, MS. Died June 5, 1993, at Springfield, MO.

UZBEKISTAN: INDEPENDENCE DAY: 10th ANNIVERSARY. Sept 1. National holiday. Commemorates independence from the Soviet Union in 1991.

WESTFEST. Sept 1–2. West, TX. West celebrates its Czech heritage with folk dances, Czech pastries, sausage, polka music, arts and crafts, children's area, 5K run, parade. Est attendance: 40,000. For info: Westfest, Box 65, West, TX 76691. Phone: (254) 826-5058. Web: www.westfest.com.

WILHELM TELL FESTIVAL. Sept 1–3. New Glarus, WI. Presentation of Schiller's Wilhelm Tell drama in German and English in natural outdoor theater. Alpine festival with Swiss entertainment. Annually, Labor Day weekend. Est attendance: 2,000. For info: New Glarus Chamber, PO Box 713, New Glarus, WI 53574. Phone: (800) 527-6838. E-mail: wilhelmtell@swisstown.com.

WORLD CHAMPIONSHIP BARBECUE GOAT COOK-OFF AND ARTS AND CRAFTS FAIR. Sept 1. Richards Park, Brady, TX. 28th annual cook-off to promote Brady/McCulloch County and the sheep and goat industry. Arts and crafts fair featuring local and statewide artists. Est attendance: 17,000. For info: Brady/McCulloch County Chamber of Commerce, 101 E First St, Brady, TX 76825. Phone: (915) 597-3491. Fax: (915) 597-2420. E-mail: evpcofc@centex.net. Web: www.bradytx.com.

BIRTHDAYS TODAY

Yvonne De Carlo (Peggy Yvonne Middleton), 79, actress ("The Munsters," *Salome*), born Vancouver, British Columbia, Canada, Sept 1, 1922.

Alan Dershowitz, 63, attorney, author, born Brooklyn, NY, Sept 1, 1938.

Gloria Estefan, 44, singer (Miami Sound Machine, "Don't Want to Lose You"), born Havana, Cuba, Sept 1, 1957.

Barry Gibb, 55, singer (with the Bee Gees, "Staying Alive"), songwriter, born Manchester, England, Sept 1, 1946.

Timothy Duane (Tim) Hardaway, 35, basketball player, born Chicago, IL, Sept 1, 1966.

Ron O'Neal, 64, actor (*Super Fly, Red Dawn*; stage: *No Place to Be Somebody* [Obie Award]), born Utica, NY, Sept 1, 1937.

Seiji Ozawa, 66, conductor, born Hoten, Japan, Sept 1, 1935.

Don Stroud, 64, actor ("Mike Hammer," *The Buddy Holly Story, License to Kill*), born Honolulu, HI, Sept 1, 1937.

Lily Tomlin, 62, actress ("Laugh-In," *The Search for Signs of Intelligent Life in the Universe*), born Detroit, MI, Sept 1, 1939.

SEPTEMBER 2 — SUNDAY

Day 245 — 120 Remaining

BELGIUM: FLANDERS FESTIVAL. Sept 2–Oct 15. Gent, Belgium. Featuring ancient music, classical music and choral music. For info: Sophie Cocquyt, Klein Gentstraat 46, Gent, Belgium B-9051. Phone: 32 (0) 9-243-94-94. Fax: 32 (0) 9-243-94-90. E-mail: sophiec@festival._von_vlaandaen.be.

BISON-TEN-YELL DAY. Sept 2. Honoring the "bicentennial" of the birth of Bison-Ten-Yell, imaginary inventor of a set of ten battle yells as signals, based on the traditional memory aid system eventually adopted by football players. For info: Bob Birch, Grand Punscorpion, Puns Corps, Box 2364, Falls Church, VA 22042-0364. Phone: (703) 533-3668.

CALENDAR ADJUSTMENT DAY: ANNIVERSARY. Sept 2. Pursuant to the British Calendar Act of 1751, Britain (and the American colonies) made the "Gregorian Correction" in 1752. The Act proclaimed that the day following Wednesday, Sept 2, should become Thursday, Sept 14, 1752. There was rioting in the streets by those who felt cheated and who demanded the eleven days back. The Act also provided that New Year's Day (and the change of year number) should fall Jan 1 (instead of Mar 25) in 1752 and every year thereafter. As a result, 1751 only had 282 days. See also: "Gregorian Calendar Adjustment: Anniversary" (Feb 24, Oct 4).

CANADA: GREAT KLONDIKE INTERNATIONAL OUTHOUSE RACE AND BATHROOM WALL LIMERICK CONTEST. Sept 2. Dawson City, YT. Crazy race of outhouses on wheels over a 1.5-mile course through the streets of downtown Dawson City. Awards presentation at Diamond Tooth Gertie's gambling hall following the race. Est attendance: 500. For info: Klondike Visitors Assn, PO Box 389V, Dawson City, YT, Canada Y0B 1G0. Phone: (867) 993-5575. Fax: (867) 993-6415. E-mail: kva@dawson.net. Web: www.dawsoncity.com.

CHEETAH RUN. Sept 2. Cincinnati Zoo, OH. The Cheetah Run is a 2.5-mile course throughout the beautiful zoo grounds. The race is followed by a Fun Run for children around Swan Lake. An awards ceremony follows the race. Est attendance: 1,500. For info: Events and Promotions Dept, Cincinnati Zoo and Botanical Garden, 3400 Vine St, Cincinnati, OH 45220. Phone: (513) 281-4701. Fax: (513) 559-7790. Web: www.cincyzoo.org.

CHINA: FESTIVAL OF HUNGRY GHOSTS. Sept 2. According to Chinese legend, during the 7th lunar month the souls of the dead are released from purgatory to roam the Earth. Joss sticks are burnt in homes; prayers, food and "ghost money" are offered to appease the ghosts. Market stallholders combine to hold celebrations to ensure that their businesses will prosper in the coming year. Wayang (Chinese street opera) and puppet shows are performed, and fruit and Chinese delicacies are offered to the spirits. Observed on the 15th day of the 7th lunar month.

DAYS OF MARATHON: ANNIVERSARY. Sept 2–9, 490 BC. Anniversary of the event during the Persian Wars from which the marathon race is derived. Phidippides, "an Athenian and by profession and practice a trained runner," according to Herodotus, was dispatched from Marathon to Sparta (26 miles), Sept 2 to seek help in repelling the invading Persian army. Help being unavailable by religious law until after the next full moon, Phidippides ran the 26 miles back to Marathon Sept 4. Without Spartan aid, the Athenians defeated the Persians at the Battle of Marathon Sept 9. According to legend Phidippides carried the news of the battle to Athens and died as he spoke the words, "Rejoice, we are victorious." The marathon race was revived at the 1896 Olympic Games at Athens. Course distance, since 1924, is 26 miles, 385 yards. See also: "Battle of Marathon: Anniversary" (Sept 9).

ENGLAND: GREAT FIRE OF LONDON: ANNIVERSARY. Sept 2–5, 1666 (OS). The fire generally credited with bringing about our system of fire insurance started Sept 2, 1666 (OS), in the wooden house of a baker named Farryner, at London's Pudding Lane, near the Tower. During the ensuing three days more than 13,000 houses were destroyed, though it is believed that only six lives were lost in the fire.

FIREWORKS DISPLAY. Sept 2. On the banks of the Ohio River, Cincinnati, OH. Nationally acclaimed 30-minute display of fireworks with a synchronized soundtrack broadcast on WEBN 102.7 FM. Blast-off is at 9:05 PM concluding the Riverfest activities. Sponsored by Toyota and WEBN-FM. Annually, the Sunday before Labor Day. Est attendance: 500,000. For info: WEBN-FM, 1111 Saint Gregory St, Cincinnati, OH 45202. Phone: (513) 621-9326. Fax: (513) 784-1249.

FORTEN, JAMES: BIRTH ANNIVERSARY. Sept 2, 1766. James Forten was born of free black parents at Philadelphia, PA. As a powder boy on an American Revolutionary warship, he escaped being sold as a slave when his ship was captured due to the intervention of the son of the British commander. While in England he became involved with abolitionists. On his return to Philadelphia, he became an apprentice to a sailmaker and eventually purchased the company for which he worked. He was active in the abolition movement, and in 1816 his support was sought by the American Colonization Society for the plan to settle American blacks at Liberia. He rejected their ideas and their plans to make him the ruler of the colony. From the large profits of his successful sailmaking company, he contributed heavily to the abolitionist movement and was a supporter of William Lloyd Garrison's anti-slavery journal, *The Liberator.* Died at Philadelphia, PA, Mar 4, 1842.

FOX VALLEY FOLK FEST. Sept 2–3. Geneva, IL. Music, dance and storytelling festival. Features food, folk art, concerts, jam sessions and an old-time community barn dance. For info: Fox Valley Folklore Society, 755 N Evanslawn Ave, Aurora, IL 60506-1905.

HARVEST WINE CELEBRATION. Sept 2–3. Livermore, CA. The Harvest Wine Celebration is an open-house event offering the public an opportunity to visit 15 wineries, listen to live music, sample wines, learn more about this historic wine region and shop for arts and crafts. Shuttle bus service is available between the wineries. Annually, Labor Day weekend. Est attendance: 10,000. For info: Erlinda Dearborn, Livermore Valley Winegrowers Assn, 1984 Railroad Ave, Ste A, Livermore, CA 94550. Phone: (925) 447-9463. Fax: (925) 447-0433. E-mail: lvwa@dnai.com. Web: www.livermorewine.com.

	S	M	T	W	T	F	S
September							1
2001	2	3	4	5	6	7	8
	9	10	11	12	13	14	15
	16	17	18	19	20	21	22
	23	24	25	26	27	28	29
	30						

IRANIAN EARTHQUAKE: ANNIVERSARY. Sept 2, 1962. Iran's biggest earthquake since 1775 destroyed 31 villages covering 8,000 square miles. More than 10,000 people died in the massive quake, 10,000 were injured and 25,000 people were left homeless.

ITALY: HISTORICAL REGATTA. Sept 2. Venice. Traditional competition among two-oar racing gondolas, preceded by a procession of Venetian ceremonial boats of the epoch of the Venetian Republic. Annually, the first Sunday in September.

ITALY: JOUST OF THE SARACEN. Sept 2. Arezzo. The first Sunday in September is set aside for the Giostra del Saracino, a tilting contest of the 13th century, with knights in armor.

JEWISH RENAISSANCE FAIR. Sept 2 (rain date Sept 3). Liberty State Park, Jersey City, NJ. Simultaneous stages of theater, music and comedy all day long, the artists' quarter, cafes and restaurants, arts and crafts expo, carnival games, golf course and storybook hay ride. Star-studded show on main stage late in the day. Annually, the Sunday of Labor Day weekend. Est attendance: 10,000. For info: Rabbi Boruch Klar, Dir of Community Outreach, Rabbinical College of America, 456 Pleasant Valley Way, West Orange, NJ 07052. Phone: (973) 731-0770. Web: www.jewishfair.com.

McAULIFFE, CHRISTA: BIRTH ANNIVERSARY. Sept 2, 1948. Christa McAuliffe, a 37-year-old Concord, NH, high school teacher, was to have been the first "ordinary citizen" in space. Born Sharon Christa Corrigan at Boston, MA, she perished with six crew members in the Space Shuttle *Challenger* explosion Jan 28, 1986. See also: "Challenger Space Shuttle Explosion: Anniversary" (Jan 28).

MOON PHASE: FULL MOON. Sept 2. Moon enters Full Moon phase at 5:43 PM, EDT.

NATIONAL RELIGIOUS REFERENCE BOOKS WEEK. Sept 2–8. To commemorate the role reference books, such as concordances, commentaries, atlases and dictionaries, play in biblical studies. Annually, the first week of September. For info: Public Relations, Zondervan Publishing House, 5300 Patterson Ave SE, Grand Rapids, MI 49530. Phone: (616) 698-6900 or (800) 9-BOOK IT. Fax: (616) 698-3223. E-mail: public.relations@zph.com. Web: www.zondervan.com/academic.

RIVERFEST FEATURING THE TOYOTA/WEBN FIREWORKS. Sept 2. Cincinnati, OH and northern Kentucky. Three-city end-of-summer celebration; entertainment on six stages. The event is capped off with one of the country's best fireworks displays. Est attendance: 500,000. For info: Rob Schoonover, Event Producer, Clear Channel Communications,

Inc, 1111 St. Gregory St, Cincinnati, OH 45202. Phone: (513) 852-1657. Fax: (513) 333-4269. E-mail: robschoonover@clear channel.com.

SCANDINAVIAN FEST. Sept 2. Waterloo Village, Stanhope, NJ. Celebrate and sample the cultures, traditions and contemporary life of the Nordic countries: Denmark, Estonia, Finland, Iceland, Norway and Sweden through food, entertainment, music, dancing, handicrafts and lectures. Est attendance: 6,000. For info: Carl Anderson, PO Box 5103, Bethlehem, PA 18015. Phone: (610) 868-7525. E-mail: info@ScanFest.org. Web: www.ScanFest.org.

SEPTEMBER SKIRMISH. Sept 2–3. Point Mallard, Decatur, AL. Staged in honor of local Confederate generals John Hunt Morgan and Joe Wheeler. More than 200 authentically clad Yankee and Rebel soldiers meet in daily battles. Visitors may join a young recruit and follow his life as a soldier during the Candlelight Camp Tour on Saturday night or join the Civil War roundtable discussion. Est attendance: 1,000. For info: Jacklyn Bailey, Decatur Conv/Visitors Bureau, 719 6th Ave SE, PO Box 2349, Decatur, AL 35602. Phone: (205) 350-2028 or (800) 524-6181. E-mail: dcvb@hiwaay.net.

SHERMAN ENTERS ATLANTA: ANNIVERSARY. Sept 2, 1864. After a four-week siege, Union General William Tecumseh Sherman entered Atlanta, GA. The city had been evacuated on the previous day by Confederate troops under General John B. Hood. Hood had mistakenly assumed Sherman was ending the siege Aug 27, when actually Sherman was beginning the final stages of his attack. Hood then sent troops to attack the Union forces at Jonesboro. Hood's troops were defeated, opening the way for the capture of Atlanta.

US TREASURY DEPARTMENT: ANNIVERSARY. Sept 2, 1789. The third presidential cabinet department, the Treasury Department, was established by Congress.

V-J DAY: ANNIVERSARY. Sept 2, 1945. Official ratification of Japanese surrender to the Allies occurred aboard the USS *Missouri* at Tokyo Bay Sept 2 (Far Eastern time) in 1945, thus prompting President Truman's declaration of this day as Victory-over-Japan Day. Japan's initial, informal agreement of surrender was announced by Truman and celebrated in the US Aug 14.

VIETNAM: INDEPENDENCE DAY: ANNIVERSARY. Sept 2. Ho Chi Minh formally proclaimed the independence of Vietnam from France and the establishment of the Democratic Republic of Vietnam on this day in 1945. National holiday.

BIRTHDAYS TODAY

Nathaniel ("Tiny") Archibald, 53, Basketball Hall of Fame guard, born New York, NY, Sept 2, 1948.

Terry Paxton Bradshaw, 53, sportscaster, Pro Football Hall of Fame quarterback, born Shreveport, LA, Sept 2, 1948.

Marge Champion, 78, dancer, actress ("Marge and Gower Champion Show," *Show Boat*), born Los Angeles, CA, Sept 2, 1923.

Jimmy Connors, 49, former tennis player, born East St. Louis, IL, Sept 2, 1952.

Eric Demetric Dickerson, 41, Pro Football Hall of Fame running back, born Sealy, TX, Sept 2, 1960.

Mark Harmon, 50, actor ("St. Elsewhere," "Chicago Hope"), born Burbank, CA, Sept 2, 1951.

Salma Hayek, 35, actress (*Fools Rush In, Frida*), born Veracruz, Mexico, Sept 2, 1966.

Linda Purl, 46, actress ("Happy Days," "Matlock"), born Greenwich, CT, Sept 2, 1955.

Keanu Reeves, 37, actor (*Bill and Ted's Excellent Adventure, My Own Private Idaho, Speed*), born Beirut, Lebanon, Sept 2, 1964.

John Thompson, 60, college basketball coach, former player, born Washington, DC, Sept 2, 1941.

Peter Victor Ueberroth, 64, former commissioner of baseball and Olympic organizer, born Evanston, IL, Sept 2, 1937.

Carlos Valderrama, 40, soccer player, born Santa Marta, Colombia, Sept 2, 1961.

SEPTEMBER 3 — MONDAY
Day 246 — 119 Remaining

AMATI, NICOLO: BIRTH ANNIVERSARY. Sept 3, 1596. Celebrated Italian violin maker, born at Cremona, Italy and died there Aug 12, 1684.

BEGINNING OF THE PENNY PRESS: ANNIVERSARY. Sept 3, 1833. Benjamin H. Day launched the *New York Sun* on this date, the first truly successful penny newspaper in the US. The *Sun* was sold on sidewalks by newspaper boys. By 1836 the paper was the largest seller in the country with a circulation of 30,000. It was possibly Day's concentration on human interest stories and sensationalism that made his publication a success while efforts at penny papers at Philadelphia and Boston had failed.

BUHL DAY. Sept 3. Buhl Farm, Sharon, PA. To honor the laboring man. Observed annually on Labor Day. Est attendance: 25,000. For info: Karen Campman-Emmett, 611 Dogwood Ln, West Middlesex, PA 16159. Phone: (724) 528-1071. E-mail: kpemmett@pgh.net.

CANADA: LABOR DAY. Sept 3. Annually, the first Monday in September.

CRANDALL, PRUDENCE: BIRTH ANNIVERSARY. Sept 3, 1803. Born to a Quaker family at Hopkinton, RI, this American schoolteacher sparked controversy in the 1830s with her efforts to educate black girls. When her private academy for girls was boycotted because she admitted a black girl, she started a school for "young ladies and misses of colour." Died Jan 28, 1890, at Elk Falls, KS.

ESCAPE TO FREEDOM: ANNIVERSARY. Sept 3, 1838. Dressed as a sailor and carrying identification papers borrowed from a retired merchant seaman, Frederick Douglass boarded a train at Baltimore, MD, a slave state, and rode to Wilmington, DE, where he caught a steamboat to the free city of Philadelphia. He then transferred to a train headed for New York City where he entered the protection of the Underground Railway network. Douglass later became a great orator and one of the leaders of the antislavery struggle.

FILENE, EDWARD ALBERT: BIRTH ANNIVERSARY. Sept 3, 1860. American merchant and philanthropist, born at Salem, MA, who established the US credit union movement in 1921. Died at Paris, France, Sept 26, 1937.

FULL EMPLOYMENT WEEK. Sept 3–9. An extension of Labor Day to include the full week beginning with that holiday.

GREAT BATHTUB RACE. Sept 3. Nome, AK. 24th annual. Bathtubs mounted on wheels are raced down Front Street. Each team has five members, one in the tub, with bubbles apparent in the bath water. Tub must be full of water at beginning and have at least 10 gallons at the finish line. The other four team members must wear large-brim hats and suspenders and carry either a bar of soap, washcloth, towel or bath mat for the entire race. Winning team claims trophy, a statue of Miss Piggy and Kermit taking a bath, which is handed down from year to year. Annually, at noon on Labor Day. Est attendance: 1,500. For info: Rasmussen's Music Mart, PO Box 2, Nome, AK 99762-0002. Phone: (907) 443-2798 or (907) 443-2919. Fax: (907) 443-5777.

INDIA: JANMASHTAMI. Sept 3. Hindu holiday. Birth anniversary of Lord Vishnu in his human incarnation as Krishna. Because there is no one universally accepted Hindu calendar, this holiday may be celebrated on a different date in some parts of India but it always falls in August or September.

ITALY SURRENDERS: ANNIVERSARY. Sept 3, 1943. General Giuseppe Castellano signed three copies of the "short armistice," effectively surrendering "unconditionally" for the Italian government. That same day the British Eighth Army, commanded by General Bernard Montgomery, invaded the Italian mainland.

JERRY LEWIS MUSCULAR DYSTROPHY ASSOCIA-TION TELETHON. Sept 3–4. The annual Labor Day weekend TV broadcast to raise money for 40 neuromuscular diseases. For info: MDA, PO Box 66002, Tucson, AZ 85728-6002. Phone: (800) 572-1717. Web: www.mdausa.org.

LABOR DAY. Sept 3. Legal public holiday. Public Law 90–363 sets Labor Day on the first Monday in September. Observed in all states. First observance believed to have been a parade on Tuesday, Sept 5, 1882, at New York, NY, probably organized by Peter J. McGuire, a Carpenters and Joiners Union secretary. In 1883 a union resolution declared "the first Monday in September of each year a Labor Day." By 1893 more than half of the states were observing Labor Day on one or another day and a bill to establish Labor Day as a federal holiday was introduced in Congress. On June 28, 1894, President Grover Cleveland signed into law an act making the first Monday in September a legal holiday for federal employees and the District of Columbia. Canada also celebrates Labor Day on the first Monday in September. In most other countries, Labor Day is observed May 1.

LABOR DAY BREAKOUT. Sept 3. The Old Jail Museum, Crawfordsville, IN. An annual event to commemorate the transfer of the deed of title of the old county jail from the county to the Montgomery County Cultural Foundation. The Foundation was organized in 1975 as a bicentennial project to preserve the unique rotary jail and operate the structure as a museum of local history and culture. Annually, on Labor Day. Est attendance: 600. For info: Montgomery County Cultural Foundation, Inc, The Old Jail Museum, 225 N Washington St, PO Box 771, Crawfordsville, IN 47933. Phone: (765) 362-5222. E-mail: oldjail@tctc.com.

MACKINAC BRIDGE WALK. Sept 3. St. Ignace, MI. Labor Day is the only day of the year pedestrians are permitted to walk across the five-mile-long span, one of the world's longest suspension bridges, connecting Michigan's two peninsulas. Walk is from St. Ignace to Mackinaw City. Est attendance: 55,000. For info: Mackinac Bridge Authority, 333 Interstate 75, St. Ignace, MI 49781. Phone: (906) 643-7600. Fax: (906) 643-7668. Web: www.mackinacbridge.org.

NEW HAVEN LABOR DAY ROAD RACE. Sept 3. New Haven Green, New Haven, CT. Men's 20K national championship, 5K race and ½-mile children's fun run. Annually, on Labor Day. Est attendance: 2,000. For info: New Haven Labor Day Road Race, (203) 481-5933 or Greater New Haven Conv & Visitors Bureau, 59 Elm St, New Haven, CT 06510. Phone: (203) 777-8550 or (800) 332-STAY. Fax: (203) 782-7755. Web: www.newhavencvb.org or www.newhavenroadrace.org/.

September
2001

S	M	T	W	T	F	S
						1
2	3	4	5	6	7	8
9	10	11	12	13	14	15
16	17	18	19	20	21	22
23	24	25	26	27	28	29
30						

QATAR: INDEPENDENCE DAY: 30th ANNIVERSARY. Sept 3. National holiday. Commemorates the severing in 1971 of treaty with Britain which had handled Qatar's foreign relations.

SAN MARINO: NATIONAL DAY. Sept 3. Public holiday. Honors St. Marinus, the traditional founder of San Marino.

"SEARCH FOR TOMORROW" TV PREMIERE: 50th ANNIVERSARY. Sept 3, 1951. This soap lasted for 35 years. It began as a 15-minute program and expanded to 30 minutes in 1968, when it also began to videotape performances instead of doing them live. "Search" was set in the town of Henderson, and its central character was Joanne Gardner Barron Tate Vincente Tourneur (played by Mary Stuart). Other notable cast members have included: Don Knotts, Robert Mandan, Ken Kercheval, Jill Clayburgh, Natalie Schafer, Susan Sarandon, Robert Loggia, Hal Linden, Morgan Fairchild, Joe Morton, Robby Benson, Kevin Kline, Cynthia Gibb and Olympia Dukakis.

SNAKE RIVER DUCK RACE. Sept 3. Nome, AK. Since 1992, thousands of plastic ducks have negotiated the historic Snake River to Nome's power plant. For info: Leo B. Rasmussen, Nome Rotary Club, PO Box 275, Nome, AK 99762. Phone: (907) 443-2798.

STEARMAN FLY-IN DAYS. Sept 3–9. Galesburg, IL. The largest gathering of Stearman airplanes—the biplane trainers that gave wings to more military pilots than any other series of aircraft in the world. Est attendance: 7,500. For info: Galesburg Area CVB, PO Box 60, Galesburg, IL 61402-0060. Phone: (309) 343-2485. Fax: (309) 343-2521. E-mail: visitors@galesburg.org. Web: www.galesburg.org/visitors.

STOCK EXCHANGE HOLIDAY (LABOR DAY). Sept 3. The holiday schedules for the various exchanges are subject to change if relevant rules, regulations or exchange policies are revised. If you have questions, phone: American Stock Exchange (212) 306-1000; Chicago Board of Trade (312) 435-3500; Chicago Board of Options Exchange (312) 786-5600; New York Stock Exchange (212) 656-2065; Pacific Stock Exchange (415) 393-4000; Philadelphia Stock Exchange (215) 496-5000.

TREATY OF PARIS ENDS AMERICAN REVOLUTION: ANNIVERSARY. Sept 3, 1783. Treaty between Britain and the US, ending the Revolutionary War, signed at Paris, France. American signatories: John Adams, Benjamin Franklin and John Jay.

WAIKIKI ROUGHWATER SWIM. Sept 3. Waikiki Beach, Honolulu, HI. The 32nd annual swim is 2.4 miles from Sans Souci Beach to Duke Kahanamoku Beach. "The World's Largest Open Water Swimming Event." Preregistration is required. Annually, Labor Day. Est attendance: 1,200. For info: Jim Anderson, One Keahole Place #1607, Honolulu, HI 96825-3414. Fax: (808) 396-8868. E-mail: waikikijim@aol.com.

BIRTHDAYS TODAY

Eileen Brennan, 64, actress (*The Last Picture Show, Private Benjamin*), born Los Angeles, CA, Sept 3, 1937.

Kitty Carlisle, 86, actress (*A Night at the Opera*, "To Tell the Truth"), singer, born New Orleans, LA, Sept 3, 1915.

Pauline Collins, 61, actress ("Upstairs, Downstairs"; stage: *Shirley Valentine* [won Olivier Award and Tony Award]), born Exmouth, England, Sept 3, 1940.

Anne Jackson, 75, actress (*Lovers and Other Strangers*), born Allegheny, PA, Sept 3, 1926.

Valerie Perrine, 58, actress (*Lenny, W.C. Fields and Me*), born Galveston, TX, Sept 3, 1943.

Charlie Sheen (Carlos Irwin Estevez), 36, actor (*Platoon, Hot Shots!*), born New York, NY, Sept 3, 1965.

Damon Stoudamire, 28, basketball player, born Portland, OR, Sept 3, 1973.

Mort Walker (Mortimer Walker Addison), 78, cartoonist ("Beetle Bailey"), born El Dorado, KS, Sept 3, 1923.

SEPTEMBER 4 — TUESDAY
Day 247 — 118 Remaining

ANOTHER LOOK UNLIMITED DAY. Sept 4. Your house, garage, barn, shed, attic or yard. Encourages everyone to look over their possessions and give surplus to charity or reuse in other projects. Lessen the flow to landfills. Annually, the day after Labor Day. For info: ENVIRA MYNYTL, PO Box 220, Holts Summit, MO 65043. E-mail: envira-myntyl@cal-a-co.com.

BRUCKNER, ANTON: BIRTH ANNIVERSARY. Sept 4, 1824. Austrian composer born at Ansfelden, Austria. Died at Vienna, Austria, Oct 11, 1896.

BURNHAM, DANIEL: BIRTH ANNIVERSARY. Sept 4, 1846. American architect and city planner born at Henderson, NY. Daniel Hudson Burnham was an advocate of tall, fireproof buildings, probably the first to be called "sky-scrapers." In 1909 he proposed a long-range city plan for Chicago, IL, that was a key factor in the "forever open, clear and free" policy which resulted in Chicago having the most beautiful lakefront of any major city in the US. Died June 1, 1912, at Heidelberg, Germany.

"CAPTAIN MIDNIGHT" TV PREMIERE: ANNIVERSARY. Sept 4, 1954. A children's show starring Richard Webb as Captain Midnight, a World War I flying ace who battled crime as part of the Secret Squadron. Webb was joined by Sid Melton as Ichabod (Ikky) Mudd, his assistant, and Olan Soule as Tut, an eccentric scientist. "Captain Midnight" moved to TV from radio, where it was sponsored by Ovaltine. In reruns the name was changed to "Jet Jackson, Flying Commando" because Ovaltine owned the rights to the Captain Midnight name.

CHATEAUBRIAND, FRANCOIS RENE DE: BIRTH ANNIVERSARY. Sept 4, 1768. French poet, novelist, historian, explorer and statesman, witness to the French Revolution. Born at St. Malo, France, he died at Paris, France, July 4, 1848.

CURACAO: ANIMALS' DAY. Sept 4. In Curaçao the Association for the Protection of Animals organizes an animal show for this day and the best-kept animals are awarded prizes.

FIRST ELECTRIC LIGHTING: ANNIVERSARY. Sept 4, 1882. Four hundred electric lights came on in offices on Spruce, Wall, Nassau and Pearl streets in lower Manhattan as Thomas Edison hooked up light bulbs to an underground cable carrying direct current electrical power. Edison had demonstrated his first incandescent light bulb in 1879. See also: "Incandescent Lamp Demonstrated: Anniversary" (Oct 21).

LETTERS FROM MOM WEEK. Sept 4–10. Letters for the new school year. Annually, the week following Labor Day. For info: Jane Boyd, 9406 Meadowbriar Ln, Houston, TX 77063. Phone: (713) 334-3370. Fax: (713) 780-0005. E-mail: janeeboyd@aol.com. Web: lettersfrommom.com.

LOS ANGELES, CALIFORNIA FOUNDED: ANNIVERSARY. Sept 4, 1781. Los Angeles founded by decree and called "El Pueblo de Nuestra Senora La Reina de Los Angeles de Porciuncula."

NEWSPAPER CARRIER DAY. Sept 4. Anniversary of the hiring of the first "newsboy" in the US, 10-year-old Barney Flaherty, who is said to have answered the following classified advertisement which appeared in *The New York Sun* in 1833: "To the Unemployed—a number of steady men can find employment by vending this paper. A liberal discount is allowed to those who buy to sell again."

PLAY DAYS. Sept 4–8. In a world filled with downsizing, rightsizing and shaftsizing, we need humor to reaffirm our humanity and sanity. This week the HUMOR Project will be spreading the word on 1,001 ways to add humor to your life and work. Jest for success—humor works. Annually, the Tuesday through Saturday after Labor Day. For a free information packet on the positive

power of humor, send a 99 cents SASE. For info: Dr. Joel Goodman, The HUMOR Project, 480 Broadway, Ste 210-C, Sarasota Springs, NY 12866-2288. Phone: (518) 587-8770. Fax: (518) 587-8771. E-mail: chase@HumorProject.com. Web: www.Humor Project.com.

POLK, SARAH CHILDRESS: BIRTH ANNIVERSARY. Sept 4, 1803. Wife of James Knox Polk, 11th president of the US. Born at Murfreesboro, TN, and died at Nashville, TN, Aug 14, 1891.

WRIGHT, RICHARD: BIRTH ANNIVERSARY. Sept 4, 1908. Novelist and short story writer whose works included *Native Son, Uncle Tom's Children* and *Black Boy*, born at Natchez, MS. Wright died at Paris, France, Nov 28, 1960.

BIRTHDAYS TODAY

Carlos Romero Barcelo, 69, US Resident Commissioner (D, Commonwealth of Puerto Rico), born San Juan, Puerto Rico, Sept 4, 1932.

Mitzi Gaynor (Franchesca Mitzi Marlene de Charney von Gerber), 70, singer, dancer, actress (*South Pacific*), born Chicago, IL, Sept 4, 1931.

Paul Harvey, 83, broadcaster, commentator ("The Rest of the Story"), born Tulsa, OK, Sept 4, 1918.

Judith Ivey, 50, actress (*Compromising Positions, Brighton Beach Memoirs*; stage: *Steaming*), born El Paso, TX, Sept 4, 1951.

Michael Joseph (Mike) Piazza, 33, baseball player, born Norristown, PA, Sept 4, 1968.

Jennifer Salt, 57, actress ("Soap"), born Los Angeles, CA, Sept 4, 1944.

Ione Skye, 31, actress (*Say Anything . . .; Gas, Food, Lodging*), born Hertfordshire, England, Sept 4, 1970.

Thomas Sturges (Tom) Watson, 52, golfer, born Kansas City, MO, Sept 4, 1949.

Damon Wayans, 41, actor, comedian ("In Living Color"), born New York, NY, Sept 4, 1960.

SEPTEMBER 5 — WEDNESDAY
Day 248 — 117 Remaining

BABE RUTH'S FIRST PRO HOMER: ANNIVERSARY. Sept 5, 1914. Babe Ruth hit his first home run as a professional while playing for Providence in the International League, a type of minor league affiliate of the Boston Red Sox. He pitched a one-hit shutout against Toronto.

BE LATE FOR SOMETHING DAY. Sept 5. To create a release from the stresses and strains resulting from a consistent need to be on time. For info: Les Waas, Pres, Procrastinators' Club of America, Inc, Box 712, Bryn Athyn, PA 19009. Phone: (215) 947-9020. Fax: (215) 947-7007. E-mail: lw518@msn.com.

CAGE, JOHN: BIRTH ANNIVERSARY. Sept 5, 1912. Avant-garde American composer John Cage was born at Los Angeles, CA. He pioneered the experimental music and performance art schools. He used non-traditional instruments such as flower pots and cowbells in innovative situations, such as performances governed by chance, in which the *I Ching* was consulted to determine the direction of the performance. In 1978 he was elected to the American Academy of Arts and Sciences, and in 1982 was awarded France's highest honor for cultural contributions, *Commandeur de l'Ordre des Arts et des Lettres.* He died Aug 12, 1992, at New York, NY.

CANADA: THE MASTERS. Sept 5–9. Spruce Meadows, Calgary, AB. International show jumping competition, along with Equi-Fair, TELUS Battle of the Breeds and the BP Amoco Festival of Nations. Feature events are the American Airlines "Evening of the Horse," the ATCO Electric Circuit "Six-Bar" and the Bank of Montreal Nations' Cup. Est attendance: 175,000. For info: Spruce Meadows, RR #9, Calgary, AB, Canada T2J 5G5. Phone: (403) 974-4200. Fax: (403) 974-4270. E-mail: smeadows@telusplanet.net. Web: www.sprucemeadows.com.

CARNOVSKY, MORRIS: BIRTH ANNIVERSARY. Sept 5, 1897. American actor Morris Carnovsky was born at St. Louis, MO. In 1931 with actor Lee Strasberg and others he founded the Group Theater at New York, NY. He was blacklisted in the 1950s by the House Un-American Activities Committee, but was still asked by John Houseman to perform in the American Shakespeare Festival in 1956 and began a successful Shakespearean career. He was elected to the Theater Hall of Fame in 1979. Carnovsky died Sept 1, 1992, at Easton, CT.

FARMERS AND THRESHERMENS JUBILEE. Sept 5–9. New Centerville, PA. Many steam engines, threshing demonstrations using manpower, horses and steam, quilt show, crafts, truck and tractor pulls. Live entertainment, good food. Est attendance: 30,000. For info: Farmers & Threshermens Jubilee, 1428 Casselman Rd, Rockwood, PA 15557. Phone: (814) 926-3142.

FIRST CONTINENTAL CONGRESS ASSEMBLY: ANNIVERSARY. Sept 5, 1774. The first assembly of this forerunner of the US Congress took place at Philadelphia, PA. Peyton Randolph, delegate from Virginia, was elected president.

September 2001	S	M	T	W	T	F	S
							1
	2	3	4	5	6	7	8
	9	10	11	12	13	14	15
	16	17	18	19	20	21	22
	23	24	25	26	27	28	29
	30						

GERALD FORD: ASSASSINATION ATTEMPTS: ANNIVERSARY. Sept 5, 1975. Lynette A. "Squeaky" Fromme, a follower of convicted murderer Charles Manson, attempted to shoot President Gerald Ford. On Sept 22 of the same year, another attempt on Ford's life occurred when Sara Jane Moore shot at him.

ISRAELI OLYMPIAD MASSACRE: ANNIVERSARY. Sept 5–6, 1972. Eleven members of the Israeli Olympic Team were killed in an attack on the Olympic Village at Munich and attempted kidnapping of team members. Four of seven guerrillas, members of the Black September faction of the Palestinian Liberation Army, were also killed. In retaliation, Israeli jets bombed Palestinian positions at Lebanon and Syria Sept 8, 1972.

JAMES, JESSE: BIRTH ANNIVERSARY. Sept 5, 1847. Western legend and bandit Jesse Woodson James was born at Centerville (now Kearney), MO. His criminal exploits were glorified and romanticized by writers for Eastern readers looking for stories of Western adventure and heroism. After the Civil War, James and his brother, Frank, formed a group of eight outlaws who robbed banks, stagecoaches and stores. In 1873 the James gang began holding up trains. The original James gang was put out of business Sept 7, 1876, while attempting to rob a bank at Northfield, MN. Every member of the gang except for the James brothers was killed or captured. The brothers formed a new gang and resumed their criminal careers in 1879. Two years later, the governor of Missouri offered a $10,000 reward for their capture, dead or alive. On Apr 3, 1882 at St. Joseph, MO, Robert Ford, a member of the gang, shot 34-year-old Jesse in the back of the head and claimed the reward.

KOESTLER, ARTHUR: BIRTH ANNIVERSARY. Sept 5, 1905. Born at Budapest, Hungary, Koestler is best known for his novel about his disillusionment with Communism, *Darkness at Noon,* and for *The God That Failed.* Died at London, England, Mar 3, 1983.

"THE MacNEIL-LEHRER NEWSHOUR" TV PREMIERE: ANNIVERSARY. Sept 5, 1983. Originally, this PBS news show was called "The MacNeil-Lehrer Report" and was on every weeknight for a half hour starting in 1976. Robert MacNeil and Jim Lehrer were joined by Charlayne Hunter-Gault and Judy Woodruff. In 1983 the show was expanded to an hour and became TV's first regularly scheduled daily hour news show. The show has been praised for its depth and objectivity. In 1995 Robert MacNeil retired and the show was retitled "The Newshour with Jim Lehrer."

MICHIGAN'S GREAT FIRE OF 1881: ANNIVERSARY. Sept 5, 1881. According to Michigan Historical Commission, "Small fires were burning in the forests of the 'Thumb area of Michigan,' tinder-dry after a long, hot summer, when a gale swept in from the southwest on Sept 5, 1881. Fanned into an inferno, the fire raged for three days. A million acres were devastated in Sanilac and Huron counties alone. At least 125 persons died, and thousands more were left destitute. The new American Red Cross won support for its prompt aid to the fire victims. This was the first disaster relief furnished by this great organization."

NIELSEN, ARTHUR CHARLES: BIRTH ANNIVERSARY. Sept 5, 1897. Marketing research engineer, founder of AC Nielsen Company, in 1923, known for radio and TV audience surveys, was born at Chicago, IL, and died there June 1, 1980.

PRIME BEEF FESTIVAL. Sept 5–8. Monmouth Park, Monmouth, IL. Princess Pageant, parade, carnival from noon to midnight, Beef and Pork Show, judging, music, food and exhibitors. Est attendance: 5,000. For info: Monmouth Chamber of Commerce, PO Box 857, 68 Public Square, Monmouth, IL 61462. Phone: (309) 734-3181. Web: www.misslink.net/macc.

SPACE MILESTONE: *VOYAGER 1* (US). Sept 5, 1977. Twin of *Voyager 2* which was launched Aug 20. On Feb 18, 1998, *Voyager* 1 set a new distance record when after more than 20 years in space it reached 6.5 billion miles from Earth.

SWITZERLAND: SAINT GOTTHARD AUTOMOBILE TUNNEL OPENING: ANNIVERSARY. Sept 5, 1980. The longest underground motorway in the world, the St. Gotthard Auto Tunnel in Switzerland, was opened to traffic. More than 10 miles long, requiring $417,000,000 and 10 years for construction, it became the most direct route from Switzerland to the southern regions of the continent. The St. Gotthard Pass, the main passage since the Middle Ages, was closed much of every year by massive snow drifts.

ZANUCK, DARRYL F.: BIRTH ANNIVERSARY. Sept 5, 1902. Born at Wahoo, NE, Darryl F. Zanuck became a celebrated—and controversial—movie producer. He was also a co-founder of Twentieth Century Studios, which later merged with Fox. His film credits include *The Jazz Singer* (the first sound picture), *Forever Amber, The Snake Pit* and *The Grapes of Wrath.* He died Dec 21, 1979, at Palm Springs, CA.

BIRTHDAYS TODAY

Kristian Alfonso, 37, actress ("Days of Our Lives," "Melrose Place"), born Brockton, MA, Sept 5, 1964.

William Devane, 62, actor (*From Here to Eternity*, "Knots Landing"), born Albany, NY, Sept 5, 1939.

Dennis Dugan, 55, actor (*The Howling, Parenthood, Problem Child*), born Wheaton, IL, Sept 5, 1946.

Cathy Lee Guisewite, 51, cartoonist (*Cathy*), born Dayton, OH, Sept 5, 1950.

Carol Lawrence (Carol Maria Laraia), 66, singer, actress (*West Side Story*), born Melrose Park, IL, Sept 5, 1935.

Bob Newhart, 72, comedian ("The Bob Newhart Show," "Newhart"), born Chicago, IL, Sept 5, 1929.

Raquel Welch, 59, actress (*The Three Musketeers, Woman of the Year*), model, born Chicago, IL, Sept 5, 1942.

Dweezil Zappa, 32, singer, actor ("Normal Life"), born Hollywood, CA, Sept 5, 1969.

SEPTEMBER 6 — THURSDAY
Day 249 — 116 Remaining

ADDAMS, JANE: BIRTH ANNIVERSARY. Sept 6, 1860. American worker for peace, social welfare, rights of women, founder of Hull House (Chicago), co-winner of Nobel Prize, 1931. Born at Cedarville, IL, she died May 21, 1935, at Chicago, IL.

BALTIC STATES' INDEPENDENCE RECOGNIZED: 10th ANNIVERSARY. Sept 6, 1991. The Soviet government recognized the independence of the Baltic states—Latvia, Estonia and Lithuania. The action came 51 years after the Baltic states were annexed by the Soviet Union. All three Baltic states had earlier declared their independence, and many nations had already recognized them diplomatically, including the US Sept 2, 1991.

BEECHER, CATHARINE ESTHER: BIRTH ANNIVERSARY. Sept 6, 1800. Catharine Esther Beecher was born at East Hampton, NY. In addition to teaching herself mathematics, philosophy and Latin, Beecher had been formally educated in art and music. An early advocate for equal education for women, she founded the Hartford Female Seminary, which was widely recognized for its advanced curriculum. She was also instrumental in the founding of women's colleges in Iowa, Illinois and Wisconsin. Beecher died May 12, 1878, at Elmira, NY.

CARRY NATION FESTIVAL. Sept 6–9. Downtown Holly, MI. 28th annual festival re-creates the historical visit of Carry Nation, the Kansas City saloon smasher. Includes pageant, parade, entertainment tent, carnival, street dance and craft show. Annually, the weekend after Labor Day. Est attendance: 25,000. For info: Holly Chamber of Commerce, PO Box 214, Holly, MI 48442. Phone: (248) 634-1055. Fax: (248) 634-1049.

DALTON, JOHN: BIRTH ANNIVERSARY. Sept 6, 1766. English chemist, physicist, teacher and developer of atomic theory, was born at Eaglesfield, near Cockermouth, England. Dalton died at Manchester, England, July 27, 1844.

DEFEAT OF JESSE JAMES DAYS. Sept 6–9. Northfield, MN. Bank raid reenactment, 5K and 15K runs, arts, crafts, bike race, parade and professional rodeo. Est attendance: 150,000. For info: Kathy Feldbrugge, Exec VP, Northfield Chamber of Commerce, PO Box 198, Northfield, MN 55057. Phone: (507) 645-5604. Fax: (507) 663-7782.

FIRST RADIO BROADCAST OF A PRIZEFIGHT: ANNIVERSARY. Sept 6, 1920. In the first boxing match broadcast on radio, Jack Dempsey knocked out Billy Miske in the third round of a scheduled 10-round fight.

GREAT PEANUT TOUR. Sept 6–9. Skippers, VA. Assorted bicycle rides from 13 to 125 miles. Special peanut tour ride to examine peanuts growing, method of harvesting and a sampling of more than 40 peanut goodies. Unique water stops, nature walks, music, campfires with marshmallow roast. Annually, the weekend following Labor Day. Est attendance: 1,500. For info: Robert C. Wrenn, Emporia Bicycle Club, PO Box 631, Emporia, VA 23847. Phone: (804) 348-4215. Fax: (804) 348-4020. E-mail: gpt@3rddoor.com. Web: www.3rddoor.com/gpt.html.

LAFAYETTE, MARQUIS DE: BIRTH ANNIVERSARY. Sept 6, 1757. French general and aristocrat, Marquis de Lafayette, whose full name was Marie-Joseph-Paul-Yves-Roch-Gilbert du Motier, came to America to assist in the revolutionary cause and volunteered to serve without compensation. He was awarded a major-generalship and began a lasting friendship with the American commander-in-chief, George Washington. After an alliance was signed with France, he returned to his native country and persuaded Louis XVI to send a 6,000-man force to assist the Americans. On his return, he was given command of an army at Virginia and was instrumental in forcing the surrender of Lord Cornwallis at Yorktown, leading to the end of the war and American independence. He was hailed as "The Hero of Two Worlds" and was appointed a brigadier general on his return to France in 1782. He became a leader of the liberal aristocrats during the early days of the French revolution, presenting to the National Assembly his draft of "A Declaration of the Rights of Man and of the Citizen." As the commander of the newly formed national guard of Paris, he rescued Louis XVI and Marie-Antoinette from a crowd that stormed Versailles Oct 6, 1789, returning them to Paris where they became hostages of the revolution. His popularity waned after his guards opened fire on angry demonstrators demanding abdication of the king in 1791. He fled to Austria with the overthrow of the monarchy in 1792, returning when Napoleon Bonaparte came to power. Born at Chavaniac, he died at Paris, May 20, 1834.

LOS ANGELES COUNTY FAIR. Sept 6–23. Pomona, CA. "America's Fair," world's largest county fair, features free stage acts and attractions, livestock, thoroughbred racing, carnival, flower and garden show, home arts, nightly fireworks, horse shows, commercial exhibits, photography and much more. Est attendance: 1,200,000. For info: Fairplex, Sharon Autry, Communications Coord, Box 2250, Pomona, CA 91769. Phone: (909) 623-3111. Fax: (909) 629-2067. E-mail: autry@fairplex.com. Web: www.fairplex.com.

MARION POPCORN FESTIVAL. Sept 6–8. Marion, OH. Performances by nationally known entertainers every evening; parade, athletic competition, arts and crafts. 11 AM to midnight daily. Annually, the Thursday, Friday and Saturday after Labor Day. Est attendance: 350,000. For info: Marion Popcorn Festival, PO Box 1101, Marion, OH 43301-1101. Phone: (740) 387-3378.

NORTH HAVEN FAIR. Sept 6–9. North Haven Fairgrounds, North Haven, CT. Large agricultural fair featuring animal and agricultural exhibits, entertainment, food and rides. Annually, the Thursday after Labor Day thru Sunday. For info: North Haven Fairgrounds Office. Phone: (203) 239-3770. Greater New Haven Conv & Visitors Bureau, 59 Elm St, New Haven, CT 06510. Phone: (203) 777-8550 or (800) 332-STAY. Fax: (203) 782-7755. Web: www.newhavencvb.org.

PAKISTAN: DEFENSE OF PAKISTAN DAY. Sept 6. National holiday.

ROSE, BILLY: BIRTH ANNIVERSARY. Sept 6, 1899. Billy Rose (William S. Rosenberg), American theatrical producer, author, songwriter and husband of Fanny Brice, was born at New York, NY. His songs include: "That Old Gang of Mine," "Me and My Shadow," "Without a Song," "It's Only a Paper Moon" and hundreds of others. Rose died at Montego Bay, Jamaica, Feb 10, 1966.

SAINT PETERSBURG NAME RESTORED: 10th ANNIVERSARY. Sept 6, 1991. Russian legislators voted to restore the name Saint Petersburg to the nation's second largest city. The city had been known as Leningrad for 67 years in honor of the Soviet Union's founder, Vladimir I. Lenin. The city, founded in 1703 by Peter the Great, has had three names in the 20th century with Russian leaders changing its German-sounding name to Petrograd at the beginning of WWI in 1914 and Soviet Communist leaders changing its name to Leningrad in 1924 following their leader's death.

SHAKESPEARE-ON-THE-ROCKS. Sept 6–30 (Thursdays–Sundays). McKelligon Canyon Amphitheater, El Paso, TX. Festival presents four Shakespeare plays in repertory. Renaissance dinner served Fridays and Saturdays at 6 PM, showtime 8 PM. Nightly backstage tours, green show. Est attendance: 16,000. For info: El Paso Assn for the Performing Arts, PO Box 31340, El Paso, TX 79931-0340. Phone: (915) 565-6900 or (800) 915-8482. Fax: (915) 565-6999. E-mail: epapa@htg.net. Web: www.viva-ep.org.

SWAZILAND: INDEPENDENCE DAY. Sept 6. Commemorates attainment of independence from Britain in 1968. National holiday.

UNITED TRIBES POWWOW. Sept 6–9. United Tribes Technical College, Bismarck, ND. Enjoy one of the largest international powwows in the nation. This colorful pageant includes Native Americans from across the country singing and dancing in friendly competition. Indian foods, artifacts and jewelry are sold on the premises. Est attendance: 8,000. For info: North Dakota Tourism, 604 E Boulevard, Bismarck, ND 58505. Phone: (701) 328-2525 or (800) 435-5663.

UTAH STATE FAIR. Sept 6–16. Utah State Fairpark, Salt Lake City, UT. PRCA Rodeo Sept 6–9. Exhibits, livestock, family contests, cook-offs, concerts and entertainment. Annually, the first Thursday after Labor Day. Est attendance: 275,000. For info: Utah State Fair Park, 155 N 1000 W, Salt Lake City, UT 84116. Phone: (801) 538-8440. Fax: (801) 538-8455. E-mail: donna@fiber.net.

WILLIAMSBURG OLD-FASHIONED TRADING DAYS. Sept 6–8. Courthouse Square, Williamsburg, KY. Arts and crafts, bluegrass and gospel singing, antique car show and more. Annually, the first Thursday, Friday and Saturday after Labor Day. Est attendance: 25,000. For info: Theresa Estes, Coord, 522 Main St, Williamsburg, KY 40769. Phone: (606) 549-2285. Fax: (606) 549-5565.

WINFIELD GOOD OLD DAYS. Sept 6–9. Winfield, IL. 34th annual festival involving current Miss Illinois USA and entire Winfield community, including live music, carnival, ladies shoe-kicking contest, bed races, horseshoes and underhand free-throw tournaments, Oakwood Pond golf challenge, pony rides, petting zoo, duck race, dunk tank, expo tent, arts and crafts, food concession, beer garden and parade. Annually, the four-day weekend following Labor Day. Est attendance: 10,000. For info: Winfield Chamber of Commerce, 0S125 Church St, Winfield, IL 60190. Phone: (630) 682-3712. Fax: (630) 682-3726. E-mail: bysina@winfield-chamber.com. Web: www.winfield-chamber.com.

"WYATT EARP" TV PREMIERE: ANNIVERSARY. Sept 6, 1955. Officially titled "The Life and Legend of Wyatt Earp," this half-hour series marked the beginning of the trend toward "adult westerns." It was loosely based on fact, with Hugh O'Brian as Earp, marshall of Dodge City, KS, and later of Tombstone, AZ. Also featured were Douglas Fowley, Morgan Woodward, Randy Stuart, Damian O'Flynn and Steve Brodie.

BIRTHDAYS TODAY

Jane Curtin, 54, actress ("Saturday Night Live," "3rd Rock from the Sun"), comedienne, born Cambridge, MA, Sept 6, 1947.

Jeff Foxworthy, 43, comedian (*You Know You're a Redneck*), actor ("The Jeff Foxworthy Show"), author (*No Shirt, No Shoes . . . No Problem*), born Atlanta, GA, Sept 6, 1958.

Swoosie Kurtz, 57, actress ("Sisters," *The World According to Garp*; Tony for *The House of Blue Leaves*), born Omaha, NE, Sept 6, 1944.

Rosie Perez, 37, actress (*King of the Jungle, White Men Can't Jump*), born Brooklyn, NY, Sept 6, 1964.

Justin Whalin, 27, actor ("Charles in Charge," "Lois & Clark"), born San Francisco, CA, Sept 6, 1974.

Jo Anne Worley, 64, comedienne, actress ("Rowan & Martin's Laugh-In"), born Lowell, IA, Sept 6, 1937.

	S	M	T	W	T	F	S
September 2001							1
	2	3	4	5	6	7	8
	9	10	11	12	13	14	15
	16	17	18	19	20	21	22
	23	24	25	26	27	28	29
	30						

SEPTEMBER 7 — FRIDAY

Day 250 — 115 Remaining

BRAZIL: INDEPENDENCE DAY. Sept 7. Declared independence from Portugal in 1822. National holiday.

CHILI AND BLUEGRASS FESTIVAL. Sept 7–8. Claremore, OK. Free concerts from the best in bluegrass and country music and tantalizing chili during the International Chili Society Mid-America Regional Chili Cookoff. Open car show, children's Kiddie Korral and arts and crafts. Annually, Friday and Saturday following Labor Day. Est attendance: 75,000. For info: Dell Davis, Fest Dir, Chili and Bluegrass Festival, 400 Veterans Pkwy, Claremore, OK 74017. Phone: (918) 342-5357. Fax: (918) 341-7275.

CORBETT-SULLIVAN PRIZE FIGHT: ANNIVERSARY. Sept 7, 1892. John L. Sullivan was knocked out by James J. Corbett in the 21st round of a prize fight at New Orleans, LA. It was the first major fight under the Marquess of Queensberry Rules.

DIAMOND GEM CITY DAYS AND PRAIRIE DAY. Sept 7–8. Diamond, MO. GEM City events include a craft fair, antique show, old-fashioned games, musical entertainment and much more. On Saturday, George Washington Carver National Monument is joining with GEM City Days for the park's annual Prairie Day event. Come take a walk back into history and celebrate life on the Missouri Prairie during the 1860s and 1870s. There will be prairie walks, wagon rides, wood carving, basket weaving, candlemaking, Dutch-oven cooking, spinning, weaving and numerous other activities. Est attendance: 1,300. For info: George Washington Carver Natl Monument, 5646 Carver Rd, Diamond, MO 64840. Phone: (417) 325-4151. Fax: (417) 325-4231.

"THE FLYING NUN" TV PREMIERE: ANNIVERSARY. Sept 7, 1967. This sitcom about a nun at a convent in Puerto Rico who discovers that she can fly starred Sally Field as Elsie Ethrington (Sister Bertrille) and featured Madeleine Sherwood, Marge Redmond, Shelley Morrison, Alejandro Rey and Vito Scotti.

GRANDMA MOSES DAY. Sept 7. Anna Mary (Robertson) Moses, modern primitive American painter born at Greenwich, NY, Sept 7, 1860. Started painting at the age of 78. Her 100th birthday was proclaimed Grandma Moses Day in New York state. Died at Hoosick Falls, NY, Dec 13, 1961.

HOLLY, BUDDY: 65th BIRTH ANNIVERSARY. Sept 7, 1936. American popular music performer, composer and bandleader. Called one of the most innovative and influential musicians of his time, he was a pioneer of rock 'n' roll. His hits included "That'll Be the Day" and "Peggy Sue." Born Charles Harden Holley, at Lubbock, TX, he died at age 22 in an airplane crash near Mason City, IA, Feb 3, 1959.

HOPPS OF FUN—A FESTIVAL OF BEER AND WINE. Sept 7–8. Mackinaw City, MI. Festival featuring a wide variety of Michigan beers and wines. Beer and wine tasting demonstrations along with live musical entertainment from some of Northern Michigan's premiere entertainers. Another highlight of this fantastic festival is a sand-sculpting competition. Watch in amazement as piles of sand are magically transformed into works of art. Est attendance: 6,000. For info: Mackinaw Area Tourist Bureau, PO Box 160, Mackinaw City, MI 49701. Phone: (800) 666-0160. Web: www.mackinawcity.com.

HUFF 'N PUFF HOT AIR BALLOON RALLY. Sept 7–9. Topeka, KS. 26th annual hot-air balloon rally. Est attendance: 10,000. For info: Great Plains Balloon Club, Box 1093, Topeka, KS 66601. Phone: (785) 235-0463.

INDIAN HERITAGE FESTIVAL AND POWWOW. Sept 7–8. Martinsville, VA. 16th annual traditional powwow, crafts, food and dancing. Annually, the Friday and Saturday after Labor Day. Est attendance: 5,000. For info: Virginia Museum of Natural History, 1001 Douglas Ave, Martinsville, VA 24112. Phone: (540) 666-8600. Fax: (540) 632-6487. Web: www.vmnh.org.

INDIAN SUMMER FESTIVAL. Sept 7–9. Maier Festival Park, Milwaukee, WI. Festival dedicated to promoting the unique culture of the American Indian. Cultural events and exhibits, competition powwow, arts and crafts, traditional and contemporary entertainment and traditional food. Est attendance: 70,000. For info: Indian Summer Festivals, Inc, 7441 W Greenfield Ave, Ste 109, Milwaukee, WI 53214. Phone: (414) 774-7119. Fax: (414) 774-6810. Web: www.indiansummer.org.

"JIM BOWIE" TV PREMIERE: 45th ANNIVERSARY. Sept 7, 1956. Also known as "The Adventures of Jim Bowie," this half-hour western about the inventor of the Bowie knife starred Scott Forbes as the title character. He was also the only regular on the show. As a result of criticism, violence was decreased on the show.

KANSAS STATE FAIR. Sept 7–16. Hutchinson, KS. Commercial and competitive exhibits, entertainment, carnival, car racing and other special attractions. Annually, beginning the first Friday after Labor Day. Est attendance: 400,000. For info: Bill Ogg, Gen Mgr, Kansas State Fair, 2000 N Poplar, Hutchinson, KS 67502. Phone: (316) 669-3600. E-mail: ksfair@southwind.net. Web: www.kansasstatefair.com.

KETTLE MORAINE JAZZ FESTIVAL. Sept 7–8. Riverside Park, West Bend, WI. Features nationally recognized jazz musicians and vocalists. Past performers have included David Sanborn, Dave Koz and Joyce Cooling. Est attendance: 5,000. For info: Dave Amoroso, Ron Sonntag Public Relations, 9406 N 107th St, Milwaukee, WI 53224. Phone: (877) 271-6903. Fax: (414) 354-5317. E-mail: dave@rspr.com. Web: www.kmjazz.com.

LAWRENCE, JACOB: BIRTH ANNIVERSARY. Sept 7, 1917. African American painter, born at Atlantic City, NJ. Lawrence was best known for his series of historical paintings on John Brown and on the migration of African Americans out of the South. A recipient of the NAACP's Spingarn Medal, he won many other awards during his lifetime. Lawrence died June 9, 2000, in Seattle, WA.

LIGONIER HIGHLAND GAMES. Sept 7–9. Ligonier, PA. Scottish bagpipe bands on parade, Highland dancers and athletes in day-long performances. Clan gatherings, dog show. Offers imported woolens, china, jewelry, records and foods. Mail SASE for schedule of events. Est attendance: 10,000. For info: David L Peet, Ligonier Highland Games, PO Box 884, Bethel Park, PA 15102-0884. Phone: (412) 851-9900. E-mail: ligdir@icubed.com. Web: www.ligoniergames.com.

LOUISIANA PASSION PLAY. Sept 7–Oct 13. Ruston, LA. Held every Friday and Saturday night. An outdoor theater presentation/interpretation of some of the major events from the life of Christ—His birth, His teachings and His death and resurrection. Est attendance: 5,000. For info: James Burns, Exec Dir, Louisiana Passion Play, 3010 S Vienna, Ruston, LA 71270. Phone: (800) 204-2101 or (318) 255-6277.

MARIGOLD FESTIVAL. Sept 7–9. Pekin, IL. Parade, flower judging, arts, crafts, golf, carnival, three-on-three basketball, Festive Foods, "Saturday Night Event" and other family-oriented activities. Est attendance: 100,000. For info: Chamber of Commerce, PO Box 636, Pekin, IL 61555-0636. Phone: (309) 346-2106. Fax: (309) 346-2104.

MONTANA STATE CHOKECHERRY FESTIVAL. Sept 7. Lewistown, MT. Taste of Lewistown, tasting and judging of jam, jelly and wine; pancake breakfast, race and run-walk, parade, farmers market, dinner train, art festival. Est attendance: 1,500. For info: Lewistown Chamber of Commerce, PO Box 818, Lewistown, MT 59457. Phone: (406) 538-5436. Fax: (406) 538-5437. E-mail: lewchamb@lewistown.net. Web: www.lewistownchamber.com.

MOUNTAIN CRAFT DAYS. Sept 7-9. Somerset, PA. Southwestern Pennsylvania's premier traditional craft festival along the Somerset Historical Center's trails. Entertainment, food, trades and crafts. Est attendance: 15,000. For info: Mark Ware, Mountain Craft Days, 10649 Somerset Pike, Somerset, PA 15501. Phone: (814) 445-6077.

MOUNTAINEER FOLK FESTIVAL. Sept 7-9. Fall Creek Falls State Park, Pikeville, TN. Handmade crafts, traditional mountain music and pioneer skills demonstrations are just part of the fun. Country cooking, bluegrass music and different exhibits round out the jam-packed schedule. Sponsored by Friends of Fall Creek Falls State Park. Est attendance: 8,000. For info: Fall Creek Falls State Park, Betty Dunn Nature Center, Rte 3, Pikeville, TN 37367. Phone: (423) 881-5708. Fax: (423) 881-5103.

MOZAMBIQUE: VICTORY DAY. Sept 7. National holiday.

MUSKIES INC INTERNATIONAL MUSKIE TOURNA-MENT. Sept 7-9. North Central, MN. 33rd annual fundraiser for nonprofit sportsman's organization. Proceeds go toward muskie stocking, rearing and research projects along with Dept of Natural Resources fisheries improvements. This tournament strongly encourages "catch and release." Annually, the Friday, Saturday and Sunday after Labor Day. The $50 entry fee entitles the contestant to participate in the Sunday banquet and compete for thousands of dollars in prizes. Grand Prize in the "Release Division" is a boat, motor and trailer with a retail value of approximately $28,000. We welcome corporate sponsorship inquiries. Est attendance: 2,400. For info: Dave Griffin, Twin Cities Chapter of Muskies, Inc, 4434 Dorchester Rd, Mound, MN 55364. Phone: (952) 472-6039.

NATIONAL CHAMPIONSHIP INDIAN POWWOW. Sept 7-9. Traders Village, Grand Prairie, TX. Hundreds of Indians gather for colorful traditional dance contests, Indian arts and crafts shows, homemade tepee competition and Indian food. Est attendance: 80,000. For info: Dallas-Fort Worth Inter-Tribal Assn, Traders Village, 2602 Mayfield Rd, Grand Prairie, TX 75052-7246. Phone: (972) 647-2331.

September *2001*	S	M	T	W	T	F	S
							1
	2	3	4	5	6	7	8
	9	10	11	12	13	14	15
	16	17	18	19	20	21	22
	23	24	25	26	27	28	29
	30						

NEITHER SNOW NOR RAIN DAY. Sept 7. Anniversary of the opening to the public on Labor Day 1914 of the New York Post Office Building at Eighth Avenue between 31st and 33rd Streets. On the front of this building was an inscription supplied by William M. Kendall of the architectural firm that planned the building. The inscription, a free translation from Herodotus, reads: "Neither snow nor rain nor heat nor gloom of night stays these couriers from the swift completion of their appointed rounds." This has long been believed to be the motto of the US Post Office and Postal Service. They have, in fact, no motto . . . but the legend remains. [Info from: New York Post Office, Public Info Office and US Postal Service.]

NEW MEXICO STATE FAIR. Sept 7-23. Albuquerque, NM. Nationally known recording artists perform at Tingley Coliseum. PRCA rodeo competitions. Thoroughbred and Quarterhorse racing. Villa Hispana and Native American villages. Free entertainment. Est attendance: 622,000. For info: New Mexico State Fair, Po Box 8546, Albuquerque, NM 87198. Phone: (505) 265-1791. Fax: (505) 266-7784.

NORDICFEST. Sept 7-9. Libby, MT. Scandinavian festival with food booths, dinners, cultural exhibits, craft shows, quilt show, art show, folk dance performances, big name performances and the international Fjord horse show. Parade on Sept 8 showcases a contingent of Norwegian fjord horses plus a variety of floats. Est attendance: 90,000. For info: Libby Nordicfest, Inc, Box 791, Libby, MT 59923. Phone: (800) 785-6541. Web: www.libby.org.

NORWALK SEAPORT OYSTER FESTIVAL. Sept 7-9. Norwalk, CT. Huge festival with vintage ships on display, 225 juried crafters, main stage with entertainment, oyster shucking and slurping contests and Kids Coves (children's entertainment). Annually, the weekend following Labor Day. Est attendance: 95,000. For info: Norwalk Seaport Assn, 132 Water St, Norwalk, CT 06854. Phone: (203) 838-9444. Fax: (203) 855-1017.

OHIO RIVER STERNWHEEL FESTIVAL. Sept 7-9. Ohio River Levee, Marietta, OH. A three-day riverfront extravaganza. More than two dozen sternwheelers line the Ohio River shore in Marietta, OH. Continuous musical entertainment for all ages, food concessions, queen coronation, sternwheel races, fireworks. Annually, the weekend following Labor Day. Est attendance: 75,000. For info: Ohio River Sternwheel Festival Committee, 316 Third St, Marietta, OH 45750. Phone: (740) 373-5178 or (740) 374- 4913. Fax: (740) 374-4959. E-mail: mtourist@ee.net. Web: www.rivertowns.org.

OKTOBERFEST. Sept 7-9. MainStrasse Village, Covington, KY. Celebration of the German "storybook wedding reception" kicks off with a beer-tapping ceremony. Features include German and American food, live Bavarian music and dancing, arts and crafts, contests, children's rides and much more. Est attendance: 300,000. For info: Donna Kramer, Promotions Coordinator, MainStrasse Village, 605 Philadelphia St, Covington, KY 41011. Phone: (606) 491-0458 or Special Events Line: (513) 357-MAIN. Fax: (606) 655-7932.

POLISH FEST. Sept 7-9. Wisconsin Dells, WI. Traditional Polish celebration with festive and colorful dance, dress, food and live music. Est attendance: 6,000. For info: Polish Fest, 400 County A & Highway 12, Wisconsin Dells, WI 53965-0390. Phone: (800) 659-6811 or (608) 253-4451.

QUEEN ELIZABETH I: BIRTH ANNIVERSARY. Sept 7, 1533. Queen of England, daughter of Henry VIII and Anne Boleyn, after whom the Elizabethan era was named, was born at Greenwich Palace. She ascended the throne in 1558 at the age of 25. During her reign, the British defeated the Spanish Armada in July 1588, the Anglican Church was essentially established and England became a world power. She died at Richmond, England, Mar 24, 1603.

REGGAE ON THE RIVER. Sept 7–8. Town Point Park, Norfolk, VA. Move to the island beat as the sounds and rhythm of reggae music sweep through Town Point Park. There will be plenty of cool, refreshing beverages and delicious island fare to round out your day in the sun. A nonstop lineup will include both regionally and nationally acclaimed artists. Est attendance: 40,000. For info: Mktg Dir, Norfolk Festevents, 120 W Main St, Norfolk, VA 23510. Phone: (757) 441-2345. Fax: (757) 441-5198. Web: www.festeventsva.org.

RIVERFEST IN MANCHESTER. Sept 7–9. Arms Park, Manchester, NH. 21st annual festival on the bank of the Merrimack River includes entertainment for the whole family, well-known national music groups, arts and crafts, special events, rowing regatta and other water activities, plus a fireworks extravaganza. Annually, the weekend following Labor Day. Admission charged. Est attendance: 100,000. For info: Riverfest, Inc, PO Box 21, Manchester, NH 03105. Phone: (603) 623-2623. Fax: (603) 624-7880.

STAR ISLAND ADVENTURE II: 2001—A STARMAN ODYSSEY. Sept 7–10. Salt Lake City, UT. A gathering of those who appreciate the "Starman" TV series/movie. Visit Antelope Island, Planetarium, other local sites. Though it lasted only one season, this TV show touched many souls and helped people change their lives in positive ways. See also: "International Starman Month (Oct 1)." For info: Bruce Jividen, 6748 Hollow Dale Dr, Salt Lake City, UT 84121-2711. Phone: (801) 944-4633. E-mail: kundar@bigfoot.com. Web: www.pobox.com/~starman.

SUGARLOAF'S FALL MANASSAS CRAFT FESTIVAL. Sept 7–9. Prince William County Fairgrounds, Manassas, VA. This show, now in its 21st year, features 350 nationally recognized craft designers and fine artists displaying and selling their original creations. Craft demonstrations, children's entertainment, live music, food, hourly gift certificate drawings and more. Est attendance: 25,000. For info: Sugarloaf Mountain Works, Inc, 200 Orchard Ridge Dr #215, Gaithersburg, MD 20878. Phone: (800) 210-9900. E-mail: smworks@sugarloafcrafts.com. Web: www.sugarloafcrafts.com.

TENNESSEE STATE FAIR. Sept 7–16. Nashville, TN. A huge variety of exhibits, carnival midway, animal and variety shows, live stage presentations, livestock, agricultural and craft competitions and food and game booths. Annually, the first Friday after Labor Day. Est attendance: 350,000. For info: Tennessee Fair Office, PO Box 40208, Melrose Station, Nashville, TN 37204. Phone: (615) 862-8980. Fax: (615) 862-8992. Web: www.nashville.org/tsf.

"TRUTH OR CONSEQUENCES" TV PREMIERE: ANNIVERSARY. Sept 7, 1950. This game show lasted for many years on both radio and TV. The half-hour show was based on a parlor game: contestants who failed to answer a question before the buzzer (nicknamed Beulah) went off had to perform stunts (i.e. pay the consequences). Ralph Edwards created and hosted the show until 1954, then it became a prime-time show hosted by Jack Bailey. Bob Barker succeeded him in 1966 and hosted it through its syndicated run. In 1977 the show was revived as "The New Truth or Consequences" with Bob Hilton as host.

WESTERN WASHINGTON FAIR. Sept 7–23. Puyallup, WA. Entertainment, animals, rides, displays and food. Est attendance: 1,300,000. For info: Western Washington Fair, PO Box 430, Puyallup, WA 98371-0162. Phone: (253) 841-5045. E-mail: info@thefair.com. Web: www.thefair.com.

WYANDOTTE HERITAGE DAYS. Sept 7–9. Bishop Park Area, Wyandotte, MI. Outdoor craft show, living history encampments, Teddy Bear picnic, costume show, Historic Home and Church Tours and colonial dinners. Est attendance: 50,000. For info: Marc Partin, Museum Dir, 2610 Biddle Ave, Wyandotte, MI 48192. Phone: (734) 324-7297. Fax: (734) 324-7283.

YELLOW DAISY FESTIVAL. Sept 7–9. Georgia's Stone Mountain Park, Stone Mountain, GA. Arts and crafts festival with more than 450 exhibitors. Continuous entertainment and foods. Annually, the weekend after Labor Day. Est attendance: 225,000. For info: PR Office, Georgia's Stone Mountain Park, PO Box 778, Stone Mountain, GA 30086. Phone: (770) 498-5633. Fax: (770) 413-5059. E-mail: mail@stonemountainpark.org. Web: www.stonemountainpark.org.

BIRTHDAYS TODAY

Corbin Bernsen, 47, actor ("LA Law," "Ryan's Hope," *Major League*), born North Hollywood, CA, Sept 7, 1954.

Susan Blakely, 51, actress (*The Way We Were, The Lords of Flatbush, Shampoo*), born Frankfurt, Germany, Sept 7, 1950.

Michael DeBakey, 93, distinguished heart surgeon, born Lake Charles, LA, Sept 7, 1908.

Michael Feinstein, 45, singer, pianist, born Columbus, OH, Sept 7, 1956.

Arthur Ferrante, 80, pianist (Ferrante and Teicher, "Exodus," "Tonight"), composer, born New York, NY, Sept 7, 1921.

Chrissie Hynde, 50, lead singer (Pretenders), songwriter, born Akron, OH, Sept 7, 1951.

Daniel Ken Inouye, 77, US Senator (D, Hawaii), born Honolulu, HI, Sept 7, 1924.

Julie Kavner, 50, actress (*Radio Days*, "Rhoda," Marge Simpson's voice on "The Simpsons"), born Los Angeles, CA, Sept 7, 1951.

Elia Kazan (Elia Kazanjoglou), 92, filmmaker (*On the Waterfront, East of Eden*), born Constantinople, Turkey, Sept 7, 1909.

John Philip Law, 64, actor (*The Russians Are Coming, the Russians Are Coming; Barbarella*), born Hollywood, CA, Sept 7, 1937.

Richard Roundtree, 59, actor (*Shaft, Q, Once upon a Time When We Were Colored*), born New Rochelle, NY, Sept 7, 1942.

Devon Sawa, 23, actor (*Wild America, The Boy's Club*), born Vancouver, British Columbia, Canada, Sept 7, 1978.

Briana Scurry, 30, soccer player, born Minneapolis, MN, Sept 7, 1971.

SEPTEMBER 8 — SATURDAY

Day 251 — 114 Remaining

ALOHA FESTIVALS ROYAL BALL. Sept 8. Hilton Hawaiian Village, Honolulu, HI. The elegant receptions of King David Kalakaua and Queen Liliuokalani are relived during Oahu's Aloha Festivals Royal Ball. Steeped in the regal traditions of Hawaii's romantic Victorian period, the Ball features the Aloha Festivals Royal Courts from all islands and marks the graceful conclusion of the statewide Aloha Festivals celebration. For info: Aloha Festivals. Phone: (800) 852-7690. Fax: (808) 589-4688. E-mail: alohafes@hula.net. Web: www.alohafestivals.com.

ANDORRA: NATIONAL HOLIDAY. Sept 8. Honors our Lady of Meritxell.

ARTIST RECEPTION & ART IN THE GARDEN. Sept 8–9. Washington, PA. Est attendance: 600. For info: Jan Bowman, Washington County Historical Soc, 49 E Maiden St, Washington, PA 15317. Phone: (724) 225-6740. Fax: (724) 225-8495. E-mail: info@wchspa.org. Web: www.wchspa.org.

☆ *Chase's 2001 Calendar of Events* ☆

BOONESBOROUGH DAYS. Sept 8–9. Shafer Memorial Park, Boonsboro, MD. Crafts, antiques, living history, demonstrations, food. Boonesborough was the original spelling of the town's name. Est attendance: 10,000. For info: Boonsboro Historical Soc, PO Box 213, Boonsboro, MD 21713. Phone: (301) 432-5889.

BOONSLICK FOLK FESTIVAL. Sept 8. Stolberg-Jackson Community Bldg, Arrow Rock, MO. Morning workshops on traditional folk instruments and afternoon concert. Contra dance in evening. Est attendance: 250. For info: Tempe McGlaughlin, H.A.R.C., PO Box M, Arrow Rock, MO 65320. Phone: (816) 837-3425. E-mail: tmcglaughlin@mid-mo.net.

CALIFORNIA PRUNE FESTIVAL. Sept 8–9. Yuba-Sutter Fairgrounds, Yuba City, CA. Food festival with celebrity chefs, five stages of entertainment, arts and crafts, children's area, 5K and 10K run/walk, petting zoo, farmers market, equipment show, floral competition, parade and more. Annually, the second weekend in September. Est attendance: 25,000. For info: Bree Gianassi, California Prune Festival, PO Box 3006, Yuba City, CA 95992. Phone: (530) 671-3100. Fax: (530) 751-8469. Web: www.prunefestival.com.

CELEBRATE PREGNANT WOMEN DAY. Sept 8. This day is set aside to honor and celebrate expectant mothers. A woman who carries life and nutures the miracle of a new life deserves recognition. Annually, the second Saturday in September. For info: Sue Battani, 1844 N Nob Hill Rd, #176, Plantation, FL 33322. Phone: (954) 474-7879. E-mail: info@miraclewithin.com. Web: miraclewithin.com.

CHADDS FORD DAYS. Sept 8–9. Chadds Ford, PA. Open-air colonial fair with 18th-century craft demonstrations, Brandywine Valley art, live old-time music, country rides and games, Colonial crafts for sale, good food. Est attendance: 10,000. For info: Chadds Ford Historical Soc, Box 27, Chadds Ford, PA 19317. Phone: (610) 388-7376. Fax: (610) 388-7480.

CIVIL WAR DAYS. Sept 8–9. Chesapeake Central Library, Chesapeake, VA. 8th annual reenactment and living history event. Skirmish both days, encampment drills, demonstrations, speakers, displays, children's activities and much more. Music groups and food vendors on site. Est attendance: 15,000. For info: Rhonda Riddick, Chesapeake Central Library, 298 Cedar Rd, Chesapeake, VA 23322. Phone: (757) 382-8571. Fax: (757) 382-8400. E-mail: rriddick@chesapeake.lib.va.us. Web: www.chesapeake.lib.va.us.

CLINE, PATSY: BIRTH ANNIVERSARY. Sept 8, 1932. Country and western singer, born Virginia Patterson Hensley at Winchester, VA. Patsy Cline got her big break in 1957 when she won an Arthur Godfrey Talent Scout show, singing "Walking After Midnight." Her career took off and she became a featured singer at the Grand Ole Opry, attaining the rank of top female country singer. She died in a plane crash Mar 5, 1963, at Camden, TN, along with singers Hawkshaw Hawkins and Cowboy Copas.

A DAY ON THE FARM. Sept 8 (tentative). Dorris Ranch, Springfield, OR. Hayrides, pony rides, homemade ice cream, entertainment, kid's crafts, petting zoo—all included in the admission fee. Take an interpretive walking tour of the Dorris Ranch Living History Filbert Farm. Costumed trappers, farmers and Kalapuyas guide the tours. Or you can browse the displays in the historic barn and watch old-time farming demonstrations. A farmer's market and refreshments will be available. You are welcome to bring a picnic lunch. For info: Willamalane Park and Recreation District, 200 S Mill St, Springfield, OR 97477. Phone: (541) 736-4544. Web: www.willamalane.org.

September 2001	S	M	T	W	T	F	S
							1
	2	3	4	5	6	7	8
	9	10	11	12	13	14	15
	16	17	18	19	20	21	22
	23	24	25	26	27	28	29
	30						

FALL IN LOVE WITH FOND DU LAC!. Sept 8–Oct 31. Fond du Lac, WI. Hike, bike or birdwatch in the Horicon National Wildlife Refuge, home to more than 260 species of birds. 200,000 Canada geese migrate to the Horicon Marsh each fall on their trip from Canada to their winter grounds. Horicon Marsh viewing area is located 12 miles south of Fond du Lac on Hwy 49. Also explore colorful Kettle Moraine State Forest. Enjoy harvest dinners, orchard hayrides, wildlife galleries and more. Annually, September and October. Est attendance: 4,500. For info: Fond du Lac Area Conv and Visitors Bureau, 19 W Scott St, Fond du Lac, WI 54935. Phone: (800) 937-9123, ext 92. Fax: (920) 929-6846. E-mail: market@fdl.com. Web: www.fdl.com.

★**FEDERAL LANDS CLEANUP DAY.** Sept 8. Presidential Proclamation 5521, of Sept 5, 1986, covers all succeeding years. The first Saturday after Labor Day. (PL99–402 of Aug 27, 1986.)

FLAX SCUTCHING FESTIVAL. Sept 8–9. Stahlstown, PA. PA Turnpike Exit 9; 4 miles north on Rte 711. Demonstrations of the art of making linen from the flax plant. Second oldest continuous complete flax demonstration festival in the world. Annually, the second weekend in September. Est attendance: 15,000. For info: Frank Newell, Flax Scutching Festival, RD #1, Rt 130W, Box 216, Stahlstown, PA 15687. Phone: (724) 593-2119.

GALVESTON HURRICANE: ANNIVERSARY. Sept 8, 1900. The worst national disaster in US history in terms of lives lost. More than 6,000 people were killed when a hurricane struck Galveston, TX, with winds of more than 120 MPH, followed by a huge tidal wave. More than 2,500 buildings were destroyed.

GARDENFEST AT LONGWOOD GARDENS. Sept 8–30. Kennett Square, PA. Longwood celebrates the beauty and bounty of late summer and early fall with harvest displays, flower shows, gardening, demonstrations, outdoor exhibits and weekend performances. Est attendance: 50,000. For info: Longwood Gardens, PO Box 501, Kennett Square, PA 19348-0501. Phone: (610) 388-1000. Web: www.longwoodgardens.org.

GUTHRIE ADULT SOAP BOX DERBY AND ROAD CELEBRATION. Sept 8. Guthrie, OK. Cruise historic Guthrie and celebrate America's infatuation with cars. Event activities include Guthrie's Adult Soap Box Derby and Classic Car Road Show. Enjoy the excitement of the races or stroll the park among vintage automobiles. Est attendance: 12,000. For info: Guthrie CVB, PO Box 995, Guthrie, OK 73044-0995. Phone: (800) 299-1889 or (405) 282-1947. Fax: (405) 282-0061.

HANG AROUND VICTOR DAY. Sept 8. Victor, NY. Festival with artists, craftsmen, antique dealers, civic and social organizations, family entertainment, pet parade and pet contest, cloggers, magicians, clowns and food vendors. Annually, the first Saturday after Labor Day. Est attendance: 12,500. For info: Susan Stehling, 31 E Main St, Victor, NY 14564. Phone: (716) 924-7260 or (716) 742-1476. Fax: (716) 924-0523.

HERITAGE DAY FESTIVAL. Sept 8 (rain date Sept 9). Lavallette, NJ. Clowns, antique cars, bands, games, food, children's games, train rides and finale with Ocean County String Band performing. 10 AM–dusk. Annually, the second Saturday in September. Est attendance: 30,000. For info: Joy Grosko, Dir, Heritage Committee Inc, 13 Camden Ave, Lavallette, NJ 08735. Phone: (732) 793-3652. Fax: (732) 854-9038. E-mail: tgrook1@juno.com.

HILLTOP FESTIVAL. Sept 8–9 (tentative). Huntington Museum of Art, Huntington, WV. Bookfair, arts and crafts and demonstrations, children's activities, popular performing groups and food booths. Annually, first weekend after Labor Day. Est attendance: 10,000. For info: Huntington Museum of Art, 2033 McCoy Rd, Huntington, WV 25701. Phone: (304) 529-2701. Fax: (304) 529-7447.

LEAVENWORTH RIVER FEST. Sept 8–9. Leavenworth, KS. Arts and crafts, antique car exhibits, parade, aircraft display and rides, children's carnival, plenty of entertainment, food and several feature attractions. Annually, the second weekend in September. Est attendance: 25,000. For info: Connie Hachenburg,

Dir, Leavenworth Conv/Visitors, 518 Shawnee, Box 44, Leavenworth, KS 66048. Phone: (913) 682-3924. Fax: (913) 682-3928.

LITTLE FALLS ARTS AND CRAFTS FAIR. Sept 8–9. Little Falls, MN. 950 artists, craftspeople and hobbyists displaying and selling their items. Est attendance: 100,000. For info: Chamber of Commerce, 200 NW First St, Little Falls, MN 56345. Phone: (320) 632-5155. Fax: (320) 632-2122. E-mail: assistance@littlefallschamber.com. Web: www.littlefallschamber.com.

LOUISIANA FOLKLIFE FESTIVAL. Sept 8–9. Monroe, LA. A festival of Louisiana's culture, heritage and music, featuring five entertainment stages, craft demonstrations and food. For info: Mike Luster. Phone: (318) 324-1665.

MALTA: SIEGE BROKEN: ANNIVERSARY. Sept 8. "Two Sieges and Regatta Day" festivities now commemorate victory over the Turks, Sept 8, 1565, when the siege that began in May 1565 was broken by the Maltese and the Knights of St. John after a loss of nearly 10,000 lives. Also commemorated is survival of the 1943 siege by the Axis Powers. Parades, fireworks, boat races, etc, especially at the capital, Valleta, and the Grand Harbour.

MARYLAND RECREATIONAL VEHICLE SHOW. Sept 8–9 (also Sept 14–16). Timonium State Fairgrounds, Timonium, MD. 10th annual outdoor show of motor homes, trailers, five-wheel trailers and pickup campers, campground booths, accessories and related items. Annually, beginning the first Saturday after Labor Day. Est attendance: 7,500. For info: Richard T. Albright, Pres, Maryland Rec Vehicle Dealers Assn, Inc, 8332 Pulaski Hwy, Baltimore, MD 21237. Phone: (410) 687-6191. Fax: (410) 686-1486.

McGWIRE HITS HIS 62nd HOME RUN: ANNIVERSARY. Sept 8, 1998. Mark McGwire of the St. Louis Cardinals hit his 62nd home run, breaking Roger Maris's 1961 record for the most home runs in a single season. McGwire hit his homer at Busch Stadium at St. Louis against pitcher Steve Trachsel of the Chicago Cubs as the Cardinals won, 6–3. McGwire finished the season with 70 home runs.

MICHIGAN WINE AND HARVEST FESTIVAL. Sept 8–10. Kalamazoo and Paw Paw, MI. An annual celebration with grape stomping, winery tours, arts and crafts, carnival rides, champagne races, a midway and a grand parade (Paw Paw). Est attendance: 80,000. For info: Michigan Wine and Harvest Festival, Inc, 128 N Kalamazoo Mall, Kalamazoo, MI 49007. Phone: (616) 655-1111 or (800) 530-9192. Fax: (616) 343-0430.

MISS AMERICA FIRST CROWNED: 80th ANNIVERSARY. Sept 8, 1921. Margaret Gorman of Washington, DC, was crowned the first Miss America at the end of a two-day pageant at Atlantic City, NJ.

MISSION SAN GABRIEL ARCHANGEL: FOUNDING ANNIVERSARY. Sept 8, 1771. California mission to the Indians founded on this date.

NANTICOKE INDIAN POWWOW. Sept 8–9. Millsboro, DE. Annual gathering of Native Americans during which Native American dances and music are presented and Native American foods and arts and crafts are sold. Dance sessions: Saturday, noon–5 PM, Sunday, 2–4:30 PM. Sunday worship service, 11 AM– noon. Annually, the weekend after Labor Day. Est attendance: 40,000. For info: Cecile Coursey, Prog Coord, Nanticoke Indian Assn, Rte 4, Box 107A, Millsboro, DE 19966. Phone: (302) 945-3400. E-mail: nanticok@bellatlantic.net.

NIXON PARDON DAY: ANNIVERSARY. Sept 8, 1974. Anniversary of the "full, free, and absolute pardon unto Richard Nixon, for all offenses against the United States which he, Richard Nixon, has committed or may have committed or taken part in during the period from January 20, 1969, through August 9, 1974." (Presidential Proclamation 4311, Sept 8, 1974, by Gerald R. Ford.)

NORSKEDALEN'S THRESHING BEE. Sept 8. Norskedalen Nature and Heritage Center, Coon Valley, WI. Antique engines and pioneer demonstrations, such as winnowing, threshing, corn shredding, shelling and grinding; cream separating and buttermaking; horsedrawn wagon rides, rope braiding, saw mill, quilt show and farm tool displays. Threshers' meal served, reservations required. Est attendance: 500. For info: Nature and Heritage Center, Inc, Norskedalen, PO Box 235, Coon Valley, WI 54623. Phone: (608) 452-3424. Fax: (608) 452-3157.

NORTHERN PACIFIC RAILROAD COMPLETED: ANNIVERSARY. Sept 8, 1883. After 19 years of construction, the Northern Pacific Railroad became the second railroad to link the two coasts. The Union Pacific and Central Pacific lines met at Utah in 1869.

"THE OPRAH WINFREY SHOW" TV PREMIERE: 15th ANNIVERSARY. Sept 8, 1986. This daytime talk show was the top-rated talk show for years and also has the distinction of being the first talk show hosted by a black woman, Oprah Winfrey. Her show is taped in front of a studio audience who are solicited for their questions and feedback. In the mid-1990s, fed up with the plethora of trashy talk shows that had sprung up everywhere, Winfrey decided to upgrade the quality of topics that her show presented.

PEPPER, CLAUDE DENSON: BIRTH ANNIVERSARY. Sept 8, 1900. US Representative and Senator, born near Dudleyville, AL. Pepper's career in politics spanned 53 years and 10 presidents, and he became the champion for America's senior citizens. He was elected to the US Senate in 1936, where he was a principal architect of many of the nation's "safety net" social programs including Social Security, the minimum wage and medical assistance for the elderly and for handicapped children. After a 14-year career in the Senate, he returned to Congress in the House of Representatives where he served 14 terms. He served as chairman of the House Select Committee on Aging, drafted legislation banning forced retirement and fought against cutting Social Security benefits. Pepper died at Washington, DC, May 30, 1989.

PIONEER POWER DAYS & ANTIQUE SHOW. Sept 8–9. Lewistown, MT. Antique tractors and equipment, operating and on display. Est attendance: 600. For info: Brian H. Sallee, Central MT Flywheelers Assn, 1015 W Washington, Lewistown, MT 59457. Phone: (406) 538-5236.

POTATO DAY FESTIVAL. Sept 8. Centennial Village Museum, Greeley, CO. Living history demonstrations, musical entertainment, square dancing, cloggers, melodrama, children's activities spread over 5-acre site. Free baked potato and trimmings. Ages 12 and over $4. Children free. Est attendance: 3,000. For info: Greeley Museums, 919 7th St, Greeley, CO 80631. Phone: (970) 350-9220. Fax: (970) 350-9700. Web: www.ci.greeley.co.us/culture/museums.

QUADRANGLE FESTIVAL. Sept 8–9 (tentative). Downtown Texarkana, TX and AR. 20th annual festival features 5K BiState Race on the Texas-Arkansas state line. Also, crafts, collectibles, antique autos, pet shows; country/western, traditional and contemporary music; folk artists and craftspeople; street dancing and food vendors. Est attendance: 45,000. For info: Dir of Mktg, Texarkana Museums System, PO Box 2343, Texarkana, TX 75504. Phone: (903) 793-4831. Fax: (903) 793-7108.

QUILTS ALONG THE BAY. Sept 8–9. Barnegat Community Center, Barnegat, NJ. Judged quilt show featuring quilts from all over the state, raffle quilt, presentations, food court, door prizes and merchants mall. Sponsored by the Barnegat Historical Society. Est attendance: 750. For info: P.A. Thorpe, 8 Forester Dr, Barnegat, NJ 08005. Phone: (609) 698-0038. E-mail: PAThorpe@aol.com.

SELLERS, PETER (RICHARD HENRY): BIRTH ANNIVERSARY. Sept 8, 1925. Award-winning British comedian and film star, born at Southsea, Hampshire, England. Sellers is especially remembered for his role as the bumbling character Inspector Clouseau in the *Pink Panther* films. Died at London, England, July 24, 1980.

SIDEWALK ARTS FESTIVAL. Sept 8. Sioux Falls, SD. Live entertainment, music, great food, cultural activities and more than 400 booths featuring the area's best art and folk displays. Est attendance: 60,000. For info: Shirley K. Sneve, Visual Arts Center at the Washington Pavilion, 301 S Main Ave, Sioux Falls, SD 57104. Phone: (605) 367-7397 ext 2353. Fax: (605) 731-2402. E-mail: vac@washingtonpavilion.org. Web: www.washington pavilion.org.

SODBUSTER DAYS—THE HARVEST. Sept 8–9. Sunne Farm, Fort Ransom State Park, Fort Ransom, ND. Demonstrations of life on a small family farm of the 1920s during the fall harvest. Activities include threshing, fall field work, gathering prairie hay, ladies' demonstrations, kids games, food, music. Most farm machinery is horse drawn. Annually, the weekend after Labor Day. Est attendance: 3,500. For info: Fort Ransom State Park, 5981 Walt Hjelle Pkwy, Fort Ransom, ND 58033-9712. Phone: (701) 973-4331. Fax: (701) 973-4271.

SPINACH AND TRAILS FESTIVAL. Sept 8. Sar-Ko-Par Trails Park, Lenexa, KS. Exhibits, food, games and more than 200 arts and crafts booths. This festival includes an 1800s Kansas prairie with settlers, traders, soldiers and emigrants setting up an encampment on their journey west. Also, a living history museum, entertainment, period concessions and an educational fair. Est attendance: 10,000. For info: Bill Nicks, Lenexa Parks & Rec, 13240 Oak St, Lenexa, KS 66215. Phone: (913) 541-8592. Fax: (913) 492-8118.

"STAR TREK" TV PREMIERE: 35th ANNIVERSARY. Sept 8, 1966. The first of 79 episodes of the TV series "Star Trek" was aired on the NBC network. Although the science fiction show set in the future only lasted a few seasons, it has remained enormously popular through syndication reruns. It has been given new life through six motion pictures, a cartoon TV series and the very popular TV series "Star Trek: The Next Generation" and "Star Trek: Deep Space Nine." It has consistently ranked among the biggest titles in the motion picture, television, home video and licensing divisions of Paramount Pictures.

"TARZAN" TV PREMIERE: 35th ANNIVERSARY. Sept 8, 1966. This hour adventure series was based on Edgar Rice Burroughs' character, who appeared for the first time on TV. Tarzan, an English lord who preferred the jungle, was played by Ron Ely. Manuel Padilla, Jr was Jai, a jungle orphan, Alan Cail-

lou was Jason Flood, Jai's tutor and Rockne Tarkington was Rao, a veterinarian. There was no Jane.

"THAT GIRL" TV PREMIERE: 35th ANNIVERSARY. Sept 8, 1966. "That Girl" was a half-hour sitcom starring Marlo Thomas as Ann Marie, an independent aspiring actress in New York City. Ted Bessell also starred as her boyfriend Don Hollinger. They were finally engaged in 1970. Also featured were Lew Parker, Rosemary De Camp and Bonnie Scott. Well-known performers who appeared on the show include Dabney Coleman, George Carlin and Bernie Kopell.

UNITED NATIONS: INTERNATIONAL LITERACY DAY. Sept 8. An international day observed by the organizations of the United Nations system. Info from: United Nations, Dept of Public Info, New York, NY 10017.

US SENIOR AMATEUR (GOLF) CHAMPIONSHIP. Sept 8–13. Norwood Country Club, St. Louis, MO. For info: US Golf Assn, Golf House, PO Box 708, Championship Dept, Far Hills, NJ 07931. Phone: (908) 234-2300. Fax: (908) 234-9687. E-mail: usga@ix.netcom.com. Web: www.usga.org.

VALPARAISO POPCORN FESTIVAL. Sept 8. Valparaiso, IN. Celebration of popcorn with a parade, the Popcorn Panic and Little Kernal Puff running races, arts, crafts, food booths, music and entertainment, kiddie carnival and a hot-air balloon show. Annually, the first Saturday after Labor Day. Est attendance: 65,000. For info: Glennas Kueck, Exec Dir, 204 E Lincolnway, PO Box 189, Valparaiso, IN 46384. Phone: (219) 464-8332. Fax: (219) 464-2343. E-mail: popcorn@netnitco.net. Web: www.popcornfest.org.

WILLOW TREE FESTIVAL. Sept 8–9. Gordon, NE. This festival is a cornucopia of arts and crafts, three quality performing stages including a children's stage, children's activities, fun and food. Annually, the second weekend in September. Est attendance: 4,600. For info: Willow Tree Festival, PO Box 303, Gordon, NE 69343-0303. Phone: (308) 327-2917. Fax: (308) 327-2166. E-mail: rwbuchan@gpcom.net.

BIRTHDAYS TODAY

David Arquette, 30, actor (*Scream, Muppets from Space*), born Winchester, VA, Sept 8, 1971.

Sid Caesar, 79, comedian, actor ("Your Show of Shows"), born Yonkers, NY, Sept 8, 1922.

Alan Feinstein, 60, actor ("Edge of Night," "Love of Life," "Search for Tomorrow"), born New York, NY, Sept 8, 1941.

Marilyn (Williamson) Mims, 47, opera singer, born Collins, MS, Sept 8, 1954.

Latrell Sprewell, 31, basketball player, born Milwaukee, WI, Sept 8, 1970.

Heather Thomas, 44, actress ("The Fall Guy"), born Greenwich, CT, Sept 8, 1957.

Henry Thomas, 30, actor (*E.T. The Extra-Terrestrial, Legends of the Fall*), born San Antonio, TX, Sept 8, 1971.

Jonathan Taylor Thomas, 20, actor ("Home Improvement"), born Bethlehem, PA, Sept 8, 1981.

Rogatien (Rogie) Vachon, 56, former hockey executive and player, born Palmarolle, Quebec, Canada, Sept 8, 1945.

	S	M	T	W	T	F	S
September							1
2001	2	3	4	5	6	7	8
	9	10	11	12	13	14	15
	16	17	18	19	20	21	22
	23	24	25	26	27	28	29
	30						

SEPTEMBER 9 — SUNDAY

Day 252 — 113 Remaining

BATTLE OF MARATHON: ANNIVERSARY. Sept 9. On the day of the ninth month's full moon in the year 490 BC, the numerically superior invading army of Persia was met and defeated on the Plain of Marathon by the Athenian army, led by Miltiades. More than 6,000 men died in the day's battle, which drove the Persians to the sea. The mound of earth covering the dead is still visible at the site. This date is in dispute. See also: "Days of Marathon: Anniversary" (Sept 2) for the legendary running of Phidippides and the origin of the marathon race.

BATTLE OF SALERNO: ANNIVERSARY. Sept 9–16, 1943. US General Mark Clark's Fifth Army made an amphibious assault on Salerno, Italy (Operation Avalanche), at 3:30 AM. The British 1st Airborne Division seized the southern Italian port of Taranto (Operation Slapstick) without opposition. Initial gains along the western coast of Italy were checked by strong German forces by Sept 12. In some places the Allied forces were pushed back to within two miles of the coast. On Sept 15 US 82nd Airborne and British 7th Armoured counter-attacked and on Sept 16 units of the American 5th Army and the British 8th Army joined up near Vallo di Lucania.

BELGIUM: HISTORICAL PROCESSION. Sept 9. Tournai. Traditional cultural observance. Annually, the Sunday closest to Sept 8.

BISCUITS AND GRAVY WEEK. Sept 9–15. Recognizes the culinary marriage of biscuits and gravy—a traditional, ever popular dish in the southern and western regions of the US. Hot biscuits can be served with a wide variety of gravies. Also, celebrates the 150th anniversary of C.H. Guenther & Son, Inc, as the oldest, continuously family-owned flour mill in the US. Consumers can find their baking products and gravies on grocers' shelves under the Pioneer, White Wings and White Lily brands. Annually, the second week of September. For info: C.H. Guenther & Son, Inc, PO Box 118, San Antonio, TX 78291. Phone: (800) 531-7912.

BONZA BOTTLER DAY™. Sept 9. To celebrate when the number of the day is the same as the number of the month. Bonza Bottler Day™ is an excuse to have a party at least once a month. For more information, see Jan 1. For info: Gail M. Berger, 109 Matthew Ave, Poca, WV 25159. Phone: (304) 776-7746. E-mail: gberger5@aol.com.

BUCKEYE TREE FESTIVAL. Sept 9. Utica, OH. Ohio's only festival recognizing the Ohio State tree, celebrating Ohio's heritage. Est attendance: 4,500. For info: Buckeye Tree Festival, PO Box 588, Utica, OH 43080. Phone: (740) 892-3921.

CALIFORNIA: ADMISSION DAY: ANNIVERSARY. Sept 9. Became 31st state in 1850.

CATONSVILLE ARTS & CRAFTS FESTIVAL. Sept 9. Catonsville, MD. Fall festival featuring handmade items by 200 artisans and crafters in the revitalized village of Catonsville. Continuous music, children's entertainment and local food vendors. Annually, the second Sunday in September. Est attendance: 30,000. For info: Maureen Sweeney Smith, Greater Catonsville Chamber of Commerce, PO Box 21100, Catonsville, MD 21228. Phone: (410) 719-9609.

CORVETTE SHOW. Sept 9 (rain date Sept 16). Wheaton Village, Millville, NJ. Presented by Corvettes Unlimited Corvette Club. Est attendance: 1,500. For info: Wheaton Village, 1501 Glasstown Rd, Millville, NJ 08332. Phone: (856) 825-6800. Fax: (856) 825-2410. E-mail: mail@wheatonvillage.org. Web: www.wheatonvillage.org.

ENCHANTED CIRCLE CENTURY BIKE TOUR. Sept 9. Red River, NM. 100-mile scenic ride and one of the longest and most difficult bicycle tours in the Southwest. Est attendance: 1,000. For info: Red River Chamber of Commerce, PO Box 870, Red River, NM 87558. Phone: (800) 348-6444. E-mail: rrinfo@redrivernewmex.com. Web: redrivernewmex.com.

"FAT ALBERT AND THE COSBY KIDS" TV PREMIERE: ANNIVERSARY. Sept 9, 1972. This cartoon series was hosted by Bill Cosby, with characters based on his childhood friends at Philadelphia. Its central characters—Fat Albert, Weird Harold, Mush Mouth and Donald—were weird-looking but very human. The show sent messages of tolerance and harmony. In 1979 the show was renamed "The New Fat Albert Show."

FESTA ITALIA. Sept 9–10. Custom House Plaza, Monterey, CA. A 65-year tradition dedicated to Santa Rosalia, patron saint of the Sicilian fishermen in Monterey, the Festival includes parade, outdoor mass, blessing of the fleet, entertainment, arts and crafts and Italian food. Benefits the Festa Italia Foundation. Est attendance: 10,000. For info: Bostrom Management, 140 Franklin, Ste 202, Monterey, CA 93940. Phone: (831) 649-6544. Fax: (831) 649-4124.

FESTIVAL-IN-THE-PARK. Sept 9 (rain date Sept 23). Memorial Park, Nutley, NJ. 28th annual festival, a craft and collectibles show to benefit the Nutley Historical Society and the Historic Restoration Trust. Annually, the first Sunday after Labor Day. Est attendance: 16,000. For info: Douglas J. Eisenfelder, Festival-in-the-Park, 51 Enclosure, Nutley, NJ 07110. Phone: (973) 667-3013.

GRANDPARENT'S DAY CELEBRATION. Sept 9. Jenkinson's Aquarium, Point Pleasant Beach, NJ. Calling all kids! Join your grandparents for a special day together at the aquarium. We will focus on families in the animal kingdom. Stories about animal families will be read throughout the day. One grandparent is admitted free with each paid child's admission (child is 3–12 years). Est attendance: 600. For info: Liz Carletta, Education Coord, Jenkinson's Aquarium, 300 Ocean Ave, Point Pleasant Beach, NJ 08742. Phone: (732) 899-1212. Fax: (732) 899-1717. E-mail: aquarium@jenkinsons.com. Web: www.jenkinsons.com.

HOMESTEADER HARVEST FESTIVAL. Sept 9. Beaver Creek Nature Area, Brandon, SD. This is a re-creation of the harvest and celebration that went with it back in the pioneer days. Annually, the second Sunday in September. Est attendance: 1,200. For info: Palisades State Park, 25495 485th Ave, Garretson, SD 57030-6117. Phone: (605) 594-3824.

INTERNATIONAL CHILDREN'S WEEK. Sept 9–15. Observed to promote the theme "Teaching Values Through Song and Music." Fairs, exhibitions, musical performances, competitions. Coordinators needed to plan and implement event at local level: vendors, advertising, sponsorships, etc. For info: Augustus Graham, Intl Children's Week Network, PO Box 551, Redan, GA 30074. Phone: (770) 822-2519. E-mail: GBQueries@aol.com.

INTERNATIONAL HOUSEKEEPERS WEEK. Sept 9–15. A week to recognize housekeeping staff, to let them know that they are appreciated and that the work they do is worthwhile, vital, commendable and acknowledged by all. Annually, the second full week in September. For info: IEHA, 1001 Eastwind Dr, Ste 301, Westerville, OH 43081-3361. Phone: (800) 200-6342. Fax: (614) 895-1248. E-mail: excel@ieha.org. Web: www.ieha.org.

ITALY: GIOSTRA DELLA QUINTANA. Sept 9. Foligno. A revival of a 17th-century joust of the Quintana, featuring 600 knights in full costume. Annually, the second Sunday in September.

JAPAN: CHRYSANTHEMUM DAY. Sept 9. Traditional chrysanthemum festival.

JCBC CENTURY RIDE. Sept 9. Junction City, Milford Lake, Fort Riley, KS. 100-mile bicycle ride (in loops) of various course routes and optional stopping points. Annually, the second Sunday in September. Sponsor: Bicycle Club. Est attendance: 200. For info: Casey Thomas, 2206 Prospect Circle, Junction City, KS 66441. Phone: (913) 762-3310. Fax: (913) 238-8351. E-mail: kspetdr@kansas.net.

KOREA, DEMOCRATIC PEOPLE'S REPUBLIC OF: NATIONAL DAY. Sept 9. National holiday in the Democratic People's Republic of [North] Korea.

LISCO OLD-TIMERS DAY. Sept 9. Lisco, NE. Local talent puts on program and skits about an honored old-timer or couple. Parade, barbecue (free-will offering), horseshoe tournament, antique tractor pull and more. Annually, Sunday after Labor Day. Sponsor: Lisco Old-timers Day Committee. Est attendance: 2,000. For info: Lisco State Bank, Lisco Old-Timers Day Committee, Lisco, NE 69148.

LUXEMBOURG: ANNIVERSARY LIBERATION CEREMONY. Sept 9. Petange. Commemoration of liberation of Grand-Duchy by the Allied forces in 1944. Ceremony at monument of the American soldier.

MAO TSE-TUNG: 25th DEATH ANNIVERSARY. Sept 9, 1976. People's Republic of China pays tribute to memory of the Chinese revolutionary leader, who died at Beijing. Memorial Hall, where his flag-draped body lies encased in crystal, was opened at Tiananmen Square at Beijing on the first anniversary of his death. Mao was born Dec 26, 1893, at Hunan Province, China.

September 2001	S	M	T	W	T	F	S
							1
	2	3	4	5	6	7	8
	9	10	11	12	13	14	15
	16	17	18	19	20	21	22
	23	24	25	26	27	28	29
	30						

NATIONAL ASSISTED LIVING WEEK. Sept 9–15. A week-long observance designed to raise awareness of the role assisted living plays in serving the nation's elderly. Annually, Grandparents' Day through the following Saturday. For info: Natl Center for Assisted Living, 1201 L St NW, Washington, DC 20005. Phone: (202) 842-4444. Fax: (202) 842-3860.

NATIONAL 5-A-DAY WEEK. Sept 9–15. To encourage all Americans to increase the amount of fruits and vegetables they eat to five or more servings per day, to better their health and reduce their risk of cancer and other chronic diseases. For info: Produce for Better Health Foundation, 5301 Limestone Rd, Ste 101, Wilmington, DE 19808. Web: www.5aday.com.

★**NATIONAL GRANDPARENTS DAY.** Sept 9. Presidential Proclamation 4679, of Sept 6, 1979, covers all succeeding years. First Sunday in September following Labor Day (PL96–62 of Sept 6, 1979). First issued in 1978 (Proc 4580 of Aug 3, 1978), requested by Public Law 325 of July 28, 1978.

NORTHEAST MISSOURI TRIATHLON CHAMPIONSHIP. Sept 9. Thousand Hills State Park, Kirksville, MO. Swim 3/4 mile, bike 18 miles, run 5 miles. USA Triathlon Federation certified. Qualifier for International Course Nationals. Annually, the Sunday after Labor Day. Est attendance: 800. For info: KRXL Radio, Box 130, Kirksville, MO 63501. Phone: (660) 626-2213. Fax: (660) 626-2483.

PROTECTING YOUR HOME FURNISHINGS WEEK. Sept 9–15. Week dedicated to taking care of the valuable furnishings in your home—furniture, window treatments, paintings, objects of art, decorative accessories, etc. A Home Furnishings laminated maintenance chart is now available: "How to Care for Your Valuable Furnishings"—weekly, monthly and annually with special prevention and repair tips ($5). Annually, the second week in September before holidays preparations begin. For info: Darvas Interiors, 1835 F Tanglewood Dr, Glenview, IL 60025. Phone: (847) 832-1414. Fax: (847) 832-1417. E-mail: DarvasInteriors@aol.com.

"RHODA" TV PREMIERE: ANNIVERSARY. Sept 9, 1974. This spin-off from "The Mary Tyler Moore Show" starred Valerie Harper as Rhoda Morgenstern, who returns to New York, finds a job and gets married (she also gets separated and divorced). Other characters included her husband Joe Gerard (David Groh), her sister Brenda (Julie Kavner), her mother Ida (Nancy Walker), her father Martin (Harold Gould) and Carlton, the heard-but-not-seen doorman (Lorenzo Music). Other regulars included Richard Masur, Ron Silver, Anne Meara and Kenneth McMillan.

SANDERS, COLONEL HARLAND DAVID: BIRTH ANNIVERSARY. Sept 9, 1890. Founder of Kentucky Fried Chicken, born near Henryville, IN. Died Dec 16, 1980, at Shelbyville, KY.

SOUTHEAST MISSOURI DISTRICT FAIR. Sept 9–15. Arena Park Fairgrounds, Cape Girardeau, MO. Oldest outdoor fair in the state. Celebrating its 146th year with beauty pageants, livestock exhibition, horse show, entertainment, carnival, food and 4-H displays. Annually, the week after Labor Day. Est attendance: 92,000. For info: SEMO District Fair Assn, PO Box 234, Cape Girardeau, MO 63702-0234. Phone: (800) 455-FAIR or (573) 334-9250.

SUBSTITUTE TEACHER APPRECIATION WEEK. Sept 9–15. Although substitute teachers get no sick days or respect, they teach when the regular teacher cannot and continually adjust to different classroom situations. Annually, the second week of September. For info: Dorothy Zjawin, Dir, 61 W Colfax Ave, Roselle Park, NJ 07204. Phone: (908) 241-6241. Fax: (908) 241-6241.

SUNDAE IN THE PARK. Sept 9. Swimming Pool Park, Yerington, NV. YTA presents a celebration of Mason Valley with an art and food festival featuring arts, crafts and food produced in the Mason Valley area. All-day entertainment and free ice cream sundaes for everyone. Est attendance: 300. For info: Mason Valley, Chamber of Commerce, 227 S Main St, Yerington, NV 89447. Phone: (775) 463-2245. Fax: (775) 463-3369. Web: www.tele-net.net/lyon.

TAJIKISTAN: INDEPENDENCE DAY: 10th ANNIVERSARY. Sept 9. National holiday commemorating independence from the Soviet Union in 1991.

TOLSTOY, LEO: BIRTH ANNIVERSARY. Sept 9, 1828. Russian novelist and moral philosopher, born at Tula Province, Russia. Best known for his novels (*War and Peace, Anna Karenina*), Tolstoy also wrote short stories, plays and essays. A member of the nobility, in his moral and religious writings he condemned private property and championed nonviolent protest. Died Nov 20, 1910, at Astapovo, Russia.

UNITED KINGDOM: BATTLE OF BRITAIN WEEK. Sept 9–15. Annually, the week of September containing Battle of Britain Day (Sept 15).

"WELCOME BACK, KOTTER" TV PREMIERE: ANNIVERSARY. Sept 9, 1975. In this half-hour sitcom, Gabe Kotter (Gabe Kaplan) returns to James Buchanan High School, his alma mater, to teach the "sweathogs," a group of hopeless underachievers. Other featured cast members included Marcia Strassman, John Travolta, Robert Hegyes, Ron Palillo, Lawrence Hilton-Jacobs and John Sylvester White. Later in the series, two new sweathogs were added, played by Melonie Haller and Stephen Shortridge. The theme song, "Welcome Back," was sung by John Sebastian. The last telecast was Aug 10, 1979.

WILLIAM, THE CONQUEROR: DEATH ANNIVERSARY. Sept 9, 1087. William I, The Conqueror, King of England and Duke of Normandy, whose image is portrayed in the Bayeux Tapestry, was born about 1028 at Falaise, Normandy. Victorious over Harold at the Battle of Hastings (the Norman Conquest) in 1066, William was crowned King of England at Westminster Abbey on Christmas Day of that year. Later, while waging war in France, William met his death at Rouen, Sept 9, 1087.

BIRTHDAYS TODAY

Benjamin Roy ("BJ") Armstrong, 34, former basketball player, born Detroit, MI, Sept 9, 1967.
Angela Cartwright, 49, actress ("Lost in Space," *The Sound of Music*), born Cheshire, England, Sept 9, 1952.
Hugh Grant, 41, actor (*Impromptu, Sense and Sensibility, Four Weddings and a Funeral*), born London, England, Sept 9, 1960.
Jane Greer, 77, actress (*Out of the Past, Prisoner of Zenda, Against All Odds*), born Washington, DC, Sept 9, 1924.
Mike Hampton, 29, baseball player, born Brooksville, FL, Sept 9, 1972.
Rachel Hunter, 32, model, born New Zealand, Sept 9, 1969.
Michael Keaton (Michael Douglas), 50, actor ("Report to Murphy," *Batman, The Dream Team*), born Pittsburgh, PA, Sept 9, 1951.
Daniel Lewis (Dan) Majerle, 36, basketball player, born Traverse City, MI, Sept 9, 1965.
Sylvia Miles, 67, actress (*Midnight Cowboy, Farewell My Lovely, She-Devil*), born New York, NY, Sept 9, 1934.

Billy Preston, 55, musician, songwriter, singer ("Nothing from Nothing"), born Houston, TX, Sept 9, 1946.
Cliff Robertson, 76, actor ("Falcon Crest," *Brainstorm, Charly, PT-109*), born La Jolla, CA, Sept 9, 1925.
Adam Sandler, 35, actor, comedian ("Saturday Night Live," *The Wedding Singer*), born Brooklyn, NY, Sept 9, 1966.
Joseph Robert (Joe) Theisman, 52, sportscaster, Pro Football Hall of Fame quarterback, born New Brunswick, NJ, Sept 9, 1949.
Goran Visnjic, 29, actor ("ER"), born Sibenik, Croatia, Sept 9, 1972.
Tom Wopat, 50, actor ("The Dukes of Hazzard," "Cybill") born Lodi, WI, Sept 9, 1951.

SEPTEMBER 10 — MONDAY
Day 253 — 112 Remaining

★**AMERICA GOES BACK TO SCHOOL.** Sept 10–16.

BELIZE: SAINT GEORGE'S CAYE DAY. Sept 10. Public holiday celebrated in honor of the battle between the European Baymen Settlers and the Spaniards for the territory of Belize.

BRAXTON, CARTER: BIRTH ANNIVERSARY. Sept 10, 1736. American revolutionary statesman and signer of the Declaration of Independence. Born at Newington, VA, he died Oct 10, 1797, at Richmond, VA.

CATS CLOSES: ANNIVERSARY. Sept 10, 2000. The longest-running production in Broadway history closed this day after more than 7,400 performances. *Cats*, which opened Oct 7, 1982, was based on a book of poetry by T.S. Eliot and had a score by Andrew Lloyd Webber. More than 10 million theatergoers saw the New York City production. It was also produced in 30 other countries.

FEARLESS FORECASTS OF TV'S FALL FLOPS. Sept 10. The 15th annual review of the new television season with a tongue-in-cheek evaluation of which shows will be cancelled. "Unbelievably accurate." Announcement will be posted prior to the event on www.boringinstitute.com to facilitate media coverage. For info: Alan Caruba, The Boring Institute, PO Box 40, Maplewood, NJ 07040. Phone: (973) 763-6492. E-mail: acaruba@aol.com. Web: www.boringinstitute.com.

FOLKFEST. Sept 10–16. Bismarck, ND. Join one of the American Bus Association's top 100 events. There is something for everyone: a parade, Gumi Race, Renaissance Feast, entertainment, downtown street fair and local events celebrating North Dakota's culture and heritage. For info: Bismarck/Mandan Conv & Visitors Bureau, PO Box 2274, Bismarck, ND 58502. Phone: (800) 767-3555. Fax: (701) 222-0647.

"GENTLE BEN" TV PREMIERE: ANNIVERSARY. Sept 10, 1967. This show was about the adventures of a boy, Mark Wedloe (Clint Howard) and his pet bear, Ben. Also featured were Dennis Weaver as his father Tom, a game warden, Beth Brickell as his mother Ellen, Jack Worley as Tom's friend Spencer and Angelo Rutherford as his friend Willie. It was filmed on location in Florida.

"GUNSMOKE" TV PREMIERE: ANNIVERSARY. Sept 10, 1955. "Gunsmoke" was TV's longest-running western, moving from radio to TV. John Wayne turned down the role of Marshall Matt Dillon but recommended James Arness, who got the role. Other regulars included Amanda Blake as Kitty Russell, saloon-owner; Dennis Weaver as Chester B. Goode, Dillon's deputy and Milburn Stone as Doc Adams. In 1962 a fifth character was added—the "rugged male." Burt Reynolds played Quint Asper, followed by Roger Ewing as Thad Greenwood, and Buck Taylor as Newly O'Brien. In 1964 Ken Curtis was added as funnyman Festus Haggen, the new deputy. "Gunsmoke" was incredibly popular, both as a half-hour and hour-long show, as the number-one rated series for four seasons, and a top ten hit for six seasons. The last telecast was Sept 1, 1975.

"KIDS ARE PEOPLE TOO" TV PREMIERE: ANNIVERSARY. Sept 10, 1978. This ABC series was a Sunday morning magazine show for kids. Hosts included Bob McAllister, Michael Young and Randy Hamilton.

KURALT, CHARLES: BIRTH ANNIVERSARY. Sept 10, 1934. TV journalist ("On the Road with Charles Kuralt") born at Wilmington, NC. Died at New York, NY, July 4, 1997.

MARIS, ROGER: BIRTH ANNIVERSARY. Sept 10, 1934. Roger Eugene Maris, baseball player born Roger Eugene Maras at Hibbing, MN. In 1961 Maris surpassed the mark set by Babe Ruth in 1927, hitting 61 home runs, a record which wasn't broken until 1998. He won the American League MVP award in 1960 and 1961 and finished his career with the St. Louis Cardinals. Died at Houston, TX, Dec 14, 1985.

MOON PHASE: LAST QUARTER. Sept 10. Moon enters Last Quarter phase at 2:59 PM, EDT.

NATIONAL BOSS/EMPLOYEE EXCHANGE DAY. Sept 10. To help bosses and employees appreciate each other by sharing each other's point of view for a day. Annually, the first Monday after Labor Day. For info: A.C. Moeller, Box 71, Clio, MI 48420-1042.

NATIONAL QUARTET CONVENTION. Sept 10–16. Freedom Hall, Kentucky Fair and Exposition Center, Louisville, KY. Six-day event with focus on the nightly Southern Gospel concerts. Daytime activities include special seminars and record company showcases, celebrity golf tournament, daily Bible study and chapel service and three-hour cruise on the *Belle of Louisville*. Est attendance: 75,000. For info: Clarke Beasley, Exec Dir, PO Box 197406, Louisville, KY 40259. Phone: (502) 961-0988. Fax: (502) 961-0987. E-mail: staff@natqc.com.

PEDDLER'S VILLAGE SCARECROW CONTEST AND OUTDOOR DISPLAY. Sept 10–Oct 28. Peddler's Village, Lahaska, PA. Contestants compete for $4,900 in cash prizes. Categories include: "A Scarecrow Whirligig"—a scarecrow that makes noise and moves with the wind; "An Extraordinary Contemporary Scarecrow"—an imaginative piece created to give a good scare in the garden; "A Traditional Scarecrow"—an outstanding example of the American Scarecrow; and "The Amateur Scarecrow"—for those who haven't won previously. Free admission. Est attendance: 650,000. For info: Peddler's Village, Routes 202 and 263, Lahaska, PA 18931. Phone: (215) 794-4000. Fax: (215) 794-4001. Web: www.peddlersvillage.com.

"THE ROAD RUNNER SHOW" TV PREMIERE: 35th ANNIVERSARY. Sept 10, 1966. Meep! Meep! The Road Runner, a clever bird who always outwitted Wile E. Coyote and his

Acme schemes, had his own cartoon series for three seasons. Other times, this character was on a show with Bugs Bunny called "The Bugs Bunny/Road Runner Hour."

SEW BE IT! DAY. Sept 10. Celebrating the anniversary of the patent on the sewing machine on Sept 10, 1846. Recognizing that when a hem loosens or a button pops off, Sew Be It! [©1995] For info: Adrienne Sioux Koopersmith, 1437 W Rosemont, #1W, Chicago, IL 60660-1319. Phone: (773) 743-5341. Fax: (773) 743-5395. E-mail: adrienne@21stcentury.net.

SWAP IDEAS DAY. Sept 10. To encourage people to explore ways in which their ideas can be put to work for the benefit of humanity, and to encourage development of incentives that will encourage use of creative imagination. For info: Robert L. Birch, Publicity Chair, Puns Corps, Box 2364, Falls Church, VA 22042-0364. Phone: (703) 533-3668.

US SENIOR WOMEN'S AMATEUR (GOLF) CHAMPIONSHIP. Sept 10–15. Allegheny Country Club, Sewickley, PA. For info: US Golf Assn, Golf House, PO Box 708, Far Hills, NJ 07931. Phone: (908) 234-2300. Fax: (908) 234-9687. Web: www.usga.org.

WERFEL, FRANZ: BIRTH ANNIVERSARY. Sept 10, 1890. Austrian author (*The Song of Bernadette, The Forty Days of Musa Dagh*), born at Prague, Czechoslovakia. Died at Hollywood, CA, Aug 26, 1945.

WOLLSTONECRAFT, MARY: DEATH ANNIVERSARY. Sept 10, 1797. Writer and advocate of equality for women, Mary Wollstonecraft died at London 11 days after giving birth to her second daughter (Mary Wollstonecraft Shelley, the author of *Frankenstein*). Wollstonecraft was born Apr 27, 1759, at London. Rebelling against her father, she left home at age 18 and served as a lady's companion, opened a school and worked as a governess. Beginning with *Thoughts on the Education of Daughters* in 1787, Wollstonecraft attracted notice as a writer in favor of women's rights. Her *A Vindication of the Rights of Woman* (1792) argued that women should be given an education that would allow them to gain economic independence.

BIRTHDAYS TODAY

José Feliciano, 56, singer, musician ("Light My Fire," "Hi-Heel Sneakers"), born Larez, Puerto Rico, Sept 10, 1945.

Colin Firth, 41, actor (*Shakespeare in Love, Valmont,* "Pride and Prejudice"), born Grayshott, Hampshire, England, Sept 10, 1960.

Judy Geeson, 53, actress (*To Sir with Love, The Eagle Has Landed*), born Arundel, Sussex, England, Sept 10, 1948.

Matt Geiger, 32, basketball player, born Salem, MA, Sept 10, 1969.

Amy Irving, 48, actress (*Carrie, Honeysuckle Rose*; singing voice of Jessica Rabbit), born Palo Alto, CA, Sept 10, 1953.

Clark Johnson, 37, actor ("Homicide"), born Philadelphia, PA, Sept 10, 1964.

Randy Johnson, 38, baseball player, born Walnut Creek, CA, Sept 10, 1963.

Karl Lagerfeld, 63, fashion designer, born Hamburg, Germany, Sept 10, 1938.

Joe Nieuwendyk, 35, hockey player, born Oshawa, Ontario, Canada, Sept 10, 1966.

Arnold Palmer, 72, golfer, born Latrobe, PA, Sept 10, 1929.

Yma Sumac, 73, singer, born Ichocan, Peru, Sept 10, 1928.

Robert Wise, 87, filmmaker (*The Curse of the Cat People, The Sound of Music*), born Winchester, IN, Sept 10, 1914.

	S	M	T	W	T	F	S
September							1
2001	2	3	4	5	6	7	8
	9	10	11	12	13	14	15
	16	17	18	19	20	21	22
	23	24	25	26	27	28	29
	30						

SEPTEMBER 11 — TUESDAY

Day 254 — 111 Remaining

ANNAPOLIS CONVENTION: ANNIVERSARY. Sept 11–14, 1786. Twelve delegates from New York, New Jersey, Delaware, Pennsylvania and Virginia met at Annapolis, MD, to discuss commercial matters of mutual interest. The delegates voted, on Sept 14, to adopt a resolution prepared by Alexander Hamilton asking all states to send representatives to a convention at Philadelphia, PA, in May 1787 "to render the constitution of the Federal Government adequate to the exigencies of the Union."

BATTLE OF BRANDYWINE: ANNIVERSARY. Sept 11, 1777. The largest engagement of the American Revolution, between the Continental Army led by General George Washington and British troops led by General William Howe. General Howe was marching to take Philadelphia when Washington chose to try and stop the British advance at the Brandywine River near Chadds Ford, PA. The American forces were defeated and the British went on to take Philadelphia Sept 26. They spent the winter in the city while Washington's troops suffered at their encampment at Valley Forge, PA.

"THE CAROL BURNETT SHOW" TV PREMIERE: ANNIVERSARY. Sept 11, 1967. This popular comedy/variety show starred comedienne Carol Burnett, who started the show by taking questions from the audience and ended with an ear tug. Sketches and spoofs included recurring characters like "The Family" (later to be spun off as "Mama's Family") and "As the Stomach Turns." Regular cast members included Harvey Korman, Lyle Waggoner and Vicki Lawrence. Later, Tim Conway joined the cast. Dick Van Dyke briefly joined after Korman left in 1977.

"DICK TRACY" TV PREMIERE: ANNIVERSARY. Sept 11, 1950. Chester Gould's famous detective appeared in the comics, on radio and in the movies before coming to TV in 1950. Ralph Byrd played Dick Tracy in the short-lived series (and in the films, too); his death in 1952 ended the series. Also featured were Joe Devlin as his partner, Sam Catchem and Angela Greene as Tess Trueheart, Tracy's wife. Warren Beatty, Madonna, Dustin Hoffman and Al Pacino starred in a 1990 feature film revival.

ETHIOPIA: NEW YEAR'S DAY. Sept 11. In the year 2001, this day will start the year 1995 on the Ethiopian Orthodox calendar. On the Coptic Orthodox calendar, it begins the year 1718.

FOOD STAMPS AUTHORIZED: ANNIVERSARY. Sept 11, 1959. Congress passed a bill authorizing food stamps for low-income Americans.

LAWRENCE, DAVID HERBERT: BIRTH ANNIVERSARY. Sept 11, 1885. English novelist, author of *Lady Chatterley's Lover*. Born at Eastwood, Nottinghamshire, England, D.H. Lawrence died Mar 2, 1930 at Vence, France.

LIND, JENNY: US PREMIERE: ANNIVERSARY. Sept 11, 1850. Jenny Lind, the "Swedish Nightingale," gave her first American performance in the Castle Garden Theatre, New York, NY, on this day.

"LITTLE HOUSE ON THE PRAIRIE" TV PREMIERE: ANNIVERSARY. Sept 11, 1974. This hour-long family drama was based on books by Laura Ingalls Wilder. It focused on the Ingalls family and their neighbors living at Walnut Grove, MN: Michael Landon as Charles (Pa), Karen Grassle as Caroline (Ma), Melissa Sue Anderson as daughter Mary, Melissa Gilbert as daughter Laura, from whose point of view the stories were told, Lindsay and Sidney Greenbush as daughter Carrie and Wendi and Brenda Turnbaugh as daughter Grace. Others featured were: Victor French, Bonnie Bartlett, Richard Bull, Katherine MacGregor, Jonathan Gilbert, Alison Arngrim, Charlotte Stewart, Dabbs Greer, Merlin Olsen, Patrick Laborteaux. The series spent one season at Winoka, Dakota. In its last season (1982), the show's name was changed to "Little House: A New Beginning." Landon appeared less often and the show centered around Laura and her husband.

MARCOS, FERDINAND EDRALIN: BIRTH ANNIVERSARY. Sept 11, 1917. Former ruler of the Philippines, born at Sarrat, Philippines. Ferdinand Marcos served as head of state from 1966 until his ouster in 1986. His authoritarian regime came under criticism for widespread corruption and suppression of democratic processes. Marcos imposed martial law in 1972 beginning a period when he wrote the constitution and laws to consolidate his power. His later years in office were marred by corruption and economic turmoil. After the assassination of Benigno Aquino, Jr, in 1983, anti-government protests increased and Marcos called for a new election in 1986, hoping to reassert his mandate. Although he defeated Corazon Aquino in the election, it was widely asserted he did so through massive vote fraud, leading to a greater decline in support at home, and Corazon Aquino became the new president of the Philippines. Marcos's health continued to decline in exile and he died Sept 28, 1989, at Honolulu, HI.

911 DAY. Sept 11. A day of recognition for our universal emergency telephone number system and the dedicated people who contribute to its success. For info: Sonya Carius, Communications Mgr, Natl Emergency Number Assn, PO Box 360960, Columbus, OH 43236. Phone: (614) 741-2080. Fax: (614) 933-0911. Web: www.nena.org.

NO NEWS IS GOOD NEWS DAY. Sept 11. Don't read, listen to or watch the news today and you'll feel better tonight. [© 2000 by WH] For info: Tom and Ruth Roy, Wellcat Holidays, 2418 Long Ln, Lebanon, PA 17046. Phone: (717) 279-0184. E-mail: wellcat@supernet.com. Web: www.wellcat.com.

O. HENRY (WILLIAM S. PORTER): BIRTH ANNIVERSARY. Sept 11, 1862. William Sydney Porter, American author, who wrote under the pen name O. Henry. Best known for his short stories, including "Gift of the Magi." Born at Greensboro, NC, he died at New York, NY, June 5, 1910.

PAKISTAN: FOUNDER'S DEATH ANNIVERSARY. Sept 11. Pakistan observes the death anniversary in 1948 of Quaid-i-Azam Mohammed Ali Jinnah (founder of Pakistan) as a national holiday.

"THE ROOKIES" TV PREMIERE: ANNIVERSARY. Sept 11, 1972. This hour crime show focused on three young police recruits: Michael Ontkean as Willie Gates, Georg Stanford Brown as Terry Webster and Sam Melville as Mike Danko. Also featured were Gerald S. O'Loughlin as Lieutenant Ed Ryker; Kate Jackson as nurse Jill Danko, Mike's wife and Bruce Fairbairn as Chris Owens. The show was produced by Aaron Spelling and Leonard Goldberg.

SPACE MILESTONE: *MARS GLOBAL SURVEYOR*
(US). Sept 11, 1997. Launched Nov 7, 1996, this unmanned vehicle was put in orbit around Mars. It is designed to compile global maps of Mars by taking high resolution photos. This mission inaugurated a new series of Mars expeditions in which NASA will launch pairs of orbiters and landers to Mars every 26 months into the next decade. *Mars Global Surveyor* was paired with the lander *Mars Pathfinder*. See also: "Space Milestone: *Mars Pathfinder*" (July 4).

TEXAS–OKLAHOMA FAIR. Sept 11–16. Multi-Purpose Events Center, Wichita Falls, TX. Largest fair in the North Texas area. Exhibits, carnival, food, arts and crafts, animal barn, special entertainment. Est attendance: 40,000. For info: Wichita Falls Conv & Visitors Bureau, 1000 5th St, Wichita Falls, TX 76301. Phone: (940) 716-5500. Fax: (940) 716-5509.

TYLER'S CABINET RESIGNS: ANNIVERSARY. Sept 11, 1841. In protest of President John Tyler's veto of the Banking Bill all of his cabinet except Secretary of State Daniel Webster resigned on this day.

BIRTHDAYS TODAY

Daniel K. Akaka, 77, US Senator (D, Hawaii), born Honolulu, HI, Sept 11, 1924.
Harry Connick, Jr, 34, singer (Grammy for *We Are in Love*), actor (*When Harry Met Sally. . .*), born New Orleans, LA, Sept 11, 1967.
Brian De Palma, 61, filmmaker (*The Untouchables, Bonfire of the Vanities, Carrie*), born Newark, NJ, Sept 11, 1940.
Lola Falana, 58, actress ("The New Bill Cosby Show," "Ben Vereen—Comin' at Ya"), born Camden, NJ, Sept 11, 1943.
William Xavier Kienzle, 73, author (*Body Count, The Rosary Murders*), former priest, born Detroit, MI, Sept 11, 1928.
Donna Lopiano, 55, women's sports executive and former softball player, born Stamford, CT, Sept 11, 1946.
Amy Madigan, 50, actress (*Places in the Heart, Field of Dreams, Uncle Buck*), born Chicago, IL, Sept 11, 1951.
Virginia Madsen, 38, actress (*Dune, The Hot Spot, Candyman*), born Winnetka, IL, Sept 11, 1963.
Kristy McNichol, 39, actress (Emmys for "Family"; "Empty Nest," *Little Darlings, Two Moon Junction*), born Los Angeles, CA, Sept 11, 1962.

SEPTEMBER 12 — WEDNESDAY
Day 255 — 110 Remaining

BATTLE OF SAINT-MIHIEL: ANNIVERSARY. Sept 12, 1918. Under the command of General John J. Pershing, the 1st US Army attacked the Germans at the Saint-Mihiel salient. This was the first major US offensive of the war. Sixteen army divisions, coupled with French II Colonial Corps tanks and artillery support forced back the Germans after 36 hours of heavy fighting and reclaimed 200 square miles of French territory that had been in the hands of the Germans since 1914. The 1st US Army lost about 7,000 soldiers in the Battle of Saint-Mihiel.

CANYONLANDS NATIONAL PARK ESTABLISHED: ANNIVERSARY. Sept 12, 1964. Area of southeastern Utah established as a national park. For further park info: Canyonlands Natl Park, 125 W—2000 S, Moab, UT 84532.

CHARLES LEROUX'S LAST JUMP: ANNIVERSARY. Sept 12, 1889. American aeronaut of French extraction, born in New York, NY, about 1857, achieved world fame as a parachutist. After his first public performance (Philadelphia, PA, 1887) he

	S	M	T	W	T	F	S
September							1
2001	2	3	4	5	6	7	8
	9	10	11	12	13	14	15
	16	17	18	19	20	21	22
	23	24	25	26	27	28	29
	30						

toured European cities where his parachute jumps attracted wide attention. Credited with 238 successful jumps. On Sept 12, 1889, he jumped from a balloon over Tallinn, Estonia, and perished in the Bay of Reval. A monument to his memory was erected at Tallinn five years after his death.

ETHIOPIA: NATIONAL REVOLUTION DAY. Sept 12. Observed as a national holiday. Commemorates 1974 overthrow of Emperor Haile Selassie.

"FRAGGLE ROCK" TV PREMIERE: ANNIVERSARY. Sept 12, 1987. This children's show was a cartoon version of the live Jim Henson puppet production on HBO. It was set in the rock underneath a scientist's house and featured characters such as the Fraggles, the Doozers and the Gorgs.

GUINEA-BISSAU: NATIONAL HOLIDAY. Sept 12. Amilcar Cabral's birthday, Sept 12, is observed as a national holiday.

"LASSIE" TV PREMIERE: ANNIVERSARY. Sept 12, 1954. This long-running series was originally about a boy and his courageous and intelligent dog, Lassie (played by more than six different dogs, all male). For the first few seasons, Lassie lived on the Miller farm. The family included Jeff (Tommy Rettig), his widowed mother Ellen (Jan Clayton) and George Cleveland as Gramps. Throughout the years there were many format and cast changes, as Lassie was exchanged from one family to another in order to have a variety of new perils and escapades. Other featured performers included Cloris Leachman, June Lockhart and Larry Wilcox.

MARYLAND: DEFENDERS DAY. Sept 12. Maryland. Annual reenactment of bombardment of Fort McHenry in 1814 that inspired Francis Scott Key to write the "Star-Spangled Banner."

"MAUDE" TV PREMIERE: ANNIVERSARY. Sept 12, 1972. Bea Arthur's character, Maude Findlay, was first introduced as Edith Bunker's cousin on "All in the Family." She was a loud, opinionated liberal, living with her fourth husband Walter (Bill Macy). Other characters on the show were her divorced daughter by a previous marriage, Carol Trainer (Adrienne Barbeau), Conrad Bain as Dr. Arthur Harmon, Rue McClanahan as Arthur's wife Vivian (Bea Arthur and McClanahan would later star in another sitcom, "The Golden Girls"), Esther Rolle as Florida Evans, Maude's maid and John Amos as her husband, Henry (in 1974 they left the series to star in "Good Times"). This was one of the first shows to tackle the controversial issue of abortion.

MENCKEN, HENRY LOUIS: BIRTH ANNIVERSARY. Sept 12, 1880. American newspaperman, lexicographer and critic, "the Sage of Baltimore" was born at Baltimore, MD, and died there Jan 29, 1956. "If, after I depart this vale," he wrote in 1921 (Epitaph, *Smart Set*), "you ever remember me and have thought to please my ghost, forgive some sinner and wink your eye at some homely girl."

"THE MONKEES" TV PREMIERE: 35th ANNIVERSARY. Sept 12, 1966. Based on a rock and roll group that was supposed to be an American version of the Beatles, this half-hour show featured a blend of comedy and music. Four young actors were chosen from more than 400 to play the group members: Micky Dolenz, Davy Jones, Mike Nesmith and Peter Tork. Dolenz and Jones had previous acting experience and Tork and Nesmith

had previous musical experience. Their first songs on the show were lip-synched but were immensely popular; later the Monkees insisted on writing and performing their own music. A Monkees album, *Headquarters*, and Monkees tours were very successful. In 1986, the Monkees, except for Nesmith, were reunited for a 20th Anniversary tour and the show was broadcast in reruns on MTV. The Monkees sans Nesmith also toured in 1996 for the 30th reunion celebration.

MORTON PUMPKIN FESTIVAL. Sept 12–15. Morton, IL. Carnival, parade, entertainment and fantastic food to celebrate the pumpkin in the "Pumpkin Capital of the World." Est attendance: 70,000. For info: Chamber of Commerce, 415 W Jefferson St, Morton, IL 61550. Phone: (309) 263-2491. Fax: (309) 263-2401. E-mail: pumpkin@dpc.net.

OMAHA PRODUCTS SHOW. Sept 12–13. Omaha Civic Auditorium, Omaha, NE. A marketing center for buyers and sellers with products, services and supplies for business and industry. Est attendance: 30,000. For info: Robert P. Mancuso, Pres, Mid-America Expositions, Inc, PO Box 24851, Omaha, NE 68124-0851. Phone: (402) 346-8003. Fax: (402) 346-5412. Web: www.showofficeonline.com.

OWENS, JESSE: BIRTH ANNIVERSARY. Sept 12, 1913. James Cleveland (Jesse) Owens, American athlete, winner of four gold medals at the 1936 Olympic Games at Berlin, Germany, was born at Oakville, AL. Owens set 11 world records in track and field. During one track meet, at Ann Arbor, MI, Owens, representing Ohio State University, broke five world records May 23, 1935, and tied a sixth in the space of 45 minutes. Died at Tucson, AZ, Mar 31, 1980.

PENDLETON ROUND-UP. Sept 12–15. Pendleton, OR. America's classic rodeo. A 91-year-old western tradition, with participating Indian tribes from the Pacific Northwest. Plus historical Happy Canyon, an outdoor pageant each evening. Est attendance: 48,000. For info: Pendleton Round-up Assn, Box 609, Pendleton, OR 97801. Phone: (800) 457-6336. Web: www.ucinet.com/~roundup/ruticks.html.

SPACE MILESTONE: *LUNA 2* (USSR). Sept 12, 1959. First spacecraft to land on moon was launched.

VIDEO GAMES DAY. Sept 12. A day for kids who love video games to celebrate the fun they have playing them and to thank their parents for all the cartridges and quarters they have provided to indulge this enthusiasm.

WARNER, CHARLES DUDLEY: BIRTH ANNIVERSARY. Sept 12, 1829. American newspaperman, born at Plainfield, MA, authored many works, but is perhaps best remembered for a single sentence (in an editorial, *Hartford Courant*, Aug 24, 1897): "Everybody talks about the weather, but nobody does anything about it." The quotation is often mistakenly attributed to his friend, Mark Twain. Died at Hartford, CT, Oct 20, 1900.

Sam Brownback, 45, US Senator (R, Kansas), born Garnett, KS, Sept 12, 1956.

Irene Dailey, 81, actress ("Another World"), born New York, NY, Sept 12, 1920.

Linda Gray, 60, actress ("Dallas," "Melrose Place"), born Santa Monica, CA, Sept 12, 1941.

Ian Holm, 70, actor (*Alien*, Academy Award for *Chariots of Fire*), born Goodmayes, England, Sept 12, 1931.

George Jones, 70, singer ("White Lightning," "Race Is On," "He Stopped Loving Her Today"), born Saratoga, TX, Sept 12, 1931.

Maria Muldaur, 58, singer ("Midnight at the Oasis," "I'm a Woman"), born New York, NY, Sept 12, 1943.

Joe Pantoliano, 47, actor (*Risky Business, The Fugitive*; stage: *Orphans*), born Jersey City, NJ, Sept 12, 1954.

Peter Scolari, 47, actor ("Bosom Buddies," "Newhart"), born New Rochelle, NY, Sept 12, 1954.

Rachel Ward, 44, actress ("The Thorn Birds," *Against All Odds*), born London, England, Sept 12, 1957.

Barry White, 57, singer ("Can't Get Enough of Your Love, Babe"), born Galveston, TX, Sept 12, 1944.

Amy Yasbeck, 38, actress (*The Mask*, "Wings"), born Cincinnati, OH, Sept 12, 1963.

SEPTEMBER 13 — THURSDAY

Day 256 — 109 Remaining

ANDERSON, SHERWOOD: 125th BIRTH ANNIVERSARY. Sept 13, 1876. American author and newspaper publisher, born at Camden, OH. His best remembered book is *Winesburg, Ohio*. Anderson died at Colon, Panama, Mar 8, 1941.

ANVIL MOUNTAIN 59 MINUTE 37 SECOND CHALLENGE. Sept 13. Nome, AK. A running event that starts at the base of Anvil Mountain, where runners must run 834 ft up the face of the mountain and return in less than 59 minutes and 37 seconds or be disqualified from the competition. Trophies awarded for first–third finishers, first woman finisher and first finisher 16 years of age and under. Record time is 25 minutes 37 seconds. Annually, the second Thursday in September. Est attendance: 1,000. For info: Rasmussen's Music Mart, PO Box 2, Nome, AK 99762-0002. Phone: (907) 443-2798 or (907) 443-2919. Fax: (907) 443-5777.

BARRY, JOHN: DEATH ANNIVERSARY. Sept 13, 1803. Revolutionary War hero John Barry, first American to hold the rank of commodore, died at Philadelphia, PA. He was born at Tacumshane, County Wexford, Ireland, in 1745. He has been called the "Father of the American Navy."

"BENSON" TV PREMIERE: ANNIVERSARY. Sept 13, 1979. This half-hour sitcom was a spin-off from the popular series "Soap." Benson, played by Robert Guillaume, went to work for Jessica's Tate's widowed cousin Governor James Gatling, played by James Noble. The series centered around Benson trying to keep the household intact while the governor performed his duties for the state. The last telecast aired Aug 30, 1986. Other cast members included Missy Gold, Rene Auberjonois, Ethan Phillips, Didi Conn, Caroline McWilliams, Inga Swenson and Lewis J. Stadlen.

BOYER, ERNEST L.: BIRTH ANNIVERSARY. Sept 13, 1928. Educator, US Commissioner of Education; president, Carnegie Foundation for the Advancement of Teaching, was born at Dayton, OH. Died Dec 8, 1995.

"CHICO AND THE MAN" TV PREMIERE: ANNIVERSARY. Sept 13, 1974. This sitcom starred Jack Albertson as Ed Brown, a cranky garage owner and Freddie Prinze as Chico Rodriguez, his Mexican-American employee. It was set in the barrio of East Los Angeles. However, the show was widely criticized for its use of the term "Chico," which was derogatory to many Chicanos, and for the lack of Mexican-Americans in the cast or crew. To remedy this, the cast was expanded to include Issac Ruiz as Chico's friend, Ramon and Rodolfo Hoyos as Ed's friend, Rudy.

Also added were Scatman Crothers as Louie Wilson, the garbage collector; Bonnie Boland as Mabel, the letter carrier; Ronny Graham as Reverend Bemis and Della Reese as Della Rogers, Ed's landlady. Prinze committed suicide in 1977 but the series continued with Gabriel Melgar as Raul Garcia, a Mexican kid adopted by Ed. Charo also joined the show as Aunt Charo.

COLBERT, CLAUDETTE: BIRTH ANNIVERSARY. Sept 13, 1903. Actress and comedienne Colbert, born Lily Claudette Chauchoin at Paris, France, was a beloved movie star of the '30s. She was best known for her films *Midnight, Cleopatra* and *It Happened One Night,* for which she won an Oscar in 1934. In addition to more than 60 movies, she appeared in Broadway shows and won a Golden Globe award for her role in the 1986 miniseries "The Two Mrs Grenvilles." She also received a Life Achievement Award from the Kennedy Center for Performing Arts in 1989. She died July 30, 1996, at Bridgetown, Barbados.

CORN ISLAND STORYTELLING FESTIVAL. Sept 13–16. Louisville, KY. More than 50 storytellers. Festival includes an "olio," mixture of tales, "Fest of Storytelling" and "ghost tales" told at Long Run Park. Est attendance: 16,000. For info: Joy Pennington, Intl Order of EARS, Inc, 12019 Donohue Ave, Louisville, KY 40243. Phone: (502) 245-0643. Fax: (502) 254-7542. E-mail: l-jpenn@prodigy.net.

DAHL, ROALD: 85th BIRTH ANNIVERSARY. Sept 13, 1916. Author (*Charlie and the Chocolate Factory, James and the Giant Peach*), born at Llandaff, South Wales, Great Britain. Died Nov 23, 1990, at Oxford, England.

HUMMER/BIRD CELEBRATION. Sept 13–16. Rockport and Fulton, TX. To celebrate the spectacular fall migration of the ruby-throated hummingbird and other birds from their summer nesting grounds in the north along the eastern Gulf Coast on the way to their winter grounds in Mexico and Central America, and its 500-mile journey across the Gulf. There are programs, workshops, booths, concessions, bus and boat tours. Est attendance: 5,000. For info: Rockport Fulton Area Chamber of Commerce, Hummer/Bird Celebration, 404 Broadway, Rockport, TX 78382. Phone: (800) 242-0071 or (361) 729-6445. Fax: (361) 729-7681. Web: www.rockport-fulton.org.

KASS KOUNTY KING KORN KARNIVAL AND MUD DRAGS. Sept 13–16. Plattsmouth, NE. Krowning of a King and Queen of Kornland, three large parades. Free street entertainment—flower show, Korn Palace, museum exhibits, Hauf Brau Garten, Ugly Pickup Contest, Cow Chip Bingo, fun run, flea market, water fights, big wheel race, art exhibit, slow tractor race, Shriners on parade, Platte Valley aviation fly-in breakfast, Mud Drag races on Sunday and much more. Annually, the second weekend in September. Est attendance: 30,000. For info: Patricia Baburek, Coord, 141 S 3rd St, PO Box 40, Plattsmouth, NE 68048. Phone: (402) 296-4155. Fax: (402) 296-4082.

"LAW & ORDER" TV PREMIERE: ANNIVERSARY. Sept 13, 1990. This hour-long series is filmed on location at New York City. Each episode shows the interaction between the police and the district attorney's office in dealing with a crime. Almost the entire cast has changed over the life of this program; Steven Hill as District Attorney Adam Schiff has been the only constant. Michael Moriarty as Assistant District Attorney Benjamin Stone was followed by Sam Waterston as ADA Jack McCoy. Richard Brooks as ADA Paul Robinette was replaced by Jill Hennessy as ADA Claire Kincaid who was replaced by Carey Lowell as ADA Jamie Ross followed by Angie Harmon as ADA Abbie Carmichael. The police have been represented by George Dzundza as Detective Max Greevey, followed by Paul Sorvino as Detective Phil Cer-

reta, followed by Jerry Orbach as Detective Lennie Briscoe. Christopher Noth playing Detective Mike Logan was replaced by Benjamin Bratt as Detective Reynaldo Curtis followed by Jesse L. Martin as Detective Edward Green. Dann Florek as Captain Donald Cragen was followed by S. Epatha Merkerson as Lieutenant Anita Van Buren.

"THE MUPPET SHOW" TV PREMIERE: 25th ANNIVERSARY. Sept 13, 1976. This comedy variety show was hosted by Kermit the Frog of "Sesame Street." The new Jim Henson puppet characters included Miss Piggy, Fozzie Bear and The Great Gonzo. Many celebrities appeared as guests on the show, which was broadcast in more than 100 countries. The show ran until 1981. "Muppet Babies" was a Saturday morning cartoon that ran from 1984 until 1992. *The Muppet Movie* (1979) was the first of five films based on "The Muppet Show." In 1996 a new show, *Muppets Tonight!*, was created.

NATIONAL CHAMPIONSHIP AIR RACES. Sept 13–16. Reno, NV. Four classes of races—Unlimited, Formula One, AT-6 and Biplane—compete. The event includes thrilling aerobatics and displays of military, vintage and contemporary aircraft. For info: Phone: (775) 972-6663.

NATIONAL CITYTRIPPING WEEK. Sept 13–20. As college students return to urban campuses all over the country, this week is a chance to celebrate and explore the urban environment. Inspired by the success of the *CityTripping New York* and *CityTripping Los Angeles* books and websites, the goal of this week is for students and young people in America's cities to explore the variety of culture—nightlife, restaurants, shopping and the arts—that each city has to offer. For info: Tom Dolby, CityTripping Productions, 151 W 25th St, 4th Fl, New York, NY 10001. Phone: (212) 924-5683. Fax: (212) 924-5845. E-mail: tdolby@citytripping .com. Web: www.citytripping.com.

NATIONAL GUITAR FLAT-PICKING CHAMPION-SHIPS AND WALNUT VALLEY FESTIVAL. Sept 13–16. Cowley County Fairgrounds, Winfield, KS. The Walnut River is the site of this 30th annual family event featuring four stages with eight contests, at least 14 workshops and many first-class concerts. The Walnut Valley Arts and Crafts Festival features handmade instruments and a large variety of art and craft items, both ornamental and functional. All-weather facilities. Est attendance: 45,000. For info: Walnut Valley Assn, Bob Redford, PO Box 245, Winfield, KS 67156. Phone: (316) 221-3250. Fax: (316) 221-3109. E-mail: wvfest@horizon.hit.net. Web: www.wvfest.com.

NEWPORT INTERNATIONAL BOAT SHOW. Sept 13–16. Newport, RI. More than 250 new sail and power boats in the water and displays of accessories, equipment and services. New product information, free sail/power boat rides in Newport harbor. Est attendance: 30,000. For info: Newport Exhibition Group, PO Box 698, 366 Thames St, Newport, RI 02840. Phone: (401) 846-1115. Web: www.newportexhibition.com.

PERSHING, JOHN J.: BIRTH ANNIVERSARY. Sept 13, 1860. US Army general who commanded the American Expeditionary Force (AEF) during World War I, Pershing was born at Laclede, MO. The AEF, as part of the inter-Allied offensive, successfully assaulted the Saint-Mihiel salient in September 1918 and later that month quickly regrouped for the Meuse-Argonne operation that led to the Armistice of Nov 11, 1918. Pershing died July 15, 1948, at Washington, DC.

REED, WALTER: 150th BIRTH ANNIVERSARY. Sept 13, 1851. American army physician (especially known for his Yellow Fever research). Born at Gloucester County, VA, he served as an army surgeon for more than 20 years and as a professor at the Army Medical College. He died at Washington, DC, Nov 22, 1902. The US Army's general hospital at Washington, DC, is named in his honor.

"SOAP" TV PREMIERE: ANNIVERSARY. Sept 13, 1977. "Soap" was a prime-time comedy that parodied soap operas. It had plots that were funny (e.g. Corinne's baby is possessed by the devil), controversial (e.g. Billy joins a cult) and downright

September *2001*	S	M	T	W	T	F	S
							1
	2	3	4	5	6	7	8
	9	10	11	12	13	14	15
	16	17	18	19	20	21	22
	23	24	25	26	27	28	29
	30						

bizarre (e.g. Burt is abducted by aliens). The show focused on two families, the wealthy Tates and the middle-class Campbells. It starred Katherine Helmond, Robert Mandan, Jennifer Salt, Diana Canova, Jimmy Baio, Robert Guillaume, Cathryn Damon, Richard Mulligan, Ted Wass, Billy Crystal, Richard Libertini, Kathryn Reynolds, Robert Urich, Arthur Peterson, Roscoe Lee Browne and Jay Johnson. Rod Roddy was the announcer who recapped what had happened on the previous episode.

"STAR-SPANGLED BANNER" INSPIRED: ANNIVERSARY.

Sept 13–14, 1814. On the night of Sept 13, Francis Scott Key was aboard a ship that was delayed in Baltimore harbor by the British attack there on Fort Henry. Key had no choice but to anxiously watch the battle. That experience and seeing the American flag still flying over the fort the next morning inspired him to pen the verses that, coupled with the tune of a popular drinking song, became our official national anthem in 1931, 117 years after the words were written.

US CAPITAL ESTABLISHED AT NEW YORK CITY: ANNIVERSARY.

Sept 13, 1788. Congress picked New York, NY, as the location of the new US government in place of Philadelphia, which had served as the capital up until this time. In 1790 the capital moved back to Philadelphia for ten years, before moving permanently to Washington, DC.

BIRTHDAYS TODAY

Jacqueline Bisset, 57, actress (*Rich & Famous, The Deep*), born Weybridge, England, Sept 13, 1944.

Nell Carter, 53, actress (Tony for *Ain't Misbehavin'*; "Gimme a Break"), born Birmingham, AL, Sept 13, 1948.

Peter Cetera, 57, singer (former lead singer of Chicago; solo hit "Glory of Love"), songwriter, born Chicago, IL, Sept 13, 1944.

Robert Indiana, 73, artist (*As I Opened Fire*), born New Castle, IA, Sept 13, 1928.

William Janklow, 62, Governor of South Dakota (R), born Chicago, IL, Sept 13, 1939.

Michael Johnson, 34, track athlete, born Dallas, TX, Sept 13, 1967.

Richard Kiel, 62, actor (*The Longest Yard, Silver Streak, The Spy Who Loved Me*), born Detroit, MI, Sept 13, 1939.

Judith Martin, 63, author, journalist ("Miss Manners"), born Washington, DC, Sept 13, 1938.

Ben Savage, 21, actor ("Boy Meets World"), born Chicago, IL, Sept 13, 1980.

Fred Silverman, 64, TV producer, born New York, NY, Sept 13, 1937.

Jean Smart, 42, actress ("Designing Women"), born Seattle, WA, Sept 13, 1959.

Bernie Williams, 33, baseball player, born Bernabe Williams, San Juan, Puerto Rico, Sept 13, 1968.

SEPTEMBER 14 — FRIDAY
Day 257 — 108 Remaining

ALOHA FESTIVALS DOWNTOWN HO'OLAULE'A.

Sept 14. Downtown Honolulu, HI. One of the best attended and most enjoyed events in Honolulu. An estimated 150,000 residents and visitors stroll through downtown Honolulu enjoying the various lei and food booths and the exciting dancing and entertainment on nine stages featuring music to suit every taste. (Also the Waikiki Ho'olaule'a on Kalakaua Avenue, Honolulu, HI, Sept 21.) Est attendance: 150,000. For info: Aloha Festivals. Phone: (808) 589-1771 or (800) 852-7690. Fax: (808) 589-1770. E-mail: alohafes@hula.net. Web: www.alohafestivals.com.

ANTIQUE AND CLASSIC CAR SHOW.

Sept 14–16. Willow Park, Bennington, VT. Classic cars, Woodies. A flea market with auto-related parts and memorabilia entices collectors seeking that elusive fender or gas running lamp. A display and demonstration of antique motorcycles, tractor and farm machinery are also featured. Annually, the second weekend after Labor Day. Est attendance: 10,000. For info: Bennington Area Chamber of Commerce, Veterans Memorial Dr, Bennington, VT 05201. Phone: (802) 447-3311. Fax: (802) 447-1163. E-mail: benncham@sover.net. Web: www.bennington.com.

BALD IS BEAUTIFUL CONVENTION.

Sept 14–16. Morehead City, NC. To cultivate a sense of pride for all bald-headed men (folks) everywhere and eliminate the vanity associated with the loss of one's hair. As seen on national television; Bald is Beautiful Contests, family events. Annually, the second weekend in September. Est attendance: 200. For info: John T. Capps III, Founder, Bald Headed Men of America, 102 Bald Dr, Morehead City, NC 28557. Phone: (252) 726-1855. Fax: (252) 726-6061. E-mail: jcapps4102@aol.com. Web: members.aol.com/BaldUSA.

THE BIG E.

Sept 14–30. West Springfield, MA. New England's Fall Classic and one of the nation's largest fairs. Each September, The Big E features all free entertainment including top-name talent, a big-top circus and horse show. Also children's attractions, daily parade with custom-built Mardi Gras floats, historic village, Avenue of States, Better Living Center and much more. Annually, beginning the second Friday after Labor Day. Est attendance: 1,000,000. For info: Eastern States Exposition, 1305 Memorial Ave, West Springfield, MA 01089. Phone: (413) 737-2443. Fax: (413) 787-0127. E-mail: info@thebige.com. Web: www.thebige.com.

"THE BOB CROSBY SHOW" TV PREMIERE: ANNIVERSARY.

Sept 14, 1953. Bob Crosby, Bing's younger brother, was a bandleader who hosted two shows. The first was a half-hour daytime show featuring the Modernaires, Joan O'Brien, Jack Narz and Cathy Crosby (his daughter). The second was a one-hour prime-time show with Gretchen Wyler, the Peter Gennaro dancers, the Clay Warnick singers, the Carl Hoff Orchestra and clown Emmett Kelly that debuted on June 14, 1958.

CANADA: BRACEBRIDGE FALL FAIR AND HORSE SHOW.

Sept 14–16. Highway 11 & Fraserburg Road—James D. Long Activity Park, Bracebridge, ON. Horse pulls, antique tractor pull, English and Western Horse Show, light and heavy horses, livestock, junior and youth fair, photography, crafts, culinary arts, fiber arts, horticulture and entertainment for all ages. 134th annual. For info: Sec, Bracebridge Agricultural Soc, PO Box 53, Bracebridge, ON, Canada P1L 1T5. Phone: (705) 645-4223.

CANADA: THUNDER BAY CHAMBER OF COMMERCE HOME SHOW: LIVING & LEISURE.

Sept 14–16. Thunder Bay, ON. For info: Mary Ann Agostino, Thunder Bay Chamber of Commerce, 857 May St North, Thunder Bay, ON, Canada P7C 3S2. Phone: (807) 622-9642. Fax: (807) 622-7752. E-mail: chamber@tb-chamber.on.ca. Web: tb-chamber.on.ca.

CASA LARGA PURPLE FOOT WEEKEND. Sept 14–16. Casa Larga, Fairport, NY. 6th annual grape stomping, music, food, tours, tastings, games and more. For info: Casa Larga Vineyards, 27 Emerald Hill Circle, Fairport, NY 14450. Phone: (716) 223-4210. Web: www.casalarga.com.

DANTE ALIGHIERI: DEATH ANNIVERSARY. Sept 14, 1321. Italian poet, author of the *Divine Comedy*, died at Ravenna, Italy. He was born in May 1265 (exact date unknown) at Florence, Italy.

DETROIT FESTIVAL OF ARTS. Sept 14–16. Detroit, MI. Detroit Cultural Center and Wayne State University become a 15-block kaleidoscope of visual, performing and literary arts: live entertainment forum with more than 300 stage and street performers, 100 visual artists. Children's Fair, Poetry Festival and more. Est attendance: 250,000. For info: Pat Borninski, PR Officer, Wayne State Univ, 3222 FAB, Detroit, MI 48202. Phone: (313) 577-2150. Fax: (313) 577-8154. E-mail: p.borninski@wayne.edu. Web: www.media.wayne.edu/

ENGLAND: HARROGATE AUTUMN FLOWER SHOW. Sept 14–16. Great Yorkshire Showground, Harrogate, N Yorkshire. See Britain's finest blooms, talk to the experts and witness the giants in the National Onion Championship. Est attendance: 35,000. For info: Roger Brownbridge, North of England Horticultural Society, 4A South Park Rd, Harrogate, North Yorkshire, England HG1 5QU. Phone: (44) (142) 356-1049. E-mail: info@flowershow.org.uk. Web: www.flowershow.org.uk.

FESTIVAL OF THE VINE. Sept 14–16. Geneva, IL. Flavors of fall are celebrated with music, wine tasting, antique carriage rides, arts and crafts, entertainment and specialties of Geneva's fine restaurants. For info: Geneva Chamber of Commerce, 8 S Third St., PO Box 481, Geneva, IL 60134. Phone: (630) 232-6060. Fax: (630) 232-6083. E-mail: chamberinfo@genevachamber.com. Web: www.genevachamber.com.

FREDERICKSBURG HINKELFEST. Sept 14–16. Fredericksburg, PA. Stage entertainment, rides, food, arts and crafts and more. Est attendance: 20,000. For info: PA Capital Regions Vacation Bureau, 1255A Harrisburg Pike, Carlisle, PA 17013. E-mail: info@parainbow.com. Web: www.parainbow.com.

FRIENDS OF LAKE FOREST LIBRARY ANNUAL BOOK SALE. Sept 14–16. Lake Forest, IL. A three-day sale of used books in excellent condition set up in 20 categories. Est attendance: 5,000. For info: Kaye Grabbe, Lake Forest Library, 360 E Deerpath, Lake Forest, IL 60045. Phone: (847) 234-0636. Fax: (847) 234-1453. E-mail: kgrabbe@lfl.alibrary.com. Web: lfkhome.northstarnet.org/FriendsofLFL.html.

September 2001	S	M	T	W	T	F	S
							1
	2	3	4	5	6	7	8
	9	10	11	12	13	14	15
	16	17	18	19	20	21	22
	23	24	25	26	27	28	29
	30						

GOAT DAYS. Sept 14–16. USA Stadium, Millington, TN. Goat contests with large cash prizes and trophies, children's area, camping, fishing, goat races, dancing, music, food, rodeo, crafts, chili and Dutch-oven cook-offs and bluegrass competition. Huge display of antique engines and tractors and national stock dog trials. Est attendance: 20,000. For info: Goat Days Intl, 4880 Navy Rd, Millington, TN 38053. Phone: (901) 872-4559. Fax: (901) 872-7700.

"THE GOLDEN GIRLS" TV PREMIERE: ANNIVERSARY. Sept 14, 1985. This comedy starred Bea Arthur, Betty White, Rue McClanahan and Estelle Getty as four divorced/widowed women sharing a house in Florida during their golden years. The last episode aired Sept 14, 1992 but the show remains popular in syndication.

"HAVE GUN WILL TRAVEL" TV PREMIERE: ANNIVERSARY. Sept 14, 1957. "Have Gun, Will Travel . . ." so read the business card of Paladin (Richard Boone), a loner whose professional services were available for a price. This western also featured Kam Tong as his servant, Hey Boy. The show was extremely popular and ranked in the top five for most of its run.

INDIANAPOLIS FALL BOAT SHOW. Sept 14–17. Indiana State Fairgrounds, Indianapolis, IN. For info: Kevin Renfro, VP, 2511 E 46th St., Ste E-2, Indianapolis, IN 46205. Phone: (317) 546-4344 or (800) 892-1723. Fax: (317) 546-3002. E-mail: insportshow@iquest.net.

"IRONSIDE" TV PREMIERE: ANNIVERSARY. Sept 14, 1967. This crime series starred Raymond Burr as Robert T. Ironside, Chief of Detectives for the San Francisco Police Department (he was in a wheelchair, paralyzed from an assassination attempt). Also featured were Don Galloway as his assistant, Detective Sergeant Ed Brown, Barbara Anderson as Officer Eve Whitfield, Don Mitchell as Mark Sanger, Ironside's personal assistant, Gene Lyons as Commissioner Dennis Randall, Elizabeth Baur as Officer Fran Belding and Joan Pringle as Diana, Mark's wife.

McKINLEY, WILLIAM: 100th DEATH ANNIVERSARY. Sept 14, 1901. President William McKinley was shot at Buffalo, NY, Sept 6, 1901. He died eight days later. Assassin Leon Czolgosz was executed Oct 29, 1901.

MOTLEY, CONSTANCE BAKER: 80th BIRTHDAY. Sept 14, 1921. New York's first black woman state senator and federal judge, and the first woman elected borough president of Manhattan, Constance Baker Motley became interested in law and civil rights when she was barred from a public beach at age 15. She went on to become one of the top civil rights lawyers of the '50s and '60s. She presented arguments before the US Supreme Court for seven cases and won them all. Motley was born at New Haven, CT.

NEW HAMPSHIRE HIGHLAND GAMES. Sept 14–16. Loon Mountain, Lincoln, NH. From the tossing of the caber to the lilting melodies of the clarsach plus massed pipe bands on parade, there's something for everyone at New Hampshire's Highland Games: a three-day Scottish festival crammed with music, dance, crafts, athletic events, Scottish food and more. For those of Scottish heritage, there's also a chance to look up one's clan connection, as more than 60 Scottish clans and societies have tents with displays. Admission charged. Est attendance: 42,000. For info: New Hampshire Highland Games, PO Box 4197, Concord, NH 03302-4197. Phone: (603) 229-1975. Fax: (603) 229-7644. E-mail: nhscot@aol.com. Web: www.nhscot.org.

NICARAGUA: BATTLE OF SAN JACINTO DAY. Sept 14. National holiday.

NORTHERN APPALACHIAN STORYTELLING FESTIVAL. Sept 14–16. Mansfield University, Mansfield, PA. 21st annual festival features five nationally-known professional storytellers who bring stories from many rich cultural traditions. Performance Friday evening, Saturday afternoon and evening and Sunday morning. Workshops and master classes will be offered. Est attendance: 4,000. For info: Dr Howard Travis, N Appalachian Storytelling Fest, PO Box 434, Mansfield, PA 16933. Phone: (570)

662-4788. Fax: (570) 662-4112. E-mail: htravis@mnsfld.edu. Web: www.wso.net/storyfest.

OKTOBERFEST. Sept 14–16 (also Sept 21–23). Larimer Square, Denver, CO. Colorado's largest German festival saluting the state's German heritage. Schuhplattler, bratwurst, authentic German entertainment, pretzels and beer are featured in this re-creation of the famous Munich festival. Est attendance: 250,000. For info: Larimer Square, 1400 Larimer St, Denver, CO 80202. Phone: (303) 534-2367. Fax: (303) 623-1041. Web: www.larimer square.com.

ON THE WATERFRONT SWAP MEET AND CAR SHOW. Sept 14–16. Downtown St. Ignace, MI. 11th anniversary. Car show, toy show, truck display and swap meet. Est attendance: 10,000. For info: Ed Reavie, President, Nostalgia Prod, Inc, 268 Hillcrest Blvd, St. Ignace, MI 49781. Phone: (906) 643-8087 or (906) 643-1USA. Fax: (906) 643-9784. E-mail: edreavie@nostalgia-prod.com. Web: www.nostalgia-prod.com or www.auto-shows.com.

POTATO FEAST DAYS. Sept 14–16. Houlton, ME. Potato Feast supper, Parade of Dolls, potato games for kids, entertainment, townwide sales, fun run, classic car show, arts and crafts fair, potato-barrel rolling contest and much more. For info: Greater Houlton Chamber of Commerce, 109 Main St, Houlton, ME 04730. Phone: (207) 532-4216. E-mail: chamber@rcn.com. Web: www.greaterhoulton.com.

RICHARD CRANE MEMORIAL TRUCK SHOW. Sept 14–16. St. Ignace, MI. 6th annual show featuring 18-wheeler competition. $2,000 cash Best of Show. Parade of Lights across the Mackinac Bridge. Est attendance: 10,000. For info: Nostalgia Productions, Inc, 268 Hillcrest Blvd, St. Ignace, MI 49781. Phone: (906) 643-8087 or (906) 643-1USA. Fax: (906) 643-9784. E-mail: edreavie@nostalgia-prod.com. Web: www.nostalgia-prod.com or www.auto-shows.com.

SAINT FRANCIS RIVER POWWOW. Sept 14–16. Park Hills, MO, 65 miles south of St. Louis. Native American Powwow and competitive dancing. Est attendance: 5,000. For info: Debby Couch, Chair, 8 Louise St, Bonne Terre, MO 63628. Phone: (573) 358-7633 or (573) 756-6702. E-mail: ymn000@mail.connect .more.net or jc63628@yahoo.com..

SANGER, MARGARET (HIGGINS): BIRTH ANNIVERSARY. Sept 14, 1879. Feminist, nurse and founder of the birth control movement in the US. Born at Corning, NY. (Note: birth year not entirely certain because, apparently, Sanger often used a later date when obliged to divulge her birthday. Best evidence now points to Sept 14, 1879, rather than the frequently used 1883 date.) She died at Tucson, AZ, Sept 6, 1966.

SETON, ELIZABETH ANN: CANONIZATION ANNIVERSARY. Sept 14, 1975. Elizabeth Ann Seton became the first native-born American to be canonized. She was declared a saint in 1974 by Pope Paul VI.

SOLO TRANSATLANTIC BALLOON CROSSING: ANNIVERSARY. Sept 14–18, 1984. Joe W. Kittinger, 56-year-old balloonist, left Caribou, ME, in a 10-story-tall helium-filled balloon named *Rosie O'Grady's Balloon of Peace* Sept 14, 1984, crossed the Atlantic Ocean and reached the French coast, above the town of Capbreton, in bad weather Sept 17 at 4:29 PM, EDT. He crashlanded amid wind and rain near Savone, Italy, at 8:08 AM, EDT, Sept 18. Kittinger suffered a broken ankle when he was thrown from the balloon's gondola during the landing. His nearly 84-hour flight, covering about 3,535 miles, was the first solo balloon crossing of the Atlantic Ocean and a record distance for a solo balloon flight.

SOUTHSIDE FALL FESTIVAL. Sept 14–16. St. Joseph, MO. The highlight of this event is a professional rodeo the United Rodeo Association named "Rodeo of the Year." Also featured are a parade, arts and crafts, street dances, food and much more. Annually, the third weekend in September. Est attendance: 30,000. For info: Beth Bush, 11330 SW State Route JJ, St. Joseph, MO, 64504. Phone: (816) 238-3515 or (816) 238-2218.

STAMP EXPO. Sept 14–16. Radisson Hotel, Anaheim, CA. Est attendance: 4,000. For info: Intl Stamp Collectors Society, PO Box 854, Van Nuys, CA 91408. Phone: (818) 997-6496. Fax: (818) 988-4337. E-mail: iibick@aol.com. Web: www.bick.net.

STATE FAIR OF OKLAHOMA. Sept 14–30. Fairgrounds, Oklahoma City, Oklahoma. Third largest fair in North America includes seven buildings of commercial exhibits; Walt Disney's World on Ice, the State Fair Super Circus, PRCA championship rodeo, livestock competitions, top-name concerts and motorsports events. Annually, second Friday after Labor Day. Est attendance: 1,300,000. For info: State Fair of Oklahoma, PO Box 74943, Oklahoma City, OK 73107. Phone: (405) 948-6700. Fax: (405) 948-6828. E-mail: oklafair@oklafair.org.

"THE WALTONS" TV PREMIERE: ANNIVERSARY. Sept 14, 1972. This epitome of the family drama spawned nearly a dozen knock-offs during its nine-year run on CBS. The drama was based on creator/writer Earl Hamner Jr's experiences growing up during the Depression in rural Virginia. It began as the TV movie "The Homecoming," which was so well-received that it was turned into a weekly series covering the years 1933–43. The cast went through numerous changes through the years; the principals were: Michael Learned as Olivia Walton, mother of the clan, Ralph Waite as John Walton, father, Richard Thomas as John-Boy, eldest son, Jon Walmsley as son Jason, Judy Norton-Taylor as daughter Mary Ellen, Eric Scott as son Ben, Mary Beth McDonough as daughter Erin, David W. Harper as son Jim-Bob and Kami Cotler as daughter Elizabeth. The Walton grandparents were played by Ellen Corby (Esther) and Will Geer (Zeb). The last telecast aired Aug 20, 1981.

WILSON, JAMES: BIRTH ANNIVERSARY. Sept 14, 1742. Signer of the Declaration of Independence and one of the first associate justices of the US Supreme Court. Born at Fifeshire, Scotland, he died Aug 21, 1798, at Edenton, NC.

WIZARD OF OZ FESTIVAL. Sept 14–16. Chesterton, IN. Parade, costumed Oz characters, meet the Munchkins, arts and crafts, food. 20th annual festival. Est attendance: 80,000. For info: Duneland Chamber of Commerce, 303 Broadway, Chesterton, IN 46304. Phone: (219) 926-5513. Fax: (219) 926-7593. E-mail: dunelandchamber@niia.net. Web: wpl.lib.in.us/chamber.

WO-ZHA-WA DAYS FALL FESTIVAL. Sept 14–16. Wisconsin Dells, WI. Celebrates the beginning of the fall season. Arts, crafts, 100-unit parade, Maxwell Street Days, Wo-Zha-Wa Run and antique flea market. Est attendance: 100,000. For info: Wisconsin Dells Visitors Bureau, PO Box 390, Wisconsin Dells, WI 53965. Phone: (800) 223-3557. E-mail: info@wisdells.com. Web: www.wisdells.com.

BIRTHDAYS TODAY

Zoe Caldwell, 68, actress (*Medea, The Prime of Miss Jean Brodie*), born Melbourne, Australia, Sept 14, 1933.

Dan Cortese, 34, actor ("Veronica's Closet," *Public Enemies*), born Sewickley, PA, Sept 14, 1967.

Mary Crosby, 42, actress ("Dallas," *Tapeheads*), born Los Angeles, CA, Sept 14, 1959.

Faith Ford, 37, actress ("Murphy Brown"), born Alexandria, LA, Sept 14, 1964.

Joey Heatherton, 57, actress (*Cry Baby, Bluebeard*, "Dean Martin and the Golddiggers"), born Rockville Centre, NY, Sept 14, 1944.

Walter Koenig, 65, actor, writer, director, producer ("Star Trek" and *Star Trek* movies), born Chicago, IL, Sept 14, 1936.

Kate Millett (Katherine Murray Millett), 67, feminist, writer (*Sexual Politics, Flying*), born St. Paul, MN, Sept 14, 1934.

Sam Neill, 54, actor (*My Brilliant Career, Jurassic Park, The Piano*), born Northern Ireland, Sept 14, 1947.

Nicol Williamson, 63, actor (*Robin and Marian, Excalibur*), born Hamilton, Scotland, Sept 14, 1938.

SEPTEMBER 15 — SATURDAY
Day 258 — 107 Remaining

ACUFF, ROY: BIRTH ANNIVERSARY. Sept 15, 1903. Grand Ole Opry "King of Country Music" Roy Acuff was born at Maynardville, TN. Singer and fiddler Acuff (who was co-founder of Acuff-Rose Publishing Company, the leading publisher of country music) was a regular host on weekly Grand Ole Opry broadcasts. He frequently appeared at the Opry with his group, the Smoky Mountain Boys. In December of 1991 Acuff became the first living member elected to the Country Music Hall of Fame. Some of his more famous songs were "The Wabash Cannonball" (his theme song), "Pins and Needles (In My Heart)" and "Night Train to Memphis." Acuff died Nov 23, 1992, at Nashville, TN.

ALABAMA COASTAL CLEANUP. Sept 15. Mobile and Baldwin County, AL. Volunteers convene to "get the trash out of the splash" by cleaning up Alabama's beaches. This event provides participants with a first-hand experience that improves the eco system. Annually, the third Saturday in September. Est attendance: 3,000. For info: Alabama Coastal Programs, 1208 Main St, Daphne, AL 36526. Phone: (334) 626-0042. Fax: (334) 626-3503.

ALOHA FESTIVALS FLORAL PARADE. Sept 15. Ala Moana Beach Park to Waikiki, Honolulu, HI. One of the most-watched televised events in the nation, the Floral Parade has become synonymous with Aloha Festivals. The colorful display is a celebration of the history and spirit of the islands, set amidst the fragrant blossoms of Hawaii. For info: Aloha Festivals. Phone: (808) 589-1771. Fax: (808) 589-1770. E-mail: alohafes@hula.net. Web: www.alohafestivals.com.

APPLEJACK FESTIVAL. Sept 15–16. Nebraska City, NE. To promote local orchards and their abundant apple harvest. Est attendance: 40,000. For info: Nebraska City Tourism & Events, 806 First Ave, Nebraska City, NE 68410. Phone: (402) 873-3000. Fax: (402) 873-6701. E-mail: necity@nebraskacity.com. Web: www.nebraskacity.com.

"BACHELOR FATHER" TV PREMIERE: ANNIVERSARY. Sept 15, 1957. John Forsythe (Bentley Gregg) and Noreen Corcoran (Kelly Gregg) starred in this sitcom about a bachelor attorney's life turning upside-down after his orphaned niece moves in with him. The series aired at different times on all three networks. The last episode aired Sept 25, 1962. Supporting players included: Sammee Tong as Peter Tong, the butler, Jimmy Boyd as Kelly's boyfriend, Howard Meechim, Bernadette Withers as Kelly's friend Ginger, Whit Bissell as Ginger's father, Bert Loomis, Alice Backes as Bentley's secretary, Vickie, Sue Ane Langdon as Bentley's secretary, Kitty Marsh and Victor Sen Yung as Peter's cousin, Charlie Fong.

BARNESVILLE BUGGY DAYS. Sept 15–16. Barnesville, GA. Arts and crafts festival with more than 180 exhibitors, food, entertainment, a parade at 4 PM and fireworks at 9:30 PM on Saturday. Annually, the third full weekend in September. Est attendance: 60,000. For info: Barnesville-Lamar Chamber of Commerce, PO Box 506, Barnesville, GA 30204. Phone: (770) 358-2732. Web: www.barnesville.org.

BELLE MEADE PLANTATION FALL FEST. Sept 15–16. Nashville, TN. Annual fundraiser, crafts, antiques, art, food, market, fine jewelry, garage treasures and children's fest. Annually, the third weekend of September. Est attendance: 20,000. For info: Belle Meade Plantation, 5025 Harding Rd, Nashville, TN 37205. Phone: (615) 356-0501 or (800) 270-3991. Fax: (615) 356-2336. Web: www.bellemeadeplantation.com.

September 2001	S	M	T	W	T	F	S
							1
	2	3	4	5	6	7	8
	9	10	11	12	13	14	15
	16	17	18	19	20	21	22
	23	24	25	26	27	28	29
	30						

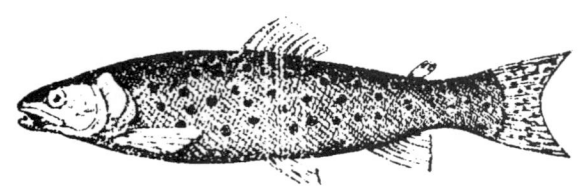

BIG WHOPPER LIAR'S CONTEST. Sept 15. Murphy Auditorium, New Harmony, IN. Thirty "story tellers" compete to see who can tell the BIGGEST Whopper. Annually, the third Saturday in September. Est attendance: 425. For info: Jeff Fleming, PO Box 598, Olney, IL 62450. Phone: (618) 395-8491. Fax: (618) 392-3174.

BORN TO BE WILD WEEKEND. Sept 15–16. Elkton, MI. Beer tent and Harley Davidson motorcycle show. Est attendance: 3,000. For info: Paul Picklo. Phone: (517) 453-4333, ext 222.

"CELEBRATE DIVERSITY" TWO RIVERS ETHNIC FESTIVAL. Sept 15. Central Memorial Park, Two Rivers, WI. A celebration of diverse cultures by bringing to Northeast Wisconsin representative musical and dance groups from around our world. Groups present a taste of these rich traditions in their music and costumes. Also included are ethnic foods, demonstrations of varied traditions, crafts and arts. Annually, the third Saturday in September. Est attendance: 27,000. For info: "Celebrate Diversity", Two Rivers Main Street, Inc, PO Box 417, Two Rivers, WI 54241. Phone: (920) 794-1482. Fax: (920) 793-4586. Web: lakefield.net/mainstreet.

CHAUTAUQUA OF THE ARTS. Sept 15–16. Columbus, IN. Fine artists and craftsmen gather to demonstrate and sell their works. Est attendance: 20,000. For info: Chautauqua of the Arts, 119 W Main St, Madison, IN 47250-3047. Phone: (812) 265-5080. Fax: (812) 265-5080. E-mail: show@chautauquaofthearts.com. Web: www.chautauquaofthearts.com.

"CHiPS" TV PREMIERE: ANNIVERSARY. Sept 15, 1977. A popular action-packed NBC police series depicting cases and chases of the motorcycle-riding California Highway Patrol. The show starred Erik Estrada as Francis "Ponch" Poncherello and Larry Wilcox as Jon Baker, two quick-witted cops. Wilcox left the show, and Estrada's new partner, Bobby "Hot Dog" Nelson, was played by Tom Reilly. Other regulars included Robert Pine, Paul Linke, Lou Wagner, Brodie Greer, Brianne Leary, Randi Oakes, Michael Dorn, Bruce Jenner, Bruce Penhall and Tina Gayle. The last telecast ran July 17, 1983.

CHRISTIE, AGATHA: BIRTH ANNIVERSARY. Sept 15, 1890. English author of nearly a hundred books (mysteries, drama, poetry and nonfiction), born at Torquay, England. Died at Wallingford, England, Jan 12, 1976. "Every murderer," she wrote, in *The Mysterious Affair at Styles,* "is probably somebody's old friend."

COOPER, JAMES FENIMORE: BIRTH ANNIVERSARY. Sept 15, 1789. American novelist, historian and social critic, born at Burlington, NJ, James Fenimore Cooper was one of the earliest American writers to develop a native American literary tradition. His most popular works are the five novels comprising *The Leatherstocking Tales,* featuring the exploits of one of the truly unique American fictional characters, Natty Bumppo. These novels, *The Deerslayer, The Last of the Mohicans, The Pathfinder, The Pioneers* and *The Prairie,* chronicle Natty Bumppo's continuing flight away from the rapid settlement of America. Other works, including *The Monikins* and *Satanstoe,* reveal him as an astute critic of American life. He died Sept 14, 1851, at Cooperstown, NY, the town founded by his father.

COSTA RICA: INDEPENDENCE DAY. Sept 15. National holiday. Gained independence from Spain in 1821.

COVERED BRIDGE FESTIVAL. Sept 15–16. Washington and Greene County, PA. Arts and crafts, entertainment and lots of homestyle food at each of nine covered bridges. Annually, the third weekend in September. Est attendance: 110,000. For info: Washington County Tourism, 1500 W Chestnut St, Washington, PA 15301. Phone: (800) 531-4114 or (724) 228-5220. E-mail: info@washpatourism.org. Web: www.washpatourism.org.

DAYTON VALLEY DAYS. Sept 15–16. Old Town Dayton, NV. A community celebration of the history and people of Nevada's first settlement. Family activities, parades, entertainment, historic portrayals and more. Annually, the third weekend in September. Est attendance: 7,000. For info: Laura Tennant, Dayton Valley Days, PO Box 1758, Dayton, NV 89403. Phone: (775) 246-3256. Fax: (775) 264-3988. E-mail: L10ant@powernet.net.

EISENHOWER WORLD WAR II WEEKEND. Sept 15–16. Eisenhower National Historic Site, Gettysburg, PA. A living history encampment featuring Allied soldiers, German prisoners of war, tanks and military vehicles of that time. Annually, the third weekend in September. Est attendance: 2,500. For info: Gettysburg CVB, PO Box 4117, Gettysburg, PA 17325. Phone: (717) 334-6274. Fax: (717) 334-1166. Web: www.gettysburg.com.

EL SALVADOR: INDEPENDENCE DAY. Sept 15. National holiday. Gained independence from Spain in 1821.

FESTIVAL OF ADVENTURES. Sept 15–16. Aitkin, MN. This 11th annual festival celebrates the area's fur trading history. Rendezvous at Depot Museum with trappers, traders, ethnic dancers, bluegrass music and food. Est attendance: 5,000. For info: Aitkin Area Chamber of Commerce, PO Box 127, Aitkin, MN 56431. Phone: (218) 927-2316 or (800) 526-8342. Fax: (218) 927-4494. E-mail: upnorth@aitkin.com. Web: www.aitkin.com.

FESTIVAL OF THE SEA. Sept 15 (rain date Sept 16). Point Pleasant Beach, NJ. Come join the fun with arts, crafts, food, games for the kids, pony rides, antiques, non-profit and commercial exhibits. Free admission. Est attendance: 55,000. For info: Point Pleasant Beach Chamber of Commerce, 517A Arnold Ave, Point Pleasant Beach, NJ 08742. Phone: (732) 899-2424. E-mail: ptpleasant@bytheshore.com. Web: www.pointpleasantbeachnj.com.

FESTIVAL 2001: FESTIVAL OF FINE ARTS AND FINE CRAFTS. Sept 15–16. Downtown, Dalton, GA. Fine arts and fine crafts festival includes outdoor artist booths, food vendors, children's arts festival, entertainment for adults and children, cash awards. 38th annual. Est attendance: 7,000. For info: Creative Arts Guild, Box 1485, Dalton, GA 30722-1485. Phone: (706) 278-0168. Fax: (706) 278-6996. E-mail: cagarts@creative artsguild.org.

FIRST NATIONAL CONVENTION FOR BLACKS: ANNIVERSARY. Sept 15, 1830. The first national convention for blacks was held at Bethel Church, Philadelphia, PA. The convention was called to find ways to better the condition of black people and was attended by delegates from seven states. Bishop Richard Allen was elected as the first convention president.

FOLKFEST. Sept 15. Dancing Bear Folk Centre, Thermopolis, WY. Music, storytelling, demonstrations and hands-on activities, frontier skills, ropemaking, knifemaking, spin-off, weave-off, sheep-shearing, quilting. Est attendance: 1,000. For info: Dancing Bear Folk Centre, PO Box 71, Thermopolis, WY 82443. Phone: (307) 864-9396. Fax: (307) 864-3582. E-mail: dancing bear@dancingbear.org. Web: www.dancingbear.org.

GREENPEACE FOUNDED: 30th ANNIVERSARY. Sept 15, 1971. The environmental organization Greenpeace, committed to a green and peaceful world, was founded by 12 members of the Don't Make a Wave committee of Vancouver, BC, Canada, when the boat *Phyllis Cormack* sailed to Amchitka, AK, to protest US nuclear testing. Greenpeace's basic principle is "that determined individuals can alter the actions and purposes of even the overwhelmingly powerful by 'bearing witness'—drawing attention to an environmental abuse through their mere unwavering presence, whatever the risk."

GUATEMALA: INDEPENDENCE DAY. Sept 15. National holiday. Gained independence from Spain in 1821.

HARVEST SHOW. Sept 15–16. Horticulture Center, Fairmount Park, Philadelphia, PA. More than 700 gardeners enter more than 350 horticultural and artistic categories. Educational exhibits and samples of freshly harvested crops and homemade preserved products judged. A series of special events, including live music and a children's activity tent. Est attendance: 5,000. For info: The Pennsylvania Horticultural Soc, 100 N 20th St, 5th Fl, Philadelphia, PA 19103-1495. Phone: (215) 988-8800. Fax: (215) 988-8810. E-mail: mdmyterk@pennhort.org. Web: www.libertynet.org/phs.

HODAG MUSKIE CHALLENGE. Sept 15–16. Rhinelander, WI. Catch and release muskie tournament. Guaranteed $15,000 first place grand prize based on full capacity of 200 teams. Annually, the third weekend in September. For info: Rhinelander Area Chamber of Commerce, PO Box 795, Rhinelander, WI 54501. Phone: (800) 236-4386. Fax: (715) 365-7467. E-mail: info@rhinelanderchamber.com. Web: www.rhinelanderchamber.com.

HONDURAS: INDEPENDENCE DAY. Sept 15. National holiday. Gained independence from Spain in 1821.

"I SPY" TV PREMIERE: ANNIVERSARY. Sept 15, 1965. Bill Cosby made television history as the first African American actor starring in a major dramatic role in this spy series. Cosby played Alexander "Scotty" Scott, an intellectual spy with a cover as a tennis trainer. Robert Culp played Kelly Robinson, the "tennis pro" and Scotty's partner in espionage. The series was notable for filming worldwide.

INTERNATIONAL COASTAL CLEANUP. Sept 15. Half a million volunteers pick up 10 million pieces of trash on 12,000 miles of beaches in 70 countries. For info: Center for Marine Conservation, 1725 DeSales St NW, Washington, DC 20036. Phone: (202) 429-5609. Fax: (202) 872-0619. E-mail: cmc@dccmc.org. Web: www.cmc-ocean.org.

JACKSON HILL CIDER DAY. Sept 15. Jackson House, Portsmouth, NH. Noon–5 PM. A harvest celebration for families and children in the orchards of the oldest house in New Hampshire. Children can wield picking poles and assist in pressing cider and cranking the paring machines. Fiddle music, beekeeping, samples of traditional sauce and pie and free tours of the house are included in the celebration. Annually, third Saturday in September. Admission: Adults $5; children $2. Est attendance: 120. For info: Soc for Preservation of New England Antiquities, 143 Pleasant St, Portsmouth, NH 03801. Phone: (603) 436-3205. Fax: (603) 436-4651.

JAPAN: OLD PEOPLE'S DAY OR RESPECT FOR THE AGED DAY. Sept 15. National holiday.

KANABEC FALL FEST. Sept 15. Kanabec History Center, Mora, MN. A beautiful setting for this 12th annual festival that showcases a diverse blend of demonstrating and performing folk artists. Arts activities and fun for all ages. Est attendance: 2,500. For info: Kanabec History Center, 805 W Forest Ave, PO Box 113, Mora, MN 55051. Phone: (320) 679-1665. Fax: (320) 679-1673. E-mail: kanabechistory@ncis.com. Web: www.kanabec history.com.

KING TURKEY DAYS (WITH TURKEY RACE). Sept 15. Worthington, MN. Community celebration which includes live turkey race between Paycheck, Worthington, MN and Ruby Begonia, Cuero, TX. Also included are a grand parade, live entertainment, free pancake breakfast and family activities. Est attendance: 15,000. For info: King Turkey Days, Inc, 1121 Third Ave, Worthington, MN 56187. Phone: (800) 279-2919 or (507) 372-2919. Fax: (507) 372-2827. E-mail: wgtncofc@prairie.lakes.com.

KRAZY WITH KUDZU. Sept 15–16. Chimney Rock Park, Chimney Rock, NC. Meet Kudzu Queen Edith Edwards, taste kudzu jelly and French-fried kudzu leaves and learn what can be done with this pesky plant. Est attendance: 2,400. For info: Mary Ritter, PR, Chimney Rock Park, PO Box 39, Chimney Rock, NC 28720. Phone: (800) 277-9611 or (828) 625-9611. Fax: (828) 625-9610. E-mail: visit@chimneyrockpark.com. Web: www.chimneyrockpark.com.

"THE LONE RANGER" TV PREMIERE: ANNIVERSARY. Sept 15, 1949. This character was created for a radio serial in 1933 by George W. Trendle. The famous masked man was the alter ego of John Reid, a Texas Ranger who was the only survivor of an ambush. He was nursed back to health by his Native-American friend, Tonto. Both men traveled around the West on their trusty steeds, Silver and Scout, fighting injustice. Clayton Moore played the Lone Ranger/John Reid and Jay Silverheels co-starred as Tonto. The theme music was Rossini's "William Tell Overture." The last episode aired Sept 12, 1957.

LOUISIANA NATIVE & CONTEMPORARY CRAFTS FESTIVAL. Sept 15–17. Lafayette, LA. A celebration of Louisiana's history through its native crafts, music, food and folklore. More than 200 juried Louisiana craftspeople, musicians, dancers, chefs, artisans and storytellers offer an inside look at the original artistry and cultural history of Louisiana, while also recognizing traditions and crafts still viable today. Est attendance: 7,000. For info: Lafayette Natural History Museum & Planetarium, 637 Girard Park Dr, Lafayette, LA 70503. Phone: (337) 291-5544. Fax: (337) 291-5464. Web: www.lnhm.org.

★**NATIONAL HISPANIC HERITAGE MONTH.** Sept 15–Oct 15. Presidential Proclamation. Beginning in 1989, always issued for Sept 15–Oct 15 of each year (PL 100–402 of Aug 17, 1988). Previously issued each year for the week including Sept 15 and 16 since 1968 at request (PL90–498 of Sept 17, 1968).

★**NATIONAL POW/MIA RECOGNITION DAY.** Sept 15.

NICARAGUA: INDEPENDENCE DAY. Sept 15. National holiday. Gained independence from Spain in 1821.

OZARK HAM AND TURKEY FESTIVAL. Sept 15. California, MO. Held each year in appreciation of the two largest industries in the county. The festival includes sand volleyball tournament, car races, parade, craft and food booths, BBQ contest, car show, folk art, live entertainment on four stages, antique tractor pull, western horse show, washerboard tournament and much more. Annually, the third Saturday in September. Est attendance: 20,000. For info: Ozark Ham and Turkey Festival, PO Box 85, California, MO 65018. Phone: (573) 796-3040. Fax: (573) 796-8309.

PEDDLER'S VILLAGE SCARECROW FESTIVAL. Sept 15–16. Peddler's Village, Lahaska, PA. Weekend festival includes scarecrow making, pumpkin-painting workshops, jack-o'-lantern and gourd art contest, musical entertainment and scarecrow competition display. Free admission. Charge for workshops. Est atten-

dance: 16,000. For info: Peddler's Village, Routes 202 & 263, Lahaska, PA 18931. Phone: (215) 794-4000. Fax: (215) 794-4001. Web: www.peddlersvillage.com.

RAINBOW OF ARTS CRAFT FESTIVAL. Sept 15 (rain or shine). Rockwood Park, Chesterfield, VA. 24th annual fest includes crafts and children's Imagination Station. Est attendance: 7,000. For info: Chesterfield Jaycees, Chesterfield, VA 23832. Phone: (804) 763-0619.

ROAD CHURCH COUNTRY FAIR. Sept 15. Road Congregational Church, Pequot Trail, Stonington, CT. White elephants, bake table, harvest table, crafts and children's midway. Famous Barnes's Chowder Luncheon at noon (served in Civil War kettles). Auction at 2 PM. 10 AM–3 PM. Est attendance: 300. For info: Libby Kennedy, 21 Roosevelt Ave, Mystic, CT 06355. Phone: (860) 536-1514.

ROAN MOUNTAIN STATE PARK FALL FESTIVAL. Sept 15–16. Roan Mountain, TN. Crafts, exhibits, music and clogging. Est attendance: 20,000. For info: Fall Fest, Ranger Naturalist, Roan Mt State Park, 1015 Hwy 143, Roan Mountain, TN 37687. Phone: (615) 772-0190, ext 108. Fax: (423) 772-0142.

SFCC STARKE FALL FESTIVAL. Sept 15–16. Starke, FL. Artists and craftsmen from all areas of Florida display their work. The Children's Creative Corner gives kids their own arts fest. Est attendance: 8,000. For info: Santa Fe Community College, Fall Arts Fest, 3000 NW 83rd St, Gainesville, FL 32606. Phone: (904) 395-5335. Fax: (352) 395-5918. E-mail: kathryn.lehman@santafe.cc.fl.us.

SOMEDAY. Sept 15. You know all those things you're going to do "someday"—lose weight, start a business, learn another language, skydive, whatever. Well, someday is here! This is the day to tackle new challenges and experience the joy of accomplishment. Free articles available for publishers and webmasters at IdeaLady.com/content.htm. For info: Cathy Stucker, Special Interests Publishing, 4646 Hwy 6, PMB 123, Sugar Land, TX 77478. Phone: (281) 265-7342. Fax: (281) 265-9727. E-mail: cathy@idealady.com. Web: www.idealady.com.

SOUTHWEST IOWA PROFESSIONAL HOT–AIR BALLOON RACES. Sept 15–16. Creston, IA. Hare and hound races held at sunrise and sunset; parade and marching band contest and much more. Annually, the third weekend in September. Est attendance: 7,000. For info: Chamber of Commerce, Box 471, Creston, IA 50801. Phone: (515) 641-7021. Web: www.mddc.com/chamber.

SPACE MILESTONE: *ARIANE-3* (ESA). Sept 15, 1987. European Space Agency rocket carrying two (Australian and European) communications satellites into Earth's orbit marked the re-entry of western nations into commercial space projects. Launched this date from Kourou, French Guiana, with Arianespace, a private company operating the rocket for the 13-nation European Space Agency.

TAFT, WILLIAM HOWARD: BIRTH ANNIVERSARY. Sept 15, 1857. The 27th president of the US was born at Cincinnati, OH. His term of office was Mar 4, 1909–Mar 3, 1913. Following his presidency he became a law professor at Yale University until his appointment as Chief Justice of the US Supreme Court in 1921. Died at Washington, DC, Mar 8, 1930, and was buried at Arlington National Cemetery.

A TASTE OF FALL FEST. Sept 15–16. Cumberland, MD. 12th annual festival featuring more than 65 craft exhibitors, entertainment, children's activities and food. Festival helps raise money to pay for equipment for the volunteer fire dept. Annually, the third weekend in September. Est attendance: 5,000. For info: Bowling Green Volunteer Fire Dept, 12420 McMullen Hwy SW, Cumberland, MD 21502. Phone: (301) 729-1522.

September 2001

S	M	T	W	T	F	S
						1
2	3	4	5	6	7	8
9	10	11	12	13	14	15
16	17	18	19	20	21	22
23	24	25	26	27	28	29
30						

TRAIL OF COURAGE LIVING-HISTORY FESTIVAL.
Sept 15–16. Rochester, IN. Portrayal of life in frontier Indiana when it was Indian territory. Historic skits, music, dancing, wigwam and tepee villages, historic encampments for Revolutionary War, French and Indian War, Voyageurs, Western Fur Trade and Plains Indians; recreated 1832 Chippeway Village, also Woodland Indian village, pioneer foods and crafts, muzzleloading and tomahawk contests, canoe rides. Museum, round barn and Living History Village on grounds. Special honored Potawatomi family from Indiana's history each year. Est attendance: 18,000. For info: Fulton County Historical Society, 37 E 375N, Rochester, IN 46975. Phone: (219) 223-4436. E-mail: wwillard@rtcol.com.

TRAIL OF TEARS COMMEMORATION AND MOTOR-
CYCLE RIDE. Sept 15–16. Waterloo, AL. A day to gather and remember the tragic Trail of Tears when Native Americans were removed from their homes in the 1830s and were forced to walk a trail to the West. Arts and crafts, museum exhibits and great entertainment. An organized motorcycle ride begins at Chattanooga the same morning and arrives in Waterloo for afternoon activities. Est attendance: 10,000. For info: Debbie Wilson, Florence/Lauderdale Tourism, One Hightower Place, Florence, AL 35630. Phone: (256) 740-4141 or (888) FLO-TOUR. Fax: (256) 740-4142. E-mail: dwilson@floweb.com. Web: www.flo-tour.org.

UNITED KINGDOM: BATTLE OF BRITAIN DAY. Sept
15. Commemorates end of biggest daylight bombing raid of Britain by German Luftwaffe, in 1940. Said to have been the turning point against Hitler's siege of Britain in WWII.

US TROOPS ENTER GERMANY: ANNIVERSARY. Sept
15, 1944. US troops of the VII and V Corps reached the southwestern frontier of Germany. The war had finally moved into the Third Reich's backyard.

VICTORIAN FAIR. Sept 15–16. Winona, MN. Southeastern Minnesota fall festival celebrating Winona's golden Victorian era. Food, music and entertainment from a time long past. Est attendance: 6,000. For info: Mark Peterson, Exec Dir, Winona County Historical Soc, 160 Johnson St, Winona, MN 55987. Phone: (507) 454-2723. Fax: (507) 454-0006. E-mail: wchs@luminet.net.

WINGS 'N' WATER FESTIVAL. Sept 15–16. Wetlands Institute, Stone Harbor, NJ. Coastal arts celebration of the environment throughout seaside towns of Stone Harbor and Avalon. 18th annual award-winning festival features Wildlife, Duck Stamp, Maritime & Landscape art. Plus bird and fish carvings, decoys, photography, crafts, quilts, music, retriever demos, boat cruises, kayaking, seafood and more. Est attendance: 5,000. For info: Nancy Morrow, Wetlands Institute, 1075 Stone Harbor Blvd, Stone Harbor, NJ 08247-1424. Phone: (609) 368-1211. Fax: (609) 368-1211. Web: www.wetlandsinstitute.org.

BIRTHDAYS TODAY

Jackie Cooper, 79, actor (*Our Gang* shorts, "The People's Choice"), producer, born Los Angeles, CA, Sept 15, 1922.
Norm Crosby, 74, comedian, host ("The Comedy Shop"), born Boston, MA, Sept 15, 1927.
Sherman Douglas, 35, basketball player, born Washington, DC, Sept 15, 1966.
Prince Harry (Henry Charles Albert David), 17, second son of Prince Charles and Princess Diana, born London, England, Sept 15, 1984.
Tommy Lee Jones, 55, actor (Oscar for *The Fugitive; Coal Miner's Daughter*), born San Saba, TX, Sept 15, 1946.
Daniel Constantine (Dan) Marino, Jr, 40, former football player, born Pittsburgh, PA, Sept 15, 1961.
Carmen Maura, 56, actress (*Women on the Verge of a Nervous Breakdown*), born Madrid, Spain, Sept 15, 1945.
Jessye Norman, 56, soprano, born Augusta, GA, Sept 15, 1945.
Merlin Jay Olsen, 61, Pro Football Hall of Fame defensive tackle, sportscaster, actor, born Logan, UT, Sept 15, 1940.
Gaylord Jackson Perry, 63, Baseball Hall of Fame pitcher, born Williamston, NC, Sept 15, 1938.
Bobby Short (Robert Waltrip), 75, singer, pianist, cafe song stylist, born Danville, IL, Sept 15, 1926.
Oliver Stone, 55, director (*Platoon, JFK, Wall Street*), screenwriter, born New York, NY, Sept 15, 1946.

SEPTEMBER 16 — SUNDAY
Day 259 — 106 Remaining

ANNE BRADSTREET DAY. Sept 16. A day to honor Anne Bradstreet and the anniversary of the publication of her book of poetry, *The Tenth Muse*. Anne Bradstreet, America's first poet who is also recognized as the first published woman poet in the English language, was born in 1612 in England and came to America in 1630 with her father, Thomas Dudley; husband, Simon Bradstreet; and the first Governor of the Commonwealth of Massachusetts, John Winthrop. Unbeknownst to Anne, her brother-in-law took her poetry back to England where it was published in 1650 as *The Tenth Muse Lately Sprung Up in America*. She died at North Andover, MA, Sept 16, 1672. For info: Sue Ellen Holmes, Dir, Stevens Memorial Library, PO Box 8, North Andover, MA 01845. Phone: (978) 688-9505. Fax: (978) 688-9507. E-mail: holmes@mvlc.lib.ma.us.

ARTS/QUINCY RIVERFEST. Sept 16. Quincy, IL. Celebration of the arts and the Mississippi River in the riverfront parks. Fine arts and crafts, jazz stage, country stage, along with children's area featuring hands-on activities and performances. Annually, the third Sunday in September. Est attendance: 20,000. For info: Kathleen Benz, Coord, Quincy Soc of Fine Arts, 300 Civic Center Plaza, Ste 244, Quincy, IL 62301-4162. Phone: (217) 222-3432. Fax: (217) 228-2787. E-mail: art@artsqcy.org. Web: www.artqcy.org.

BALANCE AWARENESS WEEK. Sept 16–22. To develop public awareness of balance and disorders of balance system (vestibular disorders); to unite professionals, educators, support groups, medical facilities in a week-long effort to focus attention of the public and the media. For info: Vestibular Disorders Assn, PO Box 4467, Portland, OR 97208-4467. Phone: (800) 837-8428. Fax: (503) 229-8064. Web: www.vestibular.org.

BALTIMORE HIGHLANDS ARTS & CRAFTS FESTI-
VAL. Sept 16. Baltimore, MD. Homemade crafts, food, children's activities, entertainment and much more. Annually, the third Sunday in September. For info: Greater Baltimore Highlands Community Assn, PO Box 18213, Halethorpe, MD 21227. Phone: (410) 789-4334.

BEL AIR FESTIVAL FOR THE ARTS. Sept 16. Bel Air, MD. Arts, crafts, photography exhibits and entertainment. Application deadline Apr 15. Est attendance: 25,000. For info: Donna Clauer, Bel Air Rec Committee, 1909 Wheel Rd, Bel Air, MD 21015. Phone: (410) 836-2395. E-mail: MrsCsWkshp@aol.com.

BUILD A BETTER IMAGE WEEK. Sept 16–22. In order to be a success, you need to look like one. This week is set aside for people to evaluate their professional image and take the steps necessary to improve on it. For "10 Steps to a Better Image" tip sheet, send #10 SASE. Annually, the third full week of September. For info: Marlys K. Arnold, Total Image Specialist, 7885 NW Roanridge Rd, Ste A, Kansas City, MO 64151. Phone: (816) 746-7888. E-mail: marnold@imagespecialist.com. Web: www.imagespecialist.com.

CHEROKEE STRIP CELEBRATION. Sept 16. Perry, OK. To commemorate the opening of the Cherokee Strip to settlement on Sept 16, 1893. Annually, the Saturday or weekend nearest Sept 16. Est attendance: 10,000. For info: Penny Murrow, Chamber of Commerce, Box 426, Perry, OK 73077. Phone: (580) 336-4684. Fax: (580) 336-3522.

CHEROKEE STRIP DAY: ANNIVERSARY. Sept 16, 1893. Optional holiday, Oklahoma. Greatest "run" for Oklahoma land in 1893.

CZECH REPUBLIC: PRAGUE AUTUMN INTERNATIONAL MUSIC FESTIVAL. Sept 16–30. Symphonic and chamber orchestras, instrumental concerts, cantatas, oratoria and recitals. For info: Prague Autumn International Music Festival, 130 00 - CZ, Prague 3, Pribenicka 20, Czech Republic. Phone: (42 2) 627 87 40. Fax: (42 2) 627 86 42. E-mail: festival@prague autumn.cz. Web: pragueautumn.cz.

FOUNDER'S DAY CORN ROAST. Sept 16. Pacific University, Forest Grove, OR. 1–5 PM. Mountain men, interactive pioneer displays, Native and other entertainment, Tug-O-War, chalk art, family activities and lots of CORN!!! Est attendance: 2,000. For info: Founder's Day Corn Roast, 2417 Pacific Ave, Forest Grove, OR 97116. Phone: (503) 357-3006. Web: www.fgchamber.com.

"FRASIER" TV PREMIERE: ANNIVERSARY. Sept 16, 1993. In this spin-off of "Cheers," psychiatrist Dr. Frasier Crane (Kelsey Grammer) has moved to Seattle where he dispenses advice on the radio. He lives with his father Martin (John Mahoney) and Martin's physical therapist Daphne Moon (Jane Leeves). His brother, Dr. Niles Crane (David Hyde Pierce), frequently asks for Frasier's advice about his love life. Roz Doyle, the producer of Frasier's show, is played by Peri Gilpin.

GENERAL MOTORS: FOUNDING ANNIVERSARY. Sept 16, 1908. The giant automobile manufacturing company was founded by William Crapo "Billy" Durant, a Flint, MI, entrepreneur.

GREAT SEAL OF THE US: FIRST USE ANNIVERSARY. Sept 16, 1782. On this date the Great Seal of the United States was, for the first time, impressed upon an official document. That document authorized George Washington to negotiate a prisoner of war agreement with the British. See also: "Great Seal of the United States: Anniversary" (Jan 28 and July 4).

INTERNATIONAL DAY OF PRAYER AND ACTION FOR HUMAN HABITAT. Sept 16. To further the goal of eliminating inadequate and poverty housing. Annually, the third Sunday in September. For info: Habitat for Humanity, 121 Habitat St, Americus, GA 31709-3498. Phone: (800) HABITAT or (912) 924-6935. Web: www.habitat.org.

	S	M	T	W	T	F	S
September							1
	2	3	4	5	6	7	8
2001	9	10	11	12	13	14	15
	16	17	18	19	20	21	22
	23	24	25	26	27	28	29
	30						

"MANNIX" TV PREMIERE: ANNIVERSARY. Sept 16, 1967. Mike Connors starred as Joe Mannix, a Los Angeles private investigator working for the computer organization Intertect, in this long-running CBS crime series. Joseph Campanella played his boss, Lou Wickersham, during the first season. The show then changed format with Mannix setting up his own agency. The new cast members were Gail Fisher as Peggy Fair, his secretary, Robert Reed as Lieutenant Adam Tobias and Ward Wood as Lieutenant Art Malcolm.

MARRIAGE CELEBRATION. Sept 16. Belleville, IL. An evening honoring married couples celebrating 10, 25, 40, 50+ and 60+ years of marriage in 2001. Sunday, 7 PM. Est attendance: 500. For info: Shrine of Our Lady of the Snows, 442 S De Mazenod Dr, Belleville, IL 62223-1094. Phone: (618) 397-6700. Fax: (618) 397-1210. Web: www.snows.org.

MAYFLOWER DAY: ANNIVERSARY. Sept 16, 1620. Anniversary of the departure of the *Mayflower* from Plymouth, England with 102 passengers and a small crew. Vicious storms were encountered en route which caused serious doubt about the wisdom of continuing, but she reached Provincetown, MA, Nov 21, and discharged the Pilgrims at Plymouth, MA, Dec 26, 1620.

MEXICO: INDEPENDENCE DAY. Sept 16. National Day. The official celebration begins at 11 PM, Sept 15 and continues through Sept 16. On the night of the 15th, the President of Mexico steps onto the balcony of the National Palace at Mexico City and voices the same "El Grito" (Cry for Freedom) that Father Hidalgo gave on the night of Sept 15, 1810 which began Mexico's rebellion from Spain.

MIDDLEMARK, MARVIN: BIRTH ANNIVERSARY. Sept 16, 1919. Marvin Middlemark was born at Long Island, NY. His passion for inventing and tinkering led to many inventions, most of which enjoyed little commercial success, like the water-driven automatic potato peeler. But it was as the inventor of a device to improve TV reception, known as "rabbit ears," that he became successful. He died Sept 14, 1989, at Old Westbury, NY.

NATIONAL CONSTITUTION CENTER CONSTITUTION WEEK. Sept 16–22. To celebrate and commemorate the signing of the US Constitution Sept 17, 1787. The National Constitution Center sponsors ceremonial signings of the Constitution nationwide. Everyone is invited to participate and receive educational materials about the world's oldest working Constitution. For info: Natl Constitution Center, The Bourse, 111 S Independence Mall East, Ste 560, Philadelphia, PA 19106. Phone: (215) 923-0004. Fax: (215) 923-1749. Web: www.constitution-center.org.

NATIONAL FARM ANIMALS AWARENESS WEEK. Sept 16–22. A week to promote awareness of farm animals and their natural behaviors. Each day of the week is dedicated to learning about a specific group of farm animals and to appreciating their many interesting and unique qualities. Annually, the third full week in September. For info: Wende Zimmerman, The Humane Society of the US, Farm Animal Section, 2100 L St NW, Washington, DC 20037. Phone: (202) 452-1100. E-mail: wzimmerman@hsus.org.

★**NATIONAL FARM SAFETY AND HEALTH WEEK.**
Sept 16–22. Presidential Proclamation issued since 1982 for the third week in September. Previously, from 1944, for one of the last two weeks in July.

NATIONAL REHABILITATION AWARENESS CELE-BRATION. Sept 16–22. The observance salutes the determination of the more than 50 million Americans with disabilities. It is a time to applaud the efforts of rehab professionals, provide a forum for education and offer an occasion to call upon our citizens to find new ways to fulfill needs that still exist. For info: Natl Rehabilitation Awareness Foundation, PO Box 71, Scranton, PA 18501. Phone: (570) 341-4637 or (800) 943-6723. Fax: (570) 341-4331. Web: wwwnraf-rehabnet.org.

NATIONAL SINGLES WEEK. Sept 16–22. To celebrate single life and to recognize singles and their contributions to society. For info: Singles Press Assn, Box 6243, Scottsdale, AZ 85261-6243. Phone: (602) 788-6001. E-mail: singles@primenet.com

OLD-FASHIONED HARVESTFEST AND FIDDLERS CONTEST. Sept 16. Woodstock, IL. A day-long celebration, Harvestfest features farmer's markets, old-time craftspeople including weavers, spinners and quilters, vintage farm equipment, blacksmithing, woodworking, wagon rides and a fiddlers contest for youth and adults. Hours: 10 AM–5 PM. Est attendance: 750. For info: Woodstock Chamber of Commerce, 136 Cass St, Woodstock, IL 60098. Phone: (815) 338-2436. Fax: (815) 338-2927. E-mail: chamber@stans.com.

★**OVARIAN CANCER AWARENESS WEEK.** Sept 16–22.

"OWEN MARSHALL: COUNSELOR AT LAW" TV PRE-MIERE: 30th ANNIVERSARY. Sept 16, 1971. "Owen Marshall" was an hour-long ABC drama with Arthur Hill as the title character, a widowed attorney in Santa Barbara. Lee Majors, Reni Santoni and David Soul played his associates. Also featured were Joan Darling as Marshall's secretary and Christine Matchett as his daughter.

PALESTINIAN MASSACRE: ANNIVERSARY. Sept 16, 1982. Christian militiamen (the Phalangists) entered Sabra and Shatila, two Palestinian refugee camps in West Beirut. They began open shooting and by Sept 18 hundreds of Palestinians, including elderly men, women and children, were dead. Phalangists had demanded blood of Palestinians since the assassination of their president, Bashir Gemayel, on Sept 14. Survivors of the massacre said they had not seen Israeli forces inside the camp; however, they claimed Israelis sealed off boundaries to the camps and allowed Christian militiamen to enter.

PANIZZI, ANTHONY: BIRTH ANNIVERSARY. Sept 16, 1797. Sir Anthony Panizzi, the only librarian ever hanged in effigy, was born Antonio Genesio Maria Panizzi at Brescello, Italy. As a young man he joined a forbidden Italian patriotic society that advocated the overthrow of the oppressive Austrians who then controlled most of northern Italy. Tried in absentia by an Austrian court in 1820, he was sentenced to death and all his property was confiscated. He fled to England in 1823, learned the language and by 1831 was employed in the British Museum where, in 1856, he was named principal librarian. Later described as the "prince of librarians," Panizzi died at London, England, Apr 8, 1879.

PAPUA NEW GUINEA: INDEPENDENCE DAY: ANNI-VERSARY. Sept 16. National holiday. Commemorates independence from Australian administration in 1975.

PARKMAN, FRANCIS: BIRTH ANNIVERSARY. Sept 16, 1823. American historian, author of *The Oregon Trail*, was born at Boston, MA, and died there Nov 8, 1893.

PROSTATE CANCER AWARENESS WEEK. Sept 16–22. Free or low-cost prostate cancer screenings for all men 50–75 and men in high risk groups such as African American men and Hispanics over age 35. Annually, the third week in September. For info: Prostate Cancer Education Council, 1800 Jackson St, Golden, CO 80401. Phone: (303) 216-0724. Web: www.pcaw.com.

"SKY KING" TV PREMIERE: 50th ANNIVERSARY.
Sept 16, 1951. This half-hour children's adventure series began on radio in 1947. Kirby Grant starred as Schuyler J. (Sky) King, owner of the Flying Crown Ranch, who used his plane, *The Songbird*, to help victims and capture criminals. To help him was a cast that included Gloria Winters as his niece, Penny, Ron Hagerthy as his nephew Clipper, Ewing Mitchell as the sheriff, Mitch, Norman Ollstead as Bob Carey and Gary Hunley as Mickey.

STAY AWAY FROM SEATTLE DAY. Sept 16. Observed worldwide, except in Seattle, WA, to give America's "Best Place to Live" city a break from the influx of people moving to the area. On this day every year, the rest of us will try to keep the appeal of Seattle from haunting us with its siren call. [© 2000 by WH] For info: Thomas and Ruth Roy, Wellcat Holidays, 2418 Long Ln, Lebanon, PA 17046. Phone: (717) 279-0184. E-mail: wellcat@supernet.com. Web: www.wellcat.com.

TOLKIEN WEEK. Sept 16–22. To promote appreciation and enjoyment of the works of J.R.R. Tolkien. For info: Phil Helms, American Tolkien Soc, PO Box 7871, Flint, MI 48507-0871. Phone: (727) 585-0985. Fax: (727) 462-6473.

TORQUEMADA, TOMAS DE: DEATH ANNIVER-SARY. Sept 16, 1498. One of history's most malevolent persons, feared and hated by millions. As Inquisitor-General of Spain, he ordered burning at the stake for more than 10,000 persons and burning in effigy for another 7,000 (according to 18th-century estimates). Torquemada persuaded Ferdinand and Isabella to rid Spain of the Jews. More than a million families were driven from the country and Spain suffered a commercial decline from which it never recovered. Torquemada was born at Valladolid, Spain, in 1420 (exact date unknown) and died at Avila, Spain.

UNITED NATIONS: INTERNATIONAL DAY FOR THE PRESERVATION OF THE OZONE LAYER. Sept 16. On Dec 19, 1994, the General Assembly proclaimed this day to commemorate the date in 1987 on which Montreal Protocol on Substances that Deplete the Ozone Layer was signed (Res 49/114). States are invited to devote the Day to promote, at the national level, activities in accordance with the objectives of the Protocol. The ozone layer filters sunlight and prevents the adverse effects of ultraviolet radiation from reaching the Earth's surface, thereby preserving life on the planet. For info: United Nations, Dept of Public Info, Public Inquiries Unit, Rm GA-57, New York, NY 10017. Phone: (212) 963-4475. E-mail: inquiries@un.org .

WOMEN'S FRIENDSHIP DAY. Sept 16. Every woman has special people that she can't live without; those people to which she tells everything and that will always listen and know just what to say. A Women's Friendship Day gives the perfect opportunity for women to praise the meaningful person/people in their lives. Annually, the third Sunday in September. For info: Kappa Delta Sorority, 3205 Players Ln, Memphis, TN 38125. Phone: (901) 748-1897. Fax: (901) 748-0949. E-mail: kappadel@ixmemphis.com.

WOOL DAY: SHEEP TO SHAWL AND BORDER COL-LIES. Sept 16. Billings Farm and Museum, Woodstock, VT. This day-long event focuses on the many aspects of wool production, including a "sheep to shawl" demonstration and sheep herding, as well as many hands-on activities for all ages to enjoy. These activities include carding wool, drop spindle spinning, weaving, knitting and rug hooking. Border Collie demonstrations will show how these natural shepherds efficiently round up sheep, drive them from one area to another and corral them. Est attendance: 1,000. For info: Billings Farm & Museum, PO Box 489, Woodstock, VT 05091. Phone: (802) 457-2355. Fax: (802) 457-4663. E-mail: billings.farm@valley.net. Web: www.billingsfarm.org.

BIRTHDAYS TODAY

Marc Anthony, 32, singer, actor (*Bringing Out the Dead*), born New York, NY, Sept 16, 1969.

Lauren Bacall (Betty Joan Perske), 77, actress (*Applause, Woman of the Year, Key Largo*), born New York, NY, Sept 16, 1924.

Elgin Gay Baylor, 67, former coach and Basketball Hall of Fame forward, born Washington, DC, Sept 16, 1934.

Ed Begley, Jr, 52, actor ("St. Elsewhere"), born Los Angeles, CA, Sept 16, 1949.

David Copperfield (Kotkin), 45, illusionist, born Metuchen, NJ, Sept 16, 1956.

Peter Falk, 74, actor (*The Great Race*, "Columbo"), born New York, NY, Sept 16, 1927.

Anne Francis, 69, actress (*Bad Day at Black Rock, Blackboard Jungle, Forbidden Planet*), born Ossining, NY, Sept 16, 1932.

Henry Louis Gates, Jr, 51, professor of African American studies at Harvard, editor of the *Norton Anthology of African American Literature*, born Keyser, WV, Sept 16, 1950.

Orel Leonard Hershiser IV, 43, baseball player, born Buffalo, NY, Sept 16, 1958.

B.B. King, 76, singer ("Rock Me Baby," "The Thrill Is Gone"), born Itta Bena, MS, Sept 16, 1925.

John Knowles, 75, writer (*A Separate Peace*), born Fairmont, WV, Sept 16, 1926.

Richard Marx, 38, singer, born Chicago, IL, Sept 16, 1963.

Mark McEwen, 47, weatherman, music editor, born San Antonio, TX, Sept 16, 1954.

Janis Paige, 78, singer, actress (stage: *The Pajama Game, Silk Stockings*), born Tacoma, WA, Sept 16, 1923.

Timothy ("Rock") Raines, 42, baseball player, born Sanford, FL, Sept 16, 1959.

Mickey Rourke, 45, actor (*9 ½ Weeks, Bar Fly*), born Schenectady, NY, Sept 16, 1956.

Susan Ruttan, 51, actress ("LA Law"), born Oregon City, OR, Sept 16, 1950.

Molly Shannon, 37, actress ("Saturday Night Live"), born Shaker Heights, OH, Sept 16, 1964.

Jennifer Tilly, 40, actress (*Johnny Be Good, Made in America*), born Los Angeles, CA, Sept 16, 1961.

Robin R. Yount, 46, Baseball Hall of Fame shortstop and outfielder, born Danville, IL, Sept 16, 1955.

SEPTEMBER 17 — MONDAY

Day 260 — 105 Remaining

ANGOLA: DAY OF THE NATIONAL HERO. Sept 17. National holiday.

BATTLE OF ANTIETAM: ANNIVERSARY. Sept 17, 1862. This date has been called America's bloodiest day in recognition of the high casualties suffered in the Civil War battle between General Robert E. Lee's Confederate forces and General George McClellan's Union army. Estimates vary, but more than 25,000 Union and Confederate soldiers were killed or wounded in this battle on the banks of the Potomac River at Maryland.

"BEWITCHED" TV PREMIERE: ANNIVERSARY. Sept 17, 1964. This sitcom centered around blonde-haired witch Samantha Stephens (Elizabeth Montgomery). Although she promises not to use her witchcraft in her daily life, Samantha finds herself twitching her nose in many situations. Her husband, Darrin Stephens, was played by Dick York and Dick Sargent, and her daughter, Tabitha Stephens, was played by Erin and Diane Murphy. The last episode aired July 1, 1972. Other cast members included Agnes Moorhead, David White, Alice Ghostley, Bernard Fox and Paul Lynde.

BURGER, WARREN E.: BIRTH ANNIVERSARY. Sept 17, 1907. Former Chief Justice of the US Warren E. Burger was born at St. Paul, MN. A conservative on criminal matters, but a progressive on social issues, he had the longest tenure (1969-86) of any chief justice in this century. Appointed by President Nixon, he voted in the majority on *Roe v Wade* (1973), which upheld a woman's right to an abortion, and on *US v Nixon* (1974), which forced Nixon to surrender audio tapes to the Watergate special prosecutor. He died June 25, 1995, at Washington, DC.

★**CITIZENSHIP DAY.** Sept 17. Presidential Proclamation always issued for Sept 17 at request (PL82–261 of Feb 29, 1952). Customarily issued as "Citizenship Day and Constitution Week." Replaces Constitution Day.

CONNOLLY, MAUREEN: BIRTH ANNIVERSARY. Sept 17, 1934. Maureen ("Little Mo") Catherine Connolly Brinker, tennis player born at San Diego, CA. Connolly became the second-youngest woman to win the US National championship at Forest Hills, NY when she captured that title in 1951. She repeated in 1952 and won Wimbledon, too. In 1953 she became the first woman to win the Grand Slam, taking the US, French, Australian and Wimbledon championships. After winning a second straight French title and a third straight Wimbledon, she suffered a crushed leg in a horseback riding accident and never competed again. Died at Dallas, TX, June 21, 1969.

CONSTITUTION COMMEMORATION DAY IN ARIZONA. Sept 17. Arizona. This state holiday commemorates the signing of the US Constitution on Sept 17, 1787.

CONSTITUTION OF THE US: ANNIVERSARY. Sept 17, 1787. Delegations from 12 states (Rhode Island did not send a delegate) at the Constitutional Convention at Philadelphia, PA, voted unanimously to approve the proposed document. Thirty-nine of the 42 delegates present signed it and the Convention adjourned, after drafting a letter of transmittal to the Congress. The proposed constitution stipulated that it would take effect when ratified by nine states. This day is a legal holiday in Florida.

★**CONSTITUTION WEEK.** Sept 17–23. Presidential Proclamation always issued for the period of Sept 17–23 each year since 1955 (PL 84–915 of Aug 2, 1956).

FOSTER, ANDREW (RUBE): BIRTH ANNIVERSARY. Sept 17, 1879. Rube Foster's efforts in baseball earned him the title of "The Father of Negro Baseball." He was a manager and star pitcher, pitching 51 victories in one year. In 1919, he called a meeting of black baseball owners and organized the first black baseball league, the Negro National League. He served as its president until his death in 1930. Foster was born at Calvert, TX, the son of a minister. He died Dec 9, 1930, at Kankakee, IL.

"THE FUGITIVE" TV PREMIERE: ANNIVERSARY. Sept 17, 1963. A nail-biting adventure series on ABC. Dr. Richard Kimble (David Janssen) was wrongly convicted and sentenced to death for his wife's murder, but escaped from his captors in a train wreck. This popular program aired for four years detailing Kimble's search for the one-armed man (Bill Raisch) who had killed his wife, Helen (Diane Brewster). In the meantime, Kimble himself was being pursued by Lieutenant Philip Gerard (Barry Morse). The final episode aired Aug 29, 1967, and featured Kimble extracting a confession from the one-armed man as they struggled from the heights of a water tower in a deserted amusement park. That single episode was the highest-rated show ever broadcast until 1976. The TV series generated a hit movie in 1993 with Harrison Ford as Kimble and Oscar-winner Tommy Lee Jones as Gerard.

"HEAD OF THE CLASS" TV PREMIERE: 15th ANNIVERSARY. Sept 17, 1986. This ABC sitcom was the antithesis of "Welcome Back, Kotter." It ran for five years, depicting the travails and triumphs of brainy students in the Individual Honors Program (IHP) of New York's Fillmore High School. One episode in 1988 was the first American prime-time program filmed entirely

		S	M	T	W	T	F	S
September								1
2001		2	3	4	5	6	7	8
		9	10	11	12	13	14	15
		16	17	18	19	20	21	22
		23	24	25	26	27	28	29
		30						

in the Soviet Union. Howard Hesseman starred as part-time actor and substitute teacher Charlie Moore (a man more adept at teaching life's lessons than history). The cast also featured William G. Schilling as Principal Samuels, Jeannetta Arnette as Assistant Principal Bernadette Meara, Leslie Bega as Maria, Dan Frischman as Arvid, Robin Givens as Darlene, Khrystyne Haje as Simone, Jory Husain as Jawarharlal, Tony O'Dell as Alan, Brian Robbins as Eric, Kimberly Russell as Sarah, Dan Schneider as Dennis, Tannis Vallely as Janice, Rain Pryor as T.J., Michael DeLorenzo as Alex, Lara Piper as Viki, De'voreaux White as Aristotle and Jonathan Ke Quan as Jasper. After Hesseman left the show in 1990, Scottish comedian Billy Connolly took over the class. The series ended with the graduation of all the characters, June 25, 1991.

HENDRICKS, THOMAS ANDREWS: BIRTH ANNIVERSARY. Sept 17, 1819. Twenty-first vice president of the US (1885) born at Muskingum County, OH. Died at Indianapolis, IN, Nov 25, 1885.

HERZOG, CHAIM: BIRTH ANNIVERSARY. Sept 17, 1918. President of Israel, an ex-general and chief delegate to the UN, author, lawyer, born at Belfast, Northern Ireland. He was a British army officer in World War II. Died at Tel Aviv, Israel, Apr 17, 1997.

"HOME IMPROVEMENT" TV PREMIERE: 10th ANNIVERSARY. Sept 17, 1991. This comedy centered around the Taylors. Tim Taylor, played by Tim Allen, was a TV host on the popular fix-it show "Tool Time." Jill, played by Patricia Richardson, was a housewife and mother going back to school to get a degree in psychology. The couple's three sons were played by Zachery Ty Bryan, Jonathan Taylor Thomas and Taran Noah Smith. Other cast members included Richard Karn, Earl Hindman, Debbe Dunning and Pamela Anderson. The last episode aired May 25, 1999.

LOVE A MENSCH WEEK. Sept 17–23. Mensches are decent, responsible men or women. During this week singles look to meet a mensch as well as take time to appreciate how mensches enhance our lives. For info: Robin Gorman Newman, Mensch Finders, 44 Somerset Dr N, Great Neck, NY 11020. Phone: (516) 773-0911. E-mail: rgnewman@aol.com.

MacNELLY, JEFF: BIRTH ANNIVERSARY. Sept 17, 1947. Pulitzer prize—winning editorial cartoonist, comic strip cartoonist ("Shoe"), born at New York, NY. Died June 9, 2000, at Baltimore, MD.

"M*A*S*H" TV PREMIERE: ANNIVERSARY. Sept 17, 1972. This popular CBS series was based on the 1970 Robert Altman movie and a book by Richard Hooker. Set during the Korean War, the show aired for 11 years (lasting longer than the war). It followed the lives of doctors and nurses on the war front with both humor and pathos. The cast included: Alan Alda as Captain Benjamin Franklin "Hawkeye" Pierce, Wayne Rogers as Captain John "Trapper John" McIntyre, McLean Stevenson as Lieutenant Colonel Henry Blake, Loretta Swit as Major Margaret "Hot Lips" Houlihan, Larry Linville as Major Frank Burns, Gary Burghoff as Corporal Walter "Radar" O'Reilly, William Christopher as Father Francis Mulcahy, Jamie Farr as Corporal Max Klinger, Harry Morgan as Colonel Sherman Potter and Mike Farrell as Captain B.J. Hunnicut. The show won numerous awards during its run. Its final episode, "Goodbye, Farewell and Amen" was the highest-rated program of all time, topping the "Who Shot J.R.?" revelation on "Dallas." See also: "M*A*S*H: The Final Episode: Anniversary" (Feb 28). The show generated two spin-offs: "Trapper John, MD" and "After M*A*S*H."

"MISSION: IMPOSSIBLE" TV PREMIERE: 35th ANNIVERSARY. Sept 17, 1966. This action-adventure espionage series was produced by Bruce Geller, appearing on CBS for seven years. The premise of the show was simple: each week the IMF (Impossible Missions Force) leader would receive instructions on a super-secret mission to be carried out by the crew. Steven Hill played the first IMF leader, Dan Briggs. He was replaced by Peter Graves who played Jim Phelps. The crew included: Martin Landau as Rollin Hand, master of disguise, Barbara Bain, real-life wife of Landau, as Cinnamon Carter, Greg Morris as Barney Collier, technical expert, Peter Lupus as Willy Armitage, tough guy, Leonard Nimoy as Hand's replacement, Paris, Lesley Ann Warren as Dana Lambert, Sam Elliott as Doug, Lynda Day George as Lisa Casey and Barbara Anderson as Mimi Davis. The show was remade for ABC in 1988; it lasted two seasons. The latest incarnation of "Mission: Impossible" was on the silver screen in 1996, starring Tom Cruise.

MOON PHASE: NEW MOON. Sept 17. Moon enters New Moon phase at 6:27 AM, EDT.

NATIONAL FOOTBALL LEAGUE FORMED: ANNIVERSARY. Sept 17, 1920. The National Football League was formed at Canton, OH.

★**NATIONAL HISTORICALLY BLACK COLLEGES AND UNIVERSITIES WEEK.** Sept 17–23.

QUARTERLY ESTIMATED FEDERAL INCOME TAX PAYERS' DUE DATE. Sept 17. For those individuals whose fiscal year is the calendar year and who make quarterly estimated federal income tax payments, today is one of the due dates. (Jan 15, Apr 16, June 15 and Sept 17, 2001.)

ROSH HASHANAH BEGINS AT SUNDOWN. Sept 17. Jewish New Year. See "Rosh Hashanah" (Sept 18).

SELFRIDGE, THOMAS E.: DEATH ANNIVERSARY. Sept 17, 1908. Lieutenant Thomas E. Selfridge, 26-year-old passenger in 740-lb biplane piloted by Orville Wright, was killed when, after four minutes in the air, the plane fell from a height of 75 feet. Nearly 2,000 spectators witnessed the crash at Fort Myer, VA. The plane was being tested for possible military use by the Army Signal Corps. Orville Wright was seriously injured in the crash. Selfridge Air Force Base, MI, was named after the young lieutenant, a West Point graduate, who was the first fatality of powered airplane travel.

SPACE MILESTONE: *PEGASUS 1* (US). Sept 17, 1978. 23,000-pound research satellite broke up over Africa and fell to Earth. Major pieces are believed to have fallen into Atlantic Ocean off the coast of Angola. The satellite had been orbiting Earth for more than 13 years since being launched Feb 16, 1965.

"SUGARFOOT" TV PREMIERE: ANNIVERSARY. Sept 17, 1957. One of three ABC westerns produced by Warner Brothers in the late 50s. The show alternated with "Cheyenne" and "Bronco." Will Hutchins starred as Tom (Sugarfoot) Brewster, an Easterner with designs on becoming a lawyer in the Wild West. All three shows later aired under the "Cheyenne" appellation in 1960.

VFW LADIES AUXILIARY ORGANIZED: ANNIVERSARY. Sept 17, 1914. This organization is loyal to the issues and actions affecting America's heroes. Its members offer assistance in addition to supporting veterans' issues in Congress. Part of the organization's mission, according to its charter, is "to assist the Posts and members thereof. . .; to foster true patriotism; and to preserve and defend the United States from all her enemies, whomsoever." For info: Veterans of Foreign Wars of the US, Women's Auxiliary, 406 W 34th St, Kansas City, MO 64111. Phone: (816) 561-8655. Fax: (816) 931-4753. Web: www.ladiesauxvfw.com.

VON STEUBEN, BARON FRIEDRICH: BIRTH ANNIVERSARY. Sept 17, 1730. Prussian-born general who volunteered to serve in the American Revolution. He died at Remsen, NY, Nov 28, 1794.

WILLIAMS, HANK, SR: BIRTH ANNIVERSARY. Sept 17, 1923. Hiram King Williams, country and western singer, born at Georgia, AL. He achieved his first major hit with "Lovesick Blues," which brought him a contract with the Grand Ole Opry. His string of hits included "Cold, Cold Heart," "Honky Tonk Blues," "Jambalaya," "Your Cheatin' Heart," "Take These Chains From My Heart" and "I'll Never Get Out of This World Alive," which was released prior to his death Jan 1, 1953, at Oak Hill, VA.

BIRTHDAYS TODAY

Anne Bancroft (Anna Maria Italiano), 70, actress (Tony and Oscar for *The Miracle Worker; The Graduate, The Turning Point*), born New York, NY, Sept 17, 1931.

Paul Benedict, 63, actor ("The Jeffersons," many stage roles), born Silver City, NM, Sept 17, 1938.

George Blanda, 74, Pro Football Hall of Fame quarterback and placekicker, born Youngwood, PA, Sept 17, 1927.

Mark Brunell, 31, football player, born Los Angeles, CA, Sept 17, 1970.

Kyle Chandler, 36, actor ("Early Edition," "Homefront"), born Buffalo, NY, Sept 17, 1965.

Charles Ernest Grassley, 68, US Senator (R, Iowa), born New Hartford, IA, Sept 17, 1933.

Philip D. (Phil) Jackson, 56, basketball coach, former player, born Deer Lodge, MT, Sept 17, 1945.

Ken Kesey, 66, author (*One Flew Over the Cuckoo's Nest*), born LaJunta, CO, Sept 17, 1935.

Dorothy Loudon, 68, actress, singer ("The Garry Moore Show"), born Boston, MA, Sept 17, 1933.

Cassandra Peterson, 50, actress (movie hostess Elvira), born Manhattan, KS, Sept 17, 1951.

John Ritter, 53, actor (Emmy for "Three's Company"; *Problem Child*), born Burbank, CA, Sept 17, 1948.

Rita Rudner, 45, comedienne, actress (*Peter's Friends*), born Miami, FL, Sept 17, 1956.

David H. Souter, 62, Associate Justice of the US Supreme Court, born Melrose, MA, Sept 17, 1939.

Rasheed Wallace, 27, basketball player, born Philadelphia, PA, Sept 17, 1974.

SEPTEMBER 18 — TUESDAY

Day 261 — 104 Remaining

"THE ADDAMS FAMILY" TV PREMIERE: ANNIVERSARY. Sept 18, 1964. Charles Addams' quirky *New Yorker* cartoon creations were brought to life in this ABC sitcom about a family full of oddballs. John Astin played lawyer Gomez Addams, with Carolyn Jones as his morbid wife Morticia, Ken Weatherwax as son Pugsley, Lisa Loring as daughter Wednesday, Jackie Coogan as Uncle Fester, Ted Cassidy as both Lurch, the butler, and Thing, a disembodied hand, Blossom Rock as Grandmama and Felix Silla as Cousin Itt. Although the last episode aired Sept 2, 1966, *The Addams Family* movie was released in 1991, starring Anjelica Huston as Morticia, Raul Julia as Gomez, Christopher Lloyd as Uncle Fester, Jimmy Workman as Pugsley and Christina Ricci as Wednesday.

BRAZZI, ROSSANO: 85th BIRTH ANNIVERSARY. Sept 18, 1916. Hollywood actor Rossano Brazzi was born at Bologna, Italy. A leading romantic figure in the 1950s and 1960s, he appeared in more than 200 films. He died Dec 24, 1994 at Rome, Italy.

		S	M	T	W	T	F	S
September								1
2001		2	3	4	5	6	7	8
		9	10	11	12	13	14	15
		16	17	18	19	20	21	22
		23	24	25	26	27	28	29
		30						

CHILE: INDEPENDENCE DAY. Sept 18. National holiday. Gained independence from Spain in 1810.

DeMILLE, AGNES: BIRTH ANNIVERSARY. Sept 18, 1905. Dancer, choreographer for ballet and Broadway shows such as *Oklahoma*, born at New York, NY. DeMille died at New York, NY, Oct 7, 1993.

DIEFENBAKER, JOHN: BIRTH ANNIVERSARY. Sept 18, 1895. Canadian lawyer, statesman and Conservative prime minister (1957–63). Born at Normandy Township, Ontario, Canada, he died at Ottawa, Ontario, Aug 16, 1979. Diefenbaker was a member of the Canadian Parliament from 1940 until his death.

GARBO, GRETA: BIRTH ANNIVERSARY. Sept 18, 1905. International film actress Greta Garbo was born Greta Lovisa Gustafsson at Stockholm, Sweden. A famous recluse, she retired temporarily, then permanently, from films after 19 years and 27 films, which spanned the late-silent era and beginning of sound movies. Her on-screen roles were characterized by an image of a seductress involved in tragic love affairs. She died Apr 15, 1990 at New York, NY.

GEIGER, RAY: BIRTH ANNIVERSARY. Sept 18, 1910. Born at Irvington, NJ, Ray Geiger became editor of the *Farmer's Almanac* in 1934, shortly after graduating from Notre Dame. He remained editor until completing the 1994 edition in the fall of 1993 (when his son Peter became editor), the longest running almanac editor in American history. He died Apr 1, 1994, at Auburn, ME. *The Farmer's Almanac* offices are in Lewiston, ME.

"GET SMART" TV PREMIERE: ANNIVERSARY. Sept 18, 1965. A spy-thriller spoof appearing on both NBC (1965–69) and CBS (1969–70). Don Adams starred as bumbling CONTROL Agent 86, Maxwell Smart. His mission was to thwart the evildoings of the KAOS organization. Agent Smart was usually successful with the help of his friends: Barbara Feldon as Agent 99 (whom Smart eventually married), Edward Platt as The Chief, Robert Karvelas as Agent Larrabee, Dick Gautier as Hymie the Robot and David Ketchum as Agent 13.

HAITI INVASION AVERTED: ANNIVERSARY. Sept 18, 1994. Just as military forces of the US were poised to invade Haiti, an agreement was reached with an American negotiating team to restore President Jean-Bertrand Aristide to power. The team consisted of former president Jimmy Carter, former chairman of the joint chiefs of staff General Colin Powell and Senator Sam Nunn, Democrat of Georgia.

HULL HOUSE OPENS: ANNIVERSARY. Sept 18, 1889. This settlement house was founded in Chicago by Jane Addams and Ellen Gates Starr. It soon became the heart of one of the country's most influential social reform movements, offering a mix of cultural and education programs to new immigrants. See also: "Addams, Jane: Birth Anniversary" (Sept 6).

IRON HORSE OUTRACED BY HORSE: ANNIVERSARY. Sept 18, 1830. In a widely celebrated race, the first locomotive built in America, the Tom Thumb, lost to a horse. Mechanical difficulties plagued the steam engine over the nine-mile course between Riley's Tavern and Baltimore, MD, and a boiler leak prevented the locomotive from finishing the race. In the early days of trains, engines were nicknamed "Iron Horses."

JACKSON COUNTY APPLE FESTIVAL. Sept 18–22. Jackson County, OH. Mountains of apples and barrels of cider. Homemade apple butter, apple pies and candy apples. Est attendance: 210,000. For info: Jackson County Apple Festival, Inc, PO Box 8, Jackson, OH 45640-0008. Phone: (740) 286-1339.

JOHNSON, SAMUEL: BIRTH ANNIVERSARY. Sept 18, 1709 (OS). English lexicographer and literary lion, creator of the first great dictionary of the English language (1755) and author of poems, novels and essays. Johnson was born at Lichfield, Staffordshire, England, and died at London, England, Dec 13, 1784. James Boswell wrote a famous biography of Johnson.

"LOVE IS A MANY SPLENDORED THING" TV PREMIERE: ANNIVERSARY. Sept 18, 1967. A soap opera created by veteran writer Irna Phillips, airing on CBS for five years. It was based on the 1955 film starring William Holden and Jennifer Jones. Irna Phillips left the show after the network nixed interracial romance in favor of political storylines. David Birney, Bibi Besch and Donna Mills appeared on the show.

NETHERLANDS: PRINSJESDAG. Sept 18. Official opening of parliament at The Hague. The queen of the Netherlands, by tradition, rides in a golden coach to the hall of knights for the annual opening of parliament. Annually, on the third Tuesday in September.

***THE NEW YORK TIMES* FIRST PUBLISHED: 150th ANNIVERSARY.** Sept 18, 1851. The *Times* debuted as *The New-York Daily Times.* The name was changed to the current one in 1857.

READ, GEORGE: BIRTH ANNIVERSARY. Sept 18, 1733. Lawyer and signer of the Declaration of Independence, born at Cecil County, MD. Died Sept 21, 1798, at New Castle, DE.

ROSH HASHANAH or JEWISH NEW YEAR. Sept 18–19. Jewish holy day; observed on following day also. Hebrew calendar date: Tishri 1, 5762. Rosh Hashanah (literally "Head of the Year") is the beginning of 10 days of repentance and spiritual renewal. (Began at sundown of previous day.)

"SHIRLEY TEMPLE THEATRE" TV PREMIERE: ANNIVERSARY. Sept 18, 1960. An NBC children's anthology of specials appearing on Sundays, hosted by Shirley Temple. Reruns were broadcast on ABC on the following Mondays. "Beauty and the Beast," "Rumplestiltskin," "Rapunzel," "Mother Goose," "The Land of Oz" and "Babes in Toyland" were among the stories presented.

SPACE MILESTONE: *SOYUZ 38* (USSR). Sept 18, 1980. Launched on this date with Cosmonauts Arnaldo Tamayo Mendes (Cuba) and Yuri Romanenko aboard and docked at *Salyut 6* for week-long mission, returning to Earth Sept 26.

"THE SPEIDEL SHOW" TV PREMIERE: ANNIVERSARY. Sept 18, 1950. Ventriloquist Paul Winchell was featured with his dummies, Jerry Mahoney and Knucklehead Smith, on this NBC comedy-variety series which ran for four years. Dorothy Claire, Hilda Vaughn and Jimmy Blaine also made appearances on the show, which included the quiz segment "What's My Name?" Winchell later hosted a variety of programs such as "Circus Time," "The Paul Winchell Show," "Cartoonies," "Winchell and Mahoney Time" and "Runaround."

STORY, JOSEPH: BIRTH ANNIVERSARY. Sept 18, 1779. Associate justice of the US Supreme Court (1811–45) was born at Marblehead, MA. "It is astonishing," he wrote a few months before his death, "how easily men satisfy themselves that the Constitution is exactly what they wish it to be." Story died Sept 10, 1845, at Cambridge, MA, having served 33 years on the Supreme Court bench.

UNITED NATIONS: INTERNATIONAL DAY OF PEACE/OPENING DAY OF GENERAL ASSEMBLY. Sept 18. The United Nations General Assembly, Nov 30, 1981, declared "that the third Tuesday of September, the opening day of the regular sessions of the General Assembly, shall be officially proclaimed and observed as International Day of Peace and shall be devoted to commemorating and strengthening the ideals of peace both within and among all nations and peoples." A Peace Month and a University for Peace have been proposed. Info from: United Nations, Dept of Public Info, New York, NY 10017.

US AIR FORCE ESTABLISHED: ANNIVERSARY. Sept 18, 1947. Although its heritage dates back to 1907 when the Army first established military aviation, the US Air Force became a separate military service on this date. Responsible for providing an Air Force that is capable, in conjunction with the other armed forces, of preserving the peace and security of the US, the department is separately organized under the Secretary of the Air Force and operates under the authority, direction and control of the Secretary of Defense.

US CAPITOL CORNERSTONE LAID: ANNIVERSARY. Sept 18, 1793. President George Washington laid the Capitol cornerstone at Washington, DC, in a Masonic ceremony. That event was the first and last recorded occasion at which the stone with its engraved silver plate was seen. In 1958, during the extension of the east front of the Capitol, an unsuccessful effort was made to find it.

US TAKES OUT ITS FIRST LOAN: ANNIVERSARY. Sept 18, 1789. The first loan taken out by the US was negotiated and secured by Alexander Hamilton on Feb 17, 1790. After beginning negotiations with the Bank of New York and the Bank of North America on Sept 18, 1789, Hamilton obtained the sum of $191,608.81 from the two banks in what became known as the Temporary Loan of 1789. The loan was obtained without authority of law and was used to pay the salaries of the president, senators, representatives and officers of the first Congress. Repayment was completed on June 8, 1790.

"WAGON TRAIN" TV PREMIERE: ANNIVERSARY. Sept 18, 1957. "Wagon Train" was a popular western on NBC and ABC, airing for eight years with its last telecast Sept 5, 1965. The series was about a journey along the wagon trail from Missouri to California. Each week the travelers encountered new surroundings and interacted with different guest stars. Ward Bond played wagonmaster Major Seth Adams until his death in 1960. He was replaced by John McIntire as Chris Hale. Other regulars were: Robert Horton as scout Flint McCullough, Frank McGrath as cook Charlie Wooster, Terry Wilson as Bill Hawks, Denny (Scott) Miller as scout Duke Shannon, Michael Burns as Barnaby West, a teen passenger and Robert Fuller as scout Cooper.

WHITE WOMAN MADE AMERICAN INDIAN CHIEF: ANNIVERSARY. Sept 18, 1891. Harriet Maxwell Converse was made a chief of the Six Nations Tribe at the Tonawanda Reservation, NY. She was given the name Ga-is-wa-noh, which means "The Watcher." She had been adopted as a member of the Seneca tribe in 1884 in appreciation of her efforts on behalf of the tribe.

BIRTHDAYS TODAY

Frankie Avalon, 62, singer ("Venus"), actor (teen flicks with Annette Funicello), born Philadelphia, PA, Sept 18, 1939.

Robert F. Bennett, 68, US Senator (R, Utah), born Salt Lake City, UT, Sept 18, 1933.

Robert Blake (Michael Gubitosi), 63, actor ("Baretta," *In Cold Blood, Little Rascals*), born Nutley, NJ, Sept 18, 1938.

Scotty Bowman, 68, Hockey Hall of Fame coach, born Montreal, Quebec, Canada, Sept 18, 1933.

Jada Pinkett Smith, 30, actress (*The Nutty Professor, Menace II Society*), born Baltimore, MD, Sept 18, 1971.

Ryne Dee Sandberg, 42, former baseball player, born Spokane, WA, Sept 18, 1959.

Jack Warden, 81, actor ("NYPD," "Bad News Bears," "Crazy Like a Fox"), born Newark NJ, Sept 18, 1920.

SEPTEMBER

SEPTEMBER 19 — WEDNESDAY

Day 262 — 103 Remaining

BATTLE OF WINCHESTER: ANNIVERSARY. Sept 19, 1864. Union General Philip Sheridan defeated Confederate General Jubal Early's forces at Winchester, VA, ending Early's raids on the North. Early's troops were again soundly beaten on Sept 22 at Fisher's Hill. After defeating Early, Sheridan turned his attention to destroying the food resources of the Shenandoah Valley.

BROUGHAM, HENRY PETER: BIRTH ANNIVERSARY. Sept 19, 1778. Scottish jurist and orator born at Edinburgh, Scotland. Died at Cannes, France, May 7, 1868. The Brougham carriage was named after him. "Education," he said, "makes a people easy to lead, but difficult to drive; easy to govern, but impossible to enslave."

CARROLL, CHARLES: BIRTH ANNIVERSARY. Sept 19, 1737 (OS). American Revolutionary leader and signer of the Declaration of Independence, born at Annapolis, MD. The last surviving signer of the Declaration, he died Nov 14, 1832, at Baltimore, MD.

"ER" TV PREMIERE: ANNIVERSARY. Sept 19, 1994. This medical drama takes place in the emergency room of the fictional County General Hospital in Chicago. Doctors and nurses take care of life and death patients while experiencing their personal traumas as well. Cast include Anthony Edwards, George Clooney, Sherry Stringfield, Noah Wylie, Laura Innes, Gloria Reubens, Eriq La Salle and Alex Kingston.

"FLIPPER" TV PREMIERE: ANNIVERSARY. Sept 19, 1964. An adventure series starring Flipper, the intelligent, communicative and helpful dolphin. The human cast members included Brian Kelly as Chief Ranger Porter Ricks, Luke Halpin as his son Sandy, Tommy Norden as his son Bud and Ulla Strömstedt as biochemist Ulla Norstrand. Although the last telecast of

September 2001	S	M	T	W	T	F	S
							1
	2	3	4	5	6	7	8
	9	10	11	12	13	14	15
	16	17	18	19	20	21	22
	23	24	25	26	27	28	29
	30						

this series was Sept 1, 1968, the series was recreated under the same title in the '90s.

GOLDEN ASPEN MOTORCYCLE RALLY. Sept 19–23. Ruidoso, NM. Trade show, bike shows, riding tours, skill events, parade, awards banquet, stunt shows and thousands in prizes. Est attendance: 20,000. For info: Golden Aspen Rally Assn, PO Box 1458, Ruidoso, NM 88355. Phone: (800) 452-8045. Web: www.motorcyclerally.com.

GOLDING, SIR WILLIAM: 90th BIRTH ANNIVERSARY. Sept 19, 1911. Born at Columb Minor at Cornwall, England, this celebrated author was recognized for his contributions to literature with a Nobel Prize in 1983. His first and most popular novel was *Lord of the Flies*. He died June 19, 1993, near Truro, Cornwall.

JAMESTOWN BURNED BY BACON'S REBELLION: 325th ANNIVERSARY. Sept 19, 1676. In the Virginia colony every adult male could vote. When Charles II was restored to the English throne, he sought to exploit the colony to the fullest. Virginia Governor Sir William Berkeley, supporting the king, adopted new laws to facilitate these efforts including measures allowing only property holders to vote, raising taxes to build up the town of Jamestown and raising the cost of shipping while lowering the price for tobacco. The resulting discontent exploded when the frontier of the colony was attacked by Indians and the governor refused to defend the settlers. Nathaniel Bacon, a colonist on the governor's council, was made leader by the frontier farmers, and his troops successfully defeated the Indians. Denounced by Berkeley as rebels, Bacon and his men occupied Jamestown, forcing the governor to call an election, the first in 15 years. The Berkeley laws were repealed and election and tax reforms were instituted. While Bacon and his troops were gone on a raiding party against the Indians, Berkeley again denounced them. They returned and attacked Berkeley's forces, defeating them and burning Jamestown on Sept 19, 1676. Berkeley again fled and Bacon became ruler of Virginia. When he died suddenly a short time later, the rebellion collapsed. Berkeley returned to power and Bacon's followers were hunted down, some executed and their property confiscated. Berkeley was replaced the next year and peace was restored.

MEXICO CITY EARTHQUAKE: ANNIVERSARY. Sept 19–20, 1985. Nearly 10,000 persons perished in the earthquakes (8.1 and 7.5 respectively, on the Richter Scale) that devastated Mexico City. Damage to buildings was estimated at more than $1 billion, and 100,000 homes were destroyed or severely damaged.

NATIONAL VISION REHABILITATION DAY. Sept 19. Because of the documented lack of knowledge about both vision loss and the availability of vision rehabilitation services, this observance has been created to promote aggressive education and treatment for people with vision problems. It is sponsored by Lighthouse International, a leading resource on vision impairment, and is commemorated throughout the nation by national organizations, eye care professionals and member agencies of The National Vision Rehabilitation Cooperative. For info: Vernice Williams, Media Mgr, Lighthouse Intl, 111 E 59th St, New York, NY 10022-1202. Phone: (212) 821-9555. Fax: (212) 821-9702. E-mail: inbox@lighthouse.org. Web: www.lighthouse.org.

PAN, HERMES: DEATH ANNIVERSARY. Sept 19, 1990. American choreographer Hermes Pan was born Hermes Panaglotopulos at Memphis, TN, 1910. He is best known for choreographing nine of the 10 films starring Fred Astaire and Ginger Rogers; he won the Academy Award in choreography for *A Damsel in Distress* (1937). He died at Beverly Hills, CA.

"PEOPLE ARE FUNNY" TV PREMIERE: ANNIVERSARY. Sept 19, 1954. This half-hour show combined audience participation and stunts. One feature was a Univac computer that played matchmaker for eligible men and women. Art Linkletter hosted the show until 1958; reruns were shown for the next few seasons. The show was revived for a short time in 1984; Flip Wilson was the host.

PETIT JEAN FALL ANTIQUE AUTO SWAP MEET. Sept 19–22. Petit Jean Mountain, Morrilton, AR. Fourth annual antique auto swap meet, car corral, flea market and arts and crafts. More than 1,400 vendor spaces. Est attendance: 30,000. For info: Buddy Hoelzeman, Museum of Automobiles, 8 Jones Ln, Morrilton, AR 72110. Phone: (501) 727-5427. Fax: (501) 727-6482. E-mail: museumofautos@mev.net. Web: museumof autos.com.

POWELL, LEWIS F., JR: BIRTH ANNIVERSARY. Sept 19, 1907. Former associate justice of the Supreme Court of the US, nominated by President Nixon Oct 21, 1971. (Took office Jan 7, 1972.) Justice Powell was born at Suffolk, VA. In 1987, he announced his retirement from the Court. He died Aug 25, 1998 at Richmond, VA.

RIVER CITY ROUNDUP. Sept 19–24. Omaha, NE. Take a moment to reflect on the Midwest's proud past. A celebration of Omaha's agricultural and western heritage; PRCA rodeo, barbecue contest, trail rides, western/wildlife art show, dances, the world's largest 4-H Livestock Expo and a downtown parade. Est attendance: 300,000. For info: Christy Aegerter, PR & Programming Mgr, River City Roundup and Rodeo, 6800 Mercy Rd, Ste 206, Omaha, NE 68106. Phone: (402) 554-9610. Fax: (402) 554-9609. E-mail: knights@aksarben.org. Web: www.aksarben .org.

ROYKO, MIKE: BIRTH ANNIVERSARY. Sept 19, 1932. Syndicated columnist to more than 600 newspapers nationwide, Pulitzer prize winner and author (*Boss, Slats Grobnick*). Born at Chicago, IL, he died there, Apr 29, 1997.

SAINT CHRISTOPHER (SAINT KITTS) AND NEVIS: INDEPENDENCE DAY. Sept 19. National holiday. Commemorates independence from Britain in 1983.

SAINT JANUARIUS (GENNARO): FEAST DAY. Sept 19. Fourth-century bishop of Benevento, martyred near Naples, Italy, whose relics in the Naples Cathedral are particularly famous because on his feast days the blood in a glass vial is said to liquefy in response to prayers of the faithful. In September 1979, the Associated Press reported that some 5,000 persons gathered at the cathedral at dawn, and that "the blood liquefied after 63 minutes of prayers." This phenomenon is said to occur also on the first Saturday in May.

TITAN II MISSILE EXPLOSION: ANNIVERSARY. Sept 19, 1980. The third major accident involving America's most powerful single weapon occurred near Damascus, AR. The explosion, at 3 AM, came nearly 11 hours after a fire had started in the missile silo. The multi-megaton nuclear warhead (a hydrogen bomb) reportedly was briefly airborne, but came to rest a few hundred feet away. One dead, 21 injured in accident. Previous major Titan Missile accidents: Aug 9, 1965, near Searcy, AR (53 dead); and Aug 24, 1978, near Rock, KS (2 dead, 29 injured).

"THE VIRGINIAN" TV PREMIERE: ANNIVERSARY. Sept 19, 1962. TV's first 90-minute western starred James Drury as the Virginian, a foreman trying to come to terms with the westward expansion of technology and civilization. It was set on the Shiloh Ranch, in Wyoming. Key players included Doug McClure (with Drury, the only cast members to stay for the entire run), Lee J. Cobb, Roberta Shore, Pippa Scott, Gary Clarke, Randy Boone, L.Q. Jones, Harlan Warde, Clu Gulager, Diane Roter, John Dehner, Charles Bickford, Don Quine, Sara Lane, Ross Elliott, John McIntire, Jeanette Nolan, David Hartman and Tim Matheson. In the last season, the title was changed to "The Men From Shiloh," and Stewart Granger and Lee Majors joined the cast.

SEPTEMBER 20 — THURSDAY
Day 263 — 102 Remaining

AMERICAN ROSE SOCIETY FALL NATIONAL CONVENTION. Sept 20–24. Cleveland, OH. Amateur growers from all over the US display thousands of their roses in this major competition. Est attendance: 600. For info: Angela Gleason, American Rose Society, PO Box 30000, Shreveport, LA 71130. Phone: (800) 637-6534. E-mail: ars@ars-hq.org. Web: www.ars.org.

BILLIE JEAN KING WINS THE "BATTLE OF THE SEXES": ANNIVERSARY. Sept 20, 1973. Billie Jean King defeated Bobby Riggs in the nationally televised "Battle of the Sexes" tennis match in three straight sets.

EQUAL RIGHTS PARTY FOUNDING: ANNIVERSARY. Sept 20, 1884. The Equal Rights Party was formed at San Francisco, CA. Its candidate for president, nominated in convention, was Mrs Belva Lockwood. The vice presidential candidate was Marietta Stow.

FAST OF GEDALYA. Sept 20. Jewish holiday. Hebrew calendar date: Tishri 3, 5762. Tzom Gedalya begins at first light of day and commemorates the 6th-century BC assassination of Gedalya Ben Achikam.

FINANCIAL PANIC OF 1873: ANNIVERSARY. Sept 20, 1873. For the first time in its history, the New York Stock Exchange was forced to close because of a banking crisis. Although the worst of the panic and crisis was over within a week, the psychological effect on businessmen, investors and the nation at large was more lasting.

"THE LORETTA YOUNG SHOW" TV PREMIERE: ANNIVERSARY. Sept 20, 1953. NBC half-hour dramatic anthology series (initially titled "Letter to Loretta") hosted by and frequently starring Oscar-winning actress Loretta Young. At the beginning of each episode Young would swirl through a door in a spectacular gown. Young garnered two Emmys during the show's eight-year run. In 1972 it was reported that Young had been awarded $559,000 in a suit against NBC for syndicating reruns of the show without her permission. Young did not want them shown because her clothes and hairstyles in the shows were long out of date by the '70s.

"LOU GRANT" TV PREMIERE: ANNIVERSARY. Sept 20, 1977. This hour-long dramatic series was a spin-off of "The Mary Tyler Moore Show." Ed Asner reprised his role as newspaper editor Lou Grant, now a city editor for the *Los Angeles Tribune*. The show tackled many serious issues, including child abuse, gun control and the plight of Vietnamese refugees. The cast included Mason Adams, Nancy Marchand, Jack Bannon, Robert Walden, Daryl Anderson, Rebecca Balding, Linda Kelsey, Allen Williams and Emilio Delgado. This series was an unusual spin-off because it was the first time a character left a sitcom to headline a drama.

"M SQUAD" TV PREMIERE: ANNIVERSARY. Sept 20, 1957. This half-hour crime series had a catchy theme song composed by Count Basie and actor Lee Marvin as Lieutenant Frank Ballinger, a Chicago cop assigned to a unit that investigates murders (the M Squad). Paul Newlan played his supervisor Captain Grey. In one episode, "The Teacher" (1959), Burt Reynolds played one of his first major roles.

MID-SOUTH FAIR. Sept 20–30. Fairgrounds, Memphis, TN. Regional fair featuring concerts, free entertainment, midway, rodeo, livestock, exhibits and special events. Est attendance: 500,000. For info: Cynthia Savage, Mid-South Fair, 940 Early Maxwell Blvd, Memphis, TN 38104. Phone: (901) 274-8800. Fax: (901) 274-8804. E-mail: libland@bellsouth.net. Web: www.mid southfair.com.

MORTON, FERDINAND "JELLY ROLL": BIRTH ANNIVERSARY. Sept 20, 1885. American jazz pianist, composer, singer and orchestra leader, was born at New Orleans, LA. Morton, subject of a biography titled *Mr Jelly Roll* by Alan Lomax, died July 10, 1941, at Los Angeles, CA.

NATIONAL RESEARCH COUNCIL: FIRST MEETING: 85th ANNIVERSARY. Sept 20, 1916. Anniversary of first meeting of National Research Council, at New York, NY. Formed at request of President Woodrow Wilson for " . . . encouraging the investigation of natural phenomena . . . ." for American business and national security.

NATIONAL STUDENT DAY™. Sept 20. Created to recognize all students from preschool through postgraduate, this is the perfect day to show the students in our lives how proud we are of them, to recognize their hard work and to show support for their efforts. For info: Ralph E Williams, Exec Dir, Natl Assn of College Students, PO Box 655, Lincolnshire, IL 60069. Phone: (800) 500-4255 or (941) 489-1530. Fax: (941) 489-1142. E-mail: nacs@collegeknowledge.com. Web: www.collegeknowledge.com.

"THE PHIL SILVERS SHOW" TV PREMIERE: ANNIVERSARY. Sept 20, 1955. This popular half-hour sitcom starred Phil Silvers as Sergeant Ernie Bilko, a scheming but good-natured con man whose schemes rarely worked out. Guest stars included Fred Gwynne, Margaret Hamilton, Dick Van Dyke and Alan Alda in his first major TV role. The character of Sergeant Bilko was featured in a movie of the same title in the mid-90s.

September	S	M	T	W	T	F	S
2001							1
	2	3	4	5	6	7	8
	9	10	11	12	13	14	15
	16	17	18	19	20	21	22
	23	24	25	26	27	28	29
	30						

ROCK OF CHICKAMAUGA: ANNIVERSARY. Sept 20, 1863. After disastrous moves by Union General William Starke Rosecrans, Confederate forces appeared to be carrying the day at the Battle of Chickamauga in Tennessee. With Rosecrans in flight to Chattanooga, Union General Henry Thomas and his men maintained their position and repeatedly turned back Southern attacks until they were reinforced. Thomas's actions saved the Union forces from a complete rout and earned him the nickname, "Rock of Chickamauga." Rosecrans was relieved of his command.

SCRIPT MAGIC DAY. Sept 20. Spirituality meets Hollywood in "Script Magic" Day. It's a time for screenwriters to forget the formulaic approach to Hollywood films and focus on the stories within. For info: Marisa D'Vari, PO Box 413, Boston, MA 02116. Phone: (617) 451-9914. Fax: (617) 351-2279. E-mail: mdvari@msn.com. Web: www.scriptmagic.com.

SEVEN SWEETS AND SEVEN SOURS FESTIVAL. Sept 20–22. Intercourse, PA. The biggest time of the year is when we put up our fruits and vegetables for the long winter. The whole Village is invaded with wonderful end-of-the-garden creations. Est attendance: 30,000. For info: Lisa Horn, Kitchen Kettle Village, Box 380, Intercourse, PA 17534. Phone: (800) 732-3538 or (717) 768-8261. Web: www.kitchenkettle.com.

SINCLAIR, UPTON (BEALL): BIRTH ANNIVERSARY. Sept 20, 1878. American novelist and politician born at Baltimore, MD. He worked for political and social reforms, and his best-known novel, *The Jungle*, prompted one of the nation's first pure food laws. Died at Bound Brook, NJ, Nov 25, 1968.

"THE THIN MAN" TV PREMIERE: ANNIVERSARY. Sept 20, 1957. The famous crime-solving duo of Nick and Nora was brought to TV after appearing in a novel by Dashiell Hammett and a film series. This half-hour crime series featured Peter Lawford as Nick Charles, a former private eye who still engaged in it for fun, and Phyllis Kirk as his wife and partner Nora. Jack Albertson played Lieutenant Harry Evans, and their pet dog Asta was played by Asta.

BIRTHDAYS TODAY

Arnold Jacob ("Red") Auerbach, 84, Basketball Hall of Fame coach, born Brooklyn, NY, Sept 20, 1917.

Joyce Brothers, 73, psychologist, author, born New York, NY, Sept 20, 1928.

Donald A. Hall, 73, poet, author (*Lucy's Christmas, Ox Cart Man*), born New Haven, CT, Sept 20, 1928.

Kristen Johnston, 34, actress ("3rd Rock from the Sun"), born Washington, DC, Sept 20, 1967.

Guy Damien LaFleur, 50, Hockey Hall of Fame right wing, born Thurso, Quebec, Canada, Sept 20, 1951.

Sophia Loren (Sofia Scicoloni), 67, actress (Oscar for *Two Women; Black Orchid, Marriage Italian Style*, "Brief Encounter"), born Rome, Italy, Sept 20, 1934.

Anne Meara, 72, actress ("Fame"), comedienne (Stiller and Meara), born New York, NY, Sept 20, 1929.

SEPTEMBER 21 — FRIDAY
Day 264 — 101 Remaining

ARMENIA: NATIONAL DAY: 10th ANNIVERSARY. Sept 21. Public holiday. Commemorates independence from Soviet Union in 1991.

BAYFEST. Sept 21–23. Corpus Christi, TX. Plenty of fun at this waterfront festival. Includes amusement rides, games, fireworks, arts and crafts displays, various musical entertainment, food booths, merchandise exhibitors and much more. Est attendance: 165,000. For info: Bayfest, PO Box 1858, Corpus Christi, TX 78403. Phone: (361) 887-0868. Fax: (361) 887-9773. E-mail: bayfest@interconnect.net. Web: www.bayfesttexas.com.

BELIZE: INDEPENDENCE DAY: 20th ANNIVERSARY. Sept 21. National holiday. Commemorates independence of the former British Honduras from Britain in 1981.

COMAL COUNTY FAIR. Sept 21–30. Comal County Fairgrounds, New Braunfels, TX. Local competition of livestock, arts and crafts, antiques, agricultural products, poultry, handwork, baked goods and plants. 107th annual fair. Est attendance: 148,000. For info: Jackie Smith-Jobela, Comal County Fair Assn, PO Box 310223, New Braunfels, TX 78131. Phone: (830) 625-1505.

COMMON GROUND COUNTRY FAIR. Sept 21–23. MOFGA's Common Ground, Unity, ME. Old-time country fair celebrating rural life with the revival of forgotten skills and demonstrations of technology appropriate for the future. Features Maine-produced food, crafts, entertainment, farming demonstrations and talks, a very special children's area with daily and ongoing participatory activities. Annually, the third weekend after Labor Day. Sponsor: Maine Organic Farmers and Gardeners Association. Est attendance: 60,000. For info: Heather Spalding, Fair Dir, PO Box 170, Unity, ME 04988. Phone: (207) 568-4142. Fax: (207) 568-4141. E-mail: cgcf@mofga.org. Web: www.mofga.org.

CORNISH FESTIVAL. Sept 21–23. Mineral Point, WI. Celebrates miners who came to southwest Wisconsin from Cornwall, England during the 1840s-50s. Bus tours of historic sites, restored Cornish stone cottages, museum tours. Plus Cornish and Celtic entertainment, genealogy workshop, Cornish food at "Taste of Mineral Point" and more. Est attendance: 1,000. For info: Mineral Point Chamber/Main St, 225 High St, Mineral Point, WI 53565. Phone: (608) 987-3201 or (888) POINT WI. E-mail: info@mineralpoint.com. Web: www.mineralpoint.com.

HOPKINSON, FRANCIS: BIRTH ANNIVERSARY. Sept 21, 1737. Signer of the Declaration of Independence. Born at Philadelphia, PA, he died there May 9, 1791.

HURRICANE HUGO HITS AMERICAN COAST: ANNIVERSARY. Sept 21, 1989. After ravaging the Virgin Islands, Hurricane Hugo hit the American coast at Charleston, SC. In its wake, Hugo left destruction totaling at least eight billion dollars.

JOSEPH, CHIEF: DEATH ANNIVERSARY. Sept 21, 1904. Admirable Nez Percé chief, whose Indian name was In-Mut-Too-Yah-Lat-Lat, was born about 1840 at Wallowa Valley, Oregon Territory, and died on the Colville Reservation at Washington. Faced with war or resettlement to a reservation, Chief Joseph led a dramatic attempt to escape to Canada. After three months and more than 1,000 miles, he and his people were surrounded 40 miles from Canada and sent to a reservation at Oklahoma. Though the few survivors were later allowed to relocate to another reservation at Washington, they never regained their ancestral lands.

LAUREL HERBSTFEST. Sept 21–23. Laurel, MT. 30th annual. Celebration of the town's German heritage. Activities include arts and crafts, dances, two full days of musical entertainment, variety of food booths, beer garden with lots of polka music and dancing. Est attendance: 1,500. For info: Laurel Herbstfest Committee, PO Box 1192, Laurel, MT 59044.

LIBERTY FALL FESTIVAL. Sept 21–23. Liberty, MO. Arts and crafts booth, food booths, children's activities, a carnival, a parade, car show, entertainment provided throughout the three-day festival. Annually, the fourth weekend in September. Est attendance: 50,000. For info: Liberty Area Chamber of Commerce, 9 S Leonard St, Liberty, MO 64068. Phone: (816) 781-5200. Fax: (816) 781-4901. E-mail: libertycoc@earthlink.net. Web: www.libertychamber.com.

MALTA: INDEPENDENCE DAY: ANNIVERSARY. Sept 21. National Day. Commemorates independence from Britain in 1964.

MONTEREY JAZZ FESTIVAL. Sept 21–23. Monterey, CA. Celebrating its 44th year, the country's oldest continuous jazz festival features the sounds of some of the world's finest jazz musicians. Est attendance: 35,000. For info: Monterey Jazz Festival, PO Box Jazz, Monterey, CA 93942. Phone: (408) 373-3366 or (925) 275-9255. Fax: (408) 373-0244.

"NYPD BLUE" TV PREMIERE: ANNIVERSARY. Sept 21, 1993. This gritty New York City police drama has had a large and changing cast. The central characters were partners Detective Bobby Simone, played by Jimmy Smits, and Detective Andy Sipowicz, played by Arthur Franz. Other cast members include Kim Delaney as Detective Diane Russell, James McDaniel as Lieutenant Arthur Fancy, Gordon Clapp as Detective Gregory Medavoy, Rick Schroder as Detective Danny Sorenson and Nicholas Turturro as Detective James Martinez.

OFFICE OLYMPICS. Sept 21. Downtown Shreveport, LA. A one-day event that spotlights the office employee! 100 teams of five (men and women) office workers compete in such zany events as The Water Break Relay, The Office Chair Roll-off, Toss the Boss, Memo Mania, Beat the Clock, The Scissor Slide, The Human Post-it-Note, Musical Office Chairs and The Pencil Push. Est attendance: 6,000. For info: Melinda R. Coyer, Office Olympics Founder, PO Box 72355, Bassier City, LA 71172. Phone: (318) 741-3100. Fax: (318) 741-3101. E-mail: melinc@aol.com.

"PERRY MASON" TV PREMIERE: ANNIVERSARY. Sept 21, 1957. Raymond Burr will forever be associated with the character of Perry Mason, a highly skilled criminal lawyer who won the great majority of his cases. Episodes followed a similar format: the action took place in the first half, with the killer's identity unknown, and the courtroom drama took place in the latter half. Mason was particularly adept at eliciting confessions from the guilty parties. Regulars and semi-regulars included Barbara Hale, William Hopper, William Talman and Ray Collins. Following the series' end, with the last telecast on Jan 27, 1974, a number of successful "Perry Mason" TV movies aired and the show remains popular in reruns.

PIONEER DAYS. Sept 21–23. Ft Worth, TX. See the Fort Worth Herd and celebrate the western heritage and pioneer spirit that is still present in the Fort Worth Stockyards National Historic District. Est attendance: 150,000. For info: Exec Dir, North Fort Worth Business Assn, 131 E Exchange Ave, #100-A, Fort Worth, TX 76106. Phone: (817) 626-7921 or (817) 654-1148. Fax: (817) 626-6204.

RACKING WORLD CELEBRATION. Sept 21–29. Decatur, AL. Week-long event featuring racking horses from across the nation. The highlight of the 75-class event is the crowning of the World Grand Racking Horse Champion on the last night. Annually, the first full week in September. Est attendance: 10,000. For info: Jacklyn Bailey, Decatur/Morgan County CVB, 719 6th Ave SE, PO Box 2349, Decatur, AL 35602. Phone: (256) 350-2028 or (800) 524-6181. E-mail: info@decaturcvb.org.

TAYLOR, MARGARET SMITH: BIRTH ANNIVERSARY. Sept 21, 1788. Wife of Zachary Taylor, 12th president of the US, born at Calvert County, MD. Died Aug 18, 1852.

"THE TEXACO STAR THEATER" TV PREMIERE: ANNIVERSARY. Sept 21, 1948. Also known as "The Milton Berle Show" and sponsored by Texaco until 1953, this popular variety show was a good sign for the fledgling TV industry. Milton Berle became a superstar. The show featured singing and comedy, especially sight gags and outrageous costumes, and guest stars. Changes were made in the fourth season: Berle cut back his appearances, new writers and a new director were added and the format was changed to a show-within-a-show. Ruth Gilbert, Fred Clark and Arnold Stang were featured, along with the new pitchman, ventriloquist Jimmy Nelson and his dummy Danny O'Day.

VIRGINIA PEANUT FESTIVAL. Sept 21–22. Emporia, VA. Annual celebration promoting peanuts and harvesting. Features musical concerts, arts and crafts, parade, corporate village, luncheon/fashion show, carnival, car show and fireworks. Sponsored by Emporia-Greensville Chamber of Commerce. Est attendance: 20,000. For info: Admit One Festivals, 425-E S Main St, PO Box 868, Emporia, VA 23847-0868. Phone: (804) 348-3378. Fax: (804) 348-0119. E-mail: vapeanutfest@admit1fest.com. Web: www.admit1fest.com.

WATTICISM DAY: ANNIVERSARY. Sept 21, 1983. Anniversary of speech by then US Interior Secretary James Watt to trade association executives at the US Chamber of Commerce. Referring to his advisory committee, Watt said: "We have every kind of mixture you can have. I have a black, I have a woman, two Jews and a cripple. And we have talent." He later apologized for an "unfortunate choice of words."

WELLS, HERBERT GEORGE: BIRTH ANNIVERSARY. Sept 21, 1866. English novelist and historian, born at Bromley, Kent, England. Among his books: *The Time Machine, The Invisible Man, The War of the Worlds* and *The Outline of History*. H.G. Wells died at London, Aug 13, 1946. "Human history," he wrote, "becomes more and more a race between education and catastrophe."

BIRTHDAYS TODAY

Ethan Coen, 44, writer, producer (*Fargo*), born Minneapolis, MN, Sept 21, 1957.

Leonard Cohen, 67, singer, songwriter, born Montreal, Quebec, Canada, Sept 21, 1934.

David James Elliott, 41, actor ("JAG"), born Toronto, Ontario, Canada, Sept 21, 1960.

Cecil Grant Fielder, 38, former baseball player, born Los Angeles, CA, Sept 21, 1963.

Fannie Flagg, 57, actress, writer (*Fried Green Tomatoes*), born Birmingham, AL, Sept 21, 1944.

Henry Gibson, 66, comedian ("Rowan and Martin's Laugh-In"), actor (*Nashville*), born Germantown, PA, Sept 21, 1935.

Artis Gilmore, 52, former basketball player, born Chipley, FL, Sept 21, 1949.

Larry Hagman, 70, actor ("I Dream of Jeannie," "Dallas"), born Fort Worth, TX, Sept 21, 1931.

Faith Hill, 34, country singer, born Jackson, MS, Sept 21, 1967.

Stephen King, 54, author (*Christine, Pet Sematary, The Shining, Misery, The Stand*), born Portland, ME, Sept 21, 1947.

Bill Kurtis, 61, TV journalist ("Investigative Reports"), born Pensacola, FL, Sept 21, 1940.

Ricki Lake, 33, talk-show host, actress (*Hairspray, Serial Mom*), born New York, NY, Sept 21, 1968.

Rob Morrow, 39, actor ("Northern Exposure," *Quiz Show*), born New Rochelle, NY, Sept 21, 1962.

September *2001*	S	M	T	W	T	F	S
							1
	2	3	4	5	6	7	8
	9	10	11	12	13	14	15
	16	17	18	19	20	21	22
	23	24	25	26	27	28	29
	30						

Bill Murray, 51, comedian ("Saturday Night Live"), actor (*Ghostbusters, Groundhog Day, Caddyshack*), born Evanston, IL, Sept 21, 1950.

Nancy Travis, 40, actress ("Almost Perfect," *Married to the Mob, Chaplin*), born New York, NY, Sept 21, 1961.

Luke Wilson, 30, actor (*Rushmore, Scream 2*), born Dallas, TX, Sept 21, 1971.

SEPTEMBER 22 — SATURDAY
Day 265 — 100 Remaining

AEROSPACE WALK OF HONOR. Sept 22. Lancaster, CA. In the tradition of the aerospace industry of the Antelope Valley, the City of Lancaster Aerospace Walk of Honor attracts visitors to Lancaster Boulevard to the unveiling of granite monuments honoring Edwards Air Force Base test pilots whose aviation careers are marked by significant achievements. Honorees such as Neil Armstrong, Chuck Yeager and William "Pete" Knight are selected because they have soared above the rest. Est attendance: 1,500. For info: Anne Aldrich, Public Information Officer, City of Lancaster, 44933 N Fern Ave, Lancaster, CA 93534. Phone: (661) 723-6053. Fax: (661) 723-6141. Web: city.lancaster.ca.us.

AMERICAN BUSINESS WOMEN'S DAY. Sept 22. A day on which all Americans can recognize the important contributions more than 57 million American working women have made and are continuing to make to this nation. Annually, Sept 22. For info: Carolyn Elman, American Business Women's Assn, 9100 Ward Pkwy, Kansas City, MO 64114. Phone: (816) 361-6621. Fax: (816) 361-4991. E-mail: cbelman@abwahq.org. Web: www.abwahq.org.

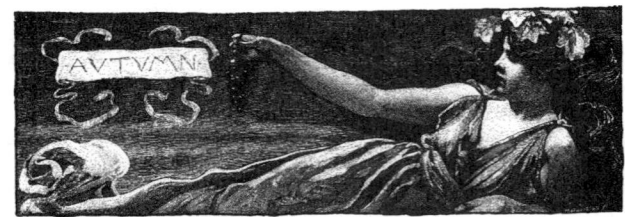

AUTUMN. Sept 22–Dec 21. In the Northern Hemisphere, autumn begins today with the autumnal equinox, at 7:04 PM, EDT. Note that in the Southern Hemisphere today is the beginning of spring. Everywhere on Earth (except near the poles) the sun rises due east and sets due west and daylight length is nearly identical—about 12 hours, 8 minutes.

BANNED BOOKS WEEK—CELEBRATING THE FREEDOM TO READ. Sept 22–29. Brings to the attention of the general public the importance of the freedom to read and the harm censorship causes to our society. Sponsors: American Library Association, American Booksellers Association, American Booksellers Association for Free Expression, American Society of Journalists and Authors, Association of American Publishers, National Association of College Stores. For info: Judith F. Krug, American Library Assn, Office for Intellectual Freedom, 50 E Huron St, Chicago, IL 60611. Phone: (312) 280-4223. Fax: (312) 280-4227. E-mail: oif@ala.org. Web: www.ala.org/bbooks.

BRIGGS AND STRATTON'S RUN AND WALK FOR CHILDREN'S HOSPITAL. Sept 22. Milwaukee, WI. Choose from an 8K run, 4-mile walk or 2.5-mile walk along the lake and through the streets. Benefit fundraiser for Children's Hospital of Wisconsin. Finish line party on Summerfest grounds with free entertainment and fitness expo. Est attendance: 16,000. For info: Children's Hospital Foundation, Briggs & Stratton Run & Walk, PO Box 1997 MS#3050, Milwaukee, WI 53201. Phone: (414) 266-6320. Fax: (414) 266-6139. Web: www.briggsrun.com.

CANADA: MUSKOKA AUTUMN STUDIO TOUR. Sept 22–23. Muskoka, ON. 23rd annual tour. Local artists and crafts-people display their studios as well as their work. For info: Bracebridge Chamber of Commerce, 1-1 Manitoba St, Bracebridge, ON, Canada P1L 2A8. Phone: (705) 645-5231 or (705) 645-8121. Fax: (705) 645-7592. E-mail: bracecha@muskoka.com.

"CHARLIE'S ANGELS" TV PREMIERE: 25th ANNIVERSARY. Sept 22, 1976. This extremely popular show of the '70s featured three attractive women solving crimes. Sabrina Duncan (Kate Jackson), Jill Munroe (Farrah Fawcett-Majors) and Kelly Garrett (Jaclyn Smith) signed on with detective agency Charles Townsend Associates. Their boss was never seen, only heard (the voice of John Forsythe); messages were communicated to the women by his associate John Bosley (David Doyle). During the course of the series, Cheryl Ladd replaced Fawcett, Shelley Hack and Tanya Roberts succeeded Kate Jackson.

CHASE'S 2002 CALENDAR OF EVENTS PUBLISHED. Sept 22. The 2002 *Chase's* is now available.

COPPER MAGNOLIA FESTIVAL. Sept 22. Washington, MS. Demonstration and sale of handmade crafts, family entertainment. Annually, in September. Est attendance: 2,500. For info: Anne L. Gray, Historian, Historic Jefferson College, Box 700, Washington, MS 39190. Phone: (601) 442-2901.

CRAFT FAIR USA: INDOOR SHOW. Sept 22–23. Wisconsin State Fair Park, Milwaukee, WI. Sale of handcrafted items: jewelry, pottery, weaving, leather, wood, glass, yulecraft and sculpture. Est attendance: 12,000. For info: Dir, Craft Fair USA, 9312 W National Ave, Milwaukee, WI 53227-1542. Phone: (414) 321-2100. Web: www.craftfairusa.com.

DEAR DIARY DAY. Sept 22. Put it on paper. You'll feel better. No need to be a professional writer. [© 2000 by WH] For info: Tom or Ruth Roy, Wellcat Holidays, 2418 Long Ln, Lebanon, PA 17046. Phone: (717) 279-0184. E-mail: wellcat@supernet.com. Web: www.wellcat.com.

ELEPHANT APPRECIATION DAY. Sept 22. Celebrate the earth's largest, most interesting and most noble endangered land animal. Free info kit from: Wayne Hepburn, WildHeart Productions, PO Box 3588, Sarasota, FL 34230-3588. Phone: (941) 365-7787. Fax: (941) 363-0273. E-mail: mail@wildheart.com. Web: www.wildheart.com.

EMANCIPATION PROCLAMATION: ANNIVERSARY. Sept 22, 1862. One of the most important presidential proclamations of American history is that of Sept 22, 1862, in which Abraham Lincoln, by executive proclamation, freed the slaves in the rebelling states. "That on . . . [Jan 1, 1863] . . . all persons held as slaves within any state or designated part of a state, the people whereof shall then be in rebellion against the United States, shall be then, thenceforward, and forever, free. . . ." See also: "13th Amendment Anniversary" (Dec 18) for abolition of slavery in all states.

"FAMILY TIES" TV PREMIERE: ANNIVERSARY. Sept 22, 1982. This popular '80s sitcom was set at Columbus, OH and focused on the Keaton family: Ex-hippies Elyse (Meredith Baxter-Birney), an architect, and Steven (Michael Gross), a station manager of the local public TV station, Alex (Michael J. Fox), their smart, conservative and financially-driven son, Mallory (Justine Bateman), their materialistic, ditzy daughter and Jennifer (Tina Yothers), their tomboy youngest daughter. Later in the series Elyse gave birth to Andrew (Brian Bonsall). Marc Price played Irwin "Skippy" Handleman, the nerdy next-door neighbor who adored the Keatons, and Mallory in particular. The last episode aired Sept 17, 1989.

FARADAY, MICHAEL: BIRTH ANNIVERSARY. Sept 22, 1791. English scientist and early experimenter with electricity, born at Newington, Surrey, England. Died at Hampton Court, Aug 25, 1867.

FIRST ALL-WOMAN JURY EMPANELED IN COLONIES. Sept 22, 1656. The General Provincial Court at Patuxent, MD, empaneled the first all-woman jury in the colonies to hear the case of Judith Catchpole, accused of murdering her child. The defendant claimed she had never even been pregnant, and after all the evidence was heard, the jury acquitted her.

"FRIENDS" TV PREMIERE: ANNIVERSARY. Sept 22, 1994. This NBC comedy brings together six single friends and their personal adult lives, ranging from their jobs to their love lives. Cast includes Courteney Cox Arquette, Lisa Kudrow, Jennifer Aniston, Matthew Perry, David Schwimmer and Matt Le Blanc.

GETTYSBURG OUTDOOR ANTIQUE SHOW. Sept 22. Gettysburg, PA. More than 175 dealers displaying their wares on the sidewalk. Annually, the fourth Saturday in September. Est attendance: 25,000. For info: Gettysburg CVB, PO Box 4117, Gettysburg, PA 17325-1899. Phone: (717) 334-6274. Fax: (717) 334-1166. Web: www.gettysburg.com.

HARVEST FESTIVAL. Sept 22–23. Cincinnati Zoo and Botanical Garden, Cincinnati, OH. Festival features a variety of crafts, demonstrations, Appalachian music, art, storytelling, a crafts village and much more. Est attendance: 12,000. For info: Events/Promo Dept, Cincinnati Zoo and Botanical Garden, 3400 Vine St, Cincinnati, OH 45220. Phone: (513) 281-4701. Fax: (513) 559-7790. Web: www.cincy.zoo.org.

HOBBIT DAY. Sept 22. To commemorate the birthdays of Frodo and Bilbo Baggins and their creator J.R.R. Tolkien. For info: American Tolkien Soc, PO Box 7871, Flint, MI 48507-0871. Phone: (727) 585-0985. Fax: (727) 462-6473.

HOUSEMAN, JOHN: BIRTH ANNIVERSARY. Sept 22, 1902. American actor and producer John Houseman was born Jacques Haussmann at Bucharest. He is best known for his collaboration with Orson Welles on the 1938 radio production of *War of the Worlds* and for his role as Professor Kingsfield in the film and television version of *The Paper Chase*. He won an Oscar for that film role in 1974 and helped establish the Juilliard drama school and the Acting Company repertory group. He died Oct 30, 1988 at Malibu, CA.

ICE CREAM CONE: BIRTHDAY. Sept 22, 1903. Italo Marchiony emigrated from Italy in the late 1800s and soon thereafter went into business at New York, NY, with a pushcart dispensing lemon ice. Success soon led to a small fleet of pushcarts, and the inventive Marchiony was inspired to develop a cone, first made of paper, later of pastry, to hold the tasty delicacy. On Sept 22, 1903, his application for a patent for his new mold was filed, and US Patent No 746971 was issued to him Dec 15, 1903.

KIWANIS KIDS' DAY. Sept 22. To honor and assist youth—our greatest resource. Annually, the fourth Saturday in September. For info: Kiwanis Intl, Program Dvmt Dept, 3636 Woodview Trace, Indianapolis, IN 46268. E-mail: kiwanismail@kiwanis.org. Web: www.kiwanis.org.

LONG COUNT DAY: ANNIVERSARY. Sept 22, 1927. Anniversary of world championship boxing match between Jack Dempsey and Gene Tunney, at Soldier Field, Chicago, IL. It was the largest fight purse ($990,446) in the history of boxing to that time. Nearly half the population of the US is believed to have listened to the radio broadcast of this fight. In the seventh round of the 10-round fight, Tunney was knocked down. Following the rules, Referee Dave Barry interrupted the count when Dempsey failed to go to the farthest corner. The count was resumed and Tunney got to his feet at the count of nine. Stopwatch records of those present claimed the total elapsed time from the beginning of the count until Tunney got to his feet at 12–15 seconds. Tunney, awarded seven of the 10 rounds, won the fight and claimed the world championship. Dempsey's appeal was denied and he never fought again. Tunney retired the following year after one more (successful) fight.

MABON. Sept 22. (Also called Alban Elfed.) One of the "Lesser Sabbats" during the Wiccan year, Mabon marks the second harvest as Nature prepares for the coming of winter. Annually, on the autumnal equinox.

MALI: INDEPENDENCE DAY: ANNIVERSARY. Sept 22. National holiday commemorating independence from France in 1960. Mali, in West Africa, was known as the French Sudan while a colony.

"MAVERICK" TV PREMIERE: ANNIVERSARY. Sept 22, 1957. This popular western, which has since been remade into a popular movie, starred James Garner as Bret Maverick, a clever man who preferred card playing to fighting. A second Maverick was introduced when production was behind schedule—Jack Kelly played his brother Bart. Garner and Kelly played most episodes separately, and when Garner left in 1961, Kelly was in almost all the episodes. Other performers included Roger Moore, Robert Colbert and Diane Brewster. This western distinguished itself by its light touch and parody of other westerns.

MITCHELL PERSIMMON FESTIVAL. Sept 22–29. Main Street, Mitchell, IN. 55th annual. Persimmon pudding and novelty contests, parade, carnival, arts and crafts, fine arts and photography shows, antique autos and machinery, pioneer village candlelight tour, free entertainment nightly. Annually, the last full week in September. Est attendance: 90,000. For info: Greater Mitchell Chamber of Commerce, PO Box 216, Mitchell, IN 47446. Phone: (800) 580-1985. Web: www.persimmonfestival.org.

NATIONAL CENTENARIANS DAY. Sept 22. A day to recognize and honor elderly individuals who have lived a century or longer. A day not only to recognize these individuals, but to listen to them discuss the memories—filled with historical information—that they have of their rich lives. Take time today to listen to a Centenarian. Special celebration held annually at Williamsport Retirement Village. For info: Beth Kirkpatrick, Mktg Dir, Williamsport Retirement Village, Founders, A Division of Brooke Grove Fdtn, 154 N Artizan St, Williamsport, MD 21795. Phone: (301) 223-7971. Fax: (301) 223-6966.

★**NATIONAL HUNTING AND FISHING DAY.** Sept 22. Presidential Proclamation 4682, of Sept 11, 1979, covers all succeeding years. Annually, the fourth Saturday of September.

RELIGIOUS FREEDOM WEEK. Sept 22–30. This date commemorates the anniversary of the Bill of Rights and the right to believe and practice the religion of one's own choice as laid out in the First Amendment. Annually, to include anniversary date. For info: Rev Susan Taylor, Religious Freedom Week Committee, c/o Church of Scientology, 1701 20th St NW, Washington, DC 20009. Phone: (202) 667-6404. Fax: (202) 667-6314.

STANHOPE, PHILIP DORMER: BIRTH ANNIVERSARY. Sept 22, 1694 (OS). Philip Dormer Stanhope, the 4th Earl of Chesterfield, was born at London, England. He was a brilliant politician and orator. On Feb 20, 1751, he brought a bill into the House of Lords that caused the "New Style" Gregorian calendar to replace the "Old Style" Julian calendar in 1752. His influential political career was eclipsed by the fame of the letters he wrote to his son Philip, giving shrewd counsel on manners, morals and the ways of the world. Published less than a year after his own death at London, Mar 24, 1773, the *Letters* became immensely popular, were translated and republished in many editions. The Chesterfield, a kind of sofa, is said to be named for him.

TACY RICHARDSON'S RIDE: ANNIVERSARY. Sept 22, 1777. Courageous 23-year-old Tacy Richardson (Jan 1, 1754–June 18, 1807) rode her favorite horse, "Fearnaught," several perilous miles from the family farm at Montgomery County, PA to the James Vaux mansion to warn General George Washington of the approach of British troops led by General William Howe. As it turned out, the British crossing of the Schuylkill at Gordon's Ford was a feint to deceive Washington who indeed hastily withdrew to Pottstown, clearing the way for General Howe to spend that night in the quarters Washington had occupied only a few hours earlier.

THRESHING BEE AND ANTIQUE SHOW. Sept 22–23. Culberston, MT. The Culberston community invites friends and neighbors from around the region to celebrate this country's heritage. Eighty plus antique tractors, many steam driven, parade on the threshing grounds. This celebration includes demonstrations of grain threshing, steam-powered sawing of lumber, tractor races, kids games and old-time fiddler music. The steam powered equipment dates back to the late 1800s and turn-of-the-century farming. Est attendance: 1,500. For info: Rodney Iverson, Threshing Bee and Antique Show, Box 168, Culberston, MT 59218. Phone: (406) 787-5265.

US POSTMASTER GENERAL ESTABLISHED: ANNIVERSARY. Sept 22, 1789. Congress established office of Postmaster General, following the Departments of State, War and Treasury.

BIRTHDAYS TODAY

Scott Baio, 40, actor ("Happy Days," "Diagnosis Murder," "Charles in Charge"), born Brooklyn, NY, Sept 22, 1961.

Shari Belafonte-Harper, 47, model, actress, born New York, NY, Sept 22, 1954.

Debbie Boone, 45, singer ("You Light Up My Life," "Baby, I'm Yours"), born Hackensack, NJ, Sept 22, 1956.

Bonnie Hunt, 37, actress (*Jerry Maguire, Jumanji*), born Chicago, IL, Sept 22, 1964.

Joan Jett, 41, singer ("I Love Rock 'n' Roll," "Crimson and Clover"), musician, born Philadelphia, PA, Sept 22, 1960.

Thomas Charles (Tommy) Lasorda, 74, Baseball Hall of Fame manager and former player, born Norristown, PA, Sept 22, 1927.

Paul Le Mat, 56, actor (*American Graffiti, Melvin and Howard, Strange Invaders*), born Rahway, NY, Sept 22, 1945.

Catherine Oxenberg, 40, actress ("Dynasty"), born New York, NY, Sept 22, 1961.

Mike Richter, 35, hockey player, born Philadelphia, PA, Sept 22, 1966.

Eugene Roche, 73, actor ("Soap," "Webster"), born Boston, MA, Sept 22, 1928.

Arthur O. Sulzberger, 50, publisher (*The New York Times*), born Mount Kisco, NY, Sept 22, 1951.

September *2001*	S	M	T	W	T	F	S
							1
	2	3	4	5	6	7	8
	9	10	11	12	13	14	15
	16	17	18	19	20	21	22
	23	24	25	26	27	28	29
	30						

SEPTEMBER 23 — SUNDAY

Day 266 — 99 Remaining

ALL ABOUT APPLES. Sept 23. Billings Farm and Museum, Woodstock, VT. Learn more about this most basic American fruit that boasts hundreds of varieties. Activities include cider pressing, making apple butter in the farm house kitchen, apples-on-a-string, harvest dolls and horse-drawn wagon rides. For info: Marjorie Wakefield, Exec Secy, Billings Farm and Museum, PO Box 489, Woodstock, VT 05091. Phone: (802) 457-2355. Fax: (802) 457-4663. E-mail: billings.farm@valley.net. Web: www.billingsfarm.org.

BASEBALL'S GREATEST DISPUTE: ANNIVERSARY. Sept 23, 1908. In the decisive game between the Chicago Cubs and the New York Giants, the National League pennant race erupted in controversy during the bottom of the ninth with the score tied 1–1, at the Polo Grounds, New York, NY. New York was at bat with two men on. The batter hit safely to center field, scoring the winning run. Chicago claimed that the runner on first, Fred Merkle, seeing the winning run scored, headed toward the dugout without advancing to second base, thus invalidating the play. The Chicago second baseman, Johnny Evers, attempted to get the ball and tag Merkle out, but was prevented by the fans streaming onto the field. Days later Harry C. Pulliam, head of the National Commission of Organized Baseball, decided to call the game a tie. The teams were forced to play a post-season playoff game, which the Cubs won 4–2. Fans invented the terms "boner" and "bonehead" in reference to the play and it has gone down in baseball history as "Merkle's Boner."

CABRILLO FESTIVAL. Sept 23–Sept 30. San Diego, CA. Colorful pageant reenacts the historic landing of explorer Juan Rodriguez Cabrillo who sailed into San Diego Bay on Sept 28, 1542. Kuneyaay basketweaving demonstrations. Reenactment of Spanish encampment. Portuguese, Spanish, Native American and Mexican dances and food. Pageant, annually the last Sunday in September. Est attendance: 9,500. For info: Cabrillo Natl Monument, 1800 Cabrillo Memorial Dr, San Diego, CA 92106. Phone: (619) 557-5450. TTY: (619) 222-8211. Fax: (619) 557-5469. Web: www.nps.gov/cabr/

CHECKERS DAY: ANNIVERSARY. Sept 23. Anniversary of the nationally televised "Checkers Speech" by then vice presidential candidate Richard M. Nixon, on Sept 23, 1952. Nixon was found "clean as a hound's tooth" in connection with a private fund for political expenses, and he declared he would never give back the cocker spaniel dog, Checkers, which had been a gift to his daughters. Other dogs prominent in American politics: Abraham Lincoln's dog, Fido; Franklin D. Roosevelt's much-traveled terrier, Fala; Harry S. Truman's dogs, Mike and Feller; Dwight D. Eisenhower's dog, Heidi; Lyndon Johnson's beagles, Him and Her; Ronald Reagan's dogs, Lucky and Rex; and George Bush's dog, Millie.

DEAF AWARENESS WEEK. Sept 23–29. Nationwide celebration to promote deaf culture, American Sign Language and deaf heritage. Activities include library displays, interpreted story hours, Open Houses in residential schools and mainstream programs, exhibit booths in shopping malls with "Five Minute Sign Language Lessons," material distribution. Annually, the last full week of September. For info: Natl Assn of the Deaf, 814 Thayer Ave, Silver Spring, MD 20910-4500. Fax: (301) 587-1791. E-mail: nadinfo@nad.org. Web: www.nad.org.

GO WILD DURING CALIFORNIA WILD RICE WEEK. Sept 23–29. To promote greater appreciation and use of cultivated wild rice. California wild rice growers want America to know that wild rice is no longer simply hiding inside a holiday turkey. This versatile grain can add a gourmet touch to meals year-round. Stuff it inside pork chop pockets and chicken breasts or toss it into soups, salads, stir-frys and even pancake and muffin batters. Let your imagination run wild! Annually, the last full week in September. For info: The Thacker Group, 1008 Second St, Courtyard Level, Old Sacramento, CA 95814. Phone: (916) 444-8363. Fax: (916) 444-3536. E-mail: info@thackergroup.com. Web: www.cawildrice.org.

INNERGIZE. Sept 23. A day set aside for anyone who has said "I don't have time to do the personal things I want to do for myself." Today is the day to set time aside for yourself to do anything you want to do. Annually, the day after autumn. For info: Michelle Porchia, inner dimensions, 4 Daniels Farm Rd, Ste 137, Trumbull, CT 06611. Phone: (203) 876-7986. Fax: (203) 876-7986. E-mail: innerdim@aol.com. Web: www.porchia.net.

JAPAN: AUTUMNAL EQUINOX DAY. Sept 23. National holiday in Japan.

"THE JETSONS" TV PREMIERE: ANNIVERSARY. Sept 23, 1962. "Meet George Jetson. His boy Elroy. Daughter Judy. Jane, his wife. . . . " These words introduced us to the Jetsons, a cartoon family living in the twenty-first century, the Flintstones of the Space Age. We followed the exploits of George and his family, as well as his work relationship with his greedy, ruthless boss Cosmo Spacely. Voices were provided by George O'Hanlon as George, Penny Singleton as Jane, Janet Waldo as Judy, Daws Butler as Elroy, Don Messick as Astro, the family dog and Mel Blanc as Spacely. New episodes were created in 1985 which also introduced a new pet, Orbity.

LIBRA, THE BALANCE. Sept 23–Oct 22. In the astronomical/astrological zodiac that divides the sun's apparent orbit into 12 segments, the period Sept 23–Oct 22 is identified traditionally as the sun sign of Libra, the Balance. The ruling planet is Venus.

LIPPMANN, WALTER: BIRTH ANNIVERSARY. Sept 23, 1889. American journalist, political philosopher and author. Born at New York, NY, he died there Dec 14, 1974. As a syndicated newspaper columnist he was the foremost and perhaps the most influential commentator in the nation. "Without criticism," he said in an address to the International Press Institute in 1965, "and reliable and intelligent reporting, the government cannot govern."

McGUFFEY, WILLIAM HOLMES: BIRTH ANNIVERSARY. Sept 23, 1800. American educator and author of the famous *McGuffey Readers*, born at Washington County, PA. Died at Charlottesville, VA, May 4, 1873.

NATIONAL DOG WEEK. Sept 23–29. To promote the relationship of dogs to mankind and emphasize the need for the proper care and treatment of dogs. Annually, the last full week in September. For info: Morris Raskin, Secy, Dogs on Stamps Study Unit (DOSSU), 202 A Newport Rd, Monroe Township, NJ 08831. Phone: (609) 655-7411.

NATIONAL GOOD NEIGHBOR DAY. Sept 23. To build a nation and world that cares by increasing appreciation and understanding of our fellow man. Annually, the fourth Sunday in September. For info: Good Neighbor Day Fdtn, Rebecca E. Mattson, Box 379, Lakeside, MT 59922. Phone: (406) 844-3000. Web: www.natgoodneighborday.com.

PAULUS, FRIEDRICH: BIRTH ANNIVERSARY. Sept 23, 1890. The German commander of the Sixth Army who led the advance on Stalingrad in 1942, Friedrich von Paulus was born at Breitenau, Germany. Paulus's troops succeeded in taking most of Stalingrad in November 1942, but eventually became trapped within the city they had captured. Paulus surrendered to the Russians Jan 31, 1943, the same day that Hitler promoted him to field marshal. He appeared as a key witness for the Soviet prosecution at the Nuremberg trials. Paulus died Feb 1, 1957, at Dresden, East Germany.

PIDGEON, WALTER: BIRTH ANNIVERSARY. Sept 23, 1897. Actor Walter Pidgeon was born at East St. John, New Brunswick, Canada. He died at age 87, Sept 25, 1984, at Santa Monica, CA. He made his film debut in 1925 in *Mannequin*. Among his films are *Saratoga* and *Mrs Miniver*.

PLANET NEPTUNE DISCOVERY: ANNIVERSARY. Sept 23, 1846. Neptune is 2,796,700,000 miles from the sun (about 30 times as far from the sun as Earth). Eighth planet from the sun, Neptune takes 164.8 years to revolve around the sun. Diameter is about 31,000 miles compared to Earth at 7,927 miles. Discovered by German astronomer Johann Galle.

REVOLUTIONARY TIMES AT BRANDYWINE. Sept 23. Brandywine Battlefield Park, Chadds Ford, PA. Reenactments of the Battle of Brandywine, an 18th-century tavern, children's activities; plus sutlers and crafters perform, display and sell their crafts. Plenty of good food. Est attendance: 5,000. For info: Tom Stolfi, Education & Outreach Coord, Brandywine Battlefield Park, PO Box 202, Chadds Ford, PA 19317. Phone: (610) 459-3342. Fax: (610) 459-9586.

	S	M	T	W	T	F	S
September							1
2001	2	3	4	5	6	7	8
	9	10	11	12	13	14	15
	16	17	18	19	20	21	22
	23	24	25	26	27	28	29
	30						

SAUDI ARABIA: ANNIVERSARY KINGDOM UNIFICATION. Sept 23. National holiday. Commemorates unification in 1932.

WOODHULL, VICTORIA CHAFLIN: BIRTH ANNIVERSARY. Sept 23, 1838. American feminist, reformer and first female candidate for the presidency of the US. Born at Homer, OH, she died at Norton Park, Bremmons, Worcestershire, England, June 10, 1927.

BIRTHDAYS TODAY

Jason Alexander, 42, actor ("Seinfeld," *Pretty Woman; Bye, Bye, Birdy*; stage: *Jerome Robbins' Broadway*), born Newark, NJ, Sept 23, 1959.

Ray Charles (Robinson), 71, singer ("Georgia on My Mind," "What'd I Say"), composer, born Albany, GA, Sept 23, 1930.

Ani DiFranco, 31, folk-punk singer and songwriter, born Buffalo, NY, Sept 23, 1970.

Julio Iglesias, 58, singer ("To All the Girls I've Loved Before" with Willie Nelson), songwriter, born Madrid, Spain, Sept 23, 1943.

Tony Joseph Mandarich, 35, football player, born Oakville, Ontario, Canada, Sept 23, 1966.

Larry Hogan Mize, 43, golfer, born Augusta, GA, Sept 23, 1958.

Elizabeth Pena, 40, actress (*Down and Out in Beverly Hills, Jacob's Ladder*, "Shannon's Deal"), born Elizabeth, NJ, Sept 23, 1961.

Paul Petersen, 56, actor ("The Donna Reed Show," *Houseboat*), born Glendale, CA, Sept 23, 1945.

Mary Kay Place, 54, writer, actress ("Mary Hartman, Mary Hartman," *The Big Chill*), born Tulsa, OK, Sept 23, 1947.

Mickey Rooney (Joe Yule, Jr), 81, actor (*Andy Hardy* movies, *The Black Stallion*), born Brooklyn, NY, Sept 23, 1920.

Bruce Springsteen, 52, singer, songwriter ("Born in the USA"), born Freehold, NJ, Sept 23, 1949.

SEPTEMBER 24 — MONDAY
Day 267 — 98 Remaining

ANGEL WEEK CELEBRATION. Sept 24–28. A celebration of the importance of angels in our lives. The feasts of the archangels and the guardian angels are celebrated during the week, the last week of September. For info: St. Joseph Hessen Cassel School, 11521 Old US 27 South, Fort Wayne, IN 46816. Fax: (219) 639-3675.

"DANIEL BOONE" TV PREMIERE: ANNIVERSARY. Sept 24, 1964. A successful show based loosely on the life of pioneer Daniel Boone, who helped settle Kentucky in the 1770s. Fess Parker starred as the American hero. Ed Ames played Mingo, Boone's friend, an educated Cherokee and Pat Blair played his wife, Rebecca. Also featured were Albert Salmi, Jimmy Dean, Roosevelt Grier, Darby Hinton, Veronica Cartwright and Dallas McKennon.

"A DIFFERENT WORLD" TV PREMIERE: ANNIVERSARY. Sept 24, 1987. In this spin-off from "The Cosby Show," Denise Huxtable (Lisa Bonet) goes off to Hillman College. The first season's cast included Marisa Tomei, Dawnn Lewis, Jasmine Guy, Loretta Devine, Amir Williams, Kadeem Hardison, Darryl Bell, Marie-Alise Recasner, Mary Alice and Sinbad. Bonet left the series and returned to "The Cosby Show." Returning for a second season were Lewis, Guy, Hardison, Bell, Alice and Sinbad, plus Charnele Brown, Cree Summer and Glynn Turman. Aretha Franklin (Turman's wife) sang the show's theme song.

FANEUIL HALL OPENED TO THE PUBLIC: ANNIVERSARY. Sept 24, 1742. On this date Faneuil Hall at Boston, MA, opened to the public. Designed by painter John Smibiert, it was enlarged in 1805 according to plans by Charles Bulfinch. Today it is on the Freedom Trail, as part of the Boston Historical Park administered by the National Park Service.

FITZGERALD, F. SCOTT: BIRTH ANNIVERSARY. Sept 24, 1896. American short story writer and novelist; author of *This Side of Paradise, The Great Gatsby* and *Tender Is the Night.* Born Francis Scott Key Fitzgerald, at St. Paul, MN, he died at Hollywood, CA, Dec 21, 1940.

GEISEL, THEODOR "DR. SEUSS": 10th DEATH ANNIVERSARY. Sept 24, 1991. Theodor Seuss Geisel, the creator of *The Cat in the Hat, If I Ran the Zoo, The Grinch Who Stole Christmas, Green Eggs and Ham, Fox in Sox, Horton Hears a Who* and dozens of other wonderful books for children, died at the age of 87 on Sept 24, 1991, at La Jolla, CA. See also: "Geisel, Theodor 'Dr. Seuss': Birth Anniversary" (Mar 2).

GUINEA-BISSAU: INDEPENDENCE DAY: ANNIVERSARY. Sept 24. National holiday. Commemorates independence from Portugal in 1974.

HENSON, JIM: 65th BIRTH ANNIVERSARY. Sept 24, 1936. Puppeteer, born at Greenville, MS. Jim Henson created a unique brand of puppetry known as the Muppets. Kermit the Frog, Big Bird, Rowlf, Bert and Ernie, Gonzo, Animal, Miss Piggy and Oscar the Grouch are a few of the puppets that captured the hearts of children and adults alike in television and film productions including "Sesame Street," "The Jimmy Dean Show," "The Muppet Show," *The Muppet Movie, The Muppets Take Manhattan, The Great Muppet Caper* and *The Dark Crystal.* Henson began his career in 1954 as producer of the TV show "Sam and Friends" at Washington, DC. He introduced the Muppets in 1956. His creativity was rewarded with 18 Emmy Awards, seven Grammy Awards, four Peabody Awards and five ACE Awards from the National Cable Television Association. Henson died unexpectedly May 16, 1990, at New York, NY.

"THE LOVE BOAT" TV PREMIERE: ANNIVERSARY. Sept 24, 1977. This one-hour comedy-drama featured guest stars aboard a cruise ship, the Pacific Princess. All stories had to do with finding or losing love. The ship's crew were the only regulars (though there were occasional recurring roles, like Charo as April): Gavin MacLeod as Captain Merrill Stubing, Bernie Kopell as the often-divorced Doctor Adam Bricker, Fred Grandy as assistant purser Burl "Gopher" Smith, Ted Lange as bartender Isaac Washington and Lauren Tewes as cruise director Julie McCoy. Also featured were Jill Whelan as Vicki, Stubing's daughter, Pat Klous as Julie, who replaced Tewes and Ted McGinley as photographer Ashley Covington "Ace" Evans. The series ended with the last telecast on Sept 5, 1986, but three two-hour specials were broadcast the next year. MacLeod, Lange, Kopell and Whelan were reunited in a Love Boat special in 1990.

"LOVE OF LIFE" TV PREMIERE: 50th ANNIVERSARY. Sept 24, 1951. This serial, which began as a 15-minute show, ran for 28 years. It was set in the town of Barrowsville at first and later moved to Rosehill; the story lines also shifted from a focus on two sisters to a larger number of characters. The diverse cast included such notables as Christopher Reeve, Karen Grassle, Roy Scheider, Dana Delaney, John Aniston, Marsha Mason, Bert Convy, Warren Beatty and Barnard Hughes.

MARSHALL, JOHN: BIRTH ANNIVERSARY. Sept 24, 1755. Fourth Chief Justice of Supreme Court, born at Germantown, VA. Served in House of Representatives and as Secretary of State under John Adams. Appointed by President Adams to the position of chief justice in January 1801, he became known as "The Great Chief Justice." Marshall's court was largely responsible for defining the role of the Supreme Court and basic organizing principles of government in the early years after adoption of the Constitution in such cases as *Marbury v Madison, McCulloch v Maryland, Cohens v Virginia* and *Gibbons v Ogden.* He died at Philadelphia, PA, July 6, 1835.

MOON PHASE: FIRST QUARTER. Sept 24. Moon enters First Quarter phase at 5:31 AM, EDT.

"THE MUNSTERS" TV PREMIERE: ANNIVERSARY. Sept 24, 1964. "The Munsters" was a half-hour sitcom about an unusual family who thought they were ordinary. Each family member resembled a different type of monster: Herman Munster (Fred Gwynne) was Frankenstein's monster, Lily, his wife (Yvonne DeCarlo) and Grandpa, her father (Al Lewis) were vampires and his son Eddie (Butch Patrick) was a werewolf. Only their niece, Marilyn (Beverly Owen and Pat Priest), looked normal, and they considered her the unattractive family member. Most of the show's laughs came from the family's interactions with outsiders. The last telecast was on Sept 1, 1966.

SCHWENKFELDER THANKSGIVING. Sept 24. On this day in 1734 members of the Schwenkfelder Society gave thanks for their deliverance from Old World persecution as they prepared to take up new lives in the Pennsylvania-Dutch counties of Pennsylvania. Still celebrated.

"60 MINUTES" TV PREMIERE: ANNIVERSARY. Sept 24, 1968. TV's longest-running prime-time program was originally hosted by Harry Reasoner and Mike Wallace. Dan Rather and Diane Sawyer were also reporters on TV's first news magazine. Today the show's correspondents include Ed Bradley, Steve Kroft, Lesley Stahl, Morley Safer, Andy Rooney and Mike Wallace.

SOUTH AFRICA: HERITAGE DAY. Sept 24. A celebration of South African nationhood, commemorating the multicultural heritage of this rainbow nation.

TAKE CHARGE OF YOUR TV WEEK. Sept 24–28. To help families make more informed television viewing choices. Co-sponsored by the National PTA, Cable in the Classroom and the National Cable Television Association. For info: Natl PTA, 330 N Wabash Ave, Ste 2100, Chicago, IL 60611. Phone: (312) 670-6782. E-mail: info@pta.org. Web: www.pta.org.

BIRTHDAYS TODAY

Gordon Clapp, 53, actor ("NYPD Blue"), born North Conway, NH, Sept 24, 1948.

Sheila MacRae, 78, singer, actress, born London, England, Sept 24, 1923.

James Kenneth (Jim) McKay (born James Kenneth McManus), 80, sportscaster, born Philadelphia, PA, Sept 24, 1921.

Rafael Corrales Palmeiro, 37, baseball player, born Havana, Cuba, Sept 24, 1964.

Kevin Sorbo, 43, actor ("Hercules"), born Mound, MN, Sept 24, 1958.

SEPTEMBER 25 — TUESDAY

Day 268 — 97 Remaining

"BEAUTY AND THE BEAST" TV PREMIERE: ANNIVERSARY. Sept 25, 1987. This updated version of the fairy tale was a romantic hit and acquired a cult following. It followed the experiences of Catherine Chandler (Linda Hamilton), a Manhattan lawyer who is beaten and abandoned and subsequently found and cared for by Vincent (Ron Perlman), a man-beast living under the city. Other cast members included Roy Dotrice, Jay Acovone, Ren Woods, Cory Danziger and David Greenlee. Hamilton left the series at the beginning of the third season; the series ended shortly thereafter.

"BROKEN ARROW" TV PREMIERE: 45th ANNIVERSARY. Sept 25, 1956. This half-hour western was one of the few to portray Native Americans in a positive light. It starred Michael Ansara as Cochise, Apache chief, and John Lupton as Indian Agent Tom Jeffords, Cochise's blood brother. The show was syndicated under the name "Cochise."

FAULKNER, WILLIAM CUTHBERT: BIRTH ANNIVERSARY. Sept 25, 1897. American novelist and short story writer William Faulkner (born Falkner) was born at New Albany, MS. A Nobel Prize winner who changed the style and structure of the American novel, he died at Byhalia, MS, on July 6, 1962. Faulkner's first novel, *Soldiers' Pay* was published in 1926. His best-known book, *The Sound and the Fury*, appeared in 1929. Shunning literary circles, Faulkner moved to a pre-Civil War house on the outskirts of Oxford, MS, in 1930. From 1930 until the onset of World War II he published an incredible body of work. *The Portable Faulkner* appeared in 1946 and *Collected Stories* in 1950. In June of 1962 Faulkner published his last novel, *The Reivers*.

FIRST AMERICAN NEWSPAPER PUBLISHED: ANNIVERSARY. Sept 25, 1690. The first (and only) edition of *Publick Occurrences Both Foreign and Domestick* was published by Benjamin Harris, at the London-Coffee-House, Boston, MA. Authorities considered this first newspaper published in the US offensive and ordered immediate suppression.

FIRST WOMAN SUPREME COURT JUSTICE: 20th ANNIVERSARY. Sept 25, 1981. Sandra Day O'Connor was sworn in as the first woman associate justice on the US Supreme Court on this date. She had been nominated by President Ronald Reagan in July 1981.

"FOUR STAR PLAYHOUSE" TV PREMIERE: ANNIVERSARY. Sept 25, 1952. The actors who founded Four Star Films—Dick Powell, Charles Boyer, Joel McCrea and Rosalind Russell—starred in this dramatic anthology series. David Niven and Ida Lupino replaced McCrea and Russell, who left shortly after the series began. Other guest actors included Ronald Colman in his first TV dramatic appearance ("The Lost Silk Hat," 1952) and Joan Fontaine in her first major dramatic TV role ("The Girl on the Park Bench," 1953).

GREENWICH MEAN TIME BEGINS: ANNIVERSARY. Sept 25, 1676 (OS). Two very accurate clocks were set in motion at the Royal Observatory at Greenwich, England. Greenwich Mean Time (now known as Universal Time) became the standard for England; in 1884 it became the standard for the world.

"THE KATE SMITH HOUR" TV PREMIERE: ANNIVERSARY. Sept 25, 1950. Kate Smith was a talented singer who hosted radio before beginning a successful but short TV career. This late afternoon show was the most successful (she also had two prime-time shows, "The Kate Smith Evening Hour" (September 1951–June 1952) and "The Kate Smith Show" (January–July 1960) that were less well-received). It included interviews, musical numbers and comedy or drama sketches. The sketches spun off many series, including "The World of Mr Sweeney" and "Ethel and Albert."

MAJOR LEAGUE BASEBALL'S FIRST DOUBLE HEADER: ANNIVERSARY. Sept 25, 1882. The first major league baseball double header was played between the Providence and Worcester teams.

NATIONAL ONE-HIT WONDER DAY. Sept 25. Honors the one-hit wonders of rock'n'roll. Anyone who ever had a hit single deserves eternal remembrance. For info: Steven Rosen, 1420 E Bates Ave, Englewood, CO 80110. Phone: (303) 783-4720 or (303) 820-1567. E-mail: srosenone@aol.com.

PACIFIC OCEAN DISCOVERED: ANNIVERSARY. Sept 25, 1513. Vasco Núñez de Balboa, a Spanish conquistador, stood high atop a peak in the Darien, in present-day Panama, becoming the first European to look upon the Pacific Ocean, claiming it as the South Sea in the name of the King of Spain.

PROWSE, JULIET: 65th BIRTH ANNIVERSARY. Sept 25, 1936. Dancer, actress, born Bombay, India. Died Sept 14, 1996.

RAMEAU, JEAN PHILLIPPE: BIRTH ANNIVERSARY. Sept 25, 1683. French composer Jean Phillippe Rameau was baptised at Dijon, France, Sept 25, 1683. Called by some the greatest French composer and musical theorist of the 18th century, Rameau died at Paris, France, Sept 12, 1764.

SEQUOIA AND KINGS CANYON NATIONAL PARK ESTABLISHED: ANNIVERSARY. Sept 25, 1890. Area in central California established as a national park. For further park info: Sequoia Natl Park, Three Rivers, CA 93271.

SHOSTAKOVICH, DMITRI: 95th BIRTH ANNIVERSARY. Sept 25, 1906. Russian composer born at St. Petersburg, Russia. Died at Moscow, USSR, Aug 9, 1975.

"SILVER SPOONS" TV PREMIERE: ANNIVERSARY. Sept 25, 1982. This half-hour sitcom was about a wealthy, immature toy company owner and his sensible son. Joel Higgins was Edward Stratton III, Rick Schroder played his son Ricky, who left military school to be with his divorced father. Erin Gray was Kate Summers, Edward's secretary and later, his wife, Leonard Lightfoot was his lawyer, Leonard Rollins, Franklyn Seales played his business manager, Dexter Stuffins, Alfonso Ribeiro was Ricky's friend and Dexter's nephew, Alfonso Spears, Jason Bateman played Derek Taylor, Ricky's sneaky friend and Corky Pigeon played geeky Freddie Lippincottleman. Ray Walston appeared as Kate's uncle, and John Houseman had a recurring role as Edward's stuffy father.

SMITH, WALTER WESLEY "RED": BIRTH ANNIVERSARY. Sept 25, 1905. Pulitzer Prize—winning sports columnist and newspaperman for 54 years, Walter Wesley (Red) Smith was born at Green Bay, WI. Called the "nation's most respected sportswriter," Smith's columns appeared in some 500 newspapers. He died at Stamford, CT, Jan 15, 1982.

WCVL/WIMC SENIOR CITIZENS HEALTH FAIR & EXPO. Sept 25. Montgomery County Fairgrounds, Crawfordsville, IN. An expo and trade show highlighting products and services of interest to seniors. Nearly 20 display booths, free health screenings for glaucoma, blood pressure, cholesterol, etc. Food service, travel logs. Annually, the last Tuesday in September. Est attendance: 1,000. For info: Mr Dick Munro, Gen Mgr, WCVL/WIMC Radio, PO Box 603, Crawfordsville, IN 47933. Phone: (765) 362-8200. Fax: (765) 364-1550.

BIRTHDAYS TODAY

Tate Donovan, 38, actor ("Friends," "Partners"), born New York, NY, Sept 25, 1963.

Michael Douglas, 57, actor ("The Streets of San Francisco," *Fatal Attraction, Basic Instinct*), director, born New York, NY, Sept 25, 1944.

Mark Hamill, 50, actor ("General Hospital," *Star Wars*), born Oakland, CA, Sept 25, 1951.

Heather Locklear, 40, actress ("T.J. Hooker," "Dynasty," "Melrose Place"), born Los Angeles, CA, Sept 25, 1961.

Michael Madsen, 42, actor (*Species II, Donnie Brasco*), born Chicago, IL, Sept 25, 1959.

Scottie Pippen, 36, basketball player, born Hamburg, AR, Sept 25, 1965.

Christopher Reeve, 49, actor (*Superman*), born New York, NY, Sept 25, 1952.

Philip Francis (Phil) Rizzuto, 84, Baseball Hall of Fame shortstop, born New York, NY, Sept 25, 1917.

September 2001

S	M	T	W	T	F	S
						1
2	3	4	5	6	7	8
9	10	11	12	13	14	15
16	17	18	19	20	21	22
23	24	25	26	27	28	29
30						

Will Smith, 33, actor (*Independence Day*, "The Fresh Prince of Bel-Air"), singer, born Philadelphia, PA, Sept 25, 1968.
Robert Walden, 58, actor ("Lou Grant," *All the King's Men*), born New York, NY, Sept 25, 1943.
Barbara Walters, 70, journalist, interviewer, TV host ("20/20"), born Boston, MA, Sept 25, 1931.
Catherine Zeta-Jones, 32, actress (*The Mask of Zorro*), born Swansea, Glamorgan, Wales, Sept 25, 1969.

SEPTEMBER 26 — WEDNESDAY
Day 269 — 96 Remaining

APPLESEED, JOHNNY: BIRTH ANNIVERSARY. Sept 26, 1774. John Chapman, better known as Johnny Appleseed, believed to have been born at Leominster, MA, Sept 26, 1774. Died at Allen County, IN, Mar 11, 1845. Planter of orchards and friend of wild animals, he was regarded as a great medicine man by the Indians.

BATTLE OF MEUSE–ARGONNE FOREST: ANNIVERSARY. Sept 26, 1918. As part of four major efforts to break the Hindenburg line, a Franco-American offensive began on this date, with the US First Army striking between the Meuse River and the Argonne Forest and the French Fourth Army to their west. After four taxing weeks of attack, the Germans were gradually pushed back. By Oct 31, the Americans had advanced 10 miles, the French had reached the Aisne River 20 miles away and the Argonne Forest was rid of the Central Power forces. This was the final great battle of World War I.

BEATLES LAST ALBUM RELEASED: ANNIVERSARY. Sept 26, 1969. The Beatles' 13th album, *Abbey Road*, was released in the United Kingdom on this date. The album zoomed to number one on the record charts and stayed there for 11 weeks. It was the last album the Beatles made together.

"THE BEVERLY HILLBILLIES" TV PREMIERE: ANNIVERSARY. Sept 26, 1962. This half-hour comedy was one of the most successful "rural" comedies on TV; in addition, according to Nielsen, the eight most-watched half-hour shows are episodes of this series. "The Beverly Hillbillies" was about an Appalachian man, Jed Clampett (Buddy Ebsen) who found oil on his property, so he moved his family to a better life in Beverly Hills, CA. Most of its jokes were based on its fish-out-of-water premise. Also in the cast were Irene Ryan as Granny, Jed's mother-in-law, Donna Douglas as his daughter Elly May, Max Baer, Jr as his nephew Jethro Bodine, Raymond Bailey as neurotic Milburn Drysdale, Jed's neighbor and the owner of the bank where Jed kept his money, Nancy Kulp as Jane Hathaway, Drysdale's secretary and right-hand-woman and Harriet MacGibbon as Margaret Drysdale, Milburn's wife.

BLACK WALNUT FESTIVAL. Sept 26–29. Stockton, MO. 40th annual. Tours of the largest, in fact the only, black walnut processing plant in the world. Also included are a parade, craft demonstrations, queen contest, carnival and musical entertainment. Est attendance: 12,000. For info: Stockton Area Chamber of Commerce, PO Box 410, Stockton, MO 65785. Phone: (417) 276-5213.

"THE BRADY BUNCH" TV PREMIERE: ANNIVERSARY. Sept 26, 1969. This popular sitcom starred Robert Reed as widower Mike Brady who has three sons and is married to Carol (played by Florence Henderson), who has three daughters. Housekeeper Alice was played by Ann B. Davis. Sons Greg (Barry Williams), Peter (Christopher Knight) and Bobby (Mike Lookinland) and daughters Marcia (Maureen McCormick), Jan (Eve Plumb) and Cindy (Susan Olsen) experienced the typical crises of youth. The program steered clear of social issues and portrayed childhood as a time of innocence. The last episode was telecast on Aug 30, 1974. The program continues to be popular in reruns in the after-school time slot. There were also many spin-offs: "The Brady Kids" (1972–74), a Saturday morning cartoon; "The Brady Bunch Hour" (1976–77), a variety series; "The Brady Brides" (1981), a sitcom about the two older daughters adjusting to marriage and "The Bradys" (1990), a short-lived dramatic series. *A Very Brady Christmas* (1988) was CBS's highest rated special for the season. In 1995, *The Brady Bunch Movie* appealed to fans who had watched the program 25 years before.

DONIZETTI'S "LUCIA DI LAMMERMOOR" PREMIERE: ANNIVERSARY. Sept 26, 1835. *Lucia di Lammermoor*, one of opera's greatest tragic love stories, premiered in Naples, Italy. The opera was composed by Gaetano Donizetti with a libretto by Salvatore Cammarano. The plot was based on Sir Walter Scott's *The Bride of Lammermoor* and takes place in 17th-century Scotland. Lucia, thwarted by a blood feud from marrying the man she loves, kills her husband and then herself.

ELIOT, T.S.: BIRTH ANNIVERSARY. Sept 26, 1888. Thomas Stearns Eliot, Nobel Prize winner, poet, playwright and critic, was born at St. Louis, MO. "There never was a time," he believed, "when those that read at all, read so many more books by living authors than books by dead authors; there never was a time so completely parochial, so shut off from the past." Eliot died at London, England, Jan 4, 1965.

FIRST TELEVISED PRESIDENTIAL DEBATE: ANNIVERSARY. Sept 26, 1960. The debate between presidential candidates John F. Kennedy and Richard Nixon was televised from a Chicago TV studio.

GERSHWIN, GEORGE: BIRTH ANNIVERSARY. Sept 26, 1898. American composer remembered for his many enduring songs and melodies, including: "The Man I Love," "Strike Up the Band," "Funny Face," "I Got Rhythm" and the opera *Porgy and Bess*. Many of his works were in collaboration with his brother, Ira. Born at Brooklyn, NY, he died of a brain tumor at Beverly Hills, CA, July 11, 1937. See also: "Gershwin, Ira: Birth Anniversary" (Dec 6).

"GILLIGAN'S ISLAND" TV PREMIERE: ANNIVERSARY. Sept 26, 1964. Seven people set sail aboard the *Minnow* for a three-hour tour and became stranded on an island. They used the resources on the island for food, shelter and entertainment. The cast included Bob Denver as Gilligan, Alan Hale, Jr, as the Skipper, Jim Backus as Thurston Howell III, Natalie Schafer as Mrs "Lovey" Howell, Russell Johnson as the Professor, Dawn Wells as Mary Ann and Tina Louise as Ginger Grant, the movie star. The last telecast aired on Sept 4, 1967.

"KNIGHT RIDER" TV PREMIERE: ANNIVERSARY. Sept 26, 1982. David Hasselhoff starred in this one-hour adventure series about a cop who was nearly killed, then brought back to life with a new identity (Michael Knight) by a mysterious millionaire. Together with a car that talked, a Pontiac Trans Am called KITT (Knight Industries Two Thousand), Knight had various adventures. Other cast members included: Edward Mulhare as Devon Miles, aide to the deceased millionaire, Patricia McPherson as mechanic Bonnie Barstow, Rebecca Holden as April Curtis, William Daniels as the voice of KITT and Peter Parros as Reginald Cornelius III, truck driver/chauffeur for KITT.

NATIONAL FOOD SERVICE EMPLOYEES DAY. Sept 26. To promote public awareness of the contributions and importance of food service employees to life in America. Annually, the Wednesday of National Food Service Employees Week. For info: Women and Infants Hospital of Rhode Island, Dietary Dept, 101 Dudley St, Providence, RI 02908.

POPE PAUL VI: BIRTH ANNIVERSARY. Sept 26, 1897. Giovanni Battista Montini, 262nd pope of the Roman Catholic Church, born at Concesio, Italy. Elected pope June 21, 1963. Died at Castel Gandolfo, near Rome, Italy, Aug 6, 1978.

"ROBIN HOOD" TV PREMIERE: ANNIVERSARY. Sept 26, 1955. This series was officially titled "The Adventures of Robin Hood" and told the story of the British hero who led a group of outlaws to steal from the rich and give to the poor. Many episodes focused on Robin Hood and his enemy, Prince John, the evil ruler of Nottingham. Cast included Richard Greene as Robin Hood, Alexander Gauge as Friar Tuck, Archie Duncan and Rufus Cruikshank as Little John, Bernadette O'Farrell and Patricia Driscoll as Maid Marian, Paul Eddington and Brian Alexis as Will Scarlett, Alan Wheatley as the Sheriff of Nottingham and Donald Pleasence as Prince John.

SHAMU'S BIRTHDAY: ANNIVERSARY. Sept 26, 1985. Shamu was born at Sea World at Orlando, FL and is the first killer whale born in captivity to survive. Shamu is now living at Sea World's Texas park.

YOM KIPPUR BEGINS AT SUNDOWN. Sept 26. Jewish Day of Atonement. See "Yom Kippur" (Sept 27).

BIRTHDAYS TODAY

Lynn Anderson, 54, singer ("Rose Garden"), born Grand Forks, ND, Sept 26, 1947.

Melissa Sue Anderson, 39, actress ("Little House on the Prairie"), born Berkeley, CA, Sept 26, 1962.

Bryan Ferry, 56, lead singer (Roxy Music, "Heart on My Sleeve"), songwriter, born Durham, England, Sept 26, 1945.

Linda Hamilton, 44, actress (*Terminator, Terminator 2*), born Salisbury, MD, Sept 26, 1957.

Mary Beth Hurt, 53, actress (*The World According to Garp, Six Degrees of Separation*), born Marshalltown, IA, Sept 26, 1948.

Olivia Newton-John, 53, singer ("Physical"), actress (*Grease*), born Cambridge, England, Sept 26, 1948.

Christine T. Whitman, 55, Governor of New Jersey (R), born New York, NY, Sept 26, 1946.

Serena Williams, 20, tennis player, born Saginaw, MI, Sept 26, 1981.

September 2001	S	M	T	W	T	F	S
							1
	2	3	4	5	6	7	8
	9	10	11	12	13	14	15
	16	17	18	19	20	21	22
	23	24	25	26	27	28	29
	30						

SEPTEMBER 27 — THURSDAY
Day 270 — 95 Remaining

ADAMS, SAMUEL: BIRTH ANNIVERSARY. Sept 27, 1722. Revolutionary leader and Massachusetts state politician Samuel Adams, cousin to President John Adams (1797–1801), was born at Boston. He died there Oct 2, 1803. As a delegate to the First and Second Continental Congresses Adams urged a vigorous stand against England. He signed the Declaration of Independence and the Articles of Confederation and supported the war for independence. Adams served as lieutenant governor of Massachusetts under John Hancock from 1789 to 1793 and then as governor until 1797.

ANCESTOR APPRECIATION DAY. Sept 27. A day to learn about and appreciate one's forebears. For info: W.D. Chase, A.A.D. Assn, PO Box 3, Montague, MI 49437-0003.

BATTLE OF CAMBRAI–SAINT QUENTIN: ANNIVERSARY. Sept 27, 1918. British General Sir Douglas Haig moved his armies toward Cambrai and St. Quentin as part of four major efforts to break the Hindenburg line in the German salient that extended from Verdun to the sea. To the south the New Zealand and Canadian divisions smashed through the Hindenburg line on Oct 6. German General Erich Ludendorff resigned Oct 16, and the line was taken between Oct 18 and 20.

CONRAD, WILLIAM: BIRTH ANNIVERSARY. Sept 27, 1920. Actor, best known for his roles in the TV series "Cannon" and "Jake and the Fat Man." Born at Louisville, KY, and died at North Hollywood, CA, Feb 11, 1994.

CRUIKSHANK, GEORGE: BIRTH ANNIVERSARY. Sept 27, 1792. English illustrator, especially known for caricatures and for illustration of Charles Dickens's books. Born at London, England and died there Feb 1, 1878.

FALL BLUEGRASS FESTIVAL. Sept 27–30. Spirit of the Suwannee Music Park, Live Oak, FL. Weekend filled with bluegrass music and other great activities. Est attendance: 7,000. For info: James Cornett, Spirit of Suwannee Music Park, 3076 95th Dr, Live Oak, FL 32060. Phone: (904) 364-1683. Fax: (904) 364-2998. E-mail: spirit@musicliveshere.com. Web: www.music liveshere.com.

NAST, THOMAS: BIRTH ANNIVERSARY. Sept 27, 1840. American political cartoonist born at Landau, Germany, best known for his cartoons attacking New York's Tweed ring. Died Dec 7, 1902, at Guayaquil, Ecuador.

OHIO PUMPKIN FESTIVAL. Sept 27–30. Downtown Barnesville, OH. This 38th annual festival features King Pumpkin contest, Queen Pageant, Giant Pumpkin Parade, classic car show, banjo & fiddle contest and more. Annually, the last full weekend of September. Est attendance: 100,000. For info: Eugene "Doc" Householder, President, Ohio Pumpkin Festival, Inc, PO Box 5, Barnesville, OH 43713. Phone: (740) 695-4359. Fax: (740) 695-6437. E-mail: beltour@aol.com.

PRESTON COUNTY BUCKWHEAT FESTIVAL. Sept 27–30. Kingwood, WV. Celebrating the fall harvest, with coronations, parades, exhibits, arts and crafts, antique cars, livestock, carnival, country music and Buckwheat Cake Dinners. Annually, beginning the last Thursday in September. Est attendance: 100,000. For info: Lucille H. Crogan, Fest Secy, Kingwood Volunteer Fire Dept, PO Box 74, Kingwood, WV 26537. Phone: (304) 329-0021. Fax: (304) 329-0021.

SAINT VINCENT DE PAUL: FEAST DAY. Sept 27. French priest, patron of charitable organizations, and co-founder of the Sisters of Charity. Canonized 1737 (lived 1581?–1660).

SEMMES, RAPHAEL: BIRTH ANNIVERSARY. Sept 27, 1809. Born at St. Charles County, MD, and died Aug 30, 1877, at Mobile, AL. Daring Confederate naval officer, best known for his incredible raids on Union merchant ships during the middle two years of the Civil War. As commander of the *Alabama*, he captured, sank or burned 82 Union ships valued at more than $6,000,000.

SPACE MILESTONE: *SOYUZ 12* (USSR). Sept 27, 1973. Because of the death of the crew of *Soyuz 11* upon reentry, it was decided that cosmonauts must wear pressurized space suits on takeoff and landing. Thus there was no longer room for three cosmonauts on a flight. Two Soviet cosmonauts (V.G. Lazarev and O.G. Makarov) made the two-day flight launched on this date.

STATE FAIR OF VIRGINIA ON STRAWBERRY HILL. Sept 27–Oct 7. Richmond, VA. The pride of Virginia's industry of agriculture can be seen in more than 3,000 exhibitions, competitions and shows. Virginia's greatest annual educational and entertainment event. Est attendance: 600,000. For info: Keith T. Hessey, Genl Mgr, PO Box 26805, Richmond, VA 23261-6805. Phone: (804) 569-3200. Fax: (804) 569-3252. Web: www.state fair.com.

"THE TONIGHT SHOW" TV PREMIERE: ANNIVERSARY. Sept 27, 1954. "The Tonight Show" has gone through numerous changes over the years it has aired, yet it has remained a top-rated show that set the standards for all variety/talk shows to come. Steve Allen served as host from 1954–57. He introduced the format of the show with an opening monologue, games or segments for the studio audience, and then the interview on a simple desk and couch set. Jack Paar hosted from 1957–62 and Johnny Carson reigned as the king of comedy from 1962–92. Comedian Jay Leno serves as its current host.

WARREN COMMISSION REPORT: ANNIVERSARY. Sept 27, 1964. On this day, the Warren Commission issued a report stating that Lee Harvey Oswald acted alone in the assassination of President John F. Kennedy on Nov 22, 1963. Congress reopened the investigation and in 1979 the House Select Committee on Assassinations issued a report stating a conspiracy was most likely involved. See also: "Committee on Assassinations Report: Anniversary" (Mar 29).

WORLD BEEF EXPO. Sept 27–30. Milwaukee, WI. World class cattle shows and sales representing 15 beef cattle breeds. Trade show featuring agribusinesses catering to the beef industry. Also includes activities for children and adults, such as Taste of Beef, Microbrewery Sampling, Scarecrow Stuffing and Kids Corral. Est attendance: 50,000. For info: Wisconsin State Fair Park, World Beef Expo, 8100 W Greenfield Ave, PO Box 14990, West Allis, WI 53214-0990. Phone: (800) 884-FAIR or (414)266-7000. Web: www.wsfp.state.wi.us.

YOM KIPPUR or DAY OF ATONEMENT. Sept 27. Holiest Jewish observance. A day for fasting, repentance and seeking forgiveness. Hebrew calendar date: Tishri 10, 5762.

BIRTHDAYS TODAY

Wilford Brimley, 67, actor (*Cocoon*, "Our House"), born Salt Lake City, UT, Sept 27, 1934.

Shaun Cassidy, 42, singer ("Da Doo Ron Ron"), actor ("The Hardy Boys," "General Hospital"), born Los Angeles, CA, Sept 27, 1959.

Claude Jarman, Jr, 67, actor (*The Yearling, Rio Grande*), born Nashville, TN, Sept 27, 1934.

Stephan Jenkins, 36, musician (Third Eye Blind), born Southern CA, Sept 27, 1965.

Steve Kerr, 36, basketball player, born Beirut, Lebanon, Sept 27, 1965.

Jayne Meadows, 77, actress ("I've Got a Secret," "The Steve Allen Show," *Lady in the Lake*), born Chang, China, Sept 27, 1924.

Meat Loaf (Marvin Lee Aday), 54, singer, musician (*The Rocky Horror Picture Show*), born Dallas, TX, Sept 27, 1947.

Arthur Heller Penn, 79, filmmaker (*Bonnie and Clyde, The Miracle Worker*), born Philadelphia, PA, Sept 27, 1922.

Michael Jack (Mike) Schmidt, 52, Baseball Hall of Fame third baseman, born Dayton, OH, Sept 27, 1949.

Delores Taylor, 62, actress, writer, producer (*Billy Jack, The Trial of Billy Jack*), born Winner, SD, Sept 27, 1939.

Sada Thompson, 72, actress (*Twigs*, "Family"), born Des Moines, IA, Sept 27, 1929.

SEPTEMBER 28 — FRIDAY
Day 271 — 94 Remaining

CABRILLO DAY: ANNIVERSARY OF DISCOVERY OF CALIFORNIA. Sept 28, 1542. California. Commemorates discovery of California by Portuguese navigator Juan Rodriguez Cabrillo who reached San Diego Bay. Cabrillo died at San Miguel Island, CA, Jan 3, 1543. His birth date is unknown. The Cabrillo National Monument marks his landfall and Cabrillo Day is still observed in California (in some areas on the Saturday nearest Sept 28).

CAPP, AL: BIRTH ANNIVERSARY. Sept 28, 1909. The creator of the fictitious village of Dogpatch, KY, Al Capp was born Alfred Gerald Caplin at New Haven, CT. The comic strip "Li'l Abner" appeared in daily newspapers from 1934 until its final episode was published Nov 13, 1977. Along with the misadventures of Abner Yokum, Capp lampooned famous public figures. The minor American institution of "Sadie Hawkins Day" made its debut in "Li'l Abner." Al Capp died Nov 5, 1979, at Cambridge, MA.

CRAFTSMEN'S CLASSIC ARTS & CRAFTS FESTIVAL. Sept 28–30 (tentative). Roanoke Civic Center, Roanoke, VA. Arts and crafts. Est attendance: 20,000. For info: Gilmore Enterprises, Inc, 1240 Oakland Ave, Greensboro, NC 27403. Phone: (336) 274-5550. Fax: (336) 274-1084.

FABULOUS 1890s WEEKEND. Sept 28–29. Mansfield, PA. Night football in America began in 1892 with a game between Mansfield University and Wyoming Seminary. Annually, Mansfield celebrates a "Fabulous 1890s Weekend" to commemorate the event. Motorless parade, period exhibits, crafts and other events, including the re-creation of the first night football game. Sponsors: Mansfield University of Pennsylvania and Greater Area Mansfield Chamber of Commerce. Est attendance: 10,000. For info: Dennis Miller, Dir PR, Mansfield University, Mansfield, PA 16933. Phone: (570) 662-4293. Fax: (570) 662-4965. E-mail: dmiller@mnsfld.edu. Web: www.mansfield.edu.

FAIRMOUNT MUSEUM DAYS/REMEMBERING JAMES DEAN FESTIVAL. Sept 28–30. Fairmount, IN. The town where James Dean grew up honors Dean and other celebrated former citizens such as Jim Davis, creator of Garfield, journalist Phil Jones and Robert Sheets, retired director of the National Hurricane Center. The Fairmount Museum boasts "the Authentic James Dean Exhibit" of memorabilia and personal items of Dean's and it sponsors the festival that also includes a parade, James Dean Look-Alike Contest, custom car show featuring the James Dean Run for pre-1970 autos, Garfield Cat Photo and Art Contest, Garfield Great Run, carnival, booths, live '50s entertainment and more. Annually, the last full weekend in September. Est attendance: 45,000. For info: Fairmount Historical Museum, Inc, 203 E Washington St, PO Box 92, Fairmount, IN 46928. Phone: (765) 948-4555. Web: www.jamesdeanartifacts.com.

FIRST NIGHT FOOTBALL GAME: ANNIVERSARY. Sept 28, 1892. The first night football game in America was played between Mansfield State Normal School (now Mansfield University) and Wyoming Seminary.

"HAZEL" TV PREMIERE: 40th ANNIVERSARY. Sept 28, 1961. "Hazel" was based on a comic strip of the same name about a maid working for the Baxter family who gets into everyone's business. Hazel was played by Shirley Booth, and the Baxters were played by Don DeFore, Whitney Blake and Bobby Buntrock. "Hazel" moved from NBC to CBS after the third season and Hazel switched families from George to younger brother, Steve Baxter. These Baxters were played by Ray Fulmer, Lynn Borden and Julia Benjamin. Buntrock and Booth remained. This very successful series also featured Mala Powers and Ann Jillian.

LAVITSEF. Sept 28–30. City-wide, Norfolk, NE. Concerts, pet show, quilt show, pancake feed, craft fair, softball/basketball tournaments, sand volleyball, ice cream social, museum events. Parade at 10 AM on Saturday. Est attendance: 10,000. For info: Lavitsef, Inc, PO Box 1512, Norfolk, NE 68702-1512.

MASTROIANNI, MARCELLO: BIRTH ANNIVERSARY. Sept 28, 1924. Actor (*White Nights, Yesterday, Today and Tomorrow*), born at Fontana Liri, Italy. Died at Paris, France, Dec 19, 1996.

MOUNT PLEASANT GLASS & ETHNIC FESTIVAL. Sept 28–30. Mount Pleasant, PA. Large outdoor street festival featuring glass blowing demos, arts and crafts, parade, entertainment and ethnic foods. Entertainment on two stages, a carnival and unique activities. Est attendance: 45,000. For info: Jeff Landy, Mount Pleasant Glass and Ethnic Festival, Municipal Bldg, Mt Pleasant, PA 15666. Phone: (724) 547-7738. Fax: (724) 547-0115.

OHIO SWISS FESTIVAL. Sept 28–29. Sugarcreek, OH. Swiss music, games, costumes, parades. Continuous entertainment and tons of Swiss cheese. Annually, the fourth Friday and Saturday following Labor Day. Est attendance: 50,000. For info: Patricia Kaser, Info Coord, Ohio Swiss Festival, PO Box 158, Sugarcreek, OH 44681. Phone: (330) 852-4113.

OKTOBERFEST. Sept 28–Oct 6. LaCrosse, WI. German fall festival featuring family events, live entertainment, lots of food, Torchlight Parade on Thursday night and Maple Leaf Parade on Saturday. Fun for the whole family. For info: Tour/Member Serv Coord, LaCrosse Area Conv & Visitors Bureau, 410 Veterans Memorial Dr, LaCrosse, WI 54601. Phone: (800) 658-9424. E-mail: info@explorelacrosse.com. Web: www.explorelacrosse.com.

PACIFIC RIM ART EXPOSITION. Sept 28–30. Seattle Center Exhibition Hall, Seattle, WA. Wildlife, western, landscape, all genres and fine art by some of the most renowned artists in North America. The show offers booth sale and auction pieces and informative seminars for the entire family. Annually, the last weekend in September. Est attendance: 10,000. For info: Bob Farrelly, PO Box 11225, Tacoma, WA 98411.

STATE FAIR OF TEXAS. Sept 28–Oct 21. Fair Park, Dallas, TX. Features a Broadway musical, college football games, new car show, concerts, livestock shows and traditional events and entertainment including exhibits, creative arts and parades. Est attendance: 3,500,000. For info: Nancy Wiley, State Fair of Texas, PO Box 150009, Dallas, TX 75315. Phone: (214) 421-8716. Fax: (214) 421-8710. E-mail: pr@greatstatefair.com. Web: www.bigtex.com.

SULLIVAN, ED: 100th BIRTH ANNIVERSARY. Sept 28, 1901. Known as the "King of TV Variety," born at New York, NY. Sullivan started his media career in 1932 as a sportswriter for the *Daily News* in New York. His popular variety show, "The Ed Sullivan Show" ("Toast of the Town"), ran from 1948 until 1971. It included such sensational acts as Elvis Presley and the Beatles. He died at New York, NY, Oct 13, 1974.

TACA FALL CRAFTS FAIR. Sept 28–30. Centennial Park, Nashville, TN. Festival of fine crafts featuring 170 selected American craft artists. 23rd annual fair. Annually, the last weekend in September. Est attendance: 35,000. For info: Alice C. Merritt, Exec Dir, Tennessee Assn of Craft Artists, PO Box 120066, Nashville, TN 37212. Phone: (615) 665-0502.

TAIWAN: CONFUCIUS'S BIRTHDAY AND TEACHERS' DAY. Sept 28. National holiday, designated as Teachers' Day. Confucius is the Latinized name of Kung-futzu, born at Shantung province on the 27th day of the tenth moon (lunar calendar) in the 22nd year of Kuke Hsiang of Lu (551 BC). He died at age 72, having spent some 40 years as a teacher. Teachers' Day is observed annually on Sept 28.

VIRGINIA BEACH NEPTUNE FESTIVAL. Sept 28–30. Virginia Beach, VA. A major mid-Atlantic regional festival. Events include sand sculpture contests, a parade, wine-tasting, sport events and more. Est attendance: 750,000. For info: Virginia Beach Neptune Festival, 265 Kings Grant Rd, #102, Virginia Beach, VA 23452. Phone: (757) 498-0215.

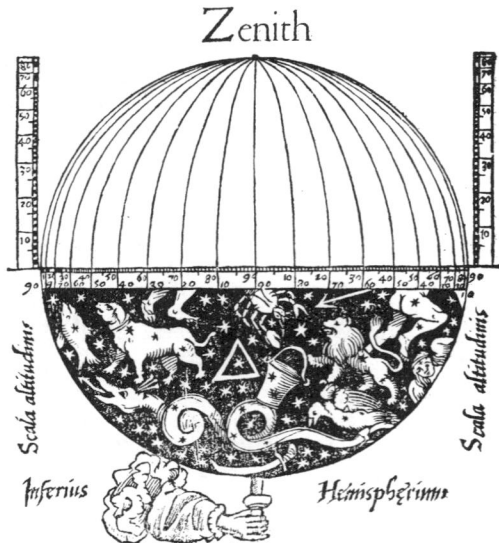

WIGGIN, KATE DOUGLAS: BIRTH ANNIVERSARY. Sept 28, 1856. Kate Wiggin was born Kate Douglas Smith at Philadelphia, PA. She helped organize the first free kindergarten on the West Coast in 1878 at San Francisco and in 1880 she and her sister established the California Kindergarten Training School. After moving back to the east coast she devoted herself to writing, producing a number of children's books including *The Birds' Christmas Carol, Polly Oliver's Problem* and *Rebecca of Sunnybrook Farm.* She died at Harrow, England, Aug 24, 1923.

WILLARD, FRANCES ELIZABETH CAROLINE: BIRTH ANNIVERSARY. Sept 28, 1839. American educator and reformer, president of the Women's Christian Temperance Union, 1879–98, and women's suffrage leader, born at Churchville, NY. Died at New York, NY, Feb 18, 1898.

BIRTHDAYS TODAY

Brigitte Bardot (Camille Javal), 67, actress (*And God Created Woman, Viva Maria*), animal rights activist, born Paris, France, Sept 28, 1934.

Jerry Clower, 75, comedian ("Nashville on the Road"), born Liberty, MS, Sept 28, 1926.

Janeane Garofalo, 37, actress (*Reality Bites, The Truth About Cats and Dogs*), born Newton, NJ, Sept 28, 1964.

Jeffrey Jones, 54, actor (*Beetlejuice, Stay Tuned*), born Buffalo, NY, Sept 28, 1947.

Ben E. King, 63, singer, musician ("There Goes My Baby"), born Henderson, NC, Sept 28, 1938.

Steve M. Largent, 47, Pro Football Hall of Fame wide receiver, born Tulsa, OK, Sept 28, 1954.

Se Ri Pak, 24, golfer, born Daejeon, South Korea, Sept 28, 1977.

Gwyneth Paltrow, 28, actress (*Emma, Shakespeare in Love*), born Los Angeles, CA, Sept 28, 1973.

William Windom, 78, actor (Emmy for "My World and Welcome to It," "Murder She Wrote"), born New York, NY, Sept 28, 1923.

	S	M	T	W	T	F	S
September							1
2001	2	3	4	5	6	7	8
	9	10	11	12	13	14	15
	16	17	18	19	20	21	22
	23	24	25	26	27	28	29
	30						

SEPTEMBER 29 — SATURDAY

Day 272 — 93 Remaining

AUTUMN IN THE LUDINGTON HARBOR AREA. Sept 29–Oct 31. Ludington, MI. Pumpkin patch, haunted fairground, hayrides, haunted Coast Guard Station, Applefest, Moonlight Madness Sale. Events are held at different times and locations, so call or write for specifics. Est attendance: 12,000. For info: Ludington Area Chamber of Commerce, 5827 W US 10, Ludington, MI 49431. Phone: (800) 842-4600. Fax: (231) 845-6857. E-mail: visitlud@carrinter.net. Web: www.ludingtoncvb.com.

BUFFALO ROUNDUP ARTS FESTIVAL. Sept 29–Oct 1. Custer, SD. South Dakota artists and craftsmen display and sell their arts and crafts. Also Western and Native American entertainment, pancake feeds, chili cookoff and much more. Est attendance: 8,000. For info: Craig Pugsley, Visitor Services Coord, Custer State Park, HC 83, Box 70, Custer, SD 57730. Phone: (605) 255-4515. Fax: (605) 255-4460. E-mail: craig.pugsley@state.sd.us.

CANDY DANCE. Sept 29–30. Genoa, NV. One of Nevada's first permanent settlements sells homemade candy instead of raising taxes to pay for improvements in the tiny community. The ingenuity shown by Genoa's town fathers has created one of the area's most popular events, which features food and an extensive fine arts and crafts show. For info: Phone: (775) 782-TOWN.

DOLLYWOOD HARVEST CELEBRATION. Sept 29–Oct 29. Dollywood, Pigeon Forge, TN. The oldest, largest and only authentic outdoor harvest festival comes alive to celebrate the fall season in the Smokies. For info: Dollywood, 1020 Dollywood Ln, Pigeon Forge, TN 37863. Phone: (865) 428-9488 or (800) DOLLYWOOD.

DYERSVILLE FESTIVAL OF THE ARTS. Sept 29–30. Beckman High School, Dyersville, IA. The "Farm Toy Capital of the World," near the film site of the movie *Field of Dreams*. Features the Dyersville Quilt & Craft Show, with hundreds of quilts and hundreds of crafts, all handmade. Dance, entertainment and food. Annually, the last full weekend in September. Est attendance: 4,000. For info: Dyersville Area Chamber of Commerce, 1100 16th Ave Ct SE, Dyersville, IA 52040. Phone: (319) 875-2311. Fax: (319) 875-8391. E-mail: dyersvillechamber@dyersville.org. Web: www.dyersville.org.

ENGLAND: SCOTLAND YARD: FIRST APPEARANCE ANNIVERSARY. Sept 29, 1829. The first public appearance of Greater London's Metropolitan Police occurred amid jeering and abuse from disapproving political opponents. Public sentiment turned to confidence and respect in the ensuing years. The Metropolitan Police had been established by an act of Parliament in June 1829, at the request of Home Secretary Sir Robert Peel, after whom the London police officers became more affectionately known as "bobbies." Scotland Yard, the site of their first headquarters near Charing Cross, soon became the official name of the force.

EVERYBODY'S DAY FESTIVAL. Sept 29. Thomasville, NC. A true hometown street festival for "everybody." Crafts, food vendors and live entertainment. Est attendance: 45,000. For info: Thomasville Area Chamber of Commerce, Box 1400, Thomasville, NC 27361. Phone: (336) 475-6134. Fax: (336) 475-4802. E-mail: tvillecoc@infoave.net. Web: www.thomasvillenc.net.

FALL FESTIVAL OF THE ARTS AND CRAFTS. Sept 29–30. Washington, MO. Juried festival featuring the creative talents of two- and three-dimensional artists and crafters. Free children's area, beer and wine garden, specialty foods, music and live entertainment. For info: Downtown Washington, Inc, PO Box 144, Washington, MO 63090. Phone: (636) 239-1743. Fax: (636) 239-4832. Web: downtownwashmo.com.

FALLASBURG FALL FESTIVAL. Sept 29–30. Fallasburg Park, Lowell, MI. A unique event that develops the potential of an extraordinary historical setting. 75 artists display their wares at the west end of Fallasburg Park spanning the Flat River. Annually, the last full weekend of September. Est attendance: 40,000. For info: Lowell Area Arts Council, 149 S Hudson St, Lowell, MI 49331. Phone: (616) 897-8545. Fax: (616) 897-3061. E-mail: lowellartscouncil@ameritech.net.

FAMILY HEALTH AND FITNESS—USA. Sept 29–30. Fifth annual national event promoting family health and fitness. During this weekend, families across the country will be involved in locally organized health promotion activities at more than 800 locations. Always held the last weekend in September. Est attendance: 80,000. For info: Pat Henze, Program Mgr, Health Info Resource Center, 1850 W Winchester Rd, Ste 213, Libertyville, IL 60048. Phone: (800) 828-8225. Fax: (847) 816-8662. E-mail: hlthinfo@aol.com. Web: www.fitnessday.com.

FERMI, ENRICO: 100th BIRTH ANNIVERSARY. Sept 29, 1901. Nuclear physicist, born at Rome, Italy. Played a prominent role in the splitting of the atom and the construction of the first American nuclear reactor. Died at Chicago, IL, Nov 28, 1954.

FESTIVAL OF QUILTS. Sept 29–30. Curry County Fairgrounds, Gold Beach, OR. Est attendance: 1,000. For info: Gold Beach Chamber of Commerce, 29279 Ellensburg Ave, #3, Gold Beach, OR 97444. Phone: (541) 247-7377 or (541) 247-9003. Fax: (541) 247-0188. E-mail: goldbeach@harborside.com. Web: www.goldbeach.org.

GENEVA AREA GRAPE JAMBOREE. Sept 29–30. Geneva, OH. Grape harvest and products. 36th annual Jamboree. Annually, the last full weekend in September. Est attendance: 250,000. For info: Geneva Grape Jamboree, Box 92, Geneva, OH 44041. Phone: (440) 466-5262. E-mail: gojamb@ncweb.com. Web: www.ncweb.com/org/grape.

GOOSE DAY. Sept 29. Lewistown, PA. Traditionally based on Michaelmas Day, the religious holiday on which the Feast of St. Michael and All Angels is celebrated, Goose Day began as a day of honor and respect for the Archangel Michael, prince of guardian angels. Today, Central Pennsylvanians everywhere go out of their way to indulge themselves in a good goose dinner, heeding the old English proverb: "If you eat goose on Michaelmas Day, you will never want money all the year round." Annually, Sept 29. For info: Juniata Valley Area Chamber of Commerce, 152 E Market St, Lewistown, PA 17044. Phone: (717) 248-6713. Fax: (717) 248-6714. E-mail: jvacc@acsworld.net.

HERITAGE DAY. Sept 29. Houston, MO. Dutch Oven cook-off, Fiddle & Jig contest, arts & crafts, demonstrations of old-time crafts. For info: Houston Area Chamber of Commerce, 111 W Main, Houston, MO 65483. Phone: (417) 967-2220. Fax: (417) 967-2178.

HOWARD, TREVOR: 85th BIRTH ANNIVERSARY.
Sept 29, 1916. British actor Trevor Howard was born at Cliftonville, England. He appeared in more than 70 films including *The Third Man* (1950) and *Mutiny on the Bounty* (1962). He died Jan 7, 1988, at Bushey, England.

JORDBRUKSDAGARNA (AGRICULTURAL DAYS).
Sept 29–30. Bishop Hill, IL. The utopian religious community at Bishop Hill was founded by immigrants from Sweden in 1846. This festival commemorates the founding, with harvest demonstrations, traditional crafts, games for children, music, special foods and farmer's market. For info: Bishop Hill Heritage Assn, 103 N Bishop Hill St, PO Box 92, Bishop Hill, IL 61419. Phone: (309) 927-3899.

LONG BEACH ISLAND CHOWDER COOK-OFF. Sept 29–30. Bayfront Park, Beach Haven, NJ. Weekend-long festival featuring unlimited tasting of up to 30 different red/white clam chowders prepared by area restaurants. Entertainment; other food/beverages available. Est attendance: 20,000. For info: Jeanne Di Paola, Exec Dir, Southern Ocean County Chamber of Commerce, 265 W 9th St, Ship Bottom, NJ 08008. Phone: (800) 292-6372. Fax: (609) 494-5807. E-mail: sochamberj@aol.com. Web: www.chowderfest.com/chamber.

"MAKE ROOM FOR DADDY" TV PREMIERE: ANNIVERSARY. Sept 29, 1953. Danny Thomas starred as Danny Williams, a nightclub singer and comedian, in this family sitcom. The series was renamed "The Danny Thomas Show" in 1956 after Jean Hagen (who played his wife, Margaret) left the show. Many cast members returned for the show's sequel, "Make Room for Granddaddy" in 1970. Thomas's co-stars were: Sherry Jackson and Penney Parker as Danny's daughter Terry, Rusty Hamer as son Rusty, Amanda Randolph as housekeeper Louise, Horace McMahon as Danny's agent, Phil Arnold, Jesse White as agent Jesse Leeds, Sid Melton as Charlie Halper, owner of the Copa Club, Ben Lessy as Danny's pianist, Ben, Mary Wickes as his publicist, Liz O'Neal, Hans Conried as Uncle Tonoose, Nan Bryant as Danny's mother-in-law and Marjorie Lord as his new wife Kathy O'Hara.

MARION COUNTY COUNTRY HAM DAYS. Sept 29–30. Lebanon, KY. Country ham breakfast, served in the streets of Lebanon. Pokey pig 10K run, a nationally certified course, PIGasus parade, antique steam and gas engine show and other specialties. Est attendance: 50,000. For info: Lebanon-Marion County Chamber of Commerce, 21 Court Sq, Lebanon, KY 40033. Phone: (502) 692-9594. Fax: (502) 692-2661. E-mail: chamber@hamdays.com. Web: www.hamdays.com.

MICHAELMAS. Sept 29. The feast of St. Michael and All Angels in the Greek and Roman Catholic Churches.

MOUNTAIN STATE FOREST FESTIVAL. Sept 29–Oct 7. Elkins, WV. Promotes the natural resources of the area with emphasis on forests. Est attendance: 100,000. For info: Mountain State Forest Festival, Box 369, Elkins, WV 26241. Phone: (304) 636-1824. Fax: (304) 636-1824.

MUSKETS IN MARYLAND. Sept 29–30. Fort Frederick State Park, Big Pool, MD. Reactivated 17th-, 18th- and 19th-century military units from several states participate in team competition. Annually, the last full weekend in September. Est attendance: 2,000. For info: Fort Frederick State Park, 11100 Fort Frederick Rd, Big Pool, MD 21711. Phone: (301) 842-2155. Fax: (301) 842-0028.

September 2001	S	M	T	W	T	F	S
							1
	2	3	4	5	6	7	8
	9	10	11	12	13	14	15
	16	17	18	19	20	21	22
	23	24	25	26	27	28	29
	30						

NELSON, HORATIO: BIRTH ANNIVERSARY. Sept 29, 1758. English naval hero of the Battle of Trafalgar, born at Burnham Thorpe, Norfolk, England. Died during a battle at sea off Cape Trafalgar, Spain, Oct 21, 1805.

OCEAN COUNTY DECOY AND GUNNING SHOW. Sept 29–30. Pinelands High & Middle Schools and Tip Seaman County Park, Tuckerton, NJ. Gathering to celebrate the local waterfowling heritage. Emphasizes traditional skills such as decoy carving, working decoy rigs, sneakbox building, gunning, retrieving and goose-calling contests. More than 500 vendors. Free rain or shine. Est attendance: 40,000. For info: Mike Mangum, PO Box 2191, Toms River, NJ 08754. Phone: (732) 270-9464. E-mail: bsteele@oceancountygov.com. Web: www.oceancountygov.com.

OCTOBERFEST. Sept 29. Lawrence University, Appleton, WI. Come enjoy a family event with ethnic foods, fun and entertainment. Annually, the last Saturday in September. Est attendance: 100,000. For info: Campus Activities, Lawrence University, PO Box 599, Appleton, WI 54912.

PANCAKE DAY. Sept 29. Centerville, IA. Free pancakes, entertainment and two-mile long parade. Est attendance: 30,000. For info: Chamber of Commerce, 128 N 12th, Centerville, IA 52544. Phone: (515) 437-4102 or (800) 611-3800. Fax: (515) 437-0527. E-mail: cntrvlle@lisco.net. Web: www.centerville-ia.com.

PUMPKIN DAY. Sept 29. Woodstock, VT. Learn about the many uses and varieties of pumpkin through activities and programs and take home a miniature pumpkin. Also harvest activities and wagon rides. For info: Billings Farm & Museum, Box 489, Woodstock, VT 05091. Phone: (802) 457-2355. Fax: (802) 457-4663. E-mail: billings.farm@valley.net.

SEPTEMBER INDIAN FEST. Sept 29–30. DeSoto Caverns Park, Childersburg, AL. 26th annual event, featuring Native American dancing, singing, flute playing, storytelling and lifeways demonstrations. Arts and crafts and great food. Est attendance: 8,000. For info: DeSoto Caverns Park, DeSoto Caverns Pkwy, Childersburg, AL 35044. Phone: (205) 378-7252 or (800) 933-2283. E-mail: fun@desotocavernspark.com. Web: www.DeSotoCaverns Park.com.

SHEYENNE VALLEY ARTS & CRAFTS FESTIVAL. Sept 29–30. Fort Ransom, ND. This 34th annual festival is one of the oldest and best in the area. Artists and crafters from several states join local people in offering 150 displays, church bazaar and dinner, turkey barbecue, cavalry performance—all in a rustic historic atmosphere. Annually, the last full weekend in September. Sponsor: Sheyenne Valley Arts and Crafts Association, Inc, a non-profit organization. Est attendance: 7,500. For info: SVACA, PO Box 21, Fort Ransom, ND 58033. Phone: (701) 973-4461.

SPACE MILESTONE: *DISCOVERY* (US). Sept 29, 1988. Space Shuttle *Discovery*, after numerous reschedulings, launched from Kennedy Space Center, FL, with a five-member crew on board, and landed Oct 3 at Edwards Air Force Base, CA. It marked the first American manned flight since the Challenger tragedy in 1986. See also: "Challenger, Space Shuttle Explosion: Anniversary" (Jan 28).

SPACE MILESTONE: *SALYUT 6* (USSR). Sept 29, 1977. Soviet space station launched this date. *Salyut* stayed in space for four years, during which 31 spacecraft docked with the space station. Burned up when it re-entered Earth's atmosphere after nearly five years on July 29, 1982.

"THIRTYSOMETHING" TV PREMIERE: ANNIVERSARY. Sept 29, 1987. This ABC drama series about a group of seven baby boomers was created by Ed Zwick and Marshall Herskovitz. The show's characters were very real to many viewers who were able to identify with their struggles—such as the death of a parent, illness, singlehood, marriage, divorce, career setbacks and the birth of a child. The cast featured Ken Olin as Michael Steadman, Mel Harris as his wife, Hope, Timothy Busfield as Michael's business partner, Elliot Weston, Patricia Wettig

(Olin's real-life wife) as Elliot's wife, Nancy, Polly Draper as Hope's friend Ellyn Warren, Melanie Mayron as Michael's cousin, Melissa Steadman and Peter Horton as family friend Gary Shepherd. The last telecast was Sept 3, 1991.

TRI-STATE BAND FESTIVAL. Sept 29. Luverne, MN. 51st annual festival with more than 2,500 high school students from Minnesota, South Dakota and Iowa; trophies awarded in four classes. Annually, the last Saturday in September. Est attendance: 10,000. For info: Dave Smith, Exec Dir, Luverne Area Chamber of Commerce, 102 E Main, Luverne, MN 56156. Phone: (507) 283-4061. Fax: (507) 283-4061. Web: luvernemn.com.

TYLENOL DEATHS: ANNIVERSARY. Sept 29, 1982. On this date the first of seven deaths, including that of a 10-year-old child, occurred as a result of the individuals unknowingly taking Tylenol capsules that had been deliberately contaminated with cyanide. After a California man was poisoned taking Tylenol laced with strychnine, Johnson and Johnson, the manufacturer of the product, recalled all capsules of the pain-reliever, some 264,000 bottles. Many lawsuits resulted. The killer has never been identified.

VETERANS OF FOREIGN WARS ESTABLISHED: ANNIVERSARY. Sept 29, 1899. This organization is loyal to the issues and actions affecting America's heroes. Its members offer assistance in addition to supporting veterans issues in Congress. Part of the organization's mission, according to its charter, is "to preserve and strengthen comradeship among its members; to foster true patriotism; and to preserve and defend the United States from all her enemies, whomsoever." For info: Veterans of Foreign Wars of the United States, 406 W 34th St, Kansas City, MO 64111. Phone: (816) 756-3390. Fax: (816) 968-1129. Web: www.vfw.org.

BIRTHDAYS TODAY

Michelangelo Antonioni, 89, filmmaker (*Blowup, Zabriskie Point*), born Ferrara, Italy, Sept 29, 1912.

Anita Ekberg, 70, actress (*La Dolce Vita*), born Malmo, Sweden, Sept 29, 1931.

Bryant Gumbel, 53, TV host ("Today," "The Public Eye," "CBS This Morning"), sportscaster, born New Orleans, LA, Sept 29, 1948.

Hersey R. Hawkins, Jr, 35, basketball player, born Chicago, IL, Sept 29, 1966.

Patricia Hodge, 55, actress ("Rumpole of the Bailey," *The Elephant Man, Betrayal*), born Cleethorpes, Lincolnshire, England, Sept 29, 1946.

Jerry Lee Lewis, 66, singer, musician ("Whole Lot of Shakin' Goin' On," "Great Balls of Fire"), born Ferriday, LA, Sept 29, 1935.

Emily Lloyd, 31, actress (*Wish You Were Here, In Country, A River Runs Through It*), born North London, England, Sept 29, 1970.

Ian McShane, 59, actor ("Lovejoy," *The Last of Sheila*), born Blackburn, England, Sept 29, 1942.

John MacBeth Paxson, 41, former basketball player, born Dayton, OH, Sept 29, 1960.

Lech Walesa, 58, Poland labor leader, Solidarity founder, born Popowo, Poland, Sept 29, 1943.

SEPTEMBER 30 — SUNDAY
Day 273 — 92 Remaining

BABE SETS HOME RUN RECORD: ANNIVERSARY. Sept 30, 1927. George Herman "Babe" Ruth hit his 60th home run of the season off Tom Zachary, of the Washington Senators. Ruth's record for the most homers in a single season stood for 34 years—until Roger Maris hit 61 in 1961. Maris's record was broken in 1998 by Mark McGwire with 62 home runs.

BABE'S LAST GAME AS YANKEE: ANNIVERSARY. Sept 30, 1934. On this date Babe played his last game for the New York Yankees. Soon after, while watching the fifth game of the World Series (between St. Louis and Detroit) and angry that he was not to be named Yankees manager, Ruth told Joe Williams, sports editor of the Scripp-Howard newspapers, that after 15 seasons he would no longer be playing for the Yankees.

BOTSWANA: INDEPENDENCE DAY: 35th ANNIVERSARY. Sept 30. National holiday. The former Bechuanaland Protectorate (British Colony) became the independent Republic of Botswana in 1966.

BUFFALO WALLOW CHILI COOKOFF. Sept 30. Custer State Park, Custer, SD. Musical entertainment, art fair and lots of chili cooking and tasting. Est attendance: 4,000. For info: Custer County Chamber of Commerce, 615 Washington St, Custer, SD 57730. Phone: (800) 992-9818. Fax: (605) 673-3726.

CAPOTE, TRUMAN: BIRTH ANNIVERSARY. Sept 30, 1924. American novelist and literary celebrity, was born Truman Streckfus Persons at New Orleans, LA. He later took the name of his stepfather and became Truman Capote. Among his best-remembered books: *Other Voices, Other Rooms, Breakfast at Tiffany's* and *In Cold Blood*. He was working on a new novel, *Answered Prayers*, at the time of his death at Los Angeles, CA, Aug 25, 1984.

"CHEERS" TV PREMIERE: ANNIVERSARY. Sept 30, 1982. NBC sitcom revolving around the owner, employees and patrons of a Beacon Street bar at Boston. Original cast: Ted Danson as owner Sam Malone, Shelley Long and Rhea Perlman as waitresses Diane Chambers and Carla Tortelli, Nicholas Colasanto as bartender Ernie "Coach" Pantusso, John Ratzenberger as mailman Cliff Clavin and George Wendt as accountant Norm Peterson. Later cast members: Woody Harrelson as bartender Woody Boyd, Kelsey Grammer as Dr. Frasier Crane, Kirstie Alley as Rebecca Howe and Bebe Neuwirth as Dr. Lilith Sternin Crane. The theme song "Where Everybody Knows Your Name," was sung by Gary Portnoy and written by he and Judy Hart Angelo. Created by Glen Charles, Les Charles and James Burrows. The last episode aired Aug 19, 1993.

COUNCIL OF LOGISTICS MANAGEMENT ANNUAL CONFERENCE. Sept 30–Oct 3. Kansas City, MO. Professional development and dialogue. Est attendance: 7,000. For info: Council of Logistics Management, 2805 Butterfield Rd, Ste 200, Oak Brook, IL 60523. Phone: (630) 574-0985. Fax: (630) 574-0989. E-mail: clmadmin@clm1.org. Web: www.clm1.org.

FALL FOLIAGE FESTIVAL. Sept 30–Oct 7. Marshfield, Walden, Cabot, Plainfield, Peacham, Barnet, Groton and St. Johnsbury, VT. Eight towns welcome visitors during Vermont's famous fall foliage season. Send self-addressed stamped envelope (SASE). Est attendance: 2,500. For info: Fall Festival Committee, PO Box 54, West Danville, VT 05873. Phone: (802) 563-2472.

FEAST OF SAINT JEROME. Sept 30. Patron saint of scholars and librarians.

FESTIFALL. Sept 30. Friendship Hill National Historic Site, Point Marion, PA. To celebrate the 19th-century arts, crafts and music of the Allegheny Plateau. Historic foods are available for purchase. Tours of the Albert Gallatin house also provided. Annually, the last Sunday in September. Est attendance: 2,000. For info: Friendship Hill Natl Historic Site, RD 1 Box 149-A, Point Marion, PA 15474. Phone: (724) 725-9190. Fax: (724) 725-1999. Web: www.nps.gov/frhi/

FIRST ANNUAL FAIR IN AMERICA: ANNIVERSARY.

Sept 30, 1641. According to the Laws and Ordinances of New Netherlands (now New York and New Jersey), on Sept 30, 1641, authorities declared that "henceforth there shall be held annually at Fort Amsterdam" a Cattle Fair (Oct 15) and a Hog Fair (Nov 1), and that "whosoever hath any things to sell or buy can regulate himself accordingly."

FIRST CRIMINAL EXECUTION IN AMERICAN COLONIES: ANNIVERSARY.

Sept 30, 1630. John Billington, one of the first pilgrims to land in America, was hanged for murder, becoming the first criminal to be executed in the American Colonies.

"THE FLINTSTONES" TV PREMIERE: ANNIVERSARY.

Sept 30, 1960. This Hanna Barbera cartoon comedy was set in prehistoric times. Characters included two Stone Age families, Fred and Wilma Flintstone and neighbors Barney and Betty Rubble. In 1994 *The Flintstones* movie was released, starring John Goodman, Rick Moranis and Rosie O'Donnell.

FRYEBURG FAIR.

Sept 30–Oct 7. Rte 5, Fryeburg, ME. Agricultural exposition, draft horse competitions, oxen and horse pulling, midway, country shows each evening, harness racing, Woodsmen's Day (always Monday), tractor pulling, baking contests, Forestry Resource Center, Firemans Muster, sheep dog trials and juried crafts show. Annually, the week that includes the first Wednesday in October. Est attendance: 325,000. For info: June Hammond, Secy, PO Box 78, Fryeburg, ME 04037. Phone: (207) 935-3268. Fax: (207) 935-3662.

★ GOLD STAR MOTHER'S DAY.

Sept 30. Presidential Proclamation always for last Sunday of each September since 1936. Proclamation 2424 of Sept 14, 1940, covers all succeeding years.

GUADALUPE MOUNTAINS NATIONAL PARK ESTABLISHED: ANNIVERSARY.

Sept 30, 1972. Area in western Texas along Texas–New Mexico border, originally authorized Oct 15, 1966, was established as a national park. For further park info: Guadalupe Mountains Natl Park, HC 60, Box 400, Salt Flat, TX 79847-9400.

GUTENBERG BIBLE PUBLISHED: ANNIVERSARY.

Sept 30, 1452. The first section of the Gutenberg Bible, the first book printed from movable type, was published at Mainz, Germany. Johann Gutenberg was the printer. The book was completed by 1456.

HALEAKALA NATIONAL PARK ESTABLISHED: 85th ANNIVERSARY.

Sept 30, 1960. Summit of a volcano on Maui in the Hawaiian Islands was authorized as a part of Hawaii National Park on Aug 1, 1916. In 1960 Haleakala was established as a separate national park. The park was expanded in 1969 to include the Kipahulu Valley. For further park info: Haleakala Natl Park, PO Box 369, Makawao, HI 96768.

MEREDITH ENROLLS AT OLE MISS: ANNIVERSARY.

Sept 30, 1962. Rioting broke out when James Meredith became the first black to enroll in the all-white University of Mississippi. President Kennedy sent US troops to the area to force compliance with the law. Three people died in the fighting and 50 were injured. On June 6, 1966, Meredith was shot while participating in a civil rights march at Mississippi. On June 25 Meredith, barely recovered, rejoined the marchers near Jackson, MS.

"MURDER, SHE WROTE" TV PREMIERE: ANNIVERSARY.

Sept 30, 1984. Angela Lansbury starred as crime novelist Jessica Fletcher from Cabot Cove, Maine, who traveled the country solving murders. This top-rated detective show was unusual in having an older female star, since young men are usually preferred in leading roles on TV. Also appearing were Tom Bosley as Sheriff Amos Tupper and William Windom as Dr. Seth Hazlett. The program ran for 12 years.

NECKER, JACQUES: BIRTH ANNIVERSARY.

Sept 30, 1732. French banker and statesman, born at Geneva, Switzerland. His dismissal from his post as head of France's Department of Finance was the immediate cause of the storming of the Bastille, July 14, 1789. Necker died near Geneva, Apr 9, 1804.

NUCLEAR MEDICINE WEEK.

Sept 30–Oct 6. In recognition of the diagnostic revolution nuclear medicine has provided to the medical profession. Special events are scheduled in thousands of nuclear medicine departments and imaging centers across the US. For info: Society of Nuclear Medicine, 1850 Samuel Morse Dr, Reston, VA 22090. Phone: (703) 708-9000. Fax: (703) 708-9015.

"THE RED SKELTON SHOW" TV PREMIERE: 50th ANNIVERSARY.

Sept 30, 1951. Vaudevillian and radio performer Red Skelton hosted several popular variety shows on NBC and CBS in a career that spanned 20 years. He was a gifted comedian, famous for his loony characters, sight gags, pantomimes and ad-libs. His show was also notable for introducing Johnny Carson and the Rolling Stones to a national audience.

"TWO FOR THE MONEY" TV PREMIERE: ANNIVERSARY.

Sept 30, 1952. A prime-time quiz show from the Mark Goodson–Bill Todman production team appearing on NBC and CBS. Herb Shriner, Walter O'Keefe, Dennis James and Sam Levenson all served as hosts during the show's five-year run.

BIRTHDAYS TODAY

Deborah Allen, 48, singer ("Baby I Lied"), songwriter ("Don't Worry 'Bout Me"), born Memphis, TN, Sept 30, 1953.

Crystal Bernard, 37, actress ("Wings"), born Garland, TX, Sept 30, 1964.

Angie Dickinson (Angeline Brown), 70, actress (Emmy for "Police Woman"; *Dressed to Kill*), born Kulm, ND, Sept 30, 1931.

Fran Drescher, 44, actress ("The Nanny," *Jack*), born Flushing, NY, Sept 30, 1957.

Jenna Elfman, 30, actress ("Dharma & Greg," "Townies"), born Los Angeles, CA, Sept 30, 1971.

Martina Hingis, 21, tennis player, born Kosice, Slovakia, Sept 30, 1980.

Deborah Kerr, 80, actress (*From Here to Eternity*, *The King and I*), born Helensburgh, Scotland, Sept 30, 1921.

Blanche Lambert Lincoln, 41, US Senator (D, Arkansas), born Helena, MT, Sept 30, 1960.

Johnny Mathis, 66, singer ("It's Not for Me to Say," "Chances Are"), born San Francisco, CA, Sept 30, 1935.

Marilyn McCoo, 58, singer (Fifth Dimension, "Up, Up and Away"), actress, born Jersey City, NJ, Sept 30, 1943.

Dominique Moceanu, 20, gymnast, born Hollywood, CA, Sept 30, 1981.

Eric Stoltz, 40, actor (*Fast Times at Ridgemont High*, *Pulp Fiction*), born Los Angeles, CA, Sept 30, 1961.

Victoria Tennant, 48, actress ("Winds of War," *All of Me*, *LA Story*), born London, England, Sept 30, 1953.

October.

OCTOBER 1 — MONDAY
Day 274 — 91 Remaining

ADOPT-A-SHELTER DOG MONTH. Oct 1–31. To promote the adoption of dogs from local shelters, the ASPCA sponsors this important observance. For info: ASPCA Public Affairs Dept, 424 E 92nd St, New York, NY 10128. Phone: (212) 876-7700. E-mail: press@aspca.org. Web: www.aspca.org.

ALTERNATE HISTORY MONTH. Oct 1–31. Bookstores nationwide celebrate Alternate Histories fiction the entire month. For info: Del Rey Books, 1540 Broadway, New York, NY 10036. Phone: (212) 782-8393. Fax: (212) 782-8442.

AUTO BATTERY SAFETY MONTH. Oct 1–31. How to properly jump-start a dead vehicle battery should be a topic for students in drivers' education classes—and something every driver should know. Prevent Blindness America will offer safety tips and instructions to new and beginning drivers. For info: Prevent Blindness America®, 500 E Remington Rd, Schaumburg, IL 60173. Phone: (800) 331-2020. Fax: (847) 843-8458. Web: www.prevent-blindness.org.

BABE CALLS HIS SHOT? ANNIVERSARY. Oct 1, 1932. In the fifth inning of game three of the World Series, with a count of two balls and two strikes and with hostile Cubs fans shouting epithets at him, Babe Ruth pointed to the center field bleachers in Chicago's Wrigley Field and followed up by hitting a soaring home run high above the very spot to which he had just gestured. With that homer Ruth squashed the Chicago Cubs' hopes of winning the game, and the Yankees went on to sweep the Series with four straight victories. For more than half a century the question has remained: Did Ruth actually call his shot that day? Even eyewitnesses disagree. Joe Williams of *The New York Times* wrote, "In no mistaken motions, the Babe notified the crowd that the nature of his retaliation would be a wallop right out of the confines of the park." But Cubs pitcher Charlie Root said, "Ruth did *not* point at the fence before he swung. If he'd made a gesture like that, I'd have put one in his ear and knocked him on his ass." Ruth's daughter has said that he denied it. But the Babe himself also claimed he had. Fact or folklore? Either way, legend!

BAYOU HURRICANE: ANNIVERSARY. Oct 1–2, 1893. Approximately 2,000 persons died Oct 1–2, 1893, when the Louisiana Bayou country was submerged in a storm that raged from the Gulf of Mexico. The unexpected arrival of this storm caught thousands of residents off guard. The coast was swept by a 10–12-ft tidal wave.

BRAZIL: FESTIVAL OF PENHA. Oct 1–31. Rio de Janeiro. Pilgrimages, especially on Saturdays during October, to the Church of Our Lady of Penha, which is built on top of a rock, requiring a climb of 365 steps (representing the days of the year), or ride in car on inclined plane (for children, invalids and aged), for those troubled and sick who seek hope or cure.

BUFFALO ROUND-UP. Oct 1. Custer, SD. To round up, brand and separate 1,500 buffalo before auction in November. Est attendance: 6,000. For info: Craig Pugsley, Custer State Park, HC 83, Box 70, Custer, SD 57730. Phone: (605) 255-4515. Fax: (605) 255-4460. E-mail: craig.pugsley@state.sd.us.

CAMPAIGN FOR HEALTHIER BABIES MONTH. Oct 1–31. A month-long concentrated effort to focus attention on the March of Dimes Birth Defects Foundation and its community health programs, public awareness messages, advocacy and fundraising efforts. This month is designated to raise awareness of how to prevent birth defects and infant mortality. For info: March of Dimes Birth Resource Center, 1275 Mamaroneck Ave, White Plains, NY 10605. Phone: (888) MODIMES or (914) 997-4764. Fax: (914) 997-4763. E-mail: rc@modimes.org. Web: www.modimes.org.

CARTER, JIMMY: BIRTHDAY. Oct 1, 1924. Thirty-ninth US president (1977–81). Born James Earl Carter at Plains, GA.

CD PLAYER DEBUTS: ANNIVERSARY. Oct 1, 1982. The first compact disc player, developed jointly by Sony, Philips and Polygram, went on sale. It cost $625 (more than $1,000 in current dollars).

★**CHILD HEALTH DAY.** Oct 1. Presidential Proclamation always issued for the first Monday of October. Proclamation has been issued since 1928. In 1959 Congress changed celebration day from May 1 to the present observance (Pub Res No. 46 of May 18, 1928, and PL86–352 of Sept 22, 1959).

CHILDREN'S DAY. Oct 1. Established by the United Nations and observed on the first Monday in October.

CHINA: MID-AUTUMN FESTIVAL. Oct 1. To worship the moon god. According to folk legend this day is also the birthday of the earth god T'u-ti Kung. The festival indicates the year's hard work in the fields will soon end with the harvest. People express gratitude to heaven as represented by the moon and earth as symbolized by the earth god for all good things from the preceding year. 15th day of eighth month of Chinese lunar calendar.

CHINA, PEOPLE'S REPUBLIC OF: NATIONAL DAY: ANNIVERSARY. Oct 1. Commemorates the founding of the People's Republic of China in 1949.

COLLINS, ALBERT: BIRTH ANNIVERSARY. Oct 1, 1932. Blues guitarist Albert Collins was born at Leona, TX. An exciting, improvisational musician, he won a Grammy for *Showdown!* (1985), which was recorded with blues guitarists Robert Cray and Johnny Copeland. He was inducted into the Blues Hall of Fame in 1989. He died Nov 24, 1993, at Las Vegas, NV.

COMPUTER LEARNING MONTH. Oct 1–31. A month-long focus of events and activities for learning new uses of computers and software, sharing ideas and helping others gain the benefits of how to prevent of computers and software. Numerous national contests are held to recognize students, educators and parents for their innovative ideas; computers and software are awarded to winning entries. Annually, the month of October. For info: Computer Learning Foundation, Dept CHS, PO Box 60007, Palo Alto, CA 94306-0007. Phone: (408) 720-8898. Fax: (408) 720-8777. E-mail: clf@computerlearning.org. Web: www.computerlearning.org.

CO-OP AWARENESS MONTH. Oct 1–31. Co-op Awareness Month was created to remind retailers of their co-op advertising funds in time for them to research and spend these remaining funds by the end of the calendar year. For info: Shannon Bryant, Sales Development Services, Inc, 445 Hutchinson Ave, Ste 800, Columbus, OH 43235. Phone: (800) MORE-ADS. Fax: (740) 548-0397. E-mail: info@sdsinc.com. Web: sdsinc.com.

CYPRUS: INDEPENDENCE DAY: ANNIVERSARY. Oct 1. National holiday. Commemorates independence from Britain in 1960.

DISNEY WORLD OPENED: 30th ANNIVERSARY. Oct 1, 1971. Disney's second theme park opened at Orlando, FL. See also "Disneyland Opened: Anniversary" (July 17).

TEA PLANT,   SUGAR CANE,   COFFEE PLANT.

DIVERSITY AWARENESS MONTH. Oct 1–31. Celebrating, promoting and appreciating the diversity of our society. Also, a month to foster and further our understanding of the inherent value of all races, genders, nationalities, age groups, religions, sexual orientations, classes and disabilities. Annually, in October. For info: Carole Copeland Thomas, C. Thomas & Assoc, 400 W Cummings Park, PMB 1725-154, Woburn, MA 01801. Phone: (800) 801-6599. Fax: (617) 361-1355. E-mail: Carole@TellCarole .com. Web: www.TellCarole.com.

DOMESTIC VIOLENCE AWARENESS MONTH. Oct 1–31. Commemorated since 1987, this month attempts to raise awareness of efforts to end violence against women and their children. The Domestic Violence Awareness Month Project is a collaborative effort of the National Resource Center on Domestic Violence, Family Violence Prevention Fund, National Coalition Against Domestic Violence, National Domestic Violence Hotline and the National Network to End Domestic Violence. For info: Natl Resource Center on Domestic Violence, 6400 Flank Dr, Ste 1300, Harrisburg, PA 17112-2778. Phone: (800) 537-2238.

DRYER VENT SAFETY AWARENESS MONTH. Oct 1–31. To promote public awareness of the dangers of unmaintained clothes dryer vent systems. There are more than 24,000 clothes dryer fires each year that could be prevented with proper vent cleaning and inspection. A free dryer vent safety checklist and information sheet is available. For info: Dr. Dryer Vent, Gregory Allaire, President, Natl Dryer Vent Safety Assn, 35 Eastfield St, Manchester, CT 06040. Phone: (860) 649-1431 or (800) 354-2392.

ENERGY MANAGEMENT IS A FAMILY AFFAIR— IMPROVE YOUR HOME. Oct 1–Mar 31, 2002. Replace energy-consuming units with new efficient home conveniences and remodel to prevent heating and cooling loss. Editorial package includes approximately 100 camera-ready stories and photos free to editors. Also available on disk. For info: James A. Stewart, Jr, Home Improvement Time Inc, PO Box 247, Oakdale, PA 15071-0247. Phone: (412) 787-2881. Fax: (412) 787-3233. E-mail: hitdirect@aol.com. Web: homeimprovementtime.com.

FAMILY HEALTH MONTH. Oct 1–31. For info: American Academy of Family Physicians, 11400 Tomahawk Creek Pkwy, Leawood, KS 66211-2672. Phone: (800) 274-2237. Web: www .familyhealthmonth.org.

FANTASY MONTH. Oct 1–31. As Halloween approaches, this is the perfect month to get out of character and into role-playing. Be daring by dressing up, have fun with your friends by making all your fantasies come true with the power of your imagination. For info: Dr. Ava Cadell, Ph.D, 9000 Sunset Blvd, #1115, Los Angeles, CA 90069. Phone: (310) 276-8623. E-mail: acadell @earthlink.net.

	S	M	T	W	T	F	S
October		1	2	3	4	5	6
2001	7	8	9	10	11	12	13
	14	15	16	17	18	19	20
	21	22	23	24	25	26	27
	28	29	30	31			

FIREPUP'S ® BIRTHDAY. Oct 1. Firepup spends his time teaching fire and life safety awareness to children and their parents in a fun-filled and non–threatening manner. For info: Natl Fire Safety Council, Inc, PO Box 378, Michigan Center, MI 49254-0378. Phone: (517) 764-2811.

GAY AND LESBIAN HISTORY MONTH. Oct 1–31. October was selected to commemorate the first two lesbian and gay marches on Washington in October 1979 and 1987.

GO HOG WILD—EAT COUNTRY HAM MONTH. Oct 1–31. Suuu-eee! It's not just a word, it is a state of mind. For more than 200 years, Americans have been curing and eating country ham. The custom of curing that began in the state of Virginia during the mid 1700s continues today from Georgia to Missouri and points in between. Discover the difference between "city ham" and "country ham" and get some great recipes to boot during National Country Ham Month. For info: Natl Country Ham Assn, PO Box 948, Conover, NC 28613. Phone: (800) 820-4HAM. E-mail: eatham@countryham.org. Web: www.country ham.org.

HARRISON, CAROLINE LAVINIA SCOTT: BIRTH ANNIVERSARY. Oct 1, 1832. First wife of Benjamin Harrison, twenty-third president of the US, born at Oxford, OH. Died at Washington, DC, Oct 25, 1892. She was the second first lady to die in the White House.

HEALTH LITERACY MONTH. Oct 1–31. Promoting understandable health information around the world. For info: Health Literacy Consulting, 31 Highland St, Ste 201, Natick, MA 01760. Phone: (508) 653-1199. Fax: (508) 650-9492. E-mail: Helen @healthliteracy.com.

HEART MAGIC DAY. Oct 1. Heart Magic Moments occur when someone gives a small child a declaration, affirmation or gesture that communicates love, respect or consideration. Heart Magic Moments are the antidote to the violence that is so destructive to the children of our country. An opportunity to build the resources for our future—our children. For info: Dr. Rita Losee, The Heart Magic Visioneer™, PO Box 163, Boxford, MA 01921. Phone: (978) 887-0952. Fax: (978) 887-9551. E-mail: ritalosee @excelonline.com. Web: heartmagic.com.

HISPANIC HERITAGE FESTIVAL. Oct 1–31. Dade County, Miami, FL. A series of special, cultural, educational and sporting events to celebrate and enhance Hispanic culture and traditions. Est attendance: 350,000. For info: Eloy Vazquez, Hispanic Heritage Council, Inc, 4011 W Flagler St, #204, Miami, FL 33134. Phone: (305) 541-5023. Fax: (305) 541-5176. Web: www.hispanic festival.com.

A HOLIDAY CELEBRATION. Oct 1–Jan 15, 2002. Myrtle Beach, SC. Featuring holiday lights, skating, special events and affordable accommodations, shopping. Est attendance: 100,000. For info: Holly Tanner, Festival Dir, Myrtle Beach Area Chamber of Commerce, PO Box 2115, Myrtle Beach, SC 29578. Phone: (843) 626-7444. Fax: (843) 626-0009. Web: www.myrtlebeach live.com.

HOROWITZ, VLADIMIR: BIRTH ANNIVERSARY. Oct 1, 1904. Virtuoso pianist, born at Berdichev, Russia. Horowitz was widely hailed as one of the world's greatest pianists, renowned for his masterful technique. His first public debut was at Kiev in 1920, and at the age of 20 he played a series of 23 recitals at Leningrad, performing a total of more than 200 works with no duplications. He made his US debut in 1928 with the New York Philharmonic. He settled in the US in 1940 and became a citizen in 1944. His career swung full circle Apr 20, 1986, when he performed his first concert in his native Russia after a self-imposed absence of 60 years. He died Nov 5, 1989, at New York, NY.

INTERNATIONAL FIRED UP MONTH. Oct 1–31. A month focusing on enthusiasm and joy, where people learn what gets them fired up and incorporate that into their lives. Seminars, workshops, parties, services, community events–especially in New England where people take action and celebrate. For info: Snowden McFall, c/o Fired Up!, 74 Northeastern Blvd, Unit 20,

Nashua, NH 03062. Phone: (603) 882-0600. Fax: (603) 882-5979. E-mail: smcfall@firedup-takeaction-now.com. Web: www.firedup-takeaction-now.com.

INTERNATIONAL STARMAN MONTH. Oct 1–31. Celebrates the TV series "Starman," which first aired in 1986 and inspired many people around the world to change their lives in positive ways. Spotlight Starman International is a group of people who appreciate the quality, consciousness and themes of the show and continue to gather annually to celebrate that spirit while raising funds for environmental, social and/or educational causes. (The organization is open to all without membership dues.) For info: Vicki Werkley, Spotlight Starman Intl, 16563 Ellen Springs, Lower Lake, CA 95457. Phone: (707) 995-1228. E-mail: spotlight_starman@bigfoot.com. Web: www.pobox.com/~starman.

JAPAN: NEWSPAPER WEEK. Oct 1–7. During this week newspapers make an extensive effort to acquaint the public with their functions and attempt to carry out the role of a newspaper in a free society. Annually, the first week in October.

KOREA: ARMED FORCES DAY. Oct 1. National holiday marked by many colorful military parades, aerial acrobatics and honor guard ceremonies, held around the reviewing plaza at Yoido, an island in the Han River.

KOREA: CHUSOK. Oct 1. Gala celebration by Koreans everywhere. Autumn harvest thanksgiving moon festival. Observed on 15th day of eighth lunar month (eighth full moon of lunar calendar) each year. Koreans pay homage to ancestors and express gratitude to guarding spirits for another year of rich crops. A time to visit tombs, leave food and prepare for coming winter season. Traditional food is "moon cake," made on eve of Chusok, with rice, chestnuts and jujube fruits. Games, dancing and gift exchanges. Observed since Silla Dynasty (beginning of First Millennium).

"KUNG FU" TV PREMIERE: ANNIVERSARY. Oct 1, 1972. David Carradine starred in this unusual ABC western as Kwai Chang Caine, a half-Chinese martial arts master drifter who was exiled from China. Appearing in flashback were: Keye Luke as Master Po, Philip Ahn as Master Kan and Radames Pera as the younger Caine. The show ran for three years. "Kung Fu" returned as a 1986 TV movie introducing the late Brandon Lee as Caine's son. A sequel series currently appears in syndication starring a much older Carradine.

LAWRENCE, JAMES: BIRTH ANNIVERSARY. Oct 1, 1781. Brilliant American naval officer, whose last battle was a defeat, but whose dying words became a most honored naval motto. Lawrence, born at Burlington, NJ, was captain of the *Chesapeake* when she engaged in a naval duel with HMS *Shannon* off Boston, June 1, 1813. The *Chesapeake* was captured and towed to Halifax as a British prize. Lawrence was mortally wounded by a musket ball during the engagement and uttered his famous last words, "Don't give up the ship," as he was being carried off the ship's deck.

LISTEN TO YOUR INNER CRITIC MONTH. Oct 1–31. Turn that nagging self-critical voice into your personal success coach. This month is set aside to explore and learn ways to overcome the negativity of self-criticism. When the negativity of your "self-critical voice" is neutralized, your inner critic can become a strong, responsive inner resource that supports your personal and professional development. For a free booklet, send a SASE to: TransformationWorks, ATTN: IC Booklet, PO Box 577, Bellaire, TX 77402-0577. Phone: (713) 667-6047. Fax: (713) 667-1745. E-mail: Transworks@aol.com. Web: www.TransformationWorks.com.

LONGWOOD GARDENS AUTUMN'S COLORS. Oct 1–19. Kennett Square, PA. Outdoor display features a harvest rainbow of brilliant foliage on 1,050 acres. Est attendance: 50,000. For info: Longwood Gardens, PO Box 501, Kennett Square, PA 19348-0501. Phone: (610) 388-1000. Web: www.longwoodgardens.org.

LUPUS AWARENESS MONTH. Oct 1–31. To promote public awareness of lupus symptoms to aid in early diagnosis and treatment of this disease. For info: Duane Peters, Dir of Communications & Advocacy, Lupus Foundation of America, 1300 Piccard Dr, Ste 200, Rockville, MD 20850-4303. Phone: (301) 670-9292. Fax: (301) 670-9486. Web: www.lupus.org.

MARIS HITS HIS 61st HOME RUN: 40th ANNIVERSARY. Oct 1, 1961. Roger Maris of the New York Yankees hit his 61st home run, breaking Babe Ruth's record for the most home runs in a season. Maris hit his homer against pitcher Tracy Stallard of the Boston Red Sox as the Yankees won, 1–0. Controversy over the record arose because the American League had adopted a 162-game schedule in 1961, and Maris played in 161 games. In 1927, when Ruth set his record, the schedule called for 154 games, and Ruth played in 151. On Sept 8, 1998, Mark McGwire of the St. Louis Cardinals hit his 62nd home run, breaking Maris's record. On Sept 13, 1998, Sammy Sosa of the Chicago Cubs hit his 62nd homer.

"THE MERV GRIFFIN SHOW" TV PREMIERE: ANNIVERSARY. Oct 1, 1962. Singer and game show king Merv Griffin's first effort as an afternoon talk-show host premiered on NBC but was later dropped for syndication. The afternoon show continued until 1969 when Griffin was tapped to host a late-night program on CBS to compete with "The Tonight Show with Johnny Carson."

MODEL T INTRODUCED: ANNIVERSARY. Oct 1, 1908. Ford introduced the Model T at a price of $850 but by 1924 the basic model sold for as little as $260. Between 1908 and 1927 Ford sold 15,007,033 Model Ts in the US. Although the first Model Ts were not built on an assembly line, the demand for the cars was so high that Ford developed a system where workers remained at their stations and cars came to them. This enabled Ford to turn out a Model T every 10 seconds.

MONTH OF THE DINOSAUR. Oct 1–31. Promoting scientific awareness and educating everyone about our environment both present and past. Special on-line forums and activities as well as educational materials available to educators. For info: Shawna Creamer, Big Horn Basin Foundation, PO Box 71, Thermopolis, WY 82443. Phone: (307) 864-2259. Fax: (307) 864-5762. E-mail: shawna@wyodino.org.

MOON FESTIVAL or MID-AUTUMN FESTIVAL. Oct 1. This festival, observed on the 15th day of the eighth moon of the lunar calendar year, is called by different names in different places, but is widely recognized throughout the Far East, including People's Republic of China, Taiwan, Korea, Singapore and Hong Kong. An important harvest festival at the time the moon is brightest, it is also a time for homage to ancestors. Special harvest foods are eaten, especially "moon cakes."

NATIONAL AIDS AWARENESS MONTH. Oct 1–31. To educate consumers, patients, students and professionals on the prevention of AIDS and sexually transmitted diseases. Kit of materials available for $15. For info: Frederick Mayer, Pres, Pharmacists Planning Service, Inc, 101 Lucas Valley Rd, #210, San Rafael, CA 94903. Phone: (415) 479-8628. Fax: (415) 479-8608. E-mail: ppsi@aol.com. Web: www.ppsinc.org.

NATIONAL ANIMAL SAFETY AND PROTECTION MONTH.
Oct 1–31. Observance to promote the appropriate ways to protect and care for domestic and wild animals and help people strengthen skills for staying safe around animals. For info: PALS Foundation, PO Box 1271, San Luis Obispo, CA 93406. Phone: (805) 544-0984. Web: www.expage.com/page/PAL Shome.

NATIONAL BREAST CANCER AWARENESS MONTH.
Oct 1–31. Entering its second decade of public and professional education and awareness. This month is promoted by 17 major national nonprofit cancer organizations to ensure that the media and communities everywhere focus a spotlight on the problem of breast cancer. For info: call the Natl Breast Cancer Awareness Month Program toll-free at (877) 88-NBCAM.

★NATIONAL BREAST CANCER AWARENESS MONTH.
Oct 1–31.

NATIONAL CAR CARE MONTH.
Oct 1–31. To educate motorists about the importance of maintaining their cars in an effort to improve air quality, highway safety and fuel conservation. For info: Car Care Council, 42 Park Dr, Port Clinton, OH 43452. Phone: (419) 734-5343. Fax: (419) 732-3780. E-mail: car care@infinet.com. Web: www.carcarecouncil.org.

NATIONAL COMMUNICATE WITH YOUR KID MONTH.
Oct 1–31. The generation gap—parents and teens are often on different wavelengths and complain that they cannot talk to each other. The purpose of this observance is to open the doors to better communication between parents and teens and to build positive teen/parent relationships. Annually, the month of October. For info send SASE to: Teresa Langston, Dir, Parenting Without Pressure, 1330 Boyer St, Longwood, FL 32750-6311. Phone: (407) 767-2524.

NATIONAL COOKIE MONTH.
Oct 1–31. Remember the aroma and tradition of fresh-baked cookies? Remember how the delicious scent filled the house? Celebrate the All-American favorite treat, the cookie, during National Cookie Month. Make, bake or buy a batch of fresh homemade cookies in any of your favorite flavors this month. Share a little love today—share a fresh-baked cookie! For info: Cookies For You, 117 S Main, Minot, ND 58701. Phone: (701) 839-4975 or (800) 814-5334. Web: www .cookiesforyou.com.

	S	M	T	W	T	F	S
October		1	2	3	4	5	6
2001	7	8	9	10	11	12	13
	14	15	16	17	18	19	20
	21	22	23	24	25	26	27
	28	29	30	31			

NATIONAL CRIME PREVENTION MONTH.
Oct 1–31. During Crime Prevention Month, individuals can commit to working on at least one of three levels—family, neighborhood or community—to drive violence and drugs from our world. It is also a time to honor individuals who have accepted personal responsibility for their neighborhoods and groups who work for the community's common good. Annually, every October. For info: Natl Crime Prevention Council, 1700 K St, Second Floor, Washington, DC 20006-3817. Phone: (202) 466-6272. Fax: (202) 296-1356. Web: www.weprevent.org or www.ncpc.org.

NATIONAL DENTAL HYGIENE MONTH.
Oct 1–31. To increase public awareness of the importance of preventive oral health care and the dental hygienist's role as the preventive professional. Annually, during the month of October. For info: Public Relations, American Dental Hygienists' Assn, 444 N Michigan Ave, Ste 3400, Chicago, IL 60611. Phone: (312) 440-8900. Web: www.adha.org.

NATIONAL DEPRESSION EDUCATION AND AWARENESS MONTH.
Oct 1–31. A nonprofit campaign to educate patients, the elderly and professionals about depression disorders. Kit of materials available for $15. Annually, the month of October. For info: Frederick Mayer, Pres, Pharmacists Planning Service, Inc, 101 Lucas Valley Rd, #210, San Rafael, CA 94903. Phone: (415) 479-8628. Fax: (415) 479-8608. E-mail: ppsi@aol .com. Web: www.ppsinc.org.

★NATIONAL DISABILITY EMPLOYMENT AWARENESS MONTH.
Oct 1–31. Presidential Proclamation issued for the month of October (PL100–630, Title III, Sec 301a of Nov 7, 1988). Previously issued as "National Employ the Handicapped Week" for a week beginning during the first week in October since 1945.

NATIONAL DISABILITY EMPLOYMENT AWARENESS MONTH.
Oct 1–31. To foster the full integration of people with disabilities into the workforce. For info: US Pres Committee on Employment of People with Disabilities, 1331 F St NW, 3rd Floor, Washington, DC 20004. Phone: (202) 376-6200 or (202) 376-6205. Fax: (202) 376-6859. E-mail: kirk-faith@pcepd.gov.

★NATIONAL DOMESTIC VIOLENCE AWARENESS MONTH.
Oct 1–31.

NATIONAL FAMILY SEXUALITY EDUCATION MONTH.
Oct 1–31. A national coalition effort to support parents as the first and primary sexuality educators of their children by providing information for parents and young people. For info: Planned Parenthood Federation of America, Education Dept, 810 Seventh Ave, New York, NY 10019. Phone: (800) 829-7732. Fax: (212) 247-6269. E-mail: education@ppfa.org. Web: www.planned parenthood.org.

NATIONAL "GAIN THE INSIDE ADVANTAGE" MONTH.
Oct 1–31. Gaining "The Inside Advantage" is how ordinary people accomplish extraordinary things. It refers to taking control of your life from the inside out. It means learning how to live deeply, joyfully and successfully. For info: Cathy W. Lauro. Phone: (800) 215-3644. E-mail: mind@CWLauro.com. Web: www.CWLauro.com.

NATIONAL HOME INSPECTION MONTH.
Oct 1–31. To raise the awareness of homeowners to the importance of having their homes annually inspected before winter sets in. By having a home inspected, the homeowner is educated on the status of the homes major systems and components and can help guard against costly repairs. An annual home inspection can also help prevent the homeowner from experiencing catastrophes due to fire, water, earthquake and pest infestation damage, alerting the homeowner to needed repairs. For info: World Inspection Network International, 6500 6th Ave NW, Seattle, WA 98117. Phone: (206) 728-8100. Fax: (206) 441-3655. E-mail: win@wini.com. Web: www.wini.com.

NATIONAL LIVER AWARENESS MONTH. Oct 1–31. To increase understanding of the importance of liver functions, to promote healthful practices and to encourage research into the causes and cures of liver disease. Annually, the month of October. For info: Public Relations Dept, American Liver Fdtn, 1425 Pompton Ave, Cedar Grove, NJ 07009. Phone: (800) 223-0179. Fax: (201) 256-3214. Web: www.liverfoundation.org.

NATIONAL LONG TERM CARE PLANNING WEEK. Oct 1–7. As lifespans increase and family structures change, this week promotes awareness and discussion of how to meet the challenge of providing compassionate long term care. Raising awareness of the importance of long term care planning in everyone's retirement plan. Annually, the first week in October. For info: Marilee Driscoll, Long Term Care Learning Institute, PO Box 956, Plymouth, MA 02362. Phone: (508) 830-9975. Fax: (508) 830-9976. E-mail: mdriscoll@longtermcarelearning.com.

NATIONAL MAKE A WILL MONTH. Oct 1–31. To encourage more Americans to make or update their will, the month is designated to focus attention on the importance of making a will—to make your wishes known, make bequests and leave a legacy. For info: Randy Berenfield, Mgr, Corporate Communications, Made E–Z Products, 384 S Military Trail, Deerfield Beach, FL 33442. Phone: (954) 480-8933. Fax: (954) 480-8906. E-mail: randyb@madeEZ.com.

NATIONAL MEDICAL LIBRARIANS MONTH. Oct 1–31. Recognizes and celebrates the importance and the achievements of these health sciences information professionals. Because more medical and health literature has been published in the past 10 years than in all previous years combined, medical librarians offer efficient access to quality medical and health-related information within a wide variety of health-care settings. Librarians representing 23 specialty groups and 14 regional chapters of the Medical Library Association (MLA) will sponsor several meetings and educational opportunities throughout the month of October. For info: Medical Library Assn, 65 E Wacker Place, Ste 1900, Chicago, IL 60601. Phone: (312) 419-9094. Fax: (312) 419-8950. E-mail: info@mlahg.org. Web: www.mlanet.org.

NATIONAL ORTHODONTIC HEALTH MONTH. Oct 1–31. A beautiful, healthy smile is only the most obvious benefit of orthodontic treatment. National Orthodontic Health Month spotlights the important role of orthodontic care in overall physical health and emotional well-being. The observance is sponsored by the American Association of Orthodontists (AAO), which supports research and education leading to quality patient care and promotes increased public awareness of the need for and benefits of orthodontic treatment. For info: Bill Beggs, Media Relations Mgr, The Hughes Group, 130 S Bemiston, St. Louis, MO 63105.

NATIONAL POPCORN POPPIN' MONTH. Oct 1–31. To celebrate the wholesome, economical, natural food snack of popcorn, America's native snack. For info: The Popcorn Board, 401 N Michigan Ave, Chicago, IL 60611-4267. Phone: (312) 644-6610. Web: www.popcorn.org.

NATIONAL PORK MONTH. Oct 1–31. The National Pork Producers Council, the National Pork Board, in cooperation with state pork producers associations, celebrates October as National Pork Month. While pork promotions are conducted throughout the year, special emphasis is placed on Pork: The Other White Meat® during October. For info: Natl Pork Producers Council, PO Box 10383, Des Moines, IA 50306. Phone: (515) 223-2600. Fax: (515) 223-2646. E-mail: pork@nppc.org. Web: www.nppc .org/

NATIONAL READING GROUP MONTH. Oct 1–31. Reading group members celebrate the joy of a book shared and inspire individuals who do not belong to a reading group to join one or start their own. Organizations, bookstores and libraries are encouraged to sponsor reading group events during this month. For info: Alice Dillon, 14511 Pfeifer Dr, Lake Oswego, OR 97035. Phone: (503) 636-1242. Fax: (503) 635-5119. E-mail: Notesinthe

Margin@aol.com or Martha Burns, 41 Park Ln, Essex Fells, NJ 07021. E-mail: mlbwrite@aol.com. .

NATIONAL ROLLER SKATING MONTH. Oct 1–31. A monthlong celebration recognizing the health benefits and recreational enjoyment of this long-loved pastime. Also includes in-line skating and an emphasis on safe skating. For info: Roller Skating Assn, 6905 Corporate Dr, Indianapolis, IN 46278. Phone: (317) 347-2626. Fax: (317) 347-2636. E-mail: rsa@rollerskating .org. Web: www.rollerskating.com.

NATIONAL SARCASTICS AWARENESS MONTH. Oct 1–31. To help people everywhere understand the positive and negative aspects of sarcasm. For info: Dr. Virginia Tooper, Dir of Barbs, Sarcastics Anonymous, 100 Bay Pl, #2112, Oakland, CA 94610. Phone: (510) 891-8479. E-mail: vtooper@ix.netcom.com.

NATIONAL SKIN CARE AWARENESS WEEK. Oct 1–7. Renée Rouleau Skin Spa, Dallas, TX. This special week focuses on providing education on caring for your skin. Topics include protecting your skin from the dangers of the sun, how diet and lifestyle affect your skin, developing a proper skin care routine and myths and facts about skin care products. All important knowledge for great-looking skin. For info: Renée Rouleau Skin Spa, 19009 Preston Rd, Ste 206, Dallas, TX 75252. Phone: (972) 248-6131. Web: www.reneerouleau.com.

NATIONAL SPINA BIFIDA AWARENESS MONTH. Oct 1–31. Promoting public awareness of current scientific, medical and educational issues related to spina bifida—the second most common birth defect. For info: Info & Referral Coord, Natl Spina Bifida Assn of America, 4590 McArthur Blvd NW, Ste 250, Washington, DC 20007-4226. Phone: (202) 944-3285 or (800) 621-3141. Fax: (202) 944-3295. E-mail: sbaa@sbaa.org. Web: www .sbaa.org.

NATIONAL SPINAL HEALTH MONTH. Oct 1–31. For info: American Chiropractic Assn, 1701 Clarendon Blvd, Arlington, VA 22209. Phone: (800) 986-4636. E-mail: memberinfo@amerchiro.org. Web: www.amerchiro.org.

NATIONAL STAMP COLLECTING MONTH. Oct 1–31. Sponsored by the US Postal Service. For info: Stamp Services, US Postal Service, 475 L'Enfant Plaza SW, Rm 4474-EB, Washington, DC 20260.

NATIONAL SUDDEN INFANT DEATH SYNDROME AWARENESS MONTH. Oct 1–31. Month-long focus on sudden infant death syndrome (also called crib death, the nation's major cause of death for infants beyond one week of age) promotes the BACK TO SLEEP CAMPAIGN to increase public awareness and funds available for medical research and family services. For info: Phipps Y. Cohe, Natl Public Affairs Dir, SIDS Alliance, 1314 Bedford Ave, Ste 210, Baltimore, MD 21208. Phone: (800) 221-7437. Fax: (410) 653-8709. E-mail: sidshg @charm.net. Web: www.sidsalliance.org.

NATIONAL TOILET TANK REPAIR MONTH. Oct 1–31. Monthlong observance dedicated to the value and benefits of a properly tuned toilet with special emphasis on do-it-yourself repairs and water conservation. For info: Greg Wisner, Mktg Mgr, Fluidmaster, Inc, 30800 Rancho Viejo Rd, San Juan Capistrano, CA 92675. Phone: (949) 728-2000. Fax: (949) 728-2205.

NIGERIA: INDEPENDENCE DAY: ANNIVERSARY. Oct 1. National holiday. Became independent of Great Britain in 1960 and a republic in 1963.

NO SALT WEEK. Oct 1–5. Give no-salt cooking and food preparation a try! This celebration will help with recipes and combinations. Annually, the first week in October. For ideas send a large self-addressed stamped envelope. For info: Make It Tasty Spice Co, Box 416, Denver, CO 80201. Phone: (303) 575-5676.

NORWAY: PAGEANTRY IN OSLO. Oct 1. The Storting (Norway's Parliament) convenes on first weekday in October, when it decides date for the ceremonial opening of the Storting—usually the following weekday—and the parliamentary session is then opened by King Harald V in the presence of Corps Diplomatique, preceded and followed by a military procession between the Royal Palace and the Storting.

OCTOBER FROZEN FOOD FESTIVAL. Oct 1–31. Promotes a national awareness of the economical and nutritional benefits of frozen foods. Annually, the month of October. For info: Julie Henderson, VP Communications, Natl Frozen Food Assn, 4755 Linglestown Rd, Ste 300, Harrisburg, PA 17112. Phone: (717) 657-8601. Fax: (717) 657-9862. E-mail: info@nffa.org. Web: www.nffa.org.

PEDIATRIC CANCER AWARENESS MONTH. Oct 1–31. Cancer is the chief cause of death by disease in children. More than 1,000 children in the US die of cancer every year, more than die of AIDS. For info: Bear Necessities Pediatric Cancer Foundation, 85 W Algonquin Rd, Ste 165, Arlington Heights, IL 60005. Phone: (847) 952-9164.

POLISH AMERICAN HERITAGE MONTH. Oct 1–31. A national celebration of Polish history, culture and pride, in cooperation with the Polish American Congress and Polonia Across America. For info: Michael Blichasz, Chair, Polish American Cultural Center, Natl HQ, 308 Walnut St, Philadelphia, PA 19106. Phone: (215) 922-1700. Fax: (215) 922-1518. E-mail: mail@polishamericancenter.org. Web: www.polishamericancenter.org.

"REMINGTON STEELE" TV PREMIERE: ANNIVERSARY. Oct 1, 1982. Laura Holt (played by Stephanie Zimbalist, daughter of Efrem Zimbalist, Jr), an imaginative private detective, could not get a case of her own—until she made up a partner, Remington Steele, who was conveniently out of the office when clients came-a-calling. Then she met the suave stranger (Pierce Brosnan) with a foreign accent who called himself Remington Steele. They began a working partnership . . . which ended in marriage. The show aired on NBC for five years, with the last telecast on Mar 9, 1987, and costarred James Read, Janet DeMay and Doris Roberts.

RETT SYNDROME AWARENESS MONTH. Oct 1–31. To promote awareness of this neurological disease. For info: Kathy Hunter, Intl Rett Syndrome Assn, 9121 Piscataway Rd, Ste 2B, Clinton, MD 20735. Phone: (301) 856-3334 or (800) 818-RETT. E-mail: irsa@rettsyndrome.org. Web: www.rettsyndrome.org.

SPINNING AND WEAVING WEEK. Oct 1–7. To celebrate the timeless craft of weaving and spinning and to honor craftsmen and women past and present who perpetuate a legacy of fine handmade textiles. Annually, the first full week in October, Monday–Sunday. For info: Handweavers Guild of America, Inc, Two Executive Concourse, Ste 201, 3327 Duluth Hwy, Duluth, GA 30096. Phone: (770) 495-7702. Fax: (770) 495-7703. E-mail: weavespindye@compuserve.com. Web: www.weavespindye.org.

	S	M	T	W	T	F	S
October		1	2	3	4	5	6
	7	8	9	10	11	12	13
2001	14	15	16	17	18	19	20
	21	22	23	24	25	26	27
	28	29	30	31			

STOCKTON, RICHARD: BIRTH ANNIVERSARY. Oct 1, 1730. Lawyer and signer of the Declaration of Independence, born at Princeton, NJ. Died there, Feb 8, 1781.

SUBSTANCE ABUSE PREVENTION MONTH. Oct 1–31. Santee, CA. Distribution of materials concerning alcohol and drug abuse. Distribution of red ribbon decals as well as attachment of red ribbons to the trees along the main thoroughfare in the city of Santee. For info: City of Santee, Santee CASA (Community Against Substance Abuse), 10601 Magnolia Ave, Santee, CA 92071-1222.

SUKKOT BEGINS AT SUNDOWN. Oct 1. Jewish Feast of Tabernacles. See "Sukkot" (Oct 2).

SUPREME COURT 2001–2002 TERM BEGINS. Oct 1. Traditionally, the Supreme Court's annual term begins on the first Monday in October and continues with seven two-week sessions of oral arguments. Between the sessions are six recesses during which the opinions are written by the Justices. Ordinarily, all cases are decided by the following June or July.

TALK ABOUT PRESCRIPTIONS MONTH. Oct 1–31. For info: Natl Council on Patient Information and Education, 4915 Saint Elmo Ave, Ste 505, Bethesda, MD 20814-6053. Phone: (301) 656-8565. Fax: (301) 656-4464. E-mail: ncpie@erols.com. Web: www.talkaboutrx.org.

TELLER APPRECIATION WEEK. Oct 1–5. An opportunity for bank management to express appreciation to the ever-pleasant and hardworking tellers who provide services to our valued customers. Expect to see balloons and posters, cakes and other treats in the breakroom and expressions of thanks all around. A great time for customers to write a note of appreciation to their favorite tellers. For info: Easy Systems, Inc, 12100 NE 195th St, Ste 300, Bothell, WA 98011. Phone: (425) 951-8300. Web: www.easysystems.com.

"THIS IS YOUR LIFE" TV PREMIERE: ANNIVERSARY. Oct 1, 1952. Ralph Edwards hosted this program that lured unsuspecting guests on the show and surprised them by detailing their lives and achievements with their family and friends. It began as a radio show in 1948.

"TOM CORBETT, SPACE CADET" TV PREMIERE: ANNIVERSARY. Oct 1, 1950. This space show was set in the 2350s at the Space Academy and starred Frankie Thomas in the title role as an eager cadet. "Tom Corbett" was one of the few shows to be aired on all four major networks, including running on two different networks (NBC and ABC) at the same time.

TUVALU: NATIONAL HOLIDAY. Oct 1. Gained independence from Britain on this day in 1978.

UNITED NATIONS: INTERNATIONAL DAY OF OLDER PERSONS. Oct 1. On Dec 14, 1990, the General Assembly designated Oct 1 as the International Day for the Elderly. It appealed for contributions to the Trust Fund for Aging (which supports projects in developing countries in implementation of the Vienna International Plan of Action on Aging adopted at the 1982 World Assembly on Aging) and endorsed an action program on aging for 1992 and beyond as outlined by the Secretary-General. (Res 45/106.) On Dec 21, 1995, the Assembly changed the name from "for the Elderly" to "of Older Persons" to conform with the 1991 UN Principles for Older Persons. Info from: United Nations, Dept of Public Info, Public Inquiries Unit, Rm GA-57, New York, NY 10017. Phone: (212) 963-4475. E-mail: inquiries@un.org.

UNITED NATIONS: WORLD HABITAT DAY. Oct 1. The United Nations General Assembly, by a resolution of Dec 17, 1985, has designated the first Monday of October each year as World Habitat Day. The first observance of this day, Oct 5, 1986, marked the 10th anniversary of the first international conference on the subject. (Habitat: United Nations Conference on Human Settlements, Vancouver, Canada, 1976.) Info from: United Nations, Dept of Public Info, Public Inquiries Unit, Rm GA-57, New York, NY 10017. Phone: (212) 963-4475. E-mail: inquiries@un.org.

UNIVERSAL CHILDREN'S WEEK. Oct 1–7. To disseminate throughout the world info on the needs of children and to distribute copies of the Declaration of the Rights of the Child. For complete info, send $4 to cover expense of printing, handling and postage. Annually, the first seven days of October. For info: Dr. Stanley Drake, Pres, Intl Soc of Friendship and Good Will, 8592 Roswell Rd, Ste 434, Atlanta, GA 30350-1870.

UNIVERSITY OF CHICAGO FIRST DAY OF CLASSES: ANNIVERSARY. Oct 1, 1892. The University of Chicago opened with an enrollment of 594 and a faculty of 103, including eight former college presidents.

US 2002 FEDERAL FISCAL YEAR BEGINS. Oct 1, 2001–Sept 30, 2002.

VEGETARIAN AWARENESS MONTH. Oct 1–31. This educational event advances awareness of the many surprising ethical, environmental, economic, health, humanitarian and other benefits of the increasingly popular vegetarian lifestyle. Each year in the US about one million more people become vegetarians. For info: Vegetarian Awareness Network, Communications Center, PO Box 321, Knoxville, TN 37901-0321. Phone: (800) USA-VEGE.

WOMEN'S NEWS DAY. Oct 1. A day for businesswomen to submit their press releases, events and articles to the media. Businesswomen who need help writing their press releases and articles can request assistance from the Women's News Bureau. Annually, the first Monday in October. For info: Jerrilynn B. Thomas. Phone: (770) 603-6521. E-mail: womensnewsbureau @hotmail.com. Web: www.womensnewsbureau.com.

WORLD VEGETARIAN DAY. Oct 1. Celebration of vegetarianism's benefits to humans, animals and our planet. In addition to individuals, participants include libraries, schools, colleges, restaurants, food services, health-care centers, health food stores, workplaces and many more. For info: North American Vegetarian Soc, Box 72, Dolgeville, NY 13329. Phone: (518) 568-7970. Fax: (518) 568-7979. E-mail: navs@telenet.net. Web: navs-online.org.

YOSEMITE NATIONAL PARK ESTABLISHED: ANNIVERSARY. Oct 1, 1890. Yosemite Valley and Mariposa Big Tree Grove, granted to the State of California June 30, 1864, were combined and established as a national park. For further park info: Yosemite Natl Park, PO Box 577, Yosemite Natl Park, CA 95389.

BIRTHDAYS TODAY

Julie Andrews (Julia Wells), 66, actress, singer (Emmy for "The Julie Andrews Hour"; Oscar for *Mary Poppins*), born Walton-on-Thames, England, Oct 1, 1935.

Tom Bosley, 74, actor ("Happy Days," "Father Dowling Mysteries"), born Chicago, IL, Oct 1, 1927.

Rodney Cline (Rod) Carew, 56, Baseball Hall of Fame infielder, born Gatun, Canal Zone, Oct 1, 1945.

Jimmy Carter (born James Earl Carter, Jr), 77, 39th US President, born Plains, GA, Oct 1, 1924.

Stephen Collins, 54, actor ("Tales of the Gold Monkey," "Tattinger's," *All the President's Men*), born Des Moines, IA, Oct 1, 1947.

Richard Harris, 71, singer ("MacArthur Park"), actor (*Camelot, Hawaii, Juggernaut*), born Limerick, Ireland, Oct 1, 1930.

Mark McGwire, 38, baseball player, born Pomona, CA, Oct 1, 1963.

Philippe Noiret, 71, actor (*The Day of the Jackal, Coup de Torchon, Il Postino*), born Lille, France, Oct 1, 1930.

Randy Quaid, 51, actor (*The Last Picture Show, Dead Solid Perfect*), born Houston, TX, Oct 1, 1950.

William Hubbs Rehnquist, 77, Chief Justice of the US Supreme Court, born Milwaukee, WI, Oct 1, 1924.

Stella Stevens, 65, actress ("Ben Casey," "Flamingo Road"), born Hot Coffee, MS, Oct 1, 1936.

Grete Waitz, 48, marathoner, born Oslo, Norway, Oct 1, 1953.

OCTOBER 2 — TUESDAY
Day 275 — 90 Remaining

"ALFRED HITCHCOCK PRESENTS" TV PREMIERE: ANNIVERSARY. Oct 2, 1955. Alfred Hitchcock was already an acclaimed director when he began hosting this mystery anthology series that aired on CBS and NBC for 10 years. Each episode began with an introduction by Hitchcock, the man with the world's most recognized profile. Hitchcock directed about 22 episodes of the series. Robert Altman was also a director for the series. Among the many stars who appeared on the show are: Barbara Bel Geddes, Brian Keith, Gena Rowlands, Dick York, Cloris Leachman, Joanne Woodward, Steve McQueen, Peter Lorre, Dick Van Dyke, Robert Redford and Katherine Ross.

GANDHI, MOHANDAS KARAMCHAND (MAHATMA): BIRTH ANNIVERSARY. Oct 2, 1869. Indian political and spiritual leader who achieved world honor and fame for his advocacy of nonviolent resistance as a weapon against tyranny was born at Porbandar, India. He was assassinated in the garden of his home at New Delhi, Jan 30, 1948. On the anniversary of Gandhi's birth (Gandhi Jayanti) thousands gather at the park on the Jumna River at Delhi where Gandhi's body was cremated. Hymns are sung, verses from the Gita, the Koran and the Bible are recited and cotton thread is spun on small spinning wheels (one of Gandhi's favorite activities). Other observances held at his birthplace and throughout India on this public holiday.

"THE GEORGE GOBEL SHOW" TV PREMIERE: ANNIVERSARY. Oct 2, 1954. George Gobel hosted this comedy-variety show for five years on NBC. Chanteuse Peggy King and Jeff Donnell were also on the show, with Eddie Fisher as "permanent guest star." In 1959 Gobel switched networks to CBS and appeared for a year with Joe Flynn, Anita Bryant and Harry von Zell.

GREENE, GRAHAM: BIRTH ANNIVERSARY. Oct 2, 1904. British author Graham Greene was born at Berkhamsted, Hertfordshire, England. He centered his works around characters facing salvation and damnation in a world of chaos, often with complex Catholic settings. His works include *The Power and The Glory* (1940) and *The Third Man* (1950). He died Apr 3, 1991, at Vevey, Switzerland.

GUINEA: INDEPENDENCE DAY. Oct 2. National Day. Guinea gained independence from France in 1958.

GUNN, MOSES: BIRTH ANNIVERSARY. Oct 2, 1929. The 1981 winner of the NAACP Image Award for his performance as Booker T. Washington in the film *Ragtime* was born at St. Louis, MO. His appearances on stage ranged from the title role in *Othello* to Jean Genet's *The Blacks*. He received an Emmy nomination for his role in *Roots* and was awarded several Obies for off-Broadway performances. On film he appeared in *Shaft* and *The Great White Hope*. He died Dec 17, 1993, at Guilford, CT.

HARVEST MOON. Oct 2. So called because the full moon nearest the autumnal equinox extends the hours of light into the evening and helps the harvester with his long day's work. Moon enters Full Moon phase at 9:49 AM, EDT.

HULL, CORDELL: BIRTH ANNIVERSARY. Oct 2, 1871. American statesman who served in both houses of the Congress and as secretary of state was born at Pickett County, TN. Noted for his contributions to the "Good Neighbor" policies of the US with regard to countries of the Americas and to the establishment of the United Nations. Hull died at Bethesda, MD, July 23, 1955.

"THE JIMMY DURANTE SHOW" TV PREMIERE: ANNIVERSARY. Oct 2, 1954. Affectionately known as "The Schnozz," Durante hosted a Saturday night variety show with his former vaudeville partner, Eddie Jackson, pianist Jules Baffano and drummer Jack Roth. It alternated with "The Donald O'Connor Show" on NBC and aired for two years.

"LUX VIDEO THEATRE" TV PREMIERE: ANNIVERSARY. Oct 2, 1950. James Mason, Otto Kruger and Gordon MacRae hosted this half-hour dramatic anthology series that aired for seven years on both CBS and NBC. Its famed guest stars included: Robert Stack in "Inside Story" (1951); Peter Lorre in "The Taste" (1952); Grace Kelly in "A Message for Janice" (1952); Edward G. Robinson in "Witness for the Prosecution" (1953) and Esther Williams in "The Armed Venus" (1957).

MAPLE LEAF RAG PREMIERE: ANNIVERSARY. Oct 2, 1990. The last work choreographed by Martha Graham premiered at City Center at New York City. One of the 181 works created by Graham, *The Maple Leaf Rag* appeared on stage for the first time just six months before the dancer and choreographer died at the age of 96.

MARSHALL, THURGOOD, SWORN IN TO SUPREME COURT: ANNIVERSARY. Oct 2, 1967. Thurgood Marshall was sworn in as the first black associate justice to the US Supreme Court. On June 27, 1991, he announced his resignation, effective upon the confirmation of his successor. See also: "Marshall, Thurgood: Birth Anniversary" (July 2).

MARX, GROUCHO: BIRTH ANNIVERSARY. Oct 2, 1890. Born Julius Henry Marx at New York, NY. Comedian, who along with his brothers, constituted the famous Marx Brothers. The Marx Brothers began as a singing group and then acted in such movies as *Duck Soup* and *Animal Crackers*. During the '40s and '50s, Groucho was the host of the television and radio show "You Bet Your Life." Died at Los Angeles, CA, Aug 19, 1977.

McFARLAND, GEORGE (SPANKY): BIRTH ANNIVERSARY. Oct 2, 1928. Chubby child star of the "Our Gang" comedy film shorts. Born at Dallas, TX, and died at Grapevine, TX, June 30, 1993.

MOON PHASE: FULL MOON. Oct 2. Moon enters Full Moon phase at 9:49 AM, EDT.

NATIONAL CUSTODIAL WORKERS DAY. Oct 2. A day to honor custodial workers—those who clean up after us. For info: Bette Tadajewski, Saint John the Baptist Church, 2425 Frederick, Alpena, MI 49707. Phone: (517) 354-3019.

NOBEL CONFERENCE XXXVII. Oct 2–3. Gustavus Adolphus College, St. Peter, MN. Annual two-day scientific symposium (37th year), and the only one sanctioned by the Nobel Foundation, Stockholm. Annually, the first Tuesday and Wednesday in October. Est attendance: 6,000. For info: Dean Wahlund, Dir of Public Affairs, Gustavus Adolphus College, 800 W College Ave, St. Peter, MN 56082-1498. Phone: (507) 933-7550.

NORTH CASCADES NATIONAL PARK ESTABLISHED: ANNIVERSARY. Oct 2, 1968.

"PEANUTS" DEBUTS: ANNIVERSARY. Oct 2, 1950. This comic strip featured Charlie Brown, Lucy, Linus, Sally, Peppermint Patty and Charlie's dog Snoopy. The last new *Peanuts* strip was published Feb 13, 2000.

PHILEAS FOGG'S WAGER DAY: ANNIVERSARY. Oct 2, 1872. Anniversary, from Jules Verne's *Around the World in Eighty Days*, of the famous wager upon which the book is based: "I will bet twenty thousand pounds against any one who wishes, that I will make the tour of the world in eighty days or less." Then, consulting a pocket almanac, Phileas Fogg said: "As today is Wednesday, the second of October, I shall be due in London, in this very room of the Reform Club, on Saturday, the twenty-first of December, at a quarter before nine PM; or else the twenty thousand pounds . . . will belong to you." See also: "Phileas Fogg Wins a Wager Day" (Dec 21).

REDWOOD NATIONAL PARK ESTABLISHED: ANNIVERSARY. Oct 2, 1968. California's Redwood National Park was established. For further park info: Redwood Natl Park, 1111 Second St, Crescent City, CA 95531.

STREETER, RUTH CHENEY: BIRTH ANNIVERSARY. Oct 2, 1895. Born at Brookline, MA, Ruth Cheney Streeter was the first director of the US Marine Corps Women's Reserve. She was active in unemployment relief, public health, welfare and old-age assistance in New Jersey during the 1930s. A student of aeronautics, she learned to fly while serving as an adjutant of a flight group in the Civil Air Patrol during the early years of World War II. She died Sept 30, 1990, at Morristown, NJ.

SUKKOT, SUCCOTH or FEAST OF TABERNACLES, FIRST DAY. Oct 2. Hebrew calendar date: Tishri 15, 5762 begins nine-day festival in commemoration of Jewish people's 40 years of wandering in the desert and thanksgiving for the fall harvest. This high holiday season closes with Shemini Atzeret (see entry on Oct 9) and Simchat Torah (see entry on Oct 10).

"THE TWILIGHT ZONE" TV PREMIERE: ANNIVERSARY. Oct 2, 1959. "The Twilight Zone" went on the air with these now-familiar words: "There is a fifth dimension, beyond that which is known to man. It is a dimension as vast as space and as timeless as infinity. It is the middle ground between light and shadow, between science and superstition, and it lies between the pit of man's fear and the summit of his knowledge. This is the dimension of imagination. It is an area which we call The Twilight Zone." The anthology program ran five seasons for 154 installments, with a one-year hiatus between the third and fourth seasons. It now is considered to have been one of the best dramas to appear on television. It was created and hosted by Rod Serling. The last episode was telecast on Sept 31, 1965.

WORLD FARM ANIMALS DAY. Oct 2. Celebrated on Gandhi's birthday. To expose and memorialize the needless suffering and death of billions of innocent, sentient animals in factories, farms and slaughterhouses. Local actions include memorial services, vigils, street theater, picketing, leafletting and information tables. For info: Farm Animal Reform Movement, Box 30654, Bethesda, MD 20824. Phone: (301) 530-1737. Fax: (301) 530-5747. E-mail: farm@farmusa.org. Web: www.farmusa.org.

BIRTHDAYS TODAY

Lorraine Bracco, 46, actress (*Goodfellas, Medicine Man*), born Brooklyn, NY, Oct 2, 1955.

Clay S. Felker, 73, publisher, born St. Louis, MO, Oct 2, 1928.

Donna Karan, 53, fashion designer, born Forest Hills, NY, Oct 2, 1948.

Don McLean, 56, singer ("Crying"), songwriter ("American Pie," "Vincent"), born New Rochelle, NY, Oct 2, 1945.

Rex Reed, 62, movie critic, born Fort Worth, TX, Oct 2, 1939.

Sting (Gordon Sumner), 50, musician, lead singer (Police), songwriter ("Every Breath You Take"), actor (*Dune*), born London, England, Oct 2, 1951.

October 2001	S	M	T	W	T	F	S
		1	2	3	4	5	6
	7	8	9	10	11	12	13
	14	15	16	17	18	19	20
	21	22	23	24	25	26	27
	28	29	30	31			

OCTOBER 3 — WEDNESDAY

Day 276 — 89 Remaining

"THE ANDY GRIFFITH SHOW" TV PREMIERE: ANNIVERSARY. Oct 3, 1960. Marks the airing of the first of 249 episodes. Set in rural Mayberry, NC, the show starred Griffith as Sheriff Andy Taylor, Ron Howard as his son Opie, Frances Bavier as Aunt Bee Taylor and Don Knotts as Deputy Barney Fife. Although the last telecast aired Sept 16, 1968, more than 12,000 members of "The Andy Griffith Show" Rerun Watchers Club and others celebrate this day with festivities every year.

BANCROFT, GEORGE: BIRTH ANNIVERSARY. Oct 3, 1800. American historian, known as "The Father of American History," born at Worcester, MA. Died at Washington, DC, Jan 27, 1891.

"CAPTAIN KANGAROO" TV PREMIERE: ANNIVERSARY. Oct 3, 1955. On the air until 1985, this was the longest-running children's TV show until it was surpassed by "Sesame Street." Starring Bob Keeshan as Captain Kangaroo, it was broadcast on CBS and PBS. Other characters included Mr Green Jeans, Grandfather Clock, Bunny Rabbit, Mr Moose and Dancing Bear. Keeshan was an advocate for excellence in children's programming and even supervised which commercials would appear on the program. In 1997 "The All New Captain Kangaroo" debuted, starring John McDonough.

"THE DICK VAN DYKE SHOW" TV PREMIERE: 40th ANNIVERSARY. Oct 3, 1961. This sitcom wasn't an immediate success but soon became a hit. It starred Dick Van Dyke as Rob Petrie, a TV show writer, and Mary Tyler Moore as his wife Laura, a former dancer. This was one of the first shows revolving around the goings-on at a TV series. Other cast members included: Morey Amsterdam, Rose Marie, Richard Deacon, Carl Reiner, Jerry Paris, Ann Morgan Guilbert and Larry Matthews. The last episode aired Sept 7, 1966 but the show remains popular in reruns. Carl Reiner created the series.

FALL SUWANEE RIVER GOSPEL JUBILEE. Oct 3–6. Live Oak, FL. Featuring well-known musical groups for a weekend of music in this beautiful park. Est attendance: 5,000. For info: James Cornett, Spirit of the Suwanee Music Park, 3076 95th Dr, Live Oak, FL 32060. Phone: (904) 364-1683. Fax: (904) 364-2998. E-mail: spirit@musicliveshere.com. Web: www.music liveshere.com.

GERMAN REUNIFICATION: ANNIVERSARY. Oct 3, 1990. After 45 years of division, East and West Germany reunited just four days short of East Germany's 41st founding anniversary (Oct 7, 1949). The new united Germany took the name the Federal Republic of Germany, the formal name of the former West Germany and adopted the constitution of the former West Germany. Today is a national holiday in Germany, Tag der Deutschen Einheit (Day of German Unity).

GORGAS, WILLIAM CRAWFORD: BIRTH ANNIVERSARY. Oct 3, 1854. Physician and sanitary engineer, born at Toulminville, AL. He eradicated yellow fever from Havana, and the Panama Canal, allowing the completion of the canal. Gorgas died at London, England, July 4, 1920.

HERRIOT, JAMES (JAMES ALFRED WIGHT): 85th BIRTH ANNIVERSARY. Oct 3, 1916. Author and veterinarian James Herriot was born at Glasgow, Scotland. Herriot wrote more than 12 books chronicling his life as a veterinarian in northern England. His *All Creatures Great and Small* (1974) was made into a TV series that was an international hit. He was made a member of the Order of the British Empire in 1979. Herriot died Feb 23, 1995, at Yorkshire, England.

HONDURAS: FRANCISCO MORAZAN HOLIDAY. Oct 3. Public holiday in honor of Francisco Morazan, national hero, who was born in 1799.

KOREA: NATIONAL FOUNDATION DAY. Oct 3. National holiday also called Tangun Day, as it commemorates day when legendary founder of the Korean nation, Tangun, established his kingdom of Chosun in 2333 BC.

KURTZMAN, HARVEY: BIRTH ANNIVERSARY. Oct 3, 1902. Cartoonist and founder of *Mad* magazine, Harvey Kurtzman was born at Brooklyn, NY. At the age of 14 he had his first cartoon published, and he began his career in comic books in 1943. His career led him to EC (Educational Comics), and with the support of William Gaines, he created *Mad* magazine, which first appeared in 1952. He died Feb 21, 1993, at Mount Vernon, NY.

"LA LAW" TV PREMIERE: 15th ANNIVERSARY. Oct 3, 1986. Set in the Los Angeles law firm of McKenzie, Brackman, Chaney and Kuzak, this drama had a large cast. Divorce lawyer Arnie Becker was played by Corbin Bernsen, public defender Victor Sifuentes by Jimmy Smits and managing partner Douglas Brackman by Alan Rachins. Other cast members included Harry Hamlin as Michael Kuzak, Richard Dysart as Leland McKenzie, Susan Dey as Grace Van Owen, Jill Eikenberry as Ann Kelsey, Michael Tucker as Stuart Markowitz and Susan Ruttan as Roxanne Melman. The last telecast was May 19, 1994.

MANSON, PATRICK: BIRTH ANNIVERSARY. Oct 3, 1844. British parasitologist and surgeon sometimes called the "father of tropical medicine." Sir Patrick's research into insects as carriers of parasites was instrumental in later understanding of mosquitoes as transmitters of malaria. Born at Aberdeen, Scotland, Manson died Apr 9, 1922, at London, England.

"MICKEY MOUSE CLUB" TV PREMIERE: ANNIVERSARY. Oct 3, 1955. This afternoon show for children was on ABC. Among its young cast members were Mouseketeers Annette Funicello and Shelley Fabares. A later version, "The New Mickey Mouse Club," starred Keri Russell and Britney Spears.

MISSISSIPPI STATE FAIR. Oct 3–14. Jackson, MS. Features nightly professional entertainment, livestock show, midway carnival, domestic art exhibits. Est attendance: 620,000. For info: Mississippi Fair Commission, PO Box 892, Jackson, MS 39205. Phone: (601) 961-4000. Fax: (601) 354-6545.

"MR AND MRS NORTH" TV PREMIERE: ANNIVERSARY. Oct 3, 1952. This half-hour murder mystery show began as a comedy radio show based on stories by Richard and Frances Lockridge. A pilot program was released in 1949, but the TV series didn't begin until 1952. It starred Richard Denning as Jerry North and Barbara Britton as his wife Pamela, a New York couple who investigated unsolved murders. Francis De Sales was also featured as Lieutenant Bill Weigand.

NETHERLANDS: RELIEF OF LEIDEN DAY. Oct 3. Celebration of the liberation of Leiden in 1574.

"OUR MISS BROOKS" TV PREMIERE: ANNIVERSARY. Oct 3, 1952. This half-hour sitcom began on the radio, and unlike many radio programs that moved to TV, most of the original radio cast was retained. It was about a favorite high school English teacher named Connie Brooks (played by Eve Arden). Also featured were Gale Gordon, Richard Crenna, Gloria McMillan and Jane Morgan. In the fall of 1955, the setting was changed, and some regulars left.

"OZZIE AND HARRIET" TV PREMIERE: ANNIVERSARY. Oct 3, 1952. "Ozzie and Harriet" was TV's longest-running sitcom. The successful radio-turned-TV show about the Nelson family starred the real-life Nelsons—Ozzie, his wife Harriet and their sons David and Ricky. Officially titled "The Adventures of Ozzie and Harriet," this show was set in the family's home. The boys were one reason the show was successful, and Ricky used the advantage to become a pop star. David and Rick's real-life wives—June Blair and Kris Nelson—also joined the cast. The show was cancelled at the end of the 1965-66 season after 435 episodes, 409 of which were in black and white and 26 in color. The last episode aired Sept 3, 1966.

"THE PAT BOONE SHOW" TV PREMIERE: ANNIVERSARY. Oct 3, 1957. Clean-cut singer Pat Boone hosted three shows between 1957 and 1969. The first was a prime-time variety series with the McGuire Sisters and the Mort Lindsey Orchestra as regulars. The second show featured the Paul Smith Orchestra and was a daytime variety and talk show. "Pat Boone in Hollywood" was the title of the third, a 90-minute talk show.

"QUINCY" TV PREMIERE: 25th ANNIVERSARY. Oct 3, 1976. This medically-oriented crime show starred Jack Klugman as Dr. Raymond Quincy, a medical examiner for the L.A. coroner's office. Quincy's curiosity about his cases led to investigative work which often solved them. Later in the series the show focused on social issues that were unrelated to forensic medicine. In the final season, Quincy got married to Dr. W. Emily Hanover (Anita Gillette). The last telecast aired on Sept 5, 1983.

"THE REAL McCOYS" TV PREMIERE: ANNIVERSARY. Oct 3, 1957. This first successful rural comedy program was one of the most popular, predating similar shows such as "The Beverly Hillbillies" by many seasons. It was set in rural California and featured the McCoys (played by Walter Brennan, Richard Crenna, Kathleen Nolan, Michael Winkelman and Lydia Reed) and their friends (played by Tony Martinez, Andy Clyde, Madge Blake, Janet DeGore, Butch Patrick and Joan Blondell).

ROBINSON NAMED BASEBALL'S FIRST BLACK MAJOR LEAGUE MANAGER: ANNIVERSARY. Oct 3, 1974. The only major league player selected most valuable player in both the American and National Leagues, Frank Robinson was hired by the Cleveland Indians as baseball's first black major league manager. During his playing career Robinson represented the American League in four World Series playing for the Baltimore Orioles, led the Cincinnati Reds to a National League pennant and hit 586 home runs in 21 years of play.

"SCARECROW AND MRS KING" TV PREMIERE: ANNIVERSARY. Oct 3, 1983. A one-hour adventure series starring Bruce Boxleitner as Lee Stetson (code name "Scarecrow"), a government agent working with Mrs Amanda King (Kate Jackson), a housewife-turned-agent. Mr King, played by Sam Melville, appeared once, but he was out of the picture when Mrs King and Scarecrow were married in the final season. Mrs King also became a trainee agent.

WORLD DAIRY EXPO. Oct 3-7. Madison, WI. World's largest dairy cattle exhibition and trade show features more than 1,200 exhibits and 1,800 head of cattle in seven breed shows at the Dane County Expo Center. About 200 animals offered for sale in four cattle breed sales. Educational forum. Open to the public. Est attendance: 70,525. For info: World Dairy Expo, 2820 Walton Commons West, Ste 101, Madison, WI 53718-6797. Phone: (608) 224-6455. Fax: (608) 224-0300. E-mail: wde@wdexpo.com. Web: www.world-dairy-expo.com.

October 2001	S	M	T	W	T	F	S
		1	2	3	4	5	6
	7	8	9	10	11	12	13
	14	15	16	17	18	19	20
	21	22	23	24	25	26	27
	28	29	30	31			

OCTOBER 4 — THURSDAY
Day 277 — 88 Remaining

"THE ALVIN SHOW" TV PREMIERE: 40th ANNIVERSARY. Oct 4, 1961. This prime-time cartoon was based on Ross Bagdasarian's novelty group called The Chipmunks, which had begun as recordings with speeded-up vocals. In the series, The Chipmunks were three chipmunks, Alvin, Simon and Theodore, who sang and had adventures along with their songwriter-manager David Seville. Bagdasarian supplied the voices. Part of the show featured the adventures of inventor Clyde Crashcup (voiced by Shepard Menken). "Alvin" was more successful as a Saturday morning cartoon. It returned in reruns in 1979 and also prompted a sequel, called "Alvin and the Chipmunks," in 1983.

CANADA: SNOW GOOSE FESTIVAL. Oct 4-14. Montmagny, QC. Come and join in the family fun which includes two parades, entertainment, meals, sports events and much more. Est attendance: 160,000. For info: Snow Goose Festival, PO Box 101, Montmagny, QC, Canada G5V 3S3. Phone: (418) 248-3954. Fax: (418) 248-3959. Web: www.festivaldeloie.qc.ca.

CITY STAGE. Oct 4-7. Greensboro, NC. A free street festival featuring the performing and visual arts, with food vendors, arts and crafts exhibitors and demonstrators, local, regional and national performers on three stages, kiddie activities, beer gardens, concessions, souvenirs, parties and a 5K fun run for the arts. Annually, the first full weekend in October. Sponsored by Miller Brewing Company. Est attendance: 150,000. For info: Tina Foxx, Community Events Dir, United Arts Council of Greensboro, PO Box 877, Greensboro, NC 27402. Phone: (336) 373-7523. Fax: (336) 373-7553.

CORSICA LIBERATED: ANNIVERSARY. Oct 4, 1943. The Island of Corsica became the first French territory in Europe freed from Nazi control when Free French troops entered the city of Bastia, thereby completing the retaking of the island, the culmination of a French uprising that had begun on the island on Sept 19.

COWBOY HALL OF FAME CEREMONY AND BANQUET. Oct 4. Willcox Community Center, Willcox, AZ. The Cowboy Hall of Fame is lead into the Rex Allen Days celebration. Open house 6 PM, Dinner 7 PM. Includes "Cowboy Hall of Fame" induction ceremony, favorite son/daughter award. Cost is $17.50 per person. Sponsored by the Willcox Chamber of Commerce & Agriculture. Est attendance: 340. For info: (520) 384-2272.

"DECEMBER BRIDE" TV PREMIERE: ANNIVERSARY. Oct 4, 1954. This sitcom was filmed before a live audience at Desilu Studios and took place mainly in a living room. It starred Spring Byington as widow Lily Ruskin, Frances Rafferty as her daughter Ruth Henshaw, Dean Miller as Ruth's husband, Matt, Harry Morgan as wisecracking next-door neighbor, Pete Porter (his wife Gladys was talked about but never seen), Verna Felton as Lily's friend Hilda Crocker and Arnold Stang as Private Marvin Fisher, Pete's brother-in-law. This series spun off "Pete and Gladys" in 1960.

EAST TEXAS POULTRY FESTIVAL. Oct 4–6. Shelby County Courthouse Square, Center, TX. County fair-style festival featuring carnival rides, food booths run by local churches and charities, art and craft exhibits, live entertainment, chicken clucking contest, street dance, 4-H broiler show and auction. Annually, the first Thursday, Friday and Saturday of October. Est attendance: 40,000. For info: David Jacobs, KDET/KCOT Radio Stations, 307 San Augustine St, Center, TX 75935. Phone: (936) 598-9537. E-mail: davidonair@hotmail.com. Web: www.listen.to /kdet.

ENGLAND: NOTTINGHAM GOOSE FAIR. Oct 4–6. Forest Recreation Ground, Nottingham. Held annually since 1284 (except during the Great Plague in 1665 and the two World Wars), the fair formerly lasted three weeks and boasted as many as 20,000 geese on display. Now lasting three days, the Nottingham Goose Fair always begins on the first Thursday in October. A traditional fair with modern amusements. For info: Markets Division, Victoria Market Offices, Glasshouse St, Nottingham, England NG1 3LP. Phone: (115) 941-7324 or (115) 924-1671.

GREGORIAN CALENDAR ADJUSTMENT: ANNIVERSARY. Oct 4, 1582. Pope Gregory XIII issued a bulletin that decreed that the day following Thursday, Oct 4, 1582, should be Friday, Oct 15, 1582, thus correcting the Julian Calendar, then 10 days out of date relative to the seasons. This reform was effective in most Catholic countries; the Julian Calendar continued in use in Britain and the American colonies until 1752, in Japan until 1873, in China until 1912, in Russia until 1918, in Greece until 1923 and in Turkey until 1925. See also: "Gregorian Calendar Adjustment: Anniversary" (Feb 24) and "Calendar Adjustment Day: Anniversary" (Sept 2).

HAYES, RUTHERFORD BIRCHARD: BIRTH ANNIVERSARY. Oct 4, 1822. Rutherford Birchard Hayes, 19th president of the US (Mar 4, 1877–Mar 3, 1881), was born at Delaware, OH. In his inaugural address, Hayes said: "He serves his party best who serves the country best." He died at Fremont, OH, Jan 17, 1893.

HISTORY ALIVE!. Oct 4–7. Norfolk Botanical Garden, Norfolk, VA. Features historical groups from various periods, with reeanctors participating in field maneuvers and constructing encampments and featuring display areas with equipment, clothing, food and bedding authentic to the era they represent. Interpreters at each site explain the life and times of the characters, providing an accurate and exciting chronicle of our past. Est attendance: 2,000. For info: Norfolk Botanical Garden, 6700 Azalea Garden Rd, Norfolk, VA 23518. Phone: (757) 441-5838. Fax: (757) 853-8294. Web: www.virginiagarden.org.

INTERNATIONAL TOOT YOUR FLUTE DAY. Oct 4. A day dedicated to selling yourself on the idea of selling yourself—and telling others how good you are. This is your day to celebrate you, to remind yourself that you're too good to be your own best secret, to accept credit where credit is due and to reject the idea that self-promotion is "bragging." For info: Fred Berns, Power Promotion, 394 Rendezvous Dr, Lafayette, CO 80026. Phone: (303) 665-6688. Fax: (303) 665-5599. E-mail: FredTalks@aol.com.

JOHNSON, ELIZA McCARDLE: BIRTH ANNIVERSARY. Oct 4, 1810. Wife of Andrew Johnson, 17th president of the US, born at Leesburg, TN. Died at Greeneville, TN, Jan 15, 1876.

KING BISCUIT BLUES FESTIVAL. Oct 4–6. Downtown Historic District, Helena, AR. 16th annual festival. Three days of the best in Delta Blues. Many of the Blues "Greats" got their start in Helena on the 1940s "King Biscuit Time" radio show and return to perform. "King Biscuit Time" first aired on station KFFA in Helena in 1941. Other activities include gospel music stage, 5K run, arm wrestling, barbecue cook-off, arts and crafts booth and games and Mississippi riverboat cruise. Est attendance: 120,000. For info: Main Street Helena, PO Box 247, Helena, AR 72342. Phone: (501) 338-8798. Fax: (501) 338-7397. Web: www.kingbiscuitfest.org.

"LEAVE IT TO BEAVER" TV PREMIERE: ANNIVERSARY. Oct 4, 1957. This family sitcom was a stereotypical portrayal of American family life. It focused on Theodore "Beaver" Cleaver (Jerry Mathers) and his family: his patient, understanding and all-knowing father, Ward (Hugh Beaumont), impeccably dressed housewife and mother June (Barbara Billingsley) and Wally (Tony Dow), Beaver's good-natured, all-American brother. The "perfectness" of the Cleaver family was balanced by other, less-than-perfect characters played by Ken Osmond, Frank Bank, Richard Deacon, Diane Brewster, Sue Randall, Rusty Stevens and Madge Blake. The last episode aired Sept 12, 1963. "Leave It to Beaver" remained popular in reruns.

LESOTHO: NATIONAL DAY: 35th ANNIVERSARY. Oct 4. National holiday. Commemorates independence from Britain in 1966. Formerly Basutoland.

OKLAHOMA INTERNATIONAL BLUEGRASS FESTIVAL. Oct 4–6. Guthrie, OK. Festival featuring top international bluegrass bands and musicians, children's activities, music workshops, RV camping, antique shopping, arts and crafts, food booths and a Celebrity Golf Tournament on Sunday. Est attendance: 45,000. For info: Guthrie Conv & Visitors Bureau, PO Box 995, Guthrie, OK 73044-0995. Phone: (800) 299-1889 or (405) 282-4446. Fax: (405) 282-0061.

REMINGTON, FREDERIC S.: BIRTH ANNIVERSARY. Oct 4, 1861. Born at Canton, NY. Frederic Remington, an artist and writer, studied at Yale Art School. He travelled extensively throughout North America and is best known for the work he did in the western US, capturing life on the plains—Indians, cowboys, horses and more. He owned a ranch near Peabody, KS. He died Dec 26, 1909, at age 48, at Ridgefield, CT, following an appendectomy. Much of his work is on display at the Frederic Reming-

ton Art Museum at Ogdensburg, NY. For museum info: Frederic Remington Art Museum, 303 Washington St, Ogdensburg, NY 13669. Phone: (315) 393-2425. Fax: (315) 393-4464. E-mail: info@remington-museum.org. Web: www.remington-museum.org.

RILEY FESTIVAL. Oct 4–7. Greenfield, IN. To celebrate the birth of Hoosier poet James Whitcomb Riley. Est attendance: 75,000. For info: Betty Wright, Riley Fest Assn, 312 E Main St, Ste C, Greenfield, IN 46140. Phone: (317) 462-2141. E-mail: rileyfst@hccn.org.

RUNYAN, DAMON: BIRTH ANNIVERSARY. Oct 4, 1884. American newspaperman and author, born at Manhattan, KS, and died at New York, NY, Dec 10, 1946. The musical *Guys and Dolls* was based on one of his short stories. ." . . always try to rub up against money," he wrote, "for if you rub up against money long enough, some of it may rub off on you."

SAINT FRANCIS OF ASSISI: FEAST DAY. Oct 4. Giovanni Francesco Bernardone, religious leader, founder of the Friars Minor (Franciscan Order), born at Assisi, Umbria, Italy, in 1181. Died at Porziuncula, Oct 3, 1226. One of the best-loved saints of all time.

SOUTH CAROLINA STATE FAIR. Oct 4–14. Columbia, SC. Conklin Shows, rides, musical entertainment, food booths and children's activities. Est attendance: 576,000. For info: South Carolina State Fair, PO Box 393, Columbia, SC 29202. Phone: (803) 799-3387. Fax: (803) 799-1760. E-mail: geninfo@scstatefair.org.

SPACE MILESTONE: *LUNA 3* (USSR). Oct 4, 1959. First satellite to photograph moon's distant side was launched on this date.

SPACE MILESTONE: *SPUTNIK* . Oct 4, 1957. Anniversary of launching of first successful man-made earth satellite. *Sputnik I* ("satellite") weighing 184 lbs was fired into orbit from the USSR's Tyuratam launch site. Transmitted radio signal for 21 days, decayed Jan 4, 1958. Beginning of Space Age and man's exploration beyond Earth. This first-in-space triumph by the Soviets resulted in a stepped-up emphasis on the teaching of science in American classrooms.

STRATEMEYER, EDWARD L.: BIRTH ANNIVERSARY. Oct 4, 1862. American author of children's books, Stratemeyer was born at Elizabeth, NJ. He created numerous series of popular children's books including "The Bobbsey Twins," "The Hardy Boys," "Nancy Drew" and "Tom Swift." He and his Stratemeyer Syndicate, using 60 or more pen names, produced more than 800 books. More than four million copies were in print in 1987. Stratemeyer died at Newark, NJ, May 10, 1930.

October 2001	S	M	T	W	T	F	S
		1	2	3	4	5	6
	7	8	9	10	11	12	13
	14	15	16	17	18	19	20
	21	22	23	24	25	26	27
	28	29	30	31			

TEN-FOUR DAY. Oct 4. The fourth day of the tenth month is a day of recognition for radio operators, whose code words, "Ten-Four," signal an affirmative reply.

UNITED NATIONS: WORLD SPACE WEEK. Oct 4–10. To celebrate the contributions of space science and technology to the betterment of the human condition. The dates recall the launch, on Oct 4, 1957, of the first artificial satellite, *Sputnik*, and the entry into force, on Oct 10, 1967, of the Treaty on Principles Governing the Activities of States in the Exploration and Use of Outer Space. For info: United Nations, Dept of Public Info, New York, NY 10017. Web: www.un.org.

YELTSIN SHELLS WHITE HOUSE: ANNIVERSARY. Oct 4, 1993. In a violent spectacle, the Russian military loyal to President Boris Yeltsin shelled the Russian White House, the symbol of Russian independence from communist rule. The parliament building had been seized by Yeltsin opponents led by Ruslan Khasbulatov and Alexander Rutskoi, who in the August 1992 coup had stood with Yeltsin on the White House balcony as he proclaimed that Russia should not submit to the coup plotters' attempts to turn back history. These former-allies-turned-foes reacted to Yeltsin's Sept 21 decision to dissolve the Russian parliament by seizing the parliament building. Yeltsin and his supporters succeeded in isolating them inside, cutting electricity and the flow of information to the building. But Rutskoi urged his followers to seize the Kremlin and other institutions, precipitating a day of bloody fighting in the streets of Moscow before the attackers retreated back into the White House.

BIRTHDAYS TODAY

Michael David (Mike) Adamle, 52, sportscaster, former football player, born Kent, OH, Oct 4, 1949.

Armand Assante, 52, actor (*Belizaire the Cajun, The Mambo Kings, Fatal Instinct*), born New York, NY, Oct 4, 1949.

Jackie Collins, 60, author (*Lucky*), born London, England, Oct 4, 1941.

Rachael Leigh Cook, 22, actress (*She's All That*, "The Baby-Sitter's Club"), born Minneapolis, MN, Oct 4, 1979.

Clifton Davis, 56, singer, actor ("That's My Mama," "Amen"), composer, born Chicago, IL, Oct 4, 1945.

Anita L. DeFrantz, 49, Olympics executive and former rower, born Philadelphia, PA, Oct 4, 1952.

Chuck Hagel, 55, US Senator (R, Nebraska), born North Platte, NE, Oct 4, 1946.

Charlton Heston, 79, actor (*The Ten Commandments, Ben-Hur, Planet of the Apes*), born Evanston, IL, Oct 4, 1922.

Tony La Russa, Jr, 57, baseball manager and former player, born Tampa, FL, Oct 4, 1944.

Jan Murray (Murry Janofsky), 84, comedian (emcee of "Dollar a Second," "Treasure Hunt"), born New York, NY, Oct 4, 1917.

Anne Rice, 60, novelist (*Interview with the Vampire*), born New Orleans, LA, Oct 4, 1941.

Susan Sarandon (Susan Tomaling), 55, actress (Oscar for *Dead Man Walking; Atlantic City, Thelma and Louise, Lorenzo's Oil*), born New York, NY, Oct 4, 1946.

Alicia Silverstone, 25, actress (*Phenomenon, Born on the Fourth of July*), born San Francisco, CA, Oct 4, 1976.

Alvin Toffler, 73, author (*Future Shock, Power Shift*), born New York, NY, Oct 4, 1928.

Jimy Williams, 58, baseball manager and former player, born Santa Maria, CA, Oct 4, 1943.

OCTOBER 5 — FRIDAY
Day 278 — 87 Remaining

ALABAMA NATIONAL FAIR. Oct 5–14. Garrett Coliseum/Fairgrounds, Montgomery, AL. A midway filled with exciting rides and games, arts and crafts, exhibits, livestock shows, racing pigs, a circus, a petting zoo, food and entertainment. Est attendance: 227,000. For info: Hazel Ashmore, PO Box 3304, Montgomery, AL 36109-0304. Phone: (334) 272-6831. Fax: (334) 272-6835.

ARKANSAS STATE FAIR AND LIVESTOCK SHOW.
Oct 5–13. Barton Coliseum and State Fairground, Little Rock, AR. Est attendance: 400,000. For info: Arkansas State Fair, PO Box 166660, Little Rock, AR 72216. Phone: (501) 372-8341. Fax: (501) 372-4197. Web: www.arkfairgrounds.com.

ARTHUR, CHESTER ALAN: BIRTH ANNIVERSARY.
Oct 5, 1829. The 21st president of the US, Chester Alan Arthur, was born at Fairfield, VT, and succeeded to the presidency following the death of James A. Garfield. Term of office: Sept 20, 1881–Mar 3, 1885. Arthur was not successful in obtaining the Republican party's nomination for the following term. He died at New York, NY, Nov 18, 1886.

CHIEF JOSEPH SURRENDER: ANNIVERSARY. Oct 5, 1877. After a 1,700-mile retreat, Chief Joseph and the Nez Perce Indians surrendered to US Cavalry troops at Bear's Paw near Chinook, MT, Oct 5, 1877. Chief Joseph made his famous speech of surrender, "From where the sun now stands, I will fight no more forever."

CIVIL WAR "SUBMARINE" ATTACK: ANNIVERSARY.
Oct 5, 1863. In an attempt to disrupt the Union blockade of Charleston Harbor, the Confederate semi-submersible *David* rammed the Federal ironclad *New Ironsides* with a spar torpedo. This was the first successful Southern attack using a submersible craft. Although both sides experimented with submarine warfare during the Civil War, the results were far from encouraging, as the submarines caused more fatalities to their own crews than to the opposing side.

COHOCTON FALL FOLIAGE FESTIVAL. Oct 5–7. Cohocton, NY. World-famous tree-sitting contest. Parade, more than 100 food, antiques, arts and crafts booths. 34th annual. Est attendance: 50,000. For info: Bob Fleishman, RD #2, Cohocton, NY 14826. Phone: (716) 384-5227 or (716) 384-5312.

COLUMBUS DAY FESTIVAL AND HOT–AIR BALLOON REGATTA. Oct 5–7. Downtown square and Industrial Park, Columbus, KS. Hot-Air Balloon Regatta starts with Balloon Glow Friday evening; prizes are awarded for both Saturday and Sunday races. Also, car show, arts and crafts fair, entertainment, children's festival and more. Est attendance: 10,000. For info: Jean Pritchett, Mgr, Columbus Chamber of Commerce, 320 E Maple, Columbus, KS 66725. Phone: (316) 429-1674. Fax: (316) 429-1674. E-mail: columbuschamber@columbus-ks.com. Web: www.columbus/ks.com.

COME AND TAKE IT DAY. Oct 5–7. Gonzales, TX. This celebration commemorating the first shot fired for Texas independence in 1835 is named for the defiant battle cry of the colonists when the Mexican military demanded the return of a cannon. Est attendance: 30,000. For info: Chamber of Commerce, Box 134, Gonzales, TX 78629. Phone: (830) 672-6532. Fax: (830) 672-6533. E-mail: info@gonzalestexas.com. Web: www.gonzales texas.com.

DALTON DEFENDERS DAY. Oct 5–6. Coffeyville, KS. Event to honor citizens killed during Dalton Gang's robbery of two banks on Oct 5, 1892. Est attendance: 10,000. For info: Coffeyville Area Chamber of Commerce, PO Box 457, Coffeyville, KS 67337. Phone: (316) 251-2550 or (800) 626-3357. Fax: (316) 251-5448. E-mail: chamber@coffeyville.com.

EDWARDS, JONATHAN: BIRTH ANNIVERSARY. Oct 5, 1703 (OS). Theologian and leader of the "Great Awakening," the religious revival in the colonies, born at East Windsor, CT. He later became president of the college of Princeton. Edwards died at Princeton, NJ, Mar 22, 1758, when he contracted smallpox from an inoculation.

ENRICO FERMI ATOMIC POWER PLANT ACCIDENT: 35th ANNIVERSARY. Oct 5, 1966. A radiation alarm and Class I alert at 3:09 PM, EST, signaled a problem at the Enrico Fermi Atomic Power Plant, Lagoona Beach, near Monroe, MI. The accident was contained, but nearly a decade was required to complete the decommissioning and disassembly of the plant.

FALL FESTIVAL (WITH OLE TIME FIDDLERS CONVENTION). Oct 5–14. Georgia Mountain Fairgrounds, Hiawassee, GA. The Fall Music Festival and the Ole Time Fiddlers Convention have been combined into a 10-day event. The first weekend will be the Fall Music Festival with country music, arts and crafts and a carnival. Open invitation to any single performers or bands who wish to participate. Amateur talent. Arts, crafts and carnival continue during the week with the Ole Time Fiddlers Convention the last weekend. Est attendance: 75,000. For info: Fall Festival, PO Box 444, Hiawassee, GA 30546. Phone: (706) 896-4191.

GEORGIA NATIONAL FAIR. Oct 5–14. Georgia National Fairgrounds, Perry, GA. Traditional state agricultural fair features thousands of entries in horse, livestock, horticultural, youth, home and fine arts categories. Family entertainment, education and fun. Sponsored by the State of Georgia. Annually, beginning the fifth Friday after Labor Day. Est attendance: 352,000. For info: John P. Webb, Jr, CFE, Georgia Natl Fair, PO Box 1367, Perry, GA 31069. Phone: (912) 987-3247. E-mail: webb1@alltel.net. Web: www.gnfa.com.

GODDARD, ROBERT HUTCHINGS: BIRTH ANNIVERSARY. Oct 5, 1882. The "father of the Space Age," born at Worcester, MA. Largely ignored or ridiculed during his lifetime because of his dreams of rocket travel, including travel to other planets. Launched a liquid-fuel-powered rocket Mar 16, 1926, at Auburn, MA. Died Aug 10, 1945, at Baltimore, MD. See also: "Goddard Day" (Mar 16).

HARVEST DAYS. Oct 5–7. Clarksville, VA, on Buggs Island, Kerr Lake. Anniversary Fall Festival marked by a time capsule. Weekend of activities including street dance, ice cream social, live musical entertainment of different types, tours of historic homes, parade, field day for children. Special feature: mock tobacco auction to highlight Clarksville's champion auctioneers and its having the oldest flue-cured tobacco market. Ethnic and traditional foods at a community meal. Annually, the first full weekend in October. For info: VLC Chamber of Commerce, Monique S. Derby, Exec Dir, PO Box 1017, Clarksville, VA 23927. Phone: (804) 374-2436.

HASENFUS, EUGENE, CAPTURED: 15th ANNIVERSARY. Oct 5, 1986. A plane carrying arms for the Nicaraguan rebels (contras) was shot down over Nicaragua on Oct 4. The only survivor was Eugene Hasenfus, ex-US Marine, of Marinette, WI, who parachuted from the doomed plane and was captured by Nicaraguan Sandinistas the following day. The US administration at first denied "any link" to the mission. Hasenfus was put on trial for violating Nicaraguan security laws. He was convicted and sentenced to 30 years in prison on Nov 15, 1986. On request of President Daniel Ortega, the Nicaraguan National Assembly pardoned Hasenfus on Dec 17, 1986, and he was flown back to the US. This episode commenced the unravelling and exposure of covert operations and possible violations of US law which in turn led to Congressional "Iran Contra" hearings and investigation by a special prosecutor.

HOLIDAY CRAFT AND GIFT SHOW. Oct 5–7. Jacob Building, Chilhowee Park, Knoxville, TN. 12th annual show featuring holiday-themed handmade crafts with an emphasis on home decor. Friday 11 AM–7 PM; Saturday 9 AM–6 PM; Sunday 12–5 PM. Est attendance: 13,000. For info: Cindy Crabtree, Esau, Inc, PO Box 50096, Knoxville, tn 37950. Phone: (865) 588-1233 or (800) 588-ESAU. Fax: (865) 588-6938. Web: www.esaushows.com.

KENTUCKY APPLE FESTIVAL. Oct 5–6. Paintsville, KY. Apple blossom beauty pageants, country music show, arts and crafts, flea market, antique car show, Corvette show, Apple Bowl, Terrapin Trot, amusement rides, food booths, clogging and square dancing. Annually, the first Friday and Saturday in October. Est attendance: 75,000. For info: Kentucky Apple Festival, Inc, Ray Tosti, Chmn, PO Box 879, Paintsville, KY 41240. Phone: (606) 789-4355 or (800) 542-5790.

LEE NATIONAL DENIM DAY. Oct 5 (or Oct 12—tentative). Companies allow employees to wear denim to work on this day in exchange for a contribution of $5 toward breast cancer research. Since this program began in 1996, more than $16 million has been raised for the Susan G. Komen Breast Cancer Foundation. Companies can register in September. Sponsored by Lee Jeans. For info: Phone: (800) 521-5533. Fax: (888) 254-4794. Web: www.denimday.com.

LITERALLY, A HAUNTED HOUSE. Oct 5–6. (Also Oct 12–13, 19–20, 26–27 & 31.) New Albany, IN. Friends of Culbertson Mansion fundraiser. Est attendance: 7,500. For info: Culbertson Mansion, 914 E Main, New Albany, IN 47150. Phone: (812) 944-9600. Web: www.ai.org/ism/sites/culbertson.

LONG GROVE APPLE FEST. Oct 5–7. Long Grove, IL. Bushels of fun and apple-inspired treats everywhere await visitors to this country village of nearly 100 specialty shops. Outdoor food booths, free music and entertainment, apple pie eating contests and special events. Admission and parking free. 10 AM–6 PM. Est attendance: 45,000. For info: Long Grove Merchants Assn, 307 Old McHenry Rd, Long Grove, IL 60047. Phone: (847) 634-0888. Fax: (847) 634-3673.

MAQUIS GRAS. Oct 5–7. Ramada Inn, Portage, IN. A fan-run Star Trek convention. A family-oriented event featuring dances, auctions, contests and a chance to meet actors from the Star Trek series and movies. Vendors are available to purchase collectibles and costuming items. Annually, the first full weekend in October. Est attendance: 450. For info: Kathy, PO Box 1101, Portage, IN 46368. Phone: (219) 464-7109. E-mail: katgar56@yahoo.com. Web: www.maquis.com/mfa.

MID-CONTINENT STEAM TRAIN AUTUMN COLOR TOURS. Oct 5–7 (also Oct 12–14). Mid-Continent Railway Museum, North Freedom, WI. Authentic steam train ride amid the brilliant hues of autumn. Annually, the first and second weekends in October. Est attendance: 3,500. For info: Angie Rizner, Wisconsin Dells Visitors Bureau, PO Box 390, Wisconsin Dells, WI 53965. Phone: (800) 223-3557. E-mail: info@wisdells.com. Web: www.wisdells.com.

★**NATIONAL DAY OF CONCERN ABOUT YOUNG PEOPLE AND GUN VIOLENCE.** Oct 5. Students across America are asked to voluntarily sign a "Student Pledge Against Gun Violence," a solemn promise never to bring a gun to school, never to use a gun to settle a dispute and to discourage their friends from using a gun.

October 2001	S	M	T	W	T	F	S
		1	2	3	4	5	6
	7	8	9	10	11	12	13
	14	15	16	17	18	19	20
	21	22	23	24	25	26	27
	28	29	30	31			

NATIONAL STORYTELLING FESTIVAL. Oct 5–7. Jonesborough, TN. Tennessee's oldest town plays host to the most dynamic storytelling event dedicated to the oral tradition. This three-day celebration showcases storytellers, stories and traditions from across America and around the world. Annually, the first full weekend in October. Est attendance: 10,000. For info: Storytelling Foundation Intl (SFI), 116 W Main, Jonesborough, TN 37659. Phone: (800) 952-8392. Fax: (423) 913-8219. Web: www.storytellingfestival.net.

OGLEBAYFEST. Oct 5–7. Oglebay, Wheeling, WV. If variety is what you enjoy, Oglebayfest is for you! Stop by and enjoy the Harvest Market, the beautiful chrysanthemums (90 varieties), a festive parade, the County Fair, German music, barbershop quartets and fireworks. Est attendance: 100,000. For info: Oglebay Visitor's Center, Oglebay Park, Wheeling, WV 26003. Phone: (304) 243-4010. Fax: (304) 243-4045. Web: www.oglebay-resort.com.

OKTOBERFEST. Oct 5–6 (also Oct 12–13). New Ulm, MN. Celebrating Minnesota's German heritage, with musical entertainment, food, horse drawn trolley rides, craft shows and dancing. Est attendance: 5,000. For info: New Ulm Chamber of Commerce, Box 384, New Ulm, MN 56073. Phone: (507) 233-4300 or (888) 4-NEWULM. E-mail: nuchamber@ic.new-ulm.mn.us.

PAUL BUNYAN SHOW. Oct 5–7. Hocking College Campus, Nelsonville, OH. Live demonstrations of forestry equipment, lumberjack contests, professional timber harvester competitions, forest industry trade show, chainsaw sculptors, Robbins Crossing interpretive history program, activities and steam show exhibits. Est attendance: 70,000. For info: Judy Sinnott, Public Info Dir, Hocking College, 3301 Hocking Pkwy, Nelsonville, OH 45764. Phone: (740) 753-3591 ext 2102. Fax: (740) 753-9018. E-mail: sinnott_j@hocking.edu.

REX ALLEN DAYS. Oct 5–7. Willcox, AZ. Annual celebration honors hometown boy Rex Allen, who gained fame as a singer, cowboy movie star and narrator for Walt Disney Productions. Celebration also honors Rex Allen, Jr, famed singer, who appeared on TNN's Yesteryears and Statler Brothers' Show. Activities include golf tournament, parade, country fair, rodeo, General Willcox Turtle Race, arts and crafts, country western concert, carnival, softball tournament, cowboy dances. Est attendance: 20,000. For info: Willcox Chamber of Commerce, 1500 N Circle I Rd, Willcox, AZ 85643. Phone: (520) 384-2272 or (800) 200-2272. Fax: (520) 384-0293. Web: www.rexallendays.com.

"SCHLITZ PLAYHOUSE OF STARS" TV PREMIERE: 50th ANNIVERSARY. Oct 5, 1951. This half-hour dramatic anthology on CBS gave many actors their first dramatic or TV role, including Amanda Blake (first major TV role), Lee Van Cleef (first major TV role), James Dean (last dramatic TV appearance), Gene Kelly (TV dramatic debut) and Janet Leigh (first dramatic American TV role). For several seasons Irene Dunne was the host, Robert Paige succeeded her.

SPACE MILESTONE: *CHALLENGER STS 41-G*. Oct 5, 1984. Space shuttle *Challenger* makes sixth mission with crew of seven, including two women. Launched from Kennedy Space Center, FL, on this date and landed there on Oct 13, 1984. Kathryn D. Sullivan became the first American woman to walk in space.

SPRINGS FOLK FESTIVAL. Oct 5–6. Springs, PA. 44th annual festival during the peak of fall foliage in Amish country. 135 craftsmen, Dutch food and continuous live music. Est attendance: 15,000. For info: Springs Folk Festival, PO Box 293, Springs, PA 15562. Phone: (814) 662-4158.

STAMP EXPO. Oct 5–7. Radisson Hotel, Anaheim, CA. Est attendance: 4,000. For info: Intl Stamp Collectors Society, PO Box 854, Van Nuys, CA 91408. Phone: (818) 997-6496. Fax: (818) 988-4337. E-mail: iibick@aol.com. Web: www.bick.net.

STONE, THOMAS: DEATH ANNIVERSARY. Oct 5, 1787. Signer of the Declaration of Independence, born 1743 (exact date unknown) at Charles County, MD. Died at Alexandria, VA.

TECUMSEH: DEATH ANNIVERSARY. Oct 5, 1813. Shawnee Indian chief and orator, born at Old Piqua near Springfield, OH, in March 1768. Tecumseh is regarded as one of the greatest of American Indians. He came to prominence between the years 1799 and 1804 as a powerful orator, defending his people against whites. He denounced as invalid all treaties by which Indians ceded their lands and condemned the chieftains who had entered into such agreements. With his brother Tenskwatawa, the Prophet, he established a town on the Tippecanoe River near Lafayette, IN, and then embarked on a mission to organize an Indian confederation to stop white encroachment. Although he advocated peaceful methods and negotiation, he did not rule out war as a last resort as he visited tribes throughout the country. While he was away, William Henry Harrison defeated the Prophet at the Battle of Tippecanoe Nov 7, 1811, and burned the town. Tecumseh organized a large force of Indian warriors and assisted the British in the War of 1812. Tecumseh was defeated and killed at the Battle of the Thames, Oct 5, 1813.

US OPEN STOCK DOG CHAMPIONSHIP. Oct 5–7. Hubert Bailey Farm, Dawsonville, GA. In the foothills of the Appalachian mountains, handlers from across the country will work both sheep and cattle. Also a petting zoo for children. Est attendance: 3,000. For info: Dawson County Chamber of Commerce, PO Box 299, Dawsonville, GA 30534. Phone: (706) 265-6278. Fax: (706) 265-6279. E-mail: info@dawson.org. Web: dawson.org.

VICTORIAN WEEK. Oct 5–14. Cape May, NJ. A 10-day celebration of Cape May's Victorian heritage, with self-guided tours of Victorian homes, antiques and crafts shows, vaudeville show and brass band concert, boisterous sing-alongs, entertaining and educational lectures. Annually, the 10 days beginning the Friday before Columbus Day. Est attendance: 15,000. For info: Mid-Atlantic Center for the Arts, PO Box 340, Cape May, NJ 08204. Phone: (609) 884-5404. E-mail: mac4arts@algorithms.com. Web: www.capemaymac.org.

WEBN HAUNTED HOUSE, CINCINNATI'S FRIGHTFUL FAVORITE!. Oct 5–28 (tentative, Thursday through Sunday only). Cincinnati, OH. Partnership with local boy scout troops featuring 20 horror-filled rooms and celebrity appearances from favorite horror movies. One of Cincinnati's top-rated haunted houses. Est attendance: 30,000. For info: Martha Izrad, Event Coord, Clear Channel Communications, Inc, 1111 St. Gregory St, Cincinnati, OH 45202. Phone: (513) 852-5876. Fax: (513) 333-4269. E-mail: marthaizard@clearchannel.com.

WORLD SMILE DAY. Oct 5. A day dedicated to good works and good cheer throughout the world. The official theme for the day is "Do an act of kindness. Help one person smile." The symbol for the day is the world famous "smiley face" icon, created in 1963 by Harvey Ball of Worcester, MA. This icon is now the international symbol of happiness and goodwill. Annually, the first Friday in October. For info: Harvey Ball, Pres, World Smile Corp, 22 Front St, PO Box 171, Worcester, MA 01614. Web: www.worldsmileday.com.

"YOU BET YOUR LIFE" TV PREMIERE: ANNIVERSARY. Oct 5, 1950. This funny game show began on radio in 1947 and moved to TV with Groucho Marx as host and George Fenneman as announcer and scorekeeper. Players tried to answer questions in the category of their choice, but Groucho's improvised interviews stole the show. Many unusual guests appeared, both professional and nonprofessional (including Phyllis Diller and Candice Bergen, who would later become famous). Players could also win money by uttering the secret word, an everyday word suspended above the stage on a duck that dropped when the word was spoken. This was one of the few shows to be filmed, because the interviews needed to be edited. Two short-lived revivals of the series aired, with Buddy Hackett as host in 1980, and with Bill Cosby in 1992.

"ZANE GREY THEATER" TV PREMIERE: 45th ANNIVERSARY. Oct 5, 1956. Officially titled "Dick Powell's Zane Grey Theater," this western anthology series was hosted by Powell and featured both stories by Grey and original telecasts. Powell occasionally starred in an episode. Guest stars included Hedy Lamarr (in her only dramatic TV role), Ginger Rogers, Claudette Colbert and Esther Williams.

BIRTHDAYS TODAY

Karen Allen, 50, actress (*The Wanderers, Raiders of the Lost Ark, Starman*), born Carrollton, IL, Oct 5, 1951.

Michael Andretti, 39, race car driver, son of Mario Andretti, born Bethlehem, PA, Oct 5, 1962.

Raymond Lester ("Trace") Armstrong, 36, football player, born Bethesda, MD, Oct 5, 1965.

Jeff Conaway, 51, actor ("Taxi," *Grease*), born New York, NY, Oct 5, 1950.

Bill Dana, 77, actor, comedian ("The Steve Allen Show," "The Bill Dana Show"), born Quincy, MA, Oct 5, 1924.

Laura Davies, 38, golfer, 1994 LPGA Championship winner, born Coventry, England, Oct 5, 1963.

Bob Geldof, 50, singer, lead singer (Boomtown Rats), born Dublin, Ireland, Oct 5, 1951.

Vaclav Havel, 65, dramatist, President of the Czech Republic, born Prague, Czechoslovakia, Oct 5, 1936.

Grant Hill, 29, basketball player, born Dallas, TX, Oct 5, 1972.

Glynis Johns, 78, actress (*Mary Poppins, The Ref, A Little Night Music*), born Pretoria, South Africa, Oct 5, 1923.

Bil Keane, 79, cartoonist ("Family Circus"), born Philadelphia, PA, Oct 5, 1922.

Mario Lemieux, 36, Hockey Hall of Famer, born Montreal, Quebec, Canada, Oct 5, 1965.

Steve Miller, 58, musician, singer (Steve Miller Band, "The Joker," "Abracadabra"), born Dallas, TX, Oct 5, 1943.

Patrick Roy, 36, hockey player, born Quebec City, Quebec, Canada, Oct 5, 1965.

Kate Winslet, 26, actress (*Titanic*), born Reading, England, Oct 5, 1975.

OCTOBER 6 — SATURDAY

Day 279 — 86 Remaining

AMERICAN LIBRARY ASSOCIATION FOUNDING: 125th ANNIVERSARY. Oct 6, 1876. Founded at Philadelphia, PA by 103 librarians attending the Centennial Exposition.

ANDERSONVILLE LIVING HISTORY AND CEMETERY DEDICATION. Oct 6–7. Andersonville, GA. Reenactment of post-Civil War Andersonville prison. Union encampment and portrayals of Clara Barton and others demonstrate efforts to identify almost 13,000 Union soldiers interred in the national cemetery. Est attendance: 1,200. For info: Andersonville Natl Historic Site, Alan Marsh, Park Ranger, Rte 1, Box 800, Hwy 49 N, Andersonville, GA 31711. Phone: (912) 924-0343.

APPLE BUTTER FESTIVAL. Oct 6–7. Berkeley Springs, WV. Fall festival with spicy apple butter simmering in copper kettles in the town square. A parade, two days of mountain music and old-fashioned contests. Fine crafts, farmer's market, down-home cooking and fall foliage. Annually, Columbus Day weekend. Est attendance: 40,000. For info: Apple Butter Festival, 304 Fairfax St, Berkeley Springs, WV 25411. Phone: (304) 258-3738.

APPLE HARVEST FESTIVAL. Oct 6–7. (also Oct 13–14) 37th annual. South Mountain Fairgrounds, Gettysburg, PA. Celebration includes tours of orchards, apple-butter boiling and antique cider press. Est attendance: 100,000. For info: Gettysburg CVB, PO Box 4117, Gettysburg, PA 17325. Phone: (717) 334-6274. Fax: (717) 334-1166. Web: www.gettysburg.com.

APPLEFEST. Oct 6–7. Downtown Weston, MO. Pressing apple cider, cooking apple butter, music, parade and Lost Arts demonstrations on Main Street. Est attendance: 8,500. For info: Weston Development Co, 502 Main, Weston, MO 64098. Phone: (816) 640-2909. Web: ci.weston.mo.us.

ARTS AND CRAFTS FAIR. Oct 6–7. Base Lodge, Jay Peak Ski Resort, Jay, VT. This annual event features more than 65 statewide artisans. The show is juried, providing many local crafters the opportunity to display their wares. Foliage tramway rides, German Bavarian buffet and entertainment are all part of this fall foliage event. Est attendance: 6,000. For info: Jay Peak Resort, Rte 242, Jay, VT 05859. Phone: (802) 988-2611. Fax: (802) 988-4049. E-mail: info@jaypeakresort.com. Web: www.jaypeakresort.com.

ARTS & CRAFTS FESTIVAL. Oct 6. Rolla, MO. Arts and craft festival held in conjunction with the University of Missouri-Rolla homecoming. Approximately 150 crafters plus food vendors. Annually, the first Saturday in October. Est attendance: 5,000. For info: Rolla Chamber of Commerce, 1301 Kingshighway, PO Box 823, Rolla, MO 65402. Phone: (573) 364-3577.

BATTLE OF GERMANTOWN REENACTMENT. Oct 6. Philadelphia, PA. Annual reenactment of the Oct 4, 1777, Battle of Germantown. Featured are more than 400 authentically costumed troops recreating the events of the original battle twice during the day, at noon and at 3 PM. Visit the nearby Germantown Country Fair for food and fun. Annually, the first Saturday in October. Est attendance: 4,000. For info: Public Relations, Cliveden of the National Trust, 6401 Germantown Ave, Philadelphia, PA 19144. Phone: (215) 848-1777. Fax: (215) 438-2892. Web: www.cliveden.org.

BIG ISLAND RENDEZVOUS. Oct 6–7. Bancroft Bay City Park, Albert Lea, MN. Named one of the top 25 festivals in Minnesota by Office of Tourism and nominated for Top 100 Festivals in North America. Fur-trade-era festival with old-time bluegrass and country music, black powder shoot, tipi village,

October	S	M	T	W	T	F	S
2001		1	2	3	4	5	6
	7	8	9	10	11	12	13
	14	15	16	17	18	19	20
	21	22	23	24	25	26	27
	28	29	30	31			

Colonial crafts for sale, workshops, traditional and ethnic foods. Est attendance: 13,000. For info: Big Island Rendezvous and Festival, Inc, 202 N Broadway, Albert Lea, MN 56007. Phone: (800) 658-2526. Fax: (507) 373-0344. E-mail: pvining@paulbunyan.net.

CELEBRATION OF FINE CRAFTS. Oct 6–7. Coolidge Park, Chattanooga, TN. Marketing the creative work of the hand by 100 select American craft artists. 6th annual fair. Annually, the first weekend in October. Est attendance: 12,000. For info: Alice C. Merritt, Exec Dir, Tennessee Assn of Craft Artists, PO Box 120066, Nashville, TN 37212. Phone: (615) 665-0502.

CHOWDERFEST. Oct 6–8. Mystic Seaport, Mystic, CT. Columbus Day weekend. A riverfront festival of New England chowders. Est attendance: 9,000. For info: Mystic Seaport, 75 Greenmanville Ave, PO Box 6000, Mystic, CT 06355-0990. Phone: (860) 572-5315 or (888) 9SEAPORT. Web: www.mysticseaport.org.

CHRYSANTHEMUM FLOWER SHOW. Oct 6–Nov 4. Garfield Park and Lincoln Park Conservatory, Chicago, IL. Mum's the word at Chicago Park District's 89th annual show. Thousands of blooms will fill the show houses with colors that vary from delicate pastel hues to the warm golden and russet colors of harvest time. The floral extravaganza offers a wide variety of different types of flowers including tiny daisy-like blooms, popular large flowering single stem mums, spidery bloom with narrow stringy petals and cascade mums. For info: Garfield Park Conservatory, 300 N Central Park Ave, Chicago, IL 60624. Phone: (312) 746-5100. Fax: (773) 638-1777. Web: www.garfield-conservatory.com. Lincoln Park Conservatory, 2400 N Stockton Dr, Chicago, IL 60614. Phone: (312) 742-7736.

CIRCLE CITY CLASSIC. Oct 6. RCA Dome, Indianapolis, IN. Bowl-style football game between two predominantly black universities is preceded by several days of related activities, including concerts, Coronation, College Fair and parade. Est attendance: 62,000. For info: Indiana Sports Corp, 201 S Capitol Ave, Ste 1200, Indianapolis, IN 46225. Phone: (317) 237-5000. Fax: (317) 237-5041. E-mail: isc@indianasportscorp.com. Web: www.indianasportscorp.com.

COWTOWN'S FALL COUNTY FAIR. Oct 6–7. Old Cowtown Museum, Wichita, KS. Re-creation of an 1870s fair with horse-drawn carriages, craft demonstrations and sales, livestock, music and reenactments. Annually, the first full weekend in October. Est attendance: 3,000. For info: Gloria G. Campbell, Dir, Old Cowtown Museum, 1871 Sim Park Dr, Wichita, KS 67203. Phone: (316) 264-0671. Fax: (316) 264-2937.

EAGLES POLKAFEST. Oct 6. Eagles Club, Dickinson, ND. Join in the fun with this all-day event. Polka, polka and more polka. Different polka bands are featured all day long with contests, food and drawings. Est attendance: 200. For info: Dennis Rixen, Eagles Club, 31 1st Ave, East, Dickinson, ND 58601. Phone: (701) 225-3561. Web: www.dickinsoncvb.com.

EGYPT: ARMED FORCES DAY. Oct 6. The Egyptian Army celebrates crossing into Sinai in 1973.

EL-SADAT, ANWAR: 20th ASSASSINATION ANNIVERSARY. Oct 6, 1981. Egyptian president and Nobel Peace Prize recipient Anwar el-Sadat was killed by assassins at Cairo while he was reviewing a military parade commemorating the 1973 Egyptian-Israeli War. At least eight other persons were reported killed in the attack on Sadat. Anwar el-Sadat was born Dec 25, 1918, at Mit Abu Al-Kom, a village near the Nile River delta.

FALL CITYWIDE GARAGE SALE. Oct 6. Electra, TX. Sales throughout the Electra area. Chamber of Commerce will provide free coffee and maps at 7 AM. The Chamber of Commerce office will close at 8 AM so that we too may enjoy all of the bargains. Est attendance: 500. For info: Dawn Dunsmore, Electra Chamber of Commerce, 112 W Cleveland, Electra, TX 76360. Phone: (940) 495-3577. E-mail: ElectraCoC@aol.com. Web: www.electratexas.org.

FELL'S POINT FUN FESTIVAL. Oct 6–7. Fell's Point National Historic District, Baltimore, MD. 35th annual popular outdoor street festival held in Baltimore's original seaport. 300+ arts and crafts vendors, antique market, carnival rides, hispanic area, five stages featuring rock and roll, bluegrass, jazz, blues, folk, gospel, dancing, etc, family and children's area, three beer gardens, international bazaar retail area, 40+ food vendors in three food courts and much more. Annually, the first full weekend in October. Sponsor: The Preservation Society. Est attendance: 700,000. For info: Fell's Point Fun Festival, 812 S Ann St, Baltimore, MD 21231. Phone: (410) 675-6756. Fax: (410) 675-6769. Web: www.preservationsociety.com.

FIESTA de COLORES. Oct 6–7. JK Northway Exposition Center, Kingsville, TX. Arts and crafts show and sale. Est attendance: 5,000. For info: Kingsville CVB, 1501 N Hwy 77, Kingsville, TX 78363. Phone: (800) 333-5032. Fax: (361) 592-3227. E-mail: cvb@kingsvilletexas.com. Web: www.kingsvilletexas.com.

HARVEST OF HARMONY. Oct 6. Downtown Grand Island, NE. Harvest of Harmony, observing its 60th annual event, is the largest high school band parade competition (115 bands last year) in the state of Nebraska. 58 float entries and 46 queen candidates also in the parade. Stadium competition for bands continues at the high school all day. Annually, the first Saturday in October. Sponsor: Grand Island Area Chamber of Commerce. Est attendance: 15,000. For info: Harvest of Harmony, Grand Island Area Chamber of Commerce, PO Box 1486, 309 W 2nd St, Grand Island, NE 68802. Phone: (308) 382-9210. Web: www.gichamber.com.

INTERNATIONAL FRUGAL FUN DAY. Oct 6. A day to celebrate that having fun doesn't have to be costly. Do at least one fun thing for yourself and/or your family that is free of cost or under $5 a person: a concert or play, a hike, a meal out, a picnic, an art gallery or museum tour, a day trip, a boat ride. Annually, the first Saturday in October. For info: Shel Horowitz, PO Box 1164, Northampton, MA 01061-1164. Phone: (413) 586-2388. Fax: (617) 249-0153. E-mail: info@frugalfun.com. Web: www.frugalfun.com/frugalfundayideas.html.

IRELAND: IVY DAY. Oct 6. The anniversary of the death of Irish nationalist leader and Home Rule advocate Charles Stewart Parnell (q.v.) is observed, especially in Ireland, as Ivy Day. A sprig of ivy is worn on the lapel to remember Parnell. James Joyce's short story "Ivy Day in the Committee Room," published in the collection titled *Dubliners*, addresses this event.

ISSAQUAH SALMON DAYS FESTIVAL. Oct 6–7. Issaquah, WA. To celebrate the return of the spawning salmon to the hatchery. Annually, the first weekend in October. Est attendance: 200,000. For info: Issaquah Salmon Days Festival, 155 NW Gilman Blvd, Issaquah, WA 98027. Phone: (425) 270-2532. Fax: (425) 392-8101.

JACKIE MAYER REHAB CENTER DAY. Oct 6. Providence Hospital, Sandusky, OH. Known as Sandusky, Ohio's "favorite daughter," Jacquelyn Jeanne Mayer, Miss America 1963 and stroke survivor since 1970, is honored on Oct 6, the anniversary of the 1997 renaming of Providence Hospital's rehab and nursing facility as the Jackie Mayer Rehab Center. After her stroke in 1970, it took Jackie Mayer seven years of self-directed rehab to regain her speech and mobility. Since then, she has been a motivational speaker and tireless advocate on behalf of stroke survivors across the US and Canada. For info: Dr Nancy Linenkugel, OSF, Pres and CEO, Providence Hospital, 1912 Hayes Ave, Sandusky, OH 44870. Phone: (419) 621-7070. Fax: (419) 621-7077. Web: www.providencehealth.org.

KNOX COUNTY SCENIC DRIVE. Oct 6–7 (also Oct 13–14). Knox County, IL. A self-conducted 100-mile driving tour through rural Spoon River Valley resplendent with fall colors. Different attractions at every stop feature food, crafts, art, antiques, fresh produce, old skills demonstrations, flea markets or games. Annually, the first two full weekends in October. Est attendance: 75,000. For info: Galesburg Area CVB, PO Box 60, Galesburg, IL 61402-0060. Phone: (309) 343-2485. Fax: (309) 343-2521. E-mail: visitors@galesburg.org. Web: www.galesburg.org/visitors.

LIND, JENNY: BIRTH ANNIVERSARY. Oct 6, 1820. Opera singer known as the "Swedish Nightingale," born at Stockholm, Sweden. She died at Malvern, England, Nov 2, 1887.

MAKOTI THRESHING BEE SHOW. Oct 6–7. Makoti, ND. To acquire, rebuild and maintain antique farm machinery and motor vehicles. Threshing and other demonstrations. Annually, the first weekend in October. Est attendance: 8,000. For info: Loren Quandt, Makoti Threshers, Inc, PO Box 124, Makoti, ND 58756. Phone: (701) 726-5649.

MAPLE LEAF FESTIVAL HERITAGE DAY. Oct 6. Hiawatha, KS. Arts and crafts on Courthouse lawn. Vendors come from all over to set up booths and show their crafts. Est attendance: 6,000. For info: Hiawatha Chamber of Commerce, 602 Oregon, Hiawatha, KS 66434. Phone: (785) 742-7136.

"MONTY PYTHON'S FLYING CIRCUS" TV PREMIERE: ANNIVERSARY. Oct 6, 1974. This series of wacky comedy skits debuted on the BBC in Great Britain in 1969 but didn't air on US TV until 1974. The cast was made up of Graham Chapman, John Cleese, Eric Idle, Terry Jones, Michael Palin and American Terry Gilliam. The troupe later went on to make three movies.

MORRO BAY HARBOR FESTIVAL. Oct 6–7. Morro Bay, CA. Celebrates a working waterfront at play! Officially launches "October Is National Seafood Month." Showcases seafood, fishing industry and diversity of marine life and coastal lifestyles. Features California Seafood Faire, wine and premium beer tasting, and a flotilla of family-oriented attractions. Annually, the first full weekend in October. Phone in California: (800) 366-6043. Est attendance: 45,000. For info: Exec Dir, Morro Bay Harbor Festival, Inc, PO Box 1869, Morro Bay, CA 93443. Phone: (805) 772-1155. E-mail: h20fest@fix.net. Web: www.harborfestival.morrobay.com.

★**NATIONAL GERMAN-AMERICAN DAY.** Oct 6. Celebration of German heritage and contributions German Americans have made to the building of the nation. A Presidential Proclamation has been issued each year since 1987. Annually, Oct 6.

OKTOBERFEST. Oct 6–7. St. Charles, MO. A citywide celebration of French and German heritage. Activities include a parade, German bands, foods and costumes. Annually, the first full weekend in October. Est attendance: 40,000. For info: Convention and Visitors Bureau, 230 S Main St, St. Charles, MO 63301. Phone: (800) 366-2427 or (636) 946-7776. Web: www.historicstcharles.com.

OYSTER FESTIVAL. Oct 6. Chincoteague Island, VA. Oysters fixed every way possible—all you can eat. Annually, Saturday of Columbus Day weekend. Tickets can be obtained in advance by contacting Chincoteague Chamber of Commerce. Est attendance: 2,600. For info: Jacklyn Russell, Chincoteague Chamber of Commerce, Box 258, Chincoteague Island, VA 23336. Phone: (757) 336-6161. Fax: (757) 336-1242. E-mail: pony@shore.intercom.net. Web: www.chincoteaguechamber.com.

"THE PEOPLE'S CHOICE" TV PREMIERE: ANNIVERSARY. Oct 6, 1955. This half-hour sitcom starred Jackie Cooper as Socrates (Sock) Miller, a government naturalist who becomes a politician and a real estate agent at New City, OK. Pat Breslin starred as Sock's girlfriend, Amanda (Mandy) Peoples, Paul Maxey as John Peoples, New City's mayor, Margaret Irving as Sock's Auntie Gus and Dick Wesson as Sock's friend Rollo. A unique characteristic of the show was a "talking" basset hound named Cleo who made comments during the episode.

PHYSICIAN ASSISTANT (PA) DAY. Oct 6. To acknowledge the unique contribution of Physician Assistants to provide access to medical care on the anniversary of the graduation of the first class of PAs from Duke University. For info: Nancy Hughes, VP, American Academy of Physician Assistants, 950 N Washington St, Alexandria, VA 22314-1534. Phone: (703) 836-2272. Fax: (703) 684-1924. E-mail: aapa@aapa.org. Web: www.aapa.org.

RENAISSANCE FAIRE. Oct 6. Belleville, IL. Come and celebrate the adventure, comedy and romance of the Renaissance in the Shrine's recreated 16th-century village. Enjoy performers, hearty food, arts and crafts, exhibits, plays and other fun activities from the days of yore. For info: Shrine of Our Lady of the Snows, 442 S DeMazenod Dr, Belleville, IL 62223-1094. Phone: (618) 397-6700. Fax: (618) 398-6549. Web: www.oblatesusa.org.

ROCKPORT SEAFAIR. Oct 6-7. Ski Basin area, Rockport, TX. Features fresh-from-the-bay seafood, gumbo cook-off, ongoing live musical entertainment, crab races, arts and crafts booths and land parade on Saturday. Annually, Columbus Day weekend. Est attendance: 40,000. For info: Rockport Seafair, 404 Broadway, Rockport, TX 78381. Phone: (800) 242-0071.

SAINT SIMONS BY THE SEA: AN ARTS FEST. Oct 6-7. St. Simons Island, GA. Sponsored by the Coastal Center for the Arts, now over a half-century of operation. Free admission for visitors; "juried to a quality level." Annually, the first full weekend in October. For info: Mittie B. Hendrix, Exec Dir, Coastal Center for the Arts, 2012 Demere Rd, St. Simons Island, GA 31522. Phone: (912) 634-0404.

SEIBERT, FLORENCE: BIRTH ANNIVERSARY. Oct 6, 1897. American physician Florence B. Seibert was born at Easton, PA. She developed the test for tuberculosis that was adopted by the US and used worldwide by the World Health Organization. She died Aug 23, 1991, at St. Petersburg, FL.

SPOON RIVER VALLEY SCENIC DRIVE. Oct 6-7 (also Oct 13-14). Fulton County, IL. Fall festival with fall foliage, arts and crafts, antiques and collectibles, demonstrations, exhibits, food and the beauty of the 140-mile-long Spoon River Valley. *Spoon River Anthology* in Lewistown. Annually, the first two weekends in October. Est attendance: 100,000. For info: Spoon River Valley Scenic Drive Assn, PO Box 525, Canton, IL 61520. Phone: (309) 647-8980.

SWAPPIN' MEETIN'. Oct 6-7. Southeast Community College, Cumberland, KY. A celebration of the rich heritage of the mountain people. Handmade goods such as quilts and woodwork are displayed; demonstrations include lye soap making, sorghum molasses making and folk singing. Est attendance: 10,000. For

info: Michael Corriston, Facility Dir, Appalachian Cntr, 700 College Rd, Cumberland, KY 40823. Phone: (606) 589-2145. Web: www.state.ky.us.

US WOMEN'S MID-AMATEUR (GOLF) CHAMPIONSHIP. Oct 6-11. Fox Run Golf Club, Eureka, MO. For info: Championship Dept, US Golf Assn, Golf House, PO Box 708, Far Hills, NJ 07931. Phone: (908) 234-2300. Web: www.usga.org.

VERMONT APPLE FESTIVAL. Oct 6-7. Riverside Middle School, Springfield, VT. Craft fair, apples, games and other family entertainment. Annually, Columbus Day weekend. Est attendance: 6,000. For info: Springfield Chamber of Commerce, 14 Clinton St, Springfield, VT 05156. Phone: (802) 885-2779. E-mail: spfldcoc@vermontel.com.

WESTINGHOUSE, GEORGE: BIRTH ANNIVERSARY. Oct 6, 1846. Engineer and inventor of the air brake for trains, born at Central Bridge, NY. He was the first employer to give his employees paid vacations. Westinghouse died at New York, NY, Mar 12, 1914.

WINFIELD ART-IN-THE-PARK FESTIVAL. Oct 6. Scenic Island Park, Winfield, KS. More than 100 artists and craftspersons display and sell their wares. Entertainment; food services available. $2 admission for those over 12 years of age. Annually, the first Saturday in October. Est attendance: 8,000. For info: Cheryl Tate, Adm Asst, Winfield Arts and Humanities Council, 700 Gary, Winfield, KS 67156-3731. Phone: (316) 221-2160. Fax: (316) 221-7232. E-mail: wahc@hit.net.

WOLLERSHEIM WINERY GRAPE STOMP FESTIVAL. Oct 6-7. Wollersheim Winery, Prairie du Sac, WI. Old-world tradition featuring wine tasting, grapespitting contests, cork-toss and "La Feet Classique Grape Stomp." Annually, the first weekend in October. Est attendance: 2,500. For info: Angie Rizner, Wisc Dells Visitors Bureau, PO Box 390, Wisconsin Dells, WI 53965. Phone: (608) 643-6515 or (800) VIP-WINE. E-mail: info@wisdells.com. Web: www.wisdells.com.

WOODLAND INDIAN CULTURAL DAYS. Oct 6. St. Mary's City, MD. Explore the lifeways of the Yaocomaco Indian people at the Woodland Indian Hamlet. Hands-on demonstrations, storytelling and more. Est attendance: 800. For info: Visitors Services, Historic St. Mary's City, PO Box 39, St. Mary's City, MD 20686. Phone: (301) 862-0990 or (800) SMC-1634. Fax: (301) 862-0968. Web: www.smcm.edu/hsmc/.

YOM KIPPUR WAR: ANNIVERSARY. Oct 6-25, 1973. A surprise attack by Egypt and Syria pushed Israeli forces several miles behind the 1967 cease-fire lines. Israel was caught off guard, partly because the attack came on the holiest Jewish religious day. After 18 days of fighting, hostilities were halted by the UN Oct 25. Israel partially recovered from the initial setback but failed to regain all the land lost in the fighting.

BIRTHDAYS TODAY

Shana Alexander, 76, journalist (formerly of "60 Minutes" Point-Counterpoint segment), author, born Boston, MA, Oct 6, 1925.

Britt Ekland, 59, actress (*The Night They Raided Minsky's*), born Stockholm, Sweden, Oct 6, 1942.

James Gilmore III, 52, Governor of Virginia (R), born Richmond, VA, Oct 6, 1949.

Thor Heyerdahl, 87, anthropologist, explorer, author (*Kon Tiki*), born Larvik, Norway, Oct 6, 1914.

Rebecca Lobo, 28, basketball player, born Southwick, MA, Oct 6, 1973.

Elisabeth Shue, 38, actress (*Adventures in Babysitting, Leaving Las Vegas*), born Wilmington, DE, Oct 6, 1963.

Fred Travalena, 59, actor ("Keep On Truckin'," "ABC Comedy Hour"), born New York, NY, Oct 6, 1942.

Stephanie Zimbalist, 45, actress ("Remington Steele"), born Encino, CA, Oct 6, 1956.

David Zucker, 54, writer, producer, with his brother Jerry, (*Naked Gun* movies, *Airplane!*), born Milwaukee, WI, Oct 6, 1947.

October 2001	S	M	T	W	T	F	S
		1	2	3	4	5	6
	7	8	9	10	11	12	13
	14	15	16	17	18	19	20
	21	22	23	24	25	26	27
	28	29	30	31			

OCTOBER 7 — SUNDAY
Day 280 — 85 Remaining

ASSOCIATION FOR DRESSINGS AND SAUCES ANNUAL MEETING. Oct 7–10. Sheraton El Conquistador, Tucson, AZ. For info: Jacque Knight, Assn for Dressings and Sauces, 5775 Peachtree-Dunwoody Rd, Ste 500-G, Atlanta, GA 30342. Phone: (404) 252-3663. Fax: (404) 252-0774. E-mail: ads @assnhq.com. Web: www.dressings-sauces.org.

BIG "C" ATTUS DAY. Oct 7. Cattus Island County Park, Toms River, NJ. Environmental organizations fair with natural history programs throughout the day. Annually, the first Sunday in October. Est attendance: 1,200. For info: Shaun O'Rourke, Cooper Environmental Center, 1170 Cattus Island Blvd, Toms River, NJ 08753. Phone: (732) 270-6960.

BLESSING OF THE FISHING FLEET. Oct 7. Church of Saints Peter and Paul and Fisherman's Wharf, San Francisco, CA. Annually, the first Sunday in October.

CIVIL WAR GARRISON DAY. Oct 7. Historic Fort Mifflin, Philadelphia, PA. Civil War reenactment and encampment with living history programs, tactical displays, medical demonstrations, costumed reenactors, 19th-century clothing displays and music. Est attendance: 500. For info: Fort Mifflin on the Delaware, Fort Mifflin Rd, Philadelphia, PA 19153. Phone: (215) 685-4192. Fax: (215) 492-1608.

DOW-JONES INDUSTRIAL AVERAGE: ANNIVERSARY. Oct 7, 1896. Dow Jones began reporting an average of the prices of 12 industrial stocks in the *Wall Street Journal* on this day. In the early years, these were largely railroad stocks. In 1928 Mr Dow expanded the number of stocks to 30, where it remains today. Today, the large, frequently-traded stocks in the DJIA represent about a fifth of the market value of all US stocks.

★ FIRE PREVENTION WEEK. Oct 7–13. Presidential Proclamation issued annually for the first or second week in October since 1925. For many years prior to 1925, National Fire Prevention Day was observed in October. Sponsored by the National Fire Protection Association. Annually, the Sunday-through-Saturday period during which the Oct 9 anniversary date falls.

FIRE PREVENTION WEEK. Oct 7–13. To increase awareness of the dangers of fire and to educate the public on how to stay safe from fire. For info: Natl Fire Protection Assn, One Batterymarch Park, Quincy, MA 02269. Phone: (617) 770-3000. Web: www.nfpa.org. and www.sparky.org.

"THE FRANK SINATRA SHOW" TV PREMIERE: ANNIVERSARY. Oct 7, 1950. Crooner Frank Sinatra's first series was a musical variety show featuring regulars Erin O'Brien and comic Ben Blue. However, during its last season this show was cut from an hour to 30 minutes as it could not compete with "The Texaco Star Theater," the most popular show of the time.

GERMANY: ERNTEDANKFEST. Oct 7. A harvest thanksgiving festival, or potato harvest festival, Erntedankfest (or Erntedanktag) is generally observed on the first Sunday in October.

GET ORGANIZED WEEK. Oct 7–13. This is an opportunity to streamline your life, create more time, lower your stress and increase your profit. Simplify your situation and make it more manageable by taking advantage of this time to get organized. Annually, the first full week in October. For info: Natl Assn of Professional Organizers, PO Box 140647, Austin, TX 78714-0647. Web: www.napo.net.

HARVEST CELEBRATION. Oct 7. Woodstock, VT. Traditional celebration of the harvest featuring a husking bee, barn dance and the arrival of the giant pumpkins. Also, farm harvest activities including food preservation, traditional toy making and cider pressing. Est attendance: 1,600. For info: Billings Farm and Museum, PO Box 489, Woodstock, VT 05091. Phone: (802) 457-2355. Fax: (802) 457-4663. E-mail: billings.farm@valley.net.

HOME-BASED BUSINESS WEEK. Oct 7–13. To celebrate, recognize and promote the home-based entrepreneur. Annually, the week including the second Tuesday of October. For info: Beverley Williams, American Assn of Home-Based Businesses, PO Box 10023, Rockville, MD 20849-0023. Phone: (800) 447-9710. Fax: (301) 963-7042. E-mail: aahbb@crosslink.net. Web: www .aahbb.org.

THE LASALLE BANK CHICAGO MARATHON. Oct 7. Grant Park, Chicago, IL. Consists of 26.2 mile marathon which attracts an international field of the world's top athletes. This marathon is ranked as one of the fastest in the world by *Runner's World* magazine. Coincides with Health and Fitness Expo at McCormick Place on Friday and Saturday. Est attendance: 25,000. For info: The LaSalle Bank Chicago Marathon, 11 East Adams, Lower Level II, Chicago, IL 60604. Phone: (312) 904-9800. Fax: (312) 904-9820. Web: www.chicagomarathon .com.

LITTLE RED SCHOOL HOUSE ART FAIR. Oct 7. Willow Springs, IL. Est attendance: 12,000. For info: Little Red School House Art Fair, Cook County Forest Preserve, 9800 S 104th Ave, Willow Springs, IL 60480. Phone: (708) 839-6897.

★ MINORITY ENTERPRISE DEVELOPMENT WEEK. Oct 7–13. Presidential Proclamation issued without request since 1983 for the first full week in October except in 1991 when issued for Sept 22–28, in 1992 for Sept 27–Oct 3, to coincide with the National Conference and in 1997 for Sept 21–27.

MYSTERY SERIES WEEK. Oct 7–13. A celebration of continuing characters in mystery fiction. Two-thirds of all new mysteries each year feature a series detective. The series tradition has been alive and well for more than 100 years. Series readers today can choose from more than 7,500 adult mysteries featuring more than 1,500 continuing characters from living writers. Mystery Series Week will celebrate fictional cops, private eyes and amateur sleuths from all walks of life—solving crimes from 55 BC to the 22nd century. Annually, the first full week in October. For info: Purple Moon Press, 3319 Greenfield Rd, Ste 317, Dearborn, MI 48120-1212. Phone: (313) 593-1033. Fax: (313) 593-4087. E-mail: PurpleMoon@prodigy.net. Web: www.mysteryseriesweek .com.

NATIONAL CHILI WEEK. Oct 7–13. National observance and celebration of chili, one of the most historical and traditional American dishes. For info: Williams Foods, Inc, 13301 W 99th St, Lenexa, KS 66215. Phone: (913) 888-4343. Fax: (913) 888-0727.

NATIONAL METRIC WEEK. Oct 7–13. To maintain an awareness of the importance of the metric system as the primary system of measurement for the US. Annually, the week of the tenth month containing the tenth day of the month. For info: US Metric Assn, 10245 Andasol Ave, Northridge, CA 91325-1504. Phone: (813) 363-5606. Web: www.metric.org.

PULASKI DAY PARADE. Oct 7. Philadelphia, PA. Parade honoring the Polish patriot known as the "Father of the American Cavalry." Begins at 19th and JFK Blvd and ends at 19th and Benjamin Franklin Parkway. For info: Polish American Congress, Eastern Pennsylvania District, 308 Walnut St, Philadelphia, PA 19106. Phone: (215) 739-3408. Fax: (215) 922-1518. Web: www.polishamericancongress.com.

RODNEY, CAESAR: BIRTH ANNIVERSARY. Oct 7, 1728 (OS). Signer of the Declaration of Independence who cast a tie-breaking vote. Born near Dover, DE, he died June 26, 1784. Rodney is on a quarter issued by the US Mint in 1999, the first in a series of quarters that will commemorate each of the 50 states.

SMITH VALLEY FUN DAYS. Oct 7. Smith Valley, NV. Car show, arts, crafts, BBQ, hay ride and more. For info: Mason Valley Chamber of Commerce, 227 S Main St, Yerington, NV 89447. Phone: (775) 463-2245. Fax: (775) 463-3369. Web: www.tele-net.net/lyon.

SQUIRREL AWARENESS WEEK (SAW). Oct 7–13. Set aside to honor one of our friendliest forms of wildlife, squirrels. "I SAW a squirrel today." Annually, the first Sunday in October through the following Saturday. For info: Gregg Bassett, The Squirrel Lover's Club, 318 W Fremont Ave, Elmhurst, IL 60126. Phone: (630) 833-1117. Fax: (630) 833-1449. E-mail: sqrlman@mediaone.net. Web: members.aol.com/sqrllovers.

WALLACE, HENRY AGARD: BIRTH ANNIVERSARY. Oct 7, 1888. Thirty-third vice president of the US (1941–45) born at Adair County, IA. Died at Danbury, CT, Nov 18, 1965.

WISE, THOMAS JAMES: BIRTH ANNIVERSARY. Oct 7, 1859. English bibliophile and literary forger, born at Gravesend, England. One of England's most distinguished bibliographic experts, he was revealed, in 1934, to have forged dozens of "first editions" and "unique" publications over a period of more than 20 years. Many of them had been sold at high prices to collectors and libraries. The forgeries in some cases purported to pre-date the real first editions. Wise, whose health was broken when the exposure came, died at Hampstead, England, May 13, 1937.

WORLD COMMUNION SUNDAY. Oct 7. Communion is celebrated by Christians all over the world. Annually, the first Sunday in October.

"YOUR HIT PARADE" TV PREMIERE: ANNIVERSARY. Oct 7, 1950. "Your Hit Parade" began as a radio show in 1935. When it finally made it to TV, the format was simple: the show's cast performed the week's top musical hits. To sustain interest, since many of the same songs appeared weekly, eye-catching production sequences were created. "YHP" was the starting point for many famous choreographers and dancers, including Tony Charmoli, Ernie Flatt, Peter Gennaro and Bob Fosse. Regulars included Dorothy Collins, Eileen Wilson, Snooky Lanson and Sue Bennett. The show was overhauled many times and switched networks before leaving the air in 1959. A summer revival in 1974 was short-lived. See also: " 'Your Hit Parade' Radio Premiere: Anniversary" (Apr 12).

BIRTHDAYS TODAY

June Allyson (Ella Geisman), 84, actress (*Little Women, The Shrike*, "The June Allyson Show"), born Lucerne, NY, Oct 7, 1917.
Imamu Amiri Baraka (Leroi Jones), 67, poet, dramatist, born Newark, NJ, Oct 7, 1934.
Toni Braxton, 34, singer, born Severn, MD, Oct 7, 1967.
Charles Dutoit, 65, Swiss conductor, born Lausanne, Switzerland, Oct 7, 1936.

	S	M	T	W	T	F	S
October		1	2	3	4	5	6
2001	7	8	9	10	11	12	13
	14	15	16	17	18	19	20
	21	22	23	24	25	26	27
	28	29	30	31			

Thomas Keneally, 66, novelist (*Schindler's List*), born New South Wales, Australia, Oct 7, 1935.
Yo-Yo Ma, 46, cellist, born Paris, France, Oct 7, 1955.
Al Martino (Alfred Cini), 74, actor, singer (*Hello Dolly, Phantom of the Opera*), born Philadelphia, PA, Oct 7, 1927.
John Mellencamp, 50, singer (*American Fool, Uh-Huh*), born Seymour, IN, Oct 7, 1951.
Oliver Laurence North, 58, US Marine Corps Lieutenant Colonel, center of Iran-Contra controversy, born San Antonio, TX, Oct 7, 1943.
Desmond Tutu, 70, South African archbishop, Nobel Peace Prize winner, born Klerksdorp, South Africa, Oct 7, 1931.

OCTOBER 8 — MONDAY
Day 281 — 84 Remaining

ALVIN C. YORK DAY. Oct 8, 1918. Sergeant Alvin C. York (while in the Argonne Forest, France, and separated from his patrol) killed 20 enemy soldiers and captured a hill, 132 enemy soldiers and 35 machine guns. He was awarded the US Medal of Honor and French Croix de Guerre. Ironically, York had petitioned for exemption from the draft as a conscientious objector, but was turned down by his local draft board.

AMERICAN INDIAN HERITAGE DAY (ALABAMA). Oct 8. First declared in 2000, this state holiday will also be observed as Columbus Day in Alabama. Annually, the second Monday in October.

CANADA: THANKSGIVING DAY. Oct 8. Observed on second Monday in October each year.

COLUMBUS DAY OBSERVANCE. Oct 8. Public Law 90–363 sets observance of Columbus Day on the second Monday in October. Applicable to federal employees and to the District of Columbia, but observed also in most states. Commemorates the landfall of Columbus in the New World, Oct 12, 1492. See also: "Columbus Day (Traditional)" (Oct 12).

★**COLUMBUS DAY.** Oct 8. Presidential Proclamation always the second Monday in October. Observed on Oct 12 from 1934 to 1970 (Pub Res No 21 of Apr 30, 1934). PL90–363 of June 28, 1968, required that beginning in 1971 it would be observed on the second Monday in October.

COLUMBUS DAY ON THE *SANTA MARIA*. Oct 8. Battelle Park, Columbus, OH. Columbus Day observances planned on board the *Santa Maria*, the only full-size replica of Columbus's flagship on permanent display in North America. Est attendance: 200. For info: Columbus Santa Maria, 90 W Broad St, 1st Floor, Columbus, OH 43215-9109. Phone: (614) 645-8760. Fax: (614) 645-8748. Web: www.SantaMaria.org.

GREAT CHICAGO FIRE: ANNIVERSARY. Oct 8, 1871. Great fire of Chicago began, according to legend, when Mrs O'Leary's cow kicked over the lantern in her barn on DeKoven Street. The fire leveled 3½ sq miles, destroying 17,450 buildings and leaving 98,500 people homeless and about 250 people dead. Financially, the loss was $200 million. On the same day a fire destroyed the entire town of Peshtigo, WI, killing more than 1,100 people.

JAPAN: HEALTH-SPORTS DAY ANNIVERSARY. Oct 8. National holiday to encourage physical activity for building sound body and mind. Created in 1966 to commemorate the day of the opening of the 18th Olympic Games at Tokyo, Oct 10, 1964. Annually, the second Monday in October.

LOVABLE LAWYERS DAY. Oct 8. Let's face it, lawyers get a lot of bad press. Yet many lawyers are warm and friendly; even lovable! They have a passion for helping others and making a difference in the world. Celebrate these exceptional men and women. For a free report, "The Top 10 Things That Make a Lawyer Lovable," e-mail LovableLawyers@sendfree.com. For info: Sheila Martin, 250 H St, Blaine, WA 98230. Phone: (604) 535-3636. E-mail: sheila@we-build-dreams.com.

★**NATIONAL CHILDREN'S DAY.** Oct 8.

NATIONAL PET PEEVE WEEK. Oct 8–12. A chance for people to make others aware of all the little things in life they find so annoying, in the hope of changing some of them. Annually, the second full week of October. When requesting info, please send SASE. For info: Ad-America, Pine Tree Center Indust Park, 2215 29th St SE, Ste B-7, Grand Rapids, MI 49508. Phone: (616) 247-3797. Fax: (616) 247-3798. E-mail: adamerica@aol.com.

NATIVE AMERICANS' DAY (SOUTH DAKOTA). Oct 8. Observed in the state of South Dakota as a legal holiday, dedicated to the remembrance of the great Native American leaders who contributed so much to the history of South Dakota. Annually, the second Monday in October.

NORMAN ROCKWELL'S SELF-PORTRAIT: ANNIVERSARY. Oct 8, 1938. For the *Saturday Evening Post* cover for this date Norman Rockwell chose to portray himself in a quandary he frequently had to grapple with—trying to come up with a cover for the *Post* on deadline.

"OZZIE AND HARRIET SHOW" RADIO DEBUT: ANNIVERSARY. Oct 8, 1944. Ozzie and Harriet Nelson made their CBS Radio debut in "The Adventures of Ozzie and Harriet." Although their sons David and Ricky were referred to frequently on air and eventually played by others, it was not until Feb 20, 1949, that David (age 12) and Rick (age 8) first appeared playing themselves on the show. "The Adventures of Ozzie and Harriet" hit television airwaves Oct 3, 1952, on ABC.

PERU: DAY OF THE NAVY. Oct 8. Public holiday in Peru.

PESHTIGO FOREST FIRE: ANNIVERSARY. Oct 8, 1871. One of the most disastrous forest fires in history began at Peshtigo, WI, the same day the Great Chicago Fire began. The Wisconsin fire burned across six counties, killing more than 1,100 persons.

"THE RAY BOLGER SHOW" TV PREMIERE: ANNIVERSARY. Oct 8, 1953. Originally titled "Where's Raymond?," the format of this half-hour sitcom allowed Bolger to play a character like himself. With Bolger playing Ray Wallace, a Broadway star living in the suburbs, there was plenty of music, dancing and comedy.

RICKENBACKER, EDWARD V.: BIRTH ANNIVERSARY. Oct 8, 1890. Aviator, auto racer, war hero, born at Columbus, OH. Died July 23, 1973, at Zurich, Switzerland.

SCHUTZ, HEINRICH: BIRTH ANNIVERSARY. Oct 8, 1585. German musician and composer sometimes called the father of German music. Born at Kostritz, Saxony, Schutz died at Dresden, Germany, Nov 6, 1672. His works enjoyed renewed attention on the occasions of the bicentennials (1885) and tricentennials (1985) of two of his most devoted followers: George Frederick Handel and Johann Sebastian Bach.

VIRGIN ISLANDS–PUERTO RICO FRIENDSHIP DAY. Oct 8. Columbus Day (second Monday in October) also celebrates historical friendship between peoples of Virgin Islands and Puerto Rico.

YORKTOWN VICTORY DAY. Oct 8. Observed as a holiday in Virginia. Annually, the second Monday in October.

BIRTHDAYS TODAY

Rona Barrett, 65, gossip columnist, born New York, NY, Oct 8, 1936.

Chevy Chase (Cornelius Crane), 58, comedian, actor ("Saturday Night Live," *Caddyshack*), born New York, NY, Oct 8, 1943.

Clodagh (Clodagh Aubry), 64, designer, born Galway, Ireland, Oct 8, 1937.

Matt Damon, 31, actor (*Good Will Hunting, The Rainmaker*), born Cambridge, MA, Oct 8, 1970.

Paul Hogan, 62, actor, writer (*Crocodile Dundee, Crocodile Dundee II*), born Lightning Ridge, Australia, Oct 8, 1939.

Jesse Jackson, 60, clergyman, civil rights leader ("I am somebody," "Keep hope alive"), born Greenville, NC, Oct 8, 1941.

Sarah Purcell, 53, TV personality ("Real People"), born Richmond, IN, Oct 8, 1948.

Faith Ringgold, 71, artist, writer (*Tar Beach, My Dream of Martin Luther King*), born New York, NY, Oct 8, 1930.

Rashaan Salaam, 27, football player, born San Diego, CA, Oct 8, 1974.

R.L. Stine, 58, author (*Goosebumps* series) books for children, born Columbus, OH, Oct 8, 1943.

Sigourney (Susan) Weaver, 52, actress (*Ghostbusters, Gorillas in the Mist, Aliens*), born New York, NY, Oct 8, 1949.

OCTOBER 9 — TUESDAY
Day 282 — 83 Remaining

ICELAND: LEIF ERIKSON DAY. Oct 9. Celebrates discovery of North America in the year 1000 by Norse explorer.

KOREA: ALPHABET DAY (HANGUL): ANNIVERSARY. Oct 9. Celebrates anniversary of promulgation of Hangul (24-letter phonetic alphabet) by King Sejong of the Yi Dynasty, in 1446.

★**LEIF ERIKSON DAY.** Oct 9. Presidential Proclamation always issued for Oct 9 since 1964 (PL88–566 of Sept 2, 1964) at request.

LENNON, JOHN: BIRTH ANNIVERSARY. Oct 9, 1940. John Winston Lennon, English composer, musician, member of "The Beatles," a sensationally popular group of musical performers who captivated audiences first in England and Germany, and later throughout the world. Born at Liverpool, England, Lennon was murdered at New York City, Dec 8, 1980.

MISSION DELORES FOUNDING: 225th ANNIVERSARY. Oct 9, 1776. The oldest building at San Francisco, CA. Formerly known as Mission San Francisco de Asis, the mission survived the great earthquake and fire of 1906.

NORSK HOSTFEST. Oct 9–13. State Fairgrounds, Minot, ND. The Northern Plains' biggest ethnic festival draws thousands of people to Minot for Scandinavian and American entertainment, Scandinavian delicacies, arts and crafts exhibits and dignitaries representing Sweden, Norway, Denmark, Iceland and Finland with big-name entertainment nightly. Est attendance: 35,000. For info: North Dakota Tourism, 604 E Boulevard, Bismarck, ND 58505. Phone: (701) 328-2525 or (800) 435-5663.

SHEMINI ATZERET. Oct 9. Hebrew calendar date: Tishri 22, 5762. The eighth day of Solemn Assembly, part of the Sukkot Festival (see entry on Oct 2), with memorial services and cycle of Biblical readings in the synagogue.

"TOPPER" TV PREMIERE: ANNIVERSARY. Oct 9, 1953. In this sitcom a man moves into a new home with his wife, only to discover that it's haunted by ghosts only he can see. Leo G. Carroll starred as Cosmo Topper and Anne Jeffreys and Robert Sterling starred as Marion and George Kerby, who had been killed in a skiing accident and returned to their former home as ghosts. The show was based on Thorne Smith's novel and used trick photography for some of the ghost scenes.

UGANDA: INDEPENDENCE DAY. Oct 9. National holiday commemorating achievement of autonomy from Britain in 1962.

UNITED NATIONS: WORLD POST DAY. Oct 9. An annual special observance of Postal Administrations of the Universal Postal Union (UPU). For info: United Nations, Dept of Public Info, Public Inquiries Unit, Rm GA-57, New York, NY 10017. Phone: (212) 963-4475. E-mail: inquiries@un.org.

BIRTHDAYS TODAY

Scott Bakula, 46, actor ("Quantum Leap," "Murphy Brown"), born St. Louis, MO, Oct 9, 1955.

Jackson Browne, 51, singer, songwriter ("Running on Empty," "Lawyers in Love"), born Heidelberg, Germany, Oct 9, 1950.

Zachery Ty Bryan, 20, actor ("Home Improvement"), born Aurora, CO, Oct 9, 1981.

Trent Lott, 60, US Senator (R, Mississippi), born Duck Hill, MS, Oct 9, 1941.

Russell Myers, 63, cartoonist ("Broom Hilda"), born Pittsburg, KS, Oct 9, 1938.

Michael Pare, 42, actor (*Streets of Fire, The Philadelphia Experiment*), born Brooklyn, NY, Oct 9, 1959.

Joseph Anthony (Joe) Pepitone, 61, former baseball player, born New York, NY, Oct 9, 1940.

Tony Shalhoub, 48, actor ("Wings," "Stark Raving Mad"), born Green Bay, WI, Oct 9, 1953.

Donald Sinden, 78, actor (*The Day of the Jackal*), born Plymouth, England, Oct 9, 1923.

Michael (Mike) Singletary, 43, Pro Football Hall of Fame linebacker, born Houston, TX, Oct 9, 1958.

Annika Sorenstam, 31, golfer, born Stockholm, Sweden, Oct 9, 1970.

Robert Wuhl, 50, writer, actor (*Bull Durham, Cobb*), born Union, NJ, Oct 9, 1951.

OCTOBER 10 — WEDNESDAY
Day 283 — 82 Remaining

AGNEW RESIGNATION: ANNIVERSARY. Oct 10, 1973. Spiro Theodore Agnew became the second person to resign the office of vice president of the United States. Agnew entered a plea of no contest to a charge of income tax evasion (on contract kickbacks received while he was governor of Maryland and after he became vice president). He was sentenced to pay a $10,000 fine and serve three years probation. Agnew was elected vice president twice, serving under President Richard M. Nixon. He died in 1996. See also "Agnew, Spiro: Birth Anniversary" (Nov 9).

"THE BOB NEWHART SHOW" TV PREMIERE: ANNIVERSARY. Oct 10, 1962. This half-hour variety series was hosted by Bob Newhart, a successful stand-up comedian famous

	S	M	T	W	T	F	S
October		1	2	3	4	5	6
2001	7	8	9	10	11	12	13
	14	15	16	17	18	19	20
	21	22	23	24	25	26	27
	28	29	30	31			

for his trademark "telephone conversation" monologues. Regulars included Jackie Joseph, Kay Westfall, Jack Grinnage, Mickey Manners, Pearl Shear, June Ericson, Andy Albin and announcer Dan Sorkin. The show was critically acclaimed, winning both an Emmy and a Peabody in its short time on the air. Newhart later starred in situation comedies. In "The Bob Newhart Show," which aired 1972–78, he played a psychologist. See also: "Newhart TV Premiere: Anniversary" (Oct 25).

BONZA BOTTLER DAY™. Oct 10. To celebrate when the number of the day is the same as the number of the month. Bonza Bottler Day™ is an excuse to have a party at least once a month. For more information, see Jan 1. For info: Gail M. Berger, 109 Matthew Ave, Poca, WV 25159. Phone: (304) 776-7746. E-mail: gberger5@aol.com.

DOUBLE TENTH DAY: 90th ANNIVERSARY. Oct 10, 1911. Tenth day of 10th month, Double Tenth Day, is observed by many Chinese as the anniversary of the outbreak of the revolution against the imperial Manchu dynasty, Oct 10, 1911. Sun Yat-sen and Huan Hsing were among the revolutionary leaders. This is a holiday in Taiwan.

FIJI: INDEPENDENCE DAY: ANNIVERSARY. Oct 10. National holiday. Commemorates independence from Britain in 1970.

GERMANY: FRANKFURT BOOK FAIR. Oct 10–15. Fairgrounds, Frankfurt. World's largest international book fair; also important event for electronic media. Best place for international rights and licenses. Open to trade for four days and to the public for two. Est attendance: 320,000. For info: Ausstellungs-und Messe (Frankfurt Book Fair), Reineckstr. 3, Frankfurt am Main, Germany D-60313. Phone: (49) 69 2102-0. Fax: (49) 69 2102-227. E-mail: marketing@book-fair.com. Web: www.frankfurt-book-fair.com.

HAYES, HELEN: BIRTH ANNIVERSARY. Oct 10, 1900. Actress Helen Hayes, often called the First Lady of the American theater, was born at Washington, DC. Hayes's greatest stage triumph was her role as the long-lived British monarch Queen Victoria in the play *Victoria Regina*. Her first great success was in *Coquette* (1927). She won an Academy Award for best actress for her first major film role in *The Sin of Madelon Claudet* (1931) and won best supporting actress for her role in *Airport* (1971). Helen Hayes died Mar 17, 1993, at Nyack, NY.

MOON PHASE: LAST QUARTER. Oct 10. Moon enters Last Quarter phase at 12:20 AM, EDT.

NATIONAL BRING YOUR TEDDY BEAR TO WORK DAY. Oct 10. A celebration and observation of the help, stress relief and joy that teddy bears bring into the lives of people of all ages and stages! Annually, the second Wednesday in October. For info: Susan E. Schwartz, Teddies Are the Answer, 454 26th Ave, San Mateo, CA 94403. Phone: (650) 349-3184. Fax: (650) 345-4944. E-mail: suwho@aol.com.

★**NATIONAL WILDLIFE WEEK.** Oct 10–16. A time for all Americans to learn about and celebrate the magnificent collection of lands set aside for wildlife and for the American spirit. This is a time for renewed awareness and commitment to wildlife conservation.

OKLAHOMA HISTORICAL DAY. Oct 10. Oklahoma.

SIMCHAT TORAH. Oct 10. Hebrew calendar date: Tishri 23, 5762. Rejoicing in the Torah concludes the nine-day Sukkot Festival (see entry on Oct 2). Public reading of the Pentateuch is completed and begun again, symbolizing the need for ever-continuing study.

TAIWAN: DOUBLE TENTH DAY. Oct 10. Commemorates the proclamation of the Chinese Republic in 1911.

TUXEDO CREATED: ANNIVERSARY. Oct 10, 1886. Griswold Lorillard of Tuxedo Park, NY, fashioned the first tuxedo for men.

UNITED NATIONS: INTERNATIONAL DAY FOR NATURAL DISASTER REDUCTION. Oct 10. The General Assembly made this designation for the second Wednesday of October each year as part of its efforts to foster international cooperation in reducing the loss of life, property damage and social and economic disruption caused by natural disasters. For info: United Nations, Dept of Public Info, New York, NY 10017.

UNITED NATIONS: WORLD MENTAL HEALTH DAY. Oct 10. For info: United Nations, Dept of Public Info, New York, NY 10017. Web: www.un.org.

"UPSTAIRS, DOWNSTAIRS" TV PREMIERE: 30th ANNIVERSARY. Oct 10, 1971. The 52 episodes of this "Masterpiece Theatre" series covered the years 1903 to 1930 in the life of a wealthy London family ("Upstairs") and their many servants ("Downstairs"). Produced by London Weekend Television, cast members included Angela Baddeley, Pauline Collins, Gordon Jackson and Jean Marsh. Won a Golden Globe for Best Drama TV Show in 1975 and an Emmy for Outstanding Limited Series in 1976.The last episode aired May 1, 1977, though the series has been rerun several times on PBS.

VERDI, GIUSEPPI: BIRTH ANNIVERSARY. Oct 10, 1813. Italian composer, born at Le Roncole, Italy. His 26 operas include *Rigoletto*, *Il Trovatore*, *La Traviata* and *Aida*, and are among the most popular of all operatic music today. Died at Milan, Italy, Jan 27, 1901.

"ZORRO" TV PREMIERE: ANNIVERSARY. Oct 10, 1957. "Zorro" was a familiar character before coming to TV; he appeared in a McCulley novel and several films. Don Diego de la Vega (Guy Williams), a Spanish nobleman, is summoned to California by his father, Don Alejandro (George J. Lewis), to fight for the people. Diego's alter ego is Zorro, a dashing and assertive defender of the people. Although the last telecast was Sept 24, 1959, the series reappeared in later years, first as a remake and then as a sequel, and once again was made as a movie, titled *The Mask of Zorro*, in 1998.

BIRTHDAYS TODAY

Charles Dance, 55, actor (*The Jewel in the Crown, White Mischief*), born Worcestershire, England, Oct 10, 1946.
Brett Favre, 32, football player, born Gulfport, MS, Oct 10, 1969.

Jessica Harper, 52, actress (*Stardust Memories, Pennies from Heaven, My Favorite Year*), born Chicago, IL, Oct 10, 1949.
Mario Lopez, 28, actor ("Saved by the Bell," "Pacific Blue"), born San Diego, CA, Oct 10, 1973.
Harold Pinter, 71, director (*Butley*), playwright (*Betrayal, The Birthday Party*), born London, England, Oct 10, 1930.
Chris Pronger, 27, hockey player, born Dryden, Ontario, Canada, Oct 10, 1974.
David Lee Roth, 46, singer, musician (Van Halen, "Jump," *Eat 'Em and Smile*), born Bloomington, IN, Oct 10, 1955.
Tanya Tucker, 43, singer ("Delta Dawn," "Lizzie and the Rain Man"), born Seminole, TX, Oct 10, 1958.
Ben Vereen, 55, actor, singer, dancer (Tony for *Pippin; Roots, All That Jazz*, "Webster"), born Miami, FL, Oct 10, 1946.

OCTOBER 11 — THURSDAY
Day 284 — 81 Remaining

BILL AND HILLARY CLINTON WEDDING: ANNIVERSARY. Oct 11, 1975. William Jefferson (Blythe) Clinton was 29 and Hillary Rodham was 27. They have one child, Chelsea Victoria Clinton, born in 1980.

BLAKEY, ART: BIRTH ANNIVERSARY. Oct 11, 1919. Born at Pittsburgh, PA, jazz musician Blakey recorded many albums with his group, The Jazz Messengers. Died at New York, NY, Oct 16, 1990.

"DAVID BRINKLEY'S JOURNAL" TV PREMIERE: 40th ANNIVERSARY. Oct 11, 1961. Newscaster David Brinkley anchored this NBC public affairs show which covered a range of issues, both serious and light. There were also filmed features. "Journal" won both an Emmy and a Peabody in 1962 and was widely respected by the critics.

★**GENERAL PULASKI MEMORIAL DAY.** Oct 11. Presidential Proclamation always issued for Oct 11 since 1929. Requested by Congressional Resolution each year from 1929–1946. (Since 1947 has been issued by custom.) Note: Proclamation 4869, of Oct 5, 1981, covers all succeeding years.

NATIONAL COMING OUT DAY. Oct 11. A project of the Human Rights Campaign. An international day of visibility for the lesbian and gay community since 1988. Local community groups sponsor activities and events which in the past have included "coming out" dances, rallies and demonstrations, educational films, fairs and workshops, literature drops, fundraisers, and religious blessings of lesbian and gay couples and families. Annually, Oct 11. For info: Candace Gingrich, Mgr, Natl Coming Out Project, 919 18th St NW, Ste 800, Washington, DC 20006. Phone: (800) 866-6263. Fax: (202) 347-5323. E-mail: ncop@hrc.org. Web: www.hrc.org.

NATIONAL DEPRESSION SCREENING DAY. Oct 11. Offers free, anonymous depression and bipolar disorder screening as well as suicide intervention training (SOS:Signs of Suicide). For info: Screening for Mental Health, One Washington St, Ste 304, Wellesley Hills, MA 02481-1706. Phone: (781) 239-0071. Fax: (781) 431-7447. Web: www.mentalhealthscreening.org.

PATENT ISSUED FOR FIRST ADDING MACHINE: ANNIVERSARY. Oct 11, 1887. A patent was granted to Dorr Eugene Felt for the Comptometer, which was the first adding machine known to be absolutely accurate at all times.

ROBBINS, JEROME: BIRTH ANNIVERSARY. Oct 11, 1918. Choreographer and ballet dancer, born at New York, NY. Robbins choreographed several Broadway musicals including *Fiddler On the Roof*, *The King and I* and *On the Town*. He died at Manhattan, NY, July 29, 1998.

ROBINSON, ROSCOE, JR: BIRTH ANNIVERSARY. Oct 11, 1928. The first black American to achieve the Army rank of four-star general. Born at St. Louis, MO, and died at Washington, DC, July 22, 1993.

ROOSEVELT, ANNA ELEANOR: BIRTH ANNIVER-SARY. Oct 11, 1884. Wife of Franklin Delano Roosevelt, 32nd president of the US, was born at New York, NY. She led an active and independent life and was the first wife of a president to give her own news conference in the White House (1933). Widely known throughout the world, she was affectionately called "the first lady of the world." She served as US delegate to the United Nations General Assembly for a number of years before her death at New York, NY, Nov 7, 1962. A prolific writer, she wrote in *This Is My Story*, "No one can make you feel inferior without your consent."

"SATURDAY NIGHT LIVE" TV PREMIERE: ANNI-VERSARY. Oct 11, 1975. Through the years this show has been through numerous cast, writing, producing and musical staff changes. However, its format has remained the same: skits, commercial parodies, recurring characters and news parodies, with a different guest host and musical guest performing every week—live. It used to be known for its outrageous comedy topics and parodies that almost bordered on slander, and for having the best in unusual musical groups. Its title was originally titled "NBC's Saturday Night," with its first host being comedian George Carlin. Notable cast members included: Chevy Chase, Dan Aykroyd, John Belushi, Jane Curtin, Garrett Morris, Laraine Newman, Gilda Radner, Bill Murray, Joe Piscopo, Eddie Murphy, Mary Gross, Tim Kazurinsky, Julia Louis-Dreyfus, Jim Belushi, Billy Crystal, Martin Short, Christopher Guest, Harry Shearer, Joan Cusack, Robert Downey, Jr, Nora Dunn, Jon Lovitz, Dana Carvey, Phil Hartman, Jan Hooks, Victoria Jackson, Dennis Miller, Chris Farley and Kevin Nealon.

STONE, HARLAN FISKE: BIRTH ANNIVERSARY. Oct 11, 1872. Former associate justice and later chief justice of the US Supreme Court who wrote more than 600 opinions and dissents for that court, Stone was born at Chesterfield, NH. He served on the Supreme Court from 1925 until his death, at Washington, DC, Apr 22, 1946.

TRAIL OF TERROR. Oct 11–13 (also Oct 18–20 and Oct 25–31). Renaissance Festival Grounds, Shakopee, MN. A family event featuring a mile-long maze through spooky corridors and haunted rooms. The night is not complete without Club Scream featuring games, music, treats and much more. Est attendance: 25,000. For info: Mid-America Festivals, 1244 S Canterbury Rd, Ste 306, Shakopee, MN 55379. Phone: (800) 966-8215 or (952) 445-7361. Fax: (952) 445-7380. Web: www.trailofterrorfest.com.

VATICAN COUNCIL II: ANNIVERSARY. Oct 11, 1962. The 21st ecumenical council of the Roman Catholic Church was convened by Pope John XXIII. It met in four annual sessions, concluding Dec 8, 1965. It dealt with the renewal of the Church and introduced sweeping changes, such as the use of the vernacular rather than Latin in the Mass.

October 2001	S	M	T	W	T	F	S
		1	2	3	4	5	6
	7	8	9	10	11	12	13
	14	15	16	17	18	19	20
	21	22	23	24	25	26	27
	28	29	30	31			

WEEMS, PARSON (MASON LOCKE): BIRTH ANNI-VERSARY. Oct 11, 1759. Mason Locke Weems was born at Anne Arundel County, MD. An Episcopal clergyman and traveling bookseller, Weems is remembered for the fictitious stories he presented as historical fact. Best known of his "fables" is the story describing George Washington cutting down his father's cherry tree with a hatchet. Weems's fictionalized histories, however, delighted many readers who accepted them as true. They became immensely popular and were bestsellers for many years. Weems died May 23, 1825, at Beaufort, SC.

WEST, DOTTIE: BIRTH ANNIVERSARY. Oct 11, 1932. American singer Dottie West was born at McMinnville, TN. In 1964 she won the first Grammy ever by a country vocalist for "Here Comes My Baby." She died Sept 4, 1991, at Nashville, TN.

BIRTHDAYS TODAY

Joan Cusack, 39, actress (*Working Girl, Sixteen Candles*), born Evanston, IL, Oct 11, 1962.

Robert Gale, 56, physician, cofounder of the International Bone Marrow Registry, born Brooklyn Heights, NY, Oct 11, 1945.

Daryl Hall, 53, singer, musician (Hall and Oates), born Pottstown, PA, Oct 11, 1948.

Orlando Hernandez, 32, baseball player, known as "El Duque," born Villa Clara, Cuba, Oct 11, 1969.

Ron Leibman, 64, actor (*Norma Rae*; stage: *We Bombed in New Haven, Angels in America* [Tony Award]), born New York NY, Oct 11, 1937.

Elmore Leonard, 76, writer (*Glitz, Get Shorty*), born New Orleans, LA, Oct 11, 1925.

David Morse, 48, actor ("St. Elsewhere," *The Indian Runner*), born Beverly, MA, Oct 11, 1953.

Patty Murray, 51, US Senator (D, Washington), born Seattle, WA, Oct 11, 1950.

Luke Perry, 35, actor ("Beverly Hills 90210," *Buffy the Vampire Slayer*), born Fredricktown, MO, Oct 11, 1966.

William Perry, 74, former US Secretary of Defense (Clinton administration), born Vandergrift, PA, Oct 11, 1927.

Steve Young, 40, former football player, born Salt Lake City, UT, Oct 11, 1961.

OCTOBER 12 — FRIDAY
Day 285 — 80 Remaining

ALGONQUIN MILL FALL FESTIVAL. Oct 12–14. Four miles south of Carrollton, OH. Presented by the Carroll County Historical Society. The event is an 1800's pioneer festival. Features include steam-powered grist and sawmill in operation. Also featured are antique tools and farm machinery and quilting, spinning and weaving demonstrations. Log buildings include a book store, print shop, souvenir shop and a two-story home. A one-room school, railroad station and stage coach station are on exhibit. More than 70 quality craftsmen will be demonstrating and selling their products. Est attendance: 35,000. For info: Jeanie Stevens, 3007 Mayham Rd NE, Carrollton, OH 44615. Phone: (330) 627-2946.

APPLE BUTTER MAKIN' DAYS. Oct 12–14. Mt Vernon, MO. A huge festival highlighting the making of apple butter in large copper kettles on the courthouse lawn. Also, 375 crafters displaying and selling handmade goods, free entertainment all three days, apple pie eating contest, hairy legs contest, log sawing contest, bubble gum blowing contest, nail driving contest, pet parade, terrapin race and fiddlers. Annually, the second full weekend in October. Est attendance: 60,000. For info: Chamber of Commerce, PO Box 373, Mt Vernon, MO 65712. Phone: (417) 466-7654.

BAHAMAS: DISCOVERY DAY. Oct 12. Commemorates the landing of Columbus in the Bahamas in 1492.

"THE BOB HOPE SHOW" TV PREMIERE: ANNI-VERSARY. Oct 12, 1953. Premiere funnyman, well-known and loved Bob Hope made monthly appearances on TV in the 1950s.

During the first season he hosted "The Colgate Comedy Hour," and during the later seasons his show was seen replacing and then alternating with Milton Berle (and in 1955-56 with Martha Raye and Dinah Shore). Leo Robin and Ralph Rainger wrote Hope's trademark show-closing song, "Thanks for the Memory."

BOER WAR: ANNIVERSARY. Oct 12, 1899. The Boers of the Transvaal and Orange Free State in southern Africa declared war on the British. The Boer states were annexed by Britain in 1900 but guerrilla warfare on the part of the Boers caused the war to drag on. It was finally ended May 31, 1902 by the Treaty of Vereeniging.

"THE BURNS AND ALLEN SHOW" TV PREMIERE: ANNIVERSARY. Oct 12, 1950. The comedic husband and wife duo of George Burns and Gracie Allen starred as themselves in this comedy series in which Burns was the straight man and Allen was known for her ditziness. The show employed the technique of speaking directly to the camera ("breaking the fourth wall"); Burns often commented on the plot, told jokes or tried to make sense of Allen's actions and statements. Also on the show were their real-life son, Ronnie Burns, Bea Benaderet, Hal March, John Brown (until blacklisted by McCarthyites in the "red scare"), Fred Clark, Larry Keating, Bill Goodwin and Harry von Zell. The show was done live for the first two seasons and included vaudeville scenes at the end of each episode.

COLUMBUS DAY (TRADITIONAL). Oct 12. Public holiday in most countries in the Americas and in most Spanish-speaking countries. Observed under different names (Dia de la Raza or Day of the Race) and on different dates (most often, as in US, on the second Monday in October). Anniversary of Christopher Columbus's arrival, Oct 12, 1492, after a dangerous voyage across "shoreless Seas," at the Bahamas (probably the island of Guanahani), which he renamed El Salvador and claimed in the name of the Spanish crown. In his *Journal*, he wrote: "As I saw that they (the natives) were friendly to us, and perceived that they could be much more easily converted to our holy faith by gentle means than by force, I presented them with some red caps, and strings of beads to wear upon the neck, and many other trifles of small value, wherewith they were much delighted, and becamed wonderfully attached to us." See also: "Columbus Day Observance" (Oct 8).

COUNTRY JAM. Oct 12–13. Live Oak, FL. A country music spectacular with award-winning performers in a beautiful outdoor setting. Est attendance: 30,000. For info: James Cornett, Spirit of the Suwannee Music Park, 3076 95th Dr, Live Oak, FL 32060. Phone: (904) 364-1683. Fax: (904) 364-2998. E-mail: spirit @musicliveshere.com. Web: www.musicliveshere.com.

CRANBERRY HARVEST WEEKEND. Oct 12–14. Nantucket Island, MA. Guided tours of bogs and craft exhibitions at this 11th annual festival. Est attendance: 10,000. For info: Nantucket Island Chamber of Commerce, 48 Main St, Nantucket, MA 02554-3595. Phone: (508) 228-1700. Web: www.nantucket chamber.org.

DAY OF THE SIX BILLION: ANNIVERSARY. Oct 12, 1999. According to the United Nations, the population of the world reached six billion on this date. More than one-third of the world's people live in China and India. It wasn't until 1804 that the world's population reached one billion; now a billion people are added to the population about every 12 years. See also: "Day of the Five Billion" (July 11).

DESTINY DAY. Oct 12. Honoring the Dutch sailor Piet de Stuini, or DeStynie, who persuaded Columbus to change the log and make it seem that Oct 12 was the date of the first New World landing. The real date, Oct 13, might have caused superstitious fear in the other sailors or in potential investors in later voyages. The change was detected by an Italian history study group named the Colombiani. For info: Bob Birch, The Puns Corps, PO Box 2364, Falls Church, VA 22042-0364. Phone: (703) 533-3668.

EQUATORIAL GUINEA: INDEPENDENCE DAY. Oct 12. National holiday. Gained independence from Spain in 1968.

FIREANT FESTIVAL. Oct 12–14. Marshall, TX. Arts and crafts, chili cook-off, Tour de FireAnt bike ride, 5K run, fireant calling contest, fireant roundup, rubber chicken chunking, gurning contest (ugly face), Diaper Derby Contest (crawling), parade, men's crazy leg contest and street dance. Est attendance: 50,000. For info: Marshall Chamber of Commerce, PO Box 520, Marshall, TX 75671. Phone: (903) 935-7868. Fax: (903) 935-9982. E-mail: cvd @internetwork.net. Web: www.marshalltxchamber.com.

FORT LIGONIER DAYS. Oct 12–14. Ligonier, PA. Commemorates the Battle of Ligonier. Reenactments, parade, outdoor entertainment, craft booths and food booths. For info: Rachel Roehrig, Ligonier Chamber of Commerce, 120 East Main St, Ligonier, PA 15658. Phone: (724) 238-4200. Fax: (724) 238-4610. E-mail: ligonier@ligonier.com.

GORDONE, CHARLES: BIRTH ANNIVERSARY. Oct 12, 1925. First black playwright to win the Pulitzer Prize for drama, for his play *No Place to Be Somebody*. Born at Cleveland, OH. Died Nov 17, 1995 at College Station, TX.

GUMBO FESTIVAL. Oct 12–14. Bridge City, LA. To promote Cajun-French culture and provide the opportunity for people from everywhere to enjoy continuous Cajun entertainment on an outdoor stage and cuisine. Gumbo cooking contests and 5K Bridge Run. Annually, the second weekend in October. Est attendance: 150,000. For info: Rev Msgr J. Anthony Luminais, Pastor, Holy Guardian Angels Church, Box 9069, Bridge City, LA 70096. Phone: (504) 436-4712. Fax: (504) 436-4070. E-mail: Gumbofest @aol.com.

INDIAN SUMMER DAYS AT AUDUBON ACRES. Oct 12–13. Audubon Acres, Chattanooga, TN. Enjoy the games of Native Americans and pioneers, participate in Native American dance, listen to stories and talk to and watch Native American craftspersons and early pioneer reacters describe how things were done. Sponsor: Chattanooga Audubon Society. Annually, the second weekend in October. Est attendance: 1,500. For info: Lynda Logan, Audubon Acres, 900 N Sanctuary Rd, Chattanooga, TN 37421. Phone: (423) 892-1499. Fax: (423) 892-6376. E-mail: caudubons@aol.com.

INTERNATIONAL MOMENT OF FRUSTRATION SCREAM DAY. Oct 12. To share any or all of our frustrations, all citizens of the world will go outdoors at twelve hundred hours Greenwich time and scream for 30 seconds. We will all feel better or Earth will go off its orbit. Annually, Oct 12. [© 2000 by WH] For info: Thomas and Ruth Roy, Wellcat Holidays, 2418 Long Ln, Lebanon, PA 17046. Phone: (717) 279-0184. E-mail: wellcat@supernet.com. Web: www.wellcat.com.

MacDONALD, ANNE THOMPSON: DEATH ANNIVERSARY. Oct 12, 1993. Born in 1896, MacDonald founded a nonprofit organization, Recording for the Blind, that produces audio tapes of books to benefit blind and learning disabled people. She founded the organization in 1948; its library currently contains more than 80,000 titles. She died at Huntington, NY.

MAGIC WOODS. Oct 12–13. Loose Park, Kansas City, MO. Join Mother Nature for an evening of magic! By way of magic fairy dust, Mother Nature will give you the power to speak to the animals. Learn about Native Missouri animals living in the Kansas City area. Great wisdom can be gained from the river otter, frogs, owls and other exciting creatures. A fun, interactive alternative to traditional Halloween activities. Each child will receive a goodie bag, as well as refreshments. Benefit for Lakeside Nature Center and Missouri Wildlife. Est attendance: 2,000. For info: Friends of Lakeside Nature Center, 4701 E Gregory Blvd, Kansas City, MO 64132. Phone: (816) 513-8960.

McNAIR, RONALD E.: BIRTH ANNIVERSARY. Oct 12, 1950. Ronald E. McNair, a 35-year-old physicist, was the second black American astronaut in space (Feb 1984). He was born at Lake City, SC. As mission specialist for the crew, he perished in the space shuttle *Challenger* explosion Jan 28, 1986. See also: "Challenger Space Shuttle Explosion: Anniversary" (Jan 28).

MEDFORD JAZZ JUBILEE. Oct 12–14. Medford, OR. 14 nationally known bands will play in various Medford locations. More than 100 performances along with fun, food and music for all ages. Est attendance: 6,000. For info: Medford Jazz Jubilee, PMB 201, 221 N Central, Medford, OR 97501. Phone: (541) 770-6972 or (800) 599-0039. E-mail: info@medfordjazz.org. Web: www.medfordjazz.org.

MEXICO: DIA DE LA RAZA. Oct 12. Columbus Day is observed as the "Day of the Race," a fiesta time to commemorate the discovery of America as well as the common interests and cultural heritage of the Spanish and Indian peoples and the Hispanic nations.

MISSISSINEWA 1812. Oct 12–14. Marion, IN. Largest War of 1812 living history event in US includes reenactment of battle. Military, trappers and woodland Indians living as they did 187 years ago. Est attendance: 32,000. For info: Mississinewa Battlefield Soc, PO Box 1812, 402 S Washington, Ste 509, Marion, IN 46952. Phone: (800) 822-1812. Fax: (765) 662-1809. E-mail: war1812@aol.com.

NATCHITOCHES PILGRIMAGE. Oct 12–14. Natchitoches, LA. Tour of homes in the National Historic Landmark District and plantation homes in Cane River Country. Candlelight tours on Friday and Saturday nights are unique and atmospheric. Est attendance: 5,000. For info: Natchitoches Parish Tourist Commission, 781 Front St., Natchitoches, LA 71457. Phone: (318) 352-8072 or 800-259-1714. Fax: (318) 352-2415. Web: www.natchitoches.net.

NATIONAL SCHOOL CELEBRATION. Oct 12. "Pledge Across America"—a synchronized recitation of the Pledge of Allegiance coast to coast, 8 AM Hawaiian time to 2 PM Eastern time. The National School Celebration will provide a high-profile celebration uniting our nation's youth during regular school hours for a patriotic observance. Every school in the nation is invited to participate. This event perpetuates the original spirit of the 1892 National School Celebration declared by President Benjamin Harrison, for which the first Pledge of Allegiance was written. Free resources available from Farmers Insurance and Celebration USA, including a CD with musical renditions of the Pledge, Constitution, Bill of Rights and other selections. Annually, the second Friday in October. For info: Paula Burton, Pres, Celebration USA, 17853 Santiago Blvd, Ste 107, Villa Park, CA 92861. Phone: (714) 283-1892. Web: www.americanpromise.com.

October 2001	S	M	T	W	T	F	S
		1	2	3	4	5	6
	7	8	9	10	11	12	13
	14	15	16	17	18	19	20
	21	22	23	24	25	26	27
	28	29	30	31			

NATIONAL WILD TURKEY CALLING CONTEST AND TURKEY TROT FESTIVAL. Oct 12–13. Town Square, Yellville, AR. 56th annual. Wild turkey calling contest, turkey shoot, Miss Turkey Trot pageant, turkey dinner, arts, crafts, musical entertainment, Gospel Sing Sunday, parade. "Oldest established turkey calling contest in the nation." Annually, the second weekend in October. Est attendance: 10,000. For info: Chamber of Commerce, PO Box 369, Yellville, AR 72687. Phone: (870) 449-4676.

NORTH CAROLINA STATE FAIR. Oct 12–21. State Fairgrounds, Raleigh, NC. Agricultural fair with livestock, arts and crafts, home arts, entertainment and carnival. Est attendance: 750,000. For info: Wesley Wyatt, Mgr, North Carolina State Fair, 1025 Blue Ridge Blvd, Raleigh, NC 27607. Phone: (919) 821-7400. Fax: (919) 733-5079. Web: www.ncstatefair.org.

OHIO ARTS & CRAFTS CHRISTMAS FESTIVAL. Oct 12–14. Cuyahoga County Fairgrounds, Berea, OH. All displays indoor in heated buildings. Est attendance: 10,000. For info: David or Debbie Stoner, Family Festivals Assn, PO Box 166, Irwin, PA 15642. Phone: (724) 863-4577. Fax: (724) 863-4577.

PARKE COUNTY COVERED BRIDGE FESTIVAL. Oct 12–21. Rockville, IN. Covered bridge capital of the world, 32 historic covered bridges. Headquarters: Courthouse Lawn, Rockville. Guided bus tours on covered bridge routes. Hundreds of booths of arts, crafts, demonstrations, old-fashioned homemade foods and a farmers' market. Annually, beginning on the second Friday in October. Est attendance: 2,000,000. For info: Anne Lynk, Exec Secy, Covered Bridge Capital, PO Box 165, Rockville, IN 47872-0165. Phone: (765) 569-5226. Fax: (765) 569-3900. E-mail: pci@ticz.com. Web: www.coverbridges.com.

RED WING SHEEP DOG TRIAL. Oct 12–14. Red Wing, MN. Farmers' and ranchers' dogs compete. Est attendance: 700. For info: Charles O'Reilly, Course Dir, Red Wing Sheep Dog Trial Assn, 33933 200 Ave, Red Wing, MN 55066-7204. Phone: (651) 923-4723. E-mail: oreillyc@aol.com. Web: www.redwingbordercollies.com.

RHINELANDER'S OKTOBERFEST. Oct 12–14. Rhinelander, WI. The entire weekend enjoy German music, dancers and food. Est attendance: 9,000. For info: Rhinelander Area Chamber of Commerce, PO Box 795, Rhinelander, WI 54501. Phone: (800) 236-4386. Fax: (715) 365-7467. Web: www.rhinelanderchamber.com.

ST. CHARLES SCARECROW FESTIVAL. Oct 12–14. St. Charles, IL. More than 100 handcrafted scarecrows invade St. Charles along with live musical entertainment, carnival, children's activities, great food, huge craft show and much more. Est attendance: 100,000. For info: St. Charles Conv & Visitors Bureau, 311 N Second St, Ste 100, St. Charles, IL 60174. Phone: (630) 377-6161 or (800) 777-4373. Web: www.visitstcharles.com.

"SNEAK PREVIEWS" TV PREMIERE: ANNIVERSARY. Oct 12, 1978. This show with film critics Gene Siskel and Roger Ebert got its start on public television in Chicago in 1975. In 1978 it went national on PBS. In 1981 the program moved to network TV and the name was changed to "At the Movies." After Siskel's death in 1999, a rotating panel of critics joined Ebert and the show's title was changed to "Roger Ebert & the Movies."

SOUTHERN FESTIVAL OF BOOKS: A CELEBRATION OF THE WRITTEN WORD. Oct 12–14. War Memorial Plaza, Nashville, TN. To promote reading, writing, the literary arts and a broader understanding of the language and culture of the South, this annual festival will feature readings, talks and panel discussions by more than 200 authors, exhibit booths of publishing companies and bookstores, autographing sessions, a comprehensive children's program and a Cafe Stage, which is a performance corner for authors, storytellers and musicians. Est attendance: 30,000. For info: Galyn Martin, Dir, Southern Festival of Books, Tennessee Humanities Council, 1003 18th Ave S, Nashville, TN 37212. Phone: 6153207001 ext 15. Fax: (615) 321-4586. E-mail: galyn@tn-humanities.org. Web: www.tn-humanities.org.

SPAIN: NATIONAL HOLIDAY. Oct 12.

SUGARLOAF'S FALL TIMONIUM CRAFT FESTIVAL. Oct 12–14. Maryland State Fairgrounds, Timonium, MD. This show, now in its 25th year, features 400 professional fine artists and craft designers displaying and selling their creations. Craft demonstrations, children's entertainment, live music, food, hourly gift certificate drawings and more. Est attendance: 31,000. For info: Sugarloaf Mountain Works, Inc, 200 Orchard Ridge Dr, Ste 215, Gaithersburg, MD 20878. Phone: (800) 210-9900. E-mail: smworks@sugarloafcrafts.com. Web: www.sugarloafcrafts.com.

TARGET TOKYO: ANNIVERSARY. Oct 12, 1944. Two months after taking the island of Guam (Aug 10, 1944), Allied forces constructed runways there long enough for B29s. On this date these fierce heavy bombers headed for their first target—Tokyo.

TRUMBULL, JONATHAN: BIRTH ANNIVERSARY. Oct 12, 1710. American patriot, counselor and friend of George Washington, governor of Connecticut Colony, born at Lebanon, CT. Died there, Aug 17, 1785.

VIRGINIA CHRISTMAS SHOW. Oct 12–14. Prince William County Fairgrounds, Manassas, VA. Artisans, crafters (displaying and selling), specialty Christmas food shops, legendary "Sgt Santa." Craft demonstrations, entertainment and more. 12th annual show. Est attendance: 10,000. For info: Virginia Show Productions, PO Box 305, Chase City, VA 23924. Phone: (804) 372-3996. Fax: (804) 372-3410.

WILLIAMS, RALPH VAUGHAN: BIRTH ANNIVERSARY. Oct 12, 1872. English composer and conductor Ralph Vaughan Williams was born at Down Ampney, Gloucestershire. He is considered England's first great truly national composer, having rooted "modern" composition techniques in traditional English folk and Tudor music and themes to create a uniquely English style. Among his many works are nine symphonies, church and choral music, film and stage music and several operas. Williams studied at the Royal College of Music as well as in Berlin under Max Bruch and in Paris under Maurice Ravel. His major compositions include the *Mass in G Minor* and the opera *The Pilgrim's Progress*. He died Aug 26, 1958, at London.

WISCONSIN DELLS AUTUMN HARVEST FEST. Oct 12–14. Tommy Bartlett Thrill Show Site, Wisconsin Dells, WI. Join us in this celebration of the autumn harvest season. A variety of events for the entire family including fall color tours, "Ghouls and Fools" haunted house, craft fair, Wisconsin Dells on Tap, live entertainment and clowns for the kids. Test your competitive edge by participating in our scarecrow stuffing, pumpkin decorating, pumpkin chuckin', straw dig and fudge eating contests. For info: Angie Rizner, Wisconsin Dells Visitors Bureau, PO Box 390, Wisconsin Dells, WI 53965. Phone: (800) 223-3557. E-mail: info@wisdells.com. Web: www.wisdells.com.

WORLD EGG DAY. Oct 12. Dedicated to the global appeal of the billions of nutritious eggs produced worldwide. Annually, the second Friday of October. For info: Linda Braun, Consumer Services Dir, American Egg Bd, 1460 Renaissance Dr, Park Ridge, IL 60068. Web: www.aeb.org.

BIRTHDAYS TODAY

Susan Anton, 51, singer ("Killin' Time" with Fred Knoblock), actress (*Goldengirl*), born Yucaipa, CA, Oct 12, 1950.

Kirk Cameron, 31, actor ("Growing Pains," "Kirk"), born Panorama City, CA, Oct 12, 1970.

Chris Chandler, 36, football player, born Everett, WA, Oct 12, 1965.

John Engler, 53, Governor of Michigan (R), born Mount Pleasant, MI, Oct 12, 1948.

Dick Gregory, 69, comedian, author, activist, born St. Louis, MO, Oct 12, 1932.

Marion Jones, 26, track runner, born Los Angeles, CA, Oct 12, 1975.

Anthony Christopher (Tony) Kubek, 65, sportscaster, former baseball player, born Milwaukee, WI, Oct 12, 1936.

Jean Nidetch, 78, founder of Weight Watchers, born Brooklyn, NY, Oct 12, 1923.

Luciano Pavarotti, 66, opera singer, one of the "Three Tenors," born Modena, Italy, Oct 12, 1935.

Adam Rich, 33, actor ("Eight Is Enough"), born Brooklyn, NY, Oct 12, 1968.

Chris Wallace, 54, broadcaster ("Dateline"), White House correspondent, born Chicago, IL, Oct 12, 1947.

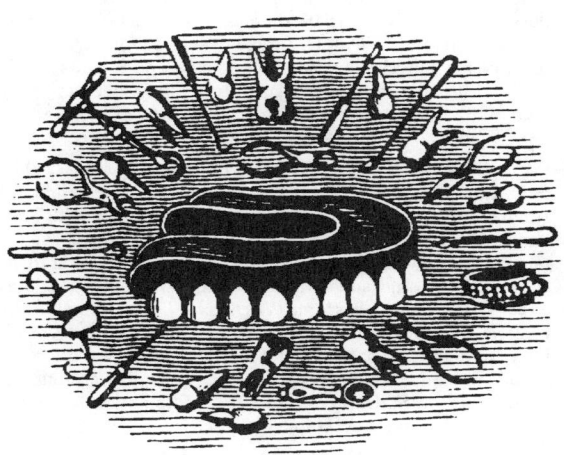

OCTOBER 13 — SATURDAY

Day 286 — 79 Remaining

AMERICAN DENTAL ASSOCIATION ANNUAL SESSIONS. Oct 13–17. Kansas City, MO. Est attendance: 26,000. For info: Vicki Guinta, American Dental Assn, 211 E Chicago Ave, Ste 200, Chicago, IL 60611. Phone: (312) 440-2581. Web: www.ada.org.

ARROW ROCK HERITAGE CRAFT FESTIVAL. Oct 13–14. Arrow Rock, MO. 1850s crafters demonstrate and sell crafts of daily living: bobbin lace making, rope braiding, candle dipping, cornshuck dolls, blacksmithing and more. Historic buildings open to tour. Annually, the second full weekend in October. Est attendance: 6,500. For info: Historic Arrow Rock Council, PO Box M, Arrow Rock, MO 65320. E-mail: tmcglaughlin@mid-mo.net.

AUTUMN GLORY 5K RUN/2 MILE WALK FOR SIGHT.
Oct 13. Broadford Park, Mountain Lake Park, MD. 5K run/2 mile walk all proceeds go for Lion's Club eye glasses and eye related treatment and operations. Cash prizes to male and female race winners. Awards to winners in various age groups. Race is held in Broadford Park in connection with the Autumn Glory festival. Annually, the Saturday of Autumn Glory Festival. Est attendance: 500. For info: Paul Shockey, 920 Broadford Rd, Mountain Lake Park, MD 21550. Phone: (301) 334-4287.

BENTONSPORT ARTS FESTIVAL. Oct 13–14. Bentonsport National Historic District, IA. Juried art show held as part of a countywide scenic drive. Variety of media represented. Held on river bank in historic and picturesque restored 1840s village. Food and lodging available locally. Guided tours via horse-drawn wagon. Demonstrations. Annually, the second full weekend in October. Est attendance: 12,000. For info: Greef General Store, Bentonsport, PO Box 9, Keosauqua, IA 52565. Phone: (319) 592-3579. E-mail: villages@netins.net. Web: www.bentonsport.com.

BROWN, JESSE LEROY: 75th BIRTH ANNIVERSARY. Oct 13, 1926. Jesse Leroy Brown was the first black American naval aviator and also the first black naval officer to lose his life in combat when he was shot down over Korea, Dec 4, 1950. On Mar 18, 1972, USS *Jesse L. Brown* was launched as the first ship to be named in honor of a black naval officer. Brown was born at Hattiesburg, MS.

CATOCTIN COLORFEST ARTS AND CRAFTS SHOW.
Oct 13–14. Thurmont, MD. Live music, food, 350 arts and crafts booths featuring artists from Maryland, Virginia, West Virginia and Pennsylvania. Annually, the second weekend in October. Est attendance: 100,000. For info send a SASE to: Catoctin Color-Fest, Inc, Box 33, Thurmont, MD 21788. Phone: (301) 271-4432.

ELDON TURKEY FESTIVAL. Oct 13. Eldon, MO. A celebration of Miller County's state and national ranking as a top producer of wild and domestic turkeys. Event includes more than 200 crafters and exhibitors, turkey events, food, quilt show and old-time machinery show. Annually, the second Saturday in October. Est attendance: 10,000. For info: Eldon Chamber of Commerce, PO Box 209, Eldon, MO 65026. Phone: (573) 392-3752. Fax: (573) 392-0634. E-mail: eldoncc@lakeozarks.net.

FAIRE ON THE SQUARE ART & CRAFT FAIR. Oct 13. Sauk County Courthouse Square Park, Downtown Baraboo, WI. Annual outdoor event. Features all handmade work of 120 artists and crafters, local cuisine food stands, farmers' market, live entertainment, carnival, kids' activities and Creation Station craft workshops for kids and adults. Held during peak fall color time for travelers in this area of scenic Wisconsin. Visit local orchards and browse the unique specialty shops in historic downtown Baraboo. Annually, the second Saturday in October. Est attendance: 5,000. For info: Cindy Doescher, Fan Faire Promotions, LLC, 1801 Jefferson St, Baraboo, WI 53913. Phone: (608) 356-7995. Web: www.baraboonow.com/downtown.

FEAST OF THE HUNTERS' MOON. Oct 13–14. Fort Ouiatenon Historic Park, Lafayette, IN. Recreation of French and Native American life at mid-1700s fur-trading outpost. 8,000 participants. Est attendance: 65,000. For info: Dir of PR, Tippecanoe County Historical Assn, 1001 South St, Lafayette, IN 47901. Phone: (765) 476-8401. Fax: (765) 476-8414. Web: www.tcha.mus.in.us.

FINE ARTS AND CRAFTS FESTIVAL. Oct 13–14. Roseland Cottage, Bowen House, Woodstock, CT. 19th annual festival features 175 juried artists and craftsmen, food court and entertainment for children and adults. Rain or shine. Admission is $4 per person with proceeds to benefit museum. Annually, the weekend after Columbus Day. Est attendance: 10,000. For info: Roseland Cottage, Bowen House, PO Box 186, Woodstock, CT 06281. Phone: (860) 928-4074. Fax: (860) 963-2208. E-mail: prusso@spnea.org. Web: www.spnea.org.

FOREST CRAFT/SCENIC DRIVE FESTIVAL. Oct 13–14. Van Buren County, IA. Scenic landscapes, historic architecture, wood carvers, buckskinners camp, flea market, quilt show, arts festival, stamp show, crafts and more. Annually, the second full weekend in October. Est attendance: 18,000. For info: Stacey Glandon, Exec Dir, Villages of Van Buren, Inc, PO Box 9, Keosauqua, IA 52565. Phone: (800) TOUR-VBC. Fax: (319) 293-7116. Web: www.800-tourvbc.com.

GOLDEN ISLES ARTS FESTIVAL. Oct 13–14. St. Simons Island, GA. 150 fine art and fine craft artists on exhibit. Also, local foods and entertainment. Annually, the second full weekend in October. Est attendance: 20,000. For info: The Glynn Art Assn, 319 Mallory St, St. Simons Island, GA 31522. Phone: (912) 638-8770. Fax: (912) 634-2787. Web: www.glynnart.org.

GRAND RAPIDS WINTER ART FAIR. Oct 13–14. Grand Rapids, MI. Fine arts and fine crafts show. Showcasing artists from a 20-state area. Est attendance: 7,000. For info: Audree Levy, 1809 Morning Glory, Carrollton, TX 75007. Phone: (972) 735-9898. Fax: (972) 735-9808. E-mail: audree@levyartfairs.com. Web: www.levyartfairs.com.

HERITAGE PARADE AND FESTIVAL. Oct 13. Tri-City Park, Placentia, CA. 37th annual parade and fair featuring entertainment, food, game and craft booths. Special car show featured. Annually, the second Saturday of October. Sponsor: Heritage Committee. Est attendance: 10,000. For info: Steve Pischel, City of Placentia, 401 E Chapman Ave, Placentia, CA 92870. Phone: (714) 993-8184. Fax: (714) 961-0283.

HONG KONG: BIRTHDAY OF CONFUCIUS. Oct 13. Religious observances are held by the Confucian Society at Confucius Temple at Causeway Bay. Observed on 27th day of 8th lunar month.

MONTAND, YVES: 80th BIRTH ANNIVERSARY. Oct 13, 1921. French actor Yves Montand was born Ivo Livi at Monsummano Alto, Italy. His career was successful in both France and America, including more than 50 films. He died Nov 9, 1991, at Senlis, France.

MOUNTAIN GLORY FESTIVAL. Oct 13. Marion, NC. A celebration of mountain heritage in western North Carolina. Arts, crafts, children's area and continuous entertainment. Also, "Mountain Glory Metric Century" bicycle ride. Annually, the second Saturday in October. Est attendance: 20,000. For info: Robert Parker, PO Drawer 700, Marion, NC 28752. Phone: (828) 652-3551. Fax: (828) 652-1983.

NORTHEAST MARBLE MEET. Oct 13–14. Radisson Inn, Marlborough, MA. Auction, exhibits; dealers and collectors buy, sell and trade marbles. Est attendance: 1,000. For info: Bert Cohen, 169 Marlborough St, Boston, MA 02116. Phone: (617) 247-4754. Fax: (617) 247-9093. E-mail: marblebert@aol.com. Web: members.aol.com/marblebert.

NORTHERN INTERNATIONAL LIVESTOCK EXPOSITION. Oct 13–20. MetraPark, Billings, MT. PRCA rodeo, trade show exhibits, cattle, sheep, swine and horse sales. Est attendance: 50,000. For info: Joyce Laughery, Genl Mgr, NILE Office, PO Box 1981, Billings, MT 59103. Phone: (406) 256-2495 or (888) NILE-TIX. Fax: (406) 256-2494. Web: www.thenile.org.

PINE BARRENS JAMBOREE. Oct 13. Wells Mills County Park, Waretown, NJ. Music of the Pines, crafts, wood carvers, nature walks, canoeing, basket weavers, children's games, food and more. Free rain or shine. Est attendance: 5,000. For info: Lillian Hoey, Show Coord, Wells Mills County Park, 905 Wells Mills Rd, Waretown, NJ 08758. Phone: (609) 971-3085. Fax: (609) 971-9540.

October 2001	S	M	T	W	T	F	S
		1	2	3	4	5	6
	7	8	9	10	11	12	13
	14	15	16	17	18	19	20
	21	22	23	24	25	26	27
	28	29	30	31			

PITCHER, MOLLY: BIRTH ANNIVERSARY. Oct 13, 1754. "Molly Pitcher," heroine of the American Revolution, was a water carrier at the Battle of Monmouth (Sunday, June 28, 1778) where she distinguished herself by loading and firing a cannon after her husband, John Hays, was wounded. Affectionately known as "Sergeant Molly" after General Washington issued her a warrant as a noncommissioned officer. Her real name was Mary Hays McCauley (née Ludwig). Born near Trenton, NJ, she died at Carlisle, PA, Jan 22, 1832.

PORTUGAL: PILGRIMAGE TO FATIMA. Oct 13. Crowds of pilgrims from Portugal and all over the world travel to Fatima to celebrate the last apparition of the Virgin to the little shepherds in 1917.

SAINT EDWARD, THE CONFESSOR: FEAST DAY. Oct 13. King of England, 1042–66, Edward was the son of King Ethelred the Unready. Born at Islip, England, in 1003, he died Jan 5, 1066, at London, England. On Oct 13, 1163, his remains were transported in a ceremony that was of national interest. Since then Oct 13 has been observed as his principal feast day.

TAMARACK TIME!. Oct 13. Bigfork, MT. Old-fashioned village celebration of harvest and autumn. Local chefs prepare their specialties for a taste treat. Est attendance: 600. For info: Elna Darrow, Box 400, Bigfork, MT 59911-0400. Phone: (406) 837-4400. E-mail: crossbow@cyberport.net.

TOMS RIVER CANOE RACE. Oct 13. Old Toms River Bus Terminal, Toms River, NJ. 8 ½ mile race, 13 categories, every skill level. Prizes awarded. Pre-registration is a must for entering the contest or come and observe. Est attendance: 500. For info: Mickey Cohen, Coord, Wells Mills County Park, 905 Wells Mills Rd, Waretown, NJ 08758. Phone: (609) 971-3085. Fax: (609) 971-9540.

US MID-AMATEUR (GOLF) CHAMPIONSHIP. Oct 13–18. San Joaquin Country Club, Fresno, CA. For info: US Golf Assn, Golf House, PO Box 708, Championship Dept, Far Hills, NJ 07931. Phone: (908) 234-2300. Fax: (908) 234-9687. Web: www.usga.org.

US NATIONAL COMMISSION ON SPACE. Oct 13, 1984. President Reagan signed executive order creating a National Commission on Space to prepare 20-year agenda for civilian space program.

US NAVY: AUTHORIZATION ANNIVERSARY. Oct 13, 1775. Commemorates legislation passed by Second Continental Congress authorizing the acquisition of ships and establishment of a navy.

VIRCHOW, RUDOLF: BIRTH ANNIVERSARY. Oct 13, 1821. German political leader, scientist, teacher and author. Called "the founder of cellular pathology." Born at Schivelbein, Prussia, died at Berlin, Sept 5, 1902.

WHITE HOUSE CORNERSTONE LAID: ANNIVERSARY. Oct 13, 1792. The presidential residence at 1600 Pennsylvania Ave NW, Washington, DC, designed by James Hoban (q.v.), observes its birthday Oct 13. The cornerstone was laid and the first presidential family to occupy it was that of John Adams, in November 1800. With three stories and more than 100 rooms, the White House is the oldest building at Washington. First described as the "presidential palace," it acquired the name "White House" about 10 years after construction was completed. Burned by British troops in 1814, it was reconstructed, refurbished and reoccupied by 1817.

WORLD WRISTWRESTLING CHAMPIONSHIPS. Oct 13. Petaluma, CA. Nationally recognized event with more than 500 entrants vying for the title of World Wristwrestling Champion. Est attendance: 1,000. For info: Bill Soberanes, c/o *Argus Courier*, 423 E Washington St, Petaluma, CA 94952. Phone: (707) 778-1430. Web: www.armwrestling.com.

ZEPHYR DAYS TRAIN SHOW. Oct 13–14. Multi-Purpose Events Center Exhibit Hall, Wichita Falls, TX. Display of model trains, tours, food, movies, buy, sell and trade. For info: Wichita Falls Conv & Visitors Bureau, 1000 5th St, Wichita Falls, TX 76301. Phone: (940) 716-5500 or (940) 692-6073. Fax: (940) 716-5509. E-mail: MPEC@WF.net. Web: www.viewscape.com or www.wf.net.

BIRTHDAYS TODAY

Chris Carter, 44, creator of "The X-Files," born Bellflower, CA, Oct 13, 1957.

Melinda Dillon, 62, actress (*Close Encounters of the Third Kind, Absence of Malice, A Christmas Story*), born Hope, AR, Oct 13, 1939.

Sammy Hagar, 52, singer, musician ("Your Love Is Driving Me Crazy"), born Monterrey, CA, Oct 13, 1949.

Nancy Kerrigan, 32, figure skater, born Woburn, MA, Oct 13, 1969.

Marie Osmond, 42, actress, singer ("Donny and Marie," "Ripley's Believe It or Not"), born Ogden, UT, Oct 13, 1959.

Kelly Preston, 39, actress (*Christine, Twins*), born Honolulu, HI, Oct 13, 1962.

Jerry Lee Rice, 39, football player, born Starkville, MS, Oct 13, 1962.

Glenn Anton ("Doc") Rivers, 40, basketball coach and former player, born Maywood, IL, Oct 13, 1961.

Nipsey Russell, 77, comedian, actor, born Atlanta, GA, Oct 13, 1924.

Paul Simon, 60, singer, songwriter (with Art Garfunkel: "The Sounds of Silence," "Mrs Robinson"; solo album: *Graceland*), born Newark, NJ, Oct 13, 1941.

Margaret Hilda Roberts Thatcher, 76, former Prime Minister of England, born Grantham, England, Oct 13, 1925.

Pamela Tiffin, 59, actress (*Harper*; stage: *Dinner at Eight* [Theatre World Award]), born Oklahoma City, OK, Oct 13, 1942.

OCTOBER 14 — SUNDAY
Day 287 — 78 Remaining

"THE ADVENTURES OF ELLERY QUEEN" TV PREMIERE: ANNIVERSARY. Oct 14, 1950. The first of many series to portray fictional detective Ellery Queen, it began on the Dumont network and later moved to ABC. Queen was played by Richard Hart. In the next four series, he would also be played by Lee Bowman, Hugh Marlowe, George Nadar, Lee Philips, Peter Lawford and Jim Hutton. In each series Queen talked to the home audience at the show's climax to see if they were able to identify the killer. Future series were titled "Ellery Queen" and "The Further Adventures of Ellery Queen." The last telecast aired on Sept 5, 1976.

AMERICAN SAMOA: WHITE SUNDAY. Oct 14. Second Sunday in October is "children's day" on the island. Children demonstrate skits, prayers, songs and special presentations for parents, friends and relatives. A feast is prepared by the parents and served to the children.

"AMERICAN WHEELS" CAR SHOW. Oct 14 (rain date Oct 28). Wheaton Village, Millville, NJ. Features cars from the '50s, '60s and '70s. Est attendance: 1,500. For info: Wheaton Village, 1501 Glasstown Rd, Millville, NJ 08332. Phone: (856) 825-6800. Fax: (856) 825-2410. E-mail: mail@wheatonvillage.org. Web: www.wheatonvillage.org.

BE BALD AND BE FREE DAY. Oct 14. For those who are bald and who either do wear or do not wear a wig or toupee, this is the day to go "shiny" and be proud. Annually, Oct 14. [© 2000 by WH] For info: Thomas or Ruth Roy, Wellcat Holidays, 2418 Long Ln, Lebanon, PA 17046. Phone: (717) 279-0184. E-mail: wellcat@supernet.com. Web: www.wellcat.com.

BELIZE: COLUMBUS DAY. Oct 14. Public holiday.

BRAZIL: CIRIO DE NAZARE. Oct 14–27. Greatest festival of northern Brazil, the Feast of Cirio starts on second Sunday of October in city of Belem (St. Mary of Bethlehem), capital of the state of Para. Festival lasts two weeks.

BURGOO FESTIVAL. Oct 14. Downtown, North Utica, IL. Only the "Burgoomeister" knows the secret recipe for this pioneer stew, burgoo, served outdoors at this annual Utica festival. Other events include arts and crafts, antiques, food, a reenactment of Civil War living conditions by uniformed volunteers and the firing of a Civil War cannon. Annually, the second Sunday in October. Est attendance: 30,000. For info: Burgoo Chairman, LaSalle Co Historical Museum, PO Box 278, Utica, IL 61373. Phone: (815) 667-4861.

DOW-JONES TOPS 6,000: 5th ANNIVERSARY. Oct 14, 1996. The Dow-Jones Index of 30 major industrial stocks topped the 6,000 mark for the first time.

EISENHOWER, DWIGHT DAVID: BIRTH ANNIVERSARY. Oct 14, 1890. The 34th president of the US, Dwight David Eisenhower, was born at Denison, TX. Serving two terms as president, Jan 20, 1953–Jan 20, 1961, Eisenhower was the first president to be baptized after taking office (Sunday, Feb 1, 1953). Nicknamed "Ike," he held the rank of five-star general of the army (resigned in 1952, and restored by act of Congress in 1961). He served as supreme commander of the Allied forces in western Europe during WWII. In his Farewell Address (Jan 17, 1961), speaking about the "conjunction of an immense military establishment and a large arms industry," he warned: "In the councils of government, we must guard against the acquisition of unwarranted influence, whether sought or unsought, by the military-industrial complex. The potential of the disastrous rise of misplaced power exists and will persist." An American hero, Eisenhower died at Washington, DC, Mar 28, 1969.

FODOR, EUGENE: BIRTH ANNIVERSARY. Oct 14, 1905. Travel writer Eugene Fodor was born at Leva, Hungary. His first travel book was published in 1936, after which he published more than 140, bringing to them a human element previously lacking in travel books. He died Feb 18, 1991, at Torrington, CT.

GETTING THE WORLD TO BEAT A PATH TO YOUR DOOR WEEK. Oct 14–20. To focus attention on improving "public relationships" in order to create success for companies, products and individuals. Free self-evaluation available. Annually, the third full week in October. For info: Barbara Gaughen, Pres, Gaughen Global Public Relations, 7456 Evergreen Dr, Santa Barbara, CA 93117. Phone: (805) 968-8567. Fax: (805) 968-5747. E-mail: barbara@rain.org.

GISH, LILLIAN: BIRTH ANNIVERSARY. Oct 14, 1893. American actress Lillian Diana Gish was born at Springfield, OH. Her film and stage career spanned more than 85 years, 100 films, the silent and sound eras of film and numerous stage productions. She was awarded an honorary Oscar in 1970 and made her last film appearance in *The Whales of August* (1987). She died Feb 27, 1993, at New York, NY.

GRANDMOTHER'S DAY IN FLORIDA. Oct 14. A ceremonial day on the second Sunday in October.

ISRA AL MI'RAJ: ASCENT OF THE PROPHET MUHAMMAD. Oct 14. Islamic calendar date: Rajab 27, 1422. Commemorates the journey of the Prophet Muhammad from Mecca to Jerusalem, his ascension into the Seven Heavens and his return on the same night. Muslims believe that on that night Muhammad prayed together with Abraham, Moses and Jesus in the area of the Al-Aqsa Mosque in Jerusalem. The rock from which he is believed to have ascended to speak with God is the one inside The Dome of the Rock. Different methods for "anticipating" the visibility of the new moon crescent at Mecca are used by different Muslim groups. US date may vary.

JAPAN: MEGA KENKA MATSURI or ROUGHHOUSE FESTIVAL. Oct 14–15. Himeji. Palanquin bearers jostle one another to demonstrate their skill and balance in handling their burdens.

KIDS CARE WEEK. Oct 14–20. A week celebrating the spirit of compassion in children. Kids will show they care by doing charitable projects for the needy in their local community. Annually, the third week in October. For info: Kids Care Clubs, PO Box 1082, New Canaan, CT 06840. Phone: (914) 533-2949. E-mail: kathy@kidscare.org. Web: www.kidscare.org.

KING AWARDED NOBEL PEACE PRIZE: ANNIVERSARY. Oct 14, 1964. Martin Luther King, Jr, became the youngest recipient of the Nobel Peace Prize when awarded the honor. Dr. King donated the entire $54,000 prize money to furthering the causes of the civil rights movement.

LEE, FRANCIS LIGHTFOOT: BIRTH ANNIVERSARY. Oct 14, 1734. Signer of the Declaration of Independence. Born at Westmoreland County, VA, he died Jan 11, 1797, at Richmond County, VA.

NATIONAL ADULT IMMUNIZATION AWARENESS WEEK. Oct 14–20. Thousands of deaths occur each year—deaths which could be easily prevented by today's available vaccines. NAIAW emphasizes the importance of appropriately vaccinating adults against measles, mumps, rubella, hepatitis A, hepatitis B, tetanus, diphtheria, influenza, pneumococcal disease and varicella. A campaign kit of materials is available. For info: Natl Coalition for Adult Immunization, 4733 Bethesda Ave, Ste 750, Bethesda, MD 20814-5228. Phone: (301) 656-0003. Fax: (301) 907-0878. E-mail: ncai@nfid.org. Web: www.NFID.org /NCAI.

October 2001	S	M	T	W	T	F	S
		1	2	3	4	5	6
	7	8	9	10	11	12	13
	14	15	16	17	18	19	20
	21	22	23	24	25	26	27
	28	29	30	31			

NATIONAL NETWORKING WEEK. Oct 14–20. Whether the goal is to grow a business or enrich your personal life, networking is invaluable. One can never meet enough new people, exchange business cards and share one's goals and desires with others who may offer leads. Cameraderie is another benefit that can result from successfully connecting with others through a concerted, consistent effort. For info: Robin Gorman Newman, Independent Business Women's Circle, 44 Somerset Dr N, Great Neck, NY 10020. Phone: (516) 773-0911. E-mail: rgnewman@aol.com.

★**NATIONAL SCHOOL LUNCH WEEK.** Oct 14–20. Presidential Proclamation issued for the week beginning with the second Sunday in October since 1962 (PL87–780 of Oct 9, 1962). Note: Not issued in 1981.

PEACE CORPS PROPOSED: ANNIVERSARY. Oct 14, 1960. At the improbable hour of 2 AM, on Oct 14, 1960, then presidential candidate John F. Kennedy spoke impromptu to several thousand students from the steps of the University of Michigan Union building. He asked: "How many of you who are going to be doctors are willing to spend your days in Ghana? How many of you (technicians and engineers) are willing to work in the Foreign Service?" The response was favorable, and 19 days later in San Francisco, Kennedy formally proposed the Peace Corps, which was created by Executive Order Mar 1, 1961.

PENN, WILLIAM: BIRTH ANNIVERSARY. Oct 14, 1644. Founder of Pennsylvania, born at London, England. Penn died July 30, 1718, at Buckinghamshire, England. Presidential Proclamation 5284 of Nov 28, 1984, conferred honorary citizenship of the USA upon William Penn and his second wife, Hannah Callowhill Penn. They were the third and fourth persons to receive honorary US citizenship (following Winston Churchill and Raoul Wallenberg).

"THE RED BUTTONS SHOW" TV PREMIERE: ANNIVERSARY. Oct 14, 1952. This comedy-variety show starred the well-known burlesque comedian Red Buttons. Regulars included Dorothy Jolliffe, Joe Silver, Jeanne Carson, Sara Seegar, Jimmy Little, Ralph Stanley, Sammy Birch and the Elliot Lawrence Orchestra. It later switched networks under a new format in 1953, as a sitcom with Phyllis Kirk and Paul Lynde.

SAMOA: WHITE SUNDAY. Oct 14. The second Sunday in October. For the children of Samoa, this is the biggest day of the year. Traditional roles are reversed, as children lead church services, are served special foods and receive gifts of new church clothes and other special items. All the children dress in white. The following Monday is an official holiday.

SHE LOVES GOD WEEK. Oct 14–20. A week for Christian women to work on growing in their relationship with God and to learn more about integrating God into their daily lives. An annual virtual conference to celebrate this week is held at www.shelovesgod.com. For info: Marnie Pehrson, 514 Old Hickory Ln, Ringgold, GA 30736. Phone: (706) 861-7936. E-mail: webmaster@shelovesgod.com.

SHOPPING CART SAFETY AWARENESS WEEK. Oct 14–20. Falls and spills from shopping carts have become the leading cause of injury for children under five. In fact, children have lost their lives due to unsafe shopping carts. The focus of this awareness week is to educate consumers and grocery and retail operators throughout the nation about the dangers of shopping carts and the simple ways to prevent accidents. For info: Four D, Inc, PO Box 3080, Burnsville, MN 55337. Phone: (800) 524-7057. Fax: (952) 894-0634. E-mail: sales@four-d.com. Web: www.four-d.com.

SOUND BARRIER BROKEN: ANNIVERSARY. Oct 14, 1947. Flying a Bell X-1 at Muroc Dry Lake Bed, CA, Air Force pilot Chuck Yeager broke the sound barrier, ushering in the era of supersonic flight.

TEEN READ WEEK. Oct 14–20. The teen years are a time when many kids reject reading as being just another dreary assignment. The goal of Teen Read Week is to encourage young adults to read for sheer pleasure as well as learning. Also to remind parents, teachers and others that reading for fun is important for teens as well as young children and to increase awareness of the resources available at libraries. For info: Young Adult Library Services Assn, American Library Assn, 50 E Huron St, Chicago, IL 60611. Phone: (800) 545-2433, ext 4390. E-mail: yalsa@ala.org. Web: www.ala.org/yalsa.

A TIME OF THANKSGIVING. Oct 14. Allentown, PA. A Native American festival to share a harvest of storytelling, dancing and crafts in a colorful fall setting. Annually, the second Sunday in October. Est attendance: 3,000. For info: Lenni Lenape Historical Soc, Museum of Indian Culture, 2825 Fish Hatchery Rd, Allentown, PA 18103-9801. Phone: (610) 797-2121. Fax: (610) 797-2801. Web: www.lenape.org.

BIRTHDAYS TODAY

Harry Anderson, 49, actor ("Night Court," "Dave's World"), born Newport, RI, Oct 14, 1952.

Beth Daniel, 45, LPGA Hall of Fame golfer, born Charleston, SC, Oct 14, 1956.

John Dean, 63, lawyer (White House counsel during Watergate), born Akron, OH, Oct 14, 1938.

Greg Evigan, 48, actor ("B.J. and the Bear," "Masquerade"), born South Amboy, NJ, Oct 14, 1953.

Gary Graffman, 73, pianist, director of the Curtis Institute of Music (Philadelphia), born New York, NY, Oct 14, 1928.

Charles Everett Koop, 85, former US Surgeon General, born Brooklyn, NY, Oct 14, 1916.

Ralph Lauren, 62, designer, born The Bronx, NY, Oct 14, 1939.

Roger Moore, 73, actor (James Bond movies, "The Saint"), born London, England, Oct 14, 1928.

OCTOBER 15 — MONDAY
Day 288 — 77 Remaining

CHINA: CANTON AUTUMN TRADE FAIR. Oct 15–Nov 15. The Guangzhou (Canton) Autumn Trade Fair is held during the same dates each year.

CROW RESERVATION OPENED FOR SETTLEMENT: ANNIVERSARY. Oct 15, 1892. By Presidential Proclamation 1.8 million acres of Crow Indian reservation were opened to settlers. The government had induced the Crow to give up a portion of their land in the mountainous western area in the state of Montana, for which they received 50 cents per acre.

FIRST MANNED FLIGHT: ANNIVERSARY. Oct 15, 1783. Jean Francois Pilatre de Rozier and Francois Laurent, Marquis d'Arlandes became the first people to fly when they ascended in a Montgolfier hot-air balloon at Paris, France, less than three months after the first public balloon flight demonstration (June 5, 1783), and only a year after the first experiments with small paper and fabric balloons by the Montgolfier brothers, Joseph and Jacques, in November 1782. The first manned free flight lasted about 4 minutes and carried the passengers at a height of about 84 feet. On Nov 21, 1783, they soared 3,000 feet over Paris for 25 minutes.

"FURY" TV PREMIERE: ANNIVERSARY. Oct 15, 1955. This popular series starred Bobby Diamond as Joey Newton, an orphan living on the streets. He is relocated to a ranch owned by recent widower Jim Newton (Peter Graves), who eventually adopts Joey. Joey's friend is a black horse given to him by Newton, called Fury. Also featured were William Fawcett, Roger Mobley and Jimmy Baird. In syndication, the series was retitled "Brave Stallion."

"I LOVE LUCY" TV PREMIERE: 50th ANNIVERSARY. Oct 15, 1951. This enormously popular sitcom, TV's first smash hit, starred the real-life husband and wife team of Cuban actor/bandleader Desi Arnaz and talented redheaded actress/comedienne Lucille Ball. They played Ricky and Lucy Ricardo, a New York bandleader and his aspiring actress/homemaker wife who was always scheming to get on stage. Costarring were William Frawley and Vivian Vance as Fred and Ethel Mertz, the Ricardos' landlords and good friends who participated in the escapades and dealt with the consequences of Lucy's often well-intentioned plans. Famous actors guest-starred on the show, including Harpo Marx, Rock Hudson, William Holden, Hedda Hopper and John Wayne. This was the first sitcom to be filmed live before a studio audience, and it did extremely well in the ratings both the first time around and in reruns. The last telecast ran Sept 24, 1961.

INTERNATIONAL INFECTION CONTROL WEEK. Oct 15–21. To promote awareness of prevention and treatment of infection. For info: Assn for Professionals in Infection Control and Epidemiology, 1275 K St NW, Ste 1000, Washington DC, 20005-4006. Phone: (202) 789-1890. Fax: (202) 789-1899. E-mail: APICinfo@apic.org. Web: www.apic.org.

JAMAICA: NATIONAL HEROES DAY. Oct 15. National holiday established in 1969. Always observed on third Monday of October.

MANN, MARTY: BIRTH ANNIVERSARY. Oct 15, 1904. American social activist and author was born at Chicago, IL. She was founder in 1944 of the National Committee for Education on Alcoholism and author of *A New Primer on Alcoholism*. She died at Bridgeport, CT, July 22, 1980.

MY MOM IS A STUDENT DAY. Oct 15. Kids can show their support to their moms by treating them with new pens, paper clips and other little school supplies. They can also fix mom a school lunch with a supportive note inside. Annually, Oct 15. For info: Patti Veld, c/o Davenport College Library, 8200 Georgia St, Merrillville, IN 46410.

NATIONAL BUSINESS WOMEN'S WEEK. Oct 15–19. National Business Women's Week recognizes the role of the working woman in American society, in the economy and in the family. It is commemorated nationwide by special activities. Annually, starting the third Monday in October. Sponsor: Business and Professional Women/USA. For info: Issues Research Mgr, BPW/USA, 2012 Massachusetts Ave NW, Washington, DC 20036. Phone: (202) 293-1100. Web: www.bpwusa.org.

★NATIONAL CHARACTER COUNTS WEEK. Oct 15–21. One of the greatest building blocks of character is citizen service. The future belongs to those who have the strength of character to live a life of service to others.

NATIONAL GROUCH DAY. Oct 15. Honor a grouch; all grouches deserve a day to be recognized. Annually, Oct 15. For info: Alan R. Miller, Carter Middle School, 300 Upland Dr, Room 207, Clio, MI 48420. Phone: (810) 591-0503.

October 2001	S	M	T	W	T	F	S
		1	2	3	4	5	6
	7	8	9	10	11	12	13
	14	15	16	17	18	19	20
	21	22	23	24	25	26	27
	28	29	30	31			

NATIONAL HEALTH EDUCATION WEEK. Oct 15–21. Annually, the third week in October. For info: Lynne Whitt, Natl Center for Health Education, 72 Spring St, Ste 208, New York, NY 10012. Phone: (212) 334-9470.

NATIONAL SCHOOL LUNCH WEEK. Oct 15–19. To celebrate good nutrition and healthy, low-cost school lunches. Annually, the second full week in October. For info: Communications Dept, American School Food Service Assn, 1600 Duke St, 7th Fl, Alexandria, VA 22314-3436. Phone: (703) 739-3900 x133.

NIETZSCHE, FRIEDRICH WILHELM: BIRTH ANNIVERSARY. Oct 15, 1844. Influential German philosopher born at Rocken. Especially remembered among his philosophical beliefs are contempt for the weak and expected ultimate triumph of a superman. Nietzsche died at Weimar, Aug 25, 1900, a decade after suffering a mental breakdown.

SENATE CONFIRMS THOMAS TO SUPREME COURT: 10th ANNIVERSARY. Oct 15, 1991. After three days of Senate Judiciary Committee hearings on charges of sexual harassment made against Judge Clarence Thomas by a former aide, Anita F. Hill, the Senate confirmed Thomas as the 106th US Supreme Court Justice with a 52–48 vote on Oct 15, 1991. The vote was the closest for a 20th-century justice and made Thomas, who would replace retired Justice Thurgood Marshall, the second African American to sit on the Supreme Court.

SPACE MILESTONE: *CASSINI* (US). Oct 15, 1997. The plutonium-powered spacecraft launched is to arrive at Saturn in July 2004. It will orbit the planet, take pictures of its 18 known moons and dispatch a probe to Titan, the largest of these moons.

VIRGIN ISLANDS: HURRICANE THANKSGIVING DAY. Oct 15. Third Monday of October is a legal holiday celebrating the end of hurricane season.

★WHITE CANE SAFETY DAY. Oct 15. Presidential Proclamation always issued for Oct 15 since 1964 (PL88–628 of Oct 6, 1964).

WILSON, EDITH BOLLING GALT: BIRTH ANNIVERSARY. Oct 15, 1872. Second wife of Woodrow Wilson, 28th president of the US, born at Wytheville, VA. Died at Washington, DC, Dec 28, 1961.

WODEHOUSE, PELHAM GRENVILLE: BIRTH ANNIVERSARY. Oct 15, 1881. English author, humorist, creator of Jeeves and Bertis Wooster. Born at Guildford, Surrey, England, P.G. Wodehouse died at Southampton, Long Island, NY, Feb 14, 1975.

BIRTHDAYS TODAY

Victor Banerjee, 55, actor (*A Passage to India*, *The Home and the World*), born Calcutta, India, Oct 15, 1946.

John Kenneth Galbraith, 93, economist, diplomat, author, born Iona Station, Ontario, Canada, Oct 15, 1908.

Lee Iacocca, 77, former automobile executive (Ford and Chrysler), born Allentown, PA, Oct 15, 1924.

Tito Jackson (Toriano Adaryll Jackson), 48, singer, musician (Jackson 5), born Gary, IN, Oct 15, 1953.

Linda Lavin, 62, actress (Tony for *Broadway Bound*; "Alice"), born Portland, ME, Oct 15, 1939.

Penny Marshall, 59, director (*Big, A League of Their Own*), actress ("Laverne & Shirley"), born New York, NY, Oct 15, 1942.

James Alvin (Jim) Palmer, 56, sportscaster, Baseball Hall of Fame pitcher, born New York, NY, Oct 15, 1945.

Sarah (Ferguson), 42, Duchess of York (former wife of Prince Andrew), born London, England, Oct 15, 1959.

Arthur Meier Schlesinger, Jr, 84, historian, author, born Columbus, OH, Oct 15, 1917.

OCTOBER 16 — TUESDAY
Day 289 — 76 Remaining

AMERICA'S FIRST DEPARTMENT STORE: ANNIVERSARY. Oct 16, 1868. Salt Lake City, UT. America's first department store, "ZCMI" (Zion's Co-Operative Mercantile Institution), is still operating at Salt Lake City. It was founded under the direction of Brigham Young. For info: Museum of Church History and Art, 45 North West Temple, Salt Lake City, UT 84150. Phone: (801) 240-4604.

BEN-GURION, DAVID: BIRTH ANNIVERSARY. Oct 16, 1886. First prime minister of the state of Israel. Born at Plonsk, Poland, died at Tel Aviv, Israel, Dec 1, 1973.

BIRTH CONTROL CLINIC OPENED: 85th ANNIVERSARY. Oct 16, 1916. Margaret Sanger, Fania Mindell and Ethel Burne opened the first birth control clinic in the US at 46 Amboy St, Brooklyn, NY. Sanger believed that the poor should be able to control the size of their families.

CRIMEAN WAR: ANNIVERSARY. Oct 16, 1853. The Ottoman Empire declared war on Russia on this day to stem Russian expansionist policies in the Empire. Britain, France and parts of Italy allied themselves with the Turks against Russia. A battle in this war was immortalized in Tennyson's poem, "The Charge of the Light Brigade." Health conditions for soldiers were scandalous, leading Florence Nightingale to work in the British hospital at Istanbul. This was the first war to be observed firsthand by newspaper reporters and photographers.

DICTIONARY DAY. Oct 16. The birthday of Noah Webster, American teacher and lexicographer, is occasion to encourage every person to acquire at least one dictionary—and to use it regularly.

DOUGLAS, WILLIAM ORVILLE: BIRTH ANNIVERSARY. Oct 16, 1898. American jurist, world traveler, conservationist, outdoorsman and author. Born at Maine, MN, he served as justice of the US Supreme Court longer than any other (36 years). Died at Washington, DC, Jan 19, 1980.

GRANT PUT IN CHARGE OF THE MISSISSIPPI REGION: ANNIVERSARY. Oct 16, 1863. After his impressive success taking Vicksburg, MS, Ulysses S. Grant, a brigadier general of the militia, was appointed a general in the regular army and, with the subsequent reorganization of the departments of war in Ohio, Cumberland and Tennessee, was placed in charge of the newly formed Military Division of the Mississippi. Grant's first priority was to save the besieged and starving Union troops at Chattanooga, TN.

JOHN BROWN'S RAID: ANNIVERSARY. Oct 16, 1859. White abolitionist John Brown, with a band of about 20 men, seized the US Arsenal at Harpers Ferry, WV. Brown was captured and the insurrection put down by Oct 19. Brown was hanged at Charles Town, WV, Dec 2, 1859.

MAPLE LEAF FESTIVAL. Oct 16–21. Carthage, MO. Brilliant fall foliage gives this Victorian city the perfect backdrop. A 150+ unit parade, four-state marching band competition, nationwide car show (more than 500 entries), historic homes tour, arts and craft show plus entertainment and much more. Est attendance: 70,000. For info: Chamber of Commerce, 107 E 3rd St, Carthage, MO 64836. Phone: (417) 358-2373. Fax: (417) 358-7479.

MARIE ANTOINETTE: EXECUTION ANNIVERSARY. Oct 16, 1793. Queen Marie Antoinette, whose extravagance and "let them eat cake" attitude toward the starving French underclass made her a target of the French Revolution, was beheaded on this date.

MILLION MAN MARCH: ANNIVERSARY. Oct 16, 1995. Hundreds of thousands of black men met at Washington, DC, for a "holy day of atonement and reconciliation" organized by Louis Farrakhan, leader of the Nation of Islam. Marchers pledged to take responsibility for themselves, their families and their communities.

MOON PHASE: NEW MOON. Oct 16. Moon enters New Moon phase at 3:23 PM, EDT.

NATIONAL BOSS DAY. Oct 16. For all employees to honor their bosses. Annually, Oct 16. For info: Mrs Patricia Bays Haroski, Originator, 2871-F-Walnut View Ct, Winston-Salem, NC 27103.

O'NEILL, EUGENE GLADSTONE: BIRTH ANNIVERSARY. Oct 16, 1888. American playwright (*Long Day's Journey into Night, Ah, Wilderness*), recipient of Pulitzer and Nobel Prize. Born at New York, NY, he died at Boston, MA, Nov 27, 1953.

UNITED NATIONS: WORLD FOOD DAY. Oct 16. Annual observance to heighten public awareness of the world food problem and to strengthen solidarity in the struggle against hunger, malnutrition and poverty. Date of observance is anniversary of founding of Food and Agriculture Organization (FAO), Oct 16, 1945, at Quebec, Canada. For info: United Nations, Dept of Public Info, New York, NY 10017.

WEBSTER, NOAH: BIRTH ANNIVERSARY. Oct 16, 1758. American teacher and journalist whose name became synonymous with the word "dictionary" after his compilations of the earliest American dictionaries of the English language. Born at West Hartford, CT, he died at New Haven, CT, May 28, 1843.

WILDE, OSCAR: BIRTH ANNIVERSARY. Oct 16, 1854. Irish poet and playwright Oscar (Fingal O'Flahertie Wills) Wilde was born at Dublin, Ireland. At the height of his career he was imprisoned for two years on a morals offense, during which time he wrote "A Ballad of Reading Gaol." Best known of his plays is *The Importance of Being Earnest*. "There is only one thing in the world worse than being talked about," he wrote in his *Picture of Dorian Gray*, "and that is not being talked about." Wilde died at Paris, France, Nov 30, 1900. His dying words are said to have been: "This wallpaper is killing me; one of us has got to go."

WORLD FOOD DAY. Oct 16. To increase awareness, understanding and informed action on hunger. Annually, on the founding date of the UN Food and Agriculture Organization. For info: Patricia Young, US Natl Committee for World Food Day, 2175 K St NW, Washington DC, 20437. Phone: (202) 653-2404.

YALE UNIVERSITY FOUNDED: 300th ANNIVERSARY. Oct 16, 1701 (OS). The Collegiate School was founded at Branford, CT by Congregationalists dissatisfied with the growing liberalism at Harvard. In 1716, the school was moved to New Haven, CT, where it became Yale College, named after Elihu Yale, a governor of the East India Company. The first degrees were awarded in 1716. Yale became a university in 1887. Founded as a school for men, Yale began admitting women undergraduates in 1969.

BIRTHDAYS TODAY

Melissa Louise Belote, 45, Olympic gold medal swimmer, born Washington, DC, Oct 16, 1956.

Manute Bol, 39, former basketball player, born Gogrial, Sudan, Oct 16, 1962.

Barry Corbin, 61, actor ("Northern Exposure," *Stir Crazy, Any Which Way You Can*), born Dawson County, TX, Oct 16, 1940.

David Albert (Dave) DeBusschere, 61, former basketball coach and executive, Basketball Hall of Fame forward, born Detroit, MI, Oct 16, 1940.

Juan Gonzalez, 32, baseball player, born Vaga Baja, Puerto Rico, Oct 16, 1969.

Gunter Grass, 74, author (*The Tin Drum, Dog Years*), born Danzig, Germany, Oct 16, 1927.

Paul Kariya, 27, hockey player, born Vancouver, British Columbia, Canada, Oct 16, 1974.

Angela Lansbury, 76, actress ("Murder She Wrote," *National Velvet*; Tony for *Sweeny Todd*), born London, England, Oct 16, 1925.

Kellie Martin, 26, actress ("Life Goes On," "ER"), born Riverside, CA, Oct 16, 1975.

Tim Robbins, 43, actor (*Top Gun, Shawshank Redemption*), born West Covina, CA, Oct 16, 1958.

Suzanne Somers, 55, actress ("Three's Company," "Step by Step," *American Graffiti*), born San Bruno, CA, Oct 16, 1946.

Kordell Stewart, 29, football player, born New Orleans, LA, Oct 16, 1972.

Bob Weir, 54, cofounder (The Grateful Dead), born San Francisco, CA, Oct 16, 1947.

OCTOBER 17 — WEDNESDAY

Day 290 — 75 Remaining

AMERICAN MASSAGE THERAPY ASSOCIATION® NATIONAL CONVENTION. Oct 17–21. Quebec Hilton, Quebec Convention Centre, Canada. American Massage Therapy Association (established 1943), the largest association of professional massage therapists, representing more than 40,000 members from all states and 30 other countries. Conventions emphasize continuing education, association governance and current research on therapeutic massage as a complement to traditional medicine. And, practical/innovative products and services pertinent to the profession are exhibited. Est attendance: 800. For info: American Massage Therapy Assn, 820 Davis St, Ste 100, Evanston, IL 60201-4444. Phone: (847) 864-0123. Fax: (847) 864-1178. E-mail: info@inet.amtamassage.org. Web: www.amtamassage.org.

October 2001	S	M	T	W	T	F	S
		1	2	3	4	5	6
	7	8	9	10	11	12	13
	14	15	16	17	18	19	20
	21	22	23	24	25	26	27
	28	29	30	31			

ARTHUR, JEAN: BIRTH ANNIVERSARY. Oct 17, 1900. American actress Jean Arthur was born Gladys Georgianna Greene at Plattsburg, NY. Her films included *Mr Deeds Goes to Town* (1936), *Mr Smith Goes to Washington* (1939) and *Shane* (1953). She died June 19, 1991, at Carmel, CA.

BLACK POETRY DAY. Oct 17 (tentative). To recognize the contribution of black poets to American life and culture and to honor Jupiter Hammon, first black in America to publish his own verse. Jupiter Hammon of Huntington, Long Island, NY, was born Oct 17, 1711. Est attendance: 200. For info: Alexis Levitin, Black Poetry Day Committee, Dept of English, SUNY-Plattsburgh, Plattsburgh, NY 12901-2681. Phone: (518) 564-2426. Fax: (518) 564-2140. E-mail: levitia@splava.cc.plattsburgh.edu.

CIRCLEVILLE PUMPKIN SHOW. Oct 17–20. Circleville, OH. More than 100,000 pounds of pumpkins, squash and gourds. Est attendance: 300,000. For info: Hugh Dresbach, Secy, Pumpkin Show Inc, 159 E Franklin St, Circleville, OH 43113. Phone: (740) 474-7000. Fax: (740) 474-6611.

EAST TEXAS YAMBOREE. Oct 17–20. Gilmer, TX. Est attendance: 100,000. For info: Joan Small, Exec Dir, Upshur County Chamber of Commerce, Box 854, Gilmer, TX 75644. Phone: (903) 843-2413 or (903) 843-3981. Fax: (903) 843-3759. E-mail: upchamber@aol.com.

HAMMON, JUPITER: BIRTH ANNIVERSARY. Oct 17, 1711. America's first published black poet, whose birth anniversary is celebrated annually as Black Poetry Day, was born into slavery, probably at Long Island, NY. He was taught to read, however, and as a trusted servant was allowed to use his master's library. "With the publication on Christmas Day, 1760, of the 88-line broadside poem 'An Evening Thought,' Jupiter Hammon, then 49, became the first black in America to publish poetry." Hammon died in 1790. The exact date and place of his death are unknown.

"THE HOLLYWOOD SQUARES" TV PREMIERE: 35th ANNIVERSARY. Oct 17, 1966. On this game show, nine celebrities sat in a giant grid. Two contestants played tic-tac-toe by determining if an answer given by a celebrity was correct. Peter Marshall hosted the show for many years with panelists Paul Lynde, Rose Marie, Cliff Arquette, Wally Cox, John Davidson and George Gobel among others. John Davidson took over as host in 1986 for a new version of the game show with Joan Rivers and, later, Shadoe Stevens at center square. In 1998 "Hollywood Squares" appeared again with Tom Bergeron as host and Whoopi Goldberg as the center square.

JOHNSON, RICHARD MENTOR: BIRTH ANNIVERSARY. Oct 17, 1780. Ninth vice president of the US (1837–41). Born at Floyd's Station, KY. Died at Frankfort, KY, Nov 19, 1850.

LITERACY VOLUNTEERS OF AMERICA CONFERENCE. Oct 17–20. Albuquerque, NM. An annual gathering of literacy providers, volunteer tutors and adult learners. Featuring: workshops, keynote and guest speakers, awards banquet, training programs and networking with experts in the adult literacy field. Est attendance: 1,000. For info: Literacy Volunteers of America, 635 James St, Syracuse, NY 13203-2214. Phone: (315) 472-0001. E-mail: info@literacyvolunteers.org. Web: literacyvolunteers.org.

MISSOURI DAY. Oct 17. Observed by teachers and pupils of schools with appropriate exercises throughout state of Missouri. Annually, the third Wednesday of October.

POPE JOHN PAUL I: BIRTH ANNIVERSARY. Oct 17, 1912. Albino Luciani, 263rd pope of the Roman Catholic Church. Born at Forno di Canale, Italy, he was elected pope Aug 26, 1978. Died at Rome, 34 days after his election, Sept 28, 1978. Shortest papacy since Pope Leo XI (Apr 1–27, 1605).

SAN FRANCISCO 1989 EARTHQUAKE: ANNIVERSARY. Oct 17, 1989. The San Francisco Bay area was rocked by an earthquake registering 7.1 on the Richter scale at 5:04 PM, EDT, just as the nation's baseball fans settled in to watch the 1989 World Series. A large audience was tuned in to the pregame coverage when the quake hit and knocked the broadcast off the air. The quake caused damage estimated at $10 billion and killed 67 people, many of whom were caught in the collapse of the double-decked Interstate 80, at Oakland, CA.

UNITED NATIONS: INTERNATIONAL DAY FOR THE ERADICATION OF POVERTY. Oct 17. The General Assembly proclaimed this observance (Res 47/196) to promote public awareness of the need to eradicate poverty and destitution in all countries, particularly the developing nations.

BIRTHDAYS TODAY

Ernie Els, 32, golfer, born Johannesburg, South Africa, Oct 17, 1969.

Beverly Garland, 75, actress ("My Three Sons," "Scarecrow and Mrs King"), born Santa Cruz, CA, Oct 17, 1926.

Mae Jemison, 45, scientist, astronaut, host ("Susan B. Anthony Slept Here"), born Decatur, AL, Oct 17, 1956.

Margot Kidder, 53, actress (Lois Lane in *Superman* movies), born Yellowknife, Northwest Territories, Canada, Oct 17, 1948.

Robert Craig ("Evel") Knievel, 63, motorcycle stunt performer, born Butte, MT, Oct 17, 1938.

Michael McKean, 54, actor ("Laverne & Shirley," *This Is Spinal Tap*), born New York, NY, Oct 17, 1947.

Arthur Miller, 86, dramatist (*Death of a Salesman, A View from the Bridge, All My Sons*), born New York, NY, Oct 17, 1915.

Tom Poston, 74, actor ("Grace Under Fire," Emmy for "The Steve Allen Show," *Soldier in the Rain*), born Columbus, OH, Oct 17, 1927.

George Wendt, 53, actor ("Cheers," "The Naked Truth"), born Chicago, IL, Oct 17, 1948.

OCTOBER 18 — THURSDAY

Day 291 — 74 Remaining

AFRICARE BISHOP JOHN T. WALKER MEMORIAL DINNER. Oct 18 (tentative). Washington, DC. Reception, dinner and program of international speakers at this annual benefit for Africare, a nonprofit African-American organization founded in 1971 that provides direct development and emergency aid Africa-wide. Est attendance: 2,500. For info: Africare Dinner Coord, Africare, 440 R St NW, Washington, DC 20001. Phone: (202) 462-3614. Fax: (202) 387-1034. Web: www.africare.org.

ALASKA DAY. Oct 18, 1867. Alaska. Anniversary of transfer of Alaska from Russia to the US which became official on Sitka's Castle Hill. This is a holiday in Alaska; when it falls on a weekend it is observed on the following Monday.

ANDREE, SALOMON AUGUSTE: BIRTH ANNIVERSARY. Oct 18, 1854. Swedish explorer and balloonist born at Grenna, Sweden. His North Pole expedition of 1897 attracted world attention but ended tragically. With two companions, Andree left Spitzbergen, July 11, 1897, in a balloon, hoping to place the Swedish flag at the North Pole. The last message from Andree, borne by carrier pigeons, was dated noon, July 13, 1897. The frozen bodies of the explorers were found 33 years later by another polar expedition in the summer of 1930. Diaries, maps and exposed photographic negatives also were found. The photos were developed successfully, providing a pictorial record of the ill-fated expedition.

THE ARC (A NATIONAL ORGANIZATION ON MENTAL RETARDATION): ANNUAL CONVENTION. Oct 18–20. New Orleans, LA. The Arc was formerly named Association for Retarded Citizens of the United States. Est attendance: 1,200. For info: L.D. Carter, Dir, The Arc Natl HQ, 500 E Border St, Ste 300, Arlington, TX 76010. Phone: (817) 261-6003. Fax: (817) 277-3491. E-mail: thearc@inetronet.com. Web: www.thearc.org/welcome.html.

AZERBAIJAN: INDEPENDENCE DAY. Oct 18. National holiday. Commemorates declaration of independence from the Soviet Union in 1991.

BELLA VISTA ARTS AND CRAFTS FESTIVAL. Oct 18–20. Bella Vista, AR. Started in 1968, this arts and crafts festival is sponsored by the Village Art Club. 325 juried exhibitors show artwork in many media and contemporary and traditional crafts. Enjoy food, music, shopping, kids' tent and petting zoo. Est attendance: 37,000. For info: Bella Vista Arts and Crafts Festival, Village Art Club, PO Box 5009, Bella Vista, AR 72714. Phone: (501) 855-2064. Fax: (501) 855-0842. E-mail: artclub@ipa.net. Web: www.villageartclub.org.

BERGSON, HENRI: BIRTH ANNIVERSARY. Oct 18, 1859. French philosopher, Nobel Prize winner and author of *Creative Evolution*, born at Paris, France. Died there Jan 4, 1941.

BIKETOBERFEST. Oct 18–21. Daytona Beach, FL. Bikers return to Daytona Beach for that last chance to ride before winter. Parades, concerts and expos highlight the weekend. Est attendance: 100,000. For info: Daytona Beach Area CVB, 126 E Orange, Daytona Beach, FL 32114. Phone: (800) 854-1234. Fax: (904) 255-5478. E-mail: info@daytonabeach.com. Web: www.biketoberfest.org.

BROOKS, JAMES DAVID: 95th BIRTH ANNIVERSARY. Oct 18, 1906. Born at St. Louis, MO, during the Depression Brooks worked as a muralist in the Federal Art Project of the Works Progress Administration. His best-known work of that period was "Flight," a mural on the rotunda of the Marine Air Terminal at La Guardia National Airport in New York. It was painted over during the 1950s but restored in 1980. Brooks served as an art correspondent with the US Army from 1942 to 1945. When he returned to New York, his interest shifted to abstract expressionism. His paintings were exhibited in the historic "Ninth Street Exhibition" as a part of the Museum of Modern Art's exhibits "Twelve Americans" and "New American Painting," among others. He died Mar 8, 1992, at Brookhaven, NY.

CANADA: PERSONS DAY. Oct 18. A day to commemorate the anniversary of the 1929 ruling that declared women to be persons in Canada. Prior to this ruling English common law prevailed ("Women are persons in matters of pains and penalties, but are not persons in matters of rights and privileges"). The celebrated cause, popularly known as the "Persons Case," was brought by five women of Alberta, Canada; leader of the courageous "Famous Five" was Emily Murphy (1868–1933). This ruling by the Judicial Committee of England's Privy Council, Oct 18, 1929, overturned a 1928 decision of the Supreme Court of Canada. Fifty years after the Persons Case decision, in 1979, the Governor General's Awards in Commemoration of the Persons Case were established to recognize deserving persons who have made outstanding contributions to the quality of life of women in Canada.

CANALETTO, GIOVANNI ANTONIO: BIRTH ANNIVERSARY. Oct 18, 1697. Italian painter Giovanni Antonio Canaletto (born Canale), who is best known for his detailed landscapes of Venice and London, was born at Venice and died there at age 70, Apr 20, 1768. He was known for his accurate use of perspective, shadow and light. He went to England in 1746 and expanded his range of subjects to include English landscapes and country homes.

"COLT .45" TV PREMIERE: ANNIVERSARY. Oct 18, 1957. Spaghetti-western actor Wayde Preston starred in this ABC western as Christopher Colt, son of the inventor of the Colt revolver, and a government agent. Character actor Donald May replaced Preston and played the role of Sam Colt, Jr, Christopher's cousin, until early 1960 when Preston returned to the show.

"JANE FROMAN'S U.S.A. CANTEEN" TV PREMIERE: ANNIVERSARY. Oct 18, 1952. Froman, "the Sweetheart of the Armed Forces," appeared in this series with talented members of the armed services.

LIEBLING, A.J.: BIRTH ANNIVERSARY. Oct 18, 1904. American journalist and author who said "Freedom of the press belongs to those who own one." Abbott Joseph Liebling was born at New York, NY, and died there Dec 28, 1963.

MERCOURI, MELINA: BIRTH ANNIVERSARY. Oct 18, 1922. Greek actress and politician Melina Mercouri was born Maria Amalia Mercouri at Athens, Greece, Oct 18, 1922 or 1925 (both reported). Of her more than 70 films and plays she is most known for her role in *Never on Sunday* (1960). In 1977 she was elected to Greece's parliament and became the first woman in Greece's senior cabinet when appointed by Premier Andreas Papandreou to the position of minister of culture in 1981. She died Mar 6, 1994, at New York, NY.

MOUNTAIN STATE APPLE HARVEST FESTIVAL. Oct 18–21. Martinsburg, WV. 22nd annual. Total family entertainment including apple pie baking contest and auction, coronation of Queen Pomona, 5K run, pancake breakfast, arts and crafts festival, tours of agricultural facilities, antique car show and the grand feature parade. Annually, the third full weekend in October. Est attendance: 75,000. For info: Mountain State Apple Harvest Festival, PO Box 1362, Martinsburg, WV 25402. Phone: (304) 263-2500. Web: www.berkeleycounty.com/MSAHF.

NORTHERN IRELAND PLOUGHING CHAMPIONSHIPS. Oct 18–19. Eglinton County, Londonderry. 57th contest. Ploughing competition for tractors, vintage ploughs and horses. Est attendance: 5,500. For info: Mrs R Adair, Sec, Northern Ireland Ploughing Assn, 475 Antrim Road, Northern Ireland BT15 3DA. Phone: (1232) 37-0222. Fax: (1232) 37-1231.

OKTOBERFEST. Oct 18–21. Tulsa, OK. This colorful ethnic festival reflects an authentic German flavor in food, music and entertainment with biergartens located at River West Festival Park. Attractions include German Bands, dancing, sing-alongs, contests, visual arts and crafts and German collectibles and children's entertainment. Est attendance: 200,000. For info: Kathy Baker, Oktoberfest Inc, 2121 S Columbia, #LL8, Tulsa, OK 74114. Phone: (918) 744-9700. Fax: (918) 744-9702.

ORPHAN TRAIN HERITAGE SOCIETY OF AMERICA: ANNUAL REUNION. Oct 18–20. Fayetteville, AR. Between 1854 and 1929, more than 150,000 homeless children and poor families were transported out of New York City, Boston and Chicago aboard trains accompanied by "agents." Agents for the New York Children's Aid Society arranged for midwestern families to take the children under a contract agreement. Infants placed by the New York Foundling Hospital were indentured. Annual reunion, plus regional reunions in Oklahoma, Missouri, Kansas, Texas, Iowa, Illinois, Indiana, California, Louisiana, Nebraska and Minnesota bring together survivors of the Orphan Trains era, their descendants and interested persons. All gatherings are open to the public, with a small registration fee charged at each. Books containing stories of the Orphan Train Riders are available at each reunion. Est attendance: 250. For info: Mary Ellen Johnson, Exec Dir, OTHSA, Inc, 614 E Emma Ave, #115, Springdale, AR 72764-4634. Phone: (501) 756-2780. Fax: (501) 756-0769. Web: pda.republic.net/othsa.

"ROSEANNE" TV PREMIERE: ANNIVERSARY. Oct 18, 1988. This comedy showed the blue-collar Conner family trying to make ends meet. Rosanne played wise-cracking Roseanne Conner, John Goodman played her husband Dan and Laurie Metcalf played her sister Jackie. The Conner children were played by Sara Gilbert (Darlene), Alicia Goranson and Sarah Chalke (Becky) and Michael Fishman (D.J). The last episode aired Nov 14, 1997 but it remains popular in reruns.

SAINT LUKE: FEAST DAY. Oct 18. Patron saint of doctors and artists, himself a physician and painter, authorship of the third Gospel and Acts of the Apostles is attributed to him. Died about AD 68. Legend says that he painted portraits of Mary and Jesus.

WAR EAGLE FAIR. Oct 18–21. War Eagle Mills Farm, War Eagle, AR. 47th annual fair with more than 350 booths of baskets, quilts, woodwork, pottery, furniture, wood carving, toys, leather, books, candles, weaving, jams, jellies and food under circus-style tents on the historic farm grounds. "One of the most highly respected shows in the country." Est attendance: 190,000. For info: Shirley Sutton, War Eagle Fair, 11036 High Sky Inn Rd, Hindsville, AR 72738. Phone: (501) 789-5398. Fax: (501) 789-2215.

WATER POLLUTION CONTROL ACT: ANNIVERSARY. Oct 18, 1972. Overriding President Nixon's veto, Congress passed a $25 billion Water Pollution Control Act.

BIRTHDAYS TODAY

Chuck Berry (Charles Edward Anderson), 75, singer, songwriter ("Johnny B. Goode," "Roll Over Beethoven"), musician, born St. Louis, MO, Oct 18, 1926.

Peter Boyle, 68, actor (*Medium Cool, The Dream Team*, "Everybody Loves Raymond"), born Philadelphia, PA, Oct 18, 1933.

Pam Dawber, 50, actress ("Mork & Mindy," "My Sister Sam"), born Farmington, MI, Oct 18, 1951.

Mike Ditka, 62, sportscaster, Pro Football Hall of Fame tight end, football coach, born Carnegie, PA, Oct 18, 1939.

Jesse Helms, 80, US Senator (R, North Carolina), born Monroe, NC, Oct 18, 1921.

Wynton Marsalis, 40, jazz musician, born New Orleans, LA, Oct 18, 1961.

Erin Moran, 40, actress ("Happy Days," "Joanie Loves Chachi"), born Burbank, CA, Oct 18, 1961.

Joe Morton, 54, actor (*The Brother from Another Planet, Trouble in Mind, City of Hope*), born New York, NY, Oct 18, 1947.

Martina Navratilova (born Martina Subertova), 45, former tennis player, born Prague, Czechoslovakia, Oct 18, 1956.

Ntozake Shange (Paulette L. Williams), 53, dramatist, poet, born Trenton, NJ, Oct 18, 1948.

Vincent Spano, 39, actor (*Baby, It's You; Rumblefish*), born New York, NY, Oct 18, 1962.

Pierre Elliott Trudeau, 82, Prime Minister of Canada, 1968–79, 1980–84, born Montreal, Quebec, Canada, Oct 18, 1919.

Jean-Claude Van Damme, 41, actor (*Kickboxer*), born Brussels, Belgium, Oct 18, 1960.

Wendy Wasserstein, 51, playwright (*The Heidi Chronicles, The Sisters Rosenzweig*), born Brooklyn, NY, Oct 18, 1950.

October 2001	S	M	T	W	T	F	S
		1	2	3	4	5	6
	7	8	9	10	11	12	13
	14	15	16	17	18	19	20
	21	22	23	24	25	26	27
	28	29	30	31			

OCTOBER 19 — FRIDAY

Day 292 — 73 Remaining

ABC/WIBC FESTIVAL OF BOWLING. Oct 19–Nov 18. Reno, NV. One-of-a-kind bowling event open to all ABC and WIBC members giving them opportunities to participate in 15 different bowling formats as often as desired. There are mixed men and women events, an event for beginner bowlers, a family event, a Baker format event, regular bowling events and senior events. For info: Michael Deering, American Bowling Congress, 5301 S 76th St, Greendale, WI 53129-0500. Phone: (414) 423-3309. Fax: (414) 421-3013.

APPLE BUTTER STIRRIN'. Oct 19–21. Coshocton, OH. Kettles of apple butter simmer over open fires; demonstrations, crafts, contests, in Roscoe Village, a restored canal town. Also, live musical entertainment. Est attendance: 35,000. For info: Roscoe Village Fdtn, 381 Hill St, Coshocton, OH 43812. Phone: (800) 877-1830 or (740) 622-9310. Fax: (740) 623-6555. E-mail: rv marketing@coshocton.com. Web: www.roscoevillage.com.

BROWNE, THOMAS: BIRTH ANNIVERSARY. Oct 19, 1605 (OS). Physician, scholar and author, Thomas Browne was born at London, England. At age 55 he wrote: "The long habit of living indisposeth us for dying." His most famous work, *Religio Medici*, was published in 1642. Browne died at Norwich, England, Oct 19, 1682 (OS).

CRAFTSMEN'S CLASSIC. Oct 19–21 (tentative). Capital Expo Center, Chantilly, VA. Arts and crafts. Est attendance: 30,000. For info: Gilmore Enterprises, Inc, 1240 Oakland Ave, Greensboro, NC 27403. Phone: (336) 274-5550. Fax: (336) 274-1084.

DOW-JONES BIGGEST DROP: ANNIVERSARY. Oct 19, 1987. The Dow-Jones Industrial Average plunged 508 points, or 22.6 percent, after frenzied selling, the largest drop in history.

EVALUATE YOUR LIFE DAY. Oct 19. To encourage everyone to check and *see* if they're really headed where they want to be. [© 2000 by WH] For info: Tom and Ruth Roy, Wellcat Holidays, 2418 Long Ln, Lebanon, PA 17042-0774. Phone: (717) 279-0184. E-mail: wellcat@supernet.com. Web: www.wellcat.com.

FALL FESTIVAL OF LEAVES. Oct 19–21. Bainbridge, Ross County, OH. Celebrating the beauty of the season and region. Folk arts, crafts, music, antique car show, log sawing contest, flea markets and parades. To obtain a map of self-guided scenic tours send SASE to sponsor. For info: Fall Festival of Leaves, Box 571, Bainbridge, Ross County, OH 45612. Phone: (740) 634-2085 or (740) 634-2997.

FALL MARYLAND HOME & GARDEN SHOW/MARYLAND HOLIDAY CRAFT SHOW. Oct 19–21. Timonium Fairgrounds, Baltimore, MD. A variety of home products and services to get your home ready for winter. Also educational exhibits, a plant market area and beautiful landscaped gardens. The Maryland Holiday Craft Show is in the same building with more than 150 artists and craftspeople selling something for everyone to fill their Christmas lists. Also a festive Christmas tree decorating contest and wonderful holiday entertainment. For info: S & L Productions, Inc, 1916 Crain Highway, Ste 16, Glen Burnie, MD 21061. Phone: (410) 863-1180. Fax: (410) 863-1187.

FANTASY FEST. Oct 19–28. Key West, FL. Ten-day adult costume festival with street parties, masked balls and nighttime grand parade. Est attendance: 75,000. For info: Fantasy Fest, Linda O'Brien, Box 230, Key West, FL 33041. Phone: (305) 296-1817. Fax: (305) 294-3335. Web: www.fantasyfest.net.

FOOTHILLS ART FESTIVAL. Oct 19–21. Jackson, OH. Visual arts exhibits with more than 600 works by 150 artists from the tri-state area. Also live music and arts activities for the entire family. Est attendance: 4,000. For info: Barbara Summers, Southern Hills Arts Council, PO Box 149, Jackson, OH 45640. Phone: (740) 286-6355. Fax: (740) 384-3063.

HAUNTED FOREST AT AUDUBON ACRES. Oct 19–20 and Oct 26–27. Audubon Acres, Chattanooga, TN. Walk the haunted trails of Audubon Acres keeping alert for ghosts, goblins, trolls and all other night creatures that like to go "Boo!" in the night. Sponsor: Chattanooga Audubon Society. Annually, the two weekends before Halloween in October. Est attendance: 2,000. For info: Lynda Logan, Audubon Acres, 900 N Sanctuary Rd, Chattanooga, TN 37421. Phone: (423) 892-1499. Fax: (423) 892-6376. E-mail: caudubons@aol.com.

JEFFERSON, MARTHA WAYLES SKELTON: BIRTH ANNIVERSARY. Oct 19, 1748. Wife of Thomas Jefferson, third president of the US. Born at Charles City County, VA, she died at Monticello, VA, Sept 6, 1782.

LEE COUNTY COTTON FESTIVAL. Oct 19–20. Bishopville, SC. Join the festivities with amusement rides, fireworks, parades, arts and crafts displays, entertainment, rodeos, sports events, food booths and much more. Annually, the third weekend in October. Est attendance: 20,000. For info: Lee County Chamber of Commerce, Lee County Cotton Fest, PO Box 187, Bishopville, SC 29010. Phone: (803) 484-5145. Fax: (803) 484-4270.

NEEWOLLAH. Oct 19–27. Independence, KS. Halloween spelled backwards means a Broadway musical presentation (local talent); Queen Neelah talent and coronation ceremonies, carnival, wide range of concessions, street acts, kiddie parade, grand parade, nationally known country western stars and concerts. Annually, the last full week in October. Est attendance: 80,000. For info: Chamber of Commerce, PO Box 386, Independence, KS 67301. Phone: (800) 882-3606. Fax: (316) 331-1899. Web: independence kschamber.org.

PECK, ANNIE S.: BIRTH ANNIVERSARY. Oct 19, 1850. World-renowned mountain climber Annie S. Peck won an international following in 1895 when she climbed the Matterhorn in the Swiss Alps. Peck climbed the Peruvian peak Huascaran (21,812 ft), giving her the record for the highest peak climbed in the Western Hemisphere by an American man or woman, and at age 61 she climbed Mt Coropuna in Peru (21,250 ft) and placed a "Votes for Women" banner at its pinnacle. Annie Peck died July 18, 1935, at New York City.

PENNSYLVANIA ARTS & CRAFTS CHRISTMAS FESTIVAL. Oct 19–20 (also Oct 27–28). Washington County Fairgrounds, Washington, PA. More than 165 exhibits of handcrafted furniture, gift items, children's toys, dolls, dried floral arrangements and clothing. Holiday food and entertainment. Est attendance: 22,000. For info: Debbie Stoner, Family Festivals Assn, Inc, PO Box 166, Irwin, PA 15642. Phone: (724) 863-4577. Fax: (724) 863-4577.

SUGARLOAF'S FALL NOVI ART FAIR. Oct 19–21. Novi Expo Center, Novi, MI. This show, now in its 7th year, features 325 nationally recognized craft designers and fine artists displaying and selling their original creations. Craft demonstration, hourly gift certificate drawings and more. Est attendance: 22,000. For info: Sugarloaf Mountain Works, Inc, 200 Orchard Ridge Dr, #215, Gaithersburg, MD 20878. Phone: (800) 210-9900. E-mail: smworks@sugarloafcrafts.com. Web: www.sugarloafcrafts.com.

YORKTOWN DAY: "AMERICA'S REAL INDEPENDENCE DAY." Oct 19. Yorktown, VA. Representatives of the US, France and other nations involved in the American Revolution gather to celebrate the anniversary of the victory (Oct 19, 1781) that assured American independence. Parade and commemorative ceremonies. Annually, Oct 19. Est attendance: 2,000. For info: Public Affairs Officer, Colonial Natl Historical Park, Box 210, Yorktown, VA 23690. Phone: (757) 898-2410. Web: www.nps.gov/colo.

YORKTOWN DAY: ANNIVERSARY. Oct 19, 1781. More than 7,000 English and Hessian troops, led by British General Lord Cornwallis, surrendered to General George Washington at Yorktown, VA, effectively ending the war between Britain and her American colonies. There were no more major battles, but the provisional treaty of peace was not signed until Nov 30, 1782, and the final Treaty of Paris, Sept 3, 1783.

OCTOBER

BIRTHDAYS TODAY

Jack Anderson, 79, journalist, columnist, author (*Japan Conspiracy, Stormin' Norman*), born Long Beach, CA, Oct 19, 1922.

Michael Gambon, 61, actor ("The Singing Detective," *The Cook, The Thief, His Wife & Her Lover*), born Dublin, Ireland, Oct 19, 1940.

Evander Holyfield, 39, boxer, born Atlanta, GA, Oct 19, 1962.

Patricia Ireland, 56, feminist, social activist, president of National Organization for Women, born Oak Park, IL, Oct 19, 1945.

John LeCarre (David John Moore Cornwell), 70, author (*The Russia House*), born Poole, England, Oct 19, 1931.

John Lithgow, 56, actor (*Twilight Zone—The Movie, I'm Dancing As Fast As I Can*, "3rd Rock from the Sun"), born Rochester, NY, Oct 19, 1945.

Peter Max, 64, artist, designer, born Berlin, Germany, Oct 19, 1937.

LaWanda Page, 81, actress ("Sanford and Son"), born Cleveland, OH, Oct 19, 1920.

Simon Ward, 60, actor (*The Three Musketeers, The Four Musketeers*), born London, England, Oct 19, 1941.

October 2001

S	M	T	W	T	F	S
	1	2	3	4	5	6
7	8	9	10	11	12	13
14	15	16	17	18	19	20
21	22	23	24	25	26	27
28	29	30	31			

OCTOBER 20 — SATURDAY
Day 293 — 72 Remaining

AMERICAN THEATRICAL PRODUCTIONS SUSPENDED: ANNIVERSARY. Oct 20, 1774. American theatrical productions were brought to an abrupt halt along with other entertainments when the Continental Congress passed an order proclaiming that the colonies "discountenance and discourage all horse racing and all kinds of gaming, cock fighting, exhibitions of shows, plays, and other expensive diversions and entertainments."

ARKALALAH FESTIVAL. Oct 20–27. Arkansas City, KS. Ark City's largest celebration features three parades (lighted evening, children's and giant Arkalalah Parade), crowning of Queen Alalah, high school band contest, street events, food concessions, crafts show, dances and reunions. Est attendance: 40,000. For info: Christie Rogers, Chamber of Commerce, PO Box 795, Arkansas City, KS 67005. Phone: (316) 442-0230 or (316) 442-6077. Fax: (316) 441-0048. E-mail: CRogers3@aol.com.

ATLANTIQUE CITY ANTIQUES AND COLLECTIBLES MEGAFAIR. Oct 20–21. Atlantic City Convention Center, Atlantic City, NJ. "World's largest" antiques and collectibles show. More than 1,600 booths with an array of memorabilia. Much weird and wonderful stuff such as Jack Benny's violin, first Superman comic book, etc. Est attendance: 65,000. For info: Mark Soifer, Press Relations, 1803 Clover Ave, Vineland, NJ 08361. Phone: (609) 691-7535. Fax: (609) 691-9458.

AUTUMN HISTORIC FOLKLIFE FESTIVAL. Oct 20–21. Downtown Historic District, Hannibal, MO. The Hannibal Arts Council sponsors its 25th annual festival celebrating heritage and tradition of the 1800s. Artisans demonstrate the folk arts of the mid-1800s, vendors prepare food and drink over wood fires and street performers play traditional tunes. Also living history and children's areas with many activities. Est attendance: 25,000. For info: Hannibal Arts Council, PO Box 1202, Hannibal, MO 63401. Phone: (573) 221-6545. E-mail: arts@nemonet.com.

BIRTH OF THE BAB: ANNIVERSARY. Oct 20, 1819. Baha'i observance of anniversary of the birth in Shiraz, Persia, of Siyyid Ali Muhammad, who later took the title "the Bab"; the Bab was the prophet-herald of the Baha'i Faith. One of the nine days of the year when Baha'is suspend work. For info: Baha'is of the US, Office of Public Information, 866 UN Plaza, Ste 120, New York, NY 10017-1822. Phone: (212) 803-2500. Fax: (212) 803-2573. E-mail: usopi-ny@bic.org. Web: www.us.bahai.org.

CANADA: ARTS FESTIVAL XVIII. Oct 20–21. Annapolis Royal, NS. Performance, workshops, art exhibits, a costume arts ball and readings by famous Canadian writers. Annually, the third weekend in October. Est attendance: 2,500. For info: Susan Tileston, Exec Dir, ARCAC, Annapolis Royal Community Arts Council, Box 534, Annapolis Royal, NS, Canada B0S 1A0. Phone: (902) 532-7069. Fax: (902) 532-7357. E-mail: arcac@ns.sympatico.ca. Web: www.arcac.ns.ca.

"CELEBRATE DIVERSITY" FESTIVAL. Oct 20. Seward County Event Center, Liberal, KS. Multi-cultural event sponsored by the City of Liberal's cultural relations advisory board. Themes: Education and Awareness. Booths representing countries of people who live in Liberal, with food, clothing, artifacts, photos, descriptive material. Also local organizations offer information connected to themes. Entertainment throughout the day. Flags of countries on display. Annually, the third Saturday in October. Est attendance: 1,300. For info: Julie Ferguson, 1120 N Tulane Ave, Liberal, KS 67901-2345. Phone: (316) 626-5184.

CHRYSLER CLASSIC SPEED FESTIVAL. Oct 20–21 (tentative). Naval Air Station, North Island, Coronado, San Diego, CA. This San Diego bayside vintage auto racing event is a presentation of the Culligan Holiday Bowl, a production of General Racing, Ltd. Est attendance: 30,000. For info: Mark Neville, Culligan Holiday Bowl, PO Box 601400, San Diego, CA 92160-1400. Phone: (619) 283-5808. Fax: (619) 281-7947. Web: holidaybowl.com.

COUNTRY AFFAIR. Oct 20–21. Ben Franklin School, Menomonee Falls, WI. Community League's 19th annual fair features antiques, folk art and country collectibles. More than 90 exhibitors; a Country Luncheon of homemade food and desserts; a Quilt Raffle; and a "Country Pantry" and silent auction. Admission charged. Est attendance: 6,000. For info: Jeanne Verbsky, Community League, Inc, Publicity—ACA, PO Box 101, Menomonee Falls, WI 53052. Phone: (414) 297-9446.

CZECH HERITAGE FESTIVAL. Oct 20 (tentative). KC Club, Dickinson, ND. Special attractions will be accordion players, Czech singers and dancers. There will be continuous music and entertainment with an ethnic supper following in the evening. Est attendance: 250. For info: Joe Kralicek, 1479 13th St W, Dickinson, ND 58601. Phone: (701) 225-2980. Web: www.dickinsoncvb.com.

DEUTSCH COUNTRY DAYS. Oct 20–21. Luxenhaus Farm, Marthasville, MO. An authentic recreation of early German life in Missouri as costumed artisans present log hewing, paper marbling, bee keeping, broom making, wood turning, quilting and more. Period music, a sorghum press driven by Missouri mules and a steam-powered sawmill add to the festivities. 19th annual. For info: Lois Mueller, Deutsch Country Days, 5437 Highway O, Marthasville, MO 63357. Phone: (314) 433-5669.

DEWEY, JOHN: BIRTH ANNIVERSARY. Oct 20, 1859. American psychologist, philosopher and educational reformer born at Burlington, VT. His philosophical views of education have been termed pragmatism, instrumentalism and experimentalism. Died at New York, NY, June 1, 1952.

EIGHTEENTH-CENTURY AUTUMN MARKET FAIR. Oct 20–21. McLean, VA. Crafts, games, music and dancing. Period food and wares. Est attendance: 5,500. For info: Publicist, Claude Moore Colonial Farm at Turkey Run, 6310 Georgetown Pike, McLean, VA 22101. Phone: (703) 442-7557. Fax: (703) 442-0714.

ESAU'S ANTIQUE AND COLLECTIBLE EXTRAVAGANZA. Oct 20–21. Chilhowee Park, Knoxville, TN. Approximately 400 local and national antique vendors showing and selling thousands of items ranging from high-price antiques to collectible bargains. Est attendance: 10,000. For info: Cindy Crabtree, Esau, Inc, PO Box 50096, Knoxville, TN 37950. Phone: (865) 588-1233 or (800) 588-ESAU. Fax: (865) 588-6938. Web: www.esaushows.com.

GRAND MILITIA MUSTER. Oct 20. St. Mary's City, MD. The largest gathering of 17th-century military reenactment groups in the US. Tacticals, contests of skill and camp life demonstrations. Est attendance: 1,000. For info: Visitors Services, Historic St. Mary's City, PO Box 39, St. Mary's City, MD 20686. Phone: (301) 862-0990 or (800) SMC-1634. Fax: (301) 862-0968. Web: www.smcm.edu/hsmc/.

GUATEMALA: REVOLUTION DAY. Oct 20. Public holiday in Guatemala.

HALLOWEEN HARVEST OF HORRORS. Oct 20. E.P. "Tom" Sawyer State Park, Louisville, KY. Storytelling performance of ghost tales, hayrides, pumpkin-carving and costume contest. Est attendance: 2,000. For info: Lee Pennington, Intl Order of EARS, Inc, 12019 Donohue Ave, Louisville, KY 40243. Phone: (502) 245-0643. Fax: (502) 254-7542.

HARTVILLE ANNUAL FALL FESTIVAL. Oct 20. Hartville, MO. Annual festival includes local entertainment, parade, games, rides for the kids and craft booths. A day of fun for all—young and old. Est attendance: 2,500. For info: Hartville Area Chamber of Commerce, PO Box 307, Hartville, MO 65667. Phone: (417) 741-7777. Fax: (417) 741-7741.

HARVEST TYME. Oct 20–21. Franklin, CT. Collections, exhibits and demonstrations of 18th and 19th century agricultural and home implements. Children's activities. Reenactors, wagon rides. Refreshments available. Annually, the weekend after Columbus weekend. For info: Blue Slope Country Museum, 138 Blue Hill

Rd, Franklin, CT 06254. Phone: (860) 642-6413. Fax: (860) 642-4424.

HORSE EXPO. Oct 20–21. Multi-Purpose Events Center, Wichita Falls, TX. Area horse show. Awards, show horses. For info: Wichita Falls CVB, 1000 5th St, Wichita Falls, TX 76301. Phone: (940) 716-5500. Fax: (940) 716-5509. E-mail: MPEC@WF.net. Web: www.viewscape.com or www.wf.net.

INTERNATIONAL GOLD CUP. Oct 20. Great Meadow, The Plains, VA. A day of steeplechasing in the heart of Virginia's hunt country. Gates open at 10 AM for special events and activities. Corporate and chalet entertainment packages available. Est attendance: 40,000. For info: Virginia Gold Cup Assn, PO Box 840, Warrenton, VA 20188. Phone: (540) 347-2612. Fax: (540) 349-1829. Web: www.vagoldcup.com.

KENYA: KENYATTA DAY. Oct 20. Public holiday.

LONGWOOD GARDENS CHRYSANTHEMUM FESTIVAL. Oct 20–Nov 18. Kennett Square, PA. 15,000 chrysanthemums and amazing topiaries are featured in indoor displays accompanied by performances and activities throughout this late autumn festival. Est attendance: 50,000. For info: Longwood Gardens, PO Box 501, Kennett Square, PA 19348-0501. Phone: (610) 388-1000. Web: www.longwoodgardens.org.

LUGOSI, BELA: BIRTH ANNIVERSARY. Oct 20, 1882. Born Bela Ferenc Denzso Blasko at Lugos, Hungary. Known best for his role as Count Dracula in *Dracula*. Lugosi died of a heart attack at Los Angeles, CA, Aug 16, 1956.

MacARTHUR RETURNS: US LANDINGS ON LEYTE, PHILIPPINES: ANNIVERSARY. Oct 20, 1944. In mid-September of 1944 American military leaders made the decision to begin the invasion of the Philippines on Leyte, a small island north of the Surigao Strait. With General Douglas MacArthur in overall command, US aircraft dropped hundreds of tons of bombs in the area of Dulag. Four divisions were landed on the east coast, and after a few hours General MacArthur set foot on Philippine soil for the first time since he was ordered to Australia Mar 11, 1942, thus fulfilling his promise, "I shall return."

MANN, JAMES ROBERT: BIRTH ANNIVERSARY. Oct 20, 1856. American lawyer and legislator, born near Bloomington, IL, Republican member of Congress from Illinois from 1896 until his death, Nov 30, 1922, at Washington, DC. Mann was the author and sponsor of the "White Slave Traffic Act," also known as the "Mann Act," passed by Congress on June 25, 1910. The act prohibited, under heavy penalties, the interstate transportation of women for immoral purposes.

MANTLE, MICKEY: 70th BIRTH ANNIVERSARY. Oct 20, 1931. Baseball Hall of Famer, born at Spavinaw, OK. Died Aug 13, 1995, at Dallas, TX.

MISSOURI DAY FESTIVAL. Oct 20–21. North Central Missouri Fairgrounds, Trenton, MO. 17th annual festival features a parade, car show, quilt show, crafts, a talent show, marching band competition and entertainment of all kinds. Est attendance: 10,000. For info: Linda Kennebeck, PO Box 84, Trenton, MO 64683. Phone: (660) 359-4324. Fax: (660) 359-4325.

MONSTER MYTHS BY MOONLIGHT. Oct 20. Milford State Park, Milford, KS. Learn the truth about spiders, snakes, bats, vultures, owls and other Halloween "monsters." Meet the real creatures as you walk our nature trail and learn the truth about them from witches, snake charmers and Little Red Riding Hood. Wear costumes. Cookies and cider served by Mother Nature. Sponsored by Friends of Milford Nature Center and State Park. Est attendance: 650. For info: Milford Nature Center, 3115 Hatchery Dr, Junction City, KS 66441. Phone: (785) 238-5323. Fax: (785) 238-5775.

MOSCOW SOCCER TRAGEDY: ANNIVERSARY. Oct 20, 1982. The world's worst soccer disaster occurred at Moscow when 340 sports fans were killed during a game between Soviet and Dutch players. Details of the event, blaming police for the tragedy in which spectators were crushed to death in an open staircase, were not published until nearly seven years later (July 1989) in *Sovietsky Sport.* In 1985, three soccer game disasters in England and Belgium took 93 lives and injured nearly 800 persons. In April 1989, 95 persons perished in a crush at a soccer match in Sheffield, England.

QUINCY PRESERVES FALL ARCHITECTURAL TOUR. Oct 20. Quincy, IL. 10 AM–5 PM. Tour historic homes decked out in their finest. Homes range in size from Quincy's grandest mansions to quaint cottages. Inside each home, ticket holders are awed by the architectural splendors. Annually, the third Saturday in October. Est attendance: 1,500. For info: Fran Cook, Quincy Preserves, 310 S 16th St, Quincy, IL 62301. Phone: (217) 224-2587.

ROMP IN THE SWAMP FUN WALK. Oct 20. Gordon Bubolz Nature Preserve, Appleton, WI. Choose to hike ¼-, 1½-, 2½- or 4-mile distances on the Preserve's beautiful trail system. Food and activities at rest stops along the way. Prizes for the most money raised. Est attendance: 1,000. For info: Joann Engel, Naturalist, 4815 N Lynndale Dr, Appleton, WI 54913. Phone: (920) 731-6041. Fax: (920) 731-9593. E-mail: bubolz@dataex.com.

SAINT MARY'S COUNTY OYSTER FESTIVAL. Oct 20–21. Fairgrounds, Leonardtown, MD. Oysters served every style, national oyster shucking contest and national oyster cook-off. Est attendance: 20,000. For info: David L. Taylor, Admin, Oyster Fest Office, Box 766, California, MD 20619-0766. Phone: (301) 863-5015. Fax: (301) 863-7788. Web: www.usoysterfest.com.

SATURDAY NIGHT MASSACRE: ANNIVERSARY. Oct 20, 1973. Anniversary of dramatic turning point in the Watergate affair. On Oct 20, 1973: White House announcement (8:24 PM, EDT), that President Richard M. Nixon had discharged Archibald Cox (Special Watergate Prosecutor) and William B. Ruckelshaus (Deputy Attorney General), the Attorney General, Elliot L. Richardson, resigned. Immediate and widespread demands for impeachment of the president ensued and were not stilled until President Nixon resigned, Aug 9, 1974.

"THE SIX MILLION DOLLAR MAN" TV PREMIERE: ANNIVERSARY. Oct 20, 1973. This action-adventure series based on the novel "Cyborg" was a monthly feature on "The ABC Suspense Movie" before becoming a regular series in 1974. Lee Majors starred as astronaut Steve Austin, who, after an accident, was "rebuilt" with bionic legs, arms and an eye. He worked for the Office of Strategic Information (OSI) carrying out sensitive missions. Also in the cast were Richard Anderson, Alan Oppenheimer and Martin E. Brooks. "The Bionic Woman," starring Lindsay Wagner, was a spin-off from this show, and the two main characters were paired for several made-for-TV sequels.

October 2001	S	M	T	W	T	F	S
		1	2	3	4	5	6
	7	8	9	10	11	12	13
	14	15	16	17	18	19	20
	21	22	23	24	25	26	27
	28	29	30	31			

SWEETEST DAY. Oct 20. Observed annually on the third Saturday in October. For info: Evans Nelson Billington, Natl Sweetest Day Committee, 1807 Glenview Rd, Glenview, IL 60025. Phone: (847) 724-6120. Fax: (847) 724-2719.

TOWN POINT VIRGINIA WINE FESTIVAL. Oct 20–21. Norfolk, VA. Join us along the Elizabeth River for one of the state's largest outdoor wine festivals. More than 25 Virginia wineries provide a sample of wines available for purchase by the glass or bottle. Specialty crafts, wine seminars and more are available for you and your friends. Call for ticket information. Est attendance: 12,000. For info: Mktg Dir, Norfolk Festevents Ltd, 120 W Main St, Norfolk, VA 23510. Phone: (757) 441-2345. Fax: (757) 441-5198. Web: www.festeventsva.org.

WOOLLY WORM FESTIVAL. Oct 20–21. Banner Elk, NC. Annual woolly worm races, mountain entertainment, crafts and food. Third full weekend in October. Est attendance: 25,000. For info: Judy Donaghy, Exec Dir, Chamber of Commerce, PO Box 335, Banner Elk, NC 28604. Phone: (828) 898-5605. Fax: (828) 898-8287. E-mail: chamber@averycounty.com. Web: www.banner-elk.com/

WREN, CHRISTOPHER: BIRTH ANNIVERSARY. Oct 20, 1632 (OS). Sir Christopher Wren, English architect, astronomer and mathematician, was born at East Knoyle, Wiltshire, England. Died Feb 25, 1723 (OS), at London, England. His epitaph, written by his son, is inscribed over the interior of the north door at St. Paul's Cathedral, London: "Si monumentum requiris, circumspice." (If you would see his monument, look about you.)

YORKTOWN VICTORY CELEBRATION. Oct 20–21. Yorktown Victory Center, Yorktown, VA. An encampment of Revolutionary War reenactors features military demonstrations, music, and games to salute the anniversary of Washington's victory at Yorktown in October 1781. Est attendance: 1,500. For info: Jamestown-Yorktown Fdtn, Media Relations, PO Box 1607, Williamsburg, VA 23187. Phone: (757) 253-4838. Fax: (757) 253-5299. Web: www.historyisfun.org.

BIRTHDAYS TODAY

Art Buchwald, 76, columnist, author (*While Reagan Slept*), born Mount Vernon, NY, Oct 20, 1925.

William Christopher, 69, actor ("M*A*S*H," *With Six You Get Eggroll*), born Evanston, IL, Oct 20, 1932.

Peter Fitzgerald, 41, US Senator (R, Illinois), born Elgin, IL, Oct 20, 1960.

Arlene Francis (Arlene Kazanjian), 93, actress, game-show panelist ("What's My Line?"), born Boston, MA, Oct 20, 1908.

Keith Hernandez, 48, former baseball player, born San Francisco, CA, Oct 20, 1953.

Eddie Jones, 30, basketball player, born Pompano Beach, FL, Oct 20, 1971.

Melanie Mayron, 49, actress (Emmy for "thirtysomething"; *Car Wash, My Blue Heaven*), born Philadelphia, PA, Oct 20, 1952.

Jerry Orbach, 66, actor ("Law & Order," *Crimes and Misdemeanors, Dirty Dancing*; stage: *The Fantasticks*; Tony for *Promises Promises*), born The Bronx, NY, Oct 20, 1935.

Tom Petty, 48, musician, singer ("Stop Draggin' My Heart Around"), born Gainesville, FL, Oct 20, 1953.

OCTOBER 21 — SUNDAY

Day 294 — 71 Remaining

ARIZONA STATE FAIR. Oct 21–Nov 7. Phoenix, AZ. Festival, concerts, flea markets, entertainment and food. For info: Marketing Dept, Arizona State Fair, PO Box 6728, Phoenix, AZ 85005. Phone: (602) 252-6771. Fax: (602) 495-1302.

BATTLE OF TRAFALGAR: ANNIVERSARY. Oct 21, 1805. This famous naval action between the British Royal Navy and the combined French and Spanish fleets removed the threat of Napoleon's invasion of England. The British victory, off Trafalgar on the coast of Spain, guaranteed the fame of Viscount Horatio Nelson who died in the battle.

CARLETON, WILL: BIRTH ANNIVERSARY. Oct 21, 1845. Anniversary of the birth of poet Will Carleton, observed (by 1919 statute) in Michigan schools where poems of Carleton must be read on this day. Best known of his poems: "Over the Hill to the Poorhouse." Carleton died in 1912.

CARVEL, TOM: DEATH ANNIVERSARY. Oct 21, 1990. American inventor and businessman Tom Carvel was born Thomas Andreas Carvelas at Greece in 1906. He invented the machine that makes soft-serve ice cream (or frozen custard). His chain of ice cream stores began with a $15 loan and grew into the third-largest ice cream chain in America. He died at Pine Plains, NY.

COLERIDGE, SAMUEL TAYLOR: BIRTH ANNIVERSARY. Oct 21, 1772. English poet ("The Rime of the Ancient Mariner") and essayist born at Ottery St. Mary, Devonshire, England. Died at Highgate, England, July 25, 1834. In *Table Talk*, he wrote: "I wish our clever young poets would remember my homely definitions of prose and poetry; that is, prose = words in their best order; poetry = the *best* words in the best order."

FILLMORE, CAROLINE CARMICHAEL McINTOSH: BIRTH ANNIVERSARY. Oct 21, 1813. Second wife of Millard Fillmore, 13th president of the US, born at Morristown, NJ. Died at New York, Aug 11, 1881.

GILLESPIE, JOHN BIRKS "DIZZY": BIRTH ANNIVERSARY. Oct 21, 1917. Dizzy Gillespie, trumpet player, composer, bandleader and one of the founding fathers of modern jazz, was born at Cheraw, SC. In the early 1940s Gillespie and alto saxophonist Charlie (Yardbird) Parker created be-bop. In the late '40s he created a second music revolution by incorporating Afro-Cuban music into jazz. In 1953 someone fell on Gillespie's trumpet and bent it. Finding he could hear the sound better, he kept it that way; his puffed cheeks and bent trumpet became his trademarks. He won a Grammy in 1975 for *Oscar Peterson and Dizzy Gillespie* and again in 1991 for *Live at the Royal Festival Hall*. He died Jan 6, 1993, at Englewood, NJ.

HARVEST FARM AUCTION. Oct 21. Smith Valley, NV. Family entertainment and some great buys on antiques. Sponsored by the Smith Valley Catholic and Methodist Churches. For info: Mason Valley, Chamber of Commerce, 227 S Main St, Yerington, NV 89447. Phone: (775) 463-2245. Fax: (775) 463-3369. Web: www.tele-net.net/lyon.

INCANDESCENT LAMP DEMONSTRATED: ANNIVERSARY. Oct 21, 1879. Thomas A. Edison demonstrated the first incandescent lamp that could be used economically for domestic purposes. This prototype, developed at his Menlo Park, NJ, laboratory, could burn for 13½ hours.

★**NATIONAL FOREST PRODUCTS WEEK.** Oct 21–27. Presidential Proclamation always issued for the week beginning with the third Sunday in October since 1960 (PL86–753 of Sept 13, 1960).

NATIONAL MASSAGE THERAPY AWARENESS WEEK. Oct 21–27. Instituted by the American Massage Therapy Association{R} (AMTA) to increase public awareness of the value of massage therapy in wellness and health. Particular attention is given to the benefits of massage therapy as a complement to traditional medicine for illness, injury and pain and in relieving stress. AMTA provides information about how to locate and choose a qualified massage therapist and chapters emphasize the importance of legislation in states that do not yet regulate the profession. Annually, the last full week of October. For info: American Massage Therapy Assn (AMTA), 820 Davis St, Ste 100, Evanston, IL 60201. Phone: (847) 864-0123. Fax: (847) 864-1178. E-mail: info@inet.amtamassage.org. Web: www.amtamassage.org.

NATIONAL SAVE YOUR BACK WEEK. Oct 21–27. To educate the population on proper back care. For info: Daniel S. Romm, MD, c/o VAMC (117), Rehab Medicine Dept, 400 Veteran's Ave, Biloxi, MS 39531. Phone: (601) 388-5541 ext 5815. Fax: (601) 385-4517.

NATIONAL SCHOOL BUS SAFETY WEEK. Oct 21–27. This week is set aside to focus attention on school bus safety—from the standpoint of the bus drivers, students and the motoring public. Annually, the third full week of October, starting on Sunday. For info: Natl School Bus Safety Week Committee, 625 Slaters Ln, Ste 205, Alexandria, VA 22314.

NATIONAL SHUT-IN VISITATION DAY. Oct 21. Visit and entertain shut-ins. Annually, the third Sunday in October. For info: Natl Shut-In Visitation Day, 237 Franklin St, Reading, PA 19602. Phone: (610) 374-2930.

NATIONAL SUNDAY SCHOOL TEACHER APPRECIATION DAY. Oct 21. Established in 1993, this is a day set aside for churches to honor the 15 million men and women who faithfully serve as Sunday School teachers—one of the largest volunteer forces in America. For info: National Sunday School Teacher Appreciation Campaign, Gospel Light, 2300 Knoll Dr, Ventura, CA 93003. Phone: (800) 354-4224. Fax: (805) 677-6818. E-mail: marlenebaer@gospellight.com. Web: www.gospellight.com.

NEW INTERNATIONAL VERSION OF THE BIBLE WEEK. Oct 21–27. To mark the anniversary of the date (Oct 27, 1973) of the publication of the New International Version of the Bible, the most popular contemporary Bible translation today, with more than 100 million copies distributed worldwide. For info: Public Relations, Zondervan Publishing House, 5300 Patterson Ave SE, Grand Rapids, MI 49530. Phone: (616) 698-6900 or (800) 9-BOOK-IT. Fax: (616) 698-3439. E-mail: public.relations @zph.com. Web: www.zondervan.com.

NOBEL, ALFRED BERNHARD: BIRTH ANNIVERSARY. Oct 21, 1833. Swedish chemist and engineer who invented dynamite was born at Stockholm, Sweden, and died at San Remo, Italy, Dec 10, 1896. His will established the Nobel Prize.

PASTORAL CARE WEEK. Oct 21–27. Honors clergy of all faiths who provide pastoral care in congregations and in such specialized settings as hospitals, correctional facilities, mental health systems, the military and counseling centers. This year's theme is "Pastoral Care: Valuing Life's Passages." For info: Pastoral Care Week Committee, PO Box 070473, Milwaukee, WI 53207-0473. Phone: (414) 483-4898. Web: www.pastoralcareweek.org.

REPTILE AWARENESS DAY. Oct 21. Jenkinson's Aquarium, Point Pleasant Beach, NJ. Learn how alligators, snakes and turtles are related. Meet our live reptiles up close! A special artifact cart and reptile stories for children will be presented throughout the day. Alligators are fed at 1:30 PM. Crafts and face painting 1–4 PM. Free buttons to the first 300 visitors. Est attendance: 600. For info: Liz Carletta, Jenkinson's Aquarium, 300 Ocean Ave, Point Pleasant Beach, NJ 08742. Phone: (732) 899-1212. Fax: (732) 899-1717. E-mail: aquarium@jenkinsons.com. Web: www.jenkinsons.com.

SHAWN, TED: BIRTH ANNIVERSARY. Oct 21, 1891. Named Edwin Myers Shawn at birth, Ted Shawn was born at Kansas City, MO. Partially paralyzed by diphtheria, Shawn was introduced to ballet for therapeutic purposes and became a professional dancer by the age of 21. The Denishawn School of Dancing was established with the help of his wife, Ruth St. Denis, and became the epicenter of much innovation in 20th-century dance and choreography. Among his many achievements is Jacob's Pillow Dance Festival, which he inaugurated and directed for the remainder of his years, and such modern ballets as *Invocation to the Thunderbird*, *Osage-Pawnee*, *Labor Symphony* and *John Brown*. He died Jan 9, 1972.

SOLTI, GEORG: BIRTH ANNIVERSARY. Oct 21, 1912. Conductor born at Budapest, Hungary. Sir Georg conducted orchestras at London (for which he was knighted), Paris and Chicago. He died at Antibes, France, Sept 5, 1997.

SOMALIA DEMOCRATIC REPUBLIC: NATIONAL DAY. Oct 21. National holiday. Anniversary of the revolution.

"THE STU ERWIN SHOW" TV PREMIERE: ANNIVERSARY. Oct 21, 1950. This often-imitated sitcom was one of the first of its kind. Stu Erwin starred as himself, a bumbling high school principal; June Collyer (his real-life wife) as his levelheaded wife, June; Ann Todd and Merry Anders as their daughter, Joyce; Sheila James Kuehl as younger daughter, Jackie; Martin Milner as Joyce's boyfriend, and later husband, Jimmy Clark; and Willie Best as Willie, the handyman. The show was also called "Life with the Erwins," "The New Stu Erwin Show" and "The Trouble with Father."

TAIWAN: OVERSEAS CHINESE DAY. Oct 21. Thousands of overseas Chinese come to Taiwan for this and other occasions that make October a particularly memorable month.

VIETNAM WAR PROTESTORS STORM PENTAGON: ANNIVERSARY. Oct 21, 1967. Some 250 protestors were arrested when thousands of the 50,000 participants in a rally against the Vietnam War at Washington, DC, crossed the Potomac River and stormed the Pentagon. No shots were fired, but many demonstrators were struck with nightsticks and rifle butts.

WSBA/WARM 103 HOLIDAY CRAFT SHOW. Oct 21. York Fairgrounds, York, PA. More than 250 crafts, from country to contemporary, Victorian and southwestern, handcrafted furniture, wood carvings, dolls, jewelry, pottery, collectibles, quilts, baskets, fine arts and much more. Admission fee. Est attendance: 5,000. For info: Joe Alfano, Asst Promo Dir, PO Box 910, York, PA 17402-0910. Phone: (717) 764-1155. Fax: (717) 252-4807. E-mail: jalfano@suscom.com.

BIRTHDAYS TODAY

Sir Malcolm Arnold, 80, composer, born Northampton, England, Oct 21, 1921.

Elvin Bishop, 59, musician, born Tulsa, OK, Oct 21, 1942.

Carrie Fisher, 45, actress (*Star Wars, Shampoo*), novelist (*Postcards from the Edge*), born Beverly Hills, CA, Oct 21, 1956.

Frances Fitzgerald, 61, journalist, author (*The Fire in the Lake*), born New York, NY, Oct 21, 1940.

Edward Charles ("Whitey") Ford, 73, Baseball Hall of Fame pitcher, born New York, NY, Oct 21, 1928.

Ursula K. LeGuin, 72, author (*The Wind's Twelve Quarters, A Wizard of Earthsea*), born Berkeley, CA, Oct 21, 1929.

☆ ☆ ☆

	S	M	T	W	T	F	S
October 2001		1	2	3	4	5	6
	7	8	9	10	11	12	13
	14	15	16	17	18	19	20
	21	22	23	24	25	26	27
	28	29	30	31			

OCTOBER 22 — MONDAY

Day 295 — 70 Remaining

BEADLE, GEORGE: BIRTH ANNIVERSARY. Oct 22, 1903. Born on a farm near Wahoo, NE, Beadle began his professional career as a professor of genetics at Harvard, eventually becoming president of the University of Chicago. Dr. Beadle won many international prizes, including the Nobel Prize for Medicine in 1958 for his work in genetic research, as well as the National Award of the American Cancer Society in 1959 and the Kimber Genetica Award of the National Academy of Science in 1960. Beadle demonstrated how the genes control the basic chemistry of the living cell. Because of his work, he has been termed "the man who did most to put modern genetics on its chemical basis." Beadle died June 9, 1989, at Pomona, CA.

"BREAK THE BANK" TV PREMIERE: ANNIVERSARY. Oct 22, 1948. As with many shows of the late '40s and '50s, this game show began on radio. Contestants had to answer up to eight questions in their area of expertise (with one wrong answer permitted) in order to answer a ninth question to "break the bank." Winners were paid on the spot. Berk Parks was the first host, followed by Bud Collyer. Parks returned as host to a revised show renamed "Break the $250,000 Bank." Family members were involved this time. After 20 years, "BTB" resurfaced with a panel of celebrities who gave different answers to the same question, while the contestants had to choose which answer was correct. Tom Kennedy hosted the network version, and Jack Barry, the syndicated version.

CUBAN MISSILE CRISIS: ANNIVERSARY. Oct 22, 1962. President John F. Kennedy, in a nationwide television address Oct 22, 1962, demanded the removal from Cuba of Soviet missiles, launch equipment and bombers, and imposed a naval "quarantine" to prevent further weaponry from reaching Cuba. On Oct 28, the USSR announced it would remove the weapons in question. In return, the US removed missiles from Turkey that were aimed at the USSR.

GROLIER, JEAN: DEATH ANNIVERSARY. Oct 22, 1565. The celebrated French bibliophile, Jean Grolier de Servieres, whose exact birthday at Lyon, France, in 1479 is unknown, died at Paris. A government official, Grolier's consuming interest was books, and he assembled one of the world's finest collections—a library of more than 3,000 elegantly bound volumes. The Grolier Club of New York City is named for him.

HOLY SEE: NATIONAL HOLIDAY. Oct 22. The state of Vatican City and the Holy See observe Oct 22 as a national holiday.

LEARY, TIMOTHY: BIRTH ANNIVERSARY. Oct 22, 1920. Timothy Francis Leary was born at Springfield, MA. Prominent psychologist and professor at Harvard, Leary became an icon of the countercultural movement in the 1960s. He lost his professorship after giving a hallucinogenic drug, psilocybin, to students. Leary was arrested numerous times, and on one occasion, while being held at a California prison, he was forced to submit to a personality test that he had designed himself several years earlier. He continued to advocate the use of LSD in the pursuit of spiritual and political freedom and simply for the fun of it, until his death, of prostate cancer, May 31, 1996, at Beverly Hills, CA.

LISZT, FRANZ: BIRTH ANNIVERSARY. Oct 22, 1811. Hungarian pianist and composer (*Hungarian Rhapsodies*). Born at Raiding, Hungary. Died July 31, 1886, at Bayreuth, Germany.

METROPOLITAN OPERA HOUSE: OPENING ANNIVERSARY. Oct 22, 1883. Grand opening of the original New York Metropolitan Opera House was celebrated with a performance of Gounod's *Faust*.

NATIONAL COLOR DAY. Oct 22. Making people aware of how color effects them and how their names are color coded. Fashion show will show how this color philosophy works. For info: D.G. Rolliet, PO Box 21, Crockett, CA 94525. E-mail: dgrolliet@aol.com. Web: www.namecolorology.com.

NATIONAL SCIENTIFIC LITERACY DAY. Oct 22. A day to honor the anniversary of the City of Chicago's first environmental museum, the Peggy Notebaert Nature Museum of the Chicago Academy of Sciences. Celebrate the work of scientists and naturalists of the past, and learn how you fit into the environment of the present. Programs, activities and online events will provide the opportunity to experience science through nature. For info: The Peggy Notebaert Nature Museum, The Chicago Academy of Sciences, 2060 N Clark St, Chicago, IL 60614. Phone: (773) 549-0606. Fax: (773) 549-5199. Web: www.chias.org.

RANDOLPH, PEYTON: DEATH ANNIVERSARY. Oct 22, 1775. First president of the Continental Congress, died at Philadelphia, PA. Born about 1721 (exact date unknown), at Williamsburg, VA.

WORLD'S END DAY: ANNIVERSARY. Oct 22, 1844. Anniversary of the day set as the one on which the world would end by followers of William Miller, religious leader and creator of a movement known as Millerism. Stories about followers disposing of all earthly possessions and climbing to high places on that date are believed to be apocryphal. (Miller was born at Pittsfield, MA, Feb 15, 1782. Died at Low Hampton, NY, Dec 20, 1849.)

ZAMBIA: INDEPENDENCE DAY. Oct 22. Zambia. National holiday commemorates the independence of what was then Northern Rhodesia from Britain in 1964. Celebrations in all cities, but main parades of military, labor and youth organizations are at capital, Lusaka. The fourth Monday in October.

BIRTHDAYS TODAY

Brian Anthony Boitano, 38, Olympic gold medal figure skater, born Mountain View, CA, Oct 22, 1963.

Jan De Bont, 58, director (*Speed, Twister*), born Amsterdam, The Netherlands, Oct 22, 1943.

Catherine Deneuve (Dorleac), 58, actress (*Repulsion, Indochine*), born Paris, France, Oct 22, 1943.

Annette Funicello, 59, singer, actress ("Mickey Mouse Club," Beach Party movies), born Utica, NY, Oct 22, 1942.

Jeff Goldblum, 49, actor (*The Big Chill, The Fly, Jurassic Park*), born Pittsburgh, PA, Oct 22, 1952.

Valeria Golino, 35, actress (*Big Top Pee-wee, Hot Shots!, Hot Shots! Part Deux*), born Naples, Italy, Oct 22, 1966.

Derek Jacobi, 63, actor ("I Claudius," *The Day of the Jackal*), born London, England, Oct 22, 1938.

Christopher Lloyd, 63, actor ("Taxi," *Back to the Future, Who Framed Roger Rabbit?*), born Stamford, CT, Oct 22, 1938.

Bill Owens, 51, Governor of Colorado (R), born Fort Worth, TX, Oct 22, 1950.

Robert Rauschenberg, 76, artist (*Monogram*), born Port Arthur, TX, Oct 22, 1925.

Tony Roberts, 62, actor (*Victor/Victoria, Annie Hall*), born New York, NY, Oct 22, 1939.

OCTOBER 23 — TUESDAY
Day 296 — 69 Remaining

APPERT, NICOLAS: BIRTH ANNIVERSARY. Oct 23, 1752. Also known as "Canning Day," this is the anniversary of the birth of French chef, chemist, confectioner, inventor and author Nicolas Appert, at Chalons-Sur-Marne. Appert, who also invented the bouillon tablet, is best remembered for devising a system of heating foods and sealing them in airtight containers. Known as the "father of canning," Appert won a prize of 12,000 francs from the French government in 1809, and the title "Benefactor of Humanity" in 1812, for his inventions which revolutionized our previously seasonal diet. Appert died at Massy, France, June 3, 1841.

BATTLE OF LEYTE GULF: ANNIVERSARY. Oct 23–26, 1944. In response to the Allied invasion of the Philippines at Leyte, the Japanese initiated "Sho-Go" (*Operation Victory*), an attempt to counter the Allies' next invasion by heavy air attacks. Four carriers were sent south from Japanese waters to lure the US aircraft carriers away from Leyte Gulf. At the same time Japanese naval forces from Singapore were sent to Brunei Bay, split up into two groups and converged on Leyte Gulf from the north and southwest. The group in the north, under Vice Admiral Kurita Takeo, was to enter the Pacific through the San Bernardino Strait between the Philippine islands of Samar and Luzon. On Oct 23 Kurita lost two of his heavy cruisers to US submarine attack, and one of Japan's greatest battleships, the *Musashi*, was sunk in an aerial attack the next day, but Kurita made his way unopposed through the San Bernardino Strait on Oct 25. The southern group commanded by Vice Admiral Nishimura Teiji was detected on its way to the Surigao Strait and was practically annihilated by the US 7th Fleet as it entered the Leyte Gulf on Oct 25. Kurita, as a result, was forced to turn back from his planned rendezvous with Nishimura. Japan's "Sho-Go," rather than inflicting damage on the Americans, resulted in serious losses for the Japanese.

BEIRUT TERRORIST ATTACK: ANNIVERSARY. Oct 23, 1983. A suicidal terrorist attack on American forces at Beirut, Lebanon, killed 240 US personnel when a truck loaded with TNT was driven into and exploded at US Headquarters there. A similar attack on French forces killed scores more.

EDERLE, GERTRUDE: 95th BIRTH ANNIVERSARY. Oct 23, 1906. American swimming champion, born at New York City, Gertrude Caroline Ederle was the first woman to swim the English Channel (from Cape Gris-nez, France, to Dover, England). At age 19 she broke the previous world record by swimming the 35-mile distance in 14 hours, 31 minutes, on Aug 6, 1926. During her swimming career she broke many other records and was a gold medal winner at the 1924 summer Olympic Games.

HUNGARY: 45th ANNIVERSARY OF 1956 REVOLUTION. Oct 23. National holiday.

HUNGARY DECLARED INDEPENDENT: ANNIVERSARY. Oct 23, 1989. Hungary declared itself an independent republic, 33 years after Russian troops crushed a popular revolt against Soviet rule. The announcement followed a week-long purge by Parliament of the Stalinist elements from Hungary's 1949 constitution, which defined the country as a socialist people's republic. Acting head of state Matyas Szuros made the declaration in front of tens of thousands of Hungarians at Parliament Square, speaking from the same balcony from which Imre Nagy addressed rebels 33 years earlier. Nagy was hanged for treason after Soviet intervention. Free elections held in March 1990 removed the Communist party to the ranks of the opposition for the first time in four decades.

MOON PHASE: FIRST QUARTER. Oct 23. Moon enters First Quarter phase at 10:58 PM, EDT.

NATIONAL MOLE DAY. Oct 23. Celebrated on Oct 23 each year from 6:02 AM to 6:02 PM in observance of the "mole." The "mole" is a way of counting the Avogadro number, 6.02×10 to the 23rd power of anything (just like a "dozen" is a way of counting 12 of anything). Mole Day owes its existence to an early-19th-century Italian physics professor named Amedeo Avogadro. He discovered that the number of molecules in a mole is the same for all substances. Because of this, chemists are able to precisely measure quantities of chemicals in the laboratory. Mole Day is celebrated to help all persons, especially chemistry students, become enthused about chemistry, which is the central science. Individual teachers develop their own ways of observing Mole Day. For 2001 the Mole Day theme is "2001—A Molar Odyssey." For info: Maurice Oehler, Exec Dir, National Mole Day Fdtn, 1220 S 5th St, Prairie du Chien, WI 53821. Fax: (608) 326-6036. E-mail: mole@mhtc.net. Web: gamstcweb.gisd.k12.mi.us/~nmdf.

SAINT JOHN OF CAPISTRANO: DEATH ANNIVERSARY. Oct 23, 1456. Giovanni da Capistrano, Franciscan lawyer, educator and preacher, was born at Capistrano, Italy, in 1386, and died of plague on Oct 23, 1456. Feast Day is Mar 28.

Scorpius

SCORPIO, THE SCORPION. Oct 23–Nov 22. In the astronomical/astrological zodiac that divides the sun's apparent orbit into 12 segments, the period Oct 23–Nov 22 is identified, traditionally, as the sun sign of Scorpio, the Scorpion. The ruling planet is Pluto or Mars.

STEVENSON, ADLAI EWING: BIRTH ANNIVERSARY. Oct 23, 1835. Twenty-third vice president of the US (1893–97) born at Christian County, KY. Died at Chicago, IL, June 14, 1914. He was grandfather of Adlai E. Stevenson, the Democratic candidate for president in 1952 and 1956. See also: "Stevenson, Adlai Ewing: Birth Anniversary" (Feb 5).

SWALLOWS DEPART FROM SAN JUAN CAPISTRANO. Oct 23. Traditional date for swallows to depart for the winter from old mission of San Juan Capistrano, CA. See also: "Swallows Return to San Juan Capistrano" (Mar 19).

THAILAND: CHULALONGKORN DAY. Oct 23. Annual commemoration of the death of King Chulalongkorn the Great, who died Oct 23, 1910, after a 42-year reign. King Chulalongkorn

October *2001*	S	M	T	W	T	F	S
		1	2	3	4	5	6
	7	8	9	10	11	12	13
	14	15	16	17	18	19	20
	21	22	23	24	25	26	27
	28	29	30	31			

abolished slavery at Thailand. Special ceremonies with floral tributes and incense at the foot of his equestrian statue in front of Bangkok's National Assembly Hall.

TV TALK-SHOW HOST DAY. Oct 23. To celebrate the many TV talk-show hosts whose personalities and intellects enable them to bring out the best in their guests. For info: Glenn Rothenberger, Blue Collar Show, 541 Clinton St, Ste 2B, Brooklyn, NY 11231. Phone: (718) 802-1689.

BIRTHDAYS TODAY

Jim Bunning, 70, US Senator (R, Kentucky), born Southgate, KY, Oct 23, 1931.

Johnny Carson, 76, former TV talk-show host ("The Tonight Show"), born Corning, IA, Oct 23, 1925.

Michael Crichton, 59, writer (*Jurassic Park, Rising Sun*), born Chicago, IL, Oct 23, 1942.

Douglas Richard (Doug) Flutie, 39, football player, born Manchester, MD, Oct 23, 1962.

Ang Lee, 47, director (*Sense and Sensibility, The Ice Storm*), born Taiwan, Oct 23, 1954.

Tiffeny Milbrett, 29, soccer player, born Portland, OR, Oct 23, 1972.

Pele (born Edson Arantes do Nascimento), 61, former soccer player, born Tres Coracoes, Brazil, Oct 23, 1940.

Juan ("Chi-Chi") Rodriguez, 67, golfer, born Rio Piedras, Puerto Rico, Oct 23, 1934.

Michael John (Mike) Tomczak, 39, football player, born Calumet City, IL, Oct 23, 1962.

Keith Van Horn, 26, basketball player, born Fullerton, CA, Oct 23, 1975.

Alfred Matthew "Weird Al" Yankovic, 42, singer, satirist, born Lynwood, CA, Oct 23, 1959.

Dwight Yoakam, 45, country singer, actor (*Sling Blade*), born Pikeville, KY, Oct 23, 1956.

OCTOBER 24 — WEDNESDAY

Day 297 — 68 Remaining

BATTLE OF VITTORIO VENETO: ANNIVERSARY. Oct 24–Nov 3, 1918. Italian forces, commanded by General Armando Diaz, began the last offensive against Austrian troops in upper Italy on this date. The battle began north of the Piave River, and on Oct 30 the Austrian headquarters at Vittorio Veneto was taken. By Nov 1 Austrian troops were breaking up into deserting mobs. A truce was signed at Villa Giusti on Nov 3, which provided for fighting to end the next day. This Allied victory led to the collapse of the Austro-Hungarian Empire.

LOCKWOOD, BELVA A. BENNETT: BIRTH ANNIVERSARY. Oct 24, 1830. Belva Lockwood, an educator, lawyer and advocate for woman's rights, was born at Royalton, NY. In 1879 she was admitted to practice before the US Supreme Court—the first woman to do so. While practicing law at Washington, DC, she secured equal property rights for women. By adding amendments to statehood bills, Lockwood helped to provide voting rights for women in Oklahoma, New Mexico and Arizona. In 1884 she was the first woman formally nominated for the US presidency. Died May 19, 1917, at Washington, DC.

NAIC NATIONAL INVESTORS CONGRESS AND EXPO. Oct 24–27. Detroit, MI. Gathering of long-term investors, with a four-day program. Includes general sessions, investment seminars, workshops, roundtable discussions, more than 150 corporate exhibits and presentations, speakers, tours, social events and more. For info: Natl Assn of Investors Corp, 711 W Thirteen Mile Rd, Madison Heights, MI 48071. Phone: (877) ASK-NAIC. Fax: (248) 583-4880. Web: www.better-investing.org.

NATIONAL FFA CONVENTION. Oct 24–27. Kentucky Fair & Exposition Center, Louisville, KY. This 74th annual convention is an opportunity for recognition, business, elections and celebration. Delegates from each state discuss topics affecting the

national agriculture education organization and elect a new team of national officers. Students compete in final rounds of leadership and career events and learn about education and career opportunities in a 350-exhibitor career show. Est attendance: 50,000. For info: Natl FFA Organization, 1410 King St, Ste 400, Alexandria, VA 22314. Phone: (800) 772-0939 or (703) 838-5889. E-mail: aboutffa@ffa.org. Web: www.ffa.org.

PIONEER DAYS. Oct 24–25. Washington, MS. Through talks and demonstrations, youngsters learn how children lived 200 years ago. Annually, in October. Est attendance: 1,500. For info: Anne L. Gray, Historian, Historic Jefferson College, PO Box 700, Washington, MS 39190. Phone: (601) 442-2901.

SHERMAN, JAMES SCHOOLCRAFT: BIRTH ANNIVERSARY. Oct 24, 1855. Twenty-seventh vice president of the US (1909–12), born at Utica, NY. Died there Oct 30, 1912.

SIOUX FALLS PRODUCTS SHOW. Oct 24–25. Sioux Falls, SD. Products show for business and industry is a marketing center for buyers and sellers with products, services and supplies for business and industry. Est attendance: 4,000. For info: Robert P. Mancuso, Pres, Mid-American Expositions, PO Box 24851, Omaha, NE 68124-0851. Phone: (402) 346-8003. Fax: (402) 346-5412. Web: www.showofficeonline.com.

STOCK MARKET PANIC: ANNIVERSARY. Oct 24, 1929. After several weeks of a downward trend in stock prices, investors began panic selling on Black Thursday, Oct 24, 1929. More than 13 million shares were dumped. Desperate attempts to support the market brought a brief rally. See also: "Stock Market Crash: Anniversary" (Oct 29).

TACOMA HOLIDAY FOOD AND GIFT FESTIVAL. Oct 24–28. Tacoma Dome, Tacoma, WA. Gifts, crafts, gourmet foods and more amidst this glittering extravaganza which transforms the Tacoma Dome into a fairyland of twinkling lights, trees and Christmas cheer. Est attendance: 50,000. For info: Showcase Northwest, Inc, PO Box 2815, Kirkland, WA 98083. Phone: (425) 889-9494 or (800) 521-7469. Fax: (425) 889-8165.

★ **UNITED NATIONS DAY.** Oct 24. Presidential Proclamation. Always issued for Oct 24 since 1948. (By unanimous request of the UN General Assembly.)

UNITED NATIONS DAY: ANNIVERSARY OF FOUNDING. Oct 24, 1945. Official United Nations holiday commemorates founding of the United Nations and effective date of the United Nations Charter. In 1971 the General Assembly recommended this day be observed as a public holiday by UN Member States (Res 2782/xxvi). For info: United Nations, Dept of Public Info, Public Inquiries Unit, Rm GA-57, New York, NY 10017. Phone: (212) 963-4475. Fax: (212) 963-0071. E-mail: inquiries @un.org.

UNITED NATIONS: DISARMAMENT WEEK. Oct 24–30. In 1978, the General Assembly called on member states to highlight the danger of the arms race, propagate the need for its cessation and increase public understanding of the urgent task of disarmament. Observed annually, beginning on the anniversary of the founding of the UN.

UNITED NATIONS: WORLD DEVELOPMENT INFORMATION DAY. Oct 24. Anniversary of adoption by United Nations General Assembly, in 1970, of the International Development Strategy for the Second United Nations Development Decade. Object is to "draw the attention of the world public opinion each year to development problems and the necessity of strengthening international cooperation to solve them." For info: United Nations, Dept of Public Info, New York, NY 10017.

BIRTHDAYS TODAY

F. Murray Abraham, 61, actor (Oscar for *Amadeus*), born El Paso, TX, Oct 24, 1940.

Kevin Kline, 54, actor (Oscar for *A Fish Called Wanda; Silverado*), born St. Louis, MO, Oct 24, 1947.

Kweisi Mfume, 53, NAACP president, born Baltimore, MD, Oct 24, 1948.

Monica, 21, singer, born Monica Arnold, Atlanta, GA, Oct 24, 1980.

David Nelson, 65, actor ("The Adventures of Ozzie and Harriet"), born New York, NY, Oct 24, 1936.

Yelberton Abraham (Y.A.) Tittle, Jr, 75, Pro Football Hall of Fame quarterback, born Marshall, TX, Oct 24, 1926.

Bill Wyman, 60, musician (Rolling Stones), born London, England, Oct 24, 1941.

OCTOBER 25 — THURSDAY

Day 298 — 67 Remaining

CARTOONISTS AGAINST CRIME DAY™. Oct 25. A day in honor of all those cartoonists, graphic designers and illustrators who join together to promote the prevention of crime through the art and medium of cartooning. Motto: "Cartoonists Against Crime: We Draw Cartoons—Not Guns!" CAC's slogan is to "Toon Out Crime" by employing comic art as an educational tool for implanting seeds of safety prevention into the minds of viewers/readers. For info: Adrienne Sioux Koopersmith, Cartoonists Against Crime, 1437 W Rosemont, #1W, Chicago, IL 60660-1319. Phone: (773) 743-5341. Fax: (773) 743-5395. E-mail: adrienne@21stcentury.net.

CHAUCER, GEOFFREY: DEATH ANNIVERSARY. Oct 25, 1400. English poet and the best-known English writer of the Middle Ages, was born at London, England, probably about 1340. His greatest work, *Canterbury Tales*, consists of some 17,000 poetic lines. Unfinished at his death, it tells the stories of 23 pilgrims. Among his lesser-known prose writings was a treatise on the Astrolabe titled *Brede and Milke for Children* (1387), written for "little Lewis, my son." Chaucer died at London and is buried at Westminster Abbey.

CHICKEN SOUP FOR THE LAUGHING SOUL TREAT WEEK. Oct 25–31. Laughing at life can be a trick to which you can treat yourself. Based on the *Chicken Soup for the Laughing Soul* book, this week reinforces the idea that "laughter is the best medicine." People are encouraged to share heartwarming and humorous stories as the best treat of all. For a free information packet on the positive power of humor send SASE (99 cents). Annually, the week before Halloween. For info: Dr. Joel Goodman, The HUMOR Project, Inc, 480 Broadway, Ste 210-C, Saratoga Springs, NY 12866-2288. Phone: (518) 587-8770. Fax: (518) 587-8771. E-mail: chase@HumorProject.com. Web: www .HumorProject.com.

FALL HOME & GARDEN EXPO. Oct 25–28. Omaha Civic Auditorium, Omaha, NE. A consumer show for indoor and outdoor living with seminars and feature areas throughout the show. There is also a "Taste of Italy" food court. Est attendance: 25,000. For info: Robert P. Mancuso, Pres, Mid-America Expositions, Inc, PO Box 24851, Omaha, NE 68124-0851. Phone: (402) 346-8003. Fax: (402) 346-5412. Web: www.showofficeonline.com.

FIRST FEMALE FBI AGENTS: ANNIVERSARY. Oct 25, 1972. The first women to become FBI agents completed training at Quantico, VA. The new agents, Susan Lynn Roley and Joanne E. Pierce, graduated from the 14-week course with 45 men.

FORT LAUDERDALE INTERNATIONAL BOAT SHOW.
Oct 25–29. Fort Lauderdale, FL. Everything from small boats to mega-yachts to boating equipment. Visitors attend from all over the world. For info: Greater Ft Lauderdale Conv/Visitors Bureau, 1850 Eller Dr, Ste 303, Ft Lauderdale, FL 33316. Phone: (954) 765-4466.

GREAT PUMPKIN CARVE. Oct 25–27. Chadds Ford, PA. Local artists carve huge pumpkins on the grounds of the Chadds Ford Historical Society, 5–9 PM. Attractions include judging and food. Est attendance: 1,500. For info: Chadds Ford Historical Soc, Box 27, Chadds Ford, PA 19317. Phone: (610) 388-7376. Fax: (610) 388-7480.

GRENADA INVADED BY US: ANNIVERSARY. Oct 25, 1983. Some 2,000 US Marines and Army Rangers invaded the Caribbean island of Grenada, taking control after a political coup the previous week had made the island a "Soviet-Cuban colony," according to President Reagan.

HONG KONG: CHUNG YEUNG FESTIVAL. Oct 25. This festival relates to the old story of the Han Dynasty, when a soothsayer advised a man to take his family to a high place on the ninth day of the ninth moon for 24 hours in order to avoid disaster. The man obeyed and found, on returning home, that all living things had died a sudden death in his absence. Part of the celebration is climbing to high places.

MACAULAY, THOMAS BABINGTON: BIRTH ANNIVERSARY. Oct 25, 1800. English essayist and historian, born at Rothley Temple, Leicestershire, England. Died at Campden Hill, London, England, Dec 28, 1859. "Nothing," he wrote, "is so useless as a general maxim."

"NEWHART" TV PREMIERE: ANNIVERSARY. Oct 25, 1982. Bob Newhart starred in this sitcom as Dick Loudon, an author of "how-to" books who moved with his wife, Joanna (Mary Frann), to Vermont to take over the Stratford Inn. Regulars included Tom Poston as George Utley, caretaker of the inn, Steven Kampmann as Kirk Devane, the owner of the Minute Man Café, Jennifer Holmes as the maid, Leslie Vanderkellen and Julia Duffy as "princess" Stephanie Vanderkellen, who, through bad luck, had to take on the maid's job. Changes in the third season introduced the characters of Michael Harris (Peter Scolari), producer of Dick's talk show and Stephanie's squeeze, and the new owners of the cafe, Larry (William Sanderson) and his silent brothers, both named Darryl (Tony Papenfuss and John Volstad). The last telecast was Sept 8, 1990.

PEACE, FRIENDSHIP AND GOOD WILL WEEK. Oct 25–31. To encourage and foster international understanding, good human relations, friendship, good will and peace throughout the world. For complete info, send $4 to cover expense of printing, handling and postage. Annually, the last seven days in October. For info: Dr. Stanley Drake, Pres, Intl Soc of Friendship and Good Will, 8592 Roswell Rd, Ste 434, Atlanta, GA 30350-1870.

PEARL, MINNIE: BIRTH ANNIVERSARY. Oct 25, 1912. Comedian, Grand Ole Opry star born at Centerville, TN. Pearl died at Nashville, TN, Mar 4, 1996.

PICASSO, PABLO RUIZ: BIRTH ANNIVERSARY. Oct 25, 1881. Called by many the greatest artist of the 20th century, Pablo Picasso excelled as a painter, sculptor and engraver. He is said to have commented once: "I am only a public entertainer who has understood his time." Born at Malaga, Spain, he died Apr 9, 1973, at Mougins, France.

October 2001	S	M	T	W	T	F	S
		1	2	3	4	5	6
	7	8	9	10	11	12	13
	14	15	16	17	18	19	20
	21	22	23	24	25	26	27
	28	29	30	31			

SAINT CRISPIN'S DAY. Oct 25. Martyr in the reign of Diocletian. Saint Crispin's Day is famous as the day in 1415 when King Henry V defeated the superior forces of France at the Battle of Agincourt. A passage in William Shakespeare's *Henry V* notes this.

SOUREST DAY. Oct 25. To emphasize the balance of things in nature. A day for sour (Sauer) people. For info: Richard Ankli, The Fifth Wheel Tavern, 639 Fifth St, Ann Arbor, MI 48103.

SOUTHERN CALIFORNIA FIRESTORMS: ANNIVERSARY. Oct 25, 1993. The Southern California fire season began viciously when fires swept from the celebrity-studded beachfront homes of Malibu to the Mexican border. Blown out of the desert by the fierce Santa Anna winds, the fires destroyed suburban enclaves south of LA at Laguna Beach and northeast of LA at Altadena. As winds died down, firefighters appeared to gain control as the flames reached the Santa Monica Mountains, but the winds roared again, spreading the fire into Malibu—often jumping the Pacific Coast Highway to destroy the beachfront homes of the wealthy celebrities who lived there. Damage from the fires was estimated at more than $1 billion.

TAIWAN EXPELLED FROM UN: ANNIVERSARY. Oct 25, 1971. The United Nations General Assembly voted to admit mainland China and expell Taiwan. This was after many years of debate about which government was the "official" government of China. In 1979 the US accorded diplomatic recognition to mainland China.

TAIWAN: RETROCESSION DAY: ANNIVERSARY. Oct 25. Commemorates restoration of Taiwan to Chinese rule in 1945, after half a century of Japanese occupation.

BIRTHDAYS TODAY

Anthony Franciosa (Anthony Papaleo), 73, actor ("The Name of the Game," "Wheels"), born New York, NY, Oct 25, 1928.

Hanna Gray, 71, educator (former president of University of Chicago), born Heidelberg, Germany, Oct 25, 1930.

Brian Kerwin, 52, actor ("Lobo," "The Blue and the Gray"), born Chicago, IL, Oct 25, 1949.

Robert Montgomery (Bobby) Knight, 61, college basketball coach and former player, born Orrville, OH, Oct 25, 1940.

Midori, 30, violinist, born Osaka, Japan, Oct 25, 1971.

Helen Reddy, 59, singer, songwriter ("I Am Woman"), born Melbourne, Australia, Oct 25, 1942.

Marion Ross, 65, actress ("Happy Days," *The Evening Star*), born Albert Lea, MN, Oct 25, 1936.

Anne Tyler, 60, author (*The Accidental Tourist, Breathing Lessons*), born Minneapolis, MN, Oct 25, 1941.

☆ ☆ ☆

OCTOBER 26 — FRIDAY
Day 299 — 66 Remaining

AUSTRIA: NATIONAL DAY. Oct 26. National holiday observed.

CLINTON, HILLARY RODHAM: BIRTHDAY. Oct 26, 1947. First Lady, wife of President Bill Clinton, attorney, born at Park Ridge, IL.

CRAFTSMEN'S CLASSIC. Oct 26–28 (tentative). Northern Kentucky Convention Center, Covington, KY. Arts and crafts. Est attendance: 20,000. For info: Gilmore Enterprises, Inc, 1240 Oakland Ave, Greensboro, NC 27403. Phone: (336) 274-5550. Fax: (336) 274-1084.

EDGAR ALLAN POE EVERMORE. Oct 26–Nov 11. Mount Hope Estate, Manheim, PA. An evening of suspense featuring the spine-chilling short stories of Edgar Allan Poe. Professionals from the Pennsylvania Renaissance Faire Actors Conservatory perform, wine served. Est attendance: 10,000. For info: Thomas Roy, Mount Hope Estate and Winery, PO Box 685, Cornwall, PA 17016. Phone: (717) 665-7021. Fax: (717) 664-3466. E-mail: Tom Roy@parenaissancefaire.com. Web: www.parenfaire.com/.

ERIE CANAL: ANNIVERSARY. Oct 26, 1825. The Erie Canal, first US major man-made waterway, was opened, providing a water route from Lake Erie to the Hudson River. Construction started July 4, 1817, and the canal cost $7,602,000. Cannons fired and celebrations were held all along the route for the opening.

FRANKENSTEIN FRIDAY. Oct 26. This holiday has been designed to honor and celebrate the "mother" and "father" of Frankenstein, Mary Shelley and Boris Karloff. Every year a different venue will be used to celebrate this occasion. In years past it has included a Torch Lighting Ceremony, film festival and FF party. This year something special has been planned to celebrate the 70th anniversary of the classic 1931 film starring Karloff. Annually, the last Friday in October. For info: Ron MacCloskey, 219 Loring Ave, Edison, NJ 08817. E-mail: ronmac55@aol.com.

GHOST TALES AROUND THE CAMPFIRE. Oct 26. Jefferson College, Washington, MS. Storytellers weave their spells of mystery, surprise and suspense as they tell tales around a bonfire. Annually, the Friday before Halloween. Est attendance: 300. For info: Anne L. Gray, Historian, Jefferson College, PO Box 700, Washington, MS 39190. Phone: (601) 442-2901.

GHOST WALK. Oct 26. Fort Frederick State Park, Big Pool, MD. Join us for a walk through the haunted forest and barracks. Guided groups. Refreshments. 7–8:30 PM. Admission fee charged. Est attendance: 1,800. For info: Fort Frederick State Park, 11100 Fort Frederick Rd, Big Pool, MD 21711. Phone: (301) 842-2155. Fax: (301) 842-0028.

HALLOWEEN PARTY. Oct 26. Canton, OH. Annual family Halloween celebration. Costume judging, science fun, crafts, refreshments, music and dancing. For info: McKinley Museum, 800 McKinley Monument Dr NW, Canton, OH 44708. Phone: (330) 455-7043. Web: www.mckinleymuseum.org.

HANSOM, JOSEPH: BIRTH ANNIVERSARY. Oct 26, 1803. English architect and inventor Joseph Aloysius Hansom registered his "Patent Safety Cab" in 1834. The two-wheeled, one-horse, enclosed cab, with driver seated above and behind the passengers, quickly became a familiar and favorite vehicle for public transportation. Hansom was born at York, England, and died at London, June 29, 1882.

HORSELESS CARRIAGE DAY. Oct 26. From James Boswell's *Life of Samuel Johnson*: Oct 26, 1769. " . . . we dined together at the Mitre tavern. . . . We went home to his house to tea. . . . There was a pretty large circle this evening. Dr. Johnson was in very good humour, lively, and ready to talk upon all subjects. Mr Ferguson, the self-taught philosopher, told him of a new-invented machine which went without horses: a man who sat in it turned a handle, which worked a spring that drove it forward. 'Then, Sir (said Johnson), what is gained is, the man has his choice whether he will move himself alone, or himself and the machine too.' . . . ."

MULE DAY. Oct 26. Anniversary of the first importation of Spanish jacks to the US, a gift from King Charles III of Spain. Mules are said to have been bred first in this country by George Washington from a pair delivered at Boston, Oct 26, 1785.

NORTHERN IRELAND: BELFAST FESTIVAL AT QUEEN'S. Oct 26–Nov 11. Queen's University, Belfast, County Antrim. International festival of the arts which includes cinema, drama, dance, opera and all types of music from folk to classical. Est attendance: 100,000. For info: Ms M McKee, Festival House, 25 College Gardens, Belfast, Northern Ireland BT9 6BS. Phone: (44) (2890) 667687. Fax: (44) (2890) 663733. E-mail: festival@qub.ac.uk. Web: www.qub.ac.uk/festival.

ROCKEFELLER, ABBY GREENE ALDRICH: BIRTH ANNIVERSARY. Oct 26, 1874. A philanthropist and art patron, Abby Rockefeller was one of the three founders of the New York Museum of Modern Art in 1929. Born at Providence, RI, she died Apr 5, 1948, at New York City.

"ST. ELSEWHERE" TV PREMIERE: ANNIVERSARY. Oct 26, 1982. A popular one-hour medical drama set in St. Eligius Hospital at Boston. Among its large and changing cast were Ed Flanders, William Daniels, Ed Begley, Jr, David Morse, Howie Mandel, Christina Pickles, Denzel Washington, Norman Lloyd, David Birney, G.W. Bailey, Kavi Raz, Stephen Furst, Mark Harmon and Alfre Woodard. The last episode of the series, aired on Aug 10, 1988, was presented in order to cast doubt on the reality of the whole series, suggesting that a child's imagination had dreamed it up.

SCARLATTI, DOMENICO: BIRTH ANNIVERSARY. Oct 26, 1685. Italian keyboard composer, born at Naples, Italy. Died July 23, 1757, at Madrid, Spain.

SEA WITCH HALLOWEEN & FIDDLERS FESTIVAL. Oct 26–28. Rehoboth Beach/Dewey Beach, DE. Sea Witch Hunt, broom tossing contest on beach, best costumed pet contest, scarecrow making, haunted house, costume parade, spook show, horse-drawn hayrides and entertainment. Annually, the last full weekend in October. Est attendance: 60,000. For info: Gina Charles, Festival Dir, PO Box 216, Rehoboth Beach, DE 19971. Phone: (800) 441-1329. Fax: (302) 227-8351. E-mail: rehoboth@beach-fun .com. Web: www.beach-fun.com.

SPACE MILESTONE: *SOYUZ 3* (USSR). Oct 26, 1968. After the crash of *Soyuz 1* and the death of its cosmonaut, *Soyuz 3* was launched this date with Colonel Georgi Beregovoy. It orbited Earth 64 times, rendezvousing but not docking with unmanned *Soyuz 2*, which had been launched the day before. Both vehicles returned to Earth under ground control. *Soyuz* means "union."

SUGARLOAF'S FALL FORT WASHINGTON CRAFT FESTIVAL. Oct 26–28. Fort Washington Expo Center, Fort Washington, PA. This show, now in its 7th year, features 375 nationally recognized craft designers and fine artists displaying and selling their original creations. Craft demonstrations, hourly gift certificate drawings and more. Est attendance: 24,000. For info: Sugarloaf Mountain Works, Inc, 200 Orchard Ridge Dr, #215, Gaithersburg, MD 20878. Phone: (800) 210-9900. E-mail: smworks@sugarloafcrafts.com. Web: www.sugarloafcrafts.com.

UGLY PICKUP PARADE AND CONTEST. Oct 26. Chadron, NE. Honors beat-up old pickups, US manufacturing prowess and ingenuity and selects the ugliest pickup in all the land. Ugly pickup queen contest held prior to the parade. Annually, the Friday before Halloween. Est attendance: 2,500. For info: *Chadron Record*, PO Box 1141, Chadron, NE 69337. Phone: (308) 432-5511. Fax: (308) 432-2385.

"VICTORY AT SEA" TV PREMIERE: ANNIVERSARY. Oct 26, 1952. This half-hour series was a documentary of naval warfare during World War II. It was narrated by Leonard Graves, produced by Henry Salomon, with a score composed by Richard Rodgers.

BIRTHDAYS TODAY

Pat Conroy, 56, writer (*The Prince of Tides, The Lords of Discipline*), born Atlanta, GA, Oct 26, 1945.

Cary Elwes, 39, actor (*The Princess Bride, Glory, Bram Stoker's Dracula*), born London, England, Oct 26, 1962.

Bob Hoskins, 59, actor (*Mona Lisa, Who Framed Roger Rabbit?*), born Bury St. Edmonds, Suffolk, England, Oct 26, 1942.

Dylan McDermott, 39, actor ("The Practice"), born Waterbury, CT, Oct 26, 1962.

Natalie Merchant, 38, singer, born Jamestown, NY, Oct 26, 1963.

Ivan Reitman, 55, filmmaker (*Ghostbusters* movies), born Komarno, Czechoslovakia, Oct 26, 1946.

Pat Sajak, 55, TV personality ("Wheel of Fortune"), born Chicago, IL, Oct 26, 1946.

Jaclyn Smith, 54, actress ("Charlie's Angels"), former Breck Girl, born Houston, TX, Oct 26, 1947.

OCTOBER 27 — SATURDAY

Day 300 — 65 Remaining

ALABAMA RENAISSANCE FAIRE. Oct 27–28. Florence, AL. Celebration in grand 16th-century style with music, arts and crafts, costumes, theater and dance. Listen to minstrels, dulcimers and autoharps, watch as knights in shining armor transform Wilson Park into "Fountain-on-the-Green," the scene of a 16th-century faire. Annually, the fourth weekend in October. Est attendance: 30,000. For info: Debbie Wilson, Dir, Florence/Lauderdale Tourism, One Hightower Pl, Florence, AL 35630. Phone: (256) 740-4141 or (800) 888-FLO-TOUR. Fax: (256) 740-4142. E-mail: dwilson@floweb.com. Web: www.flo-tour.org.

ANN ARBOR WINTER ART FAIR. Oct 27–28. Ann Arbor, MI. 28th annual. Fine art and selected craft show. Some of the best artists and craftspersons in the country. Est attendance: 15,000. For info: Audree Levy, 1809 Morning Glory, Carrollton, TX 75007. Phone: (972) 735-9898. Fax: (972) 735-9808. E-mail: audree@levyartfairs.com. Web: www.levyartfairs.com.

BLUE RIDGE FOLKLIFE FESTIVAL. Oct 27. Ferrum College/Blue Ridge Institute and Museum, Ferrum, VA. The largest celebration of authentic folkways in Virginia featuring food, crafts, music and exhibits. Annually, the fourth Saturday in October. Est attendance: 20,000. For info: Roddy Moore, BRI Dir, Ferrum College/BRI, Rte 40 West, Ferrum, VA 24088. Phone: (540) 365-4415 or (540) 365-4416. Fax: (540) 365-4419.

COOK, JAMES: BIRTH ANNIVERSARY. Oct 27, 1728 (OS). English sea captain of the ship *Endeavour* and explorer who brought Australia and New Zealand into the British Empire. Born at Marton-in-Cleveland, Yorkshire, England, he was killed Feb 14, 1779, at the Hawaiian Islands, which he discovered.

THE CRACKER LINE: ANNIVERSARY. Oct 27, 1863. In an attempt to reinforce and resupply the besieged Union troops at Chattanooga, TN, General Ulysses S. Grant ordered that a river route to Bridgeport, AL, be opened. In the early morning of Oct 27 Federal troops drifted down the Tennessee River on pontoons to Brown's Ferry. The troops reached their destination, and reinforcements and supplies crossed the bridge formed by the pontoons, opening "The Cracker Line," into Chattanooga, negating some of the Southern army's advantage in the siege.

CRAFT FAIR USA: INDOOR SHOW. Oct 27–28. Wisconsin State Fair Park, Milwaukee, WI. Sale of handcrafted items including jewelry, pottery, weaving, leather, wood, glass and sculpture. Est attendance: 16,000. For info: Dir, Craft Fair USA, 9312 W National Ave, Milwaukee, WI 53227-1542. Phone: (414) 321-2100. Web: www.craftfairusa.com.

CRANKY CO-WORKERS DAY. Oct 27. Because all of us have bad days (some more than others), here's a day when crankiness at work is actually encouraged. ©2000 Wellcat Holidays & Herbs. For info: Thomas Roy, Wellcat Holidays and Herbs, 2418 Long Ln, Lebanon, PA 17046-1708. Phone: (717) 279-0184. E-mail: wellcat@supernet.com. Web: www.wellcat.com.

DAY OF MEDITATION: 24 HOURS OF LIVING MEDITATIVELY. Oct 27. In conjunction with *USA Today's Weekend*'s Make a Difference Day, the School of Metaphysics invites people all around the world to meditate as often as possible during the 24-hour period starting midnight Oct 26 through midnight Oct 27. Meditation develops a spiritual consciousness that brings people together. Prayer, silence, contemplation and meditation promote peace, understanding and goodwill within self and among all people. For info: School of Metaphysics, HCR 1, Box 15, Windyville, MO 65783. Phone: (417) 345-8411. E-mail: som@som.org. Web: www.som.org.

EMMA CRAWFORD FESTIVAL AND MEMORIAL COFFIN RACE. Oct 27. Manitou Springs, CO. Coffin races and parade. Annually, the Saturday before Halloween. Est attendance: 3,000. For info: Manitou Springs Chamber of Commerce, 354 Manitou, Manitou Springs, CO 80829. Phone: (800) 642-2567.

FEDERALIST PAPERS: ANNIVERSARY. Oct 27, 1787. The first of the 85 "Federalist" papers appeared in print in a New York City newspaper, Oct 27, 1787. These essays, written by Alexander Hamilton, James Madison and John Jay, argued in favor of adoption of the new Constitution and the new form of federal government. The last of the essays was completed Apr 4, 1788.

HALLOWEEN FESTIVAL AND HAUNTED WALK. Oct 27. Prospect Park, Brooklyn, NY. Carnival games, musicians, storytellers and a haunted walk through Lookout Hill with many scary surprises. Est attendance: 4,500. For info: Public Info Office, Prospect Park, 95 Prospect Park W, Brooklyn, NY 11215. Phone: (718) 965-8954. Fax: (718) 965-8972. E-mail: marketing@prospectpark.org. Web: www.prospectpark.org.

HALLOWEEN HAPPENING. Oct 27–28. Cincinnati Zoo and Botanical Garden, Cincinnati, OH. Children can trick-or-treat at the zoo from 14 different treat stations. Other activities include hayrides, pumpkin giveaways, a pumpkin carving contest and the city's largest costume contest. Est attendance: 23,000. For info: Events and Promo Dept, Cincinnati Zoo and Botanical Garden, 3400 Vine St, Cincinnati, OH 45220. Phone: (513) 281-4701. Fax: (513) 559-7790. Web: www.cincyzoo.org.

HOGEYE FESTIVAL. Oct 27. Elgin, TX. The main feature of this festival is Cow Patty Bingo, buy a square painted on Depot Street and hope the cow plops on your space and win $1500. Days events also include sausage and bean cook-off, crowning of King Hog or Queen Sowpreme, crafts, kids activities and Elgin's famous hot sausage and live music. Annually, the fourth Saturday in October. Est attendance: 20,000. For info: Amy Miller, PO Box 591, Elgin, TX 78621. Phone: (512) 285-5721. Fax: (512) 285-5962. E-mail: economic@totalaccess.net. Web: www.elgintx.com.

HURRICANE MITCH: ANNIVERSARY. Oct 27, 1998. More than 7,000 people were killed at Honduras by flooding caused by Hurricane Mitch. Thousands more were killed in other Central American countries, especially Nicaragua. On Sept 21, 1974, more than 8,000 people were killed at Honduras in flooding resulting from a hurricane.

LICHTENSTEIN, ROY: BIRTH ANNIVERSARY. Oct 27, 1923. Pop artist who used comic strips and other elements of pop culture in his paintings. Born at New York City, he died there Sept 29, 1997.

October 2001	S	M	T	W	T	F	S
		1	2	3	4	5	6
	7	8	9	10	11	12	13
	14	15	16	17	18	19	20
	21	22	23	24	25	26	27
	28	29	30	31			

MAKE A DIFFERENCE DAY. Oct 27. This national day of community service is sponsored by *USA WEEKEND* magazine. Volunteer projects that take place that day are judged by well-known celebrities. More than $2.8 million in donations are awarded to charity. Key projects are honored in April during National Volunteer Week at a special Make A Difference Day awards luncheon and at the White House. Nearly two million people nationwide participate. For info: Make a Difference Day, USA Weekend, 1000 Wilson Blvd, Arlington, VA 22229-0012. Phone: (800) 416-3824. Web: www.makeadifferenceday.com.

MILL AVENUE MASQUERADE ADVENTURE. Oct 27. Tempe, AZ. A hauntingly fun time for the entire family, the Masquerade features a costume parade through the streets of downtown Tempe. Live entertainment and a costume contest. Annually, Oct 30. Est attendance: 10,000. For info: Gary Sanders, Exec Dir, Mill Avenue Merchants Assn, 520 S Mill Ave, Ste 201, Tempe, AZ 85281. Phone: (480) 967-4877. Fax: (480) 967-6638. E-mail: info@millavenue.org. Web: www.millavenue.org.

NAVY DAY. Oct 27. Observed since 1922.

NEW YORK CITY SUBWAY: ANNIVERSARY. Oct 27, 1904. Running from City Hall to West 145th Street, the New York City subway began operation. It was privately operated by the Interborough Rapid Transit Company and later became part of the system operated by the New York City Transit Authority.

OKTOBERFEST. Oct 27. Monett, MO. Street festival in historic downtown featuring live entertainment, including line dancing, cloggers, storytelling, and pancake breakfast, pork steak barbeque, last car show of the season with antique and classic vehicles from four states, food and craft booths, full carnival, children's rides, climbing wall, carriage rides, ARTExpo display, Karaoke, Little Miss & Mr Oktoberfest, best downtown window display contest and more. Annually, on the fourth Saturday of October. For info: Kris Roller, RR Western Wear, 215 E Broadway, Monett, MO 65708. Phone: (417) 235-7795. E-mail: rrwestern@sofnet.com.

PAGANINI, NICOLO: BIRTH ANNIVERSARY. Oct 27, 1782. Hailed as the greatest violin virtuoso of all time, Paganini was born at Genoa, Italy. Unusually long arms contributed to his legendary Mephistophelian appearance—and probably to his unique skills as a performer. His immensely popular concerts brought him great wealth, but his compulsive gambling repeatedly humbled the genius. Paganini died at Nice, France, May 27, 1840.

PIONEER AND INDIAN FESTIVAL. Oct 27–28 (tentative). Mississippi Crafts Center, Natchez Trace Parkway, Ridgeland, MS. Arts and crafts of the pioneer era (basket weaving, pottery, spinning), Indian stickball, dances, mules, oxen, blowguns, tomahawk throw, music and food. Annually, the fourth Saturday and Sunday in October. Sponsor: Craftsmen's Guild of Mississippi, Inc. Est attendance: 4,000. For info: Martha Garrott, Mississippi Crafts Center, PO Box 69, Ridgeland, MS 39158. Phone: (601) 856-7546 or home (601) 362-4756. Fax: (601) 856-7546.

RICHMOND HIGHLAND GAMES AND CELTIC FESTIVAL. Oct 27–28 (tentative). Richmond, VA. Celebration of Scottish and Celtic heritage featuring athletic competition, clan tents, two entertainment stages, pipe bands, sheepdog trials, dogs, livestock and horses of the British Isles, fiddle, harp and Highland and Irish dance competitions, food, pubs and whisky tasting, storytelling and more. Est attendance: 20,000. For info: Clay Roberts, Richmond Highland Games & Celtic Fest at Strawberry Hill, PO Box 26805, Richmond, VA 23261. Phone: (804) 228-3200. Fax: (804) 228-3252.

ROOSEVELT, THEODORE: BIRTH ANNIVERSARY. Oct 27, 1858. Twenty-sixth president of the US, succeeded to the presidency on the death of William McKinley. His term of office: Sept 14, 1901–Mar 3, 1909. Roosevelt was the first president to ride in an automobile (1902), to submerge in a submarine (1905) and to fly in an airplane (1910). Although his best-remembered

quote was perhaps, "Speak softly and carry a big stick," he also said: "The first requisite of a good citizen in this Republic of ours is that he shall be able and willing to pull his weight." Born at New York, NY, Roosevelt died at Oyster Bay, NY, Jan 6, 1919. His last words: "Put out the light."

SAINT VINCENT AND THE GRENADINES: INDEPENDENCE DAY. Oct 27. National Day commemorating independence from Britain in 1979.

SORGHUM DAY FESTIVAL. Oct 27. Wewoka, OK. The autumn air fills with the sweet-smelling aroma of sorghum during this old-time festival and fall tradition. Visitors can witness sorghum-making, a quilt show, antique car show and pioneer demonstrations and visit more than 100 craft booths. Annually, the fourth Saturday in October. Est attendance: 40,000. For info: Wewoka Chamber of Commerce, PO Box 719, Wewoka, OK 74884. Phone: (405) 257-5485. Fax: (405) 257-7020.

TAMBO, OLIVER REGINALD: BIRTH ANNIVERSARY. Oct 27, 1917. Former president of South Africa's antiapartheid African National Congress, Tambo was born at Transkei, South Africa, and died Apr 24, 1993, at Johannesburg.

THOMAS, DYLAN MARLAIS: BIRTH ANNIVERSARY. Oct 27, 1914. Welsh poet and playwright, born at Swansea, Wales. Died at New York, NY, Nov 9, 1953.

TURKMENISTAN: INDEPENDENCE DAY: 10th ANNIVERSARY. Oct 27. National holiday. Commemorates independence from the Soviet Union in 1991.

VIRGINIA CHILDREN'S FESTIVAL. Oct 27. Town Point Park, Norfolk, VA. An all-day family program hosted by nationally famous children's entertainers, costumed characters and five stages of entertainment. Also, magic, giant puppets, creative dance and many other activities for a day of fantasy and fun. Est attendance: 45,000. For info: Norfolk Festevents, Ltd, 120 W Main St, Norfolk, VA 23510. Phone: (757) 441-2345. Fax: (757) 441-5198. Web: www.festeventsva.org.

"WALT DISNEY" TV PREMIERE: ANNIVERSARY. Oct 27, 1954. This highly successful and long-running show appeared on different networks under different names but was essentially the same show. It was the first ABC series to break the Nielsen's Top Twenty and the first prime-time anthology series for kids. "Walt Disney" was originally titled "Disneyland" to promote the park and upcoming Disney releases. Later the title was changed to "Walt Disney Presents." When it switched networks, it was called "Walt Disney's Wonderful World of Color" to highlight its being broadcast in color. Later titles included "The Wonderful World of Disney," "Disney's Wonderful World," "The Disney Sunday Movie" and "The Magical World of Disney." Presentations included edited versions of previously released Disney films and original productions (including natural history documentaries, behind-the-scenes at Disney shows and dramatic shows, including the popular Davy Crockett segments that were the first TV miniseries). The show went off the air in December 1980 after 25 years, making it the longest-running series in prime-time TV history.

WILD FOODS DAY. Oct 27. Fall Creek Falls State Park, Pikeville, TN. Field trips demonstrating edible wild plants; and workshop on preparing wild meats. Est attendance: 100. For info: Nature Center, Fall Creek Falls State Park, Pikeville, TN 37367. Phone: (423) 881-5162. Fax: (423) 881-5103.

WMAS 94.7 FM ANNUAL HALLOWEEN BALL. Oct 27. Springfield Sheraton Hotel, Springfield, MA. Our annual listener appreciation ball, where listeners come dressed in their wildest and most creative costumes. Lots of prize categories in which people can win trips, VCRs, TVs, jewelry and more. Est attendance: 3,500. For info: Dina McMahon, PO Box 9500, Springfield, MA 01102. Phone: (413) 737-1414. Fax: (413) 737-1488.

BIRTHDAYS TODAY

Roberto Benigni, 49, actor, director (Oscar for *Life Is Beautiful*), born Arezzo, Italy, Oct 27, 1952.

Warren Christopher, 76, US Secretary of State (first Clinton administration), born Scranton, ND, Oct 27, 1925.

John Cleese, 62, actor, writer ("Monty Python's Flying Circus," *A Fish Called Wanda*), born Weston-Super-Mare, England, Oct 27, 1939.

Frederick De Cordova, 91, producer ("Tonight Show"), director, born New York, NY, Oct 27, 1910.

Ruby Dee, 77, actress ("Ossie and Rubie," *Zora Is My Name, Do the Right Thing*), born Cleveland, OH, Oct 27, 1924.

Nanette Fabray, 81, actress (Emmy for "Caesar's Hour"; "One Day at a Time," *Our Gang* comedies), born San Diego, CA, Oct 27, 1920.

Simon LeBon, 43, singer, born Bushey, England, Oct 27, 1958.

Fran Lebowitz, 51, magazine columnist famous for essays on urban life (*Social Studies*), born Morristown, NJ, Oct 27, 1950.

Marla Maples, 38, model, actress, born Dalton, GA, Oct 27, 1963.

Carrie Snodgress, 55, actress (*Diary of a Mad Housewife*), born Chicago, IL, Oct 27, 1946.

OCTOBER 28 — SUNDAY

Day 301 — 64 Remaining

BIG TEN MEN'S/WOMEN'S CROSS COUNTRY. Oct 28. University of Wisconsin, Madison, WI. For info: Dennis LaBissoniere, Big Ten Conference, 1500 W Higgins Rd, Park Ridge, IL 60068-6300. Phone: (847) 696-1010. Fax: (847) 696-1110. Web: www.bigten.org.

CZECH REPUBLIC: FOUNDATION OF THE REPUBLIC: ANNIVERSARY. Oct 28, 1918. National Day, anniversary of the bloodless revolution at Prague, after which the Czechs and Slovaks united to form Czechoslovakia (a union they dissolved without bloodshed in 1993).

DAYLIGHT SAVING TIME ENDS; STANDARD TIME RESUMES. Oct 28–Apr 7, 2002. Standard Time resumes at 2 AM on the last Sunday in October in each time zone, as provided by the Uniform Time Act of 1966 (as amended in 1986 by Public Law 99–359). Many use the popular rule: "spring forward, fall back" to remember which way to turn their clocks. See also: "Daylight Saving Time" (Apr 1).

DICKINSON, ANNA ELIZABETH: BIRTH ANNIVERSARY. Oct 28, 1842. Influential American orator and author of the Civil War era was born at Philadelphia, PA. As an advocate of abstinence, abolition and woman suffrage, she earned the nickname "American Joan of Arc." She died on Oct 22, 1932.

	S	M	T	W	T	F	S
October		1	2	3	4	5	6
2001	7	8	9	10	11	12	13
	14	15	16	17	18	19	20
	21	22	23	24	25	26	27
	28	29	30	31			

DONNER PARTY FAMINE: ANNIVERSARY. Oct 28, 1846–Apr 21, 1847. The pioneering Donner Party, a group of 90 people consisting of immigrants, families and businessmen led by George and Jacob Donner and James F. Reed, headed towards California in 1846 from Springfield, IL, in hopes of beginning a new life. They experienced the normal travails of caravan travel until their trip took several sensational twists. Indian attacks and winter weather which forced them to interrupt their journey led to famine and outright cannibalism which took their toll on members of the party whose numbers dwindled to 48 by journey's end.

ERASMUS, DESIDERIUS: BIRTH ANNIVERSARY. Oct 28, 1467. Dutch author and scholar Desiderius Erasmus was born at Rotterdam, probably Oct 28, 1467. Best known of his writings is *Encomium Moriae* (In Praise of Folly). Erasmus died at Basel, Switzerland, July 12, 1536.

ESCOFFIER, GEORGES AUGUSTE: BIRTH ANNIVERSARY. Oct 28, 1846. Celebrated French chef and author, inventor of the peche Melba (honoring the operatic singer Dame Nellie Melba), Escoffier became known as the "king of chefs and the chef of kings." Born at Villeneuve-Loubet, France. He was awarded the Legion d'Honneur in recognition of his contribution to the international reputation of French cuisine and his service at the Savoy and Carlton hotels at London, England, brought him world fame. He died at Monte Carlo, Monaco, Feb 12, 1935.

A FAMILY HALLOWEEN. Oct 28. Billings Farm and Museum, Woodstock, VT. Mystery stories, doughnuts on a string, pumpkin carving, a costume parade, plus wagon rides. Children in costume accompanied by an adult admitted free. 11 AM–3 PM. For info: Marjorie Wakefield, Exec Sec, Billings Farm and Museum, PO Box 489, Woodstock, VT 05091. Phone: (802) 457-2355. Fax: (802) 457-4663. E-mail: billings.farm@valley.net. Web: www.billingsfarm.org.

FIRST WOMAN US AMBASSADOR APPOINTED: ANNIVERSARY. Oct 28, 1949. Helen Eugenie Moore Anderson became the first woman to hold the post of US ambassador when she was sworn in by President Harry S. Truman on this date. She served as Ambassador to Denmark.

GERMAN REVOLUTION OF 1918: ANNIVERSARY. Oct 28, 1918. On this date in the final days of World War I, crews of six German battleships protested a series of planned cruiser raids. A mutiny broke out in the fleet at Kiel. All but one of the ships remaining in port ran up the red flag of revolution, 600 sailors were arrested and imprisoned on shore. The uprising spread to Hamburg, Bremen and Lubeck. On Nov 9 a general strike at Berlin brought the administration to a halt. The abdication of Kaiser Wilhelm began to be seen as the only way to avoid a full-scale revolution.

GREECE: "OHI DAY": ANNIVERSARY. Oct 28. National holiday commemorating Greek resistance and refusal to open her borders when Mussolini's Italian troops attacked Greece, Oct 28, 1940. "Ohi" means no! Celebrated with military parades, especially at Athens and Thessaloniki.

HANSON, HOWARD: BIRTH ANNIVERSARY. Oct 28, 1896. Born at Wahoo, NE, Howard Hanson in 1921 became the first American to win the Prix de Rome. In 1924 he became head of the Eastman School of Music at the University of Rochester, NY, where he served for 40 years. Best known for the music he composed, Hanson was awarded the Pulitzer Prize as outstanding contemporary composer in 1944 for his composition *Symphony No. 4*, the George Foster Peabody Award in 1946, the Laurel Leaf of the American Composers Alliance in 1957 and the Huntington Hartford Foundation Award in 1959. He died at Rochester, Feb 26, 1981.

HARVARD UNIVERSITY FOUNDED: ANNIVERSARY. Oct 28, 1636 (OS). Harvard University founded at Cambridge, MA, when the Massachusetts General Court voted to provide £400 for a "schoale or colledge."

"THE JACK BENNY PROGRAM" TV PREMIERE: ANNIVERSARY. Oct 28, 1950. One of radio's favorite comedians, Jack Benny made the transition to favorite TV personality with this situation comedy–variety show in 1950. Regulars included Eddie Anderson, Don Wilson, Dennis Day, Mel Blanc, Mary Livingstone (Benny's real-life wife) and Frank Nelson. Benny also had guest stars, including Ken Murray, Frank Sinatra, Claudette Colbert, Basil Rathbone and TV newcomers Johnny Carson, Marilyn Monroe and Humphrey Bogart. Famous for his cheapness, Benny had a guard for his vaults which created many laughs.

MOTHER-IN-LAW DAY. Oct 28. Traditionally, the fourth Sunday in October is occasion to honor mothers-in-law for their contribution to the success of families and for their good humor in enduring bad jokes.

REFORMATION SUNDAY. Oct 28. Many Protestant churches commemorate Reformation Day (Oct 31—anniversary of the day on which Martin Luther nailed his 95 theses to the door of Wittenberg's Palace church, protesting the sale of papal indulgences, in 1517), on the Sunday preceding Oct 31, each year or on the 31st, if a Sunday.

SAINT JUDE'S DAY. Oct 28. St. Jude, the saint of hopeless causes, was martyred along with St. Simon at Persia, and their feast is celebrated jointly. St. Jude was supposedly the brother of Jesus, and, like his brother, a carpenter by trade. He is most popular with those who attempt the impossible and with students, who often ask for his help on exams.

SALK, JONAS: BIRTH ANNIVERSARY. Oct 28, 1914. Dr. Jonas Salk, developer of the Salk polio vaccine, was born at New York, NY. Salk announced his development of a successful vaccine in 1953, the year after a polio epidemic claimed some 3,300 lives in the US. Polio deaths were reduced by 95 percent after the introduction of the vaccine. Salk spent the last 10 years of his life doing AIDS research. He died June 23, 1995, at La Jolla, CA.

SPACE MILESTONE: INTERNATIONAL SPACE RESCUE AGREEMENT. Oct 28, 1970. US and USSR officials agreed upon space rescue cooperation.

STATUE OF LIBERTY: DEDICATION ANNIVERSARY. Oct 28, 1886. Frederic Auguste Bartholdi's famous sculpture, the statue of *Liberty Enlightening the World*, on Bedloe's Island in New York Harbor, was dedicated. Ground breaking for the structure was in April 1883. A sonnet by Emma Lazarus, inside the pedestal of the statue, contains the words: "Give me your tired, your poor, your huddled masses yearning to breathe free, the wretched refuse of your teeming shore. Send these, the homeless, tempest-tost to me, I lift my lamp beside the golden door!"

BIRTHDAYS TODAY

Jane Alexander (Jane Quigley), 62, actress (*The Great White Hope, Kramer v Kramer*), former chair of the National Endowment for the Arts, born Boston, MA, Oct 28, 1939.

Charlie Daniels, 65, musician, singer, songwriter ("Devil Went Down to Georgia"), born Wilmington, NC, Oct 28, 1936.

Jeremy Davies, 32, actor (*Saving Private Ryan*), born Rockford, IA, Oct 28, 1969.

Terrell Davis, 29, football player, born San Diego, CA, Oct 28, 1972.

Dennis Franz, 57, actor ("Hill Street Blues," "NYPD Blue"), born Maywood, IL, Oct 28, 1944.

Bill Gates, 46, computer software executive (Microsoft), born Seattle, WA, Oct 28, 1955.

Jami Gertz, 36, actress ("ER," *Twister*), born Chicago, IL, Oct 28, 1965.

Lauren Holly, 38, actress (*Dumb & Dumber, Sabrina*), born Geneva, NY, Oct 28, 1963.

Telma Hopkins, 53, singer, actress ("Family Matters"), born Louisville, KY, Oct 28, 1948.

William Bruce Jenner, 52, sportscaster, Olympic gold medal decathlete, born Mount Kisco, NY, Oct 28, 1949.

Bowie Kent Kuhn, 75, former commissioner of baseball, born Tacoma Park, MD, Oct 28, 1926.

Annie Potts, 49, actress ("Designing Women," *Ghostbusters, Pretty in Pink*), born Nashville, TN, Oct 28, 1952.

Andy Richter, 35, former cohost ("Late Night with Conan O'Brien"), born Grand Rapids, MI, Oct 28, 1966.

Julia Roberts, 34, actress (*Steel Magnolias, Pretty Woman, My Best Friend's Wedding*), born Smyrna, GA, Oct 28, 1967.

OCTOBER 29 — MONDAY
Day 302 — 63 Remaining

BOSWELL, JAMES: BIRTH ANNIVERSARY. Oct 29, 1740 (OS). Scottish biographer, born at Edinburgh, Scotland. Died at London, England, May 19, 1795. "I think," he wrote in his monumental biography, the *Life of Samuel Johnson*, "no innocent species of wit or pleasantry should be suppressed: and that a good pun may be admitted among the smaller excellencies of lively conversation."

EMMETT, DANIEL DECATUR: BIRTH ANNIVERSARY. Oct 29, 1815. Creator of words and music for the song "Dixie," which became a fighting song for Confederate troops and unofficial "national anthem" of the South. Emmett was born at Mount Vernon, OH, and died there June 28, 1904.

"GIMME A BREAK!" TV PREMIERE: 20th ANNIVERSARY. Oct 29, 1981. Half-hour sitcom starring singer Nell Carter as Nell Harper, housekeeper, surrogate parent and confidante to a gruff cop, Carl Kanisky (Dolph Sweet) and his three daughters: Katie (Kari Michaelsen), Julie (Lauri Hendler) and Samantha (Lara Jill Miller). Also featured were Joey Lawrence and Telma Hopkins. Sweet's death in 1985 was incorporated into the storyline. Other changes included the marriage of Julie, Samantha going off to college and moving the setting to New York. The series ended with the last telecast May 12, 1987.

GOEBBELS, PAUL JOSEF: BIRTH ANNIVERSARY.
Oct 29, 1897. German Nazi leader, born at Rheydt, Germany, who became Hitler's minister of propaganda, had earlier been rejected by the military because of a limp caused by infantile paralysis. Killed himself, his wife and children May 1, 1945, in Hitler's bunker in Berlin as Russian forces advanced into the city.

INTERNET CREATED: ANNIVERSARY. Oct 29, 1969. The first connection on what would become the Internet was made on this day when bits of data flowed between computers at UCLA and the Stanford Research Institute. This was the beginning of ARPANET, the precurser to the Internet developed by the Department of Defense. By the end of 1969, four sites were connected: UCLA, the Stanford Research Institute, the University of California, Santa Barbara and the University of Utah. By the next year there were 10 sites and soon there were applications like e-mail and file transfer utilities. The @ symbol was adopted in 1972 and a year later 75 percent of ARPANET traffic was e-mail. ARPANET was decommissioned in 1990 and the National Science Foundation's NSFnet took over the role of backbone of the Internet.

SPACE MILESTONE: *DISCOVERY* (US): OLDEST MAN IN SPACE. Oct 29, 1998. Former astronaut and senator John Glenn became the oldest man in space when he traveled on the space shuttle *Discovery* at the age of 77. In 1962 on *Friendship 7* Glenn had been the first American to orbit Earth. See "Space Milestone: Friendship 7" (Feb 20).

STOCK MARKET CRASH: ANNIVERSARY. Oct 29, 1929. Prices on the New York Stock Exchange plummeted and virtually collapsed four days after President Herbert Hoover had declared "The fundamental business of the country . . . is on a sound and prosperous basis." More than 16 million shares were dumped and billions of dollars were lost. The boom was over and the nation faced nearly a decade of depression. Some analysts had warned that the buying spree, with prices 15 to 150 times above earnings, had to stop at some point. Frightened investors ordered their brokers to sell at whatever price. The resulting Great Depression, which lasted until about 1939, involved North America, Europe and other industrialized countries. In 1932 one out of four US workers was unemployed.

TURKEY: REPUBLIC DAY: ANNIVERSARY. Oct 29. Anniversary of the founding of the republic in 1923.

BIRTHDAYS TODAY

Richard Dreyfuss, 54, actor (*American Graffiti, Jaws*; Oscar for *The Goodbye Girl*), born Brooklyn, NY, Oct 29, 1947.

Joely Fisher, 36, actress ("Ellen"), born Los Angeles, CA, Oct 29, 1965.

Finola Hughes, 41, actress ("Blossom," "Pacific Palisades"), born London, England, Oct 29, 1960.

Kate Jackson, 53, actress ("Charlie's Angels," "Scarecrow and Mrs King"), born Birmingham, AL, Oct 29, 1948.

Randy Jackson (Steven Randall Jackson), 40, singer (Jackson 5), born Gary, IN, Oct 29, 1961.

Dirk Kempthorne, 50, Governor of Idaho (R), born San Diego, CA, Oct 29, 1951.

Connie Mack III, 61, US Senator (R, Florida), born Philadelphia, PA, Oct 29, 1940.

Bill Mauldin, 80, political cartoonist, born Mountain Park, NM, Oct 29, 1921.

Melba Moore, 56, singer ("You Stepped into My Life"), actress ("Melba"), born New York, NY, Oct 29, 1945.

Winona Ryder, 30, actress (*Beetlejuice, Edward Scissorhands, Little Women*), born Winona, MN, Oct 29, 1971.

	S	M	T	W	T	F	S
October		1	2	3	4	5	6
2001	7	8	9	10	11	12	13
	14	15	16	17	18	19	20
	21	22	23	24	25	26	27
	28	29	30	31			

OCTOBER 30 — TUESDAY
Day 303 — 62 Remaining

ADAMS, JOHN: BIRTH ANNIVERSARY. Oct 30, 1735. Second president of the US (term of office: Mar 4, 1797–Mar 3, 1801), had been George Washington's vice president, and was the father of John Quincy Adams (6th president of the US). Born at Braintree, MA, he once wrote in a letter to Thomas Jefferson: "You and I ought not to die before we have explained ourselves to each other." John Adams and Thomas Jefferson died on the same day, July 4, 1826, the 50th anniversary of adoption of the Declaration of Independence. Adams's last words: "Thomas Jefferson still survives." Jefferson's last words: "Is it the fourth?"

ATLAS, CHARLES: BIRTH ANNIVERSARY. Oct 30, 1893. Charles Atlas (ex-97-lb weakling), whose original name was Angelo Siciliano, was born at Acri, Calabria, Italy. A bodybuilder and physical culturist, he created a popular mail-order body-building course. The legendary sand-kicking episode used later in advertising for his course occurred at Coney Island when a lifeguard kicked sand in Atlas's face and stole his girlfriend. Three generations of comic book fans read his advertisements. He died Dec 24, 1972, at Long Beach, NY.

CLOSING OF COLUMBIAN EXPOSITION: ANNIVERSARY. Oct 30, 1893. After a rousing success, the Columbian Exposition held "American Cities Day" Oct 28, and Chicago Mayor Carter Harrison gave a speech before the visiting mayors. After he arrived home, Harrison's doorbell rang. When the mayor answered the door he was shot by Patrick Eugene Pendergast, who had been disappointed when his request for a position with the city as corporation counsel was turned down. Instead of the elaborate ceremony that had been planned to close the exposition on Oct 30, a single speech was given and the flags lowered to half-mast.

DEVIL'S NIGHT. Oct 30. Formerly a "Mischief Night" on the evening before Halloween and an occasion for harmless pranks, chiefly observed by children. However, in some areas of the US, the destruction of property and endangering of lives has led to the imposition of dusk-to-dawn curfews during the last two or three days of October. Not to be confused with "Trick or Treat," or "Beggar's Night," usually observed on Halloween. See also: "Hallowe'en" (Oct 31).

HALSEY, WILLIAM "BULL" FREDERICK: BIRTH ANNIVERSARY. Oct 30, 1882. American admiral and fleet commander who played a leading role in the defeat of the Japanese in the Pacific naval battles of WWII, William Halsey was born at Elizabeth, NJ. In April 1942, aircraft carriers under his command ferried Jimmy Doolittle's B-25s to within several hundred miles of Japan's coast. From that location the aircraft were launched from the decks of the carriers for a raid on Tokyo. In October 1942, as commander of all the South Pacific area, Halsey led naval forces in the defeat of Japan at Guadalcanal, and in November 1943, he directed the capture of Bougainville. He supported the landings in the Philippines in June 1944. In the great naval battle of Leyte (Oct 23–25, 1944) he assisted in an overwhelming defeat of the Japanese. On Sept 2, 1945, Japan's final instrument of surrender was signed in Tokyo Bay aboard Halsey's flagship, the USS *Missouri*. Halsey died at Fishers Island, NY, Aug 16, 1959.

MALLE, LOUIS: BIRTH ANNIVERSARY. Oct 30, 1932. Born at Thumeries, France, film director Louis Malle was known for his experimental approach to filmmaking and his investigation of controversial topics. *Le Souffle Au Coeur* (1971), *Lancombe, Lucien* (1974) and *Pretty Baby* (1978), for instance, dealt with the issues of incest, the collaboration of France with its Nazi occupiers and child prostitution, respectively. Of all his films, Malle wished most to be remembered for *Au Revoir Les Enfants* (1987). Died Nov 23, 1995, at Beverly Hills, CA.

POST, EMILY: BIRTH ANNIVERSARY. Oct 30, 1872. Emily Post was born at Baltimore, MD. Published in 1922, her book *Etiquette: The Blue Book of Social Usage* instantly became the American bible of manners and social behavior and established Post as the household name in matters of etiquette. It was in its 10th edition at the time of her death Sept 25, 1960, at New York, NY. *Etiquette* inspired a great many letters asking Post for advice on manners in specific situations. She used these letters as the basis for her radio show and her syndicated newspaper column, which eventually appeared in more than 200 papers.

POUND, EZRA LOOMIS: BIRTH ANNIVERSARY. Oct 30, 1885. Modernist poet, editor and critic, born at Hailey, ID. His success as a poet began in 1909 with the publication of *Personae*. In 1912 Pound initiated the Imagist movement, edited its first anthology in 1914, and collaborated with James Joyce and T.S. Eliot. He moved to Italy in 1924. As a result of his pro-Fascist radio broadcasts from Italy Pound was indicted for treason July 26, 1943 and arrested near Genoa, by the US Army. Confined to St. Elizabeth's Hospital, Washington, DC, from 1946 to 1958 as being mentally unable to stand trial, he was never tried for treason. Died at Venice, Italy, Nov 1, 1972.

SHERIDAN, RICHARD BRINSLEY: 250th BIRTH ANNIVERSARY. Oct 30, 1751. Dramatist, born at Dublin, Ireland. Died at London, England, July 7, 1816. Sheridan is said to have extended the following invitation to a young lady: "Won't you come into the garden? I would like my roses to see you."

SISLEY, ALFRED: BIRTH ANNIVERSARY. Oct 30, 1839. French impressionist painter, born at Paris, France. One of the most influential artists of his time, he died near Fontainbleau, Jan 29, 1899.

"WAR OF THE WORLDS": BROADCAST ANNIVERSARY. Oct 30, 1938. As part of a series of radio dramas based on famous novels, Orson Welles with the Mercury Players produced H.G. Wells's *War of the Worlds*. Near panic resulted when listeners believed the simulated news bulletins, which described a Martian invasion of New Jersey, to be real.

BIRTHDAYS TODAY

Dick Gautier, 64, actor (*Bye Bye Birdie*, "Here We Go Again"), born Los Angeles, CA, Oct 30, 1937.

Harry Hamlin, 50, actor ("LA Law," "Studs Lonigan"), born Pasadena, CA, Oct 30, 1951.

Ed Lauter, 61, actor (*The Longest Yard, Fat Man and Little Boy*), born Long Beach, NY, Oct 30, 1940.

Diego Armando Maradona, 41, former soccer player, born Lanus, Argentina, Oct 30, 1960.

Andrea Mitchell, 55, news correspondent, born New York, NY, Oct 30, 1946.

Kevin Pollak, 43, actor (*A Few Good Men, Grumpy Old Men*), born San Francisco, CA, Oct 30, 1958.

Grace Slick, 62, singer (Jefferson Airplane, "White Rabbit"), born Evanston, IL, Oct 30, 1939.

Charles Martin Smith, 48, actor, director (*American Graffiti, The Buddy Holly Story, The Untouchables*), born Los Angeles, CA, Oct 30, 1953.

Dick Vermeil, 65, football coach, born Calistoga, CA, Oct 30, 1936.

Henry Winkler, 56, actor ("Happy Days," "An American Christmas Carol"), coproducer ("MacGyver"), born New York, NY, Oct 30, 1945.

OCTOBER 31 — WEDNESDAY

Day 304 — 61 Remaining

AMERICAN BUSINESS WOMEN'S ASSOCIATION NATIONAL CONVENTION. Oct 31–Nov 4. Albuquerque, NM. Businesswomen gather to learn, network and elect ABWA's national board of directors for the coming year. Seminars, speakers and the announcement of the Top Ten Business Women of ABWA and the American Business Woman of ABWA are featured. Est attendance: 3,000. For info: Carolyn Elman, American Business Women's Assn, 9100 Ward Parkway, PO Box 8728, Kansas City, MO 64114-0728. Phone: (816) 361-6621. Fax: (816) 361-4991. E-mail: abwa@abwahq.org. Web: www.abwahq.org.

CANADA: BANFF MOUNTAIN BOOK FESTIVAL. Oct 31–Nov 2. Banff, AB. An international mountain book competition that features guest speakers, readings, seminars, book signings, book launches and a book fair. Est attendance: 3,000. For info: Banff Mountain Book Festival, Banff Centre, Box 1020, Banff, AB, Canada T0L 0C0. Phone: (403) 762-6369. Fax: (403) 762-6277. E-mail: CMC@banffcentre.ab.ca. Web: www.banffcentre.ab.ca/CMC/.

CANDY, JOHN: BIRTH ANNIVERSARY. Oct 31, 1950. Comedic actor who got his start in Second City improvisation at Toronto and graduated to film stardom (*Uncle Buck, Home Alone*). Born at Toronto, Ontario, Canada, and died Mar 4, 1994, while on location for a film at Chupederos, Mexico.

CHIANG KAI-SHEK: BIRTH ANNIVERSARY. Oct 31, 1887. Chinese soldier and statesman, born at Chekiang, China. Educated at the Wampoa Military Academy, Chiang led the KMT (nationalist) forces in the struggle against the Communist army led by Mao Tse-Tung and eventually had to flee mainlaind China. He died at Taipei, Taiwan, Apr 5, 1975.

FIRST BLACK PLAYS IN NBA GAME: ANNIVERSARY. Oct 31, 1950. Earl Lloyd became the first black ever to play in an NBA game when he took the floor for the Washington Capitols at Rochester, NY. Lloyd was actually one of three blacks to become an NBA player in the 1950 season, the others being Nat "Sweetwater" Clifton, who was signed by the New York Knicks, and Chuck Cooper, who was drafted by the Boston Celtics (and debuted the night after Lloyd).

HALLOWEEN. Oct 31. Arapahoe, NE. Merchants and business personnel dress in Halloween costume, children's parade and prizes, haunted house. Est attendance: 200. For info: Secretary, Chamber of Commerce, PO Box 624, Arapahoe, NE 68922.

HALLOWE'EN or ALL HALLOW'S EVE. Oct 31. An ancient celebration combining Druid autumn festival and Christian customs. Hallowe'en (All Hallow's Eve) is the beginning of Hallowtide, a season that embraces the Feast of All Saints (Nov 1) and the Feast of All Souls (Nov 2). The observance, dating from the sixth or seventh centuries, has long been associated with thoughts of the dead, spirits, witches, ghosts and devils. In fact, the ancient Celtic Feast of Samhain, the festival that marked the beginning of winter and of the New Year, was observed Nov 1. See also: "Trick or Treat or Beggar's Night" (Oct 31).

HALLOWEEN PARADE. Oct 31 (if postponed Nov 1). Toms River, NJ. Reported as the largest second Halloween parade in the nation with 8,000 participants, 118 prizes and 100,000 spectators. Parade covers a one-mile route. Est attendance: 100,000. For info: Ray Sackmann, c/o Toms River Fire Co. 1, PO Box 1035, Toms River, NJ 08754. Phone: (723) 349-0144. Fax: (732) 349-5024.

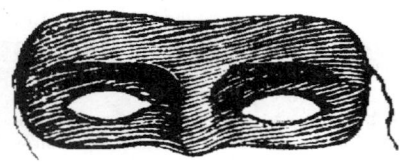

THE HALLOWEEN TRAIL. Oct 31. Pioneer Village, Worthington, MN. Open to all children, third grade and under, accompanied by their parents or a responsible adult. Treats are provided at stations located in various parts of Pioneer Village. Refreshments are available for all in the Fire Hall at the end of the trail. For info: Nobles County Historical Soc, 407 12th St, Ste 2, Worthington, MN 56187. Phone: (507) 376-4011 or (507) 376-4431.

KEATS, JOHN: BIRTH ANNIVERSARY. Oct 31, 1795. One of England's greatest poets, born at London, England. Keats wrote to Fanny Brawne (in 1820): "If I should die . . . I have left no immortal work behind me—nothing to make my friends proud of my memory—but I have loved the principle of beauty in all things, and if I had had time I would have made myself remembered." Died (of consumption) at the age of 25 at Rome, Italy, Feb 23, 1821.

LANDON, MICHAEL: 65th BIRTH ANNIVERSARY. Oct 31, 1936. American actor, born Eugene Maurice Orowitz, at Forest Hills, NY. He is best known for his roles in the television series "Bonanza" (1959–73), "Little House on the Prairie" (1974–83) and "Highway to Heaven" (1984–89). He died July 1, 1991, at Malibu, CA.

LOW, JULIET GORDON: BIRTH ANNIVERSARY. Oct 31, 1860. Founded Girl Scouts of the USA Mar 12, 1912, at Savannah, GA. Born at Savannah, Low died there Jan 17, 1927.

MOUNT RUSHMORE COMPLETION: 60th ANNIVERSARY. Oct 31, 1941. The Mount Rushmore National Memorial was completed after 14 years of work. First suggested by Jonah Robinson of the South Dakota State Historical Society, the memorial was dedicated in 1925, and work began in 1927. The memorial contains sculptures of the heads of Presidents George Washington, Thomas Jefferson, Abraham Lincoln and Theodore Roosevelt. The 60-foot-tall sculptures represent, respectively, the nation's founding, political philosophy, preservation, expansion and conservation.

NATIONAL MAGIC DAY. Oct 31. Traditionally observed on the anniversary of the death of Harry Houdini in 1926.

NATIONAL PARK OF AMERICAN SAMOA AUTHORIZED: ANNIVERSARY. Oct 31, 1988. An area of American Samoa was authorized to be developed as a national park. For further park info: Natl Park of American Samoa, c/o Pacific Area Office, PO Box 50165, Honolulu, HI 96850.

★**NATIONAL UNICEF DAY.** Oct 31. Presidential Proclamation 3817, of Oct 27, 1967, covers all succeeding years. Annually, Oct 31.

NEVADA: ADMISSION DAY: ANNIVERSARY. Oct 31. Became 36th state in 1864. Observed as a holiday in Nevada.

PACA, WILLIAM: BIRTH ANNIVERSARY. Oct 31, 1740. Signer of the Declaration of Independence and governor of Maryland. Born near Abingdon, MD, he died Oct 13, 1799, at Talbot County, MD.

REFORMATION DAY: ANNIVERSARY. Oct 31, 1517. Anniversary on which Martin Luther nailed his 95 theses to the door of Wittenberg's Palace church, denouncing the selling of papal indulgences—the beginning of the Reformation in Germany. Observed by many Protestant churches on Reformation Sunday, on this day if it is a Sunday or on the Sunday before Oct 31 (Oct 28 in 2001).

SAMHAIN. Oct 31. (Also called November Eve, Hallowmas, Hallowe'en, All Hallow's Eve, Feast of Souls, Feast of the Dead, Feast of Apples and Calan Gaeaf.) One of the "Greater Sabbats" during the Wiccan year, Samhain marks the death of the Sun-God, who then awaits his rebirth from the Mother Goddess at Yule (Dec 21 in 2001). In the Celtic tradition, the feast of Samhain was also celebrated as New Year's Eve, as their new year began on Nov 1. Annually, Oct 31.

SLEIDANUS, JOHANNES: DEATH ANNIVERSARY. Oct 31, 1556. German historian, born at Schleiden in 1506. His *Famous Chronicle of Oure Time*, called *Sleidanes Comentaries*, was first translated into English in 1560. The translator spoke thus to the book: "Go forth my painful Boke, Thou art no longer mine. Eche man may on thee loke, The Shame or praise is thine." He died at Strasbourg, Oct 31, 1556.

SWAN, JOSEPH WILSON: BIRTH ANNIVERSARY. Oct 31, 1828. English scientist and inventor born at Sunderland, Durham, England. Pioneer in photographic chemistry, incandescent electric lamp and synthetic fibers. Died at Warlingham, Surrey, England, May 27, 1914.

TAIWAN: CHIANG KAI-SHEK DAY: ANNIVERSARY. Oct 31. National holiday to honor the memory of Generalissimo Chiang Kai-Shek, the first constitutional president of the Republic of China, born Oct 31, 1887.

TRICK OR TREAT or BEGGAR'S NIGHT. Oct 31. A popular custom on Hallowe'en, in which children wearing costumes visit neighbors' homes, calling out "Trick or Treat" and "begging" for candies or gifts to place in their beggars' bags. In recent years there has been increased participation by adults, often parading in elaborate or outrageous costumes and also requesting candy.

WATERS, ETHEL: BIRTH ANNIVERSARY. Oct 31, 1896. Married when she was 13, Ethel Waters began her singing career at the urging of friends. At age 17 she was singing at Baltimore's Lincoln Center, billing herself as Sweet Mama Stringbean. Her career took her to New York, where she divided her work between the stage, nightclubs and films. She made her Broadway debut in 1927 in the revue *Africana*, and her other stage credits included *Blackbirds*, *Rhapsody in Black*, *Thousands Cheer* and *Mamba's Daughters*. Her memorable stage roles in *Cabin in the Sky* and *A Member of the Wedding* (for which she won the Drama Critics' Award) were recreated for film. Born at Chester, PA, she died Sept 9, 1977, at Chatsworth, GA.

BIRTHDAYS TODAY

Michael Collins, 70, astronaut, born Rome, Italy, Oct 31, 1931.

Dale Evans, 89, actress, evangelist ("The Roy Rogers Show"), born Uvalde, TX, Oct 31, 1912.

Deidre Hall, 53, actress ("Our House," "Days of Our Lives"), born Lake Worth, FL, Oct 31, 1948.

Frederick Stanley (Fred) McGriff, 38, baseball player, born Tampa, FL, Oct 31, 1963.

Larry Mullen, 40, musician (drummer with U2; Grammy for *The Joshua Tree*), born Dublin, Ireland, Oct 31, 1961.

Dermot Mulroney, 38, actor (*Young Guns, Longtime Companion*), born Alexandria, VA, Oct 31, 1963.

Jane Pauley, 51, TV personality, born Indianapolis, IN, Oct 31, 1950.

Dan Rather, 70, journalist (coanchor "CBS Evening News"), born Wharton, TX, Oct 31, 1931.

Stephen Rea, 58, actor (*The Crying Game, Michael Collins*), born Belfast, Northern Ireland, Oct 31, 1943.

Rob Schneider, 38, actor ("Saturday Night Live," "Men Behaving Badly"), born San Francisco, CA, Oct 31, 1963.

David Ogden Stiers, 59, actor ("M*A*S*H," *North and South*), born Peoria, IL, Oct 31, 1942.

Vanilla Ice, 34, rapper, actor (*Teenage Mutant Ninja Turtles, Cool As Ice*), born Robert Van Winkle, Miami, FL, Oct 31, 1967.

Nouember.

NOVEMBER 1 — THURSDAY
Day 305 — 60 Remaining

ALGERIA: REVOLUTION ANNIVERSARY. Nov 1. National holiday. Commemorates beginning of revolt against France in 1954.

ALL HALLOWS or ALL SAINTS' DAY. Nov 1. Roman Catholic Holy Day of Obligation. Commemorates the blessed, especially those who have no special feast days. Observed on Nov 1 since Pope Gregory IV set the date of recognition in 835. All Saints' Day is a legal holiday in Louisiana. Halloween is the evening before All Hallows Day.

AMERICAN DIABETES MONTH. Nov 1–30. American Diabetes Month is designed to communicate the seriousness of diabetes and the importance of proper diabetes control and treatment to those diagnosed with the disease and their families. Throughout the month, the ADA holds special events and programs on a variety of topics related to diabetes care and treatment. For more information, call the American Diabetes Assn at (800) DIABETES.

ANTIGUA AND BARBUDA: NATIONAL HOLIDAY: 20th ANNIVERSARY. Nov 1. Commemorates independence from Britain in 1981.

AVIATION HISTORY MONTH. Nov 1–30. Anniversary of aeronautical experiments in November 1782 (exact dates unknown), by Joseph Michel Montgolfier and Jacques Etienne Montgolfier, brothers living at Annonay, France. Inspired by Joseph Priestley's book *Experiments Relating to the Different Kinds of Air*, the brothers experimented with filling paper and fabric bags with smoke and hot air, leading to the invention of the hot-air balloon, man's first flight and the entire science of aviation and flight.

CHRISTMAS MAGIC. Nov 1–4. Multi-Purpose Events Center, Wichita Falls, TX. "A Christmas marketplace," with vendors from Texas and other states. Food, gift items, arts and crafts, entertainment. Est attendance: 15,000. For info: Wichita Falls CVB, 1000 5th St, Wichita Falls, TX 76301. Phone: (940) 716-5500. Fax: (940) 716-5509. E-mail: MPEC@WF.net. Web: www.view scape.com or www.wf.net.

CRANE, STEPHEN: BIRTH ANNIVERSARY. Nov 1, 1871. American author (*The Red Badge of Courage*), born at Newark, NJ. Died June 5, 1900, at Badenweiler, Germany.

DIABETIC EYE DISEASE MONTH. Nov 1–30. Can people with diabetes prevent the onset of diabetic eye disease? During this observance Prevent Blindness America® tells how control of diabetes can affect diabetic retinopathy, cataracts and glaucoma. For info: Prevent Blindness America®, 500 Remington Rd, Schaumburg, IL 60173. Phone: (800) 331-2020. Fax: (847) 843-8458. Web: www.preventblindness.org.

DUMMIES FOR TUMMIES. Nov 1–30. Ventriloquists' dummies mouth off where it really counts. The Ventriloquists' Association of New England raises funds and awareness for hungry people in New England. This month we work with sponsors to provide vaudeville-style shows in different locations in New England. They serve to help fill the mouths and stomachs of those less fortunate and tickle the funny bone of those who sit in the audience. For info: Judy Buch, The Ventriloquist Assn of New England, 46 Barbara Rd, Tolland, CT 06084. Phone: (860) 871-8786. Fax: (860) 870-9246.

EUROPEAN UNION ESTABLISHED: ANNIVERSARY. Nov 1, 1993. The Maastricht Treaty went into effect this day, formally establishing the European Union. The treaty was drafted in 1991. By 1993, 12 nations had ratified it. In 1995, three more nations ratified the treaty. The European Union grew out of the European Economic Community (also known as the Common Market) which was established in 1958.

FAMILY STORIES MONTH. Nov 1–30. November starts out with crisper weather and ends with the gathering of family and friends around the table which makes November the perfect month to start telling and saving family stories. For info: Scrapbook Storytelling, 3460 Hampton Ave, St. Louis, MO 63139. Phone: (314) 353-1272. E-mail: quicknews@aol.com. Web: www.scrapbookstorytelling.com.

FESTIVAL OF LIGHTS. Nov 1–Jan 6, 2002. Oglebay Resort, Wheeling , WV. This is the nations' largest light show, attracting more than a million visitors each year. The lights cover more than three hundred acres over a six-mile drive throughout the resort. Est attendance: 1,000,000. For info: Oglebay's Visitor's Center, Oglebay Park, Wheeling, WV 26003. Phone: (304) 243-4010. Fax: (304) 243-4045. Web: www.oglebay-resort.com.

GUATEMALA: KITE FESTIVAL OF SANTIAGO SACATEPEQUEZ. Nov 1. Long ago, when evil spirits disturbed the good spirits in the local cemetery, a magician told the townspeople a secret way to get rid of the evil spirits—by flying kites (because the evil spirits were frightened by the noise of wind against paper). Since then, the kite festival has been held at the cemetery each year on Nov 1 or Nov 2, and it is said that "to this day no one knows of bad spirits roaming the streets or the cemetery of Santiago Sacatepequez," a village about 20 miles from Guatemala City. Nowadays, the youth of the village work for many weeks to make the elaborate and giant kites to fly on All Saints' Day (Nov 1) or All Souls' Day (Nov 2).

HOCKEY MASK INVENTED: ANNIVERSARY. Nov 1, 1959. Tired of stopping hockey pucks with his face, Montreal Canadiens goalie Jacques Plante, having received another wound, reemerged from the locker room with seven new stitches—and a plastic face mask he had made from fiberglass and resin. Although Cliff Benedict had tried a leather mask back in the '20s, the idea didn't catch on but after Plante wore his, goalies throughout the NHL began wearing protective plastic face shields.

HUNTER'S MOON. Nov 1. The full moon following Harvest Moon. So called because the moon's light in evening extends day's length for hunters. Moon enters Full Moon phase at 12:41 AM, EST.

LUNG CANCER AWARENESS MONTH. Nov 1–30. A month created to increase awareness of the need for screening, early diagnosis, more research and compassion for lung cancer survivors. ALCASE is the only organization in the world solely dedicated to helping people with lung cancer. Support and education resources are available free of charge by phone, mail or Internet. For info: Alliance for Lung Cancer Advocacy, Support and Education, 1601 Lincoln Ave, Vancouver, WA 98660. Phone: (800) 298-2436. Fax: (360) 699-1944. E-mail: info@alcase.org. Web: www.alcase.org.

MEDICAL SCHOOL FOR WOMEN OPENED AT BOSTON: ANNIVERSARY. Nov 1, 1848. Founded by Samuel Gregory, a pioneer in medical education for women, the Boston Female Medical School opened as the first medical school exclusively for women. The original enrollment was 12 students. In 1874, the school merged with the Boston University School of Medicine and formed one of the first coed medical schools in the world.

MERLIN'S SNUG HUGS FOR KIDS. Nov 1–Dec 19. Nationwide. Each community is encouraged to provide new winter outerwear for foster and needy children. Event runs for six weeks, and includes Kids Helping Kids, scout participation and the Crochet and Knit-A-Thon. The final day (Dec 19) Merlin's caravan collects the new winter clothes and delivers them to Children's Home & Aid Society. Sponsor: Merlin's Muffler & Brake. Annually, the first week of November through the third week of December. For info: Kathleen Quinn, ProQuest/2020, PO Box 2373, Glenview, IL 60025-2373. Phone: (847) 998-9950. Fax: (847) 998-9945. E-mail: SHFK2000@aol.com. Web: www.merlins.com.

MEXICO: DAY OF THE DEAD. Nov 1–2. Observance begins during last days of October when "Dead Men's Bread" is sold in bakeries—round loaves, decorated with sugar skulls. Departed souls are remembered not with mourning but with a spirit of friendliness and good humor. Cemeteries are visited and graves are decorated.

MISSION SAN JUAN CAPISTRANO: 225th FOUNDING ANNIVERSARY. Nov 1, 1776. California mission founded on this date, collapsed during the 1812 earthquake. The swallows of Capistrano nest in the ruins of the old mission church, departing each year on Oct 23, and returning the following year on or near St. Joseph's Day (Mar 19).

MOON PHASE: FULL MOON. Nov 1. Moon enters Full Moon phase at 12:41 AM, EST.

★**NATIONAL ADOPTION MONTH.** Nov 1–30.

NATIONAL ALZHEIMER'S DISEASE MONTH. Nov 1–30. To increase awareness of Alzheimer's disease and what the Alzheimer's Association is doing to advance research and help patients, their families and their caregivers. For info: Nicolle Heller, Alzheimer's Assn, 919 N Michigan, Ste 1100, Chicago, IL 60611. Phone: (800) 272-3900 or (312) 335-4037. Fax: (312) 335-1110. E-mail: nicolle.heller@alz.org.

★**NATIONAL AMERICAN INDIAN HERITAGE MONTH.** Nov 1–30.

NATIONAL AUTHORS' DAY. Nov 1. This observance was adopted by the General Federation of Women's Clubs in 1929 and in 1949 was given a place on the list of special days, weeks and months prepared by the US Dept of Commerce. The resolution states: "by celebrating an Authors' Day as a nation, we would not only show patriotism, loyalty, and appreciation of the men and women who have made American literature possible, but would also encourage and inspire others to give of themselves in making a better America. . . ." It was also resolved "that we commemorate an Authors' Day to be observed on November First each year."

		S	M	T	W	T	F	S
November						1	2	3
2001		4	5	6	7	8	9	10
		11	12	13	14	15	16	17
		18	19	20	21	22	23	24
		25	26	27	28	29	30	

NATIONAL FAMILY CAREGIVERS MONTH. Nov 1–30. A nationwide month of recognition for the millions of family caregivers. For info: Suzanne Geffen Mintz, Pres, Natl Family Caregivers Assn, 10400 Connecticut Ave, Ste 500, Kensington, MD 20895-3944. Phone: (800) 896-3650. Fax: (301) 942-2302. E-mail: info@nfcacares.org. Web: www.nfcacares.org.

NATIONAL FAMILY LITERACY DAY®. Nov 1. Celebrated all over the country with special activities and events that showcase the importance of family literacy programs. Family literacy programs bring parents and children together in the classroom to learn and support each other in efforts to further their education and improve their life skills. Sponsored by the National Center for Family Literacy and Toyota. Annually, Nov 1. For info: Natl Center for Family Literacy, 325 W Main St, Ste 200, Louisville, KY 40202. Phone: (502) 584-1133. Fax: (502) 584-0172. E-mail: ncfl@famlit.org. Web: www.famlit.org.

NATIONAL FIG WEEK. Nov 1–7. To celebrate the completion of the California fig harvest and encourage consumers to use California figs as part of their diet for the taste, high fiber and nutritional value. For info: California Fig Advisory Board, PO Box 709, Fresno, CA 93712. Phone: (800) 588-2344. Fax: (559) 224-3449. E-mail: info@californiafigs.com. Web: www.california figs.com.

NATIONAL GEORGIA PECAN MONTH. Nov 1–30. To herald the pecan harvest and recognize Georgia's status as the nation's top pecan-producing state, providing 40 percent of the nation's supply. For info: Marcia Crowley, Georgia Agricultural Commodity Commission for Pecans (GACCP), Commodities Promotion Div, GA Dept of Agriculture, 328 Agriculture Bldg, Capitol Square, Atlanta, GA 30334. Phone: (404) 656-3678. Fax: (404) 656-9380.

NATIONAL HEALTHY SKIN MONTH. Nov 1–30. For info: American Academy of Dermatology, 930 N Meacham Rd, Schaumburg, IL 60173. Phone: (847) 330-0230 or (888) 462-DERM. Web: www.aad.org.

NATIONAL HIGHER EDUCATION CONFERENCE ON STUDENTS OF COLOR. Nov 1–3. Montego Bay, Jamaica. A forum for college and university faculty, administrators and other educators to critically review issues that influence student success in higher education. Est attendance: 100. For info: Dr. Clinita A. Ford, Dir, Higher Education Conference, PO Box 10042, Tallahassee, FL 32302-2042. Phone: (850) 222-1087. Fax: (850) 385-4673. E-mail: cnjford@aol.com.

NATIONAL HOSPICE MONTH. Nov 1–30. To promote greater awareness of hospice care and the advantages it offers; to educate physicians and other health care professionals about the concept of hospice; to honor patients and family members, as well as the thousands of dedicated professionals and volunteers who devote their time, love and support to the terminally ill and their families; and to educate public officials to ensure hospice care remains a key component in the health care delivery system. For info: Public Relations, Hospice Assn of America, 228 Seventh St, SE, Washington, DC 20003. Phone: (202) 546-4759. Fax: (202) 547-3540. Web: www.nahc.org/.

NATIONAL LIFEWRITING MONTH. Nov 1–30. An opportunity to celebrate and share ourselves by putting our lifestories in writing. Celebration by preserving our autobiographies in writing allows us to share our stories with future generations. For info: Soleil Lifestory Network, 95-33 Gould Rd, Lisbon Falls, ME 04252.

NATIONAL MARROW AWARENESS MONTH. Nov 1–30. More than 30,000 Americans are diagnosed each year with leukemia or another life-threatening blood disease for which a bone marrow or blood stem cell transplant offers hope for survival. The National Marrow Donor Program maintains a computerized registry of nearly 4,000,000 volunteer donors. For info: Natl Marrow Donor Program, 3433 Broadway St NE, Ste 500, Minneapolis, MN 55413. Phone: (800) MAR-ROW2. Web: www.marrow.org.

NATIONAL MEN MAKE DINNER DAY. Nov 1. One day set aside for "Men Only" in the kitchen. Give wives a break and let the men whip up some culinary delight with no help from family members. In the true spirit of Men Make Dinner Day, barbecues are not allowed! For info: Sandy Sharkey, KOOL FM Radio, 87 George St, Ottawa, ON, Canada K1N 9H7. Phone: (613) 738-2372. Fax: (613) 739-4040. E-mail: ssharkey@planetkool .com.

NATIONAL SLEEP COMFORT MONTH. Nov 1–30. To help a sleep deprived nation recognize the vital need for adequate sleep and the serious consequences of insufficient sleep. And to stress the importance of choosing the proper pillow, comforter and featherbed for a restful and refreshing good night's sleep. Sponsor: The Company Store, La Crosse, WI. For info: David Pipkorn, VP. Phone: (608) 791-5888. Fax: (608) 791-5892. Web: www.thecompanystore.com.

ORPHAN DISEASE MONTH. Nov 1–30. A month dedicated to the awareness of orphan/rare/uncommon diseases. Includes "Adopt-an-Orphan-Disease" and "Unsolved Cases" for public education and awareness. Goal is to spotlight no-treatment, no-cure diseases and to be an advocate for advances and cures research. For info: AmericaCares AmericanCan, Box 6783, Lafayette, IN 47903. Web: www.giftsoftime.org.

OZARK MOUNTAIN CHRISTMAS. Nov 1–Dec 31. Branson, MO. Branson theatres are alive with sounds of spectacular holiday music shows and the hills are aglow with the soft twinkling illumination of millions of holiday lights. Annually, November and December. For info: Branson Lakes Area Chamber of Commerce, PO Box 1897, Branson, MO 65615. Phone: (800) 214-3661. Web: www.bransonchamber.com.

PEANUT BUTTER LOVERS' MONTH. Nov 1–30. Celebration of America's favorite food and #1 sandwich. For info: Peanut Advisory Board, 50 Hurt Plaza, Ste 1220, Atlanta, GA 30303. Web: www.peanutbutterlovers.com.

PRESIDENT OCCUPIES THE WHITE HOUSE: ANNIVERSARY. Nov 1, 1800. Philadelphia had served as the nation's capital from 1790 to 1800. On Nov 1, 1800, President John Adams and his family moved into the newly-completed White House, as Washington, DC, became the new capital.

PRIME MERIDIAN SET: ANNIVERSARY. Nov 1, 1884. Delegates from 25 nations met in October at Washington, DC, at the International Meridian Conference to set up time zones for the world. On this day the treaty adopted by the Conference took effect, making Greenwich, England the Prime Meridian (i.e., zero° longitude) and setting the International Date Line at 180° longitude in the Pacific. Every 15° of longitude equals one hour and there are 24 meridians. While some countries do not strictly observe this system (for example, while China stretches over five time zones, it is the same time everywhere in China) this system has brought predictability and logic to time throughout the world.

US VIRGIN ISLANDS: LIBERTY DAY. Nov 1. Officially "D. Hamilton Jackson Memorial Day," commemorating establishment of the first press in the Virgin Islands in 1915.

VEGAN AWARENESS MONTH. Nov 1–30. This outreach event encourages everyone to GO VEGAN! Vegans choose to neither eat nor use any animal products (e.g., dairy products, eggs, gelatin, leather, fur, etc). A growing number of caring, compassionate people are adopting this conscientious lifestyle. Primarily ethical reasons, but also health and environmental concerns, motivate them to GO VEGAN. For info: VEGANET, PO Box 3545, Washington, DC 20007-0045. Phone: (877) GO-VEGAN.

VIRGINIA CHRISTMAS SHOW. Nov 1–4. Showplace Exhibition Center, Richmond, VA. Featuring 450 artisans and crafters, Christmas gourmet food shops and Christmas Holiday Theatre, entertainment, legendary "Sgt Santa." 16th annual show. Est attendance: 40,000. For info: Virginia Show Productions, PO Box 305, Chase City, VA 23924. Phone: (804) 372-3996. Fax: (804) 372-3410.

WORLD COMMUNICATION WEEK. Nov 1–7. To stress the importance of communication among the more than five billion human beings in the world who speak more than 3,000 languages and to promote communication by means of the international language, Esperanto. For complete info, send $4 to cover expense of printing, handling and postage. Annually, the first seven days of November. For info: Dr. Stanley Drake, Pres, Intl Society of Friendship and Goodwill, 8592 Roswell Rd, Ste 434, Atlanta, GA 30350-1870.

BIRTHDAYS TODAY

Larry Claxton Flynt, 59, publisher, born Magoffin County, KY, Nov 1, 1942.

James Jackson Kilpatrick, 81, journalist (conservative side of "60 Minutes" Point-Counterpoint segment), born Oklahoma City, OK, Nov 1, 1920.

Lyle Lovett, 44, country and western singer ("Cowboy Man"), born Klein, TX, Nov 1, 1957.

Jenny McCarthy, 29, model, actress ("Jenny"), born Chicago, IL, Nov 1, 1972.

Betsy Palmer (Patricia Bromek), 75, actress ("I've Got a Secret," "Knots Landing," "Today"), born East Chicago, IN, Nov 1, 1926.

Gary Jim Player, 66, golfer, born Johannesburg, South Africa, Nov 1, 1935.

Rachel Ticotin, 43, actress (*Total Recall, Natural Born Killers*), born The Bronx, NY, Nov 1, 1958.

Fernando Anguamea Valenzuela, 41, former baseball player, born Navojoa, Sonora, Mexico, Nov 1, 1960.

NOVEMBER 2 — FRIDAY
Day 306 — 59 Remaining

ALL SOULS' DAY. Nov 2. Commemorates the faithful departed. Catholic observance.

BIG TEN FIELD HOCKEY TOURNAMENT. Nov 2–4. Ann Arbor, MI. Est attendance: 1,000. For info: Sue Ryan, Big Ten Conference, 1500 W Higgins Rd, Park Ridge, IL 60068-6300. Phone: (847) 696-1010. Fax: (847) 696-1110. Web: www.bigten.org.

BIG TEN WOMEN'S SOCCER CHAMPIONSHIP. Nov 2–4. Illinois. Est attendance: 1,000. For info: Sue Ryan, Big Ten Conference, 1500 W Higgins Rd, Park Ridge, IL 60068-6300. Phone: (847) 696-1010. Fax: (847) 696-1110. Web: www.bigten .org.

BOONE, DANIEL: BIRTH ANNIVERSARY. Nov 2, 1734 (OS). American frontiersman, explorer and militia officer, born at Berks County, near Reading, PA. In February 1778, he was captured at Blue Licks, KY, by Shawnee Indians, under Chief Blackfish, who adopted Boone when he was inducted into the tribe as "Big Turtle." Boone escaped after five months, and in 1781 was captured briefly by the British. He experienced a series of personal and financial disasters during his life, but continued a rugged existence, hunting until his 80s. Boone died at St. Charles County, MO, Sept 26, 1820. The bodies of Daniel Boone and his wife, Rebecca, were moved to Frankfort, KY, in 1845.

CANADA: BANFF MOUNTAIN FILM FESTIVAL. Nov 2–4. Banff, AB. Mountain and adventure films and videos from around the world will be entered for this award competition at The Banff Centre. A weekend of film, seminars, guest speakers and exhibits. Est attendance: 6,000. For info: Deb Smythe, Fest Coord, Mountain Film Festival, PO Box 1020, Station 38, Banff, AB, Canada T0L 0C0. Phone: (403) 762-6125. Fax: (403) 762-6277. E-mail: CMC@banffcentre.ab.ca. Web: www.banff centre.ab.ca/CMC/.

CRAFTSMEN'S CHRISTMAS CLASSIC. Nov 2–4. Richmond Raceway Complex, Richmond, VA. Arts and crafts. Est attendance: 35,000. For info: Gilmore Enterprises, 1240 Oakland Ave, Greensboro, NC 27403. Phone: (336) 274-5550. Fax: (336) 274-1084.

FIRST SCHEDULED RADIO BROADCAST: ANNIVERSARY. Nov 2, 1920. Station KDKA at Pittsburgh, PA, broadcasted the results of the presidential election. The station got its license to broadcast Nov 7, 1921. By 1922 there were about 400 licensed radio stations in the US.

GREAT AMERICAN WARM-UP. Nov 2–4. Just as the weather outside begins to get frightful, this weekend is set aside to clean out those closets and take your warm, wearable coats and jackets that you no longer use and donate them to a homeless shelter or agency for distribution. Do it now, before it gets even colder outside. Annually, the first full weekend in November. [© 1995] For info: Adrienne Sioux Koopersmith, 1437 W Rosemont, #1W, Chicago, IL 60660-1319. Phone: (773) 743-5341. Fax: (773) 743-5395. E-mail: adrienne@21stcentury.net.

GREAT NY STATE SNOW & TRAVEL EXPO. Nov 2–4. Empire State Plaza, Albany, NY. One of the longest continuous-running snow expos in the country, the 40th annual show features ski deck shows, seminars, ski films, auction and used equipment sale. Annually, the first full weekend in November. Sponsor: Albany Times Union Newspapers. Est attendance: 20,000. For info: Tara Sullivan, Dir, Consumer Shows and Special Events, Ed Lewi Assoc, 6 Chelsea Pl, Clifton Park, NY 12065. Phone: (518) 383-6183. Fax: (518) 383-6755.

HARDING, WARREN GAMALIEL: BIRTH ANNIVERSARY. Nov 2, 1865. Twenty-ninth president of the US was born at Corsica, OH. His term of office: Mar 4, 1921–Aug 2, 1923 (died in office). His undistinguished administration was tainted by the Teapot Dome scandal, and his sudden death while on a western speaking tour (San Francisco, CA, Aug 2, 1923) prompted many rumors.

HOLIDAY MARKET. Nov 2–4. Greensboro Coliseum, Greensboro, NC. Holiday gift show with performances by local choral groups and bands and demonstrations of holiday cooking, decoration-making and holiday fashions. More than 250 exhibits—and Santa Claus! Est attendance: 20,000. For info: Gilmore Enterprises, Inc, 1240 Oakland Ave, Greensboro, NC 27403. Phone: (336) 274-5550. Fax: (336) 274-1084.

LANCASTER, BURT(ON) STEPHEN: BIRTH ANNIVERSARY. Nov 2, 1913. Distinguished American actor who began his career in show business as a circus acrobat. In a career spanning 45 years, he appeared in nearly 80 films. The first was *The Killers* (1945), in which he portrayed a tough guy, a film persona he maintained for most of his early career. Some of his more memorable roles are in *From Here to Eternity* (1953), *The Bird Man of Alcatraz* (1962) and *The Leopard* (1963); he received an Academy Award for his performance in the title role of *Elmer Gantry* (1961). Some of his later popular movies include *Atlantic*

City (1981), *Local Hero* (1983) and *Field of Dreams* (1989). Born at New York City, he died Oct 20, 1994, at Los Angeles.

NATIONAL FARM TOY SHOW. Nov 2–4. Beckman HS and National Farm Toy Museum, The Commercial Club Park, Dyersville, IA. This "granddaddy" of farm toy shows features tours of farm toy manufacturers, auction, craft bazaar, pedal pull and more than 200 vendors dealing in farm toys and implements. Annually, the first full weekend in November. For info: Dyersville Area Chamber of Commerce, 1100 16th Ave Ct SE, Dyersville, IA 52040. Phone: (319) 875-2311. Fax: (319) 875-8391. E-mail: dyersvillechamber@dyersville.org. Web: www.dyersville.org.

NEW YORK SUBWAY ACCIDENT: ANNIVERSARY. Nov 2, 1918. The Brighton Beach Express, exceeding its speed limit five times over (going 30 mph) while approaching the station near Malbone Street tunnel at Brooklyn, jumped the tracks, killing 97 people and injuring 100. The supervisor-engineer, taking the place of a striking motorman of the Brotherhood of Locomotive Engineers, was tried and acquitted of charges of negligence.

NORTH DAKOTA: ADMISSION DAY: ANNIVERSARY. Nov 2. Became 39th state in 1889.

PLAN YOUR EPITAPH DAY. Nov 2. Dedicated to the proposition that a forgettable gravestone is a fate worse than death, and that everyone can be in the same league with William Shakespeare and W.C. Fields. Annually, coincides with the Day of the Dead. For info: Lance Hardie, Dead or Alive, PO Box 4595, Arcata, CA 95518. Phone: (707) 822-6924. E-mail: sunrise @hardiehouse.org. Web: www.hardiehouse.org.

POLK, JAMES KNOX: BIRTH ANNIVERSARY. Nov 2, 1795. The 11th president of the US was born at Mecklenburg County, NC. His term of office: Mar 4, 1845–Mar 3, 1849. A compromise candidate at the 1844 Democratic Party convention, Polk was awarded the nomination on the ninth ballot. He declined to be a candidate for a second term and declared himself to be "exceedingly relieved" at the completion of his presidency. He died shortly thereafter at Nashville, TN, June 15, 1849.

SAMOA: ARBOR DAY. Nov 2. The first Friday in November is observed as Arbor Day in Samoa (formerly Western Samoa).

SENECA FALLS CONVENTION SURVIVOR VOTES: ANNIVERSARY. Nov 2, 1920. The only woman who attended the historic Seneca Falls Women's Rights Convention in 1848 who lived long enough to exercise her right to vote under the 19th Amendment, Charlotte Woodward voted at Philadelphia in the general election Nov 2, 1920.

SOUTH DAKOTA: ADMISSION DAY: ANNIVERSARY. Nov 2. Became 40th state in 1889.

SPRUCE GOOSE FLIGHT: ANNIVERSARY. Nov 2, 1947. The mammoth flying boat *Hercules*, then the world's largest airplane, was designed, built and flown (once) by Howard Hughes. Its first and only flight was about one mile and at an altitude of 70 feet over Long Beach Harbor, CA. The $25 million, 200-ton plywood craft was nicknamed the "Spruce Goose." It is now displayed near the *Queen Mary* at Long Beach, CA.

	S	**M**	**T**	**W**	**T**	**F**	**S**
November					1	2	3
2001	4	5	6	7	8	9	10
	11	12	13	14	15	16	17
	18	19	20	21	22	23	24
	25	26	27	28	29	30	

STAMP EXPO: FALL. Nov 2–4. Wilshire Ebell Convention Complex, Los Angeles, CA. Est attendance: 4,000. For info: Intl Stamp Collectors Soc, PO Box 854, Van Nuys, CA 91408. Phone: (818) 997-6496. Fax: (818) 988-4337. E-mail: iibick@aol.com. Web: www.bick.net.

SUGARLOAF'S FALL SOMERSET CRAFT FESTIVAL. Nov 2–4. Garden State Exhibit Center, Somerset, NJ. This show, now in its 8th year, features 250 nationally recognized craft designers and fine artists displaying and selling their original creations. Craft demonstrations, hourly gift certificate drawings and more. Est attendance: 16,000. For info: Sugarloaf Mountain Works, Inc, 200 Orchard Ridge Dr, #215, Gaithersburg, MD 20878. Phone: (800) 210-9900. E-mail: smworks@sugarloafcrafts.com. Web: www.sugarloafcrafts.com.

VICTORIAN HOLMES WEEKEND. Nov 2–4. Cape May, NJ. A weekend of mystery and intrigue awaits amateur sleuths when Cape May celebrates the works of Sir Arthur Conan Doyle, creator of Sherlock Holmes. Annually, the first weekend in November. Est attendance: 200. For info: Mid-Atlantic Center for the Arts, PO Box 340, 1048 Washington St, Cape May, NJ 08204. Phone: (609) 884-5404 x114 or (800) 275-4278. Fax: (609) 884-0574. Web: www.capemaymac.org.

WALSH INVITATIONAL RIFLE TOURNAMENT. Nov 2–4 (also Nov 9–11 and 16–18). Xavier University, Cincinnati, OH. To promote marksmanship and sportsmanship in the competitive spirit of collegiate athletics. International smallbore rifle and air rifle match open to all competitors. Recognized as "the largest indoor rifle match in the nation." Sponsor: Xavier University Athletic Department. Est attendance: 300. For info: Alan Joseph, O'Conner Sports Center, Dept of Athletics, Xavier Univ, 3800 Victory Pkwy, Cincinnati, OH 45207-6114. Fax: (513) 745-4390.

WURSTFEST. Nov 2–11. Landa Park, New Braunfels, TX. To honor and celebrate German heritage. Music, dancing, food, arts and crafts, historical exhibits, sporting events and special demonstrations. For accommodation info: (800) 572-2626. Est attendance: 100,000. For info: Wurstfest Assn, PO Box 310309, New Braunfels, TX 78131. Phone: (830) 625-9167 or (800) 221-4369. Fax: (830) 620-1318. E-mail: info@wurstfest.com. Web: www.wurstfest.com.

BIRTHDAYS TODAY

Patrick Buchanan, 63, political columnist, born Washington, DC, Nov 2, 1938.

Shere Hite, 59, author (*The Hite Report, Women and Love*), born St. Joseph, MO, Nov 2, 1942.

k.d. lang, 40, singer, born Consort, Canada, Nov 2, 1961.

Stefanie Powers, 59, actress ("Hart to Hart"), born Hollywood, CA, Nov 2, 1942.

David Knapp (Dave) Stockton, 60, golfer, born San Bernardino, CA, Nov 2, 1941.

NOVEMBER 3 — SATURDAY

Day 307 — 58 Remaining

AUSTIN, STEPHEN FULLER: BIRTH ANNIVERSARY. Nov 3, 1793. A principal founder of Texas, for whom its capital city was named, Austin was born at Wythe County, VA. He first visited Texas in 1821 and established a settlement there the following year, continuing a colonization project started by his father, Moses Austin. Thrown in prison when he advocated formation of a separate state (Texas still belonged to Mexico), he was freed in 1835, lost a campaign for the presidency (of the Republic of Texas) to Sam Houston (q.v.) in 1836, and died (while serving as Texas secretary of state) at Austin, TX, Dec 27, 1836.

BRYANT, WILLIAM CULLEN: BIRTH ANNIVERSARY. Nov 3, 1794. American poet (*Thanatopsis*), born at Cummington, MA. Died at New York, NY, June 12, 1878.

CANADA: FARMFAIR INTERNATIONAL. Nov 3–11. Edmonton, AB. Canada's premiere celebration of western-style living. It features more than 4,500 farm animals, a western-themed consumer trade show, interactive exhibits, dynamic team competitions and wagon loads of family entertainment. Farmfair also presents Canada's largest purebred livestock show and sale. The best-of-breed beef cattle annually entices buyers from nearly 20 countries to Farmfair. Est attendance: 60,000. For info: Kate Rogers, Marketing Coord, Northlands Park, Box 1480, Edmonton, AB, Canada T5J 2N5. Phone: (780) 471-7210. Fax: (780) 471-8176. E-mail: krogers@northlands.com. Web: www.northlands.com.

CLICHÉ DAY. Nov 3. Use clichés as much as possible today. Hey, why not? Give it a shot! Win some, lose some. You'll never know 'til you try it. Annually, Nov 3. ©1999 Wellcat Herbs & Holidays For info: Thomas & Ruth Roy, 2418 Long Ln, Lebanon, PA 17046-1708. Phone: (230) 332-4886. E-mail: wellcat@supernet.com. Web: www.wellcat.com.

DEWEY DEFEATS TRUMAN HEADLINE: ANNIVERSARY. Nov 3, 1948. This headline in the *Chicago Tribune* notwithstanding, Harry Truman defeated Republican candidate Thomas E. Dewey for the US presidency.

DOMINICA: NATIONAL DAY. Nov 3. National holiday. Commemorates independence from Britain in 1978.

FALL COUNTRY JAMBOREE. Nov 3–4. Pioneer Settlement for the Creative Arts, Barberville, FL. A celebration of pioneer life and food. More than 100 demonstrating craftsmen and tradesmen, three continuous musical stages featuring more than 75 noted artists. Historical displays include Indian and Cracker camps, antique autos, turpentine stills, flywheelers and model railroaders. For info: Pioneer Settlement for the Creative Arts, PO Box 6, Barberville, FL 32105. Phone: (904) 749-2959.

JAPAN: CULTURE DAY. Nov 3. National holiday.

JERSEY SHORE'S FINEST: MINIATURES, DOLL & DOLLHOUSE SHOW & SALE. Nov 3. Toms River Intermediate School East, Toms River, NJ. 10 AM–4 PM. Forty-five vendors, doll hospital, appraisals, collectibles, antique dolls, handmade miniatures. Admission: $3.50 adult, $1 under 18. Est attendance: 1,500. For info: Ocean County Historical Soc, PO Box 2191, 26 Hadley Ave, Toms River, NJ 08754-2191. Phone: (732) 341-1880. Fax: (732) 341-4372.

LOVINGTON FALL ARTS AND CRAFTS FESTIVAL. Nov 3–4. Lea County Fairgrounds, Lovington, NM. Displays from more than 100 local and regional crafters. No commercially manufactured items allowed. 24th annual festival. Annually, the first weekend in November. Est attendance: 10,000. For info: Lovington Chamber of Commerce, 201 S Main St, Lovington, NM 88260. Phone: (505) 396-5311. Fax: (505) 396-2823. E-mail: visitus@leaconet.com. Web: visitus.leaco.net.

MICRONESIA, FEDERATED STATES OF: INDEPENDENCE DAY: 15th ANNIVERSARY. Nov 3. National holiday commemorating independence from US in 1986.

NAGURSKI, BRONKO: BIRTH ANNIVERSARY. Nov 3, 1908. Bronislau ("Bronko") Nagurski, College Football Hall of Fame and charter member of the Pro Football Hall of Fame. Born at Rainy River, Ontario, Canada, he played football at the University of Minnesota, earning All-American honors at both tackle and fullback, and for the Chicago Bears. After retiring from football, Nagurski wrestled professionally. He died at International Falls, MN, Jan 7, 1990.

NEW INUIT TERRITORY APPROVED: ANNIVERSARY. Nov 3, 1992. Canada's Inuit people voted to accept a federal land-claim package granting them control over a new territory, Nunavut, to be carved out of the existing Northwest Territories by 1999. The voting on Nov 3–5, 1992 indicated that 69 percent of the 9,648 eligible Inuit voters accepted the settlement. In exchange for the new territory, approximately 135,000 square miles, the Inuits gave up their rights to a territory of 775,000 square miles.

NORTHERN ILLINOIS GATHERINGS POWWOW. Nov 3. Student Recreation Center, Dekalb, IL. Gathering of Native American drums, dancers and vendors. A traditional powwow—admission is free and everyone is welcome. Annually, the first Saturday in November. Est attendance: 3,500. For info: Rita Reynolds, Northern Illinois Univ, Dekalb, IL 60115. Phone: (815) 753-6366.

PANAMA: INDEPENDENCE DAY. Nov 3. Independence Day. Panama declared itself independent of Colombia in 1903.

PUBLIC TELEVISION DEBUTS: ANNIVERSARY. Nov 3, 1969. A string of local educational TV channels united on this day under the Public Broadcasting System banner. Today there are 348 PBS stations.

RESTON, JAMES: BIRTH ANNIVERSARY. Nov 3, 1909. *New York Times* journalist, born Clydebank, Scotland. Died Dec 3, 1995, at Washington, DC.

SADIE HAWKINS DAY. Nov 3. Widely observed in US, usually on the first Saturday in November. Tradition established in "Li'l Abner" comic strip in 1930s by cartoonist Al Capp. A popular occasion when women and girls are encouraged to take the initiative in inviting the man or boy of their choice for a date. A similar tradition is associated with Feb 29 in leap years.

SANDWICH DAY: BIRTH ANNIVERSARY OF JOHN MONTAGUE. Nov 3, 1718. A day to recognize the inventor of the sandwich, John Montague, Fourth Earl of Sandwich, born at London, England. England's first lord of the admiralty, secretary of state for the northern department, postmaster general and the man after whom Captain Cook named the Sandwich Islands in 1778. A rake and a gambler, he is said to have invented the sandwich as a time-saving nourishment while engaged in a 24-hour-long gambling session in 1762. He died at London, England, Apr 30, 1792.

SPACE MILESTONE: *SPUTNIK 2* **(USSR).** Nov 3, 1957. A dog named Laika became the first animal sent into space. Total weight of craft and dog was 1,121 lbs. The satellite was not capable of returning the dog to Earth and she died when her air supply was gone. Nicknamed "Muttnik" by the American press.

STEEPLECHASE AT CALLAWAY GARDENS. Nov 3. Pine Mountain, GA. A seven-race steeplechase "meet" where riders match their horses for speed and split-second timing over brush jumps. Box seating and infield tailgating spaces available. Est attendance: 12,000. For info: The Steeplechase at Callaway Gardens, PO Box 2311, Columbus, GA 31902. Phone: (706) 324-6252. Fax: (706) 324-3651.

November 2001

S	M	T	W	T	F	S
				1	2	3
4	5	6	7	8	9	10
11	12	13	14	15	16	17
18	19	20	21	22	23	24
25	26	27	28	29	30	

SWEDEN: ALL SAINTS' DAY. Nov 3. Honors the memory of deceased friends and relatives. Annually, the Saturday following Oct 30.

VERBOORT SAUSAGE AND KRAUT DINNER. Nov 3. Visitation Parish, Forest Grove, OR. 66th annual event features crafts, Bingo, raffles, beer garden, local produce, homebaked goods and, of course, famous Verboort sausage and kraut. Est attendance: 6,000. For info: Byron Schmidlkofer, Visitation Parish, 4285 NW Visitation Rd, Forest Grove, OR 97116. Phone: (503) 357-7434.

WHITE, EDWARD DOUGLASS: BIRTH ANNIVERSARY. Nov 3, 1845. Ninth Chief Justice of the Supreme Court, born at La Fourche Parish, LA. During the Civil War, he served in the Confederate Army after which he returned to New Orleans to practice law. Elected to the US Senate in 1891, he was appointed to the Supreme Court by Grover Cleveland in 1894. He became Chief Justice under President William Taft in 1910 and served until 1921. He died at Washington, DC, May 19, 1921.

BIRTHDAYS TODAY

Adam Ant (Stewart Goddard), 47, singer ("Goody Two Shoes"), born London, England, Nov 3, 1954.

Ken Berry, 68, actor ("F Troop," "Mayberry RFD," "Mama's Family"), singer, dancer, born Moline, IL, Nov 3, 1933.

Charles Bronson (Charles Buchinsky), 79, actor (*The Dirty Dozen, The Valachi Papers*), born Ehrenfeld, PA, Nov 3, 1922.

Kate Capshaw, 48, actress ("Duke of Groove," *How to Make an American Quilt*), born Fort Worth, TX, Nov 3, 1953.

Michael S. Dukakis, 68, former Governor of Massachusetts (D), 1988 presidential candidate, born Brookline, MA, Nov 3, 1933.

Robert William Andrew (Bob) Feller, 83, Baseball Hall of Fame pitcher, born Van Meter, IA, Nov 3, 1918.

Kathy Kinney, 47, actress ("The Drew Carey Show"), born Stevens Point, WI, Nov 3, 1954.

Steve Landesberg, 56, actor ("Barney Miller," "Friends and Lovers"), born The Bronx, NY, Nov 3, 1945.

Dolph Lundgren, 42, actor (*A View to a Kill, Rocky IV*), born Stockholm, Sweden, Nov 3, 1959.

Dennis Miller, 48, comedian, actor ("Saturday Night Live," "The Dennis Miller Show"), born Pittsburgh, PA, Nov 3, 1953.

Roseanne, 48, comedienne, actress ("Roseanne," *She-Devil*), born Roseanne Barr, Salt Lake City, UT, Nov 3, 1953.

Philip (Phil) Simms, 45, sportscaster, former football player, born Lebanon, KY, Nov 3, 1956.

Monica Vitti (Monica Luisa Ceciarelli), 68, actress (*The Red Desert*), born Rome, Italy, Nov 3, 1933.

NOVEMBER 4 — SUNDAY
Day 308 — 57 Remaining

ASRT RADIATION THERAPY CONFERENCE. Nov 4–7. San Francisco, CA. Premier radiation therapy conference for radiation therapists, dosimetrists, educators, managers and students. Included in the program are a vast array of continuing education and refresher courses, business meetings, career opportunities, technical exhibits, poster displays and an essay competition. Additionally, an honorary presentation is scheduled to recognize a radiation therapist who has made a significant contribution to the profession of radiation. Est attendance: 100. For info: American Soc of Radiologic Technologists, 15000 Central Ave SE, Albuquerque, NM 87123-3917. Phone: (505) 298-4500 or (800) 444-2778. Fax: (505) 298-5063. E-mail: mktg@asrt.org. Web: www.asrt.org.

BALSAM, MARTIN: BIRTH ANNIVERSARY. Nov 4, 1919. Actor ("Archie Bunker's Place," *Twelve Angry Men*), born at New York, NY. Died at Rome, Italy, Feb 13, 1996.

ENGLAND: LONDON TO BRIGHTON VETERAN CAR RUN. Nov 4. London. A 57-mile run for a maximum of 400 veteran cars, along the A23 road from Serpentine Row, Hyde Park, London, to Madiera Drive, Brighton. Celebrates emancipation—

the abolition in 1896 of English law requiring that a man walk in front of motor vehicles carrying a red flag. Annually, the first Sunday in November. Est attendance: 10,000,000. For info: Motor Sports Assn, Events Dept, Slough, Riverside Park, Colnbrook, England SL3 OHG. Phone: (44) (1753) 681736. Fax: (44) (1753) 682938. E-mail: msa_mail@compuserve.com.

"THE FALL GUY" TV PREMIERE: 20th ANNIVERSARY. Nov 4, 1981. An hourlong adventure series, the story centered around a Hollywood stuntman, Colt Seavers (Lee Majors) who also moonlighted as a bounty-hunter, catching bail-jumpers. It also starred Douglas Barr, Heather Thomas, Jo Ann Pflug, Markie Post and Nedra Volz. Lee Majors also sang the theme song for the show.

ITALY: VICTORY DAY. Nov 4. Commemorates the signing of a WWI treaty by Austria in 1918, which resulted in the transfer of Trentino and Trieste from Austria to Italy.

KING TUT TOMB DISCOVERY: ANNIVERSARY. Nov 4, 1922. In 1922, one of the most important archaeological discoveries of modern times occurred at Luxor, Egypt. It was the tomb of Egypt's child-king, Tutankhamen, who became pharaoh at the age of nine and died, probably in the year 1352 BC, when he was 19. Perhaps the only ancient Egyptian royal tomb to have escaped plundering by grave robbers, it was discovered more than 3,000 years after Tutankhamen's death by English archaeologist Howard Carter, leader of an expedition financed by Lord Carnarvon. The priceless relics yielded by King Tut's tomb were placed in Egypt's National Museum at Cairo.

MAPPLETHORPE, ROBERT: 55th BIRTH ANNIVERSARY. Nov 4, 1946. Born at Floral Park, NY, Mapplethorpe was one of photography's most controversial artists, known initially for his photographs of sadomasochistic rituals and later for his still lifes, nudes and portraits. Mapplethorpe died at Boston, Mar 9, 1989. Exhibits of his work sparked controversy in 1989 and 1990, leading to intense political debate about the funding practices of the National Endowment for the Arts when its charter was up for renewal by Congress. An exhibition of his work in Cincinnati led to the arrest of the museum's curator, causing an additional uproar over First Amendment freedoms and obscenity issues.

MISCHIEF NIGHT. Nov 4. Observed in England, Australia and New Zealand. Nov 4, the eve of Guy Fawkes Day, is occasion for bonfires and firecrackers to commemorate failure of the plot to blow up the Houses of Parliament Nov 5, 1605. See also: "England: Guy Fawkes Day" (Nov 5).

NATIONAL CHEMISTRY WEEK. Nov 4–10. To celebrate the contributions of chemistry to modern life and to help the public understand that chemistry affects every part of our lives. Activities include an array of outreach programs such as open houses, contests, workshops, exhibits and classroom visits. 10 million participants nationwide. For info: Natl Chemistry Week Office, American Chemical Soc, 1155 16th St NW, Washington, DC 20036. Phone: (202) 872-6078. Fax: (202) 833-7722. E-mail: ncw@acs.org. Web: www.acs.org/ncw.

NATIONAL OSTEOPATHIC MEDICINE WEEK. Nov 4–10 (tentative). For info: American Osteopathic Assn, 142 E Ontario St, Chicago, IL 60611. Phone: (800) 621-1773. Web: www.aoa-net.org.

NATIONAL RADIOLOGIC TECHNOLOGY WEEK. Nov 4–10. Increases public awareness of the health professionals who utilize medical radiation and diagnostic imaging techniques to aid in the diagnosis and treatment of disease. Held during the week of Nov 8 to celebrate the discovery of the X-ray in 1895 by Wilhelm Conrad Roentgen. For info: American Soc of Radiologic Technologists, 15000 Central Ave SE, Albuquerque, NM 87123-3917. Phone: (505) 298-4500 or (800) 444-2778. Fax: (505) 298-5063. Web: www.asrt.org.

NATIONAL SPLIT PEA SOUP WEEK. Nov 4–10. To promote the use and enjoyment of split pea soup. For info: Peter Klaiber, USA Dry Pea & Lentil Council, 2780 W Pullman Rd, Moscow, ID 83843-4024. Phone: (208) 882-3023. Fax: (208) 882-6406. E-mail: pulse@pea-lentil.com.

NEW YORK CITY MARATHON. Nov 4. New York, NY. 30,000 runners from all over the world gather to compete with more than two million spectators watching from the sidelines. For info: Phone: (212) 423-2249. Web: www.nycmarathon.org.

"ONE MAN'S FAMILY" TV PREMIERE: ANNIVERSARY. Nov 4, 1949. This series occurred at the same time as the popular radio continuing drama. In the first season, the cast included Bert Lytell as Henry Barbour, a wealthy San Francisco stockbroker and Marjorie Gateson as his wife Fanny. Also included were Eva Marie Saint and Tony Randall. The second time the show came to TV it was a 15-minute serial and had an entirely new cast.

PANAMA: FLAG DAY. Nov 4. Public holiday.

PHILLPOTTS, EDEN: BIRTH ANNIVERSARY. Nov 4, 1862. English novelist, poet and playwright, born at Mount Abu, Rajasthan, India. A friend of Arnold Bennett, Phillpotts wrote more than a hundred novels. He died near Exeter, England, Dec 29, 1960.

ROGERS, WILL: BIRTH ANNIVERSARY. Nov 4, 1879. William Penn Adair Rogers, American writer, actor, humorist and grassroots philosopher, born at Oologah, Indian Territory (now Oklahoma). With aviator Wiley Post, he was killed in an airplane crash near Point Barrow, AK, Aug 15, 1935. "My forefathers," he said, "didn't come over on the *Mayflower*, but they met the boat."

SEIZURE OF US EMBASSY IN TEHERAN: ANNIVERSARY. Nov 4, 1979. About 500 Iranians seized the US Embassy in Teheran, taking some 90 hostages, of whom about 60 were Americans. They vowed to hold the hostages until the former Shah, Mohammed Reza Pahlavi (in the US for medical treatments), was returned to Iran for trial. The Shah died July 27, 1980, in an Egyptian military hospital near Cairo. The remaining 52 American hostages were released and left Teheran on Jan 20, 1981, after 444 days of captivity. The release occurred on America's Presidential Inauguration Day, during the hour in which the American presidency was transferred from Jimmy Carter to Ronald Reagan.

UNESCO: 55th ANNIVERSARY. Nov 4, 1946. The United Nations Educational, Scientific and Cultural Organization was formed.

WILL ROGERS DAY. Nov 4. Oklahoma.

BIRTHDAYS TODAY

Art Carney, 83, actor (Oscar for *Harry and Tonto*; six Emmys for "The Honeymooners"), born Mount Vernon, NY, Nov 4, 1918.

Sean "Puffy" Combs, 31, rapper known as Puff Daddy, born New York, NY, Nov 4, 1970.

Walter Leland Cronkite, Jr, 85, journalist (former anchorman for "CBS Evening News"), born St. Joseph, MO, Nov 4, 1916.

Kathy Griffin, 35, comedienne, actress ("Suddenly Susan"), born Chicago, IL, Nov 4, 1966.

Ralph Macchio, 39, actor ("Eight Is Enough," *The Karate Kid*), born Huntington, NY, Nov 4, 1962.

Andrea McArdle, 38, singer, actress (Broadway's *Annie*), born Philadelphia, PA, Nov 4, 1963.

Matthew McConaughey, 32, actor (*Dazed and Confused, A Time to Kill*), born Uvalde, TX, Nov 4, 1969.

Orlando Pace, 26, football player, born Sandusky, OH, Nov 4, 1975.

Markie Post, 51, actress ("Night Court," "Hearts Afire"), born Palo Alto, CA, Nov 4, 1950.

Doris Roberts, 71, actress ("Everybody Loves Raymond," "Remington Steele"), born St. Louis, MO, Nov 4, 1930.

Loretta Swit, 64, actress ("M*A*S*H"), born Passaic, NJ, Nov 4, 1937.

NOVEMBER 5 — MONDAY
Day 309 — 56 Remaining

AUSTRALIA: RECREATION DAY. Nov 5. The first Monday in November is observed as Recreation Day at Northern Tasmania, Australia.

DEAR SANTA LETTER WEEK. Nov 5–9. Consumer advocate Bob O'Brien answers "Dear Santa" letters for the holiday season. For info: Bob O'Brien, Consumer Advocate, PO Box 2356, Secaucus, NJ 07096. Phone: (201) 860-1595. Fax: (201) 865-4775. E-mail: bobconsumeradvocate@excite.com. Web: www .consumeradvocateobrien.com.

DEBS, EUGENE VICTOR: BIRTH ANNIVERSARY. Nov 5, 1855. American politician, first president of the American Railway Union, founder of the Social Democratic Party of America, and Socialist Party candidate for president of the US in 1904, 1908, 1912 and 1920, sentenced to 10-year prison term in 1918 (for sedition) and pardoned by President Harding in 1921. Debs was born at Terre Haute, IN, and died at Elmhurst, IL, Oct 20, 1926.

DURANT, WILL: BIRTH ANNIVERSARY. Nov 5, 1885. American author and popularizer of history and philosophy. Among his books: *The Story of Philosophy* and *The Story of Civilization* (a 10-volume series of which the last four were coauthored by his wife, Ariel). Born at North Adams, MA, and died Nov 7, 1981, at Los Angeles, CA.

ENGLAND: GUY FAWKES DAY. Nov 5. United Kingdom. Anniversary of the "Gunpowder Plot." Conspirators planned to blow up the Houses of Parliament and King James I, Nov 5, 1605 (OS). Twenty barrels of gunpowder, which they had secreted in a cellar under Parliament, were discovered on the night of Nov 4, the very eve of the intended explosion, and the conspirators were arrested. They were tried and convicted, and Jan 31, 1606, eight (including Guy Fawkes) were beheaded and their heads displayed on pikes at London Bridge. Though there were at least 11

		S	M	T	W	T	F	S
November						1	2	3
2001		4	5	6	7	8	9	10
		11	12	13	14	15	16	17
		18	19	20	21	22	23	24
		25	26	27	28	29	30	

conspirators, Guy Fawkes is most remembered. In 1606, the Parliament, which was to have been annihilated, enacted a law establishing Nov 5 as a day of public thanksgiving. It is still observed, and on the night of Nov 5, "the whole country lights up with bonfires and celebration." "Guys" are burned in effigy and the old verses repeated: "Remember, remember the fifth of November,/Gunpowder treason and plot;/I see no reason why Gunpowder Treason/Should ever be forgot."

KIDS' GOALS EDUCATION WEEK. Nov 5–9. Encourage parents to foster goal-setting habits in their children's lives so that their children can make their dreams come true. For info: Gary Ryan Blair, The GoalsGuy, 911 East Klosterman Rd, Tarpon Springs, FL 34689. Phone: (877) GOALSGUY. Fax: (800) 731-GOAL. E-mail: kgew@goalsguy.com. Web: www.goalsguy .com.

LOEWY, RAYMOND: BIRTH ANNIVERSARY. Nov 5, 1893. Raymond Fernand Loewy, the "father of streamlining," an inventor, engineer and industrial designer whose ideas changed the look of 20th-century life, was born at Paris, France. His designs are evident in almost every area of modern life—the US Postal Service logo, the president's airplane, *Air Force One*, in streamlined automobiles, trains, refrigerators and pens. "Between two products equal in price, function and quality," he said, "the better looking will outsell the other." Loewy died at Monte Carlo, July 14, 1986.

MAXWELL, ROBERT: 10th DEATH ANNIVERSARY. Nov 5, 1991. Media mogul Robert Maxwell's mysterious death added more controversy to his already controversial and intriguing larger-than-life story. Born Jan Ludwig Hoch to a poor farm family in the Carpathian mountains of Czechoslovakia, he ended his life a billionaire with a media empire that included TV stations in France, Macmillan Publishing Company in the US, newspapers in Hungary and the former East Germany, MTV Europe, the only official English language newspaper in China and two of the biggest tabloids in the English-speaking world: New York's *Daily News* and London's *Daily Mirror*. He earned his first million publishing scientific books. After a brief career as a member of Parliament, he began his rise as a media baron. Maxwell died after falling overboard from his yacht near the Canary Islands. After his death, his empire was found to be in significant financial disrepair.

McCREA, JOEL: BIRTH ANNIVERSARY. Nov 5, 1905. American actor Joel McCrea was born at South Pasadena, CA. His more than 80 films include *Wells Fargo* (1937), *Union Pacific* (1939), *Sullivan's Travels* (1941) and *Foreign Correspondent* (1940). He died Oct 20, 1990, at Los Angeles, CA.

"THE NAT KING COLE SHOW" TV PREMIERE: 45th ANNIVERSARY. Nov 5, 1956. A popular African American pianist and singer, Cole hosted his own variety show for NBC. The Nelson Riddle Orchestra and the Randy Van Horne Singers also appeared as regulars on the show. It began as a 15-minute show which was expanded to half an hour. The show was dropped as a result of lack of sponsorship and because many affiliates declined to carry it.

NEW YORK WEEKLY JOURNAL: FIRST ISSUE ANNIVERSARY. Nov 5, 1733. John Peter Zenger, colonial American printer and journalist, published the first issue of the *New York Weekly Journal* newspaper. He was arrested and imprisoned on Nov 17, 1734, for libel. The trial remains an important landmark in the history of the struggle for freedom of the press. See also: "Zenger, John P.: Arrest Anniversary" (Nov 17).

ROGERS, ROY: BIRTH ANNIVERSARY. Nov 5, 1912. Known as the "King of the Cowboys," Rogers was born Leonard Slye at Cincinnati, OH. His many songs included "Don't Fence Me In" and "Happy Trails to You." He made his acting debut in *Under Western Stars* in 1935 and later hosted his own show, "The Roy Rogers Show," in 1951. Rogers died at Apple Valley, CA, July 6, 1998. See also: "The Roy Rogers Show" TV Premiere: Anniversary (Dec 30).

TARBELL, IDA M.: BIRTH ANNIVERSARY. Nov 5, 1857. American writer born at Erie County, PA. She edited the muck-raking journal, *McClure's Magazine*, which exposed the political and industrial corruption of the day and emphasized the need for reform. Died at Bethel, CT, Jan 6, 1944.

BIRTHDAYS TODAY

Bryan Adams, 42, singer ("Heaven," "Summer of '69"), songwriter ("Everything I Do"), born Vancouver, British Columbia, Canada, Nov 5, 1959.

Arthur (Art) Garfunkel, 60, singer (Simon and Garfunkel), actor (*Carnal Knowledge*), born Forest Hills, NY, Nov 5, 1941.

Javy Lopez, 31, baseball player, born Ponce, Puerto Rico, Nov 5, 1970.

Corin Nemec, 30, actor ("Parker Lewis Can't Lose," *Tucker: The Man and His Dream*), born Little Rock, AR, Nov 5, 1971.

Tatum O'Neal, 38, actress (Oscar for *Paper Moon*; *Bad News Bears*), born Los Angeles, CA, Nov 5, 1963.

Sam Shepard (Samuel Shepard Rogers), 58, dramatist, actor (*Buried Child*, *The Right Stuff*), born Ft Sheridan, IL, Nov 5, 1943.

Elke Sommer (Elke Schletze), 60, actress (*A Shot in the Dark*, *The Prize*), born Berlin, Germany, Nov 5, 1941.

Jerry Stackhouse, 27, basketball player, born Kinston, NC, Nov 5, 1974.

Ike Turner, 70, singer (Ike and Tina Turner Revue), born Clarksdale, MS, Nov 5, 1931.

Bill Walton, 49, Basketball Hall of Famer, NBA Most Valuable Player, born Mesa, CA, Nov 5, 1952.

Geoffrey Wolff, 64, author (*The Duke of Deception*, *The Age of Consent*), born Los Angeles, CA, Nov 5, 1937.

NOVEMBER 6 — TUESDAY
Day 310 — 55 Remaining

CHRISTMAS AT BILTMORE ESTATE. Nov 6–Jan 1, 2002. Biltmore Estate, Asheville, NC. Christmas is celebrated in much the same fashion as it was in 1895 when George Vanderbilt formally opened Biltmore House. The celebration includes spectacular Victorian Christmas decorations, holiday music performed daily and more than 30 Christmas trees throughout the house. Closed Nov 22 and Dec 25. Est attendance: 225,000. For info: The Biltmore Estate, 1 N Pack Square, Asheville, NC 28801. Phone: (800) 543-2961. Web: www.biltmore.com.

GENERAL ELECTION DAY. Nov 6. Annually, the first Tuesday after the first Monday in November. Many state and local government elections are held on this day, as well as presidential and congressional elections in the appropriate years. All US Congressional seats and one-third of US Senatorial seats are up for election in even-numbered years. Presidential elections are held in even-numbered years that can be divided equally by four. This day is a state holiday in 12 states.

"GOOD MORNING AMERICA" TV PREMIERE: ANNIVERSARY. Nov 6, 1975. This ABC morning program, set in a living room, is a mixture of news reports, features and interviews with newsmakers and people of interest. It was the first program to compete with NBC's "Today" show and initially aired as "A.M. America." Hosts have included David Hartman, Nancy Dussault, Sandy Hill, Charles Gibson, Joan Lunden, Lisa McRee, Kevin Newman and Diane Sawyer.

HALFWAY POINT OF AUTUMN. Nov 6. On this day, 45.5 days of autumn will have elapsed and the equivalent will remain before Dec 21, 2001, which is the winter solstice and the beginning of winter.

"MEET THE PRESS" TV PREMIERE: ANNIVERSARY. Nov 6, 1947. "Meet the Press" holds the distinction of being the oldest program on TV. It originally debuted on radio in 1945. The show has changed its format little since it began: a well-known guest (usually a politician) is questioned on current, relevant issues by a panel of journalists. The moderators throughout the years have included Martha Rountree, Lawrence E. Spivak, Ned Brooks,

Bill Monroe, Marvin Kalb, Chris Wallace and Garrick Utley with the current host being Tim Russert.

MOROCCO: ANNIVERSARY OF THE GREEN MARCH. Nov 6. National holiday. Commemorates the march into the Spanish Sahara in 1975 to claim the land for Morocco.

NAISMITH, JAMES: BIRTH ANNIVERSARY. Nov 6, 1861. Inventor of the game of basketball was born at Almonte, Ontario, Canada. Died at Lawrence, KS, Nov 28, 1939. Inducted into the Basketball Hall of Fame in 1959. Basketball became an Olympic sport in 1936.

PADEREWSKI, IGNACE JAN: BIRTH ANNIVERSARY. Nov 6, 1860. Polish composer, pianist, patriot born at Kurylowka, Podolia, Poland. He died at New York, NY, June 29, 1941. When Poland fell into the hands of the Soviets after WWII, his family decided he would remain buried in Arlington National Cemetery. In May 1963, President John F. Kennedy dedicated a plaque to Paderewski's memory and declared that the pianist would rest in Arlington until Poland was free. Paderewski's remains were returned to his native country on June 29, 1992, the 51st anniversary of his death, after Poland held its first parliamentary election following its independence from the Soviet Union.

"THE PHIL DONAHUE SHOW" TV PREMIERE: ANNIVERSARY. Nov 6, 1967. The forerunner of Oprah, Jerry, Montel, etc, this first talk show with audience participation went on the air on this date at Dayton, OH. The first guest interviewed by host Phil Donahue was atheist Madalyn Murray O'Hair. In 1970, the program went national; it moved to Chicago in 1974 and to New York in 1985. In later years the program was titled "Donahue." After winning 19 Emmy Awards, the show left daytime TV in 1996.

SAXOPHONE DAY (ADOLPHE SAX BIRTH ANNIVERSARY). Nov 6. A day to recognize the birth anniversary of Adolphe Sax, Belgian musician and inventor of the saxophone and the saxotromba. Born at Dinant, Belgium, in 1814, Antoine Joseph Sax, later known as Adolphe, was the eldest of 11 children of a musical instrument builder. Sax contributed an entire family of brass wind instruments for band and orchestra use. He was accorded fame and great wealth, but business misfortunes led to bankruptcy. Sax died in poverty at Paris, Feb 7, 1894.

SOUSA, JOHN PHILIP: BIRTH ANNIVERSARY. Nov 6, 1854. American composer and band conductor, remembered for stirring marches such as "The Stars and Stripes Forever," "Semper Fidelis," "El Capitan," born at Washington, DC. Died at Reading, PA, Mar 6, 1932. See also: "The Stars and Stripes Forever Day: Anniversary" (May 14).

SWEDEN: GUSTAVUS ADOLPHUS DAY. Nov 6. Honors Sweden's King and military leader killed in 1632.

BIRTHDAYS TODAY

Ray Conniff, 85, bandleader, born Attleboro, MA, Nov 6, 1916.

Sally Field, 55, actress (Oscars for *Norma Rae, Places in the Heart*; Emmy for *Sybil*), born Pasadena, CA, Nov 6, 1946.

Glenn Frey, 53, musician, songwriter, singer ("The Heat Is On"), born Detroit, MI, Nov 6, 1948.

Nigel Havers, 52, actor (*Chariots of Fire, Empire of the Sun*), born London, England, Nov 6, 1949.

Ethan Hawke, 31, actor (*Dead Poets Society, Reality Bites*), born Austin, TX, Nov 6, 1970.

Lance Kerwin, 41, actor ("James at 15," "The Family Holvak"), born Newport Beach, CA, Nov 6, 1960.

Mike Nichols (Michael Igor Peschkowsky), 70, comedian, actor, theater producer, director, filmmaker (Oscar for *The Graduate; Working Girl*), born Berlin, Germany, Nov 6, 1931.

Rebecca Romijn-Stamos, 29, model, host (MTV's "House of Style"), born Berkeley, CA, Nov 6, 1972.

Maria Owings Shriver, 46, broadcast journalist ("Today"), born Chicago, IL, Nov 6, 1955.

NOVEMBER 7 — WEDNESDAY

Day 311 — 54 Remaining

CAMUS, ALBERT: BIRTH ANNIVERSARY. Nov 7, 1913. French writer and philosopher, winner of the Nobel Prize for Literature in 1957, was born at Mondavi, Algeria. "The struggle to reach the top is itself enough to fulfill the heart of man. One must believe that Sisyphus is happy," he wrote, in *Le Mythe de Sisyphe*. Camus was killed in an automobile accident in France, Jan 4, 1960.

CANADA: CANADIAN FINALS RODEO. Nov 7–11. Edmonton, AB. It's always a wild ride as the top cowboys and cowgirls in the country compete for national titles and record prize money at the Canadian Finals Rodeo (CFR). CFR is one of the largest annual indoor sporting events in Canada. Each of the six performances features bull riding, bareback riding, saddle bronc riding, calf roping, steer wrestling and ladies' barrel racing. CFR's heart-stopping rodeo action sizzles with glittering western pageantry and dynamic entertainers. CFR will also be accompanied by dozens of western-related events during Be Seen In Jeans Week, an annual civic celebration. Est attendance: 90,000. For info: Kate Rogers, Marketing Coord, Northlands Park, PO Box 1480, Edmonton, AB, Canada T5J 2N5. Phone: (780) 471-7210. Fax: (780) 471-8176. E-mail: krogers@northlands.com. Web: www.northlands.com.

CANADIAN PACIFIC RAILWAY: TRANSCONTINENTAL COMPLETION ANNIVERSARY. Nov 7, 1885. At 9:30 AM the last spike was driven at Craigellachie, British Columbia, completing the Canadian Pacific Railway's 2,980-mile transcontinental railroad track between Montreal, Quebec, in the east and Port Moody, British Columbia, in the west.

November 2001	S	M	T	W	T	F	S
					1	2	3
	4	5	6	7	8	9	10
	11	12	13	14	15	16	17
	18	19	20	21	22	23	24
	25	26	27	28	29	30	

CHRISTMAS GIFT AND HOBBY SHOW. Nov 7–11. West Pavilion, Indiana State Fairgrounds, Indianapolis, IN. 52nd annual event. Selling show of arts, crafts, collectibles and other gift items. Est attendance: 60,000. For info: Debbie Bossi, Show Mgr, HSI Show Productions, Box 502797, Indianapolis, IN 46250. Phone: (317) 576-9933. Fax: (317) 576-9955.

CONTINENT-SIZED WINDSTORMS DISCOVERED: 10th ANNIVERSARY. Nov 7, 1991. A satellite that had been launched from the space shuttle *Discovery* on Sept 15, 1991, discovered large windstorms in Earth's upper atmosphere. The satellite's 10 instruments became functional on Nov 7 and detected the continent-sized windstorms, which measured up to 200 mile-per-hour velocities in areas that are 600 to 6,000 miles wide in the mesosphere. The largest storm was discovered in the Southern hemisphere and reached from western Australia eastward to points halfway across the Atlantic Ocean.

CURIE, MARIE SKLODOWSKA: BIRTH ANNIVERSARY. Nov 7, 1867. Polish chemist and physicist, born at Warsaw, Poland. In 1903 she was awarded, with her husband, the Nobel Prize for physics for their discovery of the element radium. Died near Sallanches, France, July 4, 1934.

"FACE THE NATION" TV PREMIERE: ANNIVERSARY. Nov 7, 1954. The CBS counterpart to NBC's "Meet the Press," this show employed a similar format: panelists interviewed a well-known guest. In 1983 the panel was changed to include experts in addition to journalists when Lesley Stahl succeeded George Herman as moderator. Though usually produced at Washington, DC, the show occasionally interviewed people elsewhere (such as Khrushchev in Moscow in 1957).

FIRST BLACK GOVERNOR ELECTED: ANNIVERSARY. Nov 7, 1989. L. Douglas Wilder was elected governor of Virginia, becoming the first elected black governor in US history. Wilder had previously served as lieutenant governor of Virginia.

GREAT OCTOBER SOCIALIST REVOLUTION: ANNIVERSARY. Nov 7, 1917. This holiday in the old Soviet Union was observed for two days with parades, military displays and appearances by Soviet leaders. In the mid-1990s, President Yeltsin issued a decree renaming the holiday the "Day of National Reconciliation and Agreement." According to the old Russian calendar, the revolution took place Oct 25, 1917. Soviet calendar reform causes observance to fall Nov 7 (Gregorian). The Bolshevik Revolution began at Petrograd, Russia, on the evening of Nov 6 (Gregorian), 1917. A new government headed by Nikolai Lenin took office the following day under the name Council of People's Commissars. Leon Trotsky was commissar for foreign affairs and Josef Stalin became commissar of national minorities.

JAGGER, DEAN: BIRTH ANNIVERSARY. Nov 7, 1903. American actor Dean Jagger was born at Columbus Grove, OH. Predominantly a character actor, he appeared in more than 120 films, including *Twelve O'Clock High* (1950), for which he won an Oscar for best supporting actor. He died Feb 5, 1991, at Santa Monica, CA.

NATIONAL ASSOCIATION FOR GIFTED CHILDREN CONVENTION. Nov 7–11. Cincinnati, OH. Educational sessions for administrators, counselors, coordinators, teachers and parents. Est attendance: 3,000. For info: Natl Assn for Gifted Children, 1707 L St NW, Ste 550, Washington, DC 20036. Phone: (202) 785-4268.

NIXON'S "LAST" PRESS CONFERENCE: ANNIVERSARY. Nov 7, 1962. Richard M. Nixon, having been narrowly defeated in his bid for the presidency by John F. Kennedy in the 1960 election, returned to politics two years later as a candidate for governor of California in the election of Nov 6, 1962. Defeated again (this time by incumbent governor Edmund G. Brown), Nixon held his "last" press conference with assembled reporters in Los Angeles at mid-morning the next day at which he said: ." . . just think how much you're going to be missing. You won't have Nixon to kick around any more, because, gentlemen, this is my last press conference."

NOTARY PUBLIC DAY AND NOTARY PUBLIC WEEK.
Nov 7 and Nov 1–7. To recognize the fundamental contributions made by notaries to the law and the people of the US. For info: Lisa Fisher, Exec Dir, American Soc of Notaries, PO Box 5707, Tallahassee, FL 32314-5707. Phone: (800) 522-3392 or (850) 671-5164. Fax: (850) 671-5165. E-mail: mail@notaries.org. Web: www.notaries.org.

OLD STOUGHTON MUSICAL SOCIETY: ANNIVERSARY. Nov 7, 1786. Founded at Stoughton, MA, the Stoughton Musical Society is the oldest choral society in the US. Originally consisting of 25 men, it now includes both men and women. The society performed at the Chicago World's Columbian Exposition in 1893.

REPUBLICAN SYMBOL: ANNIVERSARY. Nov 7, 1874. Thomas Nast used an elephant to represent the Republican Party in a satirical cartoon in *Harper's Weekly*. Today the elephant is still a well-recognized symbol for the Republican Party in political cartoons.

ROOSEVELT ELECTED TO FOURTH TERM: ANNIVERSARY. Nov 7, 1944. Defeating Thomas Dewey, Franklin D. Roosevelt became the first, and only, person elected to four terms as President of the US. Roosevelt was inaugurated the following Jan 20 but died in office Apr 12, 1945, serving only 53 days of the fourth term.

RUSSIA: OCTOBER REVOLUTION. Nov 7. National holiday in Russia and Ukraine. Commemorates the Great Socialist Revolution which occurred in October 1917 under the Old Style calendar. In 1997, the holiday was renamed the "Day of National Reconciliation and Agreement."

BIRTHDAYS TODAY

Billy (William Franklin) Graham, 83, evangelist, born Charlotte, NC, Nov 7, 1918.
Jeremy London, 29, actor ("I'll Fly Away," "Party of Five"), born San Diego, CA, Nov 7, 1972.
Joni Mitchell (Roberta Joan Anderson), 58, singer, songwriter ("Both Sides Now," "Big Yellow Taxi," "Woodstock"), born McLeod, Alberta, Canada, Nov 7, 1943.
Barry Newman, 63, actor ("Petrocelli," *Vanishing Point*), born Boston, MA, Nov 7, 1938.
Johnny Rivers, 59, singer ("Poor Side of Town," "Secret Agent Man"), born John Ramistella, New York, NY, Nov 7, 1942.
Joan Sutherland, 75, opera singer, born Sydney, Australia, Nov 7, 1926.
Mary Travers, 64, composer, singer (Peter, Paul and Mary, "Blowin' in the Wind"), born Louisville, KY, Nov 7, 1937.

NOVEMBER 8 — THURSDAY
Day 312 — 53 Remaining

ABET AND AID PUNSTERS DAY. Nov 8. Laugh instead of groan at incredibly dreadful puns. All-time greatest triple pun: "Though he's not very humble, there's no police like Holmes," from the register of worst puns of Punsters Unlimited. (Originated by Earl Harris, retired, and the late William Rabe.)

COOK SOMETHING BOLD AND PUNGENT DAY. Nov 8. Especially for those of us who have tightly closed up the house against chill weather for the next six months. Now is the time to create the heavenly, homey odor of pungently bold cooking. Don't

forget the sauerkraut and garlic! Sponsored by Wellcat Holidays [© 2000 WH]. For info: Thomas or Ruth Roy, 2418 Long Ln, Lebanon, PA 17046. Phone: (717) 279-0184. E-mail: wellcat @supernet.com. Web: www.wellcat.com.

CORTÉS CONQUERS MEXICO: ANNIVERSARY. Nov 8, 1519. After landing on the Yucatan peninsula in April, Spaniard Hernan Cortés and his troops marched into the interior of Mexico to the Aztec capital and took the Aztec emperor Montezuma hostage.

"DAYS OF OUR LIVES" TV PREMIERE: ANNIVERSARY. Nov 8, 1965. This popular daytime serial, like many others, has gone through many changes throughout its run. It expanded from 30 minutes to an hour; it went to number one in the ratings and slipped to nine out of 12 in the 1980s; and it dropped or deemphasized older characters, which angered its audience. The soap is set in Salem and centers around the Horton and Brady families. Notable cast members included Mary Frann, Joan Van Ark, Susan Oliver, Mike Farrell, Kristian Alfonso, Garry Marshall, John Aniston, Josh Taylor, Wayne Northrop, John DeLancie, Andrea Barber, Deidre Hall, Thaao Penghlis, Jason Bernard, Marilyn McCoo, Charles Shaughnessy, Peter Reckell, Francis Reid, Patsy Pease and Genie Francis.

HALLEY, EDMUND: BIRTH ANNIVERSARY. Nov 8, 1656 (OS). Astronomer and mathematician born at London, England. Astronomer Royal, 1721–42. Died at Greenwich, England, Jan 14, 1742 (OS). He observed the great comet of 1682 (now named for him), first conceived its periodicity and wrote in his *Synopsis of Comet Astronomy*: ." . . I may venture to foretell that this Comet will return again in the year 1758." It did, and Edmund Halley's memory is kept alive by the once-every-generation appearance of Halley's Comet. There have been 28 recorded appearances of this comet since 240 BC. Average time between appearances is 76 years. Halley's Comet is next expected to be visible in 2061.

INTERNATIONAL GIFT FESTIVAL. Nov 8–10. Fairfield, PA. Traditional handcrafts from more than 30 countries. Est attendance: 4,500. For info: Gettysburg CVB, PO Box 4117, Gettysburg, PA 17325. Phone: (717) 334-6274. Fax: (717) 334-1166. Web: www.gettysburg.com.

MERCHANT SAILING SHIP PRESERVATION DAY: 60th ANNIVERSARY. Nov 8, 1941. The whaler *Charles W. Morgan* arrived at Mystic, CT, to be restored. This was the beginning of the modern era of preservation of merchant sailing ships.

MITCHELL, MARGARET: BIRTH ANNIVERSARY. Nov 8, 1900. American novelist who won a Pulitzer Prize (1937) for her only book, *Gone with the Wind*, a romantic novel about the Civil War and Reconstruction. *Gone with the Wind* sold about 10,000,000 copies and was translated into 30 languages. Born at Atlanta, GA, Mitchell died there after being struck by an automobile Aug 16, 1949.

MONTANA: ADMISSION DAY: ANNIVERSARY. Nov 8. Became 41st state in 1889.

MOON PHASE: LAST QUARTER. Nov 8. Moon enters Last Quarter phase at 7:21 AM, EST.

MOUNT HOLYOKE COLLEGE FOUNDED: ANNIVER-SARY. Nov 8, 1837. The first college for women in the United States was founded as Mt. Holyoke Seminary in 1837 at South Hadley, MA. While many colleges for women became coeducational institutions in the 1970s and 1980s, Mt. Holyoke remains a women's college.

NATIONAL AMPLE TIME DAY. Nov 8. One day set aside each year to recognize the importance of time management, making Ample Time in one's life for priorities to make the most of each day and live a completely fulfilling life. Annually, Nov 8. For info: Lorie Hicks, Corporate Challenges Consulting, 5222 East 78th Pl, Tulsa, OK 74136. Phone: (918) 477-7779.

PAPERWORKS AND PHOTOWORKS. Nov 8–30. St. Simons Island, GA. A juried exhibit designed to showcase and explore the various artistic expressions utilizing paper as the primary medium. Also includes Photo/National exhibit which is a juried exhibit created to demonstrate the wide dimensions of the photographic world today. Deadline: Sept 18. For info: Coastal Center for the Arts, 2012 Demere Rd, St. Simons Island, GA 31522. Phone: (912) 634-0404.

PURSUIT OF HAPPINESS WEEK. Nov 8–14. The purpose of this week is to remind everyone, as stated in the Declaration of Independence, that all men and women are "endowed by their Creator with certain unalienable rights, that among them are life, liberty and the pursuit of happiness." For complete info and quotations about happiness by famous people, send $4 to cover expense of printing, handling and postage. For info: Dr. Stanley Drake, Pres, Intl Soc of Friendship and Goodwill, 8592 Roswell Rd, Ste 434, Atlanta, GA 30350-1870.

RETURN DAY. Nov 8. Georgetown, DE. The day when officially tabulated election returns are read from the balcony of Georgetown's red brick, Greek Revival courthouse to the throngs of voters assembled below. Always the second day after a general election. An official "half-holiday" in Sussex County. Reportedly Return Day has become so popular "that it is for all intents and purposes a state holiday as well."

SOUTHERN CHRISTMAS SHOW. Nov 8–18. Charlotte, NC. Show filled with exquisite art and crafts from nationally known artisans. Ideas for decorating trees, mantels, doors and wreaths; festive foods for holiday celebrations from fresh hot strudel to plum pudding. Gifts for everyone on your holiday list. Plus cooking demonstrations, Christmas Tree Lane, Santa Claus, Olde Towne Craft demonstrations and musical performances. Est attendance: 130,000. For info: Christine Swan, Asst Show Mgr, Southern Shows, Inc, PO Box 36859, Charlotte, NC 28236. Phone: (704) 376-6594. Fax: (704) 376-6345. E-mail: cswan@southern shows.com.

X-RAY DISCOVERY DAY: ANNIVERSARY. Nov 8, 1895. Physicist Wilhelm Conrad Roentgen (q.v.) discovered X-rays, beginning a new era in physics and medicine. Although X-rays had been observed previously, it was Roentgen, a professor at the University of Wurzburg (Germany), who successfully repeated X-ray experimentation and who is credited with the discovery.

☆　☆　☆

		S	M	T	W	T	F	S
November						1	2	3
2001		4	5	6	7	8	9	10
		11	12	13	14	15	16	17
		18	19	20	21	22	23	24
		25	26	27	28	29	30	

Edgardo Alfonzo, 28, baseball player, born St. Teresa, Venezuela, Nov 8, 1973.
Christiaan Barnard, 79, South African surgeon who performed the first human heart transplant in 1967, born Beaufort West, South Africa, Nov 8, 1922.
Mary Hart, 50, TV host, born Madison, SD, Nov 8, 1951.
June Havoc, 85, actress (*Brewster's Millions*, "Willy"), born Vancouver, British Columbia, Canada, Nov 8, 1916.
Christie Hefner, 49, business executive (*Playboy*), daughter of Hugh Hefner, born Chicago, IL, Nov 8, 1952.
Ricki Lee Jones, 47, singer, musician ("Chuck E.'s In Love"), born Chicago, IL, Nov 8, 1954.
Virna Lisi, 64, actress (*How to Murder Your Wife, The Secret of Santa Vittoria*), born Ancona, Italy, Nov 8, 1937.
Patti Page (Clara Ann Fowler), 74, singer ("Let Me Go Lover," "Allegheny Moon"), born Clarence, OK, Nov 8, 1927.
Parker Posey, 33, actress (*The House of Yes*), born Baltimore, MD, Nov 8, 1968.
Bonnie Raitt, 52, singer ("Sweet Forgiveness"), actress, daughter of John Raitt, born Los Angeles, CA, Nov 8, 1949.
Morley Safer, 70, journalist ("60 Minutes"), born Toronto, Ontario, Canada, Nov 8, 1931.
Courtney Thorne-Smith, 34, actress ("Melrose Place," "Ally McBeal"), born San Francisco, CA, Nov 8, 1967.
Alfre Woodard, 48, actress (*Cross Creek, Miss Evers' Boys, How to Make an American Quilt*), born Tulsa, OK, Nov 8, 1953.

NOVEMBER 9 — FRIDAY
Day 313 — 52 Remaining

AGNEW, SPIRO THEODORE: BIRTH ANNIVER-SARY. Nov 9, 1918. Thirty-ninth vice president of the US, born at Baltimore, MD. Twice elected vice president (1968 and 1972), Agnew became the second person to resign that office Oct 10, 1973. Agnew entered a plea of no contest to a charge of income tax evasion (on contract kickbacks received while he was governor of Maryland and after he became vice president). He died Sept 17, 1996, at Berlin, MD. See also: "Vice Presidential Resignation: Anniversary" (Dec 28) and "Calhoun, John Caldwell: Birth Anniversary" (Mar 18).

BANNEKER, BENJAMIN: BIRTH ANNIVERSARY. Nov 9, 1731. Astronomer, mathematician, clockmaker, surveyor and almanac author, called "first black man of science." Took part in original survey of city of Washington. Banneker's *Almanac* was published 1792–97. Born at Elliott's Mills, MD, died at Baltimore, MD, Oct 9, 1806. A fire that started during his funeral destroyed his home, library, notebooks, almanac calculations, clocks and virtually all belongings and documents related to his life.

BERLIN WALL OPENED: ANNIVERSARY. Nov 9, 1989. After 28 years as a symbol of the Cold War, the Berlin Wall was opened on this evening, and citizens of both sides walked freely through the barrier as others danced atop the structure to celebrate the end of an historic era. Coming amidst the celebration of East Germany's 40-year anniversary, pro-democracy demonstrations led to the resignation of Erich Honecker, East Germany's head of state and party chief. It was Honecker who had supervised the construction of the 27.9-mile wall across the city during the night of Aug 13, 1961, because US President John Kennedy had ordered a troop build-up in response to the blockade of West Berlin by the Soviets.

BOSTON FIRE: ANNIVERSARY. Nov 9, 1872. Though Boston had experienced several damaging fires, the worst one started on this Saturday evening in a dry-goods warehouse. Spreading rapidly in windy weather, it devastated several blocks of the business district, destroying nearly 800 buildings. Damage was estimated at more than $75 million. It was said that the fire caused a bright red glare in the sky that could be seen from nearly 100 miles away. The Boston fire came one year, one month and one day after the Great Chicago Fire of Oct 8, 1871.

CAMBODIA: INDEPENDENCE DAY: ANNIVERSARY.
Nov 9. National Day. Declared independence from France in 1949.

CHRISTKINDL MARKT. Nov 9–11. Cultural Center, Canton, OH. Fine arts and crafts show and sale with a Christmas flair. Est attendance: 8,000. For info: Canton Museum of Art, 1001 Market Ave N, Canton, OH 44702. Phone: (330) 453-7666. Fax: (330) 453-1034. Web: www.catonart.org/events.html.

DANDRIDGE, DOROTHY: BIRTH ANNIVERSARY.
Nov 9, 1923. Actress and singer Dandridge was a child star, born at Cleveland, OH, who toured with her sisters, Vivian and Etta Jones, as The Dandridge Sisters. They played at the Cotton Club, sharing the stage with artists such as Cab Calloway and W.C. Handy. Dandridge went solo in 1941 to perform in Hollywood movies and on stage with the Desi Arnaz Band. Her big break came with the lead role in Otto Preminger's musical, *Carmen Jones*. Dandridge received an Oscar nomination for her performance. Unfortunately, Dandridge could not overcome Hollywood's racism and tendency to typecast and her career foundered. She died at West Hollywood, CA, Sept 8, 1965.

DODGE PRAIRIE CIRCUIT FINALS RODEO. Nov 9–10. Lazy E Arena, Guthrie, OK. The top 12 cowboys in each event from Oklahoma, Kansas and Nebraska compete for $60,000 and Circuit Championship Titles. Est attendance: 15,000. For info: Lazy E Arena, Route 5 Box 393, Guthrie, OK 73044. Phone: (405) 282-RIDE or (800) 595-RIDE. Fax: (405) 282-3785. E-mail: arena@lazye.com. Web: www.lazye.com.

EAST COAST BLACKOUT: ANNIVERSARY. Nov 9, 1965. Massive electric power failure starting in western New York state at 5:16 PM, cut electric power to much of northeastern US and Ontario and Quebec in Canada. More than 30 million persons in an area of 80,000 square miles were affected. The experience provoked studies of the vulnerability of 20th-century technology.

FOUR CORNER STATES BLUEGRASS FESTIVAL. Nov 9–11. Wickenburg, AZ. Old-time fiddle, banjo, mandolin, flat-pick guitar championships. Clogging and gospel music. Special entertainment by nationally known bands as well as 14 competitive events. Annually, the second weekend in November. Est attendance: 5,000. For info: J Brooks, Exec Dir, Chamber of Commerce, 216 N Frontier Street, Wickenburg, AZ 85390. Phone: (520) 684-5479 or (520) 684-0977. Fax: (520) 684-5470. E-mail: info@wickenburgchamber.com. Web: www.wickenburgchamber.com.

FRIENDS OF PLANNED PARENTHOOD BOOK FAIR.
Nov 9–11. Montgomery County Fairgrounds Coliseum, Dayton, OH. More than 250,000 used books, magazines and records on display. Excellent collectibles. For info: Friends of Planned Parenthood, 224 N Wilkinson St, Dayton, OH 45402. Phone: (937) 226-0780 ext 113.

FULBRIGHT, J. WILLIAM: BIRTH ANNIVERSARY.
Nov 9, 1905. US Senator, born at Sumner, MO. He sponsored the legislation that created the Fulbright scholarships for international study for graduate students, faculty and researchers. Died Feb 9, 1995.

GREATER PITTSBURGH ARTS & CRAFTS HOLIDAY SPECTACULAR. Nov 9–11. Expo Center at Greengate Mall, Greensburg, PA. Approximately 200 booths including pottery, jewelry, quilts, furniture, tole and decorative painting, leather, toys and much more. Find that perfect gift for the holidays. Est attendance: 17,000. For info: Debbie & Steve Stoner, PO Box 166, Irwin, PA 15642. Phone: (724) 863-4577. Fax: (724) 863-4577.

GRIMES, LEONARD ANDREW: BIRTH ANNIVERSARY. Nov 9, 1815. Reverend Leonard Grimes was born at Leesburg, VA, to parents who were free. A free black man living at Washington, DC, he despised slavery and became active in assisting fugitive slaves to escape. He was caught and imprisoned at Richmond, VA. After his release he founded and became the first minister of the Twelfth Street Baptist Church at Boston, MA, where he served until his death Mar 14, 1874.

KRISTALLNACHT (CRYSTAL NIGHT): ANNIVERSARY. Nov 9–10, 1938. During the evening of Nov 9 and into the morning of Nov 10, 1938, mobs in Germany destroyed thousands of shops and homes carrying out a pogrom against Jews. Synagogues were burned down or demolished. There were bonfires in every Jewish neighborhood, fueled by Jewish prayer books, Torah scrolls and volumes of philosophy, history and poetry. More than 30,000 Jews were arrested and 91 killed. The night got its name from the smashing of glass store windows.

THE LINKS, INC: 55th ANNIVERSARY. Nov 9, 1946. Thousands of African-Americans fought in WWII, but after the war the same old injustices and hatred prevailed. In Philadelphia Margaret Roselle Hawkins and Sarah Strickland Scott founded a nonpartisan, volunteer organization called The Links, "linking" their friendship and resources in an effort to better the lives of disadvantaged African-Americans. From the first group of nine, The Links has grown to an incorporated organization of 8,000 women in 240 local chapters in 40 states plus the District of Columbia and two foreign countries. The Links promotes educational, cultural and community activities through a variety of projects here and in Africa. In May of 1985 The Links became an official Non-Governmental Organization of the UN.

LONGHORN CHAMPIONSHIP FINALS RODEO. Nov 9–10. Nashville Municipal Auditorium, Nashville, TN. One of America's Top 10 most talented rodeos. $200,000 purse and awards, including gold and silver trophy belt buckles, hand-carved trophy saddles, plus a full size $30,000 pickup truck to the Top Hand. Features top 72 contestants from more than 1,200 competing in our preceding 2001 tour of Longhorn Rodeos across the country for championships of the year in six different world class contests. Also colorful open pageantry and Big, Bad BONUS bulls. 36th annual. Est attendance: 30,000. For info: W. Bruce Lehrke, Longhorn World Chmpshp Rodeo, Inc, PO Box 70159, Nashville, TN 37207. Phone: (615) 876-1016. Fax: (615) 876-4685. E-mail: lhrodeo@idt.net. Web: www.longhornrodeo.com.

LOVEJOY, ELIJAH P.: BIRTH ANNIVERSARY. Nov 9, 1802. American newspaper publisher and abolitionist born at Albion, ME. Died Nov 7, 1837 at Alton, IL, in a fire started by a mob angry about his anti-slavery views.

NATIONAL CHILD SAFETY COUNCIL: FOUNDING ANNIVERSARY. Nov 9, 1955. National Child Safety Council (NCSC) at Jackson, MI. NCSC is the oldest and largest nonprofit organization in the US dedicated solely to child safety. Distributes comprehensive safety education materials to children through local law enforcement. For info: Barbara Handley Huggett, Dir, R & D, NCSC, Box 1368, Jackson, MI 49204-1368. Phone: (517) 764-6070.

NORSEFEST. Nov 9–10. Madison, MN. Lutefisk supper, Potato (Dumpling) Klub Luncheon and lutefisk eating contest (current record: eight pounds—we're looking for competitors from out of the area). Scandinavian Arts and Crafts Show and outhouse race, variety show and more. Est attendance: 2,500. For info: Maynard Meyer, Chamber of Commerce, PO Box 70, Madison, MN 56256. Phone: (320) 598-7301. Fax: (320) 598-7955.

"OMNIBUS" TV PREMIERE: ANNIVERSARY. Nov 9, 1952. This eclectic series deserved its name, offering a variety of presentations, including dramas, documentaries and musicals. Alistair Cooke hosted the program, which was the first major TV project to be underwritten by the Ford Foundation. Notable presentations included: James Agee's "Mr Lincoln"; "Die Fledermaus," with Eugene Ormandy conducting the Metropolitan Opera Orchestra; Agnes DeMille's ballet "Three Virgins and the Devil" (presented as "Three Maidens and the Devil"); and documentaries from underwater explorer Jacques Cousteau.

SAGAN, CARL: BIRTH ANNIVERSARY. Nov 9, 1934. Astronomer, biologist, author (*Broca's Brain, Cosmos*), born at New York, NY. Died at Seattle, WA, Dec 20, 1996.

SALT LAKE'S FAMILY CHRISTMAS GIFT SHOW. Nov 9–11. Salt Lake City, UT. A delightful holiday experience. Shoppers will find gifts and decorations from vendors across the nation. A festive shopping atmosphere with music, entertainment, Santa Claus and a Specialty Food area for all to enjoy. For info: Showcase Northwest, Inc, PO Box 2815, Kirkland, WA 98083. Phone: (800) 521-SHOW.

VIETNAM VETERANS MEMORIAL STATUE UNVEILING: ANNIVERSARY. Nov 9, 1984. The Vietnam Veterans Memorial was completed by the addition of a statue, "Three Servicemen" (sculpted by Frederick Hart), which was unveiled on this date. The statue faces the black granite wall on which are inscribed the names of more than 58,000 Americans who were killed or missing in action in the Vietnam War.

WATERFOWL FESTIVAL (WITH GOOSE-CALLING CONTEST). Nov 9–11. Easton, MD. Three-day festival of wildlife art. Five hundred of the country's most prestigious wildlife exhibitors present the finest in wildlife art, carvings, sculpture, decoys, photography, books, gifts and antique guns. Retriever and shooting demonstrations, world championship goose and regional duck-calling contests, a decoy auction, sporting clays tournament and seminars are also featured. Annually, the second full weekend in November. Proceeds contributed to conservation. Est attendance: 18,000. For info: Waterfowl Festival, PO Box 929, Easton, MD 21601. Phone: (410) 822-4567. Fax: (410) 820-9286. E-mail: facts@waterfowlfestival.org. Web: www.waterfowlfestival.org.

November	S	M	T	W	T	F	S
2001					1	2	3
	4	5	6	7	8	9	10
	11	12	13	14	15	16	17
	18	19	20	21	22	23	24
	25	26	27	28	29	30	

WHITE, STANFORD: BIRTH ANNIVERSARY. Nov 9, 1853. American architect who designed the old Madison Square Garden, the Washington Square Arch, and the Players, Century and Metropolitan Clubs at New York City. Stanford White was born at New York City and was shot to death on the roof of the Madison Square Garden by Harry Thaw, June 25, 1906.

WILHELM II ABDICATES: ANNIVERSARY. Nov 9, 1918. As World War I was coming to a close and it became clear their cause was lost, a revolt broke out in Germany. The Kaiser was advised by his military staff that the loyalty of the army could not be guaranteed. On Nov 9, 1918, it was announced in Berlin that Kaiser Wilhelm II had abdicated his throne. The former leader then fled to Holland. Philip Scheidemann, a Socialist leader, proclaimed a German Republic and became its first Chancellor.

WISCONSIN HOLIDAY MARKET. Nov 9–11. The American Club, Kohler, WI. More than 100 artists and craftspeople display their specialties in a glittering holiday market setting. Christmas shoppers can browse for crafts and collectibles to find the perfect holiday gift. Held in The American Club's Grand Hall of the Great Lakes. Est attendance: 5,000. For info: The American Club, Highland Dr, Kohler, WI 53044. Phone: (800) 344-2838. Fax: (920) 457-0299. Web: www.americanclub.com.

BIRTHDAYS TODAY

David Duval, 30, golfer, born Jacksonville, FL, Nov 9, 1971.

Lou Ferrigno, 50, actor (*Pumping Iron*, "The Incredible Hulk"), former bodybuilder, born Brooklyn, NY, Nov 9, 1951.

Robert (Bob) Gibson, 66, Baseball Hall of Fame pitcher, born Omaha, NE, Nov 9, 1935.

Robert Graham, 65, US Senator (D, Florida), born Dade County, FL, Nov 9, 1936.

Thomas Daniel (Tom) Weiskopf, 59, broadcaster and former golfer, born Massillon, OH, Nov 9, 1942.

NOVEMBER 10 — SATURDAY
Day 314 — 51 Remaining

AREA CODES INTRODUCED: 50th ANNIVERSARY. Nov 10, 1951. The 10-digit North American Numbering Plan which provides area codes for Canada, the US, and many Caribbean nations was devised in 1947 by AT&T and Bell Labs. Eighty-four area codes were assigned. However, all long-distance calls at that time were operator-assisted. On this date in 1951, the mayor of Englewood, NJ (area code 201) direct-dialed the mayor of Alameda, CA. By 1960 all telephone customers could dial long-distance calls. Currently there are 285 area codes. Because of the proliferation of faxes, modems and cell phones, the US could run out of area codes as early as 2007. The system is administered by the North American Numbering Plan Administration. For more info: www.nanpa.com

BADLANDS NATIONAL PARK ESTABLISHED: ANNIVERSARY. Nov 10, 1978. South Dakota's Badlands National Monument, authorized Mar 4, 1929, was established as a national park and preserve.

BEAVER CREEK AT IVEY STATION ARTS AND CRAFTS FESTIVAL. Nov 10–11. Ivey Station near Gordon, GA. 20th annual festival helps raise funds for preservation and restoration of historic site where festival is held. Charles Ivey settled here in 1816 and grew the first watermelons in Georgia (the Ivey Grey, named for him) and Ivey Station became the shipping center for watermelons. The area has significant Indian and Civil War history as well. Festival features arts and crafts, delicious specialty foods and entertainment. Annually, the second full weekend in November. Est attendance: 4,000. For info: Mrs Lee Korwin, Dir, Beaver Creek/Ivey Station Arts & Crafts Fest, 346 Jackson Rd, Gatlinburg, TN 37738.

BURTON, RICHARD: BIRTH ANNIVERSARY. Nov 10, 1925. Welsh-born stage and film actor. Richard Burton was never knighted and never an Oscar winner, but he was generally regarded as one of the great acting talents of his time. Born Richard Jenkins at Pontrhydyfen, South Wales, the son of a coal miner, he later took the name of his guardian, schoolmaster Philip Burton. His films include *Cleopatra, Becket, Who's Afraid of Virginia Woolf?, Anne of the Thousand Days* and *Equus.* An intense and tempestuous personal life and career suggested a self-destructive bent. Burton died at Geneva, Switzerland, Aug 5, 1984.

CALICO CRAFTS BAZAAR. Nov 10. Curry County Fairgrounds, Gold Beach, OR. 10 AM–5 PM. Est attendance: 500. For info: Gold Beach Chamber of Commerce, 29279 Ellensburg Ave, #3, Gold Beach, OR 97444. Phone: (800) 525-2334. Fax: (541) 247-0188. E-mail: goldbeach@harborside.com. Web: www.gold beach.org.

DOLL SHOW: THE DOLLMAKERS. Nov 10–11. Antique and contemporary dolls on display and for sale. Visiting artists will participate. Est attendance: 1,800. For info: Wheaton Village, 1501 Glasstown Rd, Millville, NJ 08332. Phone: (856) 825-6800 or (800) 998-4552. Fax: (856) 825-2410. E-mail: mail@wheaton village.org. Web: www.wheatonvillage.org.

DOWNTOWN FESTIVAL AND ART SHOW. Nov 10–11. Downtown Gainesville, FL. 240 fine artists display one-of-a-kind art for purchase. Two full days of live music on three stages, children's activity area, food vendors, hands-on art opportunities. 20th annual. Est attendance: 100,000. For info: Linda Piper, City of Gainesville, Dept of Cultural Affairs, PO Box 490, Gainesville, FL 32602. Phone: (352) 334-5064. Fax: (352) 334-2146.

EDMUND FITZGERALD MEMORIAL BEACON LIGHTING. Nov 10. Noon–6 PM, Two Harbors, MN. Slide presentation on *Edmund Fitzgerald* and other shipwrecks on Lake Superior; beacon lighting; lighthouse tour held at Split Rock Lighthouse. Est attendance: 1,000. For info: Lee Radzak, 3713 Split Rock Lighthouse Rd, Two Harbors, MN 55616. Phone: (218) 226-6372.

EDMUND FITZGERALD SINKING: ANNIVERSARY. Nov 10, 1975. The ore carrier *Edmund Fitzgerald* broke in two during a heavy storm in Lake Superior (near Whitefish Point). There were no survivors of this, the worst Great Lakes ship disaster of the decade, which took the lives of 29 crew members.

ENGLAND: LORD MAYOR'S SHOW. Nov 10. The City of London. Each year a colorful parade steps off at 11 AM from the Guildhall to the Royal Courts of Justice to mark the inauguration of the new Lord Mayor. Annually, the second Saturday in November. Est attendance: 500,000. For info: Pageantmaster, The Lord Mayor's Show, 1 Queens Rd, Hertford, Herts, England SG14 1EN. Phone: (44) (199) 250-5306. Web: www.lord-mayors-show .org.uk.

GOLDSMITH, OLIVER: BIRTH ANNIVERSARY. Nov 10, 1728. Irish writer, author of the play *She Stoops to Conquer.* Born at Pallas, County Longford, Ireland, he died Apr 4, 1774, at London. "A book may be amusing with numerous errors," he wrote (Advertisement to *The Vicar of Wakefield*), "or it may be very dull without a single absurdity."

HANDS-ON COLLECTOR SHOWCASE. Nov 10. Burlington, WI. Hands-on fun with items from fun, funny and elegant collections, plus meet the interesting collectors! Past events were of marbles, Victorian toys, radios, bubble blowers, sliding block logic puzzles, hat pins and other surprises. For info: Teacher Place & Parent Resources, 533 Milwaukee Ave, Burlington, WI 53105. Phone: (262) 763-3946.

HOGARTH, WILLIAM: BIRTH ANNIVERSARY. Nov 10, 1697. English painter and engraver, famed for his satiric series of engravings (*A Harlot's Progress, A Rake's Progress, Four Stages of Cruelty,* etc). Born at London, England, and died there, Oct 26, 1764.

KIRTLAND, JARED: BIRTH ANNIVERSARY. Nov 10, 1793. American physician and naturalist, Dr. Jared Potter Kirtland (for whom Kirtland's Warbler is named) was born at Wallingford, CT. The first of the now rare Kirtland's Warblers to be identified and studied was found on his farm near Cleveland, OH, in 1851. Dr. Kirtland died at Rockport, near Cleveland, Dec 10, 1877.

LUTHER, MARTIN: BIRTH ANNIVERSARY. Nov 10, 1483. Augustinian monk who was a founder and leader of the Reformation and of Protestantism was born at Eisleben, Saxony. Luther tacked his 95 Theses "On the Power of Indulgences" on the door of Wittenberg's castle church, on Oct 31, 1517, the eve of All Saints' Day. Luther asserted that the Bible was the sole authority of the church, called for reformation of abuses by the Roman Catholic Church and denied the supremacy of the Pope. Tried for heresy by the Roman Church, threatened with excommunication and finally banned by a papal bull (Jan 2, 1521), he responded by burning the bull. In 1525 he married Katherine von Bora, one of nine nuns who had left the convent due to his teaching. Luther died near his birthplace, at Eisleben, Feb 18, 1546.

MARINE CORPS BIRTHDAY: ANNIVERSARY. Nov 10, 1775. Commemorates the Marine Corps' establishment in 1775. Originally part of the navy, it became a separate unit July 11, 1789.

MICROSOFT RELEASES WINDOWS: ANNIVERSARY. Nov 10, 1983. In 1980, Microsoft signed a contract with IBM to design an operating system, MS-DOS, for a personal computer that IBM was developing. On Nov 10, 1983, Microsoft released Windows, an extension of MS-DOS with a graphical user interface. Windows 3.1 was released Apr 6, 1992.

REVOLUTIONARY SIEGE OF FORT MIFFLIN. Nov 10–11. Historic Fort Mifflin, Philadelphia, PA. A Revolutionary War reenactment and encampment with battle reenactment, black powder demonstration, living history, blacksmith demonstrations and musical presentation. Est attendance: 500. For info: Fort Mifflin on the Delaware, Fort Mifflin Rd, Philadelphia, PA 19153. Phone: (215) 685-4192. Fax: (215) 492-1608.

"SESAME STREET" TV PREMIERE: ANNIVERSARY. Nov 10, 1969. An important, successful long-running children's show, "Sesame Street" educates children while they have fun. It takes place along a city street, featuring a diverse cast of humans and puppets. Through singing, puppetry, film clips and skits, kids are taught letters, numbers, concepts and other lessons. Shows are "sponsored" by letters and numbers. Human cast members have included: Loretta Long, Matt Robinson, Roscoe Orman, Bob McGrath, Linda Bove, Buffy Sainte-Marie, Ruth Buzzi, Will Lee, Northern J. Calloway, Emilio Delgado and Sonia Manzano. Favorite Jim Henson muppets include Ernie, Bert, Grover, Oscar the Grouch, Kermit the Frog, the Cookie Monster, life-sized Big Bird and Mr Snuffleupagus.

SMOKY MOUNTAIN LIGHTS AND WINTERFEST. Nov 10–Feb 28. Gatlinburg, TN. A magical celebration of more than two million twinkling lights in animated motion. The entire city of Gatlinburg is lit up with exciting displays featuring up to 60-ft animated displays, for the entire family to enjoy. More than 100 contemporary and traditional events such as yule log burnings, living Christmas tree and festival of trees. Drive-thru and walk-thru tours available. Annually, mid-November–end of February. Est attendance: 1,000,000. For info: Deana D. Ivey, Dir Communications, Gatlinburg Chamber of Commerce, 234 Airport Rd, Gatlinburg, TN 37738. Phone: (800) 568-4748 or (423) 430-4148. Web: www.gatlinburg.com.

SPACE MILESTONE: *LUNA 17* (USSR). Nov 10, 1970. Launched in 1970, this unmanned spacecraft landed and released *Lunakhod 1* (8-wheel, radio-controlled vehicle) on Moon's Sea of Rains Nov 17, which explored lunar surface, sending data back to Earth.

STANLEY FINDS LIVINGSTONE: ANNIVERSARY. Nov 10, 1871. Having begun his search the previous March for the then two-years-missing explorer-missionary David Livingstone, explorer Henry M. Stanley found him on this day at Ujiji (Africa) and uttered those now immortal words, "Dr. Livingstone, I presume?"

BIRTHDAYS TODAY

Vanessa Angel, 38, actress (*Spies Like Us, Kingpin*), born London, England, Nov 10, 1963.

Isaac Bruce, 29, football player, born Ft Lauderdale, FL, Nov 10, 1972.

Roland Emmerich, 46, director, producer (*Independence Day, Eye of the Storm*), born Stuttgart, Germany, Nov 10, 1955.

Donna Fargo (Yvonne Vaughan), 52, singer ("Funny Face"), songwriter, born Mount Airy, NC, Nov 10, 1949.

Russell Charles Means, 61, Native American rights activist, born Pine Ridge, SD, Nov 10, 1940.

MacKenzie Phillips, 42, actress ("One Day at a Time," *American Graffiti*), daughter of John Phillips of the Mamas and Papas, born Alexandria, VA, Nov 10, 1959.

Ann Reinking, 52, dancer, actress (*Pippin*), born Seattle, WA, Nov 10, 1949.

Tim Rice, 57, lyricist (*Evita*), born Amersham, England, Nov 10, 1944.

Roy Scheider, 66, actor (*Jaws, All That Jazz, Cold Comfort Farm*, "Seaquest"), born Orange, NJ, Nov 10, 1935.

Sinbad, 45, actor (*Unnecessary Roughness*, "A Different World"), born David Adkins, Benton Harbor, MI, Nov 10, 1956.

NOVEMBER 11 — SUNDAY

Day 315 — 50 Remaining

ALDRICH, THOMAS BAILEY: BIRTH ANNIVERSARY. Nov 11, 1836. American author and editor. Best known for his book *The Story of a Bad Boy* (1870), an autobiographical work. Aldrich was born at Portsmouth, NH, and died at Boston, MA, Mar 19, 1907.

		S	M	T	W	T	F	S
November						1	2	3
2001		4	5	6	7	8	9	10
		11	12	13	14	15	16	17
		18	19	20	21	22	23	24
		25	26	27	28	29	30	

★ **AMERICAN EDUCATION WEEK.** Nov 11–17. Presidential Proclamation 5403, of Oct 30, 1985, covers all succeeding years. Always the first full week preceding the fourth Thursday in November. Issued from 1921–25 and in 1936, sometimes for a week in December and sometimes as National Education Week. After an absence of a number of years, this proclamation was issued each year from 1955–82 (issued in 1955 as a prelude to the White House Conference on Education). Previously, Proclamation 4967, of Sept 13, 1982, covered all succeeding years as the second week in November.

AMERICAN EDUCATION WEEK. Nov 11–17. Focuses attention on the importance of education and all that it stands for. Annually, the week preceding the week of Thanksgiving. For info: Natl Education Assn (NEA), 1201 16th St NW, Washington, DC 20036. Phone: (202) 833-4000. Web: www.nea.org.

AMERICAN HEART ASSOCIATION SCIENTIFIC SESSIONS: ANNUAL MEETING. Nov 11–14. Anaheim, CA. Est attendance: 30,000. For info: Public Relations, American Heart Assn, 7272 Greenville Ave, Dallas, TX 75231. Phone: (214) 706-1543. Fax: (214) 706-5262. Web: www.americanheart.org.

ANGOLA: INDEPENDENCE DAY: ANNIVERSARY. Nov 11. National holiday. Angola gained its independence from Portugal in 1975.

BONZA BOTTLER DAY™. Nov 11. To celebrate when the number of the day is the same as the number of the month. Bonza Bottler Day™ is an excuse to have a party at least once a month. For more information, see Jan 1. For info: Gail M. Berger, 109 Matthew Ave, Poca, WV 25159. Phone: (304) 776-7746. E-mail: gberger5@aol.com.

CANADA: REMEMBRANCE DAY. Nov 11. Public holiday in Alberta.

DEATH/DUTY DAY. Nov 11. Honoring soldiers on both sides who died on Nov 11, 1918, the armistice or Waffenstillstand day that ended the fighting in the First World War of 1914–18. The order was to stop fighting at 11 AM, rather than on receipt of the order. For info: Bob Birch, Punscorpion, The Puns Corps, PO Box 2364, Falls Church, VA 22042-0364. Phone: (703) 533-3668.

DOSTOYEVSKY, FYODOR MIKHAILOVICH: BIRTH ANNIVERSARY. Nov 11, 1821. Russian novelist, author of *The Brothers Karamazov, Crime and Punishment* and *The Idiot*, was born at Moscow, and died at St. Petersburg, Feb 9, 1881. A political revolutionary, he was arrested, tried, convicted and sentenced to death, but instead of execution he served a sentence in a Siberian prison and later served in the army there.

ENGLAND: REMEMBRANCE DAY SERVICE AND PARADE. Nov 11. Cenotaph, Whitehall, London. Wreath-laying ceremony to commemorate the dead of both world wars by Her Majesty The Queen, members of the Royal Family, government and service organizations. Annually, the Sunday closest to

Nov 11. For info: Public Info Office, HQ London District Military, Horse Guards, Whitehall, London, England SW1A 2AX. Phone: (44)(171) 414-2353. Fax: (44) (171) 414-2352.

FAMILYCARES WEEK. Nov 11–17. A week celebrating the spirit of compassion and volunteerism in families. Families will show they care by doing projects that help people in need in their local community. For info: FamilyCares, PO Box 1082, New Canaan, CT 06840. Phone: (914) 533-2949. E-mail: jwhiting @kidscare.org. Web: www.familycares.org.

FRENCH WEST INDIES: CONCORDIA DAY. Nov 11. St. Martin. Public holiday. Parades and joint ceremony by French and Dutch officials at the obelisk Border Monument commemorating the long-standing peaceful coexistence of both countries. For info: Ms Michel Coutosiev, Mktg Challenges Intl, 10 E 21st St, New York, NY 10010. Phone: (212) 529-9069.

"GOD BLESS AMERICA" FIRST PERFORMED: ANNIVERSARY. Nov 11, 1938. Irving Berlin wrote this song especially for Kate Smith. She first sang it during her regular radio broadcast. It quickly became a great patriotic favorite of the nation and one of Smith's most requested songs.

MARTINMAS. Nov 11. The Feast Day of St. Martin of Tours, who lived about AD 316–397. A bishop, he became one of the most popular saints of the Middle Ages. The period of warm weather often occurring about the time of his feast day is sometimes called St. Martin's Summer (especially in England).

NATIONAL E-COMMERCE WEEK. Nov 11–17. Set aside to draw attention to the convenience, security and speed associated with today's online economy. Newcomers to online shopping are encouraged to participate, as are Web-savvy shoppers. Ecount and its portfolio of e-commerce businesses will sponsor events and develop special offers that promote the benefits of e-commerce. For info: Ecount, Lee Park, Ste 457, 1100 E Hector St, Conshohocken, PA 19428. Phone: (610) 941-4600. Fax: (610) 941-4600. E-mail: info@ecount.com. Web: www.ecount.com.

NATIONAL GEOGRAPHY AWARENESS WEEK. Nov 11–17. Focus public awareness on the importance of the knowledge of geography. For information and classroom activities, visit the National Geographic Society's website at www.national geographic.com/gaw.

PATTON, GEORGE S., JR: BIRTH ANNIVERSARY. Nov 11, 1885. American military officer, graduate of West Point (1909), George Smith Patton, Jr, was born at San Gabriel, CA. Ambitious and flamboyant, he lived for combat. He served in the punitive expedition into Mexico (1916), in Europe in World War I and in North Africa and Europe in World War II. He received world attention and official censure in 1943 for slapping a hospitalized shell-shocked soldier. While a full general, owing to his critical public statements, he was relieved of his command in 1945. He died at Heidelberg, Germany, Dec 21, 1945, of injuries received in an automobile accident.

PERIOPERATIVE (OR) ROOM NURSE WEEK. Nov 11–17. To inform health care consumers that the nurse in the operating room cares for patients before, during and after surgery. Annually, the week including Nov 14. For info: Public Relations Mgr, AORN, 2170 S Parker Rd, Ste 300, Denver, CO 80231-5711. Phone: (303) 755-6300. Fax: (303) 338-4838. E-mail: jpaul son@aorn.org. Web: www.aorn.org.

POLAND: INDEPENDENCE DAY. Nov 11. Poland regained independence in 1918, after having been partitioned among Austria, Prussia and Russia for more than 120 years.

RANDOM ACTS OF KINDNESS WEEK. Nov 11–17. RAK Week is a global grassroots awareness campaign and celebration of the power of Random Acts of Kindness as a counterbalance to random acts of violence. Anyone can join in during this week and the Random Acts of Kindness Foundation can help you with ideas on how to promote this wonderful celebration! Call for a Community Coordinator Kit or a Teacher's Kit. 7th annual. For info: Random Acts of Kindness Foundation. Phone: (800) 660-2811. Web: www.actsofkindness.org.

SPACE MILESTONE: *COLUMBIA STS-5* (US). Nov 11, 1982. Shuttle *Columbia* launched from Kennedy Space Center, FL, with four astronauts: Vance Brand, Robert Overmyer, William Lenoir and Joseph Allen. "First operational mission" delivered two satellites into orbit for commercial customers. *Columbia* landed at Edwards Air Force Base, CA, Nov 16, 1982.

SPACE MILESTONE: *GEMINI 12* (US): 35th ANNIVERSARY. Nov 11, 1966. Last Project Gemini manned Earth orbit launched. Buzz Aldrin spent five hours on a space walk, setting a new record.

SWEDEN: SAINT MARTIN'S DAY. Nov 11. Originally in memory of St. Martin of Tours; also associated with Martin Luther, who is celebrated the day before. Marks the end of the autumn's work and the beginning of winter activities.

SWITZERLAND: MARTINMAS GOOSE (MARTINIGIANS). Nov 11. Sursee, Canton Lucerne. At 3 PM on Martinmas (the day on which interest is due), the "Gansabhauet" is staged in front of Town Hall. Blindfolded participants try to bring down, with a single sword stroke, a dead goose suspended on a wire.

"TOO CLOSE FOR COMFORT" TV PREMIERE: ANNIVERSARY. Nov 11, 1980. "Too Close for Comfort," based on the British series "Keep It in the Family," starred Ted Knight as San Francisco cartoonist Henry Rush, living with his wife Muriel (Nancy Dussault) in the upstairs apartment while their grown daughters, Jackie (Deborah Van Valkenburgh) and Sara (Lydia Cornell), live downstairs. This half-hour sitcom also featured Audrey Meadows as Muriel's mother, Iris, and JM J. Bullock as disaster-prone Monroe Ficus, Sara's friend. When "TCFC" was cancelled by ABC in 1983, new episodes were produced in order to assure success in syndication. The show was renamed "The Ted Knight Show" until his death in 1986.

TUNISIA: TREE FESTIVAL. Nov 11. National agricultural festival. Annually, the second Sunday in November.

VETERANS DAY. Nov 11. Veterans Day was observed on Nov 11 from 1919 through 1970. Public Law 90–363, the "Monday Holiday Law," provided that, beginning in 1971, Veterans Day would be observed on "the fourth Monday in October." This movable observance date, which separated Veterans Day from the Nov 11 anniversary of World War I Armistice, proved unpopular. State after state moved its observance back to the traditional Nov 11 date, and finally Public Law 94–97 of Sept 18, 1975, required that, effective Jan 1, 1978, the observance of Veterans Day revert to Nov 11. As Armistice Day this is a holiday in Belgium, France and other European countries. "At the eleventh hour of the eleventh day of the eleventh month" fighting ceased in World War I.

★**VETERANS DAY.** Nov 11. Presidential Proclamation. Formerly called "Armistice Day" and proclaimed each year since 1926 for Nov 11. PL83–380 of June 1, 1954, changed the name to "Veterans Day." PL90–363 of June 28, 1968, required that

beginning in 1971 it would be observed the fourth Monday in October. PL 94–97 of Sept 18, 1975, required that effective Jan 1, 1978, the observance would revert to Nov 11.

VETERANS DAY CELEBRATION. Nov 11. Mamou, LA. Memorial services, a patriotic parade and speeches, Cajun dance noon until 8 PM. Annually, on Veterans Day. Sponsor: American Legion Post 123. Est attendance: 1,000. For info: Frank Gurvis Bihm, Jr, PO Box 123, Mamou, LA 70554. Phone: (318) 468-5059. E-mail: fbihm@yahoo.com.

VICTOR EMMANUEL III: BIRTH ANNIVERSARY. Nov 11, 1869. Last king of Italy Victor Emmanuel III was born at Naples, Italy, and became king upon the assassination of his father in July 1900. For the first 20 years of his reign, Victor Emmanuel followed Italy's constitutional custom of selecting a prime minister based on the parliamentary majority, but with parliament in disarray after World War I, he named Benito Mussolini to form a cabinet and then failed to prevent Mussolini and the Fascists from seizing power. The king became little more than a figurehead. In 1946 Victor Emmanuel abdicated the throne, and he and the Crown Prince went into exile. He died at Alexandria, Egypt, Dec 28, 1947.

VIETNAM WOMEN'S MEMORIAL DEDICATION: ANNIVERSARY. Nov 11, 1993. In recognition of the 11,500 women who served in the Vietnam war, the bronze sculpture erected at Washington, DC, was dedicated this day.

VOX POPULI DAY. Nov 11. Vox Populi is the Latin term for "People's Voice." Today is the day to make your voice count. Put your voice to your ideas and opinions. [©1994] For info: Adrienne Sioux Koopersmith, 1437 W Rosemont, #1W, Chicago, IL 60660-1319. Phone: (773) 743-5341. Fax: (773) 743-5395. E-mail: adrienne@21stcentury.net.

WASHINGTON: ADMISSION DAY: ANNIVERSARY. Nov 11. Became 42nd state in 1889.

WORLD WAR I ARMISTICE: ANNIVERSARY. Nov 11, 1918. Anniversary of armistice between Allied and Central Powers ending WWI, signed at 5 AM, Nov 11, 1918, in Marshal Foch's railway car in the Forest of Compiegne, France. Hostilities ceased at 11 AM. Recognized in many countries as Armistice Day, Remembrance Day, Veterans Day, Victory Day or World War I Memorial Day. Many places observe silent memorial at the 11th hour of the 11th day of the 11th month each year. See also: "Veterans Day" (Nov 11).

November 2001	S	M	T	W	T	F	S
					1	2	3
	4	5	6	7	8	9	10
	11	12	13	14	15	16	17
	18	19	20	21	22	23	24
	25	26	27	28	29	30	

Bibi Andersson (Birgitta Anderson), 66, actress (*Story of a Woman*), born Stockholm, Sweden, Nov 11, 1935.

Barbara Boxer, 61, US Senator (D, California), born Brooklyn, NY, Nov 11, 1940.

Leonardo DiCaprio, 26, actor (*Parenthood, Titanic*), born Ridgewood, NJ, Nov 11, 1975.

Calista Flockhart, 37, actress ("Ally McBeal"), born Freeport, IL, Nov 11, 1964.

Philip McKeon, 37, actor ("Alice"), born Westbury, NY, Nov 11, 1964.

Demi Moore, 39, actress ("General Hospital," *Ghost, GI Jane*), born Roswell, NM, Nov 11, 1962.

Reynaldo Ordonez, 29, baseball player, born Havana, Cuba, Nov 11, 1972.

Kurt Vonnegut, Jr, 79, novelist (*Slaughterhouse Five, Cat's Cradle*), born Indianapolis, IN, Nov 11, 1922.

Jonathan Winters, 76, comedian, actor ("The Jonathan Winters Show," "Mork & Mindy"), born Dayton, OH, Nov 11, 1925.

Frank Urban ("Fuzzy") Zoeller, 50, golfer, born New Albany, IN, Nov 11, 1951.

NOVEMBER 12 — MONDAY
Day 316 — 49 Remaining

ARCHES NATIONAL PARK ESTABLISHED: 30th ANNIVERSARY. Nov 12, 1971. Area of natural wind-eroded formations in eastern Utah, originally proclaimed a national monument Apr 12, 1929, was established as a national park. For further park info: Arches Natl Park, PO Box 907, Moab, UT 84532.

BIRTH OF BAHA'U'LLAH. Nov 12. Baha'i observance of anniversary of the birth of Baha'u'llah (born Mirza Husayn Ali) on Nov 12, 1817, at Nur, Persia. Baha'u'llah was prophet-founder of the Baha'i Faith. One of the nine days of the year when Baha'is suspend work. For info: Dir, Baha'is of the US, Office of Public Information, 866 UN Plaza, Ste 120, New York, NY 10017-1822. Phone: (212) 803-2500. Fax: (212) 803-2573. E-mail: usopi-ny@bic.org. Web: www.us.bahai.org.

BLACKMUN, HARRY A.: BIRTH ANNIVERSARY. Nov 12, 1908. Former associate justice of the Supreme Court of the US, nominated by President Nixon Apr 14, 1970. He retired from the Court Aug 3, 1994. Justice Blackmun was born at Nashville, IL, and died at Arlington, VA, Mar 4, 1999.

KELLY, GRACE PATRICIA: BIRTH ANNIVERSARY. Nov 12, 1929. American award-winning actress (*Rear Window, To Catch a Thief*) who became Princess Grace of Monaco when she married that country's ruler, Prince Rainier III, in 1956. Born at Philadelphia, PA, she died of injuries sustained in an automobile accident, Sept 14, 1982, at Monte Carlo, Monaco.

NATIONAL CHILDREN'S BOOK WEEK. Nov 12–18. An annual event, sponsored by The Children's Book Council, to encourage the enjoyment of reading for young people. Theme: "Get Carried Away. . . Read." For info: The Children's Book Council, Inc, PO Box 2640/JAF Station, New York, NY 10116-2640. Phone: (800) 999-2160. Fax: (888) 807-9355. E-mail: joanncbc@aol.com. Web: www.cbcbooks.org.

RODIN, AUGUSTE: BIRTH ANNIVERSARY. Nov 12, 1840. French sculptor (*The Kiss, The Thinker*), born at Paris, France. Died Nov 17, 1917, near Paris.

SHALLOW PERSONS AWARENESS WEEK. Nov 12–18. This is the week to acknowledge and embrace your inner shallowness, just in time for the holidays. Annually, the second full week in November. For info: Marcus P. Meleton, Jr, Sharkbait Press, PO Box 11300, Costa Mesa, CA 92627. Phone: (949) 645-0139. E-mail: sharkbaitp@aol.com. Web: www.sharkbaitPress.com.

SPACE MILESTONE: *COLUMBIA* STS-2 (US): 20th ANNIVERSARY. Nov 12, 1981. Shuttle *Columbia*, launched from Kennedy Space Center, FL, with Joe Engle and Richard

Truly on board, became first spacecraft launched from Earth for a second orbiting mission. Landed at Edwards Air Force Base, CA, Nov 14, 1981.

STANTON, ELIZABETH CADY: BIRTH ANNIVERSARY. Nov 12, 1815. American woman suffragist and reformer, Elizabeth Cady Stanton was born at Johnstown, NY. "We hold these truths to be self-evident," she said at the first Women's Rights Convention, in 1848, "that all men and women are created equal." She died at New York, NY, Oct 26, 1902.

SUN YAT-SEN: BIRTH ANNIVERSARY (TRADITIONAL). Nov 12. Although his actual birth date in 1866 is not known, Dr. Sun Yat-Sen's traditional birthday commemoration is held Nov 12. Heroic leader of China's 1911 revolution, he died at Peking, Mar 12, 1925. The death anniversary is also widely observed. See also: "Sun Yat-Sen: Death Anniversary" (Mar 12).

TYLER, LETITIA CHRISTIAN: BIRTH ANNIVERSARY. Nov 12, 1790. First wife of John Tyler, tenth president of the US, born at New Kent County, VA. Died at Washington, DC, Sept 10, 1842.

VETERANS DAY OBSERVED. Nov 12. For federal employees, when a holiday falls on a Sunday, it is observed on the following Monday.

BIRTHDAYS TODAY

Nadia Comaneci, 40, Olympic gold medal gymnast, born Onesti, Romania, Nov 12, 1961.

Tonya Harding, 31, figure skater, born Portland, OR, Nov 12, 1970.

Kim Hunter (Janet Cole), 79, actress ("The Edge of Night," *Planet of the Apes*), born Detroit, MI, Nov 12, 1922.

Megan Mullally, 43, actress ("Will & Grace," *How to Succeed in Business Without Really Trying*), born Los Angeles, CA, Nov 12, 1958.

Jack Reed, 52, US Senator (D, Rhode Island), born Providence, RI, Nov 12, 1949.

David Schwimmer, 35, actor ("Friends"), born Queens, NY, Nov 12, 1966.

Sammy Sosa, 33, baseball player, born San Pedro de Macoris, Dominican Republic, Nov 12, 1968.

Neil Young, 56, singer with Buffalo Springfield and Crosby, Stills, Nash & Young, songwriter, born Toronto, Ontario, Canada, Nov 12, 1945.

NOVEMBER 13 — TUESDAY
Day 317 — 48 Remaining

BOOTH, EDWIN (THOMAS): BIRTH ANNIVERSARY. Nov 13, 1833. Famed American actor and founder of the Players Club, born near Bel Air, MD. His brother, John Wilkes Booth, assassinated President Lincoln. Died at New York, NY, June 7, 1893.

BRANDEIS, LOUIS DEMBITZ: BIRTH ANNIVERSARY. Nov 13, 1856. American jurist, associate justice of US Supreme Court (1916–39), born at Louisville, KY. Died at Washington, DC, Oct 5, 1941.

HOLLAND TUNNEL: ANNIVERSARY. Nov 13, 1927. The Holland Tunnel, running under the Hudson River between New York, NY, and Jersey City, NJ, was opened to traffic. The tunnel was built and operated by the New York–New Jersey Bridge and Tunnel Commission. Comprised of two tubes, each large enough for two lanes of traffic, the Holland was the first underwater tunnel built in the US.

MAXWELL, JAMES CLERK: BIRTH ANNIVERSARY. Nov 13, 1831. British physicist noted for his work in the field of electricity and magnetism. Born at Edinburgh, Scotland, he died of cancer Nov 5, 1879, at Cambridge, England.

NATIONAL COMMUNITY EDUCATION DAY. Nov 13. To recognize and promote strong relationships between public schools and the communities they serve and to help schools develop new relationships with parents, community members, local organizations and agencies. Annually, the Tuesday of American Education Week. For info: Natl Community Education Assn, 3929 Old Lee Hwy, Ste 91-A, Fairfax, VA 22030-2401. Phone: (703) 359-8973. Fax: (703) 359-0972. E-mail: ncea@ncea.com.

STEVENSON, ROBERT LOUIS: BIRTH ANNIVERSARY. Nov 13, 1850. Scottish author, born at Edinburgh, Scotland, known for his *Child's Garden of Verses* and novels such as *Treasure Island* and *Kidnapped*. Died at Samoa, Dec 3, 1894.

STOKES BECOMES FIRST BLACK MAYOR IN US: ANNIVERSARY. Nov 13, 1967. Carl Burton Stokes became the first black in the US elected mayor when he won the Cleveland, OH, mayoral election Nov 13, 1967. Died Apr 3, 1996.

TRELAWNEY, EDWARD JOHN: BIRTH ANNIVERSARY. Nov 13, 1792. English traveler and author, friend of Shelley and Byron, born at London. He died at Sompting, Sussex, Aug 13, 1881, and was buried at Rome, next to Shelley.

WORLD KINDNESS DAY. Nov 13. The Kindness Movement has gone global! The World Kindness Movement grew out of a series of Kindness Conferences convened by the Japanese Small Kindness Movement in 1996. The Random Acts of Kindness Foundation, USA has been a part of these conferences along with representatives from Japan, Singapore, Australia, Canada, Thailand and England. This day represents the pledge of each of these countries to join together to build a kinder and more compassionate world. For info: Random Acts of Kindness Foundation. Phone: (800) 660-2811. Web: www.actsofkindness.org.

BIRTHDAYS TODAY

Sheila E. Frazier, 53, actress (*Super Fly, I'm Gonna Git You Sucka*), born The Bronx, NY, Nov 13, 1948.

Whoopi Goldberg, 52, comedienne, actress (*Ghost, Sister Act, The Color Purple*), born New York, NY, Nov 13, 1949.

Joe Mantegna, 54, actor (stage: Tony for *Glengarry Glen Ross*; *House of Games, Things Change*), born Chicago, IL, Nov 13, 1947.

Garry Marshall, 67, producer, director (*Beaches, Pretty Woman*), actor ("Murphy Brown"), born New York, NY, Nov 13, 1934.

Richard Mulligan, 69, actor ("Empty Nest," *SOB*, "Soap"), born New York, NY, Nov 13, 1932.

Chris Noth, 44, actor ("Law & Order," *Burnzy's Last Call*), born Madison, WI, Nov 13, 1957.

Tracy Scoggins, 42, actress ("The Colbys," *Some Kind of Hero*), born Galveston, TX, Nov 13, 1959.

Madeline Sherwood, 79, actress ("The Flying Nun"), born Montreal, Quebec, Canada, Nov 13, 1922.

Vincent Frank (Vinny) Testaverde, 38, football player, born New York, NY, Nov 13, 1963.

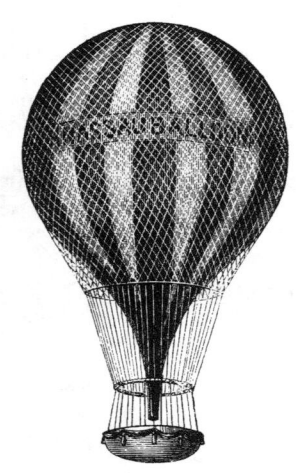

NOVEMBER 14 — WEDNESDAY

Day 318 — 47 Remaining

AROUND THE WORLD IN 72 DAYS: ANNIVERSARY.
Nov 14, 1889. Newspaper reporter Nellie Bly (pen name used by Elizabeth Cochrane Seaman) set off Nov 14, 1889, to attempt to break Jules Verne's imaginary hero Phileas Fogg's record of voyaging around the world in 80 days. She did beat Fogg's record, taking 72 days, 6 hours, 11 minutes and 14 seconds to make the trip.

BLOOD TRANSFUSION: ANNIVERSARY. Nov 14, 1666. Samuel Pepys, diarist and Fellow of the Royal Society, wrote in his diary for Nov 14, 1666: "Dr. Croone told me. . .there was a pretty experiment of the blood of one dog let out, till he died, into the body of another on one side, while all his own run out on the other side. The first died upon the place, and the other very well and likely to do well. This did give occasion to many pretty wishes, as of the blood of a Quaker to be let into an Archbishop, and such like; but, as Dr. Croone says, may, if it takes, be of mighty use to man's health, for the amending of bad blood by borrowing from a better body."

COPLAND, AARON: BIRTH ANNIVERSARY. Nov 14, 1900. American composer Aaron Copland was born at Brooklyn, NY. Incorporating American folk music and, later, the 12-tone system, he strove to create an American music style that was both popular and artistic. He composed ballets, film scores and orchestral works including *Fanfare for the Common Man* (1942), *Appalachian Spring* (1944) (for which he won the Pulitzer Prize) and the score for *The Heiress* (1948) (for which he won an Oscar). He died Dec 2, 1990, at North Tarrytown, NY.

DOW-JONES TOPS 1,000: ANNIVERSARY. Nov 14, 1972. The Dow-Jones Index of 30 major industrial stocks topped the 1,000 mark for the first time.

EISENHOWER, MAMIE DOUD: BIRTH ANNIVERSARY. Nov 14, 1896. Wife of Dwight David Eisenhower, 34th president of the US, born at Boone, IA. Died Nov 1, 1979, at Gettysburg, PA.

FULTON, ROBERT: BIRTH ANNIVERSARY. Nov 14, 1765. Inventor of the steamboat, born at Little Britain, PA. Died Feb 24, 1815, at New York, NY.

November 2001	S	M	T	W	T	F	S
					1	2	3
	4	5	6	7	8	9	10
	11	12	13	14	15	16	17
	18	19	20	21	22	23	24
	25	26	27	28	29	30	

GUINEA-BISSAU: RE-ADJUSTMENT MOVEMENT'S DAY. Nov 14. National holiday.

INDIA: CHILDREN'S DAY. Nov 14. Holiday observed throughout India.

INDIA: DIWALI (DEEPAVALI). Nov 14. Diwali, the five-day festival of lights, is the prettiest of all Indian festivals. It celebrates the return of Lord Rama to Ayodhya after a 14-year exile. Thousands of flickering lights illuminate houses and transform the drab urban landscape of cities and towns while fireworks add color and noise. The goddess of wealth, Lakshmi, is worshipped in Hindu homes on Diwali. Houses are white-washed and cleaned and elaborate designs drawn on thresholds with colored powder to welcome the fastidious goddess. Because there is no one universally accepted Hindu calendar, this holiday may be celebrated on a different date in some parts of India but it always falls in the months of October or November.

JORDAN: KING HUSSEIN: BIRTH ANNIVERSARY. Nov 14. H.M. King Hussein's birthday is honored each year on the anniversary of his birth in 1935. He died in Jordan Feb 7, 1999.

MONET, CLAUDE: BIRTH ANNIVERSARY. Nov 14, 1840. French Impressionist painter (*Water Lillies*), born at Paris. Died at Giverny, France, Dec 5, 1926.

"MURPHY BROWN" TV PREMIERE: ANNIVERSARY. Nov 14, 1988. This intelligent, timely and often acerbic sitcom set in Washington, DC, starred Candice Bergen in the title role, as an egotistical, seasoned journalist working for the fictitious TV newsmagazine show "FYI." Also featured were Grant Shaud as the show's high-strung producer, Miles Silverberg (later replaced by Lily Tomlin), Faith Ford as the former Miss America, Corky Sherwood (and later Miles' bride), Joe Regalbuto as Murphy's neurotic friend, reporter Frank Fontana, Charles Kimbrough as "FYI" 's uptight anchorman, Jim Dial and Pat Corley as Phil, owner of the local watering hole. Colleen Dewhurst appeared as Murphy's mother and Robert Pastorelli appeared as Eldin Bernecky, perfectionist housepainter and aspiring artist (he left the series for his own show). The show often blurred the lines between reality and fiction by dealing with topical issues and by including real-life journalists as guest stars playing themselves. The series ended with the May 31, 1998 episode.

NATIONAL AMERICAN TEDDY BEAR DAY. Nov 14. The Vermont Teddy Bear Company® annually celebrates the birth of America's most beloved companion, the Teddy Bear. The legend goes that President Theodore Roosevelt spared the life of a bear cub while on a big game hunt in Mississippi in 1902. Clifford Berryman, a political cartoonist, recorded the incident. President Theodore Roosevelt was most often depicted alongside a Teddy Bear and thus America's love affair with the Teddy Bear began. For info: The Vermont Teddy Bear Company®, 6655 Shelburne Rd, Shelburne, VT 05482. Web: VermontTeddyBear.com.

NATIONAL EDUCATIONAL SUPPORT PERSONNEL DAY. Nov 14. A mandate of the delegates to the 1987 National Education Association Representative Assembly called for a special day during American Education Week to honor the contributions of school support employees. Local associations and school districts salute support staff on this 14th annual observance, the Wednesday of American Education Week. For info: Connie Morris, Natl Education Assn (NEA), 1201 16th St NW, Washington, DC 20036. Phone: (202) 822-7262. Fax: (202) 822-7292. Web: www.nea.org.

NATIONAL YOUNG READER'S DAY. Nov 14. Pizza Hut and the Center for the Book in the Library of Congress established National Young Reader's Day to remind Americans of the joys and importance of reading for young people. Schools, libraries, families and communities nationwide use this day to celebrate youth reading in a variety of creative and educational ways. Ideas on ways you can celebrate this special day available. For info: Shelley Morehead, The BOOK IT! Program, PO Box 2999, Wichita, KS 67201. Phone: (800) 426-6548. Fax: (316) 685-0977. E-mail: read@bookitprogram.com.

NEHRU, JAWAHARLAL: BIRTH ANNIVERSARY. Nov 14, 1889. Indian leader and first prime minister after independence. Born at Allahabad, India, he died May 27, 1964, at New Delhi.

SALISBURY, HARRISON: BIRTH ANNIVERSARY. Nov 14, 1908. American journalist Harrison Evans Salisbury was born at Minneapolis, MN. *New York Times* Moscow correspondent from 1949 to 1954. Salisbury won the Pulitzer Prize in 1955 for a series of articles on the Soviet Union. He died July 5, 1993, at Providence, RI.

SPACE MILESTONE: *APOLLO 12* (US). Nov 14, 1969. Launched this date. This was the second manned lunar landing—in Ocean of Storms. First pinpoint landing. Astronauts Conrad, Bean and Gordon visited *Surveyor 3* and took samples. Earth splashdown Nov 24.

STEVENSON, McLEAN: BIRTH ANNIVERSARY. Nov 14, 1929. Actor, born at Bloomington, IL, Stevenson is perhaps best known for his role as the bumbling and womanizing Lieutenant Colonel Henry Blake in the long-running TV series "M*A*S*H." Other performances include "Hello, Larry." Stevenson died Feb 15, 1996, at Los Angeles, CA.

BIRTHDAYS TODAY

Boutros Boutros-Ghali, 79, former Secretary-General of the UN, born Cairo, Egypt, Nov 14, 1922.

Ben Cayetano, 62, Governor of Hawaii (D), born Honolulu, HI, Nov 14, 1939.

Prince Charles, 53, Prince of Wales, heir to the British throne, born London, England, Nov 14, 1948.

Laura San Giacomo, 39, actress (*sex, lies and videotape*, "Just Shoot Me"), born Hoboken, NJ, Nov 14, 1962.

Curt Schilling, 35, baseball player, born Anchorage, AK, Nov 14, 1966.

Joseph "Run" Simmons, 37, rapper (*Run D.M.C.*), born Queens, NY, Nov 14, 1964.

Don Stewart, 66, singer, actor ("Guiding Light"), born Staten Island, NY, Nov 14, 1935.

D.B. Sweeney, 40, actor (*Spawn, The Cutting Edge*), born Shoreham, Long Island, NY, Nov 14, 1961.

Yanni, 47, New Age composer, born Kalamata, Greece, Nov 14, 1954.

NOVEMBER 15 — THURSDAY
Day 319 — 46 Remaining

AMERICA RECYCLES DAY. Nov 15. To promote recycling and recycled products. More than 40 states will participate. For info: Environmental Defense Fund, 257 Park Ave South, New York, NY 10010. Phone: (800) CAL-LEDF. Web: www.america recyclesday.org.

AMERICAN SPEECH–LANGUAGE–HEARING ASSOCIATION CONVENTION. Nov 15–18. New Orleans, LA. Scientific sessions held on language, speech disorders, hearing science and hearing disorders and matters of professional interest to speech-language pathologists and audiologists. Est attendance: 10,000. For info: Cheryl Russell, Conv Dir, American Speech–Language–Hearing Assn, 10801 Rockville Pike, Rockville, MD 20852-3279. Phone: (301) 897-5700.

BELGIUM: DYNASTY DAY. Nov 15. National holiday in honor of Belgian monarchy.

BRAZIL: REPUBLIC DAY. Nov 15. Commemorates the Proclamation of the Republic in 1889.

FIRST BLACK PROFESSIONAL HOCKEY PLAYER: ANNIVERSARY. Nov 15, 1950. When Arthur Dorrington signed a contract to play hockey with the Atlantic City Seagulls of the Eastern Amateur League, he became the first black man to play organized hockey in the US. He played for the Seagulls during the 1950 and 1951 seasons.

GEORGE SPELVIN DAY. Nov 15. Believed to be the anniversary of George Spelvin's theatrical birth—in Charles A. Gardiner's play *Karl the Peddler* on Nov 15, 1886, in a production at New York, NY. The name (or equivalent Georgina, Georgetta, etc) is used in play programs to conceal the fact that an actor is performing in more than one role. The fictitious Spelvin is said to have appeared in more than 10,000 Broadway performances. See also: "England: Walter Plinge Day" (Dec 2) for British equivalent.

GREAT AMERICAN SMOKEOUT. Nov 15. A day observed annually to celebrate smoke-free environments. Annually, the third Thursday in November. For info: Corporate Communications Dept, American Cancer Soc, 1599 Clifton Rd NE, Atlanta, GA 30329. Phone: (404) 329-5735. Web: www.cancer.org.

GYPSY CONDEMNATION ORDER: ANNIVERSARY. Nov 15, 1943. An order was issued by Heinrich Himmler for nomadic Gypsies and part-Gypsies to be placed in concentration camps. In cases of doubt, it was up to local heads of police to determine who was a Gypsy. Some estimates put the number of Gypsies killed in the Holocaust as high as half a million.

JAPAN: SHICHI-GO-SAN. Nov 15. Annual children's festival. The *Shichi-Go-San* (Seven-Five-Three) rite is "the most picturesque event in the autumn season." Parents take their three-year-old children of either sex, five-year-old boys and seven-year-old girls to the parish shrines dressed in their best clothes. There the guardian spirits are thanked for the healthy growth of the children and prayers are offered for their further development.

MOON PHASE: NEW MOON. Nov 15. Moon enters New Moon phase at 1:40 AM, EST.

NAIA MEN'S SOCCER NATIONAL CHAMPIONSHIP. Nov 15–20. New Mexico Soccer Tournament Complex, Bernalillo, New Mexico. 12-team field competes for national championship. 43rd annual. For info: John Kehl, Natl Assn of Intercollegiate Athletics, 6120 S Yale Ave, Ste 1450, Tulsa, OK 74136-4223. Phone: (918) 494-8828. Fax: (918) 494-8841. E-mail: jkehl@naia.org. Web: www.naia.org.

NAIA WOMEN'S SOCCER NATIONAL CHAMPIONSHIP. Nov 15–20. St. Thomas University, Miami, FL. Twelve-team field competes for national championship. 18th annual. Est attendance: 3,000. For info: Natalie Cronkhite, Natl Assn of Intercollegiate Athletics, 6120 S Yale Ave, Ste 1450, Tulsa, OK 74136-4223. Phone: (918) 494-8828. Fax: (918) 494-8841. E-mail: ncronkhite@naia.org. Web: www.naia.org.

★NATIONAL GREAT AMERICAN SMOKEOUT DAY. Nov 15.

NAVRATILOVA RETIRES: ANNIVERSARY. Nov 15, 1994. Ending her professional tennis career, Martina Navratilova played a losing first round match against Gabriela Sabatini in the 1994 season-ending Virginia Slims tournament. Hardly a ripple was made in one of the most impressive records in tennis history. During 21 years of play Navratilova chalked up a career tally of 1,443–211 singles match record and 167 titles (the most ever for anyone, male or female). She recorded 18 Grand Slam singles titles, 31 Grand Slam women's doubles championships and six career Grand Slam mixed doubles championships.

NEWBERRY LIBRARY VERY MERRY HOLIDAY BAZAAR. Nov 15–18. Chicago, IL. Easy one-stop holiday shopping at booths with gifts from 40 Chicago-area cultural institutions, such as the Lincoln Park Zoo store and the Frank Lloyd Wright House at Oak Park. Est attendance: 5,500. For info: Newberry Library, 60 W Walton, Chicago, IL 60610-3380. Phone: (312) 255-3510.

O'KEEFFE, GEORGIA: BIRTH ANNIVERSARY. Nov 15, 1887. Described as one of the greatest American artists of the 20th century, Georgia O'Keeffe was born at Sun Prairie, WI. In 1924, she married the famous photographer Alfred Stieglitz. His more than 500 photographs of her have been called "the greatest love poem in the history of photography." She painted desert landscapes and flower studies. She died at Santa Fe, NM, Mar 6, 1986.

ROMMEL, ERWIN: BIRTH ANNIVERSARY. Nov 15, 1891. Field marshal and commander of the German Afrika Korps in WWII, Erwin Rommel was born at Heidenheim, in Wurttemberg, Germany. Rommel commanded the Seventh Panzer Division in the Battle of France. Considered an excellent commander, Rommel's early success in Africa made him a legend as the "Desert Fox," but in early 1943 he was outmaneuvered by Field Marshal Bernard Montgomery and Germany surrendered Tunis in May of that year. Implicated in July 1944 in an attempted assassination of Hitler, he was given the choice of suicide or a trial and chose the former. Rommel died by his own hand at age 52, Oct 14, 1944, near Ulm, Germany.

SPACE MILESTONE: *BURAN* (USSR). Nov 15, 1988. The Soviet Union's first reusable space plane, *Buran*, landed on this date, completing a smooth, unmanned mission at approximately 1:25 AM, EST, after orbiting the Earth twice in 3 hours, 25 minutes. Launched at Baikonur, Soviet central Asia, the importance of this mission was in its computer-controlled liftoff and return.

SUGARLOAF'S FALL GAITHERSBURG CRAFT FESTIVAL. Nov 15–18. Montgomery County Fairgrounds, Gaithersburg, MD. This show, now in its 26th year, features 550 nationally recognized craft designers and fine artists displaying and selling their original creations. Craft demonstrations, children's entertainment, live music, food, hourly gift certificate drawings and more. Est attendance: 48,000. For info: Sugarloaf Mountain Works, Inc, 200 Orchard Ridge Dr, #215, Gaithersburg, MD 20878. Phone: (800) 210-9900. E-mail: smworks@sugarloafcrafts .com. Web: www.sugarloafcrafts.com.

BIRTHDAYS TODAY

Ed Asner, 72, actor ("The Mary Tyler Moore Show," "Lou Grant," *Roots*), born Kansas City, MO, Nov 15, 1929.
Daniel Barenboim, 59, musician, conductor, born Buenos Aires, Argentina, Nov 15, 1942.
Joanna Barnes, 67, actress ("The Trials of O'Brien"), born Boston, MA, Nov 15, 1934.
Petula Clark, 69, singer ("Downtown," "I Know a Place," "This Is My Song"), actress, born Ewell, Surrey, England, Nov 15, 1932.
Beverly D'Angelo, 47, actress (*Hair, Coal Miner's Daughter*), born Columbus, OH, Nov 15, 1954.
Kevin Eubanks, 44, "The Tonight Show" bandleader, born Philadelphia, PA, Nov 15, 1957.
Yaphet Kotto, 64, actor ("Homicide," *Nothing But a Man, Blue Collar, Midnight Run*), born New York, NY, Nov 15, 1937.
Bill Richardson, 54, US Secretary of Energy (Clinton administration), born Pasadena, CA, Nov 15, 1947.
Joseph Wapner, 82, television personality ("People's Court"), retired judge, born Los Angeles, CA, Nov 15, 1919.
Sam Waterston, 61, actor (*The Killing Fields, The Great Gatsby*, "I'll Fly Away," "Law & Order"), born Cambridge, MA, Nov 15, 1940.

November 2001

S	M	T	W	T	F	S
				1	2	3
4	5	6	7	8	9	10
11	12	13	14	15	16	17
18	19	20	21	22	23	24
25	26	27	28	29	30	

NOVEMBER 16 — FRIDAY
Day 320 — 45 Remaining

CANADA: MUSKOKA ARTS AND CRAFTS CHRISTMAS SHOW. Nov 16–18. Bracebridge, ON. For info: Muskoka Arts and Crafts, Box 376, Bracebridge, ON, Canada P1L 1T7. Phone: (705) 645-5501. E-mail: mac@surenet.net. Web: www .muskokaartsandcrafts.com.

CHRISTMAS IN CAPE MAY. Nov 16–Jan 1, 2002. Cape May, NJ. Visit the spirit of Christmas past with tours and special events in the old-fashioned setting of Victorian Cape May. Annually, the weekend before Thanksgiving through New Year's weekend. Est attendance: 9,000. For info: Mid-Atlantic Center for the Arts, PO Box 340, 1048 Washington St, Cape May, NJ 08204. Phone: (609) 884-5404. Fax: (609) 884-0574. Web: www.capemaymac .org.

CHRISTMAS IN SEATTLE. Nov 16–18. Seattle, WA. A holiday shopper's paradise! Unique gifts and specialty foods to sample and buy. Entertainment, Santa Claus and music add a seasonal feel to the show. Crafters from across the nation and Canada await the shoppers. For info: Susie O'Brien Borer, Showcase Northwest, Inc, PO Box 2815, Kirkland, WA 98083. Phone: (800) 521-SHOW.

COLORADO RIVER CROSSING BALLOON FESTIVAL. Nov 16–18. Cibola High School, Yuma, AZ. 11th annual. 55 balloons. Sunrise balloon liftoffs on Saturday and Sunday at Cibola High School. Sunset balloon glow and fireworks on Saturday evening at Ray Kroc Complex/Desert Sun Stadium. Entertainment, food, vendors. Free admission. Est attendance: 17,000. For info: Caballeros de Yuma, Inc, PO Box 5987, Yuma, AZ 85366. Phone: (520) 343-1715. Fax: (520) 783-1609. Web: www .caballeros.org.

FANTASY OF LIGHT PARADE. Nov 16. Wheeling, WV. Night parade with more than 100 lighted floats and musical units. Est attendance: 80,000. For info: Wheeling Conv and Visitors Bureau, 1401 Main St, Wheeling, WV 26003. Phone: (800) 828-3097 or (304) 233-7709. Fax: (304) 233-1470. Web: www.wheelingcvb .com/calendar.

GARDEN OF LIGHTS. Nov 16–Dec 31. Norfolk Botanical Garden, Norfolk, VA. 8th annual. This holiday festival includes more than 500,000 twinkling lights along a 2.5-mile route through the Garden. Proceeds to benefit the Norfolk Botanical Garden Society, a non-profit organization. Est attendance: 50,000. For info: Norfolk Botanical Garden, 6700 Azalea Garden Rd, Norfolk, VA 23518. Phone: (757) 441-5830. Fax: (757) 853-8294. Web: www .virginiagarden.org.

GRAND ILLUMINATION. Nov 16. Lahaska, PA. At dusk, the Village's brilliant outdoor holiday lights display debuts. Free cider and toasted marshmallows. Preview of new gift ideas in shops. Free admission. Est attendance: 5,000. For info: Peddler's Village, Routes 202 & 263, Lahaska, PA 18931. Phone: (215) 794-4000. Fax: (215) 794-4001. Web: www.peddlersvillage.com.

HANDY, WILLIAM CHRISTOPHER: BIRTH ANNIVERSARY. Nov 16, 1873. American composer, bandleader, "Father of the Blues," W.C. Handy was born at Florence, AL. He died at New York, NY, Mar 28, 1958.

HINDEMITH, PAUL: BIRTH ANNIVERSARY. Nov 16, 1895. Prolific composer and teacher, born at Hanau, Germany. Became a resident and citizen of the US during World War II. Died at Frankfurt, Germany, Dec 28, 1963.

HOLIDAY CRAFT SHOW. Nov 16–18. Depot Lane, Schoharie, NY. Handcrafted items offered, bake sale, country kitchen. Est attendance: 1,000. For info: Paul Piela, Show Mgr, Schoharie Colonial Heritage Assn, PO Box 554, Schoharie, NY 12157. Phone: (518) 295-7505. E-mail: scha@midtel.net.

HOLIDAY FOLK FAIR INTERNATIONAL. Nov 16–18. Wisconsin Center, Milwaukee, WI. International festival featuring costumes, dancing, entertainment, exhibits, workshops, folk wares and cuisine from 65 cultures. Also children's activities. Annually,

the weekend before Thanksgiving. Est attendance: 65,000. For info: Holiday Folk Fair Intl, Intl Institute of Wisconsin, 1110 N Old World Third St, Ste 420, Milwaukee, WI 53203. Phone: (414) 225-6220. Fax: (414) 225-6235. E-mail: iiw@execpc.com.

LAND OF MARK TWAIN BLUEGRASS MUSIC FESTIVAL. Nov 16–18. Hannibal Inn, Hannibal, MO. Annually, the third weekend in November. Est attendance: 1,500. For info: Delbert Spray, Tri-State Bluegrass Assn, RR 1, Kahoka, MO 63445. Phone: (573) 853-4344.

LIGHT-UP WEEKEND. Nov 16–18. Downtown Pittsburgh, PA. A perfect spot to watch this spectacular light show would be on top of Mount Washington. Every downtown building lights up to begin the holiday season. For info: Greater Pittsburgh Conv & Visitors Bureau, 425 Sixth Ave, Pittsburgh, PA 15219-1834. Phone: (412) 281-7711 or (800) 359-0758. Fax: (412) 644-5512.

MEREDITH, BURGESS: BIRTH ANNIVERSARY. Nov 16, 1907. Actor (*Of Mice and Men, Rocky*) born at Cleveland, OH. Some sources give his year of birth as 1908 or 1909. Died at Malibu, CA, Sept 9, 1997.

★**NATIONAL FARM-CITY WEEK.** Nov 16–22. Presidential Proclamation issued for a week in November since 1956, customarily for the week ending with Thanksgiving Day. Requested by congressional resolutions from 1956–1958; since 1959 issued annually without request.

OKLAHOMA: ADMISSION DAY: ANNIVERSARY. Nov 16. Became 46th state in 1907.

PBR BULL RIDING. Nov 16–17. Multi-Purpose Events Center, Wichita Falls, TX. Professional bull riding at its best. Top riders, top bulls, top prizes. Est attendance: 3,000. For info: Wichita Falls CVB, 1000 5th St, Wichita Falls, TX 76301. Phone: (940) 716-5500. Fax: (940) 716-5509. E-mail: MPEC@WF.net. Web: www.viewscape.com or www.wf.net.

PEDDLER'S VILLAGE GINGERBREAD HOUSE COMPETITION & DISPLAY. Nov 16–Jan 6, 2002. Lahaska, PA. More than 50 gingerbread house entries from throughout the US compete for more than $4,800 in cash prizes in such categories as: Victorian, Authentic Reproduction of a Significant Building, Amateur, Incredibly Unusual 3-Dimensional and Childrens (12 and under; 13–18). The creative masterpieces are displayed throughout the holiday season in the Village Gazebo. Free admission. Est attendance: 850,000. For info: Peddler's Village, Routes 202 & 263, Lahaska, PA 18931. Phone: (215) 794-4000. Fax: (215) 794-4001. Web: www.peddlersvillage.com.

PITTSBURGH'S CHRISTMAS EXTRAVAGANZA. Nov 16–18. Pittsburgh Convention Center, Pittsburgh, PA. One of the area's finest arts and crafts festivals. More than 200 booths! Est attendance: 12,000. For info: Debbie & David Stoner, Family Festival Assn, PO Box 166, Irwin, PA 15642. Phone: (724) 863-4577. Fax: (724) 863-4577.

RAMADAN: THE ISLAMIC MONTH OF FASTING. Nov 16–Dec 15. Begins on Islamic lunar calendar date Ramadan 1, 1422. Ramadan, the ninth month of the Islamic calendar, is holy because it was during this month that the Holy Qur'an [Koran] was revealed. All adults of sound body and mind fast from dawn (before sunrise) until sunset to achieve spiritual and physical purification and self-discipline, abstaining from food, drink and intimate relations. It is a time for feeling a common bond with the poor and needy, a time of piety and prayer. Different methods for "anticipating" the visibility of the new moon crescent at Mecca are used by different Muslim groups. US date may vary.

RIEL, LOUIS: HANGING ANNIVERSARY. Nov 16, 1885. Born at St. Boniface, Manitoba, Canada, Oct 23, 1844, Louis Riel, leader of the Metis (French/Indian mixed ancestry), was elected to Canada's House of Commons in 1873 and 1874, but never seated. Confined to asylums for madness (feigned or falsely charged, some said), Riel became a US citizen in 1883. In 1885 he returned to western Canada to lead the North West Rebellion. Defeated, he surrendered and was tried for treason, convicted and hanged, at Regina, Northwest Territory, Canada. Seen as a patriot and protector of French culture in Canada, Riel's life and death became a legend and a symbol of the problems between French and English Canadians.

ROMAN CATHOLICS ISSUE NEW CATECHISM: ANNIVERSARY. Nov 16, 1992. For the first time since 1563, the Roman Catholic Church issued a new universal catechism, which addressed modern-day issues.

SAINT EUSTATIUS, WEST INDIES: STATIA AND AMERICA DAY: 225th ANNIVERSARY. Nov 16, 1776. St. Eustatius, Leeward Islands. To commemorate the first salute to an American flag by a foreign government, from Fort Oranje in 1776. Festivities include sports events and dancing. During the American Revolution St. Eustatius was an important trading center and a supply base for the colonies.

SILVER BELLS IN THE CITY. Nov 16. Lansing, MI. Michigan's capital city sparkles with hospitality on the streets of downtown Lansing's business district for this celebration of lights, music and holiday cheer including an electrical light parade and the lighting of the State of Michigan Holiday Tree. Annually, the Friday before Thanksgiving. Coordinated by Arts Council of Greater Lansing, Inc. Est attendance: 50,000. For info: Arts Council of Greater Lansing, Inc, Center for the Arts, 425 S Grand Ave, Lansing, MI 48933. Phone: (517) 372-4636 ext 3. Fax: (517) 484-2564. Web: www.lansingarts.com.

SPACE MILESTONE: *SKYLAB 4* (US). Nov 16, 1973. 30th manned US space flight launched with three astronauts, G.P. Carr, W.R. Page and E.G. Gibson who spent 84 days on the space station. Space walks totalled 22 hours. Returned to Earth on Feb 8, 1974.

SPACE MILESTONE: *VENERA 3* (USSR). Nov 16, 1965. Launched this date, this unmanned space probe crashed into Venus, Mar 1, 1966. First man-made object on another planet.

STAMP EXPO: AMERICA. Nov 16–18. Radisson Hotel, Anaheim, CA. Est attendance: 4,000. For info: Intl Stamp Collectors Soc, PO Box 854, Van Nuys, CA 91408. Phone: (818) 997-6496. Fax: (818) 988-4337. E-mail: iibick@aol.com. Web: www.bick.net.

TELLABRATION! A WEEKEND OF STORYTELLING FOR GROWN-UPS. Nov 16–18. Many sites throughout Connecticut. Simultaneous storytelling concerts for adults. Annually, the weekend before Thanksgiving. Est attendance: 1,000. For info: Ann Shapiro, Adm, Connecticut Storytelling Center, Connecticut College, Box 5295, 270 Mohegan Ave, New London, CT 06320. Phone: (860) 439-2764. Fax: (860) 439-5431. E-mail: csc@conncoll.edu.

UNITED NATIONS: INTERNATIONAL DAY FOR TOLERANCE: 5th ANNIVERSARY. Nov 16. On Dec 12, 1996, the General Assembly established the International Day for Tolerance, to commemorate the adoption by UNESCO member states of the Declaration of Principles on Tolerance in 1995. For info: United Nations, Dept of Public Info, New York, NY 10017.

UNIVERSITY OF CHICAGO'S FIRST FOOTBALL VICTORY: ANNIVERSARY. Nov 16, 1892. The University of Chicago, which played to a 0–0 tie with Northwestern in its first-ever football game on the preceding Oct 22, won its first game for Coach Amos Alonzo Stagg 10–4 against Illinois at Chicago, Nov 16, 1892. A founding member of the Big 10, Chicago eliminated its football program for many years, but now competes against the likes of New York University, Emory and Washington University at St. Louis.

WAY OF LIGHTS. Nov 16–Jan 5, 2002. Belleville, IL. Remember the birth of Christ while journeying along a path illuminated with one million white lights to the traditional crib. Indoor activities include Children's Village, choirs and a Christmas Tree display, all expressing the message of Christ's peace. Est attendance: 350,000. For info: Shrine of Our Lady of the Snows, 442 S De Mazenod Dr, Belleville, IL 62223-1094. Phone: (618) 397-6700. Fax: (618) 397-1210. Web: www.snows.org.

YORK INTERNATIONAL POSTCARD FAIR. Nov 16–17. York Fairgrounds, York, PA. Est attendance: 1,000. For info: Mary Martin Ltd, 4899 Pulaski Hwy, Rt 40, Perryville, MD 21903. Phone: (410) 575-7768. Fax: (410) 642-2053.

BIRTHDAYS TODAY

Oksana Baiul, 24, Olympic figure skater, born Dniepropetrovsk, Ukraine, Nov 16, 1977.
Lisa Bonet, 34, actress ("The Cosby Show," "A Different World," *Angel Heart*), born San Francisco, CA, Nov 16, 1967.
Elizabeth Drew, 66, journalist, born Cincinnati, OH, Nov 16, 1935.

	S	M	T	W	T	F	S
November					1	2	3
2001	4	5	6	7	8	9	10
	11	12	13	14	15	16	17
	18	19	20	21	22	23	24
	25	26	27	28	29	30	

Dwight Eugene Gooden, 37, baseball player, born Tampa, FL, Nov 16, 1964.
Marg Helgenberger, 43, actress ("China Beach"), born Fremont, NE, Nov 16, 1958.
Martha Plimpton, 31, actress ("The Defenders"), born New York, NY, Nov 16, 1970.

NOVEMBER 17 — SATURDAY
Day 321 — 44 Remaining

BALLARD'S YULEFEST AT THE NORDIC HERITAGE MUSEUM. Nov 17–18. Seattle, WA. A Scandinavian holiday extravaganza with typical Nordic Christmas foods, music and dance. Crafts throughout the museum, kid's room for decoration making, one-of-a-kind gifts. Est attendance: 5,000. For info: Marianne Forssblad, Dir, Nordic Heritage Museum, 3014 NW 67th St, Seattle, WA 98117. Phone: (206) 789-5707. Fax: (206) 789-3271.

CHRISTMAS GALLERY. Nov 17–Jan 5, 2002. Firehouse Art Center, Norman, OK. Shoppers find gifts for friends, children and family, from stocking stuffers to "executive" gifts! Original works and limited production pieces by juried and invited artists and craftspeople. Est attendance: 3,500. For info: Asst Dir, Firehouse Art Center, 444 S Flood, Norman, OK 73069. Phone: (405) 329-4523.

CHRISTMAS WALK. Nov 17–Dec 31. Pella Historical Village, Pella, IA. To celebrate an old-fashioned Christmas. Closed Sundays and Christmas Day. Est attendance: 1,000. For info: Pella Historical Soc, 507 Franklin, Pella, IA 50219. Phone: (515) 628-2409. Web: www.PellaTulipTime.com.

CUSTER STATE PARK BUFFALO AUCTION. Nov 17. Custer, SD. A live sale at 10 AM, [MST], of 300–400 surplus buffalo (calves, yearlings, mature cows and two-year-old bulls). Est attendance: 600. For info: Ron Walker, Custer State Park, HC 83, Box 70, Custer, SD 57730. Phone: (605) 255-4515 or (605) 255-4814. Fax: (605) 255-4460. E-mail: ron.walker@state.sd.us.

DELAND FALL FESTIVAL OF THE ARTS. Nov 17–18. DeLand, FL. Showcasing the works of more than 200 artists, the festival features more than $20,000 in prize money awarded during this two-day juried and judged event. Artist demonstrations, a youth art exhibition, children's workshops, specialty foods and live entertainment enhance the show. Categories featuring the traditional mediums of oil, acrylic, watercolor, pottery, sculpture and jewelry are enhanced by original video, computer and performance arts categories. Est attendance: 40,000. For info: DeLand Area Chamber of Commerce. Phone: (800) 749-4350 or (904) 734-4331.

FESTIVAL OF LIGHTS AT CINCINNATI ZOO. Nov 17–Jan 6, 2002. Cincinnati Zoo and Botanical Garden, Cincinnati, OH. More than a million lights transform the Zoo as new light displays are added each year. Ice skating at the Victorian Wonderland. Also, wagon rides, Enchanted Village, visits with Santa Claus, holiday shopping, hot chocolate and more. Est attendance: 225,000. For info: Events and Promotions Dept, Cincinnati Zoo and Botanical Garden, 3400 Vine St, Cincinnati, OH 45220. Phone: (513) 281-4701 ext 8316. Fax: (513) 559-7790. Web: www.cincyzoo.org.

HANDEL'S *MESSIAH*. Nov 17. RLDS Auditorium, Independence, MO. 85th annual performance of Handel's *Messiah* by the Independence Messiah Choir, Messiah Festival Orchestra and renowned soloists, conducted by Jack R. Ergo. Est attendance: 5,000. For info: Public Relations, RLDS Headquarters, PO Box 1059, Independence, MO 64051. Phone: (816) 521-3045. Fax: (816) 521-3043. E-mail: snaylor@rlds.org. Web: www.rlds.org.

HARVEST FESTIVAL. Nov 17–18. Dade County Youth Fairground, Miami, FL. A family-oriented festival. Crafts and quilts for sale, antique engines and cars on display, educational programs, historical reenactments, folk art demonstrations, traditional music and dance; food. Est attendance: 20,000. For info: Steve Stuempfle, Fest Coord, Historical Assn of Southern Florida, 101 W Flagler St, Miami, FL 33130. Phone: (305) 375-1492. For craft vendor info: Denise Paparella. Phone: (954) 987-4275.

HOLIDAY PARADE. Nov 17. Madison, WI. Parade around the Capitol Square with floats, bands, clowns and much more. For info: Capitol City Parade Assn, 7818 Big Sky Dr, Ste 205, Madison, WI 53719. Web: www.madfest.org.

HOLIDAYS IN THE CITY GRAND ILLUMINATION PARADE. Nov 17. Norfolk, VA. All of Norfolk's downtown skyscrapers and many of its smaller buildings outline their profiles in lights for Holidays in the City. On the first evening of the illumination a downtown lighted street parade kicks off the celebration of the season. All of the floats, bands and entries in this nighttime parade are lighted. Annually, the Saturday before Thanksgiving. Est attendance: 100,000. For info: Parade Manager, Downtown Norfolk Council, 201 Granby St, Ste 101, Norfolk, VA 23510. Phone: (757) 623-1757. Fax: (757) 623-1756. E-mail: dnc@downtownnorfolk.org.

HOMEMADE BREAD DAY. Nov 17. A day for the family to remember and enjoy the making, baking and eating of nutritious homemade bread. For info: Homemade Bread Day Committee, PO Box 3, Montague, MI 49437-0003.

IN CELEBRATION OF CHOCOLATE. Nov 17. The American Club, Kohler, WI. One of the nation's most extravagant chocolate events featuring an elegant chocolate buffet. Est attendance: 400. For info: The American Club, Highland Dr, Kohler, WI 53044. Phone: (800) 344-2838. Fax: (920) 457-0299. Web: www.americanclub.com.

KECHI'S ANTIQUE COUNTRY CHRISTMAS. Nov 17. Kechi, KS. Spend the day in "The Antique Capital of Kansas" strolling through our small quaint community of 18 antique, craft and speciality shops. Enjoy fine dining in local restaurants, Christmas caroling in the downtown area, tour Karg Art Glass & Gallery and an old-fashioned surrey ride. Motel accommodations and bed

& breakfast all located within two miles. Est attendance: 1,000. For info: Rick Eberhard, Exec Dir, Kechi Area Chamber of Commerce, 205 Heritage Ct, Kechi, KS 67067-8710. Phone: (316) 744-1337. Fax: (316) 744-1337. E-mail: kechichamber@domain diner.com. Web: www.kechikscoc.com.

LA POSADA de KINGSVILLE: A CELEBRATION OF LIGHTS. Nov 17–Dec 16. Kingsville, TX. While a celebration of lights recaptures the joy and spirit of Christmas as businesses and neighborhoods twinkle with lights from the weekend before Thanksgiving, many holiday events with a South Texas flavor are scheduled: special activities for children, nighttime parade with lighted floats and holiday music and much more. Call for dates of specific events. Est attendance: 50,000. For info: Kingsville Conv and Visitors Bureau, 1501 N Hwy 77, Kingsville, TX 78364-1562. Phone: (800) 333-5032. Fax: (361) 592-3227. Web: www .kingsvilletexas.com.

MESSINA HOF'S WINE PREMIERE. Nov 17. Bryan, TX. Traditional celebration of the new vintages. Wine aficionados' palates are treated to the premiere of all the new wines. There are several wine-related activities like Chardonnay Blending Seminars, national and international Cabernet Shoot-Outs and wine and food pairing seminars. In the evening, a new vintage reception will be followed by an elegant gourmet wine premiere dinner. Est attendance: 2,500. For info: Messina Hof Wine Cellars, 4545 Old Reliance Rd, Bryan, TX 77808. Phone: (979) 778-9463. Fax: (979) 778-1729.

MOBIUS, AUGUST: BIRTH ANNIVERSARY. Nov 17, 1790. German astronomer, mathematician, teacher and author, August Ferdinand Mobius was born at Schulpforte, Germany. Mobius was a pioneer in the field of topology, and first described the Mobius net and the Mobius strip. He died at Leipzig, Sept 26, 1868.

MONTGOMERY, BERNARD LAW: BIRTH ANNIVERSARY. Nov 17, 1887. Bernard Law Montgomery, who commanded the British Eighth Army to victory at El Alamein in north Africa in 1943, was born at St. Mark's Vicarage, Kennington Oval, London, England. He also led the Eighth Army in the Sicilian and Italian campaigns and commanded all ground forces in the 1944 Normandy landing. Montgomery died Mar 24, 1976, at Alton, Hampshire, England.

NAIA MEN'S AND WOMEN'S CROSS COUNTRY NATIONAL CHAMPIONSHIP. Nov 17. University of Wisconsin-Parkside, Kenosha, WI. Men compete on an 8K course and women compete on a 5K course with the top 25 individual finishers in each championship receiving All-America honors. 46th men's championship; 22nd women's. For info: Kevin Dee, Natl Assn of Intercollegiate Athletics, 6120 S Yale Ave, Ste 1450, Tulsa, OK 74136-4223. Phone: (918) 494-8828. Fax: (918) 494-8841. E-mail: kdee@naia.org. Web: www.naia.org.

NATIONAL COMMUNITY EDUCATION ASSOCIATION CONFERENCE. Nov 17–20. Charleston Place, Charleston, SC. 36th annual. Largest national gathering for community educators and others interested in promoting parent-community involvement in education, forming community partnerships to address community needs and expanding lifelong learning opportunities for all community residents. Est attendance: 700. For info: Ursula Ellis, Dir of Communications, Natl Community Education Assn, 3929 Old Lee Hwy, Ste 91-A, Fairfax, VA 22030-2401. Phone: (703) 359-8973. Fax: (703) 359-0972. E-mail: ncea@ncea.com.

NATIONAL DONOR SABBATH. Nov 17–19. To increase awareness about the dire need for organs and tissues for transplantation and to dispel fears that religion and tissue and organ donation are incompatible. Annually, the weekend before Thanksgiving. For info: Health Resources and Services Admin, US Dept of Health and Human Services. Phone: (301) 443-7577. Web: www.organdonor.gov.

NORDIC YULE FEST. Nov 17–18. Nordic Heritage Museum, Seattle, WA. Annual Christmas fair featuring crafts, holiday foods, beer garden, music and dance and children's activities. Est attendance: 5,000. For info: Nordic Heritage Museum, 3014 NW 67th St, Seattle, WA 98117. Phone: (206) 789-5707. Fax: (206) 789-3271.

PEALE, TITIAN RAMSEY: BIRTH ANNIVERSARY. Nov 17, 1799. American artist, naturalist, son of Charles Willson Peale, born at Philadelphia, PA. Died there Mar 13, 1885.

A PLANTATION CHRISTMAS. Nov 17–Jan 6, 2002. Belle Meade Plantation, Nashville, TN. All the splendor of an antebellum Christmas—before the onset of the Civil War. Tour guides in ca. 1860 ballgowns. For info: Belle Meade Plantation, 5025 Harding Rd, Nashville, TN 37205. Phone: (615) 356-0501. Fax: (615) 356-2336. Web: www.bellemeadeplantation.com.

QUEEN ELIZABETH I: ACCESSION ANNIVERSARY. Nov 17, 1558. Anniversary of accession of Elizabeth I to English throne; celebrated as a holiday in England for more than a century after her death in 1603.

RANCH HAND BREAKFAST. Nov 17. King Ranch, Kingsville, TX. A breakfast cooked and served outdoors at the world-famous King Ranch. See Longhorn cattle and real cowboys on horseback. Annually, the Saturday before Thanksgiving. Est attendance: 7,000. For info: Kingsville Conv and Visitors Bureau, 1501 N Hwy 77, Kingsville, TX 78364-1562. Phone: (800) 333-5032. Fax: (361) 592-3227. E-mail: cvb@kingsvilletexas.com. Web: www.kingsvilletexas.com.

REMEMBRANCE DAY. Nov 17. Gettysburg, PA. An annual event held in conjunction with the Lincoln Observance, with a parade of Civil War troops to the Albert Woolson Monument for a wreath-laying ceremony. Sponsored by the Sons of Union Veterans. Est attendance: 5,000. For info: Gettysburg CVB, PO Box 4117, Gettysburg, PA 17325. Phone: (717) 334-6274. Fax: (717) 334-1166. Web: www.gettysburg.com.

SUEZ CANAL: ANNIVERSARY. Nov 17, 1869. Formal opening of the Suez Canal. It had taken 1.5 million men a decade to dig the 100-mile canal. It shortened the sea route from Europe to India by 6,000 miles. An Anglo-French commission ran the canal until 1956, when Egypt's President Gamal Abdel Nasser seized it.

SWITZERLAND: LUCERNE PIANO FESTIVAL. Nov 17–25. Lucerne, Switzerland. A centre of piano music and a mecca for piano lovers from around the world. Meet during a prolonged weekend the world's most renowned pianists and enjoy six classical recitals and a late-night jazz performance. For info: Elisabeth Mlasko or Sheila Huber, Intl Festival of Music, PO Box CH-6002, Lucerne, Switzerland. Phone: (41) (41) 2264400. Fax: (41) (41) 2264460. E-mail: media@lucernemusic.ch. Web: www.lucernemusic.ch.

November 2001	S	M	T	W	T	F	S
					1	2	3
	4	5	6	7	8	9	10
	11	12	13	14	15	16	17
	18	19	20	21	22	23	24
	25	26	27	28	29	30	

TELLEBRATION! A NIGHT OF WORLD WIDE STORYTELLING. Nov 17. Charleston, SC. A special night of storytelling celebrating the millennium. Local storytellers from the Storytelling Troupe of Charleston and "Charleston's Storyteller of the Millennium" will give you a night you won't forget! Annually, the Saturday before Thanksgiving. Est attendance: 300. For info: Mike Miller, Pres, Storytelling Troupe of Charleston, 35 Hillcreek Blvd, Charleston, SC 29412. Phone: (843) 762-4458. E-mail: storytellingtroupe@ureach.com. Web: www.ureach.com /org/storytellingtroupe.

THAILAND: ELEPHANT ROUND-UP AT SURIN. Nov 17. Elephant demonstrations in morning, elephant races and tug-of-war between 100 men and one elephant. Observed since 1961 on third Saturday in November. Special trains from Bangkok on previous day.

WARM SPRINGS THANKSGIVING. Nov 17. Little White House, Warm Springs, GA. Dr. Tom Wentland portrays Pres Franklin D. Roosevelt in this presentation of what it was like when FDR spent the holiday here. Antique cars, harvest decor. Annually, the Saturday before Thanksgiving. Est attendance: 300. For info: Frankie Mewborn, Mgr, Little White House, 401 Little White House Rd, Warm Springs, GA 31830. Phone: (706) 655-5870.

WORLD PEACE DAY. Nov 17. World Peace Day was created to give the common person a way to demonstrate their desire for peace. To do this, people pray for peace all day, drive with their headlights on, wear a white ribbon for peace (everyday) and sign our petition for peace (available on our web page) or print our petition for peace and have 20 people sign it. Annually, Nov 17. For info: Don Morris, PO Box 565245, Miami, FL 33256-5245. Phone: (305) 270-8890. E-mail: peaceguy@peaceday.org. Web: www.peaceday.org.

ZENGER, JOHN PETER: ARREST ANNIVERSARY. Nov 17, 1734. Colonial printer and journalist who established the *New York Weekly Journal* (first issue, Nov 5, 1733). Zenger was arrested Nov 17, 1734, for libel against the colonial governor, but continued to edit his newspaper from jail. Trial was held during August 1735. Zenger's acquittal was an important early step toward freedom of the press in America. Zenger was born at Germany in 1697, came to the US in 1710 and died July 28, 1746, at New York, NY.

BIRTHDAYS TODAY

Justin Cooper, 13, actor ("Brother's Keeper," *Liar, Liar*), born Southern California, Nov 17, 1988.

Howard Dean, 53, Governor of Vermont (D), born East Hampton, NY, Nov 17, 1948.

Danny DeVito, 57, actor ("Taxi," *Twins*), director (*Throw Mama from the Train*), born Neptune, NJ, Nov 17, 1944.

Shelby Foote, 85, writer, historian (*Civil War*), born Greenville, MS, Nov 17, 1916.

Daisy Fuentes, 35, MTV veejay, host ("America's Funniest Home Videos"), born Havana, Cuba, Nov 17, 1966.

Isaac Hanson, 21, singer (Hanson), born Tulsa, OK, Nov 17, 1980.

Lauren Hutton, 57, model, actress (*American Gigolo*), born Charleston, SC, Nov 17, 1944.

James M. Inhofe, 67, US Senator (R, Oklahoma), born Des Moines, IA, Nov 17, 1934.

Gordon Lightfoot, 63, singer ("Sundown"), songwriter ("Early Morning Rain"), born Orilla, Ontario, Canada, Nov 17, 1938.

Keith Lockhart, 42, Boston Pops conductor, born Poughkeepsie, NY, Nov 17, 1959.

Sophie Marceau, 35, actress (*Braveheart*), born Paris, France, Nov 17, 1966.

Mary Elizabeth Mastrantonio, 43, actress (*The Color of Money, Thieves*), born Oak Park, IL, Nov 17, 1958.

Robert Bruce (Bob) Mathias, 71, former congressman, Olympic gold medal decathlete, born Tulare, CA, Nov 17, 1930.

Lorne Michaels, 57, producer ("Saturday Night Live"), born Toronto, Ontario, Canada, Nov 17, 1944.

RuPaul, 41, model, actor ("The RuPaul Show"), born San Diego, CA, Nov 17, 1960.

Martin Scorsese, 59, director (*Mean Streets, The Color of Money, Raging Bull, Goodfellas*), born Flushing, NY, Nov 17, 1942.

George Thomas (Tom) Seaver, 57, Baseball Hall of Fame pitcher, broadcaster, born Fresno, CA, Nov 17, 1944.

NOVEMBER 18 — SUNDAY
Day 322 — 43 Remaining

ALASCATTALO DAY. Nov 18. Anchorage, AK. To honor humor in general and Alaskan humor in particular. Event is named after "alascattalo," said to be the genetic cross between a moose and a walrus. For info: Steven C. Levi, Parsnackle Press, PO Box 241467, Anchorage, AK 99524. Phone: (907) 337-2021. Fax: (907) 337-4485. E-mail: afscl@alaska.net.

BIG D 103 CARAVAN OF CARRIAGES. Nov 18. Windsor, CT. 7th annual. "Big D Big Drive for Foodshare" consists of listeners soliciting monetary donations, purchasing a shopping cart full of food and walking a five-mile route in the "Caravan of Carriages" from a local grocery store to Foodshare in Windsor, which collects food for 200 shelters and kitchens across Connecticut. Annually, the last Sunday before Thanksgiving. Est attendance: 1,000. For info: WDRC-FM, Big D 103, 869 Blue Hills Ave, Bloomfield, CT 06002. Phone: (860) 243-1115. Fax: (860) 286-8257. Web: www.wdrc.com.

CANADA: CANADIAN WESTERN AGRIBITION. Nov 18–25. Regina, SK. Canada's premiere agricultural event is the world's largest indoor livestock show and marketplace. More than 4,000 cattle, sheep, swine and horses are brought to Agribition, plus pedigreed seed show and agricultural trade and technology show. Livestock producers from around the world come to compare breeding stocks and programs, perhaps importing new bloodlines based on what they discover. Winning at Agribition brings recognition as a producer of quality breeding stock. Also, a variety of entertainment, including the province's biggest indoor professional rodeo. Est attendance: 150,000. For info: Western Agribition, Box 3535, Regina, SK, Canada S4P 3J8. Phone: (306) 565-0565. E-mail: agribition@sk.sympatico.ca. Web: www.agribition.com.

DAGUERRE, LOUIS JACQUES MANDE: BIRTH ANNIVERSARY. Nov 18, 1789. French tax collector, theatre scene-painter, physicist and inventor, was born at Cormeilles-en-Parisis, France. He is remembered for his invention of the daguerreotype photographic process—one of the earliest to permit a photographic image to be chemically fixed to provide a permanent picture. The process was presented to the French Academy of Science Jan 7, 1839. Daguerre died near Paris, France, July 10, 1851.

EIGHTEENTH-CENTURY THRESHING DAY. Nov 18. McLean, VA. Help the farm family thresh wheat, make yeast cakes and celebrate the end of the season with light refreshment. Est attendance: 750. For info: Gretchen Brodtman, Claude Moore Colonial Farm at Turkey Run, 6310 Georgetown Pike, McLean, VA 22101. Phone: (703) 442-7557. Fax: (703) 442-0714.

GALLI-CURCI, AMELITA: BIRTH ANNIVERSARY. Nov 18, 1889. Italian-born operatic soprano, made US debut Nov 18, 1916, at Chicago, IL. Born at Milan, Italy, she died at La Jolla, CA, Nov 26, 1963.

GERMANY: VOLKSTRAUERTAG. Nov 18. Memorial Day and national day of mourning in all German states for victims of National Socialism and the dead of both world wars. Observed on the Sunday before Totensonntag. See also: "Germany: Totensonntag" (Nov 25).

GIFT SHOWCASE. Nov 18. Woodbury, CT. This 10th annual showcase includes more than 50 traditional craftsmen and artisans creating and demonstrating their talents. For info: Merry Go Round, 319 Main St S, Woodbury, CT 06798. Phone: (203) 263-2920.

GILBERT, SIR WILLIAM SCHWENCK: BIRTH ANNIVERSARY. Nov 18, 1836. English author of librettos for the famed Gilbert and Sullivan comic operas, born at London, England. Died May 29, 1911, at Harrow Weald, Middlesex, England, as a result of a heart attack experienced while saving a woman from drowning.

GINGERBREAD VILLAGE. Nov 18–Dec 22. Mormon Trail Center at Historic Winter Quarters Visitors Center, Omaha, NE. View more than 225 gingerbread houses of every shape and size delightfully decorated for the holidays. Gingerbread houses given to charities before Christmas. Est attendance: 16,000. For info: D. Spencer Nilson, Gingerbread Village, 3215 State St, Omaha, NE 68112. Phone: (402) 453-9372.

GRAY, ASA: BIRTH ANNIVERSARY. Nov 18, 1810. Botanist and natural history professor at Harvard, born at Paris, NY. Gray was known as a pioneer in the field of plant geography and a chief advocate of Darwin. Died at Cambridge, MA, Jan 30, 1888.

HAITI: ARMY DAY. Nov 18, 1803. Commemorates the Battle of Vertieres, Nov 18, 1803, in which Haitians defeated the French.

HOLIDAY RHAPSODY OF LIGHTS. Nov 18–Jan 7. Northeast Community College, Norfolk, NE. Holiday light display features more than 400,000 lights. 20 life-size animated displays reminiscent of department store windows of the '40s and '50s. Scenes include: Candy Cane Express, Elves workshop, Reindeer house, Miracle on 34th Street, Santa's mailroom and others. Also, two 12-ft nutcrackers made of 20,000 lights, plus twenty 20-ft candy canes on display. Display activated 5:30–11PM each evening. Est attendance: 100,000. For info: Sandy Wolfe, PO Box 386, Norfolk, NE 68702-0386. Phone: (402) 371-2932.

LATVIA: INDEPENDENCE DAY. Nov 18. National holiday. Commemorates the declaration of an independent Latvia from Germany and Russia in 1918.

LOMBROSO, CESARE: BIRTH ANNIVERSARY. Nov 18, 1836. Italian founder of criminology, born at Verona, Italy. A professor of psychiatry, Lombroso believed that criminality could be identified with certain physical types of people. He died at Turin, Oct 19, 1909.

MERCER, JOHN HERNDON (JOHNNY): BIRTH ANNIVERSARY. Nov 18, 1909. American songwriter, singer, radio performer and actor, born at Savannah, GA. Johnny Mercer wrote lyrics (and often the music) for some of the great American popular music from the 1930s through the 1960s, including "Autumn Leaves," "One for My Baby," "Satin Doll," "On the Achison, Topeka, and the Santa Fe," "You Must Have Been a Beautiful Baby," "Come Rain or Come Shine," "Hooray for Hollywood," "Jeepers Creepers" and countless more. Mercer died June 25, 1976, at Bel Air, CA.

MICKEY MOUSE'S BIRTHDAY. Nov 18. The comical activities of squeaky-voiced Mickey Mouse first appeared in 1928, on the screen of the Colony Theatre at New York City. The film, Walt Disney's "Steamboat Willie," was the first animated cartoon talking picture.

MITCHELL, CAMERON: BIRTH ANNIVERSARY. Nov 18, 1918. American actor Cameron Mitchell was born at Dallastown, PA. He is best-known for his role as Willy Loman's son in *Death of a Salesman* on stage and film. He died July 6, 1994, at Pacific Palisades, CA.

MOROCCO: INDEPENDENCE DAY. Nov 18. National holiday. Commemorates the return from exile in 1955 of Sultan (later King) Sidi Muhammed to form a constitutional government.

MOTHER GOOSE PARADE. Nov 18. El Cajon, CA. "A celebration of children." Floats depict Mother Goose rhymes and fairy tales. Bands, equestrians and clowns. Traditionally, the Sunday before Thanksgiving. Est attendance: 450,000. For info: Mother Goose Parade Assn, 480 N Magnolia Ave, Ste 106, El Cajon, CA 92020. Phone: (619) 444-8712. Fax: (619) 444-3971.

NATIONAL ADOPTION WEEK. Nov 18–24. To commemorate the success of three kinds of adoption—infant, special needs and intercountry—through a variety of special events. Annually, the week of Thanksgiving. For info: Natl Council for Adoption, 1930 17th St NW, Washington, DC 20009-6207. Phone: (202) 328-1200. Fax: (202) 332-0935. E-mail: info@ncfa\usa.org. Web: www.ncfa-usa.org.

NATIONAL BIBLE WEEK. Nov 18–25. An interfaith campaign to promote reading and study of the Bible. Resource packets available. Governors and mayors across the country proclaim National Bible Week observance in their constituencies. Annually, from the Sunday preceding Thanksgiving to the following Sunday. For info: Thomas R. May, Pres, Natl Bible Assn, 1865 Broadway, 7th Fl, New York, NY 10023. Phone: (212) 408-1390. E-mail: tmay @nationalbible.org. Web: www.nationalbible.org.

NATIONAL GAME AND PUZZLE WEEK. Nov 18–24. To increase appreciation of games and puzzles while preserving the tradition of investing time with family and friends. Annually, the last Sunday through Saturday of Thanksgiving week. For info: Frank Beres, Patch Products, PO Box 268, Beloit, WI 53512-0268. Phone: (608) 362-6896. Fax: (608) 362-8178. E-mail: patch @patchproducts.com. Web: www.patchproducts.com.

OMAN: NATIONAL HOLIDAY. Nov 18. Sultanate of Oman celebrates its national day.

PINCHBECK, CHRISTOPHER: DEATH ANNIVERSARY. Nov 18, 1732. English inventor, jeweler and clockmaker. Inventor of the copper and zinc alloy which looked like gold but became synonymous with cheapness. Noted manufacturer of automated musical clocks and instruments. Born at Clerkenwell, London, England, about 1670 (exact date unknown). Died at London, England, Nov 18, 1732.

PUSH-BUTTON PHONE DEBUTS: ANNIVERSARY. Nov 18, 1963. Push-button telephones went into service. Touchtone service was available as an option at an extra charge. This option was only available in two Pennsylvania cities.

"SEE IT NOW" TV PREMIERE: 50th ANNIVERSARY. Nov 18, 1951. "See It Now" was a high quality and significant public affairs show of the 1950s. Known for using its own film footage, unrehearsed interviews and no dubbing, "See It Now"

covered many relevant and newsworthy stories of its time, including desegregation, lung cancer and anti-Communist fervor. One of the most notable shows focused on Senator Joseph McCarthy, leading to McCarthy's appearance on the show which damaged his credibility. The show was hosted by Edward R. Murrow, who also produced it jointly with Fred W. Friendly. Its premiere was the first live commercial coast-to-coast broadcast.

SHEPARD, ALAN: BIRTH ANNIVERSARY. Nov 18, 1923. Former astronaut and the first American in space (in 1961), Shepard was born at East Derry, NH. He was one of only 12 Americans who have walked on the moon and was America's only lunar golfer, practicing his drive in space with a six iron. He was awarded the Medal of Honor in 1979. Shepard died near Monterey, CA, July 21, 1998.

SOUTH AFRICA ADOPTS NEW CONSTITUTION: ANNIVERSARY. Nov 18, 1993. After more than 300 years of white majority rule, basic civil rights were finally granted to blacks in South Africa. The constitution providing such rights was approved by representatives of the ruling party, as well as members of 20 other political parties.

US UNIFORM TIME ZONE PLAN: ANNIVERSARY. Nov 18, 1883. Charles Ferdinand Dowd, a Connecticut school teacher and one of the early advocates of uniform time, proposed a time zone plan of the US (four zones of 15 degrees), which he and others persuaded the railroads to adopt and place in operation on this date. Because it didn't involve the enactment of any law, some localities didn't change their clocks. A year later an international conference applied the same procedure to create time zones for the entire world. US time zones weren't nationally legalized until 1918, with the passage of the Standard Time Act. See also: "Prime Meridian Set: Anniversary" (Nov 1) and "US Standard Time Act: Anniversary" (Mar 19).

VICTORIAN CHRISTMAS WALK. Nov 18–Dec 23. Woodstock, IL. Kick off the Christmas season by visiting the merchants throughout Woodstock who will be open on this special afternoon. There will be holiday decorations, special discounts, carolers and free carriage rides on the square and Aunt Holly on hand to greet the whole family. Hours: 11 AM–5 PM. Free carriage rides every weekend. For info: Woodstock Chamber of Commerce, 136 Cass St, Woodstock, IL 60098. Phone: (815) 338-2436. Fax: (815) 338-2927. E-mail: chamber@stans.com.

WEBER, CARL MARIA VON: BIRTH ANNIVERSARY. Nov 18, 1786. Composer, "founder of German romantic school," was born at Eutin, Germany. Member of a musical family, he is remembered mainly for his operas, especially the immensely popular *Der Freischutz* (1821). He died at London, England, June 5, 1826, at age 39.

BIRTHDAYS TODAY

Margaret Eleanor Atwood, 62, author (*Cat's Eye, The Handmaid's Tale*), born Ottawa, Ontario, Canada, Nov 18, 1939.

Dante Bichette, 38, baseball player, born West Palm Beach, FL, Nov 18, 1963.

Linda Evans, 59, actress ("Dynasty," "Bachelor Father"), born Hartford, CT, Nov 18, 1942.

Wilma Mankiller, 56, Chief of the Cherokee Nation 1985–95, born Tahlequah, OK, Nov 18, 1945.

Andrea Marcovicci, 53, actress ("Trapper John, MD"), singer, born New York, NY, Nov 18, 1948.

Harold Warren Moon, 45, football player, born Los Angeles, CA, Nov 18, 1956.

Kevin Nealon, 48, comedic actor ("Champs," "Saturday Night Live"), born St. Louis, MO, Nov 18, 1953.

Jameson Parker, 54, actor ("Simon and Simon," *A Small Circle of Friends*), born Baltimore, MD, Nov 18, 1947.

Elizabeth Perkins, 41, actress (*About Last Night . . ., Big, The Flintstones*), born Queens, NY, Nov 18, 1960.

Katey Sagal, 45, actress ("Married . . . With Children"), born Los Angeles, CA, Nov 18, 1956.

November **2001**	S	M	T	W	T	F	S
					1	2	3
	4	5	6	7	8	9	10
	11	12	13	14	15	16	17
	18	19	20	21	22	23	24
	25	26	27	28	29	30	

Ted Stevens, 78, US Senator (R, Alaska), born Indianapolis, IN, Nov 18, 1923.

Susan Sullivan, 57, actress ("Falcon Crest," "Dharma & Greg"), born New York, NY, Nov 18, 1944.

Brenda Vaccaro, 62, actress (*Cactus Flower, How Now Dow Jones, The Goodbye People*), born Brooklyn, NY, Nov 18, 1939.

NOVEMBER 19 — MONDAY
Day 323 — 42 Remaining

BELIZE: GARIFUNA DAY. Nov 19. Public holiday celebrating the first arrival of Black Caribs from St. Vincent and Rotan to Southern Belize.

CAMPANELLA, ROY: 80th BIRTH ANNIVERSARY. Nov 19, 1921. Roy Campanella, one of the first black major leaguers and a star of one of baseball's greatest teams, the Brooklyn Dodgers' "Boys of Summer," was born at Philadelphia, PA. Campy, as he was often called, was named the National League MVP three times in his 10 years of play, in 1951, 1953 and 1955. Campanella had his highest batting average in 1951 (.325) and in 1953 he established three single-season records for a catcher—most putouts (807), most home runs (41) and most runs batted in (142)—as well as having a batting average of .312. His career was cut short on Jan 28, 1958, when an automobile accident left him paralyzed. Campy gained even more fame after his accident as an inspiration and spokesman for the handicapped. He was named to the Baseball Hall of Fame in 1969. Roy Campanella died June 26, 1993, at Woodland Hills, CA.

CHRISTMAS AT THE BENJAMIN HARRISON HOME. Nov 19–Dec 31. Indianapolis, IN. (Closed Thanksgiving, Christmas Eve and Christmas Day.) Daily guided tours of the 23rd President's home decorated in seasonal, Victorian style. Est attendance: 4,500. For info: PR Dept, President Benjamin Harrison Home, 1230 N Delaware St, Indianapolis, IN 46202-2598. Phone: (317) 631-1898. Fax: (317) 236-1688.

CLARK, GEORGE ROGERS: BIRTH ANNIVERSARY. Nov 19, 1752. American soldier and frontiersman, born at Albemarle County, VA. Died at Louisville, KY, Feb 13, 1818.

COLD WAR FORMALLY ENDED: ANNIVERSARY. Nov 19–21, 1990. A summit was held at Paris with the leaders of the Conference on Security and Cooperation in Europe (CSCE). The highlight of the summit was the signing of a treaty to dramatically reduce conventional weapons in Europe, thereby ending the Cold War.

FINLAND: INTERNATIONAL CHILDREN'S FILM FESTIVAL. Nov 19–25. Oulu. This one-week event gives festival visitors an opportunity to view several dozen feature-length films. Est attendance: 10,000. For info: Finnish Tourist Board, 655 Third Ave, New York, NY 10017. Phone: (212) 885-9700 or (358) (8) 881-1293. Fax: (358) (8) 881-1290. E-mail: oek@oufilm center.inet.fi. Web: www.ouka.fi/oek/

FIRST AUTOMATIC TOLL COLLECTION MACHINE: ANNIVERSARY. Nov 19, 1954. At the Union Toll Plaza on New Jersey's Garden State Parkway motorists dropped 25 cents into a wire mesh hopper and a green light would flash. The first modern toll road was the Pennsylvania Turnpike which opened in 1940.

FIRST PRESIDENTIAL LIBRARY: ANNIVERSARY. Nov 19, 1939. President Franklin D. Roosevelt laid the cornerstone for his presidential library at Hyde Park, NY. He donated the land, but public donations provided funds for the building which was dedicated on June 30, 1941.

GARFIELD, JAMES ABRAM: BIRTH ANNIVERSARY. Nov 19, 1831. Twentieth president of the US (and the first left-handed president) was born at Orange, OH. Term of office: Mar 4–Sept 19, 1881. While walking into the Washington, DC, railway station on the morning of July 2, 1881, Garfield was shot by disappointed office seeker Charles J. Guiteau. He survived, in very weak condition, until Sept 19, 1881, when he succumbed to blood poisoning at Elberon, NJ (where he had been taken for recuperation). Guiteau was tried, convicted and hanged at the jail at Washington, June 30, 1882.

GETTYSBURG ADDRESS MEMORIAL CEREMONY. Nov 19. Gettysburg, PA. 138th anniversary of Lincoln's Gettysburg Address is celebrated with brief memorial services at the Soldiers' National Monument in Gettysburg National Cemetery. Est attendance: 2,000. For info: Gettysburg CVB, PO Box 4117, Gettysburg, PA 17325. Phone: (717) 334-6274. Fax: (717) 334-1166. Web: www.gettysburg.com.

HAVE A BAD DAY DAY. Nov 19. For those who are filled with revulsion at being told endlessly to "have a nice day," this day is a brief respite. Store and business owners are to ask workers to tell customers to "have a bad day." Annually, Nov 19. [© 2000 by WH]. For info: Thomas or Ruth Roy, Wellcat Holidays, 2418 Long Ln, Lebanon, PA 17046. Phone: (717) 279-0184. E-mail: wellcat@supernet.com. Web: www.wellcat.com.

HEALTH AND HUMAN SERVICES FUNDS VETOED OVER ABORTION: 10th ANNIVERSARY. Nov 19, 1991. President George Bush vetoed a bill to appropriate $205 billion for the Departments of Health and Human Services, Labor and Education, claiming it would abrogate a rule prohibiting doctors and others who work at clinics that receive federal funding from dispensing advice about abortion.

JONESTOWN MASSACRE: ANNIVERSARY. Nov 19, 1978. On this date, Indiana-born, 47-year-old Reverend Jim Jones, leader of the "Peoples Temple," was reported to have directed the suicides of more than 900 persons at Jonestown, Guyana. US Representative Leo J. Ryan, of California, and four members of his party were killed in ambush at Port Kaituma airstrip on Nov 18, 1978, when they attempted to leave after an investigative visit to the remote jungle location of the religious cult. On the following day, Jones and his mistress killed themselves after watching the administration of Kool-Aid laced with the deadly poison cyanide to members of the cult. At least 911 persons died in the biggest murder-suicide in history.

LINCOLN'S GETTYSBURG ADDRESS: ANNIVERSARY. Nov 19, 1863. In 1863, 17 acres of the battlefield at Gettysburg, PA, were dedicated as a national cemetery. Noted orator Edward Everett spoke for two hours; the address that Lincoln delivered in less than two minutes was later recognized as one of the most eloquent of the English language. Five manuscript copies in Lincoln's hand survive, including the rough draft begun in ink at the executive Mansion at Washington and concluded in pencil at Gettysburg on the morning of the dedication (kept at the Library of Congress).

MONACO: NATIONAL HOLIDAY. Nov 19.

★**NATIONAL FAMILY WEEK.** Nov 19–25.

★**NATIONAL FAMILY CAREGIVERS WEEK.** Nov 19–25. To honor family members who care for aging relatives or those with disabilities.

PUERTO RICO: DISCOVERY DAY. Nov 19. Public holiday. Columbus discovered Puerto Rico in 1493 on his second voyage to the New World.

"ROCKY AND HIS FRIENDS" TV PREMIERE: ANNIVERSARY. Nov 19, 1959. This popular cartoon featured the adventures of a talking squirrel, Rocky (Rocket J. Squirrel), and his friend Bullwinkle, a flaky moose. The tongue-in-cheek dialogue contrasted with the simple plots in which Rocky and Bullwinkle tangled with Russian bad guys Boris Badenov and Natasha (who worked for Mr Big). Other popular segments on the show included "Fractured Fairy Tales," "Bullwinkle's Corner" and the adventures of Sherman and Mr Peabody (an intelligent talking dog). In 1961 the show was renamed "The Bullwinkle Show," but the cast of characters remained the same.

SUFFRAGISTS' VOTING ATTEMPT: ANNIVERSARY. Nov 19, 1868. Testing the wording of the 14th Amendment that says "no State shall make or enforce any law which shall abridge the privileges or immunities of citizens of the United States," 172 New Jersey suffragists, including four black women, attempted to vote in the presidential election. Denied, they cast their votes instead into a women's ballot box overseen by 84-year-old Quaker Margaret Pryer.

WOMEN'S CHRISTIAN TEMPERANCE UNION ORGANIZED: ANNIVERSARY. Nov 19, 1874. Developed out of the Women's Temperance Crusade of 1873, the Women's Christian Temperance Union was organized at Cleveland, OH. The Crusade had swept through 23 states with women going into saloons to sing hymns, pray and ask saloonkeepers to stop selling liquor. Today the temperance group, headquartered at Evanston, IL, includes more than a million members with chapters in 72 countries and continues to be concerned with educating people on the potential dangers of the use of alcohol, narcotics and tobacco.

ZION NATIONAL PARK ESTABLISHED: ANNIVERSARY. Nov 19, 1919. Utah's Mukuntuweap National Monument, proclaimed July 31, 1909, and later incorporated in Zion National Monument by proclamation Mar 18, 1918, was established as Zion National Park in 1919.

BIRTHDAYS TODAY

Dick Cavett, 65, entertainer ("The Dick Cavett Show"), born Gibbon, NE, Nov 19, 1936.

Eileen Collins, 45, first female shuttle commander, Lieutenant Colonel USAF, born Elmira, NY, Nov 19, 1956.

Gail Devers, 35, Olympic gold medal sprinter, born Seattle, WA, Nov 19, 1966.

Terry Farrell, 38, actress ("Star Trek: Deep Space Nine," "Becker"), born Cedar Rapids, IA, Nov 19, 1963.

Jodie Foster, 39, actress (Oscars for *The Accused, The Silence of the Lambs; Taxi Driver*), director (*Home for the Holidays*), born Los Angeles, CA, Nov 19, 1962.

Savion Glover, 28, dancer, choreographer (*Bring in 'Da Noise, Bring in 'Da Funk*), born Newark, NJ, Nov 19, 1973.

Thomas R. Harkin, 62, US Senator (D, Iowa), born Cumming, IA, Nov 19, 1939.

Jim Hodges, 45, Governor of South Carolina (D), born Lancaster, SC, Nov 19, 1956.

	S	M	T	W	T	F	S
November					1	2	3
2001	4	5	6	7	8	9	10
	11	12	13	14	15	16	17
	18	19	20	21	22	23	24
	25	26	27	28	29	30	

Scott Jacoby, 45, actor (*The Little Girl Who Lives Down the Lane, Return to Horror High*), born Chicago, IL, Nov 19, 1956.

Larry King, 68, talk-show host ("Larry King Live"), born Brooklyn, NY, Nov 19, 1933.

Jeane Kirkpatrick, 75, political scientist, former US ambassador to the UN, born Duncan, OK, Nov 19, 1926.

Calvin Klein, 59, fashion designer (popularized designer jeans), born New York, NY, Nov 19, 1942.

Glynnis O'Connor, 46, actress (*Ode to Billy Joe, Johnny Dangerously*), born New York, NY, Nov 19, 1955.

Kathleen Quinlan, 47, actress (*Twilight Zone: The Movie; The Doors*), born Pasadena, CA, Nov 19, 1954.

Ahmad Rashad (born Bobby Moore), 52, sportscaster, former football player, born Portland, OR, Nov 19, 1949.

Meg Ryan, 40, actress (*When Harry Met Sally . . ., Sleepless in Seattle*), born Fairfield, CT, Nov 19, 1961.

Kerri Strug, 24, Olympic gymnast, born Tucson, AZ, Nov 19, 1977.

Tommy G. Thompson, 60, Governor of Wisconsin (R), born Elroy, WI, Nov 19, 1941.

Ted Turner, 63, baseball, basketball and cable TV executive, born Cincinnati, OH, Nov 19, 1938.

Garrick Utley, 62, journalist, born Chicago, IL, Nov 19, 1939.

NOVEMBER 20 — TUESDAY
Day 324 — 41 Remaining

BATTLE OF TARAWA-MAKIN: ANNIVERSARY. Nov 20, 1943. The US began its offensive against Japan in the Central Pacific (Operation Galvanic) by attacking the Gilbert Islands, particularly the islets of Betio and Makin. The Japanese had heavily fortified the Tarawa chain of atolls, especially Tarawa, with pillboxes, blockhouses and ferroconcrete bombproofs. In the eight days it took the 5th Amphibious Corps, 2nd Marine Division and the 27th Infantry Division to take the Tarawa and Makin Islands, 1,000 US soldiers were killed and 2,311 wounded. The Japanese loss was tallied at 4,700 men killed, 17 wounded captured and 129 Koreans surrendered. The US public, who through censorship previously had been kept in the dark about the human cost of the war, was appalled by casualty figures and photographs from this battle.

BILL OF RIGHTS: ANNIVERSARY OF FIRST STATE RATIFICATION. Nov 20, 1789. New Jersey became the first state to ratify 10 of the 12 amendments to the US Constitution proposed by Congress Sept 25. These 10 amendments came to be known as the Bill of Rights.

CARRS/SAFEWAY GREAT ALASKA SHOOTOUT. Nov 20–24. Sullivan Arena, Anchorage, AK. Top NCAA basketball action as eight men's division I teams from around the country compete. Est attendance: 48,000. For info: Univ of Alaska-Anchorage, Athletic Dept, 3211 Providence Dr, Anchorage, AK 99508. Phone: (907) 786-1230. Fax: (907) 563-4565. E-mail: antlm@uaa.alaska.edu.

CHATTERTON, THOMAS: BIRTH ANNIVERSARY. Nov 20, 1752. English poet Thomas Chatterton was born at Bristol, England, and killed himself at age 17 by taking arsenic at his London garret, Aug 24, 1770. A gifted but lonely child, before he reached his teens Chatterton had created a fantasy poet-priest, Thomas Rowley, who lived in the 16th century. With his own pen, Chatterton created enough verses "by" Rowley to fill more than 600 printed pages. Chatterton's fantasy-forgery poems attracted little attention during his short life, but they were later admired by Wordsworth, Coleridge, Shelley, Keats and Byron. In addition, he became the subject of at least one play, an opera and a novel.

CHRISTMAS LIGHTS (CITY OF LIGHTS). Nov 20–Jan 6, 2002. Natchitoches, LA. A fairyland of multi-colored lights, created by 170,000 Christmas bulbs strung along city streets and incorporated into 72 unique set pieces along Cane River Lake. The lights reflect in the waters below and stretch along the historic downtown area, while the set pieces create a panoramic view on the east bank of the river. Est attendance: 150,000. For info: Natchitoches Parish Tourist Commission, Calendar of

Events, 781 Front St, Natchitoches, LA 71457. Phone: (318) 352-8072 or (800) 259-1714. Fax: (318) 352-2415.

GOULD, CHESTER: BIRTH ANNIVERSARY.
Nov 20, 1900. In 1931, Chester Gould created comic strip character Dick Tracy, the clean-cut, square-jawed, plainclothed detective who represented the code that "crime doesn't pay." The strip first appeared Oct 4, 1931, in the *Detroit Daily Mirror* and later was syndicated in nearly 1,000 newspapers worldwide. *Dick Tracy* (originally called *Plainclothes Tracy*) featured Tess Trueheart (later Mrs Tracy) and a host of bad guys with ugly names and faces to match their ugly ways—Mole, Pruneface, Flat Top, B-B Eyes, Mumbles and others. Closely following actual police methods of crime prevention, it included a "Crimestopper Notebook" with tips on self-protection. More violent than most comic strips, *Dick Tracy* was a combination of realism and science fiction. Chester Gould was born at Pawnee, OK, and died May 11, 1985, at Woodstock, IL.

HUBBLE, EDWIN POWELL: BIRTH ANNIVERSARY.
Nov 20, 1889. American astronomer Edwin Hubble was born at Marshfield, MO. His discovery and development of the concept of an expanding universe has been described as the "most spectacular astronomical discovery" of the 20th century. As a tribute, the Hubble Space Telescope, deployed Apr 25, 1990, from US Space Shuttle *Discovery*, was named for him. The Hubble Space Telescope, with a 240-centimeter mirror, was to allow astronomers to see farther into space than they had ever seen from telescopes on Earth. Hubble died at San Marino, CA, Sept 28, 1953.

KENNEDY, ROBERT FRANCIS: BIRTH ANNIVERSARY.
Nov 20, 1925. US Senator and younger brother of John F. Kennedy (thirty-fifth president) was born at Brookline, MA. An assassin shot him at Los Angeles, CA, June 5, 1968, while he was campaigning for the presidential nomination. He died the next day. Sirhan Sirhan was convicted of his murder.

LAGERLOF, SELMA: BIRTH ANNIVERSARY.
Nov 20, 1858. Author, member of the Swedish Academy and the first woman to receive the Nobel Prize for literature (1909) was born at Sweden's Varmland Province. She died there Mar 16, 1940.

LANDIS, KENESAW MOUNTAIN: BIRTH ANNIVERSARY.
Nov 20, 1866. Baseball Hall of Fame executive born at Millville, OH. Landis, a federal judge, was named the first Commissioner of Baseball in 1920. He ruled with an absolutely firm hand and imposed his view of how baseball should operate upon owners and players alike. Inducted into the Hall of Fame in 1944. Died at Chicago, IL, Nov 25, 1944.

LAURIER, SIR WILFRED: BIRTH ANNIVERSARY.
Nov 20, 1841. Canadian statesman (premier, 1896–1911), born at St. Lin, Quebec. Died Feb 17, 1919, at Ottawa, Ontario.

MARRIAGE OF ELIZABETH AND PHILIP: ANNIVERSARY.
Nov 20, 1947. The Princess Elizabeth Alexandra Mary was wed to Philip Mountbatten on Nov 20, 1947. Elizabeth was the first child of King George VI and Queen Elizabeth. Philip, the former Prince Philip of Greece, had become a British subject nine months earlier and the title Duke of Edinburgh was bestowed on him. The bride later became Elizabeth II, Queen of the United Kingdom of Great Britain and Northern Ireland and Head of the Commonwealth, upon the death of her father on Feb 6, 1952. Her coronation was at Westminster Abbey on June 2, 1953.

MEXICO: REVOLUTION: ANNIVERSARY.
Nov 20. Anniversary of the social revolution launched by Francisco I. Madero in 1910. National holiday.

NAME YOUR PC DAY.
Nov 20. Hey, why not? People name their boats! And there's a lot more PCs than boats these days. "Binky" is already taken. Annually, Nov 20. © 2000 WH. For info: Thomas and Ruth Roy, Wellcat Holidays, 2418 Long Ln, Lebanon, PA 17046. Phone: (717) 279-0184. E-mail: wellcat @supernet.com. Web: www.wellcat.com.

NUREMBERG WAR CRIMES TRIAL: ANNIVERSARY.
Nov 20, 1945. The first session of the German war crimes trials started at Berlin with indictments against 24 former Nazi leaders. Later sessions were held at Nuremberg, starting Nov 20, 1945. One defendant committed suicide during the trial, and another was excused because of his physical and mental condition. The trial lasted more than 10 months, and delivery of the judgment was completed on Oct 1, 1946. Twelve were sentenced to death by hanging, three to life imprisonment, four to lesser prison terms and three were acquitted.

TIERNEY, GENE: BIRTH ANNIVERSARY.
Nov 20, 1920. Known best for the title role in the film *Laura*, actress Gene Tierney was born at Brooklyn, NY. Her other films include *Heaven Can Wait, A Bell for Adano, Advise and Consent* and her last film, *The Pleasure Seekers*. She died Nov 6, 1991, at Houston, TX.

UNITED NATIONS: AFRICA INDUSTRIALIZATION DAY.
Nov 20. The General Assembly proclaimed this day for the purpose of mobilizing the commitment of the international community to the industrialization of the continent (Res 44/237, Dec 22, 1989). For info: United Nations, Dept of Public Info, New York, NY 10017.

UNITED NATIONS: UNIVERSAL CHILDREN'S DAY.
Nov 20. Designated by the United Nations General Assembly as Universal Children's Day. First observance was in 1953. A time to honor children with special ceremonies and festivals and to make children's needs known to governments. Observed on different days and in different ways in more than 120 nations.

WOLCOTT, OLIVER: 275th BIRTH ANNIVERSARY.
Nov 20, 1726. Signer of the Declaration of Independence, Governor of Connecticut, born at Windsor, CT. Died Dec 1, 1797, at Litchfield, CT.

BIRTHDAYS TODAY

Joseph Robinette Biden, Jr, 59, US Senator (D, Delaware), born Scranton, PA, Nov 20, 1942.

Robert C. Byrd, 84, US Senator (D, West Virginia), born North Wilkesboro, NC, Nov 20, 1917.

Steve Dahl, 47, Chicago radio personality, born La Canada, CA, Nov 20, 1954.

Richard Dawson, 69, actor, TV game-show host ("Hogan's Heroes"; Emmy for "Family Feud"), born Gosport, England, Nov 20, 1932.

Bo Derek (Cathleen Collins), 45, actress (*10, Bolero, Tarzan, A Change of Seasons*), born Long Beach, CA, Nov 20, 1956.

Nadine Gordimer, 78, writer (*July's People, Lifetimes Under Apartheid*), born Springs, South Africa, Nov 20, 1923.

Veronica Hamel, 58, actress ("Hill Street Blues"), born Philadelphia, PA, Nov 20, 1943.

Ruth Laredo, 64, concert pianist, born Detroit, MI, Nov 20, 1937.

Sabrina Lloyd, 31, actress (*Sliders*), born Mount Dora, FL, Nov 20, 1970.

Richard Masur, 53, actor ("One Day at a Time," *Who'll Stop the Rain, Under Fire, Heartburn*), born New York, NY, Nov 20, 1948.

Ricardo Montalban, 81, actor ("Fantasy Island," *Star Trek II: The Wrath of Kahn*), born Mexico City, Mexico, Nov 20, 1920.

Estelle Parsons, 74, actress ("Roseanne," *Bonnie and Clyde, Dick Tracy*; stage: *Next Time I'll Sing to You* [Obie], *In the Summer House* [Obie]), born Marblehead, MA, Nov 20, 1927.

Dick Smothers, 62, comedian, folksinger (with brother Tom, "The Smothers Brothers Comedy Hour"), born New York, NY, Nov 20, 1939.

Ming-Na Wen, 34, actress ("ER," *One Night Stand*), born Macau, China, Nov 20, 1967.

Judy Woodruff, 55, journalist, author, born Tulsa, OK, Nov 20, 1946.

Sean Young, 42, actress (*Blade Runner, No Way Out*), born Louisville, KY, Nov 20, 1959.

NOVEMBER 21 — WEDNESDAY

Day 325 — 40 Remaining

BARTLETT, JOSIAH: BIRTH ANNIVERSARY. Nov 21, 1729. Signer of the Declaration of Independence. Born at Amesbury, MA, he died at Kingston, MI, May 19, 1795.

BEAUMONT, WILLIAM: BIRTH ANNIVERSARY. Nov 21, 1785. US Army surgeon whose contribution to classic medical literature and world fame resulted from another man's shotgun wound. When Canadian fur trapper Alexis St. Martin received an apparently mortal wound June 6, 1822—a nearly point-blank blast to the abdomen—Dr. Beaumont began observing his stomach and digestive processes through an opening in his abdominal wall. His findings were published in 1833 in *Experiments and Observations on the Gastric Juice and the Physiology of Digestion*. St. Martin returned to Canada in 1834 and resisted Beaumont's efforts to have him return for further study. He outlived his doctor by 20 years and was buried at a depth of eight feet to discourage any attempt at posthumous examination. Beaumont, born at Lebanon, CT, died Apr 25, 1853, at St. Louis, MO.

CONGRESS FIRST MEETS AT WASHINGTON: ANNIVERSARY. Nov 21, 1800. Congress met at Philadelphia from 1790 to 1800, when the north wing of the new Capitol at Washington, DC, was completed. The House and the Senate had been scheduled to meet in the new building Nov 17, 1800, but a quorum wasn't achieved until Nov 21, 1800.

DOW-JONES TOPS 5,000: ANNIVERSARY. Nov 21, 1995. The Dow-Jones Index of 30 major industrial stocks topped the 5,000 mark for the first time.

FRENCHMAN ROWS ACROSS PACIFIC: 10th ANNIVERSARY. Nov 21, 1991. Gerard d'Aboville completed a four-month solo journey across the Pacific Ocean on this date. D'Aboville began rowing across the Pacific on July 11 when he left Choshi, Japan. His journey ended at Ilwaco, WA.

GERMANY: BUSS UND BETTAG. Nov 21. Buss und Bettag (Repentance Day) is observed on the Wednesday before the last Sunday of the church year. A legal public holiday in all German states except Bavaria (where it is observed only in communities with predominantly Protestant populations).

GREEN, HETTY: BIRTH ANNIVERSARY. Nov 21, 1835. Henrietta Howland Robinson Green, better known as Hetty Green, reported to have been the richest woman in America, was born at New Bedford, MA. She was an able financier who managed her own wealth, which was estimated to have been in excess of $100 million. Died at New York, NY, July 3, 1916.

MARX, HARPO: BIRTH ANNIVERSARY. Nov 21, 1893. Harpo (Adolph Arthur) Marx was born at New York, NY. He was the second born of the famed Marx brothers who were a popular comedy team of stage, screen and radio for 30 years. Harpo wore a blond curly wig and pretended to be a mute who communicated by honking a horn. He was an expert player of the harp. He died Sept 28, 1964, at Hollywood, CA. Other family members who participated in the comedy team were Groucho (Julius), Chico (Leonard) and, briefly, Zeppo (Herbert) and Gummo (Milton).

NORTH CAROLINA: RATIFICATION DAY. Nov 21. 12th state to ratify Constitution in 1789.

POPE BENEDICT XV: BIRTH ANNIVERSARY. Nov 21, 1854. Giacomo dela Chiesa, 258th pope of the Roman Catholic Church, born at Pegli, Italy, and elected pope Sept 3, 1914. Died at Rome, Italy, Jan 22, 1922.

November *2001*	S	M	T	W	T	F	S
					1	2	3
	4	5	6	7	8	9	10
	11	12	13	14	15	16	17
	18	19	20	21	22	23	24
	25	26	27	28	29	30	

PURCELL, HENRY: DEATH ANNIVERSARY. Nov 21, 1695 (OS). English composer of the early Baroque period was born at London circa 1659. Purcell's work includes more than 100 songs, the opera *Dido and Aeneas* and *The Fairy Queen*, incidental music for a version of Shakespeare's *A Midsummer Night's Dream*. Purcell died at London.

UNITED NATIONS: WORLD TELEVISION DAY: 5th ANNIVERSARY. Nov 21. On Dec 17, 1996, the General Assembly proclaimed this day as World Television Day, commemorating the date in 1996 on which the first World Television Forum was held at the UN. Info from: United Nations, Dept of Public Info, New York, NY 10017.

VOLTAIRE, JEAN FRANCOIS MARIE: BIRTH ANNIVERSARY. Nov 21, 1694. French author and philosopher to whom is attributed (perhaps erroneously) the statement: "I disapprove of what you say, but I will defend to the death your right to say it." His most famous work is the novel *Candide*. Born at Paris, he died there May 30, 1778.

WONDERLAND OF LIGHTS. Nov 21–Dec 30. Marshall, TX. More than eight million tiny white lights cover the city. Features the living Christmas tree, JC's lighted Christmas parade, candlelight home tours. Outdoor ice skating on the square and live entertainment on the square Tuesdays, Thursdays, Fridays and Saturdays. Second Saturday (Dec 8), Cowboy Christmas Celebration with breakfast, entertainment, stick-horse races, mule rides, carriage rides, bus tours and Santa Claus. Est attendance: 750,000. For info: Pam Whisenant, Dir of Conv & Visitors Dvmt, Greater Marshall Chamber of Commerce, PO Box 520, Marshall, TX 75671. Phone: (903) 935-7868. Fax: (903) 935-9982. E-mail: cvd@internetwork.net. Web: www.marshalltxchamber.com.

WORLD HELLO DAY. Nov 21. Everyone who participates greets 10 people. People in 180 countries have participated in this annual activity for advancing peace through personal communication. Heads of state of 114 countries have expressed approval of the event. 29th annual observance. For info: Michael McCormack, The McCormack Brothers, Box 993, Omaha, NE 68101. Web: www.worldhelloday.org.

BIRTHDAYS TODAY

Troy Aikman, 35, football player, born West Covina, CA, Nov 21, 1966.

Marcy Carsey, 57, television producer, born South Weymouth, MA, Nov 21, 1944.

James (Anderson) DePreist, 65, conductor (Oregon Symphony), born Philadelphia, PA, Nov 21, 1936.

Richard J. Durbin, 57, US Senator (D, Illinois), born East St. Louis, IL, Nov 21, 1944.

George Kenneth (Ken) Griffey, Jr, 32, baseball player, born Donora, PA, Nov 21, 1969.

Goldie Hawn, 56, actress ("Laugh-In," *Private Benjamin*; Oscar for *Cactus Flower*), born Washington, DC, Nov 21, 1945.

David Hemmings, 60, actor (*Blow-Up, The Charge of the Light Brigade*), born Guildford, England, Nov 21, 1941.

Laurence Luckinbill, 67, actor ("The Delphi Bureau," *The Boys in the Band, Star Trek V*), born Fort Smith, AR, Nov 21, 1934.

Lorna Luft, 49, actress ("Trapper John, MD"), daughter of Judy Garland, born Los Angeles, CA, Nov 21, 1952.

Juliet Mills, 60, (father is actor John Mills, sister is actress Hayley Mills), actress ("Nanny and the Professor," *So Well Remembered, Carry on Jack*), born London, England, Nov 21, 1941.

Stanley Frank ("Stan the Man") Musial, 81, Baseball Hall of Fame outfielder, first baseman, born Donora, PA, Nov 21, 1920.

Harold Ramis, 57, director, writer, producer (*Ghostbusters, Back to School*), born Chicago, IL, Nov 21, 1944.

Cynthia Rhodes, 45, actress, dancer (*Flashdance, Dirty Dancing*), born Nashville, TN, Nov 21, 1956.

Nicollette Sheridan, 38, actress ("Knots Landing," *The Sure Thing*), born Worthing, Sussex, England, Nov 21, 1963.

Marlo Thomas, 63, actress ("That Girl"), author (*Free to Be . . . You and Me*), born Detroit, MI, Nov 21, 1938.

NOVEMBER 22 — THURSDAY

Day 326 — 39 Remaining

ADAMS, ABIGAIL SMITH: BIRTH ANNIVERSARY. Nov 22, 1744. Wife of John Adams, second president of the US, born at Weymouth, MA. Died Oct 28, 1818, at Quincy, MA.

ATLANTA MARATHON AND ATLANTA HALF MARATHON. Nov 22. Atlanta, GA. 26.2-mile and 13.1-mile races. Advance registration only; entry forms available in July. Send SASE. Online registration available. Est attendance: 8,000. For info: Atlanta Track Club, Atlanta Marathon, 3097 E Shadowlawn Ave, Atlanta, GA 30305. Phone: (404) 231-9064. Fax: (404) 364-0708. E-mail: wft@atlantatrackclub.org. Web: www.atlanta trackclub.org.

BRITTEN, (EDWARD) BENJAMIN: BIRTH ANNIVERSARY. Nov 22, 1913. English composer born at Lowestoft, Suffolk, England. Lord Britten, Baron Britten of Aldeburgh, died at Aldeburgh, Dec 4, 1976.

CARMICHAEL, HOAGIE: BIRTH ANNIVERSARY. Nov 22, 1899. Hoagland Howard Carmichael, attorney who gave up the practice of law to become an actor and songwriter, was born at Bloomington, IN. Among his many popular songs: "Stardust," "Lazybones," "Two Sleepy People" and "Skylark." Carmichael died at Rancho Mirage, CA, Dec 27, 1981.

CHINA CLIPPER: ANNIVERSARY. Nov 22, 1935. A Pan American Martin 130 "flying boat" called the *China Clipper* began regular trans-Pacific mail service on Nov 22, 1935. The plane, powered by four Pratt and Whitney Twin Wasp engines, took off from San Francisco. It reached Manila, Philippines, 59 hours and 48 minutes later. About 20,000 persons watched the historic take-off. Commercial passenger service was established the following year (Oct 21, 1936).

CHRISTMAS IN OLD DODGE CITY. Nov 22–Dec 23. City-wide, Dodge City, KS. Home tours, bazaar, musical productions, 19th-century Christmas decorations in Old Dodge City and Dodge City Trolley City Christmas light tours. Annually, after Thanksgiving through Christmas. Est attendance: 5,000. For info: Dodge City Conv & Visitors Bureau, PO Box 1474, Dodge City, KS 67801. Phone: (800) OLD-WEST. Fax: (316) 225-8268. E-mail: dcvb@pld.com. Web: www.dodgecity.org.

DAYTONA TURKEY RUN. Nov 22–25. Daytona International Speedway, Daytona Beach, FL. 28th annual car show of all makes of 1980 and older collector vehicles. Show includes display of classics, street rods, muscle cars, race cars, customs and special trucks on the speedway infield with a large swap meet of auto parts and accessories and car sales corral. Also a craft sale. Annually, Thanksgiving weekend. Est attendance: 70,000. For info: Rick D'Louhy, Exec Dir, Daytona Beach Racing and Recreational Facilities District, PO Box 1958, Daytona Beach, FL 32115-1958. Phone: (904) 255-7355. Web: www.carshows.org.

De GAULLE, CHARLES ANDRE MARIE: BIRTH ANNIVERSARY. Nov 22, 1890. President of France from December 1958 until his resignation in April 1969, Charles de Gaulle was born at Lille, France. A military leader, he wrote *The Army of the Future* (1934) in which he predicted just the type of armored warfare that was used against his country by Nazi Germany in WW II. After France's defeat at the hands of the Germans, he declared the existence of "Free France" and made himself head of that organization. When the French Vichy government began to collaborate openly with the Germans, the French citizenry looked to de Gaulle for leadership. His greatest moment of triumph was when he entered liberated Paris on Aug 26, 1944. De Gaulle died at Colombey-les-Deux-Eglises, France, Nov 19, 1970.

ELIOT, GEORGE: BIRTH ANNIVERSARY. Nov 22, 1819. English novelist George Eliot, whose real name was Mary Ann Evans, was born at Chilvers Coton, Warwickshire, England. Her works include *Silas Marner* and *Middlemarch*. She died at Chelsea, Dec 22, 1880.

FOODS AND FEASTS OF COLONIAL VIRGINIA. Nov 22–24. Jamestown Settlement, Williamsburg, VA, and Yorktown Victory Center, Yorktown, VA. Daily activities devoted to the culinary practices of the 17th-century Jamestown colonists and Powhatan Indians at Jamestown Settlement and 18th-century Revolutionary War soldiers and Virginia farmers at Yorktown Victory Center. Est attendance: 5,000. For info: Media Relations, Jamestown-Yorktown Fdtn, PO Box 1607, Williamsburg, VA 23187. Phone: (757) 253-4838. Web: www.historyisfun.org.

GARNER, JOHN NANCE: BIRTH ANNIVERSARY. Nov 22, 1868. Thirty-second vice president of US (1933–41) born at Red River County, TX. Died at Uvalde, TX, Nov 7, 1967.

HOLIDAY LIGHTS ON THE LAKE. Nov 22–Jan 6, 2002. Altoona, PA. Drive-through displays of more than 51 acres of animated holiday lights, plus a holiday gift shop, food and visits from Santa Claus. For info: Lakemont Park, 1-99 Frankstown Exit, Altoona, PA 16602. Phone: (814) 949-7275 or (800) 434-8006. Fax: (814) 949-9207. E-mail: Lakemont99@aol.com. Web: www .lakemontparkfun.com.

KENNEDY, JOHN F.: ASSASSINATION ANNIVERSARY. Nov 22, 1963. President John F. Kennedy was slain by a sniper while riding in an open automobile at Dallas, TX. Accused assassin Lee Harvey Oswald was killed in police custody awaiting trial.

LEBANON: INDEPENDENCE DAY. Nov 22. National Day. Gained independence from France in 1943.

"LIFE WITH FATHER" TV PREMIERE: ANNIVERSARY. Nov 22, 1953. This less successful comedy followed a very successful book, Broadway play and movie based on Clarence Day, Jr's essays in *Harper's Magazine* and *The New Yorker*. The cast included Leon Ames as Clarence Day, Sr, Lurene Tuttle as his wife Vinnie, Ralph Reed and Steven Terrell as Clarence, Jr, the eldest son, Freddie Leiston and Malcolm Cassell as second son, John, Ronald Keith, B.G. Norman and Freddy Ridgeway as third son, Whitney, Harvey Grant as youngest son, Harlan and Dorothy Bernard as the maid, Margaret.

LONGWOOD GARDENS CHRISTMAS DISPLAY. Nov 22–Jan 6, 2002. Kennett Square, PA. Indoor Conservatory display of thousands of poinsettias and decorated trees. Outdoors, 400,000 lights and holiday fountain displays. Est attendance: 200,000. For info: Longwood Gardens, PO Box 501, Kennett Square, PA 19348-0501. Phone: (610) 388-1000. Web: www.long woodgardens.org.

MACY'S THANKSGIVING DAY PARADE. Nov 22. New York, NY. Starts at 9 AM, EST, in Central Park West. A part of everyone's Thanksgiving, the parade grows bigger and better each year. Featuring floats, giant balloons, marching bands and famous stars, the parade is televised for the whole country. 73rd annual parade. For info: New York Conv/Visitors Bureau, 810 7th Ave, 3rd floor, New York, NY 10019. Phone: (212) 484-1222. Web: www.nycvisit.com.

MOON PHASE: FIRST QUARTER. Nov 22. Moon enters First Quarter phase at 6:21 PM, EST.

NATIONAL STOP THE VIOLENCE DAY. Nov 22. Radio and television stations across the nation are encouraged to promote "Peace on the Streets" and help put an end to gang (and other) violence through Stop the Violence Day. Participating stations unite to call for a one-day cease-fire, the idea being, "If we can stop the violence for one day, we can stop the violence everyday, one day at a time." Stations also encourage listeners/viewers to wear and display white ribbons that day and drive with their headlights on as a show of peace. Many stations hold peace rallies with local community leaders and also conduct a moment of silence on the air in honor of the year's victims of violence. Begun in 1990. Annually, on the anniversary of President John F. Kennedy's assassination. For info: Cliff Berkowitz, Pres, Lost Coast Communications, Inc, PO Box 25, Ferndale, CA 95536. Phone: (707) 786-5104. Fax: (707) 786-5100.

PLAZA LIGHTS. Nov 22–Jan 13, 2002. Country Club Plaza, Kansas City, MO. Annual lighting ceremony heralds the beginning of the holiday season. More than 200,000 jewel-colored lights, spanning 75 miles, illuminate the outline of every tower, balcony and courtyard of a 14-square block area. Christmas shopping against a backdrop of the Plaza Lights is a Kansas City tradition that began with a single strand of lights over a store entrance in 1925. Est attendance: 250,000. For info: Plaza Merchants Assn, 450 Ward Pkwy, Kansas City, MO 64112. Phone: (816) 753-0100. Fax: (816) 753-4625. Web: www.countryclub plaza.com.

POST, WILEY: BIRTH ANNIVERSARY. Nov 22, 1898. Barnstorming aviator, stunt parachutist and adventurer, Wiley Post was born at Grand Plain, TX. Post, who taught himself to fly, and his plane, the *Winnie Mae*, were the center of world attention in the 1930s. He was co-author (with his navigator, Harold Gatty) of *Around the World in Eight Days*. In 1935, Post and friend Will Rogers started on a flight to Asia. Plane crashed near Point Barrow, AK, Aug 15, 1935; both were killed.

PRIME MINISTER THATCHER RESIGNS: ANNIVERSARY. Nov 22, 1990. Margaret Thatcher announced that she would resign from her position as England's prime minister. She was named prime minister in May 1979 and served until Nov 22, 1990. No other prime minister in the UK in the 20th century has served the post as long as she.

SAINT CECILIA: FEAST DAY. Nov 22. Roman virgin, Christian martyr and patron of music and musicians lived during third century. Survived sentences of burning and beheading. Subject of poetry and musical compositions and her feast day is still an occasion for musical events.

SCOTLAND: SCOTTISH OPEN BADMINTON CHAMPIONSHIP. Nov 22–25. Meadowbank Sports Stadium, Edinburgh. A European Badminton Union Grand Prix Tournament. Est attendance: 7,000. For info: Scottish Badminton Union, Cockburn Centre, 40 Bogmoor Pl, Glasgow, Scotland G51 4TQ. Phone: (44) (141) 445-1218. Fax: (44) (141) 425-1218. E-mail: enquiries@scotbadminton.demon.co.uk

STOCK EXCHANGE HOLIDAY (THANKSGIVING DAY). Nov 22. The holiday schedules for the various exchanges are subject to change if relevant rules, regulations or exchange policies are revised. If you have questions, phone: American Stock Exchange (212) 306-1000; Chicago Board of Trade (312) 435-3500; Chicago Board of Options Exchange (312) 786-5600; New York Stock Exchange (212) 656-2065; Pacific Stock Exchange (415) 393-4000; Philadelphia Stock Exchange (215) 496-5000.

THANKSGIVING DAY. Nov 22. Legal public holiday. (Public Law 90–363 sets Thanksgiving Day on the fourth Thursday in November.) Observed in all states. In most states, the Friday after Thanksgiving is also a holiday; in Nevada it is called Family Day.

	S	M	T	W	T	F	S
November					1	2	3
2001	4	5	6	7	8	9	10
	11	12	13	14	15	16	17
	18	19	20	21	22	23	24
	25	26	27	28	29	30	

★**THANKSGIVING DAY.** Nov 22. Presidential Proclamation. Always issued for the fourth Thursday in November. See also: "First US Holiday by Presidential Proclamation: Anniversary" (Nov 26).

TIE ONE ON FOR SAFETY. Nov 22–Jan 1, 2002. Nationwide. A holiday awareness campaign created by Mothers Against Drunk Driving in 1986 to bring attention to driving sober during the holiday season and throughout the year. MADD encourages everyone to tie a red ribbon to a visible location of their vehicle to serve as a reminder to drive sober and for others to do the same. The red ribbon also serves as a sign that the vehicle owner has chosen to "tie one on for safety" and joined MADD's campaign to make the holidays happier by making them safer. For info: MADD Natl Office, 511 E John Carpenter Frwy, #700, Irving, TX 75062. Phone: (214) 744-6233. Fax: (214) 869-2207. Web: www.madd.org.

TURKEY-FREE THANKSGIVING. Nov 22. This is a time for you to take turkey off your table, forgoing flesh foods "cold turkey" and having a harvest of health. Why not carve a compassionate celebration centerpiece—a tasty mock turkey made from tofu, tempeh or seitan? The turkeys will thank you for having a humane holiday! For info: Vegetarian Awareness Network, Communications Center, PO Box 321, Knoxville, TN 37901-0321. Phone: (800) USA-VEGE.

TURKEY TROT. Nov 22. Parkersburg City Park Pavilion, Parkersburg, WV. Three-mile fun run/walk on Thanksgiving morning. Drawings held for frozen turkeys and each participant receives a long-sleeved T-shirt. Est attendance: 700. For info: St. Joseph's Hospital, Rehab Services Dept, PO Box 327, Parkersburg, WV 26102. Phone: (304) 424-3678. Fax: (304) 424-4430.

BIRTHDAYS TODAY

Boris Becker, 34, tennis player, born Leimen, Germany, Nov 22, 1967.

Guion S. Bluford, Jr, 59, first black astronaut in space, born West Philadelphia, PA, Nov 22, 1942.

Tom Conti, 60, actor (*Reuben, Reuben*), born Paisley, Scotland, Nov 22, 1941.

Jamie Lee Curtis, 43, actress ("Anything But Love," *Love Letters, A Fish Called Wanda*), born Los Angeles, CA, Nov 22, 1958.

Rodney Dangerfield (Jacob Cohen), 80, comedian, actor (*Easy Money, Caddyshack*, "The Dean Martin Show"), born Babylon, NY, Nov 22, 1921.

Harry Edwards, 59, sports sociologist, born St. Louis, MO, Nov 22, 1942.

Allen Garfield, 62, actor (*Bananas, The Conversation, Dick Tracy*), born Newark, NJ, Nov 22, 1939.

Stephen Geoffreys, 42, actor (*Heaven Help Us, 976-EVIL*), born Cincinnati, OH, Nov 22, 1959.

Terry Gilliam, 61, actor, writer ("Monty Python's Flying Circus," *Life of Brian*), director (*Brazil*), born Minneapolis, MN, Nov 22, 1940.

Mariel Hemingway, 40, actress (*Manhattan, Personal Best, Superman IV*), born Ketchum, ID, Nov 22, 1961.

Richard Kind, 44, actor ("Spin City," "Mad About You"), born Trenton, NJ, Nov 22, 1957.

Billie Jean King, 58, former tennis player, born Long Beach, CA, Nov 22, 1943.

Robert Vaughn, 69, actor ("The Man From U.N.C.L.E.," *The Magnificent Seven*), born New York, NY, Nov 22, 1932.

NOVEMBER 23 — FRIDAY
Day 327 — 38 Remaining

ASHFORD, EMMETT LITTLETON: BIRTH ANNIVERSARY. Nov 23, 1914. Emmett Littleton Ashford, born at Los Angeles, CA, was the first black to officiate at a major league baseball game. Ashford began his pro career calling games in the minors in 1951 and went to the majors in 1966. He was noted for his flamboyant style when calling strikes and outs as well as for his dapper dress which included cuff-links with his uniform. He died Mar 1, 1980, at Marina del Rey, CA.

BILLY THE KID: BIRTH ANNIVERSARY. Nov 23, 1859. Legendary outlaw of western US. Probably named Henry McCarty at birth (New York, NY), he was better known as William H. Bonney. Ruthless killer, a failure at everything legal, he escaped from jail at age 21 while under sentence of hanging. Recaptured at Stinking Springs, NM, and returned to jail, he again escaped, only to be shot through the heart by pursuing Lincoln County Sheriff Pat Garrett at Fort Sumner, NM, during the night of July 14, 1881. His last words, answered by two shots, reportedly were "Who is there?"

BLACK FRIDAY. Nov 23. The traditional beginning of the Christmas shopping season on the Friday after Thanksgiving.

BUY NOTHING DAY. Nov 23. A 24-hour moratorium on consumer spending. A celebration of simplicity, about getting our runaway consumer culture back onto a sustainable path. Annually, on the first shopping day after Thanksgiving. For info: The Media Foundation, 1243 W 7th Ave, Vancouver, BC, Canada V6H 1B7. Phone: (800) 663-1243 or (604) 736-9401. Fax: (604) 737-6021. E-mail: buynothingday@adbusters.org. Web: www.adbusters.org/campaigns.

CHRISTMAS CANDLELIGHT TOUR. Nov 23–Dec 8. My Old Kentucky Home State Park, Bardstown, KY. Christmas in the style and flavor of the 1800s. Starts the day after Thanksgiving and runs 16 consecutive days. Est attendance: 10,000. For info: My Old Kentucky Home State Pk, PO Box 323, Hwy 150, Bardstown, KY 40004. Phone: (800) 323-7803 or (502)348-3502. Fax: (502) 349-0054. Web: www.kystateparks.com.

CHRISTMAS CANDLELIGHT TOURS. Nov 23–Dec 2 (also Dec 8–9 and 15–16). Nemacolin Castle, Brownsville, PA. Tour candlelit rooms adorned with fresh evergreen trees, flowers and holiday decorations. Hot wassail and cookies are served. For info: Tour Coordinator, Candlelight Tours at Nemacolin Castle, PO Box 24, Brownsville, PA 15417. Phone: (724) 785-6882.

CHRISTMAS CRAFT AND GIFT FESTIVAL. Nov 23–25. Cocoanut Grove, Santa Cruz, CA. A Victorian-themed festival, featuring hundreds of handmade gifts, foods and live entertainment also adorn this Santa Cruz tradition. Est attendance: 7,000. For info: Jan Bollwinkel-Smith, Communications Mgr, 400 Beach St, Santa Cruz, CA 95060-5491. Phone: (831) 423-5590. E-mail: publicity@scseaside.com. Web: www.beachboardwalk.com.

CHRISTMAS IN ROSELAND. Nov 23–Dec 30. American Rose Center, Shreveport, LA. Holiday magic transforms the American Rose Center with lights, holiday scenes, music and light sculptures. Est attendance: 40,000. For info: American Rose Center, 8877 Jefferson-Paige Rd, Shreveport, LA 71119. Phone: (318) 938-5402. Fax: (318) 938-5405. E-mail: ars@ars-hq.org. Web: www.ars.org.

CHRISTMAS TRADITIONS. Nov 23–Dec 23. St. Charles, MO. Holiday festivities include yule-log burning, caroling, chestnut roasting and authentically costumed Santas. Enjoy evening shopping on Wednesday and Friday. Annually, after Thanksgiving until Christmas. Est attendance: 50,000. For info: St. Charles CVB, 230 S Main St, St. Charles, MO 63301. Phone: (800) 366-2427. Web: www.historicstcharles.com.

CRAFTSMEN'S CHRISTMAS CLASSIC. Nov 23–25. Coliseum Special Events Center, Greensboro, NC. Arts and crafts. Est attendance: 35,000. For info: Gilmore Enterprises, 1240 Oakland Ave, Greensboro, NC 27403. Phone: (336) 274-5550. Fax: (336) 274-1084.

D & G BARREL RACE. Nov 23–25. Multi-Purpose Events Center, Wichita Falls, TX. Barrel riders from Texas, Oklahoma, New Mexico, Kansas and other areas compete in this national Barrel Racing Show. For info: Wichita Falls CVB, 1000 5th St, Wichita Falls, TX 76301. Phone: (940) 716-5500. Fax: (940) 716-5509. E-mail: MPEC@Wf.net. Web: www.viewscape.com or www.wf.net.

DICKENS CHRISTMAS FESTIVAL. Nov 23–Dec 9. Utah State Fairpark, Salt Lake City, UT. Christmas entertainment, food, booths and Father Christmas in an Old English setting with period costumes. Annually, the Friday after Thanksgiving. Est attendance: 80,000. For info: Utah State Fairpark, 155 North—1000 West, Salt Lake City, UT 84116. Phone: (801) 538-8440.

DICKENS VILLAGE FESTIVAL. Nov 23–25 (also Nov 30–Dec 1 and 7–8). Garrison, ND. Walk the streets of downtown and eat delicious hot baked potatoes and sausages on a stick, warm up with a cup of English tea, shop the Fezziwig's Warehouse, an English Market for Victorian treasures and English gifts. In the evening be outside for a parade of lights led by Christmas carolers and then attend the nightly performance of Dickens *A Christmas Carol*. Est attendance: 3,600. For info: (701) 463-2600 or North Dakota Tourism, 604 E Boulevard, Bismarck, ND 58505. Phone: (701) 328-2525 or (800) 435-5663.

"DR. WHO" TV PREMIERE: ANNIVERSARY. Nov 23, 1963. First episode of "Dr. Who" premiered on British TV with William Hartnell as the first doctor. Traveling through time and space in the TARDIS (an acronym for Time and Relative Dimensions in Space), the doctor and his companions found themselves in mortal combat with creatures such as the Daleks. "Dr. Who" didn't air in the US until Sept 29, 1975.

FAMILY DAY IN NEVADA. Nov 23. Observed annually on the Friday following the fourth Thursday in November.

FIRST PLAY-BY-PLAY FOOTBALL GAME BROADCAST: ANNIVERSARY. Nov 23, 1919. The first play-by-play football game radio broadcast in the US took place on this day. Texas A&M blanked the University of Texas 7–0.

FISH HOUSE PARADE. Nov 23. Aitkin, MN. 11th annual special parade of uniquely decorated fish houses used for ice fishing during the winter. Annually, the Friday after Thanksgiving. Est attendance: 3,000. For info: Carroll Kukowski, Exec Dir, Aitkin Area Chamber of Commerce, PO Box 127, Aitkin, MN 56431. Phone: (800) 526-8342. Fax: (218) 927-4494. E-mail: upnorth@aitkin.com. Web: www.aitkin.com.

FOLKWAYS OF THE HOLIDAYS. Nov 23–Dec 23. Shakopee, MN. Ethnic holiday traditions, presented by costumed interpreters, at historic Murphy's Landing. Weekends, excluding Christmas. Open weekdays by reservation, 10–4. Annually, beginning the Friday after Thanksgiving. Est attendance: 8,000. For info: Murphy's Landing, 2187 E Hwy 101, Shakopee, MN 55379. Phone: (952) 445-6901. Web: www.murphyslanding.com.

GETTYSBURG YULETIDE FESTIVAL. Nov 23–25 (also Nov 30–Dec 2 and Dec 7–9). Gettysburg, PA. Tours of decorated historic homes, live nativity scene, caroling and handbell choirs, Christmas parade, holiday concerts, holiday dessert tasting and candlelight walking tour. Annually, the last weekend in November and the first and second weekends in December. Est attendance: 4,000. For info: Gettysburg CVB, PO Box 4117, Gettysburg, PA 17325. Phone: (717) 334-6274. Fax: (717) 334-1166. Web: www.gettysburg.com.

GILBERT ISLANDS TAKEN: ANNIVERSARY. Nov 23, 1943. The US Second Marine Division took control of the Gilbert Islands after fierce fighting on the heavily fortified Tarawa Atoll. In the 76-hour battle the Marines beat back a "death charge" in which the Japanese ran directly at the American guns. American troops sustained 3,500 killed and wounded. The Japanese suffered 5,000 killed and 17 wounded and captured. (The Gilbert Islands are the westernmost of the Polynesians, midway between Australia and Hawaii and today are part of the nation of Kiribati.)

GIVING THANKS: HEARTH AND HOME IN EARLY MARYLAND. Nov 23–24. St. Mary's City, MD. From everyday meals to feasts, join us as we examine the colonial table. Demonstrations of food preservation and hearth cooking. 10 AM–5 PM. Est attendance: 1,000. For info: Visitors Services, Historic St. Mary's City, PO Box 39, St. Mary's City, MD 20686. Phone: (301) 862-0990 or (800) SMC-1634. Fax: (301) 862-0968. Web: www.smcm.edu/hsmc/.

HOLIDAY CRAFT AND GIFT SHOW: INDOOR SHOW. Nov 23–25. Wisconsin State Fair Park, Milwaukee, WI. Combined show with 200 commercial gift exhibitors and 400 craftsmen. Est attendance: 48,000. For info: Dir, Holiday Craft and Gift Show, 9312 W National Ave, Milwaukee, WI 53227-1542. Phone: (414) 321-2100. Web: www.craftfairusa.com.

IDAHO FESTIVAL OF LIGHTS. Nov 23–24. Preston, ID. Annual festival featuring a lighted parade, fireworks in the evenings, kids parade and international bed race. Annually, the Friday and Saturday after Thanksgiving. Est attendance: 18,000. For info: Preston Chamber of Commerce, 23 N State, Preston, ID 83263. Phone: (208) 852-2703. E-mail: pacc@idacom.net.

JAPAN: LABOR THANKSGIVING DAY. Nov 23. National holiday.

JULE FEST. Nov 23–25. Elk Horn, IA. Danish Christmas festival. Est attendance: 3,000. For info: Lisa Riggs, Danish Windmill, PO Box 245, Elk Horn, IA 51531. Phone: (712) 764-7472 or (800) 451-7960. Fax: (712) 764-7475. Web: www.danishwindmill.com.

KARLOFF, BORIS: BIRTH ANNIVERSARY. Nov 23, 1887. Born William Henry Pratt at London, England. An actor known for his portrayal of ghoulish figures, his movies included *Frankenstein, The Body Snatcher* and *The Bride of Frankenstein.* Karloff died Feb 2, 1969, at Sussex, England.

***LIFE* MAGAZINE DEBUTED: ANNIVERSARY.** Nov 23, 1936. The illustrated magazine *Life* debuted on this day. The first cover depicted a doctor slapping a baby with the caption "Life begins."

LIGHTING OF THE SQUARE. Nov 23. Woodstock, IL. Christmas will officially come alive in Woodstock with a flip of the switch that will light the buildings and trees on the square. The program starts at 7 PM and there will be caroling before and after. Est attendance: 1,000. For info: Woodstock Chamber of Commerce, 136 Cass St, Woodstock, IL 60098. Phone: (815) 338-2436. Fax: (815) 338-2497. E-mail: chamber@stans.com.

	S	M	T	W	T	F	S
November					1	2	3
2001	4	5	6	7	8	9	10
	11	12	13	14	15	16	17
	18	19	20	21	22	23	24
	25	26	27	28	29	30	

LONG GROVE COUNTRYSIDE CHRISTMAS. Nov 23–Dec 24. Long Grove, IL. Discover an old-fashioned country Christmas in historic village of nearly 100 specialty shops. Covered bridge, carriage rides, Victorian buildings outlined in lights. Breakfast and lunch with Santa, Nutcracker Teas. Fee for selected events. Free parking. 10 AM–5 PM; Sundays 11 AM–5 PM. For info: Long Grove Merchants Assn, 307 Old McHenry Rd, Long Grove, IL 60047. Phone: (847) 634-0888. Fax: (847) 634-3673.

MAYOR'S CHRISTMAS TREE. Nov 23. Crown Center Square, Kansas City, MO. The lighting of the nation's tallest Christmas tree celebrates Kansas City's 92-year-old tradition of holiday giving. Local celebrities, musical entertainment, costume characters and outdoor ice skating are all part of the evening's festivities. The Mayor's Christmas Tree stands 100 ft tall and shines with thousands of white lights and colorful ornaments. Each evening throughout the holiday season, more than 55,000 lights illuminate Crown Center Square, creating a holiday atmosphere beyond compare. Est attendance: 15,000. For info: Crown Center, 2405 Grand Blvd, Kansas City, MO 64108-2519. Phone: (816) 274-8444 or (800) 721-STAY. Fax: (816) 274-4567. Web: www.crowncenter.com.

MYSTIC SEAPORT FIELD DAYS. Nov 23–24. Mystic Seaport, Mystic, CT. Families enjoy special Thanksgiving weekend activities including wagon rides, food, entertainment and outdoor games on the green. Est attendance: 3,000. For info: Mystic Seaport Museum, 75 Greenmanville Ave, PO Box 6000, Mystic, CT 06355-0990. Phone: (860) 572-5315 or (888) 9SEAPORT. Web: www.mysticseaport.org.

OLD TYME FARM DAYS. Nov 23–27. Live Oak, FL. Festivities include cane grinding, syrup soppin', wagon trail ride, antique farm equipment, bluegrass music and many other fun-filled activities. Est attendance: 12,000. For info: James Cornett, Spirit of the Suwannee Music Park, 3076 95th Drive, Live Oak, FL 32060. Phone: (904) 364-1683. Fax: (904) 364-2998. E-mail: spirit @musicliveshere.com. Web: www.musicliveshere.com.

PIERCE, FRANKLIN: BIRTH ANNIVERSARY. Nov 23, 1804. The fourteenth president of the US was born at Hillsboro, NH. Term of office: Mar 4, 1853–Mar 3, 1857. Not nominated until the 49th ballot at the Democratic party convention in 1852, he was refused his party's nomination in 1856 for a second term. Pierce died at Concord, NH, Oct 8, 1869.

RUTLEDGE, EDWARD: BIRTH ANNIVERSARY. Nov 23, 1749. Signer of the Declaration of Independence, governor of South Carolina, born at Charleston, SC. Died there Jan 23, 1800.

SAGITTARIUS, THE ARCHER. Nov 23–Dec 21. In the astronomical/astrological zodiac that divides the sun's apparent orbit into 12 segments, the period Nov 22–Dec 21 is identified, traditionally, as the sun-sign of Sagittarius, the Archer. The ruling planet is Jupiter.

SANTALAND USA. Nov 23–Dec 23. Downtown Madison, MN. Santaland USA is a group of child-sized buildings and figures, including a church, schoolhouse, barn, bakery, ice castle, toy shop, Santa and Mrs Claus's house, Santa's Workshop, Santa's sleigh and reindeer, a mouse house, camels and a manger scene. All are built, furnished and decorated by volunteers and along with other scenes, such as a railroad train and pond, take up most of the mezzanine area of a large retail store. Santaland is sponsored by the Madison Chamber; free admission. We also have a holiday parade the first Saturday in December. Est attendance: 2,000. For info: Maynard Meyer, PO Box 70, Madison, MN 56256. Phone: (320) 598-7301. Fax: (320) 598-7955.

SINKIE DAY. Nov 23. SINKIES (people who occasionally dine over the kitchen sink) are encouraged to celebrate this time-honored, casual-yet-tasteful cuisine culture. This is a particularly appropriate day to become acquainted with the SINKIE style of dining. Christmas shopping and Thanksgiving leftovers provide the perfect reasons to enjoy a quick meal. Also the day the annual list of "Six Prominent Suspected Closet-Sinkies" is announced. Annually, the day after Thanksgiving. If it has anything to do with having a quick bite, it has everything to do with being a Sinkie. For info: Norm Hankoff, Founder, Intl Assn of People Who Dine Over the Kitchen Sink, 1579 Farmers Lane, #252, Santa Rosa, CA 95405. E-mail: normh@sinkie.com. Web: www.sinkie.com.

STAMP EXPO: CALIFORNIA. Nov 23–25. Pasadena Convention Center, Pasadena, CA. Est attendance: 4,000. For info: Intl Stamp Collectors Soc, PO Box 854, Van Nuys, CA 91408. Phone: (818) 997-6496. Fax: (818) 988-4337. E-mail: iibick@aol.com. Web: www.bick.net.

SUGARLOAF'S FALL ATLANTA CRAFT FESTIVAL. Nov 23–25. Cobb Galleria Centre, Atlanta, GA. This show, now in its 6th year, features 250 nationally recognized craft designers and fine artists displaying and selling their original creations. Craft demonstrations, hourly gift certificate drawings and more. Est attendance: 14,000. For info: Sugarloaf Mountain Works, Inc, 200 Orchard Ridge Dr, Ste 215, Gaithersburg, MD 20878. Phone: (800) 210-9900. E-mail: smworks@sugarloafcrafts.com. Web: www.sugarloafcrafts.com.

TREE LIGHTING CEREMONY. Nov 23. Town Square, Anchorage, AK. All of Anchorage turns out for this traditional start of the holiday season. 6 PM. Annually, the Friday after Thanksgiving. For info: Anchorage Downtown Partnership, 245 W Fifth Ave, Ste 124, Anchorage, AK 99501. Phone: (907) 279-5650. Fax: (907) 279-5651. E-mail: ancdp@alaska.net.

WINTERFEST. Nov 23–Jan 1, 2002. Historic Larimer Square, Denver, CO. The season brings Santa's Workshop for kids, toy train and the beautifully animated retail windows—"The Windows of the Season." Also includes Breakfast with Santa and Tuba Christmas. The festivities kick off with the tree-lighting ceremony and Christmas concert on Nov 23. Est attendance: 100,000. For info: Events, Larimer Square, 1400 Larimer St, Ste 300, Denver, CO 80202. Phone: (303) 534-2367. Fax: (303) 893-0518. Web: www.larimersquare.com.

WORLD'S CHAMPIONSHIP DUCK-CALLING CONTEST AND WINGS OVER THE PRAIRIE FESTIVAL. Nov 23–24. Stuttgart, AR. Annually, Thanksgiving weekend. Duck-calling contests, duck gumbo cookoff, carnival, 10K race, arts and crafts, beauty pageant, concessions, sporting collectibles, Sportsman's Dinner and Dance, commercial exhibitors, fun shoot. Est attendance: 65,000. For info: Stuttgart Chamber of Commerce, 507 S Main, Stuttgart, AR 72160. Phone: (870) 673-1602. Fax: (870) 673-1604. Web: www.stuttgart arkansas.com.

YOU'RE WELCOMEGIVING DAY. Nov 23. The day after Thanksgiving, to create a four-day weekend. For info: Richard Ankli, The Fifth Wheel Tavern, 639 Fifth St, Ann Arbor, MI 48103-4840.

BIRTHDAYS TODAY

Susan Anspach, 56, actress (*Five Easy Pieces, Play It Again Sam, Montenegro*), born New York, NY, Nov 23, 1945.

Vin Baker, 30, basketball player, born Lake Wales, FL, Nov 23, 1971.

Jerry Bock, 73, composer ("Fiddler on the Roof," "Fiorello"), born New Haven, CT, Nov 23, 1928.

Mary L. Landrieu, 46, US Senator (D, Louisiana), born Arlington, VA, Nov 23, 1955.

Krzysztof Penderecki, 68, composer, born Debica, Poland, Nov 23, 1933.

Charles E. Schumer, 51, US Senator (D, New York), born Brooklyn, NY, Nov 23, 1950.

Maurice Zolotow, 88, author (*Billy Wilder in Hollywood*), born New York, NY, Nov 23, 1913.

NOVEMBER 24 — SATURDAY

Day 328 — 37 Remaining

BARKLEY, ALBEN WILLIAM: BIRTH ANNIVERSARY. Nov 24, 1877. Thirty-fifth vice president of the US (1949–53), born at Graves County, KY. Died at Lexington, VA, Apr 30, 1956.

BATTLE OF CHATTANOOGA: ANNIVERSARY. Nov 24, 1863. After reinforcing the besieged Union army at Chattanooga, TN, General Ulysses S. Grant launched the Battle of Chattanooga on Nov 24, 1863. Falsely secure in the knowledge that his troops were in an impregnable position on Lookout Mountain, Confederate General Braxton Bragg and his army were overrun by the Union forces, Bragg himself barely escaping capture. The battle is famous for the Union Army's spectacular advance up a heavily fortified slope into the teeth of the enemy guns.

CAPITAL HOLIDAY. Nov 24–Dec 31. Capital-Saratoga Region, NY. More than 100 events throughout the Capital-Saratoga Region. Activities include family events at historic homes, Victorian strolls and festive holiday performances. For info: Albany Conv and Visitors Bureau, 25 Quackenbush Sq, Albany, NY 12207. Phone: (518) 434-1217 or (800) 258-3582. Fax: (518) 434-0887. E-mail: accvb@albany.org.

CARNEGIE, DALE: BIRTH ANNIVERSARY. Nov 24, 1888. American inspirational lecturer and author, Dale Carnegie was born at Maryville, MO. His best known book, *How to Win Friends and Influence People*, published in 1936, sold nearly five million copies and was translated into 29 languages. Carnegie died at New York, NY, Nov 1, 1955.

A CHARLES DICKENS VICTORIAN CHRISTMAS. Nov 24–Dec 29. Mount Hope Estate and Winery, Manheim, PA. An open house in colorfully decorated Mount Hope Mansion, wine sampling in the billiards room, actors portraying such Dickens favorites as Tiny Tim, Oliver Twist and Ebenezer Scrooge. Est attendance: 7,000. For info: Thomas Roy, Mgr, Mount Hope Estate and Winery, PO Box 685, Cornwall, PA 17016. Phone: 7176657021, ext 127. Fax: (717) 664-3466. E-mail: TomRoy@pa renaissancefaire.com. Web: www.parenfaire.com.

CUT YOUR OWN CHRISTMAS TREE. Nov 24–Dec 24. Charlottesville, VA. Est attendance: 100. For info: Ash Lawn–Highland, James Monroe Parkway, Charlottesville, VA 22902. Phone: (804) 293-9539. Fax: (804) 293-8000. E-mail: ashlawnjm@aol.com. Web: avenue.org/ashlawn.

"D.B. COOPER" HIJACKING: 30th ANNIVERSARY. Nov 24–25, 1971. A middle-aged man whose plane ticket was made out to "D.B. Cooper" parachuted from a Northwest Airlines 727 jetliner on Nov 25, 1971, carrying $200,000 which he had collected from the airline as ransom for the plane and passengers as a result of threats made during his Nov 24 flight from Portland, OR, to Seattle, WA. He jumped from the plane over an area of wilderness south of Seattle and was never apprehended. Several thousand dollars of the marked ransom money turned up in February 1980, along the Columbia River, near Vancouver, WA.

DICKENS OLDE-FASHIONED CHRISTMAS FESTIVAL. Nov 24–25 (also Dec 1–2, 8–9, 15–16 and 22–23). Holly, MI. Circa 1850 comes to life in downtown Holly. Bah humbug with Scrooge, encourage Tiny Tim, sing with the carolers, banter with the street vendors. Enjoy delicacies such as roasted chestnuts, open-flame baked potatoes and plum pudding. Entertainment on the hour. Annually, Thanksgiving weekend and each Saturday and Sunday until Christmas. Est attendance: 55,000. For info: Holly Area Chamber of Commerce, PO Box 214, Holly, MI 48442. Phone: (248) 634-1900. Fax: (248) 634-1049. Web: www.hollymi.com.

ENGLAND: ROYAL SMITHFIELD SHOW AND AGRICULTURAL MACHINERY EXHIBITION. Nov 24–27. Earls Court Exhibition Centre, Warwick Road, London. Major farming exhibition with livestock and agricultural equipment on display. Est attendance: 50,000. For info: Sue Silsby, Earls Court Exhibition Centre, Warwick Rd, London, England SW5 9TA. Phone: (44) (20) 7370 8226. Fax: (44) (20) 7370 8230.

HANGING OF THE GREENS. Nov 24. Main Street, Arrow Rock, MO. The village puts on its winter greenery as the historic boardwalk is decorated with traditional living greenery. Event includes caroling, a visit from Santa and Mrs Claus via fire truck, storytelling and merchants open house is included. Est attendance: 200. For info: HARC, PO Box M, Arrow Rock, MO 65320. E-mail: tmcglaughlin@mid-mo.net.

HOLIDAYS IN THE CITY/LIGHTED ELIZABETH RIVER BOAT PARADE. Nov 24. Norfolk, VA. Boats adorned with lights compete in this judged parade. Entries include Navy ships, pleasure craft, sailboats, Coast Guard vessels, tug boats and commercial craft. Following the parade a dockside party with live bands and refreshments is held. Est attendance: 40,000. For info: Boat Parade Mgr, Downtown Norfolk Council, 201 Granby St, Ste 101, Norfolk, VA 23510. Phone: (757) 623-1757. Fax: (757) 623-1756. E-mail: dnc@downtownnorfolk.org.

JOPLIN, SCOTT: BIRTH ANNIVERSARY. Nov 24, 1868. American musician and composer famed for his piano rags, born at Texarkana, TX. Died at New York, NY, Apr 1, 1917.

"THE LIGHT OF THE WORLD" CHRISTMAS PAGEANT. Nov 24 (also Dec 2 and 9). Courthouse square, Minden, NE. Pageant presented on three sides of the courthouse square with around 115 local citizens performing with beautiful costumes. At the climax some 10,000 Christmas lights are turned on the courthouse. 7 PM; free admission. Annually, the first Saturday after Thanksgiving and the first two Sundays in December. Est attendance: 10,000. For info: Marjorie Madsen, Mgr, Minden Chamber of Commerce, PO Box 375, Minden, NE 68959. Phone: (308) 832-1811.

MANSTEIN, ERICH von: BIRTH ANNIVERSARY. Nov 24, 1887. Considered by many to be the greatest strategist of World War II, Erich von Manstein was born at Berlin, Germany. His plan for the invasion of France in 1940 was a complete success. He was dismissed by Hitler in March 1944. Manstein died at Irschenhausen, Germany, June 10, 1973.

MEXICO: GUADALAJARA INTERNATIONAL BOOK FAIR. Nov 24–Dec 2. Mexico's largest book fair with exhibitors from all over the Spanish-speaking world. Est attendance: 275,000. For info: David Unger, Guadalajara Book Fair–US Office, Div of Hum, NAC 6293, City College, New York, NY 10031. Phone: (212) 650-7925. Fax: (212) 650-7912. E-mail: filny@aol.com.

SEMINOLE ARTS CELEBRATION. Nov 24–25. Ah-Tah-Thi-Ki Museum, Big Cypress Reservation, FL. Celebrates American Indian Heritage Month. Painting, beadwork, basketry, woodcarving, patchwork sewing, storytelling and traditional dancing. 4th annual. Annually, Thanksgiving weekend. Est attendance: 1,500. For info: Tom Gallaher, Ah-Tah-Thi-Ki Museum, HC-61, Box 21A, Clewiston, FL 33440. Phone: (954) 792-0745. Fax: (954) 583-9893. E-mail: museum@semtribe.com. Web: www.seminoletribe.com.

"SIMON & SIMON" TV PREMIERE: 20th ANNIVERSARY. Nov 24, 1981. This popular crime show about private eye brothers starred Jameson Parker as smooth, educated A.J. Simon and Gerald McRaney as brother Rick, a Vietnam vet. Other featured actors included Mary Carver as Cecilia Simon, their mother, Eddie Barth as rival detective Myron Fowler, Jeannie Wilson as Myron's daughter Janet, a district attorney, Tim Reid as undercover policeman Downtown Brown and Joan McMurtrey as Lieutenant Abby Marsh. The series was based on a 1980 made-for-TV movie called "Pirate's Key," with the series locale shifted from Florida to San Diego. The last telecast was Dec 31, 1988.

SPINOZA, BARUCH: BIRTH ANNIVERSARY. Nov 24, 1632 (OS). Dutch philosopher, born at Amsterdam. Died at The Hague, Feb 21, 1677 (OS). "Peace is not an absence of war," wrote Spinoza, in 1670, "it is a virtue, a state of mind, a disposition for benevolence, confidence, justice."

STERNE, LAURENCE: BIRTH ANNIVERSARY. Nov 24, 1713. Novelist, born at Clonmel, Ireland. Died at London, England, Mar 18, 1768. In his dedication to *Tristram Shandy*, Sterne wrote: "I live in a constant endeavour to fence against the infirmities of ill health, and other evils of life, by mirth; being firmly persuaded that every time a man smiles,—but much more so, when he laughs, that it adds something to this Fragment of Life."

TAYLOR, ZACHARY: BIRTH ANNIVERSARY. Nov 24, 1784. The soldier who became twelfth president of the US was born at Orange County, VA. Term of office: Mar 4, 1849–July 9, 1850. He was nominated at the Whig party convention in 1848, but, the story goes, he did not accept the letter notifying him of his nomination because it had postage due. He cast his first vote in 1846, when he was 62 years old. Becoming ill July 4, 1850, he died at the White House, July 9. His last words: "I am sorry that I am about to leave my friends."

TERRITORIAL CHRISTMAS CELEBRATION. Nov 24–Dec 24. Guthrie, OK. Take a step back in time and celebrate Christmas in grand Victorian style. You won't believe your eyes as you walk around Guthrie and take in many sights and sounds of Christmas past. Enjoy the Pollard's production of "A Territorial Christmas Carol," the Victorian Walk, Territorial Homes Tour, Lion's Club Christmas Parade, Christmas Light tour on the trolley, street carolers, peanut vendors, Christmas Tree Auction and Reception and Election of the Territorial Governor. Est attendance: 13,000. For info: Guthrie Conv & Visitors Bureau, PO Box 995, Guthrie, OK 73044-0995. Phone: (800) 299-1889 or (405) 282-1947. Fax: (405) 282-0061.

TOULOUSE-LAUTREC, HENRI DE: BIRTH ANNIVERSARY. Nov 24, 1864. French painter and designer of posters. Born at Albi, France, he died Sept 9, 1901, at Bordeaux, France.

November 2001	S	M	T	W	T	F	S
					1	2	3
	4	5	6	7	8	9	10
	11	12	13	14	15	16	17
	18	19	20	21	22	23	24
	25	26	27	28	29	30	

US MILITARY LEAVES PHILIPPINES: ANNIVERSARY. Nov 24, 1992. The Philippines became a US colony at the turn of the century when it was taken over from Spain after the Spanish-American War. Though President Franklin D. Roosevelt signed a bill Mar 24, 1934, granting the Philippines independence to be effective July 4, 1946, before that date Manila and Washington signed a treaty allowing the US to lease military bases on the island. In 1991 the Philippine Senate voted to reject a renewal of that lease, and Nov 24, 1992, after almost 100 years of military presence on the island, the last contingent of US marines left Subic Base.

WHAT DO YOU LOVE ABOUT AMERICA DAY. Nov 24. One day to talk about what's great about our country and its people. In the midst of cynicism, let's talk to each other about what we love. For info: Chuck Sutherland, 6906 Waggoner Place, Dallas, TX 75230. Phone: (214) 696-9214. Fax: (214) 696-2442. E-mail: sutherla@swbell.net.

WINTER FLOWER AND TRAIN SHOW. Nov 24–Jan 6, 2002. Lincoln Park Conservatory, Chicago, IL. Several model trains, including an old fashioned steam engine, freight train and trolley will wind their way through a tiny village set in a field of vibrant red, delicate pink and soft white poinsettias. The village comprised entirely of natural materials including willow spruce and birchwoods features a variety of Chicago style homes and famous buildings. For info: Lincoln Park Conservatory, 2400 N Stockton, Chicago, IL 60614. Phone: (312) 742-7736. Fax: (312) 742-5619.

BIRTHDAYS TODAY

William Frank Buckley, Jr., 76, editor (*The National Review*), author (*God and Man at Yale*), born New York, NY, Nov 24, 1925.

Dan Glickman, 57, US Secretary of Agriculture (Clinton administration), born Wichita, KS, Nov 24, 1944.

Stanley Livingston, 51, actor ("My Three Sons"), born Los Angeles, CA, Nov 24, 1950.

Keith Primeau, 30, hockey player, born Toronto, Ontario, Canada, Nov 24, 1971.

Oscar Palmer Robertson, 63, Basketball Hall of Fame guard, born Charlotte, TN, Nov 24, 1938.

Dwight Schultz, 54, actor ("Star Trek: The Next Generation," *Fat Man and Little Boy*), born Baltimore, MD, Nov 24, 1947.

Brad Sherwood, 37, comedian, actor ("Whose Line Is It Anyway?"), born Chicago, IL, Nov 24, 1964.

Rudolph (Rudy) Tomjanovich, 53, basketball coach and former player, born Hamtramck, MI, Nov 24, 1948.

NOVEMBER 25 — SUNDAY
Day 329 — 36 Remaining

AUTOMOBILE SPEED REDUCTION: ANNIVERSARY. Nov 25, 1973. Anniversary of the presidential order requiring a cutback from the 70 mile-per-hour speed limit. The 55 mile-per-hour National Maximum Speed Limit (NMSL) was established by Congress in January 1974 (PL 93–643). The National Highway Traffic Administration reported that "analysis of available data shows that the 55 mph NMSL forestalled 48,310 fatalities through 1980. There were also reductions in crash-related injuries and property damage." Motor fuel savings were estimated at 2.4 billion gallons per year. Notwithstanding, in 1987 Congress permitted states to increase speed limits on rural interstate highways to 65 miles per hour.

CARNEGIE, ANDREW: BIRTH ANNIVERSARY. Nov 25, 1835. American financier, philanthropist and benefactor of more than 2,500 libraries, was born at Dunfermline, Scotland. Carnegie Hall, Carnegie Foundation and the Carnegie Endowment for International Peace are among his gifts. Carnegie wrote in 1889, "Surplus wealth is a sacred trust which its possessor is bound to administer in his lifetime for the good of the community. . . . The man who dies . . . rich dies disgraced." Carnegie died at his summer estate, "Shadowbrook," MA, Aug 11, 1919.

CHRISTMAS PARADE. Nov 25. Woodstock, IL. Santa will officially arrive in a parade around the square at 2 PM. Est attendance: 1,000. For info: Woodstock Chamber of Commerce, 136 Cass St, Woodstock, IL 60098. Phone: (815) 338-2436. Fax: (815) 338-2497. E-mail: chamber@stans.com.

DiMAGGIO, JOSEPH PAUL (JOE): BIRTH ANNIVERSARY. Nov 25, 1914. Baseball Hall of Fame outfielder, born at Martinez, CA. In 1941 he was on "the streak," getting a hit in 56 consecutive games. He was the American League MVP for three years, was the batting champion in 1939 and led the league in RBIs in both 1941 and 1948. DiMaggio was married to actress Marilyn Monroe in 1954. He died at Harbour Island, FL, Mar 8, 1999.

GERMANY: FRANKFURT CHRISTMAS MARKET. Nov 25–Dec 23. "Weinachtsmarkt auf dem Romerberg," the Christmas market in Frankfurt, is one of Germany's best. Bells are rung simultaneously from nine downtown churches. Glockenspiels are sounded by hand and trumpets blown from the old St. Nicolas Church.

GERMANY: TOTENSONNTAG. Nov 25. In Germany, Totensonntag is the Protestant population's day for remembrance of the dead. It is celebrated on the last Sunday of the church year (the Sunday before Advent).

NATION, CARRY AMELIA MOORE: BIRTH ANNIVERSARY. Nov 25, 1846. American temperance leader, famed as hatchet-wielding smasher of saloons, born at Garrard County, KY. Died at Leavenworth, KS, June 9, 1911.

PASADENA DOO DAH PARADE. Nov 25. Pasadena, CA. No theme, no judging, no prizes, no order of march, no motorized vehicles and no animals. Annually, the Sunday following Thanksgiving Day.

POPE JOHN XXIII: BIRTH ANNIVERSARY. Nov 25, 1881. Angelo Roncalli, 261st pope of the Roman Catholic Church, born at Sotte il Monte, Italy. Elected pope, Oct 28, 1958. Died June 3, 1963, at Rome, Italy.

RADIOLOGICAL SOCIETY OF NORTH AMERICA SCIENTIFIC ASSEMBLY AND ANNUAL MEETING. Nov 25–30. McCormick Place, Chicago, IL. 87th annual. Est attendance: 61,000. For info: Radiological Soc of North America, 820 Jorie Blvd, Oak Brook, IL 60523-2251. Phone: (630) 571-2670. Fax: (630) 571-7837.

SAINT CATHERINE'S DAY. Nov 25. Patron saint of maidens, mechanics and philosophers, as well as of all who work with wheels.

SHOPPING REMINDER DAY. Nov 25. One month before Christmas, a reminder to shoppers that there are only 24 more shopping days (excluding Sundays and Christmas Eve) after today until Christmas, and that one month from today a new countdown will begin for Christmas 2002.

SURINAME: INDEPENDENCE DAY: ANNIVERSARY. Nov 25. Holiday. Gained independence from the Netherlands in 1975.

SWINE TIME. Nov 25. Climax, GA. Plenty of family fun. Past residents homecoming raises funds for the Climax Community Club.

Special events for all ages: Best Dressed Pig contest, chitterling eating, baby crawling, hog calling, bar-b-que eating, corn shucking, hog imitation and greasy pig chase contest. Plus a parade, quilt auction, pig race, petting zoo, clogging, music of all kinds, arts and crafts booths, a variety of food, kiddie rides and long distance prize. Est attendance: 25,000. For info: Climax Community Club, PO Box 131, Climax, GA 31734. Phone: (912) 248-5954. Fax: (912) 248-0273. E-mail: dshcch@planttel.net.

TRAVELERS WITH DISABILITIES AWARENESS WEEK. Nov 25–Dec 1. To promote the economic well-being of Americans with disabilities who travel and to create an environment free of obstacles throughout the tourism and travel industry for Americans with disabilities. Annually, the week following Thanksgiving. For info: Soc for the Advancement of Travel for the Handicapped, 347 Fifth Ave, Ste 610, New York, NY 10016. Phone: (212) 447-7284. E-mail: SATHTRAVEL@aol.com.

UNITED NATIONS: INTERNATIONAL DAY FOR THE ELIMINATION OF VIOLENCE AGAINST WOMEN. Nov 25. Women's activists have marked Nov 25 as a day against violence since 1981. On that date in 1961 the three Mirabel sisters, political activists in the Dominican Republic, were assassinated on orders of ruler Rafael Trujillo. For info: United Nations, Dept of Public Info, New York, NY 10017. Web: www.un.org.

VICTORIAN CHRISTMAS CELEBRATION. Nov 25–Jan 5, 2002. History House, Cumberland, MD. Victorian Christmas tea and candlelight tours with musical entertainment. Various workshops and children's programs. Theme decorating in an 1867 Victorian mansion museum. Est attendance: 1,000. For info: Sharon Nealis, Admin, History House, 218 Washington St, Cumberland, MD 21502. Phone: (301) 777-8678. Web: www.history house.allconet.org.

BIRTHDAYS TODAY

Christina Applegate, 30, actress ("Married . . . With Children," "Jesse"), born Hollywood, CA, Nov 25, 1971.
Cris Carter, 36, football player, born Troy, OH, Nov 25, 1965.
Russell Earl ("Bucky") Dent (born Russell Earl O'Dey), 50, former baseball player and manager, born Savannah, GA, Nov 25, 1951.
Joe Jackson Gibbs, 61, sportscaster, Pro Football Hall of Fame coach, born Mocksville, NC, Nov 25, 1940.
Amy Grant, 41, singer ("Baby, Baby"), born Augusta, GA, Nov 25, 1960.
Jill Hennessy, 32, actress ("Law & Order"), born Edmonton, Alberta, Canada, Nov 25, 1969.
Bernie Joseph Kosar, Jr, 38, former football player, born Boardman, OH, Nov 25, 1963.
John Larroquette, 54, actor (Emmy for "Night Court"; "Payne," "The John Larroquette Show"), born New Orleans, LA, Nov 25, 1947.
Lenny Moore, 68, Pro Football Hall of Fame halfback, born Reading, PA, Nov 25, 1933.

November 2001	S	M	T	W	T	F	S
					1	2	3
	4	5	6	7	8	9	10
	11	12	13	14	15	16	17
	18	19	20	21	22	23	24
	25	26	27	28	29	30	

NOVEMBER 26 — MONDAY
Day 330 — 35 Remaining

CASABLANCA PREMIERE: ANNIVERSARY. Nov 26, 1942. Due to the landing of the Allies in North Africa on Nov 8, the premiere and release of the film were moved up from June 1943 to Nov 26, 1942, when it premiered at New York City on Thanksgiving Day. The general nationwide release followed on Jan 23, 1943, during the Roosevelt-Churchill conferences in Casablanca.

CUSTER BATTLEFIELD BECOMES LITTLE BIGHORN BATTLEFIELD: 10th ANNIVERSARY. Nov 26, 1991. The US Congress approved a bill renaming Custer Battlefield National Monument as Little Bighorn Battlefield National Monument. The bill also authorized the construction of a memorial to the Native Americans who fought and died at the battle known as Custer's Last Stand. Introduced by then Representative Ben Nighthorse Campbell, the only Native American in Congress, the bill was signed into law by President George Bush.

FIRST US HOLIDAY BY PRESIDENTIAL PROCLAMATION: ANNIVERSARY. Nov 26, 1789. President George Washington proclaimed Nov 26, 1789, to be Thanksgiving Day. Both Houses of Congress, by their joint committee, had requested him to recommend a day of public thanksgiving and prayer, to be observed by acknowledging with grateful hearts the many and signal favors of Almighty God, especially by affording them an opportunity to peaceably establish a form of government for their safety and happiness. Proclamation issued Oct 3, 1789. Next proclaimed by President Lincoln in 1863 for the last Thursday in November. In 1939 President Roosevelt moved Thanksgiving to the fourth Thursday in November.

GRIMKE, SARAH MOORE: BIRTH ANNIVERSARY. Nov 26, 1792. American antislavery and women's rights advocate along with her sister Angelina. Born at Charleston, SC, and died Dec 23, 1873, at Hyde Park, MA.

JAPAN AGREES TO END USE OF DRIFT NETS: 10th ANNIVERSARY. Nov 26, 1991. Japan agreed to comply with a 1989 United Nations moratorium on the use of huge fishing nets in the Northern Pacific Ocean. The large nets extend up to 40 miles and have been criticized as "walls of death," causing widespread destruction of marine life, including whales, turtles, birds and many varieties of fish. Japan agreed to end half of its driftnet fishing by the June 30, 1992, deadline, and the remainder by the end of 1992.

JOHN HARVARD DAY: BIRTH ANNIVERSARY. Nov 26, 1607. English clergyman and scholar, founder of Harvard College. Born in England, he died Sept 24, 1638, at the Massachusetts Bay colony.

"THE PRICE IS RIGHT" TV PREMIERE: 45th ANNIVERSARY. Nov 26, 1956. This popular show is also TV's longest-running daily game show, surviving changes in format, networks, time slots and hosts. It began in 1956 with Bill Cullen as host, Don Pardo as announcer and a fairly rigid format: four contestants had to bid on an item and the one who bid closest to the manufacturer's suggested price without going over won the item. In 1972, after a seven-year hiatus, "The Price Is Right" came back in two versions. Bob Barker was the host of the network version, which expanded to an hour and which he hosts to this day. Johnny Olsen was the announcer until his death in 1985; Rod Roddy took his place. Also on the show are attractive women who model the prizes to be won and help set up the price-guessing games. "Price" contestants are drawn from the studio audience.

QUEEN ELIZABETH AGREES TO PAY TAXES: ANNIVERSARY. Nov 26, 1992. Prime Minister John Major announced that Britain's monarch, Queen Elizabeth, had decided to begin paying taxes on her personal income.

Corona

SCHULZ, CHARLES: BIRTH ANNIVERSARY. Nov 26, 1922. Cartoonist, born at Minneapolis, MN. Created the "Peanuts" comic strip that debuted on Oct 2, 1950. The strip included Charlie Brown, his sister Sally, his dog Snoopy, friends Linus and Lucy and a variety of other characters. Stricken with colon cancer, Schulz last daily strip was published Jan 3, 2000, and his last Sunday strip was published Feb 13, 2000. The strip ran in more than 2,500 newspapers in many different countries. Schulz won the Reuben Award in both 1955 and 1964 and was named International Cartoonist of the Year in 1978. Several TV specials were spin-offs of the strip including "It's the Great Pumpkin Charlie Brown" and "You're a Good Man Charlie Brown." Schulz died at Santa Rosa, CA Feb 12, 2000. See also "Peanuts Debuts: Anniversary" (Oct 2).

SEVAREID, ERIC: BIRTH ANNIVERSARY. Nov 26, 1912. American journalist Eric (Arnold) Sevareid was born at Velva, ND. He worked for CBS News as a radio reporter during World War II, appeared regularly on "The CBS News with Walter Cronkite" from 1964 to 1977, won the Peabody Award for news interpretations (1950, 1964 and 1967) and earned two Emmys in 1973. He died July 9, 1992, at Washington, DC.

SWITZERLAND: ONION MARKET (ZIBELEMARIT). Nov 26. Berne. Best known and most popular of Switzerland's many autumn markets. Great heaps of onions in front of Federal Palace. Fourth Monday in November commemorates granting of market right to people after great fire of Berne in 1405.

TRUTH, SOJOURNER: DEATH ANNIVERSARY. Nov 26, 1883. A former slave who had been sold four different times, Sojourner Truth became an evangelist who argued for abolition and women's rights. After a troubled early life, she began her evangelical career in 1843, traveling through New England until she discovered the utopian colony called the Northampton Association of Education and Industry. It was there she was exposed to, and became an advocate for, the cause of abolition, working with Frederick Douglass, Wendell Phillips, William Lloyd Garrison and others. In 1850 she befriended Lucretia Mott, Elizabeth Cady Stanton and other feminist leaders and actively began supporting calls for women's rights. In 1870 she attempted to petition Congress to create a "Negro State" on public lands in the west. Born at Ulster County, NY, about 1790, with the name Isabella Van Wagener, she died Nov 26, 1883, at Battle Creek, MI.

"TWENTY QUESTIONS" TV PREMIERE: ANNIVERSARY. Nov 26, 1949. This game show was based on the old guessing game. A celebrity panel had to guess the identity of an object (at the start they were told only if it was animal, vegetable or mineral) by asking up to 20 questions. Bill Slater hosted two network versions of the show on NBC and Dumont. Jay Jackson took over when it switched from NBC to ABC. "Twenty Questions" first began on radio. Regular panelists included Fred Van Deventer, Florence Rinard, Herb Polesie and Johnny McPhee.

WALKER, MARY EDWARDS: BIRTH ANNIVERSARY. Nov 26, 1832. American physician and women's rights leader, born at Oswego, NY. First female surgeon in US Army (Civil War). Spent four months in Confederate prison. First and only woman ever to receive Medal of Honor (Nov 11, 1865). Two years before her death, on June 3, 1916, a government review board asked that her award be revoked. She continued to wear it, in spite of official revocation, until her death, Feb 21, 1919, at Oswego. On June 11, 1977, the secretary of the army posthumously restored the Medal of Honor to Dr. Walker.

BIRTHDAYS TODAY

Shannon Dunn, 29, Olympic snowboarder, born Arlington Heights, IL, Nov 26, 1972.
Robert Goulet, 68, entertainer, actor (*Camelot, Naked Gun 2½*), born Lawrence, MA, Nov 26, 1933.
Shawn Kemp, 32, basketball player, member of Dream Team II, born Elkhart, IN, Nov 26, 1969.
Richard (Rich) Caruthers Little, 63, impressionist, born Ottawa, Ontario, Canada, Nov 26, 1938.
Tina Turner, 63, singer (with Ike: "A Fool in Love"; solo: "What's Love Got to Do With It"), born Nutbush, TN, Nov 26, 1938.

NOVEMBER 27 — TUESDAY
Day 331 — 34 Remaining

AGEE, JAMES: BIRTH ANNIVERSARY. Nov 27, 1909. Poet, novelist (*Let Us Now Praise Famous Men*), scriptwriter (*A Death in the Family*), born at Knoxville, TN. Died at New York, NY, May 16, 1955.

BANK BAILOUT BILL: 10th ANNIVERSARY. Nov 27, 1991. Both houses of Congress approved legislation authorizing $70 billion in additional borrowing authority for the Federal Deposit Insurance Corporation (FDIC) because of the record number of savings and loan failures.

BEARD, CHARLES A.: BIRTH ANNIVERSARY. Nov 27, 1874. American historian Charles Austin Beard who wrote many books in collaboration with his wife, Mary R. Beard, was born near Knightstown, IN. He died at New Haven, CT, Sept 1, 1948.

CHRISTMAS AT THE CAPITAL. Nov 27–Dec 28. State Capital Rotunda, Pierre, SD. More than 50 evergreens are decorated with handcrafted ornaments, each with its own theme. Est attendance: 50,000. For info: Kris Graham, Project Coord, 500 E Capital Ave, Pierre, SD 57501. Phone: (605) 773-3661.

"THE DINAH SHORE SHOW" TV PREMIERE: 50th ANNIVERSARY. Nov 27, 1951. Dinah Shore hosted a successful 15-minute musical show until 1957 and then an hour variety show from 1957 to 1962, one of the few females to have done so. The music show was sponsored by Chevrolet (and was officially known as "The Dinah Shore Chevy Show") and featured a backup group called the Skylarks. Shore also starred in specials and hosted a variety series with a guest host filling in for her every fourth week. She later moved on to hosting a talk show.

DUBCEK, ALEXANDER: BIRTH ANNIVERSARY. Nov 27, 1921. The man who attempted to give his country "socialism with a human face," Alexander Dubcek was born at Uhrocev, a village in western Slovakia. As first secretary of the Czechoslovak Communist Party during the "Prague Spring" of 1968, he moved to achieve the "widest possible democratization" and to loosen the dominant influence of the Soviet Union. As a result, Czechoslovakia was invaded by armed forces of the Warsaw Pact on Aug 21, 1968. Dubcek died Nov 7, 1992, at Prague.

HENDRIX, JIMI: BIRTH ANNIVERSARY. Nov 27, 1942. American musician and songwriter Jimi Hendrix was born at Seattle, WA. One of the greatest rock guitarists in history, he revolutionized the guitar sound with heavy use of feedback and incredible fretwork. His success first came in England, then in the US after his appearance at the Monterey Pop Festival (1967). His albums included *Are You Experienced?*, *Electric Ladyland*, *Axis: Bold as Love* (all 1968) and *Band of Gypsys* (1970). He died Sept 18, 1970, at London, England.

KEMBLE, FANNY: BIRTH ANNIVERSARY. Nov 27, 1809. Frances Anne Kemble, English actress, born at London, England, and died there Jan 15, 1893.

LIVINGSTON, ROBERT R.: BIRTH ANNIVERSARY.
Nov 27, 1746 (OS). Member of the Continental Congress, farmer, diplomat and jurist, was born at New York, NY. It was Livingston who administered the oath of office to President George Washington in 1789. He died at Clermont, NY, Feb 26, 1813.

MASTERSON, BAT: BIRTH ANNIVERSARY. Nov 27, 1853. Old American West gambler, saloonkeeper, lawman and news writer/editor. Born at Henryville, Quebec, Canada; died Oct 25, 1921, at New York, NY.

REVEREND FRANCIS GASTRELL'S EJECTMENT: ANNIVERSARY. Nov 27, 1759. The Stratford-upon-Avon town corporation gave orders to bring an "action of Ejectment" against the Reverend Francis Gastrell, Vicar of Frodsham, who lived in William Shakespeare's home. Gastrell had cut down the 150-year-old mulberry tree that had been planted by Shakespeare. Gastrell maliciously felled the tree because he was annoyed by the many Shakespeare enthusiasts who came to look at it. He sold the tree for firewood, but it was recovered by a jeweler-wood-carver, Thomas Sharp, who fashioned hundreds of relics from it. Gastrell was ejected from Stratford "amid the ragings and cursings of its people, a citizen well lost"—for one of "the meanest petty infamies in our annals."

SPACE MILESTONE: *SOYUZ T-3 (USSR).* Nov 27, 1980. Launched this date with three cosmonauts, O. Makarov, L. Kizim and G. Strekalov, docked at *Salyut 6* space station on Nov 28. Returned to Earth, Dec 10, 1980.This was the first Soviet crew of three since 1971.

WEIZMANN, CHAIM: BIRTH ANNIVERSARY. Nov 27, 1874. Israeli statesman born near Pinsk, Byelorussia. He played an important role in bringing about the British government's Balfour Declaration, calling for the establishment of a national home for Jews at Palestine. He died at Tel Aviv, Israel, Nov 9, 1952.

BIRTHDAYS TODAY

Robin Givens, 37, actress ("Head of the Class," *A Rage in Harlem*), born New York, NY, Nov 27, 1964.
Gail Henion Sheehy, 64, author, journalist (*The Silent Passage: Menopause; Pathfinders*), born Mamaroneck, NY, Nov 27, 1937.
Fisher Stevens, 38, actor (*The Brother from Another Planet, Bob Roberts*), born Chicago, IL, Nov 27, 1963.
Nick Van Exel, 30, basketball player, born Kenosha, WI, Nov 27, 1971.
Jaleel White, 25, actor ("Family Matters"), born Los Angeles, CA, Nov 27, 1976.

NOVEMBER 28 — WEDNESDAY

Day 332 — 33 Remaining

ALBANIA: INDEPENDENCE DAY. Nov 28. Commemorates independence from the Ottoman Empire in 1912.

ALSTON, CHARLES H.: BIRTH ANNIVERSARY. Nov 28, 1907. African-American painter and sculptor born at Charlotte, NC, and died at New York, NY, Apr 27, 1977. Charles Alston was celebrated in his lifetime for seminal paintings and sculptures that defy categorization. Throughout his career, he experimented with styles ranging from realism to abstraction. His realistic WPA murals at Harlem Hospital depict a narrative in the style of Diego Rivera. The Cubist painting of *The Family* (1955), is an excellent example of Alston's early work, influenced by Italian artist Amedeo Modigliani. *Black Man, Black Woman USA* has a decidedly Egyptian style of portraiture. *Walking* (1958), which depicts

a silent crowd, almost prophecies the turmoil and social agitation of the Civil Rights Movement.

BLAKE, WILLIAM: BIRTH ANNIVERSARY. Nov 28, 1757. English poet (*Songs of Innonence*), artist and philosopher, born at London, England. Died there Aug 12, 1827.

BUNYAN, JOHN: BIRTH ANNIVERSARY. Nov 28, 1628 (OS). English cleric and author of *A Pilgrim's Progress*, born at Elstow, Bedfordshire. Died at London, Aug 31, 1688 (OS).

DESERT STORM: UN DEADLINE RESOLUTION: ANNIVERSARY. Nov 28, 1990. The United Nations passed the twelfth in a series of resolutions concerning the Iraqi invasion of Kuwait. Resolution 678 authorized states "to use all necessary means" against Iraq unless it withdrew its forces from Kuwait by Jan 15, 1991. Iraq did not comply, and the Allied Forces began their attack with the code-name Operation Desert Storm within hours of the expiration of the deadline.

LULLY, JEAN BAPTISTE: BIRTH ANNIVERSARY. Nov 28, 1632. Versatile musician and composer, born at Florence, Italy, who chose France for his homeland. Noted for his quick temper, it is said that he struck his own foot with a baton while in a rage. The resulting wound led to blood poisoning, from which he died, at Paris, France, Mar 22, 1687.

MAURITANIA: INDEPENDENCE DAY: ANNIVERSARY. Nov 28. National holiday. Attained sovereignty from France in 1960.

NAIA WOMEN'S NATIONAL VOLLEYBALL CHAMPIONSHIP. Nov 28–Dec 1. Palm Beach Atlantic College, West Palm Beach, FL. 20 teams compete in a pool play tournament to determine the national champion. 22nd annual championship. For info: Lori Heeter, Natl Assn of Intercollegiate Athletics, 6120 S Yale Ave, Ste 1450, Tulsa, OK 74136-4223. Phone: (918) 494-8828. Fax: (918) 494-8841. E-mail: lheeter@naia.org. Web: www.naia.org.

PANAMA: INDEPENDENCE FROM SPAIN. Nov 28. Public holiday. Commemorates the independence of Panama (which at the time was part of Colombia) from Spain in 1821.

SPACE MILESTONE: *COLUMBIA STS-9 (US).* Nov 28, 1983. Shuttle *Columbia* launched from Kennedy Space Center, FL, with five astronauts (John Young, Brewster Shaw, Jr, Owen Garriot, Robert Parker, Byron Lichtenberg) and German physicist Ulf Merbold. Landed Edwards Air Force Base, CA, on Dec 8.

SPACE MILESTONE: *MARINER 4 (US).* Nov 28, 1964. The first successful mission to Mars. Approached within 6,118 miles of Mars on July 14, 1965. Took photographs and instrument readings.

TEHERAN CONFERENCE: ANNIVERSARY. Nov 28–Dec 1, 1943. President Franklin D. Roosevelt, British Prime Minister Winston Churchill and Soviet Premier Joseph Stalin met at Teheran, Iran, to formulate a plan for an Allied assault, a second front, in western Europe. The resulting plan was "Operation Overlord," which commenced with the landing on Normandy's beaches on June 6, 1944 ("D-Day").

BIRTHDAYS TODAY

Berry Gordy, Jr, 72, record and motion picture executive (co-founder of Motown), born Detroit, MI, Nov 28, 1929.
Ed Harris, 51, actor (*The Right Stuff, Stepmom*), born Englewood, NJ, Nov 28, 1950.
Gary Hart (Gary Hartpence), 63, former senator, presidential candidate, born Ottawa, KS, Nov 28, 1938.
Hope Lange, 68, actress ("The Ghost and Mrs Muir," *Bus Stop*), born Reading Ridge, CT, Nov 28, 1933.
S. Epatha Merkerson, 49, actress ("Law & Order"), born Detroit, MI, Nov 28, 1952.
Judd Nelson, 42, actor (*The Breakfast Club, St. Elmo's Fire,* "Suddenly Susan"), born Portland, ME, Nov 28, 1959.

November 2001

S	M	T	W	T	F	S
				1	2	3
4	5	6	7	8	9	10
11	12	13	14	15	16	17
18	19	20	21	22	23	24
25	26	27	28	29	30	

Randy Newman, 58, singer, songwriter ("Short People"), composer (film scores *Ragtime, The Natural*), born Los Angeles, CA, Nov 28, 1943.

Paul Shaffer, 52, bandleader ("Late Night with David Letterman"), comedian, born Thunder Bay, Ontario, Canada, Nov 28, 1949.

Jon Stewart, 39, comedian, host ("The Daily Show with Jon Stewart"), born Trenton, NJ, Nov 28, 1962.

Matt Williams, 36, baseball player, born Bishop, CA, Nov 28, 1965.

NOVEMBER 29 — THURSDAY
Day 333 — 32 Remaining

ALCOTT, LOUISA MAY: BIRTH ANNIVERSARY. Nov 29, 1832. American author, born at Philadelphia, PA. Died at Boston, MA, Mar 6, 1888. Her most famous novel was *Little Women*, the classic story of Meg, Jo, Beth and Amy.

BERKELEY, BUSBY: BIRTH ANNIVERSARY. Nov 29, 1895. William Berkeley Enos was born at Los Angeles, CA. After serving in World War I as an entertainment officer, he changed his name to Busby Berkeley and began a career in show business as an actor. He turned to directing in 1921, and his lavish Broadway and Hollywood creations include *Forty-Second Street, Gold Diggers of 1933, Footlight Parade, Stage Struck, Babes in Arms, Strike Up the Band, Girl Crazy* and *Take Me Out to the Ball Game*, among many others. He retired in 1962 and returned to Broadway in 1970 to supervise a revival of *No, No, Nanette*. He died Mar 14, 1976, at Palm Springs, CA.

CZECHOSLOVAKIA ENDS COMMUNIST RULE: ANNIVERSARY. Nov 29, 1989. Czechoslovakia ended 41 years of one-party communist rule when the Czechoslovak parliament voted unanimously to repeal the constitutional clauses giving the Communist Party a guaranteed leading role in the country and promoting Marxism-Leninism as the state ideology. The vote came at the end of a 12-day revolution sparked by the beating of protestors Nov 17. Although the Communist party remained in power, the tide of reform led to its ouster by the Civic Forum, headed by playwright Vaclav Havel. The Civic Forum demanded free elections with equal rights for all parties, a mixed economy and support for foreign investment.

ELECTRONIC GREETINGS DAY. Nov 29. Save a letter carrier, save a tree, save a stamp! Today's the day to send your greetings the free, electronic way, via the Internet! © 2000 Wellcat Herbs & Holidays. For info: Thomas or Ruth Roy, 2418 Long Ln, Lebanon, PA 17046. Phone: (240) 332-4886. Web: www.wellcat.com.

FESTIVAL OF TREES. Nov 29–Dec 2. Kansas Expocentre, Topeka, KS. A display of 50 artistically decorated Christmas trees is the centerpiece of the festival, which kicks off the holiday spirit in the Heartland. Live entertainment, festive foods, gift boutique. No admission charge. Est attendance: 15,000. For info: FOT, Sheltered Living Inc, 2044 SW Fillmore, Topeka, KS 66604-3093. Phone: (785) 233-2566. Fax: (785) 233-2556.

"KUKLA, FRAN AND OLLIE" TV PREMIERE: ANNIVERSARY. Nov 29, 1948. This popular children's show featured puppets created and handled by Burr Tillstrom and was equally popular with adults. Fran Allison was the only human on the show. Tillstrom's lively and eclectic cast of characters, called the "Kuklapolitans," included the bald, high-voiced Kukla, the big-toothed Oliver J. Dragon (Ollie), Fletcher Rabbit, Cecil Bill, Beulah the Witch, Colonel Crackie, Madame Ooglepuss and Dolores Dragon. Most shows were performed without scripts.

LEWIS, C.S. (CLIVE STAPLES): BIRTH ANNIVERSARY. Nov 29, 1898. British scholar, novelist and author (*The Screwtape Letters, Chronicles of Narnia*), born at Belfast, Ireland, died at Oxford, England, Nov 22, 1963.

PHILLIPS, WENDELL: BIRTH ANNIVERSARY. Nov 29, 1811. American women's suffrage, anti-slavery, prison reform leader, born at Boston, MA. Died there Feb 2, 1884.

ROSS, NELLIE TAYLOE: 125th BIRTH ANNIVERSARY. Nov 29, 1876. Nellie Tayloe Ross became the first female governor in the US when she was chosen to serve out the last month and two days of her husband's term as governor of Wyoming after he died in office. She was elected in her own right in the Nov 4, 1924, election but lost the 1927 race. Ross was appointed vice chairman of the Democratic National Committee in 1926 and named director of the US Mint by President Franklin D. Roosevelt in 1933. She served in that capacity for 20 years. Born at St. Joseph, MO, she died Dec 20, 1977, at Washington, DC.

THOMSON, CHARLES: BIRTH ANNIVERSARY. Nov 29, 1729. America's first official record keeper. Chosen secretary of the First Continental Congress Sept 5, 1774, Thomson recorded proceedings for 15 years and delivered his journals together with tens of thousands of records to the federal government in 1789. Born in Ireland, he died Aug 16, 1824. It was Thomson who notified George Washington of his election as president.

UNITED NATIONS: INTERNATIONAL DAY OF SOLIDARITY WITH THE PALESTINIAN PEOPLE. Nov 29. Annual observance proclaimed by UN General Assembly in 1977. At request of Assembly, observance is organized by secretary-general in consultation with Committee on the Exercise of the Inalienable Rights of the Palestinian People. Recommendations include a plan for return of the Palestinians to their homes and the establishment of an "independent Palestinian entity." For info: United Nations, Dept of Public Info, New York, NY 10017.

VICTORIAN CHRISTMAS SLEIGHBELL PARADE. Nov 29–Dec 2. Manistee, MI. Re-creation of Manistee history. No motorized vehicles, no amplification. Horse-drawn entries, walking entries, singers, animals and St. Nick in historic garb. Parade on Dec 1. Est attendance: 10,000. For info: Manistee Area Chamber of Commerce, 50 Filer St, Ste 224, Manistee, MI 49660. Phone: (231) 723-2575 or (800) 288-2286. E-mail: chamber@manistee.com. Web: www.manistee.com/~edo/chamber/.

WAITE, MORRISON R.: BIRTH ANNIVERSARY. Nov 29, 1816. Seventh Chief Justice of the Supreme Court, born at Lyme, CT. Appointed Chief Justice by President Ulysses S. Grant Jan 19, 1874. The Waite Court is remembered for its controversial rulings that did much to rehabilitate the idea of states' rights after the Civil War and early Reconstruction years. Waite died at Washington, DC, Mar 23, 1888.

BIRTHDAYS TODAY

Jacques Rene Chirac, 69, French President, born Paris, France, Nov 29, 1932.

Joel Coen, 47, producer, screenwriter (*Fargo*), born Minneapolis, MN, Nov 29, 1954.

Kim Delaney, 40, actress ("NYPD Blue"), born Philadelphia, PA, Nov 29, 1961.

Diane Ladd (Rose Diane Ladner), 69, actress (*Alice Doesn't Live Here Anymore, Ramblin' Rose, The Cemetery Club*), born Meridian, MS, Nov 29, 1932.

Madeleine L'Engle, 83, writer (*A Wrinkle in Time, Summer of the Great-Grandmother*), born New York, NY, Nov 29, 1918.

Howie Mandel, 46, comedic actor ("Howie Mandel's Sunny Skies," "Bobby's World"), born Toronto, Ontario, Canada, Nov 29, 1955.

Chuck Mangione, 61, musician, composer (Grammy for "Bellavia"), born Rochester, NY, Nov 29, 1940.

John Mayall, 68, musician, bandleader (The Bluesbreakers), born Manchester, England, Nov 29, 1933.

Andrew McCarthy, 39, actor (*Pretty in Pink, Weekend at Bernie's*), born Westfield, NJ, Nov 29, 1962.

Cathy Moriarty, 41, actress (*Raging Bull, The Mambo Kings*), born The Bronx, NY, Nov 29, 1960.

Mariano Rivera, 32, baseball player, born Panama City, Panama, Nov 29, 1969.

Vincent Edward (Vin) Scully, 74, sportscaster, Ford Frick award winner, born New York, NY, Nov 29, 1927.

Garry Shandling, 52, comedian ("The Larry Sanders Show"), born Chicago, IL, Nov 29, 1949.

NOVEMBER 30 — FRIDAY
Day 334 — 31 Remaining

ARTICLES OF PEACE BETWEEN GREAT BRITAIN AND THE US: ANNIVERSARY. Nov 30, 1782. These provisional articles of peace, which were to end America's War of Independence, were signed at Paris, France. The refined and definitive treaty of peace between Great Britain and the US was signed at Paris, on Sept 3, 1783. In it "His Britannic Majesty acknowledges the said United States. . .to be free, sovereign and independent states; that he treats them as such; and for himself, his heirs and successors, relinquishes all claims to the government, propriety and territorial rights of the same, and every part thereof. . . ."

BARBADOS: INDEPENDENCE DAY: 35th ANNIVERSARY. Nov 30. National holiday. Gained independence from Great Britain in 1966.

BLUE MOON. Nov 30. When two full moons fall within the same month, the second is called the "Blue Moon."

CHIMNEYVILLE CRAFTS FESTIVAL. Nov 30–Dec 2. Jackson, MS. The finest crafts for sale by more than 150 craftsmen, woodcarving, blown glass, weavings, baskets, stained glass, pottery. Est attendance: 6,500. For info: V.A. Patterson, Exec Dir, Craftsmen's Guild of Mississippi, Inc, 1150 Lakeland Dr, Jackson, MS 39216. Phone: (601) 981-0019. Web: www.mscraftsmens guild.org.

CHRISTMAS GREENS SHOW. Nov 30–Dec 2. Jackman-Long Building, State Fairgrounds, Salem, OR. Half the building houses decorated trees, large Christmas displays, hundreds of floral arrangements, wreaths and wall hangings. The other half houses 106 handcrafters and their wares, also fresh greens and wreaths. Food available. Proceeds benefit community projects. Annually, the second Friday, Saturday and Sunday after Thanks-

		November 2001					
S	**M**	**T**	**W**	**T**	**F**	**S**
				1	2	3
4	5	6	7	8	9	10
11	12	13	14	15	16	17
18	19	20	21	22	23	24
25	26	27	28	29	30	

giving. Est attendance: 15,000. For info: Linda Nelson, Willamette Christmas Assn, 1856 Dearborn Ave NE, Salem, OR 97303. Phone: (503) 393-4439. For application write to: Willamette Christmas Assn, PO Box 20817, Keizer, OR 97307.

CHURCHILL, WINSTON: BIRTH ANNIVERSARY. Nov 30, 1874. Winston Leonard Spencer Churchill, British statesman and the first man to be made an honorary citizen of the US (by an act of Congress, Apr 9, 1963), born at Blenheim Palace, Oxfordshire, England. Died Jan 24, 1965, at London, England. Dedicated to Britain and total victory over Germany, Churchill as minister of defense and prime minister was a strong leader during WWII.

CLEMENS, SAMUEL LANGHORNE (MARK TWAIN): BIRTH ANNIVERSARY. Nov 30, 1835. Celebrated American author, whose books include: *The Adventures of Tom Sawyer*, *The Adventures of Huckleberry Finn* and *The Prince and the Pauper*. Born at Florida, MO, Twain is quoted as saying, "I came in with Halley's Comet in 1835. It is coming again next year, and I expect to go out with it." He did. Twain died at Redding, CT, Apr 21, 1910 (just one day after Halley's Comet perihelion).

COMPUTER SECURITY DAY. Nov 30. The use of computers increases daily. This annual event reminds people to protect their computers, programs and data at home and at work. More than 1,500 companies participate worldwide. For info: Assn for Computer Security Day, PO Box 39110, Washington, DC 20016. E-mail: computer_security_day@acm.org. Web: www.geocities .com/siliconvalley/byte/8860.

HOFFMAN, ABBOT (ABBIE): 65th BIRTH ANNIVERSARY. Nov 30, 1936. Political activist, born at Worcester, MA, Abbie Hoffman rose to prominence during the 1968 Democratic National Convention at Chicago and at his subsequent trial as a member of the Chicago Seven, a group of radicals accused of conspiring to disrupt the convention. Combining politics and street theater was a Hoffman trait. During the 1967 march on the Pentagon, he sought a permit to allow 1,200 demonstrators to encircle and levitate the military headquarters in an attempt to end the war in Vietnam. He, Jerry Rubin and Paul Krassner conceived the Yippie movement as a youth festival of life to run concurrently with the Convention. Hoffman fled underground in 1974 to avoid trial on cocaine-possession charges and remained a fugitive for nearly seven years. Surrendering to authorities in 1980, he served his sentence in a work-release program. Hoffman died Apr 12, 1989, at New Hope, PA.

MOON PHASE: FULL MOON. Nov 30. Moon enters Full Moon phase at 3:49 PM, EST. This is the second full moon this month and is called a Blue Moon.

PARADE OF LIGHTS. Nov 30–Dec 1. Denver, CO. This 27th annual evening holiday parade features dazzling theme floats, giant helium-filled holiday balloons, magical costumed characters, the area's best marching bands, high-stepping equestrian units and much more. Friday at 8 PM, Saturday at 6 PM. Est attendance: 350,000. For info: Susan Rogers Kark, Sr Dir, Mktg & Events, Downtown Denver Partnership, Inc, 511 16th St, Ste 200, Denver, CO 80202-4250. Phone: (303) 534-6161. Fax: (303) 534-2803. Web: www.downtowndenver.com.

PHILIPPINES: BONIFACIO DAY. Nov 30. Also known as National Heroes' Day. Commemorates birth of Andres Bonifacio, leader of the 1896 revolt against Spain. Bonifacio was born in 1863.

SAINT ANDREW'S DAY. Nov 30. Feast day of the apostle and martyr, Andrew, who died about AD 60. Patron saint of Scotland.

SIDNEY, PHILIP: BIRTH ANNIVERSARY. Nov 30, 1554. English poet, statesman and soldier was born at Penshurst, Kent, England. Best known of his poems is *Arcadia* (1580). Mortally wounded as he led an English detachment aiding the Dutch near Zutphen, Sept 22, 1586, Sidney gave his water bottle to another dying soldier with the words "Thy necessity is yet greater than mine." He died at Arnheim, Oct 17, 1586, and all England mourned his death.

STATUE OF RAMSES II UNEARTHED: 10th ANNIVERSARY. Nov 30, 1991. Egyptian construction workers in the ancient provincial town of Akhimim, 300 miles south of Cairo, unearthed a statue of Ramses II. Akhimim was an important provincial district that included the city of Ipu, a mecca for worshippers of the fertility god Min. The statue was uncovered during an excavation to prepare a foundation for a post office. An additional statue was uncovered 33 feet away, but the identity of its subject was unknown.

STAY HOME BECAUSE YOU'RE WELL DAY. Nov 30. So we can call in "well," instead of faking illness and stay home from work. [© 2000 by WH]. For info: Thomas or Ruth Roy, Wellcat Holidays, 2418 Long Ln, Lebanon, PA 17046. Phone: (717) 279-0184. E-mail: wellcat@supernet.com. Web: www.wellcat.com.

SWIFT, JONATHAN: BIRTH ANNIVERSARY. Nov 30, 1667 (OS). Clergyman and satirist born at Dublin, Ireland. Died there Oct 19, 1745 (OS). Author of *Gulliver's Travels*. "I never saw, heard, nor read," Swift wrote in *Thoughts on Religion* "that the clergy were beloved in any nation where Christianity was the religion of the country. Nothing can render them popular but some degree of persecution."

TEMPE FALL FESTIVAL OF THE ARTS. Nov 30–Dec 2. Tempe, AZ. Featuring 500 artists and craftspeople, traditional and ethnic foods, continuous entertainment and a children's activity area. Annually, the first weekend in December. Est attendance: 225,000. For info: Gary Sanders, Exec Dir, Mill Avenue Merchants Assn, 520 S Mill Ave, Ste 201, Tempe, AZ 85281. Phone: (480) 967-4877. Fax: (480) 967-6638. E-mail: info@millavenue.org. Web: www.millavenue.org.

UKRAINIAN FAMINE FILM BROADCAST: 10th ANNIVERSARY. Nov 30, 1991. In the rapidly changing former Soviet Union, the film *Famine 33* produced by Oles Yanchuk, was broadcast on republic-wide TV. The film chronicled the forced collectivization of the agriculture industry in 1933 and the resulting famine which led to the death of more than seven million Ukrainians. The famine was not officially recognized until 1990, when the Central Committee of the Ukrainian Communist Party first acknowledged that the millions of deaths were caused by the seizure of crops. The airing of the film heralded a significant departure from prior Soviet handling of history.

WICHITA WINTERFEST. Nov 30–Dec 1. Wichita, KS. 10th annual festival for all ages to kick off the winter in holiday style. Carnival rides, games and horse-drawn carriage rides. 5K race for running, rolling or walking on Friday evening. Holiday food court, street carolers. Fireworks to Christmas music over the river, accompanied by the official holiday lighting ceremony. Annually, the first Friday and Saturday of December. Est attendance: 35,000. For info: Mark Chamberlin, KAKE TV-10, 1500 N West St, Wichita, KS 67203. Phone: (316) 946-1323 or (316) 946-1323. Fax: (316) 945-2802. E-mail: kake@kake.com. Web: www.kake.com.

BIRTHDAYS TODAY

Shirley Chisholm, 77, author, former congresswoman, born Brooklyn, NY, Nov 30, 1924.

Dick Clark, 72, long-time host of "American Bandstand," entertainer, producer, born Mount Vernon, NY, Nov 30, 1929.

Joan Ganz Cooney, 72, founder of the Children's Television Workshop and creator of "Sesame Street," born Nov 30, 1929.

Richard Crenna, 74, actor (*Wait Until Dark, Hot Shots! Part Deux*), born Los Angeles, CA, Nov 30, 1927.

Des'ree, 31, singer (*I Ain't Movin'*), born London, England, Nov 30, 1970.

Robert Guillaume, 74, actor ("Soap," "Benson"), born St. Louis, MO, Nov 30, 1927.

Billy Idol, 46, singer ("Mony Mony," "Eyes Without a Face"), songwriter, born Surrey, England, Nov 30, 1955.

Vincent Edward ("Bo") Jackson, 39, former baseball player, former football player, born Bessemer, AL, Nov 30, 1962.

G. Gordon Liddy, 71, Watergate participant, born New York, NY, Nov 30, 1930.

David Mamet, 54, dramatist, director (*American Buffalo, Oleanna, Things Change*), born Chicago, IL, Nov 30, 1947.

Virginia Mayo, 79, actress (*The Best Years of Our Lives*), born St. Louis, MO, Nov 30, 1922.

Colin Mochrie, 44, comedian, actor ("Whose Line Is It Anyway?"), born Ayrshire, Scotland, Nov 30, 1957.

Gordon Parks, 89, photographer, author, born Fort Scott, KS, Nov 30, 1912.

Mandy Patinkin, 49, actor (Tony for *Evita; Sunday in the Park with George*, "Chicago Hope"), born Chicago, IL, Nov 30, 1952.

Ivan "Pudge" Rodriguez, 30, baseball player, born Vega Baja, Puerto Rico, Nov 30, 1971.

Ridley Scott, 64, director (*Alien, Blade Runner, Gladiator*), born Northumberland, England, Nov 30, 1937.

Ben Stiller, 36, actor, director (*Reality Bites, The Cable Guy*), born New York, NY, Nov 30, 1965.

Paul Stookey, 64, singer, songwriter (Peter, Paul and Mary), born Baltimore, MD, Nov 30, 1937.

Lawrence Summers, 47, US Secretary of the Treasury (Clinton administration), born New Haven, CT, Nov 30, 1954.

Efrem Zimbalist, Jr, 78, actor ("The F.B.I.," *Airport*), born New York, NY, Nov 30, 1923.

December.

DECEMBER 1 — SATURDAY
Day 335 — 30 Remaining

ADELPHIAN CLUB CHRISTMAS BAZAAR. Dec 1. American Legion Building, Kennett, MO. Huge sale of arts and crafts with more than 100 exhibitors, plus a bake sale. Free admission. Annually, the first Saturday in December. For info: Adelphian Civic Club, 301 S Everett, Kennett, MO 63857. Phone: (573) 888-9472.

APPALACHIAN POTTERS MARKET. Dec 1. McDowell High School, Marion, NC. One-day display and sale of clay work only by 60 potters. Annually, the first Saturday in December. Sponsor: McDowell Arts and Crafts Association. Est attendance: 1,600. For info: Appalachian Potters Market, c/o MACA, PO Box 1387, Marion, NC 28752. Phone: (828) 652-8610.

BASKETBALL CREATED: ANNIVERSARY. Dec 1, 1891. James Naismith was a teacher of physical education at the International YMCA Training School at Springfield, MA. To create an indoor sport that could be played during the winter months, he nailed up peach baskets at opposite ends of the gym and gave students soccer balls to toss into them. Thus was born the game of basketball.

BINGO'S BIRTHDAY MONTH. Dec 1–31. To celebrate the innovation and manufacture of the game of Bingo in 1929 by Edwin S. Lowe. Bingo has grown into a five-billion-dollar-a-year charitable fund-raiser. For info: Roger Snowden, Pres, Bingo Bugle, Inc, Box 527, Vashon, WA 98070. Phone: (800) 327-6437.

CANADA: YUKON ORDER OF PIONEERS: ANNIVERSARY. Dec 1, 1894. The Yukon Order of Pioneers held its founding meeting on this date at Fortymile, Yukon. It began as a vigilante police force to deter claim jumping and later inaugurated Discovery Day (Aug 17), a statutory Yukon holiday commemorating the discovery of gold on Bonanza Creek in 1896.

CELEBRATE THE HOLIDAY SEASON. Dec 1–Jan 6, 2002. Decatur, IL. Enjoy the history, music and foods of Hanukkah, Kwanzaa and a prairie Christmas. For info: Chocolate Research Library, 202 E North St, Decatur, IL 62523. Phone: (217) 422-7933.

CHESTER GREENWOOD DAY PARADE. Dec 1. Farmington, ME. Celebration of Farmington's famous inventor of the earmuff. An earmuff-themed parade with flag raising. Annually, the first Saturday in December. Est attendance: 1,000. For info: Greater Farmington Chamber of Commerce, RR 4, PO Box 5091, Farmington, ME 04938. Phone: (207) 778-4215.

December 2001	S	M	T	W	T	F	S
							1
	2	3	4	5	6	7	8
	9	10	11	12	13	14	15
	16	17	18	19	20	21	22
	23	24	25	26	27	28	29
	30	31					

CHRISTMAS AT UNION STATION. Dec 1–31. Omaha, NE. Celebration of the Christmas holiday around a giant 45-ft Christmas tree in the splendor of Omaha's old Union Station. Est attendance: 45,000. For info: Durham Western Heritage Museum, 801 S 10th St, Omaha, NE 68108-3299. Phone: (402) 444-5701. Fax: (402) 444-5397. Web: www.dwhm.org.

CHRISTMAS CANDLELIGHT TOUR. Dec 1–2. Fredericksburg, VA. To instill the spirit of Christmases past by opening historic homes to the public. Eighteenth-century music, street dancers, carriage rides throughout the tour. Est attendance: 10,000. For info: Visitor Center, 706 Caroline St, Fredericksburg, VA 22401. Phone: (800) 678-4748. Fax: (540) 372-6587. E-mail: fburg@illuminet.net.

CHRISTMAS CRAFTS SHOW. Dec 1–2. St. Simons Island, GA. 10th annual festival features 75 fine arts and crafts artists exhibiting holiday decorations and gifts. Annually, the first weekend in December. Est attendance: 10,000. For info: The Glynn Art Assn, 319 Mallory St, PO Box 20673, St. Simons Island, GA 31522. Phone: (912) 638-8770. Fax: (912) 634-ARTS. Web: www.glynnart.org.

CHRISTMAS FESTIVAL OF LIGHTS. Dec 1. Natchitoches, LA. Featuring a parade, fireworks, food, entertainment, a fun run/walk and Christmas lighting. Listed as one of the "Top 100 Events in North America" by the American Bus Association. 75th annual. Annually, the first Saturday in December. Est attendance: 150,000. For info: Natchitoches Parish Tourist Commission, 781 Front St, Natchitoches, LA 71457. Phone: (318) 352-8072 or (800) 259-1714. Fax: (318) 352-2415. Web: www.natchitoches.net.

CHRISTMAS IN THE VILLAGES. Dec 1–2. Van Buren County, IA. Event features tour of homes, English High Tea, cookie walk, Festival of Trees, horse-drawn carriage rides, bake sales, lighting contests and displays, soup suppers and the natural beauty of the season that is found throughout the county. Est attendance: 12,000. For info: Stacey Glandon, Exec Dir, Villages of Van Buren, Inc, PO Box 9, Keosauqua, IA 52565. Phone: (800) 868-7822. Fax: (319) 293-7116. Web: www.800-tourvbc.com.

CHRISTMAS—NEW ORLEANS STYLE. Dec 1–31. New Orleans, LA. Gospel concerts, caroling in Jackson Square, parades with Papa Noel, cooking demonstrations, Celebration in the Oaks, Christmas Day Concert, tours of 19th-century houses in holiday dress, Reveillon dinners, Papa Noel hotel rates. For info: Sandra Dartus, Exec Dir, 100 Conti St, New Orleans, LA 70130. Phone: (800) 673-5725 or (504) 522-5730. E-mail: info@frenchquarterfestivals.org. Web: www.frenchquarterfestivals.org.

CHRISTMAS ON THE RIVER. Dec 1. Demopolis, AL. Fun with arts and crafts, children's parade, Alabama State BBQ Cook-off and a river boat parade. Est attendance: 35,000. For info: Kathy Leverett, Pres, Demopolis Area Chamber of Commerce, Box 667, Demopolis, AL 36732. Phone: (334) 289-0270. Fax: (334) 289-1382.

CIVIL AIR PATROL FOUNDED: ANNIVERSARY. Dec 1, 1941. The Director of Civilian Defense, former New York Mayor Fiorello H. LaGuardia, signed a formal order creating the Civil Air Patrol, a US Air Force Auxiliary. The CAP has a three-part mission: to provide an aerospace education program, a CAP cadet program and an emergency services program. For info: Civil Air Patrol, 105 S Hansell St, Maxwell AFB, AL 36112-6332. Phone: (205) 953-5463.

A COLONIAL CHRISTMAS. Dec 1–31. Jamestown Settlement, Williamsburg, VA, and Yorktown Victory Center, Yorktown, VA. Recalls traditional English Christmas customs with decorations, holiday food preparation and seasonal stories. Est attendance: 12,000. For info: Media Relations, Jamestown-Yorktown Fdtn, PO Box 1607, Williamsburg, VA 23187. Phone: (757) 253-4838. Fax: (757) 253-5299. Web: www.historyisfun.org.

COLORECTAL CANCER EDUCATION AND AWARE-NESS MONTH. Dec 1–31. To educate consumers, patients and professionals regarding the need for early diagnosis and treatment of colorectal cancer. For info: Frederick S. Mayer, Pres, Pharmacists Planning Service, Inc, 101 Lucas Valley Rd, #210, San Rafael, CA 94903. Phone: (415) 479-8628. Fax: (415) 479-8608. E-mail: ppsi@aol.com. Web: www.ppsinc.org.

COMMUNITY CHRISTMAS BAZAAR. Dec 1. Curry County Fairgrounds, Gold Beach, OR. Local non-profit organizations sell their wares with all the cheer of the Christmas season. Santa visits at 1 PM. Est attendance: 400. For info: Gold Beach Chamber of Commerce, 29279 Ellensburg Ave, #3, Gold Beach, OR 97444. Phone: (800) 525-2334. Fax: (541) 247-0188. E-mail: goldbeach@harborside.com. Web: www.goldbeach.org.

COOKIE CUTTER WEEK. Dec 1–7. The international cookie cutter collectors club celebrates a special time baking cookies and collecting cutters and what better time than the first week of December-baking season. For info: Paula W. Mullins, 207 Ash, Box 8, Lawrenceburg, KY 40342. Phone: (502) 839-4929.

COOSA RIVER CHRISTMAS. Dec 1. Rome, GA. Parade of pontoon boats decorated with Christmas scenes in lights. The night is topped off with a spectacular fireworks display. Annually, the first Saturday in December. Est attendance: 45,000. For info: Lisa Smith, Coosa River Christmas, PO Box 5823, Rome, GA 30162-5823. Phone: (706) 295-5576. Fax: (706) 236-5029. E-mail: goromega@romegeorgia.com. Web: www.romegeorgia .com.

COUNTRY CHRISTMAS. Dec 1 (also Dec 8 and 15). Roscoe Village, Coshocton, OH. 19th-century holiday atmosphere, 51-room country inn, hot mulled cider in Village. Candlelighting ceremony on the first three Saturdays in December. Special weekend activities including Christmas carriage rides, strolling carolers, visits with Mr & Mrs Santa Claus. Est attendance: 6,500. For info: Roscoe Village Fdtn, 381 Hill St, Coshocton, OH 43812. Phone: (740) 622-9310 or (800) 877-1830. Fax: (740) 623-6555. E-mail: rvmarketing@coshocton.com. Web: www.roscoevillage.com.

DAY WITH(OUT) ART. Dec 1. An annual observance about the impact of AIDS on the visual arts. Events to increase public awareness through the visual arts, direct services to artists living with HIV/AIDS. For info: Visual AIDS, 526 W 26th St, #510, New York, NY 10001. Phone: (212) 627-9855. E-mail: visualaids@earthlink.net. Web: www.thebody.com/visualaids.

DICKENS ON THE STRAND. Dec 1–2. Galveston, TX. Victorian Christmas celebration focuses on the 19th-century architecture of Galveston's Strand and ties to Charles Dickens's 19th-century London. Annually, the first Saturday–Sunday in December. Est attendance: 50,000. For info: Galveston Historical Foundation, 502 20th St, Galveston, TX 77550. Phone: (409) 765-7834. Fax: (409) 765-7851. E-mail: foundation@galveston history.org. Web: www.galvestonhistory.org.

DOWNTOWN HOLIDAY OPEN HOUSE. Dec 1–3. St. Charles, IL. A weekend-long celebration in which downtown merchants welcome residents and visitors to get festive for the holidays! Sunday: St. Charles Christmas Parade at 2 PM. For info: St. Charles CVB, 311 N Second St, Ste 100, St. Charles, IL 60174. Phone: (800) 777-4373 or (708) 377-6161. Web: www.dtown.org.

GINGERBREAD VILLAGE AND BAZAAR. Dec 1–8. St. George's Church, Middlebury, CT. Fairy land of newly baked gingerbread houses—all edible and all for sale. Bazaar, food, handicrafts and gingerbread cookie men. Groups by reservation. Handicapped access available. Est attendance: 3,000. For info: St. George's Church, Gingerbread Village and Bazaar, Tuckerhill Rd at Rte 188, Middlebury, CT 06762. Group reservations Phone: (203) 723-4143.

HERITAGE CHRISTMAS. Dec 1 (also Dec 8). Old Mill Museum Complex, Lindsborg, KS. A celebration of Christmas past with the music, drama and costumes of a traditional pioneer Christmas on the Kansas prairie. Annually, the first two Saturday evenings in December. Est attendance: 1,200. For info: McPherson County Old Mill Museum, PO Box 94, Lindsborg, KS 67456. Phone: (785) 227-3595. Web: www.lindsborg.org.

HOLIDAY ARTS AND CRAFTS FESTIVAL. Dec 1–2. Norfolk Botanical Garden, Norfolk, VA. Get in the holiday spirit with adult classes, children's programs and plenty of shopping, shopping and more shopping from the Garden's gift shop and more than 30 arts and crafts vendors. Don't get caught in a mall stampede when you can find the most unique holiday gifts for everyone on your list at Norfolk Botanical Garden. Annually, the first weekend in December. Est attendance: 3,000. For info: Norfolk Botanical Garden, 6700 Azalea Garden, Norfolk, VA 23518. Phone: (757) 441-5830. Fax: (757) 853-8294. Web: www.virginia garden.org.

HUG-A-WEEK FOR THE HEARING IMPAIRED. Dec 1–31. Give a hug to someone who doesn't hear so well, each week until the end of the year. As we approach the holiday season, start with a weekly hug and find out how you might proactively include people with hearing loss in the season's festivities. A little extra time and a few special moments may help someone who can't hear so well be included and more able to share throughout the season. Annually, the month of December. For info: Carol MacKenzie, Communicate with Care, 12 Kayla Cir, Plymouth, MA 02360. Phone: (508) 224-3640.

ICELAND: UNIVERSITY STUDENTS' CELEBRATION: ANNIVERSARY. Dec 1, 1918. Marks the day in 1918 when Iceland became an independent state from Denmark (but still remained under the king of Denmark).

INTERNATIONAL CALENDAR AWARENESS MONTH. Dec 1–31. Celebrate the vital role of the calendar in today's society. Only event of its kind to promote the calendar and its rich history, both past and present. Special events throughout month include exhibit of hundreds of 2001 calendars submitted from around the world, the 11th annual World and National Calendar Awards Program and special theme-related presentations and activities focusing on the calendar. For info: Richard Mikes, Exec Dir, Calendar Marketing Assn, 710 E Ogden Ave, Ste 600, Naperville, IL 60563. Phone: (630) 369-2406. Fax: (630) 369-2488. E-mail: cma@b-online.com. Web: www.CalendarMar ketplace.com.

LEMOYNE HOUSE CANDLELIGHT CHRISTMAS TOURS. Dec 1–2 (also Dec 7–9). Washington, PA. Evening candlelight tours of the beautifully decorated LeMoyne House. Costumed actors portray the LeMoyne family and interact with visitors. Est attendance: 500. For info: Jan Bowman, Washington County Historical Soc, 49 East Maiden St, Washington, PA 15317. Phone: (724) 225-6740. Fax: (724) 225-8495. E-mail: info @wchspa.org. Web: www.wchspa.org.

LIGHTS OF BLACKLANDS. Dec 1–31. Various sites around Texas. Lighted parades, holiday concerts, strolling carolers, Santa Claus and free hot chocolate attract folks from all over to visit the eight communities participating in this holiday showcase. The towns of Elgin, Bartlett, Lexington, Thrall, Hutto, Taylor, Granger and Thorndale display lights and banners during the month of December. Est attendance: 3,000. For info: Greater Elgin Chamber of Commerce, PO Box 408, Elgin, TX 78621. Phone: (512) 285-4515. Fax: (512) 281-3393. Web: elgintx.com.

LIGHTED BOAT PARADE ON THE TENN-TOM WATERWAY. Dec 1. Columbus, MS. Boat owners from throughout the area decorate their boats in holiday themes and parade at Lock and Dam area in Columbus. Grand finale fireworks show lights up the sky and is reflected in the water. Annually, the first Saturday in December. Est attendance: 20,000. For info: Columbus Conv and Visitors Bureau, PO Box 789, Columbus, MS 39703. Phone: (800) 327-2686. Fax: (601) 329-8969. E-mail: ccvb@tilc.com. Web: friendship.columbus.ms.us/vcb.

MADRIGAL DINNER AND CONCERT. Dec 1–2. Mount Mary College, Milwaukee, WI. Saturday dinner concert and Sunday dessert concert. Est attendance: 400. For info: Mary Cain, PR Office, Mount Mary College, 2900 N Menomonee River Pkwy, Milwaukee, WI 53222-4597. Phone: (414) 256-1210. Fax: (414) 256-1239. E-mail: mktg@mtmary.edu. Web: www.mtmary.edu.

MARTIN, MARY VIRGINIA: BIRTH ANNIVERSARY. Dec 1, 1913. American stage star Mary Martin was born at Weatherford, TX. She is best known for her title role in the Broadway and television productions of *Peter Pan*. She won Tony awards for her starring roles in *South Pacific* and *Peter Pan*. She died Nov 3, 1990, at Rancho Mirage, CA.

McCARTHY SILENCED BY SENATE: ANNIVERSARY. Dec 1, 1954. On Feb 9, 1950, Joseph McCarthy, a relatively obscure senator from Wisconsin, announced during a speech in Wheeling, WV, that he had a list of Communists in the State Department. Over the next two years he made increasingly sensational charges and in 1953 McCarthyism reached its height as he held Senate hearings in which he bullied defendants. In 1954 McCarthy's tyranny was exposed in televised hearings during which he took on the Army and on Dec 1, 1954, the Senate voted to silence him. McCarthy died May 2, 1957.

MOORE, JULIA A. DAVIS: BIRTH ANNIVERSARY. Dec 1, 1847. Julia Moore, known as the "Sweet Singer of Michigan," was born in a log cabin at Plainfield, MI. A writer of homely verse and ballads, Moore enjoyed remarkable popularity and gave many public readings before realizing that her public appearances were occasions for laughter and ridicule. Her poems were said to be "so bad, her subjects so morbid and her naivete so genuine" that they were actually gems of humorous genius. At her final public appearance she told her audience: "You people paid 50 cents to see a fool, but I got $50 to look at a house full of fools." Moore died June 17, 1920, near Manton, MI.

★**NATIONAL DRUNK AND DRUGGED DRIVING PREVENTION MONTH.** Dec 1–31.

NATIONAL DRUNK AND DRUGGED DRIVING (3D) PREVENTION MONTH. Dec 1–31. For info: Andrea M. Timbol, 3D Prevention Month Coalition, 1900 L St NW, Ste 705, Washington, DC 20036. Phone: (202) 452-6004. E-mail: tschiavone@trafficsafety.org. Web: www.ncadd.com.

NATIONAL STRESS-FREE FAMILY HOLIDAYS MONTH. Dec 1–31. The holidays are so fraught with busy schedules that families often miss out on quality time together because outside demands have left them virtually drained. This observance is a reminder for parents to strive for more stress-free holidays for their families. Annually, the month of December. For info send SASE to: Teresa Langston, Dir, Parenting Without Pressure, 1330 Boyer St, Longwood, FL 32750-6311. Phone: (407) 767-2524.

NATURE'S NOEL. Dec 1 (also Dec 8). Chimney Rock Park, Chimney Rock, NC. Holiday music, ornament making, Santa rappels the Chimney. Est attendance: 1,500. For info: Mary Ritter, PR, Chimney Rock Park, PO Box 39, Chimney Rock, NC 28720. Phone: (800) 277-9611. Fax: (828) 625-9610. E-mail: visit@chimneyrockpark.com. Web: www.chimneyrockpark.com.

NORSKEDALEN'S OLD-FASHIONED CHRISTMAS. Dec 1–2. Coon Valley, WI. Celebrate an old-fashioned Christmas with decorated pioneer log homes to view, entertainment, a la carte ethnic foods, raffle, horse-drawn wagon/sleigh rides and outdoor activities. Fun for all ages. 10 AM–4 PM. Est attendance: 500. For info: Norskedalen Nature and Heritage Center, Inc, PO Box 235, Coon Valley, WI 54623. Phone: (608) 452-3424. Fax: (608) 452-3157. E-mail: info@norskedalen.org. Web: www.norskedalen.org.

NORWEGIAN CHRISTMAS. Dec 1–2. Brooklyn Park, MN. Old-fashioned farm Christmas with turn-of-the-century decorations, carolers, making of traditional gifts, lefse and other Norwegian delicacies, visit by St. Nicholas and sleigh rides. Est attendance: 3,500. For info: Kay Grotenhuis, Site Mgr, Brooklyn Park Historical Farm, 3175 W Owasso Blvd, St. Paul, MN 55113. Phone: (763) 493-4604.

OLD-FASHIONED CHRISTMAS CELEBRATION. Dec 1–2. Historic Square, Dahlonega, GA. Festival begins with Illumination of the Square and Christmas Parade the first Saturday in December. Continues with sleighbell tour of b&bs, festival of trees and wreaths and more. Est attendance: 800. For info: Dahlonega-Lumpkin Chamber of Commerce, 13 S Park St, Dahlonega, GA 30533. Phone: (706) 864-3711. Fax: (706) 864-7917. E-mail: dahlonega@alltel.net. Web: www.dahlonega.org/festivals.

PALM HARBOR ART, CRAFT AND MUSIC FESTIVAL. Dec 1–2. Palm Harbor, FL. Juried arts and craft show with exhibitors from all over the US. Artists cash awards: $13,000. Est attendance: 30,000. For info: Connie Davis, Exec Dir, Palm Harbor Chamber of Commerce, 1151 Nebraska Ave, Palm Harbor, FL 34683. Phone: (813) 784-4287. Fax: (813) 786-2336.

***PLAYBOY* FIRST PUBLISHED: ANNIVERSARY.** Dec 1, 1953. *Playboy* magazine was launched at Chicago by publisher Hugh Hefner.

PORTUGAL: INDEPENDENCE DAY. Dec 1. Public holiday. Became independent of Spain in 1640.

ROMANIA: NATIONAL DAY. Dec 1. National holiday. Marks unification of Romania and Transylvania in 1918.

ROSA PARKS DAY: ANNIVERSARY OF ARREST. Dec 1, 1955. Anniversary of the arrest of Rosa Parks, at Montgomery, AL, for refusing to give up her seat and move to the back of a municipal bus. Her arrest triggered a yearlong boycott of the city bus system and led to legal actions which ended racial segregation on municipal buses throughout the southern US. The event has been called the birth of the modern civil rights movement. Rosa McCauley Parks was born at Tuskegee, AL, Feb 4, 1913.

SAFE TOYS AND GIFTS MONTH. Dec 1–31. What toys are dangerous to children's eyesight? Tips on how to choose age-appropriate toys will be distributed. For info: Prevent Blindness America®, 500 E Remington Rd, Schaumburg, IL 60173. Phone: (800) 331-2020. Fax: (847) 843-8458. Web: www.preventblindness.org.

SANTA BY STAGE COACH PARADE. Dec 1. El Centro, CA. Annually, the first Saturday in December. Est attendance: 25,000. For info: El Centro Chamber of Commerce, Box 3006, El Centro, CA 92244. Phone: (760) 352-3681. Fax: (760) 352-3246. Web: www.elcentrochamber.com.

SNOWFLAKE FESTIVAL. Dec 1–9. Klamath Falls, OR. Celebration of winter season in the community. Est attendance: 25,000. For info: City of Klamath Falls, Snowflake Festival, 226 S 5th St, Klamath Falls, OR 97601. Phone: (541) 883-5368. Fax: (541) 883-5395.

	S	M	T	W	T	F	S
December 2001							1
	2	3	4	5	6	7	8
	9	10	11	12	13	14	15
	16	17	18	19	20	21	22
	23	24	25	26	27	28	29
	30	31					

TOLERANCE WEEK. Dec 1–7. The purpose of this week is to promote the importance of tolerance among human beings as a means of reducing bigotry and prejudice toward those of a different religion, race or creed. For a copy of quotations about tolerance by famous people, as well as a frameable copy of the Golden Rule of ten religions, send $4 to cover printing, handling and postage. For info: Dr. Stanley Drake, Pres, Intl Soc of Friendship and Good Will, 8592 Roswell Rd, Ste 434, Atlanta, GA 30350-1870.

TWELVE VILLAGES OF CHRISTMAS. Dec 1–2 (also Dec 8–9 and 15–16). Each of 12 cities in Washington County, KS, organizes events including special lighting of entire county, craft festivals, drawings, special musical programs, home tour, retail open houses, youth Christmas coloring contest, some towns have a Christmas tree in every yard, large Christmas stocking giveaways and much more. Annually, the three weekends before Christmas. Est attendance: 7,000. For info: Washington County Economic Development, Court House, Washington, KS 66968. Phone: (785) 325-2116. Fax: (785) 325-2830. E-mail: washcoed @washington.ks.net.

UNITED NATIONS: WORLD AIDS DAY. Dec 1. In 1988 the World Health Organization of the United Nations declared Dec 1 as World AIDS Day, an international day of awareness and education about AIDS. The WHO is the leader in global direction and coordination of AIDS prevention, control, research and education. A program called UN-AIDS was created to bring together the skills and expertise of the World Bank, UNDP, UNESCO, UNICEF, UNFPA and the WHO to strengthen and expand national capacities to respond to the pandemic. Also see the World AIDS Day entry (Dec 1) for information address in US.

UNIVERSAL HUMAN RIGHTS MONTH. Dec 1–31. To disseminate throughout the world information about human rights and distribute copies of the Universal Declaration of Human Rights in English and other languages. Please send $4 to cover expense of printing, handling and postage. Annually, the month of December. For info: Dr. Stanley Drake, Pres, Intl Society of Friendship & Good Will, 8592 Roswell Rd, Ste 434, Atlanta, GA 30350-1870.

US CONGRESS PASSES GATT TREATY: ANNIVERSARY. Dec 1, 1994. Following the lead of the House of Representatives, the US Senate voted 76–24 to approve the Uruguay Round provisions of the General Agreement on Tariffs and Trade (GATT). The worldwide trade pact is intended to reduce tariffs by a third, eliminate trade quotas and protect intellectual property. The GATT agreement is expected to add $300–500 billion to the global economy through the year 2005. In Jan, 1995, the World Trade Organization (WTO) became the successor to GATT.

VICTORIAN CHRISTMAS HOME TOUR, BRUNCH AND DINNER. Dec 1. Leadville, CO. Highlight of the holiday season—annual showing off of Leadville's historic homes and buildings bedecked in Christmas trimmings. Locals and guests alike dress in period fashions. Est attendance: 350. For info: Chamber of Commerce, Box 861, Leadville, CO 80461. Phone: (719) 486-3900 or (888) 264-5344. Fax: (719) 486-8478. E-mail: leadville@leadvilleusa.com. Web: www.leadvilleusa.com.

WEIHNACHTSFEST. Dec 1. Biwabik, MN. Lighting festival, crafts, ethnic foods, entertainment, fireworks. Biwabik's population of 1,000 jumps to more than 3,000 for a day. Annually on the first Saturday in December. For info: Biwabik Area Civic Assn, PO Box 309, Biwabik, MN 55708. Phone: (218) 865-4183.

WINTERFEST. Dec 1–31. St. Joseph, MO. Experience the holiday sights and sounds in traditional St. Joseph style. From concerts to festivals, homes tours to holiday parks, it's all here for you to enjoy during Winterfest. For info: St. Joseph Convention and Visitor Bureau, 109 S 4th, St. Joseph, MO 64501. Phone: (816) 233-6688 or (800) 785-0360.

WINTERFEST. Dec 1–2. Luverne, MN. Christmas Light Parade, Parade of Homes, craft show, historical tours, dinner theater. For info: Dave Smith, Exec Dir, Luverne Area Chamber of Commerce, 102 E Main, Luverne, MN 56156. Phone: (507) 283-4061. Fax: (507) 283-4061. Web: luvernemn.com.

WORLD AIDS DAY. Dec 1. Designed to encourage public support for programs that prevent the spread of HIV/AIDS and to provide education and awareness of issues surrounding HIV/AIDS. For info: American Assn for World Health, 1825 K St NW, Ste 1208, Washington, DC 20006. Phone: (202) 466-5883. Fax: (202) 466-5896. E-mail: staff@aawhworldhealth .org. Web: www.aawhworldhealth.org.

★**WORLD AIDS DAY.** Dec 1.

YULETIDE TRADITIONS. Dec 1–31. Charlottesville, VA. Special events at Ash Lawn–Highland, Monticello and Michie Tavern circa 1784. For info: Charlottesville/Albemarle Visitors Bureau, Box 178 Dept YT, Charlottesville, VA 22902. Phone: (877) 386-1102.

BIRTHDAYS TODAY

Woody Allen (Allen Stewart Konigsberg), 66, actor, writer, producer (Oscar for *Annie Hall; Sleeper, Manhattan, Bullets over Broadway*), born Brooklyn, NY, Dec 1, 1935.

Carol Alt, 41, model, born New York, NY, Dec 1, 1960.

Nestor Carbonell, 34, actor ("Suddenly Susan"), born New York, NY, Dec 1, 1967.

Bette Midler, 56, singer ("You Are the Wind Beneath My Wings"), actress (*Beaches, For the Boys, Down and Out in Beverly Hills*), born Honolulu, HI, Dec 1, 1945.

Richard Pryor, 61, actor, comedian (*Blue Collar, Stir Crazy*, "The Richard Pryor Show"), born Peoria, IL, Dec 1, 1940.

Lou Rawls, 66, blues singer ("A Natural Man," "You've Made Me So Very Happy"), actor, born Chicago, IL, Dec 1, 1935.

Reggie Sanders, 34, baseball player, born Florence, SC, Dec 1, 1967.

Lee Buck Trevino, 62, golfer, born Dallas, TX, Dec 1, 1939.

Larry Walker, 35, baseball player, born Maple Ridge, British Columbia, Canada, Dec 1, 1966.

Treat Williams, 49, actor (*Hair, Smooth Talk*), born Rowayton, CT, Dec 1, 1952.

DECEMBER 2 — SUNDAY
Day 336 — 29 Remaining

ADVENT, FIRST SUNDAY. Dec 2. Advent includes the four Sundays before Christmas, Dec 2, Dec 9, Dec 16 and Dec 23 in 2001.

ARTIFICIAL HEART TRANSPLANT: ANNIVERSARY. Dec 2, 1982. Barney C. Clark, 61, became the first recipient of a permanent artificial heart. The operation was performed at the University of Utah Medical Center at Salt Lake City. Near death at the time of the operation, Clark survived almost 112 days after the implantation. He died Mar 23, 1983.

BROWN, JOHN: EXECUTION ANNIVERSARY. Dec 2, 1859. Abolitionist leader who is remembered for his raid on the US Arsenal at Harper's Ferry was hanged for treason at Charles Town, WV.

CALLAS, MARIA: BIRTH ANNIVERSARY. Dec 2, 1923. American opera singer born at New York, NY. Died at Paris, Sept 16, 1977.

CHRISTMAS TO REMEMBER. Dec 2. Laurel, MT. To officially open the Christmas season in Laurel, this daylong celebration includes the arrival of Santa, a community bazaar, wagon rides, children's craft activities, musical entertainment, lighting ceremony, parade of lights and fireworks. Annually, the first Sunday of December. Est attendance: 5,000. For info: Christmas to Remember Committee, Jean Carroll Thompson, 616 Sixth Ave, Laurel, MT 59044. Phone: (406) 628-4508.

CLERC-GALLAUDET WEEK. Dec 2–8. Week in which to celebrate the birth anniversaries of Laurent Clerc (Dec 26, 1785) and Thomas Hopkins Gallaudet (Dec 10, 1787). Clerc and Gallaudet pioneered education for the deaf in the US. Library activities will include a lecture on Clerc and Gallaudet and their contemporaries, storytelling for all ages and a display of books, videotapes, magazines, newspapers and posters. For info: Library for Deaf Action, 2930 Craiglawn Rd, Silver Spring, MD 20904-1816. Phone: (301) 572-5168 (TTY). Fax: (301) 572-4134. E-mail: alhagemeyer@juno.com. Web: www.LibraryDeaf.com.

DENALI NATIONAL PARK AND PRESERVE ESTABLISHED: ANNIVERSARY. Dec 2, 1980. Alaska's Mount McKinley National Park, which was established Feb 26, 1917, and Denali National Monument, which was proclaimed Dec 1, 1978, were combined and established as Denali National Park and Preserve. For info about park facilities: Denali Natl Park and Preserve, PO Box 9, McKinley Park, AK 99755.

ENGLAND: WALTER PLINGE DAY. Dec 2. A day to recognize Walter Plinge, said to have been a London pub landlord in 1900. His generosity to actors led to the use of his name as an actor, in play programs, to conceal the fact that an actor was playing more than one role. See also: "George Spelvin Day" (Nov 15) for US equivalent.

FIRST SELF-SUSTAINING NUCLEAR CHAIN REACTION: ANNIVERSARY. Dec 2, 1942. Physicist Enrico Fermi led a team of scientists at the University of Chicago in producing the first controlled, self-sustaining nuclear chain reaction. Their first simple nuclear reactor was built under the stands of the University's football stadium.

GATES OF THE ARCTIC NATIONAL PARK AND PRESERVE ESTABLISHED: ANNIVERSARY. Dec 2, 1980. Alaska's Gates of the Arctic National Monument, proclaimed Dec 1, 1978, was established as a national park and preserve. For further park info: Gates of the Arctic Natl Park and Preserve, PO Box 74680, Fairbanks, AK 99707.

GLACIER BAY NATIONAL PARK AND PRESERVE ESTABLISHED: ANNIVERSARY. Dec 2, 1980. Alaska's Glacier Bay National Monument, proclaimed Feb 25, 1925, was established as a national park and preserve. For further park info: Glacier Bay Natl Park and Preserve, Bartlett Cove, Gustavus, AK 99826.

HISTORIC HOMES PARLOR TOUR. Dec 2. Baker City, OR. Annually, the first Sunday in December. Est attendance: 300. For info: Baker County VCB, 490 Campbell St, Baker City, OR 97814. Phone: (800) 523-1235.

HOLIDAY HOUSE TOURS. Dec 2. Ashland-Highland, Home of James Monroe, Charlottesville, VA. Guides in costumes of Colonial through Victorian periods discuss Christmas customs of each period. House decorated inside and out with fresh greens, fruits and woodland seed pods. 10 AM–5 PM. Est attendance: 200. For

info: Carolyn C. Holmes, Ashlawn-Highland, 1000 James Monroe Pkwy, Charlottesville, VA 22902. Phone: (804) 293-9539. Fax: (804) 293-8000. E-mail: ashlawnjm@aol.com.

KATMAI NATIONAL PARK AND PRESERVE ESTABLISHED: ANNIVERSARY. Dec 2, 1980. Alaska's Katmai National Monument, proclaimed Sept 24, 1918, was established as a national park and preserve. For further park info: Katmai Natl Park and Preserve, PO Box 7, King Salmon, AK 99613.

KENAI FJORDS NATIONAL PARK ESTABLISHED: ANNIVERSARY. Dec 2, 1980. Alaska's Kenai Fjords National Monument, proclaimed Dec 1, 1978, was established as a national park. For further park info: Kenai Fjords Natl Park, PO Box 1727, Seward, AK 99664.

KOBUK VALLEY NATIONAL PARK ESTABLISHED: ANNIVERSARY. Dec 2, 1980. Alaska's Kobuk Valley National Monument, proclaimed Dec 1, 1978, was established as a national park. For further park info: Chief of Education and Interpretation, Kobuk Valley Natl Park, PO Box 1029, Kotzebue, AK 99752. Phone: (907) 442-3890. Fax: (907) 442-8316. Web: www.nps.gov /kova.

LAKE CLARK NATIONAL PARK AND PRESERVE ESTABLISHED: ANNIVERSARY. Dec 2, 1980. Alaska's Lake Clark National Monument, proclaimed Dec 1, 1978, was established as a national park and preserve.

LAO PEOPLE'S DEMOCRATIC REPUBLIC: NATIONAL DAY: ANNIVERSARY. Dec 2. National holiday commemorating declaration of the republic in 1975.

MONROE DOCTRINE: ANNIVERSARY. Dec 2, 1823. President James Monroe, in his annual message to Congress, enunciated the doctrine that bears his name and that was long hailed as a statement of US policy. ." . . In the wars of the European powers in matters relating to themselves we have never taken any part . . . we should consider any attempt on their part to extend their system to any portion of this hemi-sphere as dangerous to our peace and safety. . . ."

NETHERLANDS: MIDWINTER HORN BLOWING. Dec 2–Jan 6, 2002. Twente and several other areas in the Netherlands. Midwinter horn blowing, folklore custom of announcing the birth of Christ, begins with Advent and continues until Epiphany (Jan 6) of the following year.

★**PAN AMERICAN HEALTH DAY.** Dec 2. Presidential Proclamation 2447, of Nov 23, 1940, covers all succeeding years. Always Dec 2. The 1940 Pan American Conference of National Directors of Health adopted a resolution recommending that a "Health Day" be held annually in the countries of the Pan American Union.

SAFETY RAZOR PATENTED: 100th ANNIVERSARY. Dec 2, 1901. American King Camp Gillette designed the first razor with disposable blades. Up until this time, men shaved with a straight edge razor that they sharpened on a leather strap.

SEURAT, GEORGES PIERRE: BIRTH ANNIVERSARY. Dec 2, 1859. French Neo-impressionist painter born at Paris, France. Died there Mar 29, 1891. Seurat is known for his

December **2001**	S	M	T	W	T	F	S
							1
	2	3	4	5	6	7	8
	9	10	11	12	13	14	15
	16	17	18	19	20	21	22
	23	24	25	26	27	28	29
	30	31					

style of painting with small spots of color, called "pointillism," as in *Sunday Afternoon on the Island of Grand Jatte.*

SPACE MILESTONE: *SOYUZ 16* (USSR). Dec 2, 1974. Six-day mission began this date with cosmonauts A.V. Flipchenko and N.N. Rukavishnikov. Rehearsal for the *Apollo 18-Soyuz 19* US-USSR linkup July 15, 1975.

SYMS, SYLVIA: BIRTH ANNIVERSARY. Dec 2, 1917. American singer Sylvia Syms was born at New York, NY. She was called the "world's greatest saloon singer" by Frank Sinatra and recorded 15 albums. She died May 10, 1992, at New York, NY.

UNITED ARAB EMIRATES: NATIONAL DAY: 30th ANNIVERSARY OF INDEPENDENCE. Dec 2. Anniversary of the day in 1971 when a federation of seven sheikdoms known as the Trucial States declared independence from the UK and became known as the United Arab Emirates.

UNITED NATIONS: INTERNATIONAL DAY FOR THE ABOLITION OF SLAVERY. Dec 2. Recalls the date of adoption by the General Assembly in 1949 of the Convention for the Suppression of the Traffic in Persons and the Exploitation of Others.

WRANGELL–SAINT ELIAS NATIONAL PARK AND PRESERVE ESTABLISHED: ANNIVERSARY. Dec 2, 1980. Alaska's Wrangell–St. Elias National Monument, proclaimed Dec 1, 1978, was established as a national park and preserve. For further park info: Wrangell-St. Elias Natl Park and Preserve, PO Box 439, Copper Center, AK 99573. Phone: (907) 822-5234.

WSBA/WARM 103 CHRISTMAS CRAFT SHOW. Dec 2. York Fairgrounds, York, PA. More than 250 crafts, from country to contemporary, Victorian and southwestern, handcrafted furniture, wood carvings, dolls, jewelry, pottery, collectibles, quilts, baskets, fine arts and much more. Admission fee. Est attendance: 5,000. For info: Joe Alfano, Asst Promo Dir, PO Box 910, York, PA 17402-0910. Phone: (717) 764-1155. Fax: (717) 252-4807. E-mail: jalfano@suscom.com.

BIRTHDAYS TODAY

Wayne Allard, 58, US Senator (R, Colorado), born Fort Collins, CO, Dec 2, 1943.

Dan Butler, 47, actor ("Frasier"), born Huntington, IN, Dec 2, 1954.

Dennis Christopher, 46, actor (*Sweet Dreams, Breaking Away*), born Philadelphia, PA, Dec 2, 1955.

Cathy Lee Crosby, 53, actress ("That's Incredible," *Coach*), born Los Angeles, CA, Dec 2, 1948.

Randy Gardner, 43, figure skater, born Marina del Rey, CA, Dec 2, 1958.

Adolph Green, 86, composer with Betty Comden of Broadway musicals (*On the Town, Bells Are Ringing*), born New York, NY, Dec 2, 1915.

Julie Harris, 76, actress ("Knots Landing," *I Am a Camera, The Member of the Wedding*), born Grosse Pointe, MI, Dec 2, 1925.

Darryl Kile, 33, baseball player, born Garden Grove, CA, Dec 2, 1968.

Lucy Liu, 34, actress ("Ally McBeal," *Jerry Maguire*), born Queens, NY, Dec 2, 1967.

Garry Meier, 52, Chicago radio personality, born Chicago, IL, Dec 2, 1949.

Stone Phillips, 47, anchor ("Dateline," "20/20"), born Texas City, TX, Dec 2, 1954.

Harry Reid, 62, US Senator (D, Nevada), born Searchlight, NV, Dec 2, 1939.

Monica Seles, 28, tennis player, born Novi Sad, Yugoslavia, Dec 2, 1973.

Britney Spears, 20, singer, born Kentwood, LA, Dec 2, 1981.

Ray Walston, 87, actor ("Picket Fences," "My Favorite Martian," *South Pacific, The Sting*), born New Orleans, LA, Dec 2, 1914.

William Wegman, 58, artist, photographer (of dogs), born Holyoke, MA, Dec 2, 1943.

DECEMBER 3 — MONDAY
Day 337 — 28 Remaining

BHOPAL POISON GAS DISASTER: ANNIVERSARY. Dec 3, 1984. At Bhopal, India, a leak of deadly gas (methyl isocyanate) at a Union Carbide Corp plant killed more than 4,000 persons and injured more than 200,000 in the world's worst industrial accident.

CENTRAL AFRICAN REPUBLIC: NATIONAL DAY OBSERVED. Dec 3. Commemorates Proclamation of the Republic Dec 1, 1958. Usually observed on the first Monday in December.

CONRAD, JOSEPH: BIRTH ANNIVERSARY. Dec 3, 1857. English novelist, born Jozef Korzeniowski to Polish parents at Berdichev in the Ukraine. He learned English as a sailor on British ships. Author of *Lord Jim* and *Heart of Darkness*, among others. Died Aug 3, 1924 at Bishopsbourne, Kent, England.

ELECTRIC LIGHT PARADE. Dec 3. Downtown Lovington, NM. Christmas shines in Lovington with more than 60 entries including floats, motorhomes, cars and motorcycles decorated with Christmas lights. Annually, early December. Est attendance: 7,000. For info: Lovington Chamber of Commerce, 201 S Main St, Lovington, NM 88260. Phone: (505) 396-5311. E-mail: visitus@leaconet.com. Web: visitus.leaco.net.

FIRST HEART TRANSPLANT: ANNIVERSARY. Dec 3, 1967. Dr. Christiaan Barnard, a South African surgeon, performed the world's first successful heart transplantation at Cape Town, South Africa. See also: "Barnard, Christiaan Neethling: Birthday" (Nov 8).

GIANT CHRISTMAS TREE AT ROCKEFELLER CENTER. Dec 3. (Date approximate.) New York, NY. Lighting of the huge Christmas Tree in Rockefeller Plaza signals the opening of the holiday season at New York City. Date is usually a weekday during the first week of December.

ILLINOIS: ADMISSION DAY: ANNIVERSARY. Dec 3. Became 21st state in 1818.

MONTOYA, CARLOS: BIRTH ANNIVERSARY. Dec 3, 1903. Guitarist and composer renowned for popularizing flamenco guitar music. His solo performances of the Spanish folk form lifted flamenco from its traditional accompaniment role. Montoya never learned to read music and relied on the traditional improvisational nature of flamenco rooted in the Andalusian Gypsy form of music that stressed rhythms and harmonic patterns. He was born at Madrid, Spain, and died Mar 3, 1993, at Wainscott, NY.

MOST BORING CELEBRITIES OF THE YEAR. Dec 3. 18th annual list of celebrities chosen because of "massive media over-exposure" during the year. The list is posted prior to the event on our website to facilitate media coverage. For info: The Boring Institute, Alan Caruba, Founder, Box 40, Maplewood, NJ 07040. Phone: (973) 763-6392. E-mail: acaruba@aol.com. Web: www.boringinstitute.com.

STUART, GILBERT CHARLES: BIRTH ANNIVERSARY. Dec 3, 1755. American portrait painter whose most famous painting is that of George Washington. He also painted portraits of Madison, Monroe, Jefferson and other important Americans. Stuart was born near Narragansett, RI, and died July 9, 1828, at Boston, MA.

TANNEHILL VILLAGE CHRISTMAS. Dec 3–7 (also Dec 10–14). Tannehill Historical State Park, McCalla, AL. 1800s village with cabins decorated in old-fashioned Christmas style and staffed by volunteers wearing period costumes. Est attendance: 6,000. For info: Vicki Gentry, Dir, Iron and Steel Museum, Tannehill Historical State Park, 12632 Confederate Pkwy, McCalla, AL 35111. Phone: (205) 477-5711. Fax: (205) 477-9400.

UNITED NATIONS: INTERNATIONAL DAY OF DISABLED PERSONS. Dec 3. On Oct 14, 1992 (Res 47/3), at the end of the Decade of Disabled Persons, the General Assembly proclaimed Dec 3 to be an annual observance to promote the continuation of integrating the disabled into general society.

BIRTHDAYS TODAY

Brian Bonsall, 20, actor ("Family Ties," *Blank Check*), born Torrance, CA, Dec 3, 1981.

Bruno Campos, 27, actor ("Jesse"), born Rio de Janeiro, Brazil, Dec 3, 1974.

Brendan Fraser, 33, actor (*George of the Jungle*), born Indianapolis, IN, Dec 3, 1968.

Jean Luc Godard, 71, filmmaker (*Breathless, Weekend*), born Paris, France, Dec 3, 1930.

Daryl Hannah, 40, actress (*Splash, Grumpy Old Men*), born Chicago, IL, Dec 3, 1961.

Ferlin Husky, 74, singer ("Gone," "On the Wings of a Dove"), born Flat River, MO, Dec 3, 1927.

Rick Ravon Mears, 50, former auto racer, born Wichita, KS, Dec 3, 1951.

Julianne Moore, 40, actress (*The Lost World, Nine Months*), born Fort Bragg, Fayetteville, NC, Dec 3, 1961.

Jaye P. Morgan, 69, singer ("That's All I Want from You," "The Longest Walk"), born New York, NY, Dec 3, 1932.

Sven Vilhem Nykvist, 79, Swedish cinematographer (*The Unbearable Lightness of Being*), born Moheda, Sweden, Dec 3, 1922.

Ozzy Osbourne, 53, singer, songwriter (originally lead singer for Black Sabbath), born Birmingham, England, Dec 3, 1948.

Andy Williams, 71, singer (platinum album *Love Story*, 13 gold albums), born Wall Lake, IA, Dec 3, 1930.

Katarina Witt, 36, Olympic figure skater, born Karl-Marx-Stadt, East Germany, Dec 3, 1965.

DECEMBER 4 — TUESDAY

Day 338 — 27 Remaining

BUTLER, SAMUEL: BIRTH ANNIVERSARY. Dec 4, 1835. English author (*Erewhon, The Way of All Flesh*), born at Bingham, Nottinghamshire, England. Died at London, June 18, 1902.

CARLYLE, THOMAS: BIRTH ANNIVERSARY. Dec 4, 1795. Scottish essayist and historian, born at Ecclefechan, Scotland. Died at London, Feb 4, 1881. "A well-written Life is almost as rare as a well-spent one," Carlyle wrote in his *Critical and Miscellaneous Essays*.

CHASE'S CALENDAR OF EVENTS: BIRTHDAY. Dec 4, 1957. Forty-four years ago today the first copies of the first edition of *Chase's Calendar of Annual Events* (for the year 1958) were delivered by the printer at Flint, MI. Two thousand copies, consisting of 32 pages and listing 364 events, were printed. Now annual editions are more than 700 pages long and list more than 12,000 events. It has an offspring—*The Teacher's Calendar*, which debuted in 1999.

		S	M	T	W	T	F	S
December								1
2001		2	3	4	5	6	7	8
		9	10	11	12	13	14	15
		16	17	18	19	20	21	22
		23	24	25	26	27	28	29
		30	31					

EXTRAORDINARY WORK TEAM RECOGNITION DAY. Dec 4. To recognize business teams that work extraordinarily well together, producing significant results/accomplishments for their company or organization. Team leaders and management "champions" are encouraged to recognize exceptional team performance and submit their stories for a chance to win an extraordinary prize for their team! Annually, on Dec 4. For info: Kristin J. Arnold, Quality Process Consultants, 48 W Queens Way, Hampton, VA 23669. Phone: (757) 728-0191. Fax: (757) 728-0192. E-mail: karnold@qpcteam.com. Web: www.qpcteam.com.

"FALCON CREST" TV PREMIERE: 20th ANNIVERSARY. Dec 4, 1981. This nighttime serial was set in California wine country and originally focused on Angela Channing's determined efforts to gain control of the Falcon Crest vineyard and winery; later the emphasis turned to crime. Famous actors who were a part of the cast at one time or another include: Jane Wyman, Lorenzo Lamas, Billy R. Moses, Cliff Robertson, Lana Turner, Gina Lollobrigida, Parker Stevenson, Anne Archer, Apollonia, Cesar Romero, Morgan Fairchild, Ken Olin and Mary Ann Mobley. In the season finale, Angela received Falcon Crest and everyone was happy.

LAST AMERICAN HOSTAGE RELEASED IN LEBANON: 10th ANNIVERSARY. Dec 4, 1991. A sad chapter of US history came to a close when Terry Anderson, an Associated Press correspondent, became the final American hostage held in Lebanon to be freed. Anderson had been held since Mar 16, 1985, one of 15 Americans who were held hostage for from two months to as long as six years and eight months. Three of the hostages, William Buckley, Peter Kilburn and Lieutenant Colonel William Higgins, were killed during their captivity. The other hostages, released previously one or two at a time, were Jeremy Levin, Benjamin Weir, the Reverend Lawrence Martin Jenco, David Jacobsen, Thomas Sutherland, Frank Herbert Reed, Joseph Cicippio, Edward Austin Tracy, Alan Steen, Jesse Turner and Robert Polhill.

MISSION SANTA BARBARA: FOUNDING ANNIVERSARY. Dec 4, 1786. Franciscan Mission to the Indians founded at Santa Barbara, CA. Present structure is the fourth to stand on same site. Last one destroyed by 1812 earthquake.

NATIONAL GRANGE FOUNDING: ANNIVERSARY. Dec 4, 1786. The anniversary of the National Grange, the first organized agricultural movement in the US.

RUSSELL, LILLIAN: BIRTH ANNIVERSARY. Dec 4, 1861. American singer and actress who in 1881 gained fame in the comic opera *The Great Mogul*. Born Helen Louise Leonard at Clinton, IA, she died June 6, 1922, at Pittsburgh, PA.

SAINT BARBARA'S DAY. Dec 4. On this day, traditionally the feast day of St. Barbara, a young girl places a twig from a cherry tree in a glass of water. If it blooms by Christmas Eve, she is certain to marry the following year. Because the narratives of her life and martyrdom are legendary, St. Barbara was dropped from the Roman Catholic Calendar of Saints in 1970.

SPACE MILESTONE: INTERNATIONAL SPACE STATION LAUNCH (US). Dec 4, 1998. The shuttle *Endeavour* took a US component of the space station named Unity into orbit 220 miles from Earth where spacewalking astronauts fastened it to a component launched by the Russians Nov 20, 1998. It will take a total of 45 Russian and US launches over the next five years before the space station is complete. When finished, it will be 356′ across and 290′ long and will support a crew of up to seven. NASA has targeted Oct 30, 2000, for the launch of the first expedition with a three-man crew to stay aloft for four months. However, the project has had many delays so this launch may be postponed.

BIRTHDAYS TODAY

Max Baer, Jr, 64, actor, producer ("The Beverly Hillbillies," produced *Ode to Billy Joe*), born Oakland, CA, Dec 4, 1937.

Tyra Banks, 28, model, actress ("Soul Train Lady of Soul Awards"), born Los Angeles, CA, Dec 4, 1973.

Jeff Bridges, 52, actor (*The Fisher King*), born Los Angeles, CA, Dec 4, 1949.

Helen M. Chase, 77, retired chronicler of contemporary civilization as coeditor of *Chase's Annual Events*, born Whitehall, MI, Dec 4, 1924.

Deanna Durbin, 80, actress (*It Started with Eve, Can't Help Singing*), born Winnipeg, Manitoba, Canada, Dec 4, 1921.

Chris Hillman, 59, musician, born Los Angeles, CA, Dec 4, 1942.

Stewart Rawlings Mott, 64, philanthropist, born Flint, MI, Dec 4, 1937.

Marisa Tomei, 37, actress (*The Flamingo Kid, My Cousin Vinny*), born Brooklyn, NY, Dec 4, 1964.

Patricia Wettig, 50, actress ("St. Elsewhere," *City Slickers*; Emmys for "thirtysomething"), born Cincinnati, OH, Dec 4, 1951.

DECEMBER 5 — WEDNESDAY
Day 339 — 26 Remaining

"THE ABBOTT AND COSTELLO SHOW" TV PREMIERE: ANNIVERSARY.
Dec 5, 1952. Bud Abbott and Lou Costello made 52 half-hour films for television incorporating many of their best burlesque routines. The show ran for two seasons, until 1954. Costello was born at Paterson, NJ, Mar 6, 1906, and died at East Los Angeles, CA, Mar 3, 1959. In 1966 Hanna-Barbera Productions produced an animated cartoon based on the characters of Abbott and Costello. Abbott supplied his own voice while Stan Irwin imitated Costello. Bud Abbott was born at Asbury Park, NJ, Oct 2, 1895 and died at Woodland Hills, CA, Apr 24, 1974.

AFL-CIO FOUNDED: ANNIVERSARY.
Dec 5, 1955. The American Federation of Labor and the Congress of Industrial Organizations joined together in 1955, following 20 years of rivalry, to become the nation's leading advocate for trade unions.

BATHTUB PARTY DAY.
Dec 5. Almost everyone nowadays takes showers, so here's a day to recall some of the luxury of days gone by. Invite a few friends. [© 2000 WH]. For info: Tom and Ruth Roy, 2418 Long Ln, Lebanon, PA 17046. Phone: (717) 279-0184. E-mail: wellcat@desupernet.net. Web: www.wellcat.com.

DISNEY, WALT: 100th BIRTH ANNIVERSARY.
Dec 5, 1901. Animator, filmmaker, theme park developer, born at Chicago, IL. Disney died at Los Angeles, CA, Dec 15, 1966.

GRANT'S SPEECH OF APOLOGY: 125th ANNIVERSARY.
Dec 5, 1876. President Ulysses S. Grant delivered his speech of apology to Congress claiming mistakes he made while he was president were due to his inexperience. His errors, he said, were "errors of judgment, not intent." While Grant's personal integrity was never formally questioned, he was closely associated with many government scandals which became public during his presidency. He unwittingly aided Jay Gould in an attempt to corner the gold market during his first term. During the second, the Credit Mobilier affair involving many of the president's friends aired, while significant fraud was discovered in the Treasury Department and Indian Service.

HAITI: DISCOVERY DAY: ANNIVERSARY.
Dec 5. Commemorates the discovery of Haiti by Christopher Columbus in 1492. Public holiday.

MONTGOMERY BUS BOYCOTT BEGINS: ANNIVERSARY.
Dec 5, 1955. Rosa Parks was arrested at Montgomery, AL, for refusing to give up her seat on a bus to a white man. In support of Parks, and to protest the arrest, the black community of Montgomery organized a boycott of the bus system. The boycott lasted from Dec 5, 1955, to Dec 20, 1956, when a US Supreme Court ruling was implemented at Montgomery, integrating the public transportation system.

PICKETT, BILL: BIRTH ANNIVERSARY.
Dec 5, 1870. American rodeo cowboy, born at Williamson County, TX; died Apr 21, 1932, at Tulsa, OK. Inventor of bulldogging, the modern rodeo event that involves wrestling a running steer to the ground.

THAILAND: KING'S BIRTHDAY AND NATIONAL DAY.
Dec 5. Celebrated throughout the kingdom with colorful pageantry. Stores and houses decorated with spectacular illuminations at night. Public holiday.

TWENTY-FIRST AMENDMENT TO THE US CONSTITUTION RATIFIED: ANNIVERSARY.
Dec 5, 1933. Prohibition ended with the repeal of the Eighteenth Amendment, as the Twenty-First Amendment was ratified.

UNITED NATIONS: INTERNATIONAL VOLUNTEER DAY FOR ECONOMIC AND SOCIAL DEVELOPMENT.
Dec 5. In a resolution of Dec 17, 1985, the United Nations General Assembly recognized the desirability of encouraging the work of all volunteers. It invited governments to observe, annually Dec 5, the "International Volunteer Day for Economic and Social Development, urging them to take measures to heighten awareness of the important contribution of volunteer service." A day commemorating the establishment in December 1970 of the UN Volunteers program and inviting world recognition of volunteerism in the international development movement. For info: United Nations, Dept of Public Info, Public Inquiries Unit, Rm GA-57, New York, NY 10017. Phone: (212) 963-4475. E-mail: inquiries@un.org.

VAN BUREN, MARTIN: BIRTH ANNIVERSARY.
Dec 5, 1782. The eighth president of the US (term of office: Mar 4, 1837–Mar 3, 1841) was the first to have been born a citizen of the US. He was a widower for nearly two decades before he entered the White House. His daughter-in-law, Angelica, served as White House hostess during an administration troubled by bank and business failures, depression and unemployment. Van Buren was born at Kinderhook, NY, and died there July 24, 1862.

WHEATLEY, PHILLIS: DEATH ANNIVERSARY.
Dec 5, 1784. Born at Senegal, West Africa about 1753, Phillis Wheatley was brought to the US in 1761 and purchased as a slave by a Boston tailor named John Wheatley. She was allotted unusual privileges for a slave, including being allowed to learn to read and write. She wrote her first poetry at age 14, and her first work was published in 1770. Wheatley's fame as a poet spread throughout Europe as well as the US after her *Poems on Various Subjects, Religious and Moral* was published at England in 1773. She was invited to visit George Washington's army headquarters after he read a poem she had written about him in 1776. Phillis Wheatley died at about age 30, at Boston, MA.

BIRTHDAYS TODAY

Morgan Brittany (Suzanne Cupito), 51, actress ("Dallas," "Moviola," *The Birds, Marnie*), born Hollywood, CA, Dec 5, 1950.

José Carreras, 55, opera singer, one of the "Three Tenors," born Barcelona, Spain, Dec 5, 1946.

Margaret Cho, 33, actress ("All-American Girl"), born San Francisco, CA, Dec 5, 1968.

Joan Didion, 67, author, journalist (*After Henry, Run River, The White Album*), born Sacramento, CA, Dec 5, 1934.

Carrie Hamilton, 38, actress ("Fame," *Tokyo Pop*), daughter of Carol Burnett, born New York, NY, Dec 5, 1963.

Jeroen Krabbe, 57, actor (*A World Apart, King of the Hill, The Fugitive*), born Amsterdam, The Netherlands, Dec 5, 1944.

Little Richard (Penniman), 66, singer ("Tutti Frutti," "Long Tall Sally"), songwriter, born Macon, GA, Dec 5, 1935.

Jim Messina, 54, singer ("Your Mama Don't Dance"), songwriter, born Maywood, CA, Dec 5, 1947.

Chad Mitchell, 65, lead singer (Chad Mitchell trio, "Lizzie Borden"), born Portland, OR, Dec 5, 1936.

Art Monk, 44, former football player, born White Plains, NY, Dec 5, 1957.

Frankie Muniz, 16, actor ("Malcolm in the Middle," *My Dog Skip*), born Ridgewood, NJ, Dec 5, 1985.

Strom Thurmond, 99, US Senator (R, South Carolina), born Edgefield, SC, Dec 5, 1902.

Calvin Trillin, 66, author (*American Stories, Remembering Denny*), born Kansas City, MO, Dec 5, 1935.

DECEMBER 6 — THURSDAY
Day 340 — 25 Remaining

ALTAMONT CONCERT: ANNIVERSARY. Dec 6, 1969. A free concert featuring performances by the Rolling Stones, Jefferson Airplane, Santana, Crosby, Stills, Nash and Young and the Flying Burrito Brothers turned into tragedy. The "thank-you" concert for 300,000 fans was marred by overcrowding, drug overdoses and the fatal stabbing of a spectator by a member of the Hell's Angels motorcycle gang, who had been hired as security guards for the event. The concert was held at the Altamont Speedway, Livermore, CA.

BELGIUM: LOVER'S FAIR. Dec 6. Arlon, Belgium. Traditional cultural observance. Annually, the first Thursday in December.

CHRISTMAS AT PIONEER VILLAGE. Dec 6–7. Worthington, MN. Many different activities are held including Christmas carolers, sleigh rides, Santa and Mrs Claus, their elves, refreshments and the beautiful decorations. Free admission. Est attendance: 1,400. For info: Nobles County Historical Soc, 407 12th St, Ste 2, Worthington, MN 56187. Phone: (507) 376-4011 or (507) 376-4431.

	S	M	T	W	T	F	S
December							1
2001	2	3	4	5	6	7	8
	9	10	11	12	13	14	15
	16	17	18	19	20	21	22
	23	24	25	26	27	28	29
	30	31					

CHRISTMAS TOUR OF HOMES. Dec 6–7. Pella, IA. Four homes decorated for the holidays by Pella Garden Club members. Open to the public. Christmas tea at Pella Historical Village. Est attendance: 3,000. For info: Pella Historical Society, 507 Franklin, Pella, IA 50219. Phone: (515) 628-2409. Fax: (515) 628-9192. Web: www.PellaTulipTime.com.

ECUADOR: DAY OF QUITO. Dec 6. Commemorates founding of city of Quito by Spaniards in 1534.

EISENSTAEDT, ALFRED: BIRTH ANNIVERSARY. Dec 6, 1898. American photojournalist Alfred Eisenstaedt was born at Dirschau, Prussia. One of the greatest photojournalists in US history he is best known for his 86 photos that were used on covers of *Life* magazine, including the photo of the sailor kissing a nurse in New York's Times Square at the end of World War II. He died Aug 23, 1995, at Martha's Vineyard, MA.

EVERGLADES NATIONAL PARK ESTABLISHED: ANNIVERSARY. Dec 6, 1947. Part of vast marshland area on southern Florida peninsula, originally authorized May 30, 1934, was established as a national park.

FINLAND: INDEPENDENCE DAY. Dec 6. National holiday. Declaration of independence from Russia in 1917.

GERALD FORD SWEARING-IN AS VICE PRESIDENT: ANNIVERSARY. Dec 6, 1973. Gerald Ford was sworn in as vice president under Richard Nixon, following the resignation of Spiro Agnew who pled no contest to a charge of income tax evasion. See also "Agnew, Spiro Theodore: Birth Anniversary" (Nov 9) and "Ford, Gerald Rudolph: Birthday" (July 14).

GERSHWIN, IRA: BIRTH ANNIVERSARY. Dec 6, 1896. Pulitzer Prize–winning American lyricist and author who collaborated with his brother, George, and with many other composers. Among his Broadway successes: *Lady Be Good, Funny Face, Strike Up the Band* and such songs as "The Man I Love," "Someone to Watch Over Me," "I Got Rhythm" and hundreds of others. Born at New York, NY, he died at Beverly Hills, CA, Aug 17, 1983.

HALIFAX, NOVA SCOTIA, DESTROYED: ANNIVERSARY. Dec 6, 1917. More than 1,650 people were killed at Halifax when the Norwegian ship *Imo* plowed into the French munitions ship *Mont Blanc*. *Mont Blanc* was loaded with 4,000 tons of TNT, 2,300 tons of picric acid, 61 tons of other explosives and a deck of highly flammable benzene, which ignited and touched off an explosion. In addition to those killed, 1,028 were injured. A tidal wave, caused by the explosion, washed much of the city out to sea.

KILMER, JOYCE (ALFRED): BIRTH ANNIVERSARY. Dec 6, 1886. American poet most famous for his poem "Trees," which was published in 1913, was born at New Brunswick, NJ. Kilmer was killed in action near Ourcy, France, in World War I, July 30, 1918. Camp Kilmer was named for him.

LAILAT UL QADR: THE NIGHT OF POWER. Dec 6 (also Dec 8, 10, 12 or 14). "The Night of Power" falls on one of the last 10 days of Ramadan on an odd-numbered day (Islamic calendar dates: Ramadan 21, 23, 25, 27 or 29, 1422). The Holy Qur'an states that praying on this night is better than praying 1,000 months. Since it is not known which day it is, Muslims feel it is best to pray on each of the possible nights. Different methods for "anticipating" the visibility of the new moon crescent at Mecca are used by different Muslim sects or groups. US date may vary.

LANTERN LIGHT TOURS. Dec 6–23 (Thursday–Sunday evenings). Mystic, CT. Step into Christmas past. You may find yourself riding in a horse-drawn omnibus, kicking up your heels with revelers in the tavern or spying on silver-haired St. Nick. Purchase tickets for these nighttime traveling dramas by calling (888) 9SEAPORT. Est attendance: 6,000. For info: Mystic Seaport, 75 Greenmanville Ave, Box 6000, Mystic, CT 06355. Phone: (860) 572-5315 or (888) 9SEAPORT. Web: www.mysticseaport.org.

LEVINE, CHARLES A.: 10th DEATH ANNIVERSARY.
Dec 6, 1991. Charles A. Levine, whose efforts to beat Charles Lindbergh across the Atlantic by plane were stymied by a lawsuit, nevertheless became the first air passenger to cross the Atlantic Ocean. Levine's 225-horsepower plane, *The Columbia*, was grounded when one of his copilots filed a suit hours after Lindbergh took off from Roosevelt Field. Not to be overshadowed by Lindbergh's success, Levine announced that his flight, leaving June 4, 1927, would fly beyond Paris to Berlin, with himself as a passenger. Piloted by Clarence Chamberlin, the plane exhausted its fuel and landed at Eisleben, Germany, June 6, 100 miles short of his goal. The flight set a new record of 3,911 miles in 43 hours of nonstop flight, besting Lindbergh by approximately 300 miles. Levine was born at North Adams, MA, in 1897 and died at Washington, DC.

LIBERACE MUSEUM CHRISTMAS TREE LIGHTING CEREMONY. Dec 6. The Liberace Museum, Las Vegas, NV. Santa wearing Liberace's gold lamé Santa suit will pull the switch to light the tree with music of the season provided by Liberace scholars. Free admission to all who donate a new toy or nonperishable food item, which will be given to the Salvation Army for distribution to the needy. Annually, the first Thursday in December. Est attendance: 1,000. For info: Jamie G. James, The James Agency, 3630 Coldwater Canyon Ave, Studio City, CA 91604. Phone: (818) 508-4902. Fax: (818) 508-0562. E-mail: JJames@Liberace.org.

MISSOURI EARTHQUAKES: ANNIVERSARY. Dec 6, 1811. New Madrid, MO. Most prolonged series of earthquakes in US history occured not in California, but in the Midwest. Lasted until Feb 12, 1812. There were few deaths because of the sparse population. These were the most severe earthquakes in the contiguous US; those higher on the Richter scale have all occurred in Alaska.

NATIONAL PAWNBROKERS DAY. Dec 6. Celebrated on St. Nicholas Day, the patron saint of pawnbroking. Designed to acknowledge the valuable lending and retail services the pawnbroker provides his or her clientele. For info: Michael Goldstein, Empire Loan, 1130 Washington St, Boston, MA 02118. Phone: (617) 423-9366.

RENOIR, CLAUDE: BIRTH ANNIVERSARY. Dec 6, 1914. French film cameraman Claude Renoir was born at Paris, France, a grandson of painter Pierre Renoir. His films include *The River* (1951) and *The Spy Who Loved Me* (1977). He died Sept 5, 1993, at Troyes, France.

SAINT NICHOLAS DAY. Dec 6. One of the most venerated saints of both eastern and western Christian churches, of whose life little is known, except that he was Bishop of Myra (in what is today's Turkey) in the fourth century, and that from early times he has been especially noted for his charity. Santa Claus and the presentation of gifts is said to derive from Saint Nicholas.

SPAIN: CONSTITUTION DAY. Dec 6. National holiday.

"TALENT SCOUTS" TV PREMIERE: ANNIVERSARY.
Dec 6, 1948. Officially titled "Arthur Godfrey's Talent Scouts," this TV show was created when host Arthur Godfrey took his radio show to TV in 1948. On this talent show, celebrity guests introduced amateur and young professional acts. It was a weekly show until 1958. For several years beginning in 1960 it was a summer replacement series called "Celebrity Talent Scouts" and "Hollywood Talent Scouts." Hosts included Sam Levenson, Jim Backus, Merv Griffin and Art Linkletter. Pat Boone, Shari Lewis and the McGuire Sisters got their start here.

THIRTEENTH AMENDMENT TO THE US CONSTITUTION RATIFIED: ANNIVERSARY. Dec 6, 1865. The Thirteenth Amendment to the Constitution was ratified, abolishing slavery in the US. "Neither slavery nor involuntary servitude, save as a punishment for crime whereof the party shall have been duly convicted, shall exist within the United States, or any place subject to their jurisdiction." This amendment was proclaimed Dec 18, 1865. The Thirteenth, Fourteenth and Fifteenth amendments are considered the Civil War Amendments. See also: "Emancipation Proclamation: Anniversary" (Jan 1) for Lincoln's proclamation freeing slaves in the rebelling states.

WORLD'S LARGEST OUTLET SALE. Dec 6–16. Pigeon Forge, TN. Pre-holiday savings on famous brands provided by six outlet malls with almost 200 sites. For info: Pigeon Forge Dept of Tourism, 2450 Parkway, PO Box 1390, Pigeon Forge, TN 37868. Phone: (800) 251-9100 or (423) 453-8574. Fax: (423) 429-7362. Web: www.mypigeonforge.com.

BIRTHDAYS TODAY

Dave Brubeck, 81, jazz musician, born Concord, CA, Dec 6, 1920.

Andrew Cuomo, 44, US Secretary of Housing and Urban Development (Clinton administration), born Queens, NY, Dec 6, 1957.

Otto Graham, 80, former football coach and Pro Football Hall of Fame quarterback, born Waukegan, IL, Dec 6, 1921.

Thomas Hulce, 48, actor (*Amadeus, Parenthood*), born Plymouth, MI, Dec 6, 1953.

James Naughton, 56, actor (*The Paper Chase, The Good Mother*; stage: *Long Day's Journey into Night*), born Middletown, CT, Dec 6, 1945.

Don Nickles, 53, US Senator (R, Oklahoma), born Ponca City, OK, Dec 6, 1948.

Janine Turner, 39, actress ("Northern Exposure," *Cliffhanger*), born Lincoln, NE, Dec 6, 1962.

JoBeth Williams, 48, actress (*The Big Chill*, "Payne"), born Houston, TX, Dec 6, 1953.

Steven Wright, 46, comedian, born New York, NY, Dec 6, 1955.

DECEMBER 7 — FRIDAY
Day 341 — 24 Remaining

ARMENIAN EARTHQUAKE OF 1988: ANNIVERSARY. Dec 7, 1988. An earthquake measuring 6.9 on the Richter scale rocked the Soviet province of Armenia killing upwards of 60,000 people. Many of the deaths were blamed on poor construction practices as many homes had been made of adobe, mud, stones, had unreinforced masonry or were prefabricated structures made of loosely connected concrete slabs. In the quake's aftermath, Soviet President Mikhail Gorbachev cut short his trip to the US to fly home and head the massive worldwide relief efforts.

CATHER, WILLA SIBERT: BIRTH ANNIVERSARY. Dec 7, 1873. American author born at Winchester, VA. Died at New York, NY, Apr 24, 1947. Best known for her novels about the development of early 20th-century modern American life, such as *O Pioneers!* and *My Antonia*. She won a Pulitzer Prize in 1922 for her book *One of Ours*.

CHAPIN, HARRY: BIRTH ANNIVERSARY. Dec 7, 1942. Folk singer/songwriter Harry Chapin was one of only five songwriters to receive the Special Congressional Gold Medal for his devotion to the issue of hunger throughout the world. Born at New York, NY, he was killed in a car accident July 16, 1981, at Long Island, NY.

CHRISTMAS CRAFT SHOW. Dec 7–8. H.O. Weeks Recreation Center, Aiken, SC. This show consists of more than 200 Christmas exhibits and other items from the Southeast's top craftsmen. The displays range from woodwork to fine porcelain sculpture. 31st annual show. Est attendance: 14,000. For info: City of Aiken Park & Rec Dept, PO Box 1177, Aiken, SC 29802. Phone: (803) 642-7631. Fax: (803) 642-7639. E-mail: howeeks@aiken.com.

CHRISTMAS MADRIGAL EVENINGS. Dec 7–9 (also Dec 14–16). St. Mary's City, MD. Join us for an evening of feasting, music and fun at the State House. 5:30 PM-9:30 PM. Separate admission, reservations required. For info: Visitors Services, Historic St. Mary's City, PO Box 39, St. Mary's City, MD 20686. Phone: (301) 862-0990 or (800) SMC-1634. Fax: (301) 862-0968. Web: www.smcm.edu/hsmc/.

CHRISTMAS ON THE PRAIRIE. Dec 7–9. Saunders County Museum, Wahoo, NE. Old-fashioned Christmas featuring entertainment by local groups, lots of period costumes, special postal cancellation, children's activities common to the 1800s and demonstrations in the historical village decorated in the 1800s style. Annually, the first weekend of December. Sponsor: Christmas on the Prairie Steering Committee. Est attendance: 3,000. For info: Curator, Saunders County Museum, 240 N Walnut, Wahoo, NE 68066-1858. Phone: (402) 443-3090. Web: www.co.saunders.ne.us.

CHRISTMAS PAST AT AUDUBON ACRES. Dec 7–8. Audubon Acres, Chattanooga, TN. Enjoy the sights, tastes, smells and excitement of Christmas long ago; see demonstrations and reenactments of early skills; enjoy a stroll to the swinging bridge to observe signs of nature in the winter. Sponsor: Chattanooga Audubon Society. Annually, first weekend in December. Est attendance: 1,500. For info: Lynda Logan, Audubon Acres, 900 N Sanctuary Rd, Chattanooga, TN 37421. Phone: (423) 892-1499. Fax: (423) 892-6376. E-mail: caudubons@aol.com.

CHRISTMAS STROLL. Dec 7–9. Nantucket Island, MA. Christmas trees, costumed carolers, theatrical performances. Santa arrives via Coast Guard boat and is driven up Main Street in a horse-drawn carriage. Est attendance: 20,000. For info: Nantucket Island Chamber of Commerce, 48 Main St, Nantucket, MA 02554-3595. Phone: (508) 228-1700.

CHRISTMAS STROLL. Dec 7. Lewistown, MT. Christmas parade, Santa comes to Lewistown, food booths, wagon rides and buy a Christmas button for a chance to win prizes. Est attendance: 1,500. For info: Lewistown Chamber of Commerce, PO Box 818, Lewistown, MT 59457. Phone: (406) 538-5436. Fax: (406) 538-5437. E-mail: lewchamb@lewistown.net. Web: www.lewistownchamber.com.

CHRISTMAS TOWN FESTIVAL. Dec 7–8. Bethlehem, CT. More than 75 craftsmen at seven locations. Event includes entertainment, Santa, hayrides and more. Est attendance: 8,000. For info: Christmas Town Festival, PO Box 160, Bethlehem, CT 06751. Phone: (203) 266-5557.

COWBOY CHRISTMAS. Dec 7–8. Wickenburg, AZ. Gathering of cowboy poets and singers who carry on the workings of ranch life and traditional cowboy life in verse and song. Annually, the first weekend in December. Est attendance: 1,500. For info: Wickenburg Chamber of Commerce, 216 N Frontier, Wickenburg, AZ 85390. Phone: (520) 684-5479 or (520) 684-0977. Fax: (520) 684-5470. E-mail: info@wickenburgchamber.com. Web: www.wickenburgchamber.com.

DELAWARE RATIFIES CONSTITUTION: ANNIVERSARY. Dec 7, 1787. Delaware became the first state to ratify the proposed Constitution. It did so by unanimous vote.

FANTASY OF LIGHTS. Dec 7–Jan 1, 2002. Wichita Falls, TX. A spectacular light and toyland display on the Midwestern State University campus. A Wichita Falls Christmas tradition! Est attendance: 250,000. For info: Wichita Falls Conv & Visitors Bureau, 1000 Fifth St, Wichita Falls, TX 76301. Phone: (940) 716-5500. Fax: (940) 716-5509. Web: www.viewscape.com or www.wf.net.

GENEVA'S CHRISTMAS WALK. Dec 7–8. Geneva, IL. Spend the day touring charming homes aglow with holiday decorations. In the evening, Santa Lucia, the Swedish symbol of the season, arrives and Santa Claus opens his house for children's visits. Merchants graciously serve traditional holiday refreshments, including roasted chestnuts, as carolers fill the air with the sounds of the season. Annually, the first Friday and Saturday in December. Est attendance: 20,000. For info: Geneva Chamber of Commerce, 8 South Third St, PO Box 481, Geneva, IL 60134. Phone: (630) 232-6060. Fax: (630) 232-6083. E-mail: chamberinfo@genevachamber.com. Web: www.genevachamber.com.

GINGERBREAD AND LACE: A CHRISTMAS CELEBRATION. Dec 7. Ash Lawn–Highland, Charlottesville, VA. Customs of 1870s: caroling, ornament making, tree trimming and refreshments. Est attendance: 100. For info: Ash Lawn–Highland, James Monroe Parkway, Charlottesville, VA 22902. Phone: (804) 293-9539. Fax: (804) 293-8000. E-mail: ashlawnjm@aol.com. Web: avenue.org/ashlawn.

HOLLYWOOD BEACH CANDY CANE PARADE. Dec 7. Hollywood, FL. More than 200 floats and marching units line the Hollywood Beach Boardwalk. Est attendance: 15,000. For info: Roguey Doyle, City of Hollywood, Dept of Parks, Recreation & Cultural Arts, 1940 Harrison St, Ste 101, Hollywood, FL 33020. Phone: (954) 921-3404.

LIVING WINDOW CELEBRATION. Dec 7–8. Monmouth, IL. Live music and entertainment in historic downtown Monmouth. Carriage rides, contests, special Christmas promotions. 6 PM–9 PM Friday; all day Saturday. Est attendance: 10,000. For info: Monmouth Chamber of Commerce, PO Box 857, Monmouth, IL 61462. Phone: (309) 734-3181. Fax: (309) 734-6595.

MOON PHASE: LAST QUARTER. Dec 7. Moon enters Last Quarter phase at 2:52 PM, EST.

NATIONAL FINALS RODEO. Dec 7–16. Las Vegas, NV. Rodeo athletes compete for prize money and bragging rights in the sport's annual championship. In associated events, more than 300 exhibitors display Western merchandise at the Cowbow Christmas Show, and hotels book country entertainers and sponsor special events for the celebration. Est attendance: 174,000. For info: Professional Rodeo Cowboys Assn, 101 Pro Rodeo Dr, Colorado Springs, CO 80919. Phone: (702) 260-8605 or for ticket info (800) 848-4615.

NATIONAL FIRE SAFETY COUNCIL: FOUNDING ANNIVERSARY. Dec 7, 1979. Founded to promote fire prevention and life safety awareness. Distributes comprehensive material to children and adults through local fire departments. For info: Barbara Handley Huggett, Dir, R & D, Natl Fire Safety Council Inc, PO Box 378, Michigan Center, MI 49254-0378. Phone: (517) 764-2811.

★**NATIONAL PEARL HARBOR REMEMBRANCE DAY.** Dec 7.

PEARL HARBOR DAY: 60th ANNIVERSARY. Dec 7, 1941. At 7:55 AM (local time) Dec 7, 1941, "a date that will live in infamy," nearly 200 Japanese aircraft attacked Pearl Harbor, Hawaii, long considered the US "Gibraltar of the Pacific." The raid, which lasted little more than one hour, left nearly 3,000 dead. Nearly the entire US Pacific Fleet was at anchor there and few ships escaped damage. Several were sunk or disabled, while 200 US aircraft on the ground were destroyed. The attack on Pearl Harbor brought about immediate US entry into WWII, a Declaration of War being requested by President Franklin D. Roosevelt and approved by the Congress Dec 8, 1941.

December 2001	**S**	**M**	**T**	**W**	**T**	**F**	**S**
							1
	2	3	4	5	6	7	8
	9	10	11	12	13	14	15
	16	17	18	19	20	21	22
	23	24	25	26	27	28	29
	30	31					

PEGGY V. HELMERICH DISTINGUISHED AUTHOR AWARD PRESENTATION. Dec 7. Central Library, Tulsa, OK. The award is given annually by the Tulsa Library Trust to a nationally acclaimed author who has written a distinguished body of work and made a major contribution to the field of literature and letters. The award consists of a $25,000 cash prize and an engraved crystal book. The winning author will be the keynote speaker at this black-tie dinner in his or her honor. Past recipients include Neil Simon (1996), David McCullough (1995), Ray Bradbury (1994), Peter Matthiessen (1993), Norman Mailer (1992), Eudora Welty (1991) and John le Carre (1990). Est attendance: 1,000. For info: Larry Bartley, Trust and Development Mgr, Tulsa Public Library, 400 Civic Center, Tulsa, OK 74103. Phone: (918) 596-7985. Fax: (918) 596-7990.

SPACE MILESTONE: *APOLLO 17* (US). Dec 7, 1972. Launched this date with three-man crew: Eugene A. Cernan, Harrison H. Schmidt, Ronald E. Evans, who explored the moon, Dec 11–14. Lunar landing module named *Challenger*. Pacific splashdown, Dec 19. This was the last manned mission to the moon.

SPACE MILESTONE: *GALILEO* (US). Dec 7, 1995. Launched Oct 18, 1989 by the space shuttle *Atlantis*, the spacecraft *Galileo* entered the orbit of Jupiter, after a six-year journey. It orbited Jupiter for two years, sending out probes to study three of its moons. Organic compounds, the ingredients of life, were found on them.

SUGARLOAF'S WINTER GAITHERSBURG CRAFT FESTIVAL. Dec 7–9. Montgomery County Fairgrounds, Gaithersburg, MD. This show, now in its 24th year, features 325 nationally recognized craft designers and fine artists displaying and selling their original creations. Craft demonstrations, hourly gift certificate drawings, food and more. Est attendance: 17,000. For info: Sugarloaf Mountain Works, Inc, 200 Orchard Ridge Dr, #215, Gaithersburg, MD 20878. Phone: (800) 210-9900. E-mail: smworks@sugarloafcrafts.com. Web: www.sugarloafcrafts.com.

TUSSAUD, MARIE GROSHOLTZ: BIRTH ANNIVERSARY. Dec 7, 1761. Creator of Madame Tussaud's waxwork museum, born at Strasbourg, France. Some of the wax figures she created are still on view at Madame Tussaud's at London. She died at London, Apr 15, 1850.

UNITED NATIONS: INTERNATIONAL CIVIL AVIATION DAY: 5th ANNIVERSARY. Dec 7. On Dec 6, 1996, the General Assembly proclaimed Dec 7 as International Civil Aviation Day. On Dec 7, 1944, the convention on International Civil Aviation, which established the International Civil Aviation Organization, was signed. Info from: United Nations, Dept of Public Info, New York, NY 10017.

WASSAIL CELEBRATION. Dec 7–9. Woodstock, VT. Activities include a horse rider and carriage parade, Santa comes to town, Wassail Dance, concert by Revere Handbell Choir, caroling and burning the yule log on the Village Green. Est attendance: 5,000. For info: David Murison, Exec Coord, Woodstock Area Chamber of Commerce, 18 Central St, PO Box 486, Woodstock, VT 05091. Phone: (802) 457-3555 or (888) 496-6378.

WOLF POINT'S ANNUAL CHRISTMAS PARADE. Dec 7. Wolf Point, MT. The city comes alive with the Christmas spirit in this magical and enchanting evening which features a parade in which all the floats are illuminated with lights, Santa is the master of ceremonies and awards for floats are given in three categories. This event will make you remember what Christmas looks like through the eyes of a child. Est attendance: 1,000. For info: Wolf Point Chamber of Commerce, 218 3rd Ave S, Ste B, Wolf Point, MT 59201. Phone: (406) 653-2012. E-mail: wpchmber@nemontel.net.

BIRTHDAYS TODAY

Johnny Lee Bench, 54, Baseball Hall of Fame catcher, born Oklahoma City, OK, Dec 7, 1947.

Larry Joe Bird, 45, basketball coach, Basketball Hall of Famer, former player, born West Baden, IN, Dec 7, 1956.

Ellen Burstyn (Edna Rae Gilhooley), 69, actress (*Alice Doesn't Live Here Anymore; The Exorcist; Same Time, Next Year*), born Detroit, MI, Dec 7, 1932.

Thad Cochran, 64, US Senator (R, Mississippi), born Pontotoc, MS, Dec 7, 1937.

Susan M. Collins, 49, US Senator (R, Maine), born Caribou, ME, Dec 7, 1952.

Edd Hall, 43, announcer ("The Tonight Show with Jay Leno"), born Boston, MA, Dec 7, 1958.

C. Thomas Howell, 35, actor ("Two Marriages," *Soul Man, Tank*), born Los Angeles, CA, Dec 7, 1966.

Tino Martinez, 34, baseball player, born Tampa, FL, Dec 7, 1967.

Tom Waits, 52, singer, songwriter ("I Never Talk to Strangers"), actor (*Down by Law, Short Cuts*), born New York, NY, Dec 7, 1949.

Eli Wallach, 86, actor (*The Tiger Makes Out*; Emmy for "The Poppy Is Also a Flower"), born New York, NY, Dec 7, 1915.

DECEMBER 8 — SATURDAY
Day 342 — 23 Remaining

AMERICA ENTERS WORLD WAR II: ANNIVERSARY. Dec 8, 1941. One day after the surprise Japanese attack on Pearl Harbor, Congress declared war against Japan and the US entered World War II.

AMERICAN FEDERATION OF LABOR (AFL) FOUNDED: ANNIVERSARY. Dec 8, 1886. Originally founded at Pittsburgh, PA, as the Federation of Organized Trades and Labor Unions of the United States and Canada in 1881, the union was reorganized in 1886 under the name American Federation of Labor (AFL). The AFL was dissolved as a separate entity in 1955 when it merged with the Congress of Industrial Organizations to form the AFL-CIO. See also: "AFL-CIO Founded: Anniversary (Dec 5)."

BERGALIS, KIMBERLY: 10th DEATH ANNIVERSARY. Dec 8, 1991. Kimberly Bergalis, the first patient believed to have contracted the AIDS virus from a health care professional, died at Fort Pierce, FL. Her case sparked controversy over how the disease is transmitted and incited calls to ban infected health care professionals from the workplace.

CHILDREN'S VICTORIAN CHRISTMAS CELEBRATION. Dec 8–23. Washington, MS. Display of 14 or more Christmas trees decorated by fifth-grade students. Est attendance: 2,000. For info: Anne L. Gray, Historian, Historic Jefferson College, PO Box 700, Washington, MS 39190. Phone: (601) 442-2901.

CHINESE NATIONALISTS MOVE TO FORMOSA: ANNIVERSARY. Dec 8, 1949. The government of Chiang Kai–Shek moved to Formosa (Taiwan) after being driven out of Mainland China by the Communists led by Mao Tse–Tung.

CHRISTMAS BOAT PARADE ON CLEAR LAKE. Dec 8. Clear Lake, TX. Witness more than a hundred decorated boats travel across Clear Lake out to the Galveston Bay. Sponsored by the Clear Lake Area Chamber of Commerce. 40th annual parade. For info: Shari Sweeney, Clear Lake Area Chamber of Commerce, 1201 Nasa Rd One, Houston, TX 77058. Phone: (281) 488-7676. Fax: (281) 488-8981.

CHRISTMAS CRAFT FAIR USA: INDOOR SHOW. Dec 8–9. Wisconsin State Fair Park, Milwaukee, WI. Sale of hand-crafted items—jewelry, pottery, weaving, leather, wood, glass and sculpture. Est attendance: 10,000. For info: Dir, Christmas Craft Fair USA, 9312 W National Ave, Milwaukee, WI 53227-1542. Phone: (414) 321-2100. Web: www.craftfairusa.com.

CHRISTMAS IN HOPELANDS. Dec 8–26 (closed Dec 24). Aiken, SC. The pathways of Hopeland Gardens in historic Aiken are lined with thousands of sparkling lights. Visitors to the gardens can stroll along the pathways and view lighted displays throughout the gardens. Historic buildings such as the Thoroughbred Racing Hall of Fame, the Dollhouse and Rye Patch are open for the tour. Est attendance: 17,000. For info: City of Aiken Parks and Recreation Dept, PO Box 1177, Aiken, SC 29802. Phone: (803) 642-7631. Fax: (803) 642-7639. E-mail: howeeks @aiken.net.

CHRISTMAS ON THE RIVER & THE GRANDE ILLUMINATION. Dec 8. Coolidge Park, Chattanooga, TN. The Tennessee River comes alive with lighted boats decorated for the season. The Grande Illumination ceremony follows featuring a singing Santa throwing fireballs to rooftops signaling the simultaneous lighting of more than 100 downtown buildings. The evening comes to colorful close with a fireworks finale. Est attendance: 20,000. For info: Carla Pritchard, Exec Dir, Chattanooga Downtown Partnership, Christmas on the River, 850 Market St, 2nd Fl, Miller Plaza, Chattanooga, TN 37402. Phone: (423) 265-0771. Fax: (423) 265-6952.

DAVIS, SAMMY, JR: BIRTH ANNIVERSARY. Dec 8, 1925. Born at New York, NY, Sammy Davis, Jr, was the son of vaudevillians and first appeared on the stage at the age of four. He made his first film appearance in *Rufus Jones for President* in 1931. He then joined the Will Mastin Trio. The popular song-and-dance team was popular on the night club circuit; as Davis matured, his singing, dancing and impersonations became the center of the act. Davis began performing on his own in the 1950s, headlining club engagements, appearing on television variety shows and making numerous records. His Broadway debut came in 1956 in the hit musical *Mr Wonderful*, and in the late '50s and early '60s he starred in a number of films, including a series with Frank Sinatra and the Rat Pack. Davis died at Los Angeles, CA, May 16, 1990.

DICKENS CHRISTMAS FESTIVAL. Dec 8–9. Kellogg, ID. Hundreds of people in period costume, skits, plays, puppet shows and a high tea. Topped off with a parade of characters and a "town sing." Annually, the second weekend in December. Est attendance: 500. For info: Sharon Waldo, Mgr, Kellogg Chamber of Commerce, 608 Bunker Ave, Kellogg, ID 83837. Phone: (208) 784-0821. Fax: (208) 783-4343.

DICKENS OF A CHRISTMAS. Dec 8–9. Downtown Franklin, TN. 16th annual festival features living characters from *A Christmas Carol* as well as other Victorian characters including Father & Mother Christmas. Street vendors sell roasted chestnuts, plum pudding and hot chocolate. Horse-drawn carriage rides, musical, dramatic performances and town sing. Local artists and crafters create "living windows" by demonstrating their skills in shop windows. Est attendance: 20,000. For info: Laura Bustetter, PO Box 807, Franklin, TN 37065. Phone: (615) 791-9924. Fax: (615) 791-0372. E-mail: lbustetter@historicfranklin.com. Web: www.historicfranklin.com.

DURANT, WILLIAM CRAPO: BIRTH ANNIVERSARY. Dec 8, 1861. "Billy" Durant, a leading producer of carriages at Flint, MI; promoter of the Buick car; cofounder of Chevrolet and

		S	M	T	W	T	F	S
December								1
2001		2	3	4	5	6	7	8
		9	10	11	12	13	14	15
		16	17	18	19	20	21	22
		23	24	25	26	27	28	29
		30	31					

founder, in 1908, of General Motors. He lost, regained and again lost control of GM, after which he founded Durant Motors, went bankrupt in the Depression and operated a Flint bowling alley in his last working years. Durant was born at Boston, MA, and died at New York, NY, Mar 18, 1947.

FEAST OF THE IMMACULATE CONCEPTION. Dec 8. Roman Catholic Holy Day of Obligation.

FIRST STEP TOWARD A NUCLEAR-FREE WORLD: ANNIVERSARY. Dec 8, 1987. The former Soviet Union and the US signed a treaty at Washington eliminating medium-range and shorter-range missiles. This was the first treaty completely doing away with two entire classes of nuclear arms. These missiles, with a range of 500 to 5,500 kilometers, were to be scrapped under strict supervision within three years of the signing.

GUAM: LADY OF CAMARIN DAY HOLIDAY: 30th ANNIVERSARY. Dec 8. Declared a legal holiday by Guam legislature, Mar 2, 1971.

HOBAN, JAMES: DEATH ANNIVERSARY. Dec 8, 1831. Irish-born architect who designed the US President's Executive Mansion, later known as The White House. He was born at Callan, County Kilkenny, Ireland, in 1762 (exact date unknown) and died at Washington, DC. The cornerstone for the White House, Washington's oldest public building, was laid in 1792.

HOMESTEADERS HOLIDAY. Dec 8. Centennial Village Museum, Greeley, CO. Pioneer holiday family festival with candledipping, cowboy Santa, telegrams to North Pole, living history demos, musical entertainment, decorated homes, craft activities and food. Est attendance: 1,000. For info: Greeley Museums, 919 7th St, Greeley, CO 80631. Phone: (970) 350-9220. Fax: (970) 350-9700. Web: www.ci.greeley.co.us/culture/museums.

MORRISON, JIM: BIRTH ANNIVERSARY. Dec 8, 1943. Singer, songwriter, known as "The Lizard King," lead singer of The Doors, Jim Morrison is considered to be one of the fathers of contemporary rock. Born at Melbourne, FL, and died at Paris, France, July 3, 1971.

NAFTA SIGNED: ANNIVERSARY. Dec 8, 1993. President Clinton signed the North American Free Trade Agreement which cut tariffs and eliminated other trade barriers between the US, Canada and Mexico. The Agreement went into effect Jan 1, 1994.

NORMAN ROCKWELL'S 1923 CHRISTMAS COVER FOR *THE SATURDAY EVENING POST*: ANNIVERSARY. Dec 8, 1923. One of his earliest covers for the *Post* when they were still in black and red, Norman Rockwell's 1923 Christmas cover for the magazine depicted a trio performing Christmas carols. In Rockwell's biography he reveals that not one of his three models had an iota of musical talent.

OLD-FASHIONED DANISH CHRISTMAS. Dec 8. Dannebrog, NE. Days filled with Christmas Tree Fantasy, living nativity scene, crafters/working artists expo, Danish buffet luncheon, Danish pastry, Danish tree ornament cutouts demonstration, home tours and spectacular displays of holiday lights. Annually, the second Saturday in December. Est attendance: 1,200. For info: Shirley Johnson, Festival Coord, Dannebrog Area Booster Club, 522 E Roger Welsch Ave, Dannebrog, NE 68831. Phone: (308) 226-2237.

PARADE OF LIGHTS. Dec 8. Kingsville, TX. Breakfast with Santa kicks off a fun-filled day of holiday activities for children ending with an illuminated night-time parade for children of all ages in historic downtown Kingsville. Est attendance: 3,000. For info: Kingsville CVB, 1501 N Hwy 77, Kingsville, TX 78364. Phone: (800) 333-5032. Fax: (361) 592-3227. E-mail: cvb@kings villetexas.com. Web: www.kingsvilletexas.com.

POLISH CHRISTMAS OPEN HOUSE. Dec 8 (or Dec 15). Polish American Cultural Center Museum, Philadelphia, PA. Sw. Mikolaj (Polish St. Nicholas) will greet everyone with gifts for the children. Polish Christmas Tree and entertainment. Free admission. For info: Polish American Cultural Center Museum, 308 Walnut St, Philadelphia, PA 19106. Phone: (215) 922-1700. Fax: (215) 922-1518. E-mail: mail@polishamericancenter.org. Web: www.polishamericancenter.org.

RIVERA, DIEGO: BIRTH ANNIVERSARY. Dec 8, 1886. Mexican painter whose murals became center of political controversy, born at Guanajuato, Mexico. Died in his studio at San Angel, near Mexico City, Nov 25, 1957.

SEGAR, ELZIE CRISLER: BIRTH ANNIVERSARY. Dec 8, 1894. Popeye creator Elzie Crisler Segar was born at Chester, IL. Originally called *Thimble Theater*, the comic strip that came to be known as *Popeye* had the unusual format of a one-act play in cartoon form. Centered on the Oyl family, especially daughter Olive, the strip introduced a new central character in 1929. A one-eyed sailor with bulging muscles, Popeye became the strip's star attraction almost immediately. Popeye made it to the silver screen in animated form and in 1980 became a movie with Robin Williams playing the lead. Segar died Oct 13, 1938, at Santa Monica, CA.

SOVIET UNION DISSOLVED: 10th ANNIVERSARY. Dec 8, 1991. The Union of Soviet Socialist Republics ceased to exist, as the republics of Russia, Byelorussia and Ukraine signed an agreement at Minsk, Byelorussia, creating the Commonwealth of Independent States. The remaining republics, with the exception of Georgia, joined in the new Commonwealth as it began the slow and arduous process of removing the yoke of Communism and dealing with strong separatist and nationalistic movements within the various republics.

THURBER, JAMES: BIRTH ANNIVERSARY. Dec 8, 1894. James Grover Thurber, American humorist and artist, longtime contributor to the *New Yorker*, born at Columbus, OH. Died at New York, NY, Nov 2, 1961.

WHITNEY, ELI: BIRTH ANNIVERSARY. Dec 8, 1765. Inventor of the cotton gin, born at Westboro, MA. Died at New Haven, CT, Jan 8, 1825.

BIRTHDAYS TODAY

Gregg Allman, 54, singer ("Ramblin' Man"), actor (*Rush*), born Nashville, TN, Dec 8, 1947.
Kim Basinger, 48, actress (*The Natural, The Getaway, My Stepmother Is an Alien*), born Athens, GA, Dec 8, 1953.
Gordon Arthur ("Red") Berenson, 60, former hockey player and coach, born Regina, Saskatchewan, Canada, Dec 8, 1941.
David Carradine, 61, actor (*Boxcar Bertha*, "Kung-Fu" series), born Hollywood, CA, Dec 8, 1940.
James Galway, 62, flutist, born Belfast, Northern Ireland, Dec 8, 1939.
Jeff George, 34, football player, born Indianapolis, IN, Dec 8, 1967.
Teri Hatcher, 37, actress ("Lois & Clark"), born Sunnyvale, CA, Dec 8, 1964.
James MacArthur, 64, actor ("Hawaii Five-O"), born Los Angeles, CA, Dec 8, 1937.
Mike Mussina, 33, baseball player, born Williamsport, PA, Dec 8, 1968.
Sinead O'Connor, 35, singer, songwriter, born Dublin, Ireland, Dec 8, 1966.
Maximilian Schell, 71, actor (*Judgment at Nuremberg, The Odessa File*), producer, born Vienna, Austria, Dec 8, 1930.
Mary Woronov, 55, actress (*Rock 'n' Roll High School, Eating Raoul*), born Brooklyn, NY, Dec 8, 1946.

DECEMBER 9 — SUNDAY
Day 343 — 22 Remaining

AMERICA'S FIRST FORMAL CREMATION: ANNIVERSARY. Dec 9, 1792. The first formal cremation of a human body in America took place near Charleston, SC. Henry Laurens, colonial statesman and signer of the Treaty of Paris, ending the Revolutionary War, in his will provided: "I do solemnly enjoin it on my son, as an indispensable duty, that as soon as he conveniently can, after my decease, he cause my body to be wrapped in twelve yards of tow cloth and burned until it be entirely consumed, and then, collecting my bones, deposit them wherever he may think proper." Laurens died Dec 8, 1792, at his plantation, and was cremated there.

BIRDSEYE, CLARENCE: BIRTH ANNIVERSARY. Dec 9, 1886. American industrialist who developed a way of deep-freezing foods. He was marketing frozen fish by 1925 and was one of the founders of General Foods Corporation. Born at Brooklyn, NY, he died at New York City, Oct 7, 1956.

CHRISTMAS BY CANDLELIGHT. Dec 9 (also Dec 16). Ashlawn-Highland, Home of James Monroe, Charlottesville, VA. House open in evening by candlelight with fresh greens decorations both inside and outside. Costumed guides give tours focusing on Christmas customs in Colonial, Federal and Victorian periods. Refreshments served and museum shop open for visitors and shopping. For info: Carolyn C. Holmes, Ashlawn-Highland, 1000 James Monroe Pkwy, Charlottesville, VA 22902. Phone: (804) 293-9539. Fax: (804) 293-8000. E-mail: ashlawnjm @aol.com.

EIGHTEENTH-CENTURY CHRISTMAS WASSAIL. Dec 9. McLean, VA. Greet the winter solstice and Christmas season with a toast to the apple trees. Caroling and warm refreshments. Bring pots or other noisemakers to frighten off evil spirits threatening next year's apple crop. Est attendance: 800. For info: Gretchen Brodtman, Publicist, Claude Moore Colonial Farm at Turkey Run, 6310 Georgetown Pike, McLean, VA 22101. Phone: (703) 442-7557. Fax: (703) 442-0714.

ENTOMOLOGICAL SOCIETY OF AMERICA ANNUAL MEETING AND EXHIBITION. Dec 9–13. San Diego, CA. Est attendance: 2,600. For info: Judy Miller, ESA, 9301 Annapolis Rd, Lanham, MD 20706-3115. Phone: (301) 731-4535. Fax: (301) 731-4538. E-mail: meet@entsoc.org. Web: www.entsoc.org.

FOXX, REDD: BIRTH ANNIVERSARY. Dec 9, 1922. Born John Elroy Sanford at St. Louis, MO, Redd Foxx plied his comedic trade on vaudeville stages, in nightclubs, on television, in films and on record albums. His talents reached a national audience with the TV sitcom "Sanford and Son." He died after collapsing during a rehearsal for a new TV sitcom, "The Royal Family," at Los Angeles, CA, Oct 11, 1991.

GENOCIDE CONVENTION: ANNIVERSARY. Dec 9, 1948. The United Nations General Assembly unanimously approved the Convention on Prevention and Punishment of the Crime of Genocide on Dec 9, 1948. It took effect Jan 12, 1951, when ratification by 20 nations had been completed. President Truman sent it to the US Senate for approval on June 16, 1949; it was supported by Presidents Kennedy, Johnson, Nixon, Ford, Carter and Reagan. Thirty-seven years after its submission, and after approval by more than 90 nations, the Senate approved it, Feb 19, 1986, by a vote of 83–11.

HARRIS, JOEL CHANDLER: BIRTH ANNIVERSARY. Dec 9, 1848. American author, creator of the "Uncle Remus" stories, born at Eatonton, GA. Died July 3, 1908, at Atlanta, GA.

HOPPER, GRACE: 95th BIRTH ANNIVERSARY. Dec 9, 1906. Born at New York, NY. When she retired from the US Navy at the age of 79, she was the oldest naval officer ever on active duty. She attained the rank of Rear Admiral and was a leader in the computer revolution, having developed the computer language COBOL. Grace Hopper died Jan 1, 1992, at Arlington, WV.

INTERNATIONAL SHAREWARE DAY. Dec 9. A day to take the time to reward the efforts of thousands of computer programmers who trust that if we try their programs and like them, we will pay for them. Unfortunately, very few payments are received, thus stifling the programmers' efforts. This observance is meant to prompt each of us to inventory our PCs and Macs, see if we are using any shareware, and then take the time in the holiday spirit to write payment checks to the authors. Hopefully this will keep shareware coming. Annually, the second Sunday in December. For info: David Lawrence, Host, Online Today, PO Box 32320, Baltimore, MD 21282. Phone: (800) 396-6546. E-mail: david@online-today.com. Web: online-today.com.

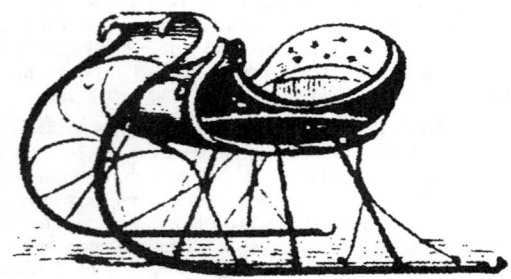

JINGLEBELL JOURNEY. Dec 9. Mount Wolf, PA. Enjoy a special holiday tour of seven creatively decorated homes and a historical landmark. They are all decked out in their holiday finery and say WELCOME to all. Enjoy more holiday atmosphere as the Northeastern Senior Community Center opens its doors and provides visitors with musical entertainment, a seniors art show, handmade crafts, homemade tea breads, cookies and wassail. Proceeds from the tour provide funding to the Senior Center to supply and improve services offered to the area's senior citizens. Annually, the third Sunday before Christmas. For info: Mrs Jackie Sprout, Dir, Northeastern Senior Community Center, 131 Center Street, PO Box 386, Mt Wolf, PA 17347. Phone: (717) 266-1400.

KELLY, EMMETT: BIRTH ANNIVERSARY. Dec 9, 1898. American circus clown and entertainer, born at Sedan, KS. Kelly was best known for "Weary Willie," a clown dressed in tattered clothes, with a beard and large nose. Died at Sarasota, FL, Mar 28, 1979.

LUCIA FEST. Dec 9. Lindsborg, KS. For info: McPherson County Old Mill Museum, PO Box 94, Lindsborg, KS 67456. Phone: (913) 227-3595. Web: www.lindsborg.org.

MILTON, JOHN: BIRTH ANNIVERSARY. Dec 9, 1608. English poet and defender of freedom of the press born at Bread Street, Cheapside, London. Died from gout, Nov 8, 1674, at London, England. "No man who knows aught," he wrote, "can be so stupid to deny that all men naturally were born free."

O'NEILL, THOMAS PHILIP, II (TIP): BIRTH ANNIVERSARY. Dec 9, 1912. Democratic congressman from Massachusetts 1953–87, Speaker of the House of Representatives 1977–87, Tip O'Neill was born at Cambridge, MA, and died Jan 5, 1994, at Boston, MA.

PERSONAL PASSION DAY. Dec 9. Rekindle and celebrate your personal passion—for life, for each other and for your fondest dream. For info: Roz Van Meter, 8588 Northwest Plaza Dr,

Ste 302, Dallas, TX 75225. Phone: (214) 361-0500. Fax: (214) 343-3299. E-mail: roz@coachroz.com. Web: www.coachroz.com.

PETRIFIED FOREST NATIONAL PARK ESTABLISHED: ANNIVERSARY. Dec 9, 1962. Arizona's Petrified Forest National Monument, proclaimed Dec 8, 1906, was established as a national park. For further park info: Petrified Forest Natl Park, Petrified Forest Natl Park, AZ 86028.

QUINCY PRESERVES CHRISTMAS CANDLELIGHT TOUR. Dec 9. Quincy, IL. Tour historic homes decked out in their Christmas finest. Each year this walking tour features a different neighborhood. Homes range in size from grand mansions to quaint cottages. Annually, the second Sunday in December. Est attendance: 1,000. For info: Fran Cook, Quincy Preserves, 310 S 16th St, Quincy, IL 62301. Phone: (217) 224-2587.

RECIPE GREETINGS FOR THE HOLIDAYS. Dec 9–15. A week in which to send recipes as great greetings. Create your own or send a large SASE for ideas. Annually, the second week in December. For info: Recipe Greetings, PO Box 416, Denver, CO 80201. Phone: (303) 575-5676.

REENACTMENT OF THE BOSTON TEA PARTY. Dec 9. Congress Street Bridge, Boston, MA. Reenactment of "Boston's most notorious protest, the single most important event leading to the American Revolution." Annually, the Sunday closest to Dec 16. Starts at Old South Meeting House 5 PM. Est attendance: 1,000. For info: Boston Tea Party Ship, Congress St Bridge, Boston, MA 02210. Phone: (617) 338-1773. Fax: (617) 338-1974.

SANDYS, EDWIN: BIRTH ANNIVERSARY. Dec 9, 1561. Sir Edwin Sandys, English statesman and one of the founders of the Virginia Colony (treasurer, the Virginia Company, 1619–20), born at Worcestershire, England. Died at Kent, England, in October 1629 (exact date unknown).

TANZANIA: INDEPENDENCE AND REPUBLIC DAY: 40th ANNIVERSARY. Dec 9. Tanganyika became independent of Britain in 1961. The republics of Tanganyika and Zanzibar joined to become one state (Apr 27, 1964), renamed (Oct 29, 1964) the United Republic of Tanzania.

BIRTHDAYS TODAY

Joan Armatrading, 51, singer, songwriter (*Me, Myself, I*), born Saint Kitts, West Indies, Dec 9, 1950.

Beau Bridges, 60, actor ("James Brady Story," *The Fabulous Baker Boys*), born Los Angeles, CA, Dec 9, 1941.

Richard Marvin (Dick) Butkus, 59, sportscaster, actor, Pro Football Hall of Fame linebacker, born Chicago, IL, Dec 9, 1942.

Thomas Andrew Daschle, 54, US Senator (D, South Dakota), born Aberdeen, SD, Dec 9, 1947.

Judi Dench, 67, actress (*Mrs Brown, Tomorrow Never Dies*), born York, England, Dec 9, 1934.

Kirk Douglas (Issur Danielovitch Demsky), 85, actor (*Champion, Lust for Life*), author, born Amsterdam, NY, Dec 9, 1916.

Morton Downey, Jr, 68, actor (*Meet Wally Sparks*), born Dec 9, 1933.

Thomas O. (Tom) Kite, Jr, 52, golfer, born Austin, TX, Dec 9, 1949.

Joe Lando, 40, actor ("Dr. Quinn Medicine Woman"), born Chicago, IL, Dec 9, 1961.

John Malkovich, 48, actor (*The Killing Fields, The Sheltering Sky*), filmmaker, born Christopher, IL, Dec 9, 1953.

Dina Merrill, 76, actress (*Desk Set, Operation Petticoat*), born New York, NY, Dec 9, 1925.

Michael Nouri, 56, actor ("Search for Tomorrow," "Love and War," *Goodbye Columbus, Flashdance*), born Washington, DC, Dec 9, 1945.

Donny Osmond, 44, actor, singer ("Donny and Marie;" stage: *Joseph and the Amazing Technicolor Dreamcoat*), born Ogden, UT, Dec 9, 1957.

Dick Van Patten, 73, actor ("Eight Is Enough," "Mama"), born Richmond Hill, NY, Dec 9, 1928.

	S	M	T	W	T	F	S
December							1
2001	2	3	4	5	6	7	8
	9	10	11	12	13	14	15
	16	17	18	19	20	21	22
	23	24	25	26	27	28	29
	30	31					

DECEMBER 10 — MONDAY
Day 344 — 21 Remaining

CHANUKAH. Dec 10–17. Feast of Lights or Feast of Dedication. Festival lasting eight days commemorates victory of Maccabees over Syrians (165 BC) and rededication of Temple of Jerusalem. Begins on Hebrew calendar date Kislev 25, 5762.

DEWEY, MELVIL: 150th BIRTH ANNIVERSARY. Dec 10, 1851. American librarian and inventor of the Dewey decimal book classification system was born at Adams Center, NY. Born Melville Louis Kossuth Dewey, he was an advocate of spelling reform, urged use of the metric system and was interested in many other education reforms. Dewey died at Highlands County, FL, Dec 26, 1931.

DICKINSON, EMILY: BIRTH ANNIVERSARY. Dec 10, 1830. One of America's greatest poets, Emily Dickinson was born at Amherst, MA. She was reclusive, mysterious and frail in health. Seven of her poems were published during her life, but after her death her sister, Lavinia, discovered almost 2,000 more poems written on the backs of envelopes and other scraps of paper locked in her bureau. They were published gradually, over 50 years, beginning in 1890. She died May 15, 1886, at Amherst, MA. The little-known Emily Dickinson who was born, lived and died at Amherst now is recognized as one of the most original poets of the English-speaking world.

FIRST GRAND OLE OPRY BROADCAST: ANNIVERSARY. Dec 10, 1927. Grand Ole Opry made its first radio broadcast from Nashville, TN.

FIRST US HEAVYWEIGHT CHAMP DEFEATED IN ENGLAND: ANNIVERSARY. Dec 10, 1810. Tom Molineaux, the first unofficial heavyweight champion of the US, was a freed slave from Virginia. He was beaten in the 40th round by Tom Cribb, the English champion, in a boxing match at Copthall Common at London.

FIRST US SCIENTIST RECEIVES NOBEL PRIZE: ANNIVERSARY. Dec 10, 1907. University of Chicago professor Albert Michelson, eminent physicist known for his research on the speed of light and optics became the first US scientist to receive the Nobel Prize.

GALLAUDET, THOMAS HOPKINS: BIRTH ANNIVERSARY. Dec 10, 1787. A hearing educator who, with Laurent Clerc, founded the first public school for deaf people, Connecticut Asylum for the Education and Instruction of Deaf and Dumb Persons (now the American School for the Deaf), at Hartford, CT, Apr 15, 1817. Gallaudet was born at Philadelphia, PA, and died Sept 9, 1851, at Hartford, CT.

HISTORICAL SOCIETY'S CHRISTMAS CANDLELIGHT TOUR. Dec 10. Crawfordsville, IN. A walking tour of fine Victorian homes at Crawfordsville. Horse sleigh rides, hot cider, cookies and musical entertainment: dulcimer players, choral groups and brass quartets. Sponsor: Montgomery County Historical Society. Est attendance: 1,500. For info: Montgomery County Visitors & Conv Bureau, Inc, 412 E Main St, Crawfordsville, IN 47933. Phone: (800) 866-3973. Fax: (317) 362-5215. E-mail: mcvcb@tctc.com. Web: www.crawfordsville.org.

★**HUMAN RIGHTS DAY.** Dec 10. Presidential Proclamation 2866, of Dec 6, 1949, covers all succeeding years. Customarily issued as "Bill of Rights Day, Human Rights Day and Week."

★**HUMAN RIGHTS WEEK.** Dec 10–16. Presidential Proclamation issued since 1958 for the week of Dec 10–16, except in 1986. See also: "Human Rights Day" (Dec 10) and "Bill of Rights Day" (Dec 15).

LAMOUR, DOROTHY: BIRTH ANNIVERSARY. Dec 10, 1914. Singer, actress (*The Hurricane, Road to Singapore*), born New Orleans, LA. Died Sept 22, 1996, at Los Angeles, CA.

"THE MIGHTY MOUSE PLAYHOUSE" TV PREMIERE: ANNIVERSARY. Dec 10, 1955. An all-time favorite of the Saturday-morning crowd (including adults). CBS had a hit with their pint-sized cartoon character Mighty Mouse, who was a tongue-in-cheek version of Superman. The show had other feature cartoons such as "The Adventures of Gandy Goose."

MISSISSIPPI: ADMISSION DAY: ANNIVERSARY. Dec 10. Became 20th state In 1817.

NOBEL PRIZE AWARDS CEREMONIES: 100th ANNIVERSARY. Dec 10. Oslo, Norway and Stockholm, Sweden. Alfred Nobel, Swedish chemist and inventor of dynamite who died in 1896, provided in his will that income from his $9 million estate should be used for annual prizes—to be awarded to people who are judged to have made the most valuable contributions to the good of humanity. The Nobel Peace Prize is awarded by a committee of the Norwegian parliament and the presentation is made at the Oslo City Hall. Five other prizes, for physics, chemistry, medicine, literature and economics, are presented in a ceremony at Stockholm, Sweden. Both ceremonies traditionally are held on the anniversary of the death of Alfred Nobel. First awarded in 1901, the current value of each prize is about $1,000,000. See also "Nobel, Alfred Bernhard: Birth Anniversary" (Oct 21).

NORTON, MARY: BIRTH ANNIVERSARY. Dec 10, 1903. British author Mary Norton was born at London, England. An author of children's books, she is best known for *Bedknob and Broomstick* (1957). She died Aug 29, 1992, at Hartland, England.

RALPH BUNCHE AWARDED NOBEL PEACE PRIZE: ANNIVERSARY. Dec 10, 1950. Dr. Ralph Johnson Bunche became the first black man awarded the Nobel Peace Prize. Bunche was awarded the prize for his efforts in mediation between Israel and neighboring Arab states in 1949.

RED CLOUD: DEATH ANNIVERSARY. Dec 10, 1909. Sioux Indian chief Red Cloud was born in 1822 (exact date unknown), near North Platte, NE. A courageous leader and defender of Indian rights, Red Cloud was the son of Lone Man and Walks as She Thinks. His unrelenting determination caused US abandonment of the Bozeman trail and of three forts that interfered with Indian hunting grounds. Red Cloud died at Pine Ridge, SD.

SPACE MILESTONE: *SOYUZ 26* (USSR). Dec 10, 1977. Launched this date with Cosmonauts Yuri Romanenko and Georgi Grechko who linked it with *Salyut 6* space station on Dec 11, after the unsuccessful attempt by *Soyuz 25* earlier that year. Returned to Earth in *Soyuz 27*, Mar 16, 1978, after record-setting 96 days in space.

THAILAND: CONSTITUTION DAY. Dec 10. A public holiday throughout Thailand.

TREATY OF PARIS ENDS SPANISH-AMERICAN WAR: ANNIVERSARY. Dec 10, 1898. Following the conclusion of the Spanish-American War in 1898, American and Spanish ambassadors met at Paris, France, to negotiate a treaty. Under the terms of this treaty, Spain granted the US the Philippine Islands and the islands of Guam and Puerto Rico, and agreed to withdraw from Cuba. Senatorial debate over the treaty centered on the US's move toward imperialism by acquiring the Philippines. A vote was taken Feb 6, 1899, and the treaty passed by a one-vote margin. President William McKinley signed the treaty Feb 10, 1899.

UNITED NATIONS: HUMAN RIGHTS DAY: ANNIVERSARY. Dec 10. Official United Nations observance day. Date is the anniversary of adoption of the "Universal Declaration of Human Rights" in 1948. The Declaration sets forth basic rights and fundamental freedoms to which all men and women everywhere in the world are entitled. For info: United Nations, Dept of Public Info, New York, NY 10017. E-mail: inquiries@un.org.

UNITED NATIONS: THIRD DECADE TO COMBAT RACISM AND RACIAL DISCRIMINATION: YEAR EIGHT. Dec 10. In 1973 the United Nations General Assembly proclaimed the years 1973–83, beginning Dec 10, UN Human Rights Day, as the Decade to Combat Racism and Racial Discrimination. Renewing its efforts, the UN designated the years

1983–93 as the Second Decade to Combat Racism and Racial Discrimination. The adopted Program of Action states the decade's goals and outlines the measures to be taken at the regional, national and international levels to achieve them. In Res 47/77 of Dec 16, 1992, the Assembly called upon the international community to provide resources for the program to be carried out during a third decade (1993–2003), particularly for the monitoring of the transition from apartheid in South Africa. Info from: United Nations, Dept of Public Info, New York, NY 10017.

BIRTHDAYS TODAY

Kenneth Branagh, 41, actor, director (*High Season, Henry V*), born Belfast, Northern Ireland, Dec 10, 1960.

Susan Dey, 49, model, actress ("The Partridge Family," "LA Law,"), born Pekin, IL, Dec 10, 1952.

Harold Gould, 78, actor ("Rhoda," "Under One Roof"), born Schenectady, NY, Dec 10, 1923.

Gloria Loring, 55, singer, actress ("Days of Our Lives"), born New York, NY, Dec 10, 1946.

DECEMBER 11 — TUESDAY
Day 345 — 20 Remaining

ALASKA'S FIRST BROADCAST TELEVISION STATION: ANNIVERSARY. Dec 11, 1953. At 6 PM, on this date, KTVA, Channel 11, at Anchorage, AK, signed on the air, becoming Alaska's first broadcast station.

BATTLE OF THE BULLS: ANNIVERSARY. Dec 11, 1846. Sandy, UT. In one of the most unusual battles in military history, US soldiers of the Mormon Battalion were attacked by a herd of wild longhorn bulls while camped on the San Pedro River in Arizona just 10 miles from present-day Tombstone. Men and mules were injured and wagons damaged. Several of the bulls were shot and killed. Lieutenant George Stoneman, one of the injured soldiers, later became Governor of California 1883–87.

BUELL, MARJORIE H.: BIRTH ANNIVERSARY. Dec 11, 1904. Cartoonist, creator of comic strip character Little Lulu, Marjorie Buell was considered a pioneer for creating a female character that outsmarted the neighborhood boys. She was born at Philadelphia, PA, and died May 30, 1993, at Elyria, OH.

BURKINA FASO: NATIONAL DAY. Dec 11. Gained independence within the French community, 1958.

CANNON, ANNIE JUMP: BIRTH ANNIVERSARY. Dec 11, 1863. American astronomer and discoverer of five stars, was born at Dover, DE. Author and winner of the National Academy of Science Draper Medal, she died at Cambridge, MA, Apr 13, 1941.

CLUTE'S CHRISTMAS IN THE PARK. Dec 11–14. Clute Municipal Park, Clute, TX. A Christmas event with nightly entertainment, Santa's Land, a beautifully decorated Christmas tree forest and a marshmallow roasting pit. Great family fun for all ages. Food and crafts. Annually, the second Tuesday through Friday in December. Est attendance: 4,500. For info: Clute Parks and Recreation, PO Box 997, Clute, TX 77531. Phone: (800) 371-2971 or (979) 265-8392. Fax: (979) 265-8767.

EDWARD VIII ABDICATION: 65th ANNIVERSARY. Dec 11, 1936. Christened Edward Albert Christian George Andrew Patrick David, King Edward VIII was born at Richmond Park, England, on June 12, 1894, and became Prince of Wales in July 1911. He ascended to the English throne upon the death of his father, George V, on Jan 20, 1936, but coronation never took place. He abdicated on Dec 11, 1936, in order to marry "the woman I love," twice-divorced American Wallis Warfield Simpson. They were married in France, June 3, 1937. Edward was named Duke of Windsor by his brother-successor, George VI. The Duke died at Paris, May 28, 1972, but was buried in England, near Windsor Castle.

"THE GABBY HAYES SHOW" TV PREMIERE: ANNIVERSARY. Dec 11, 1950. George "Gabby" Hayes, veteran of western movies, hosted two series: the first was a 15-minute weekday show; the second, a half-hour Saturday morning show. On both shows, Hayes showed clips from old westerns.

INDIANA: ADMISSION DAY: ANNIVERSARY. Dec 11. Became 19th state in 1816.

LA GUARDIA, FIORELLO HENRY: BIRTH ANNIVERSARY. Dec 11, 1882. Popularly known as the "Little Flower," Fiorello H. La Guardia was not too busy as mayor of New York City to read the "funnies" to radio listeners during the New York newspaper strike. He said of himself: "When I make a mistake it's a beaut!" La Guardia was born at New York, NY, and died there Sept 20, 1947.

"MAGNUM, PI" TV PREMIERE: ANNIVERSARY. Dec 11, 1980. Premiered on CBS starring Tom Selleck in the title role of Thomas Magnum, private investigator in Hawaii. Other cast regulars were John Hillerman as Jonathan Quayle Higgins, Roger E. Mosley as Theodore Calvin ("TC") and Larry Manetti as Orville "Rick" Wright. Final episode aired May 1, 1988. "Magnum" fans enjoy an open house at "Magnum Memorabilia" (the nonprofit research/production foundation and full-service fan information clearinghouse) in celebration of this day every year. Episode viewings and costume/prop exhibits are featured. For info: David Romas, Dir, 1581 Moorhouse, Ferndale, MI 48220. E-mail: ac2942@wayne.edu.

SPACE MILESTONE: *MARS CLIMATE ORBITER* (US). Dec 11, 1998. This unmanned craft was to track the water vapor over Mars which it was scheduled to reach in September 1999. However, it burned up just before beginning to circle the planet. Its companion, *Mars Polar Lander*, was launched Jan 3, 1999, and was to land on Mars, burrow into the ground and analyze the soil. However, on Dec 3, 1999, just before landing, all communications with the craft were lost.

UNITED NATIONS: UNICEF: 55th ANNIVERSARY. Dec 11, 1946. Anniversary of the establishment by the United Nations General Assembly of the United Nations International Children's Emergency Fund (UNICEF). For info: United Nations, Dept of Public Info, New York, NY 10017. Web: www.unicef.org.

BIRTHDAYS TODAY

Max Baucus, 60, US Senator (D, Montana), born Helena, MT, Dec 11, 1941.

Jay Bell, 36, baseball player, born Pensacola, FL, Dec 11, 1965.

Teri Garr, 52, actress (*Young Frankenstein, Tootsie, The Black Stallion*), born Lakewood, OH, Dec 11, 1949.

David Gates, 61, singer, songwriter, born Tulsa, OK, Dec 11, 1940.

Tom Hayden, 61, journalist, activist, politician, born Royal Oak, MI, Dec 11, 1940.

Jermaine Jackson, 47, singer, musician (Jackson 5, "Daddy's Home,"), born Gary, IN, Dec 11, 1954.

John F. Kerry, 58, US Senator (D, Massachusetts), born Denver, CO, Dec 11, 1943.

Brenda Lee (Brenda Mae Tarpley), 57, singer ("I'm Sorry," "All Alone Am I"), born Atlanta, GA, Dec 11, 1944.

Donna Mills, 58, actress ("Knots Landing," "Melrose Place"), born Chicago, IL, Dec 11, 1943.

Rita Moreno, 70, singer, actress (Oscar for *West Side Story*; Tony for *The Ritz*), born Hunacao, Puerto Rico, Dec 11, 1931.

Carlo Ponti, 88, producer, born Milan, Italy, Dec 11, 1913.

Susan Seidelman, 49, filmmaker (*Desperately Seeking Susan, Making Mr Right*), born Philadelphia, PA, Dec 11, 1952.

	S	M	T	W	T	F	S
December							1
2001	2	3	4	5	6	7	8
	9	10	11	12	13	14	15
	16	17	18	19	20	21	22
	23	24	25	26	27	28	29
	30	31					

Aleksandr Isayevich Solzhenitsyn, 83, author (*Cancer Ward, One Day in the Life of Ivan Denisovich, The Gulag Archipelago*), born Kislovodsk, USSR, Dec 11, 1918.

Rider Strong, 22, actor ("Boy Meets World"), born San Francisco, CA, Dec 11, 1979.

Ken Wahl, 48, actor ("Wiseguy," *The Wanderers, Fort Apache, The Bronx*), born Chicago, IL, Dec 11, 1953.

Curtis Williams, 39, musician, singer (Penguins, "Earth Angel"), born Buffalo, NY, Dec 11, 1962.

DECEMBER 12 — WEDNESDAY

Day 346 — 19 Remaining

BONZA BOTTLER DAY™. Dec 12. To celebrate when the number of the day is the same as the number of the month. Bonza Bottler Day™ is an excuse to have a party at least once a month. For more information, see Jan 1. For info: Gail M. Berger, 109 Matthew Ave, Poca, WV 25159. Phone: (304) 776-7746. E-mail: gberger5@aol.com.

DAY OF OUR LADY OF GUADALUPE. Dec 12. The legend of Guadalupe tells how in December 1531, an Indian, Juan Diego, saw the Virgin Mother on a hill near Mexico City, who instructed him to go to the bishop and have him build a shrine to her on the site of the vision. After his request was initially rebuffed, the Virgin Mother appeared to Juan Diego three days later. She instructed him to pick roses growing on a stony and barren hillside nearby and take them to the bishop as proof. Although flowers do not normally bloom in December, Juan Diego found the roses and took them to the bishop. As he opened his mantle to drop the roses on the floor, an image of the Virgin Mary appeared among them. The bishop built the sanctuary as instructed. Our Lady of Guadalupe became the patroness of Mexico City and by 1746 was the patron saint of all New Spain and by 1910 of all Latin America.

FIRST BLACK SERVES IN US HOUSE OF REPRE-SENTATIVES: ANNIVERSARY. Dec 12, 1870. Joseph Hayne Rainey of Georgetown, SC, was sworn in as the first black to serve in the US House of Representatives. Rainey filled the seat of Benjamin Franklin Whittemore, which had been declared vacant by the House. He served until Mar 3, 1879.

FLAUBERT, GUSTAVE: BIRTH ANNIVERSARY. Dec 12, 1821. French author whose works include one of the greatest French novels, *Madame Bovary*, was born at Rouen. Flaubert died at Croisset, France, May 8, 1880.

GARRISON, WILLIAM LLOYD: BIRTH ANNIVER-SARY. Dec 12, 1805. American antislavery leader, poet and journalist, was born at Newburyport, MA. Garrison died at New York, NY, May 24, 1879.

JAY, JOHN: BIRTH ANNIVERSARY. Dec 12, 1745 (OS). American statesman, diplomat and first chief justice of the US Supreme Court (1789–95), coauthor (with Alexander Hamilton and James Madison) of the influential *Federalist* papers was born at New York, NY. Jay died at Bedford, NY, May 17, 1829.

KENYA: JAMHURI DAY. Dec 12. Jamhuri Day (Independence Day) is Kenya's official National Day, commemorating proclamation of the republic and independence from Britain in 1963.

MEXICO: GUADALUPE DAY. Dec 12. One of Mexico's major celebrations. Honors the "Dark Virgin of Guadalupe," the republic's patron saint. Parties and pilgrimages, with special ceremonies at the Shrine of Our Lady of Guadalupe at Mexico City.

PENNSYLVANIA RATIFIES CONSTITUTION: ANNI-VERSARY. Dec 12, 1787. Pennsylvania became the second state to ratify the US Constitution, by a vote of 46 to 23, in 1787.

POINSETTIA DAY (JOEL ROBERTS POINSETT: DEATH ANNIVERSARY). Dec 12. A day to enjoy poinsettias and to honor Dr. Joel Roberts Poinsett, the American diplomat who introduced the Central American plant which is named for him into the US. Poinsett was born at Charleston, SC,

Mar 2, 1799. He also served as a member of Congress and as secretary of war. He died near Statesburg, SC, Dec 12, 1851. The poinsettia has become a favorite Christmas season plant.

RUSSIA: CONSTITUTION DAY. Dec 12. National holiday commemorating the adoption of a new constitution in 1993.

RUSSIAN ELECTION SURPRISE: ANNIVERSARY. Dec 12, 1993. In a shocking rebuke to Boris Yeltsin's attempts to stabilize the country, Russian voters gave Vladimir Zhironovsky and his misnamed Liberal Democratic Party 28 percent of the vote, granting them a large block of power in the new Russian Parliament and the world's imagination. Zhironovsky's platform, which has been called racist and fascist, tapped into a groundswell of nationalist fervor with calls to return Russia to the glory days of its empire and emphasizing harsh treatment for minorities and those who would stand in his way.

"SEZ WHO? SINATRA!". Dec 12. Marchinetti's Ristorante Italiano, Winfield, IL. Game show commemorating birthdate of Frank Sinatra (Dec 12, 1915), in which contestants try to complete lyrics from as many songs recorded by Sinatra. Cosponsored by Radisson Hotel & Suites Chicago. Est attendance: 100. For info: Rich Bysina, 853 Lorlyn Dr, #3D, West Chicago, IL 60185. Phone: (630) 876-9615.

SINATRA, FRANK: BIRTH ANNIVERSARY. Dec 12, 1915. Born at Hoboken, NJ, Frank Sinatra matured from a teen idol to the premiere singer of American popular music. Known as the "Chairman of the Board" to his fans, he made more than 200 albums. His signature songs included "All the Way," "New York, New York" and "My Way." His film career included musicals (*On the Town* and *Pal Joey*) and two gritty films for which he won Oscar nominations, *From Here to Eternity* and *The Man With the Golden Arm.* Died May 14, 1998, at Los Angeles, CA.

WATIE, STAND: BIRTH ANNIVERSARY. Dec 12, 1806. Born at Rome, GA, and died there Sept 9, 1871. Cherokee chief who, by signing the treaty of New Echota, surrendered his people's land in Georgia, forcing relocation to Oklahoma. Though the three other signers were murdered, Watie escaped and went on to initiate the first volunteer Cherokee regiment for the Confederates in the Civil War. Promoted to brigadier general, he was active in destroying the property of other Native Americans who supported the Union.

BIRTHDAYS TODAY

Tracy Ann Austin, 39, former tennis player, born Rolling Hills Estates, CA, Dec 12, 1962.

Bob Barker, 78, TV personality, game-show host (Emmy for "The Price Is Right"), born Darrington, WA, Dec 12, 1923.

Mayim Bialik, 26, actress ("Blossom"), born San Diego, CA, Dec 12, 1975.

Sheila E (Sheila Escoveda), 42, singer, musician ("The Glamorous Life"), born San Francisco, CA, Dec 12, 1959.

Connie Francis (Constance Franconero), 63, singer ("Where the Boys Are"), born Newark, NJ, Dec 12, 1938.

Edward Irwin Koch, 77, former mayor of New York City, born New York, NY, Dec 12, 1924.

Robert Lindsay, 52, actor (*Me and My Girl* [Olivier, Tony, Theatre World and Drama Desk Awards]), born Derbyshire, England, Dec 12, 1949.

Robert Lee (Bob) Pettit, Jr, 69, Basketball Hall of Fame forward and center, born Baton Rouge, LA, Dec 12, 1932.

Cathy Rigby, 49, former Olympic gymnast, born Long Beach, CA, Dec 12, 1952.

Dionne Warwick, 60, singer ("I Say a Little Prayer for You," "This Girl's in Love With You"), born East Orange, NJ, Dec 12, 1941.

DECEMBER 13 — THURSDAY

Day 347 — 18 Remaining

BROOKS, PHILLIPS: BIRTH ANNIVERSARY. Dec 13, 1835. American clergyman and composer born at Boston, MA. Perhaps best remembered for his lyrics for the Christmas carol "O Little Town of Bethlehem." Brooks died at Boston, Jan 23, 1893.

HEINE, HEINRICH: BIRTH ANNIVERSARY. Dec 13, 1797. German poet and critic, born at Dusseldorf. Died at Paris, France, Feb 17, 1856.

LINCOLN, MARY TODD: BIRTH ANNIVERSARY. Dec 13, 1818. Wife of Abraham Lincoln, sixteenth president of the US, born at Lexington, KY. Died at Springfield, IL, July 16, 1882.

MALTA: REPUBLIC DAY. Dec 13. National holiday. Malta became a republic in 1974.

NEW ZEALAND FIRST SIGHTED BY EUROPEANS: ANNIVERSARY. Dec 13, 1642. Captain Abel Tasman of the Dutch East India Company first sighted New Zealand but was kept from landing by Maori warriors. In 1769 Captain James Cook landed and claimed formal possession for Great Britain.

NORTH AND SOUTH KOREA END WAR: 10th ANNIVERSARY. Dec 13, 1991. North and South Korea signed a treaty of reconciliation and nonaggression, formally ending the Korean War—38 years after fighting ceased in 1953. This agreement was not hailed as a peace treaty, and the armistice that was signed July 27, 1953, between the UN and North Korea, was to remain in effect until it could be transformed into a formal peace.

SWEDEN: SANTA LUCIA DAY. Dec 13. Nationwide celebration of festival of light, honoring St. Lucia. Many hotels have their own Lucia, a young girl attired in a long, flowing white gown, who serves guests coffee and lussekatter (saffron buns) in the early morning.

THOMASVILLE'S VICTORIAN CHRISTMAS. Dec 13–14. Downtown Thomasville relives Christmas past as it celebrates the Victorian era of the late 1800s. Costumed strollers and carolers, horse-drawn carriages, bell-ringers and colorful characters from the past fill the streets of downtown. Victorian-clad merchants welcome shoppers with hot cider and confections and street vendors offer Christmas delicacies. Free—wonderful family event. Est attendance: 25,000. For info: Sharlene Celaya, Thomasville Victorian Christmas, Thomasville Main Street, PO Box 1540, Thomasville, GA 31799. Phone: (912) 227-7099. E-mail: mainstrt@rose.net. Web: www.thomasvillega.com.

December 2001	S	M	T	W	T	F	S
							1
	2	3	4	5	6	7	8
	9	10	11	12	13	14	15
	16	17	18	19	20	21	22
	23	24	25	26	27	28	29
	30	31					

BIRTHDAYS TODAY

Steve Buscemi, 43, actor (*Fargo, Pulp Fiction*), born Brooklyn, NY, Dec 13, 1958.

John Davidson, 60, singer, actor (*Edward Scissorhands*, "Hollywood Squares"), born Pittsburgh, PA, Dec 13, 1941.

Larry Doby, 77, Baseball Hall of Fame outfielder and former manager, born Camden, SC, Dec 13, 1924.

Sergei Fedorov, 32, hockey player, born Pskov, Russia, Dec 13, 1969.

Jamie Foxx, 34, actor (*The Truth About Cats and Dogs*, "The Jamie Foxx Show"), born Dallas, TX, Dec 13, 1967.

Wendie Malick, 51, actress ("Just Shoot Me"), born Buffalo, NY, Dec 13, 1950.

Ted Nugent, 52, singer (with Amboy Dukes: "Journey to the Center of the Mind"; solo: "Cat Scratch Fever"), born Detroit, MI, Dec 13, 1949.

Christopher Plummer, 72, actor (Emmy for *The Moneychangers; The Sound of Music, Dolores Claiborne*), born Toronto, Ontario, Canada, Dec 13, 1929.

Robert Prosky, 71, actor ("Hill St. Blues," "Veronica's Closet"), born Philadelphia, PA, Dec 13, 1930.

Dick Van Dyke, 76, actor, comedian (*Mary Poppins*, "The Dick Van Dyke Show," "Diagnosis Murder"), born West Plains, MO, Dec 13, 1925.

Tom Vilsack, 51, Governor of Iowa (D), born Pittsburgh, PA, Dec 13, 1950.

DECEMBER 14 — FRIDAY

Day 348 — 17 Remaining

ALABAMA: ADMISSION DAY: ANNIVERSARY. Dec 14. Became 22nd state in 1819.

DOOLITTLE, JAMES HAROLD: BIRTH ANNIVERSARY. Dec 14, 1896. American aviator and World War II hero General James Doolittle was born at Alameda, CA. A Lieutenant General in the US Army Air Force, he was the first person to fly across North America in less than a day. On Apr 18, 1942, Doolittle led a squadron of 16 B-25 bombers, launched from aircraft carriers, on the first US aerial raid on Japan of WWII. He was awarded the Congressional Medal of Honor for this accomplishment. Doolittle also headed the Eighth Air Force during the Normandy invasion. He died Sept 27, 1993, at Pebble Beach, CA.

EGYPT: MARITIME DISASTER: 10th ANNIVERSARY. Dec 14, 1991. The ferry *Salem Express* sank off the port city of Safaga, Egypt, claiming the lives of 462 passengers and crew members. 180 people survived the disaster, the worst in modern Egypt's maritime history.

HALCYON DAYS. Dec 14–28. Traditionally, the seven days before and the seven days after the winter solstice. To the ancients a time when fabled bird (called the halcyon—pronounced hal-cee-on) calmed the wind and waves—a time of calm and tranquility.

MOON PHASE: NEW MOON. Dec 14. Moon enters New Moon phase at 3:47 PM, EST.

NOSTRADAMUS: BIRTH ANNIVERSARY. Dec 14, 1503. French physician, best remembered for his astrological predictions (written in rhymed quatrains), was born Michel de Notredame, at St. Remy, Provence, France. Many believed that his book of prophecies actually foretold the future. Nostradamus died at Salon, France, July 2, 1566.

REMICK, LEE: BIRTH ANNIVERSARY. Dec 14, 1935. American actress Lee Remick was born at Quincy, MA. Her films include *A Face in the Crowd* (1957), *Anatomy of a Murder* (1959) and *Days of Wine and Roses* (1963). She died July 2, 1991, at Los Angeles, CA.

SMITH, MARGARET CHASE: BIRTH ANNIVERSARY. Dec 14, 1897. American politician Margaret Madeline Chase Smith was born at Skowhegan, ME. As the first woman to be elected to both houses of Congress (1941 to the House and 1949 to the Senate), she was also one of seven Republican senators to issue a "declaration of conscience" to denounce Senator Joseph R. McCarthy's communist witch-hunt. She died May 29, 1995, at Skowhegan, ME.

SOLAR ECLIPSE. Dec 14. Annular eclipse of the sun. Eclipse begins at 1:03 PM, EST, reaches greatest eclipse at 3:44 PM and ends at 6:40 PM. Visible in Pacific Ocean, NW South America, Central America, USA, western and southern parts of Canada.

SOUTH POLE DISCOVERY: 90th ANNIVERSARY. Dec 14, 1911. The elusive object of many expeditions dating from the 7th century, the South Pole was located and visited by Roald Amundsen with four companions and 52 sled dogs. All five men and 12 of the dogs returned to base camp safely. Next to visit the South Pole, Jan 17, 1912, was a party of five led by Captain Robert F. Scott, all of whom perished during the return trip. A search party found their frozen bodies 11 months later. See also: "Amundsen, Roald: Birth Anniversary" (July 16).

BIRTHDAYS TODAY

Craig Biggio, 36, baseball player, born Smithtown, NY, Dec 14, 1965.

Jane Birkin, 55, actress (*Blowup, Death on the Nile, Evil Under the Sun*), born London, England, Dec 14, 1946.

Leonardo Boff, 63, Brazilian Catholic theologian, born Concordia, Brazil, Dec 14, 1938.

William Joseph (Bill) Buckner, 52, former baseball player, born Vallejo, CA, Dec 14, 1949.

Patty Duke, 55, actress (Oscar for *The Miracle Worker*; Emmy for *My Sweet Charlie*), born New York, NY, Dec 14, 1946.

Don Hewitt, 79, TV news producer, born New York, NY, Dec 14, 1922.

Dee Wallace Stone, 53, actress (*10, E.T. The Extra-Terrestrial*), born Kansas City, MO, Dec 14, 1948.

DECEMBER 15 — SATURDAY
Day 349 — 16 Remaining

AFRICAN AMERICAN HOLIDAY EXPO. Dec 15–16. Washington DC. The oldest, East Coast marketplace that celebrates Christmas and the cultural holiday, Kwanzaa. The Expo offers food, fun, inner-attainment, workshops and more than 160 merchants in an African Marketplace atmosphere. Est attendance: 12,000. For info: African American Holiday Assn, 1305 Emerson St NW, Washington, DC 20011. Phone: (202) 310-1430. E-mail: aaha@aaha-info.org. Web: www.aaha-info.org.

BATTLE OF SAN PIETRO: ANNIVERSARY. Dec 15, 1943. A German panzer battalion inflicted heavy casualties on American forces trying to take the 700-year-old Italian village of San Pietro, before withdrawing from the town. San Pietro was reduced almost entirely to rubble. The American movie director John Huston, serving as an Army lieutenant, filmed the battle for the military. So graphic was the film that it was described as anti-war by the military brass at the War Department. The film was cut from five to three reels before censors allowed it to be released in 1944. It was later re-edited for the television series "The Big Picture."

BELLSOUTH WINTERFEST BOAT PARADE PRESENTED BY NOKIA. Dec 15. More than 100 decorated yachts sail up Fort Lauderdale's Intracoastal Waterway starting at Port Everglades. Est attendance: 850,000. For info: Winterfest, 512 NE 3rd Ave, Fort Lauderdale, FL 33301. Phone: (954) 767-0686. Fax: (954) 767-0665. E-mail: boats@winterfestparade .com. Web: winterfestparade.com.

★ **BILL OF RIGHTS DAY.** Dec 15. Presidential Proclamation. Has been proclaimed each year since 1962, but was omitted in 1967 and 1968. (Issued in 1941 and 1946 at Congressional request and in 1947 without request.) Since 1968 has been included in Human Rights Day and Week Proclamation.

BILL OF RIGHTS: ANNIVERSARY. Dec 15, 1791. The first 10 amendments to the US Constitution, known as the Bill of Rights, became effective following ratification by Virginia. The anniversary of ratification and of effect is observed as Bill of Rights Day.

CURACAO: KINGDOM DAY AND ANTILLEAN FLAG DAY. Dec 15. This day commemorates the Charter of Kingdom, signed in 1954 at the Knight's Hall at The Hague, granting the Netherlands Antilles complete autonomy. The Antillean Flag was hoisted for the first time on this day in 1959.

"DAVY CROCKETT" TV PREMIERE: ANNIVERSARY. Dec 15, 1954. This show, a series of five segments, can be considered TV's first miniseries. Shown on Walt Disney's "Disneyland" show, it starred Fess Parker as American western hero Davy Crockett and was immensely popular. The show spawned Crockett paraphernalia, including the famous coonskin cap (even after we found out that Boone never wore a coonskin cap).

EIFFEL, ALEXANDRE GUSTAVE: BIRTH ANNIVERSARY. Dec 15, 1832. Eiffel, the French engineer who designed the 1,000 ft-high, million-dollar, open-lattice wrought iron Eiffel Tower, and who participated in designing the Statue of Liberty, was born at Dijon, France. The Eiffel Tower, weighing more than 7,000 tons, was built for the Paris International Exposition of 1889. Eiffel died at Paris, France, Dec 23, 1923.

INTERNATIONAL LANGUAGE WEEK. Dec 15–21. To disseminate information about mankind's quest for an international language to solve the communication problem of humans, and to supply information about the international language, Esperanto. Esperanto was created in 1887 by Dr. L.L. Zamenhof as a solution to the world's language problem. For complete info, send $4 to cover expense of printing, handling and postage. Annually, Dec 15–21. For info: Dr. Stanley Drake, Pres, Intl Society of Friendship and Good Will, 8592 Roswell Rd, Ste 434, Atlanta, GA 30350-1870.

MILITARY DICTATORSHIP ENDED IN CHILE: ANNIVERSARY. Dec 15, 1989. In an election on this date, Patricio Aylwin defeated General Augusto Pinochet's former finance minister, Hernan Buchi, bringing the military dictatorship of Pinochet to an end. Fourteen months previously, Pinochet suffered defeat in a national plebiscite on eight more years of his rule. This defeat prompted democratic elections and crippled the Pinochet regime. Pinochet came to power when the military overthrew a democratically elected government and killed Marxist president Salvador Allende in a 1973 coup. Patricio Aylwin avoided a two-candidate runoff by achieving 55.2 percent of the vote. He was inaugurated on Mar 11, 1990.

NAIA FOOTBALL NATIONAL CHAMPIONSHIP GAME. Dec 15. Savannah, TN. 16-team field competes, ending with the final two teams vying for the national championship. 46th annual game. For info: Natl Assn of Intercollegiate Athletics, 6120 S Yale Ave, Ste 1450, Tulsa, OK 74136-4223. Phone: (918) 494-8828. Fax: (918) 494-8841. E-mail: thasseltine@naia .org. Web: www.naia.org.

Happy Holiday

ONE DAY. Dec 15. San Francisco, CA. Celebrating a new "melting pot" tradition of inclusiveness, Men of All Colors Together's One Day holiday echoes Martin Luther King, Jr's vision of global harmony by combining the December celebrations of Christmas, Hanukkah, Kwanzaa, Las Posadas and Winter Solstice, as well as other individual personal traditions, into One Day that celebrates diversity and embraces love among us all, as one. For info: Men of All Colors Together, San Francisco Bay Area, 2261 Market St, PMB 629, San Francisco, CA 94114. E-mail: mactsfba@go .to. Web: go.to/MACTSFBA.

PUERTO RICO: NAVIDADES. Dec 15–Jan 6. Traditional Christmas season begins mid-December and ends on Three Kings Day. Elaborate nativity scenes, carolers, special Christmas foods and trees from Canada and US. Gifts on Christmas Day and on Three Kings Day.

SALEM CHRISTMAS. Dec 15. Winston-Salem, NC. Re-creation of Christmas season as Moravian records indicate that early 19th-century Salem might have observed it. Choral and church band music, craft and trades demonstrations and special decorations. Est attendance: 5,000. For info: Bill Cissna, Old Salem, Inc, Box F, Winston-Salem, NC 27108. Phone: (888) OLD-SALEM.

SITTING BULL: DEATH ANNIVERSARY. Dec 15, 1890. Famous Sioux Indian leader, medicine man and warrior of the Hunkpapa Teton band. Known also by his native name, Tatanka-yatanka, Sitting Bull was born on the Grand River, SD. He first accompanied his father on the warpath at the age of 14 against the Crow and thereafter rapidly gained influence within his tribe. In 1886 he led a raid on Fort Buford. His steadfast refusal to go to a reservation led General Phillip Sheridan to initiate a campaign against him which led to the massacre of Lieutenant Colonel George Custer's men at the Little Bighorn, after which Sitting Bull fled to Canada, remaining there until 1881. Although many in his tribe surrendered on their return, Sitting Bull remained hostile until his death in a skirmish with US.

SPACE MILESTONE: *VEGA 1* (USSR). Dec 15, 1984. Craft launched this date to rendezvous with Halley's Comet in March 1986. *Vega 2*, launched Dec 21, 1984, was part of same mission which, in cooperation with the US, carried US-built "comet-dust" detection equipment.

34th STREET EXPRESS. Dec 15. Chartered Amtrak train leaves from Boston, MA. Christmas shopping special to New York City also takes in the Radio City Christmas Spectacular. Annually, the second Saturday in December. Est attendance: 500. For info: Mystic Valley Railway Soc, Inc, PO Box 365486, Hyde Park, MA 02136-0009. Phone: (617) 361-4445. Fax: (617) 361-4445*51 (dial all as one number).

US FORCES LAND IN MINDORO, PHILIPPINES: ANNIVERSARY. Dec 15, 1944. After the usual barrage from naval guns, the US 24th Division landed on Mindoro, the largest of the islands immediately south of Luzon (the most important island of the Philippines). American soldiers easily advanced eight miles inland, took the perimeter of their beachhead and started construction of an airfield. Japanese kamikaze counterattacks, however, sank two motor torpedo boats and damaged the escort carrier *Marcus Island*, two destroyers and a third motor torpedo boat, making Mindoro a costly conquest.

A VICTORIAN YULETIDE. Dec 15–17. Clinton, MD. Candlelight tours with holiday greenery, antique toys, cards, ornaments, music and Father Christmas. Est attendance: 800. For info: Surratt House and Tavern, PO Box 427, Clinton, MD 20735. Phone: (301) 868-1121. Fax: (301) 868-8177. Web: www.surratt.org.

ZAMENHOF, DR. L.L.: BIRTH ANNIVERSARY. Dec 15, 1859 (OS). Lazarus Ludovic Zamenhof was born at Bialystok, near the borders of Lithuania, Poland and Byelorussia, where many different languages were spoken. Zamenhof realized the need for a common tongue while a child and later developed the International Language, Esperanto, which means "he who hopes." Died Apr 14, 1917, at Warsaw, Poland. For complete information about Esperanto and this worldwide organization, please send $4 to cover expense of printing, handling and postage. For info: Dr. Stanley Drake, Pres, Intl Society of Friendship and Good Will, 8592 Roswell Rd, Ste 434, Atlanta, GA 30350-1870.

	S	M	T	W	T	F	S
December							1
	2	3	4	5	6	7	8
2001	9	10	11	12	13	14	15
	16	17	18	19	20	21	22
	23	24	25	26	27	28	29
	30	31					

DECEMBER 16 — SUNDAY
Day 350 — 15 Remaining

AUSTEN, JANE: BIRTH ANNIVERSARY. Dec 16, 1775. English novelist (*Pride and Prejudice, Sense and Sensibility*), born at Steventon, Hampshire, England. Died July 18, 1817, at Winchester, England.

BAHRAIN: INDEPENDENCE DAY: 30th ANNIVERSARY. Dec 16. National holiday. Commemorates independence from British protection in 1971.

BANGLADESH: VICTORY DAY: 30th ANNIVERSARY. Dec 16. National holiday. Commemorates victory over Pakistan in 1971. The former East Pakistan became Bangladesh.

BARBIE AND BARNEY BACKLASH DAY. Dec 16. If we have to explain this to you, you don't have kids. It's one day each year when Mom and Dad can tell the kids that Barbie and Barney don't exist. [© 2000 by WH]. For info: Tom and Ruth Roy, Wellcat Holidays, 2418 Long Ln, Lebanon, PA 17046. Phone: (717) 279-0184. E-mail: wellcat@supernet.com. Web: www.wellcat.com.

BATTLE OF NASHVILLE: ANNIVERSARY. Dec 16, 1864. On the second day of battle at Nashville, Union troops defeated Confederate forces under General John B. Hood, essentially knocking the Confederate Army of Tennessee out of the war.

BATTLE OF THE BULGE: ANNIVERSARY. Dec 16, 1944. A German offensive was launched in the Belgian Ardennes Forest, where Hitler had managed to concentrate 250,000 men. The Nazi commanders, hoping to minimize any aerial counterattack by the Allies, chose a time when foggy, rainy weather prevailed and the initial attack by eight armored divisions along a 75-mile front took the Allies by surprise, the 5th Panzer Army penetrating to within 20 miles of crossings on the Meuse River. US troops were able to hold fast at bottlenecks in the Ardennes, but by the end of December the German push had penetrated 65 miles into the Allied lines (though their line had narrowed from the initial 75 miles to 20 miles). By that time the Allies began to respond and the Germans were stopped by Montgomery on the Meuse and by Patton at Bastogne. The weather then cleared and Allied aircraft began to bomb the German forces and supply lines by Dec 26. The Allies reestablished their original line by Jan 21, 1945.

BEETHOVEN, LUDWIG VAN: BIRTH ANNIVERSARY. Dec 16, 1770. Regarded by many as the greatest orchestral composer of all time, Ludwig van Beethoven was born at Bonn, Germany. Impairment of his hearing began before he was 30, but even total deafness did not halt his composing and conducting. His last appearance on the concert stage was to conduct the premiere of his *Ninth Symphony*, at Vienna, May 7, 1824. He was unable to hear either the orchestra or the applause. Often in love, he never married. Of a stormy temperament, he is said to have died during a violent thunderstorm Mar 26, 1827, at Vienna.

BOSTON TEA PARTY: ANNIVERSARY. Dec 16, 1773. Anniversary of Boston patriots' boarding of British vessel at anchor at Boston Harbor. Contents of nearly 350 chests of tea were dumped into the harbor.

CALABRIA EARTHQUAKE: ANNIVERSARY. Dec 16, 1857. Calabria—an especially quake-prone region near Naples, Italy—experienced "a big one" that left more than 10,000 people dead and entire villages devastated. Between 1783 (the last big quake) and 1857, about 111,000 people lost their lives in the unstable region.

"DRAGNET" TV PREMIERE: 50th ANNIVERSARY. Dec 16, 1951. This famous crime show stressed authenticity, and episodes were supposedly based on real cases. It starred Jack Webb as stoic and determined Sergeant Joe Friday, a man whose life was his investigative police work and who was recognized by his recurring line, "Just the facts, ma'am." Friday had many partners: Barton Yarborough played Sergeant Ben Romero for three episodes; for the rest of the season Barney Phillips played Sergeant Ed Jacobs and Ben Alexander played his comedic sidekick, Officer Frank Smith. Dorothy Abbott and Marjie Millar played Friday's romantic interests. A new version appeared in 1967 with Webb and his new partner, Officer Bill Gannon (Harry Morgan). "Dragnet" is also known for its theme music and its narrative epilogue describing the fate of the bad guys.

EID-AL-FITR: CELEBRATING THE FAST. Dec 16. Islamic calendar date: Shawwal 1, 1422. This feast/festival celebrates the completion of the Ramadan fasting (which began Nov 16) and usually lasts for several days. Everyone wears new clothes; children receive gifts from parents and relatives; children are allowed to stay up late and participate in games, folktales, plays, puppet shows, trips to amusement parks. This holiday is known as Seker Bayram in Turkey and Hari Raya Puasa in South East Asia. Different methods for "anticipating" the visibility of the new moon crescent at Mecca are used by different Muslim groups. US date may vary.

HAWAIIAN CHRISTMAS LOOONG DISTANCE INVITATIONAL ROUGH-H2O SWIM. Dec 16. Waikiki Beach, Honolulu, HI. 7K (4.33 mile) swim across Waikiki Bay and return. Preregistration is required. Hawaii's longest open ocean race. Annually, the week following Honolulu Marathon. This is the 21st annual event. Est attendance: 90. For info: Jim Anderson, One Keahole Place #1607, Honolulu, HI 96825-3414. Fax: (808) 396-8868. E-mail: waikikijim@aol.com.

KAZAKHSTAN, REPUBLIC OF: REPUBLIC DAY: 10th ANNIVERSARY. Dec 16, 1991. National Day. Commemorates independence from the Soviet Union in 1991.

MEAD, MARGARET: 100th BIRTH ANNIVERSARY. Dec 16, 1901. American anthropologist and author, especially known for her studies of peoples of the southwest Pacific area, and for her forthright manner in speaking and writing. Born at Philadelphia, PA, Mead died at New York, NY, Nov 15, 1978.

MEXICO: POSADAS. Dec 16–24. A nine-day annual celebration throughout Mexico. Processions of "pilgrims" knock at doors asking for posada (shelter), commemorating the search by Joseph and Mary for a shelter in which the infant Jesus might be born. Pilgrims are invited inside, and fun and merrymaking ensue with blindfolded guests trying to break a "piñata" (papier mache decorated earthenware utensil filled with gifts and goodies) suspended from the ceiling. Once the piñata is broken, the gifts are distributed and celebration continues.

NEW WORLD SYMPHONY PREMIERE: ANNIVERSARY. Dec 16, 1893. Anton Dvorak's *New World Symphony* premiered at the newly erected Carnegie Hall with the New York Philharmonic playing. The composer attended and enjoyed enthusiastic applause from the audience. The symphony contains snatches from black spirituals and American folk music. Dvorak, a Bohemian, had been in the US only a year when he composed it as a greeting to his friends in Europe.

"ONE DAY AT A TIME" TV PREMIERE: ANNIVERSARY. Dec 16, 1975. This sitcom about a divorced mother raising two girls in Indianapolis starred Bonnie Franklin as Ann Romano, Mackenzie Phillips and Valerie Bertinelli as daughters Julie and Barbara Cooper. Other regulars included: Pat Harrington, Jr, as tool-belt-wearing maintenance man Dwayne Schneider, Richard Masur as David Kane, Ann's boyfriend, Mary Louise Wilson as neighbor Ginny Wroblicki, John Hillerman and Charles Siebert as Ann's bosses, John Putch as Barbara's boyfriend and Nanette Fabray as Ann's mother. During the course of the series, all three female leads got married and Ann opened her own ad agency.

PHILIPPINES: PHILIPPINE CHRISTMAS OBSERVANCE. Dec 16–Jan 6. Philippine Islands. Said to be world's longest Christmas celebration.

PHILIPPINES: SIMBANG GABI. Dec 16–25. Nationwide. A nine-day novena of predawn masses, also called "Misa de Gallo." One of the traditional Filipino celebrations of the holiday season.

SANTAYANA, GEORGE: BIRTH ANNIVERSARY. Dec 16, 1863. Philosopher and author born at Madrid, Spain. At the age of nine he emigrated to the US where he attended and later taught at Harvard University. In 1912 he returned to Europe and traveled extensively. It was Santayana who said, "Those who cannot remember the past are condemned to repeat it." He died at Rome, Italy, Sept 26, 1952.

SOUTH AFRICA: RECONCILIATION DAY. Dec 16. National holiday. Celebrates the spirit of reconciliation, national unity and peace amongst all citizens.

TELL SOMEONE THEY'RE DOING A GOOD JOB WEEK. Dec 16–22. Every day this week tell someone "you're doing a good job." For info: Joe Hoppel, Radio Station WCMS, 5589 Greenwich Rd, Virginia Beach, VA 23462. Phone: (757) 671-1000. E-mail: wcms@norfolk.infi.net. Web: www.wcms.com.

UNITED NATIONS REVOKES RESOLUTION ON ZIONISM: 10th ANNIVERSARY. Dec 16, 1991. The United Nations voted 111 to 25 to revoke Resolution 3379, which equated Zionism with racism. Resolution 3379 was approved Nov 10, 1975, with 72 countries voting in favor, 35 against and 32 abstentions. The largest block of changed votes came from the former Soviet Union and Eastern Europe.

BIRTHDAYS TODAY

Bruce N. Ames, 73, biochemist, cancer researcher, born New York, NY, Dec 16, 1928.

Steven Bochco, 58, TV writer, producer ("Hill Street Blues," "NYPD Blue"), born New York, NY, Dec 16, 1943.

Benjamin Bratt, 38, actor ("Law & Order"), born San Francisco, CA, Dec 16, 1963.

Arthur Charles Clarke, 84, author (*2001: A Space Odyssey, Islands in the Sky*), born Minehead, England, Dec 16, 1917.

Alison La Placa, 42, actress ("The John Laroquette Show"), born Lincolnshire, IL, Dec 16, 1959.

William ("The Refrigerator") Perry, 39, former football player, born Aiken, SC, Dec 16, 1962.

Clifford (Cliff) Ralph Robinson, 35, basketball player, born Buffalo, NY, Dec 16, 1966.

Lesley Stahl, 60, journalist ("60 Minutes," former White House correspondent), born Lynn, MA, Dec 16, 1941.

Jon Tenney, 40, actor ("Brooklyn South"), born Princeton, NJ, Dec 16, 1961.

Liv Johanne Ullmann, 62, actress (*The Immigrants, Scenes from a Marriage*), born Tokyo, Japan, Dec 16, 1939.

DECEMBER 17 — MONDAY

Day 351 — 14 Remaining

AZTEC CALENDAR STONE DISCOVERY: ANNIVERSARY. Dec 17, 1790. One of the wonders of the western hemisphere—the Aztec Calendar or Solar Stone—was found beneath the ground by workmen repairing Mexico City's Central Plaza. The centuries-old, intricately carved stone, 11 ft, 8 inches in diameter and weighing nearly 25 tons, proved to be a highly developed calendar monument to the sun. Believed to have been carved in the year 1479, this extraordinary time-counting basalt tablet originally stood in the Great Temple of the Aztecs. Buried along with other Aztec idols, soon after the Spanish conquest in 1521, it remained hidden until 1790. Its 52-year cycle had regulated many Aztec ceremonies, including grisly human sacrifices to save the world from destruction by the gods.

BELGIUM: NUTS FAIR. Dec 17. Bastogne. Traditional cultural observance. Annually, the third Monday in December.

CLEAN AIR ACT PASSED BY CONGRESS: ANNIVERSARY. Dec 17, 1967. A sweeping set of laws passed to protect the nation from air pollution. This was the first legislation to place pollution controls on the automobile industry.

	S	M	T	W	T	F	S
							1
December	2	3	4	5	6	7	8
2001	9	10	11	12	13	14	15
	16	17	18	19	20	21	22
	23	24	25	26	27	28	29
	30	31					

FIRST FLIGHT TRADITIONAL ANNIVERSARY CELEBRATION. Dec 17. Kill Devil Hills, NC. Each year since 1928, on the anniversary of the Wright Brothers' first successful heavier-than-air flight at Kitty Hawk, NC, Dec 17, 1903, a celebration has been held at the Wright Brothers National Memorial, with wreaths, flyover and other observances—regardless of weather.

FLOYD, WILLIAM: BIRTH ANNIVERSARY. Dec 17, 1734. Signer of the Declaration of Independence, member of Congress, born at Brookhaven, Long Island. Died at Westernville, NY, Aug 4, 1821.

HENRY, JOSEPH: BIRTH ANNIVERSARY. Dec 17, 1797. Scientist Joseph Henry was born at Albany, NY. One of his great discoveries was the principle of self-induction; the unit used in the measure of electrical inductance was named the henry in his honor. In 1831 Henry constructed the first model of an electric telegraph with an audible signal. This formed the basis of nearly all later work on commercial wire telegraphy. In 1832 Henry was named professor of natural philosophy at the College of New Jersey, now Princeton University. Henry was involved in the planning of the Smithsonian Institution and became its first secretary in 1846. President Lincoln named Henry as one of the original 50 scientists to make up the National Academy of Sciences in 1863. He served as that organization's president from 1868 until his death May 13, 1878, at Washington, DC.

"HOUSE CALLS" TV PREMIERE: ANNIVERSARY. Dec 17, 1979. This half-hour sitcom set in Kensington General Hospital starred Wayne Rogers as Dr. Charley Michaels and Lynn Redgrave as Ann Anderson, assistant administrator and Michaels's love interest. Also featured was David Wayne as flaky chief of surgery Dr. Amos Wetherby. After a dispute with the producers, Redgrave was dropped in 1982 and replaced by Sharon Gless (as assistant Jane Jeffries) for the rest of the series.

KING, W.L. MACKENZIE: BIRTH ANNIVERSARY. Dec 17, 1874. Former Canadian prime minister, born at Berlin, Ontario. Served 21 years, the longest term of any prime minister in the English-speaking world. Died at Kingsmere, July 22, 1950.

LIBBY, WILLARD FRANK: BIRTH ANNIVERSARY. Dec 17, 1908. American educator, chemist, atomic scientist and Nobel Prize winner was born at Grand Valley, CO. He was the inventor of the carbon-14 "atomic clock" method for dating ancient and prehistoric plant and animal remains and minerals. Died at Los Angeles, CA, Sept 8, 1980.

★**PAN AMERICAN AVIATION DAY.** Dec 17. Presidential Proclamation 2446, of Nov 18, 1940, covers all succeeding years (Pub Res No. 105 of Oct 10, 1940).

SAMPSON, DEBORAH: BIRTH ANNIVERSARY. Dec 17, 1760. Born at Plympton, MA, Deborah Sampson spent her childhood as an indentured servant. In 1782, wishing to participate in the Revolutionary War, she disguised herself as a man and enlisted in the Continental Army's 4th Massachusetts Regiment under the name Robert Shurtleff. She received both musket and sword wounds, but it was an attack of fever that unmasked her identity and led to her dismissal from the army in 1783. In 1802 Sampson became perhaps the first woman to lecture professionally in the US when she began giving public speeches on her experiences. Full military pension was provided for her heirs by an act of Congress in 1838. Deborah Sampson died Apr 29, 1827, at Sharon, MA.

SATURNALIA. Dec 17–23. Ancient Roman festival honoring Saturnus, the god of agriculture. It was a time of merriment at the end of harvesting and wine-making. Presents were exchanged, sacrifices offered, and masters served their slaves. Approximates the winter solstice. Some say that the date for the observance of the nativity of Jesus was selected by the early Christian church leaders to fall on Dec 25 partly to counteract the popular but disapproved of pre-Christian Roman festival of Saturnalia.

"THE SIMPSONS" TV PREMIERE: ANNIVERSARY. Dec 17, 1989. TV's hottest animated family, "The Simpsons," premiered as a half-hour weekly sitcom. The originator of Homer, Marge, Bart, Lisa and Maggie is cartoonist Matt Groening.

WHITTIER, JOHN GREENLEAF: BIRTH ANNIVERSARY. Dec 17, 1807. Poet and abolitionist, born at Haverhill, Essex County, MA. Whittier's books of poetry include *Legends of New England* and *Snowbound*. Died at Hampton Falls, NH, Sept 7, 1892.

★**WRIGHT BROTHERS DAY.** Dec 17. Presidential Proclamation always issued for Dec 17 since 1963 (PL88–209 of Dec 17, 1963). Issued twice earlier at Congressional request in 1959 and 1961.

WRIGHT BROTHERS FIRST POWERED FLIGHT: ANNIVERSARY. Dec 17, 1903. Orville and Wilbur Wright, brothers, bicycle shop operators, inventors and aviation pioneers, after three years of experimentation with kites and gliders, achieved the first documented successful powered and controlled flights of an airplane. The flights, near Kitty Hawk, NC, piloted first by Orville then by Wilbur Wright, were sustained for less than one minute but represented man's first powered airplane flight and the beginning of a new form of transportation. Orville Wright was born at Dayton, OH, Aug 19, 1871, and died there Jan 30, 1948. Wilbur Wright was born at Millville, IN, Apr 16, 1867, and died at Dayton, OH, May 30, 1912.

BIRTHDAYS TODAY

Christopher Cazenove, 56, actor (*Zulu Dawn, Eye of the Needle*), born Winchester, England, Dec 17, 1945.
Bob Guccione, 71, publisher, born Brooklyn, NY, Dec 17, 1930.
Bernard Hill, 57, actor (*Gandhi, Shirley Valentine*), born Manchester, England, Dec 17, 1944.
Ernie Hudson, 56, actor (*Ghostbusters, Ghostbusters II, The Hand That Rocks the Cradle*), born Benton Harbor, MI, Dec 17, 1945.
Eugene Levy, 55, comedian, writer ("Second City TV," "SCTV Network 90"), born Hamilton, Ontario, Canada, Dec 17, 1946.
Bill Pullman, 47, actor (*Independence Day, While You Were Sleeping*), born Delphi, NY, Dec 17, 1954.
William Safire, 72, author, journalist (*Coming to Terms, Words of Wisdom*), born New York, NY, Dec 17, 1929.
Tommy Steele, 65, actor (*The Happiest Millionaire, Half a Sixpence*), born London, England, Dec 17, 1936.

DECEMBER 18 — TUESDAY
Day 352 — 13 Remaining

BRANDT, WILLY: BIRTH ANNIVERSARY. Dec 18, 1913. Former West German chancellor Willy Brandt was born Herbert Ernst Karl Frahm at Lubeck, Germany. An anti-Nazi exile during World War II, he won the Nobel Peace Prize in 1971 for seeking better East-West relations. He died Oct 8, 1992, at Unkel, Germany.

CAPITOL REEF NATIONAL PARK ESTABLISHED: 30th ANNIVERSARY. Dec 18, 1971. Area of outstanding geological features, colorful canyons, prehistoric Fremont petroglyphs and Mormon historic fruit orchards and buildings in south central Utah, originally proclaimed a national monument Aug 2, 1937, was established as a national park. For further park info: Capitol Reef Natl Park, Box 15, Torrey, UT 84775. E-mail: care-interpretation@nps.gov. Web: www.nps.gov/care.

COBB, TYRUS RAYMOND "TY": BIRTH ANNIVERSARY. Dec 18, 1886. Famed American baseball player born at Narrows, GA. Died at Atlanta, GA, July 17, 1961. Lifetime batting average of .367 compiled over 24 years during which he played in more than 3,000 games.

GRIMALDI, JOSEPH: BIRTH ANNIVERSARY. Dec 18, 1778. Known as the "greatest clown in history" and the "king of pantomime," Joseph Grimaldi began his stage career at age two. He was an accomplished singer, dancer and acrobat. Born at London, England, he is best remembered as the original "Joey the Clown" and for the innovative humor he brought to the clown's role in theater. Illness forced his early retirement in 1823, and he died at London, May 31, 1837.

MacDOWELL, EDWARD ALEXANDER: BIRTH ANNIVERSARY. Dec 18, 1861. Composer of orchestral and piano compositions and songs, born at New York, NY. He was awarded a music professorship at Columbia University. He died at New York, NY, Jan 23, 1908.

MEXICO: FEAST OF OUR LADY OF SOLITUDE. Dec 18. Oaxaca. Pilgrims venerate the patron of the lonely.

NEW JERSEY RATIFICATION DAY: ANNIVERSARY. Dec 18, 1787. New Jersey became the third state to ratify the Constitution (following Delaware and Pennsylvania). It did so unanimously.

NIGER: REPUBLIC DAY. Dec 18. National holiday. Gained autonomy within the French community in 1958.

STRADIVARI, ANTONIO: DEATH ANNIVERSARY. Dec 18, 1737. Celebrated Italian violin maker was born probably in the year 1644, and died at Cremona, at about age 93.

"TO TELL THE TRUTH" TV PREMIERE: 45th ANNIVERSARY. Dec 18, 1956. This long-running popular game show was a production of the Mark Goodson-Bill Todman team. A celebrity panel (and the home audience) tried to guess which of three guests claiming to be the same person was telling the truth. Panelists took turns questioning the guests, and, at the conclusion, the identity of the person was revealed. Hosts have included Bud Collyer, Garry Moore, Joe Garagiola, Robin Ward, Gordon Elliott and Alex Trebek. Celebrity panelists included Dick Van Dyke, Tom Poston, Peggy Cass, Kitty Carlisle and Bill Cullen.

BIRTHDAYS TODAY

Christina Aguilera, 21, singer, born Staten Island, NY, Dec 18, 1980.
Ossie Davis, 84, actor (*A Raisin in the Sun, Grumpy Old Men*, "Evening Shade"), born Cogdell, GA, Dec 18, 1917.
Katie Holmes, 23, actress ("Dawson's Creek"), born Toledo, OH, Dec 18, 1978.
Ray Liotta, 46, actor (*Unforgettable, Goodfellas, Field of Dreams, Something Wild*), born Newark, NJ, Dec 18, 1955.
Leonard Maltin, 51, movie critic, author (*Maltin's Guide*), born New York, NY, Dec 18, 1950.
Charles Oakley, 38, basketball player, born Cleveland, OH, Dec 18, 1963.
Brad Pitt, 37, actor (*Interview with the Vampire, A River Runs Through It*), born Shawnee, OK, Dec 18, 1964.
Keith Richards, 58, musician, singer (with the Rolling Stones), born Dartford, England, Dec 18, 1943.
Steven Spielberg, 54, producer, director (*E.T. The Extra-Terrestrial, Indiana Jones* movies, *Close Encounters of the Third Kind, Jurassic Park, The Color Purple*; Oscars for *Schindler's List, Saving Private Ryan*), born Cincinnati, OH, Dec 18, 1947.
Kiefer Sutherland, 35, actor (*Flatliners, A Few Good Men*), born Los Angeles, CA, Dec 18, 1966.

DECEMBER 19 — WEDNESDAY

Day 353 — 12 Remaining

CHRISTMAS GREETINGS FROM SPACE: ANNIVERSARY. Dec 19, 1958. At 3:15 PM, EST, the US Earth satellite *Atlas* transmitted the first radio voice broadcast from space, a 58-word recorded Christmas greeting from President Dwight D. Eisenhower: "to all mankind America's wish for peace on earth and good will toward men everywhere." The satellite had been launched from Cape Canaveral Dec 18.

FISKE, MINNIE MADDERN: BIRTH ANNIVERSARY. Dec 19, 1865. American theater actress with a long, distinguished career. First stage appearance at the age of three as "Little Minnie Maddern." Born at New Orleans, LA, she died Feb 15, 1932, at Hollis, NY.

LIVERMORE, MARY ASHTON: BIRTH ANNIVERSARY. Dec 19, 1821. American reformer and women's suffrage leader, born at Boston, MA. Died May 23, 1905, at Melrose, MA.

PARRY, WILLIAM: BIRTH ANNIVERSARY. Dec 19, 1790. British explorer Sir William Edward Parry was born at Bath, England. Remembered for his Arctic expeditions and for his search for a Northwest Passage, Parry died at Ems, Germany, July 8, 1855.

SPACE MILESTONE: *INTELSAT 4 F-3 (US)*. Dec 19, 1971. Communications satellite launched by NASA on contract with COMSAT. Mission involved intercontinental relay phone and TV communications.

SUSSKIND, DAVID: BIRTH ANNIVERSARY. Dec 19, 1920. American television producer David (Howard) Susskind was born at New York, NY. In 1952 he started his own television production company and soon was producing more live programs than the three networks combined. He began to host talk shows in 1958 and was widely respected for focusing on serious matters. He died Feb 22, 1987, at New York, NY.

WOODSON, CARTER GODWIN: BIRTH ANNIVERSARY. Dec 19, 1875. Historian who introduced black studies to colleges and universities, born at New Canton, VA. His scholarly works included *The Negro in Our History*, *The Education of the Negro Prior to 1861*. Known as the father of Black history, he inaugurated Negro History Week. Woodson was working on a six-volume *Encyclopaedia Africana* when he died at Washington, DC, Apr 3, 1950.

BIRTHDAYS TODAY

Jennifer Beals, 38, actress (*Flashdance, The Bride, Into the Soup*), born Chicago, IL, Dec 19, 1963.
Janie Frickie, 49, country singer ("It Ain't Easy"), born Whitney, IN, Dec 19, 1952.
Tom Gugliotta, 32, basketball player, born Huntington Station, NY, Dec 19, 1969.
Richard E. Leakey, 57, anthropologist, born Nairobi, Kenya, Dec 19, 1944.
Kevin Edward McHale, 44, Basketball Hall of Famer, born Hibbing, MN, Dec 19, 1957.

	S	M	T	W	T	F	S
December							1
	2	3	4	5	6	7	8
2001	9	10	11	12	13	14	15
	16	17	18	19	20	21	22
	23	24	25	26	27	28	29
	30	31					

Alyssa Milano, 29, actress ("Who's the Boss," "Melrose Place"), born Brooklyn, NY, Dec 19, 1972.
Tim Reid, 57, actor ("Frank's Place," "WKRP in Cincinnati"), born Norfolk, VA, Dec 19, 1944.
Kristy Swanson, 32, actress ("Buffy the Vampire Slayer"), born Mission Viejo, CA, Dec 19, 1969.
Cicely Tyson, 62, actress (Emmy for *The Autobiography of Miss Jane Pittman; Sounder*), born New York, NY, Dec 19, 1939.
Robert Urich, 56, actor ("Marcus Welby, MD," "Spenser: For Hire"), born Toronto, Ontario, Canada, Dec 19, 1945.
Reggie White, 40, former football player, born Chattanooga, TN, Dec 19, 1961.

DECEMBER 20 — THURSDAY

Day 354 — 11 Remaining

AMERICAN POET LAUREATE ESTABLISHMENT: ANNIVERSARY. Dec 20, 1985. A bill empowering the Librarian of Congress to name, annually, a Poet Laureate/Consultant in Poetry was signed into law by President Ronald Reagan. In return for a $10,000 stipend as Poet Laureate and a salary (about $35,000) as the Consultant in Poetry, the person named will present at least one major work of poetry and will appear at selected national ceremonies. The first Poet Laureate of the US was Robert Penn Warren, appointed to that position by the Librarian of Congress Feb 26, 1986. See also: "Warren, Robert Penn: Birth Anniversary" (Apr 24).

CATHODE-RAY TUBE PATENTED: ANNIVERSARY. Dec 20, 1938. The kinescope, today known as the cathode-ray tube, was patented by Russian immigrant Vladimir Zworykin. It is still used today in computer monitors and television sets.

CLINTON IMPEACHMENT PROCEEDINGS: ANNIVERSARY. Dec 20, 1998. President Bill Clinton was impeached by a House of Representatives that was divided along party lines. He was convicted of perjury and obstruction of justice stemming from a sexual relationship with a White House intern. He was then tried by the Senate in January 1999. On Feb 12, 1999, the Senate acquitted him on both charges. Clinton was only the second US president to undergo impeachment proceedings. Andrew Johnson was impeached by the House in 1868 but the Senate voted against impeachment and he finished his term of office. See also: "Johnson Impeachment Proceedings" (Feb 24).

"THE DATING GAME" TV PREMIERE: ANNIVERSARY. Dec 20, 1965. Another game show developed by Chuck Barris, it typically featured a "bachelorette" who questioned three men who were hidden from her view and decided, based on their answers, which guy appealed to her the most. The couple was then sent on a date, courtesy of the show. Occasionally, a bachelor would question three women. Jim Lange was the host of the network series and two syndicated ones. Elaine Joyce and Jeff MacGregor hosted one season each on the retitled "The New Dating Game."

FIRESTONE, HARVEY S.: BIRTH ANNIVERSARY. Dec 20, 1868. American industrialist, businessman and founder of the Firestone Tire and Rubber Company, Harvey Samuel Firestone was born at Columbiana County, OH. A close friend of Henry Ford, Thomas Edison and John Burroughs, Firestone was also author of two books about rubber. He died at Miami Beach, FL, Feb 7, 1938.

LANGER, SUSANNE K.: BIRTH ANNIVERSARY. Dec 20, 1895. Susanne Langer, a leading American philosopher, author of *Philosophy in a New Key: A Study in the Symbolism of Reason, Rite, and Art*, was born at New York, NY. Her studies of esthetics and art exerted a profound influence on thinking in the fields of psychology, philosophy and the social sciences. She died at Old Lyme, CT, July 17, 1985.

LOUISIANA PURCHASE DAY. Dec 20, 1803. One of the greatest real estate deals in history was completed in 1803, when more than a million square miles of the Louisiana Territory were turned over to the US by France, for a price of about $20 per square mile. This almost doubled the size of the US, extending its western border to the Rocky Mountains.

MACAU REVERTS TO CHINESE CONTROL: ANNIVERSARY. Dec 20, 1999. Macau, a tiny province on the southeast coast of China, reverted to Chinese rule. It had been a Portuguese colony since 1557.

MENZIES, ROBERT GORDON: BIRTH ANNIVERSARY. Dec 20, 1894. Australian statesman and conservative leader, born at Jeparit, Victoria, Australia, Sir Robert died at Melbourne, Australia, May 14, 1978, at age 83.

MONTGOMERY BUS BOYCOTT ENDS: 45th ANNIVERSARY. Dec 20, 1956. The US Supreme Court ruling of Nov 13, 1956, calling for integration of the Montgomery, AL, public bus system was implemented. Since Dec 5, 1955, the black community of Montgomery had refused to ride on the segregated buses. The boycott was in reaction to the Dec 1, 1955, arrest of Rosa Parks for refusing to relinquish her seat on a Montgomery bus to a white man.

MUDD DAY. Dec 20, 1833. A day to remember Dr. Samuel A. Mudd (born near Bryantown, MD, Dec 20, 1833), sentenced to life imprisonment for giving medical aid to disguised John Wilkes Booth, fleeing assassin of Abraham Lincoln. Imprisoned four years before being pardoned by President Andrew Johnson. Died on Jan 10, 1883.

RICKEY, BRANCH: BIRTH ANNIVERSARY. Dec 20, 1881. Wesley Branch Rickey, Baseball Hall of Fame player, manager and executive born at Lucasville, OH. Rickey was baseball's most innovative general manager. He invented the farm system, instituted unique training and teaching methods and, most prominently, signed Jackie Robinson to play major league baseball with the Brooklyn Dodgers. Inducted into the Hall of Fame in 1967. Died at Columbia, MO, Dec 9, 1965.

SACAGAWEA: DEATH ANNIVERSARY. Dec 20, 1812. As a young Shoshone Indian woman, Sacagawea in 1805 (with her two-month-old son strapped to her back) traveled with the Lewis and Clark Expedition, serving as an interpreter. It is said that the expedition could not have succeeded without her aid. She was born about 1787 and died at Fort Manuel on the Missouri River, Dec 20, 1812. Few other women have been so often honored. There are statues, fountains and memorials of her, and her name has been given to a mountain peak. Few facts about her life are firmly established and some legends have her living to nearly a hundred years of age. In 2000 the US Mint issued a $1 coin honoring her.

SOUTH CAROLINA: SECESSION ANNIVERSARY. Dec 20, 1860. South Carolina's legislature voted to secede from the US, the first state to do so. Within six weeks, five more states seceded. On Feb 4, 1861, representatives from the six states met at Montgomery, AL to establish a government and on Feb 9 Jefferson Davis was elected president of the Confederate States of America. By June 1861, 11 states had seceded.

US INVASION OF PANAMA: ANNIVERSARY. Dec 20, 1989. The US launched operation "Just Cause," invading Panama in an attempt to seize Manuel Noriega and bring him to justice for narcotics trafficking. Seven months after Noriega had ruled unfavorable election results null and void, the US toppled the Noriega government and oversaw the installation of Guillermo Endara as president. Although the initial military action was declared a success, Noriega eluded capture. He surrendered to US troops on Jan 4, 1990, and was tried, convicted and imprisoned in the US.

VIRGINIA COMPANY EXPEDITION TO AMERICA: ANNIVERSARY. Dec 20, 1606. Three small ships, the *Susan Constant*, the *Godspeed* and the *Discovery*, commanded by Captain Christopher Newport, departed London, England bound for America, where the royally chartered Virginia Company's approximately 120 persons established the first permanent English settlement in what is now the US at Jamestown, VA, May 14, 1607.

DECEMBER 21 — FRIDAY

Day 355 — 10 Remaining

BOLL, HEINRICH: BIRTH ANNIVERSARY. Dec 21, 1917. German novelist, winner of the 1972 Nobel Prize for Literature, author of some 20 books including *Billiards at Half-Past Nine, The Clown* and *Group Portrait with Lady*, was born at Cologne, Germany. He died near Bonn, Germany, July 16, 1985.

DISRAELI, BENJAMIN: BIRTH ANNIVERSARY. Dec 21, 1804. British novelist and statesman, born at London and died there Apr 19, 1881. "No government," he wrote, "can be long secure without a formidable opposition."

FIRST CROSSWORD PUZZLE: ANNIVERSARY. Dec 21, 1913. The first crossword puzzle was compiled by Arthur Wynne and published in a supplement to the *New York World*.

FOLDES, ANDOR: BIRTH ANNIVERSARY. Dec 21, 1913. Pianist Andor Foldes was born at Budapest, Hungary. A child prodigy born to a musical family, he played a Mozart piano concerto with the Budapest Philharmonic when he was eight. He moved to the US in 1939 and is renowned for introducing the work of composer Bela Bartok to the US. He died Feb 9, 1992, at Zurich, Switzerland.

FOREFATHERS' DAY. Dec 21. Observed mainly in New England in commemoration of landing at Plymouth Rock on this day in 1620.

HUMBUG DAY. Dec 21. Allows all those preparing for Christmas to vent their frustrations. 12 "humbugs" allowed. [© 2000 by WH]. For info: Tom or Ruth Roy, Wellcat Holidays, 2418 Long Ln, Lebanon, PA 17046. Phone: (717) 279-0184. E-mail: wellcat @supernet.com. Web: www.wellcat.com.

PAN AMERICAN FLIGHT 103 EXPLOSION: ANNIVERSARY. Dec 21, 1988. Pan Am World Airways Flight 103 exploded in midair and crashed into the heart of Lockerbie, Scotland, the result of a terrorist bombing. The 259 passengers and crew members and 11 persons on the ground were killed in the disaster. The tragedy raised questions about security and the notification of passengers in the event of threatened flights. In the resultant investigation it was revealed that government agencies and the airline had known that the flight was possibly the target of a terrorist attack.

PARKINSON, JAMES: DEATH ANNIVERSARY. Dec 21, 1824. The remarkable English physician and paleontologist who first described the "shaking palsy" later had it named for him—Parkinson's disease. He was the author of numerous books and articles on a variety of subjects. His *Organic Remains of a Former World* is called the first attempt to give a scientific account of fossils—"a memorable event in the history of British paleontology." Under oath, Parkinson declared that he was a member of the group that hatched the "Pop-gun Plot" to assassinate King George III in a theater, using a poisoned dart for the deed. Parkinson was born at London about 1755, and died there, Dec 21, 1824.

PHILEAS FOGG WINS A WAGER DAY. Dec 21. Anniversary, from Jules Verne's *Around the World in Eighty Days*, of the winning of Phileas Fogg's wager, on Dec 21, 1872, when Fogg walked into the saloon of the Reform Club at London, announcing "Here I am, gentlemen!" exactly 79 days, 23 hours, 59 minutes and 59 seconds after starting his trip "around the world in 80 days," to win his £20,000 wager. See also: "Phileas Fogg's Wager Day" (Oct 2).

PILGRIM LANDING: ANNIVERSARY. Dec 21, 1620. According to Governor William Bradford's *History of Plymouth Plantation*, "On Munday," [Dec 21, 1620, New Style] the Pilgrims, aboard the *Mayflower*, reached Plymouth, MA, "sounded ye harbor, and founde it fitt for shipping; and marched into ye land, & founde diverse cornfields, and ye best they could find, and ye season & their presente necessitie made them glad to accepte of it. . . . And after wards tooke better view of ye place, and resolved wher to pitch their dwelling; and them and their goods." Plymouth Rock, the legendary place of landing since it first was "identified" in 1769, nearly 150 years after the landing, has been a historic shrine since. The landing anniversary is observed in much of New England as Forefathers' Day. See also: "Forefathers' Day" (Dec 21).

SPACE MILESTONE: *APOLLO 8* (US). Dec 21, 1968. First moon voyage launched, manned by Colonel Frank Borman, Captain James A. Lovell, Jr and Major William A. Anders. Orbited moon Dec 24, returned to Earth Dec 27. First men to orbit the moon and see the side of the moon away from Earth.

STALIN, JOSEPH: BIRTH ANNIVERSARY. Dec 21, 1879. Russian dictator whose family name was Dzhugashvili, was born at Gori, Georgia. One of the most powerful and most feared men of the 20th century, Stalin died (of a stroke) at the Kremlin, at Moscow, Mar 5, 1953.

SZOLD, HENRIETTA: BIRTH ANNIVERSARY. Dec 21, 1860. Teacher, writer, scholar, social worker, organizer and pioneer Zionist, Henrietta Szold is best remembered as founder and first president of Hadassah, the Women's Zionist Organization of America. Born at Baltimore, MD, she was influenced by her father Rabbi Benjamin Szold, an active and vocal abolitionist. She established the first "Night School" at Baltimore, one of the first to focus on teaching English and job skills to immigrants. Her trip to Palestine in 1910 sparked the genesis of Hadassah. While there, Szold was alarmed by the lack of social, medical and educational services and returned with the idea that a national women's Zionist organization must be formed to carry out practical projects. As the "Mother of Social Service in Palestine," Szold viewed volunteerism as one of the greatest human endeavors. She died at Jerusalem, Feb 13, 1945. See also: "Hadassah: Anniversary" (Feb 24).

UNDERDOG DAY. Dec 21. To salute, before the year's end, all of the underdogs and unsung heroes—the Number Two people who contribute so much to the Number One people we read about. (Sherlock Holmes's Dr. Watson and Robinson Crusoe's Friday are examples.) Observed annually on the third Friday in December since its founding in 1976 by the late Peter Moeller, THE Chief Underdog. For info: A. Moeller, Underdogs Intl, Box 71, Clio, MI 48420-1042.

WINTER. Dec 21–Mar 20, 2002. In the Northern Hemisphere winter begins today with the winter solstice, at 2:21 PM, EST. Note that in the Southern Hemisphere today is the beginning of summer. Between Equator and Arctic Circle the sunrise and sunset points on the horizon are farthest south for the year and daylight length is minimum (ranging from 12 hours, 8 minutes, at the equator to zero at the Arctic Circle).

December 2001

S	M	T	W	T	F	S
						1
2	3	4	5	6	7	8
9	10	11	12	13	14	15
16	17	18	19	20	21	22
23	24	25	26	27	28	29
30	31					

WORLD PEACE DAY–WINTER SOLSTICE. Dec 21. A day on which bells throughout the world will be rung along with prayers for World peace. Jerusalem and Tibet will be the main focal point this year. Annually, on the winter solstice. For info: Donald L. Orne, PO Box 225, Marblehead, MA 01945. Phone: (781) 631-0786. E-mail: don@yingcom.com. Web: www.yingcom.com.

YALDA. Dec 21. Yalda, the longest night of the year, is celebrated by Iranians. The ceremony has an Indo-Iranian origin, where Light and Good were considered to struggle against Darkness and Evil. With fires burning and lights lit, family and friends gather to stay up through the night helping the sun in its battle against darkness. They recite poetry, tell stories and eat special fruits and nuts until the sun, triumphant, reappears in the morning. For info: Yassaman Djalali, Librarian, West Valley Branch Library, 1243 San Tomas Aquino Rd, San Jose, CA 95117. Phone: (408) 244-4766.

YULE. Dec 21. (Also called Alban Arthan.) One of the "Lesser Sabbats" during the Wiccan year, Yule marks the death of the Sun-God and his rebirth from the Earth Goddess. Annually, on the winter solstice.

ZAPPA, FRANK: BIRTH ANNIVERSARY. Dec 21, 1940. Rock musician and composer, Zappa was noted for his satire and as a leading advocate against censorship of contemporary music. He formed the group Mothers of Invention. Born at Baltimore, MD, he died Dec 4, 1993, at Los Angeles, CA, at age 52.

BIRTHDAYS TODAY

Tina Brown, 48, former *New Yorker* editor, born London, England, Dec 21, 1953.
Andy Dick, 36, actor ("NewsRadio"), born Charleston, SC, Dec 21, 1965.
Phil Donahue, 66, former TV talk-show host ("Donahue"), born Cleveland, OH, Dec 21, 1935.
Christine Marie (Chris) Evert, 47, sportscaster, former tennis player, born Ft Lauderdale, FL, Dec 21, 1954.
Jane Fonda, 64, actress (Oscars for *Klute*, *Coming Home*; *Julia*, *On Golden Pond*), born New York, NY, Dec 21, 1937.
Samuel L. Jackson, 53, actor (*Pulp Fiction*, *Jurassic Park*), born Washington, DC, Dec 21, 1948.
Joe Paterno, 75, college football coach, born Brooklyn, NY, Dec 21, 1926.
Ray Romano, 44, comedian, actor ("Everybody Loves Raymond"), born Queens, NY, Dec 21, 1957.
Michael Tilson Thomas, 57, conductor, pianist, organist, born Hollywood, CA, Dec 21, 1944.
Andrew James (Andy) Van Slyke, 41, former baseball player, born Utica, NY, Dec 21, 1960.
Karrie Webb, 27, golfer, born Ayr, Queensland, Australia, Dec 21, 1974.
Paul Winchell, 79, ventriloquist, actor, born New York, NY, Dec 21, 1922.

DECEMBER 22 — SATURDAY
Day 356 — 9 Remaining

ASHCROFT, PEGGY: BIRTH ANNIVERSARY. Dec 22, 1907. British actress Dame Edith Margaret Emily Ashcroft was born at Croyden, England. In addition to her many accolades on the British stage she won an Oscar for her supporting role in *Passage to India* (1985) and a special British Olivier Award for lifetime achievement in 1991. She died June 14, 1991, at London, England.

CAPRICORN, THE GOAT. Dec 22–Jan 19. In the astronomical and astrological zodiac that divides the sun's apparent orbit into 12 segments, the period Dec 22–Jan 19 is identified, traditionally, as the sun-sign of Capricorn, the Goat. The ruling planet is Saturn.

"DING DONG SCHOOL" TV PREMIERE: ANNIVERSARY. Dec 22, 1952. Named by a three-year-old after watching a test broadcast of the opening sequence (a hand ringing a bell), "Ding Dong School" was one of the first children's educational series. Miss Frances (Dr. Frances Horwich, head of Roosevelt College's education department at Chicago) was the host of this weekday show.

ELLERY, WILLIAM: BIRTH ANNIVERSARY. Dec 22, 1727. Signer of the Declaration of Independence, born at Newport, RI, and died there Feb 15, 1820.

FIRST GORILLA BORN IN CAPTIVITY: 45th BIRTH ANNIVERSARY. Dec 22, 1956. "Colo" was born at the Columbus, OH, zoo, weighing in at 3 ¼ pounds, the first gorilla born in captivity.

MOON PHASE: FIRST QUARTER. Dec 22. Moon enters First Quarter phase at 3:56 PM, EST.

OGLETHORPE, JAMES EDWARD: BIRTH ANNIVERSARY. Dec 22, 1696. English general, author and colonizer of Georgia. Founder of the city of Savannah. Oglethorpe was born at London. He died June 30, 1785, at Cranham Hall, Essex, England.

PUCCINI, GIACOMO: BIRTH ANNIVERSARY. Dec 22, 1858. Italian composer of such operas as *La Boheme* and *Madame Butterfly*. Born at Lucca, Tuscany, Italy, he died Nov 29, 1924, at Brussels, Belgium.

ROBINSON, EDWIN ARLINGTON: BIRTH ANNIVERSARY. Dec 22, 1869. Three-time Pulitzer Prize winner best known for his short dramatic poems, including "Richard Cory" and "Miniver Cheevy." Born at Head Tide, ME, and died at Los Angeles, CA, Apr 6, 1935.

BIRTHDAYS TODAY

Barbara Billingsley, 79, actress ("Leave It to Beaver," *Airplane!*), born Los Angeles, CA, Dec 22, 1922.
Steven Norman (Steve) Carlton, 57, Baseball Hall of Fame pitcher, born Miami, FL, Dec 22, 1944.
Hector Elizondo, 65, actor (*Pretty Woman, Frankie and Johnny*, "Chicago Hope"), born New York, NY, Dec 22, 1936.
Ralph Fiennes, 39, actor (*Schindler's List, Wuthering Heights*), born Suffolk, England, Dec 22, 1962.

Steve Garvey, 53, former baseball player, born Tampa, FL, Dec 22, 1948.
Maurice Gibb, 52, singer, musician (The Bee Gees), born Manchester, England, Dec 22, 1949.
Robin Gibb, 52, singer, musician (The Bee Gees), born Manchester, England, Dec 22, 1949.
Claudia Alta "Lady Bird" Johnson, 89, former First Lady, born Karnack, TX, Dec 22, 1912.
Diane K. Sawyer, 55, journalist ("60 Minutes," "Prime Time Live"), born Glasgow, KY, Dec 22, 1946.
Jan Stephenson, 50, golfer, born Sydney, Australia, Dec 22, 1951.

DECEMBER 23 — SUNDAY
Day 357 — 8 Remaining

COMMUNITY CAROL SINGING. Dec 23. Mystic, CT. Lift up your voice in song to celebrate the season. Museum admission is free when you bring a canned good to be donated to charity. A brass quartet and the Mystic Seaport carolers lead an afternoon of joyous musical cheer. Est attendance: 1,000. For info: Mystic Seaport, 75 Greenmanville Ave, Box 6000, Mystic, CT 06355. Phone: (860) 572-5315 or (888) 9SEAPORT. Web: www.mysticseaport.org.

FEDERAL RESERVE SYSTEM: ANNIVERSARY. Dec 23, 1913. Established pursuant to authority contained in the Federal Reserve Act of Dec 23, 1913, the system serves as the nation's central bank, has responsibility for execution of monetary policy. It is called on to contribute to the strength and vitality of the US economy, in part by influencing the lending and investing activities of commercial banks and the cost and availability of money and credit.

FIRST NONSTOP FLIGHT AROUND THE WORLD WITHOUT REFUELING: ANNIVERSARY. Dec 23, 1987. Dick Rutan and Jeana Yeager set a new world record of 216 hours of continuous flight, breaking their own record of 111 hours set July 15, 1986. The aircraft *Voyager* departed from Edwards Air Force Base in California, Dec 14, 1987 and landed Dec 23, 1987. The journey covered 24,986 miles at an official speed of 115 miles per hour.

JAPAN: BIRTHDAY OF THE EMPEROR. Dec 23. National Day. Holiday honoring Emperor Akihito, born in 1933.

METRIC CONVERSION ACT: ANNIVERSARY. Dec 23, 1975. The Congress of the US passed Public Law 94–168, known as the Metric Conversion Act of 1975. This act declares that the SI (International System of Units) will be this country's basic system of measurement and establishes the United States Metric Board which is responsible for the planning, coordination and implementation of the nation's voluntary conversion to SI. (Congress had authorized the metric system as a legal system of measurement in the US by an act passed July 28, 1866. In 1875, the US became one of the original signers of the Treaty of the Metre, which established an international metric system.)

MEXICO: FEAST OF THE RADISHES. Dec 23. Oaxaca. Figurines of people and animals cleverly carved out of radishes are sold during festivities.

MONROE, HARRIET: BIRTH ANNIVERSARY. Dec 23, 1860. American poet, editor and founder of *Poetry* magazine. Born at Chicago, IL. Died Sept 26, 1936, at Arequipa, Peru.

SMILES, SAMUEL: BIRTH ANNIVERSARY. Dec 23, 1812. Scottish writer, born at Haddington, Berwickshire, Scotland. Died at London, England, Apr 17, 1904. "A place for everything," he wrote in *Thrift*, "and everything in its place."

TOJO HIDEKI EXECUTION: ANNIVERSARY. Dec 23, 1948. Tojo Hideki, prime minister of Japan from Oct 16, 1941, until his resignation July 19, 1944. After Japan's surrender in August 1945, Tojo was arrested as a war criminal, tried by a military tribunal and sentenced to death Nov 12, 1948. Born at Tokyo, Japan, Dec 30, 1884, Tojo was hanged (with six other Japanese wartime military leaders) at Sugamo Prison, Tokyo, Dec 23, 1948, the sentence being carried out by the US 8th Army.

TRANSISTOR INVENTED: ANNIVERSARY. Dec 23, 1947. John Bardeen, Walter Brattain and William Shockley of Bell Laboratories shared the 1956 Nobel Prize for their invention of the transistor, which led to a revolution in communications and electronics. It was smaller, lighter, more durable, more reliable and generated less heat than the vacuum tube that had been used up to this time.

BIRTHDAYS TODAY

Akihito, 68, Emperor of Japan, born Tokyo, Japan, Dec 23, 1933.
Robert Bly, 75, author (*Iron John: A Book About Men; What Have I Ever Lost by Dying?*), born Madison, MN, Dec 23, 1926.
Jose Greco, 83, dancer, born Abruzzi, Italy, Dec 23, 1918.
James Gregory, 90, actor ("Barney Miller," *The Manchurian Candidate*), born New York, NY, Dec 23, 1911.
Corey Haim, 30, actor (*Murphy's Romance, The Lost Boys*), born Toronto, Ontario, Canada, Dec 23, 1971.
James Joseph (Jim) Harbaugh, 38, football player, born Toledo, OH, Dec 23, 1963.
Susan Lucci, 52, actress ("All My Children," *Mafia Princess*), born Westchester, NY, Dec 23, 1949.
Gerald O'Loughlin, 80, actor ("The Rookies," "Our House"), born New York, NY, Dec 23, 1921.

DECEMBER 24 — MONDAY
Day 358 — 7 Remaining

AIDA PREMIERE: ANNIVERSARY. Dec 24, 1871. Giuseppe Verdi's opera *Aida* premiered at Cairo. It was commissioned by the Khedive of Egypt to celebrate the opening of the Suez Canal.

ARNOLD, MATTHEW: BIRTH ANNIVERSARY. Dec 24, 1822. English poet and essayist, born at Laleham, England. Died Apr 15, 1888, at Liverpool, England. "One has often wondered," he wrote in *Culture and Anarchy*, "whether upon the whole earth there is anything so unintelligent, so unapt to perceive how the world is really going, as an ordinary young Englishman of our upper class."

AUSTRIA: "SILENT NIGHT, HOLY NIGHT" CELEBRATIONS. Dec 24. Oberndorf, Hallein and Wagrain, Salzburg, Austria. Commemorating the creation of the Christmas carol here in 1818.

December 2001	S	M	T	W	T	F	S
							1
	2	3	4	5	6	7	8
	9	10	11	12	13	14	15
	16	17	18	19	20	21	22
	23	24	25	26	27	28	29
	30	31					

CARSON, CHRISTOPHER "KIT": BIRTH ANNIVERSARY. Dec 24, 1809. American frontiersman, soldier, trapper, guide and Indian agent best known as Kit Carson. Born at Madison County, KY, he died at Fort Lyon, CO, May 23, 1868.

CHRISTMAS BELLS RING AGAIN IN ST. BASIL'S: ANNIVERSARY. Dec 24, 1990. For the first time since the death of Lenin in 1924, the bells of St. Basil's Cathedral, on Red Square in Moscow, rang to celebrate Christmas.

CHRISTMAS EVE. Dec 24. Family gift-giving occasion in many Christian countries.

CHRISTMAS EVE TORCHLIGHT PARADE. Dec 24. Winter Park Resort, Winter Park, CO. One of Winter Park Resort's most beloved traditions, which is highlighted by Santa Claus leading a procession of torch-bearing skiers down Lower Hughs trail under a spectacular fireworks display. Est attendance: 1,500. For info: Winter Park Resort, PO Box 36, Winter Park, CO 80482. Phone: (970) 726-1580. Fax: (970) 726-1572. E-mail: wpinfo@mail.skiwinterpark.com. Web: winterparkresort.com.

FIRST SURFACE-TO-SURFACE GUIDED MISSILE: ANNIVERSARY. Dec 24, 1942. German rocket engineer Wernher von Braun launched the first surface-to-surface guided missile. Buzz bombs, a form of guided missile, were used by Germany against Great Britain starting Sept 8, 1944. On Feb 24, 1949, the first rocket to reach outer space (an altitude of 25 miles) was fired. The two-stage rocket, a Wac Corporal set in the nose of a German V-2, was launched from the White Sands Proving Grounds, NM, by a team of scientists headed by von Braun.

GARDNER, AVA: BIRTH ANNIVERSARY. Dec 24, 1922. Actress and leading sex symbol of the 1940s and '50s, Ava Lavinia Gardner was born at Smithfield, NC. Among Gardner's numerous movies are *The Barefoot Contessa, Bhowani Junction, The Sun Also Rises* and *The Life and Times of Judge Roy Bean*. Gardner was married to Mickey Rooney (1942–43), Artie Shaw (1945–46) and Frank Sinatra (1951–57). Died at London, England, Jan 25, 1990.

HUGHES, HOWARD ROBARD: BIRTH ANNIVERSARY. Dec 24, 1905. Wealthy American industrialist, aviator and movie producer who spent his latter years as a recluse. Born at Houston, TX, he died in airplane en route from Acapulco, Mexico, to Houston, Apr 5, 1976.

JOULE, JAMES PRESCOTT: BIRTH ANNIVERSARY. Dec 24, 1818. English physicist and inventor after whom Joule's Law (the first law of thermodynamics) was named was born at Salford, Lancashire, England. The unit of measurement of the mechnical equivalent of heat is known as the Joule. He died at Cheshire, England, Oct 11, 1889.

LIBYA: INDEPENDENCE DAY: 50th ANNIVERSARY. Dec 24. Libya gained its independence from Italy in 1951.

"THE PERRY COMO SHOW" TV PREMIERE: ANNIVERSARY. Dec 24, 1948. Singer Perry Como hosted "The Chesterfield Supper Club" when it came to TV from radio. Also featured were the Mitchell Ayres Orchestra and the Fontane Sisters. When the show moved from NBC to CBS in 1950, announcer Frank Gallop was added. In 1955, Como moved back to NBC, and the show was retitled "The Perry Como Show" during 1955–59 and then "The Kraft Music Hall" during 1959–63. The Ray Charles Singers and the Louis DaPron Dancers were featured. Como's theme song was "Dream Along with Me."

BIRTHDAYS TODAY

Diedrich Bader, 35, actor ("The Drew Carey Show"), born Alexandria, VA, Dec 24, 1966.

Mary Higgins Clark, 70, author (*Where Are the Children?*, *Silent Night*), born New York, NY, Dec 24, 1931.

A.P. Lutali, 82, Governor of American Samoa (D), born Aunu'u, American Samoa, Dec 24, 1919.

Ricky Martin, 30, singer, actor ("General Hospital"), born Enrique José Martín, San Juan, Puerto Rico, Dec 24, 1971.

Jeff Sessions, 55, US Senator (R, Alabama), born Hybart, AL, Dec 24, 1946.

DECEMBER 25 — TUESDAY

Day 359 — 6 Remaining

A'PHABET DAY. Dec 25. Also known as "No-L" Day, this celebration is for people who do not want to send Christmas cards but who want to greet their friends; so they send out cards listing the letters of the alphabet in order, but with a gap where L would be. For info: Bob Birch, The Puns Corps, PO Box 2364, Falls Church, VA 22042-0364. Phone: (703) 533-3668.

BARTON, CLARA: BIRTH ANNIVERSARY. Dec 25, 1821. Clarissa Harlowe Barton, American nurse and philanthropist, founder of the American Red Cross, was born at Oxford, MA. In 1881, she became first president of the American Red Cross (founded May 21, 1881). She died at Glen Echo, MD, Apr 12, 1912.

BLUE-GRAY ALL STAR FOOTBALL CLASSIC. Dec 25. Cramton Bowl, Montgomery, AL. College seniors from northern schools compete against their southern counterparts. Sponsor: Montgomery Lion's Club. Est attendance: 22,000. For info: Charles W. Jones, Exec Dir, Box 94, Montgomery, AL 36101-0094. Phone: (334) 265-1266. Fax: (334) 265-5944.

BOGART, HUMPHREY: BIRTH ANNIVERSARY. Dec 25, 1899. American stage and screen actor, Humphrey DeForest Bogart was born at New York, NY. Among his best remembered films are: *The African Queen, The Maltese Falcon, Casablanca* and *To Have and Have Not*. Bogart died Jan 14, 1957, at Hollywood, CA. A US postage stamp bearing his picture was issued in 1997.

BOOTH, EVANGELINE CORY: BIRTH ANNIVERSARY. Dec 25, 1865. Salvation Army general, active in England, Canada and the US. Author and composer of songs, Booth was born at London, England. She died at Hartsdale, NY, July 17, 1950.

CALLOWAY, CAB: BIRTH ANNIVERSARY. Dec 25, 1907. American singer and bandleader Cabell Calloway was born at Rochester, NY. George Gershwin modeled the part of Sportin' Life in *Porgy and Bess* (1953) after this jazz singer who also played the role across the US until 1956. He is best known for his song "Minnie the Moocher" (1931). He died Nov 18, 1994, at Hockessin, DE.

CEAUSESCU, NICOLAE: DEATH ANNIVERSARY. Dec 25, 1989. On Christmas evening a broadcast of a Christmas symphony on state-run television was interrupted with the report that Romanian president Nicolae Ceausescu and his wife had been executed, bringing to an end the last hard-line regime in the Soviet bloc. In a brutally fast uprising, the Romanian people ousted the Ceausescu regime, and the National Salvation Front, an ad hoc pro-democracy coalition, took charge of the country. Ceausescu's downfall began when he ordered members of his black-shirted state police, the Securitate, to use force to quell a disturbance in the town of Timisorara. The brutal crackdown led to estimates of as many as 4,500 killed. Ceausescu's rule was marked by corruption, deprivation and terror.

CHRISTMAS. Dec 25. Christian festival commemorating the birth of Jesus of Nazareth. Most popular of Christian observances, Christmas as a Feast of the Nativity dates from the 4th century. Although Jesus's birth date is not known, the Western church selected Dec 25 for the feast, possibly to counteract the non-Christian festivals of that approximate date. Many customs from non-Christian festivals (Roman Saturnalia, Mithraic sun's birthday, Teutonic yule, Druidic and other winter solstice rites) have been adopted as part of the Christmas celebration (lights, mistletoe, holly and ivy, holiday tree, wassailing and gift-giving, for example). Some Orthodox Churches celebrate Christmas Jan 7 based on the "old calendar" (Julian). Theophany (recognition of the divinity of Jesus) is observed on this date and also on Jan 6, especially by the Eastern Orthodox Church.

CHRISTMAS FIRESIDE CHAT WARNING: ANNIVERSARY. Dec 25, 1943. In his Christmas message to the American people, Franklin D. Roosevelt warned, "The war is now reaching the stage when we shall have to look forward to large casualty lists—dead, wounded and missing. War entails just that. There is no easy road to victory. And the end is not yet in sight."

CUBA: CHRISTMAS RETURNS: ANNIVERSARY. Dec 25, 1998. Christmas was celebrated in Cuba after Fidel Castro's government announced that it was again a regular holiday in the Cuban calendar. In 1997 the government had granted a Christmas holiday in deference to Pope John Paul II who was visiting the island the next month. Christmas had been abolished as a holiday in Cuba in 1969.

FARLEY, CAL: BIRTH ANNIVERSARY. Dec 25, 1895. Cal Farley, known as "America's Greatest Foster Father," started Cal Farley's Boys Ranch in 1939 with nine boys. The Ranch has grown into a modern community of 441 boys (and girls since 1992), which has housed and educated more than 4,000 boys and girls over the years. In 1996 the US Postal System issued a stamp in Farley's name. Cal Farley was born at Saxton, IA; he died Feb 19, 1967, at Boys Ranch, TX.

IT'S ABOUT TIME WEEK!. Dec 25–31. Innovative week dedicated to time-to-give, time-to-live and time-to-remember. Encourages creativity applied to problems and honors pioneers and partnerships in research and service for "ABetterWay; ABetterWorld." Awards to pioneers and partnerships. Send nominations by October. For info: The New Frontiers Univ, 427 ½ E 7th St, Michigan City, IN 46360. Web: www.giftsoftime.org.

JINNAH, MOHAMMED ALI: 125th BIRTH ANNIVERSARY. Dec 25, 1876. The founder of the Islamic Republic of Pakistan, Mohammed Ali Jinnah was born at Karachi, then part of India. When Pakistan became an independent political entity (Aug 15, 1947), Jinnah became its first governor general. He died at Karachi, Sept 11, 1948.

"THE STEVE ALLEN SHOW" TV PREMIERE: ANNIVERSARY. Dec 25, 1950. Talented actor, comedian, singer and musician, Steve Allen hosted a number of variety shows from 1950 to 1969 (with a few breaks in between to host specials and "The Tonight Show"). For two years, his television show was similar to his radio show and featured singer Peggy Lee, announcer Bern Bennett and Llemuel the llama. His next show competed with Ed Sullivan's show, though Allen's stressed comedy. Some of his "funny men" were Don Knotts, Tom Poston, Louis Nye, Gabe Dell, Pat Harrington, Jr, Dayton Allen and Bill Dana. His other shows included a talk show, a game show, a comedy show, an educational music show and a flashback-comedy show.

STOCK EXCHANGE HOLIDAY (CHRISTMAS DAY). Dec 25. The holiday schedules for the various exchanges are subject to change if relevant rules, regulations or exchange policies are revised. If you have questions, phone: American Stock Exchange (212) 306-1000; Chicago Board of Options Exchange (312) 786-5600; Chicago Board of Trade (312) 435-3500; New York Stock Exchange (212) 656-2065; Pacific Stock Exchange (415) 393-4000; Philadelphia Stock Exchange (215) 496-5000.

UNITED KINGDOM: CHRISTMAS HOLIDAY. Dec 25. Bank and public holiday in England, Wales, Scotland and Northern Ireland.

WEST, REBECCA: BIRTH ANNIVERSARY. Dec 25, 1892. English author, literary critic, prize-winning journalist and noted feminist, Dame Rebecca West was born Cicely Isabel Fairfield at London, England. She died there Mar 15, 1983.

BIRTHDAYS TODAY

Jimmy Buffett, 55, singer ("Margaritaville"), songwriter, born Pascagoula, MS, Dec 25, 1946.
Lawrence Richard (Larry) Csonka, 55, Pro Football Hall of Fame running back, born Stow, OH, Dec 25, 1946.
Rickey Henley Henderson, 43, baseball player, born Chicago, IL, Dec 25, 1958.
Annie Lennox, 47, singer (Eurythmics, "Sweet Dreams Are Made of This"), born Aberdeen, Scotland, Dec 25, 1954.
Norm MacDonald, 39, actor ("Saturday Night Live," "The Norm Show"), born Quebec City, Quebec, Canada, Dec 25, 1962.
Barbara Mandrell, 53, singer ("I Was Country When Country Wasn't Cool"), born Houston, TX, Dec 25, 1948.
Gary Sandy, 56, actor ("All That Glitters," "WKRP in Cincinnati"), born Dayton, OH, Dec 25, 1945.
Hanna Schygulla, 58, actress (*The Marriage of Maria Braun, Berlin Alexanderplatz*), born Kattowitz, Germany, Dec 25, 1943.
Sissy Spacek (Mary Elizabeth), 52, actress (Oscar for *Coal Miner's Daughter; Missing*), born Quitman, TX, Dec 25, 1949.

December 2001	S	M	T	W	T	F	S
							1
	2	3	4	5	6	7	8
	9	10	11	12	13	14	15
	16	17	18	19	20	21	22
	23	24	25	26	27	28	29
	30	31					

DECEMBER 26 — WEDNESDAY
Day 360 — 5 Remaining

BABBAGE, CHARLES: BIRTH ANNIVERSARY. Dec 26, 1792. English mathematician, born at Teignmouth, England. He developed the principles on which modern computers are designed. Babbage died at London, England, Oct 18, 1871.

BAHAMAS: JUNKANOO. Dec 26. Kaleidoscope of sound and spectacle combining a bit of Mardi Gras, mummers' parade and ancient African tribal rituals. Revelers in colorful costumes parade through the streets to sounds of cowbells, goat skin drums and many other homemade instruments. Always on Boxing Day.

BOXING DAY. Dec 26. Ordinarily observed on the first day after Christmas. A legal holiday in Canada, the United Kingdom and many other countries. Formerly (according to Robert Chambers) a day when Christmas gift boxes were "regularly expected by a postman, the lamplighter, the dustman and generally by all those functionaries who render services to the public at large, without receiving payment therefore from any individual." When Boxing Day falls on a Saturday or Sunday, the Monday or Tuesday immediately following may be proclaimed or observed as a bank or public holiday.

BOXING DAY ANNUAL CELEBRATION. Dec 26. North Star Pub, New York, NY. Annual observation of Boxing Day at an authentic British pub featuring free Bangers and Mash (sausages and mashed potatoes), Christmas crackers, games and prizes. Collection of food and clothing for homeless people. Est attendance: 500. For info: Deven Black, Genl Mgr, North Star Pub, 93 South St, New York, NY 10038. Phone: (212) 509-6757. Web: www.northstarpub.com.

CLERC, LAURENT: BIRTH ANNIVERSARY. Dec 26, 1785. The first deaf teacher in America, Laurent Clerc assisted Thomas Hopkins Gallaudet in establishing the first public school for the deaf, Connecticut Asylum for the Education and Instruction of Deaf and Dumb Persons (now the American School for the Deaf), at Hartford, CT, in 1817. For 41 years Clerc trained new teachers in the use of sign language and in methods of teaching the deaf. Clerc was born at LaBalme, France, and died July 18, 1869.

IRELAND: DAY OF THE WREN. Dec 26. Dingle Peninsula. Masked revelers and musicians go from door to door asking for money. Traditional day and night of public merrymaking.

KIDS AFTER CHRISTMAS. Dec 26–30. Mystic, CT. Everyone pays the youth admission and enjoys a full day of crafts, entertainment and the lore of the sea. Est attendance: 3,000. For info: Mystic Seaport, 75 Greenmanville Ave, Box 6000, Mystic, CT 06355. Phone: (860) 572-5315 or (888) 9SEAPORT. Web: www.mysticseaport.org.

KWANZAA. Dec 26–Jan 1, 2002. American black family observance created in 1966 by Dr. Maulana Karenga in recognition of traditional African harvest festivals. This seven-day festival stresses unity of the black family, with a harvest feast (karamu) on the first day and a day of meditation on the final one. Kwanzaa means "first fruit" in Swahili.

LOVERA, JUAN: BIRTH ANNIVERSARY. Dec 26, 1778. Venezuelan "Artist of Independence," whose best-known canvases commemorate the independence dates of Apr 19, 1810, and July 5, 1811. Known as the founder of historical painting in Venezuela. Died in 1841 (exact date unknown).

LUXEMBOURG: BLESSING OF THE WINE. Dec 26. Greiveldange, Luxembourg. Winemakers parade to the church, where a barrel of wine is blessed.

MAO TSE-TUNG: BIRTH ANNIVERSARY. Dec 26, 1893. Chinese librarian, teacher, communist revolutionist and "founding father" of the People's Republic of China, born at Hunan Province, China. Died at Beijing, Sept 9, 1976.

MILLER, HENRY (VALENTINE): BIRTH ANNIVERSARY. Dec 26, 1891. Controversial American novelist (*Tropic of Cancer*), born at New York, NY. Died at Pacific Palisades, CA, June 7, 1980.

NATIONAL WHINER'S DAY™. Dec 26. A day dedicated to whiners, especially those who return Christmas gifts and need lots of attention. People are encouraged to be happy about what they do have, rather than unhappy about what they don't have. The most famous whiner(s) of the year will be announced. Nominations accepted through Dec 15. For more info, please send SASE to: Kevin C. Zaborney, PO Box 64, Fairgrove, MI 48733. Phone: (517) 693-6666. E-mail: holidaymaker@loveslife.com. Web: holidaymaker.loveslife.com.

NELSON, THOMAS: BIRTH ANNIVERSARY. Dec 26, 1738. Merchant and signer of the Declaration of Independence, born at Yorktown, VA. Died at Hanover County, VA, Jan 4, 1789.

RADIUM DISCOVERED: ANNIVERSARY. Dec 26, 1898. French scientists Pierre and Marie Curie discovered the element radium, for which they later won the Nobel Prize for Physics.

SAINT STEPHEN'S DAY. Dec 26. One of the seven deacons named by the apostles to distribute alms. Died during 1st century. Feast Day is Dec 26 and is observed as a public holiday in Austria.

SECOND DAY OF CHRISTMAS. Dec 26. Observed as holiday in many countries.

SHENANDOAH NATIONAL PARK ESTABLISHED: ANNIVERSARY. Dec 26, 1935. Area of Blue Ridge Mountains of Virginia, originally authorized May 22, 1926, was established as a national park. For further park info: Shenandoah Natl Park, Rte 4, Box 348, Luray, VA 22835.

SOUNDS OF THE SEASON: A HOLIDAY CONCERT. Dec 26–27. Ash Lawn–Highland, Charlottesville, VA. Madrigal singers, yule log and cider. Est attendance: 150. For info: Ash Lawn–Highland, James Monroe Parkway, Charlottesville, VA 22902. Phone: (804) 293-9539. Fax: (804) 293-8000. E-mail: ashlawnjm@aol.com. Web: avenue.org/ashlawn.

SOUTH AFRICA: DAY OF GOODWILL. Dec 26. National holiday. Replaces Boxing Day.

UNITED KINGDOM: BOXING DAY BANK HOLIDAY. Dec 26. Bank and public holiday in England, Wales, Scotland and Northern Ireland.

BIRTHDAYS TODAY

Steve Allen, 80, entertainer, TV pioneer (the original "Tonight" show), composer, author, born New York, NY, Dec 26, 1921.

Evan Bayh, 46, US Senator (D, Indiana), born Shirkleville, IN, Dec 26, 1955.

Susan Butcher, 47, sled dog racer, born Cambridge, MA, Dec 26, 1954.

Gray Davis, 59, Governor of California (D), born The Bronx, NY, Dec 26, 1942.

Carlton Ernest Fisk, 54, Hall of Fame baseball player, born Bellows Falls, VT, Dec 26, 1947.

Alan King (Irwin Kniberg), 74, comedian, author ("Seventh Avenue," *Help! I'm a Prisoner in a Chinese Bakery*), born New York, NY, Dec 26, 1927.

Marcelo Rios, 26, tennis player, born Santiago, Chile, Dec 26, 1975.

Osborne Earl (Ozzie) Smith, 47, former baseball player, born Mobile, AL, Dec 26, 1954.

Phil Spector, 61, music producer, born New York, NY, Dec 26, 1940.

Richard Widmark, 87, actor (*Kiss of Death, Madigan*), born Sunrise, MN, Dec 26, 1914.

DECEMBER 27 — THURSDAY
Day 361 — 4 Remaining

CAYLEY, GEORGE: BIRTH ANNIVERSARY. Dec 27, 1773. Aviation pioneer Sir George Cayley, English scientist and inventor, was a theoretician who designed airplanes, helicopters and gliders. He is credited as the father of aerodynamics and he was the pilot of the world's first manned glider flight. Born at Scarborough, Yorkshire, England, he died at Brompton Hall, Yorkshire, Dec 15, 1857.

CHRISTMAS AT THE TOP MUSEUM. Dec 27–30. Spinning Top Museum, Burlington, WI. Enjoy the traditional, universal toys of tops and top games, well-loved Christmas gifts around the world in the 2-hour museum program: 35 hands-on games and experiments, two videos, view the exhibit of 2,000 items, plus a live show by top collector. Reservations required. For info: Spinning Top Museum, 533 Milwaukee Ave (Hwy 36), Burlington, WI 53105. Phone: (262) 763-3946.

DIETRICH, MARLENE: 100th BIRTH ANNIVERSARY. Dec 27, 1901. Marlene Dietrich was born at Berlin, Germany. A wrist injury destroyed her dream of becoming a concert violinist, and she enrolled in Max Reinhardt's drama school. Her first big break on the way to becoming a screen legend was in 1930 when Josef Von Sternberg cast her in *The Blue Angel*, the first talkie made in Germany. A year later, she and Sternberg moved to Hollywood and began a string of six films together with *Morocco*, the only film for which she received an Academy Award nomination. Some of her other films were *Destry Rides Again, Around the World in 80 Days, Touch of Evil, Judgment at Nuremberg* and *Witness for the Prosecution*. During the 1950s she was a cabaret singer in a stage revue that toured the globe. Dietrich died May 6, 1992, at Paris, France.

"HOWDY DOODY" TV PREMIERE: ANNIVERSARY. Dec 27, 1947. The first popular children's show was brought to TV by Bob Smith and was one of the first regular NBC shows to be shown in color. The show was set in the circus town of Doodyville, populated by people and puppets. Children sat in the bleachers' "Peanut Gallery" and participated in activities such as songs and stories. Human characters were Buffalo Bob (Bob

Smith), the silent clown Clarabell (Bob Keeshan, Bobby Nicholson and Lew Anderson), storekeeper Cornelius Cobb (Nicholson), Chief Thunderthud (Bill LeCornec), Princess Summerfall Winterspring (Judy Tyler and Linda Marsh), Bison Bill (Ted Brown) and wrestler Ugly Sam (Dayton Allen). Puppet costars included Howdy Doody, Phineas T. Bluster, Dilly Dally, Flub-a-Dub, Captain Scuttlebutt, Double Doody and Heidi Doody. The filmed adventures of Gumby were also featured. In the final episode, Clarabell broke his long silence to say, "Goodbye, kids."

KEPLER, JOHANNES: BIRTH ANNIVERSARY. Dec 27, 1571. One of the world's greatest astronomers, called "the father of modern astronomy," German mathematician Johannes Kepler was born at Wurttemberg, Germany; he died at Regensburg, Germany, Nov 15, 1630.

PASTEUR, LOUIS: BIRTH ANNIVERSARY. Dec 27, 1822. French chemist-bacteriologist born at Dole, Jura, France. Died at Villeneuve l'Etang, France, Sept 28, 1895. Discoverer of prophylactic inoculation against rabies. Pasteurization process named for him.

RADIO CITY MUSIC HALL: ANNIVERSARY. Dec 27, 1932. Radio City Music Hall, at New York City, opened on this date.

SAINT JOHN, APOSTLE-EVANGELIST: FEAST DAY. Dec 27. Son of Zebedee, Galilean fisherman, and Salome. Died about AD 100. Roman Rite Feast Day is Dec 27. (Observed May 8 by Byzantine Rite.)

SALK, LEE: 75th BIRTH ANNIVERSARY. Dec 27, 1926. American child psychologist Lee Salk was born at New York, NY. He became well known for proving the calming effect of a mother's heartbeat on a newborn infant. Salk's warning during the 1970s that women should not abandon full-time childrearing was met with wide opposition, especially from working mothers. He died May 2, 1992, at New York, NY.

BIRTHDAYS TODAY

Gerard Depardieu, 53, actor (*The Return of Martin Guerre, Cyrano de Bergerac*), born Chateauroux, France, Dec 27, 1948.
Tovah Feldshuh, 49, actress (*Holocaust*), born New York, NY, Dec 27, 1952.
Bernard Lanvin, 66, fashion designer, born Neuilly, France, Dec 27, 1935.
William Howell Masters, 86, physician, born Cleveland, OH, Dec 27, 1915.
Cokie Roberts, 58, news correspondent, born New Orleans, LA, Dec 27, 1943.
Anna Russell, 90, comedienne, born London, England, Dec 27, 1911.
Ernesto Zedillo Ponce de Leon, 50, former president of Mexico, born Mexico City, Mexico, Dec 27, 1951.

DECEMBER 28 — FRIDAY
Day 362 — 3 Remaining

AUSTRALIA: PROCLAMATION DAY. Dec 28. Observed in South Australia.

FROZEN FOOT RENDEZVOUS. Dec 28–30. Oakwood Lakes State Park, Bruce, SD. Treasure hunting, outdoor camping, muzzle-loading shooting contest and wild game cook-off. South Dakota State Park license required. Est attendance: 50. For info: Dave & Julie Huebner, 47826 Main St, Bushnell, SD 57276. Phone: (605) 693-4589.

December *2001*	S	M	T	W	T	F	S
							1
	2	3	4	5	6	7	8
	9	10	11	12	13	14	15
	16	17	18	19	20	21	22
	23	24	25	26	27	28	29
	30	31					

HOLY INNOCENTS DAY (CHILDERMAS). Dec 28. Commemoration of the massacre of children at Bethlehem, ordered by King Herod who wanted to destroy, among them, the infant Savior. Early and medieval accounts claimed as many as 144,000 victims, but more recent writers, noting that Bethlehem was a very small town, have revised the estimates of the number of children killed to between six and 20.

IOWA: ADMISSION DAY: ANNIVERSARY. Dec 28. Became 29th state in 1846.

MESSINA EARTHQUAKE: ANNIVERSARY. Dec 28, 1908. Messina, Sicily. The ancient town of Messina was struck by an earthquake. Nearly 80,000 persons died in the disaster, and half of the town's buildings were destroyed.

MOLSON, JOHN: BIRTH ANNIVERSARY. Dec 28, 1763. John Molson, an orphan, left his home at Lincolnshire, England, to settle in Montreal in 1782. He soon acquired a brewery and became patriarch of the Molson brewery family. Born at Lincolnshire, he died at Montreal, Quebec, Canada, Jan 11, 1836.

MOST DUBIOUS NEWS STORIES OF THE YEAR. Dec 28. An annual review of news stories based on bogus scientific and other claims, reported during the year by the nation's media. The Center monitors the media for "scare campaigns." Announcement will be posted on the website prior to the release date. For info: Alan Caruba, Founder, Natl Anxiety Center, Box 40, Maplewood, NJ 07040. Phone: (973) 763-6392. E-mail: acaruba@aol .com. Web: www.anxietycenter.com.

PLEDGE OF ALLEGIANCE RECOGNIZED: ANNIVERSARY. Dec 28, 1945. The US Congress officially recognized the Pledge of Allegiance and urged its frequent recitation in America's schools. The pledge was composed in 1892 by Francis Bellamy, a Baptist minister. At the time, Bellamy was chairman of a committee of state school superintendents of education, and several public schools adopted his pledge that year as part of the Columbus Day quadricentennial celebration that year. In 1955, the Knights of Columbus persuaded Congress to add the words "under God" to the pledge.

POOR RICHARD'S ALMANACK : ANNIVERSARY. Dec 28, 1732. The *Pennsylvania Gazette* carried the first known advertisement for the first issue of *Poor Richard's Almanack* by Richard Saunders (Benjamin Franklin) for the year 1733. The advertisement promised "many pleasant and witty verses, jests and sayings . . . new fashions, games for kisses . . . men and melons . . . breakfast in bed, &c." America's most famous almanac, *Poor Richard's* was published through the year 1758 and has been imitated many times since. From *The Autobiography of Benjamin Franklin*: "In 1732 I first publish'd my Almanack, under the name of *Richard Saunders*; it was continu'd by me about twenty-five years, commonly call'd *Poor Richard's Almanack.* I endeavor'd to make it both entertaining and useful, and it accordingly came to be in such demand, that I reap'd considerable profit from it, vending annually near ten thousand. And observing that it was generally read, scarce any neighborhood in the province being without it, I consider'd it as a proper vehicle for conveying instruction among the common people, who bought scarcely any other books; I therefore filled all the little spaces that occurr'd between the remarkable days in the calendar with proverbial sentences, chiefly such as inculcated industry and frugality, as the means of procuring wealth, and thereby securing virtue; it being more difficult for a man in want, to act always honestly, as, to use here one of those proverbs, *it is hard for an empty sack to stand upright.*"

VICE PRESIDENTIAL RESIGNATION: ANNIVERSARY. Dec 28, 1832. John C. Calhoun, who had served as vice president of the US under two presidents (John Quincy Adams and Andrew Jackson), Mar 4, 1825–Dec 28, 1832, finding himself in growing disagreement with President Jackson, resigned the office of vice president, the first to do so. He spent most of his subsequent political life as a US senator from South Carolina.

WILSON, WOODROW: BIRTH ANNIVERSARY. Dec 28, 1856. The 28th president of the US was born Thomas Woodrow Wilson at Staunton, VA. Twice elected president (1912 and

1916), it was Wilson who said, "The world must be made safe for democracy," as he asked the Congress to declare war on Germany, Apr 2, 1917. His first wife, Ellen, died Aug 6, 1914, and he married Edith Bolling Galt, Dec 18, 1915. He suffered a paralytic stroke, Sept 16, 1919, never regaining his health. There were many speculations about who (possibly Mrs Wilson?) was running the government during his illness. His second term of office ended Mar 3, 1921, and he died at Washington, DC, Feb 3, 1924.

BIRTHDAYS TODAY

Ray Bourque, 41, hockey player, born Montreal, Quebec, Canada, Dec 28, 1960.

Malcolm Gets, 37, actor ("Caroline in the City"), born near Gainesville, FL, Dec 28, 1964.

Hubert Myatt (Hubie) Green III, 55, golfer, born Birmingham, AL, Dec 28, 1946.

Lou Jacobi, 88, actor (*Irma La Douce*), born Toronto, Ontario, Canada, Dec 28, 1913.

Tim Johnson, 55, US Senator (D, South Dakota), born Canton, SD, Dec 28, 1946.

Patrick Rafter, 29, tennis player, born Mount Isa, Queensland, Australia, Dec 28, 1972.

Maggie Smith, 67, actress (*The Prime of Miss Jean Brodie*; Tony for *Lettice & Lovage*), born Ilford, England, Dec 28, 1934.

Denzel Washington, 47, actor ("St. Elsewhere," *Glory, Malcolm X*), born Mount Vernon, NY, Dec 28, 1954.

Edgar Winter, 55, singer, musician (*Edgar Winter's White Trash, They Only Come Out at Night*), born Beaumont, TX, Dec 28, 1946.

DECEMBER 29 — SATURDAY
Day 363 — 2 Remaining

ALL-COLLEGE BASKETBALL TOURNAMENT. Dec 29–30. Myriad Convention Center, Oklahoma City, OK. The oldest college basketball tournament in the world, predating the NCAA, NBA, NAIA and the NIT. 161 universities have competed. Annually, between Christmas and New Year's. Est attendance: 25,000. For info: Tim Brassfield, OK City All Sports Assn, 100 W Main, Ste 287, Oklahoma City, OK 73102. Phone: (405) 236-5000. Fax: (405) 236-5008. E-mail: info@okallsports.org. Web: www.okallsports.org.

CASALS, PABLO: 125th BIRTH ANNIVERSARY. Dec 29, 1876. Famed cellist Pablo Carlos Salvador Defillio de Casals was born at Venrell, Spain, and died at Rio Pedros, Puerto Rico, Oct 22, 1973.

GLADSTONE, WILLIAM EWART: BIRTH ANNIVERSARY. Dec 29, 1809. English statesman and author for whom the Gladstone (luggage) bag was named. Inspiring orator, eccentric individual, intensely loved or hated by all who knew him (cheered from the streets and jeered from the balconies), Gladstone is said to have left more writings (letters, diaries, journals, books) than any other major English politician. However, his preoccupation with the charitable rehabilitation of prostitutes was perhaps easily misunderstood. Born at Liverpool, England, he was four times Britain's prime minister. Gladstone died at Hawarden, Wales, May 19, 1898.

HOLIDAY BOWL PARADE AND GAME. Dec 29 (tentative; confirm after June 1). Parade along Harbor Drive; game at Qualcomm Stadium, San Diego, CA. The televised parade, the morning of the Holiday Bowl football game (teams picked from Pac 10 and Big 12), features floats, marching bands, giant balloons and unique specialty units. Parade at 10 AM, kickoff for game is 5 PM. Est attendance: 100,000. For info: Mark Neville, Holiday Bowl, PO Box 601400, San Diego, CA 92160-1400. Phone: (619) 283-5808. Fax: (619) 281-7947. Web: www.holiday bowl.com.

JOHNSON, ANDREW: BIRTH ANNIVERSARY. Dec 29, 1808. Seventeenth president of the US, Andrew Johnson, proprietor of a tailor shop at Laurens, SC, before he entered politics, was born at Raleigh, NC. Upon Abraham Lincoln's assassination Johnson became president. He was the first president to be impeached by the House and was acquitted Mar 26, 1868, by the Senate. After his term of office as president (Apr 15, 1865–Mar 3, 1869) he made several unsuccessful attempts to win public office. Finally he was elected to the US Senate from Tennessee and served in the Senate from Mar 4, 1875, until his death at Carter's Station, TN, July 31, 1875.

NEPAL: BIRTHDAY OF HIS MAJESTY THE KING. Dec 29. National holiday of Nepal. Three-day celebration of the King's birth in 1945 with huge public rally at Tundikkel, gay pageantry, musical bands and illumination in the towns at night.

RASPUTIN, GRIGORI EFIMOVICH: 85th ASSASSINATION ANNIVERSARY. Dec 29, 1916. Russian monk and mystic, born Grigori Efimovich Novjkh, about 1871, at Siberia. Rasputin gained great influence with Russian emperor Nicholas II and the empress Alexandra, urging severe measures in dealing with the peasant masses, virtually dictating government policy. Notoriously dissolute and corrupt, Rasputin was said to have possessed hypnotic powers. He claimed divine inspiration and the ability to perform miracles. His name became synonymous with corruption and evil, and he was called the "plague pot" of Russia. In fact, Rasputin was a nickname from the Russian word *rasputny*, meaning debauched, profligate, licentious. When an attempt to poison him failed, he was shot to death and his body dropped through a hole in the ice into the Neva River. It was recovered three days later and buried in a silver casket at Tsarkoe Selo. The imperial government was crushed by the 1917 Revolution within a year of his death.

SAINT THOMAS OF CANTERBURY: FEAST DAY. Dec 29. Thomas, Archbishop of Canterbury, was born at London in 1118 and was murdered at the Canterbury Cathedral on this date in 1170.

TEXAS: ADMISSION DAY: ANNIVERSARY. Dec 29. Became 28th state in 1845.

UNITED NATIONS: INTERNATIONAL DAY FOR BIOLOGICAL DIVERSITY. Dec 29. On Dec 19, 1994, the General Assembly proclaimed this observance for Dec 29, the date of entry into force of the Convention on Biological Diversity (Res 49/119). Designation of the Day had been recommended by the Conference of the Parties to the Convention, held at Nassau Nov 28–Dec 9, 1994. For info: United Nations, Dept of Public Info, New York, NY 10017.

WOUNDED KNEE MASSACRE: ANNIVERSARY. Dec 29, 1890. Anniversary of the massacre of more than 200 Native American men, women and children by the US 7th Cavalry at Wounded Knee Creek, SD. Government efforts to suppress a ceremonial religious practice, the Ghost Dance (which called for a messiah who would restore the bison to the plains, make the white men disappear and bring back the old Native American way of life), had resulted in the death of Sitting Bull, Dec 15, 1890, which further inflamed the disgruntled Native Americans and culminated in the slaughter at Wounded Knee, Dec 29.

YMCA ORGANIZED: 150th ANNIVERSARY. Dec 29, 1851. The first US branch of the Young Men's Christian Association was organized at Boston. It was modeled on an organization begun at London in 1844.

"YOU ASKED FOR IT" TV PREMIERE: ANNIVERSARY. Dec 29, 1950. Skippy Peanut Butter sponsored this half-hour human-interest show which was hosted by Art Baker until 1958 and then Jack Smith. The show answered viewers' letters requesting various types of unusual acts, heroic people and talented animals. The format of the network versions involved reading the viewer's letter prior to the feature, with the viewer's picture superimposed onto a jar of Skippy Peanut Butter.

"YOUNG DR. MALONE" TV PREMIERE: ANNIVERSARY. Dec 29, 1958. This daytime serial was first a radio show (1939–60). It was set in the town of Three Oaks at Valley Hospital. Six characters from a serial it replaced, "Today Is Ours," joined the cast. Cast members included: William Prince, Virginia Dwyer, Kathleen Widdoes, Emily McLaughlin, Peter Brandon, Lesley Woods, Martin Blaine, Zina Bethune, Patty McCormack and Diana Hyland.

BIRTHDAYS TODAY

Ted Danson, 54, actor ("Cheers," "Becker," *Three Men and a Baby*), born San Diego, CA, Dec 29, 1947.
Marianne Faithfull, 55, singer ("As Tears Go By," "Summer Nights"), actress, born London, England, Dec 29, 1946.
Thomas Edwin Jarriel, 67, broadcast journalist, born LaGrange, GA, Dec 29, 1934.
Mary Tyler Moore, 65, actress (two Emmys for "The Dick Van Dyke Show"; three Emmys for "The Mary Tyler Moore Show"; *Ordinary People*), born Brooklyn, NY, Dec 29, 1936.
Jon Polito, 51, actor ("Homicide"), born Philadelphia, PA, Dec 29, 1950.
Paula Poundstone, 42, comedienne, born Sudbury, MA, Dec 29, 1959.
Jon Voight, 63, actor (*Midnight Cowboy, Deliverance*), born Yonkers, NY, Dec 29, 1938.

DECEMBER 30 — SUNDAY
Day 364 — 1 Remaining

GUGGENHEIM, SIMON: BIRTH ANNIVERSARY. Dec 30, 1867. American capitalist and philanthropist, born at Philadelphia, PA. He established, in memory of his son, the John Simon Guggenheim Memorial Foundation, in 1925. Died Nov 2, 1941, at New York, NY.

KIPLING, RUDYARD: BIRTH ANNIVERSARY. Dec 30, 1865. English poet, novelist and short story writer, Nobel prize laureate, Kipling was born at Bombay, India. After working as a journalist at India, he traveled around the world. He married an American and lived in Vermont for several years. Kipling is best known for his children's stories, such as the *Jungle Book* and *Just So Stories* and poems such as "The Ballad of East and West" and "If." He died at London, England, Jan 18, 1936.

LEACOCK, STEPHEN: BIRTH ANNIVERSARY. Dec 30, 1869. Canadian economist and humorist, born at Swanmore, Hampshire, England. Died Mar 28, 1944, at Toronto, Canada. "Lord Ronald. . .," he wrote in *Nonsense Novels*, "flung himself upon his horse and rode madly off in all directions."

"LET'S MAKE A DEAL" TV PREMIERE: ANNIVERSARY. Dec 30, 1963. Monty Hall hosted this outrageous and no-skill-required game show. Audience members, many of whom wore costumes, were selected to sit in the trading area, and some were picked to "make a deal" with Hall by trading something of their own for something they were offered. Sometimes prizes were worthless ("zonks"). At the end of the show, the two peo-

		S	M	T	W	T	F	S
December								1
2001		2	3	4	5	6	7	8
		9	10	11	12	13	14	15
		16	17	18	19	20	21	22
		23	24	25	26	27	28	29
		30	31					

ple who had won the most were given the option to trade their winnings for a chance at the "Big Deal," hidden behind one of three doors. Jay Stewart was the announcer and Carol Merrill the assistant. The most recent revival (1990–91) was hosted by Bob Hilton.

LUNAR ECLIPSE. Dec 30. Penumbral eclipse of the moon. Moon enters penumbra at 3:25 AM, EST, reaches middle of eclipse at 5:29 AM, and leaves penumbra at 7:33 AM. Visible in Australasia, Asia except SW, N Europe, Greenland, the Americas, Pacific Ocean.

MONITOR SINKS: ANNIVERSARY. Dec 30, 1862. The Union ironclad ship USS *Monitor* (which achieved fame after her battle with the *Merrimac*) sank off Cape Hatteras during a storm. Sixteen of her crew were lost. See also: "Battle of the *Monitor* and the *Merrimac*: Anniv" (Mar 9).

MOON PHASE: FULL MOON. Dec 30. Moon enters Full Moon phase at 5:40 AM, EST.

PARKS, BERT: BIRTH ANNIVERSARY. Dec 30, 1914. Bert Parks was born at Atlanta, GA. An actor whose career spanned radio, film, television and Broadway, his name became synonymous with the Miss America pageant which he emceed for 25 years. He was fired from the Miss America post in 1980 when pageant officials wanted to acquire a younger look. Parks made a special return appearance for the 1990 pageant, once again singing his signature song "There She Is." He got his big break in show business in 1945 as the emcee for the radio quiz show "Break the Bank" and later as the host of "Stop the Music." When both shows moved to television they did so with Parks at the microphone, launching a television career that included hosting a variety of quiz shows and guest appearances on dramatic series. He died Feb 2, 1992, at La Jolla, CA.

PHILIPPINES: RIZAL DAY: ANNIVERSARY. Dec 30. Commemorates martyrdom of Dr. Jose Rizal in 1896.

"THE ROY ROGERS SHOW" TV PREMIERE: 50th ANNIVERSARY. Dec 30, 1951. This very popular TV western starred Roy Rogers and his wife, Dale Evans, as themselves. It also featured Pat Brady as Rogers's sidekick who rode a jeep named Nellybelle, the singing group Sons of the Pioneers, Rogers's horse Trigger, Evans's horse Buttermilk and a German shepherd named Bullet. This half-hour show was especially popular with young viewers.

USSR ESTABLISHED: ANNIVERSARY. Dec 30, 1922. After the Russian revolution of 1917 and the subsequent three-year civil war, the Union of Soviet Socialist Republics (or Soviet Union) was founded, a confederation of Russia, Byelorussia, the Ukraine and the Transcaucasian Federation. It was the first state in the world to be based on Marxist communism. The Soviet Union was dissolved Dec 8, 1991. See also: "Soviet Union Dissolved" (Dec 8).

VAN FLEET, JO: BIRTH ANNIVERSARY. Dec 30, 1922. Actress (Oscar for *East of Eden*; "Cinderella"), born at Oakland, CA. Died June 10, 1996.

BIRTHDAYS TODAY

Joseph Bologna, 63, actor, writer (*The Big Bus, My Favorite Year, Blame It on Rio*), born Brooklyn, NY, Dec 30, 1938.
James Burrows, 61, director ("Cheers," "Taxi"), born Los Angeles, CA, Dec 30, 1940.
Skeeter Davis, 70, singer, born Dry Ridge, KY, Dec 30, 1931.
Bo Diddley, 73, singer, songwriter ("Who Do You Love," "I'm a Man"), musician, born McCombs, MS, Dec 30, 1928.
Davy Jones, 55, actor, singer (The Monkees, "Daydream Believer"), born Manchester, England, Dec 30, 1946.
Sanford (Sandy) Koufax, 66, former sportscaster, Baseball Hall of Fame pitcher, born Brooklyn, NY, Dec 30, 1935.
Matt Lauer, 44, news anchor ("Today"), born New York, NY, Dec 30, 1957.
Michael Nesmith, 59, singer, songwriter (The Monkees), director, born Houston, TX, Dec 30, 1942.

Russ Tamblyn, 66, actor ("Twin Peaks," *Peyton Place, West Side Story*), born Los Angeles, CA, Dec 30, 1935.

Concetta Tomei, 56, actress ("Providence," "China Beach"), born Kenosha, WI, Dec 30, 1945.

Tracey Ullman, 42, actress, singer ("The Tracey Ullman Show," *I Love You to Death*), born Buckinghamshire, England, Dec 30, 1959.

Meredith Vieira, 48, TV host ("The View"), born Providence, RI, Dec 30, 1953.

Tiger (Eldrick) Woods, 26, golfer, winner of the 1997 Masters tournament, born Cypress, CA, Dec 30, 1975.

Health, Peace, and sweet content be yours. Shakespeare

DECEMBER 31 — MONDAY
Day 365 — 0 Remaining

ALBANY'S NEW YEAR'S EVE CELEBRATION. Dec 31. Downtown Albany, NY. A New Year's eve celebration of the arts in multiple locations downtown with music, dancing, children's events, fireworks, food and beverages. Annually, on New Year's Eve. Est attendance: 10,000. For info: City Hall Office of Special Events, Eagle St, Albany, NY 12207. Phone: (518) 434-2032. Web: www.albanyevents.org.

CANADA: FIRST NIGHTS. Dec 31. These Canadian cities have First Night celebrations: Banff, Drayton Valley, Edmonton and Red Deer, Alberta; Gabriola, Kamloops, Maple Ridge and Vancouver, British Columbia; Fredericton and St. John, New Brunswick; Yellowknife, Northwest Territories; and Chatham-Kent, Hamilton, Kingston, Peterborough, Toronto and Uxbridge, Ontario. For info: First Night Intl, 200 Lincoln St, Ste 301, Boston, MA 02111-2418. Phone: (617) 357-0065. Web: www.firstnightintl.org.

DENVER, JOHN: BIRTH ANNIVERSARY. Dec 31, 1943. Born Henry John Deutschendorf at Roswell, NM, this singer-songwriter ("Rocky Mountain High," "Sunshine on My Shoulder") died in a plane crash off the coast of California, Oct 12, 1997.

FIRST BANK OPENS IN US: ANNIVERSARY. Dec 31, 1781. The first modern bank in the US, the Bank of North America, was organized by Robert Morris and received its charter from the Confederation Congress. It began operations Jan 7, 1782, at Philadelphia.

FIRST NIGHT AUGUSTA. Dec 31. Staunton, VA. An alcohol/drug free community celebration of the arts for the new year designed for the whole family to enjoy. Kicks off with children's activities and performances, fireworks. Entry to any and all events via entry buttons ($5 for adults). Est attendance: 4,500. For info: Festival Dir, First Night Augusta, PO Box 716, Waynesboro, VA 22980. Phone: (540) 946-5387.

FIRST NIGHT ASHEVILLE. Dec 31. Asheville, NC. This alcohol-free celebration of art, music and entertainment includes approximately 20 indoor venues featuring magic, drama and dance, as well as interactive games and children's activities. The grand finale includes live music and a countdown to midnight that culminates with a spectacular fireworks show. Est attendance: 15,000. For info: Paul Clarke, Events Mgr, Asheville Parks & Rec/First Night, PO Box 7148, Asheville, NC 28802-7148. Phone: (828) 259-5800. Fax: (828) 259-5606.

FIRST NIGHT BOSTON. Dec 31. Boston, MA. The largest New Year's arts festival in North America, First Night Boston has grown to be a highly anticipated tradition. The festival features more than 1,000 artists in 250 performances and exhibitions in 50 venues throughout downtown Boston, a Mardi Gras-style Grand Procession, large-scale ice sculptures, music, dance, theater, family entertainment, fireworks at midnight and much more! Boston was the site of the first First Night in 1976. Est attendance: 1,500,000. For info: First Night, Inc, 20 Park Plaza, Ste 1000, Boston, MA 02116. Phone: (617) 542-1399. Web: www.firstnight.org.

FIRST NIGHT HARTFORD. Dec 31. Hartford, CT. Day-long celebration beginning at 2 PM and ending at midnight. Visual and performing arts, procession, theater, music, activities for children and fireworks to welcome the New Year. Est attendance: 30,000. For info: Pamela Amodio, Dir, Events Mgmt, Hartford Downtown Council, 250 Constitution Plaza, Hartford, CT 06103. Phone: (860) 728-3089. Fax: (860) 527-9696.

FIRST NIGHT ROANOKE. Dec 31. Downtown, Roanoke, VA. An alcohol-free New Year's Eve Celebration of the Lively Arts. First-rate entertainment and hands-on activities for the entire community, also includes fireworks, dragon processional, carriage rides. 15 site locations. Held annually on New Year's Eve. 11th annual. Est attendance: 10,000. For info: Wendi Schultz, CFE Exec Dir, Roanoke Festival in the Park, PO Box 8276, Roanoke, VA 24014. Phone: (540) 342-2640.

FIRST NIGHTS. Dec 31. The following US cities have First Night celebrations: Mobile, AL; Fayetteville, AR; Bakersfield, Escondido, Fullerton, Martinez, Monterey, San Diego, San Luis Obispo, Santa Barbara, Santa Cruz, Santa Fe Springs, Santa Rosa and Stockton, CA; Fort Collins and Pikes Peak, CO; Cheshire, Danbury, Hartford, Mystic, Torrington and Westport/Weston, CT; Dover and Wilmington, DE; Washington, DC; Atlantic Beach, Delray Beach, Dunedin, Fort Walton Beach, Miami Beach and St. Petersburg, FL; Americus, Athens, Atlanta, Gainesville, Golden Isles, Macon and Savannah, GA; Boise and Idaho Falls, ID; Aurora, Bloomington/Normal, Evanston, Pontiac, River Bend, Rockford and Springfield, IL; Evansville, IN; Owensboro, KY; Annapolis, Frederick, Montgomery County and Talbot, MD; Beverly, Chatham, Fall River, Gloucester, Lowell, Martha's Vineyard, New Bedford, Newburyport, Northampton, Pittsfield, Quincy, Sharon, Sturbridge, Twin Cities and Worcester, MA; Jackson, MS; Cadillac and Birmingham, MI; St. Paul, MN; Columbia, St. Louis and Springfield, MO; Flathead and Missoula, MT; Concord, Mount Washington Valley, Portsmouth and Wolfeboro, NH; Bridgewater/Raritan/Somerville, Flemington, Haddonfield, Manasquan, Maplewood/South Orange, Montclair, Moorestown, Morris County, Mount Holly, Newark, Oakland, Ocean City, Ocean County, Red Bank, Ridgewood, Rutherford, Summit, Teaneck and Westfield, NJ; Amsterdam, Binghamton, Buffalo, Gloversville/Johnstown, Greenport, Middletown, New York City, Norwich, Nyack, Oneonta, Rye, Saratoga, Sayville, Staten Island, Syracuse and Watertown, NY; Asheville, Piedmont, Raleigh and Sanford, NC; Grand Forks and Minot, ND; Akron, Canfield,

Columbus, North Ridgeville and Toledo, OH; Lawton, OK; Eugene, OR; Bethlehem, Bloomsburg, Bradford, Bristol, Carlisle, Doylestown, Erie, Mt. Lebanon, Newtown, Norwin, Oil City, Philipsburg, Pittsburgh, Scranton, Warren and York, PA; Providence and Westerly, RI; Charleston, Greenville and Varnville, SC; Yankton, SD; Ogden, Provo and Salt Lake City, UT; Bennington, Burlington, Montpelier, Rutland and St. Johnsbury, VT; Alexandria, Charlottesville, Fredericksburg, Harrisonburg, Leesburg, Norfolk, Warrenton, Williamsburg and Winchester, VA; Tacoma and Tri-Cities, WA; Morgantown, WV; and Jackson Hole, WY. For info: First Night Intl, 200 Lincoln St, Ste 301, Boston, MA 02111-2418. Phone: (617) 357-0065. Fax: (617) 357-0066. E-mail: mainoffice@firstnightintl.org. Web: www.firstnightintl.org.

JAPAN: NAMAHAGE. Dec 31. In evening, groups of "Namahage" men disguised as devils make door-to-door visits, growling, "Any good-for-nothing fellow hereabout?" The object of this annual event is to give sluggards an opportunity to change their minds and become diligent. Otherwise, according to legend, they will be punished by devils. Oga Peninsula, Akita Prefecture, Japan.

LEAP SECOND ADJUSTMENT TIME. Dec 31. One of the times that have been favored for the addition or subtraction of a second from clock time (to coordinate atomic and astronomical time). The determination to adjust is made by the International Earth Rotation Service of the International Bureau of Weights and Measures, at Paris, France. See also: "Leap Seconds" (see Contents).

MAKE UP YOUR MIND DAY. Dec 31. A day for all those people who have a hard time making up their minds. Make a decision today and follow through with it! Annually, Dec 31. For info: A.C. Moeller and M.A. Dufour, Box 71, Clio, MI 48420-1042.

MARSHALL, GEORGE CATLETT: BIRTH ANNIVERSARY. Dec 31, 1880. Chairman of the newly formed Joint Chiefs of Staff Committee throughout the US's involvement in WWII, General George Marshall was born at Uniontown, PA. He accompanied Roosevelt or represented the US at most Allied war conferences. He served as secretary of state and was designer of the Marshall Plan after the war. Died Oct 16, 1959, at Washington, DC.

"THE MATCH GAME" TV PREMIERE: ANNIVERSARY. Dec 31, 1962. This game show has appeared on all the major networks and in syndication, with most seasons hosted by Gene Rayburn. On the NBC version, two teams of three members each (two contestants and one celebrity) competed to try to match their answers to a fill-in-the-blank with their teammates' answers. On the CBS and syndicated versions, two contestants and a celebrity panel played; contestants won points for every celebrity's answer that matched theirs. Ross Shafer hosted the ABC revival. In 1998 the "Match Game" reappeared with host Michael Burger.

MATISSE, HENRI: BIRTH ANNIVERSARY. Dec 31, 1869. Painter born at Le Cateau, France. Matisse also designed textiles and stained glass windows. Died at Nice, France, Nov 3, 1954.

NEW YEAR'S EVE. Dec 31. The last evening of the Gregorian calendar year, traditionally a night for merrymaking to welcome in the new year.

NEW YEAR'S FEST. Dec 31. Kalamazoo, MI. Kalamazoo comes alive as families, teens and seniors come downtown to welcome the New Year. Featuring more than 25 different artists, performances are hosted in 11 different indoor sites throughout downtown Kalamazoo. The cultural celebration offers music, theatre, puppetry, dance, mime and storytelling. Artists come from throughout the Midwest to join in this non-alcoholic celebration. Est attendance: 5,500. For info: Deborah Droppers, New Year's Fest, Inc, 346 W Michigan Ave, Kalamazoo, MI 49007. Phone: (616) 388-2830. E-mail: EventKzoo@aol.com.

NIXON, JOHN: DEATH ANNIVERSARY. Dec 31, 1808. Revolutionary patriot and businessman, Commander of the Philadelphia City Guard, born 1733 (exact date unknown).

Appointed to conduct the first public reading of the Declaration of Independence, July 8, 1776. Died at Philadelphia, PA.

PANAMA: ASSUMES CONTROL OF CANAL: ANNIVERSARY. Dec 31, 1999. With the expiration of the Panama Canal Treaty of 1979 at noon, the Republic of Panama assumed full responsibility for the canal and the US Panama Canal Commission ceased to exist.

SAINT SYLVESTER'S DAY. Dec 31. Observed in Belgium, Germany, France, Switzerland. Commemorates death of Pope Sylvester I in 335. Feasting, particularly upon "St. Sylvester's Carp."

SAMOA: SAMOAN FIRE DANCE. Dec 31. New Year's Eve is occasion for Samoan bamboo fireworks, singing and traditional performances such as the Samoan Fire Dance. As the last land mass before the International Date Line, Samoa (formerly Western Samoa) was the last country in the world to usher in the year 2000.

WORLD PEACE MEDITATION. Dec 31. An opportunity for people around the world to focus their thoughts and energy on peace. The event is observed internationally, beginning at noon Greenwich Mean Time (GMT) and lasting one hour (7 AM–8 AM, EST). For info: Quartus Foundation, PO Box 1768, Boerne, TX 78006. Phone: (830) 249-3985. Fax: (830) 249-3318. E-mail: quartus@texas.net. Web: www.quartus.org.

BIRTHDAYS TODAY

Sir Anthony Hopkins, 64, actor (*The Silence of the Lambs, Legends of the Fall*), born Port Talbot, South Wales, UK, Dec 31, 1937.

Val Kilmer, 42, actor (*Batman Forever, Top Secret, The Doors, Heat*), born Los Angeles, CA, Dec 31, 1959.

Ben Kingsley (Krishna Bhanji), 58, actor (Oscar for *Gandhi; Bugsy, Schindler's List*), born Yorkshire, England, Dec 31, 1943.

Tim Matheson, 53, actor (*Animal House*, "The Virginian," "Bonanza"), born Los Angeles, CA, Dec 31, 1948.

Sarah Miles, 60, actress (*The Servant, Blow-Up, Hope and Glory*), born Ingatestone, England, Dec 31, 1941.

Bebe Neuwirth, 43, actress ("Cheers," "Frasier"; stage: *Chicago*), born Newark, NJ, Dec 31, 1958.

Odetta (Odetta Homes Felious Gordon), 71, folksinger, musician, born Birmingham, AL, Dec 31, 1930.

James Remar, 48, actor (*48HRS, Drugstore Cowboy*), born Boston, MA, Dec 31, 1953.

Patti Smith, 55, singer ("Because the Night"), born Chicago, IL, Dec 31, 1946.

Donna Summer (LaDonna Andrea Gaines), 53, singer ("Bad Girls"), born Boston, MA, Dec 31, 1948.

Diane Halfin von Furstenberg, 56, fashion designer, author, born Brussels, Belgium, Dec 31, 1945.

See ya next year!

ASTRONOMICAL PHENOMENA
FOR THE YEARS 2001–2003

All dates are given in terms of Eastern Standard or Daylight Time and the Gregorian calendar.

(Based in part on information prepared by the Nautical Almanac Office, US Naval Observatory.)

2001

PRINCIPAL PHENOMENA, 2001
EARTH

Perihelion . . . . Jan 4
Aphelion . . . . July 4
Equinoxes . . . . Mar 20, Sept 22
Solstices . . . . June 21, Dec 21

PHASES OF THE MOON

New Moon	First Quarter	Full Moon	Last Quarter
	Jan 2	Jan 9	Jan 16
Jan 24	Feb 1	Feb 8	Feb 14
Feb 23	Mar 2	Mar 9	Mar 16
Mar 24	Apr 1	Apr 7	Apr 15
Apr 23	Apr 30	May 7	May 15
May 22	May 29	June 5	June 13
June 21	June 27	July 5	July 13
July 20	July 27	Aug 4	Aug 12
Aug 18	Aug 25	Sept 2	Sept 10
Sept 17	Sept 24	Oct 2	Oct 10
Oct 16	Oct 23	Nov 1	Nov 8
Nov 15	Nov 22	Nov 30	Dec 7
Dec 14	Dec 22	Dec 30	

ECLIPSES

Total eclipse of the Moon . . . . Jan 9
Total eclipse of the Sun . . . . June 21
Partial eclipse of the Moon . . . . July 5
Annular eclipse of the Sun . . . . Dec 14
Penumbral eclipse of the Moon . . . . Dec 30

VISIBILITY OF PLANETS
IN MORNING AND EVENING TWILIGHT

	Morning	Evening
Venus	Apr 4–Dec 3	Jan 1–Mar 26
Mars	Jan 1–June 13	June 13–Dec 31
Jupiter	June 29–Dec 31	Jan 1–May 31
Saturn	June 13–Dec 3	Jan 1–May 7
		Dec 3–Dec 31

2002

PRINCIPAL PHENOMENA, 2002
EARTH

Perihelion . . . . Jan 2
Aphelion . . . . July 6
Equinoxes . . . . Mar 20, Sept 23
Solstices . . . . June 21, Dec 21

PHASES OF THE MOON

New Moon	First Quarter	Full Moon	Last Quarter
			Jan 5
Jan 13	Jan 21	Jan 28	Feb 4
Feb 12	Feb 20	Feb 27	Mar 5
Mar 13	Mar 21	Mar 28	Apr 4
Apr 12	Apr 20	Apr 26	May 4
May 12	May 19	May 26	June 2
June 10	June 17	June 24	July 2
July 10	July 17	July 24	Aug 1
Aug 8	Aug 15	Aug 22	Aug 30
Sept 6	Sept 13	Sept 21	Sept 29
Oct 6	Oct 13	Oct 21	Oct 29
Nov 4	Nov 11	Nov 19	Nov 27
Dec 4	Dec 11	Dec 19	Dec 26

ECLIPSES

Penumbral eclipse of the Moon . . . . May 26
Annular eclipse of the Sun . . . . June 10
Penumbral eclipse of the Moon . . . . June 24
Penumbral eclipse of the Moon . . . . Nov 19
Total eclipse of the Sun . . . . Dec 4

2003

PRINCIPAL PHENOMENA, 2003
EARTH

Perihelion . . . . Jan 4
Aphelion . . . . July 4
Equinoxes . . . . Mar 20, Sept 23
Solstices . . . . June 21, Dec 22

PHASES OF THE MOON

New Moon	First Quarter	Full Moon	Last Quarter
Jan 2	Jan 10	Jan 18	Jan 25
Feb 1	Feb 9	Feb 16	Feb 23
Mar 2	Mar 11	Mar 18	Mar 24
Apr 1	Apr 9	Apr 16	Apr 23
May 1	May 9	May 15	May 22
May 31	June 7	June 14	June 21
June 29	July 6	July 13	July 21
July 29	Aug 5	Aug 12	Aug 19
Aug 27	Sept 3	Sept 10	Sept 18
Sept 25	Oct 2	Oct 10	Oct 18
Oct 25	Oct 31	Nov 8	Nov 16
Nov 23	Nov 30	Dec 8	Dec 16
Dec 23	Dec 30		

ECLIPSES

Total eclipse of the Moon . . . . May 15
Annular eclipse of the Sun . . . . May 31
Total eclipse of the Moon . . . . Nov 8
Total eclipse of the Sun . . . . Nov 23

CALENDAR INFORMATION FOR THE YEAR 2001

Time shown is Eastern Standard Time. All dates are given in terms of the Gregorian calendar.
(Based in part on information prepared by the Nautical Almanac Office, US Naval Observatory.)

ERAS

	YEAR	BEGINS
Byzantine	7510	Sept 14
Jewish*	5762	Sept 18
Chinese (Year of the Snake)	4699	Jan 24
Roman (AUC)	2754	Jan 14
Nabonassar	2750	Apr 23
Japanese (Heisei)	13	Jan 1
Grecian (Seleucidae)	2313	Sept 14 (or Oct 14)
Indian (Saka)	1923	Mar 22
Diocletian	1718	Sept 12
Islamic (Hegira)**	1422	Mar 26

*Year begins at sunset.   **Year begins at moon crescent.

RELIGIOUS CALENDARS

Epiphany	Jan 6
Shrove Tuesday	Feb 27
Ash Wednesday	Feb 28
Lent	Feb 28–Apr 14
Palm Sunday	Apr 8
Good Friday	Apr 13
Easter Day	Apr 15
Ascension Day	May 24
Whit Sunday (Pentecost)	June 3
Trinity Sunday	June 10
First Sunday in Advent	Dec 2
Christmas Day (Tuesday)	Dec 25

Eastern Orthodox Church Observances

Great Lent begins	Feb 26
Pascha (Easter)	Apr 15
Ascension	May 24
Pentecost	June 3

Jewish Holy Days

Purim	Mar 9
Passover (1st day)	Apr 8
Shavuot	May 28
Tisha B'av	July 29
Rosh Hashanah (New Year)	Sept 18–19
Yom Kippur	Sept 27
Succoth	Oct 2–10
Chanukah	Dec 10–17

Islamic Holy Days

Islamic New Year (1422)	Mar 26
First Day of Ramadan (1422)	Nov 16
Eid-Al-Fitr (1422)	Dec 16

CIVIL CALENDAR—USA—2001

New Year's Day	Jan 1
Martin Luther King's Birthday (obsvd)	Jan 15
Lincoln's Birthday	Feb 12
Washington's Birthday (obsvd)/Presidents' Day	Feb 19
Memorial Day (obsvd)	May 28
Independence Day	July 4
Labor Day	Sept 3
Columbus Day (obsvd)	Oct 8
General Election Day	Nov 6
Veterans Day	Nov 11
Thanksgiving Day	Nov 22

Other Days Widely Observed in US—2001

Groundhog Day (Candlemas)	Feb 2
St. Valentine's Day	Feb 14
St. Patrick's Day	Mar 17
Mother's Day	May 13
Flag Day	June 14
Father's Day	June 17
National Grandparents Day	Sept 9
Hallowe'en	Oct 31

CIVIL CALENDAR—CANADA—2001

Victoria Day	May 21
Canada Day	July 2
Labor Day	Sept 3
Thanksgiving Day	Oct 8
Remembrance Day	Nov 11
Boxing Day	Dec 26

CIVIL CALENDAR—MEXICO—2001

New Year's Day	Jan 1
Constitution Day	Feb 5
Benito Juarez Birthday	Mar 21
Labor Day	May 1
Battle of Puebla Day (Cinco de Mayo)	May 5
Independence Day*	Sept 16
Dia de La Raza	Oct 12
Mexican Revolution Day	Nov 20
Guadalupe Day	Dec 12

*Celebration begins Sept 15 at 11:00 P.M.

CIVIL CALENDAR—UNITED KINGDOM—2001

Accession of Queen Elizabeth II	Feb 6
St. David (Wales)	Mar 1
Commonwealth Day	Mar 12
St. Patrick (Ireland)	Mar 17
Birthday of Queen Elizabeth II	Apr 21
St. George (England)	Apr 23
Coronation Day	June 2
The Queen's Official Birthday (tentative)	June 9
Birthday of Prince Philip, Duke of Edinburgh	June 10
Remembrance Sunday	Nov 11
Birthday of the Prince of Wales	Nov 14
St. Andrew (Scotland)	Nov 30

BANK AND PUBLIC HOLIDAYS—UNITED KINGDOM—2001

(Observed during 2001 in England and Wales, Scotland and Northern Ireland unless otherwise indicated)

New Year	Jan 1
Bank Holiday (Scotland)	Jan 2
St. Patrick's Day (Northern Ireland)	Mar 17
Good Friday	Apr 13
Easter Monday (except Scotland)	Apr 16
May Day Bank Holiday	May 7
Spring Bank Holiday	May 28
Orangeman's Day (Battle of the Boyne) (Northern Ireland)	July 12
Bank Holiday (Scotland)	Aug 6
Summer Bank Holiday (except Scotland)	Aug 27
Christmas Day Holiday	Dec 25
Boxing Day Holiday	Dec 26

SEASONS

Spring (Vernal Equinox)	Mar 20, 8:31 AM, EST
Summer (Summer Solstice)	June 21, 3:38 AM, EDT
Autumn (Autumnal Equinox)	Sept 22, 7:05 PM, EDT
Winter (Winter Solstice)	Dec 21, 2:22 PM, EST

DAYLIGHT SAVING TIME SCHEDULE—2001

Sunday, Apr 1, 2:00 AM–Sunday, Oct 28, 2:00 AM—in all time zones.

CHRONOLOGICAL CYCLES

Dominical Letter	G
Epact	5
Golden Number (Lunar Cycle)	VII
Julian Period (year of)	6714
Roman Indiction	9
Solar Cycle	22

CALENDAR INFORMATION FOR THE YEAR 2002

Time shown is Eastern Standard Time. All dates are given in terms of the Gregorian calendar.

(Based in part on information prepared by the Nautical Almanac Office, US Naval Observatory.)

ERAS	YEAR	BEGINS
Byzantine	7511	Sept 14
Jewish*	5763	Sept 6
Chinese (Year of the Horse)	4700	Feb 12
Roman (AUC)	2755	Jan 14
Nabonassar	2751	Apr 23
Japanese (Heisei)	14	Jan 1
Grecian (Seleucidae)	2314	Sept 14 (or Oct 14)
Indian (Saka)	1924	Mar 22
Diocletian	1719	Sept 11
Islamic (Hegira)**	1423	Mar 14

*Year begins at sunset.   **Year begins at moon crescent.

RELIGIOUS CALENDARS

Epiphany	Jan 6
Shrove Tuesday	Feb 12
Ash Wednesday	Feb 13
Lent	Feb 13–Mar 30
Palm Sunday	Mar 24
Good Friday	Mar 29
Easter Day	Mar 31
Ascension Day	May 9
Whit Sunday (Pentecost)	May 19
Trinity Sunday	May 26
First Sunday in Advent	Dec 1
Christmas Day (Wednesday)	Dec 25

Eastern Orthodox Church Observances

Great Lent begins	Mar 18
Pascha (Easter)	May 5
Ascension	June 13
Pentecost	June 23

Jewish Holy Days

Purim	Feb 26
Passover (1st day)	Mar 28
Shavuot	May 17
Tisha B'av	July 18
Rosh Hashanah (New Year)	Sept 7–8
Yom Kippur	Sept 16
Succoth	Sept 21–22
Chanukah	Nov 30–Dec 7

Islamic Holy Days

Islamic New Year (1423)	Mar 15
First Day of Ramadan (1423)	Nov 6
Eid-Al-Fitr (1423)	Dec 5

CIVIL CALENDAR—USA—2002

New Year's Day	Jan 1
Martin Luther King's Birthday (obsvd)	Jan 21
Lincoln's Birthday	Feb 12
Washington's Birthday (obsvd)/Presidents' Day	Feb 18
Memorial Day (obsvd)	May 27
Independence Day	July 4
Labor Day	Sept 2
Columbus Day (obsvd)	Oct 14
General Election Day	Nov 5
Veterans Day	Nov 11
Thanksgiving Day	Nov 28

Other Days Widely Observed in US—2002

Groundhog Day (Candlemas)	Feb 2
St. Valentine's Day	Feb 14
St. Patrick's Day	Mar 17
Mother's Day	May 12
Flag Day	June 14
Father's Day	June 16
National Grandparents Day	Sept 8
Hallowe'en	Oct 31

CIVIL CALENDAR—CANADA—2002

Victoria Day	May 20
Canada Day	July 1
Labor Day	Sept 2
Thanksgiving Day	Oct 14
Remembrance Day	Nov 11
Boxing Day	Dec 26

CIVIL CALENDAR—MEXICO—2002

New Year's Day	Jan 1
Constitution Day	Feb 5
Benito Juarez Birthday	Mar 21
Labor Day	May 1
Battle of Puebla Day (Cinco de Mayo)	May 5
Independence Day*	Sept 16
Dia de La Raza	Oct 12
Mexican Revolution Day	Nov 20
Guadalupe Day	Dec 12

*Celebration begins Sept 15 at 11:00 P.M.

CIVIL CALENDAR—UNITED KINGDOM—2002

Accession of Queen Elizabeth II	Feb 6
St. David (Wales)	Mar 1
Commonwealth Day	Mar 11
St. Patrick (Ireland)	Mar 17
Birthday of Queen Elizabeth II	Apr 21
St. George (England)	Apr 23
Coronation Day	June 2
The Queen's Official Birthday (tentative)	June 8
Birthday of Prince Philip, Duke of Edinburgh	June 10
Remembrance Sunday	Nov 10
Birthday of the Prince of Wales	Nov 14
St. Andrew (Scotland)	Nov 30

BANK AND PUBLIC HOLIDAYS—UNITED KINGDOM—2002

(Observed during 2002 in England and Wales, Scotland and Northern Ireland unless otherwise indicated)

New Year	Jan 1
Bank Holiday (Scotland)	Jan 4
St. Patrick's Day (Northern Ireland)	Mar 17
Good Friday	Mar 29
Easter Monday (except Scotland)	Apr 1
May Day Bank Holiday	May 6
Spring Bank Holiday	May 27
Orangeman's Day (Battle of the Boyne) (Northern Ireland)	July 12
Bank Holiday (Scotland)	Aug 5
Summer Bank Holiday (except Scotland)	Aug 26
Christmas Day Holiday	Dec 25
Boxing Day Holiday	Dec 26

SEASONS

Spring (Vernal Equinox)	Mar 20, 2:16 PM, EST
Summer (Summer Solstice)	June 21, 9:24 AM, EDT
Autumn (Autumnal Equinox)	Sept 23, 12:56 AM, EDT
Winter (Winter Solstice)	Dec 21, 8:15 PM, EST

DAYLIGHT SAVING TIME SCHEDULE—2002

Sunday, Apr 7, 2:00 AM–Sunday, Oct 27, 2:00 AM—in all time zones.

CHRONOLOGICAL CYCLES

Dominical Letter	F
Epact	16
Golden Number (Lunar Cycle)	VIII
Julian Period (year of)	6715
Roman Indiction	10
Solar Cycle	23

CALENDAR INFORMATION FOR THE YEAR 2003

Time shown is Eastern Standard Time. All dates are given in terms of the Gregorian calendar.

(Based in part on information prepared by the Nautical Almanac Office, US Naval Observatory.)

ERAS

	YEAR	BEGINS
Byzantine	7512	Sept 14
Jewish*	5764	Sept 26
Chinese (Year of the Sheep [Goat])	4701	Feb 1
Roman (AUC)	2756	Jan 14
Nabonassar	2752	Apr 24
Japanese (Heisei)	15	Jan 1
Grecian (Seleucidae)	2315	Sept 14 (or Oct 14)
Indian (Saka)	1925	Mar 22
Diocletian	1720	Sept 12
Islamic (Hegira)**	1424	Mar 4

*Year begins at sunset.   **Year begins at moon crescent.

RELIGIOUS CALENDARS

Epiphany . . . . Jan 6
Shrove Tuesday . . . . Mar 4
Ash Wednesday . . . . Mar 5
Lent . . . . Mar 5–Apr 19
Palm Sunday . . . . Apr 13
Good Friday . . . . Apr 18
Easter Day . . . . Apr 20
Ascension Day . . . . May 29
Whit Sunday (Pentecost) . . . . June 8
Trinity Sunday . . . . June 15
First Sunday in Advent . . . . Nov 30
Christmas Day (Thursday) . . . . Dec 25

Eastern Orthodox Church Observances

Great Lent begins . . . . Mar 10
Pascha (Easter) . . . . Apr 27
Ascension . . . . June 5
Pentecost . . . . June 15

Jewish Holy Days

Purim . . . . Mar 18
Passover (1st day) . . . . Apr 17
Shavuot . . . . June 6
Tisha B'av . . . . Aug 7
Rosh Hashanah (New Year) . . . . Sept 26–27
Yom Kippur . . . . Oct 6
Succoth . . . . Oct 11–12
Chanukah . . . . Dec 20–27

Islamic Holy Days

Islamic New Year (1424) . . . . Mar 4
First Day of Ramadan (1424) . . . . Oct 26
Eid-Al-Fitr (1424) . . . . Nov 25

CIVIL CALENDAR—USA—2003

New Year's Day . . . . Jan 1
Martin Luther King's Birthday (obsvd) . . . . . . Jan 20
Lincoln's Birthday . . . . Feb 12
Washington's Birthday (obsvd)/Presidents' Day . . . . Feb 17
Memorial Day (obsvd) . . . . May 26
Independence Day . . . . July 4
Labor Day . . . . Sept 1
Columbus Day (obsvd) . . . . Oct 13
General Election Day . . . . Nov 4
Veterans Day . . . . Nov 11
Thanksgiving Day . . . . Nov 27

Other Days Widely Observed in US—2003

Groundhog Day (Candlemas) . . . . Feb 2
St. Valentine's Day . . . . Feb 14
St. Patrick's Day . . . . Mar 17
Mother's Day . . . . May 11
Flag Day . . . . June 14
Father's Day . . . . June 15
National Grandparents Day . . . . Sept 7
Hallowe'en . . . . Oct 31

CIVIL CALENDAR—CANADA—2003

Victoria Day . . . . May 19
Canada Day . . . . July 1
Labor Day . . . . Sept 1
Thanksgiving Day . . . . Oct 13
Remembrance Day . . . . Nov 11
Boxing Day . . . . Dec 26

CIVIL CALENDAR—MEXICO—2003

New Year's Day . . . . Jan 1
Constitution Day . . . . Feb 5
Benito Juarez Birthday . . . . Mar 21
Labor Day . . . . May 1
Battle of Puebla Day (Cinco de Mayo) . . . . May 5
Independence Day* . . . . Sept 16
Dia de La Raza . . . . Oct 12
Mexican Revolution Day . . . . Nov 20
Guadalupe Day . . . . Dec 12

*Celebration begins Sept 15 at 11:00 P.M.

CIVIL CALENDAR—UNITED KINGDOM—2003

Accession of Queen Elizabeth II . . . . Feb 6
St. David (Wales) . . . . Mar 1
Commonwealth Day . . . . Mar 10
St. Patrick (Ireland) . . . . Mar 17
Birthday of Queen Elizabeth II . . . . Apr 21
St. George (England) . . . . Apr 23
Coronation Day . . . . June 2
The Queen's Official Birthday (tentative) . . . . June 14
Birthday of Prince Philip, Duke of Edinburgh . . . June 10
Remembrance Sunday . . . . Nov 9
Birthday of the Prince of Wales . . . . Nov 14
St. Andrew (Scotland) . . . . Nov 30

BANK AND PUBLIC HOLIDAYS—UNITED KINGDOM—2003

(Observed during 2003 in England and Wales, Scotland
and Northern Ireland unless otherwise indicated)

New Year . . . . Jan 1
Bank Holiday (Scotland) . . . . Jan 2
St. Patrick's Day (Northern Ireland) . . . . Mar 17
Good Friday . . . . Apr 18
Easter Monday (except Scotland) . . . . Apr 21
May Day Bank Holiday . . . . May 5
Spring Bank Holiday . . . . May 26
Orangeman's Day (Battle of the Boyne) (Northern Ireland) . July 12
Bank Holiday (Scotland) . . . . Aug 4
Summer Bank Holiday (except Scotland) . . . . . Aug 25
Christmas Day Holiday . . . . Dec 25
Boxing Day Holiday . . . . Dec 26

SEASONS

Spring (Vernal Equinox) . . . . Mar 20, 8:00 PM, EST
Summer (Summer Solstice) . . . . June 21, 3:10 PM, EDT
Autumn (Autumnal Equinox) . . . . Sept 23, 6:47 AM, EDT
Winter (Winter Solstice) . . . . Dec 22, 2:04 AM, EST

DAYLIGHT SAVING TIME SCHEDULE—2003

Sunday, Apr 6, 2:00 AM–Sunday, Oct 26, 2:00 AM—in all time zones.

CHRONOLOGICAL CYCLES

Dominical Letter . . . . E
Epact 27
Golden Number (Lunar Cycle) IX
Julian Period (year of) 6716
Roman Indiction 11
Solar Cycle 24

SOME FACTS ABOUT CANADA

Province/Territory	Capital	Population*	Flower	Land/Fresh Water (sq. mi.)	Total Area
Alberta	Edmonton	2,774,512	Wild rose	400,423/10,437	410,860
British Columbia	Victoria	3,835,748	Pacific dogwood	578,230/11,227	589,458
Manitoba	Winnipeg	1,141,727	Prairie crocus	340,834/63,129	403,964
New Brunswick	Fredericton	761,873	Purple violet	44,797/835	45,633
Newfoundland	St. John's	571,192	Pitcher plant	230,219/21,147	251,367
Northwest Territories	Yellowknife	66,164	Mountain avens	2,017,306/82,829	2,100,136
Nova Scotia	Halifax	941,235	Mayflower	32,835/1,647	34,482
Ontario	Toronto	11,209,474	White trillium	553,788/110,229	664,012
Prince Edward Island	Charlottetown	137,316	Lady's-slipper	3,515/0	3,515
Quebec	Quebec City	7,366,883	White garden lily	843,109/114,269	957,379
Saskatchewan	Regina	1,020,138	Red lily	354,365/51,347	405,712
Yukon Territory	Whitehorse	31,107	Fireweed	297,050/2,784	299,835

*1996

STATE & TERRITORY ABBREVIATIONS: UNITED STATES

Alabama . . . AL	Kentucky . . . KY	Oklahoma . . . OK
Alaska . . . AK	Louisiana . . . LA	Oregon . . . OR
Arizona . . . AZ	Maine . . . ME	Pennsylvania . . . PA
Arkansas . . . AR	Maryland . . . MD	Puerto Rico . . . PR
American Samoa . . . AS	Massachusetts . . . MA	Rhode Island . . . RI
California . . . CA	Michigan . . . MI	South Carolina . . . SC
Colorado . . . CO	Minnesota . . . MN	South Dakota . . . SD
Connecticut . . . CT	Mississippi . . . MS	Tennessee . . . TN
Delaware . . . DE	Missouri . . . MO	Texas . . . TX
District of Columbia . . . DC	Montana . . . MT	Utah . . . UT
Florida . . . FL	Nebraska . . . NE	Vermont . . . VT
Georgia . . . GA	Nevada . . . NV	Virginia . . . VA
Guam . . . GU	New Hampshire . . . NH	Virgin Islands . . . VI
Hawaii . . . HI	New Jersey . . . NJ	Washington . . . WA
Idaho . . . ID	New Mexico . . . NM	West Virginia . . . WV
Illinois . . . IL	New York . . . NY	Wisconsin . . . WI
Indiana . . . IN	North Carolina . . . NC	Wyoming . . . WY
Iowa . . . IA	North Dakota . . . ND	
Kansas . . . KS	Ohio . . . OH	

PROVINCE & TERRITORY ABBREVIATIONS: CANADA

Alberta . . . AB	Newfoundland . . . NF	Quebec . . . QC
British Columbia . . . BC	Scotia . . . NS	Saskatchewan . . . SK
Manitoba . . . MB	Ontario . . . ON	Yukon Territory . . . YT
New Brunswick . . . NB	Prince Edward Island . . . PE	Northwest Territories . . . NT

PRESIDENTIAL PROCLAMATIONS
ISSUED, JANUARY 1, 1999–JUNE 15, 2000

No. Title, Observance Dates, (Date of signing).

1999

7162 Religious Freedom Day, 1999: Jan 16, 1999 (Jan 14, 1999)

7163 Martin Luther King, Jr, Federal Holiday, 1999: Jan 18, 1999 (Jan 15, 1999)

7164 National Consumer Protection Week, 1999: Jan 31–Feb 6, 1999 (Jan 29, 1999)

7165 National African American History Month, 1999: February (Feb 1, 1999)

7166 American Heart Month, 1999: February (Feb 3, 1999)

7167 Death of King Hussein (Feb 7, 1999)

7168 American Red Cross Month, 1999: March (Feb 25, 1999)

7169 Irish-American Heritage Month, 1999: March (Mar 1, 1999)

7170 Women's History Month, 1999: March (Mar 1, 1999)

7171 Save Your Vision Week, 1999: Mar 7–13, 1999 (Mar 1, 1999)

7172 Death of Harry A. Blackmun (Mar 4, 1999)

7173 National Older Workers Employment Week, 1999: Mar 14–20, 1999 (Mar 11, 1999)

7174 National Poison Prevention Week, 1999: Mar 21–27, 1999 (Mar 19, 1999)

7175 Greek Independence Day: A National Day of Celebration of Greek and American Democracy, 1999: Mar 25, 1999 (Mar 24, 1999)

7176 Education and Sharing Day, USA, 1999: Mar 28, 1999 (Mar 25, 1999)

7177 Cancer Control Month, 1999: April (Apr 1, 1999)

7178 National Child Abuse Prevention Month, 1999: April (Apr 1, 1999)

7179 National Equal Pay Day, 1999: Apr 8, 1999 (Apr 7, 1999)

7180 National D.A.R.E. Day, 1999: Apr 8, 1999 (Apr 8, 1999)

7181 Pan American Day and Pan American Week, 1999: Apr 14, 1999, Apr 11–17, 1999 (Apr 9, 1999)

7182 National Former Prisoner of War Recognition Day, 1999: Apr 9, 1999 (Apr 9, 1999)

7183 Jewish Heritage Week, 1999: Apr 18–25, 1999 (Apr 14, 1999)

7184 National Park Week, 1999: Apr 19–25, 1999 (Apr 15, 1999)

7185 National Organ and Tissue Donor Awareness Week, 1999: Apr 18–24, 1999 (Apr 16, 1999)

7186 National Volunteer Week, 1999: Apr 18–24, 1999 (Apr 16, 1999)

7187 National Crime Victims' Awareness Week, 1999: Apr 25–May 1, 1999 (Apr 22, 1999)

7188 National Science and Technology Week, 1999: Apr 25–May 1, 1999 (Apr 23, 1999)

7189 Asian/Pacific American Heritage Month, 1999: May (Apr 30, 1999)

7190 Older Americans Month, 1999: May (Apr 30, 1999)

7191 Law Day, USA, 1999: May 1, 1999 (Apr 30, 1999)

7192 Loyalty Day, 1999: May 1, 1999 (Apr 30, 1999)

No. Title, Observance Dates, (Date of signing).

7193 National Day of Prayer, 1999: May 6, 1999 (May 5, 1999)

7194 Mother's Day, 1999: May 9, 1999 (May 5, 1999)

7195 Peace Officers Memorial Day and Police Week, 1999: May 15, 1999, May 9–15, 1999 (May 10, 1999)

7196 World Trade Week, 1999: May 16–22, 1999 (May 17, 1999)

7197 National Defense Transportation Day and National Transportation Week, 1999: May 21, 1999, May 16–22, 1999 (May 17, 1999)

7198 National Safe Boating Week, 1999: May 22–28, 1999 (May 20, 1999)

7199 National Maritime Day, 1999: May 22, 1999 (May 21, 1999)

7200 Small Business Week, 1999: May 23–29, 1999 (May 22, 1999)

7201 Prayer for Peace, Memorial Day, 1999: May 31, 1999 (May 26, 1999)

7202 To Eliminate Circumvention of the Quantitative Limitations Applicable to Imports of Wheat Gluten (May 28, 1999)

7203 Gay and Lesbian Pride Month, 1999: June (June 11, 1999)

7204 Flag Day and National Flag Week, 1999: June 14, 1999, June 13–19, 1999 (June 11, 1999)

7205 Father's Day, 1999: June 20, 1999 (June 18, 1999)

7206 To Modify Duty-Free Treatment Under the Generalized System of Preferences and for Other Purposes (June 30, 1999)

7207 To Extend Nondiscriminatory Treatment (Normal Trade Relations Treatment) to Products of Mongolia and To Implement an Agreement to Eliminate Tariffs on Certain Pharmaceuticals and Chemical Intermediates (July 1, 1999)

7208 To Facilitate Positive Adjustment to Competition From Imports of Lamb Meat (July 7, 1999)

7209 Captive Nations Week, 1999: July 18–24, 1999 (July 16, 1999)

7210 Imposition of Restraints on Imports of Certain Steel Products From the Russian Federation (July 22, 1999)

7211 Parents' Day, 1999: July 25, 1999 (July 23, 1999)

7212 25th Anniversary of the Legal Services Corporation, 1999: July 25, 1999 (July 26, 1999)

7213 National Korean War Veterans Armistice Day, 1999: July 27, 1999 (July 26, 1999)

7214 To Provide for the Efficient and Fair Administration of Action Taken With Regard to Imports of Lamb Meat and for Other Purposes (July 30, 1999)

7215 Women's Equality Day, 1999: Aug 26, 1999 (Aug 24, 1999)

7216 Minority Enterprise Development Week, 1999: Sept 19–25, 1999 (Aug 25, 1999)

7217 Small Manufacturing Week, 1999: Sept 19–25, 1999 (Aug 25, 1999)

7218 America Goes Back to School, 1999: Aug 29–Sept 11, 1999 (Aug 27, 1999)

7219 Contiguous Zone of the United States (Sept 2, 1999)

PRESIDENTIAL PROCLAMATIONS (cont'd)
ISSUED, JANUARY 1, 1999–JUNE 15, 2000

No. Title, Observance Dates, (Date of signing).

7220 National Hispanic Heritage Month, 1999: Sept 15–Oct 15, 1999 (Sept 14, 1999)

7221 National POW/MIA Recognition Day, 1999: Sept 17, 1999 (Sept 15, 1999)

7222 Citizenship Day and Constitution Week, 1999: Sept 17, 1999, Sept 17–23, 1999 (Sept 16, 1999)

7223 Ovarian Cancer Awareness Week, 1999: Sept 19–25, 1999 (Sept 17, 1999)

7224 National Farm Safety and Health Week, 1999: Sept 19–25, 1999 (Sept 17, 1999)

7225 National Historically Black Colleges and Universities Week, 1999: Sept 19–25, 1999 (Sept 17, 1999)

7226 Gold Star Mother's Day, 1999: Sept 26, 1999 (Sept 24, 1999)

7227 100th Anniversary of the Veterans of Foreign Wars, 1999: Sept 29, 1999 (Sept 29, 1999)

7228 National Breast Cancer Awareness Month, 1999: October (Sept 30, 1999)

7229 National Disability Employment Awareness Month, 1999: October (Sept 30, 1999)

7230 National Domestic Violence Awareness Month, 1999: October (Sept 30, 1999)

7231 Fire Prevention Week, 1999: Oct 3–9, 1999 (Oct 1, 1999)

7232 Child Health Day, 1999: Oct 4, 1999 (Oct 1, 1999)

7233 German–American Day, 1999: Oct 6, 1999 (Oct 5, 1999)

7234 General Pulaski Memorial Day, 1999: Oct 11, 1999 (Oct 6, 1999)

7235 To Delegate Authority for the Administration of the Tariff-Rate Quotas on Sugar-Containing Products and Other Agricultural Products to the United States Trade Representative and the Secretary of Agriculture (Oct 7, 1999)

7236 Leif Erikson Day, 1999: Oct 9, 1999 (Oct 8, 1999)

7237 National School Lunch Week, 1999: Oct 10–16, 1999 (Oct 8, 1999)

7238 National Children's Day, 1999: Oct 10, 1999 (Oct 8, 1999)

7239 Columbus Day, 1999: Oct 11, 1999 (Oct 8, 1999)

7240 White Cane Safety Day, 1999: Oct 15, 1999 (Oct 15, 1999)

7241 National Forest products Week, 1999: Oct 17–23, 1999 (Oct 15, 1999)

7242 National Character Counts Week, 1999: Oct 17–23, 1999 (Oct 16, 1999)

7243 National Day of Concern for Young People and Gun Violence, 1999: Oct 21, 1999 (Oct 21, 1999)

7244 United Nations Day, 1999: Oct 24, 1999 (Oct 22, 1999)

7245 National Adoption Month, 1999: November (Oct 28, 1999)

7246 Child Mental Health Month, 1999: November (Oct 30, 1999)

7247 National American Indian Heritage Month, 1999: November (Nov 1, 1999)

7248 Veterans Day, 1999: Nov 11, 1999 (Nov 8, 1999)

7249 Suspension of Immigrants and Nonimmigrants of Persons Responsible for Repression of the Civilian Population in Kosovo or for the Policies That Obstruct Democracy in the Federal Republic of Yugoslavia (Serbia and Montenegro) ("FRY") of Otherwise Lend Support to the Current Governments of the FRY and of the Republic of Serbia (Nov 12, 1999)

7250 America Recycles Day, 1999: Nov 15, 1999 (Nov 15, 1999)

7251 National Great American Smokeout Day, 1999: Nov 18, 1999 (Nov 18, 1999)

7252 National Farm-City Week, 1999: Nov 19–25, 1999 (Nov 18, 1999)

7253 National Family Week, 1999: Nov 21–27, 1999 (Nov 19, 1999)

7254 National Family Caregivers Week, 1999: Nov 21–27, 1999 (Nov 19, 1999)

7255 Thanksgiving Day, 1999: Nov 25, 1999 (Nov 20, 1999)

7256 World AIDS Day, 1999: Dec 1, 1999 (Nov 29, 1999)

7257 National Drunk and Drugged Driving Prevention Month, 1999: December (Nov 30, 1999)

7258 Human Rights Day, Bill of Rights Day and Human Rights Week, 1999: Dec 10, 1999, Dec 15, 1999, Dec 10–17, 1999 (Dec 6, 1999)

7259 National Pearl Harbor Remembrance Day, 1999: Dec 7, 1999 (Dec 7, 1999)

7260 Bicentennial Commemoration of the Death of George Washington: Dec 14, 1999 (Dec 13, 1999)

7261 55th Anniversary of the Battle of the Bulge: Dec 16, 1999–Jan 25, 2000 (Dec 16, 1999)

7262 Wright Brothers Day, 1999: Dec 17, 1999 (Dec 16, 1999)

2000

7263 Establishment of the Agua Fria National Monument (Jan 11, 2000)

7264 Establishment of the California Coastal National Monument (Jan 11, 2000)

7265 Establishment of the Grand Canyon-Parashant National Monument (Jan 11, 2000)

7266 Boundary Enlargement of the Pinnacles National Monument (Jan 11, 2000)

7267 Religious Freedom Day, 2000: Jan 16, 2000 (Jan 14, 2000)

7268 Martin Luther King, Jr, Federal Holiday, 2000: Jan 17, 2000 (Jan 14, 2000)

7269 National Biotechnology Month, 2000: January (Jan 19, 2000)

7270 National African American History Month, 2000: February (Jan 31, 2000)

7271 American Heart Month, 2000: February (Feb 1, 2000)

7272 National Consumer Protection Week, 2000: Feb 14–20, 2000 (Feb 11, 2000)

PRESIDENTIAL PROCLAMATIONS (cont'd) ISSUED, JANUARY 1, 1999–JUNE 15, 2000

No. Title, Observance Dates, (Date of signing).

7273 To Facilitate Positive Adjustment to Competition From Imports of Certain Steel Wire Rod (Feb 16, 2000)

7274 To Facilitate Positive Adjustment to Competition From Imports of Certain Circular Welded Carbon Quality Line Pipe (Feb 18, 2000)

7275 Registration Under the Military Selective Service Act (Feb 22, 2000)

7276 National Colorectal Cancer Awareness Month, 2000: March (Feb 29, 2000)

7277 Women's History Month, 2000: March (Feb 29, 2000)

7278 American Red Cross Month, 2000: March (Feb 29, 2000)

7279 Irish-American Heritage Month, 2000: March (Mar 1, 2000)

7280 Save Your Vision Week, 2000: Mar 5–11, 2000 (Mar 6, 2000)

7281 National Poison Prevention Week, 2000: Mar 19–25, 2000 (Mar 17, 2000)

7282 Education and Sharing Day, USA, 2000: Mar 28, 2000 (Mar 24, 2000)

7283 Greek Independence Day: A National Day of Celebration of Greek and American Democracy, 2000: Mar 25, 2000 (Mar 24, 2000)

7284 Cancer Control Month, 2000: April (Mar 31, 2000)

7285 National Child Abuse Prevention Month, 2000: April (Mar 31, 2000)

7286 Census Day, 2000: Apr 1, 2000 (Apr 1, 2000)

7287 National Volunteer Week, 2000: Apr 9–15, 2000 (Apr 7, 2000)

7288 Pan American Day and Pan American Week, 2000: Apr 14, 2000, Apr 9–15, 2000 (Apr 8, 2000)

7289 National Former Prisoner of War Recognition Day, 2000: Apr 9, 2000 (Apr 8, 2000)

7290 National Crime Victims' Rights Week, 2000: Apr 9–15, 2000 (Apr 10, 2000)

7291 National D.A.R.E. Day, 2000: Apr 13, 2000 (Apr 12, 2000)

7292 National Organ and Tissue Donor Awareness Week, 2000: Apr 16–22, 2000 (Apr 14, 2000)

7293 National Park Week, 2000: Apr 17–23, 2000 (Apr 14, 2000)

7294 National Recall Round-Up Day, 2000: Apr 18, 2000 (Apr 14, 2000)

7295 Establishment of the Giant Sequoia National Monument (Apr 15, 2000)

7296 Bicentennial of the Library of Congress, 2000: Apr 24, 2000 (Apr 21, 2000)

No. Title, Observance Dates, (Date of signing).

7297 National Charter Schools Week, 2000: May 1–5, 2000 (Apr 28, 2000)

7298 Law Day, USA, 2000: May 1, 2000 (Apr 28, 2000)

7299 Asian/Pacific American Heritage Month, 2000: May (Apr 29, 2000)

7300 Loyalty Day, 2000: May 1, 2000 (Apr 29, 2000)

7301 Older Americans Month, 2000: May (May 2, 2000)

7302 Jewish Heritage Week, 2000: May 7–14, 2000 (May 2, 2000)

7303 National Day of Prayer, 2000: May 4, 2000 (May 4, 2000)

7304 Global Science and Technology Week, 2000: May 7–13, 2000 (May 5, 2000)

7305 Mother's Day, 2000: May 14, 2000 (May 10, 2000)

7306 National Equal Pay Day, 2000: May 11, 2000 (May 11, 2000)

7307 Peace Officers Memorial Day and Police Week, 2000: May 15, 2000, May 14–20, 2000 (May 11, 2000)

7308 National Defense Transportation Day and National Transportation Week, 2000: May 19, 2000, May 14–20, 2000 (May 15, 2000)

7309 National Safe Boating Week, 2000: May 20–26, 2000 (May 18, 2000)

7310 World Trade Week, 2000: May 21–27, 2000 (May 19, 2000)

7311 Small Business Week, 2000: May 21–27, 2000 (May 19, 2000)

7312 National Maritime Day, 2000: May 22, 2000 (May 22, 2000)

7313 Day of Honor, 2000: May 25, 2000 (May 24, 2000)

7314 To Modify the Quantitative Limitations Applicable to Imports of Wheat Gluten (May 26, 2000)

7315 Prayer for Peace, Memorial Day, 2000: May 29, 2000 (May 26, 2000)

7316 Gay and Lesbian Pride Month, 2000: June (June 2, 2000)

7317 Establishment of the Canyons of the Ancients National Monument (June 9, 2000)

7318 Establishment of the Cascade-Siskiyou National Monument (June 9, 2000)

7319 Establishment of the Hanford Reach National Monument (June 9, 2000)

7320 Establishment of the Ironwood Forest National Monument (June 9, 2000)

7321 Flag Day and National Flag Week, 2000: June 14, 2000, June 11–17, 2000 (June 9, 2000)

LOOKING FORWARD

2002 • Winter Olympics (Salt Lake City)
2003 • Ohio Statehood Bicentennial
• Wright Brothers' first flight, 100th anniversary
2004 • First successful newspaper in America, 300th anniversary
• US presidential election
• Summer Olympics (Athens, Greece)
2005 • World's Fair in Aichi, Japan
2006 • Benjamin Franklin's birth, 300th anniversary
• Woodrow Wilson's birth, 150th anniversary
• Winter Olympics (Turin, Italy)
2007 • Oklahoma Statehood Centennial
• Jamestown Colony, 400th anniversary
• Sputnik launched by USSR, 50th anniversary
• William H. Taft's birth, 150th anniversary
2008 • James Monroe's birth, 250th anniversary
• Andrew Johnson's birth, 200th anniversary
• Theodore Roosevelt's birth, 150th anniversary
• Lyndon Johnson's birth, 100th anniversary
• US presidential election
2009 • Abraham Lincoln's birth, 200th anniversary
2010 • US population projected to be 298,000,000
2011 • Ronald Reagan's birth, 100th anniversary
2012 • Arizona Statehood Centennial
• Louisiana Statehood Bicentennial
• New Mexico Statehood Centennial
• US presidential election
2013 • Richard Nixon's birth, 100th anniversary
• Gerald Ford's birth, 100th anniversary
2015 • US population projected to be 310,000,000
2016 • Indiana Statehood Bicentennial
• US presidential election
2017 • Mississippi Statehood Bicentennial
• John Q. Adams's birth, 250th anniversary
• Andrew Jackson's birth, 250th anniversary
• John F. Kennedy's birth, 100th anniversary
2018 • Illinois Statehood Bicentennial
2019 • Alabama Statehood Bicentennial
• Apollo 11 astronauts walk on moon, 50th anniversary
2020 • US population projected to be 349,000,000
• Maine Statehood Bicentennial
• US presidential election
2050 • US population projected to be 403,000,000
• World population of 9 billion predicted
2061 • Halley's comet returns
2100 • US population projected to be 571,000,000

SPACE OBJECTS BOX SCORE

The Space Objects Box Score, furnished by the NASA/Goddard Space Flight Center, reflects the numbers of objects now in orbit by type—payload or debris—and by owning nation or organization. It is based on data computed at Goddard Space Flight Center, or NORAD, or provided by satellite owners. The debris includes pieces launched into space along with the functioning payloads, as well as fragments produced by in-space breakups. More current information can be found on the Web at http://www.spacecom.af.mil/usspace/boxscore.htm

CURRENT AND HISTORIC STATUS (as of 2000)

COUNTRY	OBJECTS IN ORBIT			
	SATELLITE	SPACE PROBES	DEBRIS	TOTAL
ARGENTINA	4	0	0	4
ARAB SAT. COMM. ORG.	7	0	0	7
ASIASAT CORP	3	0	0	3
AUSTRALIA	7	0	2	9
BRAZIL	9	0	0	9
CANADA	16	0	1	17
CHBZ	1	0	0	1
CHILE	1	0	0	1
CIS	1334	35	2591	3960
CZECH REPUBLIC	4	0	0	4
DEN	1	0	0	1
EGYPT	1	0	0	1
ESA	24	2	234	260
ETSO	15	0	0	15
FRANCE/GERMANY	3	0	0	3
FRANCE	31	0	17	48
GERMANY	13	2	1	16
GLOBAL	48	0	0	48
IMSO	9	0	0	9
INDIA	19	0	4	23
INDONESIA	9	0	0	9
ISRAEL	3	0	0	3
ISS	1	1	0	2
IRIDIUM	88	0	0	88
ITALY	8	0	3	11
ITSO	56	0	0	56
JAPAN	65	4	51	120
LUXEMBOURG	9	0	0	9
MALAYSIA	2	0	0	2
MEXICO	6	0	0	6
NATO	8	0	0	8
NORWAY	3	0	0	3
ORBCOM	35	0	0	35
PORTUGAL	1	0	0	1
PRC	26	0	102	128
REPUBLIC OF PHILIPPINES	2	0	0	2
ROC	1	0	0	1
SAFR	1	0	0	1
SEAL	1	0	2	3
SOUTH KOREA	7	0	0	7
SPAIN	5	0	0	5
STCT	1	1	0	2
SWEDEN	8	0	0	8
THAILAND	4	0	0	4
TURKEY	2	0	0	2
UK	17	0	1	18
USA	726	46	3014	3786
TOTAL	2645	91	6023	8758

CIS: Russia/USSR
ESA: European Space Agency
ETRO: European Telecom Satellite Organization
IMSO: International Maritime Satellite Organization
ITSO: International Telecommunications Satellite Organization
PRC: People's Republic of China
UK: United Kingdom

Note: The change in the format of this information reflects a change in what information is released to the public.

SELECTED SPECIAL YEARS: 1972–2005

Intl Book Year: 1972
World Population Year: 1974
Intl Women's Year: 1975
Intl Year of the Child: 1979
Intl Year for Disabled Persons: 1981
World Communications Year: 1983
Intl Youth Year: 1985
Intl Year of Peace: 1986
Intl Year of Shelter for the Homeless: 1987
Year of the Reader: 1987
Year of the Young Reader: 1989
Intl Literacy Year: 1990
US Decade of the Brain: 1990-99
Intl Space Year: 1992
Intl Year for World's Indigenous Peoples: 1993
Intl Year of the Family: 1994
Year for Tolerance: 1995
Intl Year for Eradication of Poverty: 1996
Intl Year of the Ocean: 1998
Intl Year of Older Persons: 1999
Intl Year for the Culture of Peace: 2000
Intl Year of Thanksgiving: 2000
Intl Year of Volunteers: 2001
Year of Dialogue Among Civilizations: 2001
Intl Decade for a Culture of Peace: 2001–10
Intl Year of Mobilization Against Racism: 2001
Intl Year of Mountains: 2002
Intl Year of Ecotourism: 2002
Intl Year of Microcredit: 2005

CHINESE CALENDAR

The Chinese lunar year is divided into 12 months of 29 or 30 days. The calendar is adjusted to the length of the solar year by the addition of extra months at regular intervals. The years are arranged in major cycles of 60 years. Each successive year is named after one of 12 animals. These 12-year cycles are continuously repeated.

1996	Rat
1997	Ox
1998	Tiger
1999	Hare
2000	Dragon
2001	Snake
2002	Horse
2003	Sheep (Goat)
2004	Monkey
2005	Rooster
2006	Dog
2007	Pig

WEDDING ANNIVERSARY GIFTS

1st	paper, plastics, clocks
2nd	cotton, china, calico
3rd	leather, crystal, glass
4th	books, electrical appliances, silk, fruit, flowers
5th	wood, silverware
6th	sugar, candy, wood, iron
7th	wool, copper, desk sets
8th	bronze, pottery, linens, laces, electrical appliances
9th	pottery, willow, leather
10th	tin, aluminum, diamond jewelry
11th	steel, fashion jewelry, accessories
12th	silk, linen, pearls, colored gems
13th	lace, textiles, furs
14th	ivory, gold jewelry
15th	crystal, watches, glass
16th	silver hollowware
17th	furniture
18th	porcelain
19th	bronze
20th	china, platinum
21st	brass, nickel
22nd	copper
23rd	silver plate
24th	musical instruments
25th	silver
26th	original pictures
27th	sculpture
28th	orchids
29th	new furniture
30th	pearl, diamond
31st	time pieces
32nd	conveyances (including automobiles)
33rd	amethyst
34th	opal
35th	coral, jade
36th	bone china
37th	alabaster
38th	beryl, tourmaline
39th	lace
40th	ruby
41st	land
42nd	improved real estate
43rd	trips
44th	groceries
45th	sapphire
46th	original poetry tributes
47th	books
48th	optical (spectacles, microscopes, telescopes)
49th	luxuries of any kind
50th	gold
55th	emerald
60th	diamond
75th	diamond

WORLD MAP OF TIME ZONES

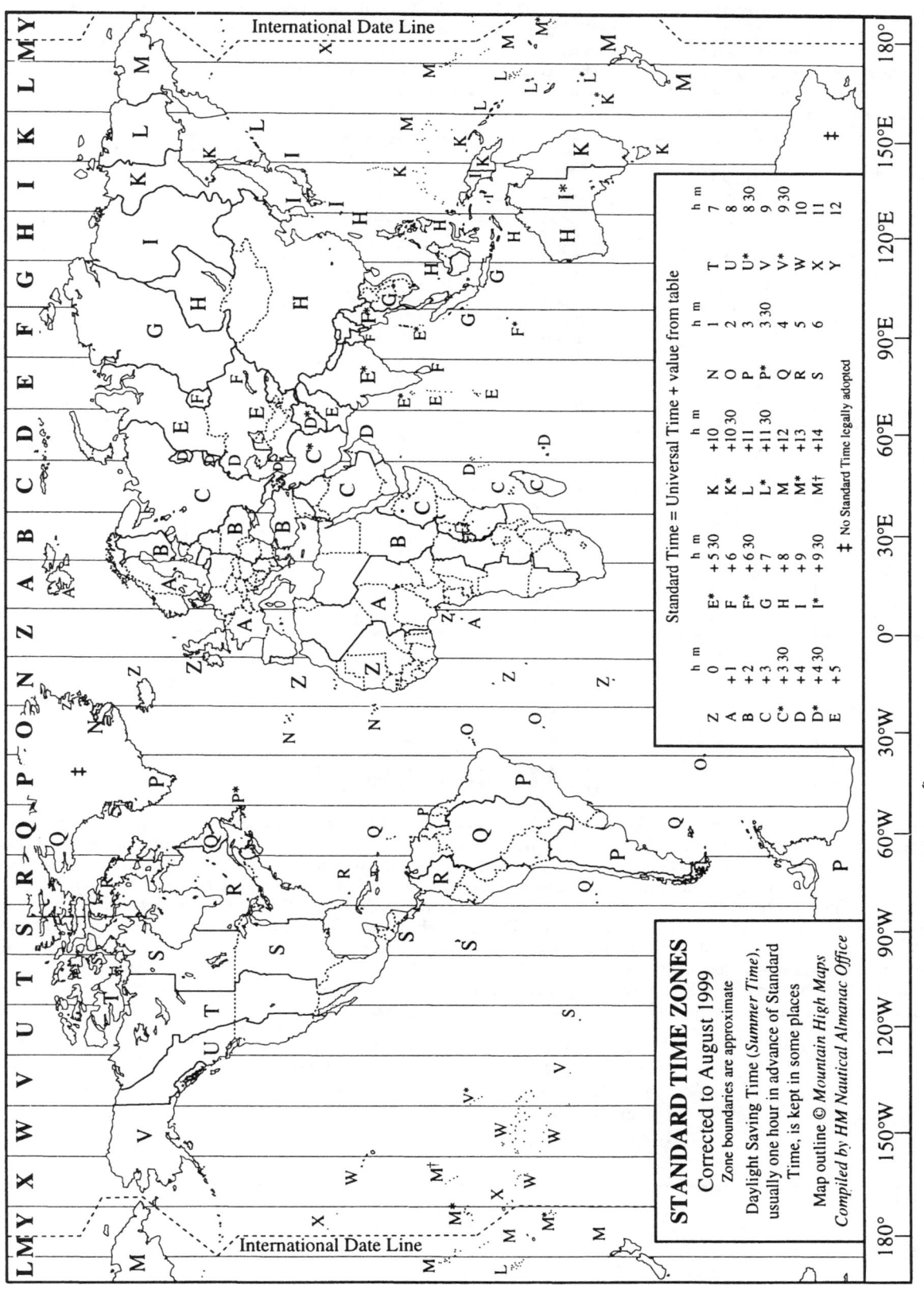

Reprinted from *Astronomical Phenomena for the Year 2002*, prepared jointly by the Nautical Almanac Office of the US Naval Observatory and Her Majesty's Nautical Almanac Office of the Royal Greenwich Observatory.

UNIVERSAL, STANDARD AND DAYLIGHT TIMES

Universal Time (UT) is also known as Greenwich Mean Time (GMT) and is the standard time of the Greenwich meridian (0° of longitude). A time given in UT may be converted to local mean time by the addition of east longitude (or the subtraction of west longitude), where the longitude of the place is expressed in time-measure at the rate of one hour for every 15°. Local clock times may differ from standard times, especially in summer when clocks are often advanced by one hour ("daylight saving" or "summer" time).

The time used in this book is Eastern Standard Time. The following table provides conversion between Universal Time and all Time Zones in the United States. An asterisk denotes that the time is on the preceding day.

Universal Time	Eastern Daylight Time	Eastern Standard Time and Central Daylight Time	Central Standard Time and Mountain Daylight Time	Mountain Standard Time and Pacific Daylight Time	Pacific Standard Time
0^h	* 8 P. M.	* 7 P. M.	* 6 P. M.	* 5 P. M.	* 4 P. M.
1	* 9	* 8	* 7	* 6	* 5
2	*10	* 9	* 8	* 7	* 6
3	*11 P. M.	*10	* 9	* 8	* 7
4	0 Midnight	*11 P. M.	*10	* 9	* 8
5	1 A. M.	0 Midnight	*11 P. M.	*10	* 9
6	2	1 A. M.	0 Midnight	*11 P. M.	*10
7	3	2	1 A. M.	0 Midnight	*11 P. M.
8	4	3	2	1 A. M.	0 Midnight
9	5	4	3	2	1 A. M.
10	6	5	4	3	2
11	7	6	5	4	3
12	8	7	6	5	4
13	9	8	7	6	5
14	10	9	8	7	6
15	11 A. M.	10	9	8	7
16	12 Noon	11 A. M.	10	9	8
17	1 P. M.	12 Noon	11 A. M.	10	9
18	2	1 P. M.	12 Noon	11 A. M.	10
19	3	2	1 P. M.	12 Noon	11 A. M.
20	4	3	2	1 P. M.	12 Noon
21	5	4	3	2	1 P. M.
22	6	5	4	3	2
23	7 P. M.	6 P. M.	5 P. M.	4 P. M.	3 P. M.

The longitudes of the standard meridians for the standard time zones are:

Eastern . . . . . 75° West   Central . . . . . 90° West   Mountain . . . . . 105° West   Pacific . . . . . 120° West

LEAP SECONDS

The information below is developed by the editors from data supplied by the International Earth Rotation Service.

Because of Earth's slightly erratic rotation and the need for greater precision in time measurement it has become necessary to add a "leap second" from time to time to man's clocks to coordinate them with astronomical time. Rotation of the Earth has been slowing since 1900, making an astronomical second longer than an atomic second. Since 1972, by international agreement, adjustments have been made to keep astronomical and atomic clocks within 0.9 second of each other. The determination to add (or subtract) seconds is made by the Central Bureau of the International Earth Rotation Service, in Paris. Preferred times for adjustment have been June 30 and December 31, but any time may be designated by the International Earth Rotation Service. The first such adjustment was made in 1972, and as of Dec 31, 1998, a total of 22 leap seconds had been added. The additions have been made at 23:59:60 UTC (Coordinated Universal Time) = 6:59:60 EST (Eastern Standard Time). Leap seconds have been inserted into the UTC time scale on the following dates:

June 30, 1972	Dec 31, 1977	June 30, 1985	June 30, 1994
Dec 31, 1972	Dec 31, 1978	Dec 31, 1987	Dec 31, 1995
Dec 31, 1973	Dec 31, 1979	Dec 31, 1989	June 30, 1997
Dec 31, 1974	June 30, 1981	Dec 31, 1990	Dec 31, 1998
Dec 31, 1975	June 30, 1982	June 30, 1992	
Dec 31, 1976	June 30, 1983	June 30, 1993	

THE NAMING OF HURRICANES

(Compiled from information issued by the US Department of Commerce, National Oceanic and Atmospheric Administration.)

Why are hurricanes named? Experience shows that the use of short, distinctive names greatly reduces confusion when two or more tropical storms occur at the same time. The use of easily remembered names in written and spoken communication is quicker and less subject to error than the older, more cumbersome latitude-longitude identification methods, advantages which are especially important in exchanging detailed storm information between hundreds of widely scattered stations, airports, coastal bases and ships at sea.

The practice of naming hurricanes began hundreds of years ago, but only relatively recently did they begin to be named solely for women. During World War II forecasters and meteorologists began using female names for storms in weather map discussions, and in 1953 the US weather services adopted the practice, creating a new international phonetic alphabet of women's names from A–W to name hurricanes. In 1978 men's names were also introduced into the storm lists.

Because hurricanes affect other nations and are tracked by their weather services, the lists have an international flavor. Names are agreed upon during international meetings of the World Meteorological Organization by the nations involved, and can be retired and replaced with new names in the event of particularly severe storms.

The National Hurricane Center near Miami, FL, keeps a constant watch on oceanic storm-breeding areas for tropical disturbances that may herald the formation of a hurricane. If a disturbance intensifies into a tropical storm—with rotary circulation and wind speeds above 39 miles per hour—the Center will give the storm a name from one of six lists. The Atlantic and Eastern Pacific lists are rotated year by year so that the 2001 set, for example, will be used again to name storms in 2007.

The lists of names for Central Pacific and Western Pacific hurricanes (tropical cyclones) are not rotated on a yearly basis. Meteorologists follow each list until all those names have been used, then go on to the next list. The name of a particularly severe storm is retired and replaced. For example, Iniki—the name of the hurricane that devastated Hawaii—has been replaced with Iolana on List 2.

ATLANTIC HURRICANE NAMES

2001	2002	2003
Allison	Arthur	Ana
Barry	Bertha	Bill
Chantal	Cristobal	Claudette
Dean	Dolly	Danny
Erin	Edouard	Erika
Felix	Fay	Fabian
Gabrielle	Gustav	Grace
Humberto	Hanna	Henri
Iris	Isidore	Isabel
Jerry	Josephine	Juan
Karen	Kyle	Kate
Lorenzo	Lili	Larry
Michelle	Marco	Mindy
Noel	Nana	Nicholas
Olga	Omar	Odette
Pablo	Paloma	Peter
Rebekah	Rene	Rose
Sebastien	Sally	Sam
Tanya	Teddy	Teresa
Van	Vicky	Victor
Wendy	Wilfred	Wanda

EASTERN PACIFIC HURRICANE NAMES

2001	2002	2003
Adolph	Alma	Andres
Barbara	Boris	Blanca
Cosme	Crisina	Carlos
Dalila	Douglas	Dolores
Erick	Elida	Enrique
Flossie	Fausto	Felicia
Gil	Genevieve	Guillermo
Henriette	Hernan	Hilda
Israel	Iselle	Ignacio
Juliette	Julio	Jimena
Kiko	Kenna	Kevin
Lorena	Lowell	Linda
Manuel	Marie	Marty
Narda	Norbert	Nora
Octave	Odile	Olaf
Priscilla	Polo	Patricia
Raymond	Rachel	Rick
Sonia	Simon	Sandra
Tico	Trudy	Terry
Velma	Vance	Vivian
Wallis	Winnie	Waldo
Xina	Xavier	Xina
York	Yolanda	York
Zelda	Zeke	Zelda

If over 24 tropical cyclones occur in a year, then the Greek alphabet will be used following Zelda or Zeke.

CENTRAL PACIFIC TROPICAL CYCLONE NAMES

LIST 1	LIST 3
Akoni (ah-KOH-nee)	Alika (ah-LEE-kah)
Ema (EH-ma)	Ele (EH-leh)
Hana (HAH-nah)	Huko (HOO-koh)
IO (EE-oo)	Ioke (ee-OH-keh)
Keli (KEH-lee)	Kika (KEE-kah)
Lala (LAH-lah)	Lana (LAH-nah)
Moke (MOH-keh)	Maka (MAH-kah)
Nele (NEH-leh)	Neki (NEH-kee)
Oka (OH-kah)	Oleka (oh-LEH-kah)
Peke (PEH-keh)	Peni (PEH-nee)
Uleki (oo-LEH-kee)	Ulia (oo-LEE-ah)
Wila (VEE-lah)	Wali (WAH-lee)

LIST 2	LIST 4
Aka (AH-kah)	Ana (AH-nah)
Ekeka (eh-KEH-kah)	Ela (EH-lah)
Hali (HAH-lee)	Halola (hah-LOH-lah)
Iolana (ee-OH-lah-nah)	Iune (ee-OO-neh)
Keoni (keh-OH-nee)	Kimo (KEE-moh)
Li (LEE)	Loke (LOH-keh)
Mele (MEH-leh)	Malia (mah-LEE-ah)
Nona (NOH-nah)	Niala (nee-AH-lah)
Oliwa (oh-LEE-vah)	Oko (OH-koh)
Paka (PAH-hak)	Pali (PAH-lee)
Upana (oo-PAH-nah)	Ulika (oo-LEE-kah)
Wene (WEH-neh)	Walaka (wah-LAH-kah)

In Hawaiian, all letters are pronounced, including double or triple vowels.

CENTRAL PACIFIC TROPICAL CYCLONE NAMES

LIST 1	LIST 2	LIST 3	LIST 4	LIST 5
Damrey	Kong-rey	Nakri	Krovanh	Sarika
Longwang	Yutu	Fengshen	Dujuan	Haima
Kirogi	Toraji	Kalmaegi	Maemi	Meari
Kai-Tak	Man-yi	Fung-wong	Choi-wan	Ma-on
Tenbin	Usagi	Kanmuri	Koppu	Tokage
Bolaven	Pabuk	Phanfone	Ketsana	Nock-ten
Chanchu	Wutip	Vongfong	Parma	Muifa
Jelawat	Sepat	Rusa	Melor	Merbok
Ewinlar	Fitow	Sinlaku	Nepartak	Nanmadol
Bilis	Danas	Hagupit	Lupit	Talas
Gaemi	Nari	Changmi	Sudal	Noru
Prapiroon	Vipa	Megkhla	Nida	Kularb
Maria	Francisco	Higos	Omais	Roke
Saomai	Lekima	Bavi	Conson	Sonca
Bopha	Krosa	Maysak	Chanthu	Nesat
Wukong	Haiyan	Haishen	Dianmu	Haitang
Sonamu	Podul	Pongsona	Mindule	Nalgae
Shanshan	Lingling	Yanyan	Tingting	Banyan
Yagi	Kaziki	Kuzira	Kompasu	Washi
Xangsane	Faxai	Chan-hom	Namtheun	Matsa
Bebinca	Vamei	Linfa	Malou	Sanvu
Rumbia	Tapah	Nangka	Meranti	Mawar
Soulik	Mitag	Soudelor	Rananin	Guchol
Cimaron	Hagibis	Imbudo	Malakas	Talim
Chebi	Noguri	Koni	Megi	Nabi
Durian	Ramasoon	Hanuman	Chaba	Khanun
Utor	Chataan	Etau	Kodo	Vicete
Trami	Halong	Vamco	Songda	Saola

BROADCASTING HALL OF FAME

The National Association of Broadcasters Broadcasting Hall of Fame, established in 1977, recognizes radio and television personalities or programs that have earned a place in broadcasting history due to outstanding programming and success.

1977
William S. Paley, entrepreneur
Jack Benny, comedian
Fred Allen, comedian
Lowell Thomas, news reporter and commentator
Edward R. Murrow, news reporter and commentator
Milton Cross, music commentator
David Sarnoff, entrepreneur
Ted Husing, sportscaster
Edwin H. Armstrong, inventor
Herbert Hoover, president of the United States
Gene Autry, singer, entertainer
Freeman F. Gosden (Amos) and Charles J. Correll
    (Andy), comedians
Bob Hope, comedian
Gordon McNamee, announcer

1978
Jim Jordan and Marian Jordan (Fibber McGee and
    Molly), comedians
Walter Winchell, commentator
Guglielmo Marconi, inventor
Arthur Godfrey, personality
Orson Welles, producer, actor, director of radio, motion
    pictures and theatre

1979
Paul Harvey, commentator

1980
George Burns, comedian
Bing Crosby, singer/entertainer

1981
Ronald Reagan (Dutch Reagan), president of the United
    States
Kate Smith, singer, entertainer

1982
Don McNeill, entertainer
Edgar Bergen, comedian

1983
Charles Lauk (Lum) and Norris Goff (Abner), comedians
Benny Goodman, entertainer

1984
Red Skelton, comedian
Bob Elliot and Ray Goulding, entertainers

1985
Fred Palmer, broadcaster, consultant
Casey Kasem, personality, announcer

1986
Mel Allen, sportscaster
Earl Nightingale, commentator

1987
Robert Trout, political journalist
Gordon B. McLendon, innovator
Robert Todd Storz, industry leader

1988
William B. Williams, personality
Roy Acuff, singer
Milton Berle, comedian
Lucille Ball, comedienne

1989
Ernie Kovacs, comedian
Sid Caesar, comedian
Red Barber, sportscaster
Nathan Safir, Spanish broadcasting pioneer

1990
Hal Jackson, entrepreneur
Charles Osgood, correspondent
"The Honeymooners" and Its Original Cast (Art Carney,
    Audrey Meadows, Joyce Randolph, Jackie Gleason),
    entertainers
Sylvester L. (Pat) Weaver, TV programming pioneer

1991
Jerry Lewis, comedian
Douglas Edwards, radio correspondent

1992
Larry King, radio personality
"Star Trek," TV series

1993
"60 Minutes," TV program
"Grand Ole Opry," radio program

1994
Harry Caray, radio program
Roone Arledge, network news president

1995
Carol Burnett, TV entertainer
Gary Owens, radio personality

1996
Don Imus, radio personality
"M*A*S*H," cast of TV series

1997
"Today," cast of TV's "Today" show
Wally Phillips, radio personality

1998
Rush Limbaugh, radio program
Bob Keeshan, TV entertainer

1999
Wolfman Jack, radio personality
"All in the Family," TV series

2000
"Saturday Night Live," TV program
Tom Joyner, radio personality

THE ACADEMY OF TELEVISION ARTS AND SCIENCES (ATAS) TELEVISION HALL OF FAME

The Academy of Television Arts & Sciences Television Academy Hall of Fame was established in 1984 to recognize the lifelong accomplishments of television's greatest contributors, including, in addition to those who appear before the camera, those who contribute to the industry as writers, executives and producers.

Bronze sculptures and bas reliefs of some of the Hall of Fame's inductees have been erected in the Hall of Fame Plaza. Located in the forecourt of the Television Academy's North Hollywood international headquarters, the plaza's centerpiece is a 27-foot Emmy statue, a replica of the internationally famous Emmy statuette, symbol of television excellence.

1984
Lucille Ball
Milton Berle
Paddy Chayefsky
Norman Lear
Edward R. Murrow
Edward S. Paley
General David Sarnoff

1985
Carol Burnett
Sid Caesar
Walter Cronkite
Joyce C. Hall
Rod Serling
Ed Sullivan
Sylvester "Pat" Weaver

1986
Steve Allen
Fred Coe
Walt Disney
Jackie Gleason
Mary Tyler Moore
Frank Stanton
Burr Tillstrom

1987
Johnny Carson
Jaques-Yves Cousteau
Leonard Goldenson
Jim Henson
Bob Hope
Ernie Kovacs

1988
Jack Benny
George Burns
Gracie Allen
Chet Huntley
David Brinkley
Red Skelton
David Susskind
David Wolper

1989
Roone Arledge
Fred Astaire
Perry Como
Joan Ganz Cooney
Don Hewitt
Carroll O'Connor
Barbara Walters

1990
Desi Arnaz
Leonard Bernstein
James Garner
"I Love Lucy"
Danny Thomas
Mike Wallace

1991
Bill Cosby
Andy Griffith
Ted Koppel
Sheldon Leonard
Dinah Shore
Ted Turner

1992
Dick Clark
John Chancellor
Phil Donahue
Mark Goodson
Bob Newhart
Agnes Nixon
Jack Webb

1993
Alan Alda
Howard Cosell
Barry Diller
Fred Friendly
William Hanna/
  Joseph Barbera
Oprah Winfrey

1994
Michael Landon
Richard Levinson and
  William Link
Jim McKay
Bill Moyers
Dick Van Dyke
Betty White

1995
Edward Asner
Steven Bochco
Marcy Carsey/Tom Werner
Charles Kuralt
Angela Lansbury
Aaron Spelling
Lew R. Wasserman

1996
James L. Brooks
Garry Marshall
Quinn Martin
Diane Sawyer
Grant Tinker

1997
No inductees

1998
Herbert Brodkin
Robert MacNeil/
  Jim Lehrer
Lorne Michaels
Carl Reiner
Fred Rogers
Fred Silverman
Ethel Winant

1999
No inductees

MAJOR AWARDS

1999–2000 SEASON TONY AWARDS

Play: *Copenhagen*
Musical: *Contact*
Book of a Musical: *James Joyce's "The Dead"*, Richard Wilson
Original Score: *Aida*, Elton John and Tim Rice
Revival of a Play: *The Real Thing*
Revival of a Musical: *Kiss Me, Kate*
Actor in a Play: Stephen Dillane, *The Real Thing*
Actress in a Play: Jennifer Ehle, *The Real Thing*
Actor in a Musical: Brian Stokes Mitchell, *Kiss Me, Kate*
Actress in a Musical: Heather Headley, *Aida*
Featured Actor in a Play: Roy Dotrice, *A Moon for the Misbegotten*
Featured Actress in a Play: Blair Brown, *Copenhagen*
Featured Actor in a Musical: Boyd Gaines, *Contact*
Featured Actress in a Musical: Karen Ziemba, *Contact*
Director of a Play: Michael Blakemore, *Copenhagen*
Director of a Musical: Michael Blakemore, *Kiss Me, Kate*
Scenery: Bob Crowley, *Aida*
Costumes: Martin Pakledinaz, *Kiss Me, Kate*
Lighting: Natasha Katz, *Aida*
Choreography: Susan Stroman, *Contact*
Orchestration: Don Sebesky, *Kiss Me, Kate*
Regional Theater: The Utah Shakespearean Festival, Cedar City

1999 ACADEMY AWARDS (OSCARS)

Picture: *American Beauty*
Actor: Kevin Spacey, *American Beauty*
Actress: Hilary Swank, *Boys Don't Cry*
Director: Sam Mendes, *American Beauty*
Supporting Actor: Michael Caine, *The Cider House Rules*
Supporting Actress: Angelina Jolie, *Girl, Interrupted*
Original Screenplay: *American Beauty*
Adapted Screenplay: *The Cider House Rules*
Cinematography: *American Beauty*
Art Direction: *Sleepy Hollow*
Film Editing: *The Matrix*
Foreign Language Film: *All About My Mother* (Spain)
Animated Short Film: *The Old Man and the Sea*
Documentary Feature: *One Day in September*
Documentary Short Subject: *King Gimp*
Costume Design: *Topsy-Turvy*
Sound Design: *The Matrix*
Visual Effects: *The Matrix*
Makeup: *Topsy-Turvy*
Sound Effects Editing: *The Matrix*
Live Action Short Film: *My Mother Dreams the Satan's Disciples in New York*
Original Score: *The Red Violin*
Original Song: "You'll Be in My Heart" from *Tarzan*

1999 AMERICAN MUSIC AWARDS
27th Annual Awards

POP/ROCK
Male Vocalist: Will Smith
Female Vocalist: Shania Twain
Band, Duo or Group: Backstreet Boys
Album: *Supernatural*, Santana
New Artist: Britney Spears

SOUL/RHYTHM & BLUES
Male Vocalist: R. Kelly
Female Vocalist: Lauryn Hill
Band, Duo or Group: TLC
Album: *The Miseducation of Lauryn Hill*, Lauryn Hill
New Artist: Tyrese

COUNTRY
Male Vocalist: Garth Brooks
Female Vocalist: Shania Twain
Band, Duo or Group: Brooks & Dunn
Album: *Double Live*, Garth Brooks
New Artist: Montgomery Gentry

LATIN MUSIC
Artist: Ricky Martin

RAP/HIP HOP
Artist: DMX

ADULT CONTEMPORARY
Artist: Phil Collins

ALTERNATIVE MUSIC
Artist: Red Hot Chili Peppers

SOUNDTRACK
Wild Wild West

AWARD OF MERIT
Gloria Estefan

AWARD OF ACHIEVEMENT
Mariah Carey

2000 GRAMMY AWARDS

Record of the Year: "Smooth," Santana
Album of the Year: *Supernatural*, Santana
Song of the Year: "Smooth," Itaal Shur and Rob Thomas
Best New Artist: Christina Aguilera
Best Female Pop Vocal Performance: "I Will Remember You," Sarah McLachlan
Best Male Pop Vocal Performance: "Brand New Day," Sting
Best Pop Performance by a Duo or Group with Vocal: "Maria Maria," Santana
Best Pop Collaboration with Vocals: "Smooth," Santana featuring Rob Thomas
Best Pop Instrumental Performance: "El Farol," Santana
Best Pop Album: *Brand New Day*, Sting
Best Traditional Pop Vocal Performance: "Bennett Sings Ellington—Hot and Cool," Tony Bennett
Best Dance Recording: "Believe," Cher
Best Female Rock Vocal Performance: "Sweet Child o' Mine," Sheryl Crow
Best Male Rock Vocal Performance: "American Woman," Lenny Kravitz
Best Rock Performance by a Duo or Group with Vocal: "Put Your Lights On," Santana featuring Everlast
Best Hard Rock Performance: "Whiskey in the Jar," Metallica
Best Metal Performance: "Iron Man," Black Sabbath
Best Rock Instrumental Performance: "The Calling," Santana featuring Eric Clapton
Best Rock Song: "Scar Tissue," Red Hot Chili Peppers
Best Rock Album: *Supernatural*, Santana
Best Alternative Music Performance: "Mutations," Beck
Best Female R&B Vocal Performance: "It's Not Right But It's Okay," Whitney Houston
Best Male R&B Vocal Performance: "Staying Power," Barry White
Best R&B Performance by a Duo or Group with Vocal: "No Scrubs," TLC
Best R&B Song: "No Scrubs," TLC
Best R&B Album: *Fanmail*, TLC
Best Traditional R&B Vocal Performance: "Staying Power," Barry White
Best Rap Solo Performance: "My Name Is," Eminem
Best Rap Performance by a Duo or Group: "You Got Me," The Roots and Erykah Badu
Best Rap Album: *The Slim Shady LP*, Eminem
Best Female Country Vocal Performance: "Man! I Feel Like a Woman!," Shania Twain
Best Male Country Vocal Performance: "Choices," George Jones
Best Country Performance by a Duo or Group with Vocal: "Ready to Run," Dixie Chicks
Best Country Collaboration with Vocals: "After the Gold Rush," Emmylou Harris, Linda Ronstadt and Dolly Parton
Best Country Instrumental Performance: "Bob's Breakdowns," Asleep at the Wheel featuring Tommy Allsup, Floyd Domino, Larry Franklin, Vince Gill and Steve Wariner
Best Country Song: "Come On Over," Robert John "Mutt" Lange and Shania Twain
Best Country Album: *Fly*, Dixie Chicks
Best Bluegrass Album: *Ancient Tones*, Ricky Skaggs and Kentucky Thunder
Best New Age Album: *Celtic Solstice*, Paul Winter and Friends
Best Contemporary Jazz Performance: "Inside," David Sanborn
Best Jazz Vocal Performance: "When I Look in Your Eyes," Diana Krall
Best Jazz Instrumental Solo: "In Walked Wayne," Wayne Shorter
Best Jazz Instrumental Performance, Individual or Group: "Like Minds," Gary Burton, Chick Corea, Pat Metheny, Roy Haynes and Dave Holland

Best Large Jazz Ensemble Performance: "Serendipity 18," The Bob Florence Limited Edition
Best Latin Jazz Performance: "Latin Soul," Poncho Sanchez
Best Rock Gospel Album: *Pray*, Rebecca St. James
Best Pop/Contemporary Gospel Album: *Speechless*, Steven Curtis Chapman
Best Southern, Country or Bluegrass Gospel Album: *Kennedy Center Homecoming*, Bill and Gloria Gaither and their Homecoming Friends
Best Traditional Soul Gospel Album: *Christmas with Shirley Caesar*, Shirley Caesar
Best Contemporary Soul Gospel Album: *Mountain High . . .Valley Low*, Yolanda Adams
Best Gospel Album by a Choir or Chorus: *High and Lifted Up*, Brooklyn Tabernacle Choir
Best Latin Pop Performance: "Tiempos," Ruben Blades
Best Latin Rock/Alternative Performance: "Resurrection," Chris Perez Band
Best Tropical Latin Performance: "Mambo Birdland," Tito Puente
Best Mexican-American Performance: "100 Anos de Mariachi," Placido Domingo
Best Tejano Music Performance: "Por Eso Te Amo," Los Palominos
Best Salsa Performance: "Llego. . .Van Van: Van Van Is Here," Los Van Van
Best Merengue Performance: "Pintame," Elvis Crespo
Best Traditional Blues Performance: "Blues on the Bayou," B.B. King
Best Contemporary Blues Album: *Take Your Shoes Off*, Robert Cray Band
Best Traditional Folk Album: *Press On*, June Carter Cash
Best Contemporary Folk Album: *Mule Variations*, Tom Waits
Best Reggae Album: *Calling Rastafari*, Burning Spear
Best World Music Album: *Livro*, Caetano Veloso
Best Polka Album: *Polkasonic*, Brave Combo
Best Musical Album for Children: *The Adventures of Elmo in Grouchland*, various artists
Best Spoken Word Album for Children: *Listen to the Storyteller*, Wynton Marsalis, Graham Greene and Kate Winslet
Best Spoken Word or Non-Musical Album: *The Autobiography of Martin Luther King, Jr*, LeVar Burton
Best Spoken Comedy Album: *Bigger and Blacker*, Chris Rock
Best Musical Show Album: *Annie Get Your Gun*
Best Instrumental Composition: "Joyful Noise Suite," Don Sebesky
Best Instrumental Composition Written for a Motion Picture or for Television: *A Bug's Life*, Randy Newman
Best Song Written Specifically for a Motion Picture or for Television: "Beautiful Stranger" (from *Austin Powers: The Spy Who Shagged Me*), Madonna and William Orbit
Best Soundtrack: *Tarzan*, Phil Collins
Best Instrumental Arrangement: "Chelsea Bridge," Don Sebesky
Best Instrumental Arrangement with Accompanying Vocal(s): "Lonely Town," Charlie Haden Quartet West featuring Shirley Horn
Best Recording Package: *Ride With Bob*, Asleep at the Wheel
Best Recording Package-Boxed: *Miles Davis—The Complete Bitches Brew Sessions*

Best Album Notes: *John Coltrane—Complete Impulse! Studio Recordings*

Best Historical Album: *The Duke Ellington Centennial Edition—The Complete RCA Victor Recordings (1927–1973)*

Best Engineered Album, Non-Classical: *When I Look in Your Eyes,* Diana Krall

Producer of the Year: Walter Afanasieff

Remixer of the Year: Club 69 (Peter Rauhofer)

Best Classical Engineered Recording: *Stravinsky: Firebird; The Rite of Spring; Persephone,* Markus Heiland

Classical Producer of the Year: Adam Abeshouse

Best Classical Album: *Stravinsky: Firebird; The Rite of Spring; Persephone*

Best Orchestral Performance: *Stravinsky: Firebird; The Rite of Spring; Persephone,* San Francisco Symphony, Michael Tilson Thomas, conductor

Best Opera Recording: *Stravinsky: The Rake's Progress,* John Eliot Gardiner, conductor

Best Choral Performance: *Britten: War Requiem,* Robert Shafer

Best Instrumental Soloist(s) Performance (With Orchestra): *Prokofiev: Piano Cons Nos 1 and 3/Bartok: Piano Con No 3,* Martha Argerich, piano

Best Instrumental Soloist Performance (Without Orchestra): *Shostakovich: 24 Preludes and Fugues, Op 87,* Vladimir Ashkenazy, piano

Best Chamber Music Performance: *Beethoven: The Violin Sonatas,* Anne-Sophie Mutter, violin, and Lambert Orkis, piano

Best Small Ensemble Album: *Colors of Love,* Chanticleer; Joseph Jennings, conductor

Best Classical Vocal Performance: *Mahler: Des Knaben Wunderhorn,* Thomas Quasthoff, baritone, Anne Sofie von Otter, mezzo soprano

Best Classical Contemporary Composition: *Boulez: Repons,* Pierre Boulez

Best Classical Crossover Album: *Schickele: Hornsmoke,* Chestnut Brass Company

Best Music Video, Short Form: *Freak on a Leash,* Korn

Best Music Video, Long Form: *Bands of Gypsies—Live at Fillmore East,* Jimi Hendrix

---

31ST ANNUAL DOVE AWARDS GOSPEL MUSIC ASSOCIATION

Song of the Year: "This Is Your Time," Michael W. Smith and Wes King

Songwriter of the Year: Michael W. Smith

Male Vocalist of the Year: Steven Curtis Chapman

Female Vocalist of the Year: Jaci Velasquez

Group of the Year: Sixpence None the Richer

Artist of the Year: Steven Curtis Chapman

New Artist of the Year: Ginny Owens

Alternative/Modern Rock Album: *Candycoatedwaterdrops,* Plumb

Rock Album: *Time,* Third Day

Hard Rock Album: *Point #1,* Chevelle

Rap/Hip Hop/Dance Album: *Power,* Raze

Pop/Contemporary Album: *Speechless,* Steven Curtis Chapman

Inspirational Album: *Selah,* Selah

Southern Gospel Album: *God Is Good,* Gaither Vocal Band

Bluegrass Album: *Kentucky Bluegrass,* The Bishops

Country Album: *A Glen Campbell Christmas,* Glen Campbell

Traditional Gospel Album: *Healing—Live in Detroit,* Richard Smallwood with Vision

Contemporary Gospel Album: *Anointed,* Anointed

Special Event Album: *Streams,* various artists

Instrumental Album: *Majesty and Wonder,* Phil Keaggy

Praise and Worship Album: *SONICFLOOd,* SONICFLOOd

Children's Music Album: *Larry Boy: The Soundtrack,* Veggie Tales

Spanish Language Album: *Llegar a Ti,* Jaci Velasquez

Rap/Hip Hop Recorded Song: "They All Fall Down," Grammatical Revolution

Alternative/Modern Rock Recorded Song: "Unforgetful You," Jars of Clay

Rock Recorded Song: "Get Down," Audio Adrenaline

Hard Music Song: "Mia," Chevelle

Pop/Contemporary Recorded Song: "Dive," Steven Curtis Chapman

Inspirational Recorded Song: "I Will Follow Christ," Clay Crosse

Southern Gospel Recorded Song: "Healing," Cathedrals

Country Recorded Song: "Angel Band," Vestal Goodman and George Jones

Urban Recorded Song: "Anything Is Possible," Anointed

Bluegrass Recorded Song: "So Fine," Lewis Family

Traditional Gospel Recorded Song: "God Can," Dottie Peoples

Contemporary Gospel Recorded Song: "Power," Fred Hammond and Radical for Christ

Producer: Brown Bannister

Musical: *A Christmas to Remember,* Claire Cloninger and Gary Rhodes

Youth/Children's Musical: *Lord, I Lift Your Name on High,* Karla Worley and Steven V. Taylor

Choral Collections: "High & Lifted Up," Brooklyn Tabernacle Music

Recorded Music Packaging: *Streams,* various artists

Enhanced CD: *Without Condition,* Ginny Owens

Short Form Video: *This Is Your Time,* Michael W. Smith

Long Form Video: *The Supernatural Experience,* dc Talk

2000 WEBBY AWARDS
4th ANNUAL

Activism: Ad Busters—www.adbusters.org
Arts: Webstalker—www.backspace.org/iod/iod4Winupdates.html
Broadband: Video Farm—www.videofarm.com
Commerce: BabyCenter—www.babycenter.com
Community: Café Utne—cafe.utne.com/cafe
Education: Merriam-Webster Word Central—
www.wordcentral.com
Fashion: Paul Smith—www.paulsmith.co.uk
Film: Atom Films—www.atomfilms.com
Finance: Gomez.com—www.gomez.com
Games: Gamespy Industries—www.gamespy.com
Health: ThriveOnline—thriveonline.com
Humor: The Onion—www.theonion.com
Kids: Scholastic.com—www.scholastic.com
Living: Epicurious—www.epicurious.com
Music: Napster—www.napster.com
News: Media News—www.medianews.org
Personal: Cocky Bastard—www.cockybastard.com
Politics/Law: Politics.com—www.politics.com
Print & Zines: Nerve—www.nerve.com
Radio: Lost and Found Sound—www.lostandfoundsound.com
Science: The Cave of Lascaux—
www.culture.fr/culture/arcnat/lascaux/en
Services: Evite—www.evite.com
Sports: ESPN—www.espn.go.com
Technical Achievements: Google—www.google.com
Travel: Outside Online—www.outsidemag.com
TV: MSNBC—www.msnbc.com
Weird: Stile Project—www.stileproject.com

PEN FAULKNER AWARD FOR FICTION (1999)

(An award given by an organization of writers to honor their peers)

Ha Jin, *Waiting*

2000 GOLDEN GLOBE AWARDS
57TH ANNUAL
For 1999 Achievement

MOVIES
Drama: *American Beauty*
Musical or Comedy: *Toy Story 2*
Director: Sam Mendes, *American Beauty*
Actor, Drama: Denzel Washington, *The Hurricane*
Actress, Drama: Hilary Swank, *Boys Don't Cry*
Actor, Musical or Comedy: Jim Carrey, *Man on the Moon*
Actress, Musical or Comedy: Janet McTeer, *Tumbleweeds*
Supporting Actor: Tom Cruise, *Magnolia*
Supporting Actress: Angelina Jolie, *Girl, Interrupted*
Screenplay: *American Beauty*

Foreign Film: Spain, *All About My Mother*
Original Score: Ennio Morricone, *The Legend of 1900*
Original Song: "You'll Be in My Heart," *Tarzan*
Cecil B. De Mille Award 2000: Barbra Streisand

TELEVISION
Series, Musical or Comedy: "Sex and the City"
Actor, Series, Musical or Comedy: Michael J. Fox, "Spin City"
Actress, Series, Musical or Comedy: Sarah Jessica Parker, "Sex and the City"
Series, Drama: "The Sopranos"
Actor, Series, Drama: James Gandolfini, "The Sopranos"
Actress, Series, Drama: Edie Falco, "The Sopranos"
Miniseries or TV Movie: *RKO 281*
Actor, Miniseries or TV Movie: Jack Lemmon, *Inherit the Wind*
Actress, Miniseries or TV Movie: Halle Berry, *Introducing Dorothy Dandridge*
Actor, Supporting Role: Peter Fonda, *The Passion of Ayn Rand*
Actress, Supporting Role: Nancy Marchand, "The Sopranos"

1999 GEORGE POLK AWARDS

(Awarded for special achievement in journalism)

Career Award: Studs Terkel
International Reporting: Sang-hun Choe, Charles J. Hanley, Martha Mendoza and Randy Herschaft, Associated Press
Local Reporting: Kevin Carmody, *Daily Southtown (Illinois)*
Regional Reporting: Todd Richissin and Andre Chung, *The Baltimore Sun*
National Reporting: Jason DeParle, *The New York Times*
Foreign Reporting: Paul Watson, *Los Angeles Times*
Medical Reporting: Andrea Gerlin, *The Philadelphia Inquirer*
Criminal Justice Reporting: Ken Armstrong and Steve Mills, *Chicago Tribune*
Financial Reporting: Ellen E. Schultz, *The Wall Street Journal*
Editorial Writing: *Daily News (New York)*
Television Foreign Reporting: Giselle Portenier, Olenka Frenkiel and Fiona Murch, "BBC News"
Local Television Reporting: The "I" Team, WWOR-TV (New Jersey)
Special Award: National Security Archive

2000 AMERICAN LIBRARY ASSOCIATION AWARDS FOR CHILDREN'S BOOKS

NEWBERY MEDAL (for most distinguished contribution to American literature for children published in 1999):
Christopher Paul Curtis, author, *Bud, Not Buddy*
Honor Books
Audrey Couloumbis, author, *Getting Near to Baby*
Tomie dePaola, author and illustrator, *26 Fairmount Avenue*
Jennifer L. Holm, author, *Our Only May Amelia*

CALDECOTT MEDAL (for most distinguished American picture book for children published in 1999):
Simms Taback, illustrator, *Joseph Had a Little Overcoat*
Honor Books
Davis Weisner, illustrator and author, *Sector 7*
Jerry Pinkney, illustrator, *The Ugly Duckling*

Molly Bang, illustrator and author, *When Sophie Gets Angry—Really, Really Angry*
Trina Schart Hyman, illustrator, *A Child's Calendar*

CORETTA SCOTT KING AWARD (for outstanding books by African American authors and illustrators):
Christopher Paul Curtis, author, *Bud, Not Buddy*
Brian Pinkney, illustrator, *In the Time of the Drums*
Honor Books—Authors
Karen English, *Francie*
Patricia C. and Fredrick L. McKissack, *Black Hands, White Sails: The Story of African-American Whalers*
Walter Dean Myers, *Monster*
Honor Books—Illustrators
E.B. Lewis, *My Rows and Piles of Coins*
Christopher Myers, *Black Cat*

MICHAEL L. PRINTZ AWARD (for excellence in writing literature for young adults):
Walter Dean Myers, *Monster*
Honor Books
Ellen Wittlinger, *Hard Love*
David Almond, *Skellig*
Laurie Halse Anderson, *Speak*

MARGARET A. EDWARDS AWARD (for lifetime achievement in writing books for young adults):
Chris Crutcher, recipient

PURA BELPRÉ AWARD (for Latino authors and illustrators whose work best portrays and celebrates Latino culture in a children's book):
Alma Flor Ada, author, *Under the Royal Palms: A Childhood in Cuba*
Carmen Lomas Garza, illustrator *Magic Windows: Cut-paper Art and Stories*
Honor Books—Author
Francisco X. Alarcón, *From the Bellybutton of the Moon and Other Summer Poems*
Juan Felipe Herrera, *Laughing Out Loud, I Fly: Poems in English and Spanish*
Honor Books—Illustrators
George Ancona, *Barrio: José's Neighborhood*
Felipe Dávalos, *The Secret Stars*
Amelia Lau Carling, *Mama & Papa Have a Store*

MILDRED L. BATCHELDER AWARD (for the best children's book first published in a foreign language in a foreign country and subsequently translated into English for publication in the US):
Walker and Company, publisher, *The Baboon King*
Honor Books
R&S Books, *Vendela in Venice*
Farrar, Straus and Giroux, *The Collector of Moments*
Front Street, *Asphalt Angels*

ANDREW CARNEGIE MEDAL FOR EXCELLENCE IN CHILDREN'S VIDEO
Paul R. Gagne, *Miss Nelson Has a Field Day*

MAY HILL ARBUTHNOT LECTURE AWARD
Susan Cooper, recipient

1999/2000 NATIONAL ENDOWMENT FOR THE HUMANITIES AWARDS

1999 National Medal of Arts:
Irene Diamond, patron of the arts
Aretha Franklin, singer
Michael Graves, architect
Juilliard School
Norman Lear, producer
Rosetta LeNoire, actress
Harvey Lichtenstein, patron of the arts
Lydia Mendoza, singer
Odetta, singer
George Segal, artist
Maria Tallchief, dancer
1999 National Medal of Humanities:
Patricia M. Battin, librarian
Taylor Branch, Pulitzer Prize-winning writer and journalist
Jacquelyn Dowd Hall, founder and director of the Southern Oral History Project at the University of North Carolina-Chapel Hill
Garrison Keillor, creator, writer and host ("A Prairie Home Companion")
Jim Lehrer, journalist, editor and anchor ("The NewsHour with Jim Lehrer")
John Rawls, political philosopher, author
Steven Spielberg, filmmaker
August Wilson, two-time Pulitzer Prize-winning playwright
2000 Jefferson Lecturer in the Humanities: James M. McPherson, Princeton University history professor, considered one of the greatest historians of the Civil War (This award is the highest honor bestowed by the federal government for distinguished intellectual achievement in the humanities.)

2000 PULITZER PRIZES

THE ARTS
Fiction: *Interpreter of Maladies*, Jhumpa Lahiri
Drama: *Dinner With Friends*, Donald Margulies
History: *Freedom From Fear: The American People in Depression and War, 1929–1945*, David M. Kennedy
Biography: *Vera*, Stacy Schiff
Poetry: *Repair*, C.K. Williams
General Nonfiction: *Embracing Defeat: Japan in the Wake of World War II*, John W. Dower

JOURNALISM
Public Service: *The Washington Post*
Breaking News Reporting: Staff, *The Denver Post*
Investigative Reporting: Sang-Hun Choe, Charles J. Hanley and Martha Mendoza, Associated Press
Explanatory Reporting: Eric Newhouse, *Great Falls Tribune*
Beat Reporting: George Dohrmann, *St. Paul Pioneer Press*
National Reporting: Staff, *The Wall Street Journal*
International Reporting: Mark Schoofs, *The Village Voice*
Feature Writing: J.R. Moehringer, *Los Angeles Times*
Commentary: Paul A. Gigot, *The Wall Street Journal*
Criticism: Henry Allen, *The Washington Post*
Editorial Writing: John C. Bersia, *The Orlando Sentinel*
Editorial Cartooning: Joel Pett, *Lexington (KY) Herald-Leader*
Breaking News Photography: Photo Staff, *Denver Rocky Mountain News*
Feature Photography: Carol Guzy, Michael Williamson and Lucian Perkins, *The Washington Post*

MUSIC
Music: *Life Is a Dream, Opera in Three Acts: Act II, Concert Version*, Lewis Spratlan

SPECIAL AWARD
Edward Kennedy "Duke" Ellington

1999 PEABODY AWARDS

"Lost & Found Sound," National Public Radio and The Kitchen Sisters
"The Mississippi: River of Song," Smithsonian Productions
"Morning Edition with Bob Edwards," National Public Radio
"ABC 2000," ABC News
Bob Simon, international reporting for CBS News
"Singled Out," WAGA-TV, Atlanta, GA
"Stadium Investigation," WCPO-TV, Cincinnati, OH
Investigative reporting by GMA Network, Manila, Philippines
"Those Were Our Children," ABC News 20/20
"BIOrhythm," MTV Networks
"Playing the China Card," Brook Lapping Productions, London
"Facing the Truth with Bill Moyers," Public Affairs Television
"The Second World War in Colour," TWI/Carlton Co-Production
"ESPN SportsCentury," ESPN
"Not for Ourselves Alone: The Story of Elizabeth Cady Stanton and Susan B. Anthony," Florentine Films with WETA-TV, Washington, DC
"FRONTLINE: The Lost Children of Rockdale County," FRONTLINE with 10/20 Productions
"Dare to Compete: The Struggle of Women in Sports," Home Box Office Sports
"Arguing the World," Riverside Films
"The Valley," Mentorn Barraclough Carey Production
"Fists of Freedom: The Story of the '68 Summer Games," Home Box Office Sports
"Murder in Purdah," BBC News, London
"I'll Make Me a World: A Century of African-American Arts," Blackside, Inc with Thirteen/WNET
"The Life of Birds by David Attenborough," BBC, London
"Good Night Moon & Other Sleepytime Tales," Home Box Office
"Annie," ABC, Storyline Entertainment, Columbia-Tristar Television and Chris Montan Productions with Walt Disney Television
"VH1 Save the Music Campaign," VH1 Public Affairs, MTV Networks
"The Sopranos," Home Box Office and Brillstein-Grey Entertainment
"Having Our Say: The Delany Sisters' First 100 Years," CBS, Televest, Columbia-Tristar Television with Dreyfuss/James Productions
"Strange Justice," Showtime and Haft Entertainment
"ExxonMobil Masterpiece Theatre: Lost for Words," Yorkshire Television Production
"A Lesson Before Dying," Home Box Office, Spanky Pictures Production with Ellen M. Krass Productions
"City Life," Thirteen/WNET, New York
"ExxonMobil Masterpiece Theatre: A Rather English Marriage," Wall to Wall Television, BBC, Carlton Television
"The West Wing," NBC, John Wells Productions with Warner Bros. Television
"American Presidents: Life Portraits," C-SPAN, Washington, DC
Sheila Nevins, Home Box Office, personal award

2000 DAYTIME EMMY AWARDS
27th Annual

Drama: "General Hospital"
Children's Animated Program: "Steven Spielberg Presents: Pinky, Elmyra & the Brain"
Children's Series: "Sesame Street"
Performer in a Children's Series: Shari Lewis, "Charlie Horse Music Pizza"
Children's Special: "Summer's End"
Talk Show: "The Rosie O'Donnell Show"
Game Show: "Who Wants to Be a Millionaire"
Lead Actress in a Drama Series: Susan Flannery, "The Bold & the Beautiful," CBS
Lead Actor in a Drama Series: Anthony Geary, "General Hospital," ABC

Supporting Actress in a Drama Series: Sarah Brown, "General Hospital," ABC
Supporting Actor in a Drama Series: Shemar Moore, "The Young and the Restless," CBS
Younger Actor in a Drama Series: David Tom, "The Young and the Restless," CBS
Younger Actress in a Drama Series: Camryn Grimes, "The Young and the Restless," CBS
Game Show Host: Bob Barker, "The Price Is Right" and Tom Bergeron, "Hollywood Squares"
Talk Show Host: Rosie O'Donnell, "The Rosie O'Donnell Show"
Drama Series Writing Team: "The Young and the Restless," CBS
Drama Series Directing Team: "General Hospital," ABC

1999 PRIME TIME EMMY AWARDS

Drama: "The Practice," ABC
Comedy: "Ally McBeal," FOX
Miniseries: *Horatio Hornblower*
Telefilm: *A Lesson Before Dying*
Lead Actress in a Drama Series: Edie Falco, "The Sopranos," HBO
Lead Actor in a Drama Series: Dennis Franz, "NYPD Blue," ABC
Supporting Actress in a Drama Series: Holland Taylor, "The Practice," ABC
Supporting Actor in a Drama Series: Michael Badalucco, "The Practice," ABC
Lead Actress in a Comedy Series: Helen Hunt, "Mad About You," NBC
Lead Actor in a Comedy Series: John Lithgow, "3rd Rock From the Sun," NBC
Supporting Actress in a Comedy Series: Kristen Johnston, "3rd Rock From the Sun," NBC
Supporting Actor in a Comedy Series: David Hyde Pierce, "Frasier," NBC
Lead Actress in a Miniseries or TV Movie: Helen Mirren, *The Passion of Ayn Rand,* Showtime
Lead Actor in a Miniseries or TV Movie: Stanley Tucci, *Winchell,* HBO
Supporting Actress in a Miniseries or TV Movie: Anne Bancroft, *Deep in My Heart,* CBS
Supporting Actor in a Miniseries or TV Movie: Peter O'Toole, *Joan of Arc,* CBS
Performance in a Variety or Music Program: John Leguizamo, "John Leguizamo's Freak," HBO
Drama Series Directing Team: "NYPD Blue," Paris Barclay, ABC
Comedy Series Directing Team: "Sports Night," Thomas Schlamme, ABC
Variety or Music Program Directing Team: "1998 Tony Awards," Paul Miller, CBS
Miniseries or TV Movie Directing Team: *The Temptations,* Allan Arkush, NBC
Variety, Music or Comedy Series: "Late Show with David Letterman," CBS
Variety, Music or Comedy Special: "1998 Tony Awards," CBS
Comedy Series Writing Team: "Frasier," NBC
Drama Series Writing Team: "The Sopranos," HBO
Variety or Music Program Writing Team: "The Chris Rock Show," HBO
Miniseries or TV Movie Writing Team: *A Lesson Before Dying,* HBO

NATIONAL FILM REGISTRY 1989–1999

The National Film Preservation Board, established by the National Film Preservation Act of 1992 (2 U.S.C. 179b), serves as a public advisory group to the Librarian of Congress. The Board consists of 36 members and alternates representing the film industry, archives, scholars, filmmakers and others who make up the diverse American motion picture industry. As its primary mission, the Board works to ensure the survival, conservation and increased public availability of America's film heritage, including advising the Librarian on the annual selection of films to be added to the National Film Registry, and counseling the Librarian on development and implementation of the national film preservation plan. Films are selected on the basis of historical, cultural and aesthetic significance. A film must be at least 10 years old to be considered. One copy in "archival quality" of each film selected is added to the National Film Registry Collection at the Library of Congress.

Adam's Rib (1949)
The Adventures of Robin Hood (1938)
The African Queen (1951)
All About Eve (1950)
All Quiet on the Western Front (1930)
All That Heaven Allows (1955)
American Graffiti (1973)
An American in Paris (1951)
Annie Hall (1977)
The Apartment (1960)
The Awful Truth (1937)
Badlands (1973)
The Band Wagon (1953)
The Bank Dick (1940)
The Battle of San Pietro (1945)
Ben Hur (1925)
The Best Years of Our Lives (1946)
Big Business (1929)
The Big Parade (1925)
The Big Sleep (1946)
The Birth of a Nation (1915)
The Black Pirate (1926)
Blacksmith Scene (1893)
Blade Runner (1982)
The Blood of Jesus (1941)
Bonnie and Clyde (1967)
Bride of Frankenstein (1935)
The Bridge on the River Kwai (1957)
Bringing Up Baby (1938)
Broken Blossoms (1919)
Cabaret (1972)
Carmen Jones (1954)
Casablanca (1942)
Castro Street (1966)
Cat People (1942)
Chan Is Missing (1982)
The Cheat (1915)
Chinatown (1974)
Chulas Fronteras (1976)
Citizen Kane (1941)
The City (1939)
City Lights (1931)
Civilization (1916)
The Conversation (1974)
The Cool World (1963)
Cops (1922)
A Corner in Wheat (1909)
The Crowd (1928)
Czechoslovakia 1968 (1968)
David Holzman's Diary (1968)
The Day the Earth Stood Still (1951)
Dead Birds (1964)
The Deer Hunter (1978)
Destry Rides Again (1939)
Detour (1946)
Do the Right Thing (1989)
The Docks of New York (1928)
Dodsworth (1936)
Dog Star Man (1964)

Don't Look Back (1967)
Double Indemnity (1944)
Dr. Strangelove or: How I Learned to Stop Worrying and Love the Bomb (1964)
Duck Amuck (1953)
Duck Soup (1933)
Easy Rider (1969)
Eaux d'Artifice (1953)
E.T. The Extra-Terrestrial (1982)
El Norte (1983)
The Emperor Jones (1933)
The Exploits of Elaine (1914)
Fantasia (1940)
Fatty's Tintype Tangle (1915)
Flash Gordon Serial (1936)
Footlight Parade (1933)
Force of Evil (1948)
The Forgotten Frontier (1931)
42nd Street (1933)
The Four Horsemen of the Apocalypse (1921)
Frank Film (1973)
Frankenstein (1931)
Freaks (1932)
The Freshman (1925)
From the Manger to the Cross (1912)
Fury (1936)
The General (1927)
Gerald McBoing Boing (1951)
Gertie the Dinosaur (1914)
Gigi (1958)
The Godfather (1972)
The Godfather, Part II (1974)
The Gold Rush (1925)
Gone with the Wind (1939)
The Graduate (1967)
The Grapes of Wrath (1940)
Grass (1925)
The Great Dictator (1940)
The Great Train Robbery (1903)
Greed (1924)
Gun Crazy (1949)
Gunga Din (1939)
Harlan County, U.S.A. (1976)
Harold and Maude (1971)
The Heiress (1949)
Hell's Hinges (1916)
High Noon (1952)
High School (1968)
Hindenburg disaster newsreel footage (1937)
His Girl Friday (1940)
The Hitch-Hiker (1953)
Hospital (1970)
The Hospital (1971)
How Green Was My Valley (1941)
How the West Was Won (1962)
The Hustler (1961)

I Am a Fugitive from a Chain Gang (1932)
The Immigrant (1917)
In the Land of the Head Hunters (1914)
Intolerance (1916)
Invasion of the Body Snatchers (1956)
It Happened One Night (1934)
The Italian (1915)
It's a Wonderful Life (1946)
Jammin' the Blues (1944)
Jazz on a Summer's Day (1959)
The Jazz Singer (1927)
Killer of Sheep (1977)
King: A Filmed Record (1970)
King Kong (1933)
The Kiss (1896)
Kiss Me Deadly (1955)
Knute Rockne, All American (1940)
The Lady Eve (1941)
Lambchops (1929)
Lassie Come Home (1943)
The Last of the Mohicans (1920)
The Last Picture Show (1972)
Laura (1944)
Lawrence of Arabia (1962)
The Learning Tree (1969)
Letter from an Unknown Woman (1948)
The Life and Death of a Hollywood Extra (1927)
Life and Times of Rosie the Riveter (1980)
The Little Fugitive (1953)
Little Miss Marker (1934)
The Lost World (1925)
Louisiana Story (1948)
Love Me Tonight (1932)
Magical Maestro (1952)
The Magnificent Ambersons (1942)
The Maltese Falcon (1941)
The Manchurian Candidate (1962)
Manhatta (1921)
March of Time: Inside Nazi Germany—1938 (1938)
Marty (1955)
M*A*S*H (1970)
Master Hands (1936)
Mean Streets (1973)
Meet Me in St. Louis (1944)
Meshes of the Afternoon (1943)
Midnight Cowboy (1969)
Mildred Pierce (1945)
Modern Times (1936)
Modesta (1956)
Morocco (1930)
Motion Painting No. 1 (1947)
A Movie (1958)
Mr. Smith Goes to Washington (1939)

The Music Box (1932)
My Darling Clementine (1946)
My Man Godfrey (1936)
The Naked Spur (1953)
Nanook of the North (1922)
Nashville (1975)
The Night of the Hunter (1955)
A Night at the Opera (1935)
Night of the Living Dead (1968)
Ninotchka (1939)
North by Northwest (1959)
Nothing But a Man (1964)
On the Waterfront (1954)
One Flew Over the Cuckoo's Nest (1975)
Out of the Past (1947)
The Outlaw Josey Wales (1976)
The Ox-Bow Incident (1943)
Pass the Gravy (1928)
Paths of Glory (1957)
Phantom of the Opera (1925)
The Philadelphia Story (1940)
Pinocchio (1940)
A Place in the Sun (1951)
The Plow that Broke the Plains (1936)
Point of Order (1964)
The Poor Little Rich Girl (1917)
Powers of Ten (1978)
Primary (1960)
The Prisoner of Zenda (1937)
The Producers (1968)
Psycho (1960)
The Public Enemy (1931)
Pull My Daisy (1959)
Raging Bull (1980)
Raiders of the Lost Ark (1981)
Rear Window (1954)
Rebel Without a Cause (1955)
Red River (1948)
Republic Steel strike riots newsreel (1937)
Return of the Secaucus 7 (1980)
Ride the High Country (1962)
Rip Van Winkle (1896)
The River (1937)
Road to Morocco (1942)
Roman Holiday (1953)
Safety Last (1923)
Salesman (1969)
Salt of the Earth (1954)
Scarface (1932)
The Searchers (1956)
Seventh Heaven (1927)
Shadow of a Doubt (1943)
Shadows (1959)
Shane (1953)

She Done Him Wrong (1933)
Sherlock, Jr. (1924)
Shock Corridor (1963)
The Shop Around the Corner (1940)
Show Boat (1936)
Singin' in the Rain (1952)
Sky High (1922)
Snow White (1933)
Snow White and the Seven Dwarfs (1937)
Some Like It Hot (1959)
Stagecoach (1939)
Star Wars (1977)
Steamboat Willie (1928)
A Streetcar Named Desire (1951)
Sullivan's Travels (1941)
Sunrise (1927)
Sunset Boulevard (1950)
Sweet Smell of Success (1957)
Tabu (1931)
Tacoma Narrows Bridge Collapse (1940)
Taxi Driver (1976)
Tevya (1939)
The Ten Commandments (1956)
The Thief of Bagdad (1924)
The Thin Man (1934)
To Be or Not to Be (1942)
To Fly (1976)
To Kill a Mockingbird (1962)
Tootsie (1982)
Top Hat (1935)
Topaz (1943–45)
Touch of Evil (1958)
Trance and Dance in Bali (1959)
The Treasure of the Sierra Madre (1948)
Trouble in Paradise (1932)
Tulips Shall Grow (1942)
Twelve O'Clock High (1949)
2001: A Space Odyssey (1968)
Verbena Tragica (1939)
Vertigo (1958)
West Side Story (1961)
Westinghouse Works, 1904 (1904)
What's Opera, Doc? (1957)
Where Are My Children? (1916)
The Wild Bunch (1969)
The Wind (1928)
Wings (1927)
Within Our Gates (1920)
The Wizard of Oz (1939)
Woman of the Year (1942)
A Woman Under the Influence (1974)
Woodstock (1970)
Yankee Doodle Dandy (1942)
Zapruder film (1963)

Perpetual Calendar, 1753–2100

A perpetual calendar lets you find the day of the week for any date in any year. Since January 1 may fall on any of the seven days of the week, and may be a leap or non-leap year, 14 different calendars are possible. The number next to each year corresponds to one of the 14 calendars. Calendar 6 will be used in 1999; calendar 14 will be used in 2000.

Year	No.	Year	No.	Year	No.	Year	No.	Year	No.	Year	No.	Year	No.	Year	No.	Year	No.
1753	2	1792	8	1831	7	1870	7	1909	6	1948	12	1987	5	2026	5	2065	5
1754	3	1793	3	1832	8	1871	1	1910	7	1949	7	1988	13	2027	6	2066	6
1755	4	1794	4	1833	3	1872	9	1911	1	1950	1	1989	1	2028	14	2067	7
1756	12	1795	5	1834	4	1873	4	1912	9	1951	2	1990	2	2029	2	2068	8
1757	7	1796	13	1835	5	1874	5	1913	4	1952	10	1991	3	2030	3	2069	3
1758	1	1797	1	1836	13	1875	6	1914	5	1953	5	1992	11	2031	4	2070	4
1759	2	1798	2	1837	1	1876	14	1915	6	1954	6	1993	6	2032	12	2071	5
1760	10	1799	3	1838	2	1877	2	1916	14	1955	7	1994	7	2033	7	2072	13
1761	5	1800	4	1839	3	1878	3	1917	2	1956	8	1995	1	2034	1	2073	1
1762	6	1801	5	1840	11	1879	4	1918	3	1957	3	1996	9	2035	2	2074	2
1763	7	1802	6	1841	6	1880	12	1919	4	1958	4	1997	4	2036	10	2075	3
1764	8	1803	7	1842	7	1881	7	1920	12	1959	5	1998	5	2037	5	2076	11
1765	3	1804	8	1843	1	1882	1	1921	7	1960	13	1999	6	2038	6	2077	6
1766	4	1805	3	1844	9	1883	2	1922	1	1961	1	2000	14	2039	7	2078	7
1767	5	1806	4	1845	4	1884	10	1923	2	1962	2	2001	2	2040	8	2079	1
1768	13	1807	5	1846	5	1885	5	1924	10	1963	3	2002	3	2041	3	2080	9
1769	1	1808	13	1847	6	1886	6	1925	5	1964	11	2003	4	2042	4	2081	4
1770	2	1809	1	1848	14	1887	7	1926	6	1965	6	2004	12	2043	5	2082	5
1771	3	1810	2	1849	2	1888	8	1927	7	1966	7	2005	7	2044	13	2083	6
1772	11	1811	3	1850	3	1889	3	1928	8	1967	1	2006	1	2045	1	2084	14
1773	6	1812	11	1851	4	1890	4	1929	3	1968	9	2007	2	2046	2	2085	2
1774	7	1813	6	1852	12	1891	5	1930	4	1969	4	2008	10	2047	3	2086	3
1775	1	1814	7	1853	7	1892	13	1931	5	1970	5	2009	5	2048	11	2087	4
1776	9	1815	1	1854	1	1893	1	1932	13	1971	6	2010	6	2049	6	2088	12
1777	4	1816	9	1855	2	1894	2	1933	1	1972	14	2011	7	2050	7	2089	7
1778	5	1817	4	1856	10	1895	3	1934	2	1973	2	2012	8	2051	1	2090	1
1779	6	1818	5	1857	5	1896	11	1935	3	1974	3	2013	3	2052	9	2091	2
1780	14	1819	6	1858	6	1897	6	1936	11	1975	4	2014	4	2053	4	2092	10
1781	2	1820	14	1859	7	1898	7	1937	6	1976	12	2015	5	2054	5	2093	5
1782	3	1821	2	1860	8	1899	1	1938	7	1977	7	2016	13	2055	6	2094	6
1783	4	1822	3	1861	3	1900	2	1939	1	1978	1	2017	1	2056	14	2095	7
1784	12	1823	4	1862	4	1901	3	1940	9	1979	2	2018	2	2057	2	2096	8
1785	7	1824	12	1863	5	1902	4	1941	4	1980	10	2019	3	2058	3	2097	3
1786	1	1825	7	1864	13	1903	5	1942	5	1981	5	2020	11	2059	4	2098	4
1787	2	1826	1	1865	1	1904	13	1943	6	1982	6	2021	6	2060	12	2099	5
1788	10	1827	2	1866	2	1905	1	1944	14	1983	7	2022	7	2061	7	2100	6
1789	5	1828	10	1867	3	1906	2	1945	2	1984	8	2023	1	2062	1		
1790	6	1829	5	1868	11	1907	3	1946	3	1985	3	2024	9	2063	2		
1791	7	1830	6	1869	6	1908	11	1947	4	1986	4	2025	4	2064	10		

Calendar 1

```
JAN                      APR                      JULY                     OCT
S  M  T  W  T  F  S       S  M  T  W  T  F  S       S  M  T  W  T  F  S       S  M  T  W  T  F  S
   1  2  3  4  5  6  7                      1                        1        1  2  3  4  5  6  7
   8  9 10 11 12 13 14    2  3  4  5  6  7  8    2  3  4  5  6  7  8    8  9 10 11 12 13 14
  15 16 17 18 19 20 21    9 10 11 12 13 14 15    9 10 11 12 13 14 15   15 16 17 18 19 20 21
  22 23 24 25 26 27 28   16 17 18 19 20 21 22   16 17 18 19 20 21 22   22 23 24 25 26 27 28
  29 30 31               23 24 25 26 27 28 29   23 24 25 26 27 28 29   29 30 31
                         30                     30 31

FEB                      MAY                      AUG                      NOV
S  M  T  W  T  F  S       S  M  T  W  T  F  S       S  M  T  W  T  F  S       S  M  T  W  T  F  S
            1  2  3  4             1  2  3  4  5  6          1  2  3  4  5                   1  2  3  4
 5  6  7  8  9 10 11    7  8  9 10 11 12 13    6  7  8  9 10 11 12    5  6  7  8  9 10 11
12 13 14 15 16 17 18   14 15 16 17 18 19 20   13 14 15 16 17 18 19   12 13 14 15 16 17 18
19 20 21 22 23 24 25   21 22 23 24 25 26 27   20 21 22 23 24 25 26   19 20 21 22 23 24 25
26 27 28               28 29 30 31            27 28 29 30 31         26 27 28 29 30

MAR                      JUNE                     SEPT                     DEC
S  M  T  W  T  F  S       S  M  T  W  T  F  S       S  M  T  W  T  F  S       S  M  T  W  T  F  S
            1  2  3  4                1  2  3                   1  2                      1  2
 5  6  7  8  9 10 11    4  5  6  7  8  9 10    3  4  5  6  7  8  9    3  4  5  6  7  8  9
12 13 14 15 16 17 18   11 12 13 14 15 16 17   10 11 12 13 14 15 16   10 11 12 13 14 15 16
19 20 21 22 23 24 25   18 19 20 21 22 23 24   17 18 19 20 21 22 23   17 18 19 20 21 22 23
26 27 28 29 30 31      25 26 27 28 29 30      24 25 26 27 28 29 30   24 25 26 27 28 29 30
                                                                     31
```

Calendar 2 (2001)

```
JAN                      APR                      JULY                     OCT
S  M  T  W  T  F  S       S  M  T  W  T  F  S       S  M  T  W  T  F  S       S  M  T  W  T  F  S
      1  2  3  4  5  6     1  2  3  4  5  6  7     1  2  3  4  5  6  7           1  2  3  4  5  6
 7  8  9 10 11 12 13    8  9 10 11 12 13 14    8  9 10 11 12 13 14    7  8  9 10 11 12 13
14 15 16 17 18 19 20   15 16 17 18 19 20 21   15 16 17 18 19 20 21   14 15 16 17 18 19 20
21 22 23 24 25 26 27   22 23 24 25 26 27 28   22 23 24 25 26 27 28   21 22 23 24 25 26 27
28 29 30 31            29 30                  29 30 31               28 29 30 31

FEB                      MAY                      AUG                      NOV
S  M  T  W  T  F  S       S  M  T  W  T  F  S       S  M  T  W  T  F  S       S  M  T  W  T  F  S
            1  2  3                1  2  3  4  5             1  2  3  4                1  2  3
 4  5  6  7  8  9 10    6  7  8  9 10 11 12    5  6  7  8  9 10 11    4  5  6  7  8  9 10
11 12 13 14 15 16 17   13 14 15 16 17 18 19   12 13 14 15 16 17 18   11 12 13 14 15 16 17
18 19 20 21 22 23 24   20 21 22 23 24 25 26   19 20 21 22 23 24 25   18 19 20 21 22 23 24
25 26 27 28            27 28 29 30 31         26 27 28 29 30 31      25 26 27 28 29 30

MAR                      JUNE                     SEPT                     DEC
S  M  T  W  T  F  S       S  M  T  W  T  F  S       S  M  T  W  T  F  S       S  M  T  W  T  F  S
            1  2  3                   1  2                         1                         1
 4  5  6  7  8  9 10    3  4  5  6  7  8  9    2  3  4  5  6  7  8    2  3  4  5  6  7  8
11 12 13 14 15 16 17   10 11 12 13 14 15 16    9 10 11 12 13 14 15    9 10 11 12 13 14 15
18 19 20 21 22 23 24   17 18 19 20 21 22 23   16 17 18 19 20 21 22   16 17 18 19 20 21 22
25 26 27 28 29 30 31   24 25 26 27 28 29 30   23 24 25 26 27 28 29   23 24 25 26 27 28 29
                                              30                     30 31
```

Calendar 3 — 2002

JAN

S	M	T	W	T	F	S
		1	2	3	4	5
6	7	8	9	10	11	12
13	14	15	16	17	18	19
20	21	22	23	24	25	26
27	28	29	30	31		

FEB

S	M	T	W	T	F	S
					1	2
3	4	5	6	7	8	9
10	11	12	13	14	15	16
17	18	19	20	21	22	23
24	25	26	27	28		

MAR

S	M	T	W	T	F	S
					1	2
3	4	5	6	7	8	9
10	11	12	13	14	15	16
17	18	19	20	21	22	23
24	25	26	27	28	29	30
31						

APR

S	M	T	W	T	F	S
	1	2	3	4	5	6
7	8	9	10	11	12	13
14	15	16	17	18	19	20
21	22	23	24	25	26	27
28	29	30				

MAY

S	M	T	W	T	F	S
			1	2	3	4
5	6	7	8	9	10	11
12	13	14	15	16	17	18
19	20	21	22	23	24	25
26	27	28	29	30	31	

JUNE

S	M	T	W	T	F	S
						1
2	3	4	5	6	7	8
9	10	11	12	13	14	15
16	17	18	19	20	21	22
23	24	25	26	27	28	29
30						

JULY

S	M	T	W	T	F	S
	1	2	3	4	5	6
7	8	9	10	11	12	13
14	15	16	17	18	19	20
21	22	23	24	25	26	27
28	29	30	31			

AUG

S	M	T	W	T	F	S
				1	2	3
4	5	6	7	8	9	10
11	12	13	14	15	16	17
18	19	20	21	22	23	24
25	26	27	28	29	30	31

SEPT

S	M	T	W	T	F	S
1	2	3	4	5	6	7
8	9	10	11	12	13	14
15	16	17	18	19	20	21
22	23	24	25	26	27	28
29	30					

OCT

S	M	T	W	T	F	S
		1	2	3	4	5
6	7	8	9	10	11	12
13	14	15	16	17	18	19
20	21	22	23	24	25	26
27	28	29	30	31		

NOV

S	M	T	W	T	F	S
					1	2
3	4	5	6	7	8	9
10	11	12	13	14	15	16
17	18	19	20	21	22	23
24	25	26	27	28	29	30

DEC

S	M	T	W	T	F	S
1	2	3	4	5	6	7
8	9	10	11	12	13	14
15	16	17	18	19	20	21
22	23	24	25	26	27	28
29	30	31				

Calendar 4 — 2003

JAN

S	M	T	W	T	F	S
			1	2	3	4
5	6	7	8	9	10	11
12	13	14	15	16	17	18
19	20	21	22	23	24	25
26	27	28	29	30	31	

FEB

S	M	T	W	T	F	S
						1
2	3	4	5	6	7	8
9	10	11	12	13	14	15
16	17	18	19	20	21	22
23	24	25	26	27	28	

MAR

S	M	T	W	T	F	S
						1
2	3	4	5	6	7	8
9	10	11	12	13	14	15
16	17	18	19	20	21	22
23	24	25	26	27	28	29
30	31					

APR

S	M	T	W	T	F	S
		1	2	3	4	5
6	7	8	9	10	11	12
13	14	15	16	17	18	19
20	21	22	23	24	25	26
27	28	29	30			

MAY

S	M	T	W	T	F	S
				1	2	3
4	5	6	7	8	9	10
11	12	13	14	15	16	17
18	19	20	21	22	23	24
25	26	27	28	29	30	31

JUNE

S	M	T	W	T	F	S
1	2	3	4	5	6	7
8	9	10	11	12	13	14
15	16	17	18	19	20	21
22	23	24	25	26	27	28
29	30					

JULY

S	M	T	W	T	F	S
		1	2	3	4	5
6	7	8	9	10	11	12
13	14	15	16	17	18	19
20	21	22	23	24	25	26
27	28	29	30	31		

AUG

S	M	T	W	T	F	S
					1	2
3	4	5	6	7	8	9
10	11	12	13	14	15	16
17	18	19	20	21	22	23
24	25	26	27	28	29	30
31						

SEPT

S	M	T	W	T	F	S
	1	2	3	4	5	6
7	8	9	10	11	12	13
14	15	16	17	18	19	20
21	22	23	24	25	26	27
28	29	30				

OCT

S	M	T	W	T	F	S
			1	2	3	4
5	6	7	8	9	10	11
12	13	14	15	16	17	18
19	20	21	22	23	24	25
26	27	28	29	30	31	

NOV

S	M	T	W	T	F	S
						1
2	3	4	5	6	7	8
9	10	11	12	13	14	15
16	17	18	19	20	21	22
23	24	25	26	27	28	29
30						

DEC

S	M	T	W	T	F	S
	1	2	3	4	5	6
7	8	9	10	11	12	13
14	15	16	17	18	19	20
21	22	23	24	25	26	27
28	29	30	31			

Calendar 5

JAN

S	M	T	W	T	F	S
				1	2	3
4	5	6	7	8	9	10
11	12	13	14	15	16	17
18	19	20	21	22	23	24
25	26	27	28	29	30	31

FEB

S	M	T	W	T	F	S
1	2	3	4	5	6	7
8	9	10	11	12	13	14
15	16	17	18	19	20	21
22	23	24	25	26	27	28

MAR

S	M	T	W	T	F	S
1	2	3	4	5	6	7
8	9	10	11	12	13	14
15	16	17	18	19	20	21
22	23	24	25	26	27	28
29	30	31				

APR

S	M	T	W	T	F	S
			1	2	3	4
5	6	7	8	9	10	11
12	13	14	15	16	17	18
19	20	21	22	23	24	25
26	27	28	29	30		

MAY

S	M	T	W	T	F	S
					1	2
3	4	5	6	7	8	9
10	11	12	13	14	15	16
17	18	19	20	21	22	23
24	25	26	27	28	29	30
31						

JUNE

S	M	T	W	T	F	S
	1	2	3	4	5	6
7	8	9	10	11	12	13
14	15	16	17	18	19	20
21	22	23	24	25	26	27
28	29	30				

JULY

S	M	T	W	T	F	S
			1	2	3	4
5	6	7	8	9	10	11
12	13	14	15	16	17	18
19	20	21	22	23	24	25
26	27	28	29	30	31	

AUG

S	M	T	W	T	F	S
						1
2	3	4	5	6	7	8
9	10	11	12	13	14	15
16	17	18	19	20	21	22
23	24	25	26	27	28	29
30	31					

SEPT

S	M	T	W	T	F	S
		1	2	3	4	5
6	7	8	9	10	11	12
13	14	15	16	17	18	19
20	21	22	23	24	25	26
27	28	29	30			

OCT

S	M	T	W	T	F	S
				1	2	3
4	5	6	7	8	9	10
11	12	13	14	15	16	17
18	19	20	21	22	23	24
25	26	27	28	29	30	31

NOV

S	M	T	W	T	F	S
1	2	3	4	5	6	7
8	9	10	11	12	13	14
15	16	17	18	19	20	21
22	23	24	25	26	27	28
29	30					

DEC

S	M	T	W	T	F	S
		1	2	3	4	5
6	7	8	9	10	11	12
13	14	15	16	17	18	19
20	21	22	23	24	25	26
27	28	29	30	31		

Calendar 6

JAN

S	M	T	W	T	F	S
					1	2
3	4	5	6	7	8	9
10	11	12	13	14	15	16
17	18	19	20	21	22	23
24	25	26	27	28	29	30
31						

FEB

S	M	T	W	T	F	S
	1	2	3	4	5	6
7	8	9	10	11	12	13
14	15	16	17	18	19	20
21	22	23	24	25	26	27
28						

MAR

S	M	T	W	T	F	S
	1	2	3	4	5	6
7	8	9	10	11	12	13
14	15	16	17	18	19	20
21	22	23	24	25	26	27
28	29	30	31			

APR

S	M	T	W	T	F	S
				1	2	3
4	5	6	7	8	9	10
11	12	13	14	15	16	17
18	19	20	21	22	23	24
25	26	27	28	29	30	

MAY

S	M	T	W	T	F	S
						1
2	3	4	5	6	7	8
9	10	11	12	13	14	15
16	17	18	19	20	21	22
23	24	25	26	27	28	29
30	31					

JUNE

S	M	T	W	T	F	S
		1	2	3	4	5
6	7	8	9	10	11	12
13	14	15	16	17	18	19
20	21	22	23	24	25	26
27	28	29	30			

JULY

S	M	T	W	T	F	S
				1	2	3
4	5	6	7	8	9	10
11	12	13	14	15	16	17
18	19	20	21	22	23	24
25	26	27	28	29	30	31

AUG

S	M	T	W	T	F	S
1	2	3	4	5	6	7
8	9	10	11	12	13	14
15	16	17	18	19	20	21
22	23	24	25	26	27	28
29	30	31				

SEPT

S	M	T	W	T	F	S
			1	2	3	4
5	6	7	8	9	10	11
12	13	14	15	16	17	18
19	20	21	22	23	24	25
26	27	28	29	30		

OCT

S	M	T	W	T	F	S
					1	2
3	4	5	6	7	8	9
10	11	12	13	14	15	16
17	18	19	20	21	22	23
24	25	26	27	28	29	30
31						

NOV

S	M	T	W	T	F	S
	1	2	3	4	5	6
7	8	9	10	11	12	13
14	15	16	17	18	19	20
21	22	23	24	25	26	27
28	29	30				

DEC

S	M	T	W	T	F	S
			1	2	3	4
5	6	7	8	9	10	11
12	13	14	15	16	17	18
19	20	21	22	23	24	25
26	27	28	29	30	31	

7

JAN

S	M	T	W	T	F	S
						1
2	3	4	5	6	7	8
9	10	11	12	13	14	15
16	17	18	19	20	21	22
23	24	25	26	27	28	29
30	31					

FEB

S	M	T	W	T	F	S
		1	2	3	4	5
6	7	8	9	10	11	12
13	14	15	16	17	18	19
20	21	22	23	24	25	26
27	28					

MAR

S	M	T	W	T	F	S
		1	2	3	4	5
6	7	8	9	10	11	12
13	14	15	16	17	18	19
20	21	22	23	24	25	26
27	28	29	30	31		

APR

S	M	T	W	T	F	S
					1	2
3	4	5	6	7	8	9
10	11	12	13	14	15	16
17	18	19	20	21	22	23
24	25	26	27	28	29	30

MAY

S	M	T	W	T	F	S
1	2	3	4	5	6	7
8	9	10	11	12	13	14
15	16	17	18	19	20	21
22	23	24	25	26	27	28
29	30	31				

JUNE

S	M	T	W	T	F	S
			1	2	3	4
5	6	7	8	9	10	11
12	13	14	15	16	17	18
19	20	21	22	23	24	25
26	27	28	29	30		

JULY

S	M	T	W	T	F	S
					1	2
3	4	5	6	7	8	9
10	11	12	13	14	15	16
17	18	19	20	21	22	23
24	25	26	27	28	29	30
31						

AUG

S	M	T	W	T	F	S
	1	2	3	4	5	6
7	8	9	10	11	12	13
14	15	16	17	18	19	20
21	22	23	24	25	26	27
28	29	30	31			

SEPT

S	M	T	W	T	F	S
				1	2	3
4	5	6	7	8	9	10
11	12	13	14	15	16	17
18	19	20	21	22	23	24
25	26	27	28	29	30	

OCT

S	M	T	W	T	F	S
						1
2	3	4	5	6	7	8
9	10	11	12	13	14	15
16	17	18	19	20	21	22
23	24	25	26	27	28	29
30	31					

NOV

S	M	T	W	T	F	S
		1	2	3	4	5
6	7	8	9	10	11	12
13	14	15	16	17	18	19
20	21	22	23	24	25	26
27	28	29	30			

DEC

S	M	T	W	T	F	S
				1	2	3
4	5	6	7	8	9	10
11	12	13	14	15	16	17
18	19	20	21	22	23	24
25	26	27	28	29	30	31

8

JAN

S	M	T	W	T	F	S
1	2	3	4	5	6	7
8	9	10	11	12	13	14
15	16	17	18	19	20	21
22	23	24	25	26	27	28
29	30	31				

FEB

S	M	T	W	T	F	S
			1	2	3	4
5	6	7	8	9	10	11
12	13	14	15	16	17	18
19	20	21	22	23	24	25
26	27	28	29			

MAR

S	M	T	W	T	F	S
			1	2	3	
4	5	6	7	8	9	10
11	12	13	14	15	16	17
18	19	20	21	22	23	24
25	26	27	28	29	30	31

APR

S	M	T	W	T	F	S
1	2	3	4	5	6	7
8	9	10	11	12	13	14
15	16	17	18	19	20	21
22	23	24	25	26	27	28
29	30					

MAY

S	M	T	W	T	F	S
		1	2	3	4	5
6	7	8	9	10	11	12
13	14	15	16	17	18	19
20	21	22	23	24	25	26
27	28	29	30	31		

JUNE

S	M	T	W	T	F	S
					1	2
3	4	5	6	7	8	9
10	11	12	13	14	15	16
17	18	19	20	21	22	23
24	25	26	27	28	29	30

JULY

S	M	T	W	T	F	S
1	2	3	4	5	6	7
8	9	10	11	12	13	14
15	16	17	18	19	20	21
22	23	24	25	26	27	28
29	30	31				

AUG

S	M	T	W	T	F	S
			1	2	3	4
5	6	7	8	9	10	11
12	13	14	15	16	17	18
19	20	21	22	23	24	25
26	27	28	29	30	31	

SEPT

S	M	T	W	T	F	S
						1
2	3	4	5	6	7	8
9	10	11	12	13	14	15
16	17	18	19	20	21	22
23	24	25	26	27	28	29
30						

OCT

S	M	T	W	T	F	S
	1	2	3	4	5	6
7	8	9	10	11	12	13
14	15	16	17	18	19	20
21	22	23	24	25	26	27
28	29	30	31			

NOV

S	M	T	W	T	F	S
				1	2	3
4	5	6	7	8	9	10
11	12	13	14	15	16	17
18	19	20	21	22	23	24
25	26	27	28	29	30	

DEC

S	M	T	W	T	F	S
						1
2	3	4	5	6	7	8
9	10	11	12	13	14	15
16	17	18	19	20	21	22
23	24	25	26	27	28	29
30	31					

9

JAN

S	M	T	W	T	F	S
	1	2	3	4	5	6
7	8	9	10	11	12	13
14	15	16	17	18	19	20
21	22	23	24	25	26	27
28	29	30	31			

FEB

S	M	T	W	T	F	S
				1	2	3
4	5	6	7	8	9	10
11	12	13	14	15	16	17
18	19	20	21	22	23	24
25	26	27	28	29		

MAR

S	M	T	W	T	F	S
					1	2
3	4	5	6	7	8	9
10	11	12	13	14	15	16
17	18	19	20	21	22	23
24	25	26	27	28	29	30
31						

APR

S	M	T	W	T	F	S
	1	2	3	4	5	6
7	8	9	10	11	12	13
14	15	16	17	18	19	20
21	22	23	24	25	26	27
28	29	30				

MAY

S	M	T	W	T	F	S
			1	2	3	4
5	6	7	8	9	10	11
12	13	14	15	16	17	18
19	20	21	22	23	24	25
26	27	28	29	30	31	

JUNE

S	M	T	W	T	F	S
						1
2	3	4	5	6	7	8
9	10	11	12	13	14	15
16	17	18	19	20	21	22
23	24	25	26	27	28	29
30						

JULY

S	M	T	W	T	F	S
	1	2	3	4	5	6
7	8	9	10	11	12	13
14	15	16	17	18	19	20
21	22	23	24	25	26	27
28	29	30	31			

AUG

S	M	T	W	T	F	S
				1	2	3
4	5	6	7	8	9	10
11	12	13	14	15	16	17
18	19	20	21	22	23	24
25	26	27	28	29	30	31

SEPT

S	M	T	W	T	F	S
1	2	3	4	5	6	7
8	9	10	11	12	13	14
15	16	17	18	19	20	21
22	23	24	25	26	27	28
29	30					

OCT

S	M	T	W	T	F	S
		1	2	3	4	5
6	7	8	9	10	11	12
13	14	15	16	17	18	19
20	21	22	23	24	25	26
27	28	29	30	31		

NOV

S	M	T	W	T	F	S
					1	2
3	4	5	6	7	8	9
10	11	12	13	14	15	16
17	18	19	20	21	22	23
24	25	26	27	28	29	30

DEC

S	M	T	W	T	F	S
1	2	3	4	5	6	7
8	9	10	11	12	13	14
15	16	17	18	19	20	21
22	23	24	25	26	27	28
29	30	31				

10

JAN

S	M	T	W	T	F	S
		1	2	3	4	5
6	7	8	9	10	11	12
13	14	15	16	17	18	19
20	21	22	23	24	25	26
27	28	29	30	31		

FEB

S	M	T	W	T	F	S
					1	2
3	4	5	6	7	8	9
10	11	12	13	14	15	16
17	18	19	20	21	22	23
24	25	26	27	28	29	

MAR

S	M	T	W	T	F	S
						1
2	3	4	5	6	7	8
9	10	11	12	13	14	15
16	17	18	19	20	21	22
23	24	25	26	27	28	29
30	31					

APR

S	M	T	W	T	F	S
		1	2	3	4	5
6	7	8	9	10	11	12
13	14	15	16	17	18	19
20	21	22	23	24	25	26
27	28	29	30			

MAY

S	M	T	W	T	F	S
				1	2	3
4	5	6	7	8	9	10
11	12	13	14	15	16	17
18	19	20	21	22	23	24
25	26	27	28	29	30	31

JUNE

S	M	T	W	T	F	S
1	2	3	4	5	6	7
8	9	10	11	12	13	14
15	16	17	18	19	20	21
22	23	24	25	26	27	28
29	30					

JULY

S	M	T	W	T	F	S
		1	2	3	4	5
6	7	8	9	10	11	12
13	14	15	16	17	18	19
20	21	22	23	24	25	26
27	28	29	30	31		

AUG

S	M	T	W	T	F	S
					1	2
3	4	5	6	7	8	9
10	11	12	13	14	15	16
17	18	19	20	21	22	23
24	25	26	27	28	29	30
31						

SEPT

S	M	T	W	T	F	S
1	2	3	4	5	6	
7	8	9	10	11	12	13
14	15	16	17	18	19	20
21	22	23	24	25	26	27
28	29	30				

OCT

S	M	T	W	T	F	S
				1	2	3	4
5	6	7	8	9	10	11
12	13	14	15	16	17	18
19	20	21	22	23	24	25
26	27	28	29	30	31	

NOV

S	M	T	W	T	F	S
						1
2	3	4	5	6	7	8
9	10	11	12	13	14	15
16	17	18	19	20	21	22
23	24	25	26	27	28	29
30						

DEC

S	M	T	W	T	F	S
1	2	3	4	5	6	
7	8	9	10	11	12	13
14	15	16	17	18	19	20
21	22	23	24	25	26	27
28	29	30	31			

11

JAN

S	M	T	W	T	F	S
			1	2	3	4
5	6	7	8	9	10	11
12	13	14	15	16	17	18
19	20	21	22	23	24	25
26	27	28	29	30	31	

FEB

S	M	T	W	T	F	S
						1
2	3	4	5	6	7	8
9	10	11	12	13	14	15
16	17	18	19	20	21	22
23	24	25	26	27	28	29

MAR

S	M	T	W	T	F	S
1	2	3	4	5	6	7
8	9	10	11	12	13	14
15	16	17	18	19	20	21
22	23	24	25	26	27	28
29	30	31				

APR

S	M	T	W	T	F	S
			1	2	3	4
5	6	7	8	9	10	11
12	13	14	15	16	17	18
19	20	21	22	23	24	25
26	27	28	29	30		

MAY

S	M	T	W	T	F	S
					1	2
3	4	5	6	7	8	9
10	11	12	13	14	15	16
17	18	19	20	21	22	23
24	25	26	27	28	29	30
31						

JUNE

S	M	T	W	T	F	S
	1	2	3	4	5	6
7	8	9	10	11	12	13
14	15	16	17	18	19	20
21	22	23	24	25	26	27
28	29	30				

JULY

S	M	T	W	T	F	S
			1	2	3	4
5	6	7	8	9	10	11
12	13	14	15	16	17	18
19	20	21	22	23	24	25
26	27	28	29	30	31	

AUG

S	M	T	W	T	F	S
						1
2	3	4	5	6	7	8
9	10	11	12	13	14	15
16	17	18	19	20	21	22
23	24	25	26	27	28	29
30	31					

SEPT

S	M	T	W	T	F	S
		1	2	3	4	5
6	7	8	9	10	11	12
13	14	15	16	17	18	19
20	21	22	23	24	25	26
27	28	29	30			

OCT

S	M	T	W	T	F	S
				1	2	3
4	5	6	7	8	9	10
11	12	13	14	15	16	17
18	19	20	21	22	23	24
25	26	27	28	29	30	31

NOV

S	M	T	W	T	F	S
1	2	3	4	5	6	7
8	9	10	11	12	13	14
15	16	17	18	19	20	21
22	23	24	25	26	27	28
29	30					

DEC

S	M	T	W	T	F	S
		1	2	3	4	5
6	7	8	9	10	11	12
13	14	15	16	17	18	19
20	21	22	23	24	25	26
27	28	29	30	31		

12

JAN

S	M	T	W	T	F	S
				1	2	3
4	5	6	7	8	9	10
11	12	13	14	15	16	17
18	19	20	21	22	23	24
25	26	27	28	29	30	31

FEB

S	M	T	W	T	F	S
1	2	3	4	5	6	7
8	9	10	11	12	13	14
15	16	17	18	19	20	21
22	23	24	25	26	27	28
29						

MAR

S	M	T	W	T	F	S
	1	2	3	4	5	6
7	8	9	10	11	12	13
14	15	16	17	18	19	20
21	22	23	24	25	26	27
28	29	30	31			

APR

S	M	T	W	T	F	S
				1	2	3
4	5	6	7	8	9	10
11	12	13	14	15	16	17
18	19	20	21	22	23	24
25	26	27	28	29	30	

MAY

S	M	T	W	T	F	S
						1
2	3	4	5	6	7	8
9	10	11	12	13	14	15
16	17	18	19	20	21	22
23	24	25	26	27	28	29
30	31					

JUNE

S	M	T	W	T	F	S
		1	2	3	4	5
6	7	8	9	10	11	12
13	14	15	16	17	18	19
20	21	22	23	24	25	26
27	28	29	30			

JULY

S	M	T	W	T	F	S
				1	2	3
4	5	6	7	8	9	10
11	12	13	14	15	16	17
18	19	20	21	22	23	24
25	26	27	28	29	30	31

AUG

S	M	T	W	T	F	S
1	2	3	4	5	6	7
8	9	10	11	12	13	14
15	16	17	18	19	20	21
22	23	24	25	26	27	28
29	30	31				

SEPT

S	M	T	W	T	F	S
			1	2	3	4
5	6	7	8	9	10	11
12	13	14	15	16	17	18
19	20	21	22	23	24	25
26	27	28	29	30		

OCT

S	M	T	W	T	F	S
					1	2
3	4	5	6	7	8	9
10	11	12	13	14	15	16
17	18	19	20	21	22	23
24	25	26	27	28	29	30
31						

NOV

S	M	T	W	T	F	S
	1	2	3	4	5	6
7	8	9	10	11	12	13
14	15	16	17	18	19	20
21	22	23	24	25	26	27
28	29	30				

DEC

S	M	T	W	T	F	S
			1	2	3	4
5	6	7	8	9	10	11
12	13	14	15	16	17	18
19	20	21	22	23	24	25
26	27	28	29	30	31	

13

JAN

S	M	T	W	T	F	S
					1	2
3	4	5	6	7	8	9
10	11	12	13	14	15	16
17	18	19	20	21	22	23
24	25	26	27	28	29	30
31						

FEB

S	M	T	W	T	F	S
	1	2	3	4	5	6
7	8	9	10	11	12	13
14	15	16	17	18	19	20
21	22	23	24	25	26	27
28	29					

MAR

S	M	T	W	T	F	S
		1	2	3	4	5
6	7	8	9	10	11	12
13	14	15	16	17	18	19
20	21	22	23	24	25	26
27	28	29	30	31		

APR

S	M	T	W	T	F	S
					1	2
3	4	5	6	7	8	9
10	11	12	13	14	15	16
17	18	19	20	21	22	23
24	25	26	27	28	29	30

MAY

S	M	T	W	T	F	S
1	2	3	4	5	6	7
8	9	10	11	12	13	14
15	16	17	18	19	20	21
22	23	24	25	26	27	28
29	30	31				

JUNE

S	M	T	W	T	F	S
			1	2	3	4
5	6	7	8	9	10	11
12	13	14	15	16	17	18
19	20	21	22	23	24	25
26	27	28	29	30		

JULY

S	M	T	W	T	F	S
					1	2
3	4	5	6	7	8	9
10	11	12	13	14	15	16
17	18	19	20	21	22	23
24	25	26	27	28	29	30
31						

AUG

S	M	T	W	T	F	S
	1	2	3	4	5	6
7	8	9	10	11	12	13
14	15	16	17	18	19	20
21	22	23	24	25	26	27
28	29	30	31			

SEPT

S	M	T	W	T	F	S
				1	2	3
4	5	6	7	8	9	10
11	12	13	14	15	16	17
18	19	20	21	22	23	24
25	26	27	28	29	30	

OCT

S	M	T	W	T	F	S
						1
2	3	4	5	6	7	8
9	10	11	12	13	14	15
16	17	18	19	20	21	22
23	24	25	26	27	28	29
30	31					

NOV

S	M	T	W	T	F	S
		1	2	3	4	5
6	7	8	9	10	11	12
13	14	15	16	17	18	19
20	21	22	23	24	25	26
27	28	29	30			

DEC

S	M	T	W	T	F	S
				1	2	3
4	5	6	7	8	9	10
11	12	13	14	15	16	17
18	19	20	21	22	23	24
25	26	27	28	29	30	31

14

2000

JAN

S	M	T	W	T	F	S
						1
2	3	4	5	6	7	8
9	10	11	12	13	14	15
16	17	18	19	20	21	22
23	24	25	26	27	28	29
30	31					

FEB

S	M	T	W	T	F	S
		1	2	3	4	5
6	7	8	9	10	11	12
13	14	15	16	17	18	19
20	21	22	23	24	25	26
27	28	29				

MAR

S	M	T	W	T	F	S
			1	2	3	4
5	6	7	8	9	10	11
12	13	14	15	16	17	18
19	20	21	22	23	24	25
26	27	28	29	30	31	

APR

S	M	T	W	T	F	S
						1
2	3	4	5	6	7	8
9	10	11	12	13	14	15
16	17	18	19	20	21	22
23	24	25	26	27	28	29
30						

MAY

S	M	T	W	T	F	S
	1	2	3	4	5	6
7	8	9	10	11	12	13
14	15	16	17	18	19	20
21	22	23	24	25	26	27
28	29	30	31			

JUNE

S	M	T	W	T	F	S
				1	2	3
4	5	6	7	8	9	10
11	12	13	14	15	16	17
18	19	20	21	22	23	24
25	26	27	28	29	30	

JULY

S	M	T	W	T	F	S
						1
2	3	4	5	6	7	8
9	10	11	12	13	14	15
16	17	18	19	20	21	22
23	24	25	26	27	28	29
30	31					

AUG

S	M	T	W	T	F	S
		1	2	3	4	5
6	7	8	9	10	11	12
13	14	15	16	17	18	19
20	21	22	23	24	25	26
27	28	29	30	31		

SEPT

S	M	T	W	T	F	S
					1	2
3	4	5	6	7	8	9
10	11	12	13	14	15	16
17	18	19	20	21	22	23
24	25	26	27	28	29	30

OCT

S	M	T	W	T	F	S
1	2	3	4	5	6	7
8	9	10	11	12	13	14
15	16	17	18	19	20	21
22	23	24	25	26	27	28
29	30	31				

NOV

S	M	T	W	T	F	S
			1	2	3	4
5	6	7	8	9	10	11
12	13	14	15	16	17	18
19	20	21	22	23	24	25
26	27	28	29	30		

DEC

S	M	T	W	T	F	S
					1	2
3	4	5	6	7	8	9
10	11	12	13	14	15	16
17	18	19	20	21	22	23
24	25	26	27	28	29	30
31						

STATE GOVERNORS/US SENATORS/US SUPREME COURT

GOVERNORS
Name (Party, State)

Don Siegelman (D, AL)
Tony Knowles (D, AK)
Jane Dee Hull (R, AZ)
Mike Huckabee (R, AR)
Gray Davis (D, CA)
Bill Owens (R, CO)
John Rowland (R, CT)
Tom Carper (D, DE)*
Jeb Bush (R, FL)
Roy Barnes (D, GA)
Ben Cayetano (D, HI)
Dirk Kempthorne (R, ID)
George Ryan (R, IL)
Frank O'Bannon (D, IN)*
Tom Vilsack (D, IA)
Bill Graves (R, KS)
Paul E. Patton (D, KY)
Mike Foster (R, LA)
Angus King, Jr (I, ME)
Parris Glendening (D, MD)
Paul Cellucci (R, MA)
John Engler (R, MI)
Jesse Ventura (I, MN)
Ronnie Musgrove (D, MS)
Mel Carnahan (D, MO)*
Marc Racicot (R, MT)*
Mike Johanns (R, NE)
Kenny Guinn (R, NV)
Jeanne Shaheen (D, NH)*
Christine T. Whitman (R, NJ)
Gary Johnson (R, NM)
George Pataki (R, NY)
James B. Hunt, Jr (D, NC)*
Edward T. Schafer (R, ND)*
Bob Taft (R, OH)
Frank Keating (R, OK)
John Kitzhaber (D, OR)
Thomas J. Ridge (R, PA)
Lincoln Almond (R, RI)
Jim Hodges (D, SC)
William Janklow (R, SD)
Don Sundquist (R, TN)
George W. Bush (R, TX)
Mike Leavitt (R, UT)*
Howard Dean (D, VT)*
James Gilmore (R, VA)
Gary Locke (D, WA)*
Cecil H. Underwood (R, WV)*
Tommy G. Thompson (R, WI)
Jim Geringer (R, WY)

*Denotes governorship or senate seat
up for reelection at press time.

SENATORS
Name (Party, State)

Jeff Sessions (R, AL)
Richard C. Shelby (R, AL)
Ted Stevens (R, AK)
Frank H. Murkowski (R, AK)
Jon Kyl (R, AZ)*
John McCain (R, AZ)
Blanche Lambert Lincoln (D, AR)
Tim Hutchinson (R, AR)
Dianne Feinstein (D, CA)*
Barbara Boxer (D, CA)
Wayne Allard (R, CO)
Ben Nighthorse Campbell (R, CO)
Christopher J. Dodd (D, CT)
Joseph I. Lieberman (D, CT)*
William V. Roth, Jr (R, DE)*
Joseph R. Biden, Jr (D, DE)
Robert Graham (D, FL)
Connie Mack III (R, FL)*
Max Cleland (D, GA)
Zell Miller (D, GA)*
Daniel K. Inouye (D, HI)
Daniel K. Akaka (D, HI)*
Larry E. Craig (R, ID)
Michael Crapo (R, ID)
Richard J. Durbin (D, IL)
Peter Fitzgerald (R, IL)
Richard G. Lugar (R, IN)*
Evan Bayh (D, IN)
Charles E. Grassley (R, IA)
Tom Harkin (D, IA)
Sam Brownback (R, KS)
Pat Roberts (R, KS)
Jim Bunning (R, KY)
Mitch McConnell (R, KY)
Mary L. Landrieu (D, LA)
John B. Breaux (D, LA)
Susan M. Collins (R, ME)
Olympia J. Snowe (R, ME)*
Paul S. Sarbanes (D, MD)*
Barbara A. Mikulski (D, MD)
Edward M. Kennedy (D, MA)*
John F. Kerry (D, MA)
Spencer Abraham (R, MI)*
Carl Levin (D, MI)
Rod Grams (R, MN)*
Paul D. Wellstone (D, MN)
Thad Cochran (R, MS)
Trent Lott (R, MS)*
John Ashcroft (R, MO)*
Christopher S. Bond (R, MO)
Max S. Baucus (D, MT)
Conrad Burns (R, MT)*
Chuck Hagel (R, NE)
J. Robert Kerrey (D, NE)*
Harry M. Reid (D, NV)
Richard H. Bryan (D, NV)*
Robert C. Smith (R, NH)

Judd Gregg (R, NH)
Robert G. Torricelli (D, NJ)
Frank R. Lautenberg (D, NJ)*
Pete V. Domenici (R, NM)
Jeff Bingaman (D, NM)*
Daniel Patrick Moynihan (D, NY)*
Charles E. Schumer (D, NY)
Jesse A. Helms (R, NC)
John Edwards (D, NC)
Kent Conrad (D, ND)*
Byron L. Dorgan (D, ND)
George Voinovich (R, OH)
Mike DeWine (R, OH)*
James M. Inhofe (R, OK)*
Don Nickles (R, OK)
Gordon Smith (R, OR)
Ron Wyden (D, OR)
Arlen Specter (R, PA)
Rick Santorum (R, PA)*
Jack Reed (D, RI)
Lincoln Chafee (R, RI)*
Strom Thurmond (R, SC)
Ernest F. Hollings (D, SC)
Tim Johnson (D, SD)
Thomas A. Daschle (D, SD)
William Frist (R, TN)*
Fred D. Thompson (R, TN)*
Phil Gramm (R, TX)
Kay Bailey Hutchison (R, TX)*
Orrin G. Hatch (R, UT)*
Robert F. Bennett (R, UT)
Patrick J. Leahy (D, VT)
James M. Jeffords (R, VT)*
John W. Warner (R, VA)
Charles S. Robb (D, VA)*
Slade Gorton (R, WA)*
Patty Murray (D, WA)
Robert C. Byrd (D, WV)*
John D. Rockefeller IV (D, WV)
Herbert H. Kohl (D, WI)*
Russell D. Feingold (D, WI)
Michael B. Enzi (R, WY)
Craig Thomas (R, WY)*

SUPREME COURT JUSTICES
Name (Appointed by, Year)

William H. Rehnquist, Chief Justice
(Reagan, 1986)
John P. Stevens (Ford, 1975)
Sandra Day O'Connor (Reagan, 1981)
Antonin Scalia (Reagan, 1986)
Anthony M. Kennedy (Reagan, 1988)
David H. Souter (Bush, 1990)
Clarence Thomas (Bush, 1991)
Ruth Bader Ginsburg (Clinton, 1993)
Stephen G. Breyer (Clinton, 1994)

ALPHABETICAL INDEX

Events are generally listed under key words; many broad categories have been created, including African American, Agriculture, Animals, Antiques, Arts—Fine and Performing, Arts and Crafts, Automobiles, Aviation, Balloons (Hot-air), Bicycle, Birds, Boats, Books, Children, Christmas, Civil Rights, Civil War, Computer, Constitution, Cowboys/Old West, Dance, Disabled, Earthquake, Education, Employment, Environment, Ethnic, Family, Film, Fire, Fishing, Flowers, Food and Beverages, Gardens, Health and Welfare, Home Shows and Tours, Horses, Human Relations, Humor, Hurricane, Journalism, Kites, Labor, Library/Librarians, Literature, Music, Native American, Parades, Peace, Photography, Poetry, Prayer, Radio, Railroad, Renaissance Fairs, Rodeos, Safety, Science/Technology, Senior Citizens, Space, Space Milestones, Storytelling, Television, Theater, United Nations, Weather, Winter Fest, World War I, World War II, Women, names of sports, types of music, etc. Events that can be attended are also listed under the states or countries where they are to be held. Index indicates only initial date for each event. See chronology for inclusive dates of events lasting more than one day.

A'phabet Day, Dec 25
Aames, Willie: Birth, July 15
Aaron, Hank: Birth, Feb 5
Aaron, Hank: Home Run Record: Anniv, Apr 8
Abbado, Claudio: Birth, June 26
Abbott and Costello Show TV Premiere: Anniv, Dec 5
Abbott, Berenice: Birth Anniv, July 17
Abbott, Jim: Birth, Sept 19
Abdul, Paula: Birth, June 19
Abdul-Jabbar, Kareem: Birth, Apr 16
Abet and Aid Punsters Day, Nov 8
Abolition Soc Founded, First American: Anniv, Apr 14
Abortion Counseling, Supreme Court Upholds Ban: Anniv, May 23
Abortion First Legalized: Anniv, Apr 25
Abortion: Roe v Wade Supreme Court Decision: Anniv, Jan 22
Abraham Baldwin Agri College Homecoming (Tifton, GA), Apr 6
Abraham, F. Murray: Birth, Oct 24
Abraham, Spencer: Birth, June 12
Absolutely Incredible Kid Day, Mar 15
Abused Women and Children's Awareness Day, June 10
Academy Awards, First: Anniv, May 16
Acadia Natl Park Established: Anniv, Jan 1
Accession of Queen Elizabeth II: Anniv, Feb 6
Accordion Awareness Month, Natl, June 1
Ace, Goodman: Birth Anniv, Jan 15
Achelis, Elisabeth: Birth Anniv, Jan 24
Ackland, Joss: Birth, Feb 29
Acuff, Roy: Birth Anniv, Sept 15
Adamle, Mike: Birth, Oct 4
Adams, Abigail: Birth Anniv, Nov 22
Adams, Ansel: Birth Anniv, Feb 20
Adams, Brooke: Birth, Feb 8
Adams, Bryan: Birth, Nov 5
Adams, Don: Birth, Apr 19
Adams, Douglas: Birth, Mar 11
Adams, Edie: Birth, Apr 16
Adams, Joey Lauren: Birth, Jan 6
Adams, John: Birth Anniv, Oct 30
Adams, John Quincy: Birth Anniv, July 11
Adams, John Quincy: Returns to Congress, Mar 4
Adams, Louisa Catherine Johnson: Birth Anniv, Feb 12
Adams, Mason: Birth, Feb 26
Adams, Maud: Birth, Feb 12
Adams, Richard C.: Death Anniv, Mar 9
Adams, Samuel: Birth Anniv, Sept 27
Adams, Scott: Birth, June 8
Addams Family TV Premiere: Anniv, Sept 18
Addams, Jane: Birth Anniv, Sept 6
Adding Machine, Patent Issued for First: Anniv, Oct 11
Addison, Joseph: Birth Anniv, May 1
Adjani, Isabelle: Birth, June 27
Administrative Professionals Day, Apr 25
Administrative Professionals Intl Conv (Toronto, Ontario, Canada), July 15
Administrative Professionals Week, Apr 22
Admission Day Holiday (Hawaii), Aug 17
Admit You're Happy Day, Aug 8
Admit You're Happy Month, Aug 1
Adolfo: Birth, Feb 15
Adopt-A-Shelter Cat Month, June 1
Adopt-a-Shelter Dog Month, Oct 1
Adoption Month, Natl, Nov 1

Adoption Week, Natl, Nov 18
Adult Immunization Awareness Week, Natl, Oct 14
Advent, First Sunday of, Dec 2
Adventures of Ellery Queen TV Premiere: Anniv, Oct 14
Advertising: Co-op Awareness Month, Oct 1
Advertising: Mobius Awards (Chicago, IL), Feb 8
Aebleskiver Days (Tyler, MN), June 20
Affleck, Ben: Birth, Aug 15
Afghanistan
  Independence Day, Aug 19
  Soviet Troop Withdrawal Deadline, Feb 15
AFL Founded: Anniv, Dec 8
AFL-CIO Founded: Anniv, Dec 5
Africa: Industrial Development Decade for Africa, Second, Jan 1
Africa: Industrialization Day (UN), Nov 20
African American History Month, Natl, Feb 1
African Methodist Episcopal Church Organized: Anniv, Apr 9
African Natl Congress Ban Lifted, Feb 2
African-American
  African American Arts Fest (Greensboro, NC), Jan 12
  African American History Month, Natl, Feb 1
  African American Holiday Expo (Washington, DC), Dec 15
  African Methodist Episcopal Church Organized: Anniv, Apr 9
  Africare Walker Memorial Dinner (Washington, DC), Oct 18
  Alpha Kappa Alpha Sorority Founded: Anniv, Jan 15
  Amistad Seized: Anniv, Aug 29
  Ashford, Emmett: Birth Anniv, Nov 23
  Attack on Fort Wagner: Anniv, July 19
  Black Heritage Parade (Monroe, LA), Feb 24
  Black History Month, Feb 1
  Black Love Day, Feb 13
  Black Page Appointed US House: Anniv, Apr 9
  Black Poetry Day, Oct 17
  Black Press Day: Anniv of First Black Newspaper in US, Mar 16
  Black Senate Page Appointed: Anniv, Apr 8
  Blacks Ruled Eligible to Vote: Anniv, Apr 3
  Bolin, Jane M.: Birth, Apr 11
  Brown, Jesse Leroy: Birth Anniv, Oct 13
  Bud Billiken Parade (Chicago, IL), Aug 11
  Civil Rights Act of 1964: Anniv, July 2
  Civil Rights Act of 1968: Anniv, Apr 11
  Civil Rights Bill of 1866: Anniv, Apr 9
  Civil Rights Workers Found Slain: Anniv, Aug 4
  Desegregation, US Army First: Anniv, July 26
  Dred Scott Decision: Anniv (St. Louis, MO), Mar 4
  Drew, Charles: Birth Anniv, June 3
  Emancipation Dream Day, Aug 28
  Emancipation of 500: Anniv, Aug 1
  Escape to Freedom (F. Douglass): Anniv, Sept 3
  First American Abolition Soc Founded: Anniv, Apr 14
  First Black Governor Elected: Anniv, Nov 7
  First Black Plays in NBA Game: Anniv, Oct 31
  First Black Pro Hockey Player: Anniv, Nov 15
  First Black Serves in US House Reps: Anniv, Dec 12
  First Black US Cabinet Member: Anniv, Jan 18
  First Black US State's Attorney: Anniv, July 6
  First Natl Convention for Blacks: Anniv, Sept 15
  Forten, James: Birth Anniv, Sept 2
  Foster, Andrew: Birth Anniv, Sept 17
  Frederick Douglass Speaks: Anniv, Aug 11

  Freedom Riders: Anniv, May 1
  Gibbs, Mifflin Wister: Birth Anniv, Apr 28
  Grimes, Leonard Andrew: Birth Anniv, Nov 9
  Harris, Patricia Roberts: Birth Anniv, May 31
  Historically Black Colleges and Universities Week, Natl (Pres Proc), Sept 17
  Hughes, Langston: Birth Anniv, Feb 1
  Joplin, Scott: Birth Anniv, Nov 24
  Juneteenth, June 19
  King Awarded Nobel: Anniv, Oct 14
  King, Martin Luther, Jr: Birth Anniv, Jan 15
  Kwanzaa Fest, Dec 26
  Links, Inc: Anniv, Nov 9
  Loving v Virginia: Anniv, June 12
  Malcolm X: Assassination Anniv, Feb 21
  Marshall, Thurgood, Resigns from Supreme Court: Anniv, June 27
  McDaniel, Hattie: Birth Anniv, June 10
  Medgar Evers Assassinated: Anniv, June 13
  Meredith (James) Enrolls at Ole Miss: Anniv, Sept 30
  Miami/Bahamas Goombay Fest (Miami, FL), June 1
  Million Man March: Anniv, Oct 16
  Minority Enterprise Development Week (Pres Proc), Oct 7
  Minority Scientists Showcase (St. Louis, MO), Jan 13
  Montgomery Boycott Arrests: Anniv, Feb 22
  Montgomery Bus Boycott Begins: Anniv, Dec 5
  Montgomery Bus Boycott Ends: Anniv, Dec 20
  Motley, Constance Baker: Birth, Sept 14
  NAACP Founded: Anniv, Feb 12
  New York Slave Revolt: Anniv, Apr 7
  Ralph Bunche Awarded Nobel Peace Prize: Anniv, Dec 10
  Robinson Named First Black Manager: Anniv, Oct 3
  Rosa Parks Day, Dec 1
  Saint Louis Race Riots: Anniv, July 2
  Scottsboro Trial: Anniv, Apr 6
  Spelman College Established: Anniv, Apr 11
  Stokes Becomes First Black Mayor in US: Anniv, Nov 13
  Tanner, Henry Ossawa: Birth Anniv, June 21
  Truth, Sojourner: Death Anniv, Nov 26
  Tuskegee Institute Opening: Anniv, July 4
  Unity in Diversity Day, Aug 11
  Wm Carney Receives Cong Medal: Anniv, May 23
Agassi, Andre: Birth, Apr 29
Agassiz, Louis: Birth Anniv, May 28
Agee, James: Birth Anniv, Nov 27
Agee, Philip: Birth, July 19
Agnew Resignation: Anniv, Oct 10
Agnew, Spiro: Birth Anniv, Nov 9
Agriculture
  Abraham Baldwin Agri College Homecoming (Tifton, GA), Apr 6
  Acton Fair (Acton, ME), Aug 23
  Ag Days—Down on the Farm (Wichita, KS), July 28
  Agriculture Day, Natl, Mar 20
  Agriculture Week, Natl, Mar 18
  Agrifair (Abbotsford, BC, Canada), Aug 2
  Alabama State Fair, South (Montgomery, AL), Oct 5
  Alaska State Fair (Palmer, AK), Aug 24
  Arizona State Fair (Phoenix, AZ), Oct 21
  Arkansas State Fair (Little Rock, AR), Oct 5
  Barn Day (Filley, NE), July 7
  Beef Empire Days (Garden City, KS), June 5
  Big E (West Springfield, MA), Sept 14
  Black Hills Steam and Gas Threshing Bee (Sturgis, SD), Aug 17

Taylor Horsefest (Taylor, ND), **July 27**
Turkey Vultures Return to the Living Sign (Canisteo, NY), **Mar 12**
Turkey-Free Thanksgiving, **Nov 22**
Turtle Derby, Canadian (Boissevain, MB, Canada), **July 13**
Turtle Races (Danville, IL), **June 2**
Veal Ban Campaign, Natl, **May 13**
Viewing the Dells Eagles (Wisconsin Dells, WI), **Jan 1**
Viola Gopher Count (Viola, MN), **June 21**
Wayne Chicken Show (Wayne, NE), **July 13**
Westminster Dog Show (New York, NY), **Feb 12**
What If Cats and Dogs Had Opposable Thumbs, **Mar 3**
Wild About Wildlife (St. Simons Island, GA), **July 12**
Wild Horse Chasing (Japan), **July 23**
Wild Turkey Calling and Fest, Natl (Yellville, AR), **Oct 12**
Wilderness Wildlife Week of Nature (Pigeon Forge, TN), **Jan 6**
Wool Day: Sheep to Shawl/Border Collies (Woodstock, VT), **Sept 16**
World Farm Animals Day, **Oct 2**
World Habitat Awareness Month, **Apr 1**
World Turtle Day, **May 23**
ZAM! Zoo and Aquarium Month, **Apr 1**
Zoo Babies (Cincinnati, OH), **June 2**
Aniston, Jennifer: Birth, Feb 11
Anka, Paul: Birth, July 30
Ann-Margret: Birth, Apr 28
Annan, Kofi: Birth, Apr 8
Annapolis Convention: Anniv, Sept 11
Anne, Princess: Birth, Aug 15
Annenberg, Walter: Birth, Mar 13
Annunciation, Feast of, Mar 25
Anonymous Giving Week, Mar 18
Another Look Unlimited Day, Sept 4
Another World TV Premiere: Anniv, May 4
Anson, Cap: Birth Anniv, Apr 17
Anspach, Susan: Birth, Nov 23
Answer Your Cat's Question Day, Jan 22
Ant, Adam: Birth, Nov 3
Anthem Day, Natl, Mar 3
Anthony, Marc: Birth, Sept 16
Anthony, Susan B.: Day, Feb 15
Anthony, Susan B.: Fined for Voting: Anniv, June 3
Anti-Boredom Month, Natl, July 1
Anti-Saloon League Founded: Anniv, May 24
Antietam, Battle of: Anniv, Sept 17
Antigua and Barbuda: August Monday, Aug 6
Antigua: National Holiday, Nov 1
Antiques
Antique & Collectibles Flea Market (Weston, MO), **Apr 28**
Antique & Collectibles Show & Sale, Mid-Summer (Millville, NJ), **July 28**
Antique Fire Apparatus Muster and Show (Millville, NJ), **Aug 19**
Antique Flea Market (Somerset, PA), **Aug 11**
Antique Marine Engine Exposition (Mystic, CT), **Aug 18**
Antique Show & Sale (Weston, MO), **Mar 3**
Antique Valentine Exhibit (Clinton, NJ), **Feb 1**
Antique/Classic Boat Rendezvous (Mystic, CT), **July 21**
Antiques in Schoharie (Schoharie, NY), **Mar 3**
Antiques on the Diamond (Ligonier, PA), **June 9**
Arrow Rock Antique Show & Sale (Arrow Rock, MO), **May 19**
Atlantique City Antiques/Collectibles (Atlantic City, NJ), **Oct 20**
Atlantique City Spring Fair (Atlantic City, NJ), **Mar 24**
Auburn Cord Duesenberg Fest (Auburn, IN), **Aug 30**
Black Hills Threshing Bee (Sturgis, SD), **Aug 17**
Blackpowder Historical Fair (Albert Lea, MN), **Feb 10**
Brush Country Antique Show & Sale (Kingsville, TX), **Mar 10**
Chelsea Antiques Fair (London, England), **Mar 16**
Chester Antiques and Fine Art Show (Cheshire, England), **Feb 15**
Cotton Pickin' Fair (Gay, GA), **May 5**
Doll Show (Millville, NJ), **Nov 10**
Esau's Antique and Collectible Extravaganza (Knoxville, TN), **Oct 20**
Flea Market-Antique-Craft Sale (Sauk Centre, MN), **July 21**
450-Mile Outdoor Fest, **Aug 16**
Getaway Gardens Weekend (CT), **May 4**
Gettysburg Outdoor Antique Show (Gettysburg, PA), **Sept 22**

Gettysburg Outdoor Antique Show (Gettysburg, PA), **May 19**
Harvest Fest (Miami, FL), **Nov 17**
Kechi's Antique Country Christmas (Kechi, KS), **Nov 17**
Landon Azalea Garden Fest/Antique Show (Bethesda, MD), **May 4**
Mid-Winter Antiques Show (Millville, NJ), **Feb 3**
New Oxford Outdoor Antique Show (Gettysburg, PA), **June 16**
Olde-Time Antiques and Collectibles Faire (Toms River, NJ), **Sept 1**
150 Years of Robinson Hats Exhib (Granville, OH), **Apr 1**
Orange Historical Society Antique Show (Orange, CT), **Feb 24**
Pec Thing (Pecatonica, IL), **May 19**
Pheasant Run Antique Show (St. Charles, IL), **Mar 9**
Premiere Antique Show (Kohler, WI), **Mar 10**
Southwest Antique Show/Sale (Yuma, AZ), **Jan 5**
Vegaspex (Anaheim, CA), **May 25**
Victorian Easter (Nashville, TN), **Mar 17**
Anton, Susan: Birth, Oct 12
Antonioni, Michelangelo: Birth, Sept 29
Ants: Carpenter Ant Awareness Week, June 24
Anvil Mountain Run (Nome, AK), Sept 13
Anwar, Gabrielle: Birth, Feb 4
Anxiety Disorders Screening Day, Natl, May 2
Apache Wars Began: Anniv, Feb 4
Apartheid Law, South Africa Repeals Last: Anniv, June 17
Apgar, Virginia: Birth Anniv, June 7
Aphelion, Earth at, July 4
Apollo I: Spacecraft Fire: Anniv, Jan 27
Appert, Nicolas: Birth Anniv, Oct 23
Apple Blossom Fest (Annapolis Valley, NS, Canada), May 30
Apple Blossom Fest (Gettysburg, PA), May 5
Apple Blossom Fest, Washington State (Wenatchee, WA), Apr 26
Apple Butter Makin' Days (Mt Vernon, MO), Oct 12
Apple Butter Stirrin' (Coshocton, OH), Oct 19
Apple Fest, Jackson County (Jackson, OH), Sept 18
Apple Fest, Kentucky (Paintsville, KY), Oct 5
Apple Fest, Vermont (Springfield, VT), Oct 6
Apple Harvest Fest (Gettysburg, PA), Oct 6
Apple II Computer Released: Anniv, June 5
Apple Week, Beatles' Natl: Anniv, Aug 11
Applefest (Weston, MO), Sept 15
Applegate, Christina: Birth, Nov 25
Applejack Fest (Nebraska City, NE), Sept 15
Appleseed, Johnny: Birth Anniv, Sept 26
Appleseed: Johnny Appleseed Day, Mar 11
April Fools' Day, Apr 1
Aquarius Begins, Jan 20
Aquino, Benigno: Assassination Anniv, Aug 21
Aquino, Corazon: Birth, Jan 25
Arab Oil Embargo Lifted: Anniv, Mar 13
Arab-Israeli War (Yom Kippur War), Oct 6
Arafat Returns to Palestine: Anniv, July 1
Arafat, Yasser: Birth, Aug 4
Arbor Day (Arizona), Apr 27
Arbor Day (Florida), Jan 19
Arbor Day, Natl (Proposed), Apr 27
Arc of the US: Anniv, Jan 1
Arcadia Daze (Arcadia, MI), July 27
Archer, Anne: Birth, Aug 25
Arches Natl Park Established: Anniv, Nov 12
Archibald, Nate: Birth, Sept 2
Architectural Feature Tours (Oak Park, IL), Apr 1
Architecture: First Skyscraper: Anniv, May 1
Area Codes Introduced: Anniv, Nov 10
Argentina
Independence Day, **July 9**
Revolution Day, **May 25**
Aries Begins, Mar 21
Arizona
Admission Day, **Feb 14**
All States Picnic (Yuma), **Jan 9**
American Family Day, **Aug 5**
Americana Indian and Western Art Show/Sale (Yuma), **Jan 26**
Apache Wars Began: Anniv, **Feb 4**
Arbor Day, **Apr 27**
Arizona Renaissance Fest (Apache Junction), **Feb 3**
Arizona State Fair (Phoenix), **Oct 21**
Assn for Dressings and Sauces Annual Meeting (Tucson), **Oct 7**
Colorado River Crossing Balloon Festival (Yuma), **Nov 16**
Constitution Commemoration Day, **Sept 17**
Cowboy Christmas (Wickenburg), **Dec 7**
Cowboy Hall of Fame Ceremony (Willcox), **Oct 4**

Desert Foothills Music Fest (Carefree), **Feb 7**
Doll Show (Yuma), **Feb 3**
Four Corner States Bluegrass Fest (Wickenburg), **Nov 9**
Gold Rush Days (Wickenburg), **Feb 9**
La Fiesta De Los Vaqueros (Tucson), **Feb 21**
Lost Dutchman Days (Apache Junction), **Feb 23**
Midnight at the Oasis (Yuma), **Mar 9**
Mill Avenue Masquerade Adventure (Tempe), **Oct 27**
Nursing Conf on Pediatric Primary Care (Phoenix), **Mar 15**
Oatman Sidewalk Egg Frying Contest (Oatman), **July 4**
Old Towne Tempe Spring Fest of Arts (Tempe), **Mar 30**
Petrified Forest Natl Park Established: Anniv, **Dec 9**
Rex Allen Days (Willcox), **Oct 5**
Scottsdale Culinary Fest (Scottsdale), **Apr 18**
Sedona Chamber Music Festival (Sedona), **May 18**
Sonora Showcase (Yuma), **Jan 23**
Southwest Antique Show/Sale (Yuma), **Jan 5**
Southwest Senior Chmpshp (Yuma), **Jan 16**
Sporting Goods Assn Mgmt Conf, Natl (Tucson), **May 20**
Tempe Fall Fest of Arts (Tempe), **Nov 30**
Wings Over Willcox—Sandhill Crane Celebration (Willcox), **Jan 19**
Winterfest (Flagstaff), **Feb 1**
World's Oldest Continuous PRCA Rodeo (Payson), **Aug 17**
Yuma Home Show (Yuma), **Jan 12**
Yuma Jaycee's Silver Spur Rodeo (Yuma), **Feb 10**
Yuma Square and Round Dance Fest (Yuma), **Feb 9**
Arkansas
Admission Day: Anniv, **June 15**
Arts and Crafts Festival (Bella Vista), **Oct 18**
Chicken and Egg Festival (Prescott), **June 2**
Chuckwagon Races, Natl Chmpshp (Clinton), **Aug 31**
Clothesline Fair (Prairie Grove), **Sept 1**
Daffodil Festival (Camden), **Mar 9**
Dermott's Annual Crawfish Fest (Dermott), **May 18**
Duck-Calling Contest/Wings Over Prairie Fest (Stuttgart), **Nov 23**
Eagles Et Cetera (Bismarck), **Jan 26**
Fordyce on the Cotton Belt Fest (Fordyce), **Apr 23**
Fox 16 3-on-3 Basketball Classic (Little Rock), **Apr 28**
Great Arkansas Pig-Out (Morrilton), **Aug 2**
Homefest (Bald Knob), **July 14**
Hope Watermelon Fest (Hope), **Aug 9**
Hot Springs Natl Park Established: Anniv, **Mar 4**
King Biscuit Blues Fest (Helena), **Oct 4**
Longhorn World Championship Rodeo (Little Rock), **Mar 2**
Magnolia Blossom Fest (Magnolia), **May 17**
NCAA Indoor Track/Field Chmpshps (Fayetteville), **Mar 9**
Orphan Train Heritage Soc Reunion (Fayetteville), **Oct 18**
Ozark UFO Conf (Eureka Springs), **Apr 6**
Petit Jean Antique Auto Show/Swap Meet (Morrilton), **June 12**
Petit Jean Fall Antique Auto Swap Meet (Morrilton), **Sept 19**
Picklefest (Atkins), **May 18**
Quadrangle Fest (Texarkana), **Sept 8**
Riverfest (Little Rock), **May 25**
Rotary Tiller Race/Purplehull Pea Fest World Chmpshp (Emerson), **June 30**
Smackover Oil Town Fest (Smackover), **June 14**
State Fair and Livestock Show (Little Rock), **Oct 5**
Steak Cookoff World Chmpshp (Magnolia), **May 19**
Tontitown Grape Fest (Tontitown), **Aug 14**
War Eagle Fair (War Eagle), **Oct 18**
Wild Turkey Calling and Fest, Natl (Yellville), **Oct 12**
Arkin, Adam: Birth, Aug 19
Arkin, Alan: Birth, Mar 26
Arledge, Roone: Birth, July 8
Arlen, Harold: Birth Anniv, Feb 15
Armani, Giorgio: Birth, July 11
Armatrading, Joan: Birth, Dec 9
Armed Forces Day (Egypt), Oct 6
Armed Forces Day (Pres Proc), May 19
Armed Forces Unified: Anniv, July 26
Armenia: Earthquake of 1988: Anniv, Dec 7
Armenia: National Day, Sept 21
Armenian Appreciation Day, Apr 3
Armenian Christmas, Jan 6
Armenian Martyrs Day, Apr 24
Armistice Day, Nov 11
Armistice Day: See Veterans Day, Nov 11

Communist Party Suspended, Soviet: Anniv, Aug 29
Community Education Day, Natl, Nov 13
Community Spirit Days, Apr 1
Como, Perry: Birth, May 18
Comoros: Independence Day, July 6
Compliment Day, Natl, Jan 24
Compliment-Your-Mirror Day, July 3
CompuFest (Orlando, FL}, June 29
Computer
American Crossword Apple II Computer Released: Anniv, **June 5**
Cathode-Ray Tube Patented: Anniv, **Dec 20**
Clean Up Your Computer Month, Natl, **Jan 1**
Computer Learning Month, **Oct 1**
Computer Security Day, **Nov 30**
E-Commerce Week, Natl, **Nov 11**
E-Mail Week, Natl, **June 11**
Eckert, J. Presper, Jr: Birth Anniv, **Apr 9**
ENIAC Introduced: Anniv, **Feb 14**
High Tech Month, Natl, **Jan 1**
IBM PC Introduced: Anniv, **Apr 24**
Internet Created: Anniv, **Oct 29**
Lotus 1-2-3 Released: Anniv, **Jan 26**
Macintosh Debuts: Anniv, **Jan 25**
Microsoft Releases Windows: Anniv, **Nov 10**
Name Your PC Day, **Nov 20**
Race Your Mouse Around the Icons Day, **Aug 28**
Religious Software Week, Natl, **Aug 19**
Shareware Day, Intl, **Dec 9**
World Wide Web: Anniv, **Aug 1**
Conaway, Jeff: Birth, Oct 5
Concorde Flight, First: Anniv, Jan 21
Concours d'Elegance (Forest Grove, OR), July 15
Condom Week, Natl, Feb 13
Cone, David: Birth, Jan 2
Confederate Heroes Day, Jan 19
Confederate Memorial Day (FL, GA), Apr 26
Confederate Memorial Day (MS), Apr 30
Confederate Memorial Day (SC), May 10
Confederate Memorial Day (VA), May 28
Confederation, Articles of: Ratification Anniv, Mar 1
Conference on Students of Color (Montego Bay, Jamaica), Nov 1
Confucius: Birthday and Teacher's Day (Taiwan), Sept 28
Confucius: Birthday Observance (Hong Kong), Oct 13
Congenital Heart Defect Awareness Day, Feb 14
Congo (Brazzaville): National Holiday, Aug 15
Congo (Kinshasa): Independence Day, June 30
Congress (House of Reps) First Quorum: Anniv, Apr 1
Congress Assembles (US), Jan 3
Congress First Meets at Washington: Anniv, Nov 21
Congress: First Meeting Anniv, Mar 4
Congress: Woman Runs the House: Anniv, June 20
Congressional Page, First Female: Anniv, Jan 3
Connecticut
American Crossword Puzzle Tournament (Stamford), **Mar 16**
Antique Marine Engine Exposition (Mystic), **Aug 18**
Antique/Classic Boat Rendezvous (Mystic), **July 21**
Big D 103 Caravan of Carriages (Windsor), **Nov 18**
Boom Box Parade (Willimantic), **July 4**
Brooklyn Fair (Brooklyn), **Aug 23**
Celebrate New Haven 4th (New Haven), **July 4**
Chowderfest (Mystic), **Oct 6**
Christmas Town Fest (Bethlehem), **Dec 7**
Community Carol Singing (Mystic), **Dec 23**
Connecticut Early Music Fest (New London), **June 8**
Connecticut Storytelling Fest (New London), **Apr 27**
Constitution Ratification: Anniv, **Jan 9**
Fest of Arts and Ideas, Intl (New Haven), **June 15**
Fine Arts and Crafts Fest (Woodstock), **Oct 13**
First Night Hartford (Hartford), **Dec 31**
Getaway Gardens Weekend, **May 4**
Gift Show Case (Woodbury), **Nov 18**
Gingerbread Village and Bazaar (Middlebury), **Dec 1**
Greenwich Arts Center Open House (Greenwich), **Jan 28**
Harvest Tyme (Franklin), **Oct 20**
Kids After Christmas (Mystic), **Dec 26**
Lantern Light Tours (Mystic), **Dec 6**
Levitt Pavilion Performing Arts/Music Fest (Westport), **June 24**
Litchfield Open House Tour (Litchfield), **July 13**
Lobsterfest (Mystic), **May 26**
Meet the Artists & Artisans Show (Milford Green), **May 19**
Milford Oyster Fest (Milford), **Aug 18**

Moby Dick Marathon (Mystic), **July 31**
Mystic Seaport Field Days (Mystic), **Nov 23**
Mystic Seaport Museum: Independence Day Celeb (Mystic), **July 4**
Nathan Hale Fife and Drum Muster (Coventry), **July 28**
New England Arts & Crafts Fest (Milford), **July 7**
New Haven Labor Day Road Race (New Haven), **Sept 3**
Norfolk Chamber Music Fest (Norfolk), **June 30**
North Haven Fair (North Haven), **Sept 6**
Norwalk Seaport Oyster Fest (Norwalk), **Sept 7**
Odyssey-A Greek Festival (Orange), **Sept 1**
Orange Historical Society Antique Show, **Feb 24**
Pilot Pen Intl Tennis Tournament (New Haven), **Aug 17**
Road Church Country Fair (Stonington), **Sept 15**
Road Church Missionary Fair (Stonington), **May 19**
Science Expo (Milford), **Jan 27**
Sea Music Fest (Mystic), **June 7**
Sharon on the Green Arts and Crafts Fair (Sharon), **Aug 4**
Small Craft Weekend (Mystic), **June 2**
Summer Tyme (Franklin), **July 7**
Supreme Court Strikes Down Law Banning Contraceptives: Anniv, **June 7**
Tag Sale on the Green (Colchester), **June 10**
Tellabration! An Evening of Storytelling for Grown-Ups, **Nov 16**
Trumball Days (New Haven), **June 29**
Whippoorwill Morgan Horse Open Barn (Old Lyme), **May 26**
Woodstock Fair (Woodstock), **Aug 31**
Connecting Week, Natl, May 1
Connery, Sean: Birth, Aug 25
Connick, Harry, Jr: Birth, Sept 11
Conniff, Ray: Birth, Nov 6
Connolly, Maureen: Birth Anniv, Sept 17
Connors, Chuck: Birth Anniv, Apr 10
Connors, Jimmy: Birth, Sept 2
Connors, Mike: Birth, Aug 15
Conrad, Joseph: Birth Anniv, Dec 3
Conrad, Kent: Birth, Mar 12
Conrad, Robert: Birth, Mar 1
Conrad, William: Birth Anniv, Sept 27
Conroy, Pat: Birth, Oct 26
Conserve Water/Detect-a-Leak Week, Mar 4
Consider Christianity Week, Apr 1
Constable, John: Birth Anniv, June 11
Constantinople Falls to the Turks: Anniv, May 29
Constitution, US
11th Amendment Ratified (States' Sov), **Feb 7**
12th Amendment Ratified, **June 15**
13th Amendment Ratified: Anniv, **Dec 6**
14th Amendment Ratified, **July 9**
15th Amendment Ratified, **Feb 3**
16th Amendment Ratified (Income Tax), **Feb 3**
17th Amendment Ratified, **Apr 8**
18th Amendment (Prohibition): Anniv, **Jan 16**
19th Amendment Ratified, **Aug 18**
20th Amendment (Inaugural, Congress opening dates), **Jan 23**
21st Amendment Ratified, **Dec 5**
22nd Amendment (Two-Term Limit): Ratified, **Feb 27**
23rd Amendment Ratified, **Mar 29**
24th Amendment (Eliminated Poll Taxes), **Jan 23**
25th Amendment (Pres Succession, Disability), **Feb 10**
26th Amendment Ratified, **June 30**
27th Amendment Ratified: Anniv, **May 19**
Bill of Rights: Anniv of First State Ratification, **Nov 20**
Constitution of the US: Anniv, **Sept 17**
Constitution Week (Pres Proc), **Sept 17**
Constitution Week, Natl, **Sept 16**
Constitutional Convention: Anniv, **May 25**
Equal Rights Amendment Sent to States for Ratification, **Mar 22**
Federalist Papers: Anniv, **Oct 27**
Great Debate (Constitutional Convention): Anniv, **Aug 6**
Presidential Succession Act: Anniv, **July 18**
Religious Freedom Day, **Jan 16**
Takes Effect: Anniv, **July 2**
Veep Day, **Aug 9**
Women's Suffrage Amendment Introduced: Anniv, **Jan 10**
Consumer Awareness Week, Apr 16
Consumer Protection Week, Natl (Pres Proc), Jan 30
Conti, Bill: Birth, Apr 13
Conti, Tom: Birth, Nov 22
Continental Congress Assembly, First: Anniv, Sept 5

Contraband Days (Lake Charles, LA), May 1
Converse, Frank: Birth, May 22
Converse, Harriet: White Woman Made Indian Chief: Anniv, Sept 18
Conway, Gary: Birth, Feb 4
Conway, Kevin: Birth, May 29
Conway, Tim: Birth, Dec 15
Coogan, Keith: Birth, Jan 13
Cook Something Bold and Pungent Day, Nov 8
Cook, James: Birth Anniv, Oct 27
Cook, Rachael Leigh: Birth, Oct 4
Cookie Cutter Week, Dec 1
Cookie Month, Natl, Oct 1
Coolidge, Calvin: Birth Anniv, July 4
Coolidge, Grace Anna Goodhue: Birth Anniv, Jan 3
Coolidge, Rita: Birth, May 1
Cooney, Gerry: Birth, Aug 24
Cooney, Joan Ganz: Birth, Nov 30
Cooper, Alice: Birth, Feb 4
Cooper, Cynthia: Birth, Apr 14
Cooper, D.B. Hijacking: Anniv, Nov 24
Cooper, Gary: Birth Anniv, May 7
Cooper, Jackie: Birth, Sept 15
Cooper, James Fenimore: Birth Anniv, Sept 15
Cooper, Justin: Birth, Nov 17
Cooper, L. Gordon: Birth, Mar 6
Cooperatives, UN Intl Day of, July 7
Copeland, Stewart: Birth, July 16
Copernicus, Nicolaus: Birth Anniv, Feb 19
Copland, Aaron: Birth Anniv, Nov 14
Copper Magnolia Fest (Washington, MS), Sept 22
Copperfield, David: Birth, Sept 16
Coppola, Francis Ford: Birth, Apr 7
Copyright Law Passed: Anniv, May 31
Copyright Revision Law: Anniv, Jan 1
Coral Sea Battle of: Anniv, May 8
Coray, Melissa Burton: Birth Anniv, Mar 2
Corbett-Sullivan Prize Fight: Anniv, Sept 7
Corbin, Barry: Birth, Oct 16
Corea, Chick: Birth, June 12
Corelli, Arcangelo: Birth Anniv, Feb 17
Corley, Pat: Birth, June 1
Corman, Roger: Birth, Apr 5
Corn Fest, Sun Prairie's Sweet (Sun Prairie, WI), Aug 16
Corn Fest, Sweet (Millersport, OH), Aug 29
Cornish Fest (Mineral Point, WI), Sept 21
Cornwell, Patricia: Birth, June 9
Corpus Christi, June 14
Corpus Christi (US): Observance, June 17
Corrigan, Mairead: Birth, Jan 27
Corrigan, Wrong Way Day, July 17
Cort, Bud: Birth, Mar 29
Cortes Conquers Mexico: Anniv, Nov 8
Cortese, Dan: Birth, Sept 14
Cortese, Valentina: Birth, Jan 1
Corvette and High Performance Meet (Puyallup, WA), Feb 10
Corvette Show (Mackinaw City, MI), Aug 24
Corvette Show (Millville, NJ), Sept 9
COSAC Annual Conference, May 4
Cosby, Bill: Birth, July 12
Cosell, Howard: Birth Anniv, Mar 25
Costa Rica: Independence Day, Sept 15
Costas, Bob: Birth, Mar 22
Costello, Elvis: Birth, Aug 25
Costner, Kevin: Birth, Jan 18
Cote D'Ivoire: Natl Day, Aug 7
Cotten, Joseph: Birth Anniv, May 15
Cotton Bowl Classic (Dallas, TX), Jan 1
Cotton Pickin' Fair (Gay, GA), May 5
Council of Logistics Mgmt Conf (Kansas City, MO), Sept 30
Council of Nicaea I: Anniv, May 20
Country Day, Colton (Colton, NY), July 21
Country Good Times (Wilberforce, ON), July 20
Country Jamboree (Fargo, ND), Aug 12
Coup Attempt in the Soviet Union: Anniv, Aug 19
Couple Appreciation Month, Apr 1
Couples, Fred: Birth, Oct 3
Coupon Month, Natl, Sept 1
Courageous Follower Day, Mar 4
Couric, Katie: Birth, Jan 7
Court TV Debut: Anniv, July 1
Courtenay, Tom: Birth, Feb 25
Cousins Day, July 24
Cousteau, Jacques: Birth Anniv, June 11
Cousy, Bob: Birth, Aug 9
Covered Bridge Fest (Washington County, PA), Sept 15
Cow Appreciation Day (Woodstock, VT), July 14
Cow Chip Throw, Wisconsin (Prairie du Sac, WI), Aug 31

Daniel Boone TV Premiere: Anniv, Sept 24
Daniel, Beth: Birth, Oct 14
Daniels, Charlie: Birth, Oct 28
Daniels, Jeff: Birth, Feb 19
Daniels, William: Birth, Mar 31
Danish
  Aebleskiver Days (Tyler, MN), June 20
  Tivoli Fest (Elk Horn, IA), **May 26**
Dankfest (Harmony, PA), Aug 25
Danner, Blythe: Birth, Feb 3
Danson, Ted: Birth, Dec 29
Dante, Alighieri: Death Anniv, Sept 14
Danza, Tony: Birth, Apr 21
Darby, Kim: Birth, July 8
Dare to Live Day, Intl, Apr 30
Dare, Virginia: Birth Anniv, Aug 18
Dark Day in New England: Anniv, May 19
Dark Shadows TV Premiere: Anniv, June 27
Darren, James: Birth, June 8
Darrow, Clarence, Death Commemoration
  (Chicago, IL), Mar 13
Darrow, Clarence: Birth Anniv, Apr 18
Darwin, Charles Robert: Birth Anniv, Feb 12
Daschle, Thomas Andrew: Birth, Dec 9
Date Fest, Natl (Indio, CA), Feb 16
Date to Create, The, Aug 8
Dating Game TV Premiere: Anniv, Dec 20
Daughters to Work Day, Take Our, Apr 26
Daumier, Honore: Birth Anniv, Feb 26
DAV Day, Natl, Feb 9
Davenport, Lindsay: Birth, June 8
David Brinkley's Journal TV Premiere: Anniv,
  Oct 11
David, Keith: Birth, June 4
Davidovich, Lolita: Birth, July 15
Davidson, John: Birth, Dec 13
Davies, Jeremy: Birth, Oct 28
Davies, Laura: Birth, Oct 5
Davies, Marion: Birth Anniv, Jan 3
Davis, Adelle: Birth Anniv, Feb 25
Davis, Al: Birth, July 4
Davis, Angela, Acquittal: Anniv, June 4
Davis, Angela: Birth, Jan 26
Davis, Bette: Birth Anniv, Apr 5
Davis, Clifton: Birth, Oct 4
Davis, Eric: Birth, May 29
Davis, Geena: Birth, Jan 21
Davis, Gray: Birth, Dec 26
Davis, Jefferson: Birth Anniv, June 3
Davis, Jefferson: Bread Riot Richmond: Anniv,
  Apr 2
Davis, Jefferson: Inauguration: Anniv, Feb 18
Davis, Jim: Birth, July 28
Davis, Judy: Birth, Apr 23
Davis, Mac: Birth, Jan 21
Davis, Miles: Birth Anniv, May 25
Davis, Ossie: Birth, Dec 18
Davis, Sammy, Jr: Birth Anniv, Dec 8
Davis, Skeeter: Birth, Dec 30
Davis, Terrell: Birth, Oct 28
Davis-Voss, Sammi: Birth, June 21
Davison, Bruce: Birth, June 28
Davy Crockett TV Premiere: Anniv, Dec 15
Dawber, Pam: Birth, Oct 18
Dawes, Charles G.: Birth Anniv, Aug 27
Dawson, Andre: Birth, July 10
Dawson, Dermontti: Birth, June 17
Dawson, Richard: Birth, Nov 20
Day for Hearts, A: CHD Awareness Days, Feb 1
Day for Tolerance, Intl, Nov 16
Day of Concern about Young People and Gun
  Violence, Natl (Pres Proc), Oct 5
Day of Meditation, Oct 27
Day of Prayer and Action for Human Habitat, Intl,
  Sept 16
Day of the Race: See Columbus Day, Oct 12
Day of the Six Billion: Anniv, Oct 12
Day on the Farm (Springfield, OR), Sept 8
Day With(out) Art, Dec 1
Day, Doris: Birth, Apr 3
Day-Lewis, Daniel: Birth, Apr 29
Dayne, Taylor: Birth, Mar 7
Days of Our Lives TV Premiere: Anniv, Nov 8
Dayton Valley Days (Dayton, NV), Sept 15
De Bont, Jan: Birth, Oct 22
De Carlo, Yvonne: Birth, Sept 1
De Cordova, Frederick: Birth, Oct 27
De Forest, Lee: Birth Anniv, Aug 26
De Gaulle, Charles: Birth Anniv, Nov 22
De Havilland, Olivia: Birth, July 1
De Klerk, Frederik: Birth, Mar 18
de la Hoya, Oscar: Birth, Feb 4
De La Renta, Oscar: Birth, July 22
De Mille, Cecil B.: Birth Anniv, Aug 12
De Mornay, Rebecca: Birth, Aug 29

De Niro, Robert: Birth, Aug 17
De Palma, Brian: Birth, Sept 11
De Rita, Joe: Birth Anniv, July 12
De Sade, Donatien: Birth Anniv, June 2
De Young, Cliff: Birth, Feb 12
Deaf Awareness Week, Sept 23
Deaf Day, Mother, Father, Apr 29
Deaf History Month, Mar 13
Deaf, First School for: Anniv, Apr 15
Dean, Dizzy: Birth Anniv, Jan 16
Dean, Howard: Birth, Nov 17
Dean, James: Birth Anniv, Feb 8
Dean, James: Fairmount Fest/Remembering
  (Fairmount, IN), Sept 28
Dean, Jimmy: Birth, Aug 10
Dean, John: Birth, Oct 14
Dear Diary Day, Sept 22
Dear Santa Letter Week, Nov 5
Death Penalty Banned: Anniv, June 29
Death/Duty Day, Nov 11
DeBakey, Michael: Birth, Sept 7
DeBarge, Eldra: Birth, June 4
Debate, Great (over Constitution): Anniv, Aug 6
Debs, Eugene V: Birth Anniv, Nov 5
DeBusschere, Dave: Birth, Oct 16
Debussy, Claude: Birth Anniv, Aug 22
Decatur, Stephen: Birth Anniv, Jan 5
December Bride TV Premiere: Anniv, Oct 4
Decide to Be Married Day, June 27
Decisions: Make Up Your Mind Day, Dec 31
Declaration of Independence
  Approval and Initial Signing: Anniv, **July 4**
  First Public Reading: Anniv, **July 8**
  Official Signing Anniv, **Aug 2**
  Resolution Anniv, **July 2**
Declaration of the Bab, May 23
Decoration Day (Memorial Day), May 28
Decoy and Wildlife Art Show (Clayton, NY),
  July 20
Decoy Fest, Chincoteague Easter (Chincoteague
  Island, VA), Apr 14
Decter, Midge: Birth, July 25
Dee, Ruby: Birth, Oct 27
Dee, Sandra: Birth, Apr 23
Deepavali (India), Nov 14
Dees, Rick: Birth, Mar 14
Defense Transportation Day, Natl (Pres Proc),
  May 18
DeFore, Don: Birth Anniv, Aug 25
DeFrantz, Anita L.: Birth, Oct 4
Degas, Edgar: Birth Anniv, July 19
DeGeneres, Ellen: Birth, Jan 26
DeHaven, Gloria: Birth, July 23
Delaney, Kim: Birth, Nov 29
Delano, Jane: Birth Anniv, Mar 26
Delany, Dana: Birth, Mar 13
DeLaurentiis, Dino: Birth, Aug 8
Delaware
  Day in Old New Castle (New Castle), **May 19**
  Delaware State Fair (Harrington), **July 19**
  Nanticoke Indian Powwow (Millsboro), **Sept 8**
  Old-Fashioned Ice Cream Fest (Wilmington), **July 7**
  Point-to-Point (Wilmington), **May 6**
  Ratification Day, **Dec 7**
  Return Day (Georgetown), **Nov 8**
  Sea Witch Halloween Fest (Rehoboth Beach/Dewey
  Beach), **Oct 26**
Delmonico, Lorenzo: Birth Anniv, Mar 13
DeLuise, Dom: Birth, Aug 1
DeMille, Agnes: Birth Anniv, Sept 18
Demme, Jonathan: Birth, Feb 22
Dempsey, Jack: Birth Anniv, June 24
Dempsey, Jack: Long Count Day, Sept 22
Dempsey, Patrick: Birth, Jan 13
DeMunn, Jeffrey: Birth, Apr 25
Denali Natl Park and Preserve Established: Anniv,
  Dec 2
Dench, Judi: Birth, Dec 9
Deneuve, Catherine: Birth, Oct 22
Denim Day, Lee Natl, Oct 5
Denmark
  Aalborg and Rebild Fest (Aalborg and Rebild),
  July 2
  Aarhus Fest Week, **Sept 1**
  Common Prayer Day, **May 11**
  Constitution Day, **June 5**
  Eel Fest (Jyllinge), **June 2**
  Ho Sheep Market, **Aug 25**
  Midsummer Eve, **June 23**
  Queen Margrethe's Birthday, **Apr 16**
  Street Urchins' Carnival, **Feb 26**
  Tivoli Gardens Season (Copenhagen), **May 1**
  Viking Fest, **June 22**
Dennehy, Brian: Birth, July 9
Dennis, Sandy: Birth Anniv, Apr 27

Dent, Bucky: Birth, Nov 25
Dental Drill Patent: Anniv, Jan 26
Dental Health Month, Natl Children's, Feb 1
Dental Hygiene Month, Natl, Oct 1
Dental School, First Woman to Graduate: Anniv,
  Feb 21
Denver, Bob: Birth, Jan 9
Denver, John: Birth Anniv, Dec 31
Depardieu, Gerard: Birth, Dec 27
Depp, Johnny: Birth, June 9
DePreist, James (Anderson): Birth, Nov 21
Depression Education and Awareness Month,
  Natl, Oct 1
Depression Screening Day, Natl, Oct 11
Derek, Bo: Birth, Nov 20
Dern, Bruce: Birth, June 4
Dern, Laura: Birth, Feb 10
Dershowitz, Alan: Birth, Sept 1
Des'ree: Birth, Nov 30
Descartes, Rene: Birth, Mar 31
Descendants Day, June 30
Desegregation, US Army First: Anniv, July 26
Desert Shield: Anniv, Aug 7
Desert Storm: Ground War Begins: Anniv, Feb 23
Desert Storm: Kuwait Liberated: Anniv, Feb 27
Desert Storm: Persian Gulf War Begins: Anniv,
  Jan 17
Desert Storm: UN Deadline Resolution: Anniv,
  Nov 28
DeShannon, Jackie: Birth, Aug 21
Designated Hitter Rule Adopted: Anniv, Jan 11
Desk Day, Natl Clean-Off-Your, Jan 8
DeSoto Caverns Park's Indian Dance Fest
  (Childersburg, AL), Apr 7
DeSoto's Winter Encampment (Tallahassee, FL),
  Jan 13
Destiny Day, Oct 12
Detroit (MI): Anniv, July 24
Detroit 300 Fest (MI), July 20
Devane, William: Birth, Sept 5
Development Information Day, World (UN), Oct 24
Devers, Gail: Birth, Nov 19
Devil's Night, Oct 30
DeVito, Danny: Birth, Nov 17
Devlin, Bernadette: Birth, Apr 23
DeVoe, Ronald: Birth, Feb 17
Dewey Defeats Truman Headline: Anniv, Nov 3
Dewey, John: Birth Anniv, Oct 20
Dewey, Melvil: Birth Anniv, Dec 10
Dewhurst, Colleen: Birth Anniv, June 3
DeWine, Mike: Birth, Jan 5
Dewitt, Joyce: Birth, Apr 23
Dey, Susan: Birth, Dec 10
Dia de la Raza (Mexico), Oct 12
Dia de la Raza: See Columbus Day, Oct 12
Diabetes Alert, American, Mar 27
Diabetes Month, American, Nov 1
Diabetic Eye Disease Month, Nov 1
Diamond GEM City Days (Diamond, MO), Sept 7
Diamond, Dustin: Birth, Jan 7
Diamond, Neil: Birth, Jan 24
Diana, Princess of Wales: Birth Anniv, July 1
Diary Day, Dear, Sept 22
Diaz, Cameron: Birth, Aug 30
DiCaprio, Leonardo: Birth, Nov 11
Dicing for Bibles (Huntingdonshire, England),
  June 4
Dick Cavett Show TV Premiere: Anniv, Mar 4
Dick Tracy TV Premiere: Anniv, Sept 11
Dick Van Dyke Show TV Premiere: Anniv, Oct 3
Dick, Andy: Birth, Dec 21
Dickens Fest (Broadstairs, England), June 16
Dickens Fest (Salt Lake City, UT), Nov 23
Dickens of a Christmas (Franklin, TN), Dec 8
Dickens on the Strand (Galveston, TX), Dec 1
Dickens, Charles: Birth Anniv, Feb 7
Dickerson, Eric: Birth, Sept 2
Dickinson, Angie: Birth, Sept 30
Dickinson, Anna: Birth Anniv, Oct 28
Dickinson, Emily: Birth Anniv, Dec 10
Dictionary Day, Oct 16
Dictionary of American English Published, First:
  Anniv, Apr 14
Diddley, Bo: Birth, Dec 30
Didion, Joan: Birth, Dec 5
Didrikson, Babe: See under Zaharias, June 26
Diefenbaker, John: Birth Anniv, Sept 18
Diego, Jose De: Birth Anniv, Apr 16
Dien Bien Phu Falls: Anniv, May 7
Diesel Engine Patented: Anniv, Feb 23
Diet Resolution Week, Jan 1
Diet: No Diet Day, May 6
Diet: Rid World Fad Diets/Gimmicks Day, Jan 23
Dietrich, Marlene: Birth Anniv, Dec 27
Different World TV Premiere: Anniv, Sept 24

Index ☆ *Chase's 2001 Calendar of Events* ☆

Herrinfesta Italiana (Herrin, IL), **May 24**

Highland County Maple Fest (Highland County, VA), **Mar 10**

Hog Capital of the World Fest (Kewanee, IL), **Aug 31**

Home of the Hamburger Celeb (Seymour, WI), **Aug 4**

Homemade Bread Day, **Nov 17**

Honey Month, Natl, **Sept 1**

Hope Watermelon Fest (Hope, AR), **Aug 9**

Hopps of Fun—A Fest of Beer and Wine (Mackinaw City, MI), **Sept 7**

Horseradish Fest (Collinsville, IL), **June 2**

Hot Dog Night (Luverne, MN), **July 12**

Hot Tea Month, Natl, **Jan 1**

Hug a Texas Chef Month, **Sept 1**

Ice Cream Cone: Birth, **Sept 22**

Ice Cream Day, Natl, **July 15**

Ice Cream Days (Le Mars, IA), **July 3**

Ice Cream Fest, Old-Fashioned (Utica, OH), **May 26**

Ice Cream Fest, Old-Fashioned (Wilmington, DE), **July 7**

Ice Cream Social (Indianapolis, IN), **July 4**

Iced Tea Month, Natl, **June 1**

Icewine Festival (Kelowna, BC, Canada), **Jan 18**

Jackson County Apple Fest (Jackson, OH), **Sept 18**

Jackson Hill Cider Day (Portsmouth, NH), **Sept 15**

Jalapeno Fest (Laredo, TX), **Feb 16**

John E. Teamer Black-Eyed Pea Dinner and Awards Ceremony (San Francisco, CA), **Jan 1**

Jose Cuervo Margarita Season, **Mar 30**

June Is Turkey Lovers' Month, **June 1**

Kool-Aid Days (Hastings, NE), **Aug 11**

Leitersburg Peach Fest (Leitersburg, MD), **Aug 11**

Lobster Fest, Maine (Rockland, ME), **Aug 1**

Lobsterfest (Mystic, CT), **May 26**

Long Beach Island Chowder Cook-Off (Beach Haven, NJ), **Sept 29**

Louisiana Peach Fest (Ruston, LA), **June 8**

Machias Wild Blueberry Fest (Machias), **Aug 17**

Maple Fair, Parke County (Rockville, IN), **Feb 24**

Maple Fest of Nova Scotia (Northern Nova Scotia, Canada), **Mar 17**

Maple Fest, Pennsylvania (Meyersdale, PSA), **Mar 31**

Maple Syrup Fest (Beaver, PA), **Apr 7**

Maple Syrup Saturday (Appleton, WI), **Mar 17**

Marion Popcorn Fest (Marion, OH), **Sept 6**

Marriage of the Port Ceremony (Bryan, TX), **Feb 3**

Marshall County Blueberry Fest (Plymouth, IN), **Aug 31**

Men Make Dinner Day, Natl, **Nov 1**

Messina Hof's Wine Premiere (Bryan, TX), **Nov 17**

Milford Oyster Fest (Milford, CT), **Aug 18**

Mint Fest, Saint Johns (St. Johns, MI), **Aug 10**

Montana State Chokecherry Fest (Lewistown), **Sept 7**

Morden Corn/Apple Fest (Morden, MB, Canada), **Aug 24**

More Herbs, Less Salt Day, **Aug 29**

Morel Mushroom Fest (Muscoda, WI), **May 18**

Morton Pumpkin Fest (Morton, IL), **Sept 12**

Mountain State Apple Harvest Fest (Martinsburg, WV), **Oct 18**

Mudbug Madness (Shreveport, LA), **May 24**

Mushroom Fest, Telluride (Telluride, CO), **Aug 23**

Mushroom Month, Natl, **Sept 1**

Mustard Day, Natl, **Aug 4**

No Salt Week, **Oct 1**

North Carolina Apple Fest (Hendersonville), **Aug 31**

North Carolina SweetPotato Month, **Feb 1**

Norwalk Seaport Oyster Fest (Norwalk, CT), **Sept 7**

Nugget Best in the West Rib Cook-Off (Sparks, NV), **Aug 31**

Nuts Fair (Bastogne, Belgium), **Dec 17**

Oatman Sidewalk Egg Frying Contest (Oatman, AZ), **July 4**

Oatmeal Month, **Jan 1**

October Frozen Food Fest, **Oct 1**

Ohio Pumpkin Fest (Barnesville, OH), **Sept 27**

Onion Market (Zibelemarit, Switzerland), **Nov 26**

Organic Harvest Month, Natl, **Sept 1**

Oscar Mayer Wienermobile: Anniv, **July 18**

Oyster Fest (Chincoteague Island, VA), **Oct 6**

Oyster Fest, St. Mary's County (Leonardtown, MD), **Oct 20**

Ozark Ham and Turkey Fest (California, MO), **Sept 15**

Pancake Day (Centerville, IA), **Sept 29**

Pancake Day, Intl (Liberal, KS), **Feb 27**

Pancake Week, Natl, **Feb 25**

Payson Golden Onion Days (Payson, UT), **Aug 31**

Peanut Butter Lover's Month, **Nov 1**

Pecan Day, **Mar 25**

Pecan Month, Natl, **Apr 1**

Pickle Week, Intl, **May 18**

Picklefest (Atkins, AR), **May 18**

Pizza Expo, **Mar 20**

Popcorn Fest (Valparaiso, IN), **Sept 8**

Popcorn Poppin' Month, Natl, **Oct 1**

Pork Expo, World (Des Moines, IA), **June 7**

Pork Month, Natl, **Oct 1**

Potato Blossom Fest, Maine (Fort Fairfield, ME), **July 14**

Potato Day Fest (Greeley, CO), **Sept 8**

Potato Feast Days (Houlton, ME), **Sept 14**

Poteet Strawberry Fest (Poteet, TX), **Apr 6**

Prairie Dog Chili Cookoff (Grand Prairie, TX), **Apr 7**

Prime Beef Fest (Monmouth, IL), **Sept 5**

Pumpkin Show, Circleville (Circleville, OH), **Oct 17**

Ranch Hand Breakfast (Kingsville, TX), **Nov 17**

Recipe Greetings for the Holidays, **Dec 9**

Restaurant Assn, Natl: Hotel/Motel Show (Chicago, IL), **May 19**

Return Shopping Carts to the Supermarket Month, **Feb 1**

Rhubarb Fest (Intercourse, PA), **May 18**

Ribfest (Kalamazoo, MI), **Aug 2**

Rice God, Day of the (Chiyoda, Japan), **June 3**

Rice Month, Natl, **Sept 1**

Rice Planting Fest (Osaka, Japan), **June 14**

Riverfront Ribfest (Huntington, WV), **Aug 16**

Roasting Ears of Corn Food Fest (Allentown, PA), **Aug 12**

Rochesterfest (Rochester, MN), **June 16**

Rockport Seafair (Rockport, TX), **Oct 6**

Root Beer Day, Stewart's, **June 16**

Salad Month, Natl, **May 1**

Salad Week, Natl, **July 25**

Salsa, Month, Natl, **May 1**

Sandwich Day, **Nov 3**

Schmeckfest (Freeman, SD), **Mar 29**

School Breakfast Week, Natl, **Mar 5**

Sea Lion Suds Fest (Gold Beach, OR), **Apr 14**

Seafood and Wine Fest, Newport (Newport, OR), **Feb 23**

Seafood Fest, Pompano Beach (Pompano Beach, FL), **Apr 27**

Seafood Month, Natl, **June 1**

Shrimp and Petroleum Fest, Louisiana (Morgan City, LA), **Aug 30**

Shrimp Fest, Low Country (McClellanville, SC), **May 5**

Shrimpfest (Roanoke, VA), **Apr 28**

Sinkie Day (eat over kitchen sink), **Nov 23**

Smith Valley Strawberry Fest (Wellington, NV), **May 27**

Snack Food Month, Natl, **Feb 1**

Sneak Some Zucchini onto Your Neighbors' Porch Night, **Aug 8**

Sour Herring Premiere (Sweden), **Aug 16**

Spam Town USA Fest (Austin, MN), **July 4**

Spinach and Trails Fest (Lenexa, KS), **Sept 8**

Split Pea Soup Week, Natl, **Nov 4**

St. Louise de Marillac Louisiana Bar-B-Q Fest (Arabi, LA), **May 18**

Steak Cookoff, World Chmpshp (Magnolia, AR), **May 19**

Strawberry Fest, West Virginia (Buckhannon, WV), **May 23**

Strawberry Fest (Long Grove, IL), **June 22**

Sun Prairie's Sweet Corn Fest (Sun Prairie, WI), **Aug 16**

Sundae in the Park (Yerington, NV), **Sept 9**

Sweet Corn Fest (Millersport, OH), **Aug 29**

Sweetcorn Fest, Natl (Hoopeston, IL), **Aug 31**

Taco Day, Chuy's Natl, **June 12**

Tacoma Holiday Food and Gift Fest (Tacoma, WA), **Oct 24**

Taste of Cincinnati (Cincinnati, OH), **May 26**

Taste of Colorado (Denver), **Aug 31**

Taste of Madison (Madison, WI), **Sept 1**

Taste of the Town (Wichita Falls, TX), **Mar 6**

Tomato Month, Fresh Florida, **Apr 1**

Tontitown Grape Fest (Tontitown, AR), **Aug 14**

Totally Chipotle Day, **May 5**

Town Point Virginia Wine Festival (Norfolk, VA), **Oct 20**

Turkey Rama (McMinnville, OR), **July 12**

University Kiwanis Pancake Fest (Wichita Falls, TX), **Jan 27**

Veal Ban Campaign, Natl, **May 13**

Vegetarian Awareness Month, **Oct 1**

Vegetarian Day, World, **Oct 1**

Verboort Sausage and Kraut Dinner (Forest Grove, OR), **Nov 3**

Virginia Peanut Fest (Emporia, VA), **Sept 21**

Virginia Wine Fest (Charlottesville, VA), **May 19**

Washington State Apple Blossom Fest (Wenatchee, WA), **Apr 26**

Watermelon Day (Vining, MN), **Aug 18**

Watermelon Fest (Rush Springs, OK), **Aug 11**

Watermelon Thump (Luling, TX), **June 21**

Whale of a Wine & Art Fest (Gold Bch, OR), **Feb 2**

Wild Foods Day (Pikeville, TN), **Oct 27**

Wine & Roses Fest (Bryan, TX), **Apr 28**

Wine Fest, Okanagan (BC, Canada), **May 3**

Wine/Harvest Fest (Kalamazoo/Paw Paw, MI), **Sept 8**

Wolf Point's Hottest Chili Weekend (Wolf Point, MT), **June 1**

Wollersheim Winery Grape Stomp Fest (Prairie du Sac, WI), **Oct 6**

World Beef Expo (Milwaukee, WI), **Sept 27**

World Chmpshp BBQ Goat Cookoff (Brady, TX), **Sept 1**

World Egg Day, **Oct 12**

World Food Day, **Oct 16**

World Grits Fest (St. George), **Apr 20**

World's Largest Breakfast Table (Battle Creek, MI), **June 8**

Food Stamps Authorized: Anniv, Sept 11

Footbag Chmpshps, World (Denver, CO), July 30

Football

Blue-Gray Classic (Montgomery, AL), **Dec 25**

Circle City Classic (Indianapolis, IN), **Oct 6**

Citrus Bowl, Florida (Orlando, FL), **Jan 1**

Delchamp's Senior Bowl Football Game (Mobile, AL), **Jan 20**

Fabulous 1890s Weekend (Mansfield, PA), **Sept 28**

First Night Football Game (Mansfield, PA), **Sept 28**

First Play-by-Play Football Game Broadcast, **Nov 23**

First Super Bowl: Anniv, **Jan 15**

Football League, Natl, Formed: Anniv, **Sept 17**

Holiday Bowl Parade/Game (San Diego, CA), **Dec 29**

Hula Bowl Game (Maui, HI), **Jan 20**

NAIA Division II Football Chmpshp Game, **Dec 15**

Nokia Sugar Bowl Classic (New Orleans, LA), **Jan 2**

Oil Bowl Football Classic (Wichita Falls, TX), **June 23**

Orange Bowl Football Game (Miami, FL), **Jan 1**

Outback Bowl Game (Tampa, FL), **Jan 1**

Rose Bowl Game (Pasadena, CA), **Jan 1**

Southwestern Bell Cotton Bowl Classic (Dallas, TX), **Jan 1**

Super Bowl, **Jan 28**

Univ of Chicago 1st Football Victory: Anniv, **Nov 16**

Foote, Shelby: Birth, Nov 17

Foothills Art Fest (Jackson, OH), Oct 19

For Pete's Sake Day, Feb 26

Forbes, Malcolm: Birth Anniv, Aug 19

Forbes, Michelle: Birth, Feb 17

Forbes, Steve: Birth, July 18

Ford, Eileen: Birth, Mar 25

Ford, Elizabeth (Betty): Birth, Apr 8

Ford, Faith: Birth, Sept 14

Ford, Gerald: Assassination Attempts: Anniv, Sept 5

Ford, Gerald: Birth, July 14

Ford, Gerald: Veep Day, Aug 9

Ford, Gerald: Vice Presidential Swearing In: Anniv, Dec 6

Ford, Glenn: Birth, May 1

Ford, Harrison: Birth, July 13

Ford, Henry: Birth Anniv, July 30

Ford, John: Birth Anniv, Feb 1

Ford, Whitey: Birth, Oct 21

Forefathers' Day, Dec 21

Foreign Language Month, Natl, July 1

Foreman, George: Birth, Jan 10

Forest Craft/Scenic Drive Fest (Van Buren Cnty, IA), Oct 13

Forest Fest, Mountain State (Elkins, WV), Sept 29

Forest Products Week, Natl (Pres Proc), Oct 21

Forgiveness Week, Natl, June 17

Forman, Milos: Birth, Feb 18

Former Prisoner of War Recognition Day, Natl (Pres Proc), Apr 9

Forrest, Nathan Bedford: Birth Anniv, July 13

Forsberg, Peter: Birth, July 20

Forster, E.M.: Birth Anniv, Jan 1

Forster, Robert: Birth, July 13

Forsyth, Frederick: Birth, Aug 25

Forsythe, John: Birth, Jan 29

Fort Ligonier Days (Ligonier, PA), Oct 12

Fort Moore Established: Anniv, Apr 24

Fort Sumter Shelled by North: Anniv, Aug 17

Fort Wayne Sports, Vacation & Boat Show (IN), Mar 15

Fortas, Abe: Birth Anniv, June 19

Forten, James: Birth Anniv, Sept 2

48 Hours TV Premiere: Anniv, Jan 19

Fosse, Robert Louis: Birth Anniv, June 23

Houseman, John: Birth Anniv, Sept 22
Housework Day, No, Apr 7
Houston, Sam: Birth Anniv, Mar 2
Houston, Whitney: Birth, Aug 9
Hovick, Rose L. (Gypsy Rose Lee): Birth Anniv, Feb 9
Howard, Juwan: Birth, Feb 7
Howard, Ken: Birth, Mar 28
Howard, Leslie: Birth Anniv, Apr 3
Howard, Moe: Birth Anniv, June 19
Howard, Ron: Birth, Mar 1
Howard, Susan: Birth, Jan 28
Howard, Traylor: Birth, June 14
Howard, Trevor: Birth Anniv, Sept 29
Howdy Doody TV Premiere: Anniv, Dec 27
Howe, Elias: Birth Anniv, July 9
Howe, Gordie: Birth, Mar 31
Howell, C. Thomas: Birth, Dec 7
Howes, Sally Ann: Birth, July 20
Hu, Kelly: Birth, Feb 13
Hubbard, Elbert: Birth Anniv, June 19
Hubbard, L. Ron: Birth Anniv, Mar 13
Hubble Space Telescope Deployed: Space Milestone, Apr 25
Hubble, Edwin Powell: Birth Anniv, Nov 20
Huckabee, Mike: Birth, Aug 24
Huckfinn Jubilee (Victorville, CA), June 15
Hudson, Ernie: Birth, Dec 17
Hudson, Kate: Birth, Apr 19
Huerta, Dolores: Birth, Apr 10
Huff 'n Puff Hot Air Balloon Rally (Topeka, KS), Sept 7
Hug a GI Day, Mar 4
Hug a Prom Sponsor Day, Apr 27
Hug a Texas Chef Month, Sept 1
Hug An Australian Day, Apr 26
Hug Holiday Week, Natl, June 3
Hug Your Cat Day, May 15
Hug Your Newsman Day, Natl, Apr 7
Hug-A-Week for the Hearing Impaired, Dec 1
Hugging Day, Natl, Jan 21
Hughes, Barnard: Birth, July 16
Hughes, Charles E.: Birth Anniv, Apr 11
Hughes, Finola: Birth, Oct 29
Hughes, Howard: Birth Anniv, Dec 24
Hughes, John: Birth, Feb 18
Hughes, Langston: Birth Anniv, Feb 1
Hugo, Victor: Birth Anniv, Feb 26
Hula Bowl, Game (Maui, HI), Jan 20
Hulce, Thomas: Birth, Dec 6
Hull House Opens: Anniv, Sept 18
Hull, Bobby: Birth, Jan 3
Hull, Brett: Birth, Aug 9
Hull, Cordell: Birth Anniv, Oct 2
Hull, Jane Dee: Birth, Aug 8
Hull, John: First Mint in America: Anniv, June 10
Human Relations
  Africare Walker Memorial Dinner (Washington, DC), Oct 18
  Amateur Radio Month, Intl, Apr 1
  American Red Cross: Founding Anniv, May 21
  Amnesty International Founded: Anniv, May 28
  Be an Angel Day, Aug 22
  Be Kind to Humankind Week, Aug 25
  Black History Month, Feb 1
  Blame Someone Else Day, Apr 13
  Brotherhood/Sisterhood Week, Feb 19
  Celebration of Love Week, Feb 11
  Day of Prayer and Action for Human Habitat, Intl, Sept 16
  Diversity Awareness Month, Oct 1
  Dump Your "Significant Jerk" Day, Feb 6
  Emancipation Proclamation: Anniv, Sept 22
  Etiquette Week, Natl, May 14
  FamilyCares Week, Nov 11
  First Natl Convention for Blacks: Anniv, Sept 15
  First US Breach of Promise Suit: Anniv, June 14
  Flirting Week, Intl, Feb 12
  Forgiveness Week, Natl, June 17
  Fourteen Points Proposed: Anniv, Jan 8
  Freedom Day, Natl (Pres Proc), Feb 1
  Freedom Week, July 4
  Friendship Week, Intl, Feb 18
  Good Neighbor Day, Natl, Sept 23
  Good Samaritan Involvement Day, Mar 13
  Goodwill Embassy Tour (Washington), May 12
  Great American Warm-Up, Nov 2
  Help Someone See Week Observance (Rockford, OH), Mar 4
  Honesty Day, Natl, Apr 30
  Hug Holiday Week, Natl, June 3
  Human Rights Day (Pres Proc), Dec 10
  Human Rights Day (UN), Dec 10
  Human Rights Month, Universal, Dec 1
  Human Rights Week (Pres Proc), Dec 10

Join Hands Day, June 16
Joygerm Day, Natl, Jan 8
Kiss-and-Make-Up-Day, Aug 25
Language Week, Intl, Dec 15
League of Nations: Anniv, Jan 10
Lost Penny Day, Feb 12
Love a Mensch Week, Sept 17
Loving v Virginia: Anniv, June 12
Lumpy Rug Day, May 3
Meet a Mate Week, June 11
Pay-a-Compliment Day, Feb 6
Peace Corps Founded: Anniv, Mar 1
Peace, Friendship and Good Will Week, Oct 25
Peace, UN Intl Day of, Sept 18
Pen-Friends Week Intl, May 1
Poverty, Intl Day for Eradication, Oct 17
Race Relations Day, Feb 14
Race Unity Day, June 10
Ralph Bunche Awarded Nobel Peace Prize: Anniv, Dec 10
Random Acts of Kindness Week, Nov 11
Red Cross Day, World, May 8
Relationship Renewal Day, May 4
Religion Day, World, Jan 21
Religious Freedom Week, Sept 22
Remembrance Day, Apr 14
Saint Louis Race Riots: Anniv, July 2
Salvation Army Founder's Day, Apr 10
Salvation Army in US: Anniv, Mar 10
Smile Week, Natl, Aug 6
Spring Fever Week, Natl, Mar 19
Stop the Violence Day, Natl, Nov 22
Swap Ideas Day, Sept 10
Thank You Days, Intl, Jan 11
UN Decade for Eradication of Poverty, Jan 1
UN Decade for Human Rights Education, Jan 1
Universal Family Week, May 9
Universal Hour of Peace, Jan 1
Universal Human Beings Week, Mar 1
Volunteer Week, Natl, Apr 22
Volunteers Week, Intl, June 1
World Day of Prayer, Mar 2
World Hello Day, Nov 21
Human Resource Week, Mar 5
Humane Education Awareness Month, Natl, Mar 1
Humanitarian Day, Jan 15
Humbug Day, Dec 21
Hummel, Sister Maria Innocentia: Birth Anniv, May 21
Humor, Comedy
  A'phabet Day, Dec 25
  Alascattalo Day (Anchorage, AK), Nov 18
  Daffynitions Month, Intl, Apr 1
  Destiny Day, Oct 12
  Gaines, William M.: Birth Anniv, Mar 1
  Holy Humor Month, Apr 1
  Humor and Stress Management Annual Intl Workshop (Raquette Lake, NY), July 22
  Humor Month, Natl, Apr 1
  Humorists Are Artists Month (HAAM), Mar 1
  Joke Day, Intl, July 1
  Kurtzman, Harvey (Mad Magazine): Birth Anniv, Oct 3
  Love May Make World Go Round but Laughter Keeps Us from Getting Dizzy Week, Feb 7
  Moment of Laughter Day, Apr 14
  O. Henry Pun-Off (Austin, TX), May 6
  Positive Power/Humor/Creativity Conf (Saratoga Spgs, NY), Mar 30
  Someday We'll Laugh About This Week, Jan 7
  Twit Award Month, Intl, Apr 1
Humperdinck, Engelbert: Birth, May 3
Humphrey, Hubert: Birth Anniv, May 27
Humphries, Barry: Birth, Feb 17
Hungary
  Anniv of 1956 Revolution, Oct 23
  Anniversary of the 1848 Revolution, Mar 15
  Hungary Declared Independent: Anniv, Oct 23
  St. Stephen's Day, Aug 20
Hungerford, Margaret Wolf: Duchess Who Wasn't Day, Aug 27
Hunnicutt, Gayle: Birth, Feb 6
Hunt, Bonnie: Birth, Sept 22
Hunt, Helen: Birth, June 15
Hunt, James B.: Birth, May 16
Hunt, Lamar: Birth, Aug 2
Hunt, Linda: Birth, Apr 2
Hunt, Nelson Bunker: Birth, Feb 22
Hunter's Moon, Nov 1
Hunter's Moon, Feast of (Lafayette, IN), Oct 13
Hunter, Catfish: Birth Anniv, Apr 8
Hunter, David: Hunter Frees the Slaves: Anniv, May 9
Hunter, Holly: Birth, Mar 20
Hunter, Kim: Birth, Nov 12

Hunter, Rachel: Birth, Sept 9
Hunter, Tab: Birth, July 11
Hunter-Gault, Charlayne: Birth, Feb 27
Hunting and Fishing Day, Natl (Pres Proc), Sept 22
Hunting: Cheltenham Hunt Fest (Prestbury, England), Mar 13
Huntington, Samuel: Birth Anniv, July 3
Huppert, Isabelle: Birth, Mar 16
Hurley, Elizabeth: Birth, June 10
Hurricanes, Tornados, Cyclones, Typhoons
  Atlantic, Caribbean and Gulf Hurricane Season, June 1
  Bayou Hurricane: Anniv, Oct 1
  Central Pacific Hurricane Season, June 1
  Eastern Pacific Hurricane Season, May 15
  Galveston, TX: Anniv, Sept 8
  Hurricane Agnes: Anniv, June 21
  Hurricane Hugo Hits American Coast: Anniv, Sept 21
  Hurricane Mitch: Anniv, Oct 27
  Hurricane Supplication Day (Virgin Islands), July 23
  Hurricane Thanksgiving Day (Virgin Islands), Oct 15
  Port Royal (Jamaica) Hurricane: Anniv, Aug 28
  Southern Cyclone: Anniv, Aug 24
  Texas Panhandle Tornado: Anniv, Apr 9
  Western Pacific Hurricane Season, Jan 1
Hurt, John: Birth, Jan 22
Hurt, Mary Beth: Birth, Sept 26
Hurt, William: Birth, Mar 20
Hus, John: Commemoration Day (Czech), July 6
Husky, Ferlin: Birth, Dec 3
Hussein, Saddam: Birth, Apr 28
Hussein: King of Jordan, Birth Anniv, Nov 14
Hussey, Olivia: Birth, Apr 17
Hustlerfest (Juneau County, WI), Aug 24
Huston, Anjelica: Birth, July 8
HutchFest (Hutchinson, KS), June 28
Hutchins, Robert Maynard: Birth Anniv, Jan 17
Hutchinson, Tim: Birth, Aug 11
Hutchison, Kay Bailey: Birth, July 22
Hutin, Mme Francisquy: Ballet Introduced to the US: Anniv, Feb 7
Hutton, Betty: Birth, Feb 26
Hutton, Lauren: Birth, Nov 17
Hutton, Timothy: Birth, Aug 16
Huxley, Aldous: Birth Anniv, July 26
Huygens, Christiaan: Birth Anniv, Apr 14
Hynde, Chrissie: Birth, Sept 7
Hypnosis: Health and Happiness with Hypnosis Day, July 24
I Am in Control Day: Anniv, Mar 30
I Forgot Day, July 2
I Hate Financial Planning Week, Feb 3
I Love Lucy TV Premiere: Anniv, Oct 15
I Spy TV Premiere: Anniv, Sept 15
I Want You to Be Happy Day, Mar 3
I've Got a Secret TV Premiere: Anniv, June 19
Iacocca, Lee: Birth, Oct 15
IBM PC Introduced: Anniv, Apr 24
Ibsen, Henrik: Birth Anniv, Mar 20
Ice Break-up: Nenana Tripod Raising Fest (Nenana, AK), Mar 3
Ice Cream Cone: Birth, Sept 22
Ice Cream Day, Natl, July 15
Ice Cream Days (Le Mars, IA), July 3
Ice Cream Fest, Old-Fashioned (Utica, OH), May 26
Ice Cream Fest, Old-Fashioned (Wilmington, DE), July 7
Ice Cream Social (Indianapolis, IN), July 4
Ice Fest (Ligonier, PA), Jan 27
Ice T: Birth, Feb 16
Icebox Days XXI (International Falls, MN), Jan 18
Iced Tea Month, Natl, June 1
Iceland
  Beer Day, Mar 1
  Bun Day, Feb 26
  Bursting Day, Feb 27
  First Day of Summer, Apr 19
  Independence Day, June 17
  Laki Volcano Eruption: Anniv, June 8
  Leif Erikson Day, Oct 9
  Shop and Office Workers' Holiday, Aug 6
  University Students' Celebration, Dec 1
Iceworm Fest, Cordova (Cordova, AK), Feb 2
Idaho
  Admission Day, July 3
  Boise River Fest (Boise), June 21
  Coeur d'Alene Tribal Pilgrimage (Cataldo), Aug 15
  Dickens Christmas Festival (Kellogg), Dec 8
  Dogwood Fest (Lewiston), Apr 20
  Eastern Idaho State Fair (Blackfoot), Sept 1
  First Security Boulder Mountain Tour (Sun Valley), Feb 3

Louisiana
Admission Day, **Apr 30**
American Speech-Lang-Hearing Assn Conv (New Orleans), **Nov 15**
ARC (Assn Retarded Citizens) Convention (New Orleans), **Oct 18**
Bayou Hurricane: Anniv, **Oct 1**
Black Heritage Parade (Monroe), **Feb 24**
Breaux Bridge Crawfish Fest (Breaux Bridge), **May 4**
Butler Issues "Woman Order": Anniv, **May 16**
Celebration on the Cane (Natchitoches), **July 4**
Christmas Fest (Natchitoches), **Dec 1**
Christmas in Roseland (Shreveport), **Nov 23**
Christmas Lights (City of Lights, Natchitoches), **Nov 20**
Christmas-New Orleans Style (New Orleans), **Dec 1**
College Stores Mtg/Expo, Natl Assn of (New Orleans), **Apr 5**
Contraband Days (Lake Charles), **May 1**
Dietary Managers Assn Mtg/Expo (New Orleans), **July 22**
Farragut Captures New Orleans: Anniv, **Apr 25**
First Bloom Fest (Shreveport), **Apr 28**
Folklife Fest (Monroe), **Sept 8**
French Quarter Fest (New Orleans), **Apr 20**
Gumbo Fest (Bridge City), **Oct 12**
Holiday in Dixie (Shreveport and Bossier City), **Apr 20**
Huey P. Long Day, **Aug 30**
Longhorn World Chmpshp Rodeo (Bossier), **Mar 30**
Louisiana Native & Contemporary Crafts Fest (Lafayette), **Sept 15**
Louisiana Passion Play (Ruston), **Sept 7**
Louisiana Purchase Day, **Dec 20**
Lousiana Sportsmen's Show (New Orleans), **Mar 7**
Marksville Easter Egg Knocking Contest (Marksville), **Apr 15**
Melrose Plantation Arts/Crafts Fest (Melrose), **June 9**
Miss Louisiana Pageant (Monroe), **June 14**
Mudbug Madness (Shreveport), **May 24**
Natchitoches Jazz Fest (Natchitoches), **Apr 7**
Natchitoches Pilgrimage (Natchitoches), **Oct 12**
Natchitoches/NW State U Folk Fest (Natchitoches), **July 20**
New Orleans Boat Show (New Orleans), **Feb 8**
New Orleans Jazz/Heritage Fest (New Orleans), **Apr 27**
Nokia Sugar Bowl Classic (New Orleans), **Jan 2**
Office Olympics (Shreveport), **Sept 21**
Peach Fest, Louisiana (Ruston), **June 8**
Red River Quilters Quiltfest (Bossier), **May 4**
Saint Patrick's Day Parade (Baton Rouge), **Mar 17**
Shrimp and Petroleum Fest, Louisiana (Morgan City), **Aug 30**
St. Louise de Marillac Louisiana Bar-B-Q Fest (Arabi), **May 18**
Twin Cities Krewe Mardi Gras Parade (Monroe), **Feb 17**
Veterans Day Celebration (Mamou), **Nov 11**
Lousma, Jack: Birth, **Feb 29**
Lovable Lawyers Day, Oct 8
Love a Mensch Week, Sept 17
Love Boat TV Premiere: Anniv, **Sept 24**
Love Is a Many Splendored Thing TV Premiere: Anniv, Sept 18
Love May Make World Go Round but Laughter Keeps Us from Getting Dizzy, Feb 7
Love of Life TV Premiere: Anniv, **Sept 24**
Love the Children Day, Mar 29
Love Week, Celebration of, Feb 11
Love Yourself Month, Jan 1
Love, Courtney: Birth, **July 9**
Love, Davis, III: Birth, **Apr 13**
Love, Mike: Birth, **Mar 15**
Lovecraft, H.P.: Birth Anniv, **Aug 20**
Lovejoy, Elijah P.: Birth Anniv, **Nov 9**
Loveladies Fair, Our (Loveladies, NJ), **June 8**
Lovell, James: Birth, **Mar 25**
Lover's Day, Book Day and (Spain), **Apr 23**
Lover's Fair (Belgium), **Dec 6**
Lovera, Juan: Birth Anniv, **Dec 26**
Lovett, Lyle: Birth, **Nov 1**
Loving TV Premiere: Anniv, **June 27**
Lovitz, Jon: Birth, **July 21**
Low, Juliet: Birth Anniv, **Oct 31**
Lowe, Chad: Birth, **Jan 15**
Lowe, Rob: Birth, **Mar 17**
Lowell, Amy: Birth Anniv, **Feb 9**
Lowell, Carey: Birth, **Feb 11**
Lowell, James R.: Birth Anniv, **Feb 22**
Lowell, Percival: Birth Anniv, **Mar 13**
Loy, Myrna: Birth Anniv, **Aug 2**
Loyalty Day (Pres Proc), May 1

Loyalty Days/Seafair Fest (Newport, OR), **May 3**
Lucas, George: Birth, **May 14**
Lucci, Susan: Birth, **Dec 23**
Luce, Clare Boothe: Birth Anniv, **Mar 10**
Luce, Henry: Birth Anniv, **Apr 3**
Lucid, Shannon: Birth, **Jan 14**
Luck: Make Your Own Luck Day, Aug 26
Luckinbill, Laurence: Birth, **Nov 21**
Ludendorff, Erick: Birth Anniv, **Apr 9**
Ludington Harbor Fest (Ludington, MI), **June 14**
Ludlum, Robert: Birth, **May 25**
Luft, Lorna: Birth, **Nov 21**
Lugar, Richard G.: Birth, **Apr 4**
Lughnasadh, Aug 1
Lugosi, Bela: Birth Anniv, **Oct 20**
Lully, Jean Baptiste: Birth Anniv, **Nov 28**
Lumet, Sidney: Birth, **June 25**
Lumpy Rug Day, May 3
Lumumba, Patrice: Death Anniv, **Jan 17**
Lunden, Joan: Birth, **Sept 19**
Lundgren, Dolph: Birth, **Nov 3**
Luner, Jaime: Birth, **May 12**
Lung Assn, American: Christmas Seal Campaign, Sept 1
Lung Cancer Awareness Month, Nov 1
Lunsford, Bascom Lamar: Birth Anniv, **Mar 21**
Lupercalia, Feb 15
LuPone, Patti: Birth, **Apr 21**
Lupus Alert Day, Apr 1
Lupus Awareness Month, Oct 1
Lusitania Sinking: Anniv, May 7
Lutali, A.P.: Birth, **Dec 24**
Luther, Martin: Birth Anniv, **Nov 10**
Lux Video Theatre TV Premiere: Anniv, **Oct 2**
Luxembourg
Beer Fest, **July 15**
Blessing of the Wine (Greiveldange), **Dec 26**
Bretzelsonndeg (Pretzel Sunday), **Mar 25**
Burgsonndeg, **Feb 12**
Candlemas, **Feb 2**
Emaishen, **Apr 16**
Ettelbruck Remembrance Day, **July 6**
Liberation Ceremony, **Sept 9**
National Holiday, **June 23**
Osweiler, **Mar 27**
Our Lady of Girsterklaus Procession, **Aug 19**
Schuebermess (Shepherd's Fair), **Aug 19**
Lydon, Johnny (Rotten): Birth, **Jan 31**
Lyman, Dorothy: Birth, **Apr 18**
Lynch, David: Birth, **Jan 20**
Lynch, Kelly: Birth, **Jan 31**
Lynch, Thomas: Birth Anniv, **Aug 5**
Lynley, Carol: Birth, **Feb 13**
Lynn, Jonathan: Birth, **Apr 3**
Lynn, Loretta: Birth, **Apr 14**
Lyon, Mary: Birth Anniv, **Feb 28**
Lyon, Sue: Birth, **July 10**
M Squad TV Premiere: Anniv, **Sept 20**
M*A*S*H TV Premiere: Anniv, **Sept 17**
M*A*S*H: Final Episode: Anniv, **Feb 28**
Ma, Yo-Yo: Birth, **Oct 7**
Maass, Clara: Birth Anniv, **June 28**
Mabon, Sept 22
MacArthur Returns: US Landing on Leyte, Philippines: Anniv, **Oct 20**
MacArthur, Douglas: Birth Anniv, **Jan 26**
MacArthur, James: Birth, **Dec 8**
Macau:Macau Day, **June 24**
Macau: Reverts to Chinese Control: Anniv, **Dec 20**
Macaulay, Thomas B.: Birth Anniv, **Oct 25**
Maccabiah Games, World (Israel), **July 16**
Macchio, Ralph: Birth, **Nov 4**
MacCorkindale, Simon: Birth, **Feb 2**
MacDonald, Anne Thompson: Death Anniv, **Oct 12**
MacDonald, John A.: Birth Anniv, **Jan 11**
MacDonald, Norm: Birth, **Dec 25**
MacDowell, Andie: Birth, **Apr 21**
MacDowell, Edward Alexander: Birth Anniv, **Dec 18**
Macedonia, Former Yugoslav Republic of: National Day, **Aug 2**
Macedonian Uprising: St. Elias Day, **Aug 2**
MacFadden, Bernarr: Birth Anniv, **Aug 16**
MacGraw, Ali: Birth, **Apr 1**
Machias Wild Blueberry Fest (Machias, ME), **Aug 17**
Machiavelli, Niccolo: Birth Anniv, **May 3**
MacInnis, Al: Birth, **July 11**
Macintosh Debuts: Anniv, Jan 25
Mack, Connie: Birth, **Oct 29**
MacKenzie, Alexander: Birth Anniv, **Jan 28**
Mackenzie, Gisele: Birth, **Jan 10**
Mackie, Bob: Birth, **Mar 24**
Mackinac Bridge Walk (St. Ignace, MI), **Sept 3**
MacLachlan, Kyle: Birth, **Feb 22**

MacLaine, Shirley: Birth, **Apr 24**
MacLeish, Archibald: Birth Anniv, **May 7**
MacLeish, Rod: Birth, **Jan 15**
MacMurray, Fred: Birth Anniv, **Aug 30**
MacNeil, Robert: Birth, **Jan 19**
MacNeil-Lehrer Newshour TV Premiere: Anniv, **Sept 5**
MacNelly, Jeff: Birth Anniv, **Sept 17**
MacNicol, Peter: Birth, **Apr 10**
Macpherson, Elle: Birth, **Mar 29**
MacRae, Sheila: Birth, **Sept 24**
Macy, William H.: Birth, **Mar 13**
Mad Magazine: Kurtzman, Harvey: Birth Anniv, **Oct 3**
Madagascar
Commemoration Day, **Mar 29**
Independence Day, **June 26**
MADD: Tie One on for Safety, **Nov 22**
Madden, John: Birth, **Apr 10**
Maddux, Greg: Birth, **Apr 14**
Madigan, Amy: Birth, **Sept 11**
Madison, Dolly: Birth Anniv, **May 20**
Madison, James: Birth Anniv, **Mar 16**
Madonna: Birth, **Aug 16**
Madsen, Michael: Birth, **Sept 25**
Madsen, Virginia: Birth, **Sept 11**
Magazine, First Published in America: Anniv, **Feb 13**
Magellan, Ferdinand: Death Anniv, **Apr 27**
Magic Day, Natl, Oct 31
Magic Get-Together, Abbott's (Colon, MI), **Aug 1**
Magna Carta Day, June 15
Magnolia Blossom Fest (Magnolia, AR), **May 17**
Magnum, PI TV Premiere: Anniv, **Dec 11**
Magnuson, Ann: Birth, **Jan 4**
Maguire, Tobey: Birth, **June 27**
Maher, Bill: Birth, **Jan 20**
Mahoney: John: Birth, **June 20**
Maifest (Covington, KY), **May 18**
Mail-Order Catalog: Anniv, Aug 18
Mail: Pony Express, Inauguration of: Anniv, Apr 3
Mail: V-Mail Delivery: Anniv, June 22
Mail: World Post Day (UN), Oct 9
Mailer, Norman: Birth, **Jan 31**
Mailorder Gardening Month, Natl, Jan 1
Maiman, Theodore: Birth, **July 11**
Maine
Acadia Natl Park Established: Anniv, **Jan 1**
Acton Fair (Acton), **Aug 23**
Admission Day, **Mar 15**
Blue Hill Fair (Blue Hill), **Aug 30**
Chester Greenwood Day Parade (Farmington), **Dec 1**
Common Ground Country Fair (Unity), **Sept 21**
Eastport "Old Home Week" Celebration (Eastport), **July 1**
Fryeburg Fair (Fryeburg), **Sept 30**
International Fest (Calais, ME/St. Stephen, NB, Canada), **Aug 5**
Kenduskeag Stream Canoe Race (Bangor), **Apr 21**
Log Driver's Weekend (Houlton), **Mar 2**
Machias Wild Blueberry Fest (Machias), **Aug 17**
Maine Fest of the Arts (Brunswick), **Aug 3**
Maine Highland Games (Brunswick), **Aug 18**
Maine Law: Anniv, **June 2**
Maine Lobster Fest (Rockland), **Aug 1**
Maine Potato Blossom Fest (Fort Fairfield), **July 14**
Moose Stompers Weekend (Houlton), **Feb 2**
Patriot's Day, **Apr 16**
Potato Feast Days (Houlton), **Sept 14**
Schooner Days (Rockland), **July 13**
Skowhegan State Fair (Skowhegan), **Aug 9**
Sundays in the Garden (South Berwick), **July 1**
Thomas Point Beach Bluegrass Fest (Brunswick), **Aug 30**
Windjammer Days (Boothbay Harbor), **June 26**
Yarmouth Clam Fest (Yarmouth), **July 20**
Majerle, Dan: Birth, **Sept 9**
Major, John: Birth, **Mar 29**
Majors, Lee: Birth, **Apr 23**
Make a Difference Day, Oct 27
Make a Will Month, Natl, Oct 1
Make Room for Daddy TV Premiere: Anniv, **Sept 29**
Make Up Your Mind Day, Dec 31
Make Up Your Own Holiday Day, Mar 26
Make Your Own Luck Day, Aug 26
Makeba, Miriam: Birth, **Mar 4**
Makepeace, Chris: Birth, **Apr 22**
Malawi
Martyr's Day, **Mar 3**
Republic Day, **July 6**
Malaysia: National Day, Aug 31
Malcolm X: Assassination Anniv, Feb 21
Malcolm X: Birth Anniv, May 19

☆ *Chase's 2001 Calendar of Events* ☆   Index

Braham Pie Day (Braham), **Aug 3**
Buffalo Days Celebration (Luverne), **June 1**
Calithumpian Parade (Biwabik), **July 4**
Catfish Days (East Grand Forks), **Aug 10**
Christmas at Pioneer Village (Worthington), **Dec 6**
Christmas Epiphany Celebration (Bradford), **Jan 7**
Defeat of Jesse James Days (Northfield), **Sept 6**
Eagle Creek Rendezvous (Shakopee), **May 26**
Edmund Fitzgerald Beacon Lighting (Two Harbors), **Nov 10**
Farm Toy Show & Auction (Sauk Centre), **Feb 10**
Fest of Adventures (Aitkin), **Sept 15**
Fest of Nations (St. Paul), **May 3**
Fish House Parade (Aitkin), **Nov 23**
Fishing Has No Boundaries (Bemidji), **June 23**
Folkways of the Holidays (Shakopee), **Nov 23**
Giants Ridge Mountain Bike Fest (Biwabik), **Aug 25**
Halloween Trail (Worthington), **Oct 31**
Heritagefest (New Ulm), **July 13**
Hot Dog Night (Luverne), **July 12**
Icebox Days XXI (International Falls), **Jan 18**
Judy Garland Fest (Grand Rapids), **June 21**
Kanabec Fall Fest (Mora), **Sept 15**
King Turkey Days (Worthington), **Sept 15**
Laura Ingalls Wilder Pageant, **July 13**
Little Arts/Crafts (Little Falls), **Sept 8**
Minnesota Renaissance Fest (Shakopee), **Aug 18**
Muskies Inc Muskie Tourn, Intl (North Central), **Sept 7**
NCAA Div I Men's Basketball Chmpshp (Minneapolis), **Mar 31**
Nobel Conference (St. Peter), **Oct 2**
Norsefest (Madison), **Nov 9**
Norwegian Christmas (Brooklyn Park), **Dec 1**
Oktoberfest (New Ulm, MN), **Oct 5**
Old Time German Social (Bradford), **June 24**
Old Time School (Cambridge), **June 11**
Old West Extravaganza (Shakopee), **June 16**
Old-Fashioned Fourth of July (Worthington), **July 1**
Paul Bunyan Sled Dog Races, Weight Pull/Mutt Races (Bemidji), **Jan 20**
Red Wing Sheep Dog Trial (Red Wing), **Oct 12**
Rochesterfest (Rochester), **June 16**
Saint Paul Winter Carnival (St. Paul), **Jan 26**
Santaland (Madison), **Nov 23**
Sinclair Lewis Days (Sauk Centre), **July 18**
Song of Hiawatha Pageant (Pipestone), **July 20**
Spam Town USA Fest (Austin), **July 4**
State Fair (St. Paul), **Aug 23**
Swedish Language and Culture Day Camp (Cambridge), **Aug 27**
Take a Kid Fishing Weekend (St. Paul), **June 9**
Tall Timbers Days Fest (Grand Rapids), **Aug 4**
Tetonkaha Rendezvous (Lake Benton), **Aug 10**
Trail of Terror (Shakopee), **Oct 11**
Tri-State Band Fest (Luverne), **Sept 29**
Uptown Art Fair (Minneapolis), **Aug 3**
Victorian Fair (Winona), **Sept 15**
Viola Gopher Count (Viola), **June 21**
Voyageurs Natl Park Established: Anniv, **Apr 8**
Watermelon Day (Vining), **Aug 18**
Weihnachtsfest (Biwabik), **Dec 1**
White Oak Rendezvous (Deer River), **Aug 4**
Winterfest (Luverne), **Dec 1**
Woodcraft Fest (Grand Rapids), **July 21**
Minority Cancer Awareness Week, Natl, Apr 12
Minority Enterprise Development Week (Pres Proc), Oct 7
Minow, Newton: Birth, Jan 17
Minow, Newton: Vast Wasteland Speech: Anniv, May 9
Mint Fest (St. Johns, MI), Aug 10
Mint, US: Anniv, Apr 2
Miou-Miou: Birth, Feb 22
Miranda Decision: Anniv, June 13
Mirren, Helen: Birth, July 26
Mirror of the World Translation: Anniv, Caxton's, Mar 8
Mirth Month, Intl, Mar 1
Mischief Night, Nov 4
Miss America Pageant, First: Anniv, Sept 8
Missile, First Surface-to-Surface Missile: Anniv, Dec 24
Missing Children's Day, Natl, May 25
Mission: Impossible TV Premiere: Anniv, Sept 17
Mission Delores Founding: Anniv, Oct 9
Mission San Antonio de Padua: Anniv, July 14
Mission San Diego de Alcala: Founding Anniv, July 16
Mission San Gabriel Archangel: Founding Anniv, Sept 8
Mission San Juan Capistrano: Founding Anniv, Nov 1
Mission San Luis Obispo de Tolosa: Founding Anniv, Sept 1

Mission San Luis Rey de Francia Founding: Anniv, June 13
Mission Santa Barbara: Anniv, Dec 4
Mission Santa Clara de Asis: Anniv, Jan 12
Missionary Fair, Road Church (Stonington, CT), May 19
Missisinewa 1812 (Marion, IN), Oct 12
Mississippi
  Admission Day, **Dec 10**
  Battle of Champion's Hill: Anniv, **May 16**
  Broiler Fest, Mississippi (Forest), **June 2**
  Children's Victorian Christmas Celeb (Washington), **Dec 8**
  Chimneyville Crafts Fest (Jackson), **Nov 30**
  Choctaw Indian Fair (Philadelphia), **July 11**
  Civil Rights Workers Found Slain: Anniv, **Aug 4**
  Confederate Memorial Day, **Apr 30**
  Copper Magnolia Fest (Washington), **Sept 22**
  Ghost Tales Around the Campfire (Washington), **Oct 26**
  Gum Tree Fest (Tupelo), **May 12**
  Lighted Boat Parade on the Tenn-Tom Waterway (Columbus), **Dec 1**
  Meredith (James) Enrolls at Ole Miss: Anniv, **Sept 30**
  Mississippi Deep Sea Fishing Tournament Rodeo (Gulfport), **July 4**
  Natchez Powwow (Natchez), **Mar 24**
  Neshoba County Fair (Philadelphia), **July 20**
  Pioneer and Indian Fest (Ridgeland), **Oct 27**
  Pioneer Days (Washington), **Oct 24**
  Pioneer Week (Washington), **June 25**
  Siege of Vicksburg: Anniv, **June 28**
  State Fair (Jackson), **Oct 3**
  Vicksburg Surrenders: Anniv, **July 3**
Missouri
  Adelphian Club Christmas Bazaar (Kennett), **Dec 1**
  Admission Day, **Aug 10**
  Albrecht-Kemper Valentine Dinner (St. Joseph), **Feb 10**
  Antique & Collectibles Flea Market (Weston), **Apr 28**
  Antique Show & Sale (Weston), **Mar 3**
  Apple Butter Makin' Days (Mt Vernon), **Oct 12**
  Applefest (Weston), **Oct 6**
  Arrow Rock Antique Show & Sale (Arrow Rock), **May 19**
  Arrow Rock Heritage Craft Fest (Arrow Rock), **Oct 13**
  Art Fair & Winefest (Washington), **May 18**
  Arts & Crafts Fest (Rolla), **Oct 6**
  Autumn Historic Folklife Fest (Hannibal), **Oct 20**
  Benton Neighbor Day (Benton), **Aug 31**
  Bess Truman Day Lecture (Independence), **Feb 13**
  Big 12 Men's Basketball Chmpshp (Kansas City), **Mar 8**
  Big 12 Women's Basketball Tourn (Kansas City), **Mar 6**
  Big Muddy Folk Music Fest (Boonville), **Apr 6**
  Black Walnut Fest (Stockton), **Sept 26**
  Blueberry Hill Open Dart Tourn (St. Louis), **Apr 27**
  Boonslick Folk Fest (Arrow Rock), **Sept 8**
  Branson Fest (Branson), **Apr 4**
  Cars in the Park (Dexter), **June 9**
  Carver Day Commemorative Celebration (Diamond), **July 21**
  Championship BBQ Cookoff (Kennett), **June 29**
  Christmas Traditions (St. Charles), **Nov 23**
  Coal Miner Days (Novinger), **May 27**
  Cow Milked While Flying: Anniv, **Feb 18**
  Dam Experience (Warsaw), **June 30**
  Deutsch Country Days (Marthasville), **Oct 20**
  Diamond GEM City Days and Prairie Day (Diamond), **Sept 7**
  Dogwood Festival (Camdenton), **Apr 27**
  Dred Scott Decision: Anniv (St. Louis), **Mar 4**
  Earth Day Community Fest (St. Louis), **Apr 21**
  Earthquakes: Anniv, **Dec 6**
  Eldon Turkey Fest (Eldon), **Oct 13**
  Elvis Presley Remembered (St. Louis), **Aug 11**
  Emmett Kelly Clown Fest (Houston), **May 4**
  Fall Fest of the Arts and Crafts (Washington), **Sept 29**
  Farmington Country Days (Farmington), **June 1**
  Fest of the Little Hills (St. Charles), **Aug 17**
  Firefall (Springfield), **June 30**
  Garden Expo (St. Louis), **Apr 21**
  Good Neighbor Award Presentation (Independence), **May 8**
  Gospel Sing (Arrow Rock), **May 6**
  Great Mississippi Riv Arts/Crafts Fest (Hannibal), **May 26**
  Groundhog Run (Kansas City), **Feb 4**
  Handel's Messiah (Independence), **Nov 17**
  Hanging of the Greens (Arrow Rock), **Nov 24**

  Harry S Truman Award for Public Service (Independence), **May 4**
  Hartville Annual Fall Fest (Hartville), **Oct 20**
  Heritage Day (Houston), **Sept 29**
  Japanese Fest (St. Louis), **Sept 1**
  Jours de Fete (Ste. Genevieve), **Aug 11**
  July 4th Celebration (Weston), **July 4**
  Kahoka Fest of Bluegrass Music (Kahoka), **Aug 17**
  Kansas City Blues and Jazz Fest (Kansas City), **July 20**
  KGBX Typewriter Toss (Springfield), **Apr 25**
  KRXL Car Cruise (Kirksville), **Aug 4**
  Land of Mark Twain Bluegrass Music Fest (Hannibal), **Nov 16**
  Lewis and Clark Rendezvous (St. Charles), **May 19**
  Liberty Fall Fest (Liberty), **Sept 21**
  Light Up the Sky—Fourth of July (St. Charles), **July 4**
  Magic Woods (Kansas City), **Oct 12**
  Maple Leaf Fest (Carthage), **Oct 16**
  Mayor's Christmas Tree (Kansas City), **Nov 23**
  Meramec Community Fair (Sullivan), **June 28**
  Midwinter Bluegrass Fest (Hannibal), **Feb 16**
  Milestones: A Miles Davis Retrospective (St. Louis), **May 1**
  Minority Scientists Showcase (St. Louis), **Jan 13**
  Missouri Day, **Oct 17**
  Missouri Day Fest (Trenton), **Oct 20**
  Missouri River Fest of Arts (Boonville), **Aug 9**
  Missouri State Chmpshp Racking Horse Show (Dexter), **June 2**
  Missouri Valley Conference Basketball Tournament (St. Louis), **Mar 2**
  Monett Old-Fashioned Fourth of July (Monett), **July 4**
  NAIA Men's Div II Basketball Chmpshp (Branson), **Mar 7**
  NCAA Div I Women's Basketball Chmpshp Finals (St. Louis), **Mar 30**
  North Central Missouri Fair (Trenton), **Aug 1**
  Northeast Missouri Triathlon Chmpshp (Kirksville), **Sept 9**
  Oktoberfest (Monett), **Oct 27**
  Oktoberfest (St. Charles), **Oct 6**
  Old Glory Jubilee (Elsberry), **July 4**
  Orchid Show (St. Louis), **Jan 27**
  Ozark Empire Fair (Springfield), **July 27**
  Ozark Ham and Turkey Festival (California), **Sept 15**
  Ozark Mountain Christmas (Branson), **Nov 1**
  Plaza Lights (Kansas City), **Nov 22**
  Presidential Wreath Laying (Independence), **May 8**
  Richmond's Mushroom Fest (Richmond), **May 5**
  Route 66 Summerfest (Rolla), **July 14**
  Saint Francis River Powwow (Park Hills), **Sept 14**
  Saint Louis Race Riots: Anniv, **July 2**
  Saint Louis Variety Club Telethon (St. Louis), **Apr 21**
  Saint Louis Walk of Fame Induction (St. Louis), **May 20**
  Saint Piran's Day Celeb (Kansas City), **Mar 3**
  Santa-Cali-Gon-Days Fest (Independence), **Aug 31**
  Show Me State Games (Columbia), **July 20**
  Southeast Missouri District Fair (Cape Girardeau), **Sept 9**
  Southside Fall Fest (St. Joseph), **Sept 14**
  State Fair (Sedalia), **Aug 9**
  Strawberry Fest (Independence), **June 2**
  Sullivan Freedom Fest (Sullivan), **July 4**
  Texas County Fair/Old Settlers Reunion (Houston), **July 31**
  Tom Sawyer Days, Natl (Hannibal), **July 4**
  Trails West! (St. Joseph), **Aug 17**
  US Senior Amateur (Golf) Chmpshp (St. Louis, MO), **Sept 8**
  US Women's Mid-Amateur (Golf) Chmpshp (Eureka), **Oct 6**
  Weston Summer Glow (Weston), **Aug 4**
  Winterfest (St. Joseph), **Dec 1**
Missouri Compromise: Anniv, Mar 3
Mister Rogers' Neighborhood TV Premiere: Anniv, May 22
Mitchell Persimmon Fest (Mitchell, IN), Sept 22
Mitchell, Andrea: Birth, Oct 30
Mitchell, Cameron: Birth Anniv, Nov 18
Mitchell, Chad: Birth, Dec 5
Mitchell, James: Birth, Feb 29
Mitchell, Joni: Birth, Nov 7
Mitchell, Margaret: Birth Anniv, Nov 8
Mitchell, Maria: Birth Anniv, Aug 1
Mitchum, Robert: Birth Anniv, Aug 6
Mix, Tom: Birth Anniv, Jan 6
Mize, Larry: Birth, Sept 23
Mobius, August: Birth Anniv, Nov 17
Mobius Awards (Chicago, IL), Feb 8

Nelson, Judd: Birth, Nov 28
Nelson, Thomas: Birth Anniv, Dec 26
Nelson, Willie: Birth, Apr 30
Nelson: Ozzie and Harriet Show Debut: Anniv,
   Oct 8
Nemec, Corin: Birth, Nov 5
Nepal
   Democracy Day, Natl, **Feb 18**
   King's Birthday National Holiday, **Dec 29**
   National Unity Day, **Jan 11**
Neptune Discovery: Anniv, Sept 23
Neptune Fest, Virginia Beach (Virginia Beach, VA),
   Sept 28
Nerve Gas Attack on Japanese Subway: Anniv,
   Mar 20
Neshoba County Fair (Philadelphia, MS), July 20
Nesmith, Michael: Birth, Dec 30
Netherlands
   European Fine Art Fair (Maastricht), **Mar 10**
   Holland Fest, **June 1**
   Liberation Day, **May 5**
   Midwinter Horn Blowing, **Dec 2**
   National Windmill Day, **May 12**
   Netherlands-United States: Diplomatic Anniv,
     Apr 19
   North Sea Jazz Fest (The Hague), **July 13**
   Prinsjesdag (Parliament opening), **Sept 18**
   Queen's Birthday, **Apr 30**
   Relief of Leiden, **Oct 3**
   Scilly Isles Peace Anniv, **Apr 17**
Network Marketing Professionals Week, Apr 8
Networking Week, Natl, Oct 14
Neuharth, Allen: Birth, Mar 22
Neurofibromatosis Awareness Month, Natl, May 1
Neutrality Appeal, American: Anniv, Aug 18
Neuwirth, Bebe: Birth, Dec 31
Nevada
   ABC/WIBC Festival of Bowling (Reno), **Oct 19**
   Admission Day, **Oct 31**
   All-Indian Rodeo and Powow (Fallon), **July 20**
   Burning Man 2001 (Black Rock Desert), **Aug 27**
   Candy Dance (Genoa), **Sept 29**
   Carson City Rendezvous (Carson City), **June 8**
   Celebrity Golf Chmpshp (Stateline), **July 6**
   Chmpshp Air Races, Natl (Reno), **Sept 13**
   Cowboy Poetry Gathering, **Jan 27**
   Coyote Chase (Wellington), **June 16**
   Dayton Valley Days (Dayton), **Sept 15**
   Family Day, **Nov 23**
   Finals Rodeo, Natl (Las Vegas), **Dec 7**
   Harvest Farm Auction (Smith Valley), **Oct 21**
   Hot August Nights (Reno and Sparks), **July 28**
   Laughlin Desert Challenge (Laughlin), **Jan 18**
   Liberace Memorial Mass (Las Vegas), **Feb 3**
   Liberace Museum Celebrated (Las Vegas), **Apr 14**
   Liberace Museum Christmas Tree Lighting (Las
     Vegas), **Dec 6**
   Liberace Play-A-Like Competition (Las Vegas),
     May 12
   Liberace Scholars Festival of the Arts (Las Vegas),
     Aug 26
   Liberace's Birthday Celebration (Las Vegas),
     May 13
   NAB 2001/National Broadcasters Conv (Las Vegas),
     Apr 21
   Nugget Best in the West Rib Cook-Off (Sparks),
     Aug 31
   Reno Birthday, **May 9**
   Reno Rodeo (Reno), **June 16**
   Smith Valley Fun Days (Smith Valley), **Oct 7**
   Smith Valley Strawberry Fest (Wellington), **May 27**
   Snowfest Winter Carnival (North Lake Tahoe),
     Mar 2
   Spirit of Wovoka Days Powwow (Yerington), **Aug 24**
   State Fair (Reno), **Aug 22**
   Sundae in the Park (Yerington), **Sept 9**
   Uptown, Downtown, Artown (Reno), **July 1**
Neville, Aaron: Birth, Jan 24
Nevis: Independence Day, Sept 19
New Beginning Fest (Coffeyville, KS), Apr 26
New England, Dark Day in: Anniv, May 19
New Friends, Old Friends Week, Natl, May 20
New Hampshire
   Artists in the Park (Wolfeboro), **Aug 15**
   Children's Day (Milton), **July 14**
   Jackson Hill Cider Day (Portsmouth), **Sept 15**
   Market Square Days (Portsmouth), **June 8**
   New England Conference on Storytelling for
     Children (Keene), **Apr 7**
   New Hampshire Highland Games (Lincoln), **Sept 14**
   Ratification Day, **June 21**
   Riverfest in Manchester, **Sept 7**
New Jersey
   American Wheels Car Show (Millville), **Oct 14**

Antique Fire Apparatus Muster and Show (Millville),
   Aug 19
Art in the Park (Bay Head), **June 9**
Arts and Crafts Fest (Loveladies), **Aug 4**
Atlantique City Antiques/Collectibles (Atlantic City),
   Oct 20
Atlantique City Spring Fair (Atlantic City), **Mar 24**
Barnegat Bay Crab Race and Fest (Seaside
   Heights), **Aug 26**
Be Nice to New Jersey Week, **July 1**
Big "C" Attus Day (Toms River), **Oct 7**
Black Maria Studio: Anniv, **Feb 1**
Blue Claw Crab Craft Show & Crab Race (Harvey
   Cedars), **Aug 18**
Cape May Music Fest (Cape May), **May 20**
Christmas in Cape May (Cape May), **Nov 16**
Corvette Show (Millville), **Sept 9**
Craft Day by the Bay (Harvey Cedars), **July 7**
Crustacean Beauty Pageant/Ocean City Creep
   (Ocean City), **Aug 1**
Day of the Seal, Intl (Point Pleasant Beach), **Mar 24**
Dog Day Road Race (Harvey Cedars), **Aug 19**
Doll Show (Millville), **Nov 10**
Earth Day Weekend (Point Pleasant Beach), **Apr 21**
Easter Parade (Atlantic City), **Apr 15**
Eggsibit (Phillipsburg), **Mar 31**
Father's Day Celebration (Point Pleasant Beach),
   June 17
Fest of the Sea (Pt Pleasant), **Sept 15**
Fest-in-the-Park (Nutley), **Sept 9**
First Black Pro Hockey Player: Anniv, **Nov 15**
Fishing Contest (Lakewood), **May 5**
Flemington Speedway Racing Season (Flemington),
   May 5
Founders' Day (Toms River), **June 9**
Grandparent's Day Celebration (Point Pleasant
   Beach), **Sept 9**
Halloween Parade (Toms River), **Oct 31**
Heritage Day Fest (Lavallette), **Sept 8**
Independence Extravaganza (Lavallette), **July 1**
Jewish Renaissance Fair (Jersey City), **Sept 2**
Lavallette Heritage Arts and Crafts Show
   (Lavallette), **July 29**
Long Beach Island Chowder Cook-Off (Beach
   Haven), **Sept 29**
Martin Z. Mollusk Day (Ocean City), **May 3**
May in Montclair (Montclair Township), **May 1**
Mid-Summer Antique & Collectibles Show & Sale
   (Millville), **July 28**
Mid-Winter Antiques Show (Millville), **Feb 3**
Miniatures, Dolls & Dollhouse Show & Sale (Toms
   River), **Nov 3**
Mother's Day Celebration (Point Pleasant Beach),
   May 13
Museum of American Glass Mid-Winter Exhibit
   (Millville), **Jan 20**
Ocean County Decoy/Gun Show (Tuckerton),
   Sept 29
Ocean County Wildfowl Art & Decoy Show (Brick),
   Feb 3
Olde-Time Antiques and Collectibles Faire (Toms
   River), **Sept 1**
Opera Fest of New Jersey (Lawrenceville), **June 24**
Our Loveladies Fair (Loveladies), **June 8**
Penguin Awareness Day (Point Pleasant Beach),
   Jan 20
PGA Seniors' Chmpshp (Paramus), **May 24**
Picatinny Peak Fall Hawkwatch (Lake Hopatong),
   Sept 1
Pine Barrens Jamboree (Waretown), **Oct 13**
Quilts Along the Bay (Barnegat), **Sept 8**
Ratification Day: Anniv, **Dec 18**
Reptile Awareness Day (Point Pleasant Beach),
   Oct 21
Saint Ann's Italian Street Fest (Hoboken), **July 20**
Scandinavian Fest (Stanhope), **Sept 2**
Seashore Open House Tour (Loveladies), **Aug 1**
Shark Awareness Day (Point Pleasant Beach),
   July 14
South Jersey Canoe/Kayak Classic (Lakewood),
   June 2
Spring Victorian Weekend (Cape May), **Apr 27**
Suffragists' Voting Attempt: Anniv, **Nov 19**
Sugarloaf's Fall Somerset Craft Fest (Somerset),
   Nov 2
Sugarloaf's Spring Somerset Craft Fest (Somerset),
   Mar 9
Sussex Farm and Horse Show/New Jersey State
   Fair (Augusta), **Aug 3**
Toms River Canoe Race (Toms River), **Oct 13**
Tour of Somerville (Somerville), **May 28**
Traditional Small Boat Fest (Berkley Township),
   June 16
Victorian Holmes Weekend (Cape May), **Nov 2**
Victorian Holmes Weekend (Cape May), **Mar 9**

Victorian Week (Cape May), **Oct 5**
Wedding of the Sea (Atlantic City), **Aug 15**
Weird Contest Week (Ocean City), **Aug 13**
Wings 'n' Water Fest (Stone Harbor), **Sept 15**
New Mexico
   ABC (Bowling) Chmpshp Tourn (Albuquerque),
     Feb 10
   ABC (Bowling) Convention (Albuquerque), **Mar 12**
   ABC Seniors Tourn (Albuquerque), **June 16**
   Admission Day, **Jan 6**
   American Business Women's Assn, Natl Conv
     (Albuquerque, NM), **Oct 31**
   AspenCash Motorcycle Rally (Ruidoso), **May 17**
   Carlsbad Caverns Natl Park Established: Anniv,
     May 14
   Chile Challenge Off-Road Bike Race (Angel Fire),
     June 23
   Electric Light Parade (Lovington), **Dec 3**
   Enchanted Circle Century Bike Tour (Red River),
     Sept 9
   Farmington Invitational Balloon Fest (Farmington),
     May 25
   Freedom Days (Farmington), **June 30**
   Golden Aspen Motorcycle Rally (Ruidoso), **Sept 19**
   Intertribal Indian Ceremonial (Gallup), **Aug 8**
   June Junque Jamboree (Lovington), **June 2**
   Literacy Volunteers America Conf (Albuquerque),
     Oct 17
   Lovington Fall Arts/Crafts Fest (Lovington), **Nov 3**
   NAIA Men's Natl Chmpshp (Bernalillo), **Nov 15**
   New Mexico State Fair (Albuquerque), **Sept 7**
   Outdoor Summer Theater (Farmington), **June 20**
   Road Runners Club Natl Conv (Albuquerque),
     May 2
   Santa Fe Chamber Music Fest (Santa Fe), **July 13**
   Show of Wheels (Lovington), **Feb 3**
   Shuttle Camp (Alamogordo), **June 4**
   Southwest Regional Sport Launch (Alamogordo),
     June 16
   Spring Gala (Lovington), **May 5**
   Taos Spring Arts Fest (Taos), **May 12**
   Totah Fest (Farmington), **Aug 31**
   World Shovel Race Chmpshp (Angel Fire), **Feb 3**
   World's Greatest Lizard Race (Lovington), **July 4**
New Orleans, Battle of: Anniv, Jan 8
New Work for the New Year (St. Simons Island,
   GA), Jan 13
New World Symphony Premiere: Anniv, Dec 16
New Year
   Albany's New Year's Eve Celebration (Albany, NY),
     Dec 31
   Chinese Lunar New Year Fest (Baltimore, MD),
     Jan 28
   Chinese New Year, **Jan 24**
   Chinese New Year Fest (San Francisco, CA),
     Jan 20
   Ethiopia: New Year's Day, **Sept 11**
   First Night (Boston, MA), **Dec 31**
   First Night Asheville (Asheville, NC), **Dec 31**
   First Night Augusta (Staunton, VA), **Dec 31**
   First Night Hartford (Hartford, CT), **Dec 31**
   First Night Roanoke (Roanoke, VA), **Dec 31**
   First Nights (Canada), **Dec 31**
   First Nights (US), **Dec 31**
   Get a Life Day, **Jan 1**
   India: New Year's Day, **Mar 22**
   Iranian New Year (Persian), **Mar 21**
   Japanese Era New Year, **Jan 1**
   Muharram (Islamic New Year), **Mar 26**
   Naw-Ruz (Baha'i New Year's Day), **Mar 21**
   New Year's Day, **Jan 1**
   New Year's Day (Gregorian), **Jan 1**
   New Year's Day Observance (Russia), **Jan 1**
   New Year's Dishonor List, **Jan 1**
   New Year's Eve, **Dec 31**
   New Year's Fest (Kalamazoo, MI), **Dec 31**
   New Year's Resolution Recommitment Day, Natl,
     June 1
   New Year's Resolutions Week, **Jan 1**
   Old New Year's Day, **Mar 25**
   Rosh Hashanah (Jewish), **Sept 18**
   Sri Lanka: Sinhala and Tamil New Year, **Apr 13**
   Stock Exchange Holiday, **Jan 1**
   United Kingdom New Year's Holiday, **Jan 1**
New York
   Albany Alive at Five (Albany), **June 7**
   Albany Riverfest (Albany), **July 21**
   Albany Tulip Fest (Albany), **May 10**
   Albany's New Year's Eve Celebration (Albany),
     Dec 31
   Antiques in Schoharie (Schoharie), **Mar 3**
   Belmont Stakes (Belmont Park), **June 9**
   Belmont Stakes, First Running of, **June 19**
   Boxing Day Annual Celebration (New York), **Dec 26**
   Brooklyn Bridge Opened: Anniv, **May 24**

Pescow, Donna: Birth, Mar 24
Peshtigo Forest Fire: Anniv, Oct 8
Pet Expo, AFRMA Fancy Rat & Mouse Display America's Family (Pomona, CA), Apr 6
Pet First Aid Awareness Month, Natl, Apr 1
Pet Owners Independence Day, Apr 18
Pet Parade (LaGrange, IL), June 2
Pet Peeve Week, Natl, Oct 8
Pet Sitters Week, Natl Prof, Mar 4
Pet Week, Natl, May 6
Peter and Paul Day, June 29
Peter I: Birth Anniv, May 30
Peters, Bernadette: Birth, Feb 28
Peters, Roberta: Birth, May 4
Petersen, Paul: Birth, Sept 23
Petersen, William: Birth, Feb 21
Peterson, Cassandra: Birth, Sept 17
Peterson, Roger Tory: Birth Anniv, Aug 28
Peterson, Seth: Birth, Aug 16
Petrified Forest Natl Park Established: Anniv, Dec 9
Petroleum Fest, Louisiana Shrimp and (Morgan City, LA), Aug 30
Pettit, Robert Lee (Bob), Jr: Birth, Dec 12
Petty, Richard: Birth, July 2
Petty, Tom: Birth, Oct 20
Pfeiffer, Michelle: Birth, Apr 29
Pharmacists Declare War on Alcoholism, June 1
Phil Donahue Show, The: Anniv, Nov 6
Phil Silvers Show TV Premiere: Anniv, Sept 20
Philadelphia Police Bombing: Anniv, May 13
Philbin, Regis: Birth, Aug 25
Philip, King: Assassination Anniv, Aug 12
Philip, Prince: Birth, June 10
Philippines
   Aquino, Benigno: Assassination Anniv, Aug 21
   Ati-Atihan Fest, Jan 20
   Bataan Day: Anniv, Apr 9
   Black Nazarene Fiesta, Jan 1
   Bonifacio Day, Nov 30
   Carabao Fest, May 14
   Christmas Observance, Dec 16
   Earthquake Jolts: Anniv, July 16
   Feast of Our Lady of Peace/Good Voyage, May 1
   Feast of the Black Nazarene, Jan 9
   Fertility Rites, May 17
   Fil-American Friendship Day, July 4
   Holy Week, Apr 8
   Independence Day, June 12
   Morione's Fest (Marinduque Island), Apr 12
   Mount Pinatubo Erupts in Philippines: Anniv, June 11
   Philippine Independence: Anniv, Mar 24
   Rizal Day, Dec 30
   Santacruzan, May 1
   Simbang Gabi, Dec 16
   US Military Leaves, Nov 24
Philips, Wendy: Birth, Jan 2
Phillips, Bobbie: Birth, Jan 29
Phillips, Chynna: Birth, Feb 12
Phillips, Julianne: Birth, May 13
Phillips, Lou Diamond: Birth, Feb 17
Phillips, MacKenzie: Birth, Nov 10
Phillips, Michelle: Birth, June 4
Phillips, Stone: Birth, Dec 2
Phillips, Wendell: Birth Anniv, Nov 29
Phillpotts, Eden: Birth Anniv, Nov 4
Photography
   Abbott, Berenice: Birth Anniv, July 17
   Bourke-White, Margaret: Birth Anniv, June 14
   First Presidential Photograph: Anniv, Feb 14
Physical Fitness and Sports Month, Natl, May 1
Piano Month, Natl, Sept 1
Piano Playing, World Chmpshp Old-Time (Decatur, IL), May 25
Piano: Kingsville Young Performers' Competition (Kingsville, TX), Apr 5
Piazza, Mike: Birth, Sept 4
Piazzetta, Giovanni Battista: Birth Anniv., Feb 13
Picasso, Pablo: Birth Anniv, Oct 25
Picatinny Peak Fall Hawkwatch (Lake Hopatong, NJ), Sept 1
Piccard, Auguste: Birth Anniv, Jan 28
Piccard, Jacques: Birth, July 28
Piccard, Jean Felix: Birth Anniv, Jan 28
Piccard, Jeannette Ridlon: Birth Anniv, Jan 5
Pickett's Charge: Battle of Gettysburg: Anniv, July 1
Pickett, Bill: Birth Anniv, Dec 5
Pickett, George: Defeat at Five Forks: Anniv, Apr 1
Pickett, Wilson: Birth, Mar 18
Pickle Week, Intl, May 18
Pickup Parade and Contest, Ugly (Chadron, NE), Oct 26

Pidgeon, Walter: Birth Anniv, Sept 23
Pied Piper of Hamelin: Anniv, July 22
Pied Piper: Rat-Catchers Day, July 22
Pierce, David Hyde: Birth, Apr 3
Pierce, Franklin: Birth Anniv, Nov 23
Pierce, Jane: Birth Anniv, Mar 12
Pieta Attacked: Anniv, May 21
Pietz, Amy: Birth, Mar 6
Pig Day, Natl, Mar 1
Pileggi, Mitch: Birth, Apr 5
Pilgrim Landing: Anniv, Dec 21
Pinchbeck, Christopher: Death Anniv, Nov 18
Pinchot, Bronson: Birth, May 20
Pine Barrens Jamboree (Waretown, NJ), Oct 13
Piniella, Lou: Birth, Aug 28
Pinkerton, Allan: Birth Anniv, Aug 25
Pinkett Smith, Jada: Birth, Sept 18
Pinochet, Augusto: Military Dictatorship Ended, Dec 15
Pinter, Harold: Birth, Oct 10
Pinzon, Martin: Arrival Anniv, Mar 1
Pioneer Days (Fort Worth, TX), Sept 21
Pioneer Week (Washington, MS), June 25
Pippen, Scottie: Birth, Sept 25
Piquet, Nelson: Birth, Aug 17
Pirates: Billy Bowlegs Fest (Ft Walton Beach, FL), June 1
Pisces Begins, Feb 20
Piscopo, Joe: Birth, June 17
Pisier, Marie-France: Birth, May 10
Pitcher, Molly: Birth Anniv, Oct 13
Pitlochry Fest Theatre, May 1
Pitt, Brad: Birth, Dec 18
Pitt, William: Birth Anniv, May 28
Pittsburgh Arts & Crafts Spring Fever Fest (PA), Mar 23
Pittsburgh Three Rivers Arts Fest (PA), June 1
Pittsburgh Three Rivers Regatta (PA), Aug 2
Piven, Jeremy: Birth, July 26
Pizarro, Francesco: Death Anniv, June 26
Pizza Bake, Great American, Feb 6
Pizza Expo (Las Vegas, NV), Mar 20
Place, Mary Kay: Birth, Sept 23
Plan to Promote Your Business Week, Natl, July 15
Plan Your Epitaph Day, Nov 2
Planck, Max: Birth Anniv, Apr 23
Planet Pluto Discovery: Anniv, Feb 18
Plant the Seeds of Greatness Month, Feb 1
Plant, Robert: Birth, Aug 20
Plantation Days (Charlottesville, VA), July 7
Plants: Natl Garden Week, Apr 8
Play Days, Sept 4
Play Presented in N American Colonies, First: Anniv, Aug 27
Play-the-Recorder Month, Mar 1
Playboy First Published: Anniv, Dec 1
Player, Gary: Birth, Nov 1
Playground Safety Day, Natl, Apr 26
Playground Safety Week, Natl, Apr 23
Pleasure Your Mate Month, Sept 1
Pledge of Allegiance Recognized: Anniv, Dec 28
Pledge of Allegiance, Pause for (Natl Flag Day USA), June 14
Pleshette, Suzanne: Birth, Jan 31
Plimpton, George: Birth, Mar 18
Plimpton, Martha: Birth, Nov 16
Plimsoll Day, Feb 10
Plough Monday (England), Jan 8
Ploughing Chmpshp, Northern Ireland (Dungannon County, Tyrone, N Ireland), Oct 18
Plumb, Eve: Birth, Apr 29
Plummer, Amanda: Birth, Mar 23
Plummer, Christopher: Birth, Dec 13
Pluto Discovery, Planet: Anniv, Feb 18
Plutonium First Weighed: Anniv, Aug 20
Plymouth Plantation Earthquake: Anniv, June 1
Pocahontas: Death Anniv, Mar 21
Poe, Edgar Allan, Evermore (Manheim, PA), Oct 26
Poe, Edgar Allan: Birth Anniv, Jan 19
Poetry
   American Poet Laureate Establishment: Anniv, Dec 20
   Bad Poetry Day, Aug 18
   Dakota Cowboy Poetry Gathering (Medora, ND), May 26
   Limerick Day, May 12
   Poetry Day in Florida, May 25
   Poetry Month, Natl, Apr 1
   Texas Cowboy Poetry Gathering (Alpine, TX), Mar 2
   Wheatley, Phillis: Death Anniv, Dec 5
Poinsett, Joel Roberts: Death Anniv, Dec 12
Poinsettia Day, Dec 12
Pointer, Bonnie: Birth, July 11
Poison Prevention Awareness Month, Mar 1

Poison Prevention Week, Natl, Mar 18
Poison Prevention Week, Natl (Pres Proc), Mar 18
Poitier, Sidney: Birth, Feb 20
Pol Pot Overthrown: Anniv, Jan 7
Poland
   Constitution Day, May 3
   Independence Day, Nov 11
   Liberation Day, Jan 17
   Solidarity Founded Anniv, Aug 31
   Solidarity Granted Legal Status: Anniv, Apr 17
Polanski, Roman: Birth, Aug 18
Polar Bear Jump Fest, Seward (Seward, AK), Jan 19
Polar Bear Swim (Sheboygan, WI), Jan 1
Pole, Pedal, Paddle (Bend, OR), May 19
Police Story TV Premiere: Anniv, Apr 4
Police Week (Pres Proc), May 13
Police Week, Natl, May 13
Police: Peace Officer Memorial Day (Pres Proc), May 15
Police: Peace Officer Memorial Day, Natl, May 15
Polio Vaccine: Anniv, Apr 12
Polish
   Polish American Heritage Month, Oct 1
   Polish Fest (Wisconsin Dells, WI), Sept 7
   Polish-American in the House (Mikulski): Anniv, Jan 4
   Polish-American Weekend (Philadelphia, PA), Aug 11
Polito, Jon: Birth, Dec 29
Polk, James: Birth Anniv, Nov 2
Polk, James: First Presidential Photograph: Anniv, Feb 14
Polk, Sarah Childress: Birth Anniv, Sept 4
Polka Fest (Wisconsin Dells, WI), Apr 6
Poll Tax Outlawed: Anniv, Apr 8
Pollack, Sydney: Birth, July 1
Pollak, Kevin: Birth, Oct 30
Pollan, Tracy: Birth, June 22
Pollard, Michael J.: Birth, May 30
Polygamists, Amnesty for: Anniv, Jan 4
Pompano Beach Seafood Fest (Pompano Beach, FL), Apr 27
Ponce de Leon Discovers Florida: Anniv, Apr 2
Ponselle, Rosa: Birth Anniv, Jan 22
Ponti, Carlo: Birth, Dec 11
Pony Express, Inauguration of: Anniv, Apr 3
Pony League World Series (Washington, PA), Aug 18
Pooh Day (A.A. Milne Birth Anniv), Jan 18
Poole, Cecil: First Black US State's Attorney: Anniv, July 6
Poor Richard's Almanack: Anniv, Dec 28
Pop Music Chart Introduced: Anniv, Jan 4
Pop, Iggy: Birth, Apr 21
Popcorn Fest (Valparaiso, IN), Sept 8
Popcorn Poppin' Month, Natl, Oct 1
Pope, Alexander: Birth Anniv, May 21
Pope, John: Birth Anniv, Mar 16
Popes, Roman Catholic
   Benedict XV: Birth Anniv, Nov 21
   John Paul I: Birth Anniv, Oct 17
   John Paul II: Assassination Attempt: Anniv, May 13
   John Paul II: Birth, May 18
   John Paul II: Nixes Ordaining of Women: Anniv, May 30
   John XXIII: Birth Anniv, Nov 25
   Paul VI: Birth Anniv, Sept 26
   Pius XI: Birth Anniv, May 31
   Pius XII: Birth Anniv, Mar 2
Population Day, World (UN), July 11
Population: Day of Five Billion: Anniv, July 11
Population: Day of the Six Billion: Anniv, Oct 12
Pork Month, Natl, Oct 1
Porter, Cole: Birth Anniv, June 9
Porter, Katherine Anne: Birth Anniv, May 15
Porter, Sylvia: Birth Anniv, June 18
Porter, Terry: Birth, Apr 8
Porter, William S. (O. Henry): Birth Anniv, Sept 11
Portman, Natalie: Birth, June 9
Portugal
   Day of Portugal, June 10
   Holy Week Festivities, Apr 8
   Independence Day, Dec 1
   Liberty Day, Apr 25
   Pilgrimage to Fatima, Oct 13
   Pilgrimage to Fatima, May 12
   Saint Anthony of Padua: Feast Day, June 13
Posey, Parker: Birth, Nov 8
Positive Alternatives for Living Day, Natl, Apr 17
Post Day, World (UN), Oct 9
Post, Emily: Birth Anniv, Oct 30
Post, Markie: Birth, Nov 4
Post, Wiley: Birth Anniv, Nov 22

Western Stock Show and Rodeo, Natl (Denver, CO), **Jan 6**
Wichita West Bullfest (Wichita Falls, TX), **Jan 20**
Wild Horse Stampede (Wolf Point, MT), **July 13**
Wonago World Chmpshp Rodeo (Milwaukee, WI), **June 15**
World's Oldest Continuous PRCA Rodeo (Payson, AZ), **Aug 17**
Yuma Jaycee's Silver Spur Rodeo (Yuma, AZ), **Feb 10**
Rodin, Auguste: Birth Anniv, Nov 12
Rodman, Dennis: Birth, May 13
Rodney, Caesar: Birth Anniv, Oct 7
Rodriguez, Alex: Birth, July 27
Rodriguez, Ivan: Birth, Nov 30
Rodriguez, Juan "Chi-Chi": Birth, Oct 23
Roe v Wade Decision: Anniv, Jan 22
Roentgen, Wilhelm K.: Birth Anniv, Mar 27
Rogation Sunday, May 20
Rogers, Edith Nourse: Birth Anniv, Mar 19
Rogers, Fred: Birth, Mar 20
Rogers, Ginger: Birth Anniv, July 16
Rogers, Kenny: Birth, Aug 21
Rogers, Mimi: Birth, Jan 27
Rogers, Roy: Birth Anniv, Nov 5
Rogers, Wayne: Birth, Apr 7
Rogers, Will: Birth Anniv, Nov 4
Roget, Peter Mark: Birth Anniv, Jan 18
Rohatyn, Felix: Birth, May 29
Roker, Al: Birth, Aug 20
Rolen, Scott: Birth, Apr 4
Roller Coaster: Santa Cruz Beach Giant Dipper: Anniv, May 17
Roller Skating Month, Natl, Oct 1
Roman Catholic/Eastern Orthodox Meeting: Anniv, Jan 5
Roman Catholic: New Catechism: Anniv, Nov 16
Romance: Kiss-Your-Mate Day, Apr 28
Romance: Sweetest Day, Oct 20
Romania: National Day, Dec 1
Romano, Ray: Birth, Dec 21
Rome Executions: Anniv, Mar 25
Rome Liberated: Anniv, June 4
Rome, Sack of: Anniv, May 6
Rome: Birthday (Italy), Apr 21
Romijn-Stamos, Rebecca: Birth, Nov 6
Rommel, Erwin: Birth Anniv, Nov 15
Ronstadt, Linda: Birth, July 15
Rookies TV Premiere: Anniv, Sept 11
Room of One's Own Day, Jan 25
Rooney, Andy: Birth, Jan 14
Rooney, Mickey: Birth, Sept 23
Roosevelt County Fair (Culbertson, MT), Aug 8
Roosevelt, Alice: Birth Anniv, July 29
Roosevelt, Edith: Birth Anniv, Aug 6
Roosevelt, Eleanor: Birth Anniv, Oct 11
Roosevelt, Franklin Delano
  Bank Holiday: Anniv, **Mar 5**
  Birth Anniv, **Jan 30**
  Christmas Fireside Chat Warning: Anniv, **Dec 25**
  Death Anniv, **Apr 12**
  Elected to Fourth Term: Anniv, **Nov 7**
  FDR Commemorative Ceremony (Warm Springs, GA), **Apr 12**
  First Fireside Chat: Anniv, **Mar 12**
  Unconditional Surrender Statement: Anniv, **Jan 24**
  Warm Springs Thanksgiving (Warm Springs, GA), **Nov 17**
Roosevelt, Theodore: Birth Anniv, Oct 27
Root Beer Day, Stewart's, June 16
Rosacea Awareness Month, Mar 1
Rose Bowl Game (Pasadena, CA), Jan 1
Rose Fest, Portland (Portland, OR), May 31
Rose Month, Natl, June 1
Rose, Billy: Birth Anniv, Sept 6
Rose, Charlie: Birth, Jan 5
Rose, Pete: Birth, Apr 14
Roseanne TV Premiere: Anniv, Oct 18
Roseanne: Birth, Nov 3
Rosenberg Execution: Anniv, June 19
Roses Indoors and Out (Granville, OH), June 1
Roses, South Carolina Fest of (Orangeburg, SC), Apr 27
Rosh Hashanah, Sept 18
Rosh Hashanah Begins, Sept 17
Ross, Betsy: Birth Anniv, Jan 1
Ross, Diana: Birth, Mar 26
Ross, George: Birth Anniv, May 10
Ross, Herbert: Birth, May 13
Ross, Katharine: Birth, Jan 29
Ross, Marion: Birth, Oct 25
Ross, Nellie Tayloe: Birth Anniv, Nov 29
Ross, Nellie Tayloe: Wyoming Inaugurates 1st US Woman Gov: Anniv, Jan 5
Rossellini, Isabella: Birth, June 18

Rossner, Judith: Birth, Mar 1
Rossovich, Rick: Birth, Aug 28
Rostropovich, Mstislav Leopoldovich: Birth, Mar 27
Rotary Tiller Race/Purplehull Pea Fest World Chmpshp (Emerson, AR), June 30
Roth, David Lee: Birth, Oct 10
Roth, Philip: Birth, Mar 19
Roth, Tim: Birth, May 14
Roth, William V., Jr: Birth, July 22
Roughhouse Fest (Japan), Oct 14
Round Barn Rendezvous & Market (Rochester, IN), June 9
Rounds Resounding Day, Aug 1
Roundtree, Richard: Birth, Sept 7
Rourke, Mickey: Birth, Sept 16
Rousseau, Henri: Birth Anniv, May 20
Rousseau, Jean J.: Birth Anniv, June 28
Route 66 Summerfest (Rolla, MO), July 14
Rowan and Martin's Laugh-In, Jan 22
Rowan, Carl: Birth, Aug 11
Rowland, John: Birth, May 24
Rowlands, Gena: Birth, June 19
Rowling, J.K.: Birth, July 31
Roy Rogers Show TV Premiere: Anniv, Dec 30
Roy, Patrick: Birth, Oct 5
Royko, Mike: Birth Anniv, Sept 19
Rozelle, Pete: Birth Anniv, Mar 1
Rubens, Paul (Pee-wee Herman): Birth, Aug 27
Rubens, Peter P.: Birth Anniv, June 28
Rubik, Erno: Birth, July 13
Ruble Becomes Convertible: Anniv, July 1
Ruck, Alan: Birth, July 1
Rucker, Darius: Birth, May 13
Rudd, Paul: Birth, Apr 6
Rudner, Rita: Birth, Sept 17
Rudolph, Wilma: Birth Anniv, June 23
Ruffin, Davis Eli (David): Birth Anniv, Jan 18
Ruffin, Edmund: Birth Anniv, Jan 5
Rukeyser, Louis: Birth, Jan 30
Rumsey Regatta (Shepherdstown, WV), July 26
Rundgren, Todd: Birth, June 22
Running
  Anvil Mountain Run (Nome, AK), **July 4**
  Anvil Mountain Challenge (Nome, AK), **Sept 13**
  Atlanta Marathon and Half Marathon (Atlanta, GA), **Nov 22**
  Autumn Glory 5K Run/2 Mile Walk (Mountain Lake Park, MD), **Oct 13**
  Beartooth Run (Red Lodge, MT), **June 30**
  Big Ten Men's/Women's Cross Country (WI), **Oct 28**
  Bolder Boulder 10K (Boulder, CO), **May 28**
  Boston Marathon (Boston, MA), **Apr 16**
  Briggs & Stratton's Run & Walk (Milwaukee, WI), **Sept 22**
  Charleston Distance Run (Charleston, WV), **Sept 1**
  Charlotte Observer Race Fest (Charlotte, NC), **Apr 21**
  Cheetah Run (Cincinnati, OH), **Sept 2**
  Coyote Chase (Wellington, NV), **June 16**
  Crater Lake Rim Runs and Marathon (Klamath Falls, OR), **Aug 11**
  Days of Marathon: Anniv, **Sept 2**
  Dog Day Road Race (Harvey Cedars, NJ), **Aug 19**
  Easter Beach Run (Daytona Beach, FL), **Apr 7**
  Egg Races (Switzerland), **Apr 16**
  Examiner Bay to Breaker Race (San Francisco, CA), **May 20**
  Governor's Cup (Helena, MT), **June 2**
  Groundhog Run (Kansas City, MO), **Feb 4**
  Hangover Handicap Run (Klamath Falls, OR), **Jan 1**
  Houston Marathon (Houston, TX), **Jan 14**
  Jimmy Stewart Relay Marathon (Los Angeles, CA), **Apr 22**
  Lakestride Half-Marathon (Ludington, MI), **June 16**
  LaSalle Bank Chicago Marathon, The (Chicago, IL), **Oct 7**
  Leadville Trail 100 Ultramarathon (Leadville, CO), **Aug 18**
  Longest Dam Run (Glasgow, MT), **June 23**
  Mackinaw City Fudge Classic (Mackinaw City, MI), **June 16**
  Mount Marathon Race (Seward, AK), **July 4**
  New Haven Labor Day Road Race (New Haven, CT), **Sept 3**
  New York City Marathon (New York, NY), **Nov 4**
  Peachtree Junior (Atlanta, GA), **June 2**
  Peachtree Road Race (Atlanta, GA), **July 4**
  Prospect Park Triple Challenge & Safety Expo (Brooklyn, NY), **Apr 7**
  Road Runners Club Natl Conv (Albuquerque, NM), **May 2**
  Romp in the Swamp Fun Walk (Appleton, WI), **Oct 20**
  Running and Fitness Week, Natl, **May 13**

  San Diego Marathon (Carlsbad, CA), **Jan 21**
  Terry Fox Day, **July 28**
  Turkey Trot (Parkersburg, WV), **Nov 22**
  YWCA Festival of Races, **May 5**
Runyan, Damon: Birth Anniv, Oct 4
RuPaul: Birth, Nov 17
Rural Life Sunday, May 20
Rush, Barbara: Birth, Jan 4
Rush, Benjamin: Birth Anniv, Jan 4
Rush, William: Death Anniv, Jan 17
Rushdie, Salman: Birth, June 19
Rusk, (David) Dean: Birth Anniv, Feb 9
Russell, Anna: Birth, Dec 27
Russell, Bill: Birth, Feb 12
Russell, Charles M.: Birth Anniv, Mar 19
Russell, Jane: Birth, June 21
Russell, Keri: Birth, Mar 23
Russell, Kurt: Birth, Mar 17
Russell, Leon: Birth, Apr 2
Russell, Lillian: Birth Anniv, Dec 4
Russell, Mark: Birth, Aug 23
Russell, Nipsey: Birth, Oct 13
Russell, Theresa: Birth, Mar 20
Russert, Tim: Birth, May 7
Russia
  Army and Navy Day, **Feb 23**
  Baltic States' Independence Recognized: Anniv, **Sept 6**
  Boris Yeltsin Inaugurated: Anniv, **July 10**
  Christmas Bells Ring Again: Anniv, **Dec 24**
  Christmas Day, **Jan 7**
  COMECON and Warsaw Pact Disband: Anniv, **June 28**
  Constitution Day, **Dec 12**
  Coup Attempt in the Soviet Union: Anniv, **Aug 19**
  Day of National Reconciliation and Agreement, **Nov 7**
  Great October Socialist Revolution: Anniv, **Nov 7**
  Independence Day, **June 12**
  Intl Labor Day, **May 1**
  KGB Founder Statue Dismantled: Anniv, **Aug 22**
  McDonald's Invades the Soviet Union: Anniv, **Jan 31**
  New Year's Day Observance, **Jan 1**
  October Revolution, **Nov 7**
  Passport Presentation, **Jan 2**
  Ruble Becomes Convertible: Anniv, **July 1**
  Russian Election Surprise: Anniv, **Dec 12**
  Soviet Communist Party Suspended: Anniv, **Aug 29**
  Soviet Cosmonaut Returns to New Country: Anniv, **Mar 26**
  Soviet Union Dissolved: Anniv, **Dec 8**
  Victory Day, **May 9**
  Women's Day, Intl, **Mar 8**
  Yeltsin Shells White House: Anniv, **Oct 4**
Russo, Rene: Birth, Feb 17
Rustin, Bayard: Birth Anniv, Mar 17
Ruth, George Herman
  Babe Calls His Shot: Anniv, **Oct 1**
  Babe Ruth Day: Anniv, **Apr 27**
  Babe Ruth's First Pro Homer: Anniv, **Sept 5**
  Babe Ruth: Death Anniv, **Aug 16**
  Babe Sets Home Run Record: Anniv, **Sept 30**
  Babe's Debut in Majors: Anniv, **July 11**
  Babe's Last Game as Yankee: Anniv, **Sept 30**
  Babe's Pitching Debut: Anniv, **Apr 22**
  Birth Anniv, **Feb 6**
  First Major League Home Run: Anniv, **May 6**
  House That Ruth Built: Anniv, **Apr 18**
  Voted into Hall of Fame: Anniv, **Feb 2**
Rutherford, Ernest: Birth Anniv, Aug 30
Rutledge, Edward: Birth Anniv, Nov 23
Rutledge, John: Death Anniv, July 18
Ruttan, Susan: Birth, Sept 16
Rwanda: Tragedy in Rwanda: Anniv, Apr 6
Rwandese Republic: Independence Day, July 1
Ryan's Hope TV Premiere: Anniv, July 7
Ryan, George: Birth, Feb 24
Ryan, Jeri: Birth, Feb 22
Ryan, Meg: Birth, Nov 19
Ryan, Nolan: Birth, Jan 31
Rydell, Bobby: Birth, Apr 26
Ryder, Albert Pinkham: Birth Anniv, Mar 19
Ryder, Winona: Birth, Oct 29
Saarinen, Eliel: Birth Anniv, Aug 20
Sabatini, Gabriela: Birth, May 16
Sabato, Antonio, Jr: Birth, Feb 29
Saberhagen, Bret: Birth, Apr 11
Sabin, Albert Bruce: Birth Anniv, Aug 26
Sacagawea: Death Anniv, Dec 20
Sacco-Vanzetti Memorial Day, Aug 23
Sacramento Jazz Jubilee (Sacramento, CA), May 25
Sadat, Anwar El: Assassination Anniv, Oct 6
Sadie Hawkins Day, Nov 3

Yes! Please send me additional copies of *Chase's 2001 Calendar of Events*.

Ship to _____

Address _____

_____

City, State, Zip _____

Phone (____) _____

Please send me _____ copies of the 2001 edition of
CHASE'S CALENDAR OF EVENTS at $49.95 each (0-8092-9554-7) $_____

or _____ copies of the 2001 edition of CHASE'S
CALENDAR OF EVENTS WITH CD-ROM at $59.95 each (0-8092-2775-4) $_____

Add applicable sales tax in AL, CA, FL, IL, NC, NJ, NY, OH, PA, TX, WA $_____

Shipping & Handling: Add $5.00 for the first copy,
$3.50 for each additional copy $_____

Total $_____

☐ Check or money order enclosed payable to: NTC/Contemporary Publishing Group, Inc.

Charge my   ☐ Visa   ☐ MasterCard   ☐ American Express   ☐ Discover Card

Acct. # _____ Exp. Date ____ / ____

X _____
                       Signature (if charging to bankcard)

Name (please print) _____

STANDING ORDER AUTHORIZATION

To make sure that I receive each year's new edition, please accept this Standing Order Authorization to ship me ____ copies of *Chase's Calendar of Events* or ____ copies of *Chase's Calendar of Events with CD-ROM*, beginning with the 2002 edition. Bill me at the address shown at the top of this order form. I understand that I may cancel my Standing Order at any time.

X _____
           Signature   Date

(____) _____

Name (please print)   Phone

GUARANTEE: Any book you order is unconditionally guaranteed and may be returned within 10 days of receipt for full refund.

Prices subject to change without notice.   9353

Mail to: **NTC/Contemporary Publishing Group, Inc.**
4255 W Touhy Ave
Lincolnwood, IL 60712-1975

There is no charge for being listed in **Chase's**. Use the form below to submit new entries for forthcoming editions of **Chase's Calendar of Events**. Background information about your entry is also appreciated. Please be sure your dates are confirmed for 2002, or clearly indicate if dates are tentative. Use a separate sheet for each entry submitted. Information selected by the editors may be used and publicized through their books, electronic formats, syndicated services and/or other related products and services. The editors reserve the right to select and edit information received. Please mail all information to: Calendar Editor, Chase's Calendar of Events, NTC/Contemporary Publishing Group, 4255 W Touhy Ave, Lincolnwood, IL 60712-1975.

☞DEADLINE FOR 2002 EDITION: MAY 10, 2001.   PLEASE TYPE OR PRINT VERY CLEARLY.

1. Exact name of entry:
2. Exact INCLUSIVE DATES for 2002:
3. If applicable, estimated attendance (one figure—grand total all days):
4. Location (site [not address], city and state):
5. Brief description:

6. Formula—ONLY if used to set date(s) each year (Example: Annually, the third Monday in May):

7. For public use, complete contact info to be printed in book—name, address, phone, fax, e-mail, web.

8. For Chase's staff use, complete address info we can use to mail our update form to you next year—name, title or department, organization name, address:

9. For Chase's staff use, name, dept and phone and fax numbers of person we can call with questions about your entry:

10. Person furnishing information: (print) _____ (sign) _____

11. PLEASE CIRCLE THE EXACT INCLUSIVE DATES FOR YOUR 2002 EVENT ON THE CALENDAR BELOW.

2002
Key dates

M. L. King Birthday, Jan 21	Passover, Mar 28	Summer, June 21	Columbus Day, Oct 14
Chinese New Year, Feb 12	Easter, Mar 31	Labor Day, Sept 2	Ramadan, Nov 6
Lent begins, Feb 13	Mother's Day, May 12	Rosh Hashanah, Sept 7–8	Thanksgiving, Nov 28
Presidents' Day, Feb 18	Memorial Day, May 27	Yom Kippur, Sept 16	Chanukah, Nov 30–Dec 7
Spring, Mar 20	Father's Day, June 16	Autumn, Sept 23	Winter, Dec 21

2002

JAN
```
 S  M  T  W  T  F  S
          1  2  3  4  5
 6  7  8  9 10 11 12
13 14 15 16 17 18 19
20 21 22 23 24 25 26
27 28 29 30 31
```

APR
```
 S  M  T  W  T  F  S
    1  2  3  4  5  6
 7  8  9 10 11 12 13
14 15 16 17 18 19 20
21 22 23 24 25 26 27
28 29 30
```

JULY
```
 S  M  T  W  T  F  S
    1  2  3  4  5  6
 7  8  9 10 11 12 13
14 15 16 17 18 19 20
21 22 23 24 25 26 27
28 29 30 31
```

OCT
```
 S  M  T  W  T  F  S
          1  2  3  4  5
 6  7  8  9 10 11 12
13 14 15 16 17 18 19
20 21 22 23 24 25 26
27 28 29 30 31
```

FEB
```
 S  M  T  W  T  F  S
                1  2
 3  4  5  6  7  8  9
10 11 12 13 14 15 16
17 18 19 20 21 22 23
24 25 26 27 28
```

MAY
```
 S  M  T  W  T  F  S
          1  2  3  4
 5  6  7  8  9 10 11
12 13 14 15 16 17 18
19 20 21 22 23 24 25
26 27 28 29 30 31
```

AUG
```
 S  M  T  W  T  F  S
             1  2  3
 4  5  6  7  8  9 10
11 12 13 14 15 16 17
18 19 20 21 22 23 24
25 26 27 28 29 30 31
```

NOV
```
 S  M  T  W  T  F  S
                1  2
 3  4  5  6  7  8  9
10 11 12 13 14 15 16
17 18 19 20 21 22 23
24 25 26 27 28 29 30
```

MAR
```
 S  M  T  W  T  F  S
                1  2
 3  4  5  6  7  8  9
10 11 12 13 14 15 16
17 18 19 20 21 22 23
24 25 26 27 28 29 30
31
```

JUNE
```
 S  M  T  W  T  F  S
                   1
 2  3  4  5  6  7  8
 9 10 11 12 13 14 15
16 17 18 19 20 21 22
23 24 25 26 27 28 29
30
```

SEPT
```
 S  M  T  W  T  F  S
 1  2  3  4  5  6  7
 8  9 10 11 12 13 14
15 16 17 18 19 20 21
22 23 24 25 26 27 28
29 30
```

DEC
```
 S  M  T  W  T  F  S
 1  2  3  4  5  6  7
 8  9 10 11 12 13 14
15 16 17 18 19 20 21
22 23 24 25 26 27 28
29 30 31
```

Note: This page may be photocopied in order to submit additional event entries to **Chase's 2002 Calendar of Events**

4255 W Touhy Ave, Lincolnwood, IL 60712-1975 • Phone (847) 745-3427 • Fax (847) 679-2595